Great Britain

Inverness &
the Highlands &
Islands
p884

Stirling &
Central Scotland
p826

⭐ Edinburgh p745

Glasgow &
Southern
Scotland
p789

Newcastle &
Northeast England
p606

The Lake District
& Cumbria
p568

Manchester, Liverpool
& Northwest England
p533

Yorkshire
p479

Snowdonia &
North Wales
p704

Brecon Beacons
& Mid-Wales
p679

Birmingham &
the Midlands
p399

Cambridge &
East Anglia
p360

Cardiff, Pembrokeshire
& South Wales
p639

⭐ London p68

Bath &
Southwest
England
p231

Oxford &
the Cotswolds
p185

Canterbury &
Southeast England
p151

Oliver Berry, Fionn Davenport, Marc Di Duca, Belinda Dixon,
Damian Harper, Catherine Le Nevez, Hugh McNaughtan,
Lorna Parkes, Andy Symington, Greg Ward, Neil Wilson

Contents

BILLY STOCK/SHUTTERSTOCK ©

CLARE COLLEGE P367,
CAMBRIDGE

CHRISNOE/SHUTTERSTOCK ©

SOUTH WEST COAST PATH
P234

Contents

ON THE ROAD

Contents

Welcome to Great Britain

The clue's in the name. Great Britain packs so much greatness into its pint-sized shores: crumbling castles, soaring cathedrals, quaint villages, timeless landscapes and history galore.

Centuries of History

Visiting Britain is like travelling in your own personal time machine. More than 5000 years of history are sown into the British soil: here you can walk around a neolithic stone circle, stand atop an Iron Age hill fort, visit a Roman bath, conquer a Norman castle, marvel at a medieval cathedral, wander around a Victorian museum and admire the view from a 21st-century skyscraper. History is everywhere – and if you want to understand what makes Britain tick, you have to gaze into its past.

Museums & Galleries

When it comes to culture, Britain is a world-beater. London is home to the nation's leading institutions, including big hitters such as the British Museum, the V&A, the Tate Modern and the Natural History Museum. But world-class museums and galleries are scattered across the island: there's Glasgow's wonderful Kelvingrove Art Gallery, Newcastle's BALTIC arts centre, Edinburgh's National Museum of Scotland and outposts of the Tate in Liverpool and St Ives. But often it's the weirdest ones that are the most fun: look around and you'll discover museums devoted to Bakelite, lawnmowers, waxworks, witchcraft and even the humble pencil. Only in Britain.

British Eccentricity

It won't take long travelling round Britain to realise that it's just a little bit, well, eccentric. Since time immemorial, this has been a country determined to do things its own way: in art, architecture, literature, engineering, music, politics and comedy, the British just never seem happy to follow the herd. Perhaps it's because Britain is an island nation; no doubt it has something to do with the infamously unpredictable weather. Whatever the case, any country that can dream up welly wanging, cheese rolling, maypole dancing, tar-barrel racing and caber tossing simply has to be worth a visit.

The Great Outdoors

It's just 874 miles from top to bottom, but Britain boasts an astonishing diversity of landscapes: moors, mountains, glens, lakes, woodlands, fields, dales and endless miles of craggy coastline. Throw in 15 national parks, numerous nature reserves and countless beauty spots, and it all adds up to a nonstop inspirational panorama – as generations of poets, painters, musicians and photographers have discovered to their, and our, advantage. Tramp the hills, cycle the lanes, bask on the beaches and wander the cliffs – the great British countryside awaits.

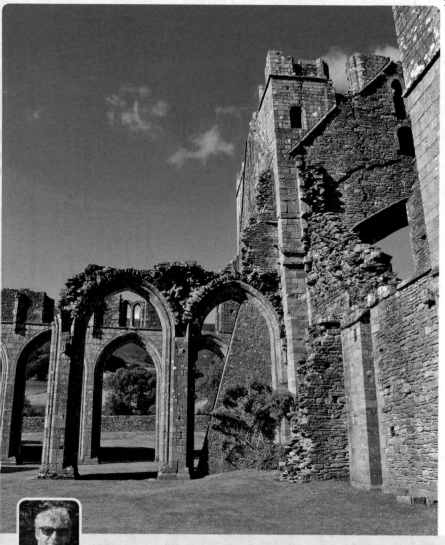

Why I Love Great Britain

By Oliver Berry, Writer

As a born-and-bred Brit, I've travelled more miles along Britain's footpaths, back lanes, byways and bridleways than anywhere on earth – and yet, somehow, every time I set out, I always seem to find something unexpected. Sometimes it's a beach I've never strolled on before, a view I've never photographed, or a hill I've never climbed; occasionally it's a museum I've not visited, a castle I've not explored, or a legend I've not heard. More often than not, it's a pub where I've never drunk a pint. I've been exploring this island for half a lifetime, and I've still only discovered a fraction of the experiences it has to offer.

For more about our writers, see p1056

Above: Llanthony Priory (p685), Black Mountains

Great Britain

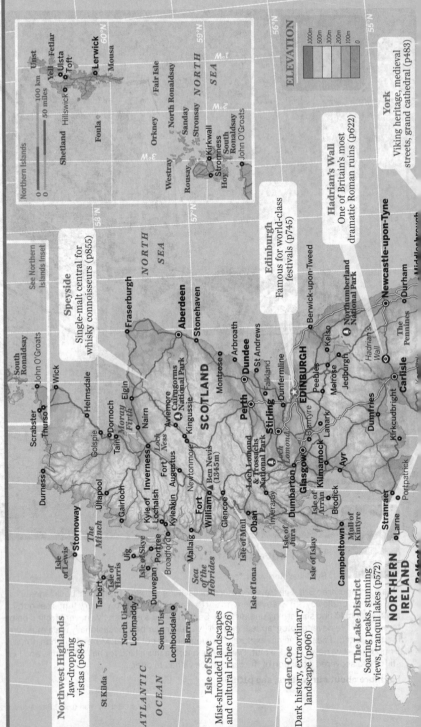

Northwest Highlands
Jaw-dropping vistas (p884)

Isle of Skye
Mist-shrouded landscapes and cultural riches (p926)

Glen Coe
Dark history, extraordinary landscape (p906)

The Lake District
Soaring peaks, stunning views, tranquil lakes (p572)

Speyside
Single-malt central for whisky connoisseurs (p855)

Edinburgh
Famous for world-class festivals (p745)

Hadrian's Wall
One of Britain's most dramatic Roman ruins (p622)

York
Viking heritage, medieval streets, grand cathedral (p483)

ATLANTIC
OCEAN

NORTH
SEA

St Kilda

Isle of Lewis
Stornoway
The Minch
Tarbert
Isle of Harris
North Uist
Lochmaddy
South Uist
Lochboisdale
Barra

Isle of Skye
Uig
Portree
Dunvegan
Broadford
Kyleakin

Durness
Scrabster
Thurso
Wick
John O'Groats
South Ronaldsay

Ullapool
Gairloch
Kyle of Lochalsh

Helmsdale
Golspie
Dornoch
Tain
Elgin
Nairn
Inverness
Moray Firth
Fort Augustus
Loch Ness
Newtonmore
Kingussie
Aviemore
Cairngorms National Park

Fraserburgh

Aberdeen
Stonehaven

Mallaig
Fort William
Ben Nevis (1345m)
Glencoe

Sea of the Hebrides
Isle of Mull
Isle of Iona
Oban
Inveraray

Loch Lomond & Trossachs National Park
Loch Lomond

Perth
Dundee
Arbroath
Montrose
St Andrews
Falkland
Dunfermline

SCOTLAND

Stirling
EDINBURGH

NORTH
SEA

Isle of Jura
Isle of Islay

Campbeltown
Mull of Kintyre

Dumbarton
Glasgow
Kilmarnock
Brodick
Isle of Arran
Ayr
Blantyre
Lanark
Peebles
Kelso
Jedburgh
Melrose
Berwick-upon-Tweed

Dumfries
Kirkcudbright

Stranraer
Portpatrick
Larne

Northumberland National Park
Hadrian's Wall
The Pennines

Newcastle-upon-Tyne
Durham
Carlisle

NORTHERN
IRELAND

Belfast

Northern Islands

Unst
Yell Fetlar
Ulsta Toft
Hillswick
Lerwick
Mousa
Shetland
Fair Isle
Foula

Westray
Rousay
Hoy
Stromness
Kirkwall
Orkney
Sanday
North Ronaldsay
Stronsay
South Ronaldsay
John O'Groats

NORTH
SEA

60°N
59°N

ELEVATION

1000m
500m
300m
200m
100m
0

56°N
55°N
57°N
58°N

0   100 km
0   50 miles

0   100 km
0   50 miles

Stratford-upon-Avon
Shakespeare's birthplace, a
shrine to the Bard (p415)

Oxford
Beautiful architecture,
ancient traditions (p187)

Cambridge
Ancient colleges, gliding
punts, dreamy spires (p364)

London
A world's-worth of
marvellous museums (p68)

Stonehenge
Britain's iconic prehistoric
site (p289)

Snowdonia
Rugged peaks,
glacier-hewn valleys (p710)

The Cotswolds
Classic chocolate-box
countryside at its best (p201)

Bath
Britain's belle of the ball
(p245)

Pembrokeshire
The best of wild and
wonderful West Wales (p667)

Cornwall
Rugged cliffs, sparkling bays,
surf and sand (p327)

FRANCE

Lille

Amiens

ENGLAND

WALES

CARDIFF

LONDON

IRELAND

Dublin

Channel Islands

0   40 km

FRANCE

Alderney

Guernsey
St Peter Port

Jersey
St Helier

Great Britain's
Top 26

Stonehenge

1 Mysterious and compelling, Stonehenge (p289) is Britain's most iconic ancient site. People have been drawn to this myth-laden ring of bluestones for the last 5000 years, and we still don't know quite why it was built. Most visitors get to gaze at the 50-tonne megaliths from behind the perimeter fence, but with enough planning you can book an early-morning or evening tour and walk around the inner ring. In the slanting sunlight, away from the crowds, it's an ethereal place – an experience that stays with you.

Edinburgh

2 Edinburgh (p745) is a city of many moods – famous for its festivals and especially lively in the summer. It's also worth visiting out of season for sights such as the castle silhouetted against a blue spring sky with a yellow haze of daffodils misting the slopes below the esplanade; or on a chill December morning with the fog snagging the spires of the Old Town, the ancient streets and alleyways more mysterious than ever, rain on the cobblestones and a warm glow beckoning from the window of a pub.

KIEV.VICTOR/SHUTTERSTOCK ©

SAMOT/SHUTTERSTOCK ©

MADANATKA/SHUTTERSTOCK ©

Bath

3 Britain has many great cities, but Bath (p245) stands out as the belle of the ball. Thanks to the natural hot springs that bubble to the surface, the Romans built a health resort here. The waters were rediscovered in the 18th century, and Bath became the place to see and be seen in by British high society. Today, the stunning Georgian architecture of grand town houses and sweeping crescents (not to mention Roman remains, a beautiful cathedral and a cutting-edge 21st-century spa) mean that Bath will demand your undivided attention. Roman Baths (p245)

Isle of Skye

4 Of all Scotland's many islands, Skye (p926) is the most famous and best loved by visitors, thanks to a mix of history (the island's link to Bonnie Prince Charlie is forever remembered by 'The Skye Boat Song'), accessibility (the ferry from the mainland has been replaced by a bridge) and sheer beauty. With jagged mountains, velvet moors and towering sea cliffs, Skye's scenery never fails to impress. And for those days when the mist comes in, there are plenty of castles and local museums to explore, and cosy pubs to enjoy. Cuillin Hills (p929)

England Coast Path

5 Britain's epic, seemingly endless coastline is without doubt one of its major draws. With its white beaches, wind-blown cliffs, lonely lighthouses and craggy headlands, it's a feast for the eyes – and it's completely free for everyone to explore, thanks to a network of public coast paths. Trails already exist around the coastlines of Wales, Scotland and the South West, and in 2020 they'll be joined by the new England Coast Path (p43) – which, at 2795 miles long, will be the longest anywhere in Europe. Path to Durdle Door (p275)

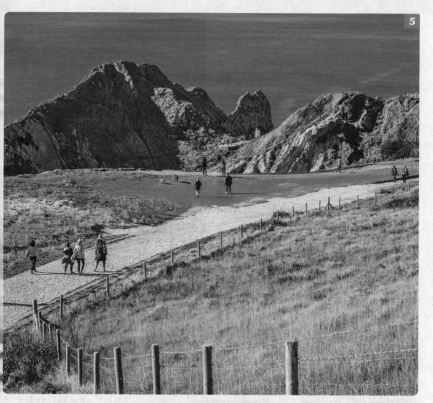

The Cotswolds

6 The most wonderful thing about the Cotswolds (p201) is that, no matter where you go or how lost you get, you'll always end up in an impossibly picturesque village complete with rose-clad cottages, an ancient church of honey-coloured stone, a pub with sloping floors and fine ales, and a view of the lush green hills. It's easy to leave the crowds behind and find your very own slice of medieval England – and some of the best boutique hotels in the country. Lords of the Manor hotel (p208), Upper Slaughter

ALTOSVIC/SHUTTERSTOCK ©

Tower of London

7 With its imposing towers and battlements overlooking the Thames, the Tower of London (p91) is an icon of the capital. The walls are nearly 1000 years old, established by William the Conqueror in the 1070s. Since then, the Tower has been a fortress, a royal residence, a treasury, a mint, an arsenal and a prison. Today it's home to the Crown Jewels, which are protected by the famous red-coated Yeoman Warders (known as Beefeaters) and a flock of fabled ravens.

Snowdonia

8 Wales is awash with wonderful scenery, but it's hard to beat Snowdonia (p710): a landscape of rocky mountain peaks, glacier-hewn valleys, sinuous ridges, sparkling lakes and rivers, and charm-infused villages. The busiest part is around Snowdon itself, where many people hike to the summit, and many more take the jolly rack-and-pinion railway, while to the south and west are rarely trod areas perfect for off-the-beaten-track exploration. And just nearby sit the lovely Llŷn Peninsula and Isle of Anglesey, where the sun often shines, even if it's raining on the mountains.

The Lake District

9 William Wordsworth and his Romantic friends were the first to champion the charms of the Lake District (p572) and it's not hard to see what stirred them. Already the UK's most popular national park, the Lake District also became a Unesco World Heritage Site in 2017, in recognition of its long history of hill farming – but for most people it's the chance to hike the hump-backed fells and drink in the gorgeous scenery that keeps them returning year after year.

Oxford

10 For centuries, the brilliant minds and august institutions of Oxford University have made Oxford (p187) famous across the globe. You'll get a glimpse of this revered world as you stroll hushed college quads and cobbled lanes roamed by cycling students and dusty academics. The beautiful college buildings, archaic traditions and stunning architecture have changed little over the centuries, coexisting with a lively, modern, working city.
Magdalen College (p193)

Hadrian's Wall

11 Hadrian's Wall (p622) is one of the country's most revealing and dramatic Roman ruins, its 2000-year-old procession of abandoned forts, garrisons, towers and milecastles marching across the wild and lonely landscape of northern England. This wall was about defence and control, but this edge-of-empire barrier also symbolised the boundary of civilised order – to the north lay the unruly land of the marauding Celts, while to the south was the Roman world of orderly taxpaying, underfloor heating and bathrooms.

Castle Howard

12 For many people, Britain's astonishing surfeit of stately homes is one of its main attractions – and they really don't get much more stately than Castle Howard (p492). Located 15 miles northeast of York, this incredible 18th-century edifice is the ancestral seat of the Earls of Carlisle, and it's a work of truly breathtaking grandeur – complete with a baroque great hall, moody mausoleum, whimsical temple and vast, peacock-filled grounds, not to mention a crowning cupola that's modelled on the one in St Paul's Cathedral.

Cornwall

13 At Britain's far southwestern extremity, the former kingdom of Cornwall (p327) boasts endless miles of coastline with rugged cliffs, sparkling bays, scenic fishing ports and white sandy beaches favoured by everyone from bucket-and-spade families to sun-bronzed surfers. Above the cliffs, the towers of former tin mines now stand like dramatic castles, while inland from the coast is a tranquil landscape of lush farmland and picturesque villages, crowned by the gigantic domes of the Eden Project – a stunning symbol of Cornwall's renaissance.

EDWARD HAYLAN/SHUTTERSTOCK ©

PAOLO PARADISO/SHUTTERSTOCK ©

Cambridge

14 Abounding with exquisite architecture and steeped in tradition, Cambridge (p364) is a university town extraordinaire. The tightly packed core of ancient colleges, the picturesque riverside 'Backs' (college gardens) and the surrounding green meadows give Cambridge a more tranquil appeal than its historic rival, Oxford. Highlights include the intricate vaulting of King's College Chapel, while no visit is complete without an attempt to steer a punt (flat-bottomed boat) along the river and under the quirky Mathematical Bridge. You'll soon wonder how you could have studied anywhere else. St John's College (p369)

Stratford-upon-Avon

15 The pretty English Midlands town of Stratford-upon-Avon (p415) is famed around the world as the birthplace of the nation's best-known dramatist, William Shakespeare. Today, the town's tight knot of Tudor streets forms a living map of Shakespeare's life and times, while crowds of fans and would-be thespians come to enjoy a play at the theatre or visit the historic houses owned by Shakespeare and his relatives, with a respectful detour to the old stone church where the Bard was laid to rest. Shakespeare's Birthplace (p415)

Canterbury Cathedral

16 Few other English cathedrals come close to Canterbury (p154), the top temple of the Anglican Church and a place of worship for over 15 centuries. Its intricate tower dominates the local skyline, its grandeur unsurpassed by later structures. At its heart lies a 12th-century crime scene, the very spot where Archbishop Thomas Becket was put to the sword – an epoch-making event that launched a million pilgrimages and still pulls in the crowds today. A lone candle mourns the gruesome deed, the pink sandstone before it smoothed by 800 years of devout kneeling.

York

17 With its Roman remains and Viking heritage, ancient city walls and maze of medieval streets, York (p483) is a living showcase for the highlights of English history. Join one of the city's many walking tours and plunge into the network of snickleways (narrow alleys), each the focus of a ghost story or historical character. Explore the intricacies of York Minster (p485; pictured), the biggest medieval cathedral in all of northern Europe, or admire the exhibits from more recent times at the National Railway Museum, the world's largest collection of historic locomotives.

Britain's Pubs

18 Despite the growth of stylish clubs and designer bars, the traditional pub is still the centre of British social life. From the ornate Victorian boozers of London, Edinburgh and Leeds, to the food-focused gastropubs of Yorkshire, Mid-Wales and Devon, and countless rustic country pubs hunkering under thatched roofs and timber beams – Ye Olde Trip to Jerusalem (p446; pictured) claims to be the country's oldest – a lunchtime or evening visit to the pub can be one of the best ways to get under the skin of the nation.

Cardiff

19 The exuberant capital of Wales, compact Cardiff (p641) has emerged as one of Britain's leading urban centres. After a mid-20th-century decline, the city entered the new millennium with vigour and confidence, flexing architectural muscles and revelling in a new-found sense of style. From the historic castle to the ultramodern waterfront, from lively street cafes to infectious nightlife, from Victorian shopping arcades to the gigantic rugby stadium that is the pulsating heart of the city on match days, Cardiff undoubtedly has buzz. St David's shopping centre (p651)

Scotland's Northwest Highlands

20 The Highlands abound in breathtaking views, but the far northwest is truly awe-inspiring. The coastal road between Durness and Kyle of Lochalsh offers jaw-dropping scenes at every turn: the rugged mountains of Assynt (p919), the desolate beauty of Torridon and the remote cliffs of Cape Wrath. Add to this Britain's finest whale-watching, and the nooks of warm Highland hospitality found in classic rural pubs and romantic hotels, and you have the makings of an unforgettable corner of the country. Eilean Donan Castle (p925)

Pembrokeshire

21 Perched at the tip of wild and wonderful West Wales, the county of Pembrokeshire (p667) has one of Britain's most beautiful and dramatic stretches of coast, with sheer cliffs, natural arches, blowholes, sea stacks, and a wonderful hinterland of tranquil villages and secret waterways. It's a landscape of Norman castles, Iron Age hill forts, holy wells and Celtic saints – including the nation's patron, St David – and intriguing stone monuments left behind by prehistoric inhabitants.

PLAN YOUR TRIP GREAT BRITAIN'S TOP 26

Liverpool

22 For many visitors, Liverpool (p551) will forever be associated with The Beatles, but a visit here proves the city has much more to offer. After a decade of redevelopment, the waterfront is once again the heart of Liverpool, with Albert Dock (p554; pictured) declared a World Heritage Site of iconic and protected buildings, a batch of top museums ensuring all sides of the city's history are not forgotten, and the Tate Liverpool gallery and The Beatles Story museum celebrating popular culture and the city's most famous musical sons.

Glen Coe

23 Scotland's most famous glen (p906) combines those two essential qualities of the Highland landscape: dramatic scenery and deep history. The peacefulness and beauty of this valley today belie the fact that it was the scene of a ruthless 17th-century massacre, when the local MacDonalds were murdered by soldiers of the Campbell clan. Some of the glen's finest walks – to the Lost Valley, for example – follow the routes used by the clanspeople trying to flee their attackers, and where many perished in the snow.

JOHNBRAID/SHUTTERSTOCK ©

YULIA_BOGOMOLOVA/SHUTTERSTOCK ©

British Museum

24 From the marvellous Tate Modern to the fascinating Natural History Museum, London is overflowing with world-leading museums and galleries – but none can quite match the British Museum (p77) in sheer scale and scope. Since 1753, this iconic institution has been amassing a vast haul of treasures from around the world, encompassing pretty much every era and culture you could care to name. You'll need a whole day (or preferably multiple visits) to do it justice – but it's the nearest most of us will ever get to feeling like Indiana Jones.

Whisky

25 After tea, Britain's best-known drink is whisky. And while this amber spirit is also made in England and Wales, it is always most associated with Scotland. There are more than 2000 whisky brands available, and distilleries are dotted all over Scotland, many open to visitors, with Speyside (p855) one of the main concentrations and a favourite spot for connoisseurs. Before enjoying your tipple, heed these warnings: never spell whisky with an 'e' (that's the Irish variety); and when ordering at the bar, never ask for 'Scotch'. What else would you drink in Scotland?

Stirling Castle

26 Scotland is littered with castles, a testament to its tempestuous and conflict-strewn past. They range from romantic ruins like Dunnottar to fairy-tale fortresses like Glamis, Braemar and Eilean Donan – but it's Stirling Castle (p827) that held the key to the Scottish throne. Until the union with England in 1706, Stirling was the seat of power for the Stuart monarchs, and, thanks to a comprehensive restoration program, now looks much as it would have done in their day. Don't miss the Royal Palace, along with the Great Hall, Royal Chapel and castle kitchens.

Need to Know

For more information, see Survival Guide (p1017)

Currency
Pound sterling (£)

Language
English; also Scottish Gaelic and Welsh

Visas
Generally not needed for stays of up to six months. Britain is not a member of the Schengen Zone, so you will need to show your passport when arriving and leaving from a UK border point.

Money
ATMs and change bureaux are widely available, especially in cities and major towns.

Mobile Phones
The UK uses the GSM 900/1800 network, which covers the rest of Europe, Australia and New Zealand, but isn't compatible with the North American GSM 1900. Most modern mobiles can function on both networks, but check before you leave home just in case.

Time
Greenwich Mean Time (UTC/GMT +00:00)

When to Go

■ Warm to hot summers, mild winters
■ Cool to mild summers, cold winters

Fort William•
GO May or Sep

• Aberdeen
GO May–Sep

• Edinburgh
GO Any time

Brecon
GO May–Sep

• Norwich
GO May–Sep

• London
GO Any time

• Exeter
GO Apr–Oct

High Season (Jun–Aug)

➡ Weather at its best. Accommodation rates peak especially for August school holidays.

➡ Roads are busy, especially in seaside areas, national parks, and popular cities such as Oxford, Bath, Edinburgh and York.

Shoulder (Mar–May, Sep & Oct)

➡ Crowds reduce. Prices drop.

➡ Weather often good. March to May has both sunny spells and sudden showers; September to October can feature balmy summers.

➡ For outdoor activities May and September are the best months.

Low Season (Nov–Feb)

➡ Wet and cold. Snow falls in mountain areas, especially up north.

➡ Opening hours reduced October to Easter; some places shut for winter. Big-city sights (particularly London's) operate all year.

Useful Websites

BBC (www.bbc.co.uk) News and entertainment from the national broadcaster.

Visit Britain (www.visitbritain.com) Comprehensive official tourism website.

Lonely Planet (www.lonelyplanet.com/great-britain) Destination information, hotel bookings, traveller forum and more.

Traveline (www.traveline.info) Great portal site for public transport in all parts of Britain.

British Arts Festivals (www.artsfestivals.co.uk) Lists hundreds of festivals – art, literature, dance, folk and more.

Important Numbers

Area codes vary in length (eg 020 for London, 01225 for Bath). Omit the code if you're inside that area. Drop the initial 0 if you're calling from abroad.

Britain (& UK) country code	☑44
International access code	☑00
Emergency (police, fire, ambulance, mountain rescue, coastguard)	☑112 or ☑999

Exchange Rates

Australia	A$1	£0.56
Canada	C$1	£0.58
Europe	€1	£0.88
Japan	¥100	£0.68
New Zealand	NZ$1	£0.51
US	US$1	£0.76

For current exchange rates, see www.xe.com.

Daily Costs

Budget: Less than £55

➡ Dorm beds: £15–30

➡ Cheap meals in cafes and pubs: £7–11

➡ Long-distance coach: £15–40 (200 miles)

Midrange: £55–120

➡ Double room in midrange hotel or B&B: £65–130 (London £100–200)

➡ Main course in midrange restaurant: £10–20

➡ Long-distance train: £20–80 (200 miles)

Top end: More than £120

➡ Four-star hotel room: from £130 (London from £200)

➡ Three-course meal in a good restaurant: around £40

➡ Car rental per day: from £35

Opening Hours

Opening hours may vary throughout the year, especially in rural areas where many places have shorter hours or close completely from October or November to March or April.

Banks 9.30am–4pm/5pm Monday to Friday; some open 9.30am–1pm Saturday

Pubs & Bars Noon–11pm Monday to Saturday (many till midnight or 1am Friday and Saturday, especially in Scotland), 12.30–11pm Sunday

Restaurants Lunch noon–3pm, dinner 6–9pm/10pm (or later in cities)

Shops 9am–5.30pm (or to 6pm in cities) Monday to Saturday, and often 11am–5pm Sunday; big-city convenience stores open 24/7

Arriving in Great Britain

Heathrow Airport (London) Trains, the London Underground (tube) and buses to central London run from just after 5am to before midnight (night buses run later); fares from £6 to £22. Taxis to central London from Heathrow cost from £48 to £90 (more at peak hours).

Gatwick Airport (London) Trains to central London run from 4.30am to 1.35am (£10 to £20); hourly buses to central London around the clock from £8. Taxis to central London from Gatwick cost £100 (more during peak times).

St Pancras International Station (Central London) Eurostar trains from Paris or Brussels arrive at this station in central London, connected by many Underground lines to other parts of the city.

Victoria Coach Station (Central London) Buses from Europe arrive at this central station; frequent Underground links to other parts of the city.

Edinburgh Airport Frequent trams (£6) and buses (£4.50) to Edinburgh city centre. Night buses every 30 minutes from 12.30am to 4am (£4). Taxis costs around £20.

For much more on **getting around**, see p1027

First Time Great Britain

For more information, see Survival Guide (p1017)

Checklist

➡ Check the validity of your passport

➡ Check visa or entry requirements

➡ Make advance bookings (sights, accommodation, theatre tickets, travel)

➡ Inform your credit-/debit-card company of your trip

➡ Organise travel insurance

➡ Check mobile (cell) phone compatibility

➡ Check rental car requirements

➡ Check airline baggage restrictions

➡ If carrying restricted items (eg liquids) in hold luggage, put them in a clear plastic bag

What to Pack

➡ Electrical plug adaptor (UK-specific)

➡ Umbrella – because the rumours about the weather are true

➡ Lightweight waterproof jacket – because sometimes the umbrella is not enough

➡ Comfortable walking shoes – Britain's towns and countryside are best explored on foot

Top Tips for Your Trip

➡ At London airports, tickets for express trains into central London are available in the baggage arrivals hall, which saves queuing at ticket machines. Alternatively you can buy in advance online.

➡ The easiest way to get currency is from an ATM (cash machine), but be aware that your bank may charge for the transaction, and the exchange rate is not always favourable.

➡ If staying more than a few days in London, get an Oyster Card, the travel card the locals use.

➡ Pickpockets and hustlers lurk in crowded tourist areas, especially in London. No need to be paranoid, but do be on your guard.

➡ Britain's electrical plugs are unlike those in the rest of Europe, so bring a UK-specific plug adaptor, or buy one when you arrive.

What to Wear

A rain jacket is essential, as is a small backpack to carry it in when the sun comes out. In summer you'll need sunscreen and an umbrella; you're bound to use both.

For sightseeing, comfortable shoes can make or break a trip. If you plan to enjoy Britain's great outdoors, suitable hiking gear is required in higher or wilder areas, but not for casual strolls in the countryside.

Casual clothes are fine for most pubs, bars and restaurants, although smarter dress is encouraged for more upmarket establishments.

Sleeping

Booking your accommodation in advance is recommended, especially in popular holiday areas and on islands. Summer and school holidays (including half-terms) are particularly busy. Book at least two months ahead for July and August.

B&Bs These small, family-run houses generally provide good value. More luxurious versions are more like boutique hotels.

Hotels British hotels range from half a dozen rooms above a pub to restored country houses and castles, with a commensurate range in rates.

Hostels There's a good choice of both institutional and independent hostels, many housed in rustic and/or historic buildings.

Money

ATMs and change bureaux are widely available, especially in cities and major towns.

Bargaining

A bit of mild haggling is acceptable at flea markets and antique shops, but everywhere else you're expected to pay the advertised price.

Tipping

Restaurants Around 10% in restaurants and teashops with table service. Nearer 15% at smarter restaurants. Tips may be added to your bill as a 'service charge'. Paying a tip or a service charge is not obligatory.

Pubs & Bars Not expected unless table service for your meal and drinks is provided, then 10% is usual.

Taxis Around 10%, or rounded up to the nearest pound, especially in London.

Camden Town (p130), London

Etiquette

Manners The British have a reputation for being polite, and good manners are considered important in most situations. When asking directions, 'Excuse me, can you tell me the way to...' is a better tactic than 'Hey, where's...'

Queues In Britain, queueing ('standing in line' to Americans), whether to board a bus, buy tickets or enter the gates of an attraction, is sacrosanct. Any attempt to 'jump the queue' will result in an outburst of tutting and hard stares.

Escalators If you take an escalator or a moving walkway (especially at tube stations in London), be sure to stand on the right, so folks in a hurry can pass on the left.

Eating

When dining out (p48) in Great Britain, it's wise to book ahead for midrange restaurants, especially at weekends, while top-end restaurants should be booked at least a couple of weeks in advance.

Restaurants Britain's restaurants range from cheap-and-cheerful to Michelin-starred options, and cover every cuisine you can imagine.

Cafes Open during daytime (rarely after 6pm), cafes are good for a casual breakfast or lunch, or simply a cup of coffee.

Pubs Most of Britain's pubs serve reasonably priced meals, and many can compete with restaurants on quality.

What's New

Crossrail

It's Britain's largest, most complex and costliest engineering project, but after years of work, London's long-awaited new rail line sent its first trains shuttling across the city in 2019.

The Lake District World Heritage Site

After intensive local lobbying (both for and against), the UK's best-known national park secured World Heritage status in 2017, in recognition of its unique landscapes and hill-farming culture. (p572)

The England Coast Path

In 2020 a long-held dream to provide walkers with a nonstop walking trail around the coastline of England will be realised – all 2795 miles of it. (p43)

Tate Modern Extension

At long last the Tate Modern can spread its expansive collection into Switch House. The views from the 10th floor are second to none, and free. (p96)

Ashmolean Museum

To mark its 400th birthday, this Oxford museum has a new exhibit celebrating its founder, Elias Ashmole, along with treasures including the hat worn by the judge at Charles I's trial and a cape belonging to the father of Pocahontas. (p192)

The Endeavour at Whitby

To coincide with the 250th anniversary of Captain Cook's voyage to Australia, a full-size replica of his ship *Endeavour* has docked in Whitby, the Yorkshire town where the original vessel was built. (p502)

Tate St Ives

In 2018 a multimillion-pound extension to the Cornish Tate has added new space for contemporary work, as well as a platform for the many famous artists of the St Ives School. (p337)

Roman Baths

The city of Bath's 1st-century bathing house now has some 21st-century tech: visual projections that illustrate what it was like to take a dip here 2000 years ago. (p245)

Great Trossachs Path

This newly designated 30-mile walking trail links Callander to Loch Lomond, with the chance to overnight in new camping pods at Loch Katrine. (p857)

New Waverley

This modern development linking Edinburgh's Old Town with Waverley train station opened in 2018 with a new public square, a gaggle of hotels, and restored railway arches housing quirky shops and bars (www.newwaverley.com).

Dundee Waterfront

The redevelopment of Dundee's waterfront continues apace, and is now graced with a stunning new building that is home to an outpost of London's Victoria & Albert Museum. (p846)

For more recommendations and reviews, see lonelyplanet.com/ great-britain

If You Like...

Castles & Stately Homes

Castle Howard A stunning baroque edifice, best known as the setting for the TV series *Brideshead Revisited*. (p492)

Tower of London Landmark of the capital, patrolled by famous Beefeaters and protected by legendary ravens. (p91)

Blenheim Palace A monumental baroque fantasy and one of Britain's greatest stately homes. (p200)

Chatsworth House The quintessential stately home, a treasure trove of heirlooms and works of art. (p476)

Burghley House Lavish mansion built by Queen Elizabeth I's chief strategist, William Cecil, with grounds by Lancelot 'Capability' Brown. (p454)

Warwick Castle Restored enough to be impressive, ruined enough to be romantic. (p413)

Beaumaris Castle The classic Welsh castle, which, along with nearby Conwy, Caernarfon and Harlech, forms a jointly listed World Heritage Site. (p740)

Carreg Cennen The most dramatically positioned fortress in Wales, standing guard over a lonely stretch of Brecon Beacons National Park. (p689)

Eilean Donan Castle Scotland's most photogenic castle, on a lonely island nestled next to a loch. (p925)

Stirling Castle Classic fortress atop a volcanic crag, with stunning views from the battlements. (p827)

Coastal Attractions

Pembrokeshire Towering cliffs, rock arches, clean waters and perfect sandy beaches at the tip of West Wales. (p667)

North Cornwall's Coast Classic coastal landscape of craggy cliffs, golden beaches and white-crest surf. (p327)

Gower Peninsula Family-friendly beaches and surfer hang-outs, backed by sand dunes and tranquil farmland. (p662)

Beachy Head & Seven Sisters Where the South Downs plunge into the sea, these mammoth chalk cliffs provide a dramatic finale. (p174)

Southwold Genteel old-style seaside town with lovely beach, charming pier and famous rows of colourful beach huts. (p387)

Brighton A favourite seaside retreat for capital-dwellers, known for its pebble beach, landmark pier and alternative vibe. (p175)

Durness to Kyle of Lochalsh This stunning Scottish coast road reveals jaw-dropping scenes at every turn. (p918)

Holkham National Nature Reserve Has a pristine expanse of sand with giant skies stretching overhead. (p396)

Royal Britain

Buckingham Palace The Queen's official London residence, best known for its royal-waving balcony and the Changing of the Guard. (p81)

Windsor Castle The largest and oldest occupied fortress in the world, a majestic vision of battlements and towers, and the Queen's weekend retreat. (p227)

Westminster Abbey Where English royalty is crowned and married – most recently William and Kate. (p76)

Royal Yacht Britannia The Royal Family's one-time floating home during foreign travels, now retired and moored near Edinburgh. (p764)

Balmoral Castle Built for Queen Victoria in 1855 and still a royal Highland hideaway. (p901)

Royal Pavilion Opulent palace built for playboy prince, later King George IV. (p177)

Althorp House Ancestral home and burial place of Diana, Princess of Wales. (p455)

Great Outdoors

Lake District The landscape that inspired William Wordsworth is a feast of mountains, valleys, views and – of course – lakes. (p572)

Northumberland National Park The dramatically empty landscape of England's far north is remote and off the beaten track. (p628)

Snowdonia The best-known slice of nature in Wales, with the grand but surprisingly accessible peak of Snowdon at its heart. (p720)

Yorkshire Dales A compact collection of moors, hills, valleys, rivers, cliffs and waterfalls, perfect for easy strolls or hardy treks. (p507)

Ben Nevis Reach for the summit of Scotland's most famous (and Britain's highest) mountain. (p909)

Cairngorms Walk through the mountains and valleys of the UK's largest national park – and Scotland's wild side. (p895)

Cathedrals & Ruined Abbeys

St Paul's Cathedral A symbol of London for centuries, and still an essential part of the city skyline. (p89)

York Minster One of the largest medieval cathedrals in all of Europe, especially renowned for its windows. (p485)

Fountains Abbey Extensive ruins set in more recently landscaped water gardens – one of the most beautiful sites in Britain. (p495)

Canterbury Cathedral The mother ship of the Anglican Church, still attracting pilgrims and visitors in their thousands. (p154)

Melrose Abbey The finest of all the great Border abbeys; Robert

Top: Ben Nevis (p909)

Bottom: Canterbury Cathedral (p154)

the Bruce's heart is buried here. (p814)

Whitby Abbey Stunning cliff-top ruin with an eerie atmosphere that inspired the author of *Dracula*. (p503)

St David's Cathedral An ancient place of worship in Britain's smallest city. (p672)

Glastonbury Abbey The legendary burial place of King Arthur and Queen Guinevere. (p257)

Tintern Abbey Riverside ruins that inspired generations of poets and artists. (p654)

Art Galleries

Tate Britain One of the best-known galleries in London, full to the brim with the finest local works. (p86)

Tate Modern London's other Tate focuses on modern art in all its wonderful permutations. (p96)

BALTIC Newcastle's very own 'Tate of the North', with work by some of contemporary art's biggest show-stoppers. (p611)

National Museum Cardiff An excellent collection of Welsh artists, plus works by Monet, Renoir, Matisse, Van Gogh, Francis Bacon and David Hockney. (p642)

Kelvingrove Art Gallery & Museum A national landmark in Glasgow – great collection, and a cracking spot to learn about Scottish art. (p797)

Yorkshire Sculpture Park England's biggest outdoor sculpture collection, dominated by the works of Henry Moore and Barbara Hepworth. (p519)

Barber Institute of Fine Arts With works by Rubens, Turner and Picasso, this Birmingham gallery is no lightweight. (p403)

V&A Dundee Brand new gallery dedicated to the best of Scottish

and international art and design. (p846)

Industrial Heritage

Ironbridge The crucible of the Industrial Revolution, where 10 museums for the price of one give fascinating insights. (p433)

Blaenavon A World Heritage Site of well-preserved ironworks and the fascinating Big Pit coal mine. (p656)

Kelham Island Museum A testament to Sheffield's steel-town heritage, anchored by the massive River Don steam engine. (p526)

New Lanark Once the largest cotton-spinning complex in Britain and a testament to enlightened capitalism. (p811)

National Railway Museum A cathedral to Britain's great days of steam; for railway fans of all ages it's the perfect place to go loco. (p485)

Brunel's SS Great Britain Isambard Kingdom Brunel's flagship ocean-going steamer, restored and now proudly installed along Bristol's harbourside. (p235)

Roman Remains

Roman Baths The city of Bath takes its name from these famous Roman remains – a complex of bathhouses around natural thermal waters. (p245)

Hadrian's Wall Snaking coast-to-coast across lonely hills, this 2000-year-old fortified line once marked the northern limit of imperial Roman jurisdiction. (p622)

Yorkshire Museum York's past as the Roman city of Eboracum is chronicled in fascinating detail. (p487)

Caerleon One of three legionary forts in Britain, with impressive remains of barracks, baths and an amphitheatre. (p654)

Corinium Museum Recounts the days when the sleepy Cotswold town of Cirencester was once Corinium, the second-largest Roman city in Britain. (p203)

Village Idylls

Lavenham A wonderful collection of exquisitely preserved medieval buildings virtually untouched since the 15th century. (p384)

Lacock Well-preserved medieval village, essentially free of modern development and – unsurprisingly – a frequent set for movies and TV period dramas. (p292)

Painswick Pretty as a painting, and one of many quintessentially English villages to be found in the Cotswolds. (p216)

Culross Scotland's best-preserved 17th-century village, familiar to fans of TV's *Outlander* as Cranesmuir. (p844)

Goathland One of Yorkshire's most attractive villages, complete with village green and traditional steam railway station. (p504)

Mousehole Southwest England overflows with picturesque pint-sized ports, but this is one of the best. (p342)

Beddgelert A conservation village of rough grey stone buildings in the heart of Snowdonia National Park. (p722)

Arts & Music Festivals

Edinburgh International Festival The world's biggest festival of art and culture. 'Nuff said. (p768)

Glastonbury Festival of Contemporary Performing Arts (p258)

Glastonbury Britain's biggest and best-loved music festival. (p258)

Hay Festival A world-class celebration of all things literary at Britain's bookshop capital. (p681)

Notting Hill Carnival London's Caribbean community shows the city how to party. (p119)

Pride Gay and lesbian street parade through London culminating in a concert in Trafalgar Sq. (p119)

Latitude Festival An eclectic mix of music, literature, dance, drama and comedy, in a stunning Suffolk location. (p387)

Festival No 6 A three-day party amongst the fantastical follies of Portmeirion. (p725)

Hebridean Celtic Festival A feast of folk, rock and Celtic music held in the grounds of Stornoway's Lews Castle. (p934)

Shopping

Portobello Rd, London One of London's best-known street markets, surrounded by quirky boutiques and gift stores. (p114)

Victoria Quarter, Leeds Lovely arcades of wrought ironwork and stained glass, home to several top fashion boutiques. (p521)

North Laine, Brighton Narrow streets lined with shops selling books, antiques, collectables, vintage clothing and more. (p180)

Cardiff Arcades Half a dozen ornate arcades branch off the city centre main streets, all with speciality shops and cafes. (p651)

Isle of Skye Home to a plethora of workshops and artists' studios, the isle is a great place to find quality handmade arts and crafts. (p926)

Hay-on-Wye The self-proclaimed secondhand-book capital of the world boasts over 30 bookshops and millions of volumes, attracting browsers, collectors and academics from afar. (p684)

Month by Month

January

January is midwinter in Britain. Festivals and events to brighten the mood are thin on the ground, but luckily some include fire – lots of it.

✺ London Parade

A ray of light in the gloom, the New Year's Day Parade in London (to use its official title; www.london-parade.co.uk) is one of the biggest events of its kind in the world, featuring marching bands, street performers, classic cars, floats and displays winding their way through the streets.

✺ Up Helly Aa

Half of Shetland dresses up with horned helmets and battleaxes in this spectacular re-enactment of a Viking fire festival, with a torchlit procession leading the burning of a full-size Viking longship. (p954)

✺ Celtic Connections

Glasgow plays host to a celebration of Celtic music, dance and culture (www.celticconnections.com), with participants from all over the globe.

February

Britain can be scenic under snow and sunshine, or more likely grey and gloomy under dark skies. Hang in there...

✺ Jorvik Viking Festival

The ancient Viking capital of York becomes home once again to invaders and horned helmets galore, with the intriguing addition of longship races. (p488)

✹ Fort William Mountain Festival

Britain's capital of the outdoors celebrates the peak of the winter season with ski workshops, mountaineering films and talks by famous climbers (www.mountainfestival.co.uk).

March

Spring finally arrives. There's a hint of better weather, and some classic sporting fixtures grace the calendar. Many locals stay hunkered down at home, though, so hotels offer special rates.

☆ Six Nations Rugby Championship

The highlight of the rugby calendar (www.rbs6nations.com) runs from late January to March, with the home nations playing at London's Twickenham, Edinburgh's Murrayfield and Cardiff's Principality stadiums.

☆ University Boat Race

Annual race down the River Thames in London between the rowing teams from Cambridge and Oxford universities; an institution since 1829 that still enthrals the country. (p119)

April

The weather slowly improves, with warmer and drier days bringing out spring blossoms. Attractions that close for the low season open around the middle of the month or at Easter.

☆ Grand National

On the first Saturday of the month half the country has a flutter on the highlight of the three-day horse race meeting at Aintree (http://aintree.thejockeyclub.co.uk) – a steeplechase with a testing course and notoriously high jumps.

🏃 London Marathon

More than 35,000 runners take to the streets; superfit athletes cover the 26.22 miles in just over two hours, while others dress up in daft costumes and take considerably longer. (p119)

🎆 Beltane

Thousands of revellers climb Edinburgh's Calton Hill for this modern revival of a pagan fire festival (www.beltane.org) marking the end of winter.

🍷 Spirit of Speyside

Based in Dufftown, a Scottish festival of whisky, food and music, with five days of art, cooking, distillery tours and outdoor activities. (p855)

May

The weather is usually good, with more events to enjoy. There are two public holidays this month (the first and last Mondays) so traffic is very busy over the those long weekends.

☆ FA Cup Final

Grand finale of the football (soccer) season for over a century. Teams from across England battle it out over the winter months, culmi-

nating in this heady spectacle at Wembley Stadium.

◉ Chelsea Flower Show

The Royal Horticultural Society flower show at Chelsea is the highlight of the gardener's year. (p119)

🎆 Hay Festival

The ever-expanding 'Woodstock of the mind' brings an intellectual influx to booktown Hay-on-Wye. (p681)

☆ Glyndebourne

Famous festival (www.glyndebourne.com) of world-class opera in the pastoral surroundings of East Sussex, running until the end of summer.

June

Now it's almost summer. You can tell because this month sees the music-festival season kick off properly, while sporting events fill the calendar.

☆ Derby Week

Horse racing, people-watching and clothes-spotting are on the agenda at this week-long meeting in Epsom, Surrey (www.epsomderby.co.uk).

🎆 Cotswolds Olimpicks

Welly-wanging, pole-climbing and shin-kicking are the key disciplines at this traditional Gloucestershire sports day, held every year since 1612. (p212)

☆ Trooping the Colour

Military bands and bear-skinned grenadiers march

down London's Whitehall in this martial pageant to mark the monarch's birthday. (p119)

☆ Royal Ascot

It's hard to tell which matters more, the fashion or the fillies, at this highlight of the horse-racing year in Berkshire. (p226)

☆ Wimbledon Tennis

The world's best-known tennis tournament, attracting all the big names, while crowds cheer and eat strawberries and cream. (p142)

☆ Glastonbury

One of Britain's favourite pop and rock gatherings is invariably muddy, and still a rite of passage for every self-respecting British music fan. (p258)

🎆 Pride

Highlight of the gay and lesbian calendar, this technicolour street parade heads through London's West End. (p119)

🎆 Glasgow's West End Festival

Scotland's second city hosts a major celebration of music and arts. (p800)

July

Proper summer. Festivals every week. School summer breaks begin, so there's a holiday tingle in the air, dulled only by busy roads on Fridays.

◉ Henley Royal Regatta

Boats of every description take to the water for

Top: Crowds at the Edinburgh Festival Fringe (p767)

Bottom: Chelsea Flower Show (p119)

Henley's upper-crust river jamboree. (p230)

⭐ TRNSMT

This new Glasgow music festival, the spiritual successor to the long-running T in the Park, has booked major names including Radiohead, London Grammar and The Killers. (p800)

⭐ Great Yorkshire Show

Harrogate plays host to one of Britain's largest county shows. This is the place for Yorkshire grit, Yorkshire tykes, Yorkshire puddings, Yorkshire beef... (p493)

⭐ Latitude

Relaxed festival in the seaside town of Southwold, with theatre, cabaret, art and literature, plus top names from the alternative music scene. (p387)

⭐ International Musical Eisteddfod

Festival of international folk music at Llangollen, with eclectic fringe and big-name evening concerts. (p709)

⭐ Royal Welsh Show

Prize bullocks and local produce at this national farm and livestock event in Builth Wells. (p692)

⭐ Cowes Week

Britain's biggest yachting spectacular on the choppy seas around the Isle of Wight. (p268)

⭐ Womad

Roots and world music take centre stage at this festival (www.womad.org) in a country park in the south Cotswolds.

☆ Port Eliot Festival

Beginning life as a literary festival, now branched out into live music, theatre and outdoor art (www.porteliot festival.com).

August

Schools and colleges are closed, parliament is in recess, the sun is shining (hopefully), most people go away for a week or two, and the nation is in holiday mood.

☆ Edinburgh Festivals

Edinburgh's most famous August happenings are the International Festival and Fringe, but this month the city also has an event for anything you care to name – books, art, theatre, comedy, marching bands... (www. edinburghfestivals.co.uk).

☆ Bestival

Quirky music festival on Dorset's Lulworth estate, with a different fancy-dress theme every year. (p276)

✵ National Eisteddfod of Wales

The largest celebration of native Welsh culture, steeped in history, pageantry and pomp; held at various venues around the country (www.eisteddfod.cymru).

🏃 World Bog Snorkelling Championships

Only in Britain – competitors, many in fancy dress, don snorkels and flippers for a swimming race along a muddy ditch in the middle of a peat bog (www. green-events.co.uk).

Top: Notting Hill Carnival (p119)

Bottom: Wimbledon Championships (p142)

☆ Brecon Fringe Festival

All musical tastes are catered for at this arts festival in the charming Mid-Wales town of Brecon. (p688)

☆ Green Man Festival

A firm favourite on the UK's summer music festival circuit, Green Man offers four days of alternative folk and rock music in a verdant Brecon Beacons setting. (p686)

🎎 Notting Hill Carnival

London's famous multicultural Caribbean-style street carnival in the district of Notting Hill. Steel drums, dancers, outrageous costumes. (p119)

September

The first week of September is still holiday time, but then schools reopen, traffic returns to normal, and the summer party's over for another year. Ironically, the weather's often better than in August, now everyone's back at work.

🎎 Braemar Gathering

The biggest and most famous Highland Games in the Scottish calendar, traditionally attended by members of the Royal Family. Highland dancing, caber tossing and bagpipe playing. (p901)

✗ Ludlow Food Festival

A great foodie festival in a great foodie town. (p441)

🏃 Great North Run

Tyneside plays host to the one of the biggest half marathons in the world (www. greatrun.org/great-north-run), with the greatest number of runners in any race at this distance.

✗ Abergavenny Food Festival

The mother of all epicurean festivals and the champion of Wales' burgeoning food scene. (p655)

October

October means autumn. The leaves on the trees are changing colour, attractions start to shut down for the low season, and accommodation rates drop as hoteliers try to entice a final few guests before winter.

✗ Falmouth Oyster Festival

The West Country port of Falmouth marks the start of the traditional oyster-catching season (www. falmouthoysterfestival. co.uk) with a celebration of local food from the sea and fields of Cornwall.

🎎 Dylan Thomas Festival

A celebration of the Welsh laureate's work with readings, events and talks in Swansea. (p659)

November

Winter's here, and November is a dull month. The weather is often cold and damp, summer is

a distant memory and Christmas is still too far away.

🎎 Guy Fawkes Night

Also called Bonfire Night (www.bonfirenight.net); on 5 November fireworks fill Britain's skies in commemoration of a failed attempt to blow up parliament, way back in 1605.

📅 Remembrance Day

Red poppies are worn and wreaths are laid in towns and cities around the country on 11 November in commemoration of fallen military personnel (www. poppy.org.uk).

December

Schools break up earlier, but shops and businesses keep going until Christmas Eve; the last weekend before Christmas Day is busy on the roads as people visit friends and family, or head for the airport.

🎎 Stonehaven Fireball Festival

The Scottish fishing town of Stonehaven celebrates Hogmanay with a spectacular procession of fireball-swinging locals (www. stonehavenfireballs.co.uk).

🎎 New Year Celebrations

The last night of December sees fireworks and street parties in town squares across the country. London's Trafalgar Sq is where the city's largest crowds gather to welcome the New Year.

Itineraries

2 WEEKS Best of Britain

This circular whistle-stop tour ticks off Britain's greatest hits in an action-packed fortnight.

Start with at least three days exploring Britain's greatest city, **London**, seeing the world-famous sights: Buckingham Palace, Tower Bridge, Trafalgar Sq, the British Museum and more. From the capital, head west for the dreaming spires of England's oldest university city, **Oxford**, before touring the lovely villages of the **Cotswolds**.

Detour south to see **Stonehenge**, the nation's most celebrated stone circle, and its lesser-known counterpart **Avebury**, then head onwards to the Georgian city of **Bath**. From here, skip across the border through two Welsh national parks: the **Brecon Beacons** and **Snowdonia**, where you can climb Wales' highest mountain. Head back into England and travel north to walk the fells of the **Lake District**, beloved by William Wordsworth and Beatrix Potter.

From here, it's easy to explore Roman Britain's most ambitious engineering project, the 73-mile **Hadrian's Wall**, before the drive north to Scotland's capital, **Edinburgh**. On the long journey back south, drive through the rolling hills and valleys of the **Yorkshire Dales**, visit the handsome city of **York** and its medieval minster, marvel at the majesty of **Chatsworth House**, or wander around the colleges and punt along the Backs of **Cambridge**.

The Full Monty

This is the big one: covering all points of the compass and all three mainland nations, it's the full-blown round-Britain adventure.

After a day or two in **London**, head southeast to **Canterbury**, then along the coast to hip and happening **Brighton**. For a change of pace, divert to the **New Forest**, then up to historic **Winchester** and **Salisbury**, with their awe-inspiring cathedrals. Next, religion of a different kind: the ancient stone circles at **Stonehenge** and **Avebury**.

Go west to **Bath**, with its grand Georgian architecture, Roman remains and famous spas, and then over the border to Wales, via the energetic little cities of **Bristol** and **Cardiff**. Head west to fall in love with the scenery of the **Pembrokeshire Coast**, and backtrack through to the whaleback hills of the **Brecon Beacons** to reach the quirky book-mad town of **Hay-on-Wye**.

Then it's back into England to visit Shakespeare's birthplace, **Stratford-upon-Avon**, and impressive castles at **Warwick**, **Ludlow** and **Shrewsbury**. Cross back into Wales via the stunning mountains of **Snowdonia**, then round the coast via the dramatic castles of **Caernarfon** and **Conwy**.

Back in England once again, have a wander round the medieval walls of **Chester** en route to **Liverpool**, with its famous musical heritage and revitalised waterfront, or **Manchester**, for a taste of northern nightlife. Cross over the moors and hills of the **Peak District**, admire the marvellous York Minster in **York**, and finish your English adventure in **Newcastle-upon-Tyne**, with its galleries, museums and Antony Gormley's monumental Angel of the North sculpture.

Hop over Hadrian's Wall en route to the historic abbey towns of **Jedburgh** and **Melrose** in Scotland. Stop off for a few days in **Edinburgh**, then head west via **Stirling Castle** to good-time **Glasgow**. Then trek to **Fort William** (and maybe up **Ben Nevis**, Britain's highest mountain), from where it's easy to reach journey's end on the beautiful **Isle of Skye**.

Island Hopscotch

10 DAYS

This route is usually done by car, but it also makes a brilliant cycling tour (270 miles, including the 60 miles from Ullapool to Inverness train station, making both start and finish accessible by rail).

From **Oban** it's a five-hour ferry crossing to **Barra**; plan to spend the night here (book ahead). On day two, after a visit to Kisimul Castle and a tour around the island, take the ferry to **South Uist**. Walk the wild beaches of the west coast, sample the local seafood and perhaps go fishing on the island's trout lochs. Continue through Benbecula and **North Uist**, prime birdwatching country.

Overnight at Lochmaddy on North Uist (if you're camping or hostelling, a night at **Berneray** is a must) before taking the ferry to **Harris**, whose west coast has some of the most spectacular beaches in Scotland. The road continues north from **Tarbert** (good hotels) through rugged hills to **Lewis**.

Don't go directly to Stornoway, but loop west via the **Callanish Standing Stones** and **Arnol Blackhouse** museum. Spend your final night in **Stornoway** (eat at Digby Chick), then take the ferry to **Ullapool** for a scenic drive to **Inverness**.

 ## Urban Odyssey

3 WEEKS

Take this ride through some of Britain's less well-known and revitalised cities.

Kick off in **Bristol**, a city with fierce pride and a rich historical legacy, then cross over to **Cardiff**, once a provincial backwater but now the lively Welsh capital.

Next stop is **Birmingham**, oozing transformation, with a renovated waterside, energised museums and a space-age shopping centre. Onwards to **Leeds**, where run-down factories and warehouses have been turned into loft apartments, ritzy boutiques and stylish department stores.

Shopping not your thing? No problem. Head for **Newcastle-upon-Tyne** and twin city **Gateshead**; both have given up on heavy industries in favour of art and architecture, and are famous for partying.

Still want more? It's got to be **Glasgow**, Scotland's other great city, boasting fabulous galleries and welcoming pubs. Then it's south to **Liverpool**, which has reinvented itself as a cultural hot spot, with a famous musical heritage. Finish your tour in **Manchester**, a long-time stage for artistic endeavour, with dramatic architecture and a rather well-known football club.

Top: Callanish Standing Stones (p935)

Bottom: Beaumaris Castle (p740)

TIM SNOW/SHUTTERSTOCK ©

Highland Fling

2 WEEKS

This itinerary is a tour of Scotland's finest and most famous sights.

Naturally it starts in **Edinburgh**, where highlights include the renowned castle, as well as the Royal Mile and the haunts of the Old Town. Hop over to **Glasgow** for a day or two as well, then head northeast to see Scotland's other great castle at **Stirling**. Next stop is **Callander**, a good base for exploring the hills and lochs of the **Trossachs**.

Continue north and the landscape becomes ever more impressive, culminating in the grandeur of **Glen Coe**. Keen hill walkers will pause for a day at **Fort William** to trek to the top of **Ben Nevis** (and another day to recover!) before taking the 'Road to the Isles' past glorious **Glenfinnan** to the fishing harbour of **Mallaig**.

Take the ferry to the **Isle of Skye**, then head back to the mainland via the Skye Bridge to reach pretty **Plockton** and magnificent **Glen Torridon**. Travelling onwards, via **Ullapool**, takes you to the remote mountain landscape of Scotland's far northwest, then continue to Highland capital **Inverness**. Conclude with a memorable drive through the **Cairngorms** and a tour of the whisky distilleries of **Speyside**.

Edge of England

2 WEEKS

If you like the outdoors, and prefer flocks of birds to crowds of people, try this backwater route along England's eastern fringe.

Start in **Colchester**, then head out into the sleepy county of Suffolk, where quaint villages and market towns such as **Sudbury** and **Lavenham** dot the landscape, while along the coast are wildlife reserves, shingly beaches, fishing ports such as **Aldeburgh**, and the delightfully retro seaside resort of **Southwold**.

Things get even quieter in **Norfolk**, especially around the misty lakes and windmill-lined rivers of the **Broads**. For beach strolls or historic country pubs, head for the coastal villages near **Wells-next-the-Sea**. Across the border in Lincolnshire lies the eerie, pan-flat landscape of the Fens, now a haven for otters and birdlife.

Continue into the heather-clad **North York Moors**, where humpbacked hills roll all the way to the coast to drop dramatically into the North Sea, and spend some time in the atmospheric seaside town of **Whitby**.

Enjoy a blustery stroll on the wild coast of Northumberland near the landmark castles of **Dunstanburgh** and **Bamburgh**, then end at the holy island of **Lindisfarne**.

Legend:
- Welsh Wander
- Way Out West

---

1 WEEK — Welsh Wander

The coast and countryside of Wales has long been a favourite with visitors, and this tour includes most of the hot spots. Continue along England's southwest coast for a longer jaunt along Britain's Celtic fringe.

Start in **Cardiff**, with its fantastical castle, gigantic rugby stadium, revitalised waterfront and stunning Millennium Centre. Head west via the beautiful **Gower Peninsula** to reach the clear waters and sandy beaches of Pembrokeshire. Don't miss the ancient cathedral at **St Davids** – Britain's smallest city. Continue up the coast to **Aberystwyth**, then through 'alternative' **Machynlleth** to reach **Harlech** and its ancient castle. Divert to the tranquil Isle of Anglesey and historic **Beaumaris Castle**, then strike through the mountains of Snowdonia to reach **Conwy** (for another stunning castle) and the seaside resort of **Llandudno**.

Southwards takes you through **Llangollen**, with its jolly steam trains and vertiginous aqueduct, then along the England–Wales borderlands to book-mad **Hay-on-Wye**. Loop inland via **Brecon Beacons** to the Welsh foodie capital of **Abergavenny**, then saunter down the **Wye Valley** to finish at the frontier town of **Chepstow** – and yet another amazing castle.

---

2 WEEKS — Way Out West

The southwest of England takes a bit of effort to reach but repays in full with a rich green landscape dotted with hills and moors, surrounded by glistening seas.

Start in **Bristol**, the capital of the West Country, then saunter south to reach **Glastonbury** – famous for its annual music festival and the best place to stock up on candles or crystals at any time of year.

West leads to the walking trails of heathery **Exmoor**, then it's south to Dorset, where highlights include picturesque **Shaftesbury** and the fossil-strewn Jurassic Coast.

Onwards into Devon, and there's a choice of coasts, as well as **Dartmoor**, the highest and wildest hills in southern Britain.

Cross into Cornwall to explore the biodomes of the **Eden Project**. Nearby, but in another era entirely, is the legendary birthplace of King Arthur, the castle at **Tintagel**. Depending on your tastes, you can hang-ten in surf-flavoured party-town **Newquay** or browse the galleries at artistic **St Ives**.

The natural finish to this wild west tour is **Land's End**, where the British mainland comes to a final full stop – but it's well worth visiting the amazing island abbey at **St Michael's Mount**.

Plan Your Trip

The Great Outdoors

What's the best way to slow down, meet the locals and get off the beaten track as you travel around Britain? Simple: go for a walk, or get on a bike. From the wild Highlands in the north to the salt-crusted coastal cliffs of the south, Britain offers an extraordinary diversity of terrain that begs to be explored.

Need to Know

Best Seasons

Summer (June–August) Weather is usually warm and dry; long evenings with plenty of daylight, too.

Late spring (May) and early autumn (September) Fewer crowds; days are often mild and sunny. In Scotland, there's drier weather and fewer midges than in high summer.

Best Maps

Ordnance Survey UK's national mapping agency; Explorer series 1:25,000 scale.

Harvey Maps Specially designed for walkers; Superwalker series 1:25,000 scale.

Best Websites

www.walkhighlands.co.uk Superb database for walks of all lengths in Scotland.

www.walkingenglishman.com Short walks in England and Wales.

www.nationaltrail.co.uk Great for specifics on long-distance trails in England and Wales.

www.scotlandsgreattrails.com Long-distance trails in Scotland.

Walking

Walking is the most popular outdoor activity in Britain – for locals and visitors alike. Firstly, because it opens up some beautiful corners of the country, and secondly, because it can be done virtually on a whim. In fact, compared to hiking and trekking in some other parts of the world, it doesn't take much planning at all.

Getting Started

An established infrastructure for walkers already exists in Britain, so everything is easy for visitors or first-timers. Most villages and country towns in areas where walking is popular have shops selling maps and local guidebooks, while the local tourist office can provide leaflets and other information. In the national parks, suggested routes or guided walks are often available. This all means you can arrive in a place for the first time, pick up some info, and within an hour you'll be walking through some of Britain's finest landscapes. No fees. No permits. No worries. It really is almost effortless.

Britain's Footpath Network

Britain is covered in a vast network of footpaths, many of which are centuries old, dating from the time when walking was the only way to get from farm to village, from village to town, from town to coast, or from valley to valley. Any walk you do today will follow these historic paths. Even Britain's longest walks simply link up many shorter paths. You'll also sometimes walk along 'bridleways', originally used for horse transport, and old unsurfaced roads called 'byways'.

Rights of Way

The absolute pleasure of walking in Britain is mostly thanks to the 'right of way' network – public paths and tracks across private property, especially in England and Wales. In Britain, nearly all land (including in national parks) is privately owned, but if there's a right of way you can follow it through fields, pastures, woods, even farmhouse yards, as long as you keep to the route and do no damage. In some mountain and moorland areas, walkers can move freely beyond the rights of way and explore at will. Known as 'freedom to roam', where permitted it's clearly advertised with markers on gates and signposts. For more information see the Access pages on www.naturalengland.org.uk.

Scotland has a different legal system, where the Scottish Outdoor Access Code (www.outdooraccess-scotland.com) allows walkers to cross most private land providing they act responsibly. There are restrictions during lambing time, bird-nesting periods and the grouse- and deer-hunting seasons.

Britain's Best Walking Areas

Although you can walk just about anywhere in Britain, some areas are better than others. Here's a rundown of favourite places, suitable for short walks of a couple of hours, or longer all-day and multi-day outings.

Britain's Coast Paths

Thanks to Britain's long-standing tradition of open access to the countryside (coupled with recent 'right to roam' laws), much of Britain's spectacular coastline is open to walkers. Several areas have dedicated long-distance trails encompassing practically the entire coastline; these include the 870-mile Wales Coast Path (www.walescoastpath.gov.uk) and the 630-mile South West Coast Path (www.southwestcoastpath.org.uk), which in 2020 will become part of the much larger 2795-mile England Coast Path (www.nationaltrail.co.uk/england-coast-path). Much – but sadly not yet all – of Scotland's coastline is also accessible; Scotland's Great Trails (www.scotlandsgreattrails.com) has advice on coastal walks, including the Ayrshire Coastal Path, Berwickshire Coastal Path, Fife Coastal Path and Moray Coast Trail.

Southern England

The chalky hills of the South Downs stride across the counties of West Sussex and East Sussex, while the New Forest in Hampshire is great for easy strolls and the nearby Isle of Wight has excellent walking options. The highest and wildest area in southern England is Dartmoor, dotted with Bronze Age remains and granite outcrops called 'tors' – looking for all the world like abstract sculptures. Exmoor has heather-covered hills cut by deep valleys and a lovely stretch of coastline, while the entire coast of the southwest peninsula from Dorset to Somerset offers dramatic walking conditions – especially along the beautiful cliff-lined shore of Cornwall.

LONG DISTANCE TRAILS

Some long-distance walking routes – such as the Pennine Way, the West Highland Way and the Pembrokeshire Coast Path – are well known and well maintained, with signposts and route-markers along the way, and are also highlighted on Ordnance Survey maps.

The most high profile of these are the national trails, usually very clearly marked on the ground and on maps – ideal for beginners or visitors from overseas (although they're easy to follow, it doesn't mean they're necessarily easy underfoot). A downside of these famous routes is that they can be crowded in holiday times, making accommodation harder to find. An upside is the great feeling of camaraderie with other walkers on the trail.

Top: Cycling in the Scottish Highlands

Bottom: Hiking to Snowdon (p720)

SIGITAS DUOBLIS/SHUTTERSTOCK ©

Central England

The gem of central England is the Cotswolds, classic English countryside with gentle paths through neat fields, mature woodland and pretty villages of honey-coloured stone. The Marches, where England borders Wales, are similarly bucolic with more good walking options. For something higher, aim for the Peak District, divided into two distinct areas: the White Peak, characterised by limestone, farmland and verdant dales, ideal for gentle strolls; and the Dark Peak, with high peaty moorlands, heather and gritstone outcrops, for more serious hikes.

Northern England

The Lake District is the heart and soul of walking in England, a wonderful area of soaring peaks, endless views, deep valleys and, of course, beautiful lakes. On the other side of the country, the rolling hills of the Yorkshire Dales make it another very popular walking area. Further north, keen walkers love the starkly beautiful hills of Northumberland National Park, while the nearby coast is less daunting but just as dramatic – perfect for wild seaside strolls.

South & Mid-Wales

The Brecon Beacons is a large range of gigantic rolling whaleback hills with broad ridges and tabletop summits, while out in the west is Pembrokeshire, a wonderful array of beaches, cliffs, islands, coves and harbours, with a hinterland of tranquil farmland and secret waterways, and a relatively mild climate year-round.

North Wales

For walkers, North Wales *is* Snowdonia, where the remains of ancient volcanoes bequeath a striking landscape of jagged peaks, sharp ridges and steep cliffs. There are challenging walks on Snowdon itself – at 1085m, the highest peak in Wales – and many more on the nearby Glyderau and Carneddau ranges, or further south around Cader Idris.

Southern & Central Scotland

This extensive region embraces several areas just perfect for keen walkers, including Ben Lomond, the best-known peak in the area, and the nearby hills of the Trossachs, lying within the Loch Lomond and The Trossachs National Park. Also here is the

splendid Isle of Arran, with a great choice of coastal rambles and high-mountain hikes.

Northern & Western Scotland

For serious walkers, heaven is the northern and western parts of Scotland, where the forces of nature have created a mountainous landscape of utter grandeur, including two of Scotland's most famous place names, Glen Coe and Ben Nevis (Britain's highest mountain at 1345m). Off the west coast lie the dramatic mountains of the Isle of Skye. Keep going north along the western coast, and things just keep getting better: it's a remote and beautiful area, sparsely populated, with scenic glens and lochs, and some of the largest, wildest and finest mountains in Britain.

> **WEATHER WATCH**
>
> While enjoying the outdoors, it's always worth remembering the fickle nature of the British weather. The countryside can appear gentle and welcoming, and often is, but sometimes conditions can turn nasty – especially on the higher ground. At any time of year, if you're walking on the hills or open moors, it's vital to be well equipped. You should carry warm and waterproof clothing (even in summer); a map and compass (that you know how to use); and drink and food, including high-energy stuff such as chocolate. If you're really going off the beaten track, leave details of your route with someone.

Cycling & Mountain Biking

A bike is the perfect mode of transport for exploring back-road Britain. Once you escape the busy main highways, a vast network of quiet country lanes winds through fields and peaceful villages, ideal for cycletouring. You can cruise through gently rolling landscapes, taking it easy and stopping for cream teas, or you can thrash all day through hilly areas, revelling in steep ascents and swooping downhill sections.

You can cycle from place to place, camping or staying in B&Bs (many of which are cyclist-friendly), or you can base yourself in one area for a few days and go out on rides in different directions. All you need is a map and a sense of adventure.

Mountain bikers can go further into the wilds on the tracks and bridleways that criss-cross Britain's hills and high moors, or head for the many dedicated mountain-bike trail centres where specially built single-tracks wind through the forests. Options at these centres vary from delightful dirt roads ideal for families to gnarly rock gardens and precipitous dropoffs for hardcore riders, all classified from green to black in ski-resort style.

www.sustrans.org.uk Details of Britain's national network of cycling trails.

www.forestry.gov.uk/england-cycling Guide to forest cycling trails in England.

www.dmbins.com Guide to mountain-biking trails in Scotland.

Surfing, SUP & Windsurfing

Britain may not seem an obvious destination for surfing, but conditions are surprisingly good and the large tidal range often means a completely different set of breaks at low and high tides. If you've come from the other side of the world, you'll be delighted to learn that summer water temperatures in southern England are roughly equivalent to winter temperatures in southern Australia (ie you'll still need a wetsuit). At the main spots, it's easy enough to hire boards and wetsuits.

Top of the list are the Atlantic-facing coasts of Cornwall and Devon (Newquay is surf central, with all the trappings from VW vans to bleached hair), and there are smaller surf scenes elsewhere, notably Pembrokeshire and the Gower in Wales, and Norfolk and Yorkshire in eastern England. Hardier souls can head for northern Scotland and the Outer Hebrides, which have some of the best and most consistent surf in Europe.

Windsurfing is hugely popular all around the coast. Top areas include Norfolk, Suffolk, Devon and Cornwall, the Isle of Wight, and the islands of Tiree, Orkney and the Outer Hebrides.

Another watersport that's growing in popularity is stand-up paddleboarding (SUP). You'll find it on offer in many coastal areas these days, as well as at a number of bays, estuaries and rivers.

www.surfinggb.com Listings of approved surf schools, courses, competitions and so on.

www.ukwindsurfing.com A good source of info.

COASTEERING

If sometimes a simple clifftop walk doesn't cut the mustard, then coasteering might appeal. It's like mountaineering, but instead of going up a mountain, you go sideways along a coast – a steep and rocky coast – with waves breaking around your feet. And if the rock gets too steep, no problem – you jump in and start swimming. Coasteering centres provide wetsuits, helmets and buoyancy aids; you provide an old pair of training shoes and a sense of adventure. The sport is available all around Britain, but the mix of sheer cliffs, sandy beaches and warmer water make Cornwall and Devon prime spots. See www.coasteering.org for info on coasteering in Devon and Cornwall.

Canoeing, Kayaking & Rafting

Britain's west coast, with its sheltered inlets, indented shoreline and countless islands, is ideal for sea kayaking, while its inland lakes and canals are great for Canadian canoeing. In addition, the turbulent spate rivers of Scotland and Wales offer some of Britain's best white-water kayaking and rafting.

Equipment rental and instruction are readily available in major centres such as Cornwall, Anglesey, the Lake District, Loch Lomond and the Isle of Skye.

www.gocanoeing.org.uk Lists approved canoeing centres in England.

www.canoescotland.org Canoe trails in Scotland.

www.ukrafting.co.uk White-water rafting in Wales.

Sailing & Boating

Scotland's west coast, with its myriad islands, superb scenery and challenging winds and tides, is widely acknowledged to be one of the finest yachting areas in the world, while the England and Wales offer a classic narrow-boating experience.

Beginners can take a Royal Yachting Association (www.rya.org.uk) training course in yachting or dinghy sailing at many sailing schools around the coast. Narrowboaters only need a quick introductory lesson at the start of their trip – for more info see www.canalholidays.com.

Skiing & Snowboarding

Britain's ski centres are all in the Scottish Highlands:

Cairngorm Mountain (www.cairngormmountain.org) 1097m; has almost 30 runs spread over an extensive area.

Glencoe (www.glencoemountain.com) 1108m; has five tows and two chairlifts.

Glenshee (www.ski-glenshee.co.uk) 920m; situated on the A93 road between Perth and Braemar; offers the largest network of lifts and the widest range of runs in Britain.

Lecht (www.lecht.co.uk) 793m; the smallest and most remote centre, on the A939 between Ballater and Grantown-on-Spey.

Nevis Range (www.nevisrange.co.uk) 1221m; near Fort William; offers the highest ski runs, the grandest setting and some of the best off-piste potential.

The high season is from January to April, but it's sometimes possible to ski from as early as November to as late as May. It's easy to turn up at the slopes, hire some kit, buy a day pass and off you go.

Weather and snow reports can be obtained from:

Ski Scotland (www.ski-scotland.com)

WinterHighland (www.winterhighland.info)

Rock Climbing

Britain has a long history of rock climbing and mountaineering, with many of the classic routes having been pioneered in

BRENDAN HOWARD/SHUTTERSTOCK ©

Snowboarding on Cairngorm Mountain (p898)

the 19th century. The main rock-climbing areas include the Scottish Highlands, the Lake District, the Peak District and North Wales, plus the sea cliffs of South Wales, Devon and Cornwall, but there are also hundreds of smaller crags situated all over the country.

Comprehensive climbing guidebooks are published by the Scottish Mountaineering Club (www.smc.org.uk), the Fell & Rock Climbing Club (www.frcc.co.uk) and the Climbers Club (www.climbers-club.co.uk).

www.ukclimbing.com Full of useful information.

Horse Riding

If you want to explore the hills and moors but walking or cycling is too much of a sweat, seeing the wilder parts of Britain from horseback is highly recommended. In rural areas and national parks like Dartmoor and Northumberland, riding centres cater to all levels of proficiency, with ponies for kids and beginners and horses for the more experienced.

www.bhs.org.uk The British Horse Society lists approved riding centres that offer day rides or longer holidays on horseback.

PLAN YOUR TRIP THE GREAT OUTDOORS

Scotch eggs

Plan Your Trip
Eat & Drink Like a Local

Britain once had a reputation for bad food, but the nation has enjoyed something of a culinary revolution in recent decades. London is recognised as having one of the best restaurant scenes in the world, while all over the country stylish eateries and gourmet gastropubs are making the most of a newfound passion for quality local produce.

The Year in Food

Best in Spring (March–May)

Spring brings fresh asparagus, new potatoes (notably Jersey Royals), pink rhubarb and tender lamb.

Best in Summer (June–August)

Strawberries, raspberries and other soft fruits are in season along with salad vegetables such as lettuce and radishes, and seafood such as scallops, langoustines, mackerel and cod.

Best in Autumn (September–November)

Apples and blackberries (often cooked together in a crumble), game including venison and wood pigeon, and shellfish – oysters, mussels and cockles. Also the main season for food festivals.

Best in Winter (December–February)

Sweet chestnuts (roasted on an open fire), and that classic Christmas combination of goose, root vegetables and Brussels sprouts.

Food Experiences

Meals of a Lifetime

Dinner by Heston Blumenthal (p127) Crazy flavours; madcap presentation. Heston's still the master.

Le Manoir aux Quat'Saisons (p197) Raymond Blanc's legendary Oxfordshire restaurant is a hymn to classic French cookery.

Ynyshir Hall (p697) Molecular gastronomy at this former royal retreat near Machynlleth.

Restaurant James Sommerin (p649) Trek across the river from Cardiff for supersophisticated fine dining.

Ninth Wave (p868) At the end of Mull, with great atmosphere and ethos.

Midsummer House (p374) Daniel Clifford's double-Michelin-starred restaurant is Cambridge's finest.

Cheap Treats

Bacon sandwich The breakfast of champions. Debate rages over the choice of sauce – red (tomato ketchup) or brown (spicy pickled fruit sauce).

Beans on toast A comforting childhood classic of tinned baked beans poured over buttered toast, served in many cafes as a breakfast or lunch dish.

Fish and chips The nation's favourite takeaway meal, served in hundreds of chip shops all over the country.

Cockles A classic seaside snack that has been enjoyed by generations of British holidaymakers, sprinkled with vinegar and eaten from a cardboard tub with a wooden fork.

Scotch egg This masterpiece of culinary engineering consists of a hardboiled egg wrapped in sausage meat, coated in breadcrumbs and deep-fried.

Dare to Try

Haggis Scotland's national dish is made from the chopped heart, liver and lungs of a sheep, mixed with oatmeal and onion, and wrapped in the sheep's stomach (or often an artificial casing).

Tripe Cow's stomach lining, traditionally poached in milk with onions. A wartime staple, but hard to find in restaurants today – though it's making a comeback.

Stinking Bishop Britain's most pungent cheese, made in Gloucestershire and redolent of old socks. Available from Harrods in London, and many specialist cheese shops.

Jellied eels Traditional London side dish that can still be found in the capital's pie and mash shops.

Black pudding Large sausage made from ground meat, offal, fat and blood, served for breakfast.

Local Specialities

Scotland

Scotland may be most famous for haggis, but seafood is where it excels. Fresh lobster, langoustine, salmon and scallops are the favourites of restaurant menus, but look out for traditional dishes such as Arbroath smokies (hot-smoked haddock) and Cullen skink (soup made with smoked haddock, onion, butter and milk). Oats have been a mainstay of the Scottish diet for centuries, appearing in the form of porridge and oatcakes, but also as a coating for fried trout or herring, and in the classic Scottish dessert known as cranachan (whipped cream flavoured with whisky and mixed with raspberries and toasted oatmeal).

Whisky (always spelt without an 'e' – whiskey with an 'e' is Irish or American) has been distilled in Scotland at least since the 15th century and probably much longer. Traditionally, Scots drink their whisky neat, or with a little water added. To appreciate the aroma and flavour to the utmost, a measure of malt whisky should be cut (diluted) with one-third to two-thirds as much spring water. At a bar, older Scots may order a 'half' or 'nip' of whisky as a chaser to a pint or half-pint of beer (called a 'hauf and a hauf').

A final word of warning: when ordering a dram in Scotland remember to ask simply for a 'whisky' – only the English and other foreigners say 'Scotch'. After all, what else would you be served in Scotland?

Wales

Tender and tasty Welsh lamb is sought after by restaurateurs all over Britain, but it also appears in the rustic local dish known as cawl (pronounced cowl) – a one-pot stew of lamb, bacon, cabbage, potato and swede. Better known is laverbread, which is not bread but seaweed, cooked with oatmeal and often served for breakfast with toast and bacon. Sweet-toothed visitors should look out for Welsh cakes (fruity

Whisky from Macallan distillery (p855)

griddle scones) and bara brith (a dense and spicy fruit cake flavoured with tea and marmalade).

Although it may not have a 'national drink' in the way that Scotland has whisky and England has ale, Wales happily partakes of both, and also produces its own real ales. Felinfoel is its oldest brewery, founded in 1878, while Newport's Tiny Rebel brewery, one of its newest, won Camra's Champion Beer of Britain award in 2015. There's also a Welsh whisky, produced by Penderyn Distillery (p689).

The Midlands

The Leicestershire town of Melton Mowbray is famed for its pork pies, always eaten cold, ideally with pickle. Only pies handmade in the eponymous town can carry the Melton Mowbray moniker – in the same way that only fizzy wine from the Champagne region of France can carry that name.

Another British speciality from this region that enjoys the same protection is Stilton – a strong white cheese, either plain or blue vein. Only five dairies in all of Britain (four of which are in Derbyshire)

Vegetarian nut roast with Yorkshire pudding

are allowed to name the cheese they produce Stilton. Bizarrely, the cheese cannot be made in the village of Stilton in Cambridgeshire, although this is where it was first sold – hence the name.

Bakewell pudding (not 'Bakewell tart' as it's sometimes called) features regularly on local dessert menus and is certainly worth sampling. It is named after the Derbyshire town where it originated in 1860, and consists of a pastry base topped with jam, egg custard and almond paste.

Northern England

The northeast of England is known for its kippers (smoked herring), traditionally grilled with butter and served for breakfast with toast and marmalade on the side, and for pease pudding (a thick stew of yellow split peas cooked in ham stock). The northwest lays claim to Lancashire hotpot (slow-cooked stew of lamb and onion topped with sliced potatoes), Eccles cakes (rounds of flaky pastry filled with currants), and Cumberland sausage (a spiral-shaped pork sausage flavoured with herbs). But the most famous of northern specialities is Yorkshire pudding, a light

and puffy batter pudding usually served as a side dish with roast beef, that's now been adopted all over Britain.

Another pudding hailing from the north is black pudding, effectively a large sausage made from ground meat, offal, fat and blood, and traditionally served for breakfast. It's known in other countries as 'blood sausage', but the British version has a high content of oatmeal so that it doesn't fall apart in the pan when fried.

Beer is England's national drink, and so-called 'real ale' – made using only natural ingredients, and allowed to mature in the cask (you'll see signs promoting 'cask-conditioned' ales) – is the country's pride and joy. It is brewed all over the country, but the north (and particularly Yorkshire) is home to many iconic brews, including Theakstons, Samuel Smith and Timothy Taylor (check out www.camra.org.uk).

Southwest England

Cows reared on the rich pastures of Devon and Cornwall create some of Britain's finest dairy produce, notably the famous clotted cream (a very thick cream made by heating full-cream milk) that forms an essential component of Cornish cream teas. Less refined but equally tasty are Cornish pasties (crimped pastry parcels containing a mix of beef and vegetables), once the lunchtime staple of miners and farm workers.

Fish and shellfish are also highlights here: there are sizeable fishing fleets at Newlyn (in west Cornwall) and Brixham (in Devon), supplemented by smaller boats at many other coastal villages. Together they haul in some of the UK's finest fish, much of which is transported upcountry to top tables in the major cities.

The alcoholic beverage traditionally associated with the southwest is cider, made with fermented apple juice. As with beer, there has been a renaissance of independent brewers producing small batches of craft cider (see www.real-cider.co.uk).

London & Southeast England

Two old-school London specialities are worth trying, if only for bragging rights – pie and mash, and jellied eels. The staple menu of working-class Londoners since the 19th century, the former consists of a small pie filled with minced beef served with mashed potato and 'liquor' – a parsley-rich gravy made from the stock in which eels have been cooked. The eels are cooled and set in the jellied stock, and served as a side dish with malt vinegar – try them out at **M Manze** (www.manze.co.uk; 87 Tower Bridge Rd, London, SE1; mains £4.30; ◷11am-2pm Mon, 10.30am-2pm Tue-Thu, 10am-2.15pm Fri, to 2.45pm Sat; ⊖Borough) or Poppies (p128).

Oysters today have an expensive reputation, but in the 19th century they were a cheap and plentiful foodstuff, eaten by all. Whitstable oysters, from Kent – the native British species, unlike the more common, farmed Pacific oysters – have been harvested since Roman times, and still grace the tables of London restaurants and oyster bars.

A new breed of microbreweries has sprung up all over Britain in the last decade, producing their own varieties of traditional and innovative brews, usually referred to as 'craft beers'. London is home to no fewer than 75 of them – check out www.craftbeerlondon.com.

How to Eat & Drink

When to Eat

Breakfast Served in most hotels and B&Bs between 7am and 9am, or perhaps 8am to 10am on weekends. In cafes, the breakfast menu might extend to 11am through the week. For many visitors, the first meal of the day is what's known as the 'Full English Breakfast' – aka Full Welsh, Scottish, Yorkshire etc – a plateful of fried food that might shock if you're expecting just a bowl of cereal. But it can fuel several hours of energetic sightseeing.

Lunch Generally taken between noon and 2pm, and can range from a sandwich and a bag of crisps to a three-course meal with wine. Many restaurants offer a set menu two-course lunch at competitive prices on weekdays, while cafes often have a daily lunch special, or offer soup and a sandwich.

Afternoon tea A tradition inherited from the British aristocracy and eagerly adopted by the middle classes, a between-meals snack now enjoying a revival in country hotels and upmarket tearooms. It consists of dainty sandwiches, cakes and pastries, plus, of course, a cup of tea, poured from a silver teapot and sipped politely from fine china cups.

Dinner Sometimes called supper, the main meal of the day is usually served in restaurants between 6pm and 9pm, and consists of two or three courses – starter, main and dessert.

CLASSIC BRITISH CHEESES

Cheddar Sharp and savoury, Britain's most popular cheese originates in Somerset but is now made all over the country (and, indeed, the world).

Stilton A pungent blue cheese, traditionally eaten after dinner with a glass of port.

Wensleydale Crumbly white cheese from Yorkshire, with a mild, honeyed flavour.

Caerphilly From the Welsh town of the same name, this hard, salty cheese has an annual festival dedicated to it.

Cornish Yarg A rich, creamy cheese characterised by its wrapping of nettle leaves.

Caboc A Highland Scottish cream cheese rolled in oatmeal, whose recipe is more than 500 years old.

BRITISH BOOZE

There's no doubt about it: the British like a drink, preferably consumed in an old, classic country pub, although these days, many craft breweries and distilleries cater for more modern tastes.

Beer Traditional British beer is more properly known as ale or bitter. It is served at room temperature, and is nearly always flat, unlike lager. It ranges in colour from light amber to dark brown, and in taste from sweet and floral to hoppy and bitter. The best quality is 'cask ale', served straight from the barrel.

Cider Served either sweet and dry. Like ale, the best are served straight from the barrel, but be warned – cider can be very alcoholic, often 10% ABV or more (nearly as strong as wine).

Spirits Whisky is the best-known tipple: the very best single malts come from Scotland's Speyside distilleries. Unsurprisingly for a nation of sailors, gin is another old and very popular British spirit.

Sunday lunch Another great British tradition. Sunday is the one day of the week when the British make lunch the main event. It's normally served between noon and 4pm. Many pubs and restaurants offer Sunday lunch, where the main course usually consists of roast beef, lamb or pork, accompanied by roast and mashed potatoes, gravy, and boiled vegetables such as carrots and peas.

Where to Eat

Cafes Traditional cafes are simple eateries serving simple food – sandwiches, pies, sausage and chips. Quality varies enormously: some cafes definitely earn their 'greasy spoon' handle, while others are neat and clean.

Tearooms The tearoom is a British institution, serving cakes, scones and sandwiches accompanied by pots of tea (though coffee is usually available, too). Upmarket tearooms may also serve afternoon tea.

Coffee shops In most cities and towns you'll also find coffee shops – both independents and international chains – serving decent lattes, cappuccinos and espressos, and continental-style snacks such as bagels, panini and ciabattas.

Restaurants London has scores of excellent restaurants that could hold their own in major cities worldwide, while eating places in other British cities can give the capital a run for its money (often for rather less money).

Pubs Many British pubs serve a wide range of food, and it's often a good-value option whether you want a toasted sandwich between museum visits in London, or a three-course meal in the evening after touring the castles of Wales.

Gastropubs The quality of food in some pubs is now so high that they have created a whole new genre of eatery – the gastropub. The finest are almost restaurants (a few have been awarded Michelin stars), but others go for a more relaxed atmosphere.

Plan Your Trip

Travel with Children

Britain is ideal for travelling with children because of its compact size, packing a lot of attractions into a small area. So when the kids in the back of the car ask 'Are we there yet?', your answer can often be 'Yes, we are'.

Best Regions for Kids

London

The capital has children's attractions galore; many are free.

Devon & Cornwall

Lovely beaches and reliable weather, though crowded in summer.

Lake District & Cumbria

Zip wires and kayaks for teens; boat rides and Beatrix Potter for youngsters; fell walks for everyone.

Oxford & the Cotswolds

Oxford has Harry Potter connections; the Cotswolds is ideal for little-leg strolls.

The Midlands

Caverns and 'show caves', plus former railways that are now traffic-free cycle routes.

Wales

Long coast of beaches, and pony trekking in the hill country. Plus loads of castles...

Southern Scotland

Edinburgh and Glasgow have kid-friendly museums; the Southern Uplands offer great mountain biking for a range of skill levels.

Scottish Highlands & Islands

Hardy teenagers plunge into outdoor activities; dolphin-spotting boat trips are fun for all the family.

Great Britain for Kids

Many places of interest cater for kids as much as adults. At historic castles, for example, mum and dad can admire the medieval architecture, while the kids will have great fun striding around the battlements. In the same way, many national parks and holiday resorts organise specific activities for children. It goes without saying that everything ramps up in the school holidays.

Bargain Hunting

Most visitor attractions offer family tickets – usually two adults plus two children – for less than the sum of the individual entrance charges. Most offer cheaper rates for solo parents and kids, too. Be sure to ask, as these are not always clearly displayed.

On the Road

If you're going by public transport, trains are great for families: intercity services have plenty of room for luggage and extra stuff like buggies (strollers), and the kids can move about a bit when bored. In contrast, they need to stay in their seats on long-distance coaches. Many train companies offer family train tickets on certain routes, and if you're doing a lot of train travel, it might be worth picking up a Family & Friends Railcard. It costs £30 and gives 33% off adult fares and 60% off children's fares for a year.

If you're hiring a car, most (but not all) rental firms can provide child seats – but you'll need to check this in advance. Most will not actually fit the child seats; you need to do that yourself, for insurance reasons.

Highlights for Kids
Best Fresh-Air Fun

If the kids tire of castles and museums, you're never far from a place for outdoor activities to blow away the cobwebs.

Wildlife Cruises, Scotland's west coast (p864) What child could resist a boat trip to see seals, porpoises and dolphins, maybe even a whale?

Puzzlewood, Forest of Dean (p222) Wonderful woodland playground with mazy paths, weird rock formations and eerie passageways.

Whinlatter Forest Park, Cumbria (p589) Highlights include a Go Ape adventure park and excellent mountain-bike trails, plus live video feeds from red-squirrel cams.

Whitby Coastal Cruises, Yorkshire (p504) If you're lucky, you'll spot minke, sei and fin whales off the north coast.

Bewilderwood, Norfolk (p393) Zip wires, jungle bridges, tree houses, marsh walks, boat trips, mazes and all sorts of old-fashioned outdoor adventure.

Lyme Regis, Dorset (p282) Guided tours to find your very own prehistoric fossil.

Tissington Trail, Derbyshire (p468) Cycling this former railway is fun and almost effortless. You can hire kids' bikes, tandems and trailers. Don't forget to hoot in the tunnels!

7Stanes Glentress, Peebles (p812) The busiest of Southern Scotland's well-run mountain-biking centres.

Best Hands-On Action

Please do not touch? No chance. Here are some places where grubby fingers and enquiring minds are positively welcomed.

Science Museum, London (p103) Seven floors of educational exhibits at the mother of all science museums.

Enginuity, Ironbridge (p433) Endless hands-on displays at the birthplace of the Industrial Revolution.

National Railway Museum, York (p485) Clambering into the driver's cab on a steam locomotive, exploring a Royal Mail train, taking part in engineering demonstrations...it's all here.

National Waterfront Museum, Swansea (p658) Great interactive family fun.

Discovery Museum, Newcastle (p610) Tyneside's rich history on display; highlights include a buzzers-and-bells science maze.

Riverside Museum, Glasgow (p801) Top-class interactive museum with a focus on transport.

Jorvik Viking Centre, York (p486) Excellent smells-and-all Viking settlement reconstruction.

Thinktank, Birmingham (p403) Every display comes with a button or a lever at this 'edutaining' science museum.

National Space Centre, Leicester (p456) Spacesuits, zero-gravity toilets and mini-astronaut training – guaranteed to boost little brains.

Best Rainy-Day Distractions

For those inevitable gloomy days, head for the indoor attractions; don't forget the nation's great collection of museums. Alternatively, try outdoor stuff like coasteering in Pembrokeshire or canyoning in the Lake District. It's always fun – wet or dry.

DINING WITH KIDS

When it comes to refuelling, most cafes and teashops are child-friendly. Restaurants are mixed: some offer high chairs and kiddy portions; others firmly say 'no children after 6pm'.

Children under 18 are usually not allowed in pubs serving just alcohol. Pubs also serving meals generally allow children of any age (with their parents) in England and Wales, but in Scotland they must be over 14 and must leave by 8pm. If in doubt, simply ask the bar staff.

And finally, a word on another kind of refuelling: Britain is still slightly buttoned up about breastfeeding. Older folks may tut-tut a bit if you give junior a top-up in public, but if done modestly it's usually considered OK.

Legoland Windsor

Cadbury World, Birmingham (p404) Dentists may cry, but kids love the story of chocolate. And yes, there are free samples.

Real Mary King's Close, Edinburgh (p749) Take a guided tour of the haunted vaults beneath the medieval Old Town.

Cheddar Gorge Caves, Somerset (p256) Finally nail the difference between stalactites and stalagmites in the West Country's deep caverns.

Underground Passages, Exeter (p303) Explore medieval catacombs – the only system of its kind open to the public in England.

National Science & Media Museum, Bradford (p521) Attractions include a TV studio where you can film yourself, a gallery of 1980s video games (yes, you can play them) and an IMAX cinema.

Honister Slate Mine, Lake District (p593) Explore the dingy depths of a former Lakeland slate mine.

Best Stealth Learning

Secretly exercise their minds while the little darlings think they are 'just' having fun.

We the Curious, Bristol (p238) One of the best interactive science museums in England, covering space, technology and the human brain.

Centre for Alternative Technology, Machynlleth (p697) Educational, fun and truly green – great for curious kids.

Natural History Museum, London (p99) Animals everywhere! Highlights include the life-size blue whale and the animatronics dinosaurs.

Glasgow Science Centre (p801) Bringing science and technology alive through hundreds of engaging exhibits.

Kielder Observatory, Northumberland National Park (p628) Attend a stargazing session at this Northumbrian astronomy centre.

National Marine Aquarium, Plymouth (p315) Gaze into the shark tank at the UK's biggest aquarium.

Best for All the Family

Sometimes a good dose of old-fashioned family fun is in order – so here are a few of our favourite days out that everyone will enjoy.

Legoland Windsor (www.legoland.co.uk; Winkfield Rd, Windsor; £47-60; ⊙open early Mar-Oct, daily in Easter holidays & late May-early Sep, less frequently otherwise, 10am-6pm in July & Aug, usually 10am-5pm otherwise) Huge Lego models and thrilling rides galore – but be prepared to queue.

Alton Towers, Staffordshire (p421) Arguably the UK's best – and certainly most popular – theme park, with a riot of roller coasters and other rides to try.

Warner Bros Studio Tour: The Making of Harry Potter, Leavesden (p224) Step behind the scenes at the Leavesden studio where the films were shot.

Warwick Castle (p413) Jousting tournaments, trebuchet launches and waxworks bring medieval times to life.

Eden Project, Cornwall (p348) Learn about all manner of environmental matters in Cornwall's spectacular space-age greenhouse.

Longleat, Wiltshire (p291) Pretend you're driving across the savannah at this Wiltshire country estate, surrounded by rhinos, giraffes, elephants and lions.

Stirling Castle (p827) Arguably the quintessential Scottish castle – good for big and little kids alike.

Planning
When to Go

The best time for families to visit Britain is pretty much the best time for everyone else: from April/May to the end of September. It's worth avoiding August – the heart of school summer holidays – when prices go up and roads are busy, especially near the coast. Other school holidays are the two weeks around Easter Sunday, and mid-December to early January, plus three week-long 'half-term' breaks – usually late February (or early March), late May and late October.

> **BABY CHANGING**
>
> Most museums and other attractions in Britain usually have good baby-changing facilities (cue old joke: I swapped mine for a nice souvenir). Elsewhere, some city-centre public toilets have baby-changing areas, although these can be a bit grimy; your best bet for clean facilities is an upmarket department store. On the road, baby-changing facilities are generally bearable at motorway service stations and OK at out-of-town supermarkets.

Accommodation

Some hotels welcome kids (with their parents) and provide cots, toys and babysitting services, while others maintain an adult atmosphere. Many B&Bs offer 'family suites' of two adjoining bedrooms with one bathroom, and an increasing number of hostels (YHA, SYHA and independent) have family rooms with four or six beds – some even with private bathroom attached. If you want to stay in one place for a while, renting a holiday cottage is ideal. Camping is very popular with British families, and there are lots of fantastic campsites, but you'll usually need all your own gear.

Resources

For all-round information and advice, check out Lonely Planet's *Travel with Children*.

Baby Goes 2 (www.babygoes2.com) Advice, tips and encouragement (and a stack of adverts) for families on holiday.

MumsNet (www.mumsnet.com) No-nonsense advice on travel and more from a vast network of UK mothers.

Regions at a Glance

From the multicultural melting pot of London to the remote islands of the Outer Hebrides, Britain's regions offer a kaleidoscope of classic experiences. Southern England is where you'll find the archetypal English countryside of lush meadows, thatched cottages and games of cricket on the village green. The southwestern counties of Devon and Cornwall are wilder in nature, known for their surf beaches and seafood restaurants. Lovers of mountain scenery will be spoilt for choice in the Scottish Highlands, the Lake District and North Wales, while those who prefer gritty industrial heritage and lively nightlife will enjoy the northern English cities of Manchester, Liverpool and Newcastle. And bang in the middle is Yorkshire, with everything from the gorgeous city of York to the rolling moors of the Yorkshire Dales.

London

History
Entertainment
Museums

Tales of London

The echoes of the footfalls of monarchs, poets, whores and saints can still be detected in places like the Tower of London, Westminster Abbey and St Paul's Cathedral, as well as the pubs that once served Dickens, Shelley and Byron.

Showtime

From West End theatres to East End clubs, from Camden's rock venues to Covent Garden's opera house, from tennis at Wimbledon, cricket at Lord's or football at Wembley, London's venues offer entertainment galore.

Museums & Galleries

While the British Museum is the crowd-puller, the capital has museums and galleries of every shape and size – from big hitters such as the V&A and Natural History Museum to little gems like the Sir John Soane's Museum.

p68

Canterbury & Southeast England

Architecture
History
Coast

Canterbury Cathedral

Canterbury Cathedral is one of the finest cathedrals in Europe, and one of the holiest places in Christendom. Write your own Canterbury tale as you explore its chapels, cloisters and crypts.

Invasion Heritage

The southeast has always been a gateway for Continental arrivals. Castles and fortresses, the 1066 battlefield and Dover's wartime tunnels tell of invasion and defence.

Brighton & the South Coast

An hour south of the capital, Brighton has long been known for its offbeat character, with its quirky shops, pebble beaches and landmark pier. Further afield, Hastings, Rye, Whitstable and Margate all have their own salty seaside charm.

p151

Oxford & the Cotswolds

Architecture
Stately Homes
Villages

Oxford Colleges

Oxford's incredible architecture can't fail to impress, whether you gaze across the 'dreaming spires' from the top of Carfax Tower, or explore the medieval streets on foot.

Blenheim Palace

Favoured by the rich and powerful for centuries, this region is scattered with some of the finest country houses in Britain. Top of the pile is the baroque masterpiece of Blenheim Palace, birthplace of Sir Winston Churchill.

The Cotswolds

Littered with picturesque 'chocolate box' scenes of honey-coloured stone cottages, thatched roofs, neat greens and cobbled lanes, the villages of the Cotswolds provide a charming snapshot of rural England.

p185

Bath & Southwest England

Coastline
History
Activities

Beaches

Devon and Cornwall are famous for their beaches, from the rocky cliffs of Kynance Cove and Crackington Haven to the golden sands of Gwithian, Perranporth, Bantham, Woolacombe and Saunton Sands.

Ancient Architecture

The southwest countryside is littered with crumbling castles, abandoned tin mines, ancient hill forts and mysterious stone circles that speak of thousands of years of human history – and don't forget Bath's eponymous Roman baths.

Hiking & Surfing

If you like to take it nice and easy, come to walk the moors or tootle along cycle trails. If you prefer life fast and furious, come to surf the best waves in England.

p231

Cambridge & East Anglia

Architecture
Coastline
Waterways

Historic Churches

From the magnificent cathedrals of Ely, Norwich and Peterborough to Cambridge's King's College Chapel and Trinity's Great Court, East Anglia's architectural splendour is second to none.

Seaside Resorts

With wide sandy beaches, great seafood, delightful old pubs, globally important bird reserves, historic villages and classic seaside resorts such as Southwold and Cromer, the coastline of East Anglia is rich and varied.

The Broads

The Norfolk and Suffolk Broads is a tranquil area of lakes and rivers, and an ideal spot for boating, birding, canoeing, cycling or walking, or just getting back to nature at a leisurely pace.

p360

Birmingham & the Midlands

Activities
Stately Homes
Food & Drink

Hiking & Biking

The Peak District National Park, Cannock Chase, the Shropshire Hills, the Roaches, the Malvern Hills, Offa's Dyke Path, the Tissington Trail and the Pennine Cycleway all make this region great for hiking and biking.

Aristocratic Architecture

Grand houses like Haddon Hall, Burghley House and especially Chatsworth promise sprawling deer-filled grounds, grand interiors full and walls dripping with oil paintings.

Curry Capital

Foodies take note: Birmingham is the curry capital of the country (and, increasingly, a magnet for Michelin-starred chefs), while the tiny town of Ludlow is an epicentre of gastronomic exploration.

p399

Yorkshire

Scenery
Food & Drink
History

National Parks

It's known as 'God's own country' for a reason: Yorkshire's landscapes are breathtaking, from its rolling hills and lonely crags to its wild moorland. It's home to two national parks – the Yorkshire Dales and the North York Moors – offering epic hiking, rock climbing and cycling.

Beer

Yorkshire's breweries turn out some of Britain's best real ales, which can readily be sampled in any of the county's traditional pubs. Just don't be surprised when the beers are served warm!

Abbeys & Industry

Several different historical narratives run through Yorkshire: York's Viking heritage, the ancient abbeys of Rievaulx, Fountains and Whitby and the Industrial Revolution in Leeds, Bradford and Sheffield.

p479

Manchester, Liverpool & Northwest England

History
Sport
Seaside Resorts

Museums

The northwest's heritage sites, from the wonderful People's History Museum in Manchester to the International Slavery Museum in Liverpool, are testament to the region's rich history and ability to keep it alive.

Football

Two cities, Liverpool and Manchester, give the world four famous clubs, including the two most successful in English history. The National Football Museum in Manchester is just another reason for fans to visit this region.

Blackpool

The epitome of the classic English seaside resort just keeps on going, thanks to the rides of the Pleasure Beach amusement park, where adrenalin junkies can always find a fix.

p533

The Lake District & Cumbria

Scenery
Activities
Literature

Lakes & Mountains

The Lake District National Park is the most mountainous part of England, home to Scafell and countless scenic lakes. Some are big and famous, while others are small and hidden.

Fell Walking

If anywhere is the heart and soul of walking in England, it's the Lake District. Casual strollers find gentle routes through foothills and valleys, while serious hikers tackle higher peaks, known locally as fells.

Literary Lakeland

Countless writers and artists have been inspired by the Lakeland scenery – most famously William Wordsworth and Beatrix Potter, whose former homes are now among the Lake District's most popular sights.

p568

Newcastle & Northeast England

History
Landscape
Castles

Hadrian's Wall

One of the world's premier Roman sites, this potent symbol of imperial power strides for over 70 miles across the neck of England, from Tyneside to the Solway Firth. You can travel its length, stopping off at forts along the way.

Northumberland National Park

If it's widescreen vistas you're after, the broad moors, stone villages and expansive views of England's most northerly national park never fail to please.

Alnwick Castle

Northumberland is dotted with some of Britain's finest castles, including the coastal fortresses of Bamburgh and Dunstanburgh, but Alnwick – setting for the Harry Potter movies – is the most famous.

p606

Cardiff, Pembrokeshire & South Wales

Architecture
Coastline
Castles

Victorian Revival

From the whimsical, fairy-tale structures of Cardiff Castle and Castell Coch to the elegant shopping arcades of the city centre, the Welsh capital has plenty to keep fans of Victorian architecture interested.

Pembrokeshire & The Gower

South Wales boasts two of Britain's most beautiful stretches of coast – the Gower Peninsula and Pembrokeshire – offering clifftop walks, family-friendly beaches, surfing hot spots and watery adventures.

Carreg Cennen

South Wales has some of the country's best castles, including Chepstow and Pembroke, but remote Carreg Cennen, is the most spectacularly positioned of them all.

p639

Brecon Beacons & Mid-Wales

Wildlife
Local Culture
Food & Drink

Red Kites

In the mountains and moors of the Brecon Beacons and many other parts of the region you can spot birds of prey – most famously the once-rare red kites, most easily spotted at feeding stations such as Gigrin Farm in Rhayader.

Market Towns

From book-obsessed Hay-on-Wye to quirky Llanwrtyd Wells and quaint Llandrindod Wells, the market towns of Mid-Wales are full of charm.

Abergavenny

Restaurants, inns and gastropubs throughout the region are at the forefront of a new Welsh gastronomy, all focused on the nation's foodie capital at Abergavenny.

p679

Snowdonia & North Wales

Mountains
Industrial Heritage
Coastline

Snowdonia

The wildest mountain scenery outside Scotland can be found in this wonderful national park, where the mountains stay snow-capped well into spring. A key target is Snowdon, Wales' highest mountain, but there are countless other peaks to seek out, too.

Seaside Resorts

From the north coast's popular resort towns to the surf spots and quiet bays of Anglesey and the Llŷn Peninsula, North Wales has plenty of beach to go round.

Welsh Slate

Welsh slate once roofed much of the world, and the region's quarries bear witness to the lives of workers, while rejuvenated railways now shunt tourists through spectacular terrain.

p704

Edinburgh

Culture
History
Food & Drink

Festival City

Dubbed the Athens of the North, the Scottish capital is a city of art and literature, home to the world's biggest arts festival. Outside festival time, there's plenty to enjoy in the city's many theatres and world-class art galleries and museums.

Edinburgh Castle

Perched on a brooding black crag overlooking the city centre, Edinburgh Castle has played a pivotal role in Scottish history, the focus of the nation's capital city since medieval times.

Scottish Cuisine

Edinburgh has more restaurants per head of population than any city in the UK, while Scottish cuisine has been given a makeover by inventive chefs using top-quality local produce.

p745

Glasgow & Southern Scotland

Museums
Historic Buildings
Stately Homes

Kelvingrove Art Gallery & Museum

Glasgow's mercantile and industrial history has left the city with a wonderful legacy of museums and art galleries, dominated by the grand Victorian cathedral of culture that is Kelvingrove.

The Border Abbeys

Rolling countryside and ruined abbeys are the big draws along the country's southern border, where you'll find the Gothic ruins of Melrose, Jedburgh and Dryburgh abbeys.

Dumfries House

This region is rich in Adam brothers'- designed mansions such as Culzean Castle and Floors Castle, but the almost perfectly preserved Chippendale time-capsule Dumfries House takes top place.

p789

Stirling & Central Scotland

Castles
Islands
Whisky

Stirling Castle

Central and northeast Scotland are home to the greatest concentration of castles in the country, from the turreted exuberance of Craigievar to the more restrained elegance of Balmoral, but topped by the regal splendour of Stirling.

Island-Hopping

Island-hopping is a great way to explore Scotland's western seaboard, and the islands of this region – wild Jura, scenic Mull and the jewel of Iona – provide a brilliant introduction.

Speyside Distilleries

No trip to Scotland is complete without a visit to a whisky distillery – the Speyside region and the isle of Islay are epicentres of the industry.

p826

Inverness & the Highlands & Islands

Activities
Scenery
History

Hill Walking

Between them, the Cairngorm resort of Aviemore, gateway to snow sports and wild hill walking, and Fort William, self-styled outdoor capital of the UK, offer enough adventure to keep you busy for a year.

Lochs & Glens

Landscape photographers are spoilt for choice, with classic views ranging from the mountain beauty of Glen Coe and the snow-patched summits of the Cairngorms to the rock pinnacles of the Cuillin Hills.

Prehistoric Sites

The region is rich in prehistoric remains, including the standing stones of Callanish, the neolithic tomb of Maeshowe, and Skara Brae – Europe's best-preserved prehistoric village.

p884

On the Road

England

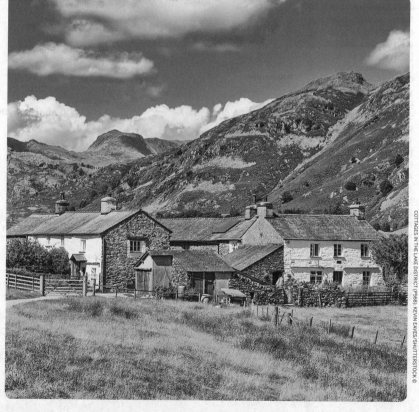

England Highlights

1 Stonehenge (p289) Marvelling at Britain's most iconic archaeological site.

2 Oxford (p187) Getting some higher education among the dreaming spires of this university town.

3 The Lake District (p572) Wandering lonely as a cloud in idyllic Lakeland.

4 York (p483) Exploring medieval walls, Viking sights and the soaring Gothic minster.

5 Bath (p245) Being a Jane Austen character for a day while exploring Roman and Georgian architecture.

6 The Cotswolds (p201) Falling in love with impossibly quaint villages.

7 Hadrian's Wall (p622) Seeing wild scenery and ancient engineering.

8 Cambridge (p364) Punting past historic colleges along the River Cam.

9 Liverpool (p551) Visiting the iconic Beatles sites and top museums along the waterfront.

10 Stratford-upon-Avon (p415) Catching a Shakespeare play or visiting the Bard's grave.

London

Best Places to Eat

➜ Hook Camden Town (p131)

➜ Glasshouse (p133)

➜ Ottolenghi (p131)

➜ Ledbury (p133)

➜ Five Fields (p129)

➜ Dinner by Heston Blumenthal (p129)

Best Places to Stay

➜ Qbic (p124)

➜ citizenM Tower of London (p123)

➜ Hoxton Hotel (p124)

➜ Main House (p125)

➜ Hazlitt's (p122)

➜ 40 Winks (p124)

Why Go?

One of the world's most visited cities, London has something for everyone: history, culture, fine food and endless good times. Immersed in history, London's rich seams of eye-opening antiquity are everywhere, with landmarks like the Tower of London, Westminster Abbey and Big Ben. Then there are modern icons like the Shard and the Tate Modern. But London is also a city of ideas and the imagination – whether it's theatrical innovation, contemporary art, music, writing, cutting-edge design or culinary adventure. Throw in charming parks, historic neighbourhoods, leafy suburbs and tranquil riverbanks and you have, quite simply, one of the world's great metropolises.

When to Go

➜ London is a place that you can visit any time of the year. That said, different months and seasons boast different charms.

➜ Spring in the city sees daffodils in bloom and blossom in the trees.

➜ In June, the parks are filled with people, there's Trooping the Colour, summer arts festivals, Field Day in Brockwell Park, other music events, gay pride and Wimbledon.

➜ Although the days are getting shorter, autumn in London is alive with festivals celebrating literature, the arts and culture.

➜ London in December is all about Christmas lights on Oxford and Regent Sts, and perhaps a whisper of snow.

History

London first came into being as a Celtic village near a ford across the River Thames, but the city only really took off after the Roman conquest in AD 43. The invaders enclosed their 'Londinium' in walls that still find refrain in the shape of the City (with a capital 'C') of London today.

By the end of the 3rd century AD, Londinium was home to some 30,000 people. Internal strife and relentless barbarian attacks wore the Romans down, however, and they abandoned Britain in the 5th century, reducing the settlement to a sparsely populated backwater. The Saxons moved in next, their 'Lundenwic' prospering and becoming a large, well-organised town.

As the city grew in importance, it caught the eye of Danish Vikings who launched numerous invasions. In 1016 the Saxons, finally beaten down, were forced to accept the Danish leader Knut (Canute) as King of England, after which London replaced Winchester as capital. In 1042, the throne reverted to the Saxon Edward the Confessor, who built Westminster Abbey.

The Norman Conquest of 1066 saw William the Conqueror march into London, where he was crowned king. He built the White Tower (the core of the Tower of London), negotiated taxes with the merchants, and affirmed the city's right to self-government. From then until the late 15th century, London politics were largely taken up by a three-way power struggle between the monarchy, the Church and city guilds.

An uneasy political compromise was reached between the factions, and the city expanded rapidly in the 16th century under the House of Tudor. In a rerun of the disease that wiped out half of London's population between 1348 and 1350, the Great Plague struck in 1665, and by the time the winter cold arrested the epidemic, 100,000 Londoners had perished.

The cataclysm was followed by further devastation when the Great Fire of 1666 sent the city skywards. One upshot of the conflagration was a blank canvas for master architect Sir Christopher Wren to build his magnificent churches. Despite these setbacks, London continued to grow, and by 1700 it was Europe's largest city, with 600,000 people. An influx of foreign workers brought expansion to the east and south, while those who could afford it headed to the more salubrious environs of the north and west.

Georgian London saw a surge in artistic creativity, with the likes of Dr Johnson, Handel, Gainsborough and Reynolds enriching the city's culture, while architects fashioned an elegant new metropolis. In 1837, 18-year-old Victoria began her epic reign, as London became the fulcrum of the British Empire. The Industrial Revolution saw the building of new docks and railways (including the first underground line in 1863), while the Great Exhibition of 1851 showcased London to the world. During the Victorian era, the city's population mushroomed from just over two million to 6.6 million.

Although London suffered a relatively minor bruising during WWI, it was devastated by the Luftwaffe in WWII, when huge swaths of the centre and East End were flattened and 32,000 people were killed. Ugly housing and low-cost developments followed, but prosperity gradually returned to the city. In the 'Swinging Sixties', London became the capital of cool in fashion and music – a party followed morosely by the austere 1970s.

Since then the city has surfed up and down the waves of global fortunes, hanging on to its position as the world's leading financial centre. In 2000, the modern metropolis won its first mayor of London, an elected role covering the City and all 32 urban boroughs. Boris Johnson was elected in 2008, and retained his post in the 2012 mayoral election. In August 2011, numerous London boroughs were rocked by riots characterised by looting and arson, triggered by the controversial shooting of a man by police in Tottenham.

Both the Olympics and the Queen's Diamond Jubilee concocted a splendid display of pageantry for London in 2012. New overground train lines opened, a cable car was flung across the Thames and a once rundown and polluted area of East London was regenerated for the Olympic Park.

Since the Olympics, the city has changed leadership, with Labour politician Sadiq Khan taking over as mayor from Boris Johnson. Scores of new high-rise buildings have transformed the London skyline. Another key development has been the Crossrail, the capital's largest and costliest construction project, which has added a new east–west train line that promises to ease congestion for commuters. In addition, the Underground's new 24-hour schedule at weekends has been warmly welcomed – but quite what effect Brexit will have on this great city's future remains to be seen.

London Highlights

1 **Regent's Park** (p109) Watching the world pass by in one of London's loveliest parks.

2 **British Museum** (p77) Marvelling at the epoch-spanning collections of the nation's flagship museum.

3 **Shakespeare's Globe** (p96) Seeing one of the Bard's plays in the theatre for which they were written.

4 **Tower of London** (p91) Viewing the dazzling Crown Jewels in this thousand year-old fortress.

5 **St Paul's Cathedral** (p89) Reaching for the heavens at the top of the dome.

6 Tate Modern (p96)
Exploring London's most adventurous and innovative art museum.

7 Hampstead Heath (p111)
Wandering the paths and

woodlands of North London's loveliest green space.

8 Kew Gardens (p116)
Stepping into a miniature rainforest inside the subtropical Palm House.

9 East End (p107) Bar-hopping, artwork-spotting and shopping in the capital's coolest neighbourhoods.

NEIGHBOURHOODS AT A GLANCE

❶ The West End (p76)

The West End is a vague term – any Londoner you meet will give you their own take on which neighbourhoods it does and doesn't include – but what is striking is its variety: from reverentially quiet in literary Bloomsbury and legal Holborn, to bustling with revellers and shoppers 24/7 in Soho, Piccadilly Circus and Oxford St. It's also the city's shopping and theatre district.

❷ The City (p89)

London's historic core is a tale of two cities: packed with office workers during the week and eerily quiet at weekends. For most of its history, the entire city was enclosed here between sturdy walls that were only dismantled in the 18th century. The current millennium has seen a profusion of daring skyscrapers sprout from the City's fringes, but the essential sights have been standing

for hundreds of years: St Paul's Cathedral and the Tower of London.

❸ South Bank (p96)

The South Bank is a must-visit area for art lovers, theatre-goers and culture hounds, and has been significantly re-energised by the renowned Tate Modern. Come for iconic Thames views, great food markets, first-rate pubs, dollops of history, striking examples of modern architecture, and a sprinkling of fine bars and restaurants.

❹ Kensington & Hyde Park (p99)

Splendidly well groomed, Kensington is one of London's most handsome neighbourhoods. You'll find three fine museums here – the V&A, the Natural History Museum and the Science Museum – as well as excellent dining and shopping, graceful parklands and elegant streets of grand period architecture.

❺ Clerkenwell, Shoreditch & Spitalfields (p107)

These historic city-fringe neighbourhoods contain a few significant sights, mainly around Clerkenwell and Spitalfields, but the area is best known for its nightlife. Shoreditch and Hoxton long ago replaced Soho and Camden as the hippest, most alternative parts of London, and although some of the action has now moved further east, they're still holding their own.

❻ East London (p107)

Anyone with an interest in multicultural London needs to visit the East End. There's standout ethnic cuisine, some interesting museums and galleries, excellent pubs, canal-side eating and drinking, some of London's hippest neighbourhoods, and the vast redeveloped expanse of Queen Elizabeth Olympic Park to explore.

❼ North London (p109)

North London is framed by Camden's famous eponymous market, its unrivalled music scene and excellent pubs. The dynamic area of King's Cross is experiencing a transformation, and is now a destination in its own right and a great place to hang out. There's plenty here for quiet enjoyment, too – from the gorgeous green spaces of Hampstead Heath and Regent's Park to overgrown Victorian cemeteries, such as Highgate and Abbeywood, and canal walks.

❽ Greenwich & South London (p112)

Regal riverside Greenwich complements its village feel with some grand architecture, grassy parkland and riverside pubs. Brixton has the creative edge in its glorious food-and-shop Village, Clapham and Battersea are full of hidden gems, while Dulwich Village is all tranquil, leafy charm.

❾ West London (p116)

Portobello Market, the Design Museum, historic cinemas, niche collections, canal-side charms, superb pubs and clubs, swish parkland and grand mansions, imposing churches, intriguing Victorian bone-yards, diverse shopping and ethnic eats all make Notting Hill and West London an eclectic must-see.

❿ Richmond, Kew & Hampton Court (p116)

To flee London's concrete urban interior and get a look at the city's leafy, riverside complexion – where the crowds thin out, the air is cleaner and the landscapes become increasingly pastoral – make a beeline to Richmond, Kew and Hampton Court. Wander by the river, explore haunted Tudor palaces (Hampton Court), get lost in beautiful Kew Gardens, go deer-spotting in Richmond Park, traipse around Wimbledon Common and down a pint waterside as the sun shimmers on the Thames at sunset.

The River Thames

A FLOATING TOUR

London's history has always been determined by the Thames. The city was founded as a Roman port nearly 2000 years ago and over the centuries since then many of the capital's landmarks have lined the river's banks. A boat trip is a great way to experience the attractions.

There are piers dotted along both banks at regular intervals where you can hop on and hop off the regular services to visit places of interest. The best place to board is Westminster Pier, from where boats head downstream, taking you from the City of Westminster, the seat of government, to the original City of London, now the financial district and dominated by a growing band of skyscrapers. Across the river, the once shabby and neglected South Bank now bristles with as many top attractions as its northern counterpart, including the slender Shard.

In our illustration we've concentrated on the top highlights you'll enjoy from a waterborne

KIEVVICTOR / SHUTTERSTOCK ©

St Paul's Cathedral
Though there's been a church here since AD 604, the current building rose from the ashes of the 1666 Great Fire and is architect Christopher Wren's masterpiece. Famous for surviving the Blitz intact and for the wedding of Charles and Diana, it's looking as good as new after a major clean-up for its 300th anniversary in 2011.

Blackfriars

Somerset House
This grand neoclassical palace was once one of many aristocratic houses lining the Thames. The huge arches at river level gave direct access to the Thames until the Embankment was built in the 1860s.

Temple

Charing Cross

Blackfriars Bridge

Blackfriars Pier

Waterloo Bridge

Victoria Embankment Gardens

One Blackfriars

National Theatre

OXO Tower

Embankment

Embankment Pier

Queen Elizabeth Hall

Southbank Centre

London Eye
Built in 2000 and originally temporary, the Eye instantly became a much-loved landmark. The 30-minute spin takes you 135m above the city from where the views are unsurprisingly amazing.

Waterloo Millennium Pier

Westminster Pier

Houses of Parliament
Rebuilt in neo-Gothic style after the old Palace of Westminster burned down in 1834, the most famous part of the British parliament is the clocktower. Generally known as Big Ben, it's named after Benjamin Hall who oversaw its construction.

Westminster

Westminster Bridge

VERDOONIE / BUDGET TRAVEL ©

vessel. These are, from west to east, the **1 Houses of Parliament**, the **2 London Eye**, **3 Somerset House**, **4 St Paul's Cathedral**, the **5 Tate Modern**, **6 Shakespeare's Globe**, the **7 Tower of London** and **8 Tower Bridge**.

In addition to covering this central section of the Thames, boats can also be taken upstream as far as Kew Gardens and Hampton Court Palace, and downstream as far as Greenwich and the Thames Barrier.

BOAT HOPPING

Thames Clippers hop-on/hop-off services are aimed at commuters but are equally useful for visitors, operating every 15 minutes on a loop from piers at Westminster, Embankment, Waterloo, Blackfriars, Bankside, London Bridge and the Tower. Oyster cardholders get a discount off the boat ticket price.

30 St Mary Axe (Gherkin)

Leadenhall Building (Cheese Grater)

Tower of London
It's not the tallest building in London anymore, but with the Crown Jewels and execution site, the 900-year-old Tower still overshadows the city's other attractions. From the river you can clearly see Traitors' Gate through which enemies of the crown entered the prison.

Cannon St ⊖

20 Fenchurch St (Walkie Talkie)

Millennium Bridge

Monument ⊖

Bankside Pier

Southwark Bridge

London Bridge

Southwark Cathedral

London Bridge Pier

HMS Belfast

Tower Pier

London Bridge ⊖

Shard

City Hall

Tate Modern
Directly across the river from St Paul's, this museum of modern art is the world's most visited. Built as a power station in the late 1940s, its industrial architecture is as popular as its artworks, while a splendid new extension was completed in 2016.

CLAUDIO DIVIZIA / SHUTTERSTOCK ©

Shakespeare's Globe
The reconstructed Globe stands on the river a few hundred metres from where the original stood (and burnt down in 1613 during a performance). The life's work of American actor Sam Wanamaker, the theatre runs a hugely popular season from April to October each year.

PRES PANAYOTOV / SHUTTERSTOCK ©

Tower Bridge
It might look as old as its namesake neighbour but one of the world's most iconic bridges was only completed in 1894. Not to be confused with London Bridge upstream, this one's famous raising bascules allowed tall ships to dock at the old wharves to the west and are still lifted up to 1000 times a year.

Sights

The West End

★ Westminster Abbey　　　CHURCH
(Map p82; ☑ 020-7222 5152; www.westminster
-abbey.org; 20 Dean's Yard, SW1; adult/child £22/9,
cloister & gardens free; ⊙ 9.30am-3.30pm Mon,
Tue, Thu & Fri, to 6pm Wed, to 1.30pm Sat; ☻ Westminster) A splendid mixture of architectural
styles, Westminster Abbey is considered
the finest example of Early English Gothic
(1190–1300). It's not merely a beautiful place
of worship – the Abbey also serves up the
country's history cold on slabs of stone. For
centuries, the country's greatest have been
interred here, including 17 monarchs from
Henry III (died 1272) to George II (1760).
Never a cathedral (the seat of a bishop),
Westminster Abbey is what is called a 'royal
peculiar', administered by the Crown.

Every monarch since William the Conqueror has been crowned here, with the exception of a couple of unlucky Eds who were
either murdered (Edward V) or abdicated
(Edward VIII) before the magic moment.

At the heart of the Abbey is the beautifully tiled **sanctuary** (sacrarium), a stage for
coronations, royal weddings and funerals.
George Gilbert Scott designed the ornate
high altar in 1873. In front of the altar is
the **Cosmati marble pavement** dating to
1268. It has intricate designs of small pieces of marble inlaid into plain marble, which

---

LONDON IN 2/4/7 DAYS

2 Days

Begin with the West End's big-draw sights: **Westminster Abbey**, then **Buckingham
Palace** (p81) for the Changing of the Guard. Walk up the Mall to **Trafalgar Square** (p80)
for its architectural grandeur and photo-op views of Big Ben down Whitehall, then take a
spin round the **National Gallery** (p80). In the afternoon, hop over to the South Bank for
a ride on the London Eye and a visit to the **Tate Modern** (p96), followed by an evening
performance at **Shakespeare's Globe** (p96).

On day two, spend the day wandering around the marvellous **British Museum** (p77),
followed by a spot of shopping around **Covent Garden** and **Oxford St**, and a night on
the tiles in **Soho**.

4 Days

On day three, head for London's finance-driven heart in the **City**, home to the sprawling
and ancient **Tower of London** (p91). Spend the morning watching the Beefeaters and
resident ravens preen and strut, and then marvel at the Crown Jewels. When you're finished, admire the iconic **Tower Bridge** (p92) from the banks of the Thames or through
the glass floors of the walkways connecting the two towers. While away the rest of the
day exploring the vibrant **East End**, with visits to **Brick Lane** (Map p138; ☻ Shoreditch High
St, Liverpool St) and **Spitalfields Market** (p147).

On day four, hop on a boat from any central London pier and make your way down to
Greenwich with its world-renowned architecture and links to time, the stars and space.
Start your visit at the legendary **Cutty Sark** (p112), a star clipper during the tea-trade
years, and have a look into the **National Maritime Museum** (p112). Stroll up through
Greenwich Park (p113) all the way to the **Royal Observatory** (p113). The views of
Canary Wharf, the business district across the river, are stunning. Spend the evening
exploring the local bars and bistros.

7 Days

With a few extra days, you'll have time to explore some of London's other neighbourhoods. On day five, head for **North London**, with a morning at **Camden Market** (p147),
a visit to **Highgate Cemetery** (p110) and a walk over **Hampstead Heath** (p111). On day
six, explore the famous **Portobello Road Market** (p116) in **Notting Hill**, then spend the
rest of the day with chic shopping in **Knightsbridge**, or visiting the museums of **South
Kensington**, such as the **Natural History Museum** (p99) and the **Science Museum**
(p103). On day seven, head out to **West London**, where you'll discover the delightful
green spaces of **Kew Gardens** (p116) and **Richmond Park** (p117), and the grand palace
of **Hampton Court** (p117).

predict the end of the world (in AD 19,693!). At the entrance to the lovely **Chapel of St John the Baptist** is a sublime alabaster Virgin and Child bathed in candlelight.

The most sacred spot in the Abbey, the **shrine of St Edward the Confessor**, lies behind the main altar; access is restricted to several prayer meetings daily to protect the 13th-century flooring. St Edward was the founder of the Abbey and the original building was consecrated a few weeks before his death. His tomb was slightly altered after the original was destroyed during the Reformation but still contains Edward's remains – the only complete saint's body in Britain. Ninety-minute **verger-led tours** (£5 plus admission) of the Abbey include a visit to the shrine.

The **quire** (choir), a space of gold, blue and red Victorian Gothic by Edward Blore, dates back to the mid-19th century. It sits where the original choir for the monks' worship would have been but bears little resemblance to the original. Nowadays, the quire is still used for singing, but its regular occupants are the Westminster Choir – 22 boys and 12 'lay vicars' (men) who sing the daily services and evensong (5pm weekdays, 3pm weekends).

Henry III began work on the new building in 1245 but didn't complete it; the Gothic nave was finished under Richard II in 1388. Henry VII's magnificent Perpendicular Gothic-style **Lady Chapel** was consecrated in 1519 after 16 years of construction.

At the west end of the nave near the **Tomb of the Unknown Warrior**, killed in WWI in northern France and laid to rest here in 1920, is St George's Chapel, which contains the rather ordinary-looking **Coronation Chair**, upon which every monarch since the early 14th century has been crowned (apart from joint-monarchs Mary II and William III, who had their own chairs fashioned for the event).

Apart from the royal graves, keep an eye out for the many famous commoners interred here, especially in **Poets' Corner**, where you'll find the resting places of Chaucer, Dickens, Hardy, Tennyson, Dr Johnson and Kipling, as well as memorials to the other greats (Shakespeare, Jane Austen, the Brontës etc). Nearby you'll find the graves of Handel and Sir Isaac Newton.

The octagonal **Chapter House** dates from the 1250s and was where the monks would meet for daily prayer and their job assignments before Henry VIII's suppression of the monasteries some three centuries later. To the right of the entrance to Chapter House is what is claimed to be the oldest door in Britain – it's been there since the 1050s. Used as a treasury and 'Royal Wardrobe', the cryptlike **Pyx Chamber** dates from about 1070, though the Altar of St Dunstan within it is even older.

Parts of the Abbey complex are free to visitors. This includes the **Cloister** and the 900-year-old **College Garden** (Map p82; ☉10am-6pm Tue-Thu Apr-Sep, to 4pm Oct-Mar). Adjacent to the abbey is **St Margaret's Church** (Map p82; ☎020-7654 4840; www.westminster-abbey.org/st-margarets-church; ☉9.30am-3.30pm Mon-Fri, to 1.30pm Sat, 2-4.30pm Sun), the House of Commons' place of worship since 1614, where windows commemorate churchgoers Caxton and Milton, and Sir Walter Raleigh is buried by the altar.

Completed in 2018, the **Queen's Diamond Jubilee Galleries** are a new museum and gallery space located in the medieval triforium, the arched gallery above the nave. Among its exhibits are the death masks of generations of royalty, wax effigies representing Charles II and William III (who is on a stool to make him as tall as his wife, Mary II), armour and stained glass. Highlights are the graffiti-inscribed Mary Chair (used for the coronation of Mary II) and the Westminster Retable, England's oldest altarpiece, from the 13th century.

★ **British Museum** MUSEUM
(Map p84; ☎020-7323 8299; www.britishmuseum. org; Great Russell St & Montague Pl, WC1; ☉10am-5.30pm Sat-Thu, to 8.30pm Fri; ⊕Russell Sq, Tottenham Court Rd) **FREE** The country's largest museum and one of the oldest and finest in the world, this famous museum boasts vast Egyptian, Etruscan, Greek, Roman, European and Middle Eastern galleries, among others. It is frequently London's most-visited attraction, drawing 6.5 million visitors annually.

Don't miss the **Rosetta Stone**, the key to deciphering Egyptian hieroglyphics, discovered in 1799; the controversial **Parthenon Sculptures**, taken from the Parthenon in Athens by Lord Elgin (then the British ambassador to the Ottoman Empire); and the large collection of **Egyptian mummies**.

Other must-see items include the Anglo-Saxon **Sutton Hoo burial relics** and the **Winged Bulls from Khorsabad**.

The British Museum

A HALF-DAY TOUR

The British Museum, with almost eight million items in its permanent collection, is so vast and comprehensive that it can be daunting for the first-time visitor. To avoid a frustrating trip – and getting lost on the way to the Egyptian mummies – set out on this half-day exploration, which takes in some of the museum's most important sights. If you want to see and learn more, join a tour or grab an audioguide (£7).

A good starting point is the ❶ Rosetta Stone, the key that cracked the code to ancient Egypt's writing system. Nearby treasures from Assyria – an ancient civilisation centred in Mesopotamia between the Tigris and Euphrates Rivers – including the colossal ❷ Winged Bulls from Khorsabad, give way to the ❸ Parthenon Sculptures, highpoints of classical Greek art that continue to influence us today. Be sure to see both the sculptures and the monumental frieze celebrating the

Winged Bulls from Khorsabad
This awesome pair of alabaster winged bulls with human heads once guarded the entrance to the palace of Assyrian King Sargon II at Khorsabad in Mesopotamia, a cradle of civilisation in present-day Iraq.

Parthenon Sculptures
The Parthenon, a white marble temple dedicated to Athena, was part of a fortified citadel on the Acropolis in Athens. There are dozens of sculptures and friezes with models and interactive displays explaining how they all once fitted together.

Ancient Greece & Rome ❸

West Stairs

Lion Hunt Reliefs from Nineveh • ❷

Audioguides Desk

Main Entrance

Great Court

Reading Room

Great Court Shop

South Stairs

❶ ❹

China, India & Southeast Asia

North America

Information Desk

Ticket Desk (Temporary Exhibitions)

GROUND FLOOR

Rosetta Stone
Written in hieroglyphic, demotic (cursive ancient Egyptian script used for everyday use) and Greek, the 762kg stone contains a decree exempting priests from tax on the first anniversary of young Ptolemy V's coronation.

Bust of Pharaoh Ramesses II
The most impressive sculpture in the Egyptian galleries, this 725kg bust portrays Ramesses the Great, scourge of the Israelites in the Book of Exodus, as great benefactor.

birth of Athena. En route to the West Stairs is a huge **④ Bust of Pharaoh Ramesses II**, just a hint of the large collection of **⑤ Egyptian mummies** upstairs. (The earliest, affectionately called Ginger because of wispy reddish hair, was preserved simply by hot sand.) The Romans introduce visitors to the early Britain galleries via the rich **⑥ Mildenhall Treasure**. The Anglo-Saxon **⑦ Sutton Hoo Ship Burial** and the medieval **⑧ Lewis Chessmen** follow.

EATING OPTIONS

Court Cafe At the northern end of the Great Court; takeaway counters with salads and sandwiches; communal tables.

Gallery Cafe Slightly out of the way off Room 12; quieter; offers hot dishes.

Great Court Restaurant Upstairs overlooking the former Reading Room; sit-down meals.

Lewis Chessmen
The much-loved 78 chess pieces portray faceless pawns, worried-looking queens, bishops with their mitres turned sideways and rooks (or castles) as 'warders', gnawing away at their shields.

ILEANA_BT / SHUTTERSTOCK ©

Egyptian Mummies
Among the rich collection of mummies and funerary objects is 'Ginger', who was buried at the site of Gebelein, in Upper Egypt, almost 5500 years ago, and Katebet, a one-time chantress (ritual performer) at the Amun temple in Karnak.

Greece & Rome

Stairs

Medieval Europe

Court Restaurant

Ancient Egypt
⑤

⑧

⑦   ⑥

Ancient Middle East

UPPER FLOOR

Sutton Hoo Ship Burial
This unique grave of an important (but unidentified) Anglo-Saxon royal has yielded drinking horns, gold buckles and a stunning helmet with face mask.

Mildenhall Treasure
Roman gods such as Neptune and Bacchus share space with early Christian symbols like the *chi-rho* (short for 'Christ') on the find's almost three dozen silver bowls, plates and spoons.

Begun in 1753 with a 'cabinet of curiosities' sold to the nation by royal physician Sir Hans Sloane, the collection mushroomed over the ensuing years partly through acquisitions, bequests and plundering the empire. The grand Enlightenment Gallery was the first section of the redesigned museum to be built in 1823.

The **Great Court**, restored and augmented by Norman Foster in 2000, has a spectacular glass-and-steel roof, making it one of the most impressive architectural spaces in the capital. In the centre is the **Reading Room**, with its stunning blue-and-gold domed ceiling made of papier mâché, where Karl Marx researched and wrote *Das Kapital*, and Mahatma Gandhi was a cardholder.

The British Museum's extension, the £135 million World Conservation and Exhibitions Centre in its northwestern corner, opened in 2014, in the same year as the Sainsbury Exhibitions Gallery, which hosts high-profile exhibitions.

The museum is huge, so make a few focused visits if you have time, and consider taking one of the free tours. There are up to 15 free 30- to 40-minute **Eye-opener tours** of individual galleries each day. The museum also has free 45-minute **lunchtime gallery talks** (1.15pm Tuesday to Friday), a

1½-hour **highlights tour** (£14; 11.30am and 2pm Friday, Saturday and Sunday) and free 20-minute **spotlight tours** on Friday evenings. Audio and family guides (adult/child £7/6) in 10 languages are available from the audio-guide desk in the Great Court.

★**Trafalgar Square**   SQUARE
(Map p84; ⊖Charing Cross) Trafalgar Sq is the true centre of London, where rallies and marches take place, tens of thousands of revellers usher in the New Year and locals congregate for anything from communal open-air cinema and Christmas celebrations to political protests. It is dominated by the 52m-high **Nelson's Column** and ringed by many splendid buildings, including the National Gallery (p80) and the church of **St Martin-in-the-Fields** (Map p84; ☏020-7766 1100; www.stmartin-in-the-fields.org; ⊗8.30am-1pm & 2-6pm Mon, Tue, Thu & Fri, 8.30am-1pm & 2-5pm Wed, 9.30am-6pm Sat, 3.30-5pm Sun).

★**National Gallery**   GALLERY
(Map p84; ☏020-7747 2885; www.nationalgallery.org.uk; Trafalgar Sq, WC2; ⊗10am-6pm Sat-Thu, to 9pm Fri; ⊖Charing Cross) `FREE`
With some 2300 European masterpieces on display, this is one of the world's great art collections, with seminal works from every important period in the history of art – from the mid-13th to the early 20th century, including masterpieces by Leonardo da Vinci, Michelangelo, Titian, Van Gogh and Renoir.

Many visitors flock to the East Wing (1700–1900), where works by 18th-century British artists such as Gainsborough, Constable and Turner, and seminal Impressionist and post-Impressionist masterpieces by Van Gogh, Renoir and Monet await.

★**Houses of Parliament**   HISTORIC BUILDING
(Palace of Westminster; Map p82; www.parliament.uk; Parliament Sq, SW1; ⊖Westminster) `FREE` A visit here is a journey to the heart of UK democracy. Officially called the Palace of Westminster, the Houses of Parliament's oldest part is 11th-century **Westminster Hall**, one of only a few sections that survived a catastrophic fire in 1834. Its roof, added between 1394 and 1401, is the earliest known example of a hammerbeam roof. The rest is mostly a neo-Gothic confection built by Charles Barry and Augustus Pugin over 20 years from 1840. The palace's most famous feature is its clock tower, officially the Elizabeth Tower but better known as **Big Ben** (Map p82).

ⓘ **LONDON TOP TIPS**

➡ London is huge – organise your visit by neighbourhood to avoid wasting time (and money) on transport.

➡ An Oyster Card is a cheaper and convenient way to use public transport, but you can also pay by credit or debit card provided it has a contactless function indicated by a wi-fi-like symbol.

➡ Walk – it's cheaper than transport and the best way to discover central London.

➡ For West End performances at bargain prices, opt for standby tickets (which you buy on the day at the venue) or last-minute tickets from the booths on Leicester Sq.

➡ To treat yourself to fine dining without breaking the bank, opt for lunch rather than dinner, or try for pre- or post-theatre dinner deals.

➡ Book online for ticketed attractions to save money and skip queues.

LOCAL KNOWLEDGE

SOHO

London's most bohemian neighbourhood was once pastureland; the name Soho is thought to have evolved from a hunting cry. While the centre of London nightlife has shifted east, and Soho has recently seen landmark clubs and music venues shut down, the neighbourhood definitely comes into its own in the evenings and remains a proud gay district. During the day you'll be charmed by the area's bohemian side and its sheer vitality.

At Soho's northern end, leafy **Soho Sq** (Map p84; ⊜ Tottenham Court Rd, Leicester Sq) is the area's back garden. It was laid out in 1681 and originally called King's Sq; a statue of Charles II stands in its northern half. In the centre is a tiny half-timbered mock-Tudor cottage built as a gardener's shed in the 1870s. The space below it was used as an underground bomb shelter during WWII.

South of the square is **Dean St**, lined with bars and restaurants. No 28 was the home of Karl Marx and his family from 1851 to 1856; they lived here in extreme poverty as Marx researched and wrote *Das Kapital* in the Reading Room of the British Museum.

Old Compton St is the epicentre of Soho's gay village. It's a street loved by all, gay or other, for its great bars, risqué shops and general good vibes.

Seducer and heart-breaker Casanova and opium-addicted writer Thomas de Quincey lived on nearby **Greek St**, while the parallel **Frith St** housed Mozart at No 20 for a year from 1764.

Big Ben is actually the 13.5-tonne bell, named after Benjamin Hall, who was First Commissioner of Works when the tower was completed in 1858.

At the business end, parliament is split into two houses. The green-hued **House of Commons** (Map p82; www.parliament.uk/business/commons; ◷ 2.30-10pm Mon & Tue, 11.30am-7.30pm Wed, 10.30am-6.30pm Thu, 9.30am-3pm Fri) is the lower house, where the 650 elected Members of Parliament sit. Traditionally the home of hereditary blue bloods, the scarlet-decorated **House of Lords** (Map p82; www.parliament.uk/business/lords; ◷ 2.30-10pm Mon & Tue, 3-10pm Wed, 11am-7.30pm Thu, 10am-close of session Fri), with over 800 members, now has peers appointed through various means. Both houses debate and vote on legislation, which is then presented to the Queen for her Royal Assent (in practice, this is a formality; the last time Royal Assent was denied was in 1708). At the annual State Opening of Parliament, which now takes place in May, the Queen takes her throne in the House of Lords, having arrived in the gold-trimmed Irish State Coach from Buckingham Palace (her crown travels alone with equerries in Queen Alexandra's State Coach).

Visitors are welcome on Saturday year-round and on most weekdays during parliamentary recesses (which includes Easter, summer and Christmas). They can choose either a self-guided audio tour (adult £18.50, one free child with each adult) in one of eight languages lasting about 75 minutes or a much more comprehensive 1½-hour **guided tour** (Map p82; ☑ 020-7219 4114; www.parliament.uk/visiting/visiting-and-tours; adult/child £28/12) of both chambers, Westminster Hall and other historic buildings conducted by qualified Blue Badge Tourist Guides in a myriad of tongues (adult/child £25.50/11). Afternoon tea (£29) in the Terrace Pavilion overlooking the River Thames is a popular add-on to the tours. Buy tickets from the office in Portcullis House on Victoria Embankment. Tour schedules change with every recess and are occasionally subject to variation or cancellation due to the State Opening of Parliament and other parliamentary business, so check ahead and book. UK residents can approach their MPs to arrange a free tour. The Elizabeth Tower, housing Big Ben, is undergoing conservation works until 2021.

Public access to the Houses of Parliament is via the Cromwell Green Entrance, next to St Stephen's Entrance. If you wish to eat here, the Palace of Westminster's principal dining rooms are open to the public on select dates (see the website for details).

★ **Buckingham Palace**   PALACE
(Map p82; ☑ 0303 123 7300; www.royalcollection.org.uk/visit/the-state-rooms-buckingham-palace;

Westminster & St James's

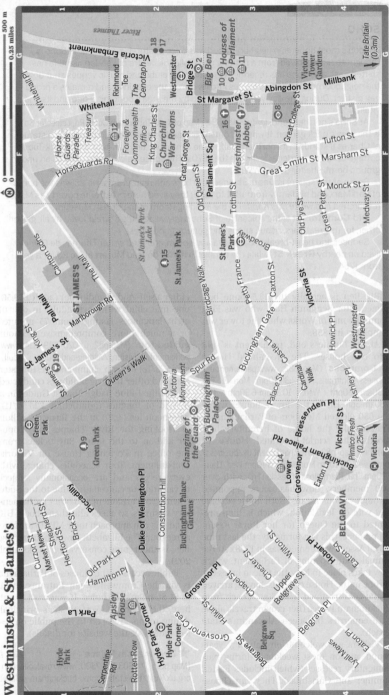

Westminster & St James's

Buckingham Palace Rd, SW1; adult/child/under 5yr £24/13.50/free; ⊙9.30am-7pm (to 6pm Sep) Jul-Sep only; ⊖Green Park, St James's Park) Built in 1703 for the Duke of Buckingham, Buckingham Palace replaced St James's Palace as the monarch's official London residence in 1837. Queen Elizabeth II divides her time between here, Windsor Castle and, in summer, Balmoral Castle in Scotland. If she's in residence, the square yellow, red and blue Royal Standard is flown; if not, it's the Union Flag. Some 19 lavishly furnished **State Rooms** are open to visitors when Her Royal Highness (HRH) takes her holidays from late July to September.

Hung with artworks by the likes of Rembrandt, Van Dyck, Canaletto, Poussin and Vermeer, the State Rooms are open for self-guided tours that include the **Throne Room**, with his-and-her pink chairs monogrammed 'ER' and 'P'. Access is by timed tickets with admission every 15 minutes (audio guide included) and visits take about two hours.

Admission includes entry to a themed special exhibition (eg royal couture during the Queen's reign, growing up at the palace) in the enormous Ballroom, which changes each summer. It also allows access to part of the palace gardens as you exit, although you must join the three-hour State Rooms & Garden Highlights Tour (adult/child/under five years £33/19.70/free) to see the wisteria-clad Summer House and other famous features, and to get an idea of the garden's full size (16 hectares).

Your ticket to Buckingham Palace is good for a return trip if bought direct from the palace ticket office (ask to have it stamped as you leave). You can even make your ticket purchase a donation and gain free access for a whole year (ask at the ticket office).

At 11am daily in June and July and on Sunday, Monday, Wednesday and Friday, weather permitting, during the rest of the year, the Old Guard (Foot Guards of the Household Regiment) comes off duty to be replaced by the New Guard on the forecourt of Buckingham Palace, an event known as the **Changing of the Guard** (Map p82; http://changing-guard.com). Highly popular, the ceremony lasts about 40 minutes (brace for crowds).

Originally designed by John Nash as a conservatory, the **Queen's Gallery** (Map p82; www.royalcollection.org.uk/visit/the-queens-gallery-buckingham-palace; South Wing, Buckingham Palace, Buckingham Gate, SW1; adult/child £10.30/5.30, incl Royal Mews £19/10; ⊙10am-5.30pm) showcases some of the palace's treasures on a rotating basis, through temporary exhibitions. Enter from Buckingham Gate.

Indulge your Cinderella fantasies while inspecting the exquisite state coaches in the **Royal Mews** (Map p82; www.royalcollection.org.uk/visit/royalmews; adult/child £11/6.40, with Queen's Gallery £19/10; ⊙10am-5pm Apr-Oct, to 4pm Mon-Sat Feb, Mar & Nov; ⊖Victoria), a working stable looking after the royals' immaculately groomed horses and the opulent vehicles they use for getting from A to B. Highlights include the magnificent Gold State Coach of 1762 and the 1911 Glass Coach.

A Royal Day Out (adult/child/under five years £42.30/23.30/free) is a combined ticket including entry to the State Rooms, Queen's Gallery and Royal Mews.

West End

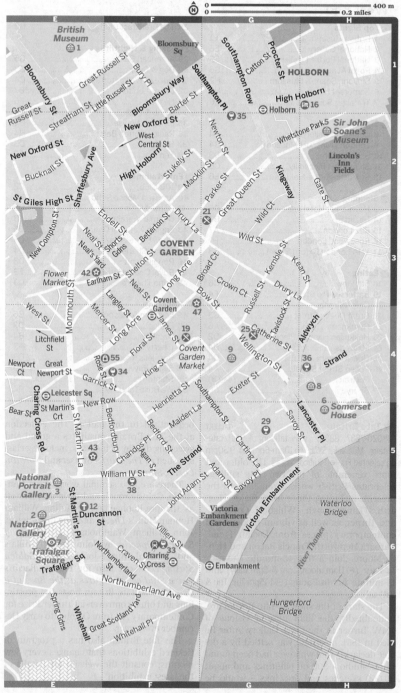

N 0 ——————————— 400 m
0 ——————————— 0.2 miles

British Museum 1

Bloomsbury Sq

HOLBORN

Great Russell St
Bloomsbury St
Streatham St
Little Russell St
Bury Pl
Great Russell St
Bloomsbury Way
Barter St
Bloomsbury Way
New Oxford St
West Central St
New Oxford St
Bucknall St
High Holborn
St Giles High St
Shaftesbury Ave
New Compton St

Southampton Row
Catton St
Procter St
Southampton Pl
High Holborn
Holborn 16
Whetstone Park 5
Sir John Soane's Museum
Lincoln's Inn Fields
Gate St
35
Newton St
Stukely St
Macklin St
Parker St
Great Queen St
Kingsway
Wild Ct
Wild St
Wild St

Endell St
Betterton St
Drury La
21
COVENT GARDEN
Neal St
Shorts Gdns
Shelton St
Long Acre
Broad Ct
Crown Ct
Russell St
Kemble St
Kean St
Drury La
Neal's Yard
Earlham St
42
Flower Market
Monmouth St
Langley St
Neal St
Mercer St
Long Acre
James St
Covent Garden 47
Bow St
25 Catherine St
Tavistock St
Aldwych
Strand
36
West St
Litchfield St
19
9
Covent Garden Market
Wellington St
8
6 Somerset House
Newport Ct
Great Newport St
Rose St 55
34
Floral St
King St
Henrietta St
Southampton St
Exeter St
Lancaster Pl
Garrick St
New Row
Leicester Sq
St Martin's Crt
Charing Cross Rd
Bear St
Bedfordbury
St Martin's La
Chandos Pl
Maiden La
Bedford St
Agar St
The Strand
Carting La
Savoy St
29
Savoy Pl
43
William IV St
38
John Adam St
Adam St
National Portrait Gallery 3
St Martin's Pl
2
National Gallery
7
12
Duncannon St
Villiers St
Victoria Embankment Gardens
Victoria Embankment
Waterloo Bridge
Trafalgar Square
Trafalgar Sq
Northumberland St
Craven St
33
Charing Cross
Embankment
River Thames
Spring Gdns
Whitehall
Northumberland Ave
Great Scotland Yard
Whitehall Pl
Hungerford Bridge

West End

★ **Tate Britain**   GALLERY
(📞020-7887 8888; www.tate.org.uk/visit/tate-britain; Millbank, SW1; ⏱10am-6pm, to 9.30pm on selected Fri; ⓔPimlico) FREE The older and more venerable of the two Tate siblings celebrates British works from 1500 to the present, including those from Blake, Hogarth, Gainsborough, Whistler, Constable and Turner, as well as vibrant modern and contemporary pieces from Lucian Freud, Barbara Hepworth, Francis Bacon and Henry Moore. Join a free 45-minute **thematic tour** (⏱11am, noon, 2pm & 3pm daily) and 15-minute **Art in Focus** (⏱1.15pm Tue, Thu & Sat) talks.

The stars of the show at Tate Britain are, undoubtedly, the light infused visions of JMW Turner in the Clore Gallery. After he died in 1851, his estate was settled by a decree declaring that whatever had been found in his studio – 300 oil paintings and about 30,000 sketches and drawings – would be bequeathed to the nation. The collection at the Tate Britain constitutes a grand and sweeping display of his work, including classics such as *The Scarlet Sunset* and *Norham Castle, Sunrise.*

There are also seminal works from Constable, Gainsborough and Reynolds, as well as the pre-Raphaelites, including William Holman Hunt's *The Awakening Conscience,* John William Waterhouse's *The Lady of Shalott, Ophelia* by John Everett Millais and Edward Burne-Jones's *The Golden Stairs.* Look out also for Francis Bacon's *Three Studies for Figures at the Base of a Crucifixion.* Tate Britain hosts the prestigious and often controversial Turner Prize for Contemporary Art from October to early December every year.

The Tate Britain also has a program of ticketed exhibitions that changes every few months; consult the website for details of the latest exhibition.

⭐**Wallace Collection** GALLERY
(Map p126; ☎020-7563 9500; www.wallace collection.org; Hertford House, Manchester Sq, W1; ⏱10am-5pm; ⊜Bond St) **FREE** Arguably London's finest smaller gallery, the Wallace Collection is an enthralling glimpse into 18th-century aristocratic life. The sumptuously restored Italianate mansion houses a treasure trove of 17th- and 18th-century paintings, porcelain, artefacts and furniture collected by generations of the same family and bequeathed to the nation by the widow of Sir Richard Wallace (1818–90) on the condition it remain displayed in the same fashion.

⭐**Churchill War Rooms** MUSEUM
(Map p82; www.iwm.org.uk/visits/churchill-war-rooms; Clive Steps, King Charles St, SW1; adult/child £21/10.50; ⏱9.30am-6pm; ⊜Westminster) Winston Churchill helped coordinate the Allied resistance against Nazi Germany on a Bakelite telephone from this underground complex during WWII. The **Cabinet War Rooms** remain much as they were when the lights were switched off in 1945, capturing the drama and dogged spirit of the time, while the multimedia **Churchill Museum** affords intriguing insights into the life and times of the resolute, cigar-smoking wartime leader.

⭐**National Portrait Gallery** GALLERY
(Map p84; ☎020-7321 0055; www.npg.org.uk; St Martin's Pl, WC2; ⏱10am-6pm Sat-Wed, to 9pm Thu & Fri; ⊜Charing Cross, Leicester Sq) **FREE** What makes the National Portrait Gallery so compelling is its familiarity; in many cases, you'll have heard of the subject (royals, scientists, politicians, celebrities) or the artist (Andy Warhol, Annie Leibovitz, Lucian Freud) but not necessarily recognise the face. Highlights include the famous 'Chandos portrait' of William Shakespeare, the first artwork the gallery acquired (in 1856) and believed to be the only likeness made during the playwright's lifetime, and a touching sketch of novelist Jane Austen by her sister.

⭐**Royal Academy of Arts** GALLERY
(Map p84; ☎020-7300 8000; www.royalacademy. org.uk; Burlington House, Piccadilly, W1; adult/child from £13.50/free, exhibition prices vary; ⏱10am-6pm Sat-Thu, to 10pm Fri; ⊜Green Park) Britain's oldest society devoted to fine arts was founded in 1768 and moved to Burlington House exactly a century later. The collection contains drawings, paintings, architectural designs, photographs and sculptures by past and present academicians, such as Joshua Reynolds, John Constable, Thomas Gainsborough, JMW Turner, David Hockney and Norman Foster.

⭐**No 10 Downing Street** HISTORIC BUILDING
(Map p82; www.number10.gov.uk; 10 Downing St, SW1; ⊜Westminster) The official office of British leaders since 1732, when George II presented No 10 to 'First Lord of the Treasury' Robert Walpole, this has also been the prime minister's London residence since refurbishment in 1902. For such a famous address, No 10 is a small-looking Georgian building on a plain-looking street, hardly warranting comparison with the White House, for example. Yet it is actually three houses joined into one and boasts roughly 100 rooms plus a 2000-sq-metre garden.

⭐**Madame Tussauds** MUSEUM
(Map p126; ☎0870 400 3000; www.madame-tussauds.com/london; Marylebone Rd, NW1; adult/child 4-15yr £35/30; ⏱10am-6pm; ⊜Baker St) It may be kitschy and pricey, but Madame Tussauds makes for a fun-filled day. There are photo ops with your dream celebrity (be it Daniel Craig, Lady Gaga, Benedict Cumberbatch, Audrey Hepburn or the Beckhams), the Bollywood gathering (sparring studs Hrithik Roshan and Salman Khan) and the Royal Appointment (the Queen, Harry and Meghan, William and Kate). Book online for much cheaper rates and check the website for seasonal opening hours.

⭐**Somerset House** HISTORIC BUILDING
(Map p84; ☎020-7845 4600; www.somerset house.org.uk; The Strand, WC2; ⏱galleries 10am-6pm, courtyard 7.30am-11pm, terrace 8am-11pm; ⊜Temple, Covent Garden) Designed by William Chambers in 1775 for government departments and royal societies – in fact, the world's first office block – Somerset House now contains several fabulous galleries. In the North Wing near the Strand entrance, the **Courtauld Gallery** (Map p84; http://court auld.ac.uk; adult/child £8/free, temporary exhibitions vary; ⏱10am-6pm) displays a wealth of 14th- to 20th-century art, including masterpieces by Rubens, Botticelli, Cézanne, Degas, Renoir, Seurat, Manet, Monet, Leger and others. The **Embankment Galleries** in the South Wing are devoted to temporary (mostly photographic, design and fashion) exhibitions; prices and hours vary.

🚶 City Walk
A Taste of the City

START ST BARTHOLOMEW-THE-GREAT
END 30 ST MARY AXE (THE GHERKIN)
LENGTH 1.5 MILES; THREE HOURS

The City of London has as much history in its square mile as the rest of London put together, and this walk picks out just a few of its many highlights.

Start by exploring the wonderful 12th-century ❶ **St Bartholomew-the-Great** (p93), whose atmospheric interior has been used frequently as a film set. Head through the Tudor gatehouse and turn right towards the colourful Victorian arches of ❷ **Smithfield Market**, London's last surviving meat market.

Head northeast along Long Lane and take a right at Aldersgate St. Follow the roundabout to the right and nip up the stairs (or take the lift) to the ❸ **Museum of London** (p93). After exploring the museum's excellent free galleries turn left onto the highwalk and pause to examine the ruins of the ❹ **Roman city walls** and behind them the distinctive towers of the ❺ **Barbican** (p93).

Descend from the highwalk and cross over to Wood St to find the ❻ **tower of St Alban** (1698), all that's left of a Wren-designed church destroyed in WWII bombing in 1940. Turn left into Love Lane and right into Aldermanbury – the impressive 15th-century ❼ **Guildhall** is on your left, behind a modern extension. Crossing its courtyard – note the black outline of the Roman amphitheatre – continue east onto Gresham St, taking a right into Prince's St and emerging onto the busy Bank intersection lined with neoclassical temples to commerce.

From the ❽ **Royal Exchange**, follow Cornhill and take a right down Gracechurch St. Turn left into wonderful ❾ **Leadenhall Market**, roughly where the Roman forum once stood. As you leave the market's far end, ❿ **Lloyd's of London** displays its innards for all to see. Once you turn left onto Lime St, ⓫ **30 St Mary Axe** (p93). Built nearly 900 years after St Bartholomew-the-Great, it's a tangible testimony to the city's ability to constantly reinvent itself.

★ **Sir John Soane's Museum**   MUSEUM
(Map p84; ☎020-7405 2107; www.soane.org; 12 Lincoln's Inn Fields, WC2; ☺10am-5pm Wed-Sun; ⊜Holborn) FREE This little museum is one of the most atmospheric and fascinating in London. The building was the beautiful, bewitching home of architect Sir John Soane (1753–1837), which he left brimming with his vast architectural and archaeological collection, as well as intriguing personal effects and curiosities. The museum represents his exquisite and eccentric tastes, persuasions and proclivities.

London Transport Museum   MUSEUM
(Map p84; ☎020-7379 6344; www.ltmuseum. co.uk; Covent Garden Piazza, WC2; adult/child £17.50/free; ☺10am-6pm; ⊜Covent Garden) This entertaining and informative museum looks at how London developed as a result of better transport and contains horse-drawn omnibuses, early taxis, underground trains you can drive yourself, a detailed look at Crossrail (a new high-frequency 75-mile rail service linking Reading with Essex), and everything in between, including signage. Start on Level 2 and don't miss the museum shop for imaginative souvenirs, including historical tube posters, 'Mind the Gap' socks and 'Way Out' T-shirts.

Charles Dickens Museum   MUSEUM
(Map p110; ☎020-7405 2127; www.dickensmuseum.com; 48 Doughty St, WC1; adult/child £9/4; ☺10am-5pm Tue-Sun; ⊜Chancery Lane, Russell Sq) A £3.5 million renovation funded by the Heritage Lottery Fund has made this museum – located in a handsome four-storey house that is the beloved Victorian novelist's sole surviving residence in London – bigger and better than ever. A period kitchen in the basement and a nursery in the attic were added, and the acquisition of 49 Doughty St increased the exhibition space substantially.

St James's Park   PARK
(Map p82; www.royalparks.org.uk/parks/st-jamess-park; The Mall, SW1; ☺5am-midnight; ⊜St James's Park, Green Park) At just 23 hectares, St James's is the second smallest of the eight royal parks after Green Park (Map p82; www. royalparks.org.uk/parks/green-park; ☺5am-midnight; ⊜Green Park). But what it lacks in size it makes up for in grooming as it is the most manicured green space in London. It has brilliant views of the London Eye, Westminster, St James's Palace, Carlton Tce and the Horse Guards Parade; the photo-perfect sight of Buckingham Palace from the footbridge spanning the central lake is the best you'll find.

◉ **The City**

★ **St Paul's Cathedral**   CATHEDRAL
(Map p90; ☎020-7246 8357; www.stpauls.co. uk; St Paul's Churchyard, EC4; adult/child £18/8; ☺8.30am-4.30pm Mon-Sat; ⊜St Paul's) Towering over diminutive Ludgate Hill in a superb position that's been a place of Christian worship for over 1400 years (and pagan before that), St Paul's is one of London's most magnificent buildings. For Londoners, the vast dome is a symbol of resilience and pride, standing tall for more than 300 years. Viewing Sir Christopher Wren's masterpiece from the inside and climbing to the top for sweeping views of the capital is an exhilarating experience.

The cathedral was designed by Wren after the Great Fire and built between 1675 and 1710; it opened the following year. The site is ancient hallowed ground, with four other cathedrals preceding Wren's English baroque masterpiece here, the first dating from 604.

The world's second-largest cathedral dome is famed for surviving Luftwaffe incendiary bombs in the 'Second Great Fire of London' of December 1940, becoming an icon of London resilience during the Blitz. Outside in the churchyard, north of the church, is a simple and elegant **monument to the people of London**, honouring the 32,000 Londoners killed.

Inside, rising 68m above the floor, is the dome, supported by eight huge columns. It actually consists of three parts: a plastered brick inner dome, a nonstructural lead outer dome visible on the skyline and a brick cone between them holding it all together. The walkway around its base, accessed via 257 steps from a staircase on the western side of the southern transept, is called the **Whispering Gallery**, because if you talk close to the wall, your words will carry to the opposite side, 32m away. A further 119 steps brings you to the exterior **Stone Gallery**, 152 iron steps above which is the **Golden Gallery** at the very top, with unforgettable views of London.

The crypt has memorials to around 300 of the great and the good, including Wellington and Nelson, whose body lies directly below the dome. But the most poignant is to

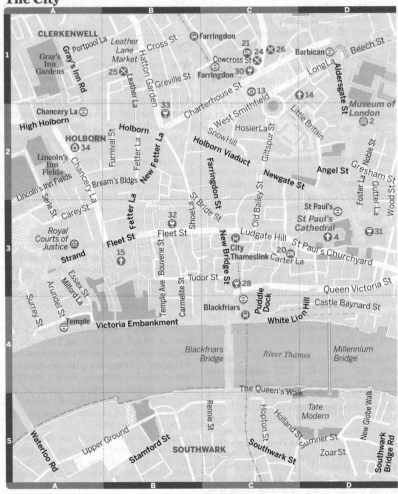

Wren himself. On a simple slab bearing his name, part of a Latin inscription translates as: 'If you seek his memorial, look around you'.

As part of its 300th anniversary celebrations in 2011, St Paul's underwent a £40-million renovation project that gave the church a deep clean. It's not looked this good since they cut the blue ribbon opening the cathedral in 1711.

There's no charge to attend a service. To hear the cathedral choir, attend the 11.30am Sunday Eucharist or Evensong (5pm Monday to Saturday and 3.15pm Sunday), but

check the website as a visiting choir may appear for the latter.

Otherwise, the standard admission price includes a free video- and audio guide. Free 1½-hour guided tours depart four times a day (10am, 11am, 1pm and 2pm); reserve a place at the tour desk, just past the entrance. Around twice a month, 60-minute tours (£8) also visit the astonishing Library, Geometric Staircase and Great Model, and include impressive views down the nave from above the Great West Doors; check the website for dates and hours and book well ahead. Filming and photography is not per-

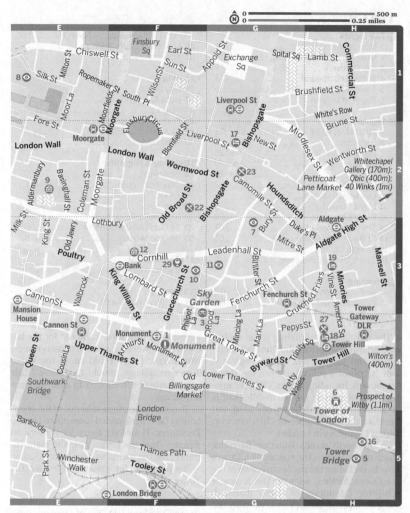

mitted within the cathedral. Book online for cheaper rates.

★ **Tower of London** CASTLE
(Map p90; ☎0844 482 7777; www.hrp.org.uk/tower-of-london; Petty Wales, EC3; adult/child £24.80/11.50, audio guide £4/3; ⊙9am-4.30pm Tue-Sat, from 10am Sun & Mon; ⊖Tower Hill) The unmissable Tower of London (actually a castle of 22 towers) offers a window into a gruesome and compelling history. A former royal residence, treasury, mint, armoury and zoo, it's perhaps now most remembered as the prison where a king, three queens and

many nobles met their deaths. Come here to see the colourful Yeoman Warders (or Beefeaters), the spectacular Crown Jewels, the soothsaying ravens and armour fit for a *very* large king.

In the 1070s, William the Conqueror started work on the White Tower to replace the stronghold he'd previously built here, in the southeast corner of the Roman walls, shortly after the Norman invasion. By 1285, two walls with towers and a moat were built around it and the defences have barely been altered since.

The City

The most striking building is the central **White Tower**, with its solid Norman architecture and four turrets. On the entrance floor it houses a collection from the **Royal Armouries**, including Henry VIII's commodious suit of armour. On the middle floor is **St John's Chapel**, dating from 1080 and therefore the oldest place of Christian worship still standing in London.

To the north stands Waterloo Barracks, which now contains the spectacular **Crown Jewels**, including the platinum crown of the late Queen Mother, set with the 106-carat Koh-i-Nûr (Mountain of Light) diamond, and the Imperial State Crown, worn by the Queen at the State Opening of Parliament. Slow-moving travelators shunt wide-eyed visitors past the collection. On the other side of the White Tower is the **Bloody Tower**, where the 12-year-old Edward V and his little brother Richard were held 'for their own safety' and later murdered, perhaps by their uncle, the future Richard III. Sir Walter Raleigh did a 13-year stretch here too under James I, where he wrote his *Historie of the World.*

In front of the **Chapel Royal of St Peter ad Vincula** stood Henry VIII's scaffold, where nobles such as Anne Boleyn and Catherine Howard (Henry's second and fifth wives) were beheaded. Look out for the latest in the Tower's long line of famous ravens, which legend says could cause the White Tower to collapse should they leave (their wing feathers are clipped in case they get any ideas).

To get your bearings, take one of the entertaining (and free) guided tours offered by the Beefeaters. Hour-long tours leave every 30 minutes from the bridge near the main entrance; the last tour is an hour before closing.

Book online for cheaper rates for the Tower.

★ **Tower Bridge**   BRIDGE
(Map p90; ⊖ Tower Hill) One of London's most recognisable sights, familiar from dozens of movies, Tower Bridge doesn't disappoint in real life. Its neo-Gothic towers and sky-blue suspension struts add extraordinary elegance to what is a supremely functional structure. London was a thriving port in 1894 when it was built as a much-needed crossing point in the east, equipped with a then-revolutionary steam-driven bascule (counter-balance) mechanism that could raise the roadway to make way for oncoming ships in just three minutes.

A lift leads up from the northern tower to the **Tower Bridge Exhibition** (Map p90;

020-7403 3761; www.towerbridge.org.uk; adult/child £9.80/4.20, incl the Monument £12/5.50; ⊙10am-5.30pm Apr-Sep, 9.30am-5pm Oct-Mar), where the story of building the bridge is recounted. Tower Bridge was designed by architect Horace Jones, who was also responsible for Smithfield and Leadenhall markets, and completed by engineer John Wolfe Barry.

The bridge is still operational, although these days it's electrically powered and rises mainly for pleasure craft. It does so around 1000 times a year and as often as 10 times a day in summer; consult the Exhibition website for times to watch it in action.

★ **Museum of London**   MUSEUM
(Map p90; 020-7001 9844; www.museumoflondon.org.uk; 150 London Wall, EC2; ⊙10am-6pm; Barbican) FREE As entertaining as it is educational, the Museum of London meanders through the various incarnations of the city, stopping off in Roman Londinium and Saxon Ludenwic before eventually ending up in the 21st-century metropolis. Interesting objects and interactive displays work together to bring each era to life, without ever getting too whiz-bang, making this one of the capital's best museums. Free themed tours take place throughout the day; check the signs by the entrance for times.

★ **Monument**   MONUMENT
(Map p90; 020-7403 3761; www.themonument.org.uk; Fish St Hill, EC3; adult/child £5/2.50, incl Tower Bridge Exhibition £12/5.50; ⊙9.30am-5.30pm Apr-Sep, to 5pm Oct-Mar; Monument) Sir Christopher Wren's 1677 column, known simply as the Monument, is a memorial to the Great Fire of London of 1666, whose impact on London's history cannot be overstated. An immense Doric column made of Portland stone, the Monument is 4.5m wide and 60.6m tall – the exact distance it stands from the bakery in Pudding Lane where the fire is thought to have started.

Note, tickets can only be purchased with cash.

★ **Sky Garden**   VIEWPOINT
(Map p90; 020-7337 2344; www.skygarden.london; L35-37, 20 Fenchurch St, EC3; ⊙10am-6pm Mon-Fri, 11am-9pm Sat & Sun; Monument) FREE The City's sixth-tallest building didn't get off to a good start when it opened in 2014. Officially called 20 Fenchurch St it was quickly dubbed the 'Walkie Talkie' by unimpressed

Londoners, and its highly reflective windows melted the bodywork of several cars parked below. However, the opening of this 155m-high, three-storey, public garden in the glass dome at the top has helped win naysayers over. Entry is free, but you'll need to book a slot in advance.

St Bartholomew-the-Great   CHURCH
(Map p90; 020-7600 0440; www.greatstbarts.com; West Smithfield, EC1; adult/child £5/3; ⊙8.30am-5pm Mon-Fri, 10.30am-4pm Sat, 8.30am-8pm Sun; Barbican) Dating to 1123 and adjoining one of London's oldest hospitals, St Bartholomew-the-Great is one of London's most ancient churches. The Norman arches and profound sense of history lend this holy space an ancient calm, while approaching from nearby Smithfield Market through the restored 13th-century half-timbered archway is like walking back in time. The church was originally part of an Augustinian priory, but became the parish church of Smithfield in 1539 when Henry VIII dissolved the monasteries.

Barbican   ARCHITECTURE
(Map p90; 020-7638 4141; www.barbican.org.uk; Silk St, EC2; tours adult/child £12.50/10; ⊙9am-11pm Mon-Sat, 11am-11pm Sun; Barbican) Londoners remain fairly divided about the architectural value of this vast complex built after WWII, but the Barbican remains the City's pre-eminent cultural centre, with the main Barbican Hall, two theatres, a state-of-the-art cinema complex and two well-regarded art galleries: the 3rd-floor **Barbican Art Gallery** (Map p90; www.barbican.org.uk/artgallery; L3 Barbican Centre; ⊙10am-6pm Sat-Wed, to 9pm Thu & Fri) and the **Curve** (Map p90; L1 Barbican Centre; ⊙11am-8pm) FREE on the ground floor. There's also a large **conservatory** (Map p90; L3 Barbican Centre, Upper Frobisher Cres, EC2; ⊙noon-5pm Sun), filled with tropical plants.

30 St Mary Axe   NOTABLE BUILDING
(Map p90; www.30stmaryaxe.info; 30 St Mary Axe, EC3; Aldgate) Nicknamed 'the Gherkin' for its unusual shape, 30 St Mary Axe is the City's most distinctive skyscraper, dominating its skyline despite actually being only the fourth tallest. Built in 2003 by award-winning architect Norman Foster, the Gherkin's futuristic exterior has become an emblem of modern London – as recognisable as Big Ben. The building is closed to the public, though in the past it has opened its

Tower of London

TACKLING THE TOWER

Although it's usually less busy in the late afternoon, don't leave your assault on the Tower until too late in the day. You could easily spend hours here and not see it all. Start by getting your bearings on one of the Yeoman Warder (Beefeater) tours; they are included in the cost of admission, entertaining and the easiest way to access the ❶ **Chapel Royal of St Peter ad Vincula**, which is where they finish up.

When you leave the chapel, the ❷ **Scaffold Site** is directly in front. The building immediately to your left is Waterloo Barracks, where the ❸ **Crown Jewels** are housed. These are the absolute highlight of a Tower visit, so keep an eye on the entrance and pick a time to visit when it looks relatively quiet. Once inside, take things at your own pace. Slow-moving travelators shunt you past the dozen or so crowns that are the treasury's centrepieces, but feel free to double-back for a second or even third pass.

Allow plenty of time for the ❹ **White Tower**, the core of the whole complex, starting with the exhibition of royal armour. As you continue onto the 1st floor, keep an eye out for ❺ **St John's Chapel**.

The famous ❻ **ravens** can be seen in the courtyard south of the White Tower. Next, visit the ❼ **Bloody Tower** and the torture displays in the dungeon of the Wakefield Tower. Head next through the towers that formed the ❽ **Medieval Palace**, then take the ❾ **East Wall Walk** to get a feel for the castle's mighty battlements. Spend the rest of your time poking around the many other fascinating nooks and crannies of the Tower complex.

BEAT THE QUEUES

➡ Buy tickets online, avoid weekends and aim to be at the Tower first thing in the morning, when queues are shortest.

➡ An annual Historic Royal Palaces membership allows you to jump the queues and visit the Tower (and four other London palaces) as often as you like.

FLIK47 / GETTY IMAGES ©

Chapel Royal of St Peter ad Vincula

This chapel serves as the resting place for the royals and other members of the aristocracy who were executed on the small green out front. Several other historical figures are buried here too, including St Thomas More.

Scaffold Site

Seven people, including three queens (Anne Boleyn, Catherine Howard and Jane Grey), lost their heads here during Tudor times, saving the monarch the embarrassment of public executions on Tower Hill. The site features a rather odd 'pillow' sculpture by Brian Catling.

Above: Execution Site Memorial, by Brian Catling

Dry Moat

Beauchamp Tower

Coins & Kings display

Main Entrance

Middle Tower

Byward Tower

Bell Tower

White Tower

Much of the White Tower is taken up with an exhibition on 500 years of royal armour. Look for the virtually cuboid suit made to match Henry VIII's bloated 49-year-old body, complete with an oversized armoured codpiece to protect, ahem, the crown jewels.

CHRISDORNEY / SHUTTERSTOCK ©

St John's Chapel
The White Tower's unadorned chapel dates from 1080, making it the oldest surviving Christian place of worship in London.

Crown Jewels
When they're not being worn for ceremonies of state, Her Majesty's bling is kept here. Among the 23,578 gems, look out for the 530-carat 1st Star of Africa diamond at the top of the Sovereign's Sceptre with cross, the largest part of what was then the largest diamond ever found.

JOSEPH M. ARSENEAU / SHUTTERSTOCK ©

Flint Tower

Bowyer Tower

Brick Tower

Martin Tower

Royal Fusiliers Museum

Constable Tower

① ②

Queen's House

④

⑤ Roman city wall

Broad Arrow Tower

Bloody Tower

⑦

⑥

Lanthorne Tower

New Armouries

⑧

Traitors' Gate & St Thomas's Tower

Wakefield Tower

⑨ Salt Tower

Cradle Tower

Well Tower

River Thames

Medieval Palace
This part of the Tower complex was begun around 1220 and was home to England's medieval monarchs. Look for the recreations of the bedchamber of Edward I (1272–1307) in St Thomas's Tower and the throne room of his father, Henry III (1216–72) in the Wakefield Tower.

CRISTIAN SANTINON / SHUTTERSTOCK ©

Ravens
This stretch of green is where the Tower's half-dozen ravens are kept, fed on raw meat and blood-soaked biscuits. According to legend, if the ravens depart the fortress, the Tower will fall.

Wall Walk
Follow the inner ramparts along the Tower's eastern and northern fortifications. Each of the seven towers along the way has themed displays, covering everything from the royal menagerie to the Tower during WWI.

doors over the **Open House London** (☏020-7383 2131; www.openhouselondon.org.uk) weekend in September.

◉ South Bank

★**Tate Modern** GALLERY
(Map p98; ☏020-7887 8888; www.tate.org.uk; Bankside, SE1; ⊙10am-6pm Sun-Thu, to 10pm Fri & Sat; 👪; ◉Blackfriars, Southwark, London Bridge) FREE One of London's most amazing attractions, this outstanding modern- and contemporary-art gallery is housed in the creatively revamped **Bankside Power Station** south of the Millennium Bridge. A spellbinding synthesis of modern art and capacious industrial brick design, Tate Modern has been extraordinarily successful in bringing challenging work to the masses, both through its free permanent collection and fee-paying big-name temporary exhibitions. The stunning Switch House extension opened in 2016, increasing the available exhibition space by 60%.

The 4.2 million bricks of the 200m-long former power house (now called Boiler House) is an imposing sight, designed by Swiss architects Herzog and de Meuron, who scooped the prestigious Pritzker Architecture Prize in 2001 for their transformation of the empty power station. Significant achievements include leaving the building's central 99m-high chimney, adding a two-storey glass box onto the roof and employing the cavernous Turbine Hall as a dramatic entrance space. Herzog and de Meuron also designed the new 10-storey extension.

As a supreme collection of modern art, the contents of the museum are, nevertheless, the main draw. At their disposal the Tate Modern curators have works by Georges Braque, Henri Matisse, Piet Mondrian, Andy Warhol, Mark Rothko and Jackson Pollock, as well as pieces by Joseph Beuys, Damien Hirst, Claes Oldenburg and Auguste Rodin.

Tate Modern's permanent collection is arranged by both theme and chronology on levels 2 and 4 of Boiler House and levels 0, 2, 3 and 4 of Switch House. The emphasis in the latter is on art from the 1960s onwards. More than 60,000 works are on constant rotation, so if there's a particular work you would like to see, check the website to see if (and where) it's hanging.

The museum's location is also supreme, made the most of by popular balconies on level 3 of Boiler House and the level 10 viewing gallery in Switch House. The magnificent view is elegantly conveyed by the **Millennium Bridge** (Map p98; ◉St Paul's, Blackfriars) directly to St Paul's Cathedral in the City on the far bank of the river.

Free guided highlights tours depart at 11am, noon, 2pm and 3pm daily. Audio guides (in five languages) are available for £4; these contain information about 50 artworks across the gallery and offer suggested tours for adults or children.

To visit the sister museum Tate Britain (p83), hop on the **Tate Boat** (Map p98; www.tate.org.uk/visit/tate-boat; one-way adult/child £8.30/4.15) from Bankside Pier.

★**Shakespeare's Globe** HISTORIC BUILDING
(Map p98; ☏020-7902 1500; www.shakespearesglobe.com; 21 New Globe Walk, SE1; adult/child £17/10; ⊙9.30am-5pm; 👪; ◉Blackfriars, London Bridge) Unlike other venues for Shakespearean plays, the new Globe was designed to resemble the original as closely as possible, which means having the arena open to the fickle London skies, leaving the 700 'groundlings' (standing spectators) to weather London's spectacular downpours. Visits to the Globe include tours of the theatre (half hourly) as well as access to the exhibition space, which has fascinating exhibits on Shakespeare and theatre in the 17th century.

★**London Eye** VIEWPOINT
(Map p98; ☏0871 222 4002; www.londoneye.com; adult/child £27/22; ⊙11am-6pm Sep-May, 10am-8.30pm Jun-Aug; ◉Waterloo, Westminster) Standing 135m high in a fairly flat city, the London Eye affords views 25 miles in every direction, weather permitting. Interactive tablets provide great information (in six languages) about landmarks as they appear in the skyline. Each rotation – or 'flight' – takes a gracefully slow 30 minutes. At peak times (July, August and school holidays) it can feel like you'll spend more time in the queue than in the capsule; book premium fast-track tickets to jump the queue.

Tickets are cheaper if purchased online, especially if you book in advance or combine the London Eye with other attractions. Feeling romantic? Hire a capsule for two (£425), with a bottle of champers (though for health and safety reasons, a 'host' needs to tag along).

The London Eye has also been the focal point of the capital's celebrated and dramatic midnight New Year's Eve fireworks display.

★ **Southbank Centre** ARTS CENTRE
(Map p98; ☑ 020-3879 9555; www.southbank
centre.co.uk; Belvedere Rd, SE1; ⚑; ⊖ Waterloo, Embankment) The flagship venue of the
Southbank Centre, Europe's largest centre
for performing and visual arts, is the **Royal Festival Hall**. Its gently curved facade
of glass and Portland stone is more hu-
mane than its 1970s brutalist neighbours.
It is one of London's leading music venues
and the epicentre of life on this part of the
South Bank, hosting cafes, restaurants,
shops and bars.

Just north, the austere Queen Elizabeth Hall (p144) is a brutalist icon, the
second-largest concert venue in the centre, hosting chamber orchestras, quartets,
choirs, dance performances and sometimes opera. Underneath its elevated floor
is a graffiti-decorated **skateboarders'
hang-out**.

The opinion-dividing 1968 **Hayward
Gallery** (£14 to £16.50; ⊙ 11am-7pm Mon & Wed,
to 9pm Thu, 11am-7pm Sat & Sun), another brutalist beauty, is a leading contemporary-art
exhibition space.

The QEH recently underwent a 21st-
century facelift, while the Hayward Gallery
reopened after a similar restoration in January 2018.

★ **London Dungeon** HISTORIC BUILDING
(Map p98; www.thedungeons.com/london; County Hall, Westminster Bridge Rd, SE1; adult/child
£30/24; ⊙ 10am-4pm Mon-Wed & Fri, 11am-4pm
Thu, 10am-6pm Sat, 10am-5pm Sun; ⚑; ⊖ Waterloo, Westminster) Older kids tend to love the

London Dungeon, as the terrifying queues
during school holidays and weekends test-
ify. It's all spooky music, ghostly boat rides,
macabre hangman's drop-rides, fake blood
and actors dressed up as torturers and
gory criminals (including Jack the Ripper
and Sweeney Todd), with interactive scares
galore.

★ **Southwark Cathedral** CHURCH
(Map p98; ☑ 020-7367 6700; www.cathedral.south
wark.anglican.org; Montague Cl, SE1; ⊙ 8am-
6pm Mon-Fri, 8.30am-6pm Sat & Sun; ⊖ London
Bridge) The earliest surviving parts of this
relatively small cathedral are the retrochoir
at the eastern end, which contains four
chapels and was part of the 13th-century
Priory of St Mary Overie, some ancient ar-
cading by the southwest door and an arch
that dates to the original Norman church.
But most of the cathedral is Victorian. Inside there are monuments galore, including
a Shakespeare memorial. Catch evensong
at 5.30pm on four weekdays a week, 4pm
on Saturdays and 3pm on Sundays.

National Theatre THEATRE
(Map p98; ☑ 020-7452 3000; www.nationalthe
atre.org.uk; South Bank, SE1; ⚑; ⊖ Waterloo) The
nation's flagship theatre complex comprises
three auditoriums for performances. Likened by Prince Charles to a nuclear power
station, the theatre's purpose-designed architecture is considered an icon of the brutalist school. Fantastic **backstage tours**
lasting 1¼ hours (adult/child £9.50/8.25)
are available. Every tour is different but
you're likely to see rehearsals and changes

GETTING HIGH IN LONDON

Not so long ago, getting a good view of London was a near-impossible endeavour. There
was the London Eye (p96), to be sure, but been-there-done-that, yeah? And **Vertigo 42**
(Map p90; ☑ 020-7877 7703; www.citysociallondon.com; L24, 25 Old Broad St, EC2; mains £26-
38; ⊙ noon-3.30pm & 6-11.30pm Mon-Fri, 5-11.30pm Sat; ⊖ Bank) involved a lot of forward
planning.

Now things are a lot more democratic and, well, the sky's the limit. The 72nd-floor
open-air platform of the Shard (p99) is as high as you'll get in the EU. For nibbles and
views head for the 40th-floor location of Duck & Waffle (p128) or to Madison (p135).
For drinks we love Sky Pod (p135) and the **Radio Rooftop Bar** (Map p84; ☑ 020-7395
3440; ME London, 10th fl, 336-337 The Strand, WC2; ⊙ noon-1am Mon-Wed, to 2am Thu-Sat,
noon-midnight Sun; ⊖ Temple, Covent Garden). The **5th View** (Map p84; ☑ 020-7851 2433;
www.5thview.co.uk; 5th fl, Waterstone's Piccadilly, 203-206 Piccadilly, W1; mains from £8.50;
⊙ 9am-9.30pm Mon-Sat, noon-5pm Sun; ⊖ Piccadilly Circus) atop Waterstones bookshop in
Piccadilly is admittedly low on the totem pole but, having taken afternoon tea there, you
can legitimately use the ultimate intellectual's chat-up line: 'I get high on books'.

South Bank

500 m
0.25 miles

A **B** **C** **D** **E** **F** **G**

Victoria Embankment

River Thames

Waterloo Bridge

Blackfriars Bridge

Millennium Bridge

Lower Thames St

Old Billingsgate Market

London Bridge

Southwark Bridge

Thames Path

Bankside

Railway App

London Bridge

Tooley St

Battle Br La

Crucifix La

Bermondsey St

Tower Bridge Rd

Grange Rd

Little Bird Gin (150m);
Maltby Street Market (150m)

White Cube

Abbey St

Bermondsey Market

Rothsay St

Law St

BERMONDSEY

Weston St

Guy St

Long La

Kipling St

Crosby Row

Snowsfields

St Thomas St

Newcomen St

Borough High St

Great Dover St

Tabard St

Trinity St

Swan St

Harper Rd

Borough

Great Guildford St

Southwark St

SOUTHWARK

Union St

Copperfield St

Great Suffolk St

Glasshill St

Webber St

Borough Rd

Lancaster St

Newington Causeway

Elephant & Castle

London Rd

Garden Row

St George's Rd

Imperial War Museum

Blackfriars Rd

Paris Garden

Hatfields St

Duchy St

Theed St

Roupell St

Meymott St

Joan St

Southwark

Surrey Row

Cut

The Cut

Mitre Rd

Pearman St

Coral St

Morley St

Westminster Bridge Rd

Lambeth Rd

BOROUGH

Waterloo Rd

Cosser St

Carlisle La

LAMBETH

Kennington Rd

Lambeth North

Bayls Rd

Lower Marsh

Addington St

York Rd

SOUTH BANK

Waterloo

Belvedere Rd

Hayward Gallery

Waterloo Rd

Southbank Centre

Hungerford Bridge & Golden Jubilee Bridge

Jubilee Gardens

London Eye

London Dungeon

Westminster Bridge Rd

Lambeth Palace Rd

Archbishop's Park

RVT (0.75mi)

Lambeth Palace Rd

Rennie St

Upper Ground

Stamford St

Coin St

Upper Ground

Stoney St

Southwark Cathedral

Borough Market

Southwark Bridge Rd

Ayres St

Redcross Way

Lant St

The Rose Playhouse

Tate Modern

Shakespeare's Globe

New Globe Walk

Park St

Sumner St

Holland St

Hopton St

Tate Boat

Southwark Bridge Rd

Great Dover St

1 · 2 · 3 · 4

South Bank

of sets or bump into actors in the corridors. There is at least one tour per day, and often more. Consult the website for exact times and make sure you book.

The Shard
NOTABLE BUILDING

(Map p98; www.theviewfromtheshard.com; 32 London Bridge St, SE1; adult/child £30.95/24.95; ◷10am-10pm; ⬤London Bridge) Puncturing the skies above London, the dramatic splinter-like form of the Shard has rapidly become an icon of London. The viewing platforms on floors 69 and 72 are open to the public and the views are, as you'd expect from a 244m vantage point, sweeping, but they come at a hefty price – book online at least a day in advance to make a big saving.

HMS Belfast
SHIP

(Map p98; www.iwm.org.uk/visits/hms-belfast; Queen's Walk, SE1; adult/child £15.45/7.70; ◷10am-5pm; ⬤London Bridge) HMS *Belfast* is a magnet for kids of all ages. This large, light cruiser – launched in 1938 – served in WWII, helping to sink the German battleship *Scharnhorst,* shelling the Normandy coast on D-Day and later participating in the Korean War. Its 6in guns could bombard a target 14 land miles distant. Displays offer a great insight into what life on board was like, in peacetimes and during military engagements.

◉ Kensington & Hyde Park

★ Natural History Museum
MUSEUM

(Map p100; www.nhm.ac.uk; Cromwell Rd, SW7; ◷10am-5.50pm; ⬤South Kensington) FREE This colossal and magnificent-looking building is infused with the irrepressible Victorian spirit of collecting, cataloguing and interpreting the natural world. The **Dinosaurs Gallery** (Blue Zone) is a must for children, who gawp at the animatronic T-Rex, fossils and excellent displays. Adults for their part will love the intriguing Treasures exhibition in the **Cadogan Gallery** (Green Zone), which houses a host of unrelated objects each telling its own unique story, from a chunk of moon rock to a dodo skeleton.

Also in the Green Zone, the **Mineral Gallery** is a breathtaking display of architectural perspective leading to the **Vault**, where you'll find the **Aurora Collection** of almost 300 coloured diamonds. In the Orange Zone, the vast **Darwin Centre** focuses on taxonomy, showcasing 28 million insects and six million plants in a giant cocoon; glass windows allow you to watch scientists at work.

At the centre of the museum is **Hintze Hall**, which resembles a cathedral nave – quite fitting, as it was built in a time when the natural sciences were challenging the

Knightsbridge, South Kensington & Chelsea

Leinster Tce

Porchester Tce

Paddington
(300m)

Lancaster Gate

Bayswater Rd

Lancaster Gate

Buck Hill Walk

Budge's Walk

7

8

The Long Water

Kensington Gardens

Lancaster Walk

Round Pond

Rockwell
(500m)

The Flower Walk

Albert Memorial

1

Kensington Gore

Kensington Rd

Kensington Rd

Palace Gate

Prince Consort Rd

Exhibition Rd

9

24

13

Bayswater Rd

W Carriage Dr

North Ride

Hyde Park

2

Hyde Park

The Serpentine

Serpentine Rd

Rotten Row

14

Ennismore Gdns

Kensington Rd

KNIGHTSBRIDGE

Knightsbridge

Rutland Gate

Montpelier St

Brompton Rd

Raphael St

28

Marble Arch (150m)

Woods Mews

Park La

Park La

Culross St

Upper Grosvenor St

Grosvenor Sq

Adam's Row

Mount St

23

Aldford St

South St

Deanery St

Mount Row

Farm St

Hill St

Hill St

Hay's Mews

Charles St

MAYFAIR

Curzon St

Curzon Sq

Shepherd St

Hertford St

Brick St

Park La

Piccadilly

Green Park

Buckingham Palace Gardens

Grosvenor Pl

Chapel St

Chester St

Halkin St

Belgrave Sq

Hyde Park Corner

Knightsbridge

18

Kinnerton St

Lowndes St

29

Knightsbridge

Sloane St

Basil St

Melcomb St

500 m
0.25 miles

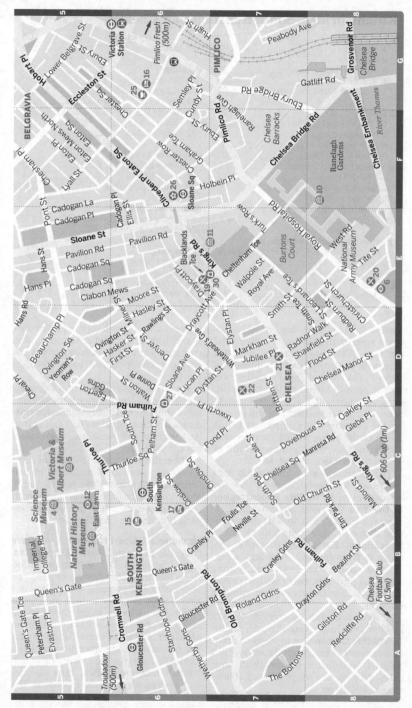

Knightsbridge, South Kensington & Chelsea

biblical tenets of Christian orthodoxy. After 81 years in the Mammals Hall, in 2017 the Blue Whale skeleton was relocated here, with the famous cast of a diplodocus skeleton (nicknamed Dippy) making way for the colossal mammal. The transfer itself was a mammoth and painstaking engineering project, disassembling and preparing the 4.5-tonne bones for reconstruction in a dramatic diving posture that greet visitors to the museum. Dippy himself will go walkabout on a long tour of the UK.

The museum hosts regular exhibitions (admission fees apply), some of them on a recurrent basis. **Wildlife Photographer of the Year** (Map p100; adult/child £13.50/8, family £28-38; ⊙ Oct-Sep), with its show-stopping images, is now in its 50th year, and **Sensational Butterflies** (Map p100; per person £5.85, family £19.80; ⊙ Apr-Sep), a tunnel tent on the East Lawn that swarms with what must originally have been called 'flutter-bys', has become a firm summer favourite.

A slice of English countryside in SW7 and due to be hugely expanded, the beautiful **Wildlife Garden** next to the West Lawn encompasses a range of British lowland habitats, including a meadow with farm gates and a bee tree where a colony of honey bees fills the air.

The museum is transforming its outdoor spaces, tripling the Wildlife Garden in size, creating a piazza in the eastern grounds and adding a geological and palaeontological timeline walk.

From Halloween to January, a section by the East Lawn of the museum is transformed into a glittering and highly popular **ice rink**, complete with a hot drinks stall. Our advice: book your slot well ahead, browse the museum and skate later.

The entire museum and its gardens cover a huge 5.7 hectares and contain 80 million specimens from across the natural world. More than five million visitors come each year, so queues can sometimes get long, especially during the school holidays.

★**Victoria & Albert Museum**   MUSEUM
(V&A; Map p100; ☏ 020-7942 2000; www.vam.ac.uk; Cromwell Rd, SW7; ⊙ 10am-5.45pm Sat-Thu, to 10pm Fri; ⊜ South Kensington) **FREE** The Museum of Manufactures, as the V&A was known when it opened in 1852, was part of Prince Albert's legacy to the nation in the aftermath of the successful Great Exhibition of 1851. It houses the world's largest collection of decorative arts, from Asian ceramics to Middle Eastern rugs, Chinese paintings, Western furniture, fashion from all ages and modern-day domestic appliances. The

(ticketed) temporary exhibitions are another highlight, covering anything from David Bowie retrospectives to designer Alexander McQueen, special materials and trends.

★ **Science Museum** MUSEUM
(Map p100; ☑ 020-7942 4000; www.sciencemuseum.org.uk; Exhibition Rd, SW7; ⊙ 10am-6pm; ⓔ South Kensington) FREE With seven floors of interactive and educational exhibits, this scientifically spellbinding museum will mesmerise adults and children alike, covering everything from early technology to space travel. A perennial favourite is **Exploring Space**, a gallery featuring genuine rockets and satellites and a full-size replica of the *Eagle*, the lander that took Neil Armstrong and Buzz Aldrin to the moon in 1969. The **Making the Modern World Gallery** next door is a visual feast of locomotives, planes, cars and other revolutionary inventions.

★ **Hyde Park** PARK
(Map p100; www.royalparks.org.uk/parks/hyde-park; ⊙ 5am-midnight; ⓔ Marble Arch, Hyde Park Corner, Queensway) At 145 hectares, Hyde Park is central London's largest open space, expropriated from the Church in 1536 by Henry VIII and turned into a hunting ground and later a venue for duels, executions and horse racing. The 1851 Great Exhibition was held here, and during WWII the park became an enormous potato field. These days, there's boating on the **Serpentine**, summer concerts (Bruce Springsteen, Florence + The Machine, Patti Smith), film nights and other warm-weather events.

★ **Kensington Palace** PALACE
(Map p106; www.hrp.org.uk/kensington-palace; Kensington Gardens, W8; adult/child £15.50/free (when booked online); ⊙ 10am-4pm Nov-Feb, to 6pm Mar-Oct; ⓔ High St Kensington) Built in 1605, the palace became the favourite royal residence under William and Mary of Orange in 1689, and remained so until George III became king and moved out. Today, it is still a royal residence, with the likes of the Duke and Duchess of Cambridge (Prince William and his wife Catherine) and the Duke and Duchess of Sussex (Prince Harry and Meghan) living there. A large part of the palace is open to the public, however, including the King's and Queen's State Apartments.

★ **Apsley House** HISTORIC BUILDING
(Map p82; ☑ 020-7499 5676; www.english-heritage.org.uk/visit/places/apsley-house; 149 Piccadilly, Hyde Park Corner, W1; adult/child £9.30/5.60, with Wellington Arch £11.20/6.70; ⊙ 11am-5pm Wed-Sun Apr-Oct, 10am-4pm Sat & Sun Nov-Mar; ⓔ Hyde Park Corner) This stunning house, containing exhibits about the Duke of Wellington, who defeated Napoleon Bonaparte at Waterloo, was once the first building to appear when entering London from the west and was therefore known as 'No 1 London'. Wellington memorabilia, including the Duke's death mask, fills the basement **gallery**, while an astonishing collection of china and silver, and paintings by Velasquez, Rubens, Van Dyck, Brueghel, Murillo and Goya awaits in the 1st-floor Waterloo Gallery.

Kensington Gardens PARK
(Map p106; ☑ 0300 061 2000; www.royalparks.org.uk/parks/kensington-gardens; ⊙ 6am-dusk; ⓔ Queensway, Lancaster Gate) A gorgeous collection of manicured lawns, tree-shaded avenues and basins immediately west of Hyde Park, the picturesque 107-hectare expanse of Kensington Gardens is technically part of Kensington Palace, located in the far west of the gardens.The large **Round Pond** is enjoyable to amble around and also worth a look are the lovely fountains in the **Italian Gardens** (Map p100; Kensington Gardens; ⓔ Lancaster Gate), believed to be a gift from Prince Albert to Queen Victoria; they are now the venue of a handy new cafe.

The **Diana, Princess of Wales Memorial Playground** (Map p106; ⓔ Queensway), in the northwest corner of the gardens, has some pretty ambitious attractions for children. Next to the playground stands the delightful **Elfin Oak** (Map p106), a 900-year-old tree stump carved with elves, gnomes, witches and small creatures. George Frampton's celebrated **Peter Pan statue** (Map p100; ⓔ Lancaster Gate) is close to the lake, while the astonishing **Albert Memorial** (Map p100; ☑ tours 020-8969 0104; tours adult/concession £9/8; ⊙ tours 2pm & 3pm 1st Sun of month Mar-Dec; ⓔ Knightsbridge, Gloucester Rd) is in the south of Kensington Gardens, facing the Royal Albert Hall.

Royal Albert Hall HISTORIC BUILDING
(Map p100; ☑ 0845 401 5034, box office 020-7589 8212; www.royalalberthall.com; Kensington Gore, SW7; tours £10.75-16.75; ⓔ South Kensington) Built in 1871, thanks in part to the proceeds of the 1851 Great Exhibition organised by Prince Albert (Queen Victoria's husband), this huge, domed, red-brick amphitheatre,

Victoria & Albert Museum

HALF-DAY HIGHLIGHTS TOUR

The art- and design-packed V&A is vast: we have devised an easy-to-follow tour of the museum highlights to help cover some signature pieces while also allowing you to appreciate some of the grandeur of the museum architecture.

Enter the V&A by the main entrance off Cromwell Rd and immediately turn left to explore the Islamic Middle East Gallery and to discover the sumptuous silk-and-wool ❶ **Ardabil Carpet**. Among the pieces from South Asia in the adjacent gallery is the terrifying automated ❷ **Tipu's Tiger**. Continue to the outstanding ❸ **Fashion Gallery** with its displays of clothing styles through the ages. The magnificent gallery opposite houses the ❹ **Raphael Cartoons**, large paintings by Raphael used to weave tapestries for the Vatican. Take the stairs to level 2 and the Britain 1500–1760 Gallery; turn left in

Raphael Cartoons
These seven drawings by Raphael, depicting the acts of St Peter and St Paul, were the full-scale preparatory works for seven tapestries that were woven for the Sistine Chapel in the Vatican.

Fashion Gallery
With clothing from the 18th century to the present day, this circular and chronologically arranged gallery showcases evening wear, undergarments and iconic fashion milestones, such as 1960s dresses designed by Mary Quant.

The Great Bed of Ware
Created during the reign of Queen Elizabeth I, its headboard and bedposts are etched with ancient graffiti; the 16th-century oak Great Bed of Ware is famously name-dropped in Shakespeare's *Twelfth Night*.

Britain 1500–1760 Gallery

Stairs from Level 1

Stairs to Level 3

5

6

Stairs to Level 2

4

3

2

1

Main Entrance

Gift Shop

John Madejski Garden

T T Tsui China Collection

Japan Gallery

Cast Courts

LEVEL 1

LEVEL 2

The Ardabil Carpet
One of the world's most beautiful carpets, the Ardabil was completed in 1540, one of a pair commissioned by Shah Tahmasp, ruler of Iran. The piece is most astonishing for the artistry of the detailing and the subtlety of design.

Tipu's Tiger
This disquieting 18th-century wood-and-metal mechanical automaton depicts a European being savaged by a tiger. When a handle is turned, an organ hidden within the feline mimics the cries of the dying man, whose arm also rises.

GREG BALFOUR EVANS / ALAMY STOCK PHOTO ©

the gallery to find the **⑤ Great Bed of Ware**, beyond which rests the exquisitely crafted artistry of **⑥ Henry VIII's Writing Box**. Head up the stairs into the Ironwork Gallery on level 3 for the **⑦ Hereford Screen**. Continue through the Ironwork and Sculpture Galleries and through the Leighton Corridor to the glittering **⑧ Jewellery Gallery**. Exit through the Stained Glass gallery, at the end of which you'll find stairs back down to level 1.

The Hereford Screen
Designed by Sir George Gilbert Scott, this awe-inspiring choir screen is a labour of love, originally fashioned for Hereford Cathedral. It's an almighty conception of wood, iron, copper, brass and hardstone, and there were few parts of the V&A that could support its great mass.

MARTIN HESKO / SHUTTERSTOCK ©

Stairs to Other Levels

20th Century Gallery

Stairs from Level 2

⑦

National Art Library

Ironwork Gallery

⑧

Leighton Corridor

Sculpture Gallery

Photographers Gallery

LEVEL 3

LEVEL 4

Jewellery Gallery
The beautifully illuminated Jewellery Gallery has a stunning collection of items from ancient Greece to the modern day, including a dazzling gold Celtic breastplate, art nouveau jewellery and animals fashioned by Fabergé.

Henry VIII's Writing Box
This exquisitely ornate walnut and oak 16th-century writing box has been added to over the centuries, but the original decorative motifs are superb, including Henry's coat of arms, flanked by Venus (holding Cupid) and Mars.

Notting Hill & Bayswater

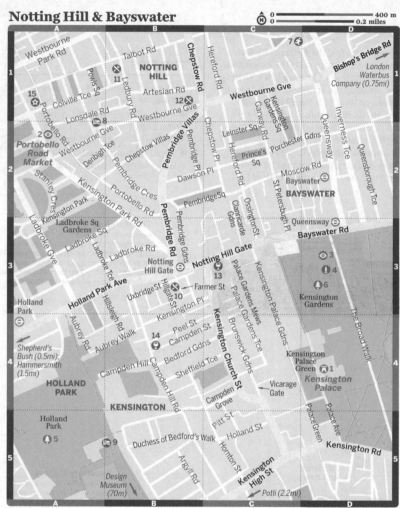

adorned with a frieze of Minton tiles, is Britain's most famous concert venue and home to the BBC's Promenade Concerts (the Proms) every summer. To find out about the hall's intriguing history and royal connections, and to gaze out from the Gallery, book an informative one-hour front-of-house **grand tour** (Map p100; ☎020-7589 8212; adult/child £14/7; ☉hourly 9.30am-4.30pm), operating most days.

Chelsea Physic Garden

GARDENS

(Map p100; ☎020-7352 5646; www.chelseaphysic garden.co.uk; 66 Royal Hospital Rd, SW3; adult/child £6.10/4.40; ☉11am-5pm Mon, to 6pm Tue-Fri & Sun Apr-Oct, 9.30am-4pm Mon-Fri Nov-Mar; ☉Sloane Sq) You may bump into a wandering duck or two as you enter this walled pocket of botanical enchantment, established by the Apothecaries' Society in 1673 for students working on medicinal plants and healing. One of Europe's oldest of its kind, the small grounds are a compendium of botany, from carnivorous pitcher plants to rich yellow flag irises, a cork oak from Portugal, the largest outdoor fruiting olive tree in the British Isles, rare trees and shrubs.

Notting Hill & Bayswater

◎ Top Sights
1 Kensington Palace D4
2 Portobello Road Market A2

◎ Sights
3 Diana, Princess of Wales
    Memorial Playground.....................D3
4 Elfin Oak D3
5 Holland Park A5
6 Kensington Gardens...........................D3

✪ Activities, Courses & Tours
7 Porchester Spa....................................C1

🛏 Sleeping
8 Main House A2
9 Safestay Holland Park........................B5

✪ Eating
10 Geales...B3
11 Ledbury...B1
12 Taquería B1

◎ Drinking & Nightlife
13 Notting Hill Arts Club.........................C3
14 Windsor Castle B4

✪ Entertainment
15 Electric Cinema A1

Royal Hospital Chelsea　　　MUSEUM
(Map p100; www.chelsea-pensioners.co.uk; Royal Hospital Rd, SW3; ◎grounds 10am-4.30pm Mon-Sat, Great Hall shuts daily noon-2pm, museum 10am-4pm Mon-Fri; ⊜Sloane Sq) FREE Designed by Christopher Wren, this superb structure was built in 1692 to provide shelter for ex-servicemen. Since the reign of Charles II, it has housed hundreds of war veterans, known as Chelsea Pensioners. They're fondly regarded as national treasures, and cut striking figures in the dark-blue greatcoats (in winter) or scarlet frock coats (in summer) that they wear on ceremonial occasions.

Serpentine Gallery　　　GALLERY
(Map p100; ☏020-7402 6075; www.serpentine galleries.org; Kensington Gardens, W2; ◎10am-6pm Tue-Sun; ⊜Lancaster Gate, Knightsbridge) FREE This gallery, looking like a 1930s tea-room amid leafy Kensington Gardens, is one of London's most important contemporary-art galleries. Damien Hirst, Andreas Gursky, Louise Bourgeois, Gabriel Orozco, Tomoko Takahashi and Jeff Koons have all exhibited here. A leading architect (who has never built in the UK) is annually commissioned to build a new 'Summer Pavilion'

nearby, open from June to October. The galleries run a full program of readings, talks and open-air cinema screenings.

◉ Clerkenwell, Shoreditch & Spitalfields

★**Geffrye Museum**　　　MUSEUM
(Map p138; ☏020-7739 9893; www.geffrye -museum.org.uk; 136 Kingsland Rd, E2; ◎10am-5pm Tue-Sun; ⊜Hoxton) FREE If you like nosing around other people's homes, you'll love this museum devoted to middle-class domestic interiors. Built in 1714 as a home for poor pensioners, these beautiful ivy-clad brick almshouses have been converted into a series of living rooms dating from 1630 to the present day. The rear garden is also organised by era, mirroring the museum's exploration of domesticity through the centuries. The Geffrye is closed until spring 2020 for major renovations.

★**Dennis Severs' House**　　　MUSEUM
(Map p138; ☏020-7247 4013; www.dennissevers house.co.uk; 18 Folgate St, E1; day/night £10/15; ◎noon-2pm & 5-9pm Mon, 5-9pm Wed & Fri, noon-4pm Sun; ⊜Liverpool St) This extraordinary Georgian House is set up as if its occupants – a family of Huguenot silk weavers – had just walked out the door. There are half-drunk cups of tea and partially consumed food, lit candles and, in perhaps unnecessary attention to detail, a full chamber pot by the bed. More than a museum, it's an opportunity to meditate on the minutiae of everyday Georgian life through silent exploration.

Old Truman Brewery　　　HISTORIC BUILDING
(Map p138; www.trumanbrewery.com; 91 Brick Lane, E1; ⊜Shoreditch High St) Founded here in the 17th century, Truman's Black Eagle Brewery was, by the 1850s, the largest brewery in the world. Spread over a series of brick buildings and yards straddling both sides of Brick Lane, the complex is now completely given over to edgy markets, pop-up fashion stores, vintage clothes shops, indie record hunters, cafes, bars and live-music venues. Beer may not be brewed here any more, but it certainly is consumed.

◉ East London

★**Whitechapel Gallery**　　　GALLERY
(☏020-7522 7888; www.whitechapelgallery.org; 77-82 Whitechapel High St, E1; ◎11am-6pm Tue, Wed & Fri-Sun, to 9pm Thu; ⊜Aldgate East) FREE A firm

favourite of art students and the avant-garde cognoscenti, this ground-breaking gallery doesn't have a permanent collection but is devoted to hosting edgy exhibitions of contemporary art. It made its name by staging exhibitions by both established and emerging artists, including the first UK shows by Pablo Picasso, Jackson Pollock, Mark Rothko and Frida Kahlo. The gallery's ambitiously themed shows change every couple of months (check online) and there's often also live music, talks and films on Thursday evenings.

★ **Museum of London Docklands** MUSEUM
(☑ 020-7001 9844; www.museumoflondon.org.uk/docklands; West India Quay, E14; ☺ 10am-6pm; ☐ DLR West India Quay) **FREE** Housed in an 1802 warehouse, this educational museum combines artefacts and multimedia displays to chart the history of the city through its river and docks. The best strategy is to begin on the 3rd floor and work your way down through the ages. Perhaps the most illuminating and certainly the most disturbing gallery is **London, Sugar and Slavery**, which examines the capital's role in the transatlantic slave trade.

★ **Columbia Road Flower Market** MARKET
(Map p138; www.columbiaroad.info; Columbia Rd, E2; ☺ 8am-3pm Sun; ☐ Hoxton) A wonderful explosion of colour and life, this weekly market sells a beautiful array of flowers, pot plants, bulbs, seeds and everything you might need for the garden. It's a lot of fun and the best place to hear proper Cockney barrow-boy banter ('We got flowers cheap enough for ya muvver-in-law's grave' etc). It gets really packed, so go as early as you can, or later on when the vendors sell off the cut flowers cheaply.

★ **Queen Elizabeth Olympic Park** PARK
(www.queenelizabetholympicpark.co.uk; E20; ☐ Stratford) The glittering centrepiece of London's 2012 Olympic Games, this vast 227-hectare expanse includes the main Olympic venues as well as playgrounds, walking and cycling trails, gardens, and a diverse mix of wetland, woodland, meadow and other wildlife habitats as an environmentally fertile legacy for the future. The main focal point is London Stadium (p143), with a Games capacity of 80,000, scaled back to 54,000 seats for its new role as the home ground for West Ham United FC.

LONDON'S LIDOS

The capital's long-running love of outdoor bathing has enjoyed a resurgence in recent years, and its lovely lidos (outdoor pools) are busier than ever. You'll see Londoners taking to the water in pretty much all weathers – even, for the real diehards, the middle of winter.

Serpentine Lido (Map p100; ☑ 020-7706 3422; Hyde Park, W2; adult/child £4.80/1.80; ☺ 10am-6pm daily Jun-Aug, to 6pm Sat & Sun May; ☐ Hyde Park Corner, Knightsbridge) Perhaps the ultimate London pool is inside the Serpentine lake. This fabulous lido is open May to August.

Hampstead Heath Ponds (www.cityoflondon.gov.uk; Hampstead Heath, NW5; adult/child £2/1; ☐ Hampstead Heath) Set in the midst of the gorgeous heath, the brown waters of Hampstead's three bathing ponds (men's, women's and mixed) offer a bracing dip. The water's tested daily, so don't be deterred by the colour.

London Fields Lido (☑ 020-7254 9038; www.better.org.uk/leisure-centre/london/hackney/london-fields-lido; London Fields West Side, E8; adult/child £4.85/2.85; ☺ 6.30am-9pm; ☐ London Fields) Built in the 1930s but abandoned by the '80s, this heated 50m Olympic-size outdoor pool reopened in 2006.

Porchester Spa (Map p106; ☑ 020-7313 3858; www.porchesterspatreatments.co.uk; Porchester Centre, Queensway, W2; admission £28.90; ☺ 10am-10pm; ☐ Bayswater, Royal Oak) Housed in a gorgeous, art deco building, the no-frills Porchester has a 30m swimming pool, a large Finnish-log sauna, two steam rooms, three Turkish hot rooms and a massive plunge pool.

London Aquatics Centre (☑ 020-8536 3150; www.londonaquaticscentre.org; Carpenters Rd, E20; adult/child from £5.20/3; ☺ 6am-10.30pm; ☐ Stratford) Not strictly a lido as it's inside, but Zaha Hadid's award-winning Aquatics Centre, built for the 2012 Olympics, is worth mentioning for its fabulous, undulating architecture.

REGENT'S CANAL

The towpath of the tranquil **Regent's Canal** (Map p132) makes an excellent shortcut across North London, either on foot or by bike. In full, the ribbon of water runs 9 miles from Little Venice (where it connects with the Grand Union Canal) to the Thames at Limehouse.

You can make do with walking from Little Venice to Camden Town in less than an hour, passing Regent's Park and London Zoo, as well as beautiful villas designed by architect John Nash and redevelopments of old industrial buildings. Allow 25 to 30 minutes between Little Venice and Regent's Park, and 15 to 20 minutes between Regent's Park and Camden Town. There are plenty of well-signed exits along the way.

If you decide to continue on, it's worth stopping at the **London Canal Museum** (☑020-7713 0836; www.canalmuseum.org.uk; 12-13 New Wharf Rd, N1; adult/child £5/2.50; ☺10am-4.30pm Tue-Sun & bank holidays; ◉King's Cross St Pancras) in King's Cross to learn more about the canal's history. Shortly afterwards you'll hit the 878m-long Islington Tunnel and have to take to the roads for a spell. After joining the path again near Colebrooke Row, you can follow the water all the way to the Thames at Limehouse Basin, or divert on to the Hertford Union Canal at Victoria Park and head to Queen Elizabeth Olympic Park.

ArcelorMittal Orbit   TOWER
(☑0333 800 8099; www.arcelormittalorbit.com; 3 Thornton St, E20; adult/child £12.50/7.50, with slide £17.50/12.50; ☺11am-5pm Mon-Fri, 10am-6pm Sat & Sun; ◉Stratford) Love it or loathe it, Turner Prize–winner Anish Kapoor's 115m-high, twisted-steel sculpture towers strikingly over the southern end of Queen Elizabeth Olympic Park. In essence it's an artwork, but at the 80m mark it also offers an impressive panorama from its mirrored viewing platform, which is accessed by a lift from the base of the sculpture (the tallest in the UK). A dramatic tunnel slide running down the tower is the world's highest and longest, coiling 178m down to ground level.

Victoria Park   PARK
(www.towerhamlets.gov.uk/victoriapark; Grove Rd, E3; ☺7am-dusk; ◉Hackney Wick) The 'Regent's Park of the East End', this 86-hectare leafy expanse of ornamental lakes, monuments, tennis courts, flower beds and lawns was opened in 1845. It was the first public park in the East End, given the go-ahead after a local MP presented Queen Victoria with a petition of 30,000 signatures. It quickly gained a reputation as the 'People's Park' when many rallies were held here.

Viktor Wynd Museum of Curiosities, Fine Art & Natural History   MUSEUM
(☑020-7998 3617; www.thelasttuesdaysociety.org; 11 Mare St, E8; £5; ☺noon-11pm Wed-Sat, to 10.30pm Sun; ◉Bethnal Green) Museum? Art project? Cocktail bar? This is not a venue that's easily classifiable. Inspired by Victorian-era cabinets of curiosities *(wunderkabinnet)*, Wynd's wilfully eccentric collection includes stuffed birds, pickled genitals, two-headed lambs, shrunken heads, a key to the Garden of Eden, dodo bones, celebrity excrement and a gilded hippo skull that belonged to Pablo Escobar. A self-confessed 'incoherent vision of the world displayed through wonder'; make of it what you will. Or stop by for a cocktail at the bar upstairs.

◉ North London

Regent's Park   PARK
(Map p126; www.royalparks.org.uk; ☺5am-dusk; ◉Regent's Park, Baker St) The most elaborate and formal of London's many parks, Regent's Park is one of the capital's loveliest green spaces. Among its many attractions are London Zoo, Regent's Canal, an ornamental lake, and sports pitches where locals meet to play football, rugby and volleyball. **Queen Mary's Gardens**, towards the south of the park, are particularly pretty, especially in June when the roses are in bloom. Performances take place here in an **open-air theatre** (☑0844 826 4242; www.openairtheatre.org; ☺May-Sep; ⊞; ◉Baker St) during summer.

★ZSL London Zoo   ZOO
(Map p132; www.zsl.org/zsl-london-zoo; Outer Circle, Regent's Park, NW1; adult/child £29.75/22; ☺10am-6pm Apr-Sep, to 5.30pm Mar & Oct, to 4pm Nov-Feb; ⊞; ▣274) Established in 1828, these 15-hectare zoological gardens are among the oldest in the world. The emphasis nowadays is firmly placed on

North Central London

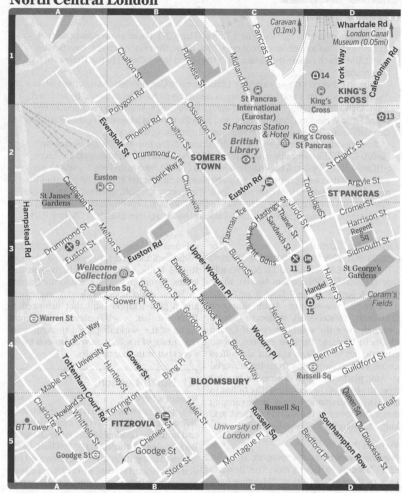

conservation, education and breeding, with fewer animals and bigger enclosures. Highlights include **Land of the Lions**, **Gorilla Kingdom**, **Tiger Territory**, the walkthrough **In with the Lemurs** and **Butterfly Paradise**. Feeding sessions and talks take place throughout the day. The zoo also organises various experiences, such as Keeper for a Day or sleepovers in the Bug House.

★ **British Library**   LIBRARY
(Map p110; www.bl.uk; 96 Euston Rd, NW1; ☺ galleries 9.30am-6pm Mon & Wed-Fri, to 8pm Tue, to 5pm Sat, 11am-5pm Sun; ⊖ King's Cross St Pancras) FREE Consisting of low-slung red-

brick terraces and fronted by a large plaza featuring an oversized statue of Sir Isaac Newton, Colin St John Wilson's British Library building is a love-it-or-hate-it affair (Prince Charles likened it to a secret-police academy). Completed in 1997, it's home to some of the greatest treasures of the written word, including the *Codex Sinaiticus* (the first complete text of the New Testament), Leonardo da Vinci's notebooks and a copy of the Magna Carta (1215).

★ **Highgate Cemetery**   CEMETERY
(www.highgatecemetery.org; Swain's Lane, N6; East Cemetery adult/child £4/free; ☺ 10am-

4pm Mon-Fri, 11am-4pm Sat & Sun; ⊖Archway) A Gothic wonderland of shrouded urns, obelisks, broken columns, sleeping angels, Egyptian-style tombs and overgrown graves, Highgate is a Victorian Valhalla spread over 20 wonderfully wild and atmospheric hectares. On the eastern side, you can pay your respects to the graves of Karl Marx and Mary Ann Evans (better known as novelist George Eliot). The real highlight, however, is the overgrown **West Cemetery**, which can only be visited on a **guided tour** (adult/child £12/6; ⊙1.45pm Mon-Fri, every 30min 11am-3pm Sat & Sun Nov-Feb, to 4pm Mar-Oct).

★**Hampstead Heath** PARK
(www.cityoflondon.gov.uk; ⊖Hampstead Heath, Gospel Oak) Sprawling Hampstead Heath, with its rolling woodlands and meadows, feels a million miles away – despite being approximately four – from the City of London. Covering 320 hectares, most of it woods, hills and meadows, it's home to about 180 bird species, 23 species of butterflies, grass snakes, bats and a rich array of flora. It's a wonderful place for a ramble, especially to the top of **Parliament Hill**, which offers expansive views across the city.

North Central London

★ **Wellcome Collection**   MUSEUM
(Map p110; www.wellcomecollection.org; 183 Euston Rd, NW1; ⊙10am-6pm Tue, Wed & Fri-Sun, to 10pm Thu; ⊜Euston Sq, Euston) FREE Focusing on the interface of art, science and medicine, this clever and resourceful museum is fascinating. The heart of the museum is Sir Henry Wellcome's collection of medical curiosities (saws for amputation, forceps through the ages, sex aids and amulets etc), which illustrate the universal fascination with health and the body across civilisations. In the **Medicine Now** gallery, interactive displays and provocative artworks are designed to make you ponder about humanity and the human body.

Abbey Road Studios   HISTORIC BUILDING
(www.abbeyroad.com; 3 Abbey Rd, NW8; ⊜St John's Wood) Beatles aficionados can't possibly visit London without making a pilgrimage to this famous recording studio in St John's Wood. The studios themselves are off-limits, so you'll have to content yourself with examining the decades of fan graffiti on the fence outside. Stop-start local traffic is long accustomed to groups of tourists lining up on the zebra crossing to re-enact the cover of the fab four's 1969 masterpiece *Abbey Road*. In 2010 the crossing was rewarded with Grade II heritage status.

For a strangely engrossing real-time view of the crossing, hit the 'live' tab for the webcam on the studio's website; you can even find your own crossing shot by punching in your time. To reach Abbey Road Studios, take the tube to St John's Wood, cross the road, follow Grove End Rd to its end and turn right. Don't do what some disappointed fans do and head to Abbey Rd Station in West Ham – it's no relation of the true site and miles off course. There are at least 10 Abbey Rds in London, adding to confusion.

Primrose Hill   PARK
(Map p132; ⊜Chalk Farm) On summer weekends, Primrose Hill park is absolutely packed with locals enjoying a picnic and the extraordinary views over the city skyline. Come weekdays, however, and there are mostly just dog walkers and nannies. It's a lovely place to enjoy a quiet stroll or an alfresco sandwich.

◉ Greenwich & South London

★ **Cutty Sark**   MUSEUM
(☏020-8312 6608; www.rmg.co.uk/cuttysark; King William Walk, SE10; adult/child £13.50/7; ⊙10am-5pm Sep-Jun, to 6pm Jul & Aug; ☐DLR Cutty Sark) The last of the great clipper ships to sail between China and England in the 19th century, the fully restored *Cutty Sark* endured massive fire damage in 2007 that occurred during a £25 million restoration. The exhibition in the ship's hold tells its story as a tea clipper at the end of the 19th century. Launched in 1869 in Scotland, she made eight voyages to China in the 1870s, sailing out with a mixed cargo and coming back with tea.

Another fire took hold in 2014, but fire crews were quick to respond and extinguish the blaze. As you make your way up, there are films, interactive maps and plenty of illustrations and props to get an idea of what life on board was like. Book online for cheaper rates.

★ **National Maritime Museum**   MUSEUM
(☏020-8312 6565; www.rmg.co.uk/national-maritime-museum; Romney Rd, SE10; ⊙10am-5pm; ☐DLR Cutty Sark) FREE Narrating the long, briny and eventful history of seafaring Britain, this excellent museum's exhibits are arranged thematically, with highlights in-

cluding *Miss Britain III* (the first boat to top 100mph on open water) from 1933, the 19m-long golden state barge built in 1732 for Frederick, Prince of Wales, the huge ship's propeller and the colourful figureheads installed on the ground floor. Families will love these, as well as the ship simulator and the 'All Hands' children's gallery on the 2nd floor.

Under eights can get to grips with all things nautical in the **'Ahoy!' gallery**, also on the ground floor. Adults are likely to prefer the other fantastic (and slightly more serene) galleries. **Voyagers: Britons and the Sea** on the ground floor is an introduction to the collection and showcases some of the museum's incredible archives. JMW Turner's largest work – controversial for its chronological inaccuracies – the huge 1824 oil painting *The Battle of Trafalgar*, is hung in its namesake gallery on the ground floor.

On the 1st floor, **Traders: the East India Company and Asia** looks back on Britain's maritime trade with the East in the 19th century, while **The Atlantic: Slavery, Trade, Empire** explores the triangular trade between Europe, Africa and America from the 1600s to the 1850s.

On the 2nd floor, the award-winning **Nelson, Navy, Nation 1688–1815** focuses on the history of the Royal Navy during the conflict-ridden 17th century. It provides an excellent look at the legendary national hero and, through documents and memorabilia, explains his achievements and dazzling celebrity. The coat in which Nelson was fatally wounded during the Battle of Trafalgar takes pride of place.

Opened in 2018, the new **Exploration Wing** contains four galleries: Pacific Exploration, Polar Worlds, Tudor and Stuart Seafarers and Sea Things, devoted to the theme of exploration and human endeavour.

★ **Royal Observatory** HISTORIC BUILDING
(☑020-8312 6565; www.rmg.co.uk/royal-observatory; Greenwich Park, Blackheath Ave, SE10; adult/child £10/6.50, incl Cutty Sark £20/11.50; ☉10am-5pm Sep-Jun, to 6pm Jul & Aug; ☒DLR Cutty Sark, DLR Greenwich, Greenwich) Rising south of Queen's House, idyllic **Greenwich Park** (☑0300 061 2380; www.royalparks.org.uk; King George St, SE10; ☉6am-around sunset; ☒DLR Cutty Sark, ☒Greenwich, Maze Hill) climbs up the hill, affording stunning views of London from the Royal Observatory, which Charles II had built in 1675 to help solve the riddle of longitude. To the north is lovely **Flamsteed House** and the **Meridian Courtyard**, where

you can stand with your feet straddling the western and eastern hemispheres; admission is by ticket. The southern half contains the highly informative and free **Weller Astronomy Galleries** and the **Peter Harrison Planetarium** (☑020-8312 6608; www.rmg.co.uk/whats-on/planetarium-shows; adult/child £8/5.50).

In 1884 Greenwich was designated as the prime meridian of the world, and Greenwich Mean Time (GMT) became the universal measurement of standard time. Becoming a Royal Museums Greenwich Member (from £44 per year) allows you unlimited access to the Royal Observatory, the Peter Harrison Planetarium, the Cutty Sark as well as exhibitions at the National Maritime Museum; see the website for details.

★ **Imperial War Museum** MUSEUM
(Map p98; ☑020-7416 5000; www.iwm.org.uk; Lambeth Rd, SE1; ☉10am-6pm; ☒Lambeth North) **FREE** Fronted by a pair of intimidating 15in naval guns, this riveting museum is housed in what was the Bethlehem Royal Hospital, a psychiatric hospital also known as Bedlam. Although the museum's focus is on military action involving British or Commonwealth troops largely during the 20th century, it rolls out the carpet to war in the wider sense. Highlights include the state-of-the-art **First World War Galleries** and **Witnesses to War** in the forecourt and atrium above.

Indeed, Witnesses to War is where you'll find everything from a Battle of Britain Spitfire and a towering German V-2 rocket to a Reuters Land Rover damaged by rocket attack in Gaza and a section of the World Trade Center in New York.

On the 1st floor **A Family in Wartime** poignantly follows WWII through the experiences of the real-life Allpress family of Stockwell. In **Secret War** on the 2nd floor, there's an intriguing rifle through the work of the Secret Operations Executive (SOE), such as rubber soles resembling feet worn underneath boots to leave 'footprints' on enemy beaches. One of the most challenging sections is the extensive and harrowing **Holocaust Exhibition** (not recommended for under 14s), the entrance of which is on the 4th floor. **Curiosities of War** is a jumble sale of fascinating items, such as a makeshift bar used by the Dam Busters crew in 1943, taken from the museum's collection. Other galleries and exhibition spaces are given over to temporary exhibitions (check the website for details).

LONDON SIGHTS

Augustus Pugin, famous Gothic Revival architect of the interior of the Houses of Parliament, was once a patient in the psychiatric wards of the former Bethlehem Royal Hospital. The hospital moved in 1930 and the building became home to the Imperial War Museum in 1936.

★ **Old Royal Naval College** HISTORIC BUILDING
(www.ornc.org; 2 Cutty Sark Gardens, SE10; ⊙10am-5pm, grounds 8am-11pm; ⊠DLR Cutty Sark) FREE Sir Christopher Wren's baroque masterpiece in Greenwich and indeed Britain's largest ensemble of baroque architecture, the Old Royal Naval College contains the Neoclassical **Chapel** and the extraordinary **Painted Hall** (�020-8269 4799) FREE. The entire Old Royal Naval College, including the Chapel, the **Visitor Centre** (www.ornc.org/visitor-centre; Pepys Bldg, King William Walk, SE10; ⊙10am-5pm, to 6pm Jun-Sep), and the grounds, can be visited for free. Volunteers lead free 45-minute tours throughout each day from the Visitor Centre.

Queen's House HISTORIC BUILDING
(www.rmg.co.uk/queens-house; Romney Rd, SE10; ⊙10am-5pm; ⊠DLR Cutty Sark) FREE The first Palladian building by architect Inigo Jones after he returned from Italy is as enticing for its form as for its art collection. The house was begun in 1616 for Anne of Denmark, wife of James I, but was not completed until 1638, when it became the home of Charles I and his queen, Henrietta Maria. The beautiful helix-shaped (and reportedly haunted) **Tulip Stairs** form England's first set of centrally unsupported stairs: they constitute a peerless photo op for upward shots.

◉ West London

★ **Portobello Road Market** MARKET
(Map p106; www.portobellomarket.org; Portobello Rd, W10; ⊙8am-6.30pm Mon-Wed, Fri & Sat, to 1pm Thu; ⊜Notting Hill Gate, Ladbroke Grove) Lovely on a warm summer's day, Portobello Road Market is an iconic London attraction with an eclectic mix of street food, fruit and veg, antiques, curios, collectables, vibrant fashion and trinkets. Although the shops along Portobello Rd open daily and the fruit and veg stalls (from Elgin Cres to Talbot Rd) only close on Sunday, the busiest day by far is Saturday, when antique dealers set up shop (from Chepstow Villas to Elgin Cres).

Design Museum MUSEUM
(⊠020-7940 8790; www.designmuseum.org; 224-238 Kensington High St, W8; ⊙10am-6pm, to 8pm 1st Fri of month; ⊜High St Kensington) FREE Relocated in 2016 from its former Thames location to a stunning new £83m home by Holland Park, this slick museum is dedicated to popularising the importance and influence of design in everyday life. With a revolving program of special exhibitions, it's a crucial pitstop for anyone with an eye for modern and contemporary aesthetics. Splendidly housed in the refitted former Commonwealth Institute (which opened in 1962), the lavish interior – all smooth oak and marble – is itself a design triumph.

◉ Richmond, Kew & Hampton Court

★ **Kew Gardens** GARDENS
(Royal Botanic Gardens, Kew; www.kew.org; Kew Rd, TW9; adult/child £17/5; ⊙10am-4.15pm Sep-Mar, closes later Apr-Aug; ⊠Kew Pier, ⊠Kew Bridge, ⊜Kew Gardens) In 1759 botanists began rummaging around the world for specimens to plant in the 3-hectare Royal Botanic Gardens at Kew. They never stopped collecting, and the gardens, which have bloomed to 121 hectares, provide the most comprehensive botanical collection on earth (including the world's largest collection of orchids). A Unesco World Heritage Site, the gardens can easily devour a day's exploration; for those pressed for time, the **Kew Explorer** (⊠020-8332 5648; www.kew.org/kew-gardens/whats-on/kew-explorer-land-train; adult/child £5/2) hop-on/hop-off road train takes in the main sights.

Don't worry if you don't know your golden slipper orchid from your fengoky or your quiver tree from your alang-alang; a visit to Kew is a journey of discovery for everyone. Highlights include the enormous early Victorian **Palm House**, a hothouse of metal and curved sheets of glass; the impressive **Princess of Wales Conservatory**; the red-brick, 1631 **Kew Palace** (www.hrp.org.uk/kewpalace; with admission to Kew Gardens; ⊙10.30am-5.30pm Apr-Sep), formerly King George III's country retreat; the celebrated **Chinese Pagoda** designed by William Chambers in 1762; the **Temperate House** the world's largest ornamental glasshouse; and the very enjoyable **Rhizotron & Xstrata Treetop Walkway**, where you can survey the tree canopy from 18m up in the air. A lattice fashioned from thousands of pieces of aluminium illuminated with hundreds of LED lights, the 17m-high **Hive** mimics activity within a real beehive. Opened in 2016, the 320m-long **Great Broad Walk Borders** is the longest double herbaceous border in the UK. The idyllic, thatched **Queen Charlotte's Cottage** (⊙11am-4pm Sat & Sun Apr-Sep) in the southwest of the gardens was popular with 'mad' George III and his wife; the beautiful carpets of bluebells around here are a draw in spring. Several long vistas (**Cedar Vista**, **Syon Vista** and **Pagoda Vista**) are channelled by trees from vantage points within Kew Gardens.

Check the website for a full list of activities at Kew, including free one-hour walking tours (daily), photography walks, theatre performances, outside cinema as well as a host of seasonal events and things to do.

Kew Gardens is easily reached by tube, but you might prefer to take a cruise on a riverboat from the Westminster Passenger Services Association (p121), which runs several daily boats from April to October, departing from Westminster Pier.

★**Hampton Court Palace**   PALACE
(www.hrp.org.uk/hamptoncourtpalace; Hampton Court Palace, KT8; adult/child/family £19/10/34; ⊙10am-4.30pm Nov-Mar, to 6pm Apr-Oct; ⊠Hampton Court Palace, ℞Hampton Court) Built by Cardinal Thomas Wolsey in 1514 but coaxed from him by Henry VIII just before Wolsey (as chancellor) fell from favour, Hampton Court Palace is England's largest and grandest Tudor structure. It was already one of Europe's most sophisticated palaces when, in the 17th century, Christopher Wren designed an extension. The result is a beautiful blend of Tudor and 'restrained baroque' architecture. You could easily spend a day exploring the palace and its 24 hectares of riverside gardens, including a 300-year-old **maze** (adult/child/family £4.20/2.60/12.30; ⊙10am-5.15pm Apr-Oct, to 3.45pm Nov-Mar).

Richmond Park   PARK
(☏0300 061 2200; www.royalparks.org.uk/parks/richmond-park; ⊙7am-dusk; ℞Richmond) At almost 1000 hectares (the largest urban parkland in Europe), this park offers everything from formal gardens and ancient oaks to unsurpassed views of central London 12 miles away. It's easy to flee the several roads slicing up the rambling wilderness, making the park perfect for a quiet walk or a picnic with the kids, even in summer when Richmond's riverside heaves. Coming from Richmond,

LONDON WETLAND CENTRE

One of Europe's largest inland wetland projects, this 42-hectare **centre** (☏020-8409 4400; www.wwt.org.uk/wetland-centres/london; Queen Elizabeth's Walk, SW13; adult/child/family £12.75/7/35.55; ⊙9.30am-5.30pm Mar-Oct, to 4.30pm Nov-Feb; ℞Barnes, ⊖Hammersmith) run by the Wildfowl & Wetlands Trust was transformed from four Victorian reservoirs in 2000 and attracts some 140 species of birds, as well as frogs, butterflies, dragonflies and lizards, plus a thriving colony of watervoles. The glass-fronted observatory affords panoramic views over the lakes, while meandering paths and boardwalks lead visitors through the watery habitats of black swans, Bewick's swans, geese, red-crested pochards, sand martins, coots, bitterns, herons and kingfishers.

it's easiest to enter via Richmond Gate or from Petersham Rd.

Strawberry Hill   HISTORIC BUILDING
(☏020-8744 1241; www.strawberryhillhouse.org.uk; 268 Waldegrave Rd, TW1; adult/child £12.50/free; ⊙house 11am-4.30pm Sun-Wed Mar-Oct, noon-4pm Sun-Mon Nov-Feb, garden 10am-5.30pm daily; ℞Strawberry Hill, ⊖Richmond Station) With its snow-white walls and Gothic turrets, this fantastical and totally restored 18th-century creation in Twickenham is the work of art historian, author and politician Horace Walpole. Studded with elaborate stained glass, the building reaches its astonishing apogee in the gallery, with its magnificent papier-mâché ceiling. For the full magic, join a twilight tour (£20). Last admission to the house is 4pm.

☞ Tours

★**London Waterbus Company**   CRUISE
(☏020-7482 2550; www.londonwaterbus.com; 32 Camden Lock Pl, NW1; adult/child one-way £9/7.50, return £14/12; ⊙hourly 10am-5pm Apr-Sep, weekends only & less frequent departures other months; ⊖Warwick Ave, Camden Town) This enclosed barge runs enjoyable 50-minute trips on Regent's Canal between Little Venice and Camden Lock, passing by Regent's Park and stopping at London Zoo. There are fewer departures outside high season; check the website for schedules. One-way tickets

Hampton Court Palace

A DAY AT THE PALACE

With so much to explore in the palace and seemingly infinite gardens, it can be tricky knowing where to begin. It helps to understand how the palace has grown over the centuries and how successive royal occupants embellished Hampton Court to suit their purposes and to reflect the style of the time.

As soon as he had his royal hands upon the palace from Cardinal Thomas Wolsey,

Henry VIII began expanding the **① Tudor architecture**, adding the **② Great Hall**, the exquisite **③ Chapel Royal**, the opulent Great Watching Chamber and the gigantic **④ Tudor kitchens**. By 1540 it had become one of the grandest and most sophisticated palaces in Europe. James I kept things ticking over, while Charles I added a new tennis court and did some serious art-collecting, including pieces that can be seen in the **⑤ Cumberland Art Gallery**.

VISITBRITAIN / GETTY IMAGES ©

⑦ The Maze

Around 150m north of the main bulding
Created from hornbeam and yew and planted in around 1700, the maze covers a third of an acre within the famous palace gardens. A must-see conclusion to Hampton Court, the maze takes the average visitor about 20 minutes to reach the centre.

Tudor Architecture

Dating to 1515, the palace serves as one of the finest examples of Tudor architecture in the nation. Cardinal Thomas Wolsey was responsible for transforming what was originally a grand medieval manor house into a stunning Tudor palace.

KIEVVICTOR / SHUTTERSTOCK ©

Tudor Kitchens

These vast kitchens were the engine room of the palace, and had a staff of 200 people. Six spit-rack-equipped fireplaces ensured roast meat was always on the menu (to the tune of 8200 sheep and 1240 oxen per year).

Information Centre

Main Entrance

Base Court

Anne Boleyn's Gateway

OPEN FOR INSPECTION

The palace was opened to the public by Queen Victoria in 1838.

After the Civil War, puritanical Oliver Cromwell warmed to his own regal proclivities, spending weekends in the comfort of the former Queen's bedroom and selling off Charles I's art collection. In the late 17th century, William and Mary employed Sir Christopher Wren for baroque extensions, chiefly the **6 King's Staircase**. William III also commissioned the world-famous **7 maze**.

TOP TIPS

➡ Ask one of the red-tunic-garbed warders for anecdotes and information.

➡ Tag along with a themed tour led by costumed historians or do a dusk till dawn sleepover at the palace.

➡ Grab one of the audio tours from the Information Centre.

The Great Hall
This grand dining hall is the defining room of the palace, displaying what is considered England's finest hammer-beam roof, 16th-century Flemish tapestries that depict the story of Abraham, and some exquisite stained-glass windows.

Chapel Royal
The blue-and-gold vaulted ceiling was originally intended for Christ Church, Oxford, but was installed here instead; the 18th-century oak reredos was carved by Grinling Gibbons. Books on display include a 1611 1st edition of the King James Bible, printed by Robert Barker.

Chapel Court Garden

2

3

The King's Staircase
One of five rooms at the palace painted by Antonio Verrio and a suitably bombastic prelude to the King's Apartments, the overblown King's Staircase adulates William III by elevating him above a cohort of Roman emperors.

Clock Court

5

Fountain Court

6

Cumberland Art Gallery
The former Cumberland Suite, designed by William Kent, has been restored to accommodate a choice selection of some of the finest works from the Royal Collection.

(adult/child £27/21), including entry to London Zoo, allowing passengers to disembark within the zoo grounds are available. Buy tickets aboard the narrowboats.

London Bicycle Tour
CYCLING

(Map p98; 020-7928 6838; www.londonbicycle.com; 1 Gabriel's Wharf, 56 Upper Ground, SE1; tour incl bike from adult/child £24.95/21.95, bike hire per day £20; Southwark, Waterloo) Three-hour tours begin in the South Bank and take in London's highlights on both sides of the river; the classic tour is available in eight languages. A night ride is available. You can also hire traditional or speciality bikes, such as tandems and folding bikes, by the hour or day.

Thames Rockets
BOATING

(Map p98; 020-7928 8933; www.thamesrockets.com; Boarding Gate 1, London Eye, Waterloo Millennium Pier, Westminster Bridge Rd, SE1; adult/child from £43.50/29.50; 10am-6pm;) Feel like James Bond on this high-speed inflatable boat that flies down the Thames at 30 knots. Tours depart from the London Eye or St Katharine Pier, including the 50-minute Ultimate London Adventure (adult/child £43.50/29.50), the 80-minute Thames Barrier Explorer's Voyage (adult/child £54.50/39.50) or Thames Lates, a 50-minute sunset trip with a cocktail on board (adults only £39.50).

Unseen Tours
WALKING

(07514 266774; www.sockmobevents.org.uk; tours £12) See London from an entirely different angle on one of these award-winning neighbourhood tours led by the London homeless covering Covent Garden, Camden Town, Brick Lane, Shoreditch and London Bridge. Sixty percent of the tour price goes to the guide.

Big Bus Tours
BUS

(020-7808 6753; www.bigbustours.com; adult/child £35/18; every 20min 8.30am-6pm Apr-Sep, to 5pm Oct & Mar, to 4.30pm Nov-Feb) Informative commentaries in 12 languages. The ticket includes a free river cruise with City Cruises and three thematic walking tours (royal London, film locations, mysteries). Good online booking discounts available. Onboard wi-fi. The ticket is valid for 24 hours; for an extra £8 (£4 for children), you can upgrade to a 48-hour ticket.

LONDON FOR FREE

Sights It costs nothing to visit the Houses of Parliament (p80) and watch debates. Another institution of public life, the Changing of the Guard (p83), is free to watch. For one weekend in September, Open House London (p96) opens the doors to some 850 buildings for free.

Museums & Galleries The permanent collections of all state-funded museums and galleries are open to the public free of charge. They include the V&A (p102), Tate Modern (p96), British Museum (p77) and National Gallery (p80). The **Saatchi Gallery** (Map p100; www.saatchigallery.com; Duke of York's HQ, King's Rd, SW3; 10am-6pm; Sloane Sq) FREE is also free.

Views Why pay good money when some of the finest viewpoints in London are free? Head up to Level 10 of Switch House at Tate Modern (p96) or the Sky Gardens atop the Walkie Talkie (p93).

Concerts A number of churches offer free lunchtime classical music concerts. Try St Martin-in-the-Fields (p80), **St James's Piccadilly** (Map p84; 020-7734 4511; www.sjp.org.uk; 197 Piccadilly, W1; 8am-8pm; Piccadilly Circus), **Temple Church** (Map p90; 020-7353 3470; www.templechurch.com; adult/child £5/3; 10am-4pm Mon, Tue, Thu & Fri, 2-4pm Wed, hours & days vary; Temple) and **St Alfege Church** (www.st-alfege.org; Greenwich Church St, SE10; 11am-4pm Mon-Fri, 10am-4pm Sat, noon-4pm Sun; Greenwich, DLR Cutty Sark).

Walks Walking around town is possibly the best way to get a sense of the city and its history. Roam through Hampstead Heath (p111) in North London, follow the Thames along the South Bank, or just walk from A to B in the compact West End.

Low-Cost Transport Bike-share your way around through Santander Cycles (p150) – the access fee is £2 for 24 hours; bike hire is then free for the first 30 minutes. Travel as much as you like on London Transport with a one-day Travelcard or an Oyster Card.

City Cruises
BOATING

(Map p82; ☑ 020-7740 0400; www.citycruises.com; adult single/return/day pass from £10.25/14.25/16.88, child £6.50/9.50/10.80; ⦿ Westminster) Ferry service departing every 30 minutes between Westminster, the London Eye, Bankside, Tower and Greenwich piers. A 24-hour Rover Ticket is as cheap as adult/child £10/5 online.

Thames River Boats
BOATING

(Map p82; ☑ 020-7930 2062; www.wpsa.co.uk; Westminster Pier, Victoria Embankment, SW1; Kew adult/child one-way £13/6.50, return £20/10, Hampton Court one-way £17/8.50, return £25/12.50; ⦿ 10am-4pm Apr-Oct; ⦿ Westminster) These boats go upriver from Westminster Pier to the Royal Botanic Gardens at Kew (1½ hours, four per day) and on to Hampton Court Palace (another 1½ hours, 11am sailing only), a distance of 22 miles. It's possible to disembark at Richmond, but it depends on the tides; check before you sail.

London Mystery Walks
WALKING

(☑ 07957 388280; www.tourguides.org.uk; £12) Tour Jack the Ripper's old haunts at 7pm on Mondays, Wednesdays, Fridays and Sundays. London chocolate tours (£40) are on Sundays at 12.30pm and gelato tours (£40) are on Fridays at 11am. You must book in advance.

Festivals & Events

Chinese New Year
CULTURAL

(⦿ late Jan/early Feb) Chinese New Year sees Chinatown snap, crackle and pop with fireworks, a colourful street parade and eating aplenty.

The Boat Race
ROWING

(www.theboatrace.org; ⦿ late Mar/early Apr) A posh-boy grudge match held annually since 1829 between the rowing crews of Oxford and Cambridge universities. Surging upstream between Putney and Mortlake, the event (which included a female crew boat race for the first time in 2015) draws huge crowds along the river.

Virgin Money London Marathon
SPORTS

(www.virginmoneylondonmarathon.com; ⦿ late Apr) Up to half a million spectators watch the whippet-thin champions and bizarrely clad amateurs take to the streets.

Chelsea Flower Show
HORTICULTURE

(☑ 020-3176 5800; www.rhs.org.uk/chelsea; Royal Hospital Chelsea, Royal Hospital Rd, SW3; admission £37-65; ⦿ May; ⦿ Sloane Sq) Held at the lovely Royal Hospital Chelsea, this is arguably the world's most renowned horticultural show, attracting green fingers from all four corners of the globe.

Field Day
MUSIC

(www.fielddayfestivals.com; Brockwell Park, SE24; ⦿ Jun; ⦿ Hackney Wick) The annual Field Day alternative music festival was held in Victoria Park (p109) from 2007, but in 2018 it moved to Brockwell Park. Performances in recent years have included Run the Jewels, PJ Harvey and James Blake.

Meltdown Festival
MUSIC

(www.southbankcentre.co.uk; ⦿ late Jun) The Southbank Centre hands over the curatorial reigns to a legend of contemporary music (Morrissey, Patti Smith, David Byrne) to pull together a full program of concerts, talks and films.

★ Trooping the Colour
PARADE

(www.trooping-the-colour.co.uk; ⦿ Jun) Celebrating the Queen's official birthday, this ceremonial procession of troops, marching along the Mall for their sovereign's inspection, is a pageantry overload, featuring 1400 officers and personnel on parade, 200 horses and 400 musicians from 10 bands.

Pride
GAY & LESBIAN

(www.prideinlondon.org; ⦿ late Jun/early Jul) The gay community paints the town pink in this annual extravaganza, featuring a smorgasbord of experiences, from talks to live events and culminating in a huge parade across London.

Summer Screen at Somerset House
FILM

(www.somersethouse.org.uk/film; tickets from £20) For a fortnight every summer, Somerset House turns its stunning courtyard into an open-air cinema screening an eclectic mix of film premieres, cult classics and popular requests.

Wireless
MUSIC

(www.wirelessfestival.co.uk; Finsbury Park, N4; ⦿ Jul) This popular pop, R&B, grime and hip-hop festival is held over three days in July every year. Recent headliners have included The Weeknd, Nas and Skepta.

Notting Hill Carnival
CARNIVAL

(www.thelondonnottinghillcarnival.com; ⦿ Aug) Every year, for three days that include the last weekend of August, Notting Hill echoes to the calypso, ska, reggae and soca sounds of the Notting Hill Carnival. Launched in 1964 by the local Afro-Caribbean community that was keen to celebrate its culture and traditions, it has grown to become Europe's largest street festival (up to two million people) and a highlight of London's calendar.

London Jazz Festival MUSIC
(www.efglondonjazzfestival.org.uk; ⊘ Nov) Musicians from around the world swing into town for 10 days of jazz. World influences are well represented, as are more conventional strands.

🛏 Sleeping

🛏 The West End

YHA London Oxford Street HOSTEL £
(Map p84; ☑ 020-7734 1618; www.yha.org.uk; 14 Noel St, W1; dm £18-36, tw £50-85; @ 🛜; ⊖ Oxford Circus) The most central of London's seven YHA hostels is also one of the most intimate with just 104 beds. The excellent shared facilities include a fuchsia-coloured kitchen and bright, funky lounge. Dormitories have three or four beds, and there are doubles and twins. The in-house shop sells coffee and beer. Free wi-fi in common areas.

Generator London HOSTEL £
(Map p110; ☑ 020-7388 7666; www.generator hostels.com/london; 37 Tavistock Pl, WC1; dm/r from £9/44; ❄ 🛜; ⊖ Russell Sq) With its industrial lines and funky decor, the huge Generator (it has more than 870 beds) is one of central London's grooviest budget spots. The bar, complete with pool tables, stays open until 3am and there are frequent themed parties. Dorm rooms have between four and 12 beds; backing it up are twins and triples.

Jesmond Hotel B&B ££
(Map p110; ☑ 020-7636 3199; www.jesmond hotel.org.uk; 63 Gower St, WC1; s £75-95, d £95-125, tr £140-165, q £150-185; @ 🛜; ⊖ Goodge St) The rooms at this popular, 15-room family-run Georgian-era hotel in Bloomsbury are basic but clean and cheerful (four are with shared bathroom); there's a small, pretty garden, and the price tag is very attractive indeed. There's also laundry service and good breakfasts for kicking off your London day. Location is highly central.

★**Haymarket Hotel** HOTEL £££
(Map p84; ☑ 020-7470 4000; www.firmdalehotels. com/hotels/london/haymarket-hotel; 1 Suffolk Pl,

off Haymarket, SW1; r/ste £335/505; ❄ 🛜 ❄ 🏊; ⊖ Piccadilly Circus) With the trademark colours and lines of hotelier/designer duo Tim and Kit Kemp, the Haymarket is scrumptious, with hand-painted Gournay wallpaper, signature fuchsia and green designs in the 50 different guest rooms, a sensational 18m pool with mood lighting, an exquisite library lounge with honesty bar, and original artwork throughout.

★**Ritz London** LUXURY HOTEL £££
(Map p84; ☑ 020-7493 8181; www.theritzlondon. com; 150 Piccadilly, W1; r/ste from £380/850; Ⓟ❄@🛜; ⊖ Green Park) What can you say about a hotel that has lent its name to the English lexicon? This 136-room caravanserai has a spectacular position overlooking Green Park and is supposedly the Royal Family's home away from home (it does have a royal warrant from the Prince of Wales and is very close to the palace). All rooms have Louis XVI–style interiors and antique furniture.

★**Rosewood London** HOTEL £££
(Map p84; ☑ 020-7781 8888; www.rosewoodho tels.com/en/london; 252 High Holborn, WC1; d/ste from £390/702; Ⓟ❄@🛜🏊; ⊖ Holborn) What was once the grand Pearl Assurance building (dating from 1914) now houses the stunning Rosewood hotel, where an artful marriage of period and modern styles thanks to designer Tony Chi can be found in its 262 rooms and 44 suites. British heritage is carefully woven throughout the bar, restaurant, deli, lobby and even the housekeepers' uniforms.

Hazlitt's HISTORIC HOTEL £££
(Map p84; ☑ 020-7434 1771; www.hazlittshotel. com; 6 Frith St, W1; s/d/ste from £200/230/600; ❄🛜; ⊖ Tottenham Court Rd) Built in 1718 and comprising four original Georgian houses, this Soho gem was the one-time home of essayist William Hazlitt (1778–1830). The 30 guest rooms have been furnished with original antiques from the appropriate era and boast a profusion of seductive details, including panelled walls, mahogany four-poster beds, antique desks, Oriental carpets, sumptuous fabrics and fireplaces in every room.

🛏 The City

London St Paul's YHA HOSTEL £
(Map p90; ☑ 020-7236 4965; www.yha.org.uk; 36 Carter Lane, EC4; dm/tw/d from £14/49/89; @ 🛜; ⊖ St Paul's) Housed in the former boarding

school for St Paul's Cathedral choir boys, this 213-bed hostel has notable period features, including Latin script in a band around the exterior. There's no kitchen, no lift and no en-suite rooms, but there is a comfortable lounge and a licensed cafe.

★ citizenM Tower of London
DESIGN HOTEL ££

(Map p90; ☑ 020-3519 4830; www.citizenm.com; 40 Trinity Sq, EC3; r from £125; ✳@🐾; ⊖Tower Hill) Downstairs it looks like a rich hipster's living room, with well-stocked bookshelves, kooky art, Beefeater knick-knacks and lots of work space. Rooms are compact but well-designed, with an iPad to open the curtains, control the TV and adjust the shower lighting. It's worth paying an extra £30 for the extraordinary Tower views, although they're even better from the 7th-floor bar.

Hotel Indigo London – Tower Hill
HOTEL ££

(Map p90; ☑ 020-7265 1014; www.hotelindigo.com; 142 Minories, EC3; r from £166; ✳🐾; ⊖Aldgate) This branch of the InterContinental group's boutique-hotel chain offers 46 differently styled rooms, all with four-poster beds and iPod docking stations. Larger-than-life drawings and photos of the neighbourhood won't let you forget where you are.

Andaz Liverpool Street
HOTEL £££

(Map p90; ☑ 020-7961 1234; https://londonliverpoolstreet.andaz.hyatt.com; 40 Liverpool St, EC2; r £295; ✳🐾; ⊖Liverpool St) Built as the Great Eastern Hotel in 1884, this is the London flagship for Hyatt's Andaz chain. There's no reception, just black-clad staff who check you in on iPads. Splashes of red add zing to the spacious, elegant rooms, and there are three restaurants, two bars, a pub, a health club and a Masonic temple hidden in the basement.

🛏 South Bank

★ citizenM
BOUTIQUE HOTEL ££

(Map p98; ☑ 020-3519 1680; www.citizenm.com/london-bankside; 20 Lavington St, SE1; r £89-329; ✳@🐾; ⊖Southwark) If citizenM had a motto, it would be 'Less fuss, more comfort'. The hotel has done away with things it considers superfluous (room service, reception, heaps of space) and instead has gone all out on mattresses and bedding (heavenly super-king-sized beds), state-of-the-art technology (everything from mood lighting to TV is controlled through a tablet computer) and superb decor.

The LaLit
BOUTIQUE HOTEL £££

(Map p98; ☑ 020-3765-0000; www.thelalit.com; 181 Tooley St, SE1; r/ste £225/1125; 🐾; ⊖London Bridge) Housed in an old Victorian grammar school, and themed on the same, this boutique hotel looks rather unassuming from the outside, but the interior is festooned in Indian decor. The rooms span varying degrees of luxury, from the Cosy Classrooms, with their marble bathrooms, to the LaLit Legacy Suite, with oak panelling, high ceilings and an impressive view of the Shard.

🛏 Kensington & Hyde Park

Lime Tree Hotel
BOUTIQUE HOTEL ££

(Map p100; ☑ 020-7730 8191; www.limetreehotel.co.uk; 135-137 Ebury St, SW1; s incl breakfast £125-165, d & tw £185-215, tr £240; @🐾; ⊖Victoria) Family run for over three decades, this beautiful 25-bedroom Georgian town-house hotel is all comfort, British designs and understated elegance. Rooms are individually decorated, many with open fireplaces and sash windows, but some are smaller than others, so enquire. There is a lovely back garden for late-afternoon rays (picnics encouraged on summer evenings). Rates include a hearty full-English breakfast. No lift.

★ Number Sixteen
HOTEL £££

(Map p100; ☑ 020-7589 5232; www.firmdalehotels.com/hotels/london/number-sixteen; 16 Sumner Pl, SW7; s from £192, d £240-396; ✳@🐾; ⊖South Kensington) With uplifting splashes of colour, choice art and a sophisticated-but-fun design ethos, Number Sixteen is simply ravishing. There are 41 individually designed rooms, a cosy drawing room and a fully stocked library. And wait till you see the idyllic, long back garden set around a fountain, or sit down for breakfast in the light-filled conservatory. Great amenities for families.

Ampersand Hotel
BOUTIQUE HOTEL £££

(Map p100; ☑ 020-7589 5895; www.ampersandhotel.com; 10 Harrington Rd, SW7; s £170-192, d £216-360; ✳@🐾; ⊖South Kensington) It feels light, fresh and bubbly in the Ampersand, where smiling staff wear denims and waistcoats rather than impersonal dark suits. The common rooms are colourful and airy, and the stylish rooms are decorated with wallpaper designs celebrating the nearby arts and sciences of South Kensington's museums.

🛏 Clerkenwell, Shoreditch & Spitalfields

★ Hoxton Hotel
HOTEL ££

(Map p138; ☑020-7550 1000; www.thehoxton. com; 81 Great Eastern St, EC2; r £69-259; ❋ 🛜; ⊖Old St) In the heart of hip Shoreditch, this sleek hotel takes the low-cost airline approach to selling its rooms – book long enough ahead and you might pay just £69. The 210 renovated rooms are small but stylish, with flat-screen TVs, desks, fridges with complimentary bottled water and milk, and breakfast (orange juice, granola, yoghurt and banana) in a bag delivered to your door.

★ citizenM
DESIGN HOTEL ££

(Map p138; www.citizenm.com; 6 Holywell Lane, EC2A; r from £119; @ 🛜; ⊖Shoreditch High St) citizenM's winning combination of awesome interior design and a no-nonsense approach to luxury (yes to king-sized beds and high-tech pod rooms; no to pillow chocolates and room service) is right at home in Shoreditch. Room rates are just right, and the convivial lounge/bar/reception downstairs always seems to be on the right side of busy.

★ Rookery
HERITAGE HOTEL £££

(Map p90; ☑020-7336 0931; www.rookeryhotel. com; 12 Peter's Lane, Cowcross St, EC1; d/ste from £249/650; ❋ 🛜; ⊖Farringdon) This charming warren of 33 rooms has been built within a row of 18th-century Georgian houses and fitted out with period furniture (including a museum-piece collection of Victorian baths, showers and toilets), original wood panelling shipped over from Ireland and artwork selected personally by the owner. Highlights: the small courtyard garden, and the library with its honesty bar and working fireplace.

Zetter Hotel
BOUTIQUE HOTEL £££

(Map p110; ☑020-7324 4444; www.thezetter.com; 86-88 Clerkenwell Rd, EC1; d from £234, studio £342-558; ❋ 🛜; ⊖Farringdon) 🌢 The Zetter Hotel is a temple of cool minimalism with an overlay of colourful kitsch on Clerkenwell's main thoroughfare. Built using sustainable materials on the site of a derelict office, its 59 rooms are relatively spacious for the area. The rooftop studios are the real treat, with terraces commanding superb views. There is a hot-drink station on every floor for guest use.

🛏 East London

Qbic
DESIGN HOTEL £

(☑020-3021 3300; www.qbichotels.com; 42 Adler St, E1; r from £54; ❋ 🛜; ⊖Aldgate East) 🌢 There's a modern feel to this snappy hotel, with white tiling, neon signs, and vibrant art and textiles. Rooms are sound-insulated, mattresses excellent and rainforest showers powerful. Prices vary widely depending on when you book, and the cheapest are windowless.

★ 40 Winks
B&B ££

(☑020-7790 0259; www.40winks.org; 109 Mile End Rd, E1; s/d/ste £120/195/295; 🛜; ⊖Stepney Green) Short on space but not on style, this 300-year-old townhouse in Stepney Green oozes quirky charm. There are just two bedrooms (a double and a compact single) that share a bathroom – or you can book both as a spacious suite. Owned by a successful designer, the rooms are uniquely and extravagantly decorated with an expert's eye. Book far ahead.

🛏 North London

★ Clink78
HOSTEL £

(Map p110; ☑020-7183 9400; www.clinkhostels. com/london/clink78; 78 King's Cross Rd, WC1; dm/r incl breakfast from £16/65; @ 🛜; ⊖King's Cross St Pancras) This fantastic 630-bed hostel is housed in a 19th-century magistrates courthouse where Charles Dickens once worked as a scribe and members of the Clash stood trial in 1978. It features pod beds (including overhead storage space) in four- to 16-bed dormitories. There's a top kitchen with a huge dining area and a busy bar – Clash – in the basement.

London St Pancras YHA
HOSTEL £

(Map p110; ☑0345 371 9344; www.yha.org.uk; 79-81 Euston Rd, NW1; dm/r from £16/59; 🛜; ⊖King's Cross St Pancras) This hostel with 186 beds spread over eight floors has modern, clean dorms sleeping four to six (nearly all with private facilities) and some private rooms. The downside is the noise from busy Euston Rd. There's a small bar and cafe, but no self-catering facilities.

🛏 West London

Safestay Holland Park
HOSTEL £

(Map p106; ☑020-3326 8471; www.safestay.co.uk; Holland Walk, W8; dm £20, r from £60; 🛜; ⊖High St Kensington, Holland Park) This fresh place replaced the long-serving YHA hostel running here since 1958. With a bright and bold colour design, the hostel has four- to eight-bunk dorm rooms, twin-bunk and single-bunk rooms, free wi-fi in the lobby and a fabulous location in the Jacobean east wing of Holland House in **Holland Park** (Map p106; Ilchester Pl; ☉ 7.30am-dusk), the only part that survived a Luftwaffe onslaught.

★ Main House
HOTEL ££

(Map p106; ☑ 020-7221 9691; www.themainhouse. co.uk; 6 Colville Rd, W11; ste £130-150; ☎; ☻ Ladbroke Grove, Notting Hill Gate, Westbourne Park) The four adorable suites at this peach of a Victorian midterrace house on Colville Rd make this a superb choice. Bright and spacious rooms are excellent value and come with vast bathrooms and endless tea and coffee. Cream of the crop is the uppermost suite, occupying the entire top floor. There's no sign, but look for the huge letters 'SIX'. Minimum three-night stay.

Rockwell
BOUTIQUE HOTEL ££

(☑ 020-7244 2000; www.therockwell.com; 181-183 Cromwell Rd, SW5; s £120-125, d £145-180, ste from £200; ☒ @ ☎; ☻ Earl's Court) With an understated-cool design ethos and some lovely floor tiling in the entrance, things are muted, dapper and more than a tad minimalist at the 'budget boutique' 40-room Rockwell. Spruce and stylish, the rooms all have showers, the mezzanine suites are peaches and the three rooms looking on to the walled garden (LG1, 2 and 3) are particularly fine.

✘ Eating

✘ The West End

★ Shoryu
NOODLES £

(Map p84; www.shoryuramen.com; 9 Regent St, SW1; mains £10-14.50; ☉ 11.15am-midnight Mon-Sat, to 10.30pm Sun; ☻ Piccadilly Circus) Compact, well-mannered and central noodle-parlour Shoryu draws in reams of noodle diners to feast at its wooden counters and small tables. It's busy, friendly and efficient, with helpful and informative staff. Fantastic *tonkotsu* (pork-broth ramen) is the name of the game here, sprinkled with nori (dried, pressed seaweed), spring onion, *nitamago* (soft-boiled eggs) and sesame seeds. No bookings.

Battersea Pie Station
BRITISH £

(Map p84; ☑ 020-7240 9566; www.batterseapie station.co.uk; lower ground fl, 28 The Market, Covent Garden, WC2; mains £6.50-9.50; ☉ 11am-7.30pm Mon-Fri, 10am-7.30pm Sat, 11am-6.30pm Sun; ☻ Covent Garden) This small, white-tiled cafe is just what Covent Garden needs. It has a terrific choice of pies (baby or big) to satisfy all levels of hunger, from careful nibblers to voracious teens. Meat is all free-range, flavours are classic and rich (lamb and mint; fish; steak and stout; chicken and mushroom; butternut squash and goat's cheese), and each pie comes with a dollop of mashed potatoes.

Mildreds
VEGETARIAN £

(Map p84; ☑ 020-7484 1634; www.mildreds.co.uk; 45 Lexington St, W1; mains £7-12; ☉ noon-11pm Mon-Sat; ☎ ☑; ☻ Oxford Circus, Piccadilly Circus) Central London's most inventive vegetarian restaurant, Mildreds is crammed at lunchtime so don't be shy about sharing a table in the sky-lit dining room. Expect the likes of Sri Lankan sweet-potato and cashew-nut curry, ricotta and truffle tortellini, Middle Eastern mezze, wonderfully exotic (and filling) salads and delicious stir-fries. There are also vegan and gluten-free options.

Monocle Cafe
CAFE £

(Map p126; ☑ 020-7135 2040; http://cafe.mono cle.com; 18 Chiltern St, W1; snacks £5.50-9, snacks £2-5.50; ☉ 7am-7pm Mon-Wed, to 8pm Thu & Fri, 8am-8pm Sat, to 7pm Sun; ☎; ☻ Baker St) A small and cool ground-floor and basement hideout for the Marylebone hipster set, Monocle Cafe (from the eponymous magazine) is a delightful addition to buzzing Chiltern St. It offers eclectic flavours from Swedish pastries to Japanese and Scandinavian breakfasts, Bircher muesli with strawberries or shrimp *katsu* (breaded shrimp) sandwiches.

The Breakfast Club
BREAKFAST £

(Map p84; ☑ 020-7434 2571; www.thebreakfast clubcafes.com; 33 D'Arblay St, W1; mains £5-12.50; ☉ 7.30am-10pm Mon-Fri, 8am-10pm Sat, 8am-7pm Sun; ☎; ☻ Oxford Circus) This fun and friendly original branch of The Breakfast Club chain has been successfully frying up since 2005. Full Monty or All American brekkies are the natural inclination, but chorizo hash browns, pancakes and delights of the El Butty also await (once you reach the front of the queue).

★ Gymkhana
INDIAN ££

(Map p84; ☑ 020-3011 5900; www.gymkhana london.com; 42 Albemarle St, W1; mains £10-38, 4-course lunch/dinner £28.50/40; ☉ noon-2.30pm

Marylebone

& 5.30-10.15pm Mon-Sat; 🔊; ⊖ Green Park) The rather sombre setting is all British Raj – ceiling fans, oak ceiling, period cricket photos and hunting trophies – but the menu is lively, bright and inspiring. For lovers of variety, there is a six-course tasting meat/vegetarian menu (£70/65). The bar is open to 1am.

Cafe Murano
ITALIAN ££
(Map p84; 📞020-3371 5559; www.cafemurano. co.uk; 33 St James's St, SW1; mains £18-25, 2-/3-course set meal £19/23; ⊙noon-3pm & 5.30-11pm Mon-Sat, 11.30am-4pm Sun; ⊖ Green Park) The setting may seem somewhat demure at

this superb and busy restaurant, but with such a sublime northern Italian menu on offer, it sees no need to be flashy and of-the-moment. You get what you come for, and the lobster linguini, pork belly and cod with mussels and samphire are as close to culinary perfection as you'll get.

North Sea Fish Restaurant
FISH & CHIPS ££
(Map p110; 📞020-7387 5892; www.northseafish restaurant.co.uk; 7-8 Leigh St, WC1; mains £9.95-24.95; ⊙noon-2.30pm & 5-10pm Mon-Sat, 5-9.30pm Sun; ⊖ Russell Sq) The North Sea sets out to cook fresh fish and potatoes – a simple

Marylebone

ambition in which it succeeds admirably. Look forward to jumbo-sized plaice or halibut fillets, deep-fried or grilled, and a huge serving of chips. There's takeaway next door with similar hours if you can't face the rather austere dining room and impersonal service.

Opera Tavern　　　　　　　　　TAPAS **££**
(Map p84; ☑020-7836-3680; www.saltyard group.co.uk/opera-tavern; 23 Catherine St, WC2; Tapas £5-10; ☺noon-11.30pm Mon-Sat, to 10.30pm Sun; ◉Covent Garden) Classy but accessible, the Opera Tavern is one of London's best tapas restaurants (no easy feat), and enjoys an unrivalled location just around the corner from Covent Garden's piazza. Regular specials adorn the menu, and the staple Spanish and Italian tapas include a variety of mouth-watering options like roasted sea bass with mussels, and Iberico pork fillet.

Wallace　　　　　　MODERN EUROPEAN **££**
(Map p126; ☑020-7563 9505; www.wallacecol lection.org/visiting/thewallacerestaurant; Hertford House, Manchester Sq, W1; mains £13.50-22.50; ☺10am-5pm Sun-Thu, to 11pm Fri & Sat; ◉Bond St) There are few more idyllically placed restaurants than this spot in the enclosed courtyard of the Wallace Collection (p87). The emphasis is on seasonal French-inspired dishes, with the daily menu offering two- or three-course meals for £22.50/24.50. Afternoon tea is £18.50.

La Fromagerie　　　　　　　　CAFE **££**
(Map p126; ☑020-7935 0341; www.lafromagerie. co.uk; 2-6 Moxon St, W1; mains £7-18; ☺8am-7.30pm Mon-Fri, 9am-7pm Sat, 10am-6pm Sun; 🛜; ◉Baker St) 🌿 This deli-cafe has bowls of delectable salads, antipasto, peppers and beans scattered about the long communal table. Huge slabs of bread invite you to tuck in, and all the while the heavenly waft from the cheese room beckons. Cheese boards come in small and large (£9.25 and £16) and breakfast is always a good choice.

Great Queen Street　　　　BRITISH **££**
(Map p84; ☑020-7242 0622; www.greatqueen streetrestaurant.co.uk; 32 Great Queen St, WC2; mains £15.80-19.80; ☺noon-2.30pm & 5.30-10.30pm Mon-Sat, noon-3.30pm Sun; ◉Holborn) The menu at one of Covent Garden's best places to eat is seasonal (and changes daily), with an emphasis on quality, hearty dishes and fine ingredients – there are always delicious stews, roasts and simple fish dishes. The atmosphere is lively, with the small **Cellar Bar** (5pm to 11pm Tuesday to Saturday) open for cocktails and drinks. Booking is essential.

⭐**Portrait**　　　　　MODERN EUROPEAN **£££**
(Map p84; ☑020-7312 2490; www.npg.org.uk/ visit/shop-eat-drink.php; 3rd fl, National Portrait Gallery, St Martin's Pl, WC2; mains £19.50-28, 2-/3-course menu £27.95/31.50; ☺10-11am, 11.45am-3pm & 3.30-4.30pm daily, 6.30-8.30pm Thu-Sat; 🛜; ◉Charing Cross) This stunningly located restaurant above the excellent National Portrait Gallery (p87) comes with dramatic views over Trafalgar Sq and Westminster. It's a fine choice for tantalising food and the chance to relax after a morning or afternoon of picture-gazing at the gallery. The breakfast/brunch (10am to 11am) and afternoon tea (3.30pm to 4.30pm) come highly recommended. Booking is advisable.

⭐**Claridge's Foyer & Reading Room**　　　　　　　　　BRITISH **£££**
(Map p126; ☑020-7107 8886; www.claridges. co.uk; 49-53 Brook St, W1; afternoon tea £60, with champagne £70; ☺afternoon tea 2.45-5.30pm; 🛜; ◉Bond St) Extend that pinkie finger to partake in afternoon tea within the classic art deco foyer and Reading Room of this landmark hotel, where the gentle clink of fine porcelain and champagne glasses could be a defining memory of your trip to London. The setting is gorgeous and dress is elegant, smart casual (ripped jeans and baseball caps won't get you served).

Pollen Street Social　MODERN EUROPEAN **£££**
(Map p84; ☑020-7290 7600; www.pollenstreet social.com; 8-10 Pollen St, W1; mains £34-38, 3-course lunch £37; ☺noon-2.30pm & 6-10.30pm

Mon-Sat; ⊖ Oxford Circus) Jason Atherton's cathedral to haute cuisine would be beyond reach of many people not on a hefty expense account, but the excellent-value set lunch (£32/37 for two/three courses) makes it fairly accessible to all. A generous two-hour slot allows ample time to linger over such delights as lime-cured salmon, braised West Country ox cheek and your choice from the dessert bar.

Hakkasan Hanway Place CANTONESE £££
(Map p84; ☑ 020-7927 7000; www.hakkasan. com; 8 Hanway Pl, W1; mains £12-63.50; ⊗ noon-3pm & 5.30-11pm Mon-Wed, noon-3pm & 5.30pm-12.30am Thu-Fri, noon-4pm & 5.30pm-12.30am Sat, noon-11.15pm Sun; ☎; ⊖ Tottenham Court Rd) This basement Michelin-starred restaurant – hidden down a back alleyway – successfully combines celebrity status, stunning design, persuasive cocktails and sophisticated Cantonese-style food. The low, nightclub-style lighting makes it a good spot for a date or a night out with friends; the bar serves seriously creative cocktails. Book far in advance or come for lunch (three courses £38, also available from 5.30pm to 6.30pm).

✖ The City

Wine Library BUFFET ££
(Map p90; ☑ 020-7481 0415; www.winelibrary. co.uk; 43 Trinity Sq, EC3; buffet £18; ⊗ buffet 11.30am-3.30pm, shop 10am-6pm Mon, to 8pm Tue-Fri; ⊖ Tower Hill) This is a great place for a light but boozy lunch opposite the Tower. Buy a bottle of wine at retail price from the large selection (£9.50 corkage fee) and then head into the vaulted cellar to snack as much as you like from the selection of delicious pâtés, charcuterie, cheeses, bread and salads.

Duck & Waffle MODERN BRITISH ££
(Map p90; ☑ 020-3640 7310; www.duckandwaffle. com; L40, 110 Bishopsgate, EC2; mains £18-19; ⊗ 24hr; ☎; ⊖ Liverpool St) If you like your views with sustenance round the clock, this is the place for you. Perched atop Heron Tower, it serves a well-waffled breakfast menu, hearty all-day sharing plates (confit duck, roast chicken, miso-glazed rabbit) and round-the-clocktails.

✖ South Bank

★ Padella ITALIAN £
(Map p98; www.padella.co; 6 Southwark St, SE1; dishes £4-11.50; ⊗ noon-3.45pm & 5-10pm Mon-

Sat, noon-3.45pm & 5-9pm Sun; ☑; ⊖ London Bridge) Yet another fantastic addition to the foodie enclave of Borough Market (p147), Padella is a small, energetic bistro specialising in handmade pasta dishes, inspired by the owners' extensive culinary adventures in Italy. The portions are small, which means that, joy of joys, you can (and should!) have more than one dish. Outstanding.

★ Watch House CAFE £
(Map p98; www.thewatchhouse.com; 199 Bermondsey St, SE1; mains from £4.95; ⊗ 7am-6pm Mon-Fri, 8am-6pm Sat, 9am-5pm Sun; ☑; ⊖ Borough, London Bridge) ✐ Saying that the Watch House nails the sandwich wouldn't really do justice to this tip-top cafe: the sandwiches really are delicious, and use artisan breads from a local baker. But there is also great coffee, and treats for the sweet-toothed. The small but lovely setting is a renovated 19th-century watch house from where guards looked out for grave robbers in the next-door cemetery.

★ Anchor & Hope GASTROPUB ££
(Map p98; www.anchorandhopepub.co.uk; 36 The Cut, SE1; mains £12-20; ⊗ noon-2.30pm Tue-Sat, 6-10.30pm Mon-Sat, 12.30-3.15pm Sun; ⊖ Southwark) A stalwart of the South Bank food scene, the Anchor & Hope is a quintessential gastropub: elegant but not formal, and utterly delicious (European fare with a British twist). The menu changes daily but think salt-marsh lamb shoulder cooked for seven hours; wild rabbit with anchovies, almonds and rocket; and panna cotta with rhubarb compote.

★ Baltic EASTERN EUROPEAN ££
(Map p98; ☑ 020-7928 1111; www.balticrestaurant. co.uk; 74 Blackfriars Rd, SE1; mains £11.50-22, 2-course lunch menu £17.50; ⊗ noon-3pm & 5.30-11.15pm Tue-Sat, noon-4.30pm & 5.30-10.30pm Sun, 5.30-11.15pm Mon; ☑; ⊖ Southwark) In a bright and airy, high-ceilinged dining room with glass roof and wooden beams, Baltic is travel on a plate: dill and beetroot, dumplings and blini, pickle and smoke, rich stews and braised meat. From Polish to Georgian, the flavours are authentic and the dishes beautifully presented. The wine and vodka lists are equally diverse.

✖ Kensington & Hyde Park

★ Pimlico Fresh CAFE £
(☑ 020-7932 0030; 86 Wilton Rd, SW1; mains from £4.50; ⊗ 7.30am-7.30pm Mon-Fri, 9am-6pm Sat & Sun; ⊖ Victoria) This friendly two-room cafe

will see you right whether you need breakfast (French toast, bowls of porridge laced with honey or maple syrup), lunch (homemade quiches and soups, 'things' on toast) or just a good old latte and cake.

⭐ Rabbit   MODERN BRITISH ££

(Map p100; ☑ 020-3750 0172; www.rabbit-restau rant.com; 172 King's Rd, SW3; mains £6-24, set lunch £13.50; ☺ noon-midnight Tue-Sat, noon-6pm Sun, 6-11pm Mon; ☑; ☻ Sloane Sq) Three brothers grew up on a farm. One became a farmer, another a butcher, while the third worked in hospitality. So they pooled their skills and came up with Rabbit, a breath of fresh air in upmarket Chelsea. The restaurant rocks the agri-chic (yes) look, and the creative, seasonal Modern British cuisine is fabulous.

⭐ Tom's Kitchen   MODERN EUROPEAN ££

(Map p100; ☑ 020-7349 0202; www.tomskitchen. co.uk/chelsea; 27 Cale St, SW3; mains £16-28; ☺ 8am-2.30pm & 6-10.30pm Mon-Fri, 9.30am-3.30pm & 6-10.30pm Sat, to 9.30pm Sun; ☎☑; ☻ South Kensington) 🍴 Recipe for success: mix one part relaxed and smiling staff, and one part light and airy decor to two parts divine food and voila: you have Tom's Kitchen. Classics such as grilled steaks, burgers, slow-cooked pork belly and chicken schnitzel are cooked to perfection, while seasonal choices such as the homemade ricotta or pan-fried scallops are sublime.

⭐ Dinner by
Heston Blumenthal   MODERN BRITISH £££

(Map p100; ☑ 020-7201 3833; www.dinnerby heston.com; Mandarin Oriental Hyde Park, 66 Knightsbridge, SW1; 3-course set lunch £45, mains £30-49; ☺ noon-2pm & 6-10.15pm Mon-Fri, noon-2.30pm & 6-10.30pm Sat & Sun; ☎; ☻ Knights-bridge) Sumptuously presented Dinner is a gastronomic tour de force, taking diners on a journey through British culinary history (with inventive modern inflections). Dishes carry historical dates to convey context, while the restaurant interior is a design triumph, from the glass-walled kitchen and its overhead clock mechanism to the large windows looking onto the park. Book ahead.

⭐ Gordon Ramsay   FRENCH £££

(Map p100; ☑ 020-7352 4441; www.gordonram sayrestaurants.com/restaurant-gordon-ramsay; 68 Royal Hospital Rd, SW3; 3-course lunch/dinner £65/110; ☺ noon-2.30pm & 6.30-11pm Mon-Fri; ☎; ☻ Sloane Sq) One of Britain's finest restaurants and London's longest-running with three Michelin stars, this is hallowed turf for those who worship at the altar of the stove. It's true that it's a treat right from the taster to the truffles, but you won't get much time to savour it all. Bookings are made in specific sittings and you dare not linger; book as late as you can to avoid that rushed feeling. The blowout Menu Prestige (£145) is seven courses of perfection.

⭐ Five Fields   MODERN BRITISH £££

(Map p100; ☑ 020-7838 1082; www.fivefieldsres taurant.com; 8-9 Blacklands Tce, SW3; 3-course set meal £65, tasting menu £85; ☺ 6.30-10pm Tue-Sat; ☎; ☻ Sloane Sq) The inventive British *prix fixe* cuisine, consummate service and enticingly light and inviting decor are hard to resist at this triumphant Chelsea restaurant – now with a Michelin star – but you'll need to plan early and book way up front.

🍴 Clerkenwell, Shoreditch & Spitalfields

⭐ Polpo   ITALIAN £

(Map p90; ☑ 020-7250 0034; www.polpo.co.uk; 3 Cowcross St, EC1M; dishes £4-12; ☺ 11.30am-11pm Mon-Thu & Sat, to midnight Fri, to 4pm Sun; ☻ Far-ringdon) Occupying a sunny spot on semi-pedestrianised Cowcross St, this sweet little place serves rustic Venetian-style meatballs, *pizzette* (small pizzas), grilled meat and fish dishes. Portions are larger than your average tapas but a tad smaller than a regular main – the perfect excuse to sample more than one of the exquisite dishes. Exceptional value for money.

Brick Lane Beigel Bake   BAKERY £

(Map p138; 159 Brick Lane, E2; bagels £1-4.10; ☺ 24hr; ☻ Shoreditch High St) This relic of the Jewish East End still makes a brisk trade serving dirt-cheap homemade bagels (filled with salmon, cream cheese and/or salt beef) to hungry shoppers and late-night boozers. The queues on Sundays are epic.

Prufrock Coffee   CAFE £

(Map p90; www.prufrockcoffee.com; 23-25 Leath-er Lane, EC1N; mains £4-7; ☺ 7.30am-6pm Mon-Fri, 10am-5pm Sat & Sun; ☎☑; ☻ Farringdon) Not content with being one of the kings of London's coffee-bean scene (it offers barista training and workshops in 'latte art'), Prufrock also dishes up delicious breakfasts, lunches and cuppa-friendly pastries and snacks. Judging by the number of laptops, plenty of customers treat it as their office.

Boiler House
MARKET £

(Map p138; www.boilerhouse-foodhall.co.uk; Old Truman Brewery, 152 Brick Lane, E1; dishes £3-8; ⊗11am-6pm Sat, 10am-5pm Sun; ⋒; ⊖Liverpool St) More than 30 food stalls selling anything from Argentinian to Vietnamese pitch up in the brewery's impressive old boiler room at the weekend. There is also a bar, and you can sit at the communal tables to tuck in. Come spring and summer, there are dozens more tables in the backyard.

Poppie's
FISH & CHIPS ££

(Map p138; www.poppiesfishandchips.co.uk; 6-8 Hanbury St, E1; mains £12.20-16.90; ⊗11am-11pm; ⊖Liverpool St) This glorious recreation of a 1950s East End chippy comes complete with waitstaff in pinnies and hairnets, and Blitz memorabilia. As well as the usual fishy suspects, it does old-time London staples – jellied eels and mushy peas – plus kid-pleasing, sweet-tooth desserts (sticky toffee pudding or apple pie with ice cream), and there's a wine list. Takeaway is a lot cheaper (£6.50 to £8.50).

St John
BRITISH ££

(Map p90; ⋒020-7251 0848; www.stjohngroup. uk.com/spitalfields; 26 St John St, EC1M; mains £14.80-24.90; ⊗noon-3pm & 6-11pm Mon-Fri, 6-11pm Sat, 12.30-4pm Sun; ⊖Farringdon) Whitewashed brick walls, high ceilings and simple wooden furniture don't make for a cosy dining space but they do keep diners free to concentrate on St John's famous nose-to-tail dishes. Serves are big, hearty and a celebration of England's culinary past. Don't miss the signature roast bone marrow and parsley salad (£8.90).

Morito
TAPAS ££

(Map p110; ⋒020-7278 7007; www.morito.co.uk; 32 Exmouth Market, EC1R; dishes £6.50-9.50; ⊗8am-4pm & 5-11pm Mon-Fri, 9am-noon & 5-11pm Sat, 9am-4pm Sun; ⋒; ⊖Farringdon) This diminutive eatery is a wonderfully authentic take on a Spanish tapas bar and has excellent eats. Seats are at the bar, along the window, or on one of the small tables inside or out. It's relaxed, convivial and often completely crammed; reservations are taken for lunch, but dinner is first come, first served, with couples generally going to the bar.

★Hawksmoor
STEAK £££

(Map p138; ⋒020-7426 4850; www.thehawks moor.com; 157 Commercial St, E1; mains £20-50; ⊗noon-2.30pm & 5-10.30pm Mon-Sat, noon-9pm Sun; ⋒; ⊖Liverpool St) You could easily miss discreetly signed Hawksmoor, but confirmed carnivores will find it worth seeking out. The dark wood, bare bricks and velvet curtains make for a handsome setting in which to gorge yourself on the best of British beef. The Sunday roasts (£20) are legendary.

✕ East London

★Towpath
CAFE £

(⋒020-7254 7606; rear 42-44 De Beauvoir Cres, N1; mains £7-9.50; ⊗9am-5pm Tue & Wed, to 9.30pm Thu-Sun; ⊖Haggerston) Occupying four small units on the Regent's Canal towpath, this simple cafe is a super place to sit in the sun and watch the ducks and narrowboats glide by. The coffee and food are excellent, too, with delicious cookies and brownies on the counter and cooked dishes chalked up on the blackboard daily.

★Corner Room
MODERN BRITISH ££

(⋒020-7871 0460; www.townhallhotel.com/food -and-drink/corner_room; Patriot Sq, E2; mains £13-14, 2-/3-course lunch £19/23; ⊗7-10am & noon-4pm Mon-Fri, 7.30-10.30am & noon-2.30pm Sat & Sun, 6-9.45pm Sun-Wed, 6-10.15pm Thu-Sat; ⊖Bethnal Green) Someone put this baby in the corner, but we're certainly not complaining. Tucked away on the 1st floor of the Town Hall Hotel, this relaxed restaurant serves expertly crafted dishes with complex yet delicate flavours, highlighting the best of British seasonal produce.

Empress
MODERN BRITISH ££

(⋒020-8533 5123; www.empresse9.co.uk; 130 Lauriston Rd, E9; mains £13.50-18.50; ⊗6-10.15pm Mon, noon-3.30pm & 6-10.15pm Tue-Sat, 10am-9.30pm Sun; ▢277) This upmarket pub conversion belts out delicious Modern British cuisine in very pleasant surroundings. On Mondays there's a £10 main-plus-drink supper deal and on weekends it serves an excellent brunch.

✕ North London

★Chin Chin Labs
ICE CREAM £

(Map p132; www.chinchinlabs.com; 49-50 Camden Lock Pl, NW1; ice cream £4-5; ⊗noon-7pm; ⊖Camden Town) This is food chemistry at its absolute best. Chefs prepare the ice-cream mixture and freeze it on the spot by adding liquid nitrogen. Flavours change regularly and match the seasons (spiced hot cross bun, passionfruit and coconut, for instance).

Sauces and toppings are equally creative. Try the ice-cream sandwich if you can: ice cream wedged inside gorgeous brownies or cookies.

★ Hook Camden Town   FISH & CHIPS £

(Map p132; www.hookrestaurants.com; 65 Parkway, NW1; mains £8-12; ⊙noon-3pm & 5-10pm Mon-Thu, noon-10.30pm Fri & Sat, to 9pm Sun; 🖰; 🔄 Camden Town) 🍴 In addition to working entirely with sustainable small fisheries and local suppliers, Hook makes all its sauces on-site and wraps its fish in recycled materials, supplying diners with extraordinarily fine-tasting morsels. Totally fresh, the fish arrives in panko breadcrumbs or tempura batter, with seaweed salted chips. Craft beers and fine wines are also on hand.

Diwana Bhel Poori House   INDIAN £

(Map p110; ☑020-7387 5556; www.diwanabph. com; 121-123 Drummond St, NW1; mains £5.10-8.95; ⊙noon-11.30pm Mon-Sat, to 10.30pm Sun; 🖋; 🔄 Euston) One of the best Indian vegetarian restaurants in London, Diwana specialises in Bombay-style *bhel poori* (a tangy, soft and crunchy 'party mix' dish) and *dosas* (filled crispy pancakes made from rice flour). Solo diners should consider a thali (a complete meal consisting of lots of small dishes). The all-you-can-eat lunchtime buffet (£7) is legendary, and there are daily specials (£6.60).

Le Mercury   FRENCH £

(☑020-7354 4088; www.lemercury.co.uk; 140a Upper St, N1; mains £10.95; ⊙noon-1am Mon-Sat, to 11pm Sun; 🔄 Highbury & Islington, Angel) An excellent and wildly popular budget French eatery, Le Mercury seems to have everything you could need in its winning formula: romantic atmosphere with candlelit, petite tables and plants everywhere, combined with superb French food at unbeatable prices. Londoners have long known about this place, so reservations are advised.

KERB Camden Market   MARKET £

(Map p132; www.kerbfood.com; Camden Lock Market; mains £6-8; ⊙noon-5pm; 🖋; 🔄 Camden Town) From Argentinian to Vietnamese, the KERB food-market collective is like an A–Z of world cuisines. Each stall looks more mouth-watering than the next, and there should be enough choice to keep even the fussiest of eaters happy. Eat on the big communal tables or find a spot somewhere along the canal.

★ Ottolenghi   BAKERY, MEDITERRANEAN ££

(☑020-7288 1454; www.ottolenghi.co.uk; 287 Upper St, N1; breakfast £5.90-12.50, mains lunch/dinner from £18.80/11.90; ⊙8am-10.30pm Mon-Sat, 9am-7pm Sun; 🖋; 🔄 Highbury & Islington) Mountains of meringues tempt you through the door of this deli-restaurant, where a sumptuous array of baked goods and fresh salads greets you. Meals are as light and bright as the brilliantly white interior design, with a strong influence from the eastern Mediterranean.

★ Trullo   ITALIAN ££

(☑020-7226 2733; www.trullorestaurant.com; 300-302 St Paul's Rd, N1; mains £12.50-21; ⊙12.30-2.45pm & 6-10.15pm Mon-Sat, 12.30-3.45pm & 6-9.15pm Sun; 🔄 Highbury & Islington) Trullo's daily homemade pasta is delicious, but the main attraction here is the charcoal grill, which churns out the likes of succulent Italian-style pork chops, steaks and fish. The extensive and all-Italian wine list is another hit. Service is excellent, although dinner time can get packed; reservations are essential.

Caravan   INTERNATIONAL ££

(☑020-7101 7661; www.caravanrestaurants.co.uk; 1 Granary Sq, N1C; mains £7-19; ⊙8am-10.30pm Mon-Fri, 10am-10.30pm Sat, 10am-4pm Sun; 🛜🖋; 🔄 King's Cross St Pancras) Housed in the lofty Granary Building, Caravan is a vast industrial-chic destination for tasty fusion bites from around the world. You can opt for several small plates to share tapas-style, or stick to main-sized plates. The outdoor seating area on Granary Sq is especially popular on warm days.

Manna   VEGETARIAN ££

(☑020-7722 8028; www.mannav.com; 4 Erskine Rd, NW3; mains £8-15; ⊙noon-3pm & 6.30-10pm Tue-Sat, noon-7.30pm Sun; 🖋; 🔄 Chalk Farm) Tucked away on a side street, this upmarket little place does a brisk trade in inventive vegetarian and vegan cooking. The menu features mouth-watering, beautifully presented dishes incorporating elements of Californian, Mexican and Asian cuisine with nods to the raw-food trend. The cheesecake of the day is always a hit.

✖ Greenwich & South London

Old Brewery   MODERN BRITISH ££

(☑020-3437 2222; www.oldbrewerygreenwich. com; Pepys Bldg, Old Royal Naval College, SE10; mains £11.50-25; ⊙10am-11pm Mon-Sat, to 10.30pm Sun; 🛜🖰; 🚇 DLR Cutty Sark) Acquired by Young's in 2016 and entirely

Camden Town

refurbished, this excellent and handsome choice within the grounds of the Old Royal Naval College (p116) is both a ravishing restaurant and a pub, with a heady range of craft beers and cocktails. There's outside seating for sunny days.

✕ West London

★ Potli
INDIAN ££

(☑020-8741 4328; www.potli.co.uk; 319-321 King St, W6; weekday 1-/2-course set lunch £7.95/10.95, mains £7.50-15; ⊘noon-2.30pm Mon-Sat, 6-10.15pm Mon-Thu, 5.30-10.30pm Fri & Sat, noon-10pm Sun; ☎; ⊜Stamford Brook, Ravenscourt Park) With its scattered pieces from Mumbai's Thieves Market, Indian-market-kitchen/bazaar cuisine, homemade pickles and spice mixes, plus an accent on genuine flavour, tantalising Potli deftly captures the aromas of its culinary home. Downstairs there's an open kitchen and service is friendly, but it's the alluring menu – where flavours are teased into a rich and authentic Indian culinary experience – that's the real crowd pleaser.

Taquería MEXICAN **£**
(Map p106; ☏ 020-7229 4734; www.taqueria.co.uk; 139-143 Westbourne Grove; tacos £7.20-10.20; ⊙ noon-11pm Mon-Thu, to 11.30pm Fri & Sat, to 10.30pm Sun; 🐾; ⊖ Notting Hill Gate) ✿ You won't find fresher or more limp (they're not supposed to be crispy!) tacos anywhere in London because these ones are made on the premises. Starting life as a stall on Portobello Rd and recently refurbished, it's a small casual place with a great vibe, committed to environmental mores: the eggs, chicken and pork are free-range, the meat British, the fish MSC-certified, and the milk and cream organic.

★Geales SEAFOOD **££**
(Map p106; ☏ 020-7727 7528; www.geales.com; 2 Farmer St, W8; 2-course express lunch £9.95, mains £9-33.50; ⊙ noon-3pm Tue-Fri, 5.30-11pm Mon-Fri, noon-11pm Sat & Sun; 🐾; ⊖ Notting Hill Gate) Frying since 1939 – a bad year for the European restaurant trade – Geales has endured with its quiet location on the corner of Farmer and Uxbridge Sts. The succulent fish in crispy batter is a fine catch, but the fish pie is also worth angling for. Look out for the good-value (two-course, one coffee) express lunch, available from Tuesday to Friday.

★Ledbury FRENCH **£££**
(Map p106; ☏ 020-7792 9090; www.theledbury. com; 127 Ledbury Rd, W11; 4-course set lunch £75, 4-course dinner £120; ⊙ noon-2pm Wed-Sun & 6.30-9.45pm daily; 🐾; ⊖ Westbourne Park, Royal Oak, Notting Hill Gate) With two Michelin stars and swooningly elegant, Brett Graham's artful French restaurant attracts well-heeled diners in jeans with designer jackets. Dishes such as hand-dived scallops, Chinese water deer, smoked bone marrow, quince and red leaves, or Herdwick lamb with salt-baked turnips, celery cream and wild garlic are triumphs. London gastronomes have the Ledbury on speed dial, so reservations well in advance are crucial.

✗ Richmond, Kew & Hampton Court

★Glasshouse MODERN EUROPEAN **££**
(☏ 020-8940 6777; www.glasshouserestaurant.co. uk; 14 Station Pde, TW9; 2-/3-course lunch Mon-Fri £30/35, 1-/2-/3-course dinner £32.50/45/55; ⊙ noon-2.30pm & 6.30-10.30pm Tue-Sat, 12.30-4pm Sun; 🐾🚆; ⊠ Kew Gardens, ⊖ Kew Gardens) A day at Kew Gardens finds a perfect conclusion at this Michelin-starred gastronomic highlight. The glass-fronted exterior envelops a delicately lit, low-key interior, where the focus remains on divinely cooked food. Diners are rewarded with a consistently accomplished menu from chef Berwyn Davies that combines English mainstays with modern European innovation.

🍷 Drinking & Nightlife

🍸 The West End

★Lamb & Flag PUB
(Map p84; ☏ 020-7497 9504; www.lambandflag coventgarden.co.uk; 33 Rose St, WC2; ⊙ 11am-11pm Mon-Sat, noon-10.30pm Sun; ⊖ Covent Garden) Everybody's favourite pub in central London, pint-sized Lamb & Flag is full of charm and history, and is on the site of a pub that dates from at least 1772. Rain or shine, you'll have to elbow your way to the bar through the merry crowd drinking outside. Inside are brass fittings and creaky wooden floors.

★American Bar COCKTAIL BAR
(Map p84; ☏ 020-7836 4343; www.fairmont. com/savoy-london/dining/americanbar; Savoy, The Strand, WC2; ⊙ 11.30am-midnight Mon-Sat, noon-midnight Sun; ⊖ Covent Garden) Home of the Hanky Panky, White Lady and other classic infusions created on-site, the seriously dishy and elegant American Bar is an icon of London, with soft blue and rust art deco lines and live piano music. Cocktails start at £17.50 and peak at a stupefying £5000 (the Original Sazerac, containing Sazerac de Forge cognac from 1857).

★Dukes London COCKTAIL BAR
(Map p82; ☏ 020-7491 4840; www.dukeshotel. com/dukes-bar; Dukes Hotel, 35 St James's Pl, SW1; ⊙ 2-11pm Mon-Sat, 4-10.30pm Sun; 🐾; ⊖ Green Park) Sip to-die-for martinis like royalty in a gentleman's-club-like ambience at this tucked-away classic bar where white-jacketed masters mix up some awesomely good preparations. Ian Fleming used to frequent the place, perhaps perfecting his 'shaken, not stirred' James Bond maxim. Smokers can ease into the secluded Cognac and Cigar Garden to light up cigars purchased here.

Swift
COCKTAIL BAR

(Map p84; ☑ 020-7437 7820; www.barswift.com; 12 Old Compton St, W1; ◷ 3pm-midnight Mon-Sat, to 10.30pm Sun; ◉ Leicester Sq, Tottenham Court Rd) Our favourite new place for cocktails, Swift (as in the bird) has a black-and-white, candlelit Upstairs Bar designed for those who want a quick tipple before dinner or the theatre, while the Downstairs Bar (open from 5pm), with its sit-down bar and art deco sofas, is a place to hang out. There's live jazz and blues at the weekend.

Connaught Bar
COCKTAIL BAR

(Map p100; ☑ 020-7314 3419; www.the-connaught. co.uk/mayfair-bars/connaught-bar; Connaught Hotel, Carlos Pl, W1; ◷ 11am-1am Mon-Sat, to midnight Sun; ◉ Bond St) Drinkers who know their stuff single out the travelling martini trolley for particular praise, but almost everything at this sumptuous bar at the exclusive and very British Connaught Hotel gets the nod: lavish art deco–inspired lines, faultless and cheerful service, and some of the best drinks in town. Cocktails, classic and those given a thoroughly contemporary twist, start at £18.

Princess Louise
PUB

(Map p84; ☑ 020-7405 8816; http://princesslou isepub.co.uk; 208 High Holborn, WC1; ◷ 11am-11pm Mon-Fri, noon-11pm Sat, noon-6.45pm Sun; ◉ Holborn) The ground-floor saloon of this pub dating from 1872 is spectacularly decorated with a riot of fine tiles, etched mirrors, plasterwork and a stunning central horseshoe bar. The old Victorian wood partitions give drinkers plenty of nooks and alcoves to hide in, and the frosted-glass 'snob screens' add further period allure.

LGBT LONDON

The West End, particularly Soho, is the visible centre of gay and lesbian London, with venues clustered around Old Compton St and its surrounds, but there are gay-friendly venues scattered all over the capital.

Heaven (Map p84; http://heaven-live.co.uk; Villiers St, WC2; ◷ 11pm-5am Mon, to 4am Thu & Fri, 10.30pm-5am Sat; ◉ Embankment, Charing Cross) This perennially popular mixed/gay club under the arches beneath Charing Cross Station is host to excellent live gigs and club nights. Monday's Popcorn (mixed dance party, with an all-welcome door policy) offers one of the best weeknight's clubbing in the capital. The celebrated G-A-Y takes place here on Thursday (G-A-Y Porn Idol), Friday (G-A-Y Camp Attack) and Saturday (plain ol' G-A-Y).

Duke of Wellington (Map p84; ☑ 020-7439 1274; www.facebook.com/Duke.Of.Welly; 77 Wardour St, W1; ◷ noon-midnight Mon-Sat, to 11.30pm Sun; ◉ Leicester Sq) This seasoned pub off Old Compton St is often busy but has few pretensions, attracting a more beardy, fun-loving gay crowd, many of whom gather outside in warmer months.

RVT (Royal Vauxhall Tavern; ☑ 020-7820 1222; www.vauxhalltavern.com; 372 Kennington Lane, SE11; entry £5-25; ◷ 7pm-midnight Mon-Thu, 9pm-3am Fri, 9pm-2am Sat, 3pm-midnight Sun; ◉ Vauxhall) A welcoming gay landmark, the Royal Vauxhall Tavern is the perfect antidote to the gleaming new wave of uppity gay venues now crowding Vauxhall's gay village. Saturday's Duckie, tagged 'London's Authentic Honky Tonk', is the club's signature queer performance night, while Sunday Social is cabaret and dance till midnight and on Monday it's the fun Big Bingo Show!

Two Brewers (☑ 020-7819 9539; www.the2brewers.com; 114 Clapham High St, SW4; after 10pm £3-8; ◷ 5pm-2am Sun-Thu, to 4am Fri & Sat; ☎; ◉ Clapham Common) Clapham exudes an inner-suburban feel, the High St in particular, but the long-standing Two Brewers endures as one of the best London gay bars outside the gay villages of Soho, Shoreditch and Vauxhall. Here there's a friendly, laid-back, local crowd who come for a quiet drink during the week and some madcap cabaret and dancing at weekends.

Dalston Superstore (☑ 020-7254 2273; www.dalstonsuperstore.com; 117 Kingsland High St, E8; ◷ 11.45am-late; ◉ Dalston Kingsland) Bar, club or diner? Gay, lesbian or straight? Dalston Superstore is hard to pigeonhole, which we suspect is the point. This two-level industrial space is open all day but really comes into its own after dark when there are club nights in the basement.

Terroirs WINE BAR

(Map p84; ☑ 020-7036 0660; www.terroirswinebar.com; 5 William IV St, WC2; ☺ noon-11pm Mon-Sat; 🖥; ☻ Charing Cross Rd) A fab two-floor spot for a pre-theatre glass and some expertly created charcuterie, with informative staff, tempting and affordable lunch specials (£10), a lively, convivial atmosphere and a breathtaking list of organic, natural and bio-dynamic wines.

Dog & Duck PUB

(Map p84; ☑ 020-7494 0697; www.nicholsonspubs.co.uk/restaurants/london/thedoganddducksoholondon; 18 Bateman St, W1; ☺ 11.30am-11pm Mon-Thu, to 11.30pm Fri, 11am-11.30pm Sat, noon-10.30pm Sun; ☻ Tottenham Court Rd) With a fine array of real ales, some stunning Victorian glazed tiling and garrulous crowds spilling onto the pavement, the Dog & Duck has attracted a host of famous regulars, including painters John Constable and pre-Raphaelite Dante Gabrielle Rossetti, dystopian writer George Orwell and musician Madonna.

🍷 The City

Blackfriar PUB

(Map p90; ☑ 020-7236 5474; www.nicholsonspubs.co.uk; 174 Queen Victoria St, EC4; ☺ 10am-11pm Mon-Fri, 9am-11pm Sat, noon-10.30pm Sun; ☻ Blackfriars) Built in 1875 on the site of a Dominican monastery (hence the name and the corpulent chap above the door), this prominent pub was famously saved from demolition in the 1960s by poet Sir John Betjeman. The unusual monastic-themed friezes date from an art nouveau makeover in 1905. It serves a good selection of ales, along with speciality sausages and chops.

Ye Olde Cheshire Cheese PUB

(Map p90; ☑ 020-7353 6170; Wine Office Court, 145 Fleet St, EC4; ☺ 11.30am-11pm Mon-Fri, noon-11pm Sat; ☻ Chancery Lane) Rebuilt in 1667 after the Great Fire, this is one of London's most famous pubs, accessed via a narrow alley off Fleet St. Over its long history, Dr Johnson, Thackeray and Dickens have all supped in its gloriously gloomy surrounds. The vaulted cellars are thought to be remnants of a 13th-century Carmelite monastery.

Sky Pod BAR

(Map p90; ☑ 0333 772 0020; www.skygarden.london; L35, 20 Fenchurch St, EC3; ☺ 7am-11pm Mon, to midnight Tue, to 1am Wed-Fri, 8am-1am Sat, 8am-11pm Sun; ☻ Monument) You'll need a booking for the Sky Garden (p93) to access this rooftop bar, and if you'd like a guaranteed table to sit at, you're best to book one at the same time. The views are extraordinary, although it does get cold up here in winter. Note, it doesn't admit patrons in shorts, sportswear, trainers or flip-flops after 5pm.

Counting House PUB

(Map p90; ☑ 020-7283 7123; www.the-counting-house.com; 50 Cornhill, EC3; ☺ 10am-11pm Mon-Fri; 🖥; ☻ Bank) With its counters and basement vaults, this award-winning pub certainly looks and feels comfortable in the former headquarters of NatWest Bank (1893), with its domed skylight and elegantly curved central bar. This is a favourite of City boys and girls, who come for the good range of real ales and the speciality pies (from £13.95).

Madison COCKTAIL BAR

(Map p90; ☑ 020-3693 5160; www.madisonlondon.net; rooftop, 1 New Change, EC4; ☺ 11am-midnight Mon-Thu, to 1am Fri & Sat, noon to 9pm Sun; ☻ St Paul's) Perched atop One New Change with a drop-dead gorgeous view of St Paul's, Madison offers a large open-air roof terrace with a restaurant on one side and a cocktail bar on the other; we come for the latter. Drinkers must be aged over 21; no trainers or flip-flops admitted, however fashionable. Expect to queue.

🍷 South Bank

★**Little Bird Gin** COCKTAIL BAR

(www.littlebirdgin.com; Maltby St, SE1; ☺ 5-10pm Thu & Fri, 10am-10pm Sat, 11am-4pm Sun; ☻ London Bridge) This South London–based distillery opens a pop-up bar in a workshop at Maltby Street Market (www.maltby.st; dishes £5-10; ☺ 9am-4pm Sat, 11am-4pm Sun; ☻ Bermondsey) to ply merry punters with devilishly good cocktails (£5 to £7), served in jam jars or apothecary's glass bottles.

★**Oblix** BAR

(Map p98; www.oblixrestaurant.com; 32nd fl, Shard, 31 St Thomas St, SE1; ☺ noon-11pm; ☻ London Bridge) On the 32nd floor of the Shard (p99), Oblix offers mesmerising vistas of London. You can come for anything from a coffee (£3.50) to a cocktail (from £13.50) and enjoy virtually the same views as the official viewing galleries of the Shard (but at a reduced cost and with the added bonus of a drink). Live music every night from 7pm.

★**Scootercaffe** BAR
(Map p98; 132 Lower Marsh, SE1; ◷8.30am-11pm Mon-Thu, to midnight Fri, 10am-midnight Sat, to 11pm Sun; ⊚; ◉Waterloo) A well-established fixture on the up-and-coming Lower Marsh road, this funky cafe-bar and former scooter-repair shop with a Piatti scooter in the window serves killer hot chocolates, coffee and decadent cocktails. Unusually, you're allowed to bring in takeaway food. The tiny patio at the back is perfect for soaking up the sun.

Skylon BAR
(Map p98; www.skylon-restaurant.co.uk; Royal Festival Hall, Southbank Centre, Belvedere Rd, SE1; ◷noon-1am Mon-Sat, to 10.30pm Sun; ⊚; ◉Waterloo) Ravishing 1950s decor and show-stopping views make Skylon a memorable choice for a drink or **meal** (Map p98; ☑020-7654 7800; 3-course menu grill/restaurant £25/30; ◷grill noon-11pm Mon-Sat, to 10.30pm Sun, restaurant noon-2.30pm & 5-10.30pm Mon-Sat, 11.30am-4pm Sun). You'll have to come early to bag one of the tables at the front with plunging views of the river. Drinks-wise, just ask: from superb seasonal cocktails to infusions and a staggering choice of wine and whiskys (plus whiskeys!).

🍷 Kensington & Hyde Park

★**Tomtom Coffee House** CAFE
(Map p100; ☑020-7730 1771; www.tomtom.co.uk; 114 Ebury St, SW1; ◷8am-5pm Mon-Fri, 9am-6pm Sat & Sun; ⊚; ◉Victoria) Tomtom has built its reputation on its amazing coffee: not only are the drinks fabulously presented (forget ferns and hearts in your latte, here it's peacocks fanning their tails), but the selection is dizzying: from the usual espresso-based suspects to filter, and a full choice of beans. You can even spice things up with a bonus tot of cognac or whisky (£3).

Queen's Arms PUB
(Map p100; www.thequeensarmskensington.co.uk; 30 Queen's Gate Mews, SW7; ◷noon-11pm Mon-Sat, to 10.30pm Sun; ◉Gloucester Rd) Just around the corner from the Royal Albert Hall is this blue-grey-painted godsend. Located in an adorable cobbled-mews setting off bustling Queen's Gate, it beckons with a cosy interior and a right-royal selection of ales – including selections from small, local cask brewers – and ciders on tap. In warm weather, drinkers

stand outside in the mews (only permitted on one side).

🍷 East London

★**Dove Freehouse** PUB
(☑020-7275 7617; www.dovepubs.com; 24-28 Broadway Market, E8; ◷noon-11pm Sun-Fri, 11am-11pm Sat; ⊚; ◉London Fields) Alluring at any time, the Dove has a rambling series of rooms and a wide range of Belgian Trappist, wheat and fruit-flavoured beers. Drinkers spill on to the street in warmer weather, or hunker down in the low-lit back room with board games when it's chilly.

★**Netil360** ROOFTOP BAR
(www.netil360.com; 1 Westgate St, E8; ◷noon-8.30pm Wed & Sun, to 10.30pm Thu-Sat Apr-Nov; ⊚; ◉London Fields) Perched atop Netil House, this uberhip rooftop cafe-bar offers incredible views over London, with brass telescopes enabling you to get better acquainted with workers in the Gherkin. In between drinks you can knock out a game of croquet on the Astroturf, or perhaps book a hot tub for you and your mates to stew in.

★**Cat & Mutton** PUB
(☑020-7249 6555; www.catandmutton.com; 76 Broadway Market, E8; ◷noon-11pm Mon, to midnight Tue-Thu, to 1am Fri, 10am-1am Sat, noon-11.30pm Sun; ◉London Fields) At this fabulous Georgian pub, Hackney hipsters sup pints under the watchful eyes of hunting trophies, black-and-white photos of old-time boxers and a large portrait of Karl Marx. If it's crammed downstairs, as it often is, head up the spiral staircase to the comfy couches. DJs spin funk, disco and soul on the weekends.

Howling Hops MICROBREWERY
(☑020-3583 8262; www.howlinghops.co.uk; 9a Queen's Yard, White Post Lane, E9; ◷noon-11pm Sun-Thu, to midnight Fri & Sat; ◉Hackney Wick) You won't find cans, bottles or barrels in this pleasantly grungy brewery bar, just 10 gleaming tanks containing ales and lagers straight from the source. It shares the old Victorian warehouse with the wonderful-smelling Billy Smokes Barbecue and there's also a counter serving excellent coffee.

Draughts CAFE, BAR
(www.draughtslondon.com; 337 Acton Mews, E8; mains £6-10; ◷10am-11pm Sun-Fri, to midnight Sat; ⊙; ◉Haggerston) London's first board-game themed cafe-bar – it has over 600 to

choose from – offers a delightfully geeky way to while away an afternoon. Food, wine and ale are served all day, and there is even a 'game guru' on hand to explain rules and advise which games are best suited to your group's wants. There's a £5 charge if you start playing a game.

Carpenter's Arms   PUB
(☑020-7739 6342; www.carpentersarmsfreehouse.com; 73 Cheshire St, E2; ⊙4-11.30pm Mon-Wed, noon-11.30pm Thu & Sun, to 12.30am Fri & Sat; ☎; ⊜Shoreditch High St) Once owned by infamous gangsters the Kray brothers (who bought it for their old ma to run), this chic yet cosy pub has been beautifully restored and its many wooden surfaces positively gleam. A back room and small yard provide a little more space for the convivial drinkers. There's a huge range of draught and bottled beers and ciders.

Prospect of Whitby   PUB
(☑020-7481 1095; www.greenekingpubs.co.uk; 57 Wapping Wall, E1; ⊙noon-11pm Mon-Thu, 11am-midnight Fri & Sat, noon-10.30pm Sun; ☎; ⊜Wapping) Once known as the Devil's Tavern due to its unsavoury clientele, the Prospect first opened its doors in 1520, although the only part of the original pub remaining is the flagstone floor. Famous patrons have included Charles Dickens and Samuel Pepys. There's a smallish terrace overlooking the Thames, a restaurant upstairs, open fires in winter and a pewter-topped bar.

🍺 Clerkenwell, Shoreditch & Spitalfields

★Worship St Whistling Shop   COCKTAIL BAR
(Map p138; ☑020-7247 0015; www.whistlingshop.com; 63 Worship St, EC2A; ⊙5pm-midnight Mon & Tue, to 1am Wed & Thu, to 2am Fri & Sat; ⊜Old St) While the name is Victorian slang for a place selling illicit booze, this subterranean drinking den's master mixologists explore the experimental limits of cocktail chemistry and aromatic science, as well as concocting the classics. Many ingredients are made with rotary evaporators in the on-site lab. Also runs cocktail masterclasses.

★Cargo   BAR, CLUB
(Map p138; www.cargo-london.com; 83 Rivington St, EC2A; ⊙noon-1am Mon-Thu, to 3am Fri & Sat, to midnight Sun; ⊜Shoreditch High St) Cargo is one of London's most eclectic clubs. Under its brick railway arches you'll find a dance

floor, a bar and an outside terrace adorned with two original Banksy images. The music policy (hip-hop, pop, R&B and club classics) is varied, with plenty of up-and-coming bands also in the line-up. Food is available throughout the day.

★Ye Olde Mitre   PUB
(Map p90; www.yeoldemitreholborn.co.uk; 1 Ely Ct, EC1N; ⊙11am-11pm Mon-Fri; ☎; ⊜Farringdon) A delightfully cosy historic pub with an extensive beer selection, tucked away in a backstreet off Hatton Garden, Ye Olde Mitre was built in 1546 for the servants of Ely Palace. There's no music, so rooms echo only with amiable chit-chat. Queen Elizabeth I danced around the cherry tree by the bar, they say.

Fabric   CLUB
(Map p90; ☑0207 336 8898; www.fabriclondon.com; 77a Charterhouse St, EC1M; cover £5-25; ⊙11pm-7am Fri, to 8am Sat, to 5.30am Sun; ⊜Farringdon, Barbican) London's leading club, Fabric's three separate dance floors in a huge converted cold store opposite Smithfield meat market draw impressive queues (buy tickets online). FabricLive (on selected Fridays) rumbles with drum 'n' bass and dubstep, while Fabric (usually on Saturdays but also on selected Fridays) is the club's signature live DJ night. Sunday's WetYourSelf! delivers house, techno and electronica.

XOYO   CLUB
(Map p138; www.xoyo.co.uk; 32-37 Cowper St, EC2A; ⊙10pm-3am Mon, Tue & Thu, 9.30pm-4am Fri & Sat; ⊜Old St) This fantastic Shoreditch warehouse club throws together a pulsing and popular mix of gigs, club nights and art events. Always buzzing, it has a varied line-up of indie bands, hip-hop, electro, dubstep and much in between, and attracts a mix of clubbers, from skinny-jeaned hipsters to more mature hedonists (but no suits).

BrewDog   BAR
(Map p138; www.brewdog.com; 51-55 Bethnal Green Rd, E1; ⊙noon-midnight Mon-Thu, to 2am Fri, 11am-2am Sat, 11am-midnight Sun; ☎; ⊜Shoreditch High St) BrewDog is an ale aficionado's paradise, with 18 different brews on tap, hundreds by the bottle and, to soak it all up, some excellent burgers (including interesting variations such as brisket and soy). Its own crowd-funded eco-brewery is located in Scotland, near Aberdeen, and it stocks other microbrewery beers, too.

Hoxton, Shoreditch & Spitalfields

Book Club BAR

(Map p138; ☏020-7684 8618; www.wearetbc. com; 100-106 Leonard St, EC2A; ⊙9am-midnight Mon-Wed, to 2am Thu & Fri, 10am-2am Sat, to midnight Sun; ☜; ⊖Old St) A creative vibe animates this fantastic one-time Victori-

an warehouse. Book Club hosts DJs and oddball events (life drawing, workshops, twerking lessons and the Crap Film Club) to complement the drinking and enthusiastic ping-pong and pool playing. Food is served

Hoxton, Shoredith & Spitalfields

throughout the day and there's a scruffy basement bar below.

Ten Bells PUB

(Map p138; www.tenbells.com; 84 Commercial St, E1; ⊙noon-midnight Sun-Wed, to 1am Thu-Sat; 🛜; ⓔShoreditch High St) This landmark Victorian pub with large windows and beautiful tiles is perfectly positioned for a pint after exploring Spitalfields Market. The most famous of London's Jack the Ripper pubs, it was patronised by his last victim before her grisly end, and possibly by the serial killer himself. Gin menu, pork scratchings and pie of the day offered.

 North London

★Proud Camden BAR

(Map p132; www.proudcamden.com; Stables Market, Chalk Farm Rd, NW1; ⊙11am-1.30am Mon-Sat, to midnight Sun; ⓔChalk Farm) Proud occupies a former horse hospital within Stables Market, with private booths in the old stalls, fantastic artworks on the walls (the main bar acts as a gallery during the day) and a kooky garden terrace complete with a hot tub. It's also one of Camden's best music venues, with live bands and DJs most nights (entry free to £15).

★Holly Bush PUB

(www.hollybushhampstead.co.uk; 22 Holly Mount, NW3; ⊙noon-11pm Mon-Sat, to 10.30pm Sun; 🛜🍴🐕; ⓔHampstead) This beautiful Grade II–listed Georgian pub opens to an antique interior, with open fires in winter. It has a knack for making you stay longer than you planned. Set above Heath St, in a secluded

hilltop location, it's reached via the Holly Bush Steps.

★Edinboro Castle PUB

(Map p132; www.edinborocastlepub.co.uk; 57 Mornington Tce, NW1; ⊙noon-11pm Mon-Sat, noon-10.30pm Sun; 🛜; ⓔCamden Town) Large and relaxed Edinboro offers a refined atmosphere, gorgeous furniture perfect for slumping into, a fine bar and a full menu. The highlight, however, is the huge beer garden, complete with warm-weather barbecues and decorated with coloured lights on long summer evenings. Patio heaters come out in winter.

🍷 Greenwich & South London

★Cutty Sark Tavern PUB

(☎020-8858 3146; www.cuttysarkse10.co.uk; 4-6 Ballast Quay, SE10; ⊙11.30am-11pm Mon-Sat, noon-10.30pm Sun; 🛜; 🚈DLR Cutty Sark) Housed in a delightful bow-windowed, wood-beamed Georgian building directly on the Thames, the Cutty Sark is one of the few independent pubs left in Greenwich. Half a dozen cask-conditioned ales on tap line the bar, there's an inviting riverside seating area opposite and an upstairs dining room looking out on to glorious views. It's a 10-minute walk from the DLR station.

★Greenwich Union PUB

(☎020-8692 6258; www.greenwichunion.com; 56 Royal Hill, SE10; ⊙noon-11pm Mon-Fri, 11.30am-11pm Sat, 11.30am-10.30pm Sun; 🛜; 🚈DLR Greenwich) The award-winning Union plies six or seven Meantime microbrewery beers, including raspberry and wheat varieties, and a strong list of ales, plus bottled international brews. It's a handsome place, with duffed-up leather armchairs and a welcoming long, narrow aspect leading to a conservatory and beer garden at the rear.

★Trafalgar Tavern   PUB
(☎020-8858 2909; www.trafalgartavern.co.uk; 6 Park Row, SE10; ☺noon-11pm Mon-Thu, noon-midnight Fri, 10am-midnight Sat, 10am-11pm Sun; ⍰DLR Cutty Sark) This elegant tavern with big windows overlooking the Thames is steeped in history. Dickens apparently knocked back a few here – and used it as the setting for the wedding breakfast scene in *Our Mutual Friend* – and prime ministers Gladstone and Disraeli used to dine on the pub's celebrated whitebait.

🍸 West London

★Troubadour   BAR
(☎020-7341 6333; www.troubadour.co.uk; 263-267 Old Brompton Rd, SW5; ☺cafe 9am-12.30am, club 8pm-12.30am or 2am; ⍰; ⍰Earl's Court) On a comparable spiritual plane to Paris' Shakespeare and Company bookshop, this eccentric, time-warped and convivial boho bar-cafe has been serenading drinkers since 1954. (Deep breath) Adele, Paolo Nutini, Ed Sheeran, Joni Mitchell and (deeper breath) Jimi Hendrix and Bob Dylan have performed here, and there's still live music (folk, blues) and a large, pleasant garden open in summer.

Windsor Castle   PUB
(Map p106; www.thewindsorcastlekensington. co.uk; 114 Campden Hill Rd, W11; ☺noon-11pm Mon-Sat, to 10.30pm Sun; ⍰; ⍰Notting Hill Gate) A classic tavern on the brow of Campden Hill Rd, this place has history, nooks and charm on tap. It's worth the search for its historic compartmentalised interior, roaring fire (in winter), delightful beer garden (in summer) and affable regulars (all seasons). According to legend, the bones of Thomas Paine (author of *Rights of Man*) are in the cellar.

Notting Hill Arts Club   CLUB
(Map p106; www.nottinghillclub.com; 21 Notting Hill Gate, W11; ☺6pm-late Mon-Fri, 4pm-late Sat & Sun; ⍰; ⍰Notting Hill Gate) London simply wouldn't be what it is without places like NHAC. Cultivating the underground-music scene, this small basement club attracts a musically curious and experimental crowd. Dress code: no suits and ties.

📍 Richmond, Kew & Hampton Court

★City Barge   PUB
(www.metropolitanpubcompany.com/our-pubs/the -city-barge; 27 Strand on the Green, W4; ☺noon-11pm Mon-Thu, to midnight Fri, 10am-midnight Sat, 10am-10.30pm Sun; ⍰; ⍰Gunnersbury) In a line of small riverside cottages facing wooded Oliver's Island (where Cromwell is alleged to have taken refuge), this excellent pub looks straight onto the muddy Thames. Once known as the Navigators Arms, there has been a pub here since the Middle Ages, although the Luftwaffe gave it a dramatic facelift (as has an attractive refurb).

★White Cross   PUB
(☎020-8940 6844; www.thewhitecrossrichmond. com; Water Lane, TW9; ☺11am-11pm Mon-Fri, 10am-11pm Sat, 10am-10.30pm Sun; ⍰; ⍰Richmond) The riverside location and fine food and ales make this bay-windowed pub on the site of a former friary a winner. There are entrances for low and high tides, but when the river is at its highest, Cholmondeley Walk running along the Thames floods and the pub is out of bounds to those not willing to wade. Wellies are provided.

☆ Entertainment

Theatre

Royal Court Theatre   THEATRE
(Map p100; ☎020-7565 5000; www.royalcourt theatre.com; Sloane Sq, SW1; tickets £12-38; ⍰Sloane Sq) Equally renowned for staging innovative new plays and old classics, the Royal Court is among London's most progressive theatres and has continued to foster major writing talent across the UK. There are two auditoriums: the main Jerwood Theatre Downstairs, and the much smaller studio Jerwood Theatre Upstairs. Tickets for Monday performances are £12.

A limited number of restricted-view standing places go on sale one hour before each Jerwood Theatre Downstairs performance for just 10p each. Contact the theatre to check on availability.

★Shakespeare's Globe   THEATRE
(Map p98; ☎020-7401 9919; www.shakespeares globe.com; 21 New Globe Walk, SE1; seats £20-45, standing £5; ⍰Blackfriars, London Bridge) If you love Shakespeare and the theatre, the Globe (p96) will knock your theatrical socks off. This authentic Shakespearean theatre is a

wooden 'O' without a roof over the central stage area, and although there are covered wooden bench seats in tiers around the stage, many people (there's room for 700) do as 17th-century 'groundlings' did, and stand in front of the stage.

Old Vic THEATRE
(Map p98; ☑ 0844 871 7628; www.oldvictheatre. com; The Cut, SE1; ⊖ Waterloo) American actor Kevin Spacey took the theatrical helm of this London theatre in 2003. He was succeeded in April 2015 by Matthew Warchus (who directed *Matilda the Musical* and the film *Pride*), whose aim is to bring eclectic programming to the theatre: expect new writing, as well as dynamic revivals of old works and musicals.

Half the seats of the first five previews of a new production are sold for just £10 each. These PwC £10 Preview Tickets go on sale five weeks before the performance.

Young Vic THEATRE
(Map p98; ☑ 020-7922 2922; www.youngvic.org; 66 The Cut, SE1; ⊖ Southwark, Waterloo) This groundbreaking theatre is as much about showcasing and discovering new talent as it is about people discovering theatre. The Young Vic features actors, directors and plays from across the world, many tackling contemporary political and cultural issues, such as the death penalty, racism or corruption, and often blending dance and music with acting.

Donmar Warehouse THEATRE
(Map p84; ☑ 020-3282 3808; www.donmarware house.com; 41 Earlham St, WC2; ⊖ Covent Garden) The cosy Donmar Warehouse is London's 'thinking person's theatre'. Josie Rourke, the artistic director until 2019, staged some intriguing and successful productions, including the well-received comedy *My Night with Reg*, George Bernard Shaw's *St Joan* and the political drama *Limehouse* by Steve Waters.

Wilton's THEATRE
(☑ 020-7702 2789; www.wiltons.org.uk; 1 Graces Alley, E1; ⊙ bar 5-11pm Mon-Sat; ⊖ Tower Hill) A gloriously atmospheric example of a Victorian music hall, Wilton's hosts a variety of shows, from comedy and classical music to theatre and opera. The **Mahogany Bar** is a great way to get a taste of the place if you're not attending a performance.

Hackney Empire THEATRE
(☑ 020-8985 2424; www.hackneyempire.co.uk; 291 Mare St, E8; ⊠ Hackney Central) One of London's most beautiful theatres, this renovated Edwardian music hall (1901) offers an extremely diverse range of performances, from hard-edged political theatre to musicals, opera and comedy. It's one of the very best places to catch a pantomime at Christmas.

Live Music

★ **Jazz Cafe** LIVE MUSIC
(Map p132; ☑ 020-7485 6834; www.thejazzcafe london.com; 5 Parkway, NW1; ⊙ live shows from 7pm, club nights 10pm-3am; ⊖ Camden Town) The name would have you think jazz is the main staple, but it's only a small slice of what's on offer. The intimate clublike space also serves up funk, hip-hop, R&B, soul and rare groove, with big-name acts regularly dropping in. Saturday club night is soul night, with two live sets from the house band.

★ **KOKO** LIVE MUSIC
(Map p132; www.koko.uk.com; 1a Camden High St, NW1; ⊖ Mornington Cres) Once the legendary Camden Palace, where Charlie Chaplin, the Goons and the Sex Pistols performed, and where Prince played surprise gigs, KOKO is maintaining its reputation as one of London's better gig venues. The theatre has a dance floor and decadent balconies, and attracts an indie crowd. There are live bands most nights and hugely popular club nights on Saturdays.

★ **Royal Albert Hall** CONCERT VENUE
(Map p100; ☑ 0845 401 5034; www.royalalbert hall.com; Kensington Gore, SW7; ⊖ South Kensington) This splendid Victorian concert hall hosts classical music, rock and other performances, but is famously the venue for the BBC-sponsored Proms. Booking is possible, but from mid-July to mid-September Proms punters queue for £5 standing (or 'promenading') tickets that go on sale one hour before curtain-up. Otherwise, the box office and prepaid-ticket collection counter are through door 12 (south side of the hall).

★ **606 Club** BLUES, JAZZ
(☑ 020-7352 5953; www.606club.co.uk; 90 Lots Rd, SW10; ⊙ 7-11.15pm Sun-Thu, 8pm-12.30am Fri & Sat; ⊠ Imperial Wharf) Named after its old address on the King's Rd that cast a spell over jazz lovers London-wide back in the '80s, this fantastic, tucked-away basement jazz club and restaurant gives centre stage to contemporary British-based jazz musicians nightly. The club can only serve alcohol to nonmembers who are dining, and it is highly advisable to book to get a table.

Roundhouse
CONCERT VENUE

(Map p132; www.roundhouse.org.uk; Chalk Farm Rd, NW1; ⊖ Chalk Farm) Built as a railway repair shed in 1847, this unusual Grade II–listed round building became an arts centre in the 1960s and hosted legendary bands before falling into near-dereliction in 1983. Its 21st-century resurrection as a creative hub has been a great success and it now hosts everything from big-name concerts to dance, circus, stand-up comedy, poetry slams and improvisation.

O2 Arena
LIVE MUSIC

(www.theo2.co.uk; Peninsula Sq, SE10; 🛜; ⊖ North Greenwich) One of the city's major concert venues, hosting all the biggies – the Rolling Stones, Paul Simon and Sting, One Direction, Ed Sheeran and many others – inside the 20,000-capacity arena. It's also a popular venue for sporting events and you can even climb the roof for ranging views with **Up at the O2** (www.theo2.co.uk/upattheo2; from £30; ⊙ hours vary).

Dublin Castle
LIVE MUSIC

(Map p132; www.thedublincastle.com; 94 Parkway, NW1; ⊙ noon-2am Fri-Sun, 1pm-2am Mon, Wed & Thu, noon-1am Tue; ⊖ Camden Town) Live punk or alternative bands play most nights in this comfortingly grungy pub's back room (cover charges are usually £4.50 to £7). DJs take over after the bands on Friday, Saturday and Sunday nights.

★Scala
LIVE MUSIC

(Map p110; ☎ 020-7833 2022; www.scala.co.uk; 275 Pentonville Rd, N1; ⊖ King's Cross St Pancras) Opened in 1920 as a salubrious golden-age cinema, Scala slipped into porn-movie hell in the 1970s, only to be reborn as a club and live-music venue in the noughties. It's one of the best places in London to catch an intimate gig and is a great dance space too, hosting a diverse range of club nights.

★Pizza Express Jazz Club
JAZZ

(Map p84; ☎ 020-7439 4962; www.pizzaexpress live.com/venues/soho-jazz-club; 10 Dean St, W1; tickets £15-40; ⊖ Tottenham Court Rd) Pizza Express has been one of the best jazz venues in London since opening in 1969. It may be a strange arrangement, in a basement beneath a branch of the chain restaurant, but it's highly popular. Lots of big names perform here and artists such as Norah Jones, Gregory Porter and the late Amy Winehouse played here in their early days.

Ronnie Scott's
JAZZ

(Map p84; ☎ 020-7439 0747; www.ronniescotts. co.uk; 47 Frith St, W1; ⊙ 7pm-3am Mon-Sat, 1-4pm & 8pm-midnight Sun; ⊖ Leicester Sq, Tottenham Court Rd) Ronnie Scott's jazz club opened in 1965 and became widely known as Britain's best. Support acts are at 7pm, with main gigs at 8.15pm (8pm Sunday) and a second house at 11.15pm Friday and Saturday (check ahead). The more informal Late, Late Show runs from 1am to 3am. Expect to pay from £25; the Late, Late Show and Sunday lunch shows are just £10.

100 Club
LIVE MUSIC

(Map p84; ☎ 020-7636 0933; www.the100club. co.uk; 100 Oxford St, W1; tickets £8-20; ⊙ check website for gig times; ⊖ Oxford Circus, Tottenham Court Rd) This heritage London venue at the same address since 1942 started off as a jazz club but now leans towards rock. Back in the day it showcased Chris Barber, BB King and the Rolling Stones, and it was at the centre of the punk revolution and the '90s indie scene. It hosts dancing gigs, the occasional big name, where-are-they-now bands and top-league tributes.

Cinemas

BFI Southbank
CINEMA

(Map p98; ☎ 020-7928 3232; www.bfi.org.uk; Belvedere Rd, SE1; tickets £8-12; ⊙ 10am-11pm; ⊖ Waterloo) Tucked almost out of sight under the arches of Waterloo Bridge, the British Film Institute (BFI) contains four cinemas that screen thousands of films each year (many art house); a gallery devoted to the moving image; and a mediatheque, where you watch film and TV highlights from the BFI National Archive.

Electric Cinema
CINEMA

(Map p106; ☎ 020-7908 9696; www.electriccinema. co.uk; 191 Portobello Rd, W11; tickets £8-22.50; ⊖ Ladbroke Grove) Having notched up its centenary in 2011, the Electric is one of the UK's oldest cinemas, updated. Avail yourself of the luxurious leather armchairs, sofas, footstools and tables for food and drink in the auditorium, or select one of the six front-row double beds! Tickets are cheapest on Mondays.

Prince Charles Cinema
CINEMA

(Map p84; www.princecharlescinema.com; 7 Leicester Pl, WC2; tickets £5-16; ⊖ Leicester Sq) Leicester Sq cinema-ticket prices are very high, so wait until the first runs have moved to the Prince Charles, central London's cheapest cinema, where nonmembers pay £5 to

£12 for new releases. Also presents mini-festivals, Q&As with film directors, classics, sleepover movie marathons, and exuberant sing-along screenings of films like *Frozen*, *The Sound of Music* and *Rocky Horror Picture Show* (£16).

Comedy

Comedy Store
COMEDY

(Map p84; ☑ 0844 871 7699; www.thecomedy store.co.uk; 1a Oxendon St, SW1; tickets £11-33.50; ⊖ Piccadilly Circus) This is one of the first (and still one of the best) comedy clubs in London. Wednesday and Sunday night's Comedy Store Players is the most famous improvisation outfit in town, with the wonderful Josie Lawrence, now a veteran of two decades. On Thursdays, Fridays and Saturdays, Best in Stand Up features the best on London's comedy circuit.

Doors at 6.30pm; show kicks off at 8pm. Tickets cost from £11 for King Gong (an open-mic night on the last Monday of the month) to £33.50 (best seats for Best in Stand Up show on Saturdays).

Amused Moose Soho
COMEDY

(Map p84; ☑ box office 020-7287 3727; www.amused moose.com; Sanctum Soho Hotel, 20 Warwick St, W1; ⊖ Piccadilly Circus, Oxford Circus) One of the city's best clubs, the peripatetic Amused Moose (the cinema in the Sanctum Soho Hotel is just one of its hosting venues) is popular with audiences and comedians alike, perhaps helped along by the fact that heckling is 'unacceptable' and all the acts are 'first-date friendly' (ie unlikely to humiliate the front row). Shows are usually at 8.15pm on Saturday.

Soho Theatre
COMEDY

(Map p84; ☑ 020-7478 0100; www.sohotheatre. com; 21 Dean St, W1; tickets £8-25; ⊖ Tottenham Court Rd) The Soho Theatre has developed a superb reputation for showcasing new comedy-writing talent and comedians. It's also hosted some top-notch stand-up or

LONDON ENTERTAINMENT

SPORTING LONDON

You may not land tickets to the FA Cup Final at Wembley Stadium or front-row seats for the Wimbledon finals, but there are plenty of ways to enjoy sport in London. You could find yourself watching the Oxford–Cambridge boat race, cheering runners at the London Marathon or hopping on a Santander Cycle – there's lots on offer. Why not check out the impressive facilities in the Queen Elizabeth Olympic Park (p108), which hosts the (former Olympic) London Stadium, the stunning Aquatics Centre and the cutting-edge Velodrome.

Alternatively, take a tour of one of the capital's great sporting stadia:

Lord's (☑ 020-7616 8500; www.lords.org; St John's Wood Rd, NW8; tours adult/child £20/12; ⊙ 4-6 tours daily; ⊖ St John's Wood) The hallowed 'home of cricket', with a fascinating museum.

Wimbledon Lawn Tennis Museum (☑ 020-8946 6131; www.wimbledon.com/museum; Gate 4, Church Rd, SW19; adult/child £13/8, museum & tour £25/15; ⊙ 10am-5pm, last admission 4.30pm; ⊠ Wimbledon, ◲ Wimbledon, ⊖ Wimbledon, ⊖ Southfields) Chart the history of lawn tennis, and see Centre Court from the 360-degree viewing box.

Wembley Stadium (☑ 0800 169 9933; www.wembleystadium.com; tours adult/child £20/12; ⊖ Wembley Park) The city's landmark national stadium, used for football test matches and mega concerts.

Twickenham Stadium (☑ 020-8892 8877; www.englandrugby.com/twickenham; Rugby Rd, Twickenham, TW1; tours adult/child/family £20/12/50; ◲ Twickenham, ⊖ Hounslow East) London's famous rugby union stadium, used for international test matches.

London Stadium (☑ 020-8522 6157; www.london-stadium.com; Queen Elizabeth Olympic Park, E20; tours adult/child £19/11; ⊙ tours 10am-4.15pm; ◲ DLR Pudding Mill Lane) Built as the centrepiece stadium for the 2012 Olympics and now home to West Ham United FC.

Arsenal Emirates Stadium (☑ 020-7619 5000; www.arsenal.com/tours; Hornsey Rd, N5; self-guided tours adult/child £22/14, guided £40; ⊙ 10am-6pm Mon-Sat, to 4pm Sun; ⊖ Holloway Rd) Offers both self-guided tours or tours led by former Arsenal players.

Stamford Bridge (☑ 0871 984 1955; www.chelseafc.com; Stamford Bridge, Fulham Rd, SW6; tours adult/child £22/15; ⊙ museum 9.30am-5pm, tours 10am-3pm; ⊖ Fulham Broadway) Home of Chelsea FC.

sketch-based comedians, including Alexei Sayle and Doctor Brown, plus cabaret. Staff don't always seem to get the joke.

Up the Creek   COMEDY

(www.up-the-creek.com; 302 Creek Rd, SE10; tickets £5-15; ⊙7-11pm Thu & Sun, to 2am Fri & Sat; ℞DLR Cutty Sark) Bizarrely enough, the hecklers can be funnier than the acts at this great club. Mischief, rowdiness and excellent comedy are the norm, with the Blackout open-mic night on Thursdays (www.the-blackout.co.uk; £5) and Sunday specials (www.sundayspecial.co.uk; £7). There's an after-party disco on Fridays and Saturdays. Check full times of acts on the website.

Classical Music

Southbank Centre   CONCERT VENUE

(Map p98; ☑0844 875 0073; www.southbank centre.co.uk; Belvedere Rd, SE1; ⊖Waterloo) The Southbank Centre comprises several venues – Royal Festival Hall, Queen Elizabeth Hall and Purcell Room – hosting a wide range of performing arts. As well as regular programming, it organises fantastic festivals, including **London Wonderground** (circus and cabaret), **Udderbelly** (a festival of comedy in all its guises) and **Meltdown** (a music event curated by the best and most eclectic names in music).

Royal Festival Hall   CONCERT VENUE

(Map p98; ☑020-7960 4200; www.southbank centre.co.uk; Southbank Centre, Belvedere Rd, SE1; ⚲; ⊖Waterloo) Royal Festival Hall's amphitheatre seats 2500 and is one of the best places for catching world- and classical-music artists. The sound is fantastic, the programming impeccable and there are frequent free gigs in the wonderfully expansive foyer.

Queen Elizabeth Hall   CONCERT VENUE

(QEH; Map p98; www.southbankcentre.co.uk; Southbank Centre, Belvedere Rd, SE1; ⊖Waterloo) This concert hall hosts music and dance performances on a smaller scale to the nearby Royal Festival Hall, both part of the Southbank Centre. The Hall reopened in April 2018 after its 21st-century facelift.

Sport

Wimbledon Championships   SPECTATOR SPORT

(☑020-8944 1066; www.wimbledon.com; Church Rd, SW19; grounds admission £8-25, tickets £41-190) For a few weeks each June and July, the sporting world's attention is fixed on the quiet southern suburb of Wimbledon, as it has been since 1877. Most show-court tickets for the Wimbledon Championships are allocated through public ballot, applications for which usually begin in early August of the preceding year and close at the end of December.

Opera & Dance

Sadler's Wells   DANCE

(Map p110; ☑020-7863 8000; www.sadlerswells. com; Rosebery Ave, EC1R; ⊖Angel) A glittering modern venue that was first established in 1683, Sadler's Wells is the most eclectic modern-dance and ballet venue in town, with experimental dance shows of all genres and from all corners of the globe. The Lilian Baylis Studio stages smaller productions.

Royal Opera House   OPERA

(Map p84; ☑020-7304 4000; www.roh.org.uk; Bow St, WC2; tickets £4-270; ⊖Covent Garden) Classic opera in London has a fantastic setting on Covent Garden Piazza and coming here for a night is a sumptuous – if pricey – affair. Although the program has been fluffed up by modern influences, the main attractions are still the opera and classical ballet – all are wonderful productions and feature world-class performers.

English National Opera   OPERA

(ENO; Map p84; ☑020-7845 9300; www.eno.org; St Martin's Lane, WC2; ⊖Leicester Sq) The English National Opera is celebrated for making opera modern and more accessible, as all productions are sung in English. It's based at the impressive London Coliseum, built in 1904 and lovingly restored a century later. The English National Ballet also does regular performances at the Coliseum. Tickets range from £12 to £125.

Barbican Centre   PERFORMING ARTS

(Map p90; ☑020-7638 8891; www.barbican.org. uk; Silk St, EC2; ⊙box office 10am-8pm Mon-Sat, 11am-8pm Sun; ⊖Barbican) Home to the London Symphony Orchestra and the BBC Symphony Orchestra, the Barbican (p93) also hosts scores of other concerts, focusing in particular on jazz, folk, world and soul artists. Dance is also performed here, while the cinema screens recent releases as well as film festivals.

🄷 Shopping

🄷 The West End

★Fortnum & Mason   DEPARTMENT STORE

(Map p84; ☑020-7734 8040; www.fortnumand mason.com; 181 Piccadilly, W1; ⊙10am-8pm Mon-Sat, 11.30am-6pm Sun; ⊖Piccadilly Circus) With its classic eau-de-Nil (pale green) colour scheme, 'the Queen's grocery store' established in 1707 refuses to yield to modern times. Its staff – men and women – still wear old-fashioned tailcoats and its glamorous food hall is supplied with hampers, cut marmalade, speciality teas, superior fruitcakes and so forth. Fortnum & Mason remains the quintessential London shopping experience.

Hamleys TOYS
(Map p84; ☑ 0371 704 1977; www.hamleys.com; 188-196 Regent St, W1; ☺ 10am-9pm Mon-Fri, 9.30am-9pm Sat, noon-6pm Sun; ☻ Oxford Circus) Claiming to be the world's oldest (and some say, the largest) toy store, Hamleys moved to its address on Regent St in 1881. From the basement's Star Wars Collection and ground floor where staff blow bubbles and glide foam boomerangs through the air with practised nonchalance to Lego World and a cafe on the 5th floor, it's a rich layer cake of playthings.

Liberty DEPARTMENT STORE
(Map p84; ☑ 020-7734 1234; www.liberty.co.uk; Great Marlborough St, W1; ☺ 10am-8pm Mon-Sat, noon-6pm Sun; ☻ Oxford Circus) An irresistible blend of contemporary styles in an old-fashioned mock-Tudor atmosphere (1875), Liberty has a huge cosmetics department and an accessories floor, along with a breathtaking lingerie section, all at sky-high prices. A classic London gift or souvenir is a Liberty fabric print, especially in the form of a scarf.

Foyles BOOKS
(Map p84; ☑ 020-7434 1574; www.foyles.co.uk; 107 Charing Cross Rd, WC2; ☺ 9.30am-9pm Mon-Sat, 11.30am-6pm Sun; ☻ Tottenham Court Rd) This is London's most legendary bookshop, where you can bet on finding even the most obscure of titles. Once synonymous with chaos, Foyles got its act together and in 2014 moved just down the road into the spacious former home of Central St Martins art school. Thoroughly redesigned, its stunning new home is a joy to explore.

Selfridges DEPARTMENT STORE
(Map p126; ☑ 0800 123 400; www.selfridges.com; 400 Oxford St, W1; ☺ 9.30am-9pm Mon-Sat, 11.30am-6pm Sun; ☻ Bond St) Selfridges loves innovation – it's famed for its inventive window displays by international artists, gala shows and, above all, its amazing range of products. It's the trendiest of London's one-stop shops, with labels such as Alexander McQueen, Tom Ford, Missoni,

Victoria Beckham and so on; an unparalleled food hall; and Europe's largest cosmetics department.

Stanford's BOOKS, MAPS
(Map p84; ☑ 020-7836 1321; www.stanfords.co.uk; 12-14 Long Acre, WC2; ☺ 9am-8pm Mon-Sat, 11.30am-6pm Sun; ☻ Leicester Sq, Covent Garden) Trading from this address since 1853, this granddaddy of travel bookshops and seasoned seller of maps, guides, globes and literature is a destination in its own right. Ernest Shackleton, David Livingstone and, more recently, Michael Palin and Brad Pitt have all popped in and shopped here.

Daunt Books BOOKS
(Map p126; ☑ 020-7224 2295; www.dauntbooks.co.uk; 83 Marylebone High St, W1; ☺ 9am-7.30pm Mon-Sat, 11am-6pm Sun; ☻ Baker St) An original Edwardian bookshop, with oak panels, galleries and gorgeous skylights, Daunt is one of London's loveliest travel bookshops. It has two floors and stocks general fiction and nonfiction titles as well. Helpful, informed staff.

Reckless Records MUSIC
(Map p84; ☑ 020-7437 4271; www.reckless.co.uk; 30 Berwick St, W1; ☺ 10am-7pm; ☻ Oxford Circus, Tottenham Court Rd) This outfit hasn't really changed in spirit since it first opened its doors in 1984. It still stocks secondhand records and CDs, from punk, soul, dance and independent to mainstream.

Skoob Books BOOKS
(Map p110; ☑ 020-7278 8760; www.skoob.com; 66 The Brunswick, off Marchmont St, WC1; ☺ 10.30am-8pm Mon-Sat, to 6pm Sun; ☻ Russell Sq) Skoob (you work out the name) has got to be London's largest secondhand bookshop, with some 55,000 titles spread over 2000 sq ft of floor space (plus more than a million further books in a warehouse outside town). If you can't find it here, it probably doesn't exist.

We Built This City GIFTS & SOUVENIRS
(Map p84; ☑ 020-3642 9650; www.webuiltthiscity.com; 56-57 Carnaby St, W1; ☺ 10am-7pm Mon-Wed, to 8pm Thu-Sat, 11am-7pm Sun; ☻ Oxford Circus) Taking a commendable stand against Union Jack hats and black-cab key rings, We Built This City is a shop selling London-themed souvenirs that the recipient might actually want. The products are artistic and thoughtful, and celebrate the city's creative side.

Sister Ray   MUSIC
(Map p84; ☑020-7734 3297; www.sisterray.co.uk;
75 Berwick St, W1; ⊙10am-8pm Mon-Sat, noon-
6pm Sun; ⊕Oxford Circus, Tottenham Court Rd)
If you were a fan of the late John Peel on
the BBC, this specialist in innovative, experimental and indie music is just right for you.
Those of you who have never heard of him
will probably also like the shop that 'sells
music to the masses'.

🄷 The City

London Silver Vaults   ARTS & CRAFTS
(Map p90; ☑020-7242 3844; www.silvervaults
london.com; 53-63 Chancery Lane, WC2; ⊙9am-
5.30pm Mon-Fri, to 1pm Sat; ⊕Chancery Lane)
The 30-odd shops that work out of these
secure subterranean vaults make up the
largest collection of silver under one roof in
the world. The different businesses tend to
specialise in particular types of silverware –
from cutlery sets to picture frames, animal
sculptures and lots of jewellery.

🄷 Kensington & Hyde Park

★John Sandoe Books   BOOKS
(Map p100; ☑020-7589 9473; www.johnsandoe.
com; 10 Blacklands Tce, SW3; ⊙9.30am-6.30pm
Mon-Sat, 11am-5pm Sun; ⊕Sloane Sq) The perfect antidote to impersonal book super-
stores, this atmospheric three-storey bookshop in 18th-century premises is a treasure
trove of literary gems and hidden surprises.
It's been in business for six decades and loyal customers swear by it, while knowledgeable booksellers spill forth with well-read
pointers and helpful advice.

Harrods   DEPARTMENT STORE
(Map p100; ☑020-7730 1234; www.harrods.com;
87-135 Brompton Rd, SW1; ⊙10am-9pm Mon-Sat,
11.30am-6pm Sun; ⊕Knightsbridge) Garish and
stylish in equal measure, perennially crowded Harrods is an obligatory stop for visitors,
from the cash-strapped to the big spenders.
The stock is astonishing, as are many of the
price tags. High on kitsch, the 'Egyptian Elevator' resembles something out of an Indiana Jones epic, while the memorial fountain
to Dodi and Di (lower ground floor) merely
adds surrealism.

Harvey Nichols   DEPARTMENT STORE
(Map p100; www.harveynichols.com; 109-125
Knightsbridge, SW1; ⊙10am-8pm Mon-Sat,
11.30am-6pm Sun; ⊕Knightsbridge) At London's
temple of high fashion, you'll find Chloé and

Balenciaga bags, the city's best denim range,
a massive make-up hall with exclusive lines
and great jewellery. The food hall and in-
house restaurant, **Fifth Floor**, are, you
guessed it, on the 5th floor. From 11.30am to
midday, it's browsing time only.

Conran Shop   DESIGN
(Map p100; ☑020-7589 7401; www.conranshop.
co.uk; Michelin House, 81 Fulham Rd, SW3; ⊙10am-
6pm Mon, Tue & Fri, to 7pm Wed & Thu, to 6.30pm
Sat, noon-6pm Sun; ⊕South Kensington) The
original design store (going strong since
1987), the Conran Shop is a treasure trove of
beautiful things – from radios to sunglasses,
kitchenware to children's toys and books,
bathroom accessories to greeting cards.
Browsing bliss. Spare some time to peruse
the magnificent art nouveau/deco Michelin
House the shop is housed in.

🄷 Clerkenwell, Shoreditch & Spitalfields

★Rough Trade East   MUSIC
(Map p138; www.roughtrade.com; Old Truman
Brewery, 91 Brick Lane, E1; ⊙9am-9pm Mon-Thu, to
8pm Fri, 10am-8pm Sat, 11am-7pm Sun; ⊛Shored-
itch High St) It's no longer directly associated
with the legendary record label (home to
The Smiths, The Libertines and The Strokes,
among many others), but this huge record
shop is still the best for music of an indie,
soul, electronica and alternative persuasion.
In addition to an impressive selection of CDs
and vinyl, it also dispenses coffee and stages
promotional gigs.

Blitz London   VINTAGE
(Map p138; www.blitzlondon.co.uk; 55-59 Hanbury
St, E1; ⊙11am-7pm; ⊕Liverpool St) One of the
capital's best secondhand clothes stores,
with more than 20,000 hand-selected items
of men's and women's clothing, shoes and
accessories spanning four decades since the
1960s. You'll find anything from mainstream
brands such as Nike to designer labels like
Burberry.

🄷 East London

Beyond Retro   VINTAGE
(☑020-7729 9001; www.beyondretro.com; 92-
100 Stoke Newington Rd, N16; ⊙10.30am-7pm
Mon, Tue & Sat, to 8pm Wed-Fri, 11.30am-6pm Sun;
⊕Dalston Kingsland) A riot of colour, furbelow,
frill, feathers and flares, this vast store has
every imaginable type of vintage clothing

LOCAL KNOWLEDGE

LONDON'S MARKETS

Perhaps the biggest draw for visitors is the capital's famed markets. A treasure trove of small designers, unique jewellery pieces, original framed photographs and posters, colourful vintage pieces and bric-a-brac, they are the antidote to impersonal, carbon-copy shopping centres.

Camden Market (Map p132; www.camdenmarket.com; Camden High St, NW1; ⊙10am-6pm; ⊕ Camden Town, Chalk Farm) London's busiest and best-known market may have stopped being cutting-edge several thousand cheap leather jackets ago, but it remains one of London's most popular attractions. There are three main market areas – Buck Street Market, Camden Lock Market and Stables Market – extending most of the way from Camden Town tube station to Chalk Farm tube station. You'll find a bit of everything: clothes (of varying quality) in profusion, bags, jewellery, arts and crafts, candles, incense and myriad decorative bits and pieces.

Sunday UpMarket (Map p138; www.sundayupmarket.co.uk; Old Truman Brewery, 91 Brick Lane, E1; ⊙11am-6pm Sat, 10am-5pm Sun; ℝ Shoreditch High St) Open all weekend, this lively market in the Old Truman Brewery offers a mix of young designers, food stalls in the Boiler House, antiques and bric-a-brac, and a huge range of vintage clothes in the basement across the street.

Old Spitalfields Market (Map p138; www.oldspitalfieldsmarket.com; Commercial St, E1; ⊙10am-5pm Mon-Fri & Sun, 10am-6pm Sat; ⊕ Liverpool St) Traders have been hawking their wares here since 1638 and it's still one of London's best markets. Sundays are the biggest and best days, but Thursdays are good for antiques and Fridays for independent fashion. There are plenty of food stalls too.

Borough Market (Map p98; www.boroughmarket.org.uk; 8 Southwark St, SE1; ⊙10am-5pm Wed & Thu, 10am-6pm Fri, 8am-5pm Sat; ⊕ London Bridge) Located in this spot since the 13th century (possibly since 1014), 'London's Larder' is always overflowing with food lovers, gastronomes and Londoners in search of dinner inspiration. The full market runs from Wednesday to Saturday, but some traders and takeaway stalls open Mondays and Tuesdays.

Brick Lane Market (Map p138; www.visitbricklane.org; Brick Lane, E1; ⊙10am-5pm Sun; ⊕ Shoreditch High St) Spilling out into its surrounding streets, this irrepressibly vibrant market fills a vast area with household goods, bric-a-brac, secondhand clothes, cheap fashion and ethnic food.

Broadway Market (www.broadwaymarket.co.uk; Broadway Market, E8; ⊙9am-5pm Sat; ▢394) There's been a market down this pretty street since the late 19th century. The focus these days is artisan food, arty knick-knacks, books, records and vintage clothing. Stock up on edible treats then head to London Fields for a picnic.

Greenwich Market (www.greenwichmarketlondon.com; College Approach, SE10; ⊙10.30am-5pm; ℝ DLR Cutty Sark) This small market has a different theme every day. On Tuesdays, Thursdays and Fridays, you'll find vintage, antiques and collectables. Wednesdays, Fridays and weekends are the best days for artists, indie designers and crafts.

South Bank Book Market (Map p98; Riverside Walk, SE1; ⊙11am-7pm, shorter hours winter; ⊕ Waterloo) Prints and secondhand books under the arches of Waterloo Bridge.

for sale, from hats to shoes. There's another branch in **Bethnal Green** (110-112 Cheshire St, E2; ⊙10am-7pm Mon-Wed, Fri & Sat, to 8pm Thu, 11.30am-6pm Sun; ℝ Shoreditch High St).

Traid   CLOTHING
(☏ 020-7923 1396; www.traid.org.uk; 106-108 Kingsland High St, E8; ⊙11am-7pm Mon-Sat, to 5pm Sun; ⊕ Dalston Kingsland) Banish every preconception you have about charity shops, for Traid is nothing like the ones you've seen before: big and bright, with not a whiff of mothball. The offerings aren't necessarily vintage but rather quality, contemporary secondhand clothes for a fraction of the

usual prices. It also sells its own creations made from offcuts.

North London

★ Camden Passage Market ANTIQUES
(www.camdenpassageislington.co.uk; Camden Passage, N1; ⊘8am-6pm Wed & Sat; ◉Angel) Not to be confused with Camden Market, Camden Passage is a pretty cobbled lane in Islington lined with antique stores, vintage-clothing boutiques and cafes. Scattered along the lane are four separate market areas devoted to antique curios and whatnots. The main market days are Wednesday and Saturday (although the shops are open all week). Stallholders know their stuff, so bargains are rare.

Harry Potter Shop at Platform 9¾ GIFTS & SOUVENIRS
(Map p110; www.harrypotterplatform934.com; King's Cross Station, N1; ⊘8am-10pm Mon-Sat, 9am-9pm Sun; ◉King's Cross St Pancras) With Pottermania refusing to die down and Diagon Alley impossible to find, when your junior witches and wizards are seeking a wand of their own, take the family directly to King's Cross Station. This little wood-panelled store also stocks jumpers sporting the colours of Hogwarts' four houses (Gryffindor having pride of place) and assorted merchandise, including, of course, the books.

ℹ Information

DANGERS & ANNOYANCES
London is a fairly safe city for its size, but exercise common sense.

➡ Several high-profile terrorist attacks have afflicted London in recent years, but the risk to individual visitors is remote. Report anything suspicious to the police by calling 999 (emergency) or 101 (nonemergency).

➡ Keep an eye on your handbag and wallet, especially in bars and nightclubs, and in crowded areas such as the Underground.

➡ Be discreet with your tablet/smartphone – snatching happens.

➡ If you're getting a cab after a night's clubbing, go for a black taxi or a licensed minicab firm.

➡ Victims of rape and sexual abuse can contact the **Rape & Sexual Abuse Support Centre** (☑ 0808 802 9999; www.rasasc.org. uk; ⊘noon-2.30pm & 7-9.30pm); anyone in emotional distress can contact **Samaritans** (☑ toll free 116 123; www.samaritans.org; ⊘24hr).

EMERGENCY

London's area code	☑020
International access code	☑00
Police, fire or ambulance	☑999
Reverse charge/collect calls	☑155

INTERNET ACCESS
➡ Virtually every hotel in London now provides wi-fi free of charge.

➡ A huge number of cafes, and many restaurants, offer free wi-fi to customers, including major chain cafes. Cultural venues such as the Barbican or the Southbank Centre also have free wi-fi.

➡ Open-air and street wi-fi access is available in areas across London, including Oxford St, Trafalgar Sq, Piccadilly Circus, the City of London and Islington's Upper St. Users have to register but there's no charge.

➡ Most major train stations, airport terminals and even some Underground stations also have wi-fi, but access isn't always free.

➡ See Time Out's Free Wi-fi Map (www.timeout. com/london/things-to-do/where-to-find-free -wi-fi-in-london-9) for more locations.

MEDICAL SERVICES
A number of hospitals have 24-hour accident and emergency departments. However, in an emergency just call an **ambulance** (☑999) and one will normally be dispatched from the hospital nearest to you.

University College London Hospital (☑020-3456 7890; www.uclh.nhs.uk; 235 Euston Rd, NW1; ◉Warren St, Euston)

Chelsea & Westminster Hospital (☑020-3315 8000; www.chelwest.nhs.uk; 369 Fulham Rd, SW10; ☐14 or 414, ◉South Kensington, Fulham Broadway)

TOURIST INFORMATION
Visit London (www.visitlondon.com) can fill you in on everything from attractions and events to tours and accommodation. Kiosks are dotted about the city and can also provide maps and brochures; some branches are able to book theatre tickets.

ℹ Getting There & Away

AIR
The city has five airports: Heathrow, which is the largest, to the west; Gatwick to the south; Stansted to the northeast; Luton to the northwest; and London City in the Docklands. For details of London's five main airports, see p1026.

BUS

Victoria Coach Station (Map p100; 164 Buckingham Palace Rd, SW1; Victoria) Long-distance and international buses arrive and depart from Victoria Coach Station, close to the Victoria tube and rail stations.

TRAIN

Main national rail routes are served by a variety of private train-operating companies. Tickets are not cheap, but trains between cities are usually quite punctual. Check National Rail (www. nationalrail.co.uk) for timetables and fares.

Eurostar (www.eurostar.com) High-speed passenger rail service linking London St Pancras International with Paris, Brussels and Lille, with up to 19 daily departures. Fares vary greatly, from £29 one-way standard class to around £245 one-way for a fully flexible business premier ticket (prices based on return journeys). New direct links between London and Amsterdam and Rotterdam commenced in 2018. There are deals on Eurostar Snap (available on Facebook), with best-value fares for those with flexibility around the specific train they travel on.

ⓘ Getting Around

TO/FROM THE AIRPORTS
Heathrow

The Underground, commonly referred to as 'the tube', is the cheapest way of getting to Heathrow; paper tickets cost one-way £6, Oyster or Contactless peak/off-peak £5.10/3.10. The journey to central London takes one hour and trains depart every three to nine minutes. Leaving from the airport, it runs from just after 5am to 11.45pm (11.28pm Sunday), and heading to the airport it runs from 5.47am to 12.32am

(11.38pm Sunday); tube trains run all night Friday and Saturday, with reduced frequency. Buy tickets at the station.

Heathrow Express (www.heathrowexpress. com; one-way/return £27/42; ☎), every 15 minutes, and **Heathrow Connect** (☎ 0345 604 1515; www.heathrowconnect.com; adult single/ open return £10.30/20.70), every 30 minutes, trains link Heathrow with Paddington train station. Heathrow Express trains take a mere 15 minutes to reach Paddington. Trains on each service run from around 5am to between 11pm and midnight.

National Express Coaches (www.national express.com; one-way from £6, 35 to 90 minutes, every 30 minutes to one hour) link the Heathrow Central bus station with London Victoria Coach Station. The first bus leaves the Heathrow Central bus station (at Terminals 2 and 3) at 4.20am, with the last departure just after 10pm. The first bus leaves Victoria at 3am, the last at around 12.30am.

At night, the **N9 bus** (£1.50, 1¼ hours, every 20 minutes) connects Heathrow Central bus station (and Heathrow Terminal 5) with central London, terminating at Aldwych.

A metered black cab trip to/from central London will cost between £48 and £90 and take 45 minutes to an hour, depending on traffic and your departure point.

Gatwick

National Rail (www.nationalrail.co.uk) Regular train services to/from London Bridge (30 minutes, every 15 to 30 minutes), London King's Cross (55 minutes, every 15 to 30 minutes) and London Victoria (30 minutes, every 10 to 15 minutes). Fares vary depending on the time of travel and the train company, but allow £10 to £20 for a single.

ⓘ OYSTER CARD

The cheapest way to get around London is with an **Oyster Card**, a smart card on which you store credit as well as Travelcards valid for periods from a day to a year. Oyster Cards are valid across the entire public transport network in London, and fares are lower than standard ones. If you make several journeys in a day, the total is capped at the appropriate Travelcard rate (peak or off-peak).

Oyster Cards can be bought (£5 refundable deposit required) and topped up at any Underground station, travel information centre or shop displaying the Oyster logo. To get your deposit back along with any remaining credit, simply return your Oyster Card at a ticket booth.

All you need to do when entering a station is touch your card on a reader (which has a yellow circle with the image of an Oyster Card on it) and then touch again on your way out. For bus journeys, you only need to touch once upon boarding. Note that some train stations don't have exit turnstiles, so you will need to tap out on the reader before leaving the station; if you forget, you will be hugely overcharged.

Contactless cards (which do not require chip and pin or a signature) are subject to the same Oyster fares, but foreign visitors should bear in mind the cost of card transactions.

Gatwick Express (www.gatwickexpress.com; one-way/return adult £19.90/35.60, child £9.95/17.75) Trains run every 15 minutes from the station near the Gatwick South Terminal to London Victoria. From the airport there are services between 5.51am and 11.20pm. From Victoria they leave between 5am and 10.30pm. The journey takes 30 minutes; book online for the best deals.

National Express (www.nationalexpress.com) Coaches run throughout the day from Gatwick to London Victoria Coach Station (one-way from £8). Services depart hourly around the clock. Journey time is between 80 minutes and two hours, depending on traffic.

EasyBus (www.easybus.co.uk) Runs 13-seater minibuses to Gatwick every 15 to 20 minutes on several routes, including from Earl's Court/West Brompton and Victoria Coach Station (one-way from £1.95). The service runs round the clock. Journey time averages 75 minutes.

Taxi A metered black-cab trip to/from central London costs around £100 and takes just over an hour. Minicabs are usually cheaper.

Stansted

Stansted Express (☑ 0345 600 7245; www.stanstedexpress.com; one-way/return £17/29) Rail service (45 minutes, every 15 to 30 minutes) links the airport and Liverpool St station. From the airport, the first train leaves at 5.30am, the last at 12.30am. Trains depart Liverpool St station from 3.40am to 11.25pm.

National Express (www.nationalexpress.com) Coaches run around the clock, offering well over 100 services per day.

Airbus A6 (☑ 0871 781 8181; www.nationalexpress.com; one-way from £10) Runs to Victoria Coach Station (around one hour to 1½ hours, every 20 minutes) via Marble Arch, Paddington, Baker St and Golders Green. **Airbus A7** (☑ 0871 781 8181; www.nationalexpress.com; one-way from £10) also runs to Victoria Coach Station (around one hour to 1½ hours, every 20 minutes), via Waterloo and Southwark. **Airbus A8** (☑ 0871 781 8181; www.nationalexpress.com; one-way from £6) runs to Liverpool St station (one-way from £6, 60 to 80 minutes, every 30 minutes), via Bethnal Green, Shoreditch High St and Mile End.

Airport Bus Express (www.airportbusexpress.co.uk; one-way from £9-10) Runs every 30 minutes to Victoria Coach Station, Baker St, Liverpool St and Stratford.

EasyBus (www.easybus.co.uk) Runs services to Baker St and Old St tube stations every 15 minutes. The journey (one-way from £4.95) takes one hour from Old St, 1¼ hour from Baker St.

Terravision (www.terravision.eu) Coaches link Stansted to Liverpool St station (one-way from £9, 55 minutes), King's Cross (from £9, 75

minutes) and Victoria Coach Station (from £10, two hours) every 20 to 40 minutes between 6am and 1am. Wi-fi on all buses.

London City

Docklands Light Railway (DLR; www.tfl.gov.uk/dlr) Stops at the London City Airport station (one-way £2.80 to £3.30). Trains depart every eight to 10 minutes from just after 5.30am to 12.15am Monday to Saturday, and 7am to 11.15pm Sunday. The journey to Bank takes just over 20 minutes.

Luton

National Rail (www.nationalrail.co.uk) Runs 24-hour services (one-way from £14, 26 to 50 minutes, departures every six minutes to one hour) from London St Pancras International to Luton Airport Parkway station, from where an airport shuttle bus (one-way/return £2.20/3.50) will take you to the airport in 10 minutes.

Airbus A1 (www.nationalexpress.com; one-way from £5) Runs over 60 times daily to London Victoria Coach Station (one-way from £5), via Portman Sq, Baker St, St John's Wood, Finchley Rd and Golders Green. It takes around 1½ hours.

Green Line Bus 757 (☑ 0344 800 4411; www.greenline.co.uk; one-way/return £10/17) Runs to Luton Airport from London Victoria Coach Station every 30 minutes on a 24-hour service via Marble Arch, Baker St, Finchley Rd and Brent Cross.

BICYCLE

London's cycle-hire scheme is called **Santander Cycles** (☑ 0343 222 6666; www.tfl.gov.uk/modes/cycling/santander-cycles). The bikes have proved as popular with visitors as with Londoners.

The idea is simple: pick up a bike from one of the 750 docking stations dotted around the capital. Cycle. Drop it off at another docking station.

The access fee is £2 for 24 hours. All you need is a credit or debit card. The first 30 minutes are free; it's then £2 for any additional period of 30 minutes.

You can take as many bikes as you like during your access period (24 hours), leaving five minutes between each trip.

The pricing structure is designed to encourage short journeys rather than longer rentals; for those, go to a hire company. You'll also find that although easy to ride, the bikes only have three gears and are quite heavy. You must be aged 18 to buy access and at least 14 to ride a bike.

CAR

London has a **congestion charge** (☑ 0343 222 2222; www.tfl.gov.uk/roadusers/congestioncharging) in place to reduce the flow of traffic into its centre.

The congestion-charge zone encompasses Euston and Pentonville Rds to the north, Park Lane to the west, Tower Bridge to the east, and Elephant and Castle and Vauxhall Bridge Rd to the south. As you enter the zone, you will see a large white 'C' in a red circle.

If you enter the zone between 7am and 6pm Monday to Friday (excluding public holidays), you must pay the £11.50 charge (payable in advance or on the day) or £14 on the first charging day after travel to avoid receiving a fine (£160, or £80 if paid within 14 days).

You can pay online or over the phone. For full details visit the website.

PUBLIC TRANSPORT
Boat

Several companies operate along the River Thames; only **Thames Clippers** (www.thames clippers.com; all zones adult/child £9.90/4.95) really offers commuter services, however. It's fast, pleasant and you're almost always guaranteed a seat and a view.

Thames Clipper boats run regular services between Embankment, Waterloo (London Eye), Blackfriars, Bankside (Shakespeare's Globe), London Bridge, Tower Bridge, Canary Wharf, Greenwich, North Greenwich and Woolwich piers from 6.55am to around midnight (from 9.29am weekends).

Thames Clipper River Roamer tickets (adult/child £19/9.50) give freedom to hop on and hop off boats on most routes all day. Book online for good discounts.

You can get a discount of one-third off the standard fare and off the price of River Roamer tickets if you're a pay-as-you-go Oyster Card holder or Travelcard holder (paper ticket or on Oyster Card). Children under five years go free on most boats.

Between April and September, Hampton Court Palace can be reached by boat on the 22-mile route along the Thames from Westminster Pier in central London (via Kew and Richmond). The trip can take up to four hours, depending on the tide. Boats are run by **Westminster Passenger Services Association** (www.wpsa.co.uk; one-way/return adult £17/25, child £8.50/12.50).

The London Waterbus Company (p117) runs canal boats between Camden Lock and Little Venice.

Bus

London's ubiquitous red double-decker buses afford great views of the city, but be aware that the going can be slow, thanks to traffic jams and dozens of commuters getting on and off at every stop.

There are excellent bus maps at every stop detailing all routes and destinations served from that particular area (generally a few bus stops

within a two- to three-minute walk, shown on a local map).

Many bus stops have LED displays listing bus arrival times, but downloading a bus app such as London Bus Live Countdown to your smartphone is the most effective way to keep track of when your next bus is due.

Bus services normally operate from 5am to 11.30pm.

Cash cannot be used on London's buses. Instead you must pay with an Oyster Card, Travelcard or a contactless payment card. Bus fares are a flat £1.50, no matter the distance travelled. If you don't have enough credit on your Oyster Card for a £1.50 bus fare, you can make one more bus journey. You must then top up your credit before you can use your Oyster Card again.

Children aged under 11 travel free; 11 to 15 year olds are half price if registered on an accompanying adult's Oyster Card (register at Zone 1 or Heathrow tube stations).

➡ More than 50 night-bus routes (prefixed with the letter 'N') run from around 11.30pm to 5am.

➡ There are also another 60 bus routes operating 24 hours; the frequency decreases between 11pm and 5am.

➡ Oxford Circus, Tottenham Court Rd and Trafalgar Sq are the main hubs for night routes.

➡ Night buses can be infrequent and stop only on request, so remember to ring for your stop.

➡ Don't forget the Night Tube, which runs along five lines for 24 hours on Friday and Saturday, and can either be used as an alternative or in concert with night buses.

Underground, DLR & Overground

The London Underground ('the tube'; 11 colour-coded lines) is part of an integrated-transport system that also includes the Docklands Light Railway (DLR; www.tfl.gov.uk/dlr; a driverless overhead train operating in the eastern part of the city) and Overground network (mostly outside of Zone 1 and sometimes underground). Despite the never-ending upgrades and 'engineering works' requiring weekend closures, it is overall the quickest and easiest way of getting around the city, if not the cheapest.

The first trains operate from around 5.30am Monday to Saturday and 6.45am Sunday. The last trains leave around 12.30am Monday to Saturday and 11.30pm Sunday.

Additionally, selected lines (the Victoria and Jubilee lines, plus most of the Piccadilly, Central and Northern lines) run all night on Friday and Saturday to get revellers home (on what is called the 'Night Tube'), with trains every 10 minutes or so. Fares are off-peak.

During weekend closures, schedules, maps and alternative route suggestions are posted in every station, and staff are at hand to help redirect you.

Some stations, most famously Leicester Sq and Covent Garden, are much closer in reality than they appear on the map.

TAXI
Black Cabs

The black cab is as much a feature of the London cityscape as the red double-decker bus. Licensed black cab drivers have the 'Knowledge', acquired after rigorous training and a series of exams. They are supposed to know 25,000 streets within a 6-mile radius of Charing Cross/Trafalgar Sq and the 100 most-visited spots of the moment, including clubs and restaurants.

➡ Cabs are available for hire when the yellow sign above the windscreen is lit; just stick your arm out to signal one.

➡ Fares are metered, with the flagfall charge of £2.60 (covering the first 235m during a weekday), rising by increments of 20p for each subsequent 117m.

➡ Fares are more expensive in the evenings and overnight.

➡ You can tip taxi drivers up to 10%, but most Londoners simply round up to the nearest pound.

➡ Apps such as mytaxi (https://uk.mytaxi.com) use your smartphone's GPS to locate the nearest black cab. You only pay the metered fare.

➡ **ComCab** (☎ 020-7908 0271; www.comcab-london.co.uk) operates one of the largest fleets of black cabs in town.

Minicabs

➡ Minicabs, which are licensed, are (usually) cheaper competitors of black cabs.

➡ Unlike black cabs, minicabs cannot legally be hailed on the street; they must be booked by phone or directly from one of the minicab offices (every high street has at least one and most clubs work with a minicab firm to send revellers home safely).

➡ Don't accept unsolicited offers from individuals claiming to be minicab drivers – they are just guys with cars.

➡ Minicabs don't have meters; there's usually a fare set by the dispatcher. Make sure you ask before setting off.

➡ Your hotel or host will be able to recommend a reputable minicab company in the neighbourhood; every Londoner has the number of at least one company. Or phone a large 24-hour operator such as **Addison Lee** (☎ 020-7387 8888; www.addisonlee.com).

➡ Apps such as Uber or Kabbee allow you to book a minicab in double-quick time and can save you money. At the time of writing, Uber had won an appeal to operate in London, but is on 15 months probation.

Canterbury & Southeast England

Best Places to Eat

➡ Royal Victoria Pavilion (p163)

➡ Allotment (p167)

➡ Iydea (p179)

➡ Terre à Terre (p180)

➡ Town House (p183)

Best Places to Stay

➡ Bleak House (p162)

➡ Jeake's House (p170)

➡ No 27 Brighton (p178)

➡ Reading Rooms (p160)

➡ Hotel Una (p179)

Why Go?

Rolling chalk hills, venerable Victorian resorts, fields of hops and grapes sweetening in the sun: welcome to England's southeast, four soothing counties' worth of country houses, fairy-tale castles and the finest food and drink. That fruit-ripening sun shines brightest and longest on the coast, warming a string of seaside towns wedged between formidable chalk cliffs. There's something for everyone here, from the medieval quaintness of Sandwich to the bohemian spirit of hedonistic Brighton and the more genteel grandeur of Eastbourne.

The southeast is also pock-marked with reminders of darker days. The region's position as the front line against Continental invaders has left a wealth of turbulent history, including the 1066 battlefield, Dover Castle's secret war tunnels and scattered Roman ruins.

England's spiritual heart is Canterbury; its cathedral and ancient Unesco-listed attractions are essential viewing for any 21st-century pilgrim.

When to Go

➡ May is a good time to get creative in Brighton at Great Britain's second-largest arts festival.

➡ During June, don your top hat and breeches to revel in frilly Victoriana at the Dickens Festival in Broadstairs.

➡ Any time between May and October is ideal for a hike along the South Downs Way, which runs the length of England's newest national park.

➡ In summer, head to the glorious beaches of Thanet in East Kent for some proper seaside fun.

➡ In late June Eastbourne hosts one of the UK's top tennis tournaments, a Wimbledon warm-up event attracting some of the biggest names in the game.

Canterbury & Southeast England Highlights

1 Brighton & Hove (p175) Shopping, tanning and partying in the hedonist capital of the southeast.

2 Canterbury (p154) Making a pilgrimage to one of England's most important religious sites.

3 Dover Castle (p165) Exploring the atmospheric WWII tunnels beneath this sprawling castle.

4 Rye (p168) Wandering the cobbled lanes of one of England's prettiest towns.

5 Leeds Castle (p159) Kicking back at this moated marvel.

A127
Stanford-le-Hope
Grays Thurrock
bbsfleet
Tilbury
Gravesend
North Feet A2
Canvey Island
Southend-on-Sea
NORTH SEA
Sheerness
Rochester
Gillingham
Chatham
M2
Isle of Sheppey
Leysdown-on-Sea
Herne Bay
Margate 7
Isle of Thanet
Birchington
ightham
Maidstone
Bearsted
5
Leeds Castle
Sittingbourne
Faversham
Whitstable
Seasalter
Broadstairs
Ramsgate
2 **Canterbury**
Richborough Roman Fort
8 **Sandwich**
Chilham
Ash
Eastry
KENT
A28
A2
M20
Staplehurst
A21
Sissinghurst
Ashford
Sutton
Ringwould
Westcliffe
Deal
Dover Castle 3
St Margaret's Bay
Tenterden
Dover
Folkestone
A259
Capel-le-Ferne
Hawkhurst
Burwash
Romney Marsh
Hythe
Romney Hythe & Dymchurch Railway
Channel Tunnel
New Romney
St Mary's Bay
EAST SUSSEX
A21
A268
Rye 4
Lydd
Lydd-on-Sea
Battle
Strait of Dover
Pevensey Castle
Bexhill
A259
Hastings

N 0 — 20 km
0 — 10 miles

6 **Beachy Head** (p174) Scrambling up this spectacular headland in snow-white chalk.

7 **Margate** (p160) Getting down with the hipsters in the art capital of the Southeast.

8 **Sandwich** (p164) Becoming hopelessly lost in crooked medieval streets.

9 **Eastbourne** (p173) Strolling the Southeast's most chic seafront to reach the dramatic cliffs of Beachy Head.

🏃 Activities

Cycling

Finding quiet roads for cycle touring takes a little extra perseverance in the southeast of England, but the effort is richly rewarded. Long-distance routes that form part of the National Cycle Network (NCN; www.sustrans.org.uk) include the Downs & Weald Cycle Route (110 miles; NCN Routes 2, 20 and 21) from London to Brighton and on to Hastings, and the Garden of England Cycle Route (172 miles; NCN Routes 1 and 2) from London to Dover and then Hastings.

You'll also find less demanding routes on the NCN website. Meanwhile, there are plenty of uppers and downers to challenge mountain bikers on walking trails, such as the South Downs Way National Trail (100 miles), which takes between two and four days to complete.

Walking

Two long-distance trails meander steadily westward through the region, and there are plenty of shorter ambles to match your schedule, stamina and scenery wish-list.

South Downs Way National Trail (www.nationaltrail.co.uk/south-downs-way) This 100-mile National Trail through England's newest national park is a beautiful roller-coaster walk along prehistoric drove roads between Winchester and Eastbourne.

North Downs Way National Trail (www.nationaltrail.co.uk/north-downs-way) This 153-mile walk begins near Farnham in Surrey, but one of its most beautiful sections runs from near Ashford to Dover; a loop takes in Canterbury near its end.

1066 Country Walk Heads from Pevensey Castle to Rye (32 miles) and serves as a continuation of the South Downs Way.

KENT

Kent isn't described as the garden of England for nothing. Within its sea-lined borders you'll find a fragrant landscape of gentle hills, fertile farmland, cultivated country estates and fruit-laden orchards. It could also be described as the beer garden of England as it produces the world-renowned Kent hops and some of the country's finest ales and wines from its numerous vineyards. At its heart is spellbinding Canterbury, crowned by its enthralling cathedral. You'll also find beautiful coastal stretches dotted with beach towns and villages, from old-school Broadstairs to gentrified Whitstable and the aesthetically challenged port town of Dover.

ℹ️ Getting There & Away

Kent is very well connected to London with two high-speed lines linking the north Kent coast and East Kent to the capital. Connections with East Sussex could be better (there's no Canterbury–Brighton coach for instance), but are still reasonably good. Ferries from Dunkirk and Calais tie up at Dover, Kent's last cross-Channel passenger port and hundreds of cruise ships call in at the town's Western Docks. The Channel Tunnel, which emerges from the chalky ground near Folkestone, is a major gateway to the Continent.

Canterbury

📞 01227 / POP 55,240

Canterbury tops the charts for English cathedral cities and is one of southern England's top attractions. Many consider the World Heritage–listed cathedral that dominates its centre to be one of Europe's finest, and the town's narrow medieval alleyways, riverside gardens and ancient city walls are a joy to explore. But Canterbury isn't just a showpiece for the past – it's a bustling, busy place with an energetic student population and a wide choice of pubs, restaurants and independent shops. Book ahead for the best hotels and eateries: pilgrims may no longer flock here in their thousands, but tourists certainly do.

◎ Sights

⭐ Canterbury Cathedral   CATHEDRAL
(www.canterbury-cathedral.org; adult/concession/child £12.50/10.50/8.50, tours adult/child £5/4, audio guide £4/3; ⊘ 9am-5.30pm Mon-Sat, 12.30-2.30pm Sun) A rich repository of more than 1400 years of Christian history, the Church of England's mother ship is a truly extraordinary place with an absorbing history. This Gothic cathedral, the highlight of the city's World Heritage Sites, is southeast England's top tourist attraction as well as a place of worship. It's also the site of English history's most famous murder: Archbishop Thomas Becket was done in here in 1170.

The cathedral is an overwhelming edifice crammed with enthralling stories, arresting architecture and a very real and enduring sense of spirituality – although visitors can't

Canterbury

Canterbury

⊙ Top Sights

⊙ Sights

✪ Activities, Courses & Tours

⬜ Sleeping

✗ Eating

⬤ Drinking & Nightlife

⬤ Shopping

help but pick up on the ominous undertones of violence and bloodshed that whisper from its walls.

This ancient structure is packed with monuments commemorating the nation's battles. Also here are the grave and heraldic tunic of one of the nation's most famous warmongers, Edward the Black Prince (1330–76). The spot in the northwest transept where Becket met his grisly end has drawn pilgrims for more than 800 years and is marked by a flickering candle and a striking modern altar.

The doorway to the crypt is beside the altar. This cavernous space is the cathedral's highlight, the only survivor from the devastating fire in 1174, which destroyed the rest of the building. Look for the amazingly well-preserved carvings among the forest of pillars.

The wealth of detail in the cathedral is immense and unrelenting, so it's well worth joining a one-hour tour (three daily, Monday to Saturday) or taking a 40-minute self-guided audio tour. Allow at least two hours to do the cathedral justice.

Roman Museum   MUSEUM

(www.canterburymuseums.co.uk; Butchery Lane; adult/concession/child £8/6/free; ⊙10am-5pm daily) This fascinating subterranean archaeological site gives an insight into Canterbury's everyday life almost two millennia ago. Visitors can stroll a reconstructed Roman marketplace and rooms, including a kitchen, as well as view Roman mosaic floors. Almost everything you see here was only discovered after WWII bombs did a bit of impromptu excavation.

A standout exhibit is an almost completely intact Roman soldier's helmet dating from Caesar's invasion, dug up near the village of Bridge in 2012. It's the best ever found in the UK.

Beaney House of
Art & Knowledge   MUSEUM

(www.canterburymuseums.co.uk; 18 High St; ⊙museum 10am-5pm Tue-Sat, noon-5pm Sun; ⊛)

FREE This mock-Tudor edifice is the grandest on the main shopping thoroughfare, if not the most authentic. Formerly called the Royal Museum & Art Gallery, it has housed Canterbury's main library, a museum and an art gallery since 1899 – its current name is in honour of the 19th-century benefactor who funded the original building. In addition to the city's main library and the tourist office (p158), the mixed bag of museum exhibits is worth half an hour between the main sights.

St Augustine's Abbey   RUINS

(EH; www.english-heritage.org.uk; Longport; adult/concession/child £6.20/5.60/4.10; ⊙10am-6pm Apr-Sep, to 5pm Oct, to 4pm Sat & Sun Nov-Mar) An integral but often overlooked part of the Canterbury World Heritage Site, St Augustine's Abbey was founded in AD 597, marking the rebirth of Christianity in southern England. Later requisitioned as a royal palace, it fell into disrepair and now only stumpy foundations remain. A small museum and a worthwhile free audio guide do their best to underline the site's importance and put flesh back onto its now-humble bones.

West Gate Towers   MUSEUM

(www.onepoundlane.co.uk; St Peter's St; adult/concession/child £4/3/2; ⊙11am-4pm) The city's only remaining medieval gateway (1380) houses a museum that focuses on the building's use as a prison. The views from the top are pretty good, but if you don't go inside, you can always entertain yourself watching buses, wing mirrors folded back, as they squeeze through the medieval archway.

Tours

Canterbury Historic River Tours   BOATING

(☑07790-534744; www.canterburyrivertours.co.uk; Kings Bridge; adult/child £10.50/9.50; ⊙10am-5pm Mar-Oct) Knowledgeable guides double

---

THE CANTERBURY TALES

If English literature has a father figure, then it is Geoffrey Chaucer (1342–1400). Chaucer was the first English writer to introduce characters – rather than 'types' – into fiction, and he did so to greatest effect in his best-known work, *The Canterbury Tales*.

Written between 1387 and his death, in the hard-to-decipher Middle English of the day, Chaucer's *Tales* is an unfinished series of 24 vivid stories told by a party of pilgrims journeying between London and Canterbury. Chaucer successfully created the illusion that the pilgrims, not Chaucer (though he appears in the tales as himself), are telling the stories, which gave him unprecedented freedom as an author. *The Canterbury Tales* remains one of the pillars of the literary canon. But more than that, it's a collection of rollicking good yarns of adultery, debauchery, crime and edgy romance, and is filled with Chaucer's witty observations about human nature.

up as energetic oarsmen on these fascinating, multi-award-winning River Stour mini-cruises, which depart from behind the Old Weaver's House.

Canterbury Guided Tours   WALKING
(☎01227-459779; www.canterburyguidedtours.com; adult/concession/child £8/7.50/6; ☻11am Feb-Oct, plus 2pm Jul-Sep) Walking tours lead by professional blue- and green-badge guides leave from opposite the Canterbury Cathedral entrance. Tickets can be purchased from the tourist office and online.

🛏 Sleeping

Kipp's Independent Hostel   HOSTEL £
(☎01227-786121; www.kipps-hostel.com; 40 Nunnery Fields; dm £12.50-24.50, s £22.50-40, d £40-68; @☻) Occupying a century-old red-brick town house in a quietish residential area less than a mile from the city centre, these superb backpacker digs enjoy a homely atmosphere, clean (though cramped) dorms, a good kitchen for self-caterers and a large TV lounge.

★ABode Canterbury   BOUTIQUE HOTEL ££
(☎01227-766266; www.abodecanterbury.co.uk; 30-33 High St; r from £64; ☻) The 72 rooms at this supercentral hotel, the only boutique hotel in town, are graded from 'comfortable' to 'fabulous' (via 'enviable'), and for the most part live up to their names. They come with features such as handmade beds, chesterfield sofas, tweed cushions and beautiful modern bathrooms. There's a splendid champagne bar, restaurant and tavern, too.

House of Agnes   HOTEL ££
(☎01227-472185; www.houseofagnes.co.uk; 71 St Dunstan's St; r £89-129; ☻) This rather wonky 13th-century beamed inn, mentioned in Dickens' *David Copperfield,* has eight themed rooms bearing names such as 'Marrakesh' (Moorish), 'Venice' (carnival masks), 'Boston' (light and airy) and 'Canterbury' (antiques and heavy fabrics). If you prefer your room to have straight lines and right angles, there are eight less exciting, but no less comfortable, 'stable' rooms in the garden annexe.

Arthouse B&B   B&B £££
(☎07976-725457; www.arthousebandb.com; 24 London Rd; r from £140; P☻) A night at Canterbury's most laid-back digs, housed in a 19th-century fire station, is a bit like sleeping over at a really cool art student's pad. The theme is funky and eclectic, with furniture by local designers and artwork by the instantly likeable artist owners, who have a house-studio out back.

🍴 Eating

Tiny Tim's Tearoom   CAFE £
(www.tinytimstearoom.com; 34 St Margaret's St; mains £6-10; ☻9.30am-5pm Mon-Sat, 10.30am-5pm Sun) It's no mean feat to be declared 'Kent Tearoom of the Year', but this swish 1930s cafe was awarded the accolade in 2015. It offers hungry shoppers big breakfasts packed with Kentish ingredients, and tiers of cakes, crumpets, cucumber sandwiches and scones plastered in clotted cream. On busy shopping days you are guaranteed to queue for a table.

Refectory Kitchen   BRITISH £
(☎01227-638766; www.refectorykitchen.com; 16 St Dunstan's St; mains around £8; ☻8am-5pm Mon-Sat, 9am-3pm Sun) This tiny, wood-beamed cafe serves popular, nutrient-packed all-day breakfasts and a short menu of light lunch and dinner mains containing Kentish ingredients as far as possible. The welcome is friendly but things get very busy at mealtimes.

Boho   INTERNATIONAL £
(www.bohocanterbury.co.uk; 27 High St; snacks £5-15; ☻9am-6pm Mon-Thu, to 9pm Fri & Sat, 10am-5pm Sun) This hip eatery in a prime spot on the main drag is extraordinarily popular and you'll be lucky to get a table on busy shopping days. Cool tunes lilt through the chic retro dining space while chilled diners chow down on humongous burgers, full-monty breakfasts and imaginative, owner-cooked international mains. Boho doesn't do bookings, so be prepared to queue.

★Goods Shed   MARKET ££
(☎01227-459153; www.thegoodsshed.co.uk; Station Rd West; mains £17.50-20; ☻market 9am-7pm Tue-Sat, to 4pm Sun, restaurant noon-2.30pm & 6pm-last customer) Aromatic farmers market, food hall and fabulous restaurant rolled into one, this converted warehouse by the Canterbury West train station is a hit with everyone from self-caterers to sit-down gourmets. The chunky wooden tables sit slightly above the market hubbub but in full view of its appetite-whetting stalls. Daily specials exploit the freshest farm goodies the Garden of England offers.

▼ Drinking & Nightlife

Foundry Brewpub   MICROBREWERY
(www.thefoundrycanterbury.co.uk; White Horse
Lane; ⊘noon–midnight Mon-Thu, til late Fri & Sat,
to 11pm Sun) Canterbury's brewpub pumps
out award-winning craft beers in the industrial setting of a former foundry where
New York's first streetlights were made. It
also stocks a wide range of local and national ales and ciders, serves light snacks
and meals and is planning its own gin and
vodka.

Steinbeck & Shaw   CLUB
(www.facebook.com/steinbeckandshaw; 41 St
George's Pl; ⊘6pm-2am Mon-Thu, to 3am Fri & Sat)
Canterbury's best city-centre nightspot has a
supercool, 21st-century interior with urban
and retro elements. The weekly program
is a mixed bag of rock and house and is as
popular with students as with tourists and
Kentish trendoids.

Thomas Becket   PUB
(www.facebook.com/thethomasbecketpubrestau
rant; 21 Best Lane; ⊘10am-midnight Mon-Thu,
to 12.30am Fri & Sat, to 11.30pm Sun) A classic
English pub with a garden's worth of hops
hanging from its timber frame, Thomas
Becket attracts many a modern-day pilgrim
to its ales. Traditional decor includes copper
pots, comfy seating and a fireplace to cosy
up to on winter nights. It also serves decent
pub grub.

Parrot   PUB
(www.parrotcanterbury.co.uk; 1-9 Church Lane;
⊘noon-11pm; 🐾) Built in 1370 on Roman
foundations, Canterbury's oldest boozer has
a snug, beam-rich, slightly upmarket pub
downstairs and a much-lauded dining room
upstairs under yet more ageing oak. Many a
local ale is pulled in both venues.

🔒 Shopping

Chaucer Bookshop   BOOKS
(www.chaucer-bookshop.co.uk; 6-7 Beer Cart Lane;
⊘10am-5pm Mon-Sat, 11am-4pm Sun) Antiquarian and used books plus interesting prints
and drawings.

ℹ Information

Tourist Office (☎01227-862162; www.canter
bury.co.uk; 18 High St; ⊘9am-6pm Mon-Wed
& Fri, to 8pm Thu, to 5pm Sat, 10am-5pm Sun;
🐾) Located in the Beaney House of Art &
Knowledge. Staff can help book accommoda-
tion, excursions and theatre tickets.

ℹ Getting There & Away

BUS
The city's **bus station** (St George's Lane) is just
within the city walls. Canterbury connections:
Dover (£5.70, 34 minutes, three hourly)
London Victoria (National Express; £10, two
hours, hourly)
Margate (£5.70, one hour, two hourly)
Ramsgate (£5.70, 45 minutes, hourly)
Sandwich (£4.20, 40 minutes, three hourly)
Whitstable (£5.20, 30 minutes, every 10
minutes)

TRAIN
There are two train stations, Canterbury East
for London Victoria and Canterbury West for
London's Charing Cross/St Pancras stations.
Canterbury connections:
Dover Priory (£8.50, 28 minutes, half-hourly)
Runs from Canterbury East train station.
London St Pancras (£38.70, one hour, hourly)
High-speed service.
London Victoria/Charing Cross (£32.60, 1¾
hours, two hourly)

Whitstable

📞 01227 / POP 32,100

Perhaps it's the oysters harvested since Roman times? Maybe it's the weatherboard
houses and shingle beach? Or perhaps it's
the pleasingly old-fashioned main street
with petite galleries, been-there-forever out-
fitters and emporia of vintage frillies? Most
likely it's for all of these reasons that Whitstable has become a bit of a weekend magnet for metropolitan types looking for refuge
from the city hassle. It's also a simple day
trip from Canterbury, to which it is linked
by regular local bus.

For a week in late July, the town hosts the
Whitstable Oyster Festival (www.whitsta
bleoysterfestival.co.uk; ⊘late Jul), a seafood, arts
and music extravaganza offering a packed
schedule of events, from history walks, crab
catching and oyster-eating competitions to a
beer festival and traditional 'blessing of the
waters'.

🛏 Sleeping

Whitstable Bay   B&B ££
(☎01227-779362; www.whitstablebay.com; 74
Joy Lane; s/d from £65/70; 🅿🐾) This much-
lauded B&B is located just a short stroll
southwest of High St and offers three very
well-appointed and stylishly decorated doubles in a quiet residential area. Continental

DON'T MISS

LEEDS CASTLE

The immense moated pile of **Leeds Castle** (www.leeds-castle.com; adult/concession/child £24.90/21.90/17.50; ⊙10am-6pm Apr-Sep, to 5pm Oct-Mar;), just east of Maidstone, is one of the most visited of Britain's fortresses. The formidable, hefty structure balancing on two islands is known as something of a 'ladies castle'. This stems from the fact that in its more than 1000 years of history, it has been home to a who's who of medieval queens, most famously Henry VIII's first wife, Catherine of Aragon.

The castle was transformed from fortress to lavish palace over the centuries, and its last owner, the high-society hostess Lady Baillie, used it as a princely family home and party pad to entertain the likes of Errol Flynn, Douglas Fairbanks and John F Kennedy. The castle's vast estate offers peaceful walks, a duckery, aviary and falconry demonstrations. You'll also find possibly the world's sole dog-collar museum, plenty of kids' attractions and a hedge maze.

Trains run from London Victoria to Bearsted, where you catch a special shuttle coach to the castle.

breakfast is free, but a full English is £6.50 extra.

Hotel Continental HOTEL ££
(☎01227-280280; www.hotelcontinental.co.uk; 29 Beach Walk; r from £75; 🐾) The bright and breezy quarters at this elegant seaside art deco building sport light-painted wood cladding, brilliant white beds and sparkling bathrooms. There's a decent restaurant and bar on the premises.

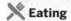 **Eating**

Samphire MODERN BRITISH ££
(☎01227-770075; www.samphirewhitstable.co.uk; 4 High St; mains £13-18; ⊙9am-9.30pm Sun-Thu, 8.30am-10pm Fri & Sat) The shabby-chic jumble of tables and chairs, big-print wallpaper and blackboard menus create the perfect stage for meticulously crafted mains containing East Kent's most flavour-packed ingredients. An interesting side dish is its namesake samphire, an asparagus-like plant that grows on sea-sprayed rocks and cliffs, often found on menus in these parts.

⭐ **Sportsman Pub** BRITISH £££
(www.thesportsmanseasalter.co.uk; Faversham Rd, Seasalter; mains around £22; ⊙restaurant noon-2pm & 7-9pm Tue-Sat, 12.30-2.45pm Sun, bar noon-3pm & 6-11pm Tue-Sat, noon-10pm Sun) The anonymous and oddly named village of Seasalter, 4 miles east of Whitstable, would hardly receive a trickle of visitors were it not for the deceivingly ramshackle Sportsman Pub, East Kent's only eatery adorned with a Michelin star. Local ingredients from sea, marsh and woods are crafted by Whitstable-born chef Stephen Harris into taste-packed Kentish creations that have food critics drooling.

Wheelers Oyster Bar SEAFOOD £££
(☎01227-273311; www.wheelersoysterbar.com; 8 High St; mains around £20; ⊙10.30am-9pm Mon & Tue, 10.15am-9pm Thu, 10.15am-9.30pm Fri, 10am-10pm Sat, 11.30am-9pm Sun) Squeeze onto a stool by the bar or into the four-table Victorian dining room of this baby-blue and pink restaurant, then choose from the seasonal menu and enjoy the best seafood in Whitstable. This place knows its stuff, as it's been serving oysters since 1856. Bookings are highly recommended unless you're travelling solo. Cash only.

ℹ **Information**

Tourist Office (☎01227-770060; www.canterbury.co.uk; 34 Harbour St; ⊙10am-4pm Mon-Fri, to 5pm Sat, 11am-5pm Sun) Run by the Whitstable Improvement Trust from its shop.

ℹ **Getting There & Away**

BUS
Whitstable has connections to Canterbury (£5.20, 30 minutes, every 10 minutes) and London Victoria (£13.70, two hours, daily).

TRAIN
Whitstable has the following connections:
London St Pancras (£28, one hour 20 minutes, hourly)
London Victoria (£22, one hour 20 minutes, hourly)
Margate (£7.20, 20 minutes, twice hourly)
Ramsgate (£9.30, 36 minutes, twice hourly)

CHATHAM HISTORIC DOCKYARD

On the riverfront in Chatham, this historic **dockyard** (☑01634-823800; www.thedockyard.co.uk; Dock Rd; adult/concession/child £24/21.50/14; ☉10am-4pm mid-Feb–Mar & Nov, to 6pm Apr-Oct), a candidate for Unesco heritage status, occupies a third of what was once the Royal Navy's main dock facility. It is possibly the most complete 18th-century dock in the world and has been transformed into a maritime museum examining the Age of Sail. Exhibits include well-restored ships, exhibitions on a variety of shipbuilding themes and a working steam railway.

Margate

☑01843 / POP 49,700

A popular resort for more than two centuries, Margate's late-20th-century slump was long and bleak as British holidaymakers ditched Victorian frump for the carefree *costas* of Spain. But this grand old seaside resort, with fine-sand beaches and artistic associations, has bounced off the bottom. Major cultural regeneration projects – including the spectacular Turner Contemporary art gallery – are slowly reversing the town's fortunes, and on busy days even the odd non-English speaker can be overheard in the hipster cafes and carefully curated junk emporia of the rejuvenated old town.

◉ Sights

★ **Turner Contemporary**　　　GALLERY
(www.turnercontemporary.org; Rendezvous; ☉10am-5pm Tue-Sun) FREE This blockbuster contemporary art gallery, bolted together on the site of the seafront guesthouse where master painter JMW Turner used to stay, is one of East Kent's top attractions. Within the strikingly featureless shell the only thing distracting the eye, apart from the artwork on display, is the sea view from the floor-to-ceiling windows. These allow you to appreciate the very thing Turner loved so much about Margate – the sea, sky and refracted light of the north Kent coast.

The gallery attracts top-notch contemporary installations by high-calibre artists such as Tracey Emin (who grew up in Margate)

and Alex Katz. When you're finished with the art, culinary creations await in the cafe and the gift shop is excellent.

Shell Grotto　　　GROTTO, CAVE
(www.shellgrotto.co.uk; Grotto Hill; adult/concession/child £4/3.50/1.50; ☉10am-5pm Apr-Oct, 11am-4pm Sat & Sun Nov-Mar) Margate's unique attraction is a mysterious subterranean grotto, discovered in 1835. It's a claustrophobic collection of rooms and passageways embedded with 4.6 million shells arranged in symbol-rich mosaics. It has inspired feverish speculation over the years; some think it a 2000-year-old pagan temple, others an elaborate 19th-century hoax. Either way, it's a one-of-a-kind place worth seeing.

Dreamland　　　AMUSEMENT PARK
(www.dreamland.co.uk; Marine Tce; entry £5, rides £1.50-5; ☉10am-6pm, days vary throughout the year; ☝) Given the kiss of life using lottery and council funds, Margate's famous amusement park has come back to life after many years of lying derelict and stop-start renovation. The main attraction here is the so-called Scenic Railway, a 1920s heritage-listed wooden roller coaster that was rebuilt after an arson attack in 2008. But there are plenty of other period rides and attractions to keep adults and kiddies thrilled, some shipped in from other defunct, 20th-century amusement parks across the country.

🛏 Sleeping

★ **Reading Rooms**　　　B&B £££
(☑01843-225166; www.thereadingroomsmargate.co.uk; 31 Hawley Sq; r £170; ☎) Occupying an unmarked 18th-century Georgian town house on a tranquil square just five minutes' walk from the sea, this luxury boutique B&B is as stylish as they come. Generously cut rooms with waxed wooden floors and beautiful French antique reproduction furniture contrast with the 21st-century bathrooms fragrant with luxury cosmetics. Breakfast is served in your room. Bookings essential.

Sands Hotel　　　BOUTIQUE HOTEL £££
(☑01843-228228; www.sandshotelmargate.co.uk; 16 Marine Dr; r £130-265; ☀☎) This beautifully styled boutique hotel sits right on the Margate seafront. It features an understated sand-hued theme throughout, the southeast's best bathrooms, and a restaurant with spectacular bay views, which around half of the rooms also share. The entrance is hidden under the arches on the seafront next to

the hotel's very own summertime ice-cream parlour.

Eating & Drinking

Old Kent Market
MARKET **£**

(www.theoldkentmarket.com; 8 Fort Hill; ⊙9am-8pm; 🚗) This resurrected indoor market a few steps from the beach is absolutely crammed with hipster eateries of every kind, from a Singapore street-food stall to a US diner, a pizzeria to an artisan coffee shop. There always seems to be someone stroking some instrument or other and the most striking feature is the red double-decker bus cafe parked in the entrance.

Hantverk & Found
SEAFOOD **££**

(☑01843-280454; www.hantverk-found.co.uk; 18 King St; mains £7-17; ⊙noon-4pm & 6.30-9.30pm Thu, to 11pm Fri, noon-11pm Sat, noon-4pm Sun) Margate's best seafood cafe plates up mussels, oysters, clams, crab and local fish in imaginative ways, be that in spicy Korean broth, *koji* miso marinated, in cider sauce or on sourdough toast. The dining space is simple, the ingredients Kent-sourced wherever possible and the H&F doubles up as a commissioning gallery with regular changing shows of top-quality art.

The Lifeboat
PUB

(1 Market St; ⊙noon-midnight) If you're looking for a pub with real atmosphere, head in the evening to this oh-so hipsterly authentic, wood-rich tavern where there's regular live jazz, craft beers and ciders on tap and a real fire. As every seafarer's drinking den should, it even has sawdust on the floor (adding spit for extra authenticity is probably not allowed).

ℹ Information

Tourist Office (☑01843-577637; www.visitthanet.co.uk; Droit House, Stone Pier; ⊙10am-5pm Easter-Oct, 10am-5pm Tue-Sat Nov-Easter) Next to the Turner Contemporary art gallery, the tourist office serves all of Planet Thanet. It hands out *The Isle*, a glossy magazine crammed with Thanet listings published twice a year and a free quarterly newspaper called the *Mercury* containing all the latest happenings.

ℹ Getting There & Away

BUS

Departure and arrival points for local buses are Queen St and adjacent Cecil St.

Broadstairs (Thanet Loop Bus; £2.20, 22 minutes, up to every 10 minutes)

Canterbury (£5.70, one hour, two hourly)

London Victoria (National Express; from £8.60, three hours, seven daily)

Ramsgate (Thanet Loop Bus; £2.70, 29 minutes, up to every 10 minutes)

TRAIN

The train station is just a few steps from the beach. There are hourly services to London Victoria (£24.40, one hour 50 minutes) and a high-speed service to London St Pancras (£43, 1½ hours) that runs twice hourly.

Broadstairs

☑01843 / POP 25,000

While its bigger, brasher neighbours seek to revive and regenerate themselves, quaint little Broadstairs quietly gets on with what it's done best for the past 150 years – wowing visitors with its tight sickle of course sand (Viking Bay) and shallow, sun-warmed sea. Charles Dickens certainly thought it an agreeable spot, spending most summers here between 1837 and 1859. The resort now plays the Victorian nostalgia card at every opportunity but this is a minor distraction for the fine-weather crowds that descend from London.

◉ Sights

Dickens House Museum
MUSEUM

(www.dickensfellowship.org; 2 Victoria Pde; adult/child £3.75/2.10; ⊙1-4.30pm Easter–mid-Jun & mid-Sep–Oct, 10am-4.30pm mid-Jun–mid-Sep, 1-4.30pm Sat & Sun Nov) This quaint museum

---

OFF THE BEATEN TRACK

ISLE OF THANET

You won't need a wetsuit or a ferry to reach the Isle of Thanet and its towns of Margate, Ramsgate and Broadstairs: the 2-mile-wide Wantsum Channel, which divides the island from the mainland, silted up in the 16th century, transforming the East Kent landscape forever. In its island days, Thanet was the springboard for several epoch-making episodes in English history. It was here that the Romans kicked off their invasion in the 1st century AD and where St Augustine landed in AD 597 to launch his conversion of the pagans. If global warming forecasts are right, Thanet could once again be an island by the end of the century.

is Broadstairs' top indoor attraction and the former home of Mary Pearson Strong – Dickens' inspiration for the character of Betsey Trotwood in *David Copperfield*. Diverse Dickensiana on display includes letters from the author.

Festivals & Events

Dickens Festival   CULTURAL
(www.broadstairsdickensfestival.co.uk; ☉mid-Jun) Broadstairs' biggest bash, this annual, week-long festival culminates in a banquet and ball in Victorian fancy dress.

Sleeping & Eating

★ Bleak House   HISTORIC HOTEL £££
(☑01843-865338; www.bleakhousebroadstairs.co.uk; Fort Rd; r £135-250, apt £300; ☎) This former Napoleonic-era fortress overlooking the beach was converted into an opulent Victorian residence just in time for one Charles Dickens to rent it for 22 summers (1837–59). From the lounge bar to the Copperfield suite with its Viking Bay views and five-star bathroom, the whole caboodle oozes unique period character. Building tours run from 11am to 5pm.

★ Wyatt & Jones   BRITISH ££
(www.wyattandjones.co.uk; 23-27 Harbour St; mains £6-21; ☉8.30am-11pm Wed-Sat, to 5pm Sun) Broadstairs' best gastronomical offering is this contemporary British restaurant

just a few steps off the beach. Savour unashamedly local dishes such as Whitstable oysters, local bream, mussels and chips, or a day-launching breakfast in the uncluttered interior of gun-metal blue and scratched timber floors. Then admire your expanding waistline in the retro mirror wall.

Getting There & Away

BUS

Broadstairs connections include the following:

Canterbury (£5.70, 1½ hours, twice hourly)

London Victoria (National Express; from £6, 3¼ hours, seven daily)

Margate (Thanet Loop Bus; £2.20, 22 minutes, up to every 10 minutes)

Ramsgate (Thanet Loop Bus; £1.70, 14 minutes, up to every 10 minutes)

TRAIN

Broadstairs is connected to London Victoria (£36.60, two hours, hourly) and by high-speed service to London St Pancras (£39.30, one hour 20 minutes to two hours, twice hourly).

Ramsgate

☑01843 / POP 40,400

The most varied of Thanet's towns, Ramsgate has a friendlier feel than rival Margate and is more vibrant than its quaint little neighbour Broadstairs. A forest of masts whistles serenely in the breeze below the handsomely

HOPS & VINES

With booze cruises over to Calais a thing of the past, many Kent and Sussex drinkers have rediscovered their counties' superb home-grown beverages. Both counties produce some of the most delicious ales in the country and the southeast's wines are even outgunning some traditional Continental vintners.

Kent's **Shepherd Neame Brewery** (☑01795-542016; www.shepherdneame.co.uk; 10 Court St, Faversham; tours £14; ☉2pm daily) is Britain's oldest and cooks up aromatic ales brewed from Kent-grown premium hops. Sussex's reply is **Harveys Brewery** (☑01273-480209; www.harveys.org.uk; Bridge Wharf), which perfumes Lewes town centre with a hop-laden scent. Book well in advance for tours of either brewery.

Mention 'English wine' not too long ago and you'd likely hear a snort of derision. Not any more. Thanks to warmer temperatures and determined winemakers, English wine, particularly of the sparkling variety, is developing a fan base all of its own.

Award-winning vineyards can be found in both Sussex and Kent, whose chalky soils are likened to France's Champagne region. Many vineyards now offer tours and wine tastings. Some of the most popular are **Biddenden Vineyards** (☑01580-291726; www.biddendenvineyards.com; £1 donation to charity; ☉10am-5pm Mon-Sat, from 11am Sun; tours 10am Sat year-round, Wed Jun-Sep), 1.2 miles from Wealden, and **Chapel Down Vinery** (☑01580-766111; www.chapeldown.com; Tenterden; tours £15; ☉tours daily Mar-Nov), located 2.5 miles south of Tenterden on the B2082.

curved walls of Britain's only royal harbour, and the seafront is surrounded by bars and cosmopolitan street cafes. Just one celebrity chef away from being described as 'up and coming', Ramsgate retains a shabbily undiscovered charm, its sweeping, environmentally sanctioned Blue Flag beaches and some spectacular Victorian architecture making it well worth the visit.

⊙ Sights

Spitfire Memorial Museum   MUSEUM

(www.spitfiremuseum.org.uk; Manston Rd; ⊙10am-5pm Apr-Oct, to 4pm Nov-Mar) **FREE** Around 4 miles northwest of Ramsgate's town centre at Manston Airport, this purpose-built museum stores two WWII planes: one a Spitfire, the other a Hurricane. Both look factory-fresh but are surprisingly delicate and so, sadly, there's no clambering on board, though you can now have a go in a rather amateurishly built simulator. Gathered around the planes are myriad flight-associated exhibits, many relating to Manston's role as an airfield during the Battle of Britain where many Spitfires were based.

The museum has a decent cafe with views of the airstrip. Take bus 38 or 11 from King St and ask the driver to drop you off as near as possible.

Ramsgate Maritime Museum   MUSEUM

(www.ramsgatemaritimemuseum.org; The Clock House, Royal Harbour; adult/child £2.50/1; ⊙10.30am-5.30pm Tue-Sun Easter-Sep) Interesting but erratically opening museum displaying loot from the more than 600 ships that have been wrecked on the notorious Goodwin Sands off this stretch of coast.

🛏 Sleeping

Glendevon Guesthouse   B&B ££

(☏01843-570909; www.glendevonguesthouse.co.uk; 8 Truro Rd; s/d from £52.50/70; ᴘ🅿🛜) ♠ Run by energetic and knowledgeable hosts, this comfy guesthouse takes the whole ecofriendly thing seriously, with guest recycling facilities, eco-showers and even energy-saving hairdryers. The hallways of this grand Victorian house, a block back from the Ramsgate seafront, are decorated with work by local artists. All rooms have kitchenettes, and breakfast is a convivial affair taken around a communal table.

Royal Harbour Hotel   BOUTIQUE HOTEL ££

(☏01843-591514; www.royalharbourhotel.co.uk; 10-12 Nelson Cres; s/d from £79/100; 🛜) Occupying two regency town houses on a glorious sea-

DOWN HOUSE

Charles Darwin's home from 1842 until his death in 1882, **Down House** (www.english-heritage.org.uk; Luxted Rd, Downe; adult/concession/child £11.80/10.60/7.20; ⊙10am-6pm Apr-Sep, to 5pm Oct, Sat & Sun only Nov-Mar) witnessed the development of Darwin's theory of evolution by natural selection. The house and gardens have been restored to look much as they would have in Darwin's time, including Darwin's study, where he undertook much of his reading and writing; the drawing room, where he tried out some of his indoor experiments; and the gardens and greenhouse, where some of his outdoor experiments are recreated.

There are three self-guided trails in the area, where you can follow in the great man's footsteps. Take bus 146 from Bromley North or Bromley South railway station, or service R8 from Orpington.

front crescent, this boutique hotel feels enveloped in warmth and quirkiness – an eclectic collection of books, magazines, games and artwork line the hotel. Rooms range from tiny nautical-esque 'cabins' to country-house style four-poster doubles, most with postcard views over the forest of masts below. All are perfectly appointed with bags of character.

🍴 Eating

★Royal Victoria Pavilion   PUB FOOD £

(www.jdwetherspoon.com; Harbour Pde; mains £5-11; ⊙8am-midnight Sun-Thu, to 1am Fri & Sat; 🛜) The old pavilion has sat on Ramsgate seafront like an upturned boat since 1904, its grand architecture, based on the Little Theatre at Versailles, a vacant symbol of the British seaside's bygone glory days. However, in 2017 the hall was brought spectacularly back to life by Wetherspoons and is now a place to eat that packs a wow factor.

Bon Appetit   FRENCH ££

(www.bonappetitramsgate.com; 4 Westcliff Arcade; mains £8-19; ⊙noon-2.30pm & 6.30pm-late Tue-Sun) The best eatery on Westcliff, this first-rate bistro serves up French-inspired dishes in a simple dining room or with al fresco harbour views. Ingredients on the menu are of the seasonal and locally sourced ilk, with finely crafted mains including delights such as venison sausages and baked camembert.

❶ Information

Tourist Office (✆ 01843-598750; www.
ramsgatetown.org; Customs House, Harbour
Pde; ⏰ 10am-4pm) A small, staffed visitor
centre with out-of-hours brochure stands.

❶ Getting There & Away

BUS

Ramsgate has the following bus connections:
Broadstairs (Thanet Loop Bus; £1.70, up to
every 10 minutes)
London Victoria (National Express; from
£8.60, three hours, six daily)
Margate (Thanet Loop Bus; £2.70, 29 minutes,
up to every 10 minutes)
Sandwich (£3.20, 28 minutes, hourly)

TRAIN

Ramsgate has many services to London Victoria,
London St Pancras and London Charing Cross.
Journey times range from 1¼ to two hours and
ticket prices from £13 to £45. There are also
services to Sandwich (£5.20, 12 minutes, hourly) and Dover (£10, 35 minutes, two hourly).

Sandwich

☏ 01304 / POP 5000

As close as you'll get to a living museum,
Sandwich was once England's fourth city
(after London, Norwich and Ipswich). It's a
fact hard to grasp as you wander its drowsy
medieval lanes, ancient churches, Dutch gables, crooked peg-tiled roofs and overhanging timber-framed houses. Once a port to
rival London, Sandwich began its decline
when the entrance to the harbour silted up
in the 16th century, and this once-vital gateway to and from the Continent spent the
next 400 years retreating into quaint rural
obscurity. Preservation is big here, with huge
local interest in period authenticity. The tiny
100-seat cinema is preserved as an art deco
museum piece and the 1920s garage deals
more in classic cars than modern vehicles.
Within the town's historical core, unlisted
buildings are the exception.

◉ Sights

Sandwich's web of medieval and Elizabethan streets is perfect for ambling through
and getting pleasantly lost (as many do).
Strand St in particular has one of the country's highest concentrations of half-timbered
buildings. Ornate brickwork on some houses
betrays the strong influence of 350 Protestant Flemish refugees (referred to as 'the

Strangers'), who settled in the town in the
16th century at the invitation of Elizabeth I.

Sandwich Quay   WATERFRONT
Several attractions line the River Stour. The
cute little flint-chequered Barbican tollgate
was built by Henry VIII and controls traffic
flow over the river's only road bridge. Nearby rises Fishergate, built in 1384 and once
the main entrance to the town, through
which goods from the Continent and beyond once passed. On fair-weather days, hop
aboard the **Sandwich River Bus** (✆ 07958-
376183; www.sandwichrb.co.uk; The Quay; adult/
child 30min trip £7/5, seal spotting £20/14; ⏰ every
30-60min 11am-6pm Thu-Sun Apr-Sep) beside the
toll bridge for seal-spotting trips along the
River Stour and in Pegwell Bay.

It's also an interesting way to reach the
Richborough Roman Fort (EH; www.english-
heritage.org.uk; Richborough Rd; adult/concession/
child £6.20/5.20/3.90; ⏰ 10am-6pm Apr-Sep, to
5pm Wed-Sun Oct, to 4pm Sat & Sun Nov-Mar).

Guildhall Museum   MUSEUM
(www.sandwichguildhallmuseum.co.uk; Guildhall;
⏰ 10am-4pm Wed-Sun) FREE Sandwich's small
but thorough museum is a good place to
start exploring the town. The exhibition
space was fully renovated in 2017 to house
a copy of the Magna Carta, accidentally discovered in Sandwich's archives in 2015. Other exhibitions examine the town's rich past
as a Cinque Port (p170), its role in various
wars, and the gruesome punishments meted
out to felons, fornicators and phoney fishers.

Salutation Gardens   GARDENS
(www.the-salutation.com; The Salutation, Knightrid-
er St; £8; ⏰ 10am-5pm Mar-Oct, to 4.30pm Nov-
Feb) Just along from Fishergate, this set of
exquisite gardens was laid out behind a 1912
mansion by leading early 20th-century garden designers Gertrude Jekyll and Edwin
Lutyens. In the mid-noughties the exquisite site was brought back to life by Dom
and Steph Parker, nationally known as minor celebrities from British TV's *Gogglebox*
show. There's a delightful little tearoom in
the grounds and you can stay with Dom and
Steph in their multimillion-pound mansion.

St Peter's   CHURCH
(✆ 01304-617295; www.stpeterschurch-sandwich.
org.uk; King St; tower adult/child £3.50/2.50;
⏰ tower noon-4pm Tue-Sun Apr-Sep, to 2pm Oct-
Mar) The oldest church in Sandwich is now
no longer used for worship. It's a real mixture of styles and years: its tower collapsed

in dramatic fashion in 1661 and it was re-built with a bulbous cupola by the Flemish 'Strangers'. In 2017 this was made accessible to the public who can now climb the narrow steps for unsurpassed views across the Kent-peg tiled roofs of Sandwich.

🛏 Sleeping & Eating

★ Bell Hotel
HOTEL £££

(☎ 01304-613388; www.bellhotelsandwich.co.uk; Sandwich Quay; s/d from £120/130; P ⛽) Today the haunt of celebrity golfers, the Bell Hotel has been sitting on the town's quay since Tudor times, though much of the remaining building is from the 19th century. A splendid sweeping staircase leads to luxurious rooms, some with pretty quay views. The Old Dining Room restaurant is one of East Kent's poshest nosh spots.

No Name Shop
DELI, BISTRO ££

(www.nonameshop.co.uk; 1 No Name St; snacks £1.90-6.25, meals £6.95-13.50; ⊗ 9am-5pm Mon-Sat, 9am-4pm Sun) The far-from-anonymous No Name Shop is a French-owned deli (downstairs) and bistro (upstairs) near the bus stop, a pleasantly aromatic spot for a quick sandwich in Sandwich or an 'oozyli-cious' *croque-monsieur*, as well as more sophisticated dishes, followed by a relaxing glass of something Gallic. Popular among locals, some of whom seem to regularly prefer it over their own kitchens.

ℹ Information

Tourist Office (☎ 01304-613565; www. open-sandwich.co.uk; Guildhall, Cattle Market; ⊗ 10am-4pm Mon-Sat Apr-Oct) Located in the historic Guildhall.

ℹ Getting There & Away

BUS

Buses go to Ramsgate (£3.20, 21 minutes, hourly), Dover (£4, 45 minutes, two hourly) and Canterbury (£4.20, 40 minutes, three hourly).

TRAIN

Trains run from Dover Priory train station (£7.50, 22 minutes, hourly), Ramsgate (£5.20, 12 minutes, hourly) and London St Pancras (£43, two hours, hourly).

Dover

☎ 01304 / POP 31,000

One of the Cinque Ports, down-in-the-dumps Dover has certainly seen better days. Its derelict postwar architecture and shabby town centre is a sad introduction to England for travellers arriving on cross-Channel ferries and cruise ships, most of whom pass through quickly. Lucky, then, that the town has a couple of stellar attractions to redeem it. The port's vital strategic position so close to mainland Europe gave rise to a sprawling hilltop castle, which has some 2000 years of history to its credit. The spectacular white cliffs, as much a symbol of English wartime resilience as Winston Churchill or the Battle of Britain, rear in chalky magnificence to the east and west.

◉ Sights

★ Dover Castle
CASTLE

(EH; www.english-heritage.org.uk; adult/concession/child £19.40/17.50/12; ⊗ 10am-6pm Apr-Jul & Sep, 9.30am-6pm Aug, to 5pm Oct, 10am-4pm Sat & Sun Nov-Mar; P) Occupying top spot, literally and figuratively, in Dover's townscape, this most

---

THE WHITE CLIFFS OF DOVER

Immortalised in song, film and literature, the iconic white cliffs of Dover are embedded in the national consciousness, and are a big 'Welcome Home' sign to generations of travellers and soldiers. The cliffs rise to 100m high and extend on either side of Dover, but the best bit is the 6-mile stretch that starts about 2 miles east of town, properly known as the **Langdon Cliffs**, now managed by the National Trust.

From the **Langdon Cliffs tourist office** (☎ 01304-202756; www.nationaltrust.org.uk; ⊗ 10am-5pm Mar-Oct, 11am-4pm Nov-Feb), follow the stony path east along the clifftops for a bracing 2-mile walk to the stout Victorian **South Foreland Lighthouse** (NT; www.nationaltrust.org.uk; adult/child £6/3; ⊗ guided tours 11am-5.30pm Fri-Mon mid-Mar–Oct). This was the first lighthouse to be powered by electricity and is the site of the first international radio transmissions, in 1898.

A trail runs along the cliffs as far as **St Margaret's Bay**, a popular spot among locals.

At the end of the trail along the cliffs at St Margaret's Bay, bus 81 shuttles back to Dover or onto Deal every hour.

Dover

Dover

impressive of castles was built to bolster the country's weakest point at the shortest sea crossing to mainland Europe. The highlights here are the unmissable **secret wartime tunnels** and the **Great Tower**, but the huge area it sprawls across has a lot of other interesting sights, so allow at least three hours for your visit, more if you stand to admire the views across the Channel to France.

The site has been in use for as many as 2000 years. On the vast grounds are the remains of a **Roman lighthouse** (Dover Castle), which dates from AD 50 and may be the oldest standing building in Britain. Beside it lies the restored Saxon **Church of St Mary** (Dover Castle) in Castro.

The robust 12th-century Great Tower, with walls up to 7m thick, is a medieval warren filled with interactive exhibits and light-and-sound shows that take visitors back to the times of Henry II.

However, the biggest draw of all is the network of secret wartime tunnels. The claustrophobic chalk-hewn passageways were first excavated during the Napoleonic Wars and then expanded to house a command post and hospital in WWII. The highly enjoyable 50-minute guided tour (every 20 minutes, included in the ticket price) tells the story of one of Britain's most famous wartime operations, code-named Dynamo, which was directed from here in 1940 and saw hundreds of thousands of soldiers evacuated from the beaches at Dunkirk. The story is told in a very effective way, with video projected sharply onto the tunnel walls and sounds rumbling through the rock. At one point, the entire passageway is consumed in flames and at others visitors are plunged into complete darkness.

★ **Banksy Brexit Mural**   PUBLIC ART
(cnr York & Townwall Sts) Despite voting leave, the poor port town of Dover is possibly the

Southeast community set to suffer most post-Brexit. It was perhaps for that reason that Banksy chose a highly visible gable end to create his Brexit mural that appeared overnight one May weekend in 2017. The huge artwork depicts a workman chipping away at one of the yellow stars of the EU flag, cracks splintering off in all directions across the image.

Roman Painted House RUINS
(www.theromanpaintedhouse.co.uk; New St; adult/child £4/3; ⊗10am-5pm Tue-Sun Apr-Sep; P) A crumbling 1960s bunker is the unlikely setting for some of the most extensive, if stunted, Roman wall paintings north of the Alps. Several scenes depict Bacchus (Roman god of wine and revelry), which makes perfect sense as this large villa was built around AD 200 as a *mansio* (hotel) for travellers needing a little lubrication to unwind.

🛏 Sleeping & Eating

Blériot's GUESTHOUSE £
(📞01304-211394; www.bleriotsguesthouse.co.uk; 47 Park Ave; s/d £38/58; P🖥) Spacious eight-room guesthouse in a quiet residential location but within walking distance of all the sights. Some of the light-filled rooms have original Victorian fireplaces, there's a cosy lounge, and the hosts are the friendliest you'll meet in the southeast. Breakfast is £7 extra.

Dover Marina Hotel HOTEL ££
(📞01304-203633; www.dovermarinahotel.co.uk; Waterloo Cres; s/d from £59/69; 🖥) Just a few steps from Dover's beach, this seafront hotel crams 81 rooms of varying dimensions into a gently curving 1870s edifice. The undulating corridors show the building's age, but there's nothing wonky about the rooms with their trendy ethnic fabrics, big-print wallpaper and contemporary artwork. Half the rooms have unrivalled sea views and 10 boast much-sought-after balconies.

★Allotment BRITISH ££
(📞01304-214467; www.theallotmentrestaurant.com; 9 High St; mains £5-17; ⊗noon-9.30pm Tue-Sat) Dover's best dining spot plates up local fish and meat from around Canterbury, seasoned with herbs from the tranquil garden out back, for breakfast, lunch and dinner. Cleanse your palette with a Kentish wine in a relaxed, understated setting as you admire the view of the Maison Dieu (13th-century pilgrims' hospital) directly opposite through the exquisite stained-glass frontage.

ℹ Information

Tourist Office (📞01304-201066; www.whitecliffscountry.org.uk; Market Sq; ⊗9.30am-5pm Mon-Sat year-round, 10am-3pm Sun Apr-Sep) Located in the Dover Museum (www.dovermuseum.co.uk; Market Sq; ⊗9.30am-5pm Mon-Sat year-round, 10am-3pm Sun Apr-Sep).

ℹ Getting There & Away

BOAT

Ferries depart for France from the Eastern Docks below the castle. Fares vary according to season and advance purchase. Services seem to be in a constant state of flux with companies rising and falling as often as the Channel's swell.

DFDS (📞0871-574 7235; www.dfdsseaways.co.uk) Services to Dunkirk (two hours, every two hours) and Calais (1½ hours, at least hourly).

P&O Ferries (📞01304-448888; www.poferries.com) Runs to Calais (1½ hours, every 40 to 60 minutes).

BUS

Dover has bus connections to the following:
Canterbury (£5.70, 34 minutes, three hourly)
London Victoria (Coach 007; from £7.70, 2½ to 3½ hours, every two hours)
Rye (Bus 100; £7.20, 2¼ hours)
Sandwich (£4, 45 minutes, two hourly)

TRAIN

Dover is connected by train to Ramsgate (£10, 35 minutes, two hourly) via Sandwich, Canterbury (£8.50, 27 minutes, two hourly) and London St Pancras, Victoria and Charing Cross (£37-45, one to 2½ hours, up to five hourly).

EAST SUSSEX

Home to rolling countryside, medieval villages and gorgeous coastline, this inspiring corner of England is besieged by weekending Londoners whenever the sun pops out. And it's not hard to see why as you explore the cobbled medieval streets of Rye; wander around historic Battle, where William the Conqueror first engaged the Saxons in 1066; and peer over the edge of the breathtaking Seven Sisters chalk cliffs and Beachy Head near the genteel seaside town of Eastbourne. Brighton, a highlight of any visit, offers some kicking nightlife, offbeat shopping and British seaside fun. Off the beaten track, you can stretch your legs on the South Downs Way, which traverses England's newest national park, the South Downs National Park.

Rye

☑ 01797 / POP 4770

Possibly southeast England's quaintest town, Rye is a little nugget of the past, a medieval settlement that looks like someone hit the pause button on time. Even the most hard-boiled cynic can't fail to be softened by Rye's cobbled lanes, mysterious passageways and crooked half-timbered Tudor buildings. Tales of resident smugglers, ghosts, writers and artists abound.

Rye was once one of the Cinque Ports, occupying a high promontory above the sea. Today the town rises 2 miles from the briny; sheep graze where the Channel's strong tides once swelled.

◎ Sights

Mermaid Street AREA

Most start their exploration of Rye on famous Mermaid St, a short walk from the Rye Heritage Centre (p171). It bristles with 15th-century timber-framed houses with quirky names such as 'The House with Two Front Doors' and 'The House Opposite'.

Lamb House HOUSE, MUSEUM

(NT; www.nationaltrust.org.uk; West St; adult/concession £6.80/3.45; ⊙ 11am-5pm Fri-Mon late Mar-Oct) This Georgian town house is a favourite stomping ground for local apparitions, but its most famous resident was American writer Henry James, who lived here from 1898 to 1916, during which time he wrote *The Wings of the Dove*. Until 2017 this was a private house but with the tenants gone, the National Trust has opened up more rooms to the public and created a more hands-on experience. For budding writers there are writing spaces and courses on offer.

Ypres Tower MUSEUM

(www.ryemuseum.co.uk; Church Sq; adult/concession/child £4/3/free; ⊙ 10.30am-5pm Apr-Oct, to 3.30pm Nov-Mar) Just off Church Sq stands the sandcastle-esque Ypres Tower (pronounced 'wipers'). You can scramble through the 13th-century building to learn about its long history as a fort, prison, mortuary and museum (the last two at overlapping times), and an annexe contains one of the last surviving Victorian women's prisons in the country. From here, there are widescreen views of Rye Bay and even France on very clear days.

Driving Tour
Dover to Rye

START DOVER EASTERN DOCKS
END RYE
LENGTH 35.5 MILES; AT LEAST FOUR HOURS (WITHOUT DUNGENESS PENINSULA DETOUR)

If you've just rolled off a cross-Channel ferry or have a day away from a cruise ship docked in Dover, instead of heading north to London, why not take this fascinating route along the white cliffs and across the flat marshes of the Kent–Sussex border to discover some of the southeast's hidden corners. Buses 100, 101 and 102 (The Wave) follow this route between Dover, Lydd and Hastings.

Starting at the exit to Dover's frantic ❶ **Eastern Docks**, where all cross-Channel ferries tie up, take the A20 along the seafront. After a few minutes, this dual carriageway begins to climb onto the famous white cliffs west of Dover. Your first stop is just outside town – take the turning for ❷ **Samphire Hoe** nature park, a ledge of parkland created between the white cliffs and the sea using 5 million cu metres of chalk excavated during the construction of the Channel Tunnel. It's a fine spot for a picnic as you watch the 30 local species of butterfly flutter by.

Back on the A20, it's a mere 1.75 miles to the exit for the village of Capel-Le-Ferne (on the B2011). Well signposted at the end of the village is the ❸ **Battle of Britain Memorial**, a striking monument to the pilots who took part in the decisive struggle with the Luftwaffe in the skies above Kent and Sussex. An airman seated at the centre of a huge Spitfire propeller looks out serenely across the Channel and there's a multimedia visitors centre and museum experience to enjoy. Returning to the B2011, a few gear changes will have you on the outskirts of ❹ **Folkestone**. Take a left at the first roundabout then the sixth right onto Dover Rd. This will take you into the centre of this formerly grand old resort, once a favourite stomping ground of royal bon viveur King Edward VII and a forgotten piece of England's seaside past. Take a stroll through the seafront Leas Coastal Park with its subtropical flora, then halt for fish and chips at the old fish market before ambling up through the Creative Quarter, Folkestone's old town, now occupied by artists' studios and craft shops.

Heading out of Folkestone to the west on the A259 Sandgate Rd, you pass through Sandgate with its antique shops and shingle beach. From there it's another 2.5 miles to fascinating little ⑤ **Hythe**. You could spend a full day in this original Cinque Port. Not only is it the eastern terminus of the fascinating narrow-gauge Romney, Hythe and Dymchurch Railway (RH&D Railway), but the Royal Military Canal also flows through the town and there's a quaint high street and beach to explore.

Heading ever west, a series of not-so-attractive shingle resorts such as Dymchurch and St Mary's are strung along the A259, cowering below their huge dykes, which keep the high tides from turning this stretch of the coast into sea bottom. You've now left the white cliffs behind and are entering the ⑥ **Romney Marsh**, a flat, sparsely populated landscape of reed beds and sheep-dotted fields. There's a visitor centre (www.kentwild lifetrust.org.uk) between St Mary's Bay and New Romney (on the A259) for those with time.

Having negotiated New Romney, another of the original five Cinque Ports, just outside the town take the turning to the left onto the B2075, which leads to ⑦ **Lydd**, a quaint former corporate member of the Cinque Ports. From here, detour along the lonely Dungeness Rd, which heads across the flats of the eerie ⑧ **Dungeness Peninsula**, a low shingle spit dominated by a brooding nuclear power station. As well as boasting the south-east's largest seabird colony, it's also the western terminus of the RH&D Railway.

Back in Lydd, stick with the B2075 heading west for 6 miles until you reach Camber. Thought the entire south coast had just shingle beaches? Well, the main attraction here is ⑨ **Camber Sands**, a wide expanse of golden grains and dunes, ideal for picnicking and strolling.

The B2075 winds through shingly, scrubby wetlands until it rejoins the A259 at the hamlet of East Guldeford, where you should turn left towards Rye. Along the roads around here you will see the main source of revenue from the Romney Marsh – thousands of sheep grazing on the verdant flats. The A259 barrels across the marshes, eventually depositing you in ⑩ **Rye**, one of the southeast's quaintest towns.

🛏 Sleeping

★ Jeake's House   HOTEL ££

(☏01797-222828; www.jeakeshouse.com; Mermaid St; r £95-200; P🛜) Situated on Mermaid St, this 17th-century town house once belonged to US poet Conrad Aitken. The 11 rooms are named after writers who stayed here. The decor was probably slightly less bold then, minus the beeswaxed antiques and lavish drapery. Take a pew in the snug book-lined bar and, continuing the theme, enjoy breakfast in an 18th-century former Quaker chapel.

Windmill Guesthouse   B&B ££

(☏01797-224027; www.ryewindmill.co.uk; Mill Lane; d from £90; P🛜) This white windmill, sails still intact, houses perhaps Rye's oddest digs. The shape of the building means room sizes vary, as do standards. The two-storey much sought-after 'Windmill Suite' is located almost at the top, enjoying 360-degree views. Breakfast is served in the former granary and the octagonal guest lounge occupies the mill's base. Book ahead.

George in Rye   HOTEL £££

(☏01797-222114; www.thegeorgeinrye.com; 98 High St; d from £135; 🛜) This old coaching inn has managed to reinvent itself as a contemporary boutique hotel while staying true to its roots. Downstairs, an old-fashioned wood-panelled lounge is warmed by roaring log fires, while the guest rooms in the main building, created by the set designer from the film *Pride & Prejudice,* are chic and understated.

The highlight of the building is the grand old ballroom, originally built in 1818 as a meeting hall for local farmers.

Mermaid Inn   HOTEL £££

(☏01797-223065; www.mermaidinn.com; Mermaid St; s/d from £90/140; P🛜) Few inns can claim to be as atmospheric as this ancient hostelry, dating from 1420. Each of the 31 rooms is different, but all are thick with dark beams and lit by leaded windows, and some are graced by secret passageways that now act as fire escapes. It also has one of Rye's best restaurants.

✗ Eating

Haydens   CAFE £

(www.haydensinrye.co.uk; 108 High St; snacks & meals £4.50-9.50; ⊘10am-5pm; 🛜) Long-time believers in organic and fair-trade produce, Haydens dishes up delicious omelettes, ploughman's lunches, salads and bagels in a light, breezy cafe. There's a wonderful elevated terrace at the back with great views over town and country. Also runs an excellent seven-room ecofriendly guesthouse upstairs.

Simon the Pieman   CAFE £

(3 Lion St; snacks £1.50-10; ⊘9.30am-4.45pm Mon-Fri, to 5.30pm Sat, 11.30am-4.45pm Sun) Many local cream-tea cognoscenti assert this traditional tearoom, Rye's oldest, does the best scone-cream-jam combo this side of Romney Marsh. Further foes of tooth and waistline tempt from the shop's window, though in the winter you may be lured in by the roaring real fire.

Webbe's at the Fish Cafe   SEAFOOD ££

(www.webbesrestaurants.co.uk; 17 Tower St; mains £13-18; ⊘noon-2pm & 6pm-late) Rye's best fish restaurant is a simple dining room flooded with natural light from large arched win-

---

CINQUE PORTS

Due to their proximity to Europe, southeast England's coastal towns were the frontline against raids and invasion during Anglo-Saxon times. In the absence of a professional army and navy, these ports were frequently called upon to defend themselves, and the kingdom, on land and at sea.

In 1278 King Edward I formalised this ancient arrangement by legally defining the Confederation of Cinque Ports (pronounced 'sink ports'). The five original ports – Sandwich, Dover, Hythe, Romney and Hastings – were awarded numerous perks and privileges in exchange for providing the king with ships and men. At their peak, the ports were considered England's most powerful institution after Crown and Church.

The importance of the ports eventually evaporated when the shifting coastlines silted up several Cinque Port harbours and a professional navy was based at Portsmouth. But still the pomp and ceremony remain. The Lord Warden of the Cinque Ports is a prestigious post now bestowed on faithful servants of the Crown. The Queen Mother was warden until she passed away, succeeded by Admiral Lord Boyce. Previous incumbents include the Duke of Wellington and Sir Winston Churchill.

WORTH A TRIP

BATTLE

'If there'd been no battle, there'd be no Battle', goes the saying in this unassuming village, which grew up around the hillside where invading French duke William of Normandy, aka William the Conqueror, scored a decisive victory over local king Harold in 1066. The epicentre of 1066 country, visitors flock here to see the spot where Harold got it in the eye, with the biggest crowd turning up mid-October to witness the annual re-enactment on the original battlefield.

The aptly named **Battle Abbey** (EH; www.english-heritage.org.uk; High St; adult/concession/child £11.20/10.10/7.80; ⊙10am-6pm Apr-Sep, to 4pm Sat & Sun Oct-Mar) marks the site of the pivotal event, which had an unparalleled impact on the country's subsequent social structure, language and, well, pretty much everything. Four years after, the Normans began constructing an abbey here, a penance ordered by the pope for the loss of life incurred. Only the foundations of the original church remain; the altar's position is supposedly the spot King Harold took an arrow in his eye.

There are train connections to Hastings (£4.30, 15 minutes, twice hourly) and London Charing Cross (£29.40, one hour and 20 minutes, twice hourly).

---

dows. The menu features local fish such as Rye Bay flounder in cider sauce and Rye cod in beer batter. The restaurant also doubles up as a cookery school and is the venue for the annual Scallop Week in March.

Landgate Bistro BRITISH ££
(☏01797-222829; www.landgatebistro.co.uk; 5-6 Landgate; mains £15-20; ⊙7-11pm Wed-Fri, noon-2.30pm & 6.30-11pm Sat, noon-2.30pm Sun) Escape the medieval excesses of Rye's central eateries to this fresh-feeling bistro, slightly off the tourist trail near the impressive 14th-century Landgate. The focus here is on competently crafted dishes using local lamb and fish. The dining space is understated with tables gathered around an ancient fireplace.

ⓘ Information

Rye Heritage Centre (☏01797-226696; www.ryeheritage.co.uk; Strand Quay; ⊙10am-5pm Apr-Oct, shorter hours Nov-Mar) See a town-model audiovisual history for £3.50 and, upstairs, a freaky collection of still-functional penny-in-the-slot novelty machines. Also runs themed walking tours of the town; see the website for details.

ⓘ Getting There & Away

BUS

There are hourly buses to Dover (bus 100; £7.20, 2¼ hours) and twice hourly services to Hastings (bus 100/101; £6.40, 40 minutes).

TRAIN

There are hourly trains to Hastings (£5.60, 18 minutes). For London St Pancras (£34.60, 1½ hours, hourly) change in Ashford.

Hastings

☏01424 / POP 98,500

Forever associated with the Norman invasion of 1066 (even though the decisive events took place 6 miles away), Hastings prospered as one of the Cinque Ports and, in its Victorian heyday, was one of Britain's most fashionable resorts. After a period of steady postwar decline, the town is enjoying a mini-renaissance, and these days is an intriguing mix of family seaside resort, working fishing port and arty hang-out.

◉ Sights

Stade AREA
(Rock-A-Nore Rd) The seafront area known as the Stade (below East Hill) is home to distinctive black clapboard structures known as Net Shops. These were built to store fishing gear back in the 17th century, but some now house fishmongers who sell off the catch of Europe's largest beach-launched fishing fleet, usually hauled up on the shingle behind. All these fishy goings-on keep the Stade very much a working place, with the combined pong of diesel and guts scenting the air.

Hastings Castle RUINS
(www.discoverhastings.co.uk; Castle Hill Rd; adult/concession/child £4.95/4.25/3.95; ⊙10am-4pm Easter-Sep) This fortress was built by William the Conquerer, and an exhibition in the grounds tells the story of the castle and the Battle of Hastings in 1066.

Jerwood Gallery
GALLERY

(www.jerwoodgallery.org; Rock-A-Nore Rd; adult/concession/child £9/6/free; ☉11am-5pm Tue-Sun) This large, purpose-built exhibition venue at the end of the Stade is used for temporary shows of contemporary British art as well as themed installations from the Jerwood collection. The building has a great cafe with sunny Channel views. The black-tiled building was designed to blend in with the adjacent net shops.

Hastings Museum & Art Gallery
MUSEUM

(www.hmag.org.uk; Johns Place, Bohemia Rd; ☉10am-5pm Tue-Sat, noon-5pm Sun Apr-Sep, shorter hours Oct-Mar) FREE A short walk west of the train station, this marvellous little museum is housed in a red-brick mansion. Highlights inside include the intricately Moorish Durbar Hall and a section on John Logie Baird, who invented television while recuperating from an illness in Hastings between February 1923 and November 1924.

Hastings Pier
LANDMARK

(www.hastingspier.org.uk; 1-10 White Rock; ☉10am-9pm daily) FREE Hastings last hit the national news in 2010 when its Victorian pier burnt down. The ballroom at the end, where the likes of The Clash, Sex Pistols, Rolling Stones, The Who, Jimi Hendrix and Pink Floyd once performed, was completely destroyed. Partially funded by the people of Hastings, the pier reopened in 2016 as a multipurpose entertainment space with a fish-and-chip shop, shops and vintage funfair rides. See the website for events such as open-air film screenings and concerts.

🛏 Sleeping

The Laindons
B&B ££

(☏01424-437710; www.thelaindons.com; 23 High St; s/d from £110/125; 🖤) Occupying a Georgian grade II–listed former coaching inn, this cosy B&B is just five minutes' amble from the seafront at the quieter end of High St. The five beautifully appointed rooms flood with sea-refracted light from the huge Georgian windows, illuminating the blend of breezy contemporary design and antique furnishings. Owner-cooked breakfasts are taken around a communal table.

★Swan House
B&B £££

(☏01424-430014; www.swanhousehastings.co.uk; 1 Hill St; s/d from £90/130; @🖤) Inside its 15th-century timbered shell, this place blends contemporary and vintage chic to perfection.

The four rooms feature organic toiletries, fresh flowers, hand-painted walls and huge beds. The guest lounge, where pale sofas, painted floorboards and striking modern sculpture rub shoulders with beams and a huge stone fireplace, is a stunner.

🍴 Eating & Drinking

St Mary in the Castle
CAFE £

(www.stmaryinthecastle.co.uk; Pelham Pl; mains £4.50-10; ☉10am-6pm Sun-Thu, to 10pm Fri & Sat; 🖤) Amid the greasy cafes that line the seafront it's a relief to find this laid-back oasis of decent food offering nutritious titbits such as tofu on toast, halloumi kebabs and a range of tempting specials. The cafe is part of a larger arts centre and gallery, the latter in the crypt of the church above and free to enter.

Hanushka Coffee House
CAFE

(28 George St; ☉9.30am-6pm) Hastings' best caffeine stop resembles a very well-stocked secondhand bookshop with every inch of wall space packed with browsable titles. The low-lit and tightly packed space in between provokes inter-table interaction, or you can seek sanctuary on the sofas and perches in the window.

ℹ Information

Tourist Office (☏01424-451111; www.visit1066country.com; Muriel Matters House, Pelham Pl; ☉9am-5pm Mon-Fri, 10am-3pm Sat & Sun)

ℹ Getting There & Away

BUS

Hastings has the following bus connections:
Battle (£3.20, 28 minutes, hourly)
Eastbourne (Bus 99; £5.20, 75 minutes, three hourly)
London Victoria (National Express; from £7.40, 2¾ hours, daily)
Rye (Bus 100/101; £6.40, 40 minutes, twice hourly)

TRAIN

Hastings has connections with Brighton (£13.90, one hour to 80 minutes, two hourly), via Eastbourne, London Charing Cross (£24.40, two hours, at least hourly), Battle (£4.30, 15 minutes, twice hourly) and Rye (£5.60, 18 minutes, hourly).

ℹ Getting Around

Hastings has two delightful old Victorian funiculars, the East Hill Cliff and West Hill Cliff Railways, useful if you need to get up onto the cliffs and don't fancy the walk. The **East Hill Cliff Railway** (Rock-A-Nore Rd; adult/child return £2.70/1.70; ⊘10am-5.30pm Apr-Sep, 11am-4pm Sat & Sun Oct-Mar) funicular ascends from the Stade to Hastings Country Park, while the **West Hill Cliff Railway** (George St; adult/child return £2.70/1.70; ⊘10am-5.30pm Mar-Sep, 11am-4pm Oct-Mar) funicular saves visitors' legs when climbing up to Hastings Castle. Otherwise the town can be easily tackled on foot.

Eastbourne

📞 01323 / POP 103,000

Despite its semi-official title as 'Britain's sunniest town', Eastbourne has been slow to throw off its unattractive image as death's waiting room by the chilly Channel, all snoozing octogenarians in deckchairs and fusty guesthouses populated by vitamin D–deprived bank-holidaying Scots. But while much of this is still to be found here, since the mid-noughties an influx of students and the arrival of the southeast's largest Portuguese and Polish communities have given the town a sprightlier feel.

Eastbourne's 3.5-mile sweeping, palm-tree-lined seafront is one of the UK's grandest. Add to this a fresh modern art gallery and the South Downs National Park that nudges its western suburbs and Eastbourne certainly makes an enjoyable day trip from London or Brighton. It's also the start and end point for a hike along the 100-mile South Downs Way.

🛏 Sleeping & Eating

Albert & Victoria   B&B ££
(📞01323-730948; www.albertandvictoria.com; 19 St Aubyns Rd; s/d from £45/80; 🖥) Book ahead to stay at this delightful Victorian terraced house, whose fragrant rooms, canopied beds, crystal chandeliers and secluded walled garden for summer breakfasts are mere paces from the seafront promenade. The four rooms are named after four of Queen Victoria's offspring.

Half Man! Half Burger!   BURGERS £
(www.halfmanhalfburger.com; 43 Grove Rd; burgers around £8; ⊘noon-10pm Wed-Sat, to 8pm Sun; 🖥) An island of cool in fusty Eastbourne, HMHB invites you to take a lifejacket-orange seat under bare lightbulbs to enjoy belly-packing burgers containing locally sourced beer, washed on its way with pricey craft beer. The half kid! half burger! £5

menu is a steal and there are several vegie/vegan burgers on the menu.

Lamb Inn   PUB FOOD ££
(📞01323-720545; www.thelambeastbourne.co.uk; 36 High St; mains £9-17; ⊘11am-11pm Sun-Thu, to midnight Fri & Sat) This ancient Eastbourne institution, less than a mile northwest of the train station in the under-visited Old Town, has been plonking Sussex ales on the bar for eight centuries, and now also serves gourmet British pub grub. A holidaying Charles Dickens left a few smudged napkins here when he stayed across the road. Buses 1, 1A and 13 stop nearby.

🛍 Shopping

⭐**Camilla's Bookshop**   BOOKS
(📞01323-736001; www.camillasbookshop.com; 57 Grove Rd; ⊘10am-5pm Mon-Sat) Literally packed to the rafters with over half a million musty volumes, this incredible secondhand-book repository, an interesting amble from the train station, fills three floors of a crumbling Victorian town house. It's the best place to source preloved reading matter on the south coast, if not the entire southeast.

❶ Information

Tourist Office (📞01323-415415; www.visiteastbourne.com; Cornfield Rd; ⊘9am-5.30pm Mon-Fri, to 5pm Sat, 10am-1pm Sun May-Sep, closed Sun & shorter hours Oct-Apr) Tourist information plus tickets to anything happening in Eastbourne.

❶ Getting There & Away

BUS
There are buses to Brighton (bus 12; £4.20, 75 minutes, up to every 10 minutes) and Hastings (bus 99; £5.20, 75 minutes, three hourly).

TRAIN
Twice-hourly trains service Brighton (£11.10, 30 to 40 minutes) and London Victoria (£18.70, 1½ hours).

South Downs National Park

The South Downs National Park (www.southdowns.gov.uk), England's newest, is more than 600 sq miles of rolling chalk downs stretching west from Eastbourne to Winchester, a distance of about 100 miles. The South Downs Way extends its entire length. The park is all about rolling English

---

DON'T MISS

CHARTWELL

The home of Sir Winston Churchill from 1924 until his death in 1965, **Chartwell** (NT; www.nationaltrust.org.uk; Westerham; £14.40; ☉ 11.30am-5pm Mar-Oct), 6 miles west of Sevenoaks, offers a breathtakingly intimate insight into the life of England's famous cigar-chomping bombast. This 19th-century house and its rambling grounds have been preserved much as Winnie left them, full of books, pictures, maps and personal mementos. Churchill was also a prolific painter and his now extremely valuable daubings are scattered throughout the house and fill the garden studio.

Transport options are limited without a car. Take a taxi from the nearest train station, Edenbridge (4 miles), accessible from London Victoria.

---

countryside and views down to the coast, a delight at any time of year, though May to October is the best time to come.

⊙ Sights & Activities

Beachy Head   LANDMARK
(www.beachyhead.org.uk) The famous cliffs of Beachy Head are the highest point of the chalky rock faces that slice across the rugged coastline at the southern end of the South Downs. It's off the B2103, from the A259 between Eastbourne and Newhaven. From here the stunning **Seven Sisters Cliffs** undulate their way west. A clifftop path (a branch of the South Downs Way) rides the waves of chalk as far as picturesque Cuckmere Haven.

Beachy Head is a spot of thrilling beauty, the brilliant white chalk rising high into the blue Sussex sky. But on a darker note, it is also known as one of Europe's most frequented suicide spots.

Along the clifftop path, you'll stumble upon the tiny seaside hamlet of **Birling Gap**. The cafe here is closed due to cliff falls but the secluded beach is still a sun-trap popular with locals and walkers taking a breather.

Pevensey Castle   RUINS
(EH; www.english-heritage.org.uk; Castle Rd, Pevensey; adult/concession/child £6.50/5.90/3.90; ☉ 10am-6pm Apr-Sep, to 5pm Oct, weekends only Nov-Mar) The ruins of William the Conqueror's first stronghold sit 5 miles east of Eastbourne, just off the A259. Regular train services between London Victoria and Hastings via Eastbourne stop at Westham, half a mile from Pevensey. Picturesquely dissolving into its own moat, the castle marks the point where William the Conqueror landed in 1066, just two weeks before the Battle of Hastings.

🛏 Sleeping & Eating

★ **Belle Tout Lighthouse**   B&B £££
(☎ 01323-423185; www.belletout.co.uk; South Downs Way, Beachy Head; d from £170) Perched precariously close to the edge of the white cliffs, this early 18th-century decommissioned lighthouse somehow manages to contain six rooms, all imaginatively done out and all rather restricted space-wise. But the highlight must be the lantern lounge, a circular guest seating area in the glass top of the building, the perfect place to enjoy a truly memorable Sussex sunset.

Tiger Inn   PUB FOOD ££
(The Green, East Dean; mains £6-14; ☉ noon-10pm; 🖥) Located back from the cliffs, in the village of East Dean, the 15th-century Tiger Inn is one of Sussex' best taverns serving a gastropub menu to walkers and day trippers alike. In summer the action spills out onto the village green. East Dean is served by bus 12.

❶ Getting There & Away

Bus 12 (up to every 10 minutes) heads through some of the South Downs National Park on the way to Brighton. A great place to alight is Cuckmere Haven from where you can walk back to Eastbourne across the Seven Sisters. Bus 99 (every 20 minutes) runs from Eastbourne to Pevensey.

Lewes

📞 01273 / POP 17,300

Strung out along an undulating High St flanked by elegant Georgian buildings, a part-ruined castle and a traditional brewery, Lewes (pronounced 'Lewis') is a charmingly affluent hillside town with a turbulent past and fiery traditions. Off the main drag, however, there's a more intimate atmosphere as you descend into twisting narrow streets called twittens – the remainder of the town's original medieval street plan.

One of Lewes' claims to fame is that it straddles the 0 degrees line of longitude. An inconspicuous plaque on Western Rd marks the meridian, though modern measuring methods have actually placed the line around 100m to the east.

Lewes also holds what it claims is the biggest Bonfire Night bash in the world with tens of thousands of people descending on the town on 5 November to watch a carnival, fireworks display and effigies of villains of the day going up in flames.

🛏 Sleeping & Eating

Shelleys HOTEL £££
(☎ 01273-472361; www.the-shelleys.co.uk; 135-136 High St; r from £130; 🛜) Lewes' top address is a 16th-century manor house full of grand old-fashioned charm. It was once home to the earl of Dorset and was owned by the Shelley family (of Percy Bysshe fame). The stylish, country rooms are the best in Lewes and there's an above standard restaurant overlooking a lovely walled garden.

Riverside FOOD HALL
(www.riverside-lewes.co.uk; Cliffe Bridge; ⊙9am-5pm) Housed in a former garage next to the river, this food hall and market is a fine place for coffee and cakes or a full sit-down brasserie meal in one of several small eateries inside.

Bill's CAFE ££
(www.bills-website.co.uk; 56 Cliffe High St; mains £10-16; ⊙8am-11pm; 🛜) Part grocers, part delicatessen, part rustic-styled cafe, this insanely popular place envelops customers in its colours and smells then dishes up melt-in-the-mouth tartlets, gourmet pizzas, salads, desserts and other artisanal snacks. Get here early at meal times, and even in-between times, as it's normally chock-a-block.

🛈 Information

Tourist Office (☎ 01273-483448; www.lewes. gov.uk; 187 High St; ⊙9.30am-4.30pm Mon-Fri, to 4pm Sat, 10am-2pm Sun Apr-Sep, closed Sun & shorter hours Sat Oct-Mar)

🛈 Getting There & Away

Lewes has the following rail connections:
Brighton (£4.40, 15 minutes, four hourly)
Eastbourne (£8, 20 minutes, four hourly)
London Victoria (£17, one hour to 1½ hours, three hourly)

Brighton & Hove

☎ 01273 / POP 260,000

Raves on the beach, Graham Greene novels, mods and rockers in bank-holiday fisticuffs, naughty weekends for Mr and Mrs Smith, the UK's biggest gay scene and the Channel's best clubbing – this coastal city evokes many images for the British. But one thing is certain: with its bohemian, hedonistic vibe, Brighton is where England's seaside experience goes from cold to cool.

Brighton is without doubt Britain's most colourful and outrageous city. Here burlesque meets contemporary design; grotty hostels share thin walls with kinky boutique hotels; microbrewed ales share bar space with 'sex on the beach'; and stags watch drag. The city returned the UK's first Green Party MP, Valentine's Day is celebrated with unusual gusto, and according to the 2001 census, it has the UK's highest Jedi population.

CANTERBURY & SOUTHEAST ENGLAND BRIGHTON & HOVE

THE CHANNEL ISLANDS

Just off the coast of France, Jersey, Guernsey, Sark, Herm and Alderney beckon with exquisite coastlines, shaded lanes and old-world charm. Not quite Britain and not quite France, the islands are proudly independent, self-governing British Crown dependencies that straddle the gap between the two. Their citizens owe their allegiance to Her Majesty, but some still speak local dialects that stem from medieval Norman French.

The warm Gulf of St Malo ensures subtropical plants and an incredible array of birdlife. The Channel Islands enjoy sunnier days and milder winters than the UK, attracting walkers and outdoorsy types for surfing, kayaking, coasteering and diving. Superb local seafood graces the tables of local restaurants in the culture hubs of St Helier (Guernsey) and St Peter Port (Jersey).

Numerous forts and castles dot the coastlines, while poignant museums – some housed in old war tunnels and bunkers – provide an insight into the islanders' fortitude during WWII.

There are daily flights to Guernsey from London Gatwick, as well as from Jersey, Manchester, Birmingham, Southampton, Bristol and London Stansted. Jersey receives daily flights from all major London airports bar Heathrow, as well as from Liverpool, Birmingham, Southampton, Cardiff, Exeter and Guernsey, as well as several flights from Europe.

Brighton & Hove

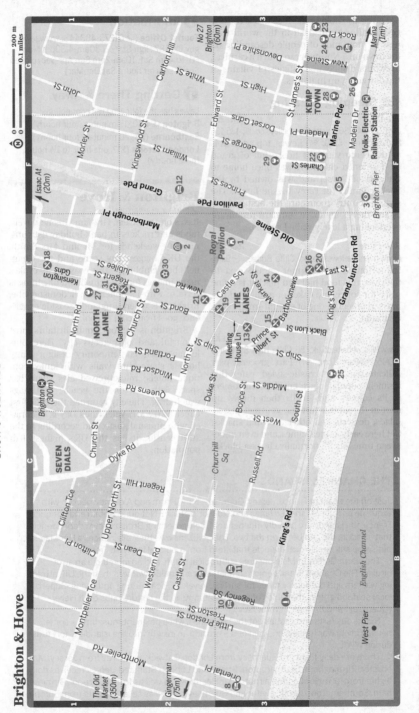

200 m
0.1 miles

The Old Market (350m)

Gingerman (75m)

Montpelier Rd

Montpelier Tce

Clifton Pl

Clifton Tce

SEVEN DIALS

Church St

Dyke Rd

Regent Hill

Upper North St

Dean St

Western Rd

Castle St

Oriental Pl

Preston St

Little Preston St

Regency Sq

West Pier

English Channel

Brighton (300m)

Queens Rd

Windsor Rd

Church St

North Rd

NORTH LAINE

Gardner St

Isaac At (20m)

Kensington Gdns

Jubilee St

Regent St

New Rd

Bond St

Ship St

Portland St

Meeting House Ln

Duke St

Middle St

Boyce St

West St

South St

Churchill Sq

Russell Rd

King's Rd

Marlborough Pl

Grand Pde

Royal Pavilion

Castle Sq

THE LANES

Market St

Prince Albert St

Black Lion St

Bartholomews

East St

King's Rd

Ship St

Old Steine

Pavilion Pde

Princes St

Charles St

George St

Dorset Gdns

Edward St

High St

St James's St

KEMP TOWN

Madeira Pl

Marine Pde

Madeira Dr

Grand Junction Rd

East St

King's Rd

Brighton Pier

Volks Electric Railway Station

Marina (1mi)

New Steine

Rock Pl

Devonshire Pl

No 27 Brighton (60m)

Carlton Hill

White St

William St

Kingswood St

Marley St

John St

1   Royal Pavilion
2
5
6
7
8
10
11
12
14
15
16
17
18
19
20
21
22
23
24
25
26
27
28
29
30
31
3
4

Brighton & Hove

The highlight for the sightseeing visitor is the Royal Pavilion, a 19th-century party palace built by the Prince Regent, who kicked off Brighton's love of the outlandish.

◎ Sights

★ **Royal Pavilion**　　　　　　　　　PALACE
(📞03000 290900; http://brightonmuseums.org.uk/royalpavilion; Royal Pavilion Gardens; adult/concession/child£13/11.50/8; ⊙9.30am-5.45pm Apr-Sep, 10am-5.15pm Oct-Mar) The Royal Pavilion is the city's must-see attraction. The glittering party pad and palace of Prince George, later Prince Regent and then King George IV, it's one of the most opulent buildings in England, and certainly the finest example of early 19th-century chinoiserie anywhere in Europe. It's an apt symbol for Brighton's reputation for decadence. An unimpressed Queen Victoria called the Royal Pavilion 'a strange, odd Chinese place', but for visitors to Brighton it's an unmissable chunk of Sussex history.

The entire palace is an eye-popping spectacle, but some interiors stand out even amid the riot of decoration. The dragon-themed banqueting hall must be the most incredible in all of England. More dragons and snakes writhe in the music room, with its ceiling of 26,000 gold scales, and the then-state-of-the-art kitchen must have wowed Georgians with its automatic spits and hot tables. Prince Albert carted away all of the

furniture, some of which has been loaned back by the present queen.

Brighton Museum & Art Gallery　　　　MUSEUM, GALLERY
(https://brightonmuseums.org.uk; Royal Pavilion Gardens; adult/concession/child £5.20/4.20/3; ⊙10am-5pm Tue-Sun) Set in the Royal Pavilion's renovated stable block, this museum and art gallery has a glittering collection of 20th-century art and design, including a crimson Salvador Dalí sofa modelled on Mae West's lips. There's also an enthralling gallery of world art, an impressive collection of Egyptian artefacts, and an 'Images of Brighton' multimedia exhibit containing a series of oral histories and a model of the defunct West Pier.

Brighton Pier　　　　　　　　　　LANDMARK
(www.brightonpier.co.uk; Madeira Dr) This grand old Edwardian pier is the place to experience Brighton's tackier side. There are plenty of stomach-churning fairground rides and noisy amusement arcades to keep you entertained, and candy floss and Brighton rock to chomp on while you're doing so. Just west are the sad remains of the West Pier (p178), a skeletal iron hulk that attracts flocks of starlings at sunset.

i360 Tower　　　　　　　　　　　TOWER
(📞03337-720360; www.britishairwaysi360.com; Lower King's Rd; adult/concession/child £16/13.50/

8.25; ⊙10am-7.30pm Sun-Thu, to 9.30pm Fri & Sat) Brighton's newest attraction opened in 2016, at the point the now defunct West Pier used to make landfall. The world's most slender tower is a brutal, 162m-tall column of reinforced steel and concrete rising like a space-age phallus (this is Brighton after all) from the seafront, with a huge, impaled, glass doughnut taking 'passengers' 138m above the city for some gob-smacking vistas of the Sussex coast.

Hove Museum & Art Gallery MUSEUM, GALLERY (https://brighton museums.org.uk; 19 New Church Rd; ⊙10am-5pm Mon, Tue & Thu-Sat, 2-5pm Sun) FREE Hove can justifiably claim to be the birthplace of British cinema, with the first short film shot here in 1898. You can see it alongside other fascinating films at this attractive Victorian villa. Another highlight is the kids' room, which is full of fairy lights and reverberates to the snores of a wizard and the whir of an underfloor train. It's 2 miles from Churchill Sq; take bus 1, 1A, 6 or 49 from there.

SEA LIFE Brighton AQUARIUM (☑01273-604234; www.visitsealife.com/brighton; Marine Pde; £19; ⊙10am-5pm; ⚑) Not just for children, this aquarium is an underground exhibition of nature's fascinating water creatures. Walking around the church-like interior, visitors can get up close to eels, tropical fish and other sealife. For those who are keen, there are opportunities to feed the animals, touch starfish and ride a glass-bottomed boat over a pool of sharks, rays and turtles.

West Pier WATERFRONT (www.westpier.co.uk) The historic West Pier, which closed in 1975, began to collapse into the sea in December 2002 and, having since caught fire twice, is just a dark shadow on the water. It's a sad end for this Victorian marvel, where the likes of Charlie Chaplin and Stan Laurel once performed. Nevertheless it's still quite an arresting, beautiful sight though the only flocks of visitors now are the thousands of starlings who swoop around it in winter.

☞ Tours

Brighton Food Tours FOOD & DRINK (☑07985 230955; www.brightonfoodtours.com; Brighton Unitarian Church, New Rd; per person £40-65; ⊙Fri & Sat) Two enthusiastic local ladies show off the best of Brighton via a trail of tasters and tales. The walking tours highlight

up to 10 small and independent businesses, in keeping with the town's creative vibe. Tour options include Very Independent Brighton, Drink Brighton and Wine Rebellion. Bring comfy shoes and an empty stomach.

✦ Festivals & Events

Brighton Festival PERFORMING ARTS (☑01273-709709; www.brightonfestival.org; ⊙May) After Edinburgh, this is the UK's biggest arts festival. It draws star performers from around the globe for three weeks by the sea.

Brighton Fringe PERFORMING ARTS (www.brightonfringe.org; ⊙May) As with the famous Edinburgh Festival, the Brighton Festival has its fringe, a month of irreverent comedy, art and theatre at numerous venues around the city.

Brighton Pride LGBT (www.brighton-pride.org; ⊙early Aug) The UK's biggest gay bash with a rainbow-hued parade and concerts in Preston Park.

🛏 Sleeping

Kipps Brighton HOSTEL £ (☑01273-604182; www.kipps-brighton.com; 76 Grand Pde; dm £15-35, d £42-92; @☎) The owners of Canterbury's award-winning hostel have created equally commendable budget digs here in Brighton. There's a real cafe vibe around reception, and facilities include a communal kitchen. Free movie, pizza and pub nights are intended to seperate guests from their wi-fi-enabled devices.

Baggies Backpackers HOSTEL £ (☑01273-733740; www.baggiesbackpackers.com; 33 Oriental Pl; dm from £16; ☎) With a warm, familial atmosphere, worn-in charm, attentive service and clean, snug dorms, this long-established hostel is a Brighton institution. There's a cosy basement music and chill-out room, and a TV lounge. The hostel has sister establishments in London and Bournemouth.

★ No 27 Brighton B&B ££ (☑01273-694951; www.brighton-bed-and-breakfast. co.uk; 27 Upper Rock Gardens; r £100-160; ☎) Brighton's top B&B has five sumptuous rooms, perfectly done out with antique flourish. All the fabrics, furniture and decoration have been painstakingly selected to fit an understated theme, based on people related to King George IV. Some rooms have sea views, but the superb decor may have you looking around more than out.

Hotel Pelirocco
HOTEL ££

(☑ 01273-327055; www.hotelpelirocco.co.uk; 10 Regency Sq; s/d from £59/89; 🛜) One of Brighton's sexiest and nuttiest places to stay, the Pelirocco has become the ultimate venue for a flirty rock-and-roll weekend. Flamboyant rooms, some designed by artists, include the 'Lord Vader's Quarters' paying homage to Star Wars, the 'Modrophenia' room on a mod and pop art theme, and the 'Pretty Vacant' double, a shrine to the Sex Pistols.

Blanch House
BOUTIQUE HOTEL ££

(☑ 01273-603504; www.blanchhouse.co.uk; 17 Atlingworth St; r from £110; 🛜) Themed rooms are the name of the game at this boutique hotel, but there's nothing tacky about them – swish art deco styling rules in the Legacia Room, while the Snowstorm is a frosty vision in white and tinkling ice. The magnificently stylish fine-dining restaurant is all white leather banquettes and space-age swivel chairs and there's a fine cocktail bar.

Snooze
HOTEL ££

(☑ 01273-605797; www.snoozebrighton.com; 25 St George's Tce; s/d from £75/95; 🛜) The retro styling at this eccentric Kemptown pad features everything from vintage posters and bright '60s and '70s wallpaper to Bollywood film ads, floral sinks and mad clashes of colour. It's more than just a gimmick – the rooms are comfortable and spotless, and there are great meat-free breakfasts. You'll find it just off St James' St, about 500m east of New Steine.

★ Artist Residence
BOUTIQUE HOTEL £££

(☑ 01273-324302; www.artistresidencebrighton. co.uk; 34 Regency Sq; d £120-290; 🛜) Eclectic doesn't quite describe the rooms at this wonderful 23-room town-house hotel, set amid the splendour of Regency Sq. As befits the name, every bedroom is a work of funky art with bold wall murals, bespoke and vintage furniture, rough wood cladding and in-room roll-top baths. The Set Restaurant downstairs has a glowing reputation.

★ Hotel Una
BOUTIQUE HOTEL £££

(☑ 01273-820464; www.hotel-una.co.uk; 55-56 Regency Sq; s £55-75, d £115-200, all incl breakfast; ❄🛜) All of the 19 generous rooms here wow guests with their bold-patterned fabrics, supersized leather sofas, in-room free-standing baths and vegan, veggie or carnivorous

breakfast in bed. Some, such as the two-level suite with its own mini-cinema, and the under-pavement chambers with their own spa, are truly show-stopping and not as expensive as you might expect.

Drakes
BOUTIQUE HOTEL £££

(☑ 01273-696934; www.drakesofbrighton.com; 43-44 Marine Pde; r £115-300; ℗❄@🛜) This stylishly minimalist boutique hotel oozes understated class. So understated is the entrance, in fact, you could easily miss it. All rooms have similar decor in bold fabrics and European elm panelling, but it's the feature rooms everyone wants – their giant free-standing tubs are set in front of full-length bay windows with widescreen Channel views. The basement restaurant is superb.

✕ Eating

★ Iydea
VEGETARIAN £

(www.iydea.co.uk; 17 Kensington Gardens; mains £5-8; ⊙9.30am-5.30pm; 🛜🖉) Even by Brighton's high standards, the food at this multi-award-winning vegetarian cafe is a treat. The daily-changing choices of curries, lasagnes, felafel, enchiladas and quiches are full of flavour and can be washed down with a selection of vegan wines, organic ales and homemade lemonades. If you're on the hop, you can get any dish to takeaway in plastic-free packaging.

Wahaca
MEXICAN £

(☑ 01273-934763; www.wahaca.co.uk; cnr North St & New Rd; mains £5-12; ⊙noon-11pm Mon-Sat, to 10.30pm Sun; 🛜) 🖉 The Brighton branch of this national chain is a bright, colourful affair where Mexican street food lands on multihued tables amid eclectic, retro decor. The recipes for the various tacos, tostados and burritos were brought home by the owner after travelling in Mexico, so authenticity is guaranteed. Lots of seats so there's always a free spot.

Choccywoccydoodah
CAFE £

(www.choccywoccydoodah.com; 3 Meeting House Lane; cakes & snacks £2-8; ⊙10am-6pm Mon-Sat, 11am-5pm Sun) Even if you're not hungry or thirsty, this incredible chocolate emporium, painted blood red inside and out, is a must-see. The downstairs is packed with outrageous chocolate creations, fake rococo mirrors, sprays of artificial flowers and tassled lampshades. Head upstairs to the small cafe where every item on sale contains chocolate. Madly popular so be prepared to queue.

THE LANES

In the market for a pair of vegan shoes, a gauche portrait of a Lego man or a letter opener in the shape of a ...? Well, whatever item you yearn for, old or new, you'll probably find it in Brighton. Visit Brighton produces a useful *Shopping, Eating and Drinking Guide* that divides the city up into its main areas.

The tightly packed Lanes is the most popular shopping district, its every twist and turn jam-packed with jewellers and gift shops, coffee shops and boutiques selling everything from antique firearms to hard-to-find vinyl.

There's another, less-claustrophobic shopping district in North Laine, a series of partially pedestrianised thoroughfares north of the Lanes, including Bond, Gardner, Kensington and Sydney Sts, lined with retro-cool boutiques and bohemian cafes.

Infinity Foods Kitchen VEGETARIAN £
(www.infinityfoodskitchen.co.uk; 50 Gardner St; mains £4-9; ⊙9am-5pm Mon-Sat, 10am-4pm Sun; 🛜🖉) The sister establishment of Infinity Foods wholefoods shop (health-food cooperative and Brighton institution) serves a wide variety of vegetarian and organic food, with many vegan and wheat- or gluten-free options including tofu burgers, mezze platters and veggie sausage sandwiches. There's seating upstairs with views of the passing hipster mob and wooden takeaway cutlery to reduce plastic waste.

★ Terre à Terre VEGETARIAN ££
(📞01273-729051; www.terreaterre.co.uk; 71 East St; mains from £15; ⊙noon-10.30pm Tue-Fri, 11am-11pm Sat, 11am-10pm Sun; 🖉🖣) Take your taste buds around the world without any meat in sight. In this vegetarian restaurant, inventive and flavourful dishes are meticulously plated and the ambience is casual and friendly. For the unconverted, there are nods to nonvegetarian favourites, including battered halloumi and chips, and KFC (Korean Fried Cauliflower). Order the sharing plate for statement elements of the main dishes.

English's of Brighton SEAFOOD ££
(📞01273-327980; www.englishs.co.uk; 29-31 East St; mains £10-30; ⊙noon-10pm) A 75-year-old institution and celebrity haunt, this local seafood paradise dishes up everything from Essex oysters to locally caught lobster and Dover sole. It's converted from fishers' cottages, with shades of the elegant style of the Edwardian era inside, and has alfresco dining on the pedestrian square outside.

Riddle & Finns SEAFOOD ££
(📞01273-721667; www.riddleandfinns.co.uk; 12b Meeting House Lane; mains £14.50-22.50; ⊙noon-10pm Sun-Fri, 11.30am-11pm Sat) Regarded as the town's most refined seafood spot, R&F is light on gimmicky interiors (think white butcher-shop tiles, marble tables and candles) but heavy on taste. With the kitchen open to the street outside, chefs put on a public cooking class with every dish as they prepare your smoked haddock in champagne sauce or some wild sea bass.

Indian Summer INDIAN ££
(📞01273-711001; www.indiansummerbrighton.co.uk; 70 East St; lunch mains £6-14, 2/3 course set dinner menu £28/33; ⊙6-10.30pm Mon-Wed, noon-3pm & 6-10.30pm Thu & Fri, noon-10.30pm Sat, noon-3pm & 6-10pm Sun; 🖉🖣) Brighton's best Indian outfit boasts typical British Indian decor (think high-back, leatherette chairs and modern fittings) and serves a multitude of dishes from across the subcontinent. There's a kids' menu, lots of meat-free choices and rare dishes such as Indian mussels and beef. Regularly voted one of the UK's best Indian restaurants.

Food for Friends VEGETARIAN ££
(📞01273-202310; www.foodforfriends.com; 17-18 Prince Albert St; mains £6-16; ⊙noon-10pm Sun-Thu, to 10.30pm Fri & Sat; 🖉) An ever-inventive choice of vegetarian and vegan food keeps bringing locals back for seconds and thirds at this place to see and be seen – literally, by every passerby through the huge street-side windows. Kept fresh-looking and as popular as it has been since 1981, you should be prepared to wait for a table on busy shopping days.

Gingerman MODERN EUROPEAN ££
(📞01273-326688; www.gingermanrestaurants.com; 21a Norfolk Sq; 2-/3-course menu £17/20; ⊙12.30-2pm & 7-10pm Tue-Sun) Hastings seafood, Sussex beef, Romney Marsh lamb, local sparkling wines and countless other seasonal, local and British treats go into the adroitly flash-fried and slow-cooked dishes served at this snug 32-cover eatery. Reservations are advised. Norfolk Sq is a short walk west along Western Rd from the Churchill Sq shopping centre.

Isaac At
BRITISH **£££**

(☑ 07765 934740; www.isaac-at.com; 2 Glouces-ter St; tasting menu £55, set menu £40; ⊘ 6.30-10.30pm Tue-Fri, 12.30-2.30pm & 6.30-10.30pm Sat) Tucked on a street corner is this in-timate fine-dining restaurant run by a small team of culinary talent, all aged under 30. Every ingredient is locally sourced, includ-ing the wines, with food miles for each in-gredient noted on the menu. It's probably the homeliest high-end dining experience in the area. First-class, fresh and thoughtful food.

Drinking & Nightlife

Concorde 2
CLUB

(www.concorde2.co.uk; Madeira Dr; ☎) Bright-on's best-known and best-loved club is a disarmingly unpretentious den, where DJ Fatboy Slim pioneered the Big Beat Bou-tique and still occasionally graces the decks. Each month there's a huge variety of club nights, live bands and concerts by interna-tional names.

Patterns
CLUB

(www.patternsbrighton.com; 10 Marine Pde; ⊘ Wed-Sat, hours vary; ☎) Some of the city's top club nights are held at this ear-numbing venue. The music is top priority here, at-tracting big name acts and a young, up-for-it crowd.

Coalition
BAR

(www.coalitionbrighton.com; 171-181 Kings Rd Arches; ⊘ 10am-5am Mon-Fri, to 7am Sat; ☎) On a summer's day, there's nowhere finer to sit and watch the world go by than at this popular beach bar, diner and club. All sorts of events happen here, from comedy to live music and club nights.

Black Dove
PUB

(www.blackdovebrighton.com; 74 St James's St; ⊘ 4pm-late) Eclectic hang-out with shab-by-chic furnishings, huge antique ceiling fans, a bar stocked with unusual tipples and a quirky basement snug. Live acoustic music and local DJs provide the soundtrack for evening quaffing that spills out onto the pavements when the mercury is high.

Dorset
PUB

(www.thedorset.co.uk; 28 North Rd; ⊘ 9.30am-mid-night Sun-Thu, to 1am Fri & Sat; ☎) In fine weath-er this laid-back Brighton institution throws open its doors and windows, and tables spill out onto the pavement. You'll be just as wel-come for a morning coffee as for an evening pint here, and should you not leave between the two, there's a decent gastropub menu.

☆ Entertainment

Komedia Theatre
COMEDY

(☑ 01273-647100; www.komedia.co.uk; 44-47 Gard-ner St) The UK's top comedy venue attracts

---

GAY & LESBIAN BRIGHTON

Brighton has the most vibrant LGBT community in the country outside London. Kemp-town (aka Camptown) on and off St James's St is where it's all at. The old Brunswick Town area of Hove is a quieter alternative to the traditionally cruisy (and sometimes seedy) scene in Kemptown.

For up-to-date information on the LGBT scene in Brighton, check out www.realbrigh ton.com, or pick up the free monthly magazine *Gscene* (www.gscene.com) from LGBT venues.

Brighton Rocks (☑ 01273-600550; www.brightonrocksbar.co.uk; 6 Rock Pl; ⊘ 4-11pm Mon-Thu, noon-1am Fri & Sat, noon-9pm Sun; ☎) Incongruously located in an alley of garages and used-car lots, this cocktail bar is firmly established on the Kemptown gay scene, but welcomes all-comers with Sussex martinis, well-executed plates of food and theme parties.

Legends Club (www.legendsbrighton.com; 31-34 Marine Pde; ⊘ bar 11am-5am, club 10pm-5am Wed & Fri-Sun; ☎) Located beneath the Legends Hotel this is arguably the best gay bar and club in town.

A Bar (☑ 01273-688826; 11-12 Marine Pde; ⊘ noon-2am; ☎) Extremely hip bar and sauna in the Amsterdam Hotel; its sun terrace is a particular hit.

Queen's Arms (www.theqabrighton.com; 7 George St; ⊘ 5pm-late Mon-Fri, from 2pm Sat & Sun) And they ain't talking Victoria or Elizabeth! Plenty of camp cabaret and karaoke at this pub.

the best stand-up acts from the English-speaking world. Book well in advance.

The Old Market   THEATRE
(☑ 01273-201801; www.theoldmarket.com; 11a Upper Market St) TOM has emerged as Hove's top venue for alternative theatre, comedy and live music, all performed in front of small crowds seated cafe-style in an informal space. The stage sees an eclectic mix to say the least with everything from grotesque mime and gay comedy to quirky Shakespeare and local bands on the programme.

Brighton Dome   THEATRE
(☑ 01273-709709; www.brightondome.org; Church St) Once the stables for King George IV's horses, this art deco complex houses three theatre venues within the Royal Pavilion estate. ABBA famously won the 1974 Eurovision Song Contest here. The Dome was under renovation at time of research.

ℹ Information

Incredibly, Brighton closed its busy tourist office in 2013, replacing it with 15 information points across the city, mostly racks of brochures in hotels, shops and museums (two of these aren't even in Brighton itself). Contact **Visit Brighton** (☑ 01273-290337; www.visitbrighton.com) for information.

ℹ Getting There & Away

BUS
Standard bus connections:
Eastbourne (Bus 12; £4.60, 75 minutes, up to every 10 minutes)
Lewes (Bus 28/29; £3.10, 30 minutes, up to every 10 minutes)
London Victoria (National Express; from £9, 2½ hours, at least every two hours)

TRAIN
London-bound services pass through Gatwick Airport (£8.80, 25 to 35 minutes, up to five hourly).
Arundel (£10.80, 1¼ hours, half-hourly) Change in Barnham.
Chichester (£13.60, 50 minutes, half-hourly)
Eastbourne (£11.10, 30 to 40 minutes, half-hourly)
Hastings (£13.90, one hour to 80 minutes, two hourly)
London St Pancras (£18.10, 1¼ hours, half-hourly)
London Victoria (£26.70, one hour, three-hourly)
Portsmouth (£16, 1½ hours, hourly)

ℹ Getting Around

Day bus tickets (£5) are available from the drivers of all Brighton & Hove buses. Alternatively, a £3.70 PlusBus ticket on top of your rail fare gives unlimited bus travel for the day.

The city operates a pricey pay-and-display parking scheme. In the town centre, it costs between £1 and £3.60 per hour for a maximum stay of two hours. Alternatively, there's a Park & Ride 2.5 miles northwest of the centre at Withdean, from where bus 27 (return £5) zips into town.

Cab companies include **Brighton Streamline Taxis** (☑ 01273-202020; www.streamline-taxis.org) and **Brighton & Hove Radio Cabs** (☑ 01273-204060; www.brightontaxis.com) and there's a taxi rank at the junction of East and Market Sts.

WEST SUSSEX

West Sussex offers a welcome respite from fast-paced adventures. The serene hills and valleys of the South Downs ripple across the county, fringed by sheltered coastline. Beautiful Arundel and cultured Chichester make good bases from which to explore the county's winding country lanes and remarkable Roman ruins.

Arundel

☑ 01903 / POP 3500

Arguably the prettiest town in West Sussex, Arundel is clustered around a vast fairy-tale castle, and its hillside streets overflow with antique emporiums, teashops and a host of eateries. While much of the town appears medieval – the whimsical castle has been home to the dukes of Norfolk for centuries – most of it dates back to Victorian times.

◎ Sights

Arundel Castle   CASTLE
(www.arundelcastle.org; adult/concession/child £22/19.50/11; ⊙ 10am-5pm Tue-Sun Easter-Oct) Arundel Castle was first built in the 11th century but all that's left of the early structure are the modest remains of the keep. It was ransacked during the English Civil War, and most of what you see today is the result of reconstruction by the eighth, 11th and 15th dukes of Norfolk between 1718 and 1900. The current Duke still lives in part of the castle, whose highlights include the atmospheric keep, the massive Great Hall and the library.

Arundel Cathedral
CATHEDRAL

(www.arundelcathedral.org; London Rd; ⊘9am-6pm Apr-Oct, to dusk Nov-Mar) FREE Arundel's ostentatious 19th-century Catholic cathedral is one of the dominating features on the town's impressive skyline. Commissioned by the 15th Duke of Norfolk in 1868, the impressive structure was designed by Joseph Aloysius Hansom (inventor of the Hansom cab) in the French Gothic style, but shows much Victorian economy and restraint. Although small for a cathedral – it holds just 500 worshippers – Hansom's clever layout makes the building seem a lot bigger.

🛏 Sleeping & Eating

Arundel House
B&B ££

(☑ 01903-882136; www.arundelhouseonline.com; 11 High St; d/ste from £90/125; ☜) The contemporary chambers at this lovely 'restaurant with rooms' may be slightly low-ceilinged, but they're clean-cut and very comfortable, with showers big enough for two. The restaurant downstairs serves some of the best food in Arundel, which, happily, extends to breakfast.

Arden Guest House
B&B ££

(☑ 01903-884184; www.ardenhousearundel.com; 4 Queens Lane; d £99, without bathroom £89; Ⓟ☜) For the classic British B&B experience, head to this seven-room guesthouse just over the river from the historical centre. Rooms are kept fresh and tick all the boxes, the hosts are amiable, and the breakfasts are cooked. Only 10% off if you're travelling solo.

★ Town House
BRITISH £££

(☑ 01903-883847; www.thetownhouse.co.uk; 65 High St; set lunch/dinner from £17.50/25.50; ⊘noon-2.30pm & 7-9.30pm Tue-Sat) The only thing that rivals the 16th-century Florentine gilded-walnut ceiling in this compact and very elegant eatery is the sparkling atmosphere and acclaimed British cuisine with a European twist. Dishes such as South Downs venison, south coast cod and roasted partridge are worth a little bit extra – but book ahead. Town House also has well-appointed rooms to let.

❶ Getting There & Away

Arundel has the following train connections:
Brighton (£10.80, 1¼ hours, half-hourly) Change at Barnham or Ford.
Chichester (£4.70, 22 minutes, twice hourly) Change at Ford or Barnham.
London Victoria (£18.70, 1½ hours, twice hourly)

Chichester
☑ 01243 / POP 26.800

A lively Georgian market town still almost encircled by its medieval town walls, the administrative capital of West Sussex keeps watch over the plains between the South Downs and the sea. Visitors flock to Chichester's splendid cathedral, streets of handsome 18th-century town houses and its famous theatre, and of course to its pedestrianised shopping streets packed with big-name and independent shops. A Roman port garrison in its early days, the town is also a launch pad to other fascinating Roman remains, as well as to Arundel and a popular stretch of coast.

⊙ Sights

Chichester Cathedral
CATHEDRAL

(www.chichestercathedral.org.uk; West St; ⊘7.15am-7pm, free tours 11.15am & 2.30pm Mon-Sat) This understated cathedral was begun in 1075 and largely rebuilt in the 13th century. The free-standing church tower went up in the 15th century; the spire dates from the 19th century, when its predecessor famously toppled over. Inside, three storeys of beautiful arches sweep upwards and Romanesque carvings are dotted around. Interesting features to track down include a smudgy stained-glass window added by artist Marc Chagall in 1978 and a glassed-over section of Roman mosaic flooring.

FISHBOURNE ROMAN PALACE

Fishbourne (www.sussexpast.co.uk; Roman Way; adult/concession/child £9.50/8.80/4.90; ⊘10am-5pm Mar-Oct, reduced hours & days rest of the year) is the largest-known Roman residence in Britain. The palace lies 1.5 miles west of Chichester, just off the A259 (take bus 700 from outside Chichester Cathedral). Happened upon by labourers in the 1960s, it's thought that this once-luxurious mansion was built around AD 75 for a romanised local king. Housed in a modern pavilion are its foundations, hypocaust and painstakingly relaid mosaics.

The centrepiece is a spectacular floor depicting Cupid riding a dolphin, flanked by sea horses and panthers. There's also a fascinating little museum and replanted Roman gardens.

Pallant House Gallery GALLERY
(www.pallant.org.uk; 9 North Pallant; adult/child £11/
free; ⊙10am-5pm Tue, Wed, Fri & Sat, to 8pm Thu,
11am-5pm Sun) A Queen Anne mansion built
by a local wine merchant, handsome Pallant
House and a 21st-century wing host this superb gallery. The focus is on mostly British,
20th-century art. Show-stoppers Patrick
Caulfield, Lucian Freud, Graham Sutherland,
Frank Auerbach and Henry Moore are interspersed with international names such as
Emil Filla, Le Corbusier and RB Kitaj. Most
of the older works are in the mansion, while
the newer wing is packed with pop art and
temporary modern and contemporary work.

Chichester City Walls ARCHITECTURE
(www.chichestercitywalls.org) Chichester's almost complete ring of Roman defensive
walls are around 1.5 miles in length, and
provide a pleasant escape from the retail
bustle they now contain. Pick up a leaflet
and booklet from the tourist office (p184)
and head out along the route, much of which
leads through parkland. Built to defend the
town of Noviomagus Reginorum 1800 years
ago, they are just about the most intact set
of Roman city walls in Britain. Best accessed
from West or East Sts.

Novium Museum MUSEUM
(www.thenovium.org; Tower St; ⊙10am-5pm
Mon-Sat, to 4pm Sun Apr-Oct, 10am-5pm Mon-Sat
Nov-Mar) FREE Chichester's purpose-built
museum provides a home for the eclectic
collections of the erstwhile District Museum,
as well as some artefacts from Fishbourne
Palace and a huge mosaic from Chilgrove Roman villa. The highlight is the set of Roman
thermae (baths) discovered in the 1970s,
around which this six-million-pound wedge
of architecture was designed.

🛏️ Sleeping & Eating

Trents B&B ££
(☑01243-773714; 50 South St; d from £64; 🛜)
One of very few places to hit the sack in the
thick of the city centre action, the five snazzy
rooms above this trendy bar-restaurant are
understandably popular. Guests heap praise
on the helpful staff and big breakfast.

Chichester
Harbour Hotel BOUTIQUE HOTEL £££
(☑01243-778000; www.chichester-harbour-hotel.
co.uk; North St; s/d from £112/162; 🛜) Big flashes of colour dominate the period rooms at
this Georgian hotel. It's the most enticing
option in town and it also boasts a stylish
restaurant. Book well ahead.

Duke & Rye AMERICAN £
(www.thedukeandrye.co.uk; 14 West St; mains £4-
14; ⊙11am-11pm Mon-Sat, noon-8pm Sun; 🛜)
Occupying a large deconsecrated church opposite Chichester Cathedral, this temple of
food and ale allows you to refuel and kick
back in an incongruously ecclesiastical setting, dotted with shabby-chic areas of funky
wallpaper, frilly standard lamps and Persian
carpets. The US diner-style menu of burgers
and sundaes is sure to bust your bible belt
and invoke a holy thirst.

ℹ️ Information

Tourist Office (☑01243-775888; www.
visitchichester.org; Tower St; ⊙10am-5pm
Mon-Sat, to 4pm Sun) Located in the Novium
Museum.

ℹ️ Getting There & Away

BUS
Chichester has bus connections to the following:
Brighton (Bus 700; three hours, £5, twice
hourly)
London Victoria (National Express; £23,
three hours 40 minutes, eight daily) Change at
Gatwick Airport.
Portsmouth (Bus 700; £4.70, one hour 10
minutes, twice hourly)

TRAIN
Chichester has train connections to the
following:
Arundel (£4.70, 22 minutes, twice hourly)
Change at Ford or Barnham.
Brighton (£13.60, 50 minutes, half-hourly)
London Victoria (£18.70, 1½ hours, half-
hourly)
Portsmouth (£7.90, 30 to 40 minutes, three
hourly)

Oxford & the Cotswolds

Best Places to Eat

➜ Hind's Head (p230)

➜ Spiced Roots (p197)

➜ Magdalen Arms (p197)

➜ Edamamé (p196)

➜ Le Champignon Sauvage (p221)

➜ Waterside Inn (p230)

Best Places to Stay

➜ Star Cottage (p205)

➜ Barnsley House (p205)

➜ Glove House (p201)

➜ Bradley (p220)

➜ Oxford Coach & Horses (p194)

➜ Wheatsheaf (p208)

Why Go?

Sprinkled with gorgeous villages and medieval towns, the part of England that stretches westwards from London to Wales comes as close to an old-world idyll as you'll ever find. It's a haven of green-cloaked hills, rose-clad cottages, graceful churches and thatched roofs. Add the university city of Oxford to this alluring mix, with its majestic architecture and youthful scene, and it's obvious why the region is a magnet for visitors.

Although the roads are busy in summer, it's easy to escape the tourist trail. The golden-hued Cotswolds work their finest magic when you find your own romantic hideaway. Splendid country houses lie tucked away throughout Buckinghamshire, Bedfordshire and Hertfordshire, while Windsor boasts the world's largest castle. Further west, the Forest of Dean offers the promise of outdoor adventure.

While individual destinations can be seen on easy day trips from London, both Oxford and the Cotswolds deserve several leisurely days.

When to Go

➜ Welcome the dawn with Oxford's Magdalen College Choir, as it sings hymns from atop the college tower to greet May Morning (1 May).

➜ In July, sip champagne and watch the rowers whizzing by at Henley Royal Regatta.

➜ Walking in the Cotswolds is ideal from April to June and in September, when the weather is (mostly) in your favour, without the July and August crowds.

➜ In early October, Cheltenham kicks into bookish action for its famous 10-day Literature Festival.

➜ Mingle with hobnobbing aristocrats in June at the country's greatest annual racing meet, Royal Ascot.

Oxford & the Cotswolds Highlights

1 Oxford (p187) Following in the inspirational footsteps of literary greats as you explore magical colleges.

2 The Cotswolds (p201) Strolling through perfect gold-tinged Cotswolds villages.

3 Windsor (p226) Catching a glimpse of how royalty relaxes at the Queen's weekend hideaway.

4 Blenheim Palace (p200) Lording it up at one of Britain's greatest stately homes, in Woodstock.

5 Stowe Gardens (p225) Getting lost in a serene world of spectacular 18th-century landscaped gardens.

6 Gloucester Cathedral (p222) Strolling the elegant cloisters of this exquisite Perpendicular Gothic creation.

7 Painswick (p216) Meandering around a beautiful and unspoilt town.

8 The Making of Harry Potter (p224) Unleashing your inner wizard in Leavesden.

ⓘ Getting There & Around

A car will give you the greatest freedom, especially if you want to explore the scattered villages of the Cotswolds.

Local buses, run by various operators, link larger towns to each other and to surrounding villages. For timetables, use the journey planner tool on Traveline (www.traveline.info).

Oxford, Moreton-in-Marsh, Stroud, Cheltenham, Gloucester, Bletchley, Hatfield, St Albans, Henley-on-Thames and Windsor are plugged into the train network; all have services to London, in most cases direct. Other direct trains go as far as Birmingham, Manchester and Newcastle (from Oxford), and Cardiff, Edinburgh and Exeter (from Cheltenham).

OXFORD

☑ 01865 / POP 161,300

A gloriously mellow ensemble of golden-hued wonders, Oxford unquestionably ranks among England's most beautiful cities. In fact, as you stroll through its historic and homogenous core, it can be hard to believe you're in modern England at all. Certain specific buildings stand out, like the domed and glowing Radcliffe Camera, and you can admire masterpieces by such great architects as Sir Christopher Wren and Nicholas Hawksmoor. Really, though, the joy of visiting Oxford lies in the sheer cumulative splendour of college after century-old college, each playing its own permutation of Gothic chapels, secluded cloisters, and tranquil quadrangles.

History

Strategically placed at the confluence of the Rivers Cherwell and Thames (called the Isis here, from the Latin Tamesis), Oxford was a key Saxon town, heavily fortified by Alfred the Great during the war against the Danes. It continued to grow under the Normans, who founded its castle in 1071.

By the 11th century, the Augustinian abbey in Oxford had begun training clerics, and when Anglo-Norman clerical scholars were expelled from the Sorbonne in 1167, the abbey began to attract students in droves. The first three colleges – University, Balliol and Merton – were founded in the mid-13th century. Alongside Oxford's growing prosperity grew the enmity between local townspeople and new students ('town and gown'), culminating in the St Scholastica's Day Massacre in 1355, which started as an argument

over beer but resulted in 90 deaths. Thereafter, the king ordered that the university be broken up into colleges, each of which developed its own traditions.

The university, largely a religious entity at the time, was rocked in the 16th century by the Reformation; the public trials and burning at the stake of Protestant heretics under Mary I; and by the subsequent hanging, drawing and quartering of Catholics under her successor Elizabeth I. As the Royalist headquarters, Oxford backed the losing side during the Civil War, but flourished after the restoration of the monarchy, with some of its most notable buildings constructed in the late 17th and early 18th centuries.

The arrival of the canal system in 1790 had a profound effect on Oxford. By creating a link with the Midlands' industrial centres, work and trade suddenly expanded beyond the academic core. This was further strengthened by the construction of the railways in the 19th century.

The city's real industrial boom came, however, when William Morris began producing cars here in 1913. With the success of his Bullnose Morris and Morris Minor, his Cowley factory went on to become one of the largest motor plants in the world. Although works have been scaled down since, Minis still run off BMW's Cowley production line today.

⊙ Sights

Oxford is a compact little town, with its major sights largely congregated in the centre. Almost all, including the Bodleian Library and the Ashmolean Museum, are connected with the university, while several of the university colleges are themselves prime visitor attractions.

⊙ City Centre

★ **Bodleian Library**   LIBRARY

(☑ 01865-287400; www.bodleian.ox.ac.uk/bodley; Catte St; Divinity School £1, with audio tour £3.50, guided tours £6-14; ⊙ 9am-5pm Mon-Sat, from 11am Sun) At least five kings, dozens of prime ministers and Nobel laureates, and luminaries such as Oscar Wilde, CS Lewis and JRR Tolkien have studied in Oxford's Bodleian Library, a magnificent survivor from the Middle Ages. Wander into its central 17th-century quad, and you can admire its ancient buildings for free, while it costs just £1 to enter the most impressive of these, the

15th-century Divinity School. To see the rest of the complex, though, you'll have to join a guided tour.

All tours, including the two most popular daily options – the 'mini-tour' (30 minutes, £6) and the 'standard tour' (one hour, £8) – start in the ornate medieval Divinity School, the university's earliest teaching room. A superb specimen of English Gothic architecture, it was founded around 1423. Inspect its fan-vaulted ceiling closely, and you'll spot the initials of benefactors, including Thomas Kemp, who features 84 times, who worked on it, as well as three 'Green Men'. In the Harry Potter films, the Divinity School served as the Hogwarts hospital wing.

Every tour also includes on the upper level, which dates from 1488. Visitors are not allowed to enter this magnificently decorated medieval room, or peruse the ancient tomes that it contains, just admire it from the adjoining 17th-century extension. It too featured in the Harry Potter films, as Hogwarts' library.

The standard tours additionally take in two grand chambers at the far end of the Divinity School – Convocation House, which hosted the English Parliament three times, once under Charles I and twice under Charles II, and the Chancellor's Court, in which Oscar Wilde and Romantic poet Percy Bysshe Shelley went on trial (for debt and promoting atheism, respectively).

Less frequent 'extended tours' cover the same ground while also offering the only public access to the nearby Radcliffe Camera, which houses part of the Bodleian's collection. The 'Upstairs, Downstairs' tour (9.15am Wednesday and Saturday, 1½ hours, £14) leads visitors along the underground Gladstone Link that connects the main library with the Camera, while the 'Explore the Reading Rooms' tour (11.15am and 1.15pm Sunday, 1½ hours, £14) spends more time in the Camera itself.

Check tour times online or at the information desk; tickets for all tours can be purchased up to two weeks in advance. Note also that a selection of 'Bodleian Treasures' is displayed in the nearby Weston Library (www.bodleian.ox.ac.uk/weston; Broad St; ⊘ 10am-5pm Mon-Sat, from 11am Sun) FREE.

★ Christ Church   COLLEGE
(☏ 01865-276492; www.chch.ox.ac.uk; St Aldate's; adult/child Jul & Aug £10/9, Sep-Jun £8/7; ⊘ 10am-5pm Mon-Sat, from 2pm Sun, last admission 4.15pm) With its compelling combination of majestic architecture, literary heritage and double identity as (parts of) Harry Potter's Hogwarts, Christ Church attracts tourists galore. Among Oxford's largest colleges – the largest, if you include its bucolic meadow – and proud possessor of its most impressive quad, plus a superb art gallery and even a cathedral, it was founded in 1525 by Cardinal Wolsey. It later became home to Lewis Carroll, whose picnic excursions with the then-dean's daughter gave us Alice in Wonderland.

The main entrance to Christ Church, Tom Gate, stands immediately below the imposing 17th-century Tom Tower. Sir Christopher Wren, who studied at Christ Church, was responsible for its topmost portions. Pass by at 9.05pm, and you'll hear 101 chimes from its 6-tonne bell, Great Tom, to commemorate the curfew inflicted on the college's original students.

All visitors, however, enter further south along St Aldate's, walking through the gardens to reach Meadow Gate (where there may be queues). From there, the self-guided tour route leads to the Renaissance Great Hall, the college's jaw-dropping dining room, with its hammer-beam roof and portraits of past scholars including Lewis Carroll and an entire troop of British prime ministers who studied here. It's often closed to visitors at lunchtime, between noon and 2pm.

If the Great Hall looks awfully familiar, that may be because it starred as Hogwarts' dining hall in the Harry Potter films. Although the movie-screen hall was mocked up in the studio, the fan-vaulted staircase via which you enter it appeared in Harry Potter and the Philosopher's Stone, as the spot where Professor McGonagall welcomes Harry.

PORT MEADOW

Although archaeologists have identified traces of Bronze and Iron Age settlements bulging from this marshy Thameside meadow, northwest of Jericho, it has remained untouched, never even ploughed, ever since. A treasure trove of rare plants, it's still grazed by cows and horses, but it's also hugely popular with walkers (heading perhaps for The Trout pub) and runners. In winter it gets so waterlogged that hikers have to go round the edge rather than cutting straight across.

The route then crosses one side of **Tom Quad** – Oxford's largest and most impressive quadrangle, overlooked by Tom Tower and with a statue of Mercury adorning its pond – to reach **Christ Church Cathedral** (📞01865-276150; www.chch.ox.ac.uk/cathedral; St Aldate's; ⊙10am-5pm Mon-Sat, from 2pm Sun, last entry 4.15) **FREE**. It stands on the site where the shrine of St Frideswide, Oxford's patron saint, was erected during the 8th century. The cathedral itself was built as the priory church during the 12th century, and became the college chapel when Cardinal Wolsey established what he called Cardinal College in 1525.

Long one of Oxford's wealthiest colleges, Christ Church has amassed an exceptional art collection. Displayed in the small **Christ Church Picture Gallery** (📞01865-276172; www.chch.ox.ac.uk/gallery; Oriel Sq; adult/child £4/2; ⊙10.30am-5pm Mon-Sat, from 2pm Sun Jul-Sep, closed Tue Jun, shorter hours Oct-May, last admission always 45min before closing), added during the 1960s, it includes painting and drawings by Tintoretto, Michelangelo and other Renaissance masters.

Stretching away south and east of the college, and accessible free of charge, **Christ Church Meadow** (www.chch.ox.ac.uk; St Aldate's; ⊙dawn-dusk) **FREE**, a verdant expanse bordered by the Cherwell and Thames (or Isis) rivers, is ideal for a leisurely half-hour walk. Look out for the college's own herd of longhorn cattle.

Bridge of Sighs
BRIDGE

(Hertford Bridge; New College Lane) As you stroll along New College Lane, look up at the steeped Bridge of Sighs linking the two halves of Hertford College. Completed in 1914, it's sometimes erroneously referred to as a copy of the famous bridge in Venice, but it looks much more like that city's Rialto Bridge.

Radcliffe Camera
LIBRARY

(📞01865-287400; www.bodleian.ox.ac.uk; Radcliffe Sq; tours £14; ⊙Bodleian tours 9.15am Wed & Sat, 11.15am & 1.15pm Sun) Surely Oxford's most photographed landmark, the sandy-gold Radcliffe Camera is a beautiful, light-filled, circular, columned library. Built between 1737 and 1749 in grand Palladian style, as 'Radcliffe Library', it's topped by Britain's third-largest dome. It's only been a 'camera', which simply means 'room', since 1860, when it lost its independence and became what it remains, a reading room of the Bodleian Li-

brary. The only way for nonmembers to see the interior is on an extended 1½-hour tour of the Bodleian (p187).

Balliol College
COLLEGE

(📞01865-277777; www.balliol.ox.ac.uk; Broad St; adult/child £3/1; ⊙10am-5pm, to dusk in winter) Dating its foundation to 'about' 1263, Balliol College claims to be the oldest college in Oxford, though its current buildings are largely 19th-century. Scorch marks on the huge Gothic wooden doors between its inner and outer quadrangles, however, supposedly date from the public burning of three Protestant bishops, including Archbishop of Canterbury Thomas Cranmer, in 1556.

Exeter College
COLLEGE

(📞01865-279600; www.exeter.ox.ac.uk; Turl St; ⊙2-5pm) **FREE** Founded in 1314, Exeter is known for its elaborate 17th-century dining hall, which celebrated its 400th birthday in 2018, and ornate Victorian Gothic chapel, a psychedelic blast of gold mosaic and stained glass that holds a tapestry created by former students William Morris and Edward Burne Jones, *The Adoration of the Magi*. Exeter also inspired former student Philip Pullman to create fictional Jordan College in *His Dark Materials*.

Merton College
COLLEGE

(📞01865-276310; www.merton.ox.ac.uk; Merton St; adult/child £3/free; ⊙2-5pm Mon-Fri, from 10am Sat & Sun) Founded in 1264, peaceful and elegant Merton is one of Oxford's three original colleges. Like the other two, Balliol and University, it considers itself the oldest, arguing that it was the first to adopt collegiate planning, bringing scholars and tutors together into a formal community and providing them with a planned residence. Its distinguishing architectural features

---

TOLKIEN'S RESTING PLACE

Lord of the Rings author JRR Tolkien (1892–1973) is buried with his wife Edith at **Wolvercote Cemetery** (Banbury Rd, Wolvercote; ⊙7am-8pm Mon-Fri, from 8am Sat & Sun Apr-Sep, to 5pm Oct-Mar) **FREE**, 2.5 miles north of Oxford city centre. Their gravestone bears the names Beren (for him) and Lúthien (for her), referencing the love between a mortal man and an elf maiden who gave up her immortality to be with him.

Oxford

include large gargoyles, whose expressions suggest that they're about to throw up, and the charming, diminutive 14th-century **Mob Quad** – the first college quad.

New College COLLEGE
(☑ 01865-279500; www.new.ox.ac.uk; Holywell St; adult/child £5/4; ⊙ 11am-5pm Easter-Oct, 2-4pm Nov-Feb) New College isn't really *that* new. Established in 1379 as Oxford's first undergraduate college, it's a glorious Perpendicular Gothic ensemble. Treasures in the chapel include superb medieval stained glass and Sir Jacob Epstein's disturbing 1951 statue of Lazarus, wrapped in his grave shroud; in

term time, visitors can attend the beautiful choral Evensong service (6.15pm nightly). The 15th-century cloisters and evergreen oak featured in *Harry Potter and the Goblet of Fire*, while the dining hall is the oldest in Oxbridge.

Trinity College COLLEGE
(☑ 01865-279900; www.trinity.ox.ac.uk; Broad St; adult/child £3/2; ⊙ 9.30am-noon & 2pm-dusk) Founded in 1555, this small college boasts a lovely 17th-century garden quad, designed by Sir Christopher Wren. Its exquisite chapel, a masterpiece of English baroque, contains a limewood altar screen adorned with

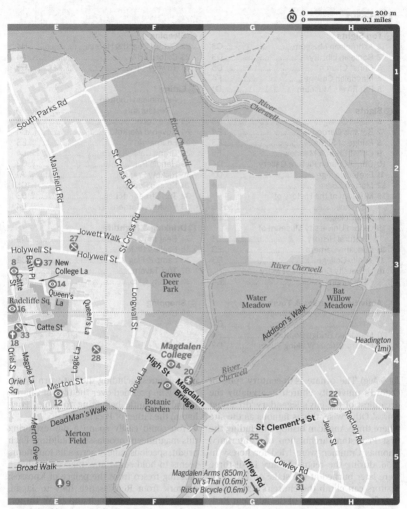

flowers and fruit carved by master craftsman Grinling Gibbons in 1694, and is looking fabulous after recent restoration work. Famous students have included Cardinal Newman, William Pitt the Elder, two other British prime ministers, and the fictional Jay Gatsby, the Great Gatsby himself.

Museum of the
History of Science
MUSEUM

(☎ 01865-277293; www.mhs.ox.ac.uk; Broad St; ⊙noon-5pm Tue-Sun) **FREE** Students of science will swoon at this fascinating museum, stuffed to the ceilings with awesome astrolabes, astonishing orreries and early electrical apparatus. Housed in the lovely 17th-century building that held the original Ashmolean Museum, it displays everything from cameras that belonged to Lewis Carroll and Lawrence of Arabia to a wireless receiver used by Marconi in 1896 and a blackboard that was covered with equations by Einstein in 1931, when he was invited to give three lectures on relativity.

University Church of
St Mary the Virgin
CHURCH

(☎ 01865-279111; www.university-church.ox.ac. uk; High St; church free, tower £4; ⊙9am-5pm Mon-Sat, from noon Sun Sep-Jun, 9am-6pm daily

Oxford

Jul & Aug) The ornate 14th-century spire of Oxford's university church is arguably the dreamiest of the city's legendary 'dreaming spires'. Otherwise, this is famous as the site where three Anglican bishops, including the first Protestant archbishop of Canterbury, Thomas Cranmer, were tried for heresy in 1556, during the reign of Mary I. All three were later burned at the stake on Broad St. Visitors can climb the church's 1280 tower (£4) for excellent views of the adjacent Radcliffe Camera (p189).

◉ Jericho & Science Area

★**Ashmolean Museum**   MUSEUM
(☎01865-278000; www.ashmolean.org; Beaumont St; ◎10am-5pm Tue-Sun, to 8pm last Fri of month) **FREE** Britain's oldest public museum, Oxford's wonderful Ashmolean Museum is surpassed only by the British Museum in London. It was established in 1683, when Elias Ashmole presented Oxford University with a collection of 'rarities' amassed by the well-travelled John Tradescant, gardener to Charles I. A new exhibition celebrates Ashmole's 400th birthday by displaying origi-

nal treasures including the hat worn by the judge who presided over the trial of Charles I, and a mantle belonging to 'Chief Powhatan', the father of Pocahontas.

You could easily spend a day exploring this magnificent neoclassical building. Each bright, spacious gallery across its four floors seems to hold some new marvel, be that a dazzling fresco from the palace of Knossos; artwork from Renaissance Italy to Japan, taking in Goya, van Gogh and JMW Turner; or, famously, the Anglo-Saxon Alfred Jewel, a glorious, golden 9th-century gem, thought to have been a sort of bookmark, that was crafted for Alfred the Great. There's a strong connection throughout with Oxford and its heritage, and upstairs there's a beautiful **rooftop restaurant** (☎01865-553823; mains £13.50-20; ◎10am-4.30pm Tue, Wed & Sun, to 10pm Thu-Sat; 🔊).

★**Pitt Rivers Museum**   MUSEUM
(☎01865-270927; www.prm.ox.ac.uk; South Parks Rd; ◎noon-4.30pm Mon, from 10am Tue-Sun; ⬦) **FREE** If exploring an enormous room full of eccentric and unexpected artefacts sounds like your idea of the perfect afternoon, wel-

come to the amulets-to-zithers extravaganza that is the Pitt Rivers museum. Tucked behind Oxford's natural-history museum (p193), and dimly lit to protect its myriad treasures, it's centred on an anthropological collection amassed by a Victorian general, and revels in exploring how differing cultures have tackled topics like 'Smoking and Stimulants' or 'Treatment of Dead Enemies'.

Oxford University Museum of Natural History MUSEUM
(☑01865-272950; www.oum.ox.ac.uk; Parks Rd; ☉10am-5pm;) FREE Housed in a glorious Victorian Gothic building, with cast-iron columns, flower-carved capitals and a soaring glass roof, this museum makes a superb showcase for some extraordinary exhibits. Specimens from all over the world include a 150-year-old Japanese spider crab, but it's the dinosaurs that really wow the crowds. As well as a towering T-rex skeleton – the second most complete ever found – you'll see pieces of Megalosaurus, which was in 1677 the first dinosaur ever mentioned in a written text.

⊙ Cowley Rd & Southeast Oxford

★Magdalen College COLLEGE
(☑01865-276000; www.magd.ox.ac.uk; High St; adult/child £6/5; ☉10am-7pm late Jun-late Sep, 1pm-dusk or 6pm late Sep-late Jun) Guarding access to a breathtaking expanse of private lawns, woodlands, river walks and even its own deer park, Magdalen ('mawd-lin'), founded in 1458, is one of Oxford's wealthiest and most beautiful colleges. Beyond its elegant Victorian gateway, you come to its medieval chapel and glorious 15th-century tower. From here, move on to the remarkable 15th-century cloisters, where the fantastic grotesques (carved figures) may have inspired CS Lewis' stone statues in *The Chronicles of Narnia*.

🏃 Activities

Magdalen Bridge Boathouse BOATING
(☑01865-202643; www.oxfordpunting.co.uk; High St; chauffeured 4-person punts per 30min £32, punt rental per hour £22; ☉9.30am-dusk Feb-Nov) Right beside Magdalen Bridge, this boathouse is the most central location to hire a punt, chauffeured or otherwise. From here you can either head downstream around the Botanic Garden and Christ Church Meadow, or upstream around Magdalen Deer Park. You can also hire rowboats and pedalos.

Salter Bros BOATING
(☑01865-243421; www.salterssteamers.co.uk; Folly Bridge; punt/rowboat/motorboat per hour £20/20/45; ☉10am-6pm Easter-Oct) As well as renting punts, rowing boats and motorboats, Salter Bros offers scenic cruises along the Thames, passing college boathouses and busy riverside pubs. Options include the 8-mile, two-hour trip to the historic market town of Abingdon (9.15am and 2.30pm, late May to early September, adult/child £20.80/11.70), and a 2½-hour Alice in Wonderland cruise (£17.50/£10).

☞ Tours

Oxford Official Walking Tours WALKING
(☑01865-686441; www.experienceoxfordshire.org; 15-16 Broad St; adult/child from £14/10; ☉10.45am & 1pm, extra tours 11am & 2pm during busy periods;) Comprehensive two-hour tours of the city and its colleges, plus several themed tours, including one devoted to *Alice in Wonderland* and Harry Potter, another to CS Lewis and JRR Tolkien, and a third to Inspector Morse. Check online for details, or book at the tourist office (p199).

Bill Spectre's Oxford Ghost Trail WALKING
(☑07941-041811; www.ghosttrail.org; Oxford Castle; adult/child £10/7; ☉6.30pm Fri & Sat;) For a theatrical and entertaining voyage through Oxford's uncanny underbelly, plus the occasional magic trick, take a 1¾-hour tour with Victorian undertaker Bill Spectre. No bookings needed, audience participation more than likely.

🛏 Sleeping

Oxford YHA HOSTEL £
(☑01865-727275; www.yha.org.uk; 2a Botley Rd; dm/r £26/110;) Set in a purpose-built modern building, behind the station, Oxford's large YHA is a cut above other local hostels, with the feel of a chain hotel – and the prices too, for a private twin or double. The simple, comfortable four- and six-bed en-suite dorms are better value. Abundant facilities include a restaurant, a library, a garden, a laundry, lounges and private lockers.

Tower House GUESTHOUSE ££
(☑01865-246828; www.towerhouseoxford.co.uk; 15 Ship St; s £100, d £125, without bathroom £110;) In a peaceful central location, this listed 17th-century town house holds eight good-value double rooms, simple but tastefully decorated. Some share bathrooms (not always on the same floor), while larger

en-suites also have attractive tongue-and-groove panelling. Run in conjunction with the excellent Turl Street Kitchen (p197) next door – slightly higher room rates include breakfast there – it donates profits to a community charity.

University Rooms Oxford

UNIVERSITY ACCOMMODATION **££**

(www.universityrooms.com; s £31-79, d £70-125, q from £189;) During university holidays – Christmas, Easter and summer – and to a lesser extent at other times, visitors can stay in a student room in one of Oxford's hallowed colleges, perhaps looking over the quad, and enjoy breakfast in a grand hall. Functional singles with basic furnishings and shared bathrooms are the most available, but you can also find en-suites, twins and apartments.

Remont

B&B **££**

(01865-311020; www.remont-oxford.co.uk; 367 Banbury Rd, Summertown; d/q £125/180;) All modern style, subtle lighting and ultra-colourful furnishings, this boutique guest-house holds 25 varying rooms decked out in cool neutrals with silky bedspreads, abstract art, vibrant bedheads, writing desks and huge TVs. There's a sunny garden and roomy breakfast hall out back. It's 2.5 miles north of the centre, in an inconspicuous residential setting, but there's good public transport.

Acorn Guest House

B&B **££**

(01865-247998; www.oxford-acorn.co.uk; 260 Iffley Rd; s/d £50/75;) Spread through two adjoining houses, the friendly Acorn offers eight comfortable rooms at very reasonable prices, close to great pubs and restaurants and a short bus ride from the centre. Single rooms and 'budget' doubles share bathrooms; en-suite facilities cost just £5 more. Everything has the feel of a family home, complete with resident labradoodle Annie (visiting dogs welcome).

★ Oxford Coach & Horses

B&B **£££**

(01865-200017; www.oxfordcoachandhorses.co.uk; 62 St Clement's St; s/d £125/135;) A former 18th-century coaching inn, this fabulous English-Mexican-owned boutique B&B hides behind a fresh powder-blue exterior, just a few metres from the Cowley Rd action. The eight light-filled rooms are cosy, spacious and individually styled in soothing pastels with exposed beams and splashes of turquoise and mauve. The converted

🏃 Walking Tour
A Riverside Stroll in Central Oxford

START CHRIST CHURCH
END MAGDALEN COLLEGE
LENGTH 2.5 MILES; TWO HOURS

Few cities can match Oxford for retaining such glorious countryside so close to its centre. Oxford's secret lies in the fact that the riverside meadows just outside the medieval city walls belonged then, and still belong today, to hugely wealthy colleges that have never felt the urge to build on them, let alone sell them. Modern visitors can therefore simply step away from the busy city streets to enjoy an idyllic stroll along delightful rural footpaths.

Start by approaching ❶ **Christ Church** (p188) via the gates on St Aldate's. There's no need to pay for admission. Follow Broad Walk straight ahead for 140m, until the college's visitor entrance is on your left, then turn right onto Poplar Walk. This broad avenue heads directly south, to reach the Thames after 410m. Turning right at the river would bring you to Folly Bridge, spanning the original 'oxen ford' for which Oxford is named, but turn left, downstream, and follow the waterfront footpath known as the Meadow Walk. You'll probably see rowing eights and pleasure boats out on the Thames; looking back the way you've come, you're now separated from Christ Church, a shimmering vision of splendour, by the broad expanse of ❷ **Christ Church Meadow** (p189), where you may see longhorn cattle grazing. After 180m, the path leaves the river, curving beside a cut-off channel that brings you in 360m to the River Cherwell. Once there, keep following the curve, and after another 450m you meet Broad Walk at its eastern end.

Across Merton Field, straight ahead, the long, high wall of ❸ **Merton College** (p189) traces the route of Oxford's medieval city wall. During the Middle Ages, the local Jewish community had to bury their dead outside the walls. Their funerals followed this self-same footpath, which became known as Dead Man's Walk. The trees that tower over it stand within Merton's enclosed Fellows' Garden. JRR Tolkien's rooms overlooked this spot when he was writing *The Lord of the Rings*; one much-loved tree, now felled, served as the model for the ents of Middle Earth.

Ninety metres north of Broad Walk, fork right along Rose Lane, which leads up to High St along Merton's eastern boundary. The former Jewish cemetery now lies on your right, though for the past four centuries it's served instead as Oxford's 4 **Botanic Garden**. If you've time, add an extra half-mile to this walk by dropping in to admire its greenhouses of rare plants, and relax in its tranquil spaces.

The visitors' entrance to 5 **Magdalen College** (p193) is directly across High St from the north end of Rose Lane. To continue your walk, pay for admission and head through the stunning 15th-century cloisters (during the university year, visitors can only enter in the afternoon). Tolkien's contemporary, CS Lewis, lived in Magdalen, and the grotesque carvings here reappeared in his *Chronicles of Narnia*.

Turn right beyond the cloisters, and you're swiftly back on the banks of the Cherwell. Get ready for the absolute highlight of the walk. Magdalen took over these riverside lands almost six centuries ago, and has left them to be enjoyed as open countryside ever since. Cross the footbridge straight ahead of you to reach the 6 **Water Meadow**, a triangular is-let in the river. The gloriously bucolic footpath known as Addison's Walk takes just under a mile to loop around its perimeter. At its southern tip, you get a head-on view of punts and rowing boats setting off below Magdalen Bridge. The Water Meadow is one of just a half-dozen places where the snakeshead fritillary still grows; you may spot its purple or white flowers in late April.

Leave the Water Meadow by its northeastern end to enter smaller 7 **Bat Willow Meadow**, where Mark Wallinger's sculpture *Y*, resembling a two-dimensional tree, was installed amid genuine willows in 2008 to mark Magdalen's 550th anniversary. Immediately south, Angel and Greyhound Meadow was named for two long-vanished coaching inns that pastured their horses here. The secluded Fellows' Garden, across another bridge beyond, was laid out in 1866, and holds an idyllic pond.

When you're ready to re-emerge into city life, retrace your footsteps back to the high street. Spare a glance, though, for the 8 **Grove Deer Park**, north of the college buildings. If you're here between July and early December, you may have encountered the college's own herd of deer browsing in the riverside meadows; before that, to spare the fritillaries, they're here in the Grove.

ground floor houses an airy, attractive breakfast room.

★ Head of the River
HOTEL £££

(☑ 01865-721600; www.headoftheriveroxford.co.uk; Folly Bridge, St Aldates; r incl breakfast £189; 🛜) A genuine jewel among Oxford hotels, this large and characterful place, at Folly Bridge immediately south of Christ Church, was originally a Thames-side warehouse. Each of its 20 good-sized rooms is individually decorated with contemporary flair, featuring exposed brickwork and/or tongue-and-groove panelling plus modern fittings, while rates include breakfast cooked to order in the (excellent) pub (p198) downstairs.

Burlington House
HOTEL £££

(☑ 01865-513513; www.burlington-hotel-oxford.co.uk; 374 Banbury Rd, Summertown; s/d incl breakfast £102/139; P🛜) This small, well-managed hotel, in a beautifully refreshed Victorian home 2 miles north of central Oxford, offers 12 elegant contemporary rooms – some in a courtyard annex – with patterned wallpaper, immaculate bathrooms and luxury touches. Personal service is as sensational as the delicious breakfast, with organic eggs, homemade bread, yoghurt, granola and fresh juice. Public transport links are good.

Oxford Townhouse
BOUTIQUE HOTEL £££

(☑ 01865-722500; www.theoxfordtownhouse.co.uk; 90 Abingdon Rd; s/d incl breakfast £136/166; P🛜) Fifteen comfortable, subtly chic, minimalist-modern rooms, with white-and-navy striped blankets, varnished-wood desks and blue flourishes, in a gorgeously restyled pair of red-brick Victorian town houses, half a mile south of the centre. Some are quite small for the price, though. Colourful paintings of Oxford adorn the walls, and the breakfasts are classy.

🍴 Eating

★ Edamamé
JAPANESE £

(☑ 01865-246916; www.edamame.co.uk; 15 Holywell St; mains £7-10.50; ⏲ 11.30am-2.30pm Wed, 11.30am-2.30pm & 5-8.30pm Thu-Sat, noon-3.30pm Sun; 🍴) No wonder a constant stream of students squeeze in and out of this tiny diner – it's Oxford's top spot for delicious, gracefully simple Japanese cuisine. Changing noodle and curry specials include fragrant chicken miso ramen, tofu stir-fries, or mackerel with soba noodles; it only serves sushi or sashimi on Thursday evenings. No

bookings; arrive early and be prepared to wait.

★ Vaults & Garden
CAFE £

(☑ 01865-279112; www.thevaultsandgarden.com; University Church of St Mary the Virgin, Radcliffe Sq; mains £7-10.50; ⏲ 9am-6pm; 🛜🍴) 🌿 This beautiful lunch venue spreads from the vaulted 14th-century Old Congregation House of the University Church into a garden facing the Radcliffe Camera. Come early, and queue at the counter to choose from wholesome organic specials such as leek and potato soup, tofu massaman curry, or slow-roasted lamb tagine. Breakfast and afternoon tea (those scones!) are equally good.

★ Covered Market
MARKET £

(www.oxford-coveredmarket.co.uk; Market St; ⏲ vary, some close Sun; 🛜🍴♿) A haven for impecunious students, this indoor marketplace holds 20 restaurants, cafes and takeaways. Let anyone loose here, and something's sure to catch their fancy. Brown's no-frills cafe, famous for its apple pies, is the longest-standing veteran. Look out too for Georgina's, serving quiches and burgers upstairs; Burt's superlative Cookies; two excellent pie shops; and good Thai and Chinese options.

Handle Bar
CAFE £

(☑ 01865-251315; www.handlebaroxford.co.uk; Bike Zone, 28-31 St Michael's St; dishes £8-13; ⏲ 8am-6pm Mon & Tue, to 11pm Wed-Fri, from 9am Sat, 10am-5pm Sun; 🛜🍴) Upstairs above a bike shop, this chatty, friendly cafe has bikes galore, including penny-farthings, dangling from its ceiling and white-painted brick walls. A tad more hippy than hipster, it's usually packed with students, professionals and lucky tourists. They're here for luscious, health-focused bites, like spiced avocado-and-feta toast, roasted chicken breast and fresh-fruit smoothie 'pots', plus tasty cakes, teas and coffees.

Grand Café
TEAHOUSE £

(☑ 01865-204463; www.thegrandcafe.co.uk; 84 High St; patisserie items £5-7, mains £9-13; ⏲ 9am-6.30pm Mon-Thu, to 7pm Fri-Sun; ♿) Boasting of being England's first-ever coffee house – though not, unlike its rival opposite, open ever since – the Grand looks very much the part, with its columns and gold leaf. While it serves sandwiches, bagels and a towering afternoon tea (from £18), it's the patisserie counter that's the real attraction: fresh, sweet pastry tarts and feather-light *mille-feuilles* pair brilliantly with tea.

Rusty Bicycle GASTROPUB **£**
(☎01865-435298; www.therustybicycle.com; 28 Magdalen Rd; mains £6.50-12; ⊗9am-11pm Sun-Thu, to midnight Fri & Sat; 🐾) This funky neighbourhood pub, tucked off Iffley Rd a mile out of town and brought to you by the people responsible for Jericho's **Rickety Press** (☎01865-424581; www.thericketypress.com; 67 Cranham St; mains £6.50-12; ⊗kitchen noon-2.30pm & 6-9.30pm Mon-Fri, 10am-3pm & 6-9.30pm Sat & Sun), serves top-notch burgers and pizzas, along with excellent local beers.

Café Coco MEDITERRANEAN **£**
(☎01865-200232; www.cafecoco.co.uk; 23 Cowley Rd; breakfast £5-9, mains £7.50-15; ⊗10am-midnight Mon-Thu, to 12.30am Fri & Sat, to 10pm Sun; 🖉) Decorated with classic posters, warm yellow walls and chunky mirrors – not to mention the plaster-cast clown – this Cowley Rd veteran is especially popular for brunch. Its global menu ranges from 'healthy' and cooked breakfasts to pizzas, salads, burgers, pastas, mezze platters, Mediterranean mains and zingy fresh juices. Or just swing by for cocktails (happy hour 5pm to 7.30pm).

★Spiced Roots CARIBBEAN **££**
(☎01865-249888; www.spicedroots.com; 64 Cowley Rd; mains £12-17.50; ⊗6-10pm Tue & Wed, noon-3pm & 6-10pm Thu-Sat, noon-8pm Sun; 🖉) From black rice with pomegranates to oxtail with mac cheese and plantains – and, of course, spicy jerk chicken – everything is just perfection at this flawless new Caribbean restaurant. There are plenty of vegetarian options too, as well as curried fish or goat, while adding a cocktail or two from the thatched rum bar is pretty much irresistible.

★Turl Street Kitchen MODERN BRITISH **££**
(☎01865-264171; www.turlstreetkitchen.co.uk; 16-17 Turl St; mains £10-16; ⊗8-10am, noon-2.30pm & 6.30-10pm; 🖉) 🍴 Whatever time you drop into this laid-back, not-quite-scruffy, seductively charming all-day bistro, with its fairy lights and faded-wood tables, you can expect to eat well. Fresh local produce is thrown into creative combinations, with the changing menu featuring the likes of roasted beetroot, braised lamb, or, on Sunday, roast beef and Yorkshire pudding. It also serves good cakes and coffee.

★Magdalen Arms BRITISH **££**
(☎01865-243159; www.magdalenarms.co.uk; 243 Iffley Rd; mains £14-42; ⊗5-11pm Mon, from 10am Tue-Sat, 10am-10.30pm Sun; 🖉🐾) A mile beyond Magdalen Bridge, this extra-special neighbourhood gastropub has won plaudits from the national press. A friendly, informal spot, it offers indoor and outdoor space for drinkers, and dining tables further back. From vegetarian specials such as broadbean tagliatelle to the fabulous sharing-size steak-and-ale pie – well, it's a stew with a suet-crust lid, really – everything is delicious, with gutsy flavours.

★Oli's Thai THAI **££**
(☎01865-790223; www.olisthai.com; 38 Magdalen Rd; mains £12-15; ⊗noon-2.30pm & 5-10pm Tue-Fri, noon-3pm Sat) This tiny Thai restaurant is a bit of a trek from town, a mile down Iffley Rd, but it's absolutely worth the effort. The short menu changes frequently, with standouts including turmeric prawns and pork belly with rice. Tables, especially on the sunny terrace, get booked up months in advance, but they usually squeeze in a few walk-ins.

Cherwell Boathouse Restaurant BRITISH **££**
(☎01865-552746; www.cherwellboathouse.co.uk; Bardwell Rd; mains £18-22; ⊗noon-2.30pm & 6-9.30pm; 🖉) With its irresistible riverside setting, 1.5 miles north of central Oxford, the century-old Cherwell Boathouse makes a perfect setting for a lazy lunch or romantic summer evening. Short seasonally changing menus feature British standards like lamb

WORTH A TRIP

LE MANOIR AUX QUAT'SAISONS

Oxford itself has no Michelin-starred restaurants, so local food-lovers make the 9-mile pilgrimage east to this impressive **manor house** (☎01844-278881; www.belmond.com/le-manoir-aux-quat-saisons-oxfordshire; Church Rd, Great Milton; 5-course lunch/7-course dinner £95/190; ⊗6.30-9.30pm Mon, 11.45am-2.15pm & 6.30-9.30pm Tue-Sun), which has two stars of its own. Chef Raymond Blanc has been working his magic here for over 30 years, presenting imaginative and complex dishes that use ingredients from the amazing on-site kitchen garden. Book well ahead and dress smart.

It also has 32 hotel rooms, the cheapest of which costs £625.50 per night.

loin with peas or plaice with shrimp sauce, and there are always a couple of vegetarian alternatives.

Oxford Kitchen MODERN BRITISH £££
(☑ 01865-511149; www.theoxfordkitchen.co.uk; 215 Banbury Rd; set menus £22.50-65; ☺ noon-2.30pm & 6-9.30pm Tue-Sat) Oxford's not renowned for high-end, cutting-edge cuisine, so if you're crying out for a few foams, mousses, funny-shaped plates and bumpy slates, make haste to Summertown's contemporary Oxford Kitchen. We jest; its Modern British food, served as set menus ranging from £22.50 for a weekday lunch up to the £65 weekend tasting menu, is superb.

🍷 Drinking & Nightlife

★ Turf Tavern PUB
(☑ 01865-243235; www.turftavern-oxford.co.uk; 4-5 Bath Pl; ☺ 11am-11pm; 🐾) Squeezed down an alleyway and subdivided into endless nooks and crannies, this medieval rabbit warren dates from around 1381. The definitive Oxford pub, this is where Bill Clinton famously 'did not inhale'; other patrons have included Oscar Wilde, Stephen Hawking and Margaret Thatcher. Home to a fabulous array of real ales and ciders, it's always pretty crowded, but there's outdoor seating, too.

★ The Perch PUB
(☑ 01865-728891; www.the-perch.co.uk; Binsey Lane, Binsey; ☺ 10.30am-11pm Mon-Sat, to 10.30pm Sun; 🐾🍽) This thatched and wonderfully rural 800-year-old inn can be reached by road, but it's more enjoyable to walk half an hour upstream along the Thames Path, then follow an enchanting footpath punctuated by floral pergolas. Its huge willow-draped garden is an idyllic spot for a pint or two of Fullers, but summer crowds can mean a long wait for food.

★ Head of the River PUB
(☑ 01865-721600; www.headoftheriveroxford. co.uk; Folly Bridge, St Aldates; ☺ 8am-10.30pm Sun-Thu, to 11.30pm Fri & Sat) For a summer-evening riverside drink, central Oxford holds no finer setting than the Thames-facing terrace of this imposing former warehouse – hence the hand-cranked crane, still outside – and later a boatyard. The beer's good, courtesy of Fullers brewery. There's plenty of room indoors – as well as decent food, and a stylish hotel upstairs – but the lure of the river is irresistible.

★ Lamb & Flag PUB
(12 St Giles; ☺ noon-11pm Mon-Sat, to 10.30pm Sun; 🐾) This relaxed 17th-century tavern remains one of Oxford's nicest pubs for a sturdy pint or glass of wine. Thomas Hardy wrote (and set) parts of *Jude the Obscure* at these very tables, while CS Lewis and JRR Tolkien shifted their custom here in later years. The food's nothing special, but buying a pint helps fund scholarships at St John's College.

Bear Inn PUB
(☑ 01865-728164; www.bearoxford.co.uk; 6 Alfred St; ☺ 11am-11pm Mon-Thu, to midnight Fri & Sat, 11.30am-10.30pm Sun) Oxford's oldest pub – there's been a pub here since 1242 – the creaky old Bear requires almost everyone to stoop while passing from room to room. An ever-expanding collection of ties, framed and fading behind glass, covers walls and ceilings alike. Affiliated with Fuller's brewery, it usually offers interesting guest ales, plus basic pub grub. There's live jazz on Tuesday.

Eagle & Child PUB
(☑ 01865-302925; www.nicholsonspubs.co.uk/ theeagleandchildoxford; 49 St Giles; ☺ 11am-11pm Mon-Sat, noon-10.30pm Sun) Affectionately nicknamed the 'Bird & Baby', and a favourite haunt of JRR Tolkien, CS Lewis and their fellow Inklings, this quirky, rambling pub dates from 1650. Its narrow wood-panelled rooms still look great, and they're still serving decent real ales, but it's lost its way recently, and owners St John's College have announced an imminent, ominous-sounding makeover.

Varsity Club COCKTAIL BAR
(☑ 01865-248777; www.tvcoxford.co.uk; 9 High St; ☺ noon-midnight; 🐾) At this sleekly minimalist rooftop cocktail bar, spectacularly located in the town centre, you can sip fruity cocktails (£7 to £10) while you soak up sensational views across Oxford's dreaming spires. Heaters, blankets and canopies keep things cosy in colder weather, while lounges and dance spaces sprawl across three floors below.

The Trout PUB
(☑ 01865-510930; www.thetroutoxford.co.uk; 195 Godstow Rd, Wolvercote; ☺ 11am-11pm Mon-Fri, from 10am Sat, 10am-10.30pm Sun; 🐾) Three miles northwest along the Thames from Oxford – a wonderful walk– this old-world pub has been drawing drinkers for around four centuries, and was popularised by TV de-

tective Inspector Morse. Its expansive riverside terrace is usually packed, and there are peckish ducks patrolling the parapet wall. If you fancy sampling its Modern British cuisine be sure to book way in advance.

Shopping

★ **Blackwell's** BOOKS
(☑ 01865-792701; www.blackwells.co.uk; 48-51 Broad St; ⊙ 9am-6.30pm Mon & Wed-Sat, from 9.30am Tue, 11am-5pm Sun) The most famous bookshop in the most studenty of cities, Blackwell's is, with its vast range of literature, treatises and guilty pleasures, a book-lover's dream. Be sure to visit the basement Norrington Room, an immense inverted step pyramid, lined with 3 miles of shelves, hailed in the Guinness Book of Records as the largest room selling books in the world.

🛈 Information

Tourist Office (☑ 01865-686430; www.experienceoxfordshire.org; 15-16 Broad St; ⊙ 9am-5.30pm Mon-Sat, 10am-4pm Sun Jul & Aug, 9.30am-5pm Mon-Sat, 10am-4pm Sun Sep-Jun) Covers the whole of Oxfordshire. Sells Oxford guidebooks, makes reservations for local accommodation and walking tours, and sells tickets for events and attractions.

🛈 Getting There & Away

BUS

Oxford's chaotic outdoor **bus station** (Gloucester Green) is in the centre, on Gloucester Green near the corner of Worcester and George Sts. The main bus companies are **Oxford Bus Company** (☑ 01865-785400; www.oxfordbus.co.uk), **Stagecoach** (☑ 01865-772250; www.stagecoachbus.com) and **Swanbrook** (☑ 01452-712386; www.swanbrook.co.uk).

Destinations:

Burford (route 853; £3.80, 45 minutes)
Cambridge (X5; £13.50, 3¾ hours)
Cheltenham (853; £8, 1½ hours)
Chipping Norton (S3; £4.70, one hour)
London Victoria (Oxford Tube/X90; £15, 1¾ hours)
Witney (11/S1/S2/853; £4.20, 40 minutes)
Woodstock (7/S3; £3.20, 30 minutes)

National Express (☑ 0871-7818181; www.nationalexpress.com) coach destinations:

Bath (£11.30, two hours)
Birmingham (£11.10, 2½ hours)
Bristol (£7.10, three hours)
London Victoria (£16, two hours)

CAR & MOTORCYCLE

Driving and parking in central Oxford is a nightmare; consider booking accommodation that offers parking. There are five Park & Ride car parks along the major routes leading into town, all at least 2 miles out. Parking costs £2 to £4 per day, with a total charge of £6.80 if you use the buses that run to/from the centre every 15 to 30 minutes, and take 12 to 25 minutes for the journey.

TRAIN

Oxford's main train station is conveniently located just west of the city centre, roughly 10 minutes' walk from, say, Broad St. Destinations include the following (note that fares vary enormously according to when you travel, when you book, and many other factors):

Birmingham (£19, 1¼ hours)
London Marylebone (£7 to £29, 1¼ hours)
London Paddington (£9.50 to £26.50, 1¼ hours)
Manchester (£38.70, 2¾ hours)
Moreton-in-Marsh (£10.50, 35 minutes)
Newcastle (£73.50, 4½ hours)
Winchester (£18.30, 1¼ hours)

Oxford Parkway station, on Banbury Rd 4 miles north of the centre, has trains to London Marylebone (£7 to £26, one hour). Convenient if you're staying in Summertown, it also has bus links to central Oxford.

🛈 Getting Around

BICYCLE

There's a real cycling culture in Oxford, and it's a popular way to get around the city for students and visitors alike. **Cyclo Analysts** (☑ 01865-424444; www.cycloanalysts.com; 150 Cowley Rd; per day/week from £10/36; ⊙ 9am-6pm Mon-Sat) and **Summertown Cycles** (☑ 01865-316885; www.summertowncycles.co.uk; 200-202 Banbury Rd, Summertown; per day/week £18/35; ⊙ 9am-5.30pm Mon-Sat, 10.30am-4pm Sun) sell, repair and rent out bikes, including hybrids.

BUS

Oxford Bus Company and Stagecoach serve an extensive local network with regular buses on major routes. Single journeys cost up to £2.20 (return £3.70); consider a day pass (£4.20). Pay when you board the bus, either in cash or with a contactless card.

TAXI

There are taxi ranks at the train station and bus station, as well as on St Giles and at Carfax. Alternatively, contact **001 Taxis** (☑ 01865-240000; www.001taxis.com; New Inn Yard, 108

WORTH A TRIP

VALE OF THE WHITE HORSE

Lying around 20 miles southwest of Oxford, this verdant valley is home to the historic market town of Wantage, birthplace of Alfred the Great (AD 849–899). Its most interesting attractions, however, are much older even than that. White Horse Hill, 7.5 miles west of Wantage, is decorated with Britain's most ancient chalk figure, the 3000-year-old **Uffington White Horse**, while the nearby hill fort known as **Uffington Castle** dates from 700 BC, and **Wayland's Smithy** is a neolithic long barrow.

The 10m-high, flat-topped mound known as **Dragon Hill** was believed by locals to be the site where St George slew the dragon. Archaeologists prefer to think that it's a natural formation, the summit of which was scraped level during the Iron Age and used for rituals.

St Aldate's) or **Oxford Cars** (☑ 01865-406070; www.oxfordcars.co.uk).

AROUND OXFORD

The Oxfordshire countryside abounds in rustic charm. To the northwest, Witney has a pretty town centre, but the major highlight is magnificent Blenheim Palace, birthplace of Sir Winston Churchill, adjoining attractive Woodstock. Southwest of Oxford, the Vale of the White Horse offers some intriguing prehistoric attractions.

Woodstock

☑ 01993 / POP 2727

Woodstock, 8 miles northwest of Oxford, is a beautiful old town that has long had close links to royalty. Fine stone houses, venerable inns and pubs, and antique shops jostle shoulder to shoulder in its well-heeled centre, but what really draws the crowds here is Blenheim Palace, a majestic baroque extravaganza that was the birthplace of Sir Winston Churchill.

◉ Sights

★ **Blenheim Palace** PALACE
(☑ 01993-810530; www.blenheimpalace.com; Woodstock; adult/child £26/14.50, park & gardens only £16/7.40; ⊙ palace 10.30am-5.30pm, park & gardens 9am-6.30pm or dusk; ℗) One of the greatest stately homes in Britain, and a Unesco World Heritage Site, Blenheim Palace is a monumental baroque fantasy, designed by Sir John Vanbrugh and Nicholas Hawksmoor, and built between 1705 and 1722. Queen Anne gave both the land, and the necessary funds, to John Churchill, Duke of Marlborough, as thanks for defeating the French at the 1704 Battle of Blenheim. Sir Winston Churchill was born here in 1874, and Blenheim (blen-num) remains home to the 12th duke.

Inside, beyond majestic oak doors, the palace is stuffed with statues, tapestries, sumptuous furniture, priceless china and giant oil paintings in elaborate gilt frames. Visits start in the **Great Hall**, a soaring space that's adorned with images of the first duke and topped by a 20m-high ceiling. From here, you can either wander through the various grand state rooms independently, or join one of the free 45-minute guided tours, which depart every 30 minutes (except on Sunday, when guides are stationed in all rooms). Highlights include the famous **Blenheim Tapestries**, a set of 10 large wall hangings commemorating the first duke's triumphs; the **State Dining Room**, with its painted walls and trompe l'œil ceilings; and the magnificent **Long Library**, overlooked by an elaborate 1738 statue of Queen Anne, where the 56m ceiling was decorated by Nicholas Hawksmoor

Upstairs, in the **Untold Story**, a phantom chambermaid leads visitors on a half-hour audio-visual tour of tableaux that recreate important scenes from Blenheim's history. Between February and September you can also join additional tours (adult/child £5/4.50) of the Duke's private apartments, the palace bedrooms or the household staff areas.

A separate sequence of rooms downstairs holds the **Churchill Exhibition**, included in the ticket price and dedicated to the life, work, paintings and writings of Winston Churchill. Official history has it that the future prime minister, grandson of the 7th duke and cousin of the 9th, was born by chance at the palace, after his mother went into premature labour. It's widely believed, however, that the tale was concocted to conceal that she was already pregnant when she married his father, seven months earlier. Winston Churchill is buried in the local parish church in Bladon, 1.5 miles south, just outside the grounds.

If the crowds in the house become too oppressive, escape into the vast, lavish **gardens and parklands**, parts of which were landscaped by the great Lancelot 'Capability' Brown. Immediately outside, two large water terraces hold fountains and sphinxes, while a minitrain (50p) takes visitors to the **Pleasure Gardens**, where features include a yew maze, adventure playground, lavender garden and butterfly house.

For quieter and longer strolls, there are glorious walks of up to 4.5 miles, leading past lakes to an arboretum, rose garden, cascade, and Vanbrugh's Grand Bridge. Look out for the Temple of Diana, where Winston Churchill proposed to his future bride, Lady Clementine, on 10 August 1908.

🛏 Sleeping

★ Glove House   B&B £££
(📞 01993-813475; www.theglovehouse.co.uk; 24 Oxford St; d/ste £170/200; 🛜) Luxuriously renovated but proudly displaying evidence of its venerable age, this elegant 400-year-old town house conceals three sumptuous rooms, all with the added bonus of a glorious rear garden. The Charlbury suite has a free-standing copper bathtub in its wonderful lounge-equipped bathroom.

Feathers   HOTEL £££
(📞 01993-812291; www.feathers.co.uk; Market St; r incl breakfast £189; 🛜) Oozing contemporary chic, this handsome 17th-century town house – previously a sanatorium, a draper's, and a butcher's – offers stylish, comfortable rooms adorned with patterned wallpaper, modern art, fuzzy throws and rich-coloured fabrics. The smart bar downstairs stocks 401 types of gin.

❶ Getting There & Away

Stagecoach buses (p199) head to/from Oxford (S3; £3.20, 30 minutes), Burford (233; £4.10, 45 minutes), Chipping Norton (S3; £4.10, 20 minutes) and Witney (233; £3.80, 30 minutes). Buses S3 and 233 stop outside Blenheim Palace.

THE COTSWOLDS

Undulating gracefully across six counties, the Cotswolds region is a delightful tangle of golden villages, thatched cottages, evocative churches and honey-coloured mansions. In 1966 it was designated an Area of Outstanding Natural Beauty, surpassed for size in England by the Lake District alone.

No one's sure what the name means, but 'wolds' are rolling hills, while 'cots' might be 'cotes', or sheep pens. Certainly the region owes its wealth, and exquisite architecture, to the medieval wool trade, when 'Cotswold Lion' sheep were prized across Europe. Attentions later turned towards textiles instead, but the Industrial Revolution passed the Cotswolds by. Hailed by William Morris in the 19th century as encapsulating a timeless English rural idyll, it remains both a prime residential area and a treasured tourist destination.

Criss-crossed by long-distance trails including the 102-mile Cotswold Way, these gentle yet dramatic hills are perfect for walking, cycling and horse riding.

🏃 Activities

Cycling
Gentle gradients and wonderfully scenic panoramas make the Cotswolds ideal for cycling. Quiet country lanes and byways criss-cross the countryside, and only the steep western escarpment poses a significant challenge to the legs. You can also follow the signposted **Thames Valley Cycle Way** (NCN Routes 4 and 5) between Oxford and Windsor (and on to London).

Companies such as **Cotswold Country Cycles** (📞 01386-438706; www.cotswoldcountrycycles.com; Longlands Farm Cottage; 3 day/2 night tours from £285) organise maps, luggage transfers and B&B stays for a range of self-guided cycling tours.

DON'T MISS

KELMSCOTT MANOR
• •
Nestling near the Thames 20 miles west of Oxford (northwest of Faringdon), **Kelmscott Manor** (📞 01367-252486; www.sal.org.uk/kelmscott-manor; Kelmscott; adult/child £10/5; ⏰ 11am-5pm Wed & Sat Apr-Oct) is a gorgeous garden-fringed Tudor pile that was bought in 1871 by a prestigious pair of artist-poets: Dante Gabriel Rossetti and William Morris, founder of the Arts and Crafts movement. The interior is true to Morris' philosophy that one should own nothing that is neither beautiful nor useful, and displays his personal effects along with fabrics and furniture designed by Morris and his associates.

The Cotswolds

Walking

The 102-mile **Cotswold Way** (www.national trail.co.uk/cotswold-way) gives walkers a wonderful overview of the region. Meandering from Chipping Campden in the northeast to Bath in the southwest, it passes through some lovely countryside, linking ancient sites and tiny villages, with no major climbs or difficult stretches. It's also easily accessible from many points en route, if you fancy tackling a shorter section or a circular walk from your village of choice.

Other long-distance trails that pass through the Cotswolds include the 100-mile **Gloucestershire Way**, which runs from Chepstow to Tewkesbury via Stow-on-the-Wold; the 55-mile **St Kenelm's Way** into Worcestershire; and the 184-mile **Thames Path** (www.nationaltrail.co.uk/thames-path), which tracks from just southwest of Cirencester all the way to London.

Local tourist offices can advise on routes and usually sell walking maps.

Cirencester

☎ 01285 / POP 19,076

Charming Cirencester (siren-sester), the most significant town in the southern Cotswolds, is just 15 miles south of Cheltenham. Amazingly, under the Romans – who knew it as Corinium – Cirencester ranked second only to London in terms of size and importance, but little now survives from that era. The medieval wool trade brought further prosperity, with wealthy merchants funding the construction of a superb church.

Cirencester today is both elegant and affluent, but refreshingly unpretentious. Upmarket boutiques and fashionable delis now line its narrow streets, but its Monday and Friday markets remain at the core of its identity. Beautiful Victorian buildings flank the busy central square, while the surrounding streets showcase a harmonious medley of historic architecture.

◎ Sights

★Corinium Museum   MUSEUM
(☑01285-655611; www.coriniummuseum.org; Park St; adult/child £5.60/2.70; ☺10am-5pm Mon-Sat, 2-5pm Sun Apr-Oct, to 4pm Nov-Mar; ♿) Most of this wonderful modern museum is, of course, dedicated to Cirencester's Roman past; reconstructed rooms, videos and interactive displays bring the era to life. Among the highlights are some beautiful floor mosaics, unearthed locally and including a 4th-century mosaic depicting the mythical lyre-player Orpheus charming animals, and the 2nd-century 'Jupiter column', a carved capital depicting Bacchus and his drunken mates. There's also an excellent Anglo-Saxon section, plus exhibits on medieval Cirencester and its prosperous wool trade.

St John the Baptist's Church   CHURCH
(☑01285-659317; www.cirenparish.co.uk; Market Sq; ☺10am-4pm) One of England's largest parish churches, the cathedral-like St John's boasts an outstanding Perpendicular Gothic tower with flying buttresses (c 1400), plus a majestic three-storey south porch, built as an office in the late 15th century but subsequently used as Cirencester's town hall. Soaring arches, magnificent fan vaulting and a Tudor nave adorn the light-filled interior, where a wall safe holds the Boleyn Cup, made for Anne Boleyn in 1535.

On some Wednesdays and summer Saturdays, it's possible to climb the tower (adult/child £3/1.50).

⊨ Sleeping

YHA Cotswolds   HOSTEL £
(Barrel Store; ☑01285-657181; www.yha.org.uk; New Arts Brewery, Brewery Ct; dm/d/q £23/65/75; ⊛) ◈ This welcome new hostel, in the heart of Cirencester, is the Cotswolds' only YHA. Part of an exciting cultural complex, it's built to the highest environmental standards, with fixtures and furnishings sourced from local artisans. All rooms, from private doubles to two- to four-bunk dorms, have en-suite bathrooms; they're quite minimal, but do have Cotswolds wool blankets.

★No 12   B&B ££
(☑01285-640232; www.no12cirencester.co.uk; 12 Park St; d/ste £130/150; Ⓟ⊛) This welcoming and very central Georgian town house offers four gloriously unfussy, very private rooms kitted out with a tasteful mix of antiques and modern furnishings. Romantic room 1 has an in-room bath, while the suite has two bathrooms and overlooks the lovely garden, with extra-long beds, piles of feather pillows and splashes of red throughout. The breakfasts are superb.

Kings Head   LUXURY HOTEL ££
(☑01285-700900; www.kingshead-hotel.co.uk; 24 Market Pl; d/ste from £119/199; ⊛⊛) A coaching inn since the 14th century, this plush spot facing the church offers slick boudoirs and super-polished service. Exposed beams, red-brick walls and wood panelling pop up between Nespresso machines and Apple TVs. The standard rooms are contemporary and comfy; suite 103, with its in-room copper bath, is a stunner. Enjoy the tucked-away spa, cosy bar and smart **restaurant** (mains £12-27, Sunday lunch £20; ☺7am-10am, noon-2.30pm & 6.30-9.30pm).

✗ Eating

Made by Bob
MODERN BRITISH ££

(☑ 01285-641818; www.foodmadebybob.com; Corn Hall, 26 Market Pl; mains £8.50-22.50; ⊘ 7.30am-5pm Mon-Sat, from 10am Sun; ⊋) Filling a substantial light-filled space inside a central mall, and focused around an enormous open-plan kitchen, Bob's is part deli, part brasserie, and popular for its casual atmosphere. The breakfast selection is excellent – granola, smashed avocado, full English – while lunch bites include salads, soups, pastas, risottos and charcuterie platters. No bookings.

Jesse's Bistro
MODERN BRITISH £££

(☑ 01285-641497; www.jessesbistro.co.uk; The Stableyard, 14 Black Jack St; mains £16-28; ⊘ 11.45am-2.45pm Mon, 11.45am-2.45pm & 6.45-9.45pm Tue-Sat, 11.45am-4.45pm Sun) Tucked away in a cobbled yard, Jesse's is a very pleasant little spot, with flagstone floors, wood-beamed ceilings and mosaic tables. Delectable dishes come fresh from the semi-open kitchen and feature seasonal produce such as Cornish fish and Cotswolds meat from the adjacent butcher.

ⓘ Information

Tourist Office (☑ 01285-654180; www.cotswolds.com; Corinium Museum, Park St; ⊘ 10am-5pm Mon-Sat, 2-5pm Sun Apr-Oct, to 4pm Nov-Mar) Doubling as the museum gift store, this helpful office can arrange accommodation, and sells a leaflet detailing a self-guided walk around Cirencester for 50p.

ⓘ Getting There & Away

The closest station to Cirencester, at Kemble 4.5 miles south, is connected by train with London Paddington (£28.10, 1¼ hours).

Stagecoach, Pulhams and Cotswold Green serve Cirencester. Most buses stop outside the Corn Hall on Market Pl. Buses run to/from the following:

Cheltenham (route 51; £3.80, 40 minutes)
Gloucester (route 882; £2.80, 50 minutes)

ⓘ COTSWOLDS DISCOVERER

The **Cotswolds Discoverer**, a great-value one-day pass that gives unlimited travel on bus or train routes throughout the region (adult/child £10/5), can be bought at all UK mainline train stations, and aboard participating buses within the Cotswolds.

Northleach (route 855; £2.90, 20 minutes)
Tetbury (route 882; £2.70, 30 minutes)

National Express (www.nationalexpress.com) coach destinations:
Birmingham (£16, 2½ hours)
London Victoria (£6, 2½ hours)

Bibury

☑ 01285 / POP 627

Memorably described as 'England's most beautiful village' by no less an authority than William Morris, Bibury, 8 miles northeast of Cirencester, epitomises the Cotswolds at its most picturesque. With a cluster of perfect cottages beside the River Coln, and a tangle of narrow streets flanked by attractive stone buildings, small wonder that it's a major halt on large-group Cotswold tours.

⊙ Sights

★ Arlington Row
STREET

Bibury's most famous attraction, this ravishing row of rustic cottages – as seen in movies like *Stardust* – was originally a 14th-century wool store, before being converted into workers' lodgings. They overlook Rack Isle, a low-lying, marshy area once used to dry cloth and graze cattle, and now a wildlife refuge. Coach parties galore arrive to admire the cottages, and stroll the flower-lined lane alongside. If you'd like to see a photo, look at the inside front cover of a UK passport.

Church of St Mary the Virgin
CHURCH

(Church Rd; ⊘ 10am-dusk) Bibury's Saxon-built church has been much altered since its original construction, but many 8th-century features are still visible among the 12th-, 13th- and 15th-century additions. It's just off the B4425 in the village centre.

⨳ Sleeping

New Inn
PUB ££

(☑ 01285-750651; www.new-inn.co.uk; Main St, Coln St Aldwyns; r incl breakfast £119-149; ℗ �ⓢ ⓧ) The jasmine-clad 16th-century New Inn, 2.5 miles southeast of Bibury, offers 15 spacious and atmospheric bedrooms divided between the main pub building and a neighbouring cottage. Idiosyncratic contemporary stylings include bold colours, fluffy throws, smart furnishings and the odd free-standing bathtub, while the pub itself, with its exposed beams, is great. Weekend rates soar in summer.

★**Barnsley House**   LUXURY HOTEL **£££**
(✆01285-740000; www.barnsleyhouse.com; B4425, Barnsley; r incl breakfast from £319; P🅿🛜⛲) For pure indulgence and romance, this 1697 country house and its famously beautiful garden take some beating. Each of its 18 rooms is individually styled; some have lavish oriental touches or in-room baths, most are elegantly understated. Facilities include a spa, a pool, a private cinema, the Potager restaurant and the knowingly re-named Village Pub. Guests must be aged 14 or over.

❶ Getting There & Away

Most drivers approach Bibury along the B4425, which passes through the village centre halfway between Burford (9 miles northeast) and Cirencester (8 miles southwest). Pulhams bus 855 heads to/from Cirencester (£2.40, 15 minutes), Barnsley (£1.70, 5 minutes) and Northleach (£2.40, 20 minutes); there's no Sunday service.

Burford
✆01993 / POP 1410

Gliding down a steep hillside to an ancient (and still single-lane) crossing point on the River Windrush, 20 miles west of Oxford, Burford has hardly changed since its medieval glory days. Locals insist it's a town not a village, having received its charter in 1090, but it's a very small town, and a very picturesque one too, home to an appealing mix of stone cottages, gold-tinged Cotswold town houses, and the odd Elizabethan or Georgian treasure.

Throw in a wonderfully preserved, centuries-old church and an array of delightful hotels and restaurants, and Burford makes an attractive stop. Antique shops, chintzy tearooms and specialist boutiques peddle nostalgia to the many summer visitors, but it's easy to escape the crowds and wander along quiet side streets, seemingly lost in time.

🛏 Sleeping & Eating

★**Star Cottage**   B&B **££**
(✆01993-822032; www.burfordbedandbreakfast. co.uk; Meadow Lane, Fulbrook; r £110-125, apt £115-140; 🛜) A mile northeast of Burford, this wonderful old Cotswold cottage holds two comfortable and character-filled en-suite rooms done up in tastefully creative blues, whites and greys, with gorgeous quilted curtains. The smaller room holds a grand canopied bed; the larger has a beautiful bath-

room; and the back barn hosts a separate four-person apartment. The home-cooked, locally sourced breakfasts are fantastic.

Lamb Inn   PUB **£££**
(✆01993-823155; www.cotswold-inns-hotels.co.uk/ the-lamb-inn; Sheep St; s/d incl breakfast from £150/160; P🅿🛜🐾) A rambling 15th-century inn, off the main street, where the flagstone floors, exposed beams and creaking stairs are complemented by 17 opulent antique-furnished rooms. A few have four-poster beds, and one even has its own private garden, while modern touches include Nespresso machines and slick bathrooms. Modern British cuisine is served in both the romantic **restaurant** (mains £14-35; ⏱7.30-10am, noon-2.30pm & 7-9pm) and the bar.

Swan Inn   PUB **£££**
(✆01993-823339; www.theswanswinbrook.co.uk; Swinbrook; s/d/ste incl breakfast £130/150/250; P🛜) All soft pastels, country comfort and dashes of colour, the Swan sits beside the River Windrush in tiny Swinbrook, 3 miles east of Burford. Six cosy, elegant rooms in a former barn overlook orchards – the plush top-floor suite is perfect for families – while five delightful rooms in the newer riverside cottage have a more contemporary style. There's an excellent **restaurant** (mains £16-26; ⏱noon-2pm & 7-9pm; P).

Downton Abbey fans: this is the pub where Lady Sybil and Branson planned their elopement.

Huffkins   BAKERY, CAFE **££**
(✆01993-824694; www.huffkins.com; 98 High St; mains £6-15; ⏱9am-4.30pm Mon-Fri, to 5pm Sat, 10am-5pm Sun; 🖶) The original outlet of a Cotswolds chain that's been baking and serving delicious scones, cakes and pies since 1890, this lively, friendly cafe is usually packed with locals enjoying quiches, soups, macaroni cheese or burgers. It also offers all-day cooked breakfasts and full-blown afternoon teas. For a quick snack, pick up baked goods in its adjoining deli.

❶ Information

Tourist Office (✆01993-823558; www.oxford shirecotswolds.org; 33a High St; ⏱9.30am-5pm Mon-Sat, 10am-4pm Sun) Information on local walks.

❶ Getting There & Away

Stagecoach and Swanbrook buses run to/from Burford. Local buses stop on High or Sheep Sts, but express services stop at the A40 roundabout, five minutes' walk south of the centre. Bus destinations include the following:

Cheltenham (route 853; £4.50, 45 minutes)

Gloucester (route 853; £6, 1¼ hours)

Oxford (route 853; £6.30, 45 minutes to 1¼ hours)

Minster Lovell (route 233/853; £2.30, 15 minutes)

Witney (route 233/853; £3.30, 19 minutes)

Woodstock (route 233; £4.10, 45 minutes)

Northleach

🗹 01451 / POP 1838

Oddly under-visited, and refreshingly uncommercialised despite holding some interesting attractions, Northleach, 14 miles southeast of Cheltenham, has been a small market town since 1227. Late-medieval cottages, imposing merchants' stores and half-timbered Tudor houses jostle for position in a wonderful melange of styles around Market Sq and the narrow laneways that lead off it.

◉ Sights

Chedworth Roman Villa ARCHAEOLOGICAL SITE
(NT; 🗹 01242-890256; www.nationaltrust.org.uk; Yanworth; adult/child £10.50/5.25; ⊙ 10am-5pm Apr-Oct, to 4pm mid-Feb–Mar & Nov; 🅿) This large and luxurious Roman villa was rediscovered by a gamekeeper in 1864. Though the earliest section dates to around AD 175, it was at its most magnificent around AD 362, equipped with two sets of bathhouses, a water shrine and a dining room with underfloor heating. A fine modern gallery preserves several exquisite mosaics, though yet more, unearthed recently, had to be reburied due to lack of resources.

It's at the far end of a dead-end rural road, 4.5 miles west of Northleach and signposted from the A429.

Mechanical Music Museum MUSEUM
(🗹 01451-860181; www.mechanicalmusic.co.uk; High St; adult/child £8/3.50; ⊙ 10am-5pm) Join an hour-long tour of this quirky collection of antique music players, and you'll hear some amazing sounds, emerging perhaps from a beautifully handcrafted 18th-century device that cost as much as a London house, or an upright piano eerily 'played' by the invisible fingers of George Gershwin himself.

Church of St Peter & St Paul CHURCH
(www.northleach.org; Church Walk; ⊙ 9am-5pm) The grandeur and complexity of this

Driving Tour
Classic Cotswolds

START BURFORD
END WINCHCOMBE
LENGTH 54 MILES; ONE TO THREE DAYS

Given the Cotswolds' intricate spider's-web of winding country lanes that connect its ancient market towns, time-warped villages and majestic stately homes, it's impossible to cover every highlight in a single day. This tour, though, spans three counties and takes in some of the most picturesque spots in the northern half of the range. You could drive it in a day, but you'll enjoy it more if you stretch it into two or three, with plentiful stop-offs along the way.

Begin in Oxfordshire at the gorgeous hillside market town of ① **Burford** (p205), then head 10 miles west on the A40 into Gloucestershire, following signs to classic Cotswolds town ② **Northleach**. The Cotswolds Discovery Centre here has excellent displays covering the history, geography, flora and fauna of the Cotswolds Area of Outstanding Natural Beauty (AONB). There's a fine church in town, and a fascinating Roman villa nearby.

From Northleach, spin 7 miles northeast on the A429 to ③ **Lower Slaughter** (p208), a serene riverside village lined with houses made of that irresistible Cotswolds golden stone. Spare the time if you can to stroll a mile northwest, along the river, to ④ **Upper Slaughter** (p208), less visited than its sibling but no less attractive, thanks to its idyllic setting between a small ford and the hills. Book ahead, and you can have lunch in an exquisite Jacobean mansion, at Lords of the Manor.

Continue 3 miles north on the A429 to ⑤ **Stow-on-the-Wold** (p208), the highest Cotswold village at 244m and a market centre since the 12th century. Explore the market square, then follow the A429 north, along the ruler-straight route of the ancient Roman Fosse Way. After 4.5 miles you'll reach busy ⑥ **Moreton-in-Marsh** (p213), known for its weekly Tuesday market and excellent shops.

Next, zip 3 miles west on the A44 to tiny ⑦ **Bourton-on-the-Hill**, filled with attractive 17th- and 18th-century cottages. It's famous for two things: the gibbeting cage in which the bodies of dead highwaymen were hung in the 19th century, and horse training – there are several stud farms in the vicinity. The Horse & Groom here is a good lunch option.

Head 3 miles west on the A44, then turn right (northeast) onto the B4081 to **8 Chipping Campden** (p210), one of the Cotswold's most bucolic towns. After admiring 15th-century St James' Church and the honey-toned buildings along High St – at least stop for cake and coffee, even if you're not tempted to stay the night – backtrack to the A44. Drive a mile northwest, crossing into the Worcestershire corner of the Cotswolds, and turn off at signposted **9 Broadway Tower** (p212), an 18th-century Gothic folly perched spectacularly atop the escarpment.

Leaving Broadway Tower, continue 1 mile south and turn right (southwest) at the crossing. You'll soon see signs to pretty little **10 Snowshill**, a mile further on and one-time film set for *Bridget Jones's Diary*. If you're visiting in June or July, you'll swing by spectacularly purple fields of flowering lavender. From Snowshill, whizz 2.5 miles north to **11 Broadway** (p211), home to an excellent museum and gallery. After cruising along broad High St, hop on the B4632 southwest towards Cheltenham.

After 3 miles, take the left (east) turn-off to **12 Stanton**, a tiny stunner of a village.

Its houses are crafted out of gold-tinged Cotswolds stone. The buildings most likely to catch your eye are Jacobean Stanton Court and St Michael & All Angels' Church, the latter with its fine Perpendicular tower and medieval interior. Stanton Court once belonged to civil architect Sir Philip Stott (1858–1937), who restored many other Stanton houses.

You're sure to see walkers passing through Stanton, heading along the Cotswold Way to **13 Stanway**, a mile south; follow the narrow road that runs parallel to the trail. There's little more to idyllic Stanway than a few thatched-roofed cottages, a church and Stanway House, a magnificent Jacobean manor house concealed behind a triple-gabled gatehouse. Its beautiful baroque water gardens feature Britain's tallest fountain. The private home of the Earls of Wemyss for 500 years, the manor has a delightful, lived-in charm, with much of its original furniture and character intact.

Traverse Stanway, turn right (west) onto the B4077 and then left (southwest) back onto the B4632. After 3.5 miles, you'll reach **14 Winchcombe** (p217), an ancient Anglo-Saxon town and walkers' favourite with good sleeping and eating options, including 5 North St. You'll probably want to stay overnight to explore wonderful Sudeley Castle in the morning.

masterpiece of the Cotswold Perpendicular style testifies to its wool-era wealth. Although the chancel and 30m tower date from the 14th century, it was extensively reworked during the 15th-century wool boom. A modern highlight is the 1964 stained-glass window depicting Christ in Glory, behind the altar, while earlier treasures include an unusual 14th-century font.

Sleeping & Eating

★ **Wheatsheaf** BOUTIQUE HOTEL ££££
(☑ 01451-860244; www.cotswoldswheatsheaf.com; West End; r incl breakfast £123-255; P 🛜 🐾) The 14 different rooms at this former coaching inn, very popular with an exclusive London set, blend atmospheric period touches, such as free-standing bathtubs, with modern comforts including power showers, organic toiletries and country-chic decor. Downstairs, an outrageously popular **restaurant** (mains £14.50-24; ◷ 8-10am, noon-3pm & 6-9pm Mon-Thu & Sun, to 10pm Fri & Sat; P 🛜 🐾) adds a contemporary twist to delightful seasonal British dishes.

ℹ Information

Cotswolds Discovery Centre (Escape to the Cotswolds; ☑ 01451-861563; www.cotswolds aonb.org.uk; Fosse Way; ◷ 9.30am-4pm Thu-Mon; P) The Cotswolds' official visitor centre.

ℹ Getting There & Away

Swanbrook or Pulhams buses head to/from the following destinations:
Burford (route 853; £2.40, 15 minutes)
Cheltenham (route 801/853; £2.90, 45 minutes)
Cirencester (route 855; £2.70; 20 minutes)
Gloucester (route 853; £3.50, one hour)
Moreton-in-Marsh (route 801; £2.40, 40 minutes)
Oxford (route 853; £8, one hour)

The Slaughters

☑ 01451 / POP 400

The picture-postcard villages of Upper and Lower Slaughter, roughly a mile apart and around 3.5 miles southwest of Stow-on-the-Wold, have somehow managed to maintain their unhurried medieval charm, despite receiving a multitude of visitors. Their names have nothing to do with abattoirs; they come from the Old English 'sloughtre', meaning slough or muddy place.

Meandering sleepily through the two villages, the River Eye passes a succession of classic gold-tinged Cotswolds houses. It's Lower Slaughter that's the real gem, with the river canalised between limestone banks to flow just a few inches below road level, and flowery footpaths to either side. If you've time for a stroll, you can follow the Eye from one village to the other – the central stretch is away from the traffic – for a round trip that typically takes around two hours.

⊙ Sights

Old Mill NOTABLE BUILDING
(☑ 01451-820052; www.oldmill-lowerslaughter. com; Lower Slaughter; adult/child £2.50/1; ◷ 10am-6pm Mar-Oct, to dusk Nov-Feb) Right on the River Eye, the Old Mill houses a cafe and crafts shop as well as a small museum, where you can find out all about the building's former life as a water-powered flour mill. A watermill is recorded as operating in this location as far back as the Domesday Book (1086).

Sleeping & Eating

Lords of the Manor HISTORIC HOTEL £££
(☑ 01451-820243; www.lordsofthemanor.com; Upper Slaughter; r incl breakfast £240-465; P 🛜 🐾) Although from the outside this 17th-century mansion appears to embody traditional rural splendour, its spacious, supremely tasteful rooms are surprisingly up to date. Expect fresh white styling, floral-print spreads and exposed beams, along with gorgeous countryside panoramas, superb service and a fantastic Michelin-starred **restaurant** (3-/7-course dinner £72.50/£90; ◷ noon-1.30pm Sat & Sun, 6.45-9pm daily; P).

ℹ Getting There & Away

Buses are not permitted in the Slaughters, so unless you're hiking or cycling, a car is your best option. To reach Lower Slaughter, detour half a mile west from the A429, 2.5 miles southwest of Stow-on-the-Wold or 6 miles northeast of Northleach. Upper Slaughter is another mile further west.

Stow-on-the-Wold

☑ 01451 / POP 2035

The highest town in the Cotswolds (244m), Stow-on-the-Wold centres on a large square surrounded by handsome buildings. The high-walled alleyways that lead into it originally served to funnel sheep into the fair, and it also witnessed a bloody massacre at the end of the English Civil War, when Roundhead soldiers dispatched defeated Royalists in 1646.

Standing on the Roman Fosse Way (now the A429), at the junction of six roads 4.5 miles south of Moreton-in-Marsh, Stow is still an important market town. It's also a major tourist destination, crowded with visitors in summer, and famous for hosting the twice-yearly Stow Horse Fair.

◎ Sights

Cotswold Farm Park   ZOO
(☑ 01451-850307; www.cotswoldfarmpark.co.uk; Guiting Power; adult/child £14/12.50; ☺ 10.30am–5pm mid-Feb–late Dec; P ⛹) ✪ Owned by TV presenter Adam Henson, Cotswold Farm Park sets out to introduce little ones to the world of farm animals, while also preserving rare breeds, such as Exmoor ponies and Cotswold Lion sheep. There are milking demonstrations, lamb-feeding sessions, an adventure playground, a 2-mile wildlife walk and pedal tractors to ride on. It's 6 miles west of Stow-on-the-Wold, signposted from the B4077 and B4068.

🛏 Sleeping & Eating

Number 9   B&B ££
(☑ 01451-870333; www.number-nine.info; 9 Park St; s £50-60, d £75-85; ☎) Centrally located and wonderfully atmospheric, set in an 18th-century town house that was once a coaching inn, this friendly B&B is all sloping floors, low ceilings and exposed beams. Two of the three comfortable en-suite rooms, styled in white and pastels, are unusually spacious, and there's a homely lounge with a crackling fire downstairs.

King's Head Inn   PUB ££
(☑ 01608-658365; www.thekingsheadinn.net; The Green, Bledington; s/d incl breakfast from £90/100; P ☎) Overlooking a peaceful green 4 miles southeast of Stow, this stylishly revamped 16th-century pub blends old and new to perfection, holding a dozen subtly luxurious, individually styled rooms plus a good **restaurant** (mains £14-25.50; ☺ noon-2pm & 6.30-9pm Mon-Sat, to 9.30pm Fri & Sat, noon-3pm & 6.30-9pm Sun; P ✿) ✪. The six cosy rooms in the original building burst with old-world character (exposed beams, check-print rugs), while the quieter courtyard rooms offer sumptuous contemporary design.

❶ Getting There & Away

Pulhams buses serve the following destinations (no Sunday service October to April):
Cheltenham (route 801; £3.20, 1¼ hours)
Moreton-in-Marsh (801; £1.90, 10 minutes)
Northleach (801; £2.30, 30 minutes)

Chipping Norton
☑ 01608 / POP 6300

Chipping Norton ('Chippy') is a handsome but slightly faded hilltop town, home to humdrum banks and businesses but with its market square still boasting stately Georgian buildings and old coaching inns as well as the pillared 19th-century town hall. The pick of the many quiet side streets is Church St, where beyond a row of honey-tinged 17th-century almshouses you'll find a fine wool-era church.

◎ Sights

Rollright Stones   ARCHAEOLOGICAL SITE
(www.rollrightstones.co.uk; off A3400, Great Rollright; suggested donation £1; ☺ 24hr) Linked by a footpath through open fields, the ancient Rollright Stones stand to either side of an unnamed road 4 miles north of Chipping Norton. The most remarkable, the King's Men, consists of the weathered remnants of a stone circle that surrounded a Neolithic ceremonial centre in around 2500BC, while the taller King Stone probably marked a Bronze Age cemetery, a millennium later.

Cotswolds Distillery   DISTILLERY
(☑ 01608-238533; www.cotswoldsdistillery.com; Phillip's Field, Whichford Rd, Stourton; tours with/without tasting £10/6; ☺ tours 11am, 1pm & 3pm,

shop 9am-5pm Mon-Sat, 11am-4pm Sun) ✐
This ambitious, ecofriendly gin and whisky distillery sits tucked into the northern Cotswolds, 8 miles north of Chipping Norton. Join a tour of the facilities to learn how its delicious Cotswolds-flavoured liquors are produced, then wrap things up with a tasting session. Reservations essential.

🛏 Sleeping & Eating

★ Falkland Arms
PUB ££
(19-21 The Green, Great Tew; s/d incl breakfast £85/90; ⊙ restaurant noon-2.30pm & 6-9pm Mon-Sat, to 8pm Sun; P 🛜) For its blissful bucolic setting and historic charm, there's no beating the thatched, 16-century Falkland Arms, in the picture-postcard village of Great Tew, 6 miles east of Chipping Norton. The half-dozen freshly restored and upgraded rooms are great value, the pub downstairs serves fine ales and decent pub grub (mains £13 to £20), and there's lovely walking in every direction.

★ Wild Thyme
MODERN BRITISH ££
(☑ 01608-645060; www.wildthymerestaurant.co.uk; 10 New St; 2-/3-course set menus lunch £20/25, dinner £32/40; ⊙ 7-9pm Tue & Wed, noon-2pm & 7-9pm Thu, noon-2pm & 6.30-9.30pm Fri & Sat) This little 'restaurant with rooms' thrills palates with top-notch creative dishes packed with flavour, such as asparagus and goat's

---

OFF THE BEATEN TRACK

MINSTER LOVELL

Eighteen miles west of Oxford, set on a gentle slope that leads down to the meandering River Windrush, **Minster Lovell** is a gorgeous village where a clutch of thatch-roofed stone cottages nestle beside an ancient pub and riverside mill. One of William Morris' favourite spots, this peaceful flower-filled hamlet has changed little since medieval times. The main sight is **Minster Lovell Hall** (EH; www.english-heritage.org.uk; Old Minster; ⊙ 24hr) **FREE**, a 15th-century riverside manor house that fell into ruins after being abandoned in 1747. You can pass through the vaulted porch to peek past blackened walls into the roofless great hall, the interior courtyard and the crumbling tower, while the wind whistles eerily through the gaping windows.

---

cheese risotto or steamed Cornish turbot with Japanese pickles. The desserts – from apple crumble to chocolate fondant – are nothing short of sublime. Hidden upstairs are three brilliantly cosy pastel-painted **rooms** (s £75-85, d £85-100; 🛜).

Jaffé & Neale Bookshop Cafe
CAFE
(☑ 01608-641033; www.jaffeandneale.co.uk; 1 Middle Row; ⊙ 9.30am-5.30pm Mon-Fri, 9am-5.30pm Sat, 11am-5pm Sun; 🛜) The cosy little cafe in this busy independent bookshop on the main square serves delicious cakes and coffees at tables squeezed between the bookshelves, or in the cosy upstairs reading lounge with sofas.

❶ Getting There & Away

Stagecoach and/or Pulhams buses head to/from the following destinations:
Oxford (route S3; £4.70, one hour)
Witney (route X9; £4, 45 minutes)
Woodstock (route S3; £4.10, 20 minutes)

Chipping Campden
☑ 01386 / POP 2308

A standout gem, even for an area of such pretty towns, Chipping Campden is a glorious reminder of Cotswolds life in medieval times. While 'Chipping' derives from the Old English 'ceapen', meaning 'market', it owes its conspicuous prosperity to its success in the wool trade. Its gracefully curving main street is flanked by a picturesque array of stone cottages, fine terraced houses, ancient inns and historic homes, most made of that beautiful honey-coloured Cotswolds stone. Westington, southwest of the centre, holds some especially striking thatch-roofed cottages.

As the northeastern end of the Cotswold Way, which rambles 102 miles southwest from here to Bath, Chipping Campden is a popular way station for walkers and cyclists, and welcomes crowds of visitors year-round. Despite its obvious allure, though, it remains surprisingly unspoiled.

◉ Sights

Hidcote
GARDENS
(NT; www.nationaltrust.org.uk/hidcote; Hidcote Bartrim; adult/child £10.90/5.45; ⊙ 10am-6pm Apr-Sep, to 5pm Oct, shorter hours Nov, Dec & mid-Feb–Mar, closed Jan; P) Hidcote, 4 miles northeast of Chipping Campden, ranks among the finest Arts and Crafts gardens in Britain. Laid out from 1907 onwards by American

horticulturalist Lawrence Johnston, and acquired by the National Trust in 1948, it consists of a series of outdoor 'rooms' filled with flowers and rare plants from across the globe. There's also a cafe and garden centre.

Grevel House
HISTORIC BUILDING

(High St; ⊘closed to the public) Built around 1380 for the supremely prosperous wool merchant William Grevel, complete with gargoyles and mullioned windows, Grevel House is Chipping Campden's oldest building. It's still a private home, but you can admire its splendid Perpendicular Gothic–style gabled window and sundial from the street.

Court Barn Museum
MUSEUM

(☑01386-841951; www.courtbarn.org.uk; Church St; adult/child £5/free; ⊘10am-5pm Tue-Sun Apr-Sep, to 4pm Oct-Mar) Ever since architect and designer Charles Robert Ashbee (1863–1942) moved his Guild of Handicraft here from east London in 1902, Chipping Campden has been linked with the Arts and Crafts movement. This small but interesting museum displays work by nine luminaries of the movement, which celebrated traditional artisans in an age of industrialisation. Sadly, robberies in 2011 and 2017 removed its prize jewellery collection, but surviving artefacts include sculpture, book-binding and ceramics. It also stages two selling exhibitions each year.

🛏 Sleeping & Eating

Eight Bells Inn
PUB ££

(☑01386-840371; www.eightbellsinn.co.uk; Church St; r incl breakfast £99-143; 🛜) This friendly and atmospheric 14th-century inn offers six bright, modern rooms with iron bedsteads, soothing neutral decor, flowery wallpaper and warm accents. Room 7 – there's no number 4 – with its chunky old-world beams, is especially striking. The cosy pub downstairs serves contemporary country cooking.

★ Badgers Hall
BAKERY £

(☑01386-840839; www.badgershall.com; High St; lunch mains £6-12, afternoon tea per person £6.50-25; ⊘8am-5.30pm Thu-Sat; 🍽) Set in a glorious old mansion facing the market hall, this definitive Cotswold tearoom is renowned for its no-holds-barred afternoon teas, served from 2.30pm onwards. Lunch is also a treat, starring the most wonderful cheese scones you've ever tasted. Guests staying in the cosy B&B rooms upstairs (£140) get to sample its baking all week; nonguests are welcome Thursday to Saturday only.

WORTH A TRIP

BATSFORD ARBORETUM

Created from 1880 onwards by Bertie Mitford (Lord Redesdale), and later briefly home to his famous granddaughters, the Mitford sisters, these exotic 22-hectare **woodlands** (☑01386-701441; www.batsarb.co.uk; Batsford Park; adult/child £7.95/3.30; ⊘9am-5pm Mon-Sat, from 10am Sun; P 🐾) 🐾, 1.5 miles west of Moreton, hold around 1600 species of labelled trees, bamboos and shrubs. Drawn especially from Nepal, China and Japan, many are rare or endangered, or were planted pre-WWI. Highlights include flowering Japanese cherries (at their best in spring), some vast North American redwoods and an enormous davidia, and the strangely churchlike 'cathedral' lime.

A 1.7-mile footpath from Moreton leads direct to the arboretum itself; motorists have to drive a mile north up the approach road from the entrance on the A44.

❶ Information

Tourist Office (☑01386-841206; www.campdenonline.org; Old Police Station, High St; ⊘9.30am-5pm mid-Mar–Oct, 9.30am-1pm Mon-Thu, to 4pm Fri-Sun Nov–mid-Mar) Pick up a town guide (£1.50) for a self-guided walk around Chipping Campden's most significant buildings. Between May and September, the Cotswold Voluntary Wardens run guided tours (suggested donation £3).

❶ Getting There & Away

From Monday to Saturday, Johnsons Excelbus services head to/from Moreton-in-Marsh (route 1/2; £3.90, 50 minutes), Broadway (route 1/2; £2.90, 20 minutes) and Stratford-upon-Avon (route 1/2; £4.40, 50 minutes).

Marchants buses 606 (Monday to Saturday) and 606S (Sunday) run to/from Broadway (£2.90, 20 minutes), Cheltenham (£8.50, one hour 20 minutes), Stratford-upon-Avon (£4.80, 25 minutes) and Winchcombe (£5.60, 35 minutes).

Broadway

☑01386 / POP 2540

The graceful, golden-hued cottages of the quintessentially English village of Broadway, set at the foot of a steep escarpment, now hold antique shops, tearooms and art galleries, interspersed with luxurious hotels. One of the Cotswolds' most popular destinations, just 5 miles west of Chipping Campden, the village attracted the likes of writer-designer William Morris and artist John Singer Sargent during the Victorian era.

The village of Snowshill, 2.5 miles south, may look familiar; a local house starred in the hit film *Bridget Jones's Diary* as Bridget's parents' home.

◉ Sights

Snowshill Manor & Garden   HOUSE

(NT; www.nationaltrust.org.uk; Snowshill; adult/child £12.80/6.40; ⊙noon-5pm mid-Mar–Oct, 11am-2.30pm Sat & Sun Nov) Once home to eccentric poet and architect Charles Paget Wade (1883–1956), this wonderful medieval mansion stands just over 2 miles south of Broadway. It now displays Wade's extraordinary collection of crafts and design, ranging from musical instruments to Southeast Asian masks and Japanese samurai armour.

Broadway Tower   TOWER

(☑01386-852390; www.broadwaytower.co.uk; Middle Hill; adult/child £5/3, with Cold War Experience £8.50/5; ⊙10am-5pm; P) Built in 1798 to resemble an imaginary Saxon fort, this turreted Gothic folly looks down on Broadway from atop the escarpment, 1 mile southeast. William Morris spent a summer here, so exhibitions on its successive levels focus on the

SHIN KICKING & CHEESE ROLLING

The medieval sport of shin kicking lives on in the extraordinary **Cotswold Olimpicks** (www.olimpickgames.co.uk; Dover's Hill; ⊙late May/early Jun), first celebrated in 1612. One of England's most bizarre and entertaining traditional sports days, it still features many of the original events, such as tug o' war. It's held in Chipping Campden.

Equally odd is the age-old (and surprisingly hazardous) pastime of **cheese-rolling** (www.cheese-rolling. co.uk; Cooper's Hill; admission free; ⊙last May bank holiday). Following a 200-year-old tradition, crowds run, tumble and slide down Cooper's Hill, 4.5 miles northeast of Painswick, pursuing an 8lb round of Double Gloucester cheese. The prize? The cheese itself – and the glory of catching it.

Arts and Crafts movement. The main reason to visit, though, is for the stunning all-round views from its rooftop platform.

Broadway Museum & Art Gallery   MUSEUM

(☑01386-859047; www.ashmoleanbroadway. org; Tudor House, 65 High St; adult/child £5/2; ⊙10am-5pm Tue-Sun Feb-Oct, to 4pm Nov & Dec, closed Jan) Set in a magnificent 17th-century coaching inn, Broadway's town museum has close links with Oxford's prestigious Ashmolean Museum (p192). Its fascinating displays of local crafts, art and antiques, and its stimulating temporary exhibitions, draw exclusively on the Ashmolean collection, so the quality is consistently high. Paintings in the sumptuous upstairs galleries include 18th-century works by Joshua Reynolds and Thomas Gainsborough.

🛏 Sleeping & Eating

Crown & Trumpet   PUB ££

(☑01386-853202; www.cotswoldholidays.co.uk; 14 Church St; r £60-90; ⊙restaurant 11am-11pm; P🛜) This very welcoming, locally loved 17th-century inn holds five good-value retro-furnished en-suite rooms, complete with sloping floors, exposed beams and low ceilings. The downstairs pub is a good bet for real ales, ciders and decent pub grub; it serves a good breakfast (to guests only) for £10 per person. Two-night minimum at weekends.

Russell's   HOTEL £££

(☑01386-853555; www.russellsofbroadway.co.uk; The Green, 20 High St; r incl breakfast from £130; ⊙restaurant noon-2.15pm & 6-9.15pm Mon-Sat, noon-2.30pm Sun; P🛜🐾) Housed in the former workshop of furniture designer Gordon Russell, this Arts and Crafts–influenced hotel offers seven sizeable rooms, some with exposed beams, four-poster beds and armchairs, and all with contemporary bathrooms and fresh white styling. The modern-British restaurant (mains £15 to £27) serves a good-value three-course menu (£24) for lunch and dinner.

★ Mount Inn   PUB FOOD ££

(☑01386-584316; www.themountinn.co.uk; Stanton; mains £13-22; ⊙noon-2pm & 6-9pm Mon-Sat, to 8pm Sun; P) Revelling in glorious hilltop views above pretty honey-washed Stanton, just off the Cotswolds Way 3.5 miles southwest of Broadway, this pub is not just idyllically located, it serves great food too: hearty country favourites, prepared with contemporary flair. Menus range over breaded local

St Eadburgha cheese, beer-battered haddock, gammon steaks, mushroom-halloumi burgers and seasonal specials.

ℹ Information

Tourist Office (☎01386-852937; www.visit-broadway.co.uk; Russell Sq; ⊙10am-5pm Mon-Sat, 11am-3pm Sun Apr-Oct, 10am-4pm Mon-Sat Nov-Mar) Sells maps of local walks.

ℹ Getting There & Away

BUS

Marchants and Johnsons ExcelBus services head to the following destinations:

Cheltenham (route 606/606S; £3.20, 40 minutes)

Chipping Campden (route 1/2/606S; £2.90, 20 minutes)

Moreton-in-Marsh (route 1/2; £3.90, 30 minutes)

Stratford-upon-Avon (route 1/2/24/606S; £4.40, 45 minutes)

Winchcombe (route 606/606S; £3, 30 minutes)

TRAIN

Rail service returned to Broadway in 2018 after a 58-year hiatus, with the reopening of the long-defunct Broadway Station, just under a mile northwest of town. Most days in summer, following an intricate schedule, the volunteer-run Gloucestershire Warwickshire Railway (p218) runs around five excursion trains between Cheltenham racecourse and Broadway, via Winchcombe, for a return fare of £18.

Moreton-in-Marsh

☎01608 / POP 3820

Graced by an ultrabroad High St that follows the die-straight line of the Roman Fosse Way (now the A429), and is lined with beautiful 17th- and 18th-century buildings, Moreton-in-Marsh is a historic Cotswolds town that's sadly rather marred by the constant heavy traffic that hurtles right through the centre. Take the time to wander around, though – ideally on a Tuesday, when the weekly market bursts into life – and you'll find plenty of tearooms, cafes and pubs, along with intriguing shops. It's 4.5 miles north of Stow-on-the-Wold.

◉ Sights

★**Cotswold Falconry Centre**   BIRD SANCTUARY
(☎01386-701043; www.cotswold-falconry.co.uk; Batsford Park; adult/child £10/5; ⊙10.30am-5pm

HIGHGROVE

The private residence of Prince Charles and the Duchess of Cornwall, a mile southwest of Tetbury, **Highgrove** (☎0303 123 7310; www.highgrovegardens.com; Doughton; tours £27.50; ⊙Apr-Sep; 🅿) 🌿 is famous for its exquisite, sustainable, organic gardens, which include rows of shape-clipped yews and a 'carpet garden' modelled on an oriental rug. Two-hour garden tours run on select summer days, detailed on the website and varying from 17 days in a month to just one. They usually sell out far in advance, but last-minute tickets are sometimes available through Highgrove Shop.

mid-Feb–mid-Nov; 🅿) Home to over 150 birds of prey (owl, vulture, eagle and, of course, falcon), this exciting spot stages displays of the ancient practice of falconry at 11.30am, 1.30pm and 3pm daily (plus 4.30pm April to October). The birds fly best on windy days. Hands-on experiences (from £40) include a one-hour 'Flying Start' during which visitors get to fly hawks.

Chastleton House   HISTORIC BUILDING
(NT; ☎01608-674355; www.nationaltrust.org.uk/chastleton-house; Chastleton; adult/child £9.50/5; ⊙1-5pm Wed-Sun Mar-Oct; 🅿) Four miles southeast of Moreton, signposted off the A44 halfway to Chipping Norton, Chastleton is one of England's finest and most complete Jacobean houses. Built between 1607 and 1612 and barely altered since, it's bursting with rare tapestries, family portraits and antique furniture; the Long Gallery is particularly resplendent. Outside, there's a wonderful topiary garden. Free garden tours run most afternoons.

🛏 Sleeping & Eating

White Hart Royal Hotel   HOTEL ££
(☎01608-650731; www.whitehartroyal.co.uk; High St; s/d £100/110; 🅿🖥) 'Royal' refers to the fact that Charles I stayed in this low-slung honey-coloured inn during the Civil War. He may not have used the iPod docks and flatscreen TVs, but he certainly walked down the atmospheric half-timbered corridors. Standard rooms these days are comfy and well equipped, even if they lack character.

Literary Britain

Britain's literary heritage is astoundingly rich and globally renowned. As the English language spread around the world in the colonial era, so too did its literature, with novelists such as Charles Dickens and George Eliot and poets including Samuel Taylor Coleridge and Robert Burns being read far from home in the late 18th and 19th centuries.

1. Radcliffe Camera (p189), Oxford
One of the most photographed landmarks in Oxford, it stores part of the Bodleian Library's collection.

2. Shakespeare's Birthplace (p415), Stratford-upon-Avon
Shakespeare was born in this house in 1564 and lived here at the beginning of his marriage to Anne Hathaway.

3. Charles Dickens Museum (p89), London
This museum is housed in Dickens' only surviving London home.

4. Statue of Robert Burns, Stirling (p827)
Burns is Scotland's most famous poet.

Martha's Coffee House
CAFE £

(☑ 01608-651999; Gavel Cottage, High St; mains £7-9; ⊙ 9am-5pm Mon-Sat, to 4pm Sun; 🛜 🚻) In an appealing historic cottage on the main road, Martha's is a local mainstay, dependable from the moment it serves the first of its all-day pancake-and-eggs breakfasts to the last of its £7.50-per-person cream teas. Lunchtime sees good-value sandwiches and toasties, but the real highlights are the £4.50 savoury scones, featuring flavours like beetroot and basil.

Horse & Groom
PUB FOOD ££

(☑ 01386-700413; www.horseandgroom.info; A44, Bourton-on-the-Hill; mains £12-23; ⊙ noon-3pm & 6.30-9.30pm Mon-Sat, to 8.30pm Sun; 🅿 🛜) 🍴 This laid-back but welcoming pub, in a tiny hamlet 2 miles west of Moreton-in-Marsh, is a firm favourite with well-heeled horsey types who appreciate its extravagant array of gins. As well as serving good food, with a menu that showcases local lamb, beef and fresh produce in general, it also has five swish rooms upstairs (£130 to £170).

🛈 Getting There & Away

BUS
Pulhams, Stagecoach and/or Johnsons Excel-bus buses head to/from the following:

Broadway (route 1/2; £3.90, 30 minutes)

Cheltenham (route 801; £3.50, 1½ hours)

Chipping Campden (route 1/2; £3.90, 50 minutes)

Northleach (route 801; £2.40, 40 minutes)

Stow-on-the-Wold (route 801; £1.90, 10 minutes)

TRAIN
The station is towards the northern end of town, just off High St. Trains head to/from the following:

Hereford (£19.60, 1¾ hours)

Ledbury (£18.50, 1½ hours)

London Paddington (£14.50, 1½ hours)

Oxford (£10.60, 35 minutes)

Worcester (£13.30, 40 minutes)

Painswick
☑ 01452 / POP 1736

Among the Cotswolds' most beautiful and unspoiled villages, hilltop Painswick sits 10 miles southwest of Cheltenham. Cars stream through, along its single-lane main road, but other than walkers on the Cotswold Way, few visitors allow themselves the pleasure of wandering its narrow winding streets to admire picture-perfect cottages, handsome stone houses and medieval inns. Keep an eye out for Bisley St, the original main drag, which was superseded by the now ancient-looking New St in medieval times.

Bucolic little Slad, 2 miles south towards Stroud in the Slad Valley, was the much-loved home of writer Laurie Lee (1914–97), who immortalised its beauty in *Cider with Rosie*.

◉ Sights

Painswick Rococo Garden
GARDENS

(☑ 01452-813204; www.rococogarden.org.uk; off B4073; adult/child £7.50/3.60; ⊙ 10.30am-5pm mid-Jan–Oct; 🅿 🚻) England's only surviving rococo garden, half a mile north of Painswick, was laid out by Benjamin Hyett in the 1740s as a vast 'outdoor room'. Restored to its original glory thanks to a contemporary painting, it's absolutely stunning. Winding paths soften its geometrical precision, leading visitors to scattered Gothic follies that include the eccentric Red House, which has Latin quotes from the Song of Solomon etched into its stained-glass windows. There's also a children's nature trail and maze.

St Mary's Church
CHURCH

(www.beaconbenefice.org.uk/painswick; New St; ⊙ 9.30am-dusk) Painswick centres on this fine 14th-century, Perpendicular Gothic wool church, surrounded by 18th-century tabletop tombs and clipped yew trees sculpted to resemble giant ice lollies. Legend has it that only 99 trees could ever grow here, as the devil would shrivel the 100th. To celebrate the millennium, they planted one anyway, and – lo and behold! – another one toppled. At the foot of the churchyard there's a rare set of iron stocks.

🛏 Sleeping & Eating

Troy House
B&B ££

(☑ 01452-812339; www.troyguesthouse.co.uk; Gloucester St; s/d £75/85; 🛜) This great little B&B sleeps guests in four sweet, spacious rooms, two of which occupy a separate rear cottage accessed across an attractive courtyard. They're prettily decked out with soothing cream decor, comfy beds and baskets of toiletries, and the freshly cooked breakfasts are excellent.

★ Painswick
LUXURY HOTEL £££

(☑ 01452-813688; www.thepainswick.co.uk; Kemps Lane; r/ste from £179/404; ⊙ restaurant noon-

2.30pm & 7-9.30pm; P ☎) Focused around an imposing 18th-century house somehow squeezed into the heart of the village, and seriously chic within its stern stone walls, the Painswick offers 16 luxurious, individually decorated, pastel-painted rooms, some with four-poster beds, that spread through assorted outbuildings. As well as massage/treatment rooms, there's a futuristic bar, a colour-popping lounge and a good modern restaurant (mains £19 to £28).

Woolpack Inn PUB FOOD ££
(☎01452-813429; www.thewoolpackslad.com; Slad; mains £12-19; ⊗noon-11pm Sun & Mon, to midnight Tue-Thu, to 1am Fri & Sat, food served 6-9pm Mon, noon-3pm & 6-9pm Tue-Sat, noon-4pm Sun; ☎) This lively little rural pub in Slad, 2 miles south of Painswick, was a favourite watering hole of local author Laurie Lee, whose portrait and books adorn its walls. Perfect for a pint, stocking excellent local beers including Uley Bitter, it also serves a daily-changing menu of classics such as gammon or fish and chips alongside pasta, burgers and curries.

ℹ Information

Tourist Office (☎01452-812278; www.painswicktouristinfo.co.uk; Gravedigger's Hut, St Mary's Church, New St; ⊗10am-4pm Mon-Fri, to 1pm Sat Mar-Oct) Beside the main road, but accessed from within the church grounds.

ℹ Getting There & Away

Stagecoach bus 66 heads to/from Cheltenham (£3.60, 36 minutes) and Stroud (£2.20, 7 minutes).

Winchcombe

☎01242 / POP 5024

Winchcombe, 8 miles northeast of Cheltenham, is very much a living, working town, where butchers, bakers and independent shops line the main streets. Capital of the Anglo-Saxon kingdom of Mercia, it remained a major trading town until the Middle Ages, and was a centre for (illegally) growing tobacco in the 17th century. Reminders of that illustrious past can still be seen in Winchcombe's dramatic stone and half-timbered buildings. Keep an eye out for the picturesque cottages on Vineyard St and Dents Tce. As Winchcombe is on the Cotswold Way and other trails, it's especially popular with walkers.

WORTH A TRIP

BERKELEY CASTLE

This superb red-stone **castle** (☎01453-810303; www.berkeley-castle.com; adult/child £12.50/7; ⊗11am-5pm Sun-Wed Apr-Oct; P ♿) has been home to the Berkeleys for nearly 900 years, and little has changed since it was built as a sturdy Norman fortress. Edward II was imprisoned here in 1327 and swiftly died, probably murdered on the orders of his wife and her lover. Highlights include its central 12th-century keep, the King's Gallery, complete with Edward's cell and dungeon, and the spectacular medieval Great Hall, lined with tapestries. Free 45-minute guided tours run every 30 minutes.

◉ Sights

Sudeley Castle CASTLE
(☎01242-604244; www.sudeleycastle.co.uk; adult/child £16.50/7.50; ⊗10am-5pm mid-Mar–Oct; P ♿) During its thousand-year history, this magnificent castle has welcomed many a monarch, including Richard III, Henry VIII and Charles I. Half a mile southeast of Winchcombe, it's most famous as the home and final resting place of Catherine Parr (Henry VIII's widow), who lived here with her fourth husband, Thomas Seymour. In fact it's the only private house in England where a queen is buried – Catherine lies in its Perpendicular Gothic St Mary's Church. It also boasts 10 splendid gardens.

Belas Knap Long Barrow ARCHAEOLOGICAL SITE
(EH; www.english-heritage.org.uk; near Charlton Abbots; ⊗dawn-dusk) FREE Dating from around 3000 BC, Belas Knap is one of the country's best-preserved neolithic burial chambers, complete with 'false' portal leading nowhere. The remains of 31 people were found when its four chambers were excavated. At 290m, views across Sudeley Castle and the surrounding countryside are breathtaking. The barrow can be accessed from Winchcombe by a 2½-mile hike south along the Cotswold Way. Alternatively, park on Corndean Lane and take a steep half-mile walk up across fields.

Hailes Abbey RUINS
(EH; www.english-heritage.org.uk; Hailes; adult/child £5.90/3.50; ⊗10am-6pm Jul & Aug, to 5pm Easter-Jun, Sep & Oct; P) Now lying in ruins

3 miles northeast of Winchcombe, this 13th-century Cistercian abbey was once, thanks to a long-running medieval scam, one of England's main pilgrimage centres. The abbey was said – by Geoffrey Chaucer in *The Canterbury Tales*, among others – to possess a vial of Christ's blood. Until that was denounced during the Reformation as containing no more than coloured water, thousands of pilgrims contributed to the abbey's wealth. Free audio guides lead visitors around.

🛏 Sleeping & Eating

Wesley House B&B **££**

(📞 01242-602366; www.wesleyhouse.co.uk; High St; s £75-85, d £95-110; ⊘ restaurant noon-2pm & 7-9pm Tue-Sat, noon-2pm Sun; 🛜🐕) Methodist founder John Wesley once stayed in this ravishing 15th-century half-timbered town house, which offers five pleasant rooms plus a warm welcome. 'Mumble Meadow', splashed with reds, overlooks the street, while 'Almsbury' has its own terrace gazing out across the countryside. Rates rise on Saturdays. Downstairs. the restaurant serves fabulous modern-British cuisine (mains £16 to £28).

★ 5 North St MODERN EUROPEAN **£££**

(📞 01242-604566; www.5northstreetrestaurant. co.uk; 5 North St; 2-/3-course lunch £26/32, 3-/7-course dinner £54/74; ⊘ 7-9pm Tue, 12.30-1.30pm & 7-9pm Wed-Sat, 12.30-1.30pm Sun; 🍴) This veteran gourmet restaurant is a treat from start to finish, from its splendid 400-year-old timbered exterior to the elegant, inventive creations you eventually find on your plate. Marcus Ashenford's cooking is rooted in traditional seasonal ingredients, but the odd playful experiment (think duck-egg pasta or malt ice cream) adds that extra magic. Vegetarians can enjoy a separate £40 menu.

ℹ Information

Tourist Office (📞 01242-602925; www.winch combe.co.uk; Town Hall, High St; ⊘ 10am-4pm daily Apr-Oct, to 3pm Sat & Sun Nov-Mar) Has maps of local walks and runs free guided town tours at 11am and 2.30pm on Sunday, from Easter to October.

ℹ Getting There & Away

BUS

Marchants buses travel to/from Broadway (route 606/606S; £3, 30 minutes) and Chel-tenham (route 606/606S/W1/W2; £2.70, 20 minutes).

TRAIN

Several days each week in summer, to a convoluted schedule, the **Gloucestershire Warwickshire Railway** (GWR; 📞 01242-621405; www. gwsr.com; day pass adult/child £18/8; ⊘ Mar-Dec; 🚼) runs around five trains that stop at Winchcombe en route between Cheltenham (£5, 25 minutes) and Broadway (£9, 20 minutes).

WESTERN GLOUCESTERSHIRE

West of the Cotswolds, Gloucestershire's greatest asset is the elegant Regency town of Cheltenham, home to tree-lined terraces, upmarket boutiques and a tempting assortment of hotels and restaurants. The county capital, Gloucester, is also worth visiting, to see its magnificent Perpendicular Gothic cathedral, while Berkeley, not far southwest, has a historic Norman castle. Further west, the Forest of Dean is a leafy backwater that's perfect for walking, cycling, kayaking and other adventurous activities.

Cheltenham

📞 01242 / POP 117,500

Cheltenham, on the western edge of the Cotswolds and the region's major town, owes its air of gracious refinement to its heyday as a spa resort during the 18th century. At that time, it rivalled Bath as *the* place for ailing aristocrats to recuperate, and it stills boast many graceful Regency buildings and manicured squares. These days, however, it's better known for its racecourse, where the upper classes still arrive in droves for the mid-March Cheltenham Cup.

Cheltenham's excellent hotel and restaurant offerings make it a much more appealing base than Gloucester (12 miles west), but in the end this mid-tier town is unlikely to be the highlight of your trip.

Central Cheltenham extends around the grand tree-lined Promenade, with the fashionable Montpellier neighbourhood at its southern end.

◎ Sights

The Promenade STREET

Famed as one of the most beautiful streets in England, this broad, tree-lined boulevard leads down from the high street to Mont-

Cheltenham

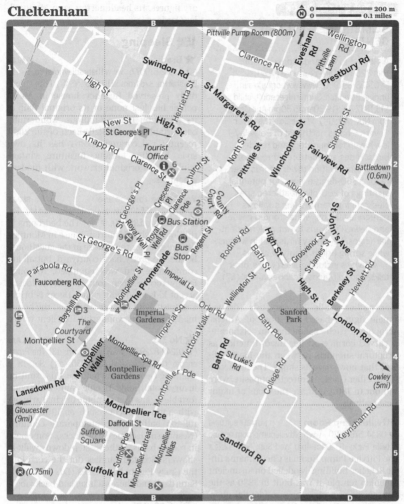

pellier, and is flanked by imposing period buildings that are now filled with fancy shops. The striking **Municipal Offices**, behind the flower-filled Long Gardens on its western side, were built in 1825 as private residences. A statue in front commemorates Cheltenham-born explorer Edward Wilson (1872–1912), who perished on Captain Scott's ill-fated second expedition to the Antarctic.

Montpellier   AREA

As well as plenty of handsome architecture, the village-y Montpellier district hosts a lively assortment of bars, restaurants, hotels, independent shops and boutiques. Along

Cheltenham

OFF THE BEATEN TRACK

SLIMBRIDGE WETLAND CENTRE

A pioneer in wetlands conservation, this 325-hectare **reserve** (WWT; ☑01453-891900; www.wwt.org.uk/slimbridge; Bowditch, Slimbridge; adult/child £13.18/7.72; ☉9.30am-5.30pm Apr-Oct, to 5pm Nov-Mar; **P**) ◢, beside the River Severn 5 miles northeast of Berkeley, is a haven for migratory and resident birds. Hides are scattered throughout, and an observation tower affords spectacular 360-degree views for potential sightings of 200-plus feathered species, ranging from visiting swallows, peregrine falcons, white-fronted geese and Bewick's swans to hot-pink resident flamingos. Migratory birds visit in winter, while spring brings plenty of chicks.

Activities include guided walks, otter talks, and self-guided 'canoe safaris' (£7).

Montpellier Walk, 32 caryatids (draped female figures based on those of Athens' Acropolis), each balancing an elaborately carved cornice on her head, function as structural supports between the 1840s edifices that now serve as shops. The attractive Montpellier Gardens, directly opposite, were laid out in 1809, and are the focus of major local festivals.

Pittville Pump Room NOTABLE BUILDING
(☑0844 576 2210; www.pittvillepumproom.org.uk; Pittville Park; ☉10am-4pm Wed-Sun; ⟳) **FREE** The Pittville Pump Room is Cheltenham's finest Regency building. Modelled on an ancient Athenian temple, it was built in 1830 as the centrepiece of a large new residential quarter a mile north of the town centre. Admire its beautiful columned exterior, then wander into the main auditorium, where, if the pump is currently operating, you can sample the pungent spa waters from the ornate fountain. The lovely surrounding ornamental park is home to a lake, lawns and an aviary.

✦ Festivals

Cheltenham Literature Festival LITERATURE
(☑01242-850270; www.cheltenhamfestivals.com; ☉early Oct) One of the world's oldest book-focused festivals kicks off over 10 days in autumn, hosting an astounding array of talks, workshops, interviews and debates by 600 top writers, actors, scholars and other literary figures. Its headquarters is in Montpellier Gardens.

⌑ Sleeping

★ Bradley B&B ££
(☑01242-519077; www.thebradleyhotel.co.uk; 19 Bayshill Rd; s/d from £110/115; ⛌⛭) This splendidly preserved Regency house in Montpellier has lost none of its original flair in its transition into a fabulous, wonderfully comfortable, luxury B&B. Each of the eight recently redecorated rooms has its own style, blending antique furniture, vintage trinkets and original artwork with modern amenities.

Wyastone Townhouse B&B ££
(☑01242-245549; www.wyastonehotel.co.uk; Parabola Rd; s/d £85/110; **P**⛌) The bedrooms in this lovely white Victorian house in Montpellier are grander than those in the guesthouse beside the pretty back courtyard, but all are comfortable and well equipped. Although family rooms sleep four guests, it doesn't accept kids aged under four. Decor is bright and fresh, with local artwork, and the homemade breakfasts wonderful. Excellent value.

★ No 131 BOUTIQUE HOTEL £££
(☑01242-822939; www.no131.com; 131 The Promenade; r incl breakfast £160-230; ⛌) Set in a stunning Georgian town house, this exquisite luxury hotel holds 11 chic, supremely comfortable rooms that combine original artwork with antique touches such as 19th-century roll-top baths and contemporary comforts (Nespresso machines, iPod docks). Some have in-room baths, others step-down walk-in showers. Scented candles dot the corridors, the Crazy Eights bar buzzes (DJs Thursday-Saturday), and there's a luxe, laid-back vibe.

✗ Eating

Boston Tea Party CAFE £
(☑01242-573935; www.bostonteaparty.co.uk; 45-49 Clarence St; dishes £4.50-11; ☉7am-8pm Mon-Sat, to 7pm Sun; ⛌⛭⛭) ◢ A spacious, friendly, vintage-chic cafe, where relaxed decor – all blue faux-leather booths and rough wood tables, fresh flowers and colourful cans – makes the perfect setting for a contemporary British-international menu focused on ethically sourced ingredients. All-day breakfasts and brunches and tasty vegan and gluten-free choices keep it buzzing. Options include halloumi- or spiced-lamb-stuffed flatbreads, grain bowls and Vietnamese Banh-Mi sandwiches.

Tavern GASTROPUB ££
(☎01242-221212; www.theluckyonion.com/property/the-tavern; 5 Royal Well Pl; mains £13-30; ⊙noon-3pm & 5.30-10pm Mon-Fri, noon-10.30pm Sat, to 9.30pm Sun; ☎🖥🍴) Behind its barebones exterior, this stylish gastropub serves Modern British food with a punch, amid exposed brick, bare wooden tables, bluevelvet booths and tile-covered floors. Classy mains – ricotta dumplings with chanterelle mushrooms, wild garlic and pine nuts; cod cheeks with Puy lentils and pancetta – plus steaks, and pub classics from mac-cheese to burgers. The warm, welcoming service is spot on.

★ **Le Champignon Sauvage** FRENCH £££
(☎01242-573449; www.lechampignonsauvage.co.uk; 24-28 Suffolk Rd; menus £28-70; ⊙12.30-1.30pm & 7.30-8.45pm Tue-Sat) For over 30 years, chef David Everitt-Matthias has been thrilling visitors and locals alike in this two-Michelin-starred Cheltenham favourite. Imaginative flavour combinations in his finely executed dishes include the likes of lamb loin with wild garlic pesto, sheep's curd and anchovy emulsion. We're not alone in thinking it's Gloucestershire's best restaurant. The set lunch and dinner menus are good value.

Daffodil BRASSERIE £££
(☎01242-700055; www.thedaffodil.com; 18-20 Suffolk Pde; mains £15-50; ⊙5-11pm Mon, Wed & Thu, noon-midnight Fri & Sat, noon-7pm Sun; ☎🍴) This breathtaking brasserie conjures its retro setting, in a 1920s cinema, into fabulous art deco glamour, with a delightful daffodil theme from its tiled floor to the plaster cornicing. Charcoal-grilled offerings range from halloumi or lobster to calves' liver and, especially, steaks, but it also has veggie options such as aubergine, coconut and lemongrass curry and open goat's-cheese ravioli.

❶ Information

Tourist Office (☎01242-387492; www.visitcheltenham.com; The Wilson, Clarence St; ⊙9.30am-5.15pm Mon-Wed, to 7.45pm Thu, to 5.30pm Fri & Sat, 10.30am-4pm Sun) A desk inside the Wilson Museum.

❶ Getting There & Away

BUS

Stagecoach, Pulhams, Marchants and Swanbrook operate local buses from Cheltenham. Most buses depart from the **bus station** (Royal Well Rd); some use stops along the Promenade. Bus destinations include the following:

Broadway (route 606/606S; £3.20, 40 minutes)
Cirencester (51; £3.80, 40 minutes)
Gloucester (10/94; £3.40, 45 minutes)
Oxford (853; £8, 1½ hours)
Stow-on-the-Wold (801; £3.20, 1¼ hours)
Stratford-upon-Avon (606S, Sunday only; £8, 1½ hours)
Stroud (66; £3.80, 45 minutes)
Winchcombe (606/606S; £2.70, 20 minutes)

National Express coach destinations:
Birmingham (£7.40, 1½ hours)
Bristol (£8.10, 1½ hours)
Leeds (£44.20, six hours)
London Victoria (£8, three hours)
Newcastle-upon-Tyne (£42.50, eight hours)
Nottingham (£23.20, 4¼ hours)

TRAIN

Cheltenham Spa train station is a mile west of the centre. The pleasant 'Honeybourne Line' footpath leads through parkland to the heart of town in around 20 minutes, while buses (D/E; £2) run every 10 minutes. Train connections include the following:

Bath (£11.90, 1¼ hours)
Bristol (£9.10, 40 minutes)
Cardiff (£19.10, 1½ hours)
Edinburgh (£159.50, six hours)
Exeter (£31.30, 1¾ hours)
Gloucester (£4.80, 10 minutes)
London Paddington (£34.30, two hours)

Forest of Dean

POP 85,400

England's oldest oak forest is a wonderfully scenic place for outdoor adventures. Designated England's first National Forest Park in 1938, this 42-sq-mile woodland had previously been a royal hunting ground and a centre of iron and coal mining. Its mysterious depths supposedly inspired the forests of JRR Tolkien's Middle Earth, while key scenes in *Harry Potter & the Deathly Hallows* were filmed here.

There's no 'Dean' in the Forest of Dean – no one knows what it means – but it also gives its name to a Gloucestershire district that includes the towns of Newent and Coleford, north and west of the forest. To the northwest, the forest spills over into Herefordshire, while the River Wye skirts its western edge, offering glorious views to canoeists who paddle from the village of Symonds Yat.

DON'T MISS

GLOUCESTER CATHEDRAL

Gloucester's spectacular **cathedral** (📞 01452-528095; www.gloucestercathedral.org.uk; 12 College Green; admission free, tours adult/child tower £7/1, crypt £3/1, library £3/1; ⏱ 7.30am-6pm) is among the first and finest examples of the English Perpendicular Gothic style.

Inside, the finest features of Norman Romanesque and Gothic design are skilfully combined, with stout columns creating a sense of gracious solidity. The **Cloister**, which featured in the first, second and sixth Harry Potter films, is a real highlight. Completed in 1367, this airy space contains the earliest example of fan vaulting in England and is matched in beauty only by Henry VII's chapel at Westminster Abbey.

From the breathtaking 14th-century wooden **choir stalls**, you'll get a good view of the imposing 22m-high Great East Window. The size of a tennis court, it was the largest in Europe when it was installed in the 1350s, and around 85% of the glass you see today is still original.

Edward II's tomb, originally gilded and bejewelled, stands beneath the window in the northern ambulatory. Behind the altar, the glorious 15th-century **Lady Chapel** was largely destroyed during the Reformation, but following restoration work, completed in 2018, it's looking wonderful once more.

Tours give access to otherwise inaccessible areas including the 15th-century library and its illuminated manuscripts (weekly, 30 minutes); the 69m tower, with its amazing views (three weekly, one hour), and the Norman crypt (daily, 30 minutes).

The Dean Heritage Centre, outside Soudley within the forest's eastern fringe, is a good place to begin exploring.

⊙ Sights

★ International Centre for Birds of Prey
BIRD SANCTUARY
(📞 01531-820286; www.icbp.org; Boulsdon House, Newent; adult/child £11.40/6.30; ⏱ 10.30am-5.30pm Feb-Nov; 🅿) Watch raptors swoop and dive at this large, long-standing countryside complex, 2 miles southwest of Newent (follow signs). There are three flyings per day (11.30am, 2pm and 4.15pm in summer; 11.30am, 1.30pm and 3.30pm in winter), along with aviaries housing 70 species of owls, falcons, kestrels, eagles, buzzards, hawks, kites and other birds of prey from all over the world. For the hands-on feel, choose from various 'experience days', devoted to specific birds (from £70).

Symonds Yat
VILLAGE
On the northwest edge of the Forest of Dean, squeezed between the River Wye and the towering limestone outcrop known as **Symonds Yat Rock** (Symonds Yat East; ⏱ 24hr; 🅿) **FREE**, Symonds Yat is a tiny, endearing tangle of pubs, guesthouses and campsites, with great walks and a couple of canoeing centres. The river splits it into two halves, one in Gloucestershire and one in Herefordshire. They're connected by an ancient hand-hauled ferry

(adult/child/bicycle £1.20/60p/60p; dawn to dusk).

Puzzlewood
FOREST, FARM
(📞 01594-833187; www.puzzlewood.net; Perrygrove Rd, Coleford; adult/child £7/6; ⏱ 10am-5pm Apr-Oct, to 3.30pm Wed, Sat & Sun mid-Feb-Mar, Nov & Dec; 🅿 ♿) A pre-Roman open-cast iron mine, overgrown with eerie moss-covered trees, Puzzlewood is a 6-hectare woodland web of paths, weird rock formations, tangled vines, rickety bridges, uneven steps and dark passageways, all seemingly designed to disorientate. Parts of hit TV shows *Doctor Who* and *Merlin*, as well as *Star Wars The Force Awakens*, were shot here. There's a mile of pathways to explore and kids will love the farm animals. Find it a mile south of Coleford on the B4228.

Clearwell Caves
CAVE
(📞 01594-832535; www.clearwellcaves.com; Clearwell; adult/child £7.50/5.50; ⏱ 10am-5pm Apr-Aug, to 4pm mid-Feb-Mar & Sep-Dec; 🅿 ♿) Descend into the damp subterranean world of a 4500-year-old iron and ochre mine, comprising a warren of dimly lit passageways, caverns and pools, and home to several species of bats. 'Deep Level Caving' sessions (adult/child £25/18) take you even further in. From November, the caves are transformed into a hugely popular Christmas grotto. They're signposted off the B4228, a mile south of Coleford.

🏃 Activities

Dean Forest Railway
RAIL

(☑ 01594-845840; www.deanforestrailway.co.uk; Forest Rd, Lydney; day ticket adult/child £13/6; ☺ Wed, Sat & Sun mid-Mar–Oct; 🚗) Three days a week for most of the year, classic steam engines ply this 4.5-mile line between Lydney and Parkend. Occasionally, though – check online – it operates diesel trains instead. The standard ride is 30 minutes, but special events range from Sunday lunch in 1st-class carriages to 'drive your own steam engine' experiences. Thomas the Tank Engine makes the occasional appearance. Book ahead.

Wyedean Canoe
& Adventure Centre
ADVENTURE SPORTS

(☑ 01600-890238; www.wyedean.co.uk; Symonds Yat East; half-day hire from £30) Hires out canoes and kayaks, and organises white-water trips, archery, high ropes, abseiling, caving, rock climbing and stand-up paddle-boarding (SUP). Hours depend on conditions.

🛏 Sleeping

YHA Wye Valley
HOSTEL £

(☑ 0345 371 9666; www.yha.org.uk; Welsh Bicknor; dm/d/camping/glamping from £13/70/10/45; ☺ hostel Mar-Oct, glamping May-Sep; 🅿🛜🐾) On the banks of the River Wye, with its own canoe landing platform, this 46-bed hostel in a Victorian former rectory is set within 16 wooded hectares. Glamping bell tents come with a double futon and three single beds, solar lighting and beanbags; premium yurts have a toasty wood burner. There's a self-catering kitchen, a laundry and wi-fi in public areas.

Garth Cottage
B&B ££

(☑ 01600-890364; www.symondsyatbandb.co.uk; Symonds Yat East; s/d £50/85; ☺ mid-Mar–Oct; 🅿🛜) An exceedingly friendly and efficiently run family-owned B&B, right by the River Wye and alongside the ferry crossing. Comfy, chintzy, spotlessly maintained rooms have floral fabrics, tea and coffee kits and gorgeous river views. Home-cooked breakfasts are excellent. Rates drop for longer stays.

Saracens Head Inn
INN ££

(☑ 01600-890435; www.saracensheadinn.co.uk; Symonds Yat East; s/d incl breakfast £70/90; 🅿🛜) Honey-toned woods, fresh cream decor and understated modern style make this revamped 16th-century riverside inn, overlooking Symond Yat's ferry crossing, a wonderful choice. Eight of its 10 bright, comfortable rooms have river views; the spacious lounge-equipped Upper Boathouse room is especially popular. The downstairs pub-restaurant is excellent.

★Tudor Farmhouse
BOUTIQUE HOTEL £££

(☑ 01594-833046; www.tudorfarmhousehotel.co.uk; High St, Clearwell; d/ste incl breakfast from £130/190; 🅿🛜) Sleep in a chic, contemporary world of whites, creams and spiralling Tudor-era staircases, inside a beautifully updated farmhouse. Stylish rooms, most with exposed beams, check-print blankets and Nespresso machines, are scattered through the main house. The spacious 'Roost' suite, with its claw-foot bath, is particularly romantic. More rooms sit in adjacent buildings. There's also an exceptional Modern British **restaurant** (mains £16-25, 2-/3-course set lunch £25/30; ☺ 7am-10pm, noon-5pm & 6.30-9pm; 🅿🛜).

ℹ Information

Dean Heritage Centre (☑ 01594-822170; www.deanheritagecentre.com; Camp Mill, Soudley; adult/child £8/6; ☺ 10am-5pm Apr-Oct, to 4pm Nov-Mar; 🅿🚗) The Forest's heritage museum doubles as its main information office.

ℹ Getting There & Away

BUS

Stagecoach is the main bus company hereabouts, while National Express coaches run to Newent from further afield.

TRAIN

Trains from Gloucester serve Lydney (£8.20, 20 minutes), on the southern side of the forest.

BUCKINGHAMSHIRE, BEDFORDSHIRE & HERTFORDSHIRE

Now poised at the edge of London's commuter belt, these three green-clad counties once served as rural boltholes for the city's rich and titled, especially when the stench and grime of the industrial age was at its peak. The sweeping valleys and forested hills remain scattered with majestic stately homes and splendid gardens, many of which are open to the public.

The 324-sq-mile Chilterns Area of Outstanding Natural Beauty (AONB; www.visitchilterns.co.uk) extends southwest from

Hitchin (Hertfordshire), through Bedfordshire and Buckinghamshire, and into Oxfordshire.

St Albans

📞 01727 / POP 151,000

As Verulamium, encircled by a 2-mile wall and 26 miles from Londinium (London), St Albans was the third-biggest city in Roman Britain. Its current name derives from Alban, a Christian Roman soldier who was beheaded here around AD 250, becoming the first English martyr. Now a bustling and prosperous market town, just beyond London's northwestern fringes, it's home to a huge and historic cathedral, amid a host of crooked Tudor buildings and elegant Georgian town houses.

👁 Sights

★ St Albans Cathedral   CATHEDRAL
(📞 01727-890210; www.stalbanscathedral.org; off High St & Holywell Hill; ⏱ 8.30am-5.45pm, free tours 11.30am & 2.30pm Mon-Fri, 11.30am & 2pm Sat, 2.30pm Sun) FREE Vast out of all proportion to the modern town, St Albans' majestic cathedral was founded as a Benedictine monastery by King Offa of Mercia in AD 793, around a shrine to St Alban, martyred five centuries earlier. It's now a glorious mash-up of Norman Romanesque and Gothic architecture, with rounded arches built using bricks salvaged from Roman Verulamium, and the country's longest medieval nave, adorned with 13th-century murals. A stone reredos screens off the restored tomb of St Alban.

Verulamium Museum   MUSEUM
(📞 01727-751810; www.stalbansmuseums.org.uk; St Michael's St; adult/child £5/2.50, combined ticket with Roman Theatre £6.50/3.50; ⏱ 10am-5.30pm Mon-Sat, from 2pm Sun) Based in what looks outside like a suburban house, this modern and highly engaging museum celebrates everyday life in Roman Verulamium. Assorted galleries cover themes like death, crafts and trade, with exhibits including farming utensils, armour, coins and pottery. Best of all are the five superb mosaic floors discovered locally, including a beautiful shell-shaped mosaic from AD 130.

🛏 Sleeping & Eating

St Michael's Manor Hotel   HOTEL £££
(📞 01727-864444; www.stmichaelsmanor.com; Fishpool St; d incl breakfast £155-200; 🅿🛜) In a lovely location, with its own lake, this 500-year-old manor offers 30 opulent rooms hidden down hushed carpeted corridors. Those in the manor itself are unshowy but

---

WORTH A TRIP

THE HOME OF HARRY POTTER

Whether you're a fair-weather fan or a full-on Potterhead, the **Warner Bros Studio Tour: The Making of Harry Potter** (📞 0345 084 0900; www.wbstudiotour.co.uk; Studio Tour Dr, Leavesden, WD25; adult/child £41/33; ⏱ 8.30am-10pm Jun-Sep, hours vary Oct-May; 🅿♿) is well worth the admittedly hefty admission price. All visitors have to book tickets online, in advance, for a specific time slot, and arrive 20 minutes beforehand; allow three hours or more to do the complex full justice. Visits begin with a short film, before you're ushered through giant doors into the actual set of Hogwarts' enormous Great Hall – just the first of many 'wow' moments.

Beyond that, you can explore the rest of the complex at your own pace. One large hangar contains the most familiar interior sets – Dumbledore's office, the Gryffindor common room, Hagrid's hut – while another holds Platform 9¾, complete with the Hogwarts Express. An outdoor section features the exterior of Privet Dr, the purple triple-decker Knight Bus, Sirius Black's motorbike and a shop selling snacks and (sickly sweet) butterbeer.

Other highlights include the animatronic workshop (say 'Hi' to the Hippogriff) and a stroll down Diagon Alley. All your favourite Harry Potter creatures are on display, from an enormous Aragog to Dobby the House-Elf, as well as props such as Harry's Invisibility Cloak. The most magical treat is saved for last – a shimmering, gasp-inducing 1:24 scale model of Hogwarts, used for exterior shots.

The Studio Tour is 20 miles northwest of London, not far off the M1 and M25 motorways. For drivers, there's a large free car park, plus extensive directions on the website. To come by rail, catch a train from London Euston to Watford Junction (£10.20, 15 minutes), then take the shuttle bus (return £2.50, 10 minutes, cash only).

BLETCHLEY PARK

During WWII, the very existence of **Bletchley Park** (☑01908-640404; www.bletchleypark. org.uk; Bletchley; adult/12-17yr £18.25/10.75; ⊙9.30am-5pm Mar-Oct, to 4pm Nov-Feb; Ⓟ) was England's best-kept secret. By breaking German and Japanese codes, as dramatised in the 2014 film *The Imitation Game*, Bletchley's team of almost 8500 scientists and technicians made a huge contribution to winning the war. Up to 20,000 enemy messages were intercepted each day, then decrypted, translated and interpreted. Inside Hut 11A, you can see the Bombe machine itself, crucial to cracking the famous Enigma code; volunteers explain its inner workings.

Entry includes an optional hour-long guided tour of the grounds – dress warm – and a multimedia guide. Both provide a real insight into the complex, frustrating and ultimately rewarding code-breaking process. The machines built here, by pioneers including Alan Turing, are now regarded as major steps in development of programmable computers.

Bletchley is just south of Milton Keynes, off the B4034. Regular trains connect Bletchley station, close to the park, with London Euston (£16, 40 minutes).

comfortable, with historic charm, while the eight more-contemporary 'luxury garden' rooms, named for plants and trees, are sumptuously sleek, with rich colours and patterned wallpaper; two have four-poster beds.

Lussmanns Fish & Grill MODERN BRITISH **££**
(☑01727-851941; www.lussmanns.com; Waxhouse Gate, off High St; mains £14-28; ⊙noon-9pm Sun-Tue, to 9.30pm Wed & Thu, to 10.30pm Fri & Sat; ☑) ✿ This bright, modern restaurant, steps from the cathedral, serves a changing, season-focused, ethically sourced menu of creative British dishes with Mediterranean touches, such as pomegranate-infused salad or chicken with pancetta. Good-value set lunches include a glass of wine (two/three courses £13.95/17.50).

ℹ Information

Tourist Office (☑01727-864511; www.enjoyst albans.com; Alban Arena, off St Peter's St; ⊙10am-4pm Mon-Sat)

ℹ Getting There & Away

Regular trains connect St Albans City, a mile east of the centre, with London King's Cross/ St Pancras (£12.20, 20 minutes) and London Blackfriars (£12.20, 30 minutes).

Stowe

Located 3 miles northwest of the market town of Buckingham, and 14 miles west of Milton Keynes, Stowe has had a manor since before the Norman conquest. While the house itself is now a private school, the ex-

traordinary Georgian gardens that surround it remain intact, and are definitely worth visiting. The most spectacular approach is via the 1.5-mile-long tree-lined Stowe Ave.

◉ Sights

★**Stowe Gardens** GARDENS
(NT; ☑01280-817156; www.nationaltrust.org.uk; New Inn Farm; adult/child £12/6; ⊙10am-5pm mid-Feb–Oct, to 4pm Nov–mid-Feb; Ⓟ) The glorious Stowe Gardens were shaped in the 18th century by Britain's greatest landscape gardeners. Among them was master landscape architect Lancelot 'Capability' Brown, who kickstarted his career here as head gardener from 1741 until 1751. The gardens are famous for the temples and follies commissioned by the superwealthy Richard Temple (1st Viscount Cobham), whose family motto was *Templa Quam Dilecta* (How Delightful are Your Temples). Paths meander past lakes, bridges, fountains and cascades, and through Capability Brown's Grecian Valley.

ℹ Getting There & Away

You'll need a car to get to Stowe House and Gardens, which are well signposted 3 miles northwest of Buckingham.

Woburn

☑01525 / POP 933
The peaceful village of Woburn has been nestling blissfully into the Bedfordshire countryside since the 10th century. Despite hosting a couple of big attractions, it's still charmingly sleepy.

◉ Sights

The Woburn Passport (adult/child £32/20.50), which gives access to both Woburn Abbey and Woburn Safari Park, can be used on two separate days between late March and October in the same calendar year.

Woburn Abbey   HOUSE
(☎01525-290333; www.woburnabbey.co.uk; Park St; adult/child £17.50/8.50; ⊙house 11am-5pm, gardens 10am-6pm mid-Mar–Oct; Ⓟ) Woburn Abbey, a wonderful country pile within a 1200-hectare deer park, stands on the site of a 12th-century Cistercian abbey that was dissolved by Henry VIII, and awarded to the Earl of Bedford; the current Duke of Bedford still calls it home. Highlights in the opulent house include Queen Victoria's bedroom, beautiful wall hangings, and paintings by Gainsborough, Reynolds and van Dyck, plus no fewer than 24 views of Venice by Canaletto, purchased for the grand sum of £188.

Woburn Safari Park   ZOO
(www.woburnsafari.co.uk; Woburn Park; adult/child £24/17; ⊙10am-6pm late Mar-Oct) Sprawling across 150 hectares, the country's largest drive-through animal reserve can only be visited in your own car (so long as it's not a convertible!). Animals such as rhinos, tigers, lions, elephants and giraffes – grouped into separate enclosures, for obvious reasons – will approach your car, or, if they're monkeys, climb on top of it. The 'foot safari' area holds sea lions, penguins, meerkats and lemurs.

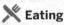 Eating

★ **Paris House**   MODERN BRITISH £££
(☎01525-290692; www.parishouse.co.uk; Woburn Park, London Rd; lunch £49, dinner £96-115;

⊙noon-1.30pm & 7-8.30pm Thu, noon-1.30pm & 6.45-9pm Fri & Sat, noon-2pm Sun) On the Woburn Estate, Paris House is a handsome, black-and-white, half-timbered structure to which the 9th duke of Bedford took a shine while visiting the French capital. He shipped it back here, and it now holds Bedfordshire's top fine-dining restaurant, serving exquisite six- to 10-course tasting menus of beautifully presented contemporary cuisine.

ⓘ Getting There & Away

Woburn is 8 miles southeast of Milton Keynes, 7 miles southeast of Bletchley Park, and 22 miles northwest of St Albans. Woburn itself does not have a train station. You can only visit Woburn Safari Park if you're driving, and no public transport serves Woburn Abbey.

THE THAMES VALLEY

The prosperous valley of the River Thames, west of London, has long served as a country getaway for the English elite, from royalty on down. Within easy reach of the capital, but utterly different in character, its pastoral landscape is peppered with handsome villages and historic houses.

It's Windsor Castle, favoured residence of the Queen, that really draws the crowds here, but Ascot, with its royal race-meet in June, and Henley-on-Thames, with its rowing regatta a month later, both boast their days in the sun. Meanwhile, bizarrely, little Bray has a genuine claim to be the country's gastronomic capital.

Windsor & Eton

☎01753 / POP 32,184

Facing each other across the Thames, with the massive bulk of Windsor Castle looming above, the twin riverside towns of Windsor and Eton have a rather surreal atmosphere. Windsor on the south bank sees the daily pomp and ritual of the changing of the guards, while schoolboys dressed in formal tailcoats wander the streets of tiny Eton to the north.

Thanks to its tourist trade, Windsor is filled with expensive boutiques, grand cafes and buzzing restaurants. Eton is far quieter, its single commercial street flanked by antique shops and art galleries. Both are easily accessible on a day trip from London.

ROYAL ASCOT

Don your finest duds and join the glitterati at the biggest racing meet of the year, **Royal Ascot** (☎08443-463000; www.ascot.co.uk; Ascot; Windsor Enclosure per day from £37, Queen Anne Enclosure per day from £75; ⊙mid-Jun), going strong since 1711. The royal family, A-list celebrities and other rich and famous folk gather for this five-day festival, 7 miles southwest of Windsor, to show off their Jimmy Choos and place the odd bet. It's essential to book tickets well in advance.

Windsor & Eton

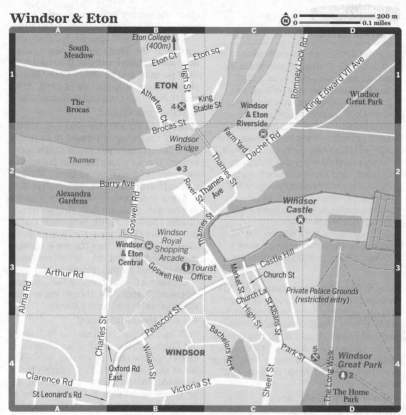

⊙ Sights & Activities

★ **Windsor Castle**   CASTLE
(☏ 03031-237304; www.royalcollection.org.uk; Castle Hill; adult/child £21.20/12.30; ⊙ 9.30am-5.15pm Mar-Oct, 9.45am-4.15pm Nov-Feb, last admission 1hr 15min before closing, all or part of castle subject to occasional closures; ♿; ➺ 702 from London Victoria, ᖴ London Waterloo to Windsor & Eton Riverside, ᖴ London Paddington to Windsor & Eton Central via Slough) The world's largest and oldest continuously occupied fortress, Windsor Castle is a majestic vision of battlements and towers. Used for state occasions, it's one of the Queen's principal residences; when she's at home, the Royal Standard flies from the Round Tower.

Frequent, free guided tours introduce visitors to the castle precincts, divided into the Lower, Middle and Upper Wards. Free audio tours guide everyone through its lavish State Apartments and beautiful chapels; certain areas may be off limits if in use.

Windsor & Eton

It was William the Conqueror, just five years after his successful invasion of England, who commanded that an earth-and-timber fortress be built beside the Thames. Completed in 1080, it was rebuilt in stone by his great-grandson, Henry II, in 1170. Successive monarchs made their own marks, with Edward III turning Windsor into a Gothic palace and Charles II adding

WORTH A TRIP

HATFIELD HOUSE

For over 400 years **Hatfield House** (☏ 01707-287010; www.hatfield-house.co.uk; Hatfield; adult/child £19/9; ⊙ house 11am-5pm Wed-Sun Apr-Sep, West Garden 10am-5.30pm Tue-Sun Apr-Sep) has been home to the Cecils, one of England's most influential political families. This magnificent Jacobean mansion was built between 1607 and 1611 for Robert Cecil, first earl of Salisbury and secretary of state to both Elizabeth I and James I. Elizabeth spent much of her childhood in the 'Old Palace' here, and the house, which is awash with tapestries, furnishings and armour, proudly displays the Rainbow Portrait, depicting her holding a rainbow. Hatfield train station has trains to London King's Cross/St Pancras (£10.10, 20 minutes).

baroque flourishes to emulate Louis XIV's Versailles outside Paris. George IV swept in with his team of artisans to establish what's still Windsor's identity, as a palace within a medieval castle. Thanks to all this rebuilding, the castle now holds almost a thousand rooms, in architectural styles that range from half-timbered fired brick to Gothic stone.

➡ **Queen Mary's Dolls' House**

Filling a side chamber as you approach the State Apartments from the North Terrace of the Upper Ward, this astonishing creation is not a toy but a masterpiece of artful miniaturisation. Designed at 1:12 scale by Sir Edwin Lutyens for Queen Mary, and completed in 1924, it displays a phenomenal attention to detail. It's equipped with fully functional plumbing, including flushing toilets, plus electric lights, tiny Crown Jewels, a silver service and wine cellar, and even a fleet of six cars in the garage.

➡ **State Apartments**

Flanked by armour and weapons, the Grand Staircase sets the tone for the spectacular State Apartments above, dripping in gilt and screaming 'royal' from every painted surface and sparkling chandelier. Presided over by a statue of Queen Victoria, the Grand Vestibule displays artefacts and treasures donated by or captured from the countries of the British Empire, while the Waterloo Chamber celebrates the 1815 victory over Napoleon. St George's Hall beyond still hosts state ban-

quets; its soaring ceiling is covered in the painted shields of the Knights of the Garter.

A succession of 10 opulent chambers, designated as the King's Rooms and Queen's Rooms and largely created by Charles II, hold royal portraits and paintings by the likes of Hans Holbein, Bruegel, Rembrandt, Peter Paul Rubens, van Dyck and Gainsborough.

➡ **St George's Chapel**

This elegant chapel, commissioned for the Order of the Garter by Edward IV in 1475, is a fine example of Perpendicular Gothic architecture. The nave and beautiful fan-vaulted roof were completed under Henry VII, and the final nail driven under Henry VIII in 1528.

Along with Westminster Abbey, it serves as a royal mausoleum. Both Henry VIII and Charles I lie beneath the beautifully carved 15th-century Quire, while the Queen's father (George VI) and mother (Queen Elizabeth) rest in a side chapel. It's also where Prince Harry married Meghan Markle in May 2018.

St George's Chapel closes on Sundays, and otherwise at 4pm daily, though visitors can attend choral evensong at 5.15pm.

➡ **Albert Memorial Chapel**

Built in 1240 and dedicated to St Edward the Confessor, the small Albert Memorial Chapel was the place of worship for the Order of the Garter until St George's Chapel, alongside, snatched away that honour. After Prince Albert died at Windsor Castle in 1861, Queen Victoria ordered the chapel to be restored as a monument to her husband, adding a magnificent vaulted roof that incorporates gold mosaic pieces from Venice.

Although the chapel holds a monument to the prince, he's actually buried, with Victoria, in the Royal Mausoleum at Frogmore House in Windsor Great Park. Their youngest son, Prince Leopold (Duke of Albany), is, however, buried here.

➡ **Changing of the Guard**

A fabulous spectacle, with triumphant tunes from a military band and plenty of foot stamping from smartly attired lads in red uniforms and bearskin caps, the changing of the guard draws crowds to Windsor Castle each day. Weather permitting, it usually takes place at 11am on Tuesdays, Thursdays and Saturdays.

★ **Windsor Great Park**　　PARK

(☏ 01753-860222; www.windsorgreatpark.co.uk; Windsor; ⊙ dawn-dusk) **FREE** Windsor Great Park stretches south from Windsor Castle almost all the way to Ascot, 7 miles southwest. Accessed via Park St, it covers just under 8 sq miles and holds a lake, walking tracks, a bridleway, gardens and a deer park where red deer roam free. Its 2.7-mile Long Walk, scene of the royal wedding procession in 2018, leads from King George IV Gate to the 1831 Copper Horse statue (of George III) on Snow Hill, the park's highest point.

Runnymede   HISTORIC SITE
(NT; 01784-432891; www.nationaltrust.org.uk; Windsor Rd, Old Windsor; parking per hour £1.50; site dawn-dusk, car park 8.30am-7pm Apr-Sep, to 5pm Oct, Nov, Feb & Mar, to 4pm Dec & Jan; P) FREE Over 800 years ago, in June 1215, King John met his barons in this unassuming field, 3 miles southeast of Windsor. Together they hammered out an agreement on a basic charter of rights that guaranteed the liberties of the king's subjects, and restricted the monarch's absolute power. The document they signed, the Magna Carta, was the world's first constitution. The field remains much as it was, plus a few modern memorials and two 1929 lodges, designed by Edwin Lutyens.

Eton College   NOTABLE BUILDING
(01753-370600; www.etoncollege.com; High St, Eton; adult/child £10/free; tours 2pm & 4pm Fri May-Aug) Eton College is England's most famous public – as in, private and fee-paying – boys' school, and arguably the most enduring symbol of the British class system. High-profile alumni include 19 British prime ministers, countless princes, kings and maharajas, Princes William and Harry, George Orwell, John Maynard Keynes, Bear Grylls and Eddie Redmayne. It can only be visited on guided tours, on summer Fridays, which take in the chapel and the Museum of Eton Life. Book online.

Tours

French Brothers   BOATING
(01753-851900; www.frenchbrothers.co.uk; Windsor Promenade, Barry Ave, Windsor; 10am-5pm mid-Feb–early Dec) Boat trips along the Thames, including cruises around Windsor (adult/child from £9/6) and voyages to/from Runnymede (return adult/child £8.75/5.85).

Eating & Drinking

Two Brewers   PUB FOOD ££
(01753-855426; www.twobrewerswindsor.co.uk; 34 Park St, Windsor; mains £14-26; 11.30am-11pm Mon-Thu, to 11.30pm Fri & Sat, noon-10.30pm Sun) This atmospheric 18th-century inn, at

the gateway to Windsor Great Park, serves tasty, well-prepped food ranging from soups, salads and fishcakes to steaks, cod loin and cheese boards. Sunny benches front the flower-covered exterior; inside are low-beamed ceilings, dim lighting and a roaring winter fire. Dinner isn't served Friday or Saturday, or after 8pm on Sunday.

Gilbey's   MODERN BRITISH £££
(01753-854921; www.gilbeygroup.com; 82-83 High St, Eton; mains £18-29.50; 6-10pm Mon, noon-3pm & 6-10pm Tue-Sun;) This bistro-restaurant, not far from the river, is Eton's best dining option. Terracotta tiling, deep-green decor and a sunny courtyard lend the feel of a European cafe, while two-/three-course set menus for both lunch (£15/20) and dinner (£22.50/28.50; not available after 6.45pm Friday and Saturday) offer Modern British favourites including pies and artisan cheeses plus good vegetarian alternatives.

Information

Tourist Office (01753-743900; www.windsor.gov.uk; Old Booking Hall, Windsor Royal Shopping Arcade, Thames St, Windsor; 10am-5pm Apr-Sep, to 4pm Oct-Mar) Tickets for attractions and events, plus guidebooks and walking maps.

Getting There & Away

BUS

Green Line buses (www.greenline.co.uk) connect Windsor and Eton with London Victoria (route 702/703; £7 to £13, 1½ hours) and Heathrow terminal 5 (route 702/703; £4, 40 minutes). Courtney Buses (www.courtneybuses.com)

READING FESTIVAL

Each August Bank Holiday weekend, up to 87,000 revellers descend on the industrial town of Reading for one of the country's biggest music events, **Reading Festival** (02070-093001; www.reading festival.com; Reading; tickets day/weekend £76.50/221.40; late Aug). The three-day extravaganza features world-class artists in all genres, with recent headliners including Kendrick Lamar, Eminem and the Red Hot Chili Peppers. Set up camp for the weekend or just book a day ticket.

Reading has regular trains to/from London Paddington (£20.20, 25 minutes to one hour).

HENLEY-ON-THAMES

The attractive commuter town of Henley, 15 miles northwest of Windsor, is synonymous with its annual rowing tournament, the **Henley Royal Regatta** (www.hrr.co.uk; tickets £25-32, on-site parking £34; ⊙ early Jul). For the rest of the year, it remains a pretty riverside town that's a delight to stroll around, particularly along the Thames.

The excellent **River & Rowing Museum** (🖉 01491-415600; www.rrm.co.uk; Mill Meadows; adult/child £12.50/10; ⊙10am-5pm; P 👶) examines why Henley is so crazy for rowing. The airy 1st-floor galleries tell the story of rowing as an Olympic sport, with striking displays that include the early-19th-century Royal Oak, Britain's oldest racing boat. Downstairs, a sweet 3D exhibition pays homage to Kenneth Grahame's *The Wind in the Willows*. The romanticised river that book so lovingly depicts was inspired by the Thames around Henley.

Trains run to/from London Paddington (£16.70, one hour); you have to change at Slough and/or Twyford.

offers services between Windsor and Bray (route 16/16A; £3.30, 30 minutes).

TRAIN

The quickest rail route from London connects London Paddington with Windsor & Eton Central, opposite the castle, but you have to change at Slough (£10.50, 30 to 45 minutes). London Waterloo has slower but direct services to Windsor & Eton Riverside, on Dachet Rd (£10.50, 45 minutes to one hour).

Bray

🖉 01628 / POP 4646

Strangely enough, this tiny village of flint, brick and half-timbered cottages, strung along the Thames 5 miles northwest of Windsor, has a real claim to be considered the gastronomic capital of Britain. Bray is home to two of the four UK restaurants to be awarded the highest possible rating of three stars by foodie bible, the Michelin guide.

There's little more to do here than to dine fabulously.

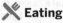 Eating

★**Fat Duck**   MODERN BRITISH £££
(🖉 01628-580333; www.thefatduck.co.uk; High St; degustation menu per person £325; ⊙ noon-1.15pm & 7-8.15pm Tue-Sat) Arguably the most famous restaurant in the country, the Fat Duck is the flagship property of whiz-bang chef Heston Blumenthal. A pioneer of 'molecular' cuisine, he transformed it from a rundown pub into a three-starred restaurant that was once voted the best in the world. Reserve four months in advance to enjoy its eye-poppingly priced, journey-themed, seasonally changing set menu.

★**Waterside Inn**   FRENCH £££
(🖉 01628-620691; www.waterside-inn.co.uk; Ferry Rd; mains £55-68, 2-/3-course lunch Wed-Fri £52/63.50; ⊙ noon-2pm & 7-10pm Wed-Sun, closed late Dec–end Jan) From the moment the uniformed valet greets you until the last tray of petit fours is served, this three-Michelin-starred riverfront restaurant is something special. For more than 40 years, chef Alain Roux has worked his magic, constructing exceptional dishes for a small army of staff to serve, in a room overlooking the Thames. It also has rooms (from £275).

★**Hind's Head**   GASTROPUB £££
(🖉 01628-626151; www.hindsheadbray.com; High St; mains £20-40, 5-course tasting menu £62; ⊙ noon-2pm & 6-9pm Mon-Sat, noon-3.30pm Sun; P) Oozing atmosphere, this 15th-century pub offers diners the chance to experience Heston Blumenthal's highly creative cuisine in a relatively affordable, informal setting. The food's less zany than you might expect from his reputation, but still has plenty of whimsical touches. Try the roast cod with mussel-and-saffron broth, or the onion-wrapped brown bread royale with Marmite emulsion.

ⓘ Getting There & Away

Courtney Buses (www.courtneybus.com) connect Bray with Windsor (route 16/16A; £3.30, 30 minutes).

Bath & Southwest England

Best Places to Eat

➡ Restaurant Nathan Outlaw (p331)

➡ Menu Gordon Jones (p253)

➡ Riverstation (p242)

➡ Black Rat (p262)

➡ Elephant (p308)

➡ Shore (p345)

Best Places to Sleep

➡ Scarlet (p334)

➡ Queensberry (p250)

➡ Hotel du Vin Exeter (p304)

➡ The Pig (p265)

➡ Number 38 (p241)

➡ Artist Residence Penzance (p344)

Why Go?

England's southwest – or the West Country, as it's often known – offers something for everyone: buzzy big cities, iconic monuments, green countryside and golden beaches galore. Stone circles and hilltop castles litter the landscape, while stately homes and serene cathedrals give way to a patchwork of green fields, wild moors, quiet villages and fishing ports. Surrounded by the sea, the region's long history of seafaring lives on in Portsmouth, Plymouth, Dartmouth, Falmouth and the dynamic city of Bristol, while beautiful Bath is a dazzling showpiece of Georgian architecture, and without doubt one of the gems in England's crown.

But it's the pleasures of coast and countryside that draw most people here: whether it's fossil-hunting on the Dorset Coast, hiking on Dartmoor, kayaking the Fowey River or surfing in Cornwall, the southwest is above all a place to enjoy England's outdoors.

When to Go

➡ Cliffs, hillsides and formal gardens burst into fragrance and blooms in April and May, when seasonal attractions also reopen and boat trips start.

➡ Music-festival fever takes hold in June at ultracool Glastonbury and the Isle of Wight.

➡ The peak holiday season and the best weather (in theory) is in July and August.

➡ The end of school summer holidays in September brings cheaper sleep spots, quieter beaches and warmer seas.

➡ Bigger waves draw surfers to Cornwall and north Devon in October; meanwhile Exmoor's deer rut sees huge stags battle for supremacy, and the winter storm-watching season begins.

Bath & Southwest England Highlights

1 **Stonehenge** (p289)
Securing a space on a magical
dawn walk inside the ring.

2 **Isles of Scilly** (p355)
Ferry-hopping around the UK's
most idyllic archipelago.

3 **Roman Baths** (p245)
Seeing how the Romans
bathed 2000 years ago.

4 **St Michael's Mount**
(p343) Crossing the causeway
to an island abbey.

5 **Dartmoor National Park**
(p318) Striding the park's
remote, high hills.

6 **Eden Project** (p348)
Marvelling at space-age

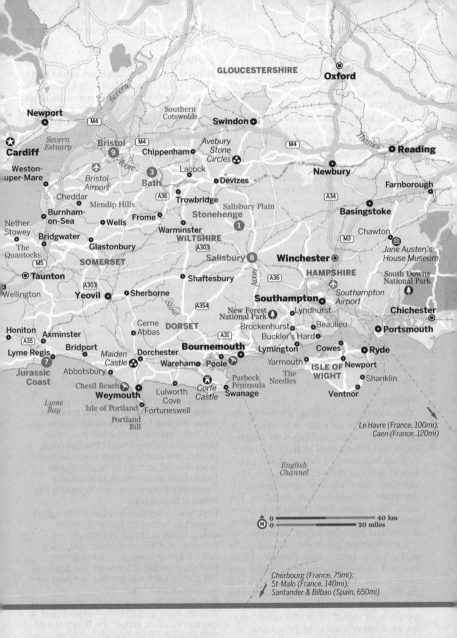

biomes in a disused Cornish claypit.

7 Jurassic Coast (p276) Foraging for 200-million-year-old fossils in the crumbling cliffs around Lyme Regis.

8 Salisbury Cathedral (p286) Savouring the city's soaring, serene house of worship.

9 SS Great Britain (p235) Stepping on the deck of

Brunel's groundbreaking steamship in Bristol.

10 Tate St Ives (p337) Getting inspired by the artistic heritage of this Cornish coastal town.

✦ Activities

Cycling

Cycling the southwest is a superb, if strenuous, way to experience England's great outdoors. The region's National Cycle Network (NCN) routes include the **West Country Way** (NCN Route 3), a 240-mile jaunt from Bristol to Padstow via Glastonbury, Taunton and Barnstaple, and the 103-mile **Devon Coast to Coast Cycle Route** between Ilfracombe and Plymouth.

The 160-mile, circular **Wiltshire Cycleway** skirts the county's borders. In Hampshire, the New Forest's hundreds of miles of cycle paths snake through a wildlife-rich environment, while the Isle of Wight boasts 62 miles of bike-friendly routes and its very own **cycling festival** (☑ 01983-299314; www.iwcyclefest.com; ☺ late-Aug).

Off-road mountain-biking highlights include the North Wessex Downs, Exmoor National Park and Dartmoor National Park. Many cycle trails trace the routes of old railway lines, including Devon's 11-mile Granite Way between Okehampton and Lydford, and Cornwall's popular 18-mile Camel Trail (p334) linking Padstow with Bodmin Moor.

For more information contact Sustrans (www.sustrans.org.uk) and local tourist offices.

Walking

Often called the 630-mile adventure, the **South West Coast Path** is Britain's longest national walking trail (until the England Coast Path is completed in 2020). It stretches from Minehead in Somerset via Land's End to Poole in Dorset. You can pick it up along the coast for short and spectacular day hikes or tackle longer stretches. The South West Coast Path Association (www.southwestcoastpath.org.uk) has a detailed website and publishes an annual guide.

For wilderness hikes, the national parks of Dartmoor (p318) and Exmoor (p295) are hard to beat. Dartmoor is bigger and more remote; Exmoor's ace in the pack is a cracking 34 miles of precipitous coast. The region's third national park, New Forest (p263), is an altogether gentler affair, offering hundreds of miles of heritage trails.

Other hiking highlights are Exmoor's 51-mile **Coleridge Way** (www.coleridgeway.co.uk), the Isle of Wight and Bodmin Moor, while Wiltshire's 87-mile **Ridgeway National Trail** (www.nationaltrail.co.uk/ridgeway) starts near Avebury and winds through chalk downland and the wooded Chiltern hills.

Surfing & Boating

North Cornwall, and to a lesser extent north Devon, serves up the best surf in England. Party town Newquay is the epicentre; other top spots are Bude in Cornwall and Croyde in Devon. Region-wide surf conditions can be found at www.magicseaweed.com.

For sailing, highlights includes Britain's 2012 Olympic sailing venues at Weymouth and Portland, and the yachting havens of the Isle of Wight, Falmouth, Dartmouth and Poole.

Other Activities

The southwest is prime territory for kitesurfing, windsurfing, diving, sea kayaking, white-water kayaking and wakeboarding. The sport of stand-up paddleboarding (SUP) continues to grow in popularity, especially in calm water spots.

Plenty of firms also offer caving, coasteering, mountainboarding, climbing and kite-buggying. Check out www.visitsouthwest.co.uk for links to the region's counties and activity operators.

ℹ Getting Around

BUS

The region's bus network is fairly comprehensive, but becomes patchy away from main towns. **National Express** (www.nationalexpress.com) often provides the quickest bus link between cities and larger towns. **PlusBus** (www.plusbus.info) adds local bus travel to your train ticket (from £2 per day). Participating cities include Bath, Bournemouth, Bristol, Exeter, Plymouth, Salisbury, Truro and Weymouth. Buy tickets at train stations.

First (www.firstgroup.com) One of the region's largest bus companies, operating in Bath, Bristol, Cornwall, Dorset, Portsmouth and Somerset. It offers subregional tickets, such as the Freedom Travelpass, covering Bath, Bristol and northeast Somerset (one day/week £13.50/59). Day Rover and Ranger tickets are available for each area.

More (www.wdbus.co.uk) Useful service across Wiltshire and Dorset and into the New Forest. It operates on a zone system: day tickets (adult/child £8.80/5.70) for Zone ABC cover the largest area and are the best value. An unlimited weekend ticket costs £7.50.

Stagecoach (www.stagecoachbus.com) A key bus provider in Devon, Hampshire and Somerset. Offers a range of Dayrider and weekly Megarider passes covering individual towns (eg

Plymouth and Exeter) as well as wider areas (eg North Devon, South Devon). Most can be purchased within the Stagecoach app.

CAR

The main car-hire firms have offices at the region's airports and main-line train stations; rates reflect those elsewhere in the UK.

TRAIN

Bristol is a main train hub with links including those to London Paddington, Scotland and Birmingham, plus services to Bath, Swindon, Chippenham, Weymouth, Southampton and Portsmouth. Trains from London Waterloo travel to Bournemouth, Salisbury, Southampton, Portsmouth and Weymouth.

Stops on the London Paddington–Penzance service include Exeter, Plymouth, Liskeard, St Austell and Truro. Spur lines run to Barnstaple, Paignton, Gunnislake, Looe, Falmouth, St Ives and Newquay.

Major companies servicing the region include **Great Western Railway** (☑ 0345 7000 125; www.gwr.com), **CrossCountry** (☑ 0844 811 0124; www.crosscountrytrains.co.uk) and **South Western Railway** (www.southwesternrailway. com). All have useful travel apps that allow you to plan journeys and purchase e-tickets that are valid for travel. South Western Railway offers travel between London and the southeast, and to southwest destinations including Bournemouth, Portsmouth, Salisbury, Bristol and Bath, as far west as Exeter.

The **Freedom of the South West Rover** (three days travel in seven days adult/child £102.60/48.20, eight days travel in 15 days £144/72) pass allows unlimited travel in an area west of, and including, Salisbury, Bath, Bristol, Portsmouth and Weymouth.

BRISTOL

POP 454,200

Bristol is on the rise. Derelict docks are becoming leisure venues, heritage attractions ooze imagination and a world-class street-art scene adds colour and spice.

History

Bristol began as a Saxon village and developed into the medieval river port of Brigstow, an important trading centre for cloth and wine. In 1497 'local hero' John Cabot (actually a Genoese sailor called Giovanni Caboto) sailed from Bristol to discover Newfoundland. By the 18th century Bristol's docks were the second largest in the country.

BRISTOL LIDO

Bristol's public **hot tub** (☑ 0117-933 9530; www.lidobristol.com; Oakfield Pl; nonmembers £20; ⊙ nonmembers 1-4pm Mon-Fri) dates back to 1849, and, after falling into disrepair during the early 20th century, this naturally heated, 24m pool has now been restored to its steamy best – with a balmy water temperature of around 24°C. Admission includes three hours' use of the pool, sauna, steam room and outdoor hot tub.

Spa treatments and massage sessions are also available, and there's a good **tapas bar** (9am to 10.30pm) and an acclaimed Mediterranean-themed **restaurant** (noon-3pm and 6pm to 10pm). Priority is given to members; if you want to visit outside the times listed, consider one of their Swim & Eat (£35 to £40) or Spa packages (from £70).

One of their activities was the so called Triangular Trade, in which Africans were enslaved, shipped to New World colonies and bartered for sugar, tobacco, cotton and rum. Much of Bristol's 18th-century splendour – including Clifton's terraces and the Old Vic theatre – were partly financed on the profits. The M Shed museum (p237) takes an honest look at the story, referencing also the local campaigners who fought for abolition.

After being usurped by rival ports, Bristol repositioned itself as an industrial and shipbuilding centre, and in 1840 became the western terminus for the newly built Great Western Railway line from London. It's audacious chief engineer was Isambard Kingdom Brunel, whose Bristol legacy includes the Clifton Suspension Bridge (p239) and SS *Great Britain*.

⊙ Sights

★ **Brunel's SS Great Britain**   HISTORIC SHIP
(☑ 0117-926 0680; www.ssgreatbritain.org; Great Western Dock, Gas Ferry Rd; adult/child/family £16.50/9.50/45; ⊙ 10am-5.30pm Apr-Oct, to 4.30pm Nov-Mar) This mighty, innovative steamship was designed by engineering genius Isambard Kingdom Brunel in 1843. You get to wander the galley, surgeon's quarters and dining saloon and see a massive replica steam engine at work. Highlights are going below the 'glass sea' on which the ship sits

Bristol

to view the screw propeller and climbing the rigging in **Go Aloft!**. The new **Being Brunel** exhibit has restored the drawing office where Brunel and his team worked to create the vessel.

The SS *Great Britain* was one of the largest and most technologically advanced steamships ever built, measuring 98m from stern to tip. The ship has had a chequered history. Between 1843 and 1886, she served her intended duty as a passenger liner, completing the transatlantic crossing between Bristol and New York in just 14 days. Unfortunately, enormous running costs and mounting debts led her towards an ignominious fate: she was eventually sold off and subsequently served as a troop vessel, quarantine ship, emigration transport and coal hulk, before finally being scuttled near Port Stanley in the Falklands in the 1930s.

Happily, that wasn't the end. The ship was towed back to Bristol in 1970, and has since undergone an impressive 30-year restoration. It's resulted in a multisensory experience: prepare to stroll the deck, peep into luxury cabins, listen to passengers' stories and catch a whiff of life on board. Those aged 10 and over can also **Go Aloft!** (£10;

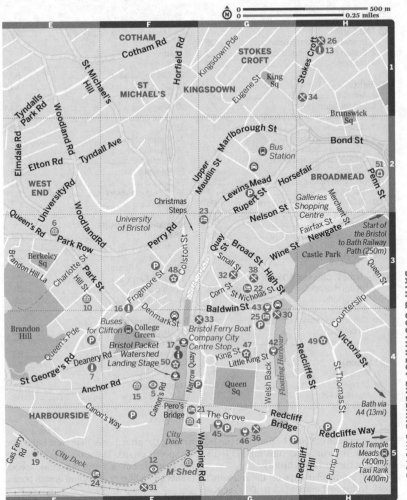

noon to 5pm daily April to October, noon to 3.45pm Saturday and Sunday November to March). This sees you donning a harness and helmet to climb 25m up the rigging and along the yard arm. Tickets for SS *Great Britain* remain valid for a year. Last entry is one hour before closing.

★ **M Shed**   MUSEUM
(☏ 0117-352 6600; www.bristolmuseums.org.uk; Princes Wharf; ◷ 10am-5pm Tue-Sun; ☏) **FREE**
Set amid the iconic cranes of Bristol's dockside, this impressive museum is a treasure trove of memorabilia. It's divided into four main sections: People, Place, Life and the vast Working Exhibits outside. They provide an absorbing overview of Bristol's history – from slaves' possessions and Wallace & Gromit figurines to a Banksy artwork and a set of decks once used by Massive Attack.

It's all highly interactive and child-friendly, especially the rides on the steam and electric cranes (tickets £2), steam trains (tickets £2) and tug and fire boats (adult/child £6/4). Another highlight is Banksy's unsettling *Grim Reaper* stencil, which used to sit on the waterline of the party boat *Thekla*. It was removed amid much

Bristol

controversy and can now be found on the 1st floor. The museum also runs guided tours exploring the harbour's history.

There are regular trips on the museum's boats, trains and cranes (£2 to £6); see the website for details.

Matthew　　　　　　　　　　　　HISTORIC SHIP
(☏ 0117-927 6868; https://matthew.co.uk; Princes Wharf; ⊙10am-4pm Tue-Sun Mar-Oct, Sat & Sun Nov-Feb) **FREE** The most striking thing about this replica of the vessel in which John Cabot made his landmark voyage from Bristol to Newfoundland in 1497 is its size. At 24m it seems far too small, but it would have carried a crew of around 18. Step aboard to climb below into their quarters, walk the deck and gaze up at the rigging.

Arnolfini　　　　　　　　　　　　　　GALLERY
(☏ 0117-917 2300; www.arnolfini.org.uk; 16 Narrow Quay; ⊙11am-6pm Tue-Sun; ☏) **FREE** At time of

writing, the art galleries here were only open for special events. The ground floor houses the Front Room, a venue for talks, special events and a library of art and design books.

Bristol Aquarium　　　　　　　　　AQUARIUM
(☏ 0117-929 8929; www.bristolaquarium.co.uk; Anchor Rd, Harbourside; adult/child/family £15/10/50; ⊙10am-4pm Mon-Fri, to 5pm Sat & Sun) The underwater habitats you'll encounter here include a Bay of Rays, Coral Sea, Shark Tank and an Amazon River Zone. The underwater viewing tunnel adds extra appeal. Tickets are 10% cheaper online.

We the Curious　　　　　　　　　　　MUSEUM
(☏ 0117-915 1000; www.wethecurious.org; Anchor Rd; adult/child/family £15/10/40; ⊙10am-5pm Mon-Fri, to 6pm Sat & Sun) Bristol's interactive science museum is a playful, hands-on space where 300 'exhibits' fly the flag for curiosity, scientific collaboration and creativity.

Which means you'll be meeting Aardman characters and becoming an animator for the day, discovering cosmic rays, walking through a tornado and exploring subjects ranging from anatomy to flight. There are also performances from the Live Science Team, immersive planetarium shows, and robots. Look out for After Hours – evenings designed for adults that feature games, activities and shows.

Georgian House
HISTORIC BUILDING

(☑ 0117-921 1362; www.bristolmuseums.org.uk; 7 Great George St; ☺ 11am-4pm Sat-Tue Apr-Dec) **FREE** Once the home of the wealthy slave plantation owner and sugar merchant John Pinney, this 18th-century house provides an insight into aristocratic life in Bristol during the Georgian era. It's decorated in period style, with a huge kitchen (complete with cast-iron roasting spit), book-lined library, grand drawing room, and cold-water plunge-pool in the basement.

There's also a small display on Pinney's involvement in the sugar trade and the life of his enslaved valet, Pedro Jones.

Bristol Museum & Art Gallery
MUSEUM

(☑ 0117-922 3571; www.bristolmuseums.org.uk; Queen's Rd; ☺ 10am-5pm Tue-Sun, plus 10am-5pm Mon school & bank holidays; 🛜) **FREE** You're in for a few surprises at this classic old Edwardian museum. Look out for the *Paint-Pot Angel* by world-famous street artist Banksy in the entrance hall; a funerary statue with an upturned pink paint pot on her head, she's designed to challenge our expectations of museum exhibits and the value of art. It's also a reminder of the artist's hugely popular 2009 exhibition here. Just above sits the Bristol Boxkite, a prototype propeller-powered biplane, which dangles from the ceiling.

⭐ Clifton Suspension Bridge
BRIDGE

(☑ 0117-974 4664; www.cliftonbridge.org.uk; Suspension Bridge Rd) Clifton's most famous (and photographed) landmark is the 76m-high Clifton Suspension Bridge, which spans the Avon Gorge. It was designed by master engineer Isambard Kingdom Brunel with construction beginning in 1836, although Brunel died before its completion in 1864. It's free to walk or cycle across; car drivers pay a £1 toll.

There's a **visitor centre** (🛜) **FREE** near the tower on the western, Leigh Woods side. The bridge **tours** (☺ 3pm Sat & Sun Easter-Oct) **FREE** are excellent.

The Downs
PARK

(🏞️🎏) The grassy parks of Clifton Down and Durdham Down (often referred to as just the Downs) fan out from the Clifton Suspension Bridge and make a fine spot for a picnic. Nearby, the **Clifton Observatory** (☑ 0117-974 1242; www.cliftonobservatory.com; Litfield Rd, Clifton Down; adult/child £2.50/1.50; ☺ 10am-5pm Feb-Oct, to 4pm Nov-Jan) houses a camera obscura and a tunnel leading down to the **Giant's Cave**, a natural cavern that emerges halfway down the cliff with dizzying views across the Avon Gorge.

Bristol Zoo Gardens
ZOO

(☑ 0117-428 5300; www.bristolzoo.org.uk; College Rd; adult/child £22/16; ☺ 9am-5.30pm; P) Highlights at the city's award-winning zoo include a family of seven western lowland gorillas (bossed by silverback Jock) and the Seal and Penguin Coast, where African penguins, eider ducks and South American fur seals lounge around. There's also a reptile and bug zone, butterfly forest, lion enclosure, monkey jungle and the **Zooropia** (adult/child £8/7) treetop adventure park. Online tickets are up to a third cheaper. To get here from the city centre, catch bus 8.

🏃 Activities

⭐ Bristol Street Art Tours
WALKING

(Where The Wall; ☑ 07748 632663; www.wherethewall.com; adult/child £9/5; ☺ 11am Sat & Sun) There's a plethora of walls dripping with skilfully applied spray paint on show in these two-hour tours that start in the city centre and end in Stokes Croft. Banksy artworks feature strongly but other highlights of the city's great graffiti offering are covered too. Afterwards they run hour-long **Stencil Art Spray Sessions** (£12.50, Saturday and Sunday 1.45pm) where you 'get your hands on the cans', producing artworks to take home.

Bristol Packet
BOATING

(☑ 0117-926 8157; www.bristolpacket.co.uk; Wapping Wharf, Gas Ferry Rd) Bristol Packet's trips include 45-minute cruises around the harbour (adult/child £7/5, six sailings daily April to October, and on winter weekends), and weekly sailings to Beese's Tea Gardens (£14/9, runs April to September). Boats depart from Wapping Wharf near SS *Great Britain*, and the Watershed landing **stage** on the Harbourside.

There are also weekly cruises to the spectacular Avon Gorge from April to September (adult/child £16/14). Cruises to Bath

(£32/24) run once a month from May to September. These two trips depart only from Wapping Wharf.

Bristol Highlights Walk WALKING

(☑ 0117-968 4638; www.bristolwalks.co.uk; adult/child £6/3; ⊙11am Sat Mar-Sep) Tours the old town, city centre and harbourside, leaving from the tourist office (p244) – there's no need to book. Themed tours exploring Clifton, medieval Bristol and the history of Bristol's slave and wine trades run on request.

🎇 Festivals & Events

★Upfest ART

(www.upfest.co.uk; ⊙Jul) Where better for a street art and graffiti festival than the city that brought us Banksy? Europe's largest event of its type sees 300 artists descending on the city to paint live, in front of audiences, at 40 venues. There are music gigs and affordable art sales too.

Bristol Shakespeare Festival THEATRE

(www.bristolshakespeare.org.uk; ⊙Jul) One of Britain's biggest outdoor festivals devoted to the Bard runs throughout July.

International Balloon Fiesta AIR SHOW

(www.bristolballoonfiesta.co.uk; ⊙Aug) More than 100 brightly coloured hot-air balloons, often of mind-boggling shapes, fill the skies at Ashton Court in what is the largest event of its type in Europe. The highlights are the fireworks and Nightglow flights.

Encounters FILM

(www.encounters-festival.org.uk; ⊙Sep) Bristol's largest short-film fest.

🛏 Sleeping

★Kyle Blue HOSTEL £

(☑ 0117-929 0609; www.kylebluebristol.co.uk; Wapping Wharf; dm/s/d £29/52/59; 🐾) What a boon for budget travellers: a boutique hostel set on a boat that's moored in easy reach of the central sights. Cabins are compact but supremely comfy, the showers and kitchen gleam and the smart lounge is the ideal spot to watch the river traffic float by.

Bristol YHA HOSTEL £

(☑ 0345 371 9726; www.yha.org.uk; 14 Narrow Quay; dm £15-35, d £59-90; @🐾) Few hostels can boast a position as good as this one,

---

BANKSY – STREET ARTIST

If there's one Bristolian nearly everyone has heard of, it's Banksy (www.banksy.co.uk) – the guerrilla street artist whose distinctive stencilled style and provocative artworks have earned him worldwide notoriety.

Banksy has tried to remain anonymous but it's believed he was born in 1974 in Yate, 12 miles from Bristol, and honed his artistic skills in a local graffiti outfit. His works take a wry view of 21st-century culture – especially capitalism, consumerism and the cult of celebrity. Among his best-known pieces are the production of spoof banknotes (featuring Princess Diana's head instead of the Queen's), a series of murals on Israel's West Bank barrier (depicting people digging holes under and climbing ladders over the wall) and a painting of a caveman pushing a shopping trolley at the British Museum (which the museum promptly claimed for its permanent collection). His documentary *Exit Through the Gift Shop*, about an LA street artist, was nominated for an Oscar in 2011.

Long despised by the authorities, Banksy's artworks have become a tourist magnet. The **Well Hung Lover** (Frogmore St) depicts an angry husband, a two-timing wife, and a naked man dangling from a window. Nearby the **Castles Stencil** points out 'you don't need planning permission to build castles in the sky'. The startling **Paint-Pot Angel** (think pink paint meets funerary monument) resides in the Bristol Museum & Art Gallery (p239) and is a reminder of the artist's hugely popular 2009 exhibition there. **Mild Mild West** (80 Stokes Croft) features a Molotov cocktail–wielding teddy bear facing three riot police and is thought to be a comment on Bristol's edgy-yet-comfy vibe. A stencil of the **Grim Reaper** rowing a boat, which used to sit on the waterline of the party boat the *Thekla*, is now in the city's M Shed Museum (p237). Hidden away near the SS *Great Britain*, **Girl With A Pierced Eardrum** FREE is the artist's 2014 take on the famous Vermeer portrait.

The tourist office (p244) sells a Banksy info sheet for 50p and can advise on other locations. The excellent Bristol Street Art Tours (p239) take in the main Banksy sites in a walk from the city centre to graffiti-central Stokes Croft.

beside the river in a red-brick warehouse. Facilities include kitchens, a cycle store, a games room and the excellent Grainshed cafe-bar. Weekends and holidays bring the highest prices.

★ Brooks
B&B ££

(☑ 0117-930 0066; www.brooksguesthousebristol. com; Exchange Ave; d £67-120, tr £90-129, trailers £80-149; ☎) Welcome to urban glamping – three vintage Airstream trailers sit in a bijou AstroTurf roof garden slap bang in the heart of Bristol. They're predictably tiny (ranging from 16ft to 20ft) but still have sleek seating areas, pocket-sized bathrooms and rooftop views. Guesthouse bedrooms are compact but smart, featuring soft tones and checked throws.

Mercure Bristol Brigstow
HOTEL ££

(☑ 0117-929 1030; www.mercure.com; 5 Welsh Back; s £85-125, d £90-210; ❄☎) A harbourside location and attractive modern design make the Mercure a sound, central option. Rooms boast 'floating' beds, curved panel walls and tiny TVs set into bathroom tiles (gimmicky, yes, but fun).

★ Number 38
B&B £££

(☑ 0117-946 6905; www.number38clifton.com; 38 Upper Belgrave Rd; s £115, d £125-180, ste £220; P☎) Set on the edge of the Downs, this up-market B&B is *the* choice for style-conscious travellers. The rooms are huge and contemporary – sombre greys and smooth blues dictate the palette – luxury is provided by waffle bathrobes and designer bath goodies, and sweeping city views unfold from most bedrooms and the roof terrace. The two suites have gleaming, old-fashioned metal baths.

Hotel du Vin
HOTEL £££

(☑ 0117-403 2979; www.hotelduvin.com; Narrow Lewins Mead; d £139-164, ste £205-270; P❄☎) The Bristol outpost of this luxury hotel brand occupies an old sugar warehouse and mixes heritage chic with smooth minimalism: exposed brick and iron pillars meet futon beds and claw-foot baths. The sumptuous split-level mezzanine suites may see you lose your heart to loft living.

The stylish bistro is great, too.

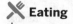 Eating

★ Primrose
CAFE £

(☑ 0117-946 6577; www.primrosecafe.co.uk; 1 Boyce's Ave; dishes £6-10; ⊙ 9am-5pm Mon-Sat,

TYNTESFIELD HOUSE

Formerly the home of the Gibbs family, **Tyntesfield** (NT; ☑ 01275-461900; www. nationaltrust.org.uk/tyntesfield; Wraxall; adult/child £15.60/7.80, gardens only £9.60/4.80; ⊙ house 11am-5pm Mar-Oct, 11am-3pm Nov-Feb, gardens 10am-5pm year-round) was purchased by the National Trust in 2002. A fairy-tale mansion bristling with pinnacles and turrets, brimful of sweeping staircases and cavernous, antique-filled rooms, the house gives an insight into the lavish lives once enjoyed by England's wealthiest families. Entry is via timed ticket and includes a guided tour. The house is 8 miles southwest of Bristol, off the B3128.

from 9.30am Sun; ☎) ✿ The Primrose richly deserves its status as a Clifton institution, thanks to decades of serving towering homemade cakes and imaginative lunches, such as halloumi and courgette burgers, and slow-cooked pheasant. Pavement tables and a secluded roof garden add to the appeal, as do belt-busting brunches that are served impressively late (to 3pm); the eggs Benedict and Belgian waffles are legendary.

Canteen
CAFE £

(☑ 0117-923 2017; www.canteenbristol.co.uk; 80 Stokes Croft; mains £5-10; ⊙ 10am-midnight Mon-Thu, to 1am Fri & Sat, to 11pm Sun; ☎) ✿ Occupying the ground floor of an old office block, this community-run cafe-bar sums up Bristol's alternative character: it's all about slow food, local suppliers and fair prices, whether you pop in for a breakfast, veggie chilli or sit-down supper. It's not signed on the outside – look out for the hipsters on the terrace and the lettering: Hamilton House.

Pieminister
FAST FOOD £

(☑ 0117-942 3322; www.pieminister.co.uk; 24 Stokes Croft; pies £5.50; ⊙ 11.30am-10pm Mon-Fri, 10am-10.30pm Sat, 10am-9.30pm Sun) This Bristol-born chain of pie shops has become a local institution. Choose from Deer Stalker (venison and cured bacon), Heidi (goat's cheese and spinach) and Moo and Blue (yes: beef and Stilton). All are drowned in lashings of gravy (meat-free if you wish).

The main shop is on Stokes Croft; there are also outlets in the city centre in St

Nicholas Market and at **Broad Quay** (📞0117-325 7616; 7 Broad Quay; ⊙11.30am-9.30pm Sun-Thu, 11.30am-11pm Fri & Sat).

St Nicholas Market
MARKET £

(St Nicks Market; www.stnicholasmarketbristol.co.uk; Corn St; ⊙9.30am-5pm Mon-Sat) The city's lively street market has a bevy of food stalls selling everything from Pieminister pies and mezze platters to pulled-pork rolls from barbecue specialists Grillstock. Lines can be long at lunchtime, but it's worth the wait. Look out, too, for the Wednesday farmers market (8am to 2.30pm).

★Riverstation
BRITISH ££

(📞0117-914 4434; www.riverstation.co.uk; The Grove; lunch 2/3 courses £14/17, dinner mains £15-18; ⊙noon-2.30pm & 6-10pm Mon-Sat, noon-3pm Sun) Riverstation's waterside location is hard to beat, with a view over the Floating Harbour, but it's the classical food that truly shines, from confit duck leg with quince and port jus, to pan fried turbot with squid ink sauce.

Cowshed
BRITISH ££

(📞0117-973 3550; www.thecowshedbristol.com; 46 Whiteladies Rd; lunch 2/3-course £12/14, dinner mains £13-28; ⊙8am-11.30am, noon-3pm & 6-10pm Mon-Sat, to 9.30pm Sun) Country food with a modern twist is served at the Cowshed. The focus is on quality, locally sourced meat – aged beef, slow-braised lamb, pork belly, plus the pièce de résistance, 'steak on stone', served sizzling on a hot lava rock. The three-course lunch is excellent value.

Shop 3
BISTRO ££

(📞0117-382 2235; www.shop3bistro.co.uk; 3a Regent St; mains £15-25; ⊙6-11pm Tue-Sat) It's a bit like heading into a French neighbourhood bistro when you step through the door at Shop 3 to encounter the rich aromas of rustic food. The focus is firmly on local and foraged – expect delicate presentation but robust flavours from ingredients such as venison, oxtail, pheasant, artichokes and kale.

Thali Café
INDIAN ££

(📞0117-974 3793; www.thethalicafe.co.uk; 1 Regent St; meals £9-12; ⊙5-10pm Mon-Fri, from noon Sat & Sun) In Thali, something of the makeshift exuberance of Indian street food comes to Clifton's hills. Richly flavoured dishes infused with spices include the eponymous thalis (multicourse meals), showcasing different curry styles. To drink? Perhaps a Jaipur IPA, dry gin with homemade tonic, or cup of chai.

Soukitchen
MIDDLE EASTERN ££

(📞0117-966 6880; www.soukitchen.co.uk; 277 North St; mains £8-14; ⊙5.30-9.30pm Mon & Tue, noon-3pm & 5.30-9.30pm Wed-Fri, 10am-2.30pm & 5.30-9.30pm Sat & Sun,) Middle Eastern market food is the stock-in-trade at this friendly diner in Southville, with characteristic dishes such as borek (filo pies stuffed with meat or vegetables), mix-and-match mezze platters and flame-grilled kebabs. Honest food with heart.

Clifton Sausage
BRITISH ££

(📞0117-973 1192; www.cliftonsausage.co.uk; 7 Portland St; mains £11-17; ⊙noon-4pm & 6-10pm Mon-Sat, 10am-4pm & 6-9pm Sun) One for Brits to go all misty-eyed over: a cool eatery that places the much-beloved sausage on a culinary pedestal. The varieties on offer here include Gloucester pork, Cotswold lamb, and beef and Butcombe ale – all come with a dollop of gourmet mash.

Fishers
SEAFOOD ££

(📞0117-974 7044; www.fishers-restaurant.com; 35 Princess Victoria St; mains £14-25; ⊙5.30-10pm Mon, noon-3pm & 5.30-10pm Tue-Sun) Bristol's top choice for fish dishes rustles up everything from garlicky pan-fried bream with pesto, to succulent grilled whole lobster. The hot shellfish platter (£46 for two people) is memorable. The simple setting, with its whitewashed walls, ship's lanterns and nautical knick-knacks, adds to the maritime vibe.

It also offers a ridiculously good-value set lunch and early-evening menu (two/three courses £9.50/13).

Ox
STEAK ££

(📞0117-922 1001; www.theoxbristol.com; The Basement, 43 Corn St; mains £13-27; ⊙noon-2.30pm Mon-Fri, 5-10.30pm Mon-Sat, noon-4pm Sun) Gorgeous, highly polished wood, glinting brass, low lighting and cool jazz ensure this sleek eatery resembles a posh Pullman dining car that's somehow been bestowed with some Pre-Raphaelite murals. The food is aimed firmly at meat eaters; expect charcuterie platters, gourmet burgers and five choices of steak cut.

Olive Shed
BISTRO ££

(📞0117-929 1960; www.theoliveshed.com; Princes Wharf; tapas £4-8.50, mains £12-19; ⊙noon-10pm Thu-Sat, to 5pm Sun) With tables right beside

Bristol harbour, this rustic eatery is a top spot for a waterfront lunch. It serves tapas and twists on Mediterranean food such as pork with manzanilla glaze, fragrant rosemary cured manchego and spicy courgette, chickpea and cumin kofta.

Glassboat FRENCH £££

(☑0117-332 3971; www.glassboat.co.uk; Welsh Back; lunch 2/3 courses £12/15, dinner mains £20-32; ☺noon-2.45pm & 5.30-9.45pm Mon-Sat, noon-4.45pm Sun) This converted river barge is an ideal spot for a romantic dinner, with candlelit tables and harbour views through a glass extension. The refined food revolves around French and Italian flavours.

The early-evening set meals (two/three courses £12/15), served between 5.30pm and 6.30pm, are great value.

 Drinking & Nightlife

★**Amoeba** CRAFT BEER

(☑0117 946 6461; www.amoebaclifton.co.uk; 10 Kings Rd; ☺1pm-1am Fri & Sat, 1pm-midnight Sun, 4pm-midnight Mon-Thu) Sixty-five craft beers, 60 cocktails (£8 to £9) and a hundred-and-something (who's counting?) spirits draw style-conscious drinkers to this chilled-out wine bar, where patrons sit on bench seats smothered in cushions and nibble on platters of charcoal crackers and artisan cheese (£8).

★**Mud Dock** PUB

(☑0117-934 9734; www.mud-dock.co.uk; 40 The Grove; ☺10am-10pm Tue-Sat, to 4pm Mon & Sun) Mud Dock epitomises the laid-back charm of Bristol's harbourside. In this long attic bikes, fairy lights and a massive metal swordfish hang from the girders. Summer sees drinkers packing the mellow waterside terrace, drinking in craft ales and cracking views.

It's set above a bike shop – head up the metal fire escape around the side to get in. The bar-food menu (mains £10 to £13) isn't massive but the quality is good.

BrewDog Bristol CRAFT BEER

(☑0117-927 9258; www.brewdog.com; 58 Baldwin St; ☺noon-midnight Sun-Wed, to 1am Thu-Sat) The Bristol outlet of Britain's punk brewery draws both the just-finished work crowd and those who want to linger at the cluster of tables out front. Expect ales such as Elvis Juice, Vagabond Pale, and Nanny State (that'll be 0.5%) on tap. Not sure which to try? Opt for the sampler of three glasses of a third of a pint (£6.70).

Thekla CLUB

(☑0117-929 3301; www.theklabristol.co.uk; The Grove, East Mud Dock; ☺Thu-Sat 9.30pm-3am or 4am) Bristol's club-boat has nights for all moods: electro-punk, indie, disco and new wave, plus regular live gigs during the week. Check the website for the latest.

Albion PUB

(www.thealbionclifton.co.uk; Boyce's Ave; ☺9am-midnight Mon-Sat, to 11pm Sun) Cliftonites make a beeline for this village local for a post-work pint, drawn by the mini armchairs, log burner, a beer terrace framed by fairy lights and Bath Ales on tap.

Grain Barge PUB

(☑0117-929 9347; www.grainbarge.com; Mardyke Wharf, Hotwell Rd; ☺noon-11pm Sun-Wed, to 11.30pm Thu-Sat) This lovingly converted 1930s cargo vessel used to transport barley and wheat. Fittingly it's now used by the Bristol Beer Factory to showcase its craft ales. The beer terrace on the barge's roof is a cool spot to watch river traffic drift by.

Apple BAR

(☑0117-925 3500; www.applecider.co.uk; Welsh Back; ☺noon-midnight Mon-Sat, to 10.30pm Sun summer, 5pm-midnight Mon-Sat winter) Around 40 varieties of cider are served on this converted barge, including raspberry, strawberry and six perries (pear cider). Best enjoyed at a table set on the canalside cobbles.

☆ **Entertainment**

Watershed CINEMA

(☑0117-927 5100; www.watershed.co.uk; 1 Canon's Rd) Bristol's digital-media centre has a three-screen, art-house cinema. Regular film-related events include talks and the Encounters Festival (p240) in September.

★**Bristol Old Vic** THEATRE

(☑0117-987 7877; www.bristololdvic.org.uk; 16 King St) Established in 1766, the much-respected Old Vic is the longest continuously running theatre in the English-speaking world, and has just had a £12.5m revamp. It hosts big touring productions in its historic Georgian auditorium, plus more experimental work in its smaller studio.

Check the website for details of its fabulous backstage and heritage tours (£12).

Fleece LIVE MUSIC

(☑0117-945 0996; www.thefleece.co.uk; 12 St Thomas St; £5-25; ☺7.30-11pm Mon-Fri, to 4am Fri & Sat) A lively gig-pub favoured by indie artists. Past performers include Oasis, Muse and Radiohead.

Colston Hall
LIVE MUSIC

(☑0117-203 4040; www.colstonhall.org; Colston St) Bristol's historic concert hall now has a gleaming five-floor annexe. Performers include rock, pop, folk and jazz bands, plus classical musicians and big-name comedy acts.

Shopping

High-street chains cluster around **Cabot Circus** (☑0117-952 9361; www.cabotcircus.com; Glass House; ☉10am-8pm Mon-Sat, 11am-5pm Sun) and Broadmead. The city centre has St Nicholas Market, plus other independent shops dotted around Corn St and Colston St.

Stokes Croft and Gloucester Rd are good for non-chain stores, especially those selling vintage clothing, crafts and secondhand music. Clifton is more upmarket, with high-end designer, homeware and antiques shops.

Information

Bristol Royal Infirmary (BRI; ☑0117-923 0000; www.uhbristol.nhs.uk; Upper Maudlin St; ☉24hr) Offers 24 hour emergency and urgent care.

Bristol Tourist Office (☑0333 321 0101; www.visitbristol.co.uk; E-Shed, 1 Canons Rd; ☉10am-5pm; ☎) Offers information and advice, plus free wi-fi, accommodation bookings, and luggage storage (£5 per item).

Getting There & Away

AIR

Bristol International Airport (☑0371 334 4444; www.bristolairport.co.uk) Bristol's airport is 8 miles southwest of the city. Destinations in the UK and Ireland include Aberdeen, Belfast, Edinburgh, Cork, Glasgow and Newcastle (mainly handled by easyJet). Direct links with cities in mainland Europe include those to Barcelona, Berlin, Milan and Paris.

BUS

Bristol's **bus station** (Marlborough St; ☉ticket office 8am-6pm) is 500m north of the city centre. From there buses shuttle into central areas and fan out around the city. There's a taxi rank nearby.

National Express (www.nationalexpress.com) coaches include those running direct to:
London (£18, 2½ hours, hourly).
London Heathrow (£30, three hours, two-hourly).
Plymouth (£14, three hours, seven daily).
Bath (£5, 45 minutes, two daily).

TRAIN

DESTINATION	COST (£)	TIME (HR)	FREQUENCY
Birmingham	30	1½	hourly
Edinburgh	90	6½	hourly
Exeter	17	1	half-hourly
Glasgow	90	6½	hourly
London	34	1¾	half-hourly
Penzance	37	5½	hourly
Truro	45	4	hourly

Getting Around

TO/FROM THE AIRPORT

Bristol Airport Flyer (http://flyer.bristolairport.co.uk) Runs shuttle buses (one-way/return £7/11, 30 minutes, every 10 minutes at peak times) from the bus station and Bristol Temple Meads train station.

Arrow (☑01275-475000; www.arrowprivatehire.co.uk) Bristol Airport's official taxi service. Prices start from around £30 (one-way) from the city centre.

BICYCLE

Bristol Cycle Shack (☑0117-955 1017; www.bristolcycleshack.co.uk; 25 Oxford St; per 24hr from £15; ☉10am-5pm Mon, Tue & Thu-Sat) Hires out bikes from its base near Bristol Temple Meads train station.

Cycle the City (☑07873 387167; www.cyclethecity.org; 1 Harbourside; tours from £18) Rents out bikes and runs cycling tours from the central harbour area.

BOAT

Bristol Ferry Boat Company (☑0117-927 3416; www.bristolferry.com) boats leave roughly hourly from the dock at Cannon's Rd near the tourist office. Its Hotwells service runs west, with stops including Millennium Sq and the SS *Great Britain*, while the Temple Meads service runs east, with stops including Welsh Back, Castle Park (for Cabot Circus) and Temple Meads (for the train station). Fares depend on distance travelled; an all-day pass is adult/child £6.50/5.50.

BUS

Bus journeys in Bristol's city centre cost £1 for up to three stops; longer trips cost £1.50. A BristolRider pass (£4.50) provides unlimited travel.

Bus 8 Runs every 15 minutes from Bristol Temple Meads train station, via College Green in the city centre, to Clifton and on to Bristol Zoo Gardens.

Bus 73/X73 Runs every 20 minutes from Bristol Parkway Station to the centre (£3.50, 30 minutes).

MetroBus The M2 service (www.metrobusbristol.co.uk; single £1.50) provides efficient links between Bristol Temple Meads train station, Long Ashton Park & Ride, the city centre and SS *Great Britain*.

CAR & MOTORCYCLE

Heavy traffic and pricey parking make driving in Bristol a headache.

Park & Ride Buses (☑ 0345-602 0121; www.travelwest.info/park-ride/bristol; peak/off-peak return £4.50/3; ⊗ 6am-9pm Mon-Sat, 9.30am-6pm Sun; ☎) run approximately every 15 to 20 minutes from Portway, Bath Rd and Long Ashton. Note that overnight parking is not allowed at the Park & Ride car parks.

TAXI

You can usually find a cab at the taxi ranks at the train and bus stations and on **St Augustine's Pde** (Narrow Quay).

To phone for a cab, try **Streamline Taxis** (☑ 0117-926 4001; www.bristolstreamlinetaxis.com) or **1st Call Taxi** (☑ 0117-955 5111; ⊗ 24hr). If you're taking a nonmetered cab, agree on the fare in advance.

BATH

POP 88,850

Bath is one of Britain's most appealing cities. Exquisite Roman and Georgian architecture, hipster hang-outs and swish spas make it hard to resist.

History

Legend has it King Bladud, a Trojan refugee and father of King Lear, founded Bath some 2800 years ago when his pigs were cured of leprosy by a dip in the muddy swamps. The Romans established the town of Aquae Sulis in AD 44 and built the extensive baths complex and a temple to the goddess Sulis-Minerva.

In 944 a monastery was founded on the site of the present abbey, helping Bath's development as an ecclesiastical centre and wool-trading town. But it wasn't until the early 18th century that Ralph Allen and the celebrated dandy Richard 'Beau' Nash made Bath the centre of fashionable society. Allen developed the quarries at Coombe Down, constructed Prior Park and employed the two John Woods (father and son) to create Bath's signature buildings.

During WWII, Bath was hit by the Luftwaffe during the so-called Baedeker raids, which targeted historic cities in an effort to sap British morale. In 1987, Bath became the only city in Britain to be declared a Unesco World Heritage Site in its entirety.

◉ Sights

★**Roman Baths**   HISTORIC BUILDING
(☑ 01225-477785; www.romanbaths.co.uk; Abbey Churchyard; adult/child/family £17.50/10.25/48; ⊗ 9.30am-5pm Nov-Feb, 9am-5pm Mar–mid-Jun, Sep & Oct, 9am-9pm mid-Jun–Aug) In typically ostentatious style, the Romans built a bathhouse complex above Bath's 46°C (115°F) hot springs. Set alongside a temple dedicated to the healing goddess Sulis-Minerva, the baths now form one of the world's best-preserved ancient Roman spas, and are encircled by 18th- and 19th-century buildings. To dodge the worst of the crowds avoid weekends, and July and August; buy fast-track tickets online to by-pass the queues. Saver tickets covering the Roman Baths and the Fashion Museum cost adult/child/family £22.50/12.25/58.

The heart of the complex is the **Great Bath**, a lead-lined pool filled with steaming, geothermally heated water from the so-called 'Sacred Spring' to a depth of 1.6m. Though now open-air, the bath would originally have been covered by a 45m-high barrel-vaulted roof.

More bathing pools and changing rooms are to the east and west, with excavated sections revealing the **hypocaust system** that heated the bathing rooms. After luxuriating in the baths, Romans would have reinvigorated themselves with a dip in the circular **cold-water pool**.

The **King's Bath** was added sometime during the 12th century around the site of the original Sacred Spring. Every day, 1.5 million litres of hot water still pour into the pool. Beneath the Pump Room are the remains of the **Temple of Sulis-Minerva**.

Digital reconstructions pop up in some sections of the complex, especially in the Temple Courtyard, and the West and East

---

ⓘ **MUSEUM DISCOUNTS**

Saver tickets covering the Roman Baths and the Fashion Museum cost adult/child/family £22.50/12.25/58.

There is also a joint ticket (adult/child/family £17/8/40) covering Beckford's Tower, No 1 Royal Crescent, the Museum of Bath Architecture and the Herschel Museum of Astronomy.

Bath

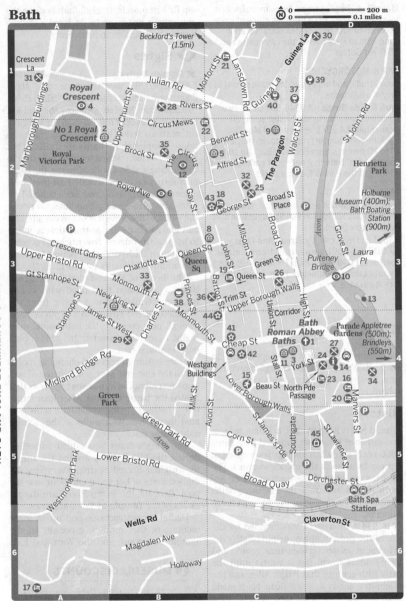

Baths, which feature projections of bathers. There is also a fascinating **museum** displaying artefacts discovered on the site. Look out for the famous gilded bronze head of Minerva and a striking carved gorgon's head, as well as some of the 12,000-odd Roman coins thrown into the spring as votive offerings to the goddess.

The complex of buildings around the baths was built in stages during the 18th and 19th centuries. John Wood the Elder and the Younger designed the buildings

Bath

⊙ Top Sights
1	Bath Abbey	D4
2	No 1 Royal Crescent	A2
3	Roman Baths	C4
4	Royal Crescent	A1

⊙ Sights
5	Bath Assembly Rooms	C2
	Fashion Museum	(see 5)
6	Georgian Garden	B2
7	Herschel Museum of Astronomy	B3
8	Jane Austen Centre	C3
9	Museum of Bath Architecture	C2
10	Pulteney Bridge	D3
11	Pump Room	C4
12	The Circus	B2

⊕ Activities, Courses & Tours
	Bath Abbey Tower Tours	(see 1)
13	Bath City Boat Trips	D3
14	Bizarre Bath Comedy Walk	D4
	Mayor's Guide Tours	(see 11)
	Pulteney Cruisers	(see 13)
15	Thermae Bath Spa	C4

⛭ Sleeping
16	Bath Backpackers	D4
17	Grays Bath	A6
18	Halcyon Apartments	C2
19	Haringtons	C3
20	Henry	D4
21	Hill House Bath	C1
22	Queensberry	B2
23	Three Abbey Green	D4

⊗ Eating
24	Acorn	D4
25	Adventure	C2
26	Bertinet Bakery	C3
27	Café Retro	D4
28	Chequers	B1
29	Farmers Market	B4
30	Hudson Steakhouse	D1
31	Marlborough Tavern	A1
	Pump Room Restaurant	(see 11)
	Sally Lunn's	(see 24)
32	Same Same But Different	C2
33	Scallop Shell	B3
34	Sotto Sotto	D4
35	The Circus	B2
36	Thoughtful Bread Company	C3

⊙ Drinking & Nightlife
37	Bell	C1
38	Colonna & Smalls	B3
39	Corkage	D1
40	Star	C1

⊙ Entertainment
41	Komedia	C4
42	Little Theatre Cinema	C4
43	Moles	C2
44	Theatre Royal	C4

⊙ Shopping
45	SouthGate	D5

around the Sacred Spring, while the famous **Pump Room** (Stall St; ⊙9.30am-5pm) FREE was built by their contemporaries, Thomas Baldwin and John Palmer, in neoclassical style, complete with soaring Ionic and Corinthian columns. The building now houses a **restaurant** (☑01225-444477; snacks £7-9, mains £13-17), where offerings include magnificent afternoon teas (£26, or £35 with champagne). You can also taste free samples of the spring waters, which were believed in Victorian times to have curative properties. If you're lucky, you might even have music provided by the Pump Room's string trio.

Admission to the Roman Baths includes an audio guide, featuring commentary in 12 languages – there's also one especially for children and a guide in sign language. One of the English guides is read by bestselling author Bill Bryson. Free hourly guided tours start at the Great Bath on the hour. The last entry to the complex is an hour before closing.

★ **Bath Abbey**　　　　CHURCH
(☑01225-422462; www.bathabbey.org; Abbey Churchyard; suggested donation adult/child £4/2; ⊙9.30am-5.30pm Mon, 9am-5.30pm Tue-Fri, to 6pm Sat, 1-2.30pm & 4.30-6pm Sun) Looming above the city centre, Bath's huge abbey church was built between 1499 and 1616, making it the last great medieval church raised in England. Its most striking feature is the west facade, where angels climb up and down stone ladders, commemorating a dream of the founder, Bishop Oliver King.

Tower tours (adult/child £8/4; ⊙10am-5pm Apr-Aug, 10am-4pm Sep & Oct, 11am-4pm Nov-Mar, closed Sun) leave on the hour from Monday to Friday, and every half-hour on Saturdays. Tours can only be booked at the Abbey shop, on the day.

Jane Austen Centre　　MUSEUM
(☑01225-443000; www.janeausten.co.uk; 40 Gay St; adult/child £12/6.20; ⊙9.45am-5.30pm Apr-Oct, 10am-4pm Sun-Fri, 9.45am-5.30pm Sat

WORTH A TRIP

PRIOR PARK ESTATE

Partly designed by the landscape architect Lancelot 'Capability' Brown, the grounds of this 18th-century **estate** (NT; ☑ 01225-833977; www.national trust.org.uk; Ralph Allen Dr; adult/child £7.40/3.70; ☉ 10am-5.30pm daily Feb-Oct, 10am-4pm Sat & Sun Nov-Jan) on Bath's southern fringe feature cascading lakes and a graceful Palladian bridge, one of only four such structures in the world (look out for the period graffiti, some of which dates back to the 1800s).

The park is a mile south of Bath's centre. Bus 2 (every 30 minutes) stops nearby, as does Bath City Sightseeing's 'City Skyline' **tour** (Bath Bus Company; ☑ 01225-444102; www.bathbuscompany. com; adult/child/family £15/9.50/43; ☉ 10am-5pm, reduced services Jan-Mar).

Nov-Mar) Bath is known to many as a location in Jane Austen's novels, including *Persuasion* and *Northanger Abbey*. Although Austen lived in Bath for only five years, from 1801 to 1806, she remained a regular visitor and a keen student of the city's social scene. Here, guides in Regency costumes regale you with Austen-esque tales as you tour memorabilia relating to the writer's life in Bath.

Herschel Museum of Astronomy   MUSEUM
(☑ 01225-446865; www.herschelmuseum.org.uk; 19 New King St; adult/child £6.50/3.20; ☉ 11am-5pm Jul & Aug, 1-5pm Mon-Fri, 10am-5pm Sat & Sun Mar-Jun & Sep) In 1781 astronomer William Herschel discovered Uranus from the garden of his home, now converted into a museum. Herschel shared the house with his wife Caroline, also an important astronomer. Their home is little changed since the 18th century; an astrolabe in the garden marks the position of the couple's telescope.

★ Royal Crescent   ARCHITECTURE
Bath is famous for its glorious Georgian architecture, and it doesn't get any grander than this semicircular terrace of majestic town houses overlooking the green sweep of Royal Victoria Park. Designed by John Wood the Younger (1728–82) and built between 1767 and 1775, the houses appear perfectly symmetrical from the outside, but the owners were allowed to tweak the interiors, so no two houses are quite the same. **No 1 Royal Crescent** (☑ 01225-428126; www.no1royalcres cent.org.uk; adult/child/family £10.30/5.10/25.40; ☉ 10am-5pm) offers you an intriguing insight into life inside.

A walk east along Brock St from the Royal Crescent leads to **the Circus**, a ring of 33 houses divided into three semicircular terraces. Plaques on the houses commemorate famous residents such as Thomas Gainsborough, Clive of India and David Livingstone. The terrace was designed by John Wood the Elder, but he died in 1754, and the terrace was completed by his son in 1768.

To the south along Gravel Walk is the **Georgian Garden** (☑ 01225-394041; off Royal Ave; ☉ 9am-7pm) **FREE**, restored to resemble a typical 18th-century town-house garden.

Bath Assembly Rooms   HISTORIC BUILDING
(NT; ☑ 01225-477786; www.nationaltrust.org.uk; 19 Bennett St; ☉ 10.30am-6pm Mar-Oct, to 5pm Nov-Feb) **FREE** When they opened in 1771, the city's stately Assembly Rooms were where fashionable Bath socialites gathered to waltz, play cards and listen to the latest chamber music. Today they're unfurnished; rooms that are open to the public include the Great Octagon, tearoom and ballroom – all lit by their original 18th-century chandeliers.

The city's fine Fashion Museum is in the basement.

Fashion Museum   MUSEUM
(☑ 01225-477789; www.fashionmuseum.co.uk; Assembly Rooms, 19 Bennett St; adult/child £9/7; ☉ 10.30am-5pm Mar-Oct, to 4pm Nov-Feb) The world-class collections on display in this museum within the basement of the city's Georgian Assembly Rooms include costumes from the 17th to late 20th centuries. Some exhibits change annually; check the website for the latest.

Pulteney Bridge   BRIDGE
Elegant Pulteney Bridge has been spanning the River Avon since the late 18th century and continues to be a much-loved and much-photographed Bath landmark (the view from Grand Parade, southwest of the bridge, is the best). Browse the shops that line both sides of the bridge or have a rest and a Bath bun in the Bridge Coffee Shop.

Museum of Bath Architecture   MUSEUM
(☑ 01225-333895; www.museumofbatharchitec ture.org.uk; The Vineyards, The Paragon; adult/child £5.50/2.50; ☉ 2-5pm Tue-Fri, 10.30am-5pm Sat

& Sun mid-Feb–Nov) The stories behind the building of Bath's most striking structures are explored here, using antique tools, displays on Georgian construction methods and a 1:500 scale model of the city.

Holburne Museum   GALLERY
(📋 01225-388569; www.holburne.org; Great Pulteney St; ⊗10am-5pm Mon-Sat, 11am-5pm Sun) FREE Sir William Holburne, the 18th-century aristocrat and art fanatic, amassed a huge collection, which now forms the core of the Holburne Museum, in a lavish mansion at the end of Great Pulteney St. The museum houses a roll call of works by artists including Turner, Stubbs, William Hoare and Thomas Gainsborough, as well as 18th-century majolica and porcelain.

American Museum in Britain   MUSEUM
(📋 01225-460503; www.americanmuseum.org; Claverton Manor; adult/child £12.50/7; ⊗10am-5pm Tue-Sun late Mar–Oct) Britain's largest collection of American folk art, including First Nations textiles, patchwork quilts and historic maps, is housed in a fine mansion a couple of miles from the city centre. Several rooms have been decorated to resemble a 17th-century Puritan house, an 18th-century tavern and a New Orleans bedroom c 1860. A free shuttle bus (11.40am to 5pm) leaves from Terrace Walk, beside Parade Gardens.

🏃 Activities

Soaking in Bath's thermal waters is a real city highlight, as are guided tours that could see you clambering up to the roof of Bath Abbey or heading out on an acclaimed comedy walk-show.

Pulteney Cruisers (📋 01225-863600; www.bathboating.com; Pulteney Bridge; adult/child £9/4; ⊗mid-Mar–Oct) and **Bath City Boat Trips** (📋 07980 335185; www.bathcityboattrips.com; Pulteney Sluice Gate; adult/child £11/9) offer cruises up and down the River Avon from the Pulteney Bridge area.

★ Thermae Bath Spa   SPA
(📋 01225-331234; www.thermaebathspa.com; Hot Bath St; spa £36-40, treatments from £65; ⊗9am-9.30pm, last entry 7pm) Taking a dip in the Roman Baths might be off limits, but you can still sample the city's curative waters at this fantastic modern spa complex, housed in a shell of local stone and plate glass. The showpiece is the open-air rooftop pool, where you can bathe in naturally heated, mineral-rich waters with a backdrop of Bath's cityscape – a don't-miss experience, best enjoyed at dusk.

Bath Boating Station   BOATING
(📋 01225-312900; www.bathboating.co.uk; Forester Rd; adult/child per hour £7/3.50, per day £18/9; ⊗10am-5.30pm Wed-Sun Easter-Sep) You can pilot your own vessel down the Avon from this Victorian-era boathouse, which rents out traditional rowing boats, punts, kayaks and Canadian canoes. It's in the suburb of Bathwick, a 20-minute walk northeast from the city centre.

🞧 Tours

★ Bizarre Bath Comedy Walk   WALKING
(www.bizarrebath.co.uk; adult/student £10/7; ⊗8pm Apr-Oct) A fabulously daft city tour mixing street theatre and live performance that bills itself as 'hysterical rather than historical'. Leaves nightly from outside the tourist office. There's no need to book.

Mayor's Guide Tours   WALKING
(www.bathguides.org.uk; ⊗10.30am & 2pm Sun-Fri, 10.30am Sat) FREE Excellent historical tours provided free by the Mayor's Corp of Honorary Guides; tours cover about 2 miles and are wheelchair accessible. They leave from within the Abbey Churchyard, outside the Pump Room. There are extra tours at 7pm on Tuesdays and Thursdays May to August.

🎊 Festivals & Events

Bath has a busy program of festivals. All bookings are handled by Bath Festival.

Bath Festival   CULTURAL
(📋 01225-614180; www.bathfestivals.org.uk; ⊗May) A new multi-arts festival that combines the Bath Literature and Bath International Music festivals, combining classical, jazz, world and folk music with fiction, debate, science, history, politics and poetry.

Bath Fringe Festival   THEATRE
(www.bathfringe.co.uk; ⊗mid-May–early Jun) Theatre-focused festival that also includes folk and world music gigs, dance and performance walks.

Great Bath Feast   FOOD & DRINK
(www.greatbathfeast.co.uk; ⊗Sep) A 15-day celebration of Bath's fine-food tradition, featuring tastings, demonstrations and markets and showcasing local producers and chefs.

🛏 Sleeping

Bath has a wide range of hotels and B&Bs, and gets extremely busy in the height of summer when prices peak. Be aware, they also rise by anything from £10 to £60 a room at weekends year-round. Few hotels have on-site parking, although some offer discounted rates at municipal car parks.

Bath YHA
HOSTEL £

(☑ 0345 371 9303; www.yha.org.uk; Bathwick Hill; dm £23, d/q from £49/69; ⊘ check in 3-11pm; 🅿 @ 🛜) Split across an Italianate mansion and modern annexes, this impressive hostel is a steep climb (or a short hop on bus U1) from the city. The listed building means the rooms are huge, and some have period features such as cornicing and bay windows.

A revamped reception, cafe-bar and new all-en suite wing opened in April 2018.

Bath Backpackers
HOSTEL £

(☑ 01225-446787; www.hostels.co.uk; 13 Pierrepont St; dm £17-21; 🛜) The showers are scarce, and it's grimy and battered, but this hostel is still on budget travellers' radars for bargain rates, a prime location and a 24-hour 'dungeon' (in truth a sound-proofed basement where you don't have to 'keep the noise down').

★ Three Abbey Green
B&B ££

(☑ 01225-428558; www.threeabbeygreen.com; 3 Abbey Green; s £108-144, d £120-200, q £240; 🛜) Rarely in Bath do you get somewhere as central as this Georgian town house with such spacious rooms. Elegant, 18th-century-style furnishings are teamed with swish wet-room bathrooms, while the opulent Lord Nelson suite features a vast four-poster bed. There's a fabulous vibe here – friendly, family-run and proud of it.

Henry
B&B ££

(☑ 01225-424052; www.thehenry.com; 6 Henry St; s £85-105, d £105-150, f £180-210; 🛜) This tall terrace has one of the best positions in Bath, literally steps from the centre. The seven rooms are jazzed up by modern floral motifs, striped cushions and mints on the pillows.

It's a great option for families – one room sleeps up to four, and cots and high chairs can be provided.

Appletree
B&B ££

(☑ 01225-337642; www.appletreebath.com; 7 Pulteney Gardens; r £95-165; 🅿 🛜) Owner, Ling, ran a city-centre hotel for 15 years, and those skills shine throughout this classy B&B. Bedrooms are named after the eponymous fruit. The best is Royal Gala, which features a sleigh bed and sofa, but even the cheaper rooms are bright and fresh and dotted with Asian art.

Hill House Bath
B&B ££

(☑ 01225-920520; www.hillhousebath.co.uk; 25 Belvedere; r £115-135; 🅿 🛜) When you walk through the door here it almost feels like you're staying with friends. The decor is quietly quirky: moustache-themed cushions, retro pictures and objets d'art abound.

Haringtons
HOTEL ££

(☑ 01225-461728; www.haringtonshotel.co.uk; 8 Queen St; r £135-200; 🛜) Bath's classical trappings aren't to everyone's taste, so things are kept strictly modern at this city-centre crash pad, with vivid colour schemes and clashing wallpapers giving it a fun, young vibe. The location is fantastic, but some rooms are a tad small. Off-site parking costs £11.

★ Queensberry
HOTEL £££

(☑ 01225-447928; www.thequeensberry.co.uk; 4 Russell St; r £112-290, ste £250-460; 🅿 🛜) Stylish but unstuffy Queensberry is Bath's best boutique spoil. In these terraced Georgian town houses heritage roots meet snazzy gingham checks, bright upholstery, original fireplaces and free-standing tubs. It's witty (see The Rules on their website), independent (and proud of it), and service is first rate.

Prices almost double on Friday and Saturday night. Valet parking is £7. The hotel's Olive Tree Restaurant is excellent, too.

★ Grays Bath
B&B £££

(☑ 01225-403020; www.graysbath.co.uk; 9 Upper Oldfield Park; r £115-245; 🅿 🛜) Boutique treat Grays is a beautiful blend of modern, pared-down design and family treasures, many picked up from the owners' travels. All the rooms are individual: choose from floral, polka dot or maritime stripes. Perhaps the pick is the curving, six-sided room 12 in the attic, with partial city views.

The owners also run **Brindleys** (☑ 01225-310444; www.brindleysbath.co.uk; 14 Pulteney Gardens; r £115-200; 🅿 🛜), a smaller but equally smart B&B on the east side of town.

Halcyon Apartments
RENTAL HOUSE £££

(☑ 01225-585100; www.thehalcyon.com/apartments; 16 George St; two-person apt £160-240, six-person apt £265; 🛜) The spacious apartments in this Georgian building blend heritage features (sash windows and high ceilings) with modern fixtures and furnishings. Quite the stylish pied-à-terre.

Walking Tour
Historic Bath

START BATH ABBEY
FINISH ROYAL CRESCENT
LENGTH 1.5 MILES; TWO HOURS

Start this architectural amble at ❶ **Bath Abbey** (p247), the city's iconic ecclesiastical edifice, built on the site of an 8th-century chapel. From the abbey square, head south along Stall St for a view of the 19th-century ❷ **Pump Room** (p247). Turn left onto York St, and follow it east to ❸ **Parade Gardens**, a landscaped Victorian park framed by the River Avon.

From here, the Grand Parade leads north; look out for the building on the corner, ❹ **The Empire**, built as a luxurious hotel in 1901. At the northern end of the Grand Parade is ❺ **Pulteney Bridge**, designed by Robert Adams in 1773, one of only a handful in the world to be lined with shops (the most famous other example is Florence's Ponte Vecchio). West of the bridge, ❻ **Upper Borough Walls** marks the northern extent of medieval Bath; if you look closely, you might spot some sections of the medieval wall that remain.

At Sawclose, you'll see the elaborate facade of Bath's ❼ **Theatre Royal** (p253), which has been staging productions since 1805. From here, follow Barton St on to ❽ **Queen Sq**, the oldest of Bath's Georgian squares, built as a showpiece development between 1728 and 1736 to demonstrate the talents of its architect, John Wood the Elder.

Head north on to Gay St, and right on to George St. Next to Clayton's Kitchen restaurant, an alley leads north, emerging next to the ❾ **Assembly Rooms** (p248), the heart of Georgian Bath's social life. Continue to Bennett St and turn left until you reach ❿ **the Circus** (p248), designed to echo the Colosseum in Rome. The three-tiered pillars exhibit the key styles of classical architecture (Doric, Ionic and Corinthian) and the facades are supposedly studded with masonic symbols.

From here, Brock St leads west to Bath's Georgian glory, the Royal Crescent. Constructed by John Wood the Younger in 1774, the terrace is now Grade I listed, making it as architecturally significant as Buckingham Palace. ⓫ **No 1 Royal Crescent** (p248) is open to the public.

✗ Eating

★ Thoughtful Bread Company
BAKERY £

(☎ 01225-471747; www.thethoughtfulbreadcompany.com; 19 Barton St; ⊙8am-5pm Tue-Fri, 8am-4pm Sat & Sun) ✔ Come lunchtime they could well be queuing out the door of this snug artisan bakery, where chunky loaves sit alongside delicate macaroons and salted caramel bombs. They also have a stall at Bath's Saturday **farmers market** (www.greenparkstation.co.uk; Green Park; ⊙9am-1.30pm Sat) ✔ – come early as they sell out fast.

Bertinet Bakery
BAKERY £

(www.bertinet.com/bertinetbakery; 1 New Bond St Pl; baked goods £2.50-5; ⊙8am-5pm Mon-Fri, 8.30am-5.30pm Sat) The flavourful fillings and light pastry of the pasties at baker Richard Bertinet's take-out shop could change your view of that foodstuff for good. You'll also be tempted by rich quiches, cheese-studded croissants, French-inspired cakes and irresistible pistachio swirls.

Café Retro
CAFE £

(☎ 01225-339347; www.caferetro.co.uk; 18 York St; mains £5-10; ⊙9am-5pm; 🖥) A poke in the eye for the corporate coffee chains. The paint job's scruffy, the crockery's ancient and none of the furniture matches, but that's all part of the charm: this is a cafe from the old school, and there are few places better for burgers, croques or cake. Takeaways (in biodegradable containers) are available from Retro-to-Go next door.

Adventure
CAFE, BAR £

(☎ 01225-462038; www.adventurecafebar.co.uk; 5 Princes Bldgs, George St; mains £5-10; ⊙8am-3am Mon-Fri, from 9am Sat & Sun; 🖥✐) This cool cafe-bar offers something for everyone at most times of the day: breakfast cappuccino, lunchtime soup and late-night beer and cocktails. There's great outdoor seating at the back.

Sally Lunn's
CAFE £

(☎ 01225-461634; www.sallylunns.co.uk; 4 North Pde Passage; afternoon tea £8-40; ⊙10am-9pm) Eating a bun at Sally Lunn's is a Bath tradition. It's all about proper English tea here, brewed in bone-china teapots, with finger sandwiches and dainty cakes served by waitresses in frilly aprons.

★ The Circus
MODERN BRITISH ££

(☎ 01225-466020; www.thecircusrestaurant.co.uk; 34 Brock St; mains lunch £12-15, dinner £16-23; ⊙10am-midnight Mon-Sat; ✐) Chef Ali Golden has turned this bistro into one of Bath's destination addresses. Her taste is for British dishes with a Continental twist, à la British food writer Elizabeth David: rabbit, Wiltshire lamb and West Country fish are all infused with herby flavours and rich sauces. It occupies an elegant town house near the Circus. Reservations recommended.

★ Acorn
VEGETARIAN ££

(☎ 01225-446059; www.acornvegetariankitchen.co.uk; 2 North Pde Passage; lunch 2/3 courses £18/23, dinner 2/3 courses £28/37; ⊙noon-3pm & 5.30-9.30pm, to 3.30pm & 10pm Sat; ✐) ✔ Proudly proclaiming 'plants taste better', Bath's premier vegetarian restaurant tempts you inside with aromas reflecting its imaginative, global-themed cuisine. The wine flights (two/three courses £15/22) matched to the set dinner menus are good value; or opt for a pear Bellini (£7) to get the liquid refreshments under way.

Scallop Shell
FISH & CHIPS ££

(☎ 01225-420928; www.thescallopshell.co.uk; 22 Monmouth Place; mains £10-15; ⊙noon-9.30pm Mon-Sat) ✔ One of Bath's best fish eateries is also one of its simplest – bags of potatoes piled up beside the door and plain wooden tables. The theme continues with the food – unfussy and unafraid to let the freshness of the ingredients and the quality of the cooking speak for themselves.

Chequers
GASTROPUB ££

(☎ 01225-360017; www.thechequersbar.com; 50 Rivers St; mains £14-25; ⊙bar noon-11pm, food noon-2.30pm & 6-9pm) A discerning crowd inhabits Chequers, a Georgian pub that's now morphed into a classy gastropub. Here the menu ranges from well-executed bar-food favourites to relative rarities such as mallard and smoked eel, and partridge with quince.

Sotto Sotto
ITALIAN ££

(☎ 01225-330236; www.sottosotto.co.uk; 10 North Pde; mains £11-25; ⊙noon-2pm & 5-10pm) The setting – an artfully lit vaulted brick chamber – is superb, and the food matches its style. Authentic Italian dishes could include herb-crusted lamb in a rich red wine sauce, and sweet potato gnocchi with fresh sea bass. Top tip: don't forgo the garlicky sautéed spinach side.

Marlborough Tavern
GASTROPUB ££

(☎ 01225-423731; www.marlborough-tavern.com; 35 Marlborough Bldgs; mains £13-25; ⊙bar noon-11pm, food noon-2pm & 6-9.30pm) The queen of

Bath's gastropubs has food that's closer to that of a fine-dining restaurant – smoked white bean puree, and crab and ginger salad rather than bog-standard meat-and-two-veg. Chunky wooden tables and racks of wine behind the bar give it an exclusive, classy feel.

Canny diners head here in the early evening to get 25% off the food bill.

★ Menu Gordon Jones   MODERN BRITISH £££

(☑ 01225-480871; www.menugordonjones.co.uk; 2 Wellsway; 5-course lunch £50, 6-course dinner £55; ⊗ 12.30-2pm & 7-9pm Tue-Sat) If you enjoy dining with an element of surprise, then Gordon Jones' restaurant will be right up your culinary boulevard. Menus are dreamt up daily and showcase the chef's taste for experimental ingredients (expect mushroom mousse and Weetabix ice cream) and eye-catching presentation (test tubes and paper bags). It's superb value given the skill on show. Reservations essential.

Hudson Steakhouse   STEAK £££

(☑ 01225-332323; www.hudsonsteakhouse.co.uk; 14 London St; mains £19-31; ⊗ 5-10.30pm Mon-Sat) Steak, steak and more steak is this acclaimed eatery's raison d'être. Tuck into top-quality cuts from porterhouse to prime fillet, all sourced from a Staffordshire farmers' co-op.

🍷 Drinking & Nightlife

★ Colonna & Smalls   CAFE

(☑ 07766 808067; www.colonnaandsmalls.co.uk; 6 Chapel Row; ⊗ 8am-5.30pm Mon-Fri, from 8.30am Sat, 10am-4pm Sun; 🛜) If you're keen on caffeinated beans, this is a cafe not to miss. A mission to explore coffee means there are three guest espresso varieties and smiley staff happy to share their expertise. They'll even tell you that black filter coffee – yes, filter coffee – is actually the best way to judge high-grade beans.

★ Star   PUB

(☑ 01225-425072; www.abbeyales.co.uk; 23 The Vineyards, off the Paragon; ⊗ noon-2.30pm & 5.30-11pm Mon-Fri, noon-midnight Sat, to 10.30pm Sun) Few pubs are registered relics, but the Star is just that, and it still has many of its 19th-century bar fittings. It's the brewery tap for Bath-based Abbey Ales; some ales are served in traditional jugs, and you can even ask for a pinch of snuff in the 'smaller bar'.

Bell   PUB

(www.thebellinnbath.co.uk; 103 Walcot St; ⊗ 11.30am-11pm Mon-Thu, to midnight Fri & Sat, noon-10.30pm Sun; 🛜) Get chatting to Bath's bohemian muso crowd around the real fire at this laid-back locals' favourite. Conversation starters include the table football, bar billiards, backgammon and chess – and live music ranging from acoustic, country and folk to blues.

Same Same But Different   CAFE ££

(☑ 01225-466856; www.same-same.co.uk; 7a Prince's Bldgs, Bartlett St; tapas £5, mains £10-12; ⊗ 8am-11pm Tue-Fri, 9am-11pm Sat, 10am-5pm Sun, 8am-6pm Mon; 🛜) In this boho hang-out for the town's trendies you can tuck into picante poached eggs for breakfast, gourmet sandwiches for lunch and afternoon cappuccino and cake. Evenings bring creative tapas – think a zesty lime and coriander octopus – best sampled with a glass from the short but strong wine list.

Corkage   WINE BAR

(☑ 01225-422577; www.corkagebath.com; 132a Walcot St; ⊗ noon-11pm Tue-Sat) There's a distinct air of a French bistro in this intimate, friendly wine bar where the aromas of flavour-packed dishes fill the air and regiments of bottles fill the shelves. It offers scaled-down versions of main courses (£4 to £8) and an extensive international wine list.

☆ Entertainment

Moles   LIVE MUSIC

(☑ 01225-437537; www.moles.co.uk; 14 George St; ⊗ 5pm-3am Mon-Thu, to 4am Fri & Sat) Bath's main music venue keeps the crowds happy with a musical diet of indie, electro pop, punk, metal, club classics, DJ sets and cheese.

Little Theatre Cinema   CINEMA

(☑ 0871 9025735; www.picturehouses.com; St Michael's Pl) Bath's excellent art-house cinema screens fringe films and foreign-language flicks in art deco surrounds.

Theatre Royal   THEATRE

(☑ 01225-448844; www.theatreroyal.org.uk; Sawclose) Bath's historic theatre dates back 200 years. Major touring productions go in the main auditorium and smaller shows appear in the Ustinov Studio.

Komedia   COMEDY

(☑ 01225-489070; www.komedia.co.uk; 22-23 Westgate St) Renowned comedy venue featuring touring shows and the sell-out Krater Saturday Comedy Club. Also live music, bingo and discos.

🛍 Shopping

Bath's shops are some of the best in the west. The city's main shopping centre is **South-Gate** (www.southgatebath.com; ⊙ shops 9am-6pm Mon-Wed, Fri & Sat, 9am-7pm Thu, 11am-5pm Sun), where you'll find all the major chain stores.

High-quality, independent shops line the narrow lanes just north of Bath Abbey and Pulteney Bridge. Milsom St is good for up-market fashion, while Walcot St has food shops, design stores, vintage-clothing retailers and artisans' workshops.

ℹ Information

Bath Tourist Office (🖉 01225-614420; www. visitbath.co.uk; 2 Terrace Walk; ⊙ 9.30am-5.30pm Mon-Sat, 10am-4pm Sun, closed Sun Nov-Jan) Offers advice and information. Also runs an accommodation booking service and sells a wide range of local books and maps.

Royal United Hospital (🖉 01225-428331; www.ruh.nhs.uk; Combe Park; ⊙ 24hr) Offers 24 hour emergency and urgent care.

ℹ Getting There & Away

BUS

Bath's **bus and coach station** (Dorchester St) is near the train station. From there regular local buses fan out into the city, there's also a taxi rank nearby, or order a cab through **Bath Taxis** (🖉 0845 003 5205; www.bath-taxis.co.uk).

National Express (www.nationalexpress.com) coaches include those running direct to:

London (£20, 2½ hours, hourly)

London Heathrow (£25, three hours, two-hourly)

Plymouth (£26, four hours, seven daily)

Bristol (£5, 45 minutes, two daily)

Services to many other destinations change at Bristol.

First Bus (www.firstgroup.com) is the biggest local bus company. Services to:

Bristol (38/39/X39; £6, 50 minutes, four per hour Monday to Saturday, half-hourly on Sunday)

Wells (172/173/174; £6, 1½ hours, two per hour Monday to Saturday, hourly Sunday)

TRAIN

Bath's train station, Bath Spa, is at the south end of Manvers St. Some services connect through Bristol, including many to the southwest and north of England. Direct services include:

Bristol (£8, 15 minutes, half-hourly)

Cardiff Central (£21, one hour, hourly)

London Paddington (from £35, 90 minutes, half-hourly)

Salisbury (£18, one hour, hourly)

There's a taxi rank at Bath Spa station, or call Bath Taxi (p254). Many city buses also leave from the train station.

ℹ Getting Around

BICYCLE

Bath is hilly. The canal paths along the Kennet and Avon Canal and the 13-mile Bristol & Bath Railway Path (www.bristolbathrailwaypath.org. uk) are great to explore by bike.

Bath Bike Hire (🖉 01225-447276; www. bath-narrowboats.co.uk; Sydney Wharf; adult/child per day £15/10; ⊙ 9am-5pm) A 10-minute walk from the centre. Handy for the canal and railway paths.

Take Charge Bikes (🖉 01225-789568; www. takechargebikes.co.uk; 1 Victoria Bldgs, Lower Bristol Rd; per day £30; ⊙ 9am-5pm Mon-Fri, to 4pm Sat) Rents electric bikes.

BUS

BathRider (adult/child £4.50/3.50) A multi-operator, all-day ticket covering a 3 mile radius of central Bath. It's valid until 3am the next day. A seven-day ticket costs adult/child £20/15.

Bus U1 Runs from the bus station, via High St and Great Pulteney St, up Bathwick Hill, past the YHA to the university every 20 minutes (£2.50).

Bus 265 Goes to Bathampton (£2.50, 10 minutes, one to two per hour).

CAR & MOTORCYCLE

Bath has serious traffic problems, especially at rush hour. **Park & Ride services** (🖉 01225-394041; return Mon-Fri £3.40, Sat & Sun £3; ⊙ 6.15am-8.30pm Mon-Sat, 9.30am-6pm Sun) operate from Lansdown to the north, Newbridge to the west and Odd Down to the south. It takes about 10 minutes to the centre; buses leave every 10 to 15 minutes.

There's a good, central car park underneath the SouthGate shopping centre (two/eight hours £3.50/11).

SOMERSET

With its pastoral landscape of hedgerows, fields and hummocked hills, sleepy Somerset is the very picture of the rural English countryside, and makes the perfect escape from the bustle of Bath and the hustle of Bristol. Things certainly move at a drowsier pace around these parts – it's a place to wander, ponder and drink in the sights at your own pace.

The cathedral city of Wells is an atmospheric base for exploring the limestone caves and gorges around Cheddar, while the hippie haven of Glastonbury is handy for venturing on to the wetlands of the Somerset Levels and the high hills of the Quantocks.

ℹ Information

→ The Taunton **tourist office** (☑ 01823-340470; www.visitsomerset.co.uk/taunton; Market House, Fore St; ⊙ 9.30am-4.30pm Mon-Sat) is the best source of information about Somerset as a whole.

→ Two websites – www.visitsomerset.co.uk and www.visitsouthsomerset.co.uk – are useful sources of information.

ℹ Getting There & Around

→ The M5 heads south past Bristol to Bridgwater and Taunton, while the A39 leads west across the Quantocks to Exmoor.

→ Key train services link Bath, Bristol, Bridgwater, Taunton and Weston-super-Mare.

→ **First** (www.firstgroup.com) is a key local bus operator.

→ For timetables and general information, contact **Traveline South West** (www.travelinesw.com).

Wells & Around

POP 11,340

In Wells, small is beautiful. This is England's smallest city, and only qualifies for the title thanks to a magnificent medieval cathedral, which sits beside the grand Bishop's Palace – the official residence of the Bishop of Bath and Wells since the 12th century.

Medieval buildings and cobbled streets radiate out from the cathedral green to a marketplace that has been the bustling heart of Wells for some nine centuries (Wednesday and Saturday are market days). Film buffs might also recognise it from the hit British comedy *Hot Fuzz* – the film's final shoot-out was filmed here.

◉ Sights

★ **Wells Cathedral**   CATHEDRAL
(Cathedral Church of St Andrew; ☑ 01749-674483; www.wellscathedral.org.uk; Cathedral Green; requested donation adult/child £6/5; ⊙ 7am-7pm Apr-Sep, to 6pm Oct-Mar) Wells' gargantuan Gothic cathedral sits plumb in the centre of the city, surrounded by one of the largest **cathedral closes** in England. It was built

in stages between 1180 and 1508, and consequently showcases several Gothic styles. Among its notable features are the **West Front**, decorated with more than 300 carved figures, and the famous **scissor arches** – an ingenious architectural solution to counter the subsidence of the central tower. Don't miss the **High Parts Tour** (adult/child £10/8; ⊙ Mon-Sat May-Oct) that heads up into the roof.

Bishop's Palace   HISTORIC BUILDING
(☑ 01749-988111; www.bishopspalace.org.uk; Market Place; adult/child £8/4; ⊙ 10am-6pm Apr-Oct, to 4pm Nov-Mar) Built for the bishop in the 13th century, this moat-ringed palace is purportedly the oldest inhabited building in England. Inside, the palace's state rooms and ruined great hall are worth a look, but it's the shady gardens that are the real draw. The natural springs after which Wells is named bubble up in the palace's grounds.

Wookey Hole   CAVE
(☑ 01749-672243; www.wookey.co.uk; Wookey Hole; adult/child £19/15; ⊙ 10am-5pm Apr-Oct, to 4pm Nov-Mar) The River Axe has gouged out this network of deep limestone caverns, which are famous for striking stalagmites and stalactites, one of which is the legendary Witch of Wookey Hole who, it's said, was turned to stone by a local priest. Admission to the caves is by guided tour; up on top you'll find 20 beyond-kitsch attractions ranging from animatronic dinosaurs to pirate adventure golf. Wookey Hole is 3 miles northwest of Wells; look out for brown tourist signs on the A371.

🛏 Sleeping

Stoberry House   B&B ££
(☑ 01749-672906;   www.stoberryhouse.co.uk; Stoberry Park; s £85, d £95-158; P 🕏) It's hard to know which is more beautiful: the lush, 2.5-hectare garden, or the house that overflows with rich fabrics, plush cushions and boutique flourishes. Expect pod coffee machines, luxury teas, books to browse and the use of a well-stocked pantry. It's all tucked away in a private estate.

Ancient Gate House Hotel   HOTEL ££
(☑ 01749-672029;   www.ancientgatehouse.co.uk; 20 Sadler St; s £95-100, d £115-130; 🕏) This old hostelry is partly built right into the cathedral's west gate. Rooms are decorated in regal reds and duck-egg blues. The best of these have four-poster beds and knockout

CHEDDAR GORGE

Carved out by glacial meltwater during the last ice age, **Cheddar Gorge** (☎01934-742343; www.cheddargorge.co.uk; adult/child £20/15; ☉10am-5pm) is England's deepest natural canyon, in places towering 138m above the twisting B3135. The gorge is riddled with subterranean caverns with impressive displays of stalactites and stalagmites. The easiest to reach are **Gough's Cave** and **Cox's Cave**; deeper caves can be explored on caving trips with **Rocksport** (☎01934-742343; www.cheddargorge.co.uk/rocksport; adult/child £22/20).

Along with its caves, Cheddar is also famous as the home of the nation's favourite cheese, produced here since the 12th century. At the **Cheddar Gorge Cheese Company** (☎01934-742810; www.cheddargorgecheeseco.co.uk; The Cliffs, Cheddar; adult/child £2/free; ☉10am-5pm Easter-Oct, winter hours vary), you can watch the cheesemaking process, sample the produce, then buy some whiffy souvenirs at the shop.

Cheddar Gorge is 20 miles northwest of Wells on the A371.

cathedral views through latticed windows; they're £15 extra, and worth it.

Beryl
B&B ££

(☎01749-678738; www.beryl-wells.co.uk; Hawkers Lane; s £75-100, d £100-170, tr from £155; P🐾☎) This grand gabled mansion offers a taste of English eccentricity. Every inch of the house is crammed with antique atmosphere, and the rooms boast grandfather clocks, chaise longues and four-posters galore. It's about a mile from Wells.

★ Babington House
LUXURY HOTEL £££

(☎01373-812266; www.babingtonhouse.co.uk; Babington, near Frome; r £255-380; P🐾☎) It's eye-poppingly pricey, but this lauded design hotel is one of Britain's most luxurious. It's a mash-up of *Homes & Gardens* and *Wallpaper*: heritage beds, antique dressers and period fireplaces meet minimalist furniture, sanded wood floors and retro lamps. There's a cool library, 45-seat private cinema and spa in the old cowshed. It's 14 miles east of Wells.

✗ Eating

Strangers with Coffee
CAFE £

(☎07728 047233; 31 St Cuthbert St; cakes £3-5; ☉7.30am-4pm Tue-Sat) 'Life is too short to drink bad coffee' says the sign – something they've taken to heart here as they work caffeinated magic with some of the best beans in town. There's a tempting selection of cakes to match.

Goodfellows Cafe & Seafood Restaurant
CAFE ££

(☎01749-673866; www.goodfellowswells.co.uk; 5 Sadler St; mains £11-24; ☉10am-3pm daily,

6-9.30pm Wed-Sat) There's a choice of eating options in Goodfellows' three vibrant rooms: the continental cafe menu offers cakes, pastries and light lunches (opt to pay either £11 or £20 for two courses and a drink). Or book for an evening fine-dining experience: £30 gets you three classy courses, while the five-course seafood tasting menu (£50) is an absolute treat.

Square Edge
BISTRO ££

(☎01749-671166; www.square-edgecafe.co.uk; 2 Town Hall Bldgs; mains £7-12; ☉9am-5pm Mon-Sat 10am-4pm Sun) There's an easygoing charm to Square Edge, a retro eatery where 1950s movie posters frame old jukeboxes and vintage radios. Treats range from full-blown cooked breakfasts and American pancakes to tangy salt beef toasties and slow-cooked ribs. The cakes are creative and great.

ℹ Information

Tourist Office (☎01749-671770; www.wellssomerset.com; Wells Museum, 8 Cathedral Green; ☉10am-5pm Mon-Sat Easter-Oct, to 4pm Nov-Easter)

ℹ Getting There & Away

The bus station is south of Cuthbert St, on Princes St. Useful services include:

Bath (bus 173; £5.80, 1¼ hours, at least hourly)

Bristol (bus 376; £5.80, 1¼ hours, half-hourly)

Cheddar (bus 126; £4.70, 25 minutes, hourly Monday to Saturday, four on Sunday); continues to Weston-super-Mare (£5.80, 1½ hours)

Glastonbury (bus 376; £3.70, 15 minutes, several hourly)

Glastonbury

POP 8900

Ley lines converge, white witches convene and every shop is filled with the aroma of smouldering joss sticks in good old Glastonbury, the southwest's undisputed capital of alternative culture. Now famous for its musical mudfest of a festival, held on Michael Eavis' farm in nearby Pilton, Glastonbury has a much more ancient past: the town's iconic tor was an important pagan site, and is rumoured by some to be the mythical Isle of Avalon, King Arthur's last resting place. It's also allegedly one of the world's great spiritual nodes, marking the meeting point of many mystical lines of power – if you feel the need to get your chakras realigned, this is definitely the place. Whatever the truth of the various legends swirling round Glastonbury, one thing's for certain – watching the sunrise from the top of the tor is an experience you won't forget in a hurry.

◉ Sights

★ **Glastonbury Tor**   LANDMARK
(NT; ⊘24hr) FREE Topped by the ruined, medieval Chapel of St Michael, the iconic hump of Glastonbury Tor is visible for miles around, and provides Somerset with one of its most unmistakable landmarks. It takes half an hour to walk up from the start of the trail on Well House Lane; the steepest sections are stepped. Between April and September a regular Tor Bus (adult/child £3/1.50) runs every half hour from St Dunstan's car park near Glastonbury Abbey to the trailhead on Well House Lane.

The tor is the focal point for a wealth of local lore. According to Celtic legend, the tor is the home of Arawn or Gwyn ap Nudd, king of the underworld and lord of the faeries. A more famous legend identifies the tor as the mythic Isle of Avalon, where King Arthur was taken after being mortally wounded in battle, and where Britain's 'once and future king' sleeps until his country calls again. Others believe that the tor marks an ancient mystical node where invisible lines of energy, known as ley lines, converge.

It's easy to see why the tor has inspired so many myths. It's a strange presence in an otherwise pan-flat landscape, and in ancient times (when the area around Glastonbury was covered by water for much of the year), the tor would indeed have appeared as an island, wreathed in mists and cut off by rivers, marshes and bogs.

Chalice Well & Gardens   GARDENS
(⌨01458-831154; www.chalicewell.org.uk; Chilkwell St; adult/child £4.30/2.15; ⊘10am-6pm Apr-Oct, to 4.30pm Nov-Mar) Shaded by yew trees and criss-crossed by quiet paths, the Chalice Well & Gardens have been sites of pilgrimage since the days of the Celts. The iron-red waters from the 800-year-old well are rumoured to have healing properties, good for everything from eczema to smelly feet; some legends also identify the well as the hiding place of the Holy Grail.

★ **Glastonbury Abbey**   RUINS
(⌨01458-832267; www.glastonburyabbey.com; Magdalene St; adult/child £7.50/4.50; ⊘9am-8pm Jun-Aug, to 6pm Mar-May, Sep & Oct, to 4pm Nov-Feb) The scattered ruins of Glastonbury Abbey give little hint that this was once one of England's great seats of ecclesiastical power. It was torn down following Henry VIII's dissolution of the monasteries in 1539, and the last abbot, Richard Whiting, was hung, drawn and quartered on the tor. Today's striking ruins include some of the nave walls, the remains of St Mary's chapel, and the crossing arches, which may have been scissor-shaped like those in Wells Cathedral.

OFF THE BEATEN TRACK

SOMERSET LEVELS

Flat as a pancake, sub-sea-level and criss-crossed with canals (known locally as rhynes), the Somerset Levels are one of England's largest native wetlands. Covering almost 250 sq miles between the Quantock and Mendip Hills, they're brilliant for bird spotters – particularly in October and November, when huge flocks of starlings (properly known as murmurations) descend on the area. Nature reserves have been established at Ham Wall, Shapwick Heath, Sedgemoor and Westhay.

The flat landscape of the Levels also makes it ideal for cycling. Several trails pass through the village of Langport, including the long-distance River Parrett Trail.

Glastonbury

Glastonbury

The grounds also contain a museum, cider orchard and herb garden. According to legend, the abbey's famous holy thorn tree sprang from the staff of Joseph of Arimathea, Jesus' great-uncle, who supposedly visited the abbey following Christ's death. It blooms at Christmas and Easter.

The abbey even has an Arthurian connection. In the 12th century, monks supposedly uncovered a tomb in the abbey grounds inscribed *Hic iacet sepultus inclitus rex arturius in insula avalonia,* or 'Here lies buried the renowned King Arthur in the Isle of Avalon'. Inside the tomb were two entwined skeletons, purportedly those of Arthur and his wife Guinevere. The bones were reburied beneath the altar in 1278, but were lost following the abbey's destruction.

★ **Lake Village Museum** MUSEUM
(The Tribunal, 9 High St; adult/child £3.50/2; ⊙10am-3pm Mon-Sat) The Lake Village Museum displays finds from a prehistoric bog village discovered in nearby Godney. The houses were clustered in about six groups and built from reeds, hazel and willow. It's thought they were occupied by summer traders who lived the rest of the year around Glastonbury Tor.

🎪 Festivals & Events

Glastonbury Festival of Contemporary Performing Arts MUSIC
(www.glastonburyfestivals.co.uk; tickets from £238; ⊙Jun or Jul) A majestic (and frequently mud-soaked) extravaganza of music, theatre, dance, cabaret, carnival, spirituality and general all-round weirdness that's been held on farmland in Pilton, just outside Glastonbury, since 1970 (bar the occasional off-year to let the farm recover). Tickets usually go on sale in the autumn, and always sell out within a matter of minutes.

🛏 Sleeping

Street YHA   HOSTEL
(☑0345-3719143; www.yha.org.uk; Ivythorn Hill, Street; dm/tr/q £20/65/75; ℗) A Swiss-chalet style building surrounded by green fields, with friendly staff and a good stock of books in the public rooms. It's set on the outskirts of the village of Street, a few miles south of Glastonbury.

★Covenstead   B&B ££
(☑01458-830278; www.covenstead.co.uk; Magdalene St; s £70, d £80-110; ℗🛜) It's as if they've distilled the wacky essence of Glastonbury and poured it all over this weirdly wonderful B&B. The downstairs is a riot of oddities: mock skeletons, witches hats, upcycled antlers and draped python skins. Bedroom themes range from fairy via green man and Gothic to Halloween honeymoon. A tad crazy, yes, but also delightfully done.

Magdalene House   B&B ££
(☑01458-830202; www.magdalenehouseglaston bury.co.uk; Magdalene St; s £75-100, d £95-110, f £130-145; ℗🛜) Artfully decorated Magdalene used to be a school run by Glastonbury's nuns, and one room still overlooks the abbey grounds. Each of the tall, light rooms is an array of olive, oatmeal and other soft tones, while tasteful knick-knacks give it all a homely feel.

Glastonbury Townhouse   B&B ££
(☑01458-831040; www.glastonburytownhouse. co.uk; Street Rd; r £95-130; ℗🛜) Nothing too outlandish about this place – just a solid, red-brick, Edwardian town house, with a clutch of quiet rooms, lots of painted furniture and a contemporary vibe. Breakfast, served overlooking the garden, can be vegetarian, vegan, or dairy- or gluten-free.

🍴 Eating

Rainbow's End   VEGETARIAN £
(☑01458-833896; www.rainbowsendcafe.com; 17b High St; mains £6-9; ⏰10am-4pm; 🖋) This psychedelic cafe sums up the Glastonbury spirit, with its all-veggie food, potted plants and mix-and-match furniture. Tuck into homity pie or a hot quiche, followed by scrumptious homemade cake. The vegan and gluten-free menu is extensive and there's a small patio out back.

★Bocabar   BRITISH ££
(☑01458-440558; http://glastonbury.bocabar. co.uk; Morland Rd; mains £8-17; ⏰9.30am-11pm Tue-Thu, to 1am Fri & Sat, 10am-5pm Sun & Mon) Formerly a sheepskin factory, now a hip hang-out, at cavernous red-brick Bocabar a pan-global menu takes in mezze platters, fish stews, gourmet burgers and adventurous puddings. Live bands play several times a week, the G&T menu boasts 22 types of gin and an industrial-chic vibe adds to the appeal.

It's about 1.5 miles southwest of the town centre along Morland Rd.

Who'd a Thought It Inn   PUB FOOD ££
(☑01458-834460; www.whodathoughtit.co.uk; 17 Northload St; mains £12-18; ⏰noon-9.30pm) In this pleasantly peculiar locals' pub vintage advertising signs sit beside an old red telephone box and an upside-down bike dangles from the ceiling. The food is solid pub fare – sausages, pies and steaks – but there are usually specials chalked above the bar.

ℹ Information

Tourist Office (☑01458-832954; www.glas tonburytic.co.uk; Magdalene St; ⏰10am-4pm Mon-Sat, 11am-3pm Sun) In the town hall.

ℹ Getting There & Away

There is no train station in Glastonbury.
Useful bus routes include:
Taunton (bus 29; £5.70, 1½ hours, four to seven daily Monday to Saturday)
Wells (bus 376; £3.70, 15 minutes, several times an hour)

MONTACUTE HOUSE

Built in the 1590s for Sir Edward Phelips, a speaker of the House of Commons, **Montacute** (NT; ☑ 01935-823289; www.nationaltrust.org.uk; Montacute; adult/child £12/6; ☺ house 11am-4pm Mar-Oct 11am-3pm Nov & Dec noon-3pm Sat & Sun Jan-Mar, gardens 10am-5pm Mar-Oct, 11am-4pm Wed-Sat Nov-Feb) contains some of the finest 16th- and 17th-century interiors in the country. It's plasterwork, chimney pieces and tapestries are renowned, but the highlight is the Long Gallery – the longest such hall in England, it's rich in Elizabethan portraits.

Montacute is 5 miles west of Yeovil off the A3088.

HAMPSHIRE

Hampshire's history is regal and rich. Kings Alfred the Great, Knut and William the Conqueror all based their reigns in its ancient cathedral city of Winchester, whose jumble of historic buildings sits in the centre of undulating chalk downs. The county's coast is awash with heritage, too – in rejuvenated Portsmouth you can clamber aboard the pride of Nelson's navy, HMS *Victory*, and wonder at the *Mary Rose* (Henry VIII's flagship), before wandering wharfs buzzing with restaurants, shops and bars. Hampshire's southwestern corner claims the open heath and woods of the New Forest National Park.

Winchester

POP 116,600

Calm, collegiate Winchester is a mellow must-see. The past still echoes strongly around the flint-flecked walls of this ancient cathedral city. It was the capital of Saxon kings and a power base of bishops, and its statues and sights evoke two of England's mightiest myth makers: Alfred the Great and King Arthur (he of the round table). Winchester's architecture is exquisite, from the handsome Elizabethan and Regency buildings in the narrow streets to the wondrous cathedral at its core, while its river valley location means there are charming waterside trails to explore.

◉ Sights

★ **Winchester Cathedral**   CATHEDRAL
(☑ 01962-857200; www.winchester-cathedral.org.uk; The Close; adult/child £8/free; ☺ 9.30am-5pm Mon-Sat, 12.30-3pm Sun) One of southern England's most awe-inspiring buildings, 11th-century Winchester Cathedral boasts a fine Gothic facade, one of the longest medieval naves in Europe (164m), and a fascinating jumble of features from all eras. Other highlights include the intricately carved medieval choir stalls, which sport everything from mythical beasts to a mischievous green man, Jane Austen's grave (near the entrance) and one of the UK's finest illuminated manuscripts. The excellent **Tower and Roof Tours** (tours £6.50; ☺ Wed 2.15pm, Sat 11.30am & 2.15pm Jan-May, Oct & Nov, Mon, Wed & Fri 2.15pm, Sat 11.30am & 2.15pm Jun-Sep) get busy – book well ahead.

As the biggest, brightest and best surviving 12th-century English Bible, the dazzling, four-volume **Winchester Bible** has vivid illuminated pages. It was commissioned in 1160, possibly by the grandson of William the Conqueror. At the time of writing, long-term conservation work meant only one volume of the Bible was on display, in a temporary exhibition in the North Transept (open from 10am to 4pm Monday to Saturday). Check online for the latest.

Today's cathedral sits beside foundations that mark Winchester's original 7th-century minster church. The cathedral was begun in 1070 and completed in 1093, and was subsequently entrusted with the bones of its patron saint, St Swithin (Bishop of Winchester from 852 to 862). He is best known for the proverb stating that if it rains on St Swithin's Day (15 July), it will rain for a further 40 days and 40 nights.

Soggy ground and poor construction spelled disaster for the early church. The original tower collapsed in 1107 and major restructuring continued until the mid-15th century. Look out for the monument at the far end of the building to diver William Walker; he saved the cathedral from collapse by delving repeatedly into its waterlogged underbelly from 1906 to 1912 to bolster rotting wooden foundations with vast quantities of concrete and brick. In the crypt, look out for *Sound II,* an enigmatic life-size depiction of a contemplative man by Antony Gormley.

The highly informative, one-hour **Cathedral Body Tours** (10am to 3pm Monday to Saturday) and atmospheric **Crypt Tours** (10.30am, 12.30pm and 2.30pm Monday

Winchester

to Saturday) are included in the admission price for Winchester Cathedral.

Choral **evensong** (5.30pm Monday to Saturday, 3.30pm Sunday) is atmospheric; other Sunday services take place at 8am, 9.45am and 11am. Listen out, too, for the magnificent peal of bells at 8.45am and 2.30pm each Sunday.

The cathedral's **tree-fringed lawns** make for tranquil spots to take time out, especially on the quieter south side beyond the cloisters; the permanent secondhand book stall in the **Deanery Porch** (⊙10am-4pm) provides great bargain hunting.

★ **Winchester College**   HISTORIC BUILDING
(✆01962-621209; www.winchestercollege.org; College St; adult/child £8/free; ⊙10.15am & 11.30am Mon-Sat, plus 2.15pm Mon, Wed & Fri-Sun) Winchester College delivers a rare chance to nosey around a prestigious English school. It was set up by William Wykeham, Bishop of Winchester, in 1393, 14 years after he founded Oxford's New College. Hour-long guided tours take in the 14th-century Gothic chapel, complete with wooden vaulted roof, the dining room (called College Hall), and a vast 17th-century open classroom (called School) where exams are still held. A revealing insight into how the other half learns.

Winchester

◉ **Top Sights**

◎ **Sights**

✪ **Activities, Courses & Tours**

⊜ **Sleeping**

⊗ **Eating**

⊜ **Drinking & Nightlife**

⊜ **Shopping**

★ **Wolvesey Castle**   CASTLE
(EH; ✆0370 333 1181; www.english-heritage. org.uk; College St; ⊙10am-5pm Apr-Oct) FREE The fantastical, crumbling remains of

early-12th-century Wolvesey Castle huddle in the protective embrace of the city's walls. Completed by Henry de Blois, it served as the Bishop of Winchester's residence throughout the medieval era, with Queen Mary I and Philip II of Spain celebrating their wedding feast here in 1554.

Round Table & Great Hall HISTORIC BUILDING
(☑01962-846476; www.hants.gov.uk/greathall; Castle Ave; suggested donation £3; ⊘10am-4.30pm) Winchester's cavernous Great Hall is the only part of 11th-century Winchester Castle that Oliver Cromwell spared from destruction. Crowning the wall like a giant-sized dartboard of green and cream spokes is what centuries of mythology have dubbed King Arthur's Round Table. It's actually a 700-year-old copy, but is fascinating nonetheless. It's thought to have been constructed in the late 13th century and then painted in the reign of Henry VIII (King Arthur's image is unsurprisingly reminiscent of Henry's youthful face).

Hospital of St Cross HISTORIC BUILDING
(☑01962-878218; www.stcrosshospital.co.uk; St Cross Rd; adult/child £4.50/2.50; ⊘9.30am-5pm Mon-Sat, 1-5pm Sun Apr-Oct, 10.30am-3.30pm Mon-Sat Nov-Mar) Welcome to the oldest charitable institution in the country, founded in 1132 by the grandson of William the Conqueror, Henry de Blois. As well as healing the sick and housing the needy, the hospital was built to care for pilgrims and crusaders en route to the Holy Land. Today, it's roamed by elderly black- and red-gowned brothers, who hand out the Wayfarer's Dole – a crust of bread and horn of ale (now a swig of beer) from the Porter's Gate.

🛏 Sleeping & Eating

St John's Croft B&B ££
(☑01962-859976; www.st-johns-croft.co.uk; St John's St; s/d/f £55/90/140; P🅿🛜) You may well fall in love with this oh-so-casually stylish, rambling Queen Anne town house, where rattan carpets are teamed with bulging bookcases, and Indian art with shabby-chic antiques. The rooms are vast, the garden is tranquil and breakfast is served beside the Aga in the country-house kitchen.

★**Hannah's** B&B £££
(☑01962-840623; www.hannahsbedandbreakfast. co.uk; 16a Parchment St; r £155-225; 🛜) The word 'boutique' gets bandied around quite freely but here it really fits. The sumptuous conversion of this old dance hall sees an antique pi-

ano and honesty bar frame a wood-burning stove. Gorgeous bedrooms feature exposed brick, lofty ceilings, vast beds, and baths on the mezzanines with views of the stars.

★**Wykeham Arms** INN £££
(☑01962-853834; www.wykehamarmswinchester. co.uk; 75 Kingsgate St; s/d/ste £85/150/200; P🛜) At 250-odd years old, the Wykeham bursts with history – it used to be a brothel and also put Nelson up for a night (some say the events coincided). Creaking stairs lead to plush bedrooms that manage to be both deeply established but also on-trend; sleigh beds meet jazzy throws, oak dressers sport stylish lights. Simply smashing.

In the eccentric **bar** tankards and school canes hang from the ceiling and worn school desks lend pint-supping an illicit air. The **menu** (served noon to 2.30pm and 6pm to 9pm) covers the bar food standards, from well-executed burgers and fish and chips, to 24oz rib-eye steaks on the bone.

★**Black Rat** MODERN BRITISH £££
(☑01962-844465; www.theblackrat.co.uk; 88 Chesil St; 3 courses £38-46; ⊘noon-2.15pm & 7-9.15pm) The aromas are irresistible, the food frankly fabulous, the cooking highly technical and the ingredients dare to surprise – expect duck pastrami to be joined by pomegranate, turbot by squid ink, and pigeon breast by pine nuts and scents of Douglas fir. That's be why the Black Rat deserves its Michelin star.

🍷 Drinking & Nightlife

Black Boy PUB
(☑01962-861754; www.theblackboypub.com; 1 Wharf Hill; ⊘noon-11pm Mon-Thu, to midnight Fri & Sat, to 10.30pm Sun) Two open fires, a random array of dented antiques, a clutch of draught ciders and five real ales make this a legendary local. Any time after noon, check to see if it still has any Black Boy Bangers (£2.50) – a sausage in a crispy roll – the fried onions and mustard are optional.

ℹ Information

Tourist Office (☑01962-840500; www.visit winchester.co.uk; Guildhall, High St; ⊘10am-5pm Mon-Sat, plus 11am-4pm Sun May-Sep) Set in Winchester's Victorian Guildhall.

ℹ Getting There & Away

➔ Winchester is 65 miles west of London.
➔ Direct National Express (www.national express.com) buses depart from the bus

PORTSMOUTH HISTORIC DOCKYARD

The world-class collection of maritime heritage at **Portsmouth Historic Dockyard** (☑ 023-9283 9766; www.historicdockyard.co.uk; Victory Gate; All Attractions ticket adult/child/family £35/15/60; ☺ 10am-5.30pm Apr-Oct, to 5pm Nov-Mar) demands a day trip.

The blockbuster draw is Henry VIII's favourite flagship, the **Mary Rose** (☑ 023-9281 2931; www.maryrose.org; adult/child/family £16/8/25; ☺ 10am-5.30pm Apr-Oct, to 5pm Nov-Mar), which sank suddenly off Portsmouth while fighting the French in 1545. She was raised from the bottom in 1982, an extraordinary feat of marine archaeology, and a £35-million, boat-shaped museum has been built around her, giving uninterrupted views of the preserved timbers of her massive hull.

Equally impressive is **HMS Victory** (☑ 023-9283 9766; www.hms-victory.com; adult/child/family £18/13/37; ☺ 10am-5.30pm Apr-Oct, to 5pm Nov-Mar), Lord Nelson's flagship at the Battle of Trafalgar (1805) and the site of his famous dying words 'Kiss me, Hardy', after victory over the French had been secured. This remarkable ship is topped by a forest of ropes and masts, and weighted by a swollen belly filled with cannons and paraphernalia for an 850-strong crew.

Other nautical sights include the Victorian **HMS Warrior** (☑ 023-9283 9766; www.hmswarrior.org; adult/child/family £18/13/37; ☺ 10am-5.30pm Apr-Oct, to 5pm Nov-Mar), the WWII-era submarine **HMS Alliance** (☑ 023-9283 9766; www.submarine-museum.co.uk; Haslar Rd, Gosport; adult/child £13.50/9; ☺ 10am-5pm Apr-Oct, 10am-4pm Wed-Sun Nov-Mar) and a wealth of imaginative museums and harbour tours. Visiting more than one exhibit makes the All Attractions ticket, not single issue tickets, the best value (although it now excludes entry to the Mary Rose Museum). There's a 20% discount for buying online.

Portsmouth is 100 miles southwest of London. Direct trains run hourly from London Victoria (£20, two hours) and half-hourly from London Waterloo (£37, 2¼ hours). For the Historic Dockyard, get off at the final stop, Portsmouth Harbour.

Other departures:

Brighton (£16, two hours, hourly)

Chichester (£8, 30 minutes, half-hourly)

Southampton (£10, one hour, half-hourly)

Winchester (£12, one hour, hourly)

station for London Victoria every two hours (£16, two hours).

➡ Trains leave half-hourly to hourly for London Waterloo (£25, 1¼ hours) and hourly for Portsmouth (£12, one hour). There are also fast links to the Midlands.

ℹ Getting Around

Bicycle Bikes can be hired from **Bespoke Biking** (☑ 07920 776994; www.bespokebiking.com; Brooks Shopping Centre; per half/full day from £15/25; ☺ 9.30am-5pm Tue-Sat).

Park & Ride car parks (per day £3) are signed off junctions 10 and 11 of the M3. Services run roughly from 6.30am to 6.30pm, Monday to Saturday.

There are taxi ranks on the High St, and outside the train station and tourist office, or call **Wintax** (☑ 01962-878727; www.wintaxcars.com).

New Forest

With typical, accidental, English irony the New Forest is anything but new – it was first proclaimed a royal hunting preserve in 1079. It's also not much of a forest, being mostly heathland ('forest' is from the Old French for 'hunting ground'). Designated a national park in 2005, the forest's combined charms make it a joy to explore. Wild ponies mooch around pretty scrubland, deer flicker in the distance and rare birds flit among the foliage. Genteel villages dot the landscape, connected by a web of walking and cycling trails.

🏃 Activities

★ **New Forest Activities** ADVENTURE SPORTS (☑ 01590-612377; www.newforestactivities.co.uk; High St, Beaulieu) Runs a wide range of sessions including canoeing (adult/child per 90 minutes from £25/19), kayaking (per 90 minutes from £20/25) and archery (adult/child per 90 minutes £22/17).

Walking

The forest is gentle, largely level hiking territory. Ordnance Survey (OS) produces a detailed, 1:25,000 Explorer map (New Forest; No OL22, £9); Crimson's *New Forest Short Walks* (£8) features 20 circular day hikes of 2 to 6 miles.

The New Forest Centre in Lyndhurst stocks maps and guides.

Ranger Walks   WALKING
(📞 0300 068 0400; www.forestry.gov.uk/newforestevents; from £6) Forestry Commission–run day walks including those themed around photography, ponies and the unique way the New Forest is managed.

Cycling

➡ The New Forest makes for superb cycling country, with 100 miles of routes linking the main villages and the key railway station at Brockenhurst.

➡ *The New Forest By Bike* map (£4.50) features 12 routes ranging from 8 to 32 miles. The *New Forest Cycling Guide* (£4) features six day-cycle routes of between 4 and 22 miles on a 1:25,000 OS map.

➡ Maps and guides can be bought from an information point in Lyndhurst's New Forest Centre.

➡ To rent bikes, you'll need to pay a deposit (usually £20 to £25) and provide identification.

AA Bike Hire   CYCLING
(📞 02380-283349; www.aabikehirenewforest.co.uk; Fern Glen, Gosport Lane, Lyndhurst; adult/child per day £10/5; ⊙ 9am-5pm Apr-Oct) Based in Lyndhurst's main car park.

The Woods Cyclery   CYCLING
(New Forest Cycle Hire; 📞 02380-282028; www.thewoodscyclery.co.uk; 56 High St, Lyndhurst; adult/child per day £18/10; ⊙ 9am-5pm) Also rents out electric bikes and kids' bike seats.

Cyclexperience   CYCLING
(New Forest Cyclehire; 📞 01590-624808; www.newforestcyclehire.co.uk; Train Station, Brockenhurst; adult/child per day £18/9; ⊙ 9am-5.30pm) Based in a vintage railway carriage – they also deliver bikes across the national park.

Forest Leisure Cycling   CYCLING
(📞 01425-403584; www.forestleisurecycling.co.uk; The Cross, Burley; adult/child per day £18/10; ⊙ 9am-5pm) Has easy links onto nine cycle routes.

Horse Riding

Arniss Equestrian Centre   HORSE RIDING
(📞 01425-654114; www.arnissequestrian.co.uk; Godshill, Fordingbridge; per hr £30) Caters for all skill levels.

Burley Villa   HORSE RIDING
(Western Riding; 📞 01425-610278; www.burleyvilla.co.uk; Bashley Common Rd, near New Milton; per hour £45) Runs rides using traditional English and also Western saddle styles (per 90 minutes £54).

ⓘ Information

Tourist Information (📞 01425-880020; www.thenewforest.co.uk; Main Car Park, Lyndhurst; ⊙ 10am-5pm Apr-Oct, to 4pm Nov-Mar) This Visitor Information Point is set inside the New Forest Centre, and features leaflets, maps and books.

🛏 Sleeping

The New Forest is a haven for campers. The Forestry Commission (www.campingintheforest.co.uk) runs 10 relatively rural sites.

The official visitor website, www.thenewforest.co.uk, has a database of accommodation options ranging from campsites and holiday parks, via B&Bs and farm stays to hotels.

ⓘ Getting There & Around

BUS
➡ National Express (www.nationalexpress.com) buses stop at Ringwood and Southampton.

➡ Bus 6 (hourly Monday to Saturday, five on Sunday) runs from Southampton to Lyndhurst (£4.70, 40 minutes), Brockenhurst (£6.30, 50 minutes) and Lymington (£6.30, 1¼ hours).

➡ Bus X1/X2 runs from Bournemouth to Lymington (£6, 1½ hours, half-hourly Monday to Saturday, four on Sunday).

➡ The **New Forest Tour** (📞 01202-338420; www.thenewforesttour.info; per 1/2/5 days adult £17/22/33, child £9/12/17; ⊙ 9am-6pm early-Jul to early-Sep) has three connecting routes of hop-on/hop-off buses, stopping at Lyndhurst's main car park, Brockenhurst train station, Lymington, Ringwood, Beaulieu and Exbury.

TRAIN
➡ Two trains an hour run to Brockenhurst from London Waterloo (£25, two hours) via Winches-

ter (£15, 30 minutes) and on to Bournemouth (£8, 20 minutes).

➤ Local trains also shuttle twice an hour between Brockenhurst and Lymington (£4, 11 minutes).

Lyndhurst, Brockenhurst & Around

The quaint country villages of Lyndhurst and Brockenhurst are separated by just 4 miles. Their picturesque accommodation options and superb eateries ensure they're atmospheric bases from which to explore the New Forest.

◉ Sights

New Forest Centre   MUSEUM
(☑02380-283444; www.newforestcentre.org.uk; Main Car Park, Lyndhurst; ⊙10am-5pm Apr-Oct, to 4pm Nov-Mar) FREE Features a local labourer's cottage (complete with socks drying beside the fire), potato dibbles and a cider press. The minifilm makes for an accessible introduction to the park – listen, too, for recordings of the autumn pony sales, which take place after the annual drifts (round-ups).

Beaulieu   HISTORIC BUILDING
(☑01590-612345; www.beaulieu.co.uk; adult/child £25/13; ⊙10am-6pm Apr-Sep, to 5pm Oct-Mar) Petrolheads, historians and ghost-hunters gravitate to Beaulieu (*bew*-lee) – a vintage car museum, stately home and tourist complex centred on a 13th-century Cistercian monastery. Motor-maniacs will be in raptures at Lord Montague's **National Motor Museum**. Tickets are valid for a year; it's up to £5 cheaper to buy in advance, online. Beaulieu is served by the New Forest Tour.

� Sleeping

★**The Pig**   BOUTIQUE HOTEL £££
(☑0345 225 9494; www.thepighotel.co.uk; Beaulieu Rd, Brockenhurst; r £185-300; ℗⊙) One of the New Forest's classiest hotels remains an utter delight: log baskets, croquet mallets and ranks of guest gumboots give things a country-house air; espresso machines and minilarders lend bedrooms a luxury touch. In fact, all this effortless elegance makes it feel like you've just dropped by a friend's (very stylish) rural retreat.

Daisybank Cottage   B&B £££
(☑01590-622086; www.bedandbreakfast-newforest.co.uk; Sway Rd, Brockenhurst; s £120-130, d £135-145; ℗⊙) The seven gorgeous themed bedrooms here are mini pamper palaces.

Expect aromatic smellies in gleaming bathrooms, stylish luxurious furnishings and lots of little extras: breakfasts laden with New Forest goodies, handmade chocolates, smartphone docks, DAB radios and range-baked cakes on arrival.

❶ Getting There & Away

➤ Bus 6 shuttles between Lyndhurst and Lymington (£4, hourly Monday to Saturday, five on Sunday), via Brockenhurst; so does the New Forest Tour (p264).

➤ Trains run twice an hour between Brockenhurst and Lymington (£3.40, 10 minutes).

Buckler's Hard

For such a tiny place, this picturesque huddle of 18th-century cottages, near the mouth of the River Beaulieu, has a big history. It started in 1722, when a duke of Montague built a port to finance a Caribbean expedition. His dream faltered, but when war with France came, this embryonic village and sheltered gravel waterfront became a secret boatyard where several of Nelson's triumphant Battle of Trafalgar warships were built. In the 20th century it played its part in the preparations for the D-Day landings.

⎞ Sleeping & Eating

★**Master Builder's House**   HOTEL £££
(☑01590-616253; www.hillbrookehotels.co.uk; d £130-175; ℗) In this beautifully restored 18th-century hotel, room styles range from crisp with hints of nauticalia to more stately, with soft lighting, burnished trunks and plush fabrics.

Your dining options range from classy restaurant to family-friendly grub in the cool hotel **bar** (mains £12-24; ⊙noon-9pm).

Lymington

POP 15,400
Yachting haven, New Forest base and jumping-off point to the Isle of Wight – the appealing Georgian harbour town of Lymington has several strings to its tourism bow. This former smuggler's port offers nautical shops, prime eating and sleeping spots and, in Quay St, an utterly quaint cobbled lane.

🏃 Activities

Puffin Cruises   BOATING
(☑07850-947618; www.puffincruiseslymington.com; Lymington Quay; from adult/child £8/4;

⊘ 10am-4pm Apr-Oct) Runs hour-long cruises on the *Puffin Billi* that meander down the winding Lymington River to saltmarshes packed with birds. Smaller swashbucklers love the pirate-themed *Black Puffin* trips that set off to search for lost treasure.

🛌 Sleeping

Auplands
B&B ££

(☑ 01590-675944; www.auplands.com; 22 Southampton Rd; s £55-65, d £75-85, f from £90; ℗ 🛜)
Your genial hosts have been running this B&B for more than 30 years, and it shows in their supremely efficient systems and easy charm. Snug rooms feature pine, bottled water and big plants, while the eateries of Lymington are only a 10-minute stroll away.

★ Mill at Gordleton
BOUTIQUE HOTEL £££

(☑ 01590-682219; www.themillatgordleton.co.uk; Silver St, Hordle; d £129-149, ste £194-295; ℗ 🛜)
Step inside here and know, instantly, you're going to be looked after beautifully. Velvet and gingham dot exquisite rooms (each one comes with a sweet soft toy duck), while the garden is a magical mix of rushing water, fairy lights and modern sculpture. The Mill is 4 miles west of Lymington.

🍽 Eating

Deep Blue
FISH & CHIPS £

(www.deepbluerestaurants.com; 130 High St; mains £9; ⊘ noon-2.30pm & 4.30-8.30pm Mon-Fri, noon-9pm Sat, noon-7.30pm Sun) They're often queuing out the door at this classic British chippy, which boasts sustainable fish, freshly cut chips, mushy peas and pickled eggs. Eat in or take away.

Ship
PUB FOOD ££

(☑ 01590-676903; www.theshiplymington.co.uk; The Quay; mains £11-24; ⊘ kitchen noon-10pm Mon-Sat, to 9pm Sun; 🍴) A pub for all seasons: knock back summertime drinks on the waterside terrace; in winter, a toasty log burner gets you warm. Well-judged food ranges from Mediterranean mezze and gooey baked camembert via pizza and koftas to pan-fried venison with port jus.

★ Elderflower
MODERN BRITISH £££

(☑ 01590-676908; www.elderflowerrestaurant.co.uk; 5 Quay St; mains £24-30, 5/7 courses £55/65; ⊘ noon-2.30pm & 6.30-9.30pm Tue-Sat) An Anglo-French feel infuses Elderflower – from the wild nettle and doc leaf velouté, to the black treacle cured ham. Innovative puddings are a real treat – where else can you get cigar-smoked chocolate with your chocolate and whisky mousse?

ℹ️ Getting There & Away

Lymington has two train stations: Lymington Town and Lymington Pier. Isle of Wight ferries connect with Lymington Pier. Trains run to Southampton (£12, 40 minutes), with a change at Brockenhurst, twice an hour.

Wightlink Ferries (☑ 0333 999 7333; www.wightlink.co.uk) has car and passenger ferries that run hourly to Yarmouth on the Isle of Wight (40 minutes). An adult/child foot-passenger single costs £11/5. Summer-time fares for a car and two passengers start at around £60 for a short-break return.

ISLE OF WIGHT

On the Isle of Wight these days there's something groovy in the air. For decades this slab of rock anchored off Portsmouth was a magnet for family holidays, and it still has seaside kitsch by the bucket and spade. But now the proms and amusement arcades are framed by pockets of pure funkiness. A long-running music festival draws party-goers, just-caught seafood is served in kooky fishers' cafes, and cool camping rules – here sites are dotted with yurts and vintage campervans. Yet still the isle's principal appeal remains: a mild climate, myriad outdoorsy activities and a 25-mile shore lined with beaches, dramatic white cliffs and tranquil sand dunes.

🏃 Activities

Cycling

With 200 miles of cycle routes, the Isle of Wight makes pedal pushers smile. The island's official visitor website (www.visitisleofwight.co.uk) lists suggested trips (complete with maps), ranging from family-friendly tootles along former railway lines, to the 60 mile **Round the Island Cycle Route**. The IW Cycle Fest is held in late-August.

Bike rentals start at around £16/60 per day/week. Many firms deliver and collect on orders over £30.

Walking

This is one of the best spots in southern England for rambling, with 500 miles of well-marked walking paths, including 67 miles of coastal routes. The island's two-week walking festival each May is billed as the UK's largest.

Isle of Wight

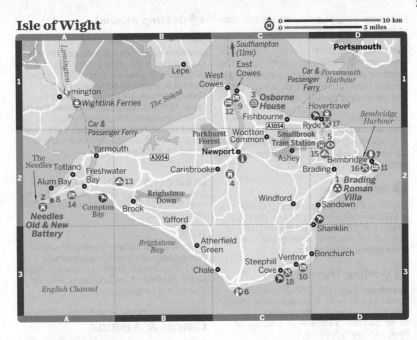

Isle of Wight

Watersports

Watersports are serious business on the Isle of Wight. Cowes is the sailing centre; surfers windsurfers and kitesurfers flock to the southwest, especially around Compton Bay; while powerboats run trips out to the Needles rocks.

Isle of Wight
Adventure Activities   ADVENTURE SPORTS
(☏0800 180 4025; www.adventureactivitiesisle ofwight.co.uk; Freshwater) Runs activities rang-
ing from surfing, stand-up paddleboarding and kayaking (per two hours adult/child £40/25) to bushcraft (per person £25) and one-hour climbing and archery taster sessions (adult/child £14/12).

🌟 Festivals

The isle's festival tradition kicked off in 1968, when an estimated 200,000 hippies came to see The Doors, The Who, Joni Mitchell and rock icon Jimi Hendrix' last performance.

Generations on, its gatherings are still some of England's top musical events.

Isle of Wight Festival
MUSIC
(www.isleofwightfestival.com; ⊘ mid-Jun) Past headline acts include Stereophonics, Muse, the Red Hot Chili Peppers, the Kings of Leon and the Rolling Stones.

Cowes Week
SAILING
(www.aamcowesweek.co.uk; ⊘ early Aug) Cowes is famous for Cowes Week; first held in 1826, it's one of the biggest and longest-running sailing regattas in the world.

ⓘ Information

The Isle of Wight's **tourist office** (☑ 01983-813813; www.visitisleofwight.co.uk; High St, Newport; ⊘ 9.30am-3.30pm Mon-Fri) is in Newport; small-scale information points include those at the main ferry ports.

ⓘ Getting There & Away

Hovertravel (☑ 01983-717700; www.hover travel.co.uk; Quay Rd, Ryde; day-return adult/child £24/12) Shuttles foot passengers between Southsea (a Portsmouth suburb) and Ryde, half-hourly to hourly.

Red Funnel (☑ 02380-248500; www.red funnel.co.uk) Runs car-and-passenger ferries between Southampton and East Cowes (same-day return adult/child £17.80/8.90, from £45 with car, 60 minutes, hourly) and high-speed passenger ferries between Southampton and West Cowes (same-day return adult/child £25.60/12.80, 25 minutes, one to two per hour).

Wightlink Ferries (☑ 0333 999 7333; www. wightlink.co.uk) Operates passenger ferries every half-hour from Portsmouth to Ryde (day-return adult/child £20/10, 22 minutes). It also runs hourly car-and-passenger ferries from Portsmouth to Fishbourne (45 minutes) and from Lymington to Yarmouth (40 minutes). For both, an adult/child foot passenger day-return costs £16/8. Car fares start at around £60 for a short-break return.

> ### ⓘ CAR FERRY COSTS
>
> The cost of car ferries to the Isle of Wight can vary enormously. Save by booking ahead, asking about special offers and travelling off-peak (midweek and later in the day). Long stays tend to be cheaper and some deals include admission to island attractions. Booking online can mean paying £20 less.

ⓘ Getting Around

BUS
Southern Vectis (www.islandbuses.info) runs buses between the eastern towns roughly every 30 minutes. Regular services to the remoter southwest, especially between Blackgang Chine and Brook, are less frequent, but between April and September, the **Island Coaster** (www.islandbuses.info; adult/child £10/5) makes one to three return circuits a day along the southern shore from Ryde in the east to Yarmouth, in the west.

CAR
1st Call (☑ 01983-400055; www.1stcallcar sales.com; 15 College Close, Sandown; per day/ week from £30/150) Collects and delivers hire cars island-wide.

TRAIN
South Western Railway (www.southwestern railway.com) runs Island Line trains twice hourly from Ryde to Shanklin (same-day return £4.60, 25 minutes), via Smallbrook Junction, Brading and Sandown.

Cowes & Around

Pack your yachting cap – the hilly Georgian harbour town of Cowes is famous for Cowes Week in early August; first held in 1826, it's one of the biggest and longest-running sailing regattas in the world. Fibreglass playthings and vintage sailing boats line Cowes' waterfronts, which are lopped into East and West Cowes by the picturesque River Medina.

The island's capital, Newport, is 5 miles south.

⊙ Sights

★ Osborne House
HISTORIC BUILDING
(EH; ☑ 01983-200022; www.english-heritage.org. uk; York Ave, East Cowes; adult/child £17.20/10/30; ⊘ 10am-6pm Apr-Sep, to 5pm Oct, 10am-4pm Sat & Sun Nov-Mar; ℗) Lemon-frosted and Italianate, Osborne House is pure Victorian pomp. Built in the 1840s at the behest of Queen Victoria, the monarch grieved here for many years after her husband's death. Extravagant rooms include the opulent Royal Apartments and Durbar Room; other highlights are horse and carriage rides, the Swiss Cottage – where the royal ankle-biters would play – and the stroll down Rhododendron Walk to Her Majesty's private beach.

Carisbrooke Castle
CASTLE
(EH; ☑ 01983-522107; www.english-heritage.org. uk; Castle Hill, Newport; adult/child £10/6;

10am-6pm Apr-Sep, to 5pm Oct, 10am-4pm Sat & Sun Nov-Mar; P) Charles I was imprisoned here before his execution in 1649. Today you can clamber the sturdy ramparts and play bowls on the very green the doomed monarch used.

Sleeping

★ onefiftycowes
B&B ££

(☎ 07795 296399; www.onefiftycowes.co.uk; 150 Park Rd, West Cowes; s/d £75/105; P 🖤) All the trappings of a luxury hotel, all the individuality of a B&B – at onefiftycowes, wicker chairs sit beside stand-alone sinks; feature fireplaces are stacked with sea-smoothed pebbles. The best room is Solent, where a pair of binoculars is waiting to help you gaze at the partial sea views.

Fountain
HOTEL ££

(☎ 0845 608 6040; www.oldenglishinns.co.uk; High St, West Cowes; s £70-97, d £90-117; 🖤) Georgian-repro style rules at this appealing harbourside inn, where mock-flock wallpaper and old, wooden furniture define comfy rooms; number 21 has slanting ceilings and prime views of the ferry quay. The snug bar and sunny terrace are good places to sample pints and pub-grub classics (mains from £10; food served 11am to 10pm).

Ryde & Around

The nippiest foot-passenger ferries between Wight and Portsmouth alight in Ryde, a workaday but appealing Victorian town rich in the trappings of the British seaside. Next come the cutesy village of Brading, with its fine Roman villa, and photogenic Bembridge Harbour, which is fringed by sandy beaches.

Further south lie the twin resort towns of Sandown and Shanklin, boasting promenades and hordes of families wielding buckets and spades.

Sights

★ Brading Roman Villa
RUINS

(☎ 01983-406223; www.bradingromanvilla.org. uk; Morton Old Rd, Brading; adult/child £9.50/4.75; 10am-5pm) The exquisitely preserved mosaics here (including a famous cockerel-headed man) make this one of the finest Romano-British sites in the UK. Wooden walkways lead over rubble walls and brightly painted tiles, allowing you to gaze right down onto the ruins below.

St Helens Duver
NATURE RESERVE

(NT; ☎ 01983-741020; www.nationaltrust.org.uk; near St Helens; 24hr; P) At this idyllic sand-and-shingle spit bordering the mouth of the River Yar, trails snake past swathes of sea pink, marram grass and rare clovers. It's signed from the village of St Helens, near Bembridge Harbour.

Isle of Wight Steam Railway
HERITAGE RAILWAY

(☎ 01983-882204; www.iwsteamrailway.co.uk; Smallbrook Junction; return adult/child from £13/6.50; mid-Apr–Sep) Regularly chugs the one-hour journey from Smallbrook Junction to Wootton Common.

Sleeping

★ Vintage Vacations
CAMPSITE ££

(☎ 07802 758113; www.vintagevacations.co.uk; Hazelgrove Farm, Ashey Rd; 2-/4-person caravans per week £620/725; Apr-Oct; P) The bevy of 1960s Airstream trailers on this farm is vintage chic personified. The gleaming aluminium shells shelter lovingly selected furnishings ranging from cheerful patchwork blankets to vivid tea cosies. Alternatively, opt for a beach-shack retreat, a 1930s scout hut, or the Mission: a late-Victorian tin chapel.

Harbourside
B&B ££

(☎ 01983-339084; www.harbourside-iow.co.uk; Embankment Rd, Bembridge Harbour; d £85-120 ste £120-170; P) How's this for a unique sleep – a boat B&B set right on the waterfront at tranquil Bembridge Harbour. The furnishings are stylish, the fixtures are often salvaged from old ships and the decked seating areas are framed by flowers. At high tides the swans drift right up to the sides.

Eating

Black Sheep
CAFE £

(☎ 01983-811006; www.theblacksheepbar.co.uk; 53 Union St, Ryde; snacks £3-6, mains £8-12; noon-3pm Mon-Fri, 6-9pm Wed-Fri, 10am-5pm Sat, 10am-3pm Sun) Chilled tunes on the music system, piles of newspapers and a palm-dotted terrace draw the locals to this laid-back Ryde venue – as do the regular live music sessions and a menu that spans homemade burgers, smoked salmon and avocado sandwiches, and steaming bowls of mussels.

Best Dressed Crab
SEAFOOD ££

(☎ 01983-874758; www.thebestdressedcrabintown. co.uk; Fisherman's Wharf, Bembridge Harbour;

mains £8-24; ☺10am-4pm daily Mar-Dec, Sat & Sun Jan & Feb) Welcome to an idyllic spot to munch your lunch. At this bijou cafe tacked on to a pontoon, the day's crab and lobster harvest is turned into supremely tasty sandwiches, salads and soups. Best eaten at one of the tables perched beside the water as local fishing boats unload their catch. It's deservedly popular – book.

Ventnor & Around

The Victorian town of Ventnor slaloms so steeply down the island's southern coast that it feels more like the south of France. The shops in the town's winding streets are worth browsing, the seafront is worth a stroll, and nearby atmospheric Steephill Cove is well worth a detour.

☉ Sights & Activities

St Catherine's Lighthouse LIGHTHOUSE
(☑01983-730435; www.trinityhouse.co.uk; near Niton; adult/child £5/3; ☺1-4.30pm Jun-Sep, hours vary Apr & May; ℗) A crenellated 19th-century navigational aid that marks the island's southernmost point. Tours climb the 90-odd steps up to the lantern room, revealing sweeping sea views.

St Catherine's Oratory LIGHTHOUSE
(near Niton) FREE Known locally as the Pepperpot, this 34ft, octagonal, 14th-century tower constitutes England's only surviving medieval lighthouse.

🛏 Sleeping & Eating

Harbour View GUESTHOUSE ££
(St Augustine Villa; ☑01983-852285; www.harbourviewhotel.co.uk; The Esplanade, Ventnor; s £74-90, d £83-99; ℗🅰) Country-house collectables dot this Italianate Victorian villa, where wing-backed chairs sit in stately bedrooms and rich red fabrics frame superb sea views. They'll have you watching the sun set from your sofa or the waves roll from your four-poster bed. The window-seated Tower Room has light pouring in from three sides.

Hambrough B&B £££
(☑01983-856333; www.thehambrough.com; Hambrough Rd, Ventnor; d £150-230 ste £190-250; 🅰) What you see from the pick of the rooms at the Hambrough is truly fabulous – the suites have balconies with wraparound sea views, while you can watch the waves from

the bathtub in room 4. The furnishings are smooth and smart, rather than stunning, and comfort comes courtesy of minifridges, underfloor heating and espresso machines.

Ale & Oyster BISTRO £££
(☑01983-857025; www.thealeandoyster.co.uk; The Esplanade, Ventnor; mains £22-25; ☺noon-2pm & 6-9pm Wed-Sun) The modern takes on Isle of Wight produce served at this top-notch little bistro have won a loyal following. Refined dishes might include crab parfait, seared scallops, confit duck, or local pigeon breast dotted with mushrooms and blackberries. Best enjoyed at a table overlooking Ventnor Bay.

Steephill Cove

Steephill Cove's tiny, sandy beach is fringed by buildings that range from stone cottages to rickety-looking shacks. Beach finds festoon porches dotted with driftwood furniture and draped with fishing nets; a tiny clapboard lighthouse presides over the scene. It's all studiedly nautical, but still very nice.

🍴 Eating

Crab Shed CAFE £
(☑01983-855819; www.steephillcove-isleofwight.co.uk; snacks from £5; ☺noon-3pm Apr-Sep) Lobster pots and fishing boats line the slipway outside a shack that's a riot of sea-smoothed spas, cork floats and faded buoys. Irresistible treats include meaty crab salads, mackerel ciabatta and crumbly crab pasties.

★Boathouse SEAFOOD £££
(☑01983-852747; www.steephill-cove.co.uk; mains £20-45; ☺noon-3pm Thu-Tue late May–early Sep) Arrive early enough, and you'll see Steephill Cove's fishers (Jimmy and Mark) landing your lunch – the sanded wooden tables here are just steps from the sea. It makes a spellbinding spot to sip chilled wine, sample succulent lobster and revel in Wight's new-found driftwood chic. Booking essential.

❶ Getting There & Away

Steephill Cove is 1 mile west of Ventnor and is off-limits to cars. Walk from the nearby Botanical Gardens (parking £5), or hike from the hillside car park 200m west of Ventnor Esplanade, then follow the (sometimes steep) coast path until you arrive.

West Wight

Rural and remote, Wight's westerly corner is where the island really comes into its own. Sheer white cliffs rear from a surging sea as the stunning coastline peels west to Alum Bay and the most famous chunks of chalk in the region: the **Needles**. These jagged rocks rise, shardlike, out of the sea, like the backbone of a prehistoric sea monster. West Wight is also home to arguably the isle's best beach: sandy, windswept **Compton Bay**.

Sights & Activities

★ Needles Old & New Battery   FORT
(NT; ☑01983-754772; www.nationaltrust.org.uk; The Needles; adult/child £6.80/3.40; ⊙11am-4pm mid-Mar–Oct) The Victorian fort complex at Wight's western tip is home to two gun emplacements where engrossing displays reveal how the site was established in 1862, served in two world wars and then became a secret Cold War rocket-testing base. Walk to the battery along the cliffs from Alum Bay (1 mile) or hop on the open-top **tourist bus** (www.islandbuses.info; per 24hr adult/child £10/5; ⊙10am-5pm mid-Mar–Oct) that runs twice hourly between battery and bay.

Needles Pleasure Cruises   BOATING
(☑01983-761587; www.needlespleasurecruises. co.uk; Alum Bay; adult/child £6/4; ⊙10.30am-4.30pm Easter-Oct) Twenty-minute voyages run half-hourly from Alum Bay beach to the towering Needles chalk stacks, providing cracking views of those soaring white cliffs.

Sleeping

Totland Bay YHA   HOSTEL £
(☑0345 260 2191; www.yha.org.uk; Hirst Hill, Totland Bay; dm/d/q £25/62/100; ⓟ@�ⓢ) Creaking, cheerfully run Victorian house with a maximum of eight beds per room and staff happy to share local info.

★ Tom's Eco Lodge   CAMPSITE ££
(☑01983-758729; www.tomsecolodge.com; Tapnell Farm, Yarmouth; 4-person pod per 3 nights £300; ⓟ�ⓢ) ⌀ Eco pods, log cabins, safari tents – the full gamut of comfy camping options sit happily on this spacious, sea-view site. They're beautifully decked out with their own showers and loos – some even have wood-fired hot tubs. Additional extras include breakfast hampers (per person £5) and food packs (for four people £40) for your own private BBQ.

DORSET

Holiday hot spot Dorset offers a checklist of charms. Its shoreline is one of Britain's best and boasts the Jurassic Coast – a World Heritage Site flecked with sea-carved bays, crumbly cliffs and beaches loaded with fossilised souvenirs. Swimming, kayaking and hiking here are memorable indeed. Inland, Thomas Hardy's lyrical landscape serves up vast Iron Age hill forts, rude chalk figures, fairy-tale castles and must-see stately homes. Then there are resorts alive with party animals, golden beaches flanked by millionaires' mansions, and sailing waters that have hosted Olympic events. Time then to add Dorset to your holiday list.

ⓘ Information

Visit Dorset (www.visit-dorset.com) The county's official tourism website.

Lonely Planet (www.lonelyplanet.com) Destination information, hotel bookings, traveller forum and more.

ⓘ Getting There & Around

TRAIN
One train route provides direct services from Bristol, via Bath and Dorchester West, to Weymouth (£20, three hours, at least six daily).

Another direct, hourly service connects London Waterloo with Weymouth (£34, three hours), via Southampton, Bournemouth, Poole and Dorchester South.

BUS
First (www.firstgroup.com/wessex-dorset-south-somerset) runs bus routes linking the main towns. A key route is bus X53 which travels regularly west from Weymouth to Axminster along the shore.

More (www.morebus.co.uk) is the key bus operator in Bournemouth, Poole and surrounding rural areas.

Bournemouth

POP 183,491

If one thing has shaped Bournemouth, it's the beach. This glorious, 7-mile strip of soft sand first drew holidaymakers in the Victorian days. Today the resort attracts both elderly coach parties and youthful stag parties – on Saturday nights fancy-dress is everywhere; angels in L-plates meet men in mankinis. But Bournemouth is more than just a full-on party town. It also boasts some hip hideaways, great restaurants, tempting watersports, and

WORTH A TRIP

KINGSTON LACY

Dorset's must-see stately home, **Kingston Lacy** (NT; ☏ 01202-883402; www.nationaltrust.org.uk; Wimborne Minster; adult/child £13.60/6.80; ☺ house 11am-5pm Mar-Oct, grounds 10am-6pm Mar-Oct, 10am-4pm Nov-Feb; P) looks every inch the setting for a period drama. It overflows with rich decor, most famously in the Spanish Room, which is smothered with gold and gilt. Other highlights are the hieroglyphics in the Egyptian Room and the elegant marble staircase and loggia. Artworks include the overwhelming ceiling fresco *The Separation of Night and Day*, by Guido Reni, and paintings by Rubens, Titian and Van Dyck.

Kingston Lacy is 2.5 miles west of Wimborne.

in Boscombe, 2 miles east of the centre, a suburb with a cool urban-surfer vibe.

◉ Sights

Bournemouth Beach   BEACH

Bournemouth's sandy shoreline regularly clocks up seaside awards. It stretches from Southbourne in the far east to Alum Chine in the west – an immense promenade backed by some 3000 deckchairs, ornamental gardens, kids' playgrounds, cafes and 200 beach huts that are available for **hire** (☏ 01202-451781; www.bournemouthbeachhuts.co.uk; per day/week from £40/115). The resort also has two piers. Around **Bournemouth Pier** you can rent deckchairs (per day £3), windbreaks (£6) and parasols (£6). **Boscombe Pier** is a focus for watersports.

Russell-Cotes   MUSEUM

(☏ 01202-451858; www.russellcotes.com; East Cliff Promenade; adult/child £7.50/4; ☺ 10am-5pm Tue-Sun) Ostentation oozes from almost every inch of this arresting structure – a mash-up of Italianate villa and Scottish baronial pile. It was built at the end of the 1800s for Merton and Annie Russell-Cotes as somewhere to showcase the remarkable range of souvenirs gathered on their world travels.

Alum Chine   GARDENS

(Mountbatten Rd; ☺ 24hr) FREE Bournemouth's 1920s heyday is beautifully evoked at a subtropical enclave containing plants from the Canary Islands, New Zealand, Mexico and

the Himalayas; their bright-red bracts, silver thistles and purple flowers are set against a glittering sea. It's 1.5 miles west of Bournemouth Pier.

🛌 Sleeping

⭐ **B&B by the Beach**   B&B ££

(☏ 01202-433632; www.bedandbreakfastbythebeach.co.uk; 7 Burtley Rd, Southbourne; s/d £70/110; P ☎) Prepare for a winning combo: charming owners and delightful rooms. Themes and colours encompass yachting, deep aquamarine and ruby red. Relaxation comes courtesy of the flower-framed terrace, posh chocs and homemade cake – best sampled with the complimentary glass of wine.

⭐ **Urban Beach**   BOUTIQUE HOTEL ££

(☏ 01202-301509; www.urbanbeach.co.uk; 23 Argyll Rd; s £58-75, d £120-140; P @ ☎) Still slumber spot of choice for Bournemouth's hip visitors, Urban Beach revels in a 'no-worries' air that sees free loans of wellingtons, umbrellas and DVDs. Soft brown, dark grey and flashes of terracotta define stylish bedrooms, while the decked terrace sees you tucking into upscale bistro fare that's served from morning (8am) till night (10pm).

Mory House   B&B ££

(☏ 01202-433553; www.moryhouse.co.uk; 31 Grand Ave, Southbourne; s/d/f £90/115/150; P ☎) In this serene, pristine B&B, stained glass and an elegant stairwell hint at the house's Edwardian age. Contemporary bedrooms are styled in muted colours; the pick is number 3, where the pint-sized balcony is an ideal spot to nibble on a home-baked cookie.

Amarillo   B&B ££

(☏ 01202-553884; www.amarillohotel.co.uk; 52 Frances Rd; s £40-45, d £70-90; P ☎) Amarillo's smart, stylish bedrooms are great value; expect jazzy wallpaper, snazzy throws and subtle lighting.

There's a three night minimum stay in summer.

✗ Eating

⭐ **Urban Reef**   BISTRO ££

(☏ 01202-443960; www.urbanreef.com; Undercliff Dr, Boscombe; snacks from £5, mains £14-22; ☺ 8am-10pm, winter times vary; ☎ ✐) On sunny weekends a cool crowd queues out the door at Urban Reef. No wonder: a waterfront deck and balcony, punchy coffee, top-notch snacks and quality, sustainable restaurant fare. On stormy days snuggle down beside the log burner and listen to the sound of the sea.

Reef Encounter
BISTRO **££**

(📞01202-280656; www.reef-encounter.com; 42 Sea Rd, Boscombe; mains £11-21; ⊙11am-10pm Mon-Fri, 9am-10pm Sat & Sun, shorter hours winter; 🛜) Big squishy sofas, a mellow soundtrack and a sea-view terrace give this chilled-out eatery a surf-bar vibe. Brunch can be healthy (avocado, salmon and egg) or decadent (maple syrup-drenched French toast). Or opt for juicy burgers and roasted veg skewers – perhaps while sipping a cool beer, watching the waves.

West Beach
SEAFOOD **££**

(📞01202-587785; www.west-beach.co.uk; Pier Approach; mains £15-40; ⊙9am-9.30pm) The seafood and setting are hard to beat – bag a chair on the decking beside the sand, watch the waves lap Bournemouth Pier and tuck into perfectly cooked, perfectly fresh fish: perhaps turbot with chorizo and capers, or a shellfish platter piled high with oysters, langoustines, cockles and clams.

Drinking & Nightlife

★ Sixty Million Postcards
PUB

(www.sixtymillionpostcards.com; 19 Exeter Rd; ⊙noon-midnight Sat-Thu, to 2am Fri) An oasis of hipster grunginess amid pound-a-pint Bournemouth, Sixty Million draws a decidedly beatnik crowd. Worn wooden floors and fringed lampshades set the scene for DJ sets, live bands and retro gaming nights.

❶ Information

Tourist Office (📞01202-451734; www. bournemouth.co.uk; Pier Approach; ⊙9am-5pm Apr-Oct, to 4pm Nov-Mar) Set right beside Bournemouth Pier.

❶ Getting There & Around

BUS

Direct National Express (www.nationalexpress. com) buses departing from Bournemouth's coach station include:

Bristol (£18, four hours, daily Monday to Saturday)

London Victoria (£15, three hours, hourly)

Oxford (£15, three hours, three daily)

Southampton (£8, 50 minutes, hourly)

Useful local buses include:

Poole (M1/M2, £2, 35 minutes, every 15 minutes)

Salisbury (X3, £6.50, 1¼ hours, at least hourly)

Morebus Zone A Dayrider (adult/child £4.10/2.60) gives a day's unlimited travel in much of Poole, Bournemouth and neighbouring Christchurch.

TRAIN

Destinations include the following:

Dorchester South (£13, 45 minutes, half-hourly)

London Waterloo (£30, 2½ hours, half-hourly)

Poole (£4, 12 minutes, half-hourly)

Weymouth (£14, one hour, hourly)

Poole

POP 147,645

In the quaint old port of Poole there's a whiff of money in the air: the town borders Sandbanks, a gorgeous beach backed by some of the world's most expensive chunks of real estate. Big bucks aside, Poole also boasts excellent eateries and is the springboard for a raft of watersports and some irresistible boat trips.

◉ Sights & Activities

Brownsea Island
ISLAND

(NT; 📞01202-707744; www.nationaltrust.org.uk; Poole Harbour; adult/child £7.20/3.60; ⊙10am-5pm late Mar–Oct) On this small, wooded island in the middle of Poole Harbour, trails weave through heath and woods, past peacocks, red squirrels, red deer and a wealth of bird life – the water-framed views

---

LAWRENCE OF ARABIA

Clouds Hill (NT; 📞01929-405616; www. nationaltrust.org.uk; King George V Rd, Bovington; adult/child £7/3.50; ⊙11am-5pm Mar-Oct; 🅿), the tiny cottage that was home to TE Lawrence (1888–1935) provides a compelling insight into a complex man. The British soldier became legendary after working with Arab forces in WWI. Look out for Lawrence's evocative desert-campaign photos, his French crusader castle sketches and the desk where he abridged *Seven Pillars of Wisdom*.

The four idiosyncratic rooms include a surprisingly comfortable cork-lined bathroom, an aluminium foil–lined bunk room and a heavily beamed music room. The house is much as Lawrence left it – he died at the age of 46 after a motorbike accident on a nearby road.

on to the Isle of Purbeck are stunning. Free guided walks focus on the wartime island, bird life, smugglers and pirates. Boats, run by **Brownsea Island Ferries** (☑ 01929-462383; www.brownseaislandferries.com; ⊙ 10am-5pm late Mar–Oct), leave from Poole Quay (adult/child return £11.50/6.75) and Sandbanks (adult/child return £7/5) at least hourly.

Poole Museum   MUSEUM
(☑ 01202-262600; www.boroughofpoole.com/museums; 4 High St; ⊙ 10am-5pm Apr-Oct) FREE The building alone is worth seeing – a beautifully restored 15th-century warehouse. The star exhibit is a 2300-year-old **Iron Age logboat** dredged up from Poole Harbour. At almost 10m long and over 12 tonnes, it's the largest to be found in southern Britain and probably carried 18 people.

Sandbanks   BEACH
A 2-mile, wafer-thin peninsula of land that curls around the expanse of Poole Harbour, Sandbanks is studded with some of the most expensive houses in the world. But the white-sand beaches that border them are free, have some of the best UK water-quality standards and are home to a host of watersports operators.

Brownsea Island Ferries shuttle from Poole to Sandbanks (adult child return £11.50/6.75), as does bus 60 (£3.60, 25 minutes, hourly).

Poole Harbour Watersports   WATER SPORTS
(☑ 01202-700503; www.pooleharbour.co.uk; 284 Sandbanks Rd) Does lessons in stand-up paddleboarding (SUP; per 1½ hours £25), windsurfing (per six hours £78) and kitesurfing (per day £99), plus memorable kayak and SUP tours (per three hours £35 to £40).

Sleeping

Old Townhouse   B&B ££
(☑ 01202-670950;   townhousepoole@btconnect.com; 7 High St; s/d £65/95; 🖤) A delightful air of old England settles cosily over this quayside B&B. It's largely down to the gleaming wood, big burnished brass taps and furnishings that aren't afraid to echo heritage styles. A central setting and tiny patio add to the appeal.

Quayside   B&B ££
(☑ 01202-683733;   www.quaysidepoole.co.uk;   9 High St; s/d £55/75; 🖤) Snug rooms in floral prints in the heart of the old harbour.

Merchant House   B&B £££
(☑ 01202-661474; www.themerchanthouse.org.uk; 10 Strand St; s £100, d £140-160) Tucked just one

street back from the water's edge, tall, red-brick Merchant House is boutiquery at its best. Hefty wood sculptures, wicker rocking chairs and crisp linen ensure it's stylish; the odd teddy bear keeps it cheery, too.

Eating

Deli on the Quay   DELI £
(☑ 01202-660022;   www.delionthequay.com;   Dolphin Quays; mains from £4.50; ⊙ 9am-5pm, to 4pm Nov-Mar) The perfect place to stock up for a beach picnic: crab cakes, old-school potato salad, and gourmet sandwiches – plus corking coffee and gooey chocolate brownies.

Storm   SEAFOOD ££
(☑ 01202-674970;   www.stormfish.co.uk;   16 High St; mains £15-21; ⊙ 6.30-9pm Mon-Sat) How rare is this? The dish you're eating could well have been caught by the chef! At chilled-out Storm, fisher Pete also rattles the pots 'n' pans, delighting in dishing up intense Goan fish curry, seafood ramen, and a classic Poole Bay Dover Sole *à la meuniére*.

Poole Arms   PUB FOOD ££
(☑ 01202-673450; www.poolearms.co.uk; 19 Poole Quay;   mains   £12-17;   ⊙ noon-9pm Sun-Thu, to 9.30pm Fri & Sat) The grub at this ancient pub is strong on locally landed seafood – try the homemade fish pie, local crab or pan-fried herring roe. Order some New Forest beer, then settle down in the snug, wood-lined bar with the locals, or on the terrace overlooking the quay.

★ **Guildhall Tavern**   FRENCH £££
(☑ 01202-671717;   www.guildhalltavern.co.uk;   15 Market St; mains £18-23; ⊙ 11.30am-3.30pm & 6-9.30pm Tue-Sat) Poole's top table consistently delights as it combines local ingredients with lashings of French flair. Predictably, fish features strongly – the spicy sautéed squid with samphire is superb; chargrilled sea bass is flambéed with Pernod – but rosemary-scented Dorset lamb also makes carnivores smile. Book.

ℹ Information

Tourist Office (☑ 01202-262600.; www.pooletourism.com; 4 High St; ⊙ 10am-5pm Apr-Oct, 10am-4pm Mon-Sat, noon-4pm Sun Nov-Mar) Set inside Poole Museum.

ℹ Getting There & Around

BOAT
Brittany Ferries (☑ 0330 159 7000; www.brittany-ferries.com) sails between Poole and

CORFE CASTLE

The startling, fractured battlements of Corfe Castle (NT; ☑ 01929-481294; www.national trust.org.uk; The Square; adult/child £9.50/4.75; ☺10am-6pm Apr-Sep, to 5pm Mar & Oct, to 4pm Nov-Feb) were once home to Sir John Bankes, Charles I's right-hand man. The Civil War saw the castle besieged by Cromwellian forces; in 1646 the plucky Lady Bankes directed a six-week defence and the castle fell only after being betrayed from within. The Roundheads then gunpowdered Corfe Castle apart; turrets and soaring walls still sheer off at precarious angles – the splayed-out gatehouse looks like it's just been blown up.

These huge fortifications also lend their name to the attractive village that has grown up alongside.

Bus 40 shuttles hourly between Poole, Wareham, Corfe Castle and Swanage. The 10-minute trip to Wareham costs £4.

Swanage Steam Railway (☑ 01929-425800; www.swanagerailway.co.uk; adult/child return £13/8; ☺daily Apr-Oct, Sat & Sun Nov, Dec & Mar) stops at Corfe Castle as it journeys between Swanage and Norden.

Cherbourg in France (4½ hours, one daily). Summer return prices start at around £80 for foot passengers and £335 for a car and two adults.

Sandbanks Ferry makes the four-minute trip from **Sandbanks** (Sandbanks Terminal; ☑ 01929-450203; www.sandbanksferry.co.uk; per pedestrian/car £1/4.50; ☺7am-11pm) to **Studland** (Studland Terminal; ☑ 01929-450203; www.sandbanksferry.co.uk; Ferry Rd; per pedestrian/car £1/4.50; ☺7am-11pm) every 20 minutes. It's a shortcut from Poole to Swanage, Wareham and the Isle of Purbeck, but the summer queues can be a pain.

BUS
A Morebus Zone A Dayrider (adult/child £4.10/2.60) gives a day's unlimited travel in much of Poole and Bournemouth.

Bournemouth (Bus M1/M2, £2, 35 minutes, every 15 minutes)

London Victoria (National Express, £18, 3½ hours, every two hours)

Sandbanks (Bus 60, £3.60, 25 minutes, hourly)

TAXI
Dial-a-Cab (☑ 01202-666822; www.pooletaxis.co.uk)

TRAIN
Bournemouth (£4, 12 minutes, half-hourly)

Dorchester South (£10, 30 minutes, hourly)

London Waterloo (£30, 2¼ hours, half-hourly)

Weymouth (£12, 45 minutes, hourly)

Lulworth Cove & Around
POP 740

In this stretch of southeast Dorset the coast steals the show. For millions of years the elements have been creating an intricate shoreline of curved bays, caves, stacks and weirdly wonderful rock formations – most notably the massive natural arch at Durdle Door.

The charismatic hamlet of Lulworth Cove is a pleasing jumble of thatched cottages and fishing gear, which winds down to a perfect crescent of white cliffs.

◉ Sights & Activities

Lulworth Cove Visitor Centre   MUSEUM
(☑ 01929-400587; www.lulworth.com; main car park; ☺10am-5pm Easter-Sep, to 4pm Oct-Easter) Excellent displays outline how geology and erosion have combined to shape the area's remarkable shoreline. Staff can advise about walks, too.

Stair Hole Bay   BAY
Stair Hole Bay sits just a few hundred metres west of Lulworth Cove. This diminutive semicircle is almost enclosed by cliffs that feature tiny rock arches – a route in that's popular with kayakers. On the landward side is the delightfully named Lulworth Crumple, where layers of rock form dramatically zigzagging folds.

★ Durdle Door   LANDMARK
The poster child of Dorset's Jurassic Coast, this immense, sea-fringed, 150-million-year-old Portland stone arch was created by a combination of massive earth movements and erosion. Today it's framed by shimmering bays; bring a swimsuit and head down the hundreds of steps for an unforgettable dip. You can park at the top of the cliffs (two hours £4, four hours £5), but it's best to hike the coast path from Lulworth Cove (1 mile).

Lulworth Castle CASTLE

(EH; ☑ 01929-400352; www.lulworth.com; adult/
child £6/4; ⏱ 10.30am-5pm Sun-Fri Apr-Dec) A
confection in creamy, dreamy white, this
baronial pile looks more like a French chateau than a traditional English castle. Built
in 1608 as a hunting lodge, it's survived
extravagant owners, extensive remodelling
and a disastrous fire in 1929. It has been
extensively restored – check out the reconstructed kitchen and cellars, then climb the
tower for sweeping coastal views. It costs £3
to park.

★ Jurassic
Coast Activities ADVENTURE SPORTS

(☑ 01305-835301; www.jurassiccoastactivities.co.
uk; per person £60-70) This unmissable, three-
hour paddle offers jaw-dropping views of
Dorset's heavily eroded coast. Starting at
Lulworth Cove, you glide through Stair
Hole's caves and stacks, across Man O'War
Bay, then under the stone arch at Durdle
Door, stopping for swims and picnics along
the way.

✵ Festivals & Events

Bestival MUSIC

(www.bestival.net; ⏱ Aug) Held in early August,
Bestival delights in an eclectic, alternative
feel, drawing the likes of the Super Furry Animals, Scissor Sisters, London Grammar and
Candi Staton to Dorset's Lulworth Estate.

For more than 10 years, Bestival was held
on the Isle of Wight.

🛏 Sleeping

Lulworth YHA HOSTEL £

(☑ 0345 371 9331; www.yha.org.uk; School Lane,
West Lulworth; dm £13-17, q £50-100; ⏱ Fri-Sun &
school holidays Mar-Oct; P) Hills stretch out
alongside, and sheep bleat outside, this cosy,
chalet-style, edge-of-the-village hostel.

Durdle Door Holiday Park CAMPSITE £

(☑ 01929-400200; www.lulworth.com; sites £28-
44; ⏱ Mar-Oct; P) Attractive, spacious site,
just minutes from the creamy cliffs, and 1.5
miles west of the hamlet of Lulworth Cove.
Opt for a good old tent, or a four-person
wooden pod (£80).

Prices rocket in the school holidays, when
there also tends to be a two night minimum
stay.

★ Lulworth Cove INN ££

(☑ 01929-400333; www.lulworth-coveinn.co.uk;
Main Rd; d £120-135; P 🖥) One to delight your
inner beachcomber. In this veritable vision
of driftwood-chic whitewashed floorboards
and aquamarine panels frame painted
wicker chairs and roll-top baths. Add cracking sea views, a mini roof terrace and top-
quality gastropub grub (mains £10 to £16;
food served from noon to 9pm) and you
have an irresistible inn.

Rudds of Lulworth B&B £££

(☑ 01929-400552; www.ruddslulworth.co.uk; Main
Rd; d £90-185; 🖥 🗷) An idyllic setting, pared-
down designs, top-notch linen and pamper-
yourself toiletries combine to make this a

JURASSIC COAST

The kind of massive, hands-on geology lesson you wish you'd had at school, the Jurassic
Coast is England's first natural World Heritage Site, putting it on a par with the Great
Barrier Reef and the Grand Canyon. This striking shoreline stretches from Exmouth in
East Devon to Swanage in Dorset, encompassing 185 million years of the Earth's history
in just 95 miles. It means you can walk, in just a few hours, many millions of years in geo-
logical time.

It began when layers of rocks formed, their varying compositions determined by different climates: desertlike conditions gave way to higher then lower sea levels. Massive
earth movements then tilted all the rock layers, forcing most of the oldest formations to
the west, and the youngest to the east. Next, erosion exposed the different strata.

The differences are very tangible. Devon's rusty-red Triassic rocks are 200–250 million years old. Lyme Regis' fossil-rich, dark-clay Jurassic cliffs are 190 million years old.
Pockets of much younger, creamy-coloured Cretaceous rocks (a mere 65–140 million
years old) pop up, notably around Lulworth Cove, where erosion has sculpted a stunning
display of bays, stacks and rock arches.

The coast's website (www.jurassiccoast.org) is a great information source; also look
out locally for the highly readable *Official Guide to the Jurassic Coast* (£4.95), or buy it
from the website's online shop.

memorable place to stay – especially if you opt for a room with Lulworth Cove views. Or just lounge beside the pool, which also overlooks that circle of bay.

✖ Eating & Drinking

Cove Fish   SEAFOOD £
(☏ 01929-400807; fish from £5; ⏱ 10am-4pm Tue-Sun Easter-Sep, plus some winter weekends) The seafood piled high in this shed by the path to the beach has been caught by ninth- and 10th-generation fishermen Joe and Levi. Bag some fish for the barbecue, or tuck into Lulworth Cove crab (from £4) or lobster – a meal that's travelled food yards not miles.

Boat Shed   CAFE £
(☏ 01929-400810; www.lulworth.com; Main Rd; snacks from £3; ⏱ 9.30am-5pm, winter hours vary) Views don't come much better than from the terrace of this converted fishers' storage shack set right beside Lulworth's glittering circular cove. The food spans fine brunches, Dorset cream teas, mezze platters and – of course – fish.

Castle   PUB
(☏ 01929-400311; www.thecastleinn-lulworthcove. co.uk; 8 Main Rd, West Lulworth; ⏱ noon-10pm; 🕾) A picture-perfect, rambling thatched inn with a swish new interior, garden and regularly changing selection of prime Dorset ciders.

❶ Getting There & Away

Bus X54 (two daily, Monday to Saturday, no service winter Sundays) stops at Lulworth Cove en route between Weymouth and Wareham and Poole.

Dorchester & Around

POP 19,143

With Dorchester, you get two towns in one: a real-life, bustling county town and Thomas Hardy's fictional Casterbridge. The Victorian writer was born nearby and his literary locations can still be found among Dorchester's Georgian terraces. Here you can also visit Hardy's former homes and see his original manuscripts. Add cracking archaeological sites and attractive places to eat and sleep and you have an appealing base for a night or two.

◉ Sights

★ Dorset County Museum   MUSEUM
(☏ 01305-262735; www.dorsetcountymuseum.org; High West St; adult/child £6.35/3.50; ⏱ 10am-5pm

Mon-Sat Apr-Oct, to 4pm Nov-Mar) The Thomas Hardy collection here is the world's largest, offering extraordinary insights into his creative process. You can see from text in Hardy's cramped handwriting where he's crossed out one word and substituted another. There's also an atmospheric reconstruction of his study at Max Gate and a letter in which Siegfried Sassoon requests permission to dedicate his first book of poems to Hardy.

Jurassic Coast fossil exhibits include a huge ichthyosaur and 1.8m plesiosaur fore paddle. Bronze and Iron Age finds from Maiden Castle include a treasure trove of coins and neck rings, while Roman artefacts include 70 gold coins, nail cleaners and (toe-curlingly) ear picks.

Roman Town House   HISTORIC BUILDING
(www.romantownhouse.co.uk; Northern Hay; ⏱ 24hr) **FREE** The knee-high flint walls and beautifully preserved mosaics here powerfully conjure up the Roman occupation of Dorchester (then Durnovaria). Peek into the summer dining room to see the underfloor heating system (hypocaust), where charcoal-warmed air circulated around pillars to produce a toasty room temperature of 18°C (64°F).

★ Maiden Castle   ARCHAEOLOGICAL SITE
(EH; www.english-heritage.org.uk; Winterborne Monkton; ⏱ dawn-dusk; 🅿) **FREE** Occupying a massive slab of horizon on the southern fringes of Dorchester, Maiden Castle is the largest and most complex Iron Age hill fort in Britain. The first defences were built on the site around 500 BC – in its heyday it was densely populated with clusters of roundhouses and a network of roads. The Romans besieged and captured Maiden Castle in AD 43 – an ancient Briton skeleton with a Roman crossbow bolt in the spine was found at the fort.

⬛ Sleeping

★ Beggars Knap   B&B ££
(☏ 07768 690691; www.beggarsknap.co.uk; 2 Weymouth Ave; s £70-80, d £90-115, f from £115; 🅿🕾) Despite the name, this altogether fabulous, vaguely decadent guesthouse is far from impoverished. Opulent rooms drip with chandeliers and gold brocades; beds draped in fine cottons range from French sleigh to four-poster. You could pay much, much more and get something half as nice.

Westwood   B&B ££
(☏ 01305-268018; www.westwoodhouse.co.uk; 29 High West St; s/d/f £80/100/140; 🕾) A skilled

LOCAL KNOWLEDGE

THOMAS HARDY'S DORCHESTER

Thomas Hardy fans can hunt down the *Mayor of Casterbridge* locations tucked away in modern Dorchester's streets. They include **Lucetta's House**, a grand Georgian affair with ornate doorposts in Trinity St, while in parallel South St, a red-brick, mid-18th-century building (now a bank) is named as the inspiration for the **house of the mayor** himself. The tourist office sells book location guides.

Max Gate (NT; ☑ 01305-262538; www.nationaltrust.org.uk; Alington Ave; adult/child £7/3.50; ⊙ 11am-5pm Mar-Oct, 11am-4pm Thu-Sat Nov-Feb; P) Hardy was a trained architect and designed this attractive house, where he lived from 1885 until his death in 1928. *Tess of the D'Urbervilles* and *Jude the Obscure* were both written here, and the house contains several pieces of original furniture. It's a mile east of Dorchester, on the A352.

Hardy's Cottage (NT; ☑ 01305-262366; www.nationaltrust.org.uk; Higher Bockhampton; adult/child £7/3.50; ⊙ 11am-5pm Mar-Oct, 11am-4pm Thu-Sun Nov-Feb; P) This picturesque cob-and-thatch house is the birthplace of Thomas Hardy. It features evocative, sparsely furnished rooms and a lush garden. It's in Higher Bockhampton, 3 miles northeast of Dorchester.

designer's been at work in this 18th-century town house, producing a contemporary-meets-Georgian style: muted greens, brass lamps, subtle checks and minisofas. The modern bathrooms glint, while tiny fridges harbour fresh milk for your tea.

Yalbury Cottage   HOTEL **££**
(☑ 01305-262382; www.yalburycottage.com; Lower Bockhampton; s/d £85/125; P � 🛜) It's almost your archetypal English cottage: framed by flowers and crowned by moss-studded thatch. Inside fresh, simple, gently rustic bedrooms overlook the garden or fields. Yalbury is in Lower Bockhampton, 3 miles east of Dorchester.

The restaurant (two/three courses £35/40) serves up top-notch takes on British classics in convivial, clublike rooms; bookings are required. Food is served from 6.30pm to 8.30pm Tuesday to Saturday, and between noon and 2pm on Sunday.

✕ Eating

 ★ **Taste**   BRASSERIE **££**
(☑ 01305-257776; www.tastebrasserie.co.uk; Trinity St; mains £9-20; ⊙ 8.30am-4pm Mon-Fri, 9am-5pm Sat, 10am-4pm Sun) One of Dorchester's best, buzziest brunch and lunch spots has fleets of fans thanks to a buy-local ethos and emphasis on superfresh sustainable ingredients. They crop up in everything from platters, tapas and melts to classy bistro dishes: grilled steak, confit duck, garlicky linguine.

Cow & Apple   BURGERS **££**
(☑ 01305-266286; www.cowandapple.co.uk; 30 Trinity St; mains £9-15; ⊙ 9am-8.30pm) Piled high and oozing all the trimmings, the dirty burgers here are decidedly good – spice things up with jalapeños, brie or a seriously sticky BBQ sauce. The cider list – more than 50 types – could take a while to work through.

Sienna   MODERN BRITISH **££**
(☑ 01305-250022; www.siennadorchester.co.uk; 36 High West St; mains £14.50, 4/6/8 courses £35/55/70; ⊙ noon-2pm Wed-Sun & 6.30-9pm Tue-Sat) The menu at sleek Sienna is peppered with rarities; expect to find fermented blackberry, jerk carrot or squid ink artfully arranged on your plate. The desserts are imaginative, too – perhaps try the chocolate pudding with surprising additions of orange and brown bread.

ⓘ Information

Tourist Office (☑ 01305-267992; www.visit-dorset.com; Dorchester Library, Charles St; ⊙ 10am-5.30pm Mon & Thu, to 1pm Wed, to 7pm Tue & Fri, to 4pm Sat)

ⓘ Getting There & Away

BUS

London Victoria (National Express, £18, four hours, one daily)

Lyme Regis (Bus X51, £4.80, 1¼ hours, hourly Monday to Saturday)

Sherborne (Bus X11, £4.70, 1¼ hours, four to seven daily Monday to Saturday)

Weymouth (Bus 10, £2, 30 minutes, half-hourly)

TRAIN

Dorchester has two train stations.

Trains leave Dorchester West for Bath and Bristol (£20, two to 2½ hours, at least six daily).

Services from Dorchester South, running at least hourly, include the following:

Bournemouth (£13, 45 minutes)
London Waterloo (£34, 2¾ hours)
Southampton (£26, 1½ hours)
Weymouth (£5, 10 minutes)

Weymouth

POP 52,168

At just over 225 years old, Weymouth is a grand dame of a resort with a couple of tricks up her faded sleeve. Candy-striped kiosks and deckchairs line a golden, 3-mile beach; chuck in cockles and chippies and prepare to promenade down seaside memory lane. But Weymouth is about more than just that sandy shore; the town boasts a historic harbour, some superb seafood restaurants and easy access to the watersports centres of the neighbouring Isle of Portland.

◉ Sights & Activities

Weymouth Beach BEACH
The nostalgia-inducing offerings along Weymouth's fine sandy shore could see you marvelling at highly skilled sand sculptors, renting a deckchair or pedalo, descending a helter-skelter, trampoline-bouncing, watching Punch & Judy shows, or taking a donkey ride.

Nothe Fort FORT
(☑ 01305-766626; www.nothefort.org.uk; Barrack Rd; adult/child £8/2; ☺ 10.30am-5.30pm Apr-Oct) Weymouth's photogenic 19th-century defences are studded with cannons, searchlights and 30cm coastal guns. Exhibits detail Dorset's Roman invasion, a Victorian soldier's drill and Weymouth in WWII.

Sea Life AQUARIUM
(☑ 01305-761070; www.visitsealife.com; Lodmoor Country Park; adult/child £23/19; ☺ 10am-5pm Apr-Oct, to 4pm Nov-Mar; ℙ) Highlights include sharks, penguins and seahorses, and talks and feeding demonstrations are held throughout the day. Tickets fall to £14 for adults and £11 for children if bought online, in advance.

Coastline Cruises BOATING
(☑ 01305-785000; www.coastlinecruises.com; Trinity Rd; adult/child return £10/6; ☺ Apr-Oct) Coastline runs the Portland Ferry, a wind-blown 90-minute sailing from Weymouth's historic fortifications, across vast Portland Harbour and on to Portland itself. Boats leave from Weymouth Harbour's west side three to four times daily from April to October.

⌣ Sleeping

★ Roundhouse B&B £££
(☑ 07825 788020; www.roundhouse-weymouth.com; 1 The Esplanade; d £105-125; 🛜) The decor here is as gently eccentric as the owner –

BATH & SOUTHWEST ENGLAND WEYMOUTH

> **WORTH A TRIP**
>
> ### THE CERNE GIANT
>
> Nude, full frontal and notoriously well endowed, the **Cerne Giant** (NT; www.nationaltrust.org.uk; Cerne Abbas; ☺ 24hr; ℙ) **FREE** chalk figure, on the hillside above the village of Cerne Abbas, is revealed in all his glory – and he's in a state of excitement that wouldn't be allowed in most magazines. The giant is around 60m high and 51m wide and his age remains a mystery; some claim he's Roman but the first historical reference comes in 1694, when three shillings were set aside for his repair. These days a car park provides grandstand views.
>
> The Victorians found it all deeply embarrassing and allowed grass to grow over his most outstanding feature. Today the hill is grazed by sheep and cattle, though only the sheep are allowed to do their nibbling over the giant – the cows would do too much damage to his lines.
>
> Down in the village, the **New Inn** (☑ 01300-341274; www.thenewinncerneabbas.co.uk; 14 Long St; d £100-140, ste £150-180; ℙ🛜) – which is actually more than 400 years old – makes a quaint place to stay.
>
> Dorchester is 8 miles south. Bus X11 (four to six daily Monday to Saturday) goes to Dorchester (£2.80, 30 minutes) and Sherborne (£3.20, 30 minutes).

vivid interiors combine sky blue, purple and shocking pink with fluffy cushions and snazzy modern art. But the best bit is the views; you can see both the beach out front and the harbour behind from all bedrooms.

Old Harbour View B&B **££**
(☑ 01305-774633; www.oldharbourviewweymouth. co.uk; 12 Trinity Rd; s/d £80/98; P 🐾) In this pristine Georgian terrace you get boating themes in the fresh, white bedrooms, and boats right outside the front door. One room overlooks the busy quay, the other faces the back.

B+B B&B **££**
(☑ 01305-761190; www.bb-weymouth.com; 68 The Esplanade; s £60-80, d £80-90; P 🐾) B+B delivers simple, streamlined rooms – some with sea views – and a first-floor lounge overlooking the bay that's stocked with guest laptop, daily newspapers, coffee and cookies. Nonnight-owls: note some of the front facing rooms can be noisy at night.

✕ Eating

Marlboro FISH & CHIPS **£**
(www.marlbororestaurant.co.uk; 46 St Thomas St; mains £7-13; ⊙ 11.30am-9.45pm) 🍃 A sustainable slant and a 40-year history help lift this traditional chippy, just metres from Weymouth's quay, above its rivals – mackerel features among the long list of super-fresh fish. Take it away and duck the seagulls or get munching in the bay-windowed, licensed cafe (open till 8pm).

★ Crustacean SEAFOOD **££**
(☑ 01305-777222; www.crustaceanrestaurant.co. uk; 59 St Mary St; mains £12-29; ⊙ noon-9pm Sun-Thu, to 9.30pm Fri & Sat) At Crustacean, you'll find an imaginative head chef with Sri Lankan heritage and a passion for French cuisine. Get cracking on a whole lobster, slurp some oysters, lunch on mussels laced with lemongrass, dine on pan-fried sea bass with a creamy saffron sauce. Or yield to temptation and go for the excellent-value threecourse set menu (£25). Book.

Manbos BISTRO **££**
(☑ 01305-839839; www.manbosbistro.com; 46 St Mary St; ⊙ noon-2.30pm & 6-9pm Tue-Sat, 6-9pm Mon) No wonder the locals love Manbos: a cosy atmosphere, great service, good prices and flavoursome, homemade bistro dishes packed with local produce. Pasta and seafood are a speciality, expect fish chowder, steaming bowls of mussels and a zesty prawn pesto linguine.

ⓘ Information

Weymouth's tourist information point has maps and brochures and is set inside the **Harbour Office** (www.visit-dorset.com; 13 Custom House Quay; ⊙ 7.30am-8pm).

ⓘ Getting There & Away

BUS

An open-top bus 501 runs to Portland Bill, Isle of Portland, from late July to August (£2.40, 45 minutes, seven daily). Four buses also run there on Saturday and Sunday from April to late July and in September.

The Jurassic Coaster (bus X53, four daily to hourly, no service winter Sundays) travels west from Weymouth to Axminster (2½ hours), via Abbotsbury (35 minutes) and Lyme Regis (1¾ hours). A Day Rider ticket costs adult/child £12/6; shorter fares are available.

Other services include:

Dorchester (Bus 10; £2, 30 minutes, halfhourly)
Fortuneswell, Isle of Portland (Bus 1; £2, 20 minutes, three to four per hour)
London Victoria (National Express; £15, 4¼ hours, one direct daily)

TRAIN

Trains running at least hourly include the following direct services:

Bournemouth (£14, one hour)
Dorchester South (£5, 10 minutes)
London Waterloo (£40, three hours)

Direct services every two hours:

Bath (£20, two hours)
Bristol (£18, 2¾ hours)

Isle of Portland

The 'Isle' of Portland is a hard, high comma of rock fused to the rest of Dorset by the ridge of Chesil Beach. On its 150m central plateau, a quarrying past still holds sway, evidenced by huge craters and large slabs of limestone. Portland offers jaw-dropping views down on to 18-mile Chesil Beach and the neighbouring Fleet – Britain's biggest tidal lagoon.

Proud, and at times bleak and rough around the edges, Portland is decidedly different from the rest of Dorset, and is all the more compelling because of it. The Isle's industrial heritage, watersport facilities, rich bird life and starkly beautiful cliffs make it worth at least a day trip.

⊙ Sights

★ Tout Quarry
SCULPTURE

(near Fortuneswell; dawn-dusk; ⊘24hr; Ⓟ) FREE
Portland's white limestone has been quarried for centuries and has been used in some of the world's finest buildings, such as the British Museum and St Paul's Cathedral. Tout Quarry's disused workings now house more than 50 sculptures that have been carved into the rock in situ, resulting in a fascinating combination of the raw material, the detritus of the quarrying process and the beauty of chiselled works.

Tout Quarry is signed off the main road, just south of Fortuneswell.

Portland Castle
CASTLE

(EH; ☑ 01305-820539; www.english-heritage.org.uk; Liberty Rd, Chiswell; adult/child £6.30/3.80; ⊘ 10am-6pm Apr-Sep, to 5pm Oct) A particularly fine product of Henry VIII's castle-building spree, with expansive views over Portland Harbour.

★ Portland Lighthouse
LIGHTHOUSE

(☑ 01305-821205; www.trinityhouse.co.uk; Portland Bill; adult/child £7/5; ⊘10am-5pm Sat-Thu Jun-Sep; Ⓟ) For a real sense of Portland's remote nature, head to its southern tip, Portland Bill, to climb the 41m-high, candy-striped lighthouse. It offers breathtaking views of rugged cliffs and the Race, a surging vortex of conflicting tides. The interactive displays in the former lighthousekeepers' cottages include Into the Dark, a recreation of sailing into stormy seas.

The lighthouse is also open on some summer Fridays and some weekends outside the main season – call for the latest times.

🏃 Activities

Andrew Simpson Water Sports Centre
BOATING

(☑ 01305-457400; www.aswc.co.uk; Osprey Quay, Portland Harbour) Activities include Royal Yachting Association (RYA) sailing lessons (adult/child per two days £199/175). Look out for their £20 taster sessions.

OTC
WATER SPORTS

(Official Test Centre; ☑ 01305-230296; http://uk.otc-windsurf.com; Osprey Quay, Portland Harbour) Offers lessons in stand-up paddleboarding (SUP; one/two hours £25/40) and windsurfing (per two hours/one day/two days £49/99/199). It also rents out SUP boards (per hour £10) and windsurfing boards and sails (per hour £30).

🛏 Sleeping & Eating

Portland YHA
HOSTEL £

(☑ 03453 719339; www.yha.org.uk; Castle Rd, Castletown; dm £25, q £49-90; Ⓟ🛜) Comfy, rambling Edwardian house with sea views from most dorms.

★ Queen Anne House
B&B ££

(☑ 01305-820028; www.queenannehouse.co.uk; 2 Fortuneswell; s/d £65/90; 🛜) It's impossible to know which room to pick: White, with skylight, beams and a hobbit-esque door; Lotus, with its grand furniture; ornate Oyster with its half-tester bed; or Garden, a suite with a French bath and miniconservatory. It doesn't matter though – they're all great value and gorgeous.

★ Crab House Cafe
SEAFOOD ££

(☑ 01305-788867; www.crabhousecafe.co.uk; Ferrymans Way, Wyke Regis; mains £14-30; ⊘ noon-2.30pm & 6-9pm Wed-Sat, noon-3.30pm Sun) This is where the locals make for on hot summer days, to sit beside the Fleet Lagoon amid beach-shack-chic tucking into fresh-as-it-gets seafood. Fish is enlivened by chilli, curry, lemon and herbs; crab comes spicy Chinese-style or whole for you to crack; and the oysters come with either pesto and parmesan or bacon and cream. Book.

Cove House
PUB FOOD ££

(☑ 01305-820895; www.thecovehouseinn.co.uk; 91 Chiswell Seafront; mains £8-18; ⊘ kitchen noon-2.30pm & 6-9pm Mon-Fri, noon-9pm Sat & Sun) Extraordinary Chesil Beach views, memorable sunsets and great grub (try the Lyme Bay scallops) in a history-rich fishers' inn.

ⓘ Getting There & Away

Bus 1 runs from Weymouth to Fortuneswell (£2, 20 minutes, three to four per hour).

From late July to August the open-top 501 bus goes from Weymouth to Portland Bill (£2.40, 45 minutes, seven daily). Four buses also run on Saturday and Sunday from April to late July and in September.

Chesil Beach

One of the most breathtaking beaches in Britain, Chesil is 18 miles long, 15m high and moving inland at the rate of 5m a century. This mind-boggling, 100-million-tonne pebble ridge is the baby of the Jurassic Coast. A mere 6000 years old, its stones range from pea-sized in the west to hand-sized in the east.

⊙ Sights

Chesil Beach Centre NATURE CENTER

(Fine Foundation; ☎01305-206191; www.dorset wildlifetrust.org.uk; Ferrybridge; parking per hr £1; ⊙10am-5pm Easter-Sep, to 4pm Oct-Easter; Ⓟ) **FREE** This centre at the start of the bridge to Portland, is a great gateway to Chesil Beach. The pebble ridge is at its highest here – 15m compared to 7m at Abbotsbury. From the car park an energy-sapping hike up sliding pebbles leads to the constant surge and rattle of waves on stones and dazzling views of the sea, with the thin pebble line and the expanse of the Fleet Lagoon behind.

★ Abbotsbury Swannery WILDLIFE RESERVE

(☎01305-871130; www.abbotsbury-tourism.co.uk; New Barn Rd, Abbotsbury; adult/child £12.50/9.50; ⊙10am-5pm late Mar–Oct) Every May some 600 free-flying swans choose to nest at this swannery, which shelters in the Fleet Lagoon, protected by the ridge of Chesil Beach. Wandering the network of trails that winds between the swans' nests is an awe-inspiring experience that's punctuated by occasional territorial displays (snuffling coughs and stand-up flapping), ensuring that even the liveliest children are stilled.

The swannery is near the picturesque village of Abbotsbury, 10 miles from Weymouth off the B3157.

Lyme Regis

POP 3637

Fantastically fossiliferous Lyme Regis packs a heavyweight historical punch. Rock-hard relics of the past pop out repeatedly from the surrounding cliffs – exposed by the landslides of a retreating shoreline. Lyme is now a pivot point of the Unesco-listed Jurassic Coast: fossil fever is definitely in the air and everyone, from proper palaeontologists to those out for a bit of fun, can engage in a spot of coastal rummaging. Add sandy beaches and some delightful places to sleep and eat, and you get a charming base for explorations.

⊙ Sights

Lyme Regis Museum MUSEUM

(☎01297-443370; www.lymeregismuseum.co.uk; Bridge St; adult/child £5/2.50; ⊙10am-5pm Mon-Sat, to 4pm Sun Apr-Oct, 10am-4pm Wed-Sun Nov-Mar) In 1814 local teenager Mary Anning found the first full ichthyosaur skeleton near Lyme Regis, propelling the town on to the world stage. An incredibly famous fossilist in her day, Miss Anning did much to pioneer the science of modern-day palaeontology. This museum, on the site of her former home, tells her story and exhibits spectacular fossils and other prehistoric finds.

The museum runs three to seven fossil-hunting walks a week (adult/child £12/6), with times dictated by the tides. It's best to book.

Cobb LANDMARK

First built in the 13th century, Lyme's iconic, curling sea defences have been strengthened and extended over the years, and so don't present the elegant line they once did, but it's still hard to resist wandering their length to the tip.

Dinosaurland MUSEUM

(☎01297-443541; www.dinosaurland.co.uk; Coombe St; adult/child £5/4; ⊙10am-4pm mid-Feb–mid-Oct, winter hours vary) This joyful, mini, indoor Jurassic Park overflows with fossil-

---

FOSSIL HUNTING

Fossil fever is catching. Lyme Regis sits in one of the most unstable sections of Britain's coast, and regular landslips mean nuggets of prehistory keep tumbling from the cliffs.

Joining a guided walk aids explorations. Three miles east of Lyme, the **Charmouth Heritage Coast Centre** (☎01297-560772; www.charmouth.org; Lower Sea Lane, Charmouth; ⊙10.30am-4.30pm daily Easter-Oct, Fri-Mon Nov-Easter) **FREE** runs one to seven trips a week (adult/child £8/4). Or, in Lyme itself, Lyme Regis Museum holds three to seven walks a week (adult/child £12/6); local expert **Brandon Lennon** (☎07854 377519; www.lymeregisfossilwalks.com; adult/child £9/7; ⊙Sat-Mon) also leads expeditions. All walks are popular, so book early.

For the best chances of a find, visit within two hours of low water. If you do hunt by yourself, official advice is to check tide times and collect on a falling tide, observe warning signs, keep away from cliffs, only pick up from the beach and always leave some behind for others. Oh, and tell the experts if you find a stunner.

ised remains; look out for belemnites, a plesiosaurus and an impressive locally found ichthyosaur. Lifelike dinosaur models will thrill youngsters – the rock-hard tyrannosaur eggs and 73kg dinosaur dung will have them in raptures.

Town Mill HISTORIC BUILDING
(☎01297-444042; www.townmill.org.uk; Mill Lane; requested donation £2.50; ☉11am-4pm Tue-Sun) An atmospheric, creaking, grinding, 14th-century working watermill. Cafes, art galleries, a jewellery workshop and micro-brewery sit alongside.

Winter hours vary; call to check.

🏃 Activities

★ Undercliff WALKING
This wildly undulating, 304-hectare nature reserve just west of Lyme was formed by massive landslides. They've left a challenging hiking landscape of slipped cliffs, fissures and ridges, where paths snake between dense vegetation, exposed tree roots and tangles of brambles. The Undercliff starts a mile west of central Lyme Regis; follow footpath signs from Holmbush Car Park.

🛏 Sleeping

Sanctuary B&B £
(☎01297-445815; www.lyme-regis.demon.co.uk; 65 Broad St; s/d £45/56) A B&B for bibliophiles: the charming, chintzy, volume-filled bedrooms here sit inside a four-floor, 18-room bookshop. Ancient tomes that just beg to be perused are everywhere – they can delay you en route to (the excellent) breakfast, but handily there's a wonderfully relaxed vibe. And yes – that price *is* right.

Coombe House B&B ££
(☎01297-443849; www.coombe-house.co.uk; 41 Coombe St; d £68-76; ℗) The airy, easygoing, stylish bedrooms in this fabulous-value guesthouse are full of bay windows, wicker and white wood. Breakfast is delivered to your room on a trolley, complete with home-made bread and a toaster – perfect for a lazy lie-in in Lyme.

★ Hix Townhouse B&B £££
(☎01297-442499; www.hixtownhouse.co.uk; 1 Pound St; s £125-135, d £135-165; ☎) With its witty designer decor, luxury flourishes and in-town location, this 18th-century terrace is hard to resist. Each room playfully conjures a leisure theme (gardening, fishing, reading etc); the pick is Sailing with its mock port-

FORDE ABBEY

Built in the 12th century as a Cistercian monastery, **Forde** (☎01460-221290; www.fordeabbey.co.uk; Chard; house adult/child £13/5, gardens £10/5; ☉house noon-4pm Tue-Fri & Sun Apr-Oct, gardens 10am-4.30pm daily year-round) has been a private home since 1649. The building boasts magnificent plasterwork ceilings and fine tapestries but the gardens steal the show: 12 hectares of lawns, ponds, shrubberies and flower beds with hundreds of rare and beautiful species.

Forde Abbey is 10 miles north of Lyme Regis; public transport is a nonstarter.

holes, artfully arranged ropes, mini roof terrace and gorgeous sea views.

🍴 Eating

★ Alexandra BRITISH £
(☎01297-442010; www.hotelalexandra.co.uk; Pound St; afternoon tea £8-30; ☉3-5.30pm; ℗⏸) It's like the setting for an Agatha Christie mystery, minus the murder. Wicker chairs dot manicured lawns, glittering Lyme Bay sweeps out behind. The perfect spot for a proper English afternoon tea, complete with scones, jam and dainty sandwiches.

Harbour Inn PUB FOOD ££
(☎01297-442299; www.harbourinnlymeregis.co.uk; 23 Marine Pde; mains £11-19; ☉noon-2.30pm & 6-9pm, closed Sun eve Oct-Mar) A flower-framed, beachside verandah, smart but snug interior and some of the best bistro–pub grub in town – the bouillabaisse is suitably intense.

Millside MODERN BRITISH ££
(☎01297-445999; www.themillside.co.uk; 1 Mill Lane; mains £13-18; ☉noon-2.30pm Tue-Sun, 6.30-9pm Tue-Sat) West Country foodstuffs pack the menu in this stylish eatery, from juicy burgers topped with cheddar from Cheddar, to fish freshly caught on the local day boats. Millside's compact terrace makes a tempting spot for lunch on a sunny day.

★ Hix Oyster & Fish House SEAFOOD £££
(☎01297-446910; www.hixoysterandfishhouse.co.uk; Cobb Rd; mains £13-23; ☉noon-10pm, closed Mon & Tue Oct-Mar; 🅿) Expect sweeping views of the Cobb and dazzling food at this

superstylish, open-plan cabin. Lyme Bay shellfish soup comes with pastis liqueur; local mackerel and ling are infused with curry and piri piri heat. Perhaps start by slurping oysters: Brownsea Island or Portland molluscs come at £2.95 a pop.

❶ Information

Tourist Office (☎ 01297-442138; www.visit-dorset.com; Church St; ⊙10am-5pm Mon-Sat, 10am-4pm Sun Apr-Oct, 10am-3pm Mon-Sat Nov-Mar)

❶ Getting There & Away

Bus X51 (£4.80, 1¼ hours, hourly Monday to Saturday) shuttles to Dorchester.

Bus X53 (four daily to hourly, no service winter Sundays) goes east to Weymouth (£7.60) via Chesil Beach, and west to Axminster (£6), with regular connections on to Exeter from there.

Sherborne

POP 9581

Sherborne gleams with a mellow, orangey-yellow stone – it's been used to build a cluster of 15th-century buildings and the impressive abbey church at their core. This serene town exudes wealth.

◉ Sights

Sherborne Abbey   CHURCH
(☎ 01935-812452; www.sherborneabbey.com; Abbey Cl; suggested donation £4; ⊙8am-6pm Apr-Sep, to 4pm Oct-Mar) At the height of its influence, the magnificent Abbey Church of St Mary the Virgin was the central cathedral of 26 succeeding Saxon bishops. Established early in the 8th century, it became a Benedictine abbey in 998 and functioned as a cathedral until 1075. The church has mesmerising fan vaulting that's the oldest in the country, a central tower supported by Saxon Norman piers and an 1180 Norman porch.

Sherborne Old Castle   CASTLE
(EH; ☎ 01935-812730; www.english-heritage.org.uk; Castleton; adult/child £4.70/2.80; ⊙10am-5pm Apr-Jun, Sep & Oct, to 6pm Jul & Aug) These days the epitome of a picturesque ruin, Sherborne's Old Castle was built by Roger, Bishop of Salisbury, in 1120 – Elizabeth I gave it to her one-time favourite Sir Walter Raleigh in the late 16th century. It became a Royalist stronghold during the English Civil War, but Cromwell reduced it to rubble after a 16-day siege in 1645, leaving just the fractured southwest gatehouse, great tower and north range.

Sherborne New Castle   CASTLE
(☎ 01935-812072; www.sherbornecastle.com; New Rd; adult/child £12/free, gardens only £6.50/free; ⊙11am-5pm Tue-Thu, Sat & Sun Apr-Oct) Sir Walter Raleigh began building the impressive Sherborne New Castle in 1594, but only got as far as the central block before being imprisoned by James I. James promptly sold the castle to Sir John Digby who added the splendid wings you see today. In 1753 the grounds received a mega-makeover at the hands of landscape-gardener extraordinaire Capability Brown who added a massive lake and the 12-hectare waterside gardens.

🛏 Sleeping & Eating

★**Cumberland House**   B&B ££
(☎ 01935-817554; www.bandbdorset.co.uk; Greenhill; d £80-85; P 🐕 �🛜) Artistry emanates from these history-rich rooms – bright scatter rugs sit on flagstone floors; lemon and oatmeal walls undulate between wonderfully wonky beams. Gourmet breakfasts include freshly squeezed orange juice, fresh fruit compote and homemade granola.

Stoneleigh Barn   B&B ££
(☎ 01935-817258; www.stoneleighbarn.co.uk; North Wootton; s £80, d £90-100, f from £120; P 🛜) Warm, weathered stone and extensive gardens ensure this 18th-century barn delights on the outside. Inside, exposed trusses frame spacious rooms named after their attractive colour schemes – choose from Lilac, Red or Blue.

Stoneleigh is some 2 miles southeast of Sherborne.

George   PUB FOOD ££
(www.thegeorgesherborne.co.uk; 4 Higher Cheap St; mains £9-13; ⊙noon-2.30pm & 6-9pm; 🛜) It's five centuries since Sherborne's oldest, cosiest inn pulled its first pint; today it signals its age with wooden settles polished smooth by countless behinds. The food is enduring pub grub fare: robust steaks, ham and egg, homemade puddings and a 'roast of the day'.

★**Green**   MODERN BRITISH £££
(☎ 01935-813821; www.greenrestaurant.co.uk; 3 The Green; mains £16-25; ⊙noon-2.30pm & 6.30-9.30pm Tue-Sat) In this affable, elegant eatery, the furniture is more chic than shabby and the food is pure West Country élan. Dorset goodies might include Dorset crab soup

with saffron aioli, or roast lamb made fragrant with wild garlic. For a great-value feed, plump for the cracking *menu du jour* (three courses £22).

ℹ Information

Tourist Office (☏ 01935-815341; www. visit-dorset.com; Digby Rd; ⊘ 9.30am-5pm Mon-Sat mid-Mar–Aug, to 4pm Sep-Nov, to 3pm Dec–mid-Mar)

ℹ Getting There & Away

BUS

Dorchester, via Cerne Abbas (Bus X11, £4.70, 1¼ hours, four to seven daily Monday to Saturday)

Yeovil (Bus 58, £2.50, 15 minutes, hourly Monday to Saturday)

TRAIN

Exeter (£18, 1¼ hours, hourly)
London Waterloo (£40, 2½ hours, hourly)
Salisbury (£14, 45 minutes, hourly)

Shaftesbury

Crowning a ridge of hogbacked hills and overlooking pastoral meadows, the agreeable market town of Shaftesbury circles around its medieval abbey ruins. A charismatic castle and a postcard-pretty, ancient street add to the town's appeal.

◉ Sights

Shaftesbury Abbey RUINS
(☏ 01747-852910; www.shaftesburyabbey.org.uk; Park Walk; adult/child £3/2.50; ⊘ 10am-5pm Apr-Oct) These hilltop ruins mark the site of what was England's largest and richest nunnery. It was founded in 888 by King Alfred the Great, and his daughter, Aethelgifu, was its first abbess. St Edward is thought to have been buried here, and King Knut died at the abbey in 1035. Most of the buildings were dismantled by Henry VIII, but you can wander the foundations and search out statuary and illuminated manuscripts in the museum.

Gold Hill STREET
The often-photographed, painfully steep, quaint cobbled slope, lined by chocolate-box cottages, that starred in a famous TV advert for Hovis bread.

Old Wardour Castle CASTLE
(EH; ☏ 01747-870487; www.english-heritage.org. uk; near Anstey; adult/child £5.40/3.20; ⊘ 10am-6pm Apr-Sep, 10am-4pm Oct, 10am-4pm Sat & Sun Nov-Mar; ℙ) Six-sided Old Wardour Castle was built around 1393 and suffered severe damage during the English Civil War, leaving these imposing remains. The views from the upper levels are fabulous while its grassy lawns make a fine spot for a picnic. It's 4 miles east of Shaftesbury.

🛏 Sleeping & Eating

Number 5 B&B ££
(☏ 01747-228490; www.fivebimport.co.uk; 5 Bimport; d £90; ℙ🐾) The restoration of this Georgian town house has clearly been a labour of love: elegant fabrics and subtle colours meet bathrooms with tiled floors and slipper baths. The breakfast is rich in food from the local farmers market – walk off a bit of it on the two-minute stroll into town.

Fleur de Lys HOTEL £££
(☏ 01747-853717; www.lafleurdelys.co.uk; Bleke St; s £95-100, d £115-160 tr £170-180; ℙ@🐾) In this bijou, delightfully romantic hotel soft lighting shines on satin throws and plump cushions, while minifridges, homemade biscuits and freshly ground coffee keep pamper levels high.

The **restaurant** (2/3courses £30/38; ⊘ 7-10pm Mon-Sat) is acclaimed.

Mitre PUB FOOD ££
(www.youngs.co.uk; 23 High St; mains £10-14; ⊘ 11am-3pm & 6-9pm Mon-Thu, noon-9pm Fri-Sun) It's the decked terrace that'll draw you into this old inn – its cracking views out over Blackmore Vale make for a memorable spot to tuck into salads and burgers or a duck egg with ham and chips.

ℹ Information

Tourist Office (☏ 01747-853514; www.shaftes burydorset.com; 8 Bell St; ⊘ 10am-4pm Mon-Sat)

ℹ Getting There & Away

Useful routes include bus 29 to Salisbury (£5, 1 hour, five daily Monday to Saturday).

WILTSHIRE

Wiltshire is rich in the reminders of ritual and packed with not-to-be-missed sights. Its verdant landscape is littered with more mysterious stone circles, processional avenues and ancient barrows than anywhere

BATH & SOUTHWEST ENGLAND SHAFTESBURY

else in Britain. It's a place that teases and tantalises the imagination – here you'll experience the prehistoric majesty of Stonehenge and the atmospheric stone ring at Avebury. Add the serene 800-year-old cathedral at Salisbury, the supremely stately homes at Stourhead and Longleat and the impossibly pretty village of Lacock, and you have a county crammed full of English charm waiting to be explored.

🛈 Getting There & Around

BUS

Wiltshire's bus coverage can be patchy, especially in the northwest.

First (www.firstgroup.com) Serves west Wiltshire.

Salisbury Reds (www.salisburyreds.co.uk) Covers Salisbury and many rural areas; offers one-day Rover Tickets (adult/child £8.50/5.50) and seven-day passes (Salisbury area £14.50, network-wide £25).

Stagecoach (www.stagecoachbus.com) Provides services around Swindon and Salisbury.

TRAIN

Rail lines run from London Waterloo to Salisbury (£23, 1½ hours, at least hourly), and beyond to Exeter and Plymouth. Another line runs north to Bath (£11, one hour, hourly) and Bristol (£11, 1¼ hours, hourly).

Salisbury
POP 40,300

Centred on a majestic cathedral that's topped by the tallest spire in England, Salisbury makes an appealing Wiltshire base. It's been an important provincial city for more than a thousand years, and its streets form an architectural timeline ranging from medieval walls and half-timbered Tudor town houses to Georgian mansions and Victorian villas.

👁 Sights

⭐ **Salisbury Cathedral**   CATHEDRAL
(☑ 01722-555120; www.salisburycathedral.org.uk; The Close; requested donation adult/child £7.50/3; ⊘ 9am-5pm Mon-Sat, noon-4pm Sun) England is endowed with countless stunning churches, but few can hold a candle to the grandeur and sheer spectacle of 13th-century Salisbury Cathedral. This early English Gothic-style structure has an elaborate exterior decorated with pointed arches and flying buttresses, and a sombre, austere interior

designed to keep its congregation suitably pious. Its statuary and tombs are outstanding; don't miss the daily **tower tours** (adult/child £13.50/8.50; ⊘ two to five daily, May-Sep) and the cathedral's original, 13th-century copy of the **Magna Carta** (⊘ 9.30am-5pm Mon-Sat, noon-4pm Sun Apr-Oct, 9.30am-4.30pm Mon-Sat, noon-3.45pm Sun Nov-Mar).

The cathedral was built between 1220 and 1258. Beyond its highly decorative **West Front**, a small passageway leads into the 70m-long **nave**, lined with handsome pillars of Purbeck stone. In the north aisle look out for a fascinating **medieval clock** dating from 1386, probably the oldest working timepiece in the world. At the eastern end of the ambulatory the glorious **Prisoners of Conscience** stained-glass window (1980) hovers above the ornate **tomb** of Edward Seymour (1539–1621) and Lady Catherine Grey. Other monuments and tombs line the sides of the nave, including that of William Longespée, son of Henry II and half-brother of King John. When the tomb was excavated a well-preserved rat was found inside Longespée's skull.

Salisbury's 123m crowning glory, its **spire**, was added in the mid-14th century, and is the tallest in Britain. It represented an enormous technical challenge for its medieval builders; it weighs around 6500 tonnes and required an elaborate system of cross-bracing, scissor arches and supporting buttresses to keep it upright. Look closely and you'll see the additional weight has buckled the four central piers of the nave.

Sir Christopher Wren surveyed the cathedral in 1668 and calculated that the spire was leaning by 75cm. A brass plate in the floor of the nave is used to measure any shift, but no further lean was recorded in 1951 or 1970. Despite this, reinforcement of the notoriously 'wonky spire' continues to this day.

The cathedral really comes into its own during **evensong**, which takes place at 5.30pm Monday to Saturday and 4.30pm on Sunday, during term time only.

⭐ **Salisbury Museum**   MUSEUM
(☑ 01722-332151; www.salisburymuseum.org.uk; 65 The Close; adult/child £8/4; ⊘ 10am-5pm Mon-Sat year-round, plus noon-5pm Sun Jun-Sep) The hugely important archaeological finds here include the Stonehenge Archer, the bones of a man found in the ditch near the stone circle – one of the arrows found alongside probably killed him. With gold coins dating

Salisbury

Salisbury

◎ Top Sights
1 Magna Carta	B4
2 Salisbury Cathedral	B3
3 Salisbury Museum	A4

⊕ Activities, Courses & Tours
Salisbury Cathedral Tower Tours	(see 2)
4 Salisbury Guides	C2

⊟ Sleeping
5 Cathedral View	C3
6 Chapter House	C3
7 Spire House	C3
8 St Ann's House	D3

⊗ Eating
9 Anokaa	A1
10 Charter 1227	C2
11 Danny's Craft Bar	C1

⊜ Drinking & Nightlife
12 Haunch of Venison	B2

⊛ Entertainment
13 Salisbury Playhouse	A1

from 100 BC and a Bronze Age gold necklace, it's a powerful introduction to Wiltshire's prehistory.

Old Sarum ARCHAEOLOGICAL SITE
(EH; ☎01722-335398; www.english-heritage.org.uk; Castle Rd; adult/child £5.20/3.10; ☺10am-6pm Mar-Sep, to 5pm Oct, to 4pm Nov-Mar; ℗) The huge ramparts of Old Sarum sit on a grass-covered hill 2 miles north of Salisbury. You can wander the grassy ramparts, see the original cathedral's stone foundations, and look across the Wiltshire countryside to the

spire of the present Salisbury Cathedral. Medieval tournaments, jousts, open-air plays and mock battles are held on selected days. Bus X5 runs hourly from Salisbury to Old Sarum (£2.30), Monday to Saturday. It's also a stop on the Stonehenge Tour bus.

★ **Wilton House**   HISTORIC BUILDING
(📞 01722-746728; www.wiltonhouse.com; Wilton; house & grounds adult/child £15.50/13.25; ⏱ 11.30am-5pm Sun-Thu May-Sep; 🅿) Stately Wilton House provides an insight into the rarefied world of the British aristocracy. One of England's finest stately homes, it's been the house of the earls of Pembroke since 1542, and has been expanded, improved and embellished by successive generations. Highlights are the Single and Double Cube Rooms, designed by the pioneering 17th-century architect Inigo Jones.

Wilton House is 2.5 miles west of Salisbury; bus R3 runs from Salisbury (£2.70, 10 minutes, one to three hourly Monday to Saturday).

☞ Tours

Salisbury Guides   WALKING
(📞 07873-212941; www.salisburycityguides.co.uk; adult/child £6/3; ⏱ 11am daily Apr-Oct, 11am Sat & Sun Nov-Mar) These 90-minute trips leave from the tourist office.

🛏 Sleeping

St Ann's House   B&B ££
(📞 01722-335657; www.stannshouse.co.uk; 32 St Ann St; s £64, d £89-110; 🛜) Utter elegance reigns at 18th century St Ann's where cast iron fireplaces, mini-chandeliers and sash windows cosy up to warm colours and well-chosen antiques. Breakfast goodies include locally baked bread and homemade orange and star anise marmalade.

Cathedral View   B&B ££
(📞 01722-502254; www.cathedral-viewbandb.co.uk; 83 Exeter St; s £85-95, d £99-140; 🅿🛜) Admirable attention to detail defines this Georgian town house, where miniature flower displays and home-baked biscuits sit in quietly elegant rooms. Breakfasts include prime Wiltshire sausages and the B&B's own bread and jam, while homemade lemon drizzle cake will be waiting for your afternoon tea.

Spire House   B&B ££
(📞 01722-339213; www.salisbury-bedandbreakfast.com; 84 Exeter St; s/d/tr £65/80/95; 🅿🛜) In

this B&B of beautifully kept rooms, the easy-going vibe extends to breakfast: croissants and freshly squeezed orange juice are delivered to your room. Bedroom styles range from a quirky tripple (tea cup lampshades) via vivid blue contemporary, to heritage chic (four-poster bed, mock oil paints and a mini leather armchair).

The price includes a free parking permit.

★ **Chapter House**   INN £££
(📞 01722-341277; www.thechapterhouseuk.com; 9 St Johns St; s £115-145 d £135-155; 🛜) In this 800-year-old boutique beauty, wood panels and wildly wonky stairs sit beside duck-your-head beams. The cheaper bedrooms are swish but the posher ones are stunning, starring slipper baths and the odd heraldic crest. The pick is room 6, where King Charles is reputed to have stayed. Lucky him.

🍴 Eating & Drinking

Anokaa   INDIAN ££
(📞 01722-414142; www.anokaa.com; 60 Fisherton St; mains £14-19; ⏱ noon-2pm & 5.30-11pm; 🍴) The pink-neon sign signals what's in store here: a modern, multilayered take on high-class Indian cuisine. The spice and flavour combos make the ingredients sing, the meat-free menu makes vegetarians gleeful, and the lunchtime buffet (£9) makes everyone smile.

Danny's Craft Bar   AMERICAN ££
(📞 01722-504416; www.dannyscraftbar.co.uk; 2 Salt Lane; burgers £7-13; ⏱ 5-9pm Mon-Thu, noon-9pm Fri, 9am-9pm Sat, 9am-5pm Sun; 🛜🍴) It's tempting to eat at this hip hang-out throughout the day: breakfast on chorizo and avocado tortilla, syrup-drenched pancakes or cheesy beans. Come evening, craft beer and cocktails usher in towering burgers and hand-cut fries. It's Tex-Mex, fun and cool.

Veggie options include a thick-sliced mushroom and halloumi sandwich, and there's occasional comedy and live music.

Charter 1227   BRITISH £££
(📞 01722-333118; www.charter1227.co.uk; 6 Ox Row, Market Pl; mains £15-30; ⏱ noon-2.30pm & 6-9.30pm Tue-Sat) Ingredients that speak of classic English dishes have a firm foothold here – feast on duck confit, beef fillet or roast lamb; the cooking and presentation are assured. Canny locals eat at lunchtime or between 6pm and 7pm Tuesday to Thursday, when mains are capped at £10 to £15.

Haunch of Venison
PUB

(www.haunchpub.co.uk; 1 Minster St; ⊙11am-11pm Mon-Sat, to 6pm Sun) Featuring wood-panelled snugs, spiral staircases and crooked ceilings, this 14th-century drinking den is packed with atmosphere – and ghosts. One is a cheating whist player whose hand was severed in a game – look out for his mummified bones on display inside.

☆ Entertainment

Salisbury Playhouse
THEATRE

(Wiltshire Creative; ☑01722-320333; www.salis buryplayhouse.com; Malthouse Lane) An acclaimed producing theatre that also hosts top touring shows and musicals.

It's merged with the Salisbury Arts Centre and International Arts Festival to form Wiltshire Creative.

ℹ Information

Tourist Office (☑01722-342860; www. visitsalisbury.co.uk; Fish Row; ⊙9am-5pm Mon-Fri, 10am-4pm Sat, 10am-2pm Sun; 🛜)

ℹ Getting There & Away

BUS

National Express (www.nationalexpress.com) services stop at Millstream Approach, near the train station. Direct services include:

Bath (£11, 1¼ hours, one daily)

Bristol (£6, 2¼ hours, one daily)

London Victoria via Heathrow (£10, three hours, three daily Monday to Saturday)

Local services leave from stops around the town; they include the following:

Devizes (bus 2; £6, one hour, hourly Monday to Saturday)

Shaftesbury (bus 29; £5, one hour, five daily Monday to Saturday)

Stonehenge (☑01202-338420; www. thestonehengetour.info; adult/child/family £30/20/90) Tour buses leave Salisbury train station regularly.

TRAIN

Salisbury's train station is half a mile northwest of the cathedral. Half-hourly connections include the following:

Bath (£10, one hour)

Bradford-on-Avon (£14, 40 minutes)

Bristol (£16, 1¼ hours)

London Waterloo (£42, 1½ hours)

Southampton (£10, 40 minutes)

Hourly connections:

Exeter (£20, two hours)

Portsmouth (£20, 1¼ hours)

Stonehenge

Welcome to Britain's most iconic archaeological site. This compelling ring of monolithic stones has been attracting a steady stream of pilgrims, poets and philosophers for the last 5000 years and is still a mystical, ethereal place – a haunting echo from Britain's forgotten past, and a reminder of those who once walked the ceremonial avenues across Salisbury Plain.

◉ Sights

★ Stonehenge
ARCHAEOLOGICAL SITE

(EH; ☑0370 333 1181; www.english-heritage.org. uk; near Amesbury; adult/child same-day tickets £19.50/11.70, advance booking £17.50/10.50; ⊙9am-8pm Jun-Aug, 9.30am-7pm Apr, May & Sep, 9.30am-5pm Oct-Mar; 🅿) An ultramodern makeover at ancient Stonehenge has brought an impressive visitor centre and the closure of an intrusive road (now restored to grassland). The result is a strong sense of historical context, with dignity and mystery returned to an archaeological gem.

A pathway frames the ring of massive stones. Although you can't walk in the circle, unless on a recommended Stone Circle Access Visit (p291), you can get fairly close. Admission is through timed tickets – secure a place well in advance.

Stonehenge is one of Britain's great archaeological mysteries: despite countless theories about the site's purpose, from a sacrificial centre to a celestial timepiece, no one knows for sure what drove prehistoric Britons to expend so much time and effort on its construction, although recent archaeological findings show the surrounding area was sacred for hundreds of years before work began.

The first phase of building started around 3000 BC, when the outer circular bank and ditch were erected. A thousand years later, an inner circle of granite stones, known

---

ℹ TICKETS FOR STONEHENGE

Stonehenge operates by timed tickets, meaning if you want to guarantee your entry you have to book in advance – even English Heritage and National Trust members entitled to free admission. If you're planning a peak-season visit, it's best to secure your ticket well in advance.

as bluestones, was added. It's thought that these mammoth 4-tonne blocks were hauled from the Preseli Mountains in South Wales, some 250 miles away – an extraordinary feat for Stone Age people equipped with only the simplest of tools. Although no one is entirely sure how the builders transported the stones so far, it's thought they probably used a system of ropes, sledges and rollers fashioned from tree trunks – Salisbury Plain was still covered by forest during Stonehenge's construction.

Around 1500 BC, Stonehenge's main stones were dragged to the site, erected in a circle and crowned by massive lintels to make the trilithons (two vertical stones topped by a horizontal one). The sarsen (sandstone) stones were cut from an extremely hard rock found on the Marlborough Downs, 20 miles from the site. It's estimated that dragging one of these 50-tonne stones across the countryside would require about 600 people.

Also around this time, the bluestones from 500 years earlier were rearranged as an inner **bluestone horseshoe** with an **altar stone** at the centre. Outside this the **trilithon horseshoe** of five massive sets of stones was erected. Three of these are intact; the other two have just a single upright. Then came the major **sarsen circle** of 30 massive vertical stones, of which 17 uprights and six lintels remain.

Much further out, another circle was delineated by the 58 Aubrey Holes, named after John Aubrey, who discovered them in the 1600s. Just inside this circle are the **South** and **North Barrows**, each originally topped by a stone. Like many stone circles in Britain (including Avebury, 22 miles away), the inner horseshoes are aligned to coincide with sunrise at the midsummer solstice, which some claim supports the theory that the site was some kind of astronomical calendar.

Prehistoric pilgrims would have entered the site via the **Avenue**, whose entrance to

Stonehenge

STONEHENGE'S RITUAL LANDSCAPE

Stonehenge actually forms part of a huge complex of ancient monuments.

North of Stonehenge and running roughly east–west is the **Cursus**, an elongated embanked oval; the smaller **Lesser Cursus** is nearby. Theories abound as to what these sites were used for, ranging from ancient sporting arenas to processional avenues for the dead. Two clusters of burial mounds, the **Old** and **New Kings Barrows**, sit beside the ceremonial pathway **the Avenue**, which originally linked Stonehenge with the River Avon, 2 miles away.

The National Trust (www.nationaltrust.org.uk) website has a downloadable 3.5-mile circular walk (search for A Kings View) that traces tracks across the chalk downland from Stonehenge, past the Cursus and Kings Barrows and along a section of the Avenue itself.

The Stonehenge visitor centre also has leaflets detailing walking routes.

the circle is marked by the **Slaughter Stone** and the **Heel Stone**, located slightly further out on one side.

Long-term plans to move the main A303 road, which runs close to the site, into a tunnel are still being debated. The proposed tunnel aims to reduce traffic around Stonehenge, although some commentators fear it could damage other, as yet undiscovered, monuments in the area.

The last admission to Stonehenge is two hours before closure. Visiting the site is free for English Heritage and National Trust members, but they still have to secure a timed ticket.

★ **Visitor Centre** MUSEUM
(EH; ☏ 0370 333 1181; www.english-heritage. org.uk; incl access to Stonehenge, adult/child same-day tickets £19.50/11.70, advance booking £17.50/10.50; ⊙ 9am-8pm Jun-Aug, 9.30am-7pm Apr, May & Sep, 9.30am-5pm Oct-Mar) The highlight here is a 360-degree projection of Stonehenge through the ages and seasons – complete with midsummer sunrise and swirling star-scape. Engaging audiovisual displays detail the transportation of the stones and the building stages, while 300 finds include flint chippings, bone pins and arrowheads. There's also a strikingly lifelike model of the face of a Neolithic man whose body was found nearby. Outside you can step into recreations of Stone Age houses and watch rope-making and flint-knapping demonstrations.

☞ Tours

★ **Stone Circle Access Visits** WALKING
(☏ 0370 333 0605; www.english-heritage.org.uk; adult/child £38.50/23.10) Visitors normally have to stay outside the stone circle itself, but on these hour-long, self-guided walks, you get to wander around the heart of the archaeological site, getting up-close views of the iconic bluestones and trilithons. Tours take place in the evening or early morning, when the quieter atmosphere and slanting sunlight add to the effect. Each visit only takes 30 people; book at least three months in advance.

Salisbury Guided Tours HISTORY
(☏ 07775 674816; www.salisburyguidedtours.com; per person from £64) Runs a wide range of expert-led trips to Stonehenge, the wider ritual landscape and Salisbury.

❶ Getting There & Away

No regular buses go to the site.

The Stonehenge Tour (p289) leaves Salisbury's railway station half-hourly from June to August, and hourly between September and May. The ticket includes admission to Stonehenge and the Iron Age hill fort at Old Sarum (p287); it stops there on the return leg.

Longleat

★ **Longleat** ZOO
(☏ 01985-844400; www.longleat.co.uk; near Warminster; all-inclusive ticket adult/child £35/26, house & grounds £19/14; ⊙ 10am-5pm Feb–mid-Oct, to 7pm late Jul & Aug; 🅿) Half ancestral mansion, half wildlife park, Longleat was transformed into Britain's first safari park in 1966, turning Capability Brown's landscaped grounds into an amazing drive-through zoo populated by a menagerie of animals more at home in the African wilderness than the fields of Wiltshire. There's a throng of attractions, too: the historic house, animatronic dinosaur exhibits, narrow-gauge railway, mazes, pets' corner, butterfly garden and bat cave.

DON'T MISS

STOURHEAD

Overflowing with vistas, temples and follies, **Stourhead** (NT; ☑ 01747-841152; www.nationaltrust.org.uk; Mere; adult/child £16.60/8.30; ⊘ 11am-4.30pm early Mar–early Nov, to 3.30pm early Nov–late-Dec; P) is landscape gardening at its finest. The Palladian house has some fine Chippendale furniture and paintings by Claude and Gaspard Poussin, but it's a sideshow to the magnificent 18th-century gardens (open 9am to 5pm), which spread out across the valley.

A picturesque 2-mile garden circuit takes you past the most ornate follies, around the lake and to the Temple of Apollo; a 3.5-mile side trip can be made from near the Pantheon to King Alfred's Tower, a 50m-high folly with wonderful views.

Stourhead is off the B3092, 8 miles south of Frome.

Longleat was the first English stately home to open its doors to the public. That decision was prompted by finance: heavy taxes and mounting post-WWII bills meant the house had to earn its keep.

The house itself contains fine tapestries, furniture and decorated ceilings, as well as seven libraries containing around 40,000 tomes. The highlight, though, is an extraordinary series of paintings and psychedelic murals by the present-day marquess, who was an art student in the '60s and upholds the long-standing tradition of eccentricity among the English aristocracy – check out his website (www.lordbath.co.uk).

Longleat is open until 7pm on many summer weekends. It's just off the A362, 3 miles from Frome. Save around 10% by booking tickets online.

Lacock

POP 1159

With its geranium-covered cottages and higgledy-piggledy rooftops, pockets of the medieval village of Lacock seem to have been preserved in mid-19th-century aspic. The village has been in the hands of the National Trust since 1944, and in many places is remarkably free of modern development – there are no telephone poles or electric street lights and the main car park on the outskirts keeps it relatively traffic-free. Unsurprisingly, it's a popular location for costume dramas and feature films – the village and its abbey pop up in the Harry Potter films, *Downton Abbey, The Other Boleyn Girl* and BBC adaptations of *Wolf Hall, Moll Flanders* and *Pride and Prejudice.*

⊙ Sights

Lacock Abbey   ABBEY
(NT; ☑ 01249-730459; www.nationaltrust.org.uk; Hither Way; adult/child £13.40/6.70; ⊘ 10.30am-5.30pm Mar-Oct, 11am-4pm Nov-Feb) Lacock Abbey is a window into a medieval world. Founded as an Augustinian nunnery in the 13th century, its deeply atmospheric rooms and stunning Gothic entrance hall are lined with bizarre terracotta figures; spot the scapegoat with a lump of sugar on its nose. Some of the original structure is evident in the cloisters and there are traces of medieval wall paintings, too.

Fox Talbot Museum   MUSEUM
(NT; ☑ 01249-730459; www.nationaltrust.org.uk; Hither Way; adult/child £13.40/6.70; ⊘ 10.30am-5.30pm Mar-Oct, 11am-4pm Nov-Feb) William Henry Fox Talbot (1800–77) pioneered the photographic negative. A prolific inventor, he began developing the system in 1834 while working at Lacock Abbey. The museum, located within the abbey, details his groundbreaking work and displays a superb collection of his images.

Entry is included with admission to the abbey.

⌷ Sleeping & Eating

★ **Sign of the Angel**   INN ££
(☑ 01249-730230; www.signoftheangel.co.uk; 6 Church St; s £110, d £110-140; P 🛜) Every inch of this gorgeous, 15th-century restaurant-with-rooms is rich in heritage pizazz. Burnished beams, slanting floors and open fires meet duck-down duvets, upcycled furniture and neutral tones, delivering a fresh provincial rustic feel. Treats include luxury toiletries, chef-baked cookies and a free glass of prosecco (if you book one of the swisher rooms).

Pear Tree   INN ££
(☑ 01225-704966; www.peartreewhitley.co.uk; Top Lane, Whitley; d £125-150, q £150; P 🛜) It takes a lot of skill to make rooms look so beautifully casual and yet so smart – the bedrooms here are a mash-up of mullioned windows, worn wooden chairs, waterfall showers and framed cartoons. Rooms in the ancient inn

have more heritage features, ones in the converted barn have a sleeker feel. It's 4 miles southwest of Lacock.

The restaurant (mains £14 to £18) is famous for its terrace, beamed sunroom and inventive dishes crammed with kitchen garden produce. Food is served from noon to 2.30pm and 6pm to 9pm.

Red Lion INN ££
(☑01249-730456; www.redlionlacock.co.uk; 1 High St; d£105-120; P⑤) In historic Lacock, where better to sleep than a Georgian coaching inn that oozes ambience. Step on flagstone floors past open fires, up a grand staircase to sweet rooms where padded cushions line stone window frames with picture-postcard views. The food's notable too (mains from £14, served noon to 8pm).

King John's Hunting Lodge CAFE £
(☑01249-730313; 21 Church St; snacks from £5; ◷11am-5pm Wed-Sun Feb–mid-Dec; P) Afternoon tea is a must at Lacock's oldest building, where a cosy, beam-lined room and a peaceful garden set the scene for dainty china, light lunches and tasty cakes.

Avebury & Around

POP 530

While the tour buses head straight for Stonehenge, prehistoric purists make for the massive stone circle at Avebury. Though it lacks the dramatic trilithons of its sister site across Salisbury Plain, Avebury is just as rewarding to visit. It's bigger and older, and a large section of the village is actually inside the stones – footpaths wind around them, allowing you to really soak up the extraordinary atmosphere. Avebury also boasts an encircling landscape that's rich in prehistoric sites and a manor house where restored rooms span five completely different eras.

◉ Sights

★ **Avebury Stone Circle** ARCHAEOLOGICAL SITE
(NT; ☑01672-539250; www.nationaltrust.org.uk; ◷24hr; P) FREE With a diameter of 348m, Avebury is the largest stone circle in the world. It's also one of the oldest, dating from 2500 to 2200 BC. Today, more than 30 stones are in place; pillars show where missing stones would have been. Wandering between them emphasises the site's sheer scale, evidenced also by the massive bank and ditch that line the circle; the quieter northwest sector is particularly atmospheric. National Trust–run guided walks (£3) are held on most days.

Avebury henge originally consisted of an outer circle of 98 standing stones of up to 6m in length, many weighing 20 tonnes. The stones were surrounded by another circle delineated by a 5m-high earth bank and a ditch up to 9m deep. Inside were smaller stone circles to the north (27 stones) and south (29 stones).

In the Middle Ages, when Britain's pagan past was an embarrassment to the Church, many of the stones were buried, removed or broken up. In 1934 wealthy businessman and archaeologist Alexander Keiller supervised the re-erection of the stones; he later bought the site for posterity using funds from his family's marmalade fortune.

Modern roads into Avebury neatly dissect the circle into four sectors. Starting at High St near the **Henge Shop** (☑01672-539229; www.hengeshop.com; High St; ◷9.30am-5pm) and walking round the circle in an anticlockwise direction, you'll encounter 11 standing stones in the southwest sector. They include the **Barber Surgeon Stone**, named after the skeleton of a man found under it – the equipment buried with him suggests he was a barber-cum-surgeon.

The southeast sector starts with huge **portal stones** marking the entry to the circle from **West Kennet Ave**. The **southern inner circle** stood in this sector and within this ring was the **obelisk** and a group of stones known as the **Z Feature**. Just outside this smaller circle, only the base of the **Ring Stone** survives.

In the **northern inner circle** in the northeast sector, three sarsens remain of what would have been a rectangular **cove**. The northwest sector has the most complete collection of standing stones, including the massive 65-tonne **Swindon Stone**, one of the few never to have been toppled.

★ **Avebury Manor** HISTORIC BUILDING
(NT; ☑01672-539250; www.nationaltrust.org.uk; adult/child £10.50/5.25; ◷11am-5pm Apr-Oct, to 4pm mid-Feb–Mar, 11am-4pm Thu-Sun Nov & Dec) The mother of all makeovers at this 16th-century manor house used original techniques and materials to recreate interiors spanning five periods. Being hands-on is encouraged here, so now you can sit on beds, play billiards and listen to the gramophone in rooms that range from Tudor, through Georgian to the 1930s. Visits are by timed ticket only; arrive early to bag a slot.

BATH & SOUTHWEST ENGLAND AVEBURY & AROUND

Avebury

Existing Stone
○ **Missing Stone**

Map labels: Swindon Rd · NORTHEAST SECTOR · Cove Stones · Northern Inner Circle · NORTHWEST SECTOR · Avebury Stone Circle · Dovecote · St James Church · Green St · SOUTHEAST SECTOR · High St · SOUTHWEST SECTOR · Southern Inner Circle · Obelisk · Z Feature · Ring Stone · Portal Stones · Portal Stones · West Kennet Avenue · Footpath to Silbury Hill (1mi); West Kennet Long Barrow (1.5mi)

Avebury

Silbury Hill   ARCHAEOLOGICAL SITE
(EH; www.english-heritage.org.uk; near Avebury; [P]) **FREE** Rising abruptly from the fields just south of Avebury, 40m-high Silbury Hill is the largest artificial earthwork in Europe, comparable in height and volume to the Egyptian pyramids. It was built in stages from around 2500 BC, but the precise reason for its construction remains unclear. Direct access to the hill isn't allowed, but you can view it from nearby footpaths and a layby on the A4.

West Kennet
Long Barrow   ARCHAEOLOGICAL SITE
(EH; ☎ 0370 333 1181; www.english-heritage.org.uk; ☉ dawn-dusk) **FREE** England's finest burial mound dates from around 3500 BC. Its entrance is guarded by huge sarsens and its roof is made out of gigantic overlapping capstones. About 50 skeletons were found when it was excavated; finds are on display at the Wiltshire Heritage Museum in Devizes. The barrow is a half-mile walk across fields from the parking layby.

A footpath also leads from Avebury Stone Circle to West Kennet (2 miles), passing the vast earthwork of Silbury Hill en route.

🛏 Sleeping & Eating

★ Manor Farm
B&B ££

(☏ 01672-539294; www.manorfarmavebury.com; High St; s/d £90/100; 🅿🛜) A rare chance to sleep in style inside a stone circle – this red-brick farmhouse snuggles just inside Ave-bury henge. The elegant, comfy rooms blend old woods with bright furnishings, while the windows provide spine-tingling views of those 4000-year-old standing stones.

Avebury Lodge
B&B £££

(☏ 01672-539023; www.aveburylodge.co.uk; High St; s/d/tr £155/195/250; 🅿🛜) It's as if gentle-manly archaeologists are still in situ: anti-quarian prints of stone circles smother the walls, pelmets and chandeliers are dotted around. And whenever you glance from a window, a bit of Avebury henge appears. It's lovely, but a bit pricey – it's the location that pushes the room rates up here.

Red Lion
PUB

(www.oldenglishinns.co.uk; High St; ⊙11am-11pm) Having a pint here means downing a drink at the only pub in the world inside a stone circle. The best table is the Well Seat where the glass tabletop covers a 26m-deep, 17th-century well – believed to be the last resting place of at least one unfortunate vil-lager.

❶ Getting There & Away

Bus 49 runs hourly to Swindon (£3, 30 minutes) and Devizes (£3, 15 minutes). There are six ser-vices on Sunday.

EXMOOR NATIONAL PARK

Exmoor is more than a little addictive, and chances are you won't want to leave its broad, russet views. In the middle sits the higher moor, an empty, expansive, oth-er-worldly landscape of tawny grasses and huge skies. Here, picturesque Exford makes an ideal village base. In the north, sheer, rock-strewn river valleys cut into the plateau and coal-black cliffs lurch towards the sea.

Amid these towering headlands, char-ismatic Porlock and the twin villages of Lynton and Lynmouth are atmospheric places to stay. Relaxed Dulverton delivers a country-town vibe, while appealing Dunster has cobbled streets and a russet-red castle. Everywhere on Exmoor life is attuned to the rhythms and colours of the seasons – new-born livestock in spring, purple heather in late summer, gold-bronze leaves in autumn, and crisp days and log fires in winter. All this ensures Exmoor delivers insights into an elemental and traditional world.

🏃 Activities

★ Exmoor Adventures
OUTDOORS

(☏ 07976 208279; www.exmooradventures.co.uk) Runs sessions in kayaking and canoeing (£35/70 per half/full day), mountain biking (from £40 per half day), coasteering (£35) and rock climbing (£65); caters to skill lev-els ranging from beginner to advanced. Also rents mountain bikes (£25 per day).

Cycling

Despite (or perhaps because of) the formi-dable hills, cycling is hugely popular on Ex-moor. Several sections of the National Cycle Network (NCN; www.sustrans.org.uk) cross the park, including the West Country Way (NCN Route 3) from Bristol to Padstow, and Devon Coast to Coast (NCN Route 27), be-tween Ilfracombe and Plymouth, via Dart-moor and Exmoor.

Exmoor is also one of the county's most exhilarating off-road cycling destinations, with a wealth of bridleways and permitted tracks. The Exmoor National Park Authority has produced a colour-coded off-road cycle map (£10); buy it at tourist offices.

Exmoor Adventures runs a five-hour mountain-biking skills course (£60) and also rents mountain bikes (£25 per day).

Pompys
CYCLING

(☏ 01643-704077; www.pompyscycles.co.uk; Mart Rd, Minehead; per day £18; ⊙9am-5pm Mon-Sat) Bike sales and hire.

Pony Trekking & Horse Riding

Exmoor is prime riding country, with stables offering pony and horse treks from around £30 to £46 for a two-hour ride.

Brendon Manor
HORSE RIDING

(☏ 01598-741246; www.brendonmanor.com) Runs a full range of horse-riding trips, from one to three hours, that head onto the open moor and down into the valleys. Prices start at £26. Based near Lynton.

Burrowhayes Farm
HORSE RIDING

(☏ 01643-862463; www.burrowhayes.co.uk; per hr £25; ⊙Apr–mid-Oct) Based near Porlock, Bur-rowhayes runs a wide range of treks that go into the Horner Valley and onto the moor.

Plus special half-hour pony rides for children (£14).

Outovercott Stables HORSE RIDING

(☑ 01598-753341; www.outovercott.co.uk; per hr £30) Outovercott's treks onto Exmoor's exposed moorland range from one-hour trips for novices to more-challenging excursions for intermediate and experienced riders, which take in views of the Valley of Rocks and the coastline.

Walking

The open moors and a profusion of marked bridleways make Exmoor an excellent area for hiking. The best-known routes are the **Somerset & North Devon Coast Path**, which is part of the **South West Coast Path** (www.southwestcoastpath.org.uk), and the Exmoor section of the **Two Moors Way**, which starts in Lynmouth and travels south to Dartmoor and beyond.

Another superb route is the **Coleridge Way** (www.coleridgeway.co.uk), which winds for 51 miles through Exmoor, the Brendon Hills and the Quantocks. Part of the 180-mile **Tarka Trail** cuts through the park: join it at Combe Martin, hike along the cliffs to Lynton and Lynmouth, then head across the moor towards Barnstaple.

Organised walks run by the national park authority (www.exmoor-national park. gov.uk) are held throughout the year and include deer safaris, nightjar birdwatching walks and dark-sky strolls.

ⓘ Information

Active Exmoor (www.visit-exmoor.co.uk/active-exmoor)

Exmoor National Park (www.exmoor-national park.gov.uk)

Lonely Planet (www.lonelyplanet.com) Destination information, hotel bookings, traveller forum and more.

Visit Exmoor (www.visit-exmoor.co.uk) The official visitor website.

There are three tourist offices run by the Exmoor National Park Authority, in **Dulverton** (☑ 01398-323841; www.visit-exmoor.co.uk; 7-9 Fore St; ⊙10am-5pm Apr-Oct, reduced hours Oct-Apr), **Dunster** (☑ 01643-821835; www.visit-exmoor. co.uk; Dunster Steep; ⊙10am-5pm Apr-Oct, reduced hours Oct-Apr) and Lynmouth (p301).

The Exmoor National Park Authority (ENPA; www.exmoor-nationalpark.gov.uk) regulates the park.

ⓘ Getting Around

Exmoor isn't that easy to get around without your own vehicle. But with some planning and patience it is possible to travel between many of the moor's main towns and villages by bus.

Dulverton

POP 1500

The southern gateway to Exmoor National Park, Dulverton sits at the base of the Barle Valley near the confluence of two key rivers: the Exe and Barle. A traditional country town, it's home to a collection of gun sellers, fishing-tackle stores and gift shops, and makes an attractive edge-of-moor base.

Exmoor's most famous landmark, is the **Tarr Steps**, an ancient stone clapper bridge shaded by gnarled old trees. Its huge slabs are propped up on stone columns embedded in the River Barle. Local folklore aside

Exmoor National Park

RED DEER SAFARIS

Exmoor supports one of England's largest wild red deer populations, best experienced in autumn when the annual 'rutting' season sees stags bellowing, charging at each other and clashing horns in an attempt to impress prospective mates.

The Exmoor National Park Authority (ENPA; www.exmoor-nationalpark.gov.uk) runs regular wildlife-themed guided walks (free), which include evening deer-spotting hikes. Or head out on an organised jeep safari to combine scenic sightseeing with a couple of hours of off-road wildlife-watching.

Barle Valley Safaris (📞07977 571494; www.exmoorwildlifesafaris.co.uk; adult/child £35/25; ⊙tours at 9.30am & 2pm) Runs half-day 4WD wildlife-watching safaris onto the moor. Trips leave from Dulverton, Dunster, Exford and Wheddon Cross.

Discovery Safaris (📞01643-863444; www.discoverysafaris.com; per person £25; ⊙tours at 10.30am & 2pm) These twice-daily jeep safaris set off from Porlock and head up onto open moorland searching for wildlife, especially Exmoor's famous red deer.

Johnny Kingdom Safaris (www.johnnykingdom.co.uk; per 4 people £100) Monthly, four-hour tours with a TV wildlife presenter and photographer. They leave from South Molton at around 8am and are popular – book well ahead.

(which declares it was used by the Devil for sunbathing), it first pops into the historical record in the 1600s, and had to be rebuilt after 21st-century floods. The steps are signed off the B3223 Dulverton–Simonsbath road, 5 miles northwest of Dulverton.

🛏 Sleeping & Eating

⭐**Streamcombe Farm**   B&B ££
(📞01398-323775; www.streamcombefarm.co.uk; Streamcombe Lane, near Dulverton; s £60-75, d £75-100; 🅿🛜) In this enchanting 18th-century farmhouse, stylish, rustic-chic bedrooms feature chimney breasts and reclaimed joists, and the only sounds are the sheep, deer and pheasants outside. Or snuggle into the bijou but beautiful two-person shepherd's hut (£85), complete with BBQ and log-burning stove.

Town Mills   B&B ££
(📞01398-323124; www.townmillsdulverton.co.uk; 1 High St; s/d/ste £95/105/140; 🅿🛜) The top choice in Dulverton town itself is a thoroughly contemporary riverside mill with creamy carpets, magnolia-coloured walls and bursts of floral art.

Tarr Farm   HOTEL £££
(📞01643-851507; www.tarrfarm.co.uk; Tarr Steps; s/d £80/160; 🅿🛜) This is the place to really lose yourself: a charming farmhouse nestled among the woods near Tarr Steps, 7 miles from Dulverton. The nine contemporary bedrooms are spacious and luxurious, with spoil-yourself extras such as organic bath

goodies and homemade biscuits. The farm is also renowned for its food.

All-comers are welcome: walkers and families arrive for cream teas (served from 11am to 5pm) and hearty lunches, while after-dark diners sample more formal country fare, such as crab rarebit and braised lamb (mains £15 to £24). Meals are served 11am to 2.30pm and 6.30pm to 9.30pm.

⭐**Woods**   BISTRO ££
(📞01398-324007; www.woodsdulverton.co.uk; 4 Bank Sq; mains £15-19; ⊙noon-2pm & 7-9.30pm) With its deer antlers, hunting prints and big wood-burning stove, multi-award-winning Woods is Exmoor to its core. No surprise then to find menus with full-bodied flavours: expect confit leg of guinea fowl, slow-roast lamb shoulder, and asparagus and wild garlic risotto. Book ahead.

The bar menu (£7 to £13, served between 6pm and 9.30pm) is simpler stuff – think steak, omelette Arnold Bennett (a fluffy omelette with smoked haddock), lamburgers, and fish and chips.

Mortimers   CAFE £
(📞01398-323850; 13 High St; mains from £9; ⊙9.30am-5pm Thu-Tue; 🛜) Chunky wooden tables and exposed brick defy traditional tearoom expectations; the menu is surprising, too. Expect homemade 'moo burgers' (beef sandwiched between brioche buns) and unusual rarebits – options for cheese-on-toast here include goats cheese or brie with added beer or Somerset cider.

Dunster

POP 820

Centred on a scarlet-walled castle and a medieval yarn market, Dunster is one of Exmoor's oldest villages, a tempting tangle of cobbled streets, bubbling brooks and packhorse bridges.

Sights

Dunster Castle   CASTLE

(NT; ☑ 01643-823004; www.nationaltrust.org. uk; Castle Hill; adult/child £11.60/5.80; ⊙ 11am-5pm Mar-Oct; [P]) Rosy-hued Dunster Castle crowns a densely wooded hill. Built by the Luttrell family, which once owned much of northern Exmoor, the oldest sections are 13th century, while the turrets and exterior walls are 19th-century additions. Look out for Tudor furnishings, 17th-century plasterwork and a ridiculously grand staircase. Leave time to explore the colourful terraced gardens, which feature riverside walks, a working watermill and views across Exmoor's shores.

Watermill   HISTORIC BUILDING

(NT; ☑ 01643-821759; www.nationaltrust.org.uk; Mill Lane; ⊙ 11am-5pm) Most of the original cogs, wheels and grinding stones continue to rotate in this working 18th-century mill. There's a picturesque riverside tearoom alongside and you can buy the mill's organic stoneground flour in the shop.

Admission to the mill is included in tickets to neighbouring Dunster Castle.

Sleeping & Eating

Dunster Castle Hotel   HOTEL ££

(☑ 01643-823030; www.thedunstercastlehotel.co. uk; 5 High St; d £90-175; ☎) Everything feels rich in this former coaching inn, from the ruby-red furnishings and tapestry-esque fabrics to the heraldic-style throws. The menu features quality pub-food classics and top-notch sweets, the chocolate and pistachio brownie is a treat. Food (mains £11 to £24) is served from 8am to 11am, noon to 2.30pm and 5.30pm to 8pm.

Millstream Cottage   B&B ££

(☑ 01643-821966; www.millstreamcottagedun-ster.co.uk; 2 Mill Lane; s £65, d £79-89) In the 1600s this was Dunster's workhouse; now it's a sweet-as-pie guesthouse with country-cottage-style rooms. Enjoy a cream tea on arrival, smoked haddock for breakfast and

an oh-so-comfy guest lounge where you can snooze in front of the wood burner.

Luttrell Arms   HISTORIC HOTEL £££

(☑ 01643-821555; www.luttrellarms.co.uk; High St; r £150-220; [P] ☎) You almost need a ladder to climb up to the high four-poster bed in the feature room at this exquisite old coaching inn. In medieval times, this was the guesthouse of the Abbots of Cleeve. Even the standard rooms are gorgeous; expect a plethora of brass plates, beams and a plaster fireplace or two.

Reeve's   BRITISH £££

(☑ 01643-821414; www.reevesrestaurantdunster. co.uk; 20 High St; mains £20-30; ⊙ 7-9pm Tue-Sat, noon-2pm Sun) The eponymous chef at seriously stylish Reeve's is an award winner. No wonder: the complex creations here truly showcase Exmoor produce. Opt for lemon sole with a tangy lobster bisque, or meltingly tender lamb roasted with rosemary and garlic. To finish? Perhaps some toasted walnut bread with local hard and soft cheeses.

ⓘ Getting There & Away

Bus 198 runs north to Minehead (£2) and south to Dulverton (£4, 1¼ hours, two to three daily, Monday to Saturday), via Wheddon Cross.

The 22-mile **West Somerset Railway** (☑ 01643-704996; www.west-somerset-railway. co.uk; 24hr rover tickets adult/child £20/10) stops at Dunster during summer, with four to seven trains daily from May to October.

Porlock & Around

The coastal village of Porlock is one of the prettiest on the Exmoor coast; the huddle of thatched cottages lining its main street is framed on one side by the sea and on the other by steeply sloping hills. Winding lanes lead to the charismatic breakwater of Porlock Weir, 2 miles to the west, with an arching pebble beach and striking coastal views.

Sights

Porlock Weir   HARBOUR

([P]) Porlock Weir's stout granite quay curves around a shingly beach, which is backed by pubs, fisherfolks' storehouses and a scattering of seasonal shops. The weir has been around for almost a thousand years (it's named in the Domesday Book as 'Portloc'). It makes a glorious place for a pub lunch and a stroll, with stirring views across the

Vale of Porlock and easy access to the South West Coast Path.

Holnicote Estate
ARCHITECTURE

(NT; ☑ 01643-862452; www.nationaltrust.org.uk; near Porlock; Ⓟ) **FREE** The 50-sq-km Holnicote Estate sweeps southeast out of Porlock, taking in a string of impossibly pretty villages. Picturesque **Bossington** leads to charming **Allerford** and its 15th-century packhorse bridge. The biggest village, **Selworthy**, offers eye-catching Exmoor views, a cafe, a shop, and cob-and-thatch cottages clustering around the village green.

🛏 Sleeping & Eating

Sea View
B&B ££

(☑ 01643-863456; www.seaviewporlock.co.uk; High Bank; s from £37, d £70-75; 🕿) Value-for-money Sea View has tiny rooms that are pleasantly packed with painted furniture, trinkets and oil paintings. Thoughtful extras include blister plasters and muscle soak for hikers tackling Porlock's precipitous hills.

Cottage
B&B ££

(☑ 01643-862996; www.cottageporlock.co.uk; High St; s/d/tr £45/£75/90; Ⓟ🕿) Evidence of the Cottage's 18th-century origins remains – a big fireplace in the guest lounge, duck-your-head lintels and quirkily shaped bedrooms. The decor though is stylishly modern, with candy-striped cushions in rooms of earthy or aquamarine tones.

Ship Inn
PUB FOOD ££

(Top Ship; ☑ 01643-862507; www.shipinnporlock. co.uk; High St; mains £10-19; ⊙noon-2.30pm & 6-8.30pm; Ⓟ) Romantic poet Samuel Taylor Coleridge and pal Robert Southey both downed pints in this 13th-century thatched Porlock inn – you can even sit in a snug still dubbed 'Southey's Corner'. Substantial pub food – mainly steaks, roasts and stews – is served in the bar.

Locanda On The Weir
ITALIAN ££

(☑ 01643-863300; www.locandaontheweir.co.uk; Porlock Weir; mains £10-24; ⊙7-9pm Wed-Sun, 12.30-2.30pm Sat & Sun, longer summer hours; Ⓟ🕿✐) The chef-proprietor hails from Italy so the dishes here are a happy fusion of Exmoor produce and flavours of the Med. Your pizza could come with gorgonzola and pear, the pasta with local beef and Tuscan tomatoes, while the fish might be *baccala' alla Livornese* (cod with capers, potatoes and olives).

ℹ Information

Tourist Office (☑ 01643-863150; www. porlock.co.uk; West End, Porlock; ⊙10am-5pm Mon-Sat Easter-Oct, to 12.30pm Mon-Sat Nov-Easter)

ℹ Getting There & Away

BUS

Bus 300 heads from Porlock east along the coast to Minehead (£6, 15 minutes), and west to Lynmouth (£10, 55 minutes). It runs from mid-July to early-September, with two buses a day, Monday to Friday only.

CAR

Drivers can choose from two picturesque routes into Porlock village. The New Rd toll road sweeps through pine forests and round U-bends, while Porlock Hill (A39) is a brake-burning 1:4 descent. A further toll road, the Porlock Scenic (Worthy) Toll Rd, provides an alternative, bouncing, route up out of Porlock Weir.

Lynton & Lynmouth

Tucked in amid precipitous cliffs and steep, tree-lined slopes, these twin coastal towns are a landscape-painter's dream. Bustling Lynmouth sits beside the shore, a busy harbour lined with pubs and souvenir shops.

STARGAZING ON EXMOOR

Exmoor holds the distinction of being named Europe's first International Dark Sky Reserve, in recognition of the night-time inky blackness overhead. But what does that mean in practice? Namely, a whole host of local organisations striving to limit light pollution, plus, for visitors, some simply spectacular star displays.

The Exmoor National Park Authority (www.exmoor-nationalpark.gov.uk) runs occasional moonlit strolls and has produced the *Dark Skies Guide*, which includes star charts and maps pinpointing the best light-free spots. Pick one up at a visitor centre or download it from the authority's website. It also runs a **Dark Skies Festival** (☑ 01398-322236; www.exmoor-nationalpark.gov.uk; ⊙late Oct) and hires out suitable telescopes (£25 per night).

For optimum stargazing, central, higher Exmoor is best – try Brandon Two Gates (on the B3223) or Webber's Post (just north of Dunkery Beacon).

On the clifftop, Lynton feels much more genteel and well to do. A cliffside railway links the two: it's powered by the rushing West Lyn River, which feeds numerous cascades and waterfalls nearby.

◎ Sights

★ Cliff Railway
HERITAGE RAILWAY

(☑ 01598-753486; www.cliffrailwaylynton.co.uk; The Esplanade, Lynmouth; one-way/return adult £2.90/3.90, child £1.80/2.40; ☺ 10am-5pm Feb, Mar & Oct, to 6pm Apr, May & Sep, to 7pm Jun-Aug) This extraordinary piece of Victorian engineering sees two cars, linked by a steel cable, descend and ascend the steeply sloping cliff face according to the weight of water in the cars' tanks. All burnished wood and polished brass, it's been running since 1890 and makes for an unmissable ride.

Flood Memorial
MUSEUM

(The Esplanade, Lynmouth; ☺ 9am-6pm Easter-Oct) FREE On 16 August 1952 a huge wave of water swept through Lynmouth following torrential rain. The devastation was immense: 34 people lost their lives, and four bridges and countless houses were washed away. This exhibition features photos of the aftermath and personal testimonies of those involved.

🏃 Activities

Popular hiking trails amid Lynton and Lynmouth's spectacular scenery include those to the lighthouse at Foreland Point; to Watersmeet, 2 miles east of Lynmouth (reached via the gorgeous East Lyn river glade); and along the scenic Glen Lyn Gorge. The dramatic Valley of the Rocks (p300), just a mile west of Lynton along the coast path, is a real highlight.

★ Valley of the Rocks
WALKING

The dramatic geology in this valley was described by poet Robert Southey as 'rock reeling upon rock, stone piled upon stone, a huge terrifying reeling mass'. Look out for the formations dubbed the Devil's Cheesewring and Ragged Jack – and also the feral goats that wander the tracks. It's a mile's walk west of Lynton along a coast path that hugs steep cliffs.

🛏 Sleeping

Bath Hotel
HOTEL ££

(☑ 01598-752238; www.bathhotellynmouth.co.uk; The Harbour, Lynmouth; d £80-130; P 🛜) A pair of third-generation hoteliers are breathing fresh life into the Bath Hotel, a feature of the town since Victorian days. To a stylish cocktail bar add revamped bedrooms teaming gorgeously nautical styling and supremely comfortable beds with expansive harbour and headland views. Standard rooms are much, much less snazzy – but they're also £50 cheaper.

Lynn Valley
B&B ££

(☑ 01598-753300; www.lynnvalleyguesthouse.com; Riverside Rd, Lynmouth; s from £60 d £80-110 q £150; 🛜) Walkers love this smart little guesthouse thanks to a setting right on the coast path, baths to soak in and the loan of flasks. Even if you're not hiking you'll like the crisp, bright decor, harbour views and minidecanters of sherry in the rooms.

Rising Sun
INN £££

(☑ 01598-753223; www.risingsunlynmouth.co.uk; Harbourside, Lynmouth; d £160-190) What was a 14th-century smugglers' haunt has been transformed into an intimate hideaway with a sleek designer feel. Elegant flourishes are all around, from the subtle lighting and local art to the soft, tasteful throws. Ask for a sea-view room to watch the tide rise and fall in the harbour just outside.

★ Old Rectory
HOTEL £££

(☑ 01598-763368; www.oldrectoryhotel.co.uk; Martinhoe; s £135-155 d £180-230 ste £230-260; P 🛜) This romantic hotel delivers beautifully in terms of style. Boutique bedrooms are supremely plush, with elegant baths, silky fabrics and luxury toiletries; the gardens are a tranquil, flower-filled delight. The hotel's chefs cook up own-grown produce for the restaurant. It's all tucked away in the village of Martinhoe, 6 miles west of Lynton.

🍴 Eating

★ Charlie Friday's
CAFE £

(☑ 07544 123324; www.charliefridays.co.uk; Church Hill, Lynton; snacks from £4; ☺ 10am-6pm Apr-Oct, reduced hours winter; 🛜🖉🚼🐾) A funky, friendly hang-out serving melt-in-your-mouth pastries, thick sarnies, tasty nachos and fair-trade two-shot espresso that really packs a punch. The cafe's guitar, knitting and board games help keep the atmosphere set to chilled.

★ Ancient Mariner
PUB FOOD ££

(☑ 01598-752238; www.bathhotellynmouth.co.uk; The Harbour, Lynmouth; mains £12-19; ☺ noon-3pm & 6-9pm; 🛜) The Mariner brings a burst of shipwreck chic to Lynmouth, thanks to a copper bar top, curved ship's decking and a figurehead that isn't entirely clothed. Drink it all in while tucking into a stacked-high Mariner Burger, complete with Exmoor ale and black-treacle-braised brisket, onion jam and blue-cheese mousse.

★ **Rising Sun** MODERN BRITISH **££**
(☑ 01598-753223; www.risingsunlynmouth.co.uk; Harbourside, Lynmouth; 2/3 courses £30/39; ⊙ noon-2.30pm & 6-9pm) At the harbourside Rising Sun, they delight in showcasing not only Exmoor meat and veg but also the seafood landed on this rugged shore. Seasonal treats might include succulent lobster, fresh sea bass and local mussels, all served up with confidence and more than a dash of élan. Booking advised.

ℹ️ Information

Lynmouth Tourist Office (☑ 01598-752509; www.visit-exmoor.co.uk; The Esplanade, Lynmouth; ⊙ 10am-5pm) An Exmoor National Park Authority visitor centre.

Lynton Tourist Office (☑ 0845 458 3775; www.lynton-lynmouth-tourism.co.uk; Lynton Town Hall, Lee Rd, Lynton; ⊙ 10am-5pm Mon-Sat, to 2pm Sun Apr-Oct, 10am-3pm Tue-Thu Nov-Mar)

DEVON

Devon offers freedom. Its rippling, beach-fringed landscape is studded with historic homes, vibrant cities and wild, wild moors. Here you can ditch schedules and to-do lists and hike a rugged coast path, take a scenic boat trip, or get lost in hedge-lined lanes that aren't even on your map.

Discover collegiate Exeter, touristy Torquay, yachting-haven Dartmouth and alternative Totnes. Or escape to wilderness Dartmoor and the remote, surf-dashed north coast. To replenish your energy, you can sample wines made from the vines beside you and food that's fresh from field, furrow or sea. However you decide to explore Devon – surfing, cycling, kayaking, horse riding, sea swimming or barefoot beachcombing – it'll feel like coming home.

ℹ️ Information

Visit Devon (www.visitdevon.co.uk) The official tourism website.

ℹ️ Getting Around

BUS

Most bus services between larger towns and villages are now run by Stagecoach (www.stagecoachbus.com), with a number of smaller coach companies offering infrequent services to other areas. Dartmoor is poorly served by buses; you'll need a car or bike to access its more remote areas.

There are several bus passes available: the **Devon Day Ticket** (adult/child/family £9.30/6.20/18.60) covers all companies, while the **Stagecoach South West Explorer** (adult/child/family £8.30/5.50/16.60) and **South West Megarider Gold** tickets (one week £30) only cover Stagecoach buses. Check the Stagecoach website for details.

Traveline South West (www.travelinesw.com) is a great online tool for travel planning, while the **Devon interactive bus map** (https://new.devon.gov.uk/travel) provides a useful visual map of bus routes.

TRAIN

Devon's main line skirts southern Dartmoor, running from Exeter to Plymouth and on to Cornwall. Branch lines include the 39-mile Exeter–Barnstaple Tarka Line, the 15-mile Plymouth–Gunnislake Tamar Valley Line and the scenic Exeter–Torquay Paignton line. There are also several lovely steam railways including Dartmouth Steam Railway (p310), Bodmin & Wenford Railway (p355) and South Devon Steam Railway (p313).

The **Freedom of Devon & Cornwall Rover** ticket (three days travel in seven days adult/child £49/24.50, eight days travel in 15 £79/39.50) is good value if you're using the train extensively.

Exeter

POP 117,800

Well-heeled and comfortable, Exeter exudes evidence of its centuries-old role as the spiritual and administrative heart of Devon. The city's Gothic cathedral presides over pockets of cobbled streets; medieval and Georgian buildings and fragments of the Roman city stretch out all around. A snazzy contemporary shopping centre brings bursts of the modern; thousands of university students ensure a buzzing nightlife; and the vibrant quayside acts as a launch pad for cycling or kayaking trips. Throw in some stylish places to stay and eat, and you have a relaxed but lively base for explorations.

History

Exeter's past can be read in its buildings. The Romans marched in around AD 55; their 17-hectare fortress included a 2-mile defensive wall, crumbling sections of which

Exeter

Exeter

◎ Top Sights

⦿ Activities, Courses & Tours

⦿ Sleeping

⦿ Eating

⦿ Drinking & Nightlife

⦿ Entertainment

remain, especially in Rougemont and Northernhay Gardens. Saxon and Norman times saw growth: a castle went up in 1068, the cathedral 40 years later. The Tudor wool boom brought Exeter an export trade, riches and half-timbered houses; prosperity continued into the Georgian era, when hundreds of merchants built genteel homes. The Blitz of WWII brought devastation; in just one night in 1942, 156 people died and 12 hectares of the city were flattened. In the 21st century, the £220-million Princesshay Shopping Centre added shimmering glass and steel lines to the architectural mix. But 2016 brought a devastating fire at the Royal Clarence Hotel – a much-loved 18th-century building in the heart of Cathedral Yard. At time of writing, plans were being discussed to rebuild the hotel and restore its iconic facade.

⊙ Sights

★ Exeter Cathedral
CATHEDRAL

(Cathedral Church of St Peter; ☑ 01392- 285983; www.exeter-cathedral.org.uk; The Close; adult/child £7.50/free; ⊙ 9am-5pm Mon-Sat, 11.30am-5pm Sun) Magnificent in warm, honey-coloured stone, Exeter's cathedral is one of Devon's most impressive ecclesiastical sights. Dating largely from the 12th and 13th centuries, the west front is framed by extraordinary medieval statuary, while inside the ceiling soars upwards to the longest span of unbroken Gothic vaulting in the world, dotted with ornate ceiling bosses in gilt and vibrant colours. Look out for the scale Lego model that's being built beside the main entrance; for £1 you can add a brick.

The site has been a religious one since at least the 5th century, but the Normans started the current building in 1114; the towers of today's cathedral date from that period. In 1270 a 90-year remodelling process began, introducing a mix of Early English and Decorated Gothic styles.

Above the Great West Front scores of weather-worn figures line a once brightly painted screen that now forms England's largest collection of 14th-century sculpture. Inside, the exquisitely symmetrical ceiling soars up and along, towards the north transept and the 15th-century Exeter Clock: in keeping with medieval astronomy, the clock shows Earth as a golden ball at the centre of the universe with the sun, a fleur-de-lys, travelling around it. Still ticking and whirring, it chimes on the hour.

The huge oak canopy over the Bishop's Throne was carved in 1312. The 1350 minstrels' gallery is decorated with 12 angels playing musical instruments. Cathedral staff will point out the famous sculpture of the lady with two left feet and the tiny St James Chapel, built to repair the one destroyed in

the Blitz. Look out for the chapel's unusual carvings: a cat, a mouse and, oddly, a rugby player.

There are free informative guided tours of the cathedral every day included in the admission price, or you can DIY with one of the free audio guides. But for the most dramatic perspective you really need to head up into one of the towers and drink in the views. Roof tours run on Tuesdays and Saturdays (you can book in advance online). There's a minimum age of eight.

Choral evensong services are held at 5.30pm from Monday to Friday, and 4pm on Saturday and Sunday.

★ RAMM
MUSEUM

(Royal Albert Memorial Museum & Art Gallery; ☑ 01392-265858; www.rammuseum.org.uk; Queen St; ⊙ 10am-5pm Tue-Sun; ☎) FREE A fixture on the city's cultural scene since Victorian times, this hulking red-brick museum recently received a £24 million revamp. It's a treasure trove of rambling rooms, filled with glass cases of curiosities and archaeological finds – from samurai armour, African masks and Egyptian mummies in the World Cultures galleries to a truly amazing echinoderm collection of starfish and sea urchins amassed by the inveterate Victorian collector Walter Percy Sladen. Exeter's own history also figures strongly.

★ Underground Passages
TUNNEL

(☑ 01392-665887; www.exeter.gov.uk/passages; 2 Paris St; adult/child £6/4; ⊙ 9.30am-5.30pm Mon-Sat, 10.30am-4pm Sun Jun-Sep, 10.30am-4.30pm Tue-Fri, 9.30am-5.30pm Sat, 11.30am-4pm Sun Oct-May) Prepare to crouch down, don a hard hat and possibly get spooked in what is the only publicly accessible system of its kind in England. These medieval vaulted

LOCAL KNOWLEDGE

CATHEDRAL ROOF TOURS

Don't miss the chance to climb up one of Exeter Cathedral's towers for panoramic views over the city's rooftops (☑ 01392-285983; www.exeter-cathedral.org.uk; incl Exeter Cathedral admission adult/child £13/5; ⊙ 2pm Tue, 10.30am Sat Jul-Sep). Quite a lot of steps are involved (251 to be precise), and there's a minimum visitor age of eight. You can book online, which is highly recommended as places are limited.

passages were built to house pipes bringing fresh water to the city. Guides lead you on a scramble through the network, relating tales of ghosts, escape routes and cholera. The last tour is an hour before closing; they're popular – book ahead.

Bill Douglas Cinema Museum
MUSEUM

(☏01392-724321; www.bdcmuseum.org.uk; Old Library, Prince of Wales Rd; ⊙10am-5pm; P) FREE This eccentric museum is a must for cinephiles. It contains a hoard of film-themed memorabilia amassed by Scottish film-maker Bill Douglas, best known for his semi-autobiographical trilogy about his childhood. Douglas was also an avid collector, amassing more than 50,000 cinematic collectables: magic lanterns, peep shows, original celluloid from Disney films, Charlie Chaplin bottle stoppers, James Bond board games, vintage film posters, *Star Wars* toys and more. It's on the Exeter University campus, a mile northwest of the city centre.

Powderham Castle
HISTORIC BUILDING

(☏01626-890243; www.powderham.co.uk; adult/child £12.95/10.95; ⊙11am-4.30pm Sun-Fri Apr-Jun, Sep & Oct, to 5.30pm Jul & Aug; P) The historic home of the Earl of Devon, Powderham is a stately but still friendly place built in 1391 and remodelled in the Victorian era. A visit takes in a fine wood-panelled Great Hall, parkland with 650 deer and glimpses of life 'below stairs' in the kitchen. Powderham is on the River Exe near Kenton, 8 miles south of Exeter.

🏃 Activities

Saddles & Paddles
OUTDOORS

(☏01392-424241; www.sadpad.com; Exeter Quay; ⊙9am-6pm) This hire shop by the quay rents out bikes (adult per hour/day £7/18), single and double kayaks (£12/45) and Canadian canoes (£18/60), and offers advice on suggested routes.

🧭 Tours

★ Redcoat Tours
WALKING

(☏01392-265203; www.exeter.gov.uk/leisure-and-culture) FREE These informative, free 1½-hour tours explore different periods of the city's history (Roman, Tudor, Georgian), with fun options like evening ghost walks and torchlit expeditions through the catacombs. Most leave from Cathedral Green; a few in summer depart from Exeter Quay.

There are at least a couple of tours per day, even in winter; there's no need to book.

🛏 Sleeping

Globe Backpackers
HOSTEL £

(☏01392-215521; www.exeterbackpackers.co.uk; 71 Holloway St; dm/d £17.50/45; ⊙reception 8.30am-noon & 3.30-11pm; P😊) Rightly a firm favourite among budget travellers, this spotlessly clean, relaxed, rambling former town house boasts three doubles, roomy dorms and six shared wet-room showers. There's a pleasant lounge, a rather undersized kitchen, free wi-fi and lockers for storage.

★ Telstar
B&B ££

(☏01392-272466; www.telstar-hotel.co.uk; 77 St David's Hill; s £35-50, d £60-85, f £85-105; P😊) 'Victoriana with a twist' best defines this excellent B&B, where stately fireplaces meet mock-flock wallpaper and stag heads wearing aviator goggles. Rooms team a heritage feel with modern comforts; bathrooms feature 19th-century-style tiles. If you like outdoors space, request the double with its own roomy deck.

Silversprings
APARTMENT ££

(☏01392-494040; www.silversprings.co.uk; 12 Richmond Rd; 1/2 bedroom apt per night £85/100; P😊) There are so many reasons to make these serviced apartments your Exeter pied-à-terre. Tucked away off a square a short walk from the city centre, they each come with a lounge and minikitchen, plus home comforts such as a DVD player and satellite TV. Furnishings are fabulous, with plush fabrics and sleek designs.

★ Hotel du Vin Exeter
BOUTIQUE HOTEL £££

(☏01392-790120; www.hotelduvin.com/locations/exeter; Magdalen St; r £105-195; @😊🏊) This grand red-brick edifice (once Exeter's eye hospital) is now part of the plush Hotel du Vin chain. Quietly stylish rooms incorporate aspects of the building's Victorian architecture (bay windows, cornicing, wood floors) into their palette of muted colours, offbeat wallpapers and Scandi-style sofas. There's a stylish octagon-shaped restaurant, an excellent bar and a sleek spa.

Headweir Mill House
B&B £££

(☏01392-210869; www.headweir-house.co.uk; Bonhay Rd; d £110-150; P😊) Overlooking the banks of the River Exe (and busy Bonhay Rd), this house has more than two centuries of history, not that you'd guess from the 11 contemporary rooms: spacious and elegant in greys, taupes, slatted wood and stripes, all seamlessly blended with the house's period

RIVER COTTAGE CANTEEN

Known for his media campaigns on sustainability and organic food, TV chef Hugh Fearnley-Whittingstall broadcasts most of his TV shows from his home base at **River Cottage HQ** (✆ 01297-630300; www.rivercottage.net; Trinity Hill Rd, Axminster; 2-course lunch £55, 4-course dinner £70), near Axminster, 30 miles from Exeter. If you fancy seeing where the magic happens, you can book in for a sumptuous four-course meal, made with produce from Hugh's own garden, or attend one of the regular cooking courses. A cheaper option is to dine at his **canteen** (✆ 01297-631715; www.rivercottage.net; Trinity Sq, Axminster; mains £7-18; ◎ 9am-5pm Sun-Tue, to 11pm Wed-Sat; ⚙) in Axminster village nearby.

features. Ask for one with a bay window and river view.

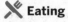

Eating

★ **Exploding Bakery**   CAFE **£**
(✆ 01392-427900; www.explodingbakery.com; 1b Central Cres, Queen St; snacks £2.50; ◎ 8am-4pm Mon-Fri, 9am-4pm Sat; 🖥) Excellent news: one of Exeter's hippest little bakeries has now added half-a-dozen tables, meaning there's even more room to sample superb flat whites, macchiato and inventive cakes – the lemon, polenta and pistachio is a hit.

Plant Cafe   VEGETARIAN **£**
(1 Cathedral Yard; mains £6-9; ◎ 8.30am-5pm Mon-Sat; 🖥⚙) Seats are at a premium at this casually cool wholefood cafe. That'll be down to its prime spot overlooking Cathedral Green and its imaginative frittata, pies and salads. When it's sunny you can sit outside.

Dinosaur Cafe   MIDDLE EASTERN **£**
(✆ 01392-490951; 5 New North Rd; mains £6-8; ◎ 10am-9pm Mon-Sat) In this cheery Turkish mezze bar, lemon-yellow walls and chunky wooden furniture set the scene for tasty couscous, kofta and spicy *mücver* fritters. The Turkish breakfasts (eggs, pepperoni and feta) are a welcome change from the norm.

Herbies   VEGETARIAN **££**
(✆ 01392-258473; 15 North St; mains £7-14; ◎ 11am-2.30pm Mon-Sat, 6.30-9.30pm Tue-Sat; ⚙) Herbies has been cheerfully feeding Exeter's vegetarians and vegans for more than 20 years. Expect the old classics here: Greek vegetable pie, mushroom and butternut-squash risotto or Moroccan tagine.

Lloyd's Kitchen   BISTRO **££**
(✆ 01392-499333; www.lloydskitchen.co.uk; 16 Catherine St; mains lunch £6.95-11.95, dinner £14-22; ◎ 9am-3pm Mon-Thu, 9am-3pm & 6.30-9.30pm Fri & Sat, 10am-3pm Sun) Squeezed in among the city-centre chains is this independent diner run by energetic owner Lloyd. With its sliding-glass frontage, bare bulbs, tiles and banquettes, it's a lovely space, and food-wise, it's classic and comforting: frittatas, open sandwiches, burgers, salads and 'British classics' by day; by night, corn-fed chicken, confit duck and steaks (Fridays and Saturdays only). Breakfasts are copious.

@Angela's   MODERN BRITISH **£££**
(✆ 01392-499038; www.angelasrestaurant.co.uk; 38 New Bridge St; mains £17-32; ◎ 6-9pm Wed-Sat) One of the most well-known of Exeter's fine-dining restaurants, good for formal, French-inspired dishes served in a starchy, white-tablecloth setting. Expect rich things like roast duck, aged Aberdeen Angus beef and steamed turbot, heavy on cream, sauce or red-wine jus.

🍷 Drinking & Nightlife

★ **Fat Pig**   MICROBREWERY
(✆ 01392-437217; www.fatpig-exeter.co.uk; 2 John St; ◎ 5-11pm Mon-Fri, noon-11pm Sat, noon-5pm Sun) There are few better spots for a pint in town than this fine craft brewery, which makes its own ales and brews its own gin, vodka and more 'experimental' spirits. It's a pleasant space, with quirky decor and fixtures, divided between a main bar and a small conservatory. Bar meals are good too, especially the Sunday roast.

Old Firehouse   PUB
(✆ 01392-277279; www.oldfirehouseexeter.co.uk; 50 New North Rd; ◎ noon-2am Mon-Wed, to 3am Thu-Sat, to 1am Sun) Step into the snug, candlelit interior of this Exeter institution and instantly feel at home. Dried hops hang from rafters above flagstone floors and walls of exposed stone. The range of draught ciders and cask ales is truly impressive, while the pizzas, served after 9pm, have kept countless students fed.

Beer Engine MICROBREWERY

(☏01392-851282; www.thebeerengine.co.uk; Newton St Cyres; mains £12; ☺11am-11pm, kitchen noon-3pm & 6-9.30pm Mon-Sat, noon-6.30pm Sun) The decor in this former railway hotel is varnished floorboards, leather settles and exposed red brick, but the best bit is downstairs: the brewery's gleaming stainless-steel tubs and tubes. The building's past is the inspiration for the brews' names: fruity Rail Ale, sharp and sweet Piston Bitter and well-rounded Sleeper Heavy.

Flavoursome food includes slow-cooked shoulder of West Country lamb, a range of ploughman's platters made with local Quickes cheddar, and steak and Sleeper Ale pie. Newton St Cyres is on the A377, 5 miles north of Exeter. Train services from Exeter (return £7) chug into the village in time for supper; the return trip just after 11pm (10.30pm on Sunday) is very handy indeed.

☆ Entertainment

Bike Shed THEATRE

(☏01392-434169; www.bikeshedtheatre.co.uk; 162 Fore St; ☺5pm-midnight Mon-Thu, to 2am Fri & Sat, to 11pm Sun) Emerging writers are profiled in the Bike Shed's rough 'n' ready subterranean, brick-lined performance space. Its vintage cocktail bar makes a hip setting for live music and DJ sets on Friday and Saturday nights.

Exeter Phoenix ARTS CENTRE

(☏01392-667080; www.exeterphoenix.org.uk; cnr Bradninch Pl & Gandy St; ☺10am-11pm Mon-Sat; ☎) Exeter's art and soul, the Phoenix is a buzzing blend of indie cinema, a performance space, galleries and a cool cafe-bar (snacks to 7pm).

Exeter Picturehouse CINEMA

(☏0871 902 5730; www.picturehouses.co.uk; 51 Bartholomew St W) An intimate, independent cinema, screening mainstream and arthouse movies.

ℹ Information

Exeter Tourist Office (☏01392-665700; www.visitexeter.com; Dix's Field; ☺9am-5pm Mon-Sat Apr-Sep, 9.30am-4.30pm Mon-Sat Oct-Mar)

ℹ Getting There & Away

AIR

Exeter International Airport (☏01392-367433; www.exeter-airport.co.uk) is 6 miles east of the city. Flights connect with several UK cities, including Manchester, Newcastle, Edinburgh and Glasgow, and with the Isles of Scilly and the Channel Islands.

Bus 56/56A/56B runs from Exeter St David's train station and Exeter bus station to Exeter International Airport (£3.90, 30 minutes), hourly between around 6.30am and 6.30pm.

BUS

Exeter's **bus station** (Paris St) is due a multi-million-pound revamp, during which time some services may depart from other locations. There's no set date. Check with the tourist office for the latest.

Services include the following.

Exmouth Bus 57 (£4.30, 35 minutes, two to four per hour).

Lyme Regis Bus 9A (£7.50, at least hourly, six on Sunday), via Beer. No Sunday service in winter.

Plymouth Bus X38 (£7.50, 1¼ hours, six daily Monday to Friday, four Saturday, two Sunday).

Sidmouth Bus 9/9A (£7, 35 minutes, two per hour Monday to Saturday, hourly on Sunday).

Topsham Bus 57 (£2.50, 10 minutes, two to four per hour).

Totnes Bus X64 (£6.10, 50 minutes, six or seven daily Monday to Saturday, two Sunday).

TRAIN

For main towns in Devon and Cornwall, it's generally much faster to take the train than the bus, though it's rarely cheaper. Main-line trains stopping at St David's train station include the following.

Bristol £29, 1¼ hours, half-hourly

London Paddington £71.20, 2½ hours, half-hourly

Paignton £7.70, 50 minutes, half-hourly

Penzance £21.80, three hours, half-hourly to hourly

Plymouth £9.70, one hour, half-hourly

Torquay £7.70, 45 minutes, half-hourly to hourly

Totnes £7, 35 minutes, half-hourly

Some branch-line services also go through Exeter Central train station.

ℹ Getting Around

BICYCLE

Saddles & Paddles (p304) Rents out bikes.

BUS

Bus H (two to four per hour) links St David's train station with Central train station (£1) and the High St, passing near the bus station.

TAXI

There are taxi ranks at St David's train station and on **High** and **Sidwell Sts**.

Apple Central Taxis ([☎] 01392-666666; www.
appletaxisexeter.co.uk)
Exeter City Cars ([☎] 01392-975808; www.
exetercitycars.com; ☻24hr)
Z Cars ([☎] 01392-595959)

Torquay & Around

POP 114,270

A seaside resort since Victorian times – and,
famously, the setting for Basil Fawlty's fictional hotel in *Fawlty Towers* – Torquay
remains a classic destination for the good,
old-fashioned British summer getaway. Rather fancifully billing itself as the heart of the
'English Riviera', a reference to its palm-lined
seafront and russet-red cliffs, it's a curious
mix: as popular as ever with coach tours,
sun-seeking families and stag- and hen parties, but with a fresh smattering of fine-dining
restaurants and boutique B&Bs that indicate
the town might be sloughing off its old image
in favour of something a bit more classy. And
in fact, it's the sprawling, bargain-basement
resort of Paignton 3 miles south that's in
more dire need of an image overhaul.

Regardless, there's plenty to see and do: a
bizarre model village, a cliff railway, Agatha
Christie connections and a bevy of impressive beaches.

⊙ Sights & Activities

Torquay boasts no fewer than 20 beaches
and an impressive 22 miles of coast. Tidal
Torre Abbey Sands (Torbay Rd) is central, locals head for the sand-and-shingle beaches
beside the 73m red-clay cliffs at **Oddicombe
Beach** and sea swimmers love picturesque
Anstey's Cove.

★**Living Coasts**   ZOO
([☎] 01803-202470; www.livingcoasts.org.uk; Beacon Quay; adult/child £11.80/3.90, joint admission
with Paignton Zoo £22.50/15.95; ☻10am-5pm
Apr-early Jul, Sep & Oct, to 6pm early Jul-Aug, to
4pm Nov-Mar; [P]) Clinging to the cliffs beside Torquay Harbour, the open-plan Living Coasts aviary brings you close to exotic
birds. The immense enclosure features a
series of underwater viewing tunnels and
mocked-up microhabitats that include Penguin Beach, Auk Cliff and Fur Seal Cove. A

AGATHA CHRISTIE

Torquay is the birthplace of one-woman publishing phenomenon **Dame Agatha Mary
Clarissa Christie** (1890–1976), a writer of murder mysteries who is beaten only by
the Bible and William Shakespeare in terms of sales. Her characters are world famous:
Hercule Poirot, the moustachioed, conceited Belgian detective; and Miss Marple, the
surprisingly perceptive busybody spinster.

Born Agatha Miller in Torquay's Barton Rd, the young writer had her first piece published by the age of 11. By WWI she'd married Lieutenant Archie Christie and was working at the Red Cross Hospital in Torquay Town Hall, acquiring a knowledge of poisons
that would lace countless plot lines, including that of her first novel, *The Mysterious
Affair at Styles* (1920). Christie made her name with *The Murder of Roger Ackroyd* six
years later with the use of what was then an innovative and cunning plot twist.

Then came 1926: in one year her mother died, Archie asked for a divorce and the
writer mysteriously disappeared for 10 days, her abandoned car prompting a massive
search. She was eventually discovered in a hotel in Harrogate, where she'd checked in
under the name of the woman her husband wanted to marry. Christie always maintained
she'd suffered amnesia; some critics saw it as a publicity stunt.

Christie later married archaeologist Sir Max Mallowan, and their trips to the Middle
East provided masses of material for her work. By the time she died in 1976, Christie had
written 75 novels and 33 plays.

Torquay's tourist office (p309) stocks the free *Agatha Christie Literary Trail* leaflet
(also available to download from the website), which guides you around significant local
sites. **Torquay Museum** ([☎]01803-293975; www.torquaymuseum.org; 529 Babbacombe Rd;
adult/child £6.45/3.95; ☻10am-4pm Mon-Sat) has a fine collection of photos, handwritten
notes and displays devoted to Christie's famous detectives. The highlight, though, is
Greenway (p309), the author's summer home near Dartmouth. Get there via the ferry
from Dartmouth (p311) or take the steam train from Paignton (p310) to Greenway Halt,
from where it's a half-mile walk through the woods to the house itself.

BATH & SOUTHWEST ENGLAND TORQUAY & AROUND

joint admission ticket with Paignton Zoo offers a 25% discount.

★ Babbacombe Model Village   MUSEUM
(☑ 01803-315315; www.model-village.co.uk; Hampton Ave; adult/child £11.95/9.95; ☉ 10am-4pm; ℗) There are 413 tiny buildings, inhabited by 13,160 even tinier people, on display at this Lilliputian attraction, the epitome of English eccentricity. Settings include a small-scale Stonehenge, a football stadium, a beach (complete with nude sunbathers), an animated circus, a castle (under attack from a fire-breathing dragon) and a thatched village where firefighters are tackling a blaze. It's all brilliantly bizarre.

★ Paignton Zoo   ZOO
(☑ 01803-697500; www.paigntonzoo.org.uk; Totnes Rd, Paignton; adult/child £16.50/12.35, joint admission with Living Coasts £22.50/15.95; ☉ 10am-6pm Apr-Oct, to 4.30pm Nov-Mar; ℗) This innovative, 32-hectare zoo is by far and away Paignton's top draw. Spacious enclosures recreate habitats from savannah and wetland to tropical forest and desert. Highlights include the orangutan island, a glass-walled big-cat enclosure and a lemur wood, where you walk over a plank suspension bridge as the primates leap around the trees. Then there's the crocodile swamp with pathways winding over and beside Nile, Cuban and saltwater crocs. Joint tickets also cover the Living Coasts seabird centre.

Babbacombe Cliff Railway   RAIL
(☑ 01803-328750; www.babbacombecliffrailway.co.uk; Babbacombe Downs Rd; adult/child return £2.80/2; ☉ 9.30am-4.30pm Feb-Oct) A marvel of engineering in its day, Babbacombe's glorious 1920s funicular railway sees you climbing into a tiny carriage and rattling up and down rails set into the cliff. At the very least, it saves you the aching legs after walking down and back up.

🛏 Sleeping

Torquay Backpackers   HOSTEL £
(☑ 01803-299924; www.torquaybackpackers.co.uk; 119 Abbey Rd; dm £18-20, d £38; @ 🛜) Set inside a Victorian terraced house, this budget stalwart is looking its age, but it's a reliably cheap option for budget travellers. There's a decent-sized kitchen, DVD den and a decked, al fresco pool-table terrace, but dorms can be noisy, as it's popular with stag and hen dos.

★ The 25   B&B ££
(☑ 01803-297517; www.the25.uk; 25 Avenue Rd; r £108-168; ℗ 🛜) 'We banished magnolia,' says the owner proudly. And how: the playful bedrooms here team zebra print with acid yellow, or burgundy with peacock blue. Pop-art flourishes, and great gadgets abound; play with the mood lighting via the iPad or watch TV in the shower. Munch on homemade brownies. Great value, great fun. There's usually a three-night minimum in summer.

Hillcroft   B&B ££
(☑ 01803-297247; www.thehillcroft.co.uk; 9 St Lukes Rd; d £89-130; ℗ 🛜) One of the better B&B options in Torquay town, with bedrooms styled after Morocco, Bali, Lombok and Tuscany. The pick is the spacious suites: Provençal, with an ormolu bed and a sitting room, or India, with Indian art and a four-poster bed.

★ Cary Arms   BOUTIQUE HOTEL £££
(☑ 01803-327110; www.caryarms.co.uk; Babbacombe Beach; d £245-395, ste £375-450; ℗ 🛜 🐾) In a dreamy spot beside Babbacombe's sands, this heritage hotel has more than a hint of a New England beach retreat. Bright, light-filled rooms with candy-stripe throws and white furniture shimmer with style, but for the best view book a stylish beach 'hut', complete with Smeg fridge, mezzanine bedroom and knockout beach-view patio. There's a divine spa, too.

🍴 Eating

Me & Mrs Jones   CAFE £
(☑ 01803-298745; www.meandmrsjonesdeli.com; 11 Ilsham Rd; dishes from £6; ☉ 8am-5.30pm Mon-Fri, 9am-4pm Sat) In this chilled-out cafe-deli, twinkling fairy lights are strung above a scattering of upcycled tables surrounded by gourmet goodies: organic sourdough, 'squealer' (pork) pies, flavoursome salads, quality charcuterie and oozing cheeses.

★ Elephant   MODERN BRITISH ££
(☑ 01803-200044; www.elephantrestaurant.co.uk; 3 Beacon Tce; lunch 2-/3-course menu £18.50/21.95, dinner mains £16.50-26.50; ☉ noon-2pm & 6.30-9pm Tue-Sat) The jumbo on Torquay's fine-dining scene: Michelin-starred and critically lauded, Elephant belongs to chef Simon Hulstone, whose taste for seasonal food (much of it grown on his own farm) and delicate presentation takes centre stage. The food is modern with classical underpinnings – though expect surpris-

ing flavour combos – and every plate looks as pretty as a painting. Lunch is a steal.

Rockfish
SEAFOOD ££

(☑ 01803-212175; www.therockfish.co.uk; 20 Victoria Pde; mains £12-20; ⊗ noon-9.30pm) The Torquay branch of award-winning chef Mitch Tonks' minichain of seafood restaurants showcases his taste for relaxed catch-of-the-day dining. Whitewashed wood and nautical knick-knacks give a shipshape ambience, while the food takes in everything from classic fish and chips and monkfish scampi to chargrilled seafood platters and seaweedy tartare sauce. For Devon lobster, preorder.

On the Rocks
BISTRO ££

(☑ 01803-203666; www.ontherocks-torquay.co.uk; 1 Abbey Cres; mains £13-26; ⊗ 11am-midnight) Sliding doors and pavement tables make the most of the seaside view at this relaxed, informal cafe-bistro – it's just a shame the main beach road gets in the way. Still, it makes a pleasant spot to tuck into a bowl of mussels, a juicy steak or a creamy monkfish fillet, and reclaimed finds give it a rustic, semi-hipster vibe.

CoCo (www.cocotorquay.co.uk; 1 Abbey Cres; 5pm-midnight Mon-Fri, 11am-midnight Sat & Sun) cocktail bar is next door.

ℹ Information

Torquay Tourist Office (☑ 01803-211211; www.theenglishriviera.co.uk; 5 Vaughan Pde; ⊗ 10am-5pm Mon-Sat) Torquay's main tourist office by the central harbour covers Torquay, Paignton and Brixham.

ℹ Getting There & Away

BUS

Services from Torquay **bus station** (Lymington Rd) are as follows.

Brixham Stagecoach Bus 12 (£4.50, 45 minutes, half-hourly) runs via Paignton.

Totnes Stagecoach Gold (£3.50, 45 minutes, half-hourly to hourly). From Totnes bus X64 goes on to Dartmouth.

FERRY

Between April and September the **Western Lady** (☑ Brixham 01803-852041, Torquay 01803-293797; www.westernladyferry.com; single/return £2/3; ⊗ Apr-Sep) shuttles between the harbours of Torquay (The Harbour) and Brixham.

TRAIN

Trains run from Exeter St David's to Torquay (£7.70, 45 minutes, half-hourly to hourly) and on to Paignton (52 minutes) for the same fare.

WORTH A TRIP

BRIXHAM

An appealing, pastel-painted tumbling of fisher cottages leads down to Brixham's horseshoe harbour, where arcades and gift shops coexist with winding streets, brightly coloured boats and one of England's busiest fishing ports.

Life in Brixham revolves around the **fish market** (www.englishriviera.co.uk; The Quay; tours incl breakfast £15; ⊗ Apr-Oct), which can be visited on an early-morning guided tour, starting at 6am. They're hugely popular – book well in advance. Down by Brixham's harbour, look out for a replica of the **Golden Hind** (☑ 01803-856223; www.goldenhind.co.uk; The Quay; adult/child £7/5; ⊗ 10.30am-4pm Mar-Oct), Francis Drake's famous globetrotting ship.

The most enjoyable way to arrive in Brixham is aboard the venerable Western Lady, which runs along the coast between Brixham Harbour and Torquay.

Dartmouth & Around

POP 10,720

Home to the nation's most prestigious naval college, the riverside town of Dartmouth is one of Devon's prettiest, awash with pastel-coloured, punch-drunk 17th- and 18th-century buildings leaning at angles, and a picturesque harbour stacked with yachts and clanking boat masts. It may be distinctly chic these days, but it's still a working port, and the triple draw of regular riverboat cruises, the art deco house of Coleton Fishacre and the former home of Agatha Christie make Dartmouth all but irresistible.

Dartmouth is on the west side of the Dart estuary. It's linked to the village of Kingswear on the east bank by fleets of car and foot ferries, also providing a key transport link to Torquay. It makes a lovely base for exploring Devon's south coast and the South Hams area.

◎ Sights

★**Greenway**
HISTORIC BUILDING

(NT; ☑ 01803-842382; www.nationaltrust.org.uk/greenway; Greenway Rd, Galmpton; adult/child £11.60/5.80; ⊗ 10.30am-5pm mid-Feb–Oct, 11am-4pm Sat & Sun Nov & Dec) High on Devon's must-see list, the captivating summer home of crime writer Agatha Christie sits beside the placid River Dart. Part-guided tours allow you to wander between rooms where the furnishings and knick-knacks are much as the author left them. The bewitching waterside gardens include features that pop up in Christie's mysteries, so you get to spot locations made notorious by fictional murders. Car parking must be prebooked; the better options are to arrive by Greenway Ferry or on foot.

★ **Coleton Fishacre** HISTORIC BUILDING
(NT; ☑ 01803-842382; www.nationaltrust.org.uk/coleton-fishacre; Brownstone Rd, near Kingswear; adult/child £11.60/5.80; ☺ 10.30am-5pm mid-Feb–Oct, 11am-4pm Sat & Sun Nov & Dec; **P**) For an evocative glimpse of jazz-age glamour, drop by the former home of the D'Oyly Carte family of theatre impresarios. Built in the 1920s, its faultless art deco embellishments include original Lalique tulip uplighters, comic bathroom tiles and a stunning saloon – complete with tinkling piano. The croquet terrace leads to deeply shelved subtropical gardens and suddenly revealed vistas of the sea. Hike the 4 miles along the cliffs from Kingswear, or drive.

Dartmouth Castle CASTLE
(EH; ☑ 01803-833588; www.english-heritage.org.uk/visit/places/dartmouth-castle; Castle Rd; adult/child £6.80/4.10; ☺ 10am-6pm Apr-Sep, to 5pm Oct, to 4pm Sat & Sun Nov-Mar; **P**) Discover maze-like passages, atmospheric guardrooms and great views from the battlements of this picturesque castle. The best way to arrive is via the tiny, open-top Castle Ferry (p311), or walk or drive along the coast road from Dartmouth (1.5 miles).

★ **Dartmouth Steam Railway** RAIL
(☑ 01803-555872; www.dartmouthrailriver.co.uk; Torbay Rd, Paignton; adult/child return £17.50/10.50; ☺ 4-9 trains daily mid-Feb–Oct) Chugging from seaside Paignton to the beautiful banks of the River Dart, these vintage trains roll back the years to the age of steam. The 7-mile, 30-minute journey puffs past Goodrington Sands, stopping at Greenway Halt (near Agatha Christie's former home), then the village of Kingswear, where ferries shuttle across to picturesque Dartmouth.

The service is run by the Dartmouth Steam Railway & Riverboat Company (p313). It operates a wealth of other trips, including coastal cruises and excursions on a paddle steamer; see the website for a full round-up.

🛏 Sleeping

Alf Resco B&B ££
(☑ 01803-835880; www.cafealfresco.co.uk; Lower St; d from £90-105, apt £125; 🛜) Not content with providing some of the town's yummiest food, Alf's also offers a couple of cosy rooms, bunk beds in the 'Crew's Quarters' and the self-contained 'Captain's Cabin', squeezed in under the rafters with all the atmosphere of a ship's cabin (lanterns, panelled walls, watery views and all).

Dartmouth Boutique B&B B&B ££
(☑ 01803-834553; www.thedartmouthbandb.co.uk; 7 Church Rd; d £95-155; **P** 🛜) Although set high on one of Dartmouth's steeply sloping streets, this exquisite B&B is only a 15-minute walk into the town centre. The gradient offers extensive views across the hills and out to sea. Bedrooms are light-filled and luxurious, all with swish fabrics, baroque flourishes and subtle tones.

★ **Bayard's Cove** B&B £££
(☑ 01803-839278; www.bayardscoveinn.co.uk; 27 Lower St; d £165-175, f £185-305; 🛜) Crammed with character and bursting with beams, Bayard's Cove has you sleeping within whitewashed stone walls and among huge church candles. The lavish family suites feature grand double beds and kids' cabins, complete with bunk beds and tiny TVs; there are even estuary glimpses from the rooms.

🍴 Eating

★ **Alf Resco** CAFE £
(☑ 01803-835880; www.cafealfresco.co.uk; Lower St; mains from £6; ☺ 7am-2pm; 🛜) This indie cafe is the preferred hang-out for a variety of discerning Dartmouthians, from yachties to families, tourists and riverboat crews. The same menu is available throughout the day: copious all-day breakfasts, toasties and chunky baguettes are the mainstays, and the coffee is great.

Crab Shell SANDWICHES £
(1 Raleigh St; sandwiches £5; ☺ 10.30am-2.30pm Apr-Dec) Sometimes all you want is a classic crab sarnie, and this little establishment will happily oblige: the shellfish is landed on the quay a few steps away. Salmon, lobster and mackerel butties also available.

Rockfish SEAFOOD ££
(☑ 01803-832800; www.therockfish.co.uk; 8 South Embankment; mains £10-18; ☺ noon-9.30pm) At the Dartmouth outpost of award-winning

chef Mitch Tonks' five-strong bistro chain, seafood is firmly the speciality, and the weathered boarding and maritime decor fit right in along Dartmouth's streets. The fish and chips are delicious.

★ **Seahorse** SEAFOOD £££
(☎01803-835147; www.seahorserestaurant.co.uk; 5 South Embankment; mains £23-34; ☺noon-2.30pm & 6-9.30 Tue-Sat) What celebrity chef Rick Stein is to Cornwall, Mitch Tonks is to Devon – a seafood supremo, with a clutch of restaurants across the county. The Seahorse is the original, and the best: a classic fish restaurant where the just-landed produce is roasted over open charcoals. Leather banquettes, wood floors and a wine wall give it a French-bistro feel. Book ahead.

ⓘ Information

Dartmouth Visitor Centre (☎01803-834224; www.discoverdartmouth.com; Mayor's Ave; ☺10.30am-2.30pm Mon-Sat) Lots of information on Dartmouth and the South Hams is available at the town's small tourist office, in a standalone building beside Mayor's Ave car park.

ⓘ Getting There & Away

BUS

Plymouth Stagecoach bus 3 (£7.30, 2½ hours, hourly Monday to Saturday) travels via Kingsbridge. On Sunday there are only two **buses** (South Embankment) that travel as far as Kingsbridge (£7, one hour).

Totnes Stagecoach bus X64 (£3.70, 50 minutes, every two hours Monday to Saturday, two Sunday) heads to Totnes and then continues to Exeter (£6.60, two hours).

FERRY

Several ferries run from Dartmouth's waterfront.

Castle Ferry (www.dartmouthcastleferry. co.uk; adult/child return £5/3; ☺10am-4.45pm Easter-Oct) Runs to Dartmouth Castle.

Dartmouth–Dittisham Ferry (☎01803-882811; www.greenwayferry.co.uk; adult/child return £8.50/6.50; ☺Easter-Oct) Shuttles upriver to the quaint village of Dittisham.

Dartsmouth–Kingswear Higher Ferry (☎07866 531687; www.dartmouthhigherferry. com; car/pedestrian one-way £5.60/60p; ☺6.30am-10.50pm Mon-Sat, from 8am Sun) Carries cars and pedestrians across the estuary every six minutes, enabling you to avoid the town's narrow streets.

Dartmouth–Kingswear Lower Ferry (www. southhams.gov.uk; per car/pedestrian £5/1.50; ☺7.10am-10.45pm) The town's oldest ferry

service, in business since the 1300s. It's a floating platform that's pulled by a tug moored alongside.

Greenway Ferry (☎01803-882811; www. greenwayferry.co.uk; adult/child return £8.50/6.50; ☺5-8 ferries daily mid–Mar-Oct) Boats to Greenway and on to Dittisham, plus scenic river cruises.

TRAIN

The Dartmouth Steam Railway links Kingswear and Paignton. The nearest mainline connections are from Totnes.

Totnes & Around

POP 8041

Totnes has such a reputation for being alternative that local jokers wrote 'twinned with Narnia' under the town sign. For decades famous as Devon's hippie haven, ecoconscious Totnes also became Britain's first 'transition town' in 2005, when it began to wean itself off a dependence on oil. Sustainability aside, Totnes boasts a tempting vineyard, a sturdy Norman castle and a mass of fine Tudor buildings, and is the springboard for a range of outdoor activities.

◉ Sights & Activities

★ **Sharpham Wine & Cheese** WINERY
(☎01803-732203; www.sharpham.com; vineyard £2.50; ☺10am-6pm May-Sep, to 5pm Mar & Apr, to 3pm Mon-Sat Oct-Dec; ℗) Three miles south of Totnes off the A381, this renowned vineyard is chiefly known for its crisp, sparkling white wines, as well as its delicious cheeses. Perched above the meandering River Dart, it's become one of the UK's best-known winemakers. You can explore the vine-covered slopes solo (£2.50), followed by a wine and/or cheese tasting in the shop (£7 and £3 respectively), or plump for the full guided tour (£20, 3pm Saturday and Sunday, April to September).

Dartington Estate HISTORIC SITE
(☎01803-847000; www.dartington.org; ☺gardens dawn-dusk, visitor centre 9am-5pm; ℗) FREE Henry VIII gave this pastoral 324-hectare estate to two of his wives (Catherines Howard and Parr). For many years it was home to the town's art college; now the 14th-century manor house hosts events, including renowned classical-music and literature festivals. There's also an art-house cinema, shops, a decent pub and B&B accommodation. The grounds are also worth exploring. It's about 2 miles northwest of Totnes.

Totnes Castle
CASTLE

(EH; ☎01803-864406; www.english-heritage.org.uk; Castle St; adult/child £4.30/2.60; ◷10am-6pm Apr-Sep, to 5pm Oct, to 4pm Sat & Sun Nov-Mar) High on a hilltop above town, Totnes' castle is among the best-preserved examples of a Norman 'motte and bailey' castle (a round keep sitting on a raised earthwork). The views over Totnes's rooftops and the South Hams beyond are captivating, but the interior is largely empty. Look out for the medieval toilet (but don't use it).

★ Dynamic Adventures
ADVENTURE SPORTS

(☎01803-862725; www.dynamicadventurescic.co.uk; Park Rd, Dartington Hall) The superb activities on offer include canoeing and kayaking (half/full day £35/70) and sea kayaking (from £75), as well as caving (half day £35), rock climbing and archery (both per hour £15). Booking is required.

It's 2 miles northwest of Totnes on the Dartington Estate.

★ Totnes Kayaks
KAYAKING

(☎07799 403788; www.totneskayaks.co.uk; The Quay, Stoke Gabriel; single kayak half/full day £30/40; ◷10am-5pm Fri-Sun Apr-Jun, Sep & Oct, daily Jul & Aug) The River Dart looks pretty enough from the bank, but to see it at its best, you really need to get out on the water. Five miles southeast of Totnes in Stoke Gabriel, this friendly outdoors company rents out single and double sit-on-top kayaks for you to explore the river – but it's worth ringing ahead to check on tide times.

🛏 Sleeping

★ Dartington Hall
B&B ££

(☎01803-847150; www.dartington.org; Dartington Estate; s/d from £55/119; 🅿�{🛜}) 🅿 The wings of this idyllic ancient manor house have been carefully converted into rooms that range from heritage themed to deluxe modern. Ask for one overlooking the grassy, cobble-fringed courtyard, and settle back for a truly tranquil night's sleep. The estate is about 1.5 miles from Totnes.

★ Cott Inn
PUB ££

(☎01803-863777; www.cottinn.co.uk; Cott Lane, Dartington; s/d £100/125; 🅿) The 14th-century Cott is pretty much the perfect English inn: rambling, thatched and lined with beams. Rooms blend undulating walls with artfully distressed furniture, crisp eco-linens, and lilac and olive tones. Ingredients for the classy gastro pub fare are sourced entirely locally –

lamb from Dartington, potatoes from Kingsbridge and crab from Salcombe.

✗ Eating
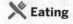

Pie Street
PIES £

(☎01803-868674; www.piestreet.co.uk; 26 High St; pies £9.95; ◷11.30am-6pm Mon, to 8pm Tue-Thu, to 9pm Fri & Sat, noon-4pm Sun) 'British soul food', runs the slogan here – in other words, poshed-up pies, served with your choice of mash or chips, and lashings of gravy. You can go classic with steak-and-ale or chicken, ham and leek, or plump for something more unusual: an Anglo-Indian curry pie or veggie homity pie, perhaps. Sit down in the bistro-style interior, or takeaway.

Willow
VEGETARIAN £

(☎01803-862605; 87 High St; mains £6-10; ◷10am-5pm Mon-Sat, plus 6.30-9pm Wed, Fri & Sat; 🅿) 🅿 Totnes simply wouldn't be Totnes if it didn't have its own veggie-friendly, wholefood hang-out – and Willow has occupied that slot handsomely for many a year. Inside, it's suitably hippy-chic, and the menu is full of quiches, pies, moussakas, salads and soups – many of which are vegan and/or gluten-free.

★ Riverford Field Kitchen
MODERN BRITISH ££

(☎01803-762074; https://fieldkitchen.riverford.co.uk; Wash Farm; 3-course lunch/dinner £23.50/27.50; ◷sittings 12.30pm Mon-Sat, noon & 3.30pm Sun, 7pm most evenings; 🅿) 🅿 This ecofriendly, organic, plough-to-plate farm is where everyone wants to eat when they visit Totnes. It began as a food-box scheme, and has now branched out into a delightful barn bistro, where diners sit communally at long wooden tables and share dishes of the day. Rustic flavours rule: expect delicious salads, roast meats and imaginative veggie options. Bookings required.

Rumour
PUB FOOD ££

(☎01803-864682; www.rumourtotnes.com; 30 High St; mains £9-18; ◷noon-3pm Mon-Sat, 6-10pm daily; 🅿) 🅿 Rumour is a local institution – a narrow, cosy pub-restaurant with low lighting, local art and newspapers for reading. It's legendary for its pizzas (£9.50), but there's plenty to choose from, such as risottos, steaks, stews and fish of the day. The bar is open from 10am to 11pm.

🍸 Drinking

★ The Totnes Brewing Co
MICROBREWERY

(☎01803-849290; www.thetotnesbrewingco.co.uk; 59a High St; ◷5pm-midnight Mon-Thu, noon-midnight Fri-Sun) There are scores of craft beers to choose from at this trendy town hang-out, from Trappist-style wheat brews to imperial stouts, all with witty names (personal favourites: Hopless Romantic, Nutty Old England and Duck Medicine). It's no dark old dive – expect stripped wood and big glass windows looking out on to the high street.

Upstairs, the **Barrel House Ballroom** hosts live gigs.

Hairy Barista COFFEE

(☑ 07916-306723; coffee@thehairybarista.co.uk; 69 High St; coffee from £2; ⊙ 8am-5pm Mon-Sat, 9am-5pm Sun) Aeropress, cold-brew, V60, flat white or just plain-old espresso, the aptly named hairy barista (aka Roe Yekutiel) will oblige – his little shop has become the town's go-to place for speciality coffee. There are cakes and pastries on offer too, but the space is a little cramped inside (and mind the step on the way in!).

ℹ Getting There & Around

BOAT

Boats shuttle downriver to Dartmouth with the **Dartmouth Steam Railway & Riverboat Company** (☑ 01803-555872; www.dartmouthrailriver.co.uk; North Embankment).

BUS

Totnes is well serviced by bus.

Exeter Stagecoach Bus X64 (£6.10, 50 minutes, six or seven daily Monday to Saturday, two Sunday). Continues to Kingsbridge and Dartmouth in the opposite direction.

Plymouth Stagecoach Gold (£3.60, one hour, half-hourly Monday to Saturday, hourly Sunday).

Torquay Stagecoach Gold (£3.50, 45 minutes, half-hourly Monday to Saturday, hourly Sunday).

TRAIN

Trains run at least hourly to Exeter (£7, 35 minutes) and Plymouth (£6.50, 30 minutes).

The quaint **South Devon Steam Railway** (☑ 01364-644370; www.southdevonrailway.co.uk; adult/child return £15/9; ⊙ Apr-Oct) chuffs to Buckfastleigh, on the edge of Dartmoor.

Plymouth & Around

POP 258,000

For decades, some have dismissed Plymouth as sprawling and ugly, pointing to its architectural eyesores and sometimes palpable poverty. But the arrival of high-profile chefs Hugh Fearnley-Whittingstall and Mitch Tonks and an ongoing waterfront regeneration begs a rethink. Yes the city, an important Royal Naval port, suffered heavy WWII bomb damage, and even today it can appear more gritty than pretty, but Plymouth is also packed with possibilities for visitors: swim in an art deco lido, tour a gin distillery, learn to SUP, kayak and sail, roam an aquarium, take a boat trip across the bay, then see a top-class theatre show and party till dawn. And the aces in the pack? The history-rich Barbican district and Plymouth Hoe – a cafe-dotted, wide, grassy headland offering captivating views of a boat-studded bay.

History

Plymouth's history is dominated by the sea. The first recorded cargo left in 1211, and by the late 16th century it was the port of choice for explorers and adventurers. It has waved off Sir Francis Drake, Sir Walter Raleigh, the fleet that defeated the Spanish Armada, the pilgrims who founded America, Charles Darwin, Captain Cook and countless boats carrying emigrants to Australia and New Zealand.

During WWII Plymouth suffered horrendously at the hands of the German Luftwaffe – more than 1000 civilians died in the Blitz, which reduced the city centre to rubble. The 21st century has brought regeneration to waterfront areas, the £200-million Drake Circus shopping centre, and a growing university, bringing with it a burst of new buildings and 30,000 students to the heart of town.

◉ Sights

★ **Plymouth Hoe** LANDMARK

Francis Drake supposedly spied the Spanish fleet from this grassy headland overlooking Plymouth Sound (the city's wide bay); the bowling green on which he continued to finish his game after the sighting was probably where his **statue** (Plymouth Hoe) now stands. The wide villa-backed promenade features scores of war memorials.

Smeaton's Tower LIGHTHOUSE

(☑ 01752-304774; www.plymhearts.org; The Hoe; adult/child £4/2; ⊙ 10am-5pm) The red-and-white stripes of Smeaton's Tower rise from the middle of the Plymouth Hoe headland. For an insight into past lighthouse keepers'

Plymouth

Plymouth

lives, head up 93 stone steps and through the circular rooms to emerge on to an open-air platform for stunning views of the city, Dartmoor and the sea.

The whole 21m structure previously stood on the Eddystone Reef, 14 miles offshore, and was transferred to its current site, brick by brick, in the 1880s.

★**Barbican** AREA
(www.barbicanwaterfront.com) For a glimpse of ancient Plymouth, head down to this historic harbour area, where part-cobbled streets are lined with Tudor and Jacobean buildings, and old dockside warehouses have been turned into bars, restaurants and art galleries. It's also famous as the point from which the Pilgrim Fathers set sail for the New World in 1620: the **Mayflower Steps** (Sutton Harbour) mark the approximate spot.

The original passenger list for the *Mayflower* can be seen on the side of **Island House** (Sutton Harbour) nearby. The steps also commemorate Captain James Cook's 1768 voyage of discovery and the first emigrant ships to depart for Australia and New Zealand.

These days the Barbican is one of the city's liveliest areas – not to mention one of its prettiest. Drink it all in, me hearties.

★**Plymouth Gin Distillery** DISTILLERY
(✆01752-665292; www.plymouthdistillery.com; 60 Southside St; tours £7) This heavily beamed distillery has been concocting gin since 1793, making it the oldest working producer of the spirit in England. Four to six tours per day thread past the stills and take in a tutored tasting before retiring to the beautiful Grade II–listed cocktail bar for a complimentary G&T.

★**Plymouth Fish Market** MARKET
(✆01752-204738; www.plymouthfisheries.co.uk; Sutton Harbour) Around 60,000 tonnes of fish pass through this market, making it the second biggest by volume in England after London's Billingsgate. It's an amazing sight when it's in full flow. Tours can be arranged with the harbourmaster (p.bromley@sutton-harbour.co.uk). There are also regular Fish in Sutton Harbour (FISH) guided tours with a local fisher; check www.facebook.com/suttonharbour for the latest.

★**National Marine Aquarium** AQUARIUM
(✆0844 893 7938; www.national-aquarium.co.uk; Rope Walk; year passes adult/child £16.95/12.95; ◷10am-5pm) The UK's biggest – and perhaps best – aquarium is lodged beside the Barbican harbour. There's a huge amount to see, but the highlight is the impressive Atlantic Ocean tank, the deepest in the UK, with over 2 million litres of water and a population of sand tiger sharks, lemon sharks, barracuda and rays, as well as a replica of a WWII Walrus Seaplane. Other zones explore the Great

Barrier Reef, and local habitats including Eddystone Reef and Plymouth Sound.

Tickets are 10% cheaper if you buy in advance online, and remain valid for a year's entry.

Activities

★**Tinside Lido** SWIMMING
(✆01752-261915; www.everyoneactive.com/centre/tinside-lido; Hoe Rd; adult/child £4.50/3.50; ◷noon-6pm Mon-Fri, from 10am Sat, Sun & school holidays late May–early Sep) This glorious outdoor swimming pool is one of Plymouth's best-loved sights. Nestled beneath the Hoe with views on to Plymouth Sound, it's a gem of the jazz age: built in 1935, with sleek white curves and candy-striped light- and dark-blue tiles – like something straight out of an F Scott Fitzgerald novel. Tinside's saltwater is unheated, but there are hot showers.

Mount Batten Centre WATER SPORTS
(✆01752-404567; www.mount-batten-centre.com; 70 Lawrence Rd) Set on the Mount Batten peninsula and linked to the Barbican by a **passenger ferry** (✆07930 838614; www.mountbattenferry.co.uk; Barbican Pontoon; adult/child return £3/1), this centre offers a range of water-sports tuition, including two-hour taster sessions in sit-on-top kayaks (£19), stand-up paddleboarding and sailing (£20).

★**Plymouth Boat Trips** BOATING
(✆01752-253153; www.plymouthboattrips.co.uk; Barbican Pontoon) The pick of this firm's trips is the **Cawsand Ferry**, a 30-minute blast across the bay to the quaint, pub-packed Cornish fishing villages of Kingsand and Cawsand (adult/child return £8/4, six daily) from Easter to October. Year-round, one-hour excursions head around Plymouth's dockyards and naval base (adult/child £8.50/5). There is also a combination cruise including entry to **Mount Edgcumbe** (✆01752-822236; www.mountedgcumbe.gov.uk; Cremyll; adult/child £7.20/3.75; ◷11am-4.30pm Sun-Thu Mar-Sep).

Festivals

★**British Fireworks Championships** FIREWORKS
(www.britishfireworks.co.uk; ◷mid-Aug) Over two nights in mid-August, six professional companies battle it out for the title, with three firms each staging 10-minute displays nightly. It's hugely popular, drawing tens of

ROYAL WILLIAM YARD

In the 1840s this imposing complex of waterfront warehouses supplied stores for countless Royal Navy vessels. Today it's home to sleek apartments, a clutch of galleries and shops, and a cluster of restaurants and bars, including the excellent social enterprise bakery, **Column Bakehouse** (☑01752-395137; www.columnbakehouse.org; Ocean Studios, Royal William Yard; dishes £4-8; ☺9am-4pm Tue-Wed, to 5pm Thu-Sat, 10am-4pm Sun) and the elegant Vignoble (p317) wine bar.

It's an atmospheric spot; roaming past a former slaughterhouse, bakery, brewery and cooperage underlines just how big the supplies operation was.

The yard is 2 miles west of the city centre. Hop on bus 34 (£1.30, nine minutes, half-hourly) or, better still, catch the hourly **ferry** (☑07979 152008; www.royalwilliamyard. com/getting-here/by-waterbus; Barbican Pontoon; one-way adult/child £3/2; ☺10am-5pm May-Sep). A 10-minute walk north of the yard, the **Cremyll Ferry** (☑01752-822105; www. cremyll-ferry.co.uk; Admirals Hard; adult/child return £3/1.50; ☺half-hourly) chugs across the Tamar to Cornwall, to the coast walks of the Mount Edgcumbe estate.

thousands of people to Plymouth's waterfront amid a carnival atmosphere.

🛌 Sleeping

Rusty Anchor
B&B £

(☑01752-663924; www.therustyanchor-plymouth.co.uk; 30 Grand Pde; s/d £40/50) One of a string of B&Bs along Grand Pde, this cute little town house makes a cosy Plymouth base. Decorative driftwood and shells lend this relaxed B&B a flavour of the sea; four rooms have views of Plymouth Sound's wide waters. Owner Jan will try to meet your breakfast requests – be that kippers, pancakes or homemade rolls.

⭐ St Elizabeth's House
BOUTIQUE HOTEL ££

(☑01752-344840; www.stelizabeths.co.uk; Longbrook St, Plympton St Maurice; d £129-149; P🐾) Prepare to be pampered. In this 17th-century manor house turned boutique bolthole, free-standing slipper baths, oak furniture and Egyptian cotton grace the rooms; the suites feature palatial bathrooms and private terraces. The only drawback is its out-of-town location: it's in the suburb-village of Plympton St Maurice, 5 miles east of Plymouth.

Imperial
HOTEL ££

(☑01752-227311; www.imperialplymouth.co.uk; Lockyer St; s £61-91, d £91-122, f £121-141; P🐾) The pick of the small hotels on Plymouth Hoe is in this 1840s town house that once belonged to an admiral. A few heritage features remain but it has been thoroughly updated and feels quite modern, with beige carpets, wooden furniture and the odd bit of Orla Kiely wallpaper.

Sea Breezes
B&B ££

(☑01752-667205; www.plymouth-bedandbreakfast.co.uk; 28 Grand Pde; s £55-65, d £85-95, f £110-125; 🐾) With its sea-themed colours and pristine rooms Sea Breezes is a supremely comfortable place to stay. Add a charming owner, cast-iron bedsteads, old-fashioned alarm clocks and sea views, and you have a winner. The two sets of interconnecting rooms are particularly good for families.

Premier Inn Sutton Harbour
HOTEL ££

(☑0871 527 8882; www.premierinn.com; 28 Sutton Rd; r £70-100; P❄🐾🐕) Yes, it's part of a national chain, and decor is corporate and functional, but it's still an eminently practical sleep. To the cream walls and MDF furniture you can add a prime location overlooking Sutton Harbour.

It won't be your most memorable night's sleep, but setting trumps posh sometimes.

🍴 Eating

⭐ Jacka Bakery
BAKERY £

(☑01752-264645; 38 Southside St; snacks £3-8; ☺9am-4pm Wed-Mon) Quietly groovy, fantastically friendly and extremely good at baking things, Jacka is much loved by locals. It excels at immense croissants, cinnamon swirls and three type of sourdough loaves. The 'on toast' options are fabulous – the wild-mushroom, tarragon and fried-egg version is something very fine indeed.

⭐ Supha's Street Emporium
ASIAN £

(☑01752-228513; www.suphas.co.uk; Unit 1, E Quay House; dishes small £2.95-4.95, large £7.50-15.95; ☺noon-9pm Tue & Sun, to 10pm Wed-Sat; 🐾) An exotic addition to the up-and-coming area around Sutton Harbour, this joint specialises in spicy, flavourful Thai-style street food: classic Massaman curry, steamed sea bass, *larb* (a meat salad) and papaya salads, and much more. Whether you opt for small street plates, platters to share or mix-and-match your curries, you'll enjoy authentic, delicious flavours. It's strong on veggie options too.

Harbourside Fish & Chips   FISH & CHIPS £
(www.barbicanfishandchips.co.uk; 35 Southside St; takeaway fish & chips from £5.65; ⊙11am-10pm, to 11pm Fri & Sat) This top-notch chip shop is renowned across the city – there are often queues out the door at peak times. If you're planning on eating al fresco, be warned – Plymouth's dive-bombing seagulls have a nasty habit of snatching your meal, so a better plan is to accompany your meal with a pint in the Dolphin next door.

★ Rock Salt   MODERN BRITISH ££
(☑01752-225522; www.rocksaltcafe.co.uk; 31 Stonehouse St; 2-/3-course lunch menu £12/16, dinner £16.95-24.95; ⊙10am-3pm & 5-9.30pm; 🐾) Local boy Dave Jenkins has worked wonders at his little brasserie, which has deservedly built up a loyal local following and scooped up foodie awards. It suits all times of day: tuck into fluffy American pancakes for breakfast, enjoy a light artichoke risotto for lunch and savour confit beef blade for dinner. A local diner par excellence.

Barbican Kitchen   MODERN BRITISH ££
(☑01752-604448; www.barbicankitchen.com; 60 Southside St; 2-/3-course lunch menu £13/16, mains £11-17.95; ⊙noon-2.30pm & 6-9.30pm Mon-Sat) Plymouth's chef brothers Chris and James Tanner have brightened up the Barbican with their relaxed-but-refined bistro at the Plymouth Gin Distillery (p315). It's a quirky, fun place to dine – turquoise banquettes and pop-art pics of Yoda and Bruce Lee on the walls – and the food is fresh and contemporary.

 Drinking & Nightlife

Like any Royal Navy city, Plymouth has a more than lively nightlife. Union St is clubland, Mutley Plain and North Hill have a studenty vibe, and the Barbican has more restaurants amid the bars. All three areas can get rowdy, especially at weekends.

★ Dolphin   PUB
(☑01752-660876; 14 The Barbican; ⊙10am-11pm) This gloriously unreconstructed Barbican boozer is all scuffed tables, padded bench seats and an authentic, no-nonsense atmosphere. Feeling peckish? Get a fish-and-chip takeaway from Harbourside Fish & Chips two doors down, then settle in with your pint.

Be sure to check out the cheeky paintings by much-loved local artist (and one-time regular) Beryl Cook on the walls.

★ Annabel's   CLUB
(www.annabelscabaret.co.uk; 88 Vauxhall St; ⊙9pm-2am Thu, 8.30pm-3am Fri & Sat) Saucy performances come to the Barbican at this late-night cabaret-nightclub. It's great fun: the DJ sets and lounge-bar vibe are spot on, and you never quite know what the entertainment might be – burlesque or blues, comedy or country.

Bread & Roses   PUB
(☑01752-659861[]; www.breadandrosesplymouth. co.uk; 62 Ebrington St; ⊙4pm-1am Mon-Fri, noon-1am Sat, noon-11pm Sun; 🐾) Plymouth's arty crowd loves this characterful combo of hip boozer, social-enterprise visionary and cultural hub. Amid its Edwardian-meets-modern decor you'll find a good pint, occasional appearances by cool local bands, and lots of people hatching creative plans.

Vignoble   WINE BAR
(☑01752-222892; www.levignoble.co.uk; Royal William Yard; ⊙noon-11.30pm, to midnight Fri & Sat) A bijou hang-out where you can sample taster-sized glasses of your chosen vintages. It's at the Royal William Yard, 2 miles west of the city centre.

ℹ️ Information

Tourist Office (☑01752-306330; www. visitplymouth.co.uk; 3 The Barbican; ⊙9am-5pm Mon-Sat, 10am-4pm Sun Apr-Oct, 10am-4pm Mon-Sat Nov-Mar) Local leaflets aplenty, plus free accommodation-booking service and advance tickets for many attractions.

ℹ️ Getting There & Away

BUS

National Express services call at Plymouth's bus station (Mayflower St). They include the following.

Bristol £13 to £24, three hours, four to six daily

Exeter £7.60 to £12.70, one to 1½ hours, four daily

London £15.50 to £28.20, five to six hours, six daily

Penzance £8, 3¼ hours, five daily

Local services include the following.

Exeter Bus X38 (£7.50, 1¼ hours, six daily Monday to Friday, four on Saturday, two on Sunday).

Totnes Stagecoach Gold (£3.60, one hour, half-hourly Monday to Saturday, hourly on Sunday).

TRAIN

Services include the following.

Bristol £41.90, two hours, two or three hourly

Exeter £9.70, one hour, half-hourly

London Paddington £79.80, 3¼ hours, half-hourly

Penzance £10.70, two hours, half-hourly

Totnes £6.50, 30 minutes, half-hourly to hourly

Dartmoor National Park

Dartmoor (✆ 01822-890414; www.visitdartmoor. co.uk) is Devon's wild heart. Covering 368 sq miles, this vast national park feels like it's tumbled straight out of a Tolkien tome, with its honey-coloured heaths, moss-smothered boulders, tinkling streams and eerie granite hills (known locally as tors).

On sunny days, Dartmoor is idyllic: ponies wander at will and sheep graze beside the road. It makes for a cinematic location, used to memorable effect in Steven Spielberg's WWI epic *War Horse*. But when sleeting rain and swirling mists arrive, you'll understand why Dartmoor is also the setting for Sir Arthur Conan Doyle's *The Hound of the Baskervilles:* the moor morphs into a bleak wilderness where tales of a phantom hound can seem very real indeed.

Dartmoor is an outdoor activities hot spot for hiking, cycling, riding, climbing and white-water kayaking, and has plenty of rustic pubs and country-house hotels where you can hunker down when the fog rolls in.

Activities

Dartmoor is a fantastic place to get out and be active, whether that means an afternoon hike or a horseback hack. For a broad-based overview, multiactivity providers such as **CRS Adventures** (✆ 01364-653444; www.crs adventures.co.uk; Holne Park; per person per day from £35) and Adventure Okehampton (p319) offer a range of ways to get your pulse racing.

Walking

Some 730 miles of public footpaths snake across Dartmoor's open heaths and rocky tors. The Ordnance Survey (OS) Pathfinder *Dartmoor Walks* (£12) guide includes 28 hikes of up to 9 miles, while its *Dartmoor Short Walks* (£8) focuses on family-friendly treks.

The 18-mile **Templer Way** is a two- to three-day stretch from Haytor to Teignmouth, while the **West Devon Way** forms a 36-mile trek linking Okehampton and Plymouth. The 95-mile **Dartmoor Way** circles from Buckfastleigh in the south, through Moretonhampstead, northwest to Okehampton and south through Lydford to Tavistock. The 117-mile **Two Moors Way** runs from Wembury on the south Devon coast, across Dartmoor and Exmoor to Lynmouth, on the north coast.

Be prepared for Dartmoor's notoriously fickle weather, and carry a map and a compass – many trails are not waymarked. The Ordnance Survey (OS) Explorer 1:25,000 map No 28, *Dartmoor* (£9), is the most comprehensive and shows park boundaries and Ministry of Defence firing-range areas.

★ **Moorland Guides**   HIKING
(www.moorlandguides.co.uk; adult/child from £2.50/free) A wide range of walks, from one-hour rambles to strenuous all-day hikes, on themes spanning heritage, geology, wildlife, myths and navigation. The walks leave from various locations – you'll be told where at the time of booking.

Cycling

Routes include the 11-mile **Granite Way** (part of NCN Route 27), which runs entirely off-road along a former railway line between Okehampton and Lydford. The 13-mile **Princetown & Burrator Mountain Bike Route** is a challenging moorland circuit along tracks and bridleways, taking in Princetown, Sheepstor village and Burrator Reservoir.

Tourist offices sell the *Dartmoor for Cyclists* map (£13).

Devon Cycle Hire   CYCLING
(✆ 01837-861141; www.devoncyclehire.co.uk; Sourton Down, near Okehampton; per day adult/child £16/12; ⏰ 9am-5pm Thu-Tue Apr-Sep, plus Wed school holidays) Located on the Granite Way (part of NCN Route 27). Will deliver bikes for a small charge.

Fox Tor Cafe Cycle Hire   CYCLING
(✆ 01822-890238; www.foxtorcafe.com/cycles; Fox Tor Cafe, Two Bridges Rd; per day adult/child £18.50/10; ⏰ 9am-5pm) This is handy for

Dartmoor National Park

Map labels: Bideford (28mi); Barnstaple (32mi); Okehampton; Okehampton Castle; Finch Foundry; Sticklepath; Cheriton Bishop; Tedburn St Mary; Granite Way; A30; Belstone Tor; Castle Drogo; Bodmin (28mi); A30; Sourton Down; Yes Tor; Gidleigh Park; Teign; Easton Cross; Granite Way; High Willhays; Scorhill; Chagford; Moretonhampstead; Exeter (6mi); White Lady; A386; Range Danger Area; Grey Wethers; Bovey; B3212; Tottiford Reservoir; A38; Lydford; West Devon Way; Warren House Inn; Grimspound; Hound Tor; Chudleigh; Lydford Gorge; Tavy; Postbridge; Haytor; Bovey Tracey; Dartmoor Way; Merrivale Stone Rows; Two Bridges; Widecombe-in-the-Moor; Dartmoor Way; Tavistock; Vixen Tor; Princetown; Brimpts Farm; Newton Abbot; A390; Walkham; Dartmeet; Poundsgate; Ashburton; Templer Way; B3212; Princetown & Burrator Mountain Bike Route; Plym; Buckfastleigh; Yelverton; Meavy; Dart; Buckland Abbey; Shaugh Prior; Yeo; A38; A385; Totnes; West Devon Way; Tamar; Erme; Two Moors Way; Paignton (1mi); Torquay (3mi); Plymouth; Plym; A38; Ivybridge; Plymouth Sound

the Princetown & Burrator Mountain Bike Route.

Horse Riding

A number of local stables across the moor cater to all abilities.

Babeny Farm   HORSE RIDING
(☑ 01364-631296; www.babenystables.co.uk; Poundsgate; rides per 30min/1hr £35/50; ⊙ Apr-Oct) A friendly, family-run farm that offers rides, lessons and 'Horse Holidays' (ie stabling) for £15 per horse, per night. It's 8 miles northwest of Ashburton.

Cholwell   HORSE RIDING
(☑ 01822-810526; www.cholwellridingstables.co.uk; near Mary Tavy; 1/2hr rides £23/42) A family-run stables that caters for novices and experts. It's near an old silver mine on the edge of the moor near the village of Mary Tavy, about halfway between Okehampton and Tavistock.

Climbing

Adventure Okehampton   OUTDOORS
(☑ 01837-53916; www.adventureokehampton.com; Klondyke Rd; per half/full day £25/50; ⊙ school holidays only) There are endless ways to get your pulse racing at this outdoors company, from standard activities like climbing, archery and kayaking to more unusual pastimes such as 'weasling' (squeezing through narrow gaps in Dartmoor's tors) and 'the Big Oke Abseil' (rappelling down from Meldon Viaduct to the Okement River).

ℹ️ Information

Dartmoor National Park Authority (DNPA; www.dartmoor.gov.uk) The main administrative body for Dartmoor has an excellent website with lots of information on sights and activities. It has also produced a few free audio guides to popular sights, including Princetown, Postbridge, Haytor and Bellever.

ℹ️ DRIVING ON DARTMOOR

Dartmoor's roads are gorgeous to drive, but large stretches have unfenced grazing, so you'll come across Dartmoor ponies, sheep and even cows in the middle of the road. Many sections have a 40mph speed limit. Car parks on the moor can be little more than lay-bys; their surface can be rough to very rough. Break-ins at isolated car parks are not unknown – keep valuables stashed out of sight.

DNPA Haytor (📞 01364-661904; www.dartmoor.gov.uk; off B3387; 🕙 10am-5pm Apr-Oct, to 3pm Thu-Sun Nov-Mar) National-park office 3 miles west of Bovey Tracey.

DNPA Postbridge (📞 01822-880272; www.dartmoor.gov.uk; car park beside B3212; 🕙 10am-5pm Apr–late Sep, to 3pm Thu-Sun late Sep–Mar) A small national-park visitor centre in Postbridge.

Higher Moorland Tourist Office (DNPA; 📞 01822-890414; www.dartmoor.gov.uk; Tavistock Rd; 🕙 10am-5pm Apr-Oct, to 3pm Tue & Thu-Sun Nov-Mar) In the same building as the visitor centre – the once-grand Duchy Hotel.

Visit Dartmoor (www.visitdartmoor.co.uk) Dartmoor's official tourism site has information on accommodation, activities, sights, events and more.

ℹ️ Getting There & Around

It is possible to get around Dartmoor by bus; however, services can be infrequent, and some are very seasonal.

Tourist offices stock bus timetables; Traveline South West (www.travelinesw.com) is a good online resource.

Bus 98 (one daily Monday to Saturday) Operated by Target Travel, this is the only regular bus into the centre of the moor. It runs from Tavistock to Princetown, Two Bridges and Postbridge, then circles back to Yelverton. A couple of afternoon buses only go as far as Princetown and back.

Bus 173 (five daily Monday to Saturday) Run by Dartline Coaches, this service goes from Exeter to Chagford, with two buses a day continuing to Moretonhampstead.

Bus 1 (four per hour Monday to Saturday, hourly Sunday) This Stagecoach service shuttles from Plymouth to Tavistock, via Yelverton.

Bus 178 (one daily Monday to Saturday) Travels from Newton Abbot to Okehampton, via Bovey Tracey, Moretonhampstead and Chagford. Operated by Country Bus.

Bus 113 (one daily Monday to Friday) Country Bus from Tavistock to Trago Mills, stopping at Yelverton, Princetown, Two Bridges, Ashburton and Newton Abbot.

Bus 6A (four per day Monday to Saturday, one Sunday) Skirts the northern edge of the moor en route from Bude to Exeter, stopping in Okehampton.

Haytor Hoppa Bus 271 Runs Saturdays between late-May and mid-September only, providing four buses between Newton Abbot, Bovey Tracey, Haytor and Widecombe-in-the-Moor (daily fare £5).

Bus 23 (📞 07580 260683; 🕙 1st Sat of month) Minibus from Tavistock to Exeter, via Princetown, Postbridge, Two Bridges and Moretonhampstead. Runs on the first Saturday of the month only; book by phone.

Princetown

POP 1770

Set in the heart of the remote higher moor, Princetown is dominated by the grey, foreboding bulk of Dartmoor Prison, and on bad-weather days the town can have a remote, even bleak, feel. But it's also an evocative reminder of the harsh realities of moorland life and makes an atmospheric base for some excellent walks.

⊙ Sights

Higher Moorland Visitor Centre MUSEUM
(DNPA; 📞 01822-890414; Tavistock Rd; 🕙 10am-5pm Apr-Sep, to 4pm Mar & Oct, 10.30am-3.30pm Thu-Sun Nov-Feb) FREE At the tourist office–visitor centre, heritage displays include those on tin workings, gunpowder factories, ecology and legends – there's also a stunning time-lapse video.

The building used to be the Duchy Hotel; one former guest was Sir Arthur Conan Doyle, who went on to write *The Hound of the Baskervilles*. Dartmoor lore recounts that local man Henry Baskerville took the novelist on a carriage tour, and the brooding landscape he encountered, coupled with legends of huge phantom dogs, inspired the thriller.

Dartmoor Prison Museum MUSEUM
(📞 01822-322130; www.dartmoor-prison.co.uk; adult/child £3.50/2.50; 🕙 9.30am-4.30pm Mon-Thu & Sat, to 4pm Fri & Sun; 🅿️) In the early 1800s, Princetown's infamous jail was home to French and American prisoners of war. It became a convict jail in 1850, and today still houses around 640 inmates. Just up from the looming gates, this museum provides a chilling glimpse of life inside. Look out for

straitjackets, manacles, escape stories and the makeshift knives made by modern-day prisoners.

In 2015, it was announced that the prison was likely to close within the next 10 years.

🛏 Sleeping & Eating

Tor Royal Farm
B&B ££

(☎01822-890189; www.torroyal.co.uk; Tor Royal Lane, near Princetown; s £60, d £80-110; P🛜) An easygoing, country-cottage-styled farmhouse packed with lived-in charm. Heritage-style rooms (cream-and-white furniture, puffy bedspreads, easy chairs) are cosy, and the free afternoon tea of Victoria sponges, cupcakes and fancies galore is reason alone to stay here.

Two Bridges
HOTEL £££

(☎01822-892300; www.twobridges.co.uk; Two Bridges; r £140-240; P🛜) This is perhaps the definitive historic moorland hotel: polished wood panels, huge inglenook fireplaces, and a guest list that includes Wallis Simpson, Winston Churchill and Vivien Leigh. The Premier and Historic rooms are positively museum worthy, with massive wooden four-poster beds and antique furniture aplenty; cheaper rooms are heavy on the florals. It's 1.5 miles northeast of Princetown.

★ Prince of Wales
PUB, HOSTEL £

(☎01822-890219; Tavistock Rd; mains £10-18; ⊙11am-11pm; P🛜) Roaring fires, low ceilings, a friendly landlord – the Prince is the place where everyone pops in for a pint of home-brewed Jail Ale and a plate of something hot and filling.

B&B accommodation is also available (double rooms from £50), and there's a bargain bunkhouse, with unexpected luxuries including central heating and a drying room.

★ Fox Tor Cafe
CAFE £

(☎01822-890238; www.foxtorcafe.com; Two Bridges Rd; mains £5-12; ⊙9am-5pm Mon-Fri, 7.30am-6pm Sat, 7.30am-5pm Sun; 🛜) Known as FTC to locals, this friendly little cafe is a favourite for hearty breakfasts, doorstep sandwiches and massive chunks of cake, but it does more-filling fare, too, such as spicy chilli and mushroom stroganoff. On cold, wet Dartmoor days the two wood-burning stoves are particularly welcoming.

There's a basic bunkhouse (dorm beds £12) out the back, where hikers and cyclists stay. Fox Tor also hires out bikes (p318).

Postbridge & Around
POP 170

The quaint hamlet of Postbridge owes its popularity, and its name, to its medieval stone slab or clapper bridge: a 13th-century structure with four, 3m-long slabs propped up on sturdy columns of stacked stones. Walking the bridge takes you across the rushing East Dart; it's a picturesque spot to whip off your boots and plunge your feet into water that's quite possibly the coldest you've ever felt.

🛏 Sleeping & Eating

Brimpts Farm
B&B £

(☎0845 034 5968; www.brimptsfarm.co.uk; Dartmeet; sites per person £5, s/d/f £40/70/105; P) A beauty of a Dartmoor farm, as traditional as afternoon tea, and all the better for it. Choose from quaint, frilly B&B rooms, basic camping fields (£5 per tent) or a timber-and-aluminium camping pod (per night £30 to £35), all with bewitching moorland views. Hearty breakfasts, packed lunches and cracking cream teas. It's on the B3357, Two Bridges–Dartmeet road.

Dartmoor YHA
HOSTEL £

(Bellever; ☎0845 371 9622; www.yha.org.uk; dm/q £25/90; P🛜) A characterful former farm on the edge of a conifer plantation, with a huge kitchen, lots of rustic stone walls and cosy dorms. It also rents out bikes. It's a mile south of Postbridge.

ⓘ WARNING

The military uses three adjoining areas of Dartmoor as training ranges where live ammunition is employed. Tourist offices can outline these locations; they're also marked on Ordnance Survey (OS) maps. You're advised to check if the hiking route you're planning falls within a range; if it does, find out if firing is taking place at the time you plan to walk via the **Firing Information Service** (☎0800 458 4868; www.mod.uk/access). During the day, red flags fly at the edges of in-use ranges, while red flares burn at night. Even when there's no firing, beware of unidentified metal objects lying in the grass. Don't touch anything you find: note its position and report it to the **Commandant** (☎01837-650010).

Driving Tour
A Dartmoor Road Trip

START TAVISTOCK
END CASTLE DROGO
LENGTH 20 MILES; ONE DAY

Driving on Dartmoor is like being inside a feature film: compelling 360-degree views are screened all around. This scenic, west-to-east transmoor traverse sweeps up and through this wilderness, taking in a bleak prison, prehistoric remains, a rustic pub and a unique castle. Start by strolling among the fine 19th-century architecture of ❶ **Tavistock**, perhaps dropping by its Pannier Market to rummage for antiques. Next take the B3357 towards Princetown. It climbs steeply (expect ears to pop), crosses a cattle grid (a sign you're on the moor 'proper') and crests a hill to reveal swaths of honey-coloured tors. Soon you're at ❷ **Merrivale**. Park up on the right, just after the Dartmoor Inn, and stroll over the rise (due south) to discover a snaking stone row; a tiny stone circle and

a standing stone are just 100m further on. Back in the car, after a short climb, turn right towards Princetown, glimpsing the brooding bulk of Dartmoor Prison (you can't stop here; there's a better vantage point later). Call in at the ❸ **Dartmoor Prison Museum** (p320) to explore the jail's grim story. Cut through rugged ❹ **Princetown**, before picking up the B3212 towards Two Bridges; the ❺ **lay-by** immediately after you leave Princetown provides prime Dartmoor Prison views. As you follow signs for Moretonhampstead, an expansive landscape unfurls. At ❻ **Postbridge**, park and stroll over the 700-year-old bridge, then dangle hot feet in the cold River Dart. A few miles further on, the ❼ **Warren House Inn** makes an atmospheric spot for lunch. Around Lettaford take one of the signed, plunging lanes to ❽ **Chagford** to visit its quaint, thatch-dotted square. Scour some of its wonderfully old-fashioned shops, then head to ❾ **Castle Drogo** to explore a unique 1920s stately home.

★**Warren House Inn** PUB FOOD **££**
(☏ 01822-880208; www.warrenhouseinn.co.uk; near Postbridge; mains £9-15; ⊙ noon-8.30pm, bar 11am-11pm, shorter hours winter; ℗) Marooned amid miles of moorland, this Dartmoor institution exudes a hospitality only found in pubs in the middle of nowhere. A fire that's been burning (apparently) since 1845 warms stone floors, trestle tables and hikers munching on robust food; the Warreners Pie (local rabbit) is legendary. It's on the B3212, some 2 miles northeast of Postbridge.

Widecombe-in-the-Moor

POP 570

With its honey-grey buildings and imposing church tower, this is archetypal Dartmoor, down to the ponies grazing on the village green. The village is commemorated in the traditional English folk song 'Widecombe Fair', a reference to the traditional country pageant that takes place on the second Tuesday of September.

◎ Sights

St Pancras Church CHURCH
(☏ 01364-621334; The Green; ⊙ 8am-5pm) St Pancras' immense 40m tower has seen it dubbed the Cathedral of the Moor. Inside, search out the boards telling the fire-and-brimstone tale of the violent storm of 1638 – it knocked a pinnacle from the roof, killing several parishioners. As ever on Dartmoor, the Devil was blamed, said to be in search of souls.

⊨ Sleeping & Eating

Manor Cottage B&B **£**
(☏ 01364-621218; www.manorcottagedartmoor. co.uk; s £45-60, d £55-70; ℗ ☎) Roses climb around the doorway of this quaint, ancient, village-centre cottage. The best billet is the bedroom-bathroom suite at the top of a private spiral staircase. Breakfasts feature berry compote, local sausages and eggs freshly laid by the hens that cluck around outside.

★**Rugglestone Inn** PUB FOOD **££**
(☏ 01364-621327; www.rugglestoneinn.co.uk; mains £11; ⊙ noon-2pm & 6.30-9pm) Just one pint at this wisteria-clad pub is enough to make you want to drop everything and move to Dartmoor. It's a classic wood-beamed, low-ceilinged, old-fashioned village boozer, full of local characters and packed with history. There are lots of real ales on tap, and

the menu features filling dishes like pies, lasagne, quiches and potted crab.

ℹ Getting There & Away

Widecombe's bus service is severely limited – bus 672 stops once a week (Wednesday) en route to Buckfastleigh, Ashburton and Newton Abbot.

On summer Saturdays Widecombe is served by the Haytor Hoppa (daily fare £5), which sees four services running to Newton Abbot, Bovey Tracey and Haytor.

Chagford & Moretonhampstead

One of the prettiest of the Dartmoor villages, Chagford's stone-walled cottages, whitewashed buildings and thatched roofs are set around a quintessential village square. It's a handsome, vibrant little village, with some great places to sleep and eat, and there are views over the tors practically everywhere you look.

◎ Sights

★**Castle Drogo** HISTORIC BUILDING
(NT; ☏ 01647-433306; www.nationaltrust.org. uk/castle-drogo; near Drewsteignton; adult/child £11.60/5.80; ⊙ 11am-5pm mid-Mar–Oct; ℗) Three miles northeast of Chagford, this outlandish architectural flight of fancy was designed by Sir Edwin Lutyens for self-made food-millionaire Julius Drewe. Built between 1911 and 1931, it was intended to be a modern-day medieval castle, with all the comforts of a country house. Unfortunately, the property hasn't worn well – it's currently the focus of a massive six-year restoration project. Parts of the house remain open, though, and imaginative midrenovation displays include a scaffolding viewing tower.

⊨ Sleeping & Eating

Sparrowhawk HOSTEL **£**
(☏ 01647-440318; www.sparrowhawkbackpackers. co.uk; 45 Ford St; dm/d/f £19/40/50; ☎) ◈ One of only a few independent hostels on Dartmoor, Sparrowhawk is a reliable budget base. It's located in a converted house, with lots of wood and exposed stone, and a central courtyard ringed by rickety outbuildings. The accommodation is basic, but serviceable. There is a kitchen, too.

★**Gidleigh Park** HOTEL **£££**
(☏ 01647-432367; www.gidleigh.co.uk; Gidleigh; r £315-545, ste £750-1095, 3-course lunch/dinner

£65/125; ◷restaurant noon-2pm & 7-9pm; P 🛜) Without doubt Devon's grandest, fanciest and priciest hotel. At the end of a long private drive, the mock-Tudor house is an unashamedly opulent pamper pad: vast suites with wet-room showers, luxurious lounges with crackling fires, and a restaurant overseen by multiple-award-winning Chris Simpson. It's 2 miles west of Chagford.

★ Horse   GASTROPUB ££
(✆ 01647-440242; www.thehorsedartmoor.co.uk; 7 George St; mains £8-20; ◷12.30-2.30pm Tue-Sat, 6.30-9pm daily) You've got to love a place that bills itself as a 'pub and nosebag'. Despite the village location, this is a hip gastropub that wouldn't feel out of place in the big city: it serves simple, well-done food including tapas, mussels, home-cured tuna, chargrilled rib-eye and lots of pizzas.

Okehampton & Lydford

Okehampton huddles on the edge of an uninhabited tract of bracken-covered slopes and granite tors – the mind-expanding landscape known as the higher moor. The town has a staging-post feel, and its traditional shops and pubs are good places to prepare for a foray into the Dartmoor wilderness.

It's also near an impressive local landmark, the 46m-high Meldon Viaduct, a remnant of the old London and South Western Railway line that ran across the moor from 1874 to 1968.

The little village of Lydford is best known for the dramatic gorge that cuts through the landscape nearby en route to a beautiful waterfall. Once a strategic stronghold, its medieval castle has long since tumbled into ruins. It's 9 miles southwest of Okehampton.

◉ Sights

★ Lydford Gorge   WATERFALL
(NT; ✆ 01822-820320; www.nationaltrust.org.uk; adult/child £9.40/4.70; ◷10am-5pm mid-Mar–Oct, 11am-3.30pm Nov & Dec) This plunging gorge is the deepest in the southwest, and can be reached via a 1.5-mile rugged riverside hike past a series of bubbling whirlpools (including the fearsome Devil's Cauldron) to the thundering 30m-high White Lady waterfall. Not quite Niagara, but quite an impressive sight nonetheless.

Okehampton Castle   CASTLE
(EH; ✆ 01837-52844; www.english-heritage.org. uk; Castle Lodge; adult/child £4.80/2.90; ◷10am-

5pm Apr-Jun, Sep & Oct, to 6pm Jul & Aug) Okehampton's castle dates back to Norman times, and is strategically sited on top of a rocky escarpment. Later it became a sumptuous residence for Hugh Courtenay, Earl of Devon, who enlarged it into Devon's largest castle. It's now a picturesque ruin; little remains of the interior, but several of the stout exterior walls still stand, some careering off at improbable angles.

Finch Foundry   HISTORIC BUILDING
(NT; ✆ 01837-840046; www.nationaltrust.org.uk; Sticklepath; adult/child £7.10/3.55; ◷11am-5pm early Mar–Oct; P) A century ago, this dramatic building would have thundered to the sound of clanging hammers and grinding metal. It was one of the busiest tool factories in the southwest, turning out hundreds of chisels, knives, shears and scythes a day. Though it's not quite the industrial powerhouse of yesteryear, it's still a working forge, powered by three working watermills. You can drive or cycle here, or follow a 4-mile (3½-hour) walk east along the Tarka Trail from Okehampton.

🛏 Sleeping & Eating

Okehampton Bracken Tor YHA   HOSTEL £
(✆ 01837-53916; www.yha.org.uk; Saxongate; dm £27; ◷reception 8-10am & 5-10pm; P @ 🛜) Budget-conscious outdoors types love this one: a 100-year-old country house, set in 1.6-hectare grounds on the fringe of the higher moor. It also offers climbing, canoeing and bike hire. It's a mile south of Okehampton; be aware, there's another YHA hostel in Okehampton itself.

★ Dartmoor Inn   INN ££
(✆ 01822-820251; www.dartmoorinn.com; Moorside; d £115; ◷restaurant noon-2.30pm & 6.45-9pm Tue-Sat; P) It looks venerable, but behind the whitewashed exterior, this coaching inn is a thoroughly modern affair: light, bright and bang up to date. Most people stop for the superb food, such as slow-cooked oxtail and butterflied lamb rump (mains £12 to £20), but it's worth spending the night: rooms sparkle with Roberts radios, sleigh beds and posh linens.

ℹ Information

Tourist Office (✆ 01837-52295; www. everythingokehampton.co.uk; 3 West St; ◷10am-3pm Mon-Fri, to 1pm Sat Apr-Oct) Based at the Museum of Dartmoor Life.

Croyde & Braunton

POP 8130

Croyde has the kind of cheerful, chilled vibe you'd expect from its role as North Devon's surf central. The old world meets a new surfing wave here: thatched roofs peep out over racks of wetsuits; crowds of hip wave-riders sip beers outside 17th-century inns; and powerful waves line up to roll in towards acres of sand.

⊙ Sights & Activities

The water's hard to resist in Croyde. **Ralph's** (☑01271-890147; Hobbs Hill; surfboard & wetsuit hire per 4/24hr £12/18, bodyboard & wetsuit £10/15; ⊙9am-dusk mid-Mar–Dec) is among those hiring out wetsuits and surfboards. Lessons are provided by **Surf South West** (☑01271-890400; www.surfsouthwest.com; Croyde Burrows car park; per half/full day £35/65; ⊙late Mar–Oct) and **Surfing Croyde Bay** (☑01271-891200; www.surfingcroydebay.co.uk; Baggy Point; per half/full day £35/70).

★**Museum of British Surfing**   MUSEUM
(☑01271-815155; www.museumofbritishsurfing.org.uk; Caen St; adult/child £2/free; ⊙11am-3pm Wed-Mon Easter-Dec) Few museums are this cool. Vibrant surfboards and vintage wetsuits line the walls; sepia images catch your eye. The stories are compelling: 18th-century British sailors riding Hawaiian waves – England's 1920s homegrown surf pioneers. Here, heritage meets hanging ten.

Braunton Burrows   WILDLIFE RESERVE
(www.explorebraunton.org; near Braunton; P)
FREE The vast network of dunes here is the UK's largest. Paths wind past sandy hummocks, salt marshes, purple thyme, yellow hawkweed and pyramidal orchids. The burrows fringe an immense sweep of sandy beach, and were the main training area for American troops before D-Day. Mock landing craft are still hidden in the tufted dunes near the car park at its southern tip.

🛏 Sleeping & Eating

★**Baggy**   HOSTEL, B&B £
(☑01271-890078; www.baggys.co.uk; Baggy Point; dm/d from £33/110; �) Forget your crammed-in beds and wetsuit-strewn dorms – this hostel and surf lodge is light, bright and enormously inviting. It has a fine coastal location, and rooms are lovely, with lots of wood and minimal clutter. There's also a surfy cafe with an outside deck where you can eat breakfast while watching the waves roll in.

Ocean Pitch   CAMPSITE £
(☑07581 024348; www.oceanpitch.co.uk; Moor Lane; sites per 2 adults £30; ⊙mid-Jun–early Sep; P�) A surfers' favourite, set at the northern end of Croyde Bay with brilliant views of the breakers. If you don't feel like pitching a tent, you can rent a luxury sleeping pod (£99 per night, two-night minimum) or even a classic VW camper (£99 per night, two-night minimum).

Thatch   INN ££
(☑01271-890349; www.thethatchcroyde.com; 14 Hobbs Hill; d £60-100, f £120) A legendary venue among surfers, this cavernous, thatched pub's trendy bedrooms feature subtle creams, stripes and checks; the owners offer extra rooms above another pub and in the cottage opposite. The pick are at the nearby (quieter) Priory, where elegant beams frame exposed stone. The Thatch also serves famously hearty pub grub (mains from £10, from 8am to 10pm).

ℹ Information

Braunton Tourist Office (☑01271-816688; www.visitbraunton.co.uk; Caen St; ⊙10am-3pm Mon-Fri year-round, plus to 1pm Sat Jun-Dec) Inside the town's (free) museum.

Ilfracombe & Around

POP 11,510

If there's anywhere that sums up the faded grandeur of the British seaside, it's surely Ilfracombe. Framed by precipitous cliffs, elegant town houses, golf greens and a promenade strung with twinkling lights, it's a place that might seem pickled in a bygone age. But look beneath the surface and you'll find there's another side to Ilfracombe – it's a favourite hang-out for the artist Damien Hirst, who's added a controversial statue to the seafront, and it's now home to some top-notch eateries. Ilfracombe more than deserves a look.

⊙ Sights & Activities

★**Verity**   LANDMARK
(The Pier) Pregnant, naked and holding aloft a huge spear, Damien Hirst's 20m statue *Verity* towers above Ilfracombe's harbour mouth. On the seaward side her skin is peeled back, revealing sinew, fat and foetus. Critics say she detracts from the scenery; the

DON'T MISS

CLOVELLY

Clovelly (☑ 01237-431781; www.clovelly.co.uk; adult/child £7.50/4.50; ☉ 9am-6pm Jun-Sep, 9.30am-5pm Apr, May & Oct, 10am-4pm Nov-Mar; ℗) is the quintessential picture-postcard Devon village. Its cottages cascade down cliffs to meet a curving claw of a harbour that is lined with lobster pots backed by a deep-blue sea. A clutch of impossibly picturesque inns and B&Bs makes it hard to leave.

Clovelly is privately owned, and admission is charged at the hilltop visitor centre. The village's cobbled streets are so steep that cars can't cope, so supplies are brought in by sledge; you'll see these big bread baskets on runners leaning outside homes. Charles Kingsley, author of the children's classic *The Water Babies*, spent much of his early life in Clovelly – don't miss his former house, or the highly atmospheric fisher's cottage and the village's twin chapels.

Guided tours (☑ 07974 134701; www.clovellyvillagetours.co.uk; tours £5) provide interesting context on the village's buildings and history.

If you don't feel up to the steep uphill slog – or you're carting luggage to one of the village B&Bs – you can book a space back to the car park on the Land Rover taxi (£2).

---

artist says she's an allegory for truth and justice. Either way, she's drawing the crowds.

Ilfracombe Aquarium AQUARIUM
(☑ 01271-864533; www.ilfracombeaquarium.co.uk; The Pier; adult/child £4.75/3.75; ☉ 10am-3pm early Feb–late May & Oct, to 5pm or 5.45pm late May–Sep) Recreates aquatic environments from Exmoor to the Atlantic, via estuary, rock pool and harbour.

★**Tunnelsbeaches** SWIMMING
(☑ 01271-879882; www.tunnelsbeaches.co.uk; Bath Pl; adult/child £2.50/1.95; ☉ 10am-5pm Apr-Jun, Sep & Oct, to 7pm Jul & Aug) In 1823 hundreds of Welsh miners hacked, by hand, the four tunnels here out of solid rock. It was a remarkable feat. The tunnels lead to a strip of beach where you can plunge into the sea from Victorian tidal bathing pools.

🛏 Sleeping & Eating

Ocean Backpackers HOSTEL £
(☑ 01271-867835; www.oceanbackpackers.co.uk; 29 St James Pl; dm £18-20, d £45-50, f from £55-80; ℗@�) Brightly painted en-suite dorms, a convivial kitchen and free coffee lend this long-established indie hostel a laid-back vibe; the giant world map in the lounge has kick-started countless traveller tales. The doubles and family rooms are great value.

★**Norbury House** B&B ££
(☑ 01271-863888; www.norburyhouse.co.uk; Torrs Park; d £85-110, f £120-145; ℗�) Each of the rooms in this gorgeous guesthouse is done up in a different style: choose from pop art, art deco or contemporary chic. Fabulous

soft furnishings, a light-filled sitting room (complete with baby grand piano), charming hosts and cracking sea-and-town views seal the deal.

★**Olive Branch & Room** BISTRO £££
(☑ 01271-867831; www.thomascarrchef.co.uk; 56 Fore St; mains £21-23; ☉ 6.30-9pm Tue-Sat; �☑) Having trained under Michelin-starred chef Nathan Outlaw, Thomas Carr has earned his own star at this Ilfracombe bistro, showcasing his skills while championing local produce and seafood. For the full experience, go for the six- or eight-course taster menu (£75 and £95). Carr has also announced plans to open a seafood grill in the town: watch this space.

Rooms are available (doubles £115 to £130), and as you'd expect, breakfast is a treat.

Quay EUROPEAN ££
(☑ 01271-868090; www.11thequay.co.uk; 11 The Quay; mains £11-25; ☉ noon-2.30pm & 6-9pm daily Apr-Sep, Wed-Sat Oct-Mar) Ilfracombe's hippest harbourside hang-out by far is owned by artist Damien Hirst (he of the cut-in-half cows and pickled sharks). His creations line the walls, so you get to tuck into a cognac-laced lobster bisque or pan-roasted Exmoor chicken breast while studying models of his local statue *Verity* and, with delicious irony, fish in formaldehyde.

ℹ Information

Tourist Office (☑ 01271-863001; www.visit ilfracombe.co.uk; The Seafront; ☉ 9.30am-4.30pm Mon-Fri, 10.30am-4.30pm Sat & Sun

Easter-Oct, closed Sun Nov-Easter) Inside the seafront Landmark Theatre building.

ⓘ Getting There & Away

Bus 21/21A Runs to Barnstaple (£2.50, 40 minutes, half-hourly) via Braunton (£1.90, 30 minutes).

Bus 300 Runs to Lynmouth in July and August only (£3, two daily Monday to Friday).

CORNWALL

You can't get further west than the ancient Celtic kingdom of Cornwall (or Kernow, as it's known to Cornish speakers). Blessed with the southwest's wildest coastline and most breathtakingly beautiful beaches, this proudly independent peninsula has always marched to its own tune.

While the staple industries of old – mining, fishing and farming – have all but disappeared, Cornwall has since reinvented itself as one of the nation's creative corners. Whether it's exploring the space-age domes of the Eden Project, sampling the culinary creations of a celebrity chef or basking on a deserted beach, you're guaranteed to feel the itch of inspiration. Time to let a little Kernow into your soul.

Since 2006, Cornwall's historic mining areas have been designated a Unesco World Heritage Site, the Cornwall and West Devon Mining Landscape (www.cornish-mining.org.uk).

ⓘ Getting There & Away

It's pretty easy to get to Cornwall these days, although its far westerly location means travel times from most locations in the UK are long.

The county's main airport (p335) is just outside Newquay, with links to London Gatwick and other major cities. First Kernow bus A5 (26 minutes, every two hours Monday to Saturday, three on Sunday) runs from Newquay's bus station to Padstow, stopping at the airport en route. Taxis cost £15 to £25 from the town centre. Various seasonal destinations around the UK and Europe are also offered during summer.

The main train line from London Paddington runs through the centre of the county before terminating at Penzance, stopping at major towns in between.

The major road into Cornwall, the A30, is very prone to traffic jams in summer. The A38 from Plymouth over the Tamar Bridge into Cornwall is another alternative, but it's a more circuitous route. You are only required to pay the bridge toll when leaving Cornwall.

ⓘ Getting Around

Bus, train and ferry timetables can be found on the **Traveline South West** (☏ 0871 200 2233; www.travelinesw.com) website.

The useful website of Great Scenic Railways (www.greatscenicrailways.com) features online booking and timetables for Cornwall's regional railways.

BUS

Cornwall's main bus provider, **First Kernow** (☏ customer service 0845 600 1420, timetables 0871 200 2233; www.firstgroup.com/cornwall), operates the majority of services between major towns. The county's other big bus company, Western Greyhound, went into administration in 2015, and although some of its routes are now operated by smaller coach companies, many were axed, leaving some rural communities stranded without a regular bus service.

A one-day ticket covering all buses costs £12/6, but it's only slightly cheaper than the Ride Cornwall Ranger (adult/child/family £13/9.75/26), which also covers train travel.

Somewhat annoyingly, First has separate apps for timetable queries and for ticket purchases (mTickets). Currently, only one-day and multiday travel passes can be bought through its mTickets ticketing app.

TRAIN

Cornwall's main railway line follows the coast as far as Penzance, with branch lines to Gunnislake, Looe, Falmouth, St Ives and Newquay.

Most trains are provided by Great Western Railway (p235), although CrossCountry Trains (p235) also run through major stations.

Both companies have useful apps that enable timetable queries and e-ticket purchases.

TRANSPORT PASSES

Several passes cover public transport in Cornwall.

Ride Cornwall Ranger (adult/child/family £13/9.75/26) is the best all-round value covering a day's bus and train travel across Cornwall, and between Cornwall and Plymouth. The ticket can be purchased from train and bus stations, and from bus drivers, and is valid after 9am Monday to Friday and weekends.

The **Freedom of Devon & Cornwall Rover** (three days travel in seven days adult/child £49/24.50, eight days travel in 15 days £79/39.50) ticket is good value if you're using the train extensively through Devon and Cornwall.

There are also Day Ranger tickets for all of Cornwall's branch railway lines, as well as 'Two Together' and 'Groupsave' tickets for two and four adults travelling together.

If you have a permanent address in Cornwall (eg a holiday home), you can also buy a **Devon & Cornwall Railcard** (£10, www.railrover.org/railcards), which qualifies you for a 30% discount on off-peak train travel within Devon and Cornwall, including all the branch lines.

Bude

POP 9240

A scant few miles from the Devon border, Bude is a breezy seaside town with a bevy of impressive beaches, as well as a lovely seawater lido built in the 1930s. The town itself isn't much to look at, but the stunning coastline on its doorstep makes it worthy of a stop.

⊙ Sights & Activities

Bude has plenty of good beaches within easy reach of the town centre, but to reach the more out-of-the-way ones, you'll need to drive or hike along the coast path. Three miles south of town is **Widemouth Bay** (*wid*-muth), a broad, sandy beach great for both families and surfers. Two miles further is the shingly beach of **Millook**, followed by the dramatic cliffs around **Crackington Haven**.

Three miles north of town are the National Trust–owned **Northcott Mouth** and **Sandymouth**.

A mile further on is pebbly **Duckpool**, often quiet even in summer.

Raven Surf School   SURFING
(☑ 07860 465499; www.ravensurf.co.uk; per lesson £35) A reliable school run by Mike Raven, a former surfing champion. It also offers surf life-saving and instructor courses, and has accommodation in 'surf pods' (ecofriendly wooden cabins) and a campsite nearby.

Big Blue Surf School   SURFING
(☑ 01288-331764;   www.bigbluesurfschool.co.uk; per lesson £30) A recommended school that offers lessons mainly to beginner and intermediate surfers. Special lessons for surfers with disabilities, and a 'women's club' on Tuesday evenings and Saturday mornings are some of its main attractions. Look for the trailer in the Summerleaze beach car park.

⌸ Sleeping & Eating

Elements Hotel   HOTEL **££**
(☑ 01288-275066; www.elements-life.co.uk; Marine Dr; s £69, d £89-130, f from £130; ▣ 🛜 ⅏ ▨) This hotel has a super clifftop position, but looks a bit bland and boxy from the outside. Fear not: inside it sports soothing sea colours, swirly patterned fabrics, big coastal views and thoughtful mod cons such as Bluetooth speakers, Playstations in the family rooms and a Finholme sauna. Surf packages are offered by Raven Surf School.

Hebasca   DESIGN HOTEL **££**
(☑ 01288-352361;   www.hebasca.co.uk;   Downs View; r £84-235; ▣ 🛜) Boutique-on-a-budget best describes this hotel, a sister establishment to **Tommy Jacks** (☑ 01288-356013; www.tommyjacks.co.uk; Crooklets Beach; r £70-165; ▣ 🛜 ⅏) at Crooklets beach. It's designed for grown-ups, with pleasant rooms blending earth tones and technicolour upholstery, bright patterned cushions and plenty of Scandi-style slate and wood. They feel efficient rather than out-and-out elegant. Downstairs there's a grill restaurant and cocktail bar, with cow-print furnishings and pop-art murals of fishermen.

★ **Beach at Bude**   HOTEL **£££**
(☑ 01288-389800;   www.thebeachatbude.co.uk; Summerleaze Cres;   r incl breakfast £179-254; ▣ 🛜 ⅏) This lovely hotel steals the show in practically every category: space, style, welcome and definitely view. It has a fine position behind Summerleaze beach, and the rooms are really attractive, with pale wood furniture, Lloyd Loom chairs and peach-and-taupe colour schemes conjuring the feel of a New England beach cabin. The **restaurant** (mains £14 to £24) is reliably good, too.

Life's a Beach   CAFE **££**
(☑ 01288-355222; www.lifesabeach.info; Summerleaze; mains lunch £5.75-9.50, 2-/3-course dinner menu £25/30; ⊙ 10.30am-3.30pm & 7-10pm Mon-Sat, 10.30am-3pm Sun) Affectionately known as LAB, this beachside bistro diner is an old favourite in Bude. It's a nice place for a baguette or a burger by day, but it's at its best as the sun goes down, when you can dine on whole salt-baked sea bream and roast halibut with the best view in town.

ⓘ Information

Bude Tourist Office (☑ 01288-354240; www.visitbude.info; The Crescent; ⊙ 10am-5pm Mon-Sat, plus to 4pm Sun summer) Beside the main car park near Bude Castle.

ⓘ Getting There & Away

First Kernow bus 95 (£3.50 to £6, six daily Monday to Saturday, four on Sunday) runs between

CORNISH VINEYARDS

Cornwall might not seem an obvious place for winemaking, but father-and-son team Bob and Sam Lindo have been producing award-winning vintages at **Camel Valley Vineyard** (☎ 01208-77959; www.camelvalley.com; ⊙ shop 10am-5pm Mon-Sat, tours 2.30pm Mon-Fri plus 5pm Wed) since 1989. The range includes whites and rosés, and a bubbly that's Champagne in all but name. Aficionados say the wines have a fresh, light quality that comes from the mild climate and pure sea air. Vineyard tours run regularly and you can taste and buy the goods in the on-site shop.

Trevibban Mill (☎ 01841-541413; www.trevibbanmill.com; Dark Lane, St Issey; ⊙ noon-5pm Wed-Thu & Sun, to 10pm Fri & Sat) has a fast-growing reputation in the wine world, and it's a fine place to sample vintages in a dreamy Cornish setting. In total there are some 11,000 vines and 1700 apple trees spread across the estate, producing a range of whites and rosés in both still and sparkling versions (there are even a couple of fruity reds on the roster). The ciders and juices are delicious, too.

Guided tours (£30) exploring the art of winemaking and the estate's organic ethos take place on Sundays and include a tasting. There's also a lovely restaurant, **Appleton's at the Vineyard** (☎ 01841-541413; www.trevibbanmill.com/appletons-at-the-vineyard; St Issey; mains £17-24; ⊙ noon-5pm Wed-Sun, 6.30-10.30pm Fri & Sat), and a wine-tasting bar.

Bude and Boscastle (30 minutes), Tintagel (40 minutes), Camelford (one hour) and Wadebridge (1½ hours).

The 96 bus (four daily Monday to Saturday) connects Camelford with Port Isaac, Polzeath and Rock. Note that on Sunday, the 95 service stops at all the places normally served by the 96.

Boscastle

POP 640

Nestled in the crook of a steep coombe (valley) at the confluence of three rivers, Boscastle's seafaring heritage stretches back to Elizabethan times. With its quaint cottages, flower-clad cliffs, tinkling streams and a sturdy quay, it's almost impossibly photogenic. But the peaceful setting belies some turbulent history: in 2004 Boscastle was hit by one of Britain's largest-ever flash floods, which carried away cars, bridges and buildings. Happily, the village has since been rebuilt, but look closely even now and you'll be able to spot reminders of the floods dotted around the village.

◉ Sights

Museum of Witchcraft & Magic MUSEUM
(☎ 01840-250111; www.museumofwitchcraftand magic.co.uk; The Harbour; adult/child £5/4; ⊙ 10.30am-6pm Mon-Sat, 11.30am-6pm Sun Mar-Nov) This oddball museum has been a fixture in Boscastle since 1960, and apparently houses the world's largest collection of witchy memorabilia, from haunted skulls to hags' bridles and voodoo dolls (known

as poppets). It's half-tacky, half-spooky, and some of the more 'controversial' exhibits might perturb kids of a sensitive disposition (and some adults, for that matter). Recent exhibitions have covered curses and ritual magic.

🍽 Sleeping & Eating

Boscastle YHA HOSTEL £
(☎ 0845 371 9006; www.yha.org.uk; Palace Stables, The Harbour; dm £19-25; ⊙ Apr-Nov) Boscastle's shoebox-sized hostel was all but washed away by the 2004 floods, but it's since been completely renovated. The dorms are very small, but in return you get a historic location in one of the village's oldest buildings, and a super harbour location. There's no food available, but you can self-cater.

Boscastle House B&B ££
(☎ 01840-250654; www.boscastlehouse.co.uk; Doctors Hill; d from £128; P 🞔) The best of Boscastle's B&Bs, in a Victorian house overlooking the valley. Five classy rooms have a bright, contemporary feel that mixes neutral colours with bold print wallpapers. Charlotte has bay-window views; Nine Windows has twin sinks and a free-standing bath; and Trelawney has ample space and its own sofa. Two-night minimum.

★ Boscastle Farm Shop CAFE £
(☎ 01840-250827; www.boscastlefarmshop.co.uk; cakes & teas £3-5; ⊙ 10am-5pm; P) Half a mile uphill from the harbour on the B3263, this excellent farm shop sells its own produce,

including ruby-red beef and possibly the best sausages on the north coast, plus a comprehensive range of Cornish goodies. In the spacious cafe, tall windows look out on to green fields and the coast – the perfect setting for a cream tea.

ℹ️ Information

Boscastle Tourist Office (📞 01840-250010; www.visitboscastleandtintagel.com; The Harbour; ⏰ 10am-5pm Mar-Oct, 10.30am-4pm Nov-Feb) Not far from the quay, and with some useful leaflets on local history and walks.

ℹ️ Getting There & Away

Coastal bus 95 (£3.20 to £5.20, six daily Monday to Saturday, four on Sunday) stops in Boscastle on its way from Bude (30 minutes), then continues on to Tintagel (13 minutes), Camelford (30 minutes) and Wadebridge (one hour).

From Camelford, you can catch the connecting bus 96 to Port Isaac.

Tintagel

POP 1820

The spectre of legendary King Arthur looms large over Tintagel and its dramatic clifftop castle. Though the present-day ruins mostly date from the 13th century, archaeological digs have revealed the foundations of a much earlier fortress, fuelling speculation that Arthur may indeed have been born at the castle, as locals like to claim. It's a stunningly romantic sight, with its crumbling walls teetering precariously above the sheer cliffs, and well worth devoting at least half a day to exploring.

A highly controversial plan has been announced to connect the mainland and the rock tower on which the castle sits by an ambitious 72m-long footbridge. Despite much local opposition, the plan was approved by councillors in late 2017, although as yet a completion date hasn't been set.

The village itself isn't terribly exciting, but if you're looking for cheesy King Arthur souvenirs, you'll find them in ample supply.

👁 Sights

★Tintagel Castle CASTLE
(EH; 📞 01840-770328; www.english-heritage.org.uk; adult/child £8.40/5; ⏰ 10am-6pm Apr-Sep, to 5pm Oct, to 4pm Nov-Mar) Famous as the supposed birthplace of King Arthur, Tintagel's epic clifftop castle has been occupied since Roman times and once served as a residence for Cornwall's Celtic kings. The present castle is largely the work of Richard, Earl of Cornwall, who built a castle here during the 1230s. Though the Arthurian links may be tenuous, it's certainly a fine spot for a fortress: clinging to black granite cliffs, surrounded by booming surf and wheeling gulls, it's the classic fairy-tale castle.

Old Post Office HISTORIC BUILDING
(NT; 📞 01840-770024; www.nationaltrust.org.uk; Fore St; adult/child £4.60/2.30; ⏰ 10.30am-5.30pm mid-Mar–Sep, 11am-4pm Oct) This is one of the best-preserved examples of a traditional 16th-century Cornish longhouse, topped by pepper-pot chimneys and a higgledy-piggledy roof, and riddled with tiny rooms. As its name suggests, it was used as a post office during the 19th century.

ℹ️ Getting There & Away

First Kernow bus 95/96 (£3.50 to £6.50, six daily Monday to Saturday, four on Sunday) stops in Tintagel en route from Camelford (15 minutes) to Bude (50 minutes).

Port Isaac

POP 720

If you're looking for a classic Cornish fishing town, you've found it in Port Isaac, where a cluster of cobbled alleyways, slender opes (lanes) and cob-walled cottages collect around a medieval harbour and slipway.

Though still a working harbour, Port Isaac is best known as a filming location: the hit TV series *Doc Martin* has used the village as a ready-made backdrop. A sign near the quayside directs visitors straight to Doc Martin's cottage. A short walk along the coast path leads to the neighbouring harbour of **Port Gaverne**, while a couple of miles west is **Port Quin**, now owned by the National Trust.

Cornwall's chef *du jour* Nathan Outlaw has made the village his culinary centre of operations.

🛏 Sleeping & Eating

Old School Hotel HOTEL **££**
(📞 01208-880721; www.theoldschoolhotel.co.uk; Fore St; s £67-101, d £119-185; 🅿🛜) A small hotel that was originally Port Isaac's schoolhouse. Eagle-eyed fans of the *Doc Martin* TV series might recognise it as the show's village school. Appropriately, rooms are named after school subjects: the best is Latin, with

its sleigh bed and cupboard bathroom; Biology, with its sofa and church-style windows; and split-level Mathematics, with a shared terrace and bunk beds.

Outlaw's Fish Kitchen
SEAFOOD £

(☑ 01208-881183; www.nathan-outlaw.com/out laws-fish-kitchen; 1 Middle St; mains £6.50-17; ⊘ noon-3pm & 6-9pm Mon-Sat Jun-Sep, Tue-Sat Oct-May) Top chef Nathan Outlaw's newest venture is this tiny fish restaurant down beside the harbour. It specialises in small seafood plates, designed to share. The exact menu is dictated by whatever's brought in on the day by Port Isaac's fishers, and the restaurant is tiny – literally just a few tables – so bookings are essential.

Fresh from the Sea
SEAFOOD ££

(☑ 01208-880849; www.freshfromthesea.co.uk; 18 New Rd; sandwiches £5.50-9.50, mains £10.50-20; ⊘ 9am-4pm Mon-Sat) Local man Callum Greenhalgh takes out his boat daily in search of crab and lobster, then brings back the catch to sell at his tiny Port Isaac shop. Seafood doesn't get any fresher; a crab salad costs £10.50, and a whole lobster is a very reasonable £20. Depending on the season, oysters from nearby Porthilly cost £1.50 each.

★ Restaurant Nathan Outlaw
SEAFOOD £££

(☑ 01208-862737; www.nathan-outlaw.com; 6 New Rd; tasting menu £130; ⊘ 7-9pm Wed-Sat, plus noon-2pm Thu-Sat) Port Isaac's prestige has skyrocketed since Cornwall's top chef, Nathan Outlaw, moved his main operation here from Rock. This is the place to experience Outlaw's passion for Cornish fish and seafood. His style is surprisingly classic, relying on top-notch ingredients rather than cheffy tricks. As you'd expect of a twice-Michelin-starred restaurant, you'll pay top dollar, but it's a tell-your-friends experience.

ⓘ Getting There & Away

First Kernow bus 95/96 stops in Port Isaac at least four times daily en route between Camelford (£4.50, 30 minutes) and St Minver (£4.50, 30 minutes).

Padstow & Rock

POP 3160

If anywhere symbolises Cornwall's increasingly chic credentials, it's Padstow. This old fishing port has become the county's most cosmopolitan corner thanks to the bevy of celebrity chefs who have set up shop here –

including Rick Stein, whose Padstow-area property portfolio encompasses several restaurants and hotels, plus a gift shop, bakery, pub, seafood school and fish-and-chip bar.

There's no doubting that Padstow has changed beyond recognition in recent years: it feels more Kensington chic than Cornish quaint these days, with restaurants and boutiques sitting alongside its pubs and pasty shops. Whether the town's held on to its soul in the gentrification process is debatable, but it's hard not to be charmed by the seaside setting.

Across the Camel Estuary from Padstow lies Rock, a small village turned uber-exclusive getaway for well-to-do holiday-makers. Nearby, the sandy sweep of Daymer Bay unfurls along the estuary, a lifelong favourite of poet John Betjeman.

◉ Sights & Activities

Padstow is surrounded by fine beaches, including the so-called Seven Bays: Trevone, Harlyn, Mother Ivey's, Booby's, Constantine, Treyarnon and Porthcothan.

In the middle of the Camel estuary runs a treacherous sandbank known as the Doom Bar, which has claimed many ships over the years, and also gave its name to a popular local ale.

Prideaux Place
HISTORIC BUILDING

(☑ 01841-532411; www.prideauxplace.co.uk; Prideaux Pl; house & grounds adult £8.50, grounds only £3; ⊘ house 1.30-4pm, grounds & tearoom 12.30-5.30pm Sun-Thu Apr-Oct) Much favoured by directors of costume dramas and period films, this stately Grade I–listed manor was built by the Prideaux-Brune family, purportedly descendants of William the Conqueror. Guided tours last around an hour and take in staterooms, staircases and Prideaux-Brune heirlooms, as well as the house's extensive collection of teddy bears.

National Lobster Hatchery
NATURE DISPLAY

(☑ 01841-533877; www.nationallobsterhatchery. co.uk; South Quay; adult/child £3.95/1.85; ⊘ 10am-7.30pm Jul & Aug, to 4pm or 5pm Sep-Jun) ✒ In an effort to combat falling lobster stocks, this harbourside hatchery rears baby lobsters in tanks before returning them to the wild. Displays detail the crustaceans' life cycle, and there are viewing tanks where you can watch the residents in action. Booking a 30-minute 'Meet the Expert' tour (adult/child £12/6) allows you a glimpse into work behind the scenes.

★**Camel Trail** CYCLING
(www.cornwall.gov.uk/cameltrail) Closed in the 1950s, the old Padstow–Bodmin railway has been turned into Cornwall's most popular bike trail. The main section starts in Padstow and runs east through Wadebridge (5.75 miles); the trail then runs on all the way to Poley Bridge on Bodmin Moor (18.3 miles).

Bikes can be hired from **Padstow Cycle Hire** (☑01841-533533; www.padstowcyclehire. com; South Quay; per day adult £16-18, child £6-11; ☉9am-5pm, to 9pm summer) or **Trail Bike Hire** (☑01841-532594; www.trailbikehire.co.uk; Unit 6, South Quay; adult £14, child £5-8; ☉9am-6pm) at the Padstow end, or from **Bridge Bike Hire** (☑01208-813050; www.bridgebikehire.co.uk; Camel Trail; adult £12-14, child £6-9; ☉10am-5pm) at the Wadebridge end.

Pumps and helmets are usually included. Tandems and kids' trailers cost extra.

Most people do the route from Padstow and back, so it's often quieter (and much easier to find parking) if you start from the Wadebridge side.

Padstow Boat Trips BOATING
(www.padstowboattrips.com; South Quay) Between Easter and October, the **Jubilee Queen** (☑07836-798457; adult/child £12/7) runs scenic trips along the coastline, while **Padstow Sealife Safaris** (☑01841-521613; www.padstowsealifesafaris.co.uk; 2hr cruises adult/child £39/25) visits local seal and seabird colonies.

For something racier, 15-minute **speedboat trips** (£7) zip past the treacherous sandbank of Doom Bar and the beaches of Daymer Bay, Polzeath, Hawkers Cove and Tregirls.

The website has listings of all the local operators.

✹ Festivals & Events

May Day CULTURAL
(☉1 May) Also known as 'Obby 'Oss Day, Padstow's biggest party is said to have its roots in an ancient pagan fertility rite, and sees two coloured 'osses (red and blue) twirl through the streets before meeting up beneath the maypole. It attracts thousands of visitors, so plan well ahead.

⌁ Sleeping

Treyarnon Bay YHA HOSTEL £
(☑0845 371 9664; www.yha.org.uk; Treyarnon Bay; dm £15-29; ☉reception 8-10am & 2-10pm; P 🗢)

A super 1930s beach hostel on the bluffs above Treyarnon Bay. Rooms are big, there's a good cafe, plus barbecues in summer, and the sunsets are spectacular. It's 4.5 miles east of Padstow: there's parking on-site, but the nearest bus stop is at Constantine, about a 20-minute walk away.

Althea Library B&B ££
(☑01841-532579; www.altheahouse-padstow. co.uk; 64 Church St; d £90-120; P 🗢) If you want to stay in Padstow proper, this charming ivy-clad house is hard to better. There are two stylish self-catering suites: Rafters is accessed via a private staircase, while Driftwood has a pine four-poster bed. It's luxurious – both suites have sofas, Nespresso coffee machines, baths and small studio kitchens. There's also a nearby cottage called Inglenook for longer stays.

Woodlands B&B ££
(☑01841-532426; www.woodlands-padstow.co.uk; Treator; d £130-150; P 🗢) Offering green fields and distant flashes of sea, this is a great B&B base for Padstow. Rooms are a bit heavy on the creams and frills, but cosy nonetheless, and the breakfasts are prodigious. It's a mile or so from Padstow's harbourside, on the A389.

Symply Padstow B&B ££
(☑01841-532814; www.symply-padstow.co.uk; 32 Dennis Rd; s £61-67, d £97-109; 🗢) There's no way around it – staying in Padstow is pricey, but this B&B turns the tables with rates that would be a bargain even in a less starry location. The three rooms are cute and feminine, decorated with florals and checks, and all come with stellar sea views. The business also runs a self-catering cottage (£400 to £920 per week).

✗ Eating

★**Chough Bakery** BAKERY £
(☑01841-533361; www.thechoughbakery.co.uk; 1-3 The Strand; pasties £3-5; ☉9am-5pm Mon-Sat) A family-run bakery right in the heart of town, renowned for its traditionally made pasties – they're among the best in the county, and several times have scooped top honours in the World Pasty Championships.

Prawn on the Lawn BISTRO ££
(☑01841-532223; www.prawnonthelawn.com; 11 Duke St; mains £7.50-45; ☉noon-midnight Tue-Sat Easter-Sep) An offshoot of a London original, this tiny seafood bar is a new addition to Padstow's dining line-up. It's a simple one-

room affair, with bare brick, white tiles and blackboards, and a handful of tables lined up along one wall. But frills aren't important here: the seafood is what counts, served as small plates, sharing platters or by weight.

Rojano's in the Square
ITALIAN ££

(☎01841-532796; www.paul-ainsworth.co.uk; 9 Mill Sq; pizza & pasta £8.50-20; ⊙10am-10pm) Under the stewardship of Michelin-starred chef Paul Ainsworth, this excellent little Italian bistro turns out fantastic wood-fired pizza, spicy pasta and antipasti. It's a fun and laid-back place to dine, and prices are very reasonable.

Cornish Arms
GASTROPUB ££

(☎01841-520288; www.rickstein.com/eat-with-us/the-cornish-arms; St Merryn; mains £10.95-17.95; ⊙11.30am-11pm) This country pub near the village of St Merryn is owned by chef Rick Stein's foodie empire, and offers pub classics such as scampi in a basket, rump steak and ham, egg and chips – all with a creative twist and firm local provenance, naturally. The Sunday roast is phenomenally popular, so arrive early. It's a 3-mile drive from Padstow.

★ Paul Ainsworth at No 6
BRITISH £££

(☎01841-532093; www.paul-ainsworth.co.uk/number6; 6 Middle St; 2-/3-course lunch £25/29, dinner mains £31-45; ⊙noon-2.30pm & 6-10pm Tue-Sat) Rick Stein might be the household name, but Paul Ainsworth is often touted as Padstow's pretender to the throne. His food combines surprising flavours and impeccable presentation with a refreshingly unpretentious approach, and the town-house setting is a relaxed, unfussy place to dine. Now Michelin-starred, this is Padstow's most sought-after table – advance bookings essential.

★ Seafood Restaurant
SEAFOOD £££

(☎01841-532700; www.rickstein.com; Riverside; 3-course lunch £40, mains £26-71; ⊙lunch 11.30am-4pm, dinner 6-9pm Sat, 6.30-9.30pm Sun-Fri) The restaurant that started the Stein dynasty, and still one of Cornwall's top places to dine. Stein senior rarely puts in any hours these days – Rick's son Jack runs the show. As ever, fish is the raison d'être: from fresh lobster to turbot, John Dory and *fruits de mer,* all served in an elegant, light-filled dining room.

❶ Information

Padstow Tourist Office (☎01841-533449; www.padstowlive.com; North Quay; ⊙10am-5pm Mon-Sat, to 4pm Sun Apr-Sep, Mon-

BEDRUTHAN STEPS

Roughly halfway between Newquay and Padstow loom the stately rock stacks of **Bedruthan** (Carnewas, NT; www.nationaltrust.org.uk) FREE. These mighty granite pillars have been carved out by the relentless action of thousands of years of wind and waves, and now provide a stirring spot for a stroll. The area is owned by the National Trust (NT), which also runs the car park and cafe. Admission to the site is free, but non-NT members have to pay for parking.

Sat Oct-Mar) In a red-brick building on the quayside.

❶ Getting There & Away

There are a couple of car parks beside the harbour in Padstow, but they fill up quickly, so it's usually better to park at one of the large car parks at the top of town and walk down.

The only useful bus serving Padstow is First Kernow bus 5A to Newquay (alternate hours Monday to Saturday, three on Sunday, one hour 25 minutes), which runs along the coast via Harlyn Bay, Constantine Bay, Porthcothan, Mawgan Porth, Newquay Cornwall Airport and Porth Beach.

Newquay

POP 19,420

Newquay: naughty, and apart from its stunning beaches, not really very nice, actually. For many years, that's been the prevailing opinion of Cornwall's surfing capital, and honestly, Newquay has no one but itself to blame for the bad rap. With a notorious nightlife, and a main street lined with trashy clubs, rowdy pubs and blinking amusement arcades, it's no surprise the town has found itself struggling to transcend its party-hard, alcohol-fuelled, bargain-basement image.

But things are changing: Newquay is making a concerted effort to smarten up its act. Several of the big clubs have closed down; trendy bistros, cafes, bakeries and health-food shops have appeared in the town centre; and along the coast, a bevy of boutique hotels are attracting a more discerning clientele. There's a way to go, but at last it feels like Newquay might be growing up. About time, too.

⊙ Sights

Newquay has a truly knockout location among some of North Cornwall's finest beaches. The trio close to town – **Towan**, **Great Western** and **Tolcarne** – are guaranteed to be packed in the middle of summer. Most surfers head for **Fistral**, but the very best beaches such as **Crantock**, **Holywell Bay** and **Watergate Bay** lie a couple of miles out of town.

Blue Reef Aquarium   AQUARIUM
(☑ 01637-878134; www.bluereefaquarium.co.uk/newquay; Towan Promenade; adult/child £10.95/8.50; ⊙ 10am-6pm; ⊕) A small aquarium on Towan beach, with touch pools and various deep-sea denizens, including reef sharks, loggerhead turtles and a giant Pacific octopus. There's a discount for online bookings.

Newquay Zoo   ZOO
(☑ 01637-873342; www.newquayzoo.org.uk; Trenance Gardens; adult/child £13.20/9.90; ⊙ 10am-5pm; ⊕) Newquay's pint-sized zoo isn't a world-beater, but its population of penguins, lemurs, parrots and snakes will keep the kids happy. The Tropical House and Toad Hall are good fun, and key events include penguin feeding at noon and lion feeding at 2.30pm.

Trerice   HISTORIC BUILDING
(NT; ☑ 01637-875404; www.nationaltrust.org.uk; adult/child £10/5; ⊙ house 11am-5pm, gardens 10.30am-5pm) Built in 1751, this National Trust–owned Elizabethan manor is most famous for the elaborate barrel-roofed ceiling of the Great Chamber, and some fantastic original 16th-century stained glass among the 576 panes that make up the great window. It's 3.3 miles southeast of Newquay.

⫯ Activities

Newquay is brimming with surf schools, but quality is variable. Choose one that offers small-group sessions, and that ideally has a no-stag-party policy. Ask about teachers' accreditation and experience, and whether they travel to beaches other than Fistral – good schools follow the best waves.

Extreme Academy   ADVENTURE SPORTS
(☑ 01637-860840; www.extremeacademy.co.uk; Watergate Bay) Owned by the nearby Watergate Bay Hotel, this watersports provider offers the full gamut: surfing lessons, of course, as well as more unusual options such as stand-up paddleboarding and hand-planing

(which involves catching a wave with a miniature surfboard attached to your wrist). A 2½-hour beginners' surf lesson costs £35, bodyboarding £25 and SUP £40.

EboAdventure   OUTDOORS
(☑ 0800 781 6861; www.eboadventure.co.uk) This multiactivity centre is based at the Penhale Training Camp, at the northern end of Holywell Bay. Surfing's definitely not the only sport on offer: you can also try kite-buggying, kayaking, power-kiting, stand-up paddleboarding and coasteering (a mix of rock climbing, scrambling and wild swimming). It also runs bushcraft training sessions.

Rip Curl English Surf School   SURFING
(☑ 01637-879571; www.englishsurfschool.com; lessons from £35) Based on Towan Beach, this is one of the most experienced and efficient large schools, linked with Rip Curl and staffed by English Surfing Federation–approved instructors (including the British team coach). Also offers coasteering and bodyboarding. Beginner lessons cost £35, or £42 if you're more advanced and want to hone your technique.

Kingsurf Surf School   SURFING
(☑ 01637-860091; www.kingsurf.co.uk; Mawgan Porth; lessons from £35) A good option for avoiding the Fistral beach hustle, this school at Mawgan Porth has five young instructors and gets a tick for personal attention and small class sizes.

⟶ Sleeping

★ **Scarlet**   HOTEL £££
(☑ 01637-861600; www.scarlethotel.co.uk; Mawgan Porth; r from £260; 🅿 🛜 🏊) For out-and-out luxury, Cornwall's fabulously chic adults-only eco-hotel takes the crown. In a regal location above Mawgan Porth, 5 miles from Newquay, it screams designer style, from the huge sea-view rooms with their funky furniture and minimalist decor to the luxurious spa, complete with meditation lounge, outdoor hot tubs and wild-swimming pool. The restaurant's a beauty, too.

★ **Watergate Bay Hotel**   HOTEL £££
(☑ 01637-860543; www.watergatebay.co.uk; Watergate Bay; d £290-440; 🅿 🛜) This stylish, popular beach hotel combines luxury with lifestyle: guests are positively encouraged to explore the many outdoor activities on offer at the in-house Extreme Academy. With beachy rooms decked out in coastal colours and slatted wood, and a glorious indoor pool

overlooking the bay, it's posh but reassuringly unpretentious: wet feet and sandy footprints are not a problem here.

✕ Eating

★ Pavilion Bakery
BAKERY £

(www.pavilionbakery.com; 37 Fore St; breads £2-4; ⊙8am-4pm) After opening three outposts in London's hippest-of-hip corners (Victoria Park, Columbia Rd and Broadway Market), this fabulous bakery has set up its first shop outside the capital in Newquay, in an A-frame building with the requisite exposed brick, rough wood and open-plan kitchen. Come for stunning sourdoughs, artisan breads and possibly Cornwall's finest croissants and pains au chocolat.

Sprout
VEGETARIAN £

(☑ 01637-875845; www.sprouthealth.co.uk; Crescent Lane; mains £3.50-5.50; ⊙9am-5pm Mon-Sat; ☑) If you like your food organic and your ingredients fair trade, then this excellent wholefood shop down an uninviting backstreet is the best address in town. The one-pot veggie meals (such as vegan African peanut stew and hearty Moroccan stew) are delicious and sell out fast – almost as fast as the delectable gluten-free cakes.

★ Fish House Fistral
SEAFOOD ££

(☑ 01637-872085; www.thefishhousefistral.com; Fistral Beach; mains lunch £8.50-16.95, dinner £12.95-19.95) This beachside seafooderie has become a firm favourite for local diners and Fistral visitors alike, and it's thoroughly deserved. Filling fishy dishes are the catch of the day, underscored by French, Italian and Asian flavours, and the beach-shack vibe is bang-on. Chef Paul Harwood trained under Rick Stein, and it shows in his seafood skills.

Beach Hut
BISTRO ££

(☑ 01637-860877; Watergate Bay; mains £12.50-22; ⊙9am-9pm) After a beach walk or a quick surf at Watergate, this cafe is where everyone tends to head for a coffee, cake or something more filling. With its wood-lined interior and big picture windows, it's a lovely spot, and the blackboards are filled with easygoing dishes such as burgers, meze, mussels, pad Thai and seafood curry.

It's underneath **Fifteen Restaurant** (☑ 01637-861000; www.fifteencornwall.co.uk; lunch mains £16-21, dinner mains £19-28, 5-course dinner £65; ⊙8.30-10am, noon-2.30pm & 6.15-9.15pm), but is owned by the Watergate Bay Hotel. Parking can be tricky in summer.

Lewinnick Lodge
BISTRO ££

(☑ 01637-878117; www.lewinnicklodge.co.uk; Pentire Head; mains £12.50-20; ⊙8am-10pm) Perched on the cliffs of Pentire Head, giving a knock-out perspective on Newquay's coastline, this gastropub is hard to better for lunch with a view. The decor is modern – lots of wood and plate glass – and the food is decent: gourmet burgers, mussels and Thai-style salads.

🍷 Drinking & Nightlife

Newquay's drinking spots aren't sophisticated. Cheesy clubs and brash bars abound, and the town centre gets notoriously rowdy on Friday and Saturday nights, especially in summer.

Tom Thumb
BAR

(☑ 01637-849180; www.tom-thumb.co.uk; 27a East St; ⊙noon-midnight) Now then Newquay: this is much, much more like it. A proper cocktail bar with reclaimed wood furniture, a cool spiral staircase and a fine selection of home-mixed drinks (divided into fun categories like 'Something Saucy' and 'Giggle Water'). A few more like this, and the days of the beer boy really will be numbered.

☆ Entertainment

Whiskers
LIVE MUSIC

(☑ 01637-498100; www.whiskersnewquay.co.uk; 5-7 Gover Lane; ⊙5pm-midnight) A grungy cool hang-out with a regular line-up of live gigs, both from local bands and a few bigger names from upcountry and further afield. The rest of the time, DJs fill in the musical gaps. Occasionally Whiskers hosts oddball events such as life drawing and spoken-word slams.

ℹ Information

Newquay Tourist Office (☑ 01637-854020; www.visitnewquay.org; Marcus Hill; ⊙9.15am-5.30pm Mon-Fri, 10am-4pm Sat & Sun) Small but well-stocked office that can help you arrange everything from accommodation to surf lessons.

ℹ Getting There & Away

AIR

Cornwall Airport Newquay (☑ 01637-860600; www.cornwallairportnewquay.com) Cornwall's main airport, 5 miles from Newquay, offers direct daily flights to Manchester and London Gatwick with Flybe (www.flybe.com) and the Isles of Scilly with Isles of Scilly Travel (p355).

BATH & SOUTHWEST ENGLAND NEWQUAY

First Kernow bus A5 (26 minutes, every two hours Monday to Saturday, three on Sunday) runs from Newquay's bus station to Padstow, stopping at the airport en route. Taxis cost £15 to £25 from the town centre.

Various seasonal destinations around the UK and Europe are also offered during summer.

BUS

Newquay's bus station is on Manor Rd.

Padstow Bus A5 (£5.20, 90 minutes, every two hours Monday to Saturday, three on Sunday) stops at the airport and then trundles up the coast via Mawgan Porth, Porthcothan, Constantine Bay and Harlyn Bay. Note that only a few buses a day stop at Bedruthan Steps.

St Agnes Bus 87 (£5.20, 50 minutes, hourly Monday to Saturday, five on Sunday) stops at Crantock, Holywell Bay and Perranporth en route to St Agnes, and continues to Truro.

Truro Bus 90/92/93 (£5.20, 70 minutes, half-hourly Monday to Saturday, five on Sunday); the various routes travel via different villages but all terminate in Truro.

Wadebridge Bus 95 (£4.20, 50 minutes, five daily Monday to Saturday).

TRAIN

Newquay is on the branch line between Newquay and Par (Atlantic Coast Line, £6.50, 45 minutes), from where you can hop aboard the main London–Penzance line.

Perranporth to Porthtowan

Southwest of Newquay, Cornwall's craggy northern coastline dips and curves through a stunning panorama of wild, sea-smacked cliffs and golden bays, including the family-friendly beach of Perranporth, the old mining town of St Agnes and the surfy hang-out of Porthtowan.

◉ Sights & Activities

★ Perranporth Beach BEACH

(P ♿) Perranporth's huge, flat, sandy beach is a favourite for everyone: dog-walkers, bucket-and-spade families, kite-buggiers and surfers alike. Its main draw is its sheer size – more than a mile long, backed by dunes and rocky cliffs – meaning there's usually space for everyone even on the busiest days. It's home to the Watering Hole, the hub of local nightlife.

★ Chapel Porth BAY

(NT; www.nationaltrust.org.uk; P) Two miles from St Agnes is one of Cornwall's most beautiful coves, Chapel Porth, a wild, rocky beach framed by steep, gorse-covered cliffs, owned by the National Trust. Above the cove is the ruined engine stack of **Wheal Coates**, which still boasts its chimney and winding house, from where the coast path winds all the way to the blustery outcrop of **St Agnes Head**. It's a panorama that graces many a postcard – don't forget your camera.

Blue Hills Tin Streams MUSEUM

(☑ 01872-553341; www.cornishtin.com; adult/child £6.50/3; ◷ 10am-2pm Tue-Sat mid-Apr–mid-Oct) A mile east of St Agnes (signed to Wheal Kitty) is the rocky valley of **Trevellas Porth**, home to one of Cornwall's last tin manufacturers. You can watch the whole tinning process, from mining and smelting through to casting and finishing. Handmade jewellery is sold in the shop.

✕ Eating & Drinking

Chapel Porth Cafe CAFE £

(Chapel Porth; sandwiches & cakes £2-5; ◷ 10am-5pm) This cafe down on the edge of Chapel Porth beach is a local institution, serving hot chocolate, cheesy baguettes, sausage butties, flapjacks and the house speciality: hedgehog ice cream (vanilla ice cream topped with clotted cream and hazelnuts).

★ Blue Bar BAR

(☑ 01209-890329; www.blue-bar.co.uk; mains £8-16; ◷ 10am-11pm) For a seaside sundowner or a lunchtime burger by the sand, this surfy Porthtowan cafe is tough to beat. There are tables outside overlooking the sand, plus more inside (arrive early to bag the prime bay window tables). The beachy decor, decent grub and regular music nights make it one of the north coast's most popular hang-outs.

Watering Hole BAR

(☑ 01872-572888; www.the-wateringhole.co.uk; Perranporth Beach; ◷ 10am-11pm) Generations of Cornish youth have passed through this venerable beach bar, and it's still going strong, despite nearly being swept away during recent storms. It's a bit shabby, but good for a morning coffee or an evening beer as the sun goes down. It also has regular live music – Tom Jones and Snoop Dogg have played shows here.

❶ Getting There & Away

Bus 87 (£6, 45 minutes, hourly in summer) stops in St Agnes on its way from Newquay, via Crantock, Holywell, Perranporth and Trevellas, to Truro.

St Ives

POP 9870

If there was a prize for the prettiest of Cornish ports, then St Ives would undoubtedly be a contender for the top spot. A tightly packed cluster of slate roofs, fishers' cottages and church towers spread out around turquoise bays – it's an unfailingly dazzling sight. Once a busy pilchard harbour, St Ives later became the centre of Cornwall's arts scene in the 1920s and '30s, when luminary figures such as Barbara Hepworth, Terry Frost, Ben Nicholson and Naum Gabo migrated here in search of artistic freedom.

The town remains an artistic centre, with numerous galleries lining its cobbled streets, as well as the renowned Tate St Ives, which recently received a multimillion pound extension. Whether the town has managed to retain its artistic soul is another matter – it's one of Cornwall's holiday home hot spots, and uncomfortably packed with tourists in summer, so visit in spring or autumn if you can.

⊙ Sights & Activities

The largest town beaches are **Porthmeor** and **Porthminster**, both of which have sand and space aplenty. Between them juts the grassy promontory known as the Island, topped by the tiny pre-14th-century **Chapel of St Nicholas**. On the peninsula's east side is the little cove of **Porthgwidden**, a smaller beach that's often a good place to escape the crowds.

As you'd expect, there are lots and lots of art galleries to visit dotted around town.

★**Tate St Ives**　　　　　　　　GALLERY
(☑01736-796226; www.tate.org.uk/stives; Porthmeor Beach; adult/child £9.50/free, joint ticket with Barbara Hepworth Museum £13/free; ⊙10am-5.20pm, last admission 4pm) After an 18-month, multimillion-pound refit, St Ives' most illustrious gallery reopened its doors, complete

BATH & SOUTHWEST ENGLAND ST IVES

West Cornwall

St Ives

with a monumental exhibition space that's been added to the museum's original, spiral-shaped core. Focusing on the coterie of experimental artists who congregated at St Ives after the WWII and turned the little seaside town into a mecca of modern art, the museum showcases the work of luminaries such as Barbara Hepworth, Terry Frost, Peter Lanyon and Patrick Heron in luminous, white-walled surroundings.

Barbara Hepworth Museum MUSEUM
(☎ 01736-796226; Barnoon Hill; adult/child £7.70/free, joint ticket with Tate St Ives £13/free; ⓧ 10am-5.20pm Mar-Oct, to 4pm Nov-Feb) Barbara Hep-

worth (1903–75) was one of the leading abstract sculptors of the 20th century and a key figure in the St Ives art scene. Her studio on Barnoon Hill has remained almost untouched since her death and the adjoining garden contains several of her most notable sculptures, many of which were inspired by the elemental forces she discovered in her adopted Cornish home: rock, sea, sand, wind, sky. Free private tours are also available to provide extra context.

★ **Leach Pottery** GALLERY
(☎ 01736-796398; www.leachpottery.com; Higher Stennack; adult/child £6/free; ⓧ 10am-5pm Mon-

St Ives

Sat year-round, 11am-4pm Sun Mar-Oct) While other St Ives artists broke new ground in sculpture and abstract art, potter Bernard Leach was hard at work reinventing British ceramics in his studio in Higher Stennack. Drawing inspiration from Japanese and oriental sculpture, and using a unique hand-built 'climbing' kiln based on ones he had seen in Japan, Leach's pottery created a unique fusion of Western and Eastern ideas.

St Ives Boats   BOATING
(☑ 0777 300 8000; www.stivesboats.co.uk; adult/child from £16/10) St Ives Boats is one of several operators along the harbour front to offer fishing trips and scenic cruises, including to the grey-seal colony on Seal Island and out to the lighthouse at Godrevy. If you're really lucky, you might even spot a porpoise or a basking shark in summer.

⊨ Sleeping

Channings   B&B ££
(☑ 01736-799500; www.channingsstives.co.uk; 3 Talland Rd; s £50-65, d £95-115; ⓟ🗐📶) This small terraced B&B would be pretty good value anywhere, but in St Ives it's an absolute bargain. If you can, book one of the panoramic suites, which have sitting areas and sloping skylights offering views over St Ives and Godrevy lighthouse. The standard seaview rooms don't have quite the same wow factor, but they're comfortable enough.

West by 5   B&B ££
(☑ 01736-794584; www.westbyfive.com; 7 Clodgy View; r £80-140; 🗐) Much recommended and reliable B&B in a stone-fronted Edwardian villa, with four rooms offering elevated views over the harbour (rooms 1 and 2 are the best of the quartet). It's simply decorat-

ed, with blue bedspreads, stripy blinds and pine bedsteads – and luxury extras including Hypnos beds and goose-down duvets add a dash of panache. The only major drawback? No parking.

Little Leaf Guest House   B&B ££
(☑ 01736-795427; www.littleleafguesthouse.co.uk; Park Ave; r £75-125; 🗐📶) Another top option to keep your St Ives spending nonstratospheric. It's small, with just six rooms – and while space isn't a strong point, rooms are attractively appointed in creams and pine furniture. Room 2 has the best view, followed by room 5 with its elevated position and dormer window.

★ Primrose Valley Hotel   HOTEL £££
(☑ 01736-794939; www.primroseonline.co.uk; Primrose Valley; r £180-230; ⓟ🗐📶) Reopened after refurbishment, this chic hotel has one massive selling point – it's a one-minute walk from Porthminster's sands. But there are more pluses – such as its light, attractive rooms in taupes, greys, checks and sea blues, and quirky design touches including wicker lamps, Scandi-style dressers, wooden cladding and model ships. It feels very modern and impeccably designed throughout.

Trevose Harbour House   B&B £££
(☑ 01736-793267; www.trevosehouse.co.uk; 22 The Warren; d £195-275; 🗐) A stylish six-room town house on the lovely backstreet known as the Warren, restored with a sea-themed combo of fresh whites and stripy blues. It's been beautifully finished – Neal's Yard bath goods, iPod docks and retro design pieces in the rooms, plus a book-lined lounge and minimalist courtyard patio. It's boutique through and through – but undeniably expensive.

BATH & SOUTHWEST ENGLAND ST IVES

✕ Eating

Moomaid of Zennor
ICE CREAM £

(www.moomaidofzennor.com; The Wharf; ice cream from £2; ⊙9am-5pm) This ice-cream maker is a local legend, and makes all its 30 flavours on the home farm just outside Zennor, using only its own milk and Rodda's clotted cream. Exotic concoctions include fig and mascarpone and pear-cider sorbet.

The Digey Food Room
CAFE £

(☑01736-799600; www.digeyfoodroom.co.uk; 6 The Digey; mains £6-8.50; ⊙9am-4pm) On one of St Ives' oldest – and loveliest – backstreets, this little cafe is a newcomer, but already a local favourite. It's small, cosy and friendly, with a well-stocked deli shop and a counter filled with homemade cakes and pastries – but it's the hearty lunches (fennel frittatas, smashed avo on toast, salmon-and-dill quiche) that really sell it.

★ Porthminster Beach Café
BISTRO ££

(☑01736-795352; www.porthminstercafe.co.uk; Porthminster Beach; mains £15-22; ⊙9am-10pm) This is no ordinary beach cafe: it's a full-blown bistro with a gorgeous sun-trap terrace and a superb Mediterranean-influenced menu, specialising in seafood. Tuck into rich bouillabaisse, seafood curry or Provençal fish soup, and settle back to enjoy the breezy beach vistas. It's published its own cookbook, too, if you fancy taking the recipes home.

Porthminster Kitchen
BISTRO ££

(☑01736-799874; www.porthminster.kitchen; The Wharf; mains lunch £7.50-16, dinner £11-19; ⊙9am-10pm) Run by the same team as Porthminster Beach Café, this is a welcome addition to the harbour front in St Ives. It's a relaxed, bistro-style kind of place, with beachy dishes such as *moules-frites,* seafood curry and hake fillet on bubble-and-squeak. The food's reliable, and the 1st-floor dining room has a hard-to-beat view of the harbour.

SILCo Searoom
CAFE ££

(☑01736-794325; www.silcosearoom.com; 1 Wharf House; tapas £3.25-12; ⊙9am-10pm Mon-Sat) Now run by the St Ives Liquor Company (makers of the town's premium craft gin), this wharfside restaurant specialises in Cornish-tinged tapas: crab gratin, mackerel fillet, mussels and the like, alongside the usual Padrón peppers and bread-and-olives combo. Richly furnished in gentlemen's club style (leather chairs, dark wood, sombre colours), it's great for cocktails and has a cracking harbour view.

Blas Burgerworks
CAFE ££

(☑01736-797272; The Warren; burgers £10-12.50; ⊙noon-9.30pm Jul & Aug, 5.30-9.30pm rest of year) 🖋 St Ives' boutique burger joint, with an ecofriendly manifesto and an imaginative menu. Go for a 6oz Classic Blasburger, or branch out with a guacamole and corn-salsa-topped Rancheros, or a Smokey with beetroot, aged cheddar and homemade piccalilli (there are plenty of veggie options, too). The owners also run the excellent Halsetown Inn (☑01736-795583; www.halsetown inn.co.uk; Halsetown; mains £13-22.50; ⊙noon-2pm & 6-9pm), just outside St Ives.

★ Alba
MODERN BRITISH £££

(☑01736-797222; www.alba-stives.co.uk; Old Lifeboat House; 2-/3-course dinner menu £24/28, mains £16-28.95; ⊙6-10pm) Other restaurants come and go, but this harbourside bistro beside the old lifeboat station continues to excel. It's in a converted boathouse, with a split-level layout: dining is upstairs, with picture windows looking over the harbour; downstairs is the sleek A-Bar. Head chef Grant Nethercott has a Michelin-starred background, so standards are high: first-class fish and seafood are the mainstays.

The set dinner menu is available from 5.30pm to 7.30pm.

🍷 Drinking & Entertainment

St Ives Brewery
MICROBREWERY

(☑01736-793467; www.stives-brewery.co.uk; Trewidden Rd; mains £3-8; ⊙9am-5pm Mon-Sat, 10am-4pm Sun) Since its foundation in 2010 St Ives' own microbrewery has expanded operations and opened its own cafe and tasting room. The flagships are Boiler's, a golden session ale, and the hoppy IPA-style Knill By Mouth; you can sample both in the cafe while enjoying an absolutely cracking outlook over the town's rooftops.

Sloop Inn
PUB

(☑01736-796584; www.sloop-inn.co.uk; The Wharf; ⊙11am-11pm) This whitewashed, beam-ceilinged boozer is as comfy as an old pair of slippers, with a few tables on the harbour and lots of local ales. On a sunny day, the picnic tables on the tiny harbourside patio are just about the best spot for a pint in town.

Hub
BAR

(www.hub-stives.co.uk; The Wharf; ⊙9am-11pm) The open-plan Hub is the heart of St Ives' (admittedly limited) nightlife: coffee and burgers by day, cocktails after dark and a great location on the harbour.

ℹ Getting There & Away

BUS

Bus 17/17A/17B (£5, 30 minutes, half-hourly Monday to Saturday, hourly Sunday) The quickest route to Penzance, via Lelant and Marazion.

Bus 16/16A (£5, hourly Monday to Saturday) An alternative route to Penzance; bus 16A travels via Zennor and the Gurnard's Head pub, while bus 16 goes via Halsetown, Ludgvan and Gulval.

TRAIN

The branch train line from St Ives is worth taking just for the coastal views.

Trains shuttle between St Ives train station via Lelant to St Erth (£3, 14 minutes, half-hourly) where you can catch connections along the Penzance–London Paddington main line.

Zennor & St Just

The B3306 coast road between St Ives and Zennor ventures into a wild corner of Cornwall, a long way from the prettified harbour towns and manicured beaches. This tiny village is set around the medieval Church of St Senara. Its main claim to fame is as the home of the legend of the Mermaid of Zennor, but it has another literary connection, too: the writer DH Lawrence sojourned here between 1915 and 1917, but his liberal habits and metropolitan tastes (not to mention a wild party or two) earned short shrift from the locals, and the writer was drummed out of the village as a suspected communist spy (an episode recounted in his novel *Kangaroo*).

◉ Sights

Church of St Senara CHURCH
This little church in the hamlet of Zennor dates from at least 1150. Inside, a famous carved chair depicts the legendary Mermaid of Zennor, who is said to have fallen in love with the singing voice of local lad Matthew Trewhella. Locals say you can still sometimes hear them singing down at nearby Pendour Cove – and even if you don't, the views along the coast path are reward enough.

★ Geevor Tin Mine MINE
(☏ 01736-788662; www.geevor.com; adult/child £14.60/8.50; ☉ 9am-5pm Sun-Fri Mar-Oct, 10am-4pm Nov-Feb) Just north of St Just near Pendeen, this historic mine closed in 1990 and now provides a powerful insight into the dark, dingy and dangerous conditions in which Cornwall's miners worked. Above ground, you can view the dressing floors and the original machinery used to sort the minerals and ores, before taking a guided tour into some of the underground shafts. Claustrophobes need not apply.

★ Botallack RUINS
(NT; www.nationaltrust.org.uk/botallack) Clinging to the cliffs near Levant, this dramatic complex of mine-workings is one of the most atmospheric sights from Cornwall's industrial past. The main mine stack, properly known as the Crowns, teeters picturesquely on the cliff edge above a cauldron of boiling surf. It's famously photogenic and a frequent filming location, most recently used by the BBC's latest version of *Poldark*. It's a steep walk down, but well worth the trek; an audio guide can be downloaded from the NT website.

During its 19th-century heyday, the mine was one of the county's richest and deepest, producing 14,500 tonnes of tin and 20,000 tonnes of copper ore from shafts that snaked out nearly half a mile out to sea. You can explore the site's history at the Count House workshop, which once contained the stables that housed the mine's pit ponies.

Levant Mine & Beam Engine HISTORIC SITE
(www.nationaltrust.org.uk/levant-mine-and-beam-engine; adult/child £8.10/4.05; ☉ 10.30am-5pm Apr-Oct) At this clifftop site, one of the world's only working beam engines is still in thunderous action. Built in 1840, these great engines were the powerhouses behind the Cornish mining boom, powering mineral trains, running lifts down into the mine shafts, and pumping water from the underground tunnels. Closed in 1930, it's since been lovingly restored by a team of enthusiasts, and is a sight to behold when it's in full steam.

Cape Cornwall LANDMARK
Jutting out from the cliffs near St Just is Cornwall's only cape, a craggy outcrop of land topped by an abandoned mine stack. Below the cape is the rocky beach of Priest's Cove, while nearby are the ruins of St Helen's Oratory, supposedly one of the first Christian chapels built in West Cornwall.

🛏 Sleeping & Eating

Zennor Chapel Guesthouse B&B ££
(☏ 01736-798307; www.zennorchapelguesthouse. com; Wayside St; r from £80; 🅿) As its name hints, this attractive B&B (previously a

WORTH A TRIP

MINACK THEATRE & PORTHCURNO

Teetering right out on Cornwall's far-western tip, the sandy wedge of **Porthcurno** is one of the best beaches in west Cornwall for swimming and sunbathing, and around the headland, the lesser-known beach of **Pednvounder** nearby is good if you like to sunbathe *au naturel* – it's one of Cornwall's few naturist beaches.

But the area is best known for its spectacular clifftop theatre, the **Minack** (☑01736-810181; www.minack.com; tickets from £10), carved out from the granite rock with sweeping views of the Atlantic waves below. Created between the 1930s and 1970s by theatre-lover Rowena Cade, there are few finer places to watch a play than this.

Porthcurno was also once an unlikely hub for transatlantic telecommunications, and a small **museum** (☑01736-810966; www.telegraphmuseum.org; adult/child £9.50/5.50; ⊙10am-5pm) explores the story.

hostel) occupies a former church on the edge of the village. There are five rooms, most of which still boast original ecclesiastical features, including beautiful arched windows. There's a range of sleeping configurations – doubles, twins and family rooms with bunk beds. There's also a cafe and gift shop downstairs.

★ **Gurnard's Head**   BRITISH **££**
(☑01736-796928; www.gurnardshead.co.uk; B3306, near Zennor; mains £11.50-24, r £125-190; ℙ�🛜🐕) On the wonderful coast road between Zennor and St Just, you can't possibly miss the Gurnard's – its name is emblazoned on the roof. It's earned a reputation as one of west Cornwall's top dining pubs, known for its classic, traditionally inspired British dishes, and a top Sunday roast. Wooden furniture, book-lined shelves and sepia prints conjure a cosy, lived-in feel.

Sennen & Land's End

Beyond St Ives, the coastline gets wilder and emptier as you near Cornwall's tip at Land's End, the westernmost point of mainland England, where the coal-black cliffs plunge into the pounding surf, and the views stretch all the way to the Isles of Scilly on a clear day.

Unfortunately, the decision to build the **Legendary Land's End** (☑0871 720 0044; www.landsend-landmark.co.uk; day ticket adult/child £12.60/9; ⊙10am-5pm Mar-Oct; ⓟ) theme park on the headland in the 1980s hasn't done much to enhance the view. Take our advice: just pay for the car park, skip the tacky multimedia shows and opt for an exhilarating clifftop stroll instead. Look for the historic Longships Lighthouse, on a reef 1.25 miles out to sea.

From Land's End, follow the coast path west to the secluded cove of **Nanjizal Bay**, or east to the old harbour of Sennen, which overlooks the glorious beach of **Whitesand Bay**, the area's most impressive stretch of sand.

Mousehole

POP 697

With a tight tangle of cottages and alleyways gathered behind the granite breakwater, Mousehole (pronounced *mowzle*) looks like something from a children's storybook (a fact not unnoticed by author Antonia Barber, who set her much-loved fairy tale *The Mousehole Cat* here). In centuries past this was Cornwall's busiest pilchard port, but the fish dried up in the late 19th century, and the village now survives mostly on tourist traffic. Packed in summer and deserted in winter (Mousehole is renowned for its high proportion of second homes), it's ripe for a wander, with a maze of slips, net lofts and courtyards.

🛏 Sleeping & Eating

★ **Old Coastguard Hotel**   HOTEL **£££**
(☑01736-731222; www.oldcoastguardhotel.co.uk; The Parade; d£140-245; ℙ🛜🐕) Run by the owners of the Gurnard's Head (p342), this coastal beauty on the edge of Mousehole ranks as one of Cornwall's top coastal hotels. Rooms are classic – restrained colour schemes, stately beds – and the best obviously have a sea view. Seafood takes prominence in the **restaurant** (mains £13.50 to £18.50), and there's a cliff garden for soaking up the rays.

2 Fore St   FRENCH **££**
(☑01736-731164; www.2forestreet.co.uk; Fore St; dinner mains £14-18.25; ⊙noon-2pm & 7-9pm)

This laid-back bistro is squeezed into a small space along Mousehole's backstreets, and majors in French-inspired classics – unsurprising, given the head chef trained under Raymond Blanc. There's a small dining room, a sweet garden and a locally focused menu strong on seafood.

Penzance

POP 21,168

Overlooking the majestic sweep of Mount's Bay, the old harbour of Penzance has a salty, sea-blown charm that feels altogether more authentic than many of Cornwall's polished-up ports. Its streets and shopping arcades still feel real and a touch ramshackle, and there's nowhere better for a windy-day walk than the town's seafront Victorian promenade.

⊙ Sights & Activities

Penlee House Gallery & Museum GALLERY
(☑ 01736-363625; www.penleehouse.org.uk; Morrab Rd; adult/child £5/4; ⊙10am-5pm Mon-Sat Easter-Sep, 10.30am-4.30pm Mon-Sat Oct-Easter) This small museum is ideal for a primer on the artistic heritage of West Cornwall. It has a fine collection of paintings by artists of the Newlyn School (including Stanhope and Elizabeth Forbes, Walter Langley and Lamorna Birch) and hosts regular exhibitions inside a handsome 19th-century building. The nearby Penlee Gardens are well worth a stroll.

Tremenheere Sculpture Garden GARDENS
(☑ 01736-448089; www.tremenheere.co.uk; adult/child £8/4.50; ⊙gardens 10am-5pm; ⊛) This inventive garden opened just outside Penzance in 2012. The landscaped gardens sit in a sheltered valley awash with artworks and installations: look out for a 'sky-view' chamber by James Turrell; 'Black Mound', a pile of tree stumps by David Nash; and 'Camera Obscura' by Billy Wynter, offering a unique panorama of the gardens and Mount's Bay.

There's also a super cafe, **Tremenheere Kitchen** (lunches £8 to £14), and family events such as den-building and art workshops during school holidays.

★ **Jubilee Pool** SWIMMING
(☑ 01736-369224; www.jubileepool.co.uk; Western Promenade Rd; adult/child £5/3.50; ⊙10.30am-6pm, to 8pm Tue, early Jun–late Sep) After being battered during recent winter storms, Penzance's glorious seawater lido has reopened and regained its rightful place as the town's

BATH & SOUTHWEST ENGLAND PENZANCE

> **DON'T MISS**
>
> ## ST MICHAEL'S MOUNT
>
> Looming up in the middle of Mount's Bay and connected to the mainland at Marazion via a cobbled causeway, **St Michael's Mount** (NT; ☑ 01736-710507; www.stmichaelsmount.co.uk; house & gardens adult/child £15/7.50; ⊙house 10.30am-5.30pm Sun-Fri Jul-Sep, to 5pm Mar-Jun & Oct) is an unforgettable sight, and one of Cornwall's most iconic images. Initially a Benedictine monastery, and later the seat of the St Aubyn family, it's a must-visit. You can catch the ferry (adult/child £2/1) from Marazion at high tide, but it's worth arriving at low tide so you can walk across the causeway, as pilgrims did centuries ago.
>
> There's been a monastery here since at least the 5th century, but the present abbey was mostly built by Benedictine monks during the 12th century (the same religious order that also constructed the island's sister abbey at Mont St-Michel in France). Highlights of the main house include the rococo drawing room, the armoury and the 14th-century church, but it's the amazing clifftop gardens that really steal the show. Thanks to the local sub-climate, many exotic flowers and shrubs flourish here, and it's all a riot of colour in summer.
>
> Recent excavations, with finds including an axe head, a dagger and a metal clasp, have proved the island has been inhabited since at least the Bronze Age, but it was almost certainly used by prehistoric people long before. According to some scholars, the island may have been a trading post for locally mined copper and tin for several thousand years.
>
> During winter, access to the island is only possible by boat, but in summer, walking across on the causeway is a magical experience: there's a useful guide to the causeway's opening hours on the website (www.stmichaelsmount.co.uk/plan-your-visit/causeway-opening-times).

Penzance

Penzance

◎ Sights
1 Penlee House Gallery & Museum.......B2

✪ Activities, Courses & Tours
2 Jubilee Pool D3

🛏 Sleeping
3 Artist Residence Penzance C2
4 Chapel House Penzance......................C2
5 Venton Vean A3

✗ Eating
6 Cornish Barn C2
7 Shore B2

🍷 Drinking & Nightlife
8 Admiral Benbow.....................................C2
9 Turk's Head C2

pride and joy. Built in 1935, it's a bold statement of art deco styling, sleek, sharp and whitewashed – the perfect backdrop for some bracing seawater bathing.

There's discounted entry after 3.30pm (adult/child £3.15/2.50).

The pool has announced an exciting project to heat part of the pool using geothermal technology: check the website for the latest announcements.

🛏 Sleeping

Penzance YHA HOSTEL £
(📞 0845 371 9653; www.yha.org.uk; Castle Horneck, Alverton; dm £19-25; 🅿 📶) Penzance's YHA is inside an 18th-century house on the edge of town. It's a rambling place, with a cafe, a laundry and four- to 10-bed dorms. It's a 15-minute walk from the harbour front.

★ Venton Vean B&B ££
(📞 01736-351294; www.ventonvean.co.uk; Trewithen Rd; r £88-100; 📶) The picture of a modern B&B, finished in stylish greys and blues, with stripped wood floors, bay windows and a keen eye for design. Rooms 1 and 2 are the most spacious; the former overlooks Penlee Memorial Park. The sumptuous breakfast choice includes pancakes, smoked Newlyn fish, avocado on sourdough toast, and a Mexican-style feast of tortillas and refried beans.

★ Artist Residence Penzance B&B £££
(📞 01736-365664; www.artistresidence.co.uk/our-hotels/cornwall; 20 Chapel St; d £135-255, deluxe ste from £315; 📶🐾🅿) Hands down Penzance's most entertaining hotel, this converted town house on Chapel St has been renovated with impeccable taste, marrying period architecture with modern boutique

style. It's full of detail: Robert's radios, roll-top baths, antique furniture, old tea chests and the odd wall mural or two. The Loft rooms are lovely, particularly the luxurious Lookout.

★ **Chapel House Penzance** B&B £££
(☑ 01736-362024; www.chapelhousepz.co.uk; Chapel St; r from £190; ☜) In one of Chapel St's most historic buildings – a sea-captain's house that was for many years an arts centre – this beautiful B&B has become a favourite of travel supplements, and it's not hard to see why. The six rooms ooze design credentials: retro furniture, waterfall baths, oak beds, sleek bathrooms, skylight windows, all carefully blended with the house's Georgian architecture.

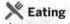 **Eating**

★ **Shore** MODERN BRITISH ££
(☑ 01736-362444; www.theshorerestaurant.uk; 13/14 Alverton St; dinner mains from £20.50, 5-/7-course tasting menu £42/60; ☻ 6.30-9pm Wed-Sat) This brilliant seafood bistro is overseen by chef Bruce Rennie, a veteran of many a Michelin-starred kitchen. It's all about classic fish and shellfish here, sourced from the Newlyn day boats and served with a strong French-Italian influence. Odds are that this is the next address in Cornwall to bag a Michelin star; get in while you can.

★ **Ben's Cornish Kitchen** BRITISH ££
(☑ 01736-719200; www.benscornishkitchen.com; West End; 2-/3-course dinner £27/33; ☻ noon-1.30pm & 7-8.30pm Tue-Sat; ☝) Blink and you'll miss Ben Prior's restaurant as you zip along Marazion's main street, but diners travel from far and wide to taste his superlative cooking, which majors in meaty Cornish flavours with a French influence. Ben's cooking has earned glowing reviews, and awards from Waitrose, the *Good Food Guide* and the *Trencherman's Guide*, so tables are scarce – book ahead.

★ **Tolcarne Inn** PUB FOOD ££
(☑ 01736-363074; www.tolcarneinn.co.uk; Tolcarne Pl; mains £15-22; ☻ noon-2.15pm & 7-9pm Tue-Sat, noon-2.15pm Sun) This Newlyn inn is run by chef Ben Tunnicliffe, a long-standing name on the Cornish dining scene. The ethos here is refreshingly honest – top-quality fish, seafood and locally sourced meat, served with minimal fuss. It's a snug space, full of smuggler's pub charm – blackboard menus, whitewashed walls and views of the har-bour. Bookings advisable, especially for Sunday lunch.

Cornish Barn BISTRO ££
(☑ 01736-339414; www.thecornishbarn.co.uk; 20 Chapel St; dishes £8-20; ☻ 7.30am-2.30pm & 5.30-9.30pm Mon-Fri, 7.30am-3pm & 5.30-9.30pm Sat, 7.30am-3.30pm & 6-9pm Sun) With its exposed brick, scuffed timber, bare bulbs and blaz-ing wood-burner, this bistro on the ground floor of the Artist Residence Penzance nails the hipster aesthetic, but it has substance as well as style. Tuck into baked eggs or but-termilk chicken burgers for lunch, and after dark go for something from the in-house smoker (think smoked steak or beer-can chicken).

🍷 Drinking & Nightlife

Admiral Benbow PUB
(☑ 01736-363448; 46 Chapel St; ☻ 11am-11pm) On historic Chapel St, the salty old Benbow looks as if it's dropped from the pages of *Treasure Island,* with nautical decor mostly reclaimed from shipwrecks: anchors, lan-terns, figureheads and all.

Turk's Head PUB
(☑ 01736-363093; Chapel St; ☻ 11am-11pm) Purportedly the town's oldest pub; there's been a tavern here since the 13th century. It was supposedly a favourite hang-out for Penzance's 'free traders' (aka smugglers); a subterranean tunnel once led to the harbour from the cellar (now the dining room). There are Skinner's and Sharp's ales on tap, and a seafood-dominated menu that features crab sandwiches and grilled lobster.

ℹ️ Getting There & Away

BUS

Buses depart from the **bus station** (Wharf Rd). Local destinations include the following.

Helston (bus U4, £6, hourly Monday to Satur-day, two hourly Sunday) Travels via Marazion and connects onward to Falmouth and Penryn.

St Ives (bus 16/16A/A17, £6, 30 minutes, hourly Monday to Saturday, five on Sunday).

Land's End (bus A1, £6, 50 minutes, every two hours Monday to Saturday, five on Sunday).

TRAIN

Penzance is the last stop on the line from Lon-don Paddington.

Truro £7, 30 minutes

St Ives £4.50, 50 minutes, change at St Erth

Exeter £40.30, three hours

London Paddington £91.10, 5½ hours

BATH & SOUTHWEST ENGLAND PENZANCE

The Lizard

Cornwall's southern coastline takes a sudden wild turn around the Lizard Peninsula, where fields and heaths plunge into a melee of black cliffs, churning surf and saw-tooth rocks. Cut off from the rest of Cornwall by the River Helford, and ringed by treacherous seas, the Lizard was once an ill-famed graveyard for ships, and the peninsula still has a raw, untamed edge. Wind-lashed in winter, in summer its clifftops blaze with wildflowers, and its beaches and coves are perfect for a bracing wild swim.

It's also a stronghold for the Cornish chough, the red-billed, crow-like bird featured on the county's coat of arms. Once all but extinct, it's slowly reestablishing itself around the Lizard's rugged cliffs.

You may catch sight of slow-worms and even an adder in summer, but the peninsula's peculiar name actually has no reptilian connections; it comes from the old Celtic words *'lys ardh'*, meaning 'high court'.

◎ Sights & Activities

★ Kynance Cove   BEACH

A mile north of Lizard Point, this National Trust–owned inlet is an absolute showstopper, studded with craggy offshore islands rising out of searingly blue seas that seem almost tropical in colour. The cliffs around the cove are rich in serpentine, a red-green rock popular with Victorian trinket-makers. It's an impossibly beautiful spot and, when the seas aren't too rough, an exhilarating place for a wild swim. Drinks and snacks are available at the ecofriendly beach cafe (☑ 01326-290436; www.kynancecovecafe.co.uk; mains £5-14; ☉ 9am-5.30pm).

Lizard Lighthouse Heritage Centre MUSEUM

(☑ 01326-290202; www.trinityhouse.co.uk/light house-visitor-centres/lizard-lighthouse-visitor-cen tre; adult/child £3.50/2.50; ☉ 11am-5pm Sun-Thu Mar-Oct) Rising above Lizard Point, the whitewashed lighthouse was built in 1751 and has protected ships from the treacherous rocks ever since. Although it's now automated, like all UK lighthouses, you can visit the heritage centre to learn more about its mechanics and the many ships that have come to grief nearby. It's also the only lighthouse in Cornwall you can actually climb; guided tours (adult/child £8/5) ascend into the tower to see the lamp room and foghorn.

★ Cornish Seal Sanctuary   ANIMAL SANCTUARY

(☑ 0871 423 2110; www.visitsealife.com/gweek; adult/child £15.50/12.50; ☉ 10am-5pm May-Sep, 9am-4pm Oct-Apr) The 'ah' factor goes into overdrive at this sea-life centre in Gweek, about 12 miles drive from Falmouth along the Helford River. It cares for sick and orphaned seals washed up along the Cornish coastline before returning them to the wild. It's a guaranteed kids' favourite, and parents will doubtless find themselves seduced by the seals' antics, too. There are regular talks and feeding sessions. Online bookings get a hefty 30% discount.

🛏 Sleeping & Eating

Lizard YHA   HOSTEL £

(☑ 0845 371 9550; www.yha.org.uk; dm £16-25; ☉ Apr-Oct) Once a Victorian hotel next to the lighthouse, now a YHA hostel, this has to rank pretty high on the 'UK's best budget beds' list. It's in a spectacular location, overlooking miles of wild cliffs and coast, and it's typically well run: a range of dorms, a self-catering kitchen and spacious lounge, but no cafe.

★ Kota   INTERNATIONAL ££

(☑ 01326-562407; www.kotarestaurant.co.uk; 2-/3-course menu £20/25, mains £14-24; ☉ 6-9pm Tue-Sat) Porthleven's top restaurant is run by half Maori, half Chinese-Malay chef Jude Kereama. Set in an old harbourside mill, the menu is spiced with Far Eastern and fusion flavours, underpinned by classic French credentials. Presentation is a strong point – the dishes look beautiful, with edible flowers and other flourishes – but some flavour combinations work better than others. Bookings essential.

There's also a more easygoing bistro, Kota Kai (☑ 01326-574411; www.kotakai.co.uk; mains £8.95-18.95; ☉ noon-2pm Thu-Tue, 5.30-9.30pm Mon-Sat; 🐾), just along the harbour.

Halzephron Inn   PUB FOOD ££

(☑ 01326-240406; www.halzephron-inn.co.uk; mains £10-22; ☉ 11am-11pm) On the cliffs above the cove of Gunwalloe, 5 miles south of Helston, this is a historic Cornish local, whitewashed and slate-topped, with brassy trinkets above the bar, stout beams and a menu of beer-battered fish, grilled gammon steak, duck breast and the like. It's cosy and stone-walled, with lots of nooks and crannies, and a small patio outside.

Falmouth & Around

POP 20,775

Few seaside towns in Cornwall boast such an arresting location as Falmouth, overlooking the broad Fal River as it empties into the English Channel. Surrounded by green hills and blue sea, Falmouth is an appealing jumble of lanes, old pubs, slate roofs and trendy cafes. It's an ideal base for exploring Cornwall's south coast, and has a wealth of bars and bistros, a trio of beaches and Cornwall's finest maritime museum.

Though it's now mainly supported by students at Falmouth University in nearby Penryn, the town made its fortune during the 18th and 19th centuries thanks to lucrative maritime trade – Falmouth has the third-deepest natural harbour in the world, and the town grew rich when tea clippers, trading vessels and mail packets stopped here to unload their cargoes. Falmouth is still an important centre for ship repairs – you can look over the dockyard cranes as you head to Pendennis Point.

◎ Sights

Falmouth's trio of bucket-and-spade beaches – **Gyllyngvase**, **Swanpool** and **Maenporth** – aren't quite up to north coast standards, but they're nice enough for paddling and sun lounging. All the beaches have car parks, but they fill up quickly in summer; a bus service (p350) is also available.

Two of Cornwall's great subtropical gardens, **Trebah** (☑ 01326-252200; www.trebah garden.co.uk; adult/child £10/5; ☉ 10.30am-5.30pm, last entry 4.30pm) and **Glendurgan** (NT; ☑ 01326-250906; www.nationaltrust.org.uk/glendurgan-garden; adult/child £9.50/4.75; ☉ 10.30am-5.30pm Tue-Sun), sit side by side along the river's northern bank, about 4 miles south of Falmouth.

★ **Potager Garden**   GARDENS
(☑ 01326-341258; www.potagergarden.org; suggested donation £3; ☉ 10am-5pm Thu-Sun) It's a bit of a drive from Falmouth but this gorgeous kitchen garden near Constantine is well worth the detour. Rescued from dilapidation by its current owners, it's been renovated by volunteers into a delightful working garden modelled on the French 'potager'. Highlights include the 30m greenhouse and the super veggie **cafe**, which is very popular with lunching locals at weekends (mains £6 to £10). There's always a good selection of plants for sale, too.

National Maritime Museum   MUSEUM
(☑ 01326-313388; www.nmmc.co.uk; Discovery Quay; adult/child £12.95/5; ☉ 10am-5pm) Falmouth's most high-profile museum is located on the revamped area around Discovery Quay. It's the sister outpost of the National Maritime Museum in Greenwich, London, and focuses on Falmouth's history as a seafaring port, supplemented by regular nautically themed exhibitions – recent shows covered the history of the Royal National Lifeboat Institution (RNLI), the exploration of the Pacific and the tradition of tattooing. The centrepiece is the impressive **Flotilla Gallery**, where an array of small boats is suspended from the ceiling.

Pendennis Castle   CASTLE
(EH; ☑ 01326-316594; www.english-heritage.org.uk; adult/child £8.40/5; ☉ 10am-6pm Mar-Sep, to 5pm Oct, to 4pm Sat & Sun Nov-Feb) Designed in tandem with its sister castle in St Mawes across the estuary, this Tudor castle sits proudly on Pendennis Point, and was built as part of Henry VIII's massive castle-building program to reinforce England's coastline. You can wander around the central keep and the Tudor gun deck, as well as the governor's bedroom, a WWI guardhouse and the WWII-era Half-Moon Battery. Listen out for the Noonday Gun, which rings out at 12pm sharp every day in July and August.

⚓ Activities

Fal River Boat Trips   BOATING
Falmouth's main pier is the departure point for boat trips along the Fal River and ferries to Flushing and St Mawes. There are several operators, all offering similar routes: Enterprise Boats (p350) is the best known, and runs regular trips to Truro and St Mawes via Trelissick Gardens.

AK Wildlife Cruises   WILDLIFE WATCHING
(☑ 01326-753389; www.akwildlifecruises.co.uk; adult/child £50/45) Run by the amiable and unfailingly enthusiastic 'Captain Keith', this specialist wildlife cruise sets out from Falmouth Harbour in search of local marine life. Depending on the season, there's a good chance of spotting dolphins, porpoises, basking sharks, puffins and seals – and it's not unheard of to spy minke whales.

Gylly Adventures   KAYAKING
(☑ 07341 890495; www.gyllyadventures.co.uk; kayak tour per person £40) Based on Gyllyngvase

THE EDEN PROJECT & THE LOST GARDENS OF HELIGAN

Five miles from St Austell, at the bottom of a china clay pit, the giant biomes of the **Eden Project** (☏01726-811911; www.edenproject.com; adult/child £27.50/14, joint ticket with Lost Gardens of Heligan £38.05/18.45; ☉9.30am-6pm, last admission 4.30pm) – the world's largest greenhouses – have become Cornwall's most famous landmark, and an absolutely essential visit. Looking rather like a lunar landing station, Eden's bubble-shaped biomes maintain miniature ecosystems that enable all kinds of weird and wonderful plants to flourish – from stinky rafflesia flowers and banana trees in the Rainforest Biome to cacti and soaring palms in the Mediterranean Biome. Book online for discounted admission.

The Eden Project is the brainchild of former record producer turned entrepreneur Tim Smit, who also rescued the **Lost Gardens of Heligan** (☏01726-845100; www.heligan.com; Pentewan; adult/child £14.50/6.50; ☉10am-6pm Mar-Oct, to 5pm Nov-Feb) from ruin. Formerly the family estate of the Tremaynes, Heligan's magnificent 19th-century gardens fell into disrepair following WWI, but have been splendidly restored by an army of gardeners and volunteers. It's a horticultural wonderland: you'll encounter formal lawns, working kitchen gardens, fruit-filled greenhouses, a secret grotto and a 25m-high rhododendron, plus a lost-world Jungle Valley of ferns, palms and tropical blooms. Heligan is 7 miles from St Austell.

Beach, this watersports company hires the usual kit – stand-up paddleboards, kayaks, bodyboards and the like – but it also offers some great guided kayaking trips. Options include a tour of Falmouth harbour, a trip down the Helford River, a pub paddle and (best of all) a night kayak trip illuminated by LED head torches (£45 per person).

✸ Festivals

Falmouth Oyster Festival　　FOOD & DRINK
(www.falmouthoysterfestival.co.uk; ☉Oct) Feast on fresh oysters, mussels and other crustaceans during this festival, which also hosts cookery classes and culinary demos.

🛏 Sleeping

★ Highcliffe Contemporary B&B　B&B ££
(☏01326-314466; www.highcliffefalmouth.com; 22 Melvill Rd; s £55-70, d £80-160; 🛜) Vintage furniture and upcycled design pieces give each of the rooms here an individual feel. The pick of the bunch is the light-filled Attic Penthouse, with skylight windows overlooking Falmouth Bay. Room-service breakfasts are served in picnic baskets, or you can tuck into pancakes and hog's pudding in the dining room.

Bosanneth　　　　　　　B&B ££
(☏01326-314649; www.bosanneth.co.uk; Gyllyngvase Hill; d from £90; 🛜) There's a mix-and-match decorative vibe running through this eight-room B&B. Some of the rooms feel vintage, with old mirrors, reclaimed furniture and classic colours, while others go for a more up-to-date look. The 'oasis' garden is a particular delight.

★ Greenbank　　　　　　HOTEL £££
(☏01326-312440; www.greenbank-hotel.co.uk; Harbourside; r £130-260; 🅿🛜) Greenbank is the queen of Falmouth's hotels, with a knockout position overlooking the boat-filled estuary towards Flushing. It feels like the setting for an Agatha Christie novel – nautical knick-knacks and ships in cabinets dot public areas, and tall windows look out on to the water. The rooms are more modern, decorated in beige and cream. Sea views command premium prices.

🍴 Eating

★ Stone's Bakery　　　　　BAKERY £
(☏07791 003183; www.stonesbakery.co.uk; 28a High St; breads £1.50-3, mains £6-9; ☉9am-4pm Mon-Sat; 🛜) Freshly baked loaves line the window like pieces of art at this gorgeous bakery, which focuses on traditional hand-shaped rustic loaves – the tangy maltster and the organic sourdough are as delicious as you'll ever taste. It recently moved up the street to new premises, and now has space to serve great breakfasts and lunchtime pizzas and tarts.

Good Vibes Café　　　　　CAFE £
(☏01326-211870; www.facebook.com/goodvibes cafefalmouth; 28 Killigrew St; sandwiches & sal-

ads £6-8; ⊗8.30am-5.30pm Mon-Sat; 🐾) This friendly, contemporary cafe on the Moor is popular for its copious breakfasts (veggie and nonveggie), as well as its creative sandwiches (which range from pulled spiced chicken to peanut-and-mackerel bagel), crunchy salads and irresistible cakes. There's free cucumber water on tap, plus smoothies and juices galore.

★**Oliver's** BISTRO ££
(📋01326-218138; www.oliversfalmouth.com; 33 High St; mains £15-24; ⊗noon-2pm & 7-9pm Tue-Sat) Run by well-respected chef Ken Symons, this little bistro is everyone's tip in Falmouth, but the tiny dining room means you'll have to book well ahead. White walls and pine tables provide a stripped-back match for Ken's imaginative, Mediterranean-inspired food. Local foragers provide many ingredients. Bookings are essential.

★**Wheelhouse** SEAFOOD ££
(📋01326-318050; Upton Slip; mains £8-15; ⊗6-10pm Wed-Sat) Hidden down a narrow alley off Church St, this tiny, nautically themed backstreet shellfish bar is all about the hands-on seafood experience: crab, scallops, mussels and lobsters are served in their shells, complete with cracking tools. There are two sittings, but both are always sold out – you will need to book well ahead, ideally a month in advance.

★**Star & Garter** GASTROPUB ££
(📋01326-316663; www.starandgarterfalmouth.com; 52 High St; dinner mains £16-23; ⊗noon-10pm) At the top of the old High St among antique shops and health-food stores, this ancient old boozer has been reincarnated as a gourmet gastropub focusing on nose-to-tail dining, locally sourced wherever possible. It's proved a great success, with a bevy of foodie awards and cracking views across the water to Flushing. The menu is meat-heavy, so veggies might struggle.

★**Ferryboat Inn** GASTROPUB ££
(📋01326-250625; www.staustellbrewery.co.uk/pub/falmouth/ferryboat-inn; Helford Passage; mains £8-20; ⊗11am-11pm) This lovely riverside pub is a Cornish classic. Outside, there are wooden picnic tables with dreamy views over the Helford River; inside, it's all wood, slate and open plan. It's great for food – oysters, shellfish and the Sunday roast are strong points – and a big blackboard is full

of fishy specials. Bus 35 passes hourly from Falmouth.

🍷 Drinking & Nightlife

★**Beerwolf Books** PUB
(📋01326-618474; www.beerwolfbooks.com; 3 Bells Ct; ⊗noon-midnight) Probably the greatest idea ever, anytime, anywhere: a prime pub and brilliant bookshop rolled into one, meaning you can browse for reading material before settling down for a pint of real ale. Beers change weekly, and you're welcome to bring in food. It feels well worn and welcoming, like a comfy pair of slippers, with old chairs and mix-and-match tables.

Chintz Symposium BAR
(📋01326-617550; www.thechintzbar.com; Old Brewery Yard; ⊗5-11.30pm; 🐾) Wine, charcuterie, cheese and cocktails take centre stage at this uber-trendy hang-out on the 1st floor above Hand Bar. Junk shop furniture and patches of reclaimed wallpaper fill the A-framed attic space, and the wine list is copious.

Hand Bar BAR
(📋01326-319888; www.facebook.com/handbeerbaruk; 3 Old Brewery Yard; ⊗noon-1am) Peter Walker's craft-beer bar showcases his knowledge, gained while running Leeds' North Bar. Esoteric choices such as New York's Brooklyn Brewery and Bodmin's Harbour Brewing Co are among the regulars on tap – although esoterica equals expensiveness. It's fittingly situated in a former brewery, with a few courtyard tables outside, but space is limited inside.

Front PUB
(📋01326-212168; Custom House Quay; ⊗11am-11.30pm) The beer-buffs' choice in Falmouth: a cosy spit-and-sawdust pub, with scuffed wood floors and a copious choice of real ales chalked up above the bar, served straight from wooden casks. The entrance is down a small hill off Arwenack St.

★**Espressini** CAFE
(📋01326-236582; www.espressini.co.uk; 39 Killigrew St; ⊗8am-6pm Mon-Sat, 10am-4pm Sun; 🐾) Cornwall's best coffee house, bar none, run by committed coffee aficionado Rupert Ellis. The choice of blends, roasts and coffees is enough to fill a 2m-long blackboard (literally) and it has recently started serving a small selection of breakfast and lunch dishes, too. There's another coffee-only branch across town on Arwenack St.

ℹ Information

The small **Fal River Information Centre** (☏ 01326-741194; www.falriver.co.uk; 11 Market Strand, Prince of Wales Pier; ⊙ 9.30am-5.30pm Mon-Sat, 10am-4pm Sun) by Prince of Wales Pier is run by the Fal River Company, and provides useful advice. It also operates most of the ferries along the Fal River, and offers an accommodation booking service.

ℹ Getting There & Away

Falmouth is at the end of the branch train line from Truro (£4.20, 24 minutes), where you can catch connections with the mainline service from Penzance to stations including Plymouth, Exeter and London Paddington.

Falmouth's **Moor Bus Station** (The Moor) is central. **First Kernow** (www.firstgroup.com/cornwall) has the following bus routes.

Helston (£5.40, hourly Monday to Saturday) Bus 35/35A stops at Glendurgan and Trebah Gardens en route.

Penzance (every two hours Monday to Saturday) Bus 2 via Helston.

Redruth (£5.40, hourly) Bus U2 via Penryn.

Truro (£5.40, half-hourly Monday to Saturday, hourly Sunday) Bus U1 via Penryn.

To reach Gyllyngvase and Swanpool beaches, bus 367 runs from the station to both (hourly Monday to Friday, four times on Saturday).

Truro

POP 17,430

Dominated by the three mighty spires of its 19th-century cathedral, which rises above town like a neo-Gothic supertanker, Truro is Cornwall's capital and its only city. It's the county's main centre for shopping and commerce: the streets here are packed with high-street chains and independent shops, and there are regular weekly markets held on the paved piazza at Lemon Quay (opposite the Hall for Cornwall).

Traces of Truro's wealthy past remain in the smart Georgian town houses and Victorian villas dotted around the city – especially along Strangways Tce, Walsingham Pl and Lemon St – although a rash of 60s and 70s architecture has somewhat marred the city's architectural appeal.

◉ Sights & Activities

Truro Cathedral   CHURCH

(www.trurocathedral.org.uk; High Cross; suggested donation £5; ⊙ 7.30am-6pm Mon-Sat, 9am-7pm Sun) Built on the site of a 16th-century parish church in soaring Gothic Revival style, Truro Cathedral was completed in 1910, making it the first cathedral built in England since St Paul's. Inside, the vast nave contains some fine Victorian stained glass and the impressive Father Willis Organ.

Royal Cornwall Museum   MUSEUM

(☏ 01872-272205; www.royalcornwallmuseum.org.uk; River St; ⊙ 10am-5pm Mon-Sat) **FREE** Collections at the county's main museum encompass everything from geological specimens to Celtic torques and a ceremonial carriage. Upstairs there's an Egyptian section and a little gallery with some surprising finds: a Turner here, a van Dyck there, and several works by the Newlyn artist Stanhope Forbes.

★ Enterprise Boats   BOATING

(☏ 01326-374241; www.falriver.co.uk/getting-about/ferries/enterprise-boats; day return adult/child £15.30/7.20) Two miles downriver from Truro's city centre, past Boscawen Park, lies the riverside hamlet Malpas, from where ferries chug out along the Fal River and on to Falmouth. Depending on the tide, boats either depart from the pontoon at Malpas, or from the Truro harbour-master's office; double-decker buses link the two.

The boats putter past wooded riverbanks and hidden inlets; some stop at Trelissick en route. It's a wonderfully scenic trip.

There's a 10% discount for online bookings.

★ Trelissick   GARDENS

(NT; ☏ 01872-862090; www.nationaltrust.org.uk/trelissick-garden; house & gardens adult/child £12/6, grounds £4; ⊙ grounds 10.30am-5.30pm, house 11am-5pm) Grandly located at the head of the Fal estuary, 4 miles south of Truro, Trelissick is one of Cornwall's most beautiful aristocratic estates, with a formal garden filled with magnolias and hydrangeas, surrounded by a huge expanse of green fields and parkland criss-crossed by trails. The grand, 19th-century neo-Palladian house has been reopened to the public, and hosts exhibitions exploring the estate's history. If you just want to explore the estate grounds, parking costs £4.

🛏 Sleeping

Mannings Hotel   HOTEL ££

(☏ 01872-270345; www.manningshotels.co.uk; Lemon St; r £115-125, apt £145; 🅿 🛜) The best place to stay in the city centre. The part-Georgian building has been tastefully modernised, with bright colours and functional furniture, even if the general vibe feels a tad corporate. There are nine self-contained apartments for longer stays, which come with small kitchens and spiral staircases. The private gated car park is very useful.

Merchant House Hotel HOTEL ££
(☑ 01872-272450; www.merchant-house.co.uk; 49 Falmouth Rd; s/d/f £79/99/119; P🛜🐕) This Victorian house is handy for town, and refurbishment has brightened up the rooms with cheery sea-blue colour schemes. Some have skylights, others overlook the garden. It's popular with business travellers and organised coach tours, however, so it's worth reserving well ahead. It's a steep walk up Lemon St past the Lander monument.

✖ Eating & Drinking

Craftworks Street Kitchen STREET FOOD £
(☑ 01872-857117; www.craftworkskitchen.co.uk; Lemon Quay; mains £6-8; ⊗11am-6pm Mon-Thu, to 8pm Fri & Sat, to 4pm Sun) Inside an old shipping container, this rough-and-ready little diner turns out the best street food in the city. Choose from delicious tacos and burritos like peri-peri chicken and beef brisket, served with taco slaw and red-onion pickle, or go the whole hog with a fish po-boy or a Korean chicken burger.

Bustopher Jones BISTRO ££
(☑ 01872-430000; www.bustophersbarbistro.com; 62 Lemon St; mains £12.95-24; ⊗noon-10pm Mon-Sat) It's been open, closed and open again over recent years, but Bustopher's is back for downtown bistro dining: expect substantial dishes like pan-seared hake with a mussel-butter sauce and duck with dauphinoise potatoes, served in an attractive, wood-panelled dining room. There's a small patio at the rear.

Thomas Daniell BRITISH ££
(☑ 01872-858110; www.tdtruro.com; 1 Infirmary Hill; mains lunch £6.95-10.95, dinner £11.95-21.50; ⊗lunch noon-5pm daily, dinner 5-10pm Mon-Sat) Run by the owners of the Old Grammar School (☑ 01872-278559; www.theoldgrammarschool.com; 19 St Mary's St; ⊗10am-late Mon-Sat) cocktail bar, this sophisticated gastropub is looking sleek and modern since its recent refurbishment, and it's become one of the city's new favourites. Big wooden tables, local ales on tap and a choice of dining spaces, plus a good wine choice. Food is fairly standard gastropub stuff, like surf-and-turf and battered fish.

★108 Coffee CAFE
(☑ 07582 339636; www.108coffee.co.uk; 109 Kenwyn St; ⊗7am-6pm Mon-Fri, 8am-6pm Sat) Set up by unapologetic coffee nuts Paul and Michelle, this is the premier place for a caffeine fix in Truro. The beans come courtesy of Cornish coffee roasters Origin, and the flat whites and espressos are as good as any the county has to offer (you can even text your order ahead to save waiting).

Old Ale House PUB
(☑ 01872-271122; www.old-ale-house.co.uk; 7 Quay St; ⊗noon-11pm) A proper ale-drinker's pub, with sawdust on the floor, beer mats on the ceiling and a menu of guest ales. Ask at the bar for a handful of peanuts to snack on – they're even happy for you to chuck your shells on the floor. Most of the beers come from Skinner's Brewery.

ℹ Information

Tourist Office (☑ 01872-274555; www.visit truro.org.uk; Boscawen St; ⊗9am-5.30pm Mon-Fri, to 5pm Sat) In a small office beside the Hall for Cornwall's rear entrance.

ℹ Getting There & Away

BUS
Truro's **bus station** is beside Lemon Quay.
Falmouth (£5.40, half-hourly Monday to Saturday, hourly Sunday) The U1 bus runs via Penryn.
St Ives (£5.40, 1½ hours, hourly Monday to Saturday) Bus 14/14A.
Penzance (£5.40, half-hourly Monday to Saturday, hourly Sunday) Bus 18.

TRAIN
Truro is on the main London Paddington–Penzance line and the branch line to Falmouth.
Bristol £49, 3½ hours
Exeter £19.60, 2¼ hours
Falmouth £4.40, 30 minutes
London Paddington £91.10, 4½ hours
Penzance £11, 30 minutes

Fowey
POP 2275

In many ways, Fowey feels like Padstow's south-coast sister; a workaday port turned well-heeled holiday town, with a tumble of pastel-coloured houses, portside pubs and tiered terraces overlooking the wooded banks of the Fowey River. The town's wealth was founded on the export of china clay from the St Austell pits, but it's been an important port since Elizabethan times, and later became the adopted home of the thriller writer Daphne du Maurier, who used the nearby house at Menabilly Barton as the inspiration for *Rebecca*.

Today it's an attractive and increasingly upmarket town, handy for exploring Cornwall's southeastern corner.

A few miles north along the creek, the riverside hamlet of **Golant** is also well worth a detour, with a waterfront pub for lunch and excellent kayaking opportunities.

◉ Sights & Activities

Polkerris Beach BEACH
(www.polkerrisbeach.com) A couple of miles west of Fowey, this is the area's largest and busiest beach. Sailing lessons, windsurfing and stand-up paddleboarding are all available.

Fowey River Expeditions KAYAKING
(☑01726-833627; www.foweyexpeditions.co.uk; 47 Fore St; adult/child £30/15; ⊙Apr-Oct) Guided trips in single- and double-seater open-top canoes, which are ideal for beginners. Standard trips last about three hours and leave from Fowey.

★Encounter Cornwall KAYAKING
(☑07976 466123; www.encountercornwall.com; Golant; adult/child £30/15) Three-hour guided kayaking trips from Golant, just north of Fowey, with a choice of exploring creek or coastline. It also offers two-hour 'sundowner' expeditions and stand-up paddleboarding trips.

⛏ Sleeping

★Coriander Cottages B&B££
(☑01726-834998; www.foweyaccommodation. co.uk; Penventinue Lane; 1-bed cottages £125-145; P 🅿🛜🐾) 🌿 A delightfully rural cottage complex on the outskirts of Fowey, with ecofriendly accommodation in open-plan, self-catering barns, all with quiet country views. The stone barns have been beautifully modernised, and use a combination of solar panels, ground-source heating and rainwater harvesting to reduce environmental impact. Handily, cottages are available

per night, so you're not restricted to weekly stays.

Old Quay House HOTEL£££
(☑01726-833302; www.theoldquayhouse.com; 28 Fore St; d £195-300, ste from £340; 🛜) The epitome of Fowey's upmarket trend, this exclusive quayside hotel is all natural fabrics, rattan chairs and tasteful monochrome tones, and the rooms are a mix of estuary-view suites and attic penthouses. It's right in the centre of town, in a handsome riverside building. The restaurant specialises in upmarket seafood.

Cormorant Hotel HOTEL££
(☑01726-833426; www.cormoranthotel.co.uk; Golant; d £90-180; P 🛜) Up the creek from Fowey in Golant (about 5 miles by road), this small hotel has a superb riverside location, and many of its rooms have water-view balconies. They're split into three comfort levels: go for a Superior overlooking the river for the premium price-to-comfort ratio. Considering the lovely view, rates are very reasonable.

✖ Eating & Drinking

Lifebuoy Cafe CAFE£
(☑07715 075869; www.thelifebuoycafe.co.uk; 8 Lostwithiel St; mains £5-10; ⊙8am-5pm) Everyone's favourite brekkie stop in Fowey, this friendly cafe is a riot of character, from the brightly coloured furniture and polka-dot bunting to the vintage Action Men on the shelves. Wolf down a Fat Buoy brekkie or a classic fish-finger butty, washed down with a mug of good old English tea.

Dwelling House CAFE£
(☑01726-833662; 6 Fore St; tea £3-6; ⊙10am-6.30pm May-Sep, to 5.30pm Wed-Sun Oct-Apr) There is no better spot for afternoon tea in town than this delightful cafe, which makes all its own cakes, from lemon drizzle to coffee and walnut, decorated with sprinkles and icing swirls, and served on a proper cake stand. Unapologetically English.

Sam's BISTRO££
(☑01726-832273; www.samscornwall.co.uk/fowey; 20 Fore St; mains £12-18; ⊙noon-9pm) Sam's has been a stalwart in Fowey for years. Booth seats, Day-Glo menus and a lively local vibe keep the feel laid-back, and the menu of burgers, fish, salads and steaks proves perennially popular – although you're not getting haute cuisine here. No bookings.

POLPERRO & MEVAGISSEY

Even in a county where picturesque fishing harbours seem to fill every cove, it's hard not to fall for **Polperro** – a warren of cottages, boat stores and alleyways, all set around a stout granite harbour. Unsurprisingly, this was once a smugglers' hideout, and it's still a place with a salty, sea-dog atmosphere, despite the inevitable summer crowds. The coast path between Polperro and Looe is particularly scenic. The main car park is 750m uphill from the village, from where it's a 15-minute stroll down to the quayside.

Just along the coast, the little village of **Mevagissey** has not been gentrified to quite the same degree as other ports along the coast, and feels all the better for it. There are alleys to wander, great pubs, secondhand bookshops and galleries to browse, and the harbour is one of the best places on the south coast for crabbing. In summer, ferries run along the coast from Mevagissey Harbour to Fowey.

King of Prussia   PUB
(☑ 01726-833694; www.kingofprussiafowey.co.uk; Town Quay; ⊙ 11am-11pm) Fowey has lots of pubs, but you might as well go for the one with the best harbour view, named after notorious 'free trader' (otherwise known as smuggler) John Carter. Head up the steps into the candy-pink building, and aim to get one of the river-view tables.

ⓘ Information

Fowey Tourist Information Centre (☑ 01726-833616; www.fowey.co.uk; 5 South St; ⊙ 9.30am-5pm Mon-Sat, 10am-4pm Sun) Lots of information on Fowey and southeast Cornwall.

ⓘ Getting There & Away

Bus services are limited: the only really useful service is bus 24 (hourly Monday to Saturday, six on Sunday), which runs to St Austell, Heligan and Mevagissey. It also stops at Par train station, where you can catch trains on the main London–Penzance line.

There are two ferry services from Fowey: the Bodinnick Ferry, which carries cars over the river to Bodinnick en route to Polruan, and the pedestrian-only Polruan Ferry.

Polruan Ferry (www.ctomsandson.co.uk/polruan-ferry; adult/child £2.80/80p, bicycle £1, dog 40p; ⊙ 7.15am-11pm May-Sep, 7.15am-7pm Mon-Sat, 10am-5pm Sun Oct-Apr) Passenger ferry to Polruan. In winter and on summer evenings, it runs from Town Quay; during the day, it runs from Whitehouse Slipway on the Esplanade.

Bodinnick Ferry (www.ctomsandson.co.uk/bodinnick-ferry; car & 2 passengers/pedestrian/bicycle £4.80/1.80/free; ⊙ 7am-7.30pm Mon-Sat, 8am-7.30pm Sun May-Sep, last ferry 7pm Oct-Apr) Car ferry crossing the river to Bodinnick.

Looe

POP 5280

Nestled in the crook of a steep-sided valley, the twin towns of East and West Looe stand on either side of a broad river estuary, connected by a multiarched Victorian bridge built in 1853. There's been a settlement here since the days of the Domesday Book, and the town thrived as a medieval port before reinventing itself as a holiday resort for well-to-do Victorians – famously, the town installed one of the county's first 'bathing machines' beside **Banjo Pier** (named for its circular shape) in around 1800, and it's been a popular beach retreat ever since.

In contrast to Fowey, Looe still feels a little behind-the-times – chip shops, souvenir sellers and chintzy B&Bs still very much rule the roost here – but if it's a classic bucket-and-spade seaside town you're looking for, you've definitely found it in Looe.

⊙ Sights

Looe Island   ISLAND
(www.cornwallwildlifetrust.org.uk/looeisland; guided walks £25) A mile offshore from Hannafore Point is densely wooded Looe Island (officially known as St George's Island), a 9-hectare nature reserve and haven for marine wildlife. You can explore on foot, or book a guided walk with the island ranger, who can help spot local wildlife including grey seals, cormorants, shags and oystercatchers. Bookings are advised for guided walks.

Between April and September, the **Moonraker** (☑ 07814 264514; Buller Quay; return adult/child £7/5, plus landing fee £4/1) putters over from Buller Quay, but trips are dependent on weather and tides.

WORTH A TRIP

COTEHELE HOUSE

At the head of the Tamar Valley sits the Tudor manor of **Cotehele** (NT; ☑ 01579-351346; www.nationaltrust.org.uk/cotehele; St Dominick; adult/child £11.60/5.80; ☺ house 11am-4pm, gardens dawn-dusk), one of the Edgcumbe dynasty's modest country retreats. The cavernous great hall is the centrepiece, and the house has an unparalleled collection of Tudor tapestries, armour and furniture.

Outside, the gardens sweep down past the 18th-century Prospect Folly to Cotehele Quay, where there's a discovery centre exploring the history of the Tamar Valley and a vintage sailing barge, the *Shamrock*.

🛌 Sleeping

Penvith Barns　　　　　　　　B&B £ £

(☑ 01503-240772; www.penvithbarns.co.uk; St-Martin-by-Looe; r £85-110; P ☑ ☎ ☀) Escape the Looe crowds at this rural barn conversion in the nearby hamlet of St-Martin-by-Looe, run by friendly owners Graham and Jules. Rooms range from small to spacious: the Piggery is tiny and tucked under the eaves, while the Dairy has enough space for a spare bed and sofa. Each room has its own private entrance. Two-night minimum in summer.

Commonwood Manor　　　　　B&B £ £

(☑ 01503-262929; www.commonwoodmanor.com; St Martins Rd; d £90-115; P ☑ ☎ ☀) In a prime position on the East Looe hillside, this elegant manor house is a cut above the bargain-basement B&Bs you'll find around the rest of Looe. Rooms are a touch frilly and pastel heavy, but if you can bag one of the bay-window bedrooms, you'll be rewarded with the best sea views in town. There's usually a two-night minimum.

ℹ Information

Looe Tourist Office (☑ 01503-262072; www.looeguide.co.uk; Guildhall, Fore St; ☺ 10am-5pm Easter-Oct) Looe's efficient and well-staffed visitor centre is the hub for all tourist things: accommodation, activities, restaurant recommendations and so on.

ℹ Getting There & Away

The branch line from Liskeard to Looe is almost a day out in itself, tracking through wooded valleys all the way out to the seaside. The Looe Valley Line Day Ranger ticket (adult/child £4.40/2.20) allows one day's unlimited travel; the journey from Liskeard to Looe takes about 40 minutes.

Bodmin Moor

It can't quite boast the wild majesty of Dartmoor, but Bodmin Moor has a bleak beauty all of its own. With its heaths and granite hills, including Rough Tor ('row-tor'; 400m) and Cornwall's highest point, Brown Willy (420m), it's a desolate place that works on the imagination, with prehistoric remains and legends of mysterious beasts.

The northern and central parts of the Moor are largely barren and treeless, while the southern section is greener. Apart from the hills, the moor's main landmark is Jamaica Inn, made famous by Daphne du Maurier's novel of the same name.

◉ Sights & Activities

★ **Lanhydrock**　　　　　　HISTORIC BUILDING

(NT; ☑ 01208-265950; www.nationaltrust.org.uk/lanhydrock; adult/child £14.35/7.20; ☺ house 11am-5.30pm, grounds 10am-5.30pm) This magnificent manor, 2.5 miles southeast of Bodmin, offers a fascinating insight into *Upstairs, Downstairs* life in Victorian England. The house was rebuilt after a devastating fire in 1881 as a home for the Agar-Robartes family, complete with mod cons such as radiators, roasting ovens, warming cupboards and flushing loos. The centrepieces are the drawing room, packed with artworks and antiques, and the enormous kitchens, complete with a pioneering refrigerator room. The ornate Long Gallery is famous for its plaster ceiling.

★ **Golitha Falls**　　　　　　WATERFALL

Around 1.25 miles west of St Cleer, these crashing waterfalls are one of the most renowned beauty spots on the moor. Around the falls are the remains of the ancient oak woodland that once covered much of the moor. There is a car park half a mile's walk from the reserve, near Draynes Bridge.

Carnglaze Caverns　　　　　　CAVE

(☑ 01579-320251; www.carnglaze.com; adult/child £7/5; ☺ 10am-5pm, to 8pm Aug; ♿ ☀) Slate was once an important local export on Bodmin Moor, and these deep caverns were cut out by hand by miners, leaving behind an atmospheric network of subterranean caves and a glittering underground pool. Concerts and plays are sometimes held inside the caves in summer. The site is just outside St Neot and well signed.

★ **Bodmin & Wenford Railway** RAIL
(☑ 01208-73555; www.bodminrailway.co.uk; Rover Pass adult/child £13.50/6.50; ☺ 3-5 daily trains May-Sep, fewer at other times) Run by enthusiasts, this steam railway – the only 'standard gauge' line of its type left in Cornwall – chuffs and clatters for 6.5 miles between Bodmin and Boscarne Junction. Many trains are still decked out in original 1950s livery. At the Boscarne end, the line links up with the Camel Trail (p332); bikes can be taken on the trains if there's space.

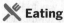 Eating

★ **St Tudy Inn** MODERN BRITISH ££
(☑ 01208-850656; www.sttudyinn.com; St Tudy; mains £14-25; ☺ meals noon-2.30pm & 6.30-9pm Mon-Sat, noon-2.30pm Sun) Run by the locally lauded chef Emily Scott, this first-rate village pub has fast become one of East Cornwall's top dining destinations. The old pub has been stripped down and smartened up, and Scott's imaginative food combines traditional British flavours with a modern, season-driven style. There is also a selection of elegant **rooms** (doubles from £135) in attached barns.

★ **Woods Cafe** CAFE ££
(☑ 01208-78111; www.woodscafecornwall.co.uk; Cardinham Woods; mains £6-12; ☺ 10.30am-4.30pm) In an old woodsman's cottage lost among the trees of Cardinham, this cracking cafe has become a dining destination in its own right – it's locally famous for its home-baked cakes, cockle-warming soups and sausage sarnies (sandwiches). Perfect for post-walk sustenance.

ISLES OF SCILLY

While only 28 miles west of the mainland, in many ways the Isles of Scilly feels like a different world. Life on this archipelago of around 140 tiny islands seems hardly to have changed in decades: there are no traffic jams, no supermarkets, no multinational hotels, and the only noise pollution comes from breaking waves and cawing gulls. That's not to say that Scilly is behind the

times – you'll find a mobile-phone signal and broadband internet on the main islands – but life ticks along at its own island pace. Renowned for its glorious beaches, there are few places better to escape.

Only five islands are inhabited: St Mary's is the largest, followed by Tresco, while only a few hardy souls remain on Bryher, St Martin's and St Agnes. Regular ferry boats run between all five islands.

Unsurprisingly, summer is by far the busiest time. Many businesses shut down completely in winter.

❶ Information

Isles of Scilly Tourist Information Centre
(☑ 01720-424031; www.visitislesofscilly.com; Porthcressa Beach; ☺ 9am-5.30pm Mon-Sat, 9am-2pm Sun Mar-Oct, 10am-2pm Mon-Fri Nov-Feb) The islands' only tourist office.

Scilly Online (www.scillyonline.co.uk) A locally run website with lots of info on the islands.

Simply Scilly (www.simplyscilly.co.uk) The official tourist site.

❶ Getting There & Away

Isles of Scilly Travel (☑ 01736-334220; www.islesofscilly-travel.co.uk) There are several flights daily from Land's End Airport, near Zennor, and from Newquay Airport. Adult fares start at £80 one way. Summer flights also run from Exeter, Bristol and Southampton. Since 2018 there has also been a helicopter service from Land's End Airport to St Mary's. The flight time is around 20 minutes.

Scillonian III (☑ 0845 710 5555; www.islesof scilly-travel.co.uk; ☺ Apr-Oct) Scilly's ferry plies the notoriously choppy waters between Penzance and St Mary's (one-way adult £49.50). There's at least one daily crossing in summer, but there are no ferries in winter. It sails in most weathers, but seasickness is a distinct possibility: be prepared.

❶ Getting Around

Inter-island ferries between St Mary's and the other islands are provided by the **St Mary's Boatmen's Association** (☑ 01720-423999; www.scillyboating.co.uk; adult/child return to any island £9.50/4.75). If you're staying at one of the hotels on Tresco, there's also a separate transfer service.

The only bus and taxi services are on St Mary's. All flights are met by **Paulgers Transport** (☑ 01720-423701; adult/child return £7.50/3.50), which will run you to wherever you're staying, or straight to the quayside if you're travelling to other islands.

St Mary's

POP 2200

First stop for every visitor to Scilly (unless you're arriving aboard your own private yacht) is St Mary's, the largest and busiest of the islands, and home to the vast majority of hotels, shops, restaurants and B&Bs. Just over 3 miles at its widest point, St Mary's is shaped like a crooked circle, with a claw-shaped peninsula at its southwestern edge – home to the island's capital, Hugh Town, and the docking point for the Scillonian ferry. The main airport is a mile east near Old Town.

◉ Sights

Isles of Scilly Museum
MUSEUM
(☑01720-422337; www.iosmuseum.org; Church St, Hugh Town; adult/child £3.50/1; ◷10am-4.30pm Mon-Fri, to noon Sat Easter-Sep, to noon Mon-Sat Oct-Easter) The small Isles of Scilly Museum explores the islands' history, with an eclectic mix of archaeological finds and artefacts from shipwrecks. Among the collection are Neolithic remains such as tools and jewellery, clay pipes left behind by generations of sailors, a couple of sailing boats and a small exhibition on Edward Heath, the British prime minister who loved Scilly so much he was buried here.

⛳ Tours

Scilly Walks
WALKING
(☑01720-423326; www.scillywalks.co.uk; adult/child £7/3.50) Three-hour archaeological and historical tours of St Mary's, plus regular guided walking trips to other islands, conducted by local historian and archaeologist Katherine Sawyer.

Island Wildlife Tours
WALKING
(☑01720-422212; www.islandwildlifetours.co.uk; half/full day £7/14) Regular birdwatching and wildlife walks with local character and resident twitcher Will Wagstaff, the undisputed authority on Scilly's natural history. Most tours start at 9.45am or 10am on St Mary's, but there are regular tours on other islands too. You need to add on the cost of the boat transfer.

Island Sea Safaris
BOATING
(☑01720-422732; www.islandseasafaris.co.uk) Trips to see local seabird and seal colonies (adult/child £34/25), plus one-hour 'island taster' tours (£25 per person). Also rents wetsuits and snorkelling gear.

🛏 Sleeping

Garrison Campsite
CAMPSITE £
(☑01720-422670; www.garrisonholidaysscilly.co.uk; Tower Cottage, Garrison; adult £10.50-12.50, child £5.25-6.25, dog £5; 🖂🐾) St Mary's main campsite sits in a lofty spot above Hugh Town, not far from the Garrison fort. It's a big site, covering 3.5 hectares, with plenty of pitches (some with electrical hook-ups), plus wi-fi, a small shop and a laundry-shower block. It also offers a couple of cottages, including an old lookout tower (£495 to £695 per week).

Mincarlo
B&B ££
(☑01720-422513; www.mincarloscilly.com; s £43-51, d £77-114; 🖂🐾) There's no better location on St Mary's than this little guesthouse in a prime spot with views all the way to Hugh Town from the western end of Town Beach. Rooms are plain and cosy (the attic's a bargain), there's a lounge with local books to browse, breakfast is great, and owners Nick and Bryony are full of local info.

Star Castle Hotel
HOTEL £££
(☑01720-422317; www.star-castle.co.uk; Garrison; s £157, d £248-327; 🖂🐾🐾) Shaped like an eight-pointed star, this former fort on Garrison Point is one of Scilly's star hotels, with heritage-style castle rooms and more-modern garden suites. It's stuffy and expensive, but the views are the best on the island, and at least prices include dinner. It gets a lot cheaper outside the peak months between May and September.

Atlantic Hotel
INN £££
(☑01720-422417; www.atlanticinnscilly.co.uk; r £175-240; 🖂🐾) Revamped courtesy of owners St Austell Brewery, this long-standing inn is looking a lot fresher. Upstairs there are summery rooms with colourful prints, pastel colours and plush fabrics; there are three categories, but here the harbour view is definitely worth the premium. Food is similar to the brewery's other inns: mussels, lobster burgers, seafood platters and other pub-style mains.

🍴 Eating

Juliet's Garden Restaurant
BISTRO ££
(☑01720-422228; www.julietsgardenrestaurant.co.uk; mains lunch £7-15, dinner £14-24.95; ◷noon-4pm & 6-9pm) St Mary's long-standing bistro, in business for over three decades, is still the best place to eat. It's in a converted barn 15 minutes' walk from town: expect gourmet

salads and sandwiches by day, plus classier plates of pan-roasted bream, slow-roasted lamb and lobster after dark, served by candlelight. The garden is glorious on a sunny day, but it gets busy.

Dibble & Grub CAFE ££
(✏01720-423719; www.dibbleandgrub.com; lunch £6-12, dinner £10-16; ⏲10am-10pm Apr-Sep) Smart beachside cafe beside Porthcressa beach, housed in the island's old fire station. The menu dabbles in tapas and Mediterranean-style classics.

❶ Getting Around

The airport bus (£3) departs from Hugh Town 40 minutes before each flight, while the **Island Rover** (✏01720-422131; www.islandrover.co.uk; tickets £9) offers sightseeing trips in a vintage bus: there are usually a couple a day, with an extra one in high summer.

For taxis on St Mary's, try **Island Taxis** (✏01720-422126), **Scilly Cabs** (✏01720-422901) or **St Mary's Taxis** (✏01720-422142), or airport taxi Paulgers Transport (p355).

Tresco

POP 175

A short boat hop across the channel from St Mary's brings you to Tresco, the second-largest island, once owned by the monks of Tavistock Abbey, and now privately leased by the Dorrien-Smith family from the Duchy of Cornwall.

The main attraction here is the island's fabulous subtropical garden, but the rest of the island is a lovely place just to explore by bike – although since the whole place is privately leased, it feels a little more manicured and packaged than the other, more community-driven islands, especially since the focus here is very much on high-end visitors.

◉ Sights

★ Tresco Abbey Garden GARDENS
(✏01720-424105; www.tresco.co.uk/enjoying/abbey-garden; adult £15, child 5-16yr £5; ⏲10am-4pm) Tresco's key attraction – and one of Scilly's must-see gems – is this subtropical estate, laid out in 1834 on the site of a 12th-century Benedictine priory by the horticultural visionary Augustus Smith. The 7-hectare gardens are now home to more than 20,000 exotic species, from towering palms to desert cacti and crimson flame trees, all nurtured by the temperate Gulf Stream. Admission also covers the **Valhal-**

la collection, made up of figureheads and nameplates salvaged from ships wrecked off Tresco.

🛏 Sleeping & Eating

★ New Inn PUB, HOTEL £££
(✏01720-422849; www.tresco.co.uk; r £130-340; ❄✈) By Tresco standards, New Inn is a bargain. The rooms are soothingly finished in buttery yellows and pale blues, although inevitably you'll have to fork out for a view. The inn itself serves good food (mains £10 to £18), mainly standards such as pollock and chips, steaks, burgers and the like, and the low-beamed bar is full of island atmosphere.

Bryher

Only around 80 people live on Bryher, Scilly's smallest and wildest inhabited island. Covered by rough bracken and heather, and fringed by white sand, this slender chunk of rock takes a fearsome battering from the Atlantic – Hell Bay hasn't earned its name for nothing. But on a bright sunny day, it's an island idyll par excellence, ideal for exploring on foot.

The island has a strong sense of community; you'll see little stalls selling freshly cut flowers, homegrown veg, jams and packets of fudge.

🛏 Sleeping & Eating

Bryher Campsite CAMPSITE £
(✏01720-422886; www.bryhercampsite.co.uk; sites £10.75; ♿✈) Bare-bones but beautiful, the island's campsite sits in a secluded spot surrounded by drystone walls and is just steps from the sea.

Hot showers and tractor transport from the quay are included in the nightly rates.

★ Hell Bay Hotel HOTEL £££
(✏01720-422947; www.hellbay.co.uk; d £140-360; 🅿❄♿) Pretty much the poshest place to stay in Scilly, and a true island getaway blending New England–style furnishings with sunny golds, sea blues and pale wood beams. It has the feel of a luxurious beach villa, with lovingly tended gardens and an excellent restaurant (three-course menu £45). Garden-view suites are the cheapest.

Fraggle Rock CAFE ££
(✏01720-422222; www.bryher.co; mains £8-15; ⏲9am-9pm; ❄) This relaxed cafe also doubles as Bryher's pub. The menu is mainly

quiches, salads and burgers, ideally served in the front garden, where chickens scratch around and there are views out to Hangman's Rock. It's a lively evening hang-out in season. There are a few timber-clad **cabins** (£620 to £1090 per week) if you feel like staying.

Bryher Shop   DELI

(☑01720-423601; www.bryhershop.co.uk; ☺9am-5.30pm Mon-Sat, 10am-1pm Sun) Pick up all your essential supplies at the island's charming general store, which also has a post office.

St Martin's

POP 136

The third-largest and furthest north of the islands, St Martin's is the main centre for Scilly's flower-growing industry, and the island's fields are a riot of colourful blooms in season. It's also blessed with gin-clear waters and the kind of untouched sands you'd more usually associate with St Lucia than Cornwall.

The main settlement is Higher Town, where you'll find the village shop and diving operation, but there are small clusters of cottages in nearby Middle and Lower Towns.

◉ Sights & Activities

St Martin's Vineyard   WINERY

(☑01720-423418; www.stmartinsvineyard.co.uk; ☺10.45am-4pm Tue-Thu, conducted tours 11am) The UK's smallest and most southwesterly vineyard produces its own range of white wines. Tours are conducted by owners Val and Graham Thomas.

★ Scilly Seal Snorkelling   SWIMMING

(☑01720-422848; www.scillysealsnorkelling.com; per person £49; ☺Mar-Sep) Now here's an experience to remember – the chance to swim with wild grey seals in the clear waters off St Martin's. the more inquisitive ones come right up close – and the boldest have even been known to nibble your fins. Trips last about three hours.

It'll collect you from your accommodation on St Martin's, but it also provides a morning transfer from Tresco or St Mary's harbour.

⊨ Sleeping

Accommodation is limited apart from a superexpensive hotel and a handful of B&Bs.

St Martin's Campsite   CAMPSITE £

(☑01720-422888; www.stmartinscampsite.co.uk; sites £11-12, dogs £3; ☺Mar-Oct) The second-largest campsite in Scilly, at the western end of Lawrence's Bay, with 50 pitches (maximum 100 people) spread across three fields. There are coin-operated washing machines and showers, and eggs and veg are available for your morning fry-up.

Polreath   B&B ££

(☑01720-422046; www.polreath.com; Higher Town; d £110-130; ☎) This friendly granite cottage has small rooms and a sunny conservatory serving cream teas, homemade lemonade and evening meals. Weekly stays required May to September.

✗ Eating & Drinking

Little Arthur Farm   CAFE £

(☑01720-422457; www.littlearthur.co.uk; cafe meals £5-8; ☺10.30am-4pm) 🍃 A little slice of the good life on tiny St Martin's, this small-scale farm has diversified in all kinds of imaginative directions. There's a cafe-bistro, it grows its own produce and even makes environmentally friendly shoes. There's an eco-cabin to stay in too (£280 to £380 per week).

Adam's Fish & Chips   SEAFOOD £

(☑01720-422457; www.adamsfishandchips.co.uk; fish & chips takeaway £9, dine-in £10.50; ☺6-8.30pm Tue-Thu & Sat, noon-2pm Sun Jul & Aug, 6-8.30pm Tue, Thu & Sat Easter-Jun & Sep) The fish here is about as fresh as it gets – whatever's caught on the day is what ends up in your batter. It's run by Adam and Emma, who live and work on Little Arthur Farm nearby. Takeaway is available, but you'll need to book if you want one of the six tables.

Seven Stones   PUB

(☑01720-423777; sevenstonesinn@gmail.com; ☺10am-11pm) A fine pub and the island's only boozer, so it's the heart of the action every night of the week. Decent grub (mains £8 to £14), Cornish ales and super views of the other islands from the terrace.

St Agnes

POP 170

Scilly's southernmost island feels really remote, with a string of empty coves and a scattering of prehistoric sites. Visitors disembark at Porth Conger, near the old lighthouse, from where you wander along the coast path around the whole island.

At low tide, a narrow sandbar appears and provides a bridge to the neighbouring island of Gugh, where many ancient burial sites and a few chamber tombs can be found.

🛏 Sleeping & Eating

★ Troytown Farm   CAMPSITE £
(☑ 01720-422360; www.troytown.co.uk; adult/child £10/5, tents £2-8) The journey to St Agnes' campsite is almost the best bit; you're picked up in a tractor trailer and rattle across the island down the hedge-lined lanes. The camping field is small, but wonderfully located on the island's sunset coast, surrounded by drystone walls and a sea-blue, big-sky horizon. There are his-and-hers loos, token-operated showers (60p) and lockers for device-charging.

Luggage transfer costs £3.50. The campsite also rents prepitched bell tents (from £420 per week) and three self-catering cottages (£385 to £1045 per week). Bring a torch, as the island gets very, very dark.

Covean Cottage   COTTAGE ££
(☑ 01720-422620; www.coveancottage.com; d £88-104) Pretty much the only B&B on the island, this little stone-walled cottage has three pretty sea-view rooms. There's also a small cafe, which serves brekkies and light meals cooked up by the owner.

★ Turk's Head   PUB FOOD ££
(☑ 01720-422434; mains £8-14; ⊙ 11am-11pm Mon-Sat, noon-10.30pm Sun) You can almost smell the history at Britain's most southerly alehouse. It's covered in maritime memorabilia – model ships in glass cabinets, vintage maps of the islands, black-and-white photos of seafarers – and there are few finer places to sup a pint. You might even be treated to a sea shanty if the local lads are in the mood.

Cambridge & East Anglia

Best Places to Eat

→ Midsummer House (p374)

→ Roger Hickman's (p391)

→ Great House (p384)

→ Eric's Fish & Chips (p397)

→ Butley Orford Oysterage (p386)

→ Orchard Tea Garden (p377)

Best Places to Stay

→ Varsity (p373)

→ Swan (p388)

→ 3 Princes (p390)

→ Victoria (p396)

→ Cley Windmill (p394)

→ Deepdale Farm (p396)

Why Go?

Unfurling gently eastwards to the sea, the vast flatlands of East Anglia are a rich web of lush farmland, melancholy Fens and sparkling rivers. The area is justly famous for its sweeping sandy beaches, big skies and the bucolic landscape that once inspired Constable and Gainsborough.

It's not all rural idyll though: rising out of the Fens is the world-famous university city of Cambridge, with its stunning classical architecture and earnest attitude, while to the east is the cosmopolitan city of Norwich. Around them, magnificent cathedral cities, pretty market towns and implausibly picturesque villages are testament to the enormous wealth amassed here during medieval times, when the wool and weaving industries flourished.

The meandering coastline is peppered with charismatic fishing villages and traditional seaside resorts, while inland lie the languid, hypnotic charms of the Norfolk Broads, an ideal location for serious relaxation.

When to Go

→ To best explore the Cambridge colleges, avoid spring (early April to mid-June), when they close to visitors as students prepare for exams.

→ June and August show the Norfolk and Suffolk beaches and the Norfolk Broads at their best. But in school holidays (late July to August) it gets busy and accommodation prices rise.

→ World-class classical music comes to Suffolk during the Aldeburgh Festival in June. In July, Southwold's eclectic Latitude Festival offers alternative rock, comedy and theatre.

→ November's Ways With Words literature festival draws big-name authors to Southwold.

→ Exquisite music fills Cambridge's King's College Chapel in December, culminating in the Festival of Nine Lessons and Carols on Christmas Eve.

History

East Anglia was a major Saxon kingdom; the dazzling treasures unearthed in the ship burial at Sutton Hoo (p383) in Suffolk have revealed how complex a society it was.

The region's heyday came during the wool boom of the Middle Ages when Flemish weavers settled in the area; many of the grand local churches date from this time – Cambridge University was founded in this period, too.

By the 17th century, much of the region's marshland and bog had been drained and converted into arable land.

It was in East Anglia's emergent, Puritan bourgeoisie that the seeds of the English Civil War were sown. Oliver Cromwell, the uncrowned king of the Parliamentarians, was a small-time merchant residing in Ely when he answered God's call to take up arms against what he saw as the fattened and corrupt monarchy of Charles I.

East Anglia's fortunes waned in the 18th century, when the Industrial Revolution flourished in northern England. During WWII the region became an ideal base for the Royal Air Force and the United States Air Force in the fight against Nazi Germany, thanks to its flat, open landscape and close proximity to mainland Europe.

🏃 Activities

East Anglia is a magnet for walkers, cyclists and kayakers. Here you can discover miles of coastline, tour vast expanses of level land and glide along snaking inland waterways – the Norfolk Broads are utterly idyllic. North Norfolk's wide, often empty beaches are ideal for land yachting and kitesurfing.

Cycling

Famously one of England's flattest regions, East Anglia offers gorgeous cycling along the Suffolk and Norfolk coastlines and in the Fens. Mountain bikers should head for Norfolk's **Thetford Forest** (www.forestry.gov.uk/thetfordforestpark), while much of the popular on- and off-road Peddars Way is also open to cyclists.

Walking

The **Peddars Way and Norfolk Coast Path** (www.nationaltrail.co.uk/peddarsway) is a seven-day, 93-mile national trail from Knettishall Heath, near Thetford, to Cromer. The first half takes in an ancient Roman road. The trail then finishes by meandering along the beaches, sea walls, salt marshes (great for birdwatching) and fishing villages of the coast.

Curving further south, the 50-mile Suffolk Coast Path links Felixstowe and Lowestoft, via Snape Maltings, Aldeburgh, Dunwich and Southwold.

Boating & Canoeing

East Anglia's coast and the Norfolk Broads are beloved by boating enthusiasts – those without their own craft can easily hire boats and arrange lessons. Alternatively, wend your way gently around the Broads in a kayak or canoe along the slow-moving rivers.

ℹ Information

Visit East of England (www.visiteastofengland.com) has more info.

ℹ Getting There & Around

Public transport links between London, the Midlands and East Anglia are excellent. Services within the region are generally good; as ever there are fewer connections to smaller towns and villages.

AIR

Key flights to Norwich International Airport (p391) include those to Amsterdam, Aberdeen, Edinburgh, Exeter and Manchester.

BUS

➡ A host of smaller firms, plus two main companies, First (www.firstgroup.com) and Stagecoach (www.stagecoachbus.com), run the region's bus networks.

➡ Traveline East Anglia (www.travelineeast anglia.org.uk) has timetables.

TRAIN

➡ Regional rail provider Greater Anglia (www.greateranglia.co.uk) offers the Anglia Plus Pass. It's valid for a week; you can pay to use it for one day (£19) or three days (£38) within that time.

CAMBRIDGESHIRE

Many visitors to Cambridgeshire never make it past the captivating university city of Cambridge, where august old buildings, student cyclists in academic gowns and glorious chapels await. But beyond this breathtaking seat of learning, the flat reclaimed Fens, lush farmland and myriad waterways make perfect walking and cycling territory, while the extraordinary cathedral at Ely and the rip-roaring Imperial War Museum at

Cambridge & East Anglia Highlights

1 Cambridge (p364) Punting past historic colleges before enjoying the heavenly evensong at King's College Chapel.

2 Sandringham (p395) Nosying around the drawing room of the Queen's country estate.

3 Norfolk Broads (p392) Canoeing your way through tranquil waterways.

4 Audley End (p380) Delighting in one of Britain's grandest stately homes.

5 Holkham Beach (p396) Wandering barefoot along immense, pine-backed golden sands.

6 Lavenham (p384) Soaking up the medieval architecture in this atmospheric market town.

7 Norwich (p388) Marvelling at the exquisite rib vaulting in the city's fine cathedral.

8 Aldeburgh (p386) Dining on sublime seafood and walking the prom in a laid-back resort.

9 Imperial War Museum (p376) Discovering the history of the British and American air forces, in Duxford.

Duxford would be headline attractions anywhere else.

ℹ️ Getting Around

Public transport radiates from Cambridge, a mere hour's train ride from London King's Cross (£25, two to four per hour). This line continues north through Ely to King's Lynn in Norfolk. Branch lines run east to Norwich and into Suffolk.

Cambridge

 01223 / POP 123,900

Abounding with exquisite architecture, exuding history and tradition, and renowned for its quirky rituals, Cambridge is a university town extraordinaire. The tightly packed core of ancient colleges, the picturesque riverside 'Backs' (college gardens) and the leafy green meadows surrounding the city give it a more tranquil appeal than its historic rival Oxford.

Like 'the Other Place', as Oxford is known locally, the buildings here seem unchanged for centuries, and it's possible to wander around the college buildings and experience them as countless prime ministers, poets, writers and scientists have done. Sheer academic achievement seems to permeate the very walls: cyclists loaded down with books negotiate cobbled passageways, students relax on manicured lawns and great minds debate life-changing research in historic pubs. First-time punters zigzag erratically across the river, and those long past their student days wonder what it would have been like to study in such splendid surroundings.

History

Despite roots stretching back to the Iron Age, Cambridge was little more than a rural backwater until the 11th century, when an Augustinian order of monks set up shop here – the first of the religious institutions that eventually became the colleges. When the university town of Oxford exploded in a riot between town and gown in 1209, a group of scholars, fed up with the constant brawling between locals and students, upped and joined what was to become the University of Cambridge. Cambridge wasn't spared by the riots, and brawls between town and gown took place with disturbing regularity here as well.

The first Cambridge college, Peterhouse (never Peterhouse *College*), was founded in 1284, and in 1318 Pope John XXII's papal bull declared Cambridge to be an official university.

By the 14th century, royalty, nobility, churches, trade guilds and anyone rich enough could court prestige by founding their own colleges, though the system was shaken up during the Reformation with the dissolution of the monasteries. It was 500 years before female students were allowed into the hallowed grounds, though, and even then they were only allowed into the women-only colleges Girton and Newnham, founded in 1869 and 1871 respectively. By 1948, Cambridge minds had broadened sufficiently to allow women to actually graduate.

The honour roll of famous Cambridge students and academics reads like an international who's who of high achievers. It's affiliates include 98 Nobel Prize winners (more than any other institution in the world), 13 British prime ministers, nine archbishops of Canterbury, an immense number of scientists, and a healthy host of poets and authors. This is the town where Newton refined his theory of gravity, Whipple invented the jet engine, and Crick and Watson (relying heavily on the work of Rosalind Franklin, also a scientist at Cambridge) discovered DNA. William Wordsworth, Lord Byron, Vladimir Nabokov, Stephen Hawking and Stephen Fry all studied here too.

Today the university remains one of the best for research worldwide. Thanks to some of the earth-shaking discoveries made here, Cambridge is inextricably linked to the history of learning.

👁️ Sights

⭐ King's College Chapel   CHURCH

(📞 01223-331212; www.kings.cam.ac.uk; King's Pde; adult/child £9/6; ⏰ 9.30am-3.15pm Mon-Sat, 1.15-2.30pm Sun term time, 9.30am-4.30pm daily university holidays) In a city crammed with showstopping buildings, this is a scene-stealer. Grandiose 16th-century King's College Chapel is one of England's most extraordinary examples of Gothic architecture. Its inspirational, intricate 80m-long fan-vaulted ceiling is the world's largest and soars upwards before exploding into a series of stone fireworks. This hugely atmospheric space is a fitting stage for the chapel's world-famous choir; hear it sing during the free and magnificent **evensong** in term time (5.30pm Monday to Saturday, 10.30am and 3.30pm Sunday).

King's **steeples** have long been a magnet for student night climbers (p372), and today images of the chapel adorn thousands of postcards, tea towels and choral CDs. But it was begun in 1446 as an act of piety by Henry VI and was only finished by Henry VIII around 1516.

The lofty **stained-glass windows** that flank the chapel's sides ensure it's remarkably light. The glass is original, a rare survivor of the excesses of the 17th-century Civil War in this region. It's said that these windows were ordered to be spared by Oliver Cromwell, who knew of their beauty from his own studies in Cambridge.

The antechapel and the choir are divided by a superbly carved **wooden screen**, designed and executed by Peter Stockton for Henry VIII. The screen bears his master's initials entwined with those of Anne Boleyn. Look closely and you may find an angry human face (possibly Stockton's) amid the elaborate jungle of mythical beasts and symbolic flowers. Above is the magnificent bat-wing **organ**, originally constructed in 1686, though much altered since.

Beyond the thickly carved dark-wood choir stalls, light suffuses the high **altar**, which is framed by Rubens' masterpiece *Adoration of the Magi* (1634) and the magnificent east window. To the left of the altar in the side chapels, an **exhibition** charts the construction stages and methods.

Note the chapel itself (but not the grounds) is open during the exam period (April to June).

Each Christmas Eve, King's College Chapel stages the **Festival of Nine Lessons & Carols**. It's broadcast globally by the BBC, and to around 300 US radio stations. You can also queue for a place – if you arrive early enough (often by around 9am), you could well get in.

★**Trinity College** COLLEGE
(☎01223-338400; www.trin.cam.ac.uk; Trinity St; adult/child £3/1; ⊙10am-4.30pm Jul-Oct, to 3.30pm Nov-Jun) The largest of Cambridge's colleges, Trinity offers an extraordinary Tudor gateway, an air of supreme elegance and a sweeping Great Court – the largest of its kind in the world. It also boasts the renowned and suitably musty **Wren Library** (⊙noon-2pm Mon-Fri year-round, plus 10.30am-12.30pm Sat term time) **FREE**, containing 55,000 books published before 1820 and more than 2500 manuscripts. Works include those by Shakespeare, St Jerome, Newton and Swift – and AA Milne's original *Winnie the Pooh;* both Milne and his son, Christopher Robin, were graduates.

As you enter Trinity through the part-gilded gate, have a look at the **statue** of the college's founder, Henry VIII, that adorns it. His left hand holds a golden orb, while his right grips not the original sceptre but a table leg, put there by student pranksters and never replaced. It's a wonderful introduction to one of Cambridge's most venerable colleges, and a reminder of who really rules the roost.

In the **Great Court** beyond, scholastic humour gives way to wonderment, thanks to its imposing architecture and sheer size. To the right of the entrance is a small tree, planted in the 1950s and reputed to be a descendant of the apple tree made famous by Trinity alumnus Sir Isaac Newton. Other alumni include Francis Bacon, Lord Byron, Tennyson, HRH Prince Charles (legend has it his bodyguard scored higher in exams than he did), at least nine prime ministers (British and international) and more than 30 Nobel Prize winners.

The college's vast **hall** has a dramatic hammer-beam roof and lantern; beyond lie the dignified cloisters of **Nevile's Court**. Henry VIII would have been proud to note, too, that his college would eventually come to throw the best party in town, the lavish May Ball (p372) in early June, though you will need a fat purse, and a friend on the inside, to get an invitation.

★**Fitzwilliam Museum** MUSEUM
(www.fitzmuseum.cam.ac.uk; Trumpington St; by donation; ⊙10am-5pm Tue-Sat, from noon Sun)

CHARIOTS OF FIRE

Trinity College's immense Great Court has been the setting for countless attempts at a feat of impressive athleticism – a 350m-sprint around the courtyard in 43 seconds (the time it takes the clock to strike 12). It's a challenge made famous by the film *Chariots of Fire*, but although many students did try it, Harold Abrahams (the hero of the movie) never did, and the run in the film was actually shot at Eton. If you fancy your chances, remember that you'll need Olympian speed to even come close.

Cambridge

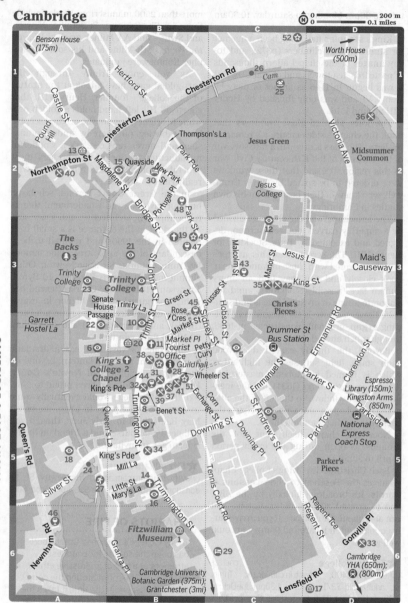

0   200 m
0   0.1 miles

Benson House
(175m)

Worth House
(500m)

Hertford St

Chesterton Rd

Castle St

Pound Hill

Chesterton La

Cam

52

26

25

36

Thompson's La

Jesus Green

Victoria Ave

Midsummer Common

13

Northampton St

Magdalene St

15 Quayside

40

New Park St

Park Pde

Portugal Pl

30

Bridge St

48

Park St

Jesus College

Jesus La

Maid's Causeway

19

47

49

Malcolm St

Manor St

12

The Backs

3

21

St John's St

43

Jesus La

35   42

King St

Trinity College

23

Trinity College

4

Senate House Passage

Trinity La

Green St

45

Rose Cres

Sussex St

Christ's Pieces

Garrett Hostel La

22

10

Market St

Sidney St

Hobson St

Drummer St Bus Station

King's College Chapel

6

20

11

Market Pl Tourist Office

38   50

Petty Cury

5

Emmanuel St

Emmanuel Rd

Clarendon St

Espresso Library (150m); Kingston Arms (850m)

Queen's Rd

King's Pde

2

44 31

28

Guildhall

Wheeler St

32

51

Corn Exchange St

St Andrew's St

9

Parkside

National Express Coach Stop

Trumpington St

8

39 37 41

Bene't St

Downing St

Downing Pl

Park Tce

Parker St

18

7

Queen's La

34

King's Pde

Mill La

Tennis Court Rd

Parker's Piece

24

27

Silver St

14

Little St Mary's La

16

Trumpington St

Fitzwilliam Museum

1

29

Regent Tce

Regent St

Gonville Pl

33

Cambridge YHA (650m); (800m)

46

Newnham Rd

Granta Pl

Cambridge University Botanic Garden (375m); Grantchester (3mi)

Lensfield Rd

17

FREE Fondly dubbed 'the Fitz' by locals, this colossal neoclassical pile was one of the first public art museums in Britain, built to house the fabulous treasures that the seventh Viscount Fitzwilliam bequeathed to his old university. Expect Roman and Egyptian grave goods, artworks by many of the great masters and some quirkier collections: banknotes, literary autographs, watches and armour.

The building's unabashedly over-the-top appearance sets out to mirror its contents;

Cambridge

◉ Top Sights

◉ Sights

◉ Activities, Courses & Tours

◉ Sleeping

◉ Eating

◉ Drinking & Nightlife

◉ Entertainment

this ostentatious jumble of styles mixes mosaic with marble, and Greek with Egyptian. The **lower galleries** are filled with priceless treasures spanning the ancient world; look out for a Roman funerary couch, an inscribed copper votive plaque from Yemen (c AD 100–200), a figurine of Egyptian cat goddess Bastet, splendid Egyptian sarcophagi and mummified animals, plus dazzling illuminated manuscripts. The **upper galleries** showcase works by Leonardo da Vinci, Titian, Rubens, the Impressionists, Gainsborough, Constable, Rembrandt and Picasso; standout works include the tender *Pietà* by Giovanni del Ponte and Salvator Rosa's dark and intensely personal *L'Umana Fragilita*.

The Fitz has a tragic footnote: although begun by George Basevi in 1837, he didn't live to see its completion. While working on Ely Cathedral he stepped back to admire his handiwork, slipped and fell to his death.

One-hour guided tours (£6) of the museum are held at 2.30pm on Saturdays.

★ **The Backs**　　　　　　　PARK
Behind the Cambridge colleges' grandiose facades and stately courts, a series of gardens and parks line up beside the river. Collectively known as the Backs, the tranquil green spaces and shimmering waters offer unparalleled views of the colleges and are often the most enduring image of Cambridge for visitors. The picture-postcard snapshots of student life and graceful bridges can be seen from the riverside pathways and pedestrian bridges – or the comfort of a chauffeur-driven punt.

For the best views of the fanciful **Bridge of Sighs** head into St John's College (p369). Built in 1831, it's best observed from the stylish bridge designed by Wren just to the south, also on St John's grounds. The oldest river crossing is at **Clare College** (☑01223-333200; www.clare.cam.ac.uk; Trinity Lane; adult/

child £5/free; ⊙ dawn-dusk, closed early Apr–mid-Jun), built in 1639 and ornamented with decorative balls. Its architect was paid a grand total of 15p for his design and, feeling aggrieved at such a measly fee, it's said he cut a chunk out of one of the balls adorning the balustrade so the bridge would never be complete.

Most curious of all is the flimsy-looking wooden construction (visible from Silver St) that joins the two halves of Queens' College (p369). Known as the **Mathematical Bridge**, it was first built in 1749. Despite what unscrupulous guides may tell you, it wasn't the handiwork of Sir Isaac Newton (he died in 1727), originally built without nails, or taken apart by academics who then couldn't figure how to put it back together.

Gonville & Caius College

COLLEGE

(☎ 01223-332400; www.cai.cam.ac.uk; Trinity St; ⊙ 8am-noon Mon-Fri mid-Jun–Sep, 9am-2pm daily Oct–mid-Apr) **FREE** Known locally as Caius (pronounced 'keys'), Gonville and Caius boasts three fascinating **gates**: Virtue, Humility and Honour. They symbolise the progress of the good student; the third gate (the Porta Honoris, a fabulous domed and sundial-sided confection) leads to the **Senate House** (Senate House Passage) and thus graduation. Former students include Francis Crick (of DNA-discoverers Crick and Watson) and Edward Wilson, of Scott's tragic Antarctic expedition. The megastar of astrophysics, the late Stephen Hawking, was a fellow here for more than 50 years.

The college was actually founded twice, first by a priest called Gonville, in 1348, and then again in 1557 by Dr Caius (his given name was Keys – it was common for academics to use the Latin form of their names), a brilliant physician who suppos-

edly spoiled his legacy by insisting in the statutes that the college admit no 'deaf, dumb, deformed, lame, chronic invalids, or Welshmen'.

Christ's College

COLLEGE

(☎ 01223-334900; www.christs.cam.ac.uk; St Andrew's St; ⊙ 9am-4pm, closed early May–mid-Jun) **FREE** Christ's College is a venerable institution at more than 500 years old. Its gleaming **Great Gate** is emblazoned with heraldic carvings of Tudor roses, a portcullis and spotted Beaufort yale (mythical antelope-like creatures). Its founder, Lady Margaret Beaufort, hovers above like a guiding spirit. A stout oak door leads into picturesque **First Court**, Cambridge's only circular front court. Hunt out the **gardens** dedicated to alumnus Charles Darwin; they feature plant species brought back from his famous Galapagos voyage.

The Second Court has a gate to the **Fellows' Garden** (open Monday to Friday only), which contains a mulberry tree under which 17th-century poet John Milton reputedly wrote *Lycidas*. Other notable alumni include Sacha Baron Cohen (aka Ali G and Borat) and historian Simon Schama.

Magdalene College

COLLEGE

(☎ 01223-332100; www.magd.cam.ac.uk; Magdalene St; ⊙ 8am-6pm, closed early Apr–mid-Jun) **FREE** Riverside Magdalene often catches people out – the college name is properly pronounced 'Maud-lyn'. This former Benedictine hostel's greatest asset is the **Pepys Library** (⊙ 2-4pm Mon-Fri, 11.30am-12.30pm & 1.30-2.30pm Sat Easter-Aug, 2-4pm Mon-Sat Oct-Easter, closed Sep) **FREE**, housing 3000 books bequeathed by the mid-17th-century diarist to his old college. This idiosyncratic collection of beautifully bound tomes is ordered by height. Treasures include vivid medieval manuscripts and the *Anthony Roll*, a 1540s depiction of the Royal Navy's ships.

Magdalene was the last college to let women study there; when they were finally admitted in 1988, some male students wore black armbands and flew the college flag at half mast.

Emmanuel College

COLLEGE

(☎ 01223-334200; www.emma.cam.ac.uk; St Andrew's St; ⊙ 9am-6pm, closed early Apr–mid-Jun) **FREE** The 16th-century Emmanuel College ('Emma' to students) is famous for its exquisite **chapel** designed by Sir Christopher Wren. Seek out the plaque commemorating John Harvard (who graduated with a BA in

---

ℹ VISITING CAMBRIDGE'S COLLEGES

Cambridge University comprises 31 colleges, though not all are open to the public. Colleges close to visitors over the two-week Christmas break, and while students are preparing for and sitting exams – between early April and mid-June. Be aware, too, that opening hours can vary from day to day, so if you have your heart set on visiting a particular college, contact it in advance to avoid disappointment.

1632), a scholar here who later settled in New England and left his money to a certain Cambridge College in Massachusetts – now Harvard University.

Queens' College
COLLEGE

(☎ 01223-335511; www.queens.cam.ac.uk; Silver St; £3.50; ☉ 10am-3pm, closed early Apr–mid-Jun) Gorgeous 15th-century Queens' College sits elegantly astride the river, connected by the unscientific-looking Mathematical Bridge (p367). Highlights include two enchanting medieval courtyards, Old Court and Cloister Court, the beautiful half-timbered President's Lodge, and the tower in which Dutch scholar and reformer Desiderius Erasmus lodged from 1510 to 1514.

Corpus Christi College
COLLEGE

(☎ 01223-338000; www.corpus.cam.ac.uk; King's Pde; £3; ☉ 10.30am-4.30pm mid-Jun–Sep, 2-4pm Oct-early Apr) Corpus Christi was founded in 1352, a heritage reflected in its exquisite buildings and a monastic atmosphere that radiates from the medieval Old Court. Look out for the fascinating sundial and plaque to playwright and past student Christopher Marlowe (1564–93), who penned *Doctor Faustus* and *Tamburlaine*. New Court (a mere 200 years old) leads to the Parker Library, which holds the world's finest collection of Anglo-Saxon manuscripts (open Monday and Thursday afternoons to tourist office–run tours only).

Note the college was closed to visitors in 2018 for building work, reopening in 2019.

Trinity Hall College
COLLEGE

(☎ 01223-332500; www.trinhall.cam.ac.uk; Trinity Lane; admission by donation; ☉ 10am-noon & 2pm-5pm Tue & Thu, 9am-noon Sun, closed Apr-Jun) Wedged cosily among the great and famous colleges (but unconnected to better-known Trinity), diminutive Trinity Hall was founded in 1350 as a refuge for lawyers and clerics escaping the ravages of the Black Death. The college's chapel is one of the most beautiful in Cambridge; you can visit for evensong during some terms; check with the college for details.

Jesus College
COLLEGE

(☎ 01223-339339; www.jesus.cam.ac.uk; Jesus Lane; ☉ 9am-5pm, closed early Apr–mid-Jun) FREE This tranquil 15th-century college was once a nunnery of St Radegund before the Bishop of Ely, John Alcock, expelled the nuns for 'improvidence, extravagance and incontinence'. Highlights include a Norman arched gallery, a 13th-century chancel and art-nouveau features by Pugin, Ford Madox Brown, William Morris (ceilings) and Burne-Jones (stained glass). Illustrious alumni include Thomas Cranmer, burnt in Oxford for his faith during the Reformation, and long-running BBC and PBS radio journalist and presenter Alistair Cooke.

St John's College
COLLEGE

(☎ 01223-33860; www.joh.cam.ac.uk; St John's St; adult/child £10/5; ☉ 10am-5pm Mar-Oct, to 3.30pm Nov-Feb, closed mid-Jun) Alma mater of six prime ministers, three saints and Douglas Adams (author of *The Hitchhiker's Guide to the Galaxy*), St John's is superbly photogenic. Founded in 1511 by Henry VII's mother, Margaret Beaufort, it sprawls along both riverbanks, joined by the Bridge of Sighs, a masterpiece of stone tracery and a focus for student pranks. Going into the college or taking a punting tour are the only ways to get a clear view of the structure.

Cambridge University Botanic Garden
GARDENS

(☎ 01223-336265; www.botanic.cam.ac.uk; 1 Brookside; adult/child £6/free; ☉ 10am-6pm Apr-Sep, to 5pm Feb, Mar & Oct, to 4pm Nov-Jan) Founded by Charles Darwin's mentor, Professor John Henslow, the beautiful Botanic Garden is home to 8000 plant species, a wonderful arboretum, glasshouses (containing both fierce carnivorous pitcher plants and the delicate slipper orchid), a winter garden and flamboyant herbaceous borders. Hour-long guided tours (free) are held at 2.30pm every Sunday from May through to September.

Free tours are also held on the first Sunday of the month from February to April and October to December. The gardens are 1200m south of the city centre via Trumpington St.

Kettle's Yard
MUSEUM

(☎ 01223-748100; www.kettlesyard.co.uk; Castle St; ☉ noon-5pm Tue-Sun) FREE An £11-million revamp has added high-tech contemporary-art galleries to much-loved Kettle's Yard. The big draw for many though will be the original collection still set in the home of HS 'Jim' Ede, a former curator at the Tate Gallery in London. Ede knocked three houses into one to create a quirky, intimate space in which to display a wealth of top-notch painting and sculpture, including works by Miró and Henry Moore, in a country-cottage atmosphere.

Round Church
CHURCH

(☑ 01223-311602; www.christianheritage.org.uk; Bridge St; £3.50; ☉ 10am-5pm Tue-Sat, from 1.30pm Sun) Cambridge's intensely atmospheric Round Church is one of only four such structures in England. It was built by the mysterious Knights Templar in 1130 and shelters an unusual circular nave ringed by chunky Norman pillars. The carved stone faces crowning the pillars bring the 12th century vividly to life.

Polar Museum
MUSEUM

(☑ 01223-336540; www.spri.cam.ac.uk/museum; Lensfield Rd; ☉ 10am-4pm Tue-Sat) FREE Tales of hostile environments, dogged determination and, sometimes, life-claiming mistakes are evoked powerfully at this compelling museum. Its focus on polar exploration charts the feats of the likes of Roald Amundsen, Fridtjof Nansen, Ernest Shackleton and Captain Robert Falcon Scott. The affecting collections include paintings, photographs, clothing, equipment, maps, journals and last messages left for loved ones by Scott's polar crew.

Corpus Clock
LANDMARK

(Bene't St) Made from 24-carat gold, the Corpus Clock displays the time through a series of concentric LED lights. A hideous-looking insect 'time-eater' crawls across the top. The clock is only accurate once every five minutes. At other times it slows or stops and then speeds up, which, according to its creator, JC Taylor, reflects life's irregularity.

Great St Mary's Church
CHURCH

(www.gsm.cam.ac.uk; Senate House Hill; ☉ 10am-4pm Mon-Sat, from 1pm Sun) FREE The foundations of Cambridge's sublime university church date from 1010. It was burnt to the ground in the 1290s and rebuilt in 1351. The major expansion of 1478–1519 resulted in the late-Gothic Perpendicular style you see today. Striking features include the mid-Victorian stained-glass windows, seating galleries and two organs – unusual in a church. The tower (adult/child £4/2.50) was added in 1690; climb it for superb vistas of Cambridge's dreamy spires.

Little St Mary's Church
CHURCH

(☑ 01223-366202; www.lsm.org.uk; Trumpington St; ☉ 7.30am-6.30pm) FREE The church's unwieldy original name was St Peter's-without-Trumpington-Gate, which gave St Peter's College (latterly Peterhouse) its name. Inside is a memorial to student Godfrey Washington, great-uncle of George. His family coat of arms was the stars and stripes, the inspiration for the US flag.

Peterhouse
COLLEGE

(☑ 01223-338200; www.pet.cam.ac.uk; Trumpington St; ☉ 9am-5pm, closed early Apr–mid-Jun) FREE The oldest and smallest college, charming Peterhouse was founded in 1284. Much of the college was rebuilt or added to over the years, including the exceptional little chapel built in 1632, but the beautifully restored main hall is bona-fide 13th century.

Rumours abound among students – vigorously denied by college authorities – of hauntings and spectral happenings on the site. Three Nobel Prize winners count themselves among Peterhouse's alumni.

Activities

Scudamore's Punting
BOATING

(☑ 01223-359750; www.scudamores.com; Mill Lane; chauffeured punts per 45 min adult/child £20/10, 6-person self-punt per hr £30; ☉ 9am-dusk) Rents punts, rowing boats, kayaks and canoes. Offers discounts if you book online.

Jesus Green Pool
SWIMMING

(☑ 01223-302579; www.cambridge.gov.uk/jesus-green-outdoor-pool; Jesus Green; adult/child £4.60/2.45; ☉ 7.30am-7.30pm Mon, Tue & Fri, noon-7.30pm Wed, Thu, Sat & Sun May-Sep) A slender, 91m, 1920s open-air swim spot; popular with poolside sunbathers too.

Tours

★ Walking Tours
WALKING

(☑ 01223-791501; www.visitcambridge.org; Peas Hill; ☉ 1-5 tours daily) The best guided tours of the city take in one of the colleges and the city's main sights. Options include the two-hour Kings College & The Backs tour (adult/child £20/10), and a 90-minute Highlights tour (adult/child £15/8), which often includes Pembroke College – the price covers college admission in both cases. They're popular – book ahead.

There's also a one-hour Essential Cambridge (adult/child £12.50/6) tour. The walks leave from the tourist office. Colourful one-hour Ghost Tours (adult/child £7/5) take place two evenings a week.

Cambridge Chauffeur Punts
BOATING

(☑ 01223-354164; www.punting-in-cambridge.co.uk; Silver St Bridge; chauffeured punts per hr adult/child £16/7, 6-person self-punt per hr £24; ☉ 9am-8pm

🚶 City Walk
The Colleges and the Backs

START KING'S COLLEGE CHAPEL
END FITZBILLIES
LENGTH 3 MILES; FOUR HOURS

From divine **1 King's** (p364), stroll north, diverting into **2 Great St Mary's Church** and climbing the tower for fine Cambridge views. Next, dodge the cyclists and tour guides before ducking into atmospheric **3 Gonville & Caius** (p368) to marvel at its ornate gates. **4 Trinity's** (p365) elaborate entranceway towers up on the left; head through it into the college's (genuinely) Great Court; marvel at the architecture, then make for the absorbing **5 Wren Library** (p365), with its extraordinary historic books. Next, pause to admire the front of gorgeous **6 St John's** (p369) before dropping into the captivating 12th-century **7 Round Church** (p370). Cut right between the sweet terraces of narrow Portugal Pl – at the end, the **8 Maypole** (p375) pub is a friendly place to eat or drink.

Next, head diagonally across Jesus Green, past lounging picnickers and tennis players, to consider a dip in the bijou open-air

9 Jesus Green Pool. Then stroll southwest beside the river, passing locks and houseboats before a waterside boardwalk leads to a punt launching pad. Cross at the bridge beside **10 Magdalene College** (p368), where the unique Pepys Library is well worth a detour.

Northampton St reminds you that the 21st century does exist, then it's on to the path through the Backs, where the stately sweep of St John's College shelters amid the trees, while Trinity sits next door. Next play zigzag with college paths and the river: nip up **11 Garrett Hostel Lane** for a closer view of punts, bridges and college facades. Then it's back to the path, before another detour left leads to the often-open gates of **12 Clare College** (p367), where the Fellow's Garden is a real must-see.

Back on the Backs, next comes the impressive west end of King's; the Palladian **13 Fellows' Building** is just to the right. After curving beside **14 Queens'** (p369), cut left. On Silver St's bridge spy the chunky **15 Mathematical Bridge** (p368) on the left, and fleets of about-to-embark punts on the right. Time to rest. Where better than **16 Fitzbillies** (p374) for a Chelsea bun and a steaming cup of tea?

PRANKSTERS & NIGHT CLIMBERS

In a city with so much concentrated mental prowess, it is perhaps inevitable that the student community would excel at all kinds of mischief. The most impressive prank ever to take place in Cambridge – lifting an Austin Seven van on to the roof of the landmark Senate House (p368) in 1958 – involved a great deal of planning from four Mechanical Sciences students and spawned a number of copycat pranks, including suspending another Austin Seven from the ornate Bridge of Sighs (p369).

King's College has long been a target of night climbers – students who get their thrills by scaling the lofty heights of out-of-bounds buildings at night. The sport is taken very seriously – to the point where a Trinity College student, Geoffrey Winthrop Young, wrote the *Roof Climber's Guide to Trinity* in 1900. If you're in Cambridge after a particularly spectacular climber excursion, you may find some out-of-place objects atop the pinnacles of King's College Chapel (p364) – anything from a traffic cone to a Santa hat.

Finally, there's the Cubes (Cambridge University Breaking and Entering Society): its objective is to access places members shouldn't be and leave distinctive calling cards – the most famous being the wooden mallard in the rafters of Trinity's Great Hall.

Jun & Aug, 10am-dusk Apr, May, Sept & Oct) Runs regular chauffeured punting tours and also offers self-hire.

Granta Moorings BOATING
(☏01223-301845; www.puntingincambridge.com; Newnham Rd; chauffeured punts per hr adult/child £14/8, 6-person self-punt per hr £22-26; ☺9.30am-dusk Apr-Oct) Conveniently situated punt-rental company if you're heading towards Grantchester (p377).

Riverboat Georgina BOATING
(☏01223-929124; www.riverboatgeorginacambridge.co.uk; Jesus Lock; 1/2hr cruises £10/20; ☺Apr-Sep) Boat cruises along the Cam. Optional extras include lunch, fish and chips, wine or a cream tea.

☆ Festivals & Events

Bumps SPORTS
(www.cucbc.org/bumps; ☺Feb & Jun) Traditional rowing races along the Cam (or the Granta, as the Cambridge stretch is called), in which college boat clubs compete to 'bump' the crew in front.

Beer Festival BEER
(www.cambridgebeerfestival.com; ☺May) Hugely popular five-day beer and cider extravaganza on Jesus Green, featuring brews from all over the country as well as a great range of British cheeses.

May Balls CULTURAL
(☺early Jun) The biggest student events of the year, the name of these formal balls doesn't match the month they're held in because college authorities decided that May's

traditional booze-fuelled revelry – just before the exams – wasn't such a great idea. Now they take place after the exams, but in a typically Cambridge quirk, they keep their old name.

Cambridge Shakespeare Festival THEATRE
(www.cambridgeshakespeare.com; ☺Jul & Aug) The bard's best-loved works performed in a handful of college gardens.

Folk Festival MUSIC
(www.cambridgefolkfestival.co.uk; ☺late Jul–early Aug) Acclaimed four-day music fest in Cherry Hinton Hall, 4 miles southeast of the city centre. It has hosted the likes of Van Morrison, Ladysmith Black Mambazo, Christy Moore, Imelda May, Paul Simon and KT Tunstall.

🛏 Sleeping

Cambridge YHA HOSTEL £
(☏0345-371 9728; www.yha.org.uk; 97 Tenison Rd; dm/d £25/60; @ 🛜) A smart, friendly and deservedly popular hostel with compact dorms and good facilities. Handily, it's very near the railway station.

Tudor Cottage B&B ££
(☏01223-565212; www.tudorcottageguesthouse.co.uk; 292 Histon Rd; s/d £55/90; P 🛜; 🚌8) Sweet features help make this neat-as-a-pin guesthouse feel like a home from home, from the tiny patio garden to the ranks of speciality teas, cereals, cakes and muffins at the breakfast table. It's just under 2 miles north of the city centre; bus 8 stops just outside.

Rosa's
B&B ££

(☑ 01223-512596; www.rosasbedandbreakfast.co.uk; 53 Roseford Rd; s £45-60; P 🛇; 🖵 8) One for solo travellers: a friendly, family-run B&B where the three bright, snug singles are decked out in neutral tones. It's 2 miles north of the city centre; there's free on-road parking outside and bus 8 runs nearby.

Worth House
B&B ££

(☑ 01223-316074; www.worth-house.co.uk; 152 Chesterton Rd; s £75-95, d £100-140, tr £165, q £192; P @ 🛇) The welcome is wonderfully warm and the great-value rooms are delightful. Soft grey and cream meets candy-stripe reds, fancy bathrooms boast clawfoot baths and tea trays are full of treats. The choice of rooms for families is particularly good.

University Rooms Cambridge
B&B ££

(www.universityrooms.com/en/city/cambridge; s/d from £50/80) For an authentic taste of university life, check into a student room in one of the colleges. Accommodation varies from functional singles (with shared bathroom) overlooking college courts to more modern, en-suite rooms in nearby annexes. Breakfast is often in hall (the students' dining room).

You'll find a bigger selection of available rooms during university holidays (June to August, Christmas, and March to April).

Benson House
B&B ££

(☑ 01223-311594; www.bensonhouse.co.uk; 24 Huntingdon Rd; s £80-120, d £120; P 🛇) Lots of little things lift Benson a cut above – sleep on feather pillows and beds made with Egyptian-cotton linen, sip tea from Royal Doulton bone china, then tuck into award-winning breakfasts featuring ground coffee, croissants and fresh fruit.

★Hotel du Vin
BOUTIQUE HOTEL £££

(☑ 01223-928991; www.hotelduvin.com; 15 Trumpington St; d £190-270, ste £290-430; @ 🛇) One of the country's swishest, coolest chains delivers again here. Achingly beautiful rooms sport roll-top baths, monsoon showers and custom-made beds, the cosy cellar bar is vaulted, the bistro (two/three courses £18/21) is chic, and the luxuriously appointed suites (expect rotating TVs, mini-cinemas and surround sound) are simply divine.

★Varsity
BOUTIQUE HOTEL £££

(☑ 01223-306030; www.thevarsityhotel.co.uk; Thompson's Lane; d £195-360; ✳ @ 🛇) In the 44 individually styled rooms of riverside Varsity, wondrous fixtures and furnishings (such as roll-top baths and travellers' trunks) sit beside floor-to-ceiling glass windows, espresso machines and smartphone docks. The views out over the colleges from the roof terrace are utterly sublime.

Valet parking costs £20 a night.

Felix
BOUTIQUE HOTEL £££

(☑ 01223-277977; www.hotelfelix.co.uk; Whitehouse Lane, Huntingdon Rd; s £220, d £165-280, ste £315-335; P @ 🛇 🛇) It's the bold modern art and imaginative design that nudge Felix into the boutique sleep spots. You'll find vividly coloured chairs set beside polished wood panels in the lounge, and silk curtains, duckdown duvets and underfloor heating in the bathrooms. Felix is 1.5 miles northwest of the city.

✗ Eating

★Urban Shed
SANDWICHES £

(☑ 01223-324888; www.theurbanshed.com; 62 King St; sandwiches from £5; ⊙ 8.30am-5pm Mon-Fri, 9am-5.30pm Sat, 10am-5pm Sun; 🖉) Unorthodox, retro Urban Shed has a personal-service ethos so strong that regular customers have a locker for their own mug. Old aeroplane seats perch beside cable-drum tables, their own-blend coffee is mellow and the choice of sandwiches is superb, with fillings including BBQ aubergine and Swiss cheese, coconut satay chicken, and grilled courgette with sunflower seeds.

Steak & Honour
BURGERS £

(www.steakandhonour.co.uk; 4 Wheeler St; burgers £6-9; ⊙ 11.30am-3pm & 5-9.30pm Mon-Fri, 11.30am-10pm Sat, to 5pm Sun) 'Don't try eating these with one hand', warns a joint that started out as a couple of burger vans. These beef patties come squished between brioche buns and dripping with cheese. You can take them away, but they're easier to manage in the bare-bones cafe (plastic trays, no cushions, Formica tables). Grab a stack of napkins and enjoy.

Aromi
ITALIAN £

(☑ 01223-300117; www.aromi.co.uk; 1 Bene't St; mains from £5; ⊙ 9am-7pm Sun-Thu, to 10pm Fri & Sat; 🖉) Sometimes you should yield to temptation. So be drawn in by a window full of stunning Sicilian pizza, and feast on light, crisp bases piled high with fresh spinach and Parma ham. Then succumb to the indecently thick hot chocolate: may as well make it a large.

Aromi also has another cafe a few doors down on Peas Hill and a *gelateria* on Fitzroy St.

Fitzbillies
CAFE **£**

(☑ 01223-352500; www.fitzbillies.com; 52 Trumpington St; mains £9-12; ☺ 8am-6pm Mon-Fri, from 9am Sat, from 9.30am Sun) Cambridge's oldest bakery has a soft, doughy place in the hearts of generations of students, thanks to its ultrasticky Chelsea buns and other sweet treats. Pick up a bagful to take away or munch in comfort in the quaint cafe.

Locker
CAFE **£**

(☑ 07566 216042; www.thelockercafe.co.uk; 54 King St; snacks from £5; ☺ 8.30am-5.30pm Mon-Fri, from 9.30am Sat, 10am-4pm Sun; ☎☑) ⚑ Ethical coffee, homemade soup, and flavoursome bread, cakes and pies from a wealth of Cambridge producers lift this artsy cafe above the crowd.

Espresso Library
CAFE **£**

(☑ 01223-367333; www.espressolibrary.com; 210 East Rd; mains £7.50-11; ☺ 7am-6pm Mon-Sat, from 8am Sun; ☎☑) A chilled soundtrack and customers with laptops at almost every table signal that this industrial-chic cafe is a student favourite. That'll be partly down to the wholesome food – dishes might include frittata with sweet potatoes and spinach, or juicy portobello mushrooms in brioche buns – and partly down to some cracking coffee.

Rainbow
VEGETARIAN **££**

(☑ 01223-321551; www.rainbowcafe.co.uk; 9a King's Pde; mains £10-13; ☺ 10am-10pm Tue-Sat, to 3pm Sun; ☑) Quite a treat for non-meat eaters: a cheery basement bistro, tucked away at the end of an alley off King's Parade. In this warren of cosy rooms, rickety tables set the scene for an eclectic range of veg that's been transformed into a variety of bakes, roasts, pasta dishes and pies.

Kingston Arms
PUB FOOD **££**

(☑ 01223-319414; www.facebook.com/pg/KingstonArms; 33 Kingston St; mains £8-14; ☺ 5-11pm Mon-Thu, noon-midnight Fri & Sat, to 11pm Sun; ☎) Great gastropub grub – from roasts to homemade risotto and gourmet sausages – keeps stomachs satisfied at the award-winning Kingston. More than 10 real ales, stacked board games and a students-meet-locals clientele deliver a contemporary Cambridge vibe. It's located 1 mile southeast of the centre.

Pint Shop
MODERN BRITISH **££**

(☑ 01223-352293; www.pintshop.co.uk; 10 Peas Hill; snacks from £5, mains £12-22; ☺ noon-10pm Mon-Fri, 11am-10.30pm Sat, 11am-10pm Sun) Popular Pint Shop's vision is to embrace eating and drinking equally. To this end, it's both a busy bar specialising in draught craft beer and a stylish dining room serving classy versions of traditional grub (dry-aged steaks, gin-cured sea trout, coal-baked fish and meat kebabs). All in all, hard to resist.

Smokeworks
BARBECUE **££**

(www.smokeworks.co.uk; 2 Free School Lane; mains £11-20; ☺ 11.30am-10pm Mon-Thu, to 10.30pm Fri & Sat, to 9.30pm Sun; ☎) This dark, industrial-themed dining spot draws discerning carnivores with its melt-in-your-mouth ribs, wings and wonderfully smoky pulled pork. The service is friendly and prompt, and the salted-caramel milkshakes come in a glass the size of your head.

Cambridge Chop House
BRITISH **££**

(☑ 01223-359506; www.cambscuisine.com/cambridge-chop-house; 1 King's Pde; mains £17-26; ☺ 9am-11.30pm, noon-10.30pm Mon-Sat, to 9.30pm Sun) The window seats here deliver some of the best views in town – onto King's College's hallowed walls. The food is pure English establishment too: hearty steaks and chops and chips, plus fish dishes and suet puddings. It's also open for breakfast (9-11.15am) and coffee and pastries (10-11.30am).

Sister restaurant **St John's Chop House** (☑ 01223-353110; www.cambscuisine.com/st-johns-chop-house; 21 Northampton St; mains £14-26; ☺ noon-3pm & 6-9.30pm Mon-Fri, noon-10.30pm Sat, to 9pm Sun) sits near the rear entrance to St John's College.

★ Midsummer House
MODERN BRITISH **£££**

(☑ 01223-369299; www.midsummerhouse.co.uk; Midsummer Common; 5/8 courses £69/145; ☺ noon-1.30pm Wed-Sat, 7-9pm Tue-Sat; ☑) At the region's top table, chef Daniel Clifford's double-Michelin-starred creations are distinguished by depth of flavour and immense technical skill. Savour transformations of pumpkin (into velouté), mackerel (with Jack Daniels), quail, sea scallops and grouse, before a coriander white-chocolate dome, served with coconut, mango and jasmine rice.

Unusually, there are vegetarian, vegan and pescatarian versions of the eight-course menu.

CAMBRIDGE & EAST ANGLIA CAMBRIDGE

Cotto
INTERNATIONAL **£££**

(☑ 01223-302010; www.cottocambridge.co.uk; Gonville Pl; 3 courses £70-75; ⊙ 6.30-9pm Tue-Sat; 🖋) 🍴 Now set inside the swish Gonville Hotel, Cotto delivers an irresistible blend of artistry and precision. Delights might include seafood velouté or the signature dish Cotto venison Wellington, perhaps followed by roasted apple with omega-3 crumble and mascarpone mousse.

🍷 Drinking & Nightlife

★ Cambridge Brew House
MICROBREWERY

(☑ 01223-855185; www.thecambridgebrewhouse. com; 1 King St; ⊙ 11am-11pm Sun-Thu, to midnight Fri & Sat) Pick a pint from the array on offer here and there's a fair chance it'll have been brewed in the gleaming vats beside the bar. Add a buzzy vibe, eclectic upcycled decor, dirty burgers and British tapas (mains £10 to £15) and you have the kind of pub you heartily wish was just down your road.

Hidden Rooms
COCKTAIL BAR

(☑ 01223-514777; www.facebook.com/pg/hidden rooms; Jesus Lane; ⊙ 7-11pm Wed & Thu, to midnight Fri & Sat) A cocktail bar for aficionados of the craft. At Hidden Rooms (if you can find it), booths and table service add an edge of exclusivity, while twice-monthly jazz and mixology lessons add another layer of class.

It's a little tricky to locate: head for the Pizza Express and drop down a floor.

Maypole
PUB

(☑ 01223-352999; www.maypolefreehouse.co.uk; 20a Portugal Pl; ⊙ 11.30am-midnight Sun-Thu, to 1am Fri & Sat) A dozen pumps dispensing real ale, 50 gins, a roomy beer garden and a friendly, unreconstructed vibe make this red-brick pub popular with the locals. That and hearty, homemade Italian food, plus festivals championing regional and micro-brewery beers.

Fez
CLUB

(www.cambridgefez.com; 15 Market Passage; ⊙ 10pm-3am Tue-Sun) Hip hop, dancehall, R&B, techno, funk, indie, house and garage; top-name DJs and club nights – you'll find it all at Cambridge's most popular club, the Moroccan-themed Fez.

Eagle
PUB

(☑ 01223-505020; www.eagle-cambridge.co.uk; Bene't St; ⊙ 11am-11pm Sun-Thu, to midnight Fri & Sat; 🖥 🍴) Cambridge's most famous pub has loosened the tongues and pickled the grey cells of many an illustrious academic; among them Nobel Prize–winning scientists Crick and Watson, who discussed their research into DNA here (note the blue plaque by the door). Fifteenth-century, wood-panelled and rambling, the Eagle's cosy rooms include one with WWII airmen's signatures on the ceiling.

The food (mains £10-15), served all day, is good too; it includes some thoughtful options for children.

Granta
PUB

(☑ 01223-505016; www.granta-cambridge.co.uk; 14 Newnham Rd; ⊙ 11am-11pm) If the exterior of this picturesque waterside pub, over-hanging a pretty mill pond, looks strangely familiar, it could be because it is the darling of many a TV director. No wonder: with its snug deck, riverside terrace and punts moored up alongside, it's a highly atmospheric spot to sit, sup and watch the world drift by.

☆ Entertainment

ADC
THEATRE

(☑ 01223-300085; www.adctheatre.com; Park St) This famous student-run theatre is home to the university's Footlights comedy troupe whose past members include Emma Thompson, Hugh Laurie and Stephen Fry.

Cambridge Arts Theatre
THEATRE

(☑ 01223-503333; www.cambridgeartstheatre. com; 6 St Edward's Passage) Cambridge's big-gest bona-fide theatre puts on everything from highbrow drama and dance, to panto and shows fresh from London's West End.

Corn Exchange
PERFORMING ARTS

(☑ 01223-357851; www.cornex.co.uk; Wheeler St) Venue attracting the top names, from pop and rock to comedy.

Junction
PERFORMING ARTS

(☑ 01223-511511; www.junction.co.uk; Clifton Way) Theatre, dance, comedy, live bands and club nights at a contemporary performance venue near the railway station.

It's 1.5 miles southeast of the city centre, down Regent St (later Hills Rd).

Portland Arms
LIVE MUSIC

(☑ 01223-357268; www.theportlandarms.co.uk; 129 Chesterton Rd; ⊙ noon-11.30pm Mon-Thu, to 12.30am Fri & Sat, to 11pm Sun) A popular student haunt, the 200-capacity Portland is the best spot in town to catch a gig and see the pick of up-and-coming bands. It has a

WORTH A TRIP

IMPERIAL WAR MUSEUM

At Europe's biggest **aviation museum** (☑ 01223-835000; www.iwm.org.uk; Duxford; adult/child £19/9.50; ⊙10am-6pm; P 👪), 200 lovingly preserved vintage aircraft are housed in several enormous hangars. The vast airfield showcases everything from dive bombers to biplanes, Spitfires and Concorde. The awe-inspiring American Air Museum hangar pays homage to US WWII servicemen, hosting the largest collection of American civil and military aircraft outside the USA.

Duxford is 9 miles south of Cambridge at Junction 10 of the M11. Buses only run to the museum on Sunday (bus 132; £3.90, 50 minutes).

wood-panelled saloon bar, a spacious terrace and monthly comedy nights too.

ⓘ Information

Tourist Office (☑ 01223-791500; www.visitcambridge.org; The Guildhall, Peas Hill; ⊙9.30am-5pm Mon-Sat Nov-Mar, plus 11am-3pm Sun Apr-Oct) Offers information plus a booking service for accommodation, walking and punting tours, events and tickets for King's College Chapel. Also sells maps, guides and souvenirs.

ⓘ Getting There & Away

BUS

Buses run by **National Express** (☑ 0871 781 8181; www.nationalexpress.com; Parkside; 🛜) leave from Parkside. Direct services include:

Gatwick £41, four hours, seven daily

Heathrow £31, 2¾ hours, hourly

London Victoria £11, 2½ hours, every two hours

Oxford £14, 3½ hours, hourly

Stansted Airport £10, 45 minutes, every two hours

CAR

Cambridge's centre is largely pedestrianised. The city's multistorey car parks charge between £2.40 and £4 for two hours.

Five Park & Ride car parks (parking per day/week £1/5) circle the city on the major routes, with buses (return tickets £3) shuttling into the city centre every 10 to 15 minutes between around 7am and 8pm Monday to Saturday, 9am to 5.45pm Sunday – check for specific times.

TRAIN

The train station is 1.5 miles southeast of the centre. Direct services include:

Birmingham New Street £35, three hours, hourly

Bury St Edmunds £11, 40 minutes, hourly

Ely £5,15 minutes, three per hour

King's Lynn £7, 50 minutes, hourly

London King's Cross £25, one hour, two to four per hour

Stansted Airport £11, 35 minutes, every 30 minutes

ⓘ Getting Around

BICYCLE

Cambridge is incredibly bike-friendly, with two wheels providing an ideal, and atmospheric, way to get around town.

Recommended bicycle-hire outfits:

City Cycle Hire (☑ 01223-365629; www.citycyclehire.com; 61 Newnham Rd; per half-day/day/week £9/12/25; ⊙9am-5.30pm Mon-Fri, plus 9am-5pm Sat Easter-Oct) A mile southwest of the city centre.

Rutland Cycling (☑ 01223-307655; www.rutlandcycling.com; Corn Exchange St; per 4hr/day £7/10; ⊙9am-6pm Mon-Fri, 10am-5pm Sun) In the heart of town at the Grand Arcade shopping centre. There's another branch just off Station Rd at the train station.

BUS

➞ Bus routes run around town from the **main bus station** (Drummer St).

➞ Many operate from 6am until around 11pm.

➞ C1, C3 and C7 stop at the train station.

➞ A city Dayrider ticket (£4.30) provides 24 hours of unlimited bus travel around Cambridge.

Ely

☑ 01353 / POP 20,256

A small but charming city dominated by a jaw-dropping cathedral, Ely makes an excellent day trip from Cambridge. It takes its name (*ee*-lee) from the eels that once inhabited the surrounding undrained Fens. From the Middle Ages onward, Ely was one of the biggest opium-producing centres in Britain, with high-class ladies holding 'poppy parties' and local mothers sedating their children with 'poppy tea'. Today, beyond the dizzying heights of its cathedral towers, Ely is a cluster of medieval streets lined with traditional tearooms and pretty Georgian houses; a quaint quayside adds extra appeal.

◉ Sights

★ Ely Cathedral
CATHEDRAL

(☑ 01353-667735; www.elycathedral.org; The Gallery; adult/child £9/free, incl tower tour £16.50/free; ☉ 7am-6.30pm) Ely Cathedral's stunning silhouette dominates the whole area; it's dubbed the 'Ship of the Fens' because it's so visible across the vast, flat sweeps of land. The early-12th-century **nave** dazzles with clean, uncluttered lines and a lofty sense of space. Look out for the entrancing ceiling, the masterly 14th-century **Octagon**, and **towers** that soar upwards in shimmering colours. Standard admission includes a ground-floor **guided tour**. The **tower tours** (four to five daily) deliver behind-the-scenes glimpses, 165 steps and remarkable views.

Ely has been a place of worship and pilgrimage since at least 673, when Etheldreda, daughter of the king of East Anglia, founded a nunnery here (shrugging off the fact that she had been twice married, in her determination to become a nun). She was canonised shortly after her death. The nunnery was sacked by the Danes, rebuilt as a monastery, demolished and then resurrected as a church after the Norman Conquest. In 1109, Ely became a cathedral. Gothic arches were added later to support the weight of the mighty walls.

The vast 14th-century **Lady Chapel** is filled with eerily empty niches that once held statues of saints and martyrs. They were hacked out unceremoniously by iconoclasts during the English Civil War. But the delicate tracery remains, overseen by a rather controversial statue of *Holy Mary* by David Wynne, unveiled in 2000 to mixed reviews. The cathedral's beauty has made it a popular film location: you may recognise some of its fine details from scenes in *Elizabeth: The Golden Age* and *The Other Boleyn Girl*. For optimum atmosphere, visit during evensong (5.30pm Monday to Saturday, 4pm Sunday) or a choral service (10.30am Sunday).

Oliver Cromwell's House
MUSEUM

(☑ 01353-662062; www.olivercromwellshouse. co.uk; 29 St Mary's St; adult/child £5/3; ☉ 10am-5pm Apr-Oct, 11am-4pm Nov-Mar) England's premier Puritan (p975) lived in this attractive, half-timbered house with his family from 1636 to 1647, when he was the local tithe collector. The interior has been restored to reflect the fixtures and fittings of their daily lives – expect flickering candles, floppy hats and writing quills.

It's engaging and entertaining, and also challenges you to answer one question: was this complex character a hero or a villain?

Ely Museum
MUSEUM

(☑ 01353-666655; www.elymuseum.org.uk; Market St; adult/child £4.50/1; ☉ 10.30am-5pm Mon-Sat, from 1pm Sun Apr-Oct, 10.30am-4pm Mon & Wed-Sat, from 1pm Sun Nov-Mar) Housed in the Old Gaol House, this quirky little museum appropriately features gruesome tableaux inside prisoners' cells, plus displays on the Romans, the Anglo-Saxons, the Long Barrow burial ground at nearby Haddlington, and the formation of the Fens. You are also initiated into the mysteries of old Ely trades such as leatherwork and eel-catching.

🛏 Sleeping

Many visitors treat Ely as a day trip from Cambridge, so it's not overrun with places to sleep, but some charming B&Bs can put you up if you do decide to stay.

OFF THE BEATEN TRACK

GRANTCHESTER

Old thatched cottages with flower-filled gardens, breezy meadows and classic cream teas aren't the only reason to make the pilgrimage along the Cam to the picture-postcard village of Grantchester. You'll also be following in the footsteps of some of the world's greatest minds on a 3-mile walk, cycle or punt from Cambridge that has changed little since Edwardian times.

After the trip, flop into a deckchair under a leafy apple tree and wolf down cakes or light lunches at the lovely **Orchard Tea Garden** (☑ 01223-840230; www.theorchard-teagarden.co.uk; 47 Mill Way; lunch mains £5-10, cakes £3; ☉ 9am-6pm Apr-Oct, to 4pm Nov-Mar), the favourite haunt of the Bloomsbury Group who came to camp, picnic, swim and discuss their work.

Bus 18 runs from Cambridge to Grantchester (£2.60, 15 minutes, hourly Monday to Saturday).

★ **Peacocks** B&B £££
(☎07900 666161; www.peacockstearoom.co.uk; 65 Waterside; s £110-135, d £135-160; �</del>) Walk into the roomy suites here and feel instantly at home. In 'Cottage', floral Laura Ashley wallpaper graces a sweet sitting area and bedroom; in 'Brewery', the vintage books, gilt mirrors and burnished antiques are reminiscent of a grand gentlemen's club.

Riverside B&B £££
(☎01353-661677; www.riversideinn-ely.co.uk; 8 Annesdale; s £72, d £129-139; P ☎) In this Georgian guesthouse on Ely's quay, rooms are enriched by dull golds, deep reds, brocade bedspreads, dark furniture and sparkling bathrooms. Just the place to gaze at the houseboats and rowers bobbing about on the River Great Ouse.

✗ Eating

★ **Peacocks** CAFE £
(☎01353-661100; www.peacockstearoom.co.uk; 65 Waterside; snacks from £8, cream teas £9-19; ⊙10.30am-4.30pm Wed-Sun, plus Tue Jun-Sep) An award-winning cafe serving a vast selection of cream teas – some include chocolate scones and sparkling rose wine. Or opt for luscious homemade soups, salads and cakes. Eat inside surrounded by fun knick-knacks and bone china, or in the bijou garden framed by drooping wisteria.

Old Fire Engine House BRITISH ££
(☎01353-662582; www.theoldfireenginehouse. co.uk; 25 St Mary's St; lunch 2/3 courses £17/22, mains £17; ⊙noon-2pm & 7-9pm Mon-Sat, noon-2pm Sun; ✍) ✎ Eating here is like sampling food from a classic East Anglian farmhouse kitchen. Seasonal and local produce rule, so dishes might include Denham Estate venison, Norfolk samphire, and – fittingly for Ely – locally smoked eels. Puddings include nursery favourites such as tangy apple and blackberry crumble with cream.

❶ Information

The **Tourist Office** (☎01353-662062; www. visitely.org.uk; 29 St Mary's St; ⊙10am-5pm Apr-Oct, 11am-4pm Nov-Mar) stocks leaflets on the picturesque 'Eel Trail' (50p) and Fen Rivers Way circular walks (£2).

❶ Getting There & Away

You can walk to Ely from Cambridge along the 17-mile riverside Fen Rivers Way. Rail connections include the following:

Cambridge £3, 20 minutes, one to three per hour

King's Lynn £7, 30 minutes, one to two per hour

Norwich £17, one hour, every 30 minutes

ESSEX

The county's inhabitants have been the butt of snobbery and some of England's cruellest jokes for years, thanks to pop-culture stereotypes. But beyond the fake tans and slots 'n' bumper-car resorts, Essex's still-idyllic medieval villages and rolling countryside provided inspiration for Constable, one of England's best-loved painters. Here, too, is the historic town of Colchester, while even Southend-on-Sea, the area's most popular resort, has a softer side in the traditional cockle-sellers and cobbled lanes of the sleepy suburb Old Leigh.

❶ Getting There & Around

➡ Essex is well served by public transport.

➡ Trains shuttle between Colchester and London Liverpool St (£25, one hour, every 15 minutes), and between Southend-on-Sea and London's Liverpool St and Fenchurch St stations (£12-15, 1¼ hours, three per hour).

➡ Regular buses head for Dedham Vale and Saffron Walden; **Traveline East Anglia** (www. travelineeastanglia.org.uk) provides timetables.

Colchester

☑ 01206 / POP 180,420
Dominated by its sturdy castle and extensive Roman walls, Colchester is Britain's oldest recorded city, dating from the 5th century BC. In AD 43 the Romans came, saw, conquered and constructed their northern capital Camulodunum. It was razed by Boudica just 17 years later. In the 11th century, the invading Normans built a mighty castle; today it's set amid narrow streets that are home to a striking new arts space and some beautiful half-timbered houses.

◉ Sights

★ **Colchester Castle** CASTLE
(www.cimuseums.org.uk; Castle Park; adult/child £7.75/4.80; ⊙10am-5pm Mon-Sat, from 11am Sun) Built in 1076 on the foundations of the Roman Temple of Claudius, England's largest surviving Norman keep is bigger than that of the Tower of London. Over the centuries

it's been a royal residence, a prison and home to the Witchfinder General. An imaginative £4-million restoration has added a cracking *son et lumière* which recreates lost internal structures.

Other highlights include the 'Fenwick Hoard' of Roman gold and silver jewellery, and guided tours onto the castle roof (adult/child £3/1.50, booking required).

firstsite
ARTS CENTRE

(☑01206-713700; www.firstsite.uk.net; Lewis Gardens; ⊙10am-5pm; ⓐ) **FREE** Colchester's shiny, curved, glass-and-copper arts centre is as striking inside as out: installations flow seamlessly into one another amid a wealth of space and light. Temporary art displays are cunningly juxtaposed with historical works; the one permanent exhibition is the magnificent **Berryfield Mosaic** – a Roman artefact found here in 1923, and now under glass in the centre of the gallery space.

Hollytrees Museum
MUSEUM

(www.cimuseums.org.uk; Castle Park; ⊙10am-5pm Mon-Sat) **FREE** In this Georgian town house, toys, costumes, watches and clocks form reminders of the domestic life of the wealthy owners and their servants. Quirky exhibits include a shipwright's baby carriage in the shape of a boat, a make-your-own Victorian silhouette feature and an intricate, envy-inducing doll's house.

Dutch Quarter
AREA

The best of the city's half-timbered houses and rickety roof lines are clustered together in this Tudor enclave just a short stroll north of High St. The area remains as a testament to the 16th-century Protestant weavers who fled here from Holland.

🛏 Sleeping & Eating

Four Sevens
B&B ££

(☑01206-546093; www.foursevens.co.uk; 28 Inglis Rd; s £55-65, d £65-80, f £90-95; ⓟ ⓡ) The far-from-frilly furnishings here include stand-alone bowl sinks, wicker chairs and platform beds. Impressive breakfasts feature eight cereal options, and guests are often welcomed with homemade cake. It's a mile southwest of the centre, off the B1022 to Maldon.

North Hill
HOTEL ££

(☑01206-574001; www.northhillhotel.com; 51 North Hill; s £65-87, d £85-107, ste £127; ⓡ) Ask for a room in the characterful, cottage-style back building of this sleek sleep spot and you'll be rewarded with wonky beams, ex-posed red brick and plush modern furnishings. Stylish, more contemporary rooms sit in the former solicitor's chambers next door – complete with ranks of law books on the shelves.

★ Company Shed
SEAFOOD ££

(☑01206-382700; http://thecompanyshed.co; 129 Coast Rd, West Mersea; mains £6-18; ⊙9am-4pm Tue-Sat, from 10am Sun) Bring your own bread and wine to this seaside shack to tuck into mussels, oysters, prawns, lobster, jellied eels, smoked fish or their signature seafood platter. It's all courtesy of the Howard family, eighth-generation oyster-harvesters. The shed is on Mersea Island, 9 miles south of Colchester. Check the times of high water – it's not accessible on particularly high tides.

Green Room
MODERN BRITISH ££

(☑01206-574001; www.northhillhotel.com; 51 North Hill; mains £8.50-26; ⊙7am-10am daily, noon-2pm & 6-9pm Mon-Sat, noon-5pm Sun) Local and seasonal comfort-food classics are given a contemporary twist at this smart, friendly restaurant, where dishes range from fish and chips or slow-roast belly pork, to a creamy crab, rocket and Parmesan risotto.

❶ Information

The **Tourist Office** (☑01206-282920; www.visitcolchester.com; Castle Park; ⊙10am-5pm Mon-Sat) is inside the Hollytrees Museum.

❶ Getting There & Away

➜ Direct National Express buses go to and from London Victoria roughly every three hours (£15, three hours).

➜ Trains run to London Liverpool St (£25, one hour, every 15 minutes).

Dedham Vale

John Constable's romantic visions of country lanes, springtime fields and babbling creeks were inspired by and painted in this serene vale. The artist was born and bred in East Bergholt in 1776 and, although you may not see the rickety old cart depicted in his renowned painting *The Hay Wain,* the picturesque cottages, rolling countryside and languid charm remain.

Now known as Constable Country, Dedham Vale centres on the villages of Dedham, East Bergholt and Flatford. With leafy lanes, arresting pastoral views and graceful old churches, it's a glorious area to explore on foot or by bike.

◉ Sights

Flatford
HISTORIC BUILDING

(NT; ☑ 01206-298260; www.nationaltrust.org. uk; Bridge Cottage, near East Bergholt; parking £4; ⊙ 10am-5pm Apr-Oct, to 3.30pm Sat & Sun Nov-Mar; Ⓟ) FREE Set right beside Flatford Mill, thatched **Bridge Cottage** has an exhibition that provides a fine introduction to the artist's life and works. Between April and October, daily **guided tours** (£3.50, noon Monday to Friday, 11.30am and 1.30pm Saturday and Sunday) take in views of Flatford Mill, Willy Lott's House (which features in *The Hay Wain*) and other sites that pop up in Constable's paintings. There are also self-guided routes.

Flatford Mill
HISTORIC BUILDING

(Flatford, near East Bergholt; Ⓟ) Constable fans will recognise red-brick Flatford Mill immediately, as it appears in many of his canvases and still looks idyllic today. It was once owned by the artist's family and is now used as an education centre, so although you can take in picture-perfect views from front and back, you can't go in.

⏹ Sleeping & Eating

★ Dedham Hall
B&B ££

(☑ 01206-323027; www.dedhamhall.co.uk; Brook St, Dedham; s/d £75/120; Ⓟ) An air of authentic old England infuses Dedham Hall, a delightfully relaxed 15th-century farmhouse where overstuffed armchairs sit beside ancient beams, candlesticks perch above red-brick fireplaces and plump pillows rest on cosy beds. Add a dappled garden dotted with chairs and it's really rather hard to leave.

Residents can also tuck into elegant, imaginative dinners (dinner and B&B for two costs £180).

Sun
INN £££

(☑ 01206-323351; www.thesuninndedham.com; High St, Dedham; s/d £90/145; Ⓟ🛜) The centuries-old Sun is the epitome of heritage-chic: creaking floors and wonky walls surround upcycled mirrors, brass bedsteads and subtle colour schemes that team terracotta with a gentle yellow and olive with green.

Milsoms
HOTEL £££

(☑ 01206-322795; www.milsomhotels.com; Stratford Rd, Dedham; d £145-190; Ⓟ✳🛜) Sure-footed design gives the rooms here a real

sense of fun: red-leather armchairs, anglepoise lamps and retro phones meet vibrant candy stripes and jazzy modern art. Their bicycle and canoe hire service enables tranquil explorations of Dedham Vale.

Drop by the buzzy restaurant (open noon to 9.30pm, mains £9 to £23) for local steaks, smoked salmon and blinis, duck tacos and lush ice cream.

ⓘ Getting There & Away

Flatford Mill is a lovely 2-mile walk from Manningtree train station.

Bus links from Colchester:

Dedham Buses 80, 81 and 102 (£2.60, 30 minutes, two to seven daily)

East Bergholt Buses 93 and 94 (£8.50, 40 minutes, hourly Monday to Saturday)

Saffron Walden

☑ 01799 / POP 15,210

The 12th-century market town of Saffron Walden is a delightful knot of half-timbered houses, narrow lanes, crooked roofs and ancient buildings. It gets its name from the purple saffron crocus (the source of the world's most expensive spice), which was cultivated in the surrounding fields between the 15th and 18th centuries. If you can, visit on a Tuesday or a Saturday morning when markets stalls fill the centre of town.

◉ Sights

★ Audley End
House & Gardens
HISTORIC BUILDING

(EH; ☑ 01799-522842; www.english-heritage.org. uk; off London Rd; adult/child £18/11; ⊙ house noon-5pm Apr-Sep, to 4pm Oct, gardens 10am-6pm Apr-Sep, to 5pm Oct) Positively palatial in its scale, style and the all-too-apparent ambition of its creator, the first Earl of Suffolk, the fabulous early-Jacobean Audley End House eventually did become a royal palace when it was bought by Charles II in 1668. Lavishly decorated rooms glitter with silverware, priceless furniture and paintings, making it one of England's grandest country homes. The fine landscaped park was designed by Lancelot 'Capability' Brown. Audley End House is 1 mile west of Saffron Walden off the B1383.

Saffron Walden Museum
MUSEUM

(☑ 01799-510333; www.saffronwaldenmuseum. org; Museum St; adult/child £2.50/free; ⊙ 10am-4.30pm Tue-Sat, from 2pm Sun; 👶) In this excellent museum dating back to 1835, you'll find eclectic collections covering everything from local history and 18th-century costumes to geology, Victorian toys and ancient Egyptian artefacts. The bramble-covered ruins of Walden Castle Keep, built around 1125, lie in the grounds.

Bridge End Gardens   GARDENS
(Bridge End; ⊗ gardens 24hr, maze & kitchen garden 9am-3.30pm Mon-Fri, plus 10am-5pm Sat & Sun Easter-Oct) FREE Careful restoration of these seven interlinked gardens has brought them back to their former Victorian glory. For extra atmosphere, try to visit when the maze and produce-packed kitchen garden are open too.

Old Sun Inn   HISTORIC BUILDING
(Church St) Saffron Walden's most famous landmark sits at a crossroads surrounded by timber-framed buildings. An ornate, 14th-century structure, it was once used as Cromwell's HQ and its exterior walls still bear intricate 17th-century pargeting (decorative plasterwork).

✕ Eating

Cafe Coucou   CAFE £
(☑ 01799-513863; www.cafecoucou.co.uk; 17 George St; mains £6-10; ⊗ 9am-5pm Mon-Sat) Delicious homemade quiches, huge scones, chunky doorstep sandwiches and imaginative salads sell like hot cakes at this cheerful family-run cafe.

Eight Bells   PUB FOOD ££
(☑ 01799-522790; www.8bells-pub.co.uk; 18 Bridge St; mains £12-19; ⊗ noon-3pm & 6-9.30pm; ☑) You'll find a warm mix of medieval character and contemporary style in this 16th-century pub. Local lamb, venison and game is teamed with southern European flavours, so expect antipasti and mezze boards as well as burgers, prime sausages, and fish and chips.

❶ Information

Tourist Office (☑ 01799-524002; www.visit saffronwalden.gov.uk; 1 Market Pl; ⊗ 9.30am-5pm Mon-Sat) Stocks a good (free) leaflet outlining a trail around the town's historic buildings.

❶ Getting There & Away

Bus 7 runs between Saffron Walden and Cambridge (£4.60, 1¼ hours), hourly between Monday and Saturday. Bus 132 makes the same journey once a day on Sunday.

The nearest train station is 2 miles west of Saffron Walden at Audley End. Bus 301 links Audley End train station with Saffron Walden (£2, 15 minutes, hourly Monday to Saturday). Train services from there include the following:

Cambridge £7, 15 minutes, every 20 minutes
London Liverpool St £10, 1¼ hours, every 30 minutes

Southend-On-Sea

☑ 01702 / POP 177,900

Full of flashing lights and fairground rides, Southend is London's weekend playground, replete with gaudy amusements and packed-out nightclubs. But as well as all that, there's a glorious stretch of sandy beach, an absurdly long pier and, in the suburb of Old Leigh, echoes of a traditional fishing village.

◎ Sights

Southend Pier   LANDMARK
(www.southend.gov.uk/pier; Western Esplanade; adult/child £2/1; ⊗ 8am-8pm late-May–Aug, to 6pm Apr–late-May & Sep-Oct, 9am-5pm Wed-Sun Nov-Mar) Welcome to the world's longest pier – a staggering 1.341 miles long, to be precise – built in 1830 and a magnet for boat crashes, storms and fires, the last of which ravaged its tip in 2005. Today, a peaceful if windy stroll to the restored Pier Head reveals a cafe, a sun deck, a gift shop, an exhibition space and an active lifeboat station. Hopping on the **Pier Railway** (one-way adult/child £4.50/2.25) saves the long slog back.

Pier Museum   MUSEUM
(☑ 01702-611214; www.southendpiermuseum.co. uk; Western Esplanade; adult/child £1.50/50p; ⊗ 11am-5pm Sat, Sun, Tue & Wed May-Oct) Southend's seaside heyday springs to life in this charming museum, where a Victorian toast-rack pier tram sits beside sepia photos and a functioning signal box. The best bits are the still-working antique penny slot machines. The museum is volunteer-run so hours can vary – call to check.

Old Leigh   AREA
Cobbled streets, cockle sheds, art galleries and craft shops define atmospheric Old Leigh. It's a long stroll west along Southend's seafront, or a short hop on the local train.

⌘ Sleeping

Hamiltons   BOUTIQUE HOTEL ££
(☑ 01702-332350; www.hamiltonsboutiquehotel. co.uk; 6 Royal Terrace; d £70-140; ☎) With its

wrought-iron mini-balconies and views of the pier, there's a sense of Southend's glamorous heyday at this Georgian retreat. The neutral tones of the pristine rooms have accents of subtle aquamarine, while the occasional French settee and crystal chandelier add to its period charm.

Roslin Beach   HOTEL **££**
(📞01702-586375; www.roslinhotel.com; Thorpe Esplanade; s £80-170, d £118-209, ste £160-325; ⊘food noon-9pm; P❄🐾🛜🐕) Seafront Roslin is all coastal chic – sand drifts up to the front steps, bedrooms have swirling seashell designs and suites feature glitzy, glass-fronted balconies. De-knot in the sauna, soak in the spa and then sample locally caught whitebait (mains £10 to £26) on the water-view terrace, framed by swaying palms.

Beaches   B&B **££**
(📞01702-585858; www.beachesguesthouse.co.uk; 192 Eastern Esplanade; s £60-70, d £95-110; 🛜) At Beaches you'll find gentle candy stripes, tasteful tones and zingy citrus-coloured cushions. Bag a bedroom with a balcony to look out over a beach dotted with boats and the slender silhouette of Southend's pier.

✴ Eating

Osborne Bros   SEAFOOD **£**
(📞01702-477233; High St, Leigh-on-Sea; snacks/mains £3/9; ⊘8am-5pm) Part fish stall, part bare-bones cafe, Osborne's is set right on Old Leigh's waterfront. It serves up expansive Thames Estuary views, best observed while tucking into crab, jellied eels or a seafood platter (cockles, mussels, prawns and crayfish; £9) and downing a pint from the pub next door.

★ Simply Seafood   SEAFOOD **£££**
(📞01702-716645; www.simply-seafood.com; 1 The Cockle Sheds, Leigh-on-Sea; mains £16-37; ⊘noon-3.30pm & 5-9.30pm Tue-Sat, to 4.30pm Sun) Tucked away under the flyover just west of Old Leigh, this light, bright little eatery lets locally sourced seafood shine. The oysters are from Essex, the crab is from Cromer and the fish is from the boats just outside. Scallops come perfectly seared and the *fruits de mer* platter is superb.

❶ Information

Tourist Office (📞01702-215620; www.visitsouthend.co.uk; Southend Pier, Western Esplanade; ⊘8am-8pm late-May–Aug, to 6pm Apr–late-May & Sep-Oct, 9am-5pm Wed-Sun Nov-Mar) At the entrance to the pier.

❶ Getting There & Away

Southend's most useful train stations are Central and Victoria (10 and 15 minutes walk from the shore, respectively). Direct services include:
Leigh-on-Sea (from Central) £3, seven minutes, every 15 minutes
London Fenchurch St (from Central) £12, 1¼ hours, three per hour
London Liverpool St (from Central) £15, 1¼ hours, two per hour

SUFFOLK

Suffolk is dotted with picturesque villages seemingly lost in time. The county made its money on the back of the medieval wool trade, and magnificent churches and lavish Tudor homes attest to its wealthy past. To the west are the picture-postcard villages of Lavenham and Long Melford. Further north, Bury St Edmunds ushers in historic buildings and a market-town vibe, while the appealing seaside resorts of Aldeburgh and Southwold overflow with genteel charm.

❶ Getting There & Around

Ipswich is the county's main transport hub. Traveline (www.travelineeastanglia.org.uk) details bus routes.

Train connections from Ipswich include the following:
Bury St Edmunds £9, 30 minutes, one to two per hour
London Liverpool St £17, 1¼ hours, two to three per hour
Norwich £16, 40 minutes, two per hour

Long Melford

📞01787 / POP 2800

Two Elizabethan manors and some good restaurants make Long Melford deserving of a detour. Its expansive village green, antiques shops and string of independent stores provide other fine reasons to meander through.

◉ Sights

Kentwell Hall   HISTORIC BUILDING
(📞01787-310207; www.kentwell.co.uk; adult/child £11.25/8.55; ⊘hours vary; P) Gorgeous, turreted Kentwell Hall may date from the 1500s and be full of Tudor grandeur, but it's still used as a private home, lending it a

SUTTON HOO

Located 11 miles northeast of Ipswich off the B1083, the site of **Sutton Hoo** (NT; ☑01394-389700; www.nationaltrust.org.uk; near Woodbridge; adult/child £8.90/4.50; ⊘10.30am-5pm Feb-Sep, to 4pm Sat & Sun Jan; P ♿) revealed one of England's greatest Anglo-Saxon treasure hoards when it was discovered in 1939. Excavations unearthed the hull of an enormous Anglo-Saxon ship belonging to the grave of Raedwald, an East-Anglian king, stuffed with Saxon riches.

A full-scale reconstruction of his ship and burial chamber can be seen in the visitor centre. The finest treasures, including the king's exquisitely crafted helmet, shields, gold ornaments and Byzantine silver, are displayed in the British Museum, but replicas are on show here, along with an original prince's sword.

Paths encircle the 18 burial mounds that make up the 'royal cemetery'. You can only walk along them as part of one-hour guided tours (adult/child £2.50/1.25). There's normally at least one tour a day; call to check for times.

The site was undergoing a dramatic £4-million redevelopment in winter 2018, closing to visitors until Spring 2019.

wonderfully lived-in feel. Kentwell is framed by a rectangular moat, lush gardens and an irresistible rare-breeds farm. During Tudor re-enactment events, the whole estate bristles with bodices, codpieces and hose. Opening hours are erratic: it tends to be open from 11am to 5pm during school summer holidays, plus other weekends; call to check.

Melford Hall   HISTORIC BUILDING
(NT; ☑01787-379228; www.nationaltrust.org.uk; Hall St; adult/child £8.20/4.10; ⊘noon-5pm Wed-Sun Easter-Oct; P) From outside, the romantic Elizabethan mansion of Melford Hall seems little changed since it entertained Queen Elizabeth I in 1578. Inside, there's a panelled banqueting hall, masses of Regency and Victorian finery, and a display on Beatrix Potter, a cousin of the Hyde Parkers, who owned the house from 1786 to 1960.

Holy Trinity   CHURCH
(☑01787-310845; www.longmelfordchurch.com; Church Walk; donation requested; ⊘10am-6pm Easter-Sept, to 4pm Oct-Easter) FREE Magnificent Holy Trinity is more cathedral- than church-sized, a spectacular example of a 15th-century wool church. The stained-glass windows and flint-and-stone flushwork are outstanding.

🛏 Sleeping & Eating

Black Lion   HOTEL ££
(☑01787-312356; www.blacklionhotel.net; The Green; s £80, d £85-95, ste £145, f £150; P 🐕) At the Black Lion, there's a heritage-meets-modern mash-up of oil paintings, antlers and log fires combined with elegant sofas, cute win-dow seats and rich throws. Colour schemes range from soothing oatmeal to vivid lime; choose to look out over the churchyard or village green.

The food (mains £10 to £18), served noon to 2.30pm and 6.30pm to 9pm, includes stone-baked pizzas, pub-food classics and classy restaurant mains.

Bull   INN ££
(☑0845 6086040; www.oldenglishinns.co.uk; Hall St; s/d £72/82-125; P 🐕) Built, probably, for a wool merchant in 1450, this cavernous pub has been pulling pints since around 1580. The carved ceilings and heraldic crests in its bars attest to its grand age. Check into a front-facing bedroom for maximum atmosphere enhanced by aged beams and dark wood.

Decent pub grub (such as slow-cooked belly pork, and stacked burgers) is served between noon and 9.30pm (mains £10 to £14).

★**Scutcher's**   MODERN BRITISH £££
(☑01787-310200; www.scutchers.com; Westgate St; mains £22-28; ⊘noon-2pm & 7-9.30pm Thu-Sat) Beautiful reinventions of traditional ingredients ensure this unpretentious place is renowned throughout the Stour Valley. Pea soup comes with a hint of curry, Parma ham has a drizzle of pomegranate molasses and local beef is given an Asian twist. It's modern, classy and assured.

ℹ Getting There & Away

Bus links include the following:
Bury St Edmunds Bus 753 (£4.30, one hour, hourly Monday to Saturday)

Sudbury Bus 753 (£1.60, 10 minutes, hourly Monday to Saturday)

Lavenham

📞 01787 / POP 1413

One of East Anglia's most beautiful and rewarding towns, the former wool-trade centre of Lavenham is home to a collection of exquisitely preserved medieval buildings that lean and lurch to dramatic effect. Lavenham's 300 half-timbered, pargeted and thatched houses have been left virtually untouched since the 15th century; many are now superb places to eat and stay.

◉ Sights

Lavenham Guildhall   HISTORIC BUILDING
(NT; 📞 01787-247646; www.nationaltrust.org.uk; Market Pl; adult/child £6.80/3.40; ⊙11am-5pm Mar-Oct, to 4pm Fri-Sun Nov-Feb) Lavenham's most enchanting buildings are clustered along High St, Water St and around the unusually triangular Market Pl. They're dominated by this early-16th-century whitewashed guildhall – a superb example of a close-studded, timber-framed building. It is now a local-history museum with displays on the wool trade and medieval guilds; in its tranquil garden you can see dye plants that produced the typical medieval colours.

Little Hall   HISTORIC BUILDING
(📞 01787-249078; www.littlehall.org.uk; Market Pl; adult/child £4/free; ⊙10am-1pm Mon, 1-4pm Tue-Sun Easter-Oct) Caramel-coloured, 14th-century Little Hall museum was once home to a successful wool merchant. Inside, you'll see how the rooms of this medieval mini-manor have been restored to period splendour through the efforts of the Gayer-Anderson twins who made it their home in the 1920s and 1930s.

St Peter & St Paul   CHURCH
(www.lavenhamchurch.onesuffolk.net; Church St; ⊙8.30am-5.30pm) This late-Perpendicular structure seems to lift into the sky, with its beautifully proportioned windows, soaring flint tower and gargoyle waterspouts. Built between 1485 and 1530, it was one of Suffolk's last great wool churches, completed on the eve of the Reformation, and is now a lofty testament to Lavenham's past prosperity.

🛏 Sleeping & Eating

Angel   HOTEL ££
(📞 01787-247388; www.cozypubs.co.uk; Market Pl; s £90-109, d £100-120; ⊙food noon-3pm & 6-10pm Mon-Fri, noon-10pm Sat, to 8pm Sun; 🅿🛜) In Lavenham's oldest building, dark-green corridors lead to gorgeously renovated, large, bright and beam-scored rooms. The eclectic decor in the bar (including theatrical spotlights and battered travelling trunks) echoes a menu that ranges confidently from pizza and English inn standards to gourmet salads and à la carte dishes (mains £12 to £26).

★ Swan   HOTEL £££
(📞 01787-247477; www.theswanatlavenham.co.uk; High St; s £180-310, d £195-375, ste £385-435; 🅿🛜) Marvellously medieval and utterly indulgent, the Swan might just spoil you in terms of other places to stay. Tasteful furnishings team oatmeal with olive and gentle reds; latticework of ancient wood climbs all around. The service is smooth, while the suites are simply stunning: soaring arched ceilings are criss-crossed with beams.

★ Great House   MODERN BRITISH £££
(📞 01787-247431; www.greathouse.co.uk; Market Pl; 3-course lunch/dinner £26/37; ⊙noon-2.30pm Wed-Sun, 7-9.30pm Tue-Sat) Contrasting cultures combine so well at this restaurant: traditional meets modern, East Anglian ingredients meet French cuisine. Dining here could see you eating roasted Norfolk (Gressingham) duck or braised Suffolk pork, then dispatching coffee and praline *millefeuille* or tangy morsels of French and Suffolk cheese.

❶ Getting There & Away

Bus 753 runs to and from Bury St Edmunds (£4.20, 30 minutes, hourly Monday to Saturday).

Bury St Edmunds

📞 01284 / POP 41,113

In Bury, the past is ever present. A centre of pilgrimage for centuries, its history-rich features include an atmospheric ruined abbey, handsome Georgian architecture and tranquil gardens. The chance to visit two breweries is tempting too.

◉ Sights

Abbey Gardens   RUINS
(Mustow St; ⊙dawn-dusk) FREE Now a picturesque ruin in parkland behind the cathedral, Bury's once-mighty abbey still impresses despite the townspeople having made off with much of the stone after the dissolution

of the monasteries. The walls are striking (especially on the west side), having crumbled and eroded into a series of fantastical shapes. Other highlights are the decorative Great Gate, the diminutive dovecote and the flower-filled gardens.

St Edmundsbury Cathedral
CATHEDRAL

(☎01284-748720; www.stedscathedral.co.uk; Angel Hill; requested donation adult/child £3/50p; ⊙7am-6pm Sun-Fri, from 8am Sat) The 45m-high tower of this cathedral was only completed in 2005 and is a vision in Lincolnshire limestone – its traditional Gothic-style construction conveys how many English cathedrals must have looked fresh from the stonemason's chisel. Most of the building is early 16th century, though the eastern end is post-1945. The overall effect is light and lofty, with a gorgeous hammerbeam roof and a striking sculpture of the crucified Christ by Dame Elisabeth Frink in the north transept.

Moyse's Hall
MUSEUM

(☎01284-706183; www.moyseshall.org; Cornhill; adult/child £4/2; ⊙10am-5pm Mon-Sat, noon-4pm Sun; ⓐ) Set in an impressive 12th-century undercroft, Moyse's Hall's rarities include a locket containing some of Mary Tudor's hair, finds from the town's ruined abbey and displays on the chilling Bury witch trials. They also run excellent talks and activities.

Theatre Royal
HISTORIC BUILDING

(NT; ☎01284-769505; www.theatreroyal.org; Westgate St) A rare treat – Britain's only working Regency playhouse features ornate gilding, sweeps of boxes and a *trompe l'oeil* ceiling, all revealed on self-led (free) and guided (£7.50) front-of-house and backstage **tours**. These guided tours tend to be held at 11am on Wednesday, Thursday and Saturday, between February and November, but times vary – call to check.

St Mary's Church
CHURCH

(☎01284-754680; www.wearechurch.net; Honey Hill; donation requested; ⊙10am-4pm Mon-Sat, to 3pm Oct-Easter) St Mary's is one of the largest parish churches in England, and it contains the tomb of Mary Tudor – Henry VIII's sister and a one-time queen of France. Built around 1430, it's famous for its hammer-beam roof, which features a host of vampire-like angels swooping from the ceiling. A bell is still rung to mark curfew, as it was in the Middle Ages.

🛏 Sleeping

★ Chantry
HOTEL ££

(☎01284-767427; www.chantryhotel.com; 8 Sparhawk St; s/ste £90/175, d £109-149; 🅿@🛜) Pretty much everything feels right about the Chantry – a family-run town house that's somewhere between a hotel and a B&B. Sash windows and cast-iron fireplaces signal its Georgian origins; French beds and walk-in showers add contemporary comfort; the convivial lounge and tiny bar help you to feel at home.

Fox
INN ££

(☎0845 6086040; www.oldenglishinns.co.uk; 1 Eastgate St; d £107-122; 🅿🛜) Slumber in these converted animal barns and be surrounded by carefully kept original features: bleached beams, weathered brick walls and even the livestock tethering rings. Painted wicker chairs and the odd chandelier add another layer of class.

Old Cannon
B&B ££

(☎01284-768769; www.oldcannonbrewery.co.uk; 86 Cannon St; s/d £105/120) In these rooms run by a hip microbrewery, converted outhouses feature smart bedrooms with subtle check patterns and terracotta walls. Each room is named after one of their beers – you get a free bottle on arrival. If you like it, have some more in the pub next door.

🍴 Eating & Drinking

★ Pea Porridge
MODERN BRITISH ££

(☎01284-700200; www.peaporridge.co.uk; 29 Cannon St; mains £13-18; ⊙noon-1.45pm Thu-Sat, 6.30-9pm Tue-Sat) Warmth, happy chatter and great aromas greet you at an intimate neighbourhood restaurant where local, seasonal produce meets ingredients from the Med – ingredients might include prosciutto, *piquillo* pepper and pomegranate. Many dishes are cooked in a charcoal oven giving the quail, veal and venison heart a smoky tang.

Maison Bleue
FRENCH £££

(☎01284-760623; www.maisonbleue.co.uk; 31 Churchgate St; mains £22-29; ⊙noon-2pm & 7-9.30pm, closed Mon) Settle into this elegant restaurant for modern French cuisine that's supremely stylish and bursting with flavour. Creative combinations might include beef with gnocchi, rabbit with snails or halibut with clams. The set menus (three-course lunch/dinner £26/36) are excellent value.

ORFORD NESS

Wind-whipped, remote **Orford Ness** (NT; ☑ 01728-648024; www.nationaltrust.org.uk; adult/child incl ferry crossing £4/2; ⊙ 10am-5pm Tue-Sat late Jun-Sep, 10am-5pm Sat Easter–late Jun & Oct) is the largest vegetated shingle spit in Europe and was once used as a secret military testing ground; now it's a nature reserve that's home to rare wading birds, animals and plants. Ferries run from Orford Quay: the last ferry from Orford (11 miles north-east of Aldeburgh) leaves at 2pm, the last ferry back from the island returns at 5pm. Spaces are limited – arrive early to reserve a seat.

The town's 12th-century **castle** (EH; www.english-heritage.org.uk; adult/child £7.30/4.40; ⊙ 10am-6pm Easter-Sep, to 5pm Oct, to 4pm Sat & Sun Nov-Easter; P) is also worth a look for its innovative 18-sided drum design. For dinner, don't miss the fresh Butley oysters, garlic-laced griddled prawns and superb seafood from **Butley Orford Oysterage** (☑ 01394-450277; www.pinneysoforford.co.uk; Market Hill; mains £9-20; ⊙ noon-2.15pm daily, plus 6.30-9pm daily Aug, Wed-Sat Apr-Jul, Sep & Oct, Fri & Sat Nov-Mar).

★**Old Cannon**   PUB
(☑ 01284-768769; www.oldcannonbrewery.co.uk; 86 Cannon St; ⊙ 11am-11pm; 🛜) 🖋 In this microbrewery, gleaming mash tuns (vats in which malt is mashed) sit alongside the funky bar – try the feisty Gunner's Daughter (ABV 5.5%) or St Edmund's Head (5%).

A fair bit of the ale goes into the food (served noon to 9pm Monday to Saturday, to 2.45pm Sunday); perhaps sample some sausages and bacon cured in stout.

Nutshell   PUB
(☑ 01284-764867; www.thenutshellpub.co.uk; The Traverse; ⊙ 11am-11pm Mon-Thu, to midnight Fri & Sat, noon-10.30pm Sun) Tiny benches and tables, a ceiling smothered in international banknotes and a suspended pufferfish: it's amazing what they've squeezed into this thimble-sized, memorabilia-packed, timber-framed pub, recognised by the *Guinness Book of Records* as one of Britain's smallest. If you're not squeamish, look out for the almost-mummified 400-year-old cat.

❶ Information

Tourist Office (☑ 01284-764667; www.visit-burystedmunds.co.uk; The Apex, Charter Sq; ⊙ 10am-5pm Mon-Sat) Set within the Arc shopping centre on the west side of town.

❶ Getting There & Away

BUS

The main bus station is on St Andrew's St North. Direct services include:

Cambridge Stagecoach bus 11 (£5.50, one hour, hourly Monday to Saturday)

London Victoria National Express (£10, 3½ hours, one daily)

TRAIN

The train station is a 10-minute walk north of the centre of town. Services include:

Cambridge £10, 40 minutes, hourly

Ely £10, 30 minutes, every two hours

Aldeburgh

☑ 01728 / POP 3225

The time-warped coastal town of Aldeburgh (pronounced *orld*-bruh) is one of the region's most charming. Pastel-coloured houses, independent shops, art galleries and ramshackle fresh-fish kiosks line its picturesque streets and sweeping shingle beach. Its two festivals and connections with composer Benjamin Britten are also a big draw.

◉ Sights

Minsmere   NATURE RESERVE
(RSPB; www.rspb.org.uk; near Westleton; adult/child £9/5; ⊙ reserve dawn-dusk, visitor centre 9am-5pm, to 4pm Nov-Jan; P) The coast near Dunwich draws ranks of birdwatchers, thanks to RSPB Minsmere. The reserve is home to one of England's rarest birds, the bittern, with hundreds of migrant birds dropping by in the autumn. Year-round, binoculars are available for rent from the visitor centre, while the hides along the reserve's trails are prime species-spotting sites.

Minsmere is 8 miles north of Aldeburgh by car. With public transport lacking you'll need to drive, cycle or walk.

Scallop   PUBLIC ART
(near Thorpe Rd car park) Maggi Hambling's sculpture commemorates Aldeburgh's links with the 20th-century composer Benjamin Britten, who spent much of his life in the

town. It manifests as two 4m-high, scallop-shell-shaped steel structures inscribed with quotes from Britten's opera *Peter Grimes*. The beachside setting of *Scallop* has proved controversial locally. It's a short stroll north of town along the seafront.

☆☆ Festivals & Events

Aldeburgh Festival   MUSIC
(www.snapemaltings.co.uk/season/aldeburgh-festival; ☉ Jun) Founded by Benjamin Britten in 1948, this exploration of classical music is one of East Anglia's biggest, taking in new, reinterpreted and rediscovered pieces, as well as the visual arts.

**Aldeburgh Food
& Drink Festival**   FOOD & DRINK
(www.aldeburghfoodanddrink.co.uk; ☉ late Sep) A two-day celebration of Suffolk produce and top-class cooking.

🛏 Sleeping & Eating

★**Ocean House**   B&B ££
(☎ 01728-452094; www.oceanhousealdeburgh. co.uk; 25 Crag Path; s £80, d £100-120, apt per week £1400) You're just seven paces (count them) from the beach at Ocean House, and many of the rustic-chic bedrooms directly overlook the surging sea. The five-person self-catering apartment comes with a homely kitchen and a pint-sized balcony, while the top-floor double is a true delight with water views on three sides and a sitting room with a baby grand piano.

Fish & Chip Shop   FISH & CHIPS £
(☎ 01728-452250; www.aldeburghfishandchips. co.uk; 226 High St; mains £5-7; ☉ noon-2pm daily, 5-8pm Thu-Mon) Aldeburgh has a reputation for the finest fish and chips in the area; this is the best place to find out why.

★**Lighthouse**   MODERN BRITISH ££
(☎ 01728-453377; www.lighthouserestaurant.co. uk; 77 High St; mains £11-19; ☉ noon-2pm & 6.30-10pm; ⊞) The owner of this bright bistro was a waiter here for years and a sense of enthusiastic friendliness pervades the place. Local fish (baked, battered or pan fried) and veg are its real strengths, although juicy steaks with peppercorn, blue cheese or garlic and herb butter sauce are also pretty hard to beat.

❶ Getting There & Away

Bus 64/65 runs hourly from Monday to Saturday, linking Aldeburgh with Ipswich (£6.50, 1½

hours). From there you can connect to the rest of the region.

Southwold

📞 01502 / POP 1090

Southwold's reputation as a well-heeled holiday getaway has earned it the nickname 'Kensington-on-Sea', after the upmarket London borough, and its lovely sandy beach, pebble-walled cottages, cannon-dotted clifftop and rows of beachfront bathing huts are undeniably picturesque. It has attracted many artists, including JMW Turner, Charles Rennie Mackintosh, Lucian Freud and Damien Hirst.

◉ Sights

Adnams   BREWERY
(☎ 01502-727225; www.adnams.co.uk; Adnams Pl; tours £20; ☉ 2-4 tours daily Mar-Sep) Spend an hour touring the high-tech kit inside this Victorian brewery, indulge in a 30-minute tutored tasting, then select a free bottle of beer to take home. Book ahead.

It's now possible to tour the Adnams gin distillery (£20) too. Under-18s can't go on the tours.

Seafront & Pier   AREA
(☎ 01502-722105; www.southwoldpier.co.uk; North Pde; ☉ pier 9am-5pm, to 8pm Fri-Sun) **FREE** Southwold's shore-front is its main attraction. Amble along the promenade, admire the squat 19th-century **lighthouse**, then drop by the 190m-long **pier**, first built in 1899 and recently reconstructed. Its **Under the Pier Show** (open 10am to 5pm, to 7pm Friday and Saturday) sports a kooky collection of handmade amusement machines combining daft fun with political satire.

Coastal Voyager   BOATING
(☎ 07887 525082; www.coastalvoyager.co.uk; Blackshore, Southwold Harbour; ☉ hourly trips, year-round) Trips include a 30-minute high-speed blast around the bay (adult/child £29/14), a leisurely 3½-hour cruise up the Blyth Estuary (£34/16) and a three-hour voyage to Scroby Sands (£44/22) to see a seal colony and wind farm.

☆☆ Festivals & Events

Latitude Festival   ART
(www.latitudefestival.co.uk; Henham Park; ☉ Jul) An eclectic mix of music, literature, dance, drama and comedy set in a country estate.

Ways with Words LITERATURE
(www.wayswithwords.co.uk; ⊙Nov) Talks and readings by big-name authors in venues around town.

🛏 Sleeping & Eating

★**Sutherland House** HOTEL £££
(✆01502-724544; www.sutherlandhouse.co.uk; 56 High St; r £100-169; P🖥) Past guests at this former mayor's residence include the prince who later became James II, and the Earl of Sandwich. They'd probably approve of its present appearance: gorgeous rooms with pargeted ceilings, exposed beams and free-standing baths – it's top-quality, luxurious and dramatic heritage-chic.

Meals (mains £12 to £23; noon to 2pm and 7pm to 9pm, closed Monday) see prime local ingredients transformed into tapas, bisque, aioli and soufflé.

Swan HOTEL £££
(✆01502-722186; www.adnams.co.uk; Market Sq; s £160-325, d £200-350; P🖥🐾) It's a boon for beer lovers – a super-stylish hotel owned by Southwold brewery giant Adnams. A bold and brilliant refurb has brought bright-pink chairs, minimalist four-poster beds and industrial-chic lights into this 17th-century building to great effect. In the Tap Room bar, staff are just itching to serve you a beer brewed right next door.

Modern British dishes (£12 to £16, served noon to 10pm) might include truffle-infused

WORTH A TRIP

THOMAS GAINSBOROUGH'S HOUSE

Thomas Gainsborough's atmospheric **birthplace** (✆01787-372958; www.gainsborough.org; 46 Gainsborough St; adult/child £7/2; ⊙10am-5pm Mon-Sat, from 11am Sun) is now home to the world's largest collection of his work. The 16th-century house and gardens feature a Georgian facade built by the artist's father. Inside, look out for *Pitminster Boy* in the entrance hall; the exquisite *Portrait of Harriett, Viscountess Tracy,* celebrated for its delicate portrayal of drapery; and the landscapes that were his passion.

Regular buses from Sudbury run to Ipswich (one hour), Long Melford (13 minutes), Lavenham (30 minutes), Bury St Edmunds (1½ hours) and Colchester (50 minutes).

baked cauliflower, ham, egg and chips, or chicken-liver parfait.

ℹ Getting There & Away

Bus 146 links Southwold with Norwich (£4.40, 1½ hours, hourly Monday to Saturday).

For services south, including those to and from Aldeburgh, catch bus 88A to Halesworth (£2.80, 30 minutes, hourly Monday to Saturday) and continue on the 521 (£4.80, one hour, four daily).

NORFOLK

Big skies, sweeping beaches, windswept marshes, meandering inland waterways and pretty flint houses combine to great effect in Norfolk. They say the locals have 'one foot on the land, and one in the sea', and you're never far from water here, whether it's beside the windmill-framed rivers of the tranquil Norfolk Broads or the wide, birdlife-rich sands of the shore. Inland, the bustling city of Norwich offers a fine castle and a cathedral, a lively market and some truly excellent places to sleep and eat.

ℹ Getting There & Around

Norwich is the county's transport hub. Train connections include a direct line to London Liverpool St (£18, two hours, two per hour).

Traveline (www.travelineeastanglia.org.uk) details bus routes. One of the most useful is the frequent Coasthopper Bus (www.sanderscoaches.com), which hugs the shore on its route between Cromer and King's Lynn.

Norwich

✆01603 / POP 132,512
The affluent and easy-going city of Norwich (*norr*-ich) is a rich tapestry of meandering alleys liberally sprinkled with architectural jewels – spoils of the city's medieval wool boom. A magnificent cathedral and impressive Norman castle bookend the city centre; in-between, crooked half-timbered buildings line quiet lanes. Thriving markets and a large student population enhance the city's relaxed vibe. Add quick access to the Broads and Norfolk's beaches, and you have an excellent base from which to explore.

◉ Sights

★**Norwich Cathedral** CATHEDRAL
(✆01603-218300; www.cathedral.org.uk; 65 The Close; donations requested; ⊙7.30am-6pm) Nor-

Norwich

Norwich

wich's most impressive landmark is a magnificent Anglican cathedral. Its barbed spire soars higher than any in England except Salisbury's, while the size of its cloisters is second to none. Highlights include the mesmerising ceiling, the ornate roof bosses, and the striking modern features of the Hostry. The 50-minute guided tours (donation re-

quested, hourly Monday to Saturday, 11am to 3pm) are an engaging way to find out more.

★ **Norwich Castle** MUSEUM
(☎ 01603-495897; www.museums.norfolk.gov.uk; Castle Hill; adult/child £9.15/7.30; ⊙10am-4.30pm Mon-Sat, from 1pm Sun) Crowning a hilltop

overlooking central Norwich, this massive 12th-century castle is one of England's best-preserved examples of Anglo-Norman military architecture. Its superb **interactive museum** crams in lively exhibits on Boudica, the Iceni, the Anglo-Saxons and the Vikings. Perhaps the best bit though is the atmospheric keep itself with its graphic displays on the grisly punishments meted out in its days as a medieval prison. **Guided tours** (adult/child £3.70/3) around the battlements and creepy dungeons run at least twice daily.

★ **Museum of Norwich**   MUSEUM
(www.museums.norfolk.gov.uk; Bridewell Alley; adult/child £5.70/4.55; ⊘10am-4.30pm Tue-Sat) Stay on your best behaviour: 14th-century Bridewell is a former house of correction, a 'prison for women, beggars and tramps'. Displays here explore Norwich's prominence as England's second city in the Middle Ages and its 19th-century industrial heritage. You can also play games in a 1950s parlour, listen to shoe-workers' memories, and watch films in a pocket-sized cinema.

Blickling Hall   HISTORIC BUILDING
(NT; ☑01263-738030; www.nationaltrust.org.uk; Blickling; adult/child £14.35/7.20; ⊘house noon-5pm Easter-Oct, 10.30am-3pm Nov-Easter, grounds 10am-5.30pm Easter-Oct, to 3pm Nov-Easter; [P][♿]) Largely remodelled in the 17th century for Sir Henry Hobart, James I's chief justice, Blickling Hall began life in the 11th century as a manor house and bishop's palace. The grand Jacobean state rooms are stuffed with fine Georgian furniture, pictures and tapestries; the plaster ceiling in the Long Gallery is spectacular. The estate's vast parklands are criss-crossed with cycling and walking routes.

Blickling Hall is 15 miles north of Norwich off the A140.

Sainsbury Centre for Visual Arts   GALLERY
(☑01603-593199; www.scva.ac.uk; University of East Anglia (UEA); ⊘10am-6pm Tue-Fri, to 5pm Sat & Sun; ☐22, 25, 26) [FREE] The region's most important centre for the arts is housed in the first major public building by renowned architect Norman Foster. Its eclectic collections include works by Picasso, Moore, Degas and Bacon, which are displayed beside curios from Africa, the Pacific and the Americas.

The gallery is in the University of East Anglia's grounds, 2 miles west of the city cen-

tre. To get there take bus 22, 25 or 26 (£2.20, 15 minutes).

Tombland & Elm Hill   AREA
Leafy Tombland, near Norwich Cathedral, is where the city's market was originally located ('tomb' is an old Norse word for empty, hence there being space for a market). From there, follow Princes St to reach Elm Hill, Norwich's prettiest street, with its medieval cobblestones, crooked timber beams and doors, intriguing shops and tucked-away cafes.

🛏 **Sleeping**

Gothic House   B&B ££
(☑01603-631879; www.gothic-house-norwich.com; King's Head Yard, Magdalen St; s/d £75/105; [P][🖦]) Step through the door to be whisked straight back to the Regency era. Original panelling, columns and cornices border the swirling stairs; fresh fruit and mini-decanters of sherry await in floral bedrooms that are studies in olive green, lemon yellow and duck-egg blue.

★ **3 Princes**   B&B £££
(☑01603-622699; www.3princes-norwich.co.uk; 3 Princes St; s/d £85/140-160; [🖦]) With its warm welcome, cosy yet minimalist decor, homemade afternoon treats and spacious rooms, 3 Princes is a perfect spot for an overnight stay. The location, on a quiet, pretty but very central street, adds to the charm, as do the help-yourself continental breakfasts (including fresh croissants and granola) and the wonderfully comfortable beds.

38 St Giles   B&B £££
(☑01603-662944; www.38stgiles.co.uk; 38 St Giles St; s/ste £95/240, d £120-150; [P][🖦]) At boutique 38 St Giles it seems everything gleams – from the highly polished floorboards to the aged cherry-red sofas. Mustard-yellow walls and rich rugs add another layer of charm. Breakfast includes local and organic meat and eggs, plus treats such as crème-fraiche pancakes with Norfolk bacon and maple syrup.

🍴 **Eating**

★ **Grosvenor Fish Bar**   FISH & CHIPS £
(www.fshshop.com; 28 Lower Goat Lane; mains from £5; ⊘11am-7.30pm Mon-Sat) At this groovy chippy-with-a-difference, chips come with fresh cod goujons, a 'Big Mack' is a crispy mackerel fillet in a bread roll, and the 'Five Quid Squid' (squid rings with garlic aioli)

really is £5. Either eat in the basement or they'll deliver to the Birdcage pub opposite, so you can have a pint with your meal.

Mustard CAFE **£**
(www.mustardcoffeebar.co.uk; 3 Bridewell Alley; snacks/mains £2/7; ⊗8am-5pm Mon-Sat; 🛜) You'll find a suitably bright-yellow colour scheme at this cool cafe set on the site of the original Colman's Mustard shop. Quality dishes might include breakfast bagels with halloumi and maple syrup, and chorizo Scotch eggs.

Library BRASSERIE **££**
(🖉01603-616606; www.thelibraryrestaurant.co.uk; 4a Guildhall Hill; mains £12-25; ⊗noon-2.30pm & 6-10pm Mon-Sat, noon-4pm Sun; 🖼) The chef here has a penchant for grilling over woodsmoke; smoky flavours infuse everything from chicken, lamb and beef to fennel seeds. It's a hit, as is the setting – with Victorian bookcases lining the walls of what was once a library; dining here has a club-like feel.

Last Wine Bar & Restaurant BRITISH **££**
(🖉01603-626626; www.lastwinebar.co.uk; 70 St George's St; mains £14-24; ⊗noon-2.30pm & 6-9.30pm Mon-Sat) The decor in the bar is fabulous and reflects the building's past life as a shoe factory, with lasts (wooden shoe moulds) as light fittings and Singer sewing machines as tables. The food lives up to the setting – top-notch burgers, steaks, gnocchi and fish pie in the bar, and creative twists on British classics in the à la carte restaurant.

★**Roger Hickman's** MODERN BRITISH **£££**
(🖉01603-633522; www.rogerhickmansrestaurant. com; 79 Upper St Giles St; dinner 2/3/7 courses £38/47/63; ⊗noon-2.30pm & 7-10pm Tue-Sat) Understated elegance is everywhere here: pale floorboards, white linen and unobtrusive service. Dishes might include confit salmon and rabbit or blow-torched mackerel – flair, imagination and a simple dedication to quality run right through. The lunches (two/three courses £20/25) are a cracking deal.

 Drinking & Nightlife

★**Birdcage** PUB
(www.thebirdcagenorwich.co.uk; 23 Pottergate; ⊗11am-midnight; 🛜) Formica tables, chilled tunes, cupcakes and cocktails make this beatnik drinking den a one-of-a-kind delight. Book for a Bums life-drawing session (yes, really; £4, Tuesday 7pm) or ferry in fish and chips from the Grosvenor Fish Bar over the lane.

Adam & Eve PUB
(Bishopsgate; ⊗11am-11pm Mon-Sat, noon-10.30pm Sun) Norwich's oldest-surviving pub has been slaking thirst since 1249, when the cathedral builders used to drop by. Tiny, with a sunken floor and part-panelled walls, it attracts a mixed band of regulars, choristers and ghost hunters, drawn by the fine malt whiskies and real ales.

🛈 **Information**

Tourist Office (🖉01603-213999; www.visit-norwich.co.uk; Millennium Plain; ⊗9.30am-5.30pm Mon-Sat, plus 10.30am-3.30pm Sun mid-Jul–mid-Sep) Inside the Forum.

🛈 **Getting There & Away**

AIR

Norwich International Airport (🖉01603-411923; www.norwichairport.co.uk; Holt Rd) is 4 miles north of town. Connections go to Amsterdam, Aberdeen, Edinburgh, Exeter and Manchester year-round; there are also summer flights to Spain and the Channel Islands.

BUS

The **bus station** (Queen's Rd) is 400m south of the castle. National Express (www.nationalexpress.com) and First (www.firstgroup.com) are among the operators:

Cromer Bus X44; £3.70, one hour, hourly Monday to Saturday

King's Lynn Excel (XL); £6.40, 1½ hours, hourly

London Victoria £12, three hours, every two hours

TRAIN

The train station is off Thorpe Rd, 600m east of Norwich Castle. Destinations include:

Cambridge £20, 1¼ hours, hourly

Ely £17, one hour, every 30 minutes

London Liverpool St £20, two hours, every 30 minutes

Cromer

🖉01263 / POP 7949
The once-fashionable Victorian resort of Cromer is a relaxed mix of an old-school English seaside holiday hotspot and an appealing fishing port. Brightly painted houses line narrow lanes dotted with independent shops. Its main attractions remain sweet-tasting Cromer crab, the atmospheric pier and an appealing stretch of pebbly shore.

THE NORFOLK BROADS

Why should I visit a swamp?

These vast wetlands were formed when the rivers Wensum, Bure, Waveney and Yare flooded the big gaping holes inland, which had been dug by 12th-century crofters looking for peat. They comprise fragile ecosystems and are protected as a **national park** (www.visit-thebroads.co.uk). They're also home to some of the UK's rarest plants and birds – the appeal to birdwatchers and naturalists is obvious. Apart from that, if you've ever envisioned yourself captaining your own boat and living afloat, there are 125 miles of lock-free waterways to explore. Or if paddling a canoe and losing yourself in lapping water away from the rest of humanity appeals, there's plenty of scope for that, too.

Exploring by boat

Launches range from large cabin cruisers to little craft with outboards; they can be hired for anything from a couple of hours' gentle messing about on the water to week-long trips. Tuition is given. Depending on boat size, facilities and the season, a four-person boat costs from around £25 per hour, from £80 for four hours and from £110 for one day. Week-long rental ranges from around £550 to £1400, including fuel and insurance.

Broadland Day Boats (☑01692-581653; www.dayboathire.com; Sutton Staithe Boatyard, Sutton Staithe; boat hire per day £95-110, canoe hire per half-/full day £25/40) hires boats and canoes. **Barnes Brinkcraft** (☑01603-782625; www.barnesbrinkcraft.co.uk; Riverside Rd, Wroxham; canoe hire per half day £30, boat hire per hr/day £18/152, 4-berth boat per week from £470; ☺Apr-Oct) offers short- and long-term rental, while **Broads Tours** (☑01603-782207; www.broads.co.uk; The Bridge, Wroxham; boat hire per hr/day/week from £20/175/1400; ☺8am-5.30pm Mar-Oct) lets out boats by the day and week, and runs boat trips. **Blakes** (☑0345 498 6184; www.blakes.co.uk; 4-berth boat per week £550-1000) arranges all manner of boating holidays.

Exploring by canoe

Paddlers can find canoes for hire for around £35 to £40 per day; **Whispering Reeds** (☑01692-598314; www.whisperingreeds.net; Staithe Rd, Hickling; canoe hire per 3/6hr £25/35; ☺Easter-Oct) and **Waveney River Centre** (☑01502-677343; www.waveneyrivercentre.co.uk; Burgh St Peter; kayak/canoe hire per day £28/36; ☺Easter-Oct) are recommended. **Mark the Canoe Man** (☑01603-783777; www.thecanoeman.com; half-day trips adult/child £25/15; ☺Apr-Oct) knows the secrets of the Broads and arranges guided trips to areas the cruisers can't reach (from £25), as well as offering canoe and kayak hire, weekend camping canoe trails, and two-day canoe and bushcraft trips (adult/child £175/125).

Exploring on foot & by bike

A web of walking trails stretches across the region, including the 61-mile **Weavers' Way**, which stretches from Cromer to Great Yarmouth, taking in some choice landscapes along

◉ Sights

Felbrigg Hall   HISTORIC BUILDING
(NT; ☑01263-837444; www.nationaltrust.org.uk; Felbrigg; adult/child £11/5.25; ☺noon-5pm late Mar-Oct, to 3pm early Feb-late Mar; ℗) An elegant Jacobean mansion boasting a fine Georgian interior, a splendid facade, an orangery and gorgeous walled gardens. It's 2 miles southwest of Cromer, off the B1436.

Henry Blogg Museum   MUSEUM
(RNLI Lifeboat Museum; ☑01263-511294; www.rnli.org; The Gangway; ☺10am-5pm Tue-Sun Apr-Sep, to 4pm Oct, Nov, Feb & Mar) **FREE** Tap out a message in Morse and spell your name in semaphore flags – hands-on gizmos add to the appeal of this excellent museum, as do the well-told tales of brave sea rescues and the WWII lifeboat sitting proudly inside.

The museum is named after one of the Royal National Lifeboat Institution's most decorated coxswains, and features accounts of his extraordinary rescues.

🛌 Sleeping & Eating

★**Red Lion**   INN ££
(☑01263-514964; www.redlioncromer.co.uk; Brook St; s £65-95, d £115-160, ste £160-180; ℗☈) Coloured floor tiles, wooden banisters and stained glass signal this seafront inn's

the way. The Broads' highest point, How Hill, is just 12m above sea level, so superhero levels of fitness are not required. The section between Aylsham and Stalham is open to bicycles.

Broadland Cycle Hire (☑ 07887 480331; www.norfolkbroadscycling.co.uk; Bewilderwood, Hoveton; bike hire per day adult/child £18/7, per week £70/45; ⏰ 10am-5pm Jul-early Sept) and Mark the Canoe Man are among those hiring out bikes. Expect to pay between £18 and £20 per day; child seats and tandems are also available.

What is there to see & do that doesn't involve water?

Museum of the Broads (☑ 01692-581681; www.museumofthebroads.org.uk; The Staithe, Stalham; adult/child £5.50/2.50; ⏰ 10am-4.30pm Sun-Fri Easter-Oct) Five miles north of Potter Heigham off the A149, this museum features fine boats and colourful displays on the local marshmen, their traditional lifestyles, peat extraction and modern conservation. You can ride on a steam launch too.

Toad Hole Cottage (☑ 01692-678555; www.howhilltrust.org.uk; How Hill; ⏰ 10.30am-5pm Apr-Oct) FREE The life of Fen dwellers is revealed at this tiny cottage, which shows how an eel-catcher's family lived and the tools they used to work the surrounding marshes.

Bewilderwood (☑ 01692-633033; www.bewilderwood.co.uk; Horning Rd, Hoveton; adult/child £16.50/14.50; ⏰ 10am-5.30pm Easter-Oct; ☒ 5B) A forest playground for children and adults alike, with zip wires, jungle bridges, tree houses and old-fashioned outdoor adventure involving plenty of mud, mazes and marsh walks.

St Helen's Church (☑ 01603-270340; Ranworth; ⏰ 9am-5pm) The Broads' most impressive ecclesiastical attraction is this 14th-century church, known locally as the 'Cathedral of the Broads'. It features a magnificent painted medieval rood screen and a 15th-century *antiphoner* – a rare illustrated book of prayers.

Bure Valley Steam Railway (☑ 01263-733858; www.bvrw.co.uk; Aylsham; adult/child return £13.50/6.50; ⏰ 2-9 trains daily Apr-Oct; ℗) Steam buffs will love this train, which puffs along 9 miles of narrow-gauge tracks between Aylsham and Wroxham. You can make the return trip by boat.

How do I get around?

Driving around the Broads is missing the point and pretty useless. The key centres of Wroxham, on the A1151 from Norwich, and Potter Heigham, on the A1062 from Wroxham, are reachable by bus from Norwich and Great Yarmouth, respectively. From there, you can either take to the water or to the trails.

18th-century heritage; stylish, sea-themed rooms bring it right up to date. All bedrooms come with baths, cafetière coffee and fresh milk – the pick is the suite (room 7), where you can see the sea from both the balcony and the roll-top tub.

★ Davies   SEAFOOD £
(☑ 01263-512727; 7 Garden St; crab £3.50-6; ⏰ 8.30am-5pm Mon-Sat, 10am-4pm Sun Apr-Oct, 8.30am-4pm Tue-Sat Nov-Mar) Less a fish shop, more a local institution – at Davies the crab is caught by its own day boat (the *Richard William*) and then boiled, cracked and dressed on-site. Other treats include cockles,

mussels and homemade pâté; the mackerel and horseradish pâté has quite a kick.

Rocket House   CAFE £
(☑ 01263-519126; www.rockethousecafe.co.uk; The Gangway; mains £6.50-11; ⏰ 9am-5pm Mon-Fri, from 10am Sat & Sun; ♿) Rocket House delivers an airy interior and widescreen sea views, thanks to a balcony that almost overhangs the waves. Light dishes include ploughman's with Norfolk Dapple and Binham Blue cheese, locally smoked mackerel salad, and their renowned Cromer crab platter.

ℹ Getting There & Away

→ Trains link Cromer with Norwich (£8, 45 minutes, hourly).

→ Cromer is on the Coasthopper (www.sanders coaches.com) bus route, with regular services to Cley-next-the-Sea, Blakeney and Wells. From Wells there are frequent connections through to King's Lynn.

Cley-next-the-Sea

☑ 01263 / POP 450

As the name suggests, the sleepy village of Cley (pronounced 'cly') huddles beside the shore. Here, a cluster of pretty cottages surrounds a photogenic windmill, and bird-rich marshes fan out all around.

◉ Sights

Cley Marshes NATURE RESERVE
(☑ 01263-740008.; www.norfolkwildlifetrust.org. uk; near Cley-next-the-Sea; adult/child £4.50/free; ☺ dawn-dusk; Ⓟ) ✔ One of England's premier birdwatching sites, Cley Marshes has more than 300 resident bird species, plentiful migrants and a network of walking trails and bird hides amid its golden reeds.

Even if you're not into birdwatching, don't miss the views from the (free) visitor centre and cafe. This is birdwatching for softies; sip a latte while enjoying zoomed-in images of marsh harriers.

🛏 Sleeping & Eating

★**Cley Windmill** B&B £££
(☑ 01263-740209; www.cleymill.co.uk; High St; d £190-205, apt per week from £560; Ⓟ) With the kind of wonky walls you'd expect from a circular 18th-century agricultural building, Cley Windmill is packed with character. Rooms are named after their former functions (the crazy-shaped Barley Bin is gorgeous), and many look out directly over reed-filled salt marshes. A sweet four-person self-catering cottage sits just next door.

George INN £££
(☑ 01263-740652; www.thegeorgehotelatcley.co. uk; High St; d £120-335) The George may be an age-old English inn, but the style is all contemporary north-Norfolk chic. Sure-footed design sees bare floorboards and feature fireplaces meet upcycled armchairs and quirky chests of drawers. Opt for a room overlooking the marshes for mesmerising views of wind-ruffled reeds.

★**Picnic Fayre** DELI £
(☑ 01263-740587; www.picnic-fayre.co.uk; High St; snacks from £3; ☺ 9am-5pm Mon-Sat, 10am-4pm Sun) A deli to ditch the diet for, crammed full of imaginative versions of English picnic classics – pork pies with chorizo, sausages smothered with sweet-chilli sauce, and home-baked lavender bread. Plus gooey homemade fudge and Portuguese custard tarts. Yum.

ℹ Information

Visitor Centre (☑ 01263-740008; www. norfolkwildlifetrust.org.uk; Cley Marshes; ☺ 10am-5pm Mar-Oct, to 4pm Nov-Feb) Seats and telescopes line up beside vast picture windows with panoramic views of the bird reserve. There's a cafe too.

ℹ Getting There & Away

Cley is on the Coasthopper (www.sanderscoach es.com) bus route, with regular services to Cromer, Blakeney and Wells. From Wells there are frequent connections through to King's Lynn.

Blakeney

☑ 01263 / POP 801

The pretty village of Blakeney was once a busy fishing and trading port before its harbour silted up. These days it offers an inviting seafront walk lined with yachts, and boat trips out to a 500-strong colony of common and grey seals that live, bask and breed on nearby Blakeney Point.

☞ Tours

Bishop's Boats BOATING
(☑ 01263-740753; www.bishopsboats.com; Blakeney Quay; adult/child £12/6; ☺ 1-4 daily Apr-Oct) Hour-long trips to see the seals at Blakeney Point; the best time to come is between June and August when the common seals pup.

Beans Seal Trips BOATING
(☑ 01263-740505; www.beansboattrips.co.uk; Morston Quay; adult/child £12/6; ☺ 1-3 daily Apr-Oct) Boat journeys out to the hundreds-strong Blakeney Point seal colony. The departure point is Morston Quay, 1.5 miles east of Blakeney.

🛏 Sleeping & Eating

Kings Arms INN ££
(☑ 01263-740341; www.blakeneykingsarms.co.uk; Westgate St; s/d £65/85; Ⓟ 🐾) Sweet, simple, old-style rooms (expect bright colours and pine) in a pub that's so welcoming you might

not want to leave. Order some substantial pub grub (its fish and chips are famous; mains from £9 to £18; meals served noon to 9pm), then, for great theatre gossip, ask landlady Marjorie about her career on the stage.

Moorings   MODERN BRITISH ££
(☑01263-740054; www.blakeney-moorings.co.uk; High St; mains £7-19; ⊙10.30am-8pm Tue-Sat, to 5pm Sun) Perfectly pitched fish dishes have won this bistro a loyal following – try the spicy Norfolk crab cake or herb-crusted local mackerel. Mustn't-miss puddings include ripe Norfolk cheese, and a rhubarb, honey and saffron tart.

❶ Getting There & Away

Blakeney is on the Coasthopper (www.sanders coaches.com) bus route, with regular services to Cromer, Cley-next-the-Sea and Wells. From Wells there are frequent connections through to King's Lynn.

Wells-next-the-Sea

☑01328 / POP 2165

Charming Wells excels at both land and sea. Rows of attractive Georgian houses and flint cottages snake down to a boat-lined quay; to the north sits a vast golden beach, backed by pine-covered dunes.

◉ Sights

Wells Beach   BEACH
(P) Fringed by dense pine forests and undulating dunes, Wells' sandy shore stretches for miles to the west, with brightly coloured beach huts clustering beside the water and wooden steps leading up into the woods. It's all tucked away at the end of a mile-long road; you can walk, drive or hop on a miniature train. Parking is available.

Wells & Walsingham Railway   HERITAGE RAILWAY
(☑01328-711630; www.wellswalsinghamrailway.co.uk; Stiffkey Rd; adult/child return £9.50/7.50; ⊙4-5 trains daily late Mar-Oct; P) The longest 10.25in narrow-gauge railway in the world puffs for 5 picturesque miles from Wells to the village of Little Walsingham, the site of religious shrines and the ruined but still impressive Walsingham Abbey.

🛏 Sleeping & Eating

Wells YHA   HOSTEL £
(☑0345 371 9544; www.yha.org.uk; Church Plain; dm/d/f £25/70/80; P🖥) Set in the heart of town in an ornately gabled early-20th-century church hall. Modern furnishings and a friendly vibe make it hard to beat.

★Old Customs House   B&B ££
(☑01328-711463; www.eastquay.co.uk; East Quay; s £85-95, d £105-115; P🖥) The stately but comfy feel here comes courtesy of worn-wood panels, alcoves full of books and gorgeous creek views. Choose from the snug 'Captain's Quarters' or a grand four-poster room. Discuss what you'd like for breakfast with the owner – perhaps locally baked bread with homemade jam or smoked haddock?

Wells Beach Cafe   CAFE £
(www.holkham.co.uk; Wells Beach; mains from £5; ⊙10am-5pm Easter-Oct, to 4pm Nov-Easter; 🖥) This locals' favourite rustles up bacon baps, homemade chilli and decadent hot chocolates. Outside there's a corral of picnic tables; inside there's a wood-burning stove for when the wind whips in.

THE QUEEN'S COUNTRY ESTATE

Both monarchists and those bemused by the English system will have plenty to mull over here at **Sandringham** (☑01485-545400; www.sandringhamestate.co.uk; adult/child £16.50/8; ⊙11am-4.30pm Easter-Sep, to 3.30pm Oct; P; 🚌35), the Queen's country estate.

Sandringham was built in 1870 by the then Prince and Princess of Wales (who later became King Edward VII and Queen Alexandra), and the house's features and furnishings remain much as they were in Edwardian days. The stables, meanwhile, now house a flag-waving museum filled with diverse royal memorabilia. The superb vintage-car collection includes the very first royal motor, from 1900, and the buggy in which the Queen Mother would bounce around race tracks. It's set in 25 hectares of beautifully landscaped gardens.

There are guided tours of the gardens (£3.50, 11am and 2pm Wednesday and Saturday). The shop stocks organic goodies produced on the vast estate.

Sandringham is 6 miles northeast of King's Lynn off the A149. Bus 35 runs from King's Lynn (£2.50, 20 minutes, hourly).

ℹ️ Information

Tourist Office (☎ 01328-710885; www.visit-northnorfolk.com; Freeman's St; ⏱10am-4pm Mon-Sat, to 1pm Sun Apr-Oct)

ℹ️ Getting There & Away

Wells is a pivot point on coastal bus services. From here regular services include:

Coasthopper (www.sanderscoaches.com) Provides links with Cromer, via Blakeney and Cley-next-the-Sea.

Coastliner (www.lynxbus.co.uk) Heads to King's Lynn, via Holkham, Burnham Deepdale, Brancaster Staithe and Titchwell.

Holkham

📞 01328 / POP 200

Little Holkham may only have two big assets, but both are highly impressive: a grand country-house estate and a spectacular stretch of sandy shore.

👁 Sights

★ Holkham National Nature Reserve   WILDLIFE RESERVE

(www.holkham.co.uk; parking per 2hr/day £3/7; ⏱ car park: 6am-9pm Apr-Sep, to 6pm Oct-Mar) Beach, dunes, salt marsh, grazing marsh, pinewoods and scrub – a high number of habitats pack into 37-sq-km Holkham Reserve. It's easily accessed from the car park at Lady Anne's Dr in Holkham village. From there, ribboning pathways lead through forests via bird hides and on to an expansive, pristine shore.

Holkham Hall & Estate   HISTORIC BUILDING

(☎ 01328-713111; www.holkham.co.uk; adult/child £16/8, parking £3; ⏱noon-4pm Sun, Mon & Thu Easter-Oct; 🅿) Holkham Hall is the ancestral seat of the original Earl of Leicester and still belongs to his descendants. A severe Palladian mansion, it's largely unadorned on the outside but the interior is sumptuous, with a red-velvet-lined saloon, copies of Greek and Roman statues, the luxurious Green State Bedroom, and fluted columns in the Marble Hall. It's set in a vast deer park (open 10am to 5pm daily), which was designed by William Kent.

🛏 Sleeping

★ Victoria   INN £££

(☎ 01328-711008; www.holkham.co.uk; Park Rd; s £135-160, d £160-250, f £260-290; ⏱food: 8-10am & noon-9pm; 🅿🛜🐾) A pint at the Victoria after a walk along sweeping Holkham Beach is pretty much a tradition. Extending your drink to an overnight stay is richly rewarding. Bathrooms gleam while sea tones and crisp modern styling are complemented by the odd antique. The food (mains £7 to £20), often sourced from Holkham Estate, is stylish country cooking at its best.

ℹ️ Getting There & Away

Holkham is on the Coastliner (www.lynxbus.co.uk) route, with regular buses linking King's Lynn and Wells. From Wells, frequent services shuttle to Cromer.

Burnham Deepdale

📞 01485 / POP 800

Walkers flock to this lovely coastal spot, with the tiny village of Burnham Deepdale (which merges seamlessly into Brancaster Staithe) strung along a rural road. Edged by the beautiful Norfolk Coast Path, surrounded by beaches and reedy marshes, alive with birdlife and criss-crossed by cycling routes, Burnham Deepdale is also the base for a whole host of water sports.

👁 Sights

Titchwell Marsh   NATURE RESERVE

(RSPB; ☎ 01485-210779; www.rspb.org.uk; Titchwell; parking £6; ⏱dawn-dusk; 🅿) The marshland, sandbars and lagoons of Titchwell Marsh Nature Reserve attract vast numbers of birds. In the spring, listen out for the booming call of the bittern; summer brings marsh harriers, avocets, terns and nesting bearded tits. In winter you'll see more than 20 species of wading birds and countless ducks and geese.

Titchwell Marsh is 3 miles west of Burnham Deepdale.

🛏 Sleeping & Eating

★ Deepdale Farm   HOSTEL £

(☎ 01485-210256; www.deepdalefarm.co.uk; Burnham Deepdale; dm/d/f/q £18/60/70/80, camping sites from £26; 🅿@🛜) 🐾 For backpackers it really doesn't get much better than Deepdale Farm: spick-and-span en-suite dorms and doubles in converted stables, a homely well-equipped kitchen, a barbecue area, and a cosy lounge warmed by a wood-burning stove. Campers can go glam in a safari-style, fully equipped tent, or bring their own – you'll find a heated shower block either way.

The hostel also operates a **tourist office** (✆ 01485-210256; www.deepdalefarm.co.uk; Burnham Deepdale; ☺9am-5pm Mon-Sat, 10am-4pm Sun), the best place to go to organise kitesurfing or windsurfing on nearby beaches.

★ **Titchwell Manor** HOTEL **£££**
(✆ 01485-210221; www.titchwellmanor.com; Titchwell, nr Brancaster; r £170-220; P@🐾) Dreamy Titchwell Manor is a swish, oh-so-contemporary hotel set in a grand Victorian house. You'll find lovingly upcycled furniture and bold colours in chic rooms ranging from those beside the herb-garden courtyard to ones with corking sea views.

The stylish restaurant and terrace set the scene for modern tapas and acclaimed à la carte dishes (mains £14 to £35; food served from noon to 2pm and 6pm to 9pm).

★ **White Horse** MODERN BRITISH **££**
(✆ 01485-210262; www.whitehorsebrancaster.co.uk; Main Rd, Brancaster Staithe; mains £14-24; ☺9am-9pm; P🐾) The White Horse gastropub's imaginative menu more than sets it apart from its competitors. Seasonal Norfolk ingredients pepper the menu – you might see foraged wild garlic, local duck *rillettes,* tempura Brancaster oysters and salt-marsh lamb. The bedrooms (doubles £160 to £250) evoke the shoreline with subtle colour schemes.

Eric's Fish & Chips FISH & CHIPS **££**
(✆ 01485-525886; www.ericsfishandchips.com; Drove Orchards; mains £9-15; ☺noon-9pm) Eric's reimagines the classic British chippy in fine north Norfolk trendy style. It has retro menus, bright tiles, bar stools and dishes that breathe fresh life into a well-established formula: Gruyère and spinach *arancini,* haddock with black garlic aioli, scallops with lime. Eat in or take away.

❶ Getting There & Away

Burnham Deepdale is on the Coastliner bus route (www.lynxbus.co.uk), which stops here frequently en route between King's Lynn and Wells.

From Wells, there are regular connections through to Cromer.

King's Lynn

✆ 01553 / POP 12,200

Once one of England's most important ports, King's Lynn was long known as 'the Warehouse on the Wash' (the Wash being the neighbouring bay). In its heyday, it was

HOUGHTON HALL

Built for Britain's first de-facto prime minister, Sir Robert Walpole, in 1730, Palladian-style **Houghton Hall** (✆ 01485-528569; www.houghtonhall.com; near King's Lynn; adult/child £15/5; ☺11am-5pm Wed, Thu & Sun May–late Sep; P) is worth seeing for the ornate staterooms alone, where stunning interiors overflow with gilt, tapestries, velvets and period furniture. The surrounding grounds, home to 600 deer, and the 2-hectare walled garden are dotted with contemporary sculptures, making for grand but pleasant rambling. Houghton Hall is just off the A148, 13 miles east of King's Lynn.

said you could cross from one side of the River Great Ouse to the other by simply stepping from boat to boat. Something of the salty port-town tang can still be sensed in old King's Lynn, with its cobbled lanes, vibrant weekly markets, and narrow streets flanked by old merchants' houses.

◉ Sights

Stories of Lynn MUSEUM
(✆ 01553-777775; www.kingslynntownhall.com; Saturday Market Pl; adult/child £4/2; ☺10am-4.30pm) A £2-million revamp has seen archive sources converted into multimedia exhibits, so you'll experience the stories of local seafarers, explorers, mayors and ne'er-do-wells. It's all set in the 15th-century Guildhall and parts of the town's Georgian jail, where you get to roam around the cells.

Lynn Museum MUSEUM
(www.museums.norfolk.gov.uk; Market St; adult/child £4.50/3.80; ☺10am-5pm Tue-Sat, plus noon-4pm Sun Apr-Sep) High points here include a large hoard of Iceni gold coins and the **Seahenge Gallery**, which tells the story behind the construction and preservation of the early Bronze Age timber circle, which survived for 4000 years, despite being submerged on the Norfolk shoreline – it was only discovered in 1998. The exhibits include a life-size replica of the monument, which you can stand inside.

True's Yard MUSEUM
(✆ 01553-770479; www.truesyard.co.uk; North St; adult/child £3/1.50; ☺10am-4pm Tue-Sat) Housed in two restored fishers' cottages –

the only legacy of the district's once bustling, fiercely independent fishing community – this museum explores the lives and traditions of the fisherfolk, who were packed like sardines into cottages such as these.

King's Lynn Minster   CHURCH
(St Margaret's Church; ☑ 01553-767090; www. stmargaretskingslynn.org.uk; St Margaret's Pl; ☺ 8am-6pm) The patchwork of styles here includes Flemish brasses and a remarkable 17th-century moon dial, which tells the tide, not the time. You'll find historic flood-level markings by the west door.

🎊 Festivals & Events

King's Lynn Festival   CULTURAL
(www.kingslynnfestival.org.uk; ☺ Jul) East Anglia's most important cultural gathering, with a diverse mix of music, from medieval ballads to opera, as well as literary talks.

🛏 Sleeping & Eating

★ Bank House   BOUTIQUE HOTEL ££
(☑ 01553-660492; www.thebankhouse.co.uk; King's Staithe Sq; s £85-120, d £115-220; ☐ ☎) 🍴 There's so much to love here: a quayside setting, gently funky decor and luxury bathrooms all make this stylish Georgian town house pretty hard to turn down. The best bedroom (the expansive Captain's Room) is gorgeous; but even cheaper, river-view 'Cosy' is still charming.

Downstairs, the hip brasserie (dishes £7 to £18; open noon to 8.30pm) serves seriously good modern British food.

Market Bistro   MODERN BRITISH ££
(☑ 01553-771483; www.marketbistro.co.uk; 11 Saturday Market Pl; mains £14-22; ☺ noon-2pm Wed-Sat, 6-8.30pm Tue-Sat) 🍴 A commitment to Norfolk ingredients has won this friendly, family-run bistro heaps of fans. Seasonal specials might include halibut with smoked cauliflower, or roast venison with beetroot relish. Their set menus (two/three/five courses £16/20/35) are creative and reveal a wide range of culinary skills.

❶ Information

Tourist Office (☑ 01553-763044; www.visit-westnorfolk.com; Purfleet Quay; ☺ 10am-5pm Mon-Sat, from noon Sun Apr-Sep, to 4pm Oct-Mar) Arranges guided heritage walks (adult/child £5/1) at 2pm on Tuesdays, Fridays and Saturdays between May and October.

❶ Getting There & Away

Bus Both Coasthopper (www.sanderscoaches. com) and Coastliner (www.lynxbus.co.uk) buses run regularly from King's Lynn along the shore all the way to Cromer (£10, 2½ hours).

Train There are hourly trains from Cambridge (£10, 50 minutes) via Ely, and also from London King's Cross (£37, 1¾ hours).

Birmingham & the Midlands

Best Places to Eat

➜ The Cross (p413)

➜ Hammer & Pincers (p459)

➜ Chatsworth Estate Farm Shop Cafe (p477)

➜ Fischer's Baslow Hall (p478)

➜ Salt (p419)

Best Places to Stay

➜ The Cow (p462)

➜ Coombe Abbey Hotel (p411)

➜ St Pauls House (p406)

➜ George Hotel (p454)

➜ Brownsover Hall (p412)

Why Go?

If you're searching for quintessentially English countryside – green valleys, chocolate-box villages of wonky black-and-white timbered houses, woodlands steeped in legend such as Nottinghamshire's Sherwood Forest, and stately homes that look like the last lord of the manor just clip-clopped out of the stables – you'll find it here in the country's heart.

You'll also find the relics of centuries of industrial history, exemplified by the World Heritage–listed mills of Ironbridge and the Derwent Valley, and by today's dynamic cities, including Britain's second-largest, Birmingham: a canal-woven industrial crucible reinvented as a cultural and creative hub, with striking 21st-century architecture and vibrant nightlife. Beyond them are tumbling hills where the air is so clean you can taste it. Walkers and cyclists flock to these pristine areas, particularly the Peak District National Park and the Shropshire Hills in the Marches, along the English–Welsh border, to vanish into the vastness of the landscape.

When to Go

➜ February or March (depending when Lent falls) sees the wonderful chaos of Shrovetide football in Ashbourne.

➜ Shakespeare takes a back seat to contemporary wordsmiths at Stratford's Literary Festival in April/May.

➜ From May to September, on weekends and bank holidays, Shropshire Hills Shuttles run from the Carding Mill Valley near Church Stretton to the villages atop the Long Mynd heath and moorland plateau in the glorious Shropshire Hills.

➜ June to September is the best season for walking and cycling in the Peak District.

➜ Foodies will want to head to Ludlow's famous Food Festival in September.

Birmingham & the Midlands Highlights

1 Library of Birmingham (p402) Surveying the buzzing city of Birmingham from its library's rooftop 'secret garden'.

2 Peak District (p466) Hiking, cycling or driving through England's inaugural national park.

3 Lincoln (p449) Strolling the William the Conqueror– built castle walls overlooking the cathedral in this history-steeped city.

4 Ironbridge Gorge (p433) Museum-hopping in the birthplace of the Industrial Revolution.

5 King Richard III: Dynasty, Death & Discovery (p456) Learning about King Richard III's life and death and the extraordinary discovery of his remains in Leicester.

6 Stratford-upon-Avon (p415) Visiting the Bard's schoolroom and reimagined town house before catching a Royal Shakespeare Company performance in his Tudor hometown.

7 Morgan Motor Company (p425) Touring Great Malvern's venerable car factory and taking a car for a spin through the surrounding hills.

8 Burghley House (p454) Wandering the opulent halls and grand gardens of this stately Stamford home.

🏃 Activities

Famous walking trails such as the **Pennine Way** and **Limestone Way** wind across the Peak District's hills, while challenging cycling routes include the **Pennine Cycleway**. The Marches, tracing the English–Welsh border, are also wonderful walking territory.

Watersports abound at Rutland Water; Hereford and Ironbridge Gorge offer canoeing and kayaking.

❶ Getting There & Around

Birmingham Airport (p409) and East Midlands Airport (p464), near Derby, are the main air hubs.

There are excellent rail connections to towns across the Midlands. **National Express** (☑ 08717 818181; www.nationalexpress.com), at Birmingham Coach Station, and local bus companies connect larger towns and villages to each other and to destinations further afield, though services are reduced in the low season. For general route information, consult Traveline for the **East Midlands** (☑ 0871 200 2233; www.travelineeastmidlands.co.uk) or the **West Midlands** (☑ 0871 200 2233; www.traveline midlands.co.uk). Ask locally about discounted all-day tickets.

BIRMINGHAM

☑ 0121 / POP 1,128,100

Regeneration, renewal and grand-scale construction continue apace in Britain's second-largest city. A state-of-the-art library, gleaming shopping centre atop revitalised New St station and beautifully restored Victorian buildings are just some of the successful initiatives of its Big City Plan, following on from the striking Mailbox and Bullring shopping malls and the iconic Selfridges building's 'bubblewrapped' facade. Work is underway on extensions to the Metro (light rail/tram) network, and on the centrepiece Paradise development's new hotels, public spaces, and glitzy residential and commercial buildings, with final completion due in 2025.

Alongside Birmingham's picturesque canals, waterside attractions, outstanding museums and galleries is an explosion of gastronomic restaurants, cool and/or secret cocktail bars and craft breweries. Thriving legacies of the city's industrial heritage include its Jewellery Quarter, Cadbury manufacturing plant and former custard factory turned cutting-edge creative hub.

And in 2022, Birmingham will host the Commonwealth Games. 'Brum', as it's locally dubbed, is buzzing.

◉ Sights

◉ City Centre

Birmingham's grandest civic buildings are clustered around pedestrianised **Victoria Square**, at the western end of New St, dominated by the stately facade of Council House, built between 1874 and 1879. Public art here includes modernist sphinxes and a fountain topped by a naked female figure, dubbed 'the floozy in the Jacuzzi', overlooked by a disapproving statue of Queen Victoria.

To the west, **Centenary Square** is bookended by the art deco Hall of Memory War Memorial, the **International Convention Centre** (ICC; ☑ 0121-644 5025; www.the-icc.co.uk; 8 Centenary Sq) and the **Symphony Hall** (☑ 0121-780 3333; www.thsh.co.uk; 8 Centenary Sq). There's a gleaming golden **statue** (Centenary Sq) of the leading lights from Birmingham's Industrial Revolution: Matthew Boulton, James Watt and William Murdoch. Centenary Sq's showpiece is the spiffing Library of Birmingham.

⭐ **Library of Birmingham**   LIBRARY
(☑ 0121-242 4242; www.birmingham.gov.uk/libraries; Centenary Sq; ⊙ ground fl 9am-9pm Mon & Tue, from 11am Wed-Fri, 11am-5pm Sat, rest of bldg 11am-7pm Mon & Tue, to 5pm Wed-Sat) Resembling a glittering stack of gift-wrapped presents, the Francine Houben–designed Library of Birmingham is an architectural triumph. The 2013-opened building features a subterranean amphitheatre, spiralling interior, viewing decks and glass elevator to the 7th-floor 'secret garden' with panoramic views over the city. In addition to its archives, and photography and rare-book collections (including Britain's most important Shakespeare collection), there are gallery spaces, 160-plus computers and a cafe. The British Film Institute Mediatheque provides free access to the National Film Archive.

Birmingham Back to Backs   HISTORIC BUILDING
(NT; ☑ 0121-666 7671; www.nationaltrust.org.uk; 55-63 Hurst St; 75min tour adult/child £8.65/5.25; ⊙ tours by reservation Tue-Sun) Quirky tours of this cluster of restored back-to-back terraced houses take you through four working-class homes, telling the stories of those who lived

here between the 1840s and the 1970s. Book ahead by phone for the compulsory guided tour.

For an even more vivid impression of what life was like here, you can book to stay in basic three-storey period cottages at 52 and 54 Inge St (doubles with wi-fi from £130). Guests receive a free Back to Backs tour.

Birmingham Museum & Art Gallery
MUSEUM, GALLERY

(📞 0121-348 8038; www.birminghammuseums. org.uk; Chamberlain Sq; ⊙ 10am-5pm Sat-Thu, from 10.30am Fri) **FREE** Major Pre-Raphaelite works by Rossetti, Edward Burne-Jones and others are among the highlights of the delightful Birmingham Museum & Art Gallery's impressive collection of ancient treasures and Victorian art. Excellent temporary exhibitions range from historical collections to emerging contemporary artists.

Its Edwardian Tearooms are an elegant spot for afternoon tea and have 'champagne buzzers' installed in its booths to order bubble at the touch of a button. There's also a casual cafe.

Birmingham Cathedral
CATHEDRAL

(📞 0121-262 1840; www.birminghamcathedral. com; Colmore Row; by donation; ⊙ 7.30am-6.30pm Mon-Fri, to 5pm Sat & Sun) Dedicated to St Philip, this small but perfectly formed cathedral was constructed in a neoclassical style between 1709 and 1715. Pre-Raphaelite artist Edward Burne-Jones was responsible for the magnificent stained-glass windows.

Thinktank
MUSEUM

(📞 0121-348 0000; www.birminghammuseums. org.uk; Millennium Point, Curzon St; adult/child £13.50/9.75, planetarium show £1.50; ⊙ 10am-5pm) Surrounded by the footprints of vanished factories, the Millennium Point development incorporates this entertaining and ambitious attempt to make science accessible to children. Highlights include galleries on the past (Birmingham's industrial breakthroughs), present (how stuff works) and future, as well as an outdoor science garden and a planetarium.

◉ Birmingham Canals

During the industrial age, Birmingham was a major hub on the English canal network and today the city has more miles of canals than Venice. Narrow boats still float through the heart of the city, passing a string of glitzy wharfside developments.

Ikon Gallery
GALLERY

(📞 0121-248 0708; www.ikon-gallery.org; 1 Oozells Sq; ⊙ 11am-5pm Tue-Sun) **FREE** Within the glitzy Brindley Pl development of banking offices and designer restaurants, a converted Gothic schoolhouse contains the cutting-edge Ikon Gallery. Prepare to be thrilled, bemused or outraged, depending on your take on conceptual art.

National Sea Life Centre
AQUARIUM

(📞 0121-643 6777; www.visitsealife.com; 3a Brindley Pl; £20, incl behind-the-scenes tour €23.50; ⊙ 10am-5pm Mon-Fri, to 6pm Sat & Sun) Exotic marine creatures including otters, jellyfish, piranhas and razor-jawed hammerhead sharks swim in the Sir Norman Foster–designed National Sea Life Centre. Prepurchase tickets online for fast-track entry and significant discounts off walk-in rates. Talks and feedings take place regularly. Book online too for 30-minute behind-the-scenes tours offering access to otherwise out-of-bounds areas, and for one-hour tours feeding turtles, penguins or (if you're game) sharks (£65 to £105; minimum age 12 to 14).

◉ Jewellery Quarter

Birmingham has been a major jewellery player since Charles II acquired a taste for it in 17th-century France. The gentrifying Jewellery Quarter, three-quarters of a mile northwest of the city centre, still produces 40% of UK-manufactured jewellery. Dozens of workshops open to the public are listed online at www.jewelleryquarter.net.

Take the Metro from Snow Hill or the train from Moor St to the Jewellery Quarter station.

Museum of the Jewellery Quarter
MUSEUM

(📞 0121-348 8140; www.birminghammuseums.org. uk; 75 Vyse St; adult/child £7/3; ⊙ 10.30am-4pm Tue-Sat) The Smith & Pepper jewellery factory is preserved as it was on its closing day in 1981 after 80 years of operation. Guided tours lasting around one hour explain the long history of the trade in Birmingham and let you watch master jewellers at work. Entry to the temporary exhibition space and shop is free.

◉ Outlying Areas

★ Barber Institute of Fine Arts
GALLERY

(📞 0121-414 7333; www.barber.org.uk; University of Birmingham, Edgbaston; ⊙ 10am-5pm Mon-Fri, from 11am Sat & Sun) **FREE** At the University of Birmingham, 3 miles south of the city centre,

Birmingham

the Barber Institute of Fine Arts has an astonishing collection of Renaissance masterpieces; European masters, such as Rubens and Van Dyck; British greats, including Gainsborough, Reynolds and Turner; and classics from modern titans Picasso, Magritte and others. Trains run from Birmingham New St to University station (£2.50, seven minutes, every 10 minutes), from where it's a 10-minute walk.

Custard Factory ARTS CENTRE
(☑0121-224 7777; www.custardfactory.co.uk; Gibb St; ☺shops 10am-6pm Tue-Sat, event times vary) Just over a mile southeast of the city centre,

Digbeth's creative quarter centres on the Custard Factory, a hip art-and-design enclave set in the converted buildings of the factory that once churned out British favourite Bird's Custard. The open-plan space is now full of artists' galleries, quirky design boutiques, vintage-clothing outlets, one-off shops such as a skateboard specialist, and affordable, offbeat cafes and pop-up street-food stalls. Regular events include cinema screenings.

Cadbury World MUSEUM
(☑0844 880 7667; www.cadburyworld.co.uk; Linden Rd, Bournville; adult/child £17/12.50; ☺11am-4.30pm, hours vary) The next best thing to

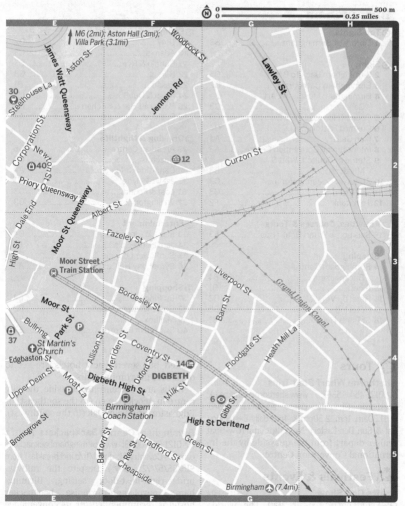

Willy Wonka's chocolate factory is Cadbury World, 4 miles south of Birmingham. It educates visitors about the history of cocoa and the Cadbury family, sweetening the deal with free samples, displays of chocolate-making machines and chocolate-themed attractions, including a 4D cinema with motion-sensor seats. Opening hours vary substantially; bookings are essential at peak times. Trains run from Birmingham New St to Bournville (£2.70, seven minutes, every 10 minutes), from where it's a signposted 10-minute walk.

Surrounding the aromatic chocolate works, pretty Bournville Village was built by the philanthropic Cadbury family to accommodate early-20th-century factory workers.

Aston Hall HISTORIC BUILDING
(☏0121-348 8100; www.birminghammuseums.org.uk; Trinity Rd, Aston; house adult/child £8/3, grounds free; ⊗11am-4pm Tue-Sun Easter-Oct) Set in lush grounds 3 miles north of the city centre, this well-preserved hall was built in extravagant Jacobean style between 1618 and 1635. The sumptuous interiors are full of friezes, moulded ceilings and tapestries. Trains run from Birmingham New St to Aston station (£2.40, seven minutes, every 10 minutes), from where it's a 10-minute walk.

Birmingham

Tours

Sherborne Wharf Boat Trips   CRUISE
(☑0121-454 5367; www.sherbornewharf.co.uk;
Sherborne St; 1hr cruise adult/child £8/6;
⊙11.30am, 1pm, 2.30pm & 4pm daily Easter-Nov,
Sat & Sun Dec-Easter) Nostalgic narrow-boat
cruises depart from the quayside by the International Convention Centre.

Festivals & Events

Crufts Dog Show   ANIMAL SHOW
(www.crufts.org.uk; ⊙early Mar) The world's
greatest collection of pooches on parade at
the National Exhibition Centre over four
days.

Birmingham Pride   LGBT
(www.birminghampride.com; ⊙late May) One of
the biggest and most colourful celebrations
of LGBTIQ culture in the country takes
place over a weekend.

Sleeping

Chains dominate Birmingham's hotel scene,
which is aimed at business travellers, ensuring high weekday prices. Look out for cheap
deals at weekends. Accommodation is often
limited but several new hotels are set to
open over the coming years.

B&Bs are concentrated outside the city
centre in Acocks Green (to the southeast) or
Edgbaston and Selly Oak (to the southwest).

Birmingham Central Backpackers HOSTEL £
(☑0121-643 0033; www.birminghambackpackers.
com; 58 Coventry St; dm/d/tr/q incl breakfast from
£15/36/57/72; @🛜) Despite the railway-
bridge-right-next-door setting, Birmingham's purple-and-turquoise backpacker
hostel is recommended for its convenience
to the bus station and for its choice of clean,
multicoloured dorms or capsule-style pods.
Excellent facilities include a lounge with
DVDs and regular movie nights, a bar (note
you can't BYO alcohol) and a self-catering
kitchen.

★**St Pauls House**   BOUTIQUE HOTEL ££
(☑0121-272 0999; www.saintpaulshouse.com;
15-20 St Paul's Sq; d from £119; P🌀🛜) Overlooking a park in the Jewellery Quarter,
this 2016-opened independent hotel has 34
fresh, contemporary rooms with welcoming
touches, such as hot-water bottles in woollen
covers. Upcycled decor in its hip bar (with

live music Friday to Sunday) and restaurant includes industrial-style ropes (as wall hangings and in furnishings) referencing the building's original use as a rope factory.

Hotel Indigo
BOUTIQUE HOTEL ££

(☑ 0121-643 2010; www.ihg.com; The Cube, Wharfside St; d from £119; ☞ ☒) A stylish operation on the 23rd and 24th floors of the Mailbox's annexe, The Cube, Birmingham's branch of the high-end Hotel Indigo chain marries a handy location with snazzy amenities, including a small swimming pool and great views from its 52 rooms (some with balconies).

Bloc
HOTEL ££

(☑ 0121-212 1223; www.blochotels.com; 77 Caroline St; d from £89; ❉☞) Located in the Jewellery Quarter, Bloc excels in sharp, contemporary pod design. Rooms are tiny but space is cleverly stretched: flatscreen TVs are built into walls; there's under-bed storage; and bathrooms are compact but with luxe shower heads. Book carefully: rooms come with window or without.

Hotel du Vin
BOUTIQUE HOTEL £££

(☑ 0121-794 3005; www.hotelduvin.com; 25 Church St; d/ste from £129/191; ❉ @ ☞) Housed in the Victorian red-brick former Birmingham Eye Hospital, this branch of the upmarket Hotel du Vin chain has real class, with wrought-iron balustrades and classical murals. Its 66 rooms have spectacular bathrooms; there's a spa and a gym, a bistro with worn floorboards and a stellar wine list, plus a pub and lounge bar with comfy, duffed-up leather furniture.

✖ Eating

Buffalo & Rye
GRILL £

(www.buffaloandrye.co.uk; 11 Bennetts Hill; dishes £7.50-17; ☺kitchen noon-11pm Mon-Thu, to midnight Fri & Sat, to 10pm Sun, bar to midnight Sun-Thu, to 2am Fri & Sat; ☞) Aromatic Buffalo & Rye specialises in smoky slow-cooked ribs, jerk-marinated poussin and Cajun-spiced buffalo wings. Beneath upturned glass jars, cocktails such as its Moonshine Margarita with peach moonshine, peach syrup and lime juice are also infused with smoke. Dozens of craft beers are sourced from small US breweries.

Pushkar
INDIAN ££

(☑ 0121-643 7978; www.pushkardining.com; 245 Broad St; 2-/3-course lunch menus £11/14, mains £8.25-19; ☺noon-2.30pm & 5-11.30pm Mon-Fri, 5-11.30pm Sat, to 11pm Sun) Classy north Indi-

an and Punjabi cuisine takes centre stage in this glass-fronted, white tableclothed, gold-trimmed dining room. The elegant presentation extends to boxed menus and serviette-wrapped naan bread as well as stunning cocktails. Lunch menus are an excellent deal. Its swanky spin-off, **Praza** (☑ 0121-456 4500; www.praza.co.uk; 94-96 Hagley Rd, Edgbaston; mains £7-18, banquet menus £29-39, Sun Indian afternoon tea adult/child £19/10; ☺5-11.30pm Mon-Sat, 1-6pm Sun), in Edgbaston, is also superb.

Purecraft Bar & Kitchen
GASTROPUB ££

(☑ 0121-237 5666; www.purecraftbars.com; 30 Waterloo St; mains £13.50-19; ☺kitchen noon-10pm Mon-Fri, from 9am Sat, noon-5pm Sun, bar 11am-11pm Mon-Thu, to midnight Fri & Sat, noon-10pm Sun) Fabulous dishes created in the open kitchen of this craft-beer-lover's paradise come with suggested beer pairings. The menu changes monthly but might include Lawless Lager–battered fish and chips (with Veltins Pilsener); Brewer's Grain asparagus and broad-bean risotto (with Odell St Lupulin American Pale Ale); or grilled plaice with beer-and-parsley butter and Jersey Royal new potatoes (with Purity Mad Goose).

Bureau
GASTROPUB ££

(☑ 0121-236 1110; www.thebureaubar.co.uk; 110 Colmore Row; mains £7-15.50, platters £16; ☺noon-10pm Mon & Tue, to 11pm Wed & Thu, to midnight Fri, to 1am Sat) While this gleaming marble ex-office building dating from 1902 serves stupendous cocktails (like hickory-smoked Bloody Marys), it's worth visiting for its food. Winning deli-style dishes include a duck Scotch egg (soft-boiled duck egg encased in confit of duck and a deep-fried breadcrumb shell, served in a nest of watercress with red-onion jam). Its roof terrace is a suntrap.

Nosh & Quaff
AMERICAN ££

(☑ 0121-236 4246; www.noshandquaff.co.uk; 130 Colmore Row; mains £8-23, whole lobster £29.50; ☺noon-10pm Sun-Thu, to 11pm Fri & Sat) North American fare at this cavernous venue spans gourmet burgers, hot dogs and slow-cooked, hickory-glazed ribs, plus sides such as charred corn on the cob and sweet-potato wedges with sour cream, but the star is the whole lobster flown in live from Canada and dressed with garlic and lemon-butter sauce. The rockin' bar serves great craft beers.

Lasan
INDIAN ££

(☑ 0121-212 3664; www.lasan.co.uk; 3-4 Dakota Bldgs, James St; mains £14.50-22; ☺noon-2.30pm

& 6-11pm Mon-Fri, 6-11pm Sat, noon-9pm Sun) Expletive-loving chef Gordon Ramsay famously proclaimed elegant, upmarket Lasan, in Birmingham's Jewellery Quarter, Britain's 'Best Local Restaurant'. Its changing menu of elevated Indian dishes are served in an intimate dining room, accompanied by cocktails (and mocktails).

1847   VEGETARIAN, VEGAN ££
(☑0121-236 2313; www.by1847.com; 26 Great Western Arcade, Colmore Row; 2-/3-course menu £22/29; ⊙noon-2.30pm & 4.30-9pm Mon-Thu, noon-2.30pm & 4.30-9.30pm Fri, noon-9.30pm Sat, to 8pm Sun; ☑) ✐ Occupying two levels in a gorgeous, heritage-listed Victorian shopping arcade, this chic spot proves that vegetarian and vegan food can be cutting-edge, from starters such as goats-cheese bonbons with kohlrabi, chilli jam and chard to mains including buttermilk-battered halloumi, and lush desserts like rhubarb with soya custard, puffed rice and coconut snow.

★ Simpsons   BRITISH £££
(☑0121-454 3434; www.simpsonsrestaurant.co.uk; 20 Highfield Rd, Edgbaston; menus lunch £45-75, dinner £75-110; ⊙noon-2pm & 7-9pm Mon-Thu, noon-2pm & 7-9.30pm Fri & Sat, noon-4.30pm Sun; ☑⛄) It's worth the 2.5-mile journey southwest of the centre to this gorgeous Georgian mansion in leafy Edgbaston for sensational Michelin-starred menus (kids and vegetarians catered for) in its contemporary dining rooms. You can also stay in one of three luxurious bedrooms upstairs (£110) or take an all-day Saturday cookery class (£150 including three-course lunch) at its Eureka Kitchen. Book ahead.

Adam's   BRITISH £££
(☑0121-643 3745; www.adamsrestaurant.co.uk; New Oxford House, 16 Waterloo St; 3-course midweek lunch menu £39.50, 3-course/tasting dinner menu £65/90; ⊙noon-2pm & 7-9pm Tue-Sat) Michelin-starred Adam's wows with intricately prepared and presented flavour combinations, such as lamb sweetbreads with goats curd, mint and radish, monkfish with wild mussels, champagne and caviar, and pear, toasted hay, caramel and praline. English vintages are represented on its excellent wine list, which has extensive by-the-glass options. Book well ahead.

🍷 Drinking & Nightlife

Independent pubs and bars proliferate throughout the city.

Nightlife hubs in Birmingham include Broad St (aka the 'golden mile' – some say for the prevalence of fake tan here) and Chinatown's **Arcadian Centre** (www.thearcadian.co.uk; Hurst St; ⊙individual venue hours vary).

Postindustrial Digbeth has alternative clubs and club events in and around the Custard Factory (p404).

★ Jekyll & Hyde   PUB
(☑0121-236 0345; www.thejekyllandhyde.co.uk; 28 Steelhouse Lane; ⊙noon-11pm Mon-Thu, to midnight Fri, to 1am Sat; ☎) Potent cocktails (or rather 'elixirs, concoctions and potions') at this trippy spot are served in sweets jars, watering cans, teapots and miniature bathtubs – even a top hat. Downstairs, Mr Hyde's emporium has a cosy drawing room and an *Alice in Wonderland*–themed courtyard; upstairs is Dr Jekyll's Gin Parlour with more than 90 different gins.

Lost & Found   BAR
(www.the-lostandfound.co.uk; 8 Bennett's Hill; ⊙11am-11pm Sun-Wed, to midnight Thu, to 1am Fri & Sat; ☎) Fictitious Victorian-era explorer/professor Hettie G Watson is the inspiration for the botanical-library theme of this bar in an 1869-built former bank. Inside the domed entrance, amid soaring columns and timber panelling, its elevated seating is surrounded by plants, books, globes and maps. Hettie's 'secret emporium' bar-within-a-bar has antique mirrors, brass and steel fixtures, and more plants.

Wellington   PUB
(www.thewellingtonrealale.co.uk; 37 Bennett's Hill; ⊙10am-midnight) The pastel wallpaper, timber bar and polished brass give the impression the Welly is frozen in time, but this spruced-up pub sheltering a timber-decked roof terrace is the best in the city for real ale. Its 27 hand-pulled beers and ciders include favourites from Black Country and Wye Valley as well as rare brews.

Bacchus   BAR
(☑0121-632 5445; www.nicholsonspubs.co.uk; Burlington Arcade, New St; ⊙11am-11pm Mon-Thu, to 1am Fri & Sat, noon-10.30pm Sun; ☎) Buried beneath the Burlington Arcade, this darkened drinking den has the ambience of a decadent underworld. Down a faux-marble-encased staircase, crumbling pillars and giant Grecian murals give way to soaring medieval-style stone arches, swords, suits of armour and candelabras. There's a great range of cask ales, gins and whiskies.

Canalside Cafe
CAFE

(☑ 0121-643 3170; 35 Worcester Bar, Gas St; ⊙ 9am-11pm Mon-Sat, to 10.30pm Sun) Narrow boats glide past the terrace of this 18th-century lock-keeper's cottage, where the low-ceilinged interior is strung with nautical paraphernalia and warmed by an open fire. Drop by for a cuppa, a real ale, or a steaming mulled cider in winter.

☆ Entertainment

Sunflower Lounge
LIVE MUSIC

(☑ 0121-632 6756; www.thesunflowerlounge.com; 76 Smallbrook Queensway; ⊙ bar noon-11.30pm Sun-Tue, to 1am Wed & Thu, to 2am Fri & Sat) This quirky little indie bar pairs a magnificent alternative soundtrack with a packed program of live gigs and DJ nights.

Electric Cinema
CINEMA

(www.theelectric.co.uk; 47-49 Station St; standard/sofa seats £10.50/12, sofa seats with waiter service £14.80) Topped by its art deco sign, this is the UK's oldest working cinema, operating since 1909. It screens mainly art-house films. Be waited upon in plush two-seater sofas, or have a drink in the small bar, which has a traditional absinthe fountain, cocktails themed around films currently showing and 'poptails' (popcorn-flavoured cocktails, in lieu of popcorn being available).

Jam House
LIVE MUSIC

(☑ 0121-200 3030; www.thejamhouse.com; 3-5 St Paul's Sq; ⊙ 6pm-midnight Tue & Wed, to 1am Thu, to 2am Fri & Sat) Pianist Jools Holland was the brains behind this moody, smart-casual music venue (dress accordingly). Acts range from jazz big bands to famous soul crooners. Over 21s only.

🛍 Shopping

Great Western Arcade
SHOPPING CENTRE

(www.greatwesternarcade.co.uk; btwn Colmore Row & Temple Row; ⊙ individual shop hours vary) Topped with a glass roof, this tile-floored Victorian-era arcade is a jewel filled with mostly independent shops.

Swordfish Records
MUSIC

(www.swordfishrecords.co.uk; 66 Dalton St; ⊙ 10am-5.30pm Mon-Sat) A Birmingham institution, this independent record shop down a tiny backstreet brims with new and secondhand vinyl (and some CDs), including its own label releases. Robert Plant, Duran Duran's John Taylor, Dave Grohl and Neil Diamond are among its past customers. It's a great place to find out about under-the-radar gigs and festivals.

Mailbox
MALL

(www.mailboxlife.com; 7 Commercial St; ⊙ mall 10am-7pm Mon-Sat, 11am-5pm Sun, individual shop hours vary) Birmingham's stylish canal-side shopping experience, the redevelopment of the former Royal Mail sorting office, comes complete with designer hotels, a fleet of upmarket restaurants, the luxury department store Harvey Nichols and designer boutiques. Its super-snazzy metallic extension, the Cube (www.thecube.co.uk), houses Marco Pierre White's panoramic Steakhouse Bar & Grill on the 25th floor.

Bullring
MALL

(www.bullring.co.uk; St Martin's Circus; ⊙ 10am-8pm Mon-Fri, from 9am Sat, 11am-5pm Sun, individual shop hours vary) Split into two vast retail spaces – the East Mall and West Mall – the Bullring has all the international brands and chain cafes you could ask for, plus the standout architectural wonder of Selfridges, which looks out over the city like the compound eye of a giant robot insect.

ℹ Information

Comprehensive tourist information is available at www.visitbirmingham.com.

The ground-floor reception of the Library of Birmingham (p402) can also provide information for tourists.

➜ The city centre, especially south of the Bullring and on and around Broad St, can get very rowdy with revellers on weekend nights.

➜ Digbeth bus station and its surrounds can be quite rough after dark.

ℹ Getting There & Away

AIR

Birmingham Airport (BHX; ☑ 0800 655 6470; www.birminghamairport.co.uk), 8 miles east of the city centre, has direct flights to destinations around the UK and Europe, as well as direct long-haul routes to Dubai, India and the USA.

Fast and convenient trains run regularly between Birmingham New St and Birmingham International stations (£3.80, 15 minutes, every 10 minutes). Birmingham International is linked to the terminal by the Air-Rail Link monorail (free, two minutes, frequent), which runs from 3.30am to 12.30am.

Alternatively, take bus X1 (£2.40, 35 minutes, up to two hourly) from Moor St Queensway, which run 24 hours.

A taxi from the airport to the city centre costs about £45.

BUS

Most intercity buses run from **Birmingham Coach Station** (☏ 0871 781 8181; Mill Lane, Digbeth), but the X20 to Stratford-upon-Avon (£5.50, 1½ hours, hourly) also leaves from a more convenient stop on Carr's Lane, opposite Moor St station.

National Express (p402) coaches link Birmingham with major cities across the country, including the following:

London Victoria £4.70 to £13.80, 3¼ hours, hourly or better

Manchester £3 to £15, three hours, hourly

Oxford £6 to £25, 2¼ hours, eight daily

TRAIN

Most long-distance trains leave from Birmingham New St station, but Chiltern Railways runs to London Marylebone (£54, two hours, hourly) from Birmingham Snow Hill, and London Midland runs to Stratford-upon-Avon (£8.30, 50 minutes, half-hourly) from Birmingham Snow Hill and Birmingham Moor St stations.

Construction on the High Speed Rail (HS2) line – connecting London with Birmingham in just 40 minutes – is set to commence in 2019 and to be completed by 2026.

Useful services from New St:

Derby £19.30, 40 minutes, four per hour

Leicester £14.50, one hour, two per hour

London Euston £54, 1½ hours, up to six per hour

Manchester £37.40, 1¾ hours, half-hourly

Nottingham £33.10, 1¼ hours, two per hour

Shrewsbury £15.30, one hour, two per hour

ⓘ Getting Around

CAR

During central Birmingham's ongoing construction, traffic into and around the city is severely disrupted and parking is limited. Check with your accommodation about access (don't rely on your satnav, or assume hotels' car parks are operational). Updated details of road closures are posted at www.visitbirmingham.com/travel/latest-travel-updates.

PUBLIC TRANSPORT

Local buses run from a convenient hub on Corporation St, just north of where it connects with New St. For routes, pick up a free copy of the *Network Birmingham Map and Guide* from the tourist office. Single-trip tickets start from £1.50.

Be aware that bus stops may change during construction works in the city centre and journey times may be extended.

Birmingham's single tram line, the Metro (www.nxbus.co.uk), links New St station with Wolverhampton via the Jewellery Quarter, West Bromwich and Dudley. Tickets start from £1.

An extension from New St to Birmingham Town Hall and Centenary Sq is due to open in 2021.

Various saver tickets covering buses and trains are available from the **Network West Midlands Travel Centre** (www.networkwestmidlands.com; New St station; ⊙ 8.30am-5.30pm Mon-Sat) at New St station.

WARWICKSHIRE

Warwickshire could have been just another picturesque county of rolling hills and market towns were it not for the English language's most famous wordsmith. William Shakespeare was born and died in Stratford-upon-Avon, and the sights linked to his life draw tourists from around the globe. Famous Warwick Castle attracts similar crowds. Elsewhere visitor numbers dwindle but Kenilworth has atmospheric castle ruins, Rugby celebrates the sport that takes its name at its World Rugby Hall of Fame, and Coventry, which will be in the spotlight in 2021 as the UK City of Culture, claims two extraordinary cathedrals and an unmissable motoring museum.

ⓘ Getting There & Around

Coventry is the main transport hub, with frequent rail connections to London Euston and Birmingham New St.

Coventry

☏ 024 / POP 352,900

Coventry was once a bustling hub for the production of cloth, clocks, bicycles, automobiles and munitions. It was this last industry that drew the German Luftwaffe in WWII: on the night of 14 November 1940, the city was so badly blitzed that the Nazis coined a new verb, *coventrieren,* meaning 'to flatten'. A handful of medieval streets that escaped the bombers offer a glimpse of old Coventry.

The city faced a further setback with the collapse of the British motor industry in the 1980s, but is undergoing a resurgence today thanks to its redeveloped and expanded university, and its vibrant cultural scene, which has seen it awarded the UK City of Culture 2021, bringing renewed investment and new openings during the run-up, and events and celebrations throughout the year.

◉ Sights

★ Coventry Transport Museum
MUSEUM

(☑024-7623 4270; www.transport-museum.com; Hales St; museum free, speed simulator adult/child £5/3.50; ⓢ10am-5pm) This stupendous museum has hundreds of vehicles, from horseless carriages to jet-powered, land-speed-record breakers. There's a brushed-stainless-steel DeLorean DMC-12 (of *Back to the Future* fame) with gull-wing doors, alongside a gorgeous Jaguar E-type, a Daimler armoured car and, for 1970s British-design-oddity enthusiasts, a Triumph TR7 and an Austin Allegro 'Special'. View the Thrust SCC, the current holder of the World Land Speed Record and the Thrust 2, the previous record holder. Kids will love the 4D Thrust speed simulator.

★ Coventry Cathedral
CATHEDRAL

(☑024-7652 1210; www.coventrycathedral.org.uk; Priory Row; cathedral & ruins by donation, tower climb £4, Blitz Experience Museum £2; ⓢcathedral & tower 10am-4pm Mon-Sat, noon-3pm Sun, ruins 9am-5pm daily, museum closed Nov–mid-Feb, hours can vary) The evocative ruins of St Michael's Cathedral, built around 1300 but destroyed by Nazi incendiary bombs in the Blitz, stand as a memorial to Coventry's darkest hour and as a symbol of peace and reconciliation. Climb the 180 steps of the Gothic spire for panoramic views.

Symbolically adjoining St Michael's Cathedral's sandstone walls is the Sir Basil Spence–designed modernist architectural masterpiece Coventry Cathedral, with a futuristic organ, stained glass, and Jacob Epstein statue of the devil and St Michael.

Fargo Village
CULTURAL CENTRE

(www.fargovillage.co.uk; Far Gosford St; ⓢhours vary) Markets, live-music gigs, moonlight cinema screenings and workshops (eg gardening or blacksmithing) are just some of the events that take place at this post-industrial cultural hub spread over a former car-radiator plant. Shops here sell everything from secondhand books to upcycled furniture; there are also art-and-craft studios, a hairdresser in a vintage Freedom Jetstream caravan, and a brilliant microbrewery, the Twisted Barrel, along with cafes, bakeries and street-food stalls.

St Mary's Guildhall
HISTORIC BUILDING

(☑024-7683 3328; www.stmarysguildhall.co.uk; Bayley Lane; ⓢ10am-4pm Sun-Thu mid-Mar–Sep) FREE One of the most evocative insights into pre-WWII Coventry is this half-timbered and brick hall where the town's trades came together in the Middle Ages to discuss town affairs. As one of England's finest guildhalls, it was chosen to be a jail for Mary Queen of Scots. Stained-glass windows glorify the kings of England; further down the hall stands WC Marshall's statue of Lady Godiva. Look out for the Coventry Tapestry, dating from 1500, depicting the Virgin Mary's assumption.

The vaulted stone undercroft houses an atmospheric cafe.

Herbert Art Gallery & Museum
GALLERY, MUSEUM

(☑024-7623 7521; www.theherbert.org; Jordan Well; ⓢ10am-4pm Mon-Sat, from noon Sun) FREE Behind Coventry's twin cathedrals, the Herbert has an eclectic collection of paintings and sculptures (including work by TS Lowry, Stanley Spencer and David Hockney), and thought-provoking history galleries spanning natural history and archaeology to Coventry's social and industrial history. Poignant and uplifting exhibits focus on conflict, peace and reconciliation. There are lots of activities aimed at kids, creative workshops for adults (calligraphy, silversmithing etc) and a light-filled cafe.

🍴 Sleeping & Eating

★ Coombe Abbey Hotel
HISTORIC HOTEL ££

(☑024-7645 0450; www.coombeabbey.com; Brinklow Rd, Binley; d incl breakfast from £105; P☎) Queen Elizabeth I lived as a child at this 200-hectare estate, 5.5 miles east of Coventry. The 12th-century abbey was converted into a stately manor in 1581, with parkland, formal gardens and a lake. Many of its 119 uniquely decorated rooms have ornate four-poster beds; some have bathrooms hidden behind bookcases. There's a glass-paned conservatory restaurant and regular themed banquets.

Golden Cross
PUB FOOD ££

(☑024-7655 1855; www.thegoldencrosscoventry.co.uk; 8 Hay Lane; mains £9-18; ⓢkitchen noon-9pm Mon-Sat, to 5pm Sun, bar 11am-11pm Mon-Thu, to 1am Fri & Sat, noon-8pm Sun; ☎) Constructed in 1583, this beautiful Tudor building with beamed ceilings, original stained glass and a toasty wood-burning stove is an inviting place for a pint, but the food (much of it gluten-free), such as ale-battered scampi with mushy peas or sirloin with Stilton

RUGBY

Warwickshire's second-largest hub, Rugby is an attractive market town whose history dates back to the Iron Age. But it's most famous for the sport that was invented here and now takes its name, and is a place of pilgrimage for fans.

The game was invented at prestigious Rugby School in 1823 when William Webb Ellis is said to have caught the ball during a football match and broken the rules by running with it. Situated just across from the **Webb Ellis Rugby Football Museum** (☑ 01788-567777; 5-6 Matthews St; ⊙ 9.30am-5pm Mon-Sat) **FREE**, the school itself is closed to the public, but you can peek at the hallowed ground through the gates on Barby Rd. A **statue of William Webb Ellis** (cnr Lawrence Sheriff St & Dunchurch Rd) stands outside the main Rugby School gates.

The whizz-bang interactive World Rugby Hall of Fame is inside the **Rugby Art Gallery & Museum** (☑ 01788-533201; www.ragm.co.uk; Little Elborow St; gallery & museum free, World Rugby Hall of Fame adult/child £6/3; ⊙ gallery & museum 10am-5pm Tue-Fri, to 4pm Sat, World Rugby Hall of Fame 10am-5pm Mon-Sat, to 4pm Sun) complex.

The top place to stay is **Brownsover Hall** (☑ 01788-546100; www.brownsoverhall.co.uk; Brownsover Lane, Old Brownsover; d from £90; **P** 🛜), a Grade II–listed Gothic Revival manor (where Frank Whittle designed the turbo jet engine). Set in 2.8 hectares of woodland and manicured gardens, it's 2.7 miles north of Rugby.

Rugby is 13 miles east of Coventry, served by regular trains (£6, 10 minutes, up to four per hour). Trains also link Rugby with Birmingham (£9.90, 40 minutes, up to four per hour) and Leicester (£14.70, 1¼ hours, hourly).

---

sauce, merits a visit in its own right. Mellow live music plays upstairs on weekends.

ℹ Information

Tourist Office (☑ 024-7623 4284; www.visitcoventryandwarwickshire.co.uk; Herbert Art Gallery & Museum, Jordan Well; ⊙10am-4pm Mon-Sat, from noon Sun) Located in the reception area of the Herbert Art Gallery & Museum (p411).

ℹ Getting There & Away

BUS

Buses X17 and X18 (every 20 minutes) go to Kenilworth (£3, 35 minutes) and Warwick (£3.20, 40 minutes).

TRAIN

Regular services include the following:
Birmingham (£4.70, 30 minutes, every 10 minutes)
London Euston (£49, 1¼ hours, every 10 to 20 minutes)
Rugby (£6, 10 minutes, up to four per hour)

Kenilworth

☑ 01926 / POP 22,413

An easy deviation off the A46 between Warwick and Coventry, the atmospheric ruin of Kenilworth Castle was the inspiration for Walter Scott's 1821 novel *Kenilworth,* and it still feels pretty inspiring today. The town is essentially split into two by Finham Brook: the historic village-like area, of most interest to visitors, is on the northern side, while the southern side is the commercial centre.

◉ Sights

Kenilworth Castle CASTLE, RUINS
(EH; ☑ 01926-852078; www.english-heritage.org.uk; Castle Green; adult/child £11.30/6.80; ⊙10am-6pm Apr-Sep, to 5pm Oct, to 4pm Sat & Sun Nov–mid-Feb, to 4pm Wed-Sun mid-Feb–Mar) This spine-tingling ruin sprawls among fields and hedges on Kenilworth's outskirts. Built in the 1120s, the castle survived the longest siege in English history in 1266, when the forces of Lord Edward (later Edward I) threw themselves at the moat and battlements for six solid months. The fortress was dramatically extended in Tudor times, but it fell in the English Civil War and its walls were breached and water defences drained. Don't miss the magnificent restored Elizabethan gardens.

Stoneleigh Abbey HISTORIC BUILDING
(☑ 01926-858535; www.stoneleighabbey.org; B4115; adult/child grounds & tour £11/4.50, grounds only £5/1; ⊙ tours 11.30am, 1pm & 2.30pm Sun-Thu Easter-Oct, grounds 11am-5pm Sun-Thu Easter-Oct; **P**) The kind of stately home that makes

film directors go weak at the knees, Stoneleigh name-drops Charles I and Jane Austen among its past visitors. Completed in 1726 and only viewable on tours (included in admission), the splendid Palladian west wing contains richly detailed plasterwork ceilings and wood-panelled rooms. A 'reflecting lake' effect is created by the widened stretch of the River Avon, which runs through the grounds. It's 2 miles east of Kenilworth.

Sleeping & Eating

The Old Bakery   B&B ££
(☑ 01926-864111; www.theoldbakery.eu; 12 High St; s/d/tr from £75/95/115; ℗ 🛜) East of the castle, with restaurants nearby, this appealing B&B has attractively attired modern rooms and a cosy, welcoming bar (open 5.30pm to 11pm Monday to Thursday, 5pm to 11pm Friday and Saturday, and 5pm to 10.30pm Sunday) serving well-kept real ales on the ground floor.

★ The Cross   GASTROPUB £££
(☑ 01926-853840; www.thecrosskenilworth.co.uk; 16 New St; 2-/3-course lunch menus £30/32.50, 5-course dinner tasting menu £75, mains £28-42; ⊙noon-2pm & 6.30-9.30pm Tue-Thu, noon-2pm & 6-9.30pm Fri, noon-2.30pm & 6-9.30pm Sat, noon-3.30pm Sun; ✍🚻) One of England's culinary jewels, this Michelin-starred gastropub occupies a romantic 19th-century inn. Prepare to be dazzled by exquisite creations like seared scallops with seaweed butter, duck breast with smoked beetroot and raspberry vinegar, and brioche pudding with apple-and-blackberry compote and bay leaf ice cream.

Vegetarian menus are available; junior gourmands have their own three-course children's menu (£12).

❶ Getting There & Away

From Monday to Saturday, buses X17 and X18 run every 20 minutes between Coventry (£3, 25 minutes) and Kenilworth and on to Warwick (£4.20, 30 minutes). There are no buses on Sunday.

Warwick
☑ 01926 / POP 31,345

Regularly name-checked by Shakespeare, Warwick was the ancestral seat of the earls of Warwick, who played a pivotal role in the Wars of the Roses. Despite a devastating fire in 1694, Warwick remains a treasure house of medieval architecture, with rich veins of history and charming streets, dominated by the soaring turrets of Warwick Castle.

◉ Sights

★ Warwick Castle   CASTLE
(☑ 01926-495421; www.warwick-castle.com; Castle Lane; castle adult/child £27/24, castle & dungeon £32/28; ⊙10am-5pm Apr-Sep, to 4pm Oct-Mar; ℗) Founded in 1068 by William the Conqueror, stunningly preserved Warwick Castle is the biggest show in town. The ancestral home of the earls of Warwick remains impressively intact, and the Tussauds Group has filled the interior with flamboyant, family-friendly attractions that bring the castle's rich history to life. Waxworks populate the private apartments; there are also jousting tournaments, daily trebuchet firings, themed evenings and a dungeon. Discounted online tickets provide fast-track entry. Great accommodation options (p414) are available on-site.

Collegiate Church of St Mary   CHURCH
(☑ 01926-403940; www.stmaryswarwick.org.uk; Old Sq; church by donation, tower adult/child £3/1.50; ⊙10am-4.30pm Mon-Sat, from 12.30pm Sun) This magnificent 1123-founded Norman church was badly damaged in the Great Fire of Warwick in 1694, but is packed with 16th- and 17th-century tombs. Highlights include the Norman crypt with a 14th-century extension; the impressive Beauchamp Chapel, built between 1442 and 1464 to enshrine the mortal remains of the earls of Warwick; and, up 134 steps, the tower, which provides supreme views over town (kids must be aged over eight).

Lord Leycester Hospital   HISTORIC BUILDING
(☑ 01926-491422; www.lordleycester.com; 60 High St; adult/child £8.50/5, garden only £2; ⊙10am-5pm Tue-Sun Apr-Sep, to 4pm Oct-Mar) A survivor of the 1694 fire, the wonderfully wonky Lord Leycester Hospital has been used as a retirement home for soldiers (but never as a hospital) since 1571. Visitors can wander around the chapel, guildhall, regimental museum and restored walled garden, which includes a knot garden and a Norman arch.

Sleeping & Eating

Tilted Wig   PUB ££
(☑ 01926-400110; www.tiltedwigwarwick.co.uk; 11 Market Pl; d £85; 🛜) Bang on the central Market Pl, this brilliantly named 17th-century

Warwick

Warwick

◎ Top Sights
1 Warwick Castle C4

◎ Sights
2 Collegiate Church of St Mary B3
3 Lord Leycester Hospital.....................A3

⊨ Sleeping
4 Rose & Crown.....................................A3
5 Tilted Wig A3

⊗ Eating
6 Old Coffee Tavern...............................B2
7 Tailors...A3

Georgian inn has four snug but comfortable rooms overlooking the square and some of the better pub food in town, such as Warwickshire rare-breed sausages with garlic mash (mains £9 to £18).

Rose & Crown   PUB ££
(☑ 01926-411117; www.roseandcrownwarwick. co.uk; 30 Market Pl; s/d/f incl breakfast from £90/100/110; ⚡) Dating from the 17th century, this family-run inn on the town square has five lovely, spacious and tastefully decorated rooms upstairs from the pub and another eight in the building across the lane, as well as great ales and bottled beers, and an excellent Modern British menu (mains £13 to £27.50). Four of its rooms are set up for families.

**★ Warwick Castle
Accommodation**   RESORT £££
(☑ 0871 097 1228; www.warwick-castle.com; Warwick Castle; tower ste/lodge/glamping per night from £550/242/212; ⊙ tower ste & lodge year-round, glamping Jul–early Sep; P ⚡) Atmospheric accommodation at Warwick Castle (p413) includes two days' castle admission. The castle itself contains two four-poster-bed Tower

Suites (including a private tour, champagne and breakfast). The riverside Knight's Village has woodland and knight-themed lodges (all with terraces and some with kitchenettes) and medieval entertainment. Themed tents (with shared bathrooms) make up the glamping ground. All sleep up to five people.

Old Coffee Tavern
BRITISH ££

(✍ 01926-679737; www.theoldcoffeetavern.co.uk; 16 Old Sq; mains £9.50-12.50; ⊙ kitchen 7am-10pm Mon-Fri, from noon Sat, noon-8pm Sun, bar 7am-11pm Mon-Thu, to 12.30am Fri, 8am-12.30am Sat, to 10pm Sun; 🕿) An 1880-built beauty with many of its Victorian features intact, this tavern was originally established as a teetotal alternative to Warwick's pubs. Today you can order real ales, craft ciders, cocktails and wines, along with elevated versions of British classics like toad-in-the-hole and chicken-and-ham-hock pie. Upstairs are 10 stylish oyster-toned guest rooms (doubles including breakfast from £92.50).

Tailors
MODERN BRITISH £££

(✍ 01926-410590; www.tailorsrestaurant.co.uk; 22 Market Pl; 2-/3-course lunch menus £17/21, 2-/3-/6-course dinner menus £29.50/39.50/60; ⊙ noon-2pm & 6.30-9pm Tue-Sat) Set in a former tailor's shop, this elegant restaurant, owned and run by two hot-shot chefs, serves prime ingredients – guinea fowl, pork belly and lamb from named farms – complemented by intricate creations like brown butter crumb, powdered coleslaw, and black truffle and fennel candy.

ℹ Information

Tourist Office (✍ 01926-492212; www.visitwarwick.co.uk; Court House, Jury St; ⊙ 9.30am-4.30pm Mon-Fri, from 10am Sat year-round, plus 10am-4pm Sun Apr–mid-Dec) Within the flagstone-floored Court House (1725).

ℹ Getting There & Away

BUS
Buses depart from outside **Westgate House** (Market St).

National Express coaches serve London Victoria (£20.50, four hours, up to four daily).

Stagecoach X17 and X18 run to Coventry (£5.80, 1¼ hours, every 20 minutes Monday to Saturday) via Kenilworth (£4.20, 30 minutes). Bus X18 also runs to Stratford-upon-Avon (£5.40, 40 minutes, two per hour Monday to Saturday, hourly Sunday).

TRAIN
The train station is half a mile northeast of the town centre on Station Rd.

Trains run to Birmingham (£7.10, 30 minutes, hourly), Stratford-upon-Avon (£6.90, 30 minutes, every two hours) and London Marylebone (£34, 1½ hours, every 30 minutes; some require a change in Leamington Spa).

Stratford-upon-Avon
🕿 01789 / POP 27,455

The author of some of the most quoted lines ever written in the English language, William Shakespeare was born in Stratford in 1564 and died here in 1616. Experiences linked to his life in this unmistakably Tudor town range from the touristy (medieval recreations and Bard-themed tearooms) to the humbling (Shakespeare's modest grave in Holy Trinity Church) and the sublime (taking in a play by the world-famous Royal Shakespeare Company).

⊙ Sights

★ Shakespeare's New Place
HISTORIC SITE

(✍ 01789-338536; www.shakespeare.org.uk; cnr Chapel St & Chapel Lane; adult/child £12.50/8; ⊙ 10am-5pm Apr-Aug, to 4.30pm Sep & Oct, to 3.30pm Nov-Feb) When Shakespeare retired, he swapped the bright lights of London for a comfortable town house at New Place, where he died of unknown causes in April 1616. The house was demolished in 1759, but an attractive Elizabethan knot garden occupies part of the grounds. A major restoration project has uncovered Shakespeare's kitchen and incorporated new exhibits in a reimagining of the house as it would have been. You can also explore the adjacent Nash's House, where Shakespeare's granddaughter Elizabeth lived.

★ Shakespeare's Birthplace
HISTORIC BUILDING

(✍ 01789-204016; www.shakespeare.org.uk; Henley St; adult/child £17.50/11.50; ⊙ 9am-5pm Apr-Aug, to 4.30pm Sep & Oct, 10am-3.30pm Nov-Mar) Start your Shakespeare quest at the house where the renowned playwright was born in 1564 and spent his childhood days. John Shakespeare owned the house for a period of 50 years. William, as the eldest surviving son, inherited it upon his father's death in 1601 and spent his first five years of marriage here. Behind a modern facade, the house has restored Tudor rooms, live presentations from famous Shakespearean

Stratford-upon-Avon

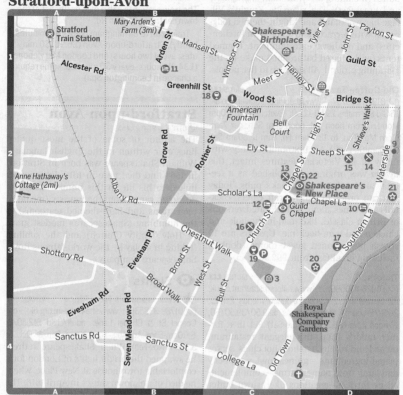

characters and an engaging exhibition on Stratford's favourite son.

Holy Trinity Church
CHURCH

(☎ 01789-266316; www.stratford-upon-avon.org; Old Town; Shakespeare's grave adult/child £3/2; ⊙ 9am-6pm Mon-Sat, 12.30-5pm Sun Apr-Sep, 9am-5pm Mon-Sat, 12.30-5pm Sun Mar & Oct, 9am-4pm Mon-Sat, 12.30-5pm Sun Nov-Feb) The final resting place of the Bard, where he was also baptised and where he worshipped, is said to be the most visited parish church in England. Inside are handsome 16th- and 17th-century tombs (particularly in the Clopton Chapel), some fabulous carvings on the choir stalls and, of course, the grave of William Shakespeare, with its ominous epitaph: 'cvrst be he yt moves my bones'.

MAD Museum
MUSEUM

(☎ 01789-269356; www.themadmuseum.co.uk; 4-5 Henley St; adult/child £7.60/5.20; ⊙ 10am-5.30pm) Fun, hands-on exhibits at Stratford's Mechanical Art & Design Museum (aka MAD) make physics accessible for kids, who can build their own gravity-propelled marble run, use their energy to light up electric panels, and pull levers and turn cranks to animate displays. Tickets are valid all day, so you can come and go as you please.

Mary Arden's Farm
HISTORIC SITE, FARM

(☎ 01789-338535; www.shakespeare.org.uk; Station Rd, Wilmcote; adult/child £15/10; ⊙ 10am-5pm Apr-Aug, to 4.30pm Sep & Oct; ⊕) Shakespeare genealogists can trace the family tree to the childhood home of the Bard's mother at Wilmcote, 3 miles west of Stratford. Aimed squarely at families, the working farm traces country life over the centuries, with nature trails, falconry displays and a collection of rare-breed farm animals. You can get here on the **City Sightseeing bus** (☎ 01789-299123; www.city-sightseeing.com; adult/child 24hr £16.82/8.41, 48hr £25.52/13; ⊙ 9.30am-5pm Apr-Sep, to 4pm Oct-Mar), or cycle via Anne

Hathaway's Cottage, following the Stratford-upon-Avon Canal towpath. Note that, unlike the other Shakespeare properties, it's closed from November to March.

Shakespeare's School Room   HISTORIC SITE
(☎ 01789-203170; www.shakespearesschoolroom. org; King Edward VI School, Church St; adult/child £8/5; ⊙ 11am-5pm) Shakespeare's alma mater, King Edward VI School (still a prestigious grammar school today), incorporates a vast black-and-white timbered building, dating from 1420, that was once the town's guild-hall, where Shakespeare's father John served as bailiff (mayor). In the Bard's former class-room, you can sit in on mock-Tudor lessons, watch a short film and test yourself on Tudor-style homework.

Anne Hathaway's Cottage   HISTORIC BUILDING
(☎ 01789-338532; www.shakespeare.org.uk; Cottage Lane, Shottery; adult/child £12.50/8; ⊙ 9am-5pm Apr-Aug, to 4.30pm Sep & Oct, 10am-3.30pm Nov-Mar) Before tying the knot with Shakespeare, Anne Hathaway lived in Shottery, 1 mile west of the centre of Stratford, in this delightful thatched farmhouse. As well as period furniture, it has gorgeous gardens and an orchard and arboretum, with examples of all the trees mentioned in Shakespeare's plays. A footpath (no bikes allowed) leads to Shottery from Evesham Pl. The City Sightseeing bus stops here.

Hall's Croft   HISTORIC BUILDING
(☎ 01789-338533; www.shakespeare.org.uk; Old Town; adult/child £8.50/5.50; ⊙ 10am-5pm Apr-Aug, to 4.30pm Sep & Oct, 11am-3.30pm Nov-Feb) The handsome Jacobean town house belonging to Shakespeare's daughter Susanna and her husband, respected doctor John

Hall, stands south of Stratford's centre. The exhibition offers fascinating insights into medicine in the 16th and 17th centuries, and the lovely walled garden sprouts with aromatic herbs employed in medicinal preparations.

Tours

Avon Boating
BOATING

(☑ 01789-267073; www.avon-boating.co.uk; The Boathouse, Swan's Nest Lane; river cruises adult/child £6/4; ◷ 9am-dusk Easter-Oct) Avon Boating runs 40-minute river cruises that depart every 20 minutes from either side of the main bridge. It also hires rowboats, canoes and punts (per hour £6) and motorboats (per hour £40).

Stratford Town Walk
WALKING

(☑ 07855 760377; www.stratfordtownwalk.co.uk; town walk adult/child £6/3, ghost walk £7/5; ◷ town walk 11am Mon-Fri, 11am & 2pm Sat & Sun, ghost walk by reservation 7.30pm Sat) Popular two-hour guided town walks depart from Waterside, opposite Sheep St (prebooking not necessary). Chilling ghost walks lasting 90 minutes leave from the same location but must be booked ahead.

Festivals & Events

Stratford Literary Festival
LITERATURE

(☑ 01789-207100; www.stratfordliteraryfestival.co.uk; ◷ late Apr/early May) A highlight of Stratford's cultural calendar is the week-long annual Stratford Literary Festival, which has attracted literary big-hitters of the cal-

---

① SHAKEPEARE HISTORIC HOMES

Five of the most important buildings associated with Shakespeare – Shakespeare's Birthplace (p415), Shakespeare's New Place (p415), Hall's Croft (p417), Anne Hathaway's Cottage (p417) and Mary Arden's Farm (p416) – contain museums that form the core of the visitor experience at Stratford. All are run by the Shakespeare Birthplace Trust (www.shakespeare.org.uk).

A Full Story ticket (adult/child £22/14.50) covering all five properties is available online or at the sites and provides up to a 60% discount off individual admission prices.

---

ibre of Robert Harris, PD James and Simon Armitage.

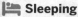

Sleeping

Stratford-upon-Avon YHA
HOSTEL £

(☑ 0345 371 9661; www.yha.org.uk; Wellesbourne Rd, Alveston; dm/d/glamping from £13/58/49; P 🖥) Set in a large 200-year-old mansion 1.5 miles east of the town centre, this superior 134-bed hostel attracts travellers of all ages. Of its 32 rooms and dorms, 16 are en suite. There's a canteen, bar and kitchen. Buses 6 and X17 (£3.50, 12 minutes, up to two per hour) run here from Bridge St. Wi-fi's in common areas only.

Stag at Red Hill
INN ££

(☑ 01789-764634; www.stagredhill.co.uk; Alcester Rd, Alcester; d/f incl breakfast from £99/109; P 🖥) Stratford's formidable one-time courthouse and prison, dating back over 500 years, is now an idyllic country inn 4 miles west of the town centre. Its nine rooms (including a family room with a pull-out sofa) are individually decorated; deluxe rooms have Chesterfield sofas. Standout pub fare includes Red Hill sausages with spring onion mash. Countryside views unfold from its beer garden.

Emsley Guesthouse
B&B ££

(☑ 01789-299557; www.theemsley.co.uk; 4 Arden St; d/f from £82/97; P 🖥) This lovely five-bedroom Victorian property has a personable owner, very clean and attractive accommodation, and a large, pretty family room at the top with an exposed-beam ceiling. Two rooms are set up for families. There's a two-night minimum stay.

Townhouse
BOUTIQUE HOTEL £££

(☑ 01789-262222; www.stratfordtownhouse.co.uk; 16 Church St; d incl breakfast from £130; 🖥) Some of the dozen rooms at this exquisite hotel have free-standing claw-foot bathtubs, and all have luxurious bedding and Temple Spa toiletries. The building is a centrally located 400-year-old gem with a first-rate restaurant (mains £9.50-24; ◷ kitchen noon-3pm & 5-10pm Mon-Fri, noon-10pm Sat, to 8pm Sun, bar 8am-midnight Mon-Sat, to 10.30pm Sun; 🖥). Light sleepers should avoid room 1, nearest the bar. There's a minimum two-night stay on weekends.

Arden Hotel
HOTEL £££

(☑ 01789-298682; www.theardenhotelstratford.com; Waterside; s/d incl breakfast from £115/130; P 🖥) Facing the Swan Theatre, this elegant property has a sleek brasserie and champagne bar. Its 45 rooms feature designer fabrics and its bathrooms are full of polished marble. Interconnecting rooms are ideal for families. Kids receive welcome bags with games.

✕ Eating

Fourteas
CAFE £

(☑ 01789-293908; www.thefourteas.co.uk; 24 Sheep St; dishes £4.60-7.55, afternoon tea with/without Prosecco £20/15; ☺ 9.30am-5pm Mon-Sat, 11am-4.30pm Sun) Breaking with Stratford's Shakespearean theme, this tearoom takes the 1940s as its inspiration with beautiful old teapots, framed posters and staff in period costume. As well as premium loose-leaf teas and homemade cakes, there are all-day breakfasts, soups, sandwiches (including a chicken and bacon 'Churchill club') and lavish afternoon teas.

Lambs
MODERN EUROPEAN ££

(☑ 01789-292554; www.lambsrestaurant.co.uk; 12 Sheep St; mains £14.50-23.50; ☺ 5-9pm Mon, noon-2pm & 5-9pm Tue-Sat, noon-2pm & 6-9pm Sun) Lambs swaps Shakespeare chintz in favour of modern elegance but throws in authentic 16th-century ceiling beams for good measure. The menu embraces Gressingham duck, Hereford steaks and, yes, lamb (a herb-crusted rack with dauphinoise potatoes, mustard green beans and rosemary jus), backed up by a strong wine list.

Edward Moon's
BRITISH ££

(☑ 01789-267069; www.edwardmoon.com; 9 Chapel St; mains £12.25-17; ☺ noon-2.30pm & 5-9.30pm Mon-Fri, noon-3pm & 5-10pm Sat, noon-3pm & 5-9pm Sun; 🖑) Named after a famous travelling chef who cooked up the flavours of home for the British colonial service, this snug independent restaurant serves hearty English dishes, such as steak-and-ale pie and meltingly tender lamb shank with redcurrant gravy. Kids get a two-course menu for £6.95.

Rooftop Restaurant
INTERNATIONAL ££

(☑ 01789-403449; www.rsc.org.uk; 3rd fl, Royal Shakespeare Theatre, Waterside; mains £12.50-25.50; ☺ 10.30am-9.30pm Mon-Thu, to 9.45pm Sat, to 3.30pm Sun; 🖘🖑) Glorious views of the River Avon extend from the dining room and outdoor terrace of this restaurant atop the Royal Shakespeare Theatre (p420). Global flavours range from crab linguine to Sri Lankan cauliflower, squash and cashew cur-

---

WORTH A TRIP

CHARLECOTE PARK

A youthful Shakespeare allegedly poached deer in the grounds of **Charlecote** (NT; ☑ 01789-470277; www.nationaltrust.org.uk; Loxley Lane, Charlecote; house & garden adult/child £11.45/5.70, garden only £7.60/3.80; ☺ house 11am-4.30pm Thu-Tue mid-Mar–Oct, noon-3.30pm Thu-Tue mid-Feb–mid-Mar, noon-3.30pm Sat & Sun Nov & Dec, garden 10.30am-5.30pm Mar-Oct, to 4.30pm Nov-Feb), a lavish Elizabethan pile on the River Avon, 5 miles east of Stratford-upon-Avon. Fallow deer still roam the grounds today. The interiors were restored from Georgian chintz to Tudor splendour in 1823. Highlights include Victorian kitchens, filled with culinary moulds, and an original 1551 Tudor gatehouse.

Bus X17 runs to Charlecote hourly from Stratford (£4.40, 30 minutes, two per hour Monday to Friday, hourly Saturday and Sunday).

---

ry; there are various set menus, including for vegans and gluten-free diners, and for kids. Its bar mixes the best cocktails in town.

★ Salt
BRITISH £££

(☑ 01789-263566; www.salt-restaurant.co.uk; 8 Church St; 2-/3-course menus lunch £33.50/37, dinner £37/45; ☺ noon-2pm & 6.30-10pm Wed-Sat, noon-2pm Sun) Stratford's gastronomic star is this intimate, beam-ceilinged bistro. In the semi-open kitchen, owner-chef Paul Foster produces stunning creations influenced by the seasons: spring might see glazed parsley root with chicory and black-truffle shavings, onglet of beef with malted artichoke, cured halibut with oyster and apple emulsion, and sea-buckthorn mille-feuille with fig and goats-milk ice cream.

🍷 Drinking & Nightlife

★ Old Thatch Tavern
PUB

(www.oldthatchtavernstratford.co.uk; Greenhill St; ☺ 11.30am-11pm Mon-Sat, from noon Sun; 🖘) To truly appreciate Stratford's olde-worlde atmosphere, join the locals for a pint at the town's oldest pub. Built in 1470, this thatch-roofed treasure has great real ales and a gorgeous summertime courtyard.

NATIONAL BREWERY CENTRE

Burton-upon-Trent grew up around its 7th-century abbey, which was famed for its healing spring waters. Brewing began here around 1700, and in the early 18th century the River Trent was opened for navigation, allowing Burton to become a major brewing centre. Its fascinating history is brought to life through two-hour guided tours of the **National Brewery Centre** (☑01283-532880; www.nationalbrewerycentre.co.uk; Horninglow St, Burton-upon-Trent; adult/child £11.95/6.95; ⊙10am-5pm, guided tours 11am & 2pm Apr-Sep; 10am-4pm, guided tours 11am & 1.30pm Oct-Mar), which contains a museum and still has a microbrewery today. Staff can point you to Burton's other breweries and traditional ale houses.

During tours, you'll learn, for example, that Burton developed pale ale to export to colonial-era India: the origins of IPA (Indian Pale Ale) today. You'll also get to taste samples (there are soft drinks for kids).

Trains run from Derby (£7.60, 15 minutes, three per hour) and Birmingham (£16.90, 30 minutes, three per hour) to Burton's train station, a half-mile walk southwest of the National Brewery Centre.

Dirty Duck PUB
(Black Swan; www.oldenglishinns.co.uk; Waterside; ⊙11am-11pm Mon-Sat, to 10.30pm Sun) Also called the 'Black Swan', this enchanting riverside alehouse is the only pub in England to be licensed under two names. It's a favourite thespian watering hole, with a roll call of former regulars (Olivier, Attenborough et al) that reads like a who's who of actors.

Windmill Inn PUB
(www.greeneking-pubs.co.uk; Church St; ⊙11am-11pm Sun-Thu, to midnight Fri & Sat; 🛜) Ale was already flowing at this low-ceilinged pub when rhyming couplets gushed from Shakespeare's quill. Flowers frame the whitewashed facade; there's a shaded rear beer garden.

☆ Entertainment

★**Royal Shakespeare Company** THEATRE
(RSC; ☑box office 01789-403493; www.rsc.org.uk; Waterside; tours adult £7-9, child £4.50-5, tower adult/child £2.50/1.25; ⊙tour times vary, tower 10am-5pm Sun-Fri, 10am-12.15 & 2-5pm Sat mid-Mar–mid-Oct, 10am-4.30pm Sun-Fri, to 12.15pm Sat mid-Oct–mid-Mar) Stratford has two grand stages run by the world-renowned Royal Shakespeare Company – the **Royal Shakespeare Theatre** and the Swan Theatre on Waterside – as well as the smaller Other Place. The theatres have witnessed performances by such legends as Lawrence Olivier, Richard Burton, Judi Dench, Helen Mirren, Ian McKellan and Patrick Stewart. Various one-hour **guided tours** take you behind the scenes.

Zipping up the lift/elevator of the Royal Shakespeare Theatre's **tower** rewards with panoramic views over the town and River Avon. Spectacular views also unfold from its 3rd-floor Rooftop Restaurant (p419), which opens to a terrace.

Contact the RSC for performance times, and book well ahead. There are often special deals for under-25-year-olds, students and seniors. A few tickets are held back for sale on the day of the performance but get snapped up fast.

Other Place THEATRE
(☑box office 01789-403493; www.rsc.org.uk; 22 Southern Lane) The smallest stage of the Royal Shakespeare Company has 200 seats. New work is presented here; it also hosts regular free live music and spoken word nights.

Swan Theatre THEATRE
(☑01789-403493; www.rsc.org.uk; Waterside) Hosting productions by the Royal Shakespeare Company, this grand stage has a capacity of 426 people.

🛍 Shopping

Chaucer Head BOOKS
(www.chaucerhead.com; 21 Chapel St; ⊙11am-5.30pm Mon-Thu, 10am-5pm Fri & Sat) Bargain-priced paperbacks through to rare antiquarian books worth thousands of pounds are stocked at the Chaucer Head, which was originally founded in Birmingham in 1830 and relocated to literary-famed Stratford in 1960.

ℹ Information

Tourist Office (☑01789-264293; www.shakespeares-england.co.uk; Bridge Foot; ⊙9am-

5.30pm Mon-Sat, 10am-4pm Sun) Just west of Clopton Bridge.

ℹ️ Getting There & Away

BUS

National Express coaches and other bus companies run from Stratford's Riverside bus station (behind the Stratford Leisure Centre on Bridgeway). National Express services include the following:

Birmingham £9, one hour, two per day

London Victoria £13.10, three hours, two direct services per day

Oxford £10.10, 1¼ hours, one per day

CAR

If you're driving, be warned that town car parks charge high fees, 24 hours a day.

TRAIN

From Stratford-upon-Avon train station, London Midland runs to Birmingham (£8, 50 minutes, two per hour), Chiltern Railways serves London Marylebone (£30.40, 2¾ hours, up to two per hour) with a change in Leamington Spa, and East Midlands runs to Warwick (£6.90, 30 minutes, every two hours).

The nostalgic **Shakespeare Express Steam Train** (☑ 0121-708 4960; www.vintagetrains. co.uk; one way/return £17.50/27.50; ☺ Sun Jul– mid-Sep) chugs twice every Sunday in summer between Stratford and Birmingham Moor St; the one-way journey time is one hour.

STAFFORDSHIRE

Wedged between the ever-expanding conurbations of Birmingham and Manchester, Staffordshire is surprisingly green, with the northern half of the county rising to meet the rugged hills of the Peak District.

Regular trains and buses serve Lichfield, Stafford and other major towns.

Lichfield

☑ 01543 / POP 32,219

Even without its magnificent Gothic cathedral – one of the most spectacular in the country – this charming cobbled market town would be worth a visit to tread in the footsteps of lexicographer and wit Samuel Johnson, and natural philosopher Erasmus Darwin, grandfather of Charles. Johnson once described Lichfield folk as 'the most sober, decent people in England', which was rather generous considering that this was the last place in the country to stop burning people at the stake.

👁 Sights

⭐ **Lichfield Cathedral**   CATHEDRAL
(☑ 01543-306100; www.lichfield-cathedral.org; 19 Cathedral Close; cathedral by donation, tower tours adult/child £6/4; ☺ cathedral 9.30am-6.15pm Mon-Sat, 12.30-5pm Sun, tower tours vary) Crowned by three dramatic towers, Lichfield Cathedral is a Gothic fantasy, constructed in stages from 1200 to 1350. The enormous vaulted nave is set slightly off line from the choir, creating a bizarre perspective when viewed from the west door, and carvings inside the cathedral still bear signs of damage caused by Civil War soldiers sharpening their swords.

Check schedules online for 45-minute tower tours climbing 160 steps for sweeping views from the central spire.

Erasmus Darwin House   HISTORIC BUILDING
(☑ 01543-306260; www.erasmusdarwin.org; Beacon St; ☺ 11am-5pm Apr-Oct, to 4pm Thu-Sun Nov-Mar) **FREE** After turning down the job of royal physician to King George III, Erasmus Darwin became a leading light in the Lunar Society, debating the origins of life with luminaries including Wedgwood, Boulton and

---

ALTON TOWERS

Phenomenally popular **Alton Towers** (☑ 0871 222 3330; www.altontowers.com; Farley Lane, Alton; adult/child amusement park £55/48, water park £18/14; ☺ hours vary), 4 miles east of Cheadle off the B5032, offers maximum G-force for your buck. Wild rides include the Th13teen, Nemesis, Oblivion, Galactica and Wickerman roller coasters. Gentler thrills span carousels and stage shows to a pirate-themed aquarium and splashtastic water park.

Check seasonal schedules online and pre-purchase tickets to skip ticket queues and take advantage of discounted entry deals. Five on-site hotels with themed rooms offer perks such as an hour's early park entry.

Your own transport is best (a monorail loops between the car park and the main entrance). In summer, one daily bus links Alton Towers with Stoke-on-Trent, Nottingham and Derby; schedules are available from Traveline (p402).

Watt decades before his grandson Charles came up with the theory of evolution. The former house of the 'Grandfather of Evolution' contains intriguing exhibits, including his notebook containing drawings of his inventions. At the back, a fragrant culinary and medicinal herb garden leads to Cathedral Close.

Samuel Johnson Birthplace Museum
MUSEUM

(☑01543-264972; www.samueljohnsonbirthplace.org.uk; Breadmarket St; ◷10.30am-4.30pm Mar-Oct, 11am-3.30pm Nov-Feb) FREE This absorbing museum charts the life of the pioneering lexicographer, wit, poet and critic Samuel Johnson, who moved to London from his native Lichfield and devoted nine years to producing the first major dictionary of the English language. Johnson's dictionary helped define the word 'dull' with this example: 'to make dictionaries is dull work'. On the 1st floor, a short dramatised film narrates Johnson's life story. It's a lovely property to explore.

Lichfield Museum
MUSEUM

(☑01543-256611; www.stmaryslichfield.co.uk; Market Sq) FREE Exhibits cover 1300 years of Lichfield history at this museum inside the revamped St Mary's Church, which also contains the town's library and art gallery. Climb the tower's 120 steps for sweeping city views.

🛏 Sleeping & Eating

George Hotel
HOTEL **££**

(☑01543-414822; www.thegeorgelichfield.co.uk; 12-14 Bird St; s/d from £90/120; P🐾) An old Georgian pub has been upgraded into a comfortable, midrange hotel with 45 rooms that scores points for location rather than atmosphere. Family rooms sleep up to four.

Swinfen Hall Hotel
HISTORIC HOTEL **£££**

(☑01543-481494; https://swinfenhallhotel.co.uk; Swinfen; s/d/ste incl breakfast from £151/165/331; P🐾) Georgian manor house Swinfen Hall, built in 1757, sits 3 miles southeast of Lichfield amid 40 wooded hectares with formal gardens, wild hay meadows and a deer park. Parkland views extend from its 17 rooms, which have either traditional or contemporary styling. Its fine-dining restaurant has multicourse tasting menus accompanied by wine flights.

THE POTTERIES – STOKE-ON-TRENT

Situated at the heart of the Potteries (the famous pottery-producing region of Staffordshire), Stoke-on-Trent is famed for its ceramics. Don't expect cute little artisanal producers: this was where pottery shifted to mass production during the Industrial Revolution, and Stoke today is a sprawl of industrial townships tied together by flyovers and bypasses. There are dozens of active potteries that you can visit in the greater area, including the famous Wedgwood factory.

The **tourist office** (☑01782-236000; www.visitstoke.co.uk; Bethesda St, Hanley; ◷10am-5pm Mon-Sat, 11am-4pm Sun) has information on all the potteries that are open to the public.

Potteries Museum & Art Gallery (☑01782-236000; www.stokemuseums.org.uk; Bethesda St, Hanley; ◷10am-5pm Mon-Sat, 11am-4pm Sun) For a thorough overview of the Potteries area's history, this museum and gallery houses an extensive ceramics display, from Toby jugs and jasperware to outrageous ornamental pieces. Other highlights include treasures from the 2009-discovered Staffordshire Hoard (the largest hoard of Anglo-Saxon gold and silver metalwork ever found, incorporating 5.1kg of gold, 1.4kg of silver and some 3500 pieces of jewellery); displays on the WWII Spitfire, created by the Stoke-born aviator Reginald Mitchell; and artworks by TS Lowry and Sir Henry Moore.

World of Wedgwood (☑01782-282986; www.worldofwedgwood.com; Wedgwood Dr, Barlaston; factory tour & museum adult/child £10/8, museum only free; ◷factory 10am-4pm Mon-Fri, museum 10am-5pm Mon-Fri, to 4pm Sat & Sun) Set in attractive parkland 8 miles south of Hanley, the modern production centre for Josiah Wedgwood's porcelain empire displays an extensive collection of historic pieces, including plenty of Wedgwood's delicate, neo-classical blue-and-white jasperware at its museum. On weekdays, there are self-guided factory tours and first-come, first-served guided factory tours lasting one hour. Pot throwing and design workshops take place at its Master Craft and Decorating studios.

Damn Fine Cafe   CAFE **£**
(www.damnfinecafelichfield.co.uk; 16 Bird St; dishes
£4.50-10; ⊘9am-3.30pm Tue-Sat, 10am-3pm Sun)
Teeming with locals, this cafe is a handy spot
for all-day bacon-and-sausage or vegetarian
toad-in-the-hole breakfasts, soup (with a
free taster of the day's special), mozzarella
melts and sandwiches on a variety of breads.

Trooper   GASTROPUB **££**
(☑01543-480413;   www.thetrooperwall.co.uk;
Watling St, Wall; mains £12-26; ⊘kitchen noon-
9.15pm Mon-Wed, to 9.45pm Thu-Sat, to 8pm Sun,
bar noon-midnight Mon-Sat, to 10pm Sun; 🖭) 🌮
Idyllically situated 3 miles southwest of Lichfield in the tiny village of Wall, this gastropub prides itself on ingredients sourced
from local suppliers and herbs from its gardens. Steaks are the house speciality, alongside contemporary twists on pub classics,
such as ham-and-cider pie. In fine weather,
enjoy its fabulous real ales in the sunny beer
garden.

Its kids' menu includes a mini 4oz steak
with fries.

Wine House   BRITISH **££**
(☑01543-419999;   www.thewinehouselichfield.
co.uk; 27 Bird St; mains £12.50-27; ⊘noon-10pm
Mon-Sat, to 6pm Sun) Well-chosen wines complement the upmarket pub fare at these
smart, red-brick premises. Choices range
from slow-cooked pork belly with apple
sauce to steaks and seafood, such as line-
caught sea bass with white wine, shallots
and clams.

🍷 Drinking & Nightlife

Beerbohm   BAR
(www.beerbohm.co.uk; 19 Tamworth St; ⊘11am-
11pm Tue-Sat; 🛜) Behind a peppermint-
painted traditional shopfront, Beerbohm's
richly coloured lounge-style interior is filled
with handmade furniture. Its discerning
drinks list includes its own brew, Dandy
Bitter, along with local ales and small-batch
gins, English wines and artisan malt whiskies plus imported craft beers (some gluten-free). It doesn't serve food but provides
plates and cutlery for you to bring your own.

Whippet Inn   PUB
(www.whippetinnmicro.co.uk; 21 Tamworth St;
⊘noon-2.30pm & 4.30-10pm Wed & Thu, noon-
10pm Fri & Sat, noon-5pm Sun) Ales and craft
keg beers from independent British breweries are the hallmark of this adorable little
one-room micropub, along with a wonderful

LORD LICHFIELD'S SHUGBOROUGH

The regal, neoclassical mansion of
Shugborough (NT; ☑01889-880160;
www.nationaltrust.org.uk; Great Haywood;
adult/child £13/6.50; ⊘house 11am-
4.30pm Mar-Oct, 10am-3pm Dec, grounds
9am-6pm Mar-Oct, 9am-4pm Nov & Dec) is
the ancestral home of royal photographer Lord Lichfield. A good proportion
of the wall space is devoted to his
work; the highlight is the staterooms'
collection of exquisite Louis XV and XVI
furniture. One-hour guided tours (included in admission) run between 11am
and 1pm. Shugborough is 6 miles east
of Stafford on the A513; bus 825 linking
Stafford and Lichfield stops 1 mile from
the manor (£4.20, 30 minutes, two per
hour Monday to Saturday).

selection of ciders and wines, but it resolutely doesn't serve lager or spirits. Artisan bar
snacks include pork pies, Scotch eggs and
sausage rolls.

ℹ Information

Tourist Office (☑01543-256611; www.stmarys
lichfield.co.uk; Market Sq) In the revamped St
Mary's Church.

ℹ Getting There & Away

The bus station is opposite the main Lichfield
City train station on Birmingham Rd. Bus 825
serves Stafford (£4.20, 1¼ hours, two per hour
Monday to Saturday).

Lichfield has two train stations:
Lichfield City Trains to Birmingham (£5.30,
35 minutes, up to four per hour) leave from
Lichfield City station in the town centre.
Lichfield Trent Valley Trains to London Euston
(£49.40, 1¾ hours, up to two per hour) run
from Lichfield Trent Valley station on the eastern side of town, 1.5 miles east of the centre.

WORCESTERSHIRE

Famed for its eponymous condiment, invented by two Worcester chemists in 1837,
Worcestershire marks the transition from
the industrial heart of the Midlands to the
peaceful countryside of the Marches along
the English–Welsh border. The southern

THE FIRS – ELGAR'S BIRTHPLACE

England's most popular classical composer, Edward Elgar, is celebrated at the humble **country cottage** (NT; www.nationaltrust.org.uk/the-firs; Crown East Lane, Lower Broadheath) where he was born in 1857. The National Trust was set to run the museum from mid-2018; check the website for prices and opening times, and details of concerts here. In the flower-filled garden there's a sculpture of Elgar, sitting on a bench looking out over the Malvern Hills; it was created by artist Jemma Pearson.

The cottage is 4 miles west of Worcester; you'll need your own transport.

and western fringes of the county burst with lush countryside and sleepy market towns, while the capital is a classic English county town, whose magnificent cathedral inspired the composer Edward Elgar to write some of his greatest works.

🏃 Activities

The 210-mile riverside **Severn Way** winds through Worcestershire en route from Plynlimon in Wales to the sea at Bristol. A shorter challenge is the 100-mile **Three Choirs Way**, linking Worcester to Hereford and Gloucester. The Malvern Hills are also prime country for walking and cycling; information is available at www.malvernhillsaonb.org.uk.

❶ Getting There & Around

Worcester is a convenient rail hub. Kidderminster is the southern railhead of the quaint Severn Valley Railway (p438).

Buses and trains connect larger towns, but bus services to rural areas can be frustratingly infrequent. Search the transport pages at www.worcestershire.gov.uk or Traveline (p402) for bus companies and timetables.

Worcester

☎ 01905 / POP 101,328

Worcester (*woos*-ter) has enough historic treasures to forgive the architectural eyesores from the postwar love affair with all things concrete. The home of the famous Worcestershire sauce (an unlikely combination of fermented tamarinds and anchovies), this ancient cathedral city was the site of the last battle of the Civil War, the Battle of Worcester, which took place on 3 September 1651. The defeated Charles II only narrowly escaped the pursuing Roundheads by hiding in an oak tree, an event still celebrated in Worcester every 29 May, when government buildings are decked out with oak sprigs.

◉ Sights

★ **Worcester Cathedral**   CATHEDRAL
(☎ 01905-732900; www.worcestercathedral.co.uk; 8 College Yard; cathedral by donation, tower adult/child £5/free, tours £5/free; ⊙ cathedral 7.30am-6pm Mon-Sat, from noon Sun, tower hours vary, tours 11am & 2.30pm Mon-Sat Mar-Nov, Sat Dec-Feb) Rising above the River Severn, Worcester's majestic cathedral is the final resting place of Magna Carta signatory King John. The strong-legged can scale 235 steps to the top of the **tower** (confirm times ahead), from where Charles II surveyed his troops during the disastrous Battle of Worcester. Hour-long **tours** run from the gift shop. Several works by local composer Edward Elgar had their first public outings here – to appreciate the acoustics, come for **evensong** (5.30pm Monday to Saturday, 4pm Sunday).

Royal Worcester Porcelain Works   MUSEUM
(☎ 01905-21247; www.museumofroyalworcester.org; Severn St; adult/child incl audio guide £6.50/free; ⊙ 10am-5pm Mon-Sat, 11am-4pm Sun) Up there with the country's most famous potteries, the Royal Worcester porcelain factory gained an edge over its rivals by picking up the contract to provide fine crockery to the British monarchy. An entertaining audio tour reveals some quirkier sides to the Royal Worcester story, including its brief foray into porcelain dentures and 'portable fonts' designed for use during cholera outbreaks. The shop has some splendid pieces, from monk-shaped candle snuffers to decorated thimbles and pill boxes.

Greyfriars   HISTORIC BUILDING
(NT; ☎ 01905-23571; www.nationaltrust.org.uk; Friar St; adult/child £5.45/2.70; ⊙ 11am-5pm Tue-Sat Mar-Oct, to 4pm Nov–mid-Dec) Friar St was largely chock-a-block with historic architecture until the iconoclastic 1960s when much was demolished, including the lovely medieval Lich Gate. Some creaky old almshouses survive and Greyfriars was saved in the nick of time by the National Trust, offering

the chance to poke around a timber-framed merchant's house from 1480. It's full of atmospheric wood-panelled rooms and is backed by a pretty walled garden.

🛏 Sleeping & Eating

Diglis House Hotel
HOTEL ££

(📞 01905-353518; www.diglishousehotel.co.uk; Severn St; s/d/ste incl breakfast from £90/115/145; P🅿🛜) Next to the boathouse in a gorgeous waterside setting, this rambling yet cosy 28-room Georgian house is a short stroll from the cathedral. The best rooms have four-poster beds, luxe bathrooms and river views. Its elegant restaurant (mains £13 to £19) opens to a terrace overlooking the river. Guests can work out at the nearby gym for free.

Mac & Jac's
DELI, CAFE £

(www.macandjacs.co.uk; 44 Friar St; dishes £4.50-18; ⊙ 9am-5pm Tue-Sat) This Friar St outfit has a lovely deli downstairs and a relaxing cafe upstairs for caffeine, sandwiches with fillings like Brie and grape, and hot dishes such as crispy pork belly with toasted almonds and coriander. Look out for gourmet supper evenings.

★Cardinal's Hat
PUB

(📞 01905-724006; www.the-cardinals-hat.co.uk; 31 Friar St; ⊙ 4-11pm Mon, from noon Tue-Sat, noon-10.30pm Sun; 🛜) Dating from the 14th century, and claiming a resident ghost, Worcester's oldest and grandest pub retains original features, including timber panelling and log-burning stoves. English craft beers and ciders dominate the taps; its menu concentrates on locally sourced British classics (Scotch eggs, pies, kippers, artisan cheese platters). Upstairs are six Georgian-style boutique guest rooms (doubles £82.50 to £125).

★Old Rectifying House
BRITISH ££

(📞 01905-619622; www.theoldrec.co.uk; North Parade; mains £9.50-18; ⊙ kitchen noon-3pm & 6-9pm Tue-Thu, noon-4pm & 6-9.30pm Fri & Sat, noon-4pm Sun, bar noon-11pm Tue-Thu & Sun, to 12.30am Fri & Sat; 🅿🛜) Worcester's hippest dining space has a candlelit, painted-brick interior and umbrella-shaded terrace tables. Its switched-on menu features dishes such as braised pork cheek with a crispy ham bonbon. DJs often hit the decks in the lounge bar, which mixes craft cocktails including a 'Hedgerow Shire' with local gin and birch liqueur.

Kids, vegetarians and vegans are catered for; vegan dishes include a Sunday nut roast (advance orders essential).

❶ Information

Tourist Office (📞 01905-726311; www.visit worcestershire.org/worcester; Guildhall, High St; ⊙ 9.30am-5pm Mon-Fri, 10am-4pm Sat) Inside the Grade I–listed Guildhall, dating from 1721.

❶ Getting There & Away

BUS
The **bus station** (Crowngate Centre, Friary Walk) is inside the Crowngate Centre on Friary Walk. National Express has services to London Victoria (£16.90, four hours, two daily).

TRAIN
Worcester Foregate is the main rail hub, but services also run from Worcester Shrub Hill. Regular trains:

Birmingham £8.50, one hour, every 20 minutes

Great Malvern £5.50, 15 minutes, up to three per hour

Hereford £9.90, 50 minutes, hourly

Ledbury £7.10, 25 minutes, hourly

London Paddington £35, 2½ hours, up to three per hour

Great Malvern

📞 01684 / POP 29,626

Tumbling down the side of a forested ridge about 7 miles southwest of Worcester, the picturesque spa town of Great Malvern is the gateway to the Malverns, a soaring 9-mile-long range of volcanic hills that rise unexpectedly from the surrounding meadows. In Victorian times, the medicinal waters were prescribed as a panacea for everything from gout to sore eyes – you can test the theory by sampling Malvern water straight from the ground at public wells dotted around the town.

◉ Sights

★Morgan Motor Company
FACTORY, MUSEUM

(📞 01684-573104; www.morgan-motor.co.uk; Pickersleigh Rd; museum free, tours adult/child £22.50/11.25; ⊙ museum 8.30am-5pm Mon-Thu, to 2pm Fri, tours by reservation) Morgan has been handcrafting elegant sports cars since 1909. You can see the mechanics at work on two-hour guided tours of the unassuming shedlike buildings comprising the factory (prebooking essential), and view a fleet of vintage classics adjacent to the museum. If buying one of these beautiful machines is beyond your budget, it's possible to hire one (per day/weekend/week from £220/595/1050, including insurance) for a spin through the Malvern Hills.

Great Malvern Priory
MONASTERY

(☑ 01684-561020; www.greatmalvernpriory.org.uk; Church St; ⊙9am-5pm) FREE The 11th-century Great Malvern Priory is packed with remarkable features, from original Norman pillars to surreal modernist stained glass. The choir is enclosed by a screen of 15th-century tiles and the monks' stalls are decorated with delightfully irreverent 14th-century misericords, depicting everything from three rats hanging a cat to the mythological reptile, the basilisk. Charles Darwin's daughter Annie is buried here.

🛏 Sleeping & Eating

Abbey Hotel
HOTEL £££

(☑ 01684-892332; www.sarova-abbeyhotel.com; Abbey Rd; d/f from £160/180; ⓟⓢⓩ) Tangled in vines like a Brothers Grimm fairy-tale castle, this stately property has 103 elegant rooms in a prime location by the local-history museum and priory.

Mac & Jac's
CAFE £

(www.macandjacs.co.uk; 23 Abbey Rd; dishes £4.50-18; ⊙9am-6pm Tue-Sat, 10am-3.30pm Sun) Creative salads, flatbreads, sharing plates, spelt risotto and a savoury tart of the day are served at this light, bright cafe set in a chic white-painted shopfront near the priory.

St Ann's Well Cafe
CAFE, VEGETARIAN £

(☑ 01684-560285; www.stannswell.co.uk; St Ann's Rd; dishes £2-4.50; ⊙11.30am-3.30pm Tue-Fri, 10am-4pm Sat & Sun Easter-Sep; ⓓ) A s-t-e-e-p climb above St Ann's Rd (so best to check opening times beforehand), this quaint cafe is set in an early-19th-century villa, with mountain-fresh spring water bubbling into a carved basin by the door. All-vegetarian food (including vegan options) spans soups to pies, filled baguettes, cakes, pastries and puddings.

Fig Tree
MEDITERRANEAN ££

(☑ 01684-569909; www.thefigtreemalvern.co.uk; 99b Church St; mains lunch £8.50-13, dinner £14-19; ⊙noon-2pm & 5.30-9.30pm Tue-Sat) Tucked down an alleyway off Church St, this 19th-century former stable serves Mediterranean-inspired fare at lunch (eg focaccia, pastas and salads) and dinner (chorizo-stuffed squid, lamb souvlaki with tzatziki and saffron rice). Day or night, don't miss its signature almond-and-lemon polenta cake with fig ice cream.

ℹ Information

Tourist Office (☑ 01684-892289; www.visitthemalverns.org; 21 Church St; ⊙10am-5pm Apr-Oct, 10am-5pm Mon-Sat, to 4pm Sun Nov-Mar) The tourist office is a mine of walking and cycling information.

ℹ Getting There & Away

Buses are limited, making trains your best bet. The train station is east of the town centre, off Avenue Rd.

Services include the following:

Hereford £8.20, 30 minutes, hourly
Ledbury £5.20, 10 minutes, hourly
Worcester £5.50, 15 minutes, up to three per hour

HEREFORDSHIRE

Adjoining the Welsh border, Herefordshire is a patchwork of fields, hills and cute little black-and-white villages, many dating back to the Tudor era and beyond.

🏃 Activities

As well as the famous **Offa's Dyke Path**, which follows the English–Welsh border for 177 miles alongside the 8th-century Offa's Dyke, walkers can follow the **Herefordshire Trail** (www.herefordshiretrail.com) on a 150-mile circular loop through Leominster, Ledbury, Ross-on-Wye and Kington.

Only slightly less ambitious is the 136-mile **Wye Valley Walk** (www.wyevalleywalk. org), which runs from Chepstow in Wales through Herefordshire and back out again to Plynlimon.

The **Three Choirs Way** is a 100-mile route connecting the cathedrals of Hereford, Worcester and Gloucester.

Cyclists can trace the **Six Castles Cycleway** (NCN Route 44) from Hereford to Leominster and Shrewsbury, or NCN Route 68 to Great Malvern and Worcester.

ℹ️ Getting Around

Trains run frequently to destinations including Hereford and Ledbury, with bus connections on to the rest of the county. For bus timetables, contact Traveline (p402).

Hereford

📞 01432 / POP 58,896

Surrounded by apple orchards and rolling pastures at the heart of the Marches, Hereford straddles the River Wye. This lively city's key draw for visitors is its magnificent cathedral.

◉ Sights

★ **Hereford Cathedral** CATHEDRAL
(📞 01432-374200; www.herefordcathedral.org; 5 College Cloisters, Cathedral Close; cathedral entry by donation, Mappa Mundi £6; ☉ cathedral 9.15am-5.30pm Mon-Sat, to 3.30pm Sun, Mappa Mundi 10am-5pm Mon-Sat mid-Mar–Oct, to 4pm Mon-Sat Nov–mid-Mar) After Welsh marauders torched the original Saxon cathedral, the Norman rulers of Hereford erected a larger, grander cathedral on the same site. The building was subsequently remodelled in a succession of medieval architectural styles.

The signature highlight is the magnificent **Mappa Mundi**, a single piece of calfskin vellum intricately painted with some rather fantastical assumptions about the layout of the globe in around 1290. The same wing contains the world's largest surviving **chained library** of rare manuscripts manacled to the shelves.

HEREFORDSHIRE CIDER

The **Herefordshire Cider Route** (www.ciderroute.co.uk) drops in on numerous local cider producers, where you can try before you buy, and then totter off to the next cidery. Mindful of road safety, tourist offices have maps and guide booklets to help you explore by bus or bicycle.

If you only have time to visit one Herefordshire cider-maker, make it **Westons Cider Mills** (📞 01531-660108; www.westons-cider.co.uk; The Bounds, Much Marcle; tours adult/child £10/4; ☉ 9am-5pm Mon-Fri, from 10am Sat & Sun), whose house brew is even served in the Houses of Parliament. Informative tours (1½ hours) start at 11am, 12.30pm, 2pm and 3.30pm, with free cider and perry tastings for the grown-ups. There's also a fascinating bottle museum. Its just under a mile west of the tiny village of Much Marcle.

Cider Museum Hereford MUSEUM
(📞 01432-354207; www.cidermuseum.co.uk; Pomona Pl; adult/child £5.50/3; ☉ 10.30am-4.30pm Mon-Sat) Mills and presses, glassware, watercolours, photographs and films are among the displays at this former cider-making factory (Bulmer's original premises), along with costrels (minibarrels) used by agricultural workers to carry their wages, which were partially paid in cider. Download brochures outlining walks through Herefordshire's orchards from its website. It's half a mile west of the city centre; follow Eign St and turn south along Ryelands St.

🛏️ Sleeping

Charades B&B £
(📞 01432-269444; www.charadeshereford.co.uk; 32 Southbank Rd; s/d from £55/61; P @ 🛜) Handy for the bus station, this imposing Victorian house dating from 1877 has six inviting rooms with high ceilings, big and bright windows, and some with soothing countryside views. The house itself has character in spades – look for old service bells in the hall and the plentiful *Titanic* memorabilia. Traditional or vegetarian breakfasts are available.

★ **Castle House** BOUTIQUE HOTEL £££
(📞 01432-356321; www.castlehse.co.uk; Castle St; s/d/ste from £140/155/190; P 🛜) In a regal

Georgian town house where the Bishop of Hereford once resided, this tranquil 16-room hotel has two sophisticated restaurants using ingredients sourced from its own nearby farm, a sunny garden spilling down to Hereford's former castle moat, and magnificent rooms and suites. Another eight newer rooms (some wheelchair accessible) are a short walk away at 25 Castle St.

Eating & Drinking

A Rule of Tum
BURGERS £

(01432-351764; www.aruleoftum.com; 32 Aubrey St; burgers £7.50-11.50; noon-10pm Mon-Sat, to 8pm Sun) Exposed brick, elongated wooden benches and a courtyard garden are the backdrop for brilliant brioche-bun burgers such as the Hereford Hop (pulled beef shin, Hereford Hop cheese, dill pickles and mustard mayo). Veggie burgers are cooked on a separate grill; you can order gluten-free buns made from quinoa flour. Alongside local ciders, kickin' cocktails include a vodka-fuelled Marmalade Mule.

Hereford Deli
DELI £

(www.thehereforddeli.com; 4 The Mews, St Owen St; sandwiches £2-3; 8am-6pm Mon-Fri, 9am-4pm Sat) At this gourmet emporium with a clutch of tables, fantastic sandwiches are a steal. Combinations include curried free-range chicken with mango chutney, Scottish smoked salmon with lemon-and-dill butter, or local roast beef with Cropwell Bishop Stilton and rosehip jelly. It's hidden down

---

BLACK & WHITE VILLAGES

A triangle of Tudor England survives almost untouched in northwest Herefordshire, where higgledy-piggledy black-and-white houses cluster around idyllic village greens, seemingly oblivious to the modern world. A delightful 40-mile circular drive follows the **Black and White Village Trail** (www.black andwhitetrail.org), meandering past the most handsome timber-framed buildings. It starts at Leominster and loops round through Eardisland and Kington, the southern terminus of the 30-mile way-marked Mortimer Trail footpath from Ludlow.

Pick up guides to exploring the villages by car, bus or bicycle at tourist offices.

---

a narrow laneway near a large public car park.

★ Beer in Hand
PUB

(www.beerinhand.co.uk; 136 Eign St; 5-10.30pm Mon, to 11pm Tue-Thu, noon-11pm Fri & Sat, 3-9pm Sun) Ciders at this independent pub are sublime and most are locally sourced. It's also the tap room for its own Odyssey beers (such as Black Out, a dark-malt, full-bodied American black ale brewed with fresh oranges, which it brews on the nearby National Trust Brockhampton Estate). There are board games but no TVs.

❶ Information

Tourist Office (01432-370514; www.rural-concierge.co.uk; Hereford Butter Market; 10am-4pm Mon-Sat) Information centre run by bespoke tour company Rural Concierge.

❶ Getting There & Away

BUS

The bus station is on Commercial Rd, 500m northeast of the city centre. Stagecoach runs to Gloucester (£4.20, 1½ hours, hourly Monday to Saturday).

Local services to destinations including Ross-on-Wye (bus 33; £3.70, 50 minutes, hourly Monday to Saturday) depart from St Owen St in the city centre.

TRAIN

The train station is 950m northeast of the city centre.

Regular services:

Birmingham £23.60, 1½ hours, hourly

Ledbury £6.50, 15 minutes, hourly

London Paddington £57.70, three hours, up to two per hour – either direct or with a change in Newport, South Wales

Ludlow £10.40, 25 minutes, up to two per hour

Worcester £13, 45 minutes, hourly

Ledbury

01531 / POP 9290

Creaking with history and dotted with antique shops, Ledbury's crooked black-and-white streets zero in on a delightfully leggy medieval Market House. The timber-framed structure is precariously balanced atop a series of wooden posts supposedly taken from the wrecked ships of the Spanish Armada.

Almost impossibly cute Church Lane, crowded with tilting timber-framed buildings, runs its cobbled way from High St to the town church.

🛌 Sleeping & Eating

Feathers Hotel
HOTEL **££**

(☑ 01531-635266; www.feathers-ledbury.co.uk; 25 High St; d incl breakfast from £89; P �🛜 🏊) A Ledbury landmark, this black-and-white Tudor hotel built in 1564 looms over the main street. Of its 22 rooms, those in the oldest part of the building come with sloping floorboards, painted beams and much more character than rooms in the modern extension. There's an atmospheric wood-panelled restaurant, Quills (mains £13.50 to £28), and an indoor swimming pool.

Verzon House Hotel
HOTEL **£££**

(☑ 01531-670381; www.verzonhouse.com; Hereford Rd, Trumpet; s/d/ste from £80/110/180; P �🛜) 🌿 The ultimate country-chic retreat, this lovely Georgian farmhouse 3.8 miles northwest of Ledbury on the A438 has eight luxuriously appointed rooms with free-standing baths, goose-down pillows and deep-pile carpets. Locally sourced produce underpins the Modern British menu at its restaurant (mains £14 to £30).

Malthouse Cafe & Gallery
CAFE **£**

(☑ 01531-634443; Church Lane; mains lunch £4.50-8, dinner £12-16; ⊙ 9am-5pm Tue-Thu, 9am-5pm & 6-11pm Fri & Sat, 10am-4pm Sun & Mon; 🖉) Set back from the street in a cobbled courtyard, this ivy-draped building is a delightful spot for breakfast (such as poached eggs with a thyme, leek and parsnip cake) or lunch (black-pudding sausage rolls, goats cheese and rosemary filo parcels). On Friday and Saturday evenings, mains might include mustard-glazed pork belly or slow-cooked Herefordshire beef ribs.

🏠 Shopping

★ Malvern Hills Vintage
ANTIQUES

(☑ 01531-633608; www.malvernhillsvintage.com; Lower Mitchell Barns, Eastnor; ⊙ shop & cafe 10am-4pm Wed-Sat, from 11am Sun) A vast timber barn 1.5 miles northeast of Ledbury is packed to the rafters with retro, antique and industrial treasures – everything from Victorian lamps and brass cash registers to mahogany dressers, oak-framed mirrors, leather Chesterfield and even classic cars, such as a 1956 Porche 356 Speedster. On the mezzanine, its tearoom serves scones, cakes and slices.

ℹ️ Getting There & Away

Buses are limited, but regular train services include the following:

Great Malvern £5.20, 10 minutes, hourly
Hereford £6.50, 15 minutes, hourly
Worcester £7.10, 25 minutes, hourly

Ross-on-Wye

☑ 01989 / POP 10,582

Set on a red sandstone bluff over a kink in the River Wye, hilly Ross-on-Wye was propelled to fame in the 18th century by Alexander Pope and Samuel Taylor Coleridge, who penned tributes to philanthropist John Kyrle, 'Man of Ross', who dedicated his life and fortune to the poor of the parish.

👁 Sights

Market House
GALLERY

(☑ 01989-769398; www.madeinross.co.uk; Market Pl; ⊙ 10am-5pm Mon-Sat, 10.30am-4pm Sun Apr-Oct, 10.30am-4pm Mon-Sat Nov-Mar) 🌿 **FREE** The 17th-century Market House sits atop weathered sandstone columns in Market Pl. The salmon-pink building is now home to artist collective Made in Ross, whose members live and work in a 20-mile radius, and exhibit and sell their arts and crafts here. Regular markets take place on the square at the front.

🛌 Sleeping & Eating

King's Head
INN **££**

(☑ 01989-763174; www.kingshead.co.uk; 8 High St; d/f from £77/95; P �🛜 🏊) Dating from the 14th century, this half-timbered inn is a charmer. Some of its 15 sage- and oyster-toned rooms have four-poster beds, and there's a timber bar serving local ales and ciders, and a candlelit, book-lined library, as well as a conservatory restaurant. Limited parking is available for guests.

Pots & Pieces
CAFE **£**

(www.potsandpieces.com; 40 High St; dishes £3-7.50; ⊙ 9am-4.45pm Mon-Fri, 10am-4.45pm Sat year-round, plus 11am-3.45pm Sun Jun-Sep) Browse ceramics and crafts at this tearoom by the marketplace, and choosing from cakes such as lemon drizzle, coffee, and walnut and carrot. Savoury options include quiches, sandwiches and a soup of the day.

Truffles Delicatessen
DELI **£**

(www.trufflesdeli.co.uk; 46 High St; dishes £2.50-5.50; ⊙ 8am-5pm Mon-Sat, from 11am Sun) Packed to the rafters with local artisan products (cheeses, breads, chutneys et al), Truffles also has stellar sandwiches, soups and salad boxes to take away for a riverside picnic.

ℹ️ Getting There & Away

The bus stand is on Cantilupe Rd. Bus 33 runs to Hereford (£3.70, 50 minutes, hourly Monday to Saturday). Bus 32 serves Gloucester (£4.20, one hour, hourly Monday to Saturday, every two hours Sunday).

SHROPSHIRE

Sleepy Shropshire is a glorious scattering of hills, castles and timber-framed villages tucked against the Welsh border. Highlights include castle-crowned Ludlow, industrial Ironbridge and the beautiful Shropshire Hills, which offer the best walking and cycling in the Marches.

🏃 Activities

The rolling Shropshire Hills call out to walkers like a siren. Between Shrewsbury and Ludlow, the landscape rucks up into dramatic folds, with spectacular trails climbing the flanks of **Wenlock Edge** and the **Long Mynd** near Church Stretton. The county is also crossed by long-distance trails, including the famous **Offa's Dyke Path** and the popular **Shropshire Way**, which meanders around Ludlow and Church Stretton.

Mountain bikers head for the muddy tracks that scramble over the **Long Mynd** near Church Stretton, while road riders aim for the **Six Castles Cycleway** (NCN 44), which runs for 58 miles from Shrewsbury to Leominster.

Tourist offices sell copies of *Cycling for Pleasure in the Marches,* a pack of five maps and guides covering the entire county.

ℹ️ Getting There & Away

Shrewsbury is the local transport hub, with good bus and rail connections. Church Stretton and Ludlow also have handy rail services.

From May to September, **Shropshire Hills Shuttles** (www.shropshirehillsaonb.co.uk; Day Rover ticket adult/child £10/4; ⏱ hourly Sat, Sun & bank holidays May-Sep) runs an hourly bus service along popular hiking routes on weekends and bank holidays.

Shrewsbury

📞 01743 / POP 71,715

A delightful jumble of winding medieval streets and timbered Tudor houses leaning at precarious angles, Shrewsbury was a crucial front in the conflict between the English and the Welsh in medieval days. Even today, the road bridge running east towards London is known as the English Bridge to mark it out from the Welsh Bridge leading northwest towards Holyhead. Shrewsbury is also the birthplace of Charles Darwin (1809–82).

The pronunciation of the town's name has long been a hot topic. A charity debate hosted by University Centre Shrewsbury in 2015 declared '*shroos*-bree' (rhyming with 'grew') the winner over the posher '*shrows*-bree' (rhyming with 'grow'), as did a survey by the *Shropshire Star,* though you'll still hear both pronunciations in the town and across British media.

◉ Sights

Shrewsbury Castle　　　　　CASTLE, MUSEUM
(📞01743-358516; www.shropshireregimentalmuseum.co.uk; Castle St; adult/child £4/1; ⏱10.30am-5pm Mon-Wed, Fri & Sat, to 4pm Sun Jun–mid-Sep, to 4pm Mon-Wed, Fri & Sat mid-Feb–May & mid-Sep–mid-Dec) Hewn from flaking red Shropshire sandstone, the town castle contains the **Shropshire Regimental Museum**. There are fine views from **Laura's Tower** and the battlements. The lower level of the **Great Hall** dates from 1150.

Shrewsbury Abbey　　　　　　　CHURCH
(📞01743-232723; www.shrewsburyabbey.com; Abbey Foregate; by donation; ⏱10am-4pm Apr-Oct, 10.30am-3pm Nov-Mar) All that remains of a vast, cruciform Benedictine monastery founded in 1083 is the lovely red-sandstone Shrewsbury Abbey. Twice used for meetings of the English Parliament, the abbey church lost its spire and two wings when the monastery was dissolved in 1540. It sustained further damage in 1826 when engineer Thomas Telford ran the London–Holyhead road right through the grounds. Nevertheless, you can still see some impressive Norman, Early English and Victorian features, including an exceptional 14th-century west window.

St Mary's Church　　　　　　　CHURCH
(www.visitchurches.org.uk; St Mary's St; by donation; ⏱10am-4pm Mon-Sat) The fabulous interior of this tall-spired medieval church contains an impressive collection of stained glass, including a 1340 window depicting the Tree of Jesse (a biblical representation of the lineage of Jesus) and a magnificent oak ceiling in the nave, which largely collapsed in a huge gale in 1894 when the top

Shrewsbury

Shrewsbury

Sights

Sleeping

Eating

Drinking & Nightlife

of the spire blew off. Much of the glass in the church is sourced from Europe, including some outstanding Dutch glass from 1500.

Shrewsbury Prison HISTORIC BUILDING
(☑01743-343100; www.shrewsburyprison.com; The Dana; prison adult/child £15/9.50, ghost tour £20; ☺prison tours 10am-5pm, ghost tours 7pm & 9pm) Built in 1793, this was a working prison as recently as 2013. Today tours are led by former prison guards: when you arrive, you're 'processed' as a prisoner and escorted into the general population wing, before having the opportunity to enter a cell, which is ominously locked behind you. Alternatively, you can take a self-guided tour. Chilling evening ghost tours (not recommended for

kids) include the prison's execution room where 11 inmates were hanged.

**Shrewsbury Museum
& Art Gallery** MUSEUM
(☑01743-258885; www.shrewsburymuseum.org.uk; The Square; adult/child £4.50/2; ☺10am-5pm Mon-Sat, 11am-4pm Sun) Diverse exhibits at Shrewsbury's town museum cover everything from Roman treasures to Shropshire gold, including the Bronze Age Perry Bracelet. Its Prehistory and Roman Gallery is free of charge.

Sleeping

Corbet Arms PUB ££
(☑01743-709232; www.thecorbetarms.com; Church Rd, Uffington; d/f incl breakfast from

WORTH A TRIP

COSFORD RAF MUSEUM

This famous aerospace **museum** (☎01902-376200; www.rafmuseum.org. uk; Shifnal; ⊘10am-5pm Mar-Oct) FREE 13 miles east of Ironbridge is run by the Royal Air Force (RAF), whose pilots steered many of the winged wonders displayed here across the skies. Among the museum's 70 aircraft are the Vulcan bomber (which carried Britain's nuclear deterrent) and the tiny helicopter-like FA330 Bachstelze glider, which was towed behind German U-boats to warn them of enemy ships. You can also try out a Black Hawk simulator. It's a half-mile walk from Cosford train station, on the Birmingham–Shrewsbury line.

The Red Arrows stunt team paint the sky with coloured smoke during the Cosford Air Show (www.cosfordairshow. co.uk) in early June.

£90/105; P⊚) Peacefully situated 4 miles east of Shrewsbury in the pint-sized village of Uffington on the banks of the River Severn, this family-friendly pub has nine stylish en-suite rooms reached by a staircase. Try for top-floor room 10, which has exposed beams, a spacious sitting area and panoramic views of the surrounding countryside. High-quality pub food includes outstanding Sunday roasts.

Lion & Pheasant   BOUTIQUE HOTEL ££
(☎01743-770345; www.lionandpheasant.co.uk; 50 Wyle Cop; s/d incl breakfast from £80/109; P⊚) This former coaching inn is now a stylish town house offering 22 individually styled rooms with comfy goose- and duck-down pillows, and some with Severn views. Original features throughout the property include magnificent exposed timber beams. Classy Modern British fare is served in the whitewashed restaurant (mains £18.50 to £25). Parking for overnight guests is first come, first served.

Lion Hotel   HOTEL ££
(☎01743-353107; www.thelionhotelshrewsbury. com; Wyle Cop; s/d/ste incl breakfast from £74/109/135; P⊚) A gilded wooden lion crowns the doorway of this famous 16th-century coaching inn, decked out inside with portraits of lords and ladies in powdered wigs. Charles Dickens was a former guest,

and the lounge is warmed by a grand stone fireplace. Its 59 rooms are lovely, right down to the period-pattern fabrics and ceramic water jugs.

✗ Eating & Drinking

Ginger & Co   CAFE £
(www.facebook.com/gingerandcocoffee; 30-31 Princess St; dishes £4.75-12; ⊘8.30am-5pm Mon-Sat, 10am-4pm Sun; ✎) A successful crowdfunding campaign propelled the opening of this airy, L-shaped cafe filled with upcycled furniture. It's a great option for a light brunch or lunch (avocado on artisan toast with oak-smoked streaky bacon), snacks (lemon and Earl Grey scones with homemade raspberry jam), good coffee and vitamin-packed smoothies. Gluten-free, dairy-free and vegan options abound.

Golden Cross   MODERN BRITISH ££
(☎01743-362507; www.goldencrosshotel.co.uk; 14 Princess St; mains £13.50-24.50; ⊘noon-2.30pm & 5.30-9.30pm Tue-Sat, noon-2.30pm Sun) Overwhelmingly romantic, this candlelit inn dating from 1428 has an upmarket pub menu (port- and clementine-glazed baked ham, pot-roast ox cheek) and five exquisite guest rooms (doubles £75 to £150) with luxurious touches like freestanding bathtubs and chaises longues.

Number Four Butcher Row   CAFE ££
(☎01743-366691; www.number-four.com; 4 Butcher Row; mains breakfast £3.25-11, lunch £7-12, 2-/3-course dinner menus £16/20; ⊘9am-4pm Mon, to 9pm Tue-Thu, to 9.30pm Fri & Sat; ✎) Tucked away near St Alkmund's Church, this bare-boards split-level cafe is best known for its fantastic breakfasts, from eggs Benedict to bacon baguettes or a full English with freshly squeezed juices. Light lunches include burgers and gourmet salads (eg black pudding with mustard vinaigrette); dinner is a more upmarket affair (slow-roast pork belly with apple and potato gratin).

Harvey's of Fish St   BISTRO ££
(☎01743-344789; www.harveysfishstreet.com; 11 Fish St; mains £13-28, 5-course tasting menu £38; ⊘11am-10.30pm Tue-Thu, to 11pm Fri & Sat, noon-4pm Sun) Foraged herbs and flowers feature in dishes such as pigeon breast with wild-garlic risotto or nettle-crusted lamb shoulder with mint and blackberry sauce at this classy bistro on charming Fish St. The sofa-strewn lounge bar is a cosy spot for cocktails.

Henry Tudor House   PUB

(www.henrytudorhouse.com; Barracks Passage; ⊙noon-11pm Mon-Thu, 11am-1am Fri & Sat, noon-10pm Sun) Tucked off Wyle Cop, this seriously overhanging black-and-white beauty was built in the early 15th century and is where Henry VII stayed before the Battle of Bosworth. Today it melds old and new with a zinc bar, a light-filled conservatory and birdcage-encased chandeliers. Live gigs regularly take to the stage. Food (mackerel with cucumber purée; Shropshire beef Wellington) is superb, too.

ℹ Information

The **tourist office** (☑01743-258888; www.originalshrewsbury.co.uk; The Square; ⊙10am-4.30pm Tue-Sat, 11am-4pm Sun) shares space with the Shrewsbury Museum and Art Gallery.

ℹ Getting There & Away

BUS

The **bus station** (Smithfield Rd) is beside the river.

Direct services include the following:

Church Stretton Bus 435; £3.70, one hour, hourly Monday to Friday, every two hours Saturday

Ironbridge Bus 96; £4.50, 35 minutes, every two hours

Ludlow Bus 435; £4.10, 1¼ hours, hourly Monday to Saturday

TRAIN

The train station is on the northeastern edge of the town centre at the bottom of Castle Foregate.

Destinations include the following:

Birmingham £15.30, one hour, two per hour

Holyhead £48.50, three hours, hourly

London Euston £74.30, 2¾ hours, every 20 minutes; change in Crewe or Wolverhampton

Ludlow £13.50, 30 minutes, up to two per hour

Ironbridge Gorge

☑ 01952 / POP 2582

Strolling or cycling through the woods, hills and villages of this leafy river gorge, it's hard to believe such a peaceful enclave could really have been the birthplace of the Industrial Revolution. Nevertheless, it was here that Abraham Darby perfected the art of smelting iron ore with coke in 1709, making it possible to mass-produce cast iron for the first time.

Abraham Darby's son, Abraham Darby II, invented a new forging process for producing single beams of iron, allowing Abraham Darby III to astound the world with the first-ever iron bridge, constructed in 1779. The bridge remains the focal point of this World Heritage Site, and 10 very different museums tell the story of the Industrial Revolution in the buildings where it took place.

◉ Sights

★ Iron Bridge   BRIDGE

(www.ironbridge.org.uk; ⊙bridge 24hr, tollhouse 10am-4pm mid-Mar–Sep, closed Mon Oct–mid-Mar) FREE The arching Iron Bridge, which gives the area its name, was built to flaunt the new technology invented by the pioneering Darby family. At the time of its construction in 1779, nobody could believe that anything so large – it weighs 384 tonnes – could be built from cast iron without collapsing under its own weight. There's a small exhibition on the bridge's history at the former **toll house**. Following restoration work completed in 2018, the bridge is illuminated at night.

★ Museum of the Gorge   MUSEUM

(www.ironbridge.org.uk; The Wharfage; adult/child £4.50/3.15; ⊙10am-4pm mid-Mar–Sep, closed Mon Oct–mid-Mar) An ideal place to kick off your Ironbridge Gorge visit is the Museum of the Gorge. Occupying a Gothic riverside warehouse, it offers an overview of the World Heritage Sites using film, photos and exhibits, including a 12m-long 3D model of the town in 1796.

Enginuity   MUSEUM

(www.ironbridge.org.uk; Wellington Rd; adult/child £9/6.95; ⊙10am-4pm mid-Mar–Sep, closed Mon Oct–mid-Mar) Kids will love this levers-and-pulleys science centre where they can control robots, move a steam locomotive with their bare hands (and a little engineering

---

ℹ IRONBRIDGE GORGE PASSPORT

The 10 Ironbridge museums are administered by the Ironbridge Gorge Museum Trust (www.ironbridge.org.uk). You'll save considerably by buying a Passport ticket (adult/child £26.50/16.50) at any of the museums or from the tourist office. Valid for 12 months, it allows unlimited entry to all of Ironbridge Gorge's sites.

Ironbridge Gorge

Ironbridge Gorge

know-how) and power up a vacuum cleaner with self-generated electricity.

Blists Hill Victorian Town MUSEUM
(☑ 01952-433424; www.ironbridge.org.uk; Legges Way; adult/child £17.95/10.90; ⊙10am-4.30pm daily mid-Mar–Sep, to 4pm Tue-Sun Oct–mid-Mar) Set at the top of the Hay Inclined Plane (a cable lift that once transported coal barges uphill from the Shropshire Canal), Blists Hill is a lovingly restored Victorian village repopulated with townsfolk in period costume, busy with day-to-day chores. There's even a bank, where you can exchange your modern pounds for shillings to use at the village shops. In summer, a Victorian fair is an added attraction for young ones.

Darby Houses MUSEUM
(☑ 01952-433424; www.ironbridge.org.uk; Darby Rd; adult/child £5.65/3.75, incl Museum of Iron £10.45/6.55; ⊙11am-3pm mid-Mar–Sep) Just uphill from the Museum of Iron (p445), these beautifully restored 18th-century homes housed generations of the Darby family in gracious but modest Quaker comfort. In the Rosehill house, kids and adults can try on Victorian dress and view china displays. The highlight of the Darby family house is the study where Abraham Darby III designed the Iron Bridge.

Coalport China Museum MUSEUM
(www.ironbridge.org.uk; Coalport High St; adult/child £9/5.50; ⊙10am-4pm daily mid-Mar–Sep, closed Mon Oct–mid-Mar) As ironmaking fell into decline, Ironbridge diversified into manufacturing china pots, using the fine clay mined around Blists Hill. Dominated by a pair of towering bottle kilns, the atmos-pheric old china-works now contains an absorbing museum tracing the history of the industry, with demonstrations of traditional pottery techniques.

Jackfield Tile Museum MUSEUM
(www.ironbridge.org.uk; Salthouse Rd; adult/child £9/5.90; ⊙10am-4pm mid-Mar–Sep, closed Mon Oct–mid-Mar) Once the largest tile factory in the world, Jackfield was famous for its encaustic tiles, with ornate designs produced using layers of different coloured clay. Tiles are still produced here today for period restorations. Gas-lit galleries recreate ornately tiled rooms from past centuries, including Victorian public conveniences. The museum is on the south bank of the Severn – cross the footbridge at the bottom of the Hay Inclined Plane.

Coalbrookdale Museum of Iron MUSEUM
(www.ironbridge.org.uk; Wellington Rd; adult/child, £9/5.90, incl Darby Houses £10.45/6.55; ⊙10am-4pm mid-Mar–Sep, closed Mon Oct–mid-Mar) Set in the brooding buildings of Abraham Darby's original iron foundry, the Coalbrookdale Museum of Iron contains some excellent interactive exhibits. As well as producing the girders for the Iron Bridge, the factory became famous for heavy machinery and extravagant ornamental castings, including the gates for London's Hyde Park.

🏃 Activities

Ironbridge Canoe & Kayak Hire CANOEING, KAYAKING
(☑ 07594 486356; www.facebook.com/ironbridge canoeandkayakhire; 31 High St; canoe/kayak rental per hour from £20; ⊙by appointment Mon-Fri, 9am-8pm Sat & Sun Easter-Oct) In summer,

Vertical right margin: BIRMINGHAM & THE MIDLANDS IRONBRIDGE GORGE when the river is at a safe level, you can rent canoes and kayaks to explore the gorge and surrounding areas.

Shropshire Raft Tours   RAFTING

(☑ 01952-427150; www.shropshirerafttours.co.uk; The Wharfage; rafting trips adult/child £14.95/6.95, canoe & kayak hire per hour/day £15/45, bike hire per half-/full day from £19/29; ☺ equipment hire 9am-5pm Easter-Oct, tours by reservation 11.30am, 2pm & 4.30pm Easter-Oct, plus 7pm Jul & Aug) ✐ Ironbridge Gorge might not have any rapids but you can take a gentle, highly enjoyable 90-minute trip along a 1.2-mile stretch of the River Severn floating past stunning gorge scenery with this eco-conscious outfit. Life jackets are provided. It also hires canoes, kayaks and bikes, including electric bikes.

🛏 Sleeping

Coalport YHA   HOSTEL £

(☑ 0845 371 9325; www.yha.org.uk; Coalport High St; dm/d from £13/50; ⓟ🛜) In a converted china factory in the quietest, prettiest corner of Ironbridge, this YHA hostel has 82 beds in 21 modern, functional rooms, but the biggest drawcard is the facilities, which include a laundry, a kitchen and a licensed cafe, with wi-fi in common areas.

★ Library House   B&B ££

(☑ 01952-432299; www.libraryhouse.com; 11 Severn Bank; s/d from £75/110; ⓟ🛜) Up an alley off the main street, this lovingly restored Georgian library building built in 1730 is hugged by vines, backed by a beautiful garden and decked out with stacks of vintage books, curios, prints and lithographs. There are three charmingly well-preserved, individually decorated rooms, named Milton, Chaucer and Eliot. The affable dog whipping around is Millie.

Calcutts House   B&B ££

(☑ 01952-882631; www.calcuttshouse.co.uk; Calcutts Rd; d from £91; ⓟ🛜) This former ironmaster's pad dates from the 18th century. Traditionally decorated rooms have heaps of character, and one is furnished with an outsized 200-year-old four-poster bed. It's tucked away on the south bank around the corner from the Jackfield Tile Museum (p445), a mile east of the bridge.

🍴 Eating & Drinking

Dale End Café   DELI £

(☑ 01952-872650; http://dale-end-cafe.business. site; Dale End, Coalbrookdale; dishes £3.50-12.50;

☺ 8.30am-4.30pm Mon, Tue & Thu-Sat, 10am-4pm Sun; 🛜🛜) This wonderful cafe is far and away the best place in the area for a light meal. Steaming soups, salads, sandwiches and pizzas are all freshly made; take them away or else dine in the cosy shop or at umbrella-shaded picnic tables in the courtyard. Kids are warmly welcomed.

Pondicherry   INDIAN ££

(☑ 01952-433055; www.pondicherryrestaurant. co.uk; 57 Waterloo St; mains £10-16; ☺ 5.30-11pm Tue-Sat, 5-9pm Sun) Original features of this 1862-built former police station and courtroom include four lock-up cells (one's now the takeaway waiting area), the magistrate's bench and blue-painted bars on the windows. Above-average contemporary Indian cuisine includes crowd-pleasers like tandoori platters and chicken tikka masala along with chef specialities, such as lamb *saag mamyam* (braised Staffordshire lamb with spinach and spices).

D'arcys at the Station   MEDITERRANEAN ££

(☑ 01952-884499; www.darcysironbridge.co.uk; Ladywood; mains £12-15, 2-course menu £13.95; ☺ 6-9.30pm Wed-Sat) Just over the bridge by the river, the handsome old station building is the backdrop for flavoursome Mediterranean dishes, from Moroccan chicken to Cypriot kebabs and Tuscan bean casserole. Kids aged over 10 are welcome.

Restaurant Severn   EUROPEAN £££

(☑ 01952-432233; www.restaurantsevern.co.uk; 33 High St; lunch mains £8.50-12.50, 2-/3-course dinner menus from £23/27, 2-/3-course Sunday lunch menus £20/25; ☺ lunch Wed-Sat by reservation, 6-11pm Wed-Sat, noon-6pm Sun) The menu at this highly praised fine-dining restaurant changes frequently but might feature dishes such as Shropshire venison medallions with cognac and sundried cranberry sauce. The setting is intimate, food is artistically presented and the riverside location beautiful.

Malthouse   PUB

(☑ 01952-433712; www.themalthouseironbridge. co.uk; The Wharfage; ☺ 11.30am-11pm Sun-Thu, to 1am Fri & Sat) Renovated in 2018, this inn on the Severn's riverbanks makes a great place to drink, eat and/or sleep. Local ales, craft gins and cocktails feature on the drinks list, the street-food-inspired menu spans fish tacos to southern fried chicken and ultra-contemporary rooms (doubles including breakfast from £75) are splashed with vibrant colours. Live music plays on weekends.

❶ Information

Tourist Office (☎ 01952-433424; www.discovertelford.co.uk/visitironbridge; Museum of the Gorge, The Wharfage; ☉10am-4pm mid-Mar–Sep, closed Mon Oct–mid-Mar) Located at the Museum of the Gorge (p433).

❶ Getting There & Away

The nearest train station is 6 miles away at Telford, from where you can travel to Ironbridge on bus 18 (£4.50, 15 minutes, every two hours Monday to Saturday). The same bus continues to Much Wenlock (£4.50, 30 minutes).

Bus 9 runs from Bridgnorth to Ironbridge (£4.50, 30 minutes, every two hours Monday to Saturday).

Bus 96 links Ironbridge with Shrewsbury (£4.50, 35 minutes, every two hours).

Much Wenlock

☑ 01952 / POP 2877

With one of those quirky names that abound in the English countryside, Much Wenlock is as charming as it sounds. Surrounding the time-worn ruins of Wenlock Priory, the streets are studded with Tudor, Jacobean and Georgian houses, and locals say hello to everyone. This storybook English village also claims to have jump-started the modern Olympics.

◉ Sights

Wenlock Priory   RUINS
(EH; ☎ 01952-727466; www.english-heritage.org.uk; 5 Sheinton St; adult/child incl audio guide £6.30/3.80; ☉10am-6pm Apr-Sep, to 5pm Oct, to 4pm Sat & Sun Nov-Mar) The maudlin Cluniac ruins of Wenlock Priory rise up from vivid green lawns, sprinkled with animal-shaped topiary. The priory was raised by Norman monks over the ruins of a Saxon monastery from AD 680, and its hallowed remains include a finely decorated chapterhouse and an unusual carved lavabo, where monks came to ceremonially wash before eating.

Guildhall   HISTORIC BUILDING
(☎ 01952-727509; www.muchwenlock-tc.gov.uk; Wilmore St; ☉11am-4pm Fri-Mon Apr-Oct) FREE
Built in classic Tudor style in 1540, the wonky Guildhall features some splendidly ornate woodcarving. One of the pillars supporting it was used for public floggings in medieval times.

🛏 Sleeping & Eating

Wilderhope Manor YHA   HOSTEL £
(☎ 0845 371 9149; www.yha.org.uk; Longville-in-the-Dale; dm/d/f from £13/50/116, camping per person £12; ☉hostel year-round, camping Apr-Oct; P@🤶) A gloriously atmospheric gabled greystone Elizabethan manor, with spiral staircases, wood-panelled walls, an impressive stone-floored dining hall and spacious, oak-beamed rooms – this is hostelling for royalty. Wi-fi's available in public areas. In the warmer months, the camping field has space for a handful of tents. It's 7.5 miles southwest of Much Wenlock, best reached by your own wheels.

Raven Hotel   INN ££
(☎ 01952-727251; https://ravenhotel.com; 30 Barrow St; d/ste incl breakfast from £120/150; P🤶) Much Wenlock's finest place to stay is this 17th-century coaching inn and converted stables with oodles of charm and country-chic styling in its spacious guest rooms. Overlooking a flower-filled courtyard, the excellent restaurant (lunch mains £12 to £22, two-/three-course dinner menus £29/39) serves Mediterranean and British fare.

Fox   PUB FOOD ££
(☎ 01952-727292; www.foxinnmuchwenlock.co.uk; 46 High St; mains £8.50-20; ☉kitchen 5-9pm Mon-Fri, from noon Sat, noon-8pm Sun, bar to 11pm; 🤶) Warm yourself by the massive fireplace, then settle down in the dining room to savour locally sourced venison, pheasant and beef, swished down with a pint of Shropshire ale, in this 16th-century inn. Candlelit dinners here are lovely. It also has five contemporary rooms (single/double/family from £50/75/115).

❶ Information

Tourist Office (☎ 01952-727679; www.visitmuchwenlock.co.uk; The Square; ☉10.30am-1pm & 1.30-4pm daily Apr-Oct, Fri-Sun Nov-Mar) Has a modest museum of local history (admission free).

❶ Getting There & Away

Bus 436 links Shrewsbury with Much Wenlock (£4.50, 35 minutes, hourly Monday to Saturday) and continues on to Bridgnorth (£4.20, 20 minutes). Bus 18 runs to Ironbridge (£4.50, 30 minutes, every two hours Monday to Saturday).

Bridgnorth

📞 01746 / POP 12,079

Cleaved into two by a dramatic sandstone bluff that tumbles down to the River Severn, Bridgnorth is one of Shropshire's finest-looking historic towns, with a wealth of architectural charm despite much of the High Town succumbing to fire in 1646 during the Civil War.

Around its namesake church, the High Town's adorable St Leonard's Close contains some of the most attractive buildings and almshouses in town, including a splendid six-gabled house, once part of the grammar school.

A 19th-century cliff railway – Britain's steepest – and several narrow lanes drop down from the High Town to the Low Town, including the vertiginous pedestrian Cartway, at the bottom of which is Bishop Percy's House, dating from 1580.

◉ Sights

★ Severn Valley Railway   RAIL

(📞 01299-403816; www.svr.co.uk; Hollybush Rd; adult/child one way £14.50/9.50, day ticket £21/14; ☺ daily May-Sep, Sat & Sun Oct-Apr) Bridgnorth is the northern terminus of the Severn Valley Railway; its historic steam or diesel locomotives chug down the valley to Kidderminster (one hour), starting from the station on Hollybush Rd. Check the calendar for additional event dates, such as afternoon teas, gin and whisky tastings, 1940s re-enactments and evening ghost trains.

Cyclists can follow a beautiful 20-mile section of the Mercian Way (NCN Route 45) beside the railway line towards the Wyre Forest; bikes are free to bring on board the trains.

'Driving experiences', during which you can learn how to drive the steam or diesel trains, start from £160.

Bridgnorth Cliff Railway   RAIL

(📞 01746-762052; www.bridgnorthcliffrailway.co.uk; entrances 6a Castle Tce & Underhill St; return £1.60; ☺ 8am-8pm Mon-Sat, from noon Sun May-Sep, to 6.30pm Oct-Apr) Britain's steepest inland railway has trundled 50m up the cliff since 1892. At the top, a pedestrian walkway (affording astonishing night-time panoramas) curves around the bluff to a pretty park dotted with scattered masonry, some leaning at an incredible angle (all that remains of Bridgnorth Castle), and passes the grand

and imposing Thomas Telford–designed and cupola-topped St Mary's Church.

Daniels Mill   HISTORIC BUILDING

(📞 01746-769793; www.danielsmill.co.uk; The Cankhorn, Eardington; adult/child £5/4; ☺ 11am-4pm Thu-Sun Apr-Oct) England's largest working water-powered mill still produces flour for local bakers. Visitors get a personal tour of the machinery in action from the resident miller. It's located 1 mile south of the town centre, reached on foot or with your own wheels.

🛏 Sleeping & Eating

Severn Arms   B&B £

(📞 01746-764616; www.thesevernarms.co.uk; 3 Underhill St; s/d/f from £50/60/80, s/d without bathroom from £36/60; 🛜) At the bottom of the bluff, conveniently positioned right next to the cliff railway, this riverside Georgian property has nine comfortable rooms, many with bridge views. The helpful owners can direct you to nearby parking. Family rooms can sleep up to two adults and two children.

Fish   SEAFOOD, TAPAS £

(📞 01746-768292; www.fishbridgnorth.co.uk; 54 High St; tapas £7-10; ☺ noon-5pm Wed, Thu & Sat, to 8pm Fri Easter-Oct, 11am-3pm Wed-Fri, to 5pm Sat Nov-Easter) Upturned wine barrels are used as tables at this stylish spot where tapas incorporates premium British seafood (Brixham oysters, dressed Whitby crab, Arbroath smokies, Dover sole, Cornish cockles, smoked North Sea mackerel and Stornoway mussels) from its adjoining fishmonger. By-the-glass wines span the globe.

ℹ Information

Tourist Office (📞 01746-763257; www.visitbridgnorth.co.uk; Listley St; ☺ 9.30am-6pm Mon, to 5pm Tue, Wed & Fri, to 3pm Sat) Inside the town library.

ℹ Getting There & Away

Bus 436 runs from Shrewsbury to Bridgnorth (£4.20, one hour, hourly Monday to Saturday), via Much Wenlock (£4.20, 20 minutes). Bus 9 runs to Ironbridge (£4.50, 30 minutes, every two hours Monday to Saturday).

Church Stretton

📞 01694 / POP 2789

Tucked in a deep valley formed by the Long Mynd and the Caradoc Hills, Church Stretton is an ideal base for walks or cycle tours through the Shropshire Hills. Although black-and-white timbers are heavily in evidence, most of the buildings in town are 19th-century fakes, built by the Victorians who flocked here to take the country air.

◉ Sights

Walking is the big draw here. The tourist office has maps and details of local mountain-biking circuits and horse-riding stables. Information on activities is also available at www.shropshiresgreatoutdoors.co.uk.

Snailbeach MINE
(☏ 07850 492036; www.shropshiremines.org.uk; tours £7.50/3; ◷ site 24hr, tours by reservation Sun & Mon Apr-Oct) The former lead- and silver-mining village of Snailbeach is littered with intriguing, rusting machinery relics. You can download a self-guided trail from the website of the **Bog Centre tourist office** (☏ 01743-792484; www.bogcentre.co.uk; The Bog, Stiperstones; ◷ noon-5pm Mon, from 10am Tue-Sun Easter-Sep, noon-4pm Mon, from 10am Tue-Sun Oct; �) to explore the site, or reserve ahead for guided tours (waterproof footwear required) that take you into the mine.

Acton Scott Estate FARM
(☏ 01694-781307; www.actonscott.com; Marshbrook; adult/child £9/5; ◷ farm 10am-4.30pm Sat-Wed, courses Apr-Dec) On the sprawling Acton Scott Estate, 4 miles south of Church Stretton, this historic working farm has traditional breeds of poultry and livestock, and daily demonstrations of Victorian farming techniques, such as barrel making, horseshoeing and cartwheel construction. Book ahead for courses including blacksmithing, beekeeping, plant identification and 19th-century cookery.

⌂ Sleeping

Bridges Long Mynd YHA HOSTEL £
(☏ 01588-650656; www.yha.org.uk; Bridges; dm from £22, camping per person from £10; ⊡) ⬭ On the Long Mynd's western side, this wonderfully isolated hiker favourite, with 38 beds (plus garden tent sites), is housed in a former school in the tiny hamlet of Bridges. No wi-fi, no mobile-phone reception, no credit cards. Cross the Mynd to Ratlinghope, from where it's 1.1 miles southwest, or take buses run by Shropshire Hills Shuttles (p430) in season.

Mynd Guest House B&B ££
(☏ 01694-722212; www.myndhouse.co.uk; Ludlow Rd, Little Stretton; s/d from £60/80; ⊡⬔) Just

under 2 miles south of Church Stretton, this inviting guesthouse has splendid views across the valley and backs directly onto the Mynd. Its eight rooms are named after local landmarks. There's a small bar and lounge stocked with local books, as well as bike storage and a room for drying your boots.

✕ Eating

Van Doesburg's DELI £
(☏ 01694-722867; www.vandoesburgs.co.uk; 3 High St; dishes £1.85-5; ◷ 9am-5pm Mon-Sat; ⬭) A fantastic place to pick up picnic ingredients, Van Doesburg's has over 80 British cheeses and other deli items, such as chutneys. Ready-to-eat dishes to take away include chicken-and-mushroom pies, salads, quiches, soups and outstanding sandwiches (eg roast beef with pickles and mustard or farmhouse cheddar with plum-and-apple relish). Phone ahead to order customised hampers.

Bridges PUB FOOD ££
(☏ 01588-650260; www.thebridgespub.co.uk; Ratlinghope; mains lunch £6-11, dinner £10.50-16; ◷ kitchen 11.30am-9pm Mon-Sat, 12.30-8.30pm Sun, bar 9.30am-11pm; ⬔⬔⬔) Some 5 miles northeast of Church Stretton, at the base of Long Mynd by the river, this is one of those secret country pubs revered for its Three Tuns ale, live music, riverside terrace, relaxed accommodation (dorm/double/family from £30/60/120) and impressive food (lamb shank and mint sauce, beef lasagne...). Mini burgers are among the choices on the kids' menu.

ⓘ Information

Tourist Office (☏ 01694-723133; www.churchstretton.co.uk; Church St; ◷ 9.30am-1pm & 1.30-5pm Mon-Sat Apr-Sep, 9.30am-1pm & 1.30-3pm Mon-Sat Oct-Mar) Adjoining the library, Church Stretton's tourist office has abundant walking information.

ⓘ Getting There & Away

BUS

Bus 435 runs from Church Stretton north to Shrewsbury (£3.80, 40 minutes, hourly Monday to Friday, every two hours Saturday) and south to Ludlow (£3.80, 40 minutes, hourly Monday to Friday, every two hours Saturday).

On summer weekends, Shropshire Hills Shuttles (p430) runs an hourly service from the Carding Mill Valley near Church Stretton to the villages atop the Long Mynd, passing the YHA at

Bridges, and Stiperstones near the Snailbeach mine.

TRAIN

Trains between Ludlow (£7.60) and Shrewsbury (£6.60) stop in Church Stretton hourly, taking 15 minutes from either end.

Bishop's Castle

✆ 01588 / POP 1630

Set amid blissfully peaceful Shropshire countryside, Bishop's Castle is a higgledy-piggledy tangle of timbered town houses and Old Mother Hubbard cottages. The High St climbs from the town church to the Georgian town hall.

◉ Sights

★ Kerry Vale Vineyard   WINERY

(✆ 01588-620627; www.kerryvalevineyard.co.uk; Pentreheyling; tours £16-35; ⊙ tours noon Thu, Sat, Sun mid-Mar–Nov, shop & cafe 10am-4pm Tue-Sun mid-Mar–Oct, to 3pm Nov & Dec) More than 6000 vines are now planted over 2.4 hectares of the former Pentreheyling Roman Fort, where pottery and metalwork have been uncovered and are displayed at the winery shop. Tours range from an hour-long guided walk through the vines, with a talk on the site's Roman history and tastings, to two-hour guided visits with tastings, a tutorial and an afternoon tea including the vineyard's own sparkling wine. Or pop by the cafe for a wine tasting flight.

House on Crutches   MUSEUM

(✆ 01588-630556; www.hocmuseum.org.uk; High St; ⊙ 2-5pm Sat & Sun Apr-Sep) FREE The crooked 16th-century House on Crutches is home to the small town museum covering Shropshire life over the past two centuries.

⌂ Sleeping

Castle Hotel   HOTEL ££

(✆ 01588-638403; www.thecastlehotelbishops castle.co.uk; Market Sq; s/d/f incl breakfast from £115/125/180; P🖥🛜🐾) This solid-looking 18th-century coaching inn was built with stones from the now-vanished Bishop's Castle, which also contributed the gorgeous wood panelling in the dining room (mains £11 to £22). All 12 en-suite rooms are lovely, with modern fabrics meeting antique furniture; three-bed family rooms and cots are available. Its bar is decidedly cosy and the garden delightful.

Poppy House   B&B ££

(✆ 01588-638443; www.poppyhouse.co.uk; 20 Market Sq; s/d/f from £50/70/90; 🛜) This sweet guesthouse has lovely individual rooms with latch doors and loads of old beams. Children are warmly welcomed; under fives stay free. Breakfast is served at the attached cafe, which opens to the public from 10am to 4pm Wednesday to Monday (dishes £4 to £8.50).

Eating & Drinking

New Deli   DELI £

(32 High St; dishes £2.50-8.50; ⊙ 9am-4pm Tue-Sat) Locally made English and Welsh cheeses and breads, along with hams, salamis and sausages, premade salads, preserves, chutneys and pickles, cakes and biscuits, and ales, wines and liqueurs at this enticing deli mean you're spoiled for choice for picnic fare to take into the surrounding hills.

Three Tuns   PUB

(www.thethreetunsinn.co.uk; Salop St; ⊙ noon-11pm Mon-Sat, to 10.30pm Sun; 🛜) Bishop's Castle's finest watering hole is attached to the tiny Three Tuns Brewery, which has been rolling barrels of nut-brown ale across the courtyard since 1642. It's a lively local, and the ales are delicious. Jazz, blues and brass bands perform regularly in summer.

ⓘ Information

Tourist Office (✆ 01588-630023; www. bishopscastletownhall.co.uk; High St; ⊙ 10am-4pm Mon-Sat) In the restored town hall (1765), Bishop's Castle's tourist office has details of walking and cycling trails in the surrounding hills. Local artists' work is exhibited in the gallery upstairs.

ⓘ Getting There & Away

Bus 553 runs to and from Shrewsbury (£3.80, one hour, five per day Monday to Saturday).

Ludlow

✆ 01584 / POP 11,003

On the northern bank of the swirling River Teme, this genteel market town fans out from the rambling ruins of its fine Norman castle, with some magnificent black-and-white Tudor buildings lining its cobbled streets. Premium produce from the lush surrounding countryside has helped the town become a gastronomic beacon, with superb markets, delis, restaurants and food festivals.

⊙ Sights

Ludlow Castle CASTLE
(☑01584-873355; www.ludlowcastle.com; Castle Sq; adult/child £6/3; ⊙10am-5pm mid-Mar–Oct, to 4pm Nov-early Jan & early Feb–mid-Mar, to 4pm Sat & Sun early Jan-early Feb) Perched in an ideal defensive location atop a cliff above a crook in the river, the town castle was built to ward off the marauding Welsh – or to enforce the English expansion into Wales, perspective depending. Founded after the Norman conquest, the castle was dramatically expanded in the 14th century.

The Norman chapel in the inner bailey is one of the few surviving round chapels in England, and the sturdy keep (built around 1090) offers wonderful views over the hills.

Ludlow Brewing Company BREWERY
(☑01584-873291; www.theludlowbrewingcompany. co.uk; The Railway Shed, Station Dr; tours £7; ⊙tours by reservation 3pm Mon-Fri, 2pm Sat, visitor centre & tap room 10am-5pm Mon-Thu & Sat, to 6pm Fri, 11am-4pm Sun) 🍺 Up an inconspicuous laneway, the Ludlow Brewing Company produces award-winning all-natural brews and sells directly from the brewery and its airy, post-industrial-style bar. Hour-long tours include one pint and six samples.

Church of St Laurence CHURCH
(www.stlaurences.org.uk; 2 College St; admission by £3 donation; ⊙10am-5pm) One of Britain's largest parish churches, the church of St Laurence contains grand Elizabethan alabaster tombs and delightfully cheeky medieval misericords carved into its medieval choir stalls, including a beer-swilling chap raiding his barrel. The Lady Chapel contains a marvellous **Jesse Window**, originally dating from 1330 (although the glass is mostly Victorian). Four windows in St John's Chapel date from the mid-15th century, including the honey-coloured **Golden Window**. Climb 200 steps up the **tower** (included in donation) for stunning views.

🎆 Festivals & Events

Ludlow Spring Festival CULTURAL
(www.ludlowspringfestival.co.uk; ⊙mid-May) The two-day Ludlow Spring Festival uses the castle as its dramatic backdrop for beer, cider and food stalls, a vintage car show and live concerts.

Ludlow Food Festival FOOD & DRINK
(www.ludlowfoodfestival.co.uk; ⊙early Sep) At Ludlow Castle, the Ludlow Food Festival spans three days in early September, with over 180 exhibitors from the town and the Welsh Marches.

🛏 Sleeping

Clive BOUTIQUE HOTEL **££**
(☑01584-856565; www.theclive.co.uk; Bromfield Rd, Bromfield; d/f incl breakfast from £115/140; P✳🕸) For foodies, this is Ludlow's ultimate place to stay. Located 4 miles northwest of town adjoining the Ludlow Food Centre (p442), it has its own top-end restaurant; breakfast is served at the Ludlow Kitchen. Many of its 15 spacious rooms are on ground level; family rooms have two sleeping areas separated by a bathroom, giving parents and kids their own space.

Charlton Arms INN **££**
(☑01584-872813; www.thecharltonarms.co.uk; Ludford Bridge; d incl breakfast £100-160; P🕸) The pick of the rooms at this landmark inn overlook the River Teme, and the pick of those have terraces (one with an outdoor hot tub as well as a four-poster bed). Its pub, also opening to a terrace, serves top-quality Modern British cuisine. Service is superb. There's a large free car park on-site.

Feathers Hotel HISTORIC HOTEL **£££**
(☑01584-875261; www.feathersatludlow.co.uk; 21 Bull Ring; s/d from £95/140; P🕸) Behind its impossibly ornate timbered Jacobean facade, this 1619-built treasure is all tapestries, creaky furniture, timber beams and stained glass: you can almost hear the cavaliers toasting the health of King Charles. The best rooms are in the old building; rooms in the newer wing lack character and romance. Dinner, bed and breakfast packages are available at its restaurant.

🍴 Eating

Ludlow Kitchen CAFE **£**
(☑01584-856020; www.ludlowkitchen.co.uk; Bromfield Rd, Bromfield; breakfast £3.50-9, lunch mains £7-13; ⊙8am-5pm Mon-Sat, to 4pm Sun; 🍴) 🌿 Produce from the Ludlow Food Centre (p442) artisanal farm shop is served at its sunlit cafe. Fantastic breakfasts (granola with homemade yoghurt; full English fry-ups with farmhouse eggs, artisan bacon and black pudding; eggs royale) are the precursor to lunch dishes such as Ludlow Brewing Company beer-battered fish with zingy tartar.

Fish House
SEAFOOD ££

(☑ 01584-879790; www.thefishhouseludlow.co.uk; 51 Bull Ring; dishes £8-15, sharing platters £25-60; ☺ noon-3pm Wed-Sat) Except on Saturdays when it's first-come, first-served, bookings are recommended for the barrel tables at this stylish fish and oyster bar. It sources Britain's best seafood – Whitby crab and lobster, Arbroath smokies, Bigbury Bay oysters – and serves it with organic bread, lemon and mayo, along with wines, local ales, ciders and champagne.

Bistro 7
BISTRO ££

(☑ 01584-877412; www.bistro7ofludlow.co.uk; 7 Corve St; mains £15.50-21.50; ☺ noon-2.30pm & 6.30-9.30pm Tue-Sat) Ludlow's red-brick former post office is the setting for creative bistro cooking. Knowledgeable staff can guide you through the regularly changing menu, which might feature dishes like wood pigeon salad, black-pudding-stuffed pork loin and red-wine-poached plums with rosemary meringue. Or finish with a platter of local cheeses served with nettle and spiced-apple chutney.

Mortimers
BRITISH £££

(☑ 01584-872325; www.mortimersludlow.co.uk; 17 Corve St; 2-/3-course lunch menu £22.50/26, 3-course dinner menu £47.50, 7-course tasting menu £62.50, with paired wines £100; ☺ noon-2pm & 6.30-9pm Tue-Sat; ☑) For fine dining, this is Ludlow's top table. Dark timber panelling and cosy nooks and crannies create a romantic backdrop for intricate dishes such as scallops with truffled pumpkin purée or lacquered Ludlow duck with pastrami-wrapped celeriac. Vegetarians can prebook a meat-free version of the seven-course tasting menu, featuring creations like asparagus with roast baby beetroot and sorrel panna cotta.

🔒 Shopping

★ Ludlow Food Centre
FOOD & DRINKS

(☑ 01584-856000; www.ludlowfoodcentre.co.uk; Bromfield Rd, Bromfield; ☺ 9am-5.30pm Mon-Sat, 10am-5pm Sun) More than 80% of the cheeses, meats, breads, fruit and vegetables are sourced from the surrounding region and tantalisingly displayed at this enormous farm shop, including many produced on the estate. Watch through viewing windows to see traditional preserves, pies, ice cream and more being made. It's signposted 2.8 miles northwest of Ludlow off Bromfield Rd (the A49).

Look out for regular events including tastings. There's a kids' playground and a picnic area. Produce is used by the adjoining cafe-restaurant, the Ludlow Kitchen (p441).

Ludlow Market
MARKET

(www.ludlowmarket.co.uk; Castle Sq; ☺ 9.30am-2pm Mon, Wed, Fri & Sat) Ludlow Market's stalls sell fresh produce, artisan food and drink, flowers, books, gifts and more. Various spin-off markets (farmers markets, flea markets, book markets and craft markets) take place on Thursdays and Sundays.

ℹ️ Information

Tourist Office (☑ 01584-875053; www.visitshropshirehills.co.uk; 1 Mill St; ☺ 10am-4pm Mon-Sat Mar-Dec, to 2pm Mon-Sat Jan & Feb) On the 3rd floor of the Ludlow Assembly Rooms.

ℹ️ Getting There & Away

BUS
Bus 435 runs to Shrewsbury (£4.10, 1¼ hours, hourly Monday to Saturday) via Church Stretton (£3.10, 35 minutes).

TRAIN
Trains run frequently from the station on the north edge of town to Hereford (£10.40, 25 minutes, up to two per hour) and Shrewsbury

---

BYRON'S NEWSTEAD ABBEY

Founded as an Augustinian priory in around 1170, lakeside **Newstead Abbey** (☑ 01623-455900; www.newsteadabbey.org.uk; Newstead; house & gardens adult/child £10/6, park free; ☺ house & gardens noon-4pm Sat & Sun, park 10am-5pm daily) was converted into a residence in 1539. It's inextricably associated with the original tortured romantic, Lord Byron (1788–1824), who inherited the house in 1798, selling it in 1818.

Byron's old living quarters are full of suitably eccentric memorabilia, and the landscaped grounds include a monument to his yappy dog, Boatswain.

Newstead Abbey is 12 miles north of Nottingham, off the A60. Pronto buses (£3.50, 25 minutes, every 10 minutes Monday to Saturday, half-hourly Sunday) from Nottingham's Victoria bus station stop at the gates, a mile from the house and gardens.

(£13.50, 30 minutes, up to two per hour), via Church Stretton (£7.60, 15 minutes).

NOTTINGHAMSHIRE

Say Nottinghamshire and people think of one thing – Robin Hood. Whether the hero woodsman existed is hotly debated, but the county plays up its connections to the outlaw. Storytelling seems to be in Nottinghamshire's blood – local wordsmiths include provocative writer DH Lawrence, of *Lady Chatterley's Lover* fame, and hedonistic poet Lord Byron. The city of Nottingham is the bustling hub; venture into the surrounding countryside and you'll discover historic towns and stately homes surrounding the green bower of Sherwood Forest.

❶ Getting There & Away

National Express and **Trent Barton** (☑ 01773-712265; www.trentbarton.co.uk) buses provide the majority of bus services. See Traveline (p402) for timetables. Trains run frequently to most large towns, and to many smaller villages in the Peak District.

Nottingham

☑ 0115 / POP 321,550

Forever associated with men in tights and a sheriff with anger-management issues (aka the Robin Hood legend), Nottingham is a dynamic county capital with big-city aspirations, evocative historical sights, and a buzzing music and club scene thanks to its spirited student population.

◉ Sights

Nottingham Castle   CASTLE, GALLERY
(www.nottinghamcity.gov.uk; Lenton Rd) Nottingham's castle crowns a sandstone outcrop worm-holed with caves and tunnels. Founded by William the Conqueror, the original castle was held by a succession of English kings before falling in the English Civil War.

Its 17th-century manor-house-like replacement is undergoing major renovations, and is closed until spring 2020. When it reopens, it will feature a new Robin Hood Gallery, a Rebellion Gallery, covering social unrest from medieval times, and displays on art and manufacturing, including salt-glazed stoneware and lacemaking.

Access to the cave system will be extended, parts of the castle grounds will be remodelled to reveal more of the medieval site, and a new visitor centre and cafe will open here. The 17th-century cottages comprising the **Museum of Nottingham Life at Brewhouse Yard** will also reopen in mid-2020.

The much-photographed **statue of Robin Hood** stands in the former moat and remains accessible while works take place.

Wollaton Hall   HISTORIC BUILDING
(☑ 0115-876 3100; www.wollatonhall.org.uk; Wollaton Park, Derby Rd; tours adult/child £5/free, grounds free; ☺ tours noon & 2pm, grounds 8am-dusk Mon-Fri, from 9am Sat & Sun) Built in 1588 for coal mogul Sir Francis Willoughby by avant-garde architect Robert Smythson, Wollaton Hall sits within 200 hectares of grounds roamed by fallow and red deer. Tours lasting 45 minutes lead you through extravagant rooms from the Tudor, Regency and Victorian periods. There's also a natural-history museum here.

Wollaton Hall is 2.5 miles west of Nottingham city centre; take bus L2, 30 or 'The 2' from Victoria bus station (£4, 15 minutes, every 15 minutes Monday to Saturday, half-hourly Sunday).

The hall starred as Wayne Manor in 2012's Batman film *The Dark Knight Rises*.

City of Caves   CAVE
(☑ 0115-952 0555; www.cityofcaves.com; Drury Walk, Upper Level, Broadmarsh shopping centre; adult/child £7.95/6.95, incl National Justice Museum £16/11.95; ☺ tours 10.30am-4pm) Over the centuries, the sandstone underneath Nottingham has been carved into a honeycomb of caverns and passageways. Tours lead you from the top level of the Broadmarsh shopping centre through a WWII air-raid shelter, a medieval underground tannery, several pub cellars and a mock-up of a Victorian slum dwelling. Book ahead.

National Justice Museum   MUSEUM
(☑ 0115-952 0555; www.nationaljusticemuseum.org.uk; High Pavement; adult/child £9.95/7.95, incl City of Caves £16/11.95; ☺ 9am-5.30pm Mon-Fri, from 10am Sat & Sun) In the grand Georgian Shire Hall, the National Justice Museum offers a ghoulish stroll through centuries of British justice, including medieval trials by fire and water. There are costumed characters representing historical figures, and activities, exhibitions and re-enacted courtroom performances regularly take place. Tickets are valid all day.

Nottingham

Nottingham

👉 Tours

★ **Ezekial Bone Tours** WALKING
(📞 07941 210986; www.ezekialbone.com; adult/
child Robin Hood Town Tour £14.50/8, Notting-

ham in a Nutshell Tour £12/6; ⊙ Robin Hood Town
Tour 2pm Sat Mar-Oct, Nottingham in a Nutshell
Tour 11am Sat Mar-Oct) Hugely entertaining,
history-focused tours led by multi-award-
winning 'modern-day Robin Hood' Ezekial

Bone (aka historian/actor/writer/local legend Ade Andrews) are a highlight of visiting Nottingham. **Robin Hood Town Tours** lasting 2½ hours depart from the **Cross Keys pub** (www.crosskeysnottingham.co.uk; 15 Byard Lane; ⊙9am-11pm Sun-Wed, to midnight Thu & Fri, to 1am Sat); whistle-stop 90-minute **Nottingham in a Nutshell** tours depart from the tourist office (p447). Tours run most Saturdays in season; confirm departures ahead.

Lace Market tours and **Robin Hood Sherwood Forest tours** are also available by request.

⚜ Festivals & Events

Goose Fair   FAIR
(⊙early Oct) The five-day Goose Fair has evolved from a medieval travelling market to a modern funfair with over 500 attractions and rides.

Robin Hood Beer & Cider Festival   DRINK
(www.beerfestival.nottinghamcamra.org; ⊙mid-Oct) This four-day tasting festival features more than 1000 beers and 250 ciders and perries.

Robin Hood Pageant   CULTURAL
(www.visit-nottinghamshire.co.uk; ⊙late Oct) The family-friendly Robin Hood Pageant takes place over two days in late October. Check with the tourist office (p447) for details of 2019's event; from 2020 the pageant is expected to return to the grounds of Nottingham Castle following its reopening after renovations.

🛏 Sleeping

Igloo Hybrid Hostel   HOSTEL £
(☎0115-948 3822; www.igloohostel.co.uk; 4-6 Eldon Chambers, Wheeler Gate; dm from £19, s/d sleep box from £32/64, s with/without en suite from £39/34, d with/without en suite £84/72; 🛜) The sister property of the much-loved **Igloo Backpackers Hostel** (☎0115-947 5250; www.igloohostel.co.uk; 110 Mansfield Rd; dm/s/d/tr from £20/29/64/78; 🛜) has a central location footsteps from the Old Market Sq. Cabin-style 'sleep boxes' incorporate USB ports and reading lights; there's a well-equipped self-catering kitchen and a sociable courtyard garden.

★**Lace Market Hotel**   BOUTIQUE HOTEL ££
(☎0115-948 4414; www.lacemarkethotel.co.uk; 29-31 High Pavement; s/d/ste incl breakfast from £76/122/184; 🅿❄🛜) In the heart of the gentrified Lace Market, this elegant Georgian town house's 42 sleek rooms have state-of-the-art furnishings and amenities; some come with air-conditioning. Its fine-dining restaurant, Merchants (p446), and adjoining pub, the **Cock & Hoop** (www.lacemarkethotel.co.uk; 25 High Pavement; ⊙noon-11pm Mon-Thu, to midnight Fri, to 1am Sat, to 10.30pm Sun, hours can vary), are both superb.

Hart's   BOUTIQUE HOTEL £££
(☎0115-988 1900; www.hartsnottingham.co.uk; Standard Hill, Park Row; d/ste incl breakfast from £139/279; 🅿🛜) Within the former Nottingham General Hospital compound, this swish hotel has ultra-contemporary rooms (some with small terraces) in a striking modernist building. Its renowned **restaurant** (mains £17.50-32.50; ⊙7am-2.30pm & 6-10pm Mon-Fri, 7.30am-2.30pm & 6-10.30pm Sat, 7.30am-2.30pm & 6-9pm Sun; 🍴) is housed in a historic red-brick wing. Work out in the small gym or unwind in the private garden.

🍴 Eating

★**Delilah Fine Foods**   DELI, CAFE £
(☎0115-948 4461; www.delilahfinefoods.co.uk; 12 Victoria St; dishes £4-10, platters £17-20; ⊙8am-7pm Mon-Fri, from 9am Sat, 11am-5pm Sun; 🍴) 🌱 Impeccably selected cheeses (more than 150 varieties), pâtés, meats and more from artisan producers are available to take away or eat on-site at this foodie's fantasy land, housed in a grand former bank with mezzanine seating. It doesn't take reservations but you can preorder customised hampers for a gourmet picnic.

Annie's Burger Shack   BURGERS, AMERICAN £
(☎0115-684 9920; www.anniesburgershack.com; 5 Broadway; burgers £8.90-13.20, breakfast £6-10; ⊙8-10.30am & noon-11pm Sun-Thu, 8-10.30am & noon-midnight Fri & Sat; 🛜🍴) More than 30 different burgers (available in vegan, veggie or meat versions) are on the menu at Annie's, a wildly popular joint in the Lace Market that stays true to its owner's US roots (and adds real ales to its offerings). Midweek breakfast menus feature American classics (blueberry pancakes with maple syrup and bacon; Boston franks 'n' beans). Book ahead.

Larder on Goosegate   BRITISH ££
(☎0115-950 0111; www.thelarderongoosegate.co.uk; 16-22 Goosegate; mains £13.50-22, afternoon tea from £16.50; ⊙5.30-10pm Tue-Thu, noon-2.30 & 5.30-11pm Fri & Sat) Floor-to-ceiling windows fill this 1st-floor restaurant with light and provide bird's-eye views of busy Goosegate

below. Blue goats cheese and beetroot cheesecake, Shetland Queen scallops with wild-garlic butter and roast spring lamb with smoked aubergine are among its superbly executed British dishes. On Fridays and Saturdays, afternoon tea is served on antique bone china. Book ahead.

Merchants
EUROPEAN £££

(☏0115-948 4414; www.lacemarkethotel.co.uk; 29-31 High Pavement; mains £16-30; ⊙7am-10pm Mon-Fri, 8-10.30am & noon-5pm Sat, 7-10.30am & noon-2pm Sun) A stunning, coffered-ceilinged dining room sets the stage for some of Nottingham's finest dining. Knock-out combinations on its changing menu might include Texel lamb with pistachio and courgette; Irish sea trout with samphire and radish; or morrels, broad beans and goats curd. Follow up with desserts such as poached-rhubarb panna cotta with black-pepper crumble and basil ice cream.

Restaurant Sat Bains
GASTRONOMY £££

(☏0115-986 6566; www.restaurantsatbains.com; Lenton Lane; 7-/10-course tasting menus £95/110; ⊙6-9pm Wed & Thu, to 9.45pm Fri & Sat; ☏) Boundary-pushing chef Sat Bains has been awarded two Michelin stars for his wildly inventive tasting menus (no à la carte; dietary restrictions can be catered for with advance notice). Book *well* ahead and beware of hefty cancellation charges. It also has chic guest rooms (double £140 to £190, suite £285). It's 2 miles southwest of the city centre off the A52.

🍸 Drinking & Nightlife

★ Ye Olde Trip to Jerusalem
PUB

(☏0115-947 3171; www.triptojerusalem.com; Brewhouse Yard, Castle Rd; ⊙11am-11pm Sun-Thu, to midnight Fri & Sat) Carved into the cliff below the castle, this atmospheric alehouse claims to be England's oldest pub. Founded in 1189, it supposedly slaked the thirst of departing crusaders, and its warren of rooms and cobbled courtyards make it the most ambient place in Nottingham for a pint.

Call ahead to ask about tours of its cellars and caves.

★ Crafty Crow
PUB

(www.craftycrownotts.co.uk; 102 Friar Lane; ⊙noon-11pm Sun-Thu, 11am-midnight Fri & Sat; ☏) ⬤ Rotating brews at this beer specialist include several from its own Nottingham-based Magpie Brewery, made from British hops and malts, plus hand-pulls from local microbreweries and craft beers and ciders on tap. Timber-planked walls line the TV-free split-level space; don't miss the bathrooms with sinks and taps made out of kegs. Gastropub food is locally sourced.

Dragon
PUB

(☏0115-941 7080; www.the-dragon.co.uk; 67 Long Row; ⊙noon-11.30pm Sun-Wed, to midnight Thu, to 1am Fri & Sat; ☏) The Dragon has a fabulous atmosphere at any time, thanks to homemade food, a good beer garden and vinyl played on weekends. But it peaks from 7.30pm on Tuesdays when it hosts Race Night (race entry £5) in the Racing Room (www.theracingroom.co.uk), with an awesome Scalextric slot-car race around a scale model of Nottingham along 180ft of track.

Boilermaker
COCKTAIL BAR

(www.boilermakerbar.co.uk; 36b Carlton St; ⊙5pm-1am Mon-Fri, from 2pm Sat, from 7pm Sun) Entering what appears to be an industrial boilermaker's shop and navigating your way through two secret doors brings you into this cavernous, low-lit speakeasy spinning chilled lounge music. Out-there cocktail combinations (eg Figgy Stardust, with tequila, artichoke-based Cynar liqueur, figs, pomegranate shrub and black walnuts) add to the unique-and-then-some experience.

Malt Cross
PUB

(www.maltcross.com; 16 St James's St; ⊙11am-11pm Mon-Thu, to 1am Fri, 10am-1am Sat, 10am-9pm Sun) A fine place for a pint, the Malt Cross occupies a stately old Victorian music hall, where past performers included Charlie Chaplin. It's now a community space run by the Christian Charity Trust hosting art exhibitions and live music. Top-notch bar food includes towering burgers.

Brass Monkey
COCKTAIL BAR

(www.brassmonkeybar.co.uk; 11 High Pavement; ⊙5pm-3am Mon-Sat) Nottingham's original cocktail bar rocks the Lace Market with DJ sets and quirky takes on favourites such as elderflower mojitos. The roof terrace gets packed on summer evenings.

Canal House
PUB

(☏0115-955 5060; www.castlerockbrewery.co.uk/pubs/the-canalhouse; 48-52 Canal St; ⊙11am-11pm Mon-Wed, to midnight Thu, to 1am Fri & Sat, to 10.30pm Sun) Split in two by a watery inlet, the Canal House is the best of the city's canal-front pubs, with plenty of waterside seating and beers by Nottingham-based

DON'T MISS

SHERWOOD FOREST NATIONAL NATURE RESERVE

If Robin Hood wanted to hide out in Sherwood Forest today, he'd have to disguise himself and his Merry Men as day trippers on mountain bikes. Now covering just 182 hectares of old-growth forest, it's nevertheless a major destination for Nottingham city dwellers. The week-long **Robin Hood Festival** (www.nottinghamshire.gov.uk; ⊙Aug) is a massive medieval reenactment that takes place in the forest in August.

The reserve's curved-timber **visitor centre** (www.visitsherwood.co.uk; Forest Corner, Edwinstowe; forest & visitor centre free, parking £4; ⊙10am-6pm Mar-Sep, to 4pm Oct-Feb) , reopened in 2018, provides information about the forest's wildlife, walking trails and Robin Hood legends – including the 800-year-old **Major Oak**, a broad-boughed oak tree (propped up by supporting rods) alleged to have sheltered Robin of Locksley.

Located 2 miles south of Sherwood Forest on the B6030, **Sherwood Pines Cycles** (☑01623-822855; www.sherwoodpinescycles.co.uk; Sherwood Pines Forest Park, Old Clipstone; bike hire adult/child per hour £9/8, per day £28/20; ⊙9am-5pm Thu-Tue, to 7pm Wed) rents mountain bikes for exploring the area's trails.

Castle Rock Brewery on tap. Regular events range from comedy to craft beer festivals.

ℹ Information

Nottingham's **tourist office** (☑0844 477 5678; www.experiencenottinghamshire.com; The Exchange, 1-4 Smithy Row; ⊙9.30am-5.30pm Mon-Sat year-round, plus 11am-5pm Sun Jul, Aug & early Dec-Christmas) has racks of information along with Robin Hood merchandise.

ℹ Getting There & Away

AIR

East Midlands Airport (p464) is 13.5 miles southwest of central Nottingham; Skylink buses pass the airport (one way/return £5.20/10.40, one hour, at least hourly, 24 hours).

BUS

Local services run from the Victoria bus station, behind the Victoria shopping centre on Milton St. Bus 100 runs to Southwell (£4.30, one hour, hourly) and bus 90 to Newark (£5.50, 50 minutes, hourly Monday to Saturday, every two hours Sunday).

Long-distance buses operate from the **Broadmarsh bus station** (Collin St).

Frequent National Express services:

Birmingham £11.10, 2¼ hours, nine daily

Derby £9, 40 minutes, seven daily

Leicester £4.60, 55 minutes, hourly or better

London Victoria £9.30, 3½ hours, every two hours

TRAIN

The train station is on the southern edge of the city centre.

Derby £7.60, 30 minutes, four hourly

Lincoln £11.80, 55 minutes, hourly

London King's Cross/St Pancras £47, 1¾ hours, two per hour

Manchester £27.50, 1¾ hours, up to two per hour

Newark-on-Trent

☑01636 / POP 27,700

Newark-on-Trent paid the price for backing the wrong side in the English Civil War. After surviving four sieges by Oliver Cromwell's men, the town was ransacked by Roundheads when Charles I surrendered in 1646. Today, the riverside town is a peaceful place worth a stop to wander its castle ruins.

◉ Sights

Newark Castle   CASTLE
(www.newark-sherwooddc.gov.uk/newarkcastle; Castle Gate; grounds free, tours adult/child £5.50/2.75; ⊙grounds dawn-dusk, tours by reservation Wed & Fri-Sun) In a pretty park overlooking the River Trent, the ruins of Newark Castle include an impressive Norman gate and a series of underground passages and chambers. The real King John, portrayed as a villain in the Robin Hood legend, died here in 1216. Book tour tickets online at www.palacenewarktickets.com. Concerts, festivals and various cultural events regularly take place in the grounds.

Newark Air Museum   MUSEUM
(☑01636-707170; www.newarkairmuseum.org; Drove Lane, Winthorpe; adult/child £9/4.50; ⊙10am-5pm Mar-Oct, to 4pm Nov-Feb) Situated 2 miles east of Newark by the Winthorpe Showground, this aviation museum has over 100 aircraft, including a fearsome Vulcan bomber, a Vampire T11, a Gloster Meteor and a de

Havilland Tiger Moth, along with a small exhibition on the Royal Air Force.

Eating & Drinking

Old Bakery Tea Rooms
CAFE £

(☑ 01636-611501; www.oldbakerytearooms.co.uk; 4 Queens Head Ct; mains £6-12; ☺ 9.30am-5pm Mon-Sat; ☑) Everything, including heavenly sweet and savoury scones, is baked fresh on the premises at the Old Bakery Tea Rooms, housed in an enchanting 15th-century Tudor building. Lunch specials include soups, frittata, bruschetta and smoked-salmon brioche. Cash only.

Castle Barge
BAR

(www.castlebarge.com; The Wharf; ☺ 10.30am-midnight) Moored on the River Trent overlooking Newark Castle, this former grain barge, which once plied the waters between Hull and Gainsborough, is an idyllic spot for a local ale inside or up on deck, with additional picnic seating on the riverbanks. Its menu includes stone-baked pizzas.

ⓘ Information

Tourist Office (☑ 01636-655765; www.newark-sherwooddc.gov.uk; 14 Appleton Gate; ☺ 10am-4pm) On the northeastern edge of the historic centre.

ⓘ Getting There & Away

Buses 28 and 29 serve Southwell (£6.70, 45 minutes, two per hour).

Newark has two train stations:

Newark Castle East Midlands trains serve Leicester (£18.30, 1¼ hours, hourly), Nottingham (£6.40, 30 minutes, two per hour) and Lincoln (£5.40, 25 minutes, two per hour).

Newark North Gate Trains on the East Coast Main Line serve London King's Cross (£34.50, 1½ hours, two per hour); destinations to the north require a change in Doncaster (£24.80, 25 minutes, hourly).

Southwell

☑ 01636 / POP 7297

A graceful scattering of grand, wisteria-draped country houses, pretty little Southwell is straight out of the pages of a novel from the English Romantic period.

◉ Sights

★ Southwell Minster
CHURCH

(www.southwellminster.org; Church St; suggested donation £5; ☺ 8am-7pm Mar-Oct, to 6.30pm Nov-Feb) Rising from the village centre, the awe-inspiring Southwell Minster, built over Saxon and Roman foundations, blends 12th- and 13th-century features, including zigzag door frames and curved arches. Its chapter-house features some unusual stained glass and detailed carvings of faces, animals and leaves of forest trees.

Southwell Workhouse
MUSEUM

(NT; ☑ 01636-817260; www.nationaltrust.org.uk; Upton Rd; adult/child £9.10/4.55; ☺ guided exteriors tours 11am, Workhouse noon-5pm Mar-early Nov) On the road to Newark, 1 mile east of the village centre, the Southwell Workhouse is a sobering reminder of the tough life faced by paupers in the 19th century. You can explore the factory floors and workers' chambers accompanied by an audio guide narrated by 'inmates' and 'officials'. One-hour guided tours of the exteriors take place at 11am.

⌖ Sleeping & Eating

Saracen's Head Hotel
HISTORIC HOTEL ££

(☑ 01636-812701; www.saracensheadhotel.com; Market Pl; s/d/f/ste incl breakfast from £90/100/130/150; ⓟ⑤🐾) Set around a flower-filled courtyard in the village heart, this rambling, black-and-white timbered coaching inn has 27 beautifully refurbished rooms (some with four-poster beds and claw-foot baths) across its old and new wings. Illustrious past guests included Charles I, Lord Byron and Dickens. Its oak-panelled restaurant serves traditional British fare (two-/three-course menus £19.50/23.50).

Family rooms sleep up to four; baby cots are available.

Old Theatre Deli
CAFE, DELI £

(www.theoldtheatredeli.co.uk; 4 Market Pl; dishes £6-12; ☺ 8.30am-6pm) Artisan breads from the Midlands' renowned Hambleton Bakery, gourmet sandwiches, quiches, pies, salads and hot specials, such as corn-and-bacon fritters, are among the treats to take away or eat inside or out on the pavement terrace. You can also order picnic hampers complete with blankets. It's housed inside a Georgian former theatre.

ⓘ Getting There & Away

Bus 100 runs from Nottingham (£4.30, one hour, hourly). For Newark-on-Trent, take bus 28 or 29 (£6.70, 45 minutes, two per hour).

LINCOLNSHIRE

Lincolnshire unfolds over low hills and the sparsely populated, pancake-flat Fens where the farmland is strewn with windmills and, more recently, wind turbines. Surrounding the history-steeped county town of Lincoln you'll find seaside resorts, scenic waterways, serene nature reserves and stone-built towns tailor-made for English period dramas.

Two of the county's most famous 'yellowbellies' (as Lincolnshire locals call themselves) were Sir Isaac Newton, whose home, Woolsthorpe Manor, can be visited, and the late former prime minister Margaret Thatcher, the daughter of a humble greengrocer from the market town of Grantham.

🏃 Activities

Traversing the area occupied by Norse invaders in the 9th century, the 147-mile **Viking Way** walking trail snakes across the gentle hills of the Lincolnshire Wolds from the banks of the River Humber to Oakham in Rutland.

Cyclists can find information on routes across the county in any of the local tourist offices. The 33-mile **Water Rail Way** is a flat, sculpture-lined on-road cycling route that follows the River Witham through classic Fens countryside along the former railway line between Lincoln and Boston.

ℹ️ Getting There & Away

East Midlands trains connect Lincoln, Newark Castle and Nottingham. Newark North Gate and Grantham lie on the East Coast Main Line between London King's Cross and Edinburgh.

Local buses link Lincolnshire's towns, but services are slow and infrequent. Check the transport pages at www.lincolnshire.gov.uk.

Comprehensive transport information is available from Traveline (p402).

Lincoln

📞 01522 / POP 97,541

Ringed by historic city gates – including the Newport Arch on Bailgate, a relic from the original Roman settlement – this beautiful city's old centre is a tangle of cobbled medieval streets surrounding its 11th-century castle and colossal 12th-century cathedral. The lanes that topple over the edge of Lincoln Cliff are lined with Tudor town houses, ancient pubs and independent shops.

BELTON HOUSE

Amid 14.2 hectares of elegant formal gardens, **Belton House** (NT; 📞 01476-566116; www.nationaltrust.org.uk; Belton; house & grounds adult/child £15.70/10, grounds only £12/8.20; ⊙ house 12.30-5pm Wed-Sun Mar-Oct, closed Nov-Feb, grounds 9.30am-5.30pm Mar-Oct, to 4pm Nov-Feb) is a dream filming location for English period dramas, *Jane Eyre*, *Tom Jones* and the Colin Firth version of *Pride and Prejudice* among them. Built in 1688 in classic Restoration style, the house retains stunning original features, including ornate woodcarvings by master Dutch carver Grinling Gibbons. It's off the A607, 2.5 miles northeast of Grantham, and is served by Stagecoach bus 1 (£2.50, 15 minutes, hourly Monday to Saturday, every two hours Sunday).

The surrounding 526-hectare grounds have been home to a fallow deer herd for more than 300 years. Also on the site are a farm shop, a restaurant, a cafe and an adventure playground.

Flanking the River Witham at the base of the hill, the new town is less absorbing, but the revitalised Brayford Waterfront development by the university is a popular spot to watch the boats go by.

◉ Sights

★ **Lincoln Cathedral**   CATHEDRAL
(📞 01522-561600;   www.lincolncathedral.com; Minster Yard; adult/child joint ticket with castle £17.20/9.60, cathedral £8/4.80 Mon-Sat, by donation before 9am, after 4.30pm & all day Sun; ⊙7.15am-8pm Mon-Fri, to 6pm Sat & Sun Jul & Aug, 7.15am-6pm Mon-Sat, to 5pm Sun Sep-Jun) Towering over the city like a medieval skyscraper, Lincoln's magnificent cathedral is a breathtaking representation of divine power on earth. The great tower rising above the crossing is the third-highest in England at 83m, but in medieval times, a lead-encased wooden spire added a further 79m, topping even the great pyramids of Giza. One-hour **guided tours** (included in admission) take place at least twice Monday to Saturday; there are also tours of the roof and tower (£4; book in advance).

The vast interior of the church is too large for modern congregations – services

Lincoln

Lincoln

take place instead in **St Hugh's Choir**, a church within a church running east from the crossing. The choir stalls are accessed through a magnificent carved stone screen;

look north to see the stunning rose window known as the Dean's Eye (c 1192), mirrored to the south by the floral flourishes of the Bishop's Eye (1330). There's more stained glass in the three Services Chapels in the north transept.

Beyond St Hugh's Choir, the **Angel Choir** is supported by 28 columns topped by carvings of angels and foliate scrollwork. Other interesting details include the 10-sided **chapterhouse** – where Edward I held his parliament and where the climax of the *Da Vinci Code* was filmed in 2005.

The best time to hear the organ resounding through the cathedral is during **evensong**; check times online.

★Lincoln Castle   CASTLE
(☑01522-554559; www.lincolncastle.com; Castle Hill; adult/child joint ticket with cathedral £17.20/9.60, castle day ticket £13.50/7.20, walls only £7.50/5, grounds free; ☺10am-5pm Apr-Sep, to 4pm Oct-Mar) One of the first castles erected by the victorious William the Conqueror, in 1068, to keep his new kingdom in line, Lincoln Castle offers awesome views over the city and miles of surrounding countryside. A major 2015-completed restoration program opened up the entire castle walls and gave the 1215 **Magna Carta** (one of only four copies) a swanky, subterranean new home. One-hour guided tours, included in the castle admission, depart from the eastern gate; check the blackboard for times.

Bishops' Palace   RUINS
(EH; ☑01522-527468; www.english-heritage.org.uk; Minster Yard; adult/child £5.90/3.50; ☺10am-6pm Wed-Sun Apr-Sep, to 5pm Wed-Sun Oct, to 4pm Sat & Sun Nov-Mar) Beside Lincoln Cathedral lie the time-ravaged but still imposing ruins of the 12th-century Bishops' Palace, gutted by parliamentary forces during the Civil War. From here, the local bishops once controlled a diocese stretching from the Humber to the Thames. Entertaining audio guides are included in admission. Grapevines are planted in its hillside terraced garden.

Museum of Lincolnshire Life   MUSEUM
(☑01522-782040; www.lincolnshire.gov.uk; Old Barracks, Burton Rd; ☺10am-4pm) FREE Displays at this charming community museum housed in an old Victorian barracks span everything from Victorian farm implements to the tin-can tank built in Lincoln for WWI.

Collection   MUSEUM
(☑01522-782040; www.thecollectionmuseum.com; Danes Tce; ☺10am-4pm, from 10.45am 1st Mon of month) FREE Archaeology bursts into life at this museum, with loads of hands-on displays. Kids can handle artefacts and dress up in period costume. Check out the crushed skull of a 4000-year-old 'yellowbelly' (as locals are dubbed), pulled from a Neolithic burial site near Sleaford. Free one-hour tours run at 2pm on Saturdays. Look out for various evening events.

Exchequergate   HISTORIC BUILDING
Located between the castle and the cathedral, the triple-arched, battlement-topped Exchequergate, where the church's tenants paid their rent, dates from the 14th century. A black-and-white chequered cloth was used to help count the payments, giving rise to the term exchequer.

☞ Tours

Ghost Walks   WALKING
(☑01673-857574; www.lincolnghostwalks.co.uk; adult/child £5/3; ☺7pm Wed-Sat) Genuinely spooky 75-minute ghost walks depart adjacent to the tourist office year-round. Bookings aren't required; turn up 10 minutes before tours begin.

Brayford Belle   CRUISE
(☑01522-881200; www.lincolnboattrips.co.uk; Brayford Wharf North; adult/child £7/4; ☺tours 11am, 12.15pm, 1.30pm, 2.45pm & 3.45pm daily Easter-Sep, hours vary Oct) Boat trips lasting around 50 minutes aboard the *Brayford Belle* travel along the River Witham and Fossdyke Navigation, a canal system dating back to Roman times. No credit cards.

◳ Sleeping

Castle Hotel   BOUTIQUE HOTEL ££
(☑01522-538801; www.castlehotel.net; Westgate; s/d/coach house incl breakfast from £90/120/220; P☎) Each of the Castle Hotel's 18 rooms have been exquisitely refurbished in olive, truffle and oyster tones, as has its family-friendly four-person coach house. Built on the site of Lincoln's Roman forum in 1852, the red-brick building's incarnations variously included a school and a WWII lookout station. Take advantage of great-value dinner, bed and breakfast deals with its award-winning restaurant **Reform** (www.reformrestaurant.co.uk; mains £15-22; ☺noon-2.30pm & 7-9pm Wed-Sat, noon-3pm Sun).

Bail House   B&B ££
(☑01522-541000; www.bailhouse.co.uk; 34 Bailgate; d/f from £84/134; P☎▩) Stone walls, worn flagstones, secluded gardens and one room with an extraordinary timber-vaulted

ceiling are just some of the charms of this lovingly restored Georgian town house in central Lincoln. There's limited on-site parking, a garden and a children's playground, and even a seasonal heated outdoor swimming pool. Family rooms sleep four.

✖ Eating

Stokes High Bridge Café
CAFE £

(www.stokes-coffee.co.uk; 207 High St; dishes £5-9; ⊙8am-5pm Mon-Sat, 11.30am-4pm Sun; 🐾🚲📶) A Lincoln landmark, this soaring 1540-built black-and-white Tudor building is England's only one atop a medieval bridge (1160). Within its preserved half-timbered interior, 1892-established, family-run roastery Stokes brews superb coffees made from speciality beans. Classic fare includes English breakfasts, traditional roasts and afternoon teas.

Cheese Society
CHEESE £

(www.thecheesesociety.co.uk; 1 St Martin's Lane; dishes £5-9, cheese boards £9-18; ⊙kitchen 11am-3.30pm Mon-Fri, to 4pm Sat, shop 10am-4.30pm Mon-Fri, to 5pm Sat) Not only does this light, bright place stock over 90 mostly British cheeses, it also serves them at its 12-seat cafe. Try its elaborate cheese boards or dishes such as twice-baked Dorset Blue Vinney soufflé or Wensleydale and herb scones with smoked salmon.

Brown's Pie Shop
PIES, BRITISH £ £

(☎01522-527330; www.brownspieshop.co.uk; 33 Steep Hill; mains £9.75-26.50; ⊙noon-2.30pm & 5-9.30pm Mon-Fri, noon-9.30pm Sat, to 8pm Sun) Hearty 'pot pies' (no pastry bottoms) at this long-established, quintessentially British restaurant are stuffed with locally sourced beef, rabbit and game. Pies aside, traditional dishes include Lincolnshire sausages with caramelised onion gravy and slow-roasted pork belly.

★ Bronze Pig
BRITISH £££

(☎01522-524817; www.thebronzepig.co.uk; 4 Burton Rd; mains £16-27; ⊙by reservation 6.30-10pm Wed-Sat, 11.30am-2pm Sun) BBC *MasterChef* finalist Irishman Eamonn Hunt and Sicilian chef Pompeo Siracusa have taken Lincoln's dining scene by storm since opening the Bronze Pig. Their exceptional Modern British cooking has an Italian accent and ingredients are locally sourced. Reserve well ahead and prepare to be wowed. It also has four deluxe guest rooms (doubles from £105).

Jews House
EUROPEAN £££

(☎01522-524851; www.jewshouserestaurant.co.uk; 15 The Strait (Steep Hill); mains £16.50-25.50; ⊙7-9.30pm Tue, noon-2pm & 7-9.30pm Wed-Sat) This local favourite serves gourmet fare (roast wood pigeon, truffle custard and bacon foam; baked lemon sole with scallop mousse) in one of England's oldest houses, the 1160-built Romanesque Jews House.

🍷 Drinking & Nightlife

Cosy Club
BAR

(www.cosyclub.co.uk; Sincil St; ⊙9am-11pm Sun-Wed, to midnight Thu, to 1am Fri & Sat; 🐾) Spectacularly converted with soaring skylit ceilings, this 1848-built corn exchange now contains one of Lincoln's liveliest bars. Along with cocktails like English Rose (gin, rosewater, strawberries and sparkling wine) and the Earl's Breakfast (vodka, Earl Grey tea and lime juice), it serves breakfast, brunch, tapas and international dishes.

Strugglers Inn
PUB

(www.strugglers-lincoln.co.uk; 83 Westgate; ⊙noon-midnight Tue & Wed, to 1am Thu-Sat, to 11pm Sun & Mon) A sunny, walled, courtyard beer garden out the back, an interior warmed by an open fire and a superb selection of real ales on tap make this the pick of Lincoln's independent pubs.

Engine Shed
LIVE MUSIC

(☎0871 220 0260; www.engineshed.co.uk; Brayford Pool) Lincoln's largest live-music venue occupies a former railway-container storage facility. Past acts have included Kings of Leon, Fat Boy Slim and Manic Street Preachers. Music aside, it also hosts sports events, comedy and pop-up markets.

❶ Information

Tourist Office (☎01522-545458; www.visitlincoln.com; 9 Castle Hill; ⊙10am-5pm Mon-Sat, 10.30am-4pm Sun) In a half-timbered, 16th-century building.

❶ Getting There & Away

BUS

The **bus station** (Melville St) is just northeast of the train station in the new town.

Stagecoach buses include bus 1 to Grantham (£5.60, 1½ hours, hourly Monday to Saturday, five on Sunday).

TRAIN

The train station is 250m east of the Brayford Waterfront development in the new town.

Boston £14.40, 1¼ hours, hourly, change at Sleaford

London King's Cross £79.50, 2¼ hours, up to three per hour; change in Newark or Peterborough

Newark-on-Trent Newark Castle; £5.40, 25 minutes, up to two per hour

Nottingham £11.90, one hour, hourly

Sheffield £15.30, 1¼ hours, hourly

Boston

☑ 01205 / POP 35,124

It's hard to believe that sleepy Boston was the inspiration for its larger and more famous American cousin. Although no Boston citizens sailed on the *Mayflower,* the port became a conduit for persecuted Puritans fleeing Nottinghamshire for religious freedom in the Netherlands and America. In the 1630s the fiery sermons of Boston vicar John Cotton inspired many locals to follow their lead, among them the ancestors of John Quincy Adams, the sixth American president. These pioneers founded a namesake town in the new colony of Massachusetts and the rest, as they say, is history.

Sights

Maud Foster Windmill   HISTORIC BUILDING

(☑ 01205-352188; www.maudfoster.co.uk; 16 Willoughby Rd; adult/child £4/2; ⊘ 10am-5pm Wed & Sat) About 800m northeast of Market Pl, England's tallest working windmill, with five sails rather than the usual four, has seven creaking, trembling floors reached by steep, ladder-like staircases; it sells bags of flour milled on-site. Self-caterers can stay in the granary next door (double from £430 for three nights including a windmill tour and parking; children not permitted).

Guildhall   MUSEUM

(☑ 01205-365954; www.bostonguildhall.co.uk; South St; ⊘ 10.30am-3.30pm Wed-Sat) **FREE** Before escaping to the New World, the Pilgrim Fathers were briefly imprisoned in the 14th-century Guildhall. It's one of Lincolnshire's oldest brick buildings, dating from the 1390s and situated close to the River

---

LINCOLNSHIRE: BOMBER COUNTY

The Royal Air Force (RAF) was formed in 1918 following WWI and two years later its college was established in Lincolnshire. During WWII, England's 'Bomber County' was home to numerous squadrons and by 1945 had more airfields (49) than any other in the country. US Navy flying boats flew antisubmarine patrols from here and B-29 bombers were also based here.

Just south of Lincoln, the 2018-opened International Bomber Command Centre has a moving memorial and an attached museum. Lincoln's tourist office has details of other aviation legacies throughout the county.

International Bomber Command Centre (☑ 01522-514755; www.internationalbcc. co.uk; Kanwick Hill; memorial free, museum adult/child £7.20/4.50; ⊘ memorial 24hr, museum 9.30am-5pm Tue-Sun) Opened in 2018, this 4.5-hectare site 1.5 miles south of Lincoln centres on a 31m-high metallic spire (at 102ft, the exact length of the wingspan of a Lancaster Bomber) surrounded by rusted-metal walls inscribed with the names of the 57,861 men and women who served and supported Britain's Bomber Command. Next to the memorial, a state-of-the-art museum has high-tech interactive displays covering the history of Bomber Command, including poignant stories from those who witnessed WWII's bombings first-hand.

Battle of Britain Memorial Flight Visitor Centre (☑ 01522-552222; www.lincolnshire. gov.uk; Dogdyke Rd, Coningsby; museum free, hangar tours adult/child £8.50/4.60; ⊘ hangar tours by reservation 10am-5pm Mon-Fri) See Spitfires and the four-engined *Lancaster City of Lincoln* at the Battle of Britain Memorial Flight Visitor Centre on 90-minute hangar tours. Bus IC5 (£4.60, one hour, hourly Monday to Saturday) runs here from Lincoln.

Lincolnshire Aviation Heritage Centre (☑ 01790-763207; www.lincsaviation.co.uk; East Kirkby, near Spilsby; adult/child £8.50/3; ⊘ 9.30am-5pm Mon-Sat Easter-Oct, 10am-4pm Mon-Sat Nov-Easter) An original WWII Bomber Command airfield complete with its original wartime control tower is now home to the Lincolnshire Aviation Heritage Centre, with wartime planes and automobiles on display. It's 30 miles southeast of Lincoln via the A153; there's no public transport.

Witham. Inside are fun interactive exhibits, as well as a restored 16th-century courtroom and a recreated Georgian kitchen. Regular temporary exhibitions are also free.

St Botolph's Church   CHURCH
(www.parish-of-boston.org.uk; Church St; tower adult/child £5/free; ⊙ church visiting hours 8.30am-4pm Mon-Sat, from 7.30am Sun, tower 10am-3.30pm Mon-Sat, from 1pm Sun, last climb 3pm) Built in the early 14th century, St Botolph's Church (the name Boston is a corruption of 'St Botolph's Stone') is known locally as the Stump, in reference to the truncated appearance of its 88m-high tower. Puff your way up the 209 steps on a clear day and you'll see out to Lincoln, 32 miles away.

❶ Getting There & Away

Trains connect Boston with Lincoln (£14.40, 1¼ hours, hourly) via a change at Sleaford, and with Nottingham (£18.20, 1½ hours, hourly).

Stamford

🎵 01780 / POP 19,704

One of England's prettiest towns, Stamford seems frozen in time, with elegant streets lined with honey-coloured limestone buildings and hidden alleyways dotted with alehouses, interesting restaurants and small independent boutiques. A forest of historic church spires rises overhead and the gently gurgling River Welland meanders through the town centre. It's a favourite with filmmakers seeking the postcard vision of Eng-

---

THE HOME OF SIR ISAAC NEWTON
....

Sir Isaac Newton fans may feel the gravitational pull of the great man's birthplace, **Woolsthorpe Manor** (NT; 🎵 01476-862823; www.nationaltrust.org.uk; Water Lane; house & grounds adult/child £7.70/3.85, grounds only £3.86/2.68; ⊙ 11am-5pm Wed-Mon mid-Mar–Oct, Fri-Sun Nov–mid-Mar), about 8 miles south of Grantham. The humble 17th-century house contains reconstructions of Newton's rooms; the apple that inspired his theory of gravity allegedly fell from the tree in the garden. There's a nifty kids' science room and a cafe. Take Centrebus 9 from Grantham (£2.80, 20 minutes, four per day Monday to Saturday).

---

land, and has appeared in everything from *Pride and Prejudice* to the *Da Vinci Code*.

◉ Sights

★ **Burghley House**   HISTORIC BUILDING
(www.burghley.co.uk; house & garden adult/child £19/10, garden only £13/9; ⊙ house 11am-5pm Sat-Thu mid-Mar–Oct, garden 11am-5pm daily mid-Mar–Oct, park 8am-6pm or dusk if earlier daily year-round) Set in more than 810 hectares of grounds, landscaped by Lancelot 'Capability' Brown, opulent Burghley House (bur-lee) was built by Queen Elizabeth's chief adviser William Cecil, whose descendants still live here. It bristles with cupolas, pavilions, belvederes and chimneys; the lavish staterooms are a particular highlight. In early September, the renowned Burghley Horse Trials take place here. The estate is 1.3 miles southeast of Stamford; follow the marked path for 15 minutes through the park by Stamford's train station.

St Mary's Church   CHURCH
(www.stamfordbenefice.com; St Mary's St; ⊙ 8am-6pm, hours can vary) An endearingly wonky 13th-century broach spire tops the 12th-century St Mary's Church. Classical concerts are held here in summer; tickets (from £14) are sold at Stamford's tourist office.

⊨ Sleeping

William Cecil at Stamford   HISTORIC HOTEL **££**
(🎵 01780-750070; www.hillbrookehotels.co.uk; High St, St Martin's; s/d/f incl breakfast from £100/110/175; P ☎) Within the Burghley Estate, this stunningly renovated hotel has 27 rooms inspired by Burghley House, with period furnishings and luxuries such as Egyptian cotton linens and complimentary organic vodka. Family rooms sleep two adults and two kids; interconnecting rooms are also available. The smart restaurant turns out stylish British classics and opens to a wicker-chair-furnished patio.

★ **George Hotel**   HISTORIC HOTEL **£££**
(🎵 01780-750750; www.georgehotelofstamford.com; 71 High St, St Martin's; s/d/ste/4-poster incl breakfast from £130/215/290/320; P ☎ ☎) Stamford's luxurious landmark inn opened its doors in 1597. Today its 45 individually sized and decorated rooms impeccably blend period charm and modern elegance. Superior Modern British cuisine is served at its oak-panelled restaurant, while its more informal garden-room restaurant hosts af-

ternoon teas in its courtyard. Its two bars include a champagne bar.

Drinking

Paten & Co
PUB

(www.kneadpubs.co.uk; 7 All Saints' Pl; ⊙11am-midnight Mon-Sat, noon-6pm Sun; 🛜) When the current owners stripped back this 18th-century building during renovations, they uncovered Paten & Co wine and spirits merchants' painted sign and got permission to use the original name. Twists on old-fashioned cocktails (eg raspberry and thyme Collins) are its speciality, along with charcoal-smoked street food. The top floor has breathtaking views of All Saints' church spires.

All Saints Brewery
BREWERY

(www.allsaintsbrewery.co.uk; 22 All Saints' St; ⊙noon-11pm Mon-Sat, to 10.30pm Sun; 🛜) 🍷 Victorian-era steam-brewing equipment is used to make organic fruit beers at this operation, which has revived the site's original 1825 brewery after it was shuttered for several decades. Try its cherry, strawberry, raspberry and apricot brews at the attached pub or in the umbrella-shaded courtyard. Bar staff can advise on informal brewery tours.

Tobie Norris
PUB

(www.kneadpubs.co.uk; 12 St Paul's St; ⊙10am-11pm Mon-Thu, to midnight Fri & Sat, noon-10.30pm Sun) A wonderful stone-walled, flagstone-floored pub, the Tobie Norris has a warren of rooms with open fireplaces, a sunny, flower-filled courtyard and local ales. Wood-fired pizzas are a highlight of its wide-ranging menu.

ⓘ Information

Tourist Office (☑ 01780-755611; www.south westlincs.com; 27 St Mary's St; ⊙9.30am-5pm Mon-Sat; 🛜) Inside the Stamford Arts Centre.

ⓘ Getting There & Away

BUS

Centrebus 4 runs to Grantham (£4.60, 1¼ hours, three per day Monday to Saturday) and Centrebus 9 serves Oakham (£3.50, 45 minutes, hourly Monday to Saturday).

TRAIN

Trains run to Birmingham (£32.80, 1½ hours, hourly), Nottingham (£25.30, 1¾ hours, hourly) with a change in Leicester (£19.10, 40 minutes), and Stansted Airport (£38.40, 1¾ hours, hourly) via Peterborough (£8.30, 15 minutes).

WORTH A TRIP

ALTHORP HOUSE

The ancestral home of the Spencer family, **Althorp House** (☑01604-770107; www.spencerofalthorp.com; adult/child £18.50/11; ⊙noon-5pm mid-Jul–early Sep) – pronounced 'altrup' – is the final resting place of Diana, Princess of Wales, commemorated by a memorial. The outstanding art collection features works by Rubens, Gainsborough and Van Dyck. Profits go to charities supported by the Princess Diana Memorial Fund.

Althorp is off the A428, 5.5 miles northwest of Northampton, and is not served by public transport; a taxi costs around £20.

LEICESTERSHIRE

Leicestershire was a vital creative hub during the Industrial Revolution, but its factories were a major target for German air raids in WWII and most towns in the county still bear the scars of war-time bombing. Nevertheless, there are some impressive remains, from Elizabethan castles to Roman ruins. The busy, multicultural capital Leicester is enjoying fame arising from the 2012 discovery and 2015 reburial of King Richard III's remains.

ⓘ Getting There & Around

Leicester is well served by buses and trains. For bus routes and timetables, visit the 'Roads and Transport' pages at www.leicestershire.gov.uk.

Regular buses connect Rutland to Leicester, Stamford and other surrounding towns.

Leicester

☑ 0116 / POP 348,300

Built over the buried ruins of two millennia of history, Leicester (*les*-ter) suffered at the hands of the Luftwaffe and postwar planners but an influx of textile workers from India and Pakistan from the 1960s transformed the city into a bustling multicultural hub.

The astonishing 2012 discovery and 2013 identification of the remains of King Richard III in a Leicester car park sparked a flurry of developments, including a spiffing visitor centre on the site, and the restoration

GEORGE WASHINGTON'S ANCESTRAL HOME

Sulgrave Manor (☑ 01295-760205; www.sulgravemanor.org.uk; Manor Rd, Sulgrave; adult/child £7.20/3.60; ⊙ 11am-5pm Thu, Fri & Sun Apr-Sep) was built by Lawrence Washington in 1539. The Washington family lived here for almost 120 years before Colonel John Washington, the great-grandfather of America's first president George Washington, sailed to Virginia in 1656.

Sulgrave Manor is 20 miles southwest of Northampton, just off the B4525 near Banbury; you'll need your own wheels to get here.

of the cathedral, where the king was reburied in 2015.

⊙ Sights

★ King Richard III: Dynasty, Death & Discovery   MUSEUM

(www.kriii.com; 4a St Martin's Pl; adult/child £8.95/4.75; ⊙ 10am-4pm Sun-Fri, to 5pm Sat) Built following the incredible 2012 discovery of King Richard III's remains, Leicester's high-tech King Richard III visitor centre encompasses three fascinating sections. Dynasty explores his rise to become the final Plantagenet king. Death delves into the Battle of Bosworth, when Richard became the last English king to be killed in battle. Discovery details the University of Leicester's archaeological dig and identification, and lets you view the site of the grave in which he was found.

Its Murder, Mystery and Mayhem exhibition covers the key players, battles and milestones of the Wars of the Roses between the House of York (symbolised by a white rose) and House of Lancaster (red rose).

★ Leicester Cathedral   CATHEDRAL

(☑ 0116-261 5357; www.leicestercathedral.org; Peacock Lane; by donation; ⊙ 10am-5pm Mon-Sat, 12.30-2.30pm Sun) Pride of place at this substantial medieval cathedral goes to the contemporary limestone tomb atop the vault where the remains of King Richard III were reburied in 2015. Look too for the striking carvings on the cathedral's roof supports.

One-hour guided tours (adult/child £5/ free) take place at 11.30am and 2.30pm from Monday to Friday. On Saturday, 30-minute

King Richard III tours (adult/child £3/free) depart on the hour from 11am to 4pm.

National Space Centre   MUSEUM

(www.spacecentre.co.uk; Exploration Drive; adult/child £14/11; ⊙ 10am-4pm Mon-Fri, to 5pm Sat & Sun) Although British space missions usually launch from French Guiana or Kazakhstan, Leicester's space museum is a fascinating introduction to the mysteries of the spheres. The ill-fated 2003 Beagle 2 mission to Mars was controlled from here. Fun, kid-friendly displays cover everything from astronomy to the status of current space missions. It's 1.5 miles north of the city centre. Take bus 54 or 54A (£1.60, 15 minutes, every 10 minutes Monday to Saturday, every 20 minutes Sunday) from Haymarket bus station (Charles St).

Leicester Castle   RUINS

(Castle View) Scattered around the Newarke Houses Museum (☑ 0116-225 4980; www.leicester.gov.uk/leisure-and-culture; The Newarke; ⊙ 10am-4pm Mon-Sat, from 11am Sun) FREE are the ruins of Leicester's medieval castle, where Richard III spent his final days before the Battle of Bosworth. The monumental gateway known as the Magazine (Newarke St) was once a storehouse for cannonballs and gunpowder. Dating from the 12th century and clad in Georgian brickwork, the Great Hall (www.dmu.ac.uk; Castle Yard) stands behind a 15th-century gate near the church of St Mary de Castro (www.stmarydecastro.co.uk; 15 Castle View; ⊙ noon-2pm Mon-Fri, 2-4pm Sat), where Geoffrey Chaucer was married in 1366.

New Walk Museum & Art Gallery   MUSEUM, GALLERY

(☑ 0116-225 4900; www.leicester.gov.uk/leisure-and-culture; 53 New Walk; ⊙ 11am-4.30pm Mon-Fri, to 5pm Sat & Sun) FREE Highlights of this grand Victorian museum include the dinosaur galleries, the painting collection (with works by Turner and Degas), ceramics by Picasso, and the Egyptian gallery, where real mummies rub shoulders with displays about Boris Karloff's 1932 film The Mummy.

Jewry Wall Museum   MUSEUM

(www.visitleicester.info; St Nicholas Circle; ⊙ 11am-4.30pm Feb-Oct) FREE This museum exploring the history of Leicester from Roman times to the modern day was undergoing renovations at the time of writing, and was expected to reopen to the public in spring 2019. In front of the museum is the Jewry

Leicester

Wall, part of Leicester's Roman baths. Tiles and masonry from the baths were incorporated in the walls of neighbouring **St Nich-** **olas Church** (www.stnicholasleicester.com; St Nicholas Circle; admission by donation; ⊙2-4pm Sat, 6.30-8.30pm Sun).

🏃 Activities

Great Central Railway
RAIL

(☑ 01509-632323; www.gcrailway.co.uk; return adult/child £17/9) Steam locomotives chug from Leicester North station on Redhill Circle to Loughborough Central, following the 8-mile route along which Thomas Cook ran the original package tour in 1841. The locos operate most weekends year-round and some summer weekdays; check timetables online.

For Leicester North station, take bus 25 (£1.60, 20 minutes, every 10 minutes) from Haymarket bus station (p456).

🛏 Sleeping

★ Hotel Maiyango
BOUTIQUE HOTEL ££

(☑ 0116-251 8898; www.maiyango.com; 13-21 St Nicholas Pl; d/ste from £79/109; ✹ �) At the end of the pedestrian High St, this sophisticated pad has 14 spacious rooms, decorated with handmade furniture, contemporary art and massive TVs. Superb cocktails are served at its rooftop bar (guests only) with city-skyline views.

Belmont Hotel
HOTEL ££

(☑ 0116-254 4773; www.belmonthotel.co.uk; 20 De Montfort St; s/d/f/ste from £62/81/105/139; P ✹ @ �) Owned and run by the same family for four generations, the 19th-century Belmont has 74 stylish, contemporary, individually designed rooms and a fantastic location overlooking leafy New Walk. Family rooms have a double bed and bunks. Its restaurant is highly regarded; the two bars, Jamie's and Bowie's, open to a terrace and a conservatory respectively.

🍴 Eating

Walkers
PIES £

(Walker & Son; www.walkerspies.co.uk; 4-6 Cheapside; dishes £1-5; ⊙ 8am-5pm Mon-Sat) For a quick lunch, you can't beat Walkers' towering pork pies. Walkers was founded in Leicester in 1824; it has since sold its famous crisp brand, but the pies remain a family business today. Other pie varieties include chicken, bacon and mushroom, farmhouse steak, game and pulled pork. There's a handful of pavement tables out the front.

Bobby's
INDIAN, VEGETARIAN £

(☑ 0116-266 0106; www.eatatbobbys.com; 154-156 Belgrave Rd; dishes £4-8; ⊙ 11am-10pm Mon-Fri, from 10am Sat & Sun; ✎) The top pick along Leicester's Indian restaurant-lined Golden Mile is 1970s-established Bobby's, serving all-vegetarian classics.

Good Earth
VEGETARIAN £

(☑ 0116-262 6260; www.facebook.com/veggiegoodearth; 19 Free Lane; mains £3.50-7; ⊙ noon-3pm Mon-Fri, to 4pm Sat; ✎) This venerable vegetarian cafe has a daily changing menu of wholesome veggie bakes, huge salads and homemade cakes, and hosts occasional evening events such as live-music gigs. Cash only.

Boot Room
BISTRO ££

(☑ 0116-262 2555; www.thebootroomeaterie.co.uk; 29 Millstone Lane; mains £13.25-25; ⊙ noon-2pm & 6-9.30pm Tue-Sat; �) A former shoe factory now houses this contemporary independent bistro. Premium ingredients are used in dishes spanning sea bass with fondant pota-

---

THE BATTLE OF BOSWORTH

Given a few hundred years, every battlefield ends up simply a field, but the site of the **Battle of Bosworth** (☑ 01455-290429; www.bosworthbattlefield.org.uk; Ambion Lane, Sutton Cheney; adult/child £8.95/5.75, guided walk £4.50/3; ⊙ heritage centre 10am-5pm, last admission 4pm, grounds 7am-dusk) – where Richard III met his maker in 1485 – is enlivened by an entertaining heritage centre full of skeletons and musket balls; guided walks around the site last 90 minutes. Enthusiasts in period costume reenact the battle each August.

Although it lasted just a few hours, the Battle of Bosworth marked the end of the Plantagenet dynasty and the start of the Tudor era. This was where the mortally wounded Richard III famously proclaimed: 'A horse, a horse, my kingdom for a horse'. (Actually, he didn't: the quote was invented by that great Tudor propagandist William Shakespeare.)

After visiting the battlefield, head for lunch at the 17th-century coaching inn, **Hercules Revived** (☑ 01455-699336; www.herculesrevived.co.uk; Sutton Cheney; mains £11.50-20; ⊙ kitchen noon-2.30pm & 6-9pm Mon-Sat, noon-4pm, bar to 11.30pm daily), which serves top-tier gastropub food.

The battlefield is 16 miles southwest of Leicester at Sutton Cheney, off the A447.

toes, king prawns, squid and prawn bisque to duck leg with Puy lentils and tamarind sauce. Save room for the soufflé of the day for dessert.

⭐ **John's House**　　　　BRITISH £££
(☑ 01509-415569; www.johnshouse.co.uk; Stonehurst Farm, 139-141 Loughborough Rd, Mountsorrel; 2-/3-course lunch menus £26/30, 2-/3-/7-course dinner menus £48/55/124; ⊘ noon-2pm & 7-9pm Tue-Sat) Chef John Duffin was born here on 16th-century Stonehurst Farm, 8 miles north of Leicester. After working in Michelin-starred restaurants, he returned in 2014 to open his restaurant, and has since gained a Michelin star of his own. Multicourse menus (no à la carte) showcase his imagination in dishes like creamed Porthilly oysters with smoked Mountsorrel eels and foraged loveage.

Still a working farm today, Stonehurst (www.stonehurstfarm.co.uk) also has a fabulous farm shop, a tearoom, a petting farm and a motor museum housing vintage vehicles.

🍷 **Drinking & Nightlife**

Gate 38　　　　COCKTAIL BAR
(38b Belvoir St; ⊘ 9pm-3.30am Fri & Sat; 🛜) Look for the tiny yellow airport-gate sign on Albion St to find this super-cool speakeasy with aeroplane-cabin seats and plane windows with pictures of Leicester's lights mimicking flying in at night. Its 'departure board' lists destinations for which cocktails are named, eg Kyoto, with sake, tomato juice and smoked pepper, or Buenos Aires, with Pisco, lime, ginger beer and cucumber.

Bread & Honey　　　　COFFEE
(www.breadnhoneycoffee.com; 15 King St; ⊘ 7.45am-3pm Mon-Fri; 🛜) Beans from single farm estates and co-ops sourced and roasted by London-based Monmouth are brewed at this little bare-boards hole in the wall; the flat whites are the best for miles around. Steaming soups, preservative-free bread, made-from-scratch hot dishes and fantastic cakes (chocolate fudge cake with white-chocolate icing; honey-glazed banana loaf) are all available, too.

Globe　　　　PUB
(www.eversosensible.com/globe; 43 Silver St; ⊘ 11am-11pm Sun-Thu, to 1am Fri & Sat) In the atmospheric Lanes – a tangle of alleys south of the High St – this old-fashioned pub has fine draught ales and a crowd that rates its drinks by quality rather than quantity.

HAMMER & PINCERS

For a mind-blowing meal, head to this idyllic **gastropub** (☑ 01509-880735; www.hammerandpincers.co.uk; 5 East Rd, Wymeswold; mains £19-27.50, 7-/10-course menu £45/60, with wine £75/100; ⊘ noon-2pm & 6-9.30pm Tue-Sat, to 4pm Sun; �) set in bucolic gardens at the edge of the cute village of Wymeswold. Everything is homemade, down to the breads and condiments; seasonal specialities might include cider-cured sea trout, gin-marinated pheasant and rosemary rhubarb sorbet. Don't miss its signature twice-baked cheese soufflé. It's 16 miles north of Leicester via the A46.

⭐ **Entertainment**

Cookie　　　　LIVE MUSIC
(☑ 0116-253 1212; www.thecookieleicester.co.uk; 68 High St; ⊘ bar 3-11pm Tue & Wed, from noon Thu, noon-1am Fri & Sat, noon-5pm Sun, concert hours vary) With a capacity of 350 in its brick cellar, this indie venue is a brilliant place to catch live bands and comedy nights in an intimate setting.

Curve Theatre　　　　THEATRE
(☑ 0116-242 3595; www.curveonline.co.uk; 60 Rutland St; backstage tours adult/child £5/4) This sleek artistic space hosts big-name shows and some innovative modern theatre, and has good accessibility for theatregoers who are aurally or visually impaired. Call the ticket office to book backstage tours.

De Montfort Hall　　　　LIVE MUSIC
(☑ 0116-233 3111; www.demonforthall.co.uk; Granville Rd) Orchestras, ballets, musicals and other big song-and-dance performances are on the bill at this huge venue.

ℹ️ **Information**

Tourist Office (☑ 0116-299 4444; www.visitleicester.info; 51 Gallowtree Gate; ⊘ 10.30am-4.30pm Mon-Fri, from 9.30am Sat, 11am-4pm Sun) Helpful office with reams of city and county info.

ℹ️ **Getting There & Away**

BUS
Intercity buses operate from **St Margaret's bus station** (Gravel St), north of the city centre. The useful Skylink bus runs to East Midlands Airport

STOKE BRUERNE & THE GRAND UNION CANAL

Brightly painted barges frequent this charming little village 8.2 miles south of Northampton on the Grand Union Canal, the main thoroughfare of England's canal network. From here, you can follow the waterways all the way to Leicester, Birmingham or London.

A converted corn mill houses the entertaining **Canal Museum** (www.canalrivertrust.org.uk/thecanalmuseum; 3 Bridge Rd; adult/child £4.75/3.10; ⊙10am-5pm Apr-Oct, shorter hours Nov-Mar), which charts the history of the canal network and its bargemen, lock-keepers and pit workers. Scale models abound; outside you can see the historic narrowboat *Sculptor*, listed on the National Historic Boat Register.

The **Boat Inn** (☏01604-862428; www.boatinn.co.uk; mains restaurant £15-25, bistro £7-13; ⊙restaurant noon-2pm & 7-9pm Tue-Sat, noon-2.30pm Sun, bar 9am-11pm Mon-Sat, to 10.30pm Sun) is a canalside landmark; with picnic tables on the quay, this sociable local pub has a relaxed bistro serving pub classics until 9pm, a more formal restaurant with refined dishes such as steaks, and a great range of ales.

(£7.30, one hour, at least hourly, 24 hours) and continues on to Derby.

National Express services:

Coventry £5.50, 45 minutes, three daily
London Victoria £11.60, 2¾ hours, hourly
Nottingham £4.60, 45 minutes, up to two per hour

TRAIN

East Midlands trains:

Birmingham £19.20, one hour, up to two per hour
London St Pancras £86.50, 1¼ hours, up to four per hour

Rutland

Tiny Rutland was merged with Leicestershire in 1974, but in 1997 regained its 'independence' as England's smallest county.

Rutland centres on Rutland Water, a vast artificial reservoir created by the damming of the Gwash Valley in 1976. Covering 4.19 sq miles, the reservoir attracts some 20,000 birds, including ospreys.

◉ Sights & Activities

Rutland Water
Nature Reserve   NATURE RESERVE

(www.rutlandwater.org.uk; Egleton; adult/child incl parking £6/3.50, binocular hire per day £5; ⊙9am-5pm Mar-Oct, to 4pm Nov-Feb) Near Oakham, the Rutland Water Nature Reserve has 31 hides throughout the reserve and a viewing section upstairs in the **Anglian Water Birdwatching Centre**, which has an exhibition on the area's abundant birdlife, including ospreys, long-tailed tits, lesser whitethroats, bullfinches, garden warblers and jays.

Look out too for water voles, which thrive here. The reserve's **Lyndon Visitor Centre** (☏01572-737378; www.rutlandwater.org.uk; Manton; adult/child incl parking £6/3.50; ⊙9am-5pm mid-Mar–early Sep), for which tickets are valid, opens during the warmer months.

Rutland Watersports   WATER SPORTS

(☏01780-460154; www.anglianwater.co.uk; Whitwell Leisure Park, Bull Brigg Lane, Whitwell; windsurf/kayak/SUP rental per hr from £20/8.50/10; ⊙9am-7pm Fri-Tue, to 8pm Wed & Thu Apr-Oct, shorter hours Nov-Mar) Aquatic activities offered by Rutland Watersports include windsurfing, kayaking and stand-up paddleboarding (SUP). You can hire gear or take lessons.

Rutland Belle   CRUISE

(☏01572-787630; www.rutlandwatercruises.com; Whitwell; adult/child £9.50/6.50; ⊙hourly noon-3pm Mon-Sat, from 11am Sun mid-Jul–Aug, shorter hours Apr–mid-Jul, Sep & Oct) Take a 45-minute round-trip cruise from Whitwell to Normanton on the southern shore of the Rutland reservoir. On some afternoons, it also runs later birdwatching cruises lasting 90 minutes (adult/child £22/13).

🛏 Sleeping & Eating

Hambleton Hall   HISTORIC HOTEL £££

(☏01572-756991; www.hambletonhall.com; Hambleton; s/d/ste incl breakfast from £225/310/625; P🅿🛜🐾🏊) One of England's finest country hotels, rambling former hunting lodge Hambleton Hall, built in 1881, sits on a peninsula jutting out into Rutland Water, 3 miles east of Oakham. Its luxuriant floral rooms and Michelin-starred restaurant (two-course lunch menu £31.50, three-/four-course dinner menus £75/95) are surrounded by gorgeous gardens, which also shelter an outdoor heated swimming pool (May to September).

Otters Fine Foods　DELI, CAFE **£**
(☑ 01572-756481; www.ottersfinefoods.co.uk; 19 Mill St, Oakham; dishes £5-8.50; ☺ 9am-5.30pm Mon-Sat) A storybook-pretty whitewashed cottage with a thatched roof houses this Oakham deli. Pick up sandwiches, quiches, soups, salads, cheeses, meats, charcuterie and more for a lakeside picnic, or preorder a hamper. If it's not picnic weather, dine at its in-store cafe.

Mill Street Pub & Kitchen　GASTROPUB **££**
(☑ 01572-729600; www.millstreetoakham.com; 6 Mill St, Oakham; mains £12.50-26.50; ☺ kitchen 7.30am-9pm Mon-Thu, to 9.45pm Fri & Sat, to 8pm Sun, bar 7.30am-11pm Mon-Thu, to midnight Fri & Sat, to 10.30pm Sun; 🛜🖉🖨) On Oakham's main shopping street, this handsome pub's dining spaces span a vaulted brick cellar, a glass conservatory and a sun-drenched terrace. Menu highlights include ham-hock and tarragon terrine with house-made piccalilli and toasted sourdough; there are vegan and kids' menus, and ales from Oakham's Grainstone brewery. Upstairs, seven contemporary rooms (doubles including breakfast from £90) are painted in beautiful countryside hues.

❶ Getting There & Away

Bus 9 links Oakham with Stamford (£3.50, 45 minutes, hourly Monday to Saturday) via Rutland Water's north shore.

Trains link Oakham with Leicester (£15.70, 30 minutes, hourly).

DERBYSHIRE

The Derbyshire countryside is painted in two distinct tones: the lush green of rolling valleys criss-crossed by dry-stone walls, and the barren mottled-brown hilltops of the high, wild moorlands. The biggest draw here is the Peak District National Park, which preserves some of England's most evocative scenery, attracting legions of hikers, climbers, cyclists and cave enthusiasts.

❶ Getting There & Away

East Midlands Airport (p464) is the nearest air hub, and Derby is well served by trains, but connecting services to smaller towns are few. In the Peak District, the Derwent Valley Line runs from Derby to Matlock. Edale and Hope lie on the Hope Valley Line from Sheffield to Manchester.

For a comprehensive list of Derbyshire bus routes, visit the 'Transport and Roads' pages at www.derbyshire.gov.uk.

Derby

☑ 01332 / POP 248,752
Gloriously sited at the southeastern edge of the Derbyshire hills that roll towards the Peak District, Derby is one of the Midlands' most energetic, creative cities. This was one of the crucibles of the Industrial Revolution: almost overnight, a sleepy market town was transformed into a major manufacturing

---

OFF THE BEATEN TRACK

CONKERS & THE NATIONAL FOREST

The National Forest (www.nationalforest.org) is an ambitious project to generate new areas of sustainable woodland by planting 30 million trees in Leicestershire, Derbyshire and Staffordshire, covering a total area of 51,800 hectares or 200 sq miles. More than 8.5 million saplings have already taken root. Visitor attractions here include the kid-friendly nature centre, **Conkers** (☑ 01283-216633; www.visitconkers.com; Rawdon Rd, Moira; adult/child £9.05/8.14; ☺ 10am-6pm Easter-Sep, to 5pm Oct-Easter). There are also several bike trails; bikes can be hired from **Hicks Lodge** (☑ 01530-274533; Willesley Wood Side, Moira; bike hire per 3hr/day adult/child £16/30; ☺ trails 8am-dusk, bike hire & cafe 9am-5pm Fri-Wed, to 9pm Thu mid-Feb-Oct, 10am-6pm Mon-Wed & Fri, 9am-9pm Thu, to 5pm Sat & Sun Nov-mid-Feb).

If you fancy overnighting, the **National Forest YHA** (☑ 0845 371 9672; www.yha.org. uk; 48 Bath Lane, Moira; dm/d/f from £13/50/70; 🅿🛜) 🍃 has impressive eco features (such as rainwater harvesting and solar biomass boiler usage), 23 spotless en-suite rooms, bike storage, and a restaurant serving local produce and organic wines. It's 300m west of Conkers along Bath Lane.

centre, producing everything from silk to bone china and, later, locomotives and Rolls-Royce aircraft engines. The city suffered the ravages of industrial decline in the 1980s, but bounced back with impressive cultural developments and a rejuvenated riverfront.

◎ Sights

Royal Crown Derby Factory MUSEUM, FACTORY
(☑01332-712800; www.royalcrownderby.co.uk; Osmaston Rd; museum & factory tour adult/child £5/2.50, museum only £2/1; ⊙museum 10am-4pm Mon-Sat, factory tours 11am & 1.30pm Mon-Thu, 11am Fri) Derby's historic potteries still turn out some of the finest bone china in England, from edgy Asian-inspired designs to the kind of stuff your grandma collects. Reservations are essential for factory tours, which last 90 minutes and include a visit to the museum. Royal Crown Derby's china (including seconds and discontinued items) is sold at its on-site shop, and is used as tableware at its elegant tearoom.

Derby Cathedral CATHEDRAL
(☑01332-341201; www.derbycathedral.org; 18 Iron-gate; cathedral by donation, tower tours adult/child £5/4; ⊙cathedral 8.30am-5.30pm, tower tours vary) Founded in AD 943 and reconstructed in the 18th century, Derby Cathedral's vaulted ceiling towers above a fine collection of medieval tombs, including the opulent grave of the oft-married Bess of Hardwick, who at various times held court at Hardwick Hall, Chatsworth House and Bolsover Castle. Check the website for dates when historians lead tours up 189 steps into the Tudor tower, the second-highest bell tower in the UK.

Peregrine falcons nest in the tower; follow their progress at www.derbyperegrines.blog-spot.com.

Derby Museum & Art Gallery MUSEUM
(www.derbymuseums.org; The Strand; ⊙10am-5pm Tue-Sat, noon-4pm Sun) FREE Local history and industry displays include fine ceramics produced by Royal Crown Derby and an archaeology gallery, along with paintings by renowned artist Joseph Wright of Derby (1734–97).

Quad GALLERY, CINEMA
(☑01332-290606; www.derbyquad.co.uk; Market Pl; gallery free, cinema tickets adult/child £9/7; ⊙gallery 11am-5pm Mon-Sat, from noon Sun) A striking modernist cube on Market Pl, Quad contains a futuristic art gallery and an art-house cinema.

🛏 Sleeping

Coach House B&B £
(☑01332-554423; www.coachhousederby.com; 185a Duffield Rd; s/d from £47/60; ℗🖤🍴) Surrounded by a rambling cottage garden, this red-brick 1860-built property 1.7 miles north of Derby has four countrified rooms with richly patterned wallpapers in the main house, and three contemporary loft-style rooms in the superbly converted stables. Personalised touches include free homemade brownies. Vegan and gluten-free breakfasts are possible (reserve ahead). Off-street parking is first come, first served.

Farmhouse at Mackworth INN £££
(☑01332-824324; www.thwfarmhouseatmackworth.com; 60 Ashbourne Rd; d/f incl breakfast from £85/110; ℗🍴) The Farmhouse at Mackworth is just 2.5 miles northwest of Derby in undulating countryside, with the bonus of plentiful free parking. The designer inn's 10 boutique rooms have checked fabrics, rustic timber cladding and chrome fittings, plus amenities including Nespresso machines and fluffy robes. There's a fabulous bar and a restaurant with a Josper charcoal oven.

Cathedral Quarter Hotel HOTEL £££
(☑01332-546080; www.cathedralquarterhotel.com; 16 St Mary's Gate; d/ste incl breakfast from £95/145; 🌀🍴) A bell's peal from the cathedral, this grand Georgian edifice houses a 38-room hotel. The service is as polished as the grand marble staircase, and there's an on-site spa and a fine-dining restaurant.

★ The Cow INN £££
(☑01332-824297; www.cowdalbury.com; The Green, Dalbury Lees; d incl breakfast from £145; ℗🖤🍴) Stunningly restored in 2017, this whitewashed 19th-century inn 6.5 miles west of Derby has solid oak floors, stone walls and timber-lined ceilings. Its 12 individually styled rooms range from Victorian and art deco to retro vintage, and feature locally handcrafted mattresses and Egyptian cotton sheets. The bar-restaurant's stools are fashioned from milk cans and food is sourced within a 30-mile radius.

🍴 Eating

Jack Rabbits CAFE £
(☑01332-206322; www.jackrabbitskitchen.com; 53-55 Queen St; dishes £4.85-9; ⊙8.30am-5pm Mon-Sat, 10am-4pm Sun; 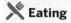) Jack Rabbits' sunlit cafe is perfect for lazy grazing on in-

KEDLESTON HALL

Sitting pretty in vast landscaped grounds, neoclassical **Kedleston Hall** (NT; ☑01332-842191; www.nationaltrust.org.uk; Kedleston Rd, Quarndon; house & gardens adult/child £13.60/6.80, garden only £6.80/3.40; ☺house noon-5pm Sat-Thu Feb-Oct, garden 10am-6pm Feb-Oct, to 4pm Nov-Jan) is a must for fans of stately homes. Entering the house through a grand portico, you'll reach the breathtaking Marble Hall with massive alabaster columns and statues of Greek deities.

The Curzon family has lived here since the 12th century, but the current wonder was built by Sir Nathaniel Curzon in 1758. Meanwhile, the poor old peasants in Kedleston village had their humble dwellings moved a mile down the road, as they interfered with the view. Ah, the good old days...

Highlights include Indian treasures amassed by Viceroy George Curzon and a domed, circular saloon modelled on the Pantheon in Rome, as well as 18th-century-style pleasure gardens.

Kedleston Hall is 5 miles northwest of Derby, off the A52. Bus 114 between Derby and Ashbourne (£3.60, 25 minutes, up to six daily Monday to Saturday) stops at the gates when the hall is open.

---

ternationally inspired dishes, from breakfast (Mexican huevos rancheros, French/American hybrid croque monsieur Benedict) through to lunch (Swedish potato pancake with a poached egg, pickled cucumber and sour cream). Breads, cakes and slices are baked in-house; coffee is from Nottingham roastery Outpost. 'Little bunnies' has a top-quality kids' menu.

Wonky Table　　　　　　　BISTRO ££

(☑01332-295000; www.wonkytable.co.uk; 32 Sadler Gate; mains lunch £8-10, dinner £13-19; ☺5-10pm Mon, noon-3pm & 5-10pm Tue-Fri, noon-3.30pm & 5-10pm Sat; ✐) Inside an inviting retro-vintage dining room with exposed-brick walls, Wonky Table features a slimmed-down daytime menu alongside salads and sandwiches, but it really comes into its own at dinner with dishes such as apricot-stuffed slow-roasted pork loin. Vegetarian options abound.

Darleys　　　　　MODERN BRITISH £££

(☑01332-364987; www.darleys.com; Waterfront, Darley Abbey Mill; mains £23-26.30, 2-/3-course lunch menus £20/25; ☺noon-2pm & 7-8.30pm Tue-Thu, noon-2pm & 7-9pm Fri & Sat, noon-2.30pm Sun; ✐) Two miles north of the city centre, this upmarket restaurant has a gorgeous setting in a bright converted mill overlooking the river, with a beautiful waterside terrace. It serves classy fare such as sea trout with cockle cream, curry oil and a samphire pakora. Vegetarian and vegan menus are available at all times.

🍷 Drinking & Nightlife

★Old Bell Hotel　　　　　　PUB

(www.bellhotelderby.co.uk; 51 Sadler Gate; ☺11.30am-11.30pm Sun-Thu, to 1.30am Fri & Sat) Dating from 1650 and hosting Bonnie Prince Charlie's soldiers in 1745, this history-steeped black-and-white inn was valiantly restored by local entrepreneur Paul Hurst in 2013, retaining original features, antiques and photographs. There's a central courtyard and, allegedly, several ghosts. Real-ale tasting flights, snacks and lunches are served in its Tavern and Tudor bars; the Belfry Bar has an upmarket steakhouse.

The Tap　　　　　　　　　　PUB

(www.brewerytap-dbc.co.uk; 1 Derwent St; ☺noon-11pm Mon-Thu, to 1am Fri, 11am-1am Sat, 11am-11pm Sun) The Tap serves its own brews, guest ales and over 80 craft beers from around the world in elegant Victorian surrounds.

🛍 Shopping

Bennetts　　　　DEPARTMENT STORE

(www.facebook.com/bennettsirongate; 8 Irongate; ☺9am-5pm Mon-Sat, 11am-4pm Sun) Founded as an ironmongers in 1734 and still retaining an ironmongery today, Derby's historic department store has evolved over the centuries to sell beautiful clothes, homewares, gifts and more.

On the 1st-floor interior balcony, **Lisa Jean at Bennetts Brasserie** (☑01332-344621; www.lisajean-bennetts.co.uk; mains £10-13, champagne breakfast £25; ☺9am-3.30pm

Mon-Sat, 11am-2pm Sun) specialises in champagne breakfasts.

❶ Information

Tourist Office (☑ 01332-643411; www.visit derby.co.uk; Market Pl; ☺ 9.30am-8pm Mon-Sat) Under the Assembly Rooms in the main square.

❶ Getting There & Away

AIR

East Midlands Airport (EMA; ☑ 0808 169 7032; www.eastmidlandsairport.com), 11.5 miles southeast of Derby, is served by regular Skylink buses (£4.70, 40 minutes, at least hourly). Buses operate 24 hours.

BUS

Local and long-distance buses run from Derby's bus station, immediately east of the Westfield shopping mall. High Peak has hourly buses between Derby and Buxton (£8, 1¾ hours), via Matlock (£4.50, 45 minutes) and Bakewell (£6.50, 1¼ hours). One bus continues to Manchester (£8, 2¼ hours).

Other services:

Leicester Skylink; £7.30, 1¾ hours, one to two hourly

Nottingham Red Arrow; £5.20, 35 minutes, every 10 minutes Monday to Saturday, three per hour Sunday

TRAIN

The train station is about half a mile southeast of the city centre on Railway Tce.

Birmingham £19.30, 40 minutes, four hourly

Leeds £35.40, 1½ hours, two hourly

London St Pancras £65.50, 1¾ hours, up to two hourly

Ashbourne

☑ 01335 / POP 8377

Perched at the southern edge of the Peak District National Park, Ashbourne is a pretty patchwork of steeply slanting stone streets lined with cafes, pubs and antique shops.

🏃 Activities

Ashbourne Cycle Hire Centre CYCLING
(☑ 01335-343156; www.peakdistrict.org; Mapleton Rd; per half-day/day standard bike from £14/17, electric bike £23/27; ☺ 9.30am-5.30pm Mar-Oct, shorter hours Nov-Feb) Situated 1km northwest of town, the Cycle Hire Centre is right on the Tissington Trail, at the end of a huge and atmospheric old railway tunnel leading under Ashbourne. Helmets, puncture repair kits and maps are included. You can also rent mountain bikes as well as children's bikes, bikes with baby seats, trailers for buggies and tandems.

🛏 Sleeping & Eating

Compton House B&B ££
(☑ 01335-343100; www.comptonhouse.co.uk; 27-31 Compton St; s/d from £55/75; ᴾ⸙) Fresh, clean, frilly rooms, a warm welcome and a central location make this the pick of Ashbourne's B&Bs. There's a minimum two-night stay on weekends.

Flower Cafe CAFE £
(www.theflowercafe.co.uk; 5 Market Pl; mains £5-12.50; ☺ 8.30am-5pm Sun-Fri, to 8pm Sat; ⸙) Soups such as parsnip, chorizo and chestnut, broccoli and Stilton, and spicy bean and lentil are a year-round speciality at this cute-as-a-button cafe where everything is homemade. In summer it also cooks delicious quiches (cheesy leek and mushroom; bacon, brie and cranberry...). Gluten-free and dairy-free dishes are plentiful.

❶ Information

Tourist Office (☑ 01335-343666; www.ash bournetowncouncil.gov.uk; Market Pl; ☺ 10am-5pm Mon-Sat Jun-Oct, shorter hours Nov-May) Inside the town hall.

❶ Getting There & Away

Bus services include the following:

Buxton High Peak routes 441 and 442; £4.50, 1¼ hours, 10 daily Monday to Friday, eight Saturday, five Sunday

Derby Trent Barton Swift; £4.30, 40 minutes, hourly Monday to Saturday, five Sunday

Matlock Bath

☑ 01629 / POP 753

Matlock Bath (not to be confused with the larger, workaday town of Matlock, 2 miles north) looks like a British seaside resort that somehow lost its way and ended up at the foot of the Peak District National Park. Following the River Derwent through a sheer-walled gorge, the main promenade is lined with amusement arcades, tearooms, fish-and-chip shops, pubs and shops catering to the motorcyclists who congregate here on summer weekends. Outside summer, the town is considerably quieter.

⊙ Sights

Peak District Lead Mining Museum
MUSEUM

(📞 01629-583834; www.peakdistrictleadmining museum.co.uk; The Grand Pavilion, South Pde; museum adult/child £4/3, mine £4.50/3.50, combined ticket £7/5; ⊙ 10am-5pm Apr-Apr, 11am-4pm Sep & Oct, 11am-4pm Sat & Sun Nov-Mar) An educational introduction to the mining history of Matlock is provided by this enthusiast-run museum set in an old Victorian dance hall. Kids can wriggle through its maze of tunnels and shafts while adults browse historical displays. At 1pm daily from April to October (at weekends only from November to March) you can go into the workings of the **Temple Mine** and pan for 'gold' (well, shiny minerals). Reservations for mine tours are recommended.

Cromford Mill
MUSEUM

(📞 01629-823256; www.cromfordmills.org.uk; Mill Lane, Cromford; audio guide or guided tour adult/child £5/free; ⊙ 9am-5pm, guided tours by reservation 11am Fri) Founded in the 1770s by Richard Arkwright, the Cromford Mill was the first modern factory, producing cotton on automated machines powered by a series of waterwheels along the River Derwent. This prototype inspired a succession of mills, ushering in the industrial age. In addition to 90-minute audio-guide tours, there are weekly one-hour guided tours. It's 1 mile south of Matlock Bath (a 20-minute walk), or you can take the train one stop to Cromford (£2.50, five minutes, hourly).

Caudwell's Mill
MUSEUM

(📞 01629-734374; www.caudwellsmill.co.uk; Rowsley; mill tours adult/child £4.50/2; ⊙ mill tours 9.30am-4.15pm, shop 9am-5pm) FREE This chugging, grinding, water-powered mill still produces flour the old-fashioned way – 20 different types are for sale, along with six different oat products, and yeast and biscuits. The mill has various craft workshops and a tearoom. You can get to Rowsley direct from Matlock Bath by bus (£3.40, 20 minutes, hourly) on the route to Bakewell, or take the Peak Rail steam train and follow the riverside path from the station.

Masson Mills
MUSEUM

(📞 01629-581001; www.massonmills.co.uk; Derby Rd; adult/child £3/2; ⊙ 10am-4pm Mon-Sat, from 11am Sun, closed Dec) A museum tells the story of the valley's textile mills at this large complex 1 mile south of Matlock Bath. The attached shopping village is full of outlet stores for big clothing brands.

🏃 Activities

Peak Rail
RAIL

(📞 01629-580381; www.peakrail.co.uk; Station Yard, Matlock; adult/child return £9.50/4.50, one-way £5/2.75; ⊙ Mar-Nov, hours vary) From a tiny platform by Sainsbury's supermarket on the outskirts of the town of Matlock (not Matlock Bath), nostalgic steam trains trundle along a 4-mile length of track to the nearby village of Rowsley, home to Caudwell's Mill.

Heights of Abraham
AMUSEMENT PARK

(📞 01629-582365; www.heightsofabraham.com; Dale Rd; adult/child £17/11.50; ⊙ 10am-4.30pm daily mid-Mar–early Nov) A spectacular cable-car ride (accessible with admission ticket only) from the bottom of the gorge brings you to this hilltop leisure park – its cave and mine tours and fossil exhibitions are a winner with kids. The cave is a constant 10ºC, so bring a jacket.

🛏 Sleeping

Grouse & Claret
INN ££

(📞 01629-733233; www.grouseclaretpub.co.uk; Station Rd, Rowsley; d incl breakfast from £90; P 📶) In the village of Rowsley, 6.2 miles northwest of Matlock Bath, this 18th-century stone inn has eight comfy, country-style wallpapered rooms, a restaurant specialising in spit-roasted chicken, and a huge, sunny beer garden with umbrella-shaded tables.

Hodgkinson's Hotel & Restaurant
HOTEL ££

(📞 01629-582170; www.hodgkinsons-hotel.co.uk; 150 South Pde; s/d/f incl breakfast from £60/110/155; P 📶) The eight rooms at this central Grade II–listed Victorian beauty conjure up Matlock's golden age with antique furnishings, cast-iron fireplaces, flowery wallpaper, handmade soaps and goose-down duvets. The restaurant (open Monday to Saturday evenings; two-/three-course menus £27/30) has just 18 seats, so bookings are advised. From April to September, there's a minimum two-night stay on weekends.

🛍 Shopping

Scarthin Books
BOOKS

(www.scarthinbooks.com; The Promenade, Cromford; ⊙ 9am-6pm Mon-Sat, from 10am Sun) More than 100,000 new and secondhand books cram 12 rooms in this biblio-paradise, which hosts regular literary events and has a vegetarian cafe (dishes £3.50 to £6.50) serving organic pizza, soups, wraps, pies and burritos.

ℹ Information

Tourist Office (☑ 01629-583834; www.visit-peakdistrict.com; The Grand Pavilion, South Pde; ⊙ 10am-5pm Apr-Aug, 11am-4pm Sep & Oct, 11am-4pm Sat & Sun Nov-Mar) At the Peak District Lead Mining Museum (p465).

ℹ Getting There & Away

Matlock is a hub for buses around the Peak District.

Bakewell High Peak; £3.80, 35 minutes, hourly
Derby High Peak; £4.60, 40 minutes, hourly

Trains run hourly between Matlock Bath and Derby (£6.30, 35 minutes, hourly).

Chesterfield

☑ 01246 / POP 103,800

The eastern gateway to the Peaks, Chesterfield is a busy service centre that's famed for the twisted spire atop its church.

Nearby is the magnificent Elizabethan mansion Hardwick Hall.

⊙ Sights

Hardwick Hall   HISTORIC BUILDING
(NT; ☑ 01246-850430; www.nationaltrust.org.uk; Doe Lea; house & garden adult/child £13.95/7, garden only £7/3.54, incl Hardwick Old Hall £20.75/11.10; ⊙ house 11am-5pm Wed-Sun mid-Feb–Oct, to 3pm Wed-Sun Nov–mid-Feb, garden 10am-6pm daily year-round) One of the most complete Elizabethan mansions in the country, Hardwick Hall was designed by eminent architect Robert Smythson. The hall featured all the latest mod-cons of the time, including fully glazed windows. The atmospheric interiors are decked out with magnificent tapestries and oil paintings of forgotten dignitaries.

Hardwick Hall is 10 miles southeast of Chesterfield, just off the M1; it's best reached by your own wheels.

The hall was home to the 16th-century's second-most powerful woman, Elizabeth, Countess of Shrewsbury (known to all as Bess of Hardwick), who amassed a staggering fortune by marrying wealthy noblemen with one foot in the grave. Hardwick Hall was constructed using her inheritance from husband number four, who shuffled off this mortal coil in 1590.

Set aside time to explore the formal gardens or the longer walking trails of Hardwick Park.

Next door to the manor are the ruins of Bess' first house, **Hardwick Old Hall** (EH; www.english-heritage.org.uk; Doe Lea; adult/child £7.50/4.60, incl Hardwick Hall £20.75/11.10; ⊙ 10am-6pm Wed-Sun Easter-Sep, to 5pm Oct, shorter hours Nov-Easter).

St Mary & All Saints Church   CHURCH
(☑ 01246-206860; www.crookedspire.org; Church Way; spire tours adult/child £6/4; ⊙ church 9am-5pm Mon-Sat, 8am-6.30pm Sun, spire tours Mon-Sat) FREE Chesterfield is worth a visit to see the astonishing crooked spire that rises atop St Mary and All Saints Church. Dating from 1360, the 68m-high spire is twisted in a right-handed corkscrew that leans several metres southwest. It's the result of the lead casing on the south-facing side having buckled in the sun. Spire tours lasting 45 minutes take you up into the tower. Tour times are posted inside the front door from Monday to Saturday, or phone ahead to check.

ℹ Information

Tourist Office (☑ 01246-345777; www.visitchesterfield.info; Rykneld Sq; ⊙ 9.30am-6pm Mon-Sat) Directly opposite St Mary and All Saints Church.

ℹ Getting There & Away

BUS

From Chesterfield coach station on Beetwell St, bus 170 serves Bakewell (£3.60, 45 minutes, hourly).

TRAIN

Chesterfield lies on the main rail line between Nottingham (£13.20, 45 minutes, up to three hourly) and Derby (£11.70, 20 minutes, up to three hourly), which continues to Sheffield (£5.50, 15 minutes). The station is just east of the centre.

PEAK DISTRICT

Rolling across the Pennines' southernmost hills is the glorious Peak District National Park. Ancient stone villages are folded into creases in the landscape, and the hillsides are littered with stately homes and rocky outcrops. The Dark Peak is dominated by exposed moorland and gritstone 'edges', while to the south, the White Peak is made up of the limestone dales.

Peak District National Park

N
0 ——————— 10 km
0 ——————— 5 miles

No one knows how the Peak District got its name – certainly not from the landscape, which has hills and valleys, gorges and lakes, wild moorland and gritstone escarpments, but no peaks. The most popular theory is that the region was named for the Pecsae-

tan, the Anglo-Saxon tribe who once populated this part of England.

Founded in 1951, the Peak District was England's first national park and is Europe's busiest. But even at peak times, there are

555 sq miles of open English countryside in which to find solitude.

Activities

Walking

The Peak District is one of the most popular walking areas in England, with awe-inspiring vistas of hills, dales and sky that attract legions of hikers in summer. The White Peak is perfect for leisurely strolls, which can start from pretty much anywhere. Be sure to close gates behind you as you go. When exploring the rugged territory of the Dark Peak, make sure your boots are waterproof and beware of slipping into rivulets and marshes.

The Peak's most famous walking trail is the **Pennine Way**, which runs north from Edale for 268 miles, finishing in the Scottish Borders. If you don't have three weeks to spare, you can reach the pretty town of Hebden Bridge in Yorkshire comfortably in three days.

The 46-mile **Limestone Way** winds through the Derbyshire countryside from Castleton to Rocester in Staffordshire, following footpaths, tracks and quiet lanes. Many people walk the 26-mile section between Castleton and Matlock in one long, tiring day, but two days is better. Tourist offices have a detailed leaflet.

Other popular routes include the **High Peak Trail**, the **Tissington Trail** and the **Monsal Trail & Tunnels**. Numerous short walks are available.

ⓘ PEAK DISTRICT TRANSPORT PASSES

Handy bus passes cover travel in the Peak District.

The Peaks Plus ticket (adult/child £7.50/5) offers all-day travel on High Peak buses, including the Transpeak between Ashbourne, Matlock Bath and Buxton. The Peaks Plus Xtra ticket (£12.50/8) includes all transport on Transpeak and TM buses between Derby, Sheffield and Buxton.

The Derbyshire Wayfarer ticket (adult/child £12.40/6.20) covers buses and trains throughout the county and as far afield as Sheffield.

The Greater Manchester Wayfarer ticket (adult/child £12/6) covers trains and buses in the Peak District, along with Greater Manchester and parts of Cheshire and Staffordshire.

Cycling

Plunging dales and soaring scarps provide a perfect testing ground for cyclists, and local tourist offices are piled high with cycling maps and trail guides. For easy traffic-free riding, head for the 17-mile **High Peak Trail**, which follows the old railway line from Cromford, near Matlock Bath, to Dowlow near Buxton. The trail winds through beautiful hills and farmland to Parsley Hay, where the **Tissington Trail**, part of NCN Route 68, heads south for 13 miles to Ashbourne. Trails are off-road on dedicated cycle paths, suitable for road bikes.

Mirroring the Pennine Way, the **Pennine Bridleway** is another top spot to put your calves through their paces. Around 120 miles of trails have been created between Middleton Top and the South Pennines, and the route is suitable for horse riders, cyclists and walkers. You could also follow the **Pennine Cycleway** (NCN Route 68) from Derby to Buxton and beyond. Other popular routes include the **Limestone Way**, running south from Castleton to Staffordshire, and the **Monsal Trail & Tunnels** between Bakewall and Wyedale, near Buxton.

The **Peak District National Park Authority** (☑01629-816200; www.peakdistrict.gov.uk) operates cycle-hire centres at Ashbourne (p464), Derwent Reservoirs (p473) and **Parsley Hay** (☑01298-84493; www.peakdistrict.gov.uk; per half-/full day standard bike £14/17, electric bike £23/27; ⊘9.30am-5pm mid-Feb–early Nov). You can hire a bike from one location and drop it off at another for no extra charge.

Peak Tours (☑01457-851462; www.peaktours.com; self-guided tour per 2 nights from £140) delivers bikes throughout the Peak District for seven different self-guided cycling tours.

Caving & Climbing

The limestone sections of the Peak District are riddled with caves and caverns, including a series of 'showcaves' in Castleton, Buxton and Matlock Bath. The website www.peakdistrictcaving.info, run by the Derbyshire Caving Association, has comprehensive information. **Peaks and Paddles** (☑07896 912871; www.peaksandpaddles.org; canoeing & caving from £55, abseiling from £25; ⊘by reservation) runs caving trips, along with canoeing and abseiling expeditions.

England's top mountaineers train in this area, which offers rigorous technical climbing on a series of limestone gorges, exposed tors (crags) and gritstone 'edges' that extend south into the Staffordshire Moorlands. Gritstone climbing in the Peak District is predominantly on old-school trad routes, requiring a decent rack of friends, nuts and hexes. Bolted sport routes are found on several limestone crags in the Peak District, but many use ancient pieces of gear and most require additional protection. Contact the British Mountaineering Council (www.thebmc.co.uk) for advice and details of local resources.

ℹ️ Getting There & Away

Buses run from regional centres such as Sheffield and Derby to destinations across the Peak District. Be aware that buses are much more frequent at weekends, and many services close down completely in winter. Bakewell and Matlock (not Matlock Bath) are the two main hubs – from these you can get anywhere in the Peak District. Timetables are available from all tourist offices as well as Traveline (p402). Trains run to Matlock Bath, Buxton, Edale and several other towns and villages.

Buxton

🎵 01298 / POP 22,115

The 'capital' of the Peak District National Park, albeit just outside the park boundary, Buxton is a confection of Georgian terraces, Victorian amusements and parks in the rolling hills of the Derbyshire dales. The town built its fortunes on its natural warm-water springs, which attracted health tourists in Buxton's turn-of-the-century heyday.

Today, visitors are drawn here by the flamboyant Regency architecture and the natural wonders of the surrounding countryside. Tuesdays and Saturdays are market days, bringing colour to the grey limestone marketplace.

◎ Sights & Activities

⭐ **Pavilion Gardens**   GARDENS
(www.paviliongardens.co.uk; ⊙10am-5pm Jul & Aug, 10am-5pm Mon-Fri, from 10.30am Sat & Sun Apr-Jun, 10.30am-5pm Sep, to 4pm Oct & Nov, 11am-4pm Dec, Feb & Mar) FREE Adjoining Buxton's opulent opera house are the equally flamboyant Pavilion Gardens. These 9.3 hectares are dotted with domed pavilions; concerts take place in the bandstand throughout the year. The main building contains a tropical greenhouse, an arts and crafts gallery, a nostalgic cafe and the tourist office (p471).

Poole's Cavern   CAVE
(🎵01298-26978; www.poolescavern.co.uk; Green Lane; adult/child £9.95/5.50; ⊙9.30am-5pm,

tours every 20min Mar-Oct; 10am-4pm, tours 10.30am, 12.30pm & 2.30pm Mon-Fri, every 20min Sat & Sun Nov-Feb) A pleasant mile-long stroll southwest from the town centre brings you to Poole's Cavern. This magnificent natural limestone cavern is reached by descending 28 steps; the temperature is a cool 7°C. Tours last 50 minutes.

From the cavern's car park, a 20-minute walk leads up through Grin Low Wood to **Solomon's Temple**, a ruined tower with fine views over the town. Built in 1896 to replace an earlier structure, it sits atop a burial mound where Bronze Age skeletons were discovered.

Buxton Crescent & Thermal Spa   HISTORIC BUILDING
(https://buxtoncrescent.com; The Crescent) In Victorian times, spa activities centred on Buxton's extravagant baths, built in Regency style in 1854 and fronted by the Crescent, a grand, curving facade inspired by the Royal Crescent in Bath. The complex was due to reopen in 2019 following extensive works. Alongside a five-star hotel and spa, its pump room, which dispensed the town's spring water for nearly a century, will be the centrepiece of a new visitor attraction, the Pump Room and Crescent Heritage Experience, covering Buxton's spa-town heritage.

Buxton Museum & Art Gallery   MUSEUM, GALLERY
(www.derbyshire.gov.uk/leisure/buxton_museum; Terrace Rd; ⊙10am-5pm Tue-Sat year-round, plus noon-4pm Sun Easter-Sep) FREE In a handsome Victorian building, the town museum has records of fossils found in the Peak District, photographs, fine arts, bric-a-brac covering the town's social history, and curiosities from Castleton's Victorian-era 'House of Wonders', including Harry Houdini's handcuffs.

Devonshire Dome   HISTORIC BUILDING
(www.devonshiredome.co.uk; 1 Devonshire Rd) A glorious piece of Victoriana, the glass Devonshire Dome, built in 1779, is the largest unsupported dome in Europe. It's home to a training restaurant run by students from the University of Derby and Buxton & Leek College, as well as the **Devonshire Spa** (🎵01298-330334; spa treatments from £40; ⊙9am-7pm Tue, Wed, Sat & Sun, to 9pm Thu & Fri, 10am-6pm Sun).

⭐ **Buxton Tram**   BUS
(🎵01298-79648; https://discoverbuxton.co.uk; adult/child £7.50/5; ⊙by reservation late Mar-

Buxton

Buxton

◎ Top Sights
1 Pavilion Gardens	A2

◎ Sights
2 Buxton Crescent & Thermal Spa	C2
3 Buxton Museum & Art Gallery	C3
4 Devonshire Dome	B1

⊕ Activities, Courses & Tours
5 Buxton Tram	B2
Devonshire Spa	(see 4)

⊜ Sleeping
6 Grosvenor House	B2

7 Old Hall Hotel	B2
8 Roseleigh Hotel	B4

⊗ Eating
9 Barbarella's	C1
10 Columbine Restaurant	C3

◉ Drinking & Nightlife
11 Old Sun Inn	B4

⊕ Entertainment
12 Opera House	B2

⊜ Shopping
13 Scrivener's Books & Bookbinding	B4

Oct) From the Pavilion Gardens (p469), this eight-seat vintage milk float takes you on a 12mph, hour-or-so circuit of the town centre on its entertaining 'Wonder of the Peak' tour.

The same company also offers several hour-long walking tours (from £7), such as Victorian Buxton, from the same departure point.

✨ Festivals & Events

Buxton Festival
ARTS

(www.buxtonfestival.co.uk; ☺ Jul) One of the largest cultural festivals in the country, the 17-day Buxton Festival attracts top names in literature, music and opera at venues including the opera house.

🛏 Sleeping

Old Hall Hotel
HISTORIC HOTEL ££

(☎ 01298-22841; www.oldhallhotelbuxton.co.uk; The Square; s/d incl breakfast from £69/79; 🛜 🖨) There's a tale to go with every creak of the floorboards at this history-soaked establishment, supposedly the oldest hotel in England. Among other esteemed residents, Mary, Queen of Scots stayed here from 1576 to 1578, albeit against her will. The rooms still retain their grandeur (some have four-poster beds), and there are several bars, lounges and dining options.

Roseleigh Hotel
B&B ££

(☎ 01298-24904; www.roseleighhotel.co.uk; 19 Broad Walk; s/d from £51/86; 🅿 📶 🛜) This gorgeous family-run B&B in a roomy old Victorian house has lovingly decorated rooms, many with fine views over the Pavilion Gardens. The owners are a welcoming couple, both seasoned travellers, with plenty of interesting stories. There's a minimum two-night stay on summer weekends.

Grosvenor House
B&B ££

(☎ 01298-72439; www.grosvenorbuxton.co.uk; 1 Broad Walk; s/d/f from £55/70/100; 🅿 🛜) Overlooking the Pavilion Gardens, the Grosvenor is an old-school Victorian guesthouse with a huge parlour overlooking the park. Its eight rooms (including one family room sleeping three people plus space for a cot) have antique furniture and patterned wallpaper and drapes. At peak times, there's a minimum two-night stay and singles aren't available.

🍴 Eating & Drinking

Barbarella's
INTERNATIONAL ££

(☎ 01298-71392; www.barbarellaswinebar.co.uk; 7 The Quadrant; mains £10-20; ☺ noon-11pm Sun-Thu, to midnight Fri & Sat; 🛜 🖨) Black-and-white paisley wallpaper, chandeliers and glossy timber tables make this sleek retro wine bar the hottest drinking den in Buxton, but it's an equally stellar place to dine on sharing boards and deli platters, or more substantial seafood dishes (including a creamy chowder) and chargrilled steaks.

Columbine Restaurant
MODERN BRITISH ££

(☎ 01298-78752; www.columbinerestaurant.co.uk; 7 Hall Bank; mains £14-23.50; ☺ 7-10pm Mon & Wed-Sat, noon-2pm Sun) 🌱 On the lane leading down beside the town hall, this understated restaurant is the top choice among discerning Buxtonites. The chef conjures up imaginative dishes primarily made from local produce, such as High Peak lamb with mint butter. Two of its three dining areas are in the atmospheric stone cellar. Bookings are recommended.

Old Sun Inn
PUB

(www.theoldsuninnbuxton.co.uk; 33 High St; ☺ noon-11pm Sun-Wed, to midnight Thu-Sat) The cosiest of Buxton's pubs, this 17th-century coaching inn has a warren of rooms full of original features, proper cask ales and a lively crowd that spans the generations.

☆ Entertainment

Opera House
OPERA

(☎ 01298-72190; https://buxtonoperahouse.org.uk; Water St; tours £10; ☺ tours by reservation) Designed by theatre architect Frank Matcham in 1903 and restored in 2001, Buxton's gorgeous opera house hosts a full program of drama, dance, concerts and comedy. Guided backstage tours lasting 90 minutes can be booked via the website. Its neighbouring **Pavilion Arts Centre** also hosts performances and has a 360-seat cinema.

🛍 Shopping

Scrivener's Books & Bookbinding
BOOKS

(☎ 01298-73100; www.scrivenersbooks.co.uk; 42 High St; ☺ 9.30am-5pm Mon-Sat, noon-4pm Sun) At this delightfully chaotic bookshop, sprawling over five floors, books are filed in piles and the Dewey system has yet to be discovered.

Cavendish Arcade
SHOPPING CENTRE

(www.cavendisharcade.co.uk; Cavendish Circus; ☺ 9am-6pm Mon-Sat, 10am-5pm Sun, individual shop hours vary) Covered by a barrel-vaulted, stained-glass canopy, Cavendish Arcade houses boutiques selling upmarket gifts.

ⓘ Information

Tourist Office (☎ 01298-25106; www.visitpeakdistrict.com; Pavilion Gardens; ☺ 10am-5pm Jul & Aug, 10am-5pm Mon-Fri, from 10.30am Sat & Sun Apr-Jun, 10.30am-5pm Sep, to 4pm Oct & Nov, 11am-4pm Dec, Feb & Mar; 🛜) Well-organised office with details of walks in the area.

Dominating the former lead-mining village of Tideswell, the massive parish church of **St John the Baptist** (☑01298-871317; https://tideswellchurch.org; Commercial Rd, Tideswell; ⊙9am-6pm) – aka the Cathedral of the Peak – has stood here virtually unchanged since the 14th century. Look out for the wooden panels inscribed with the Ten Commandments and the grand 14th-century tomb of local landowner Thurston de Bower, depicted in full medieval armour. It's 8 miles east of Buxton, linked by bus 66 (£4, 25 minutes, every two hours Monday to Saturday).

Bus 173 links Tideswell with Bakewell (£3.10, 30 minutes, every two hours daily).

❶ Getting There & Away

Buses stop on both sides of the road at Market Pl. The hourly High Peak service runs to Derby (£8, 1¾ hours), via Bakewell (£5, 30 minutes) and Matlock Bath (£5.20, one hour); five services daily continue to Manchester (£6, 1¼ hours).

Bus 66 serves Chesterfield (£5.90, 1¼ hours, every two hours Monday to Saturday) via Tideswell (£4, 25 minutes) and Eyam (£4.60, 40 minutes).

To reach Sheffield, take bus 65 (£6.40, 1¼ hours, every two hours Monday to Saturday, three services Sunday).

Northern Rail has trains to/from Manchester (£10.60, one hour, hourly).

Castleton

☑01433 / POP 742

Guarding the entrance to the forbidding Winnats Pass gorge, charming Castleton is a magnet for Midlands visitors on summer weekends – come midweek if you want to enjoy the sights in relative peace and quiet. Castleton village's streets are lined with leaning stone houses, with walking trails criss-crossing the surrounding hills. The atmospheric ruins of Peveril Castle crown the ridge above, while the bedrock below is riddled with fascinating caves.

◉ Sights

Situated at the base of 517m-high Mam Tor, Castleton is the northern terminus of the Limestone Way, which follows narrow, rocky Cave Dale, far below the east wall of the castle. The tourist office (p473) has maps and leaflets, including details of numerous easier walks.

Peveril Castle   CASTLE, RUINS
(EH; ☑01433-620613; www.english-heritage.org.uk; adult/child £5.90/3.50; ⊙10am-6pm Easter-Sep, to 5pm Oct, to 4pm Sat & Sun Nov-Easter) Topping the ridge to the south of Castleton, a 350m walk from the town centre, this evocative castle has been so ravaged by the centuries that it almost looks like a crag itself. Constructed by William Peveril, William the Conqueror's son, the castle was used as a hunting lodge by Henry II, King John and Henry III, and the crumbling ruins offer swooping views over the Hope Valley. Before heading up here, check ahead to avoid closures for maintenance.

Castleton Museum   MUSEUM
(☑01433-620679; www.peakdistrict.gov.uk; Buxton Rd; ⊙9.30am-5pm Apr-Oct, to 4.30pm Nov-Mar) **FREE** Attached to the tourist office (p473), the cute town museum has displays on everything from mining and geology to rock climbing, hang-gliding and the curious Garland Festival (p473).

Treak Cliff Cavern   CAVE
(☑01433-620571; www.bluejohnstone.com; Buxton Rd; adult/child £9.95/5.30; ⊙10am-4.15pm Mar-Oct, to 3.15pm Nov-Feb) Captivating Treak Cliff has a forest of stalactites and exposed seams of colourful Blue John stone, which is still mined to supply the jewellery trade. Tours lasting 40 minutes depart every half-hour and focus on the history of mining; kids can polish their own Blue John stone during school holidays. It's just under a mile west of Castleton's village centre.

Blue John Cavern   CAVE
(☑01433-620638; www.bluejohn-cavern.co.uk; adult/child £12/6; ⊙9.30am-4pm Mon-Fri, to 5pm Sat & Sun Apr-Oct, 9.30am-dusk Nov-Mar) Up the southeastern side of Mam Tor, 2 miles west of Castleton, Blue John is a maze of natural caverns with rich seams of Blue John stone that are still mined every winter. Access is via a one-hour guided tour that departs every 20 minutes. You can get here on foot up the closed section of the Mam Tor road.

Speedwell Cavern   CAVE
(☑01433-623018; www.speedwellcavern.co.uk; Winnats Pass; adult/child £12/10, incl Peak Cavern

£19/15.50; ⊘10am-5pm daily Apr-Oct, Sat & Sun Nov-Mar) Just over half a mile west of Castleton at the mouth of Winnats Pass, this claustrophobe's nightmare is reached by descending 106 steps for an eerie boat ride through flooded tunnels, emerging by a huge subterranean lake called the Bottomless Pit. New chambers are discovered here all the time by potholing expeditions.

Peak Cavern   CAVE
(⌀01433-620285; www.peakcavern.co.uk; Peak Cavern Rd; adult/child £11.25/9.25, incl Speedwell Cavern £19/15.50; ⊘10am-5pm daily Apr-Oct, Sat & Sun Nov-Mar) Castleton's most convenient cave is easily reached by a pretty streamside 250m walk south of the village centre. It has the largest natural cave entrance in England, known (not so prettily) as the Devil's Arse. Dramatic limestone formations are lit with fibre-optic cables. Buy tickets ahead online in the high season.

Festivals & Events

Garland Festival   CULTURAL
(www.peakdistrict.gov.uk; ⊘29 May) Castleton celebrates Oak Apple Day on 29 May (28 May if the 29th is a Sunday) as it has for centuries, with the Garland King (buried under an enormous floral headdress) and Queen parading through the village on horseback.

Sleeping & Eating

Ye Olde Nag's Head Hotel   PUB ££
(⌀01433-620248; www.yeoldenagshead.co.uk; Cross St; d £50-105; ☎☀) The cosiest of the 'residential' pubs along the main road has nine comfortable, well-appointed rooms; top-category rooms have four-poster beds and spas. Ale tasting trays are available in its bar, which has regular live music and a popular restaurant serving pub classics.

Three Roofs Cafe   CAFE £
(www.threeroofscafe.com; The Island; dishes £5-11; ⊘9.30am-4pm Mon-Fri, to 5pm Sat & Sun; ☀) Castleton's most popular purveyor of cream teas, opposite the turn-off to the tourist office, also has filling sandwiches, pies, fish and chips, burgers and jacket potatoes.

★ Samuel Fox   BRITISH £££
(⌀01433-621562; www.samuelfox.co.uk; Stretfield Rd, Bradwell; 2-/3-/7-course menus £28/35/55; ⊘6-9pm Wed-Sat, 1-4pm Sun Feb-Dec; P☀) In the Hope Valley village of Bradwell, 2.5 miles southeast of Castleton, this enchanting inn owned by pedigreed chef James Duckett

serves exceptional British cuisine: venison with pickled red cabbage, and roast pheasant with braised sprouts, bacon and parsnips. Guests staying in its four pastel-shaded guest rooms upstairs (doubles including breakfast from £130) can dine on Monday and Tuesday evenings.

Look out for dinner, bed and breakfast deals.

❶ Information

Tourist Office (⌀01433-620679; www.peakdistrict.gov.uk; Buxton Rd; ⊘9.30am-5pm Apr-Oct, 10am-4.30pm Nov-Mar) In the Castleton Museum.

❶ Getting There & Away

BUS
Bus services include the following:
Bakewell Bus 173; £3.30, 50 minutes, every two hours via Hope (£2.20, five minutes) and Tideswell (£5.30, 30 minutes)
Sheffield Buses 271 and 272; £5.90, 1¼ hours, four per day Monday to Friday, three Saturday

TRAIN
The nearest train station is at Hope, an easy 2-mile walk east of Castleton, on the line between Sheffield (£5.80, 30 minutes, hourly) and Manchester (£11.80, 55 minutes, hourly).

Derwent Reservoirs

North of the Hope Valley, the upper reaches of the Derwent Valley were flooded between 1916 and 1935 to create three huge reservoirs – the Ladybower, Derwent and Howden Reservoirs – to supply Sheffield, Leicester, Nottingham and Derby with water. These constructed lakes soon proved their worth – the Dambusters (Royal Air Force Squadron No 617) carried out practice runs over Derwent Reservoir before unleashing their 'bouncing bombs' on the Ruhr Valley in Germany in WWII.

These days, the reservoirs are popular destinations for walkers, cyclists and mountain bikers – and lots of ducks, so drive slowly!

⊙ Sights & Activities

Derwent Dam Museum   MUSEUM
(www.dambusters.org.uk; Fairholmes; ⊘10am-4pm Sun) FREE The exploits of the Royal Air Force Squadron No 617, aka the Dambusters, are detailed in the Derwent Dam Museum

in the western tower atop the dam where they tested their 'bouncing bombs'.

Derwent Cycle Hire Centre CYCLING

(☑ 01433-651261; www.peakdistrict.gov.uk; Fairholmes; per half/full day standard bike £14/17, electric bike £23/27; ⏰ 9.30am-5pm early Feb-early Nov) Fairholmes' cycle-hire centre rents wheels including mountain bikes, kids' bikes and electric bikes.

ⓘ Information

Tourist Office (☑ 01433-650953; www.peakdistrict.gov.uk; Fairholmes; ⏰ 9.30am-5pm early Feb-early Nov, 10am-3.30pm Mon-Fri, to 4.30pm Sat & Sun early Nov-early Feb) Provides walking and cycling advice.

Edale

☑ 01433 / POP 353

Surrounded by majestic Peak District countryside, this cluster of stone houses centred on a pretty parish church is an enchanting place to pass the time. Edale lies between the White and Dark Peak areas, and is the southern terminus of the Pennine Way. Despite the remote location, the Manchester–Sheffield train line passes through the village, bringing throngs of weekend visitors.

🛏 Sleeping & Eating

Fieldhead Campsite CAMPSITE £

(☑ 01433-670386; www.fieldhead-campsite.co.uk; Fieldhead; site per person/car £7/3.50; ⏰ Feb-Dec; 🅿🤶) Next to the Moorland Tourist Office, this pretty and well-equipped campsite spreads over six fields, with some pitches right by the river. Showers cost 20p. No campervans are allowed; fires and barbecues are not permitted.

Edale YHA HOSTEL £

(☑ 0845 371 9514; www.yha.org.uk; Rowland Cote, Nether Booth; dm/d/f from £13/50/70; 🅿🤶) Spectacular views across to Back Tor unfold from this country-house hostel 1.5 miles east of Edale, signposted from the Hope road. All 157 beds are bunks; wi-fi in public areas only. Check availability ahead as it's often busy with school groups.

Stonecroft B&B ££

(☑ 01433-670262; https://stonecroftguesthouse.co.uk; Grindsbrook; s/d from £60/105; 🅿🤶) 🌿 This handsomely fitted-out stone house, built in the 1900s, has three comfortable guest rooms (two doubles, one single). Host

Julia's organic breakfasts are gluten-free, with vegetarian and vegan options; packed lunches (£7.50) are available by request when booking. Bike rental costs £25 per half-day. Pick-up from the train station can be arranged. Kids aren't permitted.

Cooper's Cafe CAFE £

(☑ 01433-670401; Grindsbrook; dishes £2-11; ⏰ 9am-4pm Mon, Tue, Thu & Fri, 8am-5pm Sat & Sun; 🤶) Fuel up on soups, burgers, jacket potatoes, house-speciality vegetarian chilli and cakes at this cheerful cafe close to the village school.

Rambler Inn PUB FOOD ££

(☑ 01433-670268; www.dorbiere.co.uk; Grindsbrook; mains £7.50-11; ⏰ kitchen noon-9.30pm Mon-Sat, to 8pm Sun, bar noon-11pm Mon-Sat, to 10.30pm Sun; 🤶🐾) Opposite the train station, this stone pub warmed by open fires serves real ales and pub standards, such as stews and sausages and mash. There's a kids' menu, nine basic B&B rooms (double/triple/family from £90/110/155) and occasional live music.

ⓘ Information

Moorland Tourist Office (☑ 01433-670207; www.peakdistrict.gov.uk; Fieldhead; ⏰ 9.30am-5pm Apr-Sep, reduced hours Oct-Dec & Feb-Mar) Topped by a sedum-turf 'living roof', with a waterfall splashing across its glass panels, this eco-conscious visitor centre has maps, displays on the moors and an adjacent campsite.

ⓘ Getting There & Away

Trains run from Edale to Manchester (£11.60, 45 minutes, hourly) and Sheffield (£7.40, 30 minutes, hourly).

Eyam

☑ 01433 / POP 969

Quaint little Eyam (ee-em), a former lead-mining village, has a poignant history. In 1665 the town was infected by the dreaded Black Death plague, carried here by fleas on a consignment of cloth from London, and the village rector, William Mompesson, convinced villagers to quarantine themselves. Some 270 of Eyam's 800 inhabitants succumbed, while surrounding villages remained relatively unscathed. Today, Eyam's sloping streets of old cottages backed by rows of green hills are delightful to wander.

Driving Tour
Peak District

START BAKEWELL
END BUXTON
LENGTH 52 MILES; ONE TO TWO DAYS

Although you can drive this route in just a few hours, there's a lot to see and even more to do, so pack your hiking boots and consider breaking your journey overnight.

Fuel up at the pretty town of ① **Bakewell** (p476), famed for its distinctive Bakewell pudding. Head south on the A6 for 3.5 miles to Rowsley and turn left on winding Church Lane for 2 miles to visit the atmospheric medieval manor, ② **Haddon Hall** (p476).

Return to Rowsley, turn left on the A6 and left on the B6012 – follow it for 2.9 miles before turning right to reach the 'Palace of the Peak', ③ **Chatsworth House** (p476).

Back on the B6012, turn right to join the A619. At Baslow, home to the country hotel and Michelin-starred restaurant Fischer's Baslow Hall, turn left at the roundabout and travel along the A623 for 3.4 miles to the turn-off for ④ **Eyam**. Drive up the hill to reach its quaint museum, where you can

learn about the town's poignant plague history. There's fantastic walking here.

Continue up the hill and turn right on Edge Rd, then right on Sir William Hill Rd and left on the B601 at Grindleford. Continue to Hathersage and turn left on the A6187 to Hope Valley. From here, turn right on the A6013, passing Ladybower Reservoir, to reach the ⑤ **Derwent Dam Museum** (p473). Pop in to learn about the Dambusters squadron's 'bouncing bombs' tests here during WWII.

It's 5.8 miles back to the Hope Valley turn-off. Then turn right onto Hathersage Rd, right again on Edale Rd and follow the valley to stretch your legs at another prime walking destination, ⑥ **Edale**.

Scenery peaks when you travel towards Castleton, climbing the steep hill near 517m-high Mam Tor to Winnats Rd, then following the spectacular former coral-reef canyon Winnats Pass to explore ⑦ **Speedwell Cavern** (p472).

From Speedwell Cavern, head west along Arthurs Way on to Winnats Rd. Turning right on the A623 brings you to the riot of Victoriana in the former spa town of ⑧ **Buxton** (p469).

⊙ Sights

Eyam Parish Church
CHURCH
(St Lawrence's Church; www.eyam-church.org; Church St; by donation; ⊙9am-6pm Easter-Sep, to 4pm Oct-Easter) Many victims of the village's 1665 Black Death plague outbreak were buried at Eyam's church, whose history dates back to Saxon times. You can view stained-glass panels and moving displays telling the story of the outbreak. The churchyard contains a cross carved in the 8th century.

Eyam Museum
MUSEUM
(www.eyam.museum.org.uk; Hawkhill Rd; adult/child £2.50/2; ⊙10am-4pm Tue-Sun Easter-Oct) Vivid displays on the Eyam plague are the centrepiece of the engaging town museum, alongside exhibits on the village's history of lead mining and silk weaving.

Eyam Hall
HISTORIC BUILDING
(https://eyamhall.net; Main Rd; craft centre free, house & garden adult/child £12/6; ⊙craft centre 10am-4.30pm Wed-Sun year-round, house & garden 11am-3pm Wed, Thu & Sun mid-Feb–late Apr) Surrounded by a traditional English walled garden, this solid-looking 17th-century manor house with stone windows and door frames has a craft centre, a cheese shop, a craft-beer shop and a cafe in its grounds.

🛏 Sleeping & Eating

Miner's Arms
PUB ££
(☎01433-630853; www.theminersarmseyam.co.uk; Water Lane; s/d from £45/70; 🐾) Although its age isn't immediately obvious, this traditional village inn was built shortly before the Black Death hit Eyam in 1665. Inside you'll find beamed ceilings, affable staff, a blazing open fire, comfy en-suite rooms and good-value pub food (mains £9 to £14.50).

Village Green
CAFE £
(www.cafevillagegreen.com; The Square; dishes £2-7; ⊙9.15am-4.15pm Thu-Mon; 🐾) On the village square, with tables on the cobblestones outside, this sweet cafe has homemade soups, a mouthwatering array of cakes and slices (some gluten-free), and decent coffee.

ℹ Getting There & Away

Bus services include the following:

Bakewell Bus 275; £3.90, 20 minutes, three per day Monday to Saturday

Buxton Buses 65 and 66; £4.60, 40 minutes, every two hours Monday to Saturday

Sheffield Bus 65; £5.90, 50 minutes, every two hours Monday to Saturday

Bakewell

☎01629 / POP 3950
The second-largest town in the Peak District, charming Bakewell is a great base for exploring the limestone dales of the White Peak. Filled with storybook stone buildings, the town is ringed by famous walking trails and stately homes, but it's probably best known for its famous Bakewell pudding, a pastry shell filled with jam and a custard-like mixture of eggs, butter, sugar and almonds, invented here in 1820.

⊙ Sights

★Chatsworth House
HISTORIC BUILDING
(☎01246-565300; www.chatsworth.org; house & gardens adult/child £21/12.50, gardens only £14/7, playground £6.50, park free; ⊙10.30am-5pm late May-early Sep, shorter hours mid-Mar–late May & early Sep-early Jan) Known as the 'Palace of the Peak', this vast edifice 3 miles northeast of Bakewell has been occupied by the earls and dukes of Devonshire for centuries. Inside, the lavish apartments and mural-painted staterooms are packed with priceless paintings and period furniture. The house sits in 25 sq miles of grounds and ornamental gardens, some landscaped by Lancelot 'Capability' Brown. Kids will love the farmyard adventure playground.

From Bakewell, take bus 218 (£2.70, 15 minutes, half-hourly).

The manor was founded in 1552 by the formidable Bess of Hardwick and her second husband, William Cavendish, who earned grace and favour by helping Henry VIII dissolve the English monasteries. Mary, Queen of Scots was imprisoned at Chatsworth on the orders of Elizabeth I in 1569.

Look out for the portraits of the current generation of Devonshires by Lucian Freud.

Also on the estate is one of the country's premier farm shops (p477) and an attached cafe.

Walkers can take footpaths through Chatsworth park via the mock-Venetian village of Edensor (en-sor), while cyclists can pedal via Pilsley.

Haddon Hall
HISTORIC BUILDING
(☎01629-812855; www.haddonhall.co.uk; Haddon Rd; adult/child £15.75/free; ⊙10.30am-5pm daily late Mar-Sep, 10.30am-5pm Fri-Mon Oct, 10.30am-4pm Dec) With stone turrets, time-worn timbers and walled gardens, Haddon Hall, 2 miles south of Bakewell on the A6, looks

exactly like a medieval manor house should. Founded in the 12th century, it was expanded and remodelled throughout medieval times but lay dormant from 1700 until its restoration in the 1920s. Take the High Peak bus from Bakewell (£2.50, 10 minutes, hourly) or walk along the footpath through the fields, mostly on the east side of the river.

Spared from the more florid excesses of the Victorian period, Haddon Hall has been used as the location for numerous period blockbusters (such as 2005's *Pride and Prejudice* and 1998's *Elizabeth*).

Thornbridge Brewery
BREWERY

(☑ 01629-815999; www.thornbridgebrewery.com; Buxton Rd; tours adult/child £10/3; ☺ tours by reservation 3pm Wed, Thu & Fri, shop 9am-4.30pm Mon-Fri) Brews by this riverside brewery include bottled varieties (such as a fruity strawberry-blonde ale, I Love You Will You Marry Me), keg beers (eg its Vienna-style lager Kill Your Darlings) and cask ales (including its hoppy Brother Rabbit). Tours lasting 1½ hours take you behind the scenes and include tastings in Thornbridge glasses, which you get to keep afterwards. Under-five-year-olds aren't permitted on tours. It's half a mile from the centre of Bakewell on the northwestern edge of town.

Old House Museum
MUSEUM

(☑ 01629-813642; www.oldhousemuseum.org.uk; Cunningham Pl; adult/child £5/2.50; ☺ 11am-4pm late Mar-early Nov) Bakewell's local-history museum occupies a time-worn stone house that was built as a tax collector's premises during Henry VIII's rule and was expanded in the Elizabethan era, before being split into tiny mill workers' cottages during the Industrial Revolution. Check out the Tudor toilet and the displays on wattle and daub, a traditional technique for building walls using woven twigs and cow dung.

🏃 Activities

The scenic **Monsal Trail** follows the path of a disused railway line from Combs Viaduct on the outskirts of Bakewell to Topley Pike in Wye Dale (3 miles east of Buxton), including a number of reopened old railway tunnels, covering 8.5 miles in all.

For a rewarding shorter walk, follow the Monsal Trail for 3 miles to the dramatic viewpoint at Monsal Head, where you can pause for refreshment at the Monsal Head Hotel (p478), which serves real ales and excellent Modern British cuisine. With more time, continue to **Miller's Dale**, where viaducts give a spectacular vista across the steep-sided valley. The tourist offices at Bakewell and Buxton have full details.

Other walking routes go to the stately homes of Haddon Hall and Chatsworth House.

🛏 Sleeping

Hassop Hall Hotel
HISTORIC HOTEL ££

(☑ 01629-640488; www.hassophallhotel.co.uk; Hassop Rd, Hassop; d from £110; P ☎) Built in the 14th century and extensively remodelled in the 17th century, this magnificent property 3 miles north of Bakewell amid formal gardens and woodland is entered via a grand driveway with a gatehouse. Some of its 13 rooms have four-poster beds, decorative fireplaces and freestanding baths. Its restaurant serves refined dishes, such as salt-crusted English duckling.

Rutland Arms Hotel
HOTEL ££

(☑ 01629-338051; https://rutlandarmsbakewell.co.uk; The Square; s/d incl breakfast from £64/116; P ☎ ⚙) Jane Austen is said to have stayed in room 2 of this aristocratic, 1804-built stone coaching inn while working on *Pride and Prejudice*. Its 33 rooms are located in the main house and adjacent courtyard building; higher-priced rooms have lots of Victorian flourishes.

🍴 Eating

⭐ Chatsworth Estate
Farm Shop Cafe
CAFE, DELI £

(www.chatsworth.org; Pilsley; dishes £6-14.50; ☺ cafe & shop 9am-5pm Mon-Sat, from 10am Sun; ☑) 🍴 One of the finest places to eat in the Peak District, this bucolic cafe serves hearty breakfasts (eggs Benedict with Chatsworth-cured bacon or salmon; strawberry-and-honey Chatsworth yoghurt with muesli) until 11.30am, segueing to lunches (steak-and-kidney suet pudding; traditional roasts) until 3pm, and an afternoon menu. Over half the products at its adjacent farm shop are produced on the estate.

Old Original Bakewell
Pudding Shop
BAKERY, CAFE £

(www.bakewellpuddingshop.co.uk; The Square; dishes £7-12.50; ☺ 8.30am-6pm Mon-Sat, from 9am Sun) One of those that claims to have invented the Bakewell Pudding, this place has a lovely 1st-floor tearoom with exposed beams. It serves light meals and afternoon teas on tiered trays.

BIRMINGHAM & THE MIDLANDS BAKEWELL

Monsal Head Hotel BRITISH ££
(☎01629-640250; www.monsalhead.com; Monsal Trail; mains £11.50-16; ⏱kitchen noon-9.30pm Mon-Sat, to 9pm Sun; P🛜🐾) At the dramatic viewpoint of Monsal Head, its namesake hotel serves real ales and brilliant British cuisine, such as Cheshire cheese and horseradish soufflé, braised Derbyshire beef with smoked-garlic mash, and blackberry crumble with spiced vanilla custard and crystallised stinging nettle leaves. Book ahead to stay in its seven simple but comfortable rooms (doubles including breakfast from £110).

Juniper PIZZA ££
(☎01629-815629; www.juniperbakewell.co.uk; Rutland Sq; pizza £8-13.75; ⏱3-10pm Sun-Thu, 11am-11pm Fri & Sat; 🛜🍴) Done out with juniper-berry-coloured walls and tartan-upholstered chairs, this chic little spot combines a gin bar stocking 40-plus varieties (and Bakewell-brewed Thornbridge beers) with a contemporary pizza kitchen. Steaming pizzas include Let's Meat (salami, bacon, sausage, spiced beef and pepperoni), Billy Goat (goats cheese, caramelised red onion and mozzarella) and Mighty Brunch (black pudding, mushrooms and eggs).

Piedaniel's FRENCH ££
(☎01629-812687; www.piedaniels-restaurant.com; Bath St; mains lunch £13, dinner £16-25; ⏱noon-2pm & 7-9pm Tue-Sat) Chefs Eric and Christiana Piedaniel's Modern French cuisine is the toast of the in-town restaurants. A whitewashed dining room is the exquisite setting for the likes of Normandy onion soup with cider and Gruyère cheese, followed by pork roulade with braised red cabbage and grain-mustard sauce, and flaming crêpes Suzette.

★Fischer's Baslow Hall GASTRONOMY £££
(☎01246-583259; www.fischers-baslowhall.co.uk; 259 Calver Rd, Baslow; 2-/3-/6-course lunch menus £25/33.50/68, 2-/3-/8-course dinner menus £64.50/78.50/88; ⏱noon-2pm & 7-9pm; 🛜🍴) This 1907-built manor house, 4 miles northeast of Bakewell, has a magnificent Michelin-starred dining room showcasing British produce (Derbyshire lamb, Yorkshire game, Cornish crab...) along with vegetables from its kitchen garden. Six sumptuous floral bedrooms are in the main house, with another five in the adjacent garden house

(doubles including breakfast from £260, including a three-course dinner menu from £367).

Drinking & Nightlife

Pointing Dog & Duck PUB
(www.pointingdog.co.uk; Coombs Rd; ⏱11am-11pm; 🛜) A restored saw mill once powered by the river on which it sits now houses this pub with soaring beamed ceilings, exposed stone walls and views of the river's ducks from its waterside terrace. It's an idyllic spot for a pint or pub food, such as ale-battered fish and chips or chargrilled steaks.

Shopping

Bakewell Deli FOOD & DRINKS
(www.facebook.com/bakewelldeli; Rutland Sq; ⏱9am-5pm) Peak District–roasted Full Moon coffee, Matlock Bath honey, Bakewell puddings, and locally cured meats, chutneys, jams and pies fill the shelves of this enticing deli, along with over 50 British cheeses, including artisan varieties made nearby at the Hope Valley's Cow Close Farm. You can also pick up sandwiches, wraps and soups for a riverside picnic.

Bakewell Market MARKET
(Granby Rd; ⏱9am-4pm Mon) Local producers including Hope Valley Ice Cream, Peak Ales, Bittersweet Chocolates, Brock & Morten (cold-pressed oils) and Caudwell Mill (flour) are among the 160-plus regular stalls at Bakewell's lively Monday market.

Information

Tourist Office (☎01629-816558; www.visitpeakdistrict.com; Bridge St; ⏱9.30am-5pm Apr-Oct, 10.30am-4.30pm Nov-Mar) In the old Market Hall, with a photography gallery on the mezzanine.

Getting There & Away

Bakewell lies on the High Peak bus route. Buses run hourly to Buxton (£5, 30 minutes), Derby (£6.50, 1¼ hours) and Matlock Bath (£2.70, 35 minutes). Five services a day continue to Manchester (£8, 1¾ hours).

Other services:

Castleton Bus 173; £3.30, 50 minutes, four per day, via Tideswell (£3.10, 30 minutes)

Chesterfield Bus 170; £4.80, 50 minutes, hourly Monday to Saturday, every two hours Sunday

Yorkshire

Best Places to Eat

➡ Pipe and Glass Inn (p532)

➡ Norse (p494)

➡ Bridge Cottage Bistro (p506)

➡ Talbot Yard (p501)

➡ Ox Club (p518)

➡ Cochon Aveugle (p490)

Best Places to Stay

➡ La Rosa Hotel (p505)

➡ Talbot Hotel (p501)

➡ Grays Court (p489)

➡ Art Hostel (p517)

➡ Lister Barn (p512)

Why Go?

With a population as big as Scotland's and an area half the size of Belgium, Yorkshire is almost a country in itself. It has its own flag, its own dialect and its own celebration, Yorkshire Day (1 August).

People have long been drawn to this region for walking and cycling, framed by some of Britain's finest scenery – brooding moors and green dales rolling down to a dramatic coastline. Then there's the sheer breadth of history, from Roman times to the 21st century. Medieval York is the heartthrob of the north, but there are countless other atmospheric towns and villages to explore, via abbey ruins, craggy castles and classical gardens.

But Yorkshire refuses to fade into the past and one of its greatest charms lies in the ways innovative locals are driving its cities and towns forward. Once-derelict urban areas are seeing regeneration, and modern Britishness is being fused with Yorkshire heritage in cafes, pubs and restaurants.

When to Go

➡ The weeklong Jorvik Festival in February sees York taken over by a Viking invasion.

➡ Spring brings drifts of yellow daffodils to brighten the roadsides in the Dales and North York Moors; the Three Peaks Race takes place in Horton-in-Ribblesdale; thousands descend for Malton's annual food festival.

➡ Agriculture is celebrated at the Great Yorkshire Show in Harrogate in July. At the same time of year, Yorkshire's coastal sea cliffs become a frenzy of nesting seabirds.

➡ September is the ideal time for hiking in the Yorkshire Dales; the Walking Festival in Richmond also takes place in this month. Harrogate gets green-fingered during its Autumn Flower Show; and Whitby celebrates its biggest Goth Weekend around Halloween.

Yorkshire Highlights

1 York (p483)
Exploring the medieval streets of the city and its awe-inspiring cathedral.

2 Yorkshire Dales National Park (p507)
Getting off the beaten track and exploring lesser-known corners.

3 Fountains Abbey (p495)
Wandering among the atmospheric medieval ruins.

4 North Yorkshire Moors Railway (p502) Riding on one of England's most scenic train lines.

5 Whitby (p502)
Sitting on the pier and tucking into the world's best fish and chips.

6 Castle Howard (p492) Reliving the story of *Brideshead Revisited* amid the aristocratic splendour.

7 Malham Cove (p511) Pulling on your hiking boots and tackling the steep paths around this scenic cove.

8 Leeds (p514) Getting stuck into Yorkshire's craft-beer scene, hopping around innovative brewery taprooms.

9 Hull (p528) Exploring maritime heritage and the regenerated marina area of Yorkshire's biggest east-coast town.

10 Malton (p501) Touring artisan food and drink producers in a revitalised Georgian market town.

History

As you drive through Yorkshire on the main A1 road, you're following in the footsteps of the Roman legions who conquered northern Britain in the 1st century AD. In fact, many Yorkshire towns – including York, Catterick and Malton – were founded by the Romans, and many modern roads (including the A1, A59, A166 and A1079) follow the alignment of Roman roads.

When the Romans departed in the 5th century, native Britons battled for supremacy with the Angles, an invading Teutonic tribe, and, for a while, Yorkshire was part of the Kingdom of Northumbria. In the 9th century, the Vikings arrived and conquered most of northern Britain, an area that became known as the Danelaw. They divided the territory that is now Yorkshire into *thridings* (thirds), which met at Jorvik (York), their thriving commercial capital.

In 1066 Yorkshire was the scene of a pivotal showdown in the struggle for the English crown, when the Anglo-Saxon king, Harold II, rode north to defeat the forces of the Norwegian king, Harold Hardrada, in the Battle of Stamford Bridge, before returning south for his appointment with William the Conqueror – and a fatal arrow – in the Battle of Hastings.

The inhabitants of northern England did not take the subsequent Norman invasion lying down. In order to subdue them, the Norman nobles built a chain of formidable castles throughout Yorkshire, including those at York, Richmond, Scarborough, Skipton, Pickering and Helmsley. The Norman land grab formed the basis of the great estates that supported England's medieval aristocrats.

By the 15th century, the duchies of York and Lancaster had become so wealthy and powerful that they ended up battling for the English throne in the Wars of the Roses (1455–87). The dissolution of the monasteries by Henry VIII from 1536 to 1540 saw the wealth of the great abbeys of Rievaulx, Fountains and Whitby fall into the hands of noble families, and Yorkshire quietly prospered for 200 years, with fertile farms in the north and the Sheffield cutlery business in the south, until the big bang of the Industrial Revolution transformed the landscape.

South Yorkshire became a centre of coal mining and steel-making, while West Yorkshire nurtured a massive textile industry, and the cities of Leeds, Bradford, Sheffield and Rotherham flourished. By the late 20th century, another revolution was taking place. The heavy industries had died out, and the cities of Yorkshire were reinventing themselves as shiny, high-tech centres of finance, digital innovation and tourism.

 ## Activities

Yorkshire's varied landscape of wild hills, tranquil valleys, high moors and spectacu-

---

YORKSHIRE'S BEST WALKS

Cleveland Way (www.nationaltrail.co.uk/clevelandway) A venerable moor-and-coast classic that circles the North York Moors National Park on its 109-mile, nine-day route from Helmsley to Filey.

Coast to Coast Walk (www.wainwright.org.uk/coasttocoast.html) One of England's most popular walks: 190 miles across northern England from the Lake District through the Yorkshire Dales and North York Moors National Parks. The Yorkshire section takes a week to 10 days and offers some of the finest walking of its kind in England.

Dales Way (www.dalesway.org.uk) A charming and not-too-strenuous 80-mile amble from the Yorkshire Dales to the Lake District. It starts at Ilkley in West Yorkshire, follows the River Wharfe through the heart of the Dales and finishes at Bowness-on-Windermere.

Pennine Way (www.nationaltrail.co.uk/pennineway) The Yorkshire section of England's most famous walk runs for more than 100 miles via Hebden Bridge, Malham, Horton-in-Ribblesdale and Hawes, passing near Haworth and Skipton.

White Rose Way (www.nationaltrail.co.uk/yorkshirewoldsway) A beautiful but oft-overlooked 79-mile walk that winds through the most scenic part of Yorkshire's East Riding district. It starts at Hessle near the Humber Bridge and ends at the tip of Filey Brigg, a peninsula on the east coast just north of the town of Filey. Billed as 'Yorkshire's best-kept secret', it takes five days and is an excellent beginners' walk.

lar coastline offers plenty of opportunities for outdoor activities. See www.outdoor yorkshire.com for more details.

Cycling

Yorkshire's hosting of the start of the 2014 Tour de France saw a huge upsurge in interest in cycling, and resulted in the establishment of the Tour de Yorkshire (www.letour.york shire.com) annual cycle race from 2015. The county has a vast network of country lanes that are perfect for road cyclists, although the national parks also attract lots of motorists so even minor roads can be busy at weekends.

Mountain bikers can avail themselves of the network of bridleways, former railways and disused mining tracks now converted for two-wheel use. Dalby Forest (www.forestry.gov.uk/dalbyforest), near Pickering, sports purpose-built mountain-biking trails of all grades from green to black, and there are newly waymarked trails at the Sutton Bank National Park Centre (p499).

Walking

For shorter walks and rambles, the best area is the Yorkshire Dales, with a great selection of walks through scenic valleys or over wild hilltops, plus a few higher summits thrown in for good measure. The East Riding's Yorkshire Wolds hold hidden delights, while the quiet valleys and dramatic coast of the North York Moors are also home to some excellent trails.

ℹ Information

The Yorkshire Tourist Board (www.yorkshire. com) has plenty of general leaflets and brochures. For more detailed information, try the excellent network of local tourist offices.

ℹ Getting There & Around

BUS

Long-distance coaches operated by National Express (☑ 0871 781 8181; www.national express.com) serve most cities and large towns in Yorkshire from London, the south of England, the Midlands and Scotland.

Bus transport around Yorkshire is frequent and efficient, especially between major towns. Services are more sporadic in the national parks, but are still adequate for reaching most places if you're not in a rush, particularly in summer months (June to September).

CAR

The major north–south road transport routes – the M1 and A1 motorways – run through the middle of Yorkshire, serving the key cities of Sheffield, Leeds and York. If you're arriving by sea from northern Europe, Hull in the East Riding district is the region's main port.

Traveline Yorkshire (☑ 0871 200 2233; www. yorkshiretravel.net) provides public-transport information for all of Yorkshire.

TRAIN

The main rail line between London and Edinburgh runs through Yorkshire, with at least 10 trains calling each day at York and Doncaster, where you can change trains for other Yorkshire destinations. There are also direct links to northern cities such as Manchester and Newcastle. For timetable information, contact National Rail Enquiries (☑ 03457 48 49 50; www.nationalrail. co.uk).

NORTH YORKSHIRE

This, the largest of Yorkshire's four counties – and the largest county in England – is also the most beautiful. Unlike the rest of northern England, it has survived almost unscathed by the Industrial Revolution. Since the Middle Ages, North Yorkshire has been almost exclusively about sheep and the woolly wealth they produce.

Rather than closed-down factories, mills and mines, the human-made monuments dotting the landscape in these parts are of the stately variety – the great houses and wealthy abbeys that sit, ruined or restored, as a reminder that there was plenty of money to be made off the sheep's back.

All the same, North Yorkshire's biggest attraction is an urban one. While the genteel spa town of Harrogate and the storied seaside resort of Whitby have many fans, nothing compares to the unparalleled splendour of medieval York, England's most-visited city outside London.

York

☑ 01904 / POP 152,841

No other city in northern England says 'medieval' quite like York, a city of extraordinary cultural and historical wealth that has lost little of its pre-industrial lustre. A magnificent circuit of 13th-century walls encloses a medieval spider's web of narrow streets. At its heart lies the immense, awe-inspiring York Minster, one of the most beautiful Gothic cathedrals in the world. York's long history and rich heritage is woven into virtually every brick and beam, and the modern, tourist-oriented city – with its myriad museums,

York

Thirsk
(23mi)

Clifton

Queen Anne's Rd

Bootham Cres

Grosvenor Tce

Bootham Tce

Sycamore Pl

St Mary's

Bootham

Marygate

Longfield Tce

Frederic St

19

Lord Mayor's Walk

Deanery
Gardens

Exhibition
Square

Gillygate

29

18

8

10

12

High
Petergate

St Leonard's
Pl

York
Minster

3

Chapter
House St

11

38

Duncombe Pl

Deangate

Low Petergate

33

34

22

Grape La

Museum
Gardens

30

13

Museum St

Blake St

27

Stonegate

25

28

King's
Sq

14

St Helen's Sq

17

City War
Memorial
Gardens

36

Lendal

Lendal
Bridge

23

Davygate

Church St

Patrick
Pool

39

40

National
Railway
Museum

2

Leeman Rd

Coney St

Spurriergate

Parliament

Market St

Ouse

York
Tourist
Office

Station Rd

Rougier St

Local &
Regional
Bus Stop

Tanner Row

Ouse
Bridge

High Ousegate

Coppergate

1

Jorvik
Viking
Centre

York
Station

21

20

Micklegate

St Martin's La

Bishophill Senior

Bridge St

35

King's Staith

Castlegate

4

Clifford St

Tower St

Queen St

Toft Green

Trinity La

Fetter La

Priory St

Skeldergate

Cromwell Rd

15

Nunnery La

Blossom St

Holgate Rd

A64;
Leeds
(20mi)

Scarcroft Rd

Skeldergate
Bridge

Terry Ave

16

Bishopthorpe Rd

Middlethorpe
Hall (1.5mi)

restaurants, cafes and traditional pubs – is a carefully maintained heir to that heritage.

Try to avoid the inevitable confusion by remembering that around these parts, *gate* means street and *bar* means gate.

◉ Sights

★ York Minster CATHEDRAL

(☎01904-557200; www.yorkminster.org; Deangate; adult/child £10/free, incl tower £15/5; ⊗9am-6pm Mon-Sat, 12.30-6pm Sun, last admission 4.30pm Mon-Sat, 3pm Sun) York Minster is the largest medieval cathedral in northern Europe, and one of the world's most beautiful Gothic buildings. Seat of the archbishop of York, primate of England, it is second in importance only to Canterbury, seat of the primate of *all* England – the separate titles were created to settle a debate over the true centre of the English Church. Note that the quire, east end and undercroft close in preparation for evening service around the time of last admission.

The first church on this site was a wooden chapel built for the baptism of King Edwin of Northumbria on Easter Day 627; its location is marked in the crypt. This was replaced with a stone church built on the site of a Roman basilica, parts of which can be seen in the foundations. The first Norman minster was built in the 11th century and, again, you can see surviving fragments in the foundations and crypt.

The present minster, built mainly between 1220 and 1480, manages to encompass all the major stages of Gothic architectural development. The transepts (1220–55) were built in Early English style; the octagonal chapter house (1260–90) and nave (1291-1340) in the Decorated style; and the west towers, west front and central (or lantern) tower (1470–72) in Perpendicular style.

Don't miss the **undercroft** (open 10am to 4.15pm Monday to Saturday, 1pm to 3pm Sunday), which houses an excellent interactive exhibition – York Minster Revealed – buried within the foundations, leading visitors through 2,000 years of history on the site of the cathedral, amid Roman and Norman remains. At the heart of York's cathedral is the massive **tower**, which is well worth climbing for the unparalleled views of York; it's £5 extra for a ticket and a fairly claustrophobic climb of 275 steps.

★ National Railway Museum MUSEUM

(www.nrm.org.uk; Leeman Rd; ⊗10am-6pm Apr-Oct, to 5pm Nov-Mar; Ⓟ♿) **FREE** York's

York

National Railway Museum – the biggest in the world, with more than 100 locomotives – is well-presented and crammed with fascinating stuff. It is laid out on a vast scale and is housed in a series of giant railway sheds – allow at least two hours to do it justice. The museum also now includes a high-tech simulator experience of riding on the **Mallard** (£4), which set the world speed record for a steam locomotive in 1938 (126mph).

Highlights for trainspotters include a replica of George Stephenson's **Rocket** (1829), the world's first 'modern' steam locomotive; a 1960s Japanese **Shinkansen bullet train**; and an exhibition dedicated to the world-famous **Flying Scotsman**, the first steam engine to break the 100mph barrier (now restored to full working order and touring the UK). There's also a massive 4-6-2 loco from 1949, which has been cut in half to demonstrate how it works (daily talk at 4pm).

Even if you're not a rail nerd, you'll enjoy looking through the gleaming, silk-lined carriages of the royal trains used by Queens Mary, Adelaide and Victoria, and King Edward VII.

The museum is about 400m west of the train station. A road train (adult/child £3/2) runs between the minster and museum every 30 minutes from 11am to 4pm, weather permitting.

★ **Jorvik Viking Centre**　　　MUSEUM
(☑ ticket reservations 01904-615505; www.jorvik-viking-centre.co.uk; Coppergate; adult/child £11/8; ⏱ 10am-5pm Apr-Oct, to 4pm Nov-Mar) Interactive multimedia exhibits aimed at bringing history to life often achieve exactly the opposite, but the much-hyped Jorvik manages to pull it off with aplomb. It's a smells-and-all reconstruction of the Viking settlement unearthed here during excavations in the late 1970s, experienced via a 'time-car' monorail that transports you through 9th-century Jorvik (the Viking name for York). You can reduce time waiting in line by booking timed-entry tickets online; there is almost always a queue to get in.

While some of the 'you will now travel back in time' malarkey might seem a bit annoying, it's all done with a sense of humour tied to historical authenticity that will give you a pretty good idea of what life must have been like in Viking-era York. The museum exhibition at the end of the monorail includes items on loan from the British Museum. Look out for the Lloyds Bank coprolite, a fossilised human stool that measures an eye-watering 9in long and half a pound in weight, and might be the only turd in the world to have its own Wikipedia entry.

Dig
MUSEUM

(☎ 01904-615505; www.digyork.com; St Saviour's Church, St Saviourgate; adult/child £6.50/6; ⊙ 10am-5pm, last admission 4pm; 🖼️) Under the same management as Jorvik (p486) and housed in an atmospheric old church, Dig gives you the chance to be an 'archaeological detective', unearthing the secrets of York's distant past as well as learning something of the archaeologist's world – what they do, how they do it and so on. Aimed mainly at kids, it's much more hands-on than Jorvik and a lot of its merit depends on how good – and entertaining – your guide is.

The Shambles
STREET

The Shambles takes its name from the Saxon word *shamel,* meaning 'slaughterhouse' – in 1862 there were 26 butcher shops on this street. Today the butchers are long gone, but this narrow cobbled lane, lined with 15th-century Tudor buildings that overhang so much they seem to meet above your head, is the most picturesque in Britain, and one of the most visited in Europe, often filled with visitors wielding cameras.

Yorkshire Museum
MUSEUM

(www.yorkshiremuseum.org.uk; Museum St; adult/child £7.50/free; ⊙ 10am-5pm) Most of York's Roman archaeology is hidden beneath the medieval city, so the superb displays in the Yorkshire Museum are invaluable if you want to get an idea of what Eboracum was like. There are maps and models of Roman York, funerary monuments, mosaic floors and wall paintings, and a 4th-century bust of Emperor Constantine. Kids will enjoy the dinosaur exhibit, centred around giant ichthyosaur fossils from Yorkshire's Jurassic coast.

There are excellent galleries dedicated to Viking and medieval York as well, including priceless artefacts such as the beautifully decorated 9th-century **York helmet**.

York Castle Museum
MUSEUM

(www.yorkcastlemuseum.org.uk; Tower St; adult/child £10/free; ⊙ 9.30am-5pm) This excellent museum has displays of everyday life through the centuries, with reconstructed domestic interiors, a Victorian street and a prison cell where you can try out a condemned man's bed – and it could be that of highwayman Dick Turpin (imprisoned here

before being hanged in 1739). There's a bewildering array of evocative objects from the past 400 years, gathered together by a certain Dr Kirk from the 1920s onwards for fear the items would become obsolete and disappear completely.

York City Art Gallery
GALLERY

(☎ 01904-687687; www.yorkartgallery.org.uk; Exhibition Sq; adult/child £7.50/free; ⊙ 10am-5pm; 🖼️) As well as an impressive collection of Old Masters, York Art Gallery possesses works by LS Lowry, Pablo Picasso, Grayson Perry, David Hockney, and the controversial York artist William Etty who, in the 1820s, was the first major British painter to specialise in nudes. A unique feature is the gallery's hands-on sculpture sessions (where you can handle the works), and its brilliant interactive ceramics centre (www.centreofceramicart.org.uk), housing more than 1,000 pieces dating from Roman times to the present day.

Clifford's Tower
CASTLE

(EH; www.english-heritage.org.uk; Tower St; adult/child £5/3; ⊙ 10am-6pm Apr-Sep, to 5pm Oct, to 4pm Nov-Mar) There's precious little left of York Castle except for this evocative stone tower, a highly unusual four-lobed design built into the castle's keep after the original one was destroyed in 1190 during anti-Jewish riots. An angry mob forced 150 Jews to be locked inside the tower and the hapless victims took their own lives rather than be killed. There's not much to see inside, but the views over the city are excellent.

Richard III Experience
MUSEUM

(www.richardiiiexperience.com; Monk Bar; adult/child incl Henry VII Experience £5/3; ⊙ 10am-5pm Apr-Oct, to 4pm Nov-Mar) The best-preserved of York's medieval city gates houses this museum which explores the life and reign of Richard III (r 1483–85) and his impact on York, and sets out the case of the 'Princes in

---

ℹ️ YORK PASS

If you plan on visiting a number of sights, you can save yourself some money by using a YorkPass (https://yorkpass.com). It gives you free access to many of the best pay-to-visit sights in and around York, including York Minster, Jorvik and Castle Howard (p492). You can buy it at the York Tourist Office or online; prices for one/two/three days are adult £42/60/70, child £26/30/35.

the Tower', inviting visitors to judge whether they were murdered by Richard, who was their uncle.

Treasurer's House
HISTORIC BUILDING

(NT; www.nationaltrust.org.uk; Chapter House St; adult/child £8.10/4; ⊙11am-4.30pm Mar-Oct; 🖪) This historic home, which once housed York Minster's medieval treasures, is an anomaly: in the 19th century it was bought by Yorkshire industrialist Frank Green as a collection of rundown interconnected properties. At great expense and using historical archives, Green spent years remodelling the house to what it might once have looked like, but refused to pick just one period, resulting in a collection of authentic-looking rooms that span from medieval times to the 18th century.

The house is also the setting for one of York's most enduring ghost stories: during the 1950s a plumber working in the basement swore he saw a band of Roman soldiers marching through the walls. Regular tours (£4), including one of the haunted cellar, run every day but Wednesday.

🏃 Activities

★ Brewtown
BEER TOUR

(☑01904-636666; www.brewtowntours.co.uk; £60; ⊙11.30am-5pm) These craft-brewery minivan tours are a fuss-free way to get behind the scenes at Yorkshire's smaller breweries, some of which only open to the public for these tours. Owner Mark runs different routes (around York, Malton or Leeds) depending on the day of the week; each tour visits three breweries with tastings along the way, and sometimes even beer-pairing nibbles.

👉 Tours

Association of Voluntary Guides
WALKING

(www.avgyork.co.uk; ⊙tours 10.15am & 1.15pm year-round, 6.15pm Jun-Aug) FREE Free two-hour walking tours of the city, setting out from Exhibition Sq in front of York Art Gallery.

City Cruises York
BOATING

(www.citycruisesyork.com; Lendal Bridge; adult/child from £9.50/5.50; ⊙tours 10.30am, noon, 1.30pm & 3pm; 🖪) These hour-long cruises on the River Ouse depart from King's Staith and, 10 minutes later, Lendal Bridge. Special lunch, afternoon tea and evening cruises are also offered. You can buy tickets on board or book at the office by Lendal Bridge.

Ghost Hunt of York
WALKING

(☑01904-608700; www.ghosthunt.co.uk; adult/child £6/4; ⊙tours 7.30pm) The kids will just love this award-winning and highly entertaining 75-minute tour laced with authentic ghost stories. It begins at the top end of the Shambles, whatever the weather (it's never cancelled), and there's no need to book – just turn up and wait till you hear the handbell ringing...

✨ Festivals & Events

Jorvik Viking Festival
CULTURAL

(www.jorvik-viking-festival.co.uk) For a week in mid-February, York is invaded by Vikings as part of this festival, which features battle re-enactments, themed walks, markets and other bits of Viking-related fun.

York Food Festival
FOOD & DRINK

(www.yorkfoodfestival.com; ⊙late Sep) A 10-day celebration of all that's good to eat and drink in Yorkshire, with food stalls, tastings, a beer tent, cookery demonstrations and more. The main event is in late September, but there's a small taster festival in June and a chocolate festival on Easter weekend.

🛏 Sleeping

★ Safestay York
HOSTEL £

(☑01904-627720; www.safestay.com; 88-90 Micklegate; dm/tw/f from £15/60/75; @ 🛜) Housed in a Grade I Georgian townhouse, this is a large boutique hostel with colourful decor and good facilities including a bar with pool table. Rooms are mostly en suite and have a bit more character than you'd usually find in hostels, with the added intrigue of plaques outside doors describing the history of different rooms in the house.

It's popular with school groups and stag and hen parties – don't come here looking for peace and quiet. Family rooms are strategically positioned right at the top of the house.

York YHA
HOSTEL £

(☑0345 371 9051; www.yha.org.uk; 42 Water End, Clifton; dm/tw from £15/39; 🅿🛜) Originally the Rowntree (Quaker confectioners) mansion, this handsome Victorian house makes a spacious and child-friendly youth hostel, with more than 250 beds, a broad garden and on-site restaurant. It's often busy, so book early. It's about a mile northwest of the city centre; there's a riverside footpath from Lendal Bridge (poorly lit, so avoid after dark).

Alternatively, take bus 2 from the train station or Museum St, though be aware it doesn't run in the evenings.

Fort
HOSTEL **£**

(☎ 01904-620222; www.thefortyork.co.uk; 1 Little Stonegate; dm/d from £22/85; ☎) This boutique hostel showcases the interior design of young British talents, creating affordable accommodation with a dash of character and flair. There are six- and eight-bed dorms, along with five doubles, but don't expect a peaceful retreat – it's central and there's a lively club downstairs (earplugs are provided!). Towels are included, as well as free tea, coffee and laundry.

★ The Lawrance
APARTMENT **££**

(☎ 01904-239988; www.thelawrance.com/york/; 74 Micklegate; 1-bed/2-bed from £75/160; ❋ ☎) Set back from the road in a huddle of old red-brick buildings that once formed a factory, the Lawrance is an excellent find: super-swish serviced apartments with all mod cons on the inside and heritage character on the outside. Some apartments are split-level, all are comfy and spacious, with leather sofas, flatscreen TVs and luxurious fixtures and fittings.

Dairy Guesthouse
B&B **££**

(☎ 01904-639367; www.dairyguesthouse.co.uk; 3 Scarcroft Rd; s/d/f from £70/80/100; P ☎) This Victorian home offers tasteful rooms that mesh fresh decor and five-star bathrooms with original features like cast-iron fireplaces. The flower- and plant-filled courtyard is a lovely place to pause for a rest after a day of sightseeing. It leads to a pair of cottage-style rooms, which are not as nice as those inside but are more private.

Bar Convent
B&B **££**

(☎ 01904-643238; www.bar-convent.org.uk; 17 Blossom St; s w/without bath from £64/39, d w/without bath from £74/90, f w/without bath £102/116; ☎) This mansion just outside Micklegate Bar is less than 10 minutes' walk from the train station. It houses a working convent, a cafe, meeting rooms and an exhibition, and also offers good B&B accommodation. Open to visitors of all faiths and none. Charming bedrooms are modern and well-equipped, breakfasts are superb, and there's a garden and hidden chapel to enjoy.

Hedley House Hotel
HOTEL **££**

(☎ 01904-637404; www.hedleyhouse.com; 3 Bootham Tce; d/f from £105/130; P ☎) ✿ This large red-brick terrace-house hotel sports a variety of options including family-friendly rooms sleeping up to five and self-catering apartments. The designer lounge has the feel of a much bigger hotel, plus there's a yoga studio and Jacuzzi on the outdoor terrace at the back. It's also barely five minutes' walk from the city centre through the Museum Gardens.

★ Grays Court
HISTORIC HOTEL **£££**

(☎ 01904-612613; www.grayscourtyork.com; Chapter House St; d £190-235, ste £270-290; P ☎) This medieval mansion with just 11 rooms feels like a country-house hotel. It's set in lovely gardens with direct access to the city walls, and bedrooms combine antique furniture with modern comfort and design. The oldest part of the building was built in the 11th century, and King James I once dined in the Long Gallery.

✗ Eating

★ Mannion & Co
CAFE, BISTRO **£**

(☎ 01904-631030; www.mannionandco.co.uk; 1 Blake St; mains £7-12; ⊙ 9am-5pm Mon-Sat, 10am-4.30pm Sun) Expect to queue for a table at this busy bistro (no reservations), with its convivial atmosphere and selection of delicious daily specials. Regulars on the menu include eggs Benedict for breakfast, a chunky Yorkshire rarebit (cheese on toast) made with home-baked bread, and lunch platters of cheese and charcuterie. Oh, and pavlova for pudding.

Hairy Fig
CAFE **£**

(☎ 01904-677074; www.thehairyfig.co.uk; 39 Fossgate; mains £5-12; ⊙ 9am-4.30pm Mon-Sat) This cafe-deli is a standout in York. On the one side you've got the best of Yorkshire tripping over the best of Europe, with Italian white anchovies and truffle-infused olive oil stacked alongside York honey mead and baked pies; on the other you've got a Dickensian-style sweet store and backroom cafe serving dishes crafted from the deli.

★ No 8 Bistro
BISTRO **££**

(☎ 01904-653074; www.no8york.co.uk/bistro; 8 Gillygate; dinner mains £17-19; ⊙ noon-10pm Mon-Fri, 9am-10pm Sat & Sun; ☎ ♪) ✿ A cool little place with modern artwork mimicking the Edwardian stained glass at the front, No 8 offers a day-long menu of top-notch bistro dishes using fresh local produce, such as Jerusalem artichoke risotto with fresh herbs, and Yorkshire lamb slow-cooked in hay and lavender.

It also does breakfast (mains £6 to £9) and Sunday lunch. Booking recommended.

Mr P's Curious Tavern
BRITISH ££

(☎ 01904-521177; www.mrpscurioustavern.co.uk; 71 Low Petergate; dishes £5-14; ⏱ noon-10pm Mon-Fri, 11am-11pm Sat, noon-6pm Sun) Mr P's specialises in imaginative small plates, deli meats and cheeses, with a quality wine list – not what you'd expect from its touristy location. It's housed inside a creaky (allegedly haunted) old house, and is part of the mini-empire from Michelin-starred Yorkshire chef Andrew Pern, of Star Inn (p501) fame.

Star Inn The City
BRITISH ££

(☎ 01904-619208; www.starinnthecity.co.uk; Lendal Engine House, Museum St; mains £14-28; ⏱ 9.30-11.30am, noon-9.30pm Mon-Sat, to 7.30pm Sun; ⊕) Its riverside setting in a Grade II–listed engine house and quirky British menu make Andrew Pern's York outpost of the Star Inn (p501) an exceedingly pleasant place to while away the hours. Expect country-themed cosiness in winter, and dining out on the broad terrace in summer.

El Piano
VEGAN ££

(☎ 01904-610676; www.el-piano.com; 15 Grape Lane; lunch £12, 2-course dinner £15; ⏱ noon-10pm Mon-Sat, noon-9pm Sun; ⏱🍽⊕) ⏺ With a menu that's 100% vegan, as well as being nut-, gluten-, palm oil- and refined sugar-free, this Hispanic-style spot is a vegetarian haven. Downstairs there's a lovely cafe and suntrap patio, and upstairs, three themed rooms. The menu offers dishes such as falafel, onion bhaji, corn fritters and mushroom-and-basil salad, either in tapas-sized portions or as mixed platters. There's also a takeaway counter.

Bettys
CAFE ££

(☎ 01904-659142; www.bettys.co.uk; 6-8 St Helen's Sq; mains £6-14, afternoon tea £19.95; ⏱ 9am-9pm Sun-Fri, 8.30am-9pm Sat; ⊕) Old-school afternoon tea, with white-aproned waiters, linen tablecloths and a teapot collection ranged along the walls. The house speciality is the Yorkshire Fat Rascal, a huge fruit scone smothered in melted butter, while breakfast and lunch dishes, like bacon and raclette rösti, and Yorkshire rarebit, show off Betty's Swiss–Yorkshire heritage. No bookings, but be prepared to queue.

1331
BRITISH ££

(☎ 01904-661130; www.1331-york.co.uk; 13 Grape Lane; mains £11-20; ⏱ 8am-10pm; ⏱🍽⊕) This courtyard complex houses a bar, a cocktail lounge and even a private cinema, along with an appealing 1st-floor restaurant serving a menu of crowd-pleasing classics like sausage and mash, Sunday roasts and beef Wellington. Vegetarians are catered for, too, with a good selection of dishes such as chickpea and coriander burgers. There's a two-course set menu for £14.95.

★ Cochon Aveugle
FRENCH £££

(☎ 01904-640222; www.lecochonaveugle.uk; 37 Walmgate; 4-course lunch £40, 8-course tasting menu £60; ⏱ 6-9pm Wed-Sat, noon-1.30pm Sat) ⏺ Black-pudding macaroon? Strawberry and elderflower sandwich? Blowtorched mackerel with melon gazpacho? Fussy eaters beware – this small restaurant with huge ambition serves an ever-changing tasting menu (no à la carte) of infinite imagination and invention. You never know what will come next, except that it will be delicious. Bookings are essential.

🍷 Drinking & Nightlife

★ Blue Bell
PUB

(☎ 01904-654904; 53 Fossgate; ⏱ 11am-11pm Mon-Thu, to midnight Fri & Sat, noon-10.30pm Sun; ☎) This is what a proper English pub looks like – a tiny, 200-year-old wood-panelled room with a smouldering fireplace, decor untouched since 1903, a pile of ancient board games in the corner, friendly and efficient bar staff, and weekly cask-ale specials chalked on a board. Bliss, with froth on top – if you can get in (it's often full). Cash only.

House of Trembling Madness
BAR

(☎ 01904-640009; www.tremblingmadness.co.uk; 48 Stonegate; ⏱ 10am-midnight Mon-Sat, from 11am Sun) When a place describes itself as a 'medieval drinking hall', it clearly deserves investigation. The ground floor and basement host an impressive shop stacked with craft beers, gins, vodkas and even absinthes; but head upstairs to the first floor and you'll find the secret drinking den – an ancient timber-framed room with high ceilings, a bar and happy drinkers.

Guy Fawkes Inn
PUB

(☎ 01904-466674; www.guyfawkesinnyork.com; 25 High Petergate; ⏱ 11am-11pm Mon-Thu & Sun, to midnight Fri & Sat) The man who famously plotted to blow up the Houses of Parliament and inspired Bonfire Night in the UK was born on this site in 1570. Walk through the lovely Georgian wood-panelled pub to find

Guy Fawkes' grandmother's cottage at the far end of the back patio, watched over by a giant wall mural.

Brew York MICROBREWERY
(☑ 01904-848448; www.brewyork.co.uk; Enterprise Complex, Walmgate; ☺ 6-11pm Wed & Thu, from 4pm Fri, noon-11pm Sat, to 10pm Sun) Housed in a cavernous old warehouse, half the floor space in this craft brewery is occupied by giant brewing tanks while the rest is given over to simple wooden drinking benches and a bar with rotating keg and cask beers. At the far end of the brewery there's a small riverside terrace overlooking Rowntree Wharf.

Perky Peacock CAFE
(www.perkypeacockcoffee.co.uk; Lendal Bridge; ☺ 7am-5pm Mon-Fri, from 9am Sat, to 4pm Sun) One of York's charms is finding teeny places like this cafe, shoe-horned into historic buildings. In this case the host is a 14th-century, rotund watchtower crouched by the riverbank. Sup an excellent coffee under the ancient wood beams, or grab a street-side table for a tasty pastry.

King's Arms PUB
(☑ 01904-659435; King's Staith; ☺ noon-11pm Mon-Sat, to 10.30pm Sun) York's best-known pub enjoys a fabulous riverside location, with tables spilling out onto the quayside. It's the perfect spot on a summer evening, but be prepared to share it with a few hundred other people.

🛍 Shopping

Fossgate Books BOOKS
(☑ 01904-641389; fossgatebooks@hotmail.co.uk; 36 Fossgate; ☺ 10am-5.30pm Mon-Sat) A classic, old-school secondhand bookshop, with towers of books on the floor and a maze of floor-to-ceiling shelves crammed with titles covering every subject under the sun, from crime fiction and popular paperbacks to arcane academic tomes and 1st editions.

Red House ANTIQUES
(www.redhouseyork.co.uk; Duncombe Pl; ☺ 9.30am-5.30pm Mon-Fri, to 6pm Sat, 10.30am-5pm Sun) The goods of about 60 antiques dealers are displayed in 10 showrooms spread over two floors, with items ranging from jewellery and porcelain to clocks and furniture.

The Shop That Must Not Be Named GIFTS & SOUVENIRS
(30 The Shambles; ☺ 10am-6pm) Casting a spell over Harry Potter fans, this shop opened on the Shambles – the street said to be the inspiration for Diagon Alley – in 2017. Wands? Tick. Quidditch fan gear? Tick. Potions? Tick. Pure magic for muggles. There's now no less than three Potter shops on the Shambles, but this is the original and still the most convincing.

Shambles Market FOOD
(www.shamblesmarket.com; The Shambles; ☺ 9am-5pm) Yorkshire cheeses, Whitby fish and local meat make good fodder for self-caterers at this anything-goes market behind the Shambles, which also touts arts, crafts and Yorkshire flat caps. The food-court section near where the Shambles joins Pavement is a good spot for cheap eats, coffee and ice-cream at picnic tables.

ℹ Information

York Tourist Office (☑ 01904-550099; www.visityork.org; 1 Museum St; ☺ 9am-5pm Mon-Sat, 10am-4pm Sun) Visitor and transport info for all of Yorkshire, plus accommodation bookings (for a small fee) and ticket sales.

ℹ Getting There & Away

BUS

York does not have a bus station; intercity buses stop outside the train station, while local and regional buses stop here and also on **Rougier St** (Rougier St), about 200m northeast of the train station.

For timetable information, call **Traveline Yorkshire** (☑ 0871 200 2233; www.yorkshiretravel.net) or check the computerised 24-hour information points at the train station and Rougier St. There's a bus information point (8am to 4pm Monday to Saturday) in the train station's Travel Centre.

Birmingham £20, 3½ hours, one daily
Edinburgh £40, 5½ hours, two daily
London from £36, 5½ hours, three daily
Newcastle £12, 2¼ hours, two daily

CAR

A car is more hindrance than help in the city centre, so use one of the Park & Ride (www.itravelyork.info/park-and-ride) car parks at the edge of the city. If you want to explore the surrounding area, rental options include **Europcar** (☑ 0371 384 3458; www.europcar.co.uk; Queen St; ☺ 8am-6pm Mon-Fri, to 4pm Sat), located next to the long-stay car park at the train station.

TRAIN

York is a major railway hub, with frequent direct services to many British cities.

Birmingham £45, 2¼ hours, two per hour

Edinburgh £70, 2½ hours, two to three per hour

Leeds £7, 25 minutes, at least every 15 minutes

London King's Cross £80, two hours, every 30 minutes

Manchester £21, 1½ hours, four per hour

Newcastle £20, one hour, four to five per hour

Scarborough £11.50, 50 minutes, hourly

ⓘ Getting Around

Central York is easy to get around on foot – you're never more than 20 minutes' walk from any of the major sights.

BICYCLE

The tourist office has a useful free map showing York's cycle routes, or visit iTravel-York (www.itravelyork.info/cycling). Castle Howard (15 miles northeast of York via Haxby and Strensall) is an interesting destination, and there's also a section of the **Trans-Pennine Trail cycle path** (www.transpenninetrail.org.uk) from Bishopthorpe in York to Selby (15 miles) along the old railway line.

You can rent bikes from **Cycle Heaven** (☑ 01904-622701; www.cycle-heaven.co.uk; York Railway Station, Station Rd; 2/24hr £10/20; ⊙ 8.30am-5.30pm Mon-Fri, 9am-5pm Sat year-round, 11am-4pm Sun May-Sep) at the train station.

BUS

Local bus services are operated by First York (www.firstgroup.com/york). Single fares range from £1 to £3, and a day pass valid for all local buses is £4.50 (available on the bus or at Park & Ride car parks).

Castle Howard

Stately homes may be two a penny in England, but you'll have to try pretty damn hard to find one as breathtakingly stately as **Castle Howard** (☑ 01653-648333; www.castlehoward.co.uk; adult/child house & grounds £18.95/9.95, grounds only £11.95/7.95; ⊙ house 10am-4pm, grounds 10am-5pm, last admission 4pm; ℗), a work of theatrical grandeur and audacity set in the rolling Howardian Hills. This is one of the world's most beautiful buildings, instantly recognisable from its starring role in the 1980s TV series *Brideshead Revisited* and in the 2008 film of the same name (both based on Evelyn Waugh's 1945 novel of nostalgia for the English aristocracy).

When the Earl of Carlisle hired his pal Sir John Vanbrugh to design his new home in 1699, he was hiring a man who had no formal training and was best known as a playwright. Luckily, Vanbrugh hired Nicholas Hawksmoor, who had worked as Chris-topher Wren's clerk of works on St Paul's Cathedral. Not only did Hawksmoor have a big part to play in the design, bestowing on the house a baroque cupola modelled after St Paul's – the first on a domestic building in England – but he and Vanbrugh would later work wonders with Blenheim Palace. Today the house is still home to the Hon Nicholas Howard and his family, and he can often be seen around the place.

If you can, try to visit on a weekday when it's easier to find the space to appreciate this hedonistic marriage of art, architecture, landscaping and natural beauty. As you wander about the peacock-haunted grounds, views open up over Vanbrugh's playful Temple of the Four Winds, Hawksmoor's stately mausoleum and the distant hills. Inside, you'll find the house split into two distinct styles; the east wing, which includes the Great Hall, was built in the 1700s and is extravagantly baroque in style, whereas the west wing wasn't completed until the 1800s, by which time the fashion was for much more classical Palladian. The house is full of treasures – the breathtaking Great Hall with its soaring Corinthian pilasters, Pre-Raphaelite stained glass in the chapel, and corridors lined with classical antiquities.

Keep an eye out for talks and tours of the house and gardens, which run on an ad-hoc basis depending on what staff are available. There are also boat tours down at the lake, and the entrance courtyard has a good cafe, a gift shop and a farm shop filled with foodie delights from local producers – you could quite easily spend an entire day at the site.

Castle Howard is 15 miles northeast of York, off the A64. There are several organised tours from York; check with the tourist office for up-to-date schedules. Bus 181 from York goes to Malton via Castle Howard (£10 return, one hour, four times daily Monday to Saturday year-round).

Harrogate

☑ 01423 / POP 73,576

The quintessential Victorian spa town, prim and pretty Harrogate has long been associated with a certain kind of old-fashioned Englishness – the kind that seems the preserve of retired army majors and formidable dowagers who take the *Daily Telegraph* and always vote Tory. They come to Harrogate to enjoy the flower shows and gardens that fill the town with magnificent displays of colour, especially in spring and autumn. It is fitting that the town's most famous visitor was Agatha Christie, who fled here incognito in 1926 to escape her broken marriage.

And yet, this picture of Victoriana redux is not quite complete. While it's undoubtedly true that Harrogate remains a firm favourite of visitors in their golden years, the town has plenty of smart hotels and trendy eateries catering to the boom in Harrogate's newest trade – conferences. All those dynamic young sales-and-marketing guns have to eat and sleep somewhere.

◎ Sights & Activities

Royal Pump Room Museum   MUSEUM (www.harrogate.gov.uk; Crown Pl; adult/child £4/2.50; ⊘10.30am-5pm Mon-Sat, 2-5pm Sun Apr-Oct, to 4pm Nov-Mar) You can learn all about Harrogate's history as a spa town in the ornate Royal Pump Room, built in 1842 over the most famous of the town's sulphurous springs. It gives an insight into how the phenomenon of visiting spas to 'take the waters' shaped the town, and records the illustrious visitors it attracted. Beside the stained-glass counter where tonics would have once been dispensed, you can sit down and watch old black-and-white film of patients taking treatments such as peat baths.

The ritual of visiting spa towns as a health cure became fashionable in the 19th century and peaked during the Edwardian era in the years before WWI. Charles Dickens visited Harrogate in 1858 and described it as 'the queerest place, with the strangest people in it, leading the oddest lives of dancing, newspaper-reading and dining' – sounds quite pleasant, really.

Montpellier Quarter   AREA (www.montpellierharrogate.com) The most attractive part of town is the Montpellier Quarter, overlooking Prospect Gardens between Crescent Rd and Montpellier Hill. It's an area of pedestrianised streets lined with restored 19th-century buildings that are now home to art galleries, antique shops, fashion boutiques, cafes and restaurants – an upmarket annex to the main shopping area around Oxford and Cambridge Sts.

★**Turkish Baths**   SPA (☑01423-556746; www.turkishbathsharrogate. co.uk; Parliament St; Mon-Thu £18, Fri £21.50, Sat & Sun £29.50, guided tour per person £3.75; ⊘guided tours 9-10am Wed) Plunge into Harrogate's past at the town's fabulously tiled Turkish Baths. This mock-Moorish facility is gloriously Victorian and offers a range of watery delights: hot rooms, steam rooms, a plunge pool and so on, plus use of the original wooden changing cubicles and historic Crapper toilets. There's a complicated schedule of opening hours that are by turns single sex or mixed, so call or check online for details. The weekly guided tour of the building is fascinating and cheap – book ahead.

✦ Festivals & Events

Spring Flower Show   HORTICULTURE (www.flowershow.org.uk; £17.50; ⊘late Apr) The year's main event, held at the Great Yorkshire Show Ground. A colourful three-day extravaganza of blooms and blossoms, flower competitions, gardening demonstrations, market stalls, crafts and gardening shops.

Great Yorkshire Show   AGRICULTURE (www.greatyorkshireshow.co.uk; adult/child £25/12.50; ⊘mid-Jul) Staged over three days by the Yorkshire Agricultural Society. Expect all manner of primped and prettified farm animals competing for prizes, and entertainment ranging from showjumping and falconry to cookery demonstrations and hot-air-balloon rides. Plus a Black Sheep bar.

🛏 Sleeping

Hotel du Vin   BOUTIQUE HOTEL ££ (☑01423-856800; www.hotelduvin.com/locations/ harrogate; Prospect Pl; r/ste from £124/244, parking per night £10; 🅿🛜) An extremely stylish boutique hotel with dapper lounge – the loft suites with exposed oak beams, hardwood floors and extravagant bathrooms featuring two claw-footed baths and dual showers are among the nicest rooms in town, but even the standard bedrooms are spacious and very comfortable (though they can be noisy). Rates can plummet at quiet times, so keep an eye online.

Bijou   B&B ££ (☑01423-567974; www.thebijou.co.uk; 17 Ripon Rd; s/d from £59/74; 🅿🛜) Bijou by name, bijou by nature – this jewel of a Victorian villa sits firmly at the boutique end of the B&B spectrum, with a grand piano to tinkle on in the lounge and bottles of Prosecco for £10 a pop in the honesty bar. It's just a bit of a schlep up the hill from the conference centre.

Acorn Lodge   B&B ££ (☑01423-525630; www.acornlodgeharrogate. co.uk; 1 Studley Rd; s/d from £49/89; 🅿🛜)

Attention to detail is spot on at Acorn Lodge: stylish decor, crisp cotton sheets, powerful showers and perfect poached eggs for breakfast. Rooms 5, 6 and 7 in the eaves at the top of the house are particularly lovely. The location is good too, just 10 minutes' walk from the town centre.

★ Harrogate
Brasserie Hotel
BOUTIQUE HOTEL £££

(☎ 01423-505041; www.harrogatebrasserie.co.uk; 26-30 Cheltenham Pde; s/d £95/135, apt from £155; P 🛜) The incredibly central location makes this one of Harrogate's most appealing places to stay. Rooms are all individual, with subtle colour combinations and the occasional leather armchair; number 5 has a huge bathroom, and there's a pair of sweet studios with little balconies tucked at the top of the house; behind the main building, there's also two larger apartments that would suit families.

✗ Eating

Baltzersen's
CAFE £

(☎ 01423-202363; www.baltzersens.co.uk; 22 Oxford St; lunch £5.50-9; ⊙ 8am-5pm Mon-Sat, 10am-4pm Sun; 🛜🍴) Norse's little brother is a simple Scandi-style cafe with good coffee (from North Star in Leeds), Nordic waffles and pastries, plus Norwegian stew and open-sided sandwiches such as curried herring with potato salad on the lunch menu.

Bettys
CAFE ££

(☎ 01423-814070; www.bettys.co.uk; 1 Parliament St; mains £6-14, afternoon tea £19.95; ⊙ 9am-9pm; 🍴) A classic tearoom in a classic location with views across the park, Bettys is a local institution. It was established in 1919 by a Swiss immigrant confectioner who took the wrong train, ended up in Yorkshire and decided to stay. Everything's made in-house, and there is almost always a queue for a table for speciality tea and cake; come early or late.

Tannin Level
BISTRO ££

(☎ 01423-560595; www.tanninlevel.co.uk; 5 Raglan St; mains £13-29; ⊙ noon-2pm & 5.30-9pm Tue-Fri, to 9.30pm Sat, noon-5pm Sun) 🍸 Old terracotta floor tiles, polished mahogany tables and gilt-framed mirrors and paintings create a relaxed yet elegant atmosphere at this popular bistro. A competitively priced menu based on seasonal British produce – think Yorkshire lamb rump or heirloom courgette and Yorkshire Fettle cheese tart – means you'd best book a table on weekends.

★ Norse
SCANDINAVIAN £££

(☎ 01423-313400; www.norserestaurant.co.uk; 28a Swan Rd; mains £16-23, 9-course tasting menu £59; ⊙ 6-9pm Tue-Sat, noon-2pm Sat) 🍸 Norse injects some fun into fine dining, with a choice of tasting menus that blend the best of British produce with Scandinavian inspiration to produce unusual flavour combinations such as beetroot, cocoa and horseradish; pork, oyster and peas; and yoghurt, gooseberry and orange blossom. The drinks list includes carefully chosen craft beers and cocktails as well as wine. Bookings essential.

🍷 Drinking & Nightlife

★ Bean & Bud
COFFEE

(☎ 01423-508200; www.beanandbud.co.uk; 14 Commercial St; ⊙ 8am-5pm Mon-Sat, 10am-4pm Sun; 🛜) Small and bohemian, this cafe takes its drinks seriously, with names of coffee growers and altitudes of their plantations displayed proudly on the walls. It's also the sort of place that serves single-origin hot chocolates and puts fairtrade unrefined sugar on the tables. There's a choice of two or three freshly ground blends every day, plus top-quality white, green, oolong and black teas.

★ Major Tom's Social
CRAFT BEER

(☎ 01423-566984; www.majortomssocial.co.uk; The Ginnel, off Montpellier Gardens; ⊙ noon-11.30pm Sun-Thu, to 1am Fri & Sat) Grungy and effortlessly cool, this 1st-floor drinking den is the type of place where locals cram onto sociable wooden bench tables and talk rubbish all night, sampling far more of the interesting draft beers than they meant to. Mismatched retro sofas and walls lined with vintage film and music posters complete the picture. There's also a cheap pizza menu (£6.50 to £8.50).

Harrogate Tap
CRAFT BEER

(☎ 01423-501644; www.harrogatetap.co.uk; Station Pde; ⊙ 11am-11pm Sun-Thu, 11am-midnight Fri, 10am-midnight Sat; 🛜) Set in a restored red-brick railway-station building dating from 1862, the Tap does a grand job of conjuring up the ambience of a bustling Victorian pub, but with the added attractions of a dozen rotating hand-pulled cask ales, another dozen keg taps, and a menu of around 120 bottled craft beers from all over the world.

ⓘ Information

Harrogate Tourist Office (☎ 01423-537300; www.visitharrogate.co.uk; Crescent Rd; ⊙ 9am-

FOUNTAINS ABBEY

The alluring and strangely obsessive water gardens of the Studley Royal estate were built in the 18th century to enhance the picturesque ruins of 12th-century **Fountains Abbey** (NT; www.fountainsabbey.org.uk; adult/child £15/7.50; ⊗10am-5pm Mar-Oct, to 4pm Sat-Thu Nov-Jan, 10am-4pm Feb; P). Together, they present a breathtaking picture of pastoral elegance and tranquillity that have made them a Unesco World Heritage site and the most visited of all the National Trust's pay-to-enter properties.

After falling out with the Benedictines of York in 1132, a band of rebel monks came here to establish their own monastery. Struggling to make it alone, they were formally adopted by the Cistercians in 1135. By the middle of the 13th century, the new abbey had grown wealthy from trading wool and had become the most successful Cistercian venture in the country. After the Dissolution, when Henry VIII confiscated Church property, the abbey's estate was sold into private hands, and between 1598 and 1611 Fountains Hall was partly built using stone from the abbey ruins. The hall and ruins were united with the Studley Royal estate in 1768.

Studley Royal was owned by John Aislabie, once Chancellor of the Exchequer, who dedicated his life to creating the park after a financial scandal saw him expelled from Parliament. The main house of Studley Royal burnt down in 1946, but the superb landscaping, with its serene artificial lakes, survives almost unchanged from the 18th century.

The remains of the abbey are impressively grandiose, gathered around the sunny Romanesque cloister, with a huge vaulted cellarium leading off the west end of the church. Here, the abbey's 200 lay brothers lived, and food and wool from the abbey's farms were stored. At the east end is the soaring Chapel of Nine Altars, and on the outside of its northeast window is a green man carving (a pre-Christian fertility symbol).

A choice of scenic walking trails leads for a mile from the abbey ruins to the famous water gardens, designed to enhance the romantic views of the ruined abbey. Don't miss **St Mary's Church** (Studley Royal; ⊗noon-4pm Easter-Sep) FREE above the gardens.

Fountains Abbey is 4 miles west of Ripon off the B6265. Bus 139 travels from Ripon to Fountains Abbey visitor centre year-round (£4.40 return, 15 minutes, four times daily on Monday, Thursday and Saturday).

5.30pm Mon-Sat, 10am-1pm Sun Apr-Oct, 9.30am-5pm Mon-Sat Nov-Mar)

⊕ Getting There & Away

Bus Harrogate & District (www.harrogatebus.co.uk) bus 36 connects Harrogate with Leeds (£6.30, 45 minutes, two to four hourly) and Ripon (£6.30, 30 minutes).

Train There are trains to Harrogate from Leeds (£8.30, 35 minutes, every 30 minutes) and York (£8.90, 35 minutes, hourly).

Scarborough

📞 01723 / POP 61,750

Surveying Scarborough today, it's hard to imagine the busy medieval fishing village that flourished beneath its impressive headland castle. Much of that history has been blasted away with the salt-sea air, its castle now a toothsome ruin, but what remains is the holiday-resort atmosphere that ran away with the town in the 18th and 19th centuries, capitalising on Scarborough's natural spa waters. These days, its two attractive beaches are the main draw for loyal local holidaymakers.

Cliff-scaling tramways ferry visitors down to the South Bay promenade (where you'll find free wi-fi), lined with arcades and fish-and-chip shops. There's much to recommend a visit to Scarborough – including a redeveloped Victorian spa, grand water park, Edwardian pleasure gardens and interesting geology museum – yet the downbeat city centre still feels like it's stuck in the past, and not in a fashionably retro sort of way.

◉ Sights & Activities

Scarborough Castle　　　　　CASTLE
(EH; www.english-heritage.org.uk; Castle Rd; adult/child £6.50/3.90; ⊗10am-6pm Apr-Sep, to 5pm Oct, to 4pm Sat & Sun Nov–mid-Feb, Wed-Sun mid-Feb–Mar) The massive medieval keep of Scarborough Castle occupies a commanding position atop its headland. Legend has it that Richard I loved the views from here so much that his ghost just keeps coming back. Take

Scarborough

N 0 ____ 200 m
   0 ____ 0.1 miles

Naval Warfare (80m); Scarborough Tourist Office (170m);
North Bay Railway (450m); Sea Life Sanctuary (1mi);
Robin Hood's Bay (14mi)

North Bay

Cricket
Ground

Columbus Ravine

Queen's Pde

North Marine Rd

Royal Albert Dr

Blenheim Tce

Rutland Tce

Castle Rd

Castle
Hill

Marine Dr

St Thomas St

Queen St

Friars Way

Long Westgate

Castle Rd

North St

Princess St

Sandgate

Sandside

Old Harbour

Aberdeen Walk

Eastborough

Foreshore Rd

West
Pier

East
Pier

Northway

Newborough

Bar St

St Nicholas St

Huntriss
Row

Falconers Rd

South
Sands

Victoria Rd

The Crescent

Vernon Rd

South Bay

Mill St

Scarborough
Train Station

Valley Rd

Valley Bridge Rd

Valley
Gardens

Belmont Rd

Albion Rd

Esplanade

Foreshore Rd

Belvedere
Gardens

Scarborough

⊙ Sights
1 Peasholm Park A1
2 Rotunda Museum B3
3 Scarborough Castle D1
4 St Mary's Church C1

🛌 Sleeping
5 Windmill A3

🍴 Eating
6 Golden Grid C2
7 Jeremy's A1

🍸 Drinking & Nightlife
8 Cat's Pyjamas B3

🎭 Entertainment
9 Stephen Joseph Theatre A3

a walk out to the edge of the cliffs, where you can see the 2000-year-old remains of a **Roman signal station**. There's also a cafe and picnic tables.

Peasholm Park   PARK
(www.peasholmpark.com; Columbus Ravine; ⊙24hr) **FREE** Set back from North Bay, Scarborough's beautiful Edwardian pleasure gardens, complete with hilltop pagoda, are famous for their summer sessions of **Naval**

Warfare (adult/child £4.50/2.50; ⊙3pm Mon, Thu & Sat Jul & Aug), when large model ships reenact famous naval battles on the boating lake (check the website for dates).

Rotunda Museum   MUSEUM
(www.rotundamuseum.co.uk; Vernon Rd; adult/child £3/free; ⊙10am-5pm Tue-Sun; �i) The Rotunda Museum is dedicated to the coastal geology of northeast Yorkshire, which has yielded many of Britain's most important

dinosaur fossils. The strata in the local cliffs were also important in deciphering England's geological history. Founded by William Smith, 'the father of English geology', who lived in Scarborough in the 1820s, the museum has original Georgian exhibits as well as a hands-on gallery for kids.

Sea Life Sanctuary AQUARIUM
(www.sealife.co.uk; Scalby Mills; adult/child under 3 £19/free; ☺10am-4pm Mon-Fri, to 5pm Sat & Sun, last admission 1hr before closing; P⛺) At this family-oriented attraction you can see coral reefs, turtles, octopuses, seahorses, otters and many other fascinating creatures. The biggest draws are the talks and feeding times at the seal pool and penguin enclosure. The centre is at the far north end of North Beach; the miniature North Bay Railway (p498) runs the 0.75-mile route. Note tickets are 50% cheaper if you buy online, but you'll still have to queue to enter; at weekends and during school holidays it's swamped by kids.

Scarborough Surf School SURFING
(☑01723-585585; www.scarboroughsurfschool. co.uk; Killerby Cliff, Cayton Bay; ☺9am-5pm) Scarborough Surf School offers full-day surfing lessons from £33 per person, wetsuit and surfboard hire for £25 per day, and stand-up paddleboarding from £50 per person for a two-hour lesson. Beach parking by the school costs £3 per vehicle for the day.

🛏 Sleeping

YHA Scarborough HOSTEL £
(☑01723-361176; www.yha.org.uk; Burniston Rd; dm/q from £15/55; P) An idyllic hostel set in a converted 17th-century water mill, with bike storage and a piano in the lounge, 2 miles north of town along the A166 to Whitby. Take bus 12 from York Place to the Ivanhoe pub; it's a five-minute walk from there.

★Windmill B&B ££
(☑01723-372735; www.scarborough-windmill.co. uk; Mill St; d/f from £85/120, apt £100-130; P⛺) Quirky doesn't begin to describe this place, a beautifully converted 18th-century windmill in the middle of town. There are two self-catering apartments in the windmill itself, along with cottages, a family room and four-poster doubles around a cobbled courtyard. Try to secure the upper apartment (from £100 a night) in the windmill, which has great views from its wraparound balcony.

Waves B&B ££
(☑01723-373658; www.scarboroughwaves.co.uk; 39 Esplanade Rd, South Cliff; s/d from £54/73; P⛺) Crisp cotton sheets and powerful showers make for comfortable accommodation at this Australian-owned, retro-styled B&B, but it's the second B that's the real star – the breakfasts range from vegan-friendly kedgeree and smoothies to fry-ups and kippers. A unique selling point is the jukebox in the lounge, loaded with 1960s and '70s hits. It's 0.75 miles south of the centre, off the A165 (Ramshill Rd).

🍴 Eating & Drinking

★Jeremy's BRITISH, FRENCH ££
(☑01723-363871; www.jeremys.co; 33 Victoria Park Ave; mains £18-27, 3-course lunch Sun £27.50; ☺6-9.30pm Wed-Sat, noon-3pm Sun, plus 6-9.30pm Tue Aug; ⛺) 🍃 A fantastic bistro run by a chef who won Michelin credentials as a head chef for Marco Pierre White, this off-the-beaten-track gem sports an art-deco ambience and a menu that blends the best of Yorkshire and British produce with French inventiveness and flair. Best to book at weekends.

Golden Grid FISH & CHIPS ££
(☑01723-360922; www.goldengrid.co.uk; 4 Sandside; mains £10-20; ☺11am-8.45pm Mon-Thu, 10.30am-9.30pm Fri-Sun; ⛺) The Golden Grid is a sit-down fish restaurant that has been serving the best cod in Scarborough since 1883. Its starched white tablecloths and starched white aprons are staunchly traditional, as is the menu: as well as cod and chips, oysters, and freshly landed crab and lobster, there's sausage and mash, roast beef and Yorkshire pudding, and steak and chips.

Cat's Pyjamas CAFE
(☑01723-331721; www.thecatspyjamascafebars. co.uk; 2 St Nicholas Cliff; ☺8am-5pm Sun-Thu, 9am-10pm Fri & Sat; ⛺) Tucked inside the heritage Central Tramway shed and with sea views from its upstairs seating area, this 1920s-themed cafe and gin bar is a breath of fresh air in staid Scarborough. It serves simple brunches and lunches such as posh fish butties, plus coffee, cakes and G&Ts accompanied by jazz and swing music.

ℹ Information

Scarborough Tourist Office (☑01723-383636; www.discoveryorkshirecoast.com; Burniston Rd; ☺10am-6pm Jul & Aug, to 5pm Sep-Jun) Scarborough's staffed tourist office is part of the Open Air Theatre box office, opposite the entrance to Peasholm Park. Useful leaflets can also be found in the lobby of the **Stephen Joseph Theatre** (☑ 01723-370541; www.sjt.uk.com; Westborough).

❶ Getting There & Away

BUS

Bus 128 (www.eyms.co.uk) travels along the A170 from Helmsley to Scarborough via Pickering, while Arriva (www.arrivabus.co.uk) buses 93 and X93 come from Middlesbrough and Whitby via Robin Hood's Bay. Coastliner (www.coastliner.co.uk) bus 843 runs to Scarborough from Leeds and York.

Helmsley £8, 1¾ hours, hourly Monday to Saturday, at least four daily on Sunday

Leeds £12, 2¾ hours, hourly

Whitby £6.20, one hour, once or twice hourly

York £12, 1¾ hours, hourly

TRAIN

Book in advance for cheaper tickets to York and Leeds.

Hull £16, 1½ hours, nine daily Monday to Saturday, six on Sunday

Leeds £29.80, 1¼ hours, hourly

Malton £8.90, 25 minutes, hourly

York £17.30, 45 minutes, hourly

❶ Getting Around

Tiny Victorian-era funicular railways rattle up and down Scarborough's steep cliffs between town and beach. The **Central Tramway** (www.centraltramway.co.uk; Marine Pde; per person £1; ⊙ 9.30am-5.45pm mid-Feb–Jun, Sep & Oct, to 9.45pm Jul & Aug) connects the Grand Hotel with the promenade, while the **Spa Cliff Lift** (www.scarboroughspa.co.uk/cliff_lift; Esplanade; per person £1; ⊙ at least 10am-5pm, hours vary) runs between Scarborough Spa and the Esplanade.

Open-top bus 109 shuttles back and forth along the seafront between Scarborough Spa and the Sands complex on North Bay (£2, every 20 minutes 9.30am to 3pm). The service runs daily from Easter to September, weekends only in October. An all-day, hop on-hop off ticket costs £3.

The miniature **North Bay Railway** (☑ 01723-368791; www.nbr.org.uk; return adult/child 3yr & over £4/3; ⊙ 10.30am-3pm daily Apr-May & Sep, to 5.30pm Jul & Aug, Sat & Sun year-round) also runs to North Beach.

For a taxi, call **Station Taxis** (☑ 01723-361009, 01723-366366; www.taxisinscarborough.co.uk); £5 should get you to most places in town.

NORTH YORK MOORS NATIONAL PARK

Inland from the North Yorkshire coast, the wild and windswept North York Moors rise in desolate splendour. Three-quarters of all the world's heather moorland is found in Britain, and this is the largest expanse in England. Ridge-top roads climb up from lush green valleys to the bleak open moors, where weather-beaten stone crosses mark the lines of ancient roadways. In summer, heather blooms in billowing drifts of purple haze.

This is classic walking country. The moors are criss-crossed with footpaths old and new, and dotted with pretty, flower-bedecked villages. The national park is also home to one of England's most picturesque steam railways, and at its eastern edge lies historic Whitby – one of England's dreamiest and most haunting coastal towns.

The park produces the useful *Out & About* visitor guide, available from tourist offices and hotels, with information on things to see and do. See also www.northyorkmoors.org.uk.

🏃 Activities

Yorkshire Cycle Hub   CYCLING
(☑ 01287-669098; www.yorkshirecyclehub.co.uk; Fryup; ⊞) Wedged in the middle of the North York Moors National Park, this new centre is hell bent on making itself an indispensable aid for local and visiting cycling enthusiasts. There's cycle hire (mountain bikes and e-bikes), a repairs shop, a simple bunkhouse (£25 per night), bike wash and storage, and an excellent cafe with a log-burner and fabulous rural views.

North York Moors Guided Walks   WALKING
(☑ 01439-772738; http://northyorkmoors.eventbrite.com) **FREE** Each year the national park publishes a schedule of mostly-free guided walks led by volunteers and specialists. Some skirt high moors along ancient paths to seek out medieval sites or ruined castles; others pass through bluebell woods, track birds, or delve into the myths and mysteries of the coastal villages. Places must be booked online or by phone.

❶ Information

There are two national park visitor centres, providing information on walking, cycling, wildlife and public transport.

North York Moors National Park

Moors National Park Centre (☎ 01439-772737; www.northyorkmoors.org.uk; Lodge Lane, Danby; parking 2/24hr £2.50/4.50; ⏰10am-5pm Apr-Oct, 10.30am-4pm Nov–mid-Feb, Sat & Sun only Jan & mid-Feb; ▣)

Sutton Bank National Park Centre (☎ 01845-597426; www.northyorkmoors.org.uk; Sutton Bank, by Thirsk; ⏰10am-5pm Apr-Oct, 10.30am-4pm Nov–mid-Feb, Sat & Sun only Jan & mid-Feb; ☏)

ⓘ Getting Around

On Sundays and bank holiday Mondays from late May to September, a number of minibus services aimed at hikers shuttle around various locations within the national park; all are detailed on the Moorsbus (www.moorsbus.org) website.

For example, the **Moors Explorer** (☎ 8am-6pm Mon-Sat 01482-592929; www.eyms.co.uk; all-day hop-on, hop-off ticket £12.50.) service runs from Hull to the Moors National Park Centre in Danby with stops along the way, but only runs six or so times a year. An all-day hop-on, hop-off ticket costs £12.50. Download the EYMS app with timetables and track bus arrival times live.

The North Yorkshire Moors Railway (p502), running between Pickering and Whitby, is an excellent way of exploring the central moors in summer.

If you're planning to drive on the minor roads over the moors, beware of wandering sheep and

lambs – hundreds are killed by careless drivers every year.

Helmsley

☎ 01439 / POP 1515

Helmsley is a classic North Yorkshire market town, a handsome huddle of old stone houses, historic coaching inns and – inevitably – a cobbled market square (market day is Friday), which marks the start of the long-distance Cleveland Way (p482). It basks under the watchful gaze of a sturdy Norman castle ruin and stately home surrounded by rolling fields. Nearby are the romantic ruins of Rievaulx Abbey, several excellent restaurants and a fistful of country walks.

⊙ Sights

★ Rievaulx Abbey   RUINS

(EH; www.english-heritage.org.uk; adult/child £8.90/5.30; ⏰10am-6pm Apr-Sep, to 5pm Oct, to 4pm Sat & Sun Nov–mid-Feb, daily Mar; ℗) In the secluded valley of the River Rye about 3 miles west of Helmsley, amid fields and woods loud with birdsong, stand the magnificent ruins of Rievaulx Abbey (*ree*-voh). The extensive remains give a wonderful sense of the size and complexity of the community that once lived here, and their story

WORTH A TRIP

HUTTON-LE-HOLE

With a scatter of gorgeous stone cottages, a gurgling brook and a flock of sheep grazing contentedly on the village green, Hutton-le-Hole must be a contender for the best-looking village in Yorkshire. The dips and hollows on the green may have given the place its name – it was once called simply Hutton Hole; the Frenchified 'le' was added in Victorian times. The village is home to a couple of tearooms, a pub, ice-cream shops, and the fascinating **Ryedale Folk Museum** (www.ryedalefolkmuseum.co.uk; Hutton-le-Hole; adult/child £7.95/6.95; ⊙ 10am-5pm Apr-Sep, to 4pm Mar & Oct-Nov).

The tourist office (in the folk museum) has leaflets (£1) about walks in the area, including a 4-mile (2½-hour) circuit to the nearby village of Lastingham. The Daffodil Walk is a 3.5-mile circular walk following the banks of the River Dove. As the name suggests, the main drawcard is the daffs, usually at their best in March or April.

is fleshed out in a series of fascinating exhibits in a new museum. There's also a cafe with floor-to-ceiling windows and outdoor terrace from which to gawp at the ruins.

This idyllic spot was chosen by Cistercian monks in 1132 as a base for their missionary activity in northern Britain. St Aelred, the third abbot, famously described the abbey's setting as 'everywhere peace, everywhere serenity, and a marvellous freedom from the tumult of the world'. But the monks of Rievaulx were far from unworldly and soon created a network of commercial interests ranging from sheep farms to lead mines.

There's an excellent 3.5-mile **walking trail** from Helmsley to Rievaulx Abbey; Helmsley tourist information point can provide route leaflets and advise on buses if you don't want to walk both ways. This route is also the opening section of the Cleveland Way.

On the hillside above the abbey is **Rievaulx Terrace** (NT; www.nationaltrust.org.uk; adult/child £5.95/3; ⊙ 10am-5pm May-Sep, to 4pm Mar-Apr & Oct; P 🐾), built in the 18th century by Thomas Duncombe II as a place to admire views of the abbey. Note that there's no direct access between the abbey and the terrace, and the two sites have separate admission fees. Their entrance gates are about a mile apart along a narrow road (a 20-minute walk steeply uphill if you're heading from the abbey to the terrace).

Helmsley Castle   CASTLE
(EH; www.english-heritage.org.uk; Castlegate; adult/child £6.40/3.80; ⊙ 10am-6pm Apr-Sep, to 5pm Oct, to 4pm Fri-Sun Nov-Mar; P) The impressive ruins of 12th-century Helmsley Castle are defended by a striking series of deep ditches and banks, to which later rulers added the thick stone walls and defen-

sive towers. Only one tooth-shaped tower survives, following the dismantling of the fortress after the Civil War. The castle's tumultuous history is well explained in the 14th-century West Range at the back of the site.

Duncombe Park Gardens   GARDENS
(www.duncombepark.com; adult/child £5/3; ⊙ gardens 10.30am-5pm Sun-Fri Apr-Aug; P 🐾) On the outskirts of Helmsley lies the superb ornamental landscape of Duncombe Park estate, laid out in 1718 for Thomas Duncombe (whose son would later build Rievaulx Terrace), with the stately Georgian mansion of Duncombe Park House at its heart. From the house (not open to the public) and formal gardens, wide grassy walkways and terraces lead through woodland to mock-classical temples, while longer walking trails are set out in the landscaped parkland, now protected as a nature reserve.

🛏 Sleeping

Feathers Hotel   INN ££
(☎ 01439-770275; www.feathershotelhelmsley.co.uk; Market Pl; s/d from £80/100; P 🐶🐾) One of a number of old coaching inns on the market square that offer B&B, decent grub and a pint of hand-pumped real ale. Many of the bedrooms have been refurbished recently, and there are historical trimmings throughout.

Canadian Fields   GLAMPING ££
(☎ 01439-772409; www.canadianfields.co.uk; Gale Lane; safari tents £65-100; ⊙ Feb–mid-Nov; P 🐾) This luxury campsite 3 miles east of Helmsley offers comfortable and unusual accommodation in spacious 'safari tent' cabins with kitchens, electricity and wood-burning stoves under canvas, alongside private out-

door showers. There are also sites where you can pitch your own tent (from £15 a night), and a bar-restaurant housed in a giant tepee provides a convivial social hub.

Feversham Arms · HOTEL £££

(☑ 01439-772935; www.fevershamarms.com; High St; d/ste from £120/190; P 🔁 🛜 🌊) Just behind Helmsley's church, the Feversham Arms has a snug and sophisticated atmosphere where country charm meets boutique chic. Service is excellent and rooms are comfy (the luxury pool suites with balconies are especially light and spacious), but it's the spa and lovely heated outdoor pool that guests come from far and wide for; the on-site restaurant is not worth the money.

✕ Eating

Vine Cafe · CAFE £

(☑ 01439-771194; www.vinehousecafehelmsley.co.uk; Helmsley Walled Garden, Cleveland Way; 10am-5pm; ⏰ Apr-Oct; 🎿 🌊) Goodies plucked from the gardens take centre stage at this whimsical cafe housed in vine-draped Victorian greenhouses within creepers distance of **Helmsley Walled Garden** (www.helmsleywalledgarden.org.uk; adult/child £7.50/free; ⏰ 10am-5pm Apr-Oct). Everything on the menu is fresh and simple, like the home-made hummus and chickpea curry, organic frittata and Helmsley butcher's ham sandwich. It's licensed, too, so you can take a Yorkshire G&T with lunch in the sun.

★ Star Inn · MODERN BRITISH £££

(☑ 01439-770397; www.thestaratharome.co.uk; Harome; mains £20-32; ⏰ 11.30am-2pm Tue-Sat, 6-9.30pm Mon-Sat, noon-6pm Sun; P 🌊) This thatch-roofed country pub is home to a Michelin-starred restaurant, with a menu specialising in top-quality produce from the surrounding countryside: Whitby crab with pickled cockles and avocado 'ice', or roast English quail with braised salsify and bergamot preserve. There's also a set three-course menu for £25 (Monday to Saturday). Harome is about 2 miles southeast of Helmsley off the A170.

The Star is the sort of place you won't want to leave, and the good news is you don't have to – the adjacent lodge has nine magnificent bedrooms (£150 to £240), each decorated in classic but luxurious country style.

★ Hare Inn · MODERN BRITISH £££

(☑ 01845-597769; www.thehare-inn.com; Scawton; 6-course lunch £55, 10-course dinner £70; ⏰ noon-2.30pm & 6-9pm Wed-Sat; P) 🍴 The phrase 'hidden gem' is overused, but here it is entirely appropriate – drowsing in a secluded hamlet 4 miles west of Helmsley, the Hare is a 21st-century restaurant in a 13th-century inn, where gourmet dining is relaxed, informal and even fun. There's no à la carte, just a seasonal tasting menu – and only seven tables; bookings must be made in advance.

LOCAL KNOWLEDGE

MALTON, YORKSHIRE'S FOOD CAPITAL

It was the legendary late Italian chef Antonio Carluccio who first gave Malton the moniker of 'Yorkshire's food capital', and this sweet market town has worked hard to make the title stick – even to the extent of splashing it across road signs on the way in to town and commissioning a street mural to that effect.

The food scene is certainly extraordinary for a town of its size. The best place to start is **Talbot Yard** (www.visitmalton.com/talbot-yard-food-court; Yorkersgate; ⏰ hours vary), an extraordinary food court offering gourmet goodies from gelato, posh pork pies, award-winning ales and freshly ground coffee to Chelsea buns and macarons. Guided tours are offered by **Malton Artisan Food Tour** (www.maltoncookeryschool.co.uk; pick-up Talbot Hotel; per person £45; ⏰ Thu & Sat).

While you're here, it's worth seeking out Malton's own Shambles, where butchers would have once slaughtered the lambs brought in for the town's sheep markets. It's now crammed with vintage shops. Afterwards, head for **Brass Castle** (☑ 01653-698683; https://brasscastle.co.uk; 10 Yorkersgate; ⏰ 4-9pm Tue-Thu, noon-10pm Fri & Sat, to 8pm Sun) for fantastic craft ales, and overnight at the lovely **Talbot Hotel** (☑ 01653-639096; www.talbotmalton.co.uk; Yorkersgate; d/ste from £110/300; P 🛜).

Malton is easily accessible by train from York (£10, 25 minutes, hourly), and the train station is less than a 10-minute walk south from Market Pl.

At the time of writing the owners were also adding a pair of guest rooms, due to be completed in early 2019.

ℹ Getting There & Away

Buses stop in the main square. From Scarborough, bus 128 (£8, 1¾ hours, hourly Monday to Saturday) runs to Helmsley via Pickering, with an additional Sunday service April to October (six daily).

Pickering

📞 01751 / POP 6830

Pickering is a lively market town with an imposing Norman castle that advertises itself as the 'gateway to the North York Moors'. That gateway is also the terminus of the wonderful North Yorkshire Moors Railway, a picturesque survivor from the great days of steam.

Two scenic drives head north across the moors: the A169 to Whitby leads past the **Hole of Horcum** beauty spot and the hiking trails of Goathland (p504); and the Blakey Ridge road (beginning 6 miles west of town) passes the pretty village of Hutton-le-Hole (p500) and the famous **Lion Inn** on the way to Danby.

⦿ Sights

★ **North Yorkshire Moors Railway**   HERITAGE RAILWAY
(NYMR; www.nymr.co.uk; Park St; Pickering–Whitby day-rover ticket adult/child £30/15; ☉ Easter-Oct, reduced service Nov-Easter) This privately owned railway runs for 18 miles through beautiful countryside from Pickering to Whitby. Lovingly restored steam locos pull period carriages with wooden booths, appealing to railway buffs and day trippers alike. For visitors without wheels, it's excellent for reaching out-of-the-way spots and devising walks between stations. Book online the day before travel for a 10% discount and to sidestep ticket office queues.

Pickering Castle   CASTLE
(EH; www.english-heritage.org.uk; Castlegate; adult/child £5.40/3.20; ☉10am-6pm Apr-Sep, to 5pm Oct) Pickering Castle is a lot like the castles we drew as kids: thick stone outer walls circle the keep, and the whole lot is perched atop a high motte (mound) with great views of the surrounding countryside. Founded by William the Conqueror around 1070, it was added to and altered by later kings, but there's not much of it left.

🛏 Sleeping & Eating

★ **White Swan Hotel**   HOTEL £££
(📞01751-472288; www.white-swan.co.uk; Market Pl; s from £129, d £150-210; ℗ 🤙) 🍴 The top spot in town successfully combines a smart pub, a superb restaurant serving a daily changing menu of local produce (mains £14 to £22), and a luxurious boutique hotel. Nine rooms lie within the converted coach house itself, but the best are in a quiet, hidden block out back, where guests get the added perks of underfloor heating and free robes.

Black Swan   PUB
(📞01751-798209; www.blackswan-pickering.co.uk; 18 Birdgate; ☉11.30am-11pm Mon-Thu, to 11.30pm Fri & Sat, to 10.30pm Sun; 🤙) This 18th-century coaching inn has had an ambitious makeover to return it to its former glory. The food is recommended, the beers are brewed in-house (ask behind the bar and you might get a mini guided tour of the microbrewery), and there's also a 1920s-themed cocktail den that you enter around the back of the pub. Fresh, modern B&B rooms upstairs cost from £95.

Pickering Station Tearoom   CAFE £
(Station platform, North Yorkshire Moors Railway; mains £4-6; ☉8.30am-4pm) The vintage 1930s tearoom on platform 1 at Pickering station serves locally sourced treats such as Brymor ice cream from Masham, and simple lunches like cheese and Yorkshire ham panini; or come for a mug of Yorkshire tea to watch the train come in. Food service stops at 2.30pm.

ℹ Getting There & Away

Bus 128 between Helmsley (£5, 40 minutes) and Scarborough (£6.20, one hour) runs hourly via Pickering. Bus 840 between Leeds and Whitby also travels via Pickering (hourly).

Whitby

📞 01947 / POP 13,213

Whitby is a town of two parts, with the River Esk carving a path between a huddle of 18th-century fishermen's cottages along its East Cliff and a genteel Victorian suburb atop the West Cliff. It's also a town with two personalities – on the one hand, a busy commercial and fishing port (it was here that 18th-century explorer Captain James Cook gained his seafaring legs) with a bustling quayside awash with fish; on the other, an

Whitby

N ⬆ 0 —————— 200 m
0 —————— 0.1 miles

Whitby

⊙ Top Sights
1 Captain Cook Memorial Museum		C2
2 Whitby Abbey		D2

⊙ Sights
3 Whitby Museum		A3

⊕ Activities, Courses & Tours
4 Captain Cook Experience		C1
5 Whitby Coastal Cruises		C2
6 Whitby Ghost Walks		B1

⊜ Sleeping
7 La Rosa Hotel		B1
8 Marine Hotel		C2
9 Rosslyn House		B1

10 YHA Whitby		D2

⊗ Eating
11 Blitz		C2
12 Humble Pie 'n' Mash		C2
13 Quayside		C2
14 Rusty Shears		B2
15 Star Inn the Harbour		C3
16 White Horse & Griffin		C2

⊕ Drinking & Nightlife
17 Green Dragon		C2

⊕ Entertainment
18 Dracula Experience		C2

oh-so-pretty, traditional seaside resort complete with sandy beach, amusement arcades and promenading holidaymakers.

Keeping a watchful eye over the town is an atmospheric ruined abbey, the inspiration and setting for part of Bram Stoker's Gothic horror story *Dracula*. But tales of witchery and ghostly legends have haunted Whitby ever since Anglo-Saxon St Hilda landed here to found a monastic community in AD 657. The town embraces its reputation for the weird and wonderful, which culmi-

nates in two hugely successful Goth Weekends each year.

⊙ Sights

★ **Whitby Abbey**   RUINS
(EH; www.english-heritage.org.uk; East Cliff; adult/
child £8.70/5.20; ⊙10am-6pm Apr-Sep, to 5pm
Oct, to 4pm Tue-Sat Nov, to 4pm Sat & Sun Dec-Mar;
🅿) There are ruined abbeys, and there are
picturesque ruined abbeys. And then there's
Whitby Abbey, dominating the skyline above
the East Cliff like a great Gothic tombstone

GOATHLAND

This picture-postcard halt on the North Yorkshire Moors Railway stars as Hogsmeade train station in the Harry Potter films, while the village appeared as Aidensfield in the British TV series *Heartbeat*. It's also the starting point for lots of easy and enjoyable walks, often with the chuff-chuff-chuff of passing steam engines in the background.

The nearby hamlet of Beck Hole is home to the wonderfully atmospheric **Birch Hall Inn** (www.beckhole.info; Beck Hole; ⊙ 11am-11pm May-Sep, 11am-3pm & 7.30-11pm Wed-Mon Oct-Apr; 🚻 🐾), where it's like stepping into the past. The 'bar' is a tiny sitting room, with a hole in the wall where drinks are served; or you can sit outside by the beck. Order a pork pie and pint of ale brewed in the village. Cash only.

silhouetted against the sky. Looking as though it was built as an atmospheric film set rather than a monastic establishment, it is hardly surprising that this medieval hulk inspired the Victorian novelist Bram Stoker (who holidayed in Whitby) to make it the setting for Count Dracula's dramatic landfall.

The stately mansion beside the abbey ruins was built by the Cholmley family, who leased the Whitby estate from Henry VIII after the dissolution of England's monasteries in the 1530s. An excellent free audio guide is included with the entrance fee, and at the time of writing the visitor centre displays inside the mansion were being revamped with updated interpretations of the site's history.

From the end of Church St, the 199 steps of **Church Stairs** will lead you steeply up to Whitby Abbey. By car, you have to approach from the A171 Scarborough road to the east side of the bridge over the River Esk.

⭐ Captain Cook Memorial Museum
MUSEUM

(www.cookmuseumwhitby.co.uk; Grape Lane; adult/child £5.90/3.50; ⊙ 9.45am-5pm Apr-Oct, 11am-3pm mid-Feb–Mar) This fascinating museum occupies the house of the ship owner with whom Cook began his seafaring career. Highlights include the attic where Cook lodged as a young apprentice, Cook's own maps and letters, etchings from the South

Seas, and a wonderful model of the *Resolution*, with the crew and stores all laid out for inspection. Cook lived in Whitby for nine years and later returned to have all three of his voyage ships built in Whitby's dockyards.

Whitby Museum
MUSEUM

(www.whitbymuseum.org.uk; Pannett Park; adult/child £5/free; ⊙ 9.30am-4.30pm Tue-Sun; 🚻) Set in a park to the west of the town centre is the wonderfully eclectic Whitby Museum, with displays of fossil plesiosaurs and dinosaur footprints, Captain Cook memorabilia, ships in bottles, jet jewellery and the gruesome 'Hand of Glory', a preserved human hand reputedly cut from the corpse of an executed criminal.

🏃 Activities

Captain Cook Experience
BOATING

(☎ 01723-364100; www.endeavourwhitby.com; Fish Quay, Pier Rd; 25min trip £3.50) Take a spin out beyond Whitby harbour on this authentic replica of the *HM Bark Endeavour*, which at 40% of the size of the original still has the feel of an atmospheric large voyaging ship. The skipper will regale you with tales of Captain Cook's ordeals at sea and his long-standing associations with Whitby. Good fun for young and old.

Whitby Coastal Cruises
BOATING

(☎ 07981 712419; www.whitbycoastalcruises.co.uk; Brewery Steps; 3½hr trip £15) Spot birds, seals, dolphins or even steam trains on a coastal or River Esk boat trip with this long-running family business. September is whale-watching season, during which time you can join its sister business Whitby Whale Watching (www.whitbywhalewatching.net; trips £40) on a trip where the chances of seeing Minke whales (and more rarely humpbacks) are high.

👉 Tours

⭐ Whitby Ghost Walks
WALKING

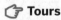

(☎ 01947-880485; www.whitbywalks.com; Whale Bone Arch, West Cliff; adult/child £5/3; ⊙ 7.30pm) Whitby wouldn't be Whitby without ghoulish tales and strange happenings, and nobody knows them better than Dr Crank, who manages to confidently keep to the right side of naff with his fascinating 75-minute tour around West Cliff's most haunted and storied alleyways. You'll learn of legends like the screaming tunnel, the hand of glory and the headless horseman, plus tidbits of local history.

Hidden Horizons
OUTDOORS

(☑ 01723-817017; www.hiddenhorizons.co.uk; adult/child from £8/5) You can get down on the beaches around Whitby to hunt for fossils (and there's plenty to find), take a dinosaur footprint walk, go rock-pooling, or join a star-gazing session with this local tour company. Sessions are entertaining but also educational. Check the online calendar for upcoming events, and book ahead.

★✶ Festivals & Events

Whitby Goth Weekends
CULTURAL

(www.whitbygothweekend.co.uk; tickets 1/2 days £34/65) Goth heaven attracting more than 8000 visitors biannually, with live-music gigs, events and the Bizarre Bazaar – dozens of traders selling Goth gear, jewellery, art and music. Held twice yearly in late April or early May and late October or early November (around Halloween).

Whitby Steampunk Weekend
CULTURAL

(www.wswofficial.com; Whitby Pavilion; ⊙ late Jul) Science fiction meets Victoriana fantasy in Whitby on the last weekend in July, when fans of the steampunk genre descend for balls, costumed promenading, entertainment and shopping at the Steampunk Emporium. A little bit Gothic, a little bit geeky; very Whitby. Events are anchored on the Whitby Pavilion on West Cliff.

⛺ Sleeping

YHA Whitby
HOSTEL £

(☑ 0845 371 9049; www.yha.org.uk; Church Lane; dm/tw/f from £13/29/25; P 📶) With an unbeatable setting in an old mansion next to the abbey, this hostel is incredibly popular – you'll have to book well in advance to get your body into one of the bunks here. Hike up the 199 steps from the town, or take bus 97 from the train station to Whitby Abbey (twice hourly Monday to Saturday).

★ La Rosa Hotel
HOTEL ££

(☑ 01947-606981; www.larosa.co.uk/hotel; 5 East Tce; d £86-135; P 📶) Weird, but wonderful. Lewis Carroll, author of *Alice in Wonderland,* once stayed in this house while holidaying in Whitby. Entering today is like stepping through the looking glass into a world of love-it-or-hate-it Victorian bric-a-brac and kitsch, peppered with vintage film props. Eight quirky and atmospheric bedrooms, great sea views, no TVs, an in-house bar and breakfast served in a basket in your room.

Rosslyn House
B&B ££

(☑ 01947-604086; www.rosslynhousewhitby.co.uk; 11 Abbey Tce; s/d/f from £65/90/100; 📶) Lovely Victorian terrace house that stands out amid the sea of B&Bs on West Cliff, with a friendly welcome and bright, modern decor. The single room is snug; the family room large (though the hotel does not admit children under 12). There's a convenient drying room for walkers.

★ Marine Hotel
INN £££

(☑ 01947-605022; www.the-marine-hotel.co.uk; 13 Marine Pde; r £150-195; 📶) Feeling more like minisuites than ordinary hotel accommodation, the four bedrooms at the Marine are quirky, stylish and comfortable; it's the sort of place that makes you want to stay in rather than go out. Ask for one of the two rooms with a balcony – they have great views across the harbour.

✕ Eating

★ Rusty Shears
BRITISH £

(☑ 01947-605383; 3 Silver St; brunch £3.50-6.50; ⊙ 9.30am-5pm; 📶) This vintage cafe covers many bases. There's an astounding drinks menu with more than 100 gins (despite the fact it's closed evenings) and gin flights, a walled courtyard for al-fresco light lunches, and a cluster of retro-styled rooms for cosy chats over excellent coffee and cakes like treacle tart or Yorkshire tea loaf. The brunches with Fortune's smoked bacon and creamy scrambled eggs deserve a medal.

Humble Pie 'n' Mash
BRITISH £

(☑ 01947-606444; www.humblepie.tccdev.com; 163 Church St; pie meal £6.99; ⊙ noon-8pm) Superb homemade gravy-laden pies with fillings ranging from lamb, leek and rosemary to roast veg and goats cheese, served in a cosy timber-framed cottage with a 1940s nostalgia vibe. No bookings, cash only.

Blitz
CAFE £

(☑ 01947-606935; www.theblitzwhitby.co.uk; 97-98 Church St; lunch £3-9, evening tapas plates £4-9; ⊙ 10am-11pm) War nostalgia is the theme of this 1940s-style cafe serving coffees, G&Ts and food on Whitby's East Cliff. London's war-ravaged night skyline is writ large on a mural, and the trenches are reimagined as walls. During the day the food menu focuses on basics like the 'Blitz Bomber' chip butty; at night there's a decent world-food tapas menu.

WORTH A TRIP

ROBIN HOOD'S BAY

Picturesque Robin Hood's Bay has nothing to do with the hero of Sherwood Forest – the origin of its name is a mystery, and the locals call it Bay Town or just Bay. But there's no denying that this fishing village is one of the prettiest spots on the Yorkshire coast.

Leave your car at the parking area in the upper village (£4 for four hours), where 19th-century ships' captains built comfortable Victorian villas, and walk downhill to Old Bay, the oldest part of the village (don't even think about driving down). This maze of narrow lanes and passages is dotted with tearooms, pubs, craft shops and artists' studios (there's even a tiny cinema), and at low tide you can go down onto the beach and fossick around in the rock pools.

Robin Hood's Bay is 6 miles southeast of Whitby. Bus 93 runs hourly between Whitby and Scarborough via Robin Hood's Bay.

★ **Bridge Cottage Bistro** BRITISH ££
(☑ 01947-893438; www.bridgecottagebistro.com; East Row, Sandsend; mains £12-28; ⊙ 10am-4pm Tue-Sun, 6.30-9pm Thu & Sat, 7-9pm Fri) This outstanding Modern British restaurant, in the pretty coastal village of Sandsend 3 miles north of Whitby, may well be the east coast's best eating experience. Its no-nonsense setting in a bare old coastal cottage lets the food sing, and the spotlight is always on Yorkshire, with delights like hay-baked lamb, Whitby sea trout with cured beetroot, and Eccles cakes with Wensleydale ice cream.

★ **White Horse & Griffin** BRITISH ££
(☑ 01947-604857; www.whitehorseandgriffin.com; 87 Church St; mains £15-24; ⊙ noon-9pm Mon-Sat, 12.30-4pm & 5.30-9pm Sun; ⛽🐕) This splendid old coaching inn is as old as Captain Cook, and indeed the man himself used it as a meeting place to fix his crews in the 17th century. Squeeze into the narrow bar and the restaurant behind it is barely noticeable, but what a find: expect elegantly presented, top-quality British cooking that celebrates both local seafood and Yorkshire meat.

Quayside FISH & CHIPS ££
(☑ 01947-825346; www.quaysidewhitby.co.uk; 7 Pier Rd; mains £9-15; ⊙ 11am-8pm; 🚗) 🐟 Top-notch fish and chips minus the 'world's best' tag line used by nearby competitor the Magpie Cafe – this place is your best bet if you want to avoid the queues there. Takeaway fish and chips are £4.60.

Star Inn the Harbour BRITISH ££
(☑ 01947-821900; www.starinntheharbour.co.uk; Langborne Rd; mains £12-24; ⊙ 11.30am-9pm Mon-Fri, from noon Sat, noon-7pm Sun) Yorkshire food hero Andrew Pern, of Michelin-starred Star Inn (p501) fame, gutted the former tourist office to create this spin-off restaurant on the harbour front in his home town of Whitby. It's no surprise that the theme is nautical and the menu leans heavily on its fishy environs, though there are also playful dishes such as Yorkshire pudding and foie gras.

🍷 Drinking & Nightlife

★ **Whitby Brewery** MICROBREWERY
(☑ 01947-228871; www.whitby-brewery.com; Abbey Lane, East Cliff; ⊙ 11am-5pm; 🅿) Walkers are pleased as punch when they find this place on the clifftop behind Whitby Abbey. There's just enough room inside the modern brew plant for three tables – half the space is taken up by a gloriously incongruous Edwardian bar counter, behind which the bartender is well and truly trapped. There's a short selection of craft ales, and extra seating out front.

Green Dragon CRAFT BEER
(www.thegreendragonwhitby.co.uk; Grape Lane; ⊙ noon-7.30pm Mon-Sat, to 6pm Sun) In a quaint old house on Whitby's most crooked lane, Green Dragon has grabbed the bull by the horns and dragged Britain's progressive craft-beer scene into this traditional real-ale town. It's part bottle shop, part teeny-weeny beer bar with five rotating taps running Yorkshire breweries like Northern Monk, Abbeydale and Vocation. Or buy any bottle (at shop price) to drink in.

☆ Entertainment

Dracula Experience THEATRE
(☑ 01947-601923; 9 Marine Pde; adult/child £3/2.50; ⊙ 9.45am-5pm Easter-Oct, Sat & Sun Nov-Easter) There's definitely an element of Gothic geekdom about this theatrical walk-

through of *Dracula*'s tale, with special effects, an occasional live actor appearing out of thin air and many a thing that goes bump in the night designed to spook you in the darkness. Wonderfully weird and very Whitby; not suitable for under eights.

ℹ️ Information

Whitby Tourist Office (☎ 01723-383636; www.visitwhitby.com; Harbour Master's Office, Langborne Rd; ⏰ 9.30am-5pm May-Oct, 10.30am-4pm Thu-Sun Nov-Apr)

ℹ️ Getting There & Away

BUS

Two buses, 93 and X93, run south to Scarborough (£6.20, one hour, every 30 minutes), with every second bus going via Robin Hood's Bay (£4.30, 15 minutes, hourly); and north to Middlesborough (£6.20, one hour, hourly), with fewer services on Sunday. The **bus station** is next to Whitby's train station.

The Coastliner service 840 runs from Leeds to Whitby (£14, 3¼ hours, four times daily Monday to Saturday, twice on Sundays, though you'll need to change at Malton) via York and Pickering.

TRAIN

Coming from the north, you can get to Whitby by train along the Esk Valley Railway from Middlesbrough (£7.10, 1½ hours, four daily), with connections from Durham and Newcastle. From the south, it's easier to get a train from York to Scarborough, and then a bus from Scarborough to Whitby.

YORKSHIRE DALES NATIONAL PARK

The Yorkshire Dales – named from the old Norse word *dalr,* meaning 'valleys', and protected as a national park since the 1950s – are beloved as one of England's best hiking and cycling areas. The park's glacial valleys are characterised by a distinctive landscape of high heather moorland, stepped skylines and flat-topped hills, punctuated by delightful country pubs and windswept trails.

Down in the green valleys, patchworked with drystone dykes and little barns, are picture-postcard villages where sheep still graze on village greens. And in the limestone country of the southern Dales you'll find England's best examples of karst scenery (created by rainwater dissolving the underlying limestone bedrock).

The whole area is seriously scenic and easy to explore. Consequently it's popular with holidaying Britons – book accommodation ahead as there are no big hotels here. Beds get particularly scarce on public holiday weekends and during events such as the annual Tour de Yorkshire.

ℹ️ Getting There & Away

About 90% of visitors to the park arrive by car, and the narrow roads can become extremely crowded in summer. Parking can also be a serious problem. If you can, try to use public transport as much as possible.

Bus services are limited, and many run in summer only, some on Sundays and bank holidays only; pick up a DalesBus timetable from tourist offices, or consult the DalesBus (www.dalesbus.org) website.

By train, the best and most interesting access to the Dales is via the famous **Settle–Carlisle Line** (SCL; ☎ 01768-353200; www.settle-carlisle.co.uk). Trains run between Leeds and Carlisle, stopping at Skipton, Settle and numerous small villages, offering unrivalled access to the hills straight from the station platform.

Skipton

☎ 01756 / POP 14,625

Home to one of England's best-preserved medieval castles and gateway to the southern Dales, this busy market town takes its name from the Anglo-Saxon *sceape ton* (sheep town). There are no prizes for

---

OFF THE BEATEN TRACK

FORBIDDEN CORNER

There can surely be no other place like **Forbidden Corner** (☎ 01969-640638; www.theforbiddencorner.co.uk; Tupgill Park Estate, near Leyburn; adult/child £12.50/10.50; ⏰ noon-dusk Mon-Sat Easter-Oct, Sun only Nov & Dec; 🅿️ 🚻) in the world: a modern walled garden furnished with Victorian-style follies, some veering into Gothic horror, others merely surreal fantasy. There's no map, so it's a case of diving in to explore the many tunnels, twisted turns and dead-ends – an experience that may make you feel like you've fallen into David Bowie's *Labyrinth*. Small children are guaranteed to feel scared witless at some turns; adults may leave feeling a little rattled, too. Tickets must be pre-booked.

guessing how it made its money. Monday, Wednesday, Friday and Saturday are market days, bringing crowds from all over and giving the town something of a festive atmosphere.

The Leeds–Liverpool Canal carves right through central Skipton, making the town a good jumping-off point for canal-boat trips.

Sights & Activities

★ Skipton Castle   CASTLE
(www.skiptoncastle.co.uk; High St; adult/child £8.30/5.20; ⊙10am-6pm Mon-Sat, noon-6pm Sun Apr-Sep, to 5pm Oct-Mar) What makes Skipton Castle so fascinating is its splendid state of preservation, providing a striking contrast to the ruins you'll see elsewhere. Although it is lauded as one of the best-preserved medieval castles in England, many of its most memorable features date to Tudor times. Entrance is through the original Norman archway, which leads to a Tudor courtyard

with a yew tree planted by Lady Anne Clifford in 1659, and beyond that a warren of rooms to explore. Grab the informative free illustrated guide to the castle from the ticket office, available in several languages.

Timber foundations were laid here in 1090 by a Norman baron, then soon replaced by a tougher stone castle after relentless attacks by marauding Scots. It was given to the Clifford family in 1310 by King Edward II and the same family ruled it for more than 350 years. During the English Civil War, the castle was the last Royalist stronghold in the North of England and was heavily damaged by a three-year siege that led to defeat in 1645. Much of what exists today is the result of restoration efforts by Lady Anne Clifford in the 17th century.

Pennine Cruisers   BOATING
(☎01756-795478; www.penninecruisers.com; The Wharf, Coach St; per person £4; ⊙10.30am-dusk Mar-Oct) No trip to Skipton is complete with-

Yorkshire Dales National Park

out a cruise along the Leeds–Liverpool Canal, which runs through the middle of town. Pennine Cruisers runs half-hour trips along the canal and back, as well as canal-boat day hire, skippered trips and longer holiday rentals.

🛏 Sleeping

★ The Pinfold
GUESTHOUSE **££**

(📞 07510 175270; http://thepinfoldskipton.wixsite.com/pinfold; Chapel Hill; r £60-80; 🅿 🛜) This petite, room-only guesthouse has three light and airy, oak-beamed rooms with a lovely fresh country feel. Forgive the tiny shower rooms, because the excellent location around the corner from Skipton Castle and the High St more than compensates. The largest room has its own sitting area, but the best deal is the Littondale room with its own entrance, parking and small grassy patio.

Park Hill
B&B **££**

(📞 01756-792772; www.parkhillskipton.co.uk; 17 Grassington Rd; d £90; 🅿 🛜) From the complimentary glass of sherry on arrival to the hearty breakfasts based on local produce, such as farm-fresh eggs and home-grown tomatoes, this B&B provides a real Yorkshire welcome. It enjoys an attractive semi-rural location half a mile north of the town centre, on the B6265 road towards Grassington. No children under 12.

🍴 Eating & Drinking

Bizzie Lizzies
FISH & CHIPS **£**

(📞 01756-701131; www.bizzielizzies.co.uk; 36 Swadford St; mains £9-12; ⊙ 11am-9pm; 🚹) An award-winning, old-fashioned fish-and-chip restaurant overlooking the canal, with a busy takeaway counter offering fish and chips for £5.80 (counter open to 11.30pm). Gluten-intolerant? No problem – Bizzie Lizzies also dishes up gluten-free chips accredited by Coeliac UK.

★ Le Caveau
BRITISH **££**

(📞 01756-794274; www.lecaveau.co.uk; 86 High St; mains £17-20; ⊙ noon-2.30pm & 7-9pm Tue-Fri, 5-9pm Sat) 🍴 Thanks to the stylish decoration there's no hint that this 16th-century cellar was once a prison for sheep rustlers. It's now one of Skipton's best bistros, offering a seasonal menu built lovingly around fresh local produce, with tempting dishes such as twice-baked smoked Ribblesdale goats cheese soufflé and slow-roasted Nidderdale lamb shoulder. On weekdays you can get a two-course lunch for £12.95.

WORTH A TRIP

BRITAIN'S HIGHEST PUB

At an elevation of 328m (1732ft) **Tan Hill Inn** (📞 01833-628246; www.tanhillinn.com; Tan Hill, Swaledale; ⊙ 8am-11.30pm Jul & Aug, 9am-9.30pm Sep-Jun; 🛜 🚹 🐕) is Britain's highest pub. Built to cater for 19th-century miners, it perches in the middle of nowhere about 11 miles northwest of Reeth. At times the howling wind can make it feel a bit wild up here, but inside it's unexpectedly comfortable and welcoming, with an ancient fireplace in the atmospheric, stone-flagged public bar and leather sofas in the lounge.

Narrow Boat
PUB

(www.markettowntaverns.co.uk; 38 Victoria St; ⊙ noon-11pm; 🛜 🚹 🐕) Down a back alley beside Skipton's canal basin, this friendly pub is essentially a modern craft beer bar but still manages to cultivate a traditional feel with wooden beams and old bar furniture. The beer selection is great; soak it up with interesting bar food such as halloumi chips, southern fried chicken burgers and a rotating range of flatbread pizzas.

ℹ Information

Tourist Office (📞 01756-792809; www.welcometoskipton.com; Town Hall, High St; ⊙ 9.30am-4pm Mon-Sat)

ℹ Getting There & Away

Skipton is the last stop on the Metro rail network from Leeds (from £5.80, 45 minutes, frequent departures). Buses 580 to 582 link Skipton with Settle Monday to Saturday (£5.50, 40 minutes, hourly during the day), with many departures continuing on to Ingleton. There are also twice daily buses from Skipton to Malham (£4, 40 minutes) Monday to Saturday, and frequent departures from Skipton to Grassington.

Grassington

📞 01756 / POP 1611

A good base for jaunts around the south Dales, Grassington's handsome Georgian centre teems with walkers and visitors throughout the summer months, soaking up an atmosphere that – despite the odd touch of faux rusticity – is as attractive and traditional as you'll find in these parts.

RIBBLESDALE & THE THREE PEAKS

Scenic Ribblesdale cuts through the southwestern corner of the Yorkshire Dales National Park, where the skyline is dominated by a trio of distinctive hills known as the Three Peaks: Whernside (735m), Ingleborough (724m) and Pen-y-ghent (694m). Easily accessible via the Settle–Carlisle railway line (p507), this is one of England's most popular areas for outdoor activities, attracting thousands of hikers, cyclists and cavers each weekend.

At the head of the valley, 5 miles north of Horton, is the spectacular 30m-high Ribblehead Viaduct, built in 1874 and, at 400m, the longest on the Settle–Carlisle Line. You can hike there along the Pennine Way and travel back by train from Ribblehead station.

A traditional cafe run by the same family since 1965, the **Pen-y-Ghent Cafe** (☑ 01729-860333; mains £3-6; ⊙ 9am-5.30pm Mon & Wed-Fri, 8am-5.30pm Sat, from 8.30am Sun; ⓟ ☑ ♿) in Horton-in-Ribblesdale fills walkers' fuel tanks with fried eggs and chips, homemade scones and pint-sized mugs of tea, and can cater for vegans and those on gluten-free diets. It also sells maps, walking guidebooks and hiking gear.

⭐ Festivals & Events

Grassington Festival   ART
(www.grassington-festival.org.uk; ⊙ Jun) Highlight of the cultural year in the Yorkshire Dales is the Grassington Festival, a two-week arts extravaganza that attracts many big names in music, theatre and comedy, and also includes offbeat events like drystone-walling workshops.

🛏 Sleeping & Eating

Ashfield House   B&B ££
(☑ 01756-752584; www.ashfieldhouse.co.uk; Summers Fold; d £80-127, ste £155-215; ⓟ ﹫) A secluded 17th-century country house with a walled garden, open fireplaces, honesty bar, and all-round cosy feel. It's just off the main square.

⭐ Devonshire Fell   HOTEL £££
(☑ 01756-718111; www.devonshirefell.co.uk; Burnsall; r from £129; ⓟ ﹫ ☀) This former gentleman's club for mill owners in the scenic village of Burnsall has a very contemporary feel and spacious rooms, many with beautiful valley views. The conservatory (used as a restaurant, breakfast room and for afternoon tea) has a stunning outlook. It's 3 miles southeast of Grassington, which can be reached via a walking path by the river.

Corner House Cafe   CAFE £
(☑ 01756-752414; www.cornerhousegrassington.co.uk; 1 Garr's Lane; mains £6-10; ⊙ 10am-4pm; ﹫ ♿ ☀) This cute little white cottage, just uphill from the village square, serves good coffee and unusual homemade cakes (citrus and lavender syrup sponge is unexpectedly delicious), as well as tasty made-to-order sandwiches and lunch specials such as Dales lamb hotpot or chicken and chorizo gratin. Breakfast, served till 11.30am, ranges from cinnamon toast to the full-English fry-up.

ℹ Information

Grassington National Park Centre (☑ 01756-751690; Hebden Rd; 2/24hr parking £2.50/5; ⊙ 10am-5pm Apr-Oct, to 4pm Sat & Sun Nov, Dec, Feb & Mar)

ℹ Getting There & Away

Grassington is 6 miles north of Skipton; take bus 72 from Skipton bus or train station (£4.20, 30 minutes, hourly Monday to Saturday), or X43 (hourly, Sunday and public holidays) from the bus station only. For onward travel, bus 72 continues up the valley to the villages of Kettlewell and Buckden.

Hawes

POP 1137

Hawes is the beating heart of Wensleydale, a thriving and picturesque market town (market day is Tuesday) surrounded by rolling hills and hiking trails. It has several antique, art and craft shops, and the added attraction of its own waterfall in the village centre. On busy summer weekends, however, Hawes' narrow arteries can get seriously clogged with traffic. Leave the car in the parking area beside the national park centre at the eastern entrance to the village.

A mile northwest of Hawes, the pretty village of Hardraw has an even more impressive waterfall, a country church and an excellent old pub offering accommodation for those who prefer a quieter rural base.

⊙ Sights

Hardraw Force WATERFALL
(www.hardrawforce.com; Hardraw; adult/child £2.50/1.50; P) About 1.5 miles north of Hawes is 30m-high Hardraw Force, the highest unbroken waterfall in England, but by international standards not that impressive (except after heavy rain). Access is via a lovely landscaped walk (400m) from the car park behind the Green Dragon Inn. There's an admission fee (cash only) to access the walk, and a cafe selling local ice cream.

Wensleydale Creamery MUSEUM
(www.wensleydale.co.uk; Gayle Lane; adult/child £3.95/2.45; ⊙10am-5pm; P⊞) Wensleydale Creamery is devoted to the production of a crumbly white cheese that's the favourite of animation characters Wallace and Gromit. You can visit the cheese museum, watch cheesemakers in action in the viewing gallery (Monday to Friday), and then try-before-you-buy in the shop (which is free to enter). An interactive exhibit for kids explains the process from grass to cow to cheese.

There's also a cafe on-site serving giant scones, Wensleydale cheese on toast and grilled-cheese sandwiches.

Dales Countryside Museum MUSEUM
(☑01969-666210; www.dalescountrysidemuseum. org.uk; Station Yard; adult/child £4.80/free; ⊙10am-5pm, closed Jan; P⊞) Sharing a building with the national park centre, the Dales Countryside Museum is a beautifully presented social history of the area that explains the forces shaping the landscape, from geology to lead mining to land enclosure and the railways.

⊨ Sleeping & Eating

★Green Dragon Inn INN ££
(☑01969-667392; www.greendragonhardraw.co. uk; Hardraw; dm/d/ste £18/97/120; P⊛≋⊛) A lovely old pub with flagstone floors, low timber beams, ancient oak furniture and Theakston's on draught. The Dragon serves up a tasty steak-and-ale pie and offers bunkhouse accommodation or B&B in pleasant, simple rooms behind the pub, as well as a pair of fancy suites above the bar. One mile northwest of Hawes.

Herriot's Guest House B&B ££
(☑01969-667536; www.herriotsinhawes.co.uk; Main St; s/d from £50/82; ⊛) This petite guesthouse in an old stone building is in a great location close to the town waterfall, with six comfy en-suite bedrooms set above a coffee shop, free homemade biscuits and walkers' packages. Top-floor rooms have lovely Dales views.

❶ Information

Hawes National Park Centre (☑01969-666210; Station Yard; parking 2/24hr £2.50/5; ⊙10am-5pm Apr-Oct, early closing Nov, Dec, Feb & Mar, closed Jan)

Malham
POP 238

Even in the Dales, where competition is fierce, Malham stands out as a strikingly attractive village. Stone cottages and inns huddle around a river that meanders through its centre and there is always a buzz about the place because of its famed hiking paths, which draw walking enthusiasts from all over the world. If you have time for only one stop in the Dales, make it here.

The village sits within the largest area of limestone country in England, stretching west from Grassington to Ingleton – a distinctive landscape pockmarked with potholes, dry valleys, limestone pavements and gorges. Two of the most spectacular features – Malham Cove and Gordale Scar – are within walking distance of Malham's centre.

⊙ Sights & Activities

★Malham Cove NATURAL FEATURE
North of Malham village, a 0.75-mile field walk beside a lovely babbling stream leads to Malham Cove, a huge rock amphitheatre lined with 80m-high vertical cliffs. A large glacial waterfall once tumbled over this cliff, but it dried up hundreds of years ago. You can hike up the steep steps on the left-hand side of the cove (follow Pennine Way signs) to see the extensive limestone pavement above the cliffs – a filming location in *Harry Potter and the Deathly Hallows*.

Peregrine falcons nest at the top in spring, when the Royal Society for the Protection of Birds (RSPB) sets up a birdwatching lookout with telescopes near the base of the cliff – call the national park centre (p512) for the schedule as it changes every year.

Malham Landscape Trail WALKING
(www.malhamdale.com) This 5-mile circular trail is one of the best day hikes in Yorkshire, linking three impressive natural features:

Malham Cove (p511); spectacular **Gordale Scar**, a deep limestone canyon with scenic cascades; and the remains of an Iron Age settlement, and **Janet's Foss** waterfall. A leaflet describing the trail in detail can be downloaded from the website or picked up at pubs and hotels in the village.

Malham Tarn   LAKE

A glacial lake and nature reserve 3.5 miles north of Malham village, accessible via a 1.5-mile walk north from Malham Cove, or by car. There are two car parks: the one at the southern edge is bigger and picks up a trail that skirts the eastern side of the lake; the one to the north (follow signs to Arncliffe/Grassington) allows easy access to an extensive bog-skimming boardwalk that wends through fen and woodland scrub. Roe deer, heron and water voles can sometimes be spotted here.

Sleeping & Eating

Malham YHA   HOSTEL £

(☑ 0845 371 9529; www.yha.org.uk; Finkle St; dm/tw from £13/49; ⊞ �📶) This purpose-built hostel has a central village location across the bridge from the main road, with a pretty garden out front and useful facilities such as bike storage, a drying room, and a shop selling beer and wine. A handful of private rooms have quite luxurious en-suite bathrooms; rates vary wildly depending on day of the week and demand.

⭐**Lister Barn**   B&B £££

(☑ 01729-830444; www.thwaites.co.uk; Cove Rd; d £140-180; ⊞ 📶 🐕) The Lister Arms pub in Malham runs this chic barn conversion on the main road through the village, with eight modern rooms centred on a lovely open-plan communal area with free herbal teas and a log burner to huddle around after long walks. One room is suitable for wheelchair users and there are two family rooms with bunks and a separate bedroom.

Lister Arms   PUB FOOD ££

(☑ 01729-830444; www.thwaites.co.uk; Cove Rd; mains £10-18; ⊗ 8am-11pm Mon-Sat, to 10.30pm Sun; ⊞ 📶 🐕) This comfy coaching inn is the best spot in Malham to kick back after a walk, with open fires for chilly days, a beer garden out back and classic pub meals plus chalkboard specials. In the busy summer months drinkers lounge out on the grass in front of the pub.

ⓘ Information

Malham National Park Centre (☑ 01729-833200; www.yorkshiredales.org.uk; parking 2/24hr £2.50/5; ⊗ 10am-5pm Apr-Oct, to 4pm Sat & Sun Nov, Dec, Feb & Mar) In the car park at the southern edge of Malham village; the walking leaflets it sells (£1.50) include more detail than the free leaflet given out around the village.

ⓘ Getting There & Away

There are at least two buses a day Monday to Saturday year-round from Skipton to Malham (£4.10, 35 minutes). The scenic Malham Tarn Shuttle bus route links Settle with Malham (£4, 30 minutes), Malham Tarn and Ingleton six times daily on Sundays and bank holidays only, Easter to October. Check the DalesBus website (www.dalesbus.org) or ask at Malham National Park Centre for details.

MASHAM

Located 9 miles northwest of Ripon, the little village of Masham is famous for producing some of Yorkshire's best beers. Yorkshire's best-known brewery, **Theakston's** (☑ 01765-680000; www.theakstons.co.uk; The Brewery, Masham; tour adult/child £8.50/4.95; ⊗ 10.30am-4.30pm Sep-Jul, to 5pm Aug), was founded way back in 1827, then taken over by global brewer Scottish & Newcastle in 1987, but since 2004 has been back in family hands. Old Peculier, its most famous ale, takes its name from the Peculier of Masham, a medieval parish court established to deal with offences such as drunkenness and brawling. There's a visitor centre that doubles as a bar, and four tours a day (five in August).

Across the village, **Black Sheep Brewery** (☑ 01765-680101; www.blacksheepbrewery.com; Wellgarth, Masham; tours adult/child £9.50/4.95; ⊗ 10am-5pm Sun-Wed, to 11pm Thu-Sat; ⊞ 🐕) was founded in 1992 by the 'black sheep' of the Theakston family, Paul Theakston, who left to start his own brewery after the controversial Scottish & Newcastle takeover. It's now almost as famous as its near neighbour, with four entertaining tours a day, an excellent casual bistro, and a bar where you can sample most of the brewery's ales and craft beers.

Note that Malham is reached via narrow roads that can get very congested in summer, so leave your car at the national park centre and walk into the village.

Richmond

📞 01748 / POP 8415

The handsome market town of Richmond perches on a rocky outcrop overlooking the River Swale and is guarded by the ruins of a massive castle, beneath which a small, frothy waterfall flows. It has been a garrison town for centuries and home to one of England's most prized regiments, which now resides nearby at modern-day Catterick Garrison.

Elegant Georgian buildings and photogenic stone cottages line the streets that radiate from the broad cobbled market square (market day is Saturday), with glimpses of the surrounding hills and dales peeking through the gaps. There are plenty of local walks, and the town makes a pleasant base for exploring the northern Dales, though it is sorely lacking decent eating and drinking options; you'll find no cute old inns here.

◉ Sights

★ **Georgian Theatre Royal** HISTORIC BUILDING
(www.georgiantheatreroyal.co.uk; Victoria Rd; adult/child £5/2; ⊙ tours hourly 10am-4pm Mon-Sat mid-Feb–mid-Nov) Built in 1788, this is the most complete Georgian playhouse in Britain. It closed in 1848 and was used as an auction house into the early 20th century, reopening as a working theatre again in 1963 after a period of restoration. Fascinating tours (starting on the hour) include a look at the country's oldest surviving stage scenery, painted between 1818 and 1836.

Richmond Castle CASTLE
(EH; www.english-heritage.org.uk; Tower St; adult/child £6.20/3.70; ⊙ 10am-6pm Easter-Sep, to 5pm Oct, to 4pm Sat & Sun Nov-Easter) The impressive heap that is Richmond Castle, founded in 1070, has had many uses through the years, including a stint as a prison for conscientious objectors during WWI (there's a small and fascinating exhibition about their part in the castle's history – enter through the shop). The best part of a visit is the view from the top of the remarkably well-preserved 30m-high keep, which dates to the late 12th century and towers over the town.

BIKING IN THE DALES

The centre of mountain biking in the Yorkshire Dales, the **Dales Bike Centre** (📞 01748-884908; www.dalesbike centre.co.uk; Fremington; mountain bike/e-bike per day from £30/50; ⊙ 9am-5pm), 12 miles west of Richmond, provides quality rentals (mountain and road bikes, as well as e-bikes), a bike shop and repair service, advice and trail maps, guided rides (£199 per day for up to seven people), a cosy cafe with decent coffee and comfortable bunkhouse accommodation (two-bunk room £58 a night).

🛏 Sleeping

Old Dairy B&B ££
(📞 01748-886057; www.olddairylowrow.wordpress. com; Low Row, Swaledale; s/d £65/80; 🅿 🛜 🐾) Guests will feel right at home in this 200-year-old village house in the heart of the Dales, where the owners have converted two rooms into comfortable, modern guest bedrooms with lovely views across the dale. There's cake in the afternoons, and the owners are a fount of knowledge on local walking, biking, stargazing and astrophotography. It's near Reeth, 15 miles west of Richmond.

Frenchgate Hotel BOUTIQUE HOTEL ££
(📞 01748-822087; www.thefrenchgate.co.uk; 59-61 Frenchgate; s/d from £88/118; 🅿 🛜) Nine elegant bedrooms occupy the upper floors of this converted Georgian town house, with flash touches such as memory-foam mattresses and heated marble floors in luxurious bathrooms. Parts of the house date to 1650, so we can forgive a crack here or peeling paint there. Downstairs there's an excellent restaurant (three-course dinner £39), an oasis of a garden and a private car park at the rear.

🍴 Eating

★ **George & Dragon** PUB FOOD £
(📞 01748-518373; www.georgeanddragonhudswell. co.uk; Hudswell; mains £8-10; ⊙ food served noon-2pm & 6-9pm Mon-Sat, noon-4pm Sun; 🛜 🌻) A mile and a half west of Richmond, the George & Dragon is a genuine local pub, owned and managed by the community. It serves a small menu of freshly prepared pub grub, including roast beef and Yorkshire pudding on Sundays, and has won awards

for its excellent rotating beer selection. The backyard terrace has gorgeous Dales views.

The Station
BRITISH £

(☑01748-850123; www.thestation.co.uk; Station Yard) Richmond's defunct Victorian railway station has been converted into a bold multipurpose space housing exhibition galleries, an independent cinema, craft brewery (offering tastings and sales) and ice-cream parlour. Locals come for takeaway lunch at Angel's Share Bakery, which bakes fresh breads, quiches and local specialities such as Yorkshire curd tart on-site. Take your goodies to a grassy picnic table outside.

Rustique
FRENCH ££

(☑01748-821565; www.rustiquerichmond.co.uk; Chantry Wynd, Finkle St; mains £11-23; ⏾noon-9pm) 🍴 Tucked away in a quirky vaulted arcade space, this bistro has consistently impressed with its mastery of French country cooking, from *confit de canard* (duck slow roasted in its own fat) to *moules marinière* (mussels with white wine, garlic and cream). Booking is recommended.

❶ Information

Richmond Tourist Office (☑01609-532980; www.richmond.org; Richmond Library, Queens Rd; ⏾10am-5pm Mon & Thu-Fri, to 7pm Tue, to noon Wed, to 1pm Sat, from 10.30am Jan & Feb) A tiny tourist office with less information than can be found at other outlets across Yorkshire.

❶ Getting There & Away

From Darlington (on the railway between London and Edinburgh) it's easy to reach Richmond on bus X26 or X27 (£5.30, 30 minutes, every half-hour, hourly on Sunday). All buses stop in Trinity Church Sq.

On Sundays and bank-holiday Mondays only, from May to September, the Northern Dalesman bus 830 runs from Richmond to Hawes (£4, 1½ hours, twice daily) via Reeth, and the afternoon bus continues to Ribblehead.

WEST YORKSHIRE

It was the tough and unforgiving textile industry that drove West Yorkshire's economy from the 18th century onward. The woollen mills, factories and canals built to transport raw materials and finished products defined much of the county's landscape. But that's all in the past, and recent years have seen the transformation of this once hard-bitten area into quite the picture postcard.

Leeds and Bradford, two adjoining cities so big they've virtually become one, are undergoing radical redevelopment and reinvention, prettifying their centres and tempting more adventurous tourists with new museums, galleries and restaurants. Beyond the cities lies a landscape of wild moorland dissected by deep valleys dotted with old mill towns and villages, scenes that were so vividly described by the Brontë sisters, West Yorkshire's most renowned literary export and biggest tourist draw.

❶ Getting There & Around

The Metro is West Yorkshire's highly efficient train and bus network, centred on Leeds and Bradford, which are also the main gateways to the county. For transport information, contact **West Yorkshire Metro** (☑0113-245 7676; www.wymetro.com).

Day Rover tickets (£8.40) are good for one day's unlimited travel on Metro buses and trains from 9.30am to 4pm and after 6.30pm on weekdays, and all day at weekends. A range of additional Rover tickets covering buses and/or trains, plus heaps of useful Metro maps and timetables, are available from bus and train stations and most tourist offices in West Yorkshire.

Leeds
☑0113 / POP 474,632

Just an hour south of the southern Dales and one of the fastest-growing cities in the UK, Leeds is the glitzy embodiment of rediscovered northern self-confidence. A decade and a half of redevelopment has transformed the city centre from a near-derelict mill town into a vision of 21st-century urban chic, with architecturally daring malls woven into the fabric of the city centre, a revitalised Victorian mill district and an innovative independent dining and drinking scene.

People come from all over the north to indulge in shopping weekends, concert trips and the lively nightlife, giving the town a decidedly confident Yorkshire swagger. There's not much in the way of tourist sights except for the national Royal Armouries museum, but excellent transport links to the Dales, York, Harrogate, Manchester and Haworth (of Brontë literary fame) can make it a good base, without the touristy veneer of neighbouring York.

Leeds

Leeds

◉ Sights
1 Henry Moore Institute	B1
2 Leeds Art Gallery	A1
3 Thornton's Arcade	C2

🛏 Sleeping
4 42 The Calls	D4
5 Art Hostel	D3
6 Chambers	A3
7 Dakota	A2
8 Quebecs	A3
9 Roomzzz Leeds City	C4

✴ Eating
10 Art's Cafe Bar & Restaurant	C3
Belgrave Music Hall & Canteen	(see 24)
11 Bundobust	B3
12 Caravanserai	C3
13 Cat's Pyjamas	D2
14 Friends of Ham	B3
15 Hansa's Gujarati	D1

Ox Club	(see 19)
16 Reliance	D1
17 Shears Yard	D3

🍷 Drinking & Nightlife
18 Bar Fibre	C3
19 Headrow House	C2
20 HiFi Club	C3
21 Laynes Espresso	B3
22 Mission	C4
23 North Bar	C2

✪ Entertainment
24 Belgrave Music Hall & Canteen	C1
25 City Varieties	C2

🛍 Shopping
26 Corn Exchange	C3
27 Harvey Nichols	C2
28 Kirkgate Market	C3
29 Victoria Quarter	C2

⊙ Sights

★ Royal Armouries   MUSEUM
(www.royalarmouries.org; Armouries Dr; ⊙10am-5pm; P ⛟) FREE Leeds' most interesting museum was originally built in 1996 to house armour and weapons from the Tower of London, but subsequently expanded to cover 3000 years of combat and self-defence, becoming home to the national collections. The exhibits are as varied as they are fascinating, covering subjects such as jousting, fencing and Indian elephant armour. To get here, walk east along the river from Centenary Footbridge (approx 10 minutes), or take the free boat from Granary Wharf outside Leeds train station's southern entrance.

Leeds Art Gallery   GALLERY
(www.leeds.gov.uk/artgallery; The Headrow; ⊙10am-5pm Tue-Sat, 11am-3pm Sun) FREE This major gallery is packed with 19th- and 20th-century British heavyweights – Turner, Constable, Stanley Spencer, Wyndham Lewis et al – along with contemporary pieces by more recent arrivals such as Antony Gormley, sculptor of the *Angel of the North*. It reopened in October 2017 after a major restoration program that uncovered a lost Victorian barrel-vaulted glass ceiling in one of its rooms.

Leeds Industrial Museum   MUSEUM
(Armley Mills; ☑0113-3783173; www.leeds.gov.uk/museumsandgalleries/armleymills; Canal Rd, Armley; adult/child £4/2; ⊙10am-5pm Tue-Sat, 1-5pm Sun; P⛟) One of the world's largest textile mills has been transformed into a museum telling the story of Leeds' industrial past, both glorious and ignominious. The city grew rich from the textile industry, but at some cost in human terms – working conditions were Dickensian. As well as a selection of mill machinery, there's an informative display about how cloth is made. The museum is 2 miles west of the city centre; take bus 15 from Vicar Lane near Kirkgate Market.

Kirkstall Abbey   CHURCH
(www.leeds.gov.uk/kirkstallabbey; Abbey Rd, Kirkstall; ⊙10am-4.30pm Tue-Sun Apr-Sep, to 4pm Oct-Mar) FREE Leeds' most impressive medieval structure is beautiful Kirkstall Abbey, founded in 1152 by Cistercian monks from Fountains Abbey in North Yorkshire. These days the city makes good use of it as an atmospheric backdrop for pop-up events and a monthly weekend food market (April to November; check online for dates). It's 3 miles northwest of the centre; take bus 33, 33A or 757.

Across the road is the **Abbey House Museum** (www.leeds.gov.uk/museumsandgalleries; Abbey Walk, Kirkstall; adult/child £4.95/2.50; ⊙10am-5pm Tue-Fri & Sun, noon-5pm Sat; P⛟), which was once the Great Gate House to the abbey. It contains meticulously reconstructed shops and houses that evoke Victorian Leeds, plus rotating exhibitions mostly aimed at kids.

Tetley   GALLERY
(☑0113-3202423; www.thetetley.org; Hunslet Rd; ⊙10am-5pm Thu-Tue, to 8pm Wed) Tetley Brewery's defunct 1930s offices have been converted into a contemporary-arts venue with a restaurant and pub on the ground floor, spilling out onto an outdoor terrace. Upstairs the old meeting rooms have been put to good use as quirky gallery spaces, housing rotating exhibitions from international and local artists and photographers. An immaculately preserved 1930s lift dominates the central stairwell shaft.

Thornton's Arcade   NOTABLE BUILDING
(enter off Briggate or Lands Lane) Though not the grandest, Thornton's Arcade was the first Victorian shopping arcade to be built in Leeds and remains one of the most interesting. Its sky-coloured, neo-Gothic arches rise up to a glass ceiling and its cupboard-sized shops host some of the city's best independent retailers and cafes. At the western end of the arcade, a giant automaton clock manned by life-sized figures of Robin Hood and Friar Tuck rings in the time on the hour.

Henry Moore Institute   GALLERY
(www.henry-moore.org/hmi; The Headrow; ⊙11am-5.30pm Tue & Thu-Sun, to 8pm Wed) FREE Housed in a converted Victorian warehouse in the city centre, this gallery showcases the work of 20th-century sculptors, but not, despite the name, anything by Henry Moore (1898–1986), who graduated from the Leeds School of Art. To see works by Moore, head to the Yorkshire Sculpture Park (p519) and Hepworth Wakefield (p519).

✦ Festivals & Events

Leeds Indie Food   FOOD & DRINK
(www.leedsindiefood.co.uk; ⊙mid-May; ⛟) This home-grown festival, launched in 2015, takes over Leeds' food scene for two weeks each May and has become one of the UK's most inventive celebrations of independent local

producers, restaurants, cafes and boozers. There are dozens of quirky events around town, such as kitchen takeovers, wine- and beer-pairing dinners, film nights, food photography workshops, foraging walks and brewery crawls.

Leeds Festival
MUSIC

(www.leedsfestival.com; ⊙end Aug) The August bank holiday weekend (the weekend preceding the last Monday in August) sees 50,000-plus music fans converge on Bramham Park, 10 miles outside the city centre, for the Leeds Festival. Spread across several stages, it's one of England's biggest rock-music extravaganzas. There are various camping/glamping options on-site, or you can buy day tickets.

🛏 Sleeping

★ Art Hostel
HOSTEL £

(☎0113-345 3363; www.arthostel.org.uk; 83 Kirkgate; dm/tw/tr £22.50/55/70; 🛜) Set in an appealingly grungy 200-year-old brick building near to Leeds' nightlife zone, this hostel is a great advert for the revitalisation of the city centre. Each room has been individually designed by a local artist, and the hostel is full of recycled furniture and innovative ideas.

Roomzzz Leeds City
APARTMENT ££

(☎0203-504 5555; www.roomzzz.com/leeds-city; 10 Swinegate; studio/2-person apt from £69/89; @🛜) This outfit offers bright and modern luxury apartments complete with fitted kitchens, with the added advantage of 24-hour hotel reception, and a great city-centre location; there are two other branches, both on Burley Rd, but this is by far the most central.

42 The Calls
BOUTIQUE HOTEL ££

(☎0113-244 0099; www.42thecalls.co.uk; 42 The Calls; r £85-160, ste from £180; @🛜) This pioneer of the boutique-hotel scene (it opened in 1991), set in a 19th-century grain mill, has been somewhat overshadowed by Leeds' clutch of new modern hotels, but its riverside setting and quirky original mill features in rooms still make it one of the city's most interesting places to stay. Breakfast costs extra and is pricey, but there are plenty of places to eat nearby.

★ Chambers
APARTMENT £££

(☎0113-386 3300; www.morethanjustabed.com; 30 Park Pl; 2-person apt £145-190, parking per night £12; 🅿🛜) This grand Edwardian office building has been converted into 63 luxury serviced apartments, ranging from two-person studios to a two-bedroom penthouse (£342 a night) that will sleep up to four adults. Simple, fresh and spotlessly clean, there's also a 24-hour reception with great service, a gym, honesty bar and pretty little patio for aperitifs or night caps.

★ Dakota
HOTEL £££

(☎0113-322 6261; http://leeds.dakotahotels.co.uk; 8 Russell St; d from £112, ste from £250; ❄🛜) Raising the bar for luxury sleeps in Leeds, this gleaming new hotel has quickly become popular thanks to its central location close to shops and bars, swanky yet muted designer interior and five-star service. Rooms are plush, modern and classic, and the suites are like mini-apartments, with open-plan lounge areas and dressing rooms with robes. Rates are room only.

Quebecs
BOUTIQUE HOTEL £££

(☎0113-244 8989; www.quebecshotel.co.uk; 9 Quebec St; d £85-165, ste £165-285; 🅿🛜) Victorian grace at its opulent best is the theme of Quebecs, a conversion of the former Leeds & County Liberal Club. The elaborate wood panelling and heraldic stained-glass windows in the public areas are mirrored by the grand design flourishes in the bedrooms, but it's a listed building (which means no double glazing) so expect some street noise.

🍴 Eating

Caravanserai
NORTH AFRICAN £

(☎0113-234 1999; www.caravanseraileeds.co.uk; 1 Crown St; dishes £3-8; ⊙10.30am-11pm Mon-Thu, to 3am or later Fri & Sat; 🛜) Emulating the traditional *caravansersai* (roadside inn) with cart wheels out front and carpets thickly draped over every inch of wall in the teeny upstairs 'banquet' room, this excellent street-food joint serves freshly prepared mezze, falafel and Ottoman barbecue from a hole in the wall. Don't miss the date-and-honey milkshake, served in a cinnamon-dusted jar. Cash only.

Belgrave Music Hall & Canteen
STREET FOOD £

(www.belgravemusichall.com; 1 Cross Belgrave St; mains £2.50-8; ⊙food served 11am-10pm; 🛜🎮) This bar and music venue has two great kitchens. One serves artisan pizza (watch out for the napalm chilli sauce); the other offers brunch and probably the best burgers in Yorkshire, all at great-value prices. Every second Saturday of the month the place hosts the **Belgrave Feast** (11am to 8pm), an art market and street-food festival.

Hansa's Gujarati   INDIAN £

(☑ 0113-244 4408; www.hansasrestaurant.com; 72-74 North St; mains £6.50-8; ⏱ 5-10pm Mon-Fri, to 11pm Sat, buffet noon-2pm Sun; ☑ 🚶) A Leeds institution, Hansa's has been dishing up wholesome Gujarati vegetarian cuisine for almost 20 years. The restaurant is plain and unassuming (save for a Hindu shrine), but the food is exquisite – specialities of the house include *khasta kachori* (fried pastries stuffed with chickpeas and potato laced with tamarind and mint), garnished with pomegranate.

Cat's Pyjamas   INDIAN £

(☑ 0113-234 0454; www.thecatspjs.co.uk; 9 Eastgate; mains £7-10; ⏱ 5-11pm Mon-Fri, from noon Sat, noon-10pm Sun) This popular suburban Indian street-food hall opened in Leeds city centre in mid-2017. Loud Bollywood wall murals offset a northern industrial aesthetic in the dining hall. The menu plays with an eclectic mash-up of subcontinent dishes (Goan chicken cafreal, tandoori grills and street-food bites like paneer tacos) and craft beers.

Bundobust   INDIAN £

(☑ 0113-243 1248; www.bundobust.com; 6 Mill Hill; dishes £3.75-6.50; ⏱ kitchen noon-9.30pm Mon-Thu, to 10pm Fri & Sat, to 8pm Sun; ☑) What could be more Yorkshire than craft beer and Indian street food rolled into one no-frills, brick-walled bar? The beers come from both local and international breweries, and food inspiration comes from vegetarian street-hawker offerings across India. The okra fries are a favourite with drinkers; more substantial bites include paneer and mushroom tikka, and biryani bhaji balls.

★ Friends of Ham   DELI ££

(☑ 0113-242 0275; www.friendsofham.co.uk; 4-8 New Station St; dishes £6-17; ⏱ 11am-11pm Mon-Wed, to midnight Thu-Sat, to 10pm Sun; ☎) This stylish bar serves the finest charcuterie and cheeses – Spanish, French, British – accompanied by fine wines and craft beers. The food is carefully selected and prepared, and utterly delicious; you can order individual tapas-like portions, or huge sharing platters with olive-oil-drizzled bread. Brunch served 11am till 2pm.

★ Ox Club   GRILL ££

(☑ 07470 359961; www.oxclub.co.uk; Bramleys Yard, The Headrow; mains £16-30; ⏱ 5-10pm Tue-Sat, brunch 11am-3pm Sat & Sun) Arguably the best restaurant in Leeds (or at least, the best without a Michelin star), Ox Club occupies an intimate, minimalist space and champions local produce with a deceptively simple menu. Though it bills itself as a grill restaurant, the Modern British dishes are far more inventive than what you'll find in your average BBQ joint – venison tartare with smoked fat, for example.

Reliance   BRITISH ££

(☑ 0113-295 6060; www.the-reliance.co.uk; 76-78 North St; mains £5-16; ⏱ noon-10pm Mon-Wed, to 10.30pm Thu-Sat, to 8.30pm Sun; ☎) ⌖ The Reliance is a comfortable-as-old-slippers bar where you can happily while away an afternoon reading or chatting with a Yorkshire beer or good glass of natural wine in hand. Yet it's also one of Leeds' best gastropubs, serving Sunday roasts, seasonal Modern British dishes like pig cheeks with beetroot and smoked apple, and platters of homemade charcuterie (yes, they make it themselves).

Shears Yard   MODERN BRITISH ££

(☑ 0113-244 4144; www.shearsyard.com; 11-15 Wharf St; mains £14-25; ⏱ 5.30-10pm Tue-Sat, 11am-3pm Sat, noon-4pm Sun; ☑) ⌖ Acres of exposed brick, concrete floors and a soaring roof provide an industrial-chic setting (it's a former rope-making yard) for painterly presentations of imaginative dishes such as ox-cheek fritter with roast-onion consommé, or squid with puffed potato and coriander emulsion. A two-/three-course dinner menu is available for £17.50/21.50 Tuesday to Thursday evenings, and before 7pm on Friday.

🍷 Drinking & Nightlife

★ Laynes Espresso   COFFEE

(☑ 07828 823189; www.laynesespresso.co.uk; 16 New Station St; ⏱ 7am-7pm Mon-Fri, 9am-6pm Sat & Sun; ☎) ⌖ Locals have Laynes to thank for the complete reinvention of the Leeds coffee scene; when it opened in 2011 there was nothing else like it in the city. Now expanded and serving excellent all-day brunch – buckwheat pancakes and smashed avocado on toast, naturally – and Yorkshire rarebit alongside strong coffee, it's still the best indie cafe in town for an espresso or flat white.

★ Northern Monk   BREWERY

(☑ 0113-243 0003; www.northernmonkbrewco.com; The Old Flax Store, Marshall St; ⏱ 11.45am-11pm Tue-Thu, to 1am Fri & Sat, 11.45am-9pm Sun)

So successful has this craft brewery become that its beers are now stocked in UK supermarkets. But it's best drunk at the source, in the brewery's Grade II–listed taproom just south of Leeds city centre in the regeneration 'hood of Holbeck. Draft options run the gamut from hoppy IPAs or rich porters to small-batch collaborations and guest beers; brewery tours also available.

★ **North Star Coffee Shop & General Store** COFFEE
(www.northstarroast.com; Unit 33, The Boulevard, Leeds Dock; ◎ 7.30am-5.30pm Mon-Fri, 9am-5pm

Sat, 10am-4pm Sun) This minimalist cafe and coffee emporium is attached to the production facility of Leeds' first independent roastery, near the Royal Armouries. Watch the daily grind through giant glass doors and inhale the aromas while sampling a flat white and cake (baked fresh on-site each day), or indulge in brunch – the slow-cooked scrambled eggs on a buttery four-cheese rye scone is small yet deliciously decadent.

★ **Headrow House** BAR
(☑ 0113-245 9370; www.headrowhouse.com; Bramleys Yard, The Headrow; ◎ noon-11pm Sun &

ART IN YORKSHIRE

Yorkshire Sculpture Park (☑ 01924-832631; www.ysp.co.uk; Bretton Park, near Wakefield; parking 2hr/all day £6/10; ◎ 10am-6pm; [P] [♿] [🐕]) One of England's most impressive collections of sculpture is scattered across the formidable 18th-century estate of Bretton Park, 200-odd hectares of lawns, fields and trees. A bit like the art world's equivalent of a safari park, the Yorkshire Sculpture Park showcases the work of dozens of sculptors both national and international. The park is partly a homage to local heroes Barbara Hepworth (1903–75), who was born in Wakefield, and Henry Moore (1898–1986), though more of their works are on display at the Hepworth Wakefield.

The rural setting is especially fitting for Moore's work, as the artist was hugely influenced by the outdoors and preferred his art to be sited in the landscape rather than indoors. Other highlights include pieces by Andy Goldsworthy and Eduardo Paolozzi, and Roger Hiorns' famous work *Seizure 2008/2013*, an apartment coated in blue copper sulphate crystals (open weekends only). There's also a program of temporary exhibitions and installations by visiting artists, plus a bookshop and cafe.

The park is 12 miles south of Leeds and 18 miles north of Sheffield, just off Junction 38 on the M1 motorway. If you're on public transport, take a train from Leeds to Wakefield (£3.90, 15 to 30 minutes, frequent departures), or from Sheffield to Barnsley (£4.30, 25 minutes, four hourly), and then take bus 96, which runs between Wakefield and Barnsley via Bretton Park (£3 to £3.40, 30 minutes, hourly Monday to Saturday).

Hepworth Wakefield (☑ 01924-247360; www.hepworthwakefield.org; Gallery Walk, Wakefield; parking £5; ◎ 10am-5pm; [P]) West Yorkshire's standing in the international arts scene got a boost in 2011 when the Yorkshire Sculpture Park was joined by this award-winning gallery of modern art, housed in a stunningly angular building on the banks of the River Calder. The gallery has been built around the works of Wakefield-born sculptor Barbara Hepworth, perhaps best known for her work *Single Form*, which graces the UN Headquarters in New York.

The gallery is smaller than it looks from the outside, but showcases more than a dozen Hepworth originals, as well as works by other 20th-century British artists including Ivon Hitchens, Paul Nash, Victor Pasmore, John Piper and Henry Moore.

The gallery is near the centre of Wakefield, a 10-minute walk south of Wakefield Kirkgate train station, easily reached from Leeds by train (£3.90, 15 to 30 minutes, three to four hourly).

Salts Mill (☑ 01274-531163; www.saltsmill.org.uk; Victoria Rd; ◎ 9.30am-5pm Mon-Fri, to 5.30pm Sat & Sun; [P]) Saltaire, a Victorian-era landmark and Unesco World Heritage Site, was an industrial village purpose-built in 1851 by philanthropic wool baron and teetotaller Titus Salt. The village's huge factory was once the largest in the world. It is now Salts Mill, a splendidly bright and airy cathedral-like building where the main draw is a permanent exhibition of works by Bradford-born artist David Hockney.

Saltaire is easily reached by train from Leeds (£4.10, 15 minutes, every 30 minutes).

Mon, to 11.30pm Tue, to midnight Wed, to 12.30am Thu, to 2am Fri, to 3am Sat) A former textile mill and one-time grotty dive pub, the historic building that now houses Headrow House was given a hefty makeover to transform it into the four-floor nightlife venue it is today. The ground-floor beer hall sells its own pilsner straight from tanks lining one wall. Upstairs there's a cocktail bar and Leeds' best roof-terrace drinking spot. It's also home to Ox Club (p518) restaurant.

North Bar   CRAFT BEER
(www.northbar.com; 24 New Briggate; ⏱11am-1am Mon & Tue, to 2am Wed-Sat, noon-midnight Sun; 🛜) This narrow bar has long been an institution in Leeds as a haven of international craft beers. It now brews its own under the banner North Brewing Co, and they're rather good. Drink them here, or visit the brewery taproom (Sheepscar Grove), which is BYO food and open Fridays 4pm to 10pm and Saturdays noon to 10pm, a 10-minute walk north of North Bar.

Water Lane Boathouse   CRAFT BEER
(📞0113-246 0985; www.waterlaneboathouse.com; Water Lane; ⏱11am-11pm Sun-Thu, to 12.30am Fri & Sat) Watch canal boats chug into Granary Wharf from the floor-to-ceiling windows or generous outside seating area at this beer bar, occupying a prime historic spot on the water close enough to clink glasses with boaters. The top-quality global craft beers are pricey, but the setting is hard to beat. There's also tasty pizza available from £5.

Bar Fibre   CLUB
(www.barfibre.com; 168 Lower Briggate; ⏱noon-1am Sun-Thu, to 3am Fri, to 4am Sat) In the heart of Leeds' LGBTIQ area, spilling out onto the cheekily named Queen's Court, this is the city's most popular gay bar although it's not just the gay crowd that loves its party atmosphere. This is where the beautiful people congregate; the dress code is...dressy, so look your best or you won't get in. Download the bar's app for deals such as buy one, get one free.

Mission   CLUB
(www.clubmission.com; Viaduct St; from £4; ⏱10.30pm-3.30am Thu, 11pm-5am Fri, 11pm-8am Sat) Describing itself as 'the home of house', this massive club redefines the term 'up for it'. Friday night Teatro hosts visiting talent from around the world, while Saturday is a feast of cutting-edge music from the resident DJs and special guests, and an af-

ter-party that keeps the beat going until the sun comes up on Sunday morning.

HiFi Club   CLUB
(📞0113-242 7353; www.thehificlub.co.uk; 2 Central Rd; ⏱11pm-4am Tue-Sun) If it's Tamla Motown or the percussive beats of dancefloor jazz that shake your booty, this is the spot for you. Also has stand-up comedy sessions (£14) on Saturdays from 7pm, which can be combined with dinner at **Art's Cafe** (📞0113-243 8243; www.artscafebar.com; 42 Call Lane; mains £13-18; ⏱noon-11pm Mon-Sat, to 9pm Sun; 🛜🍴) for £26.95 (book online).

☆ Entertainment

★**Belgrave Music**
Hall & Canteen   LIVE MUSIC
(📞0113-234 6160; www.belgravemusichall.com; 1 Cross Belgrave St; ⏱11am-midnight Sun-Thu, to 3am Fri & Sat) Belgrave is the city's best live-music venue, with a diverse roll call of acts from burlesque to comedy and folk to hip-hop. Its three floors also encompass a huge bar bristling with craft-beer taps, two kitchens (p517), loads of shared tables and sofa space, and a fantastic roof terrace with views across the city. Why would you ever leave?

City Varieties   LIVE MUSIC, COMEDY
(📞0113-243 0808; www.cityvarieties.co.uk; Swan St) Founded in 1865, City Varieties is the world's longest-running music hall, where the likes of Harry Houdini, Charlie Chaplin and Lily Langtry once trod the boards. Its programme features stand-up comedy, live music, pantomime and old-fashioned variety shows.

🛍 Shopping

Corn Exchange   SHOPPING CENTRE
(www.leedscornexchange.co.uk; Call Lane; ⏱10am-6pm Mon-Wed, Fri & Sat, to 9pm Thu, 10.30am-4.30pm Sun; 🛜) The dramatic Corn Exchange, built in 1863 to house grain-trade merchants, has a wonderful wrought-iron roof that today shelters a fine collection of independent shops and boutiques. They sell everything from vinyl and craft beer to fashion, jewellery and Yorkshire design.

Kirkgate Market   MARKET
(www.leeds.gov.uk/leedsmarkets; Kirkgate; ⏱8am-5.30pm Mon-Sat) Britain's largest covered market sells fresh meat, fish, and fruit and vegetables, as well as household goods, and now boasts a popular new street-food hall. The best section is at the top near Vicar

Lane, where the original Victorian stalls are still inhabited by traders – this was where UK retailing giant Marks & Spencer started out in 1884.

Victoria Quarter SHOPPING CENTRE (www.victorialeeds.co.uk; Vicar Lane; ☎) The mosaic-paved, stained-glass-roofed Victoria Quarter shopping arcade, between Briggate and Vicar Lane, is well worth visiting for aesthetic reasons alone, as is **County Arcade**, which runs parallel. Dedicated shoppers can join the footballers' wives browsing boutiques such as Louis Vuitton and Vivienne Westwood. The flagship store here is **Harvey Nichols** (www.harveynichols. com; 107-111 Briggate; ⊙10am-7pm Mon-Sat, 11am-5pm Sun).

ℹ Information

Leeds Tourist Office (☏ 0113-378 6977; www. visitleeds.co.uk; Leeds Art Gallery, Headrow; ⊙10am-5pm Mon-Sat, 11am-3pm Sun; ☎) In the basement of the city art gallery, next to the gallery shop.

ℹ Getting There & Away

AIR

Leeds Bradford International Airport (www. leedsbradfordairport.co.uk) is 11 miles north-west of the city via the A65, and has flights to a range of domestic and international destinations. The Flying Tiger 757 bus (£3.80, 40 minutes, every 20 to 30 minutes) runs between Leeds bus and train stations and the airport. A taxi costs about £20.

BUS

National Express (www.nationalexpress.com) serves most major cities, while Yorkshire Coastliner (www.coastliner.co.uk) buses run to York, Pickering, Malton, Scarborough and Whitby. A Daytripper Plus ticket (£16) gives unlimited travel on all Coastliner buses for a day. The **Central Bus Station** is near Victoria Gate Shopping Centre.

London £7.50 to £20, 4½ hours, hourly
Manchester £3 to £6, 1¼ hours, at least hourly
Scarborough £12, three hours, hourly
Whitby £13, 3½ hours, four daily Monday to Saturday, twice daily Sundays
York £6, 1¼ hours, at least hourly

TRAIN

Leeds train station has good rail connections with the rest of the country and Manchester's international airport. It's also the starting point for trains on the scenic Settle–Carlisle line (p507). Tickets for Manchester and York can be had for a song if you book ahead and can be flexible on times.

London King's Cross £65, 2¼ hours, at least hourly
Manchester £10, 1 to 1½ hours, every 10 to 20 minutes
Manchester Airport £24, 1½ hours, three hourly
Sheffield £11, one hour, six hourly
York £7, 25 minutes, at least every 15 minutes

ℹ Getting Around

Leeds has a compact city centre and it's quicker to walk everywhere than attempt to take a bus. CityBus 70 South Bank (50p flat fare) links the train station with Leeds Dock (for the Royal Armouries), but a nicer way to travel between the two is the free taxi ferry that runs from Granary Wharf, at the train station's southern entrance.

Various WY Metro (www.wymetro.com) Day Rover passes covering trains and/or buses are good for reaching Bradford, Haworth and Hebden Bridge.

Bradford

☏ 01274 / POP 349,561

Their suburbs may have merged into one sprawling urban conurbation, but Bradford remains far removed from its much more glamorous neighbour, Leeds. Thanks to its role as a major player in the wool trade, Bradford attracted large numbers of immigrants from Bangladesh and Pakistan during the 20th century.

Despite occasional racial tensions, these new arrivals have helped reinvigorate the city and give it new energy, plus a reputation for superb curry restaurants – Bradford has been crowned Curry Capital of Britain six times in recent years. But the main reason to visit is still the National Science & Media Museum.

◉ Sights

National Science & Media Museum MUSEUM (www.nationalmediamuseum.org.uk; off Little Horton Lane; ⊙10am-6pm) FREE Bradford's top attraction is housed in an impressive glass-fronted building and chronicles the story of photography, film, TV, radio and the web from 19th-century cameras and early animation to digital technology and the psychology of advertising. International visitors may find themselves a little lost with the British-focused TV exhibits, but there is lots of other hands-on stuff, including a trippy interactive image-and-sound tech gallery and a room crammed with 1980s video games (Pacman! Street Fighter!). There's also an **IMAX cinema** (www.picturehouses. com; adult/child from £8.50/6).

The museum looks out over **City Park**, Bradford's award-winning central square, which is home to the Mirror Pool, the country's largest urban water feature.

Eating

Bradford is famous for its curries, so don't miss out on trying one of the city's hundred or so restaurants. A great help is the Bradford Curry Guide (www.visitbradford. com/explore/Bradford_Curry_Guide.aspx), which helps sort the rogan josh from the rubbish nosh.

Kashmir   INDIAN £
(☏ 01274-726513; 27 Morley St; mains £4.50-7; ◷ 11am-2am Sun-Thu, to 4am Fri & Sat; ☂) Don't be put off by the dodgy-looking facade: Bradford's oldest curry house has top tucker, served with no frills and no booze (although it is BYO). At quieter times you'll be seated in the windowless basement, with all the character of a 1950s factory canteen, but the food is still excellent. It's just around the corner from the National Science & Media Museum.

Zouk Tea Bar   INDIAN, PAKISTANI ££
(☏ 01274-258025; www.zoukteabar.co.uk; 1312 Leeds Rd; mains £8.50-13; ◷ noon-midnight; ☏☂♿) This modern and stylish cafe-restaurant staffed by chefs from Lahore offers an upmarket menu and some unusual twists on traditional Indian and Pakistani food, such as delicious schwarma wraps and curried lamb shank slow-cooked in aromatic spices. It's in a Bradford suburb; the 72 bus that runs between Bradford Interchange and Leeds bus station will drop you outside.

Getting There & Away

Bradford is on the Metro train line from Leeds (£4.20, 20 minutes, three to five per hour) and also a stop on the line that links Leeds with Hebden Bridge.

Hebden Bridge
☏ 01422 / POP 4235
Tucked tightly into a fold of a steep-sided valley, Yorkshire's funkiest small town is a former mill centre that refused to go gently with the dying of industry's light. Instead, it raged a bit and then morphed into an attractive outdoorsy tourist trap with a distinctly bohemian atmosphere. The town is home to university academics, artists, diehard hippies and a substantial gay community. All of this explains the abundance of vintage shops, organic and vegan cafes, and secondhand bookstores. Walking trails leading from the centre of town and up into the hills are another attraction.

Sights & Activities

Gibson Mill   HISTORIC BUILDING
(NT; ☏ 01422-846236; www.nationaltrust.org.uk; parking £5; ◷ 11am-4pm mid-Mar–Oct, to 3pm Sat & Sun Nov–mid-Mar; ℗) ✐ This renovated, sustainably powered 19th-century cotton mill houses a cafe and visitor centre with exhibitions covering the industrial and social history of the mill and its former workers. It is set amid the woods and waterfalls of local beauty spot **Hardcastle Crags** (open dawn to dusk, admission free), 1.5 miles north of town, reachable via a 45-minute walk from St George's Sq, partly following the river. The route is difficult to find alone; visit www.hbwalkersaction. org.uk for directions.

Hebden Bridge Mill   HISTORIC BUILDING
(www.innovationhebdenbridge.co.uk; St George's Sq; ◷ hours vary) The spindly chimney of Hebden Bridge's old red-brick mill is a central landmark that predates the town itself, and was saved from demolition in 1974. It is now a home for vintage stores and small studios, anchored by the Innovation Shop & Cafe-Bar on the ground floor, where the mill's working water wheel and Archimedes' screw (water pump) are located. Heritage panels explain the history of the site, which is now run on sustainable water power. Shop opening hours vary; weekends are most reliable.

Heptonstall   VILLAGE
(www.heptonstall.org) Above Hebden Bridge lies the much older village of Heptonstall, its narrow cobbled street lined with 500-year-old cottages and the ruins of a beautiful **13th-century church**. But it's the churchyard of the newer **St Thomas' Church** (1854) that draws literary pilgrims, for here is buried the poet Sylvia Plath (1932–63), whose husband, poet Ted Hughes (1930–98), was born in nearby Mytholmroyd. You'll have to hunt hard to find her grave, in the new cemetery beyond the church's far wall.

WORTH A TRIP

YORKSHIRE'S BLACK GOLD

For close to three centuries, West and South Yorkshire were synonymous with coal production. The collieries shaped and scarred the landscape, and entire villages grew up around the pits. The industry came to a shuddering halt in the 1980s, but the imprint of coal is still very much in evidence, even if there's only a handful of collieries left. One of these, the former Caphouse Colliery, is now the **National Coal Mining Museum for England** (www.ncm.org.uk; Overton, near Wakefield; parking £2, tour £4, miniature train return £1.50; ⊙10am-5pm, last tour 3.15pm; P ♿) FREE.

The highlight of a visit is the underground tour (departing every 10 to 15 minutes): equipped with helmet and head-torch, you descend almost 140m in the 'cage', then follow subterranean passages to the coal seam, where massive drilling machines now stand idle. Former miners work as guides and explain the detail – sometimes with a suitably authentic and almost impenetrable mix of local dialect (known in Yorkshire as 'Tyke') and technical terminology.

The museum is 10 miles south of Leeds on the A642 between Wakefield and Huddersfield, reached via Junction 40 on the M1. By public transport, take a train from Leeds to Wakefield (£3.90, 15 to 30 minutes, three to four hourly), and then bus 232 or 128 towards Huddersfield (£3.10, 25 minutes, hourly).

Hebden Bridge Cruises CRUISE
(✆07966 808717; http://hebdenbridgecruises. com; Stubbing Wharf, King St; per person from £15; ⊙1pm & 2.15pm Sat) Join a colourful canal boat for a guided cruise along the Rochdale Canal with tea and scones or a two-course Sunday roast. Departs from the Stubbing Wharf Pub, half a mile west of the town centre.

🛏 Sleeping

Hebden Bridge Hostel HOSTEL £
(✆07786 987376, 01422-843183; www.hebden bridgehostel.co.uk; Birchcliffe Centre, Birchcliffe Rd; dm/tw/q £20/55/75; ⊙Easter-early Nov; P 🛜)
🚭 Just 10 minutes' walk uphill from the town centre, this eco-hostel is set in a peaceful stone building, complete with sunny patio, tucked behind a former Baptist chapel. There's a cosy library, comfy and clean en-suite rooms, and a vegetarian-food-only kitchen. A minor inconvenience is that the hostel locks guests out of their rooms from 10.30am to 5pm daily.

★ Thorncliffe B&B B&B ££
(✆07949 729433, 01422-842163; www.thorncliffe. uk.net; Alexandra Rd; s/d £55/75; 🛜) This delightful Victorian house is perched on the hill above town, and the guest accommodation is perched at the top of the house – a spacious and peaceful attic double with private bathroom and lovely views across the valley, and a 1st-floor en-suite double room, but without the views. A healthy vegetarian continental breakfast is served in your room.

✕ Eating & Drinking

Mooch CAFE £
(✆01422-846954; https://moochcafebar.word press.com; 24 Market St; mains £8-12; ⊙9am-8pm; 🛜🚭♿) This chilled-out little cafe-bar exemplifies Hebden's alternative atmosphere, with a menu that includes a full-vegan breakfast, brie-and-grape ciabatta, and Mediterranean lunch platters of olives, hummus, stuffed vine leaves, tabouli and more. There's also bottled beers, wine, excellent espresso, and a petite enclosed outdoor terrace through the back.

★ Green's Vegetarian Café VEGETARIAN ££
(✆01422-843587; www.greensvegetariancafe.co. uk; Old Oxford House, Albert St; mains lunch £5-9, dinner £11.95; ⊙11am-3pm Wed-Sun, 6.30-10pm Fri & Sat; ♿) 🚭 One of Yorkshire's best vegetarian restaurants, Green's adopts a gourmet attitude towards veggie and vegan world cuisine, serving dishes such as Sicilian *caponata* (aubergines, red pepper, celery, olives and capers) with spaghetti, and Thai green curry with chickpeas, squash and tofu. Breakfast (11am to noon) includes superb scrambled organic eggs on toasted focaccia. Reservations recommended for dinner.

★ Vocation & Co CRAFT BEER
(✆01422-844838; www.vocationbrewery.com; 10 New Rd; ⊙4-11pm Mon, noon-11pm Tue-Sun; 🛜) A goldmine for hopheads, the first taproom from local craft brewer Vocation Brewery is housed in an imposing Victorian building

overlooking Hebden Bridge's marina. Inside it's quite a contrast: an ultramodern, minimalist set-up with 20 draft lines including beers from other top northern breweries such as Magic Rock and Cloudwater, plus a delicious taco menu (Tuesday to Sunday).

☆ Entertainment

Trades Club
LIVE MUSIC

(☑ 01422-845265; www.thetradesclub.com; Holme St) Built in 1923 as a social club by the local trade unions, this place was revived in the 1980s and has since gone on to become one of the UK's coolest live-music venues, hosting names as big and diverse as the Buzzcocks, Patti Smith, the Fall and George Ezra in recent years, as well as a host of up-and-coming indie talent.

❶ Information

Hebden Bridge Visitor Centre (☑ 01422-843831; www.hebdenbridge.co.uk; Butlers Wharf, New Rd; ⊙ 10am-5pm) Has a good stock of maps and leaflets on local walks and bicycle routes.

❶ Getting There & Away

There's only one main road through town and it can become horribly congested on sunny days, so try to arrive by train. Hebden Bridge is on the line from Leeds (£5.80, 50 minutes, every 20 minutes Monday to Saturday, twice hourly on Sunday) to Manchester (£10, 35 minutes, three or four per hour).

Haworth

☑ 01535 / POP 6380

It seems that only Shakespeare himself is held in higher esteem than the beloved Brontë sisters – Emily, Anne and Charlotte – judging by the thousands of visitors a year who come to pay their respects at Haworth's handsome parsonage where the literary classics *Jane Eyre* and *Wuthering Heights* were penned.

Not surprisingly, the village is the beating heart of a cottage industry that has grown up around Brontë-linked tourism, but even without the literary associations Haworth is worth a visit. Its cobbled heritage high street has become a home for interesting independent vintage, craft and art shops selling work by local Yorkshire artisans, and it's possible to strike out onto the famed Brontë moors right from the parsonage's back door.

◉ Sights

Haworth Parish Church
CHURCH

(www.haworthchurch.co.uk; Church St; ⊙ 9am-5.30pm Mon-Sat) Your first stop in Haworth should be the parish church, a lovely old place of worship built in the late 19th century on the site of the older church that the Brontë sisters knew, which was demolished in 1879. The Brontë family vault lies beneath a pillar in the southeast corner, and a polished brass plaque on the floor commemorates Charlotte and Emily; Anne is buried at **St Mary's Church** (Castle Rd; ⊙ 10am-4pm Mon-Fri, 1-4pm Sun May-Sep) FREE in Scarborough.

Brontë Parsonage Museum
MUSEUM

(☑ 01535-642323; www.bronte.org.uk; Church St; adult/child £8.50/4; ⊙ 10am-5.30pm Apr-Oct, to 5pm Nov-Mar) Set in a pretty garden overlooking Haworth parish church and graveyard, the house where the Brontë family lived from 1820 to 1861 is now a museum. The rooms are meticulously furnished and decorated exactly as they were in the Brontë era, including Charlotte's bedroom, her clothes and her writing paraphernalia. There's also an informative exhibition, which includes the fascinating miniature books the Brontës wrote as children.

Keighley & Worth Valley Railway
HERITAGE RAILWAY

(www.kwvr.co.uk; Station Rd; adult/child return £12/6, Day Rover £18/9) This vintage railway runs steam and classic diesel engines between Keighley and Oxenhope via Haworth. The classic 1970 movie *The Railway Children* was shot along this line: Mr Perks was stationmaster at Oakworth, where the Edwardian look has been meticulously maintained. Trains operate about hourly every day June to August but the timetable is sporadic in other months; check the website. Tickets to view the Haworth platform and incoming trains cost 50p, but you can get a good look from the nearby pedestrian bridge.

⬛ Sleeping

YHA Haworth
HOSTEL £

(☑ 0845 371 9520; www.yha.org.uk; Longlands Dr; dm/tw £13/29; P 🛜) In keeping with Haworth's Brontë heritage, the YHA hostel is set in a brooding Victorian Gothic mansion, complete with pool table, lounge, cycle store, laundry and Black Sheep ale for sale. It's on the northeastern edge of town, off Lees Lane, and has a large garden out back.

Apothecary Guest House B&B £
(☑01535-643642; www.theapothecaryguesthouse.co.uk; 86 Main St; s/d £40/60; ☎) A quaint and ancient building at the top end of Main St, with narrow, slanted passageways that lead to simple rooms with cheerful modern decor; excellent value.

★ **Old Registry** B&B ££
(☑01535-646503; www.theoldregistryhaworth.co.uk; 2-4 Main St; d £80-135; P☎) This place is a bit special. It's an elegantly rustic guesthouse where each of the carefully themed rooms has either a four-poster bed, whirlpool bath or valley views. The Secret Garden room has a glorious view across parkland to the lower village with, if you're lucky, a steam train chuffing sedately by. Parking is £3 per night, at nearby Haworth Old Hall.

✗ Eating & Drinking

Cobbles & Clay CAFE £
(www.cobblesandclay.co.uk; 60 Main St; mains £5-8; ⊙9am-5pm; ☎✗⊞) This buzzy, child-friendly cafe not only offers fair-trade coffee and healthy salads and snacks – Tuscan bean stew, or hummus with pita bread and raw veggie sticks – but also provides the opportunity to indulge in a bit of pottery painting. Its ploughman's lunch comes with local Haworth cheese.

Hawthorn BRITISH ££
(☑01535-644477; www.thehawthornhaworth.co.uk; 103-109 Main St; lunch £5.50-11, dinner £13-20; ⊙11am-11pm Wed-Sun) A famed Georgian clockmaker used to inhabit this building, which has been given new life as a classy, candlelit restaurant-bar serving Modern British dishes such as pea-and-ham soup with quails egg, Yorkshire Dales lamb, and North Sea hake with foraged garlic. The lunch menu is a simpler affair, or come for a filter coffee and cake, or refreshing glass off dandelion and burdock.

Haworth Steam Brewery MICROBREWERY
(☑01535-646059; www.haworthsteambrewery.co.uk; 98 Main St; ⊙11am-11pm Thu-Sat, to 6pm Sun-Wed) This cosy bar must surely be one of Britain's smallest microbreweries, serving its own award-winning real ales and Haworth's Lamplighter gin, plus specials such as an IPA and gin created for Haworth's annual steampunk weekend in November. There's also a good pub grub menu featuring brewhouse lamb shank, Whitby scampi and beef brisket sandwiches.

🛍 Shopping

Cabinet of Curiosities COSMETICS, GIFTS & SOUVENIRS
(https://the-curiosity-society.myshopify.com; 84 Main St; ⊙10am-5.30pm) It was to this apothecary that Branwell Brontë staggered for his laudanum drug hits in the 1840s, contributing to his untimely death in September 1848. The current owners have restored it to its Victorian glory and it's now a fancy shop selling Gothic curios and beautiful bath products. Well worth a look inside.

ℹ Information

Haworth Tourist Office (☑01535-642329; www.visitbradford.com/discover/Haworth.aspx; 2-4 West Lane; ⊙10am-5pm Apr-Sep, to 4pm Oct-Mar) The tourist office has an excellent supply of information on the village, the surrounding area and, of course, the Brontës. At the time of writing it was expected to be taken over by the Brontë Parsonage Museum and opening hours were in flux; call ahead to check if you plan to visit.

ℹ Getting There & Away

From Leeds, the easiest approach is via Keighley, which is on the Metro rail network. The B1, B2 and B3 buses (www.keighleybus.co.uk) run from Keighley bus station to Haworth (£2.70, 20 minutes, every 20 minutes) and the hourly B3 continues to Hebden Bridge. However, the most interesting way to get from Keighley to Haworth is via the Keighley & Worth Valley Railway (p524).

SOUTH YORKSHIRE

What wool was to West Yorkshire, so steel was to South Yorkshire. A confluence of natural resources – coal, iron ore and ample water – made this part of the country a crucible of the British iron and steel industries. From the 18th to the 20th centuries, the region was the industrial powerhouse of northern England.

Sheffield's and Rotherham's blast furnaces and the coal pits of Barnsley and Doncaster may have closed long ago, but the hulking reminders of that irrepressible Victorian dynamism remain, not only in the old steelworks and pit heads (some of which have been converted into museums and exhibition spaces), but also in the grand civic buildings that grace Sheffield's city centre, fitting testaments to the untrammelled ambitions of their 19th-century patrons.

WORTH A TRIP

THE AGE OF STEEL

At its peak, the Templeborough steelworks was the world's most productive steel smelter, with six 3000°C furnaces producing 1.8 million tonnes of metal a year, and a 10,000-strong workforce. It has now been reborn as Magna (☑01709-720002; www.visit magna.co.uk; Sheffield Rd, Templeborough, Rotherham; adult/child £11.95/9.95; ☺10am-5pm, last entry 4pm; P♿), an unashamed celebration of heavy industry, and a hands-on paradise for kids of all ages. Displays are based on the themes of earth, air, water and fire. The latter section is especially impressive, with a towering tornado of flame as a centrepiece and the chance to use a real electric arc to create your own tiny puddle of molten steel (if only for a moment or two). The hourly 'Big Melt' – a massive sound, light and fireworks show – memorably reenacts the firing up of one of the original arc furnaces.

Magna is 4 miles northeast of Sheffield, just off the M1 near Rotherham; phone before visiting as it closes at 2pm some days.

Sheffield

☑0114 / POP 518,090

The steel industry that made Sheffield famous is long gone, but after many years of decline this industrious city is on the up again – like many of northern England's cities, it has grabbed the opportunities presented by urban renewal with both hands and, shored up by a thriving student population, is working hard to reinvent itself.

Some of its old foundries, mills and forges are now interesting museums celebrating South Yorkshire's industrial heyday, and Kelham Island in particular is in the throes of a fascinating redevelopment. Sheffield isn't likely to win any prizes for its looks anytime soon, but its history is interesting enough to warrant a day or two's exploration.

◉ Sights

★ **Kelham Island Museum** MUSEUM
(www.simt.co.uk; Alma St; adult/child £6/free; ☺10am-4pm Mon-Thu, 11am-4.45pm Sun; P♿)
Sheffield's prodigious industrial heritage is the subject of this excellent museum, set on a human-made island in the city's oldest industrial district. Exhibits cover all aspects of industry, from steel-making to knife-sharpening. The most impressive display is the thundering 12,000-horsepower River Don steam engine (the size of a house), which gets powered up twice a day, at noon and 2pm. The museum is 800m north of the city centre; take the tram (£1.70) from Sheffield train station to the Shalesmoor stop.

Winter Gardens GARDENS
(Surrey St; ☺8am-8pm Mon-Sat, to 6pm Sun)
Pride of place in Sheffield's city centre goes to this wonderfully ambitious public space with a soaring glass roof supported by graceful arches of laminated timber. The 21st-century architecture contrasts sharply with the nearby Victorian town hall and the Peace Gardens – complete with fountains, sculptures, and lawns full of lunching office workers.

Millennium Gallery GALLERY
(www.museums-sheffield.org.uk; Arundel Gate; ☺10am-5pm Mon-Sat, 11am-4pm Sun) FREE
Sheffield's cultural revival is embodied in this collection of four galleries under one roof. Inside, the Ruskin Collection houses an eclectic display of paintings, manuscripts and interesting objects established and inspired by Victorian artist, writer, critic and philosopher John Ruskin, who saw Sheffield as the embodiment of Britain's industrial age. The Sykes Gallery Metalwork Collection charts the transformation of Sheffield's steel industry into craft and design, with 13,000 glinting objects – the 'Sheffield steel' stamp now has the cachet of designer chic.

Graves Gallery GALLERY
(www.museums-sheffield.org.uk; Surrey St; ☺11am-4pm Tue-Sat) FREE This gallery has a neat and accessible display of British and European art from the 16th century to the present day, plus touring exhibitions; the big names represented include Turner, Sisley, Cézanne, Gaugin, Miró, Klee, LS Lowry and Damien Hirst.

Abbeydale Industrial Hamlet MUSEUM
(www.simt.co.uk; Abbeydale Rd S; adult/child £4/free; ☺10am-4pm Mon-Thu & Sat, 11am-4.45pm Sun; P♿) In the days before steel mills, metalworking was carried out in hamlet communities like Abbeydale, situated by riv-

ers and dams that were harnessed for water power. This industrial museum, now swallowed up by Sheffield's suburban sprawl, gives an excellent run-down of that innocent era, with restored 18th-century forges, workshops and machinery including the original, working water wheel. It's 4 miles southwest of the centre on the A621 (towards the Peak District).

🛏 Sleeping

Leopold Hotel
BOUTIQUE HOTEL **££**

(☎0114-252 4000; www.leopoldhotels.com; 2 Leopold St; r £70-160, ste £90-200; 🛜) Housed in a Grade II–listed former grammar-school building, Sheffield's first boutique hotel offers style and sophistication at a reasonable rate. Rooms can suffer late-night noise from the bars on Leopold Sq – ask for a quiet room at the back.

Houseboat Hotels
HOUSEBOAT **££**

(☎07776 144693; www.houseboathotels. com; Victoria Quays, Wharfe St; s/d/tr/q from £85/110/145/170; 🅿) Here's something a bit different: kick off your shoes and relax on board your very own permanently moored houseboat, complete with self-catering kitchen and patio area.

🍴 Eating

Street Food Chef
MEXICAN **£**

(☎0114-275 2390; www.streetfoodchef.co.uk; 90 Arundel St; mains £3-6; ⏱8am-10pm Mon-Sat, 10am-9pm Sun) Local students flock to this down-to-earth, healthy Mexican canteen, which started life as a street-food truck and now has several outlets in Sheffield. It focuses on freshly prepared, great-value burritos, tacos and quesadillas, available to sit in or take away. Look for its brekky and lunch deals, and gluten- or dairy-free options.

Blue Moon Cafe
VEGETARIAN **£**

(www.bluemooncafesheffield.com; 2 St James St; mains £7.70; ⏱8am-8pm Mon-Sat; 🍴) A Sheffield institution offering tasty veggie and vegan creations, breakfasts till 11am and a rotation of single-price mains with a side of rice. It's famed for the magnificent heritage room within which it sits, with high blue ceilings and an atrium glass roof – perfect for a spot of Saturday afternoon lounging.

Marmaduke's
CAFE **£**

(www.marmadukescafedeli.co.uk; 22a Norfolk Row; mains £6-12; ⏱9am-5pm Mon-Sat, 10am-4pm Sun; 🛜🍴) 🍃 This appealingly cramped and chaotic cafe, crammed with recycled furniture and fittings, and run by a young and enthusiastic crew, serves an all-day breakfast menu that highlights local and organic produce, and lunch dishes that range from deli sandwiches and quiches to vegetarian specials such as the halloumi and herb burger.

Vero Gusto
ITALIAN **££**

(☎0114-276 0004; www.verogusto.com; 12 Norfolk Row; lunch mains £9-26, dinner £15-30; ⏱11am-11pm Tue-Sat; 🛜) Gusto is a *real* Italian restaurant, from the Italian waistcoated servers dishing out homemade Italian food to the genuine Italian coffee enjoyed by Italian customers reading Italian newspapers...you get the idea. Pizza is on the menu at lunchtimes, coffee and home-baked Italian cakes and pastries are served in the afternoon, and the dinner menu focuses on exquisite Italian cuisine. Book for dinner.

🍷 Drinking & Nightlife

Fat Cat
PUB

(☎0114-249 4801; www.thefatcat.co.uk; 23 Alma St; ⏱noon-11pm Sun-Thu, to midnight Fri & Sat) This old-fashioned independent boozer is in a handy spot around the corner from Kelham Island Museum and serves Kelham Island Brewery beers and ales made in the building next door, along with pork pies (£1.50) and pub grub. Its fans are an eclectic mix of students and local fixtures.

Sheffield Tap
CRAFT BEER

(☎0114-273 7558; www.sheffieldtap.com; Sheffield Train Station; ⏱11am-11pm Sun-Thu, 10am-midnight Fri & Sat; 🛜) This lovingly restored Edwardian railway bar is a reliable stalwart for Sheffield beer drinkers. It has several bar areas, and the aroma of hops and malts gets stronger as you approach the far room where the bar produces its own Two Tapped Brew Co beers, with working brewery kit towering above drinking tables. Dozens of other local and international beers are sold here, too.

⭐ Entertainment

Showroom
CINEMA

(☎0114-275 7727; www.showroomworkstation.org. uk; 15 Paternoster Row) This is the largest independent cinema in England, set in a grand art-deco complex and screening a great mix of art-house, offbeat and not-quite-mainstream films.

Leadmill
LIVE MUSIC

(☑ 0114-272 7040; www.leadmill.co.uk; 6 Leadmill Rd) Every touring band has played the dark and dingy Leadmill on the way up (or on the way down), and it remains the best place in town to hear live rock and alternative music. There are club nights too, but they tend to play cheesy 1970s and '80s disco classics.

❶ Information

Sheffield's tourist information office closed in 2017, but www.welcometosheffield.co.uk is a good source of information on the city.

❶ Getting There & Away

For all travel-related info for Sheffield and South Yorkshire, contact **Travel South Yorkshire** (☑ 01709-515151; www.travelsouthyorkshire. com).

BUS

The bus station, called the Interchange, is just east of the centre, about 250m north of the train station. National Express coaches run from here to London (from £5, 4½ hours, eight daily).

TRAIN

Prices can double on the day of travel; book ahead.

Leeds From £6, one hour, two to five hourly
London St Pancras From £62, 2¼ hours, at least hourly
Manchester From £8, one hour, twice hourly
York From £11, 1¼ hours, twice hourly

EAST RIDING OF YORKSHIRE

The rolling farmland of the East Riding of Yorkshire meets the sea at Hull, a no-nonsense port that looks to the broad horizons of the Humber estuary and the North Sea for its livelihood. Just to its north, and in complete contrast to Hull's salt and grit, is Beverley, the East Riding's most attractive town, with lots of Georgian character and one of England's finest churches.

Hull

☑ 01482 / POP 284,321

Properly known as Kingston-upon-Hull (the ancient harbour on the River Hull was granted a royal charter in 1299 and became King's Town), Hull has long been the principal port of England's east coast, with an economy that grew up around wool, wine trading, whaling and fishing.

Its designation as UK City of Culture in 2017 has given the town a massive confidence boost, and redevelopment of its waterfront and Old Town has sparked a minor cultural flowering, particularly in the Fruit Market district around Humber St, where derelict buildings have been reclaimed as artists' studios and cool cafes and bars have flourished. Watch out: Hull is getting hip.

Though its modern centre isn't going to win prizes for prettiness, Hull's old cobbled Georgian enclave is an under-the-radar delight. Other attractions include fascinating museums, Philip Larkin heritage (the poet lived here) and an excellent aquarium – finally, the city is emerging as a great-value tourist destination.

◉ Sights

★ The Deep
AQUARIUM

(☑ 01482-381000; www.thedeep.co.uk; Tower St; adult/child £13.50/11.50; ⏰ 10am-6pm, last entry 5pm; Ⓟ⛟) Hull's biggest tourist attraction is The Deep, Britain's most dramatic aquarium, housed in a colossal angular building that appears to lunge above the muddy waters of the Humber like a giant shark's head. Inside, it's just as dramatic, with echoing commentaries and computer-generated interactive displays that guide you through the formation of the oceans, the evolution of sea life, and global conservation issues.

The largest aquarium tank is 10m deep, filled with sharks, stingrays and colourful coral fishes, with moray eels draped over rocks like scarves of iridescent slime. A glass elevator plies up and down inside the tank, though you'll get a better view by taking the stairs. Don't miss the cafe on the top floor, which has a great view of the Humber estuary.

★ Old Town
AREA

Hull's Old Town is where a grand minster and cobbled streets flush with Georgian town houses give a flashback to the prosperity the town once knew. It occupies the thumb of land between the River Hull to the east and Princes Quay to the west. Recent regeneration efforts have brought back to life the dockside **Fruit Market**, where vintage shops, art studios and independent bars and cafes are flourishing along Humber St; and the Old Town's indoor **Trinity Market**, now housing street-food vendors like Shoot the Bull.

★ **Wilberforce House** MUSEUM
(www.hullcc.gov.uk/museums; High St; ⊙10am-5pm Mon-Sat, 11am-4.30pm Sun) **FREE** The wealth that Britain amassed as the world's first industrial nation was directly aided by the transatlantic slave trade, and this important museum ensures that the facts are told, detailing the part that Britain played in bringing millions of Africans to Europe between the 17th and 19th centuries. Wilberforce House (1639) was the birthplace in 1759 of politician and antislavery crusader William Wilberforce, whose campaigning efforts eventually led to the abolition of slavery in England in 1833.

Humber St Gallery GALLERY
(www.humberstreetgallery.co.uk; 64 Humber St; ⊙10am-6pm Tue-Sun, to 8pm 1st Thu of month) **FREE** This slick three-storey contemporary gallery in a former banana-ripening warehouse anchors Hull's revamped Fruit Market. Rotating exhibitions celebrate international and local visual art, design, photography and film, but a permanent feature is a beloved piece of 1960s graffiti by Len 'Pongo' Rood saved from demolition by local campaigners. Behold *Dead Bod* – a rusty shed wall from Hull's docks that would have once signified home for returning sailors. The site was demolished in 2015, but *Dead Bod* lives on in Humber St Gallery's cafe.

Ferens Art Gallery GALLERY
(☑01482-300300; www.hullcc.gov.uk/ferens; Queen Victoria Sq; ⊙10am-5pm Mon-Sat, 1.30-4.30pm Sun; ♿) **FREE** Following extensive renovations, the Ferens Art Gallery reopened in 2017 as part of Hull's City of Culture celebrations. The permanent art collection ranges from old masters like Frans Hals to modern works by Lucian Freud, Peter Nash, Peter Blake, David Hockney and Gillian Wearing.

Humber Bridge BRIDGE
(www.humberbridge.co.uk; ℗) Opened in 1981, the Humber Bridge swoops gracefully across the broad estuary of the River Humber. Its 1410m span made it the world's longest single-span suspension bridge – until 1998 when it lost the title to Japan's Akashi Kaikyo bridge, but it is still a Grade I–listed structure. The best way to appreciate the scale of the bridge, and the vastness of the estuary, is to walk or cycle out along the footway from the Humber Bridge tourist office at its north end on Ferriby Rd.

The bridge is a mile west of the small riverside town of Hessle, about 4 miles west of Hull. It links Yorkshire to Lincolnshire along the A15, opening up what was once an often-overlooked corner of the country.

Bus 350 runs from Hull Paragon Interchange to Ferriby Rd in Hessle (25 minutes, every 30 minutes), from where it's a 300m walk to the tourist office.

Maritime Museum MUSEUM
(☑01482-300300; www.hcandl.co.uk; Queen Victoria Sq; ⊙10am-5pm Mon-Sat, 11am-4.30pm Sun; ♿) **FREE** In the early 19th century Hull had the largest whaling fleet in Britain, providing the whale oil that greased the wheels of the country's industrial revolution. This interesting museum is stuffed to the gills with seafaring artefacts from that period, including harpoons, replica boats, a whale skeleton and crow's nest (invented in Yorkshire), as well as an extensive scrimshaw collection.

Hull Pier Toilets HISTORIC BUILDING
(Nelson St) There are not too many places where a public toilet counts as a tourist attraction, but coach parties regularly stop to take photos of these Edwardian lavatories. The building is interesting but inside they're not very special. Serviceable, but no tourist attraction, that's for sure.

🛏 Sleeping

Hull Trinity Backpackers HOSTEL £
(☑01482-223229; www.hulltrinitybackpackers. com; 51-52 Market Pl; dm/s/tw from £19/30/39; 🛜) This centrally located hostel with simple rooms is just the ticket for a cheap sleep in Hull. It's clean and friendly, and the owner is passionate about showing off the city's best sides. There's a lovingly designed common area, free laundry, fluffy bedding and bike storage. Plus handy USB and plug sockets by each bed.

Garden Mews B&B £
(☑01482-215574; http://the-garden-mews-gb. book.direct; 13-14 John St; s/d/f £40/65/90, with shared bath £30/55/80; 🛜) This cheap and homely B&B is on the edge of leafy Kingston Sq, close to the New Theatre yet a bit of a hike from Hull's charming Old Town and Fruit Market. The rooms are comfortable but nothing fancy; breakfast costs an extra £5 per person.

★ **Hideout** APARTMENT ££
(☎ 01482-212222; www.hideouthotel.co.uk; North Church Side; d from £90, 1-bed apt £110-130, 2-bed apt from £130; P🐾📶) These luxury serviced apartments show just how far Hull has come since its City of Culture year. Slick and contemporary, it's the type of place where staff put retro radio on for you before check-in, and leave an easel in the living room for spontaneous creative scribbles. It's also incredibly central, in the shadow of the Old Town's minster.

🍴 Eating

★ **Thieving Harry's** CAFE £
(www.thievingharrys.co.uk; 73 Humber St; mains £6-8.50; ⊙ kitchen 10am-4pm Mon-Fri, 9am-4pm Sat, 9am-6pm Sun; 🍴) Thieving Harry's has all the trappings of a favourite local cafe: friendly faces, a breezy casual vibe, strong coffee and generous brunches, all wrapped up in a comfy warehouse conversion with mismatched retro furniture and lovely marina views of bobbing boats. The menu is interesting, with excellent dishes like fried eggs with chorizo, sourdough and coriander sourcream, plus good veggie options.

Hull Pie PIES £
(☎ 01482-345735; www.thehullpie.co.uk; 202 Newland Ave; mains £3.50-6.50; ⊙ 11am-9pm) 🍴 This famous takeaway offers award-winning freshly baked pies with a range of delicious fillings, from caramelised beer and beef brisket, to chicken, ham and mushroom with white wine and thyme, served with gravy and a choice of sides that include mushy peas, glazed carrots and chips. Look out for pop-up stalls in the city centre and at farmers markets.

★ **The Old House** BRITISH ££
(☎ 01482-210253; www.shootthebull.co.uk/the-old-house; 5 Scale Lane; mains £13-24; ⊙ 4.30-9.30pm Mon, noon-9.30pm Tue-Sun) Once an old pub, now the base of Hull street-food brand Shoot the Bull, this lovely restaurant does refined comfort food exceptionally well. Locally sourced meat and fish might translate into blow-torched mackerel followed by a rare-breed beef pie with smoked eel mash and parsley sauce. Its signature dish is on the street-food menu: a butter-lathered, rare-breed flat-iron steak sandwich in a posh bun.

A second outlet focusing solely on street food is inside Trinity Market in the Old Town.

Hitchcock's Vegetarian Restaurant VEGETARIAN ££
(☎ 01482-320233; www.hitchcocksrestaurant.co.uk; 1 Bishop Lane, High St; per person £20; ⊙ 8-10.30pm Tue-Sat; 🍴🌱) The word 'quirky' could have been invented to describe this place. It's an atmospheric maze of small rooms, with an all-you-can-eat vegetarian buffet whose theme – Mexican, Indian, Caribbean, whatever – is chosen by the first person to book that evening. But the food is excellent and the welcome is warm. Bookings necessary. There's one sitting; arrive between 8pm and 9pm.

Bait SEAFOOD ££
(☎ 01482-343088; www.baithull.co.uk; 13-15 Princes Ave; mains £12-21; ⊙ noon-2.30pm & 5-9pm Tue-Thu, noon-9pm Fri & Sat, to 9.30pm Sun) 🍴 Hull's seafaring tradition is reflected in a menu dominated by the best of British seafood, including Lindisfarne oysters au naturel and Whitby lobster bisque, but also an unexpected array of Asian-influenced dishes such as fresh sushi and nigiri. There are meat and vegetarian dishes too, and a three-course £34 midweek menu Tuesday to Thursday and on Sunday.

🍷 Drinking & Entertainment

★ **Olde Black Boy** PUB
(☎ 01482-215040; 150 High St; ⊙ 5-11.30pm Mon & Tue, noon-11.30pm Wed-Sun) A favourite watering hole of poet Philip Larkin, Hull's oldest pub has been serving ale since 1729. Oak floors and roof beams, dark-wood panelling and a snug log fire in winter make for a great atmosphere, and there's live folk music on Wednesday afternoons.

Humber St Distillery COCKTAIL BAR
(☎ 01482-219886; www.hsdc.co.uk; 18 Humber St; ⊙ noon-11pm Tue-Sun) This ambitious, gin-obsessed cocktail bar in the heart of Hull's Fruit Market area has dark-wood bar panelling offset by exposed-brick walls. The gin menu is a tome of around 150 world gins, including many local and limited-edition releases; you can take a gin flight (weeknights only); and the bar has even started producing its own gin.

Minerva PUB
(www.minerva-hull.co.uk; Nelson St; ⊙ 11.30am-11pm Mon-Sat, noon-11pm Sun; 🍴) If you're more into pubbing than clubbing, try a pint of Black Sheep at this lovely 200-year-old pub down by the waterfront. On a sunny

day you can sit outdoors and watch the ships go by, while tucking into a plate of fish and chips (£9.50). A unique feature is its real-ale and gin flights.

Früit LIVE MUSIC, COMEDY
(☑ 01482-221113; www.fruitspace.co.uk; 62-63 Humber St; ☎) A focus for the cultural revival of Hull's Fruit Market district, this former industrial space is now a multipurpose venue incorporating a bar, cinema and stage. There are regular live gigs by local bands (and occasional big names), a monthly comedy club and, on the third Sunday of the month, the Humber Street Market.

ℹ Information

Hull Tourist Office (☑ 01482-300306; www.visithullandeastyorkshire.com; Paragon Interchange, Ferensway; ☺ 8am-6.30pm Mon-Fri, from 9am Sat, 10am-5pm Sun) Inside Hull's Paragon Interchange, at the train station.

ℹ Getting There & Away

BOAT

The ferry port is 3 miles east of the centre at King George Dock; a bus connects the train station with the ferries. There are ferry services to Zeebrugge (Belgium) and Rotterdam (Netherlands).

BUS

Intercity buses depart from Hull Paragon Interchange. Mega Bus (https://uk.megabus.com) runs cheap buses to London. The X62 is a direct link to Leeds. During the summer months the X21 runs direct to Scarborough, but at other times of year you'll need to change at Bridlington. The X46/47 to York runs via Beverley.

London £10, 4½ hours, four daily
Leeds £8, two hours, three daily
York £7.70, 1¾ hours, hourly

TRAIN

The train station is part of Hull Paragon Interchange, an integrated rail and bus station.

Leeds £13, one hour, hourly
London King's Cross £85, 2¾ hours, every two hours
York £20, 1¼ hours, hourly

Beverley

☑ 01482 / POP 10,109
Handsome Beverley is one of the most attractive towns in Yorkshire, largely due to its magnificent minster – a rival to any cathedral in England – and the tangle of streets that lie beneath it, each brimming with Georgian and Victorian buildings.

All the sights are a short walk from either the train or bus station. There's a large market on Saturdays in the square called Saturday Market, and a smaller one on Wednesdays in the square called...Wednesday Market.

◉ Sights

Beverley Minster CHURCH
(www.beverleyminster.org; St John St; 1hr roof tour adult/child £10/5; ☺ 9am-5.30pm Mon-Sat, noon-5pm Sun Apr-Oct, to 4pm Nov-Mar) FREE One of the great glories of English religious architecture, Beverley Minster is the most impressive church in the country that is not a cathedral. The soaring lines of the exterior are imposing, but it is inside that the charm and beauty lie. The 14th-century north aisle is lined with original stone carvings, mostly of musicians; much of our knowledge of early musical instruments comes from these images. You'll also see goblins, devils and grotesque figures. Look out for the bagpipe player.

Construction began in 1220 – this was the third church to be built on this site, with the first dating from the 7th century – and continued for two centuries, spanning the Early English, Decorated and Perpendicular periods of the Gothic style.

Close to the altar, the elaborate and intricate **Percy Canopy** (1340), a decorative frill above the tomb of local aristocrat Lady Eleanor Percy, is a testament to the skill of the sculptor and the finest example of Gothic stone carving in England. In complete contrast, in the nearby chancel is the 10th-century Saxon **frith stool**, a plain and polished stone chair that once gave sanctuary to anyone escaping the law.

In the roof of the tower is a restored treadwheel crane, where workers ground around like hapless hamsters to lift the huge loads necessary to build a medieval church. Access to the roof is by guided tours held on Saturdays at 11am.

Beverley Westwood PARK
(Walkington Rd) The western edge of Beverley is bounded by this large area of common pasture studded with mature trees, which has been used as grazing for local livestock for centuries. The land, owned 'in common' by the community since 1380, is overseen by the Pasture Masters, a group of men elected from the Freemen of Beverley each March. Contented cows amble across the unfenced

road, while walkers stroll and enjoy the gorgeous views of Beverley Minster.

🛏 Sleeping & Eating

★ YHA Beverley Friary   HOSTEL £

(☑ 0345 371 9004; www.yha.org.uk; Friar's Lane; dm/d from £15/49; ☺ May-Dec; P 🛜) In Beverley, the cheapest accommodation also has the best setting and location. This hostel is housed in a beautifully restored 14th-century Dominican friary mentioned in Chaucer's *The Canterbury Tales*, and is only 100m from the minster and a short walk from the train station. Rooms sleep two to eight and some are en suite.

Kings Head   INN ££

(☑ 01482-868103; www.kingsheadpubbeverley.com; 38 Saturday Market; r from £90; P 🛜) A Georgian coaching inn given a modern makeover, the Kings Head is a lively pub with 10 bright and stylish rooms above the bar. The pub opens late on weekend nights, but earplugs are supplied for those who don't want to join the revelry!

Vanessa Delicafe   CAFE £

(☑ 01482-868190; www.vanessadelicafe.co.uk; 21-22 Saturday Market; mains £4.50-10; ☺ 9am-4.30pm Mon-Sat, 10am-3.30pm Sun; 🛜 ♿) This popular cafe sits above a delicatessen, with sofas and bookshelves scattered among the tables, and window seats overlooking the market square. Settle down for cappuccino and cake with the Sunday papers, or tuck into hearty lunch specials such as venison burger or a Yorkshire platter of pork pie, roast ham, cheese and chutney.

★ Pipe and Glass Inn   GASTROPUB £££

(☑ 01430-810246; www.pipeandglass.co.uk; West End, South Dalton; mains £11-30; ☺ noon-2pm & 6-9.30pm Tue-Sat, noon-4pm Sun; P 🛜 ✏ ♿) ⌀ Set in a picturesque hamlet 4 miles northwest of Beverley, this charming Michelin-starred country pub has a delightfully

informal setting, with weathered timber tables, stone hearths and leather sofas. Yet a great deal of care is lavished on the food – even seemingly simple dishes such as fish pie are unforgettable. After your meal, you can tour its herb gardens.

If you want to stay the night, there are five luxurious bedrooms to choose from (£200 to £245 per night, including breakfast), but the waiting list for a weekend night is several months long; weeknights can be booked about two months in advance.

🍷 Drinking & Nightlife

Cockpit Cafe   CAFE

(☑ 07421 225900; www.thecockpitcafe.com; 8 Wednesday Market; ☺ 10am-4.30pm Tue-Thu & Sun, 10am-midnight Fri & Sat; 🛜 ♿) What fun: preening itself on one of Beverley's Georgian market squares, this glamorous retro cafe is a throwback to the golden age of air travel with servers dressed in 1940s airline uniforms, furniture fashioned from old suitcases and nostalgic wartime ditties as background music. The drinks list includes Fentimans tonics, dandelion and burdock, coffees and cocktails, and there's a small food menu.

ⓘ Information

Beverley Tourist Office (☑ 01482-391672; www.visithullandeastyorkshire.com/beverley; Treasure House, Champney Rd; ☺ 9.30am-5pm Mon, Wed & Fri, to 8pm Tue & Thu, 9am-4pm Sat) Beverley Tourist Office lives inside Treasure House, also home to the town's art gallery, next to the library.

ⓘ Getting There & Away

There are frequent bus services from Hull, including numbers 121, 122, 246 and X46/X47 (£4.60, 30 minutes, hourly). Bus X46/X47 links Beverley with York (£7.20, 1¼ hours, hourly).

Trains run regularly to Scarborough (£14, 1¼ hours, every one to two hours) and Hull (£7, 15 minutes, twice hourly).

Manchester, Liverpool & Northwest England

Best Places to Eat

➡ 20 Stories (p544)

➡ Freemasons at Wiswell (p563)

➡ Northcote Hotel (p564)

➡ Mackie Mayor (p544)

➡ Restaurant Fraiche (p558)

Best Places to Stay

➡ Inn at Whitewell (p564)

➡ 2 Blackburne Terrace (p557)

➡ King Street Townhouse (p543)

➡ Edgar House (p549)

➡ Saba's Glen Yurt (p566)

Why Go?

Two cities brimming with history, a Tudor delight, an island that marches to the beat of its own drum and some of the most pleasant countryside in Britain...welcome to the northwest of England. Dominating the region is mighty Manchester, a city built on innovation and bursting with creativity. Just across the Pennines is perennial rival Liverpool, fiercely proud of its own heritage and well able to hold its own against its neighbour in all matters, from food to football. Between them is Chester, a Tudor gift enveloped by Roman walls. But the northwest is more than just mankind's concrete footprint: you don't have to go far to find yourself surrounded by the bucolic charms of northern Lancashire, while offshore is the Isle of Man, so pretty that Unesco gave the whole place Biosphere Reserve status.

When to Go

➡ The world's most famous steeplechase – the Aintree Grand National – is run just outside Liverpool over the first weekend in April.

➡ May and June are Tourist Trophy (TT) Festival season on the Isle of Man – beloved of motor enthusiasts the world over.

➡ In the arts, the highlight is the Manchester International Festival, a biennial showstopper held in July.

➡ Music buffs should visit Liverpool in the last week of August for madness at Creamfields dance-fest and for the Mathew St Festival, an ode to all things Beatles.

➡ The football (soccer) season runs from late August until May.

Manchester, Liverpool & Northwest England Highlights

1 Liverpool Cathedral (p553) Being overwhelmed by Sir Giles Gilbert Scott's awesome neo-Gothic masterpiece.

2 Beatles' Childhood Homes (p555) Visiting the Liverpool houses where John and Paul grew up – and wrote their earliest hits.

3 Rows (p549) Exploring Chester's Tudor-era shopping district.

4 Football (p546) Taking a tour of your favourite team's ground or – better still – going to a match.

5 Blackpool Tower (p561) Visiting the ballroom and climbing to the top of Blackpool's iconic structure.

6 Great Laxey Wheel (p567) Visiting the world's largest working waterwheel.

7 People's History Museum (p537) Learning about social justice in Manchester.

8 Philharmonic (p559) Enjoying a drink in this Liverpool pub, one of Britain's most beautiful.

ℹ Information

Visit North West (www.visitnorthwest.com) is the centralised tourist authority, but all cities and most towns have their own dedicated tourist authorities; for the Isle of Man check out **Isle of Man** (www.visitisleofman.com).

ℹ Getting There & Away

Both Manchester and Liverpool have international airports and are well served by trains from all over the UK, including London, only two hours away. The West Coast Line serves Preston, Lancaster and Blackpool. For Lancashire's smaller towns, there's an extensive bus service. The Isle of Man is accessible by ferry from Liverpool and Heysham, and there are regular flights from throughout the UK.

ℹ Getting Around

The towns and cities covered are all within easy reach of each other, and are well linked by public transport. The two main cities, Manchester and Liverpool, are only 34 miles apart and are linked by hourly bus and train services. Chester is 18 miles south of Liverpool, but is also easily accessible from Manchester by train or via the M56. Blackpool is 50 miles to the north of Manchester and Liverpool, and is also well connected on the M6.

MANCHESTER

♪ 0161 / POP 535,475

'This is Manchester, we do things differently here', declared culture catalyst and Factory Records founder Tony Wilson in 1977. It was a ballsy statement, given that Manchester's musical renaissance hadn't yet happened, the football teams were mediocre and the city was mired in economic depression.

But bold statements and ironclad self-confidence have long been a thing in Manchester, the one-time engine room of the Industrial Revolution and a city that incubated communism, suffragism, vegetarianism and a bunch of other 'isms' aimed at improving humanity's lot. In the 21st century, invention, discovery and progress remain the driving forces of this remarkable place, which responded to a terrible act of terrorism in 2017 by doubling down on the tolerant and inclusive attitudes toward all those who've made it home.

For Mancunians born or based here, it is the best home in the world; for everyone else, it's a brilliant place to visit.

History

Canals and steam-powered cotton mills were what transformed Manchester from a small, disease-infested provincial town into a big, disease-infested industrial city. It all happened in the 1760s, with the opening of the Bridgewater Canal between Manchester and the coal mines at Worsley in 1763, and with Richard Arkwright patenting his super cotton mill in 1769. Thereafter Manchester and the world would never be the same again. When the canal was extended to Liverpool and the open sea in 1776, Manchester – dubbed 'Cottonopolis' – kicked into high gear and took off on the coal-fuelled, steam-powered gravy train.

MANCHESTER IN ONE DAY

Start your exploration in the light-filled galleries of the **Manchester Art Gallery**, home to one of the most important collections in the north. The **Museum of Science & Industry** will take up at least a couple of hours – more if you've got kids or you're a science geek. Alternatively, the **People's History Museum** is a fascinating exploration of social history. Lunch on Chinese food at **Tattu** (♪ 0161-819 2060; www.tattu.co.uk; Gartside St, 3 Hardman Sq, Spinningfields; mains £14-27; ⊙ noon-3pm & 5-10.45pm Mon-Thu, noon-10.45pm Fri-Sun; 🚇 all city centre) or take your pick at **Mackie Mayor** (p544).

Hop on the tram to Salford Quays, where you can explore the **Imperial War Museum North** (p540) or take a guided tour of the northern headquarters of the **BBC** (p541); fans of Manchester United should take the tour of **Old Trafford** (p546), where they'll get to stand in the tunnel and pretend they're players. Make dinner reservations (well in advance) for **20 Stories** (p544).

After dinner, there's drinks at the **Refuge** (p545), a choice of bars in the Northern Quarter, or even a concert at the **Bridgewater Hall** (♪ 0161-907 9000; www.bridgewater-hall.co.uk; Lower Mosley St; 🚇 Deansgate-Castlefield). Alternatively, you can always head south towards Castlefield and take in a film or a play at the superb **HOME** (p546) arts centre.

There was plenty of gravy to go around, but the good burghers of 19th-century Manchester made sure that the vast majority of the city's swollen citizenry (with a population of 90,000 in 1801, and two million 100 years later) never got their hands on any of it despite producing most of it. Their reward was life in a new kind of urban settlement: the industrial slum. Working conditions were dire, with impossibly long hours, child labour, work-related accidents and fatalities all commonplace. Mark Twain commented that he would like to live here because the 'transition between Manchester and Death would be unnoticeable'. So much for Victorian values.

The wheels started to come off towards the end of the 19th century. The USA had begun to flex its own industrial muscles and was taking over a sizeable chunk of the textile trade; production in Manchester's mills began to slow, and then it stopped altogether. By WWII there was hardly enough cotton produced in the city to make a tablecloth. The postwar years weren't much better: 150,000 manufacturing jobs were lost between 1961 and 1983, and the port – still the UK's third largest in 1963 – finally closed in 1982 due to declining traffic.

Things got worse for Manchester on 15 June 1996, when an IRA bomb wrecked a chunk of the city centre, but the subsequent reconstruction proved to be the beginning of the glass-and-chrome revolution so much in evidence today.

◉ Sights

◉ City Centre

★**People's History Museum** MUSEUM
(☏0161-838 9190; www.phm.org.uk; Left Bank, Bridge St; ☺10am-5pm) FREE The story of Britain's 200-year march to democracy is told in all its pain and pathos at this superb museum, housed in a refurbished Edwardian pumping station. You clock in on the 1st floor (literally: punch your card in an old mill clock, which managers would infamously fiddle with so as to make employees work longer) and plunge into the heart of Britain's struggle for basic democratic rights, labour reform and fair pay.

Amid displays like the (tiny) desk at which Thomas Paine (1737–1809) wrote *Rights of Man* (1791), and an array of beautifully made and colourful union banners, are compelling interactive displays, including a screen where you can trace the effects of all the events covered in the museum on five generations of the same family. The 2nd floor takes up the struggle for equal rights from WWII to the current day, touching on gay rights, anti-racism initiatives and the defining British sociopolitical landmarks of the last 50 years, including the founding of the National Health Service (NHS), the Miners' Strike and the widespread protests against the Poll Tax.

★**Museum of Science & Industry** MUSEUM
(MOSI; ☏0161-832 2244; www.msimanchester.org. uk; Liverpool Rd; suggested donation £3, special exhibits £6-8; ☺10am-5pm; ☐1 or 3, ☐Deansgate-Castlefield) FREE Manchester's rich industrial legacy is explored in this excellent museum set within the enormous grounds of the old Liverpool St station, the oldest rail terminus in the world. The large collection of steam engines, locomotives and original factory machinery tell the story of the city from the sewers up, while a host of new technology looks to the future.

It's an all-ages kind of museum, but the emphasis is on making sure the young 'uns don't get bored – they could easily spend a whole day poking about, testing an early electric-shock machine here and trying out a printing press there. You can get up close and personal with fighter jets and get to grips with all kinds of space-age technology; the museum now includes an astronaut virtual-reality experience called Space Descent VR with Tim Peake. A unifying theme is that Manchester and Mancunians had a key role to play: this is the place to discover that Manchester was home to the world's first stored-program computer (a giant contraption nicknamed 'baby') in 1948 and that the world's first steam-powered submarine was built to the designs of local curate Reverend George Garrett in 1879.

★**Manchester Art Gallery** GALLERY
(☏0161-235 8888; www.manchesterartgallery.org; Mosley St; ☺10am-5pm Fri-Wed, to 9pm Thu; ☐St Peter's Square) FREE A superb collection of British art and a hefty number of European masters are the highlights at the city's top art gallery. It's home to the best assemblage of Pre-Raphaelite art as well as a permanent collection of pre-17th-century art, mostly by Dutch and early Renaissance masters. It also hosts exciting exhibitions of modern and contemporary art. The gallery runs a free

Manchester

Chetham's Library & School of Music 1

Trinity Way

Blackfriars St

Chapel St

Blackfriars St

Victoria St

Marks & Spencer

Chapel St

Dearman's Pl

River Irwell

Cross St

Salford Train Station

Stanley St

St Anne's Sq

St Anne St

29

Back Bridge St

King St

Irwell St

Bridge St 23

South King St

John Dalton St

Tib Ln

4 Left Bank

Wood St

People's History Museum

Gartside St

26 Crown Sq

Brazennose St

Princess St

Albert Sq

SPINNINGFIELDS

Hardman St

Lloyd St

Albert Sq

Town Hall

30

21

Water St

Quay St

18

Great John St

Lower Byrom St

Quay St

Byrom St

Longworth St

Deansgate

Peter St

Bootle St

St Peter's Sq

Central Library 7

Granada Studios

11

Watson St

Windmill St

24 19

Museum of Science & Industry 3

Liverpool Rd

Great Northern

G-Mex Exhibition Centre

Manchester YHA (200m)

CASTLEFIELD

Lower Mosley St

42 Bridgewater Hall 38

Great Bridgewater St

G-Mex

32

Medlock St

Rochdale Canal

Castle St

Chester Rd

Deansgate Train Station

Hewitt St

Whitworth St West

Cambridge St

DEANSGATE LOCKS

43

HOME

Chester St

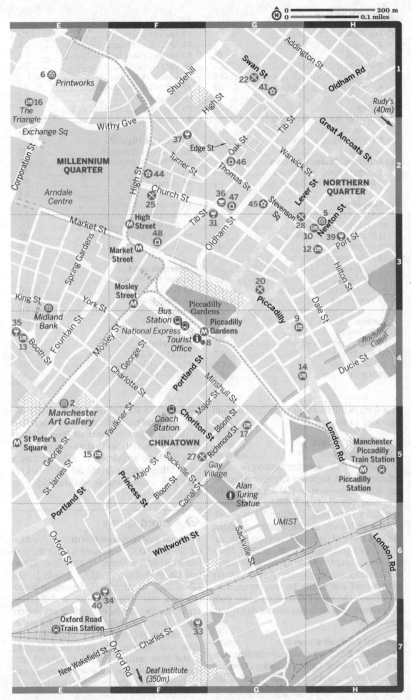

Manchester

hour-long highlights tour from 2pm to 3pm Thursday to Sunday.

★ **Chetham's Library
& School of Music** LIBRARY
(☏0161-834 7861; www.chethams.org.uk; Long Millgate; donation suggested £3; ⊙timed admission hourly 10am-noon & 1.30-3.30pm Mon-Fri; 🚇Victoria) Founded in 1653 in a building that dates from 1421, Chetham's is the oldest public library in the English-speaking world, a trove of dark shelves lined with ancient books and manuscripts. In 1845, Marx and Engels spent time studying in the alcove of the main reading room, prep work for what would eventually be the Communist Manifesto. The wider complex has its own life as part of a national school for young musicians.

National Football Museum MUSEUM
(☏0161-605 8200; www.nationalfootballmuseum.com; Urbis Building, Cathedral Gardens, Corporation St; donations welcome; ⊙10am-5pm) **FREE** This museum charts the evolution of British football from its earliest days to the multi-billion-pound phenomenon it is today. One of the highlights is **Football Plus**, a series of interactive stations that allow you to test your skills in simulated conditions; buy a credit (three for £6, eight for £10) and try your luck – it's recommended for kids over seven.

⊙ Salford Quays

Imperial War Museum North MUSEUM
(☏0161-836 4000; www.iwm.org.uk/north; Trafford Wharf Rd, The Quays; ⊙10am-5pm; 🚇Harbour City or MediaCityUK) **FREE** Inside Daniel Libeskind's aluminium-clad modern building is a war museum with a difference, exploring the effects of conflict on society rather than fetishising the instruments of destruction. Six mini exhibitions within the main hall examine war since the beginning of the 20th century from a variety of perspectives, including the role of women and the influence of science and technology.

MediaCityUK ARTS CENTRE

(☑0161-886 5300; www.mediacityuk.co.uk; Salford Quays; adult/child £11/7.25; ⊙tours 10.30am, 12.30pm & 3pm Mon-Wed, Sat & Sun; ☐Harbour City or MediaCityUK) The BBC's northern home is but one significant element of this vast 81-hectare site. Besides hosting six departments of the national broadcaster (BBC Breakfast, Children's, Sport, Radio 5 Live, Learning, and Future Media & Technology), it is also home to the set of the world's longest-running soap opera, ITV's perennially popular *Coronation Street*.

There are no plans as yet to offer tours of the Corrie set, but you can visit the BBC's impressive set-up and see the sets of some of TV's most iconic programs on a guided 90-minute tour that also includes a chance for kids to 'make' a program in an interactive studio; see www.bbc.co.uk/showsandtours. For refuelling, there are plenty of cafes and restaurants in the area.

Lowry ARTS CENTRE

(☑box office 0843-208 6000; www.thelowry.com; Pier 8, Salford Quays; ⊙gallery 11am-5pm Sun-Fri, from 10am Sat; ☐Harbour City or MediaCityUK) With multiple performance spaces, bars, restaurants and shops, this contemporary arts centre attracts more than a million visitors a year to its myriad functions, which include everything from big-name theatrical productions to comedy, kids' theatre and even weddings. The centre is also home to 300 beautifully humanistic depictions of urban landscapes by LS Lowry (1887–1976), who was born in nearby Stretford, and after whom the complex is named.

🏃 Activities

Three Rivers Gin GUIDED TOUR

(☑0161-839 2667; www.manchesterthreerivers. com; 21 Red Bank Parade; £95; ⊙7.30pm Thu-Sat, 1pm Sat & Sun) This award-winning Manchester micro-distillery cranks back the shutters a few times a week to let visitors behind the scenes with the master distiller. Its three-hour 'Gin Experience' starts with a potted history of Manchester and the city's relationship with gin, throws in several gin cocktails and culminates in mixing botanicals to cook up your own 1L batch to take home.

The distillery lives under the railway arches north of Manchester Victoria station. If you don't want to pay for the tour but still want to taste the booze you'll find it stocked in bars around town, including Impossible's gin palace.

WHITWORTH ART GALLERY

Manchester's second most important **art gallery** (☑0161-275 7450; www.whitworth.manchester.ac.uk; University of Manchester, Oxford Rd; ⊙10am-5pm Fri-Wed, to 9pm Thu; ☐15, 41, 42, 43, 140, 143 or 147 from Piccadilly Gardens) **FREE** is arguably its most beautiful, following a restoration that saw the doubling of its exhibition space through the opening of its sides and back, and the construction of glass-screened promenades. Inside is a fine collection of British watercolours, the best selection of historic textiles outside London and galleries devoted to the work of artists from Dürer and Rembrandt to Lucian Freud and David Hockney.

All this high art aside, you may find that the most interesting part of the gallery is the group of rooms dedicated to wallpaper – proof that bland pastels and horrible flowery patterns are not the final word in home decoration. There's also a lovely cafe on the grounds.

🐾 Tours

Manchester Guided Tours WALKING

(☑07505 685942; www.manchesterguidedtours. com; £10; ⊙11am) A daily walking tour of the city's highlights (departing from the Central Library at 11am), including Manchester Cathedral and the Royal Exchange. There's also a huge range of other themed tours such as Cottonopolis (looking at Manchester's industrial legacy), a John Ryland Library tour and tours of outlying suburbs like Didsbury and Chorlton.

New Manchester Walks WALKING

(☑07769 298068; www.newmanchesterwalks. com; £8-10) The complete menu of tours includes explorations of every aspect of Manchester's personality, from music to history and politics to pubs. There are a handful of football-related walks and an extensive list of 'weird and wonderful' walks, from Victorian eating habits to the history of Strangeways prison. Starting points differ.

🎊 Festivals & Events

Manchester Day ARTS, PARADE

(http://manchesterday.co.uk; ⊙mid-Jun) A day to celebrate all things Manchester inspired by New York's Thanksgiving Day parade:

MANCHESTER POLICE MUSEUM

One of the city's best-kept secrets is this superb **museum** (☐0161-856 4500; www.gmpmuseum.co.uk; 57a Newton St; ⊙10.30am-3.30pm Tue) **FREE** housed within a former Victorian police station. The original building has been magnificently – if a little creepily – brought back to life, and you can wander in and out of 19th-century cells where prisoners rested their heads on wooden pillows; visit a restored magistrates' court from 1895 and examine the case histories (complete with mugshots and photos of weapons) of some of the more notorious names to have passed through its doors.

50 performances across three city centre squares culminate in a colourful parade.

Manchester International Festival ART (☐0161-238 7300; www.mif.co.uk) A three-week-long biennial arts festival of artist-led new work across visual arts, performance and popular culture. Recent performers included Damon Albarn, Marina Abramović, Björk and Steve McQueen. The next festival is scheduled for July 2019; 2020 will see the opening of The Factory, a new multimedia arts venue that will be a flagship host of the festival.

★ **Manchester Pride Festival** LGBT (☐0161-831 7700; www.manchesterpride.com; ⊙late Aug; ⊑Piccadilly Gardens) One of England's biggest celebrations of gay, lesbian, bisexual and transgender life, held over three days of the August bank holiday weekend at the end of the month. There's music and dance (the Big Weekend); debate, films, lectures and community projects (the Superbia Weekend); a huge parade; and, on the last night, a moving candlelit vigil for all victims of HIV.

Manchester Food & Drink Festival FOOD & DRINK (www.foodanddrinkfestival.com; Albert Sq; ⊙Oct) Manchester's superb foodie scene shows off its wares over 10 days at the beginning of October. Farmers markets, pop-up restaurants and gourmet events are just part of the UK's biggest urban food fest. Much of the action takes place on Albert Square, in front of the town hall.

🛏 Sleeping

Hatters HOSTEL £ (☐0161-236 9500; http://hattershostels.com; 50 Newton St; dm/s/d from £20/40/56; ℗@☎; ⊑all city centre) The old-style lift and porcelain sinks are the only leftovers of this former millinery factory, now one of the best hostels in town. The location is a boon: smack in the heart of the Northern Quarter, you won't have to go far to get the best of alternative Manchester.

Manchester YHA HOSTEL £ (☐0345 371 9647; www.yha.org.uk; Potato Wharf; dm/d from £15/65; ℗@☎; ⊑Deansgate-Castlefield) This purpose-built canalside hostel in the Castlefield area is one of the best in the country. It's a top-class option, with four- and six-bed dorms, all with bathroom, as well as three doubles and a host of good facilities. Potato Wharf is just left off Liverpool Rd.

Roomzzz APARTMENT ££ (☐0161-236 2121; www.roomzzz.co.uk; 36 Princess St; r from £100; ❄@☎; ⊑all city centre) The inelegant name belies the designer digs inside this beautifully restored Grade II–listed building, which features serviced apartments equipped with a kitchen and the latest connectivity gadgetry, including sleek iMac computers and free wi-fi throughout. There's a small pantry, with food for sale downstairs. Highly recommended if you're planning a longer stay. There's a new **branch** (Exchange Sq; r from £119; ⊑Exchange Square) in the Corn Exchange.

Malmaison HOTEL ££ (☐0161-278 1000; www.malmaison.com; Piccadilly St; r from £110; ❄@☎; ⊑all city centre, ⊑Piccadilly Gardens) Drop-dead trendy and full of red crushed velvet, deep purples, art-deco ironwork and signature black-and-white tiles, Malmaison Manchester follows the chain's quirky design style and passion for cool, although rarely at the expense of comfort: the rooms are terrific.

ABode HOTEL ££ (☐0161-247 7744; www.abodemanchester.co.uk; 107 Piccadilly; r from £100; ❄@☎; ⊑all city centre, ⊑Piccadilly Gardens) The original fittings at this converted textile factory have been combined successfully with 61 bedrooms divided into four categories of ever-increasing luxury: Comfortable, Desirable, Enviable and Fabulous on Fifth, the latter being five seriously swanky top-floor suites.

Cow Hollow
BOUTIQUE HOTEL **££**

(☎ 07727 159727; www.cowhollow.co.uk; 57 Newton St; r/ste from £120/140; 🖵; 🖵 all city centre) Set in a stick-thin 19th-century weavers' mill, Cow Hollow offers a lot of charm in a compact space. Sixteen snug rooms are graced with original beams, brick walls and flashy bathrooms; some have original machinery incorporated into the decor. Little luxury touches include Hypnos beds, goose-down duvets, and free Prosecco and tapas each evening. Reception is in the ground-floor bar.

★ King Street Townhouse
BOUTIQUE HOTEL **£££**

(☎ 0161-667 0707; www.eclectichotels.co.uk; 10 Booth St; r/ste from £225/£335; ✳@🖵🖵; 🖵 all city centre) This beautiful 1872 Italian Renaissance–style former bank is now an exquisite boutique hotel with 40 bedrooms ranging from snug to suite. Furnishings are the perfect combination of period elegance and contemporary style. On the top floor is a small spa with an infinity pool overlooking the town hall; downstairs is a nice bar and restaurant.

Velvet Hotel
BOUTIQUE HOTEL **£££**

(☎ 0161-236 9003; www.velvetmanchester.com; 2 Canal St; r from £140; 🖵; 🖵 all city centre) Nineteen beautiful bespoke rooms each oozing style: there's the sleigh bed in room 24, the double bath of room 34, the saucy framed photographs of a stripped-down David Beckham (this is Gay Village, after all!). Despite the tantalising decor and location, this is not an exclusive hotel and is as popular with straight visitors as it is with the same-sex crowd.

Great John Street Hotel
HOTEL **£££**

(☎ 0161-831 3211; www.eclectichotels.co.uk; Great John St; r from £160; 🅿✳@🖵🖵; 🖵 2 & 3 to Museum of Science & Industry) Elegant designer luxury? Present. Fabulous rooms with all the usual delights (Egyptian cotton sheets, quality toiletries, free-standing baths and lots of high-tech electronics)? Present. This former schoolhouse (ah, now you get it) is small but sumptuous – beyond the art-deco lobby are the fabulous bedrooms, each an example of style and luxury. If only school left such comfortable memories.

Eating

Rudy's
PIZZA **£**

(www.rudyspizza.co.uk; 9 Cotton St, Ancoats; pizzas £4.90-8.90; ⊙ noon-3pm & 5-10pm Mon-Fri, noon-10pm Sat, to 9pm Sun; 🖵 Piccadilly Gardens) Makers of the best pizza in town, Rudy's can be a tough table to get (put your name down and wait) but it is oh so worth it. It makes its own dough, and uses proper San Marzano tomatoes and *fior di latte* mozzarella to create pies that a Neapolitan would approve of. There's another branch on Peter St.

Northern Soul Grilled Cheese
SANDWICHES **£**

(www.northernsoulmcr.com; 10 Church St; mains £4-7; ⊙ 11am-6pm Sun, to 8pm Mon-Wed, to 9pm Thu-Sat) Carving out a niche for artery-clogging, gooey grilled-cheese delights in Manchester's grungy Northern Quarter, Northern Soul is a great spot for a budget meal. It bills itself as 'gourmet' but there's nothing fancy about the makeshift shack it occupies, or its prices. The menu features cheese sandwiches in various guises, plus deliciously tangy mac 'n' cheese, and milkshakes.

Richmond Tea Rooms
CAFE **£**

(☎ 0161-237 9667; www.richmondtearooms.com; Richmond St; mains £5-8, afternoon teas £10.50-24.95; 🖵 all city centre) If the Mad Hatter were to have a tea party in Manchester, it would be in this wonderfully haphazard tearoom with a potpourri of period furniture and a counter painted to look like the icing on a cake. Sandwiches and light meals are the mainstay, but the real treat is the selection of afternoon teas, complete with finger sandwiches, scones and cakes.

Bundobust
INDIAN **£**

(☎ 0161-359 6757; www.bundobust.com; 61 Piccadilly; dishes £3.75-6.50; ⊙ noon-9.30pm Mon-Thu,

> **DON'T MISS**
>
> ## VICTORIA BATHS
>
> The **Victoria Baths** (☎ 0161-224 2020; www.victoriabaths.org.uk; Hathersage Rd, Chorlton-on-Medlock; adult/child £6/5; ⊙ guided tour 2pm Wed Apr-Oct; 🖵 50 or 147 from city centre) were designed to be the grandest in Britain when they opened in 1906; this Grade II–listed Edwardian classic retains much of its former grandeur despite being left virtually derelict for more than 30 years. A laborious restoration of its three pools, Turkish bath and the stunning art nouveau decor is underway, and the governing trust runs excellent hour-long guided tours of the building every Wednesday.

to 10pm Fri & Sat, to 8pm Sun; ☑; 🖵all city centre, 🖵Piccadilly Gardens) Indian veggie street food and craft beer are the order of the day at this export from Leeds. The format's the same in Manchester, right down to the pallet wall-panelling at the entrance, but this basement venue is much bigger than the original. Come for the two-dish express lunch (noon to 4pm, Monday to Friday; £7).

★ **Rosylee** CAFE ££
(www.rosylee.com; 11 Stevenson Sq; mains £10-18, 2-/3-course menu £11.95/14.95; ⊙10am-9pm Mon-Thu, to 10pm Fri-Sat, to 8pm Sun; 🖵all city centre) A touch of Edwardian and Georgian elegance in the heart of the Northern Quarter, this gorgeous tearoom has expanded its menu to offer a range of British classics like beer-battered haddock and chips, and steak suet pudding. The afternoon tea (£18.25, or £25.25 if you want a glass of bubbles) is superb.

★ **Refuge by Volta** INTERNATIONAL ££
(☑0161-233 5151; www.refugemcr.co.uk; Oxford St; ⊙noon-2.45pm & 5pm-9pm Mon-Thu, to 9.30pm Fri, noon-9.30pm Sat, noon-9pm Sun; 🖵all city centre) Manchester's snazziest dining room occupies one half of The Refuge, one of the city's best bars. The menu is made up of *voltini*, sharing plates with global influences from the Middle East to Korea (think lamb schwarma and kimchi), inspired by the travels of restaurateurs and DJs Luke Cowdrey and Justin Crawford (aka the Unabombers). Superb.

★ **Mackie Mayor** FOOD HALL ££
(www.mackiemayor.co.uk; 1 Eagle St; mains £9-15; ⊙10am-10pm Tue-Thu, to 11pm Fri, 9am-11pm Sat, 9am-8pm Sun; 🖵all city centre) This restored former meat market is now home to a superb food hall with a fine selection of 10 individual traders. The pizzas from Honest Crust are divine; the pork-belly bao from Baohouse is done just right; Nationale 7 does wonders with a basic sandwich; and Tender Cow serves really tasty steaks. Dining is communal, across two floors.

Oast House INTERNATIONAL ££
(☑0161-829 3830; www.theoasthouse.uk.com; Crown Sq, Spinningfields; mains £11-18; ⊙noon-midnight Mon-Wed & Sun, to 1am Thu, to 2am Fri-Sat; 🖵all city centre) Modelled on a Kentish oast house (a medieval kiln used to dry out hops), this Spinningfields staple was completely refurbished in 2018, including a remodelled courtyard for outdoor dining. The broad-ranging menu has burgers, ke-

babs, steaks and rotisserie chickens cooked in the BBQ oven, but you can also get a delicious fondue and a fine selection of homemade pies.

**Mr Cooper's
House & Garden** MODERN BRITISH ££
(https://mrcoopers.co.uk; Midland Hotel, 16 Peter St; mains £9.50-23; ⊙noon-10pm Mon-Sat, 1pm-10pm Sun; 🖵St Peter's Square) Rob Taylor's beautifully presented cuisine is Modern British at its tasty, unpretentious best. Interesting options include dishes like swordfish steak with edamame beans and miso butter, or slow-roasted pork belly with cavolo nero. The name comes from a local coach maker, whose house was on the land before the Midland was built.

San Carlo Cicchetti ITALIAN ££
(www.sancarlocicchetti.co.uk; King St W, House of Fraser; small plates £6.95-8.95; ⊙8am-11pm Mon-Fri, from 9am Sat, 9am-10pm Sun; 🖵all city centre) Celebrity chef Aldo Zilli has designed the superlative menu at this ornate Italian restaurant on the ground floor of House of Fraser. Instead of big plates of carb overload, though, you get smaller dishes known as *cicchetti*. The truffle and pecorino ravioli are divine. It also serves standard egg dishes for breakfast.

★ **20 Stories** BRITISH £££
(☑0161-204 3333; https://20stories.co.uk; 1 Spinningfields, Hardman Sq; mains £15-27; ⊙noon-2.45pm & 5.30-10.15pm Mon-Thu, noon-3.45pm & 5.30-10.30pm Fri-Sat, noon-3.15pm & 5.30-8.45pm Sun; 🖵all city centre) The most anticipated opening of 2018 was this rooftop restaurant atop a 20-storey tower, marshalled by local star Aiden Byrne (formerly of Manchester House). Great views and great food, courtesy of Byrne's signature style of supremely elegant, unpretentious cuisine. There's an outdoor terrace with a firepit and a grill that serves up good burgers and fish and chips.

Adam Reid at The French MODERN BRITISH £££
(☑0161-932 4198; www.the-french.co.uk; Midland Hotel, 16 Peter St; 4-/6-/9-course menu £45/65/85; ⊙noon-1.30pm & 6.30-9.30pm; 🖵St Peter's Square) 🍽 Adam Reid's exquisite Modern British cuisine is considered one of Manchester's culinary highlights, especially if you opt for one of the three tasting menus. The room is dark and moody, the soundtrack indie rock, but the food is wonderfully subtle and beautifully presented. Reservations are very much recommended.

Hawksmoor
STEAK £££

(☎ 0161-836 6980; www.thehawksmoor.com; 184-186 Deansgate; steaks £19-36; 🚇 St Peter's Square) The steakhouse that has had London's carnivores salivating landed in Manchester in 2017 and hasn't disappointed. The setting, inside a Grade II–listed courthouse, is stunning, with everything carefully put together to create an authentic 1930s-style atmosphere. The steaks – also available by weight – are prepared perfectly and the sides are just divine.

Manchester House
MODERN BRITISH £££

(www.manchesterhouse.uk.com; Tower 12, 18-22 Bridge St; mains £37, 10-/14-course tasting menu £70/95; 🖋) How would Manchester's most celebrated restaurant survive the departure of its head chef Aiden Byrne? Seamlessly, it seems, judging by the superb cooking of Nathan Tofan, who was senior sous to Byrne when he designed his menu of molecular cuisine with a Manchester twist. Tofan has made the simplified version of Blumenthal and Adrià very much his own. Reservations essential.

🍷 Drinking & Nightlife

★ Refuge
BAR

(☎ 0161-233 5151; www.refugemcr.co.uk; Oxford Rd; 🕐 8am-midnight Mon-Wed, to 1am Thu, to 2am Fri-Sat, to 11.30pm Sun; 🚇 all city centre) Occupying what was once the Victorian Gothic ground floor of the Refuge Assurance Building, this is not just Manchester's most beautiful bar, but arguably its coolest too – all thanks to the rep and aesthetic sensibilities of its creative director duo, DJs and restaurateurs Luke Cowdrey and Justin Crawford, aka the Unabombers, who run Homoelectric, the best club nights in the northwest.

★ Homoelectric
CLUB

(www.twitter.com/homoelectric; The Refuge, Oxford Rd; 🕐 10pm-4am on periodic Sat; 🚇 all city centre) The year 2018 saw the revival of one of Manchester's legendary club nights, advertised as 'a non-stop exotic disco for homos, heteros, lesbos and don't knows'. Fronted by legendary DJs, the Unabombers (Luke Cowdrey and Justin Crawford), the (roughly) monthly night takes place in the basement of The Refuge, where Cowdrey and Crawford run the bar and restaurant. Check Twitter for details.

Cloudwater Barrel Store Tap Room
BREWERY

(www.cloudwaterbrew.co; Arch 13, Sheffield St; 🕐 4-9pm Thu, 2-10pm Fri, noon-10pm Sat, noon-8pm Sun; 🚇 Piccadilly) Take a warehouse space under the arches behind Manchester Piccadilly Station, roll in a double deck of beer barrels and set out simple seating, and you've got the perfect brew for an atmospheric tap room. Cloudwater is one of England's most raved about microbreweries and this drinking den serving draft and selling cans is the bee's knees for its fans.

Fac251
CLUB

(☎ 0161-272 7251; www.factorymanchester.com; 112-118 Princess St; £1-6; 🕐 11pm-4am Mon-Sat; 🚇 all city centre) Located in Tony Wilson's former Factory Records HQ, Fac251 is one of the most popular venues in town. There are three rooms, all with a broad musical appeal, from drum and bass to Motown and indie rock. Something for everybody, from Monday's Quids In (for students) to the Big Weekender on Saturday (commercial R&B).

Peveril of the Peak
PUB

(☎ 0161-236 6364; 127 Great Bridgewater St; 🕐 11am-11pm; 🚇 Deansgate-Castlefield) The best of Manchester's collection of beautiful Victorian pubs. Check out the gorgeous glazed tilework outside.

Britons Protection
PUB

(☎ 0161-236 5895; 50 Great Bridgewater St; 🕐 noon-midnight Mon-Thu, to 1am Fri & Sat, to 11pm Sun; 🚇 Castlefield-Deansgate) Whisky – over 300 different kinds of it (the Cu Dhub 'black whisky' is a particular treat with its touch of coffee and honey) – is the beverage of choice at this liver-threatening, proper English pub that also does home-style meals (gammon, pies etc). An old-fashioned boozer with open fires in the back rooms and a cosy atmosphere...perfect on a cold evening.

Odd
BAR

(☎ 0161-833 0070; www.oddbar.co.uk; 30-32 Thomas St; 🕐 11am-midnight Sun-Wed, to 1am Thu, to 2am Fri & Sat; 🚇 Piccadilly Gardens) This eclectic little bar – with its oddball furnishings, wacky tunes and anti-establishment crew of customers – is a Northern Quarter stalwart and the perfect antidote to the increasingly similar look of so many modern bars. A slice of Mancuniana to be treasured.

Lily's Bar
COCKTAIL BAR

(☎ 0161-714 0414; www.1761mcr.co.uk; 2 Booth St; 🕐 noon-midnight; 🖋; 🚇 all city centre) This basement champagne bar inside the 1761 restaurant is named after Madame

Bollinger, whose nickname was 'Aunt Lily', though the bar itself has little association beyond selling the French champagne. It's done out like a prohibition den with chesterfield chairs, a sepia film projector screen and a giant fish tank (yes, you heard us right).

North Tea Power
CAFE

(☏ 0161-833 3073; www.northteapower.co.uk; 36 Tib St; ⊙ 8am-7pm Mon-Fri, from 9am Sat, 10am-6pm Sun; ☎) The name may say tea but the interior of this cafe screams coffee shop. North Tea Power is one of Manchester's early adopters on the artisanal coffee scene, with the requisite communal tables, industrial pillars and Macbook-wielding tribe. As well as flat whites, AeroPress and pour-overs, the menu features a load of loose-leaf teas, cakes and all-day breakfast options.

Port Street Beer House
CRAFT BEER

(www.portstreetbeerhouse.co.uk; 39-41 Port St; ⊙ noon-midnight Sun-Fri, to 1am Sat; ⬛ Piccadilly Gardens) Fans of real ale love this Northern Quarter boozer, with its seven hand pulls, 18 draught lines and more than 100 beers from around the world, including gluten-free ales and some heavy hitters: Brewdog's Tactical Nuclear Penguin is a 32% stout but at £45 a bottle you won't need more than one. It hosts regular tastings and tap takeovers.

Black Dog Ballroom
BAR

(☏ 0161-839 0664; www.blackdogballroom.co.uk; 52 Church St; ⊙ noon-4am Mon-Fri & Sun, to 5am Sat; ☎; ⬛ all city centre) A basement bar with a speakeasy vibe, but there's nothing illicit about drinking here: the cocktails are terrific (it runs occasional mixology sessions), the atmosphere is always buzzing and the music always good and loud – the resident DJs spin some great tunes Thursday through Saturday nights.

☆ Entertainment

★ HOME
ARTS CENTRE

(☏ 0161-200 1500; www.homemcr.org; 2 Tony Wilson Pl, First St; tickets £5-20; ⊙ box office noon-8pm, bar 10am-11pm Mon-Thu, to midnight Fri-Sat, 11am-10.30pm Sun; ⬛ all city centre) One of Britain's best arts centres, HOME has two theatre spaces that host provocative new work in a variety of contexts, from proscenium sets to promenade pieces. The five cinema screens show the latest indie releases as well as classics. There's also a ground-floor bar and a cafe that serves good food on the first floor.

Band on the Wall
LIVE MUSIC

(☏ 0161-834 1786; www.bandonthewall.org; 25 Swan St; ⊙ 5pm-late; ⬛ all city centre) A top-notch venue that hosts everything from rock to world music, with splashes of jazz, blues and folk thrown in.

FOOTBALL TOURS

Manchester United Museum & Tour (☏ 0161-826 1326; www.manutd.com; Sir Matt Busby Way; tours adult/child £18/12; ⊙ museum 9.30am-5pm Mon-Sat, 10am-4pm Sun, tours every 10min 9.40am-4.30pm Mon-Sat, to 3.30pm Sun, closed match days; ⬛ Old Trafford or Exchange Quay) You don't have to be a fan of the world's most famous football club to enjoy a visit to their impressive 75,000-plus capacity Old Trafford stadium, but it helps. The museum tour includes a walk down the tunnel onto the edge of the playing surface, where Manchester United's superstar footballers ply their lucrative trade.

Other highlights of the excellent tour include a seat in the stands, a stop in the changing rooms and a peek at the players' lounge (from which the manager is banned unless invited by the players) – all ecstatic experiences for a Man United devotee. The museum has a comprehensive history of the club and a state-of-the-art call-up system that means you can view your favourite goals.

Manchester City Stadium Tour (☏ 0161-444 1894; www.mcfc.co.uk; Etihad Campus; tours adult/child £17.50/12; ⊙ 9am-5pm Mon-Sat, 10am-4pm Sun except match days; ⬛ Etihad Campus) On this 90-minute tour of Manchester City's stadium you'll visit both the home and away dressing rooms (note the huge difference between the two); the pitchside dugouts; the press room; and the Tunnel Club, where VIP guests get to see the players walk through on match days. Other tours combine the stadium with the nearby academy. Online bookings are cheaper.

The tour also includes a visit to the trophy room, which has seen the addition of another Premier League title in 2018, their third since 2012 and their first under the world's most celebrated manager, the Catalan Josep 'Pep' Guardiola.

Ruby Lounge
LIVE MUSIC

(☑ 0161-834 1392; www.therubylounge.com; 28-34 High St; tickets around £8-10; ☺ noon-midnight, clubs 11pm-3am; ☒ Exchange Square) Terrific live-music venue in the Northern Quarter that features mostly rock bands. It gets very loud. After the bands there's usually a club night that runs until late.

Deaf Institute
LIVE MUSIC

(www.thedeafinstitute.co.uk; 135 Grosvenor St; ☺ 10am-midnight; ☒ all city centre) Excellent midsized venue in a former institute for deaf people; also includes a smaller venue in the basement and a cafe on the ground floor. It's where you'll hear alt rock and pop by dozens of local bands we guarantee you've never heard of (as well as some visiting bands you may have).

Soup Kitchen
LIVE MUSIC

(http://soup-kitchen.co.uk; 31-33 Spear St; £3-5; ☺ noon-11pm Mon-Wed & Sun, to 1am Thu, to 4am Fri & Sat; ☒ Market Street) By day a typical Northern Quarter canteen-style cafe, but at night this is one of the city's best places to catch live music, with a full schedule of gigs by all kinds of indie acts passing through town. When the bands are done, the excellent DJs kick in and it often goes until 6am.

🔒 Shopping

Oi Polloi
CLOTHING

(www.oipolloi.com; 63 Thomas St; ☺ 10am-6pm Mon-Sat; ☒ all city centre) Besides the impressive range of casual footwear, this hip boutique also stocks a huge range of designers including A Kind of Guise, LA Panoplie, Nudie Jeans Co and Maison Kitsuné.

Tib Street Market
MARKET

(☑ 0161-234 7357; Tib St; ☺ 10am-5pm Sat; ☒ all city centre) Up-and-coming local designers get a chance to display their wares at this weekly market where you can pick up everything from purses to lingerie and hats to jewellery.

Oxfam Originals
VINTAGE

(Unit 8, Smithfield Bldg, Oldham St; ☺ 10am-6pm Mon-Sat, noon-5pm Sun; ☒ all city centre) If you're into retro, this terrific store has high-quality gear from the 1960s and '70s. Shop in the knowledge that it's for a good cause.

ℹ Information

Tourist Office (www.visitmanchester.com; 1 Piccadilly Gardens; ☺ 9.30am-5pm Mon-Sat, 10.30am-4.30pm Sun; ☒ Piccadilly Gardens) This is mostly a self-service tourist office, with brochures and interactive maps to help guide visitors.

ℹ Getting There & Away

AIR

Manchester Airport (☑ 0808-169 7030; www.manchesterairport.co.uk) The airport is 12 miles south of the city.

BUS

National Express (☑ 08717 81 81 81; www.nationalexpress.com) serves most major cities from the **coach station** (Chorlton St), including the following:

Leeds £5.20, one hour, hourly

Liverpool £7.10, 1½ hours, hourly

London £14.10, 4¼ hours, hourly

TRAIN

Manchester Piccadilly (east of Piccadilly Gardens) is the main station for most mainline train services across Britain; Victoria Station (north of the National Football Museum) serves destinations in the northwest including Blackburn, Halifax and Huddersfield but also Leeds and Liverpool. The two stations are linked by Metrolink. Off-peak fares are considerably cheaper. Destinations include the following:

Blackpool £17.70, 1¼ hours, half-hourly

Liverpool Lime St £11.40, 45 minutes, half-hourly

London Euston £85.90, three hours, seven daily

Newcastle £69.50, three hours, six daily

ℹ Getting Around

TO/FROM THE AIRPORT

Bus £4.20, 30 minutes, every 20 minutes to Piccadilly Gardens

Metrolink £4.20, 40 minutes, every 12 minutes; change at Cornbrook or Firswood for city centre

Taxi £20 to £30, 25 to 40 minutes

Train £5, 20 minutes, every 10 minutes to Piccadilly Station

BUS

The Metroshuttle is a free service with three separate routes around the heart of Manchester every 10 minutes. Pick up a map from the tourist office. Most local buses start from Piccadilly Gardens.

METROLINK

The Metrolink (www.metrolink.co.uk) light-rail network is the best way to get between Victoria and Piccadilly train stations, as well as further afield to Salford Quays, Didsbury and other suburbs. It also serves the airport, but you need to change at either Cornbrook or Firswood. Trams run every few minutes throughout the day from 6am to 11pm. Buy your tickets from the platform machine.

TRAIN

Castlefield is served by Deansgate station with suburban rail links to Piccadilly, Oxford Rd and Salford stations.

CHESTER

☑ 01244 / POP 118,200

Chester's Tudor-and-Victorian heart is justifiably famous as one of Britain's prettiest town centres. This collection of black-and-white timber-framed beauties and red-sandstone buildings surrounded by an original set of Roman-era walls is one of the northwest's biggest tourist attractions.

Beyond the cruciform-shaped historic centre, Chester is an ordinary, residential town; it's hard to believe today, but throughout the Middle Ages Chester made its money as the most important port in the northwest. However, the River Dee silted up over time and Chester fell behind Liverpool in importance.

◉ Sights & Activities

★ City Walls
LANDMARK

A good way to get a sense of Chester's unique character is to walk the 2-mile circuit along the walls that surround the historic centre. Originally built by the Romans around AD 70, the walls were altered substantially over the following centuries but have retained their current position since around 1200. The tourist office's *Walk Around Chester Walls* leaflet is an excellent guide and you can also take a 90-minute guided walk.

Of the many features along the walls, the most eye-catching is the prominent **Eastgate**, where you can see the most famous clock in England after London's Big Ben, built for Queen Victoria's Diamond Jubilee in 1897.

At the southeastern corner of the walls are the **wishing steps**, added in 1785. Local legend claims that if you can run up and down these uneven steps while holding your breath your wish will come true.

Just inside Southgate, known here as **Bridgegate** (as it's located at the northern end of the Old Dee Bridge), is the **Bear & Billet** (www.bearandbillet.com; 94 Lower Bridge St; ☉noon-11.30pm) pub, Chester's oldest timber-framed building, built in 1664, and once a toll gate into the city.

Chester Cathedral
CATHEDRAL

(☑ 01244-324756; www.chestercathedral.com; 12 Abbey Sq; ☉9am-6pm Mon-Sat, 1-4pm Sun) **FREE** Chester Cathedral was originally a Benedictine abbey built on the remains of an earlier Saxon church dedicated to St Werburgh (the city's patron saint); it was shut down in 1540 as part of Henry VIII's Dissolution frenzy, but reconsecrated as a cathedral the following year. Despite a substantial Victorian facelift, the cathedral retains much of its original 12th-century structure. You can amble about freely, but the **tours** (adult/child full tour £8/6, short tour £6; ☉full tour 11am & 3pm daily, short tour 12.30pm & 1.15pm Mon-Tue, also 2pm & 4pm Wed-Sat) are excellent, as they take you up to the top of the panoramic bell tower.

Roman Amphitheatre
ARCHAEOLOGICAL SITE

(Little St John St) **FREE** Just outside the city walls is what was once an arena that seated 7000 spectators (making it the country's largest); some historians have suggested that it may have also been the site of King Arthur's Camelot and that his knights' 'round table' was really just this circular construction. Excavations continue; during summer months there are occasional shows held here.

Blue Planet Aquarium
AQUARIUM

(www.blueplanetaquarium.com; adult/child £17/12.25; ☉10am-5pm Mon-Fri, to 6pm Sat & Sun; ☐1 & 4 from Bus Exchange) Things aren't done by halves around Chester, where you'll find Blue Planet, which was the country's largest aquarium when it opened in 1998. It's home to 10 different kinds of shark, which can be viewed from a 70m-long moving walkway that lets you eye them up close. The aquarium is 9 miles north of Chester at Junction 10 of the M53 to Liverpool. Book online for a 10% discount.

Grosvenor Museum
MUSEUM

(☑ 01244-972197; www.grosvenormuseum.co.uk; 27 Grosvenor St; ☉10.30am-5pm Mon-Sat, 1-4pm Sun) **FREE** Excellent museum with the country's most comprehensive collection of Roman tombstones. At the back of the museum is a preserved Georgian house, complete with kitchen, drawing room, bedroom and bathroom.

Chester Boat
BOATING

(☑ 01244-325394; www.chesterboat.co.uk; Boating Station, Souters La, The Groves; tours £7-20; ☉11am-5pm) Runs hourly 30-minute and two-hour-long cruises (the latter at noon and 2.30pm Saturday and Sunday) up and down the Dee, including a foray into the gorgeous Eaton Estate, home of the Duke and Duchess of Westminster. All departures are from the riverside along the promenade known as the Groves.

🛏 Sleeping

Chester Backpackers   HOSTEL £
(☑ 01244-400185; www.chesterbackpackers.co.uk; 67 Boughton; dm/s/d from £16/22/34; ☺ reception 8am-11am & 4-7.30pm only; 🛜) Comfortable dorm and private rooms with nice pine beds in a typically Tudor white-and-black building. They're small but comfortable. It's just a short walk from the city walls and there's also a pleasant garden. Reception is only open at certain times during the day.

★ Edgar House   BOUTIQUE HOTEL ££
(☑ 01244-347007; www.edgarhouse.co.uk; 22 City Walls; ☺ r from £105) This award-winning digs is the ultimate in boutique luxury. A Georgian house with seven rooms, each decorated in its own individual style – some have free-standing claw-foot tubs and French doors that lead onto an elegant terrace. There's beautiful art on the walls and fabulous touches of the owners' gorgeous aesthetic throughout. The superb Twenty2 (www.restauranttwenty2.co.uk; tasting menu £59; ☺ 6-9pm Wed-Sat, afternoon tea noon-4pm Fri-Sun) restaurant is open to nonguests.

Stone Villa   B&B ££
(☑ 01244-345014; www.stonevillachester.co.uk; 3 Stone Pl, Hoole Rd; s/d from £60/85; 🅿🛜; 🚌9 from city centre) This award-winning, beautiful 1850 villa has everything you need for a memorable stay. Elegant bedrooms, a fabulous breakfast and welcoming, friendly owners all add up to excellent lodgings. The property is about a mile from the city centre. You can even rent the whole house – which sleeps 22 – for £900 a night.

ABode Chester   HOTEL ££
(☑ 01244-347000; www.abodechester.co.uk; Grosvenor Rd; r/ste from £89/289; 🅿✳🛜) Contemporary hotel with 84 rooms all equipped with handcrafted Vispring beds and handsome bathrooms complete with monsoon showers. Good toiletries, flat-screen TVs and cashmere throws on the bed give it a touch of elegance. Rooms come in categories: Comfortable, Desirable, Enviable, Most Enviable and Fabulous suites. South-facing

THE ROWS

Besides the City Walls, Chester's other great draw is the **Rows**, a series of two-level galleried arcades along the four streets that fan out in each direction from the Central Cross. The architecture is a handsome mix of Victorian and Tudor (original and mock) buildings that house a fantastic collection of independently owned shops.

The origin of the Rows is a little unclear, but it is believed that as the Roman walls slowly crumbled, medieval traders built their shops against the resulting rubble banks, while later arrivals built theirs on top.

rooms have great views of the Roodee racecourse.

★ Chester Grosvenor
Hotel & Spa   HOTEL £££
(☑ 01244-324024; www.chestergrosvenor.com; 58 Eastgate St; r from £200; 🅿@🛜) The black-and-white timbered Grosvenor is the city's top hotel by location – right next to the Eastgate Clock – and quality, offering a five-star experience throughout. The lobby's main feature is the chandelier, with 28,000 pieces of crystal; move on from there to the huge rooms with exquisite period furniture. There's also a top spa (open to nonguests) and a Michelin-starred restaurant (p550).

🍴 Eating

The Kitchen   LEBANESE £
(www.thekitchenstoryhouse.co.uk; Storyhouse, Hunter St; mains £8-9; ☺ 8am-9.30pm Mon-Sat, 9.30am-9pm Sun) Delicious mezze and other small plates from the Levant are the mainstay at the ground-floor restaurant in Storyhouse (p551), Chester's exciting new arts centre. The Express Lunch (£7.50) is served between noon and 3pm, and gives you the option of chicken with spices or squash and halloumi.

Joseph Benjamin   MODERN BRITISH ££
(☑ 01244-344295; www.josephbenjamin.co.uk; 134-140 Northgate St; mains £11-18; ☺ noon-3pm Tue-Sat, also 6-9.30pm Thu-Sat & noon-4pm Sun) A bright star in Chester's culinary firmament is this combo restaurant, bar and deli that delivers carefully prepared local produce to take out or eat in. Excellent sandwiches

Chester

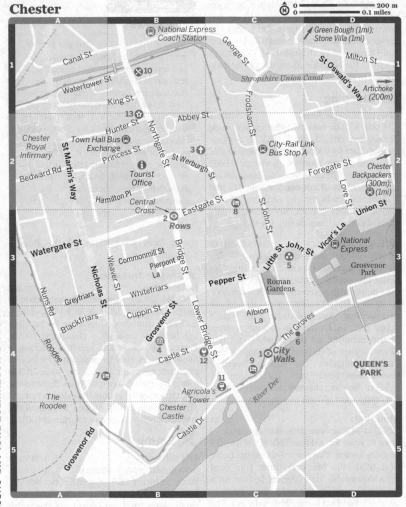

N 0 ⎯⎯⎯⎯ 200 m
0 ⎯⎯⎯⎯ 0.1 miles

and gorgeous salads are the mainstay of the takeaway menu, while the more formal dinner menu features fine examples of Modern British cuisine.

Artichoke　　　　MODERN BRITISH ££
(www.artichokechester.co.uk; The Steam Mill, Steam Mill St; mains £14-17; ⊙10am-3.30pm & 5-10pm Mon-Sat, 10am-8pm Sun) One of a number of warehouse conversions along the Shropshire Union Canal (now known as the Canal Quarter), this cafe-bar serves sandwiches and smaller bites as well as tasty main courses such as sea trout in a sweet

pea wasabi velvet cream, and confit of duck legs with Jersey potatoes, pancetta and red cabbage. It's a popular drinking spot too.

★ **Simon Radley
at the Grosvenor**　　　MODERN BRITISH £££
(☑01244-324024; www.chestergrosvenor.com; 58 Eastgate St, Chester Grosvenor Hotel; tasting menu £99, à la carte menu £75; ⊙6.30-9pm Tue-Sat) Simon Radley's formal restaurant (you're instructed to arrive 30 minutes early for drinks and canapés) has served near-perfect Modern British cuisine since 1990, when it was first awarded the Michelin star that it has kept

Chester

ever since. The food is divine and the wine list extensive. One of Britain's best, but why no second star? Note that attire must be smart and no children under 12 are permitted.

🍷 Drinking & Entertainment

Brewery Tap   PUB
(www.the-tap.co.uk; 52-54 Lower Bridge St; ⊙noon-11pm, to 10.30pm Sun) If you're looking for the best pint in the city, the aficionados at the Campaign for Real Ale (Camra) reckon you'll get it at this boozer in a Grade II–listed Jacobean banqueting hall; its seven taps offer a rotating range of quality brews from all over England.

★Storyhouse   ARTS CENTRE
(☑01244-409113; www.storyhouse.com; Hunter St) The 1930s art deco Odeon has been converted into an award-winning modern arts centre with two theatre spaces – a larger 800-seater arena and a 150-seat studio theatre – plus a cinema that screens indie and art movies. The Lebanese-inspired Kitchen (p549) restaurant on the ground floor is excellent.

ℹ Information

Tourist Office (☑01244-402111; www. visitchester.com; Town Hall, Northgate St; ⊙9am-5.30pm Mon-Sat, 10am-5pm Sun Mar-Oct, 9am-5pm Mon-Sat, 10am-4pm Sun Nov-Feb) Tourist information, accommodation booking service and brochures.

ℹ Getting There & Away

BUS

Local buses leave from the **Town Hall Bus Exchange** (Princess St). **National Express** (☑08717 81 81 81; www.nationalexpress.com)

coaches stop on Vicar's Lane, just opposite the tourist office by the Roman amphitheatre. Destinations include the following:

Birmingham £15.30, two hours, four daily
Liverpool £9.20, 45 minutes, four daily
London £33, 5½ hours, three daily
Manchester £7.60, 1¼ hours, three daily

TRAIN

The train station is about a mile from the city centre via Foregate St and City Rd, or Brook St. City-Rail Link buses are free for people with rail tickets, and operate between the station and **Bus Stop A** (Frodsham St). Destinations include the following:

Liverpool £7.30, 45 minutes, hourly
London Euston £85.90, 2½ hours, hourly
Manchester £17.60, one hour, hourly

ℹ Getting Around

Much of the city centre is closed to traffic from 10.30am to 4.30pm, so a car is likely to be a hindrance. The city is easy to walk around anyway, and most places of interest are close to the wall. There are regular buses to both the zoo and the aquarium.

LIVERPOOL

☑0151 / POP 467,500

It's hard not to be infected by a Liverpudlian's love for their own city. For decades this was a hardscrabble town beset by all manner of social ills, but still the love endured, finding its expression in a renowned gallows wit and an obsession with football.

With the worst of times now firmly behind them, it's much easier to feel the love. The city's impressive cultural heritage,

Liverpool

0 — 200 m
0 — 0.1 miles

National Express Coach Station

London Rd

Pembroke Pl

Dalby St

Hotham St

Lord Nelson St

Russell St

William Brown St

Tourist Office

Walker Art Gallery

World Museum

St George's Hall

Queen Sq

Williamson Sq

Victoria St

Hatton Gdn

Dale St

Moorfields

Tithebarn St

Old Hall St

Chapel St

Water St

New Quay

Goree Piazza

King Edward St

Bath St

William Jessop Way

Princes Dock

Mersey Tunnel

Town Hall

Rumford St

James St

Port of Mann

Brunswick St

Liverpool Building

Royal Liver Building

Cunard Building

Mersey Ferry

PIER HEAD

Mersey

The Wirral (2m)

Mersey Tunnel

Lime Street Train Station

Lime St

Clayton Sq

Church St

School La

Paradise St

Cavern Quarter

Temple La

Harrington St

Castle Cook St

Lord St

Mathew St

Ranelagh St

Central

Bold St

Renshaw St

Brownlow Hill

Mt Pleasant

Clarence St

Copperas Hill

Brownlow Hill

Metropolitan Cathedral of Christ the King

Oxford St

Hope St

Rodney St

Leece St

Roscoe Street

Berry St

Great George St

Upper Duke St

CHINATOWN

Nelson St

Liverpool Cathedral

Canning St

Blackburne Tce

Blackburne Pl

Faulkner St

Rice St

Hardman St

Hope Pl

Myrtle St

Catherine St

Seel St

Slater St

Wood St

Concert St

Campbell Sq

Par St

Duke St

Hanover St

ROPEWALKS

Liverpool ONE Bus Station

Liver St

Strand St

Strand St

Canning Dock

Salthouse Dock

Wapping Basin

Wapping

Park La

Tabley St

BALTIC TRIANGLE

District (200m); Constellations (350m)

Wapping Dock

King's Dock

Monarch's Quay

King's Pde

ALBERT DOCK

The Beatles Story

International Slavery Museum

Canning Half Tide Basin

Mersey

Liverpool

dating back to when Liverpool was Britain's second-most important city, is a source of justifiable pride to Scousers – as the locals are named, after Scouse, a fish-and-biscuit stew popular with sailors – but what really excites them is the ongoing program of urban regeneration that is transforming a once dilapidated city centre into one of the most pleasant cities in northern England.

History

Liverpool grew wealthy on the back of the triangular trading of slaves, raw materials and finished goods. From 1700 ships carried cotton goods and hardware from Liverpool to West Africa, where they were exchanged for slaves, who in turn were carried to the West Indies and Virginia, where they were exchanged for sugar, rum, tobacco and raw cotton.

As a great port, the city drew thousands of Irish and Scottish immigrants, and its Celtic influences are still apparent. Between 1830 and 1930, however, nine million emigrants – mainly English, Scots and Irish, but also Swedes, Norwegians and Russian Jews – sailed from here to the New World.

The start of WWII led to a resurgence of Liverpool's importance. More than one million American GIs disembarked here before D-Day and the port was, once again, hugely important as the western gateway for transatlantic supplies. The GIs brought with them the latest American records, and Liverpool was thus the first European port of call for the new rhythm and blues that would eventually become rock and roll. Within 20 years, the Mersey Beat was *the* sound of British pop, and four mop-topped Scousers had formed a skiffle band...

⊙ Sights

The main attractions are Albert Dock (west of the city centre) and the trendy Ropewalks area (south of Hanover St and west of the two cathedrals). Lime St station, the bus station and the Cavern Quarter – a mecca for Beatles fans – lie just to the north.

⊙ City Centre

★**Liverpool Cathedral** CHURCH
(☑ 0151-709 6271; www.liverpoolcathedral.org.uk; Upper Duke St; Tower Experience adult/student £5.50/4.50; ⊙ 8am-6pm, Tower Experience 10am-4.30pm; 🚍 82 & 86 from city centre) Britain's largest church, this magnificent neo-Gothic building is also the world's largest Anglican cathedral. It was designed by Sir Giles Gilbert Scott (creator of the red telephone box) and is a stunning bit of architecture, managing at once to provoke awe at its size as well

MANCHESTER, LIVERPOOL & NORTHWEST ENGLAND LIVERPOOL

as a profound feeling of intimacy. You can climb the tower for an unparalleled view of the city and beyond: on a clear day you can see Blackpool Tower 55 miles away.

The Tower Experience also features *Great Space,* a 10-minute, panoramic high-definition movie about the history of the cathedral, which was begun in 1904 but not completed until 1978; and a view of Great George, the world's heaviest set of bells. The vast interior is marked by a studied emptiness, but worth noting is the organ, split between two chambers on opposite sides of the Choir and comprising 10,268 pipes and 200 stops, making it most likely the world's largest operational model. The cathedral is also home to a collection of artworks, including a piece over the West Doors called *For You* by Tracey Emin: a pink neon sign that says 'I felt you and I knew you loved me'. Guides are on hand to offer tours; a donation of £3 is suggested.

★ **Walker Art Gallery**   GALLERY
(☑ 0151-478 4199; www.liverpoolmuseums.org.uk/walker; William Brown St; ☑ 10am-5pm; ☐ all city centre) FREE The city's foremost art gallery is the national gallery for northern England, housing an outstanding collection of art from the 14th to the 21st centuries. Its strong suits are Pre-Raphaelite art, modern British art and sculpture – not to mention the rotating exhibits of contemporary expression. It's a family-friendly place too: the ground-floor Big Art for Little Artists gallery is designed for under-eights and features interactive exhibits and games that will (hopefully) result in a lifelong love affair with art.

★ **World Museum**   MUSEUM
(☑ 0151-478 4399; www.liverpoolmuseums.org.uk/wml; William Brown St; ☑ 10am-5pm; ☐ all city centre) FREE Natural history, science and technology are the themes of the oldest museum in town, which opened in 1853. Its exhibits range from live bugs to human anthropology. This vastly entertaining and educational museum is spread across five themed floors, from the aquarium on the 1st floor to the planetarium on the 5th, where you'll also find exhibits dedicated to space (moon rocks, telescopes etc) and time (clocks and timepieces from the 1500s to 1960). Highly recommended.

Western Approaches Museum   MUSEUM
(www.liverpoolwarmuseum.co.uk; 1-3 Rumford St; adult/child £10.50/9; ☑ 10am-4.15pm Mon-Tue & Thu-Sun; ☐ all city centre) Between 7 February 1941 and 15 August 1945 the secret command centre for the Battle of the Atlantic was in the basement rooms of Derby House. Known as Western Approaches because its main task was to monitor enemy approaches in the Atlantic west of the British Isles, the labyrinthine nerve centre of Allied operations is pretty much as it was at war's end. Highlights include the all-important map room, where you can imagine playing a real-life, full-scale version of Risk.

◉ **Albert Dock**

Liverpool's biggest tourist attraction is Albert Dock, 2.75 hectares of water ringed by enormous cast-iron columns and impressive five-storey warehouses that make up the country's largest collection of protected

---

LIVERPOOL IN ONE DAY

Start your day at the **Beatles Story** on the Albert Dock: it's an excellent intro to the Fab Four, but fans should make sure to have booked a morning tour to **Mendips** and **20 Forthlin Road**, the childhood homes of John Lennon and Paul McCartney respectively; the tour leaves from Albert Dock. If you're not a die-hard Beatles fan, then visit the **International Slavery Museum** and then head into town for a visit to the stunning **cathedral** (p553). For lunch, try either the **Salt House** (p558) or **HOST** (p558).

If you've still got a cultural hunger, you can explore the **Walker Art Gallery** or the wonderful natural science exhibits of the **World Museum**. Football fans should make the trip to Anfield and take the tour of **Liverpool Football Club** (p560). For dinner, if you've planned it long enough in advance, go to **Restaurant Fraiche** (p558); otherwise try **Wreckfish** (p558).

After dinner, be sure to get a drink at the **Philharmonic** (p559), after which you can take in a gig across the street at the **Philharmonic Hall** (p560). If you're into something a little more adrenalised, the clubs of the Baltic Triangle are worth a punt: our favourite is **Constellations** (p560), which always has something interesting going on.

DON'T MISS

(NEVER) LET IT BE

They broke up nearly 50 years ago and two of their members are dead, but the Beatles are bigger business than ever in Liverpool.

Most of it centres around tiny Mathew St, site of the original Cavern Club, which is now the main thoroughfare of the 'Cavern Quarter', an unashamedly commercial effort to cash in on the legacy of the Fab Four. Here you can shuck oysters in the Rubber Soul Oyster Bar, buy a George pillowcase in the From Me to You shop and put it on the pillows of the Hard Days Night Hotel (p557). **The Beatles Story** (☑0151-709 1963; www.beatlesstory.com; Albert Dock; adult/child/student £15.95/9.50/12; ◷9am-7pm, last admission 5pm; ▢all city centre) in Albert Dock is the city's most visited museum, but if you really want to dig deep into Beatles lore, we strongly recommend a visit to the National Trust–owned **Mendips**, the home where John lived with his aunt from 1945 to 1963, and **20 Forthlin Road**, the plain terraced home where Paul grew up, available only by prebooking a place on the **Beatles' Childhood Homes Tour** (☑0151-427 7231; www.nationaltrust.org.uk; Jury's Inn, 31 Keel Wharf, Wapping Dock; adult/child £23/7.25; ◷10am, 11am, 2.10pm & 3pm Wed-Sun Mar-Nov).

If you'd rather do it yourself, the tourist offices stock the *Discover Lennon's Liverpool* guide and map, and Ron Jones' *The Beatles' Liverpool*.

buildings and are a World Heritage Site. A fabulous redevelopment program has really brought the dock to life – here you'll find several outstanding museums and an extension of the Tate Gallery, as well as some good restaurants and bars.

★**International Slavery Museum** MUSEUM
(☑0151-478 4499; www.liverpoolmuseums.org.uk/ism; Albert Dock; ◷10am-5pm) **FREE** Museums are, by their very nature, like a still of the past, but the extraordinary International Slavery Museum resonates very much in the present. It reveals slavery's unimaginable horrors – including Liverpool's own role in the triangular slave trade – in a clear and uncompromising manner. It does this through a remarkable series of multimedia and other displays, and it doesn't baulk at confronting racism, slavery's shadowy ideological justification for this inhumane practice.

The history of slavery is made real through a series of personal experiences, including a carefully kept ship's log and captain's diary. These tell the story of one slaver's experience on a typical trip, departing Liverpool for West Africa. The ship then purchased or captured as many slaves as it could carry before embarking on the gruesome 'middle passage' across the Atlantic to the West Indies. The slaves that survived the torturous journey were sold for sugar, rum, tobacco and raw cotton, which were then brought back to England for profit. Exhibits include original shackles, chains and instruments used to punish rebellious slaves – each piece of metal is more horrendous than the next.

Tate Liverpool GALLERY
(☑0151-702 7400; www.tate.org.uk/liverpool; Albert Dock; special exhibitions adult/child from £6/5; ◷10am-5pm; ▢all city centre) **FREE** Touted as the home of modern art in the north, this gallery features a substantial checklist of 20th-century artists across its four floors, as well as touring exhibitions from the mother ship on London's Bankside. But it's all a little sparse, with none of the energy we'd expect from the world-famous Tate.

Merseyside Maritime Museum MUSEUM
(☑0151-478 4499; www.liverpoolmuseums.org.uk/maritime; Albert Dock; ◷10am-5pm; ▢all city centre) **FREE** The story of one of the world's great ports is the theme of this excellent museum and, believe us, it's a graphic and compelling page-turner. One of the many great exhibits is Emigration to a New World (in the basement), which tells the story of nine million emigrants and their efforts to get to North America and Australia; the walk-through model of a typical ship shows just how tough conditions on board really were.

Museum of Liverpool MUSEUM
(☑0151-478 4545; www.liverpoolmuseums.org.uk/mol; Pier Head; ◷10am-5pm; ▢all city centre) **FREE** Liverpool's storied past is explored through an interactive exploration of the city's cultural and historical milestones: the railroad, poverty, wealth, *Brookside* (a popular '80s and '90s TV soap opera set in

THE THREE GRACES

The area to the north of Albert Dock is known as **Pier Head**, after a stone pier built in the 1760s. This is still the departure point for ferries across the River Mersey, and was for millions of migrants their final contact with European soil.

The Museum of Liverpool is an impressive architectural interloper, but pride of place in this part of the dock still goes to the trio of Edwardian buildings known as the 'Three Graces', dating from the days when Liverpool's star was still ascending: the Port of Liverpool Building, the Cunard Building and the Royal Liver Building, which is topped by Liverpool's symbol, the famous 5.5m copper Liver Bird.

the city), the Beatles and football (the film on the meaning of the game to the city is worth the 15 minutes). The desire to tell all of the city's rich story means there isn't a huge amount of depth, but the kids will love it.

The museum is constantly introducing new elements and temporary exhibitions, with a view towards ensuring that all visits are connected with a contemporary experience of the city. Recent exhibits include Liverpool and War (the collection of photographs taken during the Blitz in WWII is especially poignant) and Pride and Prejudice, an exploration of the city's LGBT identity.

Tours

★ **Anfield Stadium Tour**   TOUR
(www.liverpoolfc.com; Anfield Stadium; stadium tour adult/child £20/15; ⏰9am-5pm except match days; 🚌26 & 27 from Liverpool ONE Bus Station, 17 from Queens St Bus Station) For fans of Liverpool FC, Anfield is a special place, and this is reflected in the reverential tone of the hour-long self-guided audio tour that starts at the top of the new Main Stand and continues down to pitchside. Stops along the way include the home and away dressing rooms and the luxurious players' lounge.

You'll also see the press room and the home dugout, accessed via the new 'walk of champions' tunnel, where you can touch the iconic 'This is Anfield' sign. Staff positioned at various points throughout the tour are on hand to answer questions, generally with a touch of humour that makes the whole ex-

perience a memorable one for fans and especially kids. The ground is 2.5 miles northeast of the city centre.

Old Docks Tour   TOURS
(☎0151-478 4499; www.liverpoolmuseums.org.uk/maritime; Merseyside Maritime Museum, Albert Dock; ⏰10.30am, noon & 2.30pm Mon-Wed; 🚌all city centre) FREE Free and a lot of fun, the guided tours of the Old Dock – the world's first commercial enclosed wet dock – offer an insight into the history of Liverpool as a powerful port city (and the source of all its wealth). You'll also get to see the bed of the Pool, the creek that gave the city its name.

Magical Mystery Tour   CULTURAL
(☎0151-703 9100; www.cavernclub.org; per person £18.95; ⏰tours hourly 11am-4pm; 🚌all city centre) Two-hour tour that takes in all Beatles-related landmarks – their birthplaces, childhood homes, schools and places such as Penny Lane and Strawberry Field – before finishing up in the Cavern Club (which isn't the original). Departs from opposite the tourist office on Albert Dock.

★ Festivals & Events

★ **Grand National**   HORSE RACING
(☎0151-523 2600; http://aintree.thejockeyclub.co.uk; Aintree Racecourse, Ormskirk Rd; ⏰Apr; 🚌300, 311, 345, 350 & 351 from Liverpool ONE Bus Station, 🚉Aintree from Liverpool Central) The world's most famous steeplechase – and one of England's most cherished events – takes place on the first Saturday in April and is run across 4.5 miles and over the most difficult fences in world racing. Its protagonists are 40-odd veteran stalwarts of the jumps, ageing bruisers full of the oh-so-English qualities of grit and derring-do. Book tickets well in advance. Aintree is 6 miles north of the city centre.

Liverpool Sound City   MUSIC
(www.soundcity.uk.com; Baltic Triangle; ⏰May; 🚌all cross city buses) The first weekend in May sees one of the biggest alternative music festivals in town take over the Baltic Triangle and Cains Brewery.

Liverpool International Music Festival   MUSIC
(☎0151-239 9091; www.limfestival.com; Sefton Park; ⏰late Jul; 🚌75 from Lime St Station) A festival showcasing local bands and international acts during the last weekend of July. There's even a VIP experience that gives you access to private bars.

International Beatleweek
MUSIC

(www.internationalbeatleweek.com; ⊘ late Aug; 🚆 all main bus station services) Sing along to your favourite Beatles song with 70 tribute acts from 20 countries over four days in late August. Organised by the Cavern Club, there are some serious and talented acts on display; some are so good you'll wonder if they're even better than the real thing. They're not.

🛏 Sleeping

Liverpool YHA
HOSTEL £

(📞 0345-371 9527; www.yha.org.uk; 25 Tabley St; dm from £13; 🅿 🐕; 🚆 all city centre) It may have the look of an Eastern European apartment complex, but this award-winning hostel, adorned with plenty of Beatles memorabilia, is one of the most comfortable you'll find anywhere in the country – and it's recently gotten a spruce up. The dorms with en-suite bathrooms even have heated towel rails.

Tune Hotel
HOTEL £

(📞 0151-239 5070; www.tunehotels.com; 3-19 Queen Bldgs, Castle St; r from £35; ✳ @ 🐕; 🚆 all city centre) A slightly upscale version of a pod hotel, Tune offers a comfortable night's sleep (courtesy of a superb mattress and good-quality linen) in a range of en-suite rooms. The cheapest of them have no windows and are quite small, but at this price and in this location, it's an easy sacrifice to make. Bathrooms have power showers.

Titanic Liverpool
HOTEL ££

(📞 0151-559 1444; www.titanichotelliverpool.com; Stanley Dock, Regent Road; r/ste from £100/250; 🚆 135 & 235 from Liverpool ONE Bus Station) The preferred choice of visiting football teams is this fabulous warehouse conversion on Stanley Dock, now a huge hotel with massive rooms decorated in Scandi-minimalist style – lots of space, leather and earth-tones. Downstairs is the Rum Bar – a tribute to the primary stock of the 19th-century warehouse – and the basement is home to a nice spa.

Hard Days Night Hotel
HOTEL ££

(📞 0151-236 1964; www.harddaysnighthotel.com; Central Bldgs, North John St; r £90-140, ste from £350; @ 🐕; 🚆 all city centre) You don't have to be a fan to stay here, but it helps: unquestionably luxurious, the 110 ultramodern rooms are decorated with specially commissioned drawings of the Beatles. And if you opt for one of the suites, named after Lennon and McCartney, you'll get a white baby grand piano in the style of 'Imagine' and a bottle of fancy bubbly.

Hope Street Hotel
BOUTIQUE HOTEL ££

(📞 0151-709 3000; www.hopestreethotel.co.uk; 40 Hope St; r/ste from £100/165; @ 🐕; 🚆 all city centre) One of the classiest digs in town is this handsome boutique hotel on the city's most elegant street. King-sized beds draped in Egyptian cotton, oak floors with under-floor heating, LCD TVs and sleek modern bathrooms are but the most obvious touches of sophistication at this supremely cool address. Breakfast, taken in the marvellous London Carriage Works (p559), is £18.50.

62 Castle St
BOUTIQUE HOTEL ££

(📞 0151-702 7898; www.62castlest.com; 62 Castle St; r from £60; 🅿 @ 🐕) This elegant property successfully blends the traditional Victorian features of the neoclassical building with a sleek, contemporary style. The 20 fabulously different suites come with high-definition plasma-screen TVs, drench showers and luxe toiletries as standard.

Malmaison
HOTEL ££

(📞 0151-229 5000; www.malmaison.com; 7 William Jessop Way, Princes Dock; r/ste from £75/125; 🅿 @ 🐕; 🚆 135 or 235 from Liverpool ONE Bus Station) Malmaison's preferred colour scheme of plum and black is everywhere in this purpose-built hotel, which gives it an air of contemporary sophistication. Everything about the Liverpool Mal is plush, from the huge beds and the deep baths to the heavy velvet curtains and the excellent buffet breakfast. After a while, you'll ignore the constantly piped music of the Beatles.

★ 2 Blackburne Terrace
B&B £££

(www.2blackburneterrace.com; 2 Blackburne Tce; r £160-180; ✳ @ 🐕; 🚆 all city centre) This exquisite B&B, in a converted Grade II–listed Georgian townhouse from 1826, might just be the most elegant option in town. It only has four rooms, but each is impeccably appointed with a mix of period furniture and modern touches. Breakfast is fabulous and the lounge an absolute delight. Only Room 1 has a shower; all have free-standing baths.

🍴 Eating

Mowgli Street Food
INDIAN £

(www.mowglistreetfood.com; 69 Bold St; mains £3.95-6.95; ⊘ noon-9.30pm Sun-Wed, to 10.30pm Thu-Sat; 🚆 all city centre) Nisha Katona's ambition to serve authentic Indian street food has been so successful that this is just the first of a handful of restaurants spread throughout the northwest and south as far as Oxford. You'll find no stodgy curries or bland kormas

WORTH A TRIP

SPEKE HALL

A marvellous example of an Elizabethan half-timbered hall, **Speke Hall** (NT; www.national trust.org.uk; house & gardens adult/child £11.70/5.85, gardens only adult/child £8.10/4.05; ⊙12.30am-5pm Wed-Sun, also Tue Aug; ⊟500 from Liverpool ONE Bus Station) is filled with gorgeously timbered and plastered rooms. The house contains several 'priest's holes', where the hall's sympathetic owners hid Roman Catholic priests during the anti-Catholic 16th and 17th centuries.

This diagonally patterned Tudor house dates from 1490–1612 and was once surrounded by thousands of acres of land, but these days all that remains is the drive and an oasis of meticulously maintained gardens; the hall's Chapel Farm became the nucleus of nearby Liverpool Airport.

Speke Hall is about 7.5 miles from central Liverpool; the bus will drop you about half a miles from the entrance. The afternoon tours to Paul McCartney's and John Lennon's childhood homes (p555) leave from here.

here, just flavoursome dishes that would pass muster with a resident of Delhi. No bookings.

★**Wreckfish**　MODERN BRITISH **££**
(www.wreckfish.co; 60 Seel St; mains £17-25; ⊟all city centre) Restaurateur Gary Usher's crowd-funded restaurant is a marvellous example of Modern British cuisine at its best: nothing overly fussy, but everything done just right. From the open kitchen come fine dishes such as a roast wing of skate in a brown butter dressing and a near-perfect ribeye with truffle and parmesan chips.

HOST　ASIAN, FUSION **££**
(www.ho-st.co.uk; 31 Hope St; mains £10-14, Chop Chop £7; ⊙11am-11pm Mon-Sat, noon-10pm Sun; ⏰⏰; ⊟all city centre) A bright, airy room with the look of a chic, contemporary New York brasserie serves up superb pan-Asian dishes such as Indonesian braised lamb with fried rice, and red duck coconut curry with lychees. The starter nibbles are pretty delicious too. The Chop Chop single dish afternoon menu (noon to 5pm) is exceptional.

Monro　GASTROPUB **££**
(⏰0151-707 9933; www.themonro.com; 92 Duke St; 2-course lunch £12.50, dinner mains £12-18; ⊙11am-11pm; ⊟all city centre) ⏰ The Monro is one of the city's favourite spots for lunch, dinner and, especially, weekend brunch. The constantly changing menu of classic British dishes made with ingredients sourced as locally as possible has transformed this handsome old pub into a superb dining experience. It's tough to find pub grub this good elsewhere.

Etsu　JAPANESE **££**
(⏰0151-236 7530; www.etsu-restaurant.co.uk; 25 The Strand, off Brunswick St; mains £13-17, 15-piece

sashimi £15; ⊙noon-2.30pm & 5-9pm Tue, Thu & Fri, 5-9pm Wed & Sat, 4-9pm Sun; ⊟all city centre) The best Japanese food in town is in this contemporary spot on the ground floor of an office building. The speciality of the house is its fresh sushi and sashimi, but you'll find the usual selection of Japanese classics, from chicken *kara-age* (crispy fried chicken pieces marinated in soy, ginger and garlic) to *unagi don* (grilled eel over rice).

Salt House　SPANISH **££**
(www.salthousetapas.co.uk; Hanover Sq; tapas £5-8; ⊙noon-10.30pm; ⊟all city centre) Liverpool has grown fond of its Spanish tapas bars, and this gorgeous spot – half deli, half restaurant – is the best of them. The cooking is authentic, varied and delicious, from the choice of charcuterie to the wonderful fish dishes. The takeaway counter at the deli does fab sandwiches too.

The Art School　MODERN BRITISH **££**
(⏰0151-230 8600; www.theartschoolrestaurant. co.uk; 1 Sugnall St; 2-/3-course prix fixe £25/32, tasting menu £89; ⏰; ⊟all city centre) The old lantern room of a Victorian 'home for destitute children' is now one of the top spots in town for contemporary British cuisine, courtesy of chef Paul Askew (ex–London Carriage Works). Take your pick of expertly presented British classics from a series of menus, including two vegetarian and one vegan. The wine list is superb.

★**Restaurant Fraiche**　BRITISH **£££**
(www.restaurantfraiche.com; 11 Rose Mount, Oxton, Wirral; 6-course menu £88, with wine £133; ⊟Birkenhead Park) Five tables, one solitary chef and a gleaming Michelin star: Marc Wilkinson's tiny restaurant in Oxton on the Wirral is

worth the effort precisely because he goes to great lengths to provide one of the best culinary experiences in Britain. There's no menu and tables are like gold dust – try your luck up to three months in advance.

London Carriage Works MODERN BRITISH £££
(☑0151-705 2222; www.thelondoncarriageworks. co.uk; 40 Hope St; 2-/3-course meal £22/27.50, mains £17-29; ☺7-10am, noon-3pm & 5-10pm Mon-Fri, 8-11am & noon-10pm Sat, to 9pm Sun; ▣all city centre) This award-winning restaurant successfully blends ethnic influences from around the globe with staunch British favourites and serves up the result in a beautiful dining room – actually more of a bright glass box divided only by a series of sculpted glass shards. Reservations are recommended.

Drinking & Nightlife

Ropewalks is Liverpool's busiest bar district – with a lot of late-night spots that keep them drinking and dancing until the wee hours – but there's a fine selection of great bars spread throughout the city. If you're looking to hang with the city's creative crowd, you'll most likely find them in the Baltic Triangle.

★Botanical Garden BAR
(www.baltictriangle.co.uk/botanical-garden; 49 New Bird St; ☺noon-11pm Mar-Sep; ▣all city centre) A seasonal pop-up bar that specialises in gin cocktails, this is one of the city's coolest summer bars. There's a fine selection of beers if you prefer, and a kitchen that serves excellent Mexican food; in rainy weather you can retreat to the indoor greenhouse, which has a bar made from a converted VW campervan. Weekends feature top-class DJs.

★Grapes PUB
(www.thegrapesliverpool.co.uk; 60 Roscoe St; ☺3.30pm-1am Sun-Wed, to 2am Thu-Sat; ▣all city centre) One of the friendliest boozers in town is this superb old pub that serves a fine range of local ales (Bier Head, from the Liverpool Organic Brewery, is our favourite). The Beatles would stop in here during their Cavern days, but that's well down the list of reasons to stop in to this wonderful, higgledy-piggledy classic.

Roscoe Head PUB
(☑0151-709 4365; www.roscoehead.co.uk; 24 Roscoe St; ☺11.30am-midnight Tue-Sat, noon-midnight Sun, 11.30am-11pm Mon; ▣all city centre) An institution amongst Liverpool boozers is this venerable old pub, which serves a good

selection of ales to its ever-loyal clientele. It gets pretty crowded at weekends, but that just makes for an even better atmosphere.

24 Kitchen Street CLUB
(☑0780 1982583; www.facebook.com/24kitchen street; 24 Kitchen St; tickets £8-12; ☺9pm-4am Fri & Sat; ▣all city centre) This multipurpose venue splits its focus between the arts and electronic music. The converted Victorian building is one of the best places in town to dance.

Philharmonic PUB
(36 Hope St; ☺10am-midnight; ▣all city centre) This extraordinary bar, designed by the shipwrights who built the *Lusitania,* is one of the most beautiful bars in all of England. The interior is resplendent with etched and stained glass, wrought iron, mosaics and ceramic tiling – and if you think that's good, just wait until you see inside the marble men's toilets, the only heritage-listed lav in the country.

Arts Club CLUB
(☑0151-707 6171; www.academymusicgroup.com/ artsclubliverpool; 90 Seel St; £5-13; ☺7pm-3am Mon-Sat; ▣all city centre) This converted theatre is home to one of Liverpool's most beloved clubs, despite going through several name and management changes. It still hosts some fabulous nights, with a mix of live music and DJs keeping everyone entertained with some of the best music in town.

Merchant BAR
(40 Slater St; ☺noon-midnight Mon-Thu & Sun, to 2am Fri, to 3am Sat; ▣all city centre) First opening in 2016, this bar is in a converted merchant's house and has something of a Scandi feel to it – stripped-back walls, wooden bar tables – which made it the 'in' spot at the time of writing. The bar serves 50

> **THE BALTIC TRIANGLE**
>
> Forget Ropewalks – most of Liverpool's best nightlife is in the Baltic Triangle, a once-run-down area of warehouses roughly between the city centre and the docks just north of Toxteth that is now the city's self-styled creative hub. Best spots to check out include 24 Kitchen Street, pop-up gin bar Botanical Garden, the-recycling-yard-turned-multipurpose-venue Constellations (p560) and District (p560), the first venue to open in the area.

MANCHESTER, LIVERPOOL & NORTHWEST ENGLAND LIVERPOOL

different craft beers, gin by the goblet and – wait for it – Prosecco on tap. Good DJs provide the soundtrack.

☆ Entertainment

★ Liverpool Football Club
FOOTBALL

(📞0151-263 9199, ticket office 0151-220 2345; www.liverpoolfc.com; Anfield Rd; 🚌26 from Liverpool ONE Bus Station, 17 from Queen Square Bus Station or 917 from St Johns La) A dominant footballing force for most of the 1970s and 1980s, Liverpool FC remains one of the world's most famous and best-supported clubs, despite not winning a league championship since 1991. Its current crop of stars, led by the magnetic German Jürgen Klopp, play their home games at the wonderful Anfield stadium, north of the city centre.

The experience of a live match – and especially the sound of the fans singing the club's anthem, 'You'll Never Walk Alone', is one of England's sporting highlights. If you can't get a ticket for a game, you can still visit the stadium as part of the Anfield Stadium Tour (p556), which brings fans to the home dressing room and down the tunnel into the pitchside dugout. On match days, the **Soccerbus** (www.merseyrail.org; Sandhills Station; adult single/return £2/3.50, child £1/1.50; ⏱From 2hr before kick-off) runs from Sandhills Station on the Merseyrail Northern Line.

★ Constellations
LIVE PERFORMANCE

(📞0151-345 6302; www.constellations-liv.com; 35-39 Greenland St; ⏱9am-midnight Mon-Thu, to 2am Fri & Sat, 10am-midnight Sun; 🚌all city centre) Whether you're looking to join a drumming circle, take part in a martial-arts workshop or lose yourself at a rave, this terrific venue in a former recycling yard will have something worth checking out. In good weather DJs play in the garden – one of the best spots in town. It does Sunday meals in summer.

Philharmonic Hall
CLASSICAL MUSIC

(📞0151-709 3789; www.liverpoolphil.com; Hope St; 🚌75, 80, 86 from city centre) One of Liverpool's most beautiful buildings, the art deco Phil is home to the city's main orchestras and is the place to go for classical concerts and opera – as well as a broad range of other genres, from synth pop to avant-garde.

District
LIVE MUSIC

(📞07812 141936; www.facebook.com/District-473 098799400626; 61 Jordan St; ⏱7pm-4am Fri-Sat) The first venue to open in the Baltic Triangle, District is an old-school club in a warehouse, which hosts live music and cinema screenings as well as fabulous dance-floor nights. The sound system is reputed to be the best in Liverpool.

Cavern Club
LIVE MUSIC

(📞0151-236 1965; www.cavernclub.org; 8-10 Mathew St; admission before/after 2pm free/£5; ⏱10am-midnight Mon-Wed & Sun, to 1.30am Thu, to 2am Fri & Sat; 🚌all city centre) It's a faithful reconstruction of the club where the Beatles played their early gigs, and not even on the same spot (the original club was a few doors away), but the 'world's most famous club' is still a great spot to see local bands, including (invariably) Beatles cover bands.

ℹ Information

Tourist Office (www.visitliverpool.com; Liverpool Central Library, William Brown St; ⏱9.30am-5pm; 🚌all city centre) Leaflets, maps and information are provided in the small tourist office.

ℹ Getting There & Away

AIR

Liverpool John Lennon Airport (📞0870 750 8484; www.liverpoolairport.com; Speke Hall Ave; 🚌86 or 500 from city centre) serves a variety of international destinations as well as destinations in the UK (Belfast, London and the Isle of Man).

The airport is 8 miles south of the centre. **Arriva Express Bus 500** (www.arriva.co.uk; £5; ⏱4.30am-7pm) runs every 30 minutes to Liverpool ONE bus station. The journey is about 30 minutes. A taxi to the city centre should cost no more than £20.

BUS

The **National Express Coach Station** (www. nationalexpress.com; Norton St) is 300m north of Lime St train station. There are services to/from most major towns including the following:

Birmingham £14, 2½ hours, five daily

London £30.10, five to six hours, six daily

Manchester £6.10, one hour, hourly

Newcastle £16, 5½ hours, three daily

TRAIN

Liverpool's main station is Lime St. It has hourly services to almost everywhere, including the following:

Chester £7.30, 45 minutes

London Euston £44, 3¼ hours

Manchester £5.90, 45 minutes

ℹ Getting Around

If you plan on using a lot of public transport you should invest in a Walrus card, a contactless fare card available throughout the city for an initial cost of £1. You can then load up the following fare-saver passes on it:

Saveaway (adult/child £5.30/2.70) Single-day pass valid for off-peak travel on buses, trains and Mersey ferries.

Solo Ticket (1/3/5 days £4.80/13.50/21) For unlimited bus travel throughout Merseyside.

BOAT

The famous **Mersey ferry** (www.merseyferries. co.uk; one-way/return £2.70/3.50) crossing for Woodside and Seacombe departs from Pier Head Ferry Terminal, next to the Royal Liver Building (to the north of Albert Dock).

BUS

Liverpool ONE Bus Station (www.mersey travel.gov.uk; Canning Pl) is in the city centre. Local public transport is coordinated by **Merseytravel** (www.merseytravel.gov.uk).

CAR

You won't really have much use for a car in Liverpool, but if you have a car the good news is that parking in most sheltered and open car parks is relatively cheap – usually between £3 and £6 *per day*. The only exception is the huge car park at Liverpool ONE, which costs £2.50 an hour and £17 for a day. Car break-ins are a significant problem, so leave absolutely nothing of value in the car.

TRAIN

Merseyrail (www.merseyrail.org) is an extensive suburban rail service linking Liverpool with the Greater Merseyside area. There are four stops in the city centre: Lime St, Central (handy for Ropewalks), James St (close to Albert Dock) and Moorfields (for the Liverpool War Museum).

LANCASHIRE

As you travel north, past the concrete blanket that covers much of the southern half of the county, Lancashire's undulating landscape begins to reveal itself in all its bucolic glory. East of Blackpool – the faded queen of beachside holidays – the Ribble Valley is a gentle and beautiful appetiser for the Lake District that lies beyond the county's northern border. Lancaster is the county's handsome Georgian capital.

Blackpool

☑ 01253 / POP 150,331

Blackpool's enduring appeal – in the face of low-cost airlines transporting its natural constituents to sunnier coasts – is down to its defiant embrace of a more traditional kind of holiday, coupled with the high-tech adrenaline hit of its famed Pleasure Beach amusement park.

The town is also famous for its tower and its three piers. A successful ploy to extend the brief summer holiday season is the Illuminations, when, from early September to early November, 5 miles of the Promenade are illuminated with thousands of electric and neon lights.

◉ Sights

★ Blackpool Tower   AMUSEMENT PARK

(☑ 0844 856 1000; www.theblackpooltower.com; Tower Pass door price adult/child £56.45/44; ☺ from 10am, closing hours vary) Built in 1894, this 154m-high tower is Blackpool's most recognisable landmark. Watch a 4D film on the town's history in the **Blackpool Tower Eye** before taking the elevator up to the observation deck, which has splendid views and only a (thick) glass floor between you and the ant-sized people below. Visitors are *strongly* urged to buy their tickets online as buying them at the door can be up to 50% more expensive.

Down at ground level, the **dungeon** exhibit sits alongside the old Moorish circus and the magnificent rococo **ballroom**, with its extraordinary sculptured and gilded plasterwork, murals, chandeliers and couples gliding across the beautifully polished wooden floor to the melodramatic tones of a huge Wurlitzer organ. There's also **Jungle Jim's** adventure playground for kids and **Dino Golf** on level 7 – a 9-hole mini-golf course.

Blackpool Pleasure Beach   AMUSEMENT PARK

(☑ box office 0871 222 9090, enquiries 0871 222 1234; www.blackpoolpleasurebeach.com; Ocean Beach; Pleasure Beach Pass £6, 1-day Unlimited Ride wristband adult/child £39/33; ☺ hours vary, usually 10am-8pm in summer) The lifeblood of Blackpool's commercial life is the Pleasure Beach, a 16-hectare collection of more than 145 rides that attracts some seven million visitors annually. As amusement parks go, it's Britain's most popular by far.

Rides are divided into categories, and once you've gained entry to the park with your Pleasure Beach Pass you can buy tickets for individual categories or for a mixture of them all. Alternatively, an Unlimited Ride wristband includes the £6 entrance fee; there are great discounts if you book your tickets online in advance. There's also the option of a Speedy Pass (£15), which saves you the hassle of queuing for rides by allocating you a specific ride time – rent it and add as many people to it as you want. You can go one better with the VIP Speedy Pass (£25), which cuts queuing time by 50%; or with the VIP Plus Speedy Pass (£50), which reduces wait time to almost nothing. There are no set times for closing; it depends how busy it is.

North Pier   LANDMARK
(Promenade) FREE Built in 1862 and opening a year later, the most famous of Blackpool's three Victorian piers once charged a penny for admission; its plethora of unexciting rides are now free.

Sleeping

Number One   BOUTIQUE HOTEL ££
(01253-343901; www.numberoneblackpool.com; 1 St Lukes Rd; s/d from £80/110;) Far fancier than anything else around, this stunning boutique guesthouse is all luxury and contemporary style. Everything exudes a discreet elegance, from the dark-wood furniture and high-end mod cons to the top-notch breakfast. It's on a quiet road just set back from the South Promenade near the Pleasure Beach amusement park.

Big Blue Hotel   HOTEL ££
(01253-400045; www.bigbluehotel.com; Blackpool Pleasure Beach; r from £70;) A handsome family hotel with smartly kitted-out rooms. Kids are looked after with DVD players and computer games, while its location at the southern entrance to Blackpool Pleasure Beach should ensure that everyone has something to do.

Information

Tourist Office (01253-478222; www.visit blackpool.com; Festival House, Promenade; 9am-6pm Mon-Tue, to 5pm Wed-Sat, 10am-4pm Sun) The tourist office is just south of the North Pier on the Promenade.

Getting There & Away

BUS
The central coach station is on Talbot Rd, near the town centre. Services include the following:
London £39.70, seven hours, four daily
Manchester £8, 1¾ hours, four daily

TRAIN
The main train station is Blackpool North, about five blocks east of the North Pier on Talbot Rd. Most arrivals change in Preston, but there's a direct service from the following:
Liverpool £16.20, 1½ hours, seven daily

Manchester £17.70, 1¼ hours, half-hourly
Preston £7.50, 30 minutes, half-hourly

Getting Around

With more than 14,000 car-parking spaces in Blackpool, you'll have no problem parking. A host of travel-card options for trams and buses ranging from one day to a week are available at the tourist office and most newsagents. The **tramway** (one stop £1.70, up to 16 stops £2.70; from 10.30am Apr-Oct) shuttles funsters for 11 miles, including along the pier and as far as the Fylde Coast (also serving the central-corridor car parks), every eight minutes or so throughout the day.

Lancaster
 01524 / POP 143,500

Lancashire's handsome Georgian county town is a quiet enough burg these days, but its imposing castle and beautiful, honey-coloured architecture are evidence of its former power and wealth accrued in its 18th-century heyday, when it was an important trading port and a key player in the slave trade.

Sights

★Lancaster Castle   CASTLE
(01524-64998; www.lancastercastle.com; Castle Park; adult/child £8/6.50; 9.30am-5pm, guided tours hourly 10am-3pm Mon-Fri, every 30min Sat & Sun) Lancaster's most imposing building is the castle, built in 1150 but added to over the centuries: the **Well Tower** dates from 1325 and is also known as the Witches' Tower because its basement dungeon was used to imprison the accused in the infamous Pendle Witches Trial of 1612. Also dating from the early 14th century is the impressive twin-towered **gatehouse**. Visits are by guided tour only as the castle is used as a Crown Court.

Also imprisoned here was George Fox (1624–91), founder of the Quaker movement. The castle was heavily restored in the 18th and 19th centuries to suit a new function as a prison, and it continued to house Category C prisoners until 2011 – the A wing of the prison is part of the guided tour.

Williamson Park &
Tropical Butterfly House   GARDENS
(Tropical Butterfly House adult/child £4/3; 9am-5pm Apr-Sep, to 4pm Oct-Mar; 18 from bus station) Lancaster's highest point is the 22-hectare spread of this gorgeous park, the highlights of which are (besides the views)

GREAT LANCASHIRE GASTROPUBS

Freemasons at Wiswell (☎01254-822218; www.freemasonsatwiswell.com; 8 Vicarage Fold, Wiswell; mains £24-32, 2-/3-course menu £22.50/27.50; � noon-2.30pm & 6-9pm Wed-Sat, noon-6pm Sun) Steven Smith's multi-award-winning restaurant in the lovely village of Wiswell serves a proper feast of the best of New British cuisine. The room is classic English pub, with plain wooden tables and a roaring fire, in contrast to the sophisticated menu. We recommend the suckling pig, slow cooked and served with black pudding, baked sweet potato and fermented-rhubarb sauce.

The White Swan (www.whiteswanatfence.co.uk; 300 Wheatley Ln Rd, Fence, Burnley; mains £19-28; � noon-2pm & 5.30-8.30pm Tue-Thu, to 9.30pm Fri-Sat, noon-4pm Sun) It mightn't look like much from the outside, but this pub in the working village of Fence serves simply outstanding Modern British cuisine. It's all courtesy of chef Tom Parker, who cut his chops in the kitchen of Michelin-starred Nigel Haworth at Northcote (p564). The menu is deliberately small – only three mains – but oh so good.

the **Tropical Butterfly House**, full of exotic and stunning species, and the **Ashton Memorial**, a 67m-high baroque folly built by Lord Ashton (the son of the park's founder, James Williamson) for his wife. The memorial stands on what was once Lancaster Moor, the spot where until 1800 those sentenced to death at the castle were brought to meet the hangman.

Take the bus from the station, or else it's a steep, short walk up Moor Lane.

Lancaster Priory CHURCH
(☎01524-65338; www.lancasterpriory.org; Priory Cl; �a9.30am-5pm) Immediately next to Lancaster Castle is the equally fine priory church, founded in 1094 but extensively remodelled in the Middle Ages.

🛏 Sleeping

Sun Hotel & Bar HOTEL **££**
(☎01524-66006; www.thesunhotelandbar.co.uk; 63-65 Church St; r from £80; P☏) A fine hotel in a 300-year-old building with a rustic, old-world look that stops at the bedroom doors – beyond them are 16 stylish and contemporary rooms. The pub downstairs is one of the best in town and a top spot for a bit of grub; mains cost between £10 and £12.

The Borough BOUTIQUE HOTEL **££**
(☎01524-64170; www.theboroughlancaster.co.uk; 3 Dalton Sq; r from £120; P@☏) The Borough has nine beautifully appointed rooms – each with an Italian-marble wet-room bathroom for added luxury – spread over two floors of this elegant Georgian building. The downstairs bar has a microbrewery attached, so you don't have to go far to get your fill of locally made cask ales.

🍴 Eating & Drinking

★ **Bay Horse Inn** GASTROPUB **££**
(☎01524-791204; www.bayhorseinn.com; Bay Horse La, Ellel; mains £18-29; � noon-2pm & 6.30-9pm Wed-Sat, noon-3pm & 6-8pm Sun; ☒40, 41 & 42 from Lancaster Bus Station) One of Lancashire's best spots for exquisite local dishes is this handsome pub 6 miles south of Lancaster. Chef Craig Wilkinson displays his locavore links with a sign outside showing distances to the farms that supply his produce, which he then transforms into fabulous dishes like slow-cooked, maize-fed duck legs with grilled figs or a perfectly grilled hake fillet.

★ **The Hall** CAFE
(☎01524-65470; https://thecoffeehopper.com; 10 China St; �a8am-6pm Mon-Sat, 10am-5pm Sun) Nitro, Chemex, batch brew, siphon…whatever way you want it, this superb cafe in the old parish hall can satisfy even the most demanding coffee connoisseur with the perfect brew. It's part of Atkinsons Coffee Roasters, which has been roasting beans since 1840. It also does excellent sandwiches and cakes.

🛍 Shopping

★ **Charter Market** MARKET
(www.lancaster.gov.uk; Market Sq; �a9am-4.30pm Wed & Sat Apr-Oct, to 4pm Nov-Mar) Lancaster's historic market is one of the best in the northwest, a gathering place for local producers to sell their goodies. You'll find potted shrimp from Morecambe Bay, locally made hotpots and pies, as well as a range of more exotic dishes from around the world. It extends from Market Sq onto Market St and Cheapside.

ⓘ Information

Tourist Office (☎ 01524-582394; www.visit lancaster.org.uk; The Storey, Meeting House Lane; ⊙10am-4pm Mon-Sat) Books, maps, brochures and tickets for a variety of events and tours.

ⓘ Getting There & Away

Lancaster Bus Station is the main hub for transport throughout Lancashire, with regular buses to all the main towns and villages.

Lancaster is on the main west-coast railway line and on the Cumbrian coast line. Destinations include the following:

Carlisle £22.20, one hour, hourly
Manchester £18.20, one hour, hourly

Ribble Valley

Known locally as 'Little Switzerland', Lancashire's most attractive landscapes lie east of brash Blackpool and north of the sprawling urban areas of Preston and Blackburn.

Clitheroe, the Ribble Valley's largest market town is best known for its impressive Norman keep, built in the 12th century and now, sadly, standing empty; from it there are great views of the river valley below.

The northern half of the valley is dominated by the sparsely populated moorland of the Forest of Bowland, an Area of Outstanding Natural Beauty since 1964 and a fantastic place for walks. The southern half features rolling hills, attractive market towns and ruins, with the River Ribble flowing between them.

⊙ Sights & Activities

Norman Keep &
Castle Museum   HISTORIC BUILDING
(www.lancashire.gov.uk; Castle Hill; museum adult/ child £4.40/3.30; ⊙keep dawn-dusk, museum 11am-4pm Mar-Oct, noon-4pm Mon-Tue & Fri-Sun Nov-Feb) Dominating the skyline for the last 800 years is this Norman keep, England's smallest and the only remaining castle in the country to have kept a royal garrison during the Civil War. It was built in 1186 and captured by Royalist troops in 1644, but managed to avoid destruction afterwards. The extensive grounds are home to a museum that explores 350 million years of local history.

★ Cycle Adventure   CYCLING
(☎ 07518 373007; www.cycle-adventure.co.uk) A bike-hire service that will deliver and collect a bike almost anywhere in the northwest of England. Day rates range from £25 for a mountain bike to £34 for a road bike. A child's mountain bike costs from £19 a day. Helmets and other gear are also available, and it has lots of information, trail maps and other guides.

Ribble Way   WALKING
One of the most popular long-distance paths in northern England is the Ribble Way, a 70-mile footpath that follows the River Ribble from its source at Ribblehead (in the Yorkshire Dales), passing through Clitheroe to the estuary at Preston.

Lancashire Cycle Way   CYCLING
(www.visitlancashire.com) The Ribble Valley is well covered by the northern loop of the Lancashire Cycle Way; for more information about routes, safety and so on, check out Cycle Adventure.

🛏 Sleeping & Eating

★ Inn at Whitewell   INN £££
(☎ 01200-448222; www.innatwhitewell.com; Forest of Bowland; s/d from £99/137) Once the home of Bowland's forest keeper, this superb guesthouse with antique furniture, peat fires and Victorian claw-foot baths is one of the finest accommodations in northern England. Everything is top-notch, including the views: it's like being in the French countryside. Its **restaurant** (mains £15-27) is excellent too.

★ Parkers Arms   GASTROPUB ££
(☎ 01200-446236; www.parkersarms.co.uk; Newton-in-Bowland; mains £15-20; ⊙12.30-2.30pm & 6.30-8.30pm Wed-Fri, 12.30-9pm Sat, 12.30-6pm Sun) This unspoilt village pub is where you'll find the simply exceptional cooking of *terroir* chef Stosie Madi. She's best known for her superb pies, but her menus – which change up to twice daily depending on what's available – explore the very best of Lancashire cuisine, from Newton venison with local bramble and unpasteurised cheese to a superb Lancashire hotpot.

★ Northcote Hotel   MODERN BRITISH £££
(☎ 01254-240555; www.northcote.com; Northcote Rd, Langho; mains £23-48; ⊙noon-2pm & 7-9.30pm) One of the finest restaurants in northern England, Northcote's Michelin-starred menu is the unpretentious, delicious creation of chef Lisa Goodwin-Allen and sommelier Craig Bancroft. Duck, lamb, beef and chicken are given Modern British treat-

ment and the result is fantastic. Upstairs are 26 beautifully styled bedrooms (£240 to £380), making this one of the northwest's top gourmet getaways. Bookings strongly recommended.

ISLE OF MAN

Forget what you may have heard on the mainland: there's nothing odd about the Isle of Man (Ellan Vannin in the local lingo, Manx). The island's reputation for oddity is entirely down to its persistent insistence that it do its own thing, rejecting England's warm embrace in favour of a semiautonomous status (it is home to the world's oldest continuous parliament, the Tynwald).

What you'll find here is beautiful scenery in the lush valleys, barren hills and rugged coastlines. In 2016 Unesco designated the Isle of Man a biosphere reserve (one of five in the UK), marking it out as one of the most beautiful spots in Britain to enjoy nature. That bucolic charm is shattered during the world-famous Tourist Trophy (TT) motorbike racing season, which attracts 50,000 punters every May and June. Needless to say, if you want a slice of silence, avoid the high-rev bike fest.

❶ Getting There & Away

AIR
Ronaldsway Airport (www.iom-airport.com) is 10 miles south of Douglas near Castletown. The following airlines have services to the island:

Aer Lingus Regional (www.aerlingus.com; from £25)

British Airways (www.britishairways.com; from £82)

Easyjet (www.easyjet.com; from £20)

Flybe (www.flybe.com; from £25)

Loganair (www.loganair.co.uk; from £60)

BOAT
Isle of Man Steam Packet (www.steam-packet.com; foot passenger single/return from £25/42, car & 2 passengers return from £170) offers a car ferry and high-speed catamaran service from Liverpool and Heysham to Douglas. From mid-April to mid-September there's also a service to Dublin and Belfast.

❶ Getting Around

Buses link the airport with Douglas every 30 minutes between 7am and 11pm. Taxis have fixed fares to destinations throughout the island; a cab to Douglas costs £20, to Peel £25.

---

❶ MANX HERITAGE HOLIDAY PASS

The island's 11 major sights are managed by Manx Heritage (MH; www.manxnationalheritage.im), the island's version of the British National Trust. They include castles, historic homes, museums and the world's largest working waterwheel. Unless otherwise indicated, Manx Heritage sites are open 10am to 5pm daily, from Easter to October. The Manx Heritage Holiday Pass (www.manxheritageshop.com; adult/child £25/12) grants entry to all of the island's heritage attractions; it's available at tourist offices or online.

The island has a comprehensive bus service (www.gov.im); the tourist office in Douglas has timetables and sells tickets. It also sells the Go Explore ticket (one day adult/child £16/8, three day £32/16), which gives you unlimited public-transport use, including the tram to Snaefell and Douglas' horse-trams.

Bikes can be hired from **Simpsons Ltd** (☑ 01624-842472; www.simpsons.im; 15-17 Michael St, Peel; per day/week £20/100; ⊙ 9am-5pm Mon-Sat) in Peel.

Petrolheads will love the scenic, sweeping bends that make for some exciting driving – and the fact that outside of Douglas town there's no speed limit. Naturally, the most popular drive is along the Tourist Trophy route. Car-hire operators have desks at the airport, and charge from £35 per day.

The 19th-century electric and steam **rail services** (☑ 01624-663366; www.iombusandrail.info; ⊙ Mar-Oct) are a thoroughly satisfying way of getting from A to B:

Douglas–Castletown–Port Erin Steam Train Return £12.40

Douglas–Laxey–Ramsey Electric Tramway Return £12.40

Laxey–Summit Snaefell Mountain Railway Return £12

Douglas

☑ 01624 / POP 26,218

The island's largest town and most important commercial centre is a little faded around the edges and a far cry from its Victorian heyday when it was, like Blackpool across the water, a favourite with British holidaymakers. The bulk of the island's hotels and restaurants are still here – as well as most of the finance houses that are frequented so regularly by tax-allergic Brits.

👁 Sights

Manx Museum & National Art Gallery
MUSEUM

(MH; www.manxnationalheritage.im; Kingswood Grove; ⊙10am-5pm Mon-Sat) FREE This modern museum begins with an introductory film to the island's 10,000-year history and then races through it, making various stops including Viking gold and silver, the history of the Tynwald, the island's internment camps during WWII and the famous TT races. Also part of the museum is the **National Art Gallery**, which has works by the island's best-known artists including Archibald Knox and John Miller Nicholson. Overall a fine introduction to the island.

🛏 Sleeping

⭐ Saba's Glen Yurt
YURT ££

(www.sabasglenyurt.com; Close Ny Howin, Main Rd, Union Mills; 2-person yurt £110) 🍃 In the conservation area of Union Mills you can bed down in a solar-powered eco-yurt that comes equipped with a king-sized bed and a wood burner. Outside are hot tubs filled with steaming water that you can sink into up to your shoulders.

There's a two-night minimum weekend stay between April and September. It's 2.5 miles northeast of town on the road to Peel.

Inglewood
BOUTIQUE HOTEL ££

(☑01624-674734; www.inglewoodhotel-isleofman. com; 26 Palace Tce, Queens Promenade; s/d incl breakfast from £42.50/85; P@🛜) Sea-view suites in this beautifully refurbished, friendly hotel have big wooden beds and leather sofas. The homemade breakfasts are superb,

---

PEEL

Peel is the west coast's most appealing town, with a fine sandy beach. Its big attraction is the ruin of the 11th-century **Peel Castle** (MH; www.manxnational heritage.im; adult/child £6/3; ⊙10am-5pm Jun-Aug, to 4pm Mar-May & Sep-Oct), stunningly positioned atop St Patrick's Island and joined to Peel by a causeway. There's an audio guide available to help you make sense of the ruins, and you're also advised to keep your eyes open for the castle's ghost – a black dog called Moddey Dhoo.

---

and the residents' bar specialises in whisky from all over the world.

Claremont Hotel
HOTEL £££

(☑01624-617068; www.claremonthoteldouglas. com; 18-22 Loch Promenade; r from £150; P❄@🛜) The island's fanciest hotel is this classic on the promenade, with huge rooms kitted out with handsome wooden floors, seaside colours and comfortable beds with crisp linen.

🍴 Eating

⭐ Little Fish Cafe
SEAFOOD ££

(www.littlefishcafe.com; 31 North Quay; mains £11.50-14.50; ⊙11am-9pm) Superb seafood presented in a variety of ways, from hake with mustard and lemon butter to a Kerala-style fish curry. For brunch, the Queenie Po'Boy – battered Manx queenies (queen scallops), paprika mayo and avocado on sourdough brioche – is divine. It also does meat dishes, but the real focus is on the sea.

Tanroagan
SEAFOOD ££

(☑01624-472411; www.tanroagan.co.uk; 9 Ridgeway St; mains £15-21; ⊙noon-2pm & 6-9.30pm Tue-Sat) The place for all things from the sea, this elegant restaurant serves fresh fish straight off the boats, giving them the merest of continental twists or just a spell on the hot grill. Reservations are recommended.

14North
MODERN BRITISH ££

(☑01624-664414; www.14north.im; 14 North Quay; mains £16-25; ⊙noon-2.30pm & 6-9.30pm Mon-Sat) An old timber merchant's house is home to this smart restaurant specialising in local dishes including pickled herring, lamb rump and, of course, queenies – all sourced locally, of course.

ℹ Information

Tourist Office (☑01624-686766; www.visit isleofman.com; Sea Terminal Bldg, Douglas; ⊙9.15am-7pm, closed Sun Oct-Apr)

Northern Isle of Man

North of the capital, the dominant feature is Snaefell (621m), the island's tallest mountain. You can follow the Tourist Trophy circuit up and over the mountain towards Ramsey, or take the alternate route along the coast, going through Laxey, where you can also take the electric tram to near the top of Snaefell, from which it's an easy walk to the summit.

Sights

★ Great Laxey Wheel
HISTORIC SITE

(MH; https://manxnationalheritage.im/our-sites/laxey-wheel/; Mines Rd, Laxey; adult/child £8/4; ⊙9.30am-5pm Apr-Oct) It's no exaggeration to describe the Lady Isabella Laxey Wheel, built in 1854 to pump water from a mine, as a 'great' wheel: it measures 22m across and can draw 1140L of water per minute from a depth of 550m. The largest wheel of its kind in the world, it's named after the wife of the then lieutenant-governor.

Grove Museum of Victorian Life
MUSEUM

(MH; www.manxnationalheritage.im; Andreas Rd, Ramsey; adult/child £6/3; ⊙10am-5pm Jun-Aug, to 4pm Sep, 11am-3pm Sat & Sun Mar) This imposing house was built in the mid-19th century by Liverpool shipping merchant Duncan Gibb as a summer retreat for himself and his family. It has been maintained pretty much as it was in its Victorian heyday, and you can wander through its period rooms – and even learn what it was like to be a scullery maid! The house was occupied by the Gibb family until the 1970s. It's on the edge of Ramsey.

ℹ Getting There & Away

Bus Vannin services travel the 15 miles between Ramsey and Douglas either via Laxey and the coast (bus 3, 3A) or more directly inland past Snaefell (bus X3). Alternatively, there's the electric tram, which trundles up the coast to Ramsey. Another tram serves Snaefell from Laxey.

Southern Isle of Man

The quiet harbour town of Castletown, at the southern end of the island, was the Isle of Man's original capital. It is home to a fabulous castle and the old parliament.

Port Erin is a smallish Victorian seaside resort that plays host to the small **Railway Museum** (Station Rd; adult/child £2/1; ⊙9.30am-4.30pm Apr-Oct, guided tours also 7.30pm & 9.30pm Thu, 11am-1pm Sun mid-Jul–mid-Sep). Port St Mary lies across the headland and is linked to by steam train. The Calf of Man bird sanctuary is accessed from Port St Mary.

Sights

★ Castle Rushen
CASTLE

(MH; www.manxnationalheritage.im; Castletown Sq, Castletown; adult/child £8/4; ⊙10am-5pm May-Aug) Castletown is dominated by the impressive 13th-century Castle Rushen, one of the most complete medieval structures in Europe. You can visit the gatehouse, medieval kitchens, dungeons and the Great Hall. The flag tower affords fine views of the town and coast.

Cregneash Village Folk Museum
MUSEUM

(MH; www.manxnationalheritage.im; adult/child £6/3; ⊙10am-5pm Jun-Aug, to 4pm Apr-May & Sep-Oct) Until the early part of the 20th century, most farmers on the island engaged in a practice known as crofting – a social system defined by small-scale communal food production. This folk museum on a raised plateau on the island's southern tip includes a traditional Manx cottage where you can see how crofters lived, while out in the fields you can see four-horned sheep and Manx cats, which you're encouraged to pat.

Old House of Keys
MUSEUM

(MH; www.manxnationalheritage.im; Parliament Sq; debate adult/child £6/3, other times free; ⊙10am-4pm Apr-Oct) The former home of the Manx Parliament (lower house of the Tynwald) has been restored to its 1866 appearance – a key date in island history as it was then that the parliament voted to have its members elected by popular mandate. At 11am and 2.45pm visitors can participate in a debate on the hot topics of the day – gaining an insight into how this parliamentary democracy went about its business. You can also learn about the island's struggle for self-determination.

Calf of Man
BIRD SANCTUARY

(www.manxnationalheritage.im; ⊙Apr-Sep) This small island just off Cregneash is on one of western Britain's major bird migration routes, and 33 species breed annually here, including Manx shearwaters, kittiwakes, razorbills and shags. Other species normally observed on the island include peregrines, hen harriers, choughs and ravens. It's been an official bird sanctuary since 1939. **Gemini Charter** (📞01624-832761; www.geminicharter.co.uk; trips 1-4hr per person £15-30) runs birdwatching trips to the island from Port St Mary.

ℹ Getting There & Away

There is a regular Bus Vannin service between Castletown and Douglas (and the airport en route), and between Castletown, Port Erin and Port St Mary (£5.70 return). There's also the Douglas to Port Erin Steam Train (£12.40 return) which stops in Castletown. A taxi from the airport to Castletown costs around £8.

The Lake District & Cumbria

POP 499,800

Best Places to Eat

➡ L'Enclume (p599)

➡ Old Stamp House (p579)

➡ Jumble Room (p582)

➡ Punch Bowl Inn (p598)

➡ Drunken Duck (p583)

➡ Fellpack (p590)

Best Places to Stay

➡ Forest Side (p581)

➡ Brimstone Hotel (p587)

➡ Daffodil Hotel (p581)

➡ Wasdale Head Inn (p588)

➡ Cottage in the Wood (p590)

➡ Eltermere Inn (p587)

Why Go?

'No part of the country is more distinguished by its sublimity', mused the grand old bard of the lakes, William Wordsworth, and a couple of centuries on, his words still ring true. For natural splendour, nowhere in England can compare to the Lake District. For centuries, poets, painters and perambulators alike have been flocking here in search of inspiration and escape, and it's still the nation's favourite place to revel in the majesty of the English landscape.

The main draw in the region is undoubtedly the Lake District – England's largest national park (885 sq miles) and, since 2017, a Unesco World Heritage Site. Every bend in the road reveals more eye-popping views: deep valleys, plunging passes, glittering lakes, whitewashed inns, barren hills. But it's worth exploring beyond the national park's boundaries, too: the old towns of Carlisle, Kendal and Penrith are full of historical interest and Cumbria's coast has a windswept charm all of its own.

When to Go

➡ The Lake District is the UK's most popular national park; visit in early spring and late autumn for the smallest crowds.

➡ The weather is notoriously fickle – showers can strike at any time of year, so bring wet-weather gear just in case.

➡ Cumbria's largest mountain festival is held in Keswick in mid-May, while the Beer Festival in June welcomes ale aficionados from across the globe.

➡ Ambleside's traditional sports day on the last Saturday in July features events such as hound trailing and Cumbrian wrestling; Grasmere's annual sports day takes place on the August bank holiday.

➡ In November the world's greatest liars congregate on Santon Bridge for their annual fibbing contest.

History

Neolithic settlers arrived in the Lake District around 5000 BC. The region was subsequently occupied by Celts, Angles, Vikings and Romans. During the Dark Ages it was the centre of the ancient kingdom of Rheged.

During the Middle Ages, Cumbria marked the start of the 'Debatable Lands', the wild frontier between England and Scotland. Bands of raiders known as Border Reivers regularly plundered the area, prompting the construction of defensive pele towers and castles at Carlisle, Penrith and Kendal.

The area became a centre for the Romantic movement during the 19th century, largely thanks to the Cumbrian-born poet William Wordsworth, who also championed the need to protect the Lake District's landscape from overdevelopment – a dream that was achieved in 1951 when the Lake District National Park was formed.

The present-day county of Cumbria was formed from the neighbouring districts of Cumberland and Westmorland in 1974.

🏃 Activities

Cycling

Cycling is a great way to explore the Lake District and Cumbria, as long as you don't mind the hills. For short mountain-bike rides, the trails of **Grizedale Forest** (www.forestry.gov.uk/grizedale) and Whinlatter Forest Park (p589) are very popular.

Long-distance touring routes include the 70-mile **Cumbria Way** between Ulverston, Keswick and Carlisle; the 140-mile **Sea To Sea Cycle Route** (C2C, NCN 7; www.c2c-guide.co.uk), which begins in Whitehaven and cuts east across the northern Pennines to Newcastle; and the 173-mile **Reivers Route** (NCN 10; www.reivers-route.co.uk) from the River Tyne to Whitehaven.

Walking

For many people, hiking is the main reason for a visit to the Lake District. All tourist offices and bookshops sell maps and guidebooks, such as Collins' *Lakeland Fellranger* and Ordnance Survey's *Pathfinder Guides*. Purists prefer Alfred Wainwright's seven-volume *Pictorial Guides to the Lakeland Fells* (1955–66) – part walking guides, part illustrated artworks, part philosophical memoirs – with painstakingly hand-penned maps and text.

Maps are essential: the Ordnance Survey's 1:25,000 *Landranger* maps are used by most official bodies, while some hikers prefer the Harvey *Superwalker* 1:25,000 maps.

Long-distance trails that pass through Cumbria include the 54-mile **Allerdale Ramble** from Seathwaite to the Solway Firth, the 70-mile **Cumbria Way** from Ulverston to Carlisle, and the 191-mile **Coast to Coast** from St Bees to Robin Hood's Bay in Yorkshire. Door-to-door baggage services such as **Coast to Coast Packhorse** (☑ 017683-71777; www.c2cpackhorse.co.uk) or **Sherpa Van** (☑ 0871-520 0124; www.sherpavan.com) transport luggage from one destination to the next.

Other Activities

Cumbria is a haven for outdoor activities, including rock climbing, orienteering, horse riding, archery, fell (mountain) running and *ghyll* (waterfall) scrambling. Contact the **Outdoor Adventure Company** (☑ 01539-722147; www.theoutdooradventurecompany.co.uk; Old Hutton), **Rookin House** (☑ 017684-83561; www.rookinhouse.co.uk) or **Keswick Adventure Centre** (☑ 017687-75687; www.keswickadventurecentre.co.uk; Newlands).

ℹ️ Getting There & Away

The nearest major airport is in Manchester, but Carlisle's minuscule airport also now has direct flights to/from London Southend, Belfast and Dublin.

Carlisle is on the main West Coast train line from London Euston to Manchester and Glasgow. To get to the Lake District, you need to change at Oxenholme for Kendal and Windermere. The lines around the Cumbrian coast and between Settle and Carlisle are particularly scenic.

National Express coaches run direct from London Victoria and Glasgow to Windermere, Carlisle and Kendal.

ℹ️ Getting Around

BOAT

There are round-the-lake ferry services on Windermere, Coniston Water, Ullswater and Derwentwater. Windermere also has cruises and a cross-lake ferry service.

BUS

The main bus operator is **Stagecoach** (www.stagecoachbus.com). Services on most routes are reduced in winter. You can download timetables from the Stagecoach website or the Cumbria County Council website (www.cumbria.gov.uk). Bus timetables are also available from tourist offices.

Lake District & Cumbria Highlights

1 Scafell Pike (p587) Climbing to the summit of England's highest mountain.

2 Hill Top (p582) Spotting the inspirations for Beatrix Potter's tales.

3 Steam Yacht Gondola (p584) Cruising Coniston Water in stately 19th-century style.

4 Grizedale Forest (p569) Cycling woodland trails surrounded by outdoor art.

5 Honister Slate Mine (p593) Delving into the depths of the Lake District's last slate mine.

6 La'al Ratty (p598) Catching the miniature steam trains into Eskdale.

7 Dove Cottage (p580) Exploring Wordsworth's much-loved Lakeland cottage.

8 Carlisle Castle (p600) Patrolling the battlements of Carlisle's mighty medieval fortress.

9 Borrowdale & Buttermere (p594) Taking a road trip through the loveliest Lakeland valleys.

10 Lowther Estate (p602) Visiting a great Cumbrian estate in Penrith that's slowly being brought back to life.

Useful services:

Bus 555 (Lakeslink) Lancaster to Keswick, stopping at all the main towns, including Windermere and Ambleside.

Bus 505 (Coniston Rambler) Kendal, Windermere, Ambleside and Coniston.

Bus X4/X5 Penrith to Workington via Troutbeck, Keswick and Cockermouth.

CAR

Traffic can be heavy during peak season and holiday weekends. Many Cumbrian towns use timed parking permits for on-street parking, which you can pick up free from local shops and tourist offices.

If you're driving to the Lake District, National Trust membership is a good idea, as it means you can park for free at all of the National Trust's car parks (which otherwise charge extortionately high rates).

TRAVEL PASSES

Several travel passes are available in Cumbria.

Lakes Day Ranger (adult/child/family £23/11.50/45) The best-value one-day ticket, allowing a day's unlimited travel on trains and buses in the Lake District. It also includes a boat cruise on Windermere, 10% discount on the steam railways and 20% discount on the Coniston Launch, Keswick Launch and Ullswater Steamers.

Cumbria Day Ranger (adult/child £43/21.50) This pass provides one day's train travel in Cumbria and parts of Lancashire, North Yorkshire, Northumberland and Dumfries and Galloway.

Central Lakes Dayrider (adult/child/family £8.30/6.20/23) This pass covers Stagecoach buses around Bowness, Ambleside, Grasmere, Langdale and Coniston; it includes buses 599, 505 and 516. For an extra £4/2 per adult/child you can add a boat cruise on Windermere or Coniston.

Keswick & Honister Dayrider (adult/child/family £8.30/6.20/23) Covers buses from Keswick through Borrowdale, Buttermere, Lorton and the Whinlatter Forest Park.

North West Megarider Gold (per week £28) Covers seven days' travel on all Stagecoach buses operating in Lancashire, Merseyside, Cumbria, West Cheshire and Newcastle.

THE LAKE DISTRICT

POP 40,800

The Lake District (or Lakeland, as it's commonly known round these parts) is by far the UK's most popular national park. Every year, some 15 million people pitch up to explore the region's fells and countryside, and it's not hard to see why. Ever since the Romantic poets arrived in the 19th century, its postcard panorama of craggy hilltops, mountain tarns and glittering lakes has been stirring the imaginations of visitors. Since 2017 it has also been a Unesco World Heritage Site, in recognition of its unique hill-farming culture.

ℹ️ Information

The national park's main visitor centre is at Brockhole (p577), just outside Windermere, and there are tourist offices in Windermere (p577), Bowness (p577), Ambleside (p580), Keswick (p591), Coniston (p586) and Carlisle (p602).

Windermere & Around

📞 015395 / POP 5423

Stretching for 10.5 miles between Ambleside and Newby Bridge, Windermere isn't just the queen of Lake District lakes – it's also the largest body of water anywhere in England, closer in stature to a Scottish loch. It's been a centre for tourism since the first trains chugged into town in 1847 and it's still one of the national park's busiest spots.

Confusingly, the town of Windermere is split in two: Windermere Town is actually 1.5 miles from the lake, at the top of a steep hill, while touristy, overdeveloped Bowness-on-Windermere (usually shortened just to Bowness) sits on the lake's eastern shore.

Accommodation (and parking) can be hard to come by during holidays and busy periods, so plan accordingly.

◉ Sights & Activities

⭐ **Wray Castle**   HISTORIC SITE

(NT; www.nationaltrust.org.uk/wray-castle; adult/child £9.60/4.80; ⊙10am-5pm) An impressive sight with its turrets and battlements, this mock-Gothic castle was built in 1840 for James Dawson, a retired doctor from Liverpool, but it has been owned by the National Trust since 1929. Though the interior is largely empty, the lakeside grounds are glorious. It was once used as a holiday home by Beatrix Potter's family. The best way to arrive is by boat from Bowness; there's limited parking and preference is given to non-driving visitors on busy days.

Blackwell House   HISTORIC BUILDING

(📞01539-722464; www.blackwell.org.uk; adult/child under 16yr £8/free; ⊙10.30am-5pm Apr-Oct, to 4pm Feb, Mar, Nov & Dec) Two miles south of Bowness on the B5360, Blackwell House is a glorious example of the 19th-century Arts

Lake District

and Crafts Movement, which championed handmade goods and craftsmanship over the mass-produced mentality of the Industrial Revolution. Designed by Mackay Hugh Baillie Scott for Sir Edward Holt, a wealthy brewer, the house shimmers with Arts and Crafts details: light, airy rooms, bespoke craftwork, wood panelling, stained glass and delft tiles. The mock-medieval Great Hall and serene White Drawing Room are particularly fine.

The cafe has brilliant views over Windermere.

Fell Foot Park
GARDENS

(NT; www.nationaltrust.org.uk/fell-foot-park; ⊙8am-8pm Apr-Sep, 9am-5pm Oct-Mar, cafe 10am-5pm) FREE Located at the southern end of Windermere, 7 miles south of Bowness, this 7-hectare lakeside estate originally belonged to a manor house. It's now owned by the National Trust and its shoreline paths and grassy lawns are ideal for a sunny-day picnic. There's a small cafe and rowing boats are available for hire.

Lakeland Motor Museum
MUSEUM

(☑015395-30400; www.lakelandmotormuseum. co.uk; Backbarrow; adult/child £8.75/5.25; ⊙9.30am-5.30pm Apr-Sep, to 4.30pm Oct-Mar) Two miles south of Newby Bridge on the A590, this museum houses a wonderful collection of antique cars: classic (Minis, Austin Healeys, MGs), sporty (DeLoreans, Audi Quattros, Aston Martins) and downright odd (Scootacars, Amphicars). There are also quirky exhibits on the history of caravans and vintage bicycles. A separate building explores Donald and Malcolm Campbell's record attempts on Coniston Water, with replicas of the 1935 Bluebird car and 1967 *Bluebird K7* boat. Online bookings get a 10% discount.

Lakes Aquarium
AQUARIUM

(☑015395-30153; www.lakesaquarium.co.uk; Lakeside; adult/child £7.45/5.45; ⊙10am-6pm) At the southern end of the lake near Newby Bridge, this aquarium explores a range

Windermere Town

Windermere Town

🛏 Sleeping
1 1 Park Road	C3
2 Rum Doodle	B4
3 The Hideaway	B1
4 Wheatlands Lodge	B2

⊗ Eating
5 Francine's	C2
6 Homeground	C2
7 Hooked	B2

🍸 Drinking & Nightlife
8 Crafty Baa	C1

of underwater habitats from tropical Africa through to Morecambe Bay. Windermere Lake Cruises (p576) and the Lakeside & Haverthwaite Railway (p574) stop right beside the aquarium, or you could catch bus 6/X6 from Bowness. There's a £1 discount per ticket for online bookings.

Lakeside & Haverthwaite Railway   RAIL
(☑015395-31594; www.lakesiderailway.co.uk; adult/child/family return from Haverthwaite to Lakeside £6.90/3.45/19, 1-day rover ticket adult/child £10/5; ⊙mid-Mar–Oct) Built to carry ore and timber to the ports at Ulverston and Barrow, these vintage steam trains puff their way between Haverthwaite, near Ulverston, and Newby Bridge and Lakeside. There are five to seven trains a day, timed to correspond with the Windermere cruise boats – you can buy combo tickets that include an onward lake cruise to Bowness or Ambleside.

🛌 Sleeping

Windermere YHA   HOSTEL £
(☑0845-371 9352; www.yha.org.uk; Bridge Lane; dm £13-35; ⊙reception 7.30-11.30am & 3-10pm; 🅿@) Slightly misleadingly, the closest YHA to Windermere is actually about 1.5 miles from the lake, halfway between Troutbeck Bridge and Troutbeck village. Once a

mansion, the imposing building has been modernised with the usual YHA set-up: bunk-bed dorms, canteen, self-catering kitchen, lounge and gear-drying room. There are fine Windermere views from the front rooms, and space to camp outside, too.

Inconveniently, buses from Windermere stop about a mile downhill at Troutbeck Bridge.

★ Rum Doodle
B&B **££**

(☑ 015394-45967; www.rumdoodlewindermere. com; Sunny Bank Rd, Windermere Town; d £95-139; P⛛) Named after a classic travel novel about a fictional mountain in the Himalayas, this B&B zings with imagination. Its rooms are themed after places and characters in the book, with details such as book-effect wallpaper, vintage maps and old suitcases. Top of the heap is the Summit, snug under the eaves with a separate sitting room. Two-night minimum in summer.

The Hideaway
B&B **££**

(☑ 015394-43070; www.thehideawayatwindermere. co.uk; Phoenix Way; d £90-170; P⛛) There's a fine range of rooms available at this much-recommended B&B in a former schoolmaster's house. There's a choice for all budgets, from Standard Comfy (simple decor, not much space) all the way to Ultimate Comfy (claw-foot tub, split-level mezzanine, space galore). Regardless which you choose, you'll be treated to spoils such as homemade cakes and afternoon tea every day.

Wheatlands Lodge
B&B **££**

(☑ 015394-43789; www.wheatlandslodge-wind ermere.co.uk; Old College Lane; d £105-140; P⛛) There's nary a whiff of pretension about this B&B, halfway between Windermere and Bowness – it just does its job with elegance and efficiency. The house is Victorian, and rooms range from Club (a tad cramped) to Master (space and then some). Breakfast is a high point, with homemade muesli, local bacon and sausages, plus smoked salmon from Loch Ewe.

1 Park Road
B&B **££**

(☑ 015394-42107; www.1parkroad.co.uk; 1 Park Rd, Windermere Town; d £80-112; P⛛🐾) A reliable choice in Windermere Town, with six pleasant, spacious rooms (including a couple of dog-friendly ones). Thoughtful touches such as in-room DVD players, fresh (not UHT) milk for tea and welcome treats such as made-in-Cumbria fudge and marshmallow elevate it above the competition – and rates aren't bad for Windermere, especially during the week.

Gilpin Hotel
HOTEL **£££**

(☑ 015394-88818; www.gilpinlodge.co.uk; Crook Rd; r £275-465; P) Windermere's B&Bs might be pushing up their rates to silly levels, but this famously posh country-house retreat shows them how it should be done. The fabulously fancy rooms are named after fells, garden suites have their own decks and outdoor hot tubs, and the exclusive Lake House nearby comes with its own chauffeur.

A superb Michelin-starred restaurant, a lovely spa and hectares of grounds complete the high-class package.

Cranleigh
HOTEL **£££**

(☑ 015394-43293; www.thecranleigh.com; Kendal Rd, Bowness-on-Windermere; d £110-190, ste £305-525; P⛛) This super-snazzy B&B takes the prize for most-over-the-top decor in Windermere: from sleigh beds to jaguar-print throws and backlit bathroom mirrors, it's had every trick in the design book thrown at it (with varying degrees of success). Still, it's not a dull place to stay – and for extra luxury, you can book one of its boutique church suites.

✗ Eating

Homeground
CAFE **£**

(☑ 015394-44863; www.homegroundcafe.co.uk; 56 Main Rd, Windermere Town; coffee £2-4, mains £7-10; ⊗9am-5pm) Windermere gets its own boutique coffee house, serving excellent flat whites, pourovers and ristrettos, accompanied by a fine display of milk art. It's super for brunch too, with bang-on-trend options such as a lavish eggs Benedict and maple-bacon waffles. All in all, a thoroughly welcome new addition to town.

★ Mason's Arms
PUB FOOD **££**

(☑ 015395-68486; www.masonsarmsstrawberry bank.co.uk; Winster; mains £12.95-18.95) Three miles east, near Bowlands Bridge, the marvellous Mason's Arms is a local secret. The rafters, flagstones and cast-iron range haven't changed in centuries, and the patio has to-die-for views across fields and fells. The food is hearty – Cumbrian stewpot, slow-roasted Cartmel lamb – and there are lovely rooms and cottages for rent (£175 to £350). In short, a cracker.

Brown Horse Inn
PUB FOOD **££**

(☑ 015394-43443; www.thebrownhorseinn.co.uk; Winster; mains £12.95-16.95; ⊗lunch noon-2pm,

WINDERMERE & THE ISLANDS

Windermere gets its name from the old Norse, Vinandr mere (Vinandr's lake; so Lake Windermere is actually tautologous). Encompassing 5.7 sq miles between Ambleside and Newby Bridge, the lake is a mile wide at its broadest point, with a maximum depth of about 220m.

The lake's shoreline is owned by a combination of private landholders, the National Park Authority and the National Trust, but the lakebed itself (and thus the lake itself) officially belongs to the people of Windermere (local philanthropist Henry Leigh Groves purchased it on their behalf in 1938).

There are 18 islands on Windermere: the largest is Belle Isle, encompassing 16 hectares and an 18th-century Italianate mansion, while the smallest is Maiden Holme, little more than a patch of soil and a solitary tree.

Windermere Lake Cruises (☑ 015394-43360; www.windermere-lakecruises.co.uk; tickets from £2.70) offers sightseeing cruises, departing from Bowness Pier.

dinner 6-9pm) Three miles from Windermere in Winster, the Brown Horse is a popular dining pub. Produce is sourced from the Brown Horse Estate, furnishing the chefs with meat and game such as venison, spring lamb and pigeon. Beams and fireplaces conjure rustic atmosphere, and there are several ales on tap from the in-house Winster Brewery.

Angel Inn
PUB FOOD ££

(☑ 015394-44080; www.the-angelinn.com; Helm Rd, Bowness-on-Windermere; mains £10.95-16.50; ⊘11.30am-4pm & 5-9pm) This smart gastropub sits atop a grassy knoll near the Bowness shoreline and offers superior pub grub: think focaccia pizzas, sea bass with pak choi and trio of Lakeland sausage. Arrive early if you want to bag a table on the lawn – the lake views are great, so they go fast.

Upstairs are 13 bright, reasonably good-value rooms (£106 to £186).

Francine's
BISTRO ££

(☑ 015394-44088; www.francinesrestaurantwindermere.co.uk; 27 Main Rd, Windermere Town; 2-/3-course dinner menu £16.95/19.95; ⊘10am-2.30pm & 6.30-11pm Tue-Sat) The definition of a neighbourhood bistro: it's a locals' favourite and if you come more than once you'll probably be greeted by name. It's a tiny space with crammed-in tables, so watch your elbows with your neighbours. Food is solid if not stellar, with tastes tending toward the hearty, such as roast guinea fowl, confit pork belly and chicken supreme.

Hooked
SEAFOOD £££

(☑ 015394-48443; www.hookedwindermere.co.uk; Ellerthwaite Sq, Windermere Town; mains £19.95-21.95; ⊘5.30-10.30pm Tue-Sun) Seafood might not be something you immediately think of when deciding what to eat in Windermere, but Paul White's first-class fish restaurant is well worth considering. He likes to keep things classic: hake with Mediterranean veg and pesto, sea trout with peas and pancetta, or lemon sole with capers and parsley butter. It's small, so bookings are essential.

 Drinking & Nightlife

★ Crafty Baa
CRAFT BEER

(☑ 015394-88002; 21 Victoria St, Windermere Town; ⊘11am-11pm) The clue's in the name – the craft-beer revolution comes to Windermere, with a vast selection of brews: Czech pilsners, weissbiers, smoked lagers, even mango, gooseberry and coconut beers, chalked up on a wall of slates and served (if you wish) with snack platters. The space (a former house) is tiny, but plans are afoot to expand next door.

Hawkshead Brewery
BREWERY

(☑ 01539-822644; www.hawksheadbrewery.co.uk; Mill Yard, Staveley) This renowned craft brewery has its own beer hall in Staveley, 3 miles east of Windermere. Core beers include Hawkshead Bitter, dark Brodie's Prime and fruity Red. Guided tours can be arranged in advance.

Hole in T' Wall
PUB

(☑ 015394-43488; Fallbarrow Rd, Bowness-on-Windermere; ⊘11am-11pm) Bowness' oldest boozer, dating back to 1612 and offering lashings of rough-beamed, low-ceilinged atmosphere.

ℹ️ Information

There are several visitor information centres in and around Windermere.

Brockhole National Park Visitor Centre
(☑ 015394-46601; www.brockhole.co.uk;
☺10am-5pm) The lakes' main information
centre in a former country house 3 miles from
Windermere along the A591.

Windermere Information Centre (☑ 015394-
46499; www.windermereinfo.co.uk; Victoria St,
Windermere Town; ☺ 8.30am-5.30pm) A small
information point in Windermere Town, near
the railway station, run by Mountain Goat.

Bowness Visitor Information Centre (☑ 0845
901 0845; bownesstic@lake-district.gov.uk;
Glebe Rd, Bowness-on-Windermere; ☺ 9.30am-
5.30pm) Basic information point near the
Bowness jetty, with a shop and cafe.

ⓘ Getting There & Away

BOAT

To cross Windermere by car, bike or on foot,
head south of Bowness to the **Windermere
Ferry** (www.cumbria.gov.uk/roads-transport/
highways-pavements/windermereferry.asp;
car/bicycle/pedestrian £4.40/1/50p; ☺ every
20 min 6.50am-9.50pm Mon-Fri, 9.10am-
9.50pm Sat & Sun Mar-Oct, to 8.50pm Nov-Feb),
which shuttles between Ferry Nab on the east
bank to Ferry House on the west bank.

Expect car queues in summer.

BUS

There's one daily National Express coach from
London (£46, eight hours) via Lancaster and
Kendal.

Note that if you're travelling any further than
Grasmere – or if you're planning on returning
from anywhere – you're better off buying a Central Lakes Dayrider (p572) ticket.

Bus 555/556 Lakeslink (£4.70 to £9.80,
at least hourly every day) Starts at the train
station, stopping at Troutbeck Bridge (five
minutes), Brockhole Visitor Centre (seven minutes), Ambleside (£4.70, 15 minutes), Grasmere
(£7.20, 30 minutes) and Keswick (£9.80, one
hour). In the opposite direction it continues to
Kendal (£6.50, 25 minutes).

Bus 505 Coniston Rambler (hourly every day)
Travels from Bowness to Coniston (£9.80, 50
minutes) via Troutbeck, Brockhole, Ambleside,
Skelwith Fold, Hawkshead and Hawkshead Hill.
Two buses a day serve Kendal.

Bus 599 Lakes Rider (£4.20 to £7.20, three
times hourly every day) Open-top bus between
Bowness, Troutbeck, Brockhole, Rydal Church
(for Rydal Mount), Dove Cottage and Grasmere.
Some buses stop at Windermere train station.

TRAIN

Windermere is the only town inside the national
park accessible by train. It's on the branch
line to Kendal and Oxenholme, with onward
connections to Edinburgh, Manchester and
London Piccadilly.

DESTINATION	ONE-WAY FARE (£)	DURATION
Edinburgh	67	2½hr
Glasgow	68.60	2¼-2¾hr
Kendal	5.90	15min
Lancaster	14.70	45min
London Euston	108.10	3½hr
Manchester Piccadilly	37	1½hr

Ambleside

☑ 015394 / POP 2529

Once a busy mill and textile centre at Windermere's northern tip, Ambleside is an attractive little town, built from the same slate
and stern grey stone that's so characteristic
of the rest of Lakeland. Ringed by fells, it's
a favourite base for hikers, with a cluster of
outdoors shops and plenty of cosy pubs and
cafes providing fuel for adventures.

◉ Sights & Activities

★**Rydal Mount**   HISTORIC BUILDING
(☑ 015394-33002; www.rydalmount.co.uk; adult/
child £7.50/4, grounds only £5; ☺ 9.30am-5pm Mar-
Oct, 11am-4pm Nov, Dec & Feb) The poet William
Wordsworth's most famous residence in the
Lake District is undoubtedly Dove Cottage
(p580), but he actually spent a great deal
more time at Rydal Mount, 1.5 miles northwest of Ambleside, off the A591. This was the
Wordsworth family's home from 1813 until
the poet's death in 1850 and the house contains a treasure trove of Wordsworth memorabilia. Bus 555 (and bus 599 from April to
October) stops at the end of the drive.

Downstairs you can wander around the
library, dining room and drawing room (look
out for William's pen, inkstand and picnic box
in the cabinets, as well as a famous portrait
of the poet by the American painter Henry
Inman hanging above the fireplace). Upstairs
are the family bedrooms and Wordsworth's
attic study, containing his encyclopedia and
a sword belonging to his brother John, who
was lost in a shipwreck in 1805.

The gardens are lovely, too; Wordsworth
fancied himself as a landscape gardener
and much of the grounds were laid out according to his designs. Below the house is
Dora's Field, a peaceful meadow in which

Wordsworth planted daffodils in memory of his eldest daughter, who died from tuberculosis in 1847.

Armitt Museum
MUSEUM

(☎ 015394-31212; www.armitt.com; Rydal Rd; adult/child £5/free; ☉10am-5pm) Despite some damage incurred during the 2015 floods, Ambleside's excellent little museum is now back up and running. It hosts some intriguing seasonal exhibitions alongside its core collection, populated with artefacts relating to important Lakeland characters such as National Trust founder Canon Hardwicke Rawnsley, pioneering Lakeland photographers Herbert Bell and the Abraham Brothers and a certain Beatrix Potter, who bequeathed a number of botanical watercolours to the museum, along with several first editions of her books.

There are also original canvases by the modernist artist Kurt Schwitters, a German refugee who settled in Ambleside after WWII.

Stock Ghyll Force
WALKING

Ambleside's most popular walk is the half-hour stroll up to the 18m-high waterfall of Stock Ghyll Force; the trail is signposted behind the old Market Hall at the bottom of Stock Ghyll Lane. If you feel energetic, you can follow the trail beyond the falls up **Wansfell Pike** (482m), a reasonably steep walk of about two hours.

Low Wood Watersports
BOATING

(☎ 015394-39441; www.englishlakes.co.uk/low-wood-bay/watersports; Low Bay Marina) This watersports centre offers waterskiing, sailing and kayaking and has row boats and motor boats for hire. Kayaks cost from £15 per hour, canoes from £18 per hour.

🛏 Sleeping

★ Ambleside YHA
HOSTEL £

(☎ 0345 371 9620; www.yha.org.uk; Lake Rd; dm £18-32; P 🛜) One of the YHA's flagship Lake District hostels, this huge lakeside house is a fave for activity holidays (everything from kayaking to ghyll scrambling). Great facilities (kitchen, bike rental, boat jetty, bar) mean it's heavily subscribed, so book well ahead. Families can book out dorms as private rooms. It's halfway between Ambleside and Windermere on Lake Rd (A591).

Low Wray
CAMPSITE £

(NT; ☎ bookings 015394-63862; www.nationaltrust.org.uk/features/lake-district-camping; campsites

for 2 adults £16-43, ecopods £45-80; ☉campsite arrivals 3-7pm Sat-Thu, to 9pm Fri Mar-Oct) One of the most popular of the National Trust's four Lakeland campsites, in a fine spot along Windermere's shores, 3 miles from Ambleside along the B5286. There are 120 tent pitches and nine hard pitches for caravans, plus a handful of camping pods and safari tents. Choose from lake view, woodland, field or water's edge. Bus 505 stops nearby.

Waterwheel
B&B ££

(☎ 015394-33286; www.waterwheelambleside.co.uk; 3 Bridge St; d £90-110; 🛜) You'll be lulled to sleep by the sound of the river at this tiny B&B, tucked off the main street. The three rooms are small but sweet: Rattleghyll is cosily Victorian, Loughrigg squeezes under the rafters and Stockghyll features a brass bed and claw-foot bath. The drawback? The only parking is in a public car park 250m away. Two-night minimum.

Gables
B&B ££

(☎ 015394-33272; www.thegables-ambleside.co.uk; Church Walk; s £52-60, d £104-140; P 🛜) One of Ambleside's best-value B&Bs, in a double-gabled house (hence the name) in a quiet spot overlooking the recreation ground. Spotty cushions and colourful prints keep things cheery, but room sizes are variable (in this instance, bigger is definitely better). Guests receive discounts at the owner's restaurant, **Sheila's Cottage** (☎ 015394-33079; The Slack; mains £12.50-18; ☉noon-2.30pm & 6.30-10pm). There's a tiny first-come, first-served car park.

★ Nanny Brow
B&B £££

(☎ 015394-33232; www.nannybrow.co.uk; Nanny Brow, Clappersgate; d £145-280; P 🛜) There's a compelling reason to choose this premium B&B – and that's the knockout view. The whitewashed house sits on a crag with a top-drawer view down the Brathay valley, with generously sized rooms (all named after local fells) full of handsome wooden beds, gilded mirrors and antique pieces to match the house's Arts and Crafts, turn-of-the-century heritage.

Lakes Lodge
B&B £££

(☎ 015394-33240; www.lakeslodge.co.uk; Lake Rd; r £132-162; P 🛜) Halfway between a posh B&B and a midrange mini-hotel, this place makes a good Ambleside base. The rooms are all about clean lines, stark walls and zero clutter and most have a full-size wall mural featuring a local beauty spot. Some are in the main building, while others are

TOP 5 CLASSIC LAKELAND HIKES

The Lake District's most famous fell-walker, the accountant-turned-author Alfred Wainwright, recorded 214 official fells in his seven-volume *Pictorial Guides* (as if that weren't enough, he usually outlined at least two possible routes to the top or, in the case of Scafell Pike, five). If you only have limited time, here are five hikes that offer a flavour of what makes fell-walking in the Lake District so special.

Scafell Pike (978m) The daddy of Lakeland hikes, a six- to seven-hour slog to the top of England's highest peak. The classic route is from Wasdale Head.

Helvellyn (950m) Not for the faint hearted; a vertiginous scramble along the knife-edge ridge of Striding Edge. It takes at least six hours starting from Glenridding or Patterdale.

Blencathra (868m) A mountain on its own, Blencathra offers a panoramic outlook on Keswick and the northern fells. Count on four hours from Threlkeld.

Haystacks (597m) Wainwright's favourite mountain and the place where his ashes were scattered. It's a steep, three-hour return hike from Buttermere village.

Catbells (451m) The fell for everyone, accessible to six-year-olds and septuagenarians. It's on the west side of Derwentwater and takes a couple of hours to climb.

in an attached annexe. Breakfast is served buffet-style.

Waterhead Hotel
HOTEL £££

(☑08458 504503; www.englishlakes.co.uk; Lake Rd; r £142-350; P🖥📶🐾) For a proper hotel stay in Ambleside (complete with the all-essential Windermere view, of course), the Waterhead is definitely the choice. Outside, it's clad in traditional Lakeland stone; inside, there are 40-something rooms that, while perfectly comfortable, feel a tad corporate in style. Lake views command a premium, but there are often good online deals.

✗ Eating

★ Great North Pie
PIES £

(☑01625 522112; www.greatnorthpie.co; Unit 2 The Courtyard, Rothay Rd; pies £4-8; ⏰9am-5pm) Based in Wilmslow, this much-garlanded pie maker has opened an Ambleside outlet, and it's rightly become a town favourite. Go for a classic such as Swaledale beef mince or Lancashire cheese and onion, or opt for something on the seasonal pie menu: they're all delicious, and served with lashings of mash and gravy (veggie, should you wish).

Stockghyll Fine Food
DELI £

(☑015394-31865; www.stockghyllfinefood.co.uk; Rydal Rd; sandwiches £3-4; ⏰9am-5pm Wed-Sun) For premium Cumbrian cheeses, chutneys, cold cuts, beers and breadsticks, this fine food emporium is impossible to top in Ambleside – and it also does a nice line in pork pies, sausage rolls and takeaway sandwiches.

Apple Pie
CAFE £

(☑015394-33679; www.applepieambleside.co.uk; Rydal Rd; lunches £4-10; ⏰9am-5.30pm) For a quick lunch stop, you won't go far wrong at this friendly little caff, which serves stuffed sandwiches, hot pies, baked spuds and yummy cakes (the apple pie is a local legend). Everything is available either eat in or takeaway.

It also runs an excellent-value **B&B** (d £52-85; P📶).

Zeffirelli's
ITALIAN £

(☑015394-33845; www.zeffirellis.com; Compston Rd; pizzas & mains £8-15; ⏰11am-10pm) A beloved local landmark, Zeff's is often packed out for its quality pizza and pasta. The £21.75 Double Feature deal includes two courses and a ticket to the **cinema** (☑015394-33100; Compston Rd) next door.

Fellini's
VEGETARIAN ££

(☑015394-32487; www.fellinisambleside.com; Church St; mains £12-15; ⏰5.30-10pm; 🍴) Fear not, veggies: even in the land of the Cumberland sausage and the tattie hotpot (lamb, vegetable and potato stew), you won't go hungry thanks to Fellini's sophisticated 'vegeterranean' food. The dishes are creative and beautifully presented – think delicate Moroccan filo parcels, stuffed portobello mushrooms and radicchio provolne ravioli.

★ Old Stamp House
BISTRO £££

(☑015394-32775; www.oldstamphouse.com; Church St; dinner mains £24-28; ⏰12.30-2pm

Wed-Sat, 6.30-10pm Tue-Sat) In the cellar of the building where Wordsworth worked as distributor of stamps, this fine-dining bistro champions Cumbrian produce, much of it raised, caught, shot or cured within a few miles' radius. You'll find ingredients like Arctic char, Herdwick hogget and roe deer on the menu, partnered with foraged ingredients, surprising flavour combinations and delicate sauces, all impeccably presented. Outstanding.

★ **Lake Road Kitchen**   BISTRO £££
(☑015394-22012; www.lakeroadkitchen.co.uk; Lake Rd; 5-/8-course tasting menu £65/90; ⊙6-9.30pm Wed-Sun) This much-lauded bistro has brought some dazzle to Ambleside's dining scene. Its Noma-trained head chef, James Cross, explores the 'food of the north', and his multicourse tasting menus are chockfull of locally sourced, seasonal and foraged ingredients, from shore-sourced seaweed to forest-picked mushrooms. Presentation is impeccable, flavours are experimental and the Scandi-inspired decor is just so.

ℹ Information

Hub (☑015394-32582; tic@thehubofambleside.com; Central Bldgs, Market Cross; ⊙9am-5pm) Central information centre that's also home to the post office. Also has a good shop selling maps, books and souvenirs.

ℹ Getting There & Away

Bus 555 Runs at least hourly (including Sundays) to Grasmere (£4.70) and Keswick (£8.80), and to Bowness, Windermere (£4.70) and Kendal (£7.60) in the opposite direction.

Bus 599 Open-top service that leaves at least hourly (including weekends) to Grasmere, Bowness, Windermere and Brockhole Visitor Centre; four buses daily continue to Kendal. Prices as for bus 555.

Bus 505 To Hawkshead and Coniston (£5.90, hourly each day).

Bus 516 To Elterwater and Langdale (£4.40, six daily).

Grasmere

☑015394 / POP 1458

If it's Romantic connections you're looking for, the little village of Grasmere is the place to be. Huddled at the edge of an island-studded lake surrounded by woods, pastures and slate-coloured hills, it's most famous as the former home of the grand old daddy of the Romantics himself, poet William Wordsworth, who set up home at nearby Dove Cottage in 1799, and spent much of the rest of his life here. Three of the poet's former houses can be visited nearby, as well as an excellent museum – and, poignantly, his family's plot in the village churchyard.

Grasmere's literary cachet has its drawbacks, though: the village's streets are crammed to bursting throughout summer, and the modern-day rash of gift shops, tearooms and coach-tour hotels has done little to preserve the quiet country charm that drew Wordsworth here in the first place.

◉ Sights

★ **Dove Cottage & The Wordsworth Museum**   HISTORIC BUILDING
(☑015394-35544; www.wordsworth.org.uk; adult/child £8.95/free; ⊙9.30am-5.30pm Mar-Oct, 10am-4.30pm Nov, Dec & Feb) On the edge of Grasmere, this tiny, creeper-clad cottage (formerly a pub called the Dove & Olive Bough) was famously inhabited by William Wordsworth between 1799 and 1808. The cottage's cramped rooms are full of artefacts – try to spot the poet's passport, a pair of his spectacles and a portrait (given to him by Sir Walter Scott) of his favourite dog, Pepper. Entry is by timed ticket to avoid overcrowding and includes an informative guided tour.

Wordsworth lived here happily with his sister Dorothy, wife Mary and three children, John, Dora and Thomas, until 1808 when the family moved to a nearby house at Allen Bank. The cottage was subsequently rented by Thomas de Quincey (author of *Confessions of an English Opium Eater*).

Tickets also include admission to the excellent **Wordsworth Museum & Art Gallery** next door, which houses one of the nation's main collections relating to the Romantic movement, including many original manuscripts and some creepy death masks of famous Romantic figures.

Grasmere Lake & Rydal Water   LAKE
Quiet paths lead along the shores of Grasmere's twin-set lakes. Rowing boats can be hired at the northern end of Grasmere Lake from the **Grasmere Tea Gardens** (☑015394-35590; Stock Lane; ⊙9.30am-5pm), which is a five-minute walk from the village centre.

St Oswald's Church   CHURCH
(Church Stile) Named after a Viking saint, Grasmere's medieval chapel is where Wordsworth and his family attended church service every Sunday for many years. It's also their final

TROUTBECK

This out-of-the-way hamlet on the way to Kirkstone Pass is worth visiting for its National Trust-owned farmhouse of **Townend** (NT; ☑ 01539-432628; www.nationaltrust.org.uk/townend; adult/child £6.50/3.25; ⊘ 1-5pm Wed-Sun Mar-Oct, daily school holidays), which offers an insight into Lakeland life c 1700. It once belonged to farmer Ben Browne and his family, who owned the house until 1943. Now restored, the whitewashed house contains a collection of vintage farming tools, possessions and furniture. Hourly guided tours run from 11am to 1pm.

The **Mortal Man** (☑ 015394-33193; www.themortalman.co.uk; Troutbeck; mains £12.50-18.95; ℗ ⛲) makes a fine spot for a pint of ale and some grub – the views from the beer garden are epic.

Bus 508 from Windermere (£4.80, 25 minutes, five daily) stops in Troutbeck, then continues over Kirkstone Pass to Ullswater and Penrith.

resting place – under the spreading bows of a great yew tree, the Wordsworth's family graves are tucked into a quiet corner of the churchyard. A peaceful memorial garden to fund the church's restoration has recently been established next door – planted, of course, with swathes of daffodils.

Among the tombstones are those belonging to William, his wife Mary, his sister Dorothy and his children Dora, William, Thomas and Catherine. Samuel Taylor Coleridge's son Hartley is also buried here, along with several Quillinans; Edward Quillinan became Wordsworth's son-in-law in 1841, having married his beloved daughter Dora.

The church itself is worth a look. Inside you'll find Wordsworth's own prayer book and his favourite pew, marked by a plaque. The church is one of the oldest in the Lake District, mostly dating from the 13th century, but thought to have been founded sometime in the 7th century. It was restored and re-rendered in 2017.

🛏 Sleeping

Butharlyp How YHA
HOSTEL £

(☑ 0845 371 9319; www.yha.org.uk; Easedale Rd; dm £18-30; ⊘ reception 7am-11pm; ℗ ⛊ 🖥) Grasmere's YHA is in a large Victorian house set among grassy grounds, all in easy walking distance of the village. There's a good range of different-sized dorms, a licensed bar and the cafe serves breakfast and the three-course 'Supper Club' menu.

Grasmere Hostel
HOSTEL £

(☑ 015394-35055; www.grasmerehostel.co.uk; Broadrayne Farm; dm £20-24; ℗ @ ⛊ 🖥) This stylish indie hostel has a vaguely Scandi feel, with unexpected luxuries such as a Nordic sauna, skylights, two kitchens and en suite

bathrooms for each (mixed sex) dorm. Porthole windows provide impressive views over the fells. It's in a converted farmhouse on the A591 about 1.5 miles north of the village, near the Traveller's Rest pub.

Heidi's Grasmere Lodge
B&B ££

(☑ 0774 382 7252; www.heidisgrasmerelodge. co.uk; Red Lion Sq; d £99-130; 🖥) This plush B&B in the centre of the village offers six super-feminine rooms full of frilly cushions and Cath Kidston–style patterns. They're quite small but very comfy: room 6 has its own sun patio, reached via a spiral staircase.

How Foot Lodge
B&B ££

(☑ 015394-35366; www.howfootlodge.co.uk; Town End; d £78-85; ℗) Just a stroll from Dove Cottage, this stone house has six rooms finished in fawns and beiges. The nicest are the deluxe doubles, one with a sun terrace and the other with a private sitting room. Rates are an absolute bargain considering the location.

★ Forest Side
BOUTIQUE HOTEL £££

(☑ 015394-35250; www.theforestside.com; Keswick Rd; r incl full board £230-400; ℗ 🖥) For out-and-out-luxury, plump for this boutique beauty. Run by renowned hotelier Andrew Wildsmith, it's a design palace: chic interiors decorated with crushed-velvet sofas, bird-of-paradise wallpaper, stag heads and 20 swish rooms from 'Cosy' to 'Jolly Good', 'Superb', 'Grand' and 'Master'. Chef Kevin Tickle previously worked at L'Enclume (p599), and now runs the stellar restaurant here using produce from its kitchen garden.

★ Daffodil Hotel
BOUTIQUE HOTEL £££

(☑ 015394-63550; www.daffodilhotel.co.uk; d £145-260, ste £180-340; ℗ 🖥) Opened in 2012 this upscale hotel occupies a Victorian building, but the 78 rooms zing with modern style: swirly carpets, art prints and bold shades of lime, purple and turquoise. There's a choice of lake or valley views and lovely bathrooms with pan-head showers and Molton Brown bath products. A fine restaurant and luxurious spa complete the package. Rather good.

Eating

Brew CAFE £
(📞 015394-35248; www.heidisgrasmerelodge.co.uk; Red Lion Sq; mains £4-8; ⊙9am-5.30pm) This cheery village cafe is the place for a quick lunch of homemade soup and a thick-cut sandwich. The house-special flapjacks and savoury cheese smokeys are sinfully good.

★Jumble Room MODERN BRITISH ££
(📞015394-35188; www.thejumbleroom.co.uk; Langdale Rd; dinner mains £14.50-23; ⊙5.30-9.30pm Wed-Mon) Husband-and-wife team Andy and Crissy Hill have turned this village bistro into a much-loved dining landmark. It's a really fun and friendly place to eat. Spotty crockery, cow murals and primary colours set the boho tone, matched by a magpie menu that borrows flavours and ingredients from a global cookbook – Malaysian seafood curry one week, Persian lamb the next.

Lewis's BISTRO ££
(📞015394-35266; Broadgate; mains £14.95-24.95; ⊙6-9pm Tue-Sat) A reliable village bistro, Lewis's eponymous restaurant turns out hearty, classic British bistro dishes – steak, roast lamb, belly pork, sea bass and the like. It's solid rather than sensational, but a good bet for dinner all the same.

Shopping

★Sarah Nelson's Gingerbread Shop FOOD
(📞015394-35428; www.grasmeregingerbread.co.uk; Church Cottage; ⊙9.15am-5.30pm Mon-Sat, 12.30-5pm Sun) In business since 1854, this famous sweet shop next to the village church makes Grasmere's essential souvenir: traditional gingerbread with a half-biscuit, half-cakey texture (six/12 pieces for £3.50/6.70), cooked using the original top-secret recipe. Friendly service is provided by ladies dressed in frilly pinafores and starched bonnets.

❶ Getting There & Away

The regular 555 bus (at least hourly, including Sundays) runs from Windermere to Grasmere (15 minutes) via Ambleside, Rydal Church and Dove Cottage, then travels onwards to Keswick.

The open-top 599 (two or three per hour in summer) runs from Grasmere via Ambleside, Troutbeck Bridge, Windermere and Bowness.

Both buses charge the same fares: Grasmere to Ambleside is £4.70, to Bowness and Windermere is £7.20.

Hawkshead

📞 015394 / POP 1640

Lakeland villages don't come much more perfect than pint-sized Hawkshead, a jumble of whitewashed cottages, cobbled lanes and old pubs lost among bottle-green countryside between Ambleside and Coniston. The village has literary cachet, too – Wordsworth went to school here and Beatrix Potter's husband, William Heelis, worked here as a solicitor for many years (his old office is now an art gallery).

Cars are banned in the village centre.

◉ Sights

★Hill Top HISTORIC BUILDING
(NT; 📞015394-36269; www.nationaltrust.org.uk/hill-top; adult/child £10.90/5.45, admission to garden & shop free; ⊙10am-5.30pm Jun-Aug, to 4.30pm Sat-Thu Apr, May, Sep & Oct, weekends only Nov-Mar) Two miles south of Hawkshead, in the tiny village of Near Sawrey, this idyllic farmhouse was purchased in 1905 by Beatrix Potter and was used as inspiration for many of her tales: the house features directly in *Samuel Whiskers, Tom Kitten, Pigling Bland* and *Jemima Puddleduck,* among others, and you might recognise the kitchen garden from *Peter Rabbit.* Entry is by timed ticket in order to manage demand, but you can't prebook, and it's very popular, so prepare to queue.

Clad in climbing ivy and stocked with memorabilia, the house looks like something out of a storybook, but Beatrix only actually lived here until her marriage to William Heelis. In 1913 the newlywed couple moved to a larger farm at nearby Castle Cottage, where the author wrote many more tales until her death in 1943.

She bequeathed Hill Top (along with Castle Cottage and more than 1600 hectares of land) to the National Trust with the proviso that the house should be left with her belongings and decor in situ. Perhaps the most fascinating insight into the author's private life is provided by the many antiques, collectibles and objets d'art – from antique fans, delicate chinaware and butterfly collections to her own well-used paint tin. For Beatrix scholars, it's an absolute treasure trove. The house formed the centrepiece for celebrations to mark the author's 150th birthday in 2016.

The only drawback is the house's huge – and seemingly boundless – popularity. It's simply one of the must-see places for every visitor to the Lakes. Try visiting in the late afternoon or on weekdays to avoid the worst crowds.

★ Tarn Hows
LAKE

(NT; www.nationaltrust.org.uk/coniston-and-tarn-hows) Two miles off the B5285 from Hawkshead, a winding country lane leads to this famously photogenic artificial lake, now owned by the National Trust. Trails wind their way around the lakeshore and surrounding woodland – keep your eyes peeled for red squirrels in the treetops.

There's a small National Trust car park, but it fills quickly. Several buses, including the 505, stop nearby.

Beatrix Potter Gallery
GALLERY

(NT; www.nationaltrust.org.uk/beatrix-potter-gallery; Red Lion Sq; adult/child £6.50/3.25; ⊙10.30am-5pm Sat-Thu mid-Mar–Oct) As well as being a children's author, Beatrix Potter was also a talented botanical painter and amateur naturalist. This small gallery, housed in what were once the offices of Potter's husband, solicitor William Heelis, contains a collection of her watercolours depicting local flora and fauna. She was particularly fascinated by mushrooms.

Hawkshead Grammar School
HISTORIC BUILDING

(www.hawksheadgrammar.org.uk; admission £2.50; ⊙10.30am-1pm & 1.30-5pm Mon-Sat Apr-Oct) In centuries past, promising young gentlemen were sent to Hawkshead's village school for their educational foundation. Among the former pupils was a certain William Wordsworth, who attended the school from 1779 to 1787 – you can still see a desk where the naughty young poet carved his name. The curriculum was punishing: 10 hours' study a day, covering weighty subjects such as Latin, Greek, geometry, science and rhetoric. Upstairs is a small exhibition exploring the history of the school.

🛏 Sleeping & Eating

Hawkshead YHA
HOSTEL £

(☎0845 371 9321; www.yha.org.uk; dm £13-30; P @ 🛜) This impressive YHA is lodged in a Grade II–listed Regency house overlooking Esthwaite Water, a mile from Hawkshead along the Newby Bridge road. It's a fancy spot considering the bargain prices: the dorms and kitchen are large and there are camping pods outside as well as bike rentals. The 505 bus stops at the end of the lane.

Yewfield
B&B ££

(☎015394-36765; www.yewfield.co.uk; Hawkshead Hill; s £85-120, d £90-140; P 🛜) ❀ This rambling Victorian mansion is one of the best options around Hawkshead, although it's out of the way on the road to Coniston, near Tarn Hows. It's run by the owners of Zeffirelli's in Ambleside and offers a range of comfortable rooms and antique-stocked lounges, plus ecofriendly touches such as a wood-mass boiler and all-veggie breakfasts. Discounts available for three nights.

★ Drunken Duck
PUB FOOD £££

(☎015394-36347; www.drunkenduckinn.co.uk; Barngates; lunch/dinner mains £10/22; ⊙noon-2pm

---

GRIZEDALE FOREST

Stretching for 2428 hectares across the hilltops between Coniston Water and Esthwaite Water is Grizedale Forest, a dense conifer forest whose name derives from the Old Norse 'griss-dale', meaning 'valley of the pigs'. Though it looks lush and unspoilt today, the forest has been largely replanted over the last 100 years – by the late 19th century the original woodland had practically disappeared thanks to the demands of the local logging, mining and charcoal industries.

The forest has nine walking trails and seven cycling trails to explore – some are easy and designed for families, while others are geared towards hardcore hikers and cyclists. Along the way you'll spot more than 40 outdoor sculptures hidden in the undergrowth, created by artists since 1977 (there's a useful online guide at www.grizedalesculpture.org).

Trail maps are sold at the **visitors centre** (☎0300 067 4495; www.forestry.gov.uk/grizedale; ⊙10am-5pm summer, to 4pm winter), while bikes can be hired from **Grizedale Mountain Bikes** (☎01229-860335; www.grizedalemountainbikes.co.uk; adult/child per half-day from £25/15; ⊙9am-5pm).

& 6-10pm; P ⎃) Long one of the Lakes' premier dining destinations, the Drunken Duck blends historic pub and fine-dining restaurant. On a wooded crossroads on the top of Hawkshead Hill, it's renowned for its luxurious food and home-brewed ales, and the flagstones and sporting prints conjure a convincing country atmosphere. Book well ahead for dinner or take your chances at lunchtime.

If you fancy staying, you'll find the rooms (£125 to £250) are just as fancy as the food. The pub's tricky to find: drive along the B5286 from Hawkshead towards Ambleside and look out for the brown signs.

❶ Getting There & Away

Bus 505 (£4.70 to £5.90, hourly every day) links Hawkshead with Windermere, Ambleside and Coniston.

Coniston

⬛ 015394 / POP 641

Hunkered beneath the pockmarked peak known as the **Old Man of Coniston** (803m), this lakeside village was originally established to support the local mining industry, and the surrounding hilltops are littered with the remains of old copper workings. These days most people visit with two things in mind: to cruise on the lovely old Coniston Launch, or to tramp to the top of the Old Man, a steep but rewarding return hike of around 6 miles.

Coniston's other claim to fame is as the location for a string of world-record speed attempts made by Sir Malcolm Campbell and his son, Donald, between the 1930s and 1960s. Tragically, after beating the record several times, Donald was killed during an attempt in 1967 when his futuristic jetboat *Bluebird* flipped at around 320mph. The boat and its pilot were recovered in 2001, and Campbell was buried in the cemetery of St Andrew's church.

◉ Sights

Coniston Water   LAKE
Coniston's gleaming 5-mile-long lake – the third largest in the Lake District after Windermere and Ullswater – is a half-mile walk from town along Lake Rd. The best way to explore the lake is on one of the two cruise services or, better still, by paddling it yourself. Dinghies, rowing boats, canoes, kayaks and motor boats can be hired from the Coniston Boating Centre.

Along with its connections to the speed attempts made here by Malcolm and Donald Campbell, the lake is famous for inspiring Arthur Ransome's classic children's tale *Swallows and Amazons*. Peel Island, towards the southern end of Coniston Water, supposedly provided the model for Wild Cat Island in the book.

Brantwood   HISTORIC BUILDING
(☎ 015394-41396;   www.brantwood.org.uk; adult/child £7.70/free, gardens only £5.35/free; ⊙ 10.30am-5pm mid-Mar–mid-Nov, to 4pm Wed-Sun mid-Nov–mid-Mar) John Ruskin (1819–1900) was one of the great thinkers of 19th-century society. A polymath, philosopher, painter and critic, he expounded views on everything from Venetian architecture to lace making. In 1871 Ruskin purchased this lakeside house and spent the next 20 years modifying it, championing handmade crafts (he even designed the wallpaper). Look out for his vast shell collection. Boats run regularly to Brantwood from Coniston. Alternatively, look out for signs on the B5285.

Highlights include the grand but surprisingly cosy drawing room, the tome-filled study and the tiny upstairs bedroom decorated with some of his favourite watercolours (mostly by JMW Turner, and mostly copies of the originals). In the corner of the room is the little circular turret where Ruskin whiled away hours looking out across the lake and pondering the great issues of the day. Later in life he was afflicted by bouts of deep depression, and suffered some kind of mental collapse in the room. He never slept in there again.

Outside the house, 100 hectares of gardens and terraces stretch up the fellside ('Brant' derives from a Norse word meaning steep). Of particular note are the Hortus Inclusus, a herb garden modelled along medieval designs, and the Zig-Zaggy, inspired by the purgatorial mount in Dante's Inferno. The best views are from the High Walk, designed by Ruskin's cousin Joan Severn.

Afterwards, you can have lunch at the cafe in the house's former stables.

🏃 Activities

★ **Steam Yacht Gondola**   BOATING
(NT; ☎ 015394-63850; www.nationaltrust.org.uk/steam-yacht-gondola; Coniston Jetty; half lake adult/child/family £11/6/25, full lake adult/child/family £21/10/48) ✐ Built in 1859 and restored in the 1980s by the National Trust, this wonderful steam yacht looks like a cross

between a Venetian *vaporetto* and an English houseboat, complete with cushioned saloons and polished wood seats. It's a stately way to see the lake, especially if you're visiting Brantwood, and it's ecofriendly – since 2008 it's been powered by waste wood.

Coniston Launch   BOATING

([✆] 015394-36216; www.conistonlaunch.co.uk; Coniston Jetty; Red Route adult/child return £11.50/5.75, Yellow Route £12.75/6.40, Green Route £17.25/8.65) [♦] Coniston's two modern launches have been solar-powered since 2005. The regular 45-minute **Northern Service (Red Route)** calls at the Waterhead Hotel, Torver and Brantwood. The 60-minute **Wild Cat Island Cruise (Yellow Route)** tours the lake's islands.

The 105-minute **Southern Service (Green Route)** is themed: it's Swallows and Amazons on Monday and Wednesday, and the Campbell story on Tuesday and Thursday.

Coniston Boating Centre   BOATING

([✆] 015394-41366; www.conistonboatingcentre.co.uk; Coniston Jetty) Hires out rowing boats (£15 per hour), kayaks and stand-up paddleboards (£20 for two hours), Canadian canoes (£25 for two hours) and motor boats (£30 per hour). It also rents out bikes (adult/child £15/5 for two hours).

🛏 Sleeping

Hoathwaite Campsite   CAMPSITE £

(NT; [✆] bookings 015394-63862; www.nationaltrust.org.uk/holidays/hoathwaite-campsite-lake-district; adult, tent & car £8-14, extra adult/child £6/3; [⊙] Easter–Nov) This back-to-basics National Trust–owned campsite is on the A5394 between Coniston and Torver. There's a toilet block, water taps and not much else – but the views over Coniston Water are super.

Lakeland House   B&B ££

([✆] 015394-41303; www.lakelandhouse.co.uk; Tilberthwaite Ave; s £50-70, d £70-99, ste £130-190) You're smack bang in the centre of Coniston at this good-value, basic B&B above Hollands cafe. The rooms have been recently renovated with fresh colours and updated bathrooms; some have dormer windows, others have views of the Old Man. The Lookout Suite has its own sitting room and in-room bathtub.

Bank Ground Farm   B&B ££

([✆] 015394-41264; www.bankground.com; East of the Lake; d from £90; [P]) This lakeside farmhouse has literary cachet: Arthur Ransome used it as the model for Holly Howe Farm in *Swallows and Amazons*. Parts of the house date back to the 15th century, so the rooms are snug. Some have sleigh beds, others exposed beams. The tearoom is a beauty, and there are cottages for longer stays. Two-night minimum.

🍴 Eating

Herdwicks   CAFE £

([✆] 015394-41141; Yewdale Rd; mains £4-10; [⊙] 10am-4pm) Run by a local family, this bright and cheery cafe makes the perfect stop for lunch – whether you're in the mood for homemade soup, a big chunky sandwich, or a slice of sinful cake. Everything is locally sourced where possible, and the light-filled, large-windowed space is inviting.

Bluebird Cafe   CAFE £

([✆] 015394-41649; Lake Rd; mains £4-8; [⊙] 9.30am-5.30pm) This lakeside cafe does a brisk trade from people waiting for the Coniston launches. The usual salads, jacket spuds and sandwiches are on offer and there are lots of tables outside where you can look out on the lake.

Steam Bistro   BISTRO ££

([✆] 015394-41928; www.steambistro.co.uk; Tilberthwaite Ave; 2-/3-course menu £22.95/26.95; [⊙] 6-11pm Wed-Sun) This swish new bistro has become the go-to address for Coniston dining. Its magpie menu borrows lots of global flavours – you'll find everything from Japanese dumplings to Cajun pulled pork and Greek-style *kleftiko* (slow-cooked lamb) on the specials board. Even better, everything is *prix fixe* (fixed price).

🍷 Drinking & Nightlife

Sun Hotel   PUB

([✆] 015394-41248; www.thesunconiston.com; [⊙] 10am-11pm) Famously used as a headquarters by Donald Campbell during his fateful campaign, this trad boozer is a good place for a pint, with a fell-view beer garden and cosy crannies to hunker down in – look out for Campbell memorabilia. Food (mains £12 to £21) is hit-and-miss at busy times. It's up a small hill beside the bridge over Church Beck.

Black Bull   PUB

([✆] 015394-41335; www.conistonbrewery.com/black-bull-coniston.htm; Yewdale Rd; [⊙] 10am-11pm) Coniston's main meeting spot, the old

WORTH A TRIP

THE STEEPEST ROAD IN ENGLAND

Zigzagging over the fells between the valleys of Little Langdale and Eskdale, an infamous mountain road traverses England's two highest road passes: **Wrynose** and **Hardknott**. In use since ancient times, the old packhorse route was substantially improved by the Romans: at the top of Hardknott Pass, there's a ruined **Roman fort** – you can still see the remains of the walls, parade ground and commandant's house. The views from here to the coast are stunning.

A favourite of TV motoring shows and weekend bikers, the road is perfectly drivable if you take things slow and steady, but probably best avoided if you're a hesitant reverser or don't like driving next to steep drops. This is not a road to rush; you'll need to be prepared for plenty of reversing when you meet vehicles going the opposite way.

To get to the passes from Ambleside, follow road signs on the A593 to Skelwith Bridge, then turn off to Little Langdale. When you reach the Three Shires Inn, the road gets really steep. Alternatively, you can approach from the west: drive along the A595 coast road and turn off towards Eskdale, then follow the road past Boot to the passes.

Black Bull offers a warren of rooms and a popular outside terrace. The pub grub's good (mains £8 to £18), but it's mainly known for its home-brewed ales: Bluebird Bitter and Old Man Ale are always on tap and there are seasonal ones, too.

ℹ️ Information

Coniston Tourist Office (☎015394-41533; www.conistontic.org; Ruskin Ave; ⊙9.30am-4.30pm Mon-Sat, 10am-2pm Sun)

ℹ️ Getting There & Away

Bus 505 runs to Windermere (£9.80, hourly every day) via Hawkshead and Ambleside. A couple of buses a day go on to Kendal. Note that for most bus journeys, it's better value to buy a 24-hour Central Lakes Dayrider (p572) ticket instead.

The Coniston Bus-and-Boat ticket (adult/child £19/8.30) includes return bus travel on the 505, plus a trip on the launch and entry to Brantwood (p584).

Elterwater & Great Langdale

☎015394

Travelling north from Coniston, the road passes into the wild, empty landscape of Great Langdale, one of Lakeland's iconic hiking valleys. As you pass the pretty village of Elterwater, imposing fells stack up like dominoes along the horizon, looming over a pastoral patchwork of tumbledown barns and lime-green fields.

The circuit around the line-up of fells known as the **Langdale Pikes** – Pike O' Stick-

le (709m), Loft Crag (682m), Harrison Stickle (736m) and Pavey Ark (700m) – is the valley's most popular hike, allowing you to tick off between three and five Wainwrights depending on your route, and covering around six steep, hard-going miles. Allow a good six hours.

🛏️ Sleeping

Langdale YHA HOSTEL £
(☎0845 371 9748; www.yha.org.uk; High Close, Loughrigg; dm £13-32; ⊙Mar-Oct, reception 7-10am & 3-11pm; P@🛜) If you didn't know this was a hostel, you'd think it was a grand country hotel: vast, Victorian and set in private grounds with its own arboretum. Big dorms with sash windows overlook the fells and there's a cavernous kitchen and lounge (with original ornate fireplace). The cafe serves breakfast, packed lunches and a two-course 'supper club'.

Note that it's a couple of miles from Great Langdale, but the 516 bus runs right past.

Great Langdale Campsite CAMPSITE £
(NT; ☎015394-63862; www.nationaltrust.org.uk/features/great-langdale-campsite; Great Langdale; sites £12-25, extra adult £6, pods £35-70; ⊙arrivals 3-7pm Sat-Thu, to 9pm Fri; P) Quite possibly the most spectacularly positioned campsite in the Lake District, spread over grassy meadows overlooked by Langdale's fells. It gets crowded in high season, but 120 sites can be booked in advance; another 50 or so are on a first-come, first-served basis. Camping pods and yurts are also available.

Elterwater Hostel HOSTEL £
(☎015394-37245; www.elterwaterhostel.co.uk; Elterwater; dm/d/f £25/58/124; @) Formerly

owned by the YHA, this indie hostel is in a lovely spot just a short walk from Elterwater's grassy green. It was once a farmhouse but now has 40 beds split across several (mostly six-bed) dorms, some of which can be taken as private family rooms. Breakfast and dinner is available in the cafe, or there's a self-caterers' kitchen.

★ **Old Dungeon Ghyll**   HOTEL **££**

(☑ 015394-37272; www.odg.co.uk; Great Langdale; s £58, d £116-132; P ☎ ☻) Affectionately known as the ODG, this inn is awash with Lakeland heritage: many famous walkers have stayed here, including Prince Charles and mountaineer Chris Bonington. It's endearingly olde worlde (well-worn furniture, four-poster beds) and even if you're not staying, the slate-floored, fire-warmed Hiker's Bar is a must for a posthike pint – it's been the hub of Langdale's social life for decades.

★ **Brimstone Hotel**   HOTEL **£££**

(☑ 015394-38062;   www.brimstonehotel.co.uk; Langdale Estate, Great Langdale; r £340-520; P) This lavish complex on the Langdale Estate offers next-level luxury. The huge suites are more London-chic than Lakeland-cosy – mezzanine floors, sleek tiles, private patios and futuristic log burners are standard, and there's a reading room, Arc'teryx-stocked kit room, private woodland and the superb Stove restaurant. The new Brimstone Spa adds even more spoils: outdoor pool, chill-out rooms, private spa for two.

★ **Eltermere Inn**   HOTEL **£££**

(☑ 015394-37207; www.eltermere.co.uk; Elterwater; r £149-295; P ☎) This charming inn is one of Lakeland's loveliest backwater boltholes. Rooms are simple and classic, tastefully decorated in fawns and taupes with quirky features such as window seats and free-standing baths. The food's excellent, too, served in the inn's snug bar; afternoon tea is served on the lawn on sunny days.

✕ **Eating**

Sticklebarn   PUB FOOD **£**

(☑ 015394-37356; Great Langdale; lunch mains £5-8, dinner mains £11-13.50; ⊙ 11am-9pm) Now run by the National Trust, this converted barn is a walkers' favourite: it's packed with people nursing pints and aching fell-sore legs at the end of the day. Food is wholesome and hearty: herdwick and ale stew, venison ragu and ropa vieja chilli, washed down with a good ale selection.

Chesters by the River   CAFE **££**

(☑ 015394-32553;   www.chestersbytheriver.co.uk; Skelwith Bridge; lunch mains £8-15; ⊙ 9am-5pm) Beside a rattling brook at Skelwith Bridge, halfway between Ambleside and Elterwater, this smart cafe is definitely more gourmet than greasy spoon: delicious salads, specials and cakes make it well worth a stop. There's a chic gift shop, too – items include slate souvenirs from the workshop around the corner.

🛈 **Getting There & Away**

Bus 516 (six daily) is the only bus, with stops at Ambleside, Skelwith Bridge, Elterwater and the Old Dungeon Ghyll hotel in Great Langdale. The fare from Ambleside all the way into Great Langdale is £5.90.

Wasdale

☑ 019467

Carving its way for 5 miles from the Cumbrian coast, the craggy, wind-lashed valley of Wasdale is where the Lake District scenery takes a turn for the wild. Ground out by a long-extinct glacier, the valley is home to the Lake District's highest and wildest peaks, as well as the steely grey expanse of Wastwater, England's deepest and coldest lake.

Wasdale's fells are an irresistible draw for hikers, especially those looking to conquer England's tallest mountain, **Scafell Pike** (978m).

🏃 **Activities**

★ **Scafell Pike**   HIKING

At 978m, England's highest mountain features on every self-respecting hiker's bucket list. The classic route starts from Wasdale Head; it's hard going but within the reach of most moderately fit walkers, although it's steep and hard to navigate in bad weather. It's a return trip of around six to seven hours.

Proper gear is essential: raincoat, rucksack (backpack), map, food, water and hiking boots. A favourable weather forecast is preferable to make the most of the views.

🛏 **Sleeping**

★ **Wasdale Hall YHA**   HOSTEL **£**

(☑ 0845-371 9350; www.yha.org.uk; Wasdale Hall, Nether Wasdale; dm £13-30; ⊙ reception 8-10am & 5-10.30pm; P) This hostel on the shores of Wastwater has the kind of location you'd normally pay through the nose for. It's in a

19th-century mock-Tudor mansion that still has most of its period architecture, including original roof trusses and latticed windows. It has the usual self-catering facilities, plus a very decent restaurant.

Wasdale Head Campsite CAMPSITE £
(NT; ☑bookings 015394-63862; www.national trust.org.uk/features/lake-district-camping; sites £12-25, extra adult £6, pods £35-80) This National Trust campsite is in a fantastically wild spot, nestled beneath the Scafell range. Facilities are basic (laundry room, showers), but the views are out of this world. Camping pods (some with electric hook-ups) and tepees provide a bit more shelter in case Wasdale's notorious weather decides to make an appearance.

★**Wasdale Head Inn** B&B ££
(☑019467-26229; www.wasdale.com; s £59, d £118-130, tr £177; ℗🐕) A slice of hill-walking heritage here. Hunkering beneath the brooding bulk of Scafell Pike, this 19th-century hostelry is gloriously old-fashioned and covered in vintage photos and climbing memorabilia. The rooms are cosy, with roomier suites in a converted stable. The wood-panelled dining room serves fine food, with pub grub and ales from the Great Gable Brewing Co in Ritson's Bar.

Camping is also available for £5 a night.

Cockermouth

☑01900 / POP 9146

Set at the confluence of the River Cocker and River Derwent, the Georgian town of Cockermouth is best known as the birthplace of William Wordsworth and the home base of the renowned Jennings Brewery. Unfortunately, its position beside two major rivers means it has suffered frequent episodes of flooding – most recently in 2009 and 2015, when much of the town centre was swamped.

Sights

★**Wordsworth House** HISTORIC BUILDING
(NT; ☑01900-824805; www.nationaltrust.org.uk/wordsworth-house; Main St; adult/child £7.90/3.95; ⏰11am-5pm Sat-Thu Mar-Oct) The poet William Wordsworth was born on 7 April 1770 at this handsome Georgian house at the end of Main St. Built around 1745, the house has been meticulously restored based on accounts from the Wordsworth archive: the kitchen, drawing room, study and bedrooms all look much as they would have to a young

William. Costumed guides wander around the house for added period authenticity. Outside, the walled kitchen garden was mentioned in Wordsworth's autobiographical epic *The Prelude*.

The house also has some interesting hands-on experiences: you can try using a quill pen in the former clerk's office, play some chords on a harpsichord and (if the maid is in residence on the day you visit) watch meals being prepared over the kitchen's blazing fire. Exhibitions document the Wordsworth family's story and William's poetic legacy.

Jennings Brewery BREWERY
(☑01900-821011; www.jenningsbrewery.co.uk; adult/child £9/4.50; ⏰guided tours 1.30pm Wed-Sat) Real-ale aficionados will be familiar with the Jennings name – it has been brewing beers since 1874 and its pints are pulled at pubs all over the Lake District. Guided tours trace the brewing process, followed by a tasting session of Cocker Hoop and Sneck Lifter in the Old Cooperage Bar. Children must be over 12.

Sleeping

Old Homestead B&B ££
(☑01900-822223; www.byresteads.co.uk; Byresteads Farm; s £40-50, d £60-80; ℗) Byre is an old English dialect word meaning 'cowshed', but you certainly won't be roughing it with the animals at this lovely farm conversion. The rooms are sweet and traditional, blending classic pine, flagstones and rendered walls with modern luxuries like power showers and underfloor heating. The Cruck Rooms and Master's Loft are the pick of the bunch.

It's 2 miles from Cockermouth.

Croft House B&B ££
(☑01900-827533; www.croft-guesthouse.com; 6/8 Challoner St; s £68-88, d £78-98; 🐕) A pleasant little base in a lemon-yellow terraced house along a side road off the town's main street. All the rooms are decorated with great care: from tasteful tartan bedsteads and contemporary wallpapers to little posable bedside lights. Homemade granola and orange pancakes make breakfast a treat.

Eating

★**Merienda** CAFE £
(☑017687-72024; www.merienda.co.uk; 7a Station St; mains £4-8; ⏰8am-9pm Mon-Thu, to 10pm Fri & Sat, 9am-9pm Sun) This Cockermouth fave is open daily and has a second branch in

Keswick. The interior is light and airy and the Med-tinged food is packed with flavour. There's a good balance between meat and veggie-friendly dishes. Carnivores might enjoy a generous slow-cooked BBQ brisket burger, while herbivores should try the excellent baked eggs with feta and aubergine.

Quince & Medlar   VEGETARIAN **££**
(☑ 01900-823579; www.quinceandmedlar.co.uk; 13 Castlegate; mains £15.50; ☺ 7-10pm Tue-Sat; ♪) ♪ Even if you're a committed carnivore, it's well worth dining here to see that vegetarian food isn't just nut roast and baked mushrooms – here, you could find yourself feasting on courgette-wrapped cheese soufflé, root veg and puy lentil 'haggis' or French onion tartlet. The location in a Georgian house is very handsome.

Bitter End   PUB
(☑ 01900-828993; www.bitterend.co.uk; 15 Kirkgate; ☺ noon-2.30pm & 6-10pm) This brewpub produces its own award-winning beers such as Cockermouth Pride, Lakeland Honey Beer and Cuddy Lugs. You can watch the vats at work through a glass partition in the bar.

ℹ Information

Cockermouth Tourist Office (☑ 01900-822634; www.cockermouth.org.uk; 88 Main St; ☺ 10am-4pm Mon-Fri, to 2pm Sat)

ℹ Getting There & Away

Bus X4/X5 (half-hourly Monday to Saturday, hourly Sunday) travels from Cockermouth to Keswick (£6.10) and Penrith (£7.40).

Keswick

☑ 017687 / POP 4821
The most northerly of the Lake District's major towns, Keswick has perhaps the most beautiful location of all: encircled by cloud-capped fells and nestled alongside the idyllic, island-studded lake of Derwentwater, a silvery curve criss-crossed by puttering cruise boats. It's also brilliantly positioned for further adventures into the nearby valleys of Borrowdale and Buttermere, and a great base for walking – the hefty fells of Skiddaw and Blencathra rise nearby.

⊙ Sights

★**Keswick Museum**   MUSEUM
(☑ 017687-73263; www.keswickmuseum.org.uk; Station Rd; adult/child £4.50/3; ☺ 10am-4pm)

Keswick's quirky town museum explores the area's history, from ancient archaeology through to the arrival of industry in the Lakes. It's a diverse collection, taking in everything from neolithic axe heads mined in the Langdale valley to a huge collection of taxidermied butterflies. Its best-known exhibits are a 700-year-old mummified cat and the Musical Stones of Skiddaw, a weird instrument made from hornsfel rock that was once played for Queen Victoria.

Castlerigg Stone Circle   MONUMENT
FREE Set on a hilltop a mile east of town, this jaw-dropping stone circle consists of 48 stones that are between 3000 and 4000 years old, surrounded by a dramatic ring of mountain peaks.

Lakes Distillery   DISTILLERY
(☑ 017687-88850; www.lakesdistillery.com; tours £12.50; ☺ 11am-6pm) The first craft distillery in the Lake District has made a big splash since opening in 2014. It's located on a 'model farm' built during the 1850s and was founded by a team of master distillers. So far its range includes a gin, a vodka and a flagship whisky, plus liqueurs flavoured with damson plum, elderflower, rhubarb and rosehip, and salted caramel. Guided tours take you through the process and include a tasting of the three spirits.

You can also take a specialist whisky tour, and meet the distillery's resident herd of alpacas. The **Bistro at the Distillery** is worth a look for lunch, too.

Whinlatter Forest Park   FOREST
(www.forestry.gov.uk/whinlatter) **FREE** Encompassing 4.6 sq miles of pine, larch and spruce, Whinlatter is England's only true mountain forest, rising sharply to 790m about 5 miles from Keswick. The forest is a designated red squirrel reserve; you can check out live video feeds from squirrel cams at the **visitor centre** (☑ 017687-78469; ☺ 10am-4pm). It's also home to two exciting mountain-bike trails and the **Go Ape** (www.goape.co.uk/days-out/whinlatter; adult/child £33/25; ☺ 9am-5pm mid-Mar–Oct) treetop assault course. You can hire bikes from **Cyclewise** (☑ 017687-78711; www.cyclewise.co.uk; 3hr hire adult/child from £19.50/15; ☺ 10am-5pm), next to the visitor centre.

Entry to the forest is free, but you have to pay for parking (£2 for one hour, £8 all day).

Bus 77 (four daily) runs from Keswick or, if you're driving, head west on the A66 and look out for the brown signs near Braithwaite.

Derwent Pencil Museum
MUSEUM

(☎017687-73626; www.pencilmuseum.co.uk; Southy Works; adult/child £4.95/3.95; ⊙9.30am-5pm) Reopened after being badly damaged in the 2015 floods, Keswick's oddest museum is devoted to the charms of the humble pencil – with exhibits including a pencil made for the Queen's Diamond Jubilee, wartime spy pencils that were hollowed out for secret maps, and the world's largest pencil (a mighty 8m long). It all stems from the discovery of graphite in the Borrowdale valley during the 17th century, after which Keswick became a major pencil manufacturer.

🏃 Activities

Keswick Launch
BOATING

(☎017687-72263; www.keswick-launch.co.uk; round-the-lake pass adult/child/family £10.75/5.65/25.50) Shimmering to the south of Keswick, studded with islands and ringed by craggy fells, Derwentwater is undoubtedly one of the prettiest of the Lakeland lakes. As always, getting out on the water is the best way to explore. The Keswick Launch runs regular cross-lake excursions, and rowboats and motor boats (£12/27 per hour) can be hired next to the jetties.

🎊 Festivals & Events

Keswick Mountain Festival
OUTDOORS

(www.keswickmountainfestival.co.uk; ⊙May) This May festival celebrates all things mountainous.

Keswick Beer Festival
BEER

(www.keswickbeerfestival.co.uk; ⊙Jun) Lots and lots of beer is drunk during Keswick's real-ale fest in June.

🛏 Sleeping

Keswick YHA
HOSTEL £

(☎0845 371 9746; www.yha.org.uk; Station Rd; dm £15-35; ⊙reception 7am-11pm; 🛜) Refurbished after flooding in 2015, Keswick's handsome YHA looks as good as new – its premium facilities include an open-plan ground-floor cafe, a seriously smart kitchen and cracking views over Fitz Park and the rushing River Greta. The dorm decor is standard YHA, but some rooms have private riverside balconies. What a treat!

★ Howe Keld
B&B ££

(☎017687-72417; www.howekeld.co.uk; 5-7 The Heads; s £65-90, d £110-140; 🅿🛜) This gold-standard B&B pulls out all the stops: goose-down duvets, slate-floored bathrooms, chic colours and locally made furniture. The best rooms have views across Crow Park and the golf course, and the breakfast is a pick-and-mix delight. Free parking is available on The Heads if there's space.

Lookout
B&B ££

(☎017687-80407; www.thelookoutkeswick.co.uk; Chestnut Hill; d £90-120; 🅿🛜) The clue's in the name: this three-room B&B is all about the views – there's a panorama of fells filling every window. It's in a gabled 1920s house, but feels modern with cappuccino-and-cream colour schemes, wooden beds and minimalist glass showers. There's a pleasant garden, too. Take Penrith Rd west and turn right onto Chestnut Hill; the B&B is on the left.

Linnett Hill
B&B ££

(☎017687-44518; www.linnetthillkeswick.co.uk; 4 Penrith Rd; s £50, d £88-98; 🛜) Much recommended by travellers, this lovingly run B&B has lots going for it: crisp white rooms, a great location near Fitz Park and keen prices that stay the same year-round. Breakfast is good, too: there's a blackboard of specials to choose from and the dining room has gingham-check tablecloths and a crackling wood burner.

★ Cottage in the Wood
HOTEL £££

(☎017687-78409; www.thecottageinthewood.co.uk; Braithwaite; d £130-220; ⊙restaurant 6.30-9pm Tue-Sat; 🅿🛜) For a secluded spoil, head for this out-of-the-way bolthole, on the road to Whinlatter Forest, in a completely modernised coaching inn. Elegant rooms survey woods and countryside: the Mountain View rooms overlook the Skiddaw Range, but we liked the super-private Attic Suite and the Garden Room, with its wood floors and wetroom. The restaurant's fantastic, too (set dinner menu £45).

🍴 Eating

★ Fellpack
CAFE £

(☎017687-71177; www.fellpack.co.uk; 19 Lake Rd; lunches £4-8; ⊙10am-4pm Wed-Mon, 6-9pm Thu-Sat) This on-trend cafe specialises in 'fell pots' – a Lakeland-style Buddha bowl, incorporating an all-in-one meal such as sweet potato and curry, smoked macaroni and peas, or braised chilli beef, all freshly made and flavour-packed. Flatbreads and baguettes are offered for lunch to go. The owners are full of enthusiasm and the food is zingy and imaginative. We like it. It's also open three nights a week for dinner.

★ Lingholm Kitchen   CAFE £
(☑ 017687-71206; www.thelingholmkitchen.co.uk; mains £7-9; ☺ 9am-5pm) What a setting this splendid cafe has: in a delightful walled garden on the Lingholme Estate, with a 30m glass wall that presents cinematic views of Skiddaw, plus a dainty old greenhouse. For lunch, expect modern brunch dishes such as chickpea fritters, baked eggs, pork croquettes and (of course) avocado on toast.

Jasper's Coffee House   CAFE £
(☑ 017687-73366; 20 Station St; sandwiches from £4, dishes £6-8; ☺ 10am-4pm Mon-Thu, 9am-5pm Fri-Sun; 🐾) Dog fans rejoice: this popular Keswick cafe is nuts about canines. Dishes here are named after dogs of legend (The Muttley, The Old Yeller, The Huckleberry Hound), there are doggie prints on the walls, and naturally, canine companions are welcome. Food-wise, it's standard brunch-lunch fare: pittas, sausage rolls, wraps and sandwiches and cooked breakfasts.

Pheasant Inn   PUB FOOD ££
(☑ 017687-76234; www.the-pheasant.co.uk; Bassenthwaite Lake; mains £13.50-21, restaurant dinner menu £45; ☺ restaurant 7-9pm Wed-Sat, noon-2.30pm Sun, bistro noon-2.30pm & 6-9pm) A short drive along Bassenthwaite Lake is this fine-dining pub. Hunting prints and pewter tankards cover the old bar, stocked with vintage whiskies and Lakeland ales, and the two restaurants (informal bistro and very formal restaurant) serve superior country food. The afternoon tea's done in the proper English fashion too, served on a tiered cake stand with scones and cucumber sandwiches.

Square Orange   CAFE ££
(☑ 017687-73888; www.thesquareorange.co.uk; 20 St John's St; ☺ 10am-11pm Sun-Thu, to midnight Fri & Sat) This lively cafe-bar seems to have become everyone's favourite hangout in Keswick – thanks no doubt to its superb thin-based pizzas, excellent wine and craft beer selection and a regular programme of live gigs. With its big wooden bar and packed-in tables, it feels rather continental – and the coffee is hands-down the best in Keswick.

Morrel's   BRITISH ££
(☑ 017687-72666; www.morrels.co.uk; Lake Rd; 3-course menu £21.95, mains £12.50-22.50; ☺ 5.30-9pm Tue-Sun) Probably the best option in Keswick for a sit-down dinner, Morrel's is

an attractive restaurant majoring in British bistro-style food. Glossy wood, spotlights and glass give it a refined feel.

🍷 Drinking & Nightlife

Dog & Gun   PUB
(☑ 017687-73463; 2 Lake Rd; ☺ 11am-11pm) Benches, beams, hearths, rugs: the old Dog is the picture of a Lakeland pub. Look out for Thirst Rescue ale, which donates part of its proceeds to the Keswick Mountain Rescue Team.

Cafe-Bar 26   BAR
(☑ 017687-80863; 26 Lake Rd; ☺ 9am-11pm Mon-Sat, 10am-10pm Sun) A cosy corner wine bar that also serves good lunches and evening tapas (£4 to £10).

🛍 Shopping

★ George Fisher   SPORTS & OUTDOORS
(☑ 017687-72178; www.georgefisher.co.uk; 2 Borrowdale Rd; ☺ 9am-5.30pm Mon-Sat, 10am-4pm Sun) Quite possibly the most famous outdoors shop in the Lake District, founded in 1967 and still the place where discerning hikers go to buy their gear (even if it is a bit more expensive than the chains). There are three floors of boots, tents and gear, and the boot-fitting service is legendarily thorough.

ℹ Information

Keswick Tourist Office (☑ 017687-72645; www.keswick.org; Moot Hall, Market Pl; ☺ 9.30am-4.30pm; 🖫) The town's tourist office is well run and the staff are very informed. It also sells discounted tickets for the Keswick Launch, and has free wi-fi.

ℹ Getting There & Away

The Keswick & Honister Dayrider (p572) buys unlimited travel on buses in the Keswick area, including on the 77 and 78 buses to Borrowdale and Buttermere (if you're returning the same day, it's also bizarrely cheaper than buying a return). All buses leave from and arrive at the bus station.

Useful buses from Keswick:

555/556 Lakeslink Hourly to Grasmere (£8.30, 40 minutes), Ambleside (£8.80, 45 minutes), Windermere (£9.80, one hour) and Kendal (£10.60, 1½ hours).

77/77A Circular route (five to seven daily) from Keswick via Portinscale, Catbells, Grange, Seatoller, Honister Pass, Buttermere, Lorton and Whinlatter.

78 (at least hourly Monday to Friday, half-hourly weekends) The main Borrowdale bus, with stops at Lodore, Grange, Rosthwaite and Seatoller.

Borrowdale

📞 017687 / POP 417

With their patchwork of craggy hills, broad fields, tinkling streams and drystone walls, the side-by-side valleys of Borrowdale and Buttermere are many people's idea of the quintessential Lakeland landscape. Once a centre for mineral mining (especially slate, coal and graphite), this is walkers' country these days and, apart from the odd rickety barn or puttering tractor, there's precious little to spoil the view.

South of Keswick, the B5289 tracks Derwentwater into the heart of Borrowdale, winding past the small farming villages of Grange-in-Borrowdale, Rosthwaite and Stonethwaite.

◉ Sights & Activities

Watendlath Tarn   LAKE

This National Trust–owned tarn is reached via a turn-off on the B5285 south of Keswick. On the way the road passes over one of the Lake District's most photographed packhorse crossings at **Ashness Bridge**. Parking at the tarn is free for NT members, but the road is narrow and has few passing places, so it's more pleasant to walk up in summer.

Lodore Falls   WATERFALL

At the southern end of Derwentwater, this famous waterfall featured in a poem by Robert Southey, but it's only worth visiting after a good spell of rain. It's in the grounds of the Lodore Hotel; there's an honesty box for donations.

Bowder Stone   NATURAL FEATURE

A mile south from Grange, a turn-off leads up to the geological curiosity known as the Bowder Stone, a 1700-tonnes lump of rock left behind by a retreating glacier. A small stepladder leads to the top of the rock.

Platty+   BOATING

(📞 017687-76572; www.plattyplus.co.uk; kayaks & canoes per hour £8-15) Based at the Lodore Boat Landings at the southern end of Derwentwater, this company hires out kayaks, canoes, rowing boats and sailing dinghies. It also runs instruction courses.

🛏 Sleeping

Seatoller Farm   CAMPSITE £

(📞 017687-77232; www.seatollerfarm.co.uk; adult/child £7/3; ☺ Easter-Oct) A lovely, tucked-away site on a 500-year-old farm near Seatoller with a choice of riverside or woodland pitches. B&B rooms (double £75 to £90) are offered in the farmhouse.

Borrowdale YHA   HOSTEL £

(📞 0845 371 9624; www.yha.org.uk; Longthwaite; dm £15-30; ☺ Feb-Dec; P 🔊) This friendly hostel makes a super, outdoorsy base for forays around Borrowdale. It's in a lovely spot next to a babbling brook, surrounded by gardens and fells. Part timber-clad, it has the feel of a ski chalet with convivial dorms, a big kitchen and lounge, table tennis and snooker tables as well as a wildlife area outside.

Derwentwater Independent Hostel   HOSTEL £

(📞 017687-77246; www.derwentwater.org; Barrow House; dm £24, s & d £60, tr £66-75, q £83-96; P @) Built as a 19th-century mansion, this grand Grade II–listed house is one of Britain's most architecturally ostentatious hostels. Previously YHA-owned, now private, it's a thing of beauty: many rooms have original features such as plasterwork and fireplaces. The 7-hectare grounds encompass an artificial waterfall.

★ Langstrath Inn   B&B ££

(📞 017687-77239; www.thelangstrath.com; Stonethwaite; d £114-140; ☺ restaurant noon-2.30pm & 6-8.30pm Tue-Sun; P 🔊) This simple country inn makes one of the best little bases in Borrowdale. Its eight rooms are snug and simple, with crimson throws and the occasional roof beam to add character – but it's the views that really sell the place. Hearty, unpretentious food (dinner mains £13.25) and ales from Hawkshead Brewery are served in the restaurant.

Glaramara Hotel   HOTEL ££

(📞 017687-77222; www.glaramarahouse.co.uk; Seatoller; s £59, d £74-118; P 🔊 ❄) If your budget won't stretch to one of Borrowdale's plush country hotels, this great-value, activity-focused place makes a good alternative. The decor is corporate (pine-effect furniture, no-frills furnishings), but the location can't be faulted: on the doorstep of Honister Pass, surrounded by fells and greenery. The hotel has its own outdoor activities centre for ghyll scrambling, rock climbing, mine exploring and more.

ℹ Getting There & Away

Bus 77/77A (from £3.10, seven daily Monday to Saturday, five on Sunday) makes a circular route from Keswick via Portinscale, the trailhead for Catbells and all the Borrowdale villages, then heads over Honister Pass, through Buttermere and Lorton, over the Whinlatter Pass and back to Keswick.

Bus 78 (£6.20 to £8.30, at least hourly, half-hourly on weekends from July to August) shuttles through Borrowdale as far as Seatoller, then heads back the same way to Keswick.

If you're planning on making a return journey the same day, it's nearly always cheaper to buy the Keswick & Honister Dayrider (p572) than a return fare.

Buttermere

017687 / POP 121

Stretching 1.5 miles northwest of Honister Pass, the deep bowl of Buttermere was gouged out by a steamroller glacier and backed by a string of impressive peaks and emerald-green hills. The valley's twin lakes, **Buttermere** and **Crummock Water**, were once joined but became separated by glacial silt and rockfall.

The little village of Buttermere sits halfway between the two and provides a wonderfully cosy base for exploring the rest of the valley and the many nearby fells, including **Haystacks** (597m), the favourite mountain and the last resting place of the patron saint of Lakeland walkers, the author Alfred Wainwright.

🛏 Sleeping & Eating

★ Buttermere YHA
HOSTEL £

(📞 0845 371 9508; www.yha.org.uk; dm £13-32; ⊙ mid-Mar–Oct, reception 8.30-10am & 5-10.30pm; 🅿🛜) Perched in a perfect position on the Honister–Buttermere road, this excellent slate-fronted hostel (once a hotel) has rooms looking out across the lake. The decor is smart, colourful and surprisingly modern, and there's a great cafe-kitchen and plenty of four- and six-bed dorms. There's also space to pitch a tent during summer holidays.

Syke Farm
CAMPSITE £

(📞 017687-70222; www.sykefarmcampsite.com; adult/child £8/4; ⊙ Easter-Oct) Set on a bumpy riverside site, Syke Farm is back-to-basics camping, but you'll wake up to views of Red Pike, High Stile and Haystacks. Check in at the farm shop in the village first and don't forget to sample some of its homemade ice cream.

★ Kirkstile Inn
PUB FOOD ££

(📞 01900-85219; www.kirkstile.com; mains £11.50-15.95) A finer country pub you could not

HONISTER PASS

From Borrowdale, a narrow, perilously steep road snakes up the fellside to Honister Pass, home to the last working slate mine in the UK. Though you can still pick up slate souvenirs in the on-site shop, these days the **Honister Slate Mine** (📞 017687-77230; www.honister. com; mine tour adult/child £14.50/8.50, all-day pass incl mine tour & classic/extreme via ferrata £56.50/64; ⊙ tours 10.30am, 12.30pm & 3.30pm Mar-Oct) has diversified with a range of adventure activities, ranging from subterranean tours to thrilling **via ferrata** (classic route £40, extreme incl Infinity Bridge £45, all day pass incl mine tour & classic/extreme via ferrata £56.50/64) walks. An all-day pass covering all activities costs £56.50/43.50 per adult/child.

hope to find. Hidden away near the little lake of Loweswater, a mile or so north of Buttermere, the Kirkstile is a joy: crackling fires, oak beams, worn carpets, wooden bar and all. It's particularly known for its award-winning ales (try the Loweswater Gold).

Rooms (singles £85 to £105, doubles £117 to £137) are quaint; some have views across Lorton Vale.

Bridge Hotel
PUB FOOD ££

(📞 017687-70252; www.bridge-hotel.com; mains £10-16; 🅿🛜) As the name suggests, this venerable hostelry is right beside Buttermere's village bridge. There's standard pub food in the bar, or more upmarket fare in the smart-casual restaurant. Frilly rooms (singles from £84.50, doubles £169 to £189) and an antique ambience define the old Bridge.

Fish Inn
PUB FOOD ££

(📞 017687-70253; www.fishinnbuttermere.co.uk; mains £8-16; 🅿) This whitewashed inn (doubles £90 to £125) once employed the 18th-century beauty known as the 'Maid of Buttermere', but these days it's just a welcoming locals' pub serving basic staples such as lasagne and battered haddock, washed down with ales from several local breweries.

ℹ Getting There & Away

Bus 77/77A (£6.20, five to seven daily) serves Buttermere and Honister Pass from Keswick. For return journeys the same day, save a bit of

Driving Tour
Borrowdale & Buttermere

START KESWICK
END KESWICK
LENGTH 28 MILES; THREE TO FOUR HOURS

This is one of the Lakes' most beautiful road trips, a perfect day trip out of Keswick.

Begin with breakfast in ➊ **Keswick** (p589), then head along the B5289 into Borrowdale. First stop is ➋ **Lodore Falls** (p592), a pretty cascade at the southern end of Derwentwater. Next, detour to the little hamlet of ➌ **Grange-in-Borrowdale**, where a trail leads up the slate-strewn sides of Castle Crag, a small fell with great views over Borrowdale.

From Grange carry on to the huge boulder known as the ➍ **Bowder Stone** (p592), shifted into position by the long-gone glacier that carved out the Borrowdale Valley. Pootle on to ➎ **Rosthwaite** for tea and cake at the Flock In Tea-Room, or continue to ➏ **Seatoller** for lunch.

In the afternoon tackle the steep crawl up to ➐ **Honister Pass** (p593), where you can

pick up some slate souvenirs, take a tour into the depths of the old slate mine or venture out onto the hair-raising *via ferrata*.

From here the road drops down into the beautiful valley of ➑ **Buttermere** (p593). Spot the zigzag peaks of High Stile, Haystacks and Red Pike looming on your left-hand side over the lake, stop off for a drink at the Fish Inn and remember to pay your respects to hiker and author Alfred Wainwright inside St James' Church.

Continue along the shore of Crummock Water past ➒ **Loweswater**, where you could make an optional but very worthwhile detour via the excellent Kirkstile Inn. When you reach ➓ **Low Lorton**, a right-hand turn carries you over Whinlatter Pass to ⑪ **Whinlatter Forest Park** (p589).

There are a couple of great options for dinner on your way back to Keswick, such as ⑫ **Cottage in the Wood** (p590) just before Braithwaite, or the traditional Pheasant Inn on the shores of Bassenthwaite Lake.

cash by buying the Keswick & Honister Dayrider (p572).

Ullswater & Around

☑ 017684

After Windermere, the second-largest lake in the Lake District is Ullswater, stretching for 7.5 miles between Pooley Bridge at the northern end and Glenridding and Patterdale at the southern end. Carved out by a long-extinct glacier, the deep valley in which the lake sits is flanked by an impressive string of fells, most notably the razor ridge of Helvellyn, Cumbria's third-highest mountain at 950m.

The lake's eastern shore is where the three main villages are located. The remote west side is well off the beaten track, and great for crowd-free hiking around the village of Howtown and the picturesque valley of Martindale.

The villages around Ullswater were badly hit in the 2015 floods. You'll see major flood defence works in Glenridding, while the eponymous bridge in Pooley Bridge was swept away – there's a temporary one in place for now, with plans ongoing to replace it with a permanent flood-resistant structure.

⊙ Sights & Activities

★ Helvellyn   HIKING
Along with Scafell Pike (p587), this challenging hike is the one everyone wants to do. The classic ascent takes in the twin ridges of Striding and Swirral Edge, which are spectacular but very exposed and involve some scrambling and dizzyingly steep drops on either side – if you're at all nervous of heights, Helvellyn is not the fell for you.

The usual routes climb up through Glenridding or Patterdale. Always check the weather forecast and take all the necessary supplies.

Ullswater 'Steamers'   BOATING
(☑ 017684-82229; www.ullswater-steamers.co.uk; cruise all piers pass adult/child £15.95/6.95) Ullswater's historic steamers are a memorable way to explore the lake. The various vessels include the stately *Lady of the Lake*, launched in 1877 and supposedly the world's oldest working passenger boat. The boats run east–west from Pooley Bridge to Glenridding via Howtown; there are nine daily sailings in summer, three in winter.

Gowbarrow Park & Aira Force   PARK, WATERFALL
(NT) **FREE** This rolling park stretches out across the lakeshore between Pooley Bridge and Glenridding. Well-marked paths lead up to the impressive 20m waterfall of Aira Force. Another waterfall, High Force, is further up the hillside. South of Gowbarrow Park is Glencoyne Bay, where the springtime daffodils inspired William Wordsworth to pen one of his most famous poems.

🛏 Sleeping

Quiet Site   CAMPSITE £
(☑ 07768-727016; www.thequietsite.co.uk; campsites £25-44, pods £35-65, hobbit holes £65-100; ⊗year-round; 🅿🛜) Ecofriendly campsite on the fells above Ullswater, with pre-erected tents and ecopods available as well as 'hobbit holes' (timber-lined cabins built into the hillside). Camping is very pricey in summer, but there's plenty of space, and the views are outstanding.

Helvellyn YHA   HOSTEL £
(☑ 0845 371 9742; www.yha.org.uk; Greenside; dm £13-30; ⊗Easter-Oct) This back-of-beyond hostel is a favourite of hikers looking to get an early start on Helvellyn. It's in an old miner's cottage about a 900m hike up from the valley. Dorms are small and facilities are basic, but meals are provided by hostel staff. There's even a bar.

Patterdale YHA   HOSTEL £
(☑ 0845 371 9337; www.yha.org.uk; Patterdale; dm £13-30; ⊗Easter-Oct, reception 7.30-10am & 3-11pm) This 1970s hostel lacks the heritage of some of the Lakeland YHAs, but it has a great location by the lake and all the usual YHA trappings (kitchen, cafe, TV lounge) – as long as you don't mind the rather institutional architecture.

Old Water View   B&B ££
(☑ 017684-82175; www.oldwaterview.co.uk; Patterdale; d £98; 🅿🛜) Patterdale has several B&Bs, but this one's the pick. It's a simple place focusing on the essentials: friendly service, comfy rooms and good value. The split-level Bothy room is ideal for families, with attic beds for the kids, while Little Gem overlooks a stream and Place Fell was a favourite of Alfred Wainwright (his signature is on the wall).

★ Another Place, The Lake   BOUTIQUE HOTEL £££
(☑ 017684-86442; www.another.place; Watermillock; r £230-290, f £345-385; 🅿🛜🐾🏊)

Acquired by the owners of Cornwall's Watergate Bay Hotel, the former Rampsbeck Hotel has been reinvented as one of the Lakes' most luxurious, family-friendly, activity-focused getaways. A striking new wing has added an infinity pool and contemporary rooms – rooms in the old house feel more traditional. There's a restaurant, bar, well-stocked library and lakefront lawns, and activities including SUP, kayaking and wild swimming.

✕ Eating

Granny Dowbekin's   CAFE £
(☑ 017684-86453;   www.grannydowbekins.co.uk; Pooley Bridge; mains £6-12; ☺ 9am-5pm) For a filling all-day brekkie, a ploughman's lunch, chunky sandwich or a slice of something naughty and cake-shaped, this attractive cafe in Pooley Bridge is a favourite option. The homemade 'gingerbridge' makes a yummy souvenir.

Fellbites   CAFE ££
(☑ 017684-82781; Glenridding; lunch mains £3.95-9.95, dinner mains £12.50-18; ☺ 9am-8.30pm Thu-Tue, to 5.30pm Wed) This cafe beside the main car park in Glenridding has something to fill you up at any time of day: generous fry-ups for breakfast; soups, pulled-pork burgers and rarebits for lunch; lamb shanks and duck breast for dinner. It's honest, no-fuss grub.

1863   BISTRO ££
(☑ 017684-86334; www.1863ullswater.co.uk; High St, Pooley Bridge; mains £13.50-22.50; ☺dinner 6-9pm, bar 2-10pm) A classy new addition to Pooley Bridge's dining scene, overseen by head chef Phil Corrie, who has a fondness for the classics but is abreast of modern tastes, too – so you get dishes like Goosnargh Chicken with morels and truffled potato, or mead-glazed duck with sweet damson jam.

There are rooms upstairs, too (doubles £95 to £150), showcasing some adventurous wallpaper choices.

❶ Information

Lake District National Park Ullswater Information Centre (☑ 017684-82414; ullswatertic@lake-district.gov.uk; Glenridding; ☺ 9.30am-5.30pm Apr-Oct, to 3.30pm weekends Nov-Mar)

❶ Getting There & Away

Bus 508 travels from Penrith to Glenridding and Patterdale (£5.50, nine daily). Five buses continue over Kirkstone Pass to Windermere.

The Ullswater Bus-and-Boat Combo ticket (adult/child/family £16/9/34) includes a day's travel on bus 508 with a return trip on an Ullswater Steamer; buy the ticket on the bus.

Kendal
☑ 015395 / POP 28,586

Technically Kendal isn't in the Lake District, but it's a major gateway town. Often known as the 'Auld Grey Town' thanks to the sombre grey stone used for many of its buildings, Kendal is a bustling shopping centre with some good restaurants, a funky arts centre and intriguing museums. But it'll forever be synonymous in many people's minds with its famous mint cake, a staple item in the nation's hiking packs ever since Edmund Hillary and Tenzing Norgay munched it during their ascent of Everest in 1953.

◉ Sights

Abbot Hall Art Gallery   GALLERY
(☑ 01539-722464;   www.abbothall.org.uk;   adult/child £7/free, joint ticket with Museum of Lakeland Life & Industry £9; ☺ 10.30am-5pm Mon-Sat Apr-Oct, to 4pm Nov-Mar) Kendal's fine-art gallery houses one of the northwest's best collections of 18th- and 19th-century art. It's especially strong on portraiture and Lakeland landscapes: look out for works by Constable, John Ruskin and local boy George Romney, who was born in Dalton-in-Furness in 1734 and became a sought-after portraitist, as well as a key figure in the 'Kendal School'.

Kendal Museum   MUSEUM
(☑ 01539-815597;   www.kendalmuseum.org.uk; Station Rd; £2; ☺10am-4pm Tue-Sat) Founded in 1796 by the inveterate Victorian collector William Todhunter, this mixed-bag museum features everything from stuffed beasts and transfixed butterflies to medieval coin hoards. There's also a reconstruction of the office of Alfred Wainwright, who served as honorary curator at the museum from 1945 to 1974: look out for his well-chewed pipe and knapsack.

Museum of Lakeland
Life & Industry   MUSEUM
(☑ 01539-722464;   www.lakelandmuseum.org.uk; adult/child £5/free, joint ticket with Abbot Hall Art Gallery £9; ☺ 10.30am-5pm Mon-Sat Mar-Oct, to 4pm Nov-Feb) Directly opposite Abbot Hall, this museum recreates various scenes from Lakeland life during the 18th and 19th centuries, including a farmhouse parlour,

ENNERDALE

If you really want to leave the outside world behind, the remote valley of Ennerdale is definitely the place. Just to the north of Wasdale, this valley and its namesake lake were once home to slate mines and large timber plantations, but these are slowly being removed and the valley is being returned to nature as part of the Wild Ennerdale (www. wildennerdale.co.uk) project.

Needless to say, the valley is paradise if you prefer your trails quiet. Several popular routes head over the fells to Wasdale, while walking towards Buttermere takes you past the **Black Sail YHA** (☑0845-371 9680; www.yha.org.uk; dm £35; ⊙mid-Mar–Oct, check-in 5-9pm) 🍴, a marvellously remote hostel inside a shepherd's bothy. Much loved by mountaineers and hikers, it's become a YHA landmark. Space is very limited, so make sure you book ahead.

a Lakeland kitchen, an apothecary and the study of Arthur Ransome, author of *Swallows and Amazons* – look out for some of his original sketchbooks.

Levens Hall HISTORIC BUILDING
(☑015395-60321; www.levenshall.co.uk; house & gardens adult/child £13.90/5, gardens only £9.90/4; ⊙house noon-4pm, gardens 10am-5pm Sun-Thu Mar-Oct) This Elizabethan manor is built around a mid-13th-century fortified pele tower, and fine Jacobean furniture litters its interior, although the real draw is the 17th-century topiary garden – a surreal riot of pyramids, swirls, curls, pompoms and peacocks straight out of *Alice in Wonderland*.

Sizergh Castle CASTLE
(NT; ☑015395-60070; www.nationaltrust.org. uk/sizergh; adult/child £11.50/5.75, gardens only £7.50/3.75; ⊙house noon-4pm Apr-Oct, gardens 10am-5pm) Three-and-a-half miles south of Kendal along the A591, this castle is the feudal seat of the Strickland family. Set around a pele tower, its finest asset is the lavish wood panelling on display in the Inlaid Chamber, as well as a huge 650-hectare estate encompassing lakes, orchards, woods and pastureland.

🛏 Sleeping

Kendal Hostel HOSTEL £
(☑01539-724066; www.kendalhostel.com; 118-120 Highgate; dm/d £20/40; ⊙reception open 5-8pm; @🛜) An ex-YHA, this basic hostel has 14 rooms variously sleeping two to 14 people in mixed and single-sex dorms. Spread over four floors, it's a friendly place. There's a shared kitchen, lounge and a free pool table on the ground floor, plus lockers for storage (you might need your own padlock). It's next door to the Brewery Arts Centre (p598).

Sonata Guest House B&B ££
(☑01539-732290; www.sonataguesthouse.co.uk; 19 Burneside Rd; d £85-90; 🛜) Nothing too swish at this B&B in a Kendal-typical grey-stone terraced house, but it's cosy enough with feminine rooms, floral wallpapers and nice little touches such as goose-down pillows and well-stocked tea trays. Parking is a pain.

Lyth Valley Country Inn HOTEL £££
(☑015395-68295; www.lythvalley.com; Lyth; d £150-200, ste £240-300; 🅿🛜) It's seven miles west of Kendal, but there's a reason to head out so far – this hotel sits in a gorgeous spot overlooking the little-visited Lyth Valley, famous locally for its damson plums. Rooms are really attractive, with solid wooden furniture and patches of exposed brickwork (we liked the quirky names too, such as Hopping Hare and Quacking Duck).

The oak-panelled restaurant (mains £13.95 to £18.95) is high quality.

🍴 Eating

Brew Brothers CAFE £
(☑01539-722237; www.brew-brothers.co.uk; 69 Highgate; mains £8.50-10; ⊙8.30am-5.30pm Mon-Sat) The hipster cafe comes to Kendal at this new number on Highgate. With its scruffy wood furniture and black-aproned baristas, it's got the aesthetic down, but its owners are Lakeland through and through – they previously ran a cafe in Windermere. Go for smashed avocado and poached eggs for brekkie, then for lunch wolf down a hot-smoked-salmon sandwich. Yum.

Yard 46 CAFE £
(☑07585-320522; www.yard46.co.uk; Branthwaite Brow; lunches £3-8; ⊙10am-4pm Mon-Fri, to 5pm Sat) Kendal is well stocked with cafes, but

this gem is well worth seeking out. It's down a blink-and-you'll-miss-it alleyway, with a little courtyard and an old whitewashed building with cruck-framed attic dining room. Delicious soups, imaginative salads and yummy cakes, plus unusual options such as *pan con tomate* (tomato bruschetta) and veggie brunch baps with a fried duck's egg.

Baba Ganoush DELI £
(☑ 01539-738210; www.baba-ganoush.co.uk; Finkle St; mains £5-9; ☺ 10.30am-3pm Tue-Sat) Down a side alley, this Mediterranean-inspired cafe serves up delicious lunches of falafels, lamb stews, veggie meze and Moroccan tagines, plus a big range of salads. It's recently moved a little way down the street to give more space for diners.

★**Punch Bowl Inn** PUB FOOD ££
(☑ 015395-68237; www.the-punchbowl.co.uk; Crosthwaite; mains £15.95-24.50; ☺ noon-4pm & 5.30-8.30pm; [P]) If you don't mind a drive, this renowned gastropub in the village of Crosthwaite has long been known for its top-notch food. Whitewashed outside, carefully modernised inside, it's a cosy, inviting space to dine. Chef Scott Fairweather's superb food blends classic dishes with cheffy ingredients (oyster mousse, potato croquettes, pea fricassée, salsify).

The rooms (£135 to £320) are lovely, too: they're all different, but the nicest ones have reclaimed beams, sloping eaves, slate-floored bathrooms and his-and-hers claw-foot tubs.

★**The Moon Highgate** BISTRO ££
(☑ 01539-729254; www.themoonhighgate.com; 129 Highgate; lunch £6-12, dinner £17-21; ☺ 11.30am-2.15pm Tue-Sat & 5.30-9.15pm Tue-Fri, 6-9.30pm Sat) Now run by prodigiously talented chef Leon Whitehead, this smart bistro takes its cue from the seasons and the pick of Cumbrian produce. Classic flavours sit alongside surprises: watercress panna cotta, or hen's egg with onion broth. Dishes are beautifully plated, veggie choice is good and the uncluttered space is a winner. The town's top table, no question.

☆ **Entertainment**

Brewery Arts Centre THEATRE, CINEMA
(☑ 01539-725133; www.breweryarts.co.uk; Highgate) A cracking arts centre with a gallery, cafe, theatre and two cinemas, hosting the latest films as well as music, theatre, dance and much more.

🛍 **Shopping**

★**Low Sizergh Barn** FOOD
(☑ 015395-60426; www.lowsizerghbarn.co.uk; ☺ 9am-5.30pm) A prodigious selection of Lakeland goodies are available at this farm shop, just outside Kendal on the A590. There's also a farm trail and woodland walk to follow if the weather's nice, and you can watch the cows being milked – look out for the raw-milk vending machine beside the shop entrance. Only in Cumbria!

ℹ **Getting There & Away**

The train line from Windermere runs to Kendal (£5.90, 15 minutes, hourly) en route to Oxenholme.

Bus 555/556 Regular bus (half-hourly Monday to Friday, hourly at weekends) to Windermere (£6.50, 30 minutes), Ambleside (£7.60, 40 minutes) and Grasmere (£8.80, 1¼ hours).

Bus 106 To Penrith (£11.30, 80 minutes, one or two daily Monday to Friday).

CUMBRIAN COAST

☑ 01229

While the central lakes and fells pull in a never-ending stream of visitors, surprisingly few ever make the trek west to explore Cumbria's coastline. And that's a shame. While it might not compare to the wild grandeur of Northumberland, or the rugged splendour of Scotland's shores, Cumbria's coast is well worth exploring – a bleakly beautiful landscape of long sandy bays, grassy headlands, salt marshes and seaside villages stretching all the way from Morecambe Bay to the shores of the Solway Coast. There's an important seabird reserve at St Bees Head and the majestic grounds of Holker Hall are well worth a wander.

Historically, Cumbria's coast served the local mining, quarrying and shipping industries and Barrow-in-Furness remains a major shipbuilding centre. More controversial is the nuclear plant of Sellafield, a major employer but still dividing opinion half a century on from its inception.

◉ **Sights & Activities**

★**Ravenglass & Eskdale Railway** RAIL
(☑ 01229-717171; www.ravenglass-railway.co.uk; adult/child/family 24hr pass £15/9/44.95; 🚃) Affectionately known as La'al Ratty, this pocket-sized railway was built to ferry iron ore from the Eskdale mines to the coast.

CARTMEL

Tiny Cartmel is known for three things: its 12th-century **priory** (9am-5.30pm May-Oct, to 3.30pm Nov-Apr) FREE, its small **racecourse** and its world-famous sticky toffee pudding, sold at the **Cartmel Village Shop** (015395-36280; www.cartmelvillageshop.co.uk; 1 The Square; 9am-5pm Mon-Sat, 10am-4.30pm Sun).

More recently it's become known as the home of chef Simon Rogan (dubbed Cumbria's answer to Heston Blumenthal). His flagship restaurant, **L'Enclume** (015395-36362; www.lenclume.co.uk; Cavendish St; set lunch £59, lunch & dinner menu £155; noon-1.30pm & 6.30-8.30pm Tue-Sun), showcases his boundary-pushing cuisine and madcap presentation as well as his passion for foraged ingredients.

He also runs a less formal bistro, **Rogan & Company** (015395-35917; www.roganandcompany.co.uk; The Square; 2-/3-course set lunch £20/26, mains £18-25; noon-2pm & 6-9pm Mon & Wed-Sat, 12.15-3.15pm Sun), across the village. Bookings are essential for both.

These days it's one of Cumbria's most beloved family attractions, with miniature steam trains that chug for 7 miles through the Eskdale valley between the coastal town of Ravenglass and the village of Dalegarth, and several stations in between.

There are seven to 14 trains a day depending on the season; fares are cheaper outside summer. Dogs (£1.50) are welcome on board, and you can take bikes (£4), but they have to be booked in advance. You also get a 50% discount on trips on Ullswater Steamers (p595).

⭐ **Holker Hall**   HISTORIC BUILDING
(015395-58328; www.holker.co.uk; adult/child £12.50/free; house 11am-4pm, grounds 10.30am-5pm Wed-Sun Mar-Oct) Three miles east of Cartmel on the B5278, Holker Hall has been the family seat of the Cavendish family for nigh on four centuries. Though parts of it date from the 16th century, the house was almost entirely rebuilt following a devastating fire in 1871. It's a typically ostentatious Victorian affair, covered with mullioned windows, gables and copper-topped turrets outside and filled with a warren of lavishly over-the-top rooms inside.

Among the highlights are the **drawing room**, packed with Chippendale furniture and historic oil paintings, and the **library**, containing an antique microscope belonging to Henry Cavendish (discoverer of nitric acid) and more than 3500 antique books (some of which are fakes, designed to conceal light switches when the house was converted to electric power in 1911). The showstopper is the **Long Gallery**, notable for its plasterwork ceiling and fine English furniture – look for the 19th-century sphinx-

legged table and a wonderful walnut cabinet inlaid with ivory and rosewood.

Outside, Holker's grounds sprawl for more than 10 hectares, encompassing a rose garden, a woodland, ornamental fountains and a 22m-high lime tree.

There's also a food hall that stocks produce from the estate, including two renowned products: venison and salt marsh lamb.

St Bees Head   WILDLIFE RESERVE
(RSPB; stbees.head@rspb.org.uk) Five-and-a-half miles south of Whitehaven and 1½ miles north of the tiny town of St Bees, this wind-battered headland is one of Cumbria's most important reserves for nesting seabirds. Depending on the season, species nesting here include fulmars, kittiwakes and razorbills, as well as Britain's only population of resident black guillemots. There are more than 2 miles of cliff paths to explore.

Muncaster Castle   CASTLE
(01229-717614; www.muncaster.co.uk; adult/child £14.50/7.30; gardens & owl centre 10.30am-5pm, castle noon-4pm Sun-Fri) This crenellated castle, 1.5 miles east of Ravenglass, was originally built around a 14th-century pele tower, constructed to resist Reiver raids. Home to the Pennington family for seven centuries, the castle's architectural highlights are its great hall and octagonal library, and outside you'll find an ornamental maze and splendid grounds. The castle is also home to a hawk and owl centre, which stages several flying displays a day. There's a 15% discount for booking online.

Muncaster is also known for its numerous ghosts: keep your eyes peeled for the

THE LAKE DISTRICT & CUMBRIA CUMBRIAN COAST

Muncaster Boggle and a malevolent jester known as Tom Fool (hence 'tomfoolery').

Laurel & Hardy Museum
MUSEUM

(☑ 01229-582292; www.laurel-and-hardy.co.uk; Brogden St, Ulverston; adult/child £5/2.50; ⊙ 10am-5pm Easter-Oct, closed Mon & Wed rest of year) Founded by avid Laurel and Hardy collector Bill Cubin back in 1983, this madcap museum in Ulverston (the birthplace of Stan Laurel) has new premises inside the town's old Roxy cinema. It's crammed floor-to-ceiling with cinematic memorabilia, from original posters to film props, and there's a shoebox-sized cinema showing back-to-back Laurel and Hardy classics. Now run by Bill's grandson, it's a must for movie buffs.

❶ Getting There & Away

The Furness and Cumbrian Coast railway lines loop 120 miles from Lancaster to Carlisle, stopping at the coastal resorts of Grange, Ulverston, Ravenglass, Whitehaven and Workington. The **Cumbria Coast Day Ranger** (adult/child £20.20/10.10) covers a day's unlimited travel on the line and works out cheaper than a return journey from Carlisle or Lancaster.

NORTHERN & EASTERN CUMBRIA

Many visitors speed through the northern and eastern reaches of Cumbria in a headlong dash for the Lake District, but it's worth taking the time to venture inland from the national park. It might not have the big-name fells and chocolate-box villages, but it's full of interest, with traditional towns, crumbling castles, abandoned abbeys and sweeping moors set alongside the magnificent Roman engineering project of Hadrian's Wall.

Carlisle

☑ 01228 / POP 75,306

Carlisle isn't Britain's prettiest city, but it has history and heritage aplenty. Precariously perched on the frontier between England and Scotland, in the area once ominously dubbed the 'Debatable Lands', Cumbria's capital is a city with a notoriously stormy past: sacked by the Vikings, pillaged by the Scots and plundered by the Border Reivers, the city has been on the front line of England's defences for more than 1000 years.

Reminders of the past are evident in its great crimson castle and cathedral, built from the same rosy-red sandstone as most of the city's houses. On English St, you can also see two massive circular **towers** that once flanked the city's gateway.

The closest section of Hadrian's Wall begins at nearby Brampton.

⊙ Sights

★ Carlisle Castle
CASTLE

(EH; ☑ 01228-591922; www.english-heritage.org. uk/visit/places/carlisle-castle; Castle Way; adult/child £8/4.80, combined ticket with Cumbria's Museum of Military Life £9.20/5.15; ⊙ 10am-6pm Apr-Sep, to 5pm Oct-Mar) Carlisle's brooding, rust-red castle lurks on the north side of the city. Founded around a Celtic and Roman stronghold, the castle's Norman keep was added in 1092 by William Rufus, and later refortified by Henry II, Edward I and Henry VIII (who added the supposedly cannon-proof towers). From the battlements, the stirring views stretch as far as the Scottish borders. The castle also houses **Cumbria's Museum of Military Life** (☑ 01228-532774; adult/child £4.50/2.50, combined ticket with Carlisle Castle £9.20/5.15; ⊙ 10am-6pm Apr-Oct, to 5pm Sat-Thu Nov-Mar), which has collections of military memorabilia associated with the region's regiments.

The castle has witnessed some dramatic events over the centuries: Mary, Queen of Scots, was imprisoned here in 1568, and it was the site of a notorious eight-month siege during the English Civil War, when the Royalist garrison survived by eating rats, mice and the castle dogs before finally surrendering in 1645. Look out for some medieval graffiti and the 'licking stones' in the dungeon, which Jacobite prisoners supposedly lapped for moisture.

Carlisle Cathedral
CHURCH

(☑ 01228-548151; www.carlislecathedral.org.uk; 7 The Abbey; suggested donation £5, photography £1; ⊙ 7.30am-6.15pm Mon-Sat, to 5pm Sun) Built from the same red sandstone as Carlisle Castle, Carlisle's cathedral began life as a priory church in 1122 and became a cathedral when its first abbot, Athelwold, became the first bishop of Carlisle. Among its notable features are the 15th-century choir stalls, the barrel-vaulted roof and the 14th-century East Window, one of the largest Gothic windows in England. Surrounding the cathedral are other priory relics, including the 16th-century **fratry** and the **prior's tower**.

Tullie House Museum
MUSEUM

(☑01228-618718; www.tulliehouse.co.uk; Castle St; adult/child £6.50/free; ⊙10am-5pm Mon-Sat, 11am-5pm Sun) Carlisle's flagship museum covers 2000 years of the city's past. The Roman Frontier Gallery explores Carlisle's Roman foundations, while the Border Galleries cover the Bronze Age through to the Industrial Revolution. Two galleries flesh out the story: the Border Reivers covers the marauding bandits who once terrorised the area, while the Vikings Revealed exhibition displays finds from the Cumwhitton Viking cemetery, including helmets, swords and grave goods. The top-floor Lookout has cracking views of the castle.

🛌 Sleeping

★Halston Aparthotel
HOTEL ££

(☑01228-210240; www.thehalston.com; 20-34 Warwick Rd; 1-bed apt £120-140, 2-bed apt £240-280; P 🛜) For a city-centre base, this complex of self-catering apartments really has to be the pick of places to stay in Carlisle. While not huge, the apartments are well appointed with small studio kitchens, modern decor, parquet-style flooring, sash windows and zero clutter, and the setting in the Edwardian-era building (formerly Carlisle's General Post Office) is a real stunner.

★Willowbeck Lodge
B&B ££

(☑01228-513607; www.willowbeck-lodge.com; Lambley Bank, Scotby; d £100-140; P 🛜) If staying in the city centre isn't important, then this palatial B&B is the top choice in the city. The four rooms are huge, contemporary and plush, with luxuries such as underfloor heating, Egyptian-cotton bedding and tasteful shades of beige and taupe. Some rooms have balconies overlooking the gardens and pond.

Warwick Hall
B&B £££

(☑01228-561546; www.warwickhall.org; Warwick-on-Eden; s £85-150, d £90-220) This fine country house, 2 miles from the centre along Warwick Rd, is a real country retreat. With its huge rooms, high ceilings and old-fashioned decor, it feels a bit like staying on an aristocratic friend's estate. There are hectares of grounds and it even has its own stretch of river for fishing.

🍴 Eating

Foxes Cafe Lounge
CAFE £

(☑01228-491836; www.foxescafelounge.co.uk; 18 Abbey St; mains £4-8; ⊙9am-4pm Mon-Fri, 10am-4.30pm Sat) Swing by this cool cafe for a pastry and cappuccino or an Apple Refresher

smoothie – or better still, settle in for a hearty brunch (available in Full Fox carnivorous and Herbivore veggie versions).

David's
BRITISH ££

(☑01228-523578; www.davidsrestaurant.co.uk; 62 Warwick Rd; 2-course lunch £17.95, dinner mains £16.95-25.95; ⊙noon-3.30pm & 6.30-11pm Tue-Sat) For many years this town house restaurant has been the address for formal dining in Carlisle and there's no sign that's going to change. It majors in rich, traditional dishes with a strong French flavour: lamb with a pistachio crust and port gravy, roast chicken with leek and tarragon mash. The house is full of period architecture, too.

Thin White Duke
BISTRO ££

(☑01228-402334; www.thinwhiteduke.info; 1 Devonshire St; mains £9.95-14.95; ⊙11.45am-11pm) This place scores points for the name alone (at least for Bowie fans), although the Duke himself would have been most unlikely to tuck into the burgers, tandoori chicken and flat-iron steak on the menu. He might have liked the cocktails, though, and the location – in a former monastery, with plenty of exposed brick and ramshackle-chic decor.

Foxborough Smokehouse
BARBECUE ££

(☑01228-317925; www.foxboroughrestaurant.com; 52 Cecil St; lunch mains £10, dinner mains £12-16; ⊙noon-2pm & 5-9pm Wed & Thu, noon-2pm & 5-10pm Fri, 10am-10pm Sat, noon-2pm & 5-8.30pm Sun) Low and slow; pig, chicken and cow. That pretty much sums up this cellar smokehouse, where everything is spiced, full-on-flavoured and unashamedly meaty. The house special is the Jacob's Ladder – dry-aged beef short rib cooked for aeons in a 'green egg' cooker. Veggies have options – salads, chilli – but this is one for meat eaters, really.

🍷 Drinking & Nightlife

Hell Below
BAR

(☑01228-548481; 14-16 Devonshire St; ⊙noon-midnight Mon-Fri, to 2am Sat, to 6pm Sun) This brick-walled bar is a popular haunt for Carlisle's hipster drinkers, with craft beers and a bargain cocktail menu (with fun concoctions to try such as bubblegum sours and starburst cosmos). Snacky food – burgers, nachos, pizzas and the like – will fill a hole if you're hungry.

Shabby Scholar
CAFE

(☑01228-402813; 11-13 Carlyle Court; tapas £3-7, lunch mains £7-9.50; ⊙10am-midnight Mon-Sat) As its name suggests, this popular place is stylishly shabby, with scruffy furniture, a bar made out of old crates and a determinedly chilled vibe. It's fine for tapas, light bites and burgers, but many people just come for cocktails.

Entertainment

Brickyard CONCERT VENUE
(☑ 01228-512220; www.thebrickyardonline.com; 14 Fisher St) Carlisle's grungy gig venue, housed in the former Memorial Hall.

ⓘ Information

Carlisle Tourist Office (☑ 01228-598596; www.discovercarlisle.co.uk; Greenmarket; ⊙9.30am-5pm Mon-Sat, 10.30am-4pm Sun)

ⓘ Getting There & Away

AIR

From Carlisle's tiny **airport** (www.carlisleairport. co.uk), 8 miles northeast of the city centre, **Loganair** (www.loganair.co.uk) operates direct flights to/from London Southend, Dublin and Belfast.

BUS

National Express coaches depart from the bus station on Lonsdale St for destinations including London (£25.50 to £39.10, 7½ hours, two or three direct daily), Manchester (£17 to £24.40, three to 3½ hours, three daily) and Glasgow (£12 to £17.10, two hours, four to six daily).

Bus 554 goes to Keswick (£14.60, 70 minutes, four daily Monday to Saturday, three on Sunday) and bus 104 goes to Penrith (£6.30, 40 minutes, half-hourly Monday to Saturday, nine on Sunday).

TRAIN

Carlisle is on the west-coast line from London to Glasgow. It's also the terminus for the scenic Cumbrian Coast and Tyne Valley lines, as well as the historic **Settle to Carlisle Railway** (www. settle-carlisle.co.uk; adult return £28) across the Yorkshire Dales. The following are the main destinations:

Glasgow £28.50, 1¼ hours

Lancaster £32.40, 45 minutes

London Euston £119.70, 3½ hours

Manchester £56, two hours 10 minutes

Newcastle-upon-Tyne £16.70, 1½ hours

Penrith

☑ 01768 / POP 15,181

Just outside the borders of the national park, red-brick Penrith perhaps has more in common with the stout market towns of the Yorkshire Dales. It's a solid, traditional place with plenty of cosy pubs and quaint teashops and a lively market on Tuesdays. It's also the main gateway for exploring the picturesque Eden Valley.

⊙ Sights

★ Lowther Estate HISTORIC SITE
(☑ 01931-712192; www.lowthercastle.org; adult/ child £9/7; ⊙10am-5pm) This sprawling country estate once belonged to one of the Lake District's most venerable families and is currently undergoing a huge, multimillion-pound restoration project. The 400-year-old crenellated castle and the estate's grounds are now open to the public again. Though the castle itself is to remain a ruin, restoration work is gradually breathing life back into the gardens, which have been largely forgotten since the estate fell into disrepair following WWII.

Among the areas to visit are the Iris Garden, the Great Yew Walk, a restored parterre and a wealth of hidden follies, lakes and woodland areas.

Rheged VISITOR CENTRE
(☑ 01768-868000; www.rheged.com; ⊙10am-6pm) Cunningly disguised as a Lakeland hill 2 miles west of Penrith, this visitor centre houses an IMAX cinema and temporary exhibitions. There's also a large retail hall selling Cumbrian foodstuffs and souvenirs. Local chef Peter Sidwell runs cooking classes and is also responsible for the cafe menu.

🛏 Sleeping

Lounge HOTEL ££
(☑ 01768-866395; www.theloungehotelandbar. co.uk; King St; d/f from £80/110; 🛜) For a town-centre hotel at reasonable prices, you can't do any better than this chic little number. Pine furniture, laminate floors and tasteful tints of pistachio, cream and taupe feel a tad generic, but it's chintz-free and central. The three-bed apartment (£160) has its own mini-kitchen. Breakfast and dinner is served in the ground-floor bistro.

★ Augill Castle HOTEL £££
(☑ 01768-341967; www.stayinacastle.com; Kirkby Stephen; r/ste from £180/240; 🅿🛜) If you've always dreamed of staying in a bona fide British castle, this stately pile near Kirkby Stephen is definitely the place. All the trappings are here – crenellated turrets, stained-glass windows, cavernous rooms – and the design vibe inside is rather groovy, with a mix of antique furniture and contemporary

furnishings. There's even a mini-cinema. It's 25 miles southeast of Penrith.

George Hotel HOTEL **£££**
(☑ 01768-862696; www.lakedistricthotels.net/georgehotel; Devonshire St; d £125-165; P ☎) Penrith's venerable red-brick coaching inn offers classically decorated rooms in prim stripes and country patterns, plus a quaint bar and restaurant. It's not quite the heritage beauty it might appear to be at first glance – rooms are comfortable but disappointingly free of original features. The free parking's a boon.

✕ Eating

★ Four & Twenty BISTRO **££**
(☑ 01768-210231; www.fourandtwentypenrith.co.uk; 14 King St; lunch mains £14-16, dinner mains £16.50-19.50; ☺ noon-2.30pm & 6-9.30pm Tue-Sat) Proper fine dining with a reasonable price tag is the modus operandi at this bistro, which blends sleek decor with rustic wood, banquette seats and mix-and-match furniture. Expect sophisticated dishes such as pork tenderloin with garlic, sage and Parma ham, or sea bass 'bouillabaisse-style'. If you're going to eat out in Penrith town, this is the place to do it.

George & Dragon PUB FOOD **££**
(☑ 01768-865381; www.georgeanddragonclifton.co.uk; Clifton; mains £13.95-21.95; ☺ noon-2.30pm & 6-9pm) If you don't mind a drive, this pretty pub in the village of Clifton makes a good lunch or dinner stop. It's situated on the Lowther Estate and sources much of its produce (including game) from there. Fires, benches and rafters make for a cosy setting and the food is generally good, if not quite gastropub standard.

★ Allium at Askham Hall GASTRONOMY **£££**
(☑ 01931-712350; www.askhamhall.co.uk; Askham; dinner menu £50; ☺ 7-9.30pm Tue-Sat) Regal setting, royally good dining. Chef Richard Swale's passion for Cumbrian produce was learned from a childhood spent shooting, fishing and foraging (he keeps his own chickens). His food combines richness and delicacy – such as chicken, cauliflower cheese and truffles – and everything looks like a work of art. The setting inside the hall is quite formal; dress nicely.

🛍 Shopping

JJ Graham FOOD & DRINKS
(☑ 01768-862281; www.jjgraham.co.uk; 6-7 Market Sq; ☺ 8.30am-5.30pm Mon-Sat) There's been a grocer here since 1793 and this endearingly old-fashioned deli is still the place to pick up treats such as local cheeses, homemade chutneys and loose-leaf teas.

ℹ Information

Penrith Tourist Office (☑ 01768-867466; pen.tic@eden.gov.uk; Middlegate; ☺ 9.30am-5pm Mon-Sat, 1-4.45pm Sun) Also houses the town's small museum.

ℹ Getting There & Away

There are frequent train connections north to Carlisle (£5.90, 15 minutes) and south to Oxenholme (£7, 25 minutes), where you can change for branch trains to Windermere.

The bus station is northeast of the centre, off Sandgate. Bus 104 goes to Carlisle (£6.30, 40 minutes, half-hourly Monday to Saturday, nine on Sunday), and bus X4/X5 goes to the Cumbrian coast (£6.80 to £11.20, half-hourly Monday to Saturday, hourly Sunday) via Rheged, Keswick and Cockermouth.

England's Great Outdoors

The English love the great outdoors, and every weekend sees a mass exodus from the towns and cities to the hills, moors and coastline. Hiking and biking are the most popular pursuits but there's a huge range of activities available – and getting wet and muddy can actually be a highlight of your trip!

Walking

England can seem crowded, but away from the cities there are many beautiful areas, perfect for walking. You can go for a short riverside stroll or a major hike over mountain ranges – or anything in between. The best places include the Cotswolds, the Lake District and the Yorkshire Dales.

Cycling

A bike is ideal for getting to know England's countryside. Areas such as Suffolk, Yorkshire and Wiltshire offer a vast network of quiet country roads ideal for cycle touring. For off-road fun, mountain bikers can go further into the wilds in places such as the Peak District, the North Yorkshire Moors and the South Downs.

Horse Riding

If you want to explore the hills and moors at a more leisurely place, seeing the wilder parts of England from horseback is the way to go. In rural areas and national parks such as Dartmoor and Northumberland there are riding centres catering to all levels of proficiency.

Surfing

England may not be an obvious destination for surfers, but conditions can be surprisingly good at key locations. Top of the list are the west-facing coasts of Cornwall and Devon, while there are smaller scenes on the east coast, notably in Norfolk and Yorkshire.

1. Cyclists in the Peak District National Park (p466)
2. Walking in the Lake District (p569)
3. Surfing at Porthcurno (p342), Cornwall

Newcastle & Northeast England

Best Places to Eat

➡ Riley's Fish Shack (p617)

➡ House of Tides (p614)

➡ Raby Hunt (p622)

➡ Knitsley Farm Shop & Cafe (p621)

➡ Bay Horse (p622)

Best Places to Stay

➡ Lumley Castle (p619)

➡ Lord Crewe Arms (p626)

➡ Langley Castle Hotel (p627)

➡ Otterburn Castle Country House Hotel (p629)

➡ Jesmond Dene House (p612)

Why Go?

The irrepressible city of Newcastle-upon-Tyne anchors England's northeast. Set on the mighty River Tyne, this former industrial powerhouse's steep hills are lined with handsome Victorian buildings, and many of its one-time factories and warehouses have been transformed into galleries, museums, bars and entertainment venues. Newcastle's nightlife is legendary, and an evening out on the tiles is a quintessential experience.

Newcastle is also an ideal gateway for escaping into the northeast's utterly wild, starkly beautiful countryside – from the rounded Cheviot Hills to brooding Northumberland National Park and the remote North Pennines. Spectacular Hadrian's Wall cuts a lonely path through the landscape, dotted with dramatic fortress ruins that are haunting reminders of the bloody struggle with the Scots to the north, while the region's unspoilt coastline takes in long, desolate beaches, wind-worn castles and tiny, magical islands offshore.

When to Go

➡ Costumed re-enactments and Roman celebrations take place throughout the year at Hadrian's Wall.

➡ The best time to discover the region's miles of wide sandy beaches is during the summer season (June to August), although for surfers, Tynemouth's world-class waves are best (if chilliest) in winter and spring.

➡ September and October are great for losing yourself in the autumnal landscapes of Northumberland National Park.

➡ September is also the month to grab a Newkie Brown ale, or your running shoes, and join the party along the route of Tyneside's Great North Run, one of the world's biggest half-marathons.

History

Violent history has shaped this region more than any other in England, primarily because of its frontier position. Although Hadrian's Wall didn't serve as a defensive barrier, it marked the northern limit of Roman Britain and was the Empire's most heavily fortified line. Following the Romans' departure, the region became part of the Anglian kingdom of Bernicia, which united with the kingdom of Deira (encompassing much of modern-day Yorkshire) to form Northumbria in 604.

The kingdom changed hands and borders shifted several times over the next 500 years as Anglo-Saxons and Danes struggled to seize it. The land north of the River Tweed was finally ceded to Scotland in 1018, while the nascent kingdom of England kept everything below it.

The arrival of the Normans in 1066 saw William I eager to secure his northern borders against the Scots. He commissioned most of the castles you see along the coast, and cut deals with the prince bishops of Durham to ensure their loyalty. The new lords of Northumberland became very powerful because, as Marcher Lords (from the use of 'march' as a synonym of 'border'), they kept the Scots at bay.

Northumberland's reputation as a hotbed of rebellion intensified during the Tudor years, when the largely Catholic north, led by the seventh duke of Northumberland, Thomas Percy, rose up against Elizabeth I in the defeated Rising of the North in 1569. The Border Reivers, raiders from both sides of the border in the 16th century, kept the region in a perpetual state of lawlessness that only subsided after the Act of Union between England and Scotland in 1707.

Coal mines were the key to the 19th-century industrialisation of the northeast, powering steelworks, shipyards and armament works that grew up along the Tyne and Tees. In 1825 the mines also spawned the world's first steam railway, the Stockton & Darlington, built by local engineer George Stephenson. Social strife emerged in the 20th century, with mines, shipbuilding, steel production and the railway industry all winding down during the Great Depression and postwar years. Reinventing the northeast has been a mammoth task but regeneration continues apace.

🏃 Activities

Cycling

The northeast has some of England's most inspiring cycle routes.

Part of the National Cycle Network (NCN), a long-time favourite is the 200-mile **Coast & Castles Cycle Route** (www.coast-and-castles.co.uk), which runs south–north along the glorious Northumberland coast between Newcastle-upon-Tyne and Berwick-upon-Tweed and Edinburgh, Scotland.

The 140-mile **Sea to Sea Cycle Route** (www.c2c-guide.co.uk) runs across northern England between the Cumbrian coast (St Bees, Whitehaven or Workington) and Tynemouth or Sunderland via the northern Lake District and wild North Pennines' hills.

Another coast-to-coast option is the **Hadrian's Cycleway** (www.hadrian-guide.co.uk), a 174-mile route between South Shields or Tynemouth and Ravenglass in Cumbria along Hadrian's Wall.

Also running coast to coast is the 173-mile **Reivers Route** (http://reivers-route.co.uk) from Whitehaven to Tynemouth via Kielder Forest, the Scottish Borders and the Lake District.

Hiking

The North Pennines – along with the Cheviots further north – are considered 'England's last wilderness'. Long routes through the hills include the famous **Pennine Way** (www.nationaltrail.co.uk), Britain's first national trail, established in 1965, which keeps mainly to the high ground between the Yorkshire Dales and the Scottish border, but also crosses sections of river valley and some tedious patches of plantation. The whole route is 268 miles, but the 70-mile section between Bowes and Hadrian's Wall is a fine four-day taster.

Hadrian's Wall has a huge range of easy loop walks taking in forts and other historical highlights.

One of the finest walks along the windswept **Northumberland coast**, between the villages of Craster and Bamburgh via Dunstanburgh, includes two of the region's most spectacular castles. Another superb coastal trail is the 30-mile **Berwickshire Coastal Path** (www.walkhighlands.co.uk/borders/berwickshire-coastal-path.shtml) from Berwick-upon-Tweed to the village of Cockburnspath in Scotland.

ℹ️ Getting There & Around

BUS

Bus transport around the region can be sporadic, particularly around the more remote reaches of western Northumberland. Contact **Traveline**

Newcastle & Northeast England Highlights

1 Holy Island, Lindisfarne (p634) Negotiating the tidal causeway to reach this other-worldly pilgrimage site.

2 Victoria Tunnel (p611) Exploring a coal-wagon tunnel and WWII air-raid shelter beneath Newcastle's streets.

3 Kielder Observatory (p628) Stargazing from this observatory in the Northumberland International Dark Sky Park.

4 Barnard Castle (p621) Viewing extraordinary objets d'art in the chateau-housed Bowes Museum.

5 Berwick Walls (p635) Circumnavigating

---

0 --- 20 km
0 --- 10 miles

NORTH SEA

EAST LOTHIAN

SCOTLAND

Cockburnspath

Grantshouse

Coldingham

St Abbs

Eymouth

B6355

A1

Chirnside

Duns

Coldstream

BERWICKSHIRE

Berwick-upon-Tweed

Holy Island (Lindisfarne)

FARNE ISLANDS

Bamburgh

Seahouses

Low Newton-by-the-Sea

High Newton-by-the-Sea

Embleton Bay

Embleton

Dunstanburgh Castle

Craster

Alnmouth

Warkworth

Amble

Newbiggin-by-the-Sea

Ashington

A698

Earlston

Melrose

St Boswell's

A68

Kelso

A698

Kirk Yetholm

Town Yetholm

Crookham

Ford

Etal

Belford

Wooler

Bowmont Water

Tweed

Teviot

Ale Water

Kale Water

Jedburgh

A68

ROXBURGHSHIRE

Bonchester Bridge

Kielder Forest Park

Kielder Water

Kielder Observatory

Kielder Burn

Lewis Water

Liddel Water

Cheviot (815m)

Northumberland National Park

Danger Area (MOD Live Firing Range)

A697

Till

Coquet

NORTHUMBERLAND

Rothbury

Otterburn

A68

North Tyne

Bellingham

Kirkharle

A696

Morpeth

Alnwick

A1

Loftus

Saltburn-by-the-Sea

Danby

Castleton

North York Moors National Park

Esk

Seven

A171

Guisborough

Redcar

A174

Billingham

Middlesbrough

Leven

8 Hartlepool

Stokesley

Eaglescliffe

Hartlepool

Seaham

Peterlee

Sunderland

South Shields

Tynemouth

Whitley Bay

Stockton-on-Tees

Sedgefield

Darlington

Huworth-on-Tees

Northallerton

A19

Wallsend

Newcastle-upon-Tyne

Newcastle International Airport

Angel of the North

2

9 Beamish Open-Air Museum

Stanley

Ponteland

Belsay

Corbridge

Tyne

Hedley on the Hill

Consett

Knitsley

Edmundbyers

A68

Durham

6

Croxdale

A167

Bishop Auckland

Shildon

West Auckland

Crook

Wolsingham

Frosterley

DURHAM

Hamsterley Forest

Raby Castle

Summerhouse

Pierce Bridge

Teesdale

4

Barnard Castle

Bowes Castle

Tees

Catterick

A1

Bedale

NORTH YORKSHIRE

Richmond

Reeth

Middleton-in-Teesdale

Newbiggin

Langdon Beck

North Pennines

Weardale

Wear

Stanhope

B6278

Pennine Way

A66

Greta

The Pennines

Yorkshire Dales National Park

B6270

Hawes

Buttertubs Pass

Hexham

Allendale Town

Blanchland

Derwent Reservoir

Allenheads

Killhope

Ireshopeburn

Nenthead

Alston

South Tyne

A686

Haltwhistle

Hadrian's Wall

7

Hadrian's Wall

Carlisle (20mi)

CUMBRIA

Appleby

Eden

M6

Coupland

Newbiggin-on-Line

A66

Brough

Kirkby Stephen

Tebay

Ais Gill

A683

Eask

(☑ 0871-200 2233; www.travelinenortheast. info) for information on connections, timetables and prices.

TRAIN

The East Coast Main Line runs north from London King's Cross to Edinburgh via Durham, Newcastle and Berwick; Northern Rail operates local and interurban services in the north, including west to Carlisle.

There are numerous Rover tickets for single-day travel and longer periods; check http://networkonetickets.co.uk.

Newcastle-upon-Tyne

☑ 0191 / POP 293,204

Against its dramatic backdrop of Victorian elegance and industrial grit, this fiercely independent city harbours a spirited mix of heritage and urban sophistication, with excellent art galleries and a magnificent concert hall, along with boutique hotels, some exceptional restaurants and, of course, interesting bars: Newcastle is renowned throughout Britain for its thumping nightlife, bolstered by an energetic, 42,000-strong student population. The city retains deep-rooted traditions, embodied by the no-nonsense, likeable locals.

Allow at least a couple of days to explore the Victorian city centre and quayside areas along the Tyne and across the river in Gateshead, as well as the rejuvenated Ouseburn Valley to the east, gentrified Jesmond to the north, and, on the coast, the surf beaches of Tynemouth.

⊙ Sights

⊙ City Centre

Newcastle's grand Victorian centre, a compact area bordered roughly by Grainger St to the west and Pilgrim St to the east, is one of the most compelling examples of urban rejuvenation in England. Down by the quays are the city's most recognisable attractions – the iconic bridges that span the Tyne and the striking buildings that flank it.

★ **Great North Museum**   MUSEUM
(☑ 0191-208 6765; https://greatnorthmuseum.org. uk; Barras Bridge; general admission free, planetarium adult/child £3/2; ⊙10am-5pm Mon-Fri, to 4pm Sat, 11am-4pm Sun) FREE The contents of Newcastle University's museums and the prestigious Hancock Museum's natural-history exhibits come together in the latter's

neoclassical building. The result is a fascinating jumble of dinosaurs, Roman altar stones, Egyptian mummies, Samurai warriors and impressive taxidermy. Standout exhibits include a life-size *Tyrannosaurus rex* recreation and an interactive model of Hadrian's Wall showing every milecastle and fortress. There's also lots of hands-on stuff for kids and a planetarium with screenings throughout the day.

★ **Life Science Centre**   MUSEUM
(☑ 0191-243 8210; www.life.org.uk; Times Sq; adult/child £15/8; ⊙10am-6pm Mon-Sat, 11am-6pm Sun) Part of a sober-minded institute devoted to the study of genetic science, this centre lets you discover the secrets of life through a fascinating series of hands-on exhibits. The highlight is the Motion Ride, a simulator that lets you 'experience' bungee jumping and the like (the 4D film changes every year). There are lots of thought-provoking arcade-style games, and if the information sometimes gets lost on the way, never mind, kids will love it. Book ahead at busy times.

★ **Discovery Museum**   MUSEUM
(☑ 0191-232 6789; https://discoverymuseum.org. uk; Blandford Sq; ⊙10am-4pm) FREE Tyneside's rich history is explored at this unmissable museum. Exhibitions spread across three floors of the former Co-operative Wholesale Society building around the mightily impressive 30m-long *Turbinia,* the fastest ship in the world in 1897 and the first to be powered by steam turbine. Other highlights are a section on shipbuilding on the Tyne, with a scale model of the river in 1929, and the 'Story of Newcastle', spanning the city's history from Pons Aelius (Roman Newcastle) to Cheryl Cole.

Newcastle Castle   CASTLE
(☑ 0191-230 6300; www.newcastlecastle.co.uk; Castle Garth; adult/child £6.50/3.90; ⊙10am-5pm) The stronghold that put both the 'new' and 'castle' into Newcastle has been largely swallowed up by the train station, leaving only a few remaining fragments including the square Norman keep and the Black Gate. Exhibits inside the two restored buildings cover the history of the city, its castle and its residents from Roman times onwards. The 360-degree city views from the keep's rooftop are the best in town.

Laing Art Gallery   GALLERY
(☑ 0191-278 1611; www.laingartgallery.org.uk; New Bridge St; ⊙10am-5pm Tue-Sat, 2-5pm Sun) FREE

The exceptional collection at the Laing includes works by Gainsborough, Gauguin and Henry Moore, and an important collection of paintings by Northumberland-born artist John Martin (1789–1854). Check the 'What's On' section of the website for events including talks and tours. Temporary exhibitions may incur an extra charge.

Biscuit Factory GALLERY
(www.thebiscuitfactory.com; 16 Stoddart St; ⊙10am-5pm Mon-Fri, to 6pm Sat, 11am-5pm Sun) **FREE** No prizes for guessing what this commercial art gallery used to be. These days, it's the UK's biggest contemporary art, craft and design gallery/shop, where you can browse and/or buy works by more than 200 artists each season in a variety of mediums, including painting, sculpture, glassware and furniture, many with a northeast theme. There's an on-site cafe, the Factory Kitchen, and fine-dining restaurant, Artisan.

⊙ Ouseburn Valley

Now semi-regenerated, Newcastle's 19th-century industrial heartland, Ouseburn Valley, 1 mile east of the city centre, has potteries, glass-blowing studios and other creative workspaces, along with pubs, bars and entertainment venues.

★Victoria Tunnel HISTORIC SITE
(⊙9am-5pm Mon-Fri 0191-230 4210; www.ouseburntrust.org.uk; Victoria Tunnel Visitor Centre, 55 Lime St; tours adult/child £7/4; ⊙by reservation) Walking Newcastle's streets, you'd never know this extraordinary tunnel runs for 2.5 miles beneath your feet. Built between 1839 and 1842 as a coal-wagon thoroughfare, it was used as an air-raid shelter during WWII. Volunteer-led, two-hour tours take you through an atmospheric 700m-long level section of the tunnel. Book ahead as numbers are limited, and wear good shoes and a washable jacket for the limewashed walls; it's not suitable for kids under seven. Tours finish back at the Victoria Visitor Centre.

Seven Stories – The Centre for Children's Books MUSEUM
(www.sevenstories.org.uk; 30 Lime St; adult/child £7.70/6.60; ⊙10am-5pm Tue-Sat, to 4pm Sun) A marvellous conversion of a handsome Victorian mill has resulted in Seven Stories, a very hands-on museum dedicated to the wondrous world of children's literature. Across the seven floors you'll find original manuscripts and artwork from the 1930s on-

wards, and a constantly changing program of kid-oriented exhibitions, activities and events designed to encourage the AA Milnes of the new millennium. There's a bookshop, coffee shop and cafe.

⊙ Gateshead

The area of Newcastle south of the Tyne is the 'town' (neighbourhood, really) of Gateshead. Local authorities are now promoting the whole kit-and-caboodle–on-Tyne as 'NewcastleGateshead'.

★BALTIC – Centre for Contemporary Art GALLERY
(☑0191-478 1810; http://baltic.art; Gateshead Quays; ⊙10am-6pm Wed-Mon, 10.30am-6pm Tue) **FREE** Once a huge mustard-coloured grain store, BALTIC is now a huge mustard-coloured art gallery rivalling London's Tate Modern. There are no permanent exhibitions; instead, rotating shows feature the work and installations of some of contemporary art's biggest show-stoppers. The complex has artists in residence, a performance space, a cinema, a bar, a spectacular rooftop restaurant (bookings essential) and a ground-floor restaurant with riverside tables. A 4th-floor outdoor platform and 5th-floor viewing box offer fabulous panoramas of the Tyne.

⛺ Festivals & Events

Great North Run SPORTS
(www.greatrun.org; ⊙mid-Sep) Newcastle's 13.1-mile half-marathon takes place in mid-September. Entry is by ballot, with 57,000 places available. Otherwise join the locals cheering on the entrants along the route, which goes from the city centre across the Tyne Bridge and through Gateshead to South Shields.

🛌 Sleeping

Grey Street Hotel BOUTIQUE HOTEL **££**
(☑0191-230 6777; www.greystreethotel.co.uk; 2-12 Grey St; d from £89; ❄🎧🌐) On the city centre's most elegant street, this beautiful Grade II–listed former bank has been adapted for contemporary needs, including triple glazing on the sash windows. Its 49 individually designed rooms have big beds and stylish colour combinations; some have giant black-and-white photographs covering one wall.

Malmaison BOUTIQUE HOTEL **££**
(☑0191-389 8627; www.malmaison.com; 104 Quayside; d/ste from £115/190; 🅿❄🎧) The affectedly

Newcastle-upon-Tyne

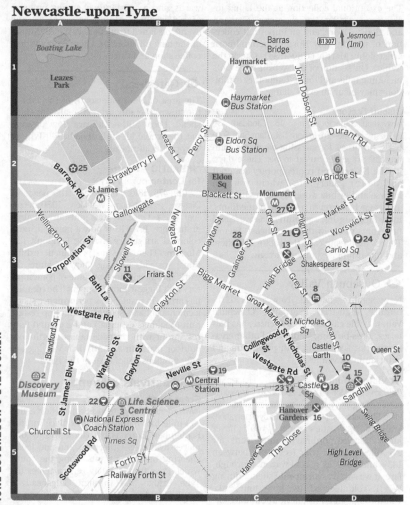

stylish Malmaison touch has been applied to this former warehouse with considerable success, even down to the French-speaking lifts. Big beds, sleek lighting and designer furniture embellish the 122 plush rooms. The best rooms have views of the Millennium Bridge. There's a spa, gym and on-site brasserie.

Newcastle Jesmond Hotel   HOTEL **££**
(☑ 0191-239 9943; www.newcastlejesmondhotel. co.uk; 105 Osborne Rd; s/d/tr from £60/77/95; Ⓟ 🛜) Rooms aren't huge at this refurbished red-brick property footsteps from the bars and restaurants of Osborne Rd, but they're

cosy, comfy and spotlessly clean, and come with the bonus of free parking (though spaces are limited, so get in quick). Wi-fi can be patchy.

★ **Jesmond Dene House**   BOUTIQUE HOTEL **£££**
(☑ 0191-212 3000; https://jesmonddenehouse.co.uk; Jesmond Dene Rd; d from £140; Ⓟ ❄ @ 🛜) Large bedrooms at this exquisite 40-room property are furnished in a modern interpretation of the Arts and Crafts style and have stunning bathrooms complete with underfloor heating, as well as the latest tech; some have private terraces. The fine-dining **restaurant** (☑ 0191-

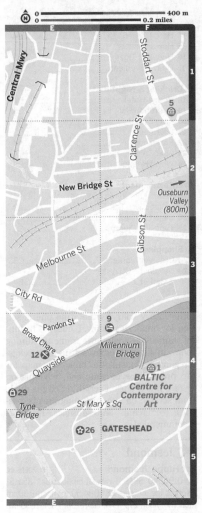

rooms and glossy timber (including interconnecting rooms for families and sumptuous suites), two bars and a smart-casual restaurant. Limited on-site parking is first-come, first-served but free. Its 11 luxury self-catering apartments are located nearby.

✖ Eating

✖ City Centre

Quay Ingredient CAFE **£**
(✆0191-447 2327; http://quayingredient.co.uk; 4 Quay St; dishes £2-8; ⊗8am-5pm; ☎) Beneath the Tyne Bridge's soaring steel girders, this chic hole-in-the-wall has a devoted following for cooked breakfasts (scrambled eggs with white truffle oil and toasted brioche, Craster kippers with lemon parsley) served until 11.30am on weekdays and all day on weekends. At lunch there are soups and spectacular sandwiches (eg hoisin confit duck wrap or Toulouse sausage with fried onions).

★ Broad Chare GASTROPUB **££**
(✆0191-211 2144; www.thebroadchare.co.uk; 25 Broad Chare; mains £10-24, bar snacks £2.25-3.85; ⊗kitchen noon-2.30pm & 5.30-10pm Mon-Sat, noon-5pm Sun, bar 11am-11pm Mon-Sat, to 10pm Sun) Spiffing English classics and splendid cask ales are served in the dark-wood bar and mezzanine of this perfect gastropub. Starters such as crispy pig ears, pork pies and venison terrine are followed by mains that might include a divine grilled pork chop with black pudding and cider sauce, and desserts like treacle tart with walnut brittle to finish.

Hop & Cleaver GASTROPUB **££**
(✆0191-261 1037; www.hopandcleaver.com; 44 Sandhill; mains £9.50-14; ⊗kitchen 5-9pm Mon-Thu, noon-10pm Fri & Sat, noon-9pm Sun, bar 5pm-midnight Mon-Thu, 11am-1am Fri-Sun) Inside the magnificent Jacobean **Bessie Surtees House** (✆0191-269 1255; https://historicengland.org.uk; ⊗10am-4pm Mon-Fri) **FREE**, this hip spot is great for a drink (it brews its own small-batch craft beers) but the food is equally outstanding: smoky brisket with apple-and-onion fritters; 12-hour cooked pulled pork with homemade slaw and BBQ sauce; charred, Bourbon-marinated ribs; beer-steamed roasted chicken. Meats are smoked in-house; veggie options exist but are limited.

Herb Garden PIZZA **££**
(✆0191-222 0491; www.theherbgardenuk.com; Arch 8, Westgate Rd; pizzas £8.50-16.50;

212 5555; mains £17.50-32, 2-/3-course menus £20/25, afternoon tea £25; ⊗7-10am, noon-5pm & 7-9pm Mon-Thu, 7-10am, noon-5pm & 7-9.30pm Fri, 7.30-10.30am, noon-5pm & 7-9.30pm Sat, 7.30-10.30am & noon-9pm Sun) ✐ is sublime; dinner, bed and breakfast packages are available.

Vermont Hotel HERITAGE HOTEL **£££**
(✆0191-233 1010; www.vermont-hotel.com; Castle Garth; d from £132, 2-/4-person apt from £169/189; 🅿☎) Early 20th-century elegance reigns at this magnificent stone building (the former County Hall), which has an art deco ballroom, 101 rooms with marble bath-

NEWCASTLE & NORTHEAST ENGLAND NEWCASTLE-UPON-TYNE

Newcastle-upon-Tyne

⊙11.30am-11.30pm; 🛜🅿) ✎ The Herb Garden lives up to its name with a wall of barrel-like cylinders where herbs and salad greens grow under glowing lights. Its 17 different pizza varieties include two calzoni; on weekends it serves breakfast pizzas, such as the Twisted English (sausages, black pudding, tomato, mushrooms and eggs) and Breakfast in Bed (chocolate, hazelnuts, banana and honey). No reservations.

★**House of Tides** GASTRONOMY £££
(☎0191-230 3720; http://houseoftides.co.uk; 28-30 The Close; tasting menus lunch £70, with paired wines £130, dinner £85, with paired wines £150; ⊙6-8.30pm Tue-Thu, noon-1.15pm & 6-8.30pm Fri, noon-1.15pm & 5-9pm Sat) A 16th-century merchant's house is now the home of Newcastle's most celebrated restaurant, the Michelin-starred House of Tides. Established by acclaimed Newcastle-born chef Kenny Atkinson, it incorporates premium ingredients – Orkney scallops, Norfolk quail, wild blackberries, black truffles and nasturtiums – in regularly changing multicourse tasting menus. Diners with dietary requirements including vegetarians (though not vegans) can be catered for by prior arrangement.

Blackfriars BRITISH £££
(☎0191-261 5945; www.blackfriarsrestaurant.co.uk; Friars St; mains £16-34; ⊙noon-2.30pm & 5.30-11pm Mon-Sat, noon-4pm Sun; 🛗) ✎ A 13th-century friary is the atmospheric setting for 'modern medieval' cuisine. Beautiful stained-glass windows frame the dining room; in summer tables set up in the cloister garden. Consult the table-mat map for the provenance of your cod, woodpigeon or rare-breed pork. Everything else is made from scratch on site, including breads, pastries, ice creams and sausages. Bookings recommended.

✕ Jesmond

Fat Hippo Jesmond BURGERS ££
(☎0191-340 8949; www.fat-hippo.co.uk; 35a St Georges Tce; burgers £8.50-14.50; ⊙noon-9.30pm Mon-Thu, noon-10pm Fri, 11am-10pm Sat, 11.30am-9.30pm Sun) Humongous burgers arrive on wooden planks with stainless-steel buckets of triple-fried, hand-cut chips at this local success story. Stinky Pete comes with blue cheese, jalapeño peppers and red-onion jam; 4x4 has a whopping four patties. Veggie burgers include spicy bean; sides span deep-fried gherkins to mac 'n cheese balls and house-made slaw. There are craft beers, ciders and boozy shakes.

Its city-centre sibling, the **Fat Hippo Underground** (☎0191-447 1161; www.fathippo.co.uk; 2-6 Shakespeare St; burgers £8-14; ⊙noon-10pm Mon-Thu, 11am-10.30pm Fri & Sat, 11.30am-10pm Sun), occupies a vaulted cellar.

Patricia
BISTRO **££**

(☑ 0191-281 4443; www.the-patricia.com; 139 Jesmond Rd; mains £16-24, sharing plates £3-10, 2-/3-course dinner menus £20/25; ⊙ 5-10pm Wed-Fri, noon-2.30pm & 6-10pm Sat, noon-4pm Sun; ☑) Named for owner-chef Nick Grieves' grandmother, the Patricia is perpetually busy; book ahead to feast on dishes like raw Orkney scallops with fermented red pepper, and roast quail with chocolate and fennel prepared in the semi-open kitchen. Excellent vegetarian choices might include roast leeks with aged feta foam. Many of its old- and new-world wines are available by the glass.

Peace & Loaf
BISTRO **£££**

(☑ 0191-281 5222; www.peaceandloaf.co.uk; 217 Jesmond Rd, Jesmond; mains £18-29, 3-course lunch/dinner menu £25/30; ⊙ noon-2pm & 5.30-9pm Mon-Wed, noon-2pm & 5.30-9.30pm Thu-Sat, noon-3.30pm Sun) A double-height space with mezzanine seating is the stage for creations by *MasterChef: The Professionals* finalist David Coulson, who subsequently worked for two-Michelin-starred chef Michel Roux Jr. Coulson's refined Modern British flavours include black pudding–stuffed guinea fowl with pear cider–braised red cabbage. Many ingredients are foraged in the Jesmond Dene woodland or grown by Coulson in his garden.

 Drinking & Nightlife

 City Centre

Lola Jeans
COCKTAIL BAR

(☑ 0191-230 1921; www.lolajeans.co.uk; 1-3 Market St; ⊙ noon-midnight Mon-Thu, to 1am Fri-Sun) At this Jazz Age–styled bar with chandeliers, velveteen chairs and dazzling murals, cocktails served in vintage glassware include locally inspired concoctions such as Fog on the Tyne (Bols Genever, Newcastle Brown Ale reduction, rose lemonade and nettle cordial) and Coal Faced Flip (Fernet Branca, coffee-infused Jagermeister, egg, stout-and-vanilla reduction and chocolate bitters).

World Headquarters
CLUB

(☑ 0191-281 3445; www.welovewhq.com; Curtis Mayfield House, Carliol Sq; ⊙ 11pm-5am Fri & Sat, weekday hours vary) Dedicated to the genius of black music – funk, rare groove, dance-floor jazz, northern soul, genuine R&B, lush disco, proper house, reggae and more – this brilliant club is a world away from commercial blandness.

Bridge Hotel
PUB

(http://sjf.co.uk/our-pubs/bridge-hotel; Castle Sq; ⊙ 11.30am-11pm Mon-Thu, to midnight Fri & Sat, noon-10.30pm Sun) Dating from 1901, this traditional pub retains original features including Victorian snugs, carved woodwork, stained-glass windows and mosaic tiles. At least 10 hand-pulled ales are on tap; there's also a great whisky selection. Its panoramic beer garden overlooking the High Level and Tyne Bridges incorporates part of Newcastle's medieval city walls.

Centurion Bar
BAR

(www.centurion-newcastle.com; Central Station; ⊙ 10am-11pm Mon-Thu, to midnight Fri & Sat, to 10.30pm Sun) With magnificent floor-to-ceiling ornate Victorian tiling, Central Station's former 1st-class waiting room – a Grade I–listed treasure dating from 1893 – is ideal for a pre-club drink in style.

Split Chimp
PUB

(www.splitchimp.pub; Arch 7, Westgate Rd; ⊙ 3-10pm Mon-Thu, noon-11pm Fri & Sat) Covered in retro chimp montages but actually named for the wood that's wedged behind ale casks to tip them, this tiny, two-level micropub inside a railway viaduct has a 31ft-long skittle alley and hosts occasional live music. Hand-pulled local ales rotate on the taps; it also has bottled craft beers, ciders and wine.

Quilliam Brothers' Tea House · TEAHOUSE

(📞0191-261 4861; www.quilliambrothers.com; Claremont Bldgs, 1 Eldon Pl; ⊙10am-midnight Mon-Fri, 9am-midnight Sat, 10am-4pm Sun) Set up by a trio of brothers as 'an alternative to Newcastle's boozy scene', this hip Hungarian-style teahouse with postindustrial decor has over 100 types of tea as well as a tiny cinema screening cult films, plus various gigs and art events.

🍷 Ouseburn Valley

★ Tyne Bar · PUB

(📞0191-265 2550; www.thetyne.com; 1 Maling St; ⊙noon-11pm Mon-Thu, to midnight Fri & Sat, to 10.30pm Sun; 📶) An outdoor stage hosting free gigs, a free jukebox, beer-garden-style seating under one of the brick arches of the Glasshouse Bridge and a sprawling expanse of grass with knockout river views make this tucked-away waterfront pub a magnet for locals. Free bar food is laid on between 7pm and 9pm on Tuesdays (you'll still need to pay for drinks).

Ship Inn · PUB

(📞0191-222 0878; www.facebook.com/ship ouseburn; Stepney Bank; ⊙noon-11pm Sun-Thu, to midnight Fri & Sat) Spilling onto a small green out front, this red-brick charmer in the Ouseburn Valley has been pouring pints since the early 1800s. Its current owners have breathed new life into its interior, with art on the walls and an excellent vegan kitchen turning out dishes from tacos to tofu pot-sticker dumplings.

☆ Entertainment

Sage Gateshead · LIVE MUSIC

(📞0191-443 4661; www.sagegateshead.com; St Mary's Square, Gateshead Quays) Norman Foster's magnificent chrome-and-glass horizontal bottle is a stunner in itself but, as the home of the Northern Sinfonia and Folkworks, also presents outstanding live music.

Tyneside Cinema · CINEMA

(📞0191-227 5500; www.tynesidecinema.co.uk; 10 Pilgrim St; adult/child from £8.75/5.25, newsreels free) Opened in 1937 as Newcastle's first newsreel cinema, this art deco picture house with plush red-velvet seats still screens newsreels (11.15am daily) as well as mainstream and offbeat movies, and archive British Pathé films. Free one-hour guided tours of the building run at 11am on Monday, Tuesday, Friday and Saturday.

Newcastle United Football Club · FOOTBALL

(NUFC; 📞0844 372 1892; www.nufc.co.uk; St James Park, Strawberry Pl; ⊙box office 10am-5pm Mon-Fri, 9am-4pm Sat, 9am until half-time on match days) NUFC is more than just a football team – it's the collective expression of Geordie hope and pride. Buy match tickets online, by phone or at the box office in the Milburn Stand of the club's hallowed ground, St James Park. Various **stadium tours** (stadium tours adult/child £15/8, rooftop tours £20/15; ⊙tours by reservation) include rooftop tours.

Cluny · LIVE MUSIC

(📞0191-230 4474; https://thecluny.com; 36 Lime St; ⊙noon-11pm Mon-Thu, to midnight Fri & Sat, to 10.30pm Sun) In the Ouseburn Valley touring acts and local talent – from experimental prog-rock heads to up-and-coming pop goddesses – fill the bill every night of the week at this beloved venue, which has been independently owned since 2017. There's a great restaurant on site.

Shopping

Grainger Market · MARKET

(www.graingermarket.org; btwn Grainger & Clayton Sts; ⊙9am-5.30pm Mon-Sat) Trading since 1835, Newcastle's gorgeous covered market has over 110 stalls selling everything from fish, farm produce, meat and vegetables to clothes, accessories and homewares. Between alleys 1 and 2, look out for the historic Weigh House, where goods were once weighed. There are some fantastic food stalls to pick up lunch on the run.

Newcastle Quayside Market · MARKET

(under the Tyne Bridge; ⊙9am-4pm Sun) Stalls displaying jewellery, photographic prints, art, clothing, homewares and more set up along the quays around the Tyne Bridge every Sunday (except in adverse weather). Buskers and food stalls add to the street-party atmosphere.

ℹ Information

Newcastle doesn't have a physical tourist office, but information is available at www.newcastlegateshead.com.

ℹ Getting There & Away

AIR

Newcastle International Airport (NCL; 📞0871 882 1121; www.newcastleairport.com; Woolsington), 7 miles north of the city off the A696, has direct services to many UK and European cities as well as long-haul flights to

Dubai. Tour operators fly charters to the USA, Middle East and Africa.

The airport is linked to town by the Metro (£3.10, 25 minutes, every 12 minutes).

A taxi to central Newcastle costs around £25.

BUS

Local and regional buses leave from **Haymarket** (Percy St) or **Eldon Sq** bus stations. National Express buses arrive and depart from the **coach station** (Churchill St). For local buses around the northeast, the excellent-value Explorer North East ticket (adult/child £10.50/5.50) is valid on most services.

Bus X15 runs north along the A1 to Berwick-upon-Tweed (£6.60, 2½ hours, hourly Monday to Saturday, every two hours Sunday). Bus X18 travels along the coast to Berwick (£6.60, four hours, three daily).

National Express operates services to Edinburgh (£11.50, 2¾ hours, three daily), London (£18.60, eight hours, three daily) and Manchester (£22.30, 4½ hours, four daily).

CAR

Two tollway vehicle tunnels (www.tt2.co.uk, one-way £1.70) travel beneath the Tyne.

TRAIN

Newcastle is on the main rail line between London and Edinburgh and is the starting point of the scenic Tyne Valley Line west to Carlisle.

Alnmouth (for bus connections to Alnwick) £10.60, 35 minutes, hourly

Berwick-upon-Tweed £10.50, 50 minutes, up to two per hour

Carlisle £8.10, 1½ hours, hourly

Durham £5.50, 20 minutes, up to five hourly

Edinburgh £33, 1½ hours, up to two hourly

Hartlepool £9.50, 50 minutes, hourly

London King's Cross £153, 3¼ hours, up to four hourly

York £21.50, 1¼ hours, up to four hourly

ⓘ Getting Around

There's a large bus network, but the best means of getting around is the excellent Metro (www.nexus.org.uk).

Single fares for public transport start from £1.50.

The DaySaver pass (£3 to £5.10) gives unlimited Metro travel for one day for travel after 9am, and the DayRover (adult/child £10.50/5.50) gives unlimited travel on all modes of transport in the Tyne and Wear county for one day for travel any time.

On weekend nights taxis can be rare; try **Noda Taxis** (☑ 0191-222 1888; www.noda-taxis.co.uk), which has a kiosk outside the entrance to Central Station.

DON'T MISS

THE ANGEL OF THE NORTH

Nicknamed the Gateshead Flasher, this extraordinary 200-tonne, rust-coloured, **winged human frame** (www.gateshead.gov.uk; Durham Rd, Low Eighton) has loomed over the A1 motorway some 6 miles south of Newcastle since 1998. Sir Antony Gormley's iconic work (which saw him knighted in 2014) stands 20m high, with a wingspan wider than a Boeing 767. Bus 21 from Newcastle's Eldon Sq (£2.20, 20 minutes) stops here. There's a free car park by the base.

Tynemouth

☑ 0191 / POP 67,520

The mouth of the Tyne, 9 miles east of Newcastle, is one of the best surf spots in England, with great all-year breaks off the immense, crescent-shaped Blue Flag beach, which occasionally hosts major surf competitions.

⊙ Sights & Activities

Tynemouth Priory RUINS
(EH; www.english-heritage.org.uk; Pier Rd; adult/child £5.90/3.50; ⊙10am-6pm Apr-Sep, to 5pm Oct, 10am-4pm Sat & Sun Nov-Mar) Built by Benedictine monks on a strategic bluff above the mouth of the Tyne in the 11th-century ruins, Tynemouth Priory was ransacked during the Dissolution in 1539. The military took over for four centuries, only leaving in 1960, and today the ruined remains of the priory church sit alongside old military installations, their guns aimed out to sea at an enemy that never came.

🛏 Sleeping & Eating

Grand Hotel HERITAGE HOTEL **££**
(☑ 0191-293 6666; www.grandhoteltynemouth.co.uk; Grand Pde; d/f incl breakfast from £98/118; 🅿@🛜) Built in 1872, the one-time summer residence of the Duke and Duchess of Northumberland is a local landmark. Many of the 46 rooms in the main building and neighbouring town house overlook the beach; some have four-poster beds and spa baths. Its Victorian-style real-ale pub, drawing room serving high tea, and brasserie are excellent. Book well ahead at peak times.

★ Riley's Fish Shack SEAFOOD **££**
(☑ 0191-257 1371; http://rileysfishshack.com; King Edward's Bay; dishes £6-18.50, mains £18.50-26.50;

9.30am-10pm Mon-Sat, to 5.30pm Sun, hours can vary) 🥾 Steep timber stairs lead from East St to the beach and this rustic, tucked-away shack. Phenomenal local seafood underpins wood-fired dishes from wraps to empanadas and mains like cod on puy lentils with pancetta and parmesan crumb, served in environmentally friendly wooden boxes. Indoor seating is limited; there's also a handful of stools outside and deckchairs spread on the sand.

Staith House GASTROPUB ££
(☑ 01912-708441; www.thestaithhouse.co.uk; 57 Low Lights; mains £15-26; ⊙ kitchen noon-3pm & 6-9pm Mon-Thu, noon-3.30pm & 6-9.30pm Fri & Sat, bar 11am-1am Mon-Sat, noon-10.30pm Sun; 🐕) 🥾 Opposite the fishing quay where catches are landed daily, gastropub Staith House has a sunny beer garden, bar made from recycled timbers and an outstanding menu drawing on local, sustainable produce including seaweed foraged from Tynemouth's beaches. Seafood is the star (South Shields crab, Lindisfarne oysters, North Sea hake...) but there are also meat dishes such as Northumberland lamb rump.

❶ Getting There & Away

From Newcastle, the easiest way to reach Tynemouth is by Metro (£3.10, 25 minutes, every 12 minutes).

Durham

☎ 0191 / POP 48,069

England's most beautiful Romanesque cathedral, a huge castle, and, surrounding them both, a cobweb of hilly, cobbled streets – filled with upper-crust students attending England's third university of choice (after Oxford and Cambridge) during term time – make Durham an ideal day trip from Newcastle or overnight stop.

◉ Sights

★ **Durham Cathedral** CATHEDRAL
(☑ 0191-386 4266; www.durhamcathedral.co.uk; Palace Green; cathedral by donation, guided tours adult/child £5/4.50; ⊙ cathedral 9.30am-6pm Mon-Sat, 12.30-5.30pm Sun, cathedral tours 10.30am, 11am & 2pm Mon-Sat) Monumental Durham Cathedral is the definitive structure of the Anglo-Norman Romanesque style, a resplendent monument to the country's ecclesiastical history and, since 1986, a Unesco World Heritage Site. Beyond the main door – and the famous **Sanctuary Knocker**,

which medieval felons would strike to gain 37 days asylum within the cathedral before standing trial or leaving the country – the interior is spectacular. Highly worthwhile guided tours last one hour. At the time of writing, the tower, reached by 325 steps, was closed for renovations until 2019.

Durham was the first European cathedral to be roofed with stone-ribbed vaulting, which upheld the heavy stone roof and made it possible to build pointed transverse arches – a great architectural achievement. The central tower dates from 1262, but was damaged in a fire caused by lightning in 1429 and unsatisfactorily patched up until it was entirely rebuilt in 1470. The western towers were added in 1217–26.

The northern side of the beautiful, 1175-built **Galilee Chapel** features rare surviving examples of 12th-century wall painting (thought to feature portraits of Sts Cuthbert and Oswald). Galilee Chapel also contains the **tomb of the Venerable Bede**, the 8th-century Northumbrian monk turned historian: his *Ecclesiastical History of the English People* is still the prime source of information on the development of early Christian Britain. Among other things, Bede introduced the AD system for the numbering of years from the birth of Jesus. He was first buried at Jarrow, but in 1022 a miscreant monk stole his remains and brought them here.

Other highlights include the 14th-century **Bishop's Throne**; the beautiful stone **Neville Screen** (1372–80), which separates the high altar from **St Cuthbert's tomb**; and the mostly 19th-century **Cloisters** where you'll find the **Monk's Dormitory**, now a library of 30,000 books, with Anglo-Saxon carved stones. There are audiovisual displays on the building of the cathedral and the life of St Cuthbert, and a rolling program of exhibitions.

★ **Durham Castle** CASTLE
(☑ 0191-334 2932; www.dur.ac.uk/durham.castle; Palace Green; admission by guided tour only, adult/child £5/4; ⊙ by reservation) Built as a standard motte-and-bailey fort in 1072, Durham Castle was the prince bishops' home until 1837, when it became the University of Durham's first college. It remains a university hall today. Highlights of the 50-minute tour include the 17th-century Black Staircase and the beautifully preserved Norman chapel (1080). Book ahead by phone, or at the Palace Green Library or the World Heritage

Durham

Site Visitor Centre (p620); tours run most days, with additional tours during university holidays.

🏃 Activities

Browns Boathouse   BOATING
(☑ 0191-386 3779; www.brownsboats.co.uk; Elvet Bridge; adult/child per hour £7/4.50; ⊗ 10am-6pm mid-Mar–late Sep) Hire a traditional, hand-built row boat for a romantic river excursion.

Prince Bishop River Cruiser   CRUISE
(☑ 0191-386 9525; www.princebishoprc.co.uk; Browns Boathouse, Elvet Bridge; adult/child £8/5; ⊗ cruises 12.30pm, 2pm & 3pm Mar-Oct) Wonderfully scenic one-hour cruises take you out on the Wear.

🛏 Sleeping

⭐ **Lumley Castle**   CASTLE £££
(☑ 0191-389 1111; www.lumleycastle.com; Ropery Lane, Chester-le-Street; d courtyard/castle from

£170/190, ste from £230; P 🛜) Spiralling stone tower steps and creaking corridors lead to richly decorated rooms with heavy drapes

BEAMISH OPEN-AIR MUSEUM

County Durham's living, breathing, working **museum** (☑ 0191-370 4000; www.beamish. org.uk; Beamish; adult/child £19/11; ⊙ 10am-5pm Easter-Oct, 10am-4pm Nov-Easter, closed Mon & Fri Jan–mid-Feb, last admission 3pm) offers an unflinching glimpse into industrial life in the northeast during the 19th and 20th centuries. Highlights include going underground, exploring mine heads, visiting a working farm, school, dentist and pub, and marvelling at how every cramped pit cottage seemed to find room for a piano. Don't miss a ride behind an 1815 Steam Elephant locomotive or a replica of Stephenson's Locomotion No 1.

Beamish is 9 miles northwest of Durham (though there are no useful bus services), and 10 miles south of Newcastle. From Newcastle, take bus 28 or 28A (£5.10, 50 minutes, every 30 minutes).

and patterned wallpapers, many with canopied four-poster beds, at this atmosphere-steeped 14th-century castle (there are also more modern courtyard rooms). Within the castle's hefty walls are a fine-dining restaurant and antiquarian book–lined library bar; regular events include Elizabethan banquets. It's 7 miles northeast of Durham.

Townhouse BOUTIQUE HOTEL £££
(☑ 0191-384 1037; www.thetownhousedurham.co. uk; 34 Old Elvet; d from £140; ☏) Each of the Townhouse's 11 luxurious rooms has a theme, from French-styled Le Jardin to ocean-liner-like Cruise and the Edwardian Express, re-creating a night in a yesteryear sleeper compartment. A couple of rooms have private outdoor hot tubs. Aged steaks are the speciality of the Modern British restaurant.

✗ Eating

Tealicious CAFE £
(☑ 0191-340 1393; www.tealicioustearoom.co.uk; 88 Elvet Bridge; dishes £2.60-6.25, high tea adult/child £13.50/8.50; ⊙ 10am-4pm Tue-Sat, noon-4pm Sun; ☑) Inside this quaint pastel-blue and white building, homemade cakes (such as white-chocolate cheesecake or ginger and lime), soups and sandwiches are complemented by 24 blends of tea served from individual pots in fine bone china. High tea here is a treat for both adults and kids. It's tiny so book ahead.

Garden House Inn BRITISH ££
(☑ 0191-386 3395; www.gardenhouseinn.com; Framwellgate; sandwiches £5-12, mains £12-18; ⊙ noon-3pm & 5-9.30pm Mon-Sat, noon-6pm Sun; ☏☑) Dating from the 18th century, rustic country-style inn Garden House does great lunchtime sandwiches, such as lobster or crab, fennel and 'Nduja (spicy pork salami)

and locavore menus at both lunch and dinner (Lindisfarne oysters with wild garlic and smoked chilli, roast Northumberland lamb with hazelnut-crusted beetroot). Its six cosy rooms (four doubles, two for families; from £85/105) have vintage-inspired decor.

Cellar Door Durham BRITISH ££
(☑ 0191-383 1856; www.thecellardoordurham. co.uk; 41 Saddler St; mains £16-24, 2-/3-course lunch menus £14/16; ⊙ noon-9.30pm) Accessed via an inconspicuous door on Saddler St, this 12th-century building has glorious river views, including from the terrace. The internationally influenced menu features starters such as crispy lamb belly with tomato couscous, coriander emulsion and aubergine followed by mains such as tandoori chicken leg, Bombay potatoes and puffed wild rice (vegetarian and vegan options available). Service is spot on.

🍷 Drinking & Nightlife

Shakespeare Tavern PUB
(63 Saddler St; ⊙ 11am-11.30pm) Built in 1190, this authentic-as-it-gets locals' boozer is complete with dartboard, cosy snugs, a terrific selection of beers and spirits, and wise-cracking characters propping up the bar – as well as, allegedly, a resident ghost. Look out for folk-music jam sessions.

ℹ Information

Durham's **World Heritage Site Visitor Centre** (World Heritage Site Visitor Centre; ☑ 0191-334 3805; www.durhamworldheritagesite. com/visit/whs-visitor-centre; 7 Owengate; ⊙ 9.30am-5pm Feb-Dec, to 4.30pm Jan) is in the shadow of the castle.

Comprehensive information on the city and county is available online at www.thisisdurham. com.

ⓘ Getting There & Away

BUS

The East Coast Main Line provides speedy connections to destinations including the following:

Edinburgh £44.90, 1¾ hours, hourly

London King's Cross £68.20, three hours, hourly

Newcastle £5.50, 18 minutes, five hourly

York £25, 55 minutes, four hourly

TRAIN

The **bus station** (North Rd) is on North Rd, on the western side of the river.

Destinations include the following:

Hartlepool Bus 57A; £7, one hour, two hourly

London National Express; £30, 6¾ hours, two daily

Newcastle Bus 21, X12 and X21; £4.40, 1¼ hours, at least four hourly

Barnard Castle

📞 01833 / POP 5495

The charming market town of Barnard Castle, better known as 'Barney', is a traditionalist's dream, full of antique and craft shops, and atmospheric old pubs. It's a wonderful setting for the town's twin draws: a daunting ruined castle and an extraordinary French chateau.

⊙ Sights

★ Bowes Museum   MUSEUM

(📞 01833-690606; www.thebowesmuseum.org. uk; Newgate; adult/child £14/5; ⊙10am-5pm) A monumental chateau half a mile east of the centre contains the lavishly furnished Bowes Museum. Funded by 19th-century industrialist John Bowes, and opened in 1892, this brainchild of his Parisian actress wife, Josephine, was built by French architect Jules Pellechet to display a collection the Bowes had travelled the world to assemble. The star attraction is the marvellous 18th-century mechanical silver swan, which performs every day at 2pm. If you miss it, a film shows it in action.

Barnard Castle   RUINS

(EH; 📞 01833-638212; www.english-heritage.org. uk; Scar Top; adult/child £5.60/3.40; ⊙10am-6pm Easter-Sep, to 5pm Oct, 10am-4pm Sat & Sun Nov-Easter) Built on a cliff above the River Tees by Guy de Bailleul and rebuilt around 1150, Barnard Castle was partly dismantled some four centuries later, but its ruins still manage to cover two very impressive hectares with wonderful river views. A sensory garden is also here.

Raby Castle   CASTLE

(📞 01833-660202; www.rabycastle.com; Staindrop; castle, gardens & park adult/child £12/6, gardens & park only £7/3; ⊙11am-4.30pm Tue-Sun Jul & Aug, 11am-4.30pm Wed-Sun late Mar-Jun & Sep) Sprawling Raby Castle was a stronghold of the Catholic Neville family until it engaged in ill-judged plotting (the 'Rising of the North') against the Protestant Queen Elizabeth in 1569. Most of the interior dates from the 18th and 19th centuries, but the exterior remains true to the original design, built around a courtyard and surrounded by a moat. It's 6.8 miles northeast of Barnard Castle; take bus 85A (£3.10, 15 minutes, eight daily Monday to Friday, six Saturday and Sunday).

🛏 Sleeping & Eating

Old Well Inn   INN ££

(📞 01833-690130; http://theoldwellinn.co.uk; 21 The Bank; s/d incl breakfast from £65/85; 🛜) Built over a huge well (not visible), this old coaching inn has 10 enormous rooms. No 9 is the most impressive with its own private entrance, flagstone floors and a bath. The pub has regional ales on tap that you can sip in the leafy beer garden in fine weather.

Cross Lanes
Organic Farm Shop   DELI, CAFE £

(📞 01833-630619; www.crosslanesorganics.co. uk; Cross Lanes, Barnard Castle; dishes £4-13; ⊙8.30am-5pm Mon-Sat, 10am-5pm Sun; 🛜♿) 🍴 Sheep graze on the grass-covered roof of

---

LOCAL KNOWLEDGE

KNITSLEY FARM SHOP

It's worth stopping off 12 miles northwest of Durham en route to Northumberland National Park and Hadrian's Wall to stock up on incredible cheeses, meats, fruits, veggies, homemade sweets, biscuits, cakes and breads at **Knitsley Farm Shop** (📞 01207-592059; www.knitsleyfarmshop.co.uk; East Knitsley Grange Farm, Knitsley; dishes £5-12.50; ⊙shop 10am-5pm Tue-Sat, to 4pm Sun, cafe 10am-5pm Tue-Fri, 9.30am-5pm Sat, 9.30am-4pm Sun) 🍴. Make time to dine at its wonderful cafe on fresh-as-it-gets soups, farmyard sausages, and pulled-pork and crackling baps.

this award-winning farm shop and cafe 1.5 miles south of Barnard Castle. The cavernous interior brims with all-organic produce; breakfasts (home-cured bacon, homemade sausages and eggs from the farm's chickens) segue into lunches including gourmet sandwiches, steak or veggie burgers and wood-fired pizzas, and 'rustic afternoon tea' with organic cream and wild-fruit jams.

★ **Raby Hunt** GASTRONOMY £££
(☑ 01325-374237; www.rabyhuntrestaurant.co.uk; Summerhouse, Darlington; tasting menu £115, chef's table £150; ⊘ 6-9.30pm Wed-Sat, noon-2pm Sun; 🛜) A two-century-old, ivy-clad drovers' inn 11 miles east of Barnard Castle is now the staging post for gastronomic expeditions by self-taught chef James Close, who received his first Michelin star in 2012 and second in 2017. Tasting menus (no à la carte) typically feature 12 to 15 intricate courses, such as in-the-shell razor clams with brown shrimp. Reserve weeks ahead.

In the former stables are three luxurious guest rooms (doubles including breakfast from £180).

★ **Bay Horse** GASTROPUB £££
(☑ 01325-720663; www.thebayhorsehurworth.com; The Green, Hurworth-on-Tees; mains lunch £8-22, dinner £20-25; ⊘ kitchen noon-2.30pm & 6-9.30pm Mon-Sat, noon-4pm Sun, bar 11am-11pm Mon-Sat, noon-10.30pm Sun; 🅿) It's well worth the 19-mile trip east of Barnard Castle to this 15th-century coaching inn in the pretty riverside village of Hurworth-on-Tees, but book ahead so you don't miss out on exceptional locally sourced dishes such as pan-fried hake with smoked apple and eel croquettes or rabbit loin with rabbit-leg pie. Wild garlic, leeks, nettles and herbs are foraged nearby.

❶ Getting There & Away

Barnard Castle is poorly served by public transport and several of its key draws are outside the town so you really need your own wheels.

Hadrian's Wall

Named in honour of the emperor who ordered it built, Hadrian's Wall was one of Rome's greatest engineering projects. This enormous 73-mile-long wall was built between AD 122 and 128 to separate Romans and Scottish Picts. Today, the awe-inspiring sections that remain are testament to Roman ambition and tenacity.

When completed, the mammoth structure ran across the island's narrow neck, from the Solway Firth in the west almost to the mouth of the Tyne in the east. Every Roman mile (0.95 miles) there was a gateway guarded by a small fort (milecastle) and between each milecastle were two observation turrets. Milecastles are numbered right across the country, starting with Milecastle 0 at Wallsend – where you can visit the wall's last stronghold, Segedunum (p626) – and ending with Milecastle 80 at Bowness-on-Solway.

A series of forts was developed as bases some distance south (and may predate the wall), and 16 lie astride it.

🕺 Activities

The **Hadrian's Wall Path** (www.nationaltrail.co.uk/hadrians-wall-path) is an 84-mile national trail that runs the length of the wall from Wallsend in the east to Bowness-on-Solway in the west. The entire route should take about seven days on foot, giving plenty of time to explore the rich archaeological heritage along the way.

❶ Information

There are tourist offices in **Hexham** (☑ 01670-620450; www.visitnorthumberland.com; Queen's Hall, Beaumont St; ⊘ 9am-5pm Mon-Fri, 9.30am-5pm Sat), Haltwhistle (p628) and Corbridge (p626). The Walltown Visitor Centre (p629), aka the Northumberland National Park Visitor Centre, is located at Greenhead, and will reopen in summer 2019 following renovations. Tourist information is also available from **The Sill** (National Landscape Discovery Centre; ☑ 01434-341200; www.thesill.org.uk; Military Rd, Once Brewed; ⊘ 9.30am-6pm Apr-early Nov), aka the National Landscape Discovery Centre, at Once Brewed.

Hadrian's Wall Country (http://hadrianswallcountry.co.uk) is the official portal for the entire area.

❶ Getting There & Around

BUS

The AD122 Hadrian's Wall bus (five daily, Easter to September) is a hail-and-ride service that runs between Hexham and Carlisle, with one bus a day starting and ending at Newcastle's Central Station; not all services cover the entire route. Bikes can be taken aboard AD122 buses, but space is limited. Bus 185 zips between Birdoswald Roman Fort and Carlisle via Haltwhistle the rest of the year (three daily, Monday to Saturday only).

Bus 10 links Newcastle with Hexham (1½ hours, every 30 minutes Monday to Saturday, hourly on Sunday).

West of Hexham the wall runs parallel to the A69, which connects Carlisle and Newcastle. Buses X84 and X85 run along the A69 every 30 minutes, passing 2 to 3 miles south of the main sites.

All these services except the X84 and X85 can be used with the **Hadrian's Wall Rover Ticket** (one day adult/child £12.50/6.50, three day £25/13). Show your Rover Ticket to get 10% off admission to all museums and attractions.

The **Hadrian's Frontier Ticket** (adult/child one day £16/8 three day £32/16) provides unlimited transport on all buses throughout Northumberland.

Both tickets are available from bus drivers and tourist offices, where you can also get timetables.

CAR & MOTORCYCLE

Your own wheels are the easiest way to get around, with one fort or garrison usually just a short hop from the next. Parking costs £5/15 per day/week; tickets are valid at all sites along the wall.

The B6318 follows the course of the wall from the outskirts of Newcastle to Birdoswald. The main A69 road and the railway line follow 3 or 4 miles to the south.

TRAIN

The railway line between Newcastle and Carlisle (Tyne Valley Line; £16.60, 1½ hours, hourly) has stations at Corbridge, Hexham, Haydon Bridge, Bardon Mill, Haltwhistle and Brampton. Not all services stop at all stations.

Corbridge

📞 01434 / POP 3011

Above a green-banked curve in the Tyne, Corbridge's shady, cobbled streets are lined with old-fashioned shops and pubs. Inhabited since Saxon times when there was a substantial monastery, many of the village's

Hadrian's Wall & Northumberland National Park

Hadrian's Wall

ROME'S FINAL FRONTIER

Of all Britain's Roman ruins, Emperor Hadrian's 2nd-century wall, cutting across northern England from the Irish Sea to the North Sea, is by far the most spectacular; Unesco awarded it World Heritage status in 1987.

We've picked out the highlights, one of which is the prime remaining Roman fort on the wall, Housesteads, which we've reconstructed here.

Housesteads' Granaries

Nothing like the clever underground ventilation system, which kept vital supplies of grain dry in Northumberland's damp and drizzly climate, would be seen again in these parts for 1500 years.

Milecastle

North Gate

Interval Tower

Birdoswald Roman Fort

Explore the longest intact stretch of the wall, scramble over the remains of a large fort then head indoors to wonder at a full-scale model of the wall at its zenith. Great fun for the kids.

Map:
- 0 — 10 km
- 0 — 5 miles
- (N) Birdoswald Roman Fort
- Irthing
- Harrow Scar Milecastle
- Greenhead
- Roman Army Museum
- Sewingshields
- Housesteads Roman Fort & Museum
- B6318
- Hadrian's Wall
- Chesters Roman Fort & Museum
- Chollerford
- Low Brunton
- Once Brewed
- Vindolanda Roman Fort & Museum
- Acomb
- A69
- Bardon Mill
- Haydon Bridge
- Hexham
- Haltwhistle
- South Tyne
- Brampton

Chesters Roman Fort

Built to keep watch over a bridge spanning the River North Tyne, Britain's best-preserved Roman cavalry fort has a terrific bathhouse, essential if you have months of nippy northern winter ahead.

Hexham Abbey

This may be the finest non-Roman sight near Hadrian's Wall, but the 7th-century parts of this magnificent church were built with stone quarried by the Romans for use in their forts.

Housesteads' Hospital

Operations performed at the hospital would have been surprisingly effective, even without anaesthetics; religious rituals and prayers to Aesculapius, the Roman god of healing, were possibly less helpful for a hernia or appendicitis.

Housesteads' Latrines
Communal toilets were the norm in Roman times and Housesteads' are remarkably well preserved – fortunately no traces remain of the vinegar-soaked sponges that were used instead of toilet paper.

ALISON ROSCOE / GETTY IMAGES ©

Commanding Officer's House

Farms

Workshop

Headquarters

Barracks

West Gate

Angle Tower

FREE GUIDES

At some sites, knowledgeable volunteer heritage guides are on hand to answer questions and put meat on the wall's stony bones.

Housesteads' Gatehouses
Unusually at Housesteads neither of the gates faces the enemy, as was the norm at Roman forts; builders aligned them east–west. Ruts worn by cart wheels are still visible in the stone.

SCALING THE WALL

The main concentration of sights is in the central and wildest part of the wall, roughly between Corbridge in the east and Brampton in the west. All our suggested stops are within this area and follow an east–west route. The easiest way to travel is by car, scooting along the B6318, but special bus AD122 will also get you there. Hiking along the designated Hadrian's Wall Path (84 miles) allows you to appreciate the achievement up close.

charming buildings feature stones nicked from nearby Corstopitum.

◉ Sights

Corbridge Roman
Site & Museum
HISTORIC SITE

(EH; www.english-heritage.org.uk; Corchester Lane; adult/child £7.60/4.60; ⊙10am-6pm Apr-Sep, to 5pm Oct, 10am-4pm Sat & Sun Nov-Mar) What's left of the Roman garrison town of Corstopitum lies about half a mile west of Market Pl on Dere St, once the main road from York to Scotland. It's the oldest fortified site in the area, predating the wall itself by some 40 years. Most of what you see here, though, dates from around AD 200, when the fort had developed into a civilian settlement and was the main base along the wall.

⌂ Sleeping & Eating

★ Lord Crewe Arms
INN £££

(⌨01434-677100; www.lordcrewearmsblanchland. co.uk; The Square, Blanchland; d from £184; P⊗🐾) An 1165-built abbot's house in the honeystone North Pennines village of Blanchland, 11 miles south of Corbridge, shelters some of this entrancing inn's 21 rooms, while others are located in former miners' cottages. Rates almost halve outside high season. Non-guests can dine on outstanding Modern British fare and drink in its vaulted bar, the Crypt, with a monumental medieval fireplace.

★ Corbridge Larder
DELI, CAFE £

(⌨01434-632948; www.corbridgelarder.co.uk; 18 Hill St; dishes £3.50-10; ⊙9am-5pm Mon-Sat, 10am-4pm Sun) Gourmet picnic fare at this fabulous deli includes bread, over 100 varieties of cheese, chutneys, cakes, chocolates and wine (you can get hampers made up) as well as made-to-order sandwiches, pies, quiches, tarts, and antipasti and mezze delicacies. Upstairs from the wonderland of provisions there's a small sit-down cafe serving dishes such as Moroccan spiced chicken.

❶ Information

Corbridge's **tourist office** (⌨01434-632815; www.visitnorthumberland.com; Hill St; ⊙10am-4.30pm Mon-Sat Apr-Oct, 11am-4pm Wed, Fri & Sat Nov-Mar) occupies a corner of the library.

❶ Getting There & Away

Buses X84 and X85 between Newcastle (£5.10, 45 minutes, hourly) and Carlisle (£7.40, 2¼ hours, hourly) come through Corbridge, as does bus 10 from Newcastle (£5.10, one hour, every

---

HADRIAN'S WALL SITES

Along with key sites such as Housesteads and Vindolanda, there are numerous other Roman remains stationed along Hadrian's Wall.

Segedunum (⌨0191-278 4217; https://segedunumromanfort.org.uk; Buddle St, Wallsend; adult/child £6/free; ⊙10am-5pm Jun–mid-Sep, to 4pm Easter-May & mid-Sep–early Nov, to 2.30pm Mon-Fri early Nov-Easter) was the last strong post of Hadrian's Wall, 5 miles east of Newcastle in the suburb of Wallsend. Beneath the 35m-high tower is an absorbing site that includes a reconstructed Roman bathhouse (with steaming pools and frescos) and a museum.

Chesters Roman Fort (EH; ⌨01434-681379; www.english-heritage.org.uk; Chollerford; adult/child £7/4.20; ⊙10am-6pm Apr-Sep, 10am-5pm Oct, 10am-4pm Sat & Sun Nov–mid-Feb, 10am-4pm Wed-Sun mid-Feb–Mar) near the village of Chollerford housed up to 500 troops from Asturias in northern Spain. It includes part of a bridge (best appreciated from the eastern bank), four gatehouses, a bathhouse and an underfloor heating system.

Birdoswald Roman Fort (EH; ⌨01697-747602; www.english-heritage.org.uk; Gilsland, Greenhead; adult/child £8.30/5; ⊙10am-6pm Apr-Sep, 10am-5pm Oct, 10am-4pm Sat & Sun Nov–mid-Feb, 10am-4pm Wed-Sun mid-Feb–Mar) (Banna to the Romans) has the longest intact stretch of wall, extending from here to Harrow's Scar Milecastle. It overlooks Irthing Gorge, 4 miles west of Greenhead in Cumbria.

Binchester Roman Fort (www.durham.gov.uk/binchester; adult/child £5/3.50; ⊙10am-5pm Jul & Aug, 11am-5pm Easter-Jun & Sep), or Vinovia, lies 9.6 miles southwest of Durham. First built in wood around AD 80 and refashioned in stone early in the 2nd century, the fort was the largest in County Durham.

30 minutes Monday to Saturday, hourly Sunday) to Hexham (£2.20, 12 minutes, every 30 minutes Monday to Saturday, hourly Sunday). At Hexham you can connect with the Hadrian's Wall bus AD122 in summer or bus 185 year-round.

Corbridge is also on the railway line between Newcastle (£6.20, 45 minutes, hourly) and Carlisle (£14.90, 1½ hours, hourly).

Haltwhistle & Around

📞 01434 / POP 3811

The village of Haltwhistle, little more than two intersecting streets, has more key Hadrian's Wall sights in its surrounds than anywhere else along the wall, but tourist infrastructure here is surprisingly underdeveloped.

Haltwhistle claims to be the geographic centre of the British mainland, although the jury is still out.

👁 Sights

★ Housesteads Roman Fort & Museum
HISTORIC SITE

(EH; 📞 01434-344363; www.english-heritage.org.uk; Haydon Bridge; adult/child £7.80/4.70; ⊙ 10am-6pm Apr-Sep, to 5pm Oct, to 4pm Nov-Mar) The most dramatic site of Hadrian's Wall – and the best-preserved Roman fort in the whole country – is at Housesteads, 4 miles north of Bardon Mill on the B6318, and 6.5 miles northeast of Haltwhistle. From here, high on a ridge and covering 2 hectares, you can survey the moors of Northumberland National Park, and the snaking wall, with a sense of awe at the landscape and the aura of the Roman lookouts.

★ Vindolanda Roman Fort & Museum
HISTORIC SITE

(📞 01434-344277; www.vindolanda.com; Bardon Mill; adult/child £7.90/4.75, with Roman Army Museum £11.60/6.80; ⊙ 10am-6pm Apr-Sep, to 5pm early Feb-Mar & Oct, to 4pm Nov-early Feb) The extensive site of Vindolanda offers a fascinating glimpse into the daily life of a Roman garrison town. The time-capsule museum is just one part of this large, extensively excavated site, which includes impressive parts of the fort and town (excavations continue) and reconstructed turrets and temple. Extraordinary finds unearthed in 2017 include the only known pair of Roman boxing gloves.

It's 1.5 miles north of Bardon Mill between the A69 and B6318, and 5.8 miles northeast of Haltwhistle.

Roman Army Museum
MUSEUM

(📞 01697-747485; www.vindolanda.com/roman-army-museum; Greenhead; adult/child £6.60/3.75 with Vindolanda £11.60/6.80; ⊙ 10am-6pm Apr-Sep, to 5pm mid-Feb–Mar & Oct) On the site of the Carvoran Roman Fort a mile northeast of Greenhead, near Walltown Crags, this revamped museum has three galleries covering the Roman army and the expanding and contracting Empire; the wall (with a 3D film illustrating what the wall was like nearly 2000 years ago and today); and colourful background detail to Hadrian's Wall life (such as how the soldiers spent their R&R time in this lonely outpost of the Empire).

🛏 Sleeping

★ Ashcroft
B&B ££

(📞 01434-320213; www.ashcroftguesthouse.co.uk; Lanty's Lonnen, Haltwhistle; s/d/f/apt from £80/94/124/140; 🅿 🛜) British B&Bs don't get better than this elegant Edwardian vicarage surrounded by nearly a hectare of beautifully manicured, terraced lawns and gardens. Some rooms open to private balconies and terraces and all have soaring ceilings and 21st-century gadgets. Breakfast (included) is cooked on a cast-iron Aga and served in a grand dining room.

Holmhead Guest House
B&B ££

(📞 01697-747402; http://bandb-hadrianswall.co.uk; Greenhead; campsites per 1/2 people £7/10, dm/s/d from £15.50/72/82; ⊙ guesthouse year-round, camping & bunk barn May-Sep; 🅿 🛜) Built using recycled bits of the wall on whose foundations it stands, this superb farmhouse half a mile north of Greenhead offers comfy rooms, a basic bunk barn and five unpowered campsites. The Pennine Way and the Hadrian's Wall Path pass through the grounds and Thirlwall Castle's jagged ruins loom above. Ask to see the 3rd-century Roman graffiti.

★ Langley Castle Hotel
CASTLE £££

(📞 01434-688888; www.langleycastle.com; Langley; d castle view/castle from £167/255; 🅿 🛜 ❄) Soaring above 12 acres of gardens, this 1350-built castle is a beauty, with creaking hallways lined by suits of armour and an alleged resident ghost. Its nine castle rooms are appointed with antique furnishings (many have four-poster beds); there are another 18 'castle view' rooms in the grounds with access to castle facilities. Check for dinner, bed and breakfast packages.

HEXHAM ABBEY

Bustling Hexham is a handsome if somewhat scuffed market town centred on its grand Augustinian **abbey** (☎ 01434-602031; www.hexhamabbey.org.uk; Beaumont St; by donation; ⊙ 9.30am-5pm), a marvellous example of Early English architecture. It cleverly escaped the Dissolution of 1537 by rebranding as Hexham's parish church, a role it still has today. The highlight is the 7th-century Saxon crypt, the only surviving element of St Wilfrid's Church, built with inscribed stones from Corstopitum in 674.

❶ Information

Tourist Office (☎ 01434-321863; www.visitnorthumberland.com; Mechanics Institute, Westgate; ⊙ 10am-4.30pm Mon-Fri, to 1pm Sat) On Haltwhistle's main street.

❶ Getting There & Away

Bus 185 runs to the Roman Army Museum (£2.60, 10 minutes, three daily) and Birdoswald Roman Fort (£3.10, 25 minutes, three daily).

Haltwhistle is also linked by train to Hexham (£6.70, 20 minutes, hourly) and Newcastle (£13.10, one hour, hourly).

Northumberland National Park

England's last great wilderness is the 405 sq miles of natural wonderland that make up the country's least populated national park. The finest sections of Hadrian's Wall run along its southern edge and the landscape is dotted with prehistoric remains and fortified houses – the thick-walled peles were the only solid buildings built here until the mid-18th century.

Adjacent to the national park, the Kielder Water & Forest Park is home to the vast artificial lake Kielder Water, holding 200,000 million litres. Surrounding its 27-mile-long shoreline is England's largest plantation forest, with 150 million spruce and pine trees.

The lack of population helped see the area awarded dark-sky status by the International Dark Skies Association in 2013 (the largest such designation in Europe), with controls to prevent light pollution.

◉ Sights & Activities

The most spectacular stretch of the **Hadrian's Wall Path** is between Sewingshields and Greenhead in the south of the park.

There are many fine walks through the Cheviots (including a clamber to the top of the 815m-high Cheviot, the highest peak in the range), frequently passing by prehistoric remnants; local tourist offices can provide maps, guides and route information.

★ **Kielder Observatory**   OBSERVATORY
(☎ 0191-265 5510; https://kielderobservatory.org; Black Fell, off Shilling Pot; adult/child from £22/20.50; ⊙ by reservation) For the best views of the Northumberland International Dark Sky Park, attend a stargazing session at this state-of-the-art, 2008-built observatory. Its program spans night-time safari observing sessions to family events and astrophotography. Book well ahead for all events, which sell out quickly, and dress as you would for the ski slopes (it's seriously chilly here at night). At the signs towards Kielder Observatory and Skyspace, turn left; it's a 2-mile drive up the track.

Chillingham Castle   CASTLE
(☎ 01668-215359; www.chillingham-castle.com; Chillingham; castle adult/child £9.50/5.50, Chillingham Wild Cattle £8/3, castle & Chillingham Wild Cattle £16/6; ⊙ castle noon-5pm Apr-Oct, Chillingham Wild Cattle tours 10am, 11am, noon, 2pm, 3pm & 4pm Mon-Fri, 10am, 11am & noon Sun Apr-Oct) Steeped in history, warfare, torture and ghosts, 13th-century Chillingham is said to be one of the country's most haunted places, with spectres from a phantom funeral to Lady Mary Berkeley seeking her errant husband. Owner Sir Humphry Wakefield has passionately restored the castle's extravagant medieval staterooms, stone-flagged banquet halls and grisly torture chambers. Chillingham is 6 miles southeast of Wooler. Bus 470 (four daily Monday to Saturday) between Alnwick (£3, 25 minutes) and Wooler (£3, 20 minutes) stops at Chillingham.

Cragside House, Garden & Woodland   HISTORIC BUILDING, GARDENS
(NT; ☎ 01669-620333; www.nationaltrust.org.uk; adult/child £18/9, gardens & woodland only £13/6.50; ⊙ house 11am-5pm, gardens & woodland

10am-6pm mid-Mar–Oct, hours can vary) Situated 1 mile northeast of Rothbury just off the B6341 is the astonishing country retreat of the first Lord Armstrong. In the 1880s the house had hot and cold running water, a telephone and alarm system, and was the world's first to be lit by electricity, generated through hydropower. The sprawling Victorian gardens feature lakes, moors and one of Europe's largest rock gardens. Visit late May to mid-June to see Cragside's famous rhododendrons in bloom.

🛌 Sleeping

Wooler YHA   HOSTEL **£**

(☑ 01668-281365; www.yha.org.uk; 30 Cheviot St, Wooler; dm/d/hut from £18/37/50; ☺ Apr-Oct; P🛜) In a low, red-brick building above Wooler, this handy hostel contains 57 beds in a variety of rooms (including handcrafted 'shepherds' huts' sleeping two to three people warmed by electric heating), a modern lounge and a small restaurant, as well as a self-catering kitchen, drying room and bike storage.

★ Otterburn Castle
Country House Hotel   CASTLE **££**

(☑ 01830-520620; www.otterburncastle.com; Main St, Otterburn; d/ste incl breakfast from £130/210; P🛜❄) Founded by William the Conqueror's cousin Robert de Umfraville in 1086 and set in almost 13 hectares of grounds, this story-book castle has 17 classically furnished rooms; some of its suites have four-poster beds and fireplaces. Modern British fare is served in its wood-panelled Oak Room Restaurant (2-/3-course menus £25/30); open fires blaze in its bar.

❶ Information

For information, contact the **Northumberland National Park** (☑ 01434-605555; www.northumberlandnationalpark.org.uk).

As well as tourist offices in towns including **Wooler** (☑ 01668-282123; www.wooler.org.uk; Cheviot Centre, 12 Padgepool Pl, Wooler; ☺10am-4.30pm Mon-Fri, to 1pm Sat) and **Rothbury** (☑ 01669-621979; www.visitkielder.com; Coquetdale Centre, Church St, Rothbury; ☺10am-4.30pm Mon-Fri, 10.30am-4pm Sat Apr-Oct, reduced hours Nov-Mar), there's a national park office, the **Walltown Visitor Centre** (Northumberland National Park Visitor Centre; ☑ 01434-344396; www.northumberlandnationalpark.org.uk; Greenhead; ☺10am-6pm Apr-Sep, to 5pm Oct, 10am-4pm Sat & Sun Nov-Mar), near Haltwhistle, reopening in summer 2019. Inside Kielder Castle, a hunting lodge built in 1775, the **Forest Park Centre** (☑ 01434-250209; www.visitkielder.com; Forest Dr, Kielder; ☺10am-4pm) has tourist information on the Northumberland National Park, including hiking, mountain biking and watersports in the Kielder area.

All offices can help find accommodation.

❶ Getting There & Away

Public transport options are limited at best – to explore properly you really need your own wheels.

Otterburn Bus 808 (£3.60, one hour, one daily Monday to Saturday) runs between Otterburn and Newcastle.

Wooler Buses 470 and 473 link Wooler and Alnwick (£3, 40 minutes, four daily Monday to Saturday). Buses 267 and 464 run between Wooler and Berwick-upon-Tweed (£4.50, one hour, every two hours Monday to Saturday).

Northumberland Coast

Northumberland's coast, like its wild and remote interior, is sparsely populated. You won't find any hurdy-gurdy seaside resorts, but instead charming, castle-crowned villages strung along miles of wide, sandy beaches that you might just have to yourself.

Alnwick

☑ 01665 / POP 8116

Northumberland's historic ducal town, Alnwick (pronounced 'annick') is an elegant maze of narrow cobbled streets around its colossal medieval castle. Alnwick is also home to an enchanting bookshop and the spectacular Alnwick Garden.

◉ Sights

★ Alnwick Castle   CASTLE

(☑ 01665-511178; www.alnwickcastle.com; The Peth; adult/child £16/8.50, with Alnwick Garden £28/12.20; ☺10am-5.30pm Apr-Oct) Set in parklands designed by Lancelot 'Capability' Brown, the imposing ancestral home of the Duke of Northumberland has changed little since the 14th century. It's a favourite set for film-makers and starred as Hogwarts for the first couple of Harry Potter films. The interior is sumptuous and extravagant; the six rooms open to the public – staterooms, dining room, guard chamber and library – have an incredible display of Italian paintings, including Titian's *Ecce Homo* and many Canalettos.

Alnwick Garden
GARDENS

(www.alnwickgarden.com; Denwick Lane; adult/child £13.20/4.95, with Alnwick Castle £28/12.20; ⊙10am-6pm Apr-Oct, to 4pm Feb-Mar) This 4.8-hectare walled garden incorporates a series of magnificent green spaces surrounding the breathtaking Grand Cascade – 120 separate jets spurting some 30,000L of water down 21 weirs. Half a dozen other gardens include a Franco-Italian-influenced Ornamental Garden (with over 15,000 plants), Rose Garden and fascinating Poison Garden, home to some of the deadliest – and most illegal – plants in the world, including cannabis, magic mushrooms, belladonna and tobacco.

Enveloped by – but not in – the treetops, the timber-lined **Treehouse** (☑01665-511852; mains £10.50-16.50; ⊙noon-2.30pm Mon & Tue, noon-2.30pm & 6-8.30pm Wed-Sat, noon-4pm Sun) restaurant serves Modern British cuisine.

⊨ Sleeping & Eating

★ Alnwick Lodge
B&B, CAMPGROUND ££

(☑01665-604363; www.alnwicklodge.com; West Cawledge Park, A1; tent sites from £15, glamping incl linen from £58, B&B s/d/f from £55/75/100; [P][☎][☻]) Situated 3 miles south of Alnwick's centre, this gorgeous Victorian farmstead has 15 antique-filled rooms with quirky touches like free-standing, lidded baths. Cooked breakfasts are served around a huge circular banqueting table. You can also go 'glamping' in restored gypsy caravans, wagons and shepherds' huts (with shared bathrooms), or pitch up on the sheltered meadow.

White Swan Hotel
HOTEL ££

(☑01665-602109; www.classiclodges.co.uk; Bondgate Within; d/f from £119/142; [P][☎][☻]) In the heart of town, this 300-year-old coaching inn has 56 superbly appointed rooms, including family rooms that sleep up to four. Its architectural showpiece is the fine-dining **Olympic restaurant** (mains £12.50-21, 2-/3-course lunch menus £14/18, 3-course dinner menu £35.50; ⊙noon-3pm & 5-9pm).

Plough Inn
GASTROPUB ££

(☑01665-602395; www.theploughalnwick.co.uk; 24 Bondgate Without; mains lunch £5.50-11.50, dinner £13-22; ⊙kitchen noon-2.30pm & 5.30-9pm Mon-Thu, noon-2.30pm & 5.30-10pm Fri &

Sat, noon-8pm Sun, bar to 11pm Sun-Thu, to 1am Fri & Sat) An 1896 coaching inn now contains this excellent gastropub styled like a contemporary hunting lodge. Evening dining is inspired: hot water crust mixed game pie, potted rabbit with gooseberry chutney, and whole grilled Amble lemon sole. Crab soups and sandwiches are the mainstays at lunch. Upstairs are seven spacious countrified rooms (doubles including breakfast from £145).

🛍 Shopping

★ Barter Books
BOOKS

(☑01665-604888; www.barterbooks.co.uk; Alnwick Station, Wagon Way Rd; ⊙9am-7pm) Coal fires, velvet ottomans, reading rooms and a cafe make this secondhand bookshop in Alnwick's Victorian former railway station wonderfully atmospheric. It's responsible for the renaissance of the WWII 'Keep Calm and Carry On' slogan: while converting the station, the owner unearthed a set of posters – the framed original is above the till – and turned it into a successful industry.

ℹ Information

Alnwick's **tourist office** (☑01670-622152; www.visitalnwick.org.uk; 2 The Shambles; ⊙9.30am-5pm Mon-Sat, 10am-4pm Sun Easter-Oct, 10am-4pm Mon-Sat Nov-Easter) is by Market Pl.

ℹ Getting There & Away

Bus X15 zips along the A1 to Berwick-upon-Tweed (£6.60, one hour, hourly Monday to Saturday, every two hours Sunday) and Newcastle (£6.60, 1½ hours, hourly Monday to Saturday, every two hours Sunday). Bus X18 follows the coast to Berwick-upon-Tweed (£6.60, two hours, three daily) and Newcastle (£6.30, two hours, hourly).

Alnwick's nearest train station is at Alnmouth, connected to Alnwick by bus X18 (£2.70, 10 minutes, hourly Monday to Saturday, every two hours Sunday). Alnmouth's train services include Berwick-upon-Tweed (£7, 20 minutes, up to two per hour), Edinburgh (£20.30, one hour, up to two per hour) and Newcastle (£10.60, 40 minutes, up to two per hour).

Craster
☑01665 / POP 305

Sandy, salty Craster is a small, sheltered fishing village about 6 miles northeast of Alnwick, and is famous for its kippers. In the early 20th century, 2500 herring were

Driving Tour
Northumberland Coast

START NEWBIGGIN-BY-THE-SEA
END BERWICK-UPON-TWEED
LENGTH 78 MILES; ONE DAY

It's possible to shadow the coast to the Scottish border from Tynemouth, but the scenery really picks up at ① **Newbiggin-by-the-Sea**. Newbiggin's beach was restored in 2007, when over 500,000 tonnes of Skegness' sand was relocated here to counteract erosion, and Sean Henry's gigantic bronze sculpture *The Couple* was installed offshore.

Continuing north along the A1068 coast road for 13 miles brings you to the fishing port of ② **Amble**, with a boardwalk along the seafront and puffin cruises (p634). Less than 2 miles north, biscuit-coloured ③ **Warkworth** is a cluster of houses around a loop in the River Coquet, dominated by the craggy ruin of 14th-century Warkworth Castle. The castle features in Shakespeare's *Henry IV* Parts I and II, and the 1998 film *Elizabeth* was shot here.

Some 5 miles north of Warkworth is ④ **Alnmouth**, with brightly painted houses and pretty beaches. It's another 5 miles inland to the bustling town of ⑤ **Alnwick** (p629) to see its imposing castle – which starred as Harry Potter's Hogwarts – and glorious Alnwick Garden. Turn back towards the coast and follow the B1339 for 4.7 miles before turning east on Windside Hill to ⑥ **Craster** (p630), famed for its smoked kippers. From Craster, there are spectacular views of brooding Dunstanburgh Castle. Around 5 miles north at ⑦ **Low Newton-by-the-Sea**, in Embleton Bay, pause for a pint brewed at the Ship Inn (p633).

Past the village of Seahouses (the jumping-off point for the Farne Islands), quaint ⑧ **Bamburgh** (p633) is home to the most dramatic castle yet. Another 17 miles on, via a tidal causeway (check tide times!), the sacred priory ruins (p634) of isolated, otherworldly ⑨ **Holy Island (Lindisfarne)** (p634) still attract spiritual pilgrims. Return to the mainland where, 14 miles north, you can walk almost the entire length of the Elizabethan walls (p635) encircling England's northernmost city, beautiful ⑩ **Berwick-upon-Tweed** (p635).

WORTH A TRIP

HARTLEPOOL

Steelworks and shipyards made this North Sea coastal town's fortunes in the 19th century, but also made it a WWI target. On 16 December 1914 it was hit by 1150 shells, killing 117 people including 29-year-old Durham Light Infantry Private Theophilus Jones, the war's first soldier killed on British soil. You can still see the town's underground magazines, parade ground and panoramic observation tower at the 19th-century **Heugh Gun Battery Museum** (☎ 01429-270746; www.heughbattery.com; Moor Tce; adult/child £6/4; ◷ 10am-5pm Fri-Mon Jun-Aug, 10am-4pm Sat & Sun Feb-May & Sep-Nov).

Also worth a visit is **Hartlepool's Maritime Experience** (☎ 01429-860077; www.hartlepoolsmaritimeexperience.com; Jackson Dock, Maritime Ave; adult/child £10/8; ◷ 10am-5pm Easter-Oct, 11am-4pm Nov-Easter), a family-friendly attraction that brings local history to life with costumed staff, intriguing historical exhibits and recreated businesses (such as a gunsmith, swordsmith and so on) along its historic quayside. It's also home to the 1817-built HMS *Trincomalee*, the oldest British warship still afloat.

smoked here daily. The kippers still produced today often grace the Queen's breakfast table.

◉ Sights

Dunstanburgh Castle CASTLE
(EH; www.english-heritage.org.uk; Dunstanburgh Rd; adult/child £5.40/3.20; ◷ 10am-6pm Apr-Aug, to 5pm Sep, to 4pm Oct, 10am-4pm Sat & Sun Nov-Mar) The dramatic 1.5-mile walk along the coast from Craster (not accessible by car) is the most scenic path to this moody, weather-beaten castle. Its construction began in 1314 and it was strengthened during the Wars of the Roses, but left to crumble, becoming ruined by 1550. Parts of the original wall and gatehouse keep are still standing and it's a tribute to its builders that so much remains.

✖ Eating

Jolly Fisherman GASTROPUB ££
(☎ 016650-576461; www.thejollyfishermancraster.co.uk; Haven Hill; mains lunch £8-14, dinner £12-25; ◷ kitchen 11am-3pm & 5-8.30pm Mon-Sat, noon-5pm Sun, bar 11am-11pm Mon-Sat, to 11pm Sun) Crab (in soup, sandwiches, fish platters and more) is the speciality of this gastropub, but it also has a variety of fish dishes, as well as a house burger and steaks served with beef-dripping chips. A strong wine list complements its wonderful real ales. There's a blazing fire in the bar and a beer garden overlooking Dunstanburgh Castle.

 Robson & Sons FOOD
(☎ 01665-576223; www.kipper.co.uk; Haven Hill; kippers per kilo from £9; ◷ 9am-4.30pm Mon-Fri,

9am-3.30pm Sat, 11am-3.30pm Sun) Four generations have operated this traditional fish smokers; loyal customers include the Royal Family. It's best known for its kippers, but also smokes salmon and other fish.

❶ Getting There & Away

Bus X18 runs to Alnwick (£5.40, 55 minutes, three daily), Berwick-upon-Tweed (£6.60, 1½ hours, three daily) and Newcastle (£6.60, 2½ hours, three daily). From Monday to Saturday, bus 418 also links Craster to Alnwick (£5.10, 30 minutes, four daily).

Embleton Bay

Beautiful Embleton Bay, a pale wide arc of sand, stretches from Dunstanburgh past the endearing, sloping village of Embleton and curves in a broad vanilla-coloured strand around to end at Low Newton-by-the-Sea, a tiny whitewashed, National Trust–preserved village.

◉ Sights

Behind the bay is a path leading to the **Newton Pool Nature Reserve**, an important spot for breeding and migrating birds such as black-headed gulls and grasshopper warblers. There are a couple of hides where you can peer out at them. You can continue walking along the headland beyond Low Newton, where you'll find **Football Hole**, a delightful hidden beach between headlands.

The easiest access to Dunstanburgh Castle is from Craster; the walk to the castle from Embleton Bay can be cut off at high tide.

NEWCASTLE & NORTHEAST ENGLAND NORTHUMBERLAND COAST

🛏 Sleeping & Eating

Joiners Arms   PUB ₤₤₤
(📞01665-576112; http://joiners-arms.com; High
Newton-by-the-Sea; d from £160; 🅿🛜🐾) Locals
love this gastropub and for good reason:
ingredients are sourced nearby, the seafood
and steaks are excellent and families are
warmly welcomed. But for visitors, it's also
a fantastic place to stay: five contemporary
guest rooms are individually and exquisitely decorated with details like exposed brick,
free-standing baths and four-poster beds.

Ship Inn   PUB FOOD ₤₤
(📞01665-576262; www.shipinnnewton.co.uk; Low
Newton-by-the-Sea; mains lunch £5.50-9, dinner
£9-22.50; ⏲kitchen noon-2.30pm & 6.45-8pm
Wed-Sat, noon-2.30pm Sun-Tue, bar 11am-11pm
Mon-Sat, 11am-10pm Sun Apr-Oct, reduced hours
Nov-Mar) 🍴 Set around a village green, this
idyllic pub brews over two dozen different
beers – blond, wheat, rye, bitter, stout and
seasonal – using local River Coquet water.
The food is first-rate, too, from crab and lobster to regional farm-sourced meat. No credit cards or lunchtime reservations (arrive
early); book ahead for dinner. Live music
often plays at weekends.

ℹ Getting There & Away

Bus X18 to Newcastle (£6.60, 2¾ hours, three
daily), Berwick-upon-Tweed (£5.60, 1¼ hours,
three daily) and Alnwick (£5.40, 45 minutes,
three daily) stops outside the Joiners Arms.
From Monday to Saturday, bus 418 (£5.10, 35
minutes, four daily) links the village of Embleton
with Alnwick.

Bamburgh

📞 01668 / POP 414
High up on a basalt crag, Bamburgh's
mighty castle looms over the quaint village
– a clutch of houses around a pleasant green
– which continues to commemorate the val-
iant achievements of local heroine Grace
Darling.

⊙ Sights

Bamburgh Castle   CASTLE
(📞01668-214515; www.bamburghcastle.com;
Links Rd; adult/child £11/5; ⏲10am-5pm early Feb-early Nov, 11am-4.30pm Sat & Sun early
Nov-early Feb) Northumberland's most dramatic castle was built around a powerful
11th-century Norman keep by Henry II. The
castle played a key role in the border wars
of the 13th and 14th centuries, and in 1464
was the first English castle to fall during the
Wars of the Roses. It was restored in the
19th century by the great industrialist Lord
Armstrong, and is still home to the Armstrong family.

RNLI Grace Darling Museum   MUSEUM
(📞01668-214910; www.rnli.org; 1 Radcliffe Rd;
⏲10am-5pm Easter-Sep, 10am-4pm Tue-Sun
Oct-Easter) FREE Born in Bamburgh, Grace
Darling was the lighthouse keeper's daughter on Outer Farne who rowed out to the
grounded, flailing SS *Forfarshire* in 1838
and saved its crew in the middle of a dread-
ful storm. This refurbished museum even
has her actual coble (row boat) as well as
a film on the events of that stormy night.
Grace was born just three houses down from
the museum and is buried in the churchyard
opposite.

🍴 Eating

★ Mizen Head   SEAFOOD ₤₤
(📞01668-214254; www.mizen-head.co.uk; Lucker Rd; mains £13-27; ⏲6-9pm Mon-Wed, noon-
1.45pm & 6-9pm Thu-Sun; 🅿🛜) Bamburgh's
best place to eat and/or stay is this stunning restaurant with rooms. Local seafood
– lobster, mussels, crab, salmon, squid and
more – is the kitchen's speciality, along with
chargrilled steaks. Its 11 rooms with chequered fabrics and black-and-white coastal
prints are light, bright and spacious (doubles from £98). Switched-on staff know
their stuff.

Potted Lobster   SEAFOOD ₤₤
(📞01668-214088; www.thepottedlobsterbam
burgh.co.uk; 3 Lucker Rd; mains £12-21, half-/full
lobster £18/33, seafood platter £70; ⏲noon-9pm
Jul & Aug, noon-3pm & 6-9pm Sep-Jun) Bamburgh lobster – served as a creamy egg
and brandy thermidor stuffed in the shell;
grilled with garlic and parsley butter; or
poached and served cold with wild garlic
mayo – is the star of this nautical-styled
gem. Seafood platters for two, piled high
with lobster, Lindisfarne oysters, Craster
crab, pickled herring and more, come with
hand-cut chips and crusty home-baked
bread.

ℹ Getting There & Away

Take bus X18 north to Berwick-upon-Tweed
(£6.60, 50 minutes, three daily) or south to
Newcastle (£6.60, 3¼ hours, three daily).

Holy Island (Lindisfarne)

There's something almost other-worldly about this tiny, 2-sq-mile island. Connected to the mainland by a narrow causeway that only appears at low tide, cutting the island off from the mainland for about five hours each day, it's fiercely desolate and isolated, scarcely different from when St Aidan arrived to found a monastery in 635.

As you cross the empty flats, it's easy to imagine the marauding Vikings who repeatedly sacked the settlement between 793 and 875, when the monks finally took the hint and left. They carried with them the illuminated *Lindisfarne Gospels* (now in the British Library in London) and the miraculously preserved body of St Cuthbert, who lived here for a couple of years but preferred the hermit's life on Inner Farne. A priory was re-established in the 11th century, but didn't survive the Dissolution in 1537.

Sights

Lindisfarne Priory   RUINS, MUSEUM

(EH; www.english-heritage.org.uk; adult/child £7.50/4.60; ⏱10am-6pm Apr-Sep, to 5pm Oct, 10am-4pm Wed-Sun Nov-Dec & mid-Feb–Mar, 10am-4pm Sat & Sun Jan–mid-Feb) The skeletal, red and grey ruins of the priory are an eerie sight and give a glimpse into the isolated life of the Lindisfarne monks. The later 13th-century St Mary the Virgin Church is built on the site of the first church between the Tees and the Firth of Forth, and the adjacent museum displays the remains of the first monastery and tells the story of the

---

THE PUFFINS OF COQUET ISLAND

For three days in late May to early June, the **Amble Puffin Festival** (http://amblepuffinfest.co.uk; ⏱late May) celebrates the hatching of puffin chicks on Coquet Island, near Amble, with events including local history talks, guided birdwatching walks, exhibitions, watersports, a craft fair, a food festival and live music.

During the breeding season, you can take a boat trip to see the birds on the island with **Dave Gray's Puffin Cruises** (☏01665-711975; www.puffincruises.co.uk; Amble Harbour, Amble; adult/child £10/5; ⏱by reservation Apr-Oct).

---

monastic community before and after the Dissolution. Hours vary according to tides.

Lindisfarne Castle   CASTLE

(NT; www.nationaltrust.org.uk; adult/child £7.30/3.60; ⏱11am-5pm Tue-Sun late May-Sep, 10am-4pm Easter-late May & Oct) Built atop a rocky bluff in 1550, this tiny, storybook castle was extended and converted by Sir Edwin Lutyens from 1902 to 1910 for Mr Edward Hudson, the owner of *Country Life* magazine – you can imagine some of the glamorous parties to have graced its alluring rooms. It's half a mile east of the village. Opening times can vary due to tide times.

Sleeping & Eating

Lindisfarne Inn   INN ££

(☏01289-381223; www.lindisfarneinn.co.uk; Beal Rd, Beal; s/d/f incl breakfast from £81/115/135; [P][🖥][⊛]) This mainland inn on the A1 next to the turn-off to the causeway is a handy alternative to island accommodation and/or dining if you're cutting it fine with crossing times. Its 23 spotless, modern rooms are set far back enough that road noise isn't a problem. Well-above-average pub food (such as suet pudding with Northumbrian game) changes seasonally.

Crown & Anchor   INN ££

(☏01289-389215; http://holyislandcrown.co.uk; Market Pl; s/d from £60/70; [P][⊛]) A cornerstone of the island's social life, this venerable pub has brightly coloured guest rooms and solid pub grub, but the biggest winner is the beer garden with a postcard panorama of the castle, priory and harbour.

Barn @ Beal   PUB FOOD ££

(☏01289-540044; http://barnatbeal.com; Beal Farm, Beal; mains lunch £9-11, dinner £14-20; ⏱cafe 9am-5pm, lunch & dinner by reservation, bar hours vary seasonally; [🖥][♿]) You can watch the causeway tides on webcam at this sociable mainland pub 1 mile northeast of the A1 turn-off (2 miles west of the island). Lindisfarne seafood, including lobster, is a menu highlight, as are house-speciality burgers utilising farm produce. There's a kids' play area. It also has 12 tent pitches (from £7) and nine caravan sites (from £25).

Shopping

St Aidan's Winery   FOOD, DRINK

(Lindisfarne Mead; ☏01289-389230; www.lindisfarne-mead.co.uk; Prior Lane; ⏱9am-5pm depending on tides) 🖉 Mead made on Lindisfarne by St Aidan's Winery to a traditional Roman recipe using locally drawn water and honey. Free tastings let you try its three varieties – original, blood orange and spiced – as well as its fortified wines, such as ginger, wild strawberry, elderberry, blackberry and cherry. Other products include mead-based chocolate truffles and jams. Check ahead for opening hours.

❶ Getting There & Away

Drivers need to pay close attention to crossing-time information, posted at tourist offices and on notice boards throughout the area, and at www.holy-island.info. Every year drivers are caught midway by the incoming tide and have to abandon their cars.

When tides permit, the Holy Island Hopper (www.berwickuponweedtaxis.co.uk; £3, 15 minutes) links the island with the mainland on the corner of Beal Rd and the A1 to connect with buses X15 and X18, serving Berwick-up-on-Tweed, Alnwick and Newcastle.

Park in the signposted car park (£4.60 per day). A shuttle bus (£2 return) runs from the car park to the castle every 20 minutes from Easter to September; alternatively it's a level 300m walk to the village centre and 1 mile to the castle.

Berwick-upon-Tweed

🖉 01289 / POP 12,043

England's northernmost city is a picturesque fortress town, cleaved by the River Tweed, which is spanned by the Grade I-listed Berwick Bridge (aka Old Bridge), built from sandstone between 1611 and 1624, and the Royal Tweed (1925–28).

Berwick is the stubborn holder of two unique honours: it is the most fought-over settlement in European history (between 1174 and 1482 it changed hands 14 times between the Scots and the English); and its football team, Berwick Rangers, is the only English team to play in the Scottish League (albeit in lowly Scottish League Two). Although firmly English since the 15th century, Berwick retains its own identity, with locals south of the border speaking with a noticeable Scottish burr.

◉ Sights & Activities

★ **Berwick Walls**   HISTORIC SITE
(EH; www.english-heritage.org.uk; ⊙dawn-dusk)
FREE You can walk almost the entire length of Berwick's hefty Elizabethan walls, begun

THE FARNE ISLANDS

During breeding season (roughly May to July), you can see feeding chicks of 20 seabird species (including puffin, kittiwake, Arctic tern, eider duck, cormorant and gull), and some 6000 grey seals, on the **Farne Islands** (NT; 🖉 01289-389244; www.nationaltrust.org.uk; adult/child excl boat transport £27.30/13.60, cheaper outside breeding season; ⊙by reservation, season & conditions permitting Mar-Oct), a rocky archipelago 3 miles offshore from the fishing village of Seahouses. Boat operators, contactable through Seahouses' **tourist office** (🖉 01670-625593; http://visitnorthumberland.com; Seafield car park, Seahouses; ⊙9.30am-4pm Thu-Tue Apr, 9.30am-4pm daily May-Oct), depart from Seahouses' dock, including **Billy Shiel** (🖉 01665-720308; www.farne-islands.com; Harbour Rd, Seahouses; adult/child excl island landing fees 2½hr tour £18/12, 6hr tour £40/25; ⊙by reservation Apr-Oct).

Crossings can be rough (impossible in bad weather); wear warm, waterproof clothing and an old hat to guard against the birds!

in 1558 to reinforce an earlier set built during the reign of Edward II. The mile-long walk is a must, with wonderful, wide-open views. Only a small fragment remains of the once-mighty border castle, most of the building having been replaced by the train station.

Berwick Barracks   MUSEUM, GALLERY
(EH; www.english-heritage.org.uk; The Parade; adult/child £4.90/2.90; ⊙10am-6pm Apr-Sep, to 4pm Wed-Sun Oct) Designed by Nicholas Hawksmoor, Britain's oldest purpose-built barracks (1717) now house an assortment of museums and art galleries, covering a history of the town and British soldiery since the 17th century. The Gymnasium Gallery hosts big-name contemporary art exhibitions.

Berwick Boat Trips   CRUISE
(🖉 07713 170845; www.berwickboattrips.co.uk; Berwick-upon-Tweed Quayside; 2hr North Sea wildlife tour adult/child £15/7, 1hr river tour £8/4, 2hr sunset estuary tour £15/7; ⊙by reservation) Choose from a North Sea cruise spotting

seals, dolphins and sea birds, a river cruise along the Tweed, or a scenic trip along the estuary at sunset. Schedules are posted online.

🛏 Sleeping & Eating

Berwick YHA   HOSTEL £

(☑ 01629-592700; www.yha.org.uk; Dewars Lane; dm/d/f from £15/59/79; P@☎) A mid-18th-century granary has been converted into a state-of-the-art hostel with 55 beds in dorms and private rooms (all with en suite bathrooms). Contemporary facilities include a TV room, a laundry and wi-fi in common areas. Staff are terrifically helpful.

★Marshall Meadows
Country House Hotel   HERITAGE HOTEL ££

(☑ 01289-331133; http://marshallmeadowshotel. co.uk; Marshall Meadows; d/f incl breakfast from £109/129; P☎☎) England's most northerly hotel, just 600m from the Scottish border, sits amid 6 hectares of woodland and or-namental gardens. The Georgian manor's 19 rooms (including a ground-floor family room) have countrified checked and flo-ral fabrics. There are two cosy bars with open fireplaces, a conservatory, and an oak-panelled restaurant serving breakfast (including kippers), and evening meals by candlelight.

Audela   BRITISH ££

(☑ 01289-308827; www.audela.co.uk; 64 Bridge St; mains £12.50-23; ☉ noon-2.30pm & 5.30-9pm Thu-Mon) Named for the last vessel to be built at Berwick Shipyard (in 1979) and set in a for-mer cockle shop, Audela is the town's top ta-ble. Local suppliers provide the ingredients for dishes like Berwick crab with pickled carrot and oysters with sea buckthorn, roast pheasant with artichoke and haggis purée, and caraway-crusted Northumberland lamb with wild garlic–wrapped potatoes.

ℹ Getting There & Away

On the East Coast Main Line linking London and Edinburgh, Berwick-upon-Tweed is almost exactly halfway between Edinburgh (£13.40, one hour, up to two per hour) and Newcastle (£8, 45 minutes, up to two per hour).

Buses stop on Golden Sq (where it meets Marygate). National Express coaches between Edinburgh (£15.70, 1¼ hours, twice daily) and London (£38.10, eight hours, twice daily) stop here.

Newcastle is served by the X15 (via Alnwick; £6.60, 2½ hours, hourly Monday to Saturday, every two hours Sunday) and X18 (£6.60, four hours, three daily).

Wales

Wales Highlights

① **Wales Coast Path** (p43) Walking the famously beautiful 870-mile route.

② **Snowdonia** (p710) Climbing Wales' highest peak, Snowdon, or taking more gentle exercise.

③ **St Davids** (p671) Enjoying tiny St Davids, with its beautiful cathedral and idyllic setting.

④ **Conwy Castle** (p733) Seeing the prettiest of Wales' many fortresses.

⑤ **Pembrokeshire** (p667) Visiting beaches, Norman castles and wildlife reserves.

⑥ **Brecon Beacons** (p681) Hiking in the mountains, then eating in a gastropub.

⑦ **Hay-on-Wye** (p681) Wandering through book-lovers heaven.

⑧ **Cardiff** (p641) Exploring the Welsh capital's castle, shopping arcades and nightlife.

⑨ **Portmeirion** (p724) Experiencing a fanciful slice of baroque Italy clinging to the North Welsh coast.

Cardiff, Pembrokeshire & South Wales

Best Places to Eat

➡ Fish at 85 (p649)

➡ The Whitebrook (p654)

➡ Walnut Tree (p655)

➡ Coast (p668)

➡ Mosaic (p659)

➡ Restaurant James Sommerin (p649)

Best Places to Stay

➡ Lincoln House (p648)

➡ Tŵr y Felin (p673)

➡ Old School Hostel (p674)

➡ Lethryd Barns (p664)

➡ Port Eynon YHA (p663)

➡ Grove (p670)

Why Go?

Stretching from historic border town Chepstow through to the jagged Pembrokeshire Coast in the west, South Wales really packs in the sights. Hugging the border, the Wye Valley is the birthplace of British tourism. For more than 200 years people have come to explore this tranquil waterway and its winding, wooded vale, where the majestic ruins of Tintern Abbey have inspired generations of poets and artists. The nation's capital, Cardiff, flies the flag for big-city sophistication in the land of the red dragon. Just out of Swansea, Wales' second city, the Gower Peninsula revels in its coastal beauty. To the north, the fecund heartland of rural Carmarthenshire offers country comfort in abundance. Beyond Cardiff, the biggest draw in South Wales remains Pembrokeshire, where almost 200 miles of magical shoreline has been declared a national park, delineated by craggy cliffs, golden sands, chocolate-box villages and seaside resorts.

When to Go

➡ January to March are the coldest months, although Wales' home matches in the Six Nations Rugby Championship warm local spirits.

➡ Many of Cardiff's big festivals are in July, including the Cardiff International Food & Drink Festival, the Everyman Open Air Theatre Festival and the Welsh Proms.

➡ For the best hiking weather on the Gower and the Pembrokeshire Coast, come in late spring, early summer or early autumn.

Cardiff, Pembrokeshire & South Wales Highlights

1 Cardiff Castle (p643) Marvelling at the Victorian extravagances grafted onto the city's citadel.

2 St Davids (p671) Exploring the little city with the spectacular cathedral and surf beach.

3 Pembrokeshire Coast Path (p671) Tracing a collision of rock and sea along the county's coast.

4 Caerphilly Castle (p657) Crossing the moat and wandering into a fairytale.

5 Tintern Abbey (p654) Strolling among romantic riverside ruins in the Wye Valley.

6 Blaenavon (p656) Feasting on industrial sites and world-class cheese.

7 National Botanic Garden of Wales (p665) Admiring glorious horticultural gardens.

8 Pentre Ifan (p678) Soaking up the views from Wales' loftiest dolmen.

9 Rhossili (p664) Watching the waves crash over Worms Head.

CARDIFF

📞 029 / POP 349,941

The capital of Wales since just 1955, Cardiff has embraced the role with vigour, emerging in the new millennium as one of Britain's leading urban centres. Spread between an ancient fort and an ultramodern waterfront, compact Cardiff seems to have surprised even itself with how interesting it has become.

Nowhere is this vitality more evident than in Cardiff's buildings – it flexes newly acquired architectural muscles as if it's still astonished to have them. Such confidence is infectious, and these days it's not just the rugby that draws crowds into the city. Come the weekend, a buzz reverberates through the streets as swarms of shoppers hit the Hayes, followed by waves of revellers descending on the capital's thriving pubs, bars and live-music venues.

Cardiff also makes an excellent base for day trips to the surrounding valleys and coast, where you'll find castles, beaches, interesting industrial sites and ancient monuments.

History

In AD 75 the Romans built a fort where Cardiff Castle now stands. The name Cardiff probably derives from Caer Tâf (Fort on the River Taff) or Caer Didi (Didius' Fort), referring to Roman general Aulus Didius. After the Romans abandoned the site around 375, it remained unoccupied until the Norman Conquest. In 1093 a Norman knight named Robert Fitzhamon (conqueror of Glamorgan and later earl of Gloucester) built himself a castle within the Roman walls and a small town grew up around it. Both were damaged in a Welsh revolt in 1183 and the town was sacked in 1404 by Owain Glyndŵr during his ill-fated rebellion against English domination.

The first of the Tudor Acts of Union in 1536 put the English stamp on Cardiff and brought some stability. But despite its importance as a port, market town and bishopric, only 1000 people were living here in 1801.

The city owes its present stature to iron and coal mining in the valleys to the north. Coal was first exported from Cardiff on a small scale as early as 1600. In 1794 the Bute family – which owned much of the land from which Welsh coal was mined – built the Glamorganshire Canal for the shipment of iron from Merthyr Tydfil down to Cardiff. In 1840 this was supplanted by the new Taff Vale Railway.

A year earlier the second marquess of Bute had completed the first docks at Butetown, just south of Cardiff, getting the jump on other South Wales ports. By the time it dawned on everyone what immense reserves of coal there were in the valleys – setting off a kind of black gold rush – the Butes were in a position to insist that it be shipped from Butetown. Cardiff was off and running.

The docklands expanded rapidly, the Butes grew staggeringly rich and the city boomed, its population mushrooming to 170,000 by the end of the 19th century and to 227,000 by 1931. A large, multiracial workers community known as Tiger Bay grew up in the harbourside area of Butetown. In 1905 Cardiff was officially designated a city, and a year later its elegant Civic Centre was inaugurated. In 1913 Cardiff became the world's top coal port, exporting over 10 million tonnes of the stuff.

The post-WWI slump in the coal trade and the Great Depression of the 1930s slowed

---

CARDIFF IN...

Two Days

Start with a stroll around the historic city centre, stopping to explore the **National Museum Cardiff** (p642) and **Cardiff Castle** (p643) along the way. Lunch could be a picnic in **Bute Park** (p645) with treats acquired at **Cardiff Market** (p651) or, if the weather's not cooperating, a meal at any of the reasonably priced central-city eateries. Spend your second day heading back to the future at **Cardiff Bay** (p646), where you can immerse yourself in remarkable architecture and have a dockside meal.

Four Days

Spend your third morning strolling through the past at **St Fagans National History Museum** (p645), then take a day trip to Penarth (p649). On your last day, head north to explore **Llandaff Cathedral** (p647), then continue on to **Castell Coch** (p645) and **Caerphilly Castle** (p657). For your last night in the Welsh capital, blast away the cobwebs in one of the city's live-music venues (p651).

Cardiff

Cardiff

this expansion. Calamities accumulated as the city was badly damaged by WWII bombing that claimed over 350 lives. Shortly afterwards the coal industry was nationalised, which led to the Butes packing their bags and leaving town in 1947, donating the castle and a large chunk of land to the city.

Wales had no official capital and the need for one was seen as an important focus for Welsh nationhood. Cardiff had the advantage of being Wales' biggest city and boasting the architectural riches of the Civic Centre. It was proclaimed the first ever capital of Wales in 1955, chosen via a ballot of the members of the Welsh authorities. Cardiff received 36 votes to Caernarfon's 11 and Aberystwyth's four.

👁 Sights

👁 City Centre

⭐ **National Museum Cardiff**   MUSEUM
(Map p644; ☎ 0300 111 2 333; www.museumwales.
ac.uk; Cathays Park; ⊙ 10am-5pm Tue-Sun; P)
FREE Devoted mainly to natural history and

art, this grand neoclassical building is the centrepiece of the seven institutions dotted around the country that together form the Welsh National Museum. It's one of Britain's best museums; you'll need at least three hours to do it justice, but it could easily consume the best part of a rainy day. On-site parking, behind the museum, is £6.50.

The Evolution of Wales exhibit whizzes onlookers through 4600 million years of geological history, its rollicking multimedia display placing Wales into a global context. Films of volcanic eruptions and aerial footage of the Welsh landscape explain how its scenery was formed, while model dinosaurs and woolly mammoths help keep the kids interested.

The natural-history displays range from brightly coloured insects to the 9m-long skeleton of a humpback whale that washed up near Aberthaw in 1982. The world's largest turtle (2.88m by 2.74m), a leatherback that was found on Harlech beach, is also here, suspended on wires from the ceiling.

Boasting one of the world's most significant impressionist collections, the gallery exhibits such treasures as a trio of Monet's *Water Lilies,* alongside his scenes of London, Rouen and Venice; Sisley's *The Cliff at Penarth* (the artist was married in Cardiff); Renoir's shimmering *La Parisienne;* a cast of Rodin's *The Kiss;* and Van Gogh's anguished *Rain: Auvers.* Welsh artists, such as Gwen and Augustus John, Richard Wilson, Thomas Jones, David Jones and Ceri Richards, are well represented, along with famous names from across the border, such as Francis Bacon, David Hockney and Rachel Whiteread.

Many of the impressionist and post-impressionist pieces were bequeathed to the museum in 1952 and 1963 by the Davies sisters, Gwendoline and Margaret, granddaughters of 19th-century coal and shipping magnate David Davies. One room is devoted to their collection of seven paintings by British master JMW Turner, which were dismissed as fakes in the 1950s but have recently been reappraised as genuine.

One of the large upstairs galleries is devoted to Welsh ceramics, while others are set aside for temporary exhibitions on subjects as wide ranging as 'Women in Photography' and 'Japanese Design'.

★ **Cardiff Castle**   CASTLE
(Map p644; ☑ 029-2087 8100; www.cardiffcastle. com; Castle St; adult/child £13/9.25, incl guided tour £16/12; ⊙ 9am-6pm Mar-Oct, to 5pm Nov-Feb) There's a medieval keep at its heart,

but it's the later additions to Cardiff Castle that really capture the imagination. In Victorian times, extravagant mock-Gothic features were grafted onto this relic, including a clock tower and a lavish banqueting hall. Some but not all of this flamboyant fantasy world can be accessed with regular castle entry; the rest can be visited as part of a (recommended) guided tour. Look for the *trebuchet* (medieval siege engine) and falcons on the grounds.

From 1766 to 1947, when it was donated to the city, the castle was the private domain of the Butes, the family who transformed Cardiff from a small town into the world's biggest coal port. It's far from a traditional Welsh castle; more a collection of disparate 'castles' scattered around a central green, encompassing practically the whole history of Cardiff. The most conventionally castle-like bits are the motte-and-bailey **Norman shell keep** at its centre (built in wood around 1081 and rebuilt in stone in 1135) and the 13th-century **Black Tower** that forms the entrance gate. William the Conqueror's eldest son, Robert, Duke of Normandy, was imprisoned in the wooden fort by his brother, England's Henry I, until his death at the age of 83.

A grand house was built into the western wall in the 1420s by the earl of Warwick and was extended in the 17th century by the Herbert family (the earls of Pembroke), but by the time the Butes acquired it, it had fallen into disrepair. The first marquess of Bute hired architect Henry Holland and Holland's father-in-law, the famous landscape architect Lancelot 'Capability' Brown, to get the house and grounds into shape.

It was only in the 19th century that it was discovered that the Normans had built their fortifications on top of Cardiff's original 1st-century Roman fort. The high walls that surround the castle now are largely a Victorian reproduction of the 3rd-century 3m-thick Roman walls. A line of red bricks, clearly visible from the city frontage, marks the point where the original Roman section ends and the reconstruction commences.

Also from the 19th century are the towers and turrets on the western side, dominated by the colourful 40m clock tower. This faux-Gothic extravaganza was dreamed up by the mind-bendingly rich third marquess of Bute and his architect William Burges, a passionate eccentric who used to dress in medieval costume and was often seen with a parrot on his shoulder. Both were obsessed with Gothic architecture, religious

Central Cardiff

symbolism and astrology, influences that were incorporated into the designs both here and at the Butes' second Welsh home at Castell Coch. Yet along with the focus on the past, the plans included all of the mod cons of the Victorian era, such as electric lighting (it was the second house in Wales to feature this newfangled wizardry) and running water in the en suite attached to the upper-floor bedroom.

A 50-minute **guided tour** takes you through the interiors, from the winter smok-

Central Cardiff

ing room in the clock tower with decor expounding on the theme of time (zodiac symbols grouped into seasons, Norse gods representing the days of the week, and a fright for anyone who dares listen at the door – look up as you pass through the doorway), to the mahogany-and-mirrors narcissism of Lord Bute's bedroom, with a gilded statue of St John the Evangelist (the marquess' name saint) and 189 bevelled mirrors on the ceiling, which reflect the name 'John' in Greek.

There's a small-but-helpful **tourist office** adjoining the ticket desk, and regular castle entry allows you access to the banqueting hall and includes an excellent audio guide (available in a children's edition and in a range of languages). Start your visit in the **WWII air-raid shelter**, preserved in a long, cold corridor within the castle walls, then proceed to the **Firing Line**, a small but interesting museum devoted to the Welsh soldier.

★**Bute Park**   PARK
(Map p644; http://parc-bute.com; ⊙ 7.30am-30min before sunset) Flanked by the castle (p643) and the River Taff, Bute Park was donated to the city along with the castle in 1947. With Sophia Gardens, Pontcanna Fields and Llandaff Fields, it forms a green corridor that stretches northwest for 1.5 miles to Llandaff. All were once part of the Butes' vast holdings.

★**Principality Stadium**   STADIUM
(Millennium Stadium; Map p644; ⊘ inquiries 0844 249 1999, tickets & tours 029-2082 2432; www. principalitystadium.wales; Westgate St; tours adult/

child £13/9; ⊙ tours 10am-5pm, to 4pm Sun) Also known as Millennium Stadium ('Principality' is the current naming-rights sponsor), this spectacular venue squats like a stranded spaceship on the River Taff's east bank. Seating 74,500 and built at a cost of £168 million, this three-tiered, retractable-roofed arena was completed in time to host the 1999 Rugby World Cup. If you can't get tickets to a match, it's well worth taking a tour – book online or at the on-site **WRU Store** (Map p644; ⊘ 0333 014 5343; www.wru.co.uk; 8 Westgate St; ⊙ 9.30am-5.30pm Mon-Sat, 10am-4pm Sun).

★**St Fagans National
History Museum**   MUSEUM
(⊘ 0300 111 2 333; www.museumwales.ac.uk; St Fagans; parking £5; ⊙ 10am-5pm; ☒ 32A) Historic buildings from all over the country have been dismantled and re-erected in the semirural surrounds of St Fagans village, 5 miles west of central Cardiff. More than 40 buildings are on show, including thatched farmhouses, barns, a watermill, a school, an 18th-century Unitarian chapel and shops selling period-appropriate goods. Buses 32, 32A and 320 (£1.80, 26 minutes) head here from Cardiff. By car it's reached from the continuation of Cathedral Rd.

Castell Coch   CASTLE
(Cadw; www.cadw.gov.wales; Castle Rd, Tongwynlais; adult/child £6.90/4.10; ⊙ 9.30am-5pm Mar-Jun, Sep & Oct, to 6pm Jul & Aug, 10am-4pm Mon-Sat, from 11am Sun Nov-Feb; ℗) Cardiff Castle's fanciful little brother sits perched atop a

thickly wooded crag on the northern fringes of Cardiff. It was the summer retreat of the third marquess of Bute and, like Cardiff Castle, was designed by oddball architect William Burges in gaudy Gothic-revival style. Raised on the ruins of Gilbert de Clare's 13th-century Castell Coch (Red Castle), the Butes' Disneyesque holiday home is a monument to high camp. An excellent audio guide is included in the admission price.

Yr Hen Lyfrgell CULTURAL CENTRE
(The Old Library; Map p644; ☑029-2022 5982; www.yrhenlyfrgell.wales; The Hayes; ☺9am-5pm Mon-Sat, 10am-4pm Sun) *Croeso* (welcome) to a bastion of the Welsh language in the overwhelmingly English-speaking capital. Cardiff's beautiful Old Library has been converted into a showcase for all things Cymraeg, with an excellent gift shop (p651), a cafe and Welsh-language lessons. Everyone's welcome, even if the only Welsh you can muster is a timid *bore da* (good morning). While you're here, check out the gorgeous Victorian tiles lining the library's original entrance and call into the **Cardiff Story museum** (Map p644; ☑029-2034 6214; www.cardiffstory.com; ☺10am-4pm) FREE.

◉ Cardiff Bay

Lined with important national institutions, Cardiff Bay is where the modern Welsh nation is put on display in an architect's playground of interesting buildings, large open spaces and public art. The bay's main commercial centre is Mermaid Quay, packed with bars, restaurants and shops.

It wasn't always this way. By 1913 more than 13 million tonnes of coal were being shipped from Cardiff's docks. Following the post-WWII slump the docklands deteriorated into a wasteland of empty basins, cut off from the city by the railway embankment. The bay outside the docks, which has one of the highest tidal ranges in the world (more than 12m between high and low water), was ringed for up to 14 hours a day by smelly, sewage-contaminated mudflats. The nearby residential area of Butetown became a neglected slum.

Since 1987 the area has been radically redeveloped. The turning point came with the completion of a state-of-the-art tidal barrage in 1999.

★ **Wales Millennium Centre** ARTS CENTRE
(Map p647; ☑029-2063 6464; www.wmc.org.uk; Bute Pl, Cardiff Bay; ☺9am-7pm, later on show nights) The centrepiece and symbol of Cardiff Bay's regeneration is the £106-million Wales Millennium Centre, an architectural masterpiece of stacked Welsh slate in shades of purple, green and grey topped with an overarching bronzed steel shell. Designed by Welsh architect Jonathan Adams, it opened in 2004 as Wales' premier arts complex, housing major cultural organisations such as the Welsh National Opera, National Dance Company, BBC National Orchestra of Wales, Literature Wales, HiJinx Theatre and Tŷ Cerdd (Music Centre Wales).

Senedd NOTABLE BUILDING
(Map p647; ☑0300 200 6565; www.assembly.wales; Cardiff Bay; ☺9.30am-4.30pm Mon-Fri, 10.30am-4.30pm Sat & Sun) FREE Designed by Lord Richard Rogers (the architect behind London's Lloyd's building and Millennium Dome and Paris' Pompidou Centre), the home of the National Assembly for Wales' Siambr (debating chamber) is a striking structure of concrete, slate, glass and steel, with an undulating canopy roof lined with red cedar. It has won awards for its environmentally friendly design, which includes a huge rotating cowl on the roof for power-free ventilation and a gutter system that collects rainwater for flushing the toilets.

◉ Roath

The bohemian heart of Cardiff lies in the suburbs immediately to the east of the city centre. Proximity to the university makes Cathays' tightly packed Victorian terrace houses popular with students, and while parts of Roath are more well heeled, the City Rd strip is a little gritty and fabulously multicultural. Few tourists make their way here, but if you want to get a broader taste of Cardiff life, take a stroll along the narrow thoroughfare that starts as City Rd, morphing into Crwys Rd and then Whitchurch Rd.

Roath Park PARK
(www.cardiff.gov.uk/parks; Lake Rd, Roath; ☺7.30am-sunset) Long, narrow Roath Park rivals Bute Park (p645) as Cardiff's favourite green space. The third marquess of Bute gifted the land to the city in 1887, when the marsh at its northern end was dammed to create the 30-acre Roath Park Lake, the park's central feature. The rest was laid out in the Victorian style, with rose gardens, tree-lined paths, lawns and wild nooks. A lighthouse was added to the lake in 1915 as

Cardiff Bay

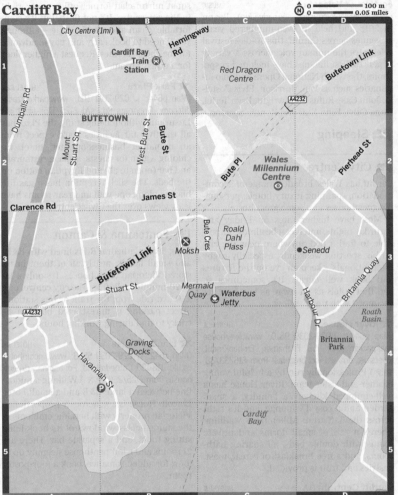

a memorial to ill-fated Antarctic explorer Robert Scott.

◉ Llandaff

Llandaff Cathedral   CATHEDRAL
(☎ 029-2056 4554; www.llandaffcathedral.org.uk; Cathedral Green, Llandaff; ⊙ 9am-6.30pm Mon-Sat, 7am-6.30pm Sun) This venerable cathedral is set in a hollow near the River Taff, on the site of a 6th-century monastery founded by St Teilo. The present building was begun in 1120, but it crumbled throughout the Middle Ages, and during the Reformation and Civil War it was used as an alehouse and then an animal shelter. Derelict by the 18th century, it was largely rebuilt in the 19th century, and then repaired again following a German bombing raid in 1941.

🎇 Festivals & Events

Six Nations   SPORTS
(www.rbs6nations.com; ⊙ Feb & Mar) The premier European rugby championship, with Wales taking on England, Scotland, Ireland, Italy and France. Cardiff normally hosts two or three home games at Millennium Stadium – the atmosphere is supercharged, and accommodation should be booked well in advance.

Festival of Voice   MUSIC
(www.festivalofvoice.wales; ⊙ early Jun) Begun in 2016 and held in even-numbered years at venues across Cardiff, this 10-day festival celebrates the human voice across a variety of genres. Past line-ups have included gospel choirs, the Welsh National Opera and solo luminaries such as Van Morrison, Elvis Costello, John Cale, Rufus Wainwright, Bryn Terfel, Anna Calvi, Femi Kuti and Ronnie Spector.

🛏 Sleeping

🛏 City Centre

Cardiff has Wales' broadest range of accommodation, spanning luxury hotels, personable guesthouses and some great hostels.

Most have higher rates on Friday and Saturday nights, and it can be almost impossible to find a bed anywhere near the city on big sporting weekends, especially rugby internationals – keep an eye on the fixtures and book well ahead. It's sometimes so bad that hotels as far away as Swansea get swamped with the overflow.

★ **River House**   HOSTEL £
(Map p644; ☑ 029-2039 9810; www.riverhouse backpackers.com; 59 Fitzhamon Embankment, Riverside; dm/s/d incl breakfast from £16/33/38; @ 🛜) Professionally run by a helpful young brother-and-sister team, River House has a well-equipped kitchen, a laundry, a small garden and a cosy TV lounge, and it's right across the Taff from Millennium Stadium. There's a mix of small dorms and private rooms with double beds, all sharing bathrooms, and a free breakfast of cereal, toast, pastries and fruit is provided.

Cardiff Central YHA   HOSTEL £
(Map p642; ☑ 0345-371 9311; www.yha.org.uk; 1 East Tyndall St; dm/r from £10/49; 🛜) Flanked by busy roads and car dealerships close to central Cardiff, this well-organised YHA has had the good sense to leave the building – a former Mercure hotel – substantially unchanged. Some of the bedrooms are now dorms and a guest kitchen, laundry and other facilities have been added, but all accommodation retains modern hotel-style bathrooms and there's plenty of parking.

Premier Inn Cardiff City Centre   HOTEL £
(Map p644; ☑ 0871 527 8196; www.premierinn. com; Helmont House, 10 Churchill Way; r without breakfast from £64; 🛜) The Cardiff branch of Britain's biggest chain has 200 beds in a squat mirror-clad former office tower, right in the city centre. It's not flash, but it's comfortable, clean and terrific value – although you'll need to book early and pay in advance for the cheapest rates. Request a higher floor for a quieter room.

★ **Park Plaza**   HOTEL £££
(Map p644; ☑ 029-2011 1111; www.parkplazacar diff.com; Greyfriars Rd; s/d £125/175; ❋ 🛜 🛜) Luxurious without being stuffy, the Plaza has all the five-star facilities you'd expect from an upmarket business-oriented hotel, including a gym for guests, a spa, a restaurant and bar (open to all) and Egyptian cotton on the beds. The slick reception has a gas fire blazing along one wall and rear rooms have leafy views over the Civic Centre.

🛏 Pontcanna & Canton

Long, leafy Cathedral Rd is lined with B&Bs and small hotels, nearly all of them in restored Victorian town houses. It's only a 15- to 20-minute walk from the city centre, or a £10 taxi ride from the train or bus stations. Street parking is unrestricted but can be tricky to find during working hours.

★ **Lincoln House**   HOTEL ££
(Map p642; ☑ 029-2039 5558; www.lincolnhotel. co.uk; 118-120 Cathedral Rd, Pontcanna; d/pent houses from £125/250; P 🛜) Walking a middle line between a large B&B and a small hotel, Lincoln House is a generously proportioned Victorian property with heraldic emblems in the stained-glass windows of its book-lined sitting room, and a separate bar. There are 21 rooms and a loft penthouse sleeping up to four; for added romance, book a four-poster room.

★ **Number 62**   GUESTHOUSE ££
(Map p642; ☑ 029-2041 2765; www.number62. com; 62 Cathedral Rd, Pontcanna; s/d from £74/83; 🛜) The only thing preventing Number 62 from being a B&B is that breakfast is only offered as an add-on (served at the Beverley Hotel across the road). The cosy rooms come with thoughtful extras such as body lotion, make-up wipes and cotton buds, and the front garden is one of the most immaculate of all the houses on this strip.

Saco Cardiff   APARTMENT ££
(Map p642; ☑ 0845 122 0405; www.sacoapart ments.co.uk; 76 Cathedral Rd, Pontcanna; apt from £120; P 🛜) This large town house has been given a contemporary makeover and con-

verted into one- and two-bedroom serviced apartments, complete with comfortable lounges and fitted kitchens. They're set up for longer visits, but one-night stays are possible midweek. The two-bedroom apartments are good value for families with kids, and there's an extra sofa bed in the lounge.

Eating

City Centre

Coffee Barker CAFE £

(Map p644; ☎029-2022 4575; Castle Arcade; mains £6-7; ⊗8.30am-5.30pm Mon-Wed, to 11pm Thu-Sat, 9.30am-4.30pm Sun; 🛜🚺) This cool cafe, a series of rooms at the entrance to one of Cardiff's Victorian arcades, is good for coffee, indulgent pancake stacks, daily soups and thick milkshakes served in glass milk bottles. Despite its size, soft chairs and quirky decor give it a cosy vibe. Usually busy, it also includes a cruisy bar, open until 11pm Thursday to Saturday.

Pettigrew Tea Rooms CAFE £

(Map p644; ☎029-2023 5486; www.pettigrew-tearooms.com; West Lodge, Castle St; mains £8-10; ⊗8.30am-5.30pm Mon-Fri, 9am-6pm Sat & Sun) Cuppas and cakes are served on delicate china at this atmospheric little tearoom within the crenellated confines of Bute Park's 1863 gatehouse. Cucumber sandwiches, cream scones, scuffed vintage furniture and crackly '20s tunes accompany the extensive range of tea on offer – or try the ploughman's platter if you're after something more hearty.

Casanova ITALIAN £££

(Map p644; ☎029-2034 4044; www.casanova cardiff.co.uk; 13 Quay St; 2-/3-course lunch £14/18, dinner £25/32; ⊗noon-2.30pm & 5.30-10pm Mon-Sat) Rather than offering generic Italian dishes or the specialities of just one region, this little charmer offers a selection of authentic regional dishes from all over Italy. The result is a varied menu with half-a-dozen options for each course, including more unusual dishes such as *carne e cappuccio*: goat braised with savoy cabbage, white wine, herbs and tomato.

Park House MODERN EUROPEAN £££

(Map p644; ☎029-2022 4343; www.parkhouse restaurant.co.uk; 20 Park Pl; mains £26-27, 2-/3-course lunch £20/25; ⊗noon-2.30pm & 6-9.30pm Tue-Sat; 🛜) The ambience is rather stuffy, but the menu at this private club is anything but conservative – subtle international

PENARTH

Well-heeled Penarth has transformed from an old-fashioned seaside resort to a virtual suburb of Cardiff, despite it being in the neighbouring county. It's connected to Cardiff Bay by the freshwater lake formed by the construction of the barrage and it now sports a busy marina on the lakefront.

It's worth making the trip solely for **Restaurant James Sommerin** (☎029-2070 6559; www.jamessommerin restaurant.co.uk; The Esplanade; mains £26-27, 6/9 courses £65/85; ⊗noon-2.30pm & 7-9.30 Tue-Sun), owned by the eponymous chef who previously earned a Michelin star at his Monmouthshire restaurant, and is surely on track for another one here. Much that issues from the kitchen looks as exquisite as it tastes, marrying multiple textures, well-balanced flavours and tricksy molecular-gastronomy techniques.

flavours meet classic European techniques and ingredients in dishes such as pan-roasted brill with Moroccan *ras el hanout* spices, heirloom carrots and local sea herbs. Dress up and push the buzzer for admittance.

Pontcanna & Canton

★ Purple Poppadom INDIAN ££

(Map p642; ☎029-2022 0026; www.purplepop padom.com; 185a Cowbridge Rd E, Canton; mains £15-17, 2-course lunch £15; ⊗noon-2pm & 5.30-11pm Tue-Sat, 1-9pm Sun) Trailblazing a path for 'nouvelle Indian' cuisine, chef and author Anand George adds his own twist to dishes from all over the subcontinent – from Kashmir to Kerala. Thankfully, the emphasis is on the perfection of tried-and-tested regional delights rather than anything unnecessarily wacky.

★ Fish at 85 SEAFOOD ££

(Map p642; ☎029-2023 5666; www.fishat85.co. uk; 85 Pontcanna St, Pontcanna; 2-/3-course lunch menu £15/18, mains £19-22; ⊗noon-2.30pm & 5.30-9.30pm Tue-Sat) By day a fishmongers (hence the fresh, lingering smell), by night an elegant restaurant with Cape Cod–ish decor and candles floating in water-filled jars, Fish at 85 is Cardiff's premier spot for a seafood dinner. Aside from the à la carte and lunch menus, there's the daily-catch menu, offering whatever is best that day from local and British waters.

Bully's
BISTRO ££

(Map p642; ☑029-2022 1905; www.bullysrestaurant.co.uk; 5 Romilly Cres, Pontcanna; mains £18-22; ⏱noon-2pm & 6.30-9pm Wed-Sat, noon-3.30pm Sun; 🅿) Eclectica (banknotes, receipts from famous restaurants etc) covers the walls of this cosy neighbourhood bistro, a quirky setting for high-quality cooking. The full *carte*, offered on Friday and Saturday nights, features dishes such as sea bass with tagliatelle, crab, samphire and lobster bisque, or curried butternut squash with polenta cake, puréed cauliflower and a sweet-potato bhaji.

✕ Cardiff Bay

Moksh
INDIAN ££

(Map p647; ☑029-2049 8120; www.moksh.co.uk; Ocean Bldg, Bute Cres, Cardiff Bay; mains £6-18; ⏱noon-2.30pm & 6-11pm Sun-Thu, noon-2.30pm & 6pm-midnight Fri & Sat; 🅿) There's a grounding Goan influence to this atypical Indian restaurant, but the kitchen shoots off on tangents such as 'Willy Wonka and the Spice Factory': a lamb chop with chilli-chocolate floss, king prawn, white-chocolate-chilli foam, whisky wood smoke, chocolate and orange chicken tikka and pork Ferrero Rocher with Jaffa Cake ice cream (!).

✕ Cathays & Roath

★ Mint & Mustard
INDIAN ££

(☑029-2062 0333; www.mintandmustard.com; 134 Whitchurch Rd, Cathays; mains £13-15; ⏱noon-2pm & 5-11pm Mon-Sat, to 10pm Sun; 🅿) Leather-backed chairs and mint and mustard decor are the sleek setting for a toothsome insight into the wonderful cuisine of the southern Indian state of Kerala. If you're not enticed by Malabar seafood moilee (prawns, mussels and squid in coconut milk, black pepper and a spicy shallot masala), there are plenty of vegetarian options and standard Indian-restaurant choices, too.

🍷 Drinking & Nightlife

Gwdihŵ
BAR

(Map p644; ☑029-2039 7933; www.gwdihw.co.uk; 6 Guildford Cres; ⏱3pm-midnight Mon-Wed, noon-2am Thu-Sat, 4pm-midnight Sun) A cute little bar with an electric-rainbow exterior, Gwdihŵ has an eclectic line-up of entertainment (comedy, DJs, quiz nights and lots of live music, including microfestivals that spill

over into the car park) and is a charming place to stop for a drink at any time. If you're wondering about the name, it's the Welsh take on an owl's call.

Buffalo Bar
BAR

(Map p644; ☑029-2031 0312; www.buffalocardiff.co.uk; 11 Windsor Pl; ⏱noon-3am Sun-Wed, to 4am Thu-Sat) A haven for cool kids about town, the Buffalo features retro furniture, tasty food, life-affirming cocktails and alternative tunes. There's a small beer garden at the rear, while upstairs cutting-edge indie bands take to the stage, interspersed with DJs for the late-night set. Interesting food such as jackfruit enchiladas is served from noon to 9pm (mains £11 to £13).

Porter's
BAR

(Map p644; ☑029-2125 0666; www.porterscardiff.com; Bute Tce; ⏱5pm-12.30am Sun-Wed, 4pm-3am Thu & Fri, noon-3am Sat) Owned by a self-confessed 'failed actor', this friendly, attitude-free bar has something on most nights, whether it's a quiz, live music, comedy, theatre or a movie screening (there's a little cinema attached). Local drama is showcased in the 'Other Room', the adjoining 44-seat theatre, while under the shadow of the railway tracks out the back is a wonderful beer garden.

Bragdy a Chegin
PUB

(Brewhouse & Kitchen; Map p642; ☑029-2037 1599; www.brewhouseandkitchen.com/venue/cardiff; Sophia Close; ⏱11am-11pm Mon-Thu, to midnight Fri & Sat, noon-10.30pm Sun; 🔊) Right by SWALEC Stadium, this outpost of the UK-wide Brewhouse and Kitchen chain is in pole position for thirsty cricket-lovers. There's an on-site microbrewery, a conservatory and beer garden, and even an 'academy' where you can learn the essentials of brewing and beer-tasting. The kitchen half of the equation (mains £11 to £15) serves barbecue food alongside pub classics.

Pen & Wig
PUB

(Map p644; ☑029-2037 1217; www.penandwigcardiff.co.uk; 1 Park Grove; ⏱11.30am-midnight Mon-Thu, to 1am Fri & Sat, to 11pm Sun) Latin legal phrases are printed on the walls of this solidly traditional pub (a nod to the many patrons from the legal fraternity), but there's nothing stuffy about the large beer garden or the entertainment roster (Cask-Ale Club Mondays, quiz Tuesdays, live-music Saturdays). The menu (mains £10 to £11) offers straightforward pub grub such as lamb shanks, lasagne and burgers.

☆ Entertainment

Pick up a copy of *Buzz* (www.buzzmag. co.uk), a free monthly magazine with up-to-date entertainment listings, available from tourist offices, bars, theatres and the like. The staff at tourist offices can also help out with recommendations.

★ Clwb Ifor Bach   LIVE MUSIC
(Map p644; ☎029-2023 2199; www.clwb.net; 11 Womanby St; cover from £5) Named for 12th-century Welsh rebel Ifor Bach, the legendary Clwb ('Club') has broken many a Welsh band since it first opened its doors as a Welsh-language social club in 1983, building a reputation as Cardiff's most important indie-music venue. It now hosts bands performing in many tongues – from young upstarts to more established acts – along with regular club nights.

★ Chapter   ARTS CENTRE
(Map p642; ☎029-2030 4400; www.chapter.org; Market Rd, Canton; ⊙8.30am-11pm Mon-Thu, to midnight Fri & Sat, to 10.30pm Sun; 🖥) Established in 1972 and now Cardiff's edgiest arts venue, Chapter has a varied rota of contemporary drama, as well as art exhibitions, arthouse cinema, workshops, alternative theatre and dance performances. There's also a very popular cafe-bar (open from 8.30am until at least 10.30pm), with a big range of European beers and real ale on tap.

🔒 Shopping

One of the most dramatic developments in the central city is the transformation of the Hayes shopping strip, with the giant, glitzy extension of the St David's shopping centre now eating up its entire eastern side. Balancing this modern mall is a historic network of Victorian and Edwardian shopping arcades spreading their wrought-iron tentacles either side of St Mary St.

★ Riverside Market   MARKET
(Map p644; ☎029-2019 0036; www.riverside market.org.uk; Fitzhamon Embankment; ⊙10am-2pm Sun) Every Sunday, the embankment across the Taff from Principality Stadium is lined with stalls for the Riverside Market. Independent producers show off their wares, from speciality cheeses, homemade sourdough bread and cured meats to fresh vegetables, jars of jam and hefty cronuts. The seats let you watch the river go by while sipping great coffee and eating your goodies.

Bodlon   GIFTS & SOUVENIRS
(Map p644; www.bodlon.com; Yr Hen Lyfrgell, The Hayes; ⊙9am-5pm Mon-Sat, 10am-4pm Sun) If you're after a properly Welsh souvenir that isn't too cheesy, this shop in the Welsh cultural centre is a great place to look. Named for the Welsh for 'happy' or 'satisfied', Bodlon stocks locally made art and craft, Welsh-language greeting cards and books, and even a range of kitchen storage containers labelled in Cymraeg.

Morgan Quarter   SHOPPING CENTRE
(Map p644; www.morganquarter.co.uk; btwn St Mary St & The Hayes) Cardiff's oldest arcade (1858), the Royal, connects with the Morgan Arcade via a series of covered lanes, forming a ritzy shopping precinct called the Morgan Quarter. Along with name-brand fashion, there are shops selling skateboards, vintage books and antiques. Look out for **Spillers Records** (Map p644; ☎029-2022 4905; www.spillersrecords.co.uk; 27 Morgan Arcade; ⊙10am-6pm Mon-Sat), art and design collective Illustrate, **The Plan** (Map p644; ☎029-2039 8764; www.theplancafe.co.uk; 28 Morgan Arcade; mains £4-9; ⊙8.30am-5pm; 🍽) cafe and the excellent **Wally's Delicatessen** (Map p644; ☎029-2022 9265; www.wallysdeli.co.uk; 38-46 Royal Arcade; ⊙8.30am-5.30pm Mon-Sat, 11am-4pm Sun).

Cardiff Market   MARKET
(Map p644; btwn St Mary & Trinity Sts; ⊙8am-5.30pm Mon-Sat) While there's been a market here since the 18th century, the current iron-framed covered market dates to 1891. Stalls sell everything from fresh fish to mobile-phone covers, and there's fresh bread, cheese, cold meats, barbecued chicken and Welsh cakes for a picnic in Bute Park. Vinyl fans should head upstairs to Kelly's Records (open 9am to 5pm Monday to Saturday).

LIVE MUSIC

Massive rock and pop concerts are staged at Principality Stadium (p645). If you're after a more intimate experience, try one of the many bars hosting live bands, such as Gwdihŵ, Buffalo Bar and **10 Feet Tall** (☎029-2022 8883; www.10feettallcardiff. com; 12 Church St; ⊙3pm-3am Mon-Thu, noon-3am Fri-Sun).

Regular classical concerts are held in Llandaff Cathedral (p647) and **St John the Baptist Church** (☎029-2039 5231; www.cardiffstjohncityparish.org.uk; 3 St John St; ⊙10am-3pm Mon-Sat).

❶ Information

Tourist Office (Map p644; ☎ 029-2087 3573; www.visitcardiff.com; Yr Hen Lyfrgell, The Hayes; ⊙10am-3pm Sun-Thu, to 5pm Fri & Sat) Information, advice and souvenirs, in the Old Library. There's also a desk next to the ticket office of Cardiff Castle, open from 9am to 5pm.

❶ Getting There & Away

AIR

Cardiff Airport (☎ 01446-711111; www.cardiff-airport.com) is 12 miles southwest of Cardiff, past Barry. Among the airlines with regular scheduled flights into Cardiff are:

Flybe (www.flybe.com) Anglesey, Berlin, Channel Islands, Cork, Dublin, Düsseldorf, Edinburgh, Glasgow, Milan, Munich, Paris, Rome, Venice

Iberia (www.iberia.com) Madrid

KLM (www.klm.com) Amsterdam

Qatar (www.qatarairways.com) Doha

Ryanair (www.ryanair.com) Faro, Tenerife South

Vueling (www.vueling.com) Alicante, Barcelona, Málaga, Palma de Mallorca

BUS

Cardiff's old central bus station was demolished in 2008; after years of planning and false starts, its replacement is due to open near the train station in a revitalised Central Sq in 2020. In the meantime, buses call at temporary stops scattered around the city. See https://www.traveline.cymru for details.

Bus destinations include the X30/30 to Newport (£2.20, 40 minutes, frequent), the X3 to Abergavenny (£8.30, 1½ hours, frequent), the T4 to Brecon (£7, 1¾ hours, eight daily), the X10 to Swansea (£5, 1¼ hours, six per day) and the T1C to Aberystwyth (£17, four hours, one daily).

Megabus (http://uk.megabus.com) offers one-way coach journeys from London to Cardiff (via Newport) from as little as £8.30.

National Express (www.nationalexpress.com) coaches depart from **Cardiff Coach Station** (Map p642; Sophia Gardens) to destinations including Tenby (£19, 2¾ hours, daily), Swansea (£5.20, 1¼ hours, frequent), Chepstow (from £6.60, one hour, six daily), Bristol (£8.70, 1¼ hours, six daily) and London (from £15, 3¾ hours, frequent).

TRAIN

Trains from major British cities arrive at Cardiff Central station, on the southern edge of the city centre. Direct services to/from Cardiff include London Paddington (from £62, 2¼ hours, two per hour), Abergavenny (£14, 40 minutes, frequent), Swansea (£11.40, one hour, two per hour), Fishguard Harbour (from £11.50, 3¼ hours, two daily) and Holyhead (£47, five hours,

seven daily). For the latest timetables and bookings, see www.thetrainline.com.

❶ Getting Around

TO/FROM THE AIRPORT

The T9 Cardiff Airport Express bus (£5, 40 minutes, every 20 minutes from 4am to 12.30am) heads between the airport and Cardiff Bay via the city centre.

The 905 shuttle bus (£1, 7 minutes) links the airport terminal to nearby Rhoose Cardiff Airport railway station. Trains from Rhoose to Cardiff Central station (£4.60, 33 minutes) run hourly Monday to Saturday and twice hourly on Sunday.

FlightLink Wales (☎ Cardiff Airport 01446-728 500, head office 029-2025 3555; www.flightlinkwales.com) has the airport taxi concession, providing minibus shuttles to the city, either on a shared basis (from £22) or for exclusive use (from £31).

BOAT

Two boats run alternating waterbus services along the River Taff from **Bute Park** (Map p644) to **Mermaid Quay** (Map p647), departing every half-hour from 10.30am to 5pm. The journey takes about 25 minutes, costs £4 each way, and is accompanied by commentary on the sights.

BUS

Local buses are operated by **Cardiff Bus** (☎ 029-2066 6444; www.cardiffbus.com; single trip/day pass £1.90/3.80); buy your ticket from the driver (cash or contactless; no change given). Useful routes from stops scattered around the city centre include the Baycar (6) to Cardiff Bay; 52 and 54 to Cathays and Roath Park; 25 and 63 via Cathedral Rd to Llandaff; and 32A to St Fagans (operated by Easyway).

TRAIN

Generally the buses are more convenient for short trips than the trains, although there are a handful of stations scattered around the city, including Cardiff Central, Cardiff Queen St, Cardiff Bay, Cathays and Grangetown. Expect to pay around £2.10.

MONMOUTHSHIRE (SIR FYNWY)

You need only ponder the preponderance of castles to realise that this pleasantly rural county was once a wild frontier. The Norman marcher lords kept stonemasons extremely busy, erecting mighty fortifications to keep the unruly Welsh at bay. Despite this stone line marking out a very clear border along the Rivers Monnow and Wye, the 1543 second Act of Union left Monmouthshire in a kind of jurisdictional limbo between England and Wales. This legal ambiguity wasn't put to rest until 1974, when Monmouthshire was definitively confirmed as part of Wales.

The River Wye, Britain's fifth longest, flows from the mountains of Mid-Wales, tootles its way into England and then returns to the middle ground – forming the border of the two countries – before emptying into the River Severn below Chepstow. Much of it is designated an Area of Outstanding Natural Beauty (AONB; www.wyevalleyaonb. org.uk), famous for its limestone gorges and dense broadleaved woodland.

Chepstow (Cas-gwent)

☑ 01291 / POP 12,418

Chepstow is an attractive market town nestled in a great S-bend in the River Wye, with a magnificent Norman castle and one of Britain's best-known racecourses. It was first developed as a base for the Norman conquest of southeast Wales (and it was only narrowly 'Welsh' in any case: the Wye that cuts its eastern edge was made the boundary between the two countries by kingdom-forming King Athelstan, in 982). Chepstow later prospered as a port for the timber and wine trades. As river-borne commerce gave way to the railways, Chepstow's importance diminished to reflect its name, which means 'market place' in Old English.

◉ Sights

★ **Chepstow Castle**　　　　　　　CASTLE
(Cadw; www.cadw.gov.wales; Bridge St; adult/child £6.90/4.10; ⊙ 9.30am-5pm Mar-Jun, Sep & Oct, to 6pm Jul & Aug, 10am-4pm Mon-Sat & 11am-4pm Sun Nov-Feb) Imposing Chepstow Castle perches atop a limestone cliff overhanging the river, guarding the main river crossing from England into South Wales. It is one of the oldest castles in Britain – building started in 1067, less than a year after William the Conqueror invaded England. The impressive Great Tower dates from this time and includes bricks plundered from the nearby Roman town of Caerwent. It was extended over the centuries, resulting in a long, narrow complex snaking along the hill.

🛏 Sleeping & Eating

Three Tuns　　　　　　　　　　PUB ££
(☑ 01291-645797; 32 Bridge St; s/d from £65/85; ⓢ) This mid-7th-century pub by the castle has had an artful makeover, with rugs and antique furniture complementing the more rugged features of the ancient building. In warm weather the flowery, castle-backed beer garden is a boon. There's a pie-heavy pub menu (mains £10) and often live music downstairs at weekends, but the noise winds down at 11pm.

Riverside Wine Bar　　　　　　TAPAS ££
(☑ 01291-628300; www.theriversidewinebar.co.uk; 18a The Back; mains £12-14; ⊙ 10.30am-11pm Mon-Thu, to midnight Fri & Sat, to 10pm Sun, food served noon-4pm & 5.30-9.30pm) Sink into a leather couch and quaff a glass of wine while grazing your way through antipasto and cheese platters, skewers, tortillas, pizza and tapas. Heavy gilt-framed mirrors and feature wallpaper set the tone, while in summer the action spills outside, where a warm-weather terrace allows views through willow curtains across the Wye to England.

❶ Getting There & Away

BUS

From Chepstow's **bus station** (Thomas St), frequent 7XP, X74 and 73 services head to/from Newport (£3.80, 30 minutes to 1¼ hours); up to 10 daily 69 services head to/from Tintern (£2.95, 19 minutes) and Monmouth (£4, 45 minutes); and up to 10 7XP services head to/from Bristol (£6, 55 minutes). Sunday services are limited.

National Express (www.nationalexpress.com) has up to four coaches a day to/from London (from £12, three hours), Cardiff (from £4.80, one hour) and Swansea (from £11, two hours).

TRAIN

There are frequent direct trains to/from Newport (£7.60, 23 minutes), Gloucester (£10, 30 minutes) and Cardiff (£10, 40 minutes), but only one direct service per day to Swansea (£17, 1¾ hours) and Fishguard Harbour (£20, 3¾ hours).

Lower Wye Valley

The A466 road follows the meandering, steep and tree-cloaked valley of the River Wye from Chepstow to Monmouth, passing through the little village of Tintern, huddled around its famous abbey as it would have done in its heyday. This is a beautiful and little-visited pocket of Wales, rendered particularly mysterious when a twilight mist rises from the river and shrouds the illuminated ruins.

It's now almost impossible to see the vestiges of the surprisingly robust industries that flourished here in the 18th and 19th

CARDIFF, PEMBROKESHIRE & SOUTH WALES ABERGAVENNY (Y FENNI)

CAERLEON ROMAN FORTRESS

Hidden in plain view beneath the small, genteel town of **Caerleon** is one of the largest and most important Roman settlements in Britain. After the Romans invaded in AD 43, they controlled their new territory through a network of forts and military garrisons. The top tier of military organisation was the legionary fort, of which there were only three in Britain – at Eboracum (York), Deva (Chester) and Isca (Caerleon).

Caerleon ('Fort of the Legion') was the headquarters of the elite 2nd Augustan Legion for more than 200 years, from AD 75 until the end of the 3rd century. It wasn't just a military camp, but a purpose-built township some 9 miles in circumference, complete with a large amphitheatre and a state-of-the-art Roman **baths complex** (Cadw; www.cadw.gov.wales; High St; ⏱ 9.30am-5pm daily Apr-Oct, 9.30am-5pm Mon-Sat, 11am-4pm Sun Nov-Mar; ℗) **FREE**.

Caerleon is 3 miles northeast of central Newport. Buses head here from Newport (£1.70, 11 minutes, frequent) and Monmouth (£4.35, 45 minutes, eight daily).

centuries: wire, paper and boat making. It's still a great place for boats, though – kayaking on the Wye provides just the pace and perspective to tune into the blissful rhythms of this special place.

◉ Sights

★ Tintern Abbey
ABBEY

(Cadw; www.cadw.gov.wales; Tintern; adult/child £6.90/4.10; ⏱ 9.30am-5pm Mar-Jun, Sep & Oct, to 6pm Jul & Aug, 10am-4pm Mon-Sat, 11am-4pm Sun Nov-Feb; ℗) The haunting riverside ruins of this sprawling monastic complex have inspired poets and artists through the centuries, most notably William Wordsworth, who penned 'Lines Composed a Few Miles Above Tintern Abbey' during a visit in 1798, and JMW Turner, who made many paintings and drawings of the site. It was founded in 1131 by the Cistercian order and left to fall into picturesque ruin after the monks were booted out by Henry VIII in 1536.

🛏 Sleeping & Eating

Tŷ Bryn
B&B ££

(☎ 01594-531330; www.wyevalleystay.co.uk; Monmouth Rd, Llandogo; s/d £85/90; ℗ 🛜) Perched on a hillside overlooking a gorgeous loop of the Wye in the village of Llandogo, this old stone house has friendly young owners and three comfortable en-suite rooms. Two of the rooms have river views, and there are a sitting room and a front-garden terrace for sociable relaxing.

★ Whitebrook
MODERN BRITISH £££

(☎ 01600-860254; www.thewhitebrook.co.uk; Whitebrook; menu 3 courses/lunch/dinner £39/53/82, d incl dinner from £250; ⏱ noon-2pm & 7-9pm Wed-Sun; ℗ 🛜) Hidden down green-canopied country lanes in a remote part of the Wye Valley, this wonderful Michelin-starred restaurant-with-rooms is well worth the effort to find. Every plate proceeding from the kitchen is a little work of art, made largely with what can be sourced from within 12 miles and adorned with foraged herbs such as monkwort, nettles, wild garlic and elderflower.

ℹ Getting There & Away

Eleven 69 buses a day (fewer on Saturday, none on Sunday) stop here on their journey between Chepstow (£1.95, 19 minutes) and Monmouth (£2.65, 30 minutes). You may want your own wheels.

Abergavenny (Y Fenni)

☏ 01873 / POP 13,283

Bustling, workaday Abergavenny has played many roles on history's stage: Roman fort, Norman stronghold, tanning and weaving centre, and prison for Hitler's deputy. Nestled between three shapely hills – the Blorenge, Ysgyryd Fawr (Skirrid) and Sugar Loaf – it's a superb base for walkers, and uplifting greenery is everywhere a glimpse away. With an annual food festival, and some acclaimed restaurants on the fringes of of town, it also attracts lovers of Welsh produce and cooking.

Its ancient name, Y Fenni (Welsh for 'place of the smiths'), was given to a stream that empties into the River Usk here, and later anglicised to Gavenny (Abergavenny means 'mouth of the Gavenny'). The Romans established Gobannium Fort here, exactly a day's march from their garrison at

Caerleon, which they maintained from AD 57 to 400. Not long after the Norman Conquest, a marcher lord, Hamelin de Ballon, built the castle and the town's importance grew.

◉ Sights

★ St Mary's Priory Church CHURCH

(☑ 01873-858787; www.stmarys-priory.org; Monk St; ⊙ 9am-4pm Mon-Sat) Although you wouldn't guess it from the outside, this large stone church has been described as the 'Westminster Abbey of South Wales' because of the remarkable treasury of aristocratic tombs that lies within. It was founded at the same time as the Norman castle (1087) as part of a Benedictine priory, but the present building dates mainly from the 14th century, with 15th- and 19th-century additions and alterations.

⚝ Festivals & Events

Abergavenny Food Festival FOOD & DRINK
(www.abergavennyfoodfestival.co.uk; ⊙ mid-Sep) The most important gastronomic event in Wales is held on the third weekend in September, with demonstrations, debates, competitions, courses, stalls and the odd celebrity. But the real drawcard is that this is an enthusiastically local festival, run by volunteers, and not some big-budget food producer's showcase. At night there's a market and events at the castle.

🛏 Sleeping & Eating

Angel Hotel HOTEL £££
(☑ 01873-857121; www.angelabergavenny.com; 15 Cross St; r/cottages from £159/300; ℗ 🛜) Abergavenny's top hotel is a fine Georgian building that was once a famous coaching inn. Choose between sleek, sophisticated rooms in the hotel itself, in an adjoining mews, in a Victorian lodge near the castle or in the 17th-century Castle Cottage (sleeping four). There's also a good **restaurant** (mains restaurant £14-18, bar £6-14; ⊙ noon-11pm) and bar, serving modern British food and elaborate afternoon and high teas.

Cwtch Cafe CAFE £
(☑ 01873-855466; 58 Cross St; mains £5-6; ⊙ 9am-5pm Mon-Sat; 🛜) Stylish and wonderfully friendly, Cwtch (Welsh for 'hug') entices a scrum of regulars through its doors with its homemade cakes, coffee, and lunchtime dishes such as rarebit, Canadian pancakes (with crispy bacon and maple syrup), quiche

and gourmet pasties. There are plenty of gluten-free options, too.

★ Walnut Tree MODERN BRITISH £££

(☑ 01873-852797; www.thewalnuttreeinn.com; Old Ross Rd, Llanddewi Skirrid; mains £27-29, 2-/3-course lunch £25/30; ⊙ noon-2.30pm & 6.30-10pm Tue-Sat) Established in 1963, the Michelin-starred Walnut Tree serves the cuisine-hopping meat and seafood creations of chef Shaun Hill, with a focus on fresh, local produce. If you're too full to move far after feasting on dishes such as John Dory and crab with summer-vegetable minestrone, elegant cottage accommodation is available (from £150).

The Walnut Tree is 3 miles northeast of Abergavenny on the B4521.

Hardwick MODERN BRITISH £££
(☑ 01873-854220; www.thehardwick.co.uk; Old Raglan Rd; mains £20-22, 2-/3-course Sunday lunch £27/34; ⊙ noon-3pm & 6.30-10pm; ℗) This traditional inn – with its old stone fireplace, low ceiling beams and burnished copper bar – has become head chef Stephen Terry's showcase for the best of unpretentious country cooking. Dishes such as braised rabbit with fried polenta are deeply satisfying, but you need to save room for the homemade ice cream. Attached are eight elegant rooms (from £140).

The Hardwick is 2 miles south of Abergavenny on the B4598.

DON'T MISS

RAGLAN CASTLE

The last great medieval castle to be built in Wales, **Raglan** (Cadw; www.cadw.wales.gov.uk; adult/child £6.90/4.10; ⊙ 9.30am-5pm Mar-Jun, Sep & Oct, to 6pm Jul & Aug, 10am-4pm Mon-Sat, 11am-4pm Sun Nov-Feb; ℗) was designed more as a swaggering declaration of wealth and power than a defensive fortress. A magnificent, sprawling complex built of dusky pink and grey sandstone, it was constructed in the 15th and 16th centuries by Sir William ap Thomas and his son William Herbert, the first earl of Pembroke.

Raglan Castle is on the busy A40, 8 miles southwest of Monmouth and 9 miles southeast of Abergavenny. Buses heading between the two stop at Raglan village, which is a five-minute walk from the castle.

ℹ Information

Tourist Office (☏ 01873-853254; www.visitabergavenny.co.uk; Tithe Barn, Monk St; ◷ 10am-4pm Mon-Sat) Located in the 12th-century Tithe Barn, once part of the Benedictine priory.

ℹ Getting There & Away

There are direct trains to/from Cardiff (£14, 45 minutes, up to nine per day), Swansea (£17, 1¾ hours, up to 14 daily), Manchester (from £31, 2¾ hours, up to 15 daily), Tenby (£30, 3¾ hours, one daily) and Holyhead (from £35, 4½ hours, up to seven daily).

Direct services at Abergavenny's **bus station** include the X3 to/from Hereford (£5.70, 55 minutes, five daily) and Cardiff (£8.30, 1¾ hours, hourly); the hourly TX4 to/from Merthyr Tydfil (£6.80, 1¾ hours); six daily 83 services to/from Monmouth (£3.80, 45 minutes); and 10 daily 43 services to/from Brecon (£3.60, one hour).

SOUTH WALES VALLEYS

The valleys fanning north from Cardiff and Newport were once the heart of industrial Wales, playing a part in national (and world) history that can't be overstated. Although the coal, iron and steel industries have withered, the valley names – Rhondda, Cynon, Rhymney, Ebbw – still evoke a world of tight-knit working-class communities, male-voice choirs and rows of neat terraced houses set amid a scarred, coal-blackened landscape. Today the region is fighting back against a very noticeable and tragic decline by creating a tourism industry celebrating and preserving its industrial heritage – places such as the Welsh Mining Experience, Big Pit and Blaenavon Ironworks are among Wales' most impressive and historically significant tourist attractions.

Blaenavon (Blaenafon)

☏ 01495 / POP 5753

Of all the valley settlements that were decimated by the demise of heavy industry, the one-time coal and iron town of Blaenavon shows the greenest shoots of regrowth, helped in large part by the awarding of Unesco World Heritage status in 2000 to its unique conglomeration of industrial sites. Its proximity to Brecon Beacons National Park and Abergavenny doesn't do it any harm either. Anyone with an interest in industrial history (or social history, for that matter) will find plenty to see and consider here.

◉ Sights

★ **Big Pit National Coal Museum**   MINE
(☏ 0300 111 2 333; www.museumwales.ac.uk; car park £3; ◷ 9.30am-5pm, guided tours 10am-3.30pm; P ♿) **FREE** Fascinating Big Pit provides an opportunity to explore a real coal mine and get a taste of what life was like for the miners who worked here from 1880 to 1980. Tours descend 90m into the mine and explore the tunnels and coalfaces in the company of an ex-miner guide. Above ground, you can visit various colliery buildings, including the 1939 pithead baths, filled with displays on the industry and the evocative reminiscences of ex-miners.

Blaenavon World
Heritage Centre   MUSEUM
(☏ 01495-742333; www.visitblaenavon.co.uk; Church Rd; ◷ 10am-5pm Tue-Sun) **FREE** Housed in an artfully converted old school, this centre contains a cafe, a tourist office, a gallery, a gift shop and, more importantly, excellent interactive audiovisual displays that explore the industrial heritage of the region. If you're going to explore much of the World Heritage Site, this is the place to start.

Blaenavon Ironworks   HISTORIC SITE
(Cadw; ☏ 01495-792615; www.cadw.gov.wales; North St; ◷ 10am-5pm Easter-Oct, to 4pm Thu-Sat Nov-Easter) **FREE** When it was completed in 1789, this ironworks was among the most advanced in the world. Today the site is one of the best preserved of all its Industrial Revolution contemporaries, with a motion-activated audiovisual display within the hulking remains of one of the blast furnaces serving to rattle the ravens that now call it home. Also on display are the ironworkers' tiny terraced cottages, furnished as they would have been at different points in history.

Pontypool &
Blaenavon Railway   HERITAGE RAILWAY
(☏ 01495-792263; www.pontypool-and-blaenavon.co.uk; day pass adult/child £9/5) Built to haul coal and passengers, this railway has been restored by local volunteers, allowing you to catch a train from the town centre to Furnace Sidings (near Big Pit) and on to Whistle Halt, which at 396m is one of the highest stations in Britain. Check online for running

WORTH A TRIP

CAERPHILLY CASTLE

You could be forgiven for thinking that **Caerphilly Castle** (Cadw; www.cadw.gov.wales; Castle St; adult/child £8.50/5.10; ⊙9.30am-5pm Mar-Jun, Sep & Oct, to 6pm Jul & Aug, 10am-4pm Mon-Sat, 11am-4pm Sun Nov-Feb; ⊕) – with its profusion of towers and crenellations reflected in a duck-filled lake – was a film set rather than an ancient monument. While it is often used as a film set, it is also one of Britain's finest examples of a 13th-century fortress with water defences, and the largest castle in Wales.

Most of the construction was completed between 1268 and 1271 by the powerful English baron Gilbert de Clare (1243–95), lord marcher of Glamorgan, in response to the threat of attack by Prince Llywelyn ap Gruffydd, prince of Gwynedd (and the last Welsh Prince of Wales), who had already united most of the country under his control. Edward I's subsequent campaign against the Welsh princes put an end to Llywelyn's ambitions and Caerphilly's short-lived spell on the front line came to an end. The leaning tower at the southeastern corner is a result of subsidence rather than battle.

In the 13th century Caerphilly was state-of-the-art, being one of the earliest castles to use lakes, bridges and a series of concentric fortifications for defence. To reach the inner court you had to overcome no fewer than three drawbridges, six portcullises and five sets of double gates. In the early 14th century it was remodelled as a grand residence and the magnificent great hall was adapted for entertaining, but from the mid-14th century the castle began to fall into ruin.

Much of what you see today is the result of restoration by the castle-loving Bute family. The third marquess of Bute purchased and demolished houses built up against the walls, and in 1870 the great hall was given a magnificent wooden ceiling. The fourth marquess instituted a major restoration from 1928 to 1939, giving jobs to many Great Depression–affected locals in the process. Work continued after 1950, when the fifth marquess gifted the castle to the state. In 1958 the dams were reflooded, creating the castle's current fairy-tale appearance.

You can enter through the outside gate and into the first tower before reaching the ticket office. Upstairs are detailed displays about the castle's history. A cartoonish film projected onto the walls of one of the inner towers tells a truncated version of the same story.

On the south dam platform you can see reconstructions of medieval siege weapons; they are working models that lob stone projectiles into the lake during battle re-enactments. Fans of toilet humour should seek out the communal latrine in a small tower nearby.

The easiest way to reach Caerphilly from Cardiff is by train (£4.60, 18 minutes, up to three per hour).

Frequent 25 and 26 buses head to/from Cardiff (£4.20, 40 to 50 minutes) and frequent 50 buses do the same with Newport (£3.80, 45 minutes). Bus 26 from Cardiff stops near Castell Coch (p645) en route, making it possible to visit both it and Cardiff Castle (p643) in one day. Sunday services are less frequent.

days and times, most of which involve restored steam locomotives.

🛏 Sleeping & Eating

Oakfield   B&B **££**
(☏01495-792829; www.oakfieldbnb.com; 1 Oakfield Tce, Varteg Rd; s/d £48/70; P🛜) Paula and Heidi, the clued-up owners of this spick-and-span B&B, are a fount of local knowledge. Their three well-appointed rooms have a fresh, modern feel. Two have en-suite bathrooms, while the third is an interconnected family suite with a bathroom on the landing.

Coffi Bean   CAFE **£**
(☏01495-790127; 76 Broad St; mains £4-5; ⊙9am-3pm Tue-Sat; 🛜) With leadlight windows, art deco fixtures and shamrock tiling on the walls, this lovely old converted shop is a great place to soak up local life. The uncomplicated food stretches to cooked breakfasts, sandwiches, jacket potatoes, stews, curries, quiches, cakes and proper Sunday lunches.

❶ Getting There & Away

Frequent X24 bus services head to/from Newport (£7.50, one hour).

WORTH A TRIP

RHONDDA VALLEY

Until its last pit closed in 1990, the **Rhondda Valley** was synonymous with coal mining. That industrial heritage is celebrated at the **Welsh Mining Experience** (Rhondda Heritage Park; ☑ 01443-682036; www.rhonddaheritagepark.com; Lewis Merthyr Colliery, Coed Cae Rd, Trehafod; tour adult/child £6.95/5.75; ☉ 10.30am-4.30pm Tue-Sun) **FREE**, within the buildings of the Lewis Merthyr coal mine, closed in 1983 and now the Rhondda Heritage Park. The highlight is the 40-minute Black Gold Experience (bookings advised), where you don a miner's helmet and lamp and, accompanied by an ex-miner, descend to the coalface. The commentary vividly recreates mine work, hammering home the social impact of the coal industry.

The mine is located just off the A4058 in Trehafod, between Pontypridd and Porth. There are regular trains from Cardiff Central station to Trehafod (£4.60, 35 minutes), from where it's a 10-minute walk to the heritage park.

SWANSEA BAY & THE GOWER

Swansea (Abertawe)

☑ 01792 / POP 241,300

Dylan Thomas called Swansea an 'ugly, lovely town', and that remains a fair description of Wales' second-largest city today. It's currently in the grip of a Cardiff-esque bout of regeneration that's slowly transforming the drab, postwar city centre into something more worthy of its setting on the glorious 5-mile sweep of Swansea Bay.

The city's Welsh name, Abertawe, describes its location at the mouth of the Tawe, where the river empties into the bay. The Vikings named the area Sveins Ey (Swein's Island), probably referring to the sandbank in the river mouth.

Swansea makes up for some visual shortcomings with a deeper charm. A hefty student population takes to the city's bars with enthusiasm, and pockets of hipness have emerged in inner suburbs such as Sketty and Uplands (which is, conveniently, where all the best B&Bs are located).

History

As they so loved to do, the Normans built a conquest-consolidating castle here in 1106, but Swansea didn't hit its stride until the Industrial Revolution, when it developed into an important copper-smelting centre. Ore was first shipped in from Cornwall, across the Bristol Channel, but by the 19th century it was arriving from Chile, Cuba and the USA in return for Welsh coal.

By the 20th century the city's industrial base had declined, although Swansea's dwindling industry was still judged a worthy target by the Luftwaffe, which devastated the city centre in 1941. It was rebuilt as a rather uninspired retail development in the 1960s, '70s and '80s, but further regeneration, more sensitive to the city's cultural and historical value, seems to be undoing some of the drabbest excesses.

◉ Sights

Dylan Thomas Centre   MUSEUM
(☑ 01792-463980; www.dylanthomas.com; Somerset Pl; ☉ 10am-4.30pm) **FREE** Housed in the former guildhall, this unassuming museum contains absorbing displays on the Swansea-born poet's life and work. It pulls no punches in examining the propensity of Dylan Thomas for puffing up his own myth; he was eventually trapped in the legend of his excessive drinking. Aside from the collection of memorabilia, what really brings his writing to life are recordings of of his work performed, part of the centre's permanent, interactive 'Love the Words' exhibition.

National Waterfront Museum   MUSEUM
(☑ 029-2057 3600, 0300 111 2 333; www.museumwales.ac.uk; South Dock Marina, Oystermouth Rd; ☉ 10am-5pm) **FREE** Housed in a 1901 dockside warehouse with a striking glass and slate extension, this museum's 15 hands-on galleries explore Wales' commercial maritime history and the impact of industrialisation on its people, making much use of interactive computer screens and audiovisual presentations. The effect can be a bit overwhelming, but there's a lot of interesting stuff here, including displays on the Welsh music industry (artefacts include Bonnie Tyler's gold and Duffy's platinum discs) and a section on 'women's work'.

Egypt Centre
MUSEUM

(📞01792-295960; www.egypt.swan.ac.uk; Swansea University Singleton Campus, Mumbles Rd; ⏱10am-4pm Tue-Sat; ♿) **FREE** Swansea University's collection of ancient Egyptian antiquities, some 5000 artefacts donated by various British institutions and collectors, includes a fascinating array of everyday and rarefied artefacts ranging from a 4000-year-old razor to a mummified crocodile. Check the website for seasonal activities for kids.

⭐ Festivals & Events

Dylan Thomas Festival
LITERATURE

(www.dylanthomas.com/festival; ⏱27 Oct-9 Nov) This festival celebrates Swansea's most famous son with poetry readings, talks, films and performances from 27 October (his birthday) to 9 November (the date he died).

🛏 Sleeping

Mirador Town House
B&B ££

(📞01792-466976; www.themirador.co.uk; 14 Mirador Cres, Uplands; s/d from £60/80; 📶) Kooky and kitsch in the extreme, all seven B&B rooms here are fancifully and elaborately themed – Roman, Mediterranean, African, Venetian, Egyptian, Asian and French – with murals on the walls and sometimes the ceilings. Comfort hasn't been sacrificed for decorative whimsy, however, and the exuberant hosts are enthusiastic cheerleaders for the bars, restaurants and general buzz of the area.

Premier Inn Swansea Waterfront
HOTEL ££

(📞0871-527 9212; www.premierinn.com; Langdon Rd; r from £62; 📶) It's hard to beat the value offered by this shiny new waterfront chain hotel, just across the river from the town centre. As at all Premier Inns, rooms are generically smart, comfortable and well equipped. Book early for discounts and request a room with a view. If you're driving, note that the parking lot next door is relatively pricey.

Dylan Thomas Birthplace
GUESTHOUSE £££

(📞01792-472555; www.dylanthomasbirthplace.com; 5 Cwmdonkin Dr; r from £150) Dylan Thomas fans now have the opportunity to stay in the house where the poet was born and spent his first 23 years. The house has been diligently maintained in period style, and you'll have the choice of staying in the bedrooms once occupied by Nancy (his sister), DJ and Florrie (his parents), and of course Dylan himself.

Booking a room entails exclusive use of the house, so solo travellers may get it all to themselves for just £150.

🍴 Eating

⭐ Square Peg
CAFE £

(📞01792-206593; www.squarepeg.org.uk; 29b Gower Rd, Sketty; mains £6-7; ⏱8am-5pm Mon-Sat; ♿) With mismatched stools re-upholstered in recycled denim and kooky local photography blanketing the walls, this is exactly the hip kind of place you'd expect to deliver seriously good coffee. With two blends on the go at any given time and monthly 'guest roasters', it doesn't disappoint. The menu includes tasty light breakfasts, salads, soups and deliciously inventive tacos.

Joe's Ice Cream Parlour
ICE CREAM £

(📞01792-653880; www.joes-icecream.com; 85 St Helen's Rd; cones/sundaes from £1.50/4.30; ⏱10am-11pm) For an ice-cream sundae or a cone, locals flock to Joe's, a Swansea institution founded in 1922 by Joe Cascarini, son of immigrants from Italy's Abruzzi mountains. So beloved is this gelato that outlets have sprung up in four other places across South Wales.

⭐ Gigi Gau's Favourite
CHINESE ££

(📞01792-653300; www.favouritechinese.co.uk; 18-23 Anchor Ct; mains £13-15; ⏱noon-10pm; 📶🍴) In a new centre-stage waterfront location, this passionately loved Chinese kitchen eschews the batters, all-purpose sauces and replica menus of many Westernised Chinese eateries to produce food that does justice to China's deep culinary treasures. Homemade organic noodles are served with unapologetically funky Beijing-style sauce, the pork is sweet braised Hunan style, and vegetarian dishes aren't just padding out the menu.

⭐ Mosaic
TAPAS ££

(📞01792-655225; www.mosaicswanseauk.com; 11 St Helen's Rd; tapas £6-7, platters per head £20; ⏱6-11pm Wed-Fri, noon-3pm & 6-11pm Sat; 🍴) Set back from the road in an old brick warehouse, and with a menu as eclectic as its decor, this chic eatery specialises in 'world fusion tapas'. This translates to small plates and tasty platters designed to be shared, striding the globe from Jamaican jerk chicken to Japanese prawn katsu curry. The attached cocktail bar is very cool indeed.

Hanson at the Chelsea
SEAFOOD ££

(📞01792-464068; www.hansonatthechelsea.co.uk; 17 St Mary's St; mains £18-22, 2/3-course lunch £15/19; ⏱noon-2pm & 7-9pm Mon-Sat) Perfect for a romantic liaison, this elegant little dining room of mustard-yellow walls and stiff napery is tucked away behind the

Swansea

frenzy of Wind St. Seafood such as hake with Provençal vegetables and raspberry pesto are the stars, but the menu also contains plenty of less challenging meaty dishes, and blackboard specials are chalked up daily. Unfortunately, vegetarians have few options.

Slice   MODERN BRITISH £££
(☑ 01792-290929; www.sliceswansea.co.uk; 73-75 Eversley Rd, Sketty; 3/6-course menu lunch £32/48, dinner £42/55; ⏰ 6.15-9.15pm Thu & Sun, 12.30-1.45pm & 6.15-9.15pm Fri & Sat) The simple decor – wooden floors and furniture, and pale walls – stands in contrast to the elaborate dishes emanating from Slice's kitchen. Its elegant-

ly presented food is terrific: locally sourced meat, fish, cheese and beer, plus homemade bread and home-grown herbs, are the foundation of successful adventures such as dressed white crab with brown-meat panna cotta, avocado and compressed watermelon.

🍷 Drinking & Nightlife

★ **No Sign Bar**   WINE BAR
(☑ 01792-465300; www.nosignwinebar.com; 56 Wind St; ⏰ 11am-midnight; ⏝) Once frequented by Dylan Thomas (it appears as the Wine Vaults in his story 'The Followers'), the No Sign stands out as the only vaguely tra-

Swansea

◎ **Sights**
1 Dylan Thomas Centre D3
2 National Waterfront Museum C4

⊗ **Eating**
3 Gigi Gau's Favourite C4
4 Hanson at the Chelsea C3
5 Mosaic A3

◎ **Drinking & Nightlife**
6 Kon-Tiki C3
7 No Sign Bar C3
8 Prohibition C3

◉ **Shopping**
9 Swansea Market B3

ditional bar left on Wind St. Once a wine merchant's, it's a long, narrow haven of dark-wood panelling, old boys in deep conversation, friendly staff, good pub grub, and great beers on cask and tap.

Kon-Tiki   COCKTAIL BAR
(☑ 01792-462896; 10 The Strand; ☺ 6pm-midnight Sun-Thu, to 1.30am Fri & Sat) Hidden down the hill from Wind St, cool Kon-Tiki offers all the requisite elements for a tropical-beach fantasy: faux Polynesian statues, cocktails served in tiki cups, flax matting on the walls and Bob Marley on the stereo. At weekends there's a clubby vibe, a £1 cover charge and DJs, and things sometimes don't wind up until the break of day.

Prohibition   COCKTAIL BAR
(☑ 07500-701866; Green Dragon Lane; ☺ 9pm-3am Wed, from 8pm Fri, from 7pm Sat) Slink down a side lane from Wind St, give a knowing nod to the bouncer lurking in the shadows, enter the corridor, push back the bookcase and enter an illicit world where attractive mixologists dispense charm and first-rate cocktails in equal serves to an appreciative, in-the-know clientele. There's no sign; look for it two doors up from Kon-Tiki bar.

Uplands Tavern   PUB
(☑ 01792-458242; www.facebook.com/theuplands tavern; 42 Uplands Cres, Uplands; ☺ 11am-11pm) A former Dylan Thomas hang-out, Uplands still serves a quiet daytime pint in the 'Dylan Thomas' snug, and is painted a sober dark green. Come nightfall it turns into a different beast altogether as the hub of the city's live-music scene, attracting a mixed crowd of students and local regulars. Check the Facebook page for upcoming events.

⛉ **Shopping**

★ **Swansea Market**   MARKET
(www.swanseaindoormarket.co.uk; Oxford St; ☺ 8am-5.30pm Mon-Sat) There's been a covered market in Swansea since 1652 and at this site since 1830. Rebuilt in 1961 after being bombed in WWII, the current version is a buzzing place to sample local specialities, like cockles, laver bread and Welsh cakes hot from the griddle. It's not local, but it's hard to go past stall 58d, Thai Taste (mains £4 to £5).

ⓘ **Information**

Morriston Hospital (☑ 01792-702222; www.wales.nhs.uk; Heol Maes Eglwys, Morriston) Has an accident and emergency department; 5 miles north of the city centre.
Police Station (☑ 101; www.south-wales.police.uk; Grove Pl)

ⓘ **Getting There & Away**

BUS
Swansea's **bus station** (Plymouth St) is at the western edge of the city centre, by the Quadrant shopping centre.

National Express (☑ 0871 781 8181; www.nationalexpress.com) coaches head to/from Tenby (£9.20, 1½ hours, two daily), Cardiff (£5.20, 1¼ hours, frequent), Chepstow (from £11, two hours, up to four daily), Bristol (£14, 2¾ hours, four daily) and London (£24, five hours, four direct daily).

Other direct bus services include the frequent X10 to/from Cardiff (£5, 1¼ hours), frequent 110 and X11 services to/from Llanelli (£5.90, one to 1½ hours), frequent X11 services to/from Carmarthen (£5.80, 1¾ hours) and the X13 to/from Llandeilo (£5.80, 1½ hours, five daily).

TRAIN
Swansea's train station is 600m north of Castle Sq along Castle St and High St. Direct services to/from Swansea include Cardiff (£11, one hour, two per hour), Abergavenny (£19, 1½ hours, up to nine per day), Tenby (£15, 1½ hours, seven daily), Llandrindod Wells (£14, 2¾ hours, four daily) and London Paddington (from £68, three hours, frequent).

The Mumbles (Y Mwmbwls)

Strung out along the shoreline at the southern end of Swansea Bay, The Mumbles has been Swansea's seaside retreat since 1807, when the Oystermouth Railway, built three years previously for transporting coal on horse-drawn carriages, was adapted for human cargo. Closed in 1960, it has the distinction of being the first passenger railway service in the world.

Once again fashionable, with bars and restaurants vying for trade along the promenade, The Mumbles received a boost to its reputation when its most famous daughter, Hollywood actor Catherine Zeta-Jones, built a £2-million luxury mansion at Limeslade, on the south side of the peninsula. Singer Bonnie Tyler also has a home here.

The origin of The Mumbles' unusual name is uncertain, although one theory is that it's a legacy of French seamen who nicknamed the twin rounded rocks at the tip of the headland *Les Mamelles* – 'the breasts'.

◎ Sights

Going west from Mumbles Head there are two small bays, **Langland Bay** and **Caswell Bay**, which are shingly at high tide but expose hectares of golden sand at low water. Both are popular with families and surfers. About 500m west of Caswell, along the coast path, is beautiful **Brandy Cove**, a tiny secluded beach away from the crowds.

★ Clyne Gardens   GARDENS
(www.swansea.gov.uk/clyne) **FREE** Spanning 20 hectares, these magnificent gardens are particularly impressive in spring, when the azaleas and rhododendrons are at their most spectacular. Plus there are delicate pieris and enkianthus, bluebell woods, wildflower meadows, a bog garden and even a dogs' graveyard to explore. The entrance is by the Woodman Pub at the Swansea end of the Mumbles Rd strip.

Oystermouth Castle   CASTLE
(☑ 01792-635478; www.swansea.gov.uk/oystermouthcastle; Castle Ave; adult/child £3/2.50; ☺ 11am-5pm Apr-Sep) It wouldn't be Wales without a castle, and sure enough the trendy shops and bars of Newton Rd are guarded broodingly by a majestic ruin. Once the stronghold of the Norman lords of Gower, it's now the focus of summer Shakespeare performances. There's a fine view over Swansea Bay from the battlements, and role-play and kids' activities days are regular.

⌕ Sleeping

Tides Reach Guest House   B&B ££
(☑ 01792-404877; www.tidesreachguesthouse.com; 388 Mumbles Rd; s/d from £65/85; ⓟ🛜) Tides Reach has maintained the same friendly service and delicious breakfasts across the years and since the arrival of new owners. Some

rooms have sea views; the best is suite-like room 9, where the dormer windows open out to create a virtual deck from within the sloping roof. Two-night minimum stays apply in peak periods.

Patricks with Rooms   HOTEL £££
(☑ 01792-360199; www.patrickswithrooms.com; 638 Mumbles Rd; s/d from £100/125; 🛜) Patricks has 16 individually styled bedrooms in bold contemporary colours, with art on the walls, fluffy robes and, in some rooms, roll-top baths and sea views. Some rooms are set back in an annexe. Downstairs are the (very good) restaurant in which Patrick cooks (mains £18 to £19) and a bar that practically insists you linger, perhaps with afternoon tea (£18).

✕ Eating

Front Room   CAFE £
(☑ 01792-362140; www.thefrontroomcafe.co.uk; 618 Mumbles Rd; mains lunch £6-7, dinner £14-16; ☺ 9.30am-4pm Tue-Sun, & 6.30-9.30pm Fri & Sat; 🛜♿) With seashell chandeliers and local art on the baby-blue walls, this convivial little cafe is a pleasant place to tuck in to a cooked breakfast, Welsh rarebit, a ploughman's lunch, a sandwich (toasted or doorstop) or traditional high tea (£14 per person for two people). More adventurous is the evening bistro menu, where you might find a fish, coconut and tamarind curry.

Munch of Mumbles   MODERN BRITISH ££
(☑ 01792-362244; http://munchofmumbles.co.uk; 650 Mumbles Rd; 2-/3-course lunch £16/20, dinner £25/30; ☺ noon-2pm & 6.30-9pm Wed-Sat, noon-2pm Sun) Small, cosy and romantic, with flowers and candles on the tables, Munch offers a top-notch bistro menu, with half a dozen choices for each course. You can bring your own wine for a small corkage charge. Dishes tend to the pleasingly nostalgic, such as butter-roasted pheasant with gratin potato and 'festive trimmings'.

❶ Getting There & Away

Regular 2B buses (and occasional 3A buses) run between Swansea and The Mumbles (£4.30, 30 to 45 minutes). Regular 2C run buses run to/from Caswell Bay (£2.60, 12 minutes).

Gower Peninsula (Y Gŵyr)

With its broad butterscotch beaches, pounding surf, precipitous cliff-top walks and rugged, untamed uplands, the Gower Peninsula feels a million miles from Swansea's urban bustle – yet it's just on the doorstep. This 15-mile-long thumb of land stretching west from The Mumbles was designated the UK's first official Area of Outstanding Natural Beauty in 1956. The National Trust owns about three-quarters of the coast and you can hike the entire length of the coastline on the Wales Coast Path. The peninsula also has the best surfing in Wales outside Pembrokeshire.

The main family beaches, patrolled by lifeguards during summer, are Langland Bay, Caswell Bay and Port Eynon. The most impressive, and most popular with surfers, is the magnificent 3-mile sweep of Rhossili Bay at the far end of the peninsula. Much of the Gower's northern coast is salt marsh, which provides an important habitat for wading birds and wildfowl.

❶ Getting There & Away

Services are relatively infrequent, but there are buses heading from Swansea to Parkmill, Port Eynon, Rhossili, Reynoldston, Llanmadoc and Llangennith. To get to Oxwich you'll need to change at Parkmill.

Carry coins if you're hoping to park anywhere near a beach.

Port Eynon

📞 01792 / POP 636

The three-quarter-mile stretch of rock-strewn Blue Flag beach at Port Eynon is the Gower's busiest summer swimming destination. The town swells dramatically with the rising mercury, as campsites, guesthouses, pubs and hostels brace themselves for the seasonal strain. Whatever the time of year, and however fierce the competition for a lunchtime table at the pub or towel space on the beach, it's a thoroughly pleasant little seaside town.

★ **Port Eynon YHA**   HOSTEL £

(📞 01792-391794; www.yha.org.uk; dm/r from £22/59; ⊙ Easter-Oct; 🐾) Worth special mention for its spectacular location, this former lifeboat station is as close as you can get to the sea without sleeping on the beach itself. It's cosier than your average hostel, with friendly owners and sea views from the lounge. There are washbasins in the rooms, but most share bathrooms.

Culver House   APARTMENT ££

(📞 01792-720300; www.culverhousehotel.co.uk; apt from £95; 🐾) Just a stone skip from the beach, this renovated 19th-century house offers eight self-contained apartments with all the mod cons. The upper apartments have balconies,

THREE CLIFFS BAY

Three Cliffs Bay is named for the pyramid-like, triple-pointed crag pierced by a natural arch that juts out into the water at its eastern point. It's regularly voted one of the most beautiful beaches in Britain, and it's particularly impressive when viewed from the impossibly picturesque ruins of 13th-century Pennard Castle.

The only way to reach the beach is on foot. For the castle view, look for the path across the road and down a bit from Shepherd's Coffee Shop in Parkmill (parking £3). Once you cross the bridge, turn right and then take the next left-hand fork heading up the hill. You'll skirt some houses and Pennard Golf Course before reaching the castle. For a flatter, quicker path, take the right-hand fork instead and follow the stream. Another approach is via the mile-long track along Pennard Cliffs from the National Trust car park in Southgate.

while most of those on the ground floor open onto cute little gardens. Two-night minimum stays may be required in busier periods.

❶ Getting There & Away

Direct buses serving Port Eynon include the 118 to/from Rhossili (£3, 13 minutes, daily), the 115, 118 and 119 to/from Reynoldston (£3.80, 15 to 35 minutes, up to seven daily), the 117 and 118 to/from Parkmill (£4.50, 30 to 45 minutes, up to five daily), the 118/119 to/from Swansea (£4.80, one hour, four daily), and the 115 to/from Llangennith (£4.80, one to 1¼ hours, three daily).

Oxwich Bay & Parkmill

Oxwich Bay is a windy, 2.5-mile-long curve of sand backed by dunes. Road access and a large car park (per day £4) make it popular with families and watersports enthusiasts (there's no lifeguard, but otherwise it's good for beginner surfers). Behind the beach lies **Oxwich Nature Reserve**, an area of salt and freshwater marshes, oak and ash woodlands and dunes; it is home to a variety of bird life and dune plants.

Some of the Gower's best and most secluded beaches are on the stretch between the Mumbles and Oxwich Bay, particularly in the area around the small tourist village of Parkmill.

★ Llethryd Barns
B&B **££**

(🖵01792-391327; www.llethrydbarns.co.uk; Llethryd; s/d from £80/105; 🅿) Arranged in a horseshoe around a central courtyard, this handsome set of late-Georgian farm buildings has been converted into seven guest suites, each with living area and mezzanine bedroom. They all have their own entrance, so there's no sense that you're intruding in someone else's house, and breakfasts are indulgent. It's 2 miles north of Parkmill on the B4271.

Parc-le-Breos House
HOTEL **££**

(🖵01792-371636; www.parc-le-breos.co.uk; Parkmill; r from £106; 🅿🛜) Set in its own private estate north of the main road, Parc-le-Breos offers 16 en-suite rooms in a Gothic Victorian hunting lodge. The majestic lounge, conservatory and dining room have grand fireplaces that crackle into action in winter, and there are great walks in the vicinity. Book ahead for the three-course dinner (£20), served 6pm to 8pm Wednesday to Sunday.

❶ Getting There & Away

Buses head to/from Swansea (36 minutes, 10 daily), Oxwich (15 minutes, seven daily), Reynoldston (14 minutes, eight daily), Port Eynon (27 minutes, four daily) and Rhossili (31 minutes, eight daily).

Rhossili
🖵 01792 / POP 236

Saving the best for last, the Gower Peninsula ends spectacularly with the 3 miles of golden sand that edges Rhossili Bay. Facing nearly due west towards the very bottom of Ireland, this is one of Britain's best and most popular surfing beaches. But be warned: when the surf's up, swimming can be dangerous. At low tide the stark, ghostly ribs of the *Helvetica,* a Norwegian barque wrecked in a storm in 1887, protrude from the sand in the middle of the beach.

South of the village is the Viel (pronounced 'vile'), a rare surviving example of a patchwork of strip fields first laid out in medieval times.

★ Worms Head
NATURAL FEATURE

The western extremity of the Gower is guarded by this mile-long promontory, which turns into an island at high tide. Worms Head takes its name from the Old English *wurm*, meaning 'dragon' – a reference to its snaking, Loch-Ness-monster profile. Seals bask around its rocks, and the cliffs are thick with razorbills, guillemots, kittiwakes, fulmars and puffins during nesting season (April to July).

There is a five-hour window of opportunity (2½ hours either side of low tide) when you can walk out across a causeway and along the narrow crest of the Outer Head to the furthest point of land. Check the tide tables posted at the **Rhossili Visitor Centre** (🖵01792-390707; www.nationaltrust.org.uk/gower; Coastguard Cottages; ⊙10.30am-4.30pm) carefully, as people are regularly rescued after being cut off by the rising waters. Among those who have spent a cold, nervous night trapped here was the young Dylan Thomas, as he relates in the story 'Who Do You Wish Was With Us?', from *Portrait of the Artist as a Young Dog.* If you do get stuck, do not try to wade or swim back: the currents are fierce and the rocks treacherous.

❶ Getting There & Away

Buses serving Rhossili include the 118 to/from Port Eynon (£3, 13 minutes, daily), the 118/119 to/from Reynoldston (£3.80, 20 to 30 minutes, up to eight daily), the 118 to/from Parkmill (£4.50, 30 to 45 minutes, up to eight daily) and the 118/119 to/from Swansea (£4.80, one to 1¼ hours, up to 11 daily).

Llangennith
🖵 01792 / POP 517

Surfers flock to this pretty village at the northern end of Rhossili Bay where there's a good local pub and a large campsite right by the beach (lovely in its own right, the campsite also offers amazing views across Rhossili Bay to Worms Head). Centred on the weathered, 12th-century church of St Cenydd, Llangennith has a local produce market every Saturday from 10am to 1pm.

🏃 Activities

PJ's Surf Shop
SURFING

(🖵01792-386669; www.pjsurfshop.co.uk; wetsuits/surfboards/stand-up paddle boards per day £12/12/30; ⊙9am-5pm Mar-Oct, 10am-5pm Mon-Fri Nov-Feb) Run by former surfing champion Peter Jones, this is a centre of activity for local surfers. Follow the website for current local surfing conditions.

Progress Surf
SURFING

(🖵07876 712106, 01792-410825; www.swanseasurfing.com; lessons 2hr/day £25/50) This mobile outfit offers introductory surf lessons at either Caswell Bay or Llangennith, depending on conditions. Also does stand-up paddle boarding, kayaking and other forms of water-based exertion.

🛏 Sleeping & Eating

King's Head HOTEL **££**

(📞 01792-386212; www.kingsheadgower.co.uk; r £99-150; 🅿🛜🐾) Up the hill behind the **pub** (mains £12-14; ⏱ 11am-11pm, kitchen noon-9.30pm) of the same name, these two stone farm buildings have been simply but stylishly fitted out with modern bathrooms and underfloor heating. As well as the 20 rooms here, there are a further seven in a nearby house. Look online for weekly and five-night deals.

ℹ Getting There & Away

Direct buses include 115 and 116 services to/ from Llanmadoc (£3, 10 minutes, up to four daily), Reynoldston (£4, 36 minutes, up to three daily) and Port Eynon (£4.80, 1¼ hours, up to three daily).

CARMARTHENSHIRE (SIR GAERFYDDIN)

Castle-dotted Carmarthenshire is home to gentle valleys washed by abundant rivers, deep-green woods and Carmarthern Bay (Bae Caerfyrddin) – a lovely crescent of coast routinely overlooked by those hurrying to Pembrokeshire, immediately west. Caught between such attractive neighbours – the Brecon Beacons lie on Carmarthenshire's eastern border – it remains a much quieter and less explored pocket of Wales than it perhaps deserves. If your interests stretch to gardens, stately homes and rural idylls, add this quiet county to your itinerary.

Llanarthne

📞 01558 / POP 870

Little Llanarthne (also spelt Llanarthney) is as pleasantly rural and slow paced as dozens of other Carmarthenshire villages, and would perhaps have remained indistinguishable from the pack if it hadn't been for the opening of the National Botanic Garden of Wales nearby. Fancy accommodation and good eating options have followed the hamlet's new-found celebrity.

◉ Sights

⭐**National Botanic Garden of Wales** GARDENS

(📞 01558-667149; www.botanicgarden.wales; adult/ child £10/4.55; ⏱ 10am-6pm Apr-Oct, to 4.30pm Nov-Mar; 🅿♿) Concealed in the rolling Tywi valley countryside, this lavish complex opened in 2000 and is still maturing. Formerly an aristocratic estate, the garden has a broad range of plant habitats, from lakes and bogs to woodland and heath, with lots of decorative areas and educational exhibits. The centrepiece is the Norman Foster–designed **Great Glasshouse**, a spectacular glass dome sunken into the earth. The garden is 2 miles southwest of Llanarthne village, signposted from the main roads.

🛏 Sleeping & Eating

Llwyn Helyg Country House B&B **£££**

(📞 01558-668778; www.llwynhelygcountryhouse. co.uk; r from £129; 🅿🛜) Although there's a Georgian look to this huge stone house at the edge of the village, it's actually a modern build. The three guest bedrooms are luxuriously decked out with dark wooden furniture, white Italian marble en suites and spa baths. To preserve the rarefied atmosphere, it doesn't take bookings for children under 16.

⭐**Wright's Food Emporium** DELI, CAFE **£**

(📞 01558-668929; www.wrightsfood.co.uk; Golden Grove Arms, B4300; mains lunch £8-9, dinner £11-13; ⏱ 11am-5pm Sun & Mon, to 7pm Wed & Thu, 9am-10pm Fri & Sat; 🅿🛜🐾) Sprawling through the rooms of an old village pub, this hugely popular deli-cafe serves sandwiches, salads and massive antipasto platters packed full of top-notch local and imported ingredients. Wash it all down with a craft beer or something from its range of small-estate, organic wine, then browse crates of vinyl records and shelves full of the area's best produce.

ℹ Getting There & Away

Up to two 278/279 buses a day stop here en route between Carmarthen (£2.40, 35 minutes) and Llandeilo (£2.40, 20 to 35 minutes). The 279 stops at the botanic garden.

Llandeilo

📞 01558 / POP 1771

Set on a hill encircled by the greenest of fields, Llandeilo is a handsome collection of narrow streets lined with grand Georgian and Victorian buildings and centred on a picturesque church and graveyard. The surrounding region was once dominated by large country estates, and though they have long gone, the deer, parkland, trees and agricultural character of the landscape are their legacy.

WORTH A TRIP

DOLAUCOTHI GOLD MINES

Set in a beautiful wooded estate near the village of Pumsaint, **Dolaucothi Gold Mines** (NT; ☑01558-650177; www.nationaltrust.org.uk; adult/child £8.40/4.20; ⊙11am-5pm Easter-Oct; P🚻) is the only known Roman goldmine in the UK. The exhibition and the mining machinery above ground are interesting, but the main attraction is the chance to go underground on a guided tour of the old mine workings. Back at the surface there's a sediment-filled water trough where you can try your hand at panning for gold. Audio guides for individual tours are included with admission.

After your visit, it's worth popping in to the lovely little **Dolaucothi Arms** (☑01558-650237; A482; mains £9-10; ⊙4-11pm Tue, noon-11pm Wed-Sat, noon-8pm Sun; P🚻📶🍽), a 16th-century drovers' inn with a friendly front bar, open fire, in-house tearoom (Doli's) and a decent pub restaurant.

The 289 bus between Lampeter (£3.50, 20 minutes) and Llandovery (£2.45, 30 minutes) stops here once every weekday.

Used by many travellers as a springboard for the wilder terrain of Brecon Beacon National Park, it's within a short drive of numerous outstanding sights – Elizabethan gardens, rolling country estates, castles and more.

👁 Sights

★ Dinefwr
HISTORIC BUILDING

(NT, Cadw; ☑01558-824512; www.nationaltrust.org.uk; adult/child £7.60/3.80; ⊙house 11am-6pm daily Easter-Oct, to 4pm Fri-Sun Nov-Easter, grounds open longer; P🚻) This idyllic, 324-hectare, beautifully landscaped estate, immediately west of Llandeilo, incorporates a **deer park**, pasture, woods, an **Iron Age fort**, the hidden remains of a **Roman fort**, a 12th-century castle and **Newton House**, a wonderful 17th-century manor with a Victorian Gothic facade. The house is presented as it was in Edwardian times, focusing particularly on the experience of servants in their downstairs domain. Other rooms recall Newton's WWII incarnation as a hospital, and the former Billiard Room is now a tearoom.

★ Aberglasney Gardens
GARDENS

(☑01558-668998; www.aberglasney.org; Llangathen; adult/child £7.73/free; ⊙10am-6pm Apr-Oct, 10.30am-4pm Nov-Mar; P) Wandering through these formal walled gardens feels a bit like walking into a Jane Austen novel. They date originally from Elizabethan times, have evolved continually, and contain a unique cloister built solely as a garden decoration. There's also a pool garden, a 250-year-old yew tunnel, a 'wild' garden in the bluebell woods to the west and various other horticultural havens. In the summer exhibitions and musical events bring further life and gaiety.

🛏 Sleeping & Eating

Cawdor
HOTEL ££

(☑01558-823500; www.thecawdor.com; Rhosmaen St; r/apt from £95/200; P🛜) Walking through the broad, slate-floored entrance to the Cawdor, you get some sense of the Georgian house of assembly it once was. Grey-and-pink-striped carpeted stairs lead to well-appointed rooms with Egyptian cotton on the beds and marble in the bathrooms, while the downstairs bar and more formal dining room both serve decent meals (mains £11 to £12).

★ Ginhaus Deli
DELI £

(☑01558-823030; www.ginhaus.co.uk; 1 Market St; mains £8-10; ⊙8am-5pm Mon-Thu, to 10pm Fri & Sat; 🛜) Specialising in two of the very finest things in life (gin and cheese), this hip deli-cafe also serves cooked breakfasts, filled baguettes, quiches, tarts, fresh juices and delicious British food such as smoked haddock with poached egg. Charcuterie and cheese platters are offered when the kitchen's having a break, and on Friday and Saturday nights there's pizza from 5pm to 8pm.

❶ Getting There & Away

Buses include up to two 278/279 services per day to/from Llanarthne (£2.40, 20 to 35 minutes), eight 280/281 services per day to/from Llandovery (£3.15, 45 minutes) and Carmarthen (£3.60, 50 minutes), and six X13 buses per day to/from Swansea (£5.80, 1½ hours).

Llandeilo is on the Heart of Wales line. Direct trains run to/from Llandovery (£3.70, 20 minutes, five daily), Swansea (£7.60, one hour, five daily), Llandrindod Wells (£8.30, 1½ hours, four daily), Cardiff (from £21, 2¼ hours, two daily) and Shrewsbury (£15, three to 3½ hours, four daily).

PEMBROKESHIRE

The Pembrokeshire coast is what you imagine the world would look like if God were a geology teacher with artistic yearnings. There are knobbly hills of volcanic rock, long, thin inlets scoured by glaciers, and stratified limestone pushed up vertically and then eroded into arches, blowholes and sea stacks. All along the shoreline towering red and grey cliffs are interleaved with perfect sandy beaches.

This wild and incredibly beautiful landscape is the county's greatest asset and in summer people flock here from all over Britain to enjoy the spectacular walking, surfing, coasteering and sea kayaking, as well as the glorious beaches, abundant marine life and comely towns.

On top of its natural assets, Pembrokeshire offers a wealth of Celtic and pre-Celtic sites, forbidding castles, fascinating islands and little St Davids – the magical mini-city with its chilled vibe, spectacular cathedral and abiding association with Wales' patron saint.

Saundersfoot

01834 / POP 2748

Cute-as-a-button Saundersfoot has a long, lovely beach with a sweet little harbour at one end, built in 1829 for the shipment of coal. Nowadays the only mining activity hereabouts is carried out by the toddlers digging in the golden sand. Well-kept old houses cling to the hilly streets radiating up from the town centre, where there are some interesting shops to peruse.

It makes for a quieter base than neighbouring Tenby, which is only an hour's walk away along the coast path.

◉ Sights

Folly Farm   ZOO
(01834-812731; www.folly-farm.co.uk; Begelly; adult/child £16/14; ⊗10am-5pm; ☷) If your toddler's tolerance for castles and churches is waning, this combination zoo, petting farm, fun fair and amusement park could

Pembrokeshire

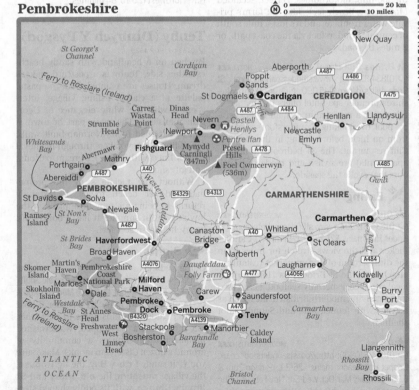

be the antidote. Once they've tired of the pirate ship, dragon playground and ride-on diggers, there's a large menagerie to explore, including farm animals, meerkats, monkeys, giraffes, zebras and an excellent penguin enclosure. Folly Farm is on the A478, 3 miles north of Saundersfoot.

Reptile Experience ZOO
(☑07940 793845; www.reptile-experience.co.uk; Waterloo House, Brewery Tce; adult/child £15/12; ☺encounters 11am, 1.30 & 4pm) Come face to face with huge snakes, hairy spiders and all sorts of other slippery, creepy and crawly critters during a two-hour-long hands-on experience.

🛏 Sleeping

★ **Trevayne Farm** CAMPGROUND £
(☑01834-813402; www.trevaynefarm.co.uk; Monkstone; sites per tent/campervan £18/28; ☺Easter-Oct; 🐾) Based on a working 40-hectare permaculture farm, this large clifftop site has beautiful sea views and two separate fields so back-to-basics campers can avoid the looming motorhomes. Perfect, secluded Monkstone Beach feels like the farm's private water frontage, and it's just a mile south of central Saundersfoot via the coast path, or 2 miles by road.

St Brides Spa Hotel HOTEL £££
(☑01834-812304; www.stbridesspahotel.com; St Brides Hill; s/d from £145/190; ℙ🛜🏊) Pembrokeshire's premier spa hotel offers the chance to relax after a massage in a small hydrotherapy pool overlooking Saundersfoot's seafront from on high, before dining in the candlelit Cliff restaurant. The 34 bedrooms (and two apartments) are stylish and modern, in colours that evoke the seaside.

🍴 Eating

★ **Cliff** MODERN BRITISH ££
(☑01834-812304; www.stbridesspahotel.com; St Brides Hill; mains £21-22; ☺6-9pm; 🛜) Candles flicker and the views stretch for miles from the dining room of this upmarket restaurant attached to the St Brides Spa Hotel. Lovely local produce, especially seafood, is finessed into satisfying modern British dishes such as halibut with fennel, kale and Saundersfoot shellfish.

★ **Coast** MODERN BRITISH £££
(☑01834-810800; http://coastsaundersfoot.co.uk; Coppet Hall Beach; mains £26-29; ☺noon-2pm & 6.30-9pm daily Mar-Oct, Wed-Sun Nov-Feb; 🅿) The spectacular beachfront setting is more than

matched by the wizardry emanating from chef Tom Hines' kitchen at this award-winning restaurant. Whether you choose from the adventurous 'Tom's menu' or opt for something simpler and slightly cheaper from the lunchtime 'Pebble menu' (£28 for three courses), prepare to be wowed. Local seafood shines, and the service is great, too.

❶ Information

Tourist Office (☑01834-813672; www.visit pembrokeshire.com; Saundersfoot Library, Regency Hall; ☺10am-1pm & 2-4pm) Saundersfoot's library also enthusiastically dispenses tourist advice.

❶ Getting There & Away

Saundersfoot's request train stop is a mile from the centre of town. Direct services head to/from Swansea (£16, 1½ hours, seven daily), Tenby (£3.60, seven minutes, nine daily) and Pembroke (£7.90, 37 minutes, nine daily).

Regular 381 buses head to/from Tenby (£2.50, 10 minutes), Narberth (£3.55, 33 minutes) and Haverfordwest (£5.10, 54 minutes).

Tenby (Dinbych Y Pysgod)
☑01834 / POP 4625

Perched on a headland with sandy beaches either side, Tenby is a postcard-maker's dream. Houses are painted from the pastel palette of a classic fishing village, interspersed with the white elegance of Georgian mansions. The main part of town is still constrained by its Norman-built walls, funnelling holidaymakers through medieval streets lined with pubs, ice-cream parlours and gift shops.

Without the tackiness of the promenade-and-pier beach towns, it tastefully returns to being a sleepy little place in the low season. In summer it has a boisterous, boozy, holiday-resort feel.

◉ Sights

Caldey Island ISLAND
(☑01834-844453; www.caldey-island.co.uk; adult/child £13/6; ☺Mon-Sat May-Sep, Mon-Thu Apr & Oct) Connected to Tenby by a seasonal boat service, Caldey Island is home to grey seals, sea birds and a red-topped, whitewashed monastery that houses a community of around a dozen Cistercian monks. Make sure you visit sandy **Priory Bay**, the **lighthouse**, the village **museum**, the **old priory** and St **Illtyd's Church**, with its oddly shaped stee-

PEMBROKESHIRE COAST NATIONAL PARK

Established in 1952, Pembrokeshire Coast National Park (Parc Cenedlaethol Arfordir Sir Benfro) takes in almost the entire coast and its offshore islands, as well as the moorland Preseli Hills in the north. Pembrokeshire's sea cliffs and islands support huge breeding populations of sea birds, while seals, dolphins, porpoises and whales are frequently spotted in coastal waters.

There are two national-park information centres (in Pembroke and St Davids) and the remaining tourist offices scattered across Pembrokeshire are well stocked with park paraphernalia. The free annual publication and app *Coast to Coast* (online at www.pembrokeshirecoast.wales) have lots of information on park attractions, a calendar of events and details of park-organised activities, including guided walks, themed tours, cycling trips, pony treks, island cruises, canoe trips and minibus tours. It's worth getting *Coast to Coast* for the tide tables alone – they're a necessity for many legs of the coast path.

ple. Inside is a stone with inscriptions in Ogham (an ancient Celtic script).

St Catherine's Island ISLAND

At low tide you can walk across the sand to little St Catherine's Island, but it's a long, cold wait if you get trapped by the tide – check tide tables in *Coast to Coast* or online at www.pembrokeshirecoast.wales, or ask at the tourist office (p670). The Victorian fort on the island is open from Easter to October.

Tudor Merchant's House HISTORIC BUILDING

(NT; ☑ 01834-842279; www.nationaltrust.org.uk; Quay Hill; adult/child £5.25/2.60; ⊙ 11am-5pm Wed-Mon Easter-Jul, Sep & Oct, daily Aug, Sat & Sun Nov-Easter) This handsomely restored 15th-century town house is set up as it would have been in its heyday, with colourful wall hangings and period-style beds and kitchen implements. The curators have drawn the line at recreating the scent of the open cesspit next to the kitchen, though.

🛏 Sleeping

Southside HOTEL £

(☑ 01834-844355; www.southsidetenby.co.uk; Picton Rd; d £60; 🛜) Rooms are spacious, comfortable and not at all chintzy at this friendly (and great-value) little private hotel just outside the town walls. Three of the four rooms have en-suite bathrooms, while the other has a private bathroom accessed from the corridor. Knock off £5 per person if you don't want breakfast.

Myrtle House Hotel HOTEL ££

(☑ 01834-842508; www.myrtlehousehoteltenby. com; St Mary's St; s/d £50/100; 🛜) There's an old-fashioned feel to this friendly, family-run hotel in a Georgian town house in the old

part of town. Don't expect anything in the way of views, but the eight en-suite rooms have all you need, and it's well located (not far from the steps leading down to Castle Beach).

Penally Abbey HOTEL £££

(☑ 01834-843033; www.penally-abbey.com; Penally; r from £165; 🅿🛜🐾) Set on a hillside overlooking Carmarthen Bay, this country-house hotel is built on the site of an ancient abbey in the village of Penally, 2 miles southwest of Tenby along the A4139. The 11 bright and comfortable rooms are spread between the main house and the neighbouring coach house, and there's an impressive restaurant attached.

🍴 Eating

Mooring CAFE ££

(☑ 01834-842502; www.themooringtenby.com; 15 High St; mains breakfast £5-6, lunch £7-8, dinner £14-18; ⊙ 8.30am-4.30pm Sun-Tue, to 9pm Wed-Sat; 🛜🐾) Although it's anchored to the High St, this fresh, modern eatery drifts breezily from a daytime cafe serving comfort food (cooked breakfasts, sandwiches, bangers and mash, mac cheese) to a sophisticated bistro in the evening, serving dishes such as spicy fish stew with tomato, cannellini beans and local mussels. The coffee's good, too.

Plantagenet House MODERN BRITISH £££

(☑ 01834-842350; www.plantagenettenby.co.uk; Quay Hill; mains lunch £10-12, dinner £25-28; ⊙ noon-2.30pm & 6-9pm, reduced hours in winter; 🐾) Atmosphere-wise, this place instantly impresses; it's perfect for a romantic, candlelit dinner. Tucked down an alley in Tenby's oldest house, parts of which date to the 10th century, it's dominated by an immense

WORTH A TRIP

PEMBROKE CASTLE

This spectacular and forbidding **castle** (☑ 01646-681510; www.pembroke-castle. co.uk; Main St; adult/child £6/5; ⊙10am-5pm; 🔄) was the home of the earls of Pembroke for over 300 years and the birthplace of Henry VII, the first Tudor king. A fort was established here in 1093 by Arnulph de Montgomery, but most of the present buildings date from the 13th century. It's a great place for both kids and adults to explore – wall walks and passages run from tower to tower, and there are vivid exhibitions detailing the castle's history.

Trains stop in both Pembroke and Pembroke Dock. There are direct services to/from Cardiff (from £10, 3¼ hours, daily), Swansea (£15, two hours, seven daily), Narberth (£8.40, 48 minutes, eight daily) and Tenby (£5.50, 20 minutes, nine daily).

12th-century Flemish chimney hearth. The menu features local seafood, organic beef, and plenty of choices for vegetarians.

ℹ️ Information

Tourist Office (☑ 01437-775603; www. visitpembrokeshire.com; Upper Park Rd; ⊙9am-5pm Mon-Fri, 10am-5pm Sat Sep-Jun, 9am-5pm Mon-Fri, 10am-5pm Sat, 10am-4pm Sun Jul & Aug)

ℹ️ Getting There & Away

BUS

The **bus station** (Upper Park Rd) is next to the tourist office.

Tenby's direct bus connections include two X49 services per day to/from Narberth (£5, 23 minutes), regular 381 buses to/from Saundersfoot (£2.50, 10 minutes), the hourly 349 to/from Manorbier (£3.60, 20 minutes) and Pembroke (£4.30, 45 minutes), and the hourly 381 to/from Haverfordwest (£5.25, 1¼ hours).

National Express (p661) coaches head to/from Swansea (£9.20, 1½ hours, two daily), Cardiff (£19, 3½ hours, one direct daily), Birmingham (£42, six hours, one direct daily) and London (£32, seven hours, one direct daily).

TRAIN

There are direct trains to/from Pembroke (£5.50, 20 minutes, nine daily), Narberth (£5.20, 20 minutes, nine daily), Swansea (£15,

1½ hours, seven daily) and Cardiff (from £12, three hours, one direct daily).

Narberth (Arberth)

☑ 01834 / POP 2412

An arty little community of independent shops, cafes, restaurants and galleries, Narberth is a charismatic South Pembrokeshire market town with a long history. Perhaps light on standout sights, it's nonetheless well worth a stop for its lively vibe, passion for food and thriving retail scene: somehow managing to beat the economic odds, butchers, delis, antique shops and boutiques line the streets. There's also a friendly food festival in September, a ruined Norman castle and an interesting town hall with a double stairway.

⊙ Sights

Narberth Museum MUSEUM
(Amgueddfa Arberth; ☑ 01834-860500; www.narberthmuseum.co.uk; The Bonded Stores, Church St; adult/child £4.50/1; ⊙10am-5pm Wed-Sat) Housed in a wonderfully atmospheric restored bonded-stores building, this volunteer-staffed and passionately well-maintained museum celebrates the rich history of Narberth and the surrounding area. You can learn about medieval siege warfare and Narberth Castle through models and interactive games; walk historic streets and visit the shops; or listen to Welsh folk stories in the story-telling chair.

🛏️ Sleeping & Eating

Max & Caroline's GUESTHOUSE £
(☑ 01834-861835; www.maxandcarolines.com; 2a St James St; s/d £50/70; 🛜) Why bother serving breakfast when you're situated directly above Narberth's best cafe? That's the philosophy at this excellent British-and-German-run guesthouse, and it means that its two handsomely furnished guest rooms can be rented a little more cheaply than you'd otherwise expect for the high standards on offer. Continental breakfast can be added for £5.

★ **Grove** HOTEL £££
(☑ 01834-860915; www.thegrove-narberth.co.uk; Molleston; r from £170, 3-/8-course dinner £69/94; ⊙restaurant noon-2.30pm & 6-9.30pm; 🅿️🛜) 🍃 A truly magical place to stay, this secluded country-house hotel is just south of Narberth, surrounded by manicured lawns, mature trees and wildflower meadows. The sumptuous rooms blend period character

with contemporary style, while the Fernery, the renowned in-house **restaurant**, is Pembrokeshire's finest, serving modern Welsh dishes such as turbot with apple-and-ginger purée and langoustine sauce.

Dragon Inn　　　　　　　　PUB FOOD ££
(☎01834-860257; www.thedragonnarberth.com; 5 Water St; mains £10-13; ⊙11am-11pm) Stone walls, slab floors and low ceilings all hint at the venerable age of this village pub. It's some 7 miles to the sea, but the kitchen specialises in 'local' seafood, including mackerel, lobster and whatever else is fresh. For Sunday lunch, three courses (including delights such 10-hour roast beef) cost just £15.

ⓘ Getting There & Away

Bus destinations include three direct 322 services to/from Haverfordwest (£4.05, 21 minutes) and Carmarthen (£5.35, 37 minutes), regular 381 buses to Saundersfoot (£3.55, 34 minutes), two X49 services per day to Tenby (£5, 23 minutes), and three 430 services per day to Cardigan (£4.15, 70 minutes).

There's one direct train per day to/from Newport Gwent (£18, 2¾ hours), two daily to Cardiff (from £12, 2½ hours), eight to Swansea (from £16, 1¼ hours), nine to Tenby (£5.20, 20 minutes) and eight to Pembroke (£8.80, 45 minutes).

St Davids (Tyddewi)

☎01437 / POP 1383

Charismatic St Davids (yes, it has dropped the apostrophe from its name) is Britain's smallest city, its enduring appeal ensured by the magnificent 12th-century cathedral that marks Wales' holiest site. The birthplace and burial place of the nation's patron saint, St Davids has been a pilgrimage site for 1500 years.

The setting itself has a mystical presence. The sea is just beyond the horizon on three sides, so you're constantly surprised by glimpses of it at the ends of streets. Then there are those strangely shaped hills in the distance, sprouting from an ancient landscape.

Today St Davids attracts hordes of non-religious pilgrims, too, drawn by the town's laid-back vibe, good sights and eating, and

---

PEMBROKESHIRE COAST PATH

Straddling the line where Pembrokeshire drops suddenly into the sea, the Pembrokeshire Coast Path is one of the most spectacular long-distance routes in Britain. Established in 1970, it meanders along 186 miles of Britain's most dramatic coastal scenery, running from Amroth to St Dogmaels, taking in vertiginous clifftops and endless beautiful beaches. If you don't have the time or the stamina for the full route, it can easily be split into smaller chunks.

The weather can be quite changeable and mobile-phone coverage is unreliable; come prepared, and bring wet-weather gear and something warm, even in summer. The path has a dedicated website, http://nt.pcnpa.org.uk, that's ideal for planning your trek.

The hiker's best friend, Pembrokeshire's **coastal buses** operate on five main routes three times a day in each direction from May to September. For the remainder of the year the Puffin Shuttle, Strumble Shuttle and Poppit Rocket operate two services a day on Thursday and Saturday only. For timetables, see www.pembrokeshire.gov.uk or pick up a copy of the national park's *Coast to Coast* magazine.

Best Sections

Marloes Sands to Broad Haven (4½ to six hours, 13 miles) A wonderful walk along dramatic cliff tops ending at an impressive beach. Many access points and regular public transport make it good for short circular walks, too.

Whitesands to Porthgain (four to five hours, 10 miles) A beautiful but taxing section worth tackling if your time is limited. It's within easy reach of St Davids and offers the reward of some excellent nosh at the end of your day.

Porthgain to Pwll Deri (four to six hours, 12 miles) An exhilarating section with sheer cliffs, rock buttresses, pinnacles, islets, bays and beaches but some steep ascents and descents in between. Magnificent views of St Davids and Strumble Head.

Newport to St Dogmaels (six to eight hours, 15.5 miles) A tough, roller-coaster section with frequent steep hills but spectacular views of the wild and rugged coast and its numerous rock formations, sheer cliffs and caves.

the excellent hiking, surfing and wildlife-watching in the surrounding area.

Sights

★ St David's Cathedral   CATHEDRAL

(www.stdavidscathedral.org.uk; The Pebbles; suggested donation £3, tours £4; ⊙8.30am-6pm Mon-Sat, 12.45-5.30pm Sun) Hidden in a hollow and behind high walls, St David's Cathedral is intentionally unassuming. The valley site was chosen in the vain hope that the church would be overlooked by Saxon raiders, but it was ransacked at least seven times. Yet once you pass through the gatehouse separating it from the town and its stone walls come into view, it's as imposing as any of its contemporaries.

★ St Davids Bishop's Palace   RUINS

(Cadw; www.cadw.gov.wales; adult/child £4/2.40; ⊙10am-6pm Jul & Aug, 9.30am-5pm Mar-Jun, Sep & Oct, 10am-4pm Nov-Feb) This atmospheric ruined palace was begun at the same time as St David's Cathedral (p672), adjacent, but its final, imposing Decorated Gothic form owes most to Henry de Gower, bishop from 1327 to 1347. The most distinctive feature is the arcaded parapet that runs around the courtyard, adorned with a chequerboard pattern of purple and yellow stone blocks. The corbels that support the arches are richly adorned with a menagerie of carved figures – animals, grotesque mythical creatures and human heads.

★ Oriel y Parc   GALLERY

(Landscape Gallery; ☑01437-720392; www.orielyparc.co.uk; cnr High St & Caerfai Rd; ⊙10am-4pm) Occupying a bold, semicircular, environmentally friendly building on the edge of town, Oriel y Parc is a winning collaboration between the Pembrokeshire Coast National Park Authority and the National Museum Wales. Not only does it function as a tourist office and national-park visitor centre (open slightly longer than the gallery), it houses changing exhibitions from the museum's art collection. The focus is on landscapes, particularly scenes from Pembrokeshire's rich cache of natural beauty.

St Davids Head   AREA

(NT) This atmospheric heather-wreathed promontory, formed from the oldest rock in Wales, was fortified by the Celts. The jumbled stones and ditch of an Iron Age rampart are still visible, as are rock circles, once the foundations of huts. The tip of the headland is a series of rock and turf ledges,

a great place for a picnic or wildlife spotting – in summer you can see gannets diving and choughs soaring. Adding to the ancient ambience, wild ponies can often be seen.

Ramsey Island   BIRD SANCTUARY

🐾 Ramsey Island (Ynys Dewi) lies off the headland to the west of St Davids, ringed by dramatic sea cliffs and an offshore armada of rocky islets and reefs. The island is a Royal Society for the Protection of Birds (RSPB) reserve famous for its large breeding population of choughs – members of the crow family with glossy black feathers and distinctive red bills and legs – and for its grey seals.

St Non's Bay   RUINS

Immediately south of St Davids, this ruggedly beautiful spot is named after St David's mother and traditionally accepted as his birthplace. A path leads to the 13th-century ruins of St Non's Chapel. Only the base of the walls remains, along with a stone marked with a cross within a circle that's believed to date from the 7th century. Standing stones in the surrounding field suggest that the chapel may have been built within an ancient pagan stone circle.

Whitesands Bay   BEACH

(Porth Mawr) This mile-long sandy beach is a popular surfing, swimming and strolling spot. At extremely low tide you can see the wreck of a paddle tugboat that ran aground here in 1882, and the fossil remains of a prehistoric forest. If Whitesands is really busy – and it often is – you can escape the worst of the crowds by walking north along the coastal path for 10 to 15 minutes to the smaller, more secluded beach at Porthmelgan.

Sleeping

YHA St Davids   HOSTEL £

(☑0800 019 1700; www.yha.org.uk; Llaethdy; dm/d from £20/45; ⊙Apr-Oct; Ⓟ) If you're an enthusiastic walker or you have your own transport, this former farmhouse tucked beneath Carn Llidi, 2 miles northwest of St Davids and near surfers' playground Whitesands Bay, is a wonderful option. The cowsheds now house snug dorms and twins, and an inviting communal kitchen. En-suite rooms sleep four people and there's bike storage available.

Bryn Awel   B&B ££

(☑01437-720082; www.brynawel-bb.co.uk; 45 High St; s/d £85/90; 🛜) Well positioned on the High St, Bryn Awel has small but cosy rooms (all en suite) spread over two floors of a handsome

St Davids

St Davids

◉ Top Sights
1 Oriel y Parc	D2
2 St Davids Bishop's Palace	A1
3 St David's Cathedral	B1

🛏 Sleeping
4 Bryn Awel	C2
5 Coach House	C1

6 Ramsey House	A2
7 Tŵr y Felin	D2

⊗ Eating
8 Bishops	B1
9 St Davids Food & Wine	C2

timber-floored Victorian. The owners are out-doors enthusiasts, and can advise on the best local spots for walking and birdwatching.

Coach House B&B ££
(☑ 01437-720632; www.thecoachhouse.biz; 15 High St; s/d from £70/95; 🛜) The 10 bright, simple rooms at the Coach House are just part of its appeal. Friendly and helpful hosts, great breakfasts and the central location all conspire to make it one of St Davids' better options. The owner sells oggies (the Welsh answer to Cornwall's pastie; £6) from his front window to passersby on the main street.

Ramsey House B&B ££
(☑ 01437-720321; www.ramseyhouse.co.uk; Lower Moor; d £135; 🅿🛜) The young owners have created a fashionable boutique-style B&B in their duck-egg-blue house on the outskirts of the little city. The six rooms are all different but feature bold wallpapers, matching chandeliers, silky throws, goose-down duvets and stylish bathrooms. Not suitable for children.

★ Tŵr y Felin HOTEL £££
(☑ 01437-725555; www.twryfelinhotel.com; Caerfai Rd; r/ste from £200/370; 🅿🛜) Incorporating an odd circular tower that was once a wind-

mill, this chic boutique hotel is St Davids' most upmarket option. The entire building is lathered with specially commissioned contemporary art, with dozens of pieces in the lounge-bar and restaurant (Blas) alone. The 21 bedrooms are all luxurious, but the most spectacular is the three-level circular suite in the tower itself.

✖ Eating

St Davids Food & Wine DELI £
(☑ 01437-721948; www.stdavidsfoodandwine.co.uk; High St; mains £3-4.50; ⊙ 8.30am-5.30pm Mon-Sat, 10am-5pm Sun, 9am-5pm Mon-Sat winter) Stock up on picnic supplies (including lavish hampers) at this delicatessen, which specialises in local organic produce. Or you can grab a pastry or a made-to-order sandwich of pulled beef braised in beer (for example) and enjoy it at the benches out the front.

Bishops PUB FOOD ££
(☑ 01437-720422; www.thebish.co.uk; 22-23 Cross Sq; mains £11-14; ⊙ 11am-midnight; 🛜) A friendly, rambling pub full of locals, walkers and blow-ins, this place serves hearty pub grub with a smile. There's a roaring fire in winter, a decent pint on offer and great cathedral

views from the beer garden. Don't be put off by table names such as 'The Bitches' – that refers to a tidal race between Ramsey Island and the mainland.

ℹ Information

National Park Visitor Centre & Tourist Office
(☑ 01437-720392; www.orielyparc.co.uk; High St; ⏱ 9.30am-5pm Apr-Oct, to 4pm Nov-Mar) Located at Oriel y Parc (St David's landscape art gallery), this office does double duty as tourist office and national-park visitor centre (as the name hints).

ℹ Getting There & Away

Public transport is limited, especially on Sunday and in winter.

The main Pembrokeshire coastal bus services (p671) stopping here are the Strumble and Puffin Shuttles. From 25 March to 25 September there's also the Celtic Coaster, which circles between St Davids, St Non's Bay, St Justinian and Whitesands.

Up to nine 411 buses per day go to/from Solva (£1.65, eight minutes), Newgale (£2.35, 21 minutes) and Haverfordwest (£3.40, 40 minutes, 10 daily), while 413 buses run to/from Fishguard (£3.80, 45 minutes, six daily).

Porthgain & Around

☑ 01348 / POP 897

For centuries the tiny harbour of Porthgain consisted of little more than a few sturdy cottages wedged into a rocky cove. From 1851 it began to prosper as the port for shipping out slate quarried just down the coast at Abereiddi, and by 1889 its own deposits of granite and fine clay had put it on the map as a source of building stone and brick. The post-WWI slump burst the bubble, and the sturdy stone quays and overgrown brick storage 'bins' are what remain, imparting a flavour of post-apocalyptic collapse.

It is, however, a delightful little port: despite having been an industrial harbour, Porthgain is surprisingly picturesque and today is home to a couple of art galleries and eateries and makes a pleasant base for day walks along the Pembrokeshire Coast Path.

◉ Sights & Activities

Blue Lagoon   BAY
(NT; Abereiddi) Slate was quarried at this site on the water's edge in Abereiddi right up until 1910 and then transported by tramway to the harbour at Porthgain. After the mining stopped, a channel was blasted through

to the sea, flooding the pit and creating a brilliantly blue-green pool surrounded by a bowl of sheer stone walls. You can certainly swim here, but be aware that the water is very deep and commensurately cold.

Preseli Venture   ADVENTURE
(☑ 01348-837709; www.preseliventure.co.uk; Parc-y-nole Fach, Mathry; coasteering & kayaking from £52; ⏱ office 9am-5pm; 🖐) 🌿 Offering coasteering, sea kayaking, surfing and coastal hiking, Preseli Ventures has its own excellent, ecofriendly backpackers' lodge (£42/58/65 per night including breakfast/ half board/full board) near Abermawr, 6 miles east of Porthgain.

🛏 Sleeping

★ **Old School Hostel**   HOSTEL £
(☑ 01348-831800; https://oldschoolhostel.com; Ffordd-yr-Afon, Trefin; s/d £30/44; 🅿🛜) 🌿 Set in a rambling old school building in Trefin, 2 miles east of Porthgain, this is one of the new breed of independent, brightly painted, personally run backpackers. The six rooms have en-suite showers but communal toilets, and there's one self-contained en-suite apartment (£50). A great collection of games and a good-quality self-service breakfast are included in the price.

Crug Glâs   HOTEL £££
(☑ 01348-831302; www.crug-glas.co.uk; Abereiddy Rd; r/houses £150/190; 🅿🛜) Set on a big beef and cereal farm that has existed here since at least the 1100s – there's a reference to it in the 12th-century Black Book of St David's – this opulent country house offers rooms decked out with rich fabrics, ornate beds, enormous bathrooms and elegant period grandeur. Five rooms are in the main house, two in converted farm buildings.

There's also a top-notch **restaurant**. Crug Glâs is 3 miles south of Porthgain, off the A487.

The Shed   SEAFOOD ££
(☑ 01348-831518; www.theshedporthgain.co.uk; mains £16-18; ⏱ 10am-9pm Jun-Aug, shorter hours rest of year, call ahead Nov-Mar; 🛜🖐) Housed in a beautifully converted machine shop right by the harbour, this simple little bistro is renowned as one of Pembrokeshire's best seafood restaurants. Fish and chips get their own separate menu, while the main menu relies where it can on the day's fresh catch, alongside favourites such as Porthgain lobster. It gets insanely busy on sunny holiday days.

Walking Tour
Whitesands to Porthgain

START WHITESANDS
END PORTHGAIN
LENGTH 10 MILES; FOUR TO SIX HOURS

Covering a beautiful but remote stretch of coast from popular Whitesands Bay near St Davids to the historic port of Porthgain, this rewarding walk takes you over rugged headlands and past dramatic cliffs, pretty coves and flooded quarries. It's a taxing route with several steep descents and ascents, but it's well worth the effort.

Start out at busy ❶ **Whitesands Bay** (p672) and head west onto wild and rocky St Davids Head. The start of the route is fairly easy, with a good path, wide open views and craggy volcanic outcrops to admire. The only signs of human habitation here are ancient, with the simple ❷ **neolithic burial chamber** on the headland predating the surrounding remnants of Celtic forts.

The path soon becomes more rugged, with a rock scramble down to and up from the lovely little cove at ❸ **Aberpwll**. Continue on past crumbling cliffs to ❹ **Abereiddi**,

looking out for seals in the coves, gannets and possibly porpoises diving for fish out at sea. The beach at Abereiddi is famous for its black sand full of tiny fossils. Ruined quarry buildings and slate workers' cottages flank the path beyond the beach that leads to the ❺ **Blue Lagoon**, a deep, turquoise flooded slate quarry. It's now popular with coasteerers and, in early September, cliff divers from all over the world, who compete here, diving 27m into the icy water below.

The 45-minute walk from Abereiddi to Porthgain is one of the best stretches along the entire coast path, following a cliff-top plateau past the often deserted ❻ **Traeth Llyfn**, an astonishingly lovely beach of fine dark sand, wave-smoothed rocks and looming cliffs. A flight of steep stairs leads down to the golden sand, but beware of strong undercurrents and the tide, which can cut off parts of the beach from the steps.

Continue on for the last descent into the tiny harbour of ❼ **Porthgain**, where you can reward yourself with some superb seafood at the Shed or a cold beverage at the welcoming Sloop Inn.

❶ Getting There & Away

The only bus heading here is the Strumble Shuttle, one of the Pembrokeshire coastal bus services (p671).

Fishguard (Abergwaun)

☑ 01348 / POP 3383

Perched on a headland between its modern ferry port and former fishing harbour, Fishguard is often overlooked by travellers, many of them rushing through on the ferries to and from Ireland. It doesn't have any standout sights, but it's an appealing and culturally vibrant town (which, incidentally, holds the distinction of being the setting for the last foreign invasion of Britain).

Fishguard is split into three distinct areas. In the middle of it all is the main town, centred on the Town Hall in Market Sq. To the east is the picturesque harbour of the Lower Town (Y Cwm), which was used as a setting for the 1971 film version of *Under Milk Wood* (starring Richard Burton, Peter O'Toole and Elizabeth Taylor). The train station and ferry terminal lie a mile northwest of the town centre, down on the bay in Goodwick (Wdig; *oo-*dig).

◉ Sights & Activities

Strumble Head   VIEWPOINT

On wild and rocky Strumble Head, a lighthouse beams out its signal as high-speed ferries thunder past on their way to Ireland. Jutting into the sea from the so-called 'Pencaer Peninsula', the headland makes a good vantage point for spotting dolphins,

seals, sharks and sunfish; below the parking area is an old coast-guard lookout that now serves as a shelter for observing wildlife. It's located 4 miles northwest of Goodwick and the route is well marked.

The Strumble Shuttle (bus 404 between St David's and Newport) stops here.

Kayak-King   KAYAKING

(☑ 07967 010203; www.kayak-king.com; tours £45) Twice-daily sea-kayaking tours, tailored to either family groups or adults. Kayak-King is a mobile outfit; its conspicuously painted van can be found in Lower Fishguard Harbour when it's running tours, but it's easier to ring or use the online form to make a booking.

🛏 Sleeping

Pwll Deri YHA   HOSTEL £

(☑ 0845 371 9536; www.yha.org.uk; Castell Mawr, Trefasser; dm/r £16/75; 🅿) Perched amid emerald fields atop a 120m-high cliff overlooking the Irish Sea, this hostel has one of the finest locations in Britain. The views from the dining room would rival those from any top hotel (sunsets are particularly spectacular) and the private rooms all have their own bathrooms. The Strumble Shuttle (bus 404 from Newport to St Davids) stops here.

★ Manor Town House   B&B ££

(☑ 01348-873260; www.manortownhouse.com; 11 Main St; s/d from £80/105; 🛜) This graceful Georgian house has a lovely garden terrace where you can gaze over the harbour (from the other direction, the view is the Preseli Hills). The charming owners take great care

---

THE LAST INVASION OF BRITAIN

While Hastings in 1066 may get all the press, the last invasion of Britain was actually at Carreg Wastad Point, northwest of Fishguard, on 22 February 1797. A ragtag collection of 1400 French mercenaries and bailed convicts, led by an Irish-American named Colonel Tate, had intended to land at Bristol and march to Liverpool, keeping English troops occupied while France mounted an invasion of Ireland. Bad weather blew them ashore at Carreg Wastad where, after scrambling up a steep cliff, they set about looting for food and drink.

The invaders had hoped that the Welsh peasants would rise up to join them in revolutionary fervour but, not surprisingly, their drunken pillaging didn't endear them to the locals. The French were quickly seen off by volunteer 'yeoman' soldiers, with help from the people of Fishguard, including, most famously, one Jemima Nicholas, who single-handedly captured 12 mercenaries armed with nothing more than a pitchfork.

The beleaguered Tate surrendered and a mere two days after their arrival the invaders laid down their weapons at Goodwick and were sent off to the jail at Haverfordwest. A curiously rough choice of landing spot, it's accessible only from the sea or the coastal path just outside Fishguard.

over the guest spaces, with continual improvements being made to the six smart en-suite rooms. Bike hire, packed lunches and other extras are never too much trouble.

Fern Villa
B&B ££

(☎ 01348-874148; www.fernvillafishguard.co.uk; Church Rd, Goodwick; s/d from £50/70; ☎) Situated on the slopes in Goodwick (head towards the church), this large cream Victorian offers clean en-suite rooms, some with exposed stone walls and sea views. It's a great option if you want to be close to the train station and ferry port, and especially to the coastal path.

✕ Eating & Drinking

Gourmet Pig
DELI, CAFE £

(☎ 01348-874404; www.gourmetpig.co.uk; 32 West St; mains £5-7; ☎ 9.30am-5.30pm Mon-Sat, 10am-4pm occasional Sun; ☎) Delicious sandwiches, samosas, Iberian-accented deli platters (laden with chorizo, *jamón*, *sobrassada* and manchego), pies and pastries are the main attractions at this relaxed deli-cafe, along with barista-made Coaltown coffee (roasted in Ammanford). Grab a window seat and watch Fishguard go about its business. There are also plenty of tempting imported (and local) treats to take away.

Peppers
BAR

(☎ 01348-874540; www.peppers-hub.co.uk; 16 West St; mains lunch £9-10, dinner £16-18; ☎ 10am-3pm & 6-10pm Thu-Sat, Mon-Sat summer) This hip hub includes an interesting gallery (the streetside West Wales Art Centre), an excellent restaurant, a peaceful terrace area and an inviting little tile-floored bar. There's a good selection of Welsh craft beer and cider, a decent choice of wine, and the staff know their way around a cocktail shaker. There are regular live gigs as well, particularly jazz.

Ship Inn
PUB

(☎ 01348-874033; 3 Old Newport Rd, Lower Town; ☎ 5-11pm Wed-Fri, noon-midnight Sat, noon-10pm Sun) This tremendously snug and convivial little 250-year-old pub has an open fire in winter and walls covered in memorabilia, including photos of Richard Burton filming *Under Milk Wood* outside (the street and nearby quay haven't changed a bit).

ℹ Information

As well as this helpful **tourist office** (☎ 01437-776636; www.visitpembrokeshire.com; Town Hall, Market Sq; ☎ 9am-5pm Mon-Fri), the Town

---

OFF THE BEATEN TRACK

PRESELI HILLS

The only upland area in Pembrokeshire Coast National Park, the **Preseli Hills** (Mynydd Preseli) rise to a height of 536m at Foel Cwmcerwyn. They encompass a fascinating prehistoric landscape, scattered with hill forts, standing stones and burial chambers, and are famous as the source of the mysterious bluestones of Stonehenge. The ancient Golden Road track, once part of a 5000-year-old trade route between Wessex and Ireland, runs along the crest of the hills, passing prehistoric cairns and the stone circle of Bedd Arthur.

Hall contains the library (handy for free internet access) and the market hall, which hosts a general market on Thursday and a farmers market on Saturday mornings.

ℹ Getting There & Away

BOAT

Stena Line (☎ 08447 707 070; www.stenaline.co.uk; Fishguard Harbour; pedestrian/car & driver from £31/79; ☎) has two ferries a day year-round between Rosslare in the southeast of Ireland and Fishguard Harbour.

BUS

Direct services to/from Fishguard include the frequent T5 to Haverfordwest (£3.50, 33 minutes), Newport (£2.50, 15 minutes), Cardigan (£3.85, 37 minutes) and Aberystwyth (£6, 2½ hours); the 413 to St Davids (£3.70, 50 minutes, up to six daily); and the useful Pembrokeshire coastal bus services (p671).

TRAIN

There are frequent direct trains between both Fishguard and Goodwick Station and Fishguard Harbour Station (both of which are actually in Goodwick) and destinations including Swansea (£16, two hours, three daily), Cardiff (from £16, 2½ to three hours, two daily), Newport (£20, 3¼ hours, daily) and Manchester (£47, 6¼ hours, daily).

Newport (Trefdraeth)

☎ 01239 / POP 880

In stark contrast to the industrial city of Newport near the English border, the Pembrokeshire Newport is a pretty cluster of flower-bedecked cottages huddled beneath a small Norman castle (now a private

PENTRE IFAN

The largest neolithic dolmen in Wales, **Pentre Ifan** (Cadw; http://cadw.gov. wales; ⏰10am-4pm) is a 5500-year-old neolithic burial chamber set on a remote hillside with superb views across the Preseli Hills and out to sea. The huge, 5m-long capstone, weighing more than 16 tonnes, is delicately poised on three tall, pointed upright stones, made of the same bluestone that was used for the menhirs at Stonehenge. The site is about 3 miles southeast of Newport, signposted off a minor road south of the A487.

residence). It sits at the foot of Mynydd Carningli, a large bump on the seaward side of the Preseli Hills, and in recent years it has gained a reputation for the quality of its restaurants and guesthouses.

Newport makes a pleasant base for walks along the coastal path or south into the Preseli Hills, but it does get crowded in summer. At the northwestern corner of the town is little **Parrog Beach**, dwarfed by the half-mile **Newport Sands** (Traeth Mawr), one of the area's finest beaches, just across the river.

◉ Sights

★ **Castell Henllys**   HISTORIC SITE
(☑01239-891319; www.castellhenllys.com; Meline; adult/child £5.50/3.50; ⏰10am-5pm Apr-Oct, reduced hours Nov-Mar) If you've ever wondered what a Celtic village looked, felt and smelt like, take a trip back in time to this Iron Age settlement, 4 miles east of Newport. From about 600 BC and right through the Roman occupation there was a thriving Celtic settlement here, and it's been reconstructed on its original foundations. Costumed staff bring the site to life, stoking the fires and performing traditional crafts, and wildlife such as bats and otters *may* appear to add verisimilitude.

Carreg Coetan Arthur   TOMB
(Cadw; http://cadw.gov.wales; 1 Carreg Coetan; ⏰10am-4pm) FREE Now surrounded by fields and houses, this little dolmen has been here for 5000 years. At first glance it looks like the capstone is securely supported by the four standing stones; closer inspection suggests that some old magic has held it together all these thousands of years, as it's balanced on only two of them. Archaeological investigations have uncovered the remains of cremated bones and urns. It's well signposted down a side road on the town's eastern edge.

🛏 Sleeping & Eating

Cnapan   B&B ££
(☑01239-820575; www.cnapan.co.uk; East St; s/d £75/98; ⏰Mar-Jan; 🅿🐾) This diligently maintained, listed Georgian town house has a flower-filled garden and five light-filled rooms. Renovations have freshened up the decor and brand-new bathrooms in their wake; ask for room 4 – it's a little bigger than the others. Downstairs was once a restaurant, and restaurant standards carry over into the excellent breakfasts.

★ **Canteen**   PIZZA, BURGERS £
(☑01239-820131; www.thecanteennewport.com; cnr Market & East Sts; mains £10-11; ⏰9.30am-2.30pm & 6-9pm; 🐾👶🍴) With names like Strumble Head, *Mae Hen Wlad Fy Nhadau* (Land of My Fathers) and Costa del Newport, the Canteen's lip-smacking range of thin, crispy, stone-baked pizza has been suitably Welshified with the addition of locally sourced quality toppings. It also serves burgers, salads and sandwiches, better-than-average coffee and a range of Welsh craft beer.

ℹ Getting There & Away

Direct services to/from Newport include the frequent T5 to Dinas Cross (£1.65, six minutes), Fishguard (£2.45, 15 minutes), Haverfordwest (£4.15, 40 minutes), Cardigan (£3.45, 23 minutes) and Aberystwyth (£6, 2¼ hours, nine daily). The Pembrokeshire coastal bus services (p671) are also useful, especially in summer.

Brecon Beacons & Mid-Wales

Why Go?

The big draw here is the magnificent upland scenery of Brecon Beacons National Park, where high mountain roads dip down to remote hamlets and whitewashed ancient churches. The hiking and mountain-biking terrain here is superb, while the book-loving town of Hay-on-Wye caters to those with more cerebral interests.

By contrast the Powys countryside is Wales at its most rural – a landscape of lustrous green fields, wooded river valleys and small market towns; it's the part that the Industrial Revolution missed. Isolated, sea-battered Ceredigion is home to some of country's most unspoiled beaches, as well as the exuberant hot spot of Aberystwyth. Thrills can be found outside urban areas along lonely trails in the hills and valleys, and on two wheels down narrow country lanes. Central Wales is thoroughly Welsh, with around 40% of people speaking the mother tongue – and more than 50% in Ceredigion.

When to Go

➡ For walking, April and July are usually the driest months; July and August are generally warmest.

➡ In May, Hay hosts its literary festival, and in June, there's philosophy and music during HowTheLightGetsIn.

➡ In August, cap off the Green Man and Brecon Fringe Festival with a spot of bog snorkelling.

➡ Face the chill to earn your laurel wreath in Llanwrtyd Wells' mountain-bike chariot race in January.

Brecon Beacons & Mid-Wales Highlights

1 Cardigan Bay (p703)
Kayaking with dolphins and seals along this rugged coast.

2 Black Mountains (p684)
Taking a hair-raising drive through the chapel-dotted Vale of Ewyas.

3 Hay-on-Wye (p681)
Visiting the Welsh town that's besotted with books.

4 Pen-y-Fan (p690)
Avoiding the crowds on the way up the region's highest mountain.

5 Cambrian Mountains (p691) Enjoying the isolation of these out-of-the-way mountains.

6 Elan Valley (p694)
Exploring mighty Victorian dams and picking wild berries.

7 Aberystwyth (p698)
Experiencing a collision of culture and student high jinks.

8 Carreg Cennen (p689)
Gazing up at Wales' most dramatically sited fortress.

BRECON BEACONS NATIONAL PARK

Rippling dramatically for 45 miles from near Llandeilo in Carmarthenshire all the way to the English border, Brecon Beacons National Park (Parc Cenedlaethol Bannau Brycheiniog) encompasses some of the finest scenery in southern Wales. High mountain plateaus of grass and heather, their northern rims scalloped with glacier-scoured hollows, rise above wooded, waterfall-splashed valleys and swooningly gorgeous rural landscapes.

There are four distinct regions within the park: the wild, lonely **Black Mountain** (Mynydd Du) in the west, with its high moors and glacial lakes; **Fforest Fawr** (Great Forest), whose rushing streams and spectacular waterfalls form the headwaters of the Rivers Tawe and Neath; the **Brecon Beacons** (Bannau Brycheiniog) proper, a group of very distinctive, flat-topped hills that includes Peny-Fan (886m), the park's highest peak; and the heathland ridges of the **Black Mountains** (Y Mynyddoedd Duon) – not to be confused with the above-mentioned Black Mountain.

🏃 Activities

The park has hundreds of walking routes, ranging from gentle strolls to strenuous climbs. Walking cards, maps and guides are available in tourist offices in the region as well as the National Park Visitor Centre near Libanus.

Likewise, there are many excellent off-road mountain-biking routes, including 14 graded and waymarked trails detailed in guides available from tourist and national-park offices.

ℹ️ Information

The park's main **visitor centre** (📞 01874-624437; www.breconbeacons.org; Libanus; ⊙ 9.30am-4.30pm Easter-Oct, 10am-4pm Nov-Easter) has details of walks, hiking and biking trails, outdoor activities, wildlife and geology, plus a cafe and souvenir shop. It's located off the A470, 4 miles southwest of Brecon and 15 miles north of Merthyr Tydfil. Any of the buses on the Merthyr Tydfil–Brecon route stop at Libanus village, a 1.25-mile walk away.

Ordnance Survey (OS) Landranger maps 160 and 161 cover most of the park, as do Outdoor Leisure maps 12 and 13. These detailed maps include walking and cycling trails.

ℹ️ Getting There & Away

There are no railway lines through the national park, but trains stop on its periphery in the towns of Abergavenny, Llandeilo, Llangadog and Llandovery.

Most bus services only operate from Monday to Saturday. The most useful routes:

T4 Cardiff, Merthyr Tydfil, Libanus, Brecon, Talgarth, Builth Wells, Llandrindod Wells, Newtown

T6 Brecon, Sennybridge, Glyntawe, Swansea

X3 Abergavenny, Llanvihangel Crucorney, Hereford

39 Brecon, Hay-on-Wye, Hereford

43/X43 Abergavenny, Crickhowell, Llangattock, Talybont-on-Usk, Llanfrynach, Brecon

63/X63 Brecon, Dan-yr-Ogof National Showcaves, Swansea

Hay-on-Wye (Y Gelli Gandryll)

📞 01497 / POP 1894

Hay-on-Wye, a pretty little town on the banks of the River Wye, just inside the Welsh border, has developed a reputation disproportionate to its size. First came the explosion in secondhand bookshops, a charge led by charismatic and forthright local maverick Richard Booth.

With Hay established as the world's secondhand-book capital, a festival of literature and culture was founded in 1988, growing in stature each year to take in all aspects of the creative arts. Today the 10-day Hay Festival is a major attraction every May and June, famously endorsed by former US president Bill Clinton, a high-profile guest in 2001, as 'the Woodstock of the mind'.

The small town centre is made up of narrow sloping lanes, peppered by interesting shops and peopled by the differing types that such individuality and so many books tend to attract. Even outside festival time its alternative ambience lingers.

🎆 Festivals & Events

★ **Hay Festival**   LITERATURE
(📞 box office 01497-822629; www.hayfestival.com; ⊙ May & Jun) **FREE** The 10-day Hay Festival is Britain's leading festival of literature and the arts – a kind of bookworms' Glastonbury. Like an iconic music festival, it has the gravity to attract the brightest stars in its corner of the artistic galaxy. Entry to the festival site is free; individual events are ticketed.

HowTheLightGetsIn   MUSIC, PHILOSOPHY
(www.howthelightgetsin.org; tickets from £108; ⊙ May & Jun) Billed as the word's largest festival of philosophy and music, HowTheLightGetsIn returned to Hay in 2018 with a

Brecon Beacons National Park

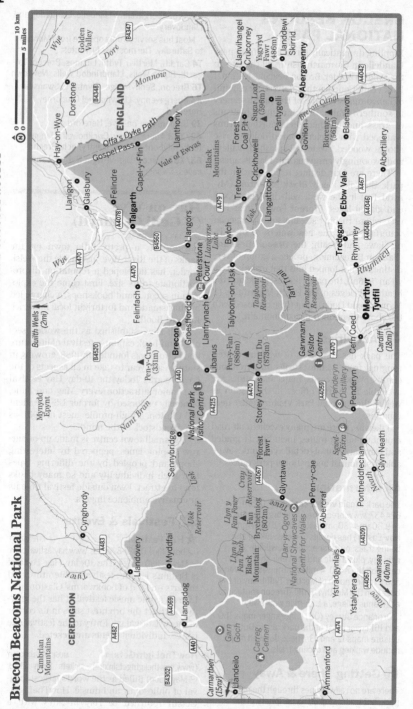

program entitled *Darkness, Authority and Dreams*, featuring speakers as diverse as linguist Noam Chomsky and Shadow Home Secretary Diane Abbott. Held to coincide with the Hay Festival, it attracts thousands to a site on the banks of the Wye.

🛌 Sleeping

Hay Stables
B&B **££**

(☎ 01497-820008; www.haystables.co.uk; Oxford Rd; s/d from £60/75; 🅿 🤖 🐾) Three modern en-suite rooms in peaceful creamy tones await you at this friendly, central guesthouse. There's a common area for guests to mingle and a large, fully equipped kitchen. Breakfast is a self-serve affair, with the ingredients provided for your own fry-up, plus yoghurts, cereals and basically anything you can think of. Check the website for last-minute deals.

Maesyronnen
B&B **££**

(☎ 01497-842763; www.maesyronnenbandb.co.uk; Glasbury; s/d £45/90; 🅿 🤖) Secluded and relaxed, this 19th-century stone house sits in pretty, rambling gardens with views of the Wye Valley and Black Mountains. Only one of the four rooms is en suite, but all feature antique furnishings and a sense of past generations of peaceful country life. Breakfast features local and homemade produce. Maesyronnen is close to Glasbury, 5 miles from Hay.

🍴 Eating

Old Electric Shop
VEGETARIAN **£**

(☎ 01497-821194; www.oldelectric.co.uk; 10 Broad St; mains £8; ⏰ 10am-5pm; 🤖 🍴) Hay's hippest cafe inhabits an eclectic junk-shop-like space crammed with studios selling new and vintage clothing, furniture and, of course, books. The blackboard menu, served until 3pm, includes tasty vegetarian soups, salads and curries. Some nights (every night during the Hay Festival; p681) the Electric Shop puts on a pop-up cocktail bar, often with live music.

★ St John's Place
MODERN BRITISH **££**

(☎ 07855 783799; www.stjohnsplacehay.tumblr.com; St. John's Chapel & Meeting Rooms, Lion St; mains £10-14; ⏰ 6-10pm Fri & Sat) St John's Place is only open two nights a week and offers only three 'plates' alongside a wider range of 'bar snacks', but this narrow focus seems to allow the kitchen plenty of room for experimentation and aspiration. The refinement of the food is offset by the simple elegance of the decor, and adventurous diners will be amply rewarded.

★ Tomatitos Tapas Bar
SPANISH **££**

(☎ 01497-820772; www.haytomatitos.co.uk; 38 Lion St; tapas £5-7; ⏰ 11am-11pm Mon-Sat, 4-11pm Sun, noon-3pm & 6-10pm Mon-Sat, 4-9pm Sun; 🤖) Friendly, bustling Tomatitos combines the atmosphere of everyone's favourite pub with an España-centric menu. Staples such as *tortilla* and chorizo in cider aside, daily specials feature guest stars such as roasted *piquillo* peppers stuffed with beef, and even lamb tagine. The food is great, and tastes even better washed down with Spanish, Portuguese and French wine by the glass.

There are also very pleasant **rooms** on the floor above (singles/doubles including breakfast £64/78).

River Cafe
BRITISH **££**

(☎ 01497-847007; www.wyevalleycanoes.co.uk; The Boat House, Glasbury; mains £15-18; ⏰ 8.30am-4pm Sun-Tue, to 9pm Wed-Sat; 🅿 🤖) River Cafe makes the most of glorious Wye frontage in the little town of Glasbury, 5 miles southwest of Hay. The dining room is open and airy, with a timbered deck perched above the gurgling flow. Inventive-yet-soothing dishes such as hake with fricasseed greens, bacon and crème fraiche are typical of a kitchen that's contemporary but not faddish.

Old Black Lion
PUB FOOD **££**

(☎ 01497-820841; www.oldblacklion.co.uk; 26 Lion St; mains lunch £9-10, dinner £16-18; ⏰ kitchen 8-9.30am, noon-2.30pm & 6.30-9pm) Walkers, book browsers and the literary glitterati all flock to this creaky 17th-century inn, with heavy black beams, low ceilings and features incorporated from a 14th-century predecessor built at the same time as Hay Castle. The atmosphere is as cosy as you'd hope such a place would be and the food is a hearty but refined take on pub fare.

🍷 Drinking & Nightlife

Baskerville Arms
PUB

(☎ 01497-820670; www.baskervillearms.co.uk; Clyro; ⏰ 11am-2.30pm & 5.50-11pm Mon-Thu, 11am-11pm Fri-Sun; 🤖 🐾) If you need to escape the festival crush for a quiet glass in an unfussy rural pub, the Baskerville in Clyro, just a mile from Hay, fits the bill. Known since at least Georgian times (when it was The Swan), it's easy to imagine it's been dispensing the same style of unadorned hospitality to wayfarers, walkers and blow-ins for generations.

BRECON BEACONS & MID-WALES HAY-ON-WYE (Y GELLI GANDRYLL)

☆ Entertainment

Globe at Hay   LIVE PERFORMANCE
(☑ 01497-821762; www.globeathay.org; Newport
St; ⊙ 9.30am-5pm Sun, Mon & Wed, to 11pm Tue
& Thu, to midnight Fri & Sat; 🐾) Run by the Institute of Art and Ideas, the people behind
Hay's HowTheLightGetsIn (p681) festival
of philosophy and music, this converted
Methodist chapel wears many hats: cafe
(mains £12 to £14), bar, live-music venue,
theatre, club and all-round community hub.
It's a wonderfully intimate place to watch a
band, catch a comedian or listen to a tub-
thumping political debate.

🛍 Shopping

There are dozens of secondhand and antiquarian bookshops in Hay, with hundreds of
thousands of tomes stacked floor-to-ceiling
across town – 500,000 in Booth's alone. Each
shop is profiled on a free map available from
the tourist office and venues around town.
There are also excellent stores selling antiques, local produce, art and historic maps.

★ Richard Booth's Bookshop   BOOKS
(☑ 01497-820322; www.boothbooks.co.uk; 44 Lion
St; ⊙ 9.30am-5.30pm Mon-Sat, 10.30am-5pm
Sun) The most famous and still the best,
Booth's is a thing of beauty – from the exquisite tiling on the outside to the immaculately catalogued shelves within (a far cry
from the teetering piles of its early years).
There's a sizeable Anglo-Welsh literature
section, a Wales travel section, a great little cafe (mains £8 to £9) and an arthouse
cinema.

Mostly Maps   MAPS
(☑ 01497-820539; www.mostlymaps.com; 2 Castle St; ⊙ 10.30am-5.30pm Tue-Sat) Behind this

boldly painted blue-and-red timber shopfront you'll find exquisite antiquarian maps
and illustrative plates, many hand-coloured.

Murder & Mayhem   BOOKS
(☑ 01497-821613; 5 Lion St; ⊙ 10am-5.30pm Mon-
Sat) Over the road from the parent store,
this specialist branch of **Addyman Books**
(☑ 01497-821136; www.hay-on-wyebooks.com; 39
Lion St; ⊙ 10am-5.30pm) has a body outline on
the floor, monsters on the ceiling and stacks
of detective fiction, true crime and horror.

Rose's Books   BOOKS
(☑ 01497-820013; www.rosesbooks.com; 14 Broad
St; ⊙ 10am-5pm) This lovely little store specialises in rare children's and illustrated books.

ℹ Information

Tourist Office (☑ 01497-820144; www.hay-
on-wye.co.uk; Chapel Cottage, Oxford Rd;
⊙ 10.30am-4.30pm Mon-Sat, 11am-2pm Sun)
Stocks a map showing all of Hay's bookshops,
as well as copious literature and advice on the
town and surrounding area..

ℹ Getting There & Away

There are up to six 39 buses per day (except on
Sunday) to/from Talgarth (£5.50, 23 minutes),
Felinfach (£6.30, 33 minutes), Brecon (£6.80,
37 minutes) and Hereford (£8.10, 57 minutes).

National Cycle Route 42 passes through
Hay-on-Wye, heading south to Abergavenny. At
nearby Glasbury it also connects with National
Cycle Route 8 (Lôn Las Cymru), which heads
southwest to Brecon and through Brecon Beacons National Park.

Black Mountains (Y Mynyddoedd Duon)

The hills that stretch northward from Abergavenny to Hay-on-Wye are untamed and
largely uninhabited (if you ignore sheep
and red kites), reaching a height of 811m at
windswept **Waun Fach**.

The scenic and secluded **Vale of Ewyas**
traces the path of the River Honddu through
the heart of the Black Mountains, from the
tiny village of **Llanvihangel Crucorney** to
the exposed **Gospel Pass** (549m), where a
single-track road winds its way through a
magically bleak landscape down to Hay-on-
Wye. Along the way it passes the picturesque
ruins of Llanthony Priory and the hamlet of
Capel-y-Ffin, where there are more monastic ruins and the 18th-century **Church of St
Mary the Virgin**.

◉ Sights

★ St Issui's Church
CHURCH

(Patrishow) Halfway up a thickly forested hillside in the Vale of Eywas, this tiny 11th-century church is like a time capsule of Welsh faith and culture, buried too deeply in these hills ever to change. Astonishing as it is in its perfectly situated, weathered simplicity, it's inside that its true wonders reveal themselves: a finely carved wooden rood screen and loft, dating from around 1500; medieval frescos of biblical texts; coats of arms and a red-ochre skeleton; and memorials to people long dead.

★ Llanthony Priory
RUINS

(Cadw; www.cadw.gov.wales; ⊙ 10am-4pm; P ♿ 🐾) FREE Halfway along the impossibly beautiful Vale of Ewyas lie the atmospheric ruins of this Augustinian priory, set among pasture and wooded hills by the River Hond-du. Perhaps the second most important abbey in Wales when completed in 1230, it was abandoned after Henry VIII dissolved Britain's monasteries in 1538. Running a close second to Tintern for grandeur, Llanthony's setting is even more stunning, and you won't have crowds to fight. JMW Turner was impressed, too: he painted the scene in 1794.

Ysgyryd Fawr
MOUNTAIN

(Skirrid) Of the glacially sculpted hills that surround Abergavenny, Skirrid (486m) is the most dramatic looking and has a history to match. A cleft in the rock near the top was once believed to have split open at the exact time of Christ's death and a chapel was built here on what was considered a particularly holy place (a couple of upright stones remain). During the Reformation as many as 100 people would attend illegal Catholic Masses at this remote spot.

🛏 Sleeping & Eating

★ Celyn Farm
B&B ££

(☎ 01873-890894; www.celynfarm.co.uk; Forest Coal Pit; s/d from £65/82) If you like to get away from all neighbours, you'll love Celyn ('Holy') Farm. Set in 120 hectares of farmland reached by narrow lanes from either Llanvihangel Crucorney or Crickhowell (make sure you print out the directions), this remote country house offers four handsome rooms, excellent breakfasts and idyllic views over Sugar Loaf and the Gwryne Fawr River below.

Skirrid Mountain Inn
PUB FOOD £

(☎ 01873-890258; www.skirridmountaininn.co.uk; Hereford Rd, Llanvihangel Crucorney; lunch £5-6, dinner £10-12; ⊙ 5.30-11pm Mon, 11am-2.30pm & 5.30-11pm Tue-Fri, 11.30am-11pm Sat, noon-10pm Sun; P ♿ 🐾) This 'may' be Wales' oldest inn; Owain Glyndŵr 'may' have rallied troops here; and Shakespeare 'may' have taken inspiration from it: whatever the conjecture, there's no doubt that the Skirrid is very old (probably pre-1110) and suitably atmospheric. Downstairs it serves hearty food in front of roaring fires.

ⓘ Getting There & Away

Bus X4 between Abergavenny (£3.10, 16 minutes) and Hereford (£4.60, 45 minutes) stops in Llanvihangel Crucorney seven times a day; no Sunday services.

Crickhowell (Crughywel)

☎ 01873 / POP 2060

This prosperous, picturesque, flower-bedecked village grew up around a Norman motte-and-bailey castle and a ford on the River Usk. All that remains of the **castle** are a few tumbledown towers, and the ford was superseded in the 17th century by the elegant **stone bridge** leading to the neighbouring village of Llangattock. The bridge is famous for having 12 arches on one side and 13 on the other.

There's not a lot to see in Crickhowell itself, but with a good clutch of independent shops to peruse it's a pleasant place for an overnight stop, and it's handily close to the Brecon Beacons and the Vale of Ewyas. The town's fiercely protective of its locally owned stores, banding together in 2015 to stymie an unwanted supermarket. Crickhowell has also staged a highly publicised tax revolt, protesting against offshore corporate tax havens by simply setting up one of its own.

◉ Sights

★ Tretower Court & Castle
HISTORIC BUILDING

(Cadw; www.cadw.gov.wales; Tretower; adult/child £6.90/4.10; ⊙ 10am-5pm Apr-Oct, to 4pm Thu-Sat Nov-Mar) Originally the home of the Vaughan family, Tretower gives you two historic buildings for the price of one: the sturdy circular Norman keep, now roofless and commanding only a sheep-nibbled bailey, and a 15th-century manor house with a fine garden and orchard (now furnished with picnic tables). Together they illustrate the transition from military stronghold to country house that took place in late-medieval times.

It's situated 3 miles northwest of Crickhowell on the A479.

Crug Hywel
MOUNTAIN

(Table Mountain) Distinctive flat-topped Crug Hywel (Hywel's Rock; 451m), better known as Table Mountain, rises to the north of Crickhowell and gave the town its name. You can do a steep but satisfying hike to the impressive remains of an Iron Age fort, which occupy the entire summit. The tourist office (p686) has a leaflet detailing the 4½-mile, three-hour round-trip route.

⚡ Festivals & Events

Green Man Festival
MUSIC

(www.greenman.net; Glanusk Park; adult/child £189/22; ⊙ mid-Aug; 🖐) This four-day music festival has a sterling reputation for its mellow vibe and green ethos and for catering well to children and people with disabilities. It attracts A-list indie acts such as The Brian Jonestown Massacre, interesting electronic artists and the occasional dead-set rock legend. Tickets include camping on the riverside site 2 miles west of Crickhowell.

Crickhowell Walking Festival
SPORTS

(www.crickhowellfestival.com; ⊙ Mar) Held in the week wrapped around St David's Day (1 March), this nine-day festival features guided treks, workshops on outdoorsy themes, and music. It's proven so popular that it's now extended for a long weekend in September, the 'Autumn Extra'.

🛏 Sleeping & Eating

Gwyn Deri
B&B ££

(☑ 01873-812494; www.gwynderibedandbreakfast.co.uk; Mill St; s/d/f £45/70/100; 🅿🛜🐾) In a quiet suburban pocket between church and river, this cosy B&B is run by a friendly couple who keep its three modern guest bedrooms immaculately clean, and are more than happy to share their knowledge of the area. Bonuses include fresh fruit in the rooms and an excellent breakfast selection. Connecting rooms are available for family groups.

Cafe at Book-ish
CAFE £

(☑ 01873-810337; www.book-ish.co.uk/cafe; 18 High St; mains £5-7; ⊙ 10am-5.30pm Mon-Sat, 11am-4pm Sun; 🛜) Attached to a great indie bookshop, this bright, licensed cafe is very popular locally, and ideal for a solo lunch – perhaps a ploughman's platter with local Perl Las cheese, ham, pork pie and pickles – over your latest paperback purchase. The

coffee's good, and the loft doubles as an event space – see the website for upcoming tastings, readings and the like.

ℹ Information

Tourist Office (☑ 01873-811970; www.visitcrickhowell.co.uk; Beaufort St; ⊙ 10am-5pm Mon-Sat, to 1.30pm Sun; 🛜) Shares a building with an art gallery and stocks leaflets for local walks.

ℹ Getting There & Away

Direct services include 12 daily 43/X43 buses to/from Abergavenny (£2, 11 minutes), Llanfrynach (£2.50, 33 minutes) and Brecon (£2.70, 45 minutes). No Sunday services.

Brecon (Aberhonddu)

☑ 01874 / POP 8403

The handsome market town of Brecon stands at the junction of the Rivers Usk and Honddu. For centuries the town thrived as a centre of wool production and weaving. Today you'll find Brecon Beacons hikers rubbing shoulders with soldiers from the town's large military base in the bars, eateries and outdoor-gear shops that dominate the old stone streets. There's a cathedral, castle ruins and old canal infrastructure to see, but its great appeal is as a base for forays into the national park.

◉ Sights

Brecon Cathedral
CHURCH

(☑ 01874-623857; www.breconcathedral.org.uk; Cathedral Close; ⊙ 8.30am-6.30pm) Perched on a hill above the River Honddu, Brecon Cathedral was founded in 1093 as part of a Benedictine monastery, though little remains of the original Norman church except the vividly carved font. Most of the Gothic structure standing today dates from the early 13th century. Modern additions include an ornate 1937 altarpiece and a cross that seems to hover in mid-air at the end of the nave. In the cathedral grounds are a **Heritage Centre** (☑ 01874-625222; ⊙ 11am-3pm Mon-Sat) FREE, cafe and gift shop.

🏃 Activities

Beacon Park Day Boats
BOATING, CANOEING

(☑ 01873-858277, 0800 612 2890; www.beaconparkdayboats.co.uk; Toll House, Canalside; boat per half-day/day £50/80, canoe per half-day/day £25/40; ⊙ 10am-5pm Easter-Oct) Rents six- to eight-seater electric-powered boats and three-seater Canadian canoes. In a day you

Brecon

Brecon

◎ Sights
1 Brecon Cathedral.................................B1
2 Heritage Centre B1

☉ Activities, Courses & Tours
3 Beacon Park Day Boats.......................C4
4 Biped Cycles B2
5 Dragonfly Cruises...............................C4

⬛ Sleeping
6 Coach House.......................................A3

✴ Eating
7 Gurkha Corner C3

◉ Drinking & Nightlife
8 Brecon Tap..C3

can cruise southeast to Llangattock and
back. It also has a fleet of luxury narrowboats for longer live-in voyages.

Dragonfly Cruises BOATING
(☏ 07831 685222; www.dragonfly-cruises.co.uk;
Canal Basin, Canal Rd; adult/child £7.80/4.50, hire
per 1/2/3hr £25/35/45; ☺ Mar-Oct; ⬚) Runs
2½-hour narrowboat cruises on the Monmouthshire and Brecon Canal. There are
trips six or seven days per week in July and
August, fewer in the cooler months – ring or
see the website to enquire. It also hires out
small boats.

Biped Cycles CYCLING
(☏ 01874-622296; www.bipedcycles.co.uk; 10 Ship
St; bike hire per day £28; ☺ 9am-5pm Mon-Sat)
Rents mountain and road bikes, performs
repairs and can arrange guided rides.

✴ Festivals & Events

Brecon Beast SPORTS
(www.breconbeast.co.uk; ☺ mid-Sep) A gruelling
mountain-bike challenge over 44 or 68 miles.
The entry fee (£35 in advance; £40 on the day)

OFF THE BEATEN TRACK

GARN GOCH

You're likely to have the impressive remains of **Garn Goch** FREE to yourself. One of the largest Iron Age sites in Wales, it comprises a smaller hill fort covering 1.5 hectares, and a much larger one of 11.2 hectares. While what you now see are immense piles of rubble, it's sobering to know that these were once 10m-high ramparts, faced with stone and 5m thick. From the top, jaw-dropping views of Black Mountain country roll to every point of the compass.

To get here, follow the signs from Llangadog through Bethlehem village and into the hills beyond.

covers camping, refreshments on the route, a 'pasta party' and a T-shirt. All proceeds go to Brecon Mountain Rescue, the Keith Morris Memorial Fund and other charities.

Brecon Fringe Festival   MUSIC
(www.breconfringe.co.uk; ⊘Aug) Started as an alternative to the famous Brecon Jazz Festival (which, sadly, blew its last note in 2015), Brecon Fringe brings a wide range of musical styles to pubs and other venues in and around town over four days in August.

🛏 Sleeping

Priory Mill Farm   CAMPGROUND £
(www.priorymillfarm.co.uk; Hay Rd; sites per adult/child £9/6; ⊘Easter-Sep; P) With a cobbled courtyard, an ancient mill building, free-range chickens and a lush camping meadow by the Honddu, this is pretty much camping heaven, all just a five-minute riverside walk from Brecon. Local wood and charcoal are supplied so you can set a campfire, plus there's a semi-enclosed shelter for cooking and chatting, and a covered bike locker for riders.

Coach House   B&B ££
(☎01874-620043; www.coachhousebrecon.com; 12 Orchard St; r/ste £84/170; 🛜) This solid 19th-century coaching inn is well attuned to the needs of walkers, with a drying room for hiking gear, generous breakfasts (including good vegetarian options), and packed lunches put together by the hosts. The six stylish, modern rooms, decorated in soothing creams, have ultra-comfy beds and good showers.

★**Peterstone Court**   HOTEL £££
(☎01874-665387; www.peterstone-court.com; Llanhamlach; r from £165; P🛜🏊) This elegant Georgian manor house on the banks of the Usk offers large, comfortable rooms with superb views across the valley to the Beacons. The boutique spa centre is another drawcard, pampering guests with organic beauty products. There's also a separate three-bedroom cottage and an excellent restaurant on the property. Llanhamlach is 3 miles southeast of Brecon, off the A40.

🍴 Eating

Gurkha Corner   NEPALI £
(☎01874-610871; 12 Glamorgan St; mains £8-9; ⊘noon-2.30pm & 5.30-11pm Tue-Sun; 🍴) Rustic scenes of the Himalayas brighten the windowless dining room of this friendly Nepalese restaurant. The delicious food dishes – curries, fried rice, lentils and rich veg side dishes – are influenced by, but not identical to, Indian food. The *sisnu* (stinging nettle) curry is a good example.

★**Felin Fach Griffin**   MODERN BRITISH £££
(☎01874-620111; www.felinfachgriffin.co.uk; Felinfach; mains lunch £15-16, dinner £20-21; ⊘noon-2.30pm & 6-9pm) With a string of awards as long as its wine list, this country pub offers gourmet dining in a relaxed and unpretentious setting. Open fires, leather sofas and timber beams create a comfortable atmosphere in which to enjoy local fish, farm produce and game in dishes such as lamb breast with white beans, sweetbreads and salsa verde. There are also excellent **rooms** (s/d from £135/193; P🏊) upstairs.

🍷 Drinking & Nightlife

Brecon Tap   BAR
(☎01874-618124; www.facebook.com/brecontap; The Bulwark; ⊘11am-11pm Sun-Thu, to midnight Fri & Sat, food served noon-3pm & 6-9pm; 🛜) Originally crowd-funded into being by the lads at Brecon Brewing, the Tap is a treasure trove of craft beer, traditional cider, estate wines and locally baked meat pies. Occasionally, live music intrudes on the happy hum of locals polishing their favourite bar stools.

ℹ Information

Visit Brecon (☎01874-620860; www.brecon beacons.org; Lion Yard; ⊘9am-5pm Mon-Sat, 10am-4pm Sun) In heartening response to the closure of the county-funded tourist office, Brecon Council found the funds for this local visitor information centre.

❶ Getting There & Away

Direct bus services run to/from Brecon's **bus interchange** (Heol Gouesnou). Services include up to 12 43/X43 buses per day to/from Crickhowell (£2.70, 30 to 45 minutes) and Abergavenny (£3.60, 45 minutes), up to six 39 buses per day to/from Hay-on-Wye (£6.80, 37 minutes), and up to eight T4 services per day to to/from Llandrindod Wells (£4.65, 1¼ hours) and Cardiff (£7, 1¾ hours). Smaller routes run no Sunday services.

The Market car park offers short-stay pay-and-display parking. There are long-stay lots on Hoel Gouesnou and near the canal basin.

Regular taxi services as well as a walkers shuttle are offered by **Ride & Hike** (☑ 07989 242550; www.rideandhike.co.uk). Indicative fares for the six-seater shuttle: National Park Visitor Centre (£20), Merthyr Tydfil (£45), Cardiff (£100).

Fforest Fawr & Black Mountain

The western half of Brecon Beacons National Park is sparsely inhabited and devoid of any towns of note. **Fforest Fawr** (Great Forest) was once a Norman hunting ground and is now a Unesco geopark (www.fforestfawr geopark.org.uk), famed for landscapes varying from bleak moorland to flower-flecked limestone pavement and lush wooded ravines replete with moss and greenery. Further west is the **Black Mountain** (Y Mynydd Du), a lonely expanse of barren peaks that throws down an irresistible gauntlet to intrepid hikers. Scoured by glaciers, shaped by human action from prehistory through the Romans to today, it's a bleak, wild and utterly captivating place.

◉ Sights

★ **Carreg Cennen**   CASTLE
(Cadw; ☑ 01558-822291; http://cadw.gov.wales; Trap; adult/child £5.50/3.50; ⊙ 9.30am-6pm Apr-Oct, to 5pm Nov-Mar) Dramatically perched atop a steep limestone crag, high above the River Cennen, are the brooding ruins of Wales' ultimate romantic castle, visible for miles in every direction. Originally a Welsh castle, the current structure dates back to Edward I's conquest of Wales in the late 13th century. It was partially dismantled in 1462 during the War of the Roses. On a working farm of the same name, Carreg Cennen is well signposted from the A483 heading south from Llandeilo.

Penderyn Distillery   DISTILLERY
(☑ 01685-810650; www.welsh-whisky.co.uk; Penderyn; tours adult/child £9/4.50; ⊙ 9.30am-5pm, to 6pm summer; ℗) Though Wales has a long history of spirit distillation, this boutique distillery released its first malt whisky only in 2004, marking the resurgence of Welsh whisky-making after an absence of more than 100 years (due to the power of the temperance movement in the late 19th century). Visitors can witness the creation of the liquid fire that's distilled with fresh spring water in a single copper still, then matured in bourbon casks and finished in rich Madeira wine casks. Tours include tastings.

Red Kite Feeding Centre   BIRD SANCTUARY
(☑ 01550-740617; www.redkiteswales.co.uk; Llanddeusant; adult/child £4/2; ⊙ 3pm Apr-Oct, 2pm Nov-Mar) A multitude of majestic birds of prey swoop in daily for their afternoon meal of manky meat scraps at this remote feeding centre. You're likely to see upwards of 50 red kites, alongside buzzards and ravens, all from a hide mere metres from the meat-munching action.

Waterfall Country   WATERFALL
A series of dramatic waterfalls lies between the villages of Pontneddfechan and Ystradfellte, where the Rivers Mellte, Hepste and Pyrddin pass through steep forested gorges. The finest is **Sgwd-yr-Eira** (Waterfall of the Snow), where you can actually walk behind the torrent. At one point the River Mellte disappears into **Porth-yr-Ogof** (Door to the Cave), the biggest cave entrance in Britain (3m high and 20m wide), only to reappear 100m further south.

BEACONS WAY

The 99-mile, eight-day Beacons Way trail wends its way across the national park from Ysgyryd Fawr (Skirrid) near Abergavenny to the village of Bethlehem on the edge of the Black Mountain, knocking off all the highest summits.

Needless to say, this is a stretching walk and requires proper walking gear as well as a good Ordnance Survey (OS) map – the moorland sections can be hard to navigate. The route is manageable in eight taxing days, but you may want to take a little longer to make it more enjoyable and less of an endurance test.

DON'T MISS

PEN-Y-FAN

Ascending **Pen-y-Fan** (886m), the tallest peak in the Brecon Beacons, is one of the most popular hikes in the park (around 350,000 people make the climb annually, giving it the nickname 'the motorway'). The shortest route begins at the Pont ar Daf car park on the A470, 10 miles southwest of Brecon. It's a steep but straightforward slog up to the summit of Corn Du (873m), followed by a short dip and final ascent to Pen-y-Fan (4.5 miles return; allow three hours).

A slightly longer (5.5 miles return) but just as crowded path starts at the Storey Arms outdoor centre, 1 mile to the north. The T4 bus stops here. (Note: the Storey Arms is not a pub!) You can avoid the crowds by choosing one of the longer routes on the north side of the mountain, which also have the advantage of more interesting views on the way up. The best starting point is the Cwm Gwdi car park, at the end of a minor road 3.5 miles southwest of Brecon. From here, you follow a path along the crest of the Cefn Cwm Llwch ridge, with great views of the neighbouring peaks, and then there's a final steep scramble to the summit. The round trip from the car park is 7 miles; allow three to four hours. Starting and finishing in Brecon, the total distance is 14 miles.

Sleeping & Eating

★ **Coed Owen Bunkhouse** HOSTEL £
(☑ 07508 544044, 01685-722628; www.brecon
beaconsbunkhouse.co.uk; Cwmtaff; dm/r £30/60;
P) On a working sheep farm just south of
the Cantref Reservoir, this excellent custom
conversion of an old stone barn offers smart
six- and 10-bed bunk rooms and two small
private rooms. There's an excellent kitch-
en, a common area, outdoor tables, a boot
room and a laundry. At weekends it's usually booked up by groups, but solo travellers
shouldn't have trouble midweek.

★ **Mandinam** CABIN ££
(☑ 01550-777368; www.mandinam.com; Llangadog; huts £100; ⊙ Easter-Oct; P) This
wonderfully remote estate on the park's
northwestern fringe offers a bohemian back-
to-nature experience in little fixed wagons,
complete with kitchens and wood-fired hot
tubs for romantic stargazing. You needn't
worry about privacy, as the huts are well
spaced within the vast, bucolic property. The
kind family that owns the farm has made
something very special here. Four-night
minimum stay.

Carreg Cennen Tearoom WELSH £
(☑ 01558-822291; www.carregcennencastle.com;
Trap; mains £6-7; ⊙ 9.30am-5.30pm; P) Possibly the best castle tearoom anywhere. The
farmer-owner's longhorn beef is on the
menu in the form of cottage pie and beef salad, plus it serves warming *cawl* (traditional
Welsh stew) and excellent homemade cakes.
The location is an impressive converted
barn that sits just below the castle (p689).

ℹ Information

Garwnant Visitor Centre (☑ 01685-387456;
www.naturalresourceswales.gov.uk/garwnant;
parking £2; ⊙ 9.30am-4.30pm; ♠) Natural
Resources Wales' visitor centre at the head of
the Llwyn-on Reservoir is the starting point for
a couple of easy forest walks. It also has a cafe
(mains £5), a mini mountain-bike course, an
adventure-play area and two puzzle trails for
kids. Fishing permits (from £6) can be bought
from a machine in the car park.

ℹ Getting There & Away

The only useful bus routes through this region
are the 63 between Brecon and Ystradgynlais,
which stops at the Dan-yr-Ogof National Showcaves Centre when it's open; and bus T4 between Cardiff and Newtown (via Merthyr Tydfil,
Brecon and Llandrindod Wells), which stops near
the Garwnant Visitor Centre.

POWYS

Small villages, quiet market towns and an
abundance of sheep litter the undulating
hills and moorland of rural Powys, by far
Wales' biggest county. Named after an ancient Welsh kingdom, this modern entity
was formed in 1974 from the historic counties of Montgomeryshire, Radnorshire and
Brecknockshire. It's an overwhelmingly rural place, ideal for walking and cycling, but
this county isn't just green in a literal sense
– Machynlleth has become a focal point for
the nation's environmentally friendly aspirations, and all over the county efforts to
restore the threatened red kite have been

met with outstanding success. The bird is now the very symbol of Powys, the county at Wales' green heart.

❶ Getting There & Around

BUS

Bus services are the most extensive means of public transport in Powys, with regular connections on major routes (such as those run by TrawsCymru) from at least Monday to Saturday (Sundays can be sparsely served) and more sporadic services on the minors. Traveline Cymru (www.traveline.cymru) is the place to plan your journey.

TRAIN

The Heart of Wales Line cuts Powys in two, entering the county near Llanwrtyd Wells and exiting at Knighton. To the north, the Cambrian Line runs from Shrewsbury in England, through Welshpool and Newtown to Machynlleth. While comparatively expensive, both lines are very scenic, and the most pleasant way to travel in Powys. Tickets and timetables can be found at www.nationalrail.co.uk.

Llanwrtyd Wells (Llanwrtyd)

📞 01591 / POP 574

Llanwrtyd (khlan-*oor*-tid) Wells is an odd little town – mostly deserted except during one of its unconventional festivals, when it's packed to the rafters with crazy contestants and their merrymaking supporters.

Apart from this recent status as the capital of wacky Wales, Llanwrtyd Wells has long been surrounded by beautiful walking, cycling and riding country, with the Cambrian Mountains to the northwest and the Mynydd Epynt to the southeast.

Theophilus Evans, the local vicar, first discovered the healing properties of the Ffynon Droellwyd (Stinking Well) in 1732 when he found it cured his scurvy. The popularity of the waters grew and Llanwrtyd became a spa town. Nowadays, however, its wells have been capped and, outside of the festivals, it's hard to find much by way of vital signs. It claims to be the smallest town in Britain, but patently isn't.

🛏️ Sleeping

Ardwyn House   B&B ££
(📞 01591-610768; www.ardwynhouse.co.uk; Station Rd; s/d £60/80; 🅿️ 🛜) The young owners have restored the Arts-and-Crafts grandeur of this once-derelict house. There are rural

views, parquet flooring and period wallpaper and furnishings throughout, and clawfoot baths in two of the three rooms. There's also an oak-panelled guest lounge with a pool table and bar, and afternoon tea on arrival. Two self-catering cottages (£495 per week) are also available.

Lasswade Country House   B&B ££
(📞 01591-610515; www.lasswadehotel.co.uk; Station Rd; s/d from £65/90; 🅿️ 🛜) 🖋️ This excellent country restaurant-with-rooms makes great use of a handsome, three-storey Edwardian house looking over the Irfon Valley towards the Brecon Beacons. Committed to green tourism (it's won a slew of awards, sources hydroelectric power and even offers electric-vehicle recharging), it's also big on gastronomy: the chef-owner's three-course menu (£34) features Cambrian lamb, Tally goat's cheese and other delights.

🍴 Eating & Drinking

★ **Carlton Riverside**   WELSH ££
(📞 01591-610248; www.carltonriverside.com; Irfon Cres; mains £19-23; ⊙ 6.30-8.30pm Mon-Sat; 🅿️ 🛜) This upscale restaurant has a boutique feel and a mantelpiece groaning under its many awards. There's an upstairs bar (open Tuesday to Sunday evenings), but the real star here is the restaurant and its

---

WORTH A TRIP

CAMBRIAN MOUNTAINS

The Cambrian Mountains are a rather desolate but starkly beautiful area of uplands covering the region roughly between Snowdonia and the Brecon Beacons. Largely unpopulated and undeveloped, this wild, empty plateau of high moorland is the source of both the Rivers Severn and Wye. Hidden in the folds of the hills are lakes, waterfalls and deserted valleys as well as hill farms home to thousands of sheep. The region sees relatively few visitors except for around the Elan Valley; if you wish to get away from it all there is no finer place in Wales in which to hike or bike in solitude. Many tracks criss-cross the area, including the 83-mile Cambrian Way; you can find details of routes at www.walkingbritain.co.uk or more information about the region at www.cambrianmountains.co.uk.

superb menu featuring plenty of local produce. Lunch can be organised from Tuesday to Saturday, with at least a day's notice.

Drovers Rest WELSH ££
(☑ 01591-610264; www.food-food-food.co.uk; Y Sgwar; 3 courses £30; ⊘ noon-2pm & 7.30-9.30pm Wed-Sun; ⊜) Increasingly recognised as one of Mid-Wales' best dining venues, this charming restaurant does fantastic things with local produce. Snugly perched by the Irfon, it has a relaxing riverside terrace and a few simple-but-cosy rooms (singles/doubles £40/80, some en suite). The owners also run regular one-day cooking courses (£165 to £195) featuring Welsh cuisine and game.

★ **Neuadd Arms Hotel** PUB
(☑ 01591-610236; www.neuaddarmshotel.co.uk; ⊘ 8.30am-midnight Sun-Thu, to 1am Fri & Sat) Like any good village pub, the Neuadd Arms is a focal point for the community. There's an interesting menu (mains £9 to £11), bed-and-breakfast rooms (singles/doubles £44/77) and excellent beers brewed in the stables out back. It's also Llanwrtyd's tourist-information point, with everything you'll need to know about mountain biking, pony trekking or hiking in the area.

❶ Getting There & Away

Bus 48 heads to Builth Wells (£3.80, 30 minutes, up to four per day).

Llanwrtyd is on the Heart of Wales Line (www.heart-of-wales.co.uk), with up to four direct services daily to Swansea (£11.90, two hours,), Llandeilo (£5.40, 45 minutes), Llandrindod Wells (£4.50, 35 minutes) and Shrewsbury (£15, 2¼ hours).

Builth Wells (Llanfair-Ym-Muallt)

☑ 01982 / POP 2738

Builth (pronounced 'bilth') Wells is perhaps the liveliest of the former spa towns of Mid-Wales, with a bustling, workaday feel. Once the playground of the Welsh working classes, it has a pretty location on the River Wye and prominence as a centre of local agriculture. While there are no attractions per se, it's a handy base for walkers or cyclists tackling any of the long-distance paths that pass through the area.

☆ Festivals & Events

Royal Welsh Show FAIR
(www.rwas.co.uk; Llanelwedd; adult/child per day £26/5; ⊘ Jul; ⊞) Over 200,000 people descend on Builth for four days every July for the Royal Welsh Show (founded in Aberystwyth in 1904) to see everything from gussied-up livestock to lumberjack competitions, falconry and a food hall bursting with farm produce.

⊨ Sleeping & Eating

Bronwye B&B ££
(☑ 04419-8250 8002; www.bronwye.co.uk; Church St; s/d from £60/75; ℗⊜) Not far from the River Wye, this imposing 19th-century house has five comfortable, modern rooms with good beds and bathrooms. It's cosily

---

LLANWRTYD FESTIVALS

While mulling over how to encourage tourism in Llanwrtyd over the dark winter, some citizens started an inspired roll call of unconventionality. There's now something on every month (see www.green-events.co.uk for more details), but these are some of the wackiest events:

World Mountain Bike Chariot Racing Championship (www.green-events.co.uk; team entry £20; ⊘ Jan) Specially designed mountain-bike chariots race off; mid-January.

Man vs Horse Marathon (www.green-events.co.uk; ⊘ mid-Jun) The first-conceived of Llanwrtyd's wacky races sees two legs take on four; mid-June.

World Bog Snorkelling Championships (www.green-events.co.uk; adult/child £15/12; ⊘ bank holiday Aug) Held over the August bank holiday; spin-off events include Mountain Bike Bog Snorkelling and the Bog Snorkelling Triathlon, both held in July.

Real Ale Wobble & Ramble (www.green-events.co.uk; 1-/2-day ride £18/25, 1-/2-day ramble £11/18; ⊘ Nov) Cyclists and walkers sup pints along a waymarked route; November.

Mari Llwyd (New Year Walk In; www.green-events.co.uk; ⊘ New Year) A celebration of Welsh poetry and the country's deep pagan past; New Year's Eve.

modern rather than rich with period character, but there's a warm welcome, a pleasant garden and excellent breakfasts, which, at these rates, make it a bargain.

Caer Beris Manor
HOTEL £££

(☎ 01982-552601; www.caerberis.com; A483; s/d from £74/143) Once home to Lord Swansea, this 1896 mock-Tudor country manor lies at the end of a long driveway, winding through 11 hectares of parkland on the River Irfon. Classic styling, log fires and spacious rooms with swag curtains, heavy fabrics and tassled lamps await. The oak-panelled Restaurant 1896 serves a fine seasonal menu featuring local produce (mains £19 to £25).

★ Drawing Room
MODERN WELSH £££

(☎ 01982-552493; www.the-drawing-room.co.uk; 3 courses £40; ◷ from 7pm, last orders 8.30pm; P 🖘) Set in a Georgian country house flanked by kitchen gardens, this two-rosette restaurant-with-rooms is one of the region's finest. Prime Welsh black beef, Brecon lamb and Cardigan Bay crab feature on the locally sourced menu, while the beautifully refurbished rooms are well worth considering (from £215, including breakfast). It's 3 miles north of Builth, on the A470.

ℹ Getting There & Away

Buses stopping here include the frequent T4 to Llandrindod Wells (£2, 20 minutes), Newtown (£5.80, 1¼ hours), Brecon (£3.70, one hour) and Cardiff (£8, 2¾ hours); one X75 per day to Crickhowell (one hour) and Abergavenny (70 minutes); and one X15 per day to Hay-on-Wye (£3.20, 30 minutes) and Hereford (£6.70, 1¼ hours).

Rhayader (Rhaeadr Gwy)

☎ 01597 / POP 1837

Rhayader is a handsome, small and fairly uneventful livestock-market town revolving around a central crossroads marked by a war-memorial clock. It's a place that appeals to walkers visiting the nearby Elan Valley and tackling the 136-mile Wye Valley Walk. Distinguished by several extremely venerable timber buildings, it's largely deserted on Thursday (when businesses trade for only half a day) but fills out on Wednesday – market day.

◉ Sights & Activities

Rhayader Museum & Gallery
MUSEUM

(☎ 01597-810561; www.carad.org.uk; East St; adult/child £4/free; ◷ 10am-4pm Tue-Fri, to 1pm Sat; P) Focusing on local history and life in and around Rhayader, this small museum uses artefacts, film and more than 50 oral histories to explore everything from folk tales to sheep farming. The attached shop sells local craft, toys and books, and has plenty of information for visitors to the area, while the theatre houses dance, drama and music.

Gigrin Farm Red-Kite Feeding Station
BIRDWATCHING

(☎ 01597-810243; www.gigrin.co.uk; South St; adult/child £7/4; ◷ 1-5pm Mon-Wed, Sat & Sun, daily school holidays; ♿) Hundreds of red kites arrive at Gigrin Farm every day at 2pm (3pm during British summer time) to gorge on meat scraps. Crows and ravens try to get in on the frenzy, but all must yield to the super-agile kites, with their 2m wingspan and raking claws – they'll mug the crows (and each other) to get the meat.

Clive Powell Mountain Bike Centre
MOUNTAIN BIKING

(☎ 01597-811343; www.clivepowell-mtb.co.uk; West St; ◷ 9am-1pm & 2-5.30pm) This centre is run by a former cycling champion and coach. You can hire a mountain/road bike here (£32/24 per day, including helmet and puncture kit; most are new Giant stock) or take it easier with an electric bike (£40 per day).

🛏 Sleeping & Eating

Camping & Caravanning Club
CAMPGROUND £

(Wyeside; ☎ 01597-810183; www.campingandcaravanningclub.co.uk; Llangurig Rd; unpowered sites for 2 adults for 2 nights £58; ◷ Apr-Oct; P 🖘) A short walk from the centre of Rhayader, this relaxed, grassy campsite has river views, lots of trees, two shower blocks and a shop. Stronger wi-fi can be bought from £3 per day.

Horseshoe Guesthouse
B&B ££

(☎ 01597-810982; www.rhayader-horseshoe.co.uk; Church St; s/d £45/78; P 🖘) This 19th-century former inn, once the Butcher's Arms, now offers comfortable modern rooms (five of seven are en suite) and plenty of communal space in the large dining room, garden, conservatory and walled courtyard. Heavy beams and other antique touches remain, there's a 20-seater restaurant (three courses for £16) and packed lunches can be arranged for £6 per person.

Triangle Inn
PUB

(☎ 01597-810537; www.triangleinn.co.uk; Cwmdauddwr; mains £8-12; ◷ noon-3pm & 6.30-11pm Tue-Sat, 6.30-11pm Sun & Mon May-Aug, noon-3pm & 6.30-11pm Thu-Sat, 6.30-11pm Sun-Wed Sep-Apr;

WORTH A TRIP

ELAN VALLEY

The Elan Valley is filled with beautiful countryside, split by imposing Victorian and Edwardian dams and the lakes they've created. In the late 19th century, dams were built on the River Elan (pronounced 'ellen'), west of Rhayader, mainly to provide a reliable water supply for Birmingham. During WWII, the earliest of the dams was used to perfect the 'bouncing bomb' used in the storied Dambusters raid on targets in Germany's Ruhr Valley. Together their reservoirs now provide over 70 million gallons of water daily for Birmingham and parts of South and Mid-Wales, and generate some 3.9 megawatts of hydroelectric power.

The valley's **visitor centre** (☑ 01597-810880; www.elanvalley.org.uk; B4518; ☉ 9am-5pm Easter-Oct, 10am-4pm Nov-Mar) houses informative exhibits, rents bicycles (£7/26 per hour/day) and offers activities such as birdwatching safaris, an autumnal 'Walking Fest' and ranger tours inside Pen y Garreg dam. It's downstream of the lowest dam, 3 miles from Rhayader on the B4518.

Unless you have your own transport, the only route to the Elan Valley is to walk, cycle or take a taxi from Rhayader.

☎) This tiny 16th-century inn, just over the bridge to Cwmdauddwr (the village adjoining Rhayader), is the pick of the local places to drink. It's so small that its toilets are across the road and there's a trapdoor in the floor so darts players don't headbutt the ceiling. A very welcoming place, it serves real ales and hearty pub classics.

❶ Getting There & Away

Buses stopping here include the X47 to Llandrindod Wells (£2.30, 17 minutes, up to seven per day), and the X75 to Newtown (£4.25, one hour, two daily), Welshpool (£6.60, two hours, two daily) and Shrewsbury (£9.50, 2¾ hours, one daily).

Montgomery

☑ 01686 / POP 966

Set around a market square lined with handsome stone and brick houses, and overlooked by the ruins of a Norman castle, genteel Montgomery is one of the prettiest small towns in the country. A charming mixture of Georgian, Victorian and timber-framed houses (many marked by helpful historical plaques) lines the streets and there are a number of excellent places to eat.

A curiosity, for travellers, is **Bunners** (☑ 01686-668308; www.bunners.co.uk; Arthur St; ☉ 9am-5.30pm Mon-Fri, to 5pm Sat), an old-fashioned ironmongers that seems to sell everything under the sun and which attracts customers from miles away. A mile east of town is one of the best-preserved sections of Offa's Dyke, with 6m-high ditches flanking the B4386.

◉ Sights

St Nicholas' Church CHURCH
(Church Bank; ☉ 9am-dusk) Evocative Norman St Nicholas' Church dates from 1226 and boasts a vaulted ceiling decorated with intricate coloured bosses, a beautifully carved pre-Reformation rood screen and striking mid-19th-century stained-glass windows. Look out for the elaborate canopied tomb of local landowner Sir Richard Herbert and his wife Magdalen, parents of Elizabethan poet George Herbert.

Cloverlands Model Car Museum MUSEUM
(☑ 01686-668004; www.cloverlandsmuseum.wales; Montgomery Institute, Arthur St; adult/child £3/free; ☉ 10am-3pm Fri, 2.15-4.15pm Sat & Sun Apr-Oct, 10am-3pm Fri, 2-4.15pm Sat Nov-Mar; ⊕) With over 3000 exhibits, Cloverlands is one of the most extensive collections of its kind in the UK, and a must for model-car lovers. Around half the cars are on loan from one collector, Gillian Rogers, including quarter-scale, working models of a Fiat 1936 Topolino and a 1935 Singer Le Mans, built especially for the collector and her sister. There are special openings on bank holidays, and appointments can be made for out-of-hours openings.

Montgomery Castle RUINS
(☉ 10am-6pm Apr-Jun, to 9pm Jul–mid-Sep) FREE
Rising from the craggy outcrop above the town are the ruins of Montgomery Castle. Work on the Norman fortress began in 1223, and in 1267, during treaty negotiations at the castle, Henry III granted Llywelyn ap Gruffydd the title of Prince of Wales. Little remains of the once-great fortress, but the

views over the chequerboard countryside are beautiful.

🛏 Sleeping & Eating

Dragon Hotel INN ££
(📞01686-668359; www.dragonhotel.com; Market Sq; s/d from £63/79; 🅿️🛜🏊) Popular with walkers, this 17th-century half-timbered coaching inn has 20 en-suite rooms, a common snug (the Den), a pool and a restaurant run by Bistro 7, formerly of Welshpool (mains £13 to £15, kitchen open 11.30am to 3pm and 6pm to 8.45pm). The bar is as good a place as any to try ales brewed at Monty's, just down the road.

Castle Kitchen CAFE £
(📞01686-668795; www.castlekitchen.org; 8 Broad St; lunch £8; ⏰9am-4.30pm Mon-Sat, from 11am Sun) This lovely little deli-cafe overlooking Monty's picturesque heart is perfect for stocking up on bottles, butter, charcuterie and other supplies for a picnic on Offa's Dyke or in the surrounding hills. Or you can just relax in-house, enjoying the unforced friendliness of the service and a wonderful selection of soups, breads, sandwiches, daily specials and, of course, luscious cakes.

★ Checkers FRENCH £££
(📞01686-669822; www.thecheckersmontgomery.co.uk; Broad St; 6 courses £65; ⏰dinner Tue-Sat; 🛜) One of the main drawcards of Montgomery is this truly excellent restaurant-with-rooms. With an inquisitive modern-French approach to fresh, locally sourced ingredients, first-rate service, and dishes such as steamed halibut with scallop mousse, pea purée, bacon and mint dressing, it's earned a loyal fan base and one of Wales' seven Michelin stars.

Upstairs, this 17th-century coaching inn once again welcomes guests, with five quietly stylish rooms with extra-comfy beds, iPod docks and blissful bathrooms. Bed-and-dinner packages are available from £285.

ℹ️ Getting There & Away

Up to six X71 and 81 buses per day run to Welshpool (18 minutes) and Newtown (23 minutes).

Welshpool (Y Trallwng)

📞01938 / POP 5994
The English originally called this place Pool, after the 'pills' – boggy, marshy ground (long since drained) along the nearby River Severn. It was changed in 1835 to Welshpool,

so nobody would get confused with Poole in Dorset. Set below a steeply wooded hill, it's a handsome market town with a mixture of Tudor, Georgian and Victorian buildings along its main streets but few other distractions in the town centre and a dearth of places to stay or eat. Perhaps its loudest contemporary claim to fame is the Monday livestock market, one of the largest in Western Europe. More compelling, to be sure, however, are the peripheral sights, such as glorious Powis Castle and the narrow-gauge Welshpool & Llanfair Light Railway.

👁 Sights & Activities

★ Powis Castle CASTLE
(NT; 📞01938-551944; www.nationaltrust.org.uk; adult/child castle & gardens £13/6.50; ⏰gardens 10am-6pm, castle 11am-5pm; 🅿️♿) Surrounded by magnificent gardens, the redbrick Powis Castle was originally constructed in the 13th century by Gruffydd ap Gwenwynwyn, prince of Powys, and subsequently enriched by generations of the Herbert and Clive families. The castle's highlight, the Clive Museum, houses exquisite treasures brought back from India and the Far East by Clive of India (British conqueror of Bengal at the Battle of Plassey in 1757) and his son Edward, who married the daughter of the first earl of Powys.

Powysland Museum & Montgomery Canal MUSEUM
(📞01938-554656; www.powys.gov.uk; Canal Wharf; ⏰10.30am-1pm & 2-5pm Mon-Fri, 11am-2pm Sat Jun-Aug, closed Wed Sep-May; ♿) FREE
The Montgomery Canal originally ran for 35 miles, starting at Newtown and ending at Frankton Junction in Shropshire, where it joined the Llangollen Canal. Beside Canal Wharf in central Welshpool is the Powysland Museum, marked outside by a big blue handbag (an Andy Hancock sculpture to commemorate the Queen's jubilee). Inside, the museum tells the story of the county, with fascinating details such as beautifully painted narrow-boat gear and a Roman coin hoard.

Welshpool & Llanfair Light Railway TOURS
(📞01938-810441; www.wllr.org.uk; Raven Sq; adult/child £13.70/4.50; ⏰Mar-Oct; ♿) This sturdy narrow-gauge railway, completed in 1903 to bring livestock to market, runs through the pretty Banwy Valley. It's an 8-mile, 50-minute journey up steep inclines from Raven Square Station to Llanfair Caereinion. Check online for departure times. Closed in 1956, the line was reopened seven years later by

enthusiastic volunteers and now even offers courses in steam-engine driving (£395).

🛏 Sleeping & Eating

Long Mountain B&B ££
(☑ 01938-553456; www.longmountainbandb.co.uk; Hope Rd, Little Hope; s/d £66/88; 🅿 🛜) Evelyn and Mike, your relaxed hosts, run this purpose-built B&B located 2 miles from Welshpool. A modern extension to a 400-year-old timber-frame house, it has three guest rooms with top-quality fittings, solid oak furniture, king-size beds with Egyptian-cotton linen, and marble bathrooms. Offa's Dyke Path runs almost past the guesthouse, and there are wonderful views. No children under 16.

To get here, head east on the B4381, turning left onto the B4388 and then right onto Hope Rd.

Corn Store INTERNATIONAL ££
(☑ 01938-554614; 4 Church St; mains £14-16, 2-course menu £17; ☺ noon-2pm & 6-9pm Tue-Sat, noon-4pm Sun) If Welshpool has a dining institution, this is it. Run by chef-proprietor Rebecca for over 25 years, it has avocado walls and cheery round, rainbow mirrors that overlook families of regulars tucking into Euro-Med-Asian dishes such as sea bass with chilli and crayfish tails or duck breast in a blackberry and sloe-gin sauce. The best and friendliest place in town.

ℹ Information

Tourist Office (☑ 01938-552043; www.visit welshpool.org.uk; 1 Vicarage Gardens, Church St; ☺ 9.30am-4.30pm Mon-Sat, 10am-4pm Sun) Has a bed-booking service and plenty of information on sights and activities in Welshpool.

ℹ Getting There & Away

Bus X75 runs to Newtown (£2.70, 48 minutes, up to nine per day) and Shrewsbury (£3.10, 48 minutes); the daily National Express runs to Aberystwyth (£15, 1¾ hours) in one direction and Birmingham (£13, 2¼ hours) in the other.

The daily National Express (www.national express.com) coach through Welshpool runs west to Aberystwyth (£12, 1¾ hours) and east to Shrewsbury (£6.40, 22 minutes), Birmingham (£13, 2¼ hours) and London (from £28, 5½ hours).

Welshpool is on the Cambrian Line, which heads east from Aberystwyth (£16, 1½ hours) to Shrewsbury (£6.10, 22 minutes) and Birmingham (£19, 1½ hours) every hour or two; in the other direction, there's Newtown (£5.50, 15 minutes) and Machynlleth (£14, 52 minutes).

Machynlleth

☑ 01654 / POP 2214

Little Machynlleth (ma-*hun*-khleth) punches well above its weight. Saturated in historical significance, the town was the site in which nationalist hero Owain Glyndŵr established the country's first parliament in 1404. Oddly, that legacy is not widely known or enthusiastically celebrated, and Machynlleth is perhaps better known as the country's green capital – thanks to the Centre for Alternative Technology, 3 miles north, and its proximity to cycle-path-laced and forested hills.

Struggling like many Welsh provincial centres to keep its economic engines firing, Machynlleth is still a surprisingly cosmopolitan local town, with some fantastic eating and sleeping options, mainly in the surrounding countryside.

◉ Sights

★ **MOMA Machynlleth** GALLERY
(☑ 01654-703355; http://moma.machynlleth.org. uk; Penrallt St; ☺ 10am-4pm Mon-Sat) 🆓 Housed partly in the **Tabernacle**, a former Wesleyan chapel, the Museum of Modern Art exhibits work by contemporary Welsh artists in a permanent collection supplemented by ever-changing temporary exhibitions. The chapel itself has the feel of a courtroom, but the acoustics are superb – it's used for concerts, theatre and August's annual celebration of international music, the Machynlleth Festival.

Owain Glyndŵr Centre MUSEUM
(Canolfan Owain Glyndŵr; ☑ 01654-702932; www. canolfanglyndwr.org; Maengwyn St; ☺ 10am-4pm Easter-Sep) 🆓 Housed in a rare example of a late-medieval Welsh town house, the Owain Glyndŵr Centre houses an exhibition telling the story of the Welsh hero's fight for independence and starring the Pennal letter, written by Glyndŵr in pursuit of an alliance with the French. Although it's called the Old Parliament Building, it was probably built around 1460, some 50 years after Glyndŵr instituted his parliament on this site, but it's believed to closely resemble the former venue.

If it's locked, ask for the key at the Caffi Alys next door.

🛏 Sleeping

★ **Beudy Banc** CABIN £
(☑ 01650-511495; www.beudybanc.co.uk; Abercegir; cabins from £75) 🅿 Set on a working sheep

farm nestled in the folds of the Dyfi Valley, this wonderful place offers cosy cabins in grassy meadows with glorious views. There's a fire pit and a walking trail across the farm that links up with **Glyndŵr's Way** (http://nationaltrail.co.uk/glyndwrs-way), but the real joy here is in the two excellent mountain-bike descents and the network of tracks and bridleways.

Beudy Banc is about 3 miles northeast of Machynlleth off the A489; look for the small turn-off signed simply 'Banc'.

★ **Glandyfi Castle**   B&B ££
(☑ 01654-781238; www.glandyficastle.co.uk; Glandyfi; r from £100; P 🛜) Built in 1820 as a gift from a slave-owning Caribbean planter to his wife, this quirky Regency Gothic castle has been brought back to life as a luxury B&B. Three rooms blend classical styling with modern sensibilities, while the turrets, towers and superb views over the 18-hectare garden to the Dyfi estuary make it an incredibly special place to stay.

The castle is 6 miles southwest of Machynlleth, off the A487.

Wynnstay Wales   HOTEL ££
(☑ 01654-702941; www.wynnstay.wales; Maengwyn St; s/d £65/115; P 🛜) This erstwhile Georgian coaching inn (1780) remains the best all-rounder in town, with 22 charming older-style rooms, one with a four-poster bed, and creaky, uneven floors. Downstairs there's a good restaurant, a wine shop with Italian single-estate varietals on tap and, in the courtyard on Friday and Saturday nights between Easter and October, a wood-fired pizzeria (pizzas £10).

★ **Living Room Treehouses**   CABIN £££
(☑ 01172-047830; www.living-room.co; d/f 3 days & 2 nights £379/399; P) Wonderfully designed, these six cosy, rustic-glam tree houses blend organically into an enchanted forest off the A470. You're as close to nature as can be (up a tree!), yet the beds are luxurious, insulation and wood-burning stoves keep you warm all year, and the seclusion is glorious (all houses are set generously apart). Arrival days are Sunday, Wednesday and Friday.

🍴 Eating

Market   MARKET £
(Maengwyn St; ⊙ Wed) Chartered by Edward I himself, in 1291, the Wednesday street market has been going ever since and remains a lively affair.

CENTRE FOR ALTERNATIVE TECHNOLOGY (CAT)

A small but dedicated band of enthusiasts have spent 40 years practising sustainability at the thought-provoking CAT (CAT; Canolfan y Dechnoleg Amgen; ☑ 01654-705950; www.cat.org.uk; Pantperthog; adult/child £8.50/4; ⊙ 10am-5pm; P 🛜) 🍴, set in the Dyfi Unesco Biosphere Reserve, north of Machynlleth. Founded in 1974 (well ahead of its time), the CAT is an education and visitor centre that demonstrates practical solutions for sustainability. There are 3 hectares of displays dealing with topics such as composting, organic gardening, environmentally friendly construction, renewable energy sources and sewage treatment and recycling.

Number Twenty One   WELSH ££
(☑ 01654-703382; www.numbertwentyone.co.uk; 21 Maengwyn St; mains £13-15; ⊙ noon-10pm Wed-Sun; 🖉 🍴) Run by a passionate young foodie couple with ambitions that exceed the usual small-town bistro, Number Twenty One has been popular since the day it opened. The food is imaginative without being fussy, the service is friendly but professional, children are welcome and nothing seems too much trouble. Space is limited, so book ahead.

★ **Ynyshir Hall**   GASTRONOMY £££
(☑ 01654-781209; www.ynyshirhall.co.uk; Eglwysfach; 12-course lunch/19-course dinner £75/125; ⊙ noon-2pm & 7-9pm Wed-Sat; P 🛜) Foraged wild foods, the best local meat and seafood and his own kitchen-garden produce give Gareth Ward of Ynyshir Hall the foundations to concoct some of Wales' most wonderful food. A Michelin-starred restaurant within a luxurious country retreat speciously associated with Queen Victoria, Yynyshir offers set menus that reach new heights for brevity ('mackerel', 'strawberry') but herald total gastronomic joy.

ℹ️ Getting There & Away

If you're on a bike, Lôn Las Cymru (Sustrans National Cycling Network Route 8) passes through Machynlleth, heading north to Corris and southeast to Rhayader.

Bus routes include the X28 to Aberystwyth (£4.25, 40 minutes, up to 10 per day); the frequent T2 to Dolgellau (£3.45, 30 minutes),

Porthmadog (£5.40, 80 minutes), Caernarfon (£5.40, 2¼ hours) and Bangor (£5.40, 2¾ hours); and up to nine 34 services per day to the Centre for Alternative Technology (p697) (£2.15, seven minutes) and Corris (£2.50, 15 minutes).

The bus stops for **Newtown** (Maengwyn St) and **other destinations** (Pentrerhedyn St) are either side of the market cross in the centre of town.

By train, Machynlleth is on the frequent Cambrian and Cambrian Coast Lines. Destinations include Aberystwyth (£6.90, 35 minutes), Porthmadog (£15, two hours), Pwllheli (£17, 2½ hours), Newtown (£10, 35 minutes) and Birmingham (£24, 2½ hours).

CEREDIGION

Bordered by Cardigan Bay on one side and the Cambrian Mountains on the other, Ceredigion (pronounced with a 'dig', not a 'didge') is an ancient Welsh kingdom founded by the 5th-century chieftain Ceredig. The rural communities here escaped the population influxes of the south's coal-mining valleys and the north's slate-mining towns, and, consequently, the Welsh language is stronger here than in any other part of the country except Gwynedd and Anglesey.

The lack of heavy industry also left Ceredigion with some of Britain's cleanest beaches that, with no train access south of Aberystwyth, tend to be pleasantly uncrowded. Adding to the isolation is the natural barrier known as the 'Green Desert of Wales' – the barren uplands of the Cambrian Mountains. Despite recent interest fuelled by the locally made bilingual detective series *Hinterland/Y Gwyll*, Ceredigion's sandy coves, river valleys, quiet market towns and arid mountains are as off-the-beaten-track as Wales gets.

ⓘ Getting There & Away

Aberystwyth is the main rail hub in Ceredigion, linking with Shrewsbury in England (£21, 1¾ hours, frequent) and Pwllheli on the Llŷn Peninsula (£16.60, 2¾ to 3¾ hours).

Aberystwyth

☑ 01970 / POP 17,183

Sweeping around the curve of Cardigan Bay, the lively university town of Aberystwyth (aber-*ist*-with) has a stunning location but a bit of an identity crisis. Student bars and cheap restaurants line the streets, and the

flashing lights of traditional amusements twinkle from the pier, but tucked away in the side streets is a handful of chichi boutiques and organic, wholefood cafes. During term time the bars are buzzing and students play football on the promenade, while in summer the bucket-and-spade brigade enjoys the beach. Meanwhile, the vestiges of a stately seaside resort can be glimpsed in the terrace of grand Georgian houses painted in subtle pastel hues that line the promenade.

Welsh is widely spoken here and the locals are proud of their heritage. Catching a show at the Arts Centre (p701), hearing the **male voice choir** (☑ 01970-623800; www.aber choir.co.uk; Plascrug Ave; ◷ 7-8.30pm Thu) perform, or simply soaking up the sunset over Cardigan Bay are quintessential experiences.

◉ Sights

Marine Tce, with its impressive sweep of imposing pastel-hued houses overlooking North Beach, harks back to the town's Victorian heyday as a fashionable resort. When you reach the bottom of the 1.5-mile prom, it's customary to kick the white bar, although the locals can't seem to explain the rationale behind this ritual.

North Beach is lined by somewhat shabby Georgian hotels, albeit with a couple of notable exceptions. **Royal Pier** (☑ 01970-636100; www.royalpier.co.uk; Marine Tce; ◷ 10am-11pm, club closes 3am Tue, Wed, Fri & Sat; ♿), the grand **Old College** (www.aber.ac.uk/en/oldcollege; 6 King St; ◷ 8am-9pm Mon-Fri, 10am-4pm Sat term time, 8am-7pm Mon-Fri holidays) and the enigmatic, sparse ruins of **Aberystwyth Castle** FREE are the major sights here.

The prom pivots before leading along **South Beach** – a more desolate but still attractive seafront. Many locals prefer the stony but emptier **Tanybwlch Beach**, just south of the harbour, where the Rivers Rheidol and Ystwyth meet. **Pen Dinas**, the upland rising behind Tanybwlch, is the site of the important Iron Age hill fort **Dinas Maelor**. While the outline of the fort is still visible, the peak is now dominated by a monument to Wellington.

National Library of Wales   LIBRARY
(☑ 01970-632800; www.llgc.org.uk; Penglais Rd; ◷ 9.30am-6pm Mon-Fri, to 5pm Sat) FREE On a hilltop east of town with a sensational view of Cardigan Bay, the National Library is a cultural powerhouse. Founded in 1916, it holds millions of books in many languages – as a copyright library it has copies of every

Aberystwyth

book published in the UK. Among its 25,000 manuscripts are such gems as the 13th-century *Black Book of Carmarthen* (the oldest existing Welsh text), a text of Chaucer penned by his scribe Adam Pinkhurst and a 1st edition of *Paradise Lost*.

Other galleries display an ever-stimulating set of changing exhibitions featuring the library's collection and Welsh heritage in general.

Ceredigion Museum   MUSEUM
(☎01970-633088; www.ceredigionmuseum.wales; Coliseum Theatre, Terrace Rd; ◷10am-5pm Mon-Sat) FREE This museum is in the three-storey Coliseum, which opened in 1905 as a theatre, then from 1932 served as a cinema promising 'amusement without vulgarity'. The elegant interior retains its stage, around which are entertaining exhibitions from the museum's collection of 60,000-plus artefacts on Aberystwyth's history – everything from old chemist furnishings and hand-knitted woollen

Aberystwyth

knickers to a mini puppet theatre and a replica 1850s cottage. There are temporary exhibitions (some with entry fees), and even yoga from 5.15pm on Thursday (£5).

🏃 Activities

★ Vale of Rheidol Railway
RAIL

(Rheilffordd Cwm Rheidol; ☏ 01970-625819; www.rheidolrailway.co.uk; Park Ave; adult/child return £22/10; ☺ up to 5 daily mid-Feb–Oct, Sun only Nov, closed Dec–mid-Feb; ♿) This scenic narrow-gauge railway is one of Aberystwyth's most popular attractions. Steam locomotives built between 1923 and 1938 have been lovingly restored by volunteers and chug for almost 12 miles up the beautiful wooded valley of the River Rheidol to Devil's Bridge. The line opened in 1902 to bring lead and timber out of the valley, but WWI and the closure of the mines it served curtailed its profitability.

Cliff Railway
CABLE CAR

(Rheilffordd y Graig; ☏ 01970-617642; www.aberystwythcliffrailway.co.uk; Cliff Tce; adult/child one-way £4/2.50, return £5/3.50; ☺ 10am-5pm Apr-Oct, to 6pm high season, shorter hours Nov-Mar; ♿) If your legs aren't up to the climb of Constitution Hill (it's 130m, and you can't drive), catch a lift on the trundling little Cliff Railway, the UK's longest electric funicular (and possibly its slowest, too, at a breakneck 4mph). It must have been glacial when first built, in 1896, when it was powered by a water-balance system.

Rheidol Cycle Trail
CYCLING

(www.discoverceredigion.co.uk; ♿) Sticking mainly to designated cycle paths and quiet country lanes, the 17-mile Rheidol Cycle Trail heads from Aberystwyth Harbour to Devil's Bridge through the beautiful Rheidol Valley. Along the way it passes the Woodland Trust's Coed Geufron, and side routes lead to Bwlch Nant yr Arian (☏ 01970-890453; www.naturalresources.wales; Ponterwyd; parking 2hr £1.50; ☺ visitor centre & cafe 10am-5pm), Rheidol Power Station and Rheidol Mines. The last section is very steep.

Ystwyth Trail
CYCLING

(www.discoverceredigion.co.uk; ♿) Suitable for cyclists and walkers, this 21-mile waymarked route mainly follows the former Great Western Railway from Aberystwyth southeast to Tregaron, shadowing the River Ystwyth for the first 12 miles and ending in the Teifi Valley. Pick up the trail from the footbridge on Riverside Tce in Aberystwyth, or start from Tregaron if you prefer heading downhill.

🛏 Sleeping

★ Gwesty Cymru
HOTEL ££

(☏ 01970-612252; www.gwestycymru.com; 19 Marine Tce; s/d from £70/90; ☺ restaurant noon-2.30pm & 6-9pm; 🛜) A real gem, the 'Wales Hotel' is a charismatic boutique property right on the waterfront with a strong sense of Welsh identity. Local slate features throughout, paired with rich aubergine carpets and contemporary styling. Of the eight en-suite rooms, four have sea views, and rooms 4 and 6 have baths.

Bodalwyn
B&B ££

(☏ 01970-612578; www.bodalwyn.co.uk; Queen's Ave; s/d from £52/82; 🛜) Simultaneously up-market and homely, this handsome Edwardian B&B offers tasteful rooms with sparkling new bathrooms and a hearty cooked breakfast (with vegetarian options). Three of the rooms have sea views, but ask for room 3, with the bay window.

🍴 Eating

Treehouse
CAFE £

(☏ 01970-615791; www.treehousewales.co.uk; 14 Baker St; mains £8-9; ☺ 10am-5pm Mon-Sat; ♿) Spread over two floors of a Victorian house above an organic grocer, this excellent cafe uses local produce in a wide range of tempting dishes catering equally to vegetarians, vegans and meat-lovers. Perhaps the best bet in town for lunch (noon to 3.30pm), it serves imaginative fare such as harissa roast chicken and brown-lentil dahl with spicy bean fritters.

★ Ultracomida
TAPAS ££

(☏ 01970-630686; www.ultracomida.co.uk; 31 Pier St; tapas £7-8; ☺ 10am-5pm Mon to 10pm Tue-Sat, noon-4pm Sun; ♿) Aber is lucky to have Ultracomida – an importer, deli and restaurant that's clearly motivated by a personal love of all things Iberian. Out front is an exceptional collection of Spanish charcuterie, cheese, dry goods and sweetmeats (with nods to France and Wales), while out back is a convivial little dining room serving great tapas and wine without pretension.

★ Y Ffarmers
PUB FOOD ££

(☏ 01974-261275; www.yffarmers.co.uk; Llanfihangel y Creuddyn; mains £15-18; ☺ 6-11pm Tue-Fri, noon-11pm Sat, noon-3pm Sun, extended hours high season) Gutted by fire in early 2018 but painstakingly restored, this outstanding pub is the main reason to visit the pretty hamlet of Llanfihangel y Creuddyn, 7 miles southeast of Aber. Ostensibly another snug, whitebrick house of assembly, it does fantastic Welsh pub food: cockle cakes with laverbread sauce, guinea fowl with tarragon and shallots, and other lip-smacking creations.

Drinking & Entertainment

White Horse PUB
(01970-615234; www.whitehorseaberystwyth. co.uk; Upper Portland St; ⊙10am-midnight Sun-Wed, to 1am Thu-Sat;) Spacious, simple and welcoming to all comers, the Horse makes the most of its plum crossroads location with its open, modern feel and picture windows for idly watching passersby outside. Relaxed and sport focused during the day, it gets rammed and rowdy on weekend nights.

Ship & Castle PUB
(07773 778785; 1 High St; ⊙4pm-midnight Mon, 2pm-midnight Tue-Thu, 2pm-1am Fri-Sun;) A sympathetic renovation has left this 1830 pub as cosy and welcoming as ever, while adding big screens for watching the rugby. It's the place to come for real ales, with a large, constantly revolving selection on tap, plus a few ciders.

Aberystwyth Arts Centre PERFORMING ARTS
(Canolfan Y Celfyddydau; box office 01970-623232; www.aberystwythartscentre.co.uk; Penglais Rd; ⊙box office 10am-8pm Mon-Sat, 1.30-5.30pm Sun) One of the largest arts centres in Wales, this happening place stages excellent opera, drama, dance and concerts, plus it has an art gallery, a quality bookshop, and a bar and cafe. The cinema shows a great range of cult and foreign-language movies, and there's always a program of workshops to sign up for.

Part of Aberystwyth University, the centre is on the Penglais campus, half a mile east of town.

Information

Tourist Office (01970-612125; www.discover ceredigion.co.uk; Terrace Rd; ⊙10am-5pm Mon-Sat;) Within the Ceredigion Museum, this office stocks maps and books on local history and has free wi-fi. The helpful staff can arrange accommodation.

Getting There & Away

BUS
Routes include the frequent T2 to Machynlleth (£4.25, 40 minutes), Dolgellau (£5.60, 1¼ hours,), Porthmadog (£5.60, 2¼ hours), Caer-

narfon (£5.60, three hours) and Bangor (£5.60, 3½ hours); the hourly T1C to Carmarthen (£6.10, 1¾ to 2½ hours) and Cardiff (£10, 3½ hours); and the hourly T5/X50 to Aberaeron (£3.80, 40 minutes) and Cardigan (£5.50, 1½ hours).

A daily National Express coach heads to/from Newtown (£13, 80 minutes), Welshpool (£15, 1¾ hours), Shrewsbury (£15, 2¼ hours), Birmingham (£21, four hours) and London (£29, seven hours).

TRAIN
Aberystwyth is the terminus of the Arriva Trains Wales Cambrian Line, which crosses Mid-Wales every two hours en route to Birmingham (£32, three hours) via Machynlleth (£6.90, 35 minutes), Newtown (£14, 1¼ hours), Welshpool (£16, 1½ hours) and Shrewsbury (£21, two hours).

Aberaeron
01545 / POP 1337
Elegant Aberaeron with its brightly painted Georgian houses was once a busy port and ship-building centre, its genteel architecture the result of planned expansion in the early 19th century. The arrival of the railway then made it a popular holiday destination. With heavy industry long gone, today Aberaeron is quietly bucking the trend of economic decline; its stylish streets and much-admired harbour are lined with independent shops and cafes, chic B&Bs and boutique hotels, and a number of excellent restaurants.

Sights

Cardigan Bay Marine
Wildlife Centre WILDLIFE RESERVE
(01545-560224; www.welshwildlife.org; Glanmor Tce, New Quay; ⊙9am-5pm Easter-Oct, to 6pm summer holidays) FREE You can learn more about Cardigan Bay's marine life here (in New Quay, 7 miles from Aberaeron) and also join a dolphin-survey boat trip, as researchers collect data on bottlenose dolphins and other local marine mammals. Trips vary in length and price (two hours aboard the *Sulaire* costs £20; four hours/a full day aboard the *Anna Lloyd* is £38/65) and dates are posted on the website. Call 01545-560032 to ensure the weather-dependent trips are on.

Llanerchaeron HISTORIC BUILDING
(NT; 01545-570200; www.nationaltrust.org.uk/ llanerchaeron; Ciliau Aeron; adult/child £7.80/4.20; ⊙garden 10.30am-5.30pm, villa 11.30am-4pm, shorter hours & villa closed winter;) This beautifully maintained Georgian country estate offers a fascinating insight into the life of the Welsh gentry and their staff 200

years ago. The villa itself was designed by John Nash and is one of his most complete early works, featuring curved walls, false windows and ornate cornices. The estate was self-sufficient and remains virtually unchanged in that respect, with staff tending to the fruit, veg and herbs in the walled garden and looking after rare-breed livestock.

🛌 Sleeping

★ Harbour Master
BOUTIQUE HOTEL **££**

(☑ 01545-570755; www.harbour-master.com; Pen Cei; s/d from £75/120; 🛜) Standing proudly at Aberaeron's harbour entrance, this boutique hotel offers food and accommodation worthy of any chic city bolthole. The striking, violet-painted Georgian buildings hold 13 singularly decorated rooms featuring Frette linens, vintage Welsh blankets, bold colour schemes and high-tech bathrooms. Those in the newly restored grain warehouse have the same contemporary styling, with excellent harbour views.

Downstairs, Harbour Master's renowned restaurant does delightful things with local ingredients such as lobster and crab, and Welsh beef, lamb and cheeses (two-/three-course dinner £28/35). The lively bar offers the same outstanding cooking in a more casual setting (mains £14 to £15). Check the website for dinner-and-room packages and be aware that two-night minimums sometimes apply.

3 Pen Cei
B&B **££**

(☑ 01545-571147; www.pen-cei-guest-house.co.uk; 3 Pen Cei; d from £95; 🛜) Affable owners John and Lesley have refurbished this grand Georgian shipping office beautifully, with crisp linens, bold colour schemes and fresh flowers in rooms all named for major local rivers. The larger ones have super-king beds (one also has a free-standing bath), and the hosts are supremely helpful and welcoming.

ℹ️ Getting There & Away

Between Monday and Saturday, buses T5 and X50 go regularly to Aberystwyth (£3.80, 40 minutes, hourly) and Cardigan (£4.40, 50 minutes to 1¼ hours, hourly).

Cardigan (Aberteifi)

☑ 01239 / POP 4191

Cardigan has the feel of a town waking from its slumber. An important entrepôt and herring fishery in Elizabethan times, it declined with the coming of the railway and the silting up of the River Teifi in the 19th century. Now its surrounding natural beauty, hip craft shops, home-grown fashion labels, gourmet food stores and homely B&Bs are bringing it back to life. Its alternative arts scene is growing and the jumble of historical architecture that lines its streets and lanes has been given a new lease of life. Most importantly, Cardigan Castle has been restored and now serves as a hub of Welsh language, culture and performance.

'Cardigan' is an anglicisation of Ceredigion, the place of Ceredig, but the Welsh name, Aberteifi, refers to its location at the mouth of the River Teifi.

◉ Sights & Activities

★ Cardigan Castle
CASTLE

(Castell Aberteifi; ☑ 01239-615131; www.cardigancastle.com; 2 Green St; adult/child £5/2.70; ⊙ 10am-4pm) Cardigan Castle holds an important place in Welsh culture, having been the venue for the first competitive National Eisteddfod, held in 1176 under the aegis of Lord Rhys ap Gruffydd. Neglected for years, it's sprung from the ashes via a multimillion-pound refurbishment and now stands as a major centre of local Welsh culture, with permanent exhibitions on the castle, Cardigan and the Eisteddfod, live performances, language classes, festivals and more taking place within its hollowed-out walls.

A Bay to Remember
WILDLIFE WATCHING

(☑ 01239-623558; www.baytoremember.co.uk; Prince Charles Quay; 1hr trip adult/child £26/13; ⊙ Mar-Oct) Running one- and two-hour trips into Cardigan Bay from St Dogmaels, Gwbert and Poppit Sands, this operation takes groups out in rigid-hulled inflatable boats to spot bottlenose dolphins, harbour porpoises, grey seals and seabirds; its sighting rate is 70% on short trips and 90% on longer. The booking office is at Prince Charles Quay, on the Teifi.

🛌 Sleeping

Gwbert Hotel
HOTEL **££**

(☑ 01239-612638; https://gwberthotel.com; Gwbert; s/d from £65/85, cottages per week from £526; P 🛜) With unspoilt views from the cliff-lined inlet through which the Teifi flows into Cardigan Bay, and 21 exceedingly comfortable, understated en-suite rooms, the Gwbert is one of Cardigan's most appealing sleeps. Add hearty breakfasts, amazing walking at your doorstep, and the Flat Rock bistro, which elevates pub and bistro classics (mains £12 to £15), and you have a wonderful package.

The Gwbert also runs five self-catering cottages in the area.

Ty-Parc B&B B&B ££
(☑01239-615452; www.ty-parc.com; Park Ave; s/d £60/75; ⓟ⛵) This appealing Edwardian house north of downtown Cardigan offers five bright en-suite rooms decked out in cream shades and blond-wood furnishings. Extra thoughtful touches include radios in the shower, fresh flowers and packed lunches on request. Not suitable for pets or children.

Eating

★Fforest Pizzatipi PIZZA £
(☑01239-612259; www.pizzatipi.co.uk; Cambrian Quay; pizza £7-9; ⊙noon-11pm daily Jul & Aug, 4-11pm Sat & Sun late Jun & Sep) Run by four young brothers, this seasonal pop-up venue is the hottest ticket in town on summer nights. Pizzas pumping from two wood-fired ovens, craft beer, music, smartly chosen events and a buzzing atmosphere all set under a candlelit tepee in a hidden riverside courtyard: what more could you ask for? Food stops at 9pm, 5pm on Sunday.

1176 BISTRO ££
(☑01239-562002; www.cardigancastle.com/dining; Cardigan Castle; lunch mains £6-8, 3-course dinner £28; ⊙10am-4pm Sun-Thu, 10am-4pm & 6.30-9.30pm Fri & Sat) Named for the year of Wales' first National Eisteddfod, held right here at Cardigan Castle, this glass-and-slate bistro is an integral part of the monument's 2015 rebirth. Popular for lunch and afternoon tea (£12 per person), it also opens for dinner on Friday and Saturday, when the produce of the castle's kitchen garden stars.

☆ Entertainment

Theatr Mwldan THEATRE
(☑01239-621200; www.mwldan.co.uk; Bath House Rd; ⊙from 5pm Mon, from 10am Tue-Sat, from noon Sun until last performance; ⛵) Located in the former slaughterhouse, Theatr Mwldan stages comedy, drama, dance, music and films, and has an art gallery and a good cafe.

CARDIGAN BAY'S DOLPHINS

Cardigan Bay is home to an amazingly rich variety of marine animals and plants, but the star attraction is Europe's largest pod of bottlenose dolphins. With reliable sightings from May to September, there are few places where these sociable creatures are more easily seen in the wild. Along with the dolphins, harbour porpoises, Atlantic grey seals and a variety of bird life are regularly seen, as well as seasonal visitors such as sunfish, basking sharks and leatherback turtles.

Some of the best places to spot bottlenose dolphins from the shore are the beaches around New Quay: New Quay North, Little Quay, Cwmtydu and Llanina are good bets, as are the beautiful sandy beaches at Penbryn and Tresaith north of Cardigan. Aberystwyth, Aberporth and Mwnt also have regular sightings.

You can learn more about Cardigan Bay's marine life at the Cardigan Bay Marine Wildlife Centre (p701), in New Quay.

In summer there are open-air productions in the castle.

ⓘ Information

Tourist Office (☑01239-613230; www.discoverceredigion.co.uk; Theatr Mwldan, Bath House Rd; ⊙10am-5pm Tue, Wed, Fri & Sat) In the lobby of the Theatr Mwldan; offers accommodation bookings and general information.

ⓘ Getting There & Away

Bus routes include the hourly T5/X50 to Aberystwyth (£5.50, 1½ hours); 407 to St Dogmaels (eight minutes) and Poppit Sands (15 minutes); 460 to Carmarthen (90 minutes); and the Poppit Rocket (405) to Fishguard (90 minutes). The **bus station** (Finch Sq) is on Finch Sq.

Bikes can be hired from **New Image Bicycles** (☑01239-621275; www.bikebikebike.co.uk; 29-30 Pendre; per half-day/day £18/23; ⊙10am-5pm Mon-Sat) for cycling around Cardigan Bay and the Teifi Valley.

Snowdonia & North Wales

Best Places to Eat

➡ Tyddyn Llan (p723)

➡ Hayloft Restaurant (p734)

➡ Watson's Bistro (p735)

➡ Tredici Italian Kitchen (p740)

➡ Y Sgwâr (p725)

Best Places to Stay

➡ Totters (p728)

➡ Bodysgallen Hall (p738)

➡ Ffynnon (p711)

➡ Ruthin Castle (p706)

➡ Tŷ Newydd (p726)

➡ Coed-y-Celyn Hall (p717)

Why Go?

Rugged mountain trails, historic train lines, World Heritage castles and rejuvenated seaside towns ensure North Wales holds its own against attractions down south. The region is dominated by Snowdonia National Park, where mighty peaks scrape moody skies.

Protected by such a formidable mountain shield, it's little wonder that the less-visited Llŷn Peninsula and the ancient island enclave of Anglesey have retained their traditional language and culture.

In fact, the whole region feels properly Welsh: you'll hear the language on the street, see the Celtic legacy in the landscape, and soak up the cultural pride in galleries, museums and attractions, all the way from the beaches of the North Coast to the river-threaded heartland of northeast Wales. In many ways, North Wales distills the very essence of Welshness – just don't mention that to the folks in Cardiff.

When to Go

➡ April to July are the driest months, while July and August are warmest.

➡ The best months to hit the mountains and coast paths are June and July.

➡ The Snowdon train runs to the summit between Easter and November.

➡ In July, hardcore runners compete during the Snowdon Race, and Llangollen holds its International Musical Eisteddfod and Fringe Festival.

➡ September is another big month for events, with Bala's triathlon, Barmouth's arts and walking festivals and Portmeirion's wonderful Festival No 6.

➡ Snow starts to fall in the mountains in October and lingers on the paths until May.

Snowdonia & North Wales Highlights

1 Cader Idris (p711)
Climbing Snowdonia's second-most-famous peak.

2 Pontcysyllte Aqueduct (p707) Marvelling at a pinnacle of Georgian civil engineering.

3 Blaenau Ffestiniog (p715) Testing your claustrophobia in gloomy slate caverns.

4 Welsh Highland Railway (p724) Taking a coast-to-coast journey on a narrow-gauge railway.

5 Braich-y-Pwll (p726) Gazing towards the magical 'Pilgrims' Island' of Bardsey.

6 Beddgelert (p722) Wandering among slate cottages and along chuckling rivers.

7 Harlech Castle (p715) Enjoying views of Cardigan Bay and Snowdon from the battlements.

8 Beaumaris (p739) Falling for the Georgian charms of Anglesey's finest town.

9 Caernarfon Castle (p727) Witnessing the castle's Byzantine beauty and strength.

NORTH WALES BORDERLANDS

The northeastern counties of Denbighshire, Wrexham and Flintshire are a baffling jumble of the gritty and the gorgeous. From 1974 to 1996 they were all part of the county of Clwyd, before being broken up and reverting to their far older names. Surprisingly, the best bits are furthest from the coast, particularly in the wild hills and lush farmland of Denbighshire's southern reaches. It's well worth pausing here as you make your way towards Snowdonia.

❶ Getting There & Away

The principal entry points to the region are **Wrexham**, with trains to Chester (£5.60, 20 minutes), Birmingham (£10.50, 1¾ hours) and London (£39, two changes, 4½ hours); and **Llangollen**, on the T3 bus route to Wrexham (30 minutes) and National Express to Wrexham (£3.60, 25 minutes), Shrewsbury (£9.40, one change, 2½ hours) and Birmingham (£17, one change, four hours).

Ruthin

📞 01824 / POP 5654

Tucked away in the bucolic Clwyd valley, well off any tourist route, Ruthin (*rith*-in) is an attractive, lost-in-time hilltop town that's somewhat surprisingly the administrative hub of Denbighshire. In the Middle Ages it was an important market town and textile producer. There are still livestock markets held here three times a week, as well as a produce market on Friday morning and a general market on Thursday.

The heart of Ruthin is St Peter's Sq, lined with an impressive collection of heritage buildings, including a 1401 half-timbered courthouse (now a bank) and St Peter's Collegiate Church, the oldest parts of which date from 1310.

◉ Sights

Nantclwyd y Dre   HISTORIC BUILDING
(📞 01824-706868; www.denbighshire.gov.uk; Castle St; adult/child £5/4; ⊗11am-4pm Mon & Wed, to 5pm Sat, to 3pm Tue & Sun Jul & Aug, shorter hours Apr-Jun & Sep) Dating from 1435, half-timbered Nantclwyd y Dre is thought to be the oldest town house in Wales. It originally belonged to a family of weavers and it retains a palpable sense of antiquity. The rooms have been restored and furnished to reflect the era of each addition, offering a window into the world of the various families that lived in them. The 13th-century Lord's Garden, behind the house, has been restored and is once again a green and pleasant place.

Ruthin Craft Centre   ARTS CENTRE
(📞 01824-704774; www.ruthincraftcentre.org.uk; Park Rd; ⊗10am-5.30pm; 🅿) FREE This is an excellent gallery and arts hub. Aside from the three galleries – which do great work bringing the best of local photography, painting and sculpture to light, and show many pieces for sale – the complex includes artists' studios, public workshops and talks, a very nice cafe and shop, and an unstaffed information centre.

Ruthin Gaol   HISTORIC BUILDING
(📞 01824-708281; www.denbighshire.gov.uk; 46 Clwyd St; adult/child £5/4; ⊗10am-5pm Wed-Mon Apr-Sep) This sombre building is the only Pentonville-style Victorian prison in Britain that's open to visitors. A free audio guide allows you to follow the sentence of an imaginary prisoner, while information panels in the cells fill you in on all the fascinating and grisly details of day-to-day prison life and the daring escapes of John Jones, the 'Welsh Houdini', banged up here in the 1870s. Pentonville-style prisons employed the 'separate system' of isolating and observing inmates.

🛏 Sleeping & Eating

★**Ruthin Castle Hotel**   HISTORIC HOTEL ££
(📞 01824-702664; www.ruthincastle.co.uk; Castle St; r/ste from £109/169; 🅿🛜) The forlorn cries of peacocks strutting the gardens of this wonderful hotel are the first hint of the offbeat luxury within. Making unabashed use of a Victorian 'castle' constructed amid the ruins of the real thing (built in the 13th century by an ally of Edward I), its over-the-top grandeur includes a spa, a wood-panelled library/bar, and even a medieval banqueting hall.

Leonardo's   DELI £
(📞 01824-707161; www.leonardosdeli.co.uk; 4 Well St; sandwiches, wraps & salads £4; ⊗9am-4pm Mon-Sat) Run by a Welsh-German couple, this drool-inducing deli offers an abundance of local cheeses, free-range eggs, preserves, spirits and top-notch pies (its chicken, leek and laverbread was champion of the 2011 British Pie Awards).

★**On the Hill**   MODERN BRITISH ££
(📞 01824-707736; www.onthehillrestaurant.co.uk; 1 Upper Clwyd St; mains £16-18, 1-/2-/3-course lunch

ERDDIG

For a glimpse of the life of the British upper class in the 18th and 19th centuries, and the 'upstairs-downstairs' social hierarchy of their bygone world, the stately house of **Erddig** (NT; ☑ 01978-355314; www.nationaltrust.org.uk/erddig; adult/child £13/6.30, grounds only £8/4; ☺ house 12.30-3.30pm, grounds 10am-5pm, shorter hours winter; P) and its gardens are highly recommended. The house, the earliest parts of which date from 1680, has hardly been altered since the early 20th century; there's no electricity and it still has extensive outbuildings. The house was the Yorke family's ancestral home for more than two centuries (until 1973).

Erddig is about 12 miles northeast of Llangollen in the village of Rhostyllen, signposted off the A483.

£14/17/20; ☺ noon-2pm & 6.30-9pm Mon-Thu, noon-2pm & 5-9pm Fri & Sat) The low ceilings and exposed beams of this 16th-century house near the square make a memorable setting for sophisticated country cooking. Meaty plates such as the Welsh pork trio (crispy belly, bacon-wrapped loin and slow-cooked cheek) are joined by a couple of fish dishes and a veggie option, and most hit the mark. The lunch menu is very good value.

ℹ Getting There & Away

Bus X51 frequently runs between Ruthin and Denbigh (£3.40, 20 minutes), with some services continuing to Wrexham (£3.90, one hour); twice a day the X1 runs to/from Chester (£3.90, one hour).

Llangollen

☑ 01978 / POP 3465

Curving confidently around the banks of the tumbling River Dee (Afon Dyfrdwy) and with the mysterious hilltop ruins of Castell Dinas Brân as a backdrop, picturesque little Llangollen (khlan-*goth*-len) has long been recognised as a scenic gem. The riverside walk, heading west from the 14th-century bridge, has been a popular promenading spot since Victorian times.

Llangollen has a growing summer walking and white-water-rafting scene, while in winter, sometimes under a thick blanket of snow, it just sits there and looks pretty. Two major arts festivals boost tourism, as do railway and engineering enthusiasts interested in the area's industrial legacy. That legacy accounts for the town's present layout: housing was relocated to make way for locomotives.

Llangollen takes its name from St Collen, a 7th-century monk who founded a religious community (*llan*) here. Centuries later it became an important stop on the London-to-Holyhead stagecoach route, linking the British capital to Ireland.

◉ Sights

★ Pontcysyllte Aqueduct & Canal World Heritage Site   CANAL

(☑ 01978-292015, visitor centre 01978-822912; www.pontcysyllte-aqueduct.co.uk; guided tours £3; ☺ visitor centre 10am-4pm Easter-Oct, long weekends Nov, Dec & late Feb-Easter) FREE The preeminent Georgian engineer Thomas Telford (1757-1834) built the Pontcysyllte Aqueduct in 1805 to carry the canal over the River Dee. At 307m long, 3.6m wide, 1.7m deep and 38m high, it is the most spectacular piece of engineering on the entire UK canal system and the highest canal aqueduct ever built. In recognition of this, the aqueduct and an 11-mile stretch of the canal have been declared a Unesco World Heritage Site. FYI, it's pronounced 'pont-kus-*sulth*-teh'.

Plas Newydd   HISTORIC BUILDING

(☑ 01978-862834; www.denbighshire.gov.uk/heritage; Hill St; adult/child £6/5; ☺ 10.30am-5pm Apr-Sep; P ♿) The 18th-century home of the Ladies of Llangollen (Irish aristocrat Lady Eleanor Butler and her companion, Sarah Ponsonby), Plas Newydd is an atmospheric step back in time. The celebrated couple transformed the house from a simple cottage into an elaborate hybrid of Gothic and Tudor styles, complete with stained-glass windows, carved-oak panels and romantic, picturesque formal gardens. Informative self-guided audio tours of the house are available for £1.50, and the tranquil gardens are free to explore.

Valle Crucis Abbey   RUINS

(Abaty Glyn y Groes; Cadw; www.cadw.wales.gov.uk; A542; adult/child Apr-Oct £4/2.40, Nov-Mar

Llangollen

Valle Crucis Abbey (1.5mi)

A542

Castell Dinas Brân (2mi)

Wharf Hill

Abbey Rd

Llangollen Railway

Llangollen Bridge

Llangollen Canal

River Dee

Dee La

Bus Stop

A539

Mill St

Princess St

East St

Greenfield St

Parade St

Bridge St

Market St

Castle St

Oak St

Chapel St

River Dee

West St

Market St Car Park

A5

Berwyn St

A539

Church St

Pontcysyllte Aqueduct (4mi)

Hall St

Victoria Sq

A5

Regent St

Willow St

Hill St

Aber-Adda

Butler's Hill

Vicarage Rd

Llangollen

free; ◷10am-5pm Apr-Oct, to 4pm Nov-Mar) The dignified ruins of this Cistercian abbey are a 2-mile walk north of Llangollen. Founded in 1201 by Madog ap Gruffydd, ruler of northern Powys, its largely Gothic form predates its more famous sibling at Tintern (which, on the eve of Valle Crucis' 1537 dissolution, was its only rival as the richest Cistercian abbey in the land). A small interpretive centre brings the monks' daily routines to life, and plays and other events sometimes animate the peaceful grounds.

Castell Dinas Brân   CASTLE

FREE The ever-visible ragged arches and tumbledown walls of Dinas Brân (Crow

Castle) mark the remnants of a short-lived 13th-century castle of which it was said 'there was not a mightier in Wales nor a better in England'. Burnt by defenders in anticipation of capture by Edward I, there's little left of it today – fabulous 360-degree views over the Dee and surrounding countryside are the real reward for the steep 1½-hour return walk from town.

🏃 Activities

Llangollen Railway   RAIL

(☎01978-860979; www.llangollen-railway.co.uk; Abbey Rd; adult/child return £16/8.50; ◷daily mid-Feb–Oct, reduced services rest of year) This 10-mile jaunt through the Dee Valley via Berwyn (near Horseshoe Falls) and Corwen on the former Ruabon to Barmouth Line is a superb day out for rail fans, families and heritage-lovers alike. There are regular *Thomas the Tank Engine*, *Paddington* and *Peppa Pig* theme days for children, while the real-ale train (£20) is popular with the mature set.

Llangollen Outdoors   OUTDOORS

(☎01978-464066; www.llangollenoutdoors.co.uk; Fringe Shed, Parade St; tubing & rafting £55; ◷8.30am-5pm, shorter hours winter) Catering to the recreational and the serious alike, this outfit runs rafting, tubing, canyoning, canoeing, rock-climbing and bushcraft tasters and trips, starting from £55 per person. Offered year-round, the program even contains such recherché activities as axe throwing.

Welsh Canal Holiday Craft BOATING
(✆01978-860702; www.horsedrawnboats.co.uk; Llangollen Wharf; ⊙mid-Mar–Oct) Peaceful horse-drawn narrowboats depart on 45-minute trips from Llangollen Wharf every half-hour during the school holidays, and hourly otherwise (adult/child £7.50/3.50). Two-hour journeys head to Horseshoe Falls and back, and motorised boats take you up to Pontcysyllte Aqueduct (p707) (adult/child £13/8.50; return journey by coach). Self-drive boats are £135/190 per day/weekend. Reservations strongly advised in busy periods.

⚜️ Festivals & Events

**International Musical
Eisteddfod** PERFORMING ARTS
(✆01978-862000; www.international-eisteddfod.co.uk; day/festival ticket £12/230; ⊙Jul) The International Musical Eisteddfod was established after WWII to promote world harmony. Each July it attracts 4000 participants and 50,000 spectators from around 50 countries, transforming lovely Llangollen into an international village. In addition to folk music and dancing competitions, gala concerts at the Royal International Pavilion feature global stars. It was nominated for the Nobel Peace Prize in 2004.

Llangollen Fringe Festival PERFORMING ARTS
(✆08001-455779; www.llangollenfringe.co.uk; festival ticket £85; ⊙Jul) This small-town, volunteer-run arts festival, held over 11 days from mid-July, manages to attract some surprisingly big names: 2018's line-up included Lee 'Scratch' Perry and Linton Kwesi Johnson. There are also poetry readings, musical narrowboat cruises and steam-train trips, and a final concert in the atmospheric ruins of Valle Crucis Abbey (p707).

🛏️ Sleeping & Eating

Llangollen Hostel HOSTEL £
(✆01978-861773; www.llangollenhostel.co.uk; Isallt, Berwyn St; dm/d £20/50; P🐾) This excellent independent hostel, based in a former family home, has friendly owners and a cared-for feel. It offers various rooms, from private en-suite doubles to a six-bed dorm, as well as an orderly kitchen and a cosy lounge. It actively welcomes cyclists, walkers and canoeists, offering laundry facilities and bike/boat storage. Prices include a self-service cereal-and-toast breakfast.

⭐ **mh Townhaus** B&B ££
(✆01978-860775; www.manorhaus.com; Hill St; d from £110; 🐾) This ultra-stylish guesthouse originally opened as a restaurant-with-rooms but now focuses solely on accommodation. Occupying a multistorey Victorian town house, it boasts nine clean-cut rooms (one sleeping six), a lounge and bar, a library and even a rooftop hot tub. There's also a semi-detached one-bedroom cottage for self-caterers.

Abbey Farm FARMSTAY ££
(✆01978-861297; www.theabbeyfarm.co.uk; pods per night from £50, cottages per week from £240; P) With three stone self-catering cottages (the largest sleeping 14), a campsite in the lee of Valle Crucis Abbey (p707), a farm shop and a tearoom-bistro (serving food 9am to 9pm high season, closed from 5pm Monday to Wednesday low season), Abbey Farm covers many bases. If you can't be bothered setting up your own tent, semifixed camping 'pods' make life easier.

Cornerstones Guesthouse B&B ££
(✆01978-861569; www.cornerstones-guesthouse.co.uk; 19 Bridge St; r from £120; P🐾📶) All stripped floorboards and oak beams, this converted 16th-century house has charm and history in spades. It's now a five-star gold B&B, with fires in winter, fantastic breakfasts and three beautifully appointed rooms. On weekdays from October to March Cornerstones offers three nights for the price of two.

Corn Mill PUB FOOD ££
(✆01978-869555; www.brunningandprice.co.uk/cornmill; Dee Lane; mains £13-17; ⊙kitchen noon-9.30pm; 🐾) The water wheel still turns at the heart of this converted mill, now a cheerful, bustling pub and eatery. The deck over the tumbling Dee is the best spot in town for an unfussy alfresco lunch, perhaps braised lamb shoulder or smoked-haddock fishcakes. The bar stays open for an hour or two longer than the kitchen.

ℹ️ Information

Tourist Office (✆01978-860828; www.northeastwales.co.uk; The Chapel, Castle St; ⊙9.30am-5pm) This helpful tourist office doubles as an art-and-craft gallery and is well stocked with maps, books and gifts. Download its *Llangollen History Trail* brochure, which details a 9.5km walking circuit taking in Valle Crucis (p707) and Dinas Brân (p708).

ℹ️ Getting There & Away

Up to 10 daily T3 buses head to/from Wrexham (£3.60, 34 minutes), Llandrillo (£4.20, 39 minutes), Bala (£5.10, one hour), Dolgellau (£6.20, 1½ hours) and Barmouth (£6.20, two hours). Buses leave from Parade St, near the museum.

Parking is at a premium in Llangollen when the summer throngs descend. If your accommodation doesn't have its own parking, check whether it can provide a pass for the council car parks.

SNOWDONIA NATIONAL PARK (PARC CENEDLAETHOL ERYRI)

Wales' best-known slice of nature became the country's first national park in 1951. Every year more than 400,000 people walk, climb or take the train to the 1085m summit of Snowdon. Yet the park offers much more – its 823 sq miles embrace stunning coastline, forests, valleys, rivers, bird-filled estuaries and Wales' biggest natural lake.

Like Wales' other national parks, this one is lived in, with sizeable towns at Bala, Dolgellau, Harlech and Betws-y-Coed, and a population touching 26,000. Two-thirds of Snowdonia is privately owned, with more than three-quarters used for raising sheep and cattle.

The park is the only home to two endangered species, an alpine plant called the Snowdon lily and the rainbow-coloured Snowdon beetle. The *gwyniad* is a species of whitefish found only in Llyn Tegid (Bala Lake), which incidentally also has probably the UK's only colony of glutinous snails.

The Welsh for Snowdonia is Eryri (*eh-ruh-ree*) – 'highlands'.

ℹ️ Information

The park authority (www.eryri-npa.gov.uk) publishes a free annual visitor newspaper, which includes information on getting around, organised walks and other activities.

ℹ️ Getting There & Away

The main points of entry for Snowdonia are Betws-y-Coed, Bala, Porthmadog and Dolgellau. For Llŷn Peninsula it's Porthmadog and Pwllheli and for the North Wales Borderlands it's Llangollen and Wrexham.

There are two major train lines into the region: the Cambrian/Cambrian Coast line (for Porthmadog and Pwllheli) and the Conwy Valley (for Betws). The narrow-gauge Welsh Highland and Ffestiniog and Welsh Highland lines run inland from Porthmadog and/or Carenarfon to Blaenau-Ffestiniog and Beddgelert.

Major bus routes include the T2 (Porthmadog and Dolgellau), T3 (Wrexham, Llangollen, Bala and Dolgellau) and a variety of services from Pwllheli across the Llŷn Peninsula.

Dolgellau

📞 01341 / POP 2679

Dolgellau (dol-*geth*-lye) is a charming little market town, steeped in history and boasting the highest concentration of heritage-listed buildings in Wales (more than 200). The county town of now-vanished Merionethshire, it was a regional centre for Wales' prosperous wool industry in the 18th and early 19th centuries and many of its finest buildings, sturdy and unadorned, were built at that time. Local mills failed to keep pace with mass mechanisation, however, and decline set in – preserving the town centre much as it was then.

The region bounced back when the Romantic Revival made Wales' wild landscapes popular with genteel travellers. There was also a minor gold rush in the 19th century. Famous for its pink tinge, Dolgellau gold became associated with royalty and the gold for the wedding rings of the current crop of senior royals was mined here. Today Dolgellau relies heavily on tourism, especially from walkers.

◉ Sights & Activities

Mawddach Estuary NATURE RESERVE
(www.mawddachestuary.co.uk) The Mawddach Estuary is a striking sight, flanked by woodlands, wetlands and the mountains of southern Snowdonia. There are two Royal Society for the Protection of Birds (RSPB) nature reserves in the valley, both easily reached on foot or by bike from Dolgellau or Barmouth via the Mawddach Trail. Arthog Bog is 8 miles west of Dolgellau on the access road to Morfa Mawddach station, off the A493, while Coed Garth Gell is 2 miles west, on the A496.

Mawddach Trail HIKING
(www.mawddachtrail.co.uk) The 9.5-mile Mawddach Trail is a flat (and in places wheelchair-accessible) walking and cycling path that

CADER IDRIS (CADAIR IDRIS)

The hulking mountain of **Cader Idris** (893m) may be named in honour of a mythical giant, a 7th-century Welsh prince, or both. It's a mystical mountain wreathed in legend: the hounds of the underworld are said to fly around its peaks, and strange light effects are often sighted. It's also said that anyone who spends the night on the summit will awaken either mad or a poet.

The usual route to the summit of Cader Idris is the 'Tŷ Nant' or **Pony Path** (6 miles return, five hours), which begins from the Tŷ Nant car park, 3 miles southwest of Dolgellau.

The easiest but longest route is the 'Tywyn' or **Llanfihangel y Pennant Path** (10 miles return, six hours), a gentle pony track that heads northeast from the hamlet of Llanfihangel y Pennant, joining the Tŷ Nant path at the latter's midpoint.

The shortest but steepest route is the **Minffordd Path** (6 miles return, five hours), which begins from the Dol Idris car park (four hours/day £2/4), 6 miles south of Dolgellau at the junction of the A487 and the B4405.

If you're summiting the mountain, you'll need stout shoes, protective clothing and a favourable weather forecast. Maps can be downloaded from the Snowdonia National Park website (www.eryri-npa.gov.uk).

If you're in need of pampering after your Cader Idris ascent, the wonderful, otter-bedecked **Old Rectory on the Lake** (☏01654-782225; www.rectoryonthelake.co.uk; Tal-y-Llyn; s/d from £70/120, 3-course meal £35; P🐕) could be just the ticket. It's on the shores of Tal-y-llyn lake, less than 2 miles from the Minffordd trailhead.

follows an old train line through woods and past wetlands on the southern side of the beautiful Mawddach Estuary, before crossing over the train viaduct to Barmouth (where you can catch the bus back). The trail starts in the car park beside the bridge in Dolgellau.

Precipice Walk HIKING

If you're not up to scaling Cader Idris, this 3.5-mile circular walk through the private Nannau estate is surprisingly varied and offers plenty of beautiful scenery. It leads you through woodland, along the side of a steeply sloped mountain and beside a lake (Llyn Cynwch). The walk starts from Saith Groesffordd car park, Llanfachreth, around 2.5 miles from Dolgellau.

🛏 Sleeping

HYB Bunkhouse HOSTEL £

(☏01341-421755; www.medi-gifts.com; 2-3 Bridge St; dm £20; P🐕) Attached to the ground-floor Medi Gift Shop, this bunkhouse has a series of oak-beamed rooms, each sleeping four people (in bunk beds, each group separated where possible), with handy kitchenettes. On the downside, there's no lounge, only one room is en suite, and during busy periods it's charged by the room rather than by the bed.

Bryn Mair House B&B ££

(☏01341-422640; www.brynmairbedandbreakfast.co.uk; Love Lane; s/d from £95/105; P🐕) This impressive stone house – a former Georgian rectory, no less – sits amid gardens on wistfully monikered Love Lane. Its three luxurious B&B rooms are all kitted out with Egyptian cotton sheets, DVD players and iPod docks; room 1 has sublime mountain views. Two-night minimums apply between Easter and September.

⭐**Ffynnon** B&B £££

(☏01341-421774; www.ffynnontownhouse.com; Love Lane; s/d from £100/160; P🐕) With an eye for contemporary design and a super-friendly welcome, this award-winning boutique B&B is both homey and stylish. French antiques mix with modern chandeliers, claw-foot tubs and electronic gadgets, and each room has a seating area for admiring the stunning views in comfort. There's a bar, a library, an outdoor hot tub, and Egyptian cotton and goose down in the bedrooms.

Penmaenuchaf Hall HOTEL £££

(☏01341-422129; www.penhall.co.uk; Penmaenpool; s/d £125/185; P🐕) With grand furnishings, sculpted gardens and superb views, this upscale country hotel is the former pile of Bolton cotton magnate James

Snowdonia & Llŷn Peninsula

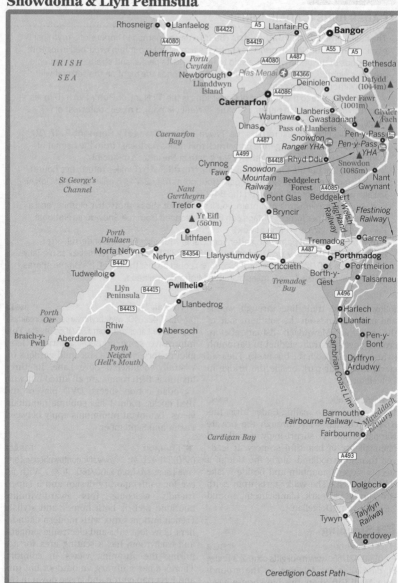

Leigh. The 14 rooms have a lavish old-world air, with all the 21st-century conveniences and four-poster beds in some. Standards are similarly high in Llygad yr Haul, the hotel's garden **restaurant**. It's 2 miles west of Dolgellau, off the A493.

✗ Eating & Drinking

TH Roberts CAFE £
(☑ 01341-423573; Parliament House, Bridge St; light mains £4-5; ☺ 9am-5.30pm Mon-Sat; ☜) Occupying a Grade II-listed building fitted with its original counter, glass cabinets and

Mawddach Restaurant   EUROPEAN **££**

(Bwyty Mawddach; ☑01341-421752; www.mawd dach.com; Llanelltyd; mains £17-20; ☺6.30-9pm Thu-Sat, noon-2.30pm Sun; ℗) Occupying a smartly renovated former barn with views of Cader Idris (p711) and the estuary (p710), Mawddach sits 2 miles west of Dolgellau on the A496. Tasteful slate floors and leather seats are matched by excellent food: poached sirloin with mushroom ragout or roasted cod with puy lentils, brown-butter breadcrumbs and salsa verde. The Sunday lunch (two/ three courses £22/25) is great value.

Dylanwad Da   WINE BAR

(☑01341-422870; www.dylanwad.co.uk; Porth Marchnad; snacks £4-7; ☺10am-6pm Tue & Wed, to 11pm Thu-Sat) The eponymous Dylan Rowlands knows how to pair tasty little plates with wine, and demonstrates this ably here, in Dolgellau's best wine bar. Cheeses, serrano ham and other small plates are still available. But – as the title of Dylan's book, *Rarebit and Rioja*, suggests – they're there as supporting cast to a personally approved selection of wines by the glass.

❶ Getting There & Away

Buses stop on the western side of Eldon Sq in the heart of town. Services include the regular T2 to/from Machynlleth (£3.45, 30 minutes), Porthmadog (£3.75, 50 minutes) and Caernarfon (£5.40 1½ hours), and the frequent T3 to Llangollen (£6.20, 1½ hours). Note that some services, such as the 28 to Tywyn (£3.40, 55 minutes), stop on the southern side of the square.

Barmouth (Abermaw)

☑01341 / POP 2279

With a Blue Flag beach and the beautiful Mawddach Estuary on its doorstep, the seaside resort of Barmouth has been a popular tourist destination since the coming of the railway in 1867. In summer it becomes a typical seaside resort – chip shops, dodgem cars, donkey rides and crabbing – catering primarily to inflowing throngs from England's West Midlands. Outside of the brash neon of high summer it's considerably mellower, allowing space to appreciate its Georgian and Victorian architecture, beautiful setting and superb walking trails.

The main commercial strip is spread out along the A496; as it passes through town it's known as Church St, High St and King Edward's St.

wooden drawers, this charismatic cafe still looks a lot like the ironmonger's it once was. The coffee and tea are proudly the best in Dolgellau, there's a reading room with books and papers, and the soup, sandwiches and rarebit (and Nan's scones) are all first rate.

COED Y BRENIN FOREST PARK

Covering 16 sq miles, this woodland park (8 miles north of Dolgellau off the A470) is the premier location for mountain biking in Wales. Ever-expanding, it's laced with more than 70 miles of purpose-built cycle trails, divided into eight graded routes to suit everyone from beginners to guns. Guidance is at hand in the form of old-fashioned waterproof trail cards or free apps: PlacesToGo and PlaceTales. Some of the more gung-ho trails – such as the Dragon's Back and the Beast of Brenin – are used for major mountain-biking events.

Wildlife here includes fallow deer; they're hard to spot but you're most likely to see them early in the morning.

You're unlikely to miss Barmouth's foremost landmark: in fact, you'll probably arrive on it, by train, on foot or on two wheels. The **Barmouth Bridge** curves scenically into town, spanning 700m of the Mawddach Estuary mouth; it was built in 1867 for the new railway and it was one of the longest wooden viaducts in Britain.

🛏 Sleeping

Hendre Mynach　　　　　　CAMPGROUND £
(📞01341-280262; www.hendremynach.co.uk; Llanaber Rd; sites/pods £28/55; 🅿 🐾) Right by the beach, this well-kept park has caravan sites marked out between manicured hedges and a couple of flat camping fields protected by windbreaks. It's just off the A496, immediately north of Barmouth.

Richmond House　　　　　　　　B&B ££
(📞01341-281366;　www.barmouthbedandbreakfast.co.uk; High St; s/d from £75/85; 🅿 🛜) This handsome stone-built Victorian town house has four comfortable, contemporary rooms (three, including the large family loft, have sea views) and an attractive garden area for summer lounging on chunky wooden furniture. There's a drying room and secure bike storage, and it's equally handy for the town centre and the beach.

🍴 Eating & Drinking

Bistro Bermo　　　　　　　　BISTRO ££
(📞01341-281284; 6 Church St; mains £19-22; ⏰6-9pm Tue-Sat, noon-3pm Sun) Discreetly hidden behind an aqua-green shopfront, this intimate restaurant delivers a sophisticated menu chock-full of Welsh farm produce and fresh fish. Featuring dishes such as duck breast with walnut crust and daily seafood specials, the cooking is classical rather than experimental, and generally excellent. There are only half a dozen tables, so book ahead.

Last Inn　　　　　　　　　　　PUB
(📞01341-280530; www.last-inn.co.uk; Church St; ⏰noon-11pm; 🪑) In a 15th-century cobbler's home now lives Barmouth's most characterful pub, full of inglenooks, old ship timber and other eclectic nautical memorabilia. Unusually, the hillside forms the rear wall, with a spring emerging to create a gaudily decorated pond inside the building itself. Kids are welcome, the menu's full of crowd-pleasers and there's live music on Tuesday and Friday nights.

ℹ Getting There & Away

Barmouth is on the Cambrian Coast Line, with up to nine direct trains per day to Fairbourne (£3, seven minutes), Harlech (£5.20, 25 minutes), Porthmadog (£7.60, 50 minutes), Machynlleth (£9.80, one hour) and Pwllheli (£12, 80 minutes).

Buses stop on Jubilee Rd, across Beach Rd from the train station. Services include the 38/39 to/from Harlech (30 minutes) and the frequent T3 to Dolgellau (£3.90, 20 minutes), Bala (£5.70, one hour), Llandrillo (£6.20, 1½ hours) and Llangollen (£6.20, two hours).

Cycle path Lôn Las Cymru passes through Barmouth, heading north to Harlech and east to Dolgellau.

Harlech

📞01766 / POP 1627

Hilly Harlech is best known for the mighty grey-stone towers of its castle, lording it over gleaming Tremadog Bay and framed sternly by the mountains of Snowdonia. Some sort of fortified structure has probably surmounted the rock since Iron Age times, but Edward I removed all traces when he commissioned the castle that currently stands. Finished in 1289, Harlech Castle is the southernmost of four fortifications grouped as the 'Castles and Town Walls of King Edward in Gwynedd' Unesco World Heritage Site.

Harlech is such a thoroughly pleasant place that it has become one of the more gentrified destinations in Snowdonia – every other shop seems to sell antiques or tea. While it's bustling in summer, it can be deliciously sleepy otherwise. It makes a great base for a beach holiday or for day trips into the national park – and those views never get boring.

◉ Sights

★ Harlech Castle
CASTLE

(Cadw; www.cadw.wales.gov.uk; Castle St; adult/child £6/4.10; ⊙ 9.30am-5pm Mar-Jun, Sep & Oct, to 6pm Jul & Aug, 10am-4pm Mon-Sat, 11am-4pm Sun Nov-Feb) Edward I finished this intimidating yet aesthetically pleasing castle in 1289, the southernmost of his 'iron ring' of fortresses designed to keep the Welsh firmly beneath his boot. The grey-sandstone castle's massive twin-towered gatehouse and outer walls are still intact and give the illusion of impregnability even now. Entry is through a well-equipped visitor centre, with interactive displays, kids' activities and films detailing the castle's history.

🛏 Sleeping & Eating

★ Maelgwyn House
B&B ££

(☑ 01766-780087; www.maelgwynharlech.co.uk; Ffordd Isaf; r from £85; ⊙ Feb-Oct; 🅿 🛜) A model B&B in an art-bedecked former boarding school, Maelgwyn has interesting hosts, delicious breakfasts and five elegant rooms stocked with DVD players and tea-making facilities (ask for one of the three with sea views – they're definitely worth it). Bridget and Derek can also help arrange birdwatching trips and fungus forays. Full marks.

Castle Cottage
COTTAGE ££

(☑ 01766-780479; www.castlecottageharlech.co.uk; Ffordd Pen Llech; s/d from £85/130; 🅿 🛜) Billing itself a 'restaurant with rooms', this 16th-century cottage has seven spacious bedrooms in a contemporary style, with exposed beams, in-room DVD players and a bowl of fresh fruit for each guest. The award-winning fine-dining **restaurant** (two-/three-/five-course dinner £39/42/45) is a great showcase for Welsh produce, featuring local rack of lamb, local line-caught sea bass and other delights.

As.Is Bistro
BISTRO ££

(☑ 01766-781208; www.asis-harlech.co.uk; The Square; pizzas/mains £11/15; ⊙ 5.30-9pm Mon, Tue & Thu-Sat) In the lee of the castle, this welcoming bistro offers a short menu of pizza and pasta alongside more adventurous fare such as seared swordfish with sweetcorn fritter and bean, tomato and coriander salsa. The space is stylish – naked wires, oversized light bulbs and rough timber tables – and the owners are very eager to please.

❶ Getting There & Away

Harlech is on the Cambrian Coast Line, with up to five direct trains per day to Fairbourne (£6.30, 34 minutes), Porthmadog (£4.20, 22 minutes), Barmouth (£5.20, 25 minutes), Pwllheli (£8.80, 47 minutes) and Machynlleth (£13, 1½ hours). The station is at the base of the rocks below the castle; it's a strenuous 20-minute climb on one of several stepped tracks up to High St, or about half a mile by road.

Bus 2 runs three times daily to/from the High St and Barmouth (30 minutes).

National Cycle Network path 8 (Lôn Las Cymru North) passes through Harlech, heading north to Porthmadog and south to Barmouth.

Blaenau Ffestiniog

📍 01766 / POP 3823

Most of the slate used to roof 19th-century Britain came from Wales, and much of that came from the mines of Blaenau Ffestiniog. However, only about 10% of mined slate is usable, so for every tonne that goes to the factory, 9 tonnes remains as rubble. Even though it's in the centre of Snowdonia National Park, the grey mountains of mine waste that surround Blaenau (*blay-nye*) prevented it from being officially included in the park – a slap in the face for this close-knit but impoverished town in the days before Wales' industrial sites were recognised as part of its heritage.

Although slate mining continues on a small scale, it's the abandoned workings of this once-mighty industry that are now Blaenau's attraction. It's by no means a 'pretty' town, but opportunities to explore the slate caverns or pursue extreme sports make it a great day trip from Porthmadog, via the historic Ffestiniog Railway.

◉ Sights

★ Cellb
ARTS CENTRE

(☑ 01766-832001; www.cellb.org; Park Sq; ⊙ cafe-bar noon-10pm Tue-Sat, kitchen noon-3pm & 6-9pm Wed-Sat) Recently opened in the Edwardian-era police station (hence 'Cell B'), this multifunction centre hosts everything from yoga to live bands to screenings in a 40-seat cinema. It's also the town's most appealing dining and drinking space, with a cafe and cocktail bar making clever use of original fittings. The final feather in Cellb's cap is hostel accommodation in three small dorms (created from the old magistrate's office and interview room; £22 per night), with a kitchen and stylish lounge.

★ **Llechwedd Slate Caverns** MINE
(☏01766-830306; www.llechwedd-slate-caverns. co.uk; tours £20; ⊙9.30am-5.30pm; P⚑) Blaenau's main attraction takes you into the bowels of a Victorian slate mine. You descend the UK's steepest mining cable railway into the 1846 network of tunnels and caverns, while 'enhanced-reality technology' brings to life the harsh working conditions of the 19th-century miners – be prepared to duck and scramble around dark tunnels. There's also a tour of the quarry in a military truck (£20 per person). The first tour each day is half price; check the website for times and prebooking.

🏃 Activities

Zip World Slate Caverns ADVENTURE SPORTS
(☏01248-601444; www.zipworld.co.uk; Llechwedd Slate Caverns; ⊙booking office 8am-6.30pm; ⚑) If you've ever wanted to practise trampoline tricks in a slate mine (and who hasn't?), then 'Bounce Below' – a 'cathedral-sized' cavern with bouncy nets, walkways, tunnels and slides – is your chance (adult/child one hour £25/20). There's also 'Titan' – 800m of zip wires over deep open pits (£50 per two hours) – and zip wires through the caverns (£65 for two hours).

Antur Stiniog MOUNTAIN BIKING
(☏01766-238007; www.anturstiniog.com; Llechwedd Slate Caverns; 1 uplift £5, day pass from £31; ⊙10am-4pm Thu-Mon) If you don't know the meaning of fear, check out these seven blue, red, black and double-black mountain-bike runs down the mountainside near the slate caverns. There's a minibus uplift service and a cafe on-site, and the same crew organises tailored activity-based holidays (walking, kayaking, climbing and wild camping) and has a cafe-shop on Blaenau Ffestiniog's High St.

ℹ Getting There & Away

Both the Conwy Valley Line from Betws-y-Coed (£5.40, 34 minutes) and Llandudno (£9.20, 1¼ hours), and the steam-powered Ffestiniog Railway (p724) from Porthmadog terminate here.

Bus services include the frequent 3/3B to/from Porthmadog (£2.30, 30 minutes); up to three 35 services per day to Dolgellau (50 minutes); and up to nine X19 services per day to Betws-y-Coed (£2.70, 25 minutes) and Llandudno (£5, 1¼ hours).

Betws-y-Coed

☐01690 / POP 532

Betws-y-Coed (*bet*-us-ee-*coyd*) sits at the junction of three river valleys (the Llugwy, the Conwy and the Lledr) and on the verge of the Gwydyr Forest. With outdoor-gear shops appearing to outnumber pubs, walking trails leaving right from the centre and guesthouses occupying a fair proportion of its slate Victorian buildings, it's the perfect base for exploring Snowdonia.

Betws has been Wales' most popular inland resort since Victorian times, when a group of countryside painters founded an artistic community to record the diversity of the landscape. The arrival of the railway in 1868 cemented its popularity, and today Betws-y-Coed is as busy with families and coach parties as it is with walkers.

◎ Sights

One of the joys of Betws is wandering its riverbanks and criss-crossing its historic bridges. The main road crosses the Conwy at the 32m-wide **Waterloo Bridge**; known locally as the 'iron bridge', it bears a large inscription celebrating its construction in the year of Wellington's victory over Boney (1815). Behind the information centre a pleasant path leads around the tongue of land framed by the convergence of the Rivers Conwy and Llugwy, and back past St Michael's Church. Nearby, **Sapper's Bridge** is a white suspension footbridge (1930) that crosses the Conwy and leads through the fields up to the A470.

At the other end of the village, the 15th-century stone **Pont-y-Pair** (Bridge of the Cauldron) crosses a set of rapids on the Llugwy. A riverside path leads about a mile downstream to the **Miners' Bridge**, named for the route miners took on their way to work in nearby lead mines. This was the oldest crossing of the Llugwy, but the original bridge is long gone.

The Rivers Conwy and Llugwy are rich with salmon in autumn. Outdoors shops are strung out along Holyhead Rd, selling equipment and specialist references for walkers, climbers and cyclists.

Swallow Falls
WATERFALL

(Rhaeadr Ewynnol; adult/child £1.50/50p) Betws-y-Coed's main natural tourist draw is located 2 miles west of town, alongside the A5 on the River Llugwy. It's a beautiful spot, with the 42m torrent, Wales' highest, weaving through the rocks into a green pool below. Outside seasonal opening hours, bring coins for the turnstile (no change is available).

Activities

★ Go Below Underground Adventures
ADVENTURE SPORTS

(✆ 01690-710108; www.go-below.co.uk; adventures from £49; ⏱ 9am-5pm) Head into the depths of an old slate mine and try your hand zip-lining across lakes and abseiling down shafts. You don't have to have caving experience, or squeeze through tiny spaces, but claustrophobes may demur. The latest challenge Go Below has devised, 'Mine to Mountain', is a 14-hour odyssey from 420m underground to the top of Snowdon.

The booking office is based at Conwy Falls, on the A5 south of Betws at the turn-off to Penmachno.

Zip World Fforest
ADVENTURE SPORTS

(✆ 01248-601444; www.zipworld.co.uk; A470; 3 'Coaster' rides £20, 2hr 'Safari' £40; ⏱ 9am-5pm; ♿) Fun in the Fforest includes the 'Safari', a network of rope ladders and zip-lines high in the treetops; the 'Coaster', a breakneck toboggan ride on rails; and 'Skyride', an 80ft, five-person swing that reaches jaw-clenching velocity. There's also a cafe for a nice, soothing hot chocolate afterwards.

Sleeping

★ Coed-y-Celyn Hall
APARTMENT £

(✆ 07821 099595; www.selfcatering-in-snowdonia.co.uk; A470, Coed-y-Celyn; apt per week from £410; P ☂) Built in the 1850s for a mining magnate, this grand pile on the banks of the Conwy was auctioned off in the 1950s and half of it has been converted into apartments. Each of the six is different, but they're all huge – and terrifically good value. Apartment 4, with moulded ceilings, grand windows and views over the front lawns, is particularly appealing.

Vagabond
HOSTEL £

(✆ 01690-710850; www.thevagabond.co.uk; Craiglan Rd; dm from £20; P ☂ ♨ ♥) On the slopes below a forested crag, from which spills its own 'private' waterfall, the Vagabond is Betws' best hostel – and the only one within

OFF THE BEATEN TRACK

GWYDYR FOREST

The 28-sq-mile **Gwydyr Forest**, planted since the 1920s with oak, beech and larch, encircles Betws-y-Coed and is scattered with the remnants of lead and zinc mine workings. Named for a more ancient forest in the same location, it's ideal for a day's walking, though it gets very muddy in wet weather. *Walks Around Betws-y-Coed* (£5), available from the National Park Information Centre, details several circular forest walks.

the town proper. It's a simple set-up, with freshly decorated six- to eight-bed dorms, two family rooms, shared bathrooms and an appealing bar (4.30pm to 11pm), kitchen and common room. Evening meals are £8.50 to £10.50.

Bod Gwynedd
B&B ££

(✆ 01690-710717; www.bodgwynedd.com; Holyhead Rd; s/d from £80/95; P ☂) Backed by towering pines and emerald fields on the western edge of town, this friendly B&B offers five tastefully furnished bedrooms in a mid-Victorian slate house. The welcoming owners keep everything spick and span and have plenty of local knowledge to impart. Not suitable for pets or under-18s.

Maes-y-Garth
B&B ££

(✆ 01690-710441; www.maes-y-garth.co.uk; Lon Muriau; d from £85; P ☂) Off the A470, and accessible from Betws by a footpath (starting behind St Michael's Church) across the river and the fields, this top-notch B&B inhabits a 1970s Clough Williams-Ellis–designed 'alpine-style' house. Inside are a warm welcome and five quietly stylish guest rooms with gorgeous views – perhaps the nicest is room 4, which has its own balcony and views of the valley.

Eating

Bwyd i Fynd
CAFE £

(Food to Go; ✆ 01690-710006; www.bwydifynd.co.uk; Station Approach; Welsh cakes 70p; ⏱ 9am-10pm, shorter hours Oct-Mar) This pint-sized spot serves Welsh cakes straight from the griddle, from traditional fare to unusually flavoured sweet and savoury ones; all are made with organic Welsh eggs and butter. Pies, homemade cakes and good coffee are also available: all ideal picnic fodder.

SURF SNOWDONIA

Lying just outside the national park's eastern border, in the lush Conwy Valley, is this unexpected little slice of Maui: the **Surf Snowdonia** (☑ 01492-353123; www.surfsnowdonia.co.uk; Conway Rd, Dolgarrog; ◎ 8am-11pm; 👶) adventure park, centred on a vast artificial wave pool (open 10am until sunset). If learning to surf (adult/child £55/45) doesn't excite, there are lagoon 'crash and splash' sessions (£25 per hour), kayaking, walking and a soft-play centre for kids.

There's also a cafe-bar, a restaurant and on-site fixed camping, if you want to dally; the Electric Wave festival is held on the 'lagoon' shore in late July. Surf Snowdonia is signposted off the A470 from Llandudno Junction to Betws-y-Coed.

★ **Bistro Betws-y-Coed**   WELSH **££**
(☑ 01690-710328; www.bistrobetws-y-coed.co.uk; Holyhead Rd; lunch £8-9, dinner £15-18; ◎ noon-2.30pm & 6.30-9pm Jun-Sep, shorter hours rest of year) Perhaps the best place to eat in town, Bistro Betws offers some interesting adaptations of national staples, such as haddock with Welsh-rarebit crumb. Watch out for possible shot pellets in the sautéed breast of wild pheasant with black-pudding potato cake and whisky sauce, and book in summer as it gets absolutely packed.

Tŷ Gwyn Hotel   EUROPEAN **££**
(☑ 01690-710383; www.tygwynhotel.co.uk; A5; mains £15-19; ◎ noon-2pm & 6-9pm; 🅿) This 400-year-old coaching inn oozes character from every one of its numerous exposed beams. The menu is full of delicious-sounding local ingredients (Pen Loyn Farm lamb loin, whole lake trout from Llyn Brenig) and a decent number of veggie options (the wild-mushroom and pine-nut stroganoff is good), but the real appeal is the quirky old building itself.

ⓘ Information

Snowdonia National Park Information Centre (☑ 01690-710426; www.eryri-npa.gov.uk; Royal Oak Stables; ◎ 9.30am-5.30pm Easter-Oct, to 4pm rest of year) More than just a repository of books, maps and local craft, this office is an invaluable source of information about walking trails, mountain conditions and more.

ⓘ Getting There & Away

Betws-y-Coed is on the Conwy Valley Line (www.conwyvalleyrailway.co.uk), with up to five trains every day to Llandudno (£6.60, 50 minutes) and Blaenau Ffestiniog (£5.40, 34 minutes).

Snowdon Sherpa bus service S2 heads to Swallow Falls (seven minutes), Capel Curig (12 minutes), Pen-y-Pass (25 minutes), Llanberis (35 minutes) and Bangor (route S6, in summer, one hour); all trips are £2.

Other buses include up to 10 19/X19 services per day to Conwy (£3.30, 45 minutes) Blaenau Ffestiniog (£2.70, 25 minutes) and Llandudno (£3.50, 50 minutes).

Llanberis

☑ 01286 / POP 1904

Llanberis is a magnet for walkers and climbers, attracting a steady flow of rugged polar-fleece wearers year-round, but especially in July and August (when accommodation is at a premium). It's positioned just outside the national park but functions as a hub, partly because the Snowdon Mountain Railway leaves from here. While not the most attractive town in the area, its offbeat charm complements the appeal of its glorious surrounds.

Llanberis originally housed workers from the Dinorwig slate quarry, and its massive waste tips are hard to miss. While tourism is the cornerstone of life these days, the town hasn't abandoned its industrial roots. Dinorwig, which once boasted the world's largest artificial cavern, is now part of Europe's biggest pumped-storage power station. Some of the old quarry workshops have been reincarnated as a slate-industry museum, and the narrow-gauge railway that once hauled slate to the coast now transports excited toddlers along Llyn Padarn.

◎ Sights & Activities

★ **National Slate Museum**   MUSEUM
(☑ 0300 111 2 333; www.museumwales.ac.uk/en/slate; ◎ 10am-5pm Easter-Oct, to 4pm Sun-Fri Nov-Easter; 🅿) **FREE** Even if you're not enraptured by industrial museums, ignore the dull-sounding name and check this one out. At Dinorwig Quarry much of the slate was carved out of the open mountainside – leaving behind a jagged, sculptural cliff face that's fascinating if not exactly beautiful. The museum, occupying the Victorian workshops beside the lake (Llyn Padarn), features video clips, a huge working water wheel, workers' cottages (progressively furnished

in period decor from 1861 to 1969, when the quarries closed) and demonstrations.

Electric Mountain
MUSEUM

(☏01286-870636; www.electricmountain.co.uk; tour adult/child £8.50/4.35; ⏱10am-4.30pm Jan-May & Sep-Dec, 9.30am-5.30pm Jun-Aug) More than just Dinorwig Power Station's public interface, Electric Mountain is a tourist hub incorporating a gallery, cafe and souvenir shop. It also has interactive exhibits on hydropower and is the starting point for a fascinating guided tour into the power station's guts, 750m under Elidir mountain.

The centre is by the lakeside on the A4086, near the southern end of High St.

🛏 Sleeping

YHA Snowdon Llanberis
HOSTEL £

(☏0845 371 9645; www.yha.org.uk; Llwyn Celyn, Ceunant St; dm/tw/pods from £24/69/109; ⏱reception 8-10am & 5-10pm; P🛜) Originally a quarry manager's house, this no-frills hostel offers great views (from an admittedly scrappy hillside locale), a self-catering kitchen, cooked meals (£8 to £10), a drying room and four-person fixed camping pods. It's about a 10-minute walk above the town, signposted from the High St.

★ Beech Bank
B&B ££

(☏01286-871085; www.beech-bank.co.uk; 2 High St; s/d £70/80; P🛜) First impressions of this double-gabled, wrought iron–trimmed stone house are great, but step inside and it just gets better. A stylish renovation has resulted in beautiful bathrooms and exuberant decor, which matches the gregarious nature of the host, and breakfasts can be packed for early-rising hikers and climbers. Highly recommended, although not set up for children.

Plas Coch Guest House
GUESTHOUSE ££

(☏01286-872122; www.plascochsnowdonia.co.uk; High St; s/d from £60/80; P🛜) More like a little hotel than a B&B, this large stone mid-Victorian guesthouse is operated by Jim and Eryl, a friendly couple with lots of local knowledge to impart. There's a cosy, slate-floored drawing room, and the bedrooms are stylish, comfortable and in some cases large enough to qualify as suites. Breakfasts, including vegetarian and vegan options, are lavish and wonderful.

🍴 Eating

★ Gallt-y-Glyn
PUB FOOD £

(☏01286-870370; www.galltyglyn.com; A4086; mains £11; ⏱kitchen 6-9pm Wed-Sat; ♿) Sure, it serves pasta, pies, burgers and salads, too, but almost everyone comes for the pizza and the free-pint-with-every-main deal. Simply tick what you want on the paper menu and hand it over at the bar. You'll find Gallt-y-Glyn on the A4086, half a mile towards Caernarfon. It's a bit shabby, slightly eccentric, very family friendly and utterly brilliant.

Pantri
CAFE £

(☏01286-238070; High St; mains £4-6; ⏱10am-5pm Wed-Sun, daily during holidays) Good coffee! After that, everything else this cruisy, pastel-hued little cafe does is a bonus. But those extras – homemade cakes, sandwiches, soups and the like – are also from the top drawer.

Pete's Eats
CAFE £

(☏01286-870117; www.petes-eats.co.uk; 40 High St; mains £5-6; ⏱8am-8pm; 🛜) Pete's Eats is a local institution – a busy, primary-coloured cafe where hikers and climbers swap tips over monster breakfasts and under photos of their knee-trembling forebears. There's bunkhouse accommodation upstairs (£16 per night), a huge noticeboard full of travellers' information, a book exchange and a map and guidebook room.

Peak Restaurant
INTERNATIONAL ££

(Bwyty'r Copa; ☏01286-872777; www.peakrestaurant.co.uk; 86 High St; mains £14-17; ⏱7-10pm Wed-Sat; ♿) A chef-patron who once clattered the pans at the legendary Chez Panisse in California is behind this restaurant's popularity and longevity. The open kitchen allows you to see her at work, turning good Welsh produce into internationally inspired dishes such as Anglesey sea bass with coriander sauce or Welsh lamb shanks with white-onion purée, rosemary and redcurrant.

A NIGHT ON SNOWDON'S DOORSTEP

This superbly situated **YHA Snowdon Pen-y-Pass** (☏08453-719534; www.yha.org.uk; A4086; dm/tw £26/79; P) has three of Snowdon's trails at its doorstep. It has a well-equipped kitchen, laundry and drying room; Mallory's Cafe/Bar (named for a past patron who perished on Everest); and quiet, comfortable rooms, 16 of which are en suite. It's 5.5 miles up the A4086 from Llanberis, and the Snowdon Sherpa bus stops right over the road.

❶ Getting There & Away

Snowdon Sherpa buses charge just £2 per ride, stopping by Joe Brown's on the High St. S1 heads to Pen-y-Pass (15 minutes), while S2 continues on to Capel Curig (35 minutes) and Betws-y-Coed (47 minutes).

Other regular buses include the 88 to/from Caernarfon (£1.80, 25 minutes) and the 85 to/from Bangor (£3, 50 minutes).

Snowdon (Yr Wyddfa)

No Snowdonia experience is complete without coming face-to-face with Snowdon (1085m), one of Britain's most awe-inspiring mountains and the highest summit in Wales (it's actually the 61st highest in Britain; the top 60 are all in Scotland). 'Yr Wyddfa' in Welsh (pronounced uhr-*with*-vuh, meaning 'the Tomb'), it's the mythical resting place of the giant Rhita Gawr, who demanded King Arthur's beard for his cloak and was killed for his temerity. On a clear day the views stretch to Ireland and the Isle of Man over Snowdon's fine jagged ridges, which drop away in great swoops to sheltered *cwms* (valleys) and deep lakes. Even on a gloomy day you could find yourself above the clouds. Thanks to the Snowdon Mountain Railway it's extremely accessible when the winds aren't too high. It's so accessible, in fact, that the summit and some of the tracks can get frustratingly crowded.

🏃 Activities

★ Snowdon Trails   HIKING

Seven paths of varying length and difficulty lead to Snowdon's summit, all taking around six hours return. That the mountain has a train station and a cafe at its summit does not mean you should underestimate it. No route is completely safe, especially in winter. People regularly come unstuck here and many have died over the years, including experienced climbers.

The most straightforward route to the summit is the **Llanberis Path** (9 miles return), running beside the train line. The two paths starting from Pen-y-Pass require the least amount of ascent but are nevertheless tougher walks: the **Miner's Track** (8 miles return) starts off wide and gentle but gets steep beyond Llyn Llydaw, and the more interesting **Pyg Track** (7 miles return) is more rugged still.

Two tracks start from the Caernarfon–Beddgelert road (A4085): the **Snowdon Ranger Path** (8 miles return) is the safest route in winter, while the **Rhyd Ddu Path** (8 miles return) is the least-used route and boasts spectacular views. The most challenging route is the **Watkin Path** (8 miles return), involving an ascent of more than 1000m on its southerly approach from Nantgwynant and finishing with a scramble across a steep-sided, scree-covered slope.

The classic **Snowdon Horseshoe** (7.5 miles return) branches off from the Pyg Track to follow the precipitous ridge of **Crib Goch** (one of the most dangerous routes on the mountain and only recommended for the very experienced), with a descent over the peak of Y Lliwedd and a final section down the Miner's Track.

★ Snowdon Mountain Railway   RAIL

(☏ 01286-870223; www.snowdonrailway.co.uk; adult/child return diesel £29/20, steam £37/27; ⊙ 9am-5pm mid-Mar–Oct) If you're not physically able to climb a mountain, short on time or just plain lazy, those industrious, railway-obsessed Victorians have gifted you an alternative. Opened in 1896, the Snowdon Mountain Railway is the UK's highest – and its only public – rack-and-pinion railway. Vintage steam and modern diesel locomotives haul carriages from Llanberis up to Snowdon's summit in an hour.

Return trips involve a scant half-hour at the top before heading back down again. Single tickets can only be booked for the journey up (adult/child £22/17); if you want to walk up and ride down, you'll have to hope there's space. Tens of thousands of people take the train to the summit each season: make sure you book well in advance or you may miss out. Departures are determined by customer demand and are weather dependent. From March to May (or during high winds) the trains can only head as far Clogwyn Station (adult/child £19/13) – an altitude of 779m.

🛏 Sleeping

YHA Snowdon Ranger   HOSTEL £

(☏ 08453-719659; www.yha.org.uk; Rhyd Ddu; dm/tw from £23/50; Ⓟ 🛜) On the A4085, 5 miles north of Beddgelert at the trailhead for the Snowdon Ranger Path, this former inn has its own adjoining beach on the shore of Llyn Cwellyn, and is close to the hiking and climbing centres of Llanberis and Beddgelert. It's basic, dependable accommodation within sight of Snowdon.

Walking Tour
Up Snowdon Ranger, Down Rhyd Ddu

START SNOWDON RANGER YHA
END RHYD DDU TRAIN STATION
LENGTH 8 MILES, SIX HOURS

This particular Snowdon route is reasonably straightforward and quiet, and it doesn't involve difficult scrambles (that said, in snowy and icy conditions, the descent on the Rhyd Ddu Path should only be undertaken by experienced mountaineers equipped with crampons and ice picks; everyone else should double back on the Snowdon Ranger Path). Both trailheads are connected by buses and trains to accommodation in Caernarfon, Beddgelert and Porthmadog.

The original 'Snowdon Ranger' was John Morton, an English mountain guide who built an inn on the site of the current YHA hostel in the early 1800s and led guests to the summit along this track. The path climbs gently along the lower slopes of ❶ **Moel Cynghorion** to ❷ **Bwlch Cwm Brwynog** before it grows steeper and heads above ❸ **Clogwyn Du'r**

Arddu. Eventually it draws parallel with the Snowdon Mountain Railway. The path crosses the tracks at a ❹ **standing stone**, turns right and merges with the Llanberis Path for the final approach to the ❺ **summit**.

When you're ready to descend, pick up the Rhyd Ddu Path below the ❻ **Hafod Eryri** (p722) visitor centre. After 200m a ❼ **standing stone** marks the point where the Watkin Path veers off; continue straight ahead. The next section, along ❽ **Bwlch Main** (meaning 'Slender Path'), is a narrow track with steep slopes on either side: if there's ice, snow or wind, this can be genuinely dangerous and is only for properly equipped and experienced walkers. Near the end of this stretch the path splits into two; keep on the right-hand track. From here the path broadens as it zigzags down and then edges along the ❾ **Llechog ridge**. It starts to flatten out after it passes the ❿ **ruins** of an old refreshment hut. The final stretch continues alongside the abandoned ⓫ **Ffridd Slate Quarry** before terminating near the Rhyd Ddu train station.

Pen-y-Gwryd
HOTEL ££

(☎01286-870211; www.pyg.co.uk; Nant Gwynant; s/d £58/115; P🐾🍽) Eccentric but full of atmosphere, this Georgian coaching inn was used as a training base by the 1953 Everest team, and memorabilia from their stay includes signatures on the restaurant ceiling. TV, wi-fi and mobile-phone signals don't penetrate here; instead, there's a comfy games room, a sauna, and a lake for those hardy enough to swim. Meals and packed lunches are available.

You'll find the hotel below Pen-y-Pass, at the junction of the A498 and A4086.

ℹ Information

Hafod Eryri (https://snowdonrailway.co.uk; ⊙10am-20min before last train departure Easter-Oct; 🍽) Clad in granite and curved to blend into the mountain, Hafod Eryri houses a cafe, toilets and ambient interpretive elements built into the structure itself. A wall of picture windows gazes down towards the west, while a small row faces the cairn. Closed in winter or if the weather's terrible, it's open whenever the train (p720) is running.

ℹ Getting There & Away

It's worth considering public transport: car parks can fill up quickly and the Pen-y-Pass car park costs £10 per day.

Before you decide which route you'll take to the summit, study the bus and train timetables. If you're based in Llanberis, you'll find it easiest to get to and from the Llanberis, Pyg and Miner's Paths. The Snowdon Ranger and Rhyd Ddu Paths are better connected to Beddgelert and Caernarfon.

The Welsh Highland Railway (p725) stops at the trailhead of the Rhyd Ddu Path, and there is a request stop (Snowdon Ranger Halt) where you can alight for the Snowdon Ranger Path.

Trailheads are accessible by Snowdon Sherpa bus services S1, S2, S4, S6 or S97 (single/day ticket £2/5).

Another option is to take the Snowdon Mountain Railway (p720) from Llanberis to the top and walk back down. It's more difficult to do this the other way around, as the train will only take on new passengers at the top if there is space.

Beddgelert
☎01766 / POP 455

Charming Beddgelert is a conservation village of dark stone cottages overlooking the River Colwyn and its ivy-covered bridge, just upstream from where it meets the River Glaslyn. Flowers festoon the village in spring and the surrounding hills are covered in a purple blaze of heather in summer. Scenes from Mark Robson's 1958 film *The Inn of the Sixth Happiness*, starring Ingrid Bergman, were shot here.

Beddgelert, meaning 'Gelert's Grave', is said to refer to the dog of 13th-century Llywelyn the Great, Prince of Gwynedd. Thinking Gelert had savaged his baby son, Llywelyn slaughtered him, only to discover Gelert had fought off a wolf attacking his owner's baby. More likely, the name Beddgelert comes from a 5th-century Irish preacher, Celert, who is believed to have founded a church here. Regardless, Gelert's 'grave' (possibly constructed by an unscrupulous 18th-century hotelier to boost business) is a popular attraction, reached by a pretty riverside trail.

◉ Sights & Activities

Sygun Copper Mine
MINE

(☎01766-890595; www.syguncoppermine.co.uk; A498; adult/child under 15yr £8.95/6.95; ⊙9.30am-5pm summer, 10am-4pm winter, closed 11 Nov-26 Dec & 3 Jan-9 Feb; P🐾) This mine dates from Roman times, although extraction was stepped up in the 19th century. Abandoned in 1903, it has since been converted into a museum, with a half-hour self-guided underground tour containing dioramas that evoke the life of Victorian miners. You can also try your hand at metal detecting (£2.50) or panning for gold (£2). It's located a mile northeast of Beddgelert, along the A498.

Craflwyn & Dinas Emrys
WALKING

(NT; ☎01766-510120; www.nationaltrust.org.uk/craflwyn-and-beddgelert) A mile northeast of

---

TYWYN

While the town falls just outside the national park, Tywyn's long sandy Blue Flag beach is one of the most popular in the region. Its other major drawcard is the narrow-gauge **Talyllyn Railway** (Rheilffordd Talyllyn; ☎01654-710472; www.talyllyn.co.uk; Wharf Station; adult/accompanied child return £18/2; ⊙Easter-Oct, varies rest of year), famous as the inspiration for Rev W Awdry's *Thomas the Tank Engine* stories. Beyond these diversions it's a quiet, pleasant town, surrounded by salt-marsh sheep pastures and strung out along a meandering High St.

BALA (Y BALA)

Kayakers, canoeists, windsurfers, sailors, rafters and hikers will appreciate the quiet Welsh-speaking town of **Bala**. Here you'll find Wales' largest natural lake, Llyn Tegid (Bala Lake), as well as the River Tryweryn, hallowed in white-water kayaking circles.

The best base hereabouts is **Tyddyn Llan** (☎01490-440264; www.tyddynllan.co.uk; Llandrillo; s/d/ste incl dinner from £185/260/320; ℙ☏), an elegant property set amid gardens in the tranquil Vale of Edeyrnion. The 12 rooms and suite each boast their own individual style: some frou-frou romantic, some shabby-chic modern. The main draw, however, is the Michelin-starred **restaurant** (2-/3-course dinner £50/60; ☉lunch Fri-Sun, dinner daily; ℙ), with a creative menu and superb produce (including live shellfish).

Tyddyn Llan is in Llandrillo, 8 miles east of Bala.

Beddgelert, near Llyn Dinas, National Trust–owned Craflwyn Farm is the starting point for several short walks, including a path to Dinas Emrys, one of the most significant yet largely unheralded sites in Welsh mythology. To stay at Pretty Craflwyn Hall, contact HF Holidays (www.hfholidays.co.uk), which leases it on behalf of the trust.

Aberglaslyn Gorge & Moel Hebog HIKING
The Aberglaslyn Gorge trail runs from Beddgelert through the pretty Glaslyn river gorge to the main road at Pont Aberglaslyn (3 miles return, two hours). The ascent of Moel Hebog hill (783m) is more strenuous (8-mile loop, five hours), and includes a lovely scenic ridge walk over two more peaks. Beddgelert's tourist office has leaflets on both hikes.

🛏 Sleeping & Eating

Sygun Fawr Country House HOTEL **££**
(☎01766-890258; www.sygunfawr.co.uk; s/d from £45/89; ℙ☏) A warm welcome awaits at this sturdy stone manor house, tucked away at the end of a narrow lane. Additions (including a conservatory) have been grafted onto the 1660s core over the centuries, so each of the 12 comfortable bedrooms is quite different; some have spectacular mountain views. It's well signposted from the A498 immediately northeast of the village.

The in-house **restaurant** deals in classic dishes such as grilled salmon in beurre blanc and slow-cooked lamb shanks.

Hebog CAFE **££**
(☎01766-890400; www.hebog-beddgelert.co.uk; Fford Caernarfon; mains £15-18; ☉10am-5pm Sun-Fri, to 7pm Sat; ☏) At the swankier end of Beddgelert's dining options, Hebog is an upmarket cafe serving the likes of braised Welsh beef in red-wine sauce and home-made spinach-and-ricotta tortellini with red-pepper pesto. A scenic summer terrace by the babbling Glaslyn seals the deal.

❶ Information

Tourist Office (☎01766-890615; www.eryri-npa.gov.uk; 3 Dolfair; ☉9.30am-12.30pm & 1-5pm Easter-Oct, 10am-4pm Sat & Sun Nov-Easter) Great for information on walks, cycling and accommodation in the area, and sells local produce.

❶ Getting There & Away

Snowdon Sherpa buses, costing just £2 per single ride, serve Beddgelert: the S4 heads to/from Caernarfon (30 minutes), Snowdon Ranger (10 minutes), Rhyd Ddu (six minutes) and Pen-y-Pass (20 minutes), and the S97 heads to Porthmadog (21 minutes), Tremadog (13 minutes) and Pen-y-Pass (18 minutes).

Beddgelert is a stop on the historic Welsh Highland Railway (p725), which runs between Caernarfon (£31 return, 1½ hours) and Porthmadog (£22 return, 40 minutes) from Easter to October, with limited winter service, and stops at the Rhyd Ddu and Snowdon Ranger trailheads.

LLŶN PENINSULA

Jutting into the Irish Sea from the rumpled massif of Snowdonia, the Llŷn (pronounced 'khleen' and sometimes spelt 'Lleyn') is a green finger of raised and rumpled land some 30 miles long and averaging 8 miles wide. This peaceful and largely undeveloped region has isolated walking and cycling routes, Iron Age forts, beaches, a scattering of small fishing villages and 70 miles of wildlife-rich coastline (much of it in the hands of the National Trust, with almost 80% designated an Area of Outstanding Natural Beauty). Over the centuries the heaviest footfalls have been those of pilgrims heading to Bardsey Island.

Welsh is the everyday language of the Llŷn. Indeed, this is about as Welsh as it gets. The peninsula and adjacent island of Anglesey were the last stops for the Romans and Normans, and both places never lost their separate identity.

ℹ Getting There & Away

The Cambrian Coast line runs as far down the Llŷn as Pwllheli, while buses run from major centres such as Caernarfon, Porthmadog and Pwllheli throughout the peninsula. Between March and October the **Llŷn Coastal Bus** (☏ 01758-721777; www.bwsarfordirllyn.co.uk) runs Thursday to Sunday, ferrying walkers and surfers to some of the peninsula's more remote and beautiful spots.

Porthmadog

☏ 01766 / POP 2910

Despite a few rough edges, busy little Porthmadog (port-mad-uk) has an arresting estuarine setting and a conspicuously friendly, mainly Welsh-speaking populace. It straddles both the Llŷn Peninsula and Snowdonia National Park, and has the fantastical village of Portmeirion at its doorstep. Throw in abundant transport connections and you have a handy place to base yourself for a couple of days.

Porthmadog is also a bona fide paradise for railway buffs. There are 'little trains' all over Wales, a legacy of Victorian industry, but Porthmadog is triply blessed: it forms the southern terminus for two of Wales' finest narrow-gauge train journeys and has a third steam-train line connected to a rail-heritage centre.

The shallow Traeth Bach estuary abounds in mullet, which in turn attract ospreys. Keep an eye out for these large birds of prey as you walk around the cliffs of Borth-y-Gest and Porthmeirion.

History

Both Porthmadog and the neighbouring village of Tremadog (the latter now virtually a suburb of the former) were founded by and named after reforming landowner William Alexander Madocks. In the early 19th century he laid down the mile-long Cob causeway, drained the 400 hectares of wetlands that lay behind it and created a brand-new

harbour. After his death the Cob became the route for the Ffestiniog Railway; at its 1873 peak, it transported more than 116,000 tonnes of slate from the mines of Blaenau Ffestiniog to the harbour. In 1888 TE Lawrence (Lawrence of Arabia) was born in Tremadog, although the Lawrence family moved to Oxford 12 years later; look for his family home (marked with a plaque) near the church.

◉ Sights & Activities

★ Portmeirion Village   VILLAGE
(☏ 01766-770000;   https://portmeirion.wales;
adult/child   £12/8.50;   ⊙ 9.30am-7.30pm;   Ⓟ)
Set on its own tranquil peninsula reaching into the estuary, this fantastical collection of colourful buildings with a heavy Italian influence was masterminded by Welsh architect Sir Clough Williams-Ellis. Starting in 1925, Sir Clough collected bits and pieces from disintegrating stately mansions and set them alongside his own creations to concoct this weird and wonderful seaside utopia. Today the buildings are all heritage listed, the site is a conservation area, and festivals, fairs, gigs and other events are frequently held here.

★ Ffestiniog Railway   RAIL
(Rheilffordd Ffestiniog; ☏ 01766-516024; www. festrail.co.uk; day ticket £25; ⊙ daily Easter-Oct, reduced service rest of year; ♿) The world's oldest surviving narrow-gauge railway, the Ffestiniog wends its way from the slate-mining town of Blaenau Ffestiniog to Porthmadog. Long past its industrial heyday, the railway's 150-year-old steam locomotives and monogrammed wooden carriages now ferry sightseers through oak woodlands, under towering peaks and beside flashing rivers. For an extra £7 each way, you can ride in giant-windowed observation carriages.

One child under 16 travels free with each ticket-buying adult; additional children travel half-price.

★ Welsh Highland Railway   RAIL
(☏ 01766-516000; www.festrail.co.uk; ⊙ Easter-Oct, limited service winter) Leaving from Porthmadog Harbour Station, the Welsh Highland Railway runs to Caernarfon (2½ hours) via Beddgelert (£22 return) and Rhyd Ddu (£26 return), and past the western slopes of Snowdon. One child under 16 travels free with each ticket-buying adult; additional children travel half-price.

🎊 Festivals & Events

★ Festival No 6 PERFORMING ARTS

(📞 0344 326 4264; www.festivalnumber6.com; Portmeirion; tickets from £180; ⊙ Sep) Started in 2012, this rock and dance-music festival with arts, culture, comedy and food components has topped many best-festival lists and makes imaginative use of Portmeirion's varied and dream-like environment over a long weekend in September. Past headliners include New Order, Fleetwood Mac and Cassius.

PortmeiriCon CULTURAL

(Prisoner Convention; www.portmeiricon.com; Portmeirion; ⊙ Apr) Here's one to either pencil in or avoid: fans of cult TV show *The Prisoner* converge on Portmeirion in April for a weekend of dress-ups and human chess. Indoor events are only open to members of the Six of One (the *Prisoner* Appreciation Society), but anyone can catch outdoor shows or glimpses of celebrities bussed in for the occasion.

🍴 Sleeping & Eating

★ Yr Hen Fecws B&B ££

(📞 01766-514625; www.henfecws.com; 16 Lombard St; s/d £80/90; 🅿 🛜) Probably Porthmadog's nicest digs, 'The Old Bakery' is a stylishly restored stone cottage containing seven simply decorated en-suite rooms with exposed slate walls and fireplaces. Breakfast is served under the marigold walls and exposed beams of the downstairs bistro (dinner mains £17 to £19, open 6pm to 9pm daily).

**Hotel Portmeirion
& Castell Deudraeth** HOTEL £££

(📞 01766-770000; https://portmeirion.wales; Portmeirion; r from £259; 🅿 🐾) Over-the-top Hotel Portmeirion, dating to 1850 but extended by Sir Clough Williams-Ellis as the original focal point of Portmeirion Village, has a plum spot by the water, 14 individually styled rooms, a restaurant, a pool and a terraced bar. Outside the village, fancifully Gothic Castell Deudraeth offers 11 comfortable, modern rooms, despite also dating to the time of Queen Victoria's reign.

★ Y Sgwâr BISTRO £££

(📞 01766-515451; www.ysgwar-restaurant. co.uk; 12-16 Market Sq, Tremadog; mains £15-25; ⊙ noon-2pm & 6-9pm) On the main square in Tremadog, Porthmadog's immediate neighbour, this cosmopolitan Welsh restaurant

CRICCIETH

This genteel, slow-moving seaside town sits above two sand-and-stone Blue Flag beaches 5 miles west of Porthmadog. Its main claim to fame is the stirringly sited, ruined **Criccieth Castle** (Cadw; www.cadw.wales.gov.uk; Castle St; adult/child £5.50/3.30; ⊙ 10am-5pm daily Apr-Oct, 10am-4pm Wed-Sat, 11am-4pm Sun Nov-Mar), perched on the seafront's most prominent headland, and offering views stretching along the peninsula's southern coast and across Tremadog Bay to Harlech.

Constructed by Welsh prince Llywelyn the Great in 1239, it was overrun in 1283 by Edward I's forces and recaptured for the Welsh in 1404 by Owain Glyndŵr, whose troops promptly sacked it. Today there is a small but informative exhibition centre at the ticket office, its angry multimedia voices raised in Welsh accents.

has the best food in either town. The service is super attentive and friendly, and dishes such as roast cod with lobster bisque and deep-fried crayfish are a delight. There's great value in the set menus offered at lunch (two/three courses £18/22) and between 6pm and 7pm.

ℹ Getting There & Away

Porthmadog is on the Cambrian Coast Line, with eight daily direct trains to/from Criccieth (£3, eight minutes), Pwllheli (£5.40, 24 minutes), Harlech (£4.20, 23 minutes), Barmouth (£7.60, one hour) and Machynlleth (£15, two hours). The **Ffestiniog & Welsh Highland Railways** (www.festrail.co.uk) run scenic services to Blaenau Ffestiniog, the Snowdon trailheads and Caernarfon.

Buses stop on High St and most services pass through the satellite town of Tremadog. Routes include the frequent T2 to/from Dolgellau (£3.75, 50 minutes), Caernarfon (£4.35, 50 minutes) and Machynlleth (£5.40, 1½ hours); the frequent 3/3B to/from Pwllheli (£3.80, 35 minutes); up to six daily S97 (Snowdon Sherpa) services to/from Beddgelert (£2, 23 minutes); and up to three T2 services to/from Caernarfon (£4.35, 45 minutes).

The Lôn Las Cymru (National Cycle Route 8) passes through Porthmadog, heading west to Criccieth and south to Harlech.

Abersoch

☑ 01758 / POP 708

Abersoch is a sweet, naturally favoured former fishing port that explodes in summer with tens of thousands of boaties, surfers, beach bums and sun-seeking families. Edged by gentle blue-green hills, the town's main attraction is its Blue Flag beach, one of the most popular on the peninsula. Surfers head further south for the Atlantic swell at **Porth Neigwl** (Hell's Mouth) and **Porth Ceiriad**.

★ **Venetia**   HOTEL **££**
(☑ 01758-713354; www.venetiawales.com; Lôn Sarn Bach; s/d from £93/128; P 🅿 🛜) No sinking Venetian palazzo here, just five luxurious rooms in a grand Victorian house decked out with designer lighting and modern art; room Cinque has a TV above its bathtub. The **restaurant** (mains £17 to £18) specialises in the traditional tastes of Venice, particularly seafood and pasta served as *cicchetti* (small plates); enjoy them under twinkling modern chandeliers.

Coconut Cove   THAI **££**
(☑ 01758-712250; www.thecoconutcove.co.uk; Lôn Port Morgan; mains £16-21; ⊙ 5.30-9pm Jul & Aug, closed Tue & Wed Sep-Jun; P) The original Thai chef and owner no longer rattles the pans at this perennially popular place (formerly Coconut Kitchen), but the replacement also hails from the mother country. As the restaurant's so close to the sea, fish dishes such as the Abersoch Bay Seafood Delight (mixed seafood stir-fried with vegetables in a spicy sauce) seem to make particular sense.

❶ Getting There & Away

Bus 18 stops on Stryd Fawr (High St), heading up to five times a day to/from Llanbedrog (seven minutes) and Pwllheli (15 to 20 minutes).

Aberdaron

☑ 01758 / POP 941

Aberdaron is an ends-of-the-earth kind of place, with whitewashed, windswept houses weathering the squalls that blow in from sweeping, cliff-lined Aberdaron Bay. It was traditionally the last resting spot before pilgrims made the treacherous crossing to Bardsey Island and the religious settlement founded by St Cadfan in the 6th century. The little Gwylan Islands, just offshore, are North Wales' most important puffin-breeding site, while choughs, peregrines,

hares and grey seals all thrive in the wild splendour of the surrounding country. Walking through this rare part of the world, with its infinite variety of light, stone and seascape, is something that stays with you.

◎ Sights

★ **Braich-y-Pwll**   AREA
(NT; www.nationaltrust.org.uk) The rugged, ethereally beautiful extremity of the Llŷn Peninsula is where medieval pilgrims set off to reach the holy island of Bardsey; one glimpse of their destination, rising out of the gunmetal-grey sea beyond the surf-pounded rocks, hints at the drama of their final voyage. A path leads down past the remains of St Mary's Abbey to a neolithic standing stone known as Maen Melyn, suggesting that this was a holy place well before the Celts or their saints arrived.

St Hywyn's Church   CHURCH
(www.st-hywyn.org.uk; ⊙ 10am-5pm) Stoically positioned above a pebbly beach, St Hywyn's Church has a left half dating from 1100 and a right half that was added 400 years later to accommodate pilgrims. Inside there's information about local history; two remnants of the original, 6th-century Christian community here (the 'Veracius' and 'Senacus' memorial stones); and a medieval font and holy-water stoup. Welsh poet RS Thomas was the minister here from 1967 to 1978 – an appropriate setting for his bleak, impassioned work.

If the church is locked during the rough opening hours, ask to borrow the key from the adjacent Tŷ Newydd hotel.

Porth Oer   BEACH
(Whistling Sands; NT; www.nationaltrust.org.uk; car park £1.50) This lovely, remote scoop of beach, 2.5 miles north of Aberdaron, has oddly shaped sand that squeaks when you walk on it, giving it its English name, Whistling Sands. From here it's a 2-mile coastal walk southwest via the twin headlands of Dinas Bach and Dinas Fawr to the cove of Porth Orion.

🛏 Sleeping & Eating

Tŷ Newydd   HOTEL **££**
(☑ 01758-760207; www.gwesty-tynewydd.co.uk; r from £110; 🛜) While the rooms are very pleasant, it's the location that really makes this friendly hotel stand out. Right on the beach, it has comfortably kitted-out, spacious and light-drenched rooms, many with wonderful

BARDSEY ISLAND (YNYS ENLLI)

This mysterious island, 2 miles long and 2 miles off the tip of the Llŷn, is a magical place. In fact, it's one of many candidates for the Isle of Avalon from the Arthurian legends. It's said that the wizard Merlin still sleeps in a glass castle somewhere on the island.

In the 6th or 7th century the obscure St Cadfan founded a monastery here, giving shelter to Celts fleeing the Saxon invaders, and medieval pilgrims followed in their wake. Three pilgrimages to Bardsey were said to be equivalent to one to Rome.

Most modern pilgrims to Bardsey are seabird-watchers; during the summer around 17,000 Manx shearwaters nest in burrows here, emerging at night. A colony of Atlantic grey seals lives here year-round; a pile of rocks by the harbour is a popular hang-out. Other sights include 6th-century **carved stones**, the remains of a 13th-century **abbey tower** and a candy-striped **lighthouse**.

The **Bardsey Island Trust** (☑ 08458-112233; www.bardsey.org) can help arrange trips to the island and holiday lets in cottages for those who wish to linger beyond a day trip.

Two private boat services are the only way to reach Bardsey. In summer **Bardsey Boat Trips** (☑ 07971-769895; www.bardseyboattrips.com; adult/child £30/20) sails to Bardsey from Porth Meudwy, near Aberdaron; **Enlli Charters** (☑ 08458-113655; www.enlli charter.co.uk; per person £45; ⊘ Apr-Sep) sails from Pwllheli.

sea views. The tide comes in right under the terraced pub restaurant (mains £12 to £17), which seems designed with an afternoon gin and tonic in mind.

Y Gegin Fawr　　　　　　　WELSH £
(The Big Kitchen; ☑ 01758-760359; mains from £7; ⊘ 9am-6pm) With their spiritual needs sorted, the Bardsey-bound pilgrims could claim a meal at Y Gegin Fawr, a little thick-walled communal kitchen with tiny windows that sits prettily at the heart of Aberdaron. Dating from 1300, it now dishes up locally caught crab and lobster, homemade cakes and scones, and, on weekend evenings in summer, barbecue pork, brisket and macaroni cheese.

ⓘ Getting There & Away

Buses calling at Aberdaron include the 8B to/from Nefyn (£2.60, 30 minutes, one direct per day), and up to eight 17/17B services per day to Llanbedrog (£2.60, 30 minutes) and Pwllheli (£2.60, 40 minutes).

THE NORTH COAST

The North Wales coast has perennial natural charms but seaside resorts of uneven appeal: some are outstanding examples of the genre, others more down at heel. The section west of Colwyn Bay includes glorious Unesco World Heritage–listed castles at Caernarfon and Conwy (p733) and the Victorian resort of Llandudno, a favourite

family-holiday hub. The sands stretch along a string of less-appealing resort towns east of the bay, but there are greater attractions to be discovered by turning south into the delightful Conwy Valley.

Caernarfon

☑ 01286 / POP 9763

Wedged between the gleaming Menai Strait and Snowdonia's deep-purple hills, Caernarfon's main claim to fame is its magnificent castle, one of the finest and doughtiest of Edward I's martial masterpieces. Given the town's crucial historical importance (it's been a key strategic site since the Roman occupation), its proximity to Snowdonia and its reputation as a centre of Welsh culture (it has a percentage of native speakers as high as anywhere), it's a winningly untouristy destination. It has an air of undemonstrative charm and there's a tangible sense of history in the streets around the castle, especially Palace St, Castle Sq and Hole in the Wall St. Within the cobbled lanes of the old walled town are some fine Georgian buildings, and the waterfront is marching inevitably towards gentrification.

⊙ Sights & Activities

★ **Caernarfon Castle**　　　　　CASTLE
(Cadw; www.cadw.wales.gov.uk; adult/child £9.50/5.70; ⊘ 9.30am-5pm Mar-Jun, Sep & Oct, to 6pm Jul & Aug, 10am-4pm Mon-Sat, from 11am Sun Nov-Feb; ♿) Majestic Caernarfon Castle was built by

Edward I between 1283 and 1330 as a military stronghold, seat of government and royal palace. Designed and mainly supervised by Master James of St George, from Savoy, its brief and scale were extraordinary. Today it remains one of the most complete and impressive castles in Britain – you can walk on and through the interconnected walls and towers gathered around the central green, most of which are well preserved but empty.

Inspired by the dream of Macsen Wledig recounted in the *Mabinogion*, Caernarfon echoes the 5th-century walls of Constantinople (İstanbul), with colour-banded masonry and polygonal towers, instead of the traditional round towers and turrets.

Despite its fairy-tale aspect it is thoroughly fortified, with a series of murder holes and a sophisticated arrangement of multiple arrow slits. It repelled Owain Glyndŵr's army in 1404 with a garrison of only 28 men, and resisted three sieges during the English Civil War before surrendering to Cromwell's army in 1646.

A year after construction began, Edward's second son was born here, becoming heir to the throne four months later when his elder brother died. To consolidate Edward junior's power he was made Prince of Wales in 1301, thus creating the tradition of English kings conferring that title on their heirs. As Edward II he came to a very nasty end, possibly via a red-hot poker; his much-eroded statue is over the King's Gate. However, the first investiture that actually took place here (rather than in London) was that of his namesake, Edward VIII, in 1911 (coincidentally, his reign was also cut short, albeit less violently).

Start your inspection at the **Eagle Tower**, the one with the flagpoles to the right of the entrance. On the turrets you can spot the weathered eagle from which it gets its name, alongside stone-helmeted figures intended to swell the garrison's apparent numbers (they're easier to spot from the quay).

There's a film tracing the history of the site since Roman times in the **North East Tower**, while in the **Queen's Tower** (named after Edward I's wife Eleanor) is the **Regimental Museum of the Royal Welch Fusiliers**, filled with medals, uniforms, weapons and historical displays.

Dinas Dinlle   BEACH
Dolphins and porpoises can sometimes be spotted from this long, sandy, rock-fringed Blue Flag beach, 6 miles southwest of Caernarfon. The flatness of the surrounding land contrasts dramatically with the sculpted Llŷn Peninsula, visible across the water, and a solitary hill capped by the remains of an Iron Age fort. Families will appreciate the cafe and toilets here.

Plas Menai   WATER SPORTS
(National Watersports Centre; ☑ 01248-670964, 0300 300 3112; www.plasmenai.co.uk; half/full day from £35/70; ☺ office 8.30am-5pm) This excellent centre offers year-round courses in sailing, power boating, kayaking, windsurfing and stand-up paddleboarding for all ability levels (weekend packages from £190, advance reservations necessary). The on-site accommodation includes B&B rooms (singles/doubles £50/80) and a bunkhouse (£32), both with pool and gym access. It's located 3 miles along the A487 towards Bangor. Bus 5C (Caernarfon to Bangor) stops here.

🛏 Sleeping & Eating

★ **Totters**   HOSTEL £
(☑ 01286-672963; www.totters.co.uk; 2 High St; dm/d £20/55; ☎) Modern, clean and very welcoming, this excellent independent hostel is Caernarfon's best-value sleep. A 14th-century arch gives a sense of history to the communal kitchen in the basement (it may once have been a street-level entrance) and continental breakfast is free. There are small dorms and doubles, a two-bed attic apartment, a TV room and a book-swap library.

★ **Victoria House**   B&B ££
(☑ 01286-678263; https://thevictoriahouse.co.uk; 13 Church St; r £90-100; @ ☎) Victoria House is pretty much the perfect guesthouse – a delightful, solid Victorian building in the middle of Caernarfon's old town, run by exceptionally hospitable and attentive hosts. The four spacious, modern rooms include lovely touches – free toiletries, a DVD on the town's history, fresh milk and a welcoming drink in the minibar – and breakfast is a joy.

Plas Dinas Country House   B&B £££
(☑ 01286-830214; www.plasdinas.co.uk; Bontnewydd; cottages/r from £109/139; P ☎) Until the 1980s this large 17th-century house belonged to Lord Snowdon's family; his wife, Princess Margaret, often stayed here. Despite the ancestral portraits in the hallway and the grand drawing room, the overall impression is surprisingly homey. The 10 bedrooms are filled with antiques and

thoughtful touches, such as quality toiletries and fluffy bathrobes, and self-catering cottages are also available.

Y Gegin Fach
CAFE £

(☎ 01286-672165; 5-9 Pool Hill; mains £6-7; ⊗ 9am-4pm Tue-Fri, from 10am Sat) 'The Little Kitchen' is a proper old-fashioned Welsh-speaking *caffi*, right down to the net curtains and cheery red-polka-dot tablecloths. It's a great spot to tuck into traditional faves like rarebit, faggots, *lobscouse* (lamb stew) and Welsh cakes, and wish you had a Welsh granny. Opens later in summer.

★Osteria
TUSCAN ££

(☎ 01286-238050; 26 Hole in the Wall St; mains £12-13; ⊗ 6-9.30pm Tue-Thu, noon-2.30pm & 6-9.30pm Fri & Sat; ✍) Two Florentine partners opened this excellent addition to Caernarfon's dining scene in a compact whitewashed-stone building hard up against the city walls. Specialising in interesting carpaccios and bruschette (try the gorgonzola with walnuts and honey), they import many of their ingredients and wines from Tuscany and prepare daily specials such as stuffed vegetables and pasta with cod and cherry-tomato ragu.

❶ Getting There & Away

BUS

Buses and coaches depart from the **bus station** (Pool Side). Buses include 1/1A to Criccieth (45 minutes), Tremadog (45 minutes) and Porthmadog (50 minutes); 5/X5 to Bangor (30 minutes), Conwy (1¼ hours) and Llandudno (1½ hours); 12 to Pwllheli (45 minutes); and 88 to Llanberis (30 minutes). Snowdon Sherpa bus S4 heads to Beddgelert (30 minutes) via the Snowdon Ranger (22 minutes) and Rhyd Ddu (24 minutes) trailheads.

Bicycle Beics Antur (☎ 01286-802222; www.anturwaunfawr.org; Porth yr Aur, High St; half/full day £12/18; ⊗ 9.30am-5pm Tue-Sat) hires bikes and can advise on local cycle routes. Information on Gwynedd recreational cycle routes including the 12.5-mile Lôn Eifion (starting near the Welsh Highland Railway station and running south to Bryncir) and the 4.5-mile Lôn Las Menai (following the Menai Strait to the village of Y Felinheli) can be found at www.gwynedd.llyw.cymru. Lôn Las Cymru passes through Caernarfon, heading northeast to Bangor and south to Criccieth.

CAR

Free street parking is at a premium, but you might snatch a park in the walled town (try Church St) and there are (highly contested) free parks by the water on the southern embankment of Victoria Dock.

TRAIN

Caernarfon is the northern terminus of the Welsh Highland Railway tourist train, which runs to Porthmadog (£40 return, 2½ hours) via Rhyd Ddu (£24 return, one hour) and Beddgelert (£31 return, 1½ hours) from Easter to October, with limited winter service. Benefiting from a £2.5-million upgrade, the station is near the river on St Helen's Rd.

Bangor

☎ 01248 / POP 18,439

While Bangor isn't the most attractive town in North Wales, it has a lively arts and cultural scene, and is the site of two of the region's best venues: Pontio and Storiel. Dominated by its university and blessed with a multicultural population, it's the largest city in Gwynedd and a major transport hub for North Wales, with plenty of onward connections to Anglesey and Snowdonia.

St Deiniol established a monastery here in the 6th century, which grew up into Bangor's sweet little cathedral. Bangor University, founded in 1884, sits on a ridge above town, its neo-Gothic contours aping those of the cathedral. During term time over 10,000 students swell the city's population, bringing youthful vigour and the area's best nightlife.

◉ Sights

Bangor Cathedral
CATHEDRAL

(https://bangorcathedral.churchinwales.org.uk; Glanrafon; ⊗ 10.30am-4.30pm Mon-Thu, to 1pm Fri & Sat) More formally known as the Cathedral Church of St Deiniol, this building occupies one of the oldest ecclesiastical sites in Britain, dating from AD 525, when the saint founded his community here. The beginning from which the city of Bangor grew, today's stone church dates to the 12th century, when Gruffudd ap Cynan rebuilt it following Viking raids. Later episodes of destruction followed, and much of today's cathedral is the work of Victorian architect Sir George Gilbert Scott.

Storiel
MUSEUM

(☎ 01248-353368; www.gwynedd.gov.uk/museums; Ffordd Gwynedd; ⊗ 11am-5pm Tue-Sat) FREE The title 'Storiel', a portmanteau of the Welsh words for 'story' and 'gallery', signals the combined historical and artistic focus of

CHRISNOE/SHUTTERSTOCK ©

1. South West Coast Path (p234), Cornwall 2. Llyn Padarn, Llanberis (p718) 3. Lake Windermere at Bowness (p572), Lake District 4. Hikers in the Scottish Highlands (p884)

LUKASZ PAJOR/SHUTTERSTOCK ©

Breathtaking Britain

Britain is best known for the historic capitals of London and Edinburgh, the university towns of Cambridge and Oxford, and the well-preserved Roman remains in Bath. However, beyond the urban sprawl lies another Britain: a landscape of high mountain vistas, dramatic valleys lined with lakes, and – as befitting an island – thousands of miles of spectacular coastline.

Lake District

The Lake District (p572) is home to the highest mountains and largest lakes in England. With summits snow-capped in winter, and spectacular at any time of year, this landscape inspired the poet William Wordsworth, and is a major magnet for hikers today. Since 2017, it's also been a Unesco World Heritage Site.

Snowdonia

Wales is crowned with Snowdonia (p710) – a range of rocky peaks and glacier-hewn valleys stretching across the north of the country. Snowdon itself is accessible by Swiss-style cog railway, while Tryfan and Glyder Fawr offer equally challenging hikes and spectacular views, as well as more chance of solitude.

Cornwall's Coast

In Britain, you're spoilt for choice when it comes to beautiful coastline, but in the far southwest, the coast of Cornwall (p327) is hard to beat, with its stunning combination of sandy beaches, tranquil coves, picture-postcard fishing ports, adrenaline-pumping surf spots and rugged cliffs carved by Atlantic waves.

Scotland's Northwest Coast

The long journey to the far northwest corner of the Scottish Highlands (p916) is repaid with some of the finest scenery anywhere in Britain. In this wild and remote region, the sheer mountainsides drop to the sea, while narrow sea lochs cut deep inland, creating a landscape that is almost other-worldly in its beauty.

this well-curated institution. Essentially a folk museum for Gwynedd county, it makes great use of the former bishop's palace, with exhibitions of local artefacts (including the Roman 'Segontium sword'), photography, art and more. Guided tours and creative workshops are offered at times, the cafe (Caffi Storiel) does good coffee, and there's a shop selling jewellery, ceramics and other handicrafts.

Garth Pier
PIER

(Garth Rd; adult/child 50/20p; ⊙8am-6pm Mon-Sat, 10am-5pm Sun) Given the large expanse of tidal mudflats here (a paradise for wading birds), it's surprising that the Victorians chose this site to build Britain's ninth-longest pleasure pier. Opened in 1896 (and narrowly escaping demolition in the 1970s), Garth Pier strides on its original iron legs 458m into the Menai Strait – most of the way to Anglesey. Ornate kiosks dot its length and there's a tearoom at the very end (closed from June 2018, to allow overdue repairs to the pier head).

You can park here for £1.50 per day.

Zip World Penrhyn Quarry
ADVENTURE SPORTS

(☑01248-601444; www.zipworld.co.uk; Penrhyn Quarry, Bethesda; single ride £89; ⊙8am-6.30pm) The old Penrhyn slate quarry, nearly a mile long and 360m deep, is home to Europe's longest (and the world's fastest) zip line – Velocity 2. Gear up in racing scarlet and build up confidence on the 'Little Zipper' before strapping in for the big one, shooting over the lake at the heart of the quarry at speeds of up to 125mph.

Bethesda is on the A5, about 4 miles southeast of Bangor.

Sleeping & Eating

Management Centre
HOTEL ££

(☑01248-365900; www.themanagementcentre. co.uk; Bangor Business School, College Rd; s/d £80/100; P☎) Bangor isn't exactly blessed with accommodation options, but this university business centre has 57 modern en-suite rooms and makes for a comfortable stay. The on-site restaurant and bar, 1884 (mains £12 to £14), serves evening meals from 6pm to 9pm if you don't fancy the steep walk down into town and back.

Blue Sky
CAFE £

(☑01248-355444; www.blueskybangor.co.uk; Ambassador Hall, rear 236 High St; mains £9-11; ⊙9.30am-5.30pm Mon-Sat; ☎☑) Blue Sky cafe hides down an alleyway in a former Jehovah's Witness Kingdom Hall, but the secret is out: it's hands down the best joint in town for breakfasts, soups, sandwiches, burgers and salads, with all ingredients sourced from local suppliers. The kitchen stops serving at 4pm, but the cafe stays open later when there's an evening gig.

☆ Entertainment

Pontio
PERFORMING ARTS

(☑01248-383838, box office 01248-382828; www. pontio.co.uk; Deiniol Rd; ⊙8.30am-11pm Mon-Sat, noon-8pm Sun) Pontio cements Bangor's place as the cultural capital of North Wales. Within the fluid, Guggenheim-esque interior of this ambitious new multimillion-pound arts and innovation centre are a 450-seat main theatre, a 120-seat studio theatre and a cinema. Run by Bangor University, it stages drama in English and Welsh, classical-music and circus performances, and other arts events, film festivals and more.

ⓘ Getting There & Away

National Express coaches head to/from Liverpool (£18, three hours), Birmingham (£19, six hours) and London Victoria (£22, 9½ hours).

The local bus station (Garth Rd) is located behind the Deiniol Shopping Centre. Bus routes include: 5C to Caernarfon (30 minutes); X5 to Conwy (40 minutes) and Llandudno (one hour); 53, 56, 57 and 58 to Menai Bridge (12 minutes) and Beaumaris (35 to 45 minutes); 85/86 to Llanberis (35 to 50 minutes); T2 to Caernarfon (25 to 35 minutes), Porthmadog (1¼ hours), Dolgellau (two hours), Machynlleth (2½ hours) and Aberystwyth (3½ hours); and X4 to Menai Bridge (18 minutes), Llangefni (40 minutes) and Holyhead (1¾ hours).

Bangor's train station is on Holyhead Rd, just off the southwestern end of the High St. Direct services head to/from Holyhead (£10, 30 to 45 minutes), Rhosneigr (£7.10, 25 minutes), Llanfair PG (£3.30, six minutes), Conwy (£7.20, 17 minutes) and London Euston (£96, 3¼ hours).

Conwy
☑01492 / POP 4839

A visit to Britain's most complete walled town should be high on the itinerary for anyone with even a mild crush on things historic. The World Heritage–listed castle continues to dominate the town and the mouth of the Conwy River, as it's done ever since Edward I first planted it here in the late 13th century.

Conwy

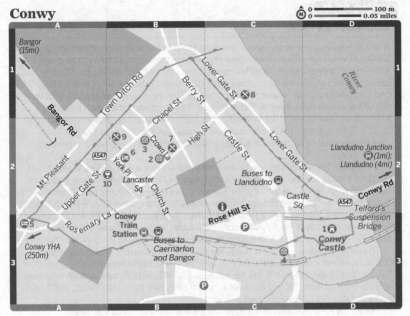

When approaching from the east, the scene is given another theatrical flourish by a tightly grouped trio of bridges crossing the Conwy, including Thomas Telford's 1826 suspension bridge (one of the first of its kind in the world) and Robert Stephenson's 1848 wrought-iron railway bridge (the first ever tubular bridge).

◎ Sights

★Conwy Castle   CASTLE
(Cadw; ☎01492-592358; www.cadw.wales.gov.uk; Castle Sq; adult/child £9.50/5.70; ⊘9.30am-5pm Mar-Jun, Sep & Oct, to 6pm Jul & Aug, 10am-4pm Mon-Sat, from 11am Sun Nov-Feb; P) Caernarfon is more complete, Harlech more dramatically positioned and Beaumaris more technically perfect, yet out of the four castles that compose the Unesco World Heritage Site, Conwy is the prettiest to gaze upon. Exploring the castle's nooks and crannies makes for a superb, living-history visit, but best of all, head to the battlements for panoramic views and an overview of Conwy's majestic complexity. Its role – to overawe and dominate the recently subjugated Welsh – couldn't be clearer.

At around £15,000 (over £45 million in today's money), Conwy was Edward I's most costly Welsh stronghold. And if its crenellat-

Conwy

◎ **Top Sights**
    1 Conwy Castle D3

◎ **Sights**
    2 Plas Mawr B2
    3 Royal Cambrian Academy B2
    4 Town Wall C3

🛏 **Sleeping**
    5 Bryn B&B A3
    6 Gwynfryn B2

🍴 **Eating**
    7 Edwards of Conwy B2
    8 Parisella's of Conwy Ice Cream C1
    9 Watson's Bistro B2

🍷 **Drinking & Nightlife**
    10 Albion Ale House B2

ed turrets and towers call to mind romance and fairy tales rather than subjugation and oppression, that certainly wasn't the intention of its builders.

Constructed between 1283 and 1287, Conwy rises from a rocky outcrop with commanding views across the mountains of Snowdonia and the mouth of the River Conwy. With two barbicans (fortified gateways),

DON'T MISS

BODNANT ESTATE

Whether you're a lover of gardens or fine food, the publicly accessible attractions on this privately owned agricultural estate (www.bodnant-estate.co.uk) should not be missed. While many large country estates fell on hard times in the 20th century, the McLaren family (holders of the title Baron Aberconway) managed to keep hold of theirs. The second Baron Aberconway, a keen horticulturist, donated **Bodnant Garden** (NT; ☑ 01492-650460; www.nationaltrust.org.uk; Ffordd Bodnant, Tal-y-Cafn; adult/child whole property £13/6.60; ☺ 10am-5pm Mar-Oct, to 4pm Nov-Feb, to 8pm Wed May-Aug; P ♦) to the National Trust in 1949, although the family continues to maintain it on the trust's behalf. Today it's a thriving seat of horticultural beauty, situated perfectly in the green and pleasant Conwy Valley.

Should you get peckish from your perambulations, there are **Bodnant Welsh Food** (☑ 01492-651931; www.bodnant-welshfood.co.uk; Furnace Farm, Tal-y-Cafn; ☺ farm shop 10am-5.30pm Mon-Sat, to 4.30pm Sun; P), the **Furnace Tea Room** (☑ 01492-651100; www.bodnant-welshfood.co.uk/eat/tea-room; Furnace Farm, Tal-y-Cafn; mains £5-8; ☺ 9am-5.30pm Mon-Sat, 10am-4.30pm Sun; P ☎) and the **Hayloft Restaurant** (☑ 01492-651102; www.bodnant-welshfood.co.uk/eat/hayloft-restaurant; Bodnant Welsh Food, Furnace Farm, Tal-y-Cafn; mains £17-20; ☺ noon-2pm & 5.30-8.30pm Wed-Sat, noon-3pm Sun) to assuage your hunger.

The estate is also home to the **National Beekeeping Centre Wales** (☑ 01492-651106; www.beeswales.co.uk; Furnace Farm, Tal-y-Cafn; tours adult/child £7/3.50; ☺ 10am-4pm Tue-Sat, from 11am Sun Apr-Oct), the **Farmhouse** (☑ 01492-651100; www.bodnant-welshfood.co.uk/accommodation; Bodnant Welsh Food, Furnace Farm, Tal-y-Cafn; s/d £70/110; P ☎) B&B and several self-contained cottages.

The estate is located east of the River Conwy, 4 miles south of Conwy town.

eight fierce, slightly tapered towers of coarse dark stone and a great bow-shaped hall all within the elongated complex, it's very solid indeed.

After the Civil War in the 17th century, the castle fell into some disrepair and the Council of State ordered it to be partly pulled down. But today it lives on and is a must-visit for anyone with an interest in Welsh history. The admission price includes a helpful audioguide; combined entry with Plas Mawr is £11.50/6.90 per adult/child.

Town Wall HISTORIC BUILDING
FREE The survival of most of its 1300m-long town wall, built concurrently with the castle (p733), makes Conwy one of the UK's prime medieval sites. The wall was erected to protect the English colonists from the Welsh, who were forbidden to live in the town and were even cleared from the surrounding countryside. You can enter the town walls at several points and walk along the battlements.

Plas Mawr HISTORIC BUILDING
(Cadw; www.cadw.wales.gov.uk; High St; adult/child £6.90/4.10; ☺ 9.30am-5pm Easter-Sep, to 4pm Oct) Completed in 1585 for merchant and courtier Robert Wynn, Plas Mawr is one of

Britain's finest surviving Elizabethan town houses. The tall, whitewashed exterior is an indication of the owner's status but gives no clue to the vivid interior, with its colourful friezes and plasterwork ceilings, and heraldic devices bearing the initials of the first owner. The admission price includes a helpful audioguide; combined entry with Conwy Castle (p733) is £11.50/6.90 per adult/child.

Royal Cambrian Academy GALLERY
(☑ 01492-593413; www.rcaconwy.org; Crown Lane; ☺ 11am-5pm Tue-Sat) FREE Founded in 1881, given the royal imprimatur by Queen Victoria in 1882, and still going strong, the Cambrian runs a full calendar of exhibitions by its members in its twin white-walled galleries, plus visiting shows from the National Museum Wales and elsewhere. Its excellent **Annual Summer Exhibition**, featuring the cream of contemporary fine art in Wales under one roof each August and September, has been a fixture from the academy's early days.

🛏 Sleeping

Conwy YHA HOSTEL £
(☑ 08453 719 732; www.yha.org.uk; Sychnant Pass Rd, Larkhill; dm/r £19/59; P ☎) Perched on a hill above the town, this former hotel

has been converted into a top-notch hostel. Dorms have two or four beds; all but one of the private rooms have an en-suite bathroom. Head up to the large dining room for awesome mountain and sea views (the bar's open from noon to 11pm). Wi-fi's in the common areas only.

★ **Gwynfryn** B&B ££

(☑ 01492-576733; www.gwynfrynbandb.co.uk; 4 York Pl; s/d from £90/105; ☎) Although it seems in danger of being engulfed by butterfly ornaments and dangling mobiles, this very friendly, nine-bedroom B&B – set in a refurbished Wesleyan chapel house and vestry – is a great place to stay. The clean, bright rooms are filled with thoughtful extras such as small fridges, biscuits, chocolates and earplugs. Guests must be 15 and over.

Bryn B&B B&B ££

(☑ 01492-592449; www.bryn.org.uk; Sychnant Pass Rd; s/d £65/95; P ☎) This sturdy Victorian house abutting the town wall have five sumptuous guest rooms decked out in soothing creams, three with king-size beds. Breakfast is a delight, with freshly baked bread and organic/fair-trade ingredients, as is the manicured garden, spreading right up to the old wall. Special diets are accommodated and nothing is too much trouble for the congenial proprietor.

✕ Eating & Drinking

★ **Parisella's of Conwy Ice Cream** ICE CREAM £

(www.parisellasicecream.co.uk; Conwy Quay; cone £2.50; ⊙ 10.30am-5.30pm, longer hours summer) This kiosk on the quay sells a selection of what may well be the best ice cream in Wales. Among Parisella's 60-plus flavours are such delights as *stracciatella*, lemon curd, and amaretto and black cherry. It also has a parlour at 12 High St (open 10am to 5pm, later in summer).

Seagulls gather outside both locations to mug unsuspecting patrons on busy days.

Edwards of Conwy DELI £

(☑ 01492-592443; www.edwardsofconwy.co.uk; 18 High St; pies £5.50; ⊙ 7am-5.30pm Mon-Sat, 10.30am-4.30pm Sun) While first and foremost a butchery with a great line in Welsh meat, Edwards also sells savoury pies, local cheeses and freshly filled baps and sandwiches. Awards are continually bestowed on the deli for everything from its sausages to its pork pies.

★ **Watson's Bistro** WELSH ££

(☑ 01492-596326; www.watsonsbistroconwy.co.uk; Bishop's Yard, Chapel St; 2-course lunch £14, mains £16-18; ⊙ 5.30-8.30pm Wed & Thu, noon-2pm & 5.30-9pm Fri & Sat, 5.30-8pm Sun) Hidden in a verdant garden setting in the lee of the town wall, Watson's marries French bistro cooking with quality local ingredients. Everything is homemade, from the ham-hock terrine, served with rarebit, to the sea bass with prawns and white wine to the ice cream. Book to arrive before 6.30pm for the early-bird set menu (three courses £22).

★ **Albion Ale House** PUB

(☑ 01492-582484; www.albionalehouse.weebly. com; 1-4 Upper Gate St; ⊙ noon-11pm Sun-Thu, to midnight Fri & Sat; ☎) Born out of a collaboration between four Welsh craft breweries (Purple Moose, Conwy, Nant and Great Orme), this heritage-listed 1920s boozer is a serious beer-drinker's nirvana. Of the 10 hand pulls, eight are loaded with real ale and two with cider. Winner of multiple Wales and North Wales pub-of-the-year awards, the Albion looks after wine and whisky drinkers, too.

ℹ Information

Tourist Office (☑ 01492-577566; www.visit llandudno.org.uk; Muriau Buildings, Rose Hill St; ⊙ 9.30am-5pm; ☎) This extremely busy office is well stocked with pamphlets and souvenirs and staffed by very helpful local experts. There's an interesting interactive exhibition on the princes of Gwynedd in the adjoining room.

ℹ Getting There & Away

BUS

Bus routes include 5/X5 to Caernarfon (1¼ hours), Bangor (40 minutes) and Llandudno (22 minutes); 14/15 to Llandudno (15 minutes); and 19 to Llandudno (20 minutes) and Betws-y-Coed (50 minutes).

Buses to Llandudno leave from the stop near Castle Sq, while those to Bangor/Caernarfon leave from outside the train station.

CAR

Through traffic bypasses town on the A55 via a tunnel under the River Conwy. The main road into town from Bangor skirts the outside of the town walls before cutting inside the walls through a gate of medieval dimensions, then crawling along Berry and Castle Sts and heading across the road bridge. The rest of the narrow grid within the walls has a one-way system and restricted parking during the day.

There are pay-and-display car parks on Mt Pleasant and by the castle. If you're after a free park and don't mind a 10-minute walk, turn right off Bangor Rd on the second-to-last street before you reach the town walls, cross the narrow rail bridge and park on residential Cadnant Park.

TRAIN

Conwy's train station is just inside the town walls on Rosemary Lane. Direct services head to/from Holyhead (£14.70, one hour), Rhosneigr (£16, 45 minutes), Llanfair PG (£8.70, 26 minutes), Bangor (£7.20, 21 minutes) and Shrewsbury (£30, two hours).

Llandudno

📞 01492 / POP 15,286

Wales' biggest seaside resort straddles a peninsula with long sandy beaches on either side. Developed as an upmarket holiday town for Victorian visitors, Llandudno still retains much of its 19th-century grandeur, with graceful wedding-cake architecture lining its sweeping waterfront promenade. Innumerable B&Bs and small private hotels cater to mainly mature-aged travellers in the low season, while young families descend with their buckets and spades in summer.

Alongside the lost-in-time charms of the British seaside (pier, promenade, Punch and Judy shows), Llandudno's main attraction is the near-wilderness of the Great Orme on its doorstep, a striking, rough-hewn headland offering breathtaking views of Snowdonia and miles of trails.

A slim connection to *Alice in Wonderland* (Alice Liddell, the inspiration for Lewis Carroll's fictional Alice, used to holiday here with her family) accounts for statues of the book's characters around the town, linked by a trail marked with 55 bronze rabbit footprints.

⊙ Sights

★ **Great Orme Bronze Age Mines** MINE
(📞 01492-870447; www.greatorme mines.info; adult/child £7/5; ⊙ 9.30am-5.30pm mid-Mar–Oct; 🅿🚼) Sitting unobtrusively near the top of the Great Orme (p736) is the largest prehistoric mine ever discovered. Nearly paved over for a car park, this site of tremendous historical importance has been developed as a must-see attraction, with a visitor centre and the chance to explore portions of the 5 miles of tunnels dug over centuries in search of copper. What is truly astounding is that

4000 years ago the tools used to excavate this maze were just stones and bones.

A 45-minute self-guided tour explains how the ancients turned rock into copper at the smelting site and then heads underground for about 200m into 3500-year-old tunnels. The site, whose discovery moved Britain's metallurgic history back a mind-boggling 2000 years, was worked again from the 17th to 19th centuries. Last entry is 4.30pm.

★ **Great Orme** NATURAL FEATURE
(Y Gogarth) From sea level it's difficult to gauge the sheer scale of the limestone chunk known as the Great Orme (Y Gogarth), yet it's 2 miles in circumference and 207m in height. Named after a Norse word for 'worm' or 'sea serpent', this gentle giant looms benevolently over Llandudno. Designated a Site of Special Scientific Interest (SSSI), the headland is home to a cornucopia of flowers, endemic butterflies and sea birds, and a herd of around 150 wild Kashmir mountain goats.

Three waymarked trails (of which the Haulfre Gardens Trail is the easiest to negotiate) lead to the summit; at various points you can find a neolithic burial chamber, a Bronze Age mine, the remains of an Iron Age fort, and an ancient church dedicated to Llandudno's namesake, St Tudno. At the summit there's a cafe, a bar, a gift shop, minigolf and other amusements, and the Great Orme Country Park Visitor Centre (p739), which has lots of fascinating displays, including a 15-minute video. Views – across the Irish Sea and its fertile wind farms in one direction, overlooking Llandudno towards Snowdonia in the other – are stunning.

Llandudno Pier PIER
(www.llandudnopier.com; North Pde; ⊙ 10am-10pm; 🚼) A trip to Llandudno isn't complete until you've strolled along the Victorian pier, eating ice cream and shooing away seagulls. At 670m, it's Wales' longest pier. When it opened in 1878 its main use was as a disembarkation point for passengers from Isle of Man steamers. Those days are long gone, and candyfloss, slot machines and views of the offshore wind farm are now the order of the day. High art it ain't, but the kids will love it.

Llandudno Promenade WATERFRONT
Llandudno's iconic 2-mile promenade is one of its distinctive sights. It was here that

Llandudno

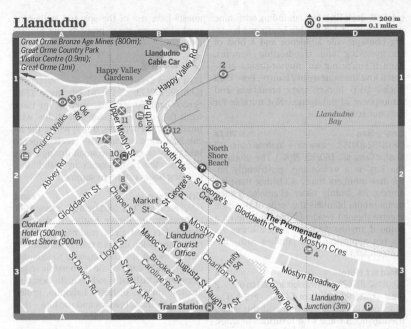

Llandudno

⊙ Sights
1 Great Orme Tramway.............................A1
2 Llandudno Pier...C1
3 Llandudno Promenade.........................C2

🛏 Sleeping
4 Can-y-Bae...D3
5 Escape B&B..A2
6 Osborne House......................................B1

🍴 Eating
7 Characters..A2
8 Cottage Loaf...B2
9 Fish Tram Chips.....................................A1
10 Orient-Express.....................................B2
11 Seahorse..B1

✪ Entertainment
12 Professor Codman's Punch &
     Judy Show...B2

Queen Victoria herself watched **Professor Codman's Punch & Judy Show** (☏07900-555515; www.punchandjudy.com/codgal.htm; The Promenade; ⊙noon-4pm Sat & Sun year-round, daily school holidays Easter–mid-Sep), performed by the same family since 1860 – let's hope she was amused. Mr Punch's iconic red-and-white-striped tent sits by the entrance to the Victorian pier.

West Shore   BEACH
When the main beach gets too frantic, go west to this considerably less built-up Blue Flag beach on Conwy Bay. The views over Anglesey and the mountains of Snowdonia can be stunning, especially as the sun sets, and there's a model-boating pool at the Orme end.

Great Orme Tramway   CABLE CAR
(☏01492-577877; www.greatormetramway.co.uk; Victoria Station, Church Walks; adult/child return £8.10/5.60; ⊙10am-6pm Easter-Oct) Head to the top of the Great Orme (p736) without breaking a sweat in an original 1902 tram-car. It's one of only three cable-operated trams in the world (the other two are in equally glamorous Lisbon and San Francisco). Trips head up the steep incline every 20 minutes, weather permitting; change to a second tram at the Halfway Station.

🛏 Sleeping

★**Escape B&B**   B&B ££
(☏01492-877776; www.escapebandb.co.uk; 48 Church Walks; r from £110; 🅿🛜) Escape is the

original sleek B&B in Llandudno, with nine individually styled double bedrooms boasting boutique-chic ambience and a host of energy-saving and trendsetting features. Even if you're not an interior-design geek, you'll love the honesty-bar lounge, Bose iPod docks, DVD library, tasty breakfasts and atmosphere of indulgence. Not suitable for kids under 10.

Can-y-Bae
HOTEL ££

(☑ 01492-874188; www.can-y-baehotel.com; 10 Mostyn Cres; s/d £60/85; ⊛✸) The 'Song of the Bay' is a welcoming, gay-friendly hotel that numbers many a visiting thespian among its mainly older clientele. Signed memorabilia blankets the walls of the little theatre-themed residents' bar and there's a piano if anyone wants to start a knees-up. It's not appropriate for families with children under 14.

Clontarf Hotel
HOTEL ££

(☑ 01492-877621; www.clontarfhotel.co.uk; 2 Great Ormes Rd; s/d from £47/67; ℗⊛) The nine individually styled rooms at this small, friendly hotel come with luxurious touches: quality showers in three of the rooms and a four-poster bed and whirlpool bath in the Romantic room. All rooms look out either onto the sea or the Great Orme (p736), a small bar contributes to evening relaxation and the friendly proprietor cooks up delicious breakfasts.

★ Bodysgallen Hall
HISTORIC HOTEL £££

(NT; ☑ 01492-584466; www.bodysgallen.com; s/d/ ste from £160/180/435; ℗⊛✸) Owned by the National Trust but privately managed, this magnificent pink-stone 1620 country house set in spectacular French-style formal gardens lets you lose yourself in the wood-panelled world of the Jacobean gentry. The rooms, split between the main hall and outlying cottages, are traditional with a nod to mod cons, and there's a fine restaurant (three courses £60) and spa centre.

Bodysgallen is 3 miles south of Llandudno, on the A470.

Osborne House
HOTEL £££

(☑ 01492-860330; www.osbornehouse.co.uk; 17 North Pde; stes from £160; ℗⊛) All marble, antique furniture and fancy drapes, the lavish Osborne House takes a classical approach to aesthetics and the results are impressive. The best suites are on the 1st floor, with Victorian-style sitting rooms and sea views. There's a restaurant (mains £14 to £17) and

guests have use of the spa and swimming pool at nearby sister property the Empire Hotel.

Eating

Fish Tram Chips
FISH & CHIPS £

(☑ 01492-872673; 22-24 Old Rd; mains £7-10; ⊙noon-7pm) Consistently serving up tasty, fresh fish and homemade side dishes with unaffected friendliness, this is where the locals head for good-value fish meals, either to take away or eat in the small dining room. Probably the best bargain in Llandudno; opening hours extend in summer.

Orient-Express
CAFE £

(☑ 01492-879990; 8 Gloddaeth St; mains £6-8; ⊙9am-5pm; ⊞) Brown leather, dark wood, chandeliers and tight confines conjure a faint impression of train travel's golden age, but above all this is simply a welcoming, child-friendly cafe. While it's possible to get standard British cafe food here, the best bets are the Turkish dishes – halloumi, grilled chicken, dolmas, baklava and the like – that draw on the owner's origins.

★ Cottage Loaf
PUB FOOD ££

(☑ 01492-870762; www.the-cottageloaf.co.uk; Market St; mains £15-19; ⊙11am-11pm, kitchen noon-9pm; ⊛✸) Tucked down an alleyway off Mostyn St, this charismatic pub has print-strewn walls, carpeted wooden floors and an atmosphere of genuine bonhomie. The delicious food ranges from the traditional – glazed Chinese pork belly, steak-and-Conwy-ale pie and their ilk – to the more exotic, and there are plenty of good beers on tap and in casks.

Characters
TEAHOUSE ££

(☑ 01492-872290; 11 Llewelyn Ave; mains lunch £6-7, dinner £17-19; ⊙11am-4pm Mon-Thu, 11am-4pm & 6.30-10.30pm Fri & Sat; ⊘) Strewn with art, decked out with wicker chairs and comfy sofas, and bedizened with glittering cake stands, Characters is Llandudno's prettiest and best tearoom. It serves three-tiered high teas (£10), along with light lunches of sandwiches, soup and jacket potatoes. Weekends sizzle with hot-stone dinners, where you cook your own meat and bring your own wine.

Seahorse
SEAFOOD £££

(☑ 01492-875315; www.the-seahorse.co.uk; 7 Church Walks; 1/2/3 courses £20/27/32; ⊙4.30-10pm) Don, the chef at Llandudno's only dedicated seafood restaurant, is a keen fisherman, and the menu reflects his passion for the local catch: Menai mussels in white wine, or Thai crab fishcakes with pickled cucumber. The restaurant is a split-level affair: upstairs is decorated with large Mediterranean murals, while the more intimate cellar room has a cosier feel.

ℹ Information

Great Orme Country Park Visitor Centre (☑ 01492-874151; www.visitllandudno.org. uk; Pyllau Rd, Great Orme; ☺10am-5.30pm Easter-Oct) The visitor centre on the summit of the **Great Orme** (p736) has 3D and interactive displays on the geology, flora and fauna of the area.

Llandudno Tourist Office (☑ 01492-577577; www.visitllandudno.org.uk; Unit 26, Victoria Centre, Mostyn St; ☺9am-4pm) In the Victoria Centre mall on Mostyn St, this tourist office has helpful staff, abundant information and an accommodation-booking service.

ℹ Getting There & Away

Llandudno's train station is centrally located on Augusta St. Frequent direct services head to/from Betws-y-Coed (£6.60, 50 minutes), Blaenau Ffestiniog (£9.20, 1¼ hours), Chester (£20, one hour) and Manchester Piccadilly (£34, 2¼ hours); for other destinations you'll need to change at Llandudno Junction (£3.10, eight minutes) or Chester.

Buses stop at the corner of Upper Mostyn and Gloddaeth Sts. National Express coaches head to/from Liverpool (£15, 2½ hours), Manchester (£17, 4½ hours), Birmingham (£24, 5½ hours) and London (£24, 8¾ hours). Other bus routes include 5/X5 to Caernarfon (1½ hours), Bangor (one hour) and Conwy (22 minutes); 14/15 to Conwy (15 minutes); and 19 to Conwy (20 minutes) and Betws-y-Coed (70 minutes).

Parking is metered during the day on the main part of the promenade, but it's free once you get past the roundabout east of Venue Cymru.

ISLE OF ANGLESEY (YNYS MÔN)

At 276 sq miles, the Isle of Anglesey is Wales' largest island, and bigger than any in England. A stronghold of Welsh language and culture, it's also a popular destination for visitors, with miles of inspiring coastline, secluded beaches and Wales' greatest concentration of ancient sites.

Over 85 sq miles of Anglesey – including almost all of its coastline – has been desig-

ORIEL YNYS MÔN

The linchpin of Anglesey's visual-arts scene, the 'Anglesey Gallery' – or Oriel Ynys Môn (☑ 01248-724444; www. orielynysmon.info; Rhosmeirch, Llangefni; ☺10.30am-5pm; P) FREE, as it's properly known – features temporary art exhibitions; a History Gallery exploring the island's past and role in the Roman invasion; licensed cafe Blas Mwy; and children's activity area the Discovery Den. But the main draw is the Oriel Kyffin Williams: exhibits change regularly but always feature some of the gallery's 400-plus works by Sir John 'Kyffin' Williams, a Llangefni boy and prolific artist whose portraits and landscapes provide a unique window into Welsh culture.

nated an Area of Outstanding Natural Beauty; hiking, beachcombing and water sports are all key attractions. Of the human-made landscape, the handsome Georgian town of Beaumaris is its most obviously appealing, but there are hidden gems scattered all over the island.

History

From prehistoric times Anglesey's fertile land was settled by small communities of farmers. The high concentration of monuments across the island – standing stones, burial chambers and circles – is testament to millennia of concentrated culture. The island was holy to the Celts and, in AD 60, was the last part of Wales to fall to the Romans. Given its outpost status and singular character, Anglesey has as fair a claim as any to being the Welsh heartland. One ancient name for the isle, bestowed by the prelate and historian Gerald of Wales in the 12th century, was Môn mam Cymru: 'Mother of Wales'.

Beaumaris (Biwmares)

☑ 01248 / POP 1274

Anglesey's prettiest town offers a winning combination of a waterfront location, everpresent views of the mainland mountains, a near-perfect castle and an elegant collection of Georgian, Victorian and Edwardian buildings, housing a growing number of boutiques, galleries, smart hotels and chic

PLAS NEWYDD

Plas Newydd (NT; ☑ 01248-714795; www.nationaltrust.org.uk; Llanfairpwll; adult/child £12/5.80, garden only £9.20/4.60; ⊙ house 11am-4.30pm Mar-early Nov, garden 10.30am-5pm Mar-Oct, 11am-3pm Nov-Feb; ℗) was the grand manor of the marquesses of Anglesey. Surrounded by tranquil gardens and pastures, with fine prospects across the Menai Strait to Snowdonia, the building has parts dating from the early 15th century, but most of today's Gothic masterpiece took shape in the 18th century. Inside, the walls are hung with gilt-framed portraits of worthy ancestors of the Paget family (William Paget was secretary of state to Henry VIII), who owned the house until 1976.

eateries. Many of the houses are painted in appealing pastels, and some are extremely old; the local real-estate agent occupies a half-timbered house dating from 1400 – one of the oldest in Britain (look for it on Castle St near the bottom of Church St).

The town's romantic name dates back to the time of French-speaking Edward I, who built the castle. It's a corruption of *beau marais* (meaning 'beautiful marsh') rather than *beau maris* (meaning 'good husbands') – although, unlike in French, the final 's' is sounded. Today, it's an understandably popular place for retirees.

⊙ Sights

★ **Beaumaris Castle**   CASTLE
(Cadw; http://cadw.gov.wales; Castle St; adult/child £6.90/4.10; ⊙ 9.30am-5pm Mar-Jun, Sep & Oct, to 6pm Jul & Aug, 11am-4pm Nov-Feb) Beaumaris is the last and most technically perfect of the ring of great castles built by Edward I of England to consolidate his Welsh conquests. Started in 1295, but never completed as fully designed, it enjoys World Heritage status. With its pleasing symmetry, water-filled moat, succession of four concentric 'walls within walls' and stout towers and gatehouse, it's what every sandcastle maker unknowingly aspires to.

Penmon Priory   CHURCH
(Cadw; www.cadw.wales.gov.uk; Penmon; parking £3; ⊙ 10am-4pm; ℗) **FREE** After the tearoom pleasantness of Beaumaris, Penmon, 4 miles north, provides a glimpse of Anglesey's long spiritual significance. An early Celtic monastery was established here in the 6th century by St Seiriol; burnt in AD 971, its last relic is the basin of the holy well, tucked behind the current simple stone church. The earliest extant parts of that church include two 10th-century Celtic crosses, a font from around the turn of the 2nd millennium and some wonderful 12th-century Romanesque arches.

Beaumaris Gaol   HISTORIC BUILDING
(www.visitanglesey.co.uk; Steeple Lane; adult/child £5.55/4.50, incl Beaumaris Courthouse £8.40/6.90, cash only; ⊙ 10.30am-5pm Sat-Thu Apr-Sep) This grim, stout-walled jail, built in the early 19th century and largely unaltered since, was modern for its time, with toilets in every cell and a treadmill water pump. However, that's not enough to dispel the gloom of the windowless punishment cell, the cell where condemned prisoners awaited their demise at the gibbet, or the stone-breaking yard where inmates were subjected to hard labour. Since it closed as a jail it's been used as a children's clinic (cheery!) and a police station.

🛏 Sleeping & Eating

Bulkeley   HERITAGE HOTEL ££
(☑ 01248-810415; www.bulkeleyhotel.co.uk; 19 Castle St; r from £102; ℗ 🛜 🐕) Grandly occupying the plum position on Beaumaris' main street, its ivied facade looking across the Menai Strait, this historic hotel was built by local grandee Richard Bulkeley expressly for the 1832 state visit of Princess (later Queen) Victoria – 450 houses were demolished in the process. Expect creaky parquet floors, stair rods on the runners and other cosy, traditional touches.

★ **Tredici Italian Kitchen**   ITALIAN ££
(☑ 01248-811230; www.tredicibeaumaris.com; 13 Castle St; mains £13-15; ⊙ noon-3pm & 6-9.30pm Sun-Thu, noon-3pm & 5-10pm Fri & Sat) Occupying an intimate 1st-floor dining room above a quality butcher and grocer, Tredici has brought a touch of the Mediterranean to wind-blown Anglesey. While local produce is used where possible (Halen Môn sea salt perks up the fries and the mussels are grown in the Menai Strait), the figs, mozzarella and the like are, naturally, imported from sunnier climes.

❶ Getting There & Away

Buses stop on Church St. Routes include the 53, 57 and 58 to Menai Bridge (18 minutes) and Bangor (35 to 45 minutes); some 57 and 58 buses continue on to Penmon (10 minutes).

There's a large pay-and-display car park on the waterfront by the castle. If you're prepared to walk, there are often free parking spots on the Menai Bridge approach to town.

Holyhead (Caergybi)

📞 01407 / POP 11,619

In the heyday of the mail coaches, Holyhead (confusingly pronounced 'holly head') was the vital terminus of the London road and the main hub for onward boats to Ireland. The coming of the railway only increased the flow of people through town, but the recent increase in cheap flights has reduced the demand for ferries and Holyhead has fallen on hard times. Regeneration funding allowed the impressive Celtic Gateway bridge to be built (linking the train station and ferry terminal to the main shopping street) and a radical waterfront redevelopment has been promised, but for now the town centre has a rather moribund air.

Holyhead isn't actually on Anglesey at all: Holy Island is divided from the west coast of Anglesey by a narrow channel, although the various bridges obstruct the views these days, and you might not realise that you're crossing onto another island.

◉ Sights

★ **South Stack**
Cliffs RSPB Reserve   WILDLIFE RESERVE
(📞 01407-762100; www.rspb.org.uk/wales; South Stack Rd; ⊙ visitor centre 10am-5pm, cafe 10am-3pm; 🅿) **FREE** Two miles west of Holyhead, the sea vents its fury against the vertiginous South Stack Cliffs, an important Royal Society for the Protection of Birds (RSPB) reserve where up to 9000 seabirds nest. Between May and June guillemots, razorbills and 15 loved-up puffin couples congregate here, while choughs, fulmars, peregrine falcons and numerous other species may be spotted throughout the year. You can get information, hire binoculars, and pre-book guided walks at the visitor centre.

South Stack Lighthouse   LIGHTHOUSE
(📞 01407-763900; www.trinityhouse.co.uk; South Stack Rd; adult/child £5.80/3.50; ⊙ 10am-4pm Easter-early Sep) The rocky islet of South Stack (Ynys Lawd) has a gloriously end-of-the-earth feel, with waves crashing around the base of the cliffs and guillemots and razorbills nesting overhead. The trail down to the rickety old bridge anchoring it to Holy Island is not for the faint-hearted, with 400 slippery steps and the promise of a steep return climb. Admission includes a tour of the 28m-high lighthouse, built in 1809, reputedly haunted and still operating. Last tickets are sold at 3.30pm.

Holyhead Maritime Museum   MUSEUM
(📞 01407-769745; www.holyheadmaritimemuseum.co.uk; Newry Beach; adult/child £5/free; ⊙ 10am-4pm Tue-Sun Easter-Oct; 🅿♿) Small but lovingly restored, this little museum is housed in what is believed to be the oldest lifeboat house in Wales (c 1858). It makes for a family-friendly outing, with model ships, photographs and exhibits on Holyhead's maritime history from Roman times onwards. Admire curiosities such as a mammoth's jawbone (unearthed in Holyhead Harbour in 1864) and the vintage hand-cranked diving pump, and catch the exhibition 'Holyhead at War' in the adjacent WWII air-raid shelter.

OFF THE BEATEN TRACK

BARCLODIAD Y GAWRES BURIAL MOUND

Squatting on a headland above gorgeous Trecastle Bay, 2 miles south of the village, Barclodiad y Gawres – the Giantess' Apronful – is the largest **neolithic tomb** (Cadw; 📞 01407-810153; www.cadw.gov.wales; ⊙ exterior 10am-4pm) **FREE** in Wales. When it was excavated in the 1950s, archaeologists were excited to find five standing stones inside, decorated in spirals and zigzags similar to those found in Ireland's Boyne Valley, along with the cremated remains of two men.

Due to problems with vandalism, the entrance to the mound is now blocked by an iron gate, but you can still peer into the murky space. If you're keen to get inside, call into Wayside Stores in Llanfaelog (1 mile up the road) to make an appointment between noon and 4pm on Saturdays, Sundays and bank holidays, and the staff will send someone down to open up.

🛏 Sleeping & Eating

Yr-Hendre
B&B ££

(📞 01407-762929; www.yr-hendre.net; Porth-y-Felin Rd; d/tw from £65; P 📶) A former minister's house set in a large garden on the quiet edge of town, Yr-Hendre is perhaps the best place to stay in Holyhead. Professionally managed and homey, the three bedrooms have a feminine touch (and names: Bethany, Amanda and Nicola) and views of the sea or Holyhead Mountain's bald pate. Walkers are welcomed and safe bicycle storage is available.

Ucheldre Kitchen
CAFE £

(www.ucheldre.org; Millbank; mains £5-6; ⏱ 10am-4.30pm Mon-Sat, 2-4.30pm Sun; P) Avoid the greasy spoons around the high street and head to the cafe attached to the arts centre (Canolfan Ucheldre; 📞 01407-763361; ⏱ 10am-5pm Mon-Sat, from 2pm Sun; P) instead. Lit by skylights and decked with art (local, and for sale), it's a relaxed spot for light lunches (wraps, toasted sandwiches, paninis, soup) or tea and cake (save room for the lemon-

meringue pie). Lunches are served from noon to 2pm only.

ℹ Getting There & Away

When the weather's poor, it always pays to check with the ferry companies – Irish Ferries (📞 0818 300 400; www.irishferries.com; foot passenger/motorcycle/car from £31/55/101) and Stena Line (📞 08447 707 070; www.stenaline.co.uk; foot passenger/bicycle/car from £31/41/99) – before heading to the ferry terminal (www.holyheadport.com), as services are sometimes cancelled. Direct trains head to/from Rhosneigr (£4.70, 12 minutes), Llanfair PG (£8.90, 29 minutes), Bangor (£10, 30 minutes), Conwy (£16, 1¼ hours) and London Euston (£100, 3¾ to 4½ hours).

National Express coaches stop at the ferry terminal, heading to/from Liverpool (£24, 2¾ hours), Manchester (£24, 4¾ hours), Birmingham (£24, four hours) and London Victoria (£59, 7½ hours).

The main local bus stop is on Summer Hill. Destinations include Trearddur (route 4; 10 minutes), Cemaes (61; 45 minutes), Llanfair PG (X4; one hour), Menai Bridge (X4; 1½ hours) and Bangor (X4; 1¾ hours).

Scotland

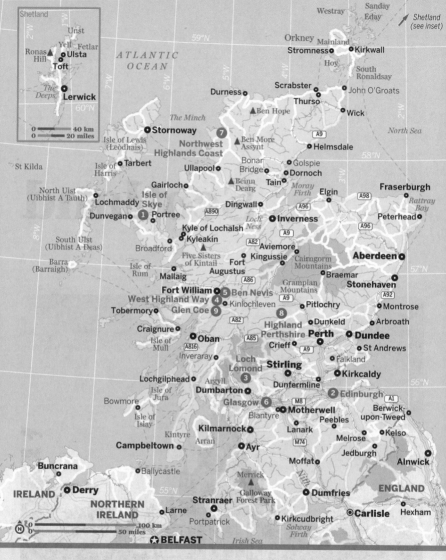

Scotland Highlights

1 **Isle of Skye** (p926)
Capturing the brooding splendour of Skye.

2 **Edinburgh** (p745)
Exploring Scotland's capital, one of the world's most fascinating cities.

3 **Loch Lomond** (p856)
Discovering one of the most scenic parts of Scotland.

4 **West Highland Way** (p857) Walking the challenging path through some of the country's finest scenery.

5 **Ben Nevis** (p909)
Climbing the highest point in Britain.

6 **Glasgow** (p792) Enjoying glorious architecture, great nightlife and friendly locals.

7 **Northwest Highlands Coast** (p916) Getting permanent jawdrop.

8 **Highland Perthshire** (p902) Admiring the magnificent forests and lochs.

9 **Glen Coe** (p906)
Uncovering scenic beauty and tragic history.

Edinburgh

☎ 0131 / POP 513,210

Best Places to Eat

➡ Kitchin (p777)
➡ Gardener's Cottage (p774)
➡ Ondine (p772)
➡ Timberyard (p777)
➡ Contini (p774)
➡ Aizle (p776)

Best Places to Stay

➡ Witchery by the Castle (p768)
➡ Pilrig House (p770)
➡ Sheridan Guest House (p770)
➡ Southside Guest House (p770)
➡ Two Hillside Crescent (p769)

Why Go?

Edinburgh is a city that begs to be explored. From the vaults and wynds (narrow lanes) that riddle the Old Town to the urban villages of Stockbridge and Cramond, it's filled with quirky, come-hither nooks that tempt you to walk just a little bit further. And every corner turned reveals sudden views and unexpected vistas – green sunlit hills, a glimpse of rust-red crags, a blue flash of distant sea.

But there's more to Edinburgh than sightseeing – there are top shops, world-class restaurants and a bacchanalia of bars to enjoy. This is a city of pub crawls and impromptu music sessions, late-night drinking, all-night parties and wandering home through cobbled streets at dawn.

All these superlatives come together at festival time in August, when it seems as if half the world descends on Edinburgh for one enormous party. If you can possibly manage it, join them.

When to Go

➡ Edinburgh is a year-round destination, but at peak periods – festival time in August and early September, and around New Year – crowds and prices reach their highest.

➡ May is a great time to visit, with generally fine weather and colourful flowers.

Edinburgh Highlights

1 **Edinburgh Castle** (p748) Admiring city-wide views from Edinburgh's dramatic fortress.

2 **Royal Yacht Britannia** (p764) Stepping on board the Queen's yacht in lively Leith.

3 **Arthur's Seat** (p761) Hiking up an extinct volcano for an unparalleled Edinburgh panorama.

4 **Real Mary King's Close** (p749) Venturing underground to see Edinburgh's hidden secrets.

5 **Palace of Holyroodhouse** (p761) Taking a tour of the city's ostentatious palace.

6 **National Museum of Scotland** (p752) Browsing the collections at Scotland's foremost museum.

7 **Rosslyn Chapel** (p783) Stepping into the real life inspiration for the Da Vinci Code.

History

Edinburgh owes its existence to the Castle Rock, the glacier-worn stump of a long-extinct volcano that provided a near-perfect defensive position guarding the coastal route from northeast England into central Scotland.

In the 7th century the Castle Rock was called Dun Eiden (meaning 'Fort on the Hill Slope'). When it was captured by invaders from the kingdom of Northumbria in northeast England in 638, they took the existing Gaelic name 'Eiden' and tacked it onto their own Old English word for fort, 'burh', to create the name Edinburgh.

Originally a purely defensive site, Edinburgh began to expand in the 12th century when King David I held court at the castle and founded the abbey at Holyrood. The royal court came to prefer Edinburgh to Dunfermline and, because parliament followed the king, Edinburgh became Scotland's capital. The city's first effective town wall was constructed around 1450, enclosing the Old Town as far east as Netherbow and south to the Grassmarket. This overcrowded area – by then the most populous town in Scotland – became a medieval Manhattan, forcing its densely packed inhabitants to build upwards instead of outwards, creating tenements five and six storeys high.

The capital played an important role in the Reformation (1560–1690), led by the Calvinist firebrand John Knox. Mary, Queen of Scots, held court in the Palace of Holyroodhouse for six brief years, but when her son James VI succeeded to the English throne in 1603 he moved his court to London. The Act of Union in 1707 further reduced Edinburgh's importance.

Nevertheless, cultural and intellectual life flourished during the Scottish Enlightenment (c 1740–1830), and Edinburgh became known as 'a hotbed of genius'. In the second half of the 18th century the New Town was built, and in the 19th century the population quadrupled to 400,000, as suburbs of Victorian tenements spread north and south.

In the 1920s the city's borders expanded again to encompass Leith in the north, Cramond in the west and the Pentland Hills in the south. Following WWII the city's cultural life blossomed, stimulated by the Edinburgh International Festival and its fellow

EDINBURGH IN...

Two Days

Edinburgh Castle (p748) is the city's number one sight, so allow a full morning to explore. Stroll down the Royal Mile via the historic **Real Mary King's Close** (p749). Have lunch at **Devil's Advocate** (p771), then spend the afternoon touring the **Scottish Parliament Building** (p759) and the **Palace of Holyroodhouse** (p761) before watching the sunset from **Calton Hill** (p757) for superb views across the city. Have dinner somewhere cosy and romantic, like **Ondine** (p772), then scare yourself silly on a ghost tour of **Greyfriars Kirkyard** (p755) and head on to the **Bongo Club** (p778) or **Cabaret Voltaire** (p778) for alternative entertainment.

Day two is all about culture: visit the **National Museum of Scotland** (p752), admire the iconic artworks of the **Scottish National Gallery** (p758), climb to the top of the **Scott Monument** (p758), then catch a bus to Leith to climb aboard the **Royal Yacht Britannia** (p764). For dinner, book a table at **Martin Wishart** (p777) for fine French dining, or **Fishers Bistro** (p777) for fresh seafood.

Four Days

With more time, you can explore further afield. Begin with a visit to the **Scottish National Gallery of Modern Art** (p765), then walk along the Water of Leith Walkway to Stockbridge and the **Royal Botanic Garden** (p765). If time allows, you could spend the afternoon hiking up **Arthur's Seat** (p761), and spend the evening sampling a few of the city's classic **pubs** (p777).

On day four, head to the southern fringes of the city and devote an entire morning to **Rosslyn Chapel** (p783). Return to the city centre to spend the afternoon browsing the boutiques and department stores of the New Town. Take an hour to wander around the **Scottish National Portrait Gallery** (p757), then enjoy an early-evening stroll through **Princes Street Gardens** (p757) en route to dinner at **Gardener's Cottage** (p774).

traveller, the Fringe, both held for the first time in 1947 and now recognised as world-class arts festivals.

Edinburgh entered a new era following the 1997 referendum vote in favour of a devolved Scottish parliament, which first convened in 1999 in a controversial modern building at the foot of the Royal Mile. The 2014 independence referendum saw Scots vote to remain part of the United Kingdom.

⊙ Sights

Edinburgh's main attractions are concentrated in the city centre – on and around the Old Town's Royal Mile between the castle and Holyrood, and in the New Town. A major exception is the Royal Yacht *Britannia,* which is in the redeveloped docklands district of Leith, 2 miles northeast of the centre.

If you tire of sightseeing, good areas for aimless wandering include the posh suburbs of Stockbridge and Morningside, the pretty riverside village of Cramond and the winding footpaths of Calton Hill and Arthur's Seat.

⊙ Old Town

Edinburgh's Old Town is a jagged, jumbled maze of historic masonry riddled with closes, stairs, vaults and wynds (narrow alleys) leading off the cobbled ravine of the Royal Mile, which links Edinburgh Castle to the Palace of Holyroodhouse. The restored 16th- and 17th-century Old Town tenements support a thriving city-centre community, crammed at street level with museums, restaurants, bars and shops.

The **Royal Mile** earned its regal nickname in the 16th century when it was used by the king to travel between the castle and the Palace of Holyroodhouse. There are five sections (the Castle Esplanade, Castlehill, Lawnmarket, High St and Canongate), the names of which reflect their historical origins.

ℹ ROYAL EDINBURGH TICKET

If you plan to visit the Royal Yacht *Britannia* as well as Edinburgh Castle and the Palace of Holyroodhouse, consider buying a Royal Edinburgh Ticket (https://edinburghtour.com/royal-edinburgh-ticket), which includes admission to all three plus unlimited travel on hop-on, hop-off tour buses among the various attractions.

★**Edinburgh Castle**   CASTLE
(Map p752; ☏ 0131-225 9846; www.edinburgh castle.gov.uk; Castle Esplanade; adult/child £18.50/11.50, audio guide £3.50/£1.50; ⊙ 9.30am-6pm Apr-Sep, to 5pm Oct-Mar, last entry 1hr before closing; ▣ 23, 27, 41, 42, 67) Edinburgh Castle has played a pivotal role in Scottish history, both as a royal residence – King Malcolm Canmore (r 1058–93) and Queen Margaret first made their home here in the 11th century – and as a military stronghold. The castle last saw military action in 1745; from then until the 1920s it served as the British army's main base in Scotland. Today it is one of Scotland's most atmospheric and popular tourist attractions.

The brooding, black crags of Castle Rock, rising above the western end of Princes St, are the very reason for Edinburgh's existence. This rocky hill was the most easily defended hilltop on the invasion route between England and central Scotland, a route followed by countless armies from the Roman legions of the 1st and 2nd centuries AD to the Jacobite troops of Bonnie Prince Charlie in 1745.

The **Entrance Gateway**, flanked by statues of Robert the Bruce and William Wallace, opens to a cobbled lane that leads up beneath the 16th-century **Portcullis Gate** to the cannons ranged along the Argyle and Mills Mount Batteries. The battlements here have great views over the New Town to the Firth of Forth.

At the far end of Mills Mount Battery is the famous **One O'Clock Gun**, where crowds gather to watch a gleaming WWII 25-pounder fire an ear-splitting time signal at exactly 1pm (every day except Sundays, Christmas Day and Good Friday).

South of Mills Mount, the road curls up leftwards through **Foog's Gate** to the highest part of Castle Rock, crowned by the tiny, Romanesque **St Margaret's Chapel**, the oldest surviving building in Edinburgh. It was probably built by David I or Alexander I in memory of their mother, Queen Margaret, sometime around 1130 (she was canonised in 1250). Beside the chapel stands **Mons Meg**, a giant 15th-century siege gun built at Mons (in what is now Belgium) in 1449.

The main group of buildings on the summit of Castle Rock is ranged around Crown Sq, dominated by the shrine of the **Scottish National War Memorial**. Opposite is the Great Hall, built for James IV (r 1488–1513) as a ceremonial hall and used as a meeting

THE STONE OF DESTINY

On St Andrew's Day 1996 a block of sandstone – 26.5 inches by 16.5 inches by 11 inches in size, with rusted iron hoops at either end – was installed with much pomp and circumstance in Edinburgh Castle. For the previous 700 years it had lain in London, beneath the Coronation Chair in Westminster Abbey. Almost all English, and later British, monarchs from Edward II in 1307 to Elizabeth II in 1953 have parked their backsides firmly over this stone during their coronation ceremony.

The legendary Stone of Destiny – said to have originated in the Holy Land, and on which Scottish kings placed their feet (not their bums; the English got that bit wrong) during their coronation – was stolen from Scone Abbey near Perth by Edward I of England in 1296. It was taken to London and there it remained for seven centuries – except for a brief removal to Gloucester during WWII air raids, and a three-month sojourn in Scotland after it was stolen by Scottish Nationalist students on Christmas in 1950 – as an enduring symbol of Scotland's subjugation by England.

The Stone of Destiny returned to the political limelight in 1996, when the then Scottish Secretary and Conservative Party MP Michael Forsyth arranged for the return of the sandstone block to Scotland. A blatant attempt to boost the flagging popularity of the Conservative Party in Scotland prior to a general election, Forsyth's publicity stunt failed miserably. The Scots said thanks very much for the stone and then, in May 1997, voted every Conservative MP in Scotland into oblivion.

Many people, however, believe Edward I was fobbed off with a shoddy imitation in 1296 and that the true Stone of Destiny remains safely hidden somewhere in Scotland. This is not impossible – some descriptions of the original stone state that it was made of black marble and decorated with elaborate carvings. Interested parties should read *Scotland's Stone of Destiny* by Nick Aitchinson, which details the history and cultural significance of Scotland's most famous lump of rock.

place for the Scottish parliament until 1639. Its most remarkable feature is the original, 16th-century hammerbeam roof.

The **Castle Vaults** beneath the Great Hall (entered via the **Prisons of War Exhibition**) were used variously as storerooms, bakeries and a prison. The vaults have been renovated to resemble 18th- and early 19th-century prisons, where graffiti carved by French and American prisoners can be seen on the ancient wooden doors.

On the eastern side of the square is the **Royal Palace**, built during the 15th and 16th centuries, where a series of historical tableaux leads to the highlight of the castle: a strongroom housing the **Honours of Scotland** (the Scottish crown jewels), among the oldest surviving crown jewels in Europe. Locked away in a chest following the Act of Union in 1707, the crown (made in 1540 from the gold of Robert the Bruce's 14th-century coronet), sword and sceptre lay forgotten until they were unearthed at the instigation of novelist Sir Walter Scott in 1818. Also on display here is the Stone of Destiny.

Among the neighbouring **Royal Apartments** is the bedchamber where Mary, Queen of Scots, gave birth to her son James

VI, who was to unite the crowns of Scotland and England in 1603.

⭐ **Real Mary King's Close**   HISTORIC BUILDING
(Map p752; ☎ 0131-225 0672; www.realmarykings close.com; 2 Warriston's Close; adult/child £15.50/9.50; ⏰ 10am-9pm Apr-Oct, 9am-5.30pm Mon-Thu, 9.30am-9pm Fri & Sat, to 6.30pm Sun Nov, 10am-5pm Sun-Thu, to 9pm Fri & Sat Dec-Mar; 🚌 23, 27, 41, 42) Edinburgh's 18th-century City Chambers were built over the sealed-off remains of Mary King's Close, and the lower levels of this medieval Old Town alley have survived almost unchanged amid the foundations for 250 years. Now open to the public, this spooky, subterranean labyrinth gives a fascinating insight into the everyday life of 17th-century Edinburgh. Costumed characters lead tours through a 16th-century town house and the plague-stricken home of a 17th-century gravedigger. Advance booking recommended.

The scripted tour, complete with ghostly tales and gruesome tableaux, can seem a little naff, milking the scary and scatological aspects of the close's history for all they're worth. But there are also things of genuine interest to see: there's something about the crumbling 17th-century **tenement room**

Royal Mile

A GRAND DAY OUT

Planning your own procession along the Royal Mile involves some tough decisions – it would be impossible to see everything in a single day, so it's wise to decide in advance what you don't want to miss and shape your visit around that. Remember to leave time for lunch, for exploring some of the Mile's countless side alleys and, during festival time, for enjoying the street theatre that is bound to be happening in High St.

The most pleasant way to reach the Castle Esplanade at the start of the Royal Mile is to hike up the zigzag path from the footbridge behind the Ross Bandstand in Princes Street Gardens (in springtime you'll be knee-deep in daffodils). Starting at ❶ **Edinburgh Castle** means that the rest of your walk is downhill. For a superb view up and down the length of the Mile, climb the ❷ **Camera Obscura's Outlook Tower** before visiting ❸ **Gladstone's Land** and ❹ **St Giles Cathedral**.

ROYAL VISITS TO THE ROYAL MILE

1561: Mary, Queen of Scots arrives from France and holds an audience with John Knox.
1745: Bonnie Prince Charlie fails to capture Edinburgh Castle, and instead sets up court in Holyroodhouse.
2004: Queen Elizabeth II officially opens the Scottish Parliament building.

CLAUDIO DIVIZIA / SHUTTERSTOCK ©

Edinburgh Castle
If you're pushed for time, visit the Great Hall, the Honours of Scotland and the Prisons of War exhibit. Head for the Half Moon Battery for a photo looking down the length of the Royal Mile.

Royal Scottish Academy

Scott Monument

Heart of Midlothian

City Chambers

NORTH BRIDGE

Scottish National Gallery

THE MOUND

Princes Street Gardens

HIGH ST

❺

❹

❷

❸

CASTLEHILL

GEORGE IV BRIDGE

❶

Scotch Whisky Experience

DE AGOSTINI / W. BUSS / GETTY IMAGES ©

Gladstone's Land
The 1st floor houses a faithful recreation of how a wealthy Edinburgh merchant lived in the 17th century. Check out the beautiful Painted Bedchamber, with its ornately decorated walls and wooden ceilings.

LUNCH BREAK

Burger and a beer at **Holyrood 9A**; steak and chips at **Maxie's Bistro**; slap-up seafood at **Ondine**.

If history's your thing, you'll want to add **⑤ Real Mary King's Close, ⑥ John Knox House** and the **⑦ Museum of Edinburgh** to your must-see list.

At the foot of the mile, choose between modern and ancient seats of power – the **⑧ Scottish Parliament** or the **⑨ Palace of Holyroodhouse.** Round off the day with an evening ascent of Arthur's Seat or, slightly less strenuously, Calton Hill. Both make great sunset viewpoints.

TAKING YOUR TIME

Minimum time needed for each attraction:
Edinburgh Castle two hours
Gladstone's Land 45 minutes
St Giles Cathedral 30 minutes
Real Mary King's Close one hour (tour)
Scottish Parliament one hour (tour)
Palace of Holyroodhouse one hour

Real Mary King's Close
The guided tour is heavy on ghost stories, but a highlight is standing in an original 17th-century room with tufts of horsehair poking from the crumbling plaster, and breathing in the ancient scent of stone, dust and history.

Canongate Kirk

CANONGATE

Our Dynamic Earth

ST MARY'S ST

SOUTH BRIDGE

Tron Kirk

Scottish Parliament
Don't have time for the guided tour? Pick up a 'Discover the Scottish Parliament Building' leaflet from reception and take a self-guided tour of the exterior, then hike up to Salisbury Crags for a great view of the complex.

Palace of Holyroodhouse
Find the secret staircase joining Mary, Queen of Scots' bedchamber with that of her husband, Lord Darnley, who restrained the queen while his henchmen stabbed to death her secretary (and possible lover), David Rizzio.

St Giles Cathedral
Look out for the Burne-Jones stained-glass window (1873) at the west end, showing the crossing of the River Jordan, and the bronze memorial to Robert Louis Stevenson in the Moray Aisle.

Old Town

that makes the hair rise on the back of your neck, with tufts of horsehair poking from collapsing lath-and-plaster walls that bear the ghost of a pattern, and the ancient smell of stone and dust thick in your nostrils.

In one of the former bedrooms off the close, a psychic once claimed to have been approached by the ghost of a little girl called Annie. It's hard to tell what's more frightening – the story of the ghostly child, or the bizarre heap of tiny dolls and teddies left by sympathetic visitors.

★**National Museum of Scotland** MUSEUM
(Map p752; ☑0300-123 6789; www.nms.ac.uk/national-museum-of-scotland; Chambers St; ⊙10am-5pm; ♿; 🚍45, 300) **FREE** Elegant Chambers St is dominated by the long facade of the National Museum of Scotland. Its extensive collections are spread between two buildings: one modern, one Victorian – the golden stone and striking architecture of the new building (1998) make it one of the city's most distinc-

tive landmarks. The museum's five floors trace the history of Scotland from geological beginnings to the 1990s, with many imaginative and stimulating exhibits. Audio guides are available in several languages. Fees apply for special exhibitions.

The modern building connects with the original Victorian museum, dating from 1861, the stolid, grey exterior of which gives way to a beautifully bright and airy, glass-roofed exhibition hall. The old building houses an eclectic collection covering natural history, archaeology, design and fashion, science and technology, and the decorative arts of ancient Egypt, the Islamic world, China, Japan, Korea and the West.

St Giles Cathedral CHURCH
(Map p752; www.stgilescathedral.org.uk; High St; ⊙9am-7pm Mon-Fri, to 5pm Sat, 1-5pm Sun Apr-Oct, 9am-5pm Mon-Sat, 1-5pm Sun Nov-Mar; 🚍23, 27,41,42) **FREE** The great grey bulk of St Giles Cathedral dates largely from the 15th centu-

ry, but much of it was restored in the 19th century. One of the most interesting corners of the kirk is the **Thistle Chapel**, built in 1911 for the Knights of the Most Ancient & Most Noble Order of the Thistle. The elaborately carved Gothic-style stalls have canopies topped with the helms and arms of the 16 knights – look out for the bagpipe-playing angel amid the vaulting.

Properly called the High Kirk of Edinburgh (it was only a true cathedral – the seat of a bishop – from 1633 to 1638 and from 1661 to 1689), the church was named after the patron saint of cripples and beggars. The interior lacks grandeur but is rich in history: a Norman-style church was built here in 1126 but was destroyed by English invaders in 1385 (the only substantial remains are the central piers that support the tower). St Giles was at the heart of the Scottish Reformation, and John Knox served as minister here from 1559 to 1572.

There are several ornate monuments in the church, including the tombs of **James Graham, Marquis of Montrose**, who led Charles I's forces in Scotland and was hanged in 1650 at the Mercat Cross; and his opponent, Covenanter (an adherent of the Scottish Presbyterian Church) **Archibald Campbell, Marquis of Argyll**, who was decapitated in 1661 after the restoration of Charles II. There's also a bronze memorial to author **Robert Louis Stevenson**, and a copy of the National Covenant of 1638.

By the side of the street, outside the western door of St Giles, is the **Heart of Midlothian**, set into the cobblestone paving. This marks the site of the Tolbooth. Built in the 15th century and demolished in the early 19th century, the Tolbooth served variously as a meeting place for parliament, the town council and the General Assembly of the Reformed Kirk, before becoming law courts and, finally, a notorious prison and place of

Old Town

execution. Passers-by traditionally spit on the heart for luck (don't stand downwind!).

At the other end of St Giles is the **Mercat Cross** (Map p752; 🚌35), a 19th-century copy of the 1365 original, where merchants and traders met to transact business and royal proclamations were read.

Camera Obscura
& World of Illusions   MUSEUM

(Map p752; www.camera-obscura.co.uk; Castlehill; adult/child £15.50/11.50; ⊙9am-10pm Jul & Aug, 9.30am-8pm Apr-Jun, Sep & Oct, 10am-7pm Nov-Mar; 🚌23, 27, 41, 42, 67) Edinburgh's camera

obscura is a curious 19th-century device – in constant use since 1853 – that uses lenses and mirrors to throw a live image of the city onto a large horizontal screen. The accompanying commentary is entertaining and the whole experience has a quirky charm, complemented by an intriguing exhibition dedicated to illusions of all kinds. Stairs lead up through various displays to the **Outlook Tower**, which offers great views over the city.

Grassmarket   STREET

(Map p752; 🚌2) The site of a cattle market from the 15th century until the start of the

20th century, the Grassmarket has always been a focal point of the Old Town. It was once the city's main place of execution, and over 100 martyred Covenanters are commemorated by a monument at the eastern end, where the gallows used to stand. The notorious murderers Burke and Hare operated from a now-vanished close off the western end.

Nowadays the broad, open square, lined by tall tenements and dominated by the looming castle, has many lively pubs and restaurants, including the **White Hart Inn** (Map p752; ✆0131-226 2806; www.whitehart-edinburgh.co.uk; 34 Grassmarket; ⊙11am-midnight Sun-Thu, to 1am Fri & Sat; ▣2), which was once patronised by Robert Burns. Claiming to be the city's oldest pub in continuous use (since 1516), it also hosted William Wordsworth in 1803. **Cowgate** – the long, dark ravine leading eastwards from the Grassmarket – was once the road along which cattle were driven from the pastures around Arthur's Seat to the safety of the city walls. Today it is the heart of Edinburgh's nightlife, with around two dozen clubs and bars within five minutes' walk of each other.

Greyfriars Kirkyard   CEMETERY
(Map p752; www.greyfriarskirk.com; Candlemaker Row; ⊙24hr; ▣2, 23, 27, 41, 42, 67) Greyfriars Kirkyard is one of Edinburgh's most evocative cemeteries, a peaceful green oasis dotted with elaborate monuments. Many famous Edinburgh names are buried here, including poet Allan Ramsay (1686–1758); architect William Adam (1689–1748); and William Smellie (1740–95), editor of the first edition of the *Encyclopaedia Britannica*. If you want to experience the graveyard at its scariest – inside a burial vault, in the dark, at night – go on a City of the Dead (p766) guided tour.

A more recent addition to the graveyard's reputation is the idea that it is the resting place of JK Rowling's famous villain Voldemort. Rowling is said to have been inspired to create the dark lord by the grave of 19th-century gentleman Thomas Riddell, who died in 1806 aged 72.

Greyfriars Bobby Statue   MONUMENT
(Map p752; cnr George IV Bridge & Candlemaker Row; ▣23, 27, 41, 42, 45, 67) Probably the most popular photo opportunity in Edinburgh, the life-size statue of Greyfriars Bobby, a Skye terrier who captured the hearts of the British public in the late 19th century,

SURGEONS' HALL MUSEUMS

Housed in a grand Ionic temple designed by William Playfair in 1832, these three fascinating **museums** (Map p752; ✆0131-527 1711; www.museum.rcsed.ac.uk; Nicolson St; adult/child £7/4; ⊙10am-5pm; ▣3, 5, 7, 8, 14, 30, 31, 33) were originally established as teaching collections. The History of Surgery Museum provides a look at surgery in Scotland from the 15th century to the present day. Highlights include the exhibit on murderers Burke and Hare, which includes Burke's death mask and a pocketbook made from his skin, and a display on Dr Joseph Bell, who was the inspiration for the character of Sherlock Holmes.

The adjacent Dental Collection, with its wince-inducing extraction tools, covers the history of dentistry, while the Pathology Museum houses a gruesome but compelling 19th-century collection of diseased organs and massive tumours pickled in formaldehyde.

EDINBURGH SIGHTS

stands outside Greyfriars Kirkyard. From 1858 to 1872 the wee dog maintained a vigil over the grave of his master, an Edinburgh police officer. The story was immortalised in a novel by Eleanor Atkinson in 1912, and in 1961 was made into a movie by – who else? – Walt Disney.

Scotch Whisky Experience   MUSEUM
(Map p752; www.scotchwhiskyexperience.co.uk; 354 Castlehill; adult/child from £15.50/7.50; ⊙10am-6pm Apr-Jul, to 5pm Aug-Mar; ▣23, 27, 41, 42) A former school houses this multimedia centre that takes you through the making of whisky, from barley to bottle, in a series of exhibits, demonstrations and talks that combine sight, sound and smell, including the world's largest collection of malt whiskies (3384 bottles!). The pricier tours include extensive whisky tastings and samples of Scottish cuisine. There's also a **restaurant** (Map p752; ✆0131-477 8477; www.scotchwhiskyexperience.co.uk/restaurant; mains £12-25; ⊙noon-8.30pm Sun-Thu, to 9pm Fri & Sat; ♠▣) that serves traditional Scottish dishes with, where possible, a dash of whisky thrown in.

Museum of Edinburgh   MUSEUM
(Map p752; ✆0131-529 4143; www.edinburgh museums.org.uk; 142 Canongate; ⊙10am-5pm

Mon & Thu-Sat, noon-5pm Sun; ⬛300) **FREE** You can't miss the colourful facade of Huntly House, brightly painted in red and yellow ochre, opposite the Tolbooth clock on the Royal Mile. Built in 1570, it houses a museum covering Edinburgh from prehistory to the present. Exhibits of national importance include an original copy of the National Covenant of 1638, but the big crowd pleaser is the dog collar and feeding bowl that once belonged to Greyfriars Bobby (p755), the city's most famous canine citizen.

Dunbar's Close Garden   GARDENS
(Map p758; Canongate; ⊘7am-7.30pm Jun-Aug, to 5.30pm May & Sep, to 4.30pm Apr & Oct, to 3.30pm Nov-Mar; ⬛300) Tucked away at the end of an Old Town close, this walled garden has been laid out in the style of the 17th century, with gravel paths, neatly trimmed shrubs, herbs, flowers and mature trees. A hidden gem,

and an oasis of tranquillity amid the bustle of the Royal Mile.

◉ New Town

Edinburgh's New Town lies north of the Old, on a ridge running parallel to the Royal Mile and separated from it by the valley of Princes Street Gardens. Its regular grid of elegant, Georgian terraces is a complete contrast to the chaotic tangle of tenements and wynds that characterises the Old Town, and is the world's most complete and unspoilt example of Georgian architecture and town planning.

Apart from the streetscape, the main sights are the art galleries and gardens on Princes St, and the Scottish National Portrait Gallery near St Andrew Sq, all within walking distance of each other.

Princes St is one of the world's most spectacular shopping streets. Built up on the

---

UNDERGROUND EDINBURGH

As Edinburgh expanded in the late 18th and early 19th centuries, many old tenements were demolished and new bridges were built to link the Old Town to the newly built areas to its north and south. South Bridge (built between 1785 and 1788) and George IV Bridge (built between 1829 and 1834) lead south from the Royal Mile over the deep valley of Cowgate, but so many buildings have been constructed around them that you can hardly tell they're bridges – George IV Bridge has a total of nine arches, but only two are visible; South Bridge has no fewer than 18 hidden arches.

These **subterranean vaults** were originally used as storerooms, workshops and drinking dens. But as Edinburgh's population swelled in the early 19th century with an influx of penniless Highlanders cleared from their lands, and Irish refugees from the potato famine, the dark, dripping chambers were given over to slum accommodation and abandoned to poverty, filth and crime.

The vaults were eventually cleared in the late 19th century, then lay forgotten until 1994, when the **South Bridge vaults** were opened to guided tours. Certain chambers are said to be haunted, and one particular vault was investigated by paranormal researchers in 2001.

Nevertheless, the most ghoulish aspect of Edinburgh's hidden history dates from much earlier – from the plague that struck the city in 1645. Legend has it that the disease-ridden inhabitants of **Mary King's Close** (a lane on the northern side of the Royal Mile, on the site of the City Chambers – you can still see its blocked-off northern end from Cockburn St) were walled up in their houses and left to perish. When the lifeless bodies were eventually cleared from the houses, they were so stiff that workers had to hack off limbs to get them through the small doorways and up the narrow, twisting stairs.

From that day on, the close was said to be haunted by the spirits of the plague victims. The few people who were prepared to live there reported seeing apparitions of severed heads and limbs, and the largely abandoned close fell into ruin. When the Royal Exchange (now the City Chambers) was constructed between 1753 and 1761, it was built over the lower levels of Mary King's Close, which were left intact and sealed off beneath the building.

Interest in the close revived in the 20th century when Edinburgh's city council began to allow occasional guided tours to enter. Visitors have reported many supernatural experiences – the most famous ghost is 'Annie', a little girl whose sad tale has prompted people to leave gifts of dolls in a corner of one of the rooms. In 2003 the close was opened to the public as the Real Mary King's Close (p749).

CALTON HILL

Calton Hill (Map p758; 🚊1, 4, 5, 15, 34, 45), which rises dramatically above the eastern end of Princes St, is Edinburgh's acropolis, its summit scattered with grandiose memorials dating mostly from the first half of the 19th century. It is also one of the best viewpoints in Edinburgh, with a panorama that takes in the castle, Holyrood, Arthur's Seat, the Firth of Forth, the New Town and the full length of Princes St. On Regent Rd, on the hill's southern side, is the **Burns Monument** (Map p758; Regent Rd; 🚊4, 5, 34) (1830), a Greek-style memorial to poet Robert Burns.

The largest structure on the summit is the **National Monument** (Map p758; Calton Hill; 🚊1, 4, 5, 15, 34, 45), a rather over-ambitious attempt to replicate the Parthenon in Athens, which was intended to honour Scotland's dead in the Napoleonic Wars. Construction – paid for by public subscription – began in 1822, but funds ran dry after only 12 columns had been erected. It became known locally as 'Edinburgh's Disgrace'.

The hill is also home to City Observatory, built in 1818 and based on the Temple of the Winds in Athens. Its original function was to provide a precise, astronomical time-keeping service for marine navigators, but it's now a stunning space for contemporary visual art.

north side only, it catches the sun in summer and allows expansive views across Princes Street Gardens to the castle and the crowded skyline of the Old Town.

The western end of Princes St is dominated by the red-sandstone edifice of the Caledonian Hotel and the tower of St John's Church (Map p752; Princes St; 🚊all Princes St buses), worth visiting for its fine Gothic Revival interior. It overlooks St Cuthbert's Parish Church (Map p752; Lothian Rd; 🚊all Lothian Rd buses), built in the 1890s on a site of great antiquity – there has been a church here since at least the 12th century, and perhaps since the 7th century. There is a circular **watchtower** in the graveyard – a reminder of the Burke and Hare days when graves had to be guarded against robbers.

At the eastern end is the prominent clock tower – traditionally three minutes fast so you don't miss your train – of the Balmoral Hotel (p769) (originally the North British Hotel, built by the railway company of the same name in 1902) and the beautiful 1788 **Register House** (Map p758; Princes St; 🚊all Princes St buses), designed by Robert Adam, with a statue of the Duke of Wellington on horseback in front. It houses the National Archives of Scotland and the **ScotlandsPeople genealogical research centre** (Map p758; ☑0131-314 4300; www.scotlandspeople.gov.uk; 2 Princes St; ☺9am-4.30pm Mon-Fri; 🚊all Princes St buses).

Princes Street Gardens (Map p752; Princes St; ☺dawn-dusk; 🚊Princes St) FREE lie in a valley that was once occupied by the Nor' Loch, a boggy depression that was drained in the early 19th century. The gardens are split in the middle by **The Mound**, which was created from around two million cartloads of earth excavated from the foundations of the New Town and dumped here to provide a road link across the valley to the Old Town. The road was completed in 1830.

★ Scottish National Portrait Gallery
GALLERY

(Map p758; ☑0131-624 6200; www.nationalgalleries.org; 1 Queen St; ☺10am-5pm; 🚼; 🚊all York Pl buses, 🚊St Andrew Sq) FREE The Venetian Gothic palace of the Scottish National Portrait Gallery is one of the city's top attractions. Its galleries illustrate Scottish history through paintings, photographs and sculptures, putting faces to famous names from Scotland's past and present, from Robert Burns, Mary, Queen of Scots, and Bonnie Prince Charlie to actor Sean Connery, comedian Billy Connolly and poet Jackie Kay. There's an admission fee for special exhibitions.

The gallery's interior is decorated in Arts and Crafts style, and nowhere more splendidly than in the **Great Hall**. Above the Gothic colonnade a processional frieze painted by William Hole in 1898 serves as a 'visual encyclopedia' of famous Scots, shown in chronological order from Calgacus (the chieftain who led the Caledonian tribes into battle against the Romans) to writer and philosopher Thomas Carlyle (1795–1881). The murals on the 1st-floor balcony depict scenes from Scottish history, while the ceiling is painted with the constellations of the night sky.

The gallery's selection of 'trails' leaflets adds a bit of background information while

New Town

leading you around the various exhibits; the Hidden Histories trail is particularly interesting.

Scott Monument
MONUMENT

(Map p758; www.edinburghmuseums.org.uk; East Princes Street Gardens; £5; ⏱10am-7pm Apr-Sep, to 4pm Oct-Mar; 🚌Princes St) The eastern half of Princes Street Gardens is dominated by the massive Gothic spire of the Scott Monument, built by public subscription in memory of novelist Sir Walter Scott after his death in 1832. The exterior is decorated with 64 carvings of characters from his novels; inside you can see an exhibition on Scott's life, and climb the 287 steps to the top for a superb view of the city.

Scottish National Gallery
GALLERY

(Map p752; ☎0131-624 6200; www.nationalgalleries.org; The Mound; ⏱10am-5pm Fri-Wed, to 7pm Thu; 🚌all Princes St buses, 🚌Princes St) FREE Designed by William Playfair, this imposing

classical building with its Ionic porticoes dates from 1850. Its octagonal rooms, lit by skylights, have been restored to their original Victorian decor of deep-green carpets and dark-red walls. The gallery houses an important collection of European art from the Renaissance to the post-Impressionism era, with works by Verrocchio (Leonardo da Vinci's teacher), Tintoretto, Titian, Holbein, Rubens, Van Dyck, Vermeer, El Greco, Poussin, Rembrandt, Gainsborough, Turner, Constable, Monet, Pissarro, Gauguin and Cézanne.

Charlotte Square
SQUARE

(Map p758; 🚌19, 36, 37, 41, 47) At the western end of George St is Charlotte Sq, the architectural jewel of the New Town, which was designed by Robert Adam shortly before his death in 1791. The northern side of the square is Adam's masterpiece and one of the finest examples of Georgian architecture anywhere. **Bute House** (Map p758), in the centre at No 6, is the official residence of Scotland's first minister.

Georgian House   HISTORIC BUILDING

(NTS; Map p758; www.nts.org.uk; 7 Charlotte Sq; adult/child £8/6; ⊙10am-5pm Apr-Oct, 11am-4pm Mar & Nov, 11am-4pm Thu-Sun 1-16 Dec; ⊒19, 36, 37, 41, 47) The National Trust for Scotland's Georgian House has been beautifully restored and furnished to show how Edinburgh's wealthy elite lived at the end of the 18th century. The walls are decorated with paintings by Allan Ramsay, Sir Henry Raeburn and Sir Joshua Reynolds, and there's a fully equipped 18th-century kitchen complete with china closet and wine cellar.

Royal Scottish Academy   GALLERY

(Map p758; ☑0131-225 6671; www.royalscottish academy.org; The Mound; ⊙10am-5pm Mon-Sat, noon-5pm Sun; ⊟Princes St) FREE This Greek Doric temple, with its northern pediment crowned by a seated figure of Queen Victo-

ria, is the home of the Royal Scottish Academy. Designed by William Playfair and built between 1823 and 1836, it was originally called the Royal Institution; the RSA took over the building in 1910. The galleries display a collection of paintings, sculptures and architectural drawings by academy members dating from 1831, and they host temporary exhibitions throughout the year (fees for these vary).

◉ Holyrood & Arthur's Seat

★Scottish
Parliament Building   NOTABLE BUILDING

(Map p762; ☑0131-348 5200; www.parliament. scot; Horse Wynd; ⊙9am-6.30pm Tue-Thu, 10am-5pm Mon, Fri & Sat in session, 10am-5pm Tue-Thu in recess; ♿; ⊒6, 300) FREE The Scottish Parliament Building, on the site of a former brewery and designed by Catalan architect Enric Miralles (1955–2000), was opened by the

New Town

Queen in October 2004. The ground plan of the complex is said to represent a 'flower of democracy rooted in Scottish soil' (best seen looking down from Salisbury Crags). Free, one-hour tours (advance bookings recommended) include visits to the Debating Chamber, a committee room, the Garden Lobby and the office of a member of parliament (MSP).

Miralles believed that a building could be a work of art. However, this weird concrete confection at the foot of Salisbury Crags initially left the good people of Edinburgh scratching their heads in confusion. What does it all mean? The strange forms of the exterior are each symbolic in some way, from the oddly shaped windows on the western wall (inspired by the silhouette of *The Reverend Robert Walker Skating on Duddingston Loch,* one of Scotland's most famous paintings) to the asymmetrical panels on the main facade (representing a curtain being drawn aside – a symbol of open government).

The **Main Hall**, inside the public entrance, has a low, triple-arched ceiling of polished concrete, like a cave, or cellar, or castle vault. It is a dimly lit space, the starting point for a metaphorical journey from this relative darkness up to the **Debating Chamber** (sitting directly above the Main Hall), which is, in contrast, a palace of light – the light of democracy. This magnificent chamber is the centrepiece of the parliament, designed not to glorify but to humble the politicians who sit within it. The windows face Calton Hill, allowing parliamentarians to look up to its monuments (reminders of the Scottish Enlightenment), while the massive, pointed oak beams of the roof are suspended by steel threads above the MSPs' heads like so many Damoclean swords.

The public areas of the building – the Main Hall, where there is an exhibition, shop and cafe, and the public gallery in the Debating Chamber – are open to visitors (free tickets are needed for the public gallery – see the website for details). If you want to see the parliament in session, check the website to see when it will be sitting – business days are normally Tuesday to Thursday year-round.

★ **Palace of Holyroodhouse** PALACE

(Map p762; ☑ 0303-123 7306; www.royalcollection. org.uk/visit/palace-of-holyroodhouse; Canongate, Royal Mile; adult/child incl audio guide £14/8.10; ◷ 9.30am-6pm, last entry 4.30pm Apr-Oct, to 4.30pm, last entry 3.15pm Nov-Mar; ▣6, 300) This palace is the royal family's official residence in Scotland but is more famous as the 16th-century home of the ill-fated Mary, Queen of Scots. The highlight of the tour is **Mary's Bedchamber**, home to the unfortunate queen from 1561 to 1567. It was here that her jealous second husband, Lord Darnley, restrained the pregnant queen while his henchmen murdered her secretary – and favourite – David Rizzio. A plaque in the neighbouring room marks the spot where Rizzio bled to death.

The palace developed from a guesthouse attached to Holyrood Abbey that was extended by James IV in 1501. The oldest surviving part of the building, the northwestern tower, was built in 1529 as a royal apartment for James V and his wife, Mary of Guise. Mary, Queen of Scots, spent six turbulent years here, during which time she debated with John Knox, married both her second and third husbands, and witnessed Rizzio's murder.

The self-guided audio tour leads you through a series of impressive royal apartments, culminating in the **Great Gallery**. The gallery's 89 portraits of Scottish kings were commissioned by Charles II and supposedly record his unbroken lineage from Scota, the Egyptian pharaoh's daughter who discovered the infant Moses in a reed basket on the banks of the Nile. The tour continues to the oldest part of the palace, which contains Mary's Bedchamber, connected by a secret stairway to her husband's bedroom, and ends with the ruins of Holyrood Abbey.

The palace is closed during royal visits; check the website for dates.

★ **Arthur's Seat** VIEWPOINT

(Holyrood Park; ▣6, 300) The rocky peak of Arthur's Seat (251m), carved by ice sheets from the deeply eroded stump of a long-extinct volcano, is a distinctive feature of Edinburgh's skyline. The view from the summit is well worth the walk, extending from the Forth bridges in the west to the distant conical hill of North Berwick Law in the east, with the Ochil Hills and the Highlands on the northwestern horizon. You can hike from Holyrood to the summit in around 45 minutes.

Holyrood Park PARK

(Map p762; ▣6, 300) In Holyrood Park Edinburgh is blessed with a little bit of wilderness in the heart of the city. The former hunting ground of Scottish monarchs, the park covers 263 hectares of varied landscape, including crags, moorland and loch, and the 251m summit of Arthur's Seat. Holyrood Park can be circumnavigated by car or bike along Queen's Dr.

Dr Neil's Garden GARDENS

(☑ 07849 187995; www.drneilsgarden.co.uk; Old Church Lane, Duddingston Village; ◷ 10am-dusk; ▣42) **FREE** Edinburgh's quintessential secret garden, in the shadow of a 12th-century kirk, is one of the most peaceful green spaces in Scotland. Cultivated in the 1960s by doctors Andrew and Nancy Neil from a scrappy piece of wilderness where Arthur's Seat slopes down to Duddingston Loch, the planting is a mixture of conifers, heathers and alpines, with a remarkable physic garden. Seek out a bench and soak up the meditative atmosphere of this special place.

Queen's Gallery GALLERY

(Map p762; www.royalcollection.org.uk/visit/the-queens-gallery-palace-of-holyroodhouse; Horse Wynd; adult/child £7/3.50, with Holyroodhouse £17.50/10; ◷ 9.30am-6pm, last entry 4.30pm Apr-Oct, to 4.30pm, last entry 3.15pm Nov-Mar; ▣6, 300) This stunning modern gallery, which occupies the shell of a former church and school, is a showcase for exhibitions of art from the Royal Collections. The exhibitions change every six months or so; for current details, check the website.

Holyrood Abbey ABBEY

(Map p762; www.historicenvironment.scot/visit-a-place/places/holyrood-abbey; Canongate; with Palace of Holyroodhouse free; ◷ 9.30am-6pm, last entry 4.30pm Apr-Oct, to 4.30pm, last entry 3.15pm Nov-Mar; ▣6, 300) David I founded this abbey

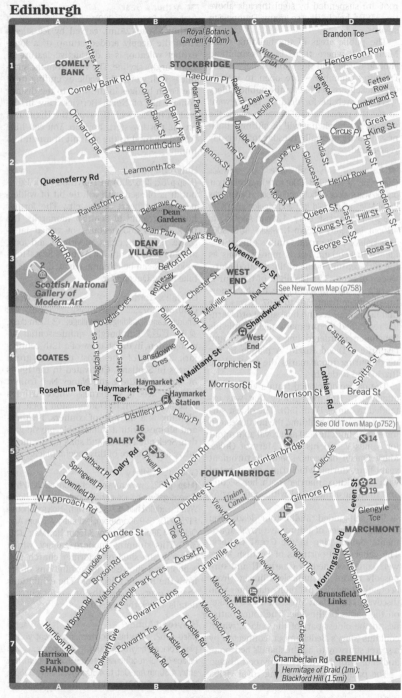

Royal Botanic Garden (400m)

Brandon Tce

Water of Leith

Henderson Row

COMELY BANK

STOCKBRIDGE

Fettes Ave

Comely Bank Rd

Raeburn Pl

Raeburn St

Dean St

Leslie Pl

Clarence St

Fettes Row

Cumberland St

Comely Bank Ave

Comely Bank St

Dean Park Mews

Danube St

Circus Pl

India St

Great King St

Howe St

Orchard Brae

S Learmonth Gdns

Lennox St

Ann St

Learmonth Tce

Eton Tce

Dune Tce

Gloucester La

Heriot Row

Frederick St

Queensferry Rd

Ravelston Tce

Belgrave Cres

Dean Gardens

Moray Pl

Queen St

Young St

Castle St

Hill St

Dean Path

DEAN VILLAGE

Bell's Brae

George St

Rose St

Belford Rd

Belford Rd

Rothesay Tce

Chester St

Melville St

WEST END

Queensferry St

Alva St

See New Town Map (p758)

Scottish National Gallery of Modern Art

2

Douglas Cres

Magdala Cres

Palmerston Pl

Manor Pl

Shandwick Pl

Castle Tce

COATES

Coates Gdns

Lansdowne Cres

W Maitland St

West End

Torphichen St

Lothian Rd

Spittal St

Bread St

Roseburn Tce

Haymarket Tce

Haymarket

Haymarket Station

Morrison St

Morrison St

See Old Town Map (p752)

Distillery La

Dalry Pl

DALRY

16

Dalry Rd

Orwell Pl

13

W Approach Rd

FOUNTAINBRIDGE

Fountainbridge

17

W Tollcross

14

Cathcart Pl

Springwell Pl

Downfield Pl

W Approach Rd

Dundee St

Viewforth

Union Canal

Gilmore Pl

11

Leven St

21

19

Glengyle Tce

MARCHMONT

Dundee Tce

Bryson Rd

Watson Cres

Dundee St

Gibson Tce

Dorset Pl

Granville Tce

Viewforth

Leamington Tce

Morningside Rd

Whitehouse Loan

Bruntsfield Links

W Bryson Rd

Temple Park Cres

Polwarth Gdns

Merchiston Park

Merchiston Ave

Viewforth

7

MERCHISTON

Forbes Rd

Harrison Rd

Harrison Park

SHANDON

Polwarth Gve

Polwarth Tce

E Castle Rd

W Castle Rd

Napier Rd

Chamberlain Rd

GREENHILL

Hermitage of Braid (1mi); Blackford Hill (1.5mi)

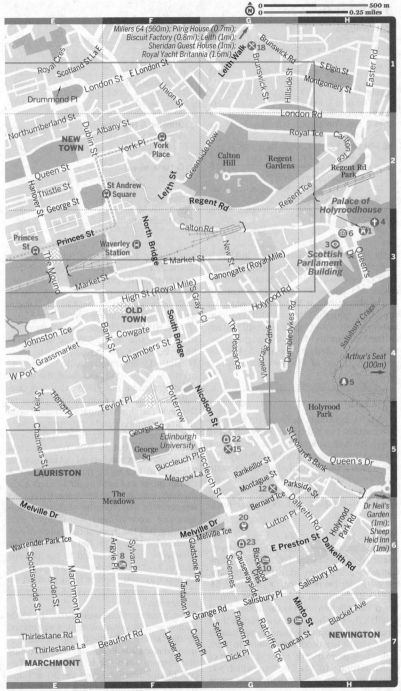

Millers 64 (560m); Pilrig House (0.7mi);
Biscuit Factory (0.8mi); Leith (1mi);
Sheridan Guest House (1mi);
Royal Yacht Britannia (1.6mi)

Edinburgh

in the shadow of Salisbury Crags in 1128. It was probably named after a fragment of the True Cross (*rood* is an old Scots word for cross), said to have been brought to Scotland by David's mother, St Margaret. Most of the ruins date from the 12th and 13th centuries, although a doorway in the far-southeastern corner has survived from the original Norman church. Admission is included in the cost of a Palace of Holyroodhouse (p761) ticket.

◉ Leith

Leith has been Edinburgh's seaport since the 14th century, but it fell into decay following WWII. It's now undergoing a steady revival, with old warehouses turned into luxury flats and a lush crop of trendy bars and restaurants sprouting along the waterfront leading to Ocean Terminal, a huge new shopping and leisure complex, and the former Royal Yacht *Britannia*.

★ **Royal Yacht Britannia** SHIP
(www.royalyachtbritannia.co.uk; Ocean Terminal; adult/child incl audio guide £16/8.50; ⊙ 9.30am-6pm Apr-Sep, to 5.30pm Oct, 10am-5pm Nov-Mar, last entry 1½hr before closing; ℗; ➂ 11, 22, 34, 36, 200, 300) Built on Clydeside, the former Royal Yacht *Britannia* was the British Royal Family's floating holiday home during their foreign travels from the time of her launch in 1953 until her decommissioning in 1997, and is now permanently moored in front of Ocean Terminal (p782). The tour, which you take at your own pace with an audio guide

(available in 30 languages), lifts the curtain on the everyday lives of the royals, and gives an intriguing insight into the Queen's private tastes.

Britannia is a monument to 1950s decor, and the accommodation reveals Her Majesty's preference for simple, unfussy surroundings. There was nothing simple or unfussy, however, about the running of the ship. When the Queen travelled, with her went 45 members of the royal household, five tonnes of luggage and a Rolls-Royce that was carefully squeezed into a specially built garage on the deck. The ship's company consisted of an admiral, 20 officers and a 220-strong crew.

The decks (of Burmese teak) were scrubbed daily, but all work near the royal accommodation was carried out in complete silence and had to be finished by 8am. A thermometer was kept in the Queen's bathroom to make sure the water was the correct temperature, and when the ship was in harbour one crew member was charged with ensuring that the angle of the gangway never exceeded 12 degrees. Note the mahogany windbreak that was added to the balcony deck in front of the bridge: it was put there to stop wayward breezes from blowing up skirts and inadvertently revealing the royal underwear.

Britannia was joined in 2010 by the 1930s racing yacht *Bloodhound,* which was owned by the Queen in the 1960s. *Bloodhound* is moored alongside *Britannia* (except in July and August, when she is away cruising) as part of an exhibition about the Royal Family's love of all things nautical.

The Majestic Tour (p767) bus runs from Waverley Bridge to *Britannia* during the ship's opening times.

Edinburgh Sculpture Workshop
ARTS CENTRE

(☑0131-551 4490; www.edinburghsculpture.org; 21 Hawthornvale; ☺9.30am-5pm Mon-Sat; [P]; ☐7, 11) FREE This state-of-the-art building located on an old railway siding is the first purpose-built centre dedicated to sculpture in the UK. There are regular exhibitions, talks and courses. Combine a visit with lunch at the top-notch on-site cafe run by Edinburgh's Milk and a stroll along the Hawthornvale path, which connects to the Water of Leith walkway.

The Shore
AREA

(☐16, 22, 36, 300) The most attractive part of Leith is this cobbled waterfront street alongside the Water of Leith, lined with pubs and restaurants. Before the docks were built in the 19th century this was Leith's original wharf. An iron plaque in front of No 30 marks the King's Landing – the spot where George IV (the first reigning British monarch to visit Scotland since Charles II in 1650) stepped ashore in 1822.

Biscuit Factory
ARTS CENTRE

(☑0131-629 0809; www.biscuitfactory.co.uk; 4-6 Anderson Pl; ☺10am-5pm; ☐11, 36) This recent addition to Leith's hipster scene is a creative arts hub housed in an old biscuit factory, also home to Edinburgh Gin's second distillery. Events range from food markets to random club nights. It's still early days, but other plans include creating 20 studios over two floors, a cafe and bar, and a community garden on the roof.

◉ Greater Edinburgh

★ Royal Botanic Garden
GARDENS

(☑0131-248 2909; www.rbge.org.uk; Arboretum Pl; ☺10am-6pm Mar-Sep, to 5pm Feb & Oct, to 4pm Nov-Jan; ☐8, 23, 27) FREE Edinburgh's Royal Botanic Garden is the second-oldest institution of its kind in Britain (after Oxford), and one of the most respected in the world. Founded near Holyrood in 1670 and moved to its present location in 1823, its 70 beautifully landscaped acres include splendid Victorian glasshouses (admission £6.50), colourful swaths of rhododendrons and azaleas, and a world-famous rock garden. There's a second entrance to the gardens at 20a Inverleith Row.

The John Hope Gateway visitor centre is housed in a striking, environmentally friendly building overlooking the main entrance on Arboretum Pl, and has exhibitions on biodiversity, climate change and sustainable development, as well as displays of rare plants from the institution's collection and a specially created biodiversity garden.

EDINBURGH SIGHTS

WORTH A TRIP

SCOTTISH NATIONAL GALLERY OF MODERN ART

Edinburgh's main modern art gallery (Map p762; ☑0131-624 6200; www.nationalgalleries. org; 75 Belford Rd; ☺10am-5pm; ☐13) FREE is surrounded by landscaped grounds some 500m west of Dean Village. As well as showcasing a stunning collection of paintings by the popular, post-Impressionist Scottish Colourists – in *Reflections, Balloch,* Leslie Hunter pulls off the improbable trick of making Scotland look like the south of France – the gallery is the starting point for a walk along the Water of Leith. Fees apply for some exhibitions.

The main collection, known as Modern One, concentrates on 20th-century art, with various European movements represented by the likes of Matisse, Picasso, Kirchner, Magritte, Miró, Mondrian and Giacometti. American and English artists are also represented, but most space is given to Scottish painters – from the Scottish Colourists of the early 20th century to contemporary artists such as Peter Howson and Ken Currie.

There's an excellent cafe (www.heritageportfolio.co.uk/cafes; mains £5-7; ☺9am-4.30pm Mon-Fri, 10am-4.30pm Sat & Sun; 🕸🏔) downstairs, and the surrounding park features sculptures by Henry Moore, Rachel Whiteread and Barbara Hepworth, among others, as well as a 'landform artwork' by Charles Jencks, and the Pig Rock Bothy, a rustic timber event and exhibition space created in 2014 as part of the Bothy Project (www.thebothy project.org).

A footpath and stairs at the rear of the gallery lead down to the Water of Leith Walkway, which you can follow along the river for 4 miles to Leith.

Edinburgh Zoo ZOO

(☑ 0131-334 9171; www.edinburghzoo.org.uk; 134 Corstorphine Rd; adult/child £19.50/9.95; ☺ 10am-6pm Apr-Sep, to 5pm Oct & Mar, to 4pm Nov-Feb; ♿; ☐ 12, 26, 31) Opened in 1913, Edinburgh Zoo is one of the world's leading conservation zoos. Edinburgh's captive breeding program has helped save many endangered species, including Siberian tigers, pygmy hippos and red pandas. The main attractions are the two **giant pandas**, Tian Tian and Yang Guang, who arrived in December 2011, and the **penguin parade** (the zoo's penguins go for a walk every day at 2.15pm). The zoo is 2.5 miles west of the city centre.

Lauriston Castle CASTLE

(☑ 0131-336 2060; www.edinburghmuseums.org.uk/Venues/Lauriston-Castle; 2a Cramond Rd S; adult/child £5/3, gardens free; ☺ gardens 8am-8pm Apr-Sep, to 5pm Oct-Mar, castle tours 2pm; Ⓟ ♿; ☐ 16, 21, 27, 29, 37, 41, 42) Lauriston Castle has one of the most remarkable Edwardian interiors in Scotland, with elements dating back to the 16th century. Gifted to the nation in the 1920s, the beautiful gardens, which remain free to the public, were originally laid out by William Playfair in the 1840s. The Italian and Japanese gardens are lovely tranquil spots for a picnic, and the views over the Firth of Forth and Cramond Island are magnificent.

🏃 Activities

Edinburgh is lucky to have several good walking areas within the city boundary, including Arthur's Seat (p761), Calton Hill (p757), **Blackford Hill** (Charterhall Rd; ☐ 24, 38, 41), **Hermitage of Braid** (www.fohb.org; ☐ 5, 11, 15, 16), **Corstorphine Hill** (www.corstorphinehill.org.uk; Clermiston Rd N; Ⓟ; ☐ 26) and the coast and river at **Cramond** (☐ 41). The **Pentland Hills** (www.pentlandhills.org) FREE, which rise to over 500m, stretch southwest from the city for over 15 miles, offering excellent high- and low-level walking.

You can follow the **Water of Leith Walkway** (www.waterofleith.org.uk/walkway) from the city centre to Balerno (8 miles), and continue across the Pentlands to Silverburn (6.5 miles) or Carlops (8 miles), and return to Edinburgh by bus. Another good walk is along the **Union Canal towpath**, which begins in Fountainbridge and runs all the way to Falkirk (31 miles). You can return to Edinburgh by bus at Ratho (8.5 miles) or Broxburn (12 miles), and by bus or train from Linlithgow (21 miles).

The **Scottish Rights of Way & Access Society** (☑ 0131-558 1222; www.scotways.com) provides information and advice on walking trails and rights of way in Scotland.

☞ Tours

Walking Tours

Edinburgh has a wealth of walking tours that allow you to explore the city by theme, as well as a number of hop-on, hop-off bus tours that run between the city's top sights.

Edinburgh Literary Pub Tour WALKING

(www.edinburghliterarypubtour.co.uk; adult/student £14/10; ☺ 7.30pm daily May-Sep, limited days Oct-Apr) An enlightening two-hour trawl through Edinburgh's literary history – and its associated howffs (pubs) – in the entertaining company of Messrs Clart and McBrain. One of the city's best walking tours.

City of the Dead Tours WALKING

(www.cityofthedeadtours.com; adult/concession £11/9; ☺ 9pm Easter-Oct, 8.30pm Nov-Easter) This nightly tour of Greyfriars Kirkyard is probably the scariest of Edinburgh's 'ghost' tours. Many people have reported encounters with the 'Mackenzie Poltergeist', the ghost of a 17th-century judge who persecuted the Covenanters and now haunts their former prison in a corner of the kirkyard. Not suitable for children under 12.

Invisible (Edinburgh) WALKING

(☑ 07500-773709; www.invisible-cities.org; per person £10) This venture trains homeless people as tour guides to explore a different side of the city. Tour themes include Crime & Punishment (includes Burke and Hare) and Powerful Women (from Maggie Dickson to JK Rowling). Must be booked in advance; check website for times.

Cadies & Witchery Tours WALKING

(Map p752; ☑ 0131-225 6745; www.witchery tours.com; 84 West Bow; adult/child £10/7.50; ☺ 7pm year-round, plus 9pm Apr-Sep; ☐ 2) The becloaked and pasty-faced Adam Lyal (deceased) leads a 'Murder & Mystery' tour of the Old Town's darker corners. These tours are famous for their 'jumper-ooters' – costumed actors who 'jump oot' when you least expect it.

Trainspotting Tours WALKING

(www.leithwalks.co.uk; per person £7.50, minimum charge £15) A tour of locations from Irvine Welsh's notorious 1993 novel *Trainspotting*, and the 1996 film of the book, delivered with wit and enthusiasm. Not suitable for kids.

Rebus Tours
WALKING
(☎0131-553 7473; www.rebustours.com; per person £15; ☉noon Sat) A two-hour guided tour of the 'hidden Edinburgh' frequented by novelist Ian Rankin's fictional detective, John Rebus. Not recommended for children under 10.

Mercat Tours
WALKING
(Map p752; ☎0131-225 5445; www.mercattours.com; Mercat Cross; adult/child £13/8; ☐35) Mercat offers a wide range of fascinating history walks and 'Ghosts & Ghouls' tours, but its most famous is a visit to the hidden, haunted underground vaults beneath South Bridge. Tours depart from the Mercat Cross (p754).

Bus Tours

Majestic Tour
BUS
(www.edinburghtour.com; adult/child £15/7.50; ☉daily year-round except 25 Dec) Hop-on, hop-off tour departing every 15 to 20 minutes from Waverley Bridge to the Royal Yacht *Britannia* at Ocean Terminal via the New Town, the Royal Botanic Garden and Newhaven, returning via Leith Walk, Holyrood and the Royal Mile.

City Sightseeing
BUS
(www.edinburghtour.com; adult/child £15/7.50; ☉daily year-round except 25 Dec) Bright-red, open-top bus tours of the Old Town and New Town, departing every 20 minutes from Waverley Bridge.

🎆 Festivals & Events

Edinburgh's Hogmanay
NEW YEAR
(☎0131-510 0395; www.edinburghshogmanay.com; street-party tickets £21; ☉30 Dec-1 Jan) Edinburgh's Hogmanay is the biggest winter festival in Europe, with events including a torchlit procession, a huge street party and the famous 'Loony Dook', a chilly sea-swimming event on New Year's Day. To get into the main party area in the city centre after 8pm on 31 December you'll need a ticket – book well in advance.

Imaginate Festival
PERFORMING ARTS
(☎0131-225 8050; www.imaginate.org.uk; late May-early Jun) Britain's biggest festival of performing arts for children, Imaginate is a week-long event suitable for kids aged three to 12. Groups from around the world perform classic tales like *Hansel and Gretel* as

well as new material written especially for a young audience.

Edinburgh International Film Festival
FILM
(☎0131-623 8030; www.edfilmfest.org.uk; ☉Jun) One of the original Edinburgh Festival trinity, having first been staged in 1947 along with the International Festival (p768) and the Fringe, the two-week June film festival is a major international event, serving as a showcase for new British and European films, and staging the European premieres of one or two Hollywood blockbusters.

Royal Highland Show
FAIR
(☎0131-335 6200; www.royalhighlandshow.org; Royal Highland Centre, Ingliston; late Jun; ☉adult/child £29/free) Scotland's hugely popular national agricultural show is a four-day feast of all things rural, with everything from show-jumping and tractor driving to sheep shearing and falconry. Countless pens are filled with coiffed show cattle and pedicured prize ewes. The show is held over a long weekend (Thursday to Sunday).

Scottish Real Ale Festival
BEER
(www.sraf.camra.org.uk; Corn Exchange, Chesser Ave; late Jun or early Jul) A celebration of the fermented and yeasty, Scotland's biggest beer fest gives you the opportunity to sample a wide range of traditionally brewed beers from Scotland and around the world. Froth-topped bliss. Held over a long weekend in June or July.

Edinburgh Food Festival
FOOD & DRINK
(www.edfoodfest.com; ☉Jul) This four-day festival, based in George Square Gardens, precedes the opening of the Edinburgh Fringe with a packed program of talks, cookery demonstrations, tastings, food stalls and entertainment.

Edinburgh International Jazz & Blues Festival
MUSIC
(☎0131-473 2000; www.edinburghjazzfestival.com; ☉Jul) Held annually since 1978, the Jazz & Blues Festival pulls in top talent from all over the world. It runs for nine days, beginning on a Friday, a week before the Fringe and Tattoo (p768) begin. The first weekend sees a carnival parade on Princes St and an afternoon of free, open-air music in Princes Street Gardens.

Edinburgh Festival Fringe
PERFORMING ARTS
(☎0131-226 0026; www.edfringe.com; ☉Aug) When the first Edinburgh International

Festival was held in 1947, eight theatre companies didn't make it onto the main program. Undeterred, they grouped together and held their own mini-festival, on the fringe, and an Edinburgh institution was born. Today the Fringe is the biggest festival of the performing arts anywhere in the world.

Edinburgh Military Tattoo
MILITARY

(☑0131-225 1188; www.edintattoo.co.uk; ☉Aug) The Military Tattoo is a spectacular display of military marching bands, massed pipes and drums, acrobats, cheerleaders and motorcycle display teams, all played out in front of the magnificent backdrop of the floodlit castle. Each show traditionally finishes with a lone piper, dramatically lit, playing a lament on the battlements. Held over the first three weeks of August.

Edinburgh International Festival
PERFORMING ARTS

(☑0131-473 2000; www.eif.co.uk; ☉Aug-Sep) First held in 1947 to mark a return to peace after the ordeal of WWII, the Edinburgh International Festival is festooned with superlatives – the oldest, the biggest, the most famous, the best in the world. The original was a modest affair, but today hundreds of the world's top musicians and performers congregate for three weeks of diverse music, opera, theatre and dance.

🛌 Sleeping

Edinburgh offers a wide range of accommodation options, from moderately priced guesthouses set in lovely Victorian villas and Georgian town houses to expensive and stylish boutique hotels. There are also plenty of chain hotels, and a few truly exceptional hotels housed in magnificent historic buildings. At the budget end of the range, there is no shortage of youth hostels and independent backpacker hostels, which often have inexpensive double and twin rooms.

🛏 Old Town

Budget Backpackers
HOSTEL £

(Map p752; ☑0131-226 6351; www.budgetback packers.com; 9 Cowgate; dm £17-24, tw £68; @🎧; 🖵2) This fun spot piles on the extras, with bike storage, pool tables, laundry and a colourful chill-out lounge. You'll pay a little more for four-bunk dorms, but the larger dorms are great value. The only downside is that prices increase at weekends, but otherwise it's a brilliant spot to doss.

Safestay Edinburgh
HOSTEL £

(Map p752; ☑0131-524 1989; www.safestay.com; 50 Blackfriars St; dm £34-40, tw £139; @🎧; 🖵300) A big, modern hostel, with a convivial cafe where you can buy breakfast, and mod cons such as keycard access and charging stations for mobile phones, MP3 players and laptops. Lockers in every room, a huge bar and a central location just off the Royal Mile make this a favourite among the young, party-mad crowd – don't expect a quiet night!

Kickass Hostel
HOSTEL ££

(Map p752; ☑0131-226 6351; https://kickasshos tels.co.uk; 2 West Port; dm £20-25, tw £74; @🎧; 🖵2) Great value and great location (the castle is just five minutes away) are the main attractions here, but the colourful decor, cheap cafe-bar and helpful staff are bonuses. Bunks have free lockers, bedside lights and phone-charging stations, too.

★ Witchery by the Castle
B&B £££

(Map p752; ☑0131-225 5613; www.thewitchery. com; Castlehill; ste from £345; P; 🖵23, 27, 41, 42) Set in a 16th-century Old Town house in the shadow of Edinburgh Castle, the Witchery's nine lavish Gothic suites are extravagantly furnished with antiques, oak panelling, tapestries, open fires, four-poster beds and roll-top baths, and supplied with flowers, chocolates and complimentary champagne. Overwhelmingly popular – you'll have to book several months in advance to be sure of getting a room.

Adagio Aparthotel
APARTMENT £££

(Map p752; ☑0131-322 8299; www.adagio-city. com; 231 Canongate; d from £214; P🎧; 🖵6, 300) One of a worldwide chain of aparthotels, this place offers luxurious, fully equipped apartments sleeping two to four, in a superb location right on the Royal Mile and just 10 minutes' walk from Waverley train station.

Grassmarket Hotel
HOTEL £££

(Map p752; ☑0131-220 2299; www.grassmarket hotel.co.uk; 94-96 Grassmarket; s/d/tr from £144/167/248; 🎧; 🖵2) An endearingly quirky hotel set in a historic Grassmarket tenement in the heart of the Old Town, this place has bedroom walls plastered with front pages from the *Dandy* (a DC Thomson comic published in Dundee) and coffee stations supplied with iconically Scottish Tunnock's teacakes and Irn-Bru. Some bargain rates available direct through the website.

🛏 New Town

Code Pod Hostel
HOSTEL **£**

(Map p758; ☑0131-659 9883; www.codehostel.com; 50 Rose St N Lane; dm from £25, d £99; ☎; 🚇Princes St) This upmarket hostel, bang in the middle of the New Town, combines cute designer decor with innovative sleeping pods that offer more privacy than bunks (four to six people per dorm, each with en suite shower room). There's also a luxurious double apartment called the Penthouse, complete with kitchenette and roof terrace.

Haystack Hostel
HOSTEL **£**

(Map p758; ☑0131-557 0036; https://haystackhostels.co.uk; 3 W Register St; dm £24-36; @☎; 🚇St Andrew Sq) The recently refurbished Haystack is a small, clean and relatively quiet hostel, with solid pine bunks and comfy new mattresses in 12-, nine- and three-bed dorms. There's a small kitchen and recreation area, and a laundry. The location is great, off the east end of Princes St and just two minutes' walk from the train and bus stations.

★ Two Hillside Crescent
B&B **££**

(Map p758; ☑0131-556 4871; www.twohillsidecrescent.com; 2 Hillside Cres; r from £115; @☎; 🚇19, 26, 44) Five spacious and individually decorated bedrooms grace this gorgeous Georgian town house – it's worth splashing out for the 'superior' room with twin floor-to-ceiling windows overlooking the gardens. Guests take breakfast around a large communal table in a stylishly modern dining room – smoked salmon and scrambled eggs is on the menu – and your hosts could not be more helpful.

★ 14 Hart Street
B&B **££**

(Map p758; ☑07795 203414; http://14hartstreet.co.uk; 14 Hart St; s/d £115/125; ☎; 🚇8) Centrally located and child friendly, 14 Hart Street is steeped in Georgian elegance and old Edinburgh charm. Run by a retired couple, the B&B has three generous bedrooms, all en suite, and a sumptuous dining room where guests can enjoy breakfast at a time of their choosing. Indulgent extras include whisky decanters and shortbread in every room.

Gerald's Place
B&B **££**

(Map p758; ☑0131-558 7017; www.geraldsplace.com; 21b Abercromby Pl; d £89-149; @☎; 🚇23, 27) Gerald is an unfailingly charming and helpful host, and his lovely Georgian garden flat (just two guest bedrooms, each with a private bathroom) has a great location across from a peaceful park, an easy stroll from the city centre. There may be a minimum three-night stay in peak season (cash or cheque only; no credit cards).

★ Principal
BOUTIQUE HOTEL **£££**

(Map p758; ☑0131-341 4932; www.phcompany.com/principal/edinburgh-charlotte-square; 38 Charlotte Sq; r from £245; 🅿☎; 🚇all Princes St buses) Arriving in this modern makeover of a classic Georgian New Town establishment (formerly the Roxburghe Hotel) feels like being welcomed into a country-house party. Service is friendly and attentive without being intrusive, and the atmosphere is informal; in the bedrooms, designer decor meets traditional tweed, and breakfast is served in a lovely glass-roofed garden courtyard.

Balmoral Hotel
HOTEL **£££**

(Map p758; ☑0131-556 2414; http://balmoralhotel.grandluxuryhotels.com; 1 Princes St; r from £295; 🅿☎🏊; 🚇all Princes St buses) The sumptuous Balmoral – a prominent landmark at the eastern end of Princes St – offers some of the best accommodation in Edinburgh, including suites with 18th-century decor, marble bathrooms and stunning sunset views of Princes St and the Scott Monument (p758). There's also a spa and gym with 20m pool in the basement.

Angels Share Hotel
HOTEL **£££**

(Map p758; ☑0131-247 7000; www.angelssharehotel.com; 9-11 Hope St; r from £135; ☎; 🚇all Princes St buses) You'll be right in the middle of the New Town action at this small but buzzing hotel, with Princes St shops and George St cocktail bars just a short stagger away. Rooms are understated but stylish, each decorated with a huge image of a Scottish celeb – fine if you don't mind Lulu or Rod Stewart looming over your bed!

🛏 South Edinburgh

Argyle Backpackers
HOSTEL **£**

(Map p762; ☑0131-667 9991; www.argyle-backpackers.co.uk; 14 Argyle Pl; dm/tw from £15/54; @☎; 🚇41) The Argyle, spread across three adjacent terrace houses, is a quiet and relaxed hostel offering triple, double and twin rooms as well as four- to six-bed dorms (mixed or female only). There's a comfortable TV lounge, an attractive little conservatory and a pleasant walled garden at the back where you can sit outside in summer.

Town House B&B ££

(Map p762; ☑0131-229 1985; www.edinburgh bedandbreakfast.com; 65 Gilmore Pl; per person £45-62; P🛜; 🚍10, 27) The five-room Town House is a plush little B&B offering the sort of quality and comfort you might expect from a much larger, more expensive place. It's an elegant Victorian terrace house with big bay windows, spacious bedrooms (all en suite) and a breakfast menu that includes salmon fishcakes and kippers alongside the more usual offerings.

Sherwood Guest House B&B ££

(Map p762; ☑0131-667 1200; www.sherwood-edinburgh.com; 42 Minto St; s/d from £75/90; P🛜; 🚍all Newington buses) One of the most attractive guesthouses on Minto St's B&B strip, the Sherwood is a refurbished Georgian terrace house decked out with hanging baskets and shrubs. Inside are six en suite rooms that combine period features with modern fabrics and neutral colours.

★**Southside Guest House** B&B £££

(Map p762; ☑0131-668 4422; www.southside guesthouse.co.uk; 8 Newington Rd; s/d from £100/140; 🛜; 🚍all Newington buses) Though set in a typical Victorian terrace, the Southside transcends the traditional guesthouse category and feels more like a modern boutique hotel. Its eight stylish rooms, featuring the clever use of bold colours and modern furniture, ooze interior design. Breakfast is an event, with Buck's Fizz (cava mixed with orange juice) on offer to ease the hangover.

Albyn Townhouse B&B £££

(Map p762; ☑0131-229 6459; https://albyn townhouse.co.uk; 16 Hartington Gardens; s/d from £101/154; P🛜; 🚍11, 15, 16, 23, 36, 45) Set in a refurbished Victorian town house tucked away at the end of a quiet cul-de-sac in the fashionable Bruntsfield district, this B&B is a real home-away-from-home. Designer-ish decor doesn't detract from the welcoming atmosphere, and the owners (plus their charming dog) are only too pleased to offer advice on where to go and what to see.

Knight Residence APARTMENT £££

(Map p752; ☑0131-622 8120; www.theknightres idence.co.uk; 12 Lauriston St; 1-/2-/3-bedroom apt from £130/160/240; P🛜; 🚍2) Works by contemporary artists adorn these modern studio, and one-, two- and three-bedroom apartments (available by the night; the three-bedroom options sleep up to seven),

each with fully equipped kitchen and comfortable lounge with cable TV, DVD and stereo. It has a good central location in a quiet street only a few minutes' walk from the Grassmarket.

🛌 Leith

Edinburgh Central SYHA HOSTEL £

(SYHA; Map p758; ☑0131-524 2090; www.syha. org.uk; 9 Haddington Pl; dm/tw £23/61; @🛜; 🚍all Leith Walk buses) This modern, purpose-built hostel, off Leith Walk about a half-mile north of Waverley train station, is a big (300-bed), flashy, five-star establishment with its own cafe-bistro as well as a self-catering kitchen, smart and comfortable eight-bed dorms and private rooms, and mod cons including keycard entry and plasma-screen TVs.

★**Sheridan Guest House** B&B ££

(☑0131-554 4107; www.sheridanedinburgh.com; 1 Bonnington Tce; s/d from £85/95; P🛜; 🚍11) Flowerpots filled with colourful blooms line the steps of this little haven hidden away north of the New Town. The eight bedrooms (all en suite) blend crisp colours with contemporary furniture, stylish lighting and colourful paintings, which complement the house's clean-cut Georgian lines. The breakfast menu adds omelettes, pancakes with maple syrup, and scrambled eggs with smoked salmon to the usual offerings.

Millers 64 B&B ££

(☑0131-454 3666; www.millers64.com; 64 Pilrig St; r £90-180; 🛜; 🚍11) Luxury textiles, colourful cushions, stylish bathrooms and fresh flowers added to a warm Edinburgh welcome make this Victorian town house a highly desirable address. There are just two bedrooms (and a minimum three-night stay during festival periods), so book well in advance.

★**Pilrig House** APARTMENT £££

(☑0131-554 4794; www.pilrighouse.com; 30 Pilrig House Close; ☺per week £945-1470; P🛜; 🚍36) 🖊 Pilrig is a gorgeous 17th-century town house that was once home to Robert Louis Stevenson's grandfather (it gets a mention in his novel *Kidnapped*). Set at the end of a quiet cul-de-sac overlooking a peaceful park, the house offers two luxurious self-catering apartments with fully equipped kitchens and private parking. Seven-night minimum stay May to August.

✖ Eating

Eating out in Edinburgh has changed beyond all recognition since the 1990s. Back then, sophisticated dining meant a visit to the Aberdeen Angus Steak House for a prawn cocktail, steak (well done) and chips, and Black Forest gateau. Today, Edinburgh has more restaurants per head of population than any other UK city, including a handful of places with Michelin stars.

✖ Old Town

★ Mums
CAFE £

(Map p752; ☑ 0131-260 9806; www.monster mashcafe.co.uk; 4a Forrest Rd; mains £9-12; ⊗ 9am-10pm Mon-Sat, 10am-10pm Sun; 🛜 🚻; ☐ 2, 23, 27, 41, 42, 300) ✈ This nostalgia-fuelled cafe serves up classic British comfort food that wouldn't look out of place on a 1950s menu – bacon and eggs, bangers and mash, shepherd's pie, fish and chips. But there's a twist – the food is all top-quality nosh freshly prepared from local produce. There's also a good selection of bottled craft beers and Scottish-brewed cider.

Scott's Kitchen
SCOTTISH, CAFE £

(Map p752; ☑ 0131-322 6868; https://scotts kitchen.co.uk; 4-6 Victoria Tce; mains £8-10; ⊗ 9am-6pm; 🅿 🛜; ☐ 23, 27, 41, 42, 67) Green tile, brown leather and arched Georgian windows lend an elegant feel to this modern cafe, which combines fine Scottish produce with great value. Fill up on a breakfast (served till 11.45am) of eggs Benedict, bacon baps or porridge with honey, banana and almonds, or linger over a lunch of Cullen skink (smoked haddock soup), venison casserole, or haggis.

Ting Thai Caravan
THAI £

(Map p752; www.tingthai-caravan.com; 8-9 Teviot Pl; mains £5-9; ⊗ 11.30am-10pm Sun-Thu, to 11pm Fri & Sat; ☐ 2, 41, 42, 47, 67) This lively, unpretentious place started as a pop-up and retains its no-frills vibe with no bookings and cash-only payments. The food, served in steaming cardboard boxes at crammed communal tables, is exceptional – aromatic curries, caramelised sticky pork with sesame, *nam pla* and palm sugar, and king-size 'bubble prawns' in grated coconut-beer batter. Service can be brusque.

★ Cannonball Restaurant
SCOTTISH ££

(Map p752; ☑ 0131-225 1550; www.contini.com/cannonball; 356 Castlehill; mains £15-25; ⊗ noon-3pm & 5.30-10pm Tue-Sat; 🛜 🚻; ☐ 23, 27, 41, 42) The historic Cannonball House next to Edinburgh Castle's esplanade has been transformed into a sophisticated restaurant (and whisky bar) where the Contini family work their Italian magic on Scottish classics to produce dishes such as haggis balls with spiced pickled turnip and whisky marmalade, and lobster with wild garlic and lemon butter.

Mother India's Cafe
INDIAN ££

(Map p752; ☑ 0131-524 9801; www.motherindia. co.uk; 3-5 Infirmary St; dishes £4-6; ⊗ noon-2pm & 5-10.30pm Mon-Wed, noon-11pm Thu-Sun; 🛜 🚻; ☐ all South Bridge buses) A simple concept pioneered in Glasgow has captured hearts and minds – and stomachs – here in Edinburgh: Indian food served in tapas-size portions, so that you can sample a greater variety of deliciously different dishes without busting a gut. Hugely popular, so book a table to avoid disappointment.

David Bann
VEGETARIAN ££

(Map p752; ☑ 0131-556 5888; www.davidbann. com; 56-58 St Mary's St; mains £12-14; ⊗ noon-10pm Mon-Fri, 11am-10pm Sat & Sun; 🍴; ☐ 300) ✈ If you want to convince a carnivorous friend that cuisine à la veg can be as tasty and inventive as a meat-muncher's menu, take them to David Bann's stylish restaurant – dishes such as puy lentil shepherd's pie, and risotto of braised leek and roasted red pepper are guaranteed to win converts.

Devil's Advocate
PUB FOOD ££

(Map p752; ☑ 0131-225 4465; http://devilsadvocate edinburgh.co.uk; 9 Advocates Close; mains £10-23; ⊗ food served noon-3pm & 5-10pm; 🛜; ☐ 6, 23, 27, 41, 42) No trip to Edinburgh is complete without exploring the narrow closes (alleys) that lead off the Royal Mile. Lucky you if your explorations lead to this cosy split-level pub-restaurant set in a converted Victorian pump house, with a menu of top-quality pub grub – the barbecue ribs are among the best in town. It gets rammed on weekends, so book ahead.

Doric
SCOTTISH ££

(Map p752; ☑ 0131-225 1084; www.the-doric. com; 15-16 Market St; mains £12-25; ⊗ noon-1am; 🚻; ☐ 6) One of Edinburgh's favourite eateries, this 1st-floor bistro (entrance stairs to the right of the Doric Bar) is handy for both Princes St and the Royal Mile. Wooden floors, white walls and a red ceiling create a smart atmosphere, while window tables with views of the Scott Monument (p758) complement a menu of fresh Scottish produce.

Maxie's Bistro
BISTRO **££**

(Map p752; ☑0131-226 7770; www.maxiesbistro. com; 5b Johnston Tce; mains £11-25; ☺noon-11pm; ⛄📶; 🚍23, 27, 41, 42) This candlelit bistro, with its cushion-lined nooks set amid stone walls and wooden beams, is a pleasant setting for a cosy dinner, but at summer lunchtimes people queue for the tables on the terrace overlooking Victoria St. The food is dependable, ranging from pasta, steak and stir-fries to seafood platters and daily specials. Best to book, especially in summer.

★ Grain Store
SCOTTISH **£££**

(Map p752; ☑0131-225 7635; www.grainstore-restaurant.co.uk; 30 Victoria St; mains £18-32; ☺noon-2.30pm & 6-9.45pm Mon-Sat, noon-2.30pm & 6-9.30pm Sun; 🚍2, 23, 27, 41, 42) An atmospheric upstairs dining room on picturesque Victoria St, the Grain Store has a well-earned reputation for serving the finest Scottish produce, perfectly prepared in dishes such as Orkney scallops with pumpkin, chestnut and pancetta, and braised venison shoulder with brambles, salsify and kale. The three-course lunch for £16 is good value.

★ Ondine
SEAFOOD **£££**

(Map p752; ☑0131-226 1888; www.ondineres taurant.co.uk; 2 George IV Bridge; mains £18-38, 2-/3-course lunch £19/24; ☺noon-3pm & 5.30-10pm Mon-Sat; ⛄; 🚍23, 27, 41, 42) Ondine is one of Edinburgh's finest seafood restaurants, with a menu based on sustainably sourced fish. Take a seat at the curved Oyster Bar and tuck into oysters Kilpatrick, smoked-haddock chowder, lobster thermidor, a roast-shellfish platter or just good old haddock and chips (with minted pea purée, just to keep things posh).

Wedgwood
SCOTTISH **£££**

(Map p752; ☑0131-558 8737; www.wedgwoodthe restaurant.co.uk; 267 Canongate; mains £18-28, 2-/3-course lunch £16/20; ☺noon-3pm & 6-10pm; 🚍35) 🌿 Fine food without the fuss is the motto at this friendly, unpretentious restaurant. Scottish produce is served with inventive flair in dishes such as beef tartare with soy, shaved egg, scurvy grass and bone-marrow crumb, or spiced monkfish with charred aubergine, pickled chilli and preserved lemon; the menu includes foraged wild salad leaves collected by the chef.

🏃 Walking Tour
Old Town Alleys

START CASTLE ESPLANADE
END COCKBURN ST
LENGTH 1 MILE; ONE TO TWO HOURS

This walk explores the alleys and side streets around the Royal Mile, and involves a bit of climbing up and down steep stairs.

Begin on the ❶ **Castle Esplanade**, which provides a grandstand view south over the Grassmarket; the prominent quadrangular building with all the turrets is George Heriot's School. Head towards Castlehill and the start of the Royal Mile.

The 17th-century house on the right is known as ❷ **Cannonball House** because of the iron ball lodged in the wall (look between, and slightly below, the two largest windows on the wall facing the castle). The ball was not fired in anger but marks the gravitation height to which water would flow naturally from the city's first piped water supply.

The low, rectangular building across the street (now a touristy tartan-weaving mill) was originally the reservoir that held the Old Town's water supply. On its western wall is the ❸ **Witches Well**, where a bronze fountain commemorates around 4000 people (mostly women) who were executed between 1479 and 1722 on suspicion of witchcraft.

Go past the reservoir and turn left down Ramsay Lane. Take a look at ❹ **Ramsay Garden** – one of Edinburgh's most desirable addresses – where late-19th-century apartments were built around the octagonal Ramsay Lodge, once home to poet Allan Ramsay. The cobbled street continues around to the right below student residences to the towers of the ❺ **New College**, home to Edinburgh University's Faculty of Divinity. Nip into the courtyard to see the statue of John Knox (a firebrand preacher who led the Protestant Reformation in Scotland, and was instrumental in the creation of the Church of Scotland in 1560).

Just past New College, turn right and climb the stairs into Milne's Court, a student residence belonging to Edinburgh University. Exit into Lawnmarket, cross the street (bearing slightly left) and duck into ❻ **Riddell's Court**, a restored Old

Town close at No 322–8. You'll find yourself in a small courtyard, but the house in front of you (built in 1590) was originally the edge of the street (the building you just walked under was added in 1726 – look for the date inscribed on the doorway on the right). The arch with the inscription *Vivendo discimus* (We live and learn) leads into the original 16th-century courtyard.

Go back into the street, turn right and right again down Fisher's Close, which leads to the delightful Victoria Tce, strung above the cobbled curve of shop-lined Victoria St. Wander right, enjoying the view – ❼ **Maxie's Bistro**, at the far end of the terrace, is a great place to stop for a drink – then descend the stairs at the foot of Upper Bow and continue downhill to the Grassmarket. At the eastern end, outside Maggie Dickson's pub, is the ❽ **Covenanters Monument**, which marks the site of the gallows where more than 100 Covenanters were martyred in the 17th century.

If you're feeling peckish, the Grassmarket has several good places to eat and a couple of good pubs – poet Robert Burns once stayed at the ❾ **White Hart Inn** (p755). Head east along the gloomy defile of the Cowgate, passing under the arch of George

IV Bridge – the buildings to your right are the new law courts, while high up to the left you can see the complex of buildings behind Parliament Sq. Past the courts, on the right, is ❿ **Tailors Hall** (built 1621, extended 1757), now a hotel and bar but formerly the meeting place of the Companie of Tailzeours (Tailors' Guild).

Turn left and climb steeply up Old Fishmarket Close, a typical cobbled Old Town wynd, and emerge once more onto the Royal Mile. Across the street and slightly downhill is ⑪ **Anchor Close**, named for a tavern that once stood there. It hosted the Crochallan Fencibles, an 18th-century drinking club that provided its patrons with an agreeable blend of intellectual debate and intoxicating liquor. The club was founded by William Smellie, editor of the 1st edition of the *Encyclopedia Britannica*; Burns was its best-known member.

Go down Anchor Close to finish the walk on ⑫ **Cockburn St**, one of the city's coolest shopping streets, lined with record shops and clothing boutiques. The street was cut through Old Town tenements in the 1850s to provide an easy route between Waverley station and the Royal Mile.

Witchery by the Castle
SCOTTISH, FRENCH £££

(Map p752; ☑0131-225 5613; www.thewitchery.com; Castlehill; mains £23-43, 2-course lunch £22; ◎noon-11.30pm; ☐23, 27, 41, 42) Set in a merchant's town house dating from 1595, the Witchery is a candlelit corner of antique splendour with oak-panelled walls, low ceilings, opulent wall hangings and red-leather upholstery; stairs lead down to a second, even more romantic, dining room called the Secret Garden. The menu ranges from oysters to Aberdeen Angus steak and the wine list runs to almost 1000 bins.

Tower
SCOTTISH £££

(Map p752; ☑0131-225 3003; www.tower-restaurant.com; National Museum of Scotland, Chambers St; mains £22-34, 2-course lunch & pre-theatre menu £20; ◎10am-10pm Sun-Thu, to 10.30pm Fri & Sat; ☐45, 300) Chic and sleek, with a great view of the castle, Tower is perched in a turret atop the National Museum of Scotland (p752) building. A star-studded guest list of celebrities has enjoyed its menu of quality Scottish food, simply prepared – try half a dozen oysters followed by a 28-day salt-aged rib-eye steak. Afternoon tea (£26) is served from 2pm to 6pm.

✖ New Town

★Urban Angel
CAFE £

(Map p758; ☑0131-225 6215; www.urban-angel.co.uk; 121 Hanover St; mains £7-11; ◎8am-5pm Mon-Fri, 9am-5pm Sat & Sun; ☑️; ☐23, 27) ✔ A wholesome deli that puts the emphasis on Fairtrade, organic and locally sourced produce, Urban Angel is also a delightfully informal cafe-bistro that serves all-day brunch (porridge with honey, French toast, eggs Benedict), mix-and-match salads, and a wide range of light, snacky meals.

Broughton Deli
CAFE £

(Map p758; ☑0131-558 7111; www.broughton-deli.co.uk; 7 Barony St; mains £7-11; ◎8am-6pm Mon-Fri, 9am-6pm Sat, 10am-5pm Sun; ☎️☑️; ☐8) Mismatched cafe tables and chairs in a bright back room behind the deli counter provide an attractive setting for brunch just off the main drag of the New Town's bohemian Broughton St. Brunch is served till 2pm weekdays or 3pm at weekends; choose from American-style pancakes, vegan burritos, and poached eggs on toast with avocado.

Henderson's
VEGETARIAN £

(Map p758; ☑0131-225 2131; www.hendersonsofedinburgh.co.uk; 94 Hanover St; mains £7-14; ◎8.30am-8.45pm Mon-Thu, to 9.15pm Fri & Sat, 10.30am-4pm Sun; ☎️☑️; ☐23, 27) ✔ Established in 1962, Henderson's is the grandmother of Edinburgh's vegetarian restaurants. The food is mostly organic and guaranteed GM-free, and special dietary requirements can be catered for. Trays and counter service lend something of a 1970s canteen feel to the place (in a good, nostalgic way), and the daily salads and hot dishes are as popular as ever.

★Dishoom
INDIAN £

(Map p758; ☑0131-202 6406; www.dishoom.com/edinburgh; 3a St Andrew Sq; mains £8-13; ◎8am-11pm Mon-Wed, to midnight Thu & Fri, 9am-midnight Sat, 9am-11pm Sun; ☎️; ☐St Andrew Sq) Dishoom is a new addition to Edinburgh's dining scene and the minichain's first opening outside London. Inspired by the Irani cafes of Bombay, this is exquisite Indian street food served in upmarket surroundings; the breakfasts, including the signature bacon naan, are legendary. Hugely popular – book well ahead, or be prepared to queue for a table.

★Gardener's Cottage
SCOTTISH ££

(Map p758; ☑0131-558 1221; www.thegardenerscottage.co; 1 Royal Terrace Gardens, London Rd; 4-course lunch £21, 7-course dinner £50; ◎noon-2pm & 5-10pm Mon-Fri, 10am-2pm & 5-10pm Sat & Sun; ☐all London Rd buses) ✔ This country cottage in the heart of the city, bedecked with flowers and fairy lights, offers one of Edinburgh's most interesting dining experiences – two tiny rooms with communal tables made of salvaged timber, and a set menu based on fresh local produce (most of the vegetables and fruit are from its own organic garden). Bookings essential; brunch served at weekends.

★Contini
ITALIAN ££

(Map p758; ☑0131-225 1550; www.contini.com/contini-george-street; 103 George St; mains £14-18; ◎8am-10pm Mon-Fri, 10am-10.30pm Sat, 11am-8pm Sun; ☎️☑️; ☐all Princes St buses) A palatial Georgian banking hall enlivened by fuchsia-pink banners and lampshades is home to this lively, family-friendly Italian bar and restaurant, where the emphasis is on fresh, authentic ingredients (produce imported weekly from Milan; homemade bread and pasta) and the uncomplicated enjoyment of food.

Dome
SCOTTISH ££

(Map p758; ☑0131-624 8624; www.thedomeedinburgh.com; 14 George St; mains £15-28; ◎10am-late; ☐St Andrew Sq) Housed in the magnificent neoclassical former headquarters of the Commercial Bank, with a lofty glass-domed ceiling, pillared arches and mosaic-tiled floor, the Grill Room at the Dome is one of the city's most impressive dining rooms. The menu is solidly modern Scottish, with great steaks, seafood and venison. Reservations strongly recommended.

Bon Vivant BISTRO ££
(Map p758; ☑0131-225 3275; http://bonvivant edinburgh.co.uk; 55 Thistle St; mains £13-17; ⊗noon-10pm; 🕿; 🚃23, 27) Candlelight reflected in the warm glow of polished wood makes for an intimate atmosphere in this New Town favourite. The food is superb value for this part of town, offering a range of tapas-style 'bites' as well as standard main courses, with a changing menu of seasonal, locally sourced dishes such as cod fillet with bacon and mussel cream.

Dogs BRITISH ££
(Map p758; ☑0131-220 1208; www.thedogson line.co.uk; 110 Hanover St; mains lunch £7, dinner £12-15; ⊗noon-2.30pm & 6-10pm Mon-Fri, noon-4pm & 6-10pm Sat & Sun; 🖉; 🚃23, 27) 🍴 This bistro-style place uses cheaper cuts of meat (smoked ox heart, devilled sweetbreads) and less well-known, more sustainable species of fish (pollack, herring) to create hearty, no-nonsense dishes; about half of the menu is vegetarian, with tasty dishes such as Scotch egg coated with skirlie (oatmeal and onion). Service can be brusque, but at these prices, who cares?

Mussel Inn SEAFOOD ££
(Map p758; ☑0131-229 5979; www.mussel-inn. com; 61-65 Rose St; mains £13-24; ⊗noon-3pm & 5.30-10pm Mon-Thu, noon-10pm Fri & Sat, 12.30-10pm Sun; 🛈; 🚃Princes St) 🍴 Owned by west-coast shellfish farmers, the Mussel Inn provides a direct outlet for fresh Scottish seafood. The busy restaurant, decorated indoors with bright beechwood, spills out onto the pavement in summer. A 1kg pot of mussels with a choice of sauces – try chilli, garlic, ginger, coriander and cumin – costs £15.

Fishers in the City SEAFOOD ££
(Map p758; ☑0131-225 5109; www.fishersbistros. co.uk; 58 Thistle St; mains £16-23; ⊗noon-10.30pm; 🕿🛈; 🚃24, 29, 42) 🍴 This more sophisticated city-centre branch of the famous Fishers Bistro (p777) in Leith, with granite-topped tables, split-level dining area and nautical theme, specialises in superior Scottish seafood – the knowledgeable staff

serve up plump and succulent oysters, meltingly sweet scallops, and sea bass that's been grilled to perfection.

Howie's SCOTTISH ££
(Map p758; ☑0131-556 5766; www.howies.uk.com; 29 Waterloo Pl; mains lunch £8-17, dinner £13-20; ⊗noon-2.30pm & 5.30-10pm; 🕿🛈; 🚃1, 4, 5, 15, 34, 45) A bright and airy Georgian corner house provides the elegant setting for this hugely popular restaurant. The recipe for success includes fresh Scottish produce simply prepared; good-value, seasonally changing menus; and eminently quaffable house wines from £18 a bottle.

Paul Kitching 21212 FRENCH £££
(Map p758; ☑0131-523 1030; www.21212res taurant.co.uk; 3 Royal Tce; 3-course lunch/dinner from £32/70; ⊗noon-1.45pm & 7-9pm Tue-Sat; 🕿; 🚃all London Rd buses) A grand Georgian town house on the side of Calton Hill is the elegant setting for one of Edinburgh's Michelin-starred restaurants. Divine decor by Timorous Beasties and Ralph Lauren provides the backdrop to an exquisitely prepared five-course dinner (£85) that changes weekly and features fresh, seasonal delights.

Number One SCOTTISH £££
(Map p758; ☑0131-557 6727; www.roccoforte hotels.com/hotels-and-resorts/the-balmoral-hotel/ restaurants-and-bars/number-one; Balmoral Hotel, 1 Princes St; 3-course dinner £80; ⊗6.30-10pm Mon-Thu, 6-10pm Fri-Sun; 🕿; 🚃all Princes St buses) This is the stylish and sophisticated chatelaine of Edinburgh's city-centre restaurants, all gold-and-velvet elegance with a Michelin star sparkling on her tiara. The food is top-notch modern Scottish (a seven-/10-course tasting menu costs £89/120 per person) and the service is just on the right side of fawning.

🍴 South Edinburgh

⭐**Brew Lab** CAFE £
(Map p752; ☑0131-662 8963; www.brewlabcof fee.co.uk; 6-8 S College St; mains £4-5; ⊗8am-6pm Mon, to 8pm Tue-Fri, 9am-8pm Sat & Sun; 🕿; 🚃all South Bridge buses) 🍴 Students with iPads lolling in armchairs, sipping carefully crafted espressos amid artfully distressed brick and plaster, recycled school-gym flooring, old workshop benches and lab stools... this is coffee-nerd heaven. There's good food, too, with hearty soups and crusty baguette sandwiches. In summer, try the refreshing cold-brew coffee.

Forest Café
VEGETARIAN £

(Map p762; ☑0131-229 4922; http://blog.the
forest.org.uk/cafe; 141 Lauriston Pl; mains £3-6;
⊙10am-11pm; ☎🅿♿; 🚍all Tollcross buses)
🍴 A chilled-out, colourful and comfortably scuffed-around-the-edges antidote to
squeaky-clean espresso bars, this volunteer-
run, not-for-profit art space and cafe serves
up humongous helpings of hearty vegetarian and vegan fodder, ranging from nachos
to falafel wraps.

Kalpna
INDIAN £

(Map p762; ☑0131-667 9890; www.kalpnarestau
rant.com; 2-3 St Patrick Sq; mains £8-13; ⊙noon-
2pm & 5.30-10.30pm; 🍴; 🚍all Newington buses)
A long-standing Edinburgh favourite, Kalp-
na is one of the best Indian restaurants in
the country, vegetarian or otherwise. The
cuisine is mostly Gujarati, with a smattering
of dishes from other parts of India. The all-
you-can-eat lunch buffet (£8.50) is superb
value.

★First Coast
SCOTTISH ££

(Map p762; ☑0131-313 4404; www.first-coast.co.uk;
97-101 Dalry Rd; mains £13-20; ⊙noon-2pm &
5-11pm Mon-Sat; ☎🅿♿; 🚍2, 3, 4, 25, 33, 44) This
popular neighbourhood bistro has a striking
main dining area with sea-blue wood panelling and stripped stonework, and a short
and simple menu offering hearty comfort
food such as fish with creamy mash, brown
shrimp and garlic butter, or pigeon breast
with black pudding, pearl barley and beetroot. Lunchtime and early evening there's an
excellent two-course meal for £13.50.

★Aizle
SCOTTISH ££

(Map p762; ☑0131-662 9349; http://aizle.co.uk;
107-109 St Leonard's St; 5-course dinner £55; ⊙5-
9pm Wed-Sat; ☎; 🚍14) If you tend to have
trouble deciding what to eat, Aizle (the
name is an old Scots word for 'spark' or 'em-
ber') will do the job for you. There's no menu
here, just a five-course dinner conjured from
a monthly 'harvest' of the finest and freshest
local produce (listed on a blackboard), and
presented beautifully – art on a plate.

★Locanda de Gusti
ITALIAN ££

(Map p762; ☑0131-346 8800; www.locandade
gusti.com; 102 Dalry Rd; mains £14-26; ⊙5.30-
10pm Mon-Wed, 12.30-2pm & 5.30-10pm Thu-Sat;
♿; 🚍2, 3, 4, 25, 33, 44) This bustling family
bistro, loud with the buzz of conversation
and the clink of glasses and cutlery, is no
ordinary Italian but a little corner of Na-
ples, complete with hearty Neapolitan home

cooking by friendly head chef Rosario. The
food ranges from light and tasty ravioli
tossed with butter and sage to delicious platters of grilled seafood.

★Loudon's Café & Bakery
CAFE ££

(Map p762; www.loudons.co.uk; 94b Fountainbridge;
mains £8-13; ⊙7.30am-5pm Mon-Fri, 8am-5pm
Sat & Sun; ☎🅿♿; 🚍1, 34, 300) Organic bread
and cakes baked on the premises, ethically
sourced coffee, daily and weekend newspapers scattered about, even some outdoor tables – what's not to like? All-day brunch (8am
to 4pm) served at weekends includes eggs
Benedict, granola with yoghurt, and specials
such as blueberry pancakes with fruit salad.

Field Southside
SCOTTISH ££

(Map p752; ☑0131-667 7010; www.fieldrestaurant.
co.uk; 41 W Nicolson St; mains £13-19; ⊙noon-2pm
& 5.30-9pm Tue-Sat; 🚍41, 42, 67) A tiny restaurant punching way above its weight, Field
pulls off that rare feat: fine dining at modest
prices. The food is Scottish, contemporary,
and beautifully plated, all eaten while overlooked by a giant cow painted on one wall.
The lunch/pre-theatre menu of three courses
for £16.95 (available noon to 2pm and 5.30pm
to 6.45pm) is extraordinarily good value.

✖ Leith

Twelve Triangles
BAKERY £

(Map p762; ☑0131-629 4664; www.twelvetrian
gles.com; 90 Brunswick St; mains £2-3; ⊙8am-
5pm Mon-Fri, 9am-5pm Sat & Sun; 🚍all Leith
Walk buses) Tucked away on an unassuming
stretch just off Leith Walk, Twelve Trian-
gles is an exceptional (and exceptionally
tiny) bakery. Some of the city's best artisan
breads, pastries and coffee come out of its
clever kitchen, and the doughnut fillings are
legendary, encompassing pistachio custard,
pink-grapefruit ricotta, and chocolate and
peanut butter. Coffee and doughnuts don't
get more sophisticated.

Quay Commons
CAFE £

(☑0131-677 0244; www.quaycommons.co; 92
Commercial Quay; mains £6-12; ⊙8am-6pm Mon-
Thu, to 10pm Fri & Sat, 9am-6pm Sun; ☎; 🚍16,
22, 36, 300) 🍴 A combined deli, bakery and
licensed cafe run by the same people behind
Gardener's Cottage (p774), this is a designer
conversion of a former bonded warehouse
where you can watch the bakers at work. It
serves healthy soups, sandwiches and salads
at lunch, plus handmade pasta dishes on
Friday and Saturday evening.

★ **Fishers Bistro**   SEAFOOD ££
(☎0131-554 5666; www.fishersbistros.co.uk; 1 The Shore; mains £14-25; ⊙noon-10.30pm Mon-Sat, 12.30-10.30pm Sun; 🐾🍽️♿; 🚇16, 22, 36, 300) This cosy little restaurant, tucked beneath a 17th-century signal tower, is one of the city's best seafood places. The menu ranges widely in price, from cheaper dishes such as classic fish cakes with lemon-and-chive mayonnaise to more expensive delights such as Fife lobster and chips (£40).

★ **A Room in Leith**   SCOTTISH ££
(☎0131-554 7427; http://teuchtersbar.co.uk; 1a Dock Pl; mains £12-25; ⊙4-11pm Mon-Thu, noon-11pm Fri-Sun; 🐾🍽️♿; 🚇16, 22, 36, 300) This restaurant – and its companion bar, **Teuchters Landing** (1c Dock Pl; ⊙10.30am-1am; 🐾) – inhabits a warren of nooks and crannies in a red-brick former waiting room (for ferries across the Firth of Forth), with a bright conservatory and outdoor tables on a floating terrace in the dock. The Scottish-flavoured menu includes haggis with whisky sauce, and Shetland scallops with crab and smoked-haddock risotto.

★ **Kitchin**   SCOTTISH £££
(☎0131-555 1755; http://thekitchin.com; 78 Commercial Quay; 3-course lunch/dinner £33/75; ⊙noon-2.30pm & 6-10pm Tue-Sat; 🍽️; 🚇16, 22, 36, 300) Fresh, seasonal, locally sourced Scottish produce is the philosophy that has won a Michelin star for this elegant but unpretentious restaurant. The menu moves with the seasons, of course, so expect fresh salads in summer and game in winter, and shellfish dishes such as baked scallops with white wine, vermouth and herb sauce when there's an 'r' in the month.

★ **Martin Wishart**   FRENCH £££
(☎0131-553 3557; www.martin-wishart.co.uk; 54 The Shore; 3-course lunch £32, 4-course dinner £90; ⊙noon-2pm & 7-10pm Tue-Fri, noon-1.30pm & 7-10pm Sat; 🍽️; 🚇16, 22, 36, 300) 🥂 In 2001 this restaurant became the first in Edinburgh to win a Michelin star, and it's retained it ever since. The eponymous chef has worked with Albert Roux, Marco Pierre White and Nick Nairn, and brings a modern French approach to the best Scottish produce, from langoustines with white asparagus and confit onion to a six-course vegetarian tasting menu (£75).

🍴 **West End & Dean Village**

L'Escargot Blanc   FRENCH ££
(Map p758; ☎0131-226 1890; www.lescargot-blanc.co.uk; 17 Queensferry St; mains £15-25; ⊙noon-2.30pm & 5.30-10pm Mon-Thu, noon-3pm & 5.30-10.30pm Fri & Sat; 🍽️; 🚇19, 36, 37, 41, 47) 🥂 This superb neighbourhood bistro, with French chef and wait staff, and two-thirds of its top-quality produce sourced in Scotland (one-third imported from France), is a true 'Auld Alliance' of culinary cultures. Choose from classics such as escargots in garlic butter, coq au vin (made with free-range Scottish chicken), and perfectly prepared Scottish rib-eye steak with cognac sauce.

★ **Timberyard**   SCOTTISH £££
(Map p752; ☎0131-221 1222; www.timberyard.co; 10 Lady Lawson St; 4-course lunch or dinner £55; ⊙noon-2pm & 5.30-9.30pm Tue-Sat; 🐾🍽️; 🚇2, 300) 🥂 Ancient, worn floorboards, cast-iron pillars, exposed joists, and tables made from slabs of old mahogany create a rustic, retro atmosphere in this slow-food restaurant where the accent is on locally sourced produce from artisan growers and foragers. Typical dishes include seared scallop with leek, fennel and cured egg yolk, and roast quail with salsify and thyme.

★ **Castle Terrace**   SCOTTISH £££
(Map p752; ☎0131-229 1222; www.castleterrace restaurant.com; 33-35 Castle Tce; 3-course lunch/dinner £33/70; ⊙noon-2.15pm & 6.30-10pm Tue-Sat; 🚇2) 🥂 It was little more than a year after opening in 2010 that Castle Terrace was awarded a Michelin star under chef-patron Dominic Jack (the star was lost in 2015). The menu is seasonal and applies honed Parisian skills to the finest of local produce, be it Ayrshire pork, Aberdeenshire lamb or Newhaven crab – even the cheese in the sauces is Scottish.

🍷 Drinking & Nightlife

Edinburgh has always been a drinkers' city. It has more than 700 pubs – more per square mile than any other UK city – and they are as varied and full of character as the people who drink in them, from Victorian palaces to stylish preclub bars, and from real-ale howffs (meeting places, often pubs) to cool cocktail lounges.

🍷 Old Town

The pubs in the Grassmarket have outdoor tables on sunny summer afternoons, but in the evenings they're favoured by boozed-up packs of party animals, so steer clear if that's not your thing. The Cowgate – the Grassmarket's extension to the east – is Edinburgh's clubland.

★ **Cabaret Voltaire** CLUB

(Map p752; www.thecabaretvoltaire.com; 36-38 Blair St; ⏰5pm-3am Tue-Sat, 8pm-1am Sun; 🛜; 🚍all South Bridge buses) An atmospheric warren of stone-lined vaults houses this self-consciously 'alternative' club, which eschews huge dance floors and egotistical DJ worship in favour of a 'creative crucible' hosting an eclectic mix of DJs, live acts, comedy, theatre, visual arts and the spoken word. Well worth a look.

★ **Bow Bar** PUB

(Map p752; www.thebowbar.co.uk; 80 West Bow; ⏰noon-midnight Mon-Sat, to 11.30pm Sun; 🚍2, 23, 27, 41, 42) One of the city's best traditional-style pubs (it's not as old as it looks), serving a range of excellent real ales, Scottish craft gins and a vast selection of malt whiskies, the Bow Bar often has standing-room only on Friday and Saturday evenings.

Bongo Club CLUB

(Map p752; www.thebongoclub.co.uk; 66 Cowgate; free-£7; ⏰11pm-3am Tue & Thu, 7pm-3am Fri-Sun; 🛜; 🚍2) Owned by a local arts charity, the weird and wonderful Bongo Club has a long history of hosting everything from wild club nights and local bands to performance art and kids comedy shows.

Edinburgh Press Club COFFEE

(Map p752; https://edinburghpressclub.coffee; 20-30 Cockburn St; ⏰7.30am-6pm Mon-Sat, 8.30am-6pm Sun; 🛜; 🚍6) Housed in the former advertising offices of the *Scotsman* newspaper, attractively refurbished with red brick, artistically arranged timber offcuts and a sprinkling of journalistic memorabilia that includes a couple of well-used manual typewriters, this popular cafe serves quality coffee and tea along with a small selection of alcoholic drinks.

Checkpoint BAR

(Map p752; ☎0131-225 9352; www.checkpoint edinburgh.com; 3 Bristo Pl; ⏰9am-1am; 🛜; 🚍2, 47) A friendly cafe, bar and restaurant with a comprehensive menu including breakfasts, bar bites and substantial mains, Checkpoint is gaining a reputation as one of the coolest spots in Edinburgh. The utilitarian white-walled space is flooded with light from floor-to-ceiling windows and is vast enough to house, of all things, an old shipping container.

BrewDog BAR

(Map p752; www.brewdog.com; 143 Cowgate; ⏰noon-1am; 🛜; 🚍45, 300) The Edinburgh outpost of Scotland's self-styled 'punk brewery', BrewDog stands out among the sticky-floored dives that line the Cowgate with its polished-concrete bar and cool, industrial-chic decor. As well as its own highly rated beers, there's a choice of guest real ales, and – a sign of a great trad pub – coat hooks under the edge of the bar.

Malt Shovel PUB

(Map p752; ☎0131-225 6843; www.maltshovel inn-edinburgh.co.uk; 11-15 Cockburn St; ⏰11am-11pm Mon-Wed, to midnight Thu & Sun, to 1am Fri & Sat; 🛜🍴; 🚍6) A traditional-looking pub with dark wood and subdued tartanry, the Malt Shovel offers a good range of real ales and more than 40 malt whiskies, and serves excellent pub grub including fish and chips, burgers, and steak-and-ale pies.

Holyrood 9A PUB

(Map p752; www.theholyrood.co.uk; 9a Holyrood Rd; ⏰9am-midnight Sun-Thu, to 1am Fri & Sat; 🛜; 🚍36) Candlelight flickering off hectares of polished wood creates an atmospheric setting for this superb real-ale bar, with more than 20 taps pouring craft beers from all corners of the country and indeed the globe. If you're peckish, it serves excellent gourmet burgers, too.

Dragonfly COCKTAIL BAR

(Map p752; ☎0131-228 4543; www.dragonfly cocktailbar.com; 52 West Port; ⏰4pm-1am; 🛜; 🚍2) A superstylish lounge bar with a Raffles of Singapore vibe – it's all crystal chandeliers, polished wood and oriental art – Dragonfly has won rave reviews for both its innovative cocktails and its designer decor. Grab a seat on the neat little mezzanine, from where you can look down on the bar as the Singapore Slings are being slung.

Jolly Judge PUB

(Map p752; www.jollyjudge.co.uk; 7a James Ct; ⏰noon-11pm Mon-Thu, to midnight Fri & Sat, 12.30-11pm Sun; 🛜; 🚍23, 27, 41, 42) A snug little howff tucked away down a close, the Judge exudes a cosy 17th-century atmosphere (low, timber-beamed painted ceilings) and has the added attraction of a cheering open fire in cold weather. No music or gaming machines, just the buzz of conversation.

📍 New Town

Café Royal Circle Bar PUB

(Map p758; ☎0131-556 1884; www.caferoyal edinburgh.co.uk; 17 W Register St; ⏰11am-11pm

Mon-Wed, to midnight Thu, to 1am Fri & Sat, to 10pm Sun; 🛜; 🚇Princes St) Perhaps *the* classic Edinburgh pub, the Café Royal's main claims to fame are its magnificent oval bar and its Doulton tile portraits of famous Victorian inventors. Sit at the bar or claim one of the cosy leather booths beneath the stained-glass windows, and choose from the seven real ales on tap.

Lucky Liquor Co   COCKTAIL BAR
(Map p758; ☑0131-226 3976; www.luckyliquorco. com; 39a Queen St; ⊙4pm-1am; 🚌24, 29, 42) This tiny, black-and-white bar is all about the number 13: 13 bottles of base spirit are used to create a daily menu of 13 cocktails. The result is a playful list with some unusual flavours, such as tonka-bean liqueur, pea purée and lavender absinthe (though not all in the same glass!), served by a fun and friendly crew.

Guildford Arms   PUB
(Map p758; ☑0131-556 4312; www.guildford arms.com; 1 W Register St; ⊙11am-11pm Mon-Thu, to 11.30pm Fri & Sat, 12.30-11pm Sun; 🛜; 🚇St Andrew Sq) Located in a side alley off the east end of Princes St, the Guildford is a classic Victorian pub full of polished mahogany, brass and ornate cornices. The range of real ales is excellent – try to get a table in the unusual upstairs gallery, with a view over the sea of drinkers below.

Artisan Roast   COFFEE
(Map p758; ☑07522 321893; www.artisanroast. co.uk; 57 Broughton St; ⊙8am-7.30pm Mon-Thu, to 6.30pm Fri, 9am-6.30pm Sat & Sun; 🚌8) Edinburgh's coffee scene punches above its weight, largely thanks to Artisan Roast. The mothership, a tiny, dark cafe on Broughton St, is now one of three branches in the city, with a 'tasting lab' in Canonmills and a roastery in Prestonfield. This is coffee for serious coffee lovers, with a richly scented atmosphere of reverence.

Bramble   COCKTAIL BAR
(Map p758; ☑0131-226 6343; www.bramblebar. co.uk; 16a Queen St; ⊙4pm-1am; 🚌23, 27) One of those places that easily earn the sobriquet 'best-kept secret', Bramble is an unmarked cellar bar (just an inconspicuous brass nameplate beneath a dry-cleaner's shop) where a maze of stone and brick hideaways conceals what is arguably the city's best cocktail venue. No beer taps, no fuss, just expertly mixed drinks.

WHISKY TASTING

If you don't have time to visit any of Scotland's distilleries, don't fret – the city has some fine places for sampling a wee dram or three.

Scotch Whisky Experience (p755) Provides a comprehensive overview of Scotland's iconic spirit.

Bow Bar Busy Grassmarket-area pub with huge selection of malt whiskies.

Malt Shovel Old-school pub with more than 100 single malts behind the bar.

Bennet's Bar (p780) A lovely setting to taste more than 100 malts.

Cumberland Bar Good summer choice; enjoy your malt while sitting in the garden.

Cumberland Bar   PUB
(Map p758; ☑0131-558 3134; www.cumberland bar.co.uk; 1-3 Cumberland St; ⊙noon-midnight Mon-Wed, to 1am Thu-Sat, 11am-11pm Sun; 🛜; 🚌23, 27) Immortalised as the stereotypical New Town pub in Alexander McCall Smith's serialised novel *44 Scotland Street*, the Cumberland has an authentic, traditional wood-brass-and-mirrors look (despite being relatively new) and serves well-looked-after, cask-conditioned ales and a wide range of malt whiskies. There's also a pleasant little beer garden.

Abbotsford   PUB
(Map p758; ☑0131-225 5276; www.theabbots ford.com; 3 Rose St; ⊙11am-11pm Mon-Thu, to midnight Fri & Sat, 12.30-11pm Sun; 🛜; 🚌all Princes St buses) One of the few pubs in Rose St that has retained its Edwardian splendour, the Abbotsford has long been a hang-out for writers, actors, journalists and media people, and has many loyal regulars. Dating from 1902, and named after Sir Walter Scott's country house, the pub's centrepiece is a splendid mahogany island bar. Good selection of real ales.

Kenilworth   PUB
(Map p758; ☑0131-226 1773; www.nicholsons pubs.co.uk; 152-154 Rose St; ⊙noon-11pm Mon-Thu, noon-midnight Fri, 11am-midnight Sat, 11am-11pm Sun; 🛜; 🚇Princes St) A gorgeous Edwardian drinking palace complete with original fittings – tile floors, mahogany circle bar and

LOCAL KNOWLEDGE

SHEIP HEID INN

Possibly the oldest inn in Edinburgh (with a licence dating back to 1360), the **Sheep Heid** (www.thesheepheid edinburgh.co.uk; 43-45 The Causeway; ⊙11am-11pm Mon-Thu, to midnight Fri & Sat, noon-11pm Sun; ⓘ; ☐42) feels more like an upmarket country pub than an Edinburgh bar. Set in the semirural shadow of Arthur's Seat, it's famous for its 19th-century skittles alley and its lovely little beer garden. It makes a great spot for a restorative pint after you've tackled the city's most famous hike.

gantry, ornate mirrors and gas lamps – the Kenilworth was Edinburgh's original gay bar in the 1970s. Today it attracts a mixed crowd of all ages, and serves a good range of real ales and malt whiskies.

Oxford Bar PUB
(Map p758; ✆0131-539 7119; www.oxfordbar.co.uk; 8 Young St; ⊙noon-midnight Mon-Thu, 11am-1am Fri & Sat, 12.30-11pm Sun; �🛜; ☐all Princes St buses) The Oxford is that rarest of things: a real pub for real people, with no 'theme', no frills and no pretensions. 'The Ox' has been immortalised by Ian Rankin, author of the Inspector Rebus novels, whose fictional detective is a regular here. Occasional live folk music.

Lulu CLUB
(Map p758; ✆0131-225 5005; www.luluedin burgh.co.uk; 125 George St; ⊙9pm-3am; 🛜; ☐all Princes St buses) Lush leather sofas, red-satin cushions, fetishistic steel-mesh curtains and dim red lighting all help to create a decadent atmosphere in this drop-dead-gorgeous club venue beneath the **Tigerlily boutique hotel** (Map p758; ✆0131-225 5005; www.tigerli lyedinburgh.co.uk; 125 George St; r from £160; 🛜; ☐all Princes St buses). Resident and guest DJs show a bit more originality than you'd find at the average club.

🍷 South Edinburgh

★Royal Dick MICROBREWERY
(Map p762; ✆0131-560 1572; www.summerhall. co.uk/the-royal-dick; 1 Summerhall; ⊙noon-1am Mon-Sat, 12.30pm-midnight Sun; ☐41, 42, 67) The decor at the Royal Dick alludes to its past as the home of Edinburgh Univer-

sity's veterinary school: there are shelves of laboratory glassware and walls covered with animal bones, even an old operating table. But rather than being creepy, it's a warm, welcoming place for a drink, serving artisan ales and craft gins produced by its own microbrewery and distillery.

★Bennet's Bar PUB
(Map p762; ✆0131-229 5143; www.bennetsbar edinburgh.co.uk; 8 Leven St; ⊙11am-1am; ☐all Tollcross buses) Situated beside the **King's Theatre** (Map p762; ✆0131-529 6000; www. capitaltheatres.com/kings; 2 Leven St; ⊙box office 10am-6pm; ☐all Tollcross buses), Bennet's (established in 1839) has managed to hang on to almost all of its beautiful Victorian fittings, from the leaded stained-glass windows and the ornate mirrors to the wooden gantry and the brass water taps on the bar (for your whisky – there are over 100 malts from which to choose).

🍷 Leith

★Roseleaf BAR
(✆0131-476 5268; www.roseleaf.co.uk; 23-24 Sandport Pl; ⊙10am-1am; 🛜ⓘ; ☐16, 22, 36, 300) Cute, quaint, and decked out in flowered wallpaper, old furniture and rose-patterned china (cocktails are served in teapots), the Roseleaf could hardly be further from the average Leith bar. The real ales and bottled beers are complemented by a range of speciality teas, coffees and fruit drinks (including rose lemonade), and well-above-average pub grub (served from 10am to 10pm).

Nobles PUB
(✆0131-629 7215; http://new.noblesbarleith.co.uk; 44a Constitution St; ⊙10am-11pm Tue, Wed & Sun, to midnight Thu, to 1am Fri & Sat; ☐12, 16) In an area stuffed with choice pubs, Nobles might be the most loved by locals. This beautifully restored Victorian cafe-bar in the heart of Leith has original stained-glass windows, wood panelling and a nautical theme that speaks to the history of this old port. The food is straightforward and modestly priced and the choice of ales excellent.

Old Chain Pier PUB
(✆0131-552 4960; http://oldchainpier.com; 32 Trinity Cres; ⊙11.30am-11pm Sun-Thu, to 1am Fri & Sat; 🛜; ☐16, 200) The delightful Old Chain Pier enjoys a brilliant location overlooking the sea – the building was once the 19th-century booking office for steamers crossing the Firth of Forth (the pier from which it

takes its name was washed away in a storm in 1898). The bar serves real ales, bottled craft beers, cocktails and wines, and the kitchen serves excellent pub grub.

Port O'Leith
PUB

(☎ 0131-554 3568; www.facebook.com/ThePortO LeithBar; 58 Constitution St; ☺ 11am-1am Mon-Sat, noon-1am Sun; 🚌 12, 16) This good old-f-ashioned local boozer has been sympathet-ically restored – it appeared in the 2013 film *Sunshine on Leith*. Its nautical history is evident in the form of flags and cap bands left behind by visiting sailors (Leith docks are just down the road). Pop in for a pint and you'll probably stay until closing time.

☆ Entertainment

☆ Old Town

★ Sandy Bell's
TRADITIONAL MUSIC

(Map p752; www.sandybellsedinburgh.co.uk; 25 Forrest Rd; ☺ noon-1am Mon-Sat, 12.30pm-midnight Sun; 🚌 2, 23, 27, 41, 42, 45) This unassuming pub has been a stalwart of the traditional-music scene since the 1960s (the founder's wife sang with the Corries). There's music every weekday evening at 9pm, and from 2pm Saturday and 4pm Sunday, plus lots of im-promptu sessions.

Caves
LIVE MUSIC

(Map p752; https://unusualvenuesedinburgh.com/ venues/the-caves-venue-edinburgh; 8-12 Niddry St S; 🚌 300) A spectacular subterranean venue set in the ancient stone vaults beneath the South Bridge, the Caves stages a series of one-off club nights and live-music gigs, as well as *ceilidh* (traditional music) nights during the Edinburgh Festival. Check the What's On link on the website for upcoming events.

Bannerman's
LIVE MUSIC

(Map p752; www.facebook.com/BannermansBar; 212 Cowgate; ☺ noon-1am Mon-Sat, 12.30pm-1am Sun; 📱; 🚌 45, 300) A long-established mu-sic venue – it seems like every Edinburgh student for the last four decades spent half their youth here – Bannerman's straggles through a warren of old vaults beneath South Bridge. It pulls in crowds of students, locals and backpackers with live rock, punk and indie bands five or six nights a week.

Royal Oak
TRADITIONAL MUSIC

(Map p752; www.royal-oak-folk.com; 1 Infirmary St; ☺ 11.30am-2am Mon-Sat, 12.30pm-2am Sun; 🚌 all

South Bridge buses) This popular folk-music pub is tiny, so get here early (9pm start weekdays, 6pm and 9.30pm sessions on Sat-urday, 4.30pm and 7pm sessions on Sunday) if you want to be sure of a place. Saturday night in the lounge is open session – bring your own instrument (and/or a good singing voice!).

Jazz Bar
JAZZ, BLUES

(Map p752; www.thejazzbar.co.uk; 1a Chambers St; £3-7; ☺ 5pm-3am Sun-Fri, 1.30pm-3am Sat; 📱; 🚌 45, 300) This atmospheric cellar bar, with its polished parquet floors, bare stone walls, candlelit tables and stylish steel-framed chairs, is owned and operated by jazz mu-sicians. There's live music every night from 9pm to 3am, and on Saturday from 3pm. As well as jazz, expect bands playing blues, funk, soul and fusion.

Whistle Binkie's
LIVE MUSIC

(Map p752; www.whistlebinkies.com; 4-6 South Bridge; admission free, except after midnight Fri & Sat; ☺ 5pm-3am Sun-Thu, 1pm-3am Fri & Sat; 🚌 all South Bridge buses) This crowded cellar bar, just off the Royal Mile, has live music most nights till 3am, from rock and blues to folk and jazz. The long-standing open-mic night on Monday is a showcase for new talent.

☆ New Town

Jam House
LIVE MUSIC

(Map p758; ☎ 0131-220 2321; www.thejamhouse. com; 5 Queen St; from £4; ☺ 6pm-3am Fri & Sat; 🚌 St Andrew Sq) The brainchild of rhythm-and-blues pianist and TV personality Jools Holland, the Jam House is set in a former BBC TV studio and offers a combination of fine dining and live jazz and blues perfor-mances. Admission is for over-21s only, and there's a smart-casual dress code.

Voodoo Rooms
LIVE MUSIC

(Map p758; ☎ 0131-556 7060; www.thevoodoo rooms.com; 19a W Register St; free-£20; ☺ 4pm-1am Mon-Thu, noon-1am Fri-Sun; 🚌 St Andrew Sq) Decadent decor of black leather, ornate plas-terwork and gilt detailing creates a stylish setting for this complex of bars and perfor-mance spaces above the Café Royal (p778) that hosts everything from classic soul and Motown to blues nights, jam sessions and live local bands.

CC Blooms
CLUB

(Map p758; ☎ 0131-556 9331; http://ccblooms. co.uk; 23 Greenside Pl; ☺ 11am-3am; 📱; 🚌 all

Leith Walk buses) The raddled old queen of Edinburgh's 1990s gay scene has been given a shot in the arm, with two floors of deafening dance and disco every night. It can get pretty crowded after 11pm and the drinks can be overpriced, but it's worth a visit – go early, or sample the wild Church of High Kicks cabaret show on Sunday nights.

Stand Comedy Club COMEDY
(Map p758; ☑ 0131-558 7272; www.thestand.co.uk; 5 York Pl; tickets £3-18; ⊗ from 7.30pm Mon-Sat, from 12.30pm Sun; ☐ St Andrew Sq) The Stand, founded in 1995, is Edinburgh's main independent comedy venue. It's an intimate cabaret bar with performances every night and a free Sunday lunchtime show.

Edinburgh Playhouse LIVE MUSIC
(Map p758; ☑ 0844 871 3014; www.atgtickets.com/venues/edinburgh-playhouse; 18-22 Greenside Pl; ⊗ box office noon-6pm Mon-Sat, to 8pm show nights; ☐ all Leith Walk buses) This restored theatre at the top of Leith Walk stages Broadway musicals, dance shows, opera and popular-music concerts.

☆ West End & Dean Village

Filmhouse CINEMA
(Map p752; ☑ 0131-228 2688; www.filmhousecinema.com; 88 Lothian Rd; 🕾; ☐ all Lothian Rd buses) The Filmhouse is the main venue for the annual Edinburgh International Film Festival (p767) and screens a full program of art-house, classic, foreign and second-run films, with lots of themes, retrospectives and 70mm screenings. It has wheelchair access to all three screens.

Henry's Cellar Bar LIVE MUSIC
(Map p752; ☑ 0131-629 2992; www.facebook.com/Henryscellarbar; 16 Morrison St; free-£10; ⊗ 9pm-3am Sun & Tue-Thu, 8pm-3am Mon, 7pm-3am Fri & Sat; ☐ all Lothian Rd buses) One of Edinburgh's most eclectic live-music venues, Henry's has something going on most nights of the week, from rock and indie to 'Balkan-inspired folk' and from funk and hip-hop to hardcore, staging both local bands and acts from around the world.

Traverse Theatre THEATRE
(Map p752; ☑ 0131-228 1404; www.traverse.co.uk; 10 Cambridge St; ⊗ box office 10am-6pm Mon-Sat, to 7pm show nights; 🕾; ☐ all Lothian Rd buses) The Traverse is the main focus for new Scottish writing; it stages an adventurous program of contemporary drama and dance.

The box office is only open on Sunday (from 4pm) when there's a show on.

Shopping

Princes St is Edinburgh's principal shopping street, lined with all the big high-street stores, with many smaller shops along pedestrianised Rose St, and more expensive designer boutiques on George St and Thistle St.

For more offbeat shopping – including fashion, music, crafts, gifts and jewellery – head for the cobbled lanes of Cockburn, Victoria and St Mary's Sts, all near the Royal Mile in the Old Town; William St in the western part of the New Town; and the Stockbridge district, immediately north of the New Town.

There are two big shopping centres in the New Town – **Waverley Mall** (Map p758; ☑ 0131-557 3759; www.waverleymall.com; Waverley Bridge; ⊗ 9am-7pm Mon-Sat, 10am-6pm Sun; ☐ all Princes St buses), at the eastern end of Princes St, and the nearby **Edinburgh St James** (Map p758; www.edinburghstjames.com; 1 Leith St; ☐ St Andrew Sq) at the top of Leith St, plus **Multrees Walk** (Map p758; www.multreeswalk.co.uk; St Andrew Sq; ☐ St Andrew Sq), a designer shopping complex with a flagship Harvey Nichols store on the eastern side of St Andrew Sq.

The huge **Ocean Terminal** (☑ 0131-555 8888; www.oceanterminal.com; Ocean Dr; ⊗ 10am-8pm Mon-Fri, to 7pm Sat, 11am-6pm Sun; 🕾; ☐ 11, 22, 34, 36, 200, 300) in Leith is the biggest shopping mall in the city.

🔒 Old Town

Armstrong's VINTAGE
(Map p752; ☑ 0131-220 5557; www.armstrongsvintage.co.uk; 83 Grassmarket; ⊗ 10am-5.30pm Mon-Thu, to 6pm Fri & Sat, noon-6pm Sun; ☐ 2) Armstrong's is an Edinburgh fashion institution (established in 1840, no less), a quality vintage-clothes emporium offering everything from elegant 1940s dresses to funky 1970s flares. Aside from the retro fashion, it's a great place to hunt for preloved kilts and Harris tweed, or to seek inspiration for that fancy-dress party.

Ragamuffin FASHION & ACCESSORIES
(Map p752; ☑ 0131-557 6007; www.facebook.com/pg/ragamuffinclothesandknitwear; 278 Canongate; ⊗ 10am-6pm Mon-Sat, noon-6pm Sun; ☐ 35) Quality Scottish knitwear and fabrics, including cashmere from Johnstons of Elgin, Fair Isle sweaters and Harris tweed.

ROSSLYN CHAPEL

Many years may have passed since Dan Brown's novel *The Da Vinci Code* and the subsequent film came out, but floods of visitors still descend on Scotland's most beautiful and enigmatic church – **Rosslyn Chapel** (Collegiate Church of St Matthew; ☑ 0131-440 2159; www.rosslynchapel.com; Chapel Loan, Roslin; adult/child £9/free; ⊙ 9.30am-6pm Mon-Sat Jun-Aug, to 5pm Sep-May, noon-4.45pm Sun year-round; 🅿; ☐ 37) 🖉 . Built in the mid-15th century for Sir William St Clair, third prince of Orkney, its ornately carved interior – at odds with the architectural fashion of its time – is a monument to the mason's art, rich in symbolic imagery. Hourly talks by qualified guides are included with admission.

As well as flowers, vines, angels and biblical figures, the carved stones include many examples of the pagan Green Man; other figures are associated with Freemasonry and the Knights Templar. Intriguingly, there are also carvings of plants from the Americas that predate Columbus' voyage of discovery. The symbolism of these images has led some researchers to conclude that Rosslyn is some kind of secret Templar repository, and it has been claimed that hidden vaults beneath the chapel could conceal anything from the Holy Grail or the head of John the Baptist to the body of Christ himself. The chapel is owned by the Scottish Episcopal Church and services are still held here on Sunday mornings.

The chapel is on the eastern edge of the village of Roslin, 7 miles south of Edinburgh's centre. Lothian Bus 37 to Penicuik Deanburn runs from Edinburgh's West End to Roslin (£1.70, one hour, every 15 minutes). Note that bus 37 to Bush does not go via Roslin – check the bus front and if in doubt ask the driver.

EDINBURGH SHOPPING

Geoffrey (Tailor) Inc   FASHION & ACCESSORIES
(Map p752; ☑ 0131-557 0256; www.geoffreykilts.co.uk; 57-59 High St; ⊙ 9.30am-6pm Mon-Sat, 10.30am-5.30pm Sun; ☐ 300) Geoffrey can fit you out in traditional Highland dress, or run up a kilt in your own clan tartan. The store's offshoot, 21st Century Kilts, offers modern fashion kilts in a variety of fabrics.

Bill Baber   FASHION & ACCESSORIES
(Map p752; ☑ 0131-225 3249; www.billbaber.com; 66 Grassmarket; ⊙ 9am-5.30pm Mon-Sat, 11am-4pm Sun; ☐ 2) This family-run designer-knitwear studio has been in the business for more than 40 years, producing stylish and colourful creations using linen, merino wool, silk and cotton.

Royal Mile Whiskies   DRINKS
(Map p752; ☑ 0131-225 3383; www.royalmilewhiskies.com; 379 High St; ⊙ 10am-7pm Sun-Wed, to 8pm Thu-Sat; ☐ 23, 27, 41, 42) If it's a drap of the cratur ye're after, this place has a selection of single malts in miniature and full-size bottles. There's also a range of blended whiskies, Irish whiskey and bourbon, and you can buy online, too.

🏠 New Town

21st Century Kilts   FASHION & ACCESSORIES
(Map p758; http://21stcenturykilts.com; 48 Thistle St; ⊙ 10am-6pm Tue & Thu-Sat; ☐ 23, 27) With celebrity customers including Alan Cummings, Robbie Williams and Vin Diesel, 21st Century Kilts offers modern fashion kilts in a variety of fabrics, both off-the-peg and made to measure.

Jenners   DEPARTMENT STORE
(Map p758; ☑ 0131-225 2442; www.houseoffraser.co.uk; 48 Princes St; ⊙ 9.30am-6.30pm Mon-Wed, to 8pm Thu, to 7pm Fri, 9am-7pm Sat, 11am-6pm Sun; ☐ Princes St) Founded in 1838, and acquired by House of Fraser in 2005, Jenners is the *grande dame* of Scottish department stores. It stocks a wide range of quality goods, both classic and contemporary.

Harvey Nichols   DEPARTMENT STORE
(Map p758; ☑ 0131-524 8388; www.harveynichols.com; 30-34 St Andrew Sq; ⊙ 10am-6pm Mon-Wed, to 8pm Thu, to 7pm Fri & Sat, 11am-6pm Sun; ☐ St Andrew Sq) The jewel in the crown of Edinburgh's shopping scene has four floors of designer labels and eye-popping price tags.

🏠 South Edinburgh

Meadows Pottery   CERAMICS
(Map p762; ☑ 0131-662 4064; www.themeadowspottery.com; 11a Summerhall Pl; ⊙ 10am-6pm Mon-Fri, to 5pm Sat; ☐ 2, 41, 42, 67) This little shop sells a range of colourful, high-fired oxidised stoneware, both domestic and decorative, all hand thrown on the premises. If you can't find what you want, you can commission custom-made pieces.

Rosslyn Chapel

DECIPHERING ROSSLYN

Rosslyn Chapel is a small building, but the density of decoration inside can be overwhelming. It's well worth buying the official guidebook by the Earl of Rosslyn first; find a bench in the gardens and have a skim through before going into the chapel – the background information will make your visit all the more interesting. The book also offers a useful self-guided tour of the chapel, and explains the legend of the Master Mason and the Apprentice.

Entrance is through the ❶ **north door**. Take a pew and sit for a while to allow your eyes to adjust to the dim interior; then look up at the ceiling vault, decorated with engraved roses, lilies and stars, (Can you spot the sun and the moon?). Walk left along the north aisle to reach the Lady Chapel, separated from the rest of the church by the ❷ **Mason's Pillar** and the ❸ **Apprentice Pillar**. Here you'll find carvings of ❹ **Lucifer**, the Fallen Angel, and the ❺ **Green Man**. Nearby are ❻ **carvings** that appear to resemble Indian corn (maize). Finally, go to the western end and look up at the wall – in the left corner is the head of the ❼ **Apprentice**; to the right is the (rather worn) head of the ❽ **Master Mason**.

ROSSLYN CHAPEL & THE DA VINCI CODE

Dan Brown was referencing Rosslyn Chapel's alleged links to the Knights Templar and the Freemasons – unusual symbols found among the carvings, and the fact that a descendant of its founder, William St Clair, was a Grand Master Mason – when he chose it as the setting for his novel's denouement. Rosslyn is indeed a coded work, written in stone, but its meaning depends on your point of view. See *The Rosslyn Hoax?* by Robert LD Cooper for an alternative interpretation of the chapel's symbolism.

Lucifer, the Fallen Angel
At head height, to the left of the second window from the left, is an upside-down angel bound with rope, a symbol often associated with Freemasonry. The arch above is decorated with the Dance of Death.

EXPLORE SOME MORE

After visiting the chapel, head downhill to see the spectacularly sited ruins of Roslin Castle, then take a walk along leafy Roslin Glen.

The Apprentice
High in the corner, beneath an empty statue niche, is the head of the murdered Apprentice, with a deep wound in his forehead above the right eye. Legend says the Apprentice was murdered in a jealous rage by the Master Mason. The worn head on the side wall to the left of the Apprentice is that of his mother.

North Door

The Master Mason
❽

Baptistry

PRACTICAL TIPS

Local guides give hourly talks throughout the day, which are included in the admission price. No photography is allowed inside the chapel.

Green Man
On a boss at the base of the arch between the second and third windows from the left is the finest example of more than a hundred 'green man' carvings in the chapel, pagan symbols of spring, fertility and rebirth.

MISTY RIVER / SHUTTERSTOCK ©

Green Man

Crypt

Lady Chapel

Mason's Pillar

North Aisle

Altar

Choir

South Aisle

The Apprentice Pillar
This is perhaps the chapel's most beautiful carving. Four vines spiral up the pillar, issuing from the mouths of eight dragons at its base. At the top is Isaac, son of Abraham, lying bound upon the altar.

DE AGOSTINI / W. BUSS / GETTY IMAGES ©

Indian Corn
The frieze around the second window on the south wall is said to represent Indian corn (maize), but it predates Columbus' discovery of the New World in 1492. Other carvings seem to resemble aloe vera.

Backbeat   MUSIC
(Map p762; ☑0131-668 2666; 31 E Crosscauseway;
⊙10am-5.30pm Mon-Sat; ☐all Newington buses) If you're hunting for secondhand vinyl
from way back, this cramped little shop has
a stunning and constantly changing collection of jazz, blues, rock and soul, plus lots of
'60s and '70s stuff, though you'll have to take
some time to hunt through the clutter.

Lighthouse   BOOKS
(Map p752; ☑0131-662 9112; http://lighthouse
bookshop.com; 43 W Nicolson St; ⊙10am-6pm
Mon-Sat, 11.30am-5pm Sun; ☐41, 42, 67) Lighthouse is a radical independent bookshop
that supports both small publishers and
local writers. It stocks a wide range of political, gay and feminist literature, as well as
non-mainstream fiction and nonfiction.

🄰 Leith

Kinloch Anderson   FASHION & ACCESSORIES
(☑0131-555 1390; www.kinlochanderson.com; 4
Dock St; ⊙9am-5.30pm Mon-Sat; ☐16, 22, 36,
300) One of the best tartan shops in Edinburgh, Kinloch Anderson was founded in
1868 and is still family run. It is a supplier of
kilts and Highland dress to the Royal Family.

🄰 Stockbridge

★Golden Hare Books   BOOKS
(Map p758; ☑0131-629 1396; https://golden
harebooks.com; 68 St Stephen St; ⊙10am-6pm;
☐24, 29, 42) Independent bookshops don't
get lovelier than this. The Golden Hare
boasts a top-notch selection of 'beautiful,
unusual and interesting books', an enchanting children's nook, and a small but perfectly formed events program. A must if you love
books, book design and beautiful shops.

Stockbridge Market   MARKET
(Map p758; www.stockbridgemarket.com; cnr Kerr
& Saunders Sts; ⊙10am-5pm Sun; ☐24, 29, 36,
42) On Sunday the local community's focus
is Stockbridge Market, set in a leafy square
next to the bridge that gives the district
its name. Wares range from fresh Scottish
produce to handmade ceramics, jewellery,
soaps and cosmetics. Grab an espresso from
Steampunk Coffee, which operates out of a
1970s VW campervan.

Galerie Mirages   JEWELLERY
(Map p758; ☑0131-315 2603; www.galeriemirag
es.com; 46a Raeburn Pl; ⊙10am-5.30pm Mon-Sat,
12-4.30pm Sun; ☐24, 29, 42) An Aladdin's cave
packed with jewellery, textiles and handicrafts from all over the world, Mirages is
best known for its silver, amber and gem-
stone jewellery in both culturally traditional
and contemporary designs.

🛈 Information

MEDICAL SERVICES

Edinburgh Royal Infirmary (☑0131-536 1000;
www.nhslothian.scot.nhs.uk/GoingToHospital/
Locations/RIE; 51 Little France Cres, Old
Dalkeith Rd; ⊙24hr; ☐7, 8, 21, 24, 38) Edinburgh's main general hospital; has 24-hour
accident and emergency department.

Western General Hospital (☑0131-537 1000;
www.nhslothian.scot.nhs.uk/GoingToHospital/
Locations/WGH; Crewe Rd S; ⊙8am-9pm;
☐19, 24, 29, 38 47) For non-life-threatening
injuries and ailments, you can attend the Minor
Injuries Clinic here without having to make an
appointment.

POST

Frederick St Post Office (Map p758; 40
Frederick St; ⊙9am-5.30pm Mon & Wed-Fri,
9.30am-5.30pm Tue, 9.30am-12.30pm Sat;
☐24, 29, 42)

Waverley Mall Post Office (Map p758; upper
level, Waverley Mall; ⊙9am-5.30pm Mon &
Wed-Sat, 9.30am-5.30pm Tue; ☐all Princes
St buses)

St Mary's St Post Office (Map p752; 46 St
Mary's St; ⊙9am-5.30pm Mon-Fri, to 12.30pm
Sat; ☐300)

TOURIST INFORMATION

Edinburgh Tourist Office (Edinburgh iCentre;
Map p758; ☑0131-473 3868; www.visitscot
land.com/info/services/edinburgh-icentre-
p234441; Waverley Mall, 3 Princes St; ⊙9am-
7pm Mon-Sat, 10am-7pm Sun Jul & Aug, to
6pm Jun, to 5pm Sep-May; 🛜; ☐St Andrew
Sq) Accommodation booking service, currency
exchange, gift shop and bookshop, internet access, and counters selling tickets for Edinburgh
city tours and Scottish Citylink bus services.

Edinburgh Airport Tourist Office (☑0131-473
3690; www.visitscotland.com; East Terminal,
Edinburgh Airport; ⊙7.30am-7.30pm Mon-Fri,
to 7pm Sat & Sun) VisitScotland Information
Centre in the airport's terminal extension.

Edinburgh Festival Fringe Office (☑0131-226
0026; www.edfringe.com; 180 High St; ⊙noon-
3pm Mon-Sat mid-Jun–mid-Jul, 10am-6pm
daily mid-Jul–1 Aug, 9am-9pm daily Aug; ☐all
South Bridge buses) Box office and information
centre for Edinburgh Festival Fringe (p767)
events.

Edinburgh Festival Guide (www.edinburgh
festivalcity.com) Everything you need to know
about Edinburgh's many festivals.

ℹ Getting There & Away

AIR

Edinburgh Airport (EDI; ☑ 0844 448 8833; www.edinburghairport.com), 8 miles west of the city, has numerous flights to other parts of Scotland and the UK, Ireland and mainland Europe. There's a VisitScotland Information Centre in the airport's terminal extension.

BUS

Edinburgh Bus Station (Map p758; left-luggage lockers per 24hr £5-10; ☉ 4.30am-midnight Sun-Thu, to 12.30am Fri & Sat; ☐ St Andrew Sq) is at the northeastern corner of St Andrew Sq, with pedestrian entrances from the square and from Elder St. For timetable information, contact **Traveline** (☑ 0871 200 22 33; www.travelinescotland.com).

Scottish Citylink (☑ 0871 266 3333; www.citylink.co.uk) buses connect Edinburgh with all of Scotland's cities and major towns. The following are sample one-way fares departing from Edinburgh.

DESTINATION	FARE (£)
Aberdeen	32.70
Dundee	17.50
Fort William	37
Glasgow	7.90
Inverness	32.20
Portree	58.30
Stirling	8.70

It's also worth checking with **Megabus** (☑ 0141-352 4444; www.megabus.com) for cheap intercity bus fares (from as little as £5) from Edinburgh to Aberdeen, Dundee, Glasgow, Inverness and Perth.

There are various buses to Edinburgh from London and the rest of the UK.

CAR

Arriving in or leaving Edinburgh by car during the morning and evening rush hours (7.30am to 9.30am and 4.30pm to 6.30pm Monday to Friday) is an experience you can live without. Try to time your journey to avoid these periods.

Major roads leading into and out of Edinburgh:
➡ M90 north to Perth
➡ M9 northwest to Stirling
➡ M8 west to Glasgow
➡ A7 south to Galashiels
➡ A68 south to Melrose and Jedburgh
➡ A1 southeast to Berwick-upon-Tweed

TRAIN

The main rail terminus in Edinburgh is **Waverley train station**, located in the heart of the city.

Trains arriving from, and departing for, the west also stop at Haymarket station, which is more convenient for the West End.

You can buy tickets, make reservations and get travel information at the **Edinburgh Rail Travel Centre** (Waverley station; ☉ 5am-midnight Mon-Sat, 7am-midnight Sun; ☐ all Princes St buses). For fare and timetable information, phone the **National Rail Enquiry Service** (☑ 03457 48 49 50; www.nationalrail.co.uk) or use the journey planner on the website.

If you're travelling as a pair, consider purchasing a **Two Together Railcard** (www.twotogether-railcard.co.uk; per year £30), which offers you up to 30% off your combined fares on train rides taken throughout Great Britain.

ScotRail (☑ 0344 811 0141; www.scotrail.co.uk) operates regular train services to the following:
Aberdeen (£35.50, 2½ hours)
Dundee (£18.90, 1¼ hours)
Glasgow (£14.40, 50 minutes, every 15 minutes)
Inverness (£40, 3½ hours)

ℹ Getting Around

TO/FROM THE AIRPORT
Bus

Lothian Buses' Airlink (https://lothianbuses.co.uk/airport) service 100 runs from Waverley Bridge, outside the train station, to the airport

QUEENSFERRY & THE FORTH BRIDGES

Queensferry, also known as South Queensferry, is at the narrowest part of the Firth of Forth, where ferries have crossed to Fife from the earliest times. The village takes its name from Queen Margaret (1046–93), who gave pilgrims free passage across the firth on their way to St Andrews. Ferries continued to operate until 1964, when the graceful **Forth Road Bridge** was opened; this was followed by a second road bridge, the **Queensferry Crossing** (2017).

Predating the first road bridge by 74 years, the magnificent **Forth Bridge** – only outsiders ever call it the Forth Rail Bridge – is one of the finest engineering achievements of the 19th century. Opened in 1890 as the world's first major steel structure, its three huge cantilevers span 1630m and took 53,000 tonnes of steel, 6.5 million rivets and the lives of 73 men to build.

(one-way/return £4.50/7.50, 30 minutes, every 10 minutes from 4am to midnight) via the West End and Haymarket. Skylink services 200 and 300 run from the airport to Ocean Terminal via north Edinburgh and west Edinburgh/the Royal Mile, respectively.

Tram

Edinburgh Trams (www.edinburghtrams.com) run from the airport to the city centre (one-way/return £6/8.50, 33 minutes, every six to eight minutes from 6am to midnight).

Taxi

An airport taxi to the city centre costs around £20 and takes about 20 to 30 minutes.

BUS

Bus timetables, route maps and fare guides are posted at all main bus and tram stops, and you can pick up a copy of the free *Lothian Buses Route Map* from Lothian Buses Travelshops on **Waverley Bridge** (Map p752; 31 Waverley Bridge; ⏰ 9am-6pm Tue, Wed & Fri, to 7pm Mon & Thu, to 5.30pm Sat, 10am-5.30pm Sun; ▢ 6) and **Hanover St** (Map p758; 27 Hanover St; ⏰ 9am-6pm Mon-Fri, to 5.30pm Sat; ▢ 23, 27).

Adult fares within the city are £1.70; purchase from the bus driver. Children aged under five travel free and those aged five to 15 pay a flat fare of 80p.

On Lothian Buses you must pay the driver the exact fare, but First buses will give change. Lothian Bus drivers also sell a day ticket (£4) that gives unlimited travel on Lothian buses and trams for a day; a family day ticket (up to two adults and three children) costs £8.50.

Night-service buses, which run hourly between midnight and 5am, charge a flat fare of £3.50.

You can also buy a Ridacard (from Travelshops; not available from bus drivers) that gives unlimited travel for one week for £19.

The Lothian Buses lost-property office is in the Hanover St Travelshop.

CAR

Though useful for day trips beyond the city, a car in central Edinburgh is more of a liability than a convenience. There is restricted access on Princes St, George St and Charlotte Sq, many streets are one way, and finding a parking place in the city centre is like striking gold. Queen's

Dr around Holyrood Park is closed to motorised traffic on Sunday.

There's no parking on main roads into the city from 7.30am to 6.30pm Monday to Saturday. Also, parking in the city centre can be a nightmare.

On-street parking is controlled by self-service ticket machines from 8.30am to 6.30pm Monday to Saturday, and costs from £2.20 to £4.20 per hour, with a 30-minute to four-hour maximum.

If you break the rules, you'll get a fine, often within minutes of your ticket expiring – Edinburgh's parking wardens are both numerous and notorious. The fine is £60, reduced to £30 if you pay up within 14 days. Cars parked illegally will be clamped or towed away. There are large, long-stay car parks at the Omni Centre, Blackfriars St, Castle Tce, Holyrood Rd and Fountain Park. Motorcycles can be parked free at designated areas in the city centre.

TAXI

Edinburgh's black taxis can be hailed in the street, ordered by phone (extra 80p charge) or picked up at one of the many central ranks. The minimum charge is £2.10 (£3.10 at night) for the first 450m, then 25p for every subsequent 184m – a typical 2-mile trip across the city centre will cost around £6 to £7. Tipping is up to you – because of the high fares, local people rarely tip on short journeys, but they occasionally round up to the nearest 50p on longer ones.

Central Taxis (☎ 0131-229 2468; www.taxis-edinburgh.co.uk)

City Cabs (☎ 0131-228 1211; www.citycabs.co.uk)

ComCab (☎ 0131-272 8001; www.comcab-edinburgh.co.uk)

TRAM

Edinburgh's tram system (www.edinburghtrams.com) consists of one line from Edinburgh Airport to York Pl, at the top of Leith Walk, via Haymarket, the West End and Princes St.

Tickets are integrated with the city's Lothian Buses, costing £1.70 for a single journey within the city boundary, or £6 to the airport. Trams run every eight to 10 minutes Monday to Saturday and every 12 to 15 minutes on Sunday, from 5.30am to 11pm.

Glasgow & Southern Scotland

Best Places to Eat

➜ Ubiquitous Chip (p806)

➜ Stravaigin (p804)

➜ Ox & Finch (p804)

➜ Cobbles (p817)

➜ Auld Alliance (p820)

➜ Coltman's (p813)

Best Places to Stay

➜ Dakota Deluxe (p801)

➜ Alamo Guest House (p802)

➜ Knockinaam Lodge (p823)

➜ Old Bank House (p814)

➜ Old Priory (p816)

➜ Edenbank House (p816)

Why Go?

Though wise folk are well aware of its charms, for many people southern Scotland is just something to drive through on the way to northern Scotland. Big mistake. But it does mean you'll find breathing room here in summer, and plenty of peaceful corners.

Proximity to England brought raiding and strife aplenty, but the ruins of many churches and abandoned abbeys now provide some of Scotland's most atmospheric historic sites. The west enjoys extensive forest cover between bustling market towns, and the rolling hills cascade down to sandy stretches of coastline. But the main draw is undoubtedly Glasgow, Scotland's biggest city, a sassy and welcoming metropolis with an infectious spirit and an excellent range of museums, restaurants and pubs. It demands several days of your time.

When to Go

➜ June is the perfect time to visit the region's numerous stately homes, with spectacular blooming gardens. The West End Festival and the Jazz Festival make Glasgow music heaven.

➜ Summer in Glasgow is a pleasure, with better weather and locals even cheerier than usual.

➜ Hit Galloway's forests in October to see red deer battling it out in the rutting season.

Glasgow & Southern Scotland Highlights

1 Glasgow (p792) Revelling in the second city's museums, restaurants, pubs and music venues.

2 Border Abbeys (p814) Exploring the noble, evocative ruins – Dryburgh is our favourite – and the area's other historic sights.

3 Culzean Castle (p817) Admiring the 18th-century architectural genius of a castle perched on wild sea cliffs.

4 Hermitage Castle (p814) Pondering the tough old life on the England–Scotland frontier at this desolate castle.

EDINBURGH

EAST LOTHIAN

MID LOTHIAN

Tyne

Cockburnspath

A1

St Abbs
Coldingham
Eyemouth

Lammermuir Hills

Duns

Tweed

Moorfoot Hills

Lauder

Lanark

New Lanark 8

SOUTH LANARKSHIRE

M8

A701

A702

Peebles

Biggar

M74

Clyde

Tweed

A72

Galashiels

Abbotsford

Selkirk

Melrose

Dryburgh Abbey 2

Coldstream

Smailholm

Kelso

A698

Kirk Yetholm

Town Yetholm

SCOTTISH BORDERS

Teviot

Jedburgh

A68

Abington

A74(M)

A708

B709

Hawick

Sanquhar

A76

Moffat

Eskdalemuir

White Esk

Teviot

Hermitage Castle 4

Border Forest Park

Northumberland National Park

Thornhill

Esk

Newcastleton

A74(M)

Langholm

Nith

Lockerbie

Cairn Water

NORTHUMBERLAND

Dumfries

Caerlaverock Castle

New Abbey

Gretna Green

Gretna

Carlisle

ENGLAND

CUMBRIA

Kirkoswald

Solway Firth

Lake District National Park

N

0   40 km
0   20 miles

5 **Kirkcudbright** (p819)
Marvelling at the creative
flair of this charming town's
inhabitants.

6 **Robert Burns Birthplace
Museum** (p818) Learning

Lallans words from the
Scottish Bard's verses.

7 **Glentrool** (p821)
Whooshing down forest trails
here and at other 7stanes
mountain-biking hubs.

8 **New Lanark** (p811)
Admiring the radical social
reform instituted in this
handsome mill community.

GLASGOW

⏴ 0141 / POP 596,500

Glasgow is a good-time city that hides behind a sober facade. Disarmingly blending sophistication and earthiness, Scotland's biggest city has evolved over the last couple of decades to become one of Britain's most intriguing metropolises. Handsomely set along the Clyde River, it's a city with a rich architectural legacy, the product of wealth generated from manufacturing and trade: stately Victorian mansions, grand public buildings and, above all, the sublime designs of Charles Rennie Mackintosh, which dot the city.

Apart from its seriously grand architecture, Glasgow is also home to some wonderful museums and galleries, super shopping, a crackling nightlife and several of Scotland's top restaurants. All in all, it's quite a place – and like many unsuspecting visitors, you'll soon find Glasgow's sheer vitality is gloriously infectious.

History

The area where Glasgow now stands was bisected by the Romans in the 2nd century AD when they built the Antonine Wall to protect the fringes of their empire from the Caledonian wildlings beyond.

Glasgow grew around the religious site established in the 6th century by St Kentigern, better known as St Mungo (originally an affectionate nickname). It became an important bishop's seat, but the cathedral that was built here is one of the few remnants of the medieval city. It was swept away by the energies of a new age – the age of capitalism, the Industrial Revolution and the British Empire.

Glasgow's west-coast position led to it becoming an important port for trade with the Americas. In the 18th century much of the tobacco trade between Europe and the USA was routed through Glasgow, providing a great source of wealth. The tobacco barons were responsible for much construction around the city that remains today. Even after the tobacco trade declined in the 19th century, the city continued to prosper as a centre of textile manufacturing, shipbuilding and the coal and steel industries. Many of the city's major buildings and monuments were constructed during the Victorian period, when Glasgow was a byword for mercantile prosperity. The outward appearance, however, was tempered by the dire working conditions in the factories.

In the first half of the 20th century Glasgow was the centre of Britain's munitions industry, supplying arms and ships for the two world wars, in the second of which the city was carpet-bombed. Post–World War II, however, the port and heavy industries began to dwindle, and by the early 1970s the city looked doomed. Glasgow became synonymous with unemployment, economic depression and urban violence, centred on high-rise housing schemes such as the infamous Gorbals.

More recently, urban development and a booming cultural sector have injected style and confidence into the city. Though the standard of living remains low for Britain and life continues to be tough for many, the ongoing regeneration process gives grounds for optimism. The successful hosting of the 2014 Commonwealth Games highlighted this regeneration to a wide global audience.

◉ Sights

◉ City Centre

Glasgow's city centre changes character as you move from east to west, going from a frenetic blend of services, transport terminals, pubs and shops to the more sedate terraces of thoroughfares like Bath St, where upmarket offices sit over basements converted into stylish bars. This is where much of the city's quality accommodation is clustered and is also a studenty zone, with a major nightlife nexus on Sauchiehall St, which runs the length of the neighbourhood.

★**Glasgow School of Art**   HISTORIC BUILDING
(Map p794; ⏴ 0141-353 4526; www.gsa.ac.uk; 167 Renfrew St) In 2018, Charles Rennie Mackintosh's greatest building was gearing up for reopening after a devastating 2014 fire when, unbelievably, another blaze destroyed the painstakingly reconstructed interiors and severely damaged the building. The school has committed to reconstructing it, but it will be a lengthy process. At time of research the visitor centre, shop and exhibitions in the neighbouring Reid building were closed to visitors; check the website to see if visits and tours have resumed.

★**City Chambers**   HISTORIC BUILDING
(Map p794; ⏴ 0141-287 2000; www.glasgow.gov. uk; George Sq; ⏱ 9am-5pm Mon-Fri) **FREE** The grand seat of local government was built in the 1880s at the high point of Glasgow's

wealth. The interior is even more extravagant than the exterior, and the chambers have sometimes been used as a movie location to represent the Kremlin or the Vatican. You can have a look at the opulent ground floor during opening hours. To see more, free guided tours are held at 10.30am and 2.30pm Monday to Friday; it's worth popping in earlier that day to prebook.

★**Sharmanka Kinetic Theatre**   THEATRE
(Map p794; ☎0141-552 7080; www.sharmanka. com; 103 Trongate; adult/child short show £8/3, long show £10/8; ⊙40-minute shows 5pm Wed & Thu, 1pm Fri, 3pm Sat & Sun, 1hr shows 7pm Thu, 5pm Sun) This extraordinary mechanical theatre is located at the Trongate 103 arts centre. Russian sculptor and mechanic Eduard Bersudsky, now resident in Scotland, has created a series of large, wondrous figures sculpted from bits of scrap and elaborate carvings. Set to haunting music, each figure performs humorous and tragic stories of the human spirit. Great for kids and very moving for adults: inspirational one moment and macabre the next, but always colourful, clever and thought provoking.

Gallery of Modern Art   GALLERY
(GoMA; Map p794; ☎0141-287 3050; www.glas gowmuseums.com; Royal Exchange Sq; ⊙10am-5pm Mon-Wed & Sat, until 8pm Thu, 11am-5pm Fri & Sun) FREE This contemporary art gallery features modern works from local and international artists, housed in a graceful neoclassical building. The original interior is

CHARLES RENNIE MACKINTOSH

Great cities have great artists, designers and architects contributing to their urban environment while expressing their soul and individuality. Charles Rennie Mackintosh was all of these and his quirky, linear and geometric designs have had an enormous influence on Glasgow. Many of the buildings Mackintosh designed are open to the public, and you'll see his tall, thin, art nouveau typeface repeatedly reproduced.

Born in 1868, Mackintosh studied at the Glasgow School of Art. It was there that he met the influential artist and designer Margaret Macdonald, whom he married; they collaborated on many projects and were major influences on each other's work. Together with her sister Frances and Herbert MacNair, the artist who married her, they formed 'The Four', a pioneering group that developed the Glasgow Style. This contribution to art nouveau incorporated influences from the Arts and Crafts movement and Japanese design.

In 1896, aged only 27, Mackintosh won a competition for his design for the new building of the Glasgow School of Art, where he had studied. This was his supreme architectural achievement. The first section was opened in 1899 and is considered to be the earliest example of art nouveau in Britain. The second section, opened a decade later, includes some of the earliest art deco. The building demonstrates his skill in combining function and style.

Another of Mackintosh's finest works is Hill House (p857), in Helensburgh. Other buildings around town include the **Daily Record Building** (Map p794; 20 Renfield Lane), **Scotland Street School** (☎0141-287 0504; www.glasgowlife.org.uk; 225 Scotland St; ⊙10am-5pm Tue-Thu & Sat, from 11am Fri & Sun) FREE, **Mackintosh Queen's Cross church** (Map p798; ☎0141-946 6600; www.mackintoshchurch.com; 870 Garscube Rd; adult/child £4/free; ⊙10am-5pm Mon-Fri Apr-Oct, to 4pm Mon, Wed & Fri Nov-Dec & Feb-Mar, closed Jan) and **House for an Art Lover** (☎0141-353 4770; www.houseforanartlover.co.uk; Bellahouston Park, Dumbreck Rd; adult/child £6/4.50; ⊙check online, roughly 10am-4pm Mon-Fri, to noon Sat, to 2pm Sun). His reconstructed Willow Tearooms (p794) feature his design concept right down to the smallest level.

Although Mackintosh's genius was quickly recognised in the rest of Europe, he did not receive the same encouragement in Scotland. His architectural career here lasted only until 1914, when he moved to England to concentrate on furniture design. He died in 1928, and it is only since the last decades of the 20th century that Mackintosh's genius has been widely recognised. For more about the man and his work, contact the **Charles Rennie Mackintosh Society** (Map p798; ☎0141-946 6600; www.crmsociety.com; Mackintosh Queen's Cross, 870 Garscube Rd). Check its website and www.glasgowmackintosh.com for special events.

Central Glasgow

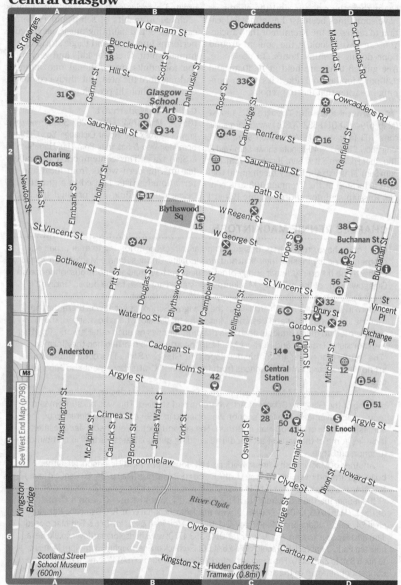

an ornate contrast to the inventive art often on display, though quality varies markedly by exhibition. There's also an effort made to keep the kids entertained. Usually the horseback statue of the Duke of Wellington outside is cheekily crowned with a traffic cone; the authorities grumble, but it keeps happening and is now an icon.

Mackintosh at the Willow HISTORIC BUILDING
(Map p794; ☑ 0141-204 1903; www.mackintoshat thewillow.com; 217 Sauchiehall St; exhibition admis-

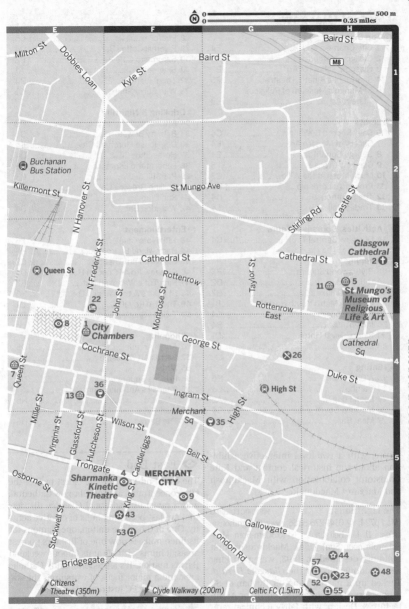

sion adult/child £5.50/3.50; ⊘Opening: Tearoom 9am-5pm, exhibition 9am-5.30pm Mon-Sat, 10am-5pm Sun, last entry 1hr before closing) Opened in 2018, this reconstruction of the original Willow tearoom that Mackintosh designed and furnished in the early 20th century for restaurateur Kate Cranston offers authentic design splendour in its original location. You can admire the architect's distinctive touch in just about every element; he had free rein and even the teaspoons were given his attention. Alongside the tearoom is a visitor

Central Glasgow

centre, with a two-level interactive exhibition about the historical context and Kate Cranston's collaboration with Mackintosh and Margaret Macdonald.

The Lighthouse   HISTORIC BUILDING
(Map p794; ☎0141-276 5365; www.thelighthouse.co.uk; 11 Mitchell Lane; ⊙10.30am-5pm Mon-Sat, from noon Sun) FREE Mackintosh's first building, designed in 1893, was a striking new headquarters for the *Glasgow Herald*. Tucked up a narrow lane off Buchanan St, it now serves as Scotland's Centre for Architecture & Design, with fairly technical temporary exhibitions (sometimes admission is payable for these), as well as the Mackintosh Interpretation Centre, a detailed (if slightly dry) overview of his life and work. On the top floor of the 'lighthouse', drink in great views over the rooftops and spires of the city centre.

◉ East End

The East End includes the oldest part of the city, concentrated around Glasgow Cathedral, and a range of traditional Glasgow districts that are fast becoming hubs of creative activity. One of these, the Calton, once famous for its linen mills, is now one of Britain's poorest areas; it hums with life at its famous weekend Barras market. It's a predominantly Catholic area and a major focus of worship is the stadium of Celtic FC just down the road.

★ Glasgow Cathedral   CATHEDRAL
(HES; Map p794; ☎0141-552 6891; www.historicenvironment.scot; Cathedral Sq; ⊙9.30am-5.30pm Mon-Sat, 1-5pm Sun Apr-Sep, 10am-4pm Mon-Sat, from 1pm Sun Oct-Mar) Glasgow Cathedral has a rare timelessness. The dark, imposing interior conjures up medieval might and can send a shiver down the spine. It's a shining

example of Gothic architecture, and unlike nearly all of Scotland's cathedrals, it survived the turmoil of the Reformation mobs almost intact. Most of the current building dates from the 15th century.

Entry is through a side door into the nave, hung with regimental colours. The wooden roof has been restored many times since its original construction, but some of the timber dates from the 14th century; note the impressive shields. Many of the cathedral's stunning, narrow stained-glass windows are modern; to your left is Francis Spear's 1958 work *The Creation*, which fills the west window.

The cathedral is divided by a late-15th-century stone choir screen, decorated with seven pairs of figures perhaps representing the seven deadly sins. The four stained-glass panels of the east window, depicting the Apostles (also by Francis Spear), are particularly evocative. At the northeastern corner is the entrance to the 15th-century upper chapter house, where the University of Glasgow was founded. It's now used as a sacristy.

The most interesting part of the cathedral, the lower church, is reached by a stairway. Its forest of pillars creates a powerful atmosphere around the tomb of St Mungo (who founded a monastic community here in the 6th century), the focus of a famous medieval pilgrimage that was believed to be as meritorious as a visit to Rome.

While here, don't miss a stroll in the **necropolis** (⊙7am-4.30pm Apr-Oct, from 8am Nov-Mar) FREE.

★**St Mungo's Museum of Religious Life & Art**   MUSEUM
(Map p794; ☑0141-276 1625; www.glasgowmuseums.com; 2 Castle St; ⊙10am-5pm Tue-Thu & Sat, from 11am Fri & Sun) FREE Set in a reconstruction of the bishop's palace that once stood in the cathedral forecourt, this museum audaciously attempts to capture the world's major religions in an artistic nutshell. A startling achievement, it presents the similarities and differences of how various religions approach common themes such as birth, marriage and death. The attraction is twofold: firstly, impressive art that blurs the lines between religion and culture, and secondly, the opportunity to delve into different faiths, as deeply or shallowly as you wish.

Provand's Lordship   HISTORIC BUILDING
(Map p794; ☑0141-276 1625; www.glasgowmuseums.com; 3 Castle St; ⊙10am-5pm Tue-Thu & Sat, from 11am Fri & Sun) FREE Near the cathedral is Provand's Lordship, the oldest house in Glasgow. This rare example of 15th-century domestic Scottish architecture was built in 1471 as a manse. The ceilings and doorways are low, and the rooms are furnished with period furniture and artefacts; upstairs a room recreates the living space of an early-16th-century chaplain. The building's biggest draw is its authentic feel, though it's a shame the original wooden floors have had to be covered for protection.

⊙ West End

★**Kelvingrove Art Gallery & Museum**   GALLERY, MUSEUM
(Map p798; ☑0141-276 9599; www.glasgowmuseums.com; Argyle St; ⊙10am-5pm Mon-Thu & Sat, from 11am Fri & Sun) FREE A magnificent sandstone building, this grand Victorian cathedral of culture is a fascinating and unusual museum, with a bewildering variety of exhibits. You'll find fine art alongside stuffed animals, and Micronesian shark-tooth swords alongside a Spitfire plane, but it's not mix 'n' match: rooms are carefully and thoughtfully themed, and the collection is of a manageable size. It has an excellent room of Scottish art, a room of fine French impressionist works, and quality Renaissance paintings from Italy and Flanders.

Salvador Dalí's superb *Christ of St John of the Cross* is also here. Best of all, nearly everything, including the paintings, has an easy-reading paragraph of interpretation. You can learn a lot about art here, and it's excellent for children, with plenty to do and displays aimed at a variety of ages. Free hour-long guided tours begin at 11am and 2.30pm. Be here at 1pm to hear the impressive organ being played. Bus 17, among many others, runs here from Renfield St.

Hunterian Museum   MUSEUM
(Map p798; ☑0141-330 4221; www.hunterian.gla.ac.uk; University Ave; ⊙10am-5pm Tue-Sat, 11am-4pm Sun) FREE Housed in the glorious sandstone university building, which is in itself reason enough to pay a visit, this quirky museum contains the collection of renowned one-time student William Hunter (1718–83). Hunter was primarily an anatomist and physician, but as one of those wonderfully well-rounded Enlightenment figures, he interested himself in everything the world had to offer.

Pickled organs in glass jars take their place alongside geological phenomena,

West End

potsherds gleaned from ancient brochs, dinosaur skeletons and a creepy case of deformed animals. The main halls of the exhibition, with their high vaulted roofs, are magnificent in themselves. Highlights include a display of artefacts from the An-

tonine Wall and the beautiful 1674 Chinese *Map of the Whole World* produced for the emperor by a Jesuit at the court.

This collection will perhaps become part of the new museum at Kelvin Hall but probably not until at least 2023.

West End

Hunterian Art Gallery GALLERY
(Map p798; ☑0141-330 4221; www.hunterian.gla.
ac.uk; 82 Hillhead St; ⊙10am-5pm Tue-Sat, 11am-
4pm Sun) **FREE** Across the road from the
Hunterian Museum (p797), and part of the
same bequest, this art gallery incorporates
Mackintosh House as well as a good selection of Dutch Old Masters. A key highlight is
a special collection of James McNeill Whistler's limpid prints, drawings and paintings.
It also has a good selection of the bold tones
of the Scottish Colourists and some works by
the Glasgow Boys, though these weren't on
display at our last visit.

★ **Mackintosh House** HISTORIC BUILDING
(Map p798; ☑0141-330 4221; www.hunterian.gla.
ac.uk; 82 Hillhead St; adult/child £6/3; ⊙10am-
5pm Tue-Sat, 11am-4pm Sun) Attached to the
Hunterian Art Gallery (p799), this is a reconstruction of the first home that Charles Rennie Mackintosh bought with his wife, noted
designer/artist Margaret Macdonald. It's
fair to say that interior decoration was one
of their strong points; Mackintosh House
is startling even today. The quiet elegance
of the hall and dining room on the ground
floor give way to a stunning drawing room
and bedroom upstairs. Visits are by guided

tour in the morning and self guided in the
afternoon.

Botanic Gardens PARK
(Map p798; ☑0141-276 1614; www.glasgowbotanic
gardens.com; 730 Great Western Rd; ⊙7am-dusk,
glasshouse 10am-6pm summer, to 4.15pm winter)
A marvellous thing about walking in here
is the way the noise of Great Western Rd
suddenly recedes into the background. The
wooded gardens follow the riverbank of the
River Kelvin and there are plenty of tropical
species to discover. **Kibble Palace**, an impressive Victorian iron and glass structure
dating from 1873, is one of the largest glasshouses in Britain; check out the herb garden, too, with its medicinal species.

Kelvin Hall MUSEUM
(Map p798; ☑0141-276 1450; www.glasgowlife.org.
uk; 1445 Argyle St; ⊙6.30am-10pm Mon-Fri, 8am-
5pm Sat, 8am-8pm Sun) **FREE** Opened in the
1920s as an exhibition centre, this enormous
sandstone palace, renovated and reopened
in 2016, is a mixed leisure-and-arts space.
In addition to a gym and sports facilities, it
hosts the audiovisual archive of the **National Library of Scotland** (Map p798; ☑0845
366 4600; www.nls.uk; Kelvin Hall; ⊙10am-5pm
Tue & Thu-Sat, 1.30-8pm Wed) **FREE** and also

stores items from the University of Glasgow's museum collection (available by appointment). The major exhibition halls are being developed and may end up holding the Hunterian collections as well as other city-related exhibits.

🏃 Activities

Clyde Walkway WALKING, CYCLING

The Clyde Walkway extends from Glasgow upriver to the Falls of Clyde near New Lanark, some 40 miles away. The Glasgow tourist office has a good leaflet pack detailing different sections of this walk. The 10-mile section through Glasgow has interesting parts, though modern buildings have replaced most of the old shipyards. The loveliest sections are upstream.

Glasgow Central Tours WALKING

(Map p794; www.glasgowcentraltours.co.uk; tour £13; ⊘ check website for tour times) A passionate, entertaining guide takes you around, behind and under Glasgow Central station (p810). Hidden spaces, an abandoned Victorian platform and lots of intriguing information make this a fascinating experience even if railways don't get you excited. It lasts about an hour; check the website for dates. The minimum age is 12 years.

Hidden Heritage Tours CYCLING

(☑ 07857 974178; www.hiddenheritagetours.co.uk; ⊘ Mar–Oct) These tours, recommencing in 2019, explore Glasgow's industrial and mercantile heritage. They offer a two-hour walking tour of Merchant City (£10), two-hour riverside bike tours (£15/20 with own/hire bike), a half-day bike tour of major attractions (£20/30 with own/hire bike), or a full-day exploration of the Clyde's shipbuilding past (£35/45 with own/hire bike).

🎊 Festivals & Events

Celtic Connections MUSIC

(☑ 0141-353 8000; www.celticconnections.com; ⊘ Jan) This two-week music festival focuses on roots music and folk from Scotland and around the world.

Glasgow Film Festival FILM

(www.glasgowfilm.org; ⊘ Feb) Two-week film festival with screenings in various locations across the city.

Glasgow International Comedy Festival COMEDY

(☑ 0844 873 7353; www.glasgowcomedyfestival.com; ⊘ Mar) Two weeks of quality comedy,

both home-grown and imported, enlivens stages across the city in March.

Southside Fringe PERFORMING ARTS

(www.southsidefringe.org.uk; ⊘ May) This increasingly popular festival focuses on the suburbs south of the Clyde with two weeks of performances in various venues.

West End Festival PERFORMING ARTS

(☑ 0141-341 0844; www.westendfestival.co.uk; ⊘ Jun) This music and arts event is Glasgow's biggest festival. Runs for three weeks.

Glasgow Jazz Festival MUSIC

(www.jazzfest.co.uk; ⊘ Jun) Excellent festival sees big-name international acts come to town, with stages set up in George Sq and Merchant City.

TRNSMT MUSIC

(www.trnsmtfest.com; ⊘ Jun–Jul) Held over two consecutive weekends in late June and early July, this festival only started in 2017 but has been a huge success, drawing major indie rock acts to Glasgow Green.

🛏 Sleeping

🛏 City Centre

Glasgow Metro Youth Hostel HOSTEL £

(Map p794; ☑ 0141-354 0109; www.hostellingscotland.org.uk; 89 Buccleuch St; s £32-45; ⊘ late Jun–Aug; 🛜) Student accommodation belonging to the nearby Glasgow School of Art provides the venue for this summer hostel. All rooms are comfortable singles, many with an en suite, there are kitchen facilities, and it's a very good deal for solo travellers or groups. Rates vary by day and month.

★ **Grasshoppers** HOTEL ££

(Map p794; ☑ 0141-222 2666; www.grasshoppersglasgow.com; 87 Union St; r £90-138; ❄🛜🐾) Discreetly hidden atop a time-worn railway administration building alongside Central station, this small, well-priced hotel is a modern, upbeat surprise. Rooms are compact (a few are larger) but well appointed, with unusual views over the station roof's glass sea. Numerous touches – friendly staff, interesting art, in-room cafetière, free cupcakes and ice cream, and weeknight suppers – make this one of the centre's homiest choices.

★ **Z Hotel** HOTEL ££

(Map p794; ☑ 0141-212 4550; www.thezhotels.com; 36 North Frederick St; r £90-165; ❄🛜) Just off George Sq, the facade of a historic build-

SOUTHSIDE & THE CLYDE

Once a thriving shipbuilding area, the Clyde sank into dereliction during the postwar era but has been subject to extensive rejuvenation. It's an intriguingly multicultural part of Glasgow, and several excellent attractions are also dotted across the area.

Glasgow Science Centre (Map p798; ☑ 0141-420 5000; www.glasgowsciencecentre.org; 50 Pacific Quay; adult/child £11.50/9.50, IMAX, Glasgow Tower or Planetarium extra £2.50-3.50; ⊙10am-5pm daily Apr-Oct, to 3pm Wed-Fri, to 5pm Sat & Sun Nov-Mar; ⊕) Brings science and technology alive through hundreds of interactive exhibits, an IMAX theatre, a rotating 127m-high observation tower, a planetarium and live science demos. To get here, take bus 89 or 90 from Union St.

Riverside Museum (☑ 0141-287 2720; www.glasgowmuseums.com; 100 Pointhouse Pl; ⊙10am-5pm Mon-Thu & Sat, from 11am Fri & Sun; ⊕) FREE Designed by the late British-Iraqi architect Zaha Hadid, this transport museum features a fascinating series of cars made in Scotland, plus assorted railway locos, trams, bikes and model Clyde-built ships.

Burrell Collection (☑ 0141-287 2550; www.glasgowlife.org.uk; Pollok Country Park; ⊙closed) FREE This outstanding museum 3 miles out of town houses everything from Chinese porcelain and medieval furniture to paintings by Cézanne. It's closed for refurbishment, and is due to reopen in 2020.

ing conceals a stylish contemporary hotel. Chambers are modern but compact – the idea is that you sleep here and socialise in the bar area, especially during the afternoon wine-and-cheese session. Big flatscreens and pleasing showers add comfort to rooms that are often overpriced but can be great value if advance booked.

Citizen M HOTEL ££
(Map p794; ☑ 020-3519 1111; www.citizenm.com; 60 Renfrew St; r £90-180; @ হ) This modern chain does away with some normal hotel accoutrements in favour of self-check-in terminals and minimalist, plasticky modern rooms with just two features: a big, comfortable king-sized bed and a decent shower with mood lighting. The idea is that guests make liberal use of the public areas, and why wouldn't you, with upbeat, supercomfortable designer furniture, a 24-hour cafe and iMacs?

Pipers' Tryst Hotel HOTEL ££
(Map p794; ☑ 0141-353 5551; www.thepipingcentre.co.uk; 30-34 McPhater St; s/d £90/120, without breakfast £78/96; হ) The name is no tartan tourist trap; rather this intimate, cosy hotel in a noble building is actually run by the adjacent bagpiping centre, and profits go towards maintaining it. Cheery staff, great value and a prime city-centre location make this a wise choice. You won't have far to migrate after a night of Celtic music and malts in the snug bar-restaurant.

★ **Dakota Deluxe** HOTEL £££
(Map p794; ☑ 0141-404 3680; www.dakotahotels.co.uk; 179 West Regent St; r £150-200; ❉ হ ❉) Suave and seductive in dark wood and grey tones, Dakota carries a strong design concept from low-lit basement restaurant to light-filled suites. Rooms are very spacious and feature appealing sitting areas as well as inviting beds. Service is excellent, and the bar area – see how many Jacks you can name – a delight.

Indigo HOTEL £££
(Map p794; ☑ 0141-226 7700; www.hinglasgow.co.uk; 75 Waterloo St; r £130-200; ❉ @ হ) Once the power station for early trams, this boutique-chain conversion of an elegant building has resulted in a satisfying, surprisingly quiet option in the city centre. Rooms have mural-style artwork, great beds and a free minibar (the contents improve as you go up the room grades). Space is good, and bathrooms have rain shower heads. Prices vary; there are usually good online deals.

Blythswood Square HOTEL £££
(Map p794; ☑ 0141-248 8888; www.blythswoodsquare.com; 11 Blythswood Sq; r £195-300; P @ হ ❉ ❉) In a gorgeous Georgian terrace, this elegant five-star offers inner-city luxury, with grey and cerise providing casual soft-toned style throughout. Rooms (recently refurbished) go from standard to penthouse with corresponding increases in comfort; it's hard to resist the traditional 'classic' rooms

with windows onto the delightful square, but at weekends you'll have a quieter sleep in the new wing at the back.

🛏 West End

The pleasant terraces of the West End are home to lots of worthwhile places to stay, from a hostel and excellent B&Bs to one of Scotland's plushest urban hotels.

Glasgow SYHA   HOSTEL £

(Map p798; ✆ 0141-332 3004; www.hostelling scotland.org.uk; 8 Park Tce; dm/s/tw £29/52/69; @ 🛜) Perched on a hill overlooking Kelvingrove Park in a charming townhouse, this place is one of Scotland's best official hostels. Dorms are mostly four to six beds with padlock lockers, and all have their own en suite. The common rooms are spacious, plush and good for lounging about. There's no curfew, it has a good kitchen, and meals are available.

Heritage Hotel   HOTEL ££

(Map p798; ✆ 0141-339 6955; www.theheritage hotel.net; 4 Alfred Tce, Great Western Rd; s/d £45/75; P 🛜) A stone's throw from all the action of the West End, this friendly hotel has an open, airy feel despite the rather dilapidated raised terrace it's located on. Generally, rooms on the 1st and 2nd floors are a bit more spacious and have a better outlook. The location, parking option and very fair prices mark it out.

★ Amadeus Guest House   B&B ££

(Map p798; ✆ 0141-339 8257; www.amadeus guesthouse.co.uk; 411 North Woodside Rd; s £60-70, s without bathroom £42-45, d £80-100; 🛜) Just off the bustle of Great Western Rd, a minute's walk from the subway but on a quiet street by the riverside pathway, this B&B has compact bright rooms, all distinct, with a cheerful, breezy feel. There's a variety of types, including several singles. It offers excellent value and a genuine welcome. A good continental breakfast is included.

★ Alamo Guest House   B&B ££

(Map p798; ✆ 0141-339 2395; www.alamoguest house.com; 46 Gray St; d £99-111, superior d £159-220, d without bathroom £69-79; @ 🛜) The Alamo may not sound like a peaceful spot, but that's exactly what this great place is. Opposite Kelvingrove Park, it feels miles from the city's hustle, but several of Glasgow's best museums and restaurants are right at hand. The decor blends antique furnishings and modern design, with excellent bathrooms, and the owners will make you very welcome.

Flower House   B&B ££

(Map p798; ✆ 0141-204 2846; www.theflower house.net; 33 St Vincent Cres; s £50-70, d £70-120; 🛜) Cosy, old-style B&B is offered in this pretty Victorian terraced house fronted by a riot of creepers and flowers – you can't miss it. Just off the Finnieston strip, its comfortably dignified interior features antiques, curios, striped wallpaper and noble furniture. Bathrooms are exterior but private: they are extraordinary, particularly the 'penny wall'. Hospitality is good humoured and exceptional, with homemade treats for breakfast.

★ 15Glasgow   B&B £££

(Map p798; ✆ 0141-332 1263; www.15glasgow.com; 15 Woodside Pl; d/ste £130/160; P 🛜) Glasgow's 19th-century merchants certainly knew how to build a beautiful house, and this 1840s terrace is a sumptuous example. Huge rooms with lofty ceilings have exquisite period detail complemented by attractive modern greys, striking bathrooms and well-chosen quality furniture. Your welcoming host makes everything easy for you: the in-room breakfast, overlooking the park, is a real treat. They prefer no under-five-year-olds.

Hotel du Vin   HOTEL £££

(✆ 0141-378 0385; www.hotelduvin.com; 1 Devonshire Gardens; r £184-304; P @ 🛜 🐾) This is traditionally Glasgow's favoured hotel of the rich and famous, and the patriarch of sophistication and comfort. A study in elegance, it's sumptuously decorated and occupies three classical sandstone terrace houses. There's a bewildering array of room types, all different in style and size. The hospitality is old-school courteous, and there's an excellent restaurant on-site with a vast wine selection.

🍴 Eating

Glasgow is the best place to eat in Scotland, with a stupendous range of restaurants and cafes. The West End is a culinary centre, with Merchant City also boasting a high concentration of quality establishments. Pubs and bars (p806) are often good mealtime options too.

The excellent *Eating & Drinking Guide,* published by *The List* every second April, covers both Glasgow and Edinburgh.

✖ City Centre

★ Riverhill Coffee Bar
CAFE £

(Map p794; ☑ 0141-204 4762; www.riverhillcafe. com; 24 Gordon St; rolls £4-5; ⊙ 7am-5pm Mon-Fri, from 8am Sat, from 10am Sun; ☎) ✐ Chain cafes plaster Glasgow's centre, so it's a joy to come across this tiny place, which offers great coffee and hot chocolate as well as delicious filled rolls and tempting pastries. Ingredients are sustainably sourced and seriously tasty. It's extremely friendly; you'd come every day if you lived nearby.

★ Saramago Café Bar
CAFE, VEGAN £

(Map p794; ☑ 0141-352 4920; www.cca-glasgow. com; 350 Sauchiehall St; mains £8-12; ⊙ food noon-10pm Sun-Wed, to 11.30pm Thu-Sat; ☎✐) In the airy atrium of the Centre for Contemporary Arts, this place does a great line in eclectic vegan fusion food, with a range of top flavour combinations from around the globe. The upstairs bar (open from 4pm) has a great deck on steep Scott St and packs out inside with a friendly arty crowd enjoying the DJ sets and quality tap beers.

Platform
STREET FOOD £

(Map p794; www.facebook.com/platformgla; 253 Argyle St; light meals £4-7; ⊙ noon-10pm Fri & Sat, to 6pm Sun) This atmospheric series of brick-arched vaults under the railway lines at Central station comes into its own at weekends, when street-food vendors open up stalls and a bar doles out pints to those seeking an escape from the weather. It's family and dog friendly. During the week the cafe is still open.

Wee Curry Shop
INDIAN £

(Map p794; ☑ 0141-353 0777; www.weecurryshop. co.uk; 7 Buccleuch St; 2-course lunch £5.95, mains £8-10; ⊙ noon-2pm & 5-10.30pm; ☎✐) This tiny place has great home-cooked curries. It's wise to book – it's a snug place with a big reputation, a limited menu and a sensational-value two-course lunch.

★ Singl-end
CAFE ££

(Map p794; ☑ 0141-353 1277; www.thesingl-end. co.uk; 265 Renfrew St; dishes £7-13; ⊙ 9am-5pm; ☎✐) There's something glorious about this long basement cafe with its cheery service and air of brunchy bonhomie. It covers a lot of bases, with good coffee, generous breakfasts and lunches, booze and baking. Dietary requirements are superbly catered for, with fine vegan choices and clear labelling. On a diet? Avert your eyes from the 'eat-me' cornucopia of meringues and pastries by the door.

Topolabamba
MEXICAN ££

(Map p794; ☑ 0141-248 9359; www.topolabamba. com; 89 St Vincent St; portions £5-11; ⊙ food noon-10pm Sun-Thu, to 10.30pm Fri & Sat; ☎✐) Lots of fun and attractively kitted-out in cool Mexican decor – all skulls, figurines and tequila crates – this place brings a real slice of authentic cuisine to Glasgow, with zingy tacos, tasty tostadas and not a plate of nachos in sight. The stuffed calamari are especially good, but it's all refreshingly flavoursome. Portions are tapa-sized, so order a few and share.

Loon Fung
CANTONESE ££

(Map p794; ☑ 0141-332 1240; www.loonfungglas-gow.com; 417 Sauchiehall St; mains £11-15; ⊙ noon-11pm; ☎✐) This elegant Cantonese oasis is one of Scotland's most authentic Chinese restaurants; indeed, it's quite a surprise after a traditional dining experience here to emerge to boisterous Sauchiehall St rather than Hong Kong. The dim-sum choices are toothsome, and the seafood – try the sea bass – really excellent.

Meat Bar
AMERICAN ££

(Map p794; ☑ 0141-204 3605; www.themeatbar. co.uk; 142 West Regent St; mains £9-20; ⊙ food noon-10pm; ☎) Like a mafia-film speakeasy where some minor henchman gets whacked, Meat Bar has underworld ambience carried off with style. As the name suggests, it's all about meat here: it even makes its way into some of the cocktails. Daily cuts of prime Scottish beef (£25 to £40) accompany a range of American-style slow-smoked meats. Tasty and atmospheric, with interesting beers.

★ Gamba
SEAFOOD £££

(Map p794; ☑ 0141-572 0899; www.gamba.co.uk; 225a West George St; mains £21-30; ⊙ noon-2.15pm & 5-9.30pm Mon-Sat, 5-9pm Sun; ☎) This business-district basement is easily missed but is actually one of the city's premier seafood restaurants. Presentation is elegant, with carefully selected flavours allowing the fish, sustainably sourced from Scotland and beyond, to shine. Service is smart and solicitous. There's a good weekday lunch deal, costing £20/22 for two/three courses.

✖ East End

McCune Smith
CAFE £

(Map p794; ☑ 0141-548 1114; www.mccunesmith. co.uk; 3 Duke St; light meals £4-8; ⊙ 8am-4pm; ☎) This stellar cafe is named after a University of Glasgow graduate who was a noted abolitionist and the first African American to hold a medical degree. The hospitable owners take their coffee seriously and offer scrumptious breakfast and brunch fare, plus delicious sandwiches and soups in a luminous, high-ceilinged interior. They bake their own bread and half the menu or more is vegan.

A'Challtainn
SEAFOOD ££

(Map p794; ☎ 0141-237 9220; www.baadglasgow.com/achalltainn; Moncur St; mains £12-19; ⊗ food noon-9pm Tue-Sat, 11am-7pm Sun) Part of the Barras markets' revitalisation, A'Challtainn is upstairs in the Art & Design Centre and is an enticing destination for quality seafood, with standout oysters and squat lobster, and superfresh fish specials. Balcony seating is great for lunch or when the market's on. There's a cocktail bar below, too, and a bakery-cafe was shortly to open at the time of research.

✗ West End

78 Cafe Bar
CAFE, VEGETARIAN £

(Map p798; ☎ 0141-576 5018; www.the78cafebar.com; 10 Kelvinhaugh St; mains £5-9; ⊗ food noon-9pm; ☎🅿) More a comfortable lounge than your typical veggie restaurant, this cafe offers cosy couch seating and reassuringly solid wooden tables, as well as an inviting range of ales. The low-priced vegan food includes hearty stews and curries, and there's regular live music in a very welcoming atmosphere.

★ Ox & Finch
FUSION ££

(Map p798; ☎ 0141-339 8627; www.oxandfinch.com; 920 Sauchiehall St; small plates £4-10; ⊗noon-10pm; ☎🅿) This fashionable place could almost sum up the thriving modern Glasgow eating scene, with a faux-pub name, sleek but comfortable contemporary decor, tapas-sized dishes and an open kitchen. Grab a cosy booth and be prepared to have your tastebuds wowed with innovative, delicious creations aimed at sharing, drawing on French and Mediterreanean influences but focusing on quality Scottish produce.

★ Mother India
INDIAN ££

(Map p798; ☎ 0141-221 1663; www.motherindia.co.uk; 28 Westminster Tce, Sauchiehall St; mains £11-16; ⊗5.30-10.30pm Mon-Thu, noon-11pm Fri, 1-11pm Sat, 1-10pm Sun; ☎🅿🅗) Glasgow curry buffs forever debate the merits of the city's numerous excellent South Asian restaurants; Mother India features in every discussion. It's been a stalwart for years, and the quality and innovation on show are superb. The three

dining areas are all attractive and it makes an effort for kids, with a separate menu.

★ Stravaigin
SCOTTISH, FUSION ££

(Map p798; ☎ 0141-334 2665; www.stravaigin.co.uk; 28 Gibson St; bar dishes £6-12, restaurant mains £15-19; ⊗food 11am-11pm; ☎) Stravaigin is a serious foodie's delight, with a menu constantly pushing the boundaries of originality and offering creative culinary excellence. With a range of eating spaces across three levels, it's pleasingly casual and easygoing. The entry level also has a buzzing bar with a separate menu. Scottish classics like haggis take their place alongside a range of Asian-influenced dishes. It's all delicious.

Alchemilla
MEDITERRANEAN ££

(Map p798; ☎ 0141-337 6060; www.thisisalchemilla.com; 1126 Argyle St; plates £5-14; ⊗food noon-10pm) The number of quality eating options opening on the Finnieston strip is phenomenal, and this is a fine example. The casual open-kitchen eatery offers small, medium and large plates with an eastern Mediterranean feel. Interesting ingredients and intriguing textures are key to delicious dishes ideal for sharing. There are lots of meat-free options and a list of hard-to-find natural wines.

The Finnieston
SEAFOOD ££

(Map p798; ☎ 0141-222 2884; www.thefinniestonbar.com; 1125 Argyle St; mains £13-23; ⊗food 11am-10pm Mon-Sat, to 9pm Sun; ☎) 🅿 A flagship of this increasingly vibrant strip, this gastropub recalls the area's sailing heritage with a cosily romantic below-decks atmosphere and artfully placed nautical motifs. It's been well thought through, with excellent G&Ts (slurp one in the little courtyard) and cocktails accompanying a short menu of high-quality upmarket pub fare focusing on sustainable Scottish seafood. Its brunches are also recommendable.

Left Bank
BISTRO ££

(Map p798; ☎ 0141-339 5969; www.theleftbank.co.uk; 33 Gibson St; mains £9-16; ⊗9am-10pm Mon-Fri, from 10am Sat & Sun; ☎🅿🅗) 🅿 Huge windows fronting the street reveal this outstanding eatery specialising in gastronomic delights and lazy afternoons. Lots of little spaces filled with couches and chunky tables make for intimacy. The wide-ranging menu is good for devising a shared meal of delightful creations using seasonal and local produce, with an eclectic variety of influences. Breakfasts and brunches are also highlights.

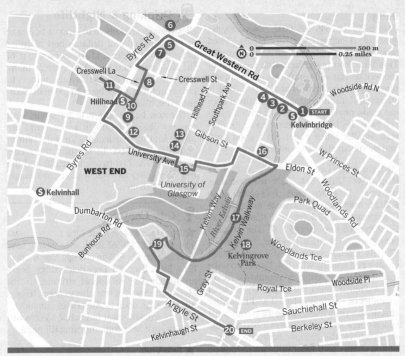

Walking Tour
West End

START KELVINBRIDGE SUBWAY STATION
END ARGYLE ST, FINNIESTON
LENGTH 3 MILES; 2 HOURS

Emerge from the subway and turn left across ❶ **Great Western Bridge (Kelvinbridge)**, emblazoned with the lion rampant of the Hillhead burgh on the south side and the city coat of arms on the north. It crosses the leafy course of the Kelvin, a tributary of the Clyde. Note the riverside bar ❷ **Inn Deep** (p807) to come back to. The coat of arms alongside the entrance is that of the Caledonian Railway Company; there was formerly a station here.

Continue along Great Western Rd, stopping for a browse in ❸ **Glasgow Vintage Company** (p810) and ❹ **Caledonia Books** (p810). At the corner of Byres Rd, a former church is now ❺ **Oràn Mór** (p807). Across the road stretch the ❻ **Botanic Gardens** (p799).

Turn left down Byres Rd; investigate interesting shops on the left in this first section, like ❼ **Demijohn** (p810). At Cresswell St, turn left and then right down Cresswell Lane to check out tiny ❽ **De Courcy's Arcade**.

Continuing down this lane brings you to the bar-heavy ❾ **Ashton Lane**, where ❿ **Ubiquitous Chip** (p806) is still one of Scotland's best places to eat. Turn right opposite Jinty McGuinty's to reach Byres Rd. Cross and examine the quirky shops down ⓫ **Ruthven Lane**, accessed directly opposite.

Back on Byres Rd, head south, then turn left up University Ave. The ugly 1960s ⓬ **Boyd Orr tower** is soon replaced by more typical sandstone terraces as you climb the hill. On the left is the ⓭ **Hunterian Art Gallery** (p799) and ⓮ **Mackintosh House** (p799); on the right, wander through the quadrangles of the University of Glasgow's main building, home to the ⓯ **Hunterian Museum** (p797).

At the bottom of University Ave, turn left, then right onto Gibson St, home to quality lunch stops like ⓰ **Stravaigin**. Cross the bridge and turn right into the park, bearing right down to the river and the ⓱ **Kelvin Walkway**. Follow this for half a mile through lovely ⓲ **Kelvingrove Park** to reach the ⓳ **Kelvingrove Art Gallery & Museum** (p797). From here it's a short hop to the Finnieston eating strip on ⓴ **Argyle St**.

Bothy
SCOTTISH ££

(Map p798; ☎0845 166 6032; www.bothyglas gow.co.uk; 11 Ruthven Lane; mains £12-20; ⊙food noon-10pm Mon-Fri, from 10am Sat & Sun; 🛜) This West End player, boasting a combo of modern design and comfy retro furnishings, blows apart the myth that Scottish food is stodgy and uninteresting. The Bothy dishes out traditional home-style fare with a modern twist. It's filling, but leave room for dessert. Smaller lunch plates are a good deal, and there's an attractive outdoor area.

★Ubiquitous Chip
SCOTTISH £££

(Map p798; ☎0141-334 5007; www.ubiquitous chip.co.uk; 12 Ashton Lane; 2-/3-course lunch £20/24, mains £20-30, brasserie mains £13-16; ⊙restaurant noon-2.30pm & 5-11pm Mon-Sat, 12.30-3pm & 5-10pm Sun; 🛜) 🍴 The original champion of Scottish produce, Ubiquitous Chip is legendary for its still-unparalleled cuisine and lengthy wine list. Named to poke fun at Scotland's culinary reputation, it offers a French touch but resolutely Scottish ingredients, carefully selected and following sustainable principles. The elegant courtyard space offers some of Glasgow's best dining, while, above, the cheaper brasserie (longer hours) offers exceptional value for money.

Cail Bruich
SCOTTISH £££

(Map p798; ☎0141-334 6265; www.cailbruich.co.uk; 725 Great Western Rd; 2-/3-course lunch £22/28, set menus £45-55; ⊙6-9pm Mon & Tue, noon-2pm & 6-9pm Wed-Sat, 1-7pm Sun; 🛜) In an elegant if rather nondescript dining room, the kitchen here turns out some memorable modern Scottish fare. The forage ethos brings surprising, tangy, herbal flavours to plates that are always interesting but never pretentious. Everything from the amuse-bouche to the homemade bread is top-notch; the degustation menu (£55) with optional wine flight (£40) combines the best on offer.

Gannet
SCOTTISH £££

(Map p798; ☎0141-204 2081; www.thegannetgla. com; 1155 Argyle St; mains £21-25; ⊙5-9.30pm Tue & Wed, noon-2pm & 5-9.30pm Thu-Sat, 1-7.30pm Sun; 🛜) 🍴 In vogue but not starchy, this jewel of the Finnieston strip offers a cosy wood-panelled ambience and gourmet food that excels on presentation and taste without venturing towards cutting-edge. The short, polished daily menu features quality produce sourced mostly from southern Scotland and the interesting wine list backs it up very well indeed. Solicitous, professional service is another plus point.

🍷 Drinking & Nightlife

Glaswegians are known to enjoy a beverage or two, and some of Britain's best nightlife is found in the din and sometimes roar of the city's pubs and bars. There are as many different styles of bar as there are punters to guzzle in them. Craft beer, single malt, Scottish gins: it's all here.

Glasgow has a vibrant LGBT scene, with the gay quarter found in and around the Merchant City (particularly Virginia, Wilson and Glassford Sts). To tap into the scene, check out *The List* (www.list.co.uk) and the free *Scots Gay* (www.scotsgay.co.uk) magazine and website.

🍷 City Centre

★DogHouse Merchant City
BAR

(Map p794; ☎0141-552 6363; www.brewdog.com; 99 Hutcheson St; ⊙11am-midnight Mon-Fri, from 10am Sat & Sun; 🛜) Brewdog's zingy beers are matched by its upbeat attitude, so this Merchant City spot was always going to be a fun place. An open kitchen doles out slidery, burgery smoked-meat fare while 25 taps run quality craft beer from morning till night.

★Sub Club
CLUB

(Map p794; ☎0141-248 4600; www.subclub.co.uk; 22 Jamaica St; ⊙typically 11pm-3am Tue, Fri & Sat) Scotland's most famous house club is still going strong several decades on. Saturday at the Sub Club is one of Glasgow's legendary nights, offering serious clubbing with a sound system that aficionados usually rate as the city's best. The claustrophobic, last-one-in vibe is not for those faint of heart. Check the website for other nights.

Shilling Brewing Co
MICROBREWERY

(Map p794; ☎0141-353 1654; www.shillingbrewing-company.co.uk; 92 West George St; ⊙noon-11pm Mon, to midnight Tue-Thu, to 1am Fri & Sat, 12.30-11pm Sun; 🛜) Drinking in former banks is a Glasgow thing and this central brewpub offers some of the best of it. The wooden, high-ceilinged space has huge windows out to the city centre and room to spare to try its beers; the almost grapefruity Unicorn IPA is a real palate cleanser. Another couple of dozen taps showcase guest craft brews from around Scotland.

Pot Still
PUB

(Map p794; ☎0141-333 0980; www.thepotstill. co.uk; 154 Hope St; ⊙11am-midnight; 🛜) The cheeriest and cosiest of places, the Pot Still has a time-warp feel with its creaky floor and old-style wrought-iron-legged tables. There's a superb whisky selection and knowledgeable staff – constantly up and down ladders to get at bottles – to back it up. Tasty pies (£4) are on hand for solid sustenance.

Laboratorio Espresso CAFE
(Map p794; ☑ 0141-353 1111; www.labespr.tumblr.com; 93 West Nile St; ◷ 7.30am-5.30pm Mon-Fri, from 9am Sat, from 11am Sun) A chic space, all concrete and glass, this cafe offers the best coffee we've tried in Glasgow. It's sourced properly, and served in delicious double-shot creations with authentically concentrated espresso; soy milk is available. There are a couple of tables outside even in the coldest weather. Pastries and biscotti are on hand, but it's all about the brew here.

ABC CLUB
(O₂ABC; Map p794; ☑ 0141-332 2232; www.o2abc glasgow.co.uk; 300 Sauchiehall St; ◷ 11pm-3am Thu-Sat; ☎) Both nightclub and venue, this reference point on Sauchiehall has two large concert spaces with big-name gigs, plus several attractive bars. It's a good all-rounder, with three well-established club nights: Jellybaby on Thursday, Propaganda on Friday and Love Music on Saturday. Admission is around £5.

Waterloo Bar PUB, GAY
(Map p794; ☑ 0141-248 7216; www.facebook.com/waterloobar1; 306 Argyle St; ◷ noon-11pm Mon-Thu, to midnight Fri & Sat, 12.30-11pm Sun) This traditional pub is Scotland's oldest gay bar. It attracts punters of all ages. It's very friendly and, with a large group of regulars, a good place to meet people away from the scene.

Babbity Bowster PUB
(Map p794; ☑ 0141-552 5055; www.babbitybow ster.com; 16-18 Blackfriars St; ◷ 11am-midnight Mon-Sat, from 12.30pm Sun; ☎) In a quiet corner of Merchant City, this handsome spot is perfect for a tranquil daytime drink, particularly in the adjoining beer garden. Service is attentive, and the smell of sausages may tempt you to lunch; it also offers accommodation. This is one of the city centre's most charming pubs, in one of its noblest buildings. There's a regular folk-music scene here.

Horse Shoe PUB
(Map p794; ☑ 0141-248 6368; www.thehorse shoebarglasgow.co.uk; 17 Drury St; ◷ 10am-midnight Sun-Fri, from 9am Sat) This legendary city pub and popular meeting place dates from the late 19th century and is largely

unchanged. It's a picturesque spot, with the longest continuous bar in the UK, but its main attraction is what's served over it – real ale and good cheer. Upstairs in the lounge is some of the best-value pub food (dishes £4 to £10) in town.

⚲ West End

★ Inn Deep BAR
(Map p798; ☑ 0141-357 1075; www.inndeep.com; 445 Great Western Rd; ◷ noon-midnight Mon-Sat, 12.30-11pm Sun) Descend the stairs to find yourself in a fabulous spot on the banks of the Kelvin. It's glorious on a fine day (and Glaswegians set that bar pretty low) to grab a craft beer and spill out onto the riverside path in a happy throng. The vaulted interior spaces under the bridge are also characterful.

Kelvingrove Café BAR, CAFE
(Map p798; ☑ 0141-221 8988; www.kelvingrove cafe.com; 1161 Argyle St; ◷ 8am-midnight Mon-Sat, from 9am Sun; ☎) A beautiful wood floor, elegant fittings and chessboard tiling give this place a stylish cosiness that perfectly matches its list of cocktails and G&Ts. It manages to straddle a few genres: the feeling of a timeworn local is offset by solicitous table service, while the food is a little more upmarket than it seems.

Brewdog Glasgow PUB
(Map p798; ☑ 0141-334 7175; www.brewdog.com; 1397 Argyle St; ◷ noon-midnight; ☎) Perfect for a pint after the Kelvingrove Art Gallery & Museum, this great spot offers the delicious range of artisanal beers from the brewery of the same name. Punk IPA is refreshingly hoppy, with other favourites, new releases and guest beers also to explore. Tasting flights mean you can try several, while burgers and dogs are on hand to soak it up.

Hillhead Bookclub BAR
(Map p798; ☑ 0141-576 1700; www.hillheadbook club.co.uk; 17 Vinicombe St; ◷ 11am-midnight Mon-Fri, from 10am Sat & Sun; ☎) Atmosphere in spades is the call sign of this easygoing West End bar. An ornate wooden ceiling overlooks two levels of well-mixed cocktails, seriously cheap drinks, comfort food and numerous intriguing decorative touches. There's even a ping-pong table in a cage.

Òran Mór BAR, CLUB
(Map p798; ☑ 0141-357 6200; www.oran-mor. co.uk; cnr Byres & Great Western Rds; ◷ 9am-2am Mon-Wed, to 3am Thu-Sat, 10am-3am Sun; ☎)

Now some may be uncomfortable with the thought of drinking in a church. But we say: the Lord giveth. This bar, restaurant, club and theatre venue is a likeable and versatile spot with an attractive interior and a fine whisky selection to replace the holy water. The lunchtime **A Play, a Pie and a Pint** (Map p798; www.playpiepint.com; Òran Mór, £10-14 incl pie & pint; ⊙1pm Mon-Sat) is an excellent feature.

☆ Entertainment

Glasgow is Scotland's entertainment city, from classical music, fine theatres and ballet to an amazing range of live music venues. To tap into the scene, check out *The List* (www.list.co.uk), an invaluable free events guide.

For theatre tickets, book directly with the venue. For concerts, a useful booking centre is **Tickets Scotland** (Map p794; ☎0141-204 5151; www.tickets-scotland.com; 237 Argyle St; ⊙9am-6pm Mon-Wed, Fri & Sat, to 7pm Thu, 11.30am-5.30pm Sun).

Live Music

★ **King Tut's Wah Wah Hut**   LIVE MUSIC
(Map p794; ☎0141-221 5279; www.kingtuts.co.uk; 272a St Vincent St; ⊙noon-midnight) One of the city's premier live-music pub venues, hosting bands every night of the week. A staple of the local scene, and a real Glasgow highlight.

Hydro   LIVE PERFORMANCE
(Map p798; ☎0844 395 4000; www.thessehydro.com; Finnieston Quay; 🛜) A spectacular modern building to keep the adjacent 'Armadillo' (Map p798; ☎0844 395 4000; www.sec.co.uk; Finnieston Quay) company, the Hydro amphitheatre is a phenomenally popular venue for big-name concerts and shows.

Hug & Pint   LIVE MUSIC
(Map p798; ☎0141-331 1901; www.thehugandpint.com; 171 Great Western Rd; ⊙noon-midnight; 🛜) With bands almost daily in the downstairs space, this comfortable local is a great destination. It would be anyway for its excellent atmosphere, highly original Asian-influenced vegan food and colourful interior.

Barrowland Ballroom   CONCERT VENUE
(The Barrowlands; Map p794; www.glasgow-barrowland.com; 244 Gallowgate) A down-at-heel but exceptional old dancehall above the Barras market catering for some of the larger acts that visit the city. It's one of Scotland's most atmospheric venues with its sprung floor and authentic character.

13th Note Café   LIVE MUSIC
(Map p794; ☎0141-553 1638; www.13thnote.co.uk; 50-60 King St; ⊙noon-11pm or midnight; 🛜) Cosy basement venue with small independent bands as well as weekend DJs and regular comedy and theatre performances. At street level the pleasant cafe does decent vegetarian and vegan food (£7 to £10, until 9pm).

St Luke's & the Winged Ox   LIVE MUSIC
(Map p794; ☎0141-552 8378; www.stlukesglasgow.com; 17 Bain St; ⊙noon-midnight; 🛜) By the Barras market area, this repurposed church – stained glass and organ still in situ – is a fantastic spot hosting live music every weekend, exhibitions, markets and more. The cosier attached space also does very well just as a pub and serves food all day until 9pm.

Cinema

★ **Glasgow Film Theatre**   CINEMA
(Map p794; ☎0141-332 6535; www.glasgowfilm.org; 12 Rose St; adult/child £10.50/5.50) This much-loved three-screener off Sauchiehall St shows art-house cinema and classics.

Grosvenor Cinema   CINEMA
(Map p798; ☎0845 166 6002; www.grosvenorwestend.co.uk; Ashton Lane) This sweet cinema puts you in the heart of West End eating and nightlife for post-show debriefings.

Theatres & Concert Halls

Glasgow Royal Concert Hall   CONCERT VENUE
(Map p794; ☎0141-353 8000; www.glasgowconcerthalls.com; 2 Sauchiehall St; 🛜) A feast of classical music is showcased at this concert hall, the modern home of the Royal Scottish National Orchestra. There are also regular pop, folk and jazz performances, typically by big-name solo artists.

Theatre Royal   CONCERT VENUE
(Map p794; ☎0844 871 7647; www.glasgowtheatreroyal.org.uk; 282 Hope St) Proudly sporting an eye-catching modern facelift, Glasgow's oldest theatre is the home of Scottish Opera.

Citizens' Theatre   THEATRE
(☎0141-429 0022; www.citz.co.uk; 119 Gorbals St) South of the Clyde, this is one of the top theatres in Scotland. It's well worth trying to catch a performance here. A major redevelopment was about to begin at last visit and the theatre will be closed until 2020.

Tramway   PERFORMING ARTS
(☎0845 330 3501; www.tramway.org; 25 Albert Dr; ⊙9.30am-8pm Mon-Sat, 10am-6pm Sun; 🛜) Occupying a former tram depot, this buzzy

cultural centre has performance and exhibition spaces as well as a popular cafe. It's a real Southside community hub, with an unusual **garden** (☑0141-433 2722; www.the hiddengardens.org.uk; 25a Albert Dr; ⊙10am-8pm Tue-Sat, noon-6pm Sun Apr-Sep, 10am-4pm Tue-Sat, noon-4pm Sun Oct-Mar) **FREE** out the back. It attracts cutting-edge theatrical groups, is the home of Scottish Ballet and hosts a varied range of artistic exhibitions. It's very close to Pollokshields East train station.

Sport

Two football clubs – **Rangers** (☑0871 702 1972; www.rangers.co.uk; Ibrox Stadium, 150 Edmiston Dr) and **Celtic** (☑0871 226 1888; www.celtic fc.net; Celtic Park, Parkhead) – totally dominate the sporting scene in Scotland, having vastly more resources than other clubs and a long history (and rivalry). This runs along traditionally partisan lines, with Rangers representing Protestant supporters, and Celtic, Catholic. It's worth going to a game; both play in magnificent arenas with great atmosphere. Games between the two (normally four a year) are fiercely contested, but tickets aren't sold to the general public; you'll need to know a season-ticket holder. In recent years, Rangers have had to work their way back up the divisions after a financial meltdown, returning to the top flight in 2016.

🔒 Shopping

With the UK's largest retail phalanx outside London, Glasgow is a shopaholic's paradise. The 'Style Mile' around Buchanan and Argyle Sts and Merchant City (particularly upmarket Ingram St) is a fashion hub, while the West End has quirkier, more bohemian shopping options: it's great for vintage clothing. The weekend Barras market in the East End is very worthwhile.

⭐ **Mr Ben**   CLOTHING
(Map p794; ☑0141-553 1936; www.mrbenretro-clothing.com; 101 King St; ⊙12.30-6pm Mon & Tue, from 10.30am Wed-Sat, 12.30-5.30pm Sun) This cute place is one of Glasgow's best destinations for vintage clothing, with a great selection of brands like Fred Perry, as well as more glam choices and even outdoor gear.

The Barras   MARKET
(Map p794; ☑0141-552 4601; www.glasgow-bar rowland.com; btwn Gallowgate & London Rd; ⊙10am-5pm Sat & Sun) Glasgow's legendary weekend flea market, the Barras on Gallowgate, is a fascinating mixture of on-trend openings and working-class Glasgow. Genuine old stalls flogging time-faded glasses, posters and DVDs that you'd struggle to give away are juxtaposed with vintage classics, very earthy traders' pubs and a street scene where fake designer gear is marked down and dodgy characters peddle smuggled cigarettes.

It's an intriguing stroll, as much for the assortment of local characters as for what's on offer. People come here just to wander, and parts of it have a real feel of a nearly vanished Britain of whelk stalls and rag-and-bone merchants. Watch your wallet.

Barras Art & Design   ARTS & CRAFTS
(BAaD; Map p794; ☑0141-237 9220; www.baad glasgow.com; Moncur St; ⊙noon-midnight Tue-Sat, 11am-10pm Sun) This workshop zone for artists and designers in the heart of the Barras has helped pep up the area and bring a new wave of folk in. It's a lovely covered courtyard with a bar, cafe and restaurant, as well as pop-up and other shops. There are events on most weekends, including a monthly farmers market.

**Randall's Antique
& Vintage Centre**   VINTAGE
(Map p794; ☑07752 658045; www.facebook.com/ randallsantiqueandvintagecentre; Stevenson St West; ⊙9am-5pm Sat & Sun) This is a real treasure trove of the once loved, the tacky, the tawdry, the magnificent and the curious from the not-so-recent past. It's an excellent set-up with several sellers and a top spot to browse. Don't take the kids; they'll make you feel ancient with their incredulity at items that you remember using not so very long ago.

Princes Square   SHOPPING CENTRE
(Map p794; ☑0141-221 0324; www.princessqu are.co.uk; 48 Buchanan St; ⊙10am-7pm Mon-Fri, 9am-6pm Sat, 11am-5pm Sun) Set in a magnificent 1841 renovated square with elaborate ironwork and an exuberant metal leaf-and-peacock facade, this place has lots of beauty and fashion outlets, including Vivienne Westwood. There's a good selection of restaurants and cafes, as well as a bar with a roof terrace.

Argyll Arcade   JEWELLERY
(Map p794; ☑0141-248 5257; www.argyll-arcade. com; Buchanan St; ⊙10am-5.30pm Mon-Sat, noon-5pm Sun) This splendid historic arcade doglegs between Buchanan and Argyle Sts and has done since before Victoria reigned. It's quite a sight with its end-to-end jewellery and watch shops. Top-hatted doorpeople

GLASGOW & SOUTHERN SCOTLAND GLASGOW

greet nervously excited couples shopping for diamond rings.

Hidden Lane
ARTS & CRAFTS

(Map p798; www.thehiddenlaneglasgow.com; 1103 Argyle St) Well concealed down a passageway off the Finnieston strip, these back alleys house a colourful mix of arty shops and studios well worth investigating. There's a tearoom, jewellery store, yoga centre and plenty more.

Caledonia Books
BOOKS

(Map p798; ☑ 0141-334 9663; www.caledonia books.co.uk; 483 Great Western Rd; ☺10.30am-6pm Mon-Sat) This characterful spot is just what a secondhand bookshop should be, with a smell of dust and venerability and a wide range of intriguing volumes on the slightly chaotic shelves.

Slanj Kilts
CLOTHING

(Map p794; ☑ 0141-248 5632; www.slanjkilts.com; 80 St Vincent St; ☺9.30am-5.30pm Mon-Wed, Fri & Sat, to 6.30pm Thu, 11am-4pm Sun) This upbeat shop is a top spot to hire or buy kilts both traditional and modern, as well as other tartan wear and a range of T-shirts and other accessories. Always worth a look.

Glasgow Vintage Company
VINTAGE

(Map p798; ☑ 0141-338 6633; www.facebook.com/theglasgowvintagecompany; 453 Great Western Rd; ☺11am-6pm Mon-Sat, to 5pm Sun) With a little more breathing room than some of Glasgow's vintage shops, this one offers relaxed browsing.

Demijohn
FOOD & DRINKS

(Map p798; ☑ 0141-337 3600; www.demijohn.co.uk; 382 Byres Rd; ☺10am-6pm Mon-Sat, 11.30am-5pm Sun) Unusual and intriguing, this shop is lined with large glass bottles stocking artisanal vinegars, oils, liqueurs and distillates. Try before you buy, then pick a quirky receptacle to bottle it in.

ℹ Information

INTERNET ACCESS

There's a free wi-fi zone across the city centre. You can get a local SIM card for about a pound and data packages are cheap.

MEDICAL SERVICES

Glasgow Dental Hospital (☑ 0141-211 9600; www.nhsggc.org.uk; 378 Sauchiehall St)

Glasgow Royal Infirmary (☑ 0141-211 4000; www.nhsggc.org.uk; 84 Castle St) Medical emergencies and outpatient facilities.

Queen Elizabeth University Hospital (☑ 0141-201 1100; www.nhsggc.org.uk; 1345 Govan Rd) Modern; south of the river.

TOURIST INFORMATION

Useful websites with tourist information include www.glasgowlife.org.uk, www.peoplemakeglas gow.com and www.list.co.uk, which publishes entertainment listings and restaurant reviews.

Glasgow Tourist Office (Map p794; www.visitscotland.com; 158 Buchanan St; ☺9am-5pm Mon-Sat, 10am-4pm Sun Nov-Apr, 9am-6pm Mon-Sat, 10am-4pm Sun May, Jun, Sep & Oct, 9am-7pm Mon-Sat, 10am-5pm Sun Jul & Aug; �) The city's tourist office is in the centre of town. It opens at 9.30am on Thursday mornings.

ℹ Getting There & Away

AIR

Glasgow International Airport (GLA; ☑ 0344 481 5555; www.glasgowairport.com; ☎) Ten miles west of the city, Glasgow International Airport handles domestic traffic and international flights. Facilities include car hire, ATMs, free wi-fi and internet terminals.

Glasgow Prestwick Airport (PIK; ☑ 0871 223 0700; www.glasgowprestwick.com) Glasgow Prestwick Airport, 30 miles southwest of Glasgow, is used by Ryanair and some other budget airlines, with many connections to mostly holiday destinations in southern Europe.

BUS

All long-distance buses arrive at and depart from **Buchanan bus station** (Map p794; ☑ 0141-333 3708; www.spt.co.uk; Killermont St; ☎), which has pricey lockers, ATMs and wi-fi.

Megabus (☑ 0141-352 4444; www.megabus.com) Your first port of call if you're looking for the cheapest fare. Megabus offers very cheap demand-dependent prices on many major bus routes, including to Edinburgh and London.

National Express (☑ 0871 781 8181; www.nationalexpress.com) Runs daily to several English cities.

Scottish Citylink (☑ 0871 266 3333; www.citylink.co.uk) Has buses to Edinburgh (£7.90, 1¼ hours, every 15 minutes) and most major towns in Scotland.

There are also buses from Buchanan bus station direct to/from Edinburgh Airport (£12, one hour, half-hourly).

TRAIN

As a general rule, **Glasgow Central station** (www.scotrail.co.uk; Gordon St) serves southern Scotland, England and Wales, and **Queen Street station** (www.scotrail.co.uk; George St) serves the north and east (including Edinburgh). Buses run between the two stations every 10 minutes.

LANARK & NEW LANARK

Below the market town of Lanark, in an attractive gorge by the River Clyde, is the World Heritage Site of **New Lanark** (☎01555-661345; www.newlanark.org; adult/child/family £12.50/9/38; ☺10am-5pm Apr-Oct, to 4pm Nov-Mar; ♿). Once Britain's largest cotton-spinning complex, it's better known for the pioneering social experiments of Robert Owen, who managed the mill from 1800. Now a World Heritage Site, New Lanark is really a memorial to this enlightened capitalist. He provided his workers with housing, a cooperative store, the world's first nursery school, adult-education classes, a sick-pay fund for workers and a social centre he called the New Institute for the Formation of Character.

Admission includes access to a huge working spinning mule, producing woollen yarn, and the Historic Schoolhouse, which contains an innovative, high-tech journey to New Lanark's past via a 3D hologram of the spirit of Annie McLeod, a 10-year-old mill girl who describes life here in 1820. You can also see a millworker's house, Robert Owen's own home and a 1920s-style village store.

Lanark is 25 miles southeast of Glasgow. Express bus 240X runs hourly Monday to Saturday (£6.50, one hour); trains from Glasgow Central also run (£7.30, 55 minutes, every 30 minutes, hourly on Sundays).

It's a pleasant walk to New Lanark, but there's also a half-hourly bus service from the train station (daily).

There are direct trains more than hourly to London Euston station; they're much quicker (4½ hours) and more comfortable than the bus. The fare is £65/142/183 for advance/off-peak/any-time singles.

ScotRail (p787) runs Scottish trains. Destinations include the following:

Aberdeen (£41.80, 2½ to 3½ hours, hourly)

Dundee (£23.20, 1½ hours, hourly)

Edinburgh (£14.40, 50 minutes, every 15 minutes)

Fort William (£30.80, 3¾ hours, four daily)

Inverness (£92.50; 3½ to four hours; five direct daily, three on Sunday)

Oban (£25.30, three hours, three to six daily)

❶ Getting Around

TO/FROM THE AIRPORT

Bus 500 runs every 10 or 15 minutes (half-hourly or hourly late at night) from Glasgow International Airport to Buchanan bus station via Central and Queen Street train stations (single/return £8/12, 25 minutes). This is a 24-hour service. You can include a day ticket on the bus network for £12 total or a four-day ticket for £18.

Another bus, the 77, covers the same route via the West End twice hourly, taking longer.

A taxi costs around £25.

BUS

City bus services, mostly run by **First Glasgow** (☎0141-420 7600; www.firstglasgow.com), are frequent. You can buy tickets when you board buses, but on most you must have the exact change. Short journeys in town cost £1.60 or

£2.30; a day ticket (£4.50) is good value and is valid until 1am, when a night network starts. A weekly ticket is £17. Check route maps online at www.spt.co.uk.

CAR

The most difficult thing about driving in Glasgow is the sometimes-confusing one-way system. For short-term parking (up to two hours), you've got a decent chance of finding something on the street, paying at the meters, which cost up to £4 per hour. Otherwise, multistorey car parks are probably your best bet and are not so expensive. Ask your hotel in advance if it offers parking discounts.

There are numerous car-rental companies; both big names and discount operators have airport offices.

Arnold Clark (☎0141-423 9559; www.arnold clarkrental.com; 43 Allison St; ☺8am-5.30pm Mon-Fri, to 4pm Sat, 11am-4pm Sun)

Avis (☎0344 544 6064; www.avis.co.uk; 70 Lancefield St; ☺8am-6pm Mon-Fri, to 3pm Sat, 10am-2pm Sun)

Enterprise (☎0141-221 2124; www.enterprise. co.uk; 40 Oswald St; ☺7am-9pm Mon-Fri, 8am-4pm Sat, 10am-3pm Sun)

Europcar (☎0371 384 3471; www.europcar. co.uk; 76 Lancefield Quay; ☺8am-6pm Mon-Fri, to 4pm Sat)

Hertz (☎0141-229 6120; www.hertz.co.uk; Jury's Inn, 80 Jamaica St; ☺8am-6pm Mon-Fri, to 1pm Sat, 10am-2pm Sun)

TAXI

There's no shortage of taxis, and if you want to know anything about Glasgow, striking up a conversation with a cabbie is a good place to start. Fares are very reasonable – you can get across the city centre for around £6, and there's no surcharge for calling a taxi. You can pay by credit card with **Glasgow Taxis** (☑ 0141-429 7070; www.glasgowtaxis.co.uk) if you order by phone; most of its taxis are wheelchair accessible. Download its app to make booking easy.

TRAIN

There's an extensive suburban network of trains in and around Glasgow; tickets should be purchased before travel if the station is staffed, or from the conductor if it isn't.

There's also an underground line, the subway, that serves 15 stations in the city centre, and west and south of the city (single £1.70). The train network connects with the subway at Buchanan Street underground station, next to **Queen Street overground station** (p810), and St Enoch underground station, near **Glasgow Central station** (p810). The All Day Ticket (£4.10) gives unlimited travel on the subway for a day, while the Roundabout ticket gives a day's unlimited train and subway travel for £7. The subway runs roughly from 6.30am to 11.30pm Monday to Saturday but annoyingly runs only from 10am to 6pm on Sunday.

BORDERS REGION

The Borders has had a rough history: centuries of war and plunder have left a battle-scarred landscape, exemplified by the magnificent ruins of the Border abbeys. Their

---

WORTH A TRIP

PAXTON HOUSE

Paxton House (☑ 01289-386291; www.paxtonhouse.co.uk; B6461; adult/child £10/4; ☺ 10am-5pm Easter-Oct, grounds 10am-sunset; 🚗), 6 miles west of Berwick-upon-Tweed, is beside the River Tweed and surrounded by parkland and gardens. It was built in 1758 by Patrick Home for his intended wife, the daughter of Prussia's Frederick the Great. Unfortunately, she stood him up, but it was her loss; designed by the Adam family – brothers John, James and Robert – it's acknowledged as one of the finest 18th-century Palladian houses in Britain. Four tours run daily; see the website for limited winter visiting.

Bus 32 runs past here every couple of hours from Berwick.

---

wealth was an irresistible magnet during cross-frontier wars, and they were destroyed and rebuilt numerous times. Today these massive stone shells are the region's finest attraction. And don't miss Hermitage Castle: nothing encapsulates the region's turbulent history like this spooky stronghold.

But the Borders is also genteel. Welcoming villages with ancient traditions pepper the countryside and grandiose mansions await exploration. It's fine walking and cycling country too, the hills lush with shades of green. Offshore you'll find some of Europe's best cold-water diving.

Peebles

☑ 01721 / POP 8600

With a picturesque main street set on a ridge between the River Tweed and the Eddleston Water, Peebles is one of the most handsome of the Border towns. Though it lacks a major sight, the agreeable atmosphere and good walking options in the rolling, wooded hills thereabouts will entice you to linger for a couple of days.

◉ Sights & Activities

The riverside walk along the River Tweed has plenty of grassed areas ideal for a picnic, and there's a children's playground (near the main road bridge).

Nearby in Glentress forest is the busiest of the 7stanes mountain-biking **hubs** (www.7stanesmountainbiking.com) FREE, as well as osprey viewing and marked walking trails. There are also swing and zip-line **forest routes** (www.goape.co.uk; Glentress Forest; adult/child £33/25; ☺ Feb-Nov), not to mention camping huts (see www.glentressforest-lodges.co.uk). In town, you can hire bikes to explore the region from **Bspoke Cycles** (☑ 01721-723423; www.bspokepeebles.co.uk; Old Tweeddale Garage, Innerleithen Rd; bikes per day from £25; ☺ 9am-5.30pm Mon-Sat).

There are further mountain-biking trails at Innerleithen, 7 miles east of Peebles.

🛏 Sleeping & Eating

Lindores Guest House   B&B ££
(☑ 01721-729040; www.lindoresgh.co.uk; 60 Old Town; s £50-60, d £70-80; 🖥) Run by an interesting, kind couple, this rather striking house offers commodious, flowery rooms. Both en-suite and shared bathrooms are available and showers are great. Breakfast features really delicious home-baked bread

TRAQUAIR HOUSE

One of Scotland's great country houses, **Traquair House** (☑ 01896-830323; www.traquair.
co.uk; Innerleithen; adult/child/family £9/4.50/25; ☉ 11am-5pm Easter-Sep, to 4pm Oct, to 3pm
Sat & Sun Nov) has a powerful, ethereal beauty, and exploring it is like time travelling. Odd,
sloping floors and a musty odour bestow a genuine feel, and parts of the building are believed to have been constructed long before the first official record of its existence in 1107.
The massive tower house was gradually expanded but has remained virtually unchanged
since the 17th century. Traquair is about 6 miles southeast of Peebles.

Since the 15th century, the house has belonged to various branches of the Stuart family,
and the family's unwavering Catholicism and loyalty to the Stuart cause led to famous visitors like Mary, Queen of Scots, and Bonnie Prince Charlie, but also to numerous problems
after the deposal of James II of England in 1688. The family's estate, wealth and influence
were gradually whittled away, as life as a Jacobite became a furtive, clandestine affair.

One of Traquair's most interesting places is the concealed room where priests secretly
lived and performed Mass – up until 1829 when the Catholic Emancipation Act was finally passed. Other beautiful, time-worn rooms hold fascinating relics, including the cradle
used by Mary for her son, James VI of Scotland (who also became James I of England),
and fascinating letters from the Jacobite Earls of Traquair and their families, including
one particularly moving one written from death row in the Tower of London.

In addition to the house, there's a garden maze, a small brewery producing the tasty
Bear Ale, and a series of craft workshops. You can also stay here in one of three opulent
B&B rooms (single/double £130/190).

Bus X62 runs from Edinburgh via Peebles to Innerleithen and on to Galashiels and
Melrose.

among other goodies. There's secure parking
for bikes and motorbikes.

Tontine Hotel　　　　　　　　　　HOTEL **££**
(☑ 01721-720892; www.tontinehotel.com; High St;
s £70-90, d £100-130; [P][☎][☺][🌐]) Right in the
heart of things, this is a bastion of Borders
hospitality. Refurbished rooms have high
comfort levels, modish colours and top-
notch bathrooms, while service couldn't be
more helpful. There's a small supplement
for rooms with four-poster beds and/or
river views. Good **restaurant** (mains £11-19;
☉ noon-2.30pm & 6-8.45pm; [☎]) and bar, too.

Cocoa Black　　　　　　　　　　　　CAFE **£**
(☑ 01721-723764; www.cocoablack.com; 1 Cuddy
Bridge; sweets £2-5; ☉ 9.30am-5pm Mon-Fri, 9am-
5pm Sat, 10.30am-5pm Sun; [☎][♿]) Chocaholics
should make a beeline for this friendly cafe,
where exquisite cakes and other patisserie
offerings will satisfy any cacao-focused crav-
ings. It also runs a school where you can
learn to make them yourself.

★ **Coltman's**　　　　　　　BISTRO, DELI **££**
(☑ 01721-720405; www.coltmans.co.uk; 71 High St;
mains £13-16; ☉ 10am-5pm Sun-Wed, to 10pm Thu-
Sat; [☎]) 🍃 This main-street deli has numerous temptations, such as excellent cheeses
and Italian smallgoods, as well as perhaps

Scotland's tastiest sausage roll. Behind the
shop, the good-looking dining area serves up
confident bistro fare and light snacks with
a variety of culinary influences, using top-
notch local ingredients. Upstairs is a cosy bar.

ℹ Information

Peebles Tourist Office (☑ 01721-728095;
www.visitscottishborders.com; 23 High St;
☉ 9am-5pm Mon-Sat, 11am-4pm Sun Apr-Jun,
Sep & Oct, 9am-5.30pm Mon-Sat, 10am-4pm
Sun Jul & Aug, 9am-5pm Mon-Fri, 9.30am-4pm
Sat, 11am-5pm Sun Nov & Dec, 9.30am-5pm Mon-
Fri, 9.30am-4pm Sat Jan-Mar) Helpful office in
the centre of town. Future was in doubt at the
time of research.

ℹ Getting There & Away

The bus stop is beside the post office on
Eastgate. Bus X62 runs half-hourly (hourly on
Sundays) to Edinburgh (£5.60, 1¼ hours). In the
other direction it heads for Melrose (£6.20, 1¼
hours).

Melrose

☑ 01896 / POP 2500

Tiny, charming Melrose is a polished village
running on the well-greased wheels of tourism. Sitting at the feet of the three heath-

HERMITAGE CASTLE

The 'guardhouse of the bloodiest valley in Britain', **Hermitage Castle** (HES; ☑ 01387-376222; www.historicenvironment.scot; B6357; adult/child £5/3; ⊙ 9.30am-5.30pm Apr-Sep) embodies the brutal history of the Scottish Borders. Desolate but proud with its massive squared stone walls, it looks more like a lair for orc raiding parties than a home for Scottish nobility, and is one of the bleakest and most stirring of Scottish ruins. The castle is about 12 miles south of Hawick on the B6357.

Strategically crucial, the castle was the scene of many a dark deed and dirty deal with the English invaders, all of which rebounded heavily on the perfidious Scottish lord in question. Here, in 1338, Sir William Douglas imprisoned his enemy Sir Alexander Ramsay and deliberately starved him to death. Ramsay survived for 17 days by eating grain that trickled into his pit (which can still be seen) from the granary above. In 1566 Mary, Queen of Scots, famously visited the wounded tenant of the castle, Lord Bothwell, here. Fortified, he recovered to (probably) murder her husband, marry her himself, then abandon her months later and flee into exile.

er-covered Eildon Hills, Melrose has a classic market square and one of the great abbey ruins. Just outside town is Abbotsford, the home of Sir Walter Scott, which makes another superb visit.

◉ Sights

★ Melrose Abbey
RUINS

(HES; ☑ 01896-822562; www.historicenvironment. scot; adult/child £6/3.60; ⊙ 9.30am-5.30pm Apr-Sep, 10am-4pm Oct-Mar) Perhaps the most interesting of the Border abbeys, red-sandstone Melrose was repeatedly destroyed by the English in the 14th century. The remaining broken shell is pure Gothic and the ruins are famous for their decorative stonework – look out for the pig gargoyle playing the bagpipes. Though Melrose had a monastery way back in the 7th century, this abbey was founded by David I in 1136 for Cistercian monks, and later rebuilt by Robert the Bruce, whose heart is buried here.

★ Abbotsford
HISTORIC BUILDING

(☑ 01896-752043; www.scottsabbotsford.com; visitor centre free, house adult/child £11/5; ⊙ 10am-5pm Apr-Oct, to 4pm Nov-Mar, house closed Dec-Feb) Just outside Melrose, this is where to discover the life and works of Sir Walter Scott, to whom we arguably owe both the modern novel and our mind's-eye view of Scotland. This whimsical, fabulous house where he lived – and which ruined him when his publishers went bust – really brings this 19th-century writer to life. The grounds on the banks of the Tweed are lovely, and Scott drew much inspiration from rambles in the surrounding countryside.

★ Dryburgh Abbey
RUINS

(HES; ☑ 01835-822381; www.historicenvironment. scot; adult/child £6/3.60; ⊙ 9.30am-5.30pm Apr-Sep, 10am-4pm Oct-Mar) This is the most beautiful and complete of the Border abbeys, partly because the neighbouring town of Dryburgh no longer exists (another victim of the wars) and partly because of its lovely site by the Tweed in a sheltered birdsong-filled valley. Dating from about 1150, the abbey belonged to the Premonstratensians, a religious order founded in France, and evokes 12th-century monastic life more successfully than its nearby counterparts. The pink-hued stone ruins are the burial place of Sir Walter Scott.

🛌 Sleeping & Eating

Dunfermline House
B&B ££

(☑ 01896-822411; www.dunfermlinehouse.co.uk; Buccleuch St; d £65; 🐾) Very close to Melrose Abbey (p814), this place offers a genuinely warm welcome and comfortable, flowery rooms in classic B&B style. It's very walker- and cyclist-friendly and breakfast is well above average, with plenty of fruit on hand.

★ Old Bank House
B&B ££

(☑ 01896-823712; www.oldbankhousemelrose. co.uk; 27 Buccleuch St; s/d £55/70; 🐾🐕) Right in the centre, this is a superb B&B in a charming old building. The owner's artistic touch is evident throughout, from walls covered with paintings, some his own, to a house full of curios and tasteful art nouveau features, and a sumptuous breakfast room. Rooms are spacious with comfortable furniture and modern bathrooms; they're complemented by a generous can-do attitude.

★**Townhouse** BOUTIQUE HOTEL **£££**
(☑01896-822645; www.thetownhousemelrose.co.
uk; Market Sq; s/d/superior d £100/138/159;
🅿🛜) The classy Townhouse exudes warmth
and professionalism, and has some of the
best rooms in town, tastefully furnished
with attention to detail. The superior rooms
are enormous with lavish furnishings and
excellent en suites. Standard rooms are a
fair bit smaller but they're refurbished and
very comfortable. It's well worth the price.

There is an excellent **restaurant** (mains
£14-18; ⊘noon-2pm & 6-9pm; 🛜) located
on-site.

Cellar CAFE **£**
(Abbey Fine Wines, Rhymer's Fayre; ☑01896-
823224; www.abbeyfinewines.co.uk; 17 Market Sq;
mains £5-8; ⊘9.30am-4.30pm Mon-Sat Apr-Oct,
10am-4pm Mon-Sat Nov-Mar) Drop into the
Cellar for a caffeine hit. It's also a good spot
for a glass of wine on the town square, as
well as food platters and speciality cheeses.
Out front is a more-than-decent shop selling
wine and whisky.

❶ Getting There & Away

The Borders Railway runs from Edinburgh to
Tweedbank (£10.70, one hour, half-hourly),
which is 1.5 miles from Melrose. Buses run
half-hourly from here into Melrose.

Regular X62 buses run to/from Edinburgh
(£7.50, 2½ hours, half-hourly Monday to Saturday) via Peebles. On Sundays this service runs
hourly but only from nearby Galashiels, connected to Melrose by regular buses.

For other Borders destinations, you'll most
likely need to change in Galashiels.

Jedburgh

☑01835 / POP 4000

Attractive Jedburgh, where many old buildings and wynds (narrow alleys) have been
intelligently restored, invites exploration by
foot. It's centred on the noble skeleton of its
ruined abbey.

◉ Sights

★**Jedburgh Abbey** RUINS
(HES; ☑01835-863925; www.historicenvironment.
scot; Abbey Rd; adult/child £6/3.60; ⊘9.30am-
5.30pm Apr-Sep, 10am-4pm Oct-Mar; 🐾) Dominating the town skyline, this was the first
of the great Border abbeys to be passed into
state care, and it shows – audio and visual
presentations telling the abbey's story are

scattered throughout the carefully preserved
ruins (good for the kids). The red-sandstone
ruins are roofless but relatively intact, and
the ingenuity of the master mason can be
seen in some of the rich (if somewhat faded)
stone carvings in the nave.

The abbey was founded in 1138 by David I
as a priory for Augustinian canons.

**Mary, Queen of
Scots' Visitor Centre** HISTORIC BUILDING
(Queen St; ⊘9.30am-4.30pm Mon-Sat, 10.30am-
4pm Sun early Mar–late Nov) **FREE** Mary stayed
at this beautiful 16th-century tower house
in 1566 after her famous ride to visit the in-
jured Earl of Bothwell, her future husband,
at Hermitage Castle. The interesting exhibition evokes the sad saga of Mary's life and
death. Various objects associated with her –
including a lock of her hair – are on display.

🛏 Sleeping & Eating

Maplebank B&B **£**
(☑01835-862051; maplebank3@btinternet.com;
3 Smiths Wynd; s/d £30/50; 🅿🛜🐾) It's pleasing to come across places where it feels like
you're staying in someone's home. Here, that
someone is like your favourite aunt: friendly,
chaotic and generous. There's lots of clutter
and it's very informal. Rooms are comfortable and large, sharing a good bathroom.
Breakfast (including fruit, yoghurts and
homemade jams) is brilliant – much better
than at most posher places.

Glenbank House Hotel HOTEL **££**
(☑01835-862258; www.jedburgh-hotel.com; Castlegate; d £65-99; 🅿🛜) This lovely old building
has modernised, comfortable rooms – some
of which are rather compact – shiny contemporary bathrooms, and nice views over
the town and hills. It's a likeable place, with
very welcoming people running it. There's no
restaurant service but you're in the centre of
town.

Capon Tree SCOTTISH **££**
(☑01835-869596; www.thecapontree.com; 61
High St; mains £14-20; ⊘food 6-9pm Mon-Fri,
noon-2.30pm & 5.30-9pm Sat, noon-2.30pm &
5.30-8pm Sun; 🛜) Attractively combining
smart and casual, this welcoming bistro and
bar does modern Scottish cuisine. Plates
are beautifully, though not fussily, presented and ingredients are of high quality. The
overall package is appealing, the service
good and the ambience romantic. There are
handsome rooms available, too.

ℹ️ Information

Jedburgh Tourist Office (📞 01835-863170; www.visitscotland.com; Murray's Green; ⏰ 9am-5pm Mon-Sat, 10am-4pm Sun Apr-Jun, Sep & Oct, 9am-5.30pm Mon-Sat, 10am-5pm Sun Jul & Aug, 10am-4pm Mon-Sat Nov-Mar; 🖥️) Head tourist office for the Borders region. Very helpful.

ℹ️ Getting There & Away

Jedburgh has good bus connections to Hawick, Melrose and Kelso (all around 25 minutes, roughly hourly, two-hourly on Sunday). Buses also run to Edinburgh (£7.80, two hours, six daily, three on Sunday).

Kelso

📳 01573 / POP 5600

Kelso, a prosperous market town with a broad, cobbled square flanked by Georgian buildings, has a cheery feel and historic appeal. During the day it's a busy little place, but after 8pm you'll have the streets to yourself. The town has a lovely site at the junction of the Tweed and Teviot, and is one of the most enjoyable places in the Borders.

👁️ Sights

Floors Castle   HISTORIC BUILDING
(📞 01573-223333; www.floorscastle.com; adult/child castle & grounds £11.50/6; ⏰ 10.30am-5pm May-Sep, Sat & Sun Oct) Grandiose Floors Castle is Scotland's largest inhabited mansion, home to the Duke of Roxburghe, and overlooks the Tweed about a mile west of Kelso. Built by William Adam in the 1720s, the original Georgian simplicity was 'improved' in the 1840s with the addition of somewhat

---

OFF THE BEATEN TRACK

SMAILHOLM TOWER

Perched on a rocky knoll above a small lake, this narrow stone **tower** (HES; 📞 01573-460365; www.historicenviron-ment.scot; Sandyknowe Farm, Smailholm; adult/child £5/3; ⏰ 9.30am-5.30pm Apr-Sep) provides one of the most evocative sights in the Borders and keeps its bloody history alive. Although displays inside are sparse, the panoramic view from the top is worth the climb. The tower is 6 miles west of Kelso, a mile south of Smailholm village on the B6397.

OTT battlements and turrets. Inside, view the vivid colours of 17th-century Brussels tapestries in the drawing room and intricate oak carvings in the ornate ballroom. The walled garden is a highlight of the extensive grounds.

Mellerstain House   HISTORIC BUILDING
(📞 01573-410225; www.mellerstain.com; Gordon; adult/child £10/5; ⏰ noon-5pm Fri-Mon Easter & May-Sep) Finished in 1778, this is considered to be Scotland's finest Robert Adam–designed mansion. It is huge and famous for its classic elegance, ornate interiors and plaster ceilings; the library in particular is outstanding. The upstairs bedrooms are less attractive, but have a peek at the bizarre puppet-and-doll collection in the gallery.

It's about 6 miles northwest of Kelso, near Gordon. There are concerts held here through the summer months.

Kelso Abbey   RUINS
(HES; www.historicenvironment.scot; Bridge St; ⏰ 9.30am-5.30pm Apr-Sep, 10am-4pm Sat-Wed Oct-Mar) **FREE** Once one of the richest abbeys in southern Scotland, Kelso Abbey was built by the Tironensians, an order founded in Picardy and brought to the Borders around 1113 by David I. English raids in the 16th century reduced it to ruins, though what little remains today is some of the finest surviving Romanesque architecture in Scotland.

🛏️ Sleeping

⭐ **Edenbank House**   B&B ££
(📞 01573-226734; www.edenbank.co.uk; Stichill Rd; s/d £50/90; 🅿️🖥️) A half-mile down the Stichill road, this grand Victorian house sits in spacious grounds where only bleating lambs in the fields and birds in the garden break the silence. It's a fabulous place, with huge opulent rooms, lovely views over the fields and incredibly warm hospitality. Breakfast features homemade produce, and a laissez-faire attitude makes for an utterly relaxing stay.

⭐ **Old Priory**   B&B ££
(📞 01573-223030; www.theoldpriorykelso.com; 33 Woodmarket; s/d £80/90; 🅿️🖥️) Fantastic rooms here are allied with numerous personal details – the operators turn down the beds at night and make you feel very welcome. Doubles are top-notch and the family room really excellent. The huge windows flood the rooms with natural light. The wonderful li-

CULZEAN CASTLE

The Scottish National Trust's flagship property, magnificent **Culzean** (NTS; ☑ 01655-884455; www.nts.org.uk; Culzean; castle adult/child/family £16.50/12.25/41; ⊗ castle 10.30am-5pm Apr-Oct, last entry 4pm, park 9.30am-sunset year-round; ⦿) (kull-ane) is one of the most impressive of Scotland's stately homes. On approach the castle floats into view like a mirage. It was designed by Robert Adam, the most influential architect of his time, renowned for his meticulous attention to detail and the elegant classical embellishments with which he decorated his ceilings and fireplaces.

The 18th-century mansion is perched dramatically on a clifftop. The beautiful oval staircase here is regarded as one of his finest achievements. On the 1st floor, the opulence of the circular saloon contrasts violently with the views of the wild sea below. Lord Cassillis' bedroom is said to be haunted by a lady in green, mourning for a lost baby. Even the bathrooms are palatial: the dressing room beside the state bedroom is equipped with a Victorian state-of-the-art shower.

There's a great play area for kids, which replicates the castle on a smaller scale, as well as a recreation of a Victorian vinery, an orangery, a deer park and an aviary. It's even possible to stay in the castle from April to October, and there's also a campsite.

Stagecoach buses running between Ayr and Girvan stop outside the gates, from where it's a 1-mile walk to the castle itself

---

brary room (£120) is huge and luxurious, with a super bathroom. Top-class B&B.

✗ Eating & Drinking

★**Cobbles**　　　　　　　　　　BISTRO ££
(☑ 01573-223548; www.thecobbleskelso.co.uk; 7 Bowmont St; mains £10-17; ⊗ food noon-2.30pm & 5.45-9pm Mon-Fri, noon-9pm Sat, noon-8.30pm Sun; ☎) This inn off the main square is so popular you will need to book a table at weekends. It's cheery, very welcoming and warm, and serves excellent upmarket pub food in generous portions. Pick and mix from bar menu, steaks and gourmet options. Leave room for cheese and/or dessert. The bar's own microbrewed ales are excellent. A cracking place.

★**Rutherfords**　　　　　　　　　　PUB
(☑ 07803-208460; www.rutherfordsmicropub.co.uk; 38 The Square; ⊗ noon-10pm Sun-Thu, to 11pm Fri & Sat, reduced hours Nov-Mar) This enchanting small bar prioritises conversation and has no TV or music. It's a charming place with gin on tap poured through a microscope, carefully selected craft beers and spirits, and a warm, convivial atmosphere. Unusual and excellent.

❶ Getting There & Away

There are six daily direct bus services to Edinburgh (£7.70, two hours, two on Sunday) and regular routes to other Borders towns and Berwick-upon-Tweed.

DUMFRIES & GALLOWAY

Some of southern Scotland's finest attractions lie in the gentle hills and lush valleys of Dumfries and Galloway. It's an ideal destination for families, as there's plenty on offer for the kids. Galloway Forest – with its sublime views, mountain-biking and walking trails, red deer, kites and other wildlife – is a highlight, as are the dream-like ruins of Caerlaverock Castle. Adding to the appeal of this enticing region is a string of southern Scotland's most idyllic towns, which are charming when the sun shines. And shine it does. This is the mildest region in Scotland and is warmed by the Gulf Stream, a phenomenon that has allowed the development of some famous gardens.

Dumfries

☑ 01387 / POP 32,900

Lovely, red-hued sandstone bridges crisscross the wide, grassy-banked River Nith, which runs through the centre of pleasant Dumfries. Historically the town held a strategic position in the path of vengeful English armies; consequently, although it has existed since Roman times, the oldest standing building dates from the 17th century. Plenty of famous names have passed through: Robert Burns lived here and worked as a tax collector, Peter Pan creator JM Barrie was schooled here and DJ Calvin Harris hails from the town.

ROBERT BURNS

Best remembered for penning the words of 'Auld Lang Syne', Robert Burns (1759–96) is Scotland's most famous poet and a popular hero; his birthday (25 January) is celebrated as Burns Night by Scots around the world.

The pretty, lush village of Alloway (3 miles south of Ayr) should be on the itinerary of every Burns fan – he was born here on 25 January 1759. The **Robert Burns Birthplace Museum** (NTS; 01292-443700; www.burnsmuseum.org.uk; Murdoch's Lone; adult/child £10.50/7.50; 10am-5pm) has collected a solid range of memorabilia, including manuscripts and possessions of the poet, like the pistols he packed for his work as a tax collector. There's plenty of humour that the poet surely would have approved of, and entertaining audio and visual performances will keep the kids amused.

The admission ticket also covers the atmospheric Burns Birthplace Cottage (open 11am to 5pm), connected via a walkway to the Birthplace Museum. Born in the little boxbed in this cramped thatched dwelling, the poet spent the first seven years of his life here.

The Burns connection in southern Scotland is milked for all it's worth and tourist offices have a Burns Heritage Trail leaflet leading you to every place that can claim some link with the bard. Burns fans should have a look at www.robertburns.org.

◉ Sights

★ **Burns House**　　　　　　　　MUSEUM
(01387-255297; www.dumgal.gov.uk; Burns St; 10am-5pm Mon-Sat, 2-5pm Sun Apr-Sep, 10am-1pm & 2-5pm Tue-Sat Oct-Mar) FREE This is a place of pilgrimage for Burns enthusiasts. It's here that the poet spent the last years of his life, and there are various possessions of his in glass cases, as well as manuscripts and, entertainingly, letters: make sure you have a read.

Robert Burns Centre　　　　MUSEUM
(01387-264808; www.dumgal.gov.uk; Mill Rd; audiovisual presentation £2.30; 10am-5pm Mon-Sat, 2-5pm Sun Apr-Sep, 10am-1pm & 2-5pm Tue-Sat Oct-Mar) FREE A worthwhile Burns exhibition in an old mill on the banks of the River Nith; it tells the story of the poet and Dumfries in the 1790s. The optional audiovisual presentations give more background on Dumfries, and explain the exhibition's contents. The centre functions as a cinema in the evenings.

Robert Burns Mausoleum　　　TOMB
(St Michael's Kirk, Brooms Rd) FREE Burns' mausoleum is in the graveyard at **St Michael's Kirk** (www.stmichaelschurchdumfries.org; 10.30am-3.30pm Mon-Fri Apr-Sep). It's in the far corner (ie eastern corner) from the entrance. There's a grisly account of his reburial on the information panel.

⌂ Sleeping & Eating

★ **Ferintosh Guest House**　　　B&B ££
(01387-252262; www.ferintosh.net; 30 Lovers Walk; s £35-42, d £66-74;) A typically lovely Dumfries sandstone Victorian villa opposite the train station, Ferintosh is a good-humoured place with excellent rooms and a warm welcome. These people have the right attitude towards hospitality, with comfortable plush beds, a free dram on arrival, and plenty of good chat on distilleries. The owner's original artwork complements the decor.

Huntingdon　　　　　　　　B&B ££
(01387-249071; www.thehuntingdonbandb.co.uk; 32 Lovers Walk; r £90;) This smart modernisation of a sturdy sandstone former day hospital offers high-standard B&B in four attractive, very commodious rooms with good modern bathrooms right by the train station. There's a pleasant front lawn and a gracious host. Room-only rates are available.

Cavens Arms　　　　　　PUB FOOD £
(01387-252896; www.facebook.com/cavens.arms.9; 20 Buccleuch St; mains £8-12; food 11.30am-8.30pm Tue-Sat, noon-8.30pm Sun;) Engaging staff, 10 real ales on tap and a warm, contented buzz make this a legendary Dumfries pub. Generous portions of typical pub nosh backed by a long list of more adventurous daily specials make it one of the town's most enjoyable places to eat, too. Gets packed on weekends (but staff will still try to find you a table).

Kings　　　　　　　　　　CAFE £
(01387-254444; www.kings-online.co.uk; 12 Queensberry St; snacks £2-6; 8am-5.30pm Mon-Sat, noon-4pm Sun;) This buzzy cafe in the centre of town doubles as a bookshop. It does tasty fair-trade coffee, has big windows for observing Dumfries life passing by and

serves toothsome sweet things, breakfasts and filled rolls.

ℹ️ Information

Dumfries Tourist Office (📞 01387-253862; www.visitscotland.com; 64 Whitesands; ⏰ 9.30am-4.30pm Mon-Sat Nov-Mar, 9.30am-5pm or 5.30pm Mon-Sat, 11am-4pm Sun Apr-Oct) By the river. Offers plenty of information on the region including a leaflet on the local Robert Burns trail. You can get a parking disc here to use in the riverside car park opposite.

ℹ️ Getting There & Away

BUS

Buses (Whitesands) run via towns along the A75 to Stranraer (£7.80, 2¼ hours, seven daily Monday to Saturday, three on Sunday) as well as to Castle Douglas and Kirkcudbright. Buses 101 and 102 run to/from Edinburgh (£10, 2¾ to three hours, four to seven daily), via Moffat and Biggar.

TRAIN

There are trains between Carlisle and Dumfries (£11.40, 40 minutes, every hour or two), and direct trains between Dumfries and Glasgow (£17.10, 1¾ hours, nine daily Monday to Saturday). Services are reduced on Sundays.

South of Dumfries

The scenic area south of Dumfries, with a picturesque coastline, is well worth exploring. Several excellent sights dot the region; there are also good family-friendly activities.

👁 Sights & Activities

★ Caerlaverock Castle   CASTLE

(HES; 📞 01387-770244; www.historicenvironment.scot; Glencaple; adult/child £6/3.60; ⏰ 9.30am-5.30pm Apr-Sep, 10am-4pm Oct-Mar) The ruins of Caerlaverock Castle, by Glencaple on a beautiful stretch of the Solway coast, are among the loveliest in Britain. Surrounded by a moat, lawns and stands of trees, the unusual pink-stoned triangular castle looks impregnable. In fact, it fell several times, most famously when it was attacked in 1300 by Edward I: the siege became the subject of an epic poem, 'The Siege of Caerlaverock'.

Caerlaverock
Wetland Centre   NATURE RESERVE

(📞 01387-770200; www.wwt.org.uk/caerlaverock; Eastpark Farm; adult/child £7.90/4.54, free for WWT members; ⏰ 10am-5pm; 🚼) This protects 546 hectares of salt marsh and mudflats, the habitat for numerous birds, including barnacle

geese. There are various activities, including badger-watching, dawn goose flights and child-focused events. It also has a good bookshop for nature watchers, and a coffee shop that serves organic food. Accommodation in private rooms with a shared kitchen (double £60 to £84) is available, too.

Mabie Farm Park   FARM

(📞 01387-259666; www.mabiefarmpark.co.uk; Burnside Farm, Mabie; adult/child/family £8/7.50/30; ⏰ 10am-5pm Apr-Oct, plus Sat & Sun Mar; 🚼) If your kids are complaining about historic sights and Robert Burns, pack up the clan and get down to this spot, between Dumfries and New Abbey off the A710. It's a brilliantly run complex with plenty of animals and activities, including petting-and-feeding sessions, donkey rides, go-karting, slides, a soft play area, picnic spots...the list goes on. Put a full day aside.

7stanes Mabie   MOUNTAIN BIKING

(www.7stanesmountainbiking.com; A710) **FREE** Mabie Forest Park is one of southern Scotland's 7stanes mountain-biking hubs, set among forested hills a couple of miles north of New Abbey. There are nearly 40 miles of trails for all levels; the closest bike hire is in Dumfries. It's very close to the Mabie Farm Park, which is handy if you've got kids of different ages.

🛏 Sleeping

Mabie House Hotel   HOTEL **££**

(📞 01387-263188; www.mabiehousehotel.co.uk; s £45, d £90-120, ste £170; 🅿️ 🛜 🐾) Four miles north of New Abbey, this welcoming country-house hotel (built in 1715) is a great base, especially for families, as the farm park and mountain-biking trails are nearby. Rooms are stylish and luxurious, offering excellent comfort at fair prices. It often books out for weddings at weekends. Food is served from midday to 2.30pm and 5pm to 9pm.

ℹ️ Getting There & Away

Stagecoach (📞 01387-253496; www.stagecoachbus.com) buses run from Dumfries south to Caerlaverock and southeast to Annan via Ruthwell. New Abbey is served regularly from Dumfries.

Kirkcudbright

📞 01557 / POP 3400

Kirkcudbright (kirk-*coo*-bree), with its dignified streets of 17th- and 18th-century merchants' houses and appealing harbour, is the

DUMFRIES HOUSE

A Palladian mansion designed in the 1750s by the Adam brothers, **Dumfries House** (☑ 01290-425959; www.dumfries-house.org.uk; Cumnock; house tour adult/child £9/4; ⊙ tours 10.45am-3.30pm Sun-Fri, 10.45am & noon Sat Easter-Oct, 12.15pm & 1.45pm Sat & Sun Nov-Feb, closed mid-Dec–early Jan) is an architectural jewel: such is its preservation that Prince Charles personally intervened to ensure its protection. It contains an extraordinarily well-preserved collection of Chippendale furniture and numerous objets d'art. Visits are by guided tour; book ahead. There's a discount for Historic Environment Scotland members. The daily Grand Tour (adult/child £13/4) also takes you to the bedrooms upstairs and the grounds. There's a cafe here.

The house is located 13 miles east of Ayr, near Cumnock. Bus it from Ayr or Dumfries to Cumnock and walk or cab it the 2 miles to the house; you can also get a train from Glasgow to Auchinleck.

ideal base from which to explore the south coast. Look out for the nook-and-cranny closes and wynds in the elbow of beautifully restored High St. With its architecture and setting, it's easy to see why Kirkcudbright has been an artists colony since the late 19th century.

◉ Sights

Broughton House GALLERY
(NTS; ☑ 01557-330437; www.nts.org.uk; 12 High St; adult/child £7.50/6.50; ⊙ 10am-5pm Apr-Oct) The 18th-century Broughton House displays paintings by EA Hornel, one of the Glasgow Boys (he lived and worked here). The library, with its wood panelling and stone carvings, is probably the most impressive room. Behind the house is a lovely Japanese-style garden (also open 11am to 4pm Monday to Friday in February and March).

MacLellan's Castle CASTLE
(HES; ☑ 01557-331856; www.historicenvironment. scot; Castle St; adult/child £5/3; ⊙ 9.30am-1pm & 2-5.30pm Apr-Sep) Near the harbour, this is a large, atmospheric ruin built in 1577 by Thomas MacLellan, then provost of Kirkcudbright, as his town residence. Inside, look for the 'lairds' lug', a 16th-century hidey-hole designed for the laird to eavesdrop on his guests.

🛏 Sleeping & Eating

Anchorlee B&B ££
(☑ 01557-330197; www.anchorlee.co.uk; 95 St Mary St; s/d £68/80; ⊙ Easter-Dec; 🅿 🛜 🐾) This elegant residence on the main road offers great hospitality from its cordial hosts. Four lovely rooms offer plenty of space; number four is an appealing split-level affair overlooking the garden. Breakfast is excellent.

★**Selkirk Arms Hotel** HOTEL ££
(☑ 01557-330402; www.selkirkarmshotel.co.uk; High St; s/d £90/120, compact d £99; 🅿 @ 🛜 🐾) What a haven of hospitality this is. Rooms look great with a stylish purply finish and slate-floored bathrooms. Wood furnishings and views over the back garden give some of them an extra rustic appeal. There's a good **restaurant** (mains £11-17; ⊙ noon-2pm & 6-9pm; 🅿 🛜 🐾) as well as a cute gin and prosecco bar. Staff are happy to be there, and you will be, too.

Garret BOUTIQUE HOTEL ££
(☑ 01557-330797; www.thegarrethotel.co.uk; 116 High St; s/d £75/95, superior d £105; 🛜) This hotel wasn't quite open when we last passed by but should be well worth a look. It's a noble Georgian town house with eight spacious, light rooms. There's also a cafe-bar with garden seating. The location on this lovely street is excellent.

★**Auld Alliance** SCOTTISH, FRENCH ££
(☑ 01557-330888; www.auldalliancekirkcudbright. co.uk; 29 St Cuthbert St; mains £14-23; ⊙ 6-9pm Thu-Sat, plus Wed Jul-Sep; 🛜) Overlooking the heart of town, this restaurant's cuisine is true to its name, which refers to the historic bond between Scotland and France. Local produce is given a Gallic and Mediterranean twist, with dishes like Galloway lamb tagine or local haddock encrusted with oatmeal and black olive tapenade.

ℹ Information

Kirkcudbright Tourist Office (☑ 01557-330494; www.visitscotland.com; Harbour Sq; ⊙ 11am-3pm Mon-Sat, 11am-5pm Sun Apr–mid-Jun, 9.30am-6pm Mon-Sat, 10am-5pm Sun mid-Jun–Aug, 10am-5pm Mon-Sat, 11am-3pm Sun Sep & Oct, 11am-4pm Mon-Sat Nov-Mar) Handy office with useful brochures detailing walks and road tours in the surrounding district. Its future was in doubt at the time of research.

ℹ Getting There & Away

Kirkcudbright is 28 miles southwest of Dumfries. Buses run to Dumfries (£4.50, 1¼ hours) via or changing in Castle Douglas (£2.50, 15 minutes). Change at Ringford or Gatehouse of Fleet for Stranraer.

Galloway Forest Park

South and northwest of the small town of New Galloway is 300-sq-mile Galloway Forest Park, with numerous lochs and great whale-backed mountains covered in heather and pine. The highest point is **Merrick** (843m). The park is criss-crossed by off-road bike routes and some superb signposted walking trails, from gentle strolls to long-distance paths, including the **Southern Upland Way** (☑ 01387-273987; www.southernuplandway.gov.uk).

Walkers and cyclists should head for **Glentrool** in the park's west, accessed by the forest road east from Bargrennan off the A714, north of Newton Stewart. Located just over a mile from Bargrennan is the **Glentrool Visitor Centre** (☑ 01671-840302; https://scotland.forestry.gov.uk; ⊙ 10.30am-4.30pm). The road then winds and climbs up to Loch Trool, where there are magnificent views.

The park is very family focused; look out for the booklet of annual events in tourist offices. It's also great for **stargazing**; it has been named a Dark Sky Park by the International Dark-Sky Association (www.darksky.org).

🏃 Activities

7stanes Glentrool   MOUNTAIN BIKING
(www.7stanesmountainbiking.com; Visitor Centre, Glentrool) **FREE** One of the 7stanes mountain-biking hubs. The Blue Route here is 5.6 miles in length and is a lovely ride climbing up to Green Torr Ridge overlooking Loch Trool. The Big Country Route is 36 miles of challenging ascents and descents that afford magnificent views of the Galloway Forest. It takes a full day and is not for wimps.

Galloway Red Deer Range   WILDLIFE WATCHING
(https://scotland.forestry.gov.uk; A712) **FREE** At the Galloway Red Deer Range you can observe Britain's largest land-based beast from a hide and viewing area. During rutting season in autumn, it's a bit like watching a bullfight as snorting, charging stags compete for the harem. From April to September there are guided ranger-led visits (adult/child £8/5) to see these impressive beasts.

Raiders' Road   SCENIC DRIVE
(http://scotland.forestry.gov.uk; per vehicle £2; ⊙ vehicles Apr-Oct; 🚗) About a mile west of Clatteringshaws Visitor Centre, Raiders' Rd is a 10-mile drive through the forest with various picnic spots, child-friendly activities and short walks marked along the way. Drive slowly as there's plenty of wildlife about. One of the nicest spots is a cascade where you might spot otters. Walkers and cyclists can access the road year-round.

Red Kite Feeding Station   BIRDWATCHING
(☑ 01644-450202; www.bellymackhillfarm.co.uk; Bellymack Hill Farm, Laurieston; adult/child £5/free; ⊙ noon-4pm) Just off the B795, this farm has daily feedings of red kites at 2pm. There's a visitor centre (with cafe) here, from which you can observe these beautiful raptors, which congregate from about 1pm. There are often RSPB (Royal Society for the Protection of Birds) volunteers present who can inform you about the birds' lifestyles.

Stargazing Scotland   OUTDOORS
(☑ 07340 518498; www.stargazingscotland.com) The couple here will take you out under the dark skies of Galloway Forest Park for a stargazing session. They run a few public sessions through the year (adult/child £15/8) so check their online calendar, but you're more likely to have to book a private tour (for one/two £75/89).

ℹ️ Information

Clatteringshaws Visitor Centre (☑ 01644-420285; https://scotland.forestry.gov.uk; A712; ⊙ 10am-4pm) On Clatteringshaws Loch's shore, 6 miles west of New Galloway, this is basically a cafe but has the odd display panel. From here you can walk to a replica of a Romano-British homestead (0.5 miles), and to Bruce's Stone (1 mile), where Robert the Bruce is said to have rested after defeating the English at the Battle of Rapploch Moss.

Kirroughtree Visitor Centre (☑ 01671-402165; https://scotland.forestry.gov.uk; off A75, Palnure; ⊙ 10am-5pm) This park information office 3 miles east of Newton Stewart has a cafe and a nature-watching hide. This is one of the **7stanes mountain-biking hubs** (www.7stanesmountainbiking.com; Visitor Centre, Kirroughtree), and there's a good bike shop here (open 10am to 4pm) that does hires and repairs.

ℹ️ Getting There & Away

The scenic 19-mile A712 (Queen's Way) between New Galloway and Newton Stewart slices through the southern section of the park. It's the only road through the park, but no buses run along it. The nearest public-transport point for the western part of this road is Newton Stewart, for the east New Galloway. There's **bike hire**

(🚲 01671-401529; www.kirkcowancycles.co.uk; Victoria Lane; half-/full day £13/20; ⊙9am-5pm Mon-Sat) available in Newton Stewart.

Stranraer

📞 01776 / POP 10,400

The friendly but somewhat ramshackle port of Stranraer has seen its tourist mainstay, the ferry traffic to Northern Ireland, move up the road to Cairnryan. The town's still wondering what to do with itself, but there are good places to stay and lots to explore in the surrounding area.

◉ Sights

Castle Kennedy Gardens   GARDENS, CASTLE
(📞 01776-702024; www.castlekennedygardens. com; Sheuchan; adult/child £5.50/2; ⊙10am-5pm Apr-Oct, Sat & Sun Feb & Mar) Three miles east of Stranraer, these magnificent gardens are among Scotland's most renowned. They cover 30 hectares and are set on an isthmus between two lochs and two castles. The landscaping was undertaken in 1730 by the Earl of Stair, who used unoccupied soldiers to do the work. Buses heading east from Stranraer stop at the gate on the main road; it's a pleasant 20-minute stroll from here to the gardens' entrance.

Stranraer Museum   MUSEUM
(📞 01776-705088; www.dumgal.gov.uk; 55 George St; ⊙10am-5pm Mon-Fri, 10am-1pm & 1.30-4.30pm Sat) FREE This museum houses exhibits on local history and you can learn about Stranraer's polar explorers. The highlight is the carved stone pipe from Madagascar. Temporary exhibitions by local artists are also on display.

🛏 Sleeping & Eating

Ivy House   B&B £
(📞 01776-704176; www.ivyhouse-ferrylink.co.uk; 3 Ivy Pl; s/d £35/55, s without bathroom £30; 🖥) This is a great guesthouse that does Scottish hospitality proud, with excellent facilities, tidy en-suite rooms and a smashing breakfast. Nothing is too much trouble for the genial host, who always has a smile for her guests. Prices are excellent. The room at the back overlooking the churchyard is particularly light and quiet.

★**Thornbank House**   B&B ££
(📞 01776-706168; www.thornbankhouse.co.uk; Thornbank Rd; r £80; 🅿🖥🚳🐾) An exceptional place offering extremely comfortable and well-furnished modern rooms (one with a jacuzzi), Thornbank also offers excellent breakfasts and friendly, casual hospitality. It's already well out of the ordinary before you even consider the large indoor swimming pool and absolutely sensational vista over the bay to Ailsa Craig. One room has an outdoor deck to enjoy the view.

Henrys Bay House   SCOTTISH ££
(📞 01776-707388; www.henrysbayhouse.co.uk; Cairnryan Rd; mains £11-20; ⊙noon-2pm & 5-9pm Tue-Sat) Just east of the centre, this is Stranraer's best place to eat, with hearty portions of well-sourced meat and seafood and a welcoming vibe. There's a pleasingly old-fashioned feel to some of the dishes, while others have a more contemporary style. If the weather's fine, the deck is a great spot to be, overlooking the bay.

ℹ Getting There & Away

Stranraer is 6 miles south of the ferry port of Cairnryan, which is on the eastern side of Loch Ryan. A bus service coinciding with **Stena Line** (📞 08447 70 70 70; www.stenaline.co.uk) ferries runs between Stranraer and Cairnryan. Buses running frequently between Stranraer and Ayr also stop in Cairnryan. For a taxi, call **McLean's Taxis** (📞 01776-703343; www.mcleanstaxis. com; 21 North Strand St; ⊙24hr) (about £8).

Rhinns of Galloway

The Rhinns (or Rhins) of Galloway is a hammerhead-shaped peninsula west of Stranraer that runs 25 miles from north to south. Its coastal scenery includes rugged cliffs, tiny harbours and sandy beaches. Dairy cattle graze on the greenest grass you've ever seen, and the warm waters of the Gulf Stream give the peninsula the mildest climate in Scotland.

Pretty Portpatrick, set around a harbour, is a big drawcard. Further south, sleepy **Port Logan** has an excellent sandy beach and a famous botanical garden. From **Drummore**, a fishing village on the east coast, it's another 5 miles to the spectacular **Mull of Galloway**, Scotland's most southerly point.

Buses from Stranraer cover the peninsula.

◉ Sights

★**Mull of Galloway**   NATURE RESERVE
(www.mull-of-galloway.co.uk) Scotland's southernmost point is a spectacular spot, with windswept green grass and views of Scotland, England, the Isle of Man and Northern

THE MACHARS

South of Newton Stewart, the Galloway Hills give way to the softly rolling pastures of the triangular peninsula known as the **Machars**. The south has many early Christian sites and the 25-mile Pilgrims Way walk.

It's a little-visited area that's well worth exploring. Little **Wigtown** is officially Scotland's National Book Town, with more than a dozen bookshops offering an astonishingly wide selection of volumes, while **Whithorn** was the site of the first Christian mission beyond Hadrian's Wall, established in 397 by St Ninian. As such, the priory here is the earliest recorded church in Scotland, and now forms part of the fascinating **Whithorn Timescape** (The Whithorn Trust; ☑01988-500508; www.whithorn.com; 45 George St; adult/child £6/3.60; ☺10.30am-5pm Apr-Oct).

The nearby **Isle of Whithorn** was once an island but is now linked to the mainland by a causeway. It has an attractive natural harbour and colourful houses.

Bus 415 runs every hour or so (only twice on Sundays) between Newton Stewart and the Isle of Whithorn (£3.20, one hour) via Wigtown (15 minutes) and Whithorn.

Ireland. The lighthouse here was built by Robert Stevenson, grandfather of the writer, in 1826. The Mull of Galloway RSPB nature reserve, home to thousands of seabirds, is also important for its wildflowers. At the entrance to the reserve is a spectacular clifftop cafe. The former homes of the lightkeepers are available as accommodation; check out www.lighthouseholidaycottages.co.uk.

Logan Botanic Garden   GARDENS
(☑01776-860231; www.rbge.org.uk/logan; Port Logan; adult/child £6.50/free; ☺10am-5pm Mar-Oct, to 4pm early Nov) The mild climate in this southwestern part of Scotland is demonstrated at Logan Botanic Garden, a mile north of Port Logan, where an array of subtropical flora includes tree ferns and cabbage palms. The garden is an outpost of the Royal Botanic Garden in Edinburgh. There's a good cafe here.

Mull of Galloway Lighthouse   LIGHTHOUSE
(www.mull-of-galloway.co.uk; Mull of Galloway; adult/child £5/1.50; ☺10am-4pm Sat & Sun Apr-Oct, daily Jul & Aug) You can climb the lighthouse at the Mull of Galloway for views over four different political entities: Northern Ireland, Scotland, England and the Isle of Man. Check the website to coincide with a blast on the newly restored foghorn (outside of seabird nesting season).

🛏 Sleeping & Eating

★**Corsewall Lighthouse Hotel**   HOTEL £££
(☑01776-853220; www.lighthousehotel.co.uk; Kirkcolm; d £140-250; ⓟ🛜) It's just you and the cruel sea out here at this fabulously romantic 200-year-old lighthouse. On a

sunny day, the water shimmers with light, and you can see Ireland, Kintyre, Arran and Ailsa Craig. But when wind and rain beat in, it's just great to be cosily holed up in the bar-restaurant or snuggling under the covers in your room.

★**Knockinaam Lodge**   HOTEL £££
(☑01776-810471; www.knockinaamlodge.com; dinner & B&B s £215, d £360-460; ⓟ🛜🐾) For a real dose of luxury, head 3 miles southeast to this former hunting lodge in a dramatic, secluded location with grassy lawns rolling down to a sandy cove. It's where Churchill plotted the endgame of WWII – you can stay in his suite – and it's a very romantic place to get away from it all.

Gallie Craig   CAFE £
(☑01776-840558; www.galliecraig.co.uk; Mull of Galloway; light meals £3-8; ☺11am-4pm Sat-Wed Feb & Mar, 10am-5pm daily Apr-Oct, 11am-4pm Sat & Sun Nov) Invisible from above, thanks to its turf roof, this clifftop cafe offers spectacular vistas, great cakes and tasty savouries.

Campbell's   SEAFOOD ££
(☑01776-810314; www.campbellsrestaurant.co.uk; 1 South Crescent; mains £13-23; ☺noon-2.30pm & 6-9pm Tue-Sat, noon-2.30pm & 6.30-9pm Sun; 🛜) Fresh local seafood is the stock-intrade of this unpretentious local favourite. With Melba toast, prawn cocktails and curious cutlery, it's got a retro vibe, and the old-fashioned portion sizes are impressive, too. Choose one of the sharing platters and enjoy the flavour burst of locally caught fish or shellfish with harbour views. For sale at time of research.

1. Stilton cheese **2.** Sunday roast with Yorkshire pudding
3. Haggis **4.** Cream tea

WICKED DIGITAL/SHUTTERSTOCK ©

2

4

Flavours of Britain

Food fans know that Britain has finally shaken off its reputation for bland meals. Wherever you go it's easy to find quality dishes, celebrating tradition – often with a modern twist – with local ingredients.

For many visitors, the culinary day begins in a hotel or B&B with the 'Full English Breakfast' – also available as the Full Welsh, Full Scottish, Full Yorkshire etc – a plate full of mainly fried meat that might shock, but there's enough fuel here for several hours of energetic sightseeing.

Lunch or dinner is the time to try regional specialities such as haggis or salmon in Scotland, lamb or laver bread in Wales, Cumberland sausage in northern England, Stilton cheese in the Midlands, curry in Birmingham's Balti Triangle or London's Brick Lane, and seafood just about anywhere on the coast.

And if you're feeling peckish in between meals, look out for country cafes serving cream teas: scones, jam and cream, with that other British classic, a hot cup of tea.

BRITISH CLASSICS

Fish and Chips Longstanding favourite, best sampled in coastal towns.

Haggis Scottish icon, mainly offal and oatmeal, traditionally served with 'tatties and neeps' (potatoes and turnips).

Sandwich Global snack today, but an English 'invention' from the 18th century.

Laverbread Laver is a type of seaweed, mixed with oatmeal and fried to create this traditional Welsh speciality.

Ploughman's lunch Bread and cheese – pub menu regular, perfect with a pint.

Roast beef & Yorkshire pudding Traditional lunch on Sunday for the English.

Cornish pasty Savoury pastry, southwest speciality, now available country-wide.

Stirling &
Central Scotland

Best Places to Eat

➜ Cellar Restaurant (p842)

➜ Peat Inn (p840)

➜ Loch Leven's Larder (p841)

➜ Adamson (p839)

➜ Ninth Wave (p868)

Best Places to Stay

➜ Old Fishergate House (p837)

➜ Spindrift (p842)

➜ Victoria Square Guesthouse (p834)

➜ Monachyle Mhor (p860)

➜ Iona Hostel (p869)

Why Go?

The country's historic roots are deeply embedded in central Scotland. Key battles around Stirling shaped the nation's fortunes; significant castles from the region's history pepper the landscape; and Perth, the former capital, is where kings were crowned on the Stone of Destiny.

Arriving from Glasgow and Edinburgh, visitors begin to get a sense of the country further north as the Lowland scenery ramps up towards Highland splendour. It is here that the majesty of Scotland's landscape begins to unfold among woodlands and waterfalls, craggy hills and rushing rivers, with the silhouettes of soaring, sentinel-like peaks on the northern horizon.

Whether in the softly wooded country of lowland Perthshire or the green Fife coastline dotted with fishing villages, opportunities to enjoy the outdoors abound: walking, cycling and angling are all easy possibilities. The region also has some of the country's best pubs and restaurants, which greet weary visitors at day's end.

When to Go

➜ May is a magical time to explore before summer crowds arrive.

➜ July and August are the best times to enjoy seafood feasts in Fife and fresh raspberries in Blairgowrie.

➜ Autumn colours enliven walks in the Perthshire woods around Crieff, Comrie and Blairgowrie in October and November.

STIRLING REGION

Covering Scotland's wasp-like waist, this region has always been a crucial strategic point connecting the Lowlands to the Highlands. Scotland's two most important independence battles were fought here, within sight of Stirling's hilltop castle. William Wallace's victory over the English at Stirling Bridge in 1297, followed by Robert the Bruce's triumph at Bannockburn in 1314, established Scottish nationhood, and the region remains a focus of much national pride.

ℹ Getting There & Around

Stirling lies on the main rail lines north from Glasgow and Edinburgh to Perth and Inverness, and is also linked to Glasgow and Edinburgh by fast motorways and frequent bus services.

Trains serve Stirling and Dunblane but not the rest of the region, so you'll be relying on buses if you don't have your own transport. **First** (☑ 01324-602200; www.firstgroup.com) is the main operator.

Stirling

☑ 01786 / POP 36,150

With an impregnable position atop a mighty wooded crag (the plug of an extinct volcano), Stirling's beautifully preserved Old Town is a treasure trove of historic buildings and cobbled streets winding up to the ramparts of its impressive castle, which offer views for miles around. Clearly visible is the brooding Wallace Monument, a strange Victorian Gothic creation honouring the legendary freedom fighter of *Braveheart* fame. Nearby is Bannockburn, scene of Robert the Bruce's pivotal triumph over the English in 1314.

The castle makes a fascinating visit, but make sure you also spend time exploring the Old Town and the picturesque Back Walk footpath that encircles it. Below the Old Town, retail-oriented modern Stirling doesn't offer the same appeal; stick to the high ground as much as possible and you'll love the place.

◉ Sights

★ **Stirling Castle**   CASTLE

(HES; www.stirlingcastle.gov.uk; Castle Wynd; adult/child £15/9; ⊙ 9.30am-6pm Apr-Sep, to 5pm Oct-Mar, last entry 45min before closing; Ⓟ) Hold Stirling and you control Scotland. This maxim has ensured that a fortress of some kind has existed here since prehistoric times.

You cannot help drawing parallels with Edinburgh Castle, but many find Stirling's fortress more atmospheric – the location, architecture, historical significance and commanding views combine to make it a grand and memorable sight. It's best to visit in the afternoon; many tourists come on day trips, so you may have the castle almost to yourself by about 4pm.

The current castle dates from the late 14th to the 16th century, when it was a residence of the Stuart monarchs. The undisputed highlight of a visit is the fabulous **Royal Palace**, which underwent a major restoration in 2011. The idea was that it should look brand new, just as when it was constructed by French masons under the orders of James V in the mid-16th century with the aim of impressing his new (also French) bride and other crowned heads of Europe.

The suite of six rooms – three for the king, three for the queen – is a sumptuous riot of colour. Particularly notable are the **Stirling Heads** – reproductions of painted oak roundels in the ceiling of the king's audience chamber (originals are in the Stirling Heads Gallery). The **Stirling tapestries** are modern reproductions, painstakingly woven by expert hands over many years, and based on 16th-century originals in New York's Metropolitan Museum. They depict the hunting of a unicorn – an event ripe with Christian metaphor – and are breathtakingly beautiful. An exhibition at the far end of the Nether Bailey (at the castle's northern end) describes their creation, often with a weaver on hand to demonstrate the techniques used.

The **Stirling Heads Gallery**, above the royal chambers, displays some of the original carved oak roundels that decorated the king's audience chamber – a real rogue's gallery of royals, courtiers, and biblical and classical figures. In the vaults beneath the palace is a child-friendly **exhibition** on various aspects of castle life.

The other buildings surrounding the main castle courtyard are the vast **Great Hall**, built by James IV; the **Royal Chapel**, remodelled in the early 17th century by James VI and with the colourful original mural painting intact; and the King's Old Building. The latter is now home to the **Argyll & Sutherland Highlanders Regimental Museum** (www.argylls.co.uk; with Stirling Castle admission free; ⊙ 9.30am-5pm Apr-Sep, 10am-4.15pm Oct-Mar).

Stirling & Central Scotland Highlights

❶ Stirling Castle
(p827) Admiring the views across ancient independence battlefields from this magnificent castle.

❷ St Andrews
(p836) Pacing through the historic birthplace of golf to play the famous Old Course.

❸ Scone Palace
(p847) Strutting with the peacocks at this elegant palace, near where Scottish kings were once crowned.

❹ East Neuk of Fife (p840) Feasting on local seafood in picturesque fishing villages.

❺ Culross (p844) Exploring the set of TV series *Outlander* in this perfectly preserved medieval village.

❻ Loch Leven Heritage Trail (p841) Hiking or biking around lovely Loch Leven on a scenic all-abilities trail.

❼ Glamis Castle (p848) Exploring the legendary setting for Shakespeare's *Macbeth*.

Stirling Castle

A FORTRESS TOUR

Stirling's a sizeable fortress, but not so huge that you'll have to decide what to leave out – there's time to see it all. Unless you've got a working knowledge of Scottish monarchs, head to the **1 Castle Exhibition** first: it'll help you sort one James from another. That done, take on the sights at leisure. First, stop and look around you from the **2 ramparts**; the views high over this flat valley, a key strategic point in Scotland's history, are magnificent.

Track back towards the citadel's heart, stopping for a quick tour through the **3 Great Kitchens**; looking at all that fake food might make you seriously hungry, though. Then enter the main courtyard. Around you are the principal castle buildings, including the **4 Royal Chapel**. During summer there are events (such as Renaissance dancing) in the **5 Great Hall** – get details at the entrance. The **6 Museum of the Argyll & Sutherland Highlanders** is a treasure trove if you're interested in regimental history, but missable if you're not. Leave the best for last – crowds thin in the afternoon – and enter the sumptuous **7 Royal Palace**. Take time to admire the beautiful **8 Stirling Tapestries**, skillfully woven by hand on-site between 2001 and 2014.

THE WAY UP & DOWN

If you have time, take the atmospheric Back Walk, a peaceful, shady stroll around the Old Town's fortifications and up to the castle's imposing crag-top position. Afterwards, wander down through the Old Town to admire its facades.

FAST FACTS

➡ Admission is free for Historic Scotland members. If you'll be visiting several Historic Scotland sites a membership will save you plenty.

➡ Vital Statistics: first constructed: before 1110; number of sieges: at least nine; last besieger: Bonnie Prince Charlie (unsuccessful); money spent refurbishing the Royal Palace: £12 million.

BRIAN JANNSEN / GETTOTOSTOCK ©

Museum of the Argyll & Sutherland Highlanders
The history of one of Scotland's legendary regiments – now subsumed into the Royal Regiment of Scotland – is on display here, featuring memorabilia, weapons and uniforms.

Prince's Tower

Guard Room Sq (Shop & Tickets)

Forework

Entrance

Robert the Bruce statue

Castle Exhibition
A great overview of the Stewart dynasty here will get your facts straight, and also offers the latest archaeological titbits from the ongoing excavations under the citadel. Analysis of skeletons has revealed surprising amounts of biographical data.

Royal Palace
The impressive highlight of a visit to the castle is this recreation of the royal lodgings originally built by James V. The finely worked ceiling, ornate furniture and sumptuous unicorn tapestries dazzle.

Great Hall & Royal Chapel
Creations of James IV and VI, respectively, these elegant spaces around the central courtyard have been faithfully restored. The vast Great Hall, with its imposing beamed roof, was the largest medieval hall in Scotland.

King's Old Building

Nether Bailey

⑥ ④

⑦ ⑧

⑤

③

Grand Battery

② ①

Great Kitchens
Dive into this original display that brings home the massive enterprise of organising, preparing and cooking a feast fit for a Renaissance king. Your stomach may rumble at the lifelike haunches of meat, loaves of bread, fowl and fishes.

The Stirling Tapestries
Copies of an exquisite series of 16th-century tapestries hang in the Royal Palace. They were painstakingly reproduced by hand using medieval techniques – each one took four years to make – and depict a unicorn hunt rich with Christian symbolism.

Ramparts
Perched on the wall you can appreciate the utter dominance of the castle's position atop this lofty volcanic crag. From its vantage points, you can see the site of Robert the Bruce's victory at Bannockburn and the monument to William Wallace.

Stirling

Stirling

Other displays include the **Great Kitchens**, bringing to life the bustle and scale of the enterprise of cooking for the king, and, near the entrance, the **Castle Exhibition**, which gives good background information on the Stuart kings and updates on current archaeological investigations. There are magnificent vistas from the ramparts towards the Highlands and the Ochil Hills.

Admission includes an audio guide, and free guided tours leave regularly from near the entrance. Your ticket also includes admission to nearby Argyll's Lodging.

★ Old Town Jail
HISTORIC BUILDING

(http://oldtownjail.co.uk; St John St; adult/child £6.50/4.50; ☉10.15am-5.15pm Jul–mid-Sep) This impressive Victorian prison building lay derelict from the 1960s until 2015, when it was reopened as a visitor attraction. Costumed guides lead tours around the former prison cells and up to the top of the observation tower, recounting gruesome tales of prisoners, punishments and executions along with fascinating facts about Stirling's history. Tours depart every 30 minutes.

National Wallace Monument
MONUMENT

(☎01786-472140; www.nationalwallacemonument. com; Abbey Craig; adult/child £9.99/6.25; ☉9.30am-5pm Apr-Jun, Sep & Oct, to 6pm Jul & Aug, 10am-4pm Nov-Feb, 10am-5pm Mar; P⊕) Perched high on a crag above the floodplain of the River Forth, this Victorian monument is so Gothic it deserves circling bats and croaking ravens. In the shape of a medieval tower, it commemorates William Wallace, the hero of the bid for Scottish independence depicted in the film *Braveheart*. The view from the top over the flat, green gorgeousness of the Forth Valley, including the site of Wallace's 1297 victory over the English at Stirling Bridge, almost justifies the steep entry fee.

The climb up the narrow staircase inside leads through a series of galleries, including the Hall of Heroes, a marble pantheon of lugubrious Scottish luminaries. Admire Wallace's 66 inches of broadsword and see the man himself recreated in a 3D audiovisual display.

Buses run from Stirling bus station to the visitor centre (£2.60, 10 minutes, every 30 minutes). From the visitor centre, walk or shuttle-bus up the hill to the monument itself.

Bannockburn Heritage Centre
MUSEUM

(NTS; http://battleofbannockburn.com; Glasgow Rd; adult/child £11.50/8.50; ☉10am-5.30pm Mar-Oct, to 5pm Nov-Feb; P⊕) Robert the Bruce's defeat of the English army on 24 June 1314 at Bannockburn established Scotland as a separate nation. The Bannockburn Heritage Centre uses interactive technology to bring the battle to life. The highlight is a digital projection of the battlefield onto a 3D landscape that shows the movements of infantry and cavalry (entry is by prebooked time slots). Bannockburn is 2 miles south of

Stirling; buses run from Stirling bus station (£2.20, 10 minutes, three per hour).

Outside the centre, the 'battlefield' itself is no more than an expanse of neatly trimmed grass, crowned with a circular monument inscribed with a poem by Kathleen Jamie, and a Victorian statue of the victor astride his horse. There has been much debate over exactly where the Battle of Bannockburn took place, but it was definitely somewhere near here on the southern edge of Stirling's urban sprawl. Exploiting the marshy ground around the Bannock Burn, Bruce won a great tactical victory against a much larger and better-equipped force.

Argyll's Lodging
HISTORIC BUILDING

(www.stirlingcastle.gov.uk; Castle Wynd; with Stirling Castle admission free; ☉12.45-4pm) This elegant building is Scotland's most impressive 17th-century town house, built for a wealthy local merchant and later acquired by the Earl of Argyll when he thought that Charles II might use Stirling Castle as a royal residence. It has been tastefully restored and gives an insight into the lavish lifestyle of 17th-century aristocrats. You can join a 20-minute guided tour (included in the Stirling Castle admission fee) or wander through the house at your leisure.

🛏 Sleeping

Stirling SYHA
HOSTEL £

(☎01786-473442; www.syha.org.uk; St John St; dm/tw £17.50/44; P@⑨) This hostel has an unbeatable location and great facilities. Though its facade is that of a former church, the interior is modern and efficient. The dorms are compact but comfortable, with lockers and en suite bathrooms; other highlights include pool table, bike shed and, at busy times, cheap meals on offer. Lack of atmosphere is a possible downside.

Willy Wallace Backpackers Hostel
HOSTEL £

(☎01786-446773; www.willywallacehostel.com; 77 Murray Pl; dm/tw from £16/48; @⑨) This highly convenient, central hostel is friendly, roomy and sociable – there's a piano and guitar in the common room. The colourful, spacious dormitories are clean and light, and it has free tea and coffee, a good kitchen and a laissez-faire atmosphere. Other amenities include bicycle hire and laundry service.

McGregor B&B
B&B £

(Sruighlea; ☎01786-471082; www.sruighlea.com; 27 King St; s/d £48/65; ⑨❀) This place feels

WORTH A TRIP

DOUNE

Magnificent **Doune Castle** (HES; www.
historicenvironment.scot; adult/child
£6/3.60; ⊙ 9.30am-5.30pm Apr-Sep,
10am-4pm Oct-Mar; P) is one of the best-
preserved medieval fortresses in Scotland, having remained largely unchanged
since it was built for the duke of Albany
in the 14th century. It has been used as
a set for the movie *Monty Python and
the Holy Grail* (1975) – the audio guide
is narrated by Python member Terry
Jones – and the TV series *Outlander* and
Game of Thrones. Highlights include the
cathedral-like Great Hall, and a kitchen
fireplace big enough to roast a whole ox.

The castle was a favourite royal
hunting lodge, but it was also of great
strategic importance because it controlled the route between the Lowlands
and Highlands. Mary, Queen of Scots,
once stayed here, as did Bonnie Prince
Charlie. There are great views from the
castle walls, and the lofty gatehouse is
very impressive, rising nearly 30m.

like a secret hideaway – there's just 'McGregor B&B' on the doorbell – but it's conveniently located smack bang in the centre of
town. You'll feel like a local staying here, and
there are eating and drinking places practically on the doorstep. It's a B&B that welcomes guests with the kind of warmth that
keeps them returning.

★**Victoria Square Guesthouse**   B&B **££**
(☑ 01786-473920; www.victoriasquareguesthouse.
com; 12 Victoria Sq; s/d from £84/120; P🛜)
Though close to the centre of town, Victoria Sq is a quiet oasis of elegant Victorian
buildings surrounding a verdant park. This
luxury guesthouse's huge rooms, bay windows and period features make it a winner –
there's a great four-poster room (from £145)
for romantic getaways, and some bedrooms
have views to the castle towering above. No
children.

Castlecroft Guest House   B&B **££**
(☑ 01786-474933; www.castlecroft-uk.co.uk; Bal-
lengeich Rd; d/tr £85/105; P🛜) Nestling into
the hillside behind the castle, this hideaway
feels like a rural retreat but is a short, spectacular walk from the heart of Stirling. The
lounge and deck area enjoy views over green

fields to the nearby hills, the rooms have
excellent modern bathrooms, and the welcome couldn't be warmer. Breakfast features
homemade bread, among other delights.

★**Friars Wynd**   HOTEL **££**
(☑ 01786-473390; www.friarswynd.co.uk; 17 Friars
St; r from £119; 🛜) Set in a lovingly restored
19th-century town house just a short walk
from the train station, Friars Wynd offers
eight bedrooms of varying size, many with
period features such as Victorian cast-iron
fire surrounds or exposed patches of original
red-brick walls. The 1st-floor rooms are directly above the bar and restaurant, so they
can be a little noisy at weekends.

✖ Eating

Darnley Coffee House   CAFE **£**
(☑ 01786-474468; www.facebook.com/Darnley
CoffeeHouse; 18 Bow St; mains £4-6; ⊙ 10am-4pm;
🛜⚙) Just down the hill from Stirling Castle,
this is a good pit stop for home baking, soup,
vegan food and speciality coffees (no espresso machine, though) during a walk around
the Old Town. The cafe is in the vaulted cellars of a 16th-century house where Darnley,
the lover and later husband of Mary, Queen
of Scots, once stayed.

Birds & Bees   PUB FOOD **££**
(☑ 01786-473663; www.thebirdsandthebees-stir
ling.com; Easter Cornton Rd, Causewayhead; mains
£11-22; ⊙ food served noon-2.30pm & 5-10pm;
P🛜♿) This pub is a bit of a local secret; it's
in a converted barn, hidden away on a back
road on the city's northern fringes. There's
faux-rustic decor and a crowd-pleasing pub-
grub menu that runs from nachos and tempura king prawns to steaks, burgers, ribs
and fish and chips. Outdoor seating and
plenty of space for kids to run around.

Breá   SCOTTISH **££**
(www.brea-stirling.co.uk; 5 Baker St; mains £15-22;
⊙ noon-9pm Sun-Thu, to 10pm Fri & Sat; 🛜⚙♿)
🍴 Bringing a bohemian touch to central
Stirling, this busy bistro has pared-back contemporary decor and a short menu showcasing carefully sourced Scottish produce,
including beef, venison, seafood, haggis and
Brewdog beers, as well as gourmet burgers,
pizza and a handful of vegetarian dishes.

Portcullis   PUB FOOD **££**
(☑ 01786-472290; www.theportcullishotel.com;
Castle Wynd; mains £10-18; ⊙ food served noon-
3.30pm & 5.30-9pm; 🛜) Built in stone as solid
as the castle that it stands below, this for-

mer school is just the spot for a pint and a pub lunch after your castle (p827) visit. With bar meals that would have had even William Wallace loosening his belt a couple of notches, a little beer garden and a cosy buzz indoors, it's well worth a visit.

Hermann's AUSTRIAN, SCOTTISH **££**
(✆01786-450632; www.hermanns.co.uk; 58 Broad St; mains £12-20, 2-/3-course lunch £12.50/15.50; ⊙noon-3pm & 6-10pm; ⚑⛄) This elegant Scottish-Austrian restaurant is a reliable and popular choice, with conservative decor oddly offset by magazine-spread skiing photos, but the food doesn't miss a beat and ranges from Scottish favourites such as Cullen skink (smoked haddock soup) to Austrian schnitzel and *spätzle* noodles. Vegetarian options are good, and quality Austrian wines provide an out-of-the-ordinary accompaniment.

🍷 Drinking & Nightlife

Brewdog BAR
(✆01786-440043; www.brewdog.com/bars/uk/ stirling; 7 Baker St; ⊙noon-midnight Sun-Thu, to 1am Fri & Sat; 🛜) The burgeoning Brewdog empire has come to Stirling, with a cool bar done out in designer-distressed timber offering no fewer than 16 taps dispensing craft beers from all over the world, including several from its own famously crowdfunded brewery near Fraserburgh in Aberdeenshire.

Settle Inn PUB
(✆01786-474609; 91 St Mary's Wynd; ⊙11am-11pm Mon-Sat, 12.30-11pm Sun; 🛜) A warm welcome is guaranteed at Stirling's oldest pub (1733), a spot redolent with atmosphere, with its log fire, vaulted back room, low-slung ceilings and Friday-night folk-music sessions. Guest ales, atmospheric nooks where you can settle in for the night, and a blend of local characters make it a classic of its kind.

❶ Information

Stirling Tourist Office (✆01786-475019; www.destinationstirling.com; Old Town Jail, St John St; ⊙10am-5pm) Accommodation bookings and internet access.

❶ Getting There & Away

BUS

The **bus station** (Goosecroft Rd) is on Goosecroft Rd. **Citylink** (✆0871 266 3333; www.citylink.co.uk) offers a number of services to/from Stirling, including:

Dundee £15.20, 1¾ hours, hourly
Edinburgh £8.70, 1¼ hours, hourly
Glasgow £8.20, 45 minutes, hourly
Perth £9.70, 50 minutes, at least hourly

Some buses continue to Aberdeen, Inverness and Fort William; more frequently a change will be required.

TRAIN

ScotRail (www.scotrail.co.uk) has services to/ from a number of destinations, including:

Aberdeen £34.40, 2¼ hours, hourly weekdays, every two hours Sunday
Dundee £15, one hour, hourly weekdays, every two hours Sunday
Edinburgh £9.10, one hour, twice hourly Monday to Saturday, hourly Sunday
Glasgow £8.30, 40 minutes, twice hourly Monday to Saturday, hourly Sunday
Perth £8.30, 35 minutes, hourly weekdays, every two hours Sunday

FIFE

The Kingdom of Fife (www.visitfife.com) as it calls itself – it was home to Scottish monarchs for 500 years – is a tongue of land protruding between the Firths of Forth and Tay that has managed to maintain an individual Lowland identity quite separate from the rest of the country. Though southern Fife is part of Edinburgh's commuter-belt territory, eastern Fife's rolling green farmland and quaint fishing villages are prime turf for exploration, and the fresh sea air feels like it's doing you a power of good. Fife's biggest attraction, St Andrews, has Scotland's most venerable university and a wealth of historic buildings. It's also, of course, the headquarters of golf and draws professionals and keen slashers alike to take on the Old Course – the classic links experience.

The **Fife Coastal Path** (www.fifecoastal path.co.uk) runs for 117 miles, following the entire Fife coastline from Kincardine to Newburgh. It's well waymarked, picturesque and not too rigorous, though winds can buffet. It's easily accessed for shorter sections or day walks, and long stretches of it can also be tackled on a mountain bike.

❶ Getting There & Around

The main bus operator here is Stagecoach East Scotland (www.stagecoachbus.com). The Fife Dayrider ticket (£9.10) gives one day's unlimited travel around Fife on Stagecoach buses.

LOCAL KNOWLEDGE

FIFE DISTILLERIES

There are several distilleries around Fife that are well worth a detour, and much less busy than the better-known ones on Speyside. All offer guided tours and tasting experiences.

Lindores Abbey Distillery (☑ 01337-842547; http://lindoresabbeydistillery.com; Abbey Rd, Newburgh; tours per person £12.50; ⊙10am-4pm Apr-Sep, 11am-4pm Oct-Mar; ℗) Opened in 2017, this distillery stands beside the ruins of Lindores Abbey, the site of the earliest written reference to Scotch whisky, which dates from 1494.

Eden Mill Distillery (☑ 01334-834038; www.edenmill.com; Main St, Guardbridge; tours per person £10; ⊙10am-6pm) This brewery-distillery produces beer and whisky but is best known for its range of craft gins made using locally grown botanicals. It's 4 miles north-west of St Andrews, towards Leuchars.

Kingsbarns Distillery (☑ 01333-451300; www.kingsbarnsdistillery.com; East Newhall Farm, Kingsbarns; guided tour £10; ⊙10am-6pm Apr-Sep, to 5pm Mar & Oct, shorter hours Nov-Feb; ℗) This distillery in Crail opened in 2015 and uses Fife-grown barley to create a distinctive Lowland whisky.

Fife Council produces a useful transport map, *Getting Around Fife*, available from tourist offices. Good public-transport information can be found at www.fifedirect.org.uk.

If you are driving from the Forth bridges to St Andrews, a slower but much more scenic route than the M90/A91 is along the signposted Fife Coastal Tourist Route.

St Andrews

☑ 01334 / POP 16,900

For a small town, St Andrews has made a big name for itself: firstly as a religious centre and place of pilgrimage, then as Scotland's oldest (and Britain's third-oldest) university town. But it is its status as the home of golf that has propelled it to even greater fame, and today's pilgrims mostly arrive with a set of clubs in hand. Nevertheless, it's a lovely place to visit even if you've no interest in the game, with impressive medieval ruins, stately university buildings, idyllic white sands and excellent guesthouses and restaurants.

The Old Course, the world's most famous golf links, has a striking seaside location at the western end of town – it's a thrilling experience to stroll the hallowed turf. Nearby is magnificent West Sands beach, made famous by the film *Chariots of Fire*.

◉ Sights

St Andrews Cathedral RUINS
(HES; www.historicenvironment.scot; The Pends; adult/child £5/3, incl castle £9/5.40; ⊙9.30am-5.30pm Apr-Sep, 10am-4pm Oct-Mar) All that's left of one of Britain's most magnificent medieval buildings are ruined fragments of wall and arch, and a single towering gable, but you can still appreciate the scale and majesty of the edifice from these scant remains. There's also a **museum** with a collection of superb 17th- and 18th-century grave slabs, 9th- and 10th-century Celtic crosses, and the late-8th-century **St Andrews Sarcophagus**, Europe's finest example of early medieval stone carving.

Founded in 1160 and consecrated in 1318, the cathedral stood as the focus of this important pilgrimage centre until 1559, when it was pillaged during the Reformation. The bones of St Andrew himself lie beneath the altar; until the cathedral was built, they had been enshrined in the nearby **Church of St Regulus** (or Rule). All that remains of this church is **St Rule's Tower**, worth the claustrophobic climb for the view across St Andrews. The admission fee only applies for the museum and tower; you can wander freely around the atmospheric ruins.

St Andrews Castle CASTLE
(HES; www.historicenvironment.scot; The Scores; adult/child £6/3.60, incl cathedral £9/5.40; ⊙9.30am-5.30pm Apr-Sep, 10am-4pm Oct-Mar) The castle is mainly in ruins, but the site itself is evocative and has dramatic coastline views. It was founded around 1200 as a fortified home for the bishop of St Andrews. After the execution of Protestant reformers in 1545, other reformers retaliated by murdering Cardinal Beaton and taking over the castle. They spent almost a year holed up, during which time they and their attackers dug a complex of **siege tunnels**; you can walk (or stoop) along their damp, mossy lengths.

British Golf Museum MUSEUM
(www.britishgolfmuseum.co.uk; Bruce Embankment; adult/child £8.50/free; ⊙9.30am-5pm Mon-Sat, 10am-5pm Sun Apr-Oct, 10am-4pm daily Nov-Mar) This museum provides a comprehensive overview of the history and development of the game and the role of St Andrews in it. The huge collection ranges from the world's oldest set of clubs (late 17th century, used with feather-stuffed golf balls) to modern equipment, trophies and clothing, and there's a large collection of memorabilia from Open winners both male and female, including Tiger Woods' sweat-stained Nike cap.

✨ Festivals & Events

Open Championship SPORTS
(www.theopen.com; ⊙Jul) One of international golf's four major championships. The tournament venue changes from year to year, and comes to St Andrews every five years (next in 2021) – check the website for future venues.

St Andrews Highland Games CULTURAL
(www.standrewhighlandgames.co.uk; adult/child £7/4; ⊙Jul) Held on the North Haugh on the last Sunday in July.

🛏 Sleeping

St Andrews Tourist Hostel HOSTEL £
(☑01334-479911; www.hostelsstandrews.com; St Marys Pl; dm £14.50-18.50; @📶) Laid back and central, this hostel is the only backpacker accommodation in town. Occupying a stately old building, it has high corniced ceilings, especially in the huge lounge. There's

a laissez-faire approach that can verge on chaotic at times, but the staff and location can't be beaten. Reception closed between 2pm and 5pm.

★**Fairways of St Andrews** B&B ££
(☑01334-479513; www.fairwaysofstandrews.co.uk; 8a Golf Pl; d £105-140; 📶) Just a few paces from golf's most famous 18th green, this is more like a boutique hotel than a B&B, despite its small size. There are just three superstylish rooms; the best, on the top floor, is huge and has its own balcony with views over the Old Course.

★**Old Fishergate House** B&B ££
(☑01334-470874; www.oldfishergatehouse.co.uk; North Castle St; r £115-125; 📶) This historic 17th-century town house, furnished with period pieces, is in the oldest part of town, close to the cathedral. The two twin rooms are very spacious and even have their own sitting room. On a scale of one to 10 for quaintness, we'd rate it a 9½. The cracking breakfast menu features pancakes with maple syrup, and smoked-haddock omelette.

Five Pilmour Place B&B ££
(☑01334-478665; www.5pilmourplace.com; 5 Pilmour Pl; s/d from £80/120; 📶) Just around the corner from the Old Course (p837), this luxurious and intimate spot offers stylish, compact rooms with plenty of designer touches. The king-size beds are especially comfortable, and the lounge area is an Edwardian-style retreat of leather armchairs, polished wood and swagged curtains.

ST ANDREWS OLD COURSE

The **Old Course** (☑Reservations Department 01334-466718; www.standrews.com; Golf Pl) is the oldest and most famous golf course in the world. Golf has been played here since the 15th century – by 1457 it was apparently so popular that James II had to ban it because it was interfering with his troops' archery practice.

To play the Old Course, you'll need to book in advance via the website, or by contacting the Reservations Department. Reservations open on the last Wednesday in August the year before you wish to play. No bookings are taken for weekends or for September (check the latest guidelines on the website).

Unless you've booked months in advance, getting a tee-off time is literally a lottery; enter the ballot at the **caddie office** (☑01334-466666; West Sands Rd) (or by phone) before 2pm two days before you wish to play (there's no Sunday play). Be warned that applications by ballot are normally heavily oversubscribed, and green fees are £180 in summer.

A caddie for your round costs £50 plus tip. If you play on a windy day, expect those scores to balloon: Nick Faldo famously stated, 'When it blows here, even the seagulls walk'.

There are also **guided walks** (www.standrews.com/walk; per person £10; ⊙11am & 2pm daily Apr-Sep), and you are free to walk over the course on Sunday, or follow the footpaths around the edge at any time.

St Andrews

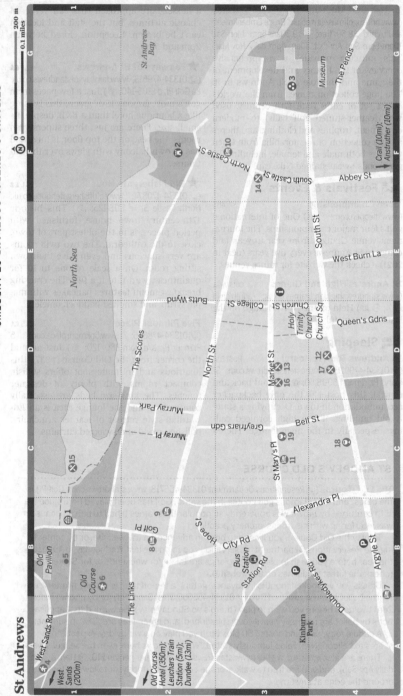

0 — 200 m
0 — 0.1 miles

West Sands (200m)
West Sands Rd
Old Course Hotel (350m); Leuchars Train Station (5mi); Dundee (13mi)
Crail (10mi); Anstruther (10mi)

St Andrews Bay
North Sea

Old Pavilion
Old Course
The Links
Golf Pl
The Scores
North St
Murray Park
Murray Pl
Murray Pl
Greyfriars Gdn
St Mary's Pl
Bell St
Hope St
City Rd
Station Rd
Bus Station
Alexandra Pl
Doubledykes Rd
Argyle St
Kinburn Park
Butts Wynd
Market St
College St
Church St
Church Sq
Holy Trinity Church
Queen's Gdns
South St
West Burn La
North Castle St
South Castle St
Abbey St
Museum
The Pends

St Andrews

★ **34 Argyle St**   B&B **£££**
(☏07712 863139; www.34argylestreet.com; 34 Argyle St; r from £150; ☎) Set in a fine old stone-built house just west of the town centre, the Argyle has four luxurious, hotel-quality bedrooms with huge modern bathrooms of dark tile, chrome and glass (two of the four have free-standing bath tubs). Little touches like drinks offered on arrival, fresh flowers and sweets add to the atmosphere of hospitality.

Old Course Hotel   HOTEL **£££**
(☏01334-474371; www.oldcoursehotel.co.uk; Old Station Rd; r from £399; P☎✈) A byword for golfing luxury, this hotel is right alongside the famous 17th green (Road Hole) on the Old Course (p837) and has huge rooms, excellent service and a raft of facilities, including a spa complex. Fork out the extra £50 or so for a view over the Old Course. You can usually find good deals online.

✕ **Eating**

Tailend   FISH & CHIPS **£**
(www.thetailend.co.uk; 130 Market St; takeaway £5-9; ⊗11.30am-10pm) ✐ Delicious fresh fish sourced from Arbroath, just up the coast, puts this place a class above most chippies. It fries to order and the food's worth the wait. The array of exquisite smoked delicacies at the counter will have you planning a picnic or fighting for a table in the licensed cafe out the back.

Northpoint Cafe   CAFE **£**
(☏01334-473997; www.facebook.com/northpoint cafe; 24 North St; mains £4-8; ⊗8.30am-5pm Mon-Fri, 9am-5pm Sat, 10am-4pm Sun; ☎) The cafe where Prince William famously met his future wife, Kate Middleton, while they were both students at St Andrews serves good coffee and a broad range of breakfast fare, from porridge topped with banana to toasted bagels, pancake stacks and classic fry-ups. It's a bit too busy for its own good these days, so get in early for lunch.

★ **Adamson**   BRASSERIE **££**
(☏01334-479191; http://theadamson.com; 127 South St; mains £13-27; ⊗noon-3pm & 5pm-midnight Mon-Fri, 11am-midnight Sat & Sun; ☎⚑) Housed in the former post-office building, this loud and bustling brasserie panders to a youngish clientele of local families, well-heeled students and tourists with a crowd-pleasing menu of steaks and seafood. Service can be overeager or occasionally chaotic, but it all adds to the hectic buzz.

Mitchell's Deli   DELI, SCOTTISH **££**
(☏01334-441396; www.mitchellsdeli.co.uk; 110-112 Market St; mains £8-20; ⊗8am-10pm Sun-Thu, to 11pm Fri & Sat; ☎⚑) ✐ Railway-sleeper floors, cut-down-workbench tables and seats upholstered with old tweed jackets lend a utilitarian air to this excellent deli-cafe-restaurant where local produce is king. Breakfast (served till noon, 2pm on Sunday) includes free-range eggs Benedict, and avocado on sourdough toast, while the evening menu runs to fish and chips, mac and cheese, and burgers.

★ **Vine Leaf**   SCOTTISH **£££**
(☏01334-477497; www.vineleafstandrews.co.uk; 131 South St; 2-/3-course dinner £28/33; ⊗6-11pm Tue-Sat; ✐) ✐ Classy, comfortable and well established, the friendly Vine Leaf offers a changing menu of sumptuous Scottish seafood, game and vegetarian dishes. There's a wide selection within the set-price menu, all well presented, and an interesting, mostly old-world wine list. Reservations recommended.

★ **Peat Inn** SCOTTISH £££
(☑ 01334-840206; www.thepeatinn.co.uk; 3-course
lunch/dinner £25/55; ⊙ 12.30-2pm & 6.30-9pm
Tue-Sat; ℗) ✦ This superb Michelin-starred
restaurant, backed by a commodious suite
of **bedrooms** (s/d £230/250; ℗ 🤎), makes an
ideal gourmet break. The chef makes a great
effort to source premium-quality Scottish produce and presents it in innovative ways that
never feel pretentious or overmodern. The inn
is 6 miles from St Andrews; head southwest
on the A915, then turn right onto the B940.

The split-level bedrooms look over the
garden and fields beyond. Various all-
inclusive offers are available.

Seafood Ristorante SEAFOOD £££
(☑ 01334-479475; www.theseafoodrestaurant.com;
The Scores; mains £25-36; ⊙ noon-9.30pm Mon-
Sat, 12.30-9.30pm Sun) ✦ This stylish restaurant occupies a glass-walled room, built out
over the sea, with polished wooden floors,
crisp white linen, an open kitchen and panoramic views of St Andrews Bay. It offers top-
notch seafood and an excellent wine list; an
all-day menu offers smaller dishes between
lunch and dinner service. There's a three-
course lunch (£25) on weekdays only.

🍸 Drinking & Nightlife

St Andrews Brewing Co MICROBREWERY
(www.standrewsbrewingcompany.com; 177 South
St; ⊙ 11am-midnight; 🤎🚻🌮) Good beer, good
food and good company are the order of the
day in this friendly, modern brewpub, with
18 beers and ciders on tap (including several
of its own brews), more than 170 varieties in
bottles, and around 30 craft gins.

Vic BAR
(www.vicstandrews.co.uk; 1 St Mary's Pl; ⊙ 10am-
2am; 🤎) Warehouse chic meets medieval
conviviality in this strikingly restored student favourite. Walls plastered with black-
and-white pop culture give way to a handsome, high-ceilinged bar with sociable long
tables down the middle and an eclectic assortment of seating. Other spaces include a
more romantic bar, a dance floor and a deck
for smokers. There are regular events, including weekend club nights.

❶ Information

St Andrews Tourist Office (☑ 01334-472021;
www.visitscotland.com; 70 Market St; ⊙ 9.15am-
6pm Mon-Sat, 10am-5pm Sun Jul & Aug, reduced hours rest of year) Helpful staff with good
knowledge of St Andrews and Fife.

❶ Getting There & Away

BUS
All buses leave from the **bus station** (Station
Rd). Services include:

Anstruther £4.50, 25 minutes, hourly
Crail £4.50, 25 minutes, hourly
Dundee £8, 40 minutes, at least half-hourly
Edinburgh £12.50, two hours, hourly
Glasgow £12.50, 2½ hours, hourly
Stirling £9, two hours, every two hours Mon-
day to Saturday

TRAIN
There is no train station in St Andrews itself,
but you can take a train from Edinburgh (grab
a seat on the right-hand side of the carriage
for great sea views) to Leuchars (£14.70, one
hour, half-hourly), 5 miles to the northwest.
From here, buses leave regularly for St Andrews
(£3.20, 10 minutes, every 10 minutes), or a taxi
costs around £13.

East Neuk

This charming stretch of coast runs south
from St Andrews to the headland at Fife
Ness, then as far west as Earlsferry. Neuk
is an old Scots word for 'corner', and it's certainly an appealing nook of the country to
investigate, with picturesque fishing villages whose distinctive red pantiled roofs and
crowstep gables are a legacy of centuries-old
trading links with the Low Countries.

The Fife Coastal Path's most scenic
stretches are in this area. It's easily visited
from St Andrews, or even as a day trip from
Edinburgh, but also offers many pleasant
places to stay.

Crail
☑ 01333 / POP 1640
Pretty and peaceful, little Crail has a
much-photographed stone-built harbour
surrounded by quaint cottages with red-tiled
roofs. The village's history is outlined in the
Crail Museum (www.crailmuseum.org.uk; 62
Marketgate; ⊙ 11am-4pm Mon-Sat, 1.30-4pm Sun
Jun-Oct, Sat & Sun only Apr & May) **FREE**, but the
main attraction is just wandering the winding streets and hanging out by the harbour.
There are views across to the Isle of May.

◉ Sights

Cambo Walled Garden GARDENS
(www.camboestate.com; Cambo Estate; adult/child
£5.50/free; ⊙ 10am-5pm; ℗🚻🌮) Cambo Es-

LOCH LEVEN HERITAGE TRAIL

One of the best all-abilities hiking and biking routes in Scotland, this scenic 14-mile circuit (www.lochlevenheritagetrail.co.uk) of Loch Leven links Kinross Pier, the RSPB Loch Leven nature reserve, and the excellent **Loch Leven's Larder** (☑01592-841000; http://lochlevenslarder.com; Channel Farm; mains £6-11; ⊗9.30am-5.30pm; P 🗟 🛗 🐕) 🖉 farm shop and restaurant. Allow two hours to cycle the trail or five hours to walk it; you can hire bikes and mobility scooters at Kinross Pier. The circuit offers great views of the Lomond Hills, and there's a sandy beach northeast of Kinross.

You can also visit **Lochleven Castle** (HES; www.historicenvironment.scot; Kinross Pier; adult/child incl boat ride £7.50/4.50; ⊗10am-5.15pm Apr-Sep, to 4.15pm Oct, last sailing 1hr before closing; P), an island fortress and prison from the late 14th century, where Mary, Queen of Scots, was incarcerated in 1567. The castle is now roofless but basically intact and makes for an atmospheric destination – you cross to the island by boat (included in admission fee).

tate, 2.5 miles north of Crail, is the country seat of the Erskine family. Its walled garden, with an ornamental stream running through the middle, is famously beautiful in spring and summer, but also in January and February, when its spectacular displays of snowdrops are in flower. There's a visitor centre and cafe, and woodland walks that lead to the Fife Coastal Path, plus the kids can feed potatoes to the estate's pigs.

🛏 Sleeping & Eating

Selcraig House　　　　　B&B ££
(☑01333-450697; www.selcraighouse.co.uk; 47 Nethergate; s/d £40/80; 🗟🐕) Eighteenth-century Selcraig House is a characterful, well-run place with a variety of rooms and a friendly resident cat. Curiously shaped top-floor chambers will appeal to those who appreciate the quirky, while the fantastic four-poster-bed rooms will charm those with a taste for luxury and beautiful furnishings.

Lobster Store　　　　　SEAFOOD ££
(☑01333-450476; 34 Shoregate; mains £4-15; ⊗noon-4pm Tue-Sun Jun-Sep, Sat & Sun only Oct-Apr) This quaint little shack overlooking Crail harbour serves dressed crab and freshly boiled lobster that has been caught locally. You can have a whole lobster (split) or lobster rolls. This is no-fuss takeaway – there's a single table out the front, but you can find a place to sit and eat your catch anywhere around the harbour.

🛈 Getting There & Away

Crail is 10 miles southeast of St Andrews. Stagecoach (www.stagecoachbus.com) bus 95 linking Leven, Anstruther, Crail and St Andrews passes

through Crail hourly every day (£4.50, 35 minutes to St Andrews).

Anstruther

☑01333 / POP 3450

Once among Scotland's busiest fishing ports, cheery Anstruther (pronounced *en*-ster by locals) has ridden the tribulations of the declining fishing industry better than some, and now offers a pleasant mixture of bobbing boats, historic streets, and visitors ambling around the harbour grazing on fish and chips or contemplating a boat trip to the Isle of May.

👁 Sights

Scotland's Secret Bunker　　　MUSEUM
(www.secretbunker.co.uk; Troywood; adult/child £12.50/8.50; ⊗10am-6pm Mar-Oct, last entry 5pm; P) This fascinating – and chilling – monument to Cold War paranoia was built in the 1950s to serve as one of Britain's regional command centres in the event of a nuclear war. Hidden 30m underground and encased in nearly 5m of reinforced concrete, it houses two levels of austere operations rooms, communication centres, broadcasting studios, weapons stores and dormitories, filled with period artefacts and museum displays. The bunker is 3 miles north of Anstruther, off the B9131 to St Andrews.

Scottish Fisheries Museum　　　MUSEUM
(www.scotfishmuseum.org; East Shore; adult/child £9/free; ⊗10am-5.30pm Mon-Sat, 11am-5pm Sun Apr-Sep, 10am-4.30pm Mon-Sat, noon-4.30pm Sun Oct-Mar) This excellent museum covers the history of the Scottish fishing industry in fascinating detail, including plenty of

hands-on exhibits for kids. Displays include the **Zulu Gallery**, which houses the huge, partly restored hull of a traditional 19th-century Zulu-class fishing boat, redolent with the scents of tar and timber. Afloat in the harbour outside the museum is the **Reaper**, a fully restored Fifie-class fishing boat built in 1902.

Isle of May   NATURE RESERVE
(www.nature.scot) The mile-long Isle of May, 6 miles southeast of Anstruther, is a spectacular nature reserve. Between April and July the island's cliffs are packed with breeding kittiwakes, razorbills, guillemots, shags and more than 80,000 puffins. Inland are the remains of the 12th-century St Adrian's Chapel, dedicated to a monk who was murdered on the island by the Danes in 875. Several boats operating out of Anstruther harbour offer trips to the island.

Kellie Castle   CASTLE
(NTS; www.nts.org.uk; adult/child £10.50/7.50; ⊙ castle 11am-5pm daily Jun-Aug, Sat-Thu Apr, May, Sep & Oct; P) An authentic example of Lowland Scottish domestic architecture, Kellie Castle has creaky floors, crooked little doorways, superb decorative plasterwork and some marvellous works of art. The original part of the building dates from 1360; it was enlarged to its present dimensions around 1606. It's set amid beautiful gardens (open year-round from 9.30am to 6pm or dusk), 3 miles northwest of Pittenweem on the B9171.

🛏 Sleeping

★ Murray Library Hostel   HOSTEL £
(☏ 01333-311123; http://murraylibraryhostel.com; 7 Shore St; dm/d from £20/52; ☎) Set in a handsome, red-sandstone waterfront building that once housed the local library, this hostel is beautifully furnished and equipped. There are four- to six-bed dorms, many with sea views, plus private twins and doubles, a gorgeous modern kitchen and a comfortable lounge.

★ Spindrift   B&B ££
(☏ 01333-310573; www.thespindrift.co.uk; Pittenweem Rd; d/f £100/150; P☎🐾) Arriving from the west, there's no need to go further than Anstruther's first house on the left, a redoubt of Scottish cheer and warm hospitality. The rooms are elegant and extremely comfortable – some have views across to Edinburgh, and one is a wood-panelled recreation of a ship's cabin, courtesy of the sea captain who once owned the house.

Bank   INN ££
(☏ 01333-310189; www.thebank-anstruther.co.uk; 23 High St; s/d £60/100; ☎) Rooms at this modernised central pub, housed in a converted Victorian bank, offer loads of space, big beds and spotless bathrooms. The building backs onto the river mouth, meaning pleasant views from many of the rooms. The bar is enticing, with craft beers on tap and a glass-walled dining room overlooking the sea, which serves good pub grub (mains £11 to £20).

🍴 Eating

Anstruther Fish Bar   FISH & CHIPS £
(☏ 01333-310518; www.anstrutherfishbar.co.uk; 42-44 Shore St; mains £5-9; ⊙ 11.30am-9.30pm Sun-Thu, to 10pm Fri & Sat; 🖐) An award-winning chippie famous for its deep-fried haddock and chips, this place also offers classy takes on traditional takeaway dishes, including dressed crab and battered prawns (both locally caught).

Waterfront   INTERNATIONAL ££
(☏ 01333-312200; www.anstruther-waterfront.co.uk; 20 Shore St; mains £11-20; ⊙ 8am-10pm; 🖐) With tables spilling onto the pavement in summer, this perennially popular restaurant is a family favourite, offering a wide-ranging but top-quality menu that covers all bases from Tex-Mex fajitas and Italian lasagne to steaks, burgers and crispy Cajun chicken. But it also has a fine selection of Scottish seafood fresh from the local markets, including mussels, scallops, haddock and hake.

★ Cellar Restaurant   SCOTTISH £££
(☏ 01333-310378; www.thecellaranstruther.co.uk; 24 East Green; 5-course lunch/7-course dinner £35/60; ⊙ 6.30-9pm Wed, 12.30-1.45pm & 6.30-9pm Thu-Sun, no lunch Thu Oct-Mar) 🍃 Tucked away in an alley behind the Scottish Fisheries Museum (p841), the elegant and upmarket Cellar has been famous for its superb food and fine wines since 1982. The recipient of a Michelin star in 2015, it is at the top of its game, offering a creative menu built around Scottish seafood, lamb, pork and beef. Advance booking essential.

ℹ Getting There & Away

Stagecoach (www.stagecoachbus.com) bus X60 runs hourly from Edinburgh to Anstruther (£12.50, 2¼ hours) and on to St Andrews (£4.50, 25 minutes). Bus 95 links Anstruther to all the other East Neuk villages, including Crail (£2.40, 15 minutes, hourly).

Driving Tour
The Fife Coast

START STIRLING
END ST ANDREWS
LENGTH 76 MILES; ONE DAY

This tour links two of the most popular tourist towns in Central Scotland via the scenic delights of the Fife coast.

Head south from **1 Stirling** (p827) on the M9 and at Junction 7 turn east towards Kincardine Bridge. As you approach the bridge, follow signs for Kincardine and Kirkcaldy; then once across the Firth of Forth, follow the Fife Coastal Tourist Rte signposts to the historic village of **2 Culross** (p844). Spend an hour or so exploring the medieval buildings of Culross before continuing via the A994 to **3 Dunfermline** (p844), for a look at its fine abbey and palace ruins.

From Dunfermline take the M90 towards the Forth Road Bridge, but leave at Junction 1 (signposted A921 Dalgety Bay) and continue to the attractive seaside village of **4 Aberdour** for lunch at the Aberdour Hotel or the Room with a View restaurant. Stay on the A921 as far as Kirkcaldy, then take the faster A915 (signposted St Andrews) as far as Upper Largo, where you'll follow the A917 towards Elie; from here on, you will be following the brown Fife Coastal Tourist Rte signs.

5 Elie, with its sandy beaches and coastal footpaths, is a great place to stretch your legs and take in some bracing sea air before driving just a couple of miles further on to explore the neighbouring fishing villages of **6 St Monans** and **7 Pittenweem**. Just 1 mile beyond Pittenweem, **8 Anstruther** (p841) deserves a slightly longer stop for a visit to the Scottish Fisheries Museum, a stroll by the harbour and an ice cream. If time allows, you may want to detour inland a couple of miles to visit Kellie Castle or Scotland's Secret Bunker.

The final stop before St Andrews is the pretty fishing village of **9 Crail** (p840), where the late-afternoon or early-evening light will provide ideal conditions for capturing one of Scotland's most photographed harbours. A brisk hike along the coastal path towards Fife Ness, keeping an eye out for seals and seabirds, will round off the day before you drive the last 10 miles into **10 St Andrews** (p836).

DON'T MISS

FALKLAND

A 16th-century country residence of the Stuart monarchs, **Falkland Palace** (NTS; www.nts.org.uk; High St; adult/child £13/9; ⏰11am-5pm Mon-Sat, noon-5pm Sun Mar-Oct) is prettier and in many ways more impressive and interesting than the Palace of Holyroodhouse in Edinburgh. Mary, Queen of Scots, is said to have spent the happiest days of her life here 'playing the country girl' in the surrounding woods and parks, and James V, James VI and Charles II all stayed here on various occasions. Don't miss the world's oldest surviving real tennis court, dating from 1539.

Falkland village is 11 miles north of Kirkcaldy. Stagecoach (www.stagecoachbus.com) bus 64 links St Andrews to Falkland direct (£6.50, 1¾ hours, hourly Monday to Saturday, five on Sunday).

Dunfermline

☎ 01383 / POP 49,700

Dunfermline is a large and unlovely town, but it's rich in history, boasting the evocative Dunfermline Abbey, its neighbouring palace and the attractive grounds of Pittencrieff Park, the latter gifted to the city by local boy made good Andrew Carnegie (1835–1919), of US-steel-industry fame.

⊙ Sights

Dunfermline Abbey & Palace   RUINS
(HES; www.historicenvironment.scot; St Catherine's Wynd; adult/child £5/3; ⏰9.30am-5.30pm Apr-Sep, 10am-4pm Sat-Wed Oct-Mar) Dunfermline Abbey was founded by David I in the 12th century as a Benedictine monastery. The abbey and its neighbouring palace were already favoured by religious royals: Malcolm III married the exiled Saxon princess Margaret here in the 11th century, and both chose to be interred here. More royal burials followed, none more notable than that of Robert the Bruce, whose remains were interred here in 1329.

What remains of the abbey are the ruins of the impressive three-tiered refectory building, and the atmosphere-laden nave of the old church, endowed with geometrically patterned columns and fine Romanesque and Gothic windows. It adjoins the 19th-century **abbey church** (https://dunfermlineabbey.com; ⏰10am-4.30pm Mon-Sat, 2-4.30pm Sun Apr-Oct) **FREE** where Robert the Bruce lies entombed beneath the ornate pulpit.

Next to the refectory (and included in your abbey admission) is **Dunfermline Palace**. Once the abbey guesthouse, it was converted for James VI, whose son, the ill-fated Charles I, was born here in 1600. Below stretches the leafy, strollable **Pittencrieff Park**.

**Andrew Carnegie
Birthplace Museum**   MUSEUM
(www.carnegiebirthplace.com; Moodie St; ⏰10am-5pm Jul & Aug, 10am-5pm Mon-Sat, 1-4pm Sun Mar-Jun, Sep & Oct, reduced hours Nov) **FREE** The cottage where the great American industrialist and philanthropist Andrew Carnegie was born in 1835 is now a museum. Carnegie emigrated to the United States in 1848 and by the late 19th century had become the richest man in the world, but he gave away 90% of his wealth to build libraries, universities and schools all around the world. Dunfermline benefited by his purchase of Pittencrieff Park, beside the palace.

**Dunfermline Carnegie
Library & Galleries**   MUSEUM
(www.onfife.com/venues/dunfermline-carnegie-library-galleries; 1-7 Abbot St; ⏰10am-7pm Mon & Thu, to 5pm Tue & Fri, to 2pm Wed, to 4pm Sat, noon-4pm Sun) **FREE** Opened in 2017, this award-winning building houses a museum that charts the history of Dunfermline, with a massive Meldrum weaving loom as its centrepiece. There are also galleries that host art exhibitions, and a decent cafe.

❶ Getting There & Away

There are frequent buses between Dunfermline and Edinburgh (£6.50, 50 minutes), Stirling (£5.50, 1¼ hours) and St Andrews (£11.50, 1½ hours), plus trains to/from Edinburgh (£5.60, 35 minutes, half-hourly).

Culross

☎ 01383 / POP 400

Instantly familiar to fans of the TV series *Outlander*, in which it appears as the fictional village of Cranesmuir, Culross (*koo-ross*) is Scotland's best-preserved example of a 17th-century town. Limewashed white and yellow-ochre houses with red-tiled roofs stand amid a maze of cobbled streets, and the winding Back Causeway to the abbey is lined with whimsical cottages. The National Trust for Scotland (NTS) owns no fewer than 20 of the town's buildings.

As the birthplace of St Mungo, Glasgow's patron saint, Culross was an important religious centre from the 6th century. The burgh developed under local laird Sir George Bruce by extracting coal through ingenious tunnels extending under the seabed. When mining was ended by flooding of the tunnels, the town switched to making linen and shoes.

◉ Sights

Culross Palace   HISTORIC SITE
(NTS; www.nts.org.uk; Low Causewayside; adult/child £10.50/7.50; ☉11am-5pm Jul & Aug, to 4pm Apr-Jun, Sep & Oct) More large house than palace, the 17th-century residence of local laird Sir George Bruce features an interior largely unchanged since his time. The decorative wood panelling and painted timber ceilings are of national importance, particularly the allegorical scenes in the Painted Chamber, which survive from the early 1600s. Don't miss the recreation of a 17th-century garden at the back, with gorgeous views from the top terrace.

Culross Abbey   RUINS
(HES; www.historicenvironment.scot; Back Causeway; ☉dawn-dusk) FREE Ruined Culross Abbey, founded by the Cistercians in 1217, sits atop a hill in a lovely peaceful spot with vistas of the firth. The choir was converted into the parish church in the 16th century; it's worth a peek inside for the stained glass and the Gothic Argyll tomb.

❶ Getting There & Away

Culross is 16 miles east of Stirling, and 12 miles west of the Forth bridges. Buses run from Dunfermline (£3.20, 30 minutes, hourly) to Culross. Buses from Stirling (£9, 1½ hours, three daily) require a change at Falkirk.

DUNDEE & ANGUS

Angus is a fertile farming region stretching north from Dundee – Scotland's fourth-largest city – to the Highland border. It's an attractive area of broad straths (valleys) and low, green hills contrasting with the rich, red-brown soil of freshly ploughed fields. The romantic Angus Glens finger their way into the foothills of the Grampian Mountains, while the scenic coastline ranges from the red-sandstone cliffs of Arbroath to the long, sandy beaches around Montrose. This was the Pictish heartland of the 7th and 8th centuries, and many interesting Pictish symbol stones survive here.

Apart from the crowds visiting newly confident Dundee and the coach parties shuffling through Glamis Castle, Angus is a bit of a tourism backwater and a good place to escape the crowds.

Dundee

📞 01382 / POP 147,300
London's Trafalgar Sq has Nelson, Edinburgh's Princes St has Sir Walter Scott and Belfast has Queen Victoria outside City Hall. Dundee's City Sq, on the other hand, is graced – rather endearingly – by the bronze figure of Desperate Dan. Familiar to generations of British schoolchildren, Dan is one of the best-loved cartoon characters from the comic *Dandy,* published by Dundee firm DC Thomson since 1937.

Dundee enjoys perhaps the finest location of any Scottish city, spreading along the northern shore of the Firth of Tay, and has tourist attractions of national importance in Discovery Point and Verdant Works. Add attractive seaside town Broughty Ferry, and the Dundonians themselves – among the friendliest, most welcoming and entertaining people you'll meet – and Dundee is definitely worth a stopover.

The waterfront around Discovery Point has undergone a massive redevelopment, centred on the construction of the architecturally outstanding V&A Dundee museum of design, opened in 2018.

History

During the 19th century Dundee grew from its trading-port origins to become a major player in the shipbuilding, whaling, textile and railway engineering industries. Dundonian firms owned and operated most of the jute mills in India (jute is a natural fibre used to make ropes and sacking), and the city's textile industry employed as many as 43,000 people – little wonder Dundee earned the nickname 'Juteopolis'.

Dundee is often called the city of the 'Three Js' – jute, jam and journalism. According to legend, it was a Dundee woman, Janet Keillor, who invented marmalade in the late 18th century; her son founded the city's famous Keillor jam factory. Jute is no longer produced, and when the Keillor factory was taken over in 1988, production was transferred to England. Journalism still thrives, however, led by the family firm of DC Thomson. Best known for children's comics such as the *Beano* and the *Dandy,* and regional newspapers including the *Press and Journal,* Thomson is now the city's largest employer.

In the late 19th and early 20th centuries Dundee was one of the richest cities in the country – there were more millionaires per head of population here than anywhere else in Britain – but the textile and engineering industries declined in the second half of the 20th century, leading to high unemployment and urban decay.

In the 1960s and '70s Dundee's cityscape was scarred by ugly blocks of flats, office buildings and shopping centres linked by unsightly concrete walkways; most visitors passed it by. Since the mid-1990s, however, Dundee has reinvented itself as a tourist destination, and a centre for banking, insurance and high-tech industries, while its waterfront has undergone a major redevelopment. It also has more university students – one in seven of the population – than any other town in Europe, except Heidelberg.

⊙ Sights

★**V&A Dundee**   MUSEUM
(☏01382-305665; www.vandadundee.org; Riverside Esplanade; ⊗10am-5pm) FREE The centrepiece of Dundee's revitalised waterfront is this stunning building designed by Japanese architect Kengo Kuma. Opening in September 2018, it houses an outpost of London's Victoria & Albert Museum of art and design with exhibitions showcasing the work of Scottish designers past and present, from famous names such as Charles Rennie Mackintosh to modern creatives such as fashion designer Holly Fulton, alongside the best of art and design from around the world.

★**Discovery Point**   MUSEUM
(www.rrsdiscovery.com; Discovery Quay; adult/child £11.25/6.25; ⊗10am-6pm Mon-Sat, 11am-6pm Sun Apr-Oct, to 5pm Nov-Mar; P⌖) The three masts of Captain Robert Falcon Scott's famous polar expedition vessel the RRS *Discovery* provide a historic counterpoint to the modern architecture of the V&A Design Museum (p846). Exhibitions and audiovisual displays

in the neighbouring visitor centre provide a fascinating history of both the ship and Antarctic exploration, but *Discovery* is the star attraction. You can visit the bridge, the galley and the mahogany-panelled officers' wardroom, and poke your nose into the cabins used by Scott and his crew.

The ship was built in Dundee in 1900, with a wooden hull at least half a metre thick to survive the pack ice, and sailed for the Antarctic in 1901 where it spent two winters trapped in the ice. From 1931 it was laid up in London where its condition steadily deteriorated, until it was rescued by the efforts of Peter Scott (Robert's son) and the Maritime Trust, and restored to its 1925 condition. In 1986 the ship was given a berth in its home port of Dundee, where it became a symbol of the city's regeneration.

A joint ticket that gives entry to both Discovery Point and the Verdant Works costs £18.25/10.25/46 per adult/child/family.

★**Verdant Works**   MUSEUM
(www.verdantworks.com; West Henderson's Wynd; adult/child £11.25/6.25; ⊗10am-6pm Mon-Sat, 11am-6pm Sun Apr-Oct, reduced hours Nov-Mar; ⌖) One of the finest industrial museums in Europe, the Verdant Works explores the history of Dundee's jute industry. Housed in a restored jute mill, complete with original machinery in working condition, the museum's exhibits follow the raw material from its origins in India through to the manufacture of a wide range of finished products, from sacking to sailcloth to wagon covers for the pioneers of the American West. The museum is 250m west of the city centre.

Dundee Contemporary Arts   ARTS CENTRE
(www.dca.org.uk; Nethergate; ⊗10am-6pm Fri-Wed, to 8pm Thu) FREE Pioneering the development of the city's Cultural Quarter from its opening in 1999, Dundee Contemporary Arts is a centre for modern art, design and cinema. The galleries here exhibit work by contemporary UK and international artists, and there are printmakers' studios where you can watch artists at work, or even take part in craft demonstrations and workshops. There's also the Jute Café-Bar (☏01382-909246; www.jutecafebar.co.uk; 152 Nethergate; mains £8-18; ⊗10am-9.30pm; 🛜⌖).

McManus Galleries   MUSEUM
(www.mcmanus.co.uk; Albert Sq; ⊗10am-5pm Mon-Sat, 12.30-4.30pm Sun) FREE Housed in a solid Victorian Gothic building designed

SCONE PALACE

'So thanks to all at once and to each one, whom we invite to see us crowned at Scone.' This line from Macbeth indicates the importance of **Scone** (☑ 01738-552300; www. scone-palace.co.uk; Scone Estate; adult/child £12/8.50, grounds only £7.50/5.50; ⊙ 9.30am-6pm May-Sep, 10am-5pm Apr & Oct, last entry 1hr before closing; P), pronounced 'skoon', as the coronation place of Scottish monarchs. The original palace of 1580, laying claim to this historic site, was rebuilt in the early 19th century as a Georgian mansion of extreme elegance and luxury. Scone has belonged for centuries to the Murray family, earls of Mansfield, and many of the objects have a fascinating history attached to them (friendly guides are on hand to explain).

Ancient kings were crowned on **Moot Hill**, now topped by a chapel next to the palace. It's said that the hill was created by bootfuls of earth, brought by nobles attending the coronations as an acknowledgement of the king's rights over their lands, although it's more likely the site of an ancient motte-and-bailey castle. Here in 838 Kenneth MacAlpin became the first king of a united Scotland and brought to Scone the **Stone of Destiny**, on which Scottish kings were ceremonially invested. In 1296 Edward I of England carted this talisman off to Westminster Abbey, where it remained for 700 years before being returned to Scotland in 1997 (it now sits in Edinburgh Castle, but there are plans afoot to return it to Perth).

Scone Palace is 2 miles north of Perth; from the town centre, cross the bridge, turn left, and bear left along the footway beside the A93 until you reach the gates of the estate. From here, it's another half-mile to the palace (about 45 minutes' walk). Various buses from town stop here; the **tourist office** (☑ 01738-450600; www.perthshire.co.uk; 45 High St; ⊙ 9.30am-4.30pm Mon-Sat, 11am-4pm Sun, longer hours Jul & Aug) can advise.

by Gilbert Scott in 1867, the McManus Galleries are a city museum on a human scale – you can see everything there is to see in a single visit, without feeling rushed or overwhelmed. The exhibits cover the history of the city from the Iron Age to the present day, including relics of the Tay Bridge Disaster and the Dundee whaling industry.

Dundee Law   PARK

It's worth making the climb up Dundee Law (174m) for great views of the city, the two Tay bridges and across to Fife. The **Tay Rail Bridge** – at just over 2 miles long, it was the world's longest when it was built – was completed in 1887. The 1.5-mile **Tay Road Bridge** was opened in 1966. Dundee Law is a steep 1.5-mile walk northwest of the city centre, or you can drive to the summit.

HM Frigate Unicorn   MUSEUM

(www.frigateunicorn.org; Victoria Dock; adult/child £6.50/2.50; ⊙ 10am-5pm Apr-Oct, noon-4pm Thu-Sun Nov-Mar) Dundee's second floating tourist attraction – unlike the polished and much-restored RRS *Discovery* – retains the authentic atmosphere of a salty old sailing ship. Built in 1824, the 46-gun *Unicorn* is the oldest British-built ship still afloat – she was mothballed soon after launching and

never saw action. Wandering around below deck gives you an excellent impression of what it must have been like for the crew forced to live in such cramped conditions.

🛏 Sleeping

Athollbank   B&B £

(☑ 01382-801118; www.atholllbank.com; 19 Thomson St; s/d £30/48; 🐾🐾) A great-value B&B set on a quiet side street in the city's West End, Athollbank has smart, good-sized bedrooms (none are en suite, though) and is close to local pubs and restaurants.

Dundee Backpackers   HOSTEL £

(☑ 01382-224646; www.hoppo.com/dundee; 71 High St; dm £18, s/tw from £25/45; @🐾) This hostel is set in a beautifully converted historic building, with a clean, modern kitchen, a pool room and an ideal location right in the city centre. It can get a bit noisy at night, but that's because it's close to pubs and nightlife.

★ Malmaison   BOUTIQUE HOTEL ££

(☑ 01382-339715; www.malmaison.com/locations/dundee; 44 Whitehall Cres; r from £85; 🐾) Housed in a Victorian hotel building, this place has been refurbished in typical Malmaison style with period features such as intricate

GLAMIS CASTLE

Looking every inch the Scottish Baronial castle, with its roofline sprouting a forest of pointed turrets and battlements, **Glamis Castle** (www.glamis-castle.co.uk; adult/child £12.50/9; ⏰10am-5.30pm Apr-Oct, last entry 4.30pm; 🅿️🚼) claims to be the legendary setting for Shakespeare's Macbeth. A royal residence since 1372, it is the family home of the earls of Strathmore and Kinghorne – the Queen Mother (born Elizabeth Bowes-Lyon, 1900–2002) spent her childhood at Glamis (pronounced 'glams') and Princess Margaret (the Queen's sister, 1930–2002) was born here.

The five-storey, L-shaped castle was given to the Lyon family in 1372, but was significantly altered in the 17th century. Inside, the most impressive room is the drawing room, with its vaulted plasterwork ceiling. There's a display of armour and weaponry in the haunted crypt and frescoes in the chapel (also haunted). Duncan's Hall is named for the murdered King Duncan from Macbeth (though the scene actually takes place in Macbeth's castle in Inverness). As with Cawdor Castle, the claimed Shakespeare connection is fictitious – the real Macbeth had nothing to do with either castle, and died long before either was built.

You can also look around the royal apartments, including the Queen Mother's bedroom. Hour-long guided tours (included in admission) depart every 15 minutes; the last tour is at 4.30pm.

Glamis Castle is 12 miles north of Dundee. There are two to four buses a day from Dundee (£6.85, 1½ hour) to Glamis; change at Forfar.

wrought-iron balustrades complemented by delightfully over-the-top modern decor. The rooms on the south side overlook the redeveloped waterfront and the V&A museum. Room rates are excellent value; check website for special offers.

Shaftesbury Lodge HOTEL ££
(📞01382-669216; www.shaftesburylodge.co.uk; 1 Hyndford St; s/d from £60/80; 📶) The family-run, 12-room Shaftesbury is set in a Victorian mansion that was built for a jute baron and has many authentic period features, including a fine marble fireplace in the dining room. It's 1.5 miles west of the city centre, just off Perth Rd.

🍴 Eating & Drinking

★Bach CAFE £
(https://the-bach.com; 31 Meadowside; mains £5-11; ⏰9am-5pm; 📶📷🚼🐶) Easily the best breakfast spot in town (served till 11.45am weekdays, all-day brunch at weekends), this place sports a mix of Scottish, New Zealand, Asian and Mexican influences with delightful dishes such as Hebridean eggs (with Stornoway black pudding), homemade Kiwi burgers, nachos and *banh mi* (Vietnamese baguette sandwiches).

Parlour Cafe CAFE £
(📞01382-203588; 58 West Port; mains £6-9; ⏰8am-6pm Mon-Sat, 10am-3pm Sun; 📶📷) 🌿

Tiny but terrific, this friendly neighbourhood cafe is bursting with good things to eat including filled tortillas, savoury tarts, bean burgers, bagels and homemade soup, all freshly prepared using seasonal produce. Great coffee and cakes, too, but be prepared to wait for a table or squeeze in among the locals.

Pacamara CAFE £
(📞01382-527666; www.facebook.com/espressoh coffee; 302 Perth Rd; mains £6-9; ⏰9.30am-5pm Mon-Sat, to 4pm Sun; 📶📷) 🌿 Lots of locals will tell you that this cool cafe serves the best coffee in Dundee, but it also does a roaring trade in tasty and inventive breakfasts (served till 11.30am) such as free-range scrambled eggs with avocado and sourdough toast, and superb-value lunch dishes such as chicken and sriracha burger. Best to book a table.

★Castlehill MODERN SCOTTISH ££
(📞01382-220008; www.castlehillrestaurant.co.uk; 22 Exchange St; 3-course dinner £38; ⏰noon-2.30pm Fri & Sat, 5.30-10pm Wed-Sat) Thought by many to be worthy of earning Dundee's first Michelin star, the Castlehill is passionate about Scottish produce (the chef is a keen forager for wild herbs and fungi) and invests a lot of imagination into turning out beautifully presented dishes made with Angus lamb, Perthshire pork and Shetland

scallops – art on a plate. Five-course tasting menu is £55.

★**Newport**   SCOTTISH **££**
(📞01382-541449; http://thenewportrestaurant.co.
uk; 1 High St, Newport-on-Tay; small plates £6-14;
⏱noon-2.30pm Thu-Sat, noon-3pm Sun, 6-9.30pm
Wed-Sat; 🅿🖺) ✔ The setting is fabulous,
with vast windows overlooking the Firth of
Tay, and quirky 'recycled' decor that includes
the clever use of an old piano to store cutlery
and wine glasses. Graze on an assortment of
'small plates' showcasing the best of local
produce, or opt for the six-course tasting
menu (per person £55). It has vegetarian
and pescatarian options.

D'Arcy Thompson   BAR
(http://thedarcythompson.co.uk; 21-23 Old Hawkhill; ⏱11.30am-11pm Sun-Thu, to midnight Fri &
Sat; 🛜🖺) Bentwood chairs, old laboratory
stools and a handful of discreetly displayed
Victorian zoological specimens pay tribute
to the eponymous Dundee professor of natural history (1860–1948) who once worked
at the university across the road. Craft
beers, coffee and cocktails are on the menu,
as well as an above-average choice of pub
grub.

ℹ Information

Dundee Tourist Office (📞01382-527527;
www.angusanddundee.co.uk; 16 City Sq;
⏱9.30am-5pm Mon-Sat)

ℹ Getting There & Away

AIR
Two and a half miles west of the city centre, **Dundee Airport** (www.hial.co.uk/dundee-airport)
has daily scheduled services to London Stansted
airport, Jersey and Amsterdam. A taxi from the
city centre to the airport takes 10 minutes and
costs around £5.

BUS
The bus station is northeast of the city centre.
Some Aberdeen buses travel via Arbroath, oth-
ers via Forfar.
Aberdeen £18.30, 1½ hours, hourly
Edinburgh £17.50, 1½ hours, hourly, some
change at Perth
Glasgow £17.50, 1¾ hours, hourly
London from £21, 11 to 12 hours, National
Express, daily
Oban £38.20, 5½ hours, three daily, change at
Glasgow
Perth £8.20, 35 minutes, hourly

TRAIN
Trains from Dundee to Aberdeen travel via Ar-
broath and Stonehaven.
Aberdeen £20.90, 1¼ hours, twice hourly
Edinburgh £18.90, 1¼ hours, at least hourly
Glasgow £23.20, 1½ hours, hourly
Perth £8.30, 20 minutes, hourly

Arbroath
📞01241 / POP 23,900

Arbroath is an old-fashioned seaside resort
and fishing harbour, home of the famous Arbroath smokie (a form of smoked haddock).
The humble smokie achieved European
Union 'Protected Geographical Indication'
status in 2004 – the term 'Arbroath smokie'
can only be used legally to describe haddock
smoked in the traditional manner within an
8km radius of Arbroath.

◉ Sights

Arbroath Abbey   HISTORIC BUILDING
(HES; www.historicenvironment.scot; Abbey St;
adult/child £6/3.60; ⏱9.30am-5.30pm Apr-
Sep, 10am-4pm Oct-Mar) The picturesque,
red-sandstone ruins of Arbroath Abbey,
founded in 1178 by King William the Lion,
dominate the town of Arbroath. It is thought
that Bernard of Linton, the abbot here in the
early 14th century, wrote the famous Declaration of Arbroath in 1320, asserting Scotland's right to independence; an exhibition
in the beautifully preserved Abbot's House
includes a replica of the declaration. You can
climb part way up one of the towers for a
grand view over the ruins.

St Vigeans Museum   MUSEUM
(HES; 📞01241-878756; www.historicenvironment.
scot; St Vigeans Lane; adult/child £5/3; ⏱by appointment) About a mile north of Arbroath
town centre, this cottage museum houses
a superb collection of Pictish and medieval sculptured stones. The museum's masterpiece is the **Drosten Stone**, beautifully
carved with animal figures and hunting
scenes on one side, and an interlaced Celtic
cross on the other (look for the devil perched
in the top left corner). Check the website for
open days; otherwise phone ahead or ask at
Arbroath Abbey to arrange a visit.

🛏 Sleeping & Eating

Harbour Nights Guest House   B&B **££**
(📞01241-434343; www.harbournights-scotland.
com; 4 The Shore; s/d from £55/75; 🛜) With a

superb location overlooking the harbour, four stylishly decorated bedrooms and a gourmet breakfast menu, Harbour Nights is our favourite place to stay in Arbroath. Rooms 2 and 3, with harbour views, are a bit more expensive (from £80), but well worth asking for when booking.

But'n'Ben Restaurant　　　SCOTTISH **££**
(☑ 01241-877223; www.thebutnben.com; 1 Auchmithie; mains £8-26; ⊙noon-2pm Wed-Mon, 6-9pm Wed-Sat, 4-5.30pm Sun; Ｐ✿) 🍴 Above the harbour in Auchmithie, this cosy cottage restaurant with open fireplace, rustic furniture and sea-themed art serves the best of local seafood – the Arbroath smokie pancakes are recommended – plus great homemade cakes and desserts, and high teas on Sunday (£16). Best to book.

Gordon's Restaurant　　　SCOTTISH **£££**
(☑ 01241-830364; www.gordonsrestaurant.co.uk; Main St, Inverkeillor; 3-course lunch £35, 4-course dinner £65; ⊙12.30-1.30pm Sun, 7-8.30pm Tue-Sun, closed Sun dinner Oct-Apr) 🍴 Six miles north of Arbroath, in the tiny and unpromising-looking village of Inverkeillor, lies this intimate and rustic eatery serving gourmet-quality Scottish cuisine. There are five comfortable **bedrooms** (single/double from £85/110) for those who don't want to drive after dinner.

❶ Getting There & Away

BUS
Bus 140 runs from Arbroath to Auchmithie (£1.60, 15 minutes, six daily Monday to Friday, three daily on Saturday and Sunday).

TRAIN
Trains from Dundee to Arbroath (£5.90, 20 minutes, two per hour) continue to Aberdeen (£20.50, 55 minutes) via Montrose and Stonehaven.

ABERDEENSHIRE

Since medieval times Aberdeenshire and its northwestern neighbour Moray have been the richest and most fertile regions of the Highlands. Aberdeenshire is famed for its Aberdeen Angus beef cattle, its many fine castles and the prosperous 'granite city' of Aberdeen.

North of Aberdeen, the Grampian Mountains fall away to rolling agricultural plains pocked with small, craggy volcanic hills.

This fertile lowland corner of northeastern Scotland is known as Buchan; the old Scots dialect, the Doric, is in everyday use here (if you think the Glaswegian accent is difficult to understand, just try listening in on a conversation in Fraserburgh).

The Buchan coast alternates between rugged cliffs and long, long stretches of sand, dotted with picturesque little fishing villages such as Pennan, where parts of the film *Local Hero* were shot.

❶ Getting There & Around

The main bus routes link Aberdeen to Fraserburgh, Elgin, and Inverness via Huntly. There's a good network of rural bus services, too.

The only railway line runs from Aberdeen to Elgin and Inverness via Huntly and Keith.

Aberdeen

☑ 01224 / POP 195,000

Aberdeen is northeast Scotland's powerhouse, fuelled by the North Sea petroleum industry. Oil money made the city as expensive as London, with prices charged to match the depth of oil-wealthy pockets, though regular downturns in the industry see prices fall. Fortunately, most cultural attractions, such as the Maritime Museum and Aberdeen Art Gallery, are free.

Known throughout Scotland as the granite city, much of the town was built using silvery-grey granite hewn from the now-abandoned Rubislaw Quarry, at one time the biggest artificial hole in the ground in Europe. On a sunny day the granite lends an attractive glitter to the city, but when low, grey rain clouds scud in off the North Sea it can be hard to tell where the buildings stop and the sky begins.

Royal Deeside is easily accessible to the west, Dunnottar Castle to the south, sandy beaches to the north and whisky country northwest.

◎ Sights & Activities

★ **Aberdeen Maritime Museum**　　　MUSEUM
(☑ 01224-337700; www.aagm.co.uk; Shiprow; ⊙10am-5pm Mon-Sat, noon-3pm Sun) **FREE**
Overlooking the nautical bustle of Aberdeen harbour is the Maritime Museum, centred on a three-storey replica of a North Sea oil-production platform, which explains all you ever wanted to know about the petroleum industry. Other galleries, some situated in **Provost Ross's House**, the oldest

building in the city and part of the museum, cover the shipbuilding, whaling and fishing industries.

★ **Gordon Highlanders Museum** MUSEUM
(www.gordonhighlanders.com; St Lukes, Viewfield Rd; adult/child £8/4.50; ⊘ 10am-4.30pm Tue-Sat Feb-Nov; P ★) This excellent museum records the history of one of the British Army's most famous fighting units, described by Winston Churchill as 'the finest regiment in the world'. Originally raised in the northeast of Scotland by the 4th Duke of Gordon in 1794, the regiment was amalgamated with the Seaforths and Camerons to form the Highlanders regiment in 1994. The museum is about a mile west of the western end of Union St – take bus 11 or X17 from Union St.

Aberdeen Art Gallery GALLERY
(☎ 01224-523700; www.aagm.co.uk; Schoolhill; ⊘ 10am-5pm Tue-Sat, 2-5pm Sun) FREE Behind the grand facade of Aberdeen Art Gallery (closed for a major redevelopment until early 2019) is a cool, marble-lined space exhibiting the work of contemporary Scottish and English painters, such as Gwen Hardie, Stephen Conroy, Trevor Sutton and Tim Ollivier. There are also several landscapes by Joan Eardley, who lived in a cottage on the cliffs near Stonehaven in the 1950s and '60s and painted tempestuous oils of the North Sea and poignant portraits of slum children.

St Machar's Cathedral CATHEDRAL
(www.stmachar.com; The Chanonry; ⊘ 9.30am-4.30pm) FREE The 15th-century St Machar's, with its massive twin towers, is a rare example of a fortified cathedral. According to legend, St Machar was ordered to establish a church where the river takes the shape of a bishop's crook, which it does just here. The cathedral is best known for its impressive **heraldic ceiling**, dating from 1520, which has 48 shields of kings, nobles, archbishops and bishops. Sunday services are held at 11am and 6pm.

Clyde Cruises WILDLIFE WATCHING
(☎ 01475-722204; www.clydecruises.com; Commercial Quay; adult/child from £16/8; ⊘ Tue-Sun Jul-Aug, Fri-Sun Apr-Jun & Sep-Oct) Operates 45-minute cruises around Aberdeen's bustling commercial harbour, and 1½-hour trips (adult/child £25/12) outside the harbour to look for dolphins and other marine wildlife. If you're driving, park in Commer-

WORTH A TRIP

DUNNOTTAR CASTLE

A pleasant, 20-minute walk along the clifftops south of Stonehaven harbour leads to the spectacular ruins of **Dunnottar Castle** (☎ 01569-762173; www.dunnottarcastle.co.uk; adult/child £7/3; ⊘ 9am-5.30pm Apr-Sep, 10am-4.30pm or dusk Oct-Mar; P), spread out across a grassy promontory 50m above the sea. As dramatic a film set as any director could wish for, it provided the backdrop for Franco Zeffirelli's Hamlet (1990), starring Mel Gibson. The original fortress was built in the 9th century; the keep is the most substantial remnant, but the drawing room (restored in 1926) is more interesting.

cial Quay car park or Union Sq car park (both paid parking) across Market St from the harbour.

🛏 Sleeping

Aberdeen SYHA HOSTEL £
(SYHA; ☎ 01224-646988; www.syha.org.uk; 8 Queen's Rd; dm/tw from £15.50/36; @ 🕱) This unexceptional but good-value hostel, set in a granite Victorian villa, is a mile west of the train station. Walk west along Union St and take the right fork along Albyn Pl until you reach a roundabout; Queen's Rd continues on the western side of the roundabout.

★ **Dutch Mill Hotel** HOTEL ££
(☎ 01224-322555; www.dutchmill.co.uk; 7 Queen's Rd; s £60-85, d £70-95; P 🕱) The grand, granite-hewn, Victorian-era mansions that line Queens Rd house financial offices, private schools, medical practices and the occasional hotel – this one has nine bedrooms with beautifully understated modern decor, a popular bar and a conservatory restaurant. Rates are cheaper at weekends.

★ **Globe Inn** B&B ££
(☎ 01224-624258; www.the-globe-inn.co.uk; 13-15 North Silver St; s/d £72/78; 🕱) This popular pub has seven appealing, comfortable guest bedrooms upstairs, done out in dark wood with burgundy bedspreads. There's live music in the pub on weekends so it's not a place for early-to-bed types, but the price versus location factor can't be beaten. No dining room, so breakfast is continental, served on a tray in your room. Cheaper at weekends.

STIRLING & CENTRAL SCOTLAND ABERDEEN

Aberdeen

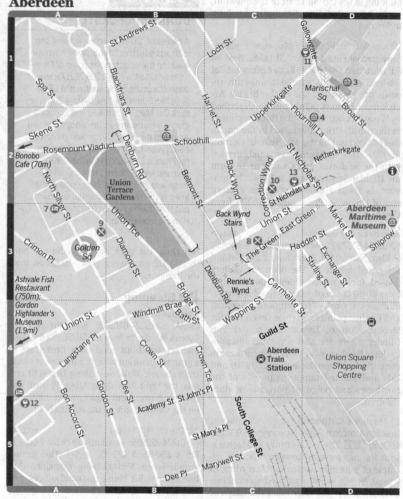

★ **Jays**   B&B **££**
(☎01224-638295; www.jaysguesthouse.co.uk; 422
King St; s/d from £70/100; ☺Mon-Thu; P🛜)
Located halfway between the city centre
(a 15-minute walk) and Old Aberdeen (a
10-minute walk), this elegantly decorated
Edwardian villa is a cosy nest of hospitality,
with welcoming owners who seemingly can't
do enough to help their guests enjoy their
stay. Popular, so book well in advance (note –
open Monday to Thursday nights only).

Bauhaus Hotel   BOUTIQUE HOTEL **££**
(☎01224-212122; www.thebauhaus.co.uk; 52-60
Langstane Pl; d/ste from £75/120; 🛜) Decor of

exposed brick and leather wall panels, slate-
lined bathrooms, and Corbusier armchairs
in the more expensive suites add a designer's
touch to this centrally located, good-value
hotel. Rates vary hugely, so check the website for special offers.

✕ Eating

Bonobo Cafe   VEGAN **£**
(www.bonobotribe.co.uk; 73-75 Skene St; mains £4-
7; ☺8am-4pm Tue-Fri, 9am-5pm Sat, 10am-4pm
Sun; ✎) ✿ Aberdeen has lagged behind a
bit in the vegetarian-restaurant stakes, so it
was good to see this 100% vegan cafe open in

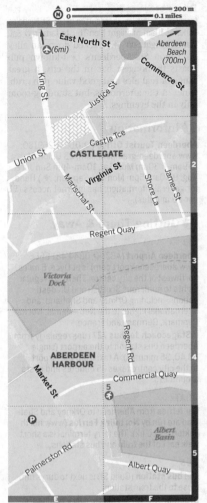

Aberdeen

◎ Top Sights
1 Aberdeen Maritime Museum D3

◎ Sights
2 Aberdeen Art Gallery B2
3 Marischal College D1
4 Provost Skene's House D2

◆ Activities, Courses & Tours
5 Clyde Cruises F4

⌂ Sleeping
6 Bauhaus Hotel A4
7 Globe Inn A3

✕ Eating
8 Café 52 .... C3
9 Granite Park A3
10 Moonfish Café C2

◎ Drinking & Nightlife
11 BrewDog D1
   Globe Inn .... (see 7)
12 Orchid A5
13 Prince of Wales C2

get a second one free (as if you'd want one by then!). It's 300m southwest of the west end of Union St.

★ **Café 52**   BISTRO **££**
(☑ 01224-590094; www.cafe52.co.uk; 52 The Green; mains lunch £5, dinner £13; ⊗ noon-midnight Mon-Sat, to 4pm Sun; ⊠🖉) This little haven of laid-back industrial chic – a high, narrow space lined with bare stonework, rough plaster and exposed ventilation ducts – serves some of the finest and best-value cuisine in the northeast (beetroot falafel with crispy capers and red-pepper aioli), and at incredible prices considering the quality on offer.

Granite Park   MODERN SCOTTISH **££**
(☑ 01224-478004; www.granitepark.co.uk; 8 Golden Sq; 2-/3-course lunch £23/28, dinner mains £18-33; ⊗ noon-2.30pm & 5-9.30pm Tue-Sat) 🖉 This smart and sophisticated restaurant and cocktail bar, tucked away on a quiet square, takes Scottish favourites such as sea trout, scallops and Aberdeen Angus beef and gives them a sprinkling of French or Mediterranean flair. Best to book.

★ **Silver Darling**   SEAFOOD **££**
(☑ 01224-576229; www.thesilverdarling.co.uk; Pocra Quay, North Pier; mains £15-21; ⊗ noon-2pm & 5.30-9.30pm Mon-Fri, noon-9.30pm Sat, noon-

2017. The menu runs from breakfast (served till noon, and all day on Sunday) of avocado on toast or smoked carrot and cream-cheese bagel, to lunch dishes such as smoky pinto bean and sweetcorn wraps.

Ashvale Fish Restaurant   FISH & CHIPS **£**
(www.theashvale.co.uk; 42-48 Great Western Rd; takeaway £5-10, sit-in £9-17; ⊗ 11.45am-10pm; 🖪) This is the flagship, 200-seat branch of the Ashvale, an award-winning fish-and-chips restaurant famed for its quality haddock. The Ashvale Whale – a 1lb fish fillet in batter (£12.45) – is a speciality; finish it and you

8pm Sun;) The Silver Darling (an old Scottish nickname for herring) is the place for a special meal, housed in a former Customs office at the entrance to Aberdeen harbour with picture windows overlooking the sea. Here you can enjoy fresh Scottish seafood while you watch the porpoises playing in the harbour mouth. Bookings are recommended.

★ **Moonfish Café**   MODERN SCOTTISH £££
(☑ 01224-644166; www.moonfishcafe.co.uk; 9 Correction Wynd; 2-/3-course dinner £30/36; ⊙ noon-2pm & 6-9.30pm Tue-Sat) The menu of this funky little eatery hidden on a backstreet concentrates on good-quality Scottish produce but draws its influences from cuisines all around the world, from simple scallops with chorizo, pine kernels and fennel, to rump of lamb with Jerusalem artichoke, mint and hazelnuts. Two-course lunch £16.50.

🍷 Drinking & Nightlife

★ **Orchid**   COCKTAIL BAR
(www.orchidaberdeen.com; 51 Langstane Pl; ⊙ 6pm-2am Sun-Thu, 5pm-3am Fri, 6pm-3am Sat) The winner of Scotland's Best Cocktail Bar 2017 is a relaxed and welcoming spot, quietly confident in its wide-ranging knowledge and expertise. Offers regular gin- and whisky-tasting sessions as well as mixology classes – the house cocktail is the Pink Orchid (vanilla vodka, black raspberry liqueur, cranberry, lime, sugar and egg white, shaken with ice and strained into a chilled glass).

BrewDog   BAR
(www.brewdog.com/bars/aberdeen; 17 Gallowgate; ⊙ noon-midnight Mon-Thu, to 1am Fri & Sat, 12.30pm-midnight Sun; 🕸) The original flagship bar of northeast Scotland's most innovative craft brewery brings a bit of industrial chic to Aberdeen's pub scene along with a vast range of guest beers from around the world.

Globe Inn   PUB
(www.the-globe-inn.co.uk; 13-15 North Silver St; ⊙ 11am-midnight, to 1am Fri & Sat) This lovely Edwardian-style pub with wood panelling, marble-topped tables and walls decorated with old musical instruments is a great place for a quiet afternoon drink. It serves good coffee, as well as real ales and malt whiskies, and has live folk music Tuesdays, and rock bands Friday and Saturday. It also has probably the poshest pub toilets in the country.

Prince of Wales   PUB
(www.princeofwales-aberdeen.co.uk; 7 St Nicholas Lane; ⊙ 10am-midnight Mon-Thu, to 1am Fri & Sat, 11am-midnight Sun;) Tucked down an alley off Union St, Aberdeen's best-known pub boasts the longest bar in the city, a great range of real ales and good-value pub grub. Quiet in the afternoons, but standing-room only in the evenings.

ℹ Information

Aberdeen Tourist Office (☑ 01224-269180; www.aberdeen-grampian.com; 23 Union St; ⊙ 9am-6.30pm Mon-Sat, 10am-4pm Sun Jul & Aug, 9.30am-5pm Mon-Sat Sep-Jun; 🛜) Handy for general information; has internet access (£1 per 20 minutes).

ℹ Getting There & Away

AIR

Aberdeen Airport (ABZ; ☑ 0844 481 6666; www.aberdeenairport.com) is at Dyce, 6 miles northwest of the city centre. There are regular flights to numerous Scottish and UK destinations, including Orkney and Shetland, and international flights to the Netherlands, Norway, Denmark, Germany and France.

Stagecoach Jet bus 727 runs regularly from Aberdeen bus station to the airport (single £3.40, 35 minutes). A taxi from the airport to the city centre takes 25 minutes and costs around £15.

BOAT

Car ferries from Aberdeen to Orkney and Shetland are run by **Northlink Ferries** (www.northlinkferries.co.uk). The ferry terminal is a short walk east of the train and bus stations.

BUS

The **bus station** (Guild St) is next to Jurys Inn, close to the train station.

Braemar £12.10, 2¼ hours, every two hours; via Ballater and Balmoral

Dundee £18.30, 1½ hours, hourly

Edinburgh £32.70, three hours, three daily direct, more frequent changing at Perth

Glasgow £32.70, three hours, at least hourly

Inverness £13.45, four hours, hourly; via Huntly, Keith, Fochabers, Elgin and Nairn

London from £36, 13½ hours, twice daily; National Express

Perth £25.70, two hours, hourly

TRAIN

The **train station** is south of the city centre, next to the massive Union Sq shopping mall.

Dundee £20.90, 1¼ hours, twice an hour

Edinburgh £35.50, 2½ hours, hourly

Glasgow £35.50, 2¾ hours, hourly

Inverness £29.70, 2¼ hours, eight daily

London King's Cross £175, seven to 11 hours, hourly; some direct, most change at Edinburgh

MORAY

The old county of Moray (*murr*-ay), centred on the county town of Elgin, lies at the heart of an ancient Celtic earldom and is famed for its mild climate and rich farmland – the barley fields of the 19th century once provided the raw material for the Speyside whisky distilleries, one of the region's main attractions for present-day visitors.

Elgin

📞 01343 / POP 23,130

Elgin has been the provincial capital of Moray for over eight centuries and was an important town in medieval times. Dominated by a hilltop monument to the 5th Duke of Gordon, Elgin's main attractions are its impressive ruined cathedral, where the tombs of the duke's ancestors lie, and its fine museum.

◉ Sights

★ **Elgin Museum** MUSEUM

(www.elginmuseum.org.uk; 1 High St; donations accepted; ⊙10am-5pm Mon-Fri, 11am-4pm Sat Apr-Oct) **FREE** Scotland's oldest independent museum is an old-fashioned cabinet of curiosities, a captivating collection artfully displayed in a beautiful, purpose-built Victorian building. Exhibits range from Ecuadorian shrunken heads to Peruvian mummies, and include mysterious Pictish carved stones and internationally important fish and reptile fossils discovered in local rocks.

Elgin Cathedral CATHEDRAL

(HES; www.historicenvironment.scot; King St; adult/child £7.50/4.50; ⊙9.30am-5.30pm Apr-Sep, 10am-4pm Oct-Mar) Many people think that the ruins of Elgin Cathedral, known as the 'lantern of the north', are the most beautiful and evocative in Scotland; its octagonal chapter house is the finest in the country. Consecrated in 1224, the cathedral was burned down in 1390 by the infamous Wolf of Badenoch, the illegitimate son of Robert II, following his excommunication by the Bishop of Moray. Guided tours are available on weekdays.

STIRLING & CENTRAL SCOTLAND ELGIN

THE SPEYSIDE WHISKY TRAIL

Visiting a distillery can be memorable, but only hardcore malthounds will want to go to more than one or two. Here are the top five whisky sights in the area.

Aberlour (📞01340-881249; www.aberlour.com; tours from £15; ⊙9.30am-5pm daily Apr-Oct, 10am-4pm Mon-Fri Nov-Mar; **P**) Has an excellent, detailed tour with a proper tasting session. It's on the main street in Aberlour.

Glenfarclas (📞01807-500257; https://glenfarclas.com; tours £7.50; ⊙10am-5pm Mon-Fri Apr-Sep, to 4pm Sat Jul-Sep, Mon-Fri Oct-Mar; **P**) Small, friendly and independent, Glenfarclas is 5 miles south of Aberlour on the Grantown road; the last tour leaves 90 minutes before closing. The in-depth Connoisseur's Tour (Fridays only, July to September) is £40.

Glenfiddich (📞01340-820373; www.glenfiddich.co.uk; admission free, tours from £10; ⊙9.30am-4.30pm; **P**) It's big and busy, but handiest for Dufftown and foreign languages are available. The standard tour (£10) starts with an overblown video, but it's fun and informative. The in-depth half-day Pioneer's Tour (£95) must be prebooked.

Macallan (📞01340-872280; www.themacallan.com; Easter Elchies, Craigellachie; tours £15; ⊙9.30am-5pm Mon-Fri; **P**) Macallan opened a new distillery and visitor centre in 2018. The 1¾-hour tours (maximum group of 10) should be prebooked. Lovely location 1 mile west of Craigellachie.

Speyside Cooperage (📞01340-871108; www.speysidecooperage.co.uk; tours £4; ⊙9am-5pm Mon-Fri, closed Christmas–early Jan) Here you can see the fascinating art of barrel-making in action. It's a mile from Craigellachie on the Dufftown road.

The biannual **Spirit of Speyside** (www.spiritofspeyside.com; ⊙May & Sep) whisky festival in Dufftown has a number of great events. It takes place in early May and late September; both accommodation and events should be booked well ahead.

🛏 Sleeping & Eating

Moraydale B&B **££**

(☑ 01343-546381; www.moraydaleguesthouse. com; 276 High St; s/d/f from £70/85/95; ⓟ 🛜 🐾) The Moraydale is a spacious Victorian mansion filled with period features – check out the stained glass and the cast-iron and tile fireplaces. The bedrooms are all en suite and equipped with modern bathrooms – the three large family rooms are particularly good value.

Southbank Guest House B&B **££**

(☑ 01343-547132; www.southbankguesthouse.co. uk; 36 Academy St; s/d/f from £70/90/145; ⓟ 🛜) The family-run, 15-room Southbank is set in a large Georgian town house in a quiet street south of Elgin's centre, just five minutes' walk from the cathedral and other sights. There may be a three-night minimum stay in high season.

★ **Drouthy Cobbler** CAFE, BAR **££**

(☑ 01343-596000; http://thedrouthycobbler.uk; 48a High St; mains £10-18; ⊙ food served 5-9.30pm daily, noon-4.30pm Sat & Sun; 🛜 🎵 🐾) This cafe-bar has a bistro-style menu that changes regularly but includes quality versions of popular dishes such as Cullen skink, mussels, bangers and mash, fish and chips and homemade burgers. It's tucked away up a side alley. It also hosts live music and comedy gigs in the evenings.

ℹ Getting There & Away

BUS

Aberdeen £13.45, 2½ hours, hourly
Banff & Macduff £11.30, 1¾ hours, hourly
Dufftown £5.95, 50 minutes, hourly Monday to Saturday
Inverness £11.30, 1½ hours, hourly

TRAIN

Aberdeen £19.90, 1¾ hours, five daily
Inverness £13.10, 40 minutes, five daily

Dufftown & Aberlour

Rome may be built on seven hills, but Dufftown's built on seven stills, say the locals. Founded in 1817 by James Duff, 4th Earl of Fife, Dufftown is 17 miles south of Elgin and lies at the heart of the Speyside whisky-distilling region. With seven working distilleries nearby, Dufftown has been dubbed Scotland's malt-whisky capital and is host to the biannual Spirit of Speyside (p855)

whisky festival. Ask at the whisky museum about the **Malt Whisky Trail** (www.maltwhisky trail.com), a self-guided tour around the local distilleries.

Aberlour (www.aboutaberlour.co.uk) – or Charlestown of Aberlour, to give it its full name – is even prettier than Dufftown, straggling along the banks of the River Spey. It is famous as the home of Walkers Shortbread, and has the Aberlour Distillery right on the main street. Attractions include salmon fishing on the Spey, nearby Knockando Woolmill and some lovely walks along the Speyside Way.

ℹ Getting There & Away

Buses link Elgin to Dufftown (£6.25, 50 minutes) hourly Monday to Saturday, continuing to Huntly and Aberdeen.

On summer weekends, you can take a train from Inverness or Aberdeen to Keith (£16.30, one hour, five daily), and then ride the Keith and Dufftown Railway to Dufftown.

LOCH LOMOND & THE TROSSACHS

The 'bonnie banks' and 'bonnie braes' of Loch Lomond have long been Glasgow's rural retreat – a scenic region of hills, lochs and healthy fresh air within easy reach of Scotland's largest city. Today the loch's popularity shows no sign of decreasing. The scenic Trossachs have likewise long been popular for their wild Highland beauty, set so close to the southern population centres.

Together, they are conjoined by the **Loch Lomond & the Trossachs National Park** (☑ 01389-722600; www.lochlomond-trossachs. org) – Scotland's first national park, created in 2002. The park extends over a huge area, from Balloch north to Tyndrum and Killin, and from Callander west to the forests of Cowal. The length of Loch Lomond means that access between the western part of the park and the Trossachs is either in the far north of the region via Crianlarich or the far south via Drymen. Walkers and cyclists can link the two more easily via the waterbuses that criss-cross Loch Lomond.

Loch Lomond

Loch Lomond is mainland Britain's largest lake and, after Loch Ness, the most famous of Scotland's lochs. Its proximity to Glasgow (20 miles away) means that the tourist honey pots of Balloch and Luss get pretty crowded in summer. The eastern shore, which is followed by the West Highland Way long-distance footpath, is quieter and offers a better chance to appreciate the loch away from the busy main road.

Loch Lomond straddles the Highland border. The southern part is broad and is-land-studded, fringed by woods and Low-land meadows. However, north of Luss the loch narrows, occupying a deep trench gouged out by glaciers during the Ice Age, with 900m mountains crowding either side.

🏃 Activities

The **West Highland Way** (www.west-highland-way.org) runs along the loch's eastern shore, while the **Rob Roy Way** (www.robroyway.com) heads from Drymen to Pitlochry via the Trossachs. The **Three Lochs Way** (www.threelochsway.co.uk) loops west from Balloch through Helensburgh and Arrochar before returning to Loch Lomond at Inveruglas. The **Great Trossachs Path** (www.lochlomond-trossachs.org) links the loch with the Trossachs. There are numerous shorter walks around: get further information from tourist offices.

Rowardennan is the starting point for ascents of **Ben Lomond** (www.nts.org.uk; 974m), a popular and relatively straightforward (if strenuous) climb.

The mostly traffic-free **Clyde and Loch Lomond Cycle Way** links Glasgow to Balloch (20 miles), where it joins the **West Loch Lomond Cycle Path**, which continues along the loch shore to Tarbet (10 miles). The park website (www.lochlomond-trossachs.org) details some other local routes.

Cruise Loch Lomond   BOATING
(☏ 01301-702356; www.cruiselochlomond.co.uk; Tarbet; ⊗ 8.30am-5.30pm Easter-Oct) With departures from Tarbet and Luss, this operator runs short cruises and two-hour trips to Arklet Falls and Rob Roy's Cave (adult/child £15/8). There are several options. You can also be dropped off at Rowardennan to climb Ben Lomond (£15/9), getting picked up in the afternoon, or after a 7-mile hike along the West Highland Way (£15/9).

🛏 Sleeping & Eating

Rowardennan SYHA   HOSTEL £
(☏ 01360-870259; www.syha.org.uk; Rowardennan; dm/tw/q £23.50/60/112; ⊗ mid-Mar–mid-

HILL HOUSE

Built in 1902 for Glasgow publisher Walter Blackie, **Hill House** (☏ 01436-673900; www.nts.org.uk; Upper Colquhoun St, Helensburgh; adult/child £10.50/7.50; ⊗ 11.30am-5pm Mar-Oct) is perhaps architect Charles Rennie Mackintosh's finest creation – its timeless elegance still feels chic today. The interiors are stunning, with rose motifs and fabulous furniture. Water soaking through the rendered cement exterior means that you'll find the house enclosed in a giant covering structure. You can stay on the top floor here – check the Holidays section of the NTS website. It's near Upper Helensburgh station, though not all trains stop there.

If you're arriving at Helensburgh Central station, it's about a 1-mile uphill walk to Hill House. Buses 302 and 306 can get you close.

Oct; ℗ 🤝) Where the road ends on the eastern side of Loch Lomond is this postcard-quality retreat in an elegant ex-hunting lodge with lawns stretching right down to the water's edge. Whether you're walking the West Highland Way, climbing Ben Lomond or just putting your feet up, it's a great choice, with a huge lounge that has windows overlooking the loch.

Oak Tree Inn   INN ££
(☏ 01360-870357; www.theoaktreeinn.co.uk; Balmaha; s/d £80/100; ℗ 🤝) An attractive traditional inn built in slate and timber, this place offers bright, modern bedrooms for pampered hikers, plus super-spacious superior chambers, self-catering cottages and glamping pods with their own deck. The rustic restaurant brings locals, tourists and walkers together and dishes up hearty meals that cover lots of bases (mains £10 to £13; noon to 9pm). There's plenty of outdoor seating.

Drover's Inn   PUB FOOD ££
(☏ 01301-704234; www.thedroversinn.co.uk; Inverarnan; bar meals £9-14; ⊗ 11.30am-10pm Mon-Sat, to 9.30pm or 10pm Sun; ℗ 🤝) Don't miss this low-ceilinged howff (drinking den), just north of Ardlui, with its smoke-blackened stone, kilted bartenders, and walls festooned with moth-eaten stags' heads and stuffed

birds. The convivial bar, where Rob Roy allegedly dropped by for pints, serves hearty hill-walking fuel and hosts live folk music on weekends.

ℹ Tourist Information

Balloch Tourist Office (☑ 01389-753533; www.visitscotland.com; Balloch Rd; ◐ 9.30am-6pm Jul & Aug, to 5.30pm Jun & Sep, 10am-5pm Oct-May) Opposite Balloch train station.

Balmaha National Park Centre (☑ 01389-722100; www.lochlomond-trossachs.org; Balmaha; ◐ 9.30am-4pm Apr-Oct, 9.30am-4pm Sat & Sun Nov-Mar) Has maps showing local walking routes.

ℹ Getting There & Around

BOAT

From mid-March to October a network of boats criss-crosses Loch Lomond, allowing you to explore the loch's hiking and biking trails using public transport. The Loch Lomond Water Bus timetable is available from tourist offices and online (www.lochlomond-trossachs.org).

Arden to Inchmurrin (☑ 07748 823243; www.inchmurrin-lochlomond.com; return £5) On demand.

Ardlui to Ardleish (☑ 01301-704243; www.ardlui.com; solo passengers £6 or per person £4; ◐ 9am-7pm Apr-Oct) On demand; operated by Ardlui Hotel.

Balloch to Luss (☑ 01389-752376; www.sweeneyscruises.com; single/return £13.50/19) Three daily May to September.

Balmaha to Inchcailloch (☑ 01360-870214; www.balmahaboatyard.co.uk; return £5; ◐ 9.30am-5pm mid-Mar–Oct) On demand.

Inveruglas to Inversnaid (☑ 01301-702356; www.cruiselochlomond.co.uk; single/return £10/13; ◐ mid-Mar–Oct) Must be booked.

Inveruglas to Tarbet (☑ 01301-702356; www.cruiselochlomond.co.uk; single/return £8/12; ◐ May-Sep) One daily via Inversnaid.

Luss to Balmaha (☑ 01389-752376; www.sweeneyscruises.com; single/return £8.50/12; ◐ May-Sep) Four to five daily with Sweeneys.

An **additional service** (☑ 01301-702356; www.cruiselochlomond.co.uk; single/return £10/13; ◐ mid-Mar–Oct) is run by Cruise Loch Lomond.

Luss to Inchcailloch (☑ 01301-702356; www.cruiselochlomond.co.uk; single/return £10/13; ◐ mid-Mar–Oct) Four daily.

Rowardennan to Luss (☑ 01301-702356; www.cruiselochlomond.co.uk; single/return £10/13; ◐ mid-Mar–Oct) One daily; must be booked.

Tarbet to Inversnaid (☑ 01301-702356; www.cruiselochlomond.co.uk; single/return £10/13; ◐ mid-Mar–Oct) Five to six daily.

Tarbet to Luss (☑ 01301-702356; www.cruiselochlomond.co.uk; single/return £10/13; ◐ mid-Mar–Oct) One daily.

Tarbet to Rowardennan (☑ 01301-702356; www.cruiselochlomond.co.uk; single/return £10/13; ◐ mid-Mar–Oct) One daily at 8.45am.

BUS

Bus 309 runs from Balloch to Drymen and Balmaha (£2.60, 20 minutes, nine to 10 daily), while bus 305 heads to Luss (£2.80, 20 minutes, nine to 10 daily). Bus 207 connects Balloch with Loch Lomond Shores and Alexandria. An **SPT Daytripper ticket** gives a family group unlimited travel for a day on most bus and train services in the Glasgow, Loch Lomond and Helensburgh area. Buy the ticket (£12.30 for one adult and two children, £21.80 for two adults and up to four children) from any train station or Glasgow bus station.

Tarbet and Ardlui are accessible by train and by Citylink buses between Glasgow and north-western destinations.

Local buses run from Helensburgh to Arrochar via Luss and Tarbet four times daily Monday to Friday.

The Trossachs

The Trossachs region has long been a favourite weekend getaway, offering outstanding natural beauty and excellent walking and cycling routes within easy reach of the country's southern population centres. With thickly forested hills, romantic lochs, national-park status and an interesting selection of places to stay and eat, its popularity is sure to continue.

The Trossachs first gained cachet in the early 19th century, when curious visitors came from across Britain, drawn by the romantic language of Walter Scott's poem 'Lady of the Lake', inspired by Loch Katrine, and novel *Rob Roy,* about the derring-do of the region's most famous son.

In summer, the Trossachs can be overburdened with coach tours, but many of these are for day trippers – peaceful, long evenings gazing at the reflections in the nearest loch are still possible. If you can, it's worth timing your visit to avoid weekends.

Callander

☑ 01877 / POP 3100

Callander, the principal Trossachs town, has been pulling in tourists for over 150 years, and has a laid-back ambience along its main thoroughfare that quickly lulls visitors into lazy pottering. There's an excellent array of accommodation options here, and some intriguing places to eat. Good walking and cycling routes are close at hand.

◎ Sights & Activities

★ Hamilton Toy Collection MUSEUM
(☏ 01877-330004; www.thehamiltontoycollection.co.uk; 111 Main St; adult/child £3/1; ⊙ 10.30am-5pm Mon-Sat, noon-5pm Sun Apr-Oct; ⊙) The Hamilton Toy Collection is a powerhouse of 20th-century juvenile memorabilia, chock-full of dolls houses, puppets and toy soldiers. It's an amazing collection and a guaranteed nostalgia trip. Phone ahead in winter as it opens some weekends.

Bracklinn Falls & Callander Crags WALKING
Impressive Bracklinn Falls are reached by track and footpath from Bracklinn Rd (30 minutes each way from the car park). Also off Bracklinn Rd, a woodland trail leads up to Callander Crags, with great views over the surroundings; a return trip from the car park is about 4 miles.

Wheels Cycling Centre CYCLING
(☏ 01877-331100; www.scottish-cycling.com; bike per hour/day/week from £8/20/90; ⊙ 10am-6pm Mar-Oct) The Trossachs is a lovely area to cycle around. On a cycle route, excellent Wheels Cycling Centre has a wide range of hire bikes. To get here from the centre of Callander, take Bridge St off Main St, turn right onto Invertrossachs Rd and continue for a mile.

⌒ Sleeping

★ Callander Hostel HOSTEL £
(☏ 01877-331465; www.callanderhostel.co.uk; 6 Bridgend; dm/d £19.50/60; ⓟ⊙⊙) ⊘ This hostel in a mock-Tudor building has been a major labour of love by a local youth project and is now a top-class facility. Well-furnished dorms offer bunks with individual lights and USB charge ports, while en suite doubles have super views. Staff are lovely, and it has a spacious common area and share kitchen as well as a cafe and garden.

Abbotsford Lodge HOTEL ££
(☏ 01877-330066; www.abbotsfordlodge.com; Stirling Rd; d £75-85; ⊙ mid-Feb-early Nov; ⓟ⊙) Offering excellent value for stylish contemporary rooms in a handsome Victorian house, this main-road choice has energetic owners who provide first-class hospitality and have a real eye for design. There are fabulous, spacious superiors (from £125) as well as cheaper top-floor rooms – with shared bathroom – that have lovably offbeat under-roof shapes. It caters to cyclists and walkers with bike storage and packed lunches.

Arden House B&B ££
(☏ 01877-339405; www.ardenhouse.org.uk; Bracklinn Rd; d £100-125; ⊙ Mar-Oct; ⓟ⊙) This elegant home has a fabulous hillside location with verdant garden and lovely vistas; it's close to Callander's centre but far from the crowds. The rooms are impeccable, with lots of natural light, and include large upstairs doubles with great views. Welcoming owners, noble architectural features – super bay windows – and a self-catering studio make this a top option.

★ Roman Camp Hotel HOTEL £££
(☏ 01877-330003; www.romancamphotel.co.uk; off Main St; s/d/superior £135/160/260; ⓟ⊙⊙) Callander's best hotel is centrally located but feels rural, set by the river in beautiful grounds. Endearing features include a lounge with blazing fire and a library with a tiny secret chapel. It's an old-fashioned warren of a place with four grades of rooms; standards are certainly luxurious, but superiors are even more appealing, with period furniture, excellent bathrooms, armchairs and fireplace.

✕ Eating

★ Callander Meadows SCOTTISH ££
(☏ 01877-330181; www.callandermeadows.co.uk; 24 Main St; dinner mains £13-19; ⊙ 10am-2.30pm & 6-8.30pm Thu-Sun year-round, plus Mon May-Sep; ⊙) Informal and cosy, this well-loved restaurant in the centre of Callander occupies the front rooms of a Main St house. It's truly excellent; there's a contemporary flair for presentation and unusual flavour combinations, but a solidly British base underpins the cuisine. There's a great beer/coffee garden out the back, where you can also eat.

ⓘ TRANSPORT IN THE TROSSACHS

DRT (Demand Responsive Transport; ☏ 01786-404040; www.stirling.gov.uk) covers the Trossachs area. It sounds complex, but basically it means for the price of a bus you get a taxi to where you want to go. There are various zones. Taxis should preferably be booked 24 hours in advance by phone.

MONACHYLE MOOR

A luxury hideaway with a fantastically peaceful location overlooking two lochs, **Monachyle Mhor** (📞01877-384622; www.monachylemhor.net; d £195-285, wagon £125; ☻Feb-Dec; 🅿🛏🐕) 🍴 is a great fusion of country Scotland and contemporary attitudes to design and food. Rooms are superb and feature quirkily original decor, particularly the fabulous 'feature rooms'. Otherwise, go glamping in a retro wagon or kip in a romantic…ferry waiting room. The restaurant is excellent.

It's an enchanting combination of top-class hospitality with a relaxed rural atmosphere: dogs and kids happily romp on the lawns, and no one looks askance if you come in flushed and muddy after a day's fishing or walking.

It's in Balquhidder, reached via a turn-off on the main road between Callander and Killin.

Lighter lunches such as sandwiches are also available.

⭐**Venachar Lochside** SCOTTISH ££
(📞01877-330011; www.venachar-lochside.com; Loch Venachar; mains £13-18; ☻noon-4pm Jan-Nov, plus 5.30-8.30pm Fri & Sat Jun-Sep; 📶🐕) On lovely Loch Venachar, 4.5 miles west of Callander, this cafe-restaurant has a stunning waterside setting and does a nice line in carefully sourced produce (including delicious local trout) prepared in innovative ways. It opens from 10am for coffees, teas and baked goods. You can also hire boats and tackle to go fishing for trout on the loch.

Mhor Fish SEAFOOD ££
(📞01877-330213; www.mhorfish.net; 75 Main St; mains £9-18; ☻noon-9pm Tue-Sun, closed Tue Nov–mid-Feb; 📶) 🍴 This simply decorated spot, with formica tables and a hodgepodge of chairs, sources brilliant sustainable seafood. Browse the fresh catch then eat it panseared in the dining area accompanied by a decent wine selection, or fried and wrapped in paper with chips to take away. It's all great, and calamari and oysters are wonderfully toothsome starters.

Poppy Seed SCOTTISH ££
(📞01877-330329; www.poppyseedrestaurant.co.uk; Leny Rd; mains £12-18; ☻noon-9pm Thu-Tue; 📶)

A revamp has seen this restaurant of a small main-road hotel invigorated by young owners. Start with an aperitif from the fine spirit selection of the handsome bar, then move through to dine on a short menu of quality ingredients prepared with imagination and deftly presented. In winter it's closed lunchtimes except on Sundays.

ℹ️ Getting There & Away

First (www.firstgroup.com) operates buses from Stirling (£5.80, 45 minutes, hourly Monday to Saturday, every two hours Sunday).

Kingshouse (📞01877-384768; www.kingshousetravel.com) has buses between Callander and Killin (£5.30, 40 minutes, five to six Monday to Saturday).

For Aberfoyle, use DRT (p859) or get off a Stirling-bound bus at Blair Drummond safari park, cross the road and pick up an Aberfoyle-bound bus.

Lochs Katrine & Achray

This rugged area, 7 miles north of Aberfoyle and 10 miles west of Callander, is the heart of the Trossachs. **Loch Katrine Cruises** (📞01877-376315; www.lochkatrine.com; Trossachs Pier, Loch Katrine; 1hr cruise adult £12-14, child £6.50-7.50) run from Trossachs Pier at the eastern tip of beautiful Loch Katrine. One of these is the fabulous centenarian steamship *Sir Walter Scott;* check the website for departures, as it's worth taking a trip on this veteran if possible. There are various one-hour afternoon sailings, and at 10.30am (plus additional summer departures) there's a trip to Stronachlachar at the other end of the loch. From Stronachlachar (accessible by car via a 12-mile road from Aberfoyle), you can reach Loch Lomond's eastern shore at isolated Inversnaid. A tarmac path links Trossachs Pier with Stronachlachar, so you can take the boat out and walk/cycle back (14 miles). At Trossachs Pier, **Katrinewheelz** (📞01877-376366; www.katrinewheelz.co.uk; Trossachs Pier, Loch Katrine; bike hire per half-/full day from £15/20; ☻9am-5pm Apr-Oct, 11am-3pm Sat & Sun Nov-Dec & Feb-Mar) hires out good bikes. The cafe is mediocre so bring a picnic or eat at the other end of the loch.

Killin
📞01567 / POP 800

A fine base for the Trossachs or Perthshire, this lovely village sits at the western end of Loch Tay and has a spread-out, relaxed feel, particularly around the scenic **Falls of Dochart**, which tumble through the centre. On a sunny day people sprawl over the rocks by the bridge, with pint or picnic in hand. Killin offers fine walking around the town, and there are mighty mountains and glens close by.

◉ Sights & Activities

Five miles northeast of Killin, **Ben Lawers** (1214m) rises above Loch Tay. Walking routes abound; one rewarding **circular walk** heads up into the Acharn forest south of town, emerging above the treeline to great views of Loch Tay and Ben Lawers. **Killin Outdoor Centre** (☑ 01567-820652; www.killinoutdoor. co.uk; Main St; bike per 24hr £25, kayak/canoe per 2hr £25; ⊗ 8.45am-5.30pm) provides walking advice.

Glen Lochay runs westwards from Killin into the hills of Mamlorn. You can take a **mountain bike** up the glen; the scenery is impressive and the hills aren't too difficult. It's possible, on a nice summer day, to climb over the top of **Ben Challum** (1025m) and descend to Crianlarich, but it's hard work. A potholed road, not maintained and no longer suitable for cars, also connects Glen Lochay with Glen Lyon.

Killin is on the **Lochs & Glens Cycle Way** from Glasgow to Inverness. Hire bikes from helpful Killin Outdoor Centre (which also has canoes and kayaks and, in winter, crampons and snowshoes).

🛏 Sleeping & Eating

★ Courie Inn INN ££

(☑ 01567-831000; www.thecourieinn.com; Main St; d £99-140; 🅿🛜) An excellent all-round choice, Courie Inn has quality, comfortable rooms decorated with restrained modern elegance; they come in a variety of sizes, including a sumptuous suite with views. It artfully blends the traditional and contemporary. Downstairs, the restaurant does smart bistro food (mains £11 to £15; daily 5pm to 8.30pm, plus noon to 3pm Friday to Sunday), and there's a bar.

Old Bank B&B ££

(☑ 01567-829317; www.theoldbankkillin.co.uk; Manse Rd; s/d £55/80; 🅿🛜) This four-square building with a pretty garden stands proud above the main street in Killin. It's a genuinely welcoming place, with a host who does everything in her power to make you feel welcome. Breakfast is abundant and the rooms are super-comfortable, with contemporary colours, hill views and thoughtful extras.

ℹ Getting There & Away

Kingshouse runs five to six buses Monday to Saturday to Callander (£5.30, 40 minutes), where you can change for Stirling.

ARGYLLSHIRE

Oban

☑ 01631 / POP 8600

Oban, the main gateway to many of the Hebridean islands, is a waterfront town on a delightful bay, with sweeping views to Kerrera and Mull. It's peaceful in winter, but in summer the town centre is jammed with traffic and crowded with holidaymakers and travellers headed for the archipelago. But the setting is still lovely, and Oban's brilliant seafood restaurants are marvellous places to be as the sun sets over the bay. There's a real magic to the location.

◉ Sights

Dunollie Castle CASTLE

(☑ 01631-570550; www.dunollie.org; Dunollie Rd; adult/child £6/3; ⊗ 10am-5pm Mon-Sat, noon-5pm Sun Apr-Oct) A pleasant 1-mile stroll north along the coast road leads to Dunollie Castle, built by the MacDougalls of Lorn in the 13th century and unsuccessfully besieged for a year during the 1715 Jacobite rebellion. It's ruined, but ongoing conservation work is offering increasing access. The nearby 1745 House – seat of Clan MacDougall – is an intriguing museum of local and clan history, and there are pleasant wooded grounds and a cafe. Free tours run twice daily.

Oban Distillery DISTILLERY

(☑ 01631-572004; www.malts.com; Stafford St; tours £10; ⊗ noon or 12.30-4.30pm Dec-Feb, 9.30am-5pm Mar-Jun & Oct-Nov, 9.30am-7.30pm Mon-Fri & 9.30am-5pm Sat & Sun Jul-Sep) This handsome distillery has been in operation since 1794. The standard guided tour leaves regularly (worth booking) and includes a dram, a take-home glass and a taste straight from the cask. Specialist tours (£40) run once on Mondays to Fridays in summer. Even without a tour, it's still worth looking at the small exhibition in the foyer.

McCaig's Tower   HISTORIC BUILDING

(cnr Laurel & Duncraggan Rds; ⊘24hr) Crowning the hill above town is this Colosseum-like Victorian folly, commissioned in 1890 by local worthy John Stuart McCaig, with the philanthropic intention of providing work for unemployed stonemasons. To reach it on foot, make the steep climb up Jacob's Ladder (a flight of stairs) from Argyll St; the bay views are worth the effort.

Activities

⭐ **Basking Shark Scotland**   BOATING

(☎07975 723140; www.baskingsharkscotland. co.uk; ⊘Apr-Oct) Runs boat trips focused on finding and observing basking sharks – the world's second-largest fish – and other notable marine species. The one-day options leave from Coll, synchronised with the ferry from Oban, and cost £140, or £195 with swimming/snorkelling. Multiday trips are available, as are low-season research trips. It also offers excursions allowing you to swim or kayak with seals.

Sea Kayak Oban   KAYAKING

(National Kayak School; ☎01631-565310; www. seakayakoban.com; Argyll St; ⊘10am-5pm Mon-Fri, 9am-5pm Sat, 10am-4pm Sun, winter hours greatly reduced) Sea Kayak Oban has a well-stocked shop, great route advice and sea-kayaking courses, including an all-inclusive two-day intro for beginners (£170 per person). It also has full equipment rental for experienced paddlers – trolley your kayak from the shop to the ferry (kayaks carried free) to visit the islands. Three-hour excursions (adult/child £50/35) leave regularly in season.

Sleeping

Despite having lots of B&B accommodation, Oban can still fill up quickly in July and August, so try to book ahead. Avoid the substandard, tourist-trap B&Bs south of the roundabout on Dunollie Rd. If you can't find a bed in Oban, consider Connel, 4 miles north.

⭐ **Backpackers Plus**   HOSTEL £

(☎01631-567189; www.backpackersplus.com; Breadalbane St; dm/s/tw/d incl bathroom & breakfast £20/29/54/60; @🖙) This is a friendly place in an old church with a good vibe and a large and attractive communal lounge with lots of sofas and armchairs. A buffet breakfast is included, plus there's free tea and coffee, a laundry service and powerful showers. Private rooms are available in adjacent buildings: they are a very good deal.

Oban SYHA   HOSTEL £

(☎01631-562025; www.syha.org.uk; Corran Esplanade; dm/tw £24/58, plus £3 per person for non-members; 🅿@🖙) Set in a grand Victorian villa on the Esplanade, 0.75 miles north of Oban's train station, this hostel is modernised to a high standard, with comfy wooden bunks, lockers, good showers and a lounge with great views across Oban Bay. All dorms are en suite; the neighbouring lodge has three- and four-bedded rooms. Breakfast is available. Dorm rates drop substantially in low season.

⭐ **Elderslie Guest House**   B&B ££

(☎01631-570651; www.obanbandb.com; Soroba Rd; s £50-56, d £75-88; ⊘Apr-mid-Oct; 🅿🖙) A B&B can be a difficult balancing act: making things modern without losing cosiness, being friendly and approachable without sacrificing privacy. At this spot a mile south of Oban the balance is absolutely right, with a variety of commodious rooms with big showers, large towels and lovely outlooks over greenery. Breakfast is great, there's outdoor lounging space and the hosts are excellent.

Barriemore Guest House   GUESTHOUSE ££

(☎01631-566356; www.barriemore.co.uk; Corran Esplanade; s from £100, d £120-135; ⊘Mar-Nov; 🅿🖙) With a grand location overlooking the entrance to Oban Bay, this place offers top-notch hospitality with tartan carpets on the stairs and plump Loch Fyne kippers on the breakfast menu. Rooms are all spacious, refurbished and full of features. The front ones – pricier but enormous – have fabulous vistas; there's also a great family suite up the back (£165) and solicitous service.

Kathmore Guest House   B&B ££

(☎01631-562104; www.kathmore.co.uk; Soroba Rd; s £50, d £65-75; 🅿🖙) A 10-minute stroll from Oban's centre, this warmly welcoming place mixes traditional Highland hospitality and hearty breakfasts with a wee touch of boutique flair in its stylish bedspreads and colourful artwork. It's actually two adjacent houses combined. There's a comfortable lounge and outdoor garden deck where you can enjoy a glass of wine on long summer evenings.

Manor House   HOTEL £££

(☎01631-562087; www.manorhouseoban.com; Gallanach Rd; r £195-270; 🅿🖙🍽) Built in 1780 for the Duke of Argyll, the old-fashioned Manor House is Oban's finest hotel. It has small but elegant Georgian-style rooms – the majority with lovely sea views – with antiques and period-style wallpaper, plus a classy restaurant serving Scottish/French cuisine (table d'hôte dinner £49). Rates include access to a local gym and golf course. No under-12s.

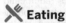
Eating

Oban Seafood Hut
SEAFOOD £
(☑07881 418565; www.facebook.com/obanseafood.hut.9; Railway Pier; mains £3-13; ⊙10am-6pm mid-Mar–Oct) If you want to savour superb Scottish seafood without the expense of an upmarket restaurant, head for Oban's famous seafood stall – it's the green shack on the quayside near the ferry terminal. Here you can buy fresh and cooked seafood to take away, such as excellent prawn sandwiches, dressed crab and fresh oysters, for a pittance.

Little Potting Shed Cafe
CAFE, VEGETARIAN £
(☑01631-358150; www.facebook.com/thelittlepottingshedcafeoban; 5 John St; light meals £4-9; ⊙9am-5pm daily, to 9pm Fri & Sat Jul & Aug; ☜☑☻) Up a side alley off Oban's main street, this sweet spot has wooden tables and an excellent choice of vegetarian and vegan savoury and sweet bites. The vegan breakfast is also tasty, the coffee is good and strong, there's a wide selection of teas, and the non-dairy ice-cream is perfect for a summer's day. It's dog-friendly.

★ Ee-Usk
SEAFOOD ££
(☑01631-565666; www.eeusk.com; North Pier; mains £14-24; ⊙noon-3pm & 5.45-9.30pm Apr-Oct, noon-2.30pm & 5.45-9pm Nov-Mar; ☜) ✿ Bright and modern Ee-Usk (how you pronounce *iasg*, Gaelic for fish) occupies a prime pier location. Floor-to-ceiling windows allow diners on two levels to enjoy sweeping views while sampling local sustainable seafood ranging from fragrant fish cakes to langoustines and succulent fresh fish. A bevy of serving staff make it swift and efficient, and they'll try to give you the best view available.

Waterfront Fishouse Restaurant
SEAFOOD ££
(☑01631-563110; www.waterfrontfishouse.co.uk; 1 Railway Pier; mains £13-20; ⊙noon-2pm & 5.30-9pm, extended hours Jun-Aug; ☜☻) Waterfront is housed on the top floor of a converted seamen's mission, and the stylish, unfussy

decor, bathed by the summer evening sun, does little to distract from the seafood freshly landed at the quay just a few metres away. The menu ranges from classic haddock and chips to fresh oysters, scallops and langoustines. It's best to book for dinner.

Drinking & Nightlife

Aulay's Bar
PUB
(☑01631-562596; www.aulaysbar.com; 8 Airds Cres; ⊙11.30am-11pm; ☜) An authentic Scottish pub, Aulay's is cosy and low-ceilinged, its walls covered with old photographs of Oban ferries and other ships. It pulls in a mixed crowd of locals and visitors with its warm atmosphere and wide range of malt whiskies. There are two sides: the left door leads to a quieter lounge bar.

Oban Inn
PUB
(☑01631-567441; www.facebook.com/theobaninn; 1 Stafford St; ⊙11am-1am; ☜) It's a pleasure to see this four-square 18th-century pub open again after some years closed, with its solid walls, flagstone floor and roof beams in the cosy front bar. It has Fyne Ales on tap, making it a prime spot for a waterfront pint, with a good mix of locals, visitors and yachties.

ⓘ Information

Oban Tourist Office (☑01631-563122; www.oban.org.uk; 3 North Pier; ⊙10am-5pm Mon-Sat, 11am-3pm Sun Nov-Mar, 9am-5.30pm Mon-Sat, 10am-5pm Sun Apr-Oct) A helpful tourist office on the waterfront.

ⓘ Getting There & Away

AIR
Hebridean Air Services (☑0845 805 7465; www.hebrideanair.co.uk; Oban Airport, North Connel) Flies from North Connel airfield to the islands of Coll, Tiree, Colonsay and Islay.

BOAT
Oban is a major gateway to the Hebrides. The **CalMac Ferry Terminal** (☑01631-562244; www.calmac.co.uk; Railway Pier) is in the centre, close to the train station, with ferries running from here to Mull, Islay, Colonsay, Coll, Tiree, Barra and Lismore.

BUS
Scottish Citylink (☑0871 266 3333; www.citylink.co.uk) has two to five buses connecting Glasgow (£20.50, three hours) with Oban. Most of these travel via Tarbet and Inveraray; in

summer, one goes via Crianlarich. Two buses Monday to Saturday head north to Fort William (£9.40, 1½ hours).

TRAIN

ScotRail trains run to Oban from Glasgow (£25.30, three hours, three to six daily). Change at Crianlarich for Fort William.

Mull

POP 2800

From the rugged ridges of Ben More and the black basalt crags of Burg to the blinding white sand, rose-pink granite and emerald waters that fringe the Ross, Mull can lay claim to some of the finest and most varied scenery in the Inner Hebrides. Noble birds of prey soar over mountain and coast, while the western waters provide good whale watching. Add a lovely waterfront 'capital', an impressive castle, the sacred island of Iona and easy access from Oban, and you can see why it's sometimes impossible to find a spare bed on the island.

🏃 Activities

There's some standout walking on Mull, including the popular climb of **Ben More** and the spectacular **Carsaig Arches Walk**. More information on these and other walks can be obtained from the tourist offices in Oban (p863), Craignure and Tobermory.

Mull Eagle Watch   BIRDWATCHING
(✎01680-812556; www.mulleaglewatch.com; adult/child £8/4; ⊘Apr-Sep) Britain's largest bird of prey, the white-tailed eagle, or sea eagle, has been successfully reintroduced to Mull, and the island is crowded with bird-watchers raptly observing the raptor. Two-hour tours to observe this bird are held in the mornings and afternoons, and must be booked in advance.

Nature Scotland   WILDLIFE
(✎07743 956380; www.naturescotland.com) Young, enthusiastic guides offer a range of excellent wildlife tours, including afternoon trips that can link to ferries (adult/child £30/25, four hours), evening otter-spotting trips (£40/35, three to four hours), all-day walking trips (£60/50, seven hours) and winter stargazing excursions (£40/30, two to three hours).

Turus Mara   BOATING
(✎01688-400242; www.turusmara.com; ⊘Apr–mid-Oct) Offers trips from Ulva Ferry in central Mull to Staffa and the Treshnish Isles (adult/child £65/32.50, six hours), with an hour ashore on Staffa and two hours on Lunga, where you can see seals, puffins, kittiwakes, razorbills and many other species of seabird. There are also trips to Staffa alone (£32.50/18, 3¾ hours) and birdwatching-focused trips (£75/37.50, eight hours).

Staffa Tours   BOATING
(✎07831 885985; www.staffatours.com; ⊘Apr–mid-Oct) Runs boat trips from Fionnphort and Iona to Staffa (adult/child £35/17.50, three hours), or Staffa plus the Treshnish Isles (also available from Tobermory and Ardnamurchan; £65/32.50, six hours). Before and after the seabird season, the trip is shorter (£50/30, five hours), not landing on Lunga. There are also connection-plus-tour options leaving from Oban.

WILDLIFE WATCHING ON MULL

The North Atlantic Drift – a swirling tendril of the Gulf Stream – carries warm water into the cold, nutrient-rich seas off the Scottish coast, resulting in huge plankton blooms. Small fish feed on the plankton, and bigger fish feed on the smaller fish; this huge seafood smorgasbord attracts large numbers of marine mammals, from harbour porpoises and dolphins to minke whales and even – though sightings are rare – humpback and sperm whales.

There are dozens of operators around the coast offering **whale-watching** boat trips lasting from a couple of hours to all day; some have sighting success rates of 95% in summer.

While seals, porpoises and dolphins can be seen year-round, minke whales are migratory. The best time to see them is from June to August, with August being the peak month for sightings. The website of the **Hebridean Whale & Dolphin Trust** (www.whaledolphintrust.co.uk) has lots of information on the species you are likely to see, and how to identify them.

Mull, Coll & Tiree

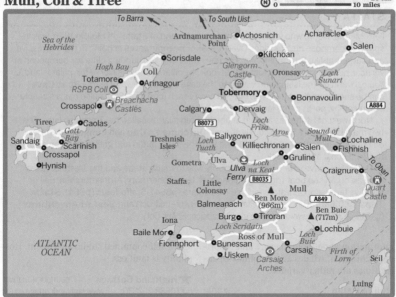

ℹ Information

There's a bank with an ATM in Tobermory; otherwise you can get cash back with a purchase from Co-op food stores.

Craignure Tourist Office (☑ 01680-812377; www.visitscotland.com; Craignure; ⊙ 9am-5pm Mon, 8.30am-5pm Tue-Sat, 10am-5pm Sun Sep-Jun, 9am-6.15pm Mon, 8.30am-6.15pm Tue-Sat, 10am-4.15pm Sun Jul & Aug) Opposite the ferry slip.

Explore Mull (☑ 01688-302875; www.isle-of-mull.net; Ledaig; ⊙ 9am-5pm Easter-Jun & Sep–mid-Oct, to 7pm Jul & Aug; ☎) In Tobermory car park. Has local information, can book all manner of island tours and hires bikes.

ℹ Getting There & Away

CalMac (☑ 0800 066 5000; www.calmac.co.uk) has three car ferries that link Mull with the mainland:

Oban to Craignure (adult/car £3.60/13.40, 40 minutes, every two hours) The busiest route – bookings are advised if you have a car.

Lochaline to Fishnish (adult/car £2.40/7.15, 15 minutes, at least hourly, except four daily on winter Sundays) On the east coast of Mull.

Tobermory to Kilchoan (adult/car £2.75/8.65, 35 minutes, seven daily Monday to Saturday, five Sunday April to October, three Monday to Saturday November to March) Links to the Ardnamurchan peninsula.

Tobermory

☑ 01688 / POP 1000

Mull's main town is a very picturesque little fishing and yachting port with brightly painted houses arranged around a sheltered harbour. It's a great base, with good places to eat, inviting pubs and an array of quality accommodation both along the harbourfront and on the hill behind.

◉ Sights & Activities

Sea Life Surveys WILDLIFE
(☑ 01688-302916; www.sealifesurveys.com; Ledaig) Whale-watching trips head from Tobermory harbour to the waters north and west of Mull. An all-day whale-watch allows up to seven hours at sea (£80), and has a 95% success rate for sightings. The four-hour Whale-watch cruise (adult/child £60/30) is better for families. Shorter seal-spotting excursions are also available (£25/12.50, two hours).

Hebridean Whale & Dolphin Trust MUSEUM
(☑ 01688-302620; www.whaledolphintrust.co.uk; 28 Main St; ⊙ 10.30am-4.30pm Mar-Nov) ✐ FREE
This place has displays, videos and interactive exhibits on whale and dolphin biology and ecology, and is a great place for kids to learn about sea mammals. It also provides

STAFFA

Felix Mendelssohn, who visited the uninhabited island of Staffa, off Mull, in 1829, was inspired to compose his 'Hebrides Overture' after hearing waves echoing in the impressive and cathedral-like **Fingal's Cave**. The cave walls and surrounding cliffs are composed of vertical, hexagonal basalt columns that look like pillars (Staffa is Norse for 'pillar island'). You can land on the island and walk into the cave via a causeway. Nearby **Boat Cave** can be seen from the causeway, but you can't reach it on foot. Staffa also has a sizeable puffin colony, north of the landing place.

Northwest of Staffa lies a chain of uninhabited islands called the Treshnish Isles. The two main islands are the curiously shaped **Dutchman's Cap** and **Lunga**. You can land on Lunga, walk to the top of the hill, and visit the shag, puffin and guillemot colonies on the west coast at Harp Rock.

Unless you have your own boat, the only way to reach Staffa and the Treshnish Isles is on an organised boat trip from Fionnphort, Iona, Tobermory, Ardnamurchan, Seil or the Ulva ferry slip. Operators include Turus Mara (p864), Staffa Tours (p864), **Staffa Trips** (☑ 01681-700358; www.staffatrips.co.uk; ⊙ Apr–mid-Oct) and **Seafari Adventures** (☑ 01852-300003; www.seafari.co.uk; Ellenabeich; ⊙ Apr–Oct).

information about volunteering and reporting sightings of whales and dolphins. Opening times are rather variable.

Mull Museum MUSEUM
(☑ 01688-301100; www.mullmuseum.org.uk; Main St; ⊙ 10am-4pm Mon-Sat Easter-Oct) **FREE** Mull Museum, which records the history of the island, is a good place to go on a rainy day. There are interesting exhibits on crofting, and on the *Tobermory Galleon,* a ship from the Spanish Armada that sank in Tobermory Bay in 1588 and has been the object of treasure seekers ever since. Donations are appreciated in this volunteer-run set-up.

🛏 Sleeping

Tobermory SYHA HOSTEL **£**
(☑ 01688-302481; www.syha.org.uk; Main St; dm/tw/q £20/60/112; ⊙ Mar-Oct; @ 🛜) This hostel has a great location in a Victorian house right on the waterfront. It's got an excellent kitchen and spotless if somewhat austere dorms, as well as good triples and quads for families. It books out fast in summer.

★ Sonas House B&B **££**
(☑ 01688-302304; www.sonashouse.co.uk; Fairways, Erray Rd; s/d £90/130; apt for 2 excl/incl breakfast £100/130; 🅿 🛜 🏊) Here's a treat: a B&B with a heated, indoor 10m swimming pool! Sonas is a large, modern house (follow signs to the golf course) offering luxury in a beautiful setting with superb Tobermory Bay views. Both rooms are beautifully done out with blond wood and other colours; 'Blue Poppy' has its own balcony. There's

also a self-contained studio apartment. Hospitality is faultless.

★ Highland Cottage BOUTIQUE HOTEL **£££**
(☑ 01688-302030; www.highlandcottage.co.uk; Breadalbane St; d £160-175; ⊙ Apr–mid-Oct; 🅿 🛜 🐾) Antique furniture, four-poster beds, embroidered bedspreads, fresh flowers and candlelight lend this small hotel (only six rooms) an appealingly old-fashioned cottage atmosphere, but with all mod cons, including cable TV, full-size baths and room service. There's also an excellent restaurant here (dinner £42.50), and the personable owners are experts in guest comfort.

🍴 Eating & Drinking

Fish & Chip Van FISH & CHIPS **£**
(☑ 01688-301109; www.tobermoryfishandchipvan. co.uk; Main St; fish & chips £6-10; ⊙ 12.30-9pm Mon-Sat Apr-May, 12.30-9pm daily Jun-Sep, 12.30-7pm Mon-Thu, to 8pm Fri & Sat Oct-Mar) If it's takeaway you're after, you can tuck into some of Scotland's best gourmet fish and chips down on the Tobermory waterfront. And where else will you find a chip van selling freshly cooked scallops?

★ Café Fish SEAFOOD **££**
(☑ 01688-301253; www.thecafefish.com; The Pier; mains £15-26; ⊙ noon-3pm & 5.30-11pm mid-Mar–Oct; 🛜) 🍴 Seafood doesn't come much fresher than the stuff served at this warm and welcoming little restaurant overlooking Tobermory harbour. Crustaceans go straight from boat to kitchen to join rich seafood stew, fat scallops, fish pie and catch-of-the-

day on the daily-changing menu, where confident use of Asian ingredients adds an extra dimension. Book ahead.

Hebridean Lodge
SCOTTISH ££

(📱01688-301207; www.hebrideanlodge.co.uk; Salen Rd, Baliscate; mains £17-21; ⊙6.30-8.30pm Mon-Fri Easter-Dec) Above a gallery and shop, this mezzanine restaurant offers delicious local produce at chunky wooden tables. There's a warm welcome and fine, fresh seafood and lamb, with daily specials complementing the short menu of generous-spirited Scottish cuisine. Book ahead.

★Mishnish Hotel
PUB

(📱01688-302500; www.mishnish.co.uk; Main St; ⊙11am-1am; 🛜) 'The Mish', near the pier on the harbourfront, is a favourite hang-out for visiting yachties and a great place for a pint, with a very convivial atmosphere. Wood-panelled and flag-draped, this is a good old traditional pub where you can listen to live folk music, toast your toes by the open fire or challenge locals to a game of pool.

❶ Getting There & Away

Summer ferries head from Tobermory to Kilchoan on the Ardnamurchan peninsula.

Buses connect Tobermory with Craignure (single/return £7/10, five to eight daily, 40 to 50 minutes) via Salen. To explore North Mull, there's a bus service from Tobermory to Calgary via Dervaig.

North Mull

The road from Tobermory west to Calgary cuts inland, leaving most of Mull's north coast wild and inaccessible. It continues through the settlement of Dervaig to the glorious beach at Calgary. From here onwards you are treated to spectacular coastal views; it's worth doing the route in reverse from Gruline for the best vistas.

◉ Sights

Glengorm Castle
GALLERY, PARK

(📱01688-302321; www.glengormcastle.co.uk; Glengorm; ⊙buildings 10am-5pm Easter-Oct) FREE A long, single-track road leads north for 4 miles from Tobermory to majestic Glengorm Castle, with views across the sea to Ardnamurchan, Rum and the Outer Hebrides. The castle outbuildings house a nature centre, farm shop and the excellent Glengorm Coffee Shop (light meals £3-9;

⊙10am-5pm Easter-Oct; 🛜🍴) 🍃. The castle, which also has upmarket B&B acccommodation (r £135-290; P🛜🐾), is not open to the public, but you're free to explore the beautiful grounds, where several good walks are signposted. Guided nature walks also run from here; check the website for times.

Calgary Beach
BEACH

Mull's best (and busiest) silver-sand beach, flanked by cliffs and with views out to Coll and Tiree, is about 12 miles west of Tobermory. And yes – this is the place from which Canada's more famous Calgary takes its name.

🛏 Sleeping & Eating

Dervaig Hostel
HOSTEL £

(📱01688-400313; dervaigbunkrooms@gmail.com; Dervaig; dm/q £18/60; ⊙Apr-Oct; P🛜) Comfortable bunkhouse accommodation in Dervaig's village hall, with self-catering kitchen and sitting room. The dorms have good en suite bathrooms and comfortable bunks.

★Calgary Farmhouse
COTTAGE ££

(📱01688-400256; www.calgary.co.uk; Calgary; per week summer apt & cottages £500-2000, per 3 days studios & cabin £200-270; P🛜🐾) 🍃 This brilliant complex near Calgary beach offers a number of fantastic apartments, cottages and houses, beautifully designed and fitted out with timber furniture and wood-burning stoves. The Hayloft is spectacular, with noble oak and local art, while the wood-clad longhall-like Beach House has luxury and dreamy views. Romantic Kittiwake, a beautiful wooden camping cabin among trees, has bay views and a boat ceiling.

Am Birlinn
SCOTTISH ££

(📱01688-400619; www.ambirlinn.com; Penmore, Dervaig; mains £14-24; ⊙noon-2.30pm & 5-9pm Wed-Sun mid-Mar–Oct; 🛜) 🍃 Occupying a spacious and modern wooden building between Dervaig and Calgary, this is an interesting dining option. Locally caught crustaceans and molluscs are the way to go here, though there are burgers, venison and other meat dishes available. Free pick-up and drop-off from Tobermory or other nearby spots is offered. There's also a bar.

❶ Getting There & Away

There are four buses Monday to Friday and two on Saturday from Tobermory to Calgary (£3, 45 minutes) via Dervaig (£2.50, 30 minutes).

South Mull

The road from Craignure to Fionnphort climbs through wild and desolate scenery before reaching the southwestern part of the island, which consists of a long peninsula called the Ross of Mull. The Ross has a spectacular south coast lined with black basalt cliffs that give way further west to white-sand beaches and pink granite crags. The cliffs are highest at Malcolm's Point, near the superb Carsaig Arches.

The village of Bunessan is home to a cottage museum; a minor road leads south from here to the beautiful white-sand bay of Uisken, with views of the Paps of Jura.

At the western end of the Ross, 35 miles from Craignure, is Fionnphort (*finn*-a-fort) and the Iona ferry. The coast here is a beautiful blend of pink granite rocks, white sandy beaches and vivid turquoise sea.

🛏 Sleeping

Ross of Mull Bunkhouse HOSTEL £
(☑ 07759 615200; www.rossofmullbunkhouse. co.uk; Fionnphort; dm/s/tw £24/48/70; P🛜) Run by enthusiastic young owners, this excellent year-round bunkhouse about a mile from the Iona ferry offers a rural atmosphere, top-notch modern bathrooms and spacious, comfortable four-berth rooms with sturdy metal bunks, USB ports and bedside lights. There's an attractive common room with fireplace, guitars and loch views, plus a brilliant kitchen and a drying room.

⭐ Seaview B&B ££
(☑ 01681-700235; www.iona-bed-breakfast-mull. com; Fionnphort; s £65, d £90-105; ⊙mid-Mar–Oct; P🛜🐾) 🌿 Just up from the ferry, Seaview has beautifully decorated bedrooms and a breakfast conservatory with grand views across to Iona. The rooms are compact and charming, with gleaming modern bathrooms. The owners are incredibly helpful and also offer tasty three-course dinners (not in summer), often based around local seafood, while breakfasts include locally sourced produce.

Achaban House B&B ££
(☑ 01681-700205; www.achabanhouse.co.uk; Fionnphort; s/d £46/75; P🛜) This super refurbished rural house has very pleasing contemporary rooms with modern fabrics and a light, uncluttered feel. Some rooms look over the loch below. It's casual and friendly, and the ideal base for visiting Iona with the ferry less than a mile away. Guests have use of an excellent kitchen and a lounge with woodburning stove. Continental breakfasts feature homemade bread.

🍴 Eating

Creel Seafood Bar SEAFOOD £
(☑ 07864 605682; Fionnphort; light meals £4-8; ⊙8.30am-7pm Apr-Oct) There's no better way to wait for the Iona ferry than to munch on a crab sandwich or langoustine cocktail from this little seafood shack by the boat ramp. Run by a fishing family, it's got tasty, simply cooked crustaceans and a daily fish special at a sharp price. The seafood platter is a bargain.

⭐ Ninth Wave SCOTTISH £££
(☑ 01681-700757; www.ninthwaverestaurant.co.uk; Bruach Mhor, Fionnphort; 3-/4-/5-course dinner £48/56/68; ⊙sittings 7pm Wed-Sun May-Oct) 🌿 This excellent croft restaurant is owned and operated by a lobster fisherman and his Canadian wife. The daily menu makes use of locally landed shellfish and crustaceans, vegetables and salad grown in the garden, and quality local meats with a nose-to-tail ethos. It's all served in a stylishly converted bothy. Advance bookings (a couple of weeks at least) are essential. No under-12s.

❶ Getting There & Away

Buses run from Craignure to Fionnphort three to four times Monday to Saturday and once on Sunday (single/return £9/14, 1¼ hours).

Iona

☑ 01681 / POP 200

Like an emerald teardrop off Mull's western shore, enchanting, idyllic Iona, holy island and burial ground of kings, is a magical place that lives up to its lofty reputation. From the moment you embark on the ferry towards its sandy shores and green fields, you'll notice something different about it. To appreciate its charms, spend the night: there are some excellent places to stay. Iona has declared itself a fair-trade island and actively promotes ecotourism.

St Columba sailed from Ireland and landed on Iona in 563, establishing a monastic community with the aim of Christianising Scotland. It was here that the *Book of Kells* – the prize attraction of Dublin's Trinity College – is believed to have been transcribed.

◉ Sights & Activities

Past the abbey, look for a footpath on the left signposted **Dun I** (dun-ee). An easy 15-minute walk leads to Iona's highest point, with fantastic 360-degree views.

★ Iona Abbey
HISTORIC BUILDING
(☑ 01681-700512; www.historicenvironment.scot; adult/child £7.50/4.50; ⊙ 9.30am-5.30pm Apr-Sep, 10am-4pm Oct-Mar) Iona's ancient but heavily reconstructed abbey is the spiritual heart of the island. The spectacular **nave**, dominated by Romanesque and early Gothic vaults and columns, is a powerful space; a door on the left leads to the beautiful **cloister**, where medieval grave slabs sit alongside modern religious sculptures. Out the back, the **museum** displays fabulous carved high crosses and other inscribed stones, along with lots of background information. A replica of the intricately carved St John's Cross stands outside the abbey.

Iona Heritage Centre
MUSEUM
(☑ 01681-700576; www.ionaheritage.co.uk; entry by donation; ⊙ 10am-5.15pm Mon-Sat Easter-Oct) This place covers the history of Iona, crofting and lighthouses; there's also a craft shop and a cafe serving delicious home baking.

⌸ Sleeping & Eating

There are B&B options, camping, a hostel and a pair of hotels on the island. It's imperative to book accommodation well ahead in spring and summer. Very little is open in winter apart from the hostel.

★ Iona Hostel
HOSTEL £
(☑ 01681-700781; www.ionahostel.co.uk; dm adult/child £21/17.50, tw £42, bothy s/d £40/60; P 🛜) 🖉 This working ecological croft and environmentally sensitive hostel is one of Scotland's most rewarding and tranquil places to stay. Lovable black Hebridean sheep surround the building, which features pretty, practical and comfy dorms and an excellent kitchen-lounge. There's a fabulous beach nearby, and a hill to climb for views. It's just over a mile from the ferry on Iona, past the abbey.

Iona Campsite
CAMPSITE £
(☑ 07747 721275; www.ionacampsite.co.uk; tent site per adult/child £7.50/4; ⊙ Apr-Sep; 🛁) This basic, welcoming grassy campsite is about 1 mile west of the ferry on Iona. Sleeping bags and mats are available for hire.

DUART CASTLE

The ancestral seat of the Maclean clan, **Duart Castle** (☑ 01680-812309; www.duartcastle.com; adult/child £7/3.50; ⊙ 10.30am-5pm daily May–mid-Oct, 11am-4pm Sun-Thu Apr) enjoys a spectacular position on a rocky outcrop overlooking the Sound of Mull. Originally built in the 13th century, it was abandoned for 160 years before a 1912 restoration. As well as dungeons, courtyard and battlements with memorable views, there's lots of clan history.

A bus to the castle meets some of the incoming ferries at Craignure (£11 return including castle entrance), but it's a pretty walk to get here, too.

★ Argyll Hotel
HOTEL ££
(☑ 01681-700334; www.argyllhoteliona.co.uk; s £79, d £99-119; ⊙ mid-Mar–mid-Oct; 🛜🛁) 🖉 This lovable, higgledy-piggledy warren of a hotel has great service and appealing snug rooms (those with sea views cost more – £174 for a double), including good-value family options. The rooms offers simple comfort and relaxation rather than luxury. Most look out to the rear, where a huge organic garden supplies the restaurant. This is a relaxing and amiably run Iona haven.

❶ Getting There & Away

The ferry from Fionnphort to Iona (£3.40 adult return, five minutes, hourly) runs daily. Cars can only be taken with a permit. There are also various day trips available to Iona from Tobermory and Oban.

Inveraray
☑ 01499 / POP 600
There's no fifty shades of grey around here: this historic planned village is all black and white – even logos of high-street chain shops conform. Spectacularly set on the shores of Loch Fyne, Inveraray was built by the Duke of Argyll in Georgian style when he revamped his nearby castle in the 18th century.

◉ Sights

Inveraray Castle
CASTLE
(☑ 01499-302203; www.inveraray-castle.com; adult/child/family £11/8/32; ⊙ 10am-5.45pm

Apr-Oct) This visually stunning castle on the north side of town has been the seat of the Dukes of Argyll – chiefs of Clan Campbell – since the 15th century. The 18th-century building, with its fairy-tale turrets and fake battlements, houses an impressive armoury hall, its walls patterned with more than 1000 pole arms, dirks, muskets and Lochaber axes. Entry is slightly cheaper if you book online.

Inveraray Jail   MUSEUM
(☑ 01499-302381; www.inverarayjail.co.uk; Church Sq; adult/child £11.50/7; ☉ 9.30am-6pm Apr-Oct, 10am-5pm Nov-Mar; ꘈ) At this entertaining interactive tourist attraction you can sit in on a trial, try out a cell and discover the harsh tortures that were meted out to unfortunate prisoners. The attention to detail – including a life-sized model of an inmate squatting on a 19th-century toilet – is excellent, and actors enliven things during busy periods. Last admission is an hour before closing.

🛏 Sleeping & Eating

★George Hotel   INN ££
(☑ 01499-302111; www.thegeorgehotel.co.uk; Main St E; d £90-135; 🅿🛜🐕) The George boasts a magnificent choice of opulent, individual rooms decorated with sumptuous period furniture. Some feature four-poster beds, Victorian roll-top baths and/or private jacuzzis (superior rooms and suites cost £145 to £180 per double; the library suite is quite a sight). Some rooms are in an annexe opposite and there are also self-catering options.

★Loch Fyne Oyster Bar   SEAFOOD ££
(☑ 01499-600482; www.lochfyne.com; Clachan, Cairndow; mains £13-26; ☉ 9am-5pm; 🛜) 🖉 The success of this cooperative is such that it now lends its name to dozens of restaurants throughout the UK. But the original is still the best, with large, salty, creamy oysters straight out of the lake, and fabulous salmon dishes. The atmosphere and decor is simple, friendly and unpretentious; it also has a shop and deli where you can eat casually.

Samphire   SEAFOOD ££
(☑ 01499-302321; www.samphireseafood.com; 6a Arkland; dinner mains £11-21; ☉ noon-2.30pm & 5.30-9pm Wed-Fri, noon-2.30pm & 5-11pm Sat, noon-2.30pm & 5-9pm Sun; 🛜) 🖉 There's lots to like about this compact restaurant that makes an effort to source sustainable local seafood. There's a fairly light touch from

the kitchen, which tends to let the natural flavours shine through, with very pleasing results.

ℹ️ Getting There & Away

Scottish Citylink (p863) has buses running from Glasgow to Inveraray (£13, 1¾ hours, up to nine daily). Some continue to Campbeltown (£14.20, 2¼ hours); others to Oban (£10.80, 1¼ hours). There are also buses to Dunoon (£3.90, 1¼ hours, three daily Monday to Saturday)

Kilmartin Glen

This magical glen is the focus of one of the biggest concentrations of prehistoric sites in Scotland. Burial cairns, standing stones, stone circles, hill forts and cup-and-ring-marked rocks litter the countryside. Within a 6-mile radius of Kilmartin village there are 25 sites with standing stones and more than 100 rock carvings.

In the 6th century, Irish settlers arrived in this part of Argyll and founded the kingdom of Dál Riata (Dalriada), which eventually united with the Picts in 843 to create the first Scottish kingdom. Their capital was the hill fort of Dunadd, on the plain to the south of Kilmartin.

Kilmartin House Museum   MUSEUM
(☑ 01546-510278; www.kilmartin.org; Kilmartin; adult/child £6.50/2.50; ☉ 10am-5.30pm Mar-Oct, 11am-4pm Nov-late Dec) This museum, in Kilmartin village, is a fascinating interpretive centre that provides a context for the ancient monuments you can go on to explore, alongside displays of artefacts recovered from various sites. Funding has nearly been achieved for a major redevelopment of the museum, so check the website for the latest details before visiting. It also has a **cafe** (☑ 01546-510278; www.kilmartin.org; Kilmartin; mains £5-9; ☉ 10am-5pm Mar-Oct, 11am-4pm Nov-late Dec; 🛜🖉) 🖉 and a good shop with handicrafts and books on Scotland.

Dunadd Fort   ARCHAEOLOGICAL SITE
(☉ 24hr) FREE This hill fort, 3.5 miles south of Kilmartin village, was the seat of power of the first kings of Dál Riata, and may have been where the Stone of Destiny was originally located. Faint rock carvings of a boar and two footprints with an ogham inscription may have been used in inauguration ceremonies. The prominent little hill rises straight out of the boggy plain of Moine Mhor Nature Reserve.

ℹ Getting There & Away

Bus 423 between Oban and Ardrishaig (three to five Monday to Friday, two on Saturday) stops at Kilmartin (from Oban £5.60, one hour).

You can walk or cycle along the **Crinan Canal** from Ardrishaig, then turn north at Bellanoch on the minor B8025 road to reach Kilmartin (12 miles one way). It's a lovely journey.

Kintyre

The 40-mile-long Kintyre peninsula is almost an island, with only a narrow isthmus at Tarbert connecting it to Knapdale. During the Norse occupation of the Western Isles, the Scottish king decreed that the Vikings could claim as their own any island they circumnavigated in a longship. So in 1098 the wily Magnus Barefoot stood at the helm while his men dragged their boat across this neck of land, validating his claim to Kintyre.

The coastline is spectacular on both sides, with stirring views of Arran, Islay, Jura and Northern Ireland. On a sunny day the water shimmers beyond the stony shore. Hiking the Kintyre Way is a great means of experiencing the peninsula, which has a couple of cracking golf courses at Machrihanish near Campbeltown.

ℹ Getting There & Away

Scottish Citylink (p863) has buses running along the whole length of the peninsula from Glasgow. Campbeltown is also connected by ferry to Ardrossan, Ayrshire in summer. Local buses are run by West Coast Motors (www. westcoastmotors.co.uk).

Tarbert

✆ 01880 / POP 1100

The attractive fishing village and yachting centre of Tarbert is the gateway to Kintyre, and is most scenic, with buildings strung around its excellent natural harbour. A crossroads for nearby ferry routes, it's a handy stepping stone to Arran or Islay, but is well worth a stopover on any itinerary.

The picturesque harbour is overlooked by the crumbling, ivy-covered ruins of **Tarbert Castle** (⊙ 24hr) **FREE**, rebuilt by Robert the Bruce in the 14th century. You can hike up via a signposted footpath beside **Loch Fyne Gallery** (✆ 01880-820390; www.lochfynegallery. com; Harbour St; ⊙ 10am-5pm Mon-Sat, 10.30am-5pm Sun), which showcases the work of local artists.

MULL OF KINTYRE

A narrow winding road, 15 miles long, leads south from Campbeltown to the **Mull of Kintyre**, passing good sandy beaches near Southend. This remote headland was immortalised in the famous song by Paul McCartney and Wings; the former Beatle owns a farmhouse in the area. From the road's end, a 30-minute steep downhill walk leads to a clifftop lighthouse, with Northern Ireland, only 12 miles away, visible across the channel. Don't leave the road when the frequent mists roll in; it's easy to become disoriented.

🛏 Sleeping & Eating

★ **Knap Guest House**   B&B ££

(✆ 01880-820015;   www.knapguesthouse.co.uk; Campbeltown Rd; d £90-99; 🔊) This cosy upstairs spot at the bend in the main road offers faultless hospitality, luxurious furnishings and an attractive blend of Scottish and Far Eastern decor, with wooden elephants especially prominent. The welcome is warm, and there are great harbour views from the breakfast room, where the open kitchen allows you to admire the host at work. Prices drop in low season.

Moorings   B&B ££

(✆ 01880-820756; www.themooringsbb.co.uk; Pier Rd; s £50-60, d £80; 🅿🔊) Follow the harbour just past Tarbert's centre to this spot, which is beautifully maintained and decorated by one man and his dogs. It has great views over the water and an eclectic menagerie of ceramic and wooden animals and offbeat artwork; you can't miss it from the street.

Starfish Rooms   B&B ££

(✆ 01880-820304; www.starfishtarbert.com; Castle St; s/d without breakfast £35/70; 🔊) Above the restaurant of the same name, but run separately, this corridor of compact, floorboarded en suite rooms is a good deal, particularly for single travellers. Rooms 6 and 7 are doubles with attractive exposed stone walls. Breakfast isn't included, but there are cafes very close at hand.

Ca' Dora   CAFE £

(✆ 01880-820258; www.facebook.com/cafecadora; Harbour St; mains £6-16; ⊙ 8am-9pm; 🔊) A welcome spot among the somewhat tired line of pubs around this part of Tarbert's waterfront, this cheerful, locally popular cafe has bright and breezy staff and walls attractively adorned with nautical charts. As well as some standard Scottish cafe fare such as macaroni cheese and baked potatoes, it also offers some innovative daily specials based around local seafood.

★ **Starfish** SEAFOOD **££**
(☑ 01880-820733; www.starfishtarbert.com; Castle St; mains £12-23; ☺ 6-9pm Sun-Thu, noon-2pm & 6-9pm Fri & Sat mid-Mar–Oct; ☎) ✐ This attractive, very welcoming restaurant does simple, stylish seafood of brilliant quality. A great variety of specials – anything from classic French fish dishes to Thai curries – are prepared with whatever's fresh off the Tarbert boats that day. There are options for vegetarians and meat-eaters, too, and decent cocktails. Closed Sunday and Monday early and late in the season.

❶ Getting There & Away

BOAT

CalMac (☑ 0800 066 5000; www.calmac.co.uk) operates a car ferry from Tarbert to Portavadie on the Cowal Peninsula (adult/car £2.70/8.40, 25 minutes, six to 12 daily). From late October to March there are also ferries to Lochranza on Arran (adult/car £2.90/9.70, 1¼ hours, one daily) that must be booked in advance.

Ferries to Islay and Colonsay depart from Kennacraig ferry terminal, 5 miles southwest.

BUS

Tarbert is served by four to five daily coaches with Scottish Citylink (p863), between Campbeltown (£8.40, one hour) and Glasgow (£17.70, 3¼ hours).

Campbeltown

☑ 01586 / POP 4800

Blue-collar Campbeltown is set around a beautiful harbour. It still suffers from the decline of its fishing and whisky industries and the closure of the nearby air-force base, but is rebounding on the back of golf tourism, increased distillery action and a ferry link to Ayrshire. The spruced-up seafront backed by green hills lends the town a distinctly optimistic air.

◉ Sights & Activities

Springbank DISTILLERY
(☑ 01586-551710; www.springbankwhisky.com; 85 Longrow; tours from £7; ☺ tours 10am, 11.30am, 1.30pm & 3pm Mon-Fri, 10am & 11.30am Sat)

There were once no fewer than 32 distilleries around Campbeltown, but most closed in the 1920s. Today this is one of only three still in operation. It is also one of the few around that distills, matures and bottles all its whisky on the one site, making for an interesting tour. It produces a quality malt, one of Scotland's finest. Various premium tours take you deeper into the process.

Davaar Cave CAVE
(☺ 24hr) FREE A very unusual sight awaits in this cave on the southern side of Davaar island, at the mouth of Campbeltown Loch. On the wall of the cave is an eerie painting of the Crucifixion by local artist Archibald MacKinnon, dating from 1887. You can walk to the island at low tide: check tide times with the tourist office.

🛏 Sleeping

★ **Campbeltown Backpackers** HOSTEL **£**
(☑ 01586-551188; www.campbeltownbackpackers. co.uk; Big Kiln St; dm £20; ℗ ☎) ✐ This beautiful hostel occupies a central former school building: it's great, with a modern kitchen, state-of-the-art wooden bunks and access for people with disabilities. Profits go to maintain the Heritage Centre (opposite) that runs it. Rates are £2 cheaper if you book ahead.

Argyll Hotel INN **££**
(☑ 01583-421212; www.argylehotelkintyre.co.uk; A83, Bellochantuy; s £45, d £80-90; ℗ ☎ ☒) Right on a fine stretch of beach with a magnificent outlook to Islay and Jura, this traditional inn 10 miles north of Campbeltown on the main road is run with cheery panache. Rooms are cosy and breakfast is a highlight, with creative egg dishes and a wealth of homemade jams, as you gaze over the water.

🍷 Drinking & Nightlife

Ardshiel Hotel BAR
(☑ 01586-552133; www.ardshiel.co.uk; Kilkerran Rd; ☺ noon-11pm Mon-Sat, from 12.30pm Sun; ☎) This friendly hotel has one of Scotland's best whisky bars, the perfect place to learn more about the Campbeltown distilling tradition and to taste the local malts. With over 700 whiskies to choose from, it's not a place for the indecisive.

❶ Getting There & Away

AIR

Loganair (www.loganair.co.uk) flies between Glasgow and Campbeltown's mighty runway at Machrihanish.

BOAT

Kintyre Express (☎ 01586-555895; www.kintyreexpress.com; ☺ Apr-Sep) operates a small, high-speed passenger ferry from Campbeltown to Ballycastle in Northern Ireland (£50/90 one-way/return, 1½ hours, daily May to August, Friday to Sunday April and September). You must book in advance. From Ballycastle it heads on to Islay (£60/95 one-way/return from Ballycastle) and back before the return trip to Campbeltown. It also runs charters.

CalMac (☎ 0800 066 5000; www.calmac.co.uk) runs thrice weekly May to September between Ardrossan in Ayrshire and Campbeltown (adult/car £7.90/41.70, 2¾ hours); the Saturday return service stops at Brodick on Arran.

BUS

Scottish Citylink (p863) runs from Campbeltown to Glasgow (£21.60, 4¼ hours, four to five daily) via Tarbert, Inveraray and Loch Lomond. Change at Inveraray for Oban.

Islay

☎ 01496 / POP 3200

The home of some of the world's greatest and peatiest whiskies, whose names reverberate on the tongue like a pantheon of Celtic deities, Islay (*eye*-lah) is a wonderfully friendly place whose welcoming inhabitants offset its lack of scenic splendour compared to Mull or Skye. The distilleries are well geared-up for visits, but even if you're not a fan of single malt, the birdlife, fine seafood, turquoise bays and basking seals are ample reasons to visit. Locals are among Britain's most genial: a wave or cheerio to passers-by is mandatory, and you'll soon find yourself unwinding to relaxing island pace. The only drawback is that the waves of well-heeled whisky tourists have induced many sleeping options to raise prices to eye-watering levels.

In late May, the island hosts Fèis Ìle (Islay Festival; www.islayfestival.com; ☺ late May), a weeklong celebration of traditional Scottish music and whisky. Events include *ceilidhs*, pipe-band performances, distillery tours, barbecues and whisky tastings. The island packs out; book accommodation well in advance.

❶ Getting There & Away

There are two ferry terminals: Port Askaig on the east coast, and Port Ellen in the south. Islay airport lies midway between Port Ellen and Bowmore.

AIR

Loganair (www.loganair.co.uk) flies up to three times daily from Glasgow to Islay, while

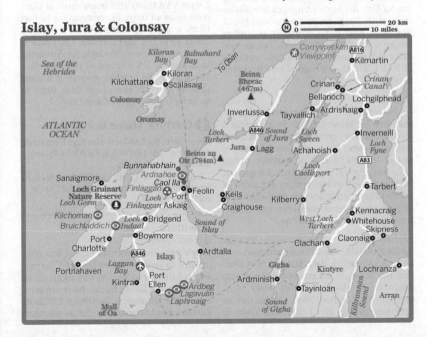

Islay, Jura & Colonsay

N 0 ——————— 20 km
   0 ——————— 10 miles

Sea of the Hebrides
Kiloran Bay
Balnahard Bay
To Oban
Corryvreckan Viewpoint
Kilmartin
Kiloran
Kilchattan
Scalasaig
Beinn Bhreac (467m)
Crinan
Crinan Canal
Bellanoch
Lochgilphead
Colonsay
Oronsay
Inverlussa
Tayvallich
Ardrishaig
ATLANTIC OCEAN
Loch Tarbert
Sound of Jura
Loch Sween
Inverneill
Loch Fyne
Jura
Lagg
Achahoish
Beinn an Oir (784m)
Loch Caolisport
Bunnahabhain
Ardnahoe
Caol Ila
Finlaggan
Sanaigmore
Loch Gruinart Nature Reserve
Loch Gorm
Feolin
Port Askaig
Keils
Craighouse
Kilberry
Tarbert
Loch Finlaggan
Kilchoman
Bridgend
Sound of Islay
Kennacraig
Bruichladdich
Loch Indaal
Bowmore
West Loch Tarbert
Whitehouse
Skipness
Port Charlotte
Islay
Ardtalla
Clachan
Claonaig
Portnahaven
Laggan Bay
Gigha
Kintyre
Lochranza
Kintra
Port Ellen
Ardbeg
Lagavulin
Laphroaig
Ardminish
Tayinloan
Arran
Mull of Oa
Sound of Gigha
Kilbrannan Sound
A816
A846
A83
A846

Hebridean Air Services (p863) operates twice daily on Tuesday and Thursday from Oban to Colonsay and Islay.

BOAT

CalMac (p873) runs ferries from Kennacraig to Port Ellen or Port Askaig (adult/car £6.70/33.45, two hours, three to five daily). On Wednesday and Saturday in summer you can travel to Colonsay (adult/car £4.15/17.30, 1¼ hours, day trip possible) and Oban (adult/car £9.60/51.45, four hours).

Book car space on ferries several days in advance.

Port Ellen & Around

Port Ellen is Islay's principal entry point. The coast stretching northeast is one of the loveliest parts of the island, where within 3 miles you'll find three of whisky's biggest names: Laphroaig, Lagavulin and Ardbeg.

The kelp-fringed skerries (small rocky islands or reefs) of the **Ardmore Islands**, near Kildalton, are a wildlife haven and home to Europe's second-largest colony of common seals.

⦿ Sights

Ardbeg   DISTILLERY
(☑ 01496-302244; www.ardbeg.com; tours from £6; ⊙ 9.30am-5pm Mon-Fri year-round, plus Sat & Sun Apr-Oct) Ardbeg's iconic peaty whiskies start with their magnificent 10-year-old. The basic tour is good, and it also offers longer tours involving walks, stories and extended tastings. It's 3 miles northeast of Port Ellen; there's a good cafe for lunch here, too.

Lagavulin   DISTILLERY
(☑ 01496-302749;   www.lagavulindistillery.com; tours from £6; ⊙ 9am-6pm Mon-Fri, to 5pm Sat & Sun May-Sep, 9am-5pm daily Apr & Oct, 10am-4pm Mon-Sat Nov-Mar) Peaty and powerful, this is one of the triumvirate of southern distilleries near Port Ellen. The Core Range tour (£15) is a good option, cutting out much of the distillery mechanics that you might have already experienced elsewhere and replacing it with an extended tasting.

Laphroaig   DISTILLERY
(☑ 01496-302418; www.laphroaig.com; tours from £10; ⊙ 9.45am-5pm daily Mar-Oct, to 4.30pm daily Nov & Dec, to 4.30pm Mon-Fri Jan & Feb) Laphroaig produces famously peaty whiskies just outside Port Ellen. Of the various premium tastings that it offers, the 'Water to

Whisky' tour (£100) is recommended – you see the water source, dig peat, have a picnic and try plenty of drams.

🛏 Sleeping & Eating

Askernish B&B   B&B ££
(☑ 01496-302536; www.askernishbandb.co.uk; 49 Frederick Cres, Port Ellen; s £50, d £90-100; 🛜) Very handy for the Port Ellen ferry slip, this dark-stone Victorian house was once the local medical practice; indeed, one of the rooms is in the former surgery, while another is the waiting room. Rooms are generous, with old-style flowery decor but modern bathroom fittings. The owner takes real interest in her guests and is a delight.

Old Kiln Café   CAFE £
(☑ 01496-302244;   www.ardbeg.com;   Ardbeg; mains £8-13; ⊙ 10am-3.45pm Mon-Fri year-round, plus Sat & Sun Apr-Oct; 🛜) Housed in the former malting kiln at Ardbeg distillery, this cafe serves homemade soups, tasty light meals, heartier daily specials and a range of desserts, including traditional clootie dumpling (a rich steamed pudding filled with currants and raisins).

SeaSalt   BISTRO, PIZZA ££
(☑ 01496-300300; www.seasalt-bistro.co.uk; 57 Frederick Cres, Port Ellen; mains £10-16; ⊙ noon-2.30pm & 5-8.45pm) This buzzy modern place represents an unusual combination in Port Ellen: a takeaway doing kebabs, pizzas and bacon rolls, but also a bistro. High-backed dining chairs are comfortable for devouring local seafood off a menu of daily specials. The prawn and crayfish cocktail is a great place to start. It also opens from 10am to noon for coffee and breakfasty fare.

ⓘ Getting There & Away

About half of the CalMac ferries from Kennacraig dock in Port Ellen (adult/car £6.70/33.45, two hours).

Buses run to Port Ellen from Bowmore six to 10 times Monday to Saturday (25 minutes); some continue to Ardbeg.

Bowmore

☑ 01496 / POP 700

Islay's attractive Georgian capital was built in 1768 to replace the village of Kilarrow, which just had to go – it was spoiling the view from the laird's house. Its centrepieces are the **Bowmore Distillery** (☑ 01496-810441; www.bowmore.com; School St; tours from £10; ⊙9.30am-5pm Mon-Sat, noon-4pm Sun Mar-Oct, 10am-5pm Mon-Sat Nov-Feb) and distinctive **Round Church** at the top of Main St, built in circular form to ensure that the devil had no corners to hide in. He was last seen in one of the island's distilleries.

Sleeping & Eating

★ Lambeth House
B&B ££

(☑01496-810597; lambethguesthouse@tiscali.co. uk; Jamieson St; s/d £70/98; ☎) Cheerily welcoming, and with smart modern rooms with top-notch en suite bathrooms, this is a sound option in the centre of town. The host is a long-time expert in making guests feel at home, and her breakfasts are reliably good. Rooms vary substantially in size but their prices are the same, so ask for a larger one when booking.

Dha Urlar
B&B ££

(☑07967 505991; www.dha-urlar-bed-and-break fast.co.uk; Cruach; r £125-150; ℗☎) Just a mile out of Bowmore, this place sits in an elevated position granting spectacular perspectives across moorland to Jura, the Mull of Kintyre and the coast of Ireland. Rooms have lots of space, comfortable beds and modern bathrooms. Breakfast is served from an open kitchen while your hosts helpfully supply you with lots of local information.

Bowmore House
B&B £££

(☑01496-810324; www.thebowmorehouse.co.uk; Shore St; s/d from £85/135; ℗☎) This stately former bank building has plenty of character and super water views. It's a top-level B&B, with coffee machines in the rooms, an honesty minibar with bottles of wine and local ales, and plush king-sized beds. Rooms are spacious, high-ceilinged and light. Further rooms are in adjacent cottages, also available on a self-catering basis.

Harbour Inn
BOUTIQUE HOTEL £££

(☑01496-810330; www.bowmore.com/harbour-inn; The Square; s/d from £115/145; ☎) The plush seven-room Harbour Inn, owned by Bowmore Distillery, offers friendly service, a good restaurant, a snug bar and prime location a few steps from the water in Islay's capital. The chambers are well appointed with modern comforts, quality amenities – including whisky soaps and gels – and plush fabrics, though some are on the small side for the price.

✕ Eating & Drinking

Harbour Inn
BRITISH ££

(☑01496-810330; www.bowmore.com; The Square; mains £15-20; ⊙noon-2.30pm & 6-9.30pm; ☎) Owned by the Bowmore Distillery, this restaurant at the Harbour Inn is the classiest in town. The conservatory-style dining area offers wonderful sunset views over the water. Islay oysters are a delicious and obvious choice; the rest of the menu could benefit from a little more seasonal and local focus, but is competently prepared and presented.

Peatzeria
ITALIAN ££

(☑01496-810810; www.peatzeria.com; 22 Shore St; mains £11-18; ⊙noon-10pm, closed Mon in winter; ☎) This is one of those names that just had to be. Nice work, punsters! An impressively realised church conversion has created a warmly welcoming Italian restaurant that specialises in toothsome stone-baked pizzas, but it also does a great line in antipasti, lasagne and other pasta dishes. The weatherproof conservatory seating area has special views over the bay.

Lochside Hotel
PUB

(☑01496-810244; www.lochsidehotel.co.uk; 20 Shore St; ⊙11am-midnight; ☎) One of Islay's key whisky bars, Lochside Hotel has a fine selection of local malts and a good atmosphere, with locals rubbing shoulders with distillery tourists looking for a taste of a hard-to-find dram. It also does decent bar meals.

❶ Information

Bowmore Tourist Office (☑01496-305165; www.islayinfo.com; The Square; ⊙10am-5pm Mon-Sat, noon-3pm Sun Mar-Jun, 9.30am-5.30pm Mon-Sat, noon-3pm Sun Jul & Aug, 10am-5pm Mon-Sat Sep-Oct, 10am-3pm Mon-Fri Nov-Feb) One of the nation's best tourist offices. The staff will bend over backwards to find you accommodation if things look full up.

❶ Getting There & Away

Bowmore is connected by bus (Monday to Saturday) to the ferry terminals and Islay's major settlements.

Port Charlotte & Around

Eleven miles from Bowmore, on the opposite shore of Loch Indaal, is attractive Port Charlotte, a former distillery town that appeals as a base. Museums in town and distilleries close by mean there's plenty to do.

Six miles southwest of Port Charlotte the road ends at **Portnahaven**, a picturesque fishing village. For seal-spotting, you can't do better; there are frequently dozens of the portly beasts basking in the small harbour.

◉ Sights

★ Bruichladdich   DISTILLERY

(☑ 01496-850190; www.bruichladdich.com; Bruichladdich; tours from £5; ⊙ 9am-6pm Mon-Fri, to 5pm Sat, 10am-4pm Sun Apr-Sep, reduced hours Oct-Mar) A couple of miles from Port Charlotte, Bruichladdich (brook-*lad*-dy) is an infectiously fun distillery to visit and produces a mind-boggling range of bottlings; there's always some new experiment cooking. The standard expression is lightly peated, but they turn out some phenolic monsters under the Port Charlotte and Octomore labels. They also make a gin here, the Botanist, infused with local herbs. A generous attitude to tastings makes for an uplifting visit.

Kilchoman   DISTILLERY

(☑ 01496-850011; www.kilchomandistillery.com; Rockfield Farm, Kilchoman; tours from £7; ⊙ 9.45am-5pm Apr-Oct, closed Sat & Sun Nov-Mar) ✎ Likeable Kilchoman, set on a farm, is one of Scotland's smallest distilleries. It grows and malts some of its own barley here and does its own bottling by hand. It has a wide variety of attractively packaged expressions: the 100% Islay whiskies are the ones produced from the home-grown barley. The tour is informative and the tasting generous. There's also a good cafe.

Museum of Islay Life   MUSEUM

(☑ 01496-850358; www.islaymuseum.org; Port Charlotte; adult/child £4/1; ⊙ 10.30am-4.30pm Mon-Fri Apr-Oct) Islay's long history is lovingly recorded in this museum, housed in the former Free Church. Prize exhibits include an illicit still, 19th-century crofters' furniture, and a set of leather boots once worn by the horse that pulled the lawnmower at Islay House (so it wouldn't leave hoof prints on the lawn!).

🛏 Sleeping & Eating

Islay SYHA   HOSTEL £

(☑ 01496-850385; www.syha.org.uk; Main St, Port Charlotte; dm/tw/q £20/48/90; ⊙ Apr-Oct; @ 🛜) This clean and modern brick hostel has spotless dorms with washbasins and a large kitchen and living room. It's housed in a former distillery building with views over the loch. The bus stops nearby. Breakfast and

heatable dinners are available. Have a crack at Islay Monopoly, one of the board games on hand.

Distillery House   B&B £ial£

(☑ 01496-850495; mamak@sky.com; Main St, Port Charlotte; s/d £38/80, tw without bathroom £76; P 🛜) For genuine islander hospitality at a fair price, head to this homely B&B, on the right as you enter Port Charlotte from the north. Set in part of the former Lochindaal distillery, it's run by a kindly local couple who make their own delicious marmalade and oatcakes. Rooms are well kept and most comfortable. The cute single has sea views. Minimum two-night stay.

Port Charlotte Hotel   HOTEL £££

(☑ 01496-850360; www.portcharlottehotel.co.uk; Main St, Port Charlotte; s/d/f £175/240/290; P 🛜 🍽) This lovely old Victorian hotel has individually decorated bedrooms – modern but classic in style – with crisp white sheets, good toiletries and sea views. It's a friendly place with a plush lounge, cosy bar and quality restaurant.

Yan's Kitchen   BISTRO ££

(☑ 01496-850230; www.yanskitchen.co.uk; Main St, Port Charlotte; tapas £4-7, mains £13-22; ⊙ food noon-3pm & 5.30-9pm Tue-Sun Apr-Oct; ✎) On the left as you enter Port Charlotte from the north, this cabin-like restaurant offers confident bistro cuisine, using ingredients like duck breast and local scallops to create satisfying, well-presented plates, whether Spanish tapas or evening seafood specials. The appealing wooden-floored interior takes full advantage of the coastal views. It's also open from 10.30am to noon for coffee and scones.

ⓘ Getting There & Away

Six buses run Monday to Saturday from Bowmore to Port Charlotte (30 minutes) via Bruichladdich, and continue to Portnahaven.

Jura

☑ 01496 / POP 200

Jura lies long, dark and low off the coast like a vast Viking longship, its billowing sail the distinctive triple peaks of the Paps of Jura. A magnificently wild and lonely island, it's the perfect place to get away from it all – as George Orwell did in 1948. Orwell wrote his masterpiece *Nineteen Eighty-Four* while living at the remote farmhouse of Barnhill in the north of the island.

Jura takes its name from the Old Norse *dyr-a* (deer island) – an apt appellation, as the island supports a population of around 6000 red deer, outnumbering their human cohabitants by about 30 to one.

Sights & Activities

There are few proper footpaths, and off-path exploration often involves rough going through giant bracken, knee-deep bogs and thigh-high tussocks. Hill access may be restricted during the deer-stalking season (July to February); the Jura Hotel can provide details. Look out for adders – the island is infested with them, but they're shy snakes and will move away as you approach.

Isle of Jura Distillery   DISTILLERY
(☑ 01496-820385; www.jurawhisky.com; Craighouse; tours from £6; ⊙10am-4.30pm Mon-Sat Apr-Oct, to 4pm Mon-Fri Nov-Mar) There aren't a whole lot of indoor attractions on the island of Jura apart from visiting the Isle of Jura Distillery. The standard tour runs twice a day, while specialist tours (£15 to £25) take you deeper into the production process and should be booked in advance.

Sleeping & Eating

Places to stay are very limited, so book ahead.

Jura Hotel   HOTEL ££
(☑ 01496-820243; www.jurahotel.co.uk; Craighouse; s £65, d £100-130; P⊋) The heart of Jura's community is this hotel, which is warmly welcoming and efficiently run. Rooms vary in size and shape, but all are renovated and inviting. The premier rooms, which all have sea views, are just lovely, with understated elegance and polished modern bathrooms. Eat in the restaurant or the convivial pub.

Barnhill   COTTAGE ££
(☑ 01786 850274; www.escapetojura.com; per week from £1200; P⊋) The cottage where George Orwell stayed in is in a gloriously remote location in Jura's north. It sleeps eight and is 7 miles from the main road on a rough 4WD track, and 25 miles from the pub. It's pretty basic but has a generator.

Antlers   CAFE £
(☑ 01496-820496; www.facebook.com/antlers. jura; Craighouse; light meals £4-9; ⊙10am-4pm Easter-Oct) ⌀ This community-owned cafe has a craft shop and displays on Jura heritage. It does tasty home baking, venison burgers, sandwiches and more. Sit out on

THE PAPS OF JURA

Climbing the **Paps** is a truly tough hill walk over ankle-breaking scree requiring good fitness and navigational skills. It's 11 hard miles (allow eight hours). The first peak you reach is Beinn a'Chaolais (734m), the second Beinn an Oir (784m), then Beinn Shiantaidh (755m). Most hikers also climb Corra Bheinn (569m), before joining Evans' Walk to return.

The most popular starting place is by the bridge over the River Corran, 3 miles north of Craighouse. If you succeed in bagging all four hills, reflect on the fact that the record for the annual **Isle of Jura Fell Race** (www.jurafellrace.org.uk; ⊙late May) is just three hours; and that includes cresting seven hills!

the deck to enjoy the view. It does takeaway dinners on Fridays and sometimes opens for sit-ins. Not licensed – £3 corkage.

Getting There & Around

A **car ferry** (☑ 01496-840681; www.argyll-bute. gov.uk) shuttles between Port Askaig on Islay and Feolin on Jura (adult/car/bicycle £1.85/9.60/free, five minutes, hourly Monday to Saturday, every two hours Sunday). There is no direct car-ferry connection to the mainland.

From April to September, **Jura Passenger Ferry** (☑ 07768 450000; www.jurapassenger ferry.com; one-way £20; ⊙Apr-Sep) runs from Tayvallich on the mainland to Craighouse on Jura (one hour, one or two daily except Wednesday). Booking is recommended (you can do this online).

The island's only **bus service** (☑ 01436-810200; www.garelochheadcoaches.co.uk) runs between the ferry slip at Feolin and Craighouse (20 minutes, six to seven Monday to Saturday), timed to coincide with ferry arrivals and departures. Some of the runs continue north as far as Inverlussa.

ARRAN

☑ 01770 / POP 4600

Enchanting Arran is a jewel in Scotland's scenic crown. The island is a visual feast, and boasts culinary delights, its own brewery and distillery, and stacks of accommodation options. The variations in Scotland's dramatic landscape can all be experienced

Arran

STIRLING & CENTRAL SCOTLAND BRODICK & AROUND

on this one island, best explored by pulling on the hiking boots or jumping on a bicycle. Arran offers some challenging walks in the mountainous north, while the island's circular coastal road is very popular with cyclists.

ℹ Information

The **tourist office** (☑ 01770-303774; www.visitscotland.com; ☉9am-5pm Mon-Sat Mar-Oct, plus 10am-5pm Sun Apr-Sep, 10am-4pm Mon-Sat Nov-Feb) is in Brodick. The ferry from Ardrossan also has some tourist information. Useful websites include www.visitarran.com.

ℹ Getting There & Around

CalMac (p873) runs ferries between Ardrossan and Brodick (adult/car £3.90/15.55, 55 minutes, four to nine daily). From April to late October services also run between Claonaig on the Kintyre peninsula and Lochranza (adult/car £2.90/9.70, 30 minutes, seven to nine daily). In winter this service runs to Tarbert (1¼ hours) once daily and must be reserved.

Four to seven buses daily go from Brodick pier to Lochranza (£3.15, 45 minutes), and many head the other way to Lamlash (£2) and Whiting Bay (£2.75, 30 minutes), then on to Kildonan and Blackwaterfoot. Pick up a timetable from the tourist office.

An Arran Dayrider costs £6.30 from the driver, giving a day's travel. Download a bus timetable from www.spt.co.uk.

Brodick & Around

☑ 01770 / POP 800

Most visitors arrive in Brodick, the beating heart of the island of Arran, and congregate along the coastal road to admire the town's long curving bay. On a clear day it's a spectacular vista, with Goatfell looming over the forested shore.

◉ Sights & Activities

Brodick Castle   CASTLE
(NTS; ☑ 01770-302202; www.nts.org.uk; castle & park adult/child £14/10, park only £7.50/6.50; ☉ castle 11am-4pm May-Aug, 11am-3pm Apr & Sep, park 9.30am-sunset year-round) This elegant castle 2 miles north of Brodick evolved from 13th-century origins into a stately home and hunting lodge for the Dukes of Hamilton. You enter via the hunting gallery, wallpapered with deer heads. The rest of the interior is characterised by fabulous 19th-century wooden furniture and an array of horses 'n' hounds paintings. Helpful guides and laminated sheets – the kids' ones are more entertaining – add info. At last visit it was closed for renovations, due to reopen in spring 2019.

Isle of Arran Brewery   BREWERY
(☑ 01770-302353; www.arranbrewery.com; tours £5; ☉ 10am-5pm Mon-Sat, 12.30-5pm Sun Apr-Sep, 10am-3.30pm Mon & Wed-Sat Oct-Mar) This brewery, 1.5 miles from Brodick off the Lochranza road, produces the excellent Arran beers, which include the addictive Arran Dark. Tours run daily: call for times as they vary by season. They last about 45 minutes and include a tasting of all the beers.

Isle of Arran Heritage Museum   MUSEUM
(☑ 01770-302636; www.arranmuseum.co.uk; Rosaburn; adult/child £4/2; ☉ 10.30am-4.30pm Apr-Oct) This museum has a varied collection of historical and ethnographic items, from prehistoric stone tools to farming implements. There's quite a bit to see across several heritage buildings, with good background on the island and its people. Gardens and a cafe round out the experience. It's on the way to the castle from Brodick.

★ Goatfell   HIKING
The walk up and down Goatfell (874m), the island's highest point, is 8 miles return (up

to eight hours), with trailheads at Brodick and Brodick Castle among others. In fine weather there are superb views to Ben Lomond and Northern Ireland. It can, however, be very cold and windy up here; take appropriate maps (available at the tourist office), waterproofing and a compass.

Sleeping & Eating

Brodick Bunkhouse HOSTEL £
(☎01770-302968; www.brodickbunkhouse.co.uk; Alma Rd; dm £25; 🅿🛜) A short stroll from the ferry, behind the Douglas hotel, this handy hostel has attractive, comfortable triple-decker bunks with individual plugs and USB ports. It's generally unstaffed, with keycode entry. It has a simple kitchen and access for people with disabilities. No under-18s are admitted.

⭐ **Glenartney** B&B ££
(☎01770-302220; www.glenartney-arran.co.uk; Mayish Rd; d £75-100; ⊗Easter-Oct; 🅿🛜🍽) ♻
Uplifting bay views and genuine, helpful hosts make this a cracking option. Airy, stylish rooms make the most of the natural light at the top of the town. Comfortable lounges, help-yourself home baking and pod coffee plus a sustainable ethos make for a very pleasurable stay. Top facilities for cyclists, plus drying rooms and trail advice for hikers are added bonuses.

Douglas HOTEL £££
(☎01770-302968; www.thedouglashotel.co.uk; Shore Rd; r £160-200, ste £230; 🅿🛜🍽) Opposite the ferry, the Douglas is a smart, stylish haven of island hospitality. Views are magnificent and luxurious rooms with smart contemporary fabrics make the most of them. There are numerous thoughtful touches such as binoculars to admire the vistas, and bathrooms are great. The downstairs **bar and bistro** (bistro mains £13-20, bar meals £10-15; ⊗bistro 6-9.30pm, bar noon-9.30pm; 🛜♻) are also recommended. Prices drop midweek and in winter.

⭐ **Brodick Bar & Brasserie** BRASSERIE ££
(☎01770-302169; www.brodickbar.co.uk; Alma Rd; mains £13-22; ⊗noon-2.30pm & 5.30-9pm Mon-Sat; 🛜) This is one of Arran's most enjoyable eating experiences. The regularly changing blackboard menu brings modern French flair to a Brodick pub, with great presentation, efficient service and delicious flavour combinations. You'll have a hard time choosing, as it's all brilliant. It's very buzzy

on weekend evenings. It was for sale at the time of research so things may change.

ℹ Getting There & Away

CalMac (p873) runs ferries between Ardrossan and Brodick (adult/car £3.90/15.55, 55 minutes, four to nine daily), and buses depart from here to the rest of the island.

Lochranza

☎01770 / POP 200

The village of Lochranza has a stunning location in a small bay on Arran island's north coast. It's characterised by the ruined 13th-century **Lochranza Castle** (www.historicenvironment.scot; ⊗24hr) **FREE**, a ruin standing proud on a little promontory. The nearby **Isle of Arran Distillery** (☎01770-830264; www.arranwhisky.com; tours adult/child £8/free; ⊗10am-5pm Mar-Oct, 10.30am-4pm Nov-Feb) produces a light, aromatic single malt. The Lochranza area bristles with red deer, who wander insouciantly into the village to crop the grass.

Sleeping & Eating

⭐ **Lochranza SYHA** HOSTEL £
(☎01770-830631; www.syha.org.uk; dm/d/q £24.50/64/108; ⊗mid-Mar–Oct, plus Sat & Sun year-round; 🅿@🛜🍽) ♻ An excellent hostel in a charming spot with lovely views. Rooms sport chunky wooden furniture, keycards and lockers. Rainwater toilets, energy-saving heating solutions and a wheelchair-accessible room show thoughtful design, while plush lounging areas, a kitchen you could run a restaurant out of, a laundry, a drying room, red deer in the garden and welcoming management combine for a top option.

⭐ **Butt Lodge** B&B ££
(☎01770-830333; www.buttlodge.co.uk; s from £72, d £85-95, ste £110-125; ⊗Mar–mid-Oct; 🅿🛜) Down a short potholed road, this Victorian hunting lodge has been adapted by keen young owners to offer contemporary comfort with relaxed style and genuine hospitality. Rooms give perspectives over hills, garden and the rustic village golf course, with its red deer greenkeepers. The Castle suite is a fabulous space with views three ways and a mezzanine seating area.

Stags Pavilion BISTRO ££
(☎01770-830600; www.stagspavilion.com; mains £11-20; ⊗5.30-8.15pm Mon, Tue & Thu-Sat, noon-2.30pm Sun; ♻) The best restaurant up this

---

OFF THE BEATEN TRACK

KING'S CAVE

Arran is one of several islands that claim the cave where Robert the Bruce had his famous arachnid encounter: the story goes that watching a persistent spider finally manage to swing itself to its goal gave him heart to continue the independence struggle. The seaside grotto known as **King's Cave** (⊘24hr) FREE can be reached from Blackwaterfoot (6 miles) or on a 3-mile circuit from a car park on the road north of town. Take a torch to spot early Christian carvings and typical Pictish symbols within it.

The walk can easily be extended to **Machrie Moor Stone Circle** (Machrie; ⊘24hr) FREE, erected around 4000 years ago.

---

end of Arran island, Stags Pavilion is unassumingly set in the former clubhouse of the rustic Lochranza golf course. There's a strong emphasis on local seafood, and dishes are created with a marked Italian influence. You'll likely see red deer munching the grass nearby. It's almost always booked out; reserve ahead if possible. BYO booze.

ⓘ Getting There & Away

From April to late October ferries run between Claonaig on the Kintyre peninsula and Lochranza (adult/car £2.90/9.70, 30 minutes, seven to nine daily). In winter this service runs to Tarbert (1¼ hours) once daily and must be reserved.

Buses run regularly between Brodick and Lochranza (£3.15, 45 minutes).

South Coast

The landscape in the south of Arran is gentler than in the north; the road drops into little wooded valleys, and it's particularly lovely around **Kilmory** and **Lagg**, from where a 10-minute walk will take you to **Torrylinn Cairn**, a chambered tomb over 4000 years old. **Kildonan** has pleasant sandy beaches, a gorgeous water outlook, a hotel, a campsite and an ivy-clad ruined castle.

In genteel **Whiting Bay**, strung out along the water, you'll find small sandy beaches and easy one-hour walks through the forest to the **Giant's Graves** and **Glenashdale**

Falls – keep an eye out for golden eagles and other birds of prey.

🛏 Sleeping & Eating

★**Sealshore Campsite**   CAMPSITE £
(☎01770-820320; www.campingarran.com; Kildonan; 1-/2-person tents £9/16, pods for 2 people £35; ⊘Mar-Oct; P🐕📶🐶) Living up to its name, this excellent small campsite is right by the sea (and the Kildonan Hotel) and has one of Arran's finest views from its grassy camping area. There are good facilities, including BBQs, power showers and a day room; the breeze keeps the midges away. Cosy camping pods or a fabulously refurbished Roma caravan offer non-tent choices.

Kilmory Haven   HOSTEL £
(☎01770-870345; www.kilmoryhaven.com; Village Hall, Kilmory; r per adult £25.20; P📶) This community project in Kilmory's village hall is run with great enthusiasm and makes a recommendable place to stay. Comfortable upstairs dorms and family bunk rooms are hostel-style, but you won't share. Bedding is included in the price and there's a decent kitchen and eating area. Downstairs is a friendly seasonal cafe, the Wee Bite, and a weekend bar.

Kildonan Hotel   HOTEL ££
(☎01770-820207; www.kildonanhotel.com; Kildonan; s/d/ste £85/109/135; P@📶🐶) The Kildonan's position, with dreamy views over the water and seals basking on the rocks, is unbeatable. Appealing rooms, nearly all of which have sea vistas, have been renovated; suites – with private terrace or small balcony – are just great. Rooms are gradually being converted into smart modern apartments, which look fab but will have a minimumstay requirement.

Coast   BISTRO ££
(☎01770-700308; www.facebook.com/coastarran; Shore Rd, Whiting Bay; lunches £5-7, dinner mains £11-16; ⊘10am-3pm & 5-9pm Wed-Sat, 10am-4pm Sun-Tue, hours vary by season; 📶🐕) Offering a sun-drenched conservatory on the water's edge, this place serves dinners in the evening, with lighter offerings during the day. It has changed hands quite a bit in recent years but is always a pleasurable spot to sit. Hours vary substantially by season.

ⓘ Getting There & Away

Buses head from Brodick and Lamlash to Whiting Bay and on to Kildonan and beyond.

Lamlash

📞 01770 / POP 1000

Lamlash, just 3 miles south of Brodick, is in a dazzling setting strung along the beachfront. The bay was used as a safe anchorage by the navy during WWI and WWII.

◉ Sights

Holy Island   ISLAND

Just off Lamlash, this island is owned by the Samye Ling Tibetan Centre and used as a retreat, but day visits are allowed. A tide-dependent ferry zips across from Lamlash. No dogs, bikes, alcohol or fires are allowed on Holy Island. A good walk to the top of the hill (314m) takes two or three hours return. You can stay at the **Holy Island Centre for World Peace & Health** (📞01770-601100; www.holyisle.org; dm/s/d incl full board £32/55/80; ⊙Apr-Oct). Prices include full (vegetarian) board.

🛏️ Sleeping & Eating

Lilybank Guest House   B&B ££

(📞01770-600230; www.lilybank-arran.co.uk; Shore Rd; s/d £60/80; ⊙Apr-Sep; 🅿️🛜) Built in the 17th century, Lilybank retains its heritage but has been refurbished for 21st-century needs. Rooms are clean and comfortable, with one that's good for those with limited mobility. The front rooms have great views over Holy Island. Breakfast includes organic porridge, oak-smoked kippers and other Arran goodies.

★Glenisle Hotel   HOTEL £££

(📞01770-600559; www.glenislehotel.com; Shore Rd; s/d/superior d £102/157/207; 🛜) This stylish hotel offers great service and high comfort levels. Rooms are decorated with contemporary fabrics; 'cosy' rooms under the sloping roof are a little cheaper. All feel fresh and include binoculars for scouring the seashore; upgrade to a 'superior' for the best water views. Downstairs is excellent **food** (📞01770-600559; www.glenislehotel.com; Shore Rd; mains £12-18; ⊙noon-8.45pm; 🛜🍴) and lovely outdoor seating by the garden.

ℹ️ Getting There & Away

Lamlash is served by regular buses from Brodick (£2, 10 minutes).

A **ferry** (📞01770-700463, 07970 771960; tomin10@btinternet.com; return adult/child £12/6; ⊙daily Apr-Oct; by arrangement Tue & Fri Nov-Mar) to Holy Island makes three daily trips (15 minutes) between April and October.

CATUNCIA/SHUTTERSTOCK ©

1. Dunvegan Castle (p931), Dunvegan
Seat of the chief of Clan MacLeod and a popular attraction on Isle of Skye.

2. Highland cow, Perthshire (p902)
Though a small island, Britain has a diverse range of wildlife.

3. Rosslyn Chapel (p783), Roslin
Crowds of tourists come to see the church made famous by Dan Brown's *The Da Vinci Code*.

4. Glen Coe (p906), West Highlands
The grandest and most famous glen in Scotland and the site of a 17th-century massacre.

Inverness & the Highlands & Islands

Best Places to Eat

➜ Loch Bay (p931)

➜ Côte du Nord (p917)

➜ Captain's Galley (p915)

➜ Machair Kitchen (p939)

➜ Three Chimneys (p931)

Best Places to Stay

➜ Torridon (p924)

➜ Hillstone Lodge (p931)

➜ Brinkies Guest House (p949)

➜ Albert Hotel (p946)

➜ Rocpool Reserve (p888)

Why Go?

Scotland's vast and melancholy soul is here, in an epic landscape whose stark beauty imprints the hearts of those who journey through it. Mist, peat, rock, heather...and long, sun-blessed summer evenings that compensate for the occasional days of horizontal rain.

The hills and glens of Highland Perthshire offer a memorable first taste. The region's capital, Inverness, is backed by the craggy Cairngorms, which draw hikers and skiers to their slopes. Further north, ancient stones stand testament to prehistoric builders on the magical islands of Orkney and Shetland, where squadrons of seabirds wheel above huge nesting colonies.

The most epic mountain scenery – you really need an orchestra to do it justice – is in the northwest Highlands, and it continues into Skye, where the mighty Cuillin Hills tower jaggedly in the setting sun. Beyond, on the Atlantic fringe, the Outer Hebrides offer the nation's most beautiful beaches and a glimpse of traditional island life.

When to Go

➜ May, June and September are the ideal times to visit: you have the best chance for dry weather, and fewer midges.

➜ September is also the month of the Braemar Gathering, Scotland's best-known Highland Games.

➜ Snow covers the hills from November to March, and in December it gets dark at 4pm.

➜ In January, there's great skiing in the Cairngorms, and Shetland hosts the Viking-themed Up Helly Aa festival.

History

From the decline of the Vikings onwards, Scottish history has been predictably and often violently bound to that of its southern neighbour. Battles and border raids were commonplace until shared kingship, then political union, drew the two together. However, there has often been as much – if not more – of a cultural divide between Highland and Lowland Scotland than ever between Lowland Scotland and England.

INVERNESS & THE GREAT GLEN

Inverness, one of Britain's fastest growing cities, is the capital of the Highlands. It's a transport hub and jumping-off point for the central, western and northern Highlands, the Moray Firth coast and the Great Glen.

The Great Glen is a geological fault running in a line across Scotland from Fort William to Inverness. The glaciers of the last Ice Age eroded a deep trough along the fault line, which is now filled by four lochs – Linnhe, Lochy, Oich and Ness. The glen has always been an important communication route – General George Wade built a military road along the southern side of Loch Ness in the early 18th century, and in 1822 the various lochs were linked by the Caledonian Canal to create a cross-country waterway. The A82 road along the glen was completed in 1933 – a date that coincides neatly with the first modern sightings of the Loch Ness Monster.

❶ Getting There & Away

There are regular bus services along the Great Glen between Inverness and Fort William. Inverness is connected by train to Glasgow and Edinburgh.

Inverness

☑ 01463 / POP 61,235

Inverness has a great location astride the River Ness at the northern end of the Great Glen. In summer it overflows with visitors intent on monster hunting at nearby Loch Ness, but it's worth a visit in its own right for a stroll along the picturesque River Ness, a cruise on Loch Ness, and a meal in one of the city's excellent restaurants.

Inverness was probably founded by King David in the 12th century, but thanks to its often violent history few buildings of real age or historical significance have survived – much of the older part of the city dates from the period following the completion of the Caledonian Canal in 1822. The broad and shallow River Ness, famed for its salmon fishing, runs through the heart of the city.

◉ Sights & Activities

★**Ness Islands**   PARK

The main attraction in Inverness is a leisurely stroll along the river to the Ness Islands. Planted with mature Scots pine, fir, beech and sycamore, and linked to the river banks and each other by elegant Victorian footbridges, the islands make an appealing picnic spot. They're a 20-minute walk south of the castle – head upstream on either side of the river (the start of the Great Glen Way), and return on the opposite bank.

Inverness Museum & Art Gallery   MUSEUM

(☑ 01463-237114; www.inverness.highland.museum; Castle Wynd; ⊙10am-5pm Tue-Sat Apr-Oct, noon-4pm Thu-Sat Nov-Mar) FREE Inverness Museum & Art Gallery has wildlife dioramas, geological displays, period rooms with historic weapons, Pictish stones and exhibitions of contemporary Highland arts and crafts.

Inverness Castle   CASTLE

(Castle St) The hill above the city centre is topped by the picturesque Baronial turrets of Inverness Castle, a pink-sandstone confection dating from 1847 that replaced a medieval castle blown up by the Jacobites in 1746; it serves today as the Sheriff's Court. It's not open to the public, but there are good views from the surrounding gardens.

Dolphin Spirit   WILDLIFE WATCHING

(☑ 07544 800620; www.dolphinspirit.co.uk; Inverness Marina, Stadium Rd; adult/child £18.50/12; ⊙Easter-Oct) Four times a day in season, this outfit runs cruises from Inverness into the Moray Firth to spot the UK's largest pod of bottlenose dolphins – around 130 animals. The dolphins feed on salmon heading for the rivers at the head of the firth, and can often be seen leaping and bow-surfing.

Loch Ness by Jacobite   BOATING

(☑ 01463-233999; www.jacobite.co.uk; Glenurquhart Rd; adult/child £23/15; ⊙Jun-Sep; ❄) Boats depart from Tomnahurich Bridge twice daily for a three-hour cruise along the Caledonian Canal to Loch Ness and back, with a live commentary on local history and wildlife. Buy tickets at the tourist

Inverness & the Highlands & Islands Highlights

1 North Coast 500 (p921) Road-tripping through quintessential Scottish scenery.

2 Harris (p936) Admiring the most beautiful beaches in the Western Isles.

3 Cuillin Hills (p929) Hiking over the top of Skye for a stunning skyscape.

4 Glen Affric (p891) Traversing the hills and lochs of Scotland's most beautiful glen.

5 Rothiemurchus Estate (p898) Wandering through ancient Caledonian forest in the Cairngorms.

6 Ben Nevis (p909) Summiting the UK's highest mountain.

7 Glen Coe (p906) Snapping a shot of this photogenic glen (when you can see it!).

8 Knoydart Peninsula (p911) Venturing into Britain's most remote and rugged wilderness.

9 Skara Brae (p948) Marvelling at monuments that predate the pyramids.

10 Orkney (p942) Island-hopping through a wild, beach-studded archipelago.

office (p890) and catch a free minibus to the boat. Other cruises and combined cruise and coach tours, from one to 6½ hours, are also available, some year-round.

🛏 Sleeping

Inverness has a good range of backpacker accommodation, and also some excellent boutique hotels. There are lots of guesthouses and B&Bs along Old Edinburgh Rd and Ardconnel St on the east side of the river, and on Kenneth St and Fairfield Rd on the west bank; all are within 10 minutes' walk of the city centre.

Black Isle Bar & Rooms HOSTEL £
(✆01463-229920; www.blackislebar.com; 68 Church St; dm/s/d £25/55/100; 🛜) It's a beer drinker's dream come true – top-quality hostel accommodation in a central location, upstairs from a bar that serves real ales from the local Black Isle Brewery.

Bazpackers Backpackers Hotel HOSTEL £
(✆01463-717663; www.bazpackershostel.co.uk; 4 Culduthel Rd; dm/d £18/60; @🛜) 🍃 This may be Inverness' smallest hostel (34 beds), but it's hugely popular. It's a friendly, quiet place – the main building has a convivial lounge centred on a wood-burning stove, and a small garden and great views (some rooms are in a separate building with no garden). The dorms and kitchen can be a bit cramped, but the showers are great.

Inverness SYHA HOSTEL £
(SYHA; ✆01463-231771; www.syha.org.uk; Victoria Dr; dm/d £19/77; P@🛜) Inverness' modern 166-bed hostel is 10 minutes' walk northeast of the city centre. Clean and well equipped, with comfy beds and a flashy stainless-steel kitchen. Booking is essential, especially at Easter and in July and August.

Ardconnel House B&B ££
(✆01463-240455; www.ardconnel-inverness.co.uk; 21 Ardconnel St; r per person £45-50; 🛜) The six-room Ardconnel is one of our favourites (advance booking is essential, especially in July and August) – a terraced Victorian house with comfortable en suite rooms, a dining room with crisp white table linen, and a breakfast menu that includes Vegemite for homesick Antipodeans. Kids under 10 years not allowed.

⭐ Heathmount Hotel BOUTIQUE HOTEL £££
(✆01463-235877; www.heathmounthotel.com; Kingsmills Rd; r from £160; P🛜) Small and

friendly, the Heathmount combines a popular local bar and restaurant with eight designer hotel rooms, each one different, ranging from a boldly coloured family room in purple and gold to a slinky black velvet four-poster double. Five minutes' walk east of the city centre.

⭐ Rocpool Reserve BOUTIQUE HOTEL £££
(✆01463-240089; www.rocpool.com; Culduthel Rd; r from £270; P🛜) Boutique chic meets the Highlands in this slick and sophisticated little hotel, where an elegant Georgian exterior conceals an oasis of contemporary cool. A gleaming white entrance hall lined with red carpet and contemporary art leads to designer rooms in shades of chocolate, cream and gold. A restaurant by Albert Roux completes the luxury package.

⭐ Trafford Bank B&B £££
(✆01463-241414; www.traffordbankguesthouse.co.uk; 96 Fairfield Rd; d £130-150; P🛜) Lots of rave reviews for this elegant Victorian villa, which was once home to a bishop, just a mitre's-toss from the Caledonian Canal and 10 minutes' walk west from the city centre. The luxurious rooms include fresh flowers and fruit, bathrobes and fluffy towels – ask for the Tartan Room, which has a wrought-iron king-size bed and Victorian roll-top bath.

🍴 Eating

Velocity Cafe CAFE £
(✆01463-419956; www.velocitylove.co.uk; 1 Crown Ave; mains £4-7; ⏰8am-5pm Mon-Wed & Fri, to 9pm Thu, 9am-5pm Sat, 10am-5pm Sun; 🛜🍼♿) 🍃 This cyclists' cafe serves soups, sandwiches and salads prepared with organic, locally sourced produce, as well as yummy cakes and coffee. There's also a workshop where you can repair your bike or book a session with a mechanic.

⭐ Café 1 BISTRO ££
(✆01463-226200; www.cafe1.net; 75 Castle St; mains £12-28; ⏰noon-2.30pm & 5-9.30pm Mon-Fri, 12.30-3pm & 6-9.30pm Sat; 🍼♿) 🍃 Café 1 is a friendly, appealing bistro with candle-lit tables amid elegant blonde-wood and wrought-iron decor. There is an international menu based on quality Scottish produce, from Aberdeen Angus steaks to crisp pan-fried sea bass and meltingly tender pork belly. There's a separate vegan menu.

Sam's Indian Cuisine INDIAN ££
(✆01463-713111; www.samsindian.com; 77-79 Church St; mains £9-17; ⏰noon-10.30pm Sat-Thu,

Inverness

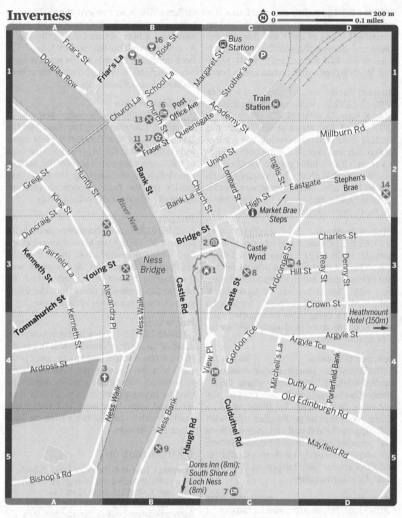

Inverness

◎ Sights
1 Inverness Castle	C3
2 Inverness Museum & Art Gallery	C3
3 St Andrew's Cathedral	B4

🛏 Sleeping
4 Ardconnel House	C3
5 Bazpackers Backpackers Hotel	C4
6 Black Isle Bar & Rooms	B1
7 Rocpool Reserve	C5

✕ Eating
8 Café 1	C3
9 Contrast Brasserie	B5
10 Kitchen Brasserie	B3
11 Mustard Seed	B2
12 Rocpool	B3
13 Sam's Indian Cuisine	B1
14 Velocity Cafe	D2

🍷 Drinking & Nightlife
15 MacGregor's	B1
16 Phoenix	B1

✪ Entertainment
17 Hootananny	B2

4-10.30pm Fri) The stylish decor in Sam's is a cut above your average curry shop, and so is the food – lots of fresh and flavoursome spices and herbs make dishes such as *jeera* chicken (cooked with cumin seed) really zing. Wash it down with Indian Cobra beer.

Mustard Seed   BISTRO **££**
(☑ 01463-220220; www.mustardseedrestaurant. co.uk; 16 Fraser St; mains £13-23; ⊙ noon-3pm & 5.30-10pm) ∅ The menu at this bright and bustling bistro changes weekly, but focuses on Scottish and French cuisine with a modern twist. Grab a table on the upstairs balcony if you can – it's the best outdoor lunch spot in Inverness, with a great view across the river. And a two-course lunch for £10 – yes, that's right – is hard to beat.

Kitchen Brasserie   MODERN SCOTTISH **££**
(☑ 01463-259119; www.kitchenrestaurant.co.uk; 15 Huntly St; mains £11-22; ⊙ noon-3pm & 5-10pm; ☎ ♿) This spectacular glass-fronted restaurant offers a great menu of top Scottish produce with a Mediterranean or Asian touch, and a view over the River Ness – try to get a table upstairs. Great value two-course lunch (£10, noon to 3pm) and early bird menu (£14, 5pm to 7pm).

Contrast Brasserie   BRASSERIE **££**
(☑ 01463-223777; www.glenmoristontownhouse. com/restaurant; 20 Ness Bank; mains £16-24; ⊙ noon-10pm) Book early for one of the best-value restaurants in Inverness – a dining room that drips designer style, with smiling professional staff and truly delicious food prepared using fresh Scottish produce. The two-/three-course lunch menu (£13/16) and three-course early bird menu (£18, 5pm to 6.30pm) are bargains.

Rocpool   MEDITERRANEAN **£££**
(☑ 01463-717274; www.rocpoolrestaurant.com; 1 Ness Walk; mains £14-31; ⊙ noon-2.30pm & 5.45-10pm Mon-Sat) ∅ Lots of polished wood, crisp white linen and leather booths and banquettes lend a sophisticated nautical air to this relaxed bistro, which offers a Mediterranean-influenced menu that makes the most of quality Scottish produce, especially seafood. The two-course lunch is £17.

🍷 Drinking & Nightlife

MacGregor's   BAR
(www.macgregorsbars.com; 113 Academy St; beer set menu for 2 from £21; ⊙ 11am-midnight Mon-Thu, 11am-1am Fri & Sat, noon-midnight Sun) Decked out in timber and tweed, this bar

strikes a distinctly modern chord. There's a huge selection of Scottish craft beers on tap, and even a beer 'set menu' described as 'a journey through the basics of craft beer'. The beer nerdiness extends to the gents' toilets, where urinals and washbasins have been fashioned out of beer kegs.

Clachnaharry Inn   PUB
(☑ 01463-239806; www.clachnaharryinn.co.uk; 17-19 High St, Clachnaharry; ⊙ 11am-11pm Mon-Thu, 11am-1am Fri & Sat, noon-11pm Sun; ☎) Just over a mile northwest of the city centre, on the bank of the Caledonian Canal just off the A862, is this delightful old coaching inn (with beer garden out the back) serving an excellent range of real ales and good pub grub.

Phoenix   PUB
(☑ 01463-233685; www.phoenixalehouse.co.uk; 108 Academy St; ⊙ 11am-1am Mon-Sat, noon-midnight Sun) Beautifully refurbished, this is the most traditional of the pubs in the city centre, with a mahogany horseshoe bar and several real ales on tap, including beers from the Cairngorm, Cromarty and Isle of Skye breweries.

Hootananny   LIVE MUSIC
(☑ 01463-233651; www.hootanannyinverness. co.uk; 67 Church St; ⊙ noon-1am Mon-Thu, to 3am Fri & Sat, 4pm-midnight Sun) Hootananny is the city's best live-music venue, with traditional folk- and/or rock-music sessions nightly, including big-name bands from all over Scotland (and, indeed, the world). The bar is well stocked with a range of beers from the local Black Isle Brewery.

ℹ Information

Inverness Tourist Office (☑ 01463-252401; www.visithighlands.com; 36 High St; ⊙ 9am-5pm Mon & Wed-Sat, from 10am Tue, 10am-3pm Sun, longer hours Mar-Oct; ☎) Accommodation booking service; also sells tickets for tours and cruises.

ℹ Getting There & Away

AIR

Inverness Airport (INV; ☑ 01667-464000; www.invernessairport.co.uk) is at Dalcross, 10 miles east of the city, off the A96 towards Aberdeen. There are scheduled flights to Amsterdam, London, Manchester, Dublin, Orkney, Shetland and the Outer Hebrides, as well as other places in the UK.

Stagecoach (☑ 01463-233371; www.stagecoachbus.com) bus 11/11A runs from the airport to Inverness bus station (£4.40, 25 minutes, every 30 minutes).

BUS

Services depart from **Inverness bus station** (Margaret St). Most intercity routes are served by **Scottish Citylink** (☑ 0871 266 3333; www.citylink.co.uk) and Stagecoach (p890). **National Express** (☑ 08717 818181; www.nationalexpress.com) has services to London (from £30, 13½ hours, one daily – more frequent services require changing at Glasgow).

Aberdeen (Stagecoach) £13.45, four hours, hourly

Aviemore £10.80, 45 minutes, eight daily

Edinburgh £32.20, 3½ to 4½ hours, seven daily

Fort William £12.20, two hours, six daily

Glasgow £32.20, 3½ to 4½ hours, hourly

Portree £26.40, 3¼ hours, two daily

Thurso (Stagecoach) £21, 3½ hours, three daily

Ullapool £14, 1½ hours, two daily except Sunday

If you book far enough in advance, **Megabus** (☑ 0141-352 4444; www.megabus.com) offers fares from as little as £1 for buses from Inverness to Glasgow and Edinburgh, and £10 to London.

TRAIN

Aberdeen £29.70, 2¼ hours, eight daily

Edinburgh £40, 3½ hours, eight daily

Glasgow £40, 3½ hours, eight daily

Kyle of Lochalsh £20, 2½ hours, four daily Monday to Saturday, two Sunday; one of Britain's great scenic train journeys

London £180, up to nine hours, one daily direct; others require a change at Edinburgh

Wick £18, 4½ hours, four daily Monday to Saturday, one or two on Sunday; via Thurso

ⓘ Getting Around

BICYCLE

Ticket to Ride (☑ 01463-419160; www.ticketoridehighlands.co.uk; Bellfield Park; per day from £30; ⊙ 9am-6pm Apr-Aug, Wed-Mon Sep & Oct) Hires out mountain bikes, hybrids and tandems; bikes can be dropped off in Fort William. Will deliver bikes free to local hotels and B&Bs.

BUS

City services and buses to places around Inverness, including Nairn, Forres, the Culloden battlefield, Beauly, Dingwall and Lairg, are operated by Stagecoach. An Inverness Zone 2 Dayrider ticket costs £6.80 and gives unlimited travel for a day on buses as far afield as Culloden, Fortrose and Drumnadrochit.

TAXI

Inverness Taxis (☑ 01463-222222; www.inverness-taxis.com) There's a taxi rank outside the train station.

Around Inverness

Culloden Battlefield

The Battle of Culloden in 1746 – the last pitched battle ever fought on British soil – saw the defeat of Bonnie Prince Charlie and

---

OFF THE BEATEN TRACK

STRATHGLASS & GLEN AFFRIC

The broad valley of Strathglass extends about 18 miles inland from Beauly, followed by the A831 to **Cannich** (the only village in the area), where there's a grocery store and a post office.

Glen Affric (www.glenaffric.org), one of the most beautiful glens in Scotland, extends deep into the hills beyond Cannich. The upper reaches of the glen are designated as the **Glen Affric National Nature Reserve** (www.nnr.scot).

About 4 miles southwest of Cannich is **Dog Falls**, a scenic spot where the River Affric squeezes through a narrow, rocky gorge. A circular walking trail (red waymarks) leads from Dog Falls car park to a footbridge below the falls and back on the far side of the river (2 miles, allow one hour).

The road continues beyond Dog Falls to a parking area and picnic site at the eastern end of **Loch Affric**, where there are several short walks along the river and the loch shore. The circuit of Loch Affric (10 miles, allow five hours walking, two hours by mountain bike) follows good paths right around the loch and takes you deep into the heart of some very wild scenery.

Stagecoach buses 17 and 117 run from Inverness to Cannich (£5.90, one hour, two daily Monday to Friday) via Drumnadrochit. D&E Coaches (www.decoaches.co.uk) runs a service from Inverness to Cannich that continues to Tomich (£6.50, 1¼ hours, three daily, weekdays only).

the end of the Jacobite dream when 1200 Highlanders were slaughtered by government forces in a 68-minute rout. The Duke of Cumberland, son of the reigning King George II and leader of the Hanoverian army, earned the nickname 'Butcher' for his brutal treatment of the defeated Jacobite forces. The battle sounded the death knell for the old clan system, and the horrors of the Clearances, when tenants were evicted from their lands, soon followed. The sombre moor where the conflict took place has scarcely changed in the ensuing 260 years.

The impressive **visitor centre** (NTS; www. nts.org.uk/culloden; adult/child £11/9.50; ⊙ 9am-7pm Jun-Aug, to 6pm Mar-May, Sep & Oct, 10am-4pm Nov-Feb; P) provides plenty of historical context through film, audio presentations and an audio guide (included in the admission price).

Culloden is 6 miles east of Inverness. Bus 5 runs from Eastgate shopping centre in Inverness to Culloden battlefield (£3.15, 30 minutes, hourly except Sunday).

Fort George

One of the finest artillery fortifications in Europe, **Fort George** (HES; ☑ 01667-462777; www.historicenvironment.scot; adult/child £9/5.40; ⊙ 9.30am-5.30pm Apr-Sep, 10am-4pm Oct-Mar; P) was established in 1748 in the aftermath of the Battle of Culloden as a base for George II's army of occupation in the Highlands. By the time of its completion in 1769 it had cost the equivalent of around £1 billion in today's money. It still functions as a military barracks; public areas have exhibitions on 18th-century soldiery, and the mile-plus walk around the ramparts offers fine views.

The fort is off the A96 about 11 miles northeast of Inverness; there is no public transport.

Cawdor Castle

Cawdor Castle (☑ 01667-404615; www.cawdor castle.com; Cawdor; adult/child £11.50/7.20; ⊙ 10am-5.30pm May-Sep; P), 5 miles southwest of Nairn, was once the seat of the Thane of Cawdor, one of the titles bestowed on Shakespeare's Macbeth. The real Macbeth – an ancient Scottish king – couldn't have lived here, though, since he died in 1057, 300 years before the castle was begun. Nevertheless the tour gives a fascinating insight into the lives of the Scottish aristocracy.

Loch Ness

Deep, dark and narrow, Loch Ness stretches for 23 miles between Inverness and Fort Augustus. Its bitterly cold waters have been extensively explored in search of Nessie, the elusive Loch Ness monster, but most visitors see her only in the form of a cardboard cut-out at Drumnadrochit's monster exhibitions. The busy A82 road runs along the northwestern shore, while the more tranquil and picturesque B862 follows the southeastern shore. A complete circuit of the loch is about 70 miles – travel anticlockwise for the better views.

❶ Getting There & Away

Scottish Citylink (p902) and Stagecoach (p890) buses from Inverness to Fort William run along the shores of Loch Ness (six to eight daily, five on Sunday); those headed for Skye turn off at Invermoriston. There are bus stops at Drumnadrochit (£3.70, 30 minutes) and Urquhart Castle car park (£4, 35 minutes) and Fort Augustus (£8 to £11.20, one hour, five to eight daily Monday to Saturday, five on Sunday).

Drumnadrochit

POP 1100

Seized by Loch Ness Monster madness, its gift shops bulging with Nessie cuddly toys, Drumnadrochit is a hotbed of beastie fever, with two monster exhibitions battling it out for the tourist dollar.

◉ Sights & Activities

Loch Ness Centre & Exhibition MUSEUM
(☑ 01456-450573; www.lochness.com; adult/child £7.95/4.95; ⊙ 9.30am-6pm Jul & Aug, to 5pm Easter-Jun, Sep & Oct, 10am-4pm Nov-Easter; P ♿) This Nessie-themed attraction adopts a scientific approach that allows you to weigh the evidence for yourself. Exhibits include original equipment – sonar survey vessels, miniature submarines, cameras and sediment coring tools – used in various monster hunts, plus original photographs and film footage of sightings. You'll find out about hoaxes and optical illusions, as well as learning a lot about the ecology of Loch Ness – is there enough food in the loch to support even one 'monster', let alone a breeding population?

Urquhart Castle CASTLE
(HES; ☑ 01456-450551; adult/child £9/5.40; ⊙ 9.30am-8pm Jun-Aug, to 6pm Apr, May & Sep, to

Driving Tour
A Loch Ness Circuit

START INVERNESS
END INVERNESS
LENGTH 130 MILES; SIX TO SEVEN HOURS

Head out of Inverness on the A862 to **1** **Beauly**, arriving in time for breakfast at Corner on the Square. Backtrack a mile and turn right on the A831 to Cannich, passing **2** **Kilmorack Gallery**, which exhibits contemporary art in a converted church. The scenery gets wilder as you approach **3** **Cannich**; turn right and follow the single-track road to the car park at **4** **Dog Falls**. Take a stroll along the rushing river, or hike to the viewpoint (about one-hour round trip; 2.5 miles) for a glimpse of remote Glen Affric.

Return to Cannich and turn right on the A831 to Drumnadrochit, then right on the A82 past picturesque **5** **Urquhart Castle** (p892) and along the shores of Loch Ness. At **6** **Invermoriston**, pause to look at the old bridge, built by Thomas Telford in 1813, then head west on the A887 towards Kyle of Loch-

alsh; after 16 miles go left on the A87 towards Invergarry. You are now among some of the finest mountain scenery in the Highlands; as the road turns east above Loch Garry, stop at the famous **7** **viewpoint** (layby on right, signposted Glengarry Viewpoint). Through a quirk of perspective, the lochs to the west appear to form the map outline of Scotland.

At Invergarry, turn left on the A82 to reach **8** **Fort Augustus** and a late lunch at the Lovat (p895) or Lock Inn (p895). Take the B862 out of town, following the line of General Wade's 18th-century military road, to another viewpoint at **9** **Suidhe Chuimein**. A short (800m) walk up the well-worn path to the summit affords an even better panorama.

Ahead, you can choose the low road via the impressive **10** **Falls of Foyers**, or stay on the high road (B862) for more views; both converge on Loch Ness at **11** **Dores** and the Dores Inn, where you can sip a pint with a view along Loch Ness, and even stay for dinner before returning to Inverness.

5pm Oct, to 4.30pm Nov-Mar; ℗) Commanding a superb location 1.5 miles east of Drumnadrochit, with outstanding views (on a clear day), Urquhart Castle is a popular Nessie-hunting hot spot. A huge visitor centre (most of which is beneath ground level) includes a video theatre (with a dramatic 'reveal' of the castle at the end of the film) and displays of medieval items discovered in the castle. The site includes a huge gift shop and a restaurant, and is often very crowded in summer.

Nessie Hunter
BOATING

(☑01456-450395; www.lochness-cruises.com; adult/child £16/10; ☺Easter-Oct) One-hour monster-hunting cruises, complete with sonar and underwater cameras. Cruises depart from Drumnadrochit hourly (except 1pm) from 10am to 6pm daily.

🛏 Sleeping

BCC Loch Ness Hostel
HOSTEL £

(☑07780 603045; www.bcclochnesshostel.co.uk; Glen Urquhart; tr/q from £60/75, tent sites per person £5, 2-person pods £70; ℗ 🛜) Clean, modern, high-quality budget accommodation located 6.5 miles west of Drumnadrochit, halfway between Cannich and Loch Ness; booking well in advance is recommended. There's also a good campsite with the option of luxury glamping pods.

★ Loch Ness Inn
INN ££

(☑01456-450991; www.staylochness.co.uk; Lewiston; s/d/f £99/120/140; ℗🛜) Loch Ness Inn ticks all the weary traveller's boxes, with comfortable bedrooms (the family suite sleeps two adults and two children), a cosy bar pouring real ales from the Cairngorm and Isle of Skye breweries, and a rustic res-

---

THE NESSIE LEGEND

Highland folklore is filled with tales of strange creatures living in lochs and rivers, notably the kelpie (water horse) that lures unwary travellers to their doom. The use of the term 'monster', however, is a relatively recent phenomenon, whose origins lie in an article published in the *Inverness Courier* on 2 May 1933, entitled 'Strange Spectacle on Loch Ness'.

The article recounted the sighting of a disturbance in the loch by Mrs Aldie Mackay and her husband: 'There the creature disported itself, rolling and plunging for fully a minute, its body resembling that of a whale, and the water cascading and churning like a simmering cauldron.'

The story was taken up by the London press and sparked a flurry of sightings that year, including a notorious on-land encounter with London tourists Mr and Mrs Spicer on 22 July 1933, again reported in the *Inverness Courier*:

'It was horrible, an abomination. About 50 yards ahead, we saw an undulating sort of neck, and quickly followed by a large, ponderous body. I estimated the length to be 25ft to 30ft, its colour was dark elephant grey. It crossed the road in a series of jerks, but because of the slope we could not see its limbs. Although I accelerated quickly towards it, it had disappeared into the loch by the time I reached the spot. There was no sign of it in the water. I am a temperate man, but I am willing to take any oath that we saw this Loch Ness beast. I am certain that this creature was of a prehistoric species.'

The London newspapers couldn't resist. In December 1933 the *Daily Mail* sent Marmaduke Wetherell, a film director and big-game hunter, to Loch Ness to track down the beast. Within days he found 'reptilian' footprints in the shoreline mud (soon revealed to have been made with a stuffed hippopotamus foot). Then in April 1934 came the famous long-necked monster photograph taken by the seemingly reputable Harley St surgeon Robert Kenneth Wilson. The press went mad and the rest, as they say, is history.

In 1994, however, Christian Spurling – Wetherell's stepson, by then 90 years old – revealed that the most famous photo of Nessie ever taken was in fact a hoax, perpetrated by his stepfather with Wilson's help. Today, of course, there are those who claim that Spurling's confession is itself a hoax. And, ironically, the researcher who exposed the surgeon's photo as a fake still believes wholeheartedly in the monster's existence.

There have been regular sightings of the monster through the years (see www.lochnesssightings.com), with a peak in 1996–97 (the Hollywood movie *Loch Ness* was released in 1996), but reports have tailed off in recent years.

Hoax or not, the bizarre mini-industry that has grown up around Loch Ness and its mysterious monster since that eventful summer last century is a spectacle in itself.

taurant (mains £10 to £20) serving wholesome fare. It's conveniently located in the quiet hamlet of Lewiston, between Drumnadrochit and Urquhart Castle.

Drumbuie Farm B&B **££**
(☑ 01456-450634; www.loch-ness-farm.co.uk; s/d from £54/68; P 🖟) A B&B in a modern house on a working farm surrounded by fields full of sheep and highland cattle, with views over Urquhart Castle and Loch Ness. Walkers and cyclists are welcome.

🍷 Drinking & Nightlife

Benleva Hotel MICROBREWERY
(☑ 01456-450080; www.benleva.co.uk; Kilmore Rd; ⊙ noon-midnight Mon-Thu, to 1am Fri, to 12.45am Sat, 12.30-11pm Sun; 🖟) Set in an 18th-century manse a half-mile east of the main road, the Benleva is a rough diamond of a pub – a bit frayed around the edges but with a heart of gold. The beer is the main event, with a selection of real ales from around the country, including those from their own Loch Ness Brewery, located nearby.

Fort Augustus

POP 620

Fort Augustus, at the junction of four old military roads, was originally a government garrison and the headquarters of General George Wade's road-building operations in the early 18th century. Today it's a neat and picturesque little place bisected by the Caledonian Canal, and often overrun by coach-tour crowds in summer.

◉ Sights & Activities

Caledonian Canal CANAL
(www.scottishcanals.co.uk) At Fort Augustus, boats using the Caledonian Canal are raised and lowered 13m by a 'ladder' of five consecutive locks. It's fun to watch, and the neatly landscaped canal banks are a great place to soak up the sun or compare accents with fellow tourists. The **Caledonian Canal Centre** (Ardchattan House, Canalside; ⊙ 9am-6pm) **FREE**, beside the lowest lock, has information on the history of the canal.

Cruise Loch Ness BOATING
(☑ 01320-366277; www.cruiselochness.com; adult/child £14.50/8.50; ⊙ hourly 10am-4pm Apr-Oct, 1pm & 2pm Nov-Mar) One-hour cruises on Loch Ness are accompanied by the latest high-tech sonar equipment so you can keep an underwater eye open for Nessie. There are also one-hour evening cruises, departing 8pm

daily (except Friday) April to August, and 90-minute speedboat tours.

🛏 Sleeping & Eating

Morag's Lodge HOSTEL **£**
(☑ 01320-366289; www.moragslodge.com; Bunoich Brae; dm/tw from £24.50/62; P @ 🖟) This large, well-run hostel is based in a big Victorian house with great views of Fort Augustus' hilly surrounds, and has a convivial bar with open fire. It's hidden away in the trees up the steep side road just north of the tourist office car park.

Lorien House B&B **££**
(☑ 01320-366576; www.lorien-house.co.uk; Station Rd; s/d £70/80; P 🖟) Lorien is a cut above your usual B&B – the bedrooms are spick and span, the house is set up to accommodate walkers and cyclists, the breakfasts include smoked salmon, and there's a library of walking, cycling and climbing guides in the lounge. No children under 10 years.

★ **Lovat** HOTEL **£££**
(☑ 01456-459250; www.thelovat.com; Main Rd; d from £173; P @ 🖟) 🍴 A boutique-style makeover has transformed this former huntin'-and-shootin' hotel into a luxurious but eco-conscious retreat set apart from the tourist crush around the canal. The bedrooms are spacious and stylishly furnished, while the lounge is equipped with a log fire, comfy armchairs and grand piano.

Lock Inn PUB FOOD **££**
(☑ 01320-366302; Canal Side; mains £10-15; ⊙ meals noon-8pm) A superb little pub right on the canal bank, the Lock Inn has a vast range of malt whiskies and a tempting menu of bar meals, which includes Orkney salmon, Highland venison and daily seafood specials; the house speciality is beer-battered haddock and chips.

THE CAIRNGORMS

The Cairngorms National Park (www.cairngorms.co.uk) is the largest national park in the UK, more than twice the size of the Lake District. It stretches from Aviemore in the north to the Angus Glens in the south, and from Dalwhinnie in the west to Ballater and Royal Deeside in the east.

The park encompasses the highest landmass in Britain – a broad mountain plateau, riven only by the deep valleys of the Lairig Ghru and Loch Avon, with an average

The Cairngorms

altitude of more than 1000m and including five of the six highest summits in the UK. This wild mountain landscape of granite and heather has a sub-Arctic climate and supports rare alpine tundra vegetation and high-altitude bird species, such as snow bunting, ptarmigan and dotterel.

This is prime hill-walking territory, but even couch potatoes can enjoy a taste of the high life by riding the Cairngorm Mountain Railway (p898).

🛈 Getting There & Away

The main A9 Perth to Inverness road and railway line run along the western and northern boundaries of the national park, while the A93 Aberdeen–Braemar road provides the main access to the eastern part. The Angus Glens in the south are reached along minor roads branching out from the small towns of Kirriemuir and Brechin, to the north of Dundee.

The nearest airport (p890) is at Inverness, an hour's drive north of Aviemore.

Aviemore

📞 01479 / POP 3150

The gateway to the Cairngorms, Aviemore is the region's main centre for transport, accommodation, restaurants and shops. It's not the prettiest town in Scotland by a long stretch – the main attractions are in the surrounding area – but when bad weather puts the hills off limits, Aviemore fills up with hikers, cyclists and climbers (plus skiers and snowboarders in winter) cruising the outdoor-equipment shops or recounting their latest adventures in the cafes and bars. Add in tourists and locals and the eclectic mix makes for a lively little town.

Aviemore is on a loop off the A9 Perth–Inverness road. Almost everything of note is to be found along the main drag, Grampian Rd; the train station and bus stop are towards its southern end.

The Cairngorm Mountain funicular railway and ski area lie 10 miles southeast of Aviemore along the B970 (Ski Rd) and its continuation, past Coylumbridge and Glenmore.

◉ Sights & Activities

Strathspey Steam Railway HERITAGE RAILWAY
(📞01479-810725; www.strathspeyrailway.co.uk; Station Sq; return ticket adult/child £15/11.80; 🅿)
The Strathspey railway runs steam trains on a section of restored line between Aviemore and Broomhill, 10 miles to the northeast, via Boat of Garten. There are four or five trains daily from June to August, and a more limit-

ed service in April, May, September, October and December, with the option of enjoying afternoon tea, Sunday lunch or a five-course dinner on board.

Craigellachie Nature Reserve
NATURE RESERVE

(www.nnr.scot; Grampian Rd) `FREE` This reserve is a great place for short hikes across steep hillsides covered in natural birch forest where you can spot wildlife such as the peregrine falcons that nest on the crags from April to July. A trail leads west from Aviemore SYHA and passes under the A9 into the reserve.

Bothy Bikes
MOUNTAIN BIKING

(01479-810111; www.bothybikes.co.uk; 5 Granish Way, Dalfaber; per half-/full day from £16/20; 9am-5.30pm) Located in northern Aviemore, this place rents out mountain bikes and can also advise on routes and trails; a good choice for beginners is the Old Logging Way, which runs from Aviemore to Glenmore, where you can make a circuit of Loch Morlich before returning. For experienced bikers, the whole of the Cairngorms is your playground. Booking recommended.

Sleeping

Aviemore SYHA
HOSTEL £

(SYHA; 01479-810345; www.syha.org.uk; 25 Grampian Rd; dm £23; P@) Upmarket hostelling in a spacious, well-equipped modern building, five minutes' walk south of the village centre. There are four- and six-bed rooms, and a comfortable lounge with views of the mountains.

Cairngorm Hotel
HOTEL ££

(01479-810233; www.cairngorm.com; Grampian Rd; s/d from £84/118; P) Better known as 'the Cairn', this long-established hotel is set in the fine old granite building with the pointy turret opposite the train station. It's a welcoming place with comfortable rooms and a determinedly Scottish atmosphere, with tartan carpets and stags' antlers. There's live music on weekends, so it can get a bit noisy – not for early-to-bedders.

Ardlogie Guest House
B&B ££

(01479-810747; www.ardlogie.co.uk; Dalfaber Rd; s/d £80/100, bothy per 3 nights £360; P) Handy to the train station, the welcoming five-room Ardlogie has great views over the River Spey towards the Cairngorms, and the chance of spotting red squirrels from your bedroom window. There's also self-catering accommodation in the Bothy, a cosy, two-person timber cabin. Facilities include a boules pitch in the garden. Two-night minimum stay.

Hilton Coylumbridge
HOTEL £££

(01479-810661; www.coylumbridge.hilton.com; Ski Rd, Coylumbridge; d from £139; P) This modern, low-rise hotel, set amid the pine woods just outside Aviemore, is a wonderfully family friendly place, with bedrooms for up to two adults and two children, indoor and outdoor play areas, a crèche and a baby-sitting service. The hotel is 1.5 miles east of Aviemore, on the road to Loch Morlich.

Eating & Drinking

★ Route 7 Cafe
CAFE £

(01479-812433; http://highlandhomecentre.com/route-7-cafe.html; 18 Dalfaber Industrial Estate; mains £6-10; 9am-4pm; P) This place, named for the cycle route that passes the door, takes a bit of finding (at the end of the side road that passes Cairngorm Brewery), but is well worth seeking out for its hearty menu of burgers, grilled sandwiches and salads; also wood-fired pizzas (noon to 3pm weekends only). Cyclists can use the power washer and tools outside.

Roo's Leap
AMERICAN ££

(01479-811161; www.roosleap.com; Station Sq; mains £8-15, steaks £22-25; noon-2.30pm & 5-9pm Mon-Fri, noon-9pm Sat & Sun;) Friendly service, cold bottled beer and great barbecue contribute to the antipodean atmosphere at this lively restaurant set in the old railway station building. However, the menu is more like classic American and Tex Mex – sizzling steaks, juicy burgers, fajitas and nachos.

Mountain Cafe
CAFE ££

(www.mountaincafe-aviemore.co.uk; 111 Grampian Rd; mains £10-15; 8.30am-5pm Mon-Fri, to 5.30pm Sat & Sun; P) The Mountain Cafe offers freshly prepared local produce with a Kiwi twist (the owner is from New Zealand): healthy breakfasts of muesli, porridge and fresh fruit (till 11.30am); hearty lunches of seafood chowder, burgers and imaginative salads; and home-baked breads, cakes and biscuits. Caters for vegan, coeliac and nut-allergic diets.

Ski-ing Doo
STEAK ££

(01479-810392; 9 Grampian Rd; mains £8-14, steaks £19-23; noon-9pm;) A long-standing Aviemore institution, the

WORTH A TRIP

ROTHIEMURCHUS ESTATE

The **Rothiemurchus Estate** (www.rothiemurchus.net), which extends from the River Spey at Aviemore to the Cairngorm summit plateau, is famous for having one of Scotland's largest remnants of **Caledonian forest**, the ancient forest of Scots pine that once covered most of the country. The forest is home to a large population of red squirrels, and is one of the last bastions of the capercaillie and the Scottish wildcat.

The **Rothiemurchus Centre** (☑ 01479-812345; www.rothiemurchus.net; Ski Rd, Inverdruie; ⊘ 9.30am-5.30pm; P) FREE, a mile southeast of Aviemore along the B970, sells an Explorer Map detailing more than 50 miles of footpaths and cycling trails, including the wheelchair-accessible 4-mile trail around Loch an Eilein, with its ruined castle and peaceful pine woods.

child-friendly Ski-ing Doo (it's a pun...ask the waiter!) is a favourite with family skiers and hikers. It's an informal place offering a range of hearty, homemade burgers, chicken dishes and juicy steaks; the Doo Below cafe-bar is open from 3pm to 11pm.

Winking Owl   PUB
(www.thewinkingowl.co; Grampian Rd; ⊘ noon-11pm Mon-Thu, 11am-1am Fri & Sat, 12.30-11pm Sun; 🐾) Lively local pub that operates under the wing of the Cairngorm Brewery. It's popular with hikers and climbers, and serves a good range of real ales and malt whiskies.

ⓘ Information

Aviemore Tourist Office (☑ 01479-810930; www.visitaviemore.com; The Mall, Grampian Rd; ⊘ 9am-5pm Mon-Sat, 10am-4pm Sun year-round, longer hours Jul & Aug)

ⓘ Getting There & Away

BUS
Buses stop on Grampian Rd opposite the train station; buy tickets at the tourist office. Services include the following:
Edinburgh £28.50, four hours, five daily
Glasgow £28.50, 2¾ hours, five daily
Grantown-on-Spey £4, 35 minutes, five daily weekdays, two Saturday

Inverness £10.80, 45 minutes, eight daily
Perth £20.90, 2¼ hours, five daily

Bus 31 links Aviemore to Cairngorm Mountain car park (£2.90, 30 minutes, hourly) via Coylumbridge and Glenmore. A Strathspey Dayrider/Megarider ticket (£7.30/18.40) gives one/seven days unlimited bus travel from Aviemore as far as Cairngorm, Carrbridge and Kingussie; buy it from the bus driver.

TRAIN
The train station is on Grampian Rd.
Edinburgh £41, three hours, six daily
Glasgow £41, three hours, six daily
Inverness £12.80, 40 minutes, 12 daily

Around Aviemore

Cairngorm Mountain

Cairn Gorm (1245m), 10 miles southeast of Aviemore, is the sixth-highest summit in the UK and home to Scotland's most popular ski area, Cairngorm Mountain. A funicular railway ferries skiers almost to the top of the mountain, and continues to operate throughout the summer so that visitors can get a taste of the high mountain plateau.

Cairngorm Mountain Railway   FUNICULAR
(☑ 01479-861261; www.cairngormmountain.org; adult/child return £13.90/9.30; ⊘ every 20min 10am-4pm May-Nov, 9am-4.30pm Dec-Apr; P) The national park's most popular attraction is this funicular railway that will whisk you to the edge of the Cairngorm plateau (altitude 1085m) in just eight minutes. The bottom station is at the Coire Cas car park at the end of Ski Rd; at the top is an exhibition, a shop (of course) and a restaurant. Unfortunately, for environmental and safety reasons, you're not allowed out of the top station in summer unless you book a guided walk.

From May to October, a 90-minute guided walk to the summit of Cairn Gorm (£21.60 per person) departs twice a day, while a four-hour guided hill walk runs four days a week. Check the website for details.

Loch Morlich

Six miles east of Aviemore, Loch Morlich is surrounded by some 8 sq miles of pine and spruce forest that make up the Glenmore Forest Park. Its attractions include a sandy beach (at the east end) and a watersports centre.

🏃 Activities

⭐ Glenmore Lodge
ADVENTURE SPORTS

(📞01479-861256; www.glenmorelodge.org.uk; Glenmore; 1-day courses from £65) One of Britain's leading adventure-sports training centres, offering courses in hill walking, rock climbing, ice climbing, canoeing, mountain biking and mountaineering. The centre's comfortable **B&B accommodation** (s/tw £60/83; 📵🖂🛜🐕) is available to all, even if you're not taking a course, as is the indoor climbing wall, gym and sauna.

Cairngorm Reindeer Centre
TOURS

(www.cairngormreindeer.co.uk; Glenmore; adult/child £15/9; ⊙closed early Jan–mid-Feb; 🐾) The warden here leads guided walks to see and feed Britain's only herd of reindeer, which are very tame and will even eat out of your hand. Walks take place at 11am daily (weather-dependent), plus there's another at 2.30pm from May to September, and a third at 3.30pm Monday to Friday in July and August.

Loch Morlich
Watersports Centre
WATER SPORTS

(📞01479-861221; www.lochmorlich.com; ⊙9am-5pm Easter-Oct) This popular outfit rents out Canadian canoes (£23 an hour), kayaks (£9), sailboards (£18), sailing dinghies (£25) and stand-up paddle boards (£15), and also offers instruction.

Boat of Garten

Boat of Garten is known as the Osprey Village because these rare and beautiful birds of prey nest nearby at the **RSPB Loch Garten Osprey Centre** (📞01479-831694; www.rspb.org.uk/lochgarten; Tulloch; osprey hide adult/child £5/2; ⊙osprey hide 10am-6pm Apr-Aug). The ospreys migrate here each spring from Africa and nest in a tall pine tree.

Boat of Garten is 5 miles northeast of Aviemore. The most interesting way to get here is on the Strathspey Steam Railway (p896) from Aviemore, or you can ride or walk along National Cycle Network Route 7 (allow 30 to 40 minutes by bike, two hours on foot).

Kingussie & Newtonmore

The old Speyside towns of Kingussie (kin-yew-see) and Newtonmore sit at the foot of the great heather-clad humps known as the Monadhliath Mountains. Newtonmore is best known as the home of the excellent Highland Folk Museum, Kingussie for one of the Highlands' best restaurants.

The road west from Newtonmore to Spean Bridge passes Ardverikie Estate and Loch Laggan, famous as the setting for the BBC TV series *Monarch of the Glen*.

⊙ Sights & Activities

Highland Folk Museum
MUSEUM

(📞01540-673551; www.highlandfolk.museum; Kingussie Rd, Newtonmore; ⊙10.30am-5.30pm Apr-Aug, 11am-4.30pm Sep & Oct; 📵) **FREE** This open-air museum comprises a collection of historical buildings and artefacts revealing many aspects of Highland culture and lifestyle. Laid out like a farming township, it has a community of traditional thatch-roofed cottages, a sawmill, a schoolhouse, a shepherd's bothy (hut) and a rural post office. Actors in period costume give demonstrations of woodcarving, wool-spinning and peat-fire baking. You'll need at least two to three hours to make the most of a visit here.

Laggan Wolftrax
MOUNTAIN BIKING

(http://scotland.forestry.gov.uk/visit/laggan-wolftrax; Strathmashie Forest; trails free, parking per day £3; ⊙10am-6pm Mon, 9.30am-5pm Tue, Thu & Fri, 9.30am-6pm Sat & Sun) Ten miles southwest of Newtonmore, on the A86 road towards Spean Bridge, this is one of Scotland's top mountain-biking centres with purpose-built trails ranging from open-country riding to black-diamond downhills with rock slabs and drop-offs. Includes bike hire outlet and a good cafe (open 10am to 5pm April to October).

🛏️ Sleeping & Eating

⭐ Eagleview Guest House
B&B ££

(📞01540-673675; Perth Rd, Newtonmore; r £78-85; 📵🖂🛜) Welcoming Eagleview is one of the most pleasant places to stay in the area, with beautifully decorated bedrooms, super-king-size beds, spacious bathrooms with power showers (except room 4, which has a Victorian slipper bath!), and nice little touches such as cafetières (coffee plungers) with real coffee – and fresh milk – on your hospitality tray.

⭐ Restaurant at the Cross
SCOTTISH £££

(📞01540-661166; www.thecross.co.uk; Tweed Mill Brae, off Ardbroilach Rd, Kingussie; 3-course lunch/dinner £30/55; ⊙noon-2pm & 7-8.30pm; 📵🛜) 🌿 Housed in a converted watermill, the Cross is one of the finest restaurants in the Highlands. The intimate, low-raftered dining room has an open fire and a patio overlooking the stream, and serves a daily changing menu of fresh Scottish produce accompanied by a superb wine list (booking essential).

If you want to stay the night, there are eight stylish rooms (double or twin £110 to £200) to choose from.

ℹ Getting There & Away

BUS

Kingussie and Newtonmore are served by **Scottish Citylink** (☑ 0871 266 3333; www.citylink. co.uk) coaches on the main Perth-to-Inverness bus route, as well as local Stagecoach buses.
Aviemore £3.70, 20 minutes, hourly
Inverness £10.70, 1½ hours, three daily, change at Carrbridge
Perth £17.10, 1¾ hours, one daily

TRAIN

Kingussie and Newtonmore are on the Edinburgh/Glasgow-to-Inverness railway line.
Edinburgh £37.50, 2¾ hours, seven daily Monday to Saturday, two Sunday
Inverness £12.80, one hour, eight daily Monday to Saturday, four Sunday

Royal Deeside

The upper valley of the River Dee stretches west from Aboyne and Ballater to Braemar, closely paralleled by the A93 road. Made famous by its long association with the monarchy – today's Royal Family still holiday at Balmoral Castle, built for Queen Victoria in 1855 – the region is often called Royal Deeside.

The River Dee, renowned world-over for its salmon fishing, has its source in the Cairngorm Mountains west of Braemar, the starting point for long walks into the hills. The FishDee website (www.fishdee.co.uk) has all you need to know about fishing on the river.

Ballater

☑ 01339 / POP 1530
The attractive little village of Ballater owes its 18th-century origins to the curative waters of nearby Pannanich Springs (now bottled commercially as Deeside Natural Mineral Water), and its prosperity to nearby Balmoral Castle.

The village received a double dose of misfortune when the Old Royal Station (its main tourist attraction) burned down in May 2015, followed by the worst flooding in living memory in January 2016. The restored station building reopened in 2018 with a museum, restaurant and tourist office.

🛏 Sleeping & Eating

Ballater Hostel HOSTEL £
(☑ 01339-753752; www.ballater-hostel.com; Bridge Sq; dm/tw from £22/50; ☎) ⌀ Tucked up a lane near the bridge over the River Dee, this is an attractive, ecofriendly hostel with six en suite private rooms (sleeping two to eight). Rooms have personal lockers and reading lamps, and there's a comfortable lounge with big, soft sofas and a wood-burning stove.

★ **Auld Kirk** HOTEL ££
(☑ 01339-755762; www.theauldkirk.com; Braemar Rd; r from £85; P☎❄) Here's something a little out of the ordinary – a seven-bedroom hotel housed in a converted 19th-century church. The interior blends original features with sleek modern decor – the pulpit now serves as the reception desk, while the lounge is bathed in light from leaded Gothic windows. Breakfast not included, but guests can buy it at the hotel's coffee shop.

Rock Salt & Snails CAFE £
(☑ 07834 452583; www.facebook.com/rocksalt andsnailsballater; 2 Bridge St; mains £4-9; ◔ 10am-5pm Mon-Fri, to 9pm Sat, to 6pm Sun May-Sep, 10am-5pm Mon-Sat, 11am-5pm Sun Oct-Apr; ☎❄) A great little cafe serving excellent coffee and tempting lunch platters featuring locally sourced deli products (cheese, ham, salads etc), including a kids' platter.

ℹ Getting There & Away

Bus 201 runs from Aberdeen to Ballater (£12.10, 1¾ hours, hourly Monday to Saturday, six on Sunday) via Crathes Castle, and continues to Braemar (£6.25, 35 minutes) every two hours.

Braemar

POP 450
Braemar is a pretty little village with a grand location on a broad plain ringed by mountains where the Dee valley and Glen Clunie meet. In winter this is one of the coldest places in the country – temperatures as low as -29°C have been recorded – and during spells of severe cold, hungry deer wander

WORTH A TRIP

BALMORAL CASTLE

Built for Queen Victoria in 1855 as a private residence for the Royal Family, **Balmoral** (☑ 01339-742534; www.balmoralcastle.com; Crathie; adult/child £11.50/6; ⊙ 10am-5pm Apr-Jul, last admission 4.30pm; ℙ) kicked off the revival of the Scottish Baronial style of architecture that characterises so many of Scotland's 19th-century country houses. The admission fee includes an interesting and well-thought-out audio guide, but the tour is very much an outdoor one through garden and grounds.

As for the castle itself, only the ballroom, which displays a collection of Sir Edwin Landseer paintings and royal silver, is open to the public. Don't expect to see the Queen's private quarters!

You can buy a booklet that details several waymarked walks within Balmoral Estate; the best is the climb to Prince Albert's Cairn, a huge granite pyramid that bears the inscription 'To the beloved memory of Albert the great and good, Prince Consort. Erected by his broken hearted widow Victoria R. 21st August 1862'.

the streets looking for a bite to eat. Braemar is an excellent base for hill walking, and there's also skiing at nearby Glenshee.

⊙ Sights

Mar Lodge Estate   NATURE RESERVE
(www.nts.org.uk; ⊙ 24hr) FREE West of Braemar spreads the National Trust for Scotland's Mar Lodge Estate, one of the country's most important nature conservation areas, covering 7% of the Cairngorms National Park. The £4 million legacy that allowed the trust to purchase the property in 1995 stipulated that, as well as promoting conservation and public access, the trust should continue to run Mar Lodge as a sporting estate. So alongside walking trails and forest regeneration there is salmon fishing and deer stalking.

Braemar Castle   CASTLE
(www.braemarcastle.co.uk; adult/child £8/4; ⊙ 10am-5pm Jul & Aug, Wed-Sun Apr-Jun, Sep & Oct; ℙ) Just north of Braemar village, turreted Braemar Castle dates from 1628 and served as a government garrison after the 1745 Jacobite rebellion. It was taken over by the local community in 2007, which now offers guided tours of the historic castle apartments. There's a short walk from the car park to the castle.

🎎 Festivals & Events

Braemar Gathering   SPORTS
(☑ 01339-755377; www.braemargathering.org; adult/child from £12/2; ⊙ Sep) There are Highland games in many towns and villages throughout the summer, but the best known is the Braemar Gathering, which takes place on the first Saturday in Septem-

ber. It's a major occasion, organised every year since 1817 by the Braemar Royal Highland Society.

🛏 Sleeping

Braemar SYHA   HOSTEL £
(☑ 01339-741659; www.syha.org.uk; 21 Glenshee Rd; dm/tw £21/49; ⊙ Feb-Oct; ℙ @ 🐾 🛜 🐕) This hostel is housed in a grand former shooting lodge just south of Braemar village centre on the A93 to Perth. It has a comfy lounge with pool table, and a barbecue in the garden.

Braemar Cabins   CABIN ££
(☑ 01339-741242; http://braemarcabins.com; 7-9 Invercauld Rd; 3 nights from £285; ℙ 🛜 🐕) These attractive larch-clad cabins at the entrance to the village can sleep up to four people in two double or twin bedrooms (some wheelchair accessible). They have underfloor heating, well-equipped kitchens and outdoor decks. In high season the minimum stay is one week (£695).

Braemar Lodge Hotel   HOTEL ££
(☑ 01339-741627; www.braemarlodge.co.uk; Glenshee Rd; dm/s/d from £15/80/120; ℙ 🛜) This Victorian shooting lodge on the southern outskirts of Braemar has bags of character, not least in the wood-panelled Malt Room bar, which is as well stocked with mounted deer heads as it is with single malt whiskies. There's a good restaurant with views of the hills, plus a 12-berth hikers' bunkhouse (book in advance) in the hotel grounds.

❶ Information

Braemar Tourist Office (☑ 01399-741600; The Mews, Mar Rd; ⊙ 9am-6pm Aug, to 5pm Jun, Jul, Sep & Oct, reduced hours Nov-May)

Opposite the Fife Arms Hotel; has lots of useful info on walks in the area.

ℹ Getting There & Away

Bus 201 runs from Aberdeen to Braemar (£12.10, 2¼ hours, every two hours Monday to Saturday, five on Sunday). The 50-mile drive from Perth to Braemar is beautiful, but there's no public transport on this route.

HIGHLAND PERTHSHIRE

The Highland border cuts diagonally across Scotland from Dumbarton to Stonehaven, dividing the county of Perthshire into two distinctive regions. Highland Perthshire, spreading north of a line from Comrie to Blairgowrie, is a land of mountains, forest and lochs, with some of the finest scenery in the UK. The ancient city of Dunkeld, on the main A9 road from Perth to Inverness, is the main gateway to the region.

ℹ Getting There & Around

Citylink (🖉 0871 266 3333; www.citylink. co.uk) buses from Edinburgh or Glasgow to Inverness stop at Birnam and Pitlochry. There are regular buses from Perth to most of the towns in the area. Trains running between Perth and Inverness stop at Blair Atholl and Pitlochry.

Dunkeld & Birnam

POP 1005

The Tay runs like a storybook river through the heart of Perthshire's Big Tree Country, where the twin towns of Dunkeld and Birnam are linked by Thomas Telford's graceful bridge of 1808. As well as Dunkeld's ancient cathedral, there's much walking to be done in this area of magnificent forested hills. These same walks were one of the inspirations for Beatrix Potter to create her children's tales.

There's less to see in Birnam, a name made famous by Macbeth. There's not much left of Birnam Wood, but a riverside path leads to the **Birnam Oak**, a venerable 500-year-old survivor from Shakespeare's time, its ageing boughs propped up with timber supports. Nearby is the 300-year-old Birnam Sycamore.

◉ Sights & Activities

Dunkeld Cathedral   CHURCH
(HS;   www.dunkeldcathedral.org.uk;   High St;
⊘ 9.30am-5.30pm Apr-Sep, 10am-4pm Oct-Mar)
FREE Situated on the grassy banks of the River Tay, Dunkeld Cathedral is one of the most beautifully sited churches in Scotland; don't miss it on a sunny day, when there are few lovelier places to be. Half the cathedral is still in use as a church; the rest is a romantic ruin. It partly dates from the 14th century, having suffered damage during the Reformation and the battle of Dunkeld (Jacobites versus the government) in 1689.

Dunkeld House Grounds   GARDENS
(⊘ 24hr) **FREE** Waymarked walks lead upstream from Dunkeld Cathedral through the gorgeous grounds of Dunkeld House Hotel, formerly a seat of the dukes of Atholl. In the 18th and early 19th centuries the 'planting dukes', as they became known, planted more than 27 million conifers on their estates 'for beauty and profit', introducing species such as larch, Douglas fir and sequoia, and sowing the seeds of Scottish forestry.

Loch of the Lowes
Wildlife Centre   WILDLIFE RESERVE
(🖉 01350-727337;   www.swt.org.uk;   adult/child
£4/50p; ⊘ 10am-5pm Mar-Oct, 10.30am-4pm Fri-Sun Nov-Feb; P) Loch of the Lowes, 2 miles east of Dunkeld off the A923, has a visitor centre devoted to red squirrels and the majestic osprey. There's a birdwatching hide (with binoculars provided), where you can see the birds nesting during breeding season (late April to August), complete with a live video link to the nest.

Hermitage   WALKING
One of the most popular walks near Dunkeld is the Hermitage, where a well-marked trail follows the River Braan to Ossian's Hall, a quaint folly built by the Duke of Atholl in 1758 overlooking the spectacular Falls of Braan (salmon can be seen leaping here, especially in September and October). It's signposted off the A9 just west of the village.

🛏 Sleeping & Eating

★**Jessie Mac's**   HOSTEL, B&B £
(🖉 01350-727324; www.jessiemacs.co.uk; Murthly Tce, Birnam; dm/d from £20/59; 🖙🐾) 🍴 Set in a Victorian manse complete with baronial turret, Jessie Mac's is a glorious cross between B&B and luxury hostel, with three gorgeous doubles and four shared or family rooms with bunks. Guests make good use of the country-style lounge, sunny dining room and well-equipped kitchen, and breakfasts are composed of local produce, from organic eggs to Dunkeld smoked salmon.

Erigmore Estate
LODGE **££**

(☑ 01350-727236; www.erigmore.co.uk; Birnam; d 3 nights from £273; P ☎ 🐾) Scattered around the wooded, riverside grounds of Erigmore House, the former country retreat of a wealthy clipper ship's captain, these luxury timber lodges provide cosseted comfort complete with outdoor deck and – at the more expensive end of the range – a private hot tub. The house itself contains shared facilities, including a bar, restaurant and swimming pool.

★ Taybank
PUB FOOD **££**

(☑ 01350-727340; www.thetaybank.co.uk; Tay Tce, Dunkeld; mains £9-13; ⊙ food served noon-9pm; P) 🍴 Top choice for a sun-kissed pub lunch by the river is the Taybank, a regular meeting place and performance space for folk musicians and a wonderfully welcoming bar serving ales from the local Strathbraan Brewery. There's live music several nights per week, and the menu features local produce with dishes such as smoked venison or grilled sea trout.

ℹ️ Information

Dunkeld Tourist Office (☑ 01350-727688; www.dunkeldandbirnam.org.uk; The Cross; ⊙ 10.30am-4.30pm Mon-Sat, 11am-4pm Sun Apr-Oct, longer hours Jul & Aug, Fri-Sun only Nov-Mar) Has information on local hiking and biking trails.

ℹ️ Getting There & Away

Citylink (p891) buses running between Glasgow/Edinburgh and Inverness stop at the Birnam Hotel (£18.10, two hours, two or three daily). **Stagecoach** (www.stagecoachbus.com) runs hourly buses (only five on Sunday) between Perth and Dunkeld (£2.80, 45 minutes), continuing to Aberfeldy.

Pitlochry

☑ 01796 / POP 2780

Pitlochry, with the scent of the Highlands already in the air, is a popular stop on the way north. In summer the main street can be a conga line of tour groups, but linger a while and it can still charm – on a quiet spring evening it's a pretty place with salmon leaping in the Tummel and good things brewing at the Moulin Hotel.

⊙ Sights

One of Pitlochry's attractions is its beautiful riverside; the River Tummel is dammed here, and if you're lucky you might see salmon swimming up the fish ladder to Loch Faskally above (May to November; best month is October).

★ Pitlochry Dam Visitor Centre
VISITOR CENTRE

(www.pitlochrydam.com; Armoury Rd; ⊙ 9.30am-5.30pm; P) **FREE** Opened in 2017, this architecturally stunning visitor centre is perched above the dam on the River Tummel, and houses an exhibition that details the history of hydroelectricity in Scotland, alongside the life cycle of the Atlantic salmon (all hydro stations need a fish ladder to allow salmon to migrate upstream past the dams). Includes an excellent cafe.

★ Edradour Distillery
DISTILLERY

(☑ 01796-472095; www.edradour.co.uk; Moulin Rd; tour adult/child £10/5; ⊙ 10am-5pm Mon-Sat Apr-Oct, to 4.30pm Mon-Fri Nov-Mar; P 🚗) This is proudly Scotland's smallest and most picturesque distillery and one of the best to visit: you can see the whole process, easily explained, in one building. It's 2.5 miles east of Pitlochry by car, along the Moulin road, or a pleasant 1-mile walk.

Pass of Killiecrankie
HISTORIC SITE

(NTS; parking £2; ⊙ 24hr; P 🚗) **FREE** The beautiful, rugged Pass of Killiecrankie, 3.5 miles north of Pitlochry, where the River Garry tumbles through a narrow gorge, was the site of the 1689 Battle of Killiecrankie that ignited the Jacobite rebellion. The visitor centre (NTS; ☑ 01796-473233; www.nts.org.uk; ⊙ 10am-5pm Apr-Sep, 11am-4pm Oct; P 🚗) **FREE** has great interactive displays on Jacobite history and local flora and fauna. There's plenty to touch, pull and open – great for kids. There are some stunning walks along the wooded gorge, too; keep an eye out for red squirrels.

Explorers Garden
GARDENS

(☑ 01796-484600; www.explorersgarden.com; Foss Rd; adult/child £4/1; ⊙ 10am-5pm Apr-Oct; P) This gem of a garden is based around plants brought to Scotland by 18th- and 19th-century Scottish botanists and explorers such as David Douglas (after whom the Douglas fir is named), and celebrates 300 years of collecting and the 'plant hunters' who tracked down these exotic species.

🛏️ Sleeping

Pitlochry Backpackers Hotel
HOSTEL **£**

(☑ 01796-470044; www.scotlands-top-hostels.com; 134 Atholl Rd; dm/tw £20/53; ⊙ Apr–mid-Nov;

P @ ?) Friendly, laid-back and very comfortable, this is a cracking hostel smack bang in the middle of town, with three- to eight-bed dorms that are in mint condition. There are also good-value en suite twins and doubles, with beds, not bunks. Cheap breakfast and a pool table add to the convivial party atmosphere. No extra charge for linen.

Pitlochry SYHA   HOSTEL £
(☑ 01796-472308; www.syha.org.uk; Knockard Rd; dm/tw £19/46; ☺ Mar-Oct; P @ ?) Great location overlooking the town centre. Popular with families and walkers.

★Craigatin House   B&B ££
(☑ 01796-472478; www.craigatinhouse.co.uk; 165 Atholl Rd; d from £107, ste £134; P @ ?) Several times more tasteful than the average Scottish B&B, this elegant house and garden is set back from the main road. Chic contemporary fabrics covering expansive beds offer a standard of comfort above and beyond the reasonable price; the rooms in the converted stable block are particularly inviting. A fabulous breakfast and lounge area gives views over the lush garden.

★Fonab Castle Hotel   HISTORIC HOTEL £££
(☑ 01796-470140; www.fonabcastlehotel.com; Foss Rd; r from £225; P ?) This Scottish Baronial fantasy in red sandstone was built in 1892 as the country house of Lt Col George Sandeman, a scion of the famous port and sherry merchants. Now a luxury hotel and spa, it has a tasteful modern extension with commanding views over Loch Faskally, and a superb restaurant serving the finest Scottish venison, beef and seafood.

Killiecrankie Hotel   HOTEL £££
(☑ 01796-473220; www.killiecrankiehotel.co.uk; d incl dinner from £125; ☺ Mar-Dec; P ? ?) This standout choice offers faultless hospitality in a peaceful setting, with interesting art on the walls, and relaxing rooms with views over the lovely gardens. The best things about the Scottish country-house experience are here, without the musty feel that sometimes goes with it; the food is also excellent. Two-night minimum stay at busy times; B&B-only rates are sometimes available.

✖ Eating

★Moulin Hotel   PUB FOOD ££
(☑ 01796-472196; www.moulinhotel.co.uk; Kirkmichael Rd; mains £9-16; ☺ food served noon-9.30pm; P ? ?) A mile away from town but a world apart, this atmospheric inn has low ceilings, ageing wood and snug booths. It's a wonderfully romantic spot for a home-brewed ale (there's a microbrewery out back) and some Highland comfort food: try the mince and tatties, or game casserole. It's a pleasant uphill stroll from Pitlochry, and an easy roll down afterwards.

Port-na-Craig Inn   BISTRO ££
(☑ 01796-472777; www.portnacraig.com; Port-na-Craig; mains £8-17; ☺ 11am-8.30pm; P ?) Across the river from the town centre, this cute little cottage sits in what was once a separate hamlet. Top-quality main meals are prepared with confidence and panache; there are also simpler sandwiches, kids' meals and light lunches. Or you could just sit outdoors by the river with a pint and watch the salmon anglers.

☆ Entertainment

★Pitlochry Festival Theatre   THEATRE
(☑ 01796-484626; www.pitlochryfestivaltheatre. com; Port-na-Craig; tickets £6-35) Founded in 1951 (in a tent!), this famous and much-loved theatre is the focus of Highland Perthshire's cultural life. The summer season, from May to mid-October, stages a different production each night of the week except Sunday.

❶ Information

Pitlochry Tourist Office (☑ 01796-472215; www.perthshire.co.uk; 22 Atholl Rd; ☺ 9.30am-5.30pm Mon-Sat, 10am-4pm Sun Mar-Oct, longer hours Jul & Aug, reduced hours Nov-Feb) Good information on local walks.

❶ Getting There & Away

BUS

Scottish Citylink (p902) Buses run two to four times daily to Inverness (£18.10, 1¾ hours), Perth (£11.50, 50 minutes), Edinburgh (£18.10, two to 2½ hours) and Glasgow (£18.10, 2¼ hours).

Megabus (☑ 0871 266 3333; www.megabus. com) Offers discounted fares to Inverness, Perth, Edinburgh and Glasgow.

Stagecoach (p903) Buses run to Aberfeldy (£3, 40 minutes, hourly Monday to Saturday, three Sunday), Dunkeld (£2.60, 40 minutes, hourly Monday to Saturday) and Perth (£4.10, 1¼ hours, hourly Monday to Saturday).

TRAIN

Pitlochry is on the main railway line from Perth (£14.40, 30 minutes, nine daily Monday to Saturday, five on Sunday) to Inverness (£23.40, 1¾ hours, same frequency).

Blair Castle

One of the most popular tourist attractions in Scotland, magnificent **Blair Castle** (☑01796-481207; www.blair-castle.co.uk; adult/child £12/7.70; ⊙9.30am-5.30pm Easter-Oct, 10am-4pm Sat & Sun Nov-Mar; Ⓟ🐾) – and its surrounding estates – is the seat of the Duke of Atholl, head of the Murray clan. (The current duke visits every May to review the **Atholl Highlanders**, Britain's only private army.) It's an impressive white heap set beneath forested slopes above the River Garry. Thirty rooms are open to the public and they present a wonderful picture of upper-class Highland life from the 16th century on.

The original tower was built in 1269, but the castle underwent significant remodelling in the 18th and 19th centuries. Highlights include the 2nd-floor **drawing room** with its ornate Georgian plasterwork and Zoffany portrait of the fourth duke's family, complete with a pet lemur (yes, you read that correctly) called Tommy; and the **tapestry room** draped with 17th-century wall hangings created for Charles I. The **dining room** is sumptuous – check out the 9-pint wine glasses – and the **ballroom** is a vast oak-panelled chamber hung with hundreds of stag antlers.

Lochs Tummel & Rannoch

The scenic route along Lochs Tummel and Rannoch (www.rannochandtummel.co.uk) is worth doing any way you can – by foot, bicycle or car. Hillsides shrouded with ancient birchwoods and forests of spruce, pine and larch make up the fabulous **Tay Forest Park**, whose wooded hills roll into the glittering waters of the lochs; a visit in autumn, when the birch leaves are at their finest, is recommended.

Eighteen miles west of Kinloch Rannoch the road ends at romantic and isolated **Rannoch Station**, which lies on the Glasgow–Fort William railway line. Beyond sprawls the desolate expanse of Rannoch Moor. There's an excellent **tearoom** (☑01882-633247; www.rannochstationtearoom.co.uk; Rannoch Station; mains £4-6; ⊙8.30am-4.30pm Mon-Thu & Sat, 10am-4.30pm Sun; Ⓟ🍽) on the station platform, and a welcoming small hotel alongside. Be aware that Rannoch Station is a dead end, and the nearest service station is at Aberfeldy.

There are two to four trains daily from Rannoch Station north to Fort William (£11.10, one hour) and Mallaig, and south to Glasgow (£25.30, 2¾ hours).

Loch Tay

Loch Tay is the heart of the ancient region known as Breadalbane (from the Gaelic Bràghad Albainn, 'the heights of Scotland') – mighty **Ben Lawers** (1214m), looming over the loch, is the highest peak outside the Ben Nevis and Cairngorms regions. Much of the land to the north of Loch Tay falls within the **Ben Lawers National Nature Reserve** (www.nnr.scot), known for its rare alpine flora.

A mile south of Kenmore on the banks of Loch Tay is the fascinating **Scottish**

RANNOCH MOOR

Beyond Rannoch Station, civilisation fades away and Rannoch Moor begins. This is the largest area of moorland in Britain, stretching west for eight barren, bleak and uninhabited miles to the A82 Glasgow–Fort William road. A triangular plateau of blanket bog occupying more than 50 sq miles, the moor is ringed by high mountains and puddled with countless lochs, ponds and peat hags. Water covers 10% of the surface, and it has been canoed across, swum across, and even skated across in winter.

Despite the appearance of desolation, the moor is rich in wildlife, with curlew, golden plover and snipe darting among the tussocks, black-throated diver, goosander and merganser on the lochs, and – if you're lucky – osprey and golden eagle overhead. Herds of red deer forage alongside the railway, and otters patrol the loch shores. Keep an eye out for the sundew, a tiny, insect-eating plant with sticky-fingered leaves.

A couple of excellent (and challenging) walks start from Rannoch Station – north to Corrour Station (11 miles, four to five hours) from where you can return by train; and west along the northern edge of the moor to the **Kings House Hotel** (☑01855-851259; www.kingshousehotel.co.uk; Kingshouse; s/d £45/100; Ⓟ) at the eastern end of Glen Coe (11 miles, four hours).

Crannog Centre (☑01887-830583; www.crannog.co.uk; tours adult/child £10/7; ⊙10am-5.30pm Apr-Oct; 🅿♿), perched on stilts above the loch. Crannogs – effectively artificial islands – were a favoured form of defensive dwelling from the 3rd millennium BC onwards. This superb recreation (based on studies of Oakbank crannog, one of 18 discovered in Loch Tay) offers a guided tour that includes fire making and Iron Age crafts.

Loch Tay is also famous for its fishing – salmon, trout and pike are all caught here. Fish 'n' Trips (☑07967 567347; www.lochtayfishntrips.co.uk) can kit you out for a day's fishing with boat, tackle and guide for £120 for two people, or rent you a boat for £60 a day.

The main road from Kenmore to Killin runs along the north shore of Loch Tay. The minor road along the south shore is narrow and twisting (unsuitable for large vehicles), but offers great views of the hills to the north.

WEST HIGHLANDS

This region extends from the bleak blanket-bog of the Moor of Rannoch to the west coast beyond Glen Coe and Fort William, and includes the southern reaches of the Great Glen. The scenery is grand throughout, with high, rocky mountains rising above wild glens. Great expanses of moor alternate with lochs and patches of commercial forest. Fort William, at the inner end of Loch Linnhe, is the only sizeable town in the area.

Since 2007 the region has been promoted as Lochaber Geopark (www.lochabergeopark.org.uk), an area of outstanding geology and scenery.

❶ Getting There & Away

The scenic West Highland railway line from Glasgow to Fort William and Mallaig – the departure point for ferries to the Small Isles, Skye and the Outer Hebrides – runs through the heart of the region, and is an ideal way of travelling between the main centres. A good network of local bus services fills in the gaps.

Glen Coe

Scotland's most famous glen is also one of its grandest and – in bad weather – its grimmest. The approach to the glen from the east is guarded by the rocky pyramid of **Buachaille Etive Mor** – the Great Shepherd of Etive – and the lonely **Kings House Hotel**

(closed for renovation until 2019). After the Battle of Culloden in 1745 it was used as a Hanoverian garrison – hence the name.

The A82 road leads over the Pass of Glencoe and into the narrow upper glen. The southern side is dominated by three massive, brooding spurs, known as the **Three Sisters**, while the northern side is enclosed by the continuous steep wall of the knife-edged **Aonach Eagach** ridge, a classic mountaineering challenge. The road threads its way past deep gorges and crashing waterfalls to the more pastoral lower reaches of the glen around Loch Achtriochtan and the only settlement here, **Glencoe village**.

Two miles west of **Glencoe Mountain** (☑01855-851226; www.glencoemountain.com; Kingshouse; chairlift adult/child £12/6; ⊙9am-4.30pm) ski centre, a minor road leads along peaceful and beautiful **Glen Etive**, which runs southwest for 12 miles to the head of Loch Etive. On a hot summer's day the River Etive contains many tempting pools for swimming in, and there are lots of good picnic sites.

🛏 Sleeping & Eating

Glencoe Independent Hostel HOSTEL £
(☑01855-811906; www.glencoehostel.co.uk; farmhouse/bunkhouse dm £17/15; 🅿@🛜) This handily located hostel, just 1.5 miles southeast of Glencoe village, is set in an old farmhouse with six- and eight-bed dorms, and a bunkhouse with another 16 bed spaces in communal, alpine-style bunks. There's also a cute little wooden cabin that sleeps up to three (£80 per night).

Glencoe SYHA HOSTEL £
(☑08155-811219; www.syha.org.uk; dm/tr £19/83; 🅿@🛜🛜) Very popular with hikers, though the atmosphere can be a little institutional. It's a 1.5-mile walk from Glencoe village along the minor road on the northern side of the river.

Clachaig Inn HOTEL ££
(☑01855-811252; www.clachaig.com; s/d £57/114; 🅿🛜) The Clachaig, 2 miles east of Glencoe village, has long been a favourite haunt of hill walkers and climbers. As well as comfortable en suite accommodation, there's a smart, modern lounge bar with snug booths and high refectory tables, mountaineering photos and bric-a-brac, and climbing magazines to leaf through.

Climbers usually head for the lively Boots Bar on the other side of the hotel – it has log fires, serves real ale and good pub grub (mains £10 to £21, served noon to 9pm), and has live Scottish music on Saturday nights.

★ **Glencoe Café** CAFE £
(📞 01855-811168; www.glencoecafe.co.uk; Glencoe village; mains £4-8; ⊙ 10am-4pm, to 5pm May-Sep, closed Nov; P 🛜) This friendly cafe is the social hub of Glencoe village, serving breakfast fry-ups till 11.30am (including vegetarian versions), light lunches based on local produce (think Cullen skink, smoked salmon quiche, venison burgers), and the best cappuccino in the glen.

ℹ️ Getting There & Away

Scottish Citylink (p902) buses run between Fort William and Glencoe (£8.50, 30 minutes, four to eight daily) and from Glencoe to Glasgow (£22.70, 2¾ hours, four to eight daily). Buses stop at Glencoe village, Glencoe Visitor Centre and Glencoe Mountain Resort.

Stagecoach (p903) bus 44 links Glencoe village with Fort William (£4.10, 40 minutes, hourly Monday to Saturday, three on Sunday) and Kinlochleven (£2.20, 15 minutes).

Fort William

📞 01397 / POP 9910

Basking on Loch Linnhe's shores amid magnificent mountain scenery, Fort William has one of the most enviable settings in all of Scotland. If it weren't for the busy dual carriageway crammed between the less-than-attractive town centre and the loch, and one of the highest rainfall records in the country, it would be almost idyllic. Even so, the Fort has carved out a reputation as the 'Outdoor Capital of the UK' (www.outdoorcapital.co.uk), and easy access by rail and bus makes it a good base for exploring the surrounding mountains and glens.

Magical Glen Nevis begins near the northern end of the town and wraps itself around the southern flanks of Ben Nevis (1345m) – Britain's highest mountain and a magnet for hikers and climbers. The glen is also popular with movie makers – parts of *Braveheart* (1995), *Pokemon: Detective Pikachu* (2018), the Harry Potter movies and the *Outlander* TV series were filmed here.

👁️ Sights

★ **Jacobite Steam Train** HERITAGE RAILWAY
(📞 0844 850 4685; www.westcoastrailways.co.uk; day return adult/child from £35/20; ⊙ daily mid-Jun–Aug, Mon-Fri mid-May–mid-Jun, Sep & Oct) The Jacobite Steam Train, hauled by a former LNER K1 or LMS Class 5MT locomotive, travels the scenic two-hour run between Fort William and Mallaig. Classed as one of the great railway journeys of the world, the route crosses the historic Glenfinnan Viaduct, made famous in the Harry Potter films – the Jacobite's owners supplied the steam locomotive and rolling stock used in the film.

Trains depart from Fort William train station in the morning and return from Mallaig in the afternoon. There's a brief stop at Glenfinnan station, and you get 1½ hours in Mallaig.

West Highland Museum MUSEUM
(📞 01397-702169; www.westhighlandmuseum.org. uk; Cameron Sq; ⊙ 10am-5pm Mon-Sat May-Sep, to 4pm Oct-Apr, 11am-3pm Sun Jul & Aug) FREE This small but fascinating museum is packed with all manner of Highland memorabilia. Look out for the secret portrait of Bonnie Prince Charlie – after the Jacobite rebellions, all things Highland were banned, including pictures of the exiled leader, and this tiny painting looks like nothing more than a smear of paint until viewed in a cylindrical mirror, which reflects a credible likeness of the prince.

🛏️ Sleeping

Calluna APARTMENT £
(📞 01397-700451; www.fortwilliamholiday.co.uk; Heathercroft, Connochie Rd; dm/tw £20/44, 6-person apt per 3 nights £124; P 🛜) Run by well-known mountain guide Alan Kimber and wife Sue, the Calluna offers self-catering apartments geared to groups of hikers and climbers, but also takes individual travellers prepared to share. There's a fully equipped kitchen and an excellent drying room for your soggy hiking gear.

Fort William Backpackers HOSTEL £
(📞 01397-700711; www.scotlands-top-hostels.com; Alma Rd; dm/tw £21/50; P @ 🛜) A 10-minute walk from the bus and train stations, this lively and welcoming hostel is set in a grand Victorian villa, perched on a hillside with great views over Loch Linnhe.

6 Caberfeidh B&B ££
(📞 01397-703756; www.6caberfeidh.com; 6 Caberfeidh, Fassifern Rd; d/f £78/108; 🛜) Friendly owners and comfortable accommodation make a great combination; add a good central location and you're all set. Choose from

one of two family rooms (one double and one single bed) or a romantic double with four-poster. Freshly prepared breakfasts include scrambled eggs with smoked salmon.

★ **Grange** B&B £££
(☎ 01397-705516; www.grangefortwilliam.com; Grange Rd; d from £180; P �ᔕ) An exceptional 19th-century villa set in its own landscaped grounds, the Grange is crammed with antiques and warmed by log fires, and has two luxury suites fitted with leather sofas, handcrafted furniture and roll-top baths, one situated in a charming self-contained cottage in the sprawling gardens, all with a view over Loch Linnhe. No children.

Lime Tree HOTEL £££
(☎ 01397-701806; www.limetreefortwilliam.co.uk; Achintore Rd; r from £140; P ᔕ ᔕ) Much more interesting than your average guesthouse, this former Victorian manse overlooking Loch Linnhe is an 'art gallery with rooms', decorated throughout with the artist-owner's atmospheric Highland landscapes. Foodies rave about the restaurant, and the gallery space – a triumph of sensitive design – stages everything from serious exhibitions (works by David Hockney and Andy Goldsworthy have appeared) to folk concerts.

Ashburn House B&B £££
(☎ 01397-706000; www.ashburnhouse.co.uk; Achintore Rd; r per person from £65; ⊙ Mar-Oct; P ᔕ) Gorgeously bright and spacious bedrooms – some with views over Loch Linnhe – are the norm at this grand Victorian villa south of the centre. The leather sofas in the residents' lounge and the breakfast tables in the dining room enjoy sea views. No children under 12; two-night minimum May to September.

✗ Eating & Drinking

DeliCraft DELI £
(☎ 01397-698100; www.delicraft.co.uk; 61 High St; mains £3-10; ⊙ 8am-6.30pm Mon-Sat, 10am-4pm Sun; ᔕ) This deli serves great coffee, excellent pizza and delicious sandwiches, including deli classics such as pastrami on rye, to eat in or take away, as well as a range of Scottish cheeses, craft beers and gins.

★ **Lime Tree** SCOTTISH ££
(☎ 01397-701806; www.limetreefortwilliam.co.uk; Achintore Rd; mains £16-20; ⊙ 6.30-9.30pm; P ᔕ) ✐ Fort William is not over-endowed with great places to eat, but the restaurant at this small hotel and art gallery has put

the UK's Outdoor Capital on the gastronomic map. The chef turns out delicious dishes built around fresh Scottish produce, ranging from Loch Fyne oysters to Loch Awe trout and Ardnamurchan venison.

★ **Crannog**
Seafood Restaurant SEAFOOD ££
(☎ 01397-705589; www.crannog.net; Town Pier; mains £15-24; ⊙ noon-2.30pm & 6-9pm) ✐ The Crannog wins the prize for the best location in town – perched on the Town Pier, giving window-table diners an uninterrupted view down Loch Linnhe. Informal and unfussy, it specialises in fresh local fish – there are three or four daily fish specials plus the main menu – though there are lamb, venison and vegetarian dishes, too. Two-/three-course lunch costs £16/19.

Grog & Gruel PUB
(☎ 01397-705078; www.grogandgruel.co.uk; 66 High St; ⊙ noon-midnight; ᔕ) The Grog & Gruel is a traditional-style, wood-panelled pub with an excellent range of cask ales from regional Scottish and English microbreweries.

ⓘ Information

Fort William Tourist Office (☎ 01397-701801; www.visithighlands.com; 15 High St; internet per 20min £1; ⊙ 9am-5pm Mon-Sat, 10am-3pm Sun, longer hours Jun-Aug; ᔕ) Internet access.

ⓘ Getting There & Away

The bus and train stations are next to the huge Morrisons supermarket, reached from the town centre via an underpass next to the Nevisport shop.

BUS

Scottish Citylink (☎ 0871 266 3333; www.citylink.co.uk) buses link Fort William with other major towns and cities:

Edinburgh £37, 5¼ hours, four daily with a change at Glasgow; via Glencoe and Crianlarich

Glasgow £25, three hours, four daily

Inverness £12.20, two hours, six daily

Oban £9.40, 1½ hours, two daily

Portree £32.20, three hours, three daily

Shiel Buses (☎ 01397-700700; www.shielbuses.co.uk) service 500 runs to Mallaig (£6.10, 1½ hours, four daily Monday to Friday, plus one daily Saturday and Sunday) via Glenfinnan and Arisaig (£5.60, one hour).

TRAIN

The spectacular West Highland line runs from Glasgow to Mallaig via Fort William. The overnight **Caledonian Sleeper** (www.sleeper.

scot) service connects Fort William and London Euston (from £135 sharing a twin-berth cabin, 13 hours).

There's no direct rail connection between Oban and Fort William – you have to change at Crianlarich, so it's faster to use the bus.

Edinburgh £40, five hours; change at Glasgow's Queen St station, three daily, two on Sunday

Glasgow £30, 3¾ hours, three daily, two on Sunday

Mallaig £13, 1½ hours, four daily, three on Sunday

Around Fort William

Glen Nevis

Scenic Glen Nevis – used as a filming location for *Braveheart* and the Harry Potter movies – lies just an hour's walk from Fort William town centre.

Glen Nevis Caravan & Camping Park
CAMPGROUND £

(☏01397-702191; www.glen-nevis.co.uk; tent sites per person £9.50, campervan £26; ⊙mid-Mar–early Nov; ☎) This big, well-equipped site is a popular base camp for Ben Nevis and the surrounding mountains. The site is 2.5 miles from Fort William, along the Glen Nevis road.

Glen Nevis SYHA
HOSTEL £

(SYHA; ☏01397-702336; www.syha.org.uk; dm £24; P@☎) Benefitting from a complete overhaul in early 2018, this hostel is 3 miles from Fort William, right beside one of the starting points for the tourist track up Ben Nevis. Cooked breakfasts (£7) and packed lunches (£6) are available.

Achintee Farm
B&B, HOSTEL ££

(☏01397-702240; www.achinteefarm.com; Achintee; B&B d £110, hostel tw/tr £54/81; ⊙B&B May-Sep, hostel year-round; P☎) This attractive farmhouse offers excellent B&B accommodation

---

CLIMBING BEN NEVIS

As the highest peak in the British Isles, **Ben Nevis** (1345m) attracts many would-be ascensionists who would not normally think of climbing a Scottish mountain – a staggering (often literally) 100,000 people reach the summit each year.

Although anyone who is reasonably fit should have no problem climbing Ben Nevis on a fine summer's day, an ascent should not be undertaken lightly; every year people have to be rescued from the mountain. You will need proper walking boots (the path is rough and stony, and there may be snow on the summit), warm clothing, waterproofs, a map and compass, and plenty of food and water. And don't forget to check the weather forecast (www.bennevisweather.co.uk).

Here are a few facts to mull over before you go racing up the tourist track: the summit plateau is bounded by 700m-high cliffs and has a sub-Arctic climate; at the summit it can snow on any day of the year; the summit is wrapped in cloud nine days out of 10; in thick cloud, visibility at the summit can be 10m or less; and in such conditions the only safe way off the mountain requires careful use of a map and compass to avoid walking over those 700m cliffs.

The tourist track (the easiest route to the top) was originally called the Pony Track. It was built in the 19th century for the pack ponies that carried supplies to a meteorological observatory on the summit (now in ruins), which was in use continuously from 1883 to 1904.

There are three possible starting points for the tourist track ascent – Achintee Farm ; the footbridge at Glen Nevis SYHA hostel; and, if you have a car, the car park at Glen Nevis Visitor Centre (p910). The path climbs gradually to the shoulder at Lochan Meall an t-Suidhe (known as the Halfway Lochan), then zigzags steeply up beside the Red Burn to the summit plateau. The highest point is marked by a trig point on top of a huge cairn beside the ruins of the old observatory; the plateau is scattered with countless smaller cairns, stones arranged in the shape of people's names and, sadly, a fair bit of litter.

The total distance to the summit and back is 8 miles; allow at least four or five hours to reach the top, and another 2½ to three hours for the descent. Afterwards, as you celebrate in the Ben Nevis Inn (p910) with a pint, consider the fact that the record time for the annual Ben Nevis Hill Race is just under 1½ hours – up and down. Then have another pint.

and also has a small hostel attached. It's at the start of the path up Ben Nevis.

⭐ **Ben Nevis Inn** SCOTTISH **££**
(☑01397-701227; www.ben-nevis-inn.co.uk; Achintee; mains £10-15; ⊙noon-11pm Apr-Oct, Thu-Sun Dec-Mar, closed Nov; P) This great barn of a pub serves real ale and tasty bar meals (till 9pm), and has a comfy 24-bed bunkhouse downstairs (beds £17 per person). It's at the start of the path from Achintee up Ben Nevis, and only a mile from the end of the West Highland Way.

❶ Information

Glen Nevis Visitor Centre (☑01397-705922; www.bennevisweather.co.uk; ⊙8.30am-6pm Jul & Aug, 9am-5pm Apr-Jun, Sep & Oct, 9am-3pm Nov-Mar) The Glen Nevis Visitor Centre is situated 1.5 miles up the glen, and provides information on walking, weather forecasts, and specific advice on climbing Ben Nevis.

❶ Getting There & Away

Bus 41 runs from Fort William bus station to the Glen Nevis SYHA (p909) hostel (£2.30, 15 or 20 minutes, two daily year-round, five daily Monday to Saturday June to September). Check at the tourist office for the latest timetable, which is liable to alteration.

Nevis Range

Six miles to the north of Fort William lies **Nevis Range ski area** (☑01397-705825; www.nevisrange.co.uk; day ticket per adult/child £21/12; ⊙10am-6pm Jul & Aug, to 5pm Apr-Jun, Sep & Oct, 9.30am-dusk Nov-Mar), where a gondola gives access to the upper part of Aonach Mor mountain. The facility operates year-round, allowing visitors to access mountain paths and downhill mountain-biking **trails** (☑01397-705825; www.nevisrange.co.uk/bike; single/multitrip ticket £18.50/34.50; ⊙downhill course 10.15am-3.45pm Apr-Oct, forest trails 24hr year-round) outside of the ski season.

Bus 41 runs from Fort William bus station to Nevis Range (£2.30, 25 minutes, three daily Monday to Saturday, limited service October to April). Check at Fort William's tourist office (p908) for the latest timetable, which is liable to alteration.

Road to the Isles

The 46-mile A830 road from Fort William to Mallaig is traditionally known as the Road to the Isles, as it leads to the jump-ing-off point for ferries to the Small Isles and Skye, itself a stepping stone to the Outer Hebrides. This is a region steeped in Jacobite history, having witnessed both the beginning and the end of Bonnie Prince Charlie's doomed attempt to regain the British throne in 1745–46.

The final section of this scenic route, between Arisaig and Mallaig, has been upgraded to a fast straight road. Unless you're in a hurry, opt instead for the more scenic old road (signposted Alternative Coastal Route).

Between the A830 and the A87 far to the north lie Knoydart and Glenelg – Scotland's 'Empty Quarter'.

❶ Getting There & Away

BOAT

A passenger ferry operated by Western Isles Cruises (p911) links Mallaig to Inverie on the Knoydart Peninsula (25 to 40 minutes) four times daily Monday to Saturday (three on Sunday) from April to October.

CalMac (☑0800 066 5000; www.calmac. co.uk) operates the passenger-only ferry from Mallaig to the following destinations in the Small Isles:

Canna £10.90 return, two hours, six weekly
Eigg £8 return, 1¼ hours, five weekly
Muck £9.20 return, 1½ hours, five weekly
Rum £8.60 return, 1¼ hours, five weekly

There are CalMac car ferry services to Armadale in Skye (car/passenger £9.70/2.90, 30 minutes, eight daily Monday to Saturday, five to seven on Sunday), and Lochboisdale in South Uist (car/passenger £57.65/10.45, 3½ hours, one daily).

BUS

Shiel Buses (☑01397-700700; www.shiel-buses.co.uk) service 500 runs from Fort William to Mallaig (£6.10, 1½ hours, four daily Monday to Friday, plus one daily Saturday and Sunday) via Glenfinnan (£3.30, 30 minutes) and Arisaig (£5.60, one hour).

TRAIN

The West Highland train line runs between Fort William and Mallaig, stopping at Glenfinnan (£6.70, 35 minutes, four daily, three on Sunday), Arisaig (£11.20, one hour) and Morar (£12.40, 1¼ hours).

Glenfinnan

POP 100

Glenfinnan is hallowed ground for fans of Bonnie Prince Charlie; the monument here marks where he raised his Highland army. It is also a place of pilgrimage for steam train

KNOYDART PENINSULA

The Knoydart peninsula – a rugged landscape of wild mountains and lonely sea lochs – is the only sizeable area in Britain that remains inaccessible to the motor car, cut off by miles of rough country and the embracing arms of Lochs Nevis and Hourn (Gaelic for the lochs of Heaven and Hell). The main reasons for visiting are to climb the 1020m peak of **Ladhar Bheinn** (laar-ven), or just to enjoy the feeling of remoteness. There's no TV and no mobile-phone reception; electricity is provided by a private hydroelectric scheme.

No road penetrates this wilderness of rugged hills – **Inverie**, its sole village, can only be reached by ferry from Mallaig, or on foot from the remote road's end at Kinloch Hourn (a tough 16-mile hike). A 4WD track leads northwest from Inverie for 7 miles to the outposts of **Doune** and **Airor**, which offer even more remote accommodation options.

All accommodation is listed on www.visitknoydart.co.uk. Options include the **Knoydart Foundation Bunkhouse** (☑ 01687-462163; www.knoydart-foundation.com; Inverie; dm adult/child £18/10; @🖲) 🖉 and **Knoydart Lodge** (☑ 01687-460129; www.knoydart lodge.co.uk; Inverie; r per person from £30; 🖲🖲) 🖉, while the homely **Old Forge** (☑ 01687-462267; www.theoldforge.co.uk; Inverie; mains £16-24; ⊘ 12.30-11.30pm Thu-Tue mid-Mar–Oct, 4-11pm Thu-Tue Nov–mid-Mar; 🖲🖮) 🖉 is listed in the *Guinness World Records* as Britain's remotest pub. Because of Knoydart's remote location, accommodation should be booked unless you're planning on camping.

Western Isles Cruises (☑ 01687-462233; https://westernislescruises.co.uk; one-way/ day return £10/20, bike £3) operates a passenger ferry from Mallaig to Inverie (25 to 40 minutes) four times daily Monday to Saturday and three on Sunday from April to October. Taking the morning boat gives you up to 10 hours ashore in Knoydart before the return trip (first and last boats of the day should be booked in advance). There's also an afternoon sailing between Inverie and Tarbet on the south side of Loch Nevis, allowing walkers to hike along the northern shore of Loch Morar to Tarbet and return by boat (£15 Tarbet–Inverie–Mallaig).

It's also possible to join the boat just for the cruise, without going ashore (£22 for Mallaig–Inverie–Tarbet–Inverie–Mallaig).

enthusiasts and Harry Potter fans – the famous railway viaduct features in the Potter films, and is regularly traversed by the Jacobite Steam Train (p907).

⊙ Sights & Activities

Glenfinnan Monument
MONUMENT

FREE This tall column, topped by a statue of a kilted Highlander, was erected in 1815 on the spot where Bonnie Prince Charlie first raised his standard and rallied the Jacobite clans on 19 August 1745, marking the start of his ill-fated campaign, which would end in disaster at Culloden 14 months later. The setting, at the north end of Loch Shiel, is hauntingly beautiful.

Glenfinnan Station Museum
MUSEUM

(www.glenfinnanstationmuseum.co.uk; admission by donation, suggested £1; ⊘ 9am-5pm Easter-Oct; 🅿) This fascinating little museum records the epic tale of building the West Highland railway line. The famous 21-arch **Glenfinnan viaduct**, just east of the station, was built in 1901, and featured in several Harry

Potter movies. A pleasant walk of around 0.75 miles east from the station (signposted) leads to a viewpoint for the viaduct and for Loch Shiel.

Glenfinnan Visitor Centre
MUSEUM

(NTS; www.nts.org.uk; adult/child £3.50/2.50; ⊘ 9am-7pm Jul & Aug, to 6pm Mar-Jun, Sep & Oct, 10am-4pm Nov-Feb; 🅿) This centre recounts the story of the '45, as the Jacobite rebellion of 1745 is known, when Bonnie Prince Charlie's loyal clansmen marched and fought their way from Glenfinnan south via Edinburgh to Derby, then back north to final defeat at Culloden.

Loch Shiel Cruises
CRUISE

(☑ 07801 537617; www.highlandcruises.co.uk; per person £12-22; ⊘ Apr-Sep) Boat trips along Loch Shiel, with the opportunity of spotting golden eagles and other wildlife. There are one- to 2½-hour cruises on Tuesday and Thursday. On Wednesday the boat goes the full length of the loch to Acharacle (one-way/return £20/30), calling at Polloch and

WORTH A TRIP

DUNROBIN CASTLE

In both landscape and character, the east coast is where the real barrenness of the Highlands begins to unfold. A gentle splendour and a sense of escapism mark the route along the twisting A9, as it heads north for the last of Scotland's far-flung, mainland population outposts. With only a few exceptions the tourism frenzy is left behind once the road traverses Cromarty Firth and snakes its way along wild and pristine coastline.

The main reason to make a detour along this windswept coast is magnificent **Dunrobin Castle** (☑ 01408-633177; www.dunrobincastle.co.uk; A9; adult/child £11.50/7; ☉ 10.30am-4.30pm Apr, May & Oct, 10am-5pm Jun-Sep), a mile past Golspie, the Highlands' largest house. Although it dates to 1275, most of what you see was built in French style between 1845 and 1850. The beautiful castle inspires mixed feelings locally; it was once the seat of the first Duke of Sutherland, notorious for some of the cruellest episodes of the Highland Clearances.

The classic fairy-tale castle is adorned with towers and turrets, but only 22 of its 187 rooms are on display, with hunting trophies much to the fore. Beautiful formal gardens, where impressive falconry displays take place two or three times a day, extend down to the sea. In the gardens is a museum with an eclectic mix of archaeological finds, natural-history exhibits, more non-PC animal remains and an excellent collection of Pictish stones.

Trains (£19.90, 2¼ hours) and buses (£12.05, 1½ hours) from Inverness towards Wick/Thurso stop in Golspie and at Dunrobin Castle.

Dalilea, allowing for walks and bike rides using the forestry track on the eastern shore.

The boat departs from a jetty near Glenfinnan House Hotel.

🛏 Sleeping & Eating

★ Prince's House Hotel INN £££
(☑ 01397-722246; www.glenfinnan.co.uk; s/d from £95/160; ℗) A delightful old coaching inn dating from 1658, the Prince's House is a great place to pamper yourself – ask for the spacious, tartan-draped Stuart Room (£225), complete with four-poster bed, if you want to stay in the oldest part of the hotel. The relaxed but well-regarded restaurant specialises in Scottish produce (four-course dinner £46).

Dining Car Tearoom CAFE £
(☑ 01397-722300; www.glenfinnanstationmuseum. co.uk; mains £6-10; ☉ 9am-4.30pm May-Oct; ℗) This atmospheric tearoom, set in a 1960s railway coach, serves soup and sandwiches, scones with cream and jam, and pots of tea, with superb views of the mountains above Loch Shiel. It is also possible to stay in a **sleeping car** (☑ 01397-722295; Glenfinnan Station; per person £15, entire coach £130; ☉ May-Oct; ℗).

Arisaig & Morar

The 5 miles of coast between the tiny villages of Arisaig and Morar is a fretwork of rocky islets, inlets and gorgeous silver-sand beaches backed by dunes and machair, with stunning sunset views across the sea to the silhouetted peaks of Eigg and Rum. The **Silver Sands of Morar**, as they are known, draw crowds of bucket-and-spade holidaymakers in July and August, when the many campsites scattered along the coast are filled to overflowing.

🛏 Sleeping & Eating

Old Library Lodge & Restaurant SCOTTISH ££
(☑ 01687-450651; www.oldlibrary.co.uk; Arisaig; mains £10-21; ☉ noon-2pm & 6-8.30pm; ℗ 🛜) 🍴 The Old Library is a charming restaurant with rooms (singles/doubles £75/120) set in converted 200-year-old stables overlooking the waterfront in Arisaig village. The lunch menu concentrates on soups, burgers and smoked fish or meat platters, while dinner is a more sophisticated affair offering local seafood, beef and lamb.

Mallaig

☑ 01687 / POP 800

If you're travelling between Fort William and Skye, you may find yourself overnighting in the bustling fishing and ferry port of Mallaig (*mahl*-ig). Indeed, it makes a good base for a series of day trips by ferry to the Small Isles and Knoydart.

Mallaig has a post office, a bank with an ATM and a co-op supermarket.

Seafari (☑ 01471-833316; Harbour Pontoons; adult/child £42/34; ☉ Easter-Sep) runs three-hour whale-watching cruises around Skye and the Small Isles aboard the single-hulled *Amelia* and the 36-seat catamaran *Orion*. These trips have a high success rate for spotting minke whales in summer (an average of 180 sightings a year), with rarer sightings of bottlenose dolphins and basking sharks.

🛏 Sleeping & Eating

Seaview Guest House B&B ££

(📞 01687-462059; www.seaviewguesthousemallaig.com; Main St; s/d £65/90, cottage per week £600; 🅿🛜) This comfortable B&B has grand views over the harbour, not only from the upstairs bedrooms but from the breakfast room, too. There's also a cute little cottage next door that offers self-catering accommodation (www.selfcateringmallaig.com; one double and one twin room).

Springbank Guest House B&B ££

(📞 01687-462459; www.springbank-mallaig.co.uk; East Bay; s/d from £45/75; 🛜) The Springbank is a traditional West Highland house with six homely guest bedrooms, with superb views across the harbour to the Cuillin of Skye.

Fish Market Restaurant SEAFOOD ££

(📞 01687-462299; www.thefishmarketrestaurant. co.uk; Station Rd; mains £12-28; ⊙noon-3pm & 6-9pm) 🥢 At least half-a-dozen signs in Mallaig advertise 'seafood restaurant', but this bright, modern, bistro-style place next to the harbour is our favourite, serving simply prepared scallops, smoked salmon, mussels, and fresh Mallaig haddock fried in breadcrumbs, as well as the tastiest Cullen skink on the west coast.

Upstairs is a **coffee shop** (Station Rd; mains £4-8; ⊙11am-4pm, to 6pm Jun-Aug).

CAITHNESS

Once you pass Helmsdale, you are entering Caithness, a place of jagged gorse-and-grass-topped cliffs hiding tiny fishing harbours. Scotland's top corner was once Viking territory, historically more connected to Orkney and Shetland than the rest of the mainland. It's a mystical, ancient land dotted with old monuments and peopled by folk who are proud of their Norse heritage.

❶ Getting There & Away

Despite being so far north, Caithness is easily reached. Flybe and Loganair service Wick's airport, and there are trains to both Wick and Thurso. Buses run between towns up the east and along the north coast.

Wick

📞 01955 / POP 7100

Wick is worth a visit, particularly for its excellent museum and attractive, spruced-up harbour area, and it has some very good places to stay. More gritty than pretty, however, it's been a little down on its luck since the collapse of the herring industry. It was once the world's largest fishing port for the 'silver darlings', but when the market dropped off after WWII, job losses were huge and the town hasn't ever totally recovered.

◎ Sights

★**Wick Heritage Centre** MUSEUM

(📞 01955-605393; www.wickheritage.org; 20 Bank Row; adult/child £4/50p; ⊙10am-5pm Apr-Oct, last entry 3.45pm) Tracking the rise and fall of the herring industry, this great town museum displays everything from fishing equipment to complete herring boats. It's absolutely huge inside, and is crammed with memorabilia and extensive displays describing Wick's heyday in the mid-19th century. The Johnston collection is the star exhibit. From 1863 to 1977, three generations photographed everything that happened around Wick and the 70,000 photographs are an amazing record.

Old Pulteney DISTILLERY

(📞 01955-602371; www.oldpulteney.com; Huddart St; tours £10; ⊙10am-4pm Mon-Fri Oct-Apr, 10am-5pm Mon-Fri, 10am-4pm Sat May-Sep) Though it can no longer claim to be the most northerly whisky distillery on mainland Scotland (that goes to the upstart Wolfburn in Thurso), friendly Pulteney still runs excellent tours twice or more daily (normally at 11am and 2pm), with more expensive visits available for aficionados. Its Stroma whisky liqueur is dangerously more-ish.

🛏 Sleeping & Eating

Bank Guesthouse B&B ££

(📞 01955-604001; www.guesthousewick.co.uk; 28 Bridge St; s £50-60, d £75-85; 🅿🛜) In the very centre of Wick, this striking Victorian building contains a warmly welcoming B&B run by a local family. Rooms have plenty of space and feature attractive carpets, wallpaper and fabrics along with modern bathrooms with great showers. Breakfast is well above average. Stairs might be a problem for the less mobile.

Mackays Hotel HOTEL ££
(☑01955-602323; www.mackayshotel.co.uk; Union St; s/d £93/129; 🕸) Hospitable Mackays is Wick's best hotel by a long stretch. Attractive, mostly refurbished rooms vary in layout and size, so ask to see a few; prices are usually lower than the rack rates. On-site No 1 Bistro (mains £17-24; ☺noon-2pm & 5-9pm; 🕸) is a fine option for lunch or dinner. The world's shortest street, 2.06m-long Ebenezer Place, is on one side of the hotel.

Bord de l'Eau FRENCH ££
(☑01955-604400; 2 Market St; mains £16-24; ☺noon-2pm & 6-9pm Tue-Sat, 6-9pm Sun) This serene, relaxed French restaurant is Wick's best place to eat. It overlooks the river and serves a changing menu of mostly meat and game French classics, backed up by daily fish specials. Starters are great value, and mains include a huge assortment of vegetables. The conservatory dining room with water views is lovely on a sunny evening.

ℹ Getting There & Away

AIR
Wick is a Caithness transport gateway. Loganair flies to Edinburgh and Flybe/Eastern Airways to Aberdeen (three daily, Monday to Friday).

BUS
Stagecoach and Citylink operate to/from Inverness (£20.15, three hours, six daily) and Stagecoach to Thurso (£3.90, 40 minutes, hourly). There's also connecting service to John O'Groats and Gills Bay (£3.60, 30 minutes, four to five Monday to Saturday) for the passenger and car ferries to Orkney.

TRAIN
Trains service Wick from Inverness (£21.10, 4¼ hours, four daily Monday to Saturday, one on Sunday).

John O'Groats

POP 300

Though not the northernmost point of the British mainland (that's Dunnet Head), John O'Groats still serves as the end point of the 874-mile trek from Land's End in Cornwall, a popular if arduous route for cyclists and walkers, many of whom raise money for charitable causes. Most of the settlement is taken up by a stylish modern self-catering

complex. There's a passenger ferry from here to Orkney.

Two miles east of John O'Groats, **Duncansby Head** has a small lighthouse and 60m-high cliffs sheltering nesting fulmars. A 15-minute walk through a sheep paddock yields spectacular views of the sea-surrounded monoliths known as Duncansby Stacks.

For sustenance, **Stacks Coffee House & Bistro** (☑01955-611582; www.facebook.com/stacksbistro; mains £10-13; ☺10am-4pm Tue-Sun) does really excellent home baking and tasty home-cooked meals.

ℹ Getting There & Away

Stagecoach (p903) runs between John O'Groats and Wick (£3.60, 30 minutes, four to five Monday to Saturday) or Thurso (£4.25, 40 minutes, five to eight Monday to Saturday).

From May to September, a passenger ferry (p942) shuttles across to Burwick in Orkney. Three miles west, a car ferry (p942) runs all year from Gills Bay to St Margaret's Hope in Orkney.

Mey

The **Castle of Mey** (☑01847-851473; www.castleofmey.org.uk; adult/child £11.75/6.50; ☺10.20am-5pm May-Sep, last entry 4pm), a big crowd-puller for its Queen Mother connections, is 6 miles west of John O'Groats. The exterior is grand but inside it feels domestic and everything is imbued with the Queen Mum's character. The highlight is the genteel guided tour, with various anecdotes recounted by staff who once worked for her. In the grounds there's a farm zoo, an unusual walled garden that's worth a stroll and lovely views over the Pentland Firth.

Buses running between Thurso (50 minutes) and John O'Groats (15 minutes) will stop in Mey. Call the castle ahead of time if you need assistance, and they'll try to pick you up.

Dunnet Head

Eight miles east of Thurso a minor road leads to dramatic Dunnet Head, the most northerly point on the British mainland. There are majestic cliffs dropping into the turbulent Pentland Firth, inspiring views of Orkney, basking seals and nesting seabirds below, and a lighthouse built by Robert Louis Stevenson's grandad. Just south, the excellent curving strand of Dunnet Bay is one of Scotland's finest beaches.

Buses running between Thurso (20 minutes) and John O'Groats (45 minutes) stop in Dunnet on the A836, but there's no public transport further north into the promontory.

Thurso & Scrabster

☑ 01847 / POP 7600

Britain's most northerly mainland town, Thurso makes a handy overnight stop if you're heading west or across to Orkney. There's a pretty town beach, riverside strolls and a good museum. Ferries for Orkney leave from Scrabster, 2.5 miles away.

🛏 Sleeping & Eating

Waterside House　　　　　B&B £

(☑ 01847-894751; www.watersidehouse.org; 3 Janet St; s £35-40, d £50-70; 🛜🐾) Easy to find, and easy to park outside, this welcoming budget guesthouse offers rooms of varying sizes with good en suites – try for one of the renovated chambers. Breakfast choices include egg-and-bacon rolls, or a takeaway pack if you've got an early ferry. To get here, turn left just after the bridge coming into town from the east.

★ Pennyland House　　　　B&B ££

(☑ 01847-891194; www.pennylandhouse.co.uk; A9; s £80, d £90-100; 🅿🛜🐾) A super conversion of a historic house, this is a standout B&B choice. It offers phenomenal value for this level of accommodation, with huge oak-furnished rooms named after golf courses: we especially loved St Andrews – super-spacious, with a great chessboard-tiled bathroom. Hospitality is enthusiastic and helpful, and there's an inviting breakfast space, garden and terraced area with views across to Hoy.

Two-night minimum stay in summer.

Camfield House　　　　　B&B ££

(☑ 01847-891118; www.riversideaccommodation. co.uk; Janet St; r £125-145; 🅿🛜) A Narnia-style portal leads from central Thurso through a gate and you're suddenly in what feels like an opulent rural estate. The garden is sumptuous and extravagantly features a manicured par-3 golf hole, complete with bunker and water hazard. The interior lacks nothing by comparison, with spacious rooms with huge TVs, quality linen and excellent bathrooms. There's even a full-sized billiard table.

Holborn Hotel　　　　　BISTRO ££

(☑ 01847-892771; www.holbornhotelthurso.co.uk; 16 Princes St; bar meals £9-13, restaurant mains £13-19; ⊙ noon-2pm & 6-8pm Mon-Thu, to 9pm Fri, noon-2.30pm & 6-9pm Sat & Sun; 🛜) A trendy, comfortable place decked out in light wood, the Holborn contrasts starkly with more traditional Thurso watering holes. Uncomplicated but decent meals are available in the bar, while quality seafood – including delicious home-smoked salmon – is the mainstay of a short menu fleshed out by specials at the evening-only Red Pepper restaurant, where desserts are excellent too. Service can be slow when busy.

It also has decent accommodation (singles/doubles £65/90).

★ Captain's Galley　　　SEAFOOD £££

(☑ 01847-894999; www.captainsgalley.co.uk; Scrabster; 5-course dinner £53.50, with wine flight £77; ⊙ 6.30-9pm Thu-Sat) 🍃 Classy but friendly Captain's Galley, by the Scrabster ferry, offers a short, seafood-based menu featuring local and sustainably sourced produce prepared in delicious ways that let the natural flavours shine through. The chef picks the best fish off the local boats, and the menu describes exact-

---

MIDGES

Forget Nessie, the Highlands have a real monster: a voracious bloodsucking female fully 3mm long named the Highland midge (*Culicoides impunctatus*). The bane of campers and as much a symbol of Scotland as the kilt or dram, they drive sane folk to distraction, descending in biting clouds.

Though normally vegetarian, the female midge needs a dose of blood in order to lay her eggs. And, like it or not, if you're in the Highlands between June and August, you just volunteered as a donor. Midges especially congregate near water, and are most active in the early morning, though squadrons also patrol in the late evening.

Repellents and creams are reasonably effective, though some walkers favour midge veils. Light-coloured clothing also helps. Many pubs and campsites have midge-zappers. Check www.smidgeup.com/midge-forecast for activity levels by area, but don't blame us: we've been eaten alive when the forecast said moderate, too.

ly which fishing grounds your morsel came from. It's worth scheduling a night in Thurso to eat here.

ⓘ Getting There & Away

BUS

Stagecoach/Citylink buses link Thurso/ Scrabster with Inverness (£20.15, three hours, five daily). There are also buses roughly every hour to Wick (£3.90, 40 minutes), as well as every couple of hours to John O'Groats (£4.25, 40 minutes, five to eight Monday to Saturday).

TRAIN

There are four daily trains (one on Sunday) from Inverness (£21.10, 3¾ hours), with a connecting bus to Scrabster.

NORTH & WEST COAST

Quintessential Highland country such as this, with breathtaking emptiness, a wild, fragile beauty and single-track roads, is a rarity on the modern, crowded, highly urbanised island of Britain. You could get lost up here for weeks – and that still wouldn't be enough time.

Carving its way from Thurso to Glencoul, the north and northwest coastline is a feast of deep inlets, forgotten beaches and surging peninsulas. Within the rugged confines, the interior is home to vast, empty spaces, enormous lochs and some of Scotland's highest peaks.

Whether in blazing sunshine or murky greyness, the character of the land is totally unique and constantly changing – for that window of time in which you can glimpse it, you'll capture an exclusive snapshot of this ancient area in your mind. Park the car and gaze. This northernmost slab of the Highlands is the stuff of coastal-drive dreams.

Thurso to Durness

It's 80 winding – and utterly spectacular – coastal miles from Thurso to Durness.

Ten miles west of Thurso, the Dounreay nuclear power station was the first in the world to supply mains electricity; it's currently being decommissioned. The clean-up is planned to be finished by 2025; it's still a major source of employment for the region.

Beyond, Melvich overlooks a fine beach and there are great views from Strathy Point (a 2-mile drive from the coast road, then a 15-minute walk).

Bettyhill is a pretty village that overlooks a magnificent stretch of coastline, and the scenery just improves as you head west through Coldbackie and Tongue, with a succession of gorgeous sea lochs, stunning beaches and striking rock formations backed by imposing hills and mountains.

◉ Sights

Strathnaver Museum   MUSEUM
(☑ 01641-521418; www.strathnavermuseum.org. uk; adult/child £2/1; ⊙ 10am-5pm Mon-Sat Apr-Oct) Housed in an old church, this museum tells the sad story of the Strathnaver Clearances through posters created by local kids. The museum contains memorabilia of Clan Mackay, various items of crofting equipment and a 'St Kilda mailboat', a small wooden boat-shaped container bearing a letter that was used by St Kildans to send messages to the mainland.

Outside the back door of the church is the **Farr Stone**, a fine carved Pictish cross-slab.

🛏 Sleeping & Eating

Bettyhill Hotel   INN ££
(☑ 01641-521202; www.bettyhillhotel.com; s/d without bathroom £60/90, d with bathroom £140; ⊙ Apr-Oct, check for winter opening; 🅿 ◉ 🕸) This historic hotel has a fabulous position overlooking the marvellous perspective of the sandy beach fringing Torrisdale Bay. The owners have been doing a great renovation and the excellent updated rooms are bright, with top-grade mattresses. Rooms come in many different types (some have super views), with lots of singles as well as a cottage. Bar and restaurant meals are available.

★ **Cloisters**   B&B ££
(☑ 01847-601286; www.cloistersbandb.co.uk; Talmine; s/d £40/70; 🅿 ◉ 🕸) Superbly located Cloisters has three en suite rooms by an artistically converted church and absolutely brilliant views over the Kyle of Tongue and offshore islands; you'll never tire of the vista. The breakfast room takes advantage of it; the courteous hosts can also arrange evening meals. From Tongue, cross the causeway and turn right towards Melness; Cloisters is a couple of miles.

Altnaharra Hotel   INN ££
(☑ 01549-411222; www.altnaharra.com; Altnaharra; s £70,d £109-120, superior d £140-160; ⊙ Mar-Dec; 🅿 ◉ 🕸) With two centuries of history as an angling destination, this remote, upmarket hotel has bags of character and is popular

with fisherfolk. The variety of rooms are decorated in plush classical fabrics. The restaurant serves excellent food (two-/three-course dinners £29/35), and there's also a convivial bar. It's worth coming here just for the drive: the route from Tongue is spectacular.

There are also refurbished self-catering cottages available.

Tigh-nan-Ubhal   B&B **££**

(📞01847-611281; www.tigh-nan-ubhal.com; Main St, Tongue; d £70-80; 🅿️🛜) In the middle of Tongue and within a minute's stumbling distance of two pubs is this charming B&B. There are snug, loft-style rooms with plenty of natural light, a great basement double with an enormous en suite and other lovely rooms with renovated bathrooms, colourful fabrics and plenty of comfort. Reliable, friendly and hospitable, it makes a great year-round choice.

⭐**Côte du Nord**   MODERN SCOTTISH **£££**

(📞01641-521773; www.cotedunord.co.uk; The School House, Kirtomy; degustation £35-45; ⏰7.30pm Wed, Fri & Sat Apr-Sep; 🍷) 🌿 Brilliantly innovative cuisine, wonderfully whimsical presentation and an emphasis on local ingredients are the highlights of the excellent gastronomic degustation menu here. It's an unlikely spot to find such a gourmet experience; the chef is none other than the local GP who forages for wild herbs and flavours in between surgery hours. Top value. It's tiny, so reserve well ahead.

Kirtomy is signposted off the main road about 2.5 miles east of Bettyhill; the restaurant is about a mile down this road.

Durness

📞01971 / POP 400

Scattered Durness (www.durness.org) is wonderfully located, strung out along cliffs rising from a series of pristine beaches. When the sun shines, the effects of blinding white sand, the cry of seabirds and the spring-green-coloured seas combine in a magical way.

👁 Sights

Walking the sensational sandy coastline is a highlight, as is a visit to **Cape Wrath**. Durness' beautiful beaches include **Rispond** to the east, **Sango Sands** below town and **Balnakeil** to the west. At Balnakeil, a craft village occupies a one-time early-warning radar station. A northerly beach walk leads to **Faraid Head**, where there are puffins in early summer.

Bikes can be hired from a shed on the square.

Smoo Cave   CAVE

(www.smoocave.org) FREE A mile east of the centre of Durness is a path down to Smoo Cave. From the vast main chamber, you can head through to a smaller flooded cavern where a waterfall sometimes cascades from the roof. There's evidence the cave was inhabited about 6000 years ago. You can take a **tour** (📞01971-511704; www.smoocavetours. weebly.com; adult/child £5/2; ⏰11am-4pm May & Sep, 10am-5pm Jun-Aug) to explore a little further into the interior.

🛏 Sleeping & Eating

Lazy Crofter Bunkhouse   HOSTEL **£**

(📞01971-511202; www.visitdurness.com/bunkho use; dm £20; 🛜) Durness' best budget accommodation is here, opposite the supermarket. A bothy vibe gives it a very Highland feel. Inviting dorms have plenty of room and lockers, and there's also a sociable shared table for meals and board games, and a great wooden deck with sea views, perfect for midge-free evenings.

⭐**Mackays Rooms**   HOTEL **££**

(📞01971-511202; www.visitdurness.com; d standard £129, deluxe £149-159; ⏰May-Oct; 🅿️🛜🏊) You really feel you're at the furthest corner of Scotland here, where the road turns through 90 degrees. But whether heading south or east, you'll go far before you find a better place to stay than this haven of Highland hospitality. With its big beds, soft fabrics and contemporary colours, it's a romantic spot with top service and numerous boutique details.

There's also a self-contained cabin here, which can be rented on a self-catering or B&B basis. With two rooms, it sleeps up to four.

Smoo Lodge   B&B **£££**

(📞01971-511423; www.smoolodge.co.uk; r £135-155; 🅿️🛜) A sizeable former shooting lodge on ample grounds has been lovingly restored to a very high standard. Excellent rooms feature high-quality mattresses and bedding as well as great modern bathrooms. Asian-inflected evening meals are available, and breakfast features an excellent Korean option – a nice change from bacon and eggs. No under-12s.

⭐**Cocoa Mountain**   CAFE **£**

(📞01971-511233; www.cocoamountain.co.uk; Balnakeil; hot chocolate £4, 10 truffles £10; ⏰9am-6pm

WORTH A TRIP

CAPE WRATH

Though its name actually comes from the Norse word *hvarf* ('turning point'), there is something daunting and primal about Cape Wrath, the remote northwesternmost point of the British mainland.

The danger of the hazardous, stormy seas led to the building of the lighthouse at the cape by Robert and Alan Stevenson in 1828. The last keepers had left by 1998, when people were replaced by automation. Three miles to the east are the seabird colonies of Clo Mor, the British mainland's highest vertical sea cliffs (195m).

Part of the moorland has served for decades as a bombing range. The island of An Garbh-Eilean, 5 miles from the cape, has the misfortune to be around the same size as an aircraft carrier and is regularly ripped up by RAF bombs and missiles. There is no public access when the range is in use; times are displayed on www.visitcapewrath.com.

Getting to Cape Wrath involves taking a **ferry** (☑ 07719 678729; www.capewrathferry. co.uk; single/return trip £5/7; ☺ Easter–mid-Oct) – passengers and bikes only – across the Kyle of Durness (10 minutes). It connects with the **Cape Wrath Minibus** (☑ 01971-511284; www.visitcapewrath.com; single/return trip £7/12; ☺ Easter–mid-Oct), which runs the very slow and bumpy 11 miles to the cape (50 minutes).

This combination is a friendly but eccentric and sometimes shambolic service with limited capacity, so plan on waiting in high season, and call ahead to make sure the ferry is running. The ferry leaves from 2 miles southwest of Durness, and runs twice or more daily from Easter to mid-October. If you eschew the minibus, it's a spectacular 11-mile ride or hike from boat to cape over bleak scenery.

Easter-Oct) ✐ At the Balnakeil craft village, this upbeat cafe and chocolate maker offers handmade treats including a chilli, lemongrass and coconut white-chocolate truffle, plus many more unique flavours. Tasty espresso and hot chocolate warm the cockles on those blowy horizontal-drizzle days. It offers light lunches and home-baking too, plus chocolate-making workshops.

❶ Getting There & Away

A year-round service with **Far North Bus** (☑ 07782 110007; www.thedurnessbus.com) heads to Lairg (£9, 2½ hours, Monday to Friday), where there is a train station. On Saturday buses head to Inverness (£13.40, three hours) and Thurso (£10.30, 2½ hours). In summer school holidays, there's also an Ullapool service (£10, 2½ hours). All these services should be prebooked; some have bicycle capacity.

There are also two Tuesday services with **Transport for Tongue** (☑ 01847-611766; www. transportfortongue.co.uk) between Tongue and Durness (£7, one hour).

Durness to Ullapool

Perhaps Scotland's most spectacular road, the 69 miles connecting Durness to Ullapool is a smorgasbord of dramatic scenery, almost too much to take in. From Durness you pass through a broad heathered valley with the looming grey bulk of Foinaven and Arkle to the southeast. Heather gives way to a rockier landscape of Lewisian gneiss pockmarked with hundreds of lochans (small lochs). This is the most interesting zone geologically in the UK, with Britain's oldest rock. Next come gorse-covered hills prefacing the magnificent Torridonian sandstone mountains of Assynt and Coigach, including Suilven's distinctive sugarloaf, ziggurat-like Quinag and pinnacled Stac Pollaidh. The area has been named as the **Northwest Highlands Geopark** (www.nwhgeopark.com).

Kylesku & Loch Glencoul

Hidden away on the shores of Loch Glencoul, tiny Kylesku served as a ferry crossing on the route north until it was made redundant by beautiful Kylesku Bridge in 1984. It's a good base for walks; you can hire bikes, too.

Five miles southeast of Kylesku, in wild, remote country, lies 213m-high **Eas a'Chual Aluinn**, Britain's highest waterfall. You can hike to the top of the falls from a parking area at a sharp bend in the main road 3 miles south of Kylesku; allow five hours for the 6-mile return trip. It can also be seen on boat trips from Kylesku.

🛏 Sleeping

Kylesku Hotel INN **££**
(📞01971-502231; www.kyleskuhotel.co.uk; Kylesku; s £75-110, d £115-170; ⊗mid-Feb–Nov; 🅿🛜🐾) Looking very spruce after renovations, and run with pride and enthusiasm, this hotel is a great place to stay and eat. There's a variety of rooms, including some stunning ones with balconies in a modern annexe. It's worth paying the small extra fee to get a loch view, though the cosy, secluded attic rooms also have appeal.

❶ Getting There & Away

In summer school holidays, there's a bus service with Far North Bus from Monday to Saturday between Durness and Ullapool, stopping in Kylesku. Book ahead.

Lochinver & Assynt

With its otherworldly scenery of isolated peaks rising above a sea of crumpled, lochan-spattered gneiss, Assynt epitomises the northwest's wild magnificence. Glaciers have sculpted the hills of Suilven (731m), Canisp (846m), Quinag (808m) and Ben More Assynt (998m) into strange, wonderful silhouettes.

Lochinver is the main settlement, a busy little fishing port that's a popular port of call with its laid-back atmosphere, good facilities and striking scenery. Just north of Lochinver (or if coming from the north, not far south of Kylesku), a 23-mile detour on the narrow B869 rewards with spectacular views and fine beaches. From the lighthouse at Point of Stoer, a one-hour cliff walk leads to the Old Man of Stoer, a spectacular sea stack.

🛏 Sleeping & Eating

An Cala Bunkhouse HOSTEL **£**
(Lochinver Bunkhouse; 📞01571-844598; www.ancalacafeandbunkhouse.co.uk; Culag Park, Lochinver; s/d bunk £25/45; 🅿🛜) Housed near the harbour in the former fishermen's mission, this is an appealing modern hostel with three functional dorms and a good kitchen and lounge. Call ahead on Sunday (plus Monday and Tuesday in the low season) when the cafe downstairs is closed and there's nobody on the premises.

Clachtoll Beach Campsite CAMPSITE **£**
(📞01571-855377; www.clachtollbeachcampsite.co.uk; B869, Clachtoll; site £6-12, plus per adult/child £5/2; ⊗Apr–mid-Oct; 🅿🛜🐾) Set among the machair beside a lovely white-sand beach and emerald seas, Clachtoll is a divine coastal camping spot, though somewhat overwhelmed by the adjacent self-catering development. It's 6 miles northwest of Lochinver by road.

Achmelvich Beach SYHA HOSTEL **£**
(📞01571-844480; www.syha.org.uk; dm/tw £21/53; ⊗Apr-Sep) Off the B869, this whitewashed cottage is set beside a great beach at the end of a side road. Dorms are simple, and there's a sociable common kitchen and eating area. Heat-up meals are available as is a basic shop in summer; otherwise, there's a chip van at the adjacent campsite, or you can take the 4-mile walk to Lochinver.

⭐**Albannach** HOTEL **£££**
(📞01571-844407; www.thealbannach.co.uk; Baddidarroch, Lochinver; s/d/ste £135/170/235; ⊗mid-Feb–mid-Dec; 🅿🛜) 🍴 The Albannach combines old-fashioned country-house elements – steep creaky stairs, stuffed animals, fireplaces and noble antique furniture – with strikingly handsome rooms that range from a sumptuous four-poster to more modern spaces with underfloor heating and, in one case, a private deck with outdoor spa. Glorious views, spacious grounds and great walks in easy striking distance make this a perfect place to base yourself.

The renowned restaurant is closed but the welcoming owners do food at the Caberfeidh in town. The Albannach was for sale at the time of research so things may change.

Caberfeidh PUB FOOD **££**
(📞01571-844321; www.thecaberfeidh.co.uk; Main St, Lochinver; tapas £5-8, mains £12-18; ⊗kitchen 6-9pm Tue-Sat, 12.30-8pm Sun Easter-Oct, plus noon-2.30pm Tue-Sat in summer, 6-8pm Thu-Sat, 12.30-8pm Sun Nov-Mar; 🛜) 🍴 This convivial pub with riverside beer garden serves a range of real ales, decent wines and some excellent food. The menu is based around tapas-sized portions including venison meatballs and local langoustines. A sustainable, low-food-mile philosophy is at work and the quality shines through.

Lochinver Larder
& Riverside Bistro CAFE, BISTRO **££**
(📞01571-844356; www.lochinverlarder.co.uk; 3 Main St, Lochinver; pies £5-6, mains £12-16; ⊗10am-7.45pm Mon-Sat, to 5.30pm Sun Apr-Oct, 10am-4pm Mon-Sat Nov-Mar; 🛜) An outstanding menu of inventive food made with local produce

is on offer here. The bistro turns out delicious seafood dishes in the evening, while the takeaway counter sells tasty pies with a wide range of gourmet fillings (try the wild boar and apricot). It also does quality meals to take away and heat up: great for hostellers and campers.

ℹ️ Getting There & Away

There are buses from Ullapool to Lochinver (£5.10, one hour, two to three Monday to Saturday) and a summer bus that goes on to Durness.

Ullapool

📞 01854 / POP 1500

This pretty port on the shores of Loch Broom is the largest settlement in Wester Ross and one of the most alluring spots in the Highlands, a wonderful destination in itself as well as a gateway to the Western Isles. Offering a row of whitewashed cottages arrayed along the harbour and special views of the loch and its flanking hills, the town has a very distinctive appeal. The harbour served as an emigration point during the Clearances, with thousands of Scots watching Ullapool recede behind as they began a journey to a new continent.

👁️ Sights & Activities

Ullapool Museum   MUSEUM
(📞 01854-612987; www.ullapoolmuseum.co.uk; 7 West Argyle St; adult/child £4/free; ⏰ 11am-4pm Mon-Sat Apr-Oct) Housed in a converted Telford church, this museum relates the prehistoric, natural and social history of the town and Lochbroom area, with a particular focus on the emigration to Nova Scotia and other places. There's also a genealogy section if you want to trace your Scottish roots.

Seascape   BOATING
(📞 07511 290081; www.sea-scape.co.uk; ⏰ May-Sep) Leaving from Ullapool's harbour, Seascape runs enjoyable two-hour tours (adult/child £30/20) out to the Summer Isles in an orange rigid inflatable boat (RIB). It also runs shorter trips (adult/child £25/15), as well as excursions to nearby Isle Martin, with time ashore (adult/child £15/10).

🛏️ Sleeping

Ullapool SYHA   HOSTEL £
(📞 01854-612254; www.syha.org.uk; Shore St; dm/tw/q £21.50/55/96; ⏰ Apr-Oct; 🛜) You've got to hand it to the SYHA – it's chosen some

very sweet locations for its hostels. This one is right in the heart of town on the pretty waterfront; some rooms have harbour views and the busy dining area and little lounge are also good spots for contemplating the water.

★ Tamarin Lodge   B&B ££
(📞 01854-612667; www.tamarinullapool.com; 9 The Braes; s/d £45/90; 🅿️🛜🐾) Effortlessly elegant modern architecture in this hilltop house is noteworthy in its own right, but the glorious vistas over the hills opposite and water far below are unforgettable. All rooms face the view; some have a balcony, and all are very spacious, quiet and utterly relaxing, with unexpected features and gadgets. The great lounge and benevolent hosts are a delight.

Follow signs for Braes from the Inverness road.

★ West House   B&B ££
(📞 01854-613126; www.westhousebandb.co.uk; West Argyle St; d without breakfast £75-85; ⏰ May-Sep; 🅿️🛜) 🐾 Slap bang in Ullapool's centre, this solid house, once a manse, has excellent rooms with contemporary style and great bathrooms. There's no breakfast, but you get a fridge, juice and decent coffee, plus there are two good cafes close by. Most rooms have great views, as well as lots of conveniences. The genial owners also have tempting self-catering options in the area.

There's a minimum two-night stay.

★ Ceilidh Place   HOTEL £££
(📞 01854-612103; www.theceilidhplace.com; 14 West Argyle St; s £70-96, d £140-170; 🅿️🛜🐾) This hotel is a celebration of Scottish culture: we're talking literature and traditional music, not tartan and Nessie dolls. Rooms go for character over modernity; instead of TVs they come with a selection of books chosen by Scottish literati, plus eclectic artwork and cosy touches. The sumptuous lounge has sofas, chaise longues and an honesty bar. There's a bookshop here, too.

It's not luxurious but it's one of the Highlands' more unusual and delightful places to stay.

🍴 Eating & Drinking

Seafood Shack   SEAFOOD £
(📞 07876 142623; www.seafoodshack.co.uk; West Argyle St; takeaways £4-9; ⏰ noon-6pm Apr-late Oct) High-quality fresh seafood is served out of a trailer in this vacant lot by two cheery lasses. There's a wide range of tasty fare

available, from hand-dived scallops to calamari to mussels, crab, oysters and fish.

Ceilidh Place
SCOTTISH ££

(☎01854-612103; www.theceilidhplace.com; 14 West Argyle St; mains £10-18; ⊙8am-9pm Feb-Dec; ☎) The restaurant in this hub of culture and good cheer serves inventive dishes that focus on fresh local seafood backed up by stews, plus lighter meals like pies and burgers during the day. Quality depends a bit on staffing, but it's an atmospheric, cosy place with outdoor seating, good wines by the glass and regular live music and events.

Arch Inn
PUB FOOD ££

(☎01854-612454; www.thearchinn.co.uk; West Shore St; mains £10-18; ⊙kitchen noon-2.30pm & 5-9pm Mon-Sat, 12.30-2.30pm & 5-9pm Sun Apr-Oct, to 8.30pm daily Nov-Mar; ☎) There's pleasing pub food at this shorefront establishment, where the cosy bar and restaurant area dishes up generously proportioned, well-presented mains that range from tender chicken and fish dishes to more advanced blackboard specials with local seafood a highlight. Service is helpful and efficient. The outdoor tables right beside the lapping water are a top spot for a pint.

Ferry Boat Inn
PUB

(☎01854-612431; www.fbiullapool.com; Shore St; ⊙bar 11am-midnight; ☎) Known as the FBI, this character-laden waterfront inn is a popular spot where locals and visitors go to mingle. The food isn't anything special but it's still a decent, friendly place to drop by for a drink.

❶ Getting There & Away

Citylink has buses from Inverness to Ullapool (£14, 1½ hours, one to three daily), connecting with the Lewis ferry.

Two daily ferries (only one on winter Sundays) with **CalMac** (☎0800 066 5000; www.calmac.co.uk) run from Ullapool to Stornoway on Lewis in the Outer Hebrides (adult/car £9.50/50.95, 2½ hours).

Ullapool to Kyle of Lochalsh

Although it's less than 50 miles as the crow flies from Ullapool to Kyle of Lochalsh, it's more like 150 miles along the circuitous coastal road – but don't let that put you off. It's a deliciously remote region and there are fine views of beaches and bays backed by mountains all the way along.

THE NORTH COAST 500

The drive along Scotland's far northern coastline is one of Europe's finest road trips. Words fail to describe the sheer variety of the scenic splendour, which unfolds before you as you cross this empty landscape that combines desolate moorlands, brooding mountains, fertile coastal meadows and stunning white-sand beaches.

In a clever piece of recent marketing, it's been dubbed the **North Coast 500** (www.northcoast500.com), as the round trip from Inverness is roughly that many miles, though you'll surely clock up a few more if you follow your heart down narrow byroads and seek perfect coastal vistas at the end of dead-end tracks.

In our opinion, the scenery is best viewed by taking the route anticlockwise, heading north from Inverness up the east coast to Caithness, then turning west across the top of Scotland before descending down the west coast. This way, you'll make the most of the coastal vistas, the light and the awesome backdrop of the Assynt mountains.

Much of the drive is along single-track road, so it's important to pull over to let both oncoming vehicles and faster traffic behind you pass. Though Inverness companies hire out prestige sports cars for the journey, these really aren't roads where you want to open the throttle; a lazy pace with plenty of photo stops makes for the best journey. It's worth taking several days to do it; in fact you could easily spend a week between Inverness and Ullapool, stopping off for leisurely seafood lunches, tackling some emblematic hills, detouring down valleys to explore the legacy of the Clearances or daring a dip in the North Sea.

While the drive hasn't actually changed, the new name has caught the imagination of tourists, so visitor numbers are well up. The villages along the way aren't overstocked with accommodation, so it's well worth reserving everything in advance if you're travelling the route in the spring or summer months. In winter lots of accommodation is closed so it's a good idea to book then, too.

Twelve miles southeast of Ullapool at Braemore, the A832 doubles back towards the coast as it heads for Gairloch (the A835 continues southeast across the wild, sometimes snowbound, Dirrie More pass to Garve and Inverness). If you're hurrying to Skye, use the A835 and catch up with the A832 further south, near Garve.

Falls of Measach   WATERFALL

Just west of the junction of the A835 and A832, 2 miles south of Braemore, a car park gives access to the Falls of Measach, which spill 45m into spectacularly deep and narrow Corrieshalloch Gorge. You can cross the gorge on a swaying suspension bridge, and walk west for 250m to a viewing platform that juts out dizzyingly above a sheer drop. The thundering falls and misty vapours rising from the gorge are very impressive.

Gairloch & Around

01445 / POP 1000

Gairloch is a group of villages (comprising Achtercairn, Strath and Charlestown) around the inner end of a loch of the same name. Gairloch is a good base for whale- and dolphin-watching excursions and the surrounding area has beautiful sandy beaches, good trout fishing and birdwatching. Hill walkers also use Gairloch as a base for the Torridon hills and An Teallach.

Sights & Activities

Inverewe Garden   GARDENS

(NTS; 01445-712952; www.nts.org.uk; adult/concession £11/9.50; 9.30am-6pm Jun-Aug, to 5pm Mar, Apr & Sep, to 5.30pm May, to 4pm Oct, 10am-4pm Nov-Feb) Six miles north of Gairloch, this splendid place is a welcome splash of colour on this otherwise bleak coast. The climate here is warmed by the Gulf Stream, which allowed Osgood MacKenzie to create this exotic woodland garden in 1862. There are free guided tours on weekdays at 1.30pm from March to October. The licensed cafe-restaurant serves great cakes.

Hebridean Whale Cruises   WILDLIFE, CRUISE

(01445-712458; www.hebridean-whale-cruises.com; Pier Rd; cruises 2½/4hr £50/80; Apr-Oct) Based at Gairloch's harbour, this set-up runs three trips: a standard 2½-hour whale-watching excursion (from May), a three-hour visit to the seabird-rich Shiant Islands and a four-hour excursion to further-flung feeding grounds in search of orca. Other wildlife it's possible to see includes otters, dolphins and seals. Trips are in a zippy rigid inflatable.

Gairloch Marine Wildlife
Centre & Cruises   WILDLIFE, CRUISE

(01445-712636; www.porpoise-gairloch.co.uk; Pier Rd; cruises adult/child £20/15; 10am-4pm Easter-Oct) This small visitor centre has audiovisual and interactive displays, lots of charts, photos and knowledgable staff. From here, cruises run three times daily (weather permitting); during the two-hour trips you may see basking sharks, porpoises and minke whales. The crew collects data on water temperature and conditions, and monitors cetacean populations, so you are subsidising important research.

Sleeping

Gairloch Sands Youth Hostel   HOSTEL £

(01445-712219; www.hostellingscotland.org.uk; Carn Dearg; dm/tw/q £22/55/96; Apr-Sep; P) Located 2.5 miles west of Gairloch in a stunning coastal position, this hostel is close to beaches and well set up for walkers. Wood-panelled rooms and a large dining room/lounge offer comfort, but the real star is that view...magic!

Rua Reidh Lighthouse   LODGE ££

(01445-771263; www.stayatalighthouse.co.uk; Melvaig; s £75-90, d £100-120; Easter-Oct; P) Three miles down a narrow private road beyond Melvaig (11 miles north of Gairloch), this simple yet excellent lodge gives a taste of a lighthouse keeper's life. It's a wild, lonely location great for walking and birdwatching. Breakfast is included and tasty evening meals are available. There's no mobile-phone signal or wi-fi and there's usually a two-night minimum stay: book well ahead.

Shieldaig Lodge   HOTEL £££

(01445-741333; www.shieldaiglodge.com; Badachro; s £150, d £200-300; P) This refurbished hunting lodge has a super waterside position on a sizeable estate offering good walking and fishing as well as falconry and archery. It's a cosy place – think drams and a log fire – with a good restaurant, a very well-stocked bar and tasteful rooms, the best of which have water views. There's also a snooker table and a lovely library.

Eating

Mountain Coffee Company   CAFE £

(01445-712316; www.facebook.com/mountain-coffee.gairloch; Strath Sq, Strath; light meals £4-7;

☺9am-5.30pm, reduced hours low season) 🛈 More the sort of place you'd expect to find on the gringo trail in the Andes, this off-beat and cosy (if brusque) spot is a shrine to mountaineering and travelling. It serves tasty savoury bagels, home baking and sustainably sourced coffees. The conservatory is the place to lap up the sun, while the attached Hillbillies Bookshop is well worth a browse.

Spiral BISTRO ££
(📞01445-712397; www.facebook.com/spiralcafe andbistro; Strath Sq, Strath; mains £11-18; ☺5.30-9pm Tue-Sat, noon-2pm Sun late Feb-Dec, plus noon-2pm Tue-Sat Jun-Aug; 🛜🍽️) On the square in Strath, this place pleases locals and visitors alike with its upbeat, cheerful atmosphere and range of tasty bistro fare, with a variety of influences. Local seafood features; the monkfish curry is a signature dish. Vegetarian choices show more imagination than the norm. Opening hours vary widely according to staffing availability; check its Facebook page.

🛈 Information

Gairloch Information Centre (📞01445-712071; www.galeactionforum.co.uk; Achtercairn; ☺9.30am-5.30pm Mon-Sat, 10.30am-5pm Sun Jun-Sep, 10am-5.30pm Mon-Sat, 10.30am-4.30pm Sun Oct-May) Community-run information centre in the wooden Gale Centre, on the road through town. Has good walking pamphlets; there's also a cafe here.

🛈 Getting There & Away

Public transport to Gairloch is very limited. **Westerbus** (📞01445-712255) runs to/from Inverness (£10.30, 2¼ hours, Monday to Saturday) and Ullapool (£5.15, 1¾ hours, Thursday).

Loch Maree & Around

Stretching 12 miles between Poolewe and Kinlochewe, Loch Maree is considered one of Scotland's prettiest lochs, with the imposing bulk of Slioch on its northeastern side and Beinn Eighe on the southwestern. Look out for black-throated divers on the lake in summer. At its southern end, tiny Kinlochewe makes a good base for outdoor activities.

Beinn Eighe Mountain Trail WALKING
This waymarked 4-mile loop walk to a plateau and cairn on the side of Beinn Eighe has magnificent views over Loch Maree. It's

quite exposed up here, so take some warm clothing. The walk starts from a car park on the A832 about 1.5 miles northwest of the Beinn Eighe Visitor Centre.

From the same trailhead there's a shorter 1-mile trail through Scots pine forest.

Kinlochewe Hotel INN, HOSTEL ££
(📞01445-760253; www.kinlochewehotel.co.uk; Kinlochewe; dm £17.50, s £60, d £100-110; 🅿🛜🐕) 🛈 This is a welcoming hotel that's very walker-friendly, with features such as a handsome lounge well stocked with books, a great bar with several real ales on tap and a menu of locally sourced food. There are 'economy' rooms that share a bath-only bathroom (£90) and also a bunkhouse with one no-frills 12-bed dorm, plus a decent kitchen and clean bathrooms.

★Whistle Stop Cafe CAFE, BISTRO ££
(📞01445-760423; www.facebook.com/Whistle-Stop-Cafe-Kinlochewe-223096744444313; Kinlochewe; meals £8-16; ☺8am-8pm Mon-Sat, 10am-5pm Sun Apr-Sep, reduced hours mid-Feb–Mar & Oct–mid-Nov) A colourful presence in the former village hall, this is a tempting place to drop by for anything from a coffee to enticing bistro fare. There are great daily specials and delicious home baking, juices and smoothies. It's very friendly, and used to pumping life back into chilly walkers and cyclists. It's unlicensed, but you can take your own wine (£1 corkage).

Torridon

📞01445
The road southwest from Kinlochewe passes through Glen Torridon, amid some of Britain's most beautiful scenery. Carved by ice from massive layers of ancient sandstone that takes its name from the region, the mountains here are steep, shapely and imposing, whether flirting with autumn mists, draped in dazzling winter snows, or reflected in the calm blue waters of Loch Torridon on a summer day.

The road reaches the sea at spectacularly sited Torridon village, then continues westwards to lovely Shieldaig, which boasts an attractive main street of whitewashed houses right on the water.

🏃 Activities

Torridon Activities ADVENTURE SPORTS
(📞01445-791242; www.thetorridon.com/activities; activities half-/full day £40/60) This activity

centre organises sea kayaking, canyoning, mountain biking and climbing among several other outdoor pursuits. It also rents bikes, including mountain bikes.

🛏 Sleeping & Eating

Torridon SYHA
HOSTEL £

(☑ 01445-791284; www.syha.org.uk; Torridon; dm/tw £21.50/55; ☺ daily Mar-Oct, Fri & Sat nights Nov-Feb; ℗ @ 🛜 🐾) This spacious hostel has enthusiastic, can-do management and sits in a magnificent location, surrounded by spectacular mountains. Roomy dorms and privates (twins have single beds) are allied to a huge kitchen and convivial lounge area, with ales on sale. It's a very popular walking base, with great advice from the in-house mountain rescue team, so book ahead.

Torridon Inn
INN ££

(☑ 01445-791242; www.thetorridon.com; Torridon; s/d/q £110/140/215; ☺ daily Easter-Oct, Thu-Sun Nov & mid-Feb–Easter, closed Dec–mid-Feb; ℗ 🛜 🐾) This convivial but upmarket walkers hang-out has excellent modern rooms that vary substantially in size and layout. Rooms for groups (of up to six) offer more value than the commodious but overpriced doubles. The sociable bar serves all-day food and there are numerous activities (p923) on offer.

★ Torridon
HOTEL £££

(☑ 01445-791242; www.thetorridon.com; Torridon; r standard/superior/deluxe/master £265/320/390/450; ☺ closed Jan, plus Mon & Tue Nov, Dec, Feb & Mar; ℗ @ 🛜 🐾) If you prefer the lap of luxury to the sound of rain beating on your tent, head for this lavish Victorian shooting lodge with a romantic lochside location. Sumptuous contemporary rooms with awe-inspiring views, top bathrooms and a cheery Highland cow atop the counterpane couldn't be more inviting. This is one of Scotland's top country hotels, always luxurious but never pretentious.

Tigh an Eilean
HOTEL £££

(☑ 01520-755251; www.tighaneilean.co.uk; Shieldaig; s/d £72.50/145; ☺ Feb-Dec; 🛜) With a lovely waterfront position in the pretty village of Shieldaig, this is an appealing destination for a relaxing stay, offering old-style rooms that are comfortable, not luxurious. Loch-view rooms – with gloriously soothing vistas – are allocated on a first-booked basis, so it's worth reserving ahead. Service is very helpful, and there's a cosy lounge with an honesty bar.

Shieldaig Bar & Coastal Kitchen
SEAFOOD ££

(☑ 01520-755251; www.shieldaigbarandcoastalkit chen.co.uk; Shieldaig; mains £10-21; ☺ food noon-2.30pm & 6-8.30pm or 9pm, closed some winter lunchtimes; 🛜) This attractive pub has real ales and waterside tables plus a great upstairs dining room and an outdoor deck. There's an emphasis on quality local seafood as well as wood-fired pizzas and bistro-style meat dishes such as steak-frites or sausages and mash. Blackboard specials feature the daily catch.

ℹ Information

Torridon Countryside Centre (NTS; ☑ 01445-791221; www.nts.org.uk; Torridon; ☺ 10am-5pm Sun-Fri Easter-Sep) Offers information on wildlife, geology and walks in the area, and sells walking maps. You can buy food here for a nearby red deer herd.

ℹ Getting There & Away

On schooldays there's a bus from Shieldaig to Torridon and Gairloch and back. Two weekly bus services with **Lochcarron Garage** (☑ 01520-722997; www.facebook.com/BCSLochcarron Garage) from Inverness to Lochcarron can be extended to Shieldaig (from Inverness £9.90, 2½ hours) by prior booking.

Applecross

POP 200

The delightfully remote seaside village of Applecross feels like an island retreat due to its isolation and the magnificent views of Raasay and the hills of Skye that set the pulse racing, particularly at sunset. On a clear day it's an unforgettable place. The campsite and pub fill to the brim in school holidays.

A road leads here 25 winding miles from Shieldaig, but more spectacular (accessed from further south on the A896) is the magnificent Bealach na Bà (626m; Pass of the Cattle), the third-highest motor road in the UK, and the longest continuous climb. Originally built in 1822, it climbs steeply and hair-raisingly via hairpin bends perched over sheer drops, with gradients of up to 25%, then drops dramatically to the village with views of Skye.

Applecross Inn
INN £££

(☑ 01520-744262; www.applecross.uk.com; Shore St; s/d £90/140; ℗ 🛜 🐾) 🍴 The hub of the spread-out Applecross community, this inn is a great spot to hole up, but you'll need to book ahead. Seven snug bedrooms all have a view of the Skye hills and the sea. It's a

EILEAN DONAN CASTLE

Photogenically sited at the entrance to Loch Duich, **Eilean Donan** (☎01599-555202; www.eileandonancastle.com; A87, Dornie; adult/child/family £7.50/4/20; ☉10am-6pm Apr-May & Oct, 9.30am-6pm Jun & Sep, 9am-6pm Jul & Aug, 10am-4pm Nov-Dec & Feb-Mar, closed Jan) is one of Scotland's most evocative castles and must now be represented in millions of photo albums. It's on an offshore islet, elegantly linked to the mainland by a stone-arched bridge. It's very much a recreation inside, with an excellent introductory exhibition. Citylink buses from Fort William and Inverness to Portree stop opposite the castle. The last entry is strictly one hour before closing.

Keep an eye out for the photos of castle scenes from the movie *Highlander*; there's also a sword used at the battle of Culloden in 1746. The castle was bombarded into ruins by government ships in 1719 when Jacobite forces were defeated at the Battle of Glenshiel; it was rebuilt between 1912 and 1932.

magical spot and there's a cracking pub and **restaurant** (mains £10-18; ☉noon-9pm; ☎) 🖉, too. It also has some cottage accommodation along the waterfront.

Applecross Walled Garden　　CAFE ££
(The Potting Shed; ☎01520-744440; www.applecrossgarden.co.uk; mains £11-15; ☉11am-8.30pm early Mar-Oct; 🖉) On the grounds of the local mansion in Applecross is a pretty walled garden, and in a building at the end of the garden is this lovely licensed cafe-restaurant, serving sandwiches, soups and more filling meals, with plenty of vegetarian options and good daily specials. The garden itself is open from 8.30am.

❶ Getting There & Away

There are two buses a week (Wednesday and Saturday) with Lochcarron Garage (p924) from Inverness to Lochcarron that continue to Applecross (£11.10, 3½ hours) via Shieldaig on prior request.

Plockton

☎01599 / POP 400

Idyllic little Plockton, with its perfect cottages lining a perfect bay, looks like it was designed as a film set. And it has indeed served as just that – scenes from *The Wicker Man* (1973) were filmed here, and the village became famous as the location for the 1990s TV series *Hamish Macbeth*.

With all this picture-postcard perfection, it's hardly surprising that Plockton is a tourist hot spot, crammed with day trippers and holidaymakers in summer. But there's no denying its appeal, with 'palm trees' (actually hardy New Zealand cabbage palms) lining the waterfront, a thriving small-boat sailing

scene and several good places to stay, eat and drink. The big event of the year is the **Plockton Regatta** (www.plockton-sailing.com; ☉Jul/Aug).

🏄 Activities

Sea Kayak Plockton　　KAYAKING
(☎01599-544422; www.seakayakplockton.co.uk; 1-day beginner course £85) Sea Kayak Plockton offers everything from beginner lessons to multiday trips around Skye and right out to St Kilda.

☞ Tours

Calum's Seal Trips　　BOATING
(☎01599-544306; www.calums-sealtrips.com; adult/child £12/6; ☉Apr-Oct) Seal-watching cruises visit swarms of the slippery suckers just outside the harbour. There's excellent commentary and you may even spot otters as well. Trips leave several times daily. There's also a longer dolphin-watching trip available.

🛏 Sleeping & Eating

Plockton Station Bunkhouse　　HOSTEL £
(☎01599-544235; www.visitplockton.com/stay/bunkhouse; dm £18; ℗⤬) Airily set in the former train station (the new one is opposite), this hostel has cosy four-bed dorms, a garden and kitchen-lounge with plenty of light and good perspectives over the frenetic comings-and-goings of the platforms below (OK, that last bit's a lie). The owners also have good-value B&B accommodation (single/double £35/60) next door in the inaccurately named 'Nessun Dorma'.

★Tigh Arran　　B&B ££
(☎01599-544307; www.plocktonbedandbreakfast.com; Duirinish; s/d £70/80; ℗⤬⤬) It's hard

to decide which is better at this sweet spot 2 miles from the Plockton shorefront – the warm personal welcome or the absolutely stunning views across to Skye. All three of the en suite rooms – with appealing family options – enjoy the views, as does the comfy lounge. A top spot, far from stress and noise, it's great value as well.

★ **Plockton Hotel** INN ££
(☑ 01599-544274; www.plocktonhotel.co.uk; 41 Harbour St; s/d £100/150, cottage s/d £65/100; 🐾) ✿ Black-painted Plockton Hotel is one of those classic Highland spots that manages to make everyone happy, whether it's thirst, hunger or fatigue that brings people knocking. Assiduously tended rooms are a real delight, with excellent facilities and thoughtful touches. Those without a water view are consoled with more space and a balcony with rock-garden perspectives. The cottage nearby offers simpler comfort.

★ **Plockton Shores** SEAFOOD ££
(☑ 01599-544263; www.plocktonshoresrestaurant. com; 30 Harbour St; restaurant mains £14-19; ⊘ cafe 9am-5.30pm Mon-Sat, noon-4pm Sun, restaurant 5-9pm Tue-Sat; 🍴) ✿ This restaurant attached to a shop has a tempting menu of local seafood, including good-value platters with langoustines, mussels, crab, squat lobster and more, and succulent hand-dived tempura scallops. There's also a very tasty line in venison, steaks and a small selection of good vegetarian dishes that are more than an afterthought. The licensed cafe does home baking and light lunches.

❶ Getting There & Away

Trains running between Kyle of Lochalsh (£2.80, 15 minutes) and Inverness (£23.10, 2½ hours) stop in Plockton up to four times daily each way.

SKYE

POP 10,000

The Isle of Skye (an t-Eilean Sgiathanach in Gaelic) takes its name from the old Norse *sky-a*, meaning 'cloud island', a Viking reference to the often-mist-enshrouded Cuillin Hills. It's the second-largest of Scotland's islands, a 50-mile-long patchwork of velvet moors, jagged mountains, sparkling lochs and towering sea cliffs.

The stunning scenery is the main attraction, but when the mist closes in there are plenty of castles, crofting museums and cosy pubs and restaurants; there are also dozens of art galleries and craft studios.

Along with Edinburgh and Loch Ness, Skye is one of Scotland's top-three tourist destinations. However, the crowds tend to stick to Portree, Dunvegan and Trotternish – it's almost always possible to find peace and quiet in the island's further-flung corners. Come prepared for changeable weather: when it's fine it's very fine indeed, but all too often it isn't.

🏃 Activities

Walking

Skye offers some of the finest – and in places, the roughest and most difficult – walking in Scotland. There are many detailed guidebooks available, including a series of four walking guides by Charles Rhodes, available from the **Aros Centre** (☑ 01478-613750; www. aros.co.uk; Viewfield Rd; exhibition £5; ⊘ 9am-5pm; P ♿) FREE and the tourist office (p930) in Portree. You'll need Ordnance Survey (OS) 1:50,000 maps 23 and 32, or Harvey's 1:25,000 *Superwalker – The Cuillin*. Don't attempt the longer walks in bad weather or in winter.

Easy, low-level routes include: through **Strath Mor** from Luib (on the Broadford–Sligachan road) and on to Torrin (on the Broadford–Elgol road; allow 1½ hours, 4 miles); from **Sligachan to Kilmarie** via Camasunary (four hours, 11 miles); and from **Elgol to Kilmarie** via Camasunary (2½ hours, 6.5 miles). The walk from Kilmarie to Coruisk and back via Camasunary and the 'Bad Step' is superb but slightly harder (11 miles round trip; allow at least six hours). The **Bad Step** is a rocky slab poised above the sea that you have to scramble across; it's easy in fine, dry weather, but some walkers find it intimidating.

Skye Wilderness Safaris (☑ 01470-552292; www.skye-wilderness-safaris.com; per person £95-120; ⊘ May-Sep) runs one-day guided hiking trips for small groups (four to six people) through the Cuillin Hills, into the Quiraing or along the Trotternish ridge; transport to/from Portree is included.

Climbing

The Cuillin Hills are a playground for rock climbers, and the two-day traverse of the **Cuillin Ridge** is the finest mountaineering expedition in the British Isles. There are several mountain guides in the area who can provide instruction and safely introduce inexperienced climbers to the more difficult routes.

Skye & Outer Hebrides

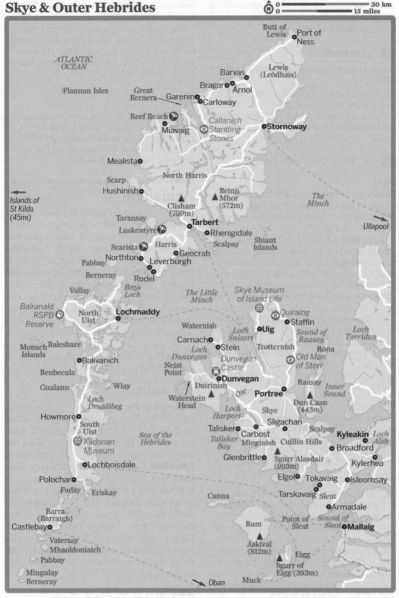

Skye Guides (☏01471-822116; www.skye guides.co.uk) offers a one-day introduction-to-rock-climbing course for around £260; a private mountain guide can be hired for £280 a day (both rates are for two clients).

Sea Kayaking

Whitewave Outdoor Centre KAYAKING (☏01470-542414; www.white-wave.co.uk; 19 Lini-cro, Kilmuir; half-day kayak session per person £40-50; ☺Mar-Oct) Provides sea kayaking instruction and guiding for both beginners and experts; prices include equipment hire. Other activities include mountain-boarding, bushcraft and rock climbing.

ℹ Information

Only Portree and Broadford have banks and ATMs.

Portree Tourist Office (p930) is the only tourist office on the island. It provides internet access and an accommodation booking service. Ask for the free *Art Skye – Gallery & Studio Trails* booklet.

ℹ Getting There & Away

BOAT

Despite the bridge, there are still a couple of ferry links between Skye and the mainland. Ferries also operate from Uig on Skye to the Outer Hebrides.

The **CalMac** (☑ 0800 066 5000; www.calmac.co.uk) ferry between Mallaig and Armadale (passenger/car £2.90/9.70, 30 minutes, eight daily Monday to Saturday, five to seven on Sunday) is very popular on weekends and in July and August. Book ahead if you're travelling by car.

The **Glenelg-Skye Ferry** (☑ 07881 634726; www.skyeferry.co.uk; car with up to 4 passengers £15; ☉ Easter-mid-Oct) runs a tiny vessel (six cars only) on the short Kylerhea to Glenelg crossing (five minutes, every 20 minutes). The ferry operates from 10am to 6pm daily (till 7pm June to August).

BUS

There are buses from Glasgow to Portree (£44, seven hours, three daily), and Uig (£44, 7½ hours, two daily) via Crianlarich, Fort William and Kyle of Lochalsh, plus a service from Inverness to Portree (£26.40, 3¼ hours, three daily).

CAR

The Isle of Skye became permanently tethered to the Scottish mainland when the Skye Bridge opened in 1995. The controversial bridge tolls were abolished in 2004 and the crossing is now free.

Much of the driving is on single-track roads – remember to use passing places to allow any traffic behind you to overtake. There are petrol stations at Broadford (open 24 hours), Armadale, Portree, Dunvegan and Uig.

ℹ Getting Around

BUS

Getting around the island by public transport can be a pain, especially if you want to explore away from the main Kyleakin–Portree–Uig road. Here, as in much of the Highlands, there are fewer buses on Saturday and only a handful of Sunday services.

Stagecoach (p903) operates the main bus routes on the island, linking all the main villages and towns. Its Skye Dayrider/Megarider ticket gives unlimited bus travel for one/seven days for £9.20/34.60. For timetable info, call Traveline (p787).

TAXI

You can order a taxi or hire a car (arrange for the car to be waiting at Kyle of Lochalsh train station) from **Kyle Taxi Company** (☑ 01599-534323; www.skyecarhire.co.uk; car hire per day/week from around £40/240).

Armadale

If you cross over the sea to Skye on the ferry from Mallaig you arrive in Armadale, at the southern end of the long, low-lying peninsula known as Sleat (pronounced 'slate'). The landscape of Sleat itself is not exceptional, but it provides a grandstand for ogling the magnificent scenery on either side – take the steep and twisting minor road that loops through Tarskavaig and Tokavaig for stunning views of the Isle of Rum, the Cuillin Hills and Bla Bheinn.

Armadale is little more than a store, a post office, a cluster of craft shops and a scattering of houses.

◉ Sights

Museum of the Isles   MUSEUM
(☑ 01471-844305; www.clandonald.com; adult/child £8.50/7; ☉ 10am-5.30pm Apr-Oct, occasionally shorter hours Oct; 🅿 🐾) Just along the road from Armadale pier is the part-ruined **Armadale Castle**, former seat of Lord MacDonald of Sleat. The neighbouring museum will tell you all you ever wanted to know about Clan Donald, and also provides an easily digestible history of the Lordship of the Isles. Prize exhibits include rare portraits of clan chiefs, and a wine glass that was once used by Bonnie Prince Charlie. The ticket also gives admission to the lovely castle gardens.

ℹ Getting There & Away

From late May to August there are three to five buses a day Monday to Saturday (three on Sunday) from Armadale to Broadford (£4.10, 30 minutes) and Portree (£7.70, 1¼ hours), timed to meet the arrival of ferries from Mallaig. Outside the summer season, services are less frequent and may not coincide with ferry times.

Broadford (An T-Ath Leathann)

🖉 01471 / POP 750

The long, straggling village of Broadford is a service centre for the scattered communities of southern Skye. It has a 24-hour petrol station, a bank and a large Co-op supermarket with an ATM.

🛏 Sleeping

Skye Basecamp HOSTEL £
(🖉 01471-820044; www.skyebasecamp.co.uk; Lime Park; dm/q from £20/70; P 🛜) Run by the mountaineers at Skye Guides (p927), this well-equipped hostel is set in a converted residential house with great views across the sea towards the Crowlin Islands. Maps, guidebooks, weather forecasts and walking advice are all to hand.

★**Tigh an Dochais** B&B ££
(🖉 01471-820022; www.skyebedbreakfast.co.uk; 13 Harrapool; d £105; P 🛜) 🖉 A cleverly designed modern building, Tigh an Dochais is one of Skye's best B&Bs – a little footbridge leads to the front door, which is on the 1st floor. Here you'll find the dining room (gorgeous breakfasts) and lounge offering a stunning view of sea and hills; the bedrooms (downstairs) open onto an outdoor deck with that same wonderful view.

🍴 Eating

★**Cafe Sia** CAFE, PIZZERIA ££
(🖉 01471-822616; www.cafesia.co.uk; Rathad na h-Atha; mains £7-17; ⊙10am-9pm; 🛜🖐) 🖉 Serving everything from eggs Benedict and cappuccino to cocktails and seafood specials, this appealing cafe specialises in wood-fired pizzas (also available to take away) and superb artisan coffee. There's also an outdoor deck with great views of the Red Cuillin. Takeaway coffee from 8am.

★**Creelers** SEAFOOD ££
(🖉 01471-822281; www.skye-seafood-restaurant. co.uk; Lower Harrapool; mains £14-20; ⊙noon-8.30pm Tue-Sat Mar-Nov; 🖐) 🖉 Broadford has several places to eat but one really stands out: Creelers is a small, bustling restaurant (refurbished in 2018) that serves some of the best seafood on Skye. The house speciality is traditional Marseille bouillabaisse (a rich, spicy seafood stew). Best to book ahead.

ℹ Getting There & Away

There are Scottish Citylink buses every day from Inverness to Broadford (£24.40, 2½ hours, three daily) via Kyle of Lochalsh, continuing to Portree and Uig. Stagecoach buses run from Broadford to Portree (£6, 45 minutes) four or five times a day.

Cuillin Hills

The Cuillin Hills are Britain's most spectacular mountain range (the name comes from the Old Norse *kjöllen,* meaning 'keelshaped'). Though small in stature – Sgurr Alasdair, the highest summit, is only 993m – the peaks are near-alpine in character, with knife-edge ridges, jagged pinnacles, scree-filled gullies and hectares of naked rock. The higher reaches of the Cuillins are off limits except to experienced climbers, but there are plenty of lower-level hiking routes, too.

One of the best hikes (on a fine day) is the steep climb from **Glenbrittle Campsite** (🖉 01478-640404; www.dunvegancastle.com; Glenbrittle; sites per adult/child incl car £10/6; ⊙Apr-Sep) to **Coire Lagan** (6 miles round trip; allow at least three hours). The impressive upper corrie contains a lochan for bathing (for the hardy!).

Even more spectacular, but much harder to reach on foot, is **Loch Coruisk** (from the Gaelic Coir'Uisg, the Water Corrie), a remote loch ringed by the highest peaks of the Cuillin. Accessible by **boat trip** (🖉 0800 731 3089; www.bellajane.co.uk; Elgol Pier; adult/child £28/16; ⊙Apr-Oct) from Elgol, or via an arduous 5.5-mile hike from Kilmarie, Coruisk was popularised by Sir Walter Scott in his 1815 poem 'Lord of the Isles'.

There are two main bases – Sligachan to the north (on the Kyle of Lochalsh–Portree bus route), and Glenbrittle to the south (no public transport). The **Sligachan Hotel** (🖉 01478-650204; www.sligachan.co.uk; Sligachan; r from £170; P 🛜) is perhaps the best-known base, beloved by generations of walkers and climbers.

Bus 54 runs from Portree to Carbost via Sligachan (£4.25, 50 minutes) twice daily on school days only; from there, you'll have to walk the remaining 8 miles to Glenbrittle.

Portree (Port Righ)

🖉 01478 / POP 2320

Portree is Skye's largest and liveliest town. It has a pretty harbour lined with brightly painted houses, and there are great views of the surrounding hills. Its name (from the Gaelic for King's Harbour) commemorates James V, who came here in 1540 to pacify the local clans.

Activities

MV Stardust
BOATING

(☎07798 743858; www.skyeboat-trips.co.uk; Portree Harbour; adult/child £20/10) MV *Stardust* offers 1½-hour boat trips around Portree Bay, with the chance to see seals, porpoises and – if you're lucky – white-tailed sea eagles. There are longer two-hour cruises to the Sound of Raasay (£25/15). You can also arrange fishing trips, or to be dropped off for a hike on the Isle of Raasay and picked up again later.

Sleeping

Portree Youth Hostel
HOSTEL £

(SYHA; ☎01478-612231; www.syha.org.uk; Bayfield Rd; dm/tw £26/78; P☎) This SYHA hostel (formerly Bayfield Backpackers) was completely renovated in 2015 and offers brightly decorated dorms and private rooms, a stylish lounge with views over the bay, and outdoor seating areas. Its location in the town centre just 100m from the bus stop is ideal.

Torvaig Campsite
CAMPGROUND £

(☎01478-611849; www.portreecampsite.co.uk; Torvaig; tent sites per person £9, campervan £21; ⊘Apr-Oct; ☎) An attractive, family-run campsite located 1.5 miles north of Portree, on the road to Staffin.

Rosedale Hotel
HOTEL ££

(☎01478-613131; www.rosedalehotelskye.co.uk; Beaumont Cres; s/d from £70/90; ⊘Easter-Oct; P☎) The Rosedale is a cosy, old-fashioned hotel delightfully situated down by the waterfront – you'll be welcomed with a glass of whisky when you check-in. Its three converted fishers' cottages are linked by a maze of narrow stairs and corridors, the spruced-up bedrooms include a couple with four-poster beds, and the dining room has a view of the harbour.

Cuillin Hills Hotel
HOTEL £££

(☎01478-612003; www.cuillinhills-hotel-skye.co.uk; Scorrybreac Rd; r from £295; P☎) Located on the eastern fringes of Portree, this luxury hotel enjoys a superb outlook across the harbour towards the Cuillin mountains. The more expensive rooms cosset guests with four-poster beds and panoramic views, but everyone can enjoy the scenery from the glass-fronted restaurant and well-stocked whisky bar.

Bosville Hotel
HOTEL £££

(☎01478-612846; www.bosvillehotel.co.uk; 9-11 Bosville Tce; r from £233; ☎) The Bosville brings a little bit of metropolitan style to Portree with its designer fabrics and furniture, fluffy bathrobes and bright, spacious bathrooms. It's worth splashing out a bit for the 'premium' rooms, with leather recliner chairs from which you can lap up the view over the town and harbour.

Eating

Café Arriba
CAFE £

(☎01478-611830; www.cafearriba.co.uk; Quay Brae; mains £6-12; ⊘7am-6pm May-Sep, 8am-5pm Tue-Sat Oct-Apr; ☎) Arriba is a funky little cafe, brightly decked out in primary colours and offering delicious flatbread melts (bacon, leek and cheese is a favourite), as well as the best choice of vegetarian grub on the island, ranging from a veggie breakfast fry-up to felafel wraps with hummus and chilli sauce. Also serves excellent coffee.

★ Scorrybreac
MODERN SCOTTISH ££

(☎01478-612069; www.scorrybreac.com; 7 Bosville Tce; 3-course dinner £42; ⊘5-9pm Wed-Sun year-round, noon-2pm mid-May–mid-Sep) Set in the front rooms of what was once a private house, and with just eight tables, Scorrybreac is snug and intimate, offering fine dining without the faff. Chef Calum Munro (son of Donnie Munro, of Gaelic rock band Runrig fame) sources as much produce as possible from Skye, including foraged herbs and mushrooms, and creates the most exquisite concoctions.

Dulse & Brose
MODERN SCOTTISH ££

(☎01478-612846; www.bosvillehotel.co.uk; Bosville Hotel, 7 Bosville Tce; mains £17-23; ⊘noon-3pm & 6-10pm May-Sep, 6-8.15pm Oct-Apr; ☎) This hotel restaurant sports a relaxed atmosphere, an award-winning chef and a menu that makes the most of Skye produce – including lamb, game, seafood, cheese, organic vegetables and berries – and adds a French twist to traditional dishes. The neighbouring Merchant Bar (food served noon to 5pm), also part of the Bosville Hotel, serves tapas-style bar snacks through the afternoon.

Information

Portree Tourist Office (☎01478-612992; www.visitscotland.com; Bayfield Rd; ⊘9am-

6pm Mon-Sat, 10am-4pm Sun Jun-Aug, shorter hours Sep-May; 🛈) The only tourist office on the island; provides internet access and currency exchange.

🛈 Getting There & Away

The main bus stop is at Somerled Sq. There are five or six Scottish Citylink buses every day from Kyle of Lochalsh to Portree (£7.10, one hour) continuing to Uig.

Local buses (mostly six to eight Monday to Saturday, three on Sunday) run from Portree to:

Armadale (£7.70, 1¼ hours) Connecting with the ferry to Mallaig late May to August.

Broadford (£6, 45 minutes) Four or five daily.

Dunvegan Castle (£5.35, 50 minutes) Four daily on Saturday year-round; also four daily Monday to Friday from May to September.

There are also three buses a day on a circular route around Trotternish (in both directions), taking in Flodigarry (£4.10, 35 minutes), Kilmuir (£4.80, 45 minutes) and Uig (£3.60, 30 minutes).

You can hire bikes at **Island Cycles** (☏ 01478-613121; www.islandcycles-skye.co.uk; The Green; bike hire per 24hr £20; ◷ 9am-5pm Mon-Sat).

Dunvegan (Dun Bheagain)

Dunvegan, an unremarkable village on the western side of Skye, is famous for its historic namesake castle that has links to Sir Walter Scott and Bonnie Prince Charlie.

◉ Sights

Dunvegan Castle   CASTLE
(☏ 01470-521206; www.dunvegancastle.com; adult/child £14/9; ◷ 10am-5.30pm Easter–mid-Oct; 🅿) Skye's most famous historic building, and one of its most popular tourist attractions, Dunvegan Castle is the seat of the chief of Clan MacLeod. In addition to the usual castle stuff – swords, silver and family portraits – there are some interesting artefacts, including the Fairy Flag, a diaphanous silk banner that dates from some time between the 4th and 7th centuries, and Bonnie Prince Charlie's waistcoat and a lock of his hair, donated by Flora MacDonald's granddaughter.

Coral Beaches   BEACH
From the end of the minor road beyond Dunvegan Castle entrance, an easy 1-mile walk leads to the Coral Beaches – a pair of blindingly white beaches composed of the bleached exoskeletons of coralline algae known as *maerl*.

🛏 Sleeping & Eating

★Hillstone Lodge   B&B £££
(☏ 01470-511434; www.hillstonelodge.com; 12 Colbost; r from £140; 🅿🛈) 🍴 You can't help notice the many new houses on Skye that bear the hallmarks of award-winning local architects Rural Design – weathered timber walls and modern materials used with traditional shapes and forms. Hillstone is one of the best, with tasteful modern styling and stunning views across Loch Dunvegan. It's about 1km north of the Three Chimneys, above the pier.

★Three Chimneys   MODERN SCOTTISH £££
(☏ 01470-511258; www.threechimneys.co.uk; Colbost; 3-course lunch/dinner £40/68; ◷ 12.15-1.45pm Mon-Sat mid-Mar–Oct, plus Sun Easter-Sep, 6.30-9.15pm daily year-round; 🅿🛈) 🍴 Halfway between Dunvegan and Waterstein, the Three Chimneys is a superb romantic retreat combining a gourmet restaurant in a candlelit crofter's cottage with sumptuous five-star rooms (double £345) in the modern house next door. Book well in advance, and note that children are not welcome in the restaurant in the evenings.

★Loch Bay   SEAFOOD £££
(☏ 01470-592235; www.lochbay-restaurant.co.uk; Stein, Waternish; 3-course dinner £43.50; ◷ 12.15-1.45pm Wed-Sun, 6.15-9pm Tue-Sat Apr-early Oct; 🅿) 🍴 This cosy farmhouse kitchen of a place, with terracotta tiles and a wood-burning stove, is one of Skye's most romantic restaurants and was awarded a Michelin star in 2018. The menu includes most things that swim in the sea or live in a shell, but there are non-seafood choices too. Best to book ahead.

🛈 Getting There & Away

A limited bus service runs from Portree via Dunvegan and Colbost to Glendale (£6.60, 1½ hours, two daily Monday to Friday) during parts of May, June, August and September; check times in advance at Portree tourist office. There are no bus services to Stein and Waternish.

Trotternish

The Trotternish peninsula to the north of Portree has some of Skye's most beautiful – and bizarre – scenery. A loop road allows a circular driving tour of the peninsula from Portree, passing through the village of Uig, where the ferry to the Outer Hebrides departs.

THE QUIRAING

Staffin Bay is dominated by the dramatic basalt escarpment of the **Quiraing**: its impressive land-slipped cliffs and pinnacles constitute one of Skye's most remarkable landscapes. From a parking area at the highest point of the minor road between Staffin and Uig you can walk north to the Quiraing in half an hour.

⊙ Sights

Staffin Dinosaur Museum MUSEUM
(www.staffindinosaurmuseum.com; 3 Ellishadder, Staffin; adult/child £2/1; ⊘9.30am-5pm; ℗) In an old stone barn by the roadside, this museum houses an interesting collection of dinosaur footprints, ammonites and other fossils discovered in the local Jurassic sandstones, which have become a focus for dinosaur research in recent years.

Fairy Glen AREA
Just south of Uig, a minor road (signposted 'Sheader and Balnaknock') leads a mile or so to the Fairy Glen, a strange and enchanting natural landscape of miniature conical hills, rocky towers, ruined cottages and a tiny roadside lochan.

Old Man of Storr NATURAL FEATURE
(℗) The 50m-high, pot-bellied pinnacle of crumbling basalt known as the Old Man of Storr is prominent above the road 6 miles north of Portree. Walk up to its foot from the car park at the northern end of Loch Leathan (2-mile round trip). This seemingly unclimbable pinnacle was first scaled in 1955 by English mountaineer Don Whillans, a feat that has been repeated only a handful of times since.

Skye Museum of Island Life MUSEUM
(☑01470-552206; www.skyemuseum.co.uk; Kilmuir; adult/child £2.50/50p; ⊘9.30am-5pm Mon-Sat Easter-late Sep; ℗) The peat-reek of crofting life in the 18th and 19th centuries is preserved in the thatched cottages, croft houses, barns and farm implements of the Skye Museum of Island Life. Behind the museum is **Kilmuir Cemetery**, where a tall Celtic cross marks the grave of Flora MacDonald; the cross was erected in 1955 to replace the original monument, of which 'every fragment was removed by tourists'.

⊫ Sleeping & Eating

★**Cowshed Boutique Bunkhouse** HOSTEL£
(☑07917 536820; www.skyecowshed.co.uk; Uig; dm/tw £20/80, pod £70; ℗⊛⊛⊛) This hostel enjoys a glorious setting overlooking Uig Bay, with superb views from its ultra-stylish lounge. The dorms have custom-built wooden bunks that offer comfort and privacy, while the camping pods (sleeping up to four, but more comfortable with two) have heating and en suite shower rooms; there are even mini 'dog pods' for your canine companions.

Flodigarry Hotel HOTEL£££
(☑01470-552203; www.hotelintheskye.co.uk; Flodigarry; r £175-295; ⊘Easter-Oct; ℗⊛) From 1751–59 Flora MacDonald lived in a cottage that is now part of this atmospheric hotel, given a new lease of life by adventurous owners. You can stay in the cottage itself (there are four bedrooms), or in the more spacious rooms in the main hotel; nonguests are welcome at the stylish bar and restaurant, with great sea views.

Single Track CAFE£
(www.facebook.com/singletrackskye; Kilmaluag; snacks £3-4; ⊘10.30am-5pm Sun-Thu mid-May–late Oct; ℗⊛) This turf-roofed, timber-clad art gallery and espresso bar will be familiar to fans of British TV's *Grand Designs* – it was featured on the Channel 4 series in 2012. The owners are serious about their coffee, and it's seriously good, as are the accompanying cakes and scones. Art by the owners and other Skye artists is on display, and for sale.

ⓘ Getting There & Away

Two or three daily buses (four on Saturday) follow a circular route (in both directions) around the Trotternish peninsula, taking in Flodigarry (£4.60, 35 minutes), Kilmuir (£5.35, 45 minutes) and Uig (£4, 30 minutes).

Car ferries run from Uig to Tarbert (Harris; car/pedestrian £31/6.30, 1½ hours) and Lochmaddy (North Uist; car/pedestrian £31/6.30, 1¾ hours) in the Outer Hebrides, with one or two crossings a day.

OUTER HEBRIDES

POP 27,670

The Western Isles, or Na h-Eileanan an Iar in Gaelic – also known as the Outer Hebrides – are a 130-mile-long string of islands lying off the northwest coast of Scotland.

There are 119 islands in total, of which the five main inhabited islands are Lewis and Harris (two parts of a single island, although often described as if they are separate islands), North Uist, Benbecula, South Uist and Barra. The middle three (often referred to simply as 'the Uists') are connected by road-bearing causeways.

The ferry crossing from Ullapool or Uig to the Western Isles marks an important cultural divide – more than a third of Scotland's registered crofts are in the Outer Hebrides, and no less than 60% of the population are Gaelic speakers.

If your time is limited, head straight for the west coast of Lewis with its prehistoric sites, preserved blackhouses and beautiful beaches.

ℹ Information

The only tourist offices are in Stornoway and Tarbert. See www.visitouterhebrides.co.uk for tourist information.

ℹ Getting There & Away

AIR

There are airports at Stornoway (Lewis), Benbecula and Barra. Flights operate to Stornoway from Edinburgh, Inverness, Glasgow, Aberdeen and Manchester. There are also two flights a day (Tuesday to Thursday only) between Stornoway and Benbecula.

There are daily flights from Glasgow to Barra, and from Tuesday to Thursday to Benbecula. At Barra, the planes land on the hard-sand beach at low tide, so the schedule depends on the tides.
Eastern Airways (☏ 0870 366 9100; www.easternairways.com)
Loganair (☏ 0344 800 2855; www.loganair.co.uk)

BOAT

Standard one-way fares on **CalMac** (☏ 0800 066 5000; www.calmac.co.uk) ferries:

CROSSING	DURA-TION (HOURS)	CAR (£)	DRIVER/PASSENGER (£)
Ullapool–Stornoway	2¾	51	9.50
Uig–Lochmaddy	1¾	31	6.30
Uig–Tarbert	1½	31	6.30
Oban–Castlebay	4¾	68	14.75
Mallaig–Lochboisdale	3½	58	10.45

There are two or three ferries a day to Stornoway, one or two a day to Tarbert and Lochmaddy, and one a day to Castlebay and Lochboisdale. See www.calmac.co.uk for ferry timetables.

Advance booking for cars is recommended (essential in July and August); foot and bicycle passengers should have no problems. Bicycles are carried free.

ℹ Getting Around

Despite their separate names, Lewis and Harris are actually one island. Berneray, North Uist, Benbecula, South Uist and Eriskay are all linked by road bridges and causeways. There are car ferries between Leverburgh (Harris) and Berneray and between Eriskay and Castlebay (Barra).

The local council publishes timetables of all bus and ferry services within the Outer Hebrides, which are available at tourist offices. Timetables can also be found online at www.cne-siar.gov.uk.

BICYCLE

Bikes can be hired for around £10 to £20 a day in Stornoway (Lewis), Leverburgh (Harris), Howmore (South Uist) and Castlebay (Barra).

BUS

The bus network covers almost every village in the islands, with around four to six buses a day on all the main routes; however, there are no buses at all on Sunday. You can pick up timetables from Stornoway tourist office (p935), or call Stornoway bus station (p935) for information.

CAR

Apart from the fast, two-lane road between Tarbert and Stornoway, most roads are single track (p1030). The main hazard is posed by sheep wandering about or sleeping on the road. Petrol stations are far apart (almost all of those on Lewis and Harris are closed on Sunday), and fuel is about 10% more expensive than on the mainland.

There are petrol stations at Stornoway, Barvas, Borve, Uig, Breacleit (Great Bernera), Ness, Tarbert and Leverburgh on Lewis and Harris; Lochmaddy and Cladach on North Uist; Balivanich on Benbecula; Howmore, Lochboisdale and Daliburgh on South Uist; and Castlebay on Barra.

Cars can be hired from around £35/170 per day/week from **Car Hire Hebrides** (☏ 01851-706500; www.carhire-hebrides.co.uk; Ferry Terminal, Shell St).

Lewis (Leodhais)

POP 21,000 (INCLUDING HARRIS)

The northern part of Lewis is dominated by the desolate expanse of the Black Moor, a vast, undulating peat bog dimpled with glittering lochans, seen clearly from the Stornoway–Barvas road. But Lewis' finest scenery is on the west coast, from Barvas southwest to Mealista, where the rugged landscape of hill, loch and sandy strand is reminiscent of the northwestern Highlands. The Outer Hebrides' most evocative historic sites – Callanish Standing Stones, **Dun Carloway** (Dun Charlabhaigh; P) and Arnol Blackhouse (p935) – are also to be found here.

Stornoway (Steornabhagh)

📞 01851 / POP 5715

Stornoway is the bustling 'capital' of the Outer Hebrides and the only real town in the whole archipelago. It's a surprisingly busy little place, with cars and people swamping the centre on weekdays. Though set on a beautiful natural harbour, the town isn't going to win any prizes for beauty or atmosphere, but it's a pleasant enough introduction to this remote corner of the country.

👁 Sights

Museum nan Eilean   MUSEUM
(www.lews-castle.co.uk; Lews Castle; ⊙10am-5pm Mon-Wed, Fri & Sat Apr-Sep, 1-4pm same days Oct-Mar; P) **FREE** The 'Museum of the Isles' opened in 2017, occupying a modern extension built onto the side of Lews Castle (p934). Artefacts, photos and videos celebrate the culture and history of the Outer Hebrides and explore traditional island life. The highlights of the collection are six of the famous **Lewis chess pieces**, discovered at Uig in west Lewis in 1831. Carved from whale and walrus ivory, they are thought to have been made in Norway more than 800 years ago.

Lews Castle   CASTLE
(📞01851-822750; www.lews-castle.co.uk; ⊙8am-5pm; P) **FREE** The Baronial mansion across the harbour from Stornoway town centre was built in the 1840s for the Matheson family, then owners of Lewis; it was gifted to the community by Lord Leverhulme in 1923. A major redevelopment completed in 2017 saw it converted to luxury self-catering accommodation, but the grand public rooms on the ground floor are free to visit when not in use. There's also an excellent **cafe** (mains £7-15; ⊙8am-4pm; 🛜🚻), one of the few local eateries to open on Sundays.

The beautiful wooded grounds, crisscrossed with walking trails, are open to the public and host the **Hebridean Celtic Festival** (www.hebceltfest.com; ⊙Jul).

🏃 Activities

Hebridean Adventures   WILDLIFE WATCHING
(📞07871 463755; www.hebrideanadventures.co.uk; Stornoway Harbour; per person £95; ⊙Apr-Sep) Seven-hour whale-watching trips (Wednesdays only) out of Stornoway harbour in a converted fishing boat with a cosy saloon to shelter from any wild weather.

🛏 Sleeping

★ **Heb Hostel**   HOSTEL £
(📞01851-709889; www.hebhostel.com; 25 Kenneth St; dm/f £19/75; @🛜) The Heb is an easygoing hostel close to the ferry, with comfy wooden bunks, a convivial living room with peat fire and a welcoming owner who can provide all kinds of advice on what to do and where to go.

Park Guest House   B&B ££
(📞01851-702485; www.the-parkguesthouse.com; 30 James St; s/d from £79/110; 🛜) A charming Victorian villa with a conservatory and six luxurious rooms (mostly en suite), the Park Guest House is comfortable and central and has the advantage of an excellent restaurant specialising in Scottish seafood, beef and game plus one or two vegetarian dishes (three-course dinner £38). Rooms overlooking the main road can be noisy on weekday mornings.

Royal Hotel   HOTEL ££
(📞01851-702109; www.royalstornoway.co.uk; Cromwell St; s/d from £82/105; P🛜) The 19th-century Royal is the most appealing of Stornoway's hotels – the rooms at the front retain period features such as wood panelling and enjoy a view across the harbour to Lews Castle (p934). Ask to see your room first, though, as some are a bit cramped.

🍴 Eating

Artizan Cafe   CAFE £
(📞01851-706538; www.facebook.com/artizanstornoway; 12-14 Church St; mains £4-7; ⊙10am-6pm Mon-Fri, 9am-6pm Sat; 🛜🚻) Recycled timber and cool colours mark out this cafe-gallery as one of Stornoway's hip hang-outs, serving great coffee and cake and tapas-style lunches (noon to 2.30pm). Hosts cultural events, including poetry nights on Saturday.

Lido   INTERNATIONAL ££
(📞01851-703354; 5 Cromwell St; mains £8-13; ⊙noon-3pm & 5-9pm Mon-Sat; 🛜🚻) Black-and-chrome decor and grey-granite table-

tops lend an art deco air to this busy diner, whose menu covers all bases from gourmet burgers to smoked-salmon salads to Italian meatballs. Speciality of the house is pizza, though, and these are excellent – thin, crispy and well-fired.

★**Digby Chick**   BISTRO **£££**
(☑ 01851-700026; www.digbychick.co.uk; 5 Bank St; mains £19-26, 2-course lunch £15; ☺ noon-2pm & 5.30-9pm Mon-Sat; ☒) 🖉 A modern restaurant that dishes up bistro cuisine such as haddock and chips, slow-roast pork belly or roast vegetable panini at lunchtime, the Digby Chick metamorphoses into a candlelit gourmet restaurant in the evening, serving dishes such as grilled langoustines, seared scallops, venison and steak. Three-course early-bird menu (5.30pm to 6.30pm) for £24.

ⓘ Information

Stornoway Tourist Office (☑ 01851-703088; www.visitouterhebrides.co.uk; 26 Cromwell St; ☺ 9am-6pm Mon-Sat Apr-Oct, to 5pm Mon-Fri Nov-Mar)

ⓘ Getting There & Away

The **bus station** (☑ 01851-704327; South Beach) is on the waterfront next to the ferry terminal (left luggage 25p to £1.30 per piece). Bus W10 runs from Stornoway to Tarbert (£4.80, one hour, four or five daily Monday to Saturday) and Leverburgh (£6.80, two hours).

The Westside Circular bus W2 runs a circular route from Stornoway through Callanish (£2.70, 30 minutes), Carloway, Garenin and Arnol; the timetable allows you to visit one or two of the sites in a day.

The bus network covers almost every village in the islands, with around four to six buses a day on all the main routes; however, there are no buses at all on Sunday. You can pick up timetables from the tourist offices, or call Stornoway bus station for information.

Callanish (Calanais)

Callanish, on the western side of Lewis, is famous for its prehistoric standing stones. One of the most atmospheric prehistoric sites in the whole of Scotland, its ageless mystery, impressive scale and undeniable beauty leave a lasting impression.

◉ Sights

Callanish Standing Stones   HISTORIC SITE
(HES; www.historicenvironment.scot; ☺ 24hr) **FREE** The Callanish Standing Stones, 15

ARNOL BLACKHOUSE

Not so much a museum as a perfectly preserved fragment of a lost world, this traditional **blackhouse** (HES; ☑ 01851-710395; www.historicenvironment.scot; Arnol; adult/child £5/3; ☺ 9.30am-5.30pm Mon-Sat Apr-Sep, 10am-4pm Mon, Tue & Thu-Sat Oct-Mar; ℗) – a combined byre, barn and home – was built in 1885 and inhabited until 1964. Staff faithfully rekindle the central peat fire every morning so you can experience the distinctive peat-reek; there's no chimney, and the smoke finds its own way out through the turf roof, windows and door – spend too long inside and you might feel like you've been kippered!

The museum is about 3 miles west of Barvas.

miles west of Stornoway on the A858 road, form one of the most complete stone circles in Britain. It is one of the most atmospheric prehistoric sites anywhere. Sited on a wild and secluded promontory overlooking Loch Roag, 13 large stones of beautifully banded gneiss are arranged, as if in worship, around a 4.5m-tall central monolith.

Some 40 smaller stones radiate from the circle in the shape of a cross, with the remains of a chambered tomb at the centre. Dating from 3800 to 5000 years ago, the stones are roughly contemporary with the pyramids of Egypt.

Calanais Visitor Centre   MUSEUM
(☑ 01851-621422; www.callanishvisitorcentre.co.uk; admission free, exhibition £2.50; ☺ 9.30am-8pm Mon-Sat Jun-Aug, 10am-6pm Mon-Sat Apr, May, Sep & Oct, 10am-4pm Tue-Sat Nov-Mar; ℗) This visitor centre near the Callanish Standing Stones (p935) is a tour de force of discreet design. Inside is a small exhibition that speculates on the origins and purpose of the stones, and an excellent **cafe** (mains £4-7; ☺ 9.30am-8pm Mon-Sat Jun-Aug, 10am-6pm Mon-Sat Apr, May, Sep & Oct, 10am-4pm Tue-Sat Nov-Mar; ℗).

ⓘ Getting There & Away

Bus W2 (Westside Circular) runs from Stornoway to Callanish (£2.70, 30 minutes) twice daily Monday to Saturday, allowing enough time to visit the stones.

THE BUTT OF LEWIS

The **Butt of Lewis** (P) – the extreme northern tip of the Hebrides – is windswept and rugged, with a very imposing lighthouse, pounding surf and large colonies of nesting fulmars on the high cliffs. There's a bleak sense of isolation here, with nothing but the grey Atlantic between you and Canada. The main settlement is Port of Ness (Port Nis), which has an attractive harbour. To the west is the sandy beach of Traigh, which is popular with surfers.

Just before the turn-off to the Butt at Eoropie (Eoropaidh), you'll find St Moluag's Church (Teampull Mholuidh), an austere, barnlike structure believed to date from the 12th century but still used by the Episcopal Church.

Garenin (Na Gearrannan)

The picturesque and fascinating Gearrannan Blackhouse Village is a cluster of nine restored thatch-roofed blackhouses perched above the exposed Atlantic coast. One of the cottages is home to the **Blackhouse Museum** (☑ 01851-643416; www.gearrannan.com; adult/child £3.60/1.20; ☺ 9.30am-5.30pm Mon-Sat Apr-Sep; P), a 1955 blackhouse with displays on the village's history, while another houses a cafe (mains £3-6; ☺ 9.30am-5.30pm Mon-Sat).

The W2 (Westside Circular) bus runs from Stornoway to Carloway village (£3.40, 45 minutes), a mile from Garenin, twice a day, Monday to Saturday.

Western Lewis

The B8011 road (signposted Uig, on the A858 Stornoway–Callanish road) from Garrynahine to Timsgarry (Timsgearraidh) meanders through scenic wilderness to some of Scotland's most stunning beaches. At **Miavaig**, a loop road detours north through the Bhaltos Estate to the pretty, mile-long white strand of **Reef Beach**; there's a basic but spectacular campsite (Cnip; Traigh na Beirigh; tent sites £10; ☺ May-Sep) in the machair behind the beach.

From Miavaig, the road continues west through a rocky defile to Timsgarry and the vast, sandy expanse of **Traigh Uige** (Uig Sands). The famous 12th-century **Lewis chess pieces**, made of walrus ivory, were discovered in the sand dunes here in 1831.

The minor road that continues south from Timsgarry to **Mealista** passes a few smaller, but still spectacular, white-sand and boulder beaches on the way to a remote dead end; on a clear day you can see St Kilda on the horizon.

Buses head from Stornoway to Uig (£4.80, one hour, two or three daily); some services continue (by request) to Ardroil and Brenish, a mile or so short of Mealista.

Harris (Na Hearadh)
POP 2000

Harris, to the south of Lewis, is the scenic jewel in the necklace of islands that comprise the Outer Hebrides. It has a spectacular blend of rugged mountains, pristine beaches, flower-speckled machair and barren rocky landscapes. The isthmus at Tarbert splits Harris neatly in two: North Harris is dominated by mountains that rise forbiddingly above the peat moors to the south of Stornoway – Clisham (799m) is the highest point. South Harris is lower-lying, fringed by beautiful white-sand beaches in the west and a convoluted rocky coastline to the east.

Harris is famous for Harris Tweed, a high-quality woollen cloth still hand-woven in islanders' homes. The industry employs around 400 weavers; staff at Tarbert tourist office can tell you about weavers and workshops you can visit.

❶ Getting There & Around

Harris and neighbouring Lewis are actually part of the same island, and Tarbert is linked to Stornoway by a good, fast road (37 miles). Car ferries sail between Tarbert and Uig (on the isle of Skye), and between Leverburgh and Berneray (North Uist).

Tarbert (An Tairbeart)
POP 480

Tarbert is a harbour village with a spectacular location, tucked into the narrow neck of land that links North and South Harris. It is one of the main ferry ports for the Outer Hebrides, and home to the Isle of Harris Distillery.

Village facilities include two petrol stations, a bank, an ATM, two general stores and a tourist office.

◉ Sights

Isle of Harris Distillery   DISTILLERY
(☑ 01859-502212; www.harrisdistillery.com; Main St; tours £10; ☺ 10am-5pm Mon-Sat; P) This distillery started production in 2015, so its first

batch of single malt whisky will be ready in 2019; meanwhile, it's producing Isle of Harris gin, too. The modern building is very stylish – the lobby feels like a luxury hotel – and 75-minute tours depart two or three times daily (weekdays only) in summer; they're popular, so book in advance. There's a **cafe** (mains £6-9; ☺ 10am-4pm Mon-Sat) here, too.

🛏 Sleeping & Eating

Tigh na Mara   B&B £

(☏ 01859-502270; flora@tigh-na-mara.co.uk; East Tarbert; per person £30-35; P) Excellent-value B&B (though the single room is a bit cramped) just five minutes' walk from the ferry – head up the hill above the tourist office and turn right. The owner bakes fresh cakes every day, which you can enjoy in the conservatory with a view over the bay.

Harris Hotel   HOTEL ££

(☏ 01859-502154; www.harrishotel.com; s/d from £90/115; P🐾) Run since 1903 by four generations of the Cameron family, Harris Hotel is a 19th-century sporting hotel, built in 1865 for visiting anglers and deer stalkers, and retains a distinctly old-fashioned atmosphere. It has spacious, comfy rooms and a decent restaurant; look out for JM Barrie's initials on the dining-room window (the author of *Peter Pan* visited in the 1920s).

Hebscape   CAFE £

(www.hebscapegallery.co.uk; Ardhasaig; mains £3-7; ☺ 10.30am-4.30pm Tue-Sat Apr-Oct; P🐾) 🥗 This stylish cafe and art gallery, a couple of miles outside Tarbert on the road north towards Stornoway, occupies a hilltop site with breathtaking views over Loch A Siar. Enjoy home-baked cakes or scones with Suki tea or freshly brewed espresso, or a hearty bowl of homemade soup, while admiring the gorgeous landscape photography of co-owner Darren Cole.

ℹ Information

Tarbert Tourist Office (☏ 01859-502011; www.visithebrides.com; Pier Rd; ☺ 9am-5pm Mon-Sat Apr-Oct)

ℹ Getting There & Away

There are four or five daily buses, Monday to Saturday, from Tarbert to Stornoway (£4.80, one hour) and Leverburgh (£3.20, 50 minutes) via the west coast road.

Tarbert also has ferry connections to Uig (car/pedestrian £31/6.30, 1½ hours, one or two daily) on Skye.

South Harris

South Harris' west coast has some of the most beautiful beaches in Scotland. The blinding white sands and turquoise waters of **Luskentyre** and **Scarasta** would be major holiday resorts if they were transported to somewhere with a warm climate; as it is, they're usually deserted.

The east coast is a complete contrast to the west – a strange, rocky moonscape of naked gneiss pocked with tiny lochans, the bleakness lightened by the occasional splash of green around the few crofting communities. Film buffs will know that the psychedelic sequences depicting an alien landscape in *2001: A Space Odyssey* were shot from an aircraft flying over Harris' east coast.

The narrow, twisting road that winds along this coast is known locally as the **Golden Road** because of the vast amount of money it cost per mile. It was built in the 1930s to link all the tiny communities known as 'The Bays'.

◉ Sights

★ **Luskentyre**   BEACH

(Losgaintir) Luskentyre is one of the biggest and most beautiful beaches in Scotland, famed for its acres of low-tide white sands and turquoise waters. A minor road leads along the northern side of the bay to a parking area beside an ancient graveyard; from here you can walk west along the beach or through the grassy dunes with gorgeous views across the sea to the island of Taransay.

LOCAL KNOWLEDGE

HARRIS' GOLDEN EAGLES

Magnificent North Harris is the most mountainous region of the Outer Hebrides. There are few roads here, but many opportunities for climbing, walking and birdwatching.

Between the old whaling station and Amhuinnsuidhe Castle, at Miavaig, a parking area and gated track gives hikers access to a **golden eagle observatory**, a 1.3-mile walk north from the road. On Wednesday from April to September, local rangers lead a 3½-hour guided walk (£5 per person) in search of eagles; details from Tarbert tourist office or www.north-harris.org.

ST KILDA

St Kilda is a collection of spectacular sea stacks and cliff-bound islands about 45 miles west of North Uist. The largest island, **Hirta**, measures only 2 miles by 1 mile, with huge cliffs along most of its coastline. Owned by the National Trust for Scotland (NTS), the islands are a Unesco World Heritage Site and are the biggest seabird nesting site in the North Atlantic, home to more than a million birds.

Hirta is the only island on which visitors can land. In addition to watching the bird life, you can explore the remains of the island's only settlement at **Village Bay**, where there's a ranger's office and small museum, and climb to the summit of Conachair (430m), the island's highest point.

Boat tours to St Kilda are a major undertaking – day trips are at least seven-hour affairs, involving a minimum 2½-hour crossing each way, often in rough seas; all must be booked in advance and are weather-dependent (April to September only).

Tour operators include **Go To St Kilda** (☑ 07789 914144; www.gotostkilda.co.uk; Stein Jetty; per person £260), Kilda Cruises, Uist Sea Tours (p940) and Sea Harris.

Talla na Mara   ARTS CENTRE
(☑ 01859-503900; www.tallanamara.co.uk; Pairc Niseaboist; ⊙ 9am-5pm Mon-Sat; P) **FREE** Opened in 2017 as a community enterprise, this beautiful modern building houses several artists' studios and an exhibition space that displays works celebrating the landscapes and culture of Scotland's Western Isles.

Clò Mòr   MUSEUM
(☑ 01859-502040; Old School, Drinishader; ⊙ 9am-5.30pm Mon-Sat Mar-Oct; P) **FREE** The Campbell family has been making Harris tweed for 90 years, and this exhibition (behind the family shop) celebrates the history of the fabric known in Gaelic as *clò mòr* (the 'big cloth'); ask about live demonstrations of tweed weaving on the 70-year-old Hattersley loom. Drinishader is 5 miles south of Tarbert on the east coast road.

Leverburgh   VILLAGE
(An t-Ob) The village of Leverburgh is named after Lord Leverhulme (creator of Sunlight Soap, and founder of Unilever), who bought Lewis and Harris in 1918. He had grand plans for An t-Ob, as Leverburgh was then known – it was to be a major fishing port with a population of 10,000 – but the plans died with him in 1925 and the village reverted to a sleepy backwater.

🏃 Activities

Sea Harris   BOATING
(☑ 01859-502007; www.seaharris.com; Leverburgh Pier; ⊙ Apr-Sep) Operates private-hire boat trips to spot wildlife around the Sound of Harris (from £40 per person), and also runs 10-hour day trips to St Kilda (£185 per person) with four to five hours ashore.

Kilda Cruises   BOATING
(☑ 01859-502060; www.kildacruises.co.uk; Leverburgh Pier; per person £215) Operates 12-hour day trips to the remote and spectacular island group of St Kilda. Daily from mid-April to mid-September.

🛏 Sleeping

Am Bothan   HOSTEL £
(☑ 01859-520251; www.ambothan.com; Ferry Rd, Leverburgh; dm £25; P🕙) An attractive, chalet-style hostel, Am Bothan has small, neat dorms and a great porch where you can enjoy morning coffee with views over the bay. The hostel has bike hire and can arrange wildlife-watching boat trips.

Sorrel Cottage   B&B ££
(☑ 01859-520319; www.sorrelcottage.co.uk; 2 Glen, Leverburgh; s/d from £70/90; P🕙🌐) Sorrel Cottage is a pretty crofter's house with beautifully modernised rooms, about 1.5 miles west of the ferry at Leverburgh. Vegetarians and vegans are happily catered for. Bike hire available.

★ Borve Lodge Estate   COTTAGE £££
(☑ 01859-550358; www.borvelodge.com; per 3/7 nights £900/1850; P🕙) This estate on the west side of South Harris has developed some of the most spectacular self-catering accommodation in the Outer Hebrides, including the Rock House, a turf-roofed nook built into the hillside with sweeping views over the sea, and the stunning Broch, a

three-storey rock tower based on Iron Age designs (both sleep two persons).

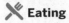

Eating

★ Skoon Art Café
CAFE **£**

(☏01859-530268; www.skoon.com; Geocrab; mains £5-9; ☉10am-4.30pm Tue-Sat Apr-Sep, reduced hours Oct-Mar; **P**) 🦋 Set halfway along the Golden Road, this neat little art gallery doubles as an excellent cafe serving delicious homemade soups, sandwiches, cakes and desserts (try the gin-and-tonic cake).

Temple Cafe
CAFE **£**

(☏07876 340416; www.facebook.com/thetemple cafe; Northton; mains £5-12; ☉10.30am-5pm Tue-Sun Apr-Sep, reduced hours Oct-Mar; **P** 🐾) Set in a cute stone-and-timber 'hobbit house' that was originally a visitor centre, and strewn with cushions covered in Harris tweed, this rustic cafe serves homemade scones, soups, salads and hot lunch specials to a soundtrack of '70s tunes. Evening meals 6.30pm to 8pm Friday to Sunday in summer (must be booked in advance).

★ Machair Kitchen
SCOTTISH **££**

(☏01859-550333; www.tallanamara.co.uk; Talla na Mara; mains £7-15; ☉noon-4pm & 6-9pm) The restaurant in this community centre and art gallery enjoys a stunning location, with views across the sea to the island of Taransay, and an outdoor deck that makes the most of any sunny weather. The menu includes local mussels, crab and smoked salmon, plus sandwiches, fish and chips and burgers. Open for coffee and cake from 10am to 5pm.

❶ Getting There & Around

A CalMac (p933) car ferry zigzags through the reefs of the Sound of Harris from Leverburgh to Berneray (pedestrian/car £3.60/13.55, one hour, three or four daily Monday to Saturday, two or three Sunday).

You can rent bikes from Sorrel Cottage (p938).

North Uist (Uibhist A Tuath) & Berneray (Bearnaraigh)

North Uist, an island half-drowned by lochs, is famed for its trout fishing (www.nuac.co.uk) but also has some magnificent beaches on its north and west coasts. For birdwatchers this is an earthly paradise, with regular sightings of waders and wildfowl ranging from redshank to red-throated diver to red-necked phalarope. The landscape is less wild and mountainous than Harris but it has a sleepy, subtle appeal.

Little **Lochmaddy** is the first village you hit after arriving on the ferry from Skye. It has a couple of stores, a bank with an ATM, a petrol station, a post office and a pub.

Berneray was linked to North Uist by a causeway in October 1998, but that hasn't altered the peace and beauty of the island. The beaches on its west coast are some of the most beautiful and unspoilt in Britain, and seals and otters can be seen in Bays Loch on the east coast.

◉ Sights

St Kilda Viewpoint
VIEWPOINT

(**P**) From the westernmost point of the road that runs around North Uist, a minor, drivable track leads for 1.5 miles to the summit of Clettraval hill where a lookout point with telescope affords superb views west to the distant peaks of St Kilda and the Monach Isles.

Balranald RSPB Reserve
WILDLIFE RESERVE

(www.rspb.org.uk; **P**) **FREE** Birdwatchers flock to this Royal Society for the Protection of Birds (RSPB) nature reserve, 18 miles west of Lochmaddy, in the hope of spotting the rare red-necked phalarope or hearing the distinctive call of the corncrake. There's a visitor centre with a resident warden who offers 1½-hour guided walks (£6), departing at 10am Tuesday from May to September.

Taigh Chearsabhagh
ARTS CENTRE, MUSEUM

(☏01870-603970; www.taigh-chearsabhagh.org; Lochmaddy; arts centre free, museum £3; ☉10am-5pm Mon-Sat Apr-Oct, to 4pm Nov-Mar; **P**) Taigh Chearsabhagh is a museum and arts centre that preserves and displays the history and culture of the Uists, and is also a thriving community centre, post office and meeting place. The centre's cafe (mains £4 to £6, closes at 3pm) dishes up homemade soups, sandwiches and cakes.

🛏 Sleeping & Eating

Balranald Campsite
CAMPGROUND **£**

(☏01876-510304; www.balranaldhebrideanholi days.com; Balranald Nature Reserve, Hougharry; tent sites £8-10, plus per person £2; 🛜) You can birdwatch from your tent at this lovely campsite set on the machair alongside the RSPB's Balranald nature reserve, and listen to rare corncrakes calling as the sun goes down beyond the neighbouring white-sand beach.

★ Langass Lodge
HOTEL **££**

(☑ 01876-580285; www.langasslodge.co.uk; Locheport; s/d from £95/115; [P][☎]) The delightful Langass Lodge hotel is a former shooting lodge set in splendid isolation overlooking Loch Langais. Refurbished and extended, it now offers a dozen appealing rooms, many with sea views, as well as one of the Hebrides' best **restaurants** (mains £15-25, 3-course dinner £38; ⊙ 6-8.30pm), noted for its fine seafood and game.

Hamersay House
HOTEL **£££**

(☑ 01876-500700; www.hamersayhouse.co.uk; Lochmaddy; s/d £95/135; [P][☎]) Hamersay is Lochmaddy's most luxurious accommodation, with eight designer bedrooms, a lounge with leather sofas set around an open fire, and a good restaurant (mains £13 to £21, open 6pm to 8.30pm) with sea views from the terrace.

❶ Getting There & Away

Buses from Lochmaddy to Lochboisdale (£5.30, 1¾ hours) and Eriskay Pier (£6.20, 2½ hours) run five to eight times a day Monday to Saturday.

CalMac (p933) ferries run from Lochmaddy to Uig (per car/pedestrian £31/6.30, 1¾ hours, one or two daily) on Skye, and from Berneray to Leverburgh on Harris.

South Uist (Uibhist A Deas)

POP 1755

South Uist is the second-largest island in the Outer Hebrides and saves its choicest corners for those who explore away from the main north–south road. The low-lying west coast is an almost unbroken stretch of white-sand beach and flower-flecked machair – a waymarked hiking trail, the **Hebridean Way**, follows the coast – while the multitude of inland lochs provide excellent trout fishing (www.southuistfishing. com). The east coast, riven by four large sea lochs, is hilly and remote, with spectacular **Beinn Mhor** (620m) the highest point.

Driving south from Benbecula you cross from the predominantly Protestant northern half of the Outer Hebrides into the mostly Roman Catholic south, a religious transition marked by the granite statue of **Our Lady of the Isles** on the slopes of Rueval and the presence of many roadside shrines.

The ferry port of **Lochboisdale** is the island's largest settlement, with a bank, ATM, grocery store and petrol station.

◉ Sights & Activities

Kildonan Museum
MUSEUM

(☑ 01878-710343; www.kildonanmuseum.co.uk; Kildonan; adult/child £3/free; ⊙ 10am-5pm Apr-Oct; [P]) Six miles north of Lochboisdale, Kildonan Museum explores the lives of local crofters through its collection of artefacts, an absorbing exhibition of B&W photography and firsthand accounts of harsh Hebridean conditions. There's also an excellent tearoom (mains £4 to £8, open 11am to 4pm) and craft shop.

Loch Druidibeg
NATURE RESERVE

FREE The northern part of South Uist is mostly occupied by the watery expanses of Loch Bee and Loch Druidibeg. The area is a Site of Special Scientific Interest and an important breeding ground for birds such as dunlin, redshank, ringed plover, greylag goose and corncrake; you can take a 5-mile self-guided walk through the reserve. Ask for details at the Scottish Natural Heritage office on the main road beside the loch.

Uist Sea Tours
BOATING

(☑ 07810 238752; www.uistseatours.com; The Pier, Lochboisdale) From mid-April to mid-September this outfit runs two-hour boat trips (£40 per person) from Lochboisdale to spot bottlenose dolphins in the Sound of Barra (Monday, Wednesday and Friday evenings), and six-hour trips from Eriskay harbour (£85 per person) to see nesting puffins on the island of Mingulay (Friday). There are also seven-hour day trips to St Kilda (£175 per person).

🛏 Sleeping

Uist Storm Pods
CAMPGROUND **£**

(☑ 01878-700845; www.uiststormpods.co.uk; Lochboisdale; per pod £70; [P][🐾]) This place has two Scandinavian-style timber camping pods set on a hillside on a working farm. Each has an outdoor deck and barbecue overlooking the sea; a mini-kitchen, fridge and chemical toilet; and can sleep up to four people. The pods are a short walk from the ferry; take the second road on the left, immediately before the RBS bank.

Wireless Cottage
B&B **£**

(☑01878-700660; www.wirelesscottage.co.uk; Lochboisdale; s/d/f from £37/60/90; 🛜) This pretty little cottage, which once housed the local telephone exchange, is now a welcoming and good-value B&B with just two bedrooms (one double, one family). It's a short (300m) walk from the ferry.

★ Polochar Inn
INN **££**

(☑01878-700215; www.polocharinn.com; Polochar; s/d from £80/95; P🛜) This 18th-century inn has been transformed into a stylish, welcoming hotel with a stunning location looking out across the sea to Barra. The excellent restaurant and bar menu (mains £11 to £20; booking recommended) includes seafood chowder, venison casserole, local salmon and scallops, and Uist lamb. Polochar is 7 miles southwest of Lochboisdale, on the way to Eriskay.

❶ Getting There & Away

Rothan Cycles (☑07740 364093; www.rothan.scot; Howmore; per day from £10; ⊘9am-5pm) offers bike hire, and a delivery and pick-up service (extra charge on top of rental) at various points between Eriskay and Stornoway.

Bus W17 runs about four times a day (except Sunday) between Berneray and Eriskay via Lochmaddy, Balivanich and Lochboisdale. The trip from Lochboisdale to Lochmaddy (£5.30) takes 1¾ hours.

CalMac (p933) ferries run between Lochboisdale and Mallaig.

Barra (Barraigh)

POP 1175

With its beautiful beaches, wildflower-clad dunes, rugged little hills and strong sense of community, diminutive Barra – just 14 miles in circumference – is the Outer Hebrides in miniature. For a great view of the island, walk up to the top of **Heaval** (383m), a mile northeast of **Castlebay** (Bagh a'Chaisteil), the largest village.

◉ Sights

Traigh Mor
BEACH

This vast expanse of firm golden sand (the name means 'Big Strand') serves as Barra's airport (a mile across at low tide, and big enough for three 'runways'), the only beach airport in the world that handles scheduled flights. Watching the little Twin Otter aircraft come and go is a popular specta-

tor sport. In between flights, locals gather cockles, a local seafood speciality, from the sands.

Kisimul Castle
CASTLE

(HES; ☑01871-810313; www.historicenvironment.scot; Castlebay; adult/child incl ferry £6/3.60; ⊘9.30am-5.30pm Apr-Sep) Castlebay takes its name from the island fortress of Kisimul Castle, first built by the MacNeil clan in the 11th century. A short boat trip (weather permitting) takes you out to the island, where you can explore the fortifications and soak up the view from the battlements.

🛏 Sleeping

Dunard Hostel
HOSTEL **£**

(☑01871-810443; www.dunardhostel.co.uk; Castlebay; dm/tw from £20/48; P🛜) Dunard is a friendly, family-run hostel just a five-minute walk from the ferry terminal. The owners can help to organise sea-kayaking trips.

Tigh na Mara
B&B **££**

(☑01871-810304; www.tighnamara-barra.co.uk; Castlebay; s/d £45/75; ⊘Apr-Oct; P🛜) A lovely cottage B&B with a brilliant location just above the ferry pier, looking out over the bay and Kisimul Castle (p941). Ask for the en suite double bedroom with bay view.

Castlebay Hotel
HOTEL **££**

(☑01871-810223; www.castlebayhotel.com; Castlebay; s/d from £70/125; P🛜) The Castlebay Hotel has spacious bedrooms decorated with a subtle tartan motif – it's worth paying a bit extra for a sea view – and there's a comfy lounge and conservatory with grand views across the harbour to the islands south of Barra. The hotel bar is the hub of island social life, with regular sessions of traditional music.

❶ Getting There & Away

There are two daily flights from Glasgow to Barra airport.

CalMac (p933) ferries link Eriskay with Ardmhor (pedestrian/car £3.05/10.55, 40 minutes, three to five daily) at the northern end of Barra. Ferries also run from Castlebay to Oban.

A bus service links ferry arrivals and departures at Ardmhor with Castlebay (£1.80, 20 minutes). Bus W32 makes a circuit of the island up to five times daily (except Sunday), and also connects with flights at the airport.

You can hire bikes from **Barra Bike Hire** (☑07876 402842; www.barrabikehire.co.uk; Vatersay Rd, Castlebay; per half-/full day £10/16; ⊘9am-5pm Mon-Sat).

ORKNEY

POP 21,670

There's a magic to Orkney that you begin to feel as soon as the Scottish mainland slips astern. Only a few short miles of ocean separate the chain of islands from Scotland's north coast, but the Pentland Firth is one of Europe's most dangerous waterways, a graveyard of ships that adds an extra mystique to these islands shimmering in the sea mists.

An archipelago of mostly flat, green-topped islands stripped bare of trees and ringed with red sandstone cliffs, its heritage dates back to the Vikings, whose influence is still strong today. Famed for ancient standing stones and prehistoric villages, for sublime sandy beaches and spectacular coastal scenery, it's a region whose ports tell of lives shared with the blessings and rough moods of the sea, and a destination where seekers can find melancholy wrecks of warships and the salty clamour of remote seabird colonies.

☞ Tours

Orkney Archaeology Tours TOURS
(☑ 01856-721450; www.orkneyarchaeologytours.co.uk) Specialises in all-inclusive multiday tours focusing on Orkney's ancient sites, with an archaeologist guide. These tours should be booked far ahead (a year or two). Also runs customisable private tours outside of the main season.

Wildabout Orkney BUS
(☑ 01856-877737; www.wildaboutorkney.com) Operates tours covering Orkney's history, ecology, folklore and wildlife. Day trips operate year-round and cost £59, with pick-ups in Stromness (to meet the morning ferry) and Kirkwall.

❶ Information

There's an excellent range of tourist information on Orkney, including a useful annual guide, as well as a separate guide to the smaller islands. The Kirkwall Information Centre (p946) has a good range of info and very helpful staff.

❶ Getting There & Away

AIR

Loganair (☑ outside UK 0141-642 9407, within UK 0344 800 2855; www.loganair.co.uk) flies daily from Kirkwall to Aberdeen, Edinburgh, Glasgow, Inverness and Sumburgh (Shetland). There are summer services to Manchester, Fair Isle and Bergen (Norway).

BOAT

During summer, book car spaces ahead. Peak-season fares are quoted here. At the time of research, the road-equivalent tariff (RET) scheme was due to be rolled out on Orkney services, so prices should drop.

Northlink Ferries (☑ 0845 6000 449; www.northlinkferries.co.uk) Operates from Scrabster to Stromness (passenger/car £19.40/59, 1½ hours, two to three daily), from Aberdeen to Kirkwall (passenger/car £31.50/111, six hours, three or four weekly) and from Kirkwall to Lerwick (passenger/car £24.65/103, six to eight hours, three or four weekly) on Shetland. Fares are up to 35% cheaper in the low season.

Pentland Ferries (☑ 0800 688 8998; www.pentlandferries.co.uk; adult/child/car/bike £16/8/38/free) Leave from Gills Bay, 3 miles west of John O'Groats, and head to St Margaret's Hope on South Ronaldsay three to four times daily. The crossing takes a little over an hour.

John O'Groats Ferries (☑ 01955-611353; www.jogferry.co.uk; s £19, incl bus to Kirkwall £20; ☉ May-Sep) Has a passenger-only service from John O'Groats to Burwick, on the southern tip of South Ronaldsay, with connecting buses to Kirkwall. A 40-minute crossing, with two to three departures daily.

❶ Getting Around

The *Orkney Transport Guide* details all island transport and is free from tourist offices. There's a winter and summer version; ferry sailings, flights and some bus services are reduced from October to April.

The largest Orkney island, Mainland, is linked by causeways to four southern islands; others are reached by air and ferry.

AIR

Loganair Inter-Isles Air Service (☑ 01856-873457; www.loganair.co.uk) operates interisland flights from Kirkwall to Eday, Stronsay, Sanday, Westray, Papa Westray and North Ronaldsay. Fares are reasonable, with some special discounted tickets if you stay a night on the outer islands. You have to book by email or phone.

BICYCLE

Various locations on Mainland hire out bikes, including **Cycle Orkney** (☑ 01856-875777; www.cycleorkney.com; Tankerness Lane, Kirkwall; per day/3 days/week £20/40/80; ☉ 9am-5.30pm Mon-Sat) and **Orkney Cycle Hire** (☑ 01856-850255; www.orkneycyclehire.co.uk; 54 Dundas St; per day £10-15; ☉ 8am-5pm). Both offer out-of-hours pick-ups and options for kids.

BOAT

Orkney Ferries (☑ 01856-872044; www.orkneyferries.co.uk) operates car ferries from

Orkney

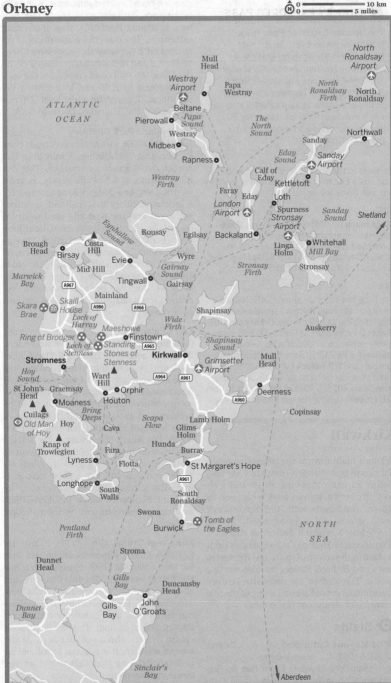

0   10 km
0   5 miles

North Ronaldsay Airport

North Ronaldsay Firth

North Ronaldsay

Mull Head

Westray Airport

Papa Westray

Beltane

Pierowall

Papa Sound

The North Sound

Sanday

Northwall

Westray

Eday Sound

Sanday Airport

Midbea

Rapness

Calf of Eday

Kettletoft

Loth

Whitehall

Mill Bay

ATLANTIC OCEAN

Westray Firth

Faray

Eday

London Airport

Spurness

Stronsay Airport

Linga Holm

Sanday Sound

Shetland

Brough Head

Costa Hill

Birsay

Evie

Rousay

Egilsay

Backaland

Stronsay

Mid Hill

Wyre

Tingwall

Gairsay Sound

Gairsay

Stronsay Firth

Marwick Bay

A967

Mainland

A986

A966

Shapinsay

Auskerry

Skara Brae

Skaill House

Loch of Harray

Maeshowe

Wide Firth

Ring of Brodgar

Standing Stones of Stenness

Finstown

Shapinsay Sound

Loch of Stenness

Kirkwall

A965

Stromness

Ward Hill

A964

A961

Grimsetter Airport

Mull Head

Hoy Sound

Graemsay

Orphir

Houton

Deerness

A960

St John's Head

Moaness

Bring Deeps

Copinsay

Cuilags

Old Man of Hoy

Hoy

Cava

Scapa Flow

Lamb Holm

Glims Holm

Knap of Trowiegien

Fara

Hunda

Burray

Lyness

Flotta

St Margaret's Hope

Longhope

South Walls

A961

South Ronaldsay

Swona

Burwick

Tomb of the Eagles

NORTH SEA

Pentland Firth

Stroma

Dunnet Head

Gills Bay

Duncansby Head

Dunnet Bay

Gills Bay

John O'Groats

Aberdeen

Sinclair's Bay

ⓘ ORKNEY EXPLORER PASS

The **Orkney Explorer Pass** (www.
historicenvironment.scot; adult/child/
family £19/11.40/38; ☺ Apr-Oct) covers
all Historic Environment Scotland sites
in Orkney, including Maeshowe, Skara
Brae, the Broch of Gurness, the Brough
of Birsay and the Bishop's Palace and
Earl's Palace in Kirkwall. It lasts for 30
consecutive days and is only available
from April to October.

Mainland to the islands. An Island Explorer
pass costs £42 for a week's passenger travel in
summer. Bikes are carried free.

BUS

Stagecoach (☏ 01856-870555; www.stage-
coachbus.com) runs buses on Mainland and
connecting islands. Most don't operate on
Sunday. Dayrider (£8.65) and 7-Day Megarider
(£19.25) tickets allow unlimited travel.

CAR

Small-car hire rates are around £45/240 per
day/week, although there are sometimes specials for as low as £30 per day. **Orkney Car Hire**
(James D Peace & Co; ☏ 01856-872866; www.
orkneycarhire.co.uk; Junction Rd, Kirkwall; per
day/week £45/240; ☺ 8am-5pm Mon-Fri, 9am-
1pm Sat) and **WR Tullock** (☏ 01856-875500;
www.orkneycarrental.co.uk; Castle St; per day/
week £45/240; ☺ 8.30am-6pm Mon-Fri, to 5pm
Sat) are both close to the bus station in Kirkwall.

Kirkwall

☏ 01856 / POP 7000

Orkney's main town is the islands' commercial centre and there's a comparatively busy
feel to its main shopping street and ferry
dock. It's set back from a wide bay, and its
vigour, combined with the atmospheric
paved streets and twisting wynds (lanes),
give Orkney's capital a distinctive character.
Magnificent St Magnus Cathedral takes pride
of place in the centre of town, and the nearby
Earl's and Bishop's Palaces are also worth a
ramble. Founded in the early 11th century,
the original part of Kirkwall is one of the best
examples of an ancient Norse town.

◉ Sights

★**St Magnus Cathedral**　　　CATHEDRAL
(☏ 01856-874894; www.stmagnus.org; Broad
St; ☺ 9am-6pm Mon-Sat, 1-6pm Sun Apr-Sep,
9am-1pm & 2-5pm Mon-Sat Oct-Mar) FREE Constructed from local red sandstone, Kirkwall's
centrepiece, dating from the early 12th century, is among Scotland's most interesting
cathedrals. The powerful atmosphere of an
ancient faith pervades the impressive interi-
or. Lyrical and melodramatic epitaphs of the
dead line the walls and emphasise the serious business of 17th- and 18th-century be-
reavement. Tours of the upper level (£8) run
on Tuesday and Thursday; phone to book.

★**Highland Park Distillery**　　　DISTILLERY
(☏ 01856-874619; www.highlandpark.co.uk; Holm
Rd; tours adult/child £10/free; ☺ tours 10am-4pm
Apr-Oct, 2pm & 3pm Mon-Fri Nov-Mar) This distillery, South of Kirkwall's centre, is great
to visit. Despite a dodgy Viking rebrand, it's
a serious distillery that malts its own barley; see it and the peat kiln used to dry it
on the excellent, well-informed hour-long
tour (book ahead). The standard 12-year-
old is a soft, balanced malt, great for novices and aficionados alike; the 18-year-old is
among the world's finest drams. This and
older whiskies can be tasted on more specialised tours (£20 to £75), which you can
prearrange.

Earl's Palace　　　RUINS
(☏ 01856-871918; www.historicenvironment.scot;
Watergate; adult/child £5/3; ☺ 9.30am-5.30pm
Apr-Sep) The intriguing Earl's Palace was
once known as the finest example of French
Renaissance architecture in Scotland. One
room features an interesting history of its
builder, Earl Patrick Stewart, a bastard in
every sense of the word, who was beheaded in Edinburgh for treason. He started
construction in about 1600, but ran out of
money and never completed it. When it's
closed you can still get a good look at it
from the garden. Admission includes the
adjacent **Bishop's Palace** (☏ 01856-871918;
www.historicenvironment.scot; ☺ 9.30am-5.30pm
Apr-Sep).

Kirkjuvagr Orkney Gin　　　DISTILLERY
(☏ 01856-875338; www.orkneydistilling.com; Ayre
Rd; tours adult/child £15/8; ☺ tours 11am & 2pm
Mon-Sat) Opened in 2018, this distillery and
visitor centre on the waterfront is a new
showcase for this tasty Orkney spirit. Tours
run for an hour and include an audiovisual
display and a tasting; it's wise to prebook
online. There's also a cafe-bar here. At the
time of research, it was about to roll out an
in-depth day-long tour that would let you
create your own gin.

Kirkwall

Kirkwall

Orkney Museum MUSEUM
(☏ 01856-873191; www.orkney.gov.uk; Broad St; ☉ 10.30am-5pm Mon-Sat year-round, closed 12.30-1.30pm Oct-Apr) **FREE** This labyrinthine display in a former merchant's house gives an overview of Orcadian history and prehistory, including Pictish carvings and a display on the ba' (p946). Most engaging are the last rooms, covering 19th- and 20th-century social history.

🛏 Sleeping

Orcades Hostel HOSTEL £
(☏ 01856-873745; www.orcadeshostel.com; Muddisdale Rd; dm/s/d £20/40/52; P@🛜) Book ahead to get a bed in this cracking hostel on the western edge of Kirkwall. It's a guesthouse conversion, so there's a very smart kitchen and lounge, and great-value doubles. Comfortable, spacious en suite dorms with just four bunks make for sound sleeping;

THE BA'

Every Christmas Day and New Year's Day, Kirkwall holds a staggering spectacle: a crazy ball game known as the ba'. Two enormous teams, the Uppies and the Doonies, fight their way, no holds barred, through the streets, trying to get a leather ball to the other end of town. The ball is thrown from the Mercat Cross to the waiting teams; the Uppies have to get the ba' to the corner of Main St and Junction Rd, the Doonies must get it to the water. Violence, skulduggery and other stunts are common, and the event, fuelled by plenty of strong drink, can last hours.

enthusiastic owners give the place spark. There are lockers for valuables at reception.

Peedie Hostel HOSTEL £
(☑ 01856-877177; www.stayinkirkwall.co.uk; Ayre Rd; dm/s/tw £15/20/35; P ☎) Nestling into a corner at the end of the Kirkwall waterfront, this marvellously located hostel set in former fisherfolk's cottages has a cute, tiny downstairs section and a more sizeable upper area. Most of the dorms have just two beds, and there are three separate kitchen areas. It's normally unstaffed, but the keen new owner is giving it a gradual facelift.

Royal Oak Guest House B&B ££
(☑ 01856-877177; www.royaloakhouse.co.uk; Holm Rd; s £55-64, d £80; P ☎) This likeable spot south of Kirkwall's centre has eight bright rooms, all with modern en suite bathrooms. Photos of Orkney decorate the guesthouse, which features a luminous dining room and guest access to fridge, microwave and lounge. Best is having a great chat with owner Liz.

★ **Albert Hotel** HOTEL £££
(☑ 01856-876000; www.alberthotel.co.uk; Mounthoolie Lane; s £97, d £146-181; ☎) Stylishly refurbished in plum and grey, this central but peaceful hotel is Kirkwall's finest address. Comfortable contemporary rooms in a variety of categories sport super-inviting beds and smart bathrooms. Staff are helpful, and will pack you a breakfast box if you've got an early ferry. A great Orkney base, with the more-than-decent **Bothy Bar** (mains £7-12; ⏱ noon-2pm & 5-9pm; ☎) downstairs. Walk-in prices are often cheaper.

Ayre Hotel HOTEL £££
(☑ 01856-873001; www.ayrehotel.co.uk; Ayre Rd; s/d £96/136; P ☎) Right on the waterfront, this welcoming 200-year-old hotel with spruce, inviting, large-bedded rooms makes a great Kirkwall base. It's definitely worth paying the extra few pounds to grab one with a sea view. The bar-restaurant downstairs is convivial and friendly, though doesn't excel food-wise.

✗ Eating

Reel CAFE £
(www.facebook.com/thereelkirkwall; Albert St; sandwiches £3-6; ⏱ 9am-6pm Mon-Sat; ☎) Part music shop, part cafe, the Reel is Kirkwall's best coffee stop and sits alongside St Magnus Cathedral (p944), bravely putting tables outside at the slightest promise of sunshine. It's a relaxed spot, good for a morning-after debriefing, a quiet Orkney ale, or lunchtime panini and musically named sandwiches (plus the cheese-and-mushroom Skara Brie).

★ **Foveran** SCOTTISH ££
(☑ 01856-872389; www.thefoveran.com; St Ola; mains £15-26; ⏱ 6.30-8.30pm mid-May–mid-Sep, Fri & Sat only plus other days by arrangement low season; ☎) ✔ Three miles down the Orphir road, one of Orkney's best dining options is surprisingly affordable for its quality. Tranquilly located, with a cosy eating area overlooking the sea, it shines with its classic Orcadian ingredients – the steak with haggis and whisky sauce is feted, while North Ronaldsay lamb comes in four different, deliciously tender cuts.

★ **The Shore** SCOTTISH ££
(☑ 01856-872200; www.theshore.co.uk; 6 Shore St; bar meals £9-11, restaurant mains £17-22; ⏱ food noon-2pm & 6-9pm Mon-Fri, 10am-9pm Sat & Sun, reduced hours winter; ☎) This popular harbourside place is a convivial spot with a helpful attitude. It offers high-standard bar meals and excellent evening meals in the restaurant section, which features local seafood and beautifully prepared meat dishes. Upstairs are some very decent rooms.

ⓘ Information

Kirkwall Information Centre (☑ 01856-872856; www.visitorkney.com; West Castle St; ⏱ 9am-5pm Mon-Sat Nov-Mar, to 6pm Mon-Sat Apr & Sep-Oct, to 6pm daily May-Aug) Has a good range of Orkney info and helpful staff. Shares a building with the bus station.

❶ Getting There & Away

Kirkwall Airport (☏ 01856-872421; www.hial.co.uk) is located 2.5 miles southeast of town and is served regularly by bus 4 (15 minutes).

Ferries to Orkney's northern islands depart from the **pier** (www.orkneyferries.co.uk; Shore St) in the centre of town. Here, too, is the **Orkney Ferries Office** (☏ 01856-872044; www.orkneyferries.co.uk; Shore St; ⊗7am-5pm Mon-Fri, 7am-noon & 1-3pm Sat) for bookings. **Ferries to Shapinsay** (www.orkneyferries.co.uk; Shore St) depart from the next pier to the west.

Ferries to Aberdeen and Shetland use the **Hatston Ferry Terminal** (www.northlinkferries.co.uk; Grainshore Rd; ☎), 2 miles northwest. Bus X10 heads there to coincide with departures.

❶ Getting Around

All services leave from the **bus station** (West Castle St):

Bus X1 Stromness (£3.20, 30 minutes, hourly Monday to Saturday, seven on Sunday); in the other direction to St Margaret's Hope (£3).

Bus 2 Orphir and Houton (£2.35, 20 minutes, four or five daily Monday to Saturday, five on Sunday from mid-June to mid-August).

Bus 6 Evie (£3.50, 30 minutes, three to five daily Monday to Saturday) and Tingwall (Rousay ferry). Runs Sunday in summer to Tingwall only.

East Mainland to South Ronaldsay

After a German U-boat sank battleship HMS *Royal Oak* in 1939, Winston Churchill had causeways of concrete blocks erected across the channels on the eastern side of Scapa Flow, linking Mainland to the islands of Lamb Holm, Glims Holm, Burray and South Ronaldsay. The Churchill Barriers, flanked by rusting wrecks of blockships, now support the main road from Kirkwall to Burwick.

◉ Sights

⭐**Fossil & Heritage Centre**   MUSEUM
(☏ 01865-731255; www.orkneyfossilcentre.co.uk; adult/child £4.50/3; ⊗10am-5pm mid-Apr–Sep) This eclectic museum is a great visit, combining some excellent 360-million-year-old Devonian fish fossils found locally with a well-designed exhibition on the World Wars and Churchill Barriers. Upstairs is a selection of household and farming implements. There's a good little gift shop and an enjoyable coffee shop. Coming from Kirkwall it's on the left half a mile after crossing onto Burray.

⭐**Tomb of the Eagles**   ARCHAEOLOGICAL SITE
(☏ 01856-831339; www.tomboftheeagles.co.uk; Cleat; adult/child £7.50/3.50; ⊗ 9.30am-5.30pm Apr-Sep, 10am-noon Mar, 9.30am-12.30pm Oct) Two significant archaeological sites were found here by a farmer on his land. The first is a Bronze Age stone building with a firepit, indoor well and plenty of seating (a communal cooking site or the original Orkney pub?). Beyond, in a spectacular clifftop position, the neolithic tomb (wheel yourself in prone on a trolley) is an elaborate stone construction that held the remains of up to 340 people who died some five millennia ago.

Banks Chambered Tomb   ARCHAEOLOGICAL SITE
(Tomb of the Otters; ☏ 01856-831605; www.bankschamberedtomb.co.uk; Cleat; adult/child £6/3; ⊗11am-5pm Apr-Sep) Discovered while digging was under way for a car park, this 5000-year-old chambered tomb has yielded a vast quantity of human bones, well preserved thanks to the saturation of the earth. The tomb, dug into bedrock, is an atmospheric if claustrophobic visit. The guided tour mixes homespun archaeological theories with astute observations. Within the adjacent bistro, you can handle discoveries of stones and bones, including the remains of otters, who presumably used this as a den. Follow signs for Tomb of the Eagles.

Italian Chapel   CHURCH
(☏ 01865-781268; Lamb Holm; adult/child £3/free; ⊗ 9am-6.30pm Jun-Aug, to 5pm May & Sep, 10am-4pm Mon-Sat, to 3pm Sun Apr & Oct, 10am-1pm Nov-Mar) The Italian Chapel is all that remains of a POW camp that housed the Italian soldiers who worked on the Churchill Barriers. They built the chapel in their spare time, using two Nissen huts, scrap metal and their considerable artistic skills. It's quite extraordinary inside and the charming back story makes it an Orkney highlight. One of the artists returned in 1960 to restore the paintwork.

West & North Mainland

This part of Mainland island is sprinkled with outstanding prehistoric monuments: the journey to Orkney is worth it for these alone and they stand proud as some of the world's most important neolithic sites.

It would take a day to see all of them – if pushed for time, visit Skara Brae then Maeshowe, but book your visit to the latter in advance.

◎ Sights

★ Maeshowe   ARCHAEOLOGICAL SITE
(☑ 01856-761606; www.historicenvironment. scot; adult/child £5.50/3.30; ⊘ 9.30am-5pm Apr-Sep, 10am-4pm Oct-Mar, tours hourly 10am-4pm, plus 6pm & 7pm Jul & Aug) Constructed about 5000 years ago, Maeshowe is an extraordinary place, a Stone Age tomb built from enormous sandstone blocks, some of which weighed many tonnes and were brought from several miles away. Creeping down the long stone passageway to the central chamber, you feel the indescribable gulf of years that separate us from the architects of this mysterious tomb.

Entry is by 45-minute guided tours (prebooking online is strongly advised) that leave by bus from the visitor centre at nearby Stenness.

★ Skara Brae   ARCHAEOLOGICAL SITE
(www.historicenvironment.scot; Sandwick; adult/ child Nov-Mar £6.50/3.90, Apr-Oct incl Skaill House £7.50/4.50; ⊘ 9.30am-5.30pm Apr-Sep, 10am-4pm Oct-Mar) Idyllically situated by a sandy bay 8 miles north of Stromness, and predating Stonehenge and the pyramids of Giza, extraordinary Skara Brae, one of the world's most evocative prehistoric sites, is northern Europe's best-preserved neolithic village. Even the stone furniture – beds, boxes and dressers – has survived the 5000 years since a community lived and breathed here. It was hidden until 1850, when waves whipped up by a severe storm eroded the sand and grass above the beach, exposing the houses underneath.

There's an excellent interactive exhibit and short video, arming visitors with facts and theory, which will enhance the impact of the site. You then enter a reconstructed house, giving the excavation (which you head to next) more meaning. The official guidebook, available from the visitor centre, includes a good self-guided tour.

In the summer months, your ticket also gets you into Skaill House (☑ 01856-841501; www.skaillhouse.co.uk; Sandwick; ⊘ 9.30am-5.30pm Apr-Sep, 10am-4pm Oct), an important step-gabled Orcadian mansion built for the bishop in 1620. It may feel a bit anticlimactic catapulting straight from the neolithic to the 1950s decor, but it's an interesting sight in its own right. You can see a smart hidden compartment in the library as well as the bishop's original 17th-century four-poster bed.

At the time of research, a trial bus route (8S) was running to Skara Brae from Kirkwall and Stromness a few times weekly, but not all were useful to visit the site. It's possible to walk along the coast from Stromness to Skara Brae (9 miles), or it's an easy taxi (£15), hitch or cycle from Stromness. Mobility scooters are available at the visitor centre to cut out the walk to the site.

Ring of Brodgar   ARCHAEOLOGICAL SITE
(www.historicenvironment.scot; ⊘ 24hr) **FREE** A mile northwest of Stenness is this wide circle of standing stones, some over 5m tall. The last of the three Stenness monuments to be built (2500–2000 BC), it remains a most atmospheric location. Twenty-one of the original 60 stones still stand among the heather. On a grey day with dark clouds thudding low across the sky, the stones are a spine-tingling sight.

Broch of Gurness   ARCHAEOLOGICAL SITE
(www.historicenvironment.scot; Evie; adult/child £6/3.60; ⊘ 9.30am-5.30pm Apr-Sep, 10am-4pm Oct) Here is a fine example of the drystone fortified towers that were both a status symbol for powerful farmers and useful protection from raiders some 2200 years ago. The imposing entranceway and sturdy stone walls – originally 10m high – are impressive; inside you can see the hearth and where a mezzanine floor would have fitted. Around the broch are a number of well-preserved outbuildings, including a curious shamrock-shaped house. The visitor centre has some interesting displays on the culture that built these remarkable fortifications.

The broch is on an exposed headland at Aikerness, a 1.5-mile walk northeast from the strung-out village of Evie.

Ness of Brodgar   ARCHAEOLOGICAL SITE
(www.nessofbrodgar.co.uk; ⊘ tours 2-3 times Mon-Fri early Jul-late Aug) **FREE** The spectacular finds from ongoing excavations at this archaeological site between the Standing Stones of Stenness and the Ring of Brodgar have revolutionised understanding of the neolithic in Britain. Evidence of a major settlement centred on a monumental building has been revealed, dating from the fourth and third millennia BC. There have been

some spectacular finds. During the summer dig season, there are free guided tours Monday to Friday; check the website for times and dates.

Standing Stones of Stenness
ARCHAEOLOGICAL SITE

(www.historicenvironment.scot; ⊙24hr) FREE Part of this Mainland area's concentration of neolithic monuments, four mighty stones remain of what was once a circle of 12. Recent research suggests they were perhaps erected as long ago as 3300 BC, and they impose by their sheer size; the tallest measures 5.7m in height. The narrow strip of land they're on, the Ness of Brodgar, separates the Harray and Stenness lochs and was the site of a large settlement inhabited throughout the neolithic period (3500–1800 BC).

Barnhouse Neolithic Village
ARCHAEOLOGICAL SITE

(www.historicenvironment.scot; ⊙24hr) FREE Alongside the Standing Stones of Stenness are the excavated remains of a village thought to have been inhabited by the builders of Maeshowe. Don't skip this: it brings the area to life. The houses are well preserved and similar to Skara Brae with their stone furnishings. One of the buildings was entered by crossing a fireplace: possibly an act of ritual significance.

❶ Getting There & Away

The regular bus service between Kirkwall and Stromness is good for accessing several of the ancient sites, though not Skara Brae. At the time of research there were buses on a trial route between Kirkwall, Stromness and Skara Brae (line 8S) but not all services are well timed for visiting. The south coast and Birsay are also serviced by buses.

Stromness

☑ 01856 / POP 1800

This appealing grey-stone port has a narrow, elongated, flagstone-paved main street and tiny alleys leading down to the waterfront between tall houses. It lacks the size of Kirkwall, Orkney's main town, but makes up for that with bucketloads of character, having changed little since its heyday in the 18th century, when it was a busy staging post for ships avoiding the troublesome English Channel during European wars. Stromness is ideally located for trips to Orkney's major prehistoric sites.

◉ Sights

★ Stromness Museum
MUSEUM

(☑ 01856-850025; www.stromnessmuseum.co.uk; 52 Alfred St; adult/child £5/1; ⊙10am-5pm daily Apr-Sep, 10am-5pm Mon-Sat Oct, 11am-3.30pm Mon-Sat Nov-Mar) This superb museum, run with great passion, is full of knick-knacks from maritime and natural-history exhibitions covering whaling, the Hudson's Bay Company and the German fleet sunk after WWI. Recent finds from the jaw-dropping excavations at the Ness of Brodgar are on display and there's always an excellent summer exhibition, too. You can happily nose around for a couple of hours. Across the street is the house where local poet and novelist George Mackay Brown lived.

⬛ Sleeping

Hamnavoe Hostel
HOSTEL £

(☑ 01856-851202; www.hamnavoehostel.co.uk; 10a North End Rd; dm/s/tw £22/24/48; 🛜) This well-equipped hostel is efficiently run and has excellent facilities, including a fine kitchen and a lounge room with great perspectives over the water. The dorms are very spacious, with duvets, decent mattresses and reading lamps (bring a pound coin for the heating), and the showers are good. Ring ahead as the owner lives off site.

★ Brinkies Guest House
B&B ££

(☑ 01856-851881; www.brinkiesguesthouse.co.uk; Brownstown Rd; s £65, d £80-90; 🅿🛜) Just a short walk from the centre of Stromness, but with a lonely, king-of-the-castle position overlooking the town and bay, this exceptional place offers five-star islander hospitality. Compact, modern rooms are handsome, stylish and comfortable, and the public areas are done out attractively in wood, but above all it's the charming owner's flexibility and can-do attitude that makes this place so special.

Burnside Farm
B&B ££

(☑ 01856-850723; www.burnside-farm.com; North End Rd/A965; s £60, d £80-90; 🅿🛜) On a working dairy farm on the edge of Stromness, this place has lovely views over green fields, town and harbour. Rooms are elegant and maintain the style from when the house was built in the late 1940s, with attractive period furnishings. The top-notch bathrooms, however, are sparklingly contemporary. Breakfast comes with views, and the kindly owner couldn't be more welcoming.

✕ Eating

★ Hamnavoe Restaurant   SEAFOOD ££

(☑ 01856-851226, 01856-850606; 35 Graham Pl; mains £15-24; ⊗ 7-9pm Tue-Sun Jun-Aug) Tucked away off the main street, this Stromness favourite specialises in excellent local seafood in an intimate, cordial atmosphere. There's always something good off the boats, and the chef prides himself on his lobster. Booking is a must. It opens some weekends in low season; it's worth calling ahead to check.

Ferry Inn   PUB FOOD ££

(☑ 01856-850280; www.ferryinn.com; 10 John St; mains £10-19; ⊗ food 7am-9pm Apr-Oct; 🔊) Every port has its pub, and in Stromness it's the Ferry. Convivial and central, it warms the cockles with folk music, local beers and characters, and all-day food that offers decent value in a dining area done out like the deck of a ship. The fish and chips are excellent, and a few blackboard specials fill things out.

ⓘ Getting There & Away

Northlink Ferries (p942) runs services from Stromness to Scrabster on the mainland (passenger/car £19.40/59, 1½ hours, two to three daily). At the time of research, the road-equivalent tariff scheme was due to be rolled out on Orkney services, so prices should drop.

Bus X1 runs regularly to Kirkwall (£3.20, 30 minutes, hourly Monday to Saturday, seven

---

OLD MAN OF HOY

Hoy's best-known sight is this 137m-high **rock stack** jutting from the ocean off the tip of an eroded headland. It's a tough ascent and for experienced climbers only, but the walk to see it is a Hoy highlight, revealing much of the island's most spectacular scenery. You can also spot the Old Man from the Scrabster–Stromness ferry.

The easiest approach to the Old Man is from Rackwick Bay, a 5-mile walk by road from Moaness Pier. You'll pass the 5000-year-old **Dwarfie Stane** (Rackwick Glen; ⊗ 24hr) **FREE**, the only example of a rock-cut tomb in Scotland. On your return you can take the path via the Glens of Kinnaird and Berriedale Wood, Scotland's most northerly tuft of native forest. Allow seven hours for the return trip from Moaness Pier, or three hours from Rackwick Bay.

Sunday), with some going on to St Margaret's Hope (£5.90, 1¼ hours).

Hoy

POP 400

Orkney's second-largest island, Hoy (meaning 'High Island'), got the lion's share of the archipelago's scenic beauty. Shallow turquoise bays lace the east coast and massive seacliffs guard the west, while peat and moorland cover Orkney's highest hills. Much of the north is a reserve for breeding seabirds. The Scrabster–Stromness ferry gives you a decent perspective of the island's wild good looks.

Lyness was an important naval base during both World Wars, when the British Grand Fleet was based in Scapa Flow. The fascinating **Scapa Flow Visitor Centre & Museum** (☑ 01856-791300; www.orkney.gov.uk; Lyness; ⊗ 10am-4.30pm Mon-Sat Mar, Apr & Oct, 9am-4.30pm Mon-Sat, 1st to last ferry Sun May-Sep) **FREE**, located in an old pumphouse that once fed fuel to the ships, is a must-see for anyone interested in Orkney's military history.

🛏 Sleeping

Hoy Centre   HOSTEL £

(☑ office hours 01856-873535, warden 01856-791315; https://orkney.campstead.com; dm/tw £20/57.70; 🅿🔊) This clean, bright, modern hostel has an enviable location, around 15 minutes' walk from Moaness Pier, at the base of the rugged Cuilags. Rooms are all en suite and include good-value family options; it also has a spacious kitchen and DVD lounge. It's open year-round: book via the website to avoid an admin fee (private rooms only).

Stromabank Hotel   INN ££

(☑ 01856-701494; www.stromabank.co.uk; Longhope; s/d £55/90; 🅿🔊) Perched on the hill above Longhope, the small atmospheric Stromabank Hotel has very acceptable, refurbished en suite rooms, as well as tasty home-cooked meals, including seafood and steaks (£8 to £14) using lots of local produce. (Served 6pm to 8pm Friday to Wednesday, plus noon to 2pm Sunday. It does meals for residents only on Thursday and takeaways on Saturday evenings.)

ⓘ Getting There & Away

Orkney Ferries (p942) runs a passenger/bike ferry (adult £4.25, 30 minutes, two to six daily) between Stromness and Moaness at Hoy's northern end, and a car ferry to Lyness (with one service to/from Longhope) from Houton on Mainland (passenger/car £4.25/13.60, 40 minutes, up to seven daily Monday to Friday, two or three Saturday and Sunday); book cars well in advance. Sunday service is from May to September only.

The Moaness ferry also stops at Graemsay. The Houton service also links to Flotta.

Northern Islands

The group of windswept islands north of Mainland is a haven for birds, rich in archaeological sites and blessed with wonderful white-sand beaches and azure seas. Though some are hillier than others, all offer a broadly similar landscape of flattish green farmland running down to scenic coastline. Some give a real sense of what Orkney was like before the modern world impinged upon island life.

Accessible by reasonably priced ferry or plane, the islands are well worth exploring. Though you can see 'the sights' in a matter of hours, the key is to stay a day or two and relax into the pace of island life.

Note that the 'ay' at the end of island names (from the Old Norse for 'island') is pronounced closer to 'ee'.

❶ Getting There & Away

Orkney Ferries (p942) and Loganair Inter-Isles Air Service (p942) enable you to make day trips to many of the islands from Kirkwall.

Most islands offer a bus service that meets ferries: you may have to call to book this. The same operator often offers island tours.

Westray

POP 600

If you've time to visit only one of Orkney's Northern Islands, make Westray (www.west raypapawestray.co.uk) the one. The largest of the group, it has rolling farmland, handsome sandy beaches, great coastal walks and several appealing places to stay.

◉ Sights

★ **Noltland Castle**   CASTLE
(www.historicenvironment.scot; ⊙8am-8pm) **FREE**
A half-mile west of Pierowall stands this sturdy ruined tower house, built in the 16th century by Gilbert Balfour, aide to Mary, Queen of Scots. The castle is super-atmospheric and bristles with shot holes, part of the defences of the deceitful Balfour, who plotted to murder Cardinal Beaton and, after being exiled, the

king of Sweden. Like a pantomime villain, he met a sticky end.

Noup Head   NATURE RESERVE
FREE This bird reserve at Westray's northwestern tip is a dramatic area of sea cliffs, with vast numbers of breeding seabirds from April to July. You can walk here along the clifftops from a car park, passing the impressive chasm of Ramni Geo, and return via the lighthouse access road (4 miles).

🛏 Sleeping & Eating

Chalmersquoy & the Barn   B&B, HOSTEL £
(☑01857-677214; www.chalmersquoywestray.co. uk; Pierowall; dm/s/q £24/32/72, B&B s/d £58/80, apt for 4/6 £60/100, tent sites £9-12 plus per adult/child £2/1; ℗🛜) This excellent, intimate, modern hostel is an Orcadian gem. It's heated throughout and has pristine kitchen facilities and an inviting lounge; rooms sleep two or three in comfort. Out front, the lovely owners have top self-catering apartments with great views, and spacious en suite B&B rooms. There's also a campsite and a fabulous byre that hosts atmospheric concerts. A recommended all-round choice.

★ **West Manse**   B&B £
(☑01857-677482; www.westmanse.co.uk; Westside; r per person £25; ℗🛜🐕) 🍃 No timetables reign at this imposing house with arcing coastal vistas; make your own breakfast when you feel like it. Your welcoming hosts have introduced a raft of green solutions for heating, fuel and more. Kids will love this unconventional place, with its play nooks and hobbit house, while art exhibitions, eclectic workshops, venerably comfortable furniture and clean air are drawcards for parents.

Pierowall Hotel   PUB FOOD £
(☑01857-677472; www.pierowallhotel.co.uk; Pierowall; mains £9-14; ⊙food noon-2pm & 5-9pm May-Sep, noon-1.30pm & 6-8pm Oct-Apr; 🛜) The heart of the Westray community, this refurbished local pub is famous throughout Orkney for its popular fish and chips – whatever has turned up in the day's catch from the hotel's boats is displayed on the blackboard. There are also some curries available, but the sea is the way to go here. It also has rooms, and hires out bikes (£10 per day).

❶ Getting There & Away

AIR
There are daily flights with Loganair (p942) from Kirkwall to Westray (one-way £37, 20 minutes).

BOAT

Orkney Ferries (p942) links Kirkwall with Rapness (passenger/car £8.35/19.70, 1½ hours, daily). A bus to the main town, Pierowall, meets the ferry.

Rousay

POP 200

Just off the north coast of Mainland, hilly Rousay merits exploration for its fine assembly of prehistoric sites, great views and relaxing away-from-it-all ambience. Connected by regular ferry from Tingwall, it makes a great little day trip, but you may well feel a pull to stay longer. A popular option is to hire a bike from Trumland Farm (p952) near the ferry and take on the 14-mile circuit of the island.

The island's principal sight is mighty **Midhowe Cairn & Broch** (www.historicenvironment.scot; ⊙24hr) FREE, dubbed the 'Great Ship of Death'. Built around 3500 BC and enormous, it's divided into compartments, in which the remains of 25 people were found. The site is 6 miles from the ferry on Rousay.

🛏 Sleeping

Trumland Farm HOSTEL **£**
(☑01856-821252; trumland@btopenworld.com; sites £7, dm £15-16; P 🐕) 🐾 An easy stroll from the ferry (turn left at the main road), this organic farm has a wee hostel with two dorms and a pretty little kitchen and common area. You can pitch tents and use the facilities; there's also well-equipped self-catering in a cottage and various farm buildings. Linen is £2 extra. Bikes can be hired here.

Taversoe INN **££**
(☑01856-821325; www.taversoehotel.co.uk; s £40-50, d £80-95; P 🛜) Two miles west from the ferry pier, Rousay's only hotel is an attractively low-key place, with renovated rooms offering excellent bathrooms – one suitable for people with disabilities – and beautiful water vistas. The best views are from the dining room, which serves good-value meals. The friendly owners will collect you from the ferry.

ℹ Getting There & Away

A small ferry connects Tingwall on Mainland with Rousay (passenger/bicycle/car £4.25/free/13.60, 30 minutes, up to six daily) and the nearby islands of Egilsay and Wyre.

Papa Westray

Known locally as Papay, this exquisitely peaceful, tiny island (4 miles by 1 mile) is home to possibly Europe's oldest domestic building, the 5500-year-old **Knap of Howar** (⊙24hr) FREE, and largest Arctic tern colony. Plus the two-minute hop from Westray is the world's shortest scheduled air service. It's a charming island with seals easily spotted while walking its coast.

🛏 Sleeping

Beltane House GUESTHOUSE, HOSTEL **£**
(☑01857-644224; www.papawestray.co.uk; Beltane; dm/s/d £20/28/44; P 🛜 🐕) Owned by the local community, this is Papa Westray's hub. It has the only shop, and functions as a makeshift pub on Saturday nights. One wing is a hostel with bunks, the other a guesthouse with immaculate rooms with en suites. There are two kitchens, zippy wi-fi (when it works), a big lounge/eating area and views over grassy fields to the sea beyond.

It's just over a mile north of the ferry. You can also camp here (£8/4 per adult/child) and there are camping pods available that sleep two (£20 per person plus £5 for bedding).

ℹ Getting There & Away

AIR

There are two or three daily flights with Loganair (p942) to Papa Westray (£18, 20 minutes) from Kirkwall. The £21 return offer (you must stay overnight) is great value. Some of the Kirkwall flights go via Westray (£17, two minutes, the world's shortest scheduled flight) or North Ronaldsay (£17, 10 minutes).

BOAT

A passenger-only ferry with Orkney Ferries (p942) runs from Pierowall on Westray to Papa Westray (£4.15, 25 minutes, three to six daily in summer); the crossing is free if you've come straight from the Kirkwall–Westray ferry. From October to April the boat sails by arrangement (call 01857-677216). On Tuesday and Friday a car ferry from Kirkwall makes the journey to Papa Westray.

SHETLAND

Close enough to Norway geographically and historically to make nationality an ambiguous concept, the Shetland Islands are Britain's most northerly outpost. There's a Scandinavian lilt to the local accent, and

Shetland

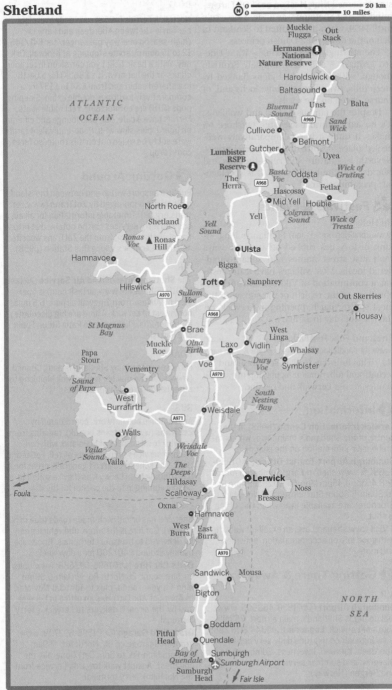

0 — 20 km
0 — 10 miles

Muckle Flugga
Out Stack
Hermaness National Nature Reserve
Haroldswick
Baltasound
Balta
Bluemull Sound
Unst
Sand Wick
Cullivoe
Belmont
Gutcher
Uyea
Lumbister RSPB Reserve
Oddsta
Wick of Gruting
Basta Voe
The Herra
Hascosay
Fetlar
Mid Yell
Houbie
North Roe
Yell
Colgrave Sound
Wick of Tresta
Shetland
Yell Sound
Ronas Voe
▲ Ronas Hill
Hamnavoe
Ulsta
ATLANTIC OCEAN
Bigga
Hillswick
Toft
Samphrey
Sullom Voe
Out Skerries
Housay
St Magnus Bay
Brae
West Linga
Muckle Roe
Olna Firth
Laxo
Vidlin
Whalsay
Papa Stour
Vementry
Voe
Dury Voe
Symbister
Sound of Papa
West Burrafirth
South Nesting Bay
Weisdale
Walls
Vaila Sound
Weisdale Voe
Vaila
The Deeps
Hildasay
Lerwick
Foula
Scalloway
Noss
Oxna
Bressay
Hamnavoe
West Burra
East Burra
Sandwick
Mousa
Bigton
NORTH SEA
Boddam
Fitful Head
Quendale
Bay of Quendale
Sumburgh
Sumburgh Airport
Sumburgh Head
Fair Isle

streets named King Haakon or St Olaf are reminders that Shetland was under Norse rule until 1469, when it was gifted to Scotland in lieu of the dowry of a Danish princess.

The stirringly bleak setting – it's a Unesco geopark – still feels uniquely Scottish, though, with deep, naked glens flanked by steep hills, twinkling, sky-blue lochs and, of course, sheep on the roads.

Despite the famous ponies and woollens, it's no agricultural backwater. Offshore oil makes it quite a busy, comparatively well-heeled place, despite drops in barrel prices. Nevertheless nature still rules the seas and islands, and the birdlife (p955) is spectacular: pack binoculars.

⭐ Festivals & Events

Up Helly Aa   CULTURAL
(www.uphellyaa.org; ⊘ Jan) Shetland's long Viking history has rubbed off in more ways than just street names and square-shouldered locals. Most villages have a fire festival, a continuation of Viking midwinter celebrations of the rebirth of the sun, with the most spectacular happening in Lerwick, on the last Tuesday in January.

Shetland Folk Festival   MUSIC
(www.shetlandfolkfestival.com; ⊘ late Apr or early May) This four-day festival sees local and international folk musicians playing in various venues across Lerwick and beyond.

ⓘ Information

Lerwick Information Centre (p958) In the centre of the Shetland's main town, with comprehensive information on the islands.

Sumburgh Airport Tourist Office (☑ 01950-460905; www.shetland.org; Sumburgh Airport; ⊘ 8.45am-4.45pm Mon-Fri, 10.15am-4pm Sat, 10.30am-5.30pm Sun, closed Sat Nov-Mar) Brochures are available even when this office is shut.

Visit www.shetland.org, an excellent website with good info on accommodation, activities and more.

ⓘ Getting There & Away

AIR

Sumburgh Airport (☑ 01950-460905; www.hial.co.uk) is Shetland's main airport, 25 miles south of Lerwick. **Loganair** (☑ 0344 800 2855; www.loganair.co.uk) runs daily services to Aberdeen, Kirkwall, Inverness, Edinburgh and Glasgow, and summer services to Manchester and Bergen (Norway).

BOAT

Northlink Ferries (p958) runs daily overnight car ferries between Aberdeen and Lerwick (high-season one-way passenger/car £41/146, 12 to 15 hours), some stopping at Kirkwall, Orkney. With a basic ticket you can sleep in recliner chairs or the bar area. It's £36.50 for a berth in a shared cabin and from £84 to £137 for a comparatively luxurious double cabin. Sleeping pods (£18) are comfortable, reclinable seats. Ferries have a cafe, bar, paid lounge and cinema on board, plus slow wi-fi. Road-equivalent tariffs were set to be rolled out on this route, so fares could drop.

ⓘ Getting Around

Public transport within and between the islands of Shetland is managed by **ZetTrans** (www.zettrans.org.uk). Timetable information for all air, bus and ferry services can be obtained at http://travel.shetland.org, from the ZetTrans website and from Lerwick's Viking Bus Station (p958).

AIR

The **Shetland Inter-Island Air Service** (Airtask; ☑ 01595-840246; www.airtask.com) is operated by Airtask from Tingwall airport, 6.5 miles northwest of Lerwick. There are big discounts for under-25s. Flights run to Papa Stour, Foula and Fair Isle.

BOAT

Ferry services run by Shetland Islands Council (www.shetland.gov.uk/ferries) link Mainland to other islands from various points.

BUS

An extensive bus network, coordinated by **ZetTrans** (www.zettrans.org.uk), radiates from Lerwick to all corners of Mainland, with connecting services to the islands of Yell, Fetlar and Unst. The schedules aren't generally great for day tripping from Lerwick as they're suited to people coming in to the capital for the day.

CAR

Shetland has broad, well-made roads (due to oil money). Car hire is fuss-free, and vehicles can be delivered to transport terminals. Prices are usually around £40/200 for a day/week.

Bolts Car Hire (☑ 01595-693636; www.boltscarhire.co.uk; 26 North Rd; ⊘ 9am-5.30pm Mon-Fri year-round, plus to 1pm Sat Nov-Mar, to 4pm Sat Apr-Oct) Has an office in Lerwick and by the airport; delivers to Lerwick's ferry terminal.

Grantfield Garage (☑ 01595-692709; www.grantfieldgarage.co.uk; North Rd; ⊘ 9am-5.30pm Mon-Fri, to 5pm Sat) Generally the cheapest. A short walk towards Lerwick from the Northlink ferry terminal.

Star Rent-a-Car (☑ 01595-692075; www.star rentacar.co.uk; 22 Commercial Rd; ⊙ 8am-7pm Mon-Fri, to 6pm Sat, noon-5pm Sun) Opposite Lerwick's Viking Bus Station. Has an office at Sumburgh Airport as well.

TAXI

Allied Taxis (☑ 01595-690069; www.shetlandtaxis.co.uk) Reliable taxi service across Mainland.

Lerwick

☑ 01595 / POP 7000

Built on the herring trade and modernised by the oil trade, Lerwick is Shetland's only real town, home to a third of the islands' population. It has a solidly maritime feel, with aquiline oil boats competing for space in the superb natural harbour with the dwindling fishing fleet. Wandering along atmospheric Commercial St is a delight, and the excellent Shetland Museum provides cultural background.

⊙ Sights & Activities

★ Shetland Museum   MUSEUM

(☑ 01595-695057; www.shetlandmuseumandarchives.org.uk; Hay's Dock; ⊙ 10am-4pm Mon-Sat, noon-5pm Sun Sep-Apr) **FREE** This museum houses an impressive collection of 5000 years' worth of culture, people and their interaction with this ancient landscape. Comprehensive but never dull, it covers everything from the archipelago's geology to its fishing industry, via local mythology – find out about scary *nyuggles* (ghostly horses), or detect *trows* (fairies). Pictish carvings and replica jewellery are among the finest pieces. The museum also includes a working lighthouse mechanism, a small gallery, a boat-building workshop and an archive for tracing Shetland ancestry.

Shetland Textile Museum   MUSEUM

(Böd of Gremista; ☑ 01595-694386; www.shetlandtextilemuseum.com; Gremista Rd; adult/child £3/free; ⊙ noon-5pm Tue-Sat, to 7pm Thu late-Apr–early Oct) A mile north of the centre of Lerwick, this four-square stone house, birthplace of P&O founder Arthur Anderson, was also once a fish-curing station. It now holds a good display on the knitted and woven textiles and patterns that Shetland is famous for.

Shetland Wildlife Boat Tours   BOATING

(☑ 07876-522292; www.thule-charters.co.uk; adult/child £45/35; ⊙ Apr-Sep) This outfit runs two daily trips to Noss in summer in a small

---

NATURE WATCHING IN SHETLAND

For birdwatchers, Shetland is paradise – a stopover for migrating Arctic species and host to vast seabird breeding colonies. June is the height of the season.

Every bird has its own name here: rain geese are red-throated divers, bonxies are great skuas, and alamooties are storm petrels. Clownish puffin antics are a highlight. The **Royal Society for the Protection of Birds** (RSPB; www.rspb.org.uk) maintains several reserves, plus there are National Nature Reserves at **Hermaness**, **Keen of Hamar** and **Noss**. **Foula** and **Fair Isle** also support large seabird populations.

Keep an eye on the sea: sea otters, orcas and other cetaceans are regularly sighted. Latest sightings are logged at useful www.nature-shetland.co.uk.

Shetland Nature Festival (www.shetlandnaturefestival.co.uk; ⊙ early Jul) has guided walks, talks, boat trips, open days and workshops.

---

catamaran. An underwater camera offers glimpses of the birds diving in the depths.

Shetland Seabird Tours   BIRDWATCHING

(☑ 07767 872260; www.shetlandseabirdtours.com; adult/child £45/25; ⊙ Apr-Oct) With two daily departures, these three-hour cruises head out to watch gannets feeding, observe the raucous seabird colonies of Bressay and Noss, and do a bit of seal-spotting. You can book at the Lerwick Information Centre (p958).

🛏 Sleeping

Woosung   B&B £

(☑ 01595-693687; conroywoosung@hotmail.com; 43 St Olaf St; d £70, s/d without bathroom £40/65; 🛜🍽) A budget gem in the heart of Lerwick B&B-land, this place has a wise and welcoming host, and comfortable, clean, good-value rooms with fridge and microwave. Two of them share a compact but spotless bathroom. The solid stone house dates from the 19th century, built by a clipper captain who traded tea out of the Chinese port it's named after.

Islesburgh House Hostel   HOSTEL £

(☑ 01595-745100; www.islesburgh.org.uk; King Harald St; dm/s/tw/q £21.50/39/43/61; 🅿@🛜) This typically grand Lerwick mansion houses an excellent hostel, with comfortable dorms, a shop, a laundry, a cafe and an industrial kitchen. Electronic keys offer reliable security and no curfew. It's wise to book ahead in summer. If nobody's about you can check in at the nearby community centre.

★**Fort Charlotte Guesthouse** B&B ££
(☎01595-692140; www.fortcharlotte.co.uk; 1 Charlotte St; s/d £40/80; ☎☎) Sheltering under Fort Charlotte's walls, this friendly place offers summery en suite rooms, including great singles. Views down the pedestrian

Lerwick

street are on offer in some; sloping ceilings and Asian touches add charm to others. It has local salmon for breakfast and a bike shed. Very popular; book ahead. There's also a self-catering option available.

Aald Harbour   B&B **££**
(☑01595-840689; www.aaldharbourbedandbreakfast.com; 7 Church Rd; s/d £55/80; ☞) With a handy location just off the pedestrian street, this upbeat spot has four cute rooms decked out in IKEA furniture with Shetland fabrics and toiletries creating a cosy Nordic fusion. Rooms have fridges and good showers and wi-fi; there are good public areas downstairs. Breakfast includes fresh fruit and smoked fish options; an on-site tearoom operates some days.

Rockvilla Guest House   B&B **££**
(☑01595-695804; www.rockvillaguesthouse.com; 88 St Olaf St; s/d £65/90; ☞☒) Some of Shetland's B&Bs are aimed more at oil workers than visitors, but this is quite the reverse: a relaxing, welcoming spot in a fine house behind a pretty garden. The three rooms are colour themed: Blue is bright, with a front-and-back outlook, Red is sultry, with a sofa in the window, and smaller Green is shyer, under the eaves.

Kveldsro House Hotel   HOTEL **£££**
(☑01595-692195; www.shetlandhotels.com; Greenfield Pl; s/d £118/145; ℗☞) Lerwick's best hotel overlooks the harbour and has a quiet but central setting. It's a dignified small set-up that will appeal to older visitors or couples. All doubles cost the same, but some are markedly better than others, with four-poster beds or water views. All boast new stylish bathrooms. The bar area is elegant and has fine perspectives.

🍴 Eating

Mareel Cafe   CAFE **£**
(☑01595-745500; www.mareel.org; Hay's Dock; light meals £3-5; ⊙9am-11pm Sun-Thu, 9am-1am Fri & Sat, food to 9pm; ☞) Buzzy, arty and colourful, this cheery venue in Mareel overlooks the water and does sandwiches and snacks by day, and shared platters, burgers and nachos in the evenings. The coffee is decent, too, and it's a nice place for a drink. Cocktail mixing at weekends, DJs and other events spice it up.

Peerie Shop Cafe   CAFE **£**
(☑01595-692816; www.peerieshop.co.uk; Esplanade; light meals £3-8; ⊙8am-6pm Mon-Sat; ☞) If you've been craving proper espresso since leaving the mainland, head to this gem, with art exhibitions, wire-mounted halogens and industrial-gantry chic. Newspapers, scrumptious cakes and sandwiches, hot chocolate that you deserve after that blasting wind outside, and – less often – outdoor seating give everyone a reason to be here.

★ Fjarå   CAFE, BISTRO **££**
(☑01595-697388; www.fjaracoffee.com; Sea Rd; mains £8-22; ⊙8am-10pm Tue-Sat, 10am-6pm Sun, food until 8pm; ☞) A cute wooden building in a super location, Fjarå is perched above a rocky shore and takes full advantage, with big picture windows looking out over the water and occasionally some basking seals. It does a bit of everything, with breakfasts, sandwiches, salads and bagels, plus beers, cocktails and some excellent dinner offerings, including creative burgers, game and local seafood.

★ Hay's Dock   SCOTTISH, CAFE **££**
(☑01595-741569; www.haysdock.co.uk; Hay's Dock, Shetland Museum; mains lunch £8-13, dinner

£17-24; ⊙ 10am-3pm Mon-Thu, 10am-3pm & 5-9pm Fri & Sat; 🛜🖩) 🖉 Upstairs in the Shetland Museum, this place sports a wall of picture windows and a fair-weather balcony that overlooks the harbour. Clean lines and pale wood recall Scandinavia, but the menu relies on carefully selected local and Scottish produce, with a substantial dash of international influence. Lunch ranges from delicious fish and chips to chowder, while evening menus concentrate on seafood and steak.

Drinking & Nightlife

Captain Flint's   PUB
(🖉 01595-692249; 2 Commercial St; ⊙ 11am-1am; 🛜) This upstairs port-side bar has a distinctly nautical, creaky-wooden feel. There's a cross-section of young 'uns, tourists, boat folk and older locals. It has live music some nights and a pool table tucked away on another level. Try a G&T with the seaweed-infused version of the local Reel gin.

Mareel   ARTS CENTRE
(🖉 01595-745500; www.mareel.org; Hay's Dock) Modern Mareel is a thriving arts centre, with a cinema, concert hall and cafe in a great waterside location.

❶ Information

Lerwick Information Centre (🖉 01595-693434; www.shetland.org; cnr Commercial & Mounthooly Sts; ⊙ 9am-5pm Mon-Sat & 10am-4pm Sun Apr-Sep, 10am-4pm Mon-Sat Oct-Mar) Helpful, with a good range of books and maps.

❶ Getting There & Away

BOAT

Northlink Ferries (🖉 0845 600 0449; www.northlinkferries.co.uk; 🛜) from Aberdeen and Kirkwall dock at **Holmsgarth Terminal** (Holmsgarth Rd), a 15-minute walk northwest from the town centre.

BUS

From **Viking Bus Station** (🖉 01595-744868; Commercial Rd), buses service various corners of the archipelago, including regular services to/from Sumburgh Airport.

Sumburgh

With sea cliffs, and grassy headlands jutting out into sparkling blue waters, Sumburgh is one of the most scenic places on Mainland, with a far greener landscape than the peaty north. It has a handful of excellent attractions clustered near Shetland's major airport.

◉ Sights & Activities

★ Sumburgh Head
Visitor Centre   LIGHTHOUSE, MUSEUM
(🖉 01595-694688; www.sumburghhead.com; adult/child £6/2; ⊙ 11am-5.30pm Apr-Sep) High on the cliffs at Sumburgh Head, this excellent attraction is set across several buildings. Displays explain about the lighthouse, foghorn and radar station that operated here, and there's a good exhibition on the local marine creatures and birds. You can visit the lighthouse itself on a guided tour for an extra charge.

Jarlshof   ARCHAEOLOGICAL SITE
(🖉 01950-460112; www.historicenvironment.scot; adult/child £6/3.60; ⊙ 9.30am-5.30pm Apr-Sep, to 4.30pm Oct-Mar) Old and new collide here, with Sumburgh airport right by this picturesque, instructive archaeological site. Various periods of occupation from 2500 BC to AD 1500 can be seen; the complete change upon the Vikings' arrival is obvious: their rectangular longhouses present a marked contrast to the preceding brochs, roundhouses and wheelhouses. Atop the site is 16th-century Old House, named 'Jarlshof' in a novel by Sir Walter Scott. There's an informative audio tour included with admission.

Old Scatness   ARCHAEOLOGICAL SITE
(🖉 01595-694688; www.shetland-heritage.co.uk/old-scatness; adult/child £5/4; ⊙ 10.15am-4.30pm Fri mid-May–Aug; 🖩) This dig brings Shetland's prehistory vividly to life; it's a must-see for archaeology buffs, but fun for kids, too. Clued-up guides in Iron Age clothes show you the site, which has provided important clues on the Viking takeover and dating of Shetland material. It has an impressive broch from around 300 BC, roundhouses and later wheelhouses. Best of all is the reconstruction with peat fire and working loom. At the time of research, a lack of funding had badly restricted the opening hours.

★ Sumburgh Head   BIRDWATCHING
(www.rspb.org.uk) At Mainland's southern tip, these cliffs offer a good chance to get up close to puffins, and huge nesting colonies of fulmars, guillemots and razorbills. If you're lucky, you might spot dolphins, minke whales or orcas. Also here is

FOULA

Out in the Atlantic Ocean, about 15 miles southwest of Walls, stands the remote, wind-swept island of Foula (Bird Island). Seen from Mainland it has a distinctive outline, rising to a series of peaks – the highest point is **Da Sneug** (418m) – then dropping dramatically to the sea at the cliffs of **Da Kame** (376m). It competes with Fair Isle for the title of Britain's most isolated community, with just a handful of human inhabitants, a scattering of Shetland ponies and 1500 sheep, plus 500,000 seabirds, including the rare Leach's petrel and Manx shearwater, and the world's largest colony of great skuas.

Accommodation is very limited: the best option is **Ristie** (☑01595-753293; www.face-book.com/ristieselfcatering; studio/house from £35/50), at the northern end of Foula, which offers comfortable self-catering accommodation.

There are flights with Shetland Inter-Island Air Service (p954) to Foula from Tingwall (£79 return), with day trips possible.

BK Marine (☑01595-840208; www.bkmarine.co.uk) has ferries from Walls (adult/car and driver one-way £5.50/7.20, two hours) two to three times a week; bookings are essential.

the excellent Sumburgh Head Visitor Centre (p958), in the lighthouse buildings.

ℹ️ Getting There & Away

Bus 6 runs to Sumburgh and Sumburgh Airport from Lerwick (£2.90 to Sumburgh, £3.30 to the airport; one hour, five to seven daily).

The North Isles

Yell, Unst and Fetlar make up the North Isles of the Shetlands, which are connected to each other by ferry, as is Yell to Mainland. All are great for nature-watching; Unst has the most to offer overall.

ℹ️ Getting There & Away

An integrated bus and ferry connection runs once daily Monday to Saturday from Lerwick to Yell and on to Unst and Fetlar. Smaller local buses serve island destinations off the principal bus route.

If you're going to spend a night on both Yell and Fetlar or Unst, consider visiting Yell on the way back, as the second ferry is free if you are coming from Mainland that same day.

Yell

☑ 01957 / POP 1000

Yell if you like but nobody will hear; the desolate peat moors here are typical Shetland scenery. The bleak landscape has an appeal, though. Yell is all about colours: the browns and vivid, lush greens of the bogland, grey clouds thudding through the skies and the steely blue waters of the North Atlantic,

which are never far away. The peat makes the ground look cracked and parched, although it's swimming most of the year. Though many folk fire on through to Unst, Yell offers several good hill walks, especially around the Herra peninsula, about halfway up the west coast.

🛏️ Sleeping & Eating

Quam B&B B&B ££

(☑01957-766256; www.quambandbyellshetland.co.uk; Westsandwick; d £80; P ☎) Just off the main road through Yell island, this farm B&B has friendly owners and three good rooms. Breakfast features eggs from the farm, which also has cute ponies that you can meet. Dinners (£15 per person) can be arranged.

Gutcher Goose CAFE £

(☑01957-744783; www.facebook.com/gutchercafe; Gutcher; light meals £3-6; ☻9am-5pm Mon-Sat Apr-early Oct; ☎) Just by the Unst ferry slip, this place is a fine spot to wait for the boat. Mostly operating as a shop, it also offers decent coffee plus sandwiches, panini and breakfast fare.

Unst

POP 600

You're fast running out of Scotland once you cross to rugged Unst (www.unst.org). Scotland's most northerly inhabited island is prettier than nearby Yell, with bare, velvety-smooth hills and settlements clinging to waterside locations, fiercely resisting the buffeting winds.

◉ Sights

★ Hermaness National
Nature Reserve   NATURE RESERVE
(www.nnr-scotland.org.uk) At marvellous Hermaness headland, a 4.5-mile round walk takes you to cliffs where gannets, fulmars and guillemots nest, and numerous puffins frolic. You can also see Scotland's most northerly point, the rocks of **Out Stack**, and **Muckle Flugga**, with its lighthouse built by Robert Louis Stevenson's uncle. Duck into the **Hermaness Visitor Centre** (☑01595-711278; ⊗9am-5pm Apr-early Sep) `FREE`, with its poignant story about one-time resident Albert Ross.

★ Unst Bus Shelter   LANDMARK
(Bobby's Bus Shelter; www.unstbusshelter.shetland.co.uk; Baltasound) At the turn-off to Littlehamar, just past Baltasound, is Britain's most impressive bus stop. Enterprising locals, tired of waiting in discomfort, decided to do a job on it, and it now boasts posh seating, novels, numerous decorative features and a visitors' book to sign. The theme and colour scheme changes yearly.

Unst Boat Haven   MUSEUM
(☑01957-711809; Haroldswick; adult/child £3/free, combined ticket with Unst Heritage Centre £5; ⊗11am-4pm Mon-Sat, 2-4pm Sun May-Sep) This large shed is a boatie's delight, packed with a beautifully cared for collection of Shetland rowing and sailing boats, all with a backstory. Old photos and maritime artefacts speak of the glory days of Unst fishing. There's a seasonal tearoom out front.

⊨ Sleeping

★ Gardiesfauld Hostel   HOSTEL, CAMPSITE £
(☑01957-755279; www.gardiesfauld.shetland.co.uk; 2 East Rd, Uyeasound; per adult/child tent sites £8/4, dm £16/9; ⊗Apr-Sep; **P** ⊗) This spotless hostel has very spacious dorms with lockers, family rooms, a garden, an elegant lounge and a wee conservatory dining area with great bay views. You can camp here, too; there are separate areas for tents and vans. The bus stops right outside. Bring 20p coins for the showers. It will open in winter if you prebook.

Baltasound Hotel   HOTEL ££
(☑01957-711334; www.baltasoundhotel.co.uk; Baltasound; s £68-75, d £125-135; ⊗Apr–mid-Oct; **P** ⊗) Brightly decorated rooms – some bigger than others – are complemented by wooden chalets arrayed around the lawn here. Rooms feel a little overpriced so it's worth the small upgrade to the 'large doubles', which sport modern bathrooms. There's a lovely country outlook, and evening bar meals in a dining room dappled by the setting sun. Contact the hotel for winter opening details.

Understand Great Britain

Great Britain Today

Britain is a nation poised on the brink of seismic change. For the first time in four decades, it will no longer be part of the EU (European Union), and despite two years of long and bitter negotiations, still no one has the faintest idea quite what the future holds. Major questions loom: over the state of the union, the prospects for the economy, the direction of UK politics and the future of the monarchy. Hold on to your hats: it looks like Britain's in for a bumpy ride.

Best on Film

Brief Encounter (1945) Classic tale of a buttoned-up English love affair.

Whisky Galore! (1949) Classic Ealing comedy about Scots outfoxing the government when a cargo of whisky gets shipwrecked; remade in 2016.

Trainspotting (1996) The gritty underbelly of life among Edinburgh drug addicts.

Withnail & I (1987) Cult comedy about two out-of-work actors on a disastrous Lake District holiday.

Hope and Glory (1987) Moving tale of life in London during the Blitz, based on director John Boorman's own experiences.

Submarine (2010) Scabrous coming-of-age tale set in 1980s-era Swansea.

Best in Print

Notes from a Small Island (Bill Bryson; 1995) An American's fond and astute take on Britain.

Raw Spirit (Iain Banks; 2003) An enjoyable jaunt around Scotland in search of the perfect whisky.

Slow Coast Home (Josie Drew; 2003) The chatty tale of a 5000-mile cycle tour through England and Wales.

On the Black Hill (Bruce Chatwin; 1982) Traces 20th-century Welsh rural life through the lens of oddball twins.

On the Slow Train (Michael Williams; 2011) A paean to the pleasure of British rail travel.

The Brexit Question

The fallout from Britain's decision to withdraw from the EU rumbles on across the UK. Decided by a narrow 52% to 48% vote in favour in the 2016 referendum, Britain's exit from the EU (colloquially known as Brexit) looms large wherever you care to look or listen: on every news bulletin, talk show and phone-in, and it's the prevailing topic of conversation in pubs, parks and workplaces up and down the land. With negotiations ongoing, so much remains up in the air: heavyweight questions over immigration, trade, investment and the hot-button topic of the Northern Irish border have yet, at the time of writing, to be decided. After the March 2019 deadline (when the UK ceased to be a voting member of the EU), a two-year transition period has been agreed to that will smooth the separation, at least for a while – but politicians can only dodge the really difficult questions for so long. In the meantime, supporters of Brexit (or Brexiteers, as they're dubbed by the press) maintain the nation can look forward to a bright global future, while opponents point out a swath of negative economic forecasts. In truth, no one can really say with certainty how the long-term story will play out.

What's most surprising about the Brexit issue is that so far, no one has addressed the fact that of Britain's four constituent nations, the vote was split precisely down the middle: 54% of English voters and 53% of Welsh voters returned a vote to leave, while 62% of Scots and 56% of Northern Irish voted to remain. The split raises a tricky question: can it really be democratically legitimate for the will of English and Welsh voters to supersede that of their neighbours in Scotland and Northern Ireland? So far, it's a question that remains unanswered – and if nothing else, paints an unhappy picture of a nation more divided than ever. It also underlines the peculiar truth that England and Britain, and notions of

Englishness and Britishness, are two very different – and not necessarily compatible – things.

So where does all this leave Britain, and Europe for that matter? All we know for sure is that on Friday 29 March 2019, Britain gave up being a member of the EU. Exactly what that means for the nation, and its future, is still really anyone's guess.

North & South

Another perennially thorny topic is the intractable divide between Britain's north and south. For decades, the north has lagged behind the south in nearly every significant economic indicator you could care to mention: employment, wages, life expectancy and average house prices have remained significantly lower in northern England's cities and counties than in the prosperous, London-centric south. It's been an issue since the late 1970s and '80s, propelled by the ongoing decline of traditional heavy industries such as shipbuilding, coal mining and steel-making. So far, the much mooted idea of recreating a 'northern powerhouse', by improving transport links and boosting industry, hasn't amounted to much – but there are signs that the north is regaining something of its old swagger. House prices are rising. Unemployment is falling. The HS2 high-speed rail link is underway. Manchester and Liverpool have both appointed their first directly elected mayors, while Hull was named UK City of Culture in 2017, and Newcastle hosted the high-profile Great Exhibition of the North in 2018.

The topic of England's north–south divide ties in to another larger divide, one that's rumbled on for three centuries – the fraught and sometimes fractious relationship between Scotland and England. Though 55% of Scots voted to remain part of the UK in the 2014 independence referendum, Scotland's anti-Brexit stance has opened yet another political gulf between north and south – and raised the potential prospect of a second referendum (catchily dubbed 'indyref2') in the not-too-distant future. Once again, the 300-year-old union looks far from secure, and this time no one has any compelling solutions on how to bridge the great divide.

A Green & Pleasant Land?

Despite its reputation as a green and pleasant land, trouble is afoot in Britain's beloved countryside. Many wildlife species are in serious decline, affected by construction, habitat loss, pesticides and farming methods. A major report in 2016 stated that more than one in 10 of the UK's wildlife species are threatened with extinction, including much-loved icons such as the hedgehog. But it's not all doom and gloom: while many species are struggling, some – such as the badger and fox – are increasing in number, while others, such as the once-endangered otter, have staged unlikely comebacks. But with the prospect of climate

POPULATION: **66 MILLION**

AREA: **88,500 SQ MILES**

GDP PER CAPITA: **£29,670**

GDP GROWTH: **0.2%**

INFLATION: **2.3%**

UNEMPLOYMENT: **4.2%**

if Great Britain were 100 people

87 would be white
7 would be Asian
3 would be black
3 would be mixed/other

belief systems
(% of population)

59 — Christian

33 — no religion or not stated

4.5 — Muslim

1.5 — Hindu

2 — other

population per sq km

BRITAIN

USA

FRANCE

≈ 40 people

Best in Music

Waterloo Sunset (The Kinks; 1967) Ray Davies' love letter to a London sunset.

A Day in the Life (The Beatles; 1967) The standout from *Sgt Pepper's*.

God Save The Queen (The Sex Pistols; 1977) The Pistols do the national anthem.

Ghost Town (The Specials; 1981) Classic track from the maestros of two-tone.

Parklife (Blur; 1994) Britpop-meets-Barnet courtesy of Damon Albarn and co.

Common People (Pulp; 1994) Jarvis Cocker's wry commentary on British class.

Teardrop (Massive Attack; 1998) The quintessential trip-hop track.

Best Blogs

Guido Fawkes (www.order-order. com) The hottest gossip from Westminster politics.

CaughtOffside (www.caughtoffside. com) The blog of choice for British football fanatics.

Elizabeth's Kitchen Diary (www. elizabethskitchendiary.co.uk) Hugely popular food blog from a Canadian expat living in the Shetland Islands.

The Londoner (www.londoner.me) Lifestyle blog from capital-dweller Rosie Jones.

The Quietus (www.thequietus.com) Music, art, film and cultural comment with a British slant.

change, major house-building programs and infrastructure projects on the horizon – including the controversial HS2 high-speed railway and a third Heathrow runway – the need to protect Britain's precious wildlife is now more urgent than ever.

Thankfully, the UK's network of 15 national parks and numerous AONBs (Areas of Outstanding Natural Beauty) have provided a much-needed safe haven for many threatened species, and plans are currently being considered to increase their number – not least because the Lake District became the first UK national park to be recognised as a Unesco World Heritage Site, in 2017. But prestige and popularity bring their own pressures – just ask the Isle of Skye, which has pondered limiting visitor numbers in order to protect the island's natural environment.

A Right Royal Affair

With HM Queen Elizabeth II in her 10th decade and Prince Harry's wedding to American actress Meghan Markle in 2018, thoughts are beginning to turn to the next generation of the British monarchy – particularly the question of succession. Officially, the next in line to the throne is the Queen's eldest son, Prince Charles, although some commentators believe that, thanks to his strong political views and controversial second marriage to Camilla Parker Bowles, he may perhaps pass over the throne in favour of his eldest son, Prince William. Despite the uncertainty, one thing seems clear – British support for the Royal Family remains high, with most opinion polls suggesting that more than three-quarters of people still support the idea of constitutional monarchy.

History

Britain may be a small country on the edge of Europe, but it has rarely been on the sidelines of history. For thousands of years, invaders and immigrants have arrived, settled and made their mark. The result is Britain's fascinating mix of landscape, culture and language. That rich historic legacy – everything from Stonehenge to Culloden, via Hadrian's Wall, Canterbury Cathedral, Caernarfon Castle and the Tower of London – is one of the country's most absorbing aspects.

First Arrivals

Around 4000 BC, as glaciers retreated in the wake of the Ice Age, a group of migrants arrived from Europe, but instead of hunting and moving on, they settled in one place and started farming. Alongside their fields, Britain's Stone Age people used rocks and turf to build massive burial mounds; the remains of many of these can still be seen, including West Kennet Long Barrow in Wiltshire, Pentre Ifan in Pembrokeshire and Maeshowe in Orkney. But the most impressive legacies left by these nascent Britons were the enigmatic stone circles of Callanish, Avebury and Stonehenge.

> Probably built around 3000 BC, Stonehenge has stood on Salisbury Plain for more than 5000 years and is older than the famous Great Pyramids of Egypt.

Iron & Celts

During the Iron Age (from 800 BC to AD 100) the population expanded and began to divide into specific tribes. Forests were cleared as more land was used for farming. This led to a patchwork pattern of fields, woods and small villages that still exists today in many parts of rural Britain. As the population grew, territorial defence became an issue, so the Iron Age people left another legacy: the great 'earthwork' castles of southern England, stone forts in northern England and brochs (defensive towers) in Wales and Scotland.

The Celts, a people who originally migrated from Central Europe, had settled across much of Britain by around 500 BC. A Celtic-British population developed, comprising about 20 tribes, including the Cantiaci (in today's county of Kent), the Iceni (Norfolk), the Brigantes (northern

TIMELINE	4000 BC	c 500 BC	c 55 BC
	Neolithic peoples migrate from continental Europe. They differ significantly from previous arrivals: instead of hunting and moving on, they settle in one place and start farming.	The Celts, a group originally from Central Europe, arrive in Britain, and by the middle of the 1st millennium BC have settled across much of the island, absorbing the indigenous people.	Relatively small groups of Roman invaders under the command of Julius Caesar make forays into southern England from the northern coast of Gaul (today's France).

Boudica was queen of the Iceni, a Celtic-British tribe whose territory was invaded by the Romans around AD 60. A year later, she led an army against the Roman settlements of Camulodunum (now Colchester) and Londinium (London), but was eventually defeated at the Battle of Watling Street (in today's Shropshire).

England), the Picts and Caledonii (Scotland), the Ordivices (parts of Wales) and the Scotti (Ireland).

You noticed the Latin-sounding names? That's because the tribal tags were first handed out by the next arrivals on Britain's shores...

Enter the Romans

Julius Caesar, the Roman ruler everyone remembers, made forays to the island of Britain in 55 BC. But the real Roman invasion happened a century later, when Emperor Claudius led a ruthless campaign resulting in the Romans controlling pretty much everywhere in southern England by AD 50.

Much of the occupation was straightforward: several Celtic-British tribal kings realised collaboration was more profitable than battle. It wasn't all plain sailing, though, and some locals fought back. The most famous freedom fighter was warrior-queen Boudica, who led an army as far as Londinium, the Roman port on the present site of London.

However, opposition was mostly sporadic and no real threat to the legions' military might. By around AD 80 the new province of Britannia (much of today's England and Wales) was firmly under Roman rule.

Exit the Romans

Settlement by the Romans in Britain lasted almost four centuries. Intermarriage was common between locals and incomers (many from other parts of the empire, including today's Belgium, Spain and Syria), and a Romano-British population evolved, particularly in the towns, while indigenous Celtic-British culture remained in some areas, including parts of Wales, Scotland and Cornwall.

To control the territory they'd occupied, the Romans built forts and garrisons across Britain, especially in Wales and England. Many of these developed into towns, which can be recognised by names ending in 'chester' or 'caster' (from the Latin *castrum*, meaning 'military camp'), such as Lancaster, Winchester, Manchester, Cirencester and Chester.

Along with stability and wealth, the Romans introduced a new religion called Christianity, officially recognised by Emperor Constantine in AD 313. Although Romano-British culture was thriving by this time, back in its Mediterranean heartland the empire was already in decline.

It was an untidy finale. Britannia was simply dumped by Rome, and the colony slowly fizzled out of existence. But historians are tidy folk, and the end of Roman power in Britain is generally dated at AD 410.

The Emergence of England

Britain's post-Roman power vacuum didn't go unnoticed and once again invaders arrived from the European mainland. Angles and Saxons (Teutonic tribes from the lands we now call Germany, Denmark and the Netherlands) advanced across the former Roman turf.

Historians disagree on exactly what happened next. Either the Anglo-Saxons largely replaced or absorbed the Romano-British and Celtic pop-

AD 43	60	60	122
Emperor Claudius leads the first proper Roman invasion of England. His army wages a ruthless campaign, and the Romans control most of southern England by AD 50.	Warrior-queen Boudica leads an army against the Romans, destroys the Roman town of Colchester and gets as far as Londinium, the Roman port on the present site of London.	In Wales the Celts, led by their mystic faith healers, the druids, fight a last stand on Anglesey against the Roman army; they are beaten but not totally conquered.	Rather than conquer wild north British tribes, Emperor Hadrian settles for building a coast-to-coast barricade. For nearly 300 years, Hadrian's Wall marks the northernmost limit of the Roman Empire.

ulation, or the indigenous tribes simply adopted Anglo-Saxon language and culture. Either way, by the late 6th century much of the area we now call England was dominated by the Anglo-Saxons and divided into three main kingdoms: Wessex (in today's southern England), Mercia (the Midlands) and Northumbria (northeastern England and southeastern Scotland).

In many areas the original inhabitants lived alongside the Anglo-Saxons and remained unaffected by the incomers (the Celtic language was still being spoken in parts of southern England when the Normans invaded 500 years later), but the overall impact was immense: the core of the modern English language is Anglo-Saxon, many place names have Anglo-Saxon roots, and the very term 'Anglo-Saxon' has become a (much abused and factually incorrect) byword for 'pure English'.

The Waking of Wales

The Celts on the western fringes of the British Isles (particularly in Ireland) kept alive their own distinct yet Roman-influenced culture. And while the Anglo-Saxons occupied eastern Britain, towards the end of the 5th century the Scotti (from today's Ireland) invaded what is today Wales and western Scotland.

In response to the invasion, people from the kingdom of Gododdin (near today's Edinburgh) moved to northwest Wales to drive out the invaders, then stayed and settled in the area, which became the kingdom of Gwynedd. (The modern county in northern Wales still proudly bears this name.) More settlers came to Wales from Cornwall and western France, and Christian missionaries arrived from Ireland in the 6th and 7th centuries.

The people of Wales were also under pressure to the east, harassed by the Anglo-Saxons. In response, by the 8th century the disparate tribes of Wales had started to band together and sow the seeds of nationhood. They called themselves *cymry* (fellow countrymen), and today Cymru is the Welsh word for Wales.

The Stirring of Scotland

While Wales was becoming established in the west of Britain, similar events were taking place to the north. The Picts were the region's dominant indigenous tribe (in the north and east) and named their kingdom Alba, which remains to this day the Gaelic word for Scotland. Ancient Britons inhabited the southwest.

Following the end of Roman rule in Britannia, Alba was invaded from two sides: first, towards the end of the 5th century, the Scotti crossed the sea from Ireland and established the kingdom of Dalriada (in what is

HISTORY THE WAKING OF WALES

History Websites

www.royal.uk

www.bbc.co.uk/history

www.english monarchs.co.uk

www.victorianweb. org

Christianity was introduced to Britain by the Romans and adopted by the Celts, but the Anglo-Saxons were pagans, and their invasion of Britain forced the Christian religion, along with other aspects of Celtic culture, to the edges of the British Isles – today's Wales, Scotland and Ireland.

c 410	5th century	Late 5th century	597
As the classical world's greatest empire finally declines after centuries of relative peace and prosperity, Roman rule ends in Britain with more of a whimper than a bang.	Teutonic tribes (known today as the Anglo-Saxons) from modern Germany, Denmark and the Netherlands migrate to England and quickly spread across much of the country.	The Scotti people (from today's Ireland) invade Alba, the land of the Picts (today's Scotland). Where Argyll stands today they establish the kingdom of Dalriada.	Pope Gregory sends missionary St Augustine to southern England to revive interest in Christianity among the southern Anglo-Saxons. His colleague St Aidan similarly converts many people in northern England.

now Argyll); then in the 7th century Anglo-Saxons from the expanding English kingdom of Northumbria moved in to colonise the southeast. But by this time the Scotti were well dug in alongside the Picts, foreshadowing the time when yet another name – Scotland – would be applied to northern Britain.

Myths and Legends of the British Isles by Richard Barber is an ideal read if you want a break from firm historical facts. Learn about King Arthur and the Knights of the Round Table, plus much more from the mists of time.

The Viking Era

In the 9th century, just as the new territories of England, Wales and Scotland were becoming established, Britain was yet again invaded by a bunch of pesky continentals. This time, it was the Vikings – Nordic people from today's Scandinavia.

It's another classic historical image: blonde hair, horned helmets, big swords, square-sailed longboats, rape and pillage. Tradition has it that Vikings turned up, killed everyone, took everything and left. There's *some* truth in some of that, but in reality many Vikings settled in Britain, and their legacy is especially evident in today's northern England (notably Yorkshire), Orkney and Shetland.

After conquering northern and eastern areas, the Vikings started to expand into central England. Blocking their route were the Anglo-Saxon armies led by Alfred the Great, the king of Wessex and one of English history's best-known characters.

The battles that followed were seminal to the foundation of the nation-state of England, but the fighting didn't all go Alfred's way. For a few months he was on the run, wading through swamps, hiding in peasant hovels and famously burning cakes while distracted by his predicament. It was the stuff of legend, and by 886 Alfred had gathered his strength and pushed the Vikings back to the north.

United England?

Thus England was divided in two: north and east was the Viking 'Danelaw', while south and west was Anglo-Saxon territory. Alfred was hailed as king of the English – the first time the Anglo-Saxons regarded themselves as a truly united people.

Alfred's son and successor was Edward the Elder. After more battles, he gained control of the Danelaw, and thus became the first king to rule the whole of England. His son, Athelstan, took the process a stage further and was specifically crowned King of England in 927. But it was hardly cause for celebration: the Vikings were still around, and later in the 10th century more raids from Scandinavia threatened this fledgling English unity. Over the following decades, control swung from English (King Edgar) to Dane (King Knut) and back to English again (King Edward the Confessor). As the country came to the end of the 1st millennium AD, the future was anything but certain.

685	8th century	850	9th century
The Pictish king Bridei defeats the Northumbrians at Nechtansmere in Angus, an against-the-odds victory that sets the foundations for Scotland as a separate entity.	King Offa of Mercia orders the construction of a clear border between his kingdom and Wales – a defensive ditch called Offa's Dyke, still visible today.	Vikings come from today's Scandinavia and conquer east and northeast England. They establish their capital at Jorvik, modern-day York.	Kenneth MacAlpin, the king of the Scotti, declares himself ruler of both the Scots *and* the Picts, thus uniting Scotland north of the Firth of Forth into a single kingdom.

Highs & Lows in Wales

Meanwhile, as England fought off the Viking threat, Wales was also dealing with the Nordic intruders. Building on the initial cooperation forced upon them by Anglo-Saxon oppression, in the 9th and 10th centuries the small kingdoms of Wales began cooperating, through necessity, to repel the Vikings.

King Rhodri Mawr (who died in 878) defeated a Viking force off the Isle of Anglesey and began the unification process. His grandson Hywel the Good is thought to have been responsible for drawing up a set of laws to bind the disparate Welsh tribes. But just as Wales was becoming a recognisable entity, the fledgling country was faced with more destructive onslaughts than it could handle and in 927 the Welsh kings recognised the Anglo-Saxon King Athelstan as their overlord, in exchange for an anti-Viking alliance.

Scotland Becomes a Kingdom

In the 9th century, the king of the Scotti of Dalriada was one Kenneth MacAlpin. His father was a Scot, but his mother was a Pictish princess, so MacAlpin took advantage of the Pictish custom of matrilineal succession to declare himself ruler of both the Scots *and* the Picts, and therefore king of all Alba.

In a surprisingly short time, the Scots gained cultural and political ascendancy. The Picts were absorbed, and their culture disappeared; from the union of Alba and Pictland came the beginnings of a Scottish kingdom.

In the 11th century, Scottish nation-building was further consolidated by King Malcolm III (whose most famous act was the 1057 murder of Macbeth, immortalised by William Shakespeare). With his English queen, Margaret, he founded the Canmore dynasty that would rule Scotland for the next two centuries.

1066 & All That

Back in England things were unsettled, as the royal pendulum swung between Saxon and Viking monarchs. When King Edward the Confessor died, the crown passed to Harold, his brother-in-law. That should've settled things, but Edward had a cousin in Normandy (the northern part of today's France) called William, who thought that *he* had a right to the throne of England.

The result was the Battle of Hastings in 1066, the most memorable of dates for anyone who's studied English history – or for anyone who hasn't. William sailed from Normandy with an army of Norman soldiers, the Saxons were defeated and Harold was killed (although not, despite popular belief, by an arrow in the eye).

The story of William Wallace is told in the Mel Gibson epic *Braveheart*. In devolution debates of the 1990s, the patriotic pride engendered by this movie did more for Scottish nationalism than any politician's speech.

The Year 1000 by Robert Lacey and Danny Danziger looks long and hard at English life a millennium ago. Apparently it was cold and damp then, too.

927	1040	1066	1085–86
Athelstan, grandson of Alfred the Great, son of Edward the Elder, is the first monarch to be specifically crowned King of England, building on his ancestors' success in regaining Viking territory.	Macbeth takes the Scottish throne after defeating Duncan in battle. This, and the fact that he was later killed by Duncan's son Malcolm, are the only parallels with the Shakespeare play.	Battle of Hastings – a crucial date in English history. Incumbent King Harold is defeated by an invading Norman army, and England has a new monarch: William the Conqueror.	The new Norman rulers establish the Domesday Book census. Within three years they have a snapshot of England's current stock and future potential.

Norman Wisdom

William became king of England, earning the title William the Conqueror. It was no idle nickname – to control the Anglo-Saxons, the Norman invaders wisely built castles across their newly won territory, and by 1086 the Domesday Book provided a census of England's current stock and future potential.

In the years after the invasion, the French-speaking Normans and the English-speaking Anglo-Saxons kept pretty much to themselves. A strict hierarchy of class developed, known as the feudal system.

Intermarriage was not completely unknown; William's son, Henry I, married a Saxon princess. Nonetheless, such unifying moves stood for nothing after Henry's death: a bitter struggle for succession followed, finally won by Henry II, who took the throne as the first king of the Plantagenet dynasty.

At the top of the feudal system came the monarch, followed by nobles (barons, dukes and bishops), then earls, knights, lords and ladies. At the bottom were peasants or 'serfs'. This strict hierarchy became the basis of a class system that still exists in Britain today.

Post-Invasion Wales & Scotland

To secure his new kingdom, and keep the Welsh in theirs, William the Conqueror built castles and appointed feudal barons along the border. The Lords Marcher, as they were known, became massively rich and powerful, and the parts of western England along the Welsh border are still called the Marches today.

In Scotland, King Malcolm III and Queen Margaret were more accommodating to Norman ways. Malcolm's successor, David I (1124–53), adopted the Norman feudal system, as well as granting land to great Norman families. By 1212 a courtier called Walter of Coventry remarked on how French-influenced the Scottish court was.

But while the French-Norman effect changed England and lowland Scotland over the following centuries, further north the Highland clans remained inaccessible in their glens, and were a law unto themselves for another 600 years.

Royal & Holy Squabbling

When the reign of England's Henry I came to an end, the enduring British habit of competition for the throne introduced an equally enduring tendency for bickering between royalty and the church. Things came to a head in 1170 when Henry II had the 'turbulent priest' Thomas Becket murdered in Canterbury Cathedral, where a memorial to Becket can still be seen today.

Perhaps the next king, Richard I, wanted to make amends for his forebears' unholy sentiments by leading a crusade (a Christian 'holy war') to liberate Jerusalem and the Holy Land from occupation by Muslim 'heathens' under their leader Saladin. The campaign became known as

1095	12th century	1215	13th century
The start of the First Crusade – a campaign of Christian European armies against the Muslim occupation of Jerusalem and the 'Holy Land'. A series of crusades continues until 1272.	Oxford University is founded. There's evidence of teaching in the area since 1096, but King Henry II's 1167 ban on students attending the University of Paris solidified Oxford's importance.	King John signs the Magna Carta, limiting the monarch's power for the first time in English history in an early step along the path towards constitutional rule.	Wales is invaded by English King Edward I, bringing to an end the rule of Welsh leader 'Llywelyn the Last'. Edward builds a ring of castles to suppress further Welsh uprisings.

MAGNA CARTA

In 1215 the barons found King John's erratic rule increasingly hard to swallow and forced him to sign a document called Magna Carta (the Great Charter), limiting the monarch's power for the first time in British history. Although originally intended as a set of handy ground rules, the Magna Carta was a fledgling bill of human rights that eventually led to the creation of parliament – a body to rule the country, independent of the throne. The signing took place at Runnymede, near Windsor, and you can still visit the site today.

the Third Crusade, and although the Christian armies captured the cities of Acre and Jaffa, they did not take Jerusalem.

Unfortunately, Richard's overseas activities meant he was too busy crusading to bother about governing England and in his absence the country fell into disarray, although his bravery and ruthlessness earned him the sobriquet Richard the Lionheart.

Richard was succeeded by his brother John, but under his harsh rule things got even worse for the general population. According to legend, during this time a nobleman called Robert of Loxley, better known as Robin Hood, hid in Sherwood Forest and engaged in a spot of wealth redistribution.

Expansionist Edward

Edward I of England (1272–1307) was a skilled ruler and ambitious general. During a busy 35-year reign he was unashamedly expansionist in his outlook, leading campaigns into Wales and Scotland.

Some decades earlier, the Welsh king Llywelyn the Great (d 1240) had attempted to set up a state in Wales, and his grandson Llywelyn the Last was recognised by Henry III as the first Prince (but not King) of Wales. But Edward I had no time for such niceties, and descended on Wales in a bloody invasion that lasted much of the 1270s. In the end, Wales became a dependent principality, owing allegiance to England. There were no more Welsh kings, and Edward made his own son Prince of Wales. Ever since, the British sovereign's eldest son has automatically been given the title. (Most recently, Prince Charles was formally proclaimed Prince of Wales at Caernarfon Castle in 1969, much to the displeasure of Welsh nationalists.)

Edward I then looked north. For 200 years, Scotland had been ruled by the Canmores, but the dynasty effectively ended in 1286 with the death of Alexander III. He was succeeded by his four-year-old granddaughter Margaret ('the Maid of Norway'), who was engaged to the son of Edward I, but she died in 1290 before the wedding could take place.

Great Britain consists of the countries of England, Wales and Scotland. The United Kingdom (UK) is Great Britain plus Northern Ireland. The British Isles is a *geographical* term for the islands that make up the UK and the Republic of Ireland, plus others such as the Channel Islands.

1295	1296	1298–1305	1314
John Balliol of Scotland and Philip IV of France sign a mutual defence treaty that establishes the 'Auld Alliance' – this predominantly anti-English agreement remains in place for several centuries.	King Edward I marches on Scotland with an army of 30,000 men and in a brutal invasion captures the castles of Berwick, Edinburgh, Roxburgh and Stirling.	William Wallace is proclaimed Guardian of Scotland in 1298. After Edward's army defeats the Scots at the Battle of Falkirk, Wallace goes into hiding but is betrayed and executed in 1305.	An army under Robert the Bruce wins against the English at the Battle of Bannockburn – a victory that consolidated Scottish independence for the next 400 years.

Scotland Wins Independence

There followed a dispute for the Scottish throne between John Balliol and Robert Bruce of Annandale. Arbitration was needed and the nobles asked Edward I, who chose Balliol. Edward then sought to formalise his feudal overlordship and travelled through Scotland forcing local leaders to swear allegiance. In a final blow to Scottish pride, Edward removed the Stone of Destiny, on which the kings of Scotland had been crowned for centuries, and sent it to London.

That was too much. In response, Balliol got in touch with Edward's old enemy, France, and arranged a treaty of cooperation, the start of an anti-English partnership, the 'Auld Alliance', which was to last for many centuries (and to the present day when it comes to rugby or football).

Edward wasn't the sort of bloke to brook opposition, though. In 1296 the English army defeated Balliol, forcing the Scottish barons to accept Edward's rule, and his ruthless retaliation earned him the title 'Hammer of the Scots'. But still the Scottish people refused to lie down; in 1297, at the Battle of Stirling Bridge, the English were defeated by a Scots army under the leadership of William Wallace. Over 700 years later, Wallace is still remembered as a Scottish hero.

By this time, Robert the Bruce (grandson of Bruce of Annandale) had crowned himself king of Scotland (1290), been beaten in battle, gone on the run and, while hiding in a cave, been famously inspired to renew his efforts by a spider persistently spinning its web. Bruce's army went on to defeat Edward II's superior English forces at the Battle of Bannockburn in 1314, a famous victory that led to the official recognition of Scotland as an independent nation, with Bruce as its king, in 1328.

Stewarts Enter the Scene

While the Hundred Years' War (1337–1453) rumbled on between England and France, things weren't much better in Scotland. After the death of Robert the Bruce in 1329, the country was ravaged by endless internal conflicts and plague epidemics.

WHO'D WANT TO BE KING?

Despite immense power and privilege, the position of monarch (or, perhaps worse, *potential* monarch) probably ranks as one of history's most dangerous occupations. English kings have been killed in battle (Harold), beheaded (Charles I), assassinated (William II), murdered by a wicked uncle (allegedly; Edward V), and bumped off by their queen and her lover (Edward II). Life was just as uncertain for the rulers of Wales and Scotland: some murdered by a wicked uncle (James I of Scotland), others killed in battle (Llywelyn the Last of Wales, and James IV of Scotland, the last British monarch to die on the battlefield).

1337–1453	1348	1371	1381
England battles France in a long conflict known as the Hundred Years' War. It was actually a series of small conflicts. And it lasted for more than a century, too...	The bubonic plague (called the Black Death) arrives, ultimately killing more than a third of the population. For peasant labourers who survived, an upside was a rise in wages.	The last of the Bruce dynasty dies, succeeded by the Stewards (Stewarts), who rule Scotland and then Britain for the next three centuries.	Richard II is confronted by the Peasants' Revolt. This attempt by commoners to overthrow the feudal system is brutally suppressed, further injuring an already deeply divided country.

Bruce's son became David II of Scotland, but he was soon caught up in battles against fellow Scots disaffected by his father and aided by England's Edward III. So when David died in 1371, the Scots quickly crowned Robert Stewart (Robert the Bruce's grandson) as king, marking the start of the House of Stewart, which was to crop up again in England a bit further down the line.

Houses of York & Lancaster

In 1399 the ineffectual Richard II of England was ousted by a powerful baron called Henry Bolingbroke, who became Henry IV, the first monarch of the House of Lancaster. Less than a year later, his rule was disrupted by a final cry of resistance from the downtrodden Welsh, led by royal descendant Owain Glyndŵr (Owen Glendower). But the rebellion was crushed, Glyndŵr died an outlaw and the Welsh elite were barred from public life for many years.

Henry IV was followed by Henry V, who stirred up the dormant Hundred Years' War and defeated France at the Battle of Agincourt. The patriotic speech penned for him by Shakespeare in *Henry V* ('Cry "God for Harry, England, and St George!"') has ensured his position among the most famous English kings of all time.

When the Hundred Years' War finally ground to a halt in 1453, you'd have thought things would be calm for a while, but no. The English forces returning from France threw their energies into a civil war dubbed the Wars of the Roses.

Briefly it went like this: Henry VI of the House of Lancaster (emblem, a red rose) was challenged by Richard, Duke of York (emblem, a white rose). Henry was weak and it was almost a walkover for Richard. But Henry's wife, Margaret of Anjou, was made of sterner stuff and her forces defeated the challenger. It didn't rest there. Richard's son Edward entered the scene with an army, turned the tables and finally drove out Henry. He became King Edward IV, first monarch of the House of York.

Dark Deeds in the Tower

Edward IV hardly had time to catch his breath before Richard Neville, Earl of Warwick, and Margaret of Anjou teamed up in 1471 to force him into exile and bring Henry VI back to the throne. But a year later Edward IV came bouncing back: he killed Warwick, captured Margaret and had Henry snuffed out in the Tower of London.

Although Edward IV's position seemed secure, he ruled for only a decade before being succeeded by his 12-year-old son, Edward V. But the boy-king's reign was even shorter than his dad's. In 1483 he was mysteriously murdered, along with his brother, and once again the Tower of London was the scene of the crime.

Shakespeare's *Henry V* (1989) was filmed as a superb epic starring Kenneth Branagh as the eponymous king. Also worth catching is the earlier movie of the same name starring Laurence Olivier, made in 1944 as a patriotic rallying cry.

Walks Through Britain's History (published by the Automobile Association) guides you on foot to castles, battlefields and hundreds of other sites with a link to the past. Take the air. Breathe in history!

1400	1455–85	1468–69	1485
Welsh nationalist hero Owain Glyndŵr leads the Welsh in rebellion, declaring a parliament in Machynlleth, but his rebellion is short-lived and victory fleeting.	The Wars of the Roses – an ongoing conflict between two competing dynasties, the Houses of Lancaster and York. The Yorkists are eventually successful, enabling King Edward IV to gain the throne.	Orkney and then Shetland are mortgaged to Scotland as part of a dowry from Danish King Christian I, whose daughter is to marry the future King James III of Scotland.	Henry Tudor defeats Richard III at the Battle of Bosworth to become King Henry VII, establishing the Tudor dynasty and ending York–Lancaster rivalry for the throne.

With the 'princes in the Tower' dispatched, this left the throne open for their dear old Uncle Richard. Whether he was the princes' killer is still the subject of debate, but his rule as Richard III was short-lived. Despite being given another famous Shakespearean sound bite ('A horse, a horse! My kingdom for a horse!'), few tears were shed in 1485 when he was tumbled from the top job by a nobleman from Wales called Henry Tudor, who became Henry VII.

Moves Towards Unity

Six Wives: The Queens of Henry VIII, by historian David Starkey, is an accessible modern study of the multi-marrying monarch.

After the Wars of the Roses, Henry VII's Tudor neutrality was important. He mended fences with his northern neighbours by marrying his daughter to James IV of Scotland, linking the Tudor and Stewart lines, though this didn't stop James IV invading England in 1513, only to be killed at the Battle of Flodden. Henry VII married Edward IV's daughter, Elizabeth of York (daughter of Edward IV and niece of Richard III), further cementing his claim to the throne.

Matrimony may have been more useful than warfare for Henry VII, but the multiple marriages of his successor, Henry VIII, were a very different story. Fathering a male heir was his problem, hence the famous six wives, but the Pope's disapproval of divorce and remarriage led to a split with the Roman Catholic Church. Parliament made Henry the head of the Protestant Church of England – the beginning of a pivotal division between Catholics and Protestants that still exists in some areas of Britain.

In 1536 Henry followed this up by 'dissolving' many monasteries in Britain and Ireland, a blatant takeover of their land and wealth rather than a symptom of the struggle between church and state. Nonetheless, the general populace felt little sympathy for the wealthy (and often corrupt) abbeys, and in 1539–40 another monastic land grab swallowed the larger ones as well.

The 1998 film *Elizabeth*, directed by Shekhar Kapur and starring Cate Blanchett, covers the early years of the Virgin Queen's rule, as she graduates from princess to commanding monarch – a time of forbidden love, unwanted suitors, intrigue and death.

At the same time, Henry signed the Acts of Union (1536 and 1543), formally uniting England and Wales for the first time. Meanwhile, in Scotland, James IV had been succeeded by James V, who died in 1542. His baby daughter Mary became queen, and Scotland was ruled by regents.

The Elizabethan Age

Henry VIII died in 1547, succeeded by his son Edward VI, then by his daughter Mary I, but their reigns were short. So, unexpectedly, Elizabeth, third in line, came to the throne.

As Elizabeth I, she inherited a nasty mess of religious strife and divided loyalties, but after an uncertain start she gained confidence and turned the country around. Refusing marriage, she borrowed biblical

1509–47	1536 & 1543	1558–1603	1560
The reign of King Henry VIII. The Pope's disapproval of Henry's serial marriage and divorce results in the English Reformation – the founding of the Church of England.	English authority is exerted over Wales; the Laws in Wales Acts, also known as the Acts of Union, formally tie the two countries as a single political entity.	The reign of Queen Elizabeth I, a period of boundless English optimism. Enter stage right playwright William Shakespeare. Exit due west navigators Walter Raleigh and Francis Drake.	The Scottish Parliament creates a Protestant Church that is independent of Rome and the monarchy, as a result of the Reformation. The Latin Mass is abolished and the Pope's authority denied.

MARY, QUEEN OF SCOTS

During Elizabeth I's reign, her cousin Mary (the Catholic daughter of Scottish King James V) had become known as Mary, Queen of Scots. She'd spent her childhood in France and had married the French *dauphin* (crown prince), thereby becoming Queen of France as well. Why stop at two? After her husband's death, Mary returned to Scotland, where she claimed the English throne as well, on the grounds that Elizabeth I was illegitimate.

However, Mary's plans failed. She was imprisoned and forced to abdicate in favour of her son (a Protestant, who became James VI of Scotland), but she escaped to England and appealed to Elizabeth for help. This was a bad move; Mary was seen, not surprisingly, as a security risk and imprisoned once again. In an uncharacteristic display of indecision, Elizabeth held Mary under arrest for nearly 19 years before finally ordering her execution. As a prisoner, Mary was frequently moved from house to house, so that today Britain has many stately homes (and even a few pubs) claiming 'Mary, Queen of Scots slept here'.

imagery and became known as the Virgin Queen, making her perhaps the first British monarch to create a cult image.

It paid off. Her 45-year reign was a period of boundless optimism, characterised by the naval defeat of the Spanish Armada, the expansion of trade due to the global explorations of seafarers such as Walter Raleigh and Francis Drake, not to mention a cultural flourishing thanks to writers such as William Shakespeare and Christopher Marlowe.

United & Disunited Britain

Elizabeth I died in 1603 without an heir, and was succeeded by her closest relative, James, the safely Protestant son of the executed Mary. Already James VI of Scotland, he became James I of England, the first English monarch of the House of Stuart (Mary's time in France had Gallicised the Stewart name). Most importantly, James united England, Wales and Scotland into one kingdom for the first time in history – another step towards British unity.

James' attempts to smooth religious relations were set back by the anti-Catholic outcry that followed the infamous Guy Fawkes Gunpowder Plot, a terrorist attempt to blow up parliament in 1605. The event is still celebrated every 5 November with fireworks, bonfires and burning effigies of Guy himself.

Alongside the Catholic–Protestant rift, the divide between king and parliament continued to smoulder. The power struggle worsened during the reign of the next king, Charles I, and eventually degenerated into the Civil War of 1642–49. The antiroyalist (or 'parliamentarian') forces were led by Oliver Cromwell, a Puritan who preached against the excesses of

1588	1603	1642–49	1688
The first complete translation of the Bible into Welsh helps the cause of Protestantism and also helps the survival of the neglected Welsh language.	James VI of Scotland inherits the English throne in the so-called Union of the Crowns, becoming James I of England and James VI of Scotland.	English Civil War between the king's Cavaliers and Oliver Cromwell's Roundheads establishes the Commonwealth of England.	William of Orange and his wife, Mary, daughter of King James II, jointly ascend the throne after William defeats his father-in-law in the Glorious Revolution.

the monarchy and established Church. His army (known as the Round-heads) was pitched against the king's forces (the Cavaliers) in a conflict that tore Britain, and especially England, apart. The Civil War extended into Scotland where the main struggle was between royalists and radical 'Covenanters', who sought freedom from state interference in church government.

On the chilly day of his execution, dethroned King Charles I reputedly wore two shirts to avoid shivering and being regarded as a coward.

It all ended with victory for the Roundheads, with the king executed, the country declared a republic and Cromwell hailed as 'Protector'.

The Return of the King

By 1653 Cromwell was finding parliament too restrictive and he assumed dictatorial powers, much to his supporters' dismay. On his death in 1658, he was followed half-heartedly by his son, but in 1660 parliament decided to re-establish the monarchy, as republican alternatives were proving far worse.

Charles II (the exiled son of Charles I) came to the throne, and his rule, known as 'the Restoration', saw scientific and cultural activity bursting forth. Exploration and expansion were also on the agenda. Backed by the army and navy (modernised, ironically, by Cromwell), British colonies stretched down the American coast, while the East India Company set up headquarters in Bombay (now Mumbai), laying foundations for what was to become the British Empire.

The next king, James II/VII, had a harder time. Attempts to ease restrictive laws on Catholics ended with his overthrow and defeat at the Battle of the Boyne by William III, ruler of the Netherlands, better known as William of Orange. William was married to James' own daughter Mary, but it didn't stop him (and her) attacking James.

William and Mary came to the throne as King and Queen, each in their own right (Mary had more of a claim, but William would not agree to be a mere consort), and their joint accession in 1688 was known as the Glorious Revolution.

Act of Union

In 1694 Mary died, leaving William as sole monarch. He died a few years later and was succeeded by his sister-in-law Anne (the second daughter of James II). In 1707, during Anne's reign, the Act of Union was passed, bringing an end to the independent Scottish Parliament and linking the countries of England, Wales and Scotland under one parliament (based in London) for the first time. The nation of Great Britain was now established as a single state, with a bigger, more powerful parliament, and a constitutional monarchy with clear limits on the king or queen.

1707	1745–46	1749	1775–83
The Act of Union brings England and Scotland under one parliament, one sovereign and one flag.	The culmination of the Jacobite uprisings sees Bonnie Prince Charlie land in Scotland, gather an army and march southwards, to be eventually defeated at the Battle of Culloden.	Author and magistrate Henry Fielding founds the Bow Street Runners, cited as London's first professional police force. A 1792 Act of Parliament allows the Bow Street model to spread across England.	The American War of Independence is the British Empire's first major reversal, a fact not missed by French ruler Napoléon.

The new-look parliament didn't wait long to flex its muscles. The Act of Union banned any Catholic, or anyone married to a Catholic, from ascending the throne – a rule still in force today. In 1714 Anne died without leaving an heir, marking the end of the Stuart line. The throne was then passed to distant (but still safely Protestant) German relatives: the House of Hanover, better known as the Georgians.

The Jacobite Rebellions

Despite, or perhaps because of, the 1707 Act of Union, anti-English feeling in Scotland refused to disappear. The Jacobite rebellions, most notably those of 1715 and 1745, were attempts to overthrow the Hanoverian monarchy and bring back the Stuarts. Although these are iconic events in Scottish history, in reality there was never much support for the Jacobite cause outside the Highlands: the people of the lowlands were mainly Protestant and feared a return to the Catholicism that the Stuarts represented.

The 1715 rebellion was led by James Edward Stuart (the Old Pretender), the son of the exiled James II of England (James VII of Scotland), but when the attempt failed he fled to France. To impose control on the Highlands, General George Wade was commissioned to build a network of military roads through many previously inaccessible glens.

In 1745 James' son Charles Edward Stuart (Bonnie Prince Charlie, the Young Pretender) landed in Scotland to claim the crown for his father. He was initially successful, moving south into England as far as Derby, but the prince and his Highland army suffered a catastrophic defeat at the Battle of Culloden in 1746; his legendary escape to the western isles is remembered in *The Skye Boat Song*. General Wade is remembered, too, as many of the roads his troops built are still in use today.

The Empire Strikes Out

By the mid-18th century, struggles for the British throne seemed a thing of the past, and the Georgian kings increasingly relied on parliament to govern the country. As part of the process, from 1721 to 1742 a senior parliamentarian called Sir Robert Walpole effectively became Britain's first prime minister.

Meanwhile, the British Empire continued to grow in America, Canada and India. The first claims were made on Australia after Captain James Cook's epic voyage of exploration in 1768.

The empire's first major reversal came when the American colonies won the War of Independence (1775–83). This setback forced Britain to withdraw from the world stage for a while, a gap not missed by French ruler Napoléon. He threatened to invade Britain and hinder the power

A History of Britain by historian and TV star Simon Schama is a highly accessible set of three books, examining events from 3000 BC to AD 2000.

1799–1815	1837–1901	1847	1858 & 1860
In the Napoleonic Wars, Napoléon threatens invasion on a weakened Britain, but his ambitions are curtailed by Nelson and Wellington at the famous battles of Trafalgar (1805) and Waterloo (1815).	The reign of Queen Victoria, during which the British Empire – 'on which the sun never sets' – expands from Canada through Africa and India to Australia and New Zealand.	Publication of a government report, dubbed the 'Treason of the Blue Books', suggests the Welsh language is detrimental to education in Wales, and fuels the Welsh-language struggle.	The first modern national eisteddfods are held in Llangollen and Denbigh – although earlier ones had been organised from the end of the 18th century as part of a Welsh cultural revival.

of the British overseas, before his ambitions were curtailed by naval hero Admiral Nelson and military hero the Duke of Wellington at the famous battles of Trafalgar (1805) and Waterloo (1815).

The Industrial Age

While the empire expanded abroad, at home Britain became the crucible of the Industrial Revolution. Steam power (patented by James Watt in 1781) and steam trains (launched by George Stephenson in the 1820s) transformed methods of production and transport, and the towns of the English Midlands became the first industrial cities.

From about 1750, much of the Scottish Highlands was emptied of people, as landowners casually expelled entire farms and villages to make way for more profitable sheep, a seminal event in Scotland's history known as the Clearances. Although many of the dispossessed left for the New World, others headed to the burgeoning cotton mills of Lanarkshire and the shipyards of Glasgow.

By the early 19th century, copper, iron and slate were being extracted in the Merthyr Tydfil and Monmouth areas of Wales. The 1860s saw the Rhondda valleys opened up for coal mining, and Wales soon became a major exporter of coal, as well as the world's leading producer of tin plate.

Across Britain, industrialisation meant people were on the move as never before, leaving the farms and villages their families had occupied for generations. The rapid change from rural to urban society caused great dislocation, and although knowledge of science and medicine also improved alongside industrial advances, for many people the adverse side effects of Britain's economic blossoming were poverty and deprivation.

Age of Empire

Despite the social turmoil of the early 19th century, by the time Queen Victoria took the throne in 1837 Britain's factories dominated world trade and British fleets dominated the oceans. The rest of the 19th century was seen as Britain's Golden Age.

Victoria ruled a proud nation at home and great swaths of territories abroad, from Canada through much of Africa and India to Australia and New Zealand, trumpeted as 'the empire on which the sun never sets'.

The times were optimistic, but it wasn't all tub-thumping jingoism. Prime Minister Disraeli, who rose to office in 1868, and his successor William Gladstone, also introduced social reforms to address the worst excesses of the Industrial Revolution. Education became universal, trade unions were legalised and the right to vote was extended in a series of

Captain James Cook's voyage to the southern hemisphere was primarily a scientific expedition. His objectives included monitoring the transit of Venus, an astronomical event that happens only twice every 180 years or so (most recently in 2004 and 2012). 'Discovering' Australia was just a sideline.

At its height, the British Empire covered 20% of the land area of the earth and contained a quarter of the world's population.

1900	1914	1916	1939–45
James Keir Hardie (usually known as just Keir Hardie) becomes the first Labour MP, winning a seat in the Welsh mining town of Merthyr Tydfil.	Archduke Franz Ferdinand of Austria is assassinated in the Balkan city of Sarajevo – the final spark in a decade-long crisis that starts the Great War, now called World War I.	The Welsh Liberal MP David Lloyd George becomes the British prime minister in an alliance with the Conservative Party, having built a reputation for championing the poor and needy.	WWII rages across Europe, and much of Africa and Asia. Britain and the Allies, including America, Russia, Australia, India and New Zealand, eventually defeat the armies of Germany, Japan and Italy.

reform acts, finally being granted to all men over the age of 21 in 1918, and to all women in 1928.

World War I

When Queen Victoria died in 1901, it seemed Britain's energy fizzled out too. The new king, Edward VII, ushered in the relaxed Edwardian era – and a long period of decline.

Meanwhile, in continental Europe, other states were more active: four restless military powers (Russia, Austria-Hungary, Turkey and Germany) focused their sabre-rattling on the Balkan states, and the assassination of Archduke Ferdinand in Sarajevo in 1914 finally sparked a clash that became the 'Great War' we now call World War I. Soldiers from Britain and Allied countries were drawn into a conflict of horrendous slaughter, most infamously on the killing fields of Flanders and the beaches of Gallipoli.

By the war's weary end in 1918, over a million Britons had died, plus millions more from many other countries, and there was hardly a street or village untouched by death, as the sobering lists of names on war memorials all over Britain still show.

Disillusion & Depression

For the soldiers that did return from WWI, the war had created disillusion and a questioning of the social order. Many supported the ideals of relatively new political force, the Labour Party, to represent the working class.

Meanwhile, the bitter Anglo-Irish War (1919–21) saw most of Ireland achieving full independence from Britain. Six counties in the north remained British, creating a new political entity called the United Kingdom of Great Britain and Northern Ireland. But the decision to partition the island of Ireland was to have long-term repercussions that still dominate political agendas in both the UK and the Republic of Ireland today.

The Labour Party won for the first time in the 1923 election, in coalition with the Liberals. James Ramsay MacDonald was the first Labour prime minister, but by the mid-1920s the right-wing Conservatives were back. The world economy was soon in decline and in the 1930s the Great Depression meant another decade of misery and political upheaval.

World War II

In 1933 Adolf Hitler came to power in Germany and in 1939 Germany invaded Poland, once again drawing Britain into war. The German army swept through Europe and pushed back British forces to the beaches of Dunkirk (northern France) in June 1940. An extraordinary flotilla of

One of the finest novels about WWI is *Birdsong* by Sebastian Faulks. Understated, perfectly paced and intensely moving, it tells of passion, fear, waste, incompetent generals and the poor bloody infantry.

HISTORY WORLD WAR I

In 2017's *Dunkirk*, British director Christopher Nolan delivered a haunting depiction of the evacuation of British troops from northern France in May 1940. Its stars included Kenneth Branagh, Mark Rylance, Tom Hardy, and pop singer Harry Styles in his first film role.

1946–48	1948	1952	1955 & 1959
The Labour Party nationalises key industries such as shipyards, coal mines and steel foundries. Britain's 'big four' train companies are combined into British Railways.	Aneurin Bevan, the health minister in the Labour government, launches the National Health Service – the core of Britain as a 'welfare state'.	Princess Elizabeth becomes Queen Elizabeth II when her father, George VI, dies. Her coronation takes place in Westminster Abbey in June 1953.	Cardiff is declared the Welsh capital in 1955, and Wales gets its own official flag (the red dragon on a green and white field) in 1959.

D-Day in Figures

Largest military armada in history

More than 5000 ships

Approximately 150,000 Allied troops landed

Campaign time: four days

rescue vessels turned total disaster into a brave defeat, and an event that is still remembered with pride and sadness every year in Britain.

By mid-1940 most of Europe was controlled by Germany. In Russia, Stalin had negotiated a peace agreement. The USA was neutral, leaving Britain virtually isolated. Into this arena came a new prime minister, Winston Churchill.

Between September 1940 and May 1941, the German air force launched the Blitz, a series of (mainly night-time) bombing raids on London and other cities. Despite this, morale in Britain remained strong, thanks partly to Churchill's regular radio broadcasts. In late 1941 the USA entered the war, and the tide began to turn.

By 1944 Germany was in retreat. Russia pushed back from the east, and Britain, the USA and other Allies were again on the beaches of France. The Normandy landings (or D-Day, as they are better remembered) marked the start of the liberation of Europe's western side. By 1945 Hitler was dead and the war was finally over.

Swinging & Sliding

Despite victory in WWII, there was an unexpected swing on the political front in 1945. An electorate tired of war and hungry for change tumbled Churchill's Conservatives in favour of the Labour Party.

In 1952 George VI was succeeded by his daughter Elizabeth II and, following the trend set by earlier queens Elizabeth I and Victoria, she has remained on the throne for over six decades, overseeing a period of massive social and economic change.

WINSTON CHURCHILL

Born in 1874 to an aristocratic family, Winston Churchill is Britain's most famous prime minister. As a young man he joined the British Army and saw action in India and Africa. He was first elected to parliament as a Conservative MP (Member of Parliament) in 1900, and held various ministerial positions through the 1920s.

In 1939 Britain entered WWII, and by 1940 Churchill was prime minister, taking additional responsibility as minister of defence. Hitler had expected an easy victory, but Churchill's extraordinary dedication, not to mention his radio speeches (most famously offering nothing but 'blood, toil, tears and sweat' and promising to 'fight on the beaches'), inspired the British people to resist.

Between July and October 1940 the Royal Air Force withstood Germany's aerial raids to win what became known as the Battle of Britain, a major turning point in the war – in Churchilll's words of praise for the RAF, 'never was so much owed by so many to so few'. It was an audacious strategy, but it paid off and Churchill was rightly lauded as a national hero.

1960s	1970s	1979	1982
It's the era of African and Caribbean independence, for Nigeria (1960), Tanzania (1961), Jamaica and Trinidad & Tobago (1962), Kenya (1963), Malawi (1964), the Gambia (1965) and Barbados (1966).	The discovery of oil and gas in the North Sea brings new prosperity to Aberdeen in Scotland and the surrounding area, and also to the Shetland Islands.	A Conservative government led by Margaret Thatcher wins the national election, a major milestone of Britain's 20th-century history, ushering in a decade of dramatic political and social change.	Britain is victorious in a war against Argentina over the invasion of the Falkland Islands, leading to a rise in patriotic sentiment.

By the late 1950s, recovery was strong enough for Prime Minister Harold Macmillan to famously remind the British people they had 'never had it so good'. By the time the 1960s had started, grey old Britain was suddenly more fun and lively than it had been for generations. In 1965, Britain's wartime saviour, Sir Winston Churchill, died at the age of 91. He was given a full state funeral, a ceremony usually reserved for the nation's sovereign – one of only a handful of non-royals ever to receive the honour.

Although the 1960s were swinging, the 1970s saw an economic slide thanks to a grim combination of inflation, the oil crisis and international competition. The rest of the decade was marked by strikes, disputes and all-round gloom.

Neither the Conservatives (also known as the Tories), under Edward Heath, nor Labour, under Harold Wilson and Jim Callaghan, proved capable of controlling the strife. The British public had had enough, and in the elections of 1979 the Conservatives won a landslide victory, led by a little-known politician named Margaret Thatcher.

The Thatcher Years

Soon everyone had heard of Margaret Thatcher. Love her or hate her, no one could argue that her methods weren't dramatic. Looking back from a 21st-century vantage point, most commentators agree that by economic measures the Thatcher government's policies were largely successful, but by social measures they were a failure and created a polarised Britain: on one side were the people who gained from the prosperous wave of opportunities in the 'new' industries, while on the other side were those left unemployed and dispossessed by the decline of the 'old' industries such as coal mining and steel production.

Despite, or perhaps thanks to, policies that were frequently described as uncompromising, Margaret Thatcher was, by 1988, the longest-serving British prime minister of the 20th century.

For detail on the 1980s, read *No Such Thing as Society* by Andy McSmith. Drawing on Margaret Thatcher's famous proclamation, this book studies the era dominated by the Iron Lady.

New Labour, New Millennium, New Start

Margaret Thatcher was replaced as leader by John Major in 1990 and voters, still regarding Labour with suspicion, gave the Conservatives an unexpected win in the 1992 election. Labour reinvented itself in the succeeding years and in the 1997 election 'New' Labour swept to power under a fresh-faced leader called Tony Blair.

Blair and the Labour Party enjoyed an extended honeymoon period, and the next election (in 2001) was another walkover. The Conservative Party continued to struggle, allowing Labour to win a historic third term in 2005, and a year later Blair became the longest-serving Labour prime minister in British history.

1990	1997	1999	1999–2004
Mrs Thatcher is ousted as leader and the Conservative Party enters a period of decline but remains in power thanks to inept Labour opposition.	The general election sees Tony Blair lead 'New' Labour to victory in the polls, with a record-breaking parliamentary majority, ending almost 20 years of Tory rule.	The first National Assembly is elected for Wales, with the members sitting in a new building in Cardiff; Rhodri Morgan becomes First Minister.	Scottish Parliament is convened for the first time on 12 May 1999. Five years later, after plenty of scandal and huge sums of money, a new parliament building is opened at Holyrood in Edinburgh.

In May 2010 a record 13 years of Labour rule came to an end, and a coalition government (the first in the UK since WWII) was formed between the Conservatives and the Liberal Democrats. It was an experiment that ended disastrously for the Lib Dems at the 2015 general election: they lost 49 seats, and were left with just eight MPs. The same vote left the defeated Labour Party searching for a new identity, and the Conservatives back in sole charge under David Cameron.

Just over a year later a referendum saw the people of the UK vote, by 52% to 48%, to leave the EU – in defiance of the main parties, who had wanted the country to stay in. Cameron resigned almost immediately after the vote, and was succeeded by former home secretary Theresa May, whose premiership was marred by wrangling over the Brexit issue – as well as a misjudged decision to hold a snap general election in 2017, which resulted in her losing her majority in a hung parliament in the House of Commons.

May's plan had been to exploit the apparent unpopularity of the Labour leader, Jeremy Corbyn, whose strongly socialist policies had caused division in his own party. But unexpectedly, Corbyn's leftist agenda proved popular with the public – particularly disillusioned younger voters.

The six decades since the end of WWII are neatly covered in *A History of Modern Britain*, a handy overview focusing on political events, by TV presenter and commentator Andrew Marr.

2007	2016	2017	2018
The Government of Wales Bill heralds the largest transfer of power from Westminster to Cardiff since the founding of the National Assembly.	A referendum is held asking the question 'Should the UK remain a member of the EU or leave the EU?' The result was: 52% voted Leave, 48% voted Remain.	Conservatives call a snap general election, which results in a hung parliament. Northern Ireland's Democratic Unionist Party (DUP) agrees to support the Conservatives in forming a minority government.	Prince Harry marries American actress Meghan Markle, to become the first member of the royal family to wed a person of mixed race.

The British Table

The idea of British cuisine was once a bit of a joke. But a culinary landmark came in 2005, when food bible *Gourmet* magazine famously singled out London as having the best collection of restaurants in the world. In the years since then the choice for food lovers – whatever their budget – has continued to improve. London is now regarded as a global gastronomic capital, and it's increasingly easy to find great food all over Great Britain.

Eating in Britain

The infamous outbreaks of 'mad cow' disease in the 1990s are ancient history now, and British beef is once again exported to the world, but an upside of the bad press at the time was a massive surge in demand for good-quality food. That means wherever you go in Britain today, you'll find a plethora of organic, natural, unadulterated, chemical-free, free-range, hand-reared, locally farmed, nonintensive foods available in shops, markets, cafes and restaurants.

Alongside this greater awareness of quality and provenance, there have been other changes to British food thanks to outside influences. For decades most towns have boasted Italian, Chinese and Indian restaurants, so spaghetti carbonara, chow mein and vindaloo are no longer considered exotic, but in more recent times dishes from Japan, Korea, Thailand and other Asian countries have also become widely available.

The overall effect of these foreign influences has been the introduction to 'traditional' British cuisine of new techniques, new ingredients and new herbs and spices. So now we have 'modern British cuisine', where even humble bangers and mash (sausages with mashed potato) are raised to new heights when handmade pork, apple and thyme-scented sausages are paired with fennel and red wine gravy.

Britain's most popular restaurant dish is chicken tikka masala, an 'Indian' curry dish created specifically for the British palate and unheard of in India itself.

The Full British

Although grazing on a steady supply of snacks is increasingly commonplace in Britain, as it is in many other industrialised nations, the British culinary day is still punctuated by the three traditional meals of breakfast, lunch and dinner. And just to keep you on your toes, dinner is sometimes known as tea or supper, depending on social class and geographical location.

Breakfast

Many people in Britain make do with toast or a bowl of cereal before dashing to work, but visitors staying in hotels and B&Bs will undoubtedly encounter a phenomenon called the 'full English Breakfast' – or one of its regional equivalents. This usually consists of bacon, sausages, eggs, tomatoes, mushrooms, baked beans and fried bread. In Scotland the 'full Scottish breakfast' might include tattie scones (potato bread) instead of fried bread. In Wales you may be offered laver bread, which is not a bread at all but seaweed – a tasty speciality often served with oatmeal and bacon on toast. In northern England you may get black pudding (blood

Few British foods are as divisive as Marmite – a strong, tangy spread made from yeast extract, which many people love to spread on buttered toast in the morning. An equal number simply can't stand the stuff – something that Marmite's makers embraced with their 'love it or hate it' ad campaign.

The Scottish dish of haggis is a staple at celebrations like Hogmanay and Burns Night, but it has the most unappetising ingredient list of any British dish (offal minced with oatmeal, suet and spices, wrapped up in a sheep's stomach and boiled). It's traditionally eaten with 'neeps and tatties' (turnips and potatoes).

sausage). And just in case you thought this insufficient, it's still preceded by cereal, and followed by toast and marmalade or jam.

If you don't feel like eating half a farmyard first thing in the morning, most places offer a lighter alternative or local speciality such as kippers (smoked fish) or a 'continental breakfast', which completely omits the cooked stuff and may even add something once thought of as exotic such as croissants.

Lunch

One of the many great inventions that Britain gave the world is the sandwich, often eaten as a midday meal. Slapping a slice of cheese or ham between two bits of bread may seem a simple concept, but no one apparently thought of it until the 18th century, when the Earl of Sandwich (his title comes from the southeast England town of Sandwich that originally got its name from the Viking word for sandy beach) ordered his servants to bring cold meat between bread so he could keep working at his desk, or, as some historians claim, continue playing cards late at night.

Another lunch classic that perhaps epitomises British food more than any other – especially in pubs – is the ploughman's lunch. Basically it's bread and cheese, and although hearty yokels probably did carry such food to the fields (no doubt wrapped in a red-spotted handkerchief) in days of yore, the meal is actually a modern phenomenon. It was invented in the 1960s by the marketing chief of the national cheesemakers' organisation as a way to boost consumption, neatly cashing in on public nostalgia and fondness for tradition.

You can still find a basic ploughman's lunch offered in some pubs – and it undeniably goes well with a pint or two of local ale at lunchtime – but these days the meal has usually been smartened up to include butter, salad, pickle, pickled onion and dressings. At some pubs you get a selection of cheeses. You'll also find other variations, such as a farmer's lunch (bread and chicken), stockman's lunch (bread and ham), Frenchman's lunch (brie and baguette) and fisherman's lunch (you guessed it, with fish).

For cheese and bread in a different combination, try Welsh rarebit – a sophisticated variation on cheese on toast, seasoned and flavoured with butter, milk and sometimes a little beer. For a takeaway lunch in

THE CORNISH PASTY

A favourite speciality in southwest England is the Cornish pasty. A mix of cooked meat and vegetables wrapped in pastry, it originated as an all-in-one-lunch pack that tin miners carried underground and left on a ledge ready for mealtime. So that pasties weren't mixed up, they were marked with their owner's initials – always at one end, so the miner could eat half and safely leave the rest to snack on later without it mistakenly disappearing into the mouth of a workmate. Before going back to the surface, the miners traditionally left the last few crumbs of the pasty as a gift for the spirits of the mine, known as 'knockers', to ensure a safe shift the next day.

Since 2015, the Cornish pasty has had Protected Geographical Indication status – meaning that by law, only pasties made in Cornwall according to a strict set of guidelines can call themselves Cornish pasties. Beware pale imitations – if you want to taste a proper pasty, to Cornwall you must go. Other protected UK products include Melton Mowbray pork pie, Newmarket sausage, Stornoway black pudding, Cumberland sausage, Arbroath smokies, Gloucestershire Old Spot pork, Isle of Man lamb and a whole smorgasbord of cheeses (Buxton Blue, Yorkshire Wensleydale and Westcountry farmhouse cheddar cheese, to name a few).

Fish and chips

Scotland, look out for Forfar bridies (pastry turnovers filled with minced beef and onion).

Dinner

While the traditional idea of 'meat and two veg' was an evening staple for many decades, the British have embraced global cuisine with gusto, and you're now just as likely to find a curry, a pizza or a bowl of pasta on the dinner table as you are a serving of chops, chips and peas. The popularity of TV cooking shows and the profusion of celebrity chef cookbooks has helped expand Britain's culinary repertoire exponentially in recent years, and these days most Brits are pretty cosmopolitan in their tastes.

One tradition that hasn't changed all that much is the roast dinner, customarily eaten for Sunday lunch. The classic is roast beef (always roast, never 'roasted') accompanied by Yorkshire pudding (portions of crispy baked batter), a selection of vegetables, and gravy. Another classic dish brings Yorkshire pudding and sausages together, with the delightful name of 'toad-in-the-hole'.

The nation's most revered beef comes from Scotland's Aberdeen Angus cattle, while the best-known meat from Wales is lamb. Venison – usually from red deer – is readily available in Scotland, as well as in parts of Wales and England, most notably in the New Forest.

Perhaps the best-known British meal is fish and chips, often bought from the 'chippie' wrapped in paper to carry home. Late at night, epicures may order their fish and chips 'open' to eat immediately while walking back from the pub. It has to be said that quality varies outrageously across the country; sometimes the chips are limp and soggy, and the fish greasy and tasteless, especially once you get away from the sea,

> Britain's best-known cheese is cheddar – a strong, nutty hard cheese that's aged for several months and is an essential part of a ploughman's lunch. It gets its name from the village of Cheddar in Somerset; the cheese used to be kept in limestone caves nearby.

Apple crumble

but in towns with salt in the air, this classic deep-fried delight is always worth trying.

Puddings & Desserts

In British English, 'pudding' has two meanings: the course that comes after the main course (ie dessert); and a type of food that might be sweet (such as Bakewell pudding) or savoury (such as Yorkshire pudding).

A classic British dessert is crumble: a fruit base (often apple or rhubarb), stewed and sweetened, then topped with a crunchy mix of flour, butter and more sugar, and served with custard or ice cream.

Scotland's classic pudding is 'clootie dumpling' (a rich fruit pudding that is wrapped in a cotton cloth, or *cloot* in Scots dialect, while being steamed). Other sweet temptations include cranachan, whipped cream flavoured with whisky and mixed with toasted oatmeal and raspberries, and Atholl brose, a mixture of cream, whisky and honey, flavoured with oatmeal.

Other favourite British puddings include treacle sponge, bread-and-butter pudding and plum pudding, a dome-shaped cake with fruit, nuts and brandy or rum, traditionally eaten at Christmas, when it's called – surprise, surprise – Christmas pudding. This pudding is steamed (rather than baked), cut into slices and served with brandy butter.

While key ingredients of most puddings are self-explanatory, they are perhaps not so obvious for another well-loved favourite: spotted dick. The origin of 'dick' in this context is unclear (it may be a corruption of 'dough' or derived from the German *dicht,* meaning 'thick', or even from 'spotted dog'), but the ingredients are easy: it's just a white suet pudding dotted with blackcurrants. Plus sugar, of course. Most British puddings have loads of butter or loads of sugar, preferably both. Light, subtle and healthy? No chance.

Many towns and cities in England hold regular farmers markets – a chance for food producers large and small to sell direct to the public. For more info and a database, see www.localfoods.org.uk.

Drinking in Britain

The drinks most associated with Britain are tea, beer and whisky. The first two are unlike drinks of the same name found elsewhere in the world, and all three are well worth sampling on your travels around the country.

Tea & Coffee

In Britain, if a local asks 'Would you like a drink?', don't automatically expect a gin and tonic. They may well mean a 'cuppa' – a cup of tea – Britain's best-known beverage. It's usually made with dark tea leaves to produce a strong, brown drink, more bitter in taste than tea served in some other Western countries, which is partly why it's usually served with a dash of milk.

Although tea is sometimes billed as the national drink, coffee is equally popular these days; the Brits consume 165 million cups a day and the British coffee market is worth almost £700 million a year – but with the prices some coffee shops charge, maybe that's not surprising.

A final word of warning: when you're ordering a coffee and the server says 'white or black', don't panic. It simply means 'Do you want milk in it?'

Beer & Cider

British beer typically ranges from dark brown to amber in colour, and is often served at room temperature. Technically it's ale, and often known as 'bitter' (or 'heavy' in Scotland). This is to distinguish it from lager – the drink that most of the rest of the world calls 'beer', which is generally yellow and served cold.

Bitter that's brewed and served traditionally is called 'real ale' to distinguish it from mass-produced brands, and there are many regional varieties. But be ready! If you're used to the 'amber nectar' or 'king of beers', a British brew may be a surprise – it's nearly always flat (uncarbonated) and is served at room temperature. This is partly to do with Britain's climate, and partly to do with the beer being served by hand pump rather than gas pressure. Most important, though, is the integral flavour: traditional British beer doesn't need to be chilled or fizzed to make it palatable.

The increasing popularity of real ales and a backlash against the bland conformity of globalised multinational brewing conglomerates has seen a huge rise in the number of artisan brewers and microbreweries springing up all over Britain – by 2016 there were around 1500 in operation, with around 75 in London alone. They take pride in using only natural ingredients, and many try to revive ancient recipes, such as heather- and seaweed-flavoured ales.

Another key feature is that real ale must be properly stored and looked after, which usually means a willingness on the part of the pub manager or landlord to put in extra effort to ensure the ale tastes as it should.

If beer doesn't tickle your palate, try cider – available in sweet and dry varieties and, increasingly, as craft cider, often with various fruit or herbal flavours added. In western parts of England, notably Herefordshire

In medieval times, labourers often received some of their wages as 'small beer' – a weak ale typically between 0.5% and 2% ABV. Since the ale had been fermented and brewed, it was usually very safe to drink – unlike water, which in pre-sanitation days frequently carried all kinds of diseases and pathogens.

WHERE THERE'S SMOKE...

All restaurants and cafes in Britain are nonsmoking throughout. Virtually all pubs have the same rule, which is why there's often a small crowd of smokers standing on the pavement outside, though some places provide specific outdoor smoking areas. Smoking is permitted in pub gardens, so nonsmokers sometimes need to go *inside* to escape the fumes.

Top: BrewDog, London

Bottom: Macallan distillery (p855)

JOHNBRAID/SHUTTERSTOCK ©

and the southwestern counties of Devon and Somerset, you could try 'scrumpy', a very strong dry cider traditionally made from local apples. Many pubs serve it straight from the barrel.

On hot summer days, you could go for shandy – beer and lemonade mixed in equal quantities. You'll usually need to specify 'lager shandy' or 'bitter shandy'.

Wine

Many visitors are surprised to learn that wine is produced in Britain, and has been since the time of the Romans. Today, more than 400 vineyards produce between three and four million bottles a year – many highly regarded and frequently winning major awards. English sparkling wines have been a particular success story, especially those produced in southeast England where the chalky soil and climatic conditions are similar to those of the Champagne region in France.

Whisky

The spirit most visitors associate with Britain – and especially Scotland – is whisky (note the spelling – it's Irish whiskey that has an 'e'). There's a big difference between single-malt whisky, made purely from malted barley in a single distillery, and blended whisky, made from a blend of cheaper grain whisky and malt whiskies from several distilleries.

A single malt, like a fine wine, somehow captures the terroir or essence of the place where it was made and matured – a combination of the water, the barley, the peat smoke, the oak barrels in which it was aged and (in the case of certain coastal distilleries) the sea air and salt spray. Each distillation varies from the one before, like different vintages from the same vineyard.

Bars & Pubs

In Britain the difference between a bar and a pub is sometimes vague, but generally bars are smarter, larger and louder than pubs, possibly with a younger crowd. Drinks are more expensive, too, unless there's a gallon-of-vodka-and-Red-Bull-for-a-fiver promotion – which there often is.

As well as beer, cider and wine, pubs and bars offer the usual choice of spirits, often served with a 'mixer', producing British favourites such as gin and tonic, rum and coke, and vodka and lime. These drinks are served in measures called 'singles' and 'doubles'. A single can be either 25mL or 35mL (depending on the bar) – just over one US fluid ounce. A double is, of course, 50mL or 70mL – still disappointingly small when compared with measures in other countries. To add further to your disappointment, the vast array of cocktail options, as found in America, is generally restricted to more upmarket city bars in Britain.

And while we're serving up warnings, here are two more. First, if you see a pub calling itself a 'free house', it's simply a place that doesn't belong to a brewery or pub company, and thus is 'free' to sell any brand of beer. Unfortunately, it doesn't mean the booze is free of charge. Second, remember that drinks in British pubs are ordered and paid for at the bar. You can always spot the freshly arrived tourists – they're the ones sitting forlornly at a table hoping to spot a waiter.

When it comes to gratuities, it's not usual to tip pub and bar staff. However, if you're ordering a large round, or the service has been good all evening, you can say to the person behind the bar '…and one for yourself'. They may not have a drink, but they'll add the monetary equivalent to the total you pay and keep it as a tip.

The Campaign for Real Ale promotes the understanding of traditional British beer. Look for endorsement stickers on pub windows, and for more info, see www.camra.org.uk.

To help you find the best ales and a fine pub to drink them in, check out the *Good Beer Guide to Great Britain*, by the Campaign for Real Ale, and the *Good Pub Guide*, by Fiona Stapley.

Architecture in Britain

The history of British architecture spans more than four millennia, from the mysterious stone circles of Stonehenge and Callanish to the glittering skyscrapers of modern London. The country's built heritage includes Roman baths and parish churches, mighty castles and magnificent cathedrals, humble cottages and grand stately homes, and exploring it all is one of the great joys of a visit to Britain.

Early Foundations

The oldest surviving structures in Britain are the grass-covered mounds of earth called 'tumuli' or 'barrows', used as burial sites by the country's prehistoric residents. These mounds, measuring anything from a rough hemisphere just 2m high to oval domes around 5m high and 10m long, are dotted across the countryside and are especially common in areas of chalk such as Salisbury Plain and the Wiltshire Downs in southern England.

Perhaps the most famous mound, and certainly the largest and most mysterious, is Silbury Hill near Marlborough. Historians are not sure exactly why this huge conical mound was built – there's no evidence of it actually being used for burials. Theories include the possibility it was used at cultural ceremonies or in the worship of deities in the style of South American pyramids. Whatever its original purpose, it's still awe-inspiring today.

Even more impressive than the giant tumuli are the most prominent legacies of the neolithic era – the iconic stone circles of Stonehenge and Avebury, both in Wiltshire. Again, their original purpose is a mystery, providing fertile ground for hypothesis and speculation. The most recent theories suggest that Stonehenge may have been a place of pilgrimage for the sick, like modern-day Lourdes, though it was also used as a burial ground and a place of ancestor worship.

Bronze Age & Iron Age

After the neolithic era's great stone circles, the Bronze Age architecture we can see today is more domestic in scale. Hut circles from this period can still be seen in parts of Britain, most notably on Dartmoor in Devon. The Scottish islands hold many of Europe's best surviving Bronze and Iron Age remains, in places like the stone villages of Skara Brae in Orkney and Jarlshof in Shetland.

During the Iron Age, the early peoples of Britain began organising themselves into clans or tribes. Their legacy includes forts built to defend territory and protect from rival tribes or other invaders. Most forts consisted of a steep mound of earth behind a large circular or oval ditch; a famous example is Maiden Castle in Dorset.

The Roman Era

Remains of the Roman Empire are found in many towns and cities (mostly in England and Wales, as the Romans didn't colonise most of what is now Scotland). There are impressive remains in Chester, Exe-

---

The Callanish Standing Stones on Scotland's Isle of Lewis, dating from 3800 to 5000 years ago, are even older than those at Stonehenge and Avebury.

Heritage Organisations

National Trust (www.national trust.org.uk)

National Trust for Scotland (www. nts.org.uk)

English Heritage (www.english-heritage.org.uk)

Cadw (www.cadw. wales.gov.uk)

Historic Environment Scotland (www.historic environment.scot) ter and St Albans, as well as in the lavish Roman spa and bath-house complex in Bath. Britain's largest and most impressive Roman relic is the 73-mile-long sweep of Hadrian's Wall, built in the 2nd century as a defensive line stretching from coast to coast across the island. Originally intended to defend the empire's territories in the south from the marauding tribes further north, it became as much a symbol of Roman power as a fortification.

Medieval Masterpieces

In the centuries following the Norman Conquest of 1066, the perfection of the mason's art saw an explosion of architecture in stone, inspired by the two most pressing concerns of the day: religion and defence. Early structures of timber and rubble were replaced with churches, abbeys and monasteries built in dressed stone. The round arches, squat towers and chevron decoration of the Norman or Romanesque style (11th to 12th centuries) slowly evolved into the tall pointed arches, ribbed vaults and soaring spires of the Gothic (13th to 16th centuries), a history that can often be seen all in the one church – construction often took a couple of hundred years to complete. Many cathedrals remain modern landmarks, such as Salisbury, Winchester, Canterbury and York.

Stone was also put to good use in the building of elaborate defensive structures. Castles range from the atmospheric ruins of Tintagel and Dunstanburgh, and the sturdy ramparts of Conwy and Beaumaris, to the stunning crag-top fortresses of Stirling and Edinburgh. And then there's the most impressive of them all: the Tower of London, guarding the capital for more than 900 years.

Stately Homes

The medieval period was tumultuous, but by the start of the 17th century life had become more settled and the nobility had less need for fortifications. While they were excellent for keeping out the riff-raff, castles were often too cold and draughty for comfortable aristocratic living.

Many castles underwent the home improvements of the day, with larger windows, wider staircases and better drainage installed. Others were simply abandoned for a brand-new dwelling next door, as at Hardwick Hall in Derbyshire.

Following the Civil War, the trend away from castles gathered pace, and throughout the 17th century the landed gentry developed a taste for fine 'country houses' designed by famous architects of the day. Many became the stately homes that are a major feature of the British landscape and a major attraction for visitors. Among the most extravagant are Chatsworth House and Blenheim Palace in England, Powis Castle in Wales and Floors Castle in Scotland.

The great stately homes all display the proportion, symmetry and architectural harmony that was in vogue during the 17th and 18th centuries. These styles were later reflected in the fashionable town houses of the Georgian era, most notably in the city of Bath, where the stunning Royal Crescent is the ultimate example of the genre.

Britain's Best Castles

....
Alnwick
....
Balmoral
....
Beaumaris
....
Berkeley
....
Caernarfon
....
Caerphilly
....
Carlisle
....
Chepstow
....
Conwy
....
Edinburgh
....
Eilean Donan
....
Glamis
....
Harlech
....
Ludlow
....
Pembroke
....
Raglan
....
Richmond
....
Skipton
....
Stirling
....
Tintagel

ARCHITECTURE IN BRITAIN MEDIEVAL MASTERPIECES

HOUSE & HOME

In Britain, it's not all about big houses. Alongside the stately homes, ordinary domestic architecture can still be seen in rural areas. Black-and-white 'half-timbered' houses characterise counties such as Worcestershire, brick-and-flint buildings pepper Suffolk and Sussex, and hardy, centuries-old cottages and farm buildings of slate and local stone are a feature of North Wales. In northern Scotland, the blackhouse is a classic basic dwelling, with walls of dry, unmortared stone packed with earth and a roof of straw and turf.

Houses of Parliament and Big Ben (p80), London

Victoriana

The Victorian era was a time of great building activity. A style called Victorian Gothic developed, imitating the tall, narrow windows and ornamented spires featured in the original Gothic cathedrals. The most famous example is London's Houses of Parliament and the clock tower that everyone knows as Big Ben, which was officially renamed Elizabeth Tower in 2012 to celebrate the Queen's diamond jubilee (although the name doesn't quite seem to have caught on with the general public). A restoration program means that Big Ben's noon-time bongs (the clock by which most clocks and watches in Britain are set) won't ring out again until at least 2021.

Other Victorian Gothic highlights in England's capital include the Natural History Museum and St Pancras train station. The style was copied all around the country, especially for civic buildings, with the finest examples including Manchester Town Hall and Glasgow City Chambers.

Industrialisation

Through the late 19th and early 20th centuries, as Britain's cities grew in size and stature, the newly moneyed middle classes built smart town houses in streets and squares. Elsewhere, the first town planners oversaw the construction of endless terraces of 'back-to-back' and 'two-up-two-down' houses to accommodate the massive influx of workers required for the country's factories. In South Wales, similar, though often single-storeyed, houses were built for the burgeoning numbers of coal miners. The industrial areas of Scotland saw the construction of tenements, usually three or four storeys high, with a central communal staircase and two dwellings on each floor. In many cases the terraced houses and basic

Founded by German immigrant Nikolaus Pevsner after WWII, the Pevsner Architectural Guides are the classic travellers' handbooks of British architecture. Around 80 volumes, published between 1951 and the present day, lovingly document the significant buildings of England, Scotland and Wales.

Scottish Parliament Building (p759), Edinburgh

tenements are not especially scenic, but they are perhaps the most enduring mark on the British architectural landscape.

Postwar Pains & Pride

WWII bombing damaged many of Britain's cities and the rebuilding that followed showed little regard for the overall appearance of the cities or for the lives of people who lived in them. Rows of terraces were swept away in favour of high-rise tower blocks, while the brutalist architecture of the 1950s and '60s embraced the modern and efficient building materials of steel and concrete.

Perhaps this is why the British are largely conservative in their architectural tastes. They often resent ambitious or experimental designs, especially applied to public buildings or when a building's form appears more important than its function. However, a familiar pattern unfolds: after a few years of resentment, the building is given a nickname, then it gains grudging acceptance, and finally it becomes a source of pride and affection. The British just don't like to be rushed, that's all.

The 21st Century

During the first decade of this century, many areas of Britain placed new importance on having progressive, popular architecture as part of a wider regeneration. Top examples include Manchester's Imperial War Museum North, Birmingham's Bullring shopping centre, Edinburgh's Scottish Parliament Building, the Welsh National Assembly building and the Wales Millennium Centre (both on the Cardiff waterfront), the overlapping arches of Glasgow's Scottish Exhibition and Conference Centre (affectionately called 'the Armadillo') and the Sage concert hall in Gateshead in northeast England.

One enduring feature of the British landscape is the boundaries that have been used to divide fields since ancient times. The most common are hedgerows (mostly made of native trees and shrubs such as hazel, ash, blackthorn and alder) and drystone walls (hand-built stone walls, traditionally built without mortar).

DOMINATING THE LANDSCAPE

If you're travelling through Wales, it won't take you long to notice the country's most striking architectural asset: castles. There are about 600 in all, giving Wales the dubious honour of being Europe's most densely fortified country. Most were built in medieval times, first by William the Conqueror and then by other Anglo-Norman kings, to keep the Welsh in check. In the late 13th century Edward I built spectacular castles at Caernarfon, Harlech, Conwy and Beaumaris, now jointly listed as a Unesco World Heritage Site. Other castles to see include Rhuddlan, Denbigh, Criccieth, Raglan, Pembroke, Kidwelly, Chepstow and Caerphilly. While undeniably great for visitors, the castles are a sore point for patriotic Welsh; the writer Thomas Pennant called them the 'magnificent badge of our subjection'.

Perhaps the best-known example of 1950/60s brutalist architecture is London's Southbank Centre. A building of its time, it was applauded when finished, then reviled for its ugliness, and is now regarded by Londoners with something close to pride and affection.

Britain's largest and highest-profile architectural project of recent times was the Olympic Park, the centrepiece of the 2012 Olympic Games. Situated in the London suburb of Stratford, it was renamed the Queen Elizabeth Olympic Park after the games. The main Olympic Stadium – now home to West Ham United football club – and other arenas, including the much-admired Velodrome and Aquatics Centre, were built using cutting-edge techniques and are all dramatic structures in their own right.

Meanwhile, in the centre of the capital, the Shard – a giant, pointed glass skyscraper – dominates the South Bank; at 306m, it's one of Europe's tallest buildings. On the other side of the River Thames, two more giant skyscrapers were completed in 2014: 20 Fenchurch St (thanks to its shape, nicknamed 'the Walkie-Talkie') and the slanting-walled Leadenhall Building (dubbed, inevitably, 'the Cheese Grater').

London continues to grow upwards and British architecture continues to push new boundaries of style and technology. The buildings may look a little different, but they're still iconic and impressive.

The Arts

Britain's contributions to the worlds of literature, drama, cinema and music are celebrated around the world, thanks in no small part to the global dominance of the English language. As you travel around Britain today you can explore artists' childhood homes and the landscapes and locations made famous in lyrics, movie backdrops and literary settings – from the centuries-old birthplace of Shakespeare in Stratford-upon-Avon to Abbey Road of The Beatles fame.

Literature

First Stars

The first big name in Britain's literary history is Geoffrey Chaucer, best known for *The Canterbury Tales*. This mammoth collection of fables, stories and morality tales, using travelling pilgrims (the Knight, the Wife of Bath, the Nun's Priest and so on) as a narrative hook, is considered an essential of the canon.

After Chaucer, two centuries passed before Britain's next major literary figure rose to prominence: enter stage left William Shakespeare. Best known for his many world-famous plays, he was also a prolific and influential poet – although debate rumbles on about whether he actually wrote every word of his work, or whether (as some scholars and performers claim) they are more likely to have been the result of collaborative work.

A collection of folk tales discovered in medieval Welsh manuscripts of the 14th century, *The Mabinogion* was translated into English in the mid-19th century. Drawing on pre-Christian Celtic myths, several of the stories deal with the legendary feats of King Arthur and the Knights of the Round Table.

The 17th & 18th Centuries

The 17th century saw the publication of John Milton's epic blank verse poem *Paradise Lost,* a literary landmark inspired by the biblical tale of Adam and Eve's expulsion from the Garden of Eden. This was followed a few years later by the equally seminal *Pilgrim's Progress* by John Bunyan, an allegorical tale of the everyday Christian struggle. For mere mortals, reading these books in their entirety can be hard going, but they're worth dipping into for a taste of the rich language.

More familiar to most British people are the words of *Auld Lang Syne,* penned by Scotland's national poet Robert Burns, and traditionally sung at New Year. His more unusual *Address to a Haggis* is also still recited annually on Burns Night, a Scottish celebration held on 25 January (the poet's birthday).

Another milestone work of this period is Daniel Defoe's *Robinson Crusoe*. On one level it's an adventure story about a man shipwrecked on an uninhabited island, but it's also a discussion on civilisation, colonialism and faith, and is regarded by many scholars as the first English-language novel. It's also been an armchair travellers' favourite since its publication in 1719.

The *Oxford Guide to Literary Britain & Ireland,* edited by Daniel Hahn and Nicholas Robins, gives details of towns, villages and the countryside immortalised by writers, from Chaucer's Canterbury and Austen's Bath to Scott's Highlands.

The painter, writer, poet and visionary William Blake (1757–1827) mixed fantastical landscapes and mythological scenes with motifs drawn from classical art, religious iconography and legend. For more, see www.blakearchive.org.

LITERARY LOCATIONS

Bath Grandeur that never tired Jane Austen's heroines.

Canterbury Synonymous with Chaucer's *Canterbury Tales*.

Edinburgh Unesco's first City of Literature, with links to Burns, Scott and Stevenson (and even JK Rowling).

Haworth Home of the Brontë sisters, surrounded by wuthering moors.

Lake District Source of inspiration for William Wordsworth.

Laugharne Dylan Thomas' home.

Stratford-upon-Avon Birthplace of William Shakespeare.

The Romantic Era

As industrialisation began to take hold in Britain during the late 18th and early 19th centuries, a new generation of writers, including William Blake, John Keats, Percy Bysshe Shelley, Lord Byron and Samuel Taylor Coleridge, drew inspiration from human imagination and the natural world (in some cases aided by a healthy dose of laudanum). Known as the 'Romantics', the best known of all was William Wordsworth; his famous line from the poem commonly known as 'Daffodils' – 'I wandered lonely as a cloud' – was inspired by a walk along the shores of Ullswater in the Lake District.

Victoriana

During the reign of Queen Victoria (1837–1901), key novels of the time explored social themes. Charles Dickens is the best-known writer of the period: *Oliver Twist* is a tale of child pickpockets surviving in the London slums, while *Hard Times* is a critique of the excesses of capitalism.

At around the same time, but in a rural setting, George Eliot (the pen name of Mary Anne Evans) wrote *The Mill on the Floss,* whose central character, Maggie Tulliver, searches for true love and struggles against society's expectations.

Meanwhile, Thomas Hardy's classic *Tess of the D'Urbervilles* deals with the peasantry's decline, and *The Trumpet Major* paints a picture of idyllic English country life interrupted by war and encroaching modernity. Many of Hardy's works are in the fictionalised county of Wessex, largely based on today's Dorset and surrounding counties, where towns such as Dorchester are popular stops on tourist itineraries today.

Displaying similarly close links to the landscape is *Waverley* by Scotland's greatest historical novelist, Sir Walter Scott. Written in the early 19th century and set in the mountains and glens of Scotland during the time of the Jacobite rebellion, it is usually regarded as the first historical novel in the English language. Scott's bestselling works, which include the narrative poem 'The Lady of the Lake' and the novel *Rob Roy,* are often credited with kick-starting the Scottish tourist industry.

Graham Greene's novel *Brighton Rock* (1938) is a classic account of wayward English youth. For an even more shocking take, try *A Clockwork Orange* by Anthony Burgess, later infamously filmed by Stanley Kubrick in 1971.

The Modern World

Britain – and its literature – changed forever following WWI and the social disruption of the period. This fed into the modernist movement, with DH Lawrence perhaps its finest exponent. *Sons and Lovers* follows the lives and loves of generations in the English Midlands as the country changes from rural idyll to industrial landscape, while his controversial exploration of sexuality in *Lady Chatterley's Lover* was banned until 1960 because of its 'obscenity'.

Other highlights of this period included Daphne du Maurier's romantic suspense novel *Rebecca,* with close connections to Cornwall; Evelyn

Waugh's *Brideshead Revisited,* an exploration of moral and social disintegration among the English aristocracy in the 1920s and '30s; and Richard Llewellyn's Welsh classic *How Green Was My Valley.* A decade or so later, after WWII, Compton Mackenzie lifted postwar spirits with *Whisky Galore,* a comic novel about a cargo of booze shipwrecked on a Scottish island.

In the 1950s, the poet Dylan Thomas found fame with his *Portrait of The Artist As A Young Dog,* although his most celebrated work is a radio play *Under Milk Wood* (1954), exposing the social tensions of small-town Wales.

Then came the swinging '60s. Liverpool poet Roger McGough and friends determined to make art relevant to daily life produced *The Mersey Sound* – landmark pop poetry for the streets. Other new writers included Muriel Spark, who introduced the world to a highly unusual Edinburgh school mistress in *The Prime of Miss Jean Brodie.*

The 1970s saw the arrival of two novelists who went on to become prolific through the rest of the century and beyond. Martin Amis produced a string of novels whose common themes include the absurdity and unappealing nature of modern life, such as *London Fields* (1989). Ian McEwan made his debut with *The Cement Garden* (1978), and earned critical acclaim for finely observed studies of the English character in works such as *Atonement* (2001) and *On Chesil Beach* (2007).

Kate Roberts explored the experiences of working men and women in rural Wales, often evoking qualities of a time since past with *Feet in Chains* (1977). The elegant *On the Black Hill* (1982), by Bruce Chatwin, also evokes the joys and hardships of small-town life, exploring Welsh spirit and cross-border antipathy through the lives of torpid twin-brother farmers.

Modern novels in a different vein include 1993's *Trainspotting* by Irvine Welsh, a dark look at Edinburgh's drug culture, while the grim realities of modern Glasgow are vividly conjured in the 1983 short-story collection *Not Not While the Giro* by James Kelman, whose controversial novel *How Late It Was, How Late* won the 1994 Booker Prize.

Other well-known Scots writers of this period include Janice Galloway (*The Trick Is To Keep Breathing*) and Liz Lochhead (*Mary Queen of Scots Got Her Head Chopped Off*).

For a taste of surreal humour, try two of Britain's funniest (and most successful) writers: Douglas Adams (*The Hitchhiker's Guide to the Galaxy* plus sequels) and Terry Pratchett (the *Discworld* series).

The New Millennium

As the 20th century came to a close, and the new millennium dawned, Britain's multicultural landscape proved a rich inspiration for contemporary novelists. Hanif Kureishi sowed the seeds with his ground-breaking 1990 novel *The Buddha of Suburbia,* followed by Zadie Smith's acclaimed debut *White Teeth* (2000) and a string of subsequent bestsellers. Andrea Levy found acclaim with *Small Island* (2004), and Monica Ali's *Brick*

CHILDREN'S FAVOURITES

Britain's greatest literary phenomenon of the 21st century is JK Rowling's *Harry Potter* series, a set of other-worldly adventures that have entertained millions of children (and many grown-ups too), from the publication of the first book in 1996 to the stage play, *Harry Potter and the Cursed Child,* in 2016. The magical tales, brought vividly to life in the Harry Potter movies, are the latest in a long line of British children's classics that are also enjoyed by adults. The pedigree stretches back to the works of Lewis Carroll (*Alice's Adventures in Wonderland*), E Nesbit (*The Railway Children*), AA Milne (*Winnie-the-Pooh*), CS Lewis (*The Chronicles of Narnia*) and Roald Dahl (*Charlie and the Chocolate Factory, Matilda*). Newcastle's Seven Stories – The Centre for Children's Books is a wonderful place to get acquainted, or reacquainted, with favourites old and new.

Lane was shortlisted for the 2003 Man Booker Prize, a high-profile literary award.

Also popular is Julian Barnes, whose book *England, England* is a darkly ironic study of nationalism and tourism, while *The Sense of an Ending* won the 2011 Man Booker Prize. Hilary Mantel, author of many novels on an astoundingly wide range of subjects, has won the Man Booker Prize twice, first in 2009 for historical blockbuster *Wolf Hall* (about Henry VIII and his ruthless advisor Thomas Cromwell), and then 2012 for its sequel *Bring Up the Bodies;* the third and final instalment, *The Mirror and the Light,* is still a work in progress.

Meanwhile, the genre known as 'Tartan Noir' – crime fiction set in Scottish cities – continues to grow. Ian Rankin, best known for his Edinburgh-set Inspector Rebus novels, is a master of the form, but Val McDermid, Louise Welsh and Christopher Brookmyre are right up there with him.

Cinema

British cinema has a long history, with many early directors cutting their teeth in the silent-film industry. Perhaps the best-known of these was Alfred Hitchcock, who directed *Blackmail,* one of the first British 'talkies' in 1929, and who went on to direct a string of films during the 1930s, before migrating to Hollywood in the early 1940s.

No comedy has captured the British sense of humour better than *Monty Python's Flying Circus,* the surreal, supremely silly sketch show that still inspires legions of fans across the world more than half a century after it first aired.

Early Days

During WWII, British films were dominated by patriotic stories designed to raise morale: *Went the Day Well?* (1942), *In Which We Serve* (1942) and *We Dive at Dawn* (1943) are prime examples of the genre. During this period David Lean directed the classic tale of repressed passion, *Brief Encounter* (1945), before graduating to Hollywood epics, including *Lawrence of Arabia* and *Doctor Zhivago.*

Another great film of the 1940s is *How Green Was My Valley,* a tale of everyday life in the coal-mining villages of Wales. Perhaps the best-known movie about Wales, it manages to annoy more Welsh people than any other with its stereotyped characters, absence of Welsh actors, and the fact that it was shot in a Hollywood studio. It's worth seeing, though, for its period flavour.

After the War

The Ladykillers (1955) is a classic Ealing comedy about a band of hapless bank robbers holed up in a London guesthouse, and features Alec Guinness sporting quite possibly the most outrageous set of false teeth ever captured on celluloid.

Following the hardships of WWII, British audiences were in the mood for escape and entertainment. During the late 1940s and early '50s, the domestic film industry specialised in eccentric British comedies epitomised by the output of Ealing Studios: notable titles include *Passport to Pimlico* (1949), *Kind Hearts and Coronets* (1949) and *The Titfield Thunderbolt* (1953).

Dramatic box-office hits of the time included *Hamlet* (1948; the first British film to win an Oscar in the Best Picture category), starring Laurence Olivier, and Carol Reed's *The Third Man* (1949). In a post-war Britain still struggling with rationing and food shortages, tales of heroic derring-do such as *The Dam Busters* (1955) and comedies like *Whisky Galore!* (1949; a remake was filmed in 2016) helped lighten the national mood.

Swinging Sixties

In the late 1950s, 'British New Wave' and 'Free Cinema' explored the gritty realities of life in an intimate, semidocumentary style, with Lindsay Anderson and Tony Richardson crystallising the movement with films such as *This Sporting Life* (1963) and *A Taste of Honey* (1961).

HAMMER HORROR

The British company Hammer Film Productions produced low-budget horror films in the 1950s and '60s, still revered by fans around the globe. Early flicks included *The Quatermass Xperiment* (1955) and *The Curse of Frankenstein* (1957). The stars of the latter – Peter Cushing as Dr Frankenstein and Christopher Lee as the Monster – would feature in many of Hammer's best films over the next 20 years, including a string of nine *Dracula* films (most of which star Lee as Dracula and Cushing as Van Helsing or his descendants) and six *Frankenstein* sequels.

The studio also launched the careers of several other notable actors (including Oliver Reed, who made his debut in *The Curse of the Werewolf,* 1961) and even spawned its very own spoof, *Carry On Screaming* (1966) – the ultimate British seal of approval. From 1979 the company went into hibernation, but its fortunes revived in 2012 with the release of *The Woman in Black,* starring Harry Potter lead Daniel Radcliffe.

At the other end of the spectrum were the *Carry On* films, packed with bawdy gags and double entendres, and starring a troupe of 'national treasures' including Barbara Windsor, Sid James and Kenneth Williams.

The 1960s saw the birth of another classic British icon: super-spy James Bond, adapted from the Ian Fleming novels and first played by Sean Connery in *Dr No* (1962). Since then over 20 Bond movies have been made, with Bond played by a series of actors from Roger Moore and George Lazenby to Pierce Brosnan and Daniel Craig.

Burning Gold

After the boom of the 1960s, British cinema entered troubled waters for a decade or so, but was revived in the 1980s thanks partly to David Puttnam's *Chariots of Fire,* the Oscar-winning tale of two British athletes competing at the 1924 Olympics.

The newly established (1982) Channel 4 invested in edgy films such as *My Beautiful Laundrette* (1985), while the British producing duo of Ismail Merchant and James Ivory played Hollywood at its own game with period epics such as *Heat and Dust* (1983) and *A Room With A View* (1985), capitalising on the success of Richard Attenborough's big-budget *Gandhi* (1982), which bagged eight Academy Awards.

Brit Flicks

In the 1990s, the massively successful *Four Weddings and a Funeral* (1994), which introduced Hugh Grant in his trademark role as the likeable, self-deprecating Englishman (an archetype he reprised in subsequent hits *Notting Hill,* 1999, and *Love Actually,* 2003) spearheaded the 'Brit flick' genre. *The Full Monty* (1997), about a troupe of laid-off steel workers turned male strippers, was Britain's most successful film ever (until overtaken by the Harry Potter franchise in 2001), while *The English-man Who Went Up a Hill and Came Down a Mountain* (1995), is an affectionate story about a hill in North Wales.

Grittier films of the 1990s included *Trainspotting* (1996), a visually innovative, hard-hitting film about Edinburgh's drugged-out underworld, which launched the careers of Scottish actors Ewan McGregor and Robert Carlyle, while Mike Leigh's *Secrets and Lies* (1996), a Palme d'Or winner at Cannes, tells the story of an adopted black woman who seeks out her white mother.

Other landmark films of the decade included gangster movie *Lock, Stock and Two Smoking Barrels* (1998), which spawned a host of copycats; *Breaking the Waves* (1996), a perfect study of culture clash in 1970s

Withnail and I (1987) is one of the great British cult comedies. Directed by Bruce Robinson, it stars Paul McGann and Richard E Grant as a pair of hapless out-of-work actors on a disastrous holiday to the Lake District.

The British Film Institute (BFI) is dedicated to promoting film and cinema in Britain, and publishes the monthly academic journal *Sight & Sound.* See www.bfi. org.uk and www. screenonline.org. uk for complete coverage of Britain's film and TV industry.

Scotland; *Human Traffic* (1999), an edgy romp through Cardiff's club-land; and the Oscar-winning Austen adaptation *Sense and Sensibility* (1995) starring English doyennes Emma Thompson and Kate Winslet as the Dashwood sisters, with Hugh Grant as (you guessed it) a likeable and self-deprecating Englishman.

Award-winning Welsh-language films of the time include *Hedd Wynn* (1992), a heartbreaking story of a poet killed in WWI, and *Solomon and Gaenor* (1999), a passionate tale of forbidden love at the turn of the 20th century, starring Ioan Gruffudd and filmed twice; once in the Welsh language and once in English.

The decade ended with films such as *East Is East* (1999), a beautifully understated study of the clash between first- and second-generation immigrant Pakistanis in Britain, and *Billy Elliott* (2000), about a boy's quest to learn ballet and escape the slag heaps of post-industrial northern England.

Britain's main broadcasters are known for their long-running 'soaps' (soap operas) such as *EastEnders* (BBC), *Emmerdale* and *Coronation Street* (both ITV), which have collectively been running on British screens for well over a century.

The 21st Century

In the early part of the 21st century, literature continued to provide the richest seam mined by the British film industry. Hits include the blockbuster *Harry Potter* franchise (based on the books of JK Rowling, and the most financially successful film series of all time) starring Daniel Radcliffe, as well as 2005's *The Constant Gardener* (based on a John Le Carré novel), 2007's *Atonement* (based on Ian McEwan's novel), 2011's *War Horse* (directed by Stephen Spielberg and based on Michael Morpurgo's novel), and 2012's *Anna Karenina,* directed by Joe Wright and starring Keira Knightley. *T2* (2017), the much anticipated sequel to *Trainspotting,* was based on Irvine Welsh's novel *Porno.*

Biopics are a perennial favourite, with recent highlights including the stories of Queen Elizabeth II (*The Queen,* 2006), Queen Elizabeth I (*Elizabeth: The Golden Age,* 2007), Margaret Thatcher (*The Iron Lady,* 2011), scientist Stephen Hawking (*The Theory of Everything,* 2014) and 19th-century artist JMW Turner (*Mr Turner,* 2014).

The BBC is a public-service broadcaster, financed by the licence fee of £150.50, paid annually by every house in Britain with a TV set, rather than by advertising. This means shows are not interrupted by commercial breaks.

Comedy continues to thrive: building on the success of zombie-spoof *Shaun of the Dead* (2004) and cop-movie spoof *Hot Fuzz* (2007), Simon Pegg (who stars as Scotty in the most recent Star Trek movies) and Nick Frost returned in alien-invasion spoof *The World's End* (2013), while Richard Curtis produced another crowd-pleasing romantic comedy with *About Time* (2013).

Meanwhile, the oldest of British film franchises rolls on, with James Bond played as a tough, toned and occasionally fallible character by Daniel Craig in *Casino Royale (2006), Quantum of Solace* (2008), *Skyfall* (2012) and *Spectre* (2015). Craig has signed up for a final time for the 25th instalment in 2019; after that, the role will be up for grabs, with many commentators speculating that it may go next to an ethnic minority actor or, perhaps, a woman.

Pop & Rock Music

Britain's been putting the world through its musical paces ever since a mop-haired four-piece from Liverpool tuned up their Rickenbackers and created The Beatles. And while some may claim that Elvis invented rock 'n' roll, it was the Fab Four who transformed it into a global phenomenon, backed by the other bands of the 1960s 'British Invasion' – The Rolling Stones, The Who, Cream, The Kinks and soul man Tom Jones.

Glam to Punk

Glam rock swaggered onto the stage at the start of the 1970s, led by the likes of Marc Bolan and David Bowie in their tight-fitting jumpsuits and chameleon guises, and succeeded by early boy band Bay City Rollers, art-rockers Roxy Music, outrageously costumed Elton John and anthemic popsters Queen. In the same era, Led Zeppelin, Deep Purple and Black Sabbath laid down the blueprint for heavy metal, while the psychedelia of the previous decade morphed into the spacey noodlings of prog rock, epitomised by Pink Floyd, Genesis and Yes.

By the late '70s, glam and prog bands were looking out of touch in a Britain wracked by rampant unemployment and industrial unrest, and punk rock exploded onto the scene, summing up the air of doom with nihilistic lyrics and three-chord tunes. The Sex Pistols remain the best-known band of the era, while other punk pioneers included The Clash, The Damned, The Buzzcocks and The Stranglers.

Punk begat New Wave, with acts such as The Jam and Elvis Costello blending spiky tunes and sharp lyrics into a more radio-friendly sound. A little later, along came bands like The Specials and baggy-trousered rude boys Madness, mixing punk, reggae and ska sounds. Meanwhile, another punk-and-reggae-influenced band called The Police – fronted by bassist Sting – became one of the biggest names of the decade.

Mode, Metal & Miserabilism

The conspicuous consumption of Britain in the early 1980s was reflected in the decade's pop scene. Big hair and shoulder pads became the uniform of New Romantics such as Spandau Ballet, Duran Duran and Culture Club, while the increased use of synthesizers led to the development of a new electronic sound in the music of Depeche Mode and The Human League. More hits and highlights were supplied by Texas, Eurythmics and Wham! – a boyish duo headed by a bright young fellow named George Michael.

Away from the glitz, fans enjoyed the doom-laden lyrics of The Cure, Bauhaus and Siouxsie & the Banshees, while Britain's heavy rock heritage inspired acts such as Iron Maiden. In a different tone entirely, the disaffection of mid-1980s Britain was summed up by the arch-priests of 'miserabilism', The Smiths, fronted by quiffed wordsmith Morrissey.

Raves, Indie & Britpop

The beats and bleeps of 1980s electronica fuelled the burgeoning dance-music scene of the early '90s. An eruption of ecstasy-saturated rave culture, centred on famous clubs like Manchester's Haçienda and London's Ministry of Sound, overflowed into the mainstream through chart-topping artists such as The Prodigy and Fatboy Slim. Manchester was also a focus for the burgeoning British 'indie' scene, driven by guitar-based bands such as The Charlatans, The Stone Roses, James and Happy Mondays.

Indie grew up in the mid- to late 1990s, and the term 'Britpop' was coined, with Oasis at the forefront, and including a wide range of bands

The Spice Girls were one of the most famous pop creations of the 1990s, and they became the world's best-selling all-female group. Sporty, Scary, Baby, Ginger and Posh famously reunited in 2012 to perform at the London Olympics closing ceremony.

POP ON FILM

If you want to combine British pop music with British cinema, try some of these films:

Backbeat (1994) A look at the early days of The Beatles.

Sid and Nancy (1986) The demise of Sex Pistols bassist Sid Vicious and his American girlfriend.

Velvet Goldmine (1998) A tawdry glimpse of the 1970s glam-rock scene.

24 Hour Party People (2002) A totally irreverent and suitably chaotic film about the 1990s Manchester music scene.

Control (2007) Biopic about Joy Division's lead singer Ian Curtis.

Nowhere Boy (2009) About John Lennon in his pre-Beatles days.

ROCK 'N' ROLL LOCATIONS

Fans buy the music, then the T-shirt. However, true fans visit the locations featured on album covers. Here are some favourites, many in London, plus a few others around the country:

Abbey Rd, St John's Wood, London – *Abbey Road,* The Beatles

Battersea Power Station, London – *Animals,* Pink Floyd

Berwick St, Soho, London – *(What's the Story) Morning Glory?,* Oasis

Big Ben, London – *My Generation* (US version), The Who

Camden Market, London – *The Clash,* The Clash

Heddon St, off Regent St, London – *The Rise and Fall of Ziggy Stardust & the Spiders from Mars,* David Bowie

Porthmadog (Black Rock Sands) – *This is My Truth Tell Me Yours,* Manic Street Preachers

Salford Lads Club, Manchester – *The Queen is Dead,* The Smiths

Thor's Cave, Manifold Valley, near Ashbourne, Peak District National Park – *A Storm In Heaven,* The Verve

Yes Tor, Dartmoor, Devon – *Tormato,* Yes

---

such as Blur, Pulp, Elastica, Suede, Supergrass, Ocean Colour Scene, The Verve, Travis, Super Furry Animals, Stereophonics, Catatonia and the Manic Street Preachers.

Pop Today, Gone Tomorrow

The new millennium saw no let-up in the British music scene's shape-shifting and reinvention. Jazz, soul, R&B and hip hop have fused into an 'urban' sound epitomised by artists like Dizzee Rascal, Tinie Tempah and Plan B.

In a totally different genre, British folk and roots music, and folk-influenced acoustic music, is enjoying its biggest revival since the 1960s, with major names including Eliza Carthy, Mumford & Sons and Welsh band Allan Yn Y Fan.

Meanwhile, the singer-songwriter, exemplified by Katie Melua, Ed Sheeran, the late Amy Winehouse, James Bay and the all-conquering Adele, has made a comeback, and the spirit of British punk and indie stays alive thanks to the likes of Florence & the Machine, Muse, Kasabian, Radiohead, The Horrors and breakthrough grunge-pop band Wolf Alice.

But the biggest commercial success of all has been boy band One Direction, becoming the first artists ever to have each of their four albums debut at number one in the US charts, having the biggest grossing concert tour ever in 2014, and being named Billboard Artist of the Year in 2014.

Painting & Sculpture

For many centuries, continental Europe – especially Holland, Spain, France and Italy – set the artistic agenda. The first artist with a truly British style and sensibility was arguably William Hogarth, whose riotous canvases exposed the vice and corruption of 18th-century London. His most celebrated work is *A Rake's Progress,* which kick-started a long tradition of British caricatures that can be traced right through to the work of modern-day cartoonists such as Gerald Scarfe and Steve Bell. It's displayed at Sir John Soane's Museum in London.

Portraits & Landscapes

While Hogarth was busy satirising society, other artists were hard at work showing it in its best light. The leading figures of 18th-century British portraiture were Sir Joshua Reynolds, Thomas Gainsborough and George Romney, while George Stubbs is best known for his intricate studies of animals (particularly horses). Works by these artists are displayed at the Tate Britain and the National Gallery in London.

In the 19th century, leading painters favoured the landscape. John Constable's best-known works include *Salisbury Cathedral* and *The Hay Wain*, depicting a mill in Suffolk (and now on show in the National Gallery, London), while JMW Turner was fascinated by the effects of light and colour, with his works becoming almost entirely abstract by the 1840s – vilified at the time but prefiguring the Impressionist movement that was to follow 50 years later.

Fables & Flowers

In the mid- to late 19th century, the Pre-Raphaelite movement harked back to the figurative style of classical Italian and Flemish art, tying in with the prevailing Victorian taste for fables, myths and fairy tales. Key members of the movement included Sir John Everett Millais and William Holman Hunt. Millais' *Ophelia,* showing the damsel picturesquely drowned in a river, is an excellent example of their style, and can be seen at the Tate Britain. However, one of the best collections of Pre-Raphaelite art is in the Birmingham Museum and Art Gallery.

A good friend of the Pre-Raphaelites was William Morris; he saw late-19th-century furniture and interior design as increasingly vulgar, and with Dante Gabriel Rossetti and Edward Burne-Jones founded the Arts and Crafts movement to encourage the revival of a decorative approach to features such as wallpaper, tapestries and windows. Many of his designs are still used today.

North of the border, Charles Rennie Mackintosh, fresh from the Glasgow School of Art, fast became a renowned artist, designer and architect. He is still Scotland's greatest art nouveau exponent, and much of his work remains in Glasgow. He also influenced a group of artists from the 1890s that became known as the Glasgow School (often divided into two groups: the Glasgow Boys and the Glasgow Girls), among them Margaret and Frances MacDonald, James Guthrie and EA Walton. Much of their work can be seen in the Kelvingrove Art Gallery in Glasgow.

Stone & Sticks

In the tumultuous 20th century, British art became increasingly experimental, with key painters including Francis Bacon, whose work was influenced by Freudian psychoanalysis, and the group known as the Scottish Colourists – Francis Cadell, SJ Peploe, Leslie Hunter and JD Fergusson. Meanwhile, pioneering sculptors such as Henry Moore and Barbara Hepworth experimented with natural forms in stone and new materials.

At around the same time, Welsh artist Gwen John painted introspective portraits of women friends, cats and nuns (and famously became the model and lover of French artist Rodin), while her brother Augustus John became Britain's leading portrait painter, with famous sitters such as Thomas Hardy and George Bernard Shaw. One place to admire the Johnses' works is at the Glynn Vivian Art Gallery in Swansea.

Pop Art

The mid-1950s and early '60s saw an explosion of British artists plundering TV, music, advertising and popular culture for inspiration. Leaders of this new 'pop art' movement included David Hockney, who used bold

The works of Henry Moore and Barbara Hepworth can be seen at the Yorkshire Sculpture Park, between Sheffield and Leeds, in northern England. Hepworth is also forever associated with St Ives in Cornwall, while the Hepworth Wakefield gallery is dedicated to her life and work.

Antony Gormley's *Angel of the North* is one of the most viewed works of art in the world. It stands beside the busy A1 London–Edinburgh road, where millions of drivers each year can't help but see it.

colours and simple lines to depict his dachshunds and swimming pools, and Peter Blake, who designed the collage cover for The Beatles' landmark *Sgt. Pepper's Lonely Hearts Club Band* album.

The '60s also saw the rise of sculptor Anthony Caro, who held his first ground-breaking exhibition at the Whitechapel Art Gallery in 1963. Creating large abstract works in steel and bronze, he remains one of Britain's most influential sculptors.

Britart & Beyond

Thanks partly to the support (and money) of advertising tycoon Charles Saatchi, a new wave of British artists came to the fore in the 1990s. The movement was dubbed, inevitably, 'Britart'; its leading members included Damien Hirst, initially famous (or infamous) for works involving pickled sharks, semidissected human figures and a diamond-encrusted skull entitled *For the Love of God*. His pregnant, naked and half-flayed *Verity* towers 20m high beside the harbour mouth at Ilfracombe in north Devon.

A contemporary is Tracey Emin. Once considered an enfant terrible, she incurred the wrath of the tabloids for works such as *My Bed,* a messed-up bedroom scene that sold for £2.2 million in 2014, but is now a respected figure and patron of the Turner Gallery in Margate. Her recent work, the 20m neon sculpture 'I Want My Time With You', was installed at London's St Pancras Station in 2018, and has been interpreted by some commentators as Emin's comment on the Brexit debate.

The Turner Prize (named after JMW Turner) is a high-profile (and frequently controversial) annual award for British visual artists. As well as Hirst, other winners and their works have included Martin Creed (a room with lights going on and off), Mark Wallinger (a collection of anti-war objects), Simon Starling (a shed converted to a boat and back again), Rachel Whiteread (a plaster cast of a house) and Antony Gormley (best known for his gigantic *Angel of the North*).

Theatre

Theatre in Britain has its roots in medieval morality plays, court jesters and travelling storytellers. Its origins can possibly be traced all the way back to dramas during Roman times in amphitheatres, a few of which still remain at places such as Chester and Cirencester. Most scholars agree that the key milestone in the story is the opening of England's first theatre, called simply The Theatre, in London in 1576. A few years later, two more theatres appeared, the Rose and the Globe, and the stage was set for the entrance of Britain's best-known playwright.

Jez Butterworth is one of the UK's most successful playwrights. His 2009 state-of-England tale *Jerusalem* was one of the most successful and acclaimed plays in West End history. His 2017 work *The Ferryman*, a moving tale set in IRA-era Northern Ireland, was another smash hit, winning awards and becoming the Royal Court Theatre's fastest-selling play.

Shakespeare

For most visitors to Britain (and for many locals) drama means just one name: Shakespeare. Born in 1564 in the Midlands town of Stratford-upon-Avon, William Shakespeare made his name in London, where most of his plays were performed at the Globe Theatre.

He started writing plays around 1585, and his early theatrical works are grouped together as 'comedies' and 'histories', many of which are household names today – such as *All's Well that Ends Well, The Taming of the Shrew, A Midsummer Night's Dream, Richard III* and *Henry V*. Later in his career Shakespeare wrote the plays known collectively as the 'tragedies', including *Romeo and Juliet, Macbeth, Julius Caesar, Hamlet* and *King Lear*. His brilliant plots and spectacular use of language, plus the sheer size of his body of work, have turned him into a national – and international – icon.

Today, 400 years after he shuffled off his mortal coil, the Bard's plays still pull in big crowds, and can be enjoyed at the rebuilt Globe on London's South Bank and at the Royal Shakespeare Company's own theatre in his original hometown of Stratford-upon-Avon.

The debate rages on, however, about precisely how Shakespeare penned his plays. Some academics maintain he was the sole author, while others (including the well-known actor and former director of the RSC, Mark Rylance) maintain that the plays were much more likely to have been written as a collaborative effort – perhaps with other writers, or in collaboration with his troupe of actors, or perhaps both. The truth will probably never be known, but the plays will endure.

British Theatre Today

However you budget your time and money during your visit to Britain, be sure to see some theatre. It easily lives up to its reputation as the finest in the world, especially in London (whatever New Yorkers may say), while other big cities around the country boast their own top-class venues, such as the Birmingham Repertory Theatre, the Bristol Old Vic, the Chichester Festival Theatre, the Playhouse in Nottingham, the New Theatre in Cardiff and the Royal Lyceum in Edinburgh.

For big names, most people head for London's West End, where famous spots include the Shaftsbury, the Adelphi, and the Theatre Royal, Drury Lane. Such venues are mostly the preserve of classic plays, including *The Mousetrap,* the legendary whodunnit and world's longest-running play, showing continuously since 1952.

West End Musicals

As well as drama, London's West End means big musicals, with a long history of crowd-pullers such as *Cats, The Wizard of Oz, Les Misérables, Sweeney Todd, The Phantom of the Opera* and *The Lion King,* with many of today's shows raiding the pop world for material, such as *We Will Rock You,* inspired by the music of Queen, and Abba-based *Mamma Mia!*

Around Britain, buildings associated with notable people are marked with a (usually blue) plaque. In early 2012, a plaque was placed at 23 Heddon St in London to commemorate David Bowie's fictional pop character Ziggy Stardust.

THE ARTS THEATRE

The British Landscape

When it comes to landscapes, Britain is not a place of extremes; there are no Alps or Himalaya here, no Amazon or Sahara. But there's plenty to keep you enthralled. The country may be small, but even a relatively short journey takes you through a surprising mix of scenery. Seeing the change as you travel – subtle in some areas, dramatic in others – is one of this country's great attractions.

Location, Location, Location

Geologically at least, Britain is part of Europe. It's on the edge of the Eurasian landmass, separated from the mother continent by the shallow English Channel. (The French are not so proprietorial, and call it La Manche – 'the sleeve'.) Until about 10,000 years ago, Britain was connected to Europe by land, but then sea levels rose and created the island we know today. Only in more recent times has there been a reconnection, in the form of the Channel Tunnel.

Wildlife of Britain by George McGavin et al is subtitled 'the definitive visual guide'. Although too heavy to carry around, this beautiful photographic book is great for pre-trip inspiration or post-trip memories.

Southern England is covered in a mix of cities, towns and gently undulating countryside. Eastern England (especially the area called East Anglia) is almost entirely low and flat, while southwest England has wild moors, granite outcrops and rich pastures (Devon's cream is world famous), plus a rugged coast with sheltered beaches, making it a favourite holiday destination.

In the north of England, farmland is interspersed with towns and cities, but the landscape is noticeably more rugged. A spine of large hills called the Pennines (fondly tagged 'the backbone of England') runs from Derbyshire to the Scottish border, and includes the peaty plateau of the Peak District, the wild moors around Haworth (immortalised in Brontë novels), the delightful valleys of the Yorkshire Dales and the frequently windswept but starkly beautiful hills of Northumberland.

Perhaps England's best-known landscape is the Lake District, a small but spectacular cluster of mountains and lakes in the northwest, where Scafell Pike (978m) is England's highest peak.

The landscape of Wales is also defined by hills: notably the rounded Black Mountains and Brecon Beacons in the south, and the spiky peaks of Snowdonia in the north, with Snowdon (1085m) the highest Welsh summit. In between lie the wild Cambrian Mountains of central Wales, rolling to the west coast of spectacular cliffs and shimmering river estuaries.

For real mountains, you need to head to Scotland, especially the wild, remote and thinly populated northwest Highlands – separated from the rest of the country by a diagonal gash in the earth's crust called the Great Glen Fault. Ben Nevis (1345m) is Scotland's – and Britain's – highest summit, but there are many more to choose from. The Highlands are further enhanced by the vast cluster of beautiful islands that lie off the loch-indented west coast.

South of the Scottish Highlands is the relatively flat central Lowlands, home to the bulk of Scotland's population. Further south, down to the border with England, things get hillier again; this is the southern Uplands, an area of rounded heather-clad hills and fertile farms.

National Parks

Back in 1810, English poet and outdoor fan William Wordsworth suggested that the wild landscape of the Lake District in Cumbria, northwest England, should be 'a sort of national property, in which every man has a right'. More than a century later, in 1951, the Lake District did indeed become a national park along with the Peak District, Dartmoor and Snowdonia, followed in later years by the Brecon Beacons, Cairngorms, Exmoor, Loch Lomond and The Trossachs, New Forest, Norfolk and Suffolk Broads, Northumberland, North York Moors, Pembrokeshire Coast, South Downs and Yorkshire Dales. In 2017 the Lake District was also named the UK's newest World Heritage Site by Unesco.

Britain's national parks combined cover over 10% of its area, but the term 'national park' can cause confusion. First, these areas are not state owned: nearly all land in Britain is privately owned, belonging mostly to aristocratic families, private trusts and conservation organisations. Second, they are not areas of wilderness as in many other countries. In Britain's national parks you'll see crop fields in lower areas and grazing sheep on the uplands, as well as roads, railways and villages. Some national parks even contain towns, quarries and factories. It's a reminder of the balance that needs to be struck in this crowded country between protecting the natural environment and catering for the people who live in it.

But don't be put off. Despite these apparent anomalies, Britain's national parks still contain mountains, hills, downs, moors, woods, river valleys and other areas of quiet countryside, all ideal for long walks, easy rambles, cycle rides, sightseeing or just lounging around. To help you get the best from the parks, they all have information centres, and all provide various recreational facilities (trails, car parks, campsites etc) for visitors.

Finally, it's worth noting that there are many beautiful parts of Britain that are *not* national parks (such as central Wales, the North Pennines in England, and many parts of Scotland). These can be just as good for outdoor activities or simply exploring by car or foot, and are often less crowded than the popular national parks.

Wildlife

For a small country, Britain has a very diverse range of plants and animals. Many native species are hidden away, but there are some undoubted gems, from lowland woods carpeted in shimmering bluebells to stately herds of deer on the high moors. Taking the time to have a closer look will enhance your trip enormously, especially if you have the time and inclination to enjoy some walking or cycling through the British landscape.

BRITAIN'S BEST BEACHES

Britain has a great many beaches, each with their own distinct character, from tiny hidden coves in Cornwall and Pembrokeshire to vast neon-lined strands in resorts such as Brighton and Blackpool. Favourite spots line the entire southwest peninsula and much of the south coast.

Other great beaches can be found in Suffolk, Norfolk, Lancashire, Yorkshire and Northumberland in England, and pretty much anywhere on the Welsh coast between the Gower Peninsula and Llandudno. Scotland offers even more choice, from the rocky bays of the west coast to the gorgeous white-sand beaches of the Outer Hebrides.

Britain's best resort beaches earn the coveted international Blue Flag (www.blueflag. global) award, meaning sand and water are clean and unpolluted. Other parameters include the presence of lifeguards, litter bins and recycling facilities – meaning some wild beaches may not earn the award, but are still stunning nonetheless.

BRITAIN'S NATIONAL PARKS

NATIONAL PARK	FEATURES	ACTIVITIES	BEST TIME TO VISIT
Brecon Beacons (p681)	great green ridgelines, waterfalls; Welsh mountain ponies, otters, red kites, buzzards, peregrine falcons, kingfishers	horse riding, cycling, caving, canoeing, hang-gliding	Mar & Apr (spring lambs on the hills)
Cairngorms (p895)	snowy mountains, pine forests; ospreys, pine martens, wildcats, grouse, capercaillies	skiing, climbing, birdwatching, walking	Feb (for the snow)
Dartmoor (p318)	rolling hills, rocky outcrops, serene valleys; wild ponies, deer, peregrine falcons	walking, mountain biking, horse riding	May & Jun (wildflowers in bloom)
Exmoor (p295)	sweeping moors, craggy sea cliffs; red deer, wild ponies, horned sheep	horse riding, walking	Sep (heather in bloom)
Lake District (p572)	majestic fells, rugged mountains, shimmering lakes; red squirrels, osprey, golden eagles	watersports, walking, mountaineering, climbing	Sep & Oct (summer crowds depart, autumn colours abound)
Loch Lomond & The Trossachs (p856)	sparkling lochs, brooding mountains; deer, squirrels, badgers, foxes, otters, buzzards	climbing, walking, cycling, canoeing	May (bluebell woods; before the summer rush)
New Forest (p263)	woods, heathland; wild ponies, otters, Dartford warblers, southern damselflies	walking, cycling, horse riding	Apr-Sep (lush vegetation)
Norfolk & Suffolk Broads (p392)	shallow lakes, rivers, marshlands, water lilies; otters, wildfowl	walking, cycling, boating	Apr & May (birds most active)
North York Moors (p498)	heather-clad hills, deep-green valleys; merlins, curlews, golden plovers	walking, mountain biking	Aug & Sep (heather flowering)
Northumberland (p628)	wild rolling moors, heather, gorse; red squirrels, black grouse; Hadrian's Wall	walking, cycling, climbing	Apr & May (lambs), Sep (heather flowering)
Peak District (p466)	high moors, tranquil dales, limestone caves; badgers, kestrels, grouse	walking, cycling, mountain biking, hang-gliding, climbing	Apr & May (even more lambs)
Pembrokeshire Coast (p669)	wave-ravaged shorelines, cliffs, beaches; puffins, fulmars, shearwaters, grey seals, dolphins, porpoises	walking, kayaking, coasteering, mountain biking, horse riding	Apr & May (lambs again)
Snowdonia (p710)	major mountain ranges, lakes, estuaries, Snowdon lilies; wild goats, polecats, curlews, choughs, red kites, buzzards	walking, kayaking, climbing, mountain biking, horse riding	May-Sep (better weather)
South Downs (p173)	rolling chalky hills, tranquil farmland, sheer white sea cliffs, bastard toadflax; Adonis Blue butterflies, buzzards, red kites, peregrine falcons	walking, mountain biking, cycling, horse riding	any time of year (thanks to mild climate)
Yorkshire Dales (p507)	rugged hills, lush valleys, limestone pavements; red squirrels, hares, curlews, lapwings, buzzards	walking, cycling, mountain biking, climbing	Apr & May (you guessed it, lambs)

Farmland

In farmland areas, rabbits are everywhere, but if you're hiking through the countryside be on the lookout for brown hares, an increasingly rare species. They're related to rabbits, but much larger. Males who battle for territory by boxing on their hind legs in early spring are, of course, as 'mad as a March hare'.

Although hare numbers are on the decline, otters are making a comeback. In southern Britain they inhabit the banks of rivers and lakes, and in Scotland they frequently live on the coast where they are easier to spot. Although their numbers are growing, they are mainly nocturnal, but keep your eyes peeled in the daytime and you might be lucky.

You're much more likely to see a red fox. This classic British mammal was once seen only in the countryside, but these wily beasts adapt well to any situation, so these days you're just as likely to see them scavenging in towns and even in city suburbs.

Elsewhere, another British classic, the badger, is under threat from farmers who believe they transmit bovine tuberculosis to cattle, although conservationists say the case is far from proven.

Common birds of farmland and similar landscapes (and urban gardens) include the robin, with its instantly recognisable red breast and cheerful whistle; the wren, whose loud trilling song belies its tiny size; and the yellowhammer, with a song that sounds like (if you use your imagination) 'a-little-bit-of-bread-and-no-cheese'. In open fields, the warbling cry of a skylark is another classic, but now threatened, sound of the British outdoors. You're more likely to see a pheasant, a large bird originally introduced from Russia to the nobility's shooting estates, but now considered naturalised.

Between the fields, hedges provide cover for flocks of finches, but these seed-eaters must watch out for sparrowhawks – birds of prey that come from nowhere at tremendous speed. Other predators include barn owls, a wonderful sight as they fly silently along hedgerows listening for the faint rustle of a vole or shrew. In rural Wales or Scotland you will see plenty of buzzards, Britain's most common large raptor.

Woodland

In woodland areas, mammals include the small white-spotted fallow deer and the even smaller roe deer. Woodlands are full of birds too, but you'll hear them more than see them. Listen out for willow warblers (which, as the name suggests, have a warbling song with a descending cadence) and chiffchaffs (once again, the clue's in the name: they make a repetitive 'chiff chaff' noise).

If you hear rustling among the fallen leaves it might be a hedgehog – a cute-looking, spiny-backed insect eater – but it's an increasingly rare sound these days; conservationists say they'll be extinct in Britain by 2025, due to insecticides in farming, increased building in rural areas and hedgehogs' notoriously poor ability to cross roads safely.

In no such danger are grey squirrels, originally introduced from North America. They have proved very adaptable, to the extent that native red squirrels are severely endangered because the greys eat all the food. Pockets of red squirrels survive in the English Lake District and in many parts of Scotland, especially north of the central Lowlands.

Much larger than squirrels are pine martens, which are seen in some forested regions, especially in Scotland. With beautiful brown coats, they were once hunted for their fur, but are now fully protected.

Mountain & Moorland

On mountains and high moors – including Exmoor, Dartmoor, the Lake District, Northumberland and much of Scotland – the most visible

Herds of 'wild' ponies roam the New Forest, Exmoor and Dartmoor; these animals certainly roam free, but in reality they are privately owned and managed.

Britain's most wooded county is Surrey, despite its proximity to London. The soil is too poor for agriculture, so Surrey's trees were spared. But almost half of all Britain's forested areas are in Scotland. The Woodland Trust (www.woodlandtrust.org.uk) campaigns to protect Britain's remaining woodlands.

mammal is the red deer. Males of the species grow their famous large antlers between April and July, and shed them again in February.

Also on the high ground, well known and easily recognised birds include the red grouse, which often hides in the heather until almost stepped on then flies away with a loud warning call. On the high peaks of Scotland you may see the grouse's northern cousin, the ptarmigan, dappled brown in summer but white in winter.

Look out, too, for the curlew, with its stately long legs and elegant curved bill. With luck you may see beautifully camouflaged golden plovers, while the spectacular aerial displays of lapwings are impossible to miss.

Other mountain birds include red kites (there have been various successful projects around the country to reintroduce these spectacular fork-tailed raptors). Also in the Scottish mountains, keep an eye peeled for golden eagles, Britain's second-largest birds of prey, as they glide and soar along ridges.

> Would-be twitchers can easily spot majestic red kites in the mountains and moors of the Brecon Beacons, particularly at feeding stations such as Gigrin Farm in Rhayader, Wales.

Rivers & Coasts

If you're near inland water, you have a chance of spotting an osprey; the best places in Britain to see this magnificent bird include Rutland Water in the English Midlands and the Cairngorms in Scotland. You could also look along the riverbanks for signs of water voles, endearing rodents that were once very common but have been all but wiped out by wild mink (fur farm escapees first introduced from America).

On the coasts of Britain, particularly in Cornwall, Pembrokeshire and northwest Scotland, the dramatic cliffs are a marvellous sight in early summer (around May), when they are home to hundreds of thousands of breeding seabirds. Guillemots, razorbills and kittiwakes, among others, fight for space on impossibly crowded rock ledges. The cliffs become white with droppings and the air is filled with their shrill calls. Even if you're not into bird spotting, this is one of Britain's finest wildlife spectacles.

Another bird to look out for in coastal areas is the comical puffin (especially common in Shetland), with its distinctive rainbow beak and 'nests' burrowed in sandy soil. In total contrast, gannets are one of the largest seabirds and make dramatic dives for fish, often from a great height. The biggest tick in coastal birdwatching, though, is the white-tailed eagle, Britain's largest bird of prey, which can be seen in the west of Scotland, notably on Mull and Skye.

WILDLIFE IN YOUR POCKET

Is it a rabbit or a hare? A gull or a tern? Buttercup or cowslip? If you need to know a bit more about Britain's plant and animal kingdoms the following field guides are ideal for entry-level naturalists:

➡ *Complete Guide to British Wildlife* by Paul Sterry is portable and highly recommended, and covers mammals, birds, fish, plants, snakes, insects and even fungi, with brief descriptions and excellent photos.

➡ If feathered friends are enough, the *Complete Guide to British Birds* by Paul Sterry combines clear photos and descriptions, plus when and where each species may be seen.

➡ *Wildlife of the North Atlantic* by world-famous film-maker Tony Soper beautifully covers the animals seen from beach, boat and clifftop in the British Isles and beyond.

➡ The Collins Gem series includes handy little books on wildlife topics such as *Birds, Trees, Fish* and *Wild Flowers*.

Estuaries and mudflats are feeding grounds for numerous migrant wading birds; easily spotted are black-and-white oystercatchers with their long red bills, while flocks of small ringed plovers skitter along the sand.

And finally, the sea mammals. There are two species of seal that frequent British waters; the larger grey seal is more often seen than the (misnamed) common (or harbour) seal. Boat trips to see their offshore colonies are available at various points around the coast, and are especially popular when the seal pups are born.

Dolphins, porpoises and minke whales can all be seen off the west coast of Britain, particularly off Scotland, and especially from May to September when viewing conditions are better. Whale-watching trips (also good for seeing other marine wildlife such as basking sharks) are available from harbour towns, especially in Scotland.

Plants

In any part of Britain, the best places to see wildflowers are areas that have escaped large-scale farming. In the chalky downs of southern England and in limestone areas such as the Peak District and Yorkshire Dales, for example, many fields erupt with great profusions of cowslips and primroses in April and May.

Some flowers prefer woodland and, again, the best time for seeing these is April and May. This is because the leaf canopy of the woods is not yet fully developed, allowing sunlight to break through to encourage plants such as bluebells (a beautiful and internationally rare species). Another classic British plant is gorse – you can't miss the swaths of this spiky bush in heath areas, most notably in the New Forest in southern England, and all over Scotland.

In contrast, the blooming season for heather is quite short. On the Scottish mountains, the Pennine moors of northern England, and Dartmoor in the south, the landscape is covered in a riot of purple in August and September.

Britain's natural deciduous trees include oak, ash, beech, birch, hazel and rowan, with seeds and leaves supporting a vast range of insects and birds. The New Forest in southern England and the Forest of Dean on the Wales–England border are good examples of this type of habitat. In some parts of Scotland, most notably Glen Affric, remnants of indigenous Caledonian pine forest can still be seen. As you travel through Britain you're also likely to see non-native conifers, often in vast plantations without any wildlife, although an increasing number of deciduous trees are also planted these days.

Environmental Issues

With Britain's long history, it's not surprising that the country's appearance is almost totally the result of human interaction with the environment. Since the earliest times, people have been chopping down trees and creating fields for crops or animals, but the most dramatic changes in rural areas came in the late 1940s, continuing into the '50s and '60s, when a postwar drive to be self-reliant in food meant new and intensive large-scale farming methods. The result was lowland Britain's ancient patchwork of small meadows becoming a landscape of vast fields, as walls were demolished, woodlands felled, ponds filled, wetlands drained and, most notably, hedgerows ripped out.

In most cases the hedgerows were lines of dense bushes, shrubs and trees forming a network that stretched across the countryside, protecting fields from erosion, supporting a varied range of flowers, and providing shelter for numerous insects, birds and small mammals. But in the rush to improve farm yields, thousands of miles of hedgerows were destroyed

THE BRITISH LANDSCAPE PLANTS

Several of Britain's native species are threatened by introduced diseases – most notably the ash, which is facing the ominous prospect of 'ash dieback', caused by a fungus called *Hymenoscyphus fraxineus*. Some experts believe it could wipe out more than 90% of the UK's ash trees, as it has in several other European countries.

in the postwar decades, and between the mid-1980s and the early 2000s another 25% disappeared.

In addition to hedgerow clearance, other farming techniques remain hot environmental issues. Studies have shown that the use of pesticides and intensive irrigation results in rivers running dry or being poisoned by run-off. In 2014 scientists announced that neonicotinoid pesticides – introduced in the 1990s to replace harmful chemicals such as DDT – may actually be even more dangerous, and are implicated in the collapse of the bee population.

Meanwhile, monocropping means vast fields with one type of grass, dubbed 'green deserts' by conservationists as they support no insects, are causing wild bird populations to plummet. This is not a case of wizened old peasants recalling the idyllic days of their forebears; you only have to be over about 40 in Britain to remember a countryside where birds such as skylarks or lapwings were visibly much more numerous.

In fact, a recent report by State of Nature found that one in 10 of the UK's wildlife species is threatened with extinction, and around one-sixth of the nation's animals, birds, fish and plants has been lost since 1970. But it's not all doom and gloom – while populations of many native species such as the hedgehog have crashed, others, such as the otter, have staged an impressive comeback. Another recent returnee is the beaver, once a native resident of England, but trapped out of existence long ago. The animals have now been reintroduced to several locations around England, although the exact sites have been kept secret to ensure their safety.

Up-to-the-minute statistics on the UK's electricity generation are provided by Drax (www.electric insights.co.uk), one of the nation's largest power stations.

Sporting Britain

If you want a shortcut into the heart of British culture, then watch the British at play. They're passionate about their sport – as participants and spectators. Every weekend thousands of people turn out to cheer their favourite team, and sporting highlights such as Wimbledon keep the entire nation enthralled.

Playing the Game

The British invented many of the world's favourite team sports – or at least codified their modern rules – including cricket, tennis, rugby, golf and football (soccer), although, it has to be said, the national teams in the high-profile sports aren't always that successful internationally. This applies mainly to the male teams – the women's national teams have a better record of success, with the England women's football team taking third place in the FIFA Women's World Cup in 2015, and the England women's cricket team winning the World Cup in 2009 and 2017.

But whether the British 'home teams' are winning or losing – be they the individual teams of England, Wales or Scotland, or national teams representing Great Britain or the whole of the UK – nothing dulls the enthusiasm of the fans.

Football (Soccer)

Despite what the football fans may say in Madrid or São Paulo, the English Premier League has some of the finest teams in the world, dominated in recent years by Arsenal and Chelsea (both based in London), the two top Manchester clubs (United and City) and Liverpool. Their big pockets weren't enough in 2016, however, when unfancied Leicester City stunned the pundits and delighted neutrals by winning the league title, only for Chelsea and Manchester City to return to form by winning titles in 2017 and 2018.

One step down from the Premier League, 72 other teams play in the English divisions called the Championship, League One and League Two.

The Scottish football scene has a similar pattern: the best teams in the Scottish Premiership, the rest in the Scottish Football League. The top flight has long been dominated by Glasgow teams Celtic and Rangers, although the latter were forced into liquidation in 2012 over a tax dispute

The word 'soccer', often used outside Britain, derives from the sport's official name Association Football (as opposed to rugby football), or possibly from 'sock' – a leather foot-cover worn in medieval times, ideal for kicking a pig's bladder around the park on a Saturday afternoon.

BRITAIN AT THE OLYMPICS

For many people, the high-water mark of British athletics was thought to be the outstanding achievements by Team GB at the 2012 Olympic and Paralympic Games in London, which resulted in a haul of 65 medals (including 29 golds and third place on the medals table behind China and the USA). The British Paralympic athletes exceeded even this impressive total by winning 120 medals, and notching up another third place in the medals table behind China and Russia.

But at the 2016 Olympics in Rio, Team GB went even better: 27 golds, 23 silvers and 17 bronzes, finishing in second place behind the USA, an achievement equalled by the GB Paralympians (64 golds, 39 silvers, 44 bronzes and another second place overall).

THE FA CUP

The Football Association (FA) held its first interclub knockout tournament in 1871. Fifteen clubs took part, playing for a nice piece of silverware called the FA Cup – then worth about £20.

Nowadays, around 600 clubs compete for this legendary and priceless trophy. It differs from many other competitions in that every team – from the lowest-ranking part-timers to the stars of the Premier League – is in with a chance. The preliminary rounds begin in August, and the world-famous Cup Final is held the following May at the iconic Wembley Stadium in London.

Unsurprisingly, the big teams such as Manchester United, Arsenal and Chelsea have all won the cup on many occasions – but public attention and affection is invariably focused on the 'giant killers', minor clubs that claw their way up through the rounds, unexpectedly beating higher-ranked competitors. The best-known giant-killing event occurred in 1992, when Wrexham, then ranked 24th in Division 3, famously beat league champions Arsenal.

and kicked out of the premier league. Celtic had an easy run while their traditional rivals clawed their way back to the top, eventually gaining readmittance to the premiership in 2016.

Football is less popular in Wales (rugby is the national sport) and the main Welsh football teams, such as Wrexham, Cardiff and Swansea, play in the lower English leagues.

The football season is the same for all divisions (August to May), so seeing a match can easily be tied into most visitors' itineraries. However, tickets for Premier League matches are like gold dust – your chances of bagging one are pretty much zilch unless you're a club member or know someone who is – you're better off buying tickets for a lower-division game, which are cheaper. You can often buy tickets on the spot at stadiums, or go to club websites or online agencies such as www.ticketmaster.co.uk and www.myticketmarket.com.

Each of Britain's four nations fields its own national football team at international competitions such as the FIFA World Cup and the European Championships, although it's been a long time indeed since any of them have won anything – famously, the last time England won the World Cup was in 1966, and the nation's hopes have been dashed at nearly every championships since (often as the result of an excruciating penalty shoot-out). At the 2018 World Cup a young, inexperienced England team fared better than expected, reaching the semi-finals before being knocked out by Croatia. Unfortunately, Scotland, Wales and Northern Ireland failed to even qualify.

For the dates and details of major football and cricket matches, horse racing and other sporting fixtures across Britain, a great place to start is the sports pages of www.brit events.com.

Golf

Golf is a very popular sport in Britain, with millions taking to the fairways every week. The main tournament for spectators is the Open Championship, often referred to simply as The Open (or the 'British Open' outside the UK). It's the oldest of professional golf's major championships (dating back to 1860) and the only one held outside the USA, and is watched by many thousands of golf fans. It is usually played over the third weekend in July and the location changes each year, using nine courses around the country – check www.theopen.com for details of past, present and future championships.

Perhaps Great Britain's most famous golfing destination is the Old Course at St Andrews, often dubbed the 'home of golf' as it was one of the first places the sport was played, all the way back in the early 1400s. Playing here is almost a spiritual experience for golf enthusiasts, but you'll need to plan well ahead to get a game. If you fancy a round as part of your visit to Britain, there are around 2000 private and public golf courses to choose from, with 500 in Scotland alone. (There are more golf courses per capita in Scotland than in any other country in the world.) Some private clubs admit members or golfers with a handicap certificate, but most welcome visitors. Public golf courses are open to anyone. A round costs around £10 to £30 on public courses, and up to £200 on famous championship courses.

Rugby

A wit once said that football was a gentlemen's game played by hooligans, while rugby was a hooligans' game played by gentlemen. That may be true, but rugby is very popular, especially since England became world champions in 2003. It's worth catching a game for the display of skill (OK, and brawn) and the fun atmosphere in the grounds. Tickets for games cost around £15 to £50 depending on the club's status and fortunes.

There are two versions of the game in Britain: rugby union (www. englandrugby.com) is played more in southern England, Wales and Scotland, and is traditionally the game of the middle and upper classes, while rugby league (www.rugby-league.com) is played predominantly in northern England, traditionally by the working classes – although these days there's a lot of crossover.

Both rugby codes trace their roots back to a football match in 1823 at Rugby School, in Warwickshire. A player called William Webb Ellis, frustrated at the limitations of mere kicking, reputedly picked up the ball and ran with it towards the opponents' goal. True to the British tradition of fair play, rather than Ellis being dismissed from the game, a whole new sport was developed around his tactic, and the Rugby Football Union was formally inaugurated in 1871. Today, the Rugby World Cup is named the Webb Ellis trophy after this enterprising young tearaway.

The highlight of rugby union's international calendar is the annual Six Nations Championship (www.rbs6nations.com), between teams from England, Wales, Scotland, Ireland, France and Italy. A simple points system sees teams compete to win the Grand Slam or Triple Crown, or at least avoid the Wooden Spoon award for coming last.

The Rugby League World Cup is dominated by Australia and New Zealand; the next Rugby Union World Cup will be hosted by Japan in 2019. For details, see www.rugbyworldcup.com.

Cricket

Although it is played in Wales and Scotland too, cricket is a quintessentially English sport. Dating from the 18th century – although its roots are much older – the sport spread throughout the Commonwealth during Britain's colonial era. Australia, the Caribbean and the Indian subcontinent took to the game with gusto, and today the former colonies delight in giving the old country a good spanking on the cricket pitch.

While many English people follow cricket like a religion, to the uninitiated it's an impenetrable spectacle. Spread over one-day games or five-day test matches, progress seems so *slow* (surely, say the unbelievers, this is the game for which TV highlights were invented) and dominated by arcane terminology such as innings, over, googly, out-swinger, leg-bye and silly-mid-off. Nonetheless, at least one cricket match should feature in your travels. If you're patient and learn the intricacies, you could find cricket as absorbing and enriching as all the fans who remain glued to their radio or computer all summer, 'just to see how England are getting on'.

One-day games and international tests are played at grounds including Lord's in London, Edgbaston in Birmingham and Headingley in Leeds. Tickets cost from £30 to well over £200. The County Championship pits the best teams from around the country against each other; tickets cost £5 to £25, and only the most crucial games tend to sell out. Details are on the website of the English Cricket Board (www.ecb.co.uk).

Causing ructions in the cricket world, the fast-paced Twenty20 format emphasises big-batting scores, rather than slow and careful run-building. Traditionalists say it's changing the character of the game, but there's no doubting its popularity – many Twenty20 matches are quickly sold out.

THE ASHES

The historic test cricket series between England and Australia known as the Ashes has been played every other year since 1882, bar a few interruptions during wartime (women's cricket has its own Ashes series, played intermittently since the 1930s). It is played alternately in England and Australia with each of the five matches in the series held at a different cricket ground, always in the summer in the host location.

The contest's name dates back to the landmark test match of 1882, won (for the very first time) by the Australians. Defeat of the mother country by the colonial upstarts was a source of profound national shock: a mock obituary in the *Sporting Times* lamented the death of English cricket and referred to the game's ashes being taken to Australia.

Later the name was given to a terracotta urn presented the following year to the English captain Ivo Bligh, purportedly containing the cremated ashes of a stump or bail used in this landmark match. Since 1953 this hallowed relic has resided at the Marylebone Cricket Club (MCC) Museum at Lord's Cricket Ground. Despite the vast importance given to winning the series, the urn itself is a diminutive 15cm high.

The recent history of the Ashes has not been without drama. In the 2010–11 series England beat Australia, winning on Australian turf for the first time in 24 years. Then in 2013–14 Australia thrashed England 5–0, the third time in Ashes history that the Aussies have had a clean sweep. In 2015 England won again 3–2, only to be humiliated with another whitewash 4–0 loss in 2017–18. The next series will be held in England in 2019.

The easiest way to watch cricket – and often the most enjoyable – is stumbling across a local game on a village green as you travel around the country. There's no charge for spectators, and no one will mind if you nip into the pub during a quiet period.

Horse Racing

The tradition of horse racing in Britain stretches back centuries, and there's a 'race meeting' somewhere pretty much every day. For all but the major events you should be able to get a ticket on the day, or buy in advance from the British Horse Racing Authority's website (www.greatbritishracing.com), which also has lots of information about social events such as music festivals that coincide with the races.

The top event in the calendar is Royal Ascot at Ascot Racecourse in mid-June, where the rich and famous come to see and be seen, and the fashion is almost as important as the nags. Even the Queen turns up to put a fiver each way on Lucky Boy in the 3.15.

Over 27 tonnes of strawberries and 7000L of cream are consumed during the two weeks of the annual Wimbledon Tennis Championships.

Other highlights include the Grand National steeplechase at Aintree in early April and the Derby at Epsom on the first Saturday in June. The latter is especially popular with the masses so, unlike at Ascot, you won't see many morning suits or outrageous hats.

Tennis

Tennis is widely played in Britain, but the best-known tournament for spectators is the All England Championships – known to everyone as Wimbledon – when tennis fever sweeps through Britain in June/July every year. Although there's something more English than British about the combination of grass courts, polite applause and umpires in straw hats, it was a Scotsman, Andy Murray, who in 2013 became the first British men's singles champion since 1936, winning again in 2016.

Demand for seats at Wimbledon always outstrips supply, but to give everyone an equal chance tickets are sold through a public ballot. You can also take your chance on the spot; about 6000 tickets are sold each day (excluding the final four days), but you'll need to be an early riser: dedicated fans start queuing before dawn. For more information, see www.wimbledon.com.

Survival Guide

Directory A–Z

Accessible Travel

All new buildings have wheelchair access, and even hotels in grand old country houses often have lifts, ramps and other facilities. Hotels and B&Bs in historic buildings are often harder to adapt, so you'll have less choice here.

Modern city buses and trams have low floors for easy access, but few have conductors who can lend a hand when you're getting on or off. Many taxis take wheelchairs, or just have more room in the back.

For long-distance travel, coaches may present problems but the main operator, **National Express** (www.nationalexpress.com) has wheelchair-friendly coaches on many routes. For details, see the website or ring the dedicated Disabled Passenger Travel Helpline (☏0371 781 8181).

On most intercity trains there's more room and better facilities, compared with travel by coach, and usually station staff around; just have a word and they'll be happy to help. A **Disabled Person's**

Railcard (www.disabled persons-railcard.co.uk) costs £20 and gets you 33% off most train fares.

The following are some useful organisations:

Disability Rights UK (www.disa bilityrightsuk.org) Published titles include a holiday guide. Services include a key for 7000 public disabled toilets across the UK.

Good Access Guide (www. goodaccessguide.co.uk)

Tourism for All (www.tourism forall.org.uk)

Accommodation

B&Bs

The B&B (bed and breakfast) is a great British institution. At smaller places it's pretty much a room in somebody's house; larger places may be called a 'guesthouse' (halfway between a B&B and a full hotel). Prices start from around £40 per person for a simple bedroom and shared bathroom; for around £45 to £55 per person you get a private bathroom, either down the hall or en suite.

In country areas, most B&Bs cater for walkers and cyclists, but some don't, so let them know if you'll be turning up with dirty boots or wheels.

When booking, check where your B&B actually is. In country areas, postal addresses include the nearest town, which may be 20 miles away – important if you're walking! Some B&B owners will pick you up by car for a small charge.

Prices Usually quoted per person, based on two people sharing a room. Single rooms for solo travellers are harder to find, and attract a 20% to 50% premium. Some B&Bs simply won't take single people (unless you pay the full double-room price), especially in summer.

Booking Advance reservations are preferred at B&Bs and are essential during popular periods. You can book many B&Bs via online agencies, but rates may be cheaper if you book directly. If you haven't booked in advance, most towns have a main drag of B&Bs; those with spare rooms hang up a 'Vacancies' sign. Many B&Bs require a minimum two-night stay at weekends. Some places reduce rates for longer stays (two or three nights) mid-week. If a B&B is full, owners may recommend another place nearby (possibly a private house taking occasional guests, not in tourist listings).

Food Most B&Bs serve enormous breakfasts; some offer packed lunches (around £6) and evening meals (around £15 to £20).

BOOK YOUR STAY ONLINE

For more accommodation reviews by Lonely Planet authors, check out http://lonelyplanet.com/hotels/. You'll find independent reviews, as well as recommendations on the best places to stay. Best of all, you can book online.

Bed & Breakfast Nationwide (www.bedandbreakfastnationwide.com)

Camping & Bunkhouses

Campsites range from farmers' fields with a tap and basic toilet, costing from £5 per person per night, to smarter affairs with hot showers and many other facilities, charging up to £15, sometimes more. Make sure you know what you're getting for the price; some campsites charge per pitch, others per person, with extra costs added on for having a car, pets, children, larger tents, electrical hook-ups and so on.

Many campsites (except the most back-to-basics ones) have a small shop, but otherwise you will need all your own camping kit.

A few campsites also offer self-catering accommodation in chalets, caravans, tepees, yurts and stylish wooden camping 'pods', often dubbed 'glamping'.

If you're touring Britain with a tent or campervan (motorhome), consider joining the **Camping & Caravanning Club** (www.campingandcaravanningclub.co.uk), which provides up to 30% discount on its sites for an annual membership fee of £37. The club owns almost 100 campsites and lists thousands more in the invaluable *Big Sites Book* (free to members).

A bunkhouse in Britain is a simple place to stay, usually in country areas, with a communal sleeping area and bathroom, plus stoves for self-catering. You provide a sleeping bag and possibly cooking gear. Most charge around £12 to £15 per person per night.

Some basic places are called 'camping barns' – usually converted farm buildings. Take everything you'd need to camp except the tent. Charges are from around £6 to £10 per person.

Hostels

There are two types of hostel in Britain: those run by the **Youth Hostels Association** (www.yha.org.uk) and **Scottish Youth Hostels Association** (www.syha.org.uk); and independent hostels, most listed in the **Independent Hostel Guide** (www.independenthostelguide.co.uk).

Hostels can be found in rural areas, towns and cities, and are aimed at all types of traveller, young and old. Some hostels are converted cottages, country houses and even castles – often in wonderful locations. Sleeping is usually in dormitories; most hostels also have twin- or four-bed rooms.

YHA & SYHA HOSTELS

The simplest YHA and SYHA hostels cost around £13 to £18 per person per night. Larger hostels with more facilities are £18 to £30.

London's YHA hostels cost from around £35. Advance bookings and payments with credit card are usually possible.

You don't have to be a member of the YHA or SYHA (or another Hostelling International organisation) to stay, but most hostels charge extra if you're not a member (usually a surcharge of £3), so it's usually worth joining. Annual YHA membership costs £15, or £5 if you're aged from 16 to 25. Annual SYHA membership costs £15 (£6 for those aged 16 to 25).

Most hostel prices vary according to demand and season. Book early for a Tuesday night in May and you'll get the best rate. Book late for a weekend in August and you'll pay top price – if there's space at all.

YHA hostels tend to have complicated opening times and days, especially in remote locations or out of tourist season, so check before turning up.

INDEPENDENT HOSTELS

In rural areas some independent hostels are little more than simple bunkhouses (charging around £13), or almost up to B&B standard (£20 or more). In cities, independent backpacker hostels are usually aimed at young budget travellers. Most are open 24 hours, with a lively atmosphere, a range of rooms (doubles or dorms), bar, cafe, wi-fi and laundry. Prices go from around £20 for a dorm bed to £40 for a bed in a private room.

Hotels

There's a massive choice of hotels in Britain, from

EATING PRICE RANGES

The following price ranges refer to a main dish.

CATEGORY	LONDON	ELSEWHERE
£	less than £12	less than £10
££	£12–25	£10–20
£££	more than £25	more than £20

small town houses to grand country mansions, from no-frills locations to boutique hideaways. At the bargain end, single/double rooms cost from £45/60. Move up the scale and you'll pay £100/150 or beyond.

If all you want is a place to put your head down, budget chain hotels can be a good option. Most are lacking in ambience, but who cares? You'll be there for 12 hours, and eight of them you'll be asleep. Prices vary on demand: at quiet times twin-bed rooms start from £30; at the height of the tourist season you'll pay £60 or more. Some options:

Ibis Hotels (www.ibis.com)

Premier Inn (www.premierinn. com)

Travelodge (www.travelodge. co.uk)

RATES

There's no such thing as a 'standard' hotel rate in Britain. Many hotels, especially larger places or chains, vary prices according to demand – or have different rates for online, phone or walk-in bookings – just like airlines and train operators. So if you book early for a night when the hotel is likely to be quiet, rates are cheap. If you book late, or aim for a public holiday weekend, you'll pay a lot. But wait until the very last minute, and you can *sometimes* get a bargain as rates drop again. The end result: you can pay anything from £25 to £200 for the very same hotel room. (In contrast, B&B prices tend to be much more consistent.)

Houseboats

A popular English holiday option is renting a houseboat on one of England's picturesque waterways, combining accommodation and transport for a few days or a week.

ABC Boat Hire (www.abcboathire. com)

Hoseasons (www.hoseasons. co.uk)

Wandering Duck (www.wandering duck.co.uk) 'Floating hostels' for budget travellers.

Pubs & Inns

As well as selling drinks, many pubs and inns offer lodging, particularly in country areas. For bed and breakfast you'll pay around £35 per person for a basic room, around £45 to £50 per person for something better. An advantage for solo tourists: pubs often have single rooms.

Rental Accommodation

If you want to stay in one place, renting for a week can be ideal. Choose from neat apartments in cities or quaint old houses (always called 'cottages', whatever the size) in country areas. Cottages for four people cost between £275 and £700 in high season. Rates fall at quieter times and you may be able to rent for a long weekend. Some handy websites include the following:

Cottages & Castles (www. cottages-and-castles.co.uk)

Cottages4you (www.cottages4you.co.uk)

Hoseasons (www.hoseasons. co.uk)

National Trust (www.nationaltrust.org.uk/holidays)

Stilwell's (www.stilwell.co.uk)

Sleeping Price Ranges

The following price ranges refer to a double room with private bathroom in high season. Hotels in London are more expensive than the rest of the country, so have different price ranges.

Climate

London

Newquay

York

CATE-GORY	LONDON	ELSE-WHERE
£	less than £100	less than £65
££	£100–£200	£65–£130
£££	more than £200	more than £130

Customs Regulations

Travellers arriving in the UK from EU countries don't have to pay tax or duty on goods for personal use, and can bring in as much EU du-ty-paid alcohol and tobacco as they like. However, if you bring in more than the follow-ing, you'll probably be asked some questions:

➜ 800 cigarettes
➜ 1kg of tobacco
➜ 10L of spirits
➜ 90L of wine
➜ 110L of beer

Travellers from outside the EU can bring in, duty-free:

➜ 200 cigarettes or 100 cigarillos or 50 cigars or 250g of tobacco
➜ 16L of beer
➜ 4L of non-sparkling wine
➜ 1L of spirits or 2L of fortified wine or sparkling wine
➜ £390 worth of all other goods, including perfume, gifts and souvenirs

Anything over this limit must be declared to customs of-ficers on arrival. For further details, and for information on reclaiming VAT on items purchased in the UK by non-EU residents, go to www.gov.uk and search for 'Bringing goods into the UK'.

Electricity

**Type G
230V/50Hz**

Health
Health Insurance

➜ If you're an EU citizen, a European Health Insurance Card (EHIC) – available from health centres or, in the UK, post offices – covers you for most medical care. An EHIC will not cover you for non-urgent cases, or emergency repatriation. This arrangement could change once Britain exits the EU; check the latest situation with your own national health service before travelling.

➜ Citizens from non-EU countries should find out if there is a reciprocal arrangement for free medical care between their country and the UK.

➜ If you do need health insurance, make sure you get a policy that covers you for the worst possible scenarios, including emergency flights home.

Cardiff

Inverness

Edinburgh

Availability & Cost of Health Care

➔ Chemists (pharmacies) can advise on minor ailments such as sore throats and earaches. In large cities there's always at least one 24-hour chemist.

➔ For medical advice that is not an emergency you can call the NHS 111 service (phone ☏111).

Vaccinations

➔ No jabs (vaccinations) are required to travel to Britain. For more information, check with your medical provider in your own country before you travel.

Insurance

Although everyone receives free emergency treatment, regardless of nationality, travel insurance is still highly recommended in Britain. It will usually cover medical and dental consultation and treatment at private clinics, which can be quicker than NHS places – as well as the cost of any emergency flights – plus all the usual stuff like loss of baggage.

Worldwide travel insurance is available at www.lonelyplanet.com/travel-insurance. You can buy, extend and claim online anytime – even if you're already on the road.

Internet Access

➔ 3G and 4G mobile broadband coverage is good in large population centres, but limited or sometimes nonexistent in rural areas.

➔ EU citizens can now use their own mobile/cellphone data roaming allowance in the UK for no charge, but travellers from non-EU countries will usually incur high charges – check with your provider before travelling.

➔ Most hotels, B&Bs, hostels, stations and coffee shops (even some trains and buses) have wi-fi access, charging anything from nothing to £6 per hour.

➔ Internet cafes are surprisingly rare in Britain, especially away from big cities and tourist spots. Most charge from £1 per hour, but out in the sticks you can pay £5 per hour.

➔ Public libraries often have computers with free internet access, but only for 30-minute slots, and demand is high. All the usual warnings apply about keystroke-capturing software and other security risks.

Legal Matters

➔ Police have the power to detain, for up to six hours, anyone suspected of having committed an offence punishable by imprisonment (including drugs offences). Police have the right to search anyone they suspect of possessing drugs.

➔ You must be over 18 to buy alcohol and cigarettes. You usually have to be 18 to enter a pub or bar, although rules are different for under-18s if eating. Some bars and clubs are over-21 only.

➔ Illegal drugs are widely available, especially in clubs. Cannabis possession is a criminal offence; punishment for carrying a small amount may be a warning, a fine or imprisonment. Dealers face stiffer penalties, as do people caught with other drugs.

➔ On buses and trains (including the London Underground), people without a valid ticket are fined on the spot (£80,

reduced to £40 if you pay within 21 days).

LGBT+ Travellers

Britain is a generally tolerant place for gays and lesbians. London, Manchester and Brighton have flourishing gay scenes, and in other sizeable cities (even some small towns), you'll find communities not entirely in the closet. That said, you'll still find pockets of homophobic hostility in some areas. Resources include the following:

Diva (www.divamag.co.uk)

Gay Times (www.gaytimes.co.uk)

Switchboard LGBT+ Helpline (www.switchboard.lgbt; ☏0300 330 0630)

Money

ATMs

ATMs (usually called 'cash machines' in Britain) are common in cities and even small towns. Cash withdrawals from some ATMs may be subject to a small charge, but most are free. If you're not from the UK, your home bank will likely charge you for withdrawing money overseas. Watch out for tampered ATMs; a common ruse is to attach a card reader or mini camera.

Credit & Debit Cards

Visa and Mastercard credit and debit cards are widely accepted in Britain. Other credit cards, including Amex, are not so widely accepted. Most businesses will assume your card is 'Chip and PIN' enabled (using a PIN instead of signing). If it isn't, you should be able to sign instead, but some

---

SCOTTISH BANKNOTES

Scottish banks issue their own sterling banknotes. They are interchangeable with Bank of England notes, but you'll sometimes run into problems outside Scotland – shops in the south of England may refuse to accept them. They are also harder to exchange once you get outside the UK, though British banks will always exchange them.

places may not accept your card. Some smaller country B&Bs don't take cards, so you'll need to pay with cash.

Currency

The currency of Britain is the pound sterling (£). Paper money ('notes') comes in £5, £10, £20 and £50 denominations. Some shops don't accept £50 notes because fakes circulate.

Other currencies are rarely accepted, except at some gift shops in London, which may take euros, US dollars, yen and other major currencies.

Money Changers

Cities and larger towns have banks and exchange bureaux for changing your money into pounds. Check rates first; some bureaux offer poor rates or levy outrageous commissions. You can also change money at some post offices – very handy in country areas, and exchange rates are fair.

Tipping

Restaurants Around 10% in restaurants and teashops with table service. Nearer 15% at smarter restaurants. Tips may be added to your bill as a 'service charge'. Paying a tip or a service charge is not obligatory.

Pubs & Bars Not expected unless table service for your meal and drinks is provided, then 10% is usual.

Taxis Around 10%, or rounded up to the nearest pound, especially in London.

Opening Hours

Opening hours may vary throughout the year, especially in rural areas where many places have shorter hours or close completely from October or November to March or April.

Banks 9.30am to 4pm/5pm Monday to Friday; some open 9.30am to 1pm Saturday

Pubs & Bars Noon to 11pm Monday to Saturday (many till midnight or 1am Friday and

---

Saturday, especially in Scotland), 12.30 to 11pm Sunday

Shops 9am to 5.30pm (or to 6pm in cities) Monday to Saturday, and often 11am to 5pm Sunday; big-city convenience stores open 24/7

Restaurants Lunch noon to 3pm, dinner 6 to 9pm/10pm (or later in cities)

Museums & Sights

➡ Large museums and sights usually open daily.

➡ Some smaller places open Saturday and Sunday but close Monday and/or Tuesday.

➡ Smaller places open daily in high season but operate weekends only or completely close in low season.

Post

The British postal service is generally efficient and reliable. Information on post office locations and postage rates can be found at www.postoffice.co.uk.

Public Holidays

Holidays for the whole of Britain:

New Year's Day 1 January (plus 2 January in Scotland)

Easter March/April (Good Friday to Easter Monday inclusive)

May Day First Monday in May

Spring Bank Holiday Last Monday in May

Summer Bank Holiday Last Monday in August

Christmas Day 25 December

Boxing Day 26 December

If a public holiday falls on a weekend, the nearest Monday is usually taken instead. In England and Wales most businesses and banks close on official public holidays (hence the quaint term 'bank holiday'). In Scotland, bank holidays are just for the banks, and many businesses stay open. Many Scottish towns normally have a spring and autumn holiday, but the dates vary.

On public holidays, some small museums and places of interest close, but larger attractions have their busiest times. If a place closes on Sunday, it'll probably be shut on bank holidays as well.

Virtually everything – attractions, shops, banks, offices – closes on Christmas Day, although pubs are open at lunchtime. There's usually no public transport on Christmas Day, and a very minimal service on Boxing Day.

Safe Travel

Britain is a remarkably safe country, but crime is not unknown – especially in London and other cities.

→ Watch out for pickpockets and hustlers in crowded areas popular with tourists, such as around Westminster Bridge in London.

→ When travelling by tube, tram or urban train services at night, choose a carriage containing other people.

→ Many town centres can be rowdy on Friday and Saturday nights when the pubs and clubs are emptying.

→ Unlicensed minicabs – a driver with a car earning money on the side – operate in large cities, and are worth avoiding unless you know what you're doing.

Telephone

Mobile Phones

The UK uses the GSM 900/1800 network, which covers the rest of Europe, Australia and New Zealand, but isn't compatible with the North American GSM 1900. Most modern mobiles can function on both networks, but check before you leave home just in case.

Roaming charges within the EU were removed from June 2017, meaning that EU citizens can use their home call, SMS and data allowances for no extra cost.

Roaming charges for non-EU citizens can be prohibitively high, however, and you'll probably find it cheaper to get a UK number. This is easily done by buying a SIM card (from £5 including calling credit) and sticking it in your phone. Your phone may be locked to your home network, however, so you'll have to either get it unlocked, or buy a cheap pay-as-you-go phone along with your SIM card (from £10 including calling credit).

Pay-as-you-go phones can be recharged by buying vouchers from any post office or at supermarkets and convenience stores where you see the green 'top-up' sign.

Phone Codes

Dialling into the UK Dial your country's international access code then 44 (the UK country code), then the area code (dropping the first 0) followed by the telephone number.

Dialling out of the UK The international access code is 00; dial this, then add the code of the country you wish to dial.

Making a reverse-charge (collect) international call Dial 155 for the operator. It's an expensive option, but not for the caller.

Area codes in the UK Do not have a standard format or length, eg Edinburgh 0131, London 020, Ambleside 015394.

Directory Assistance A host of agencies offer this service – numbers include 118 118, 118 500 and 118 811 – but fees are extortionate (around £6 for a 45-second call); search online for free at www.thephonebook. bt.com.

Mobile phones Codes usually begin with 07.

Free calls Numbers starting with 0800 or 0808 are free.

National operator 100

International operator 155

Time

Britain is on GMT/UTC. The clocks go forward one hour for 'summer time' at the end of March, and go back at the end of October. The 24-hour clock is used for transport timetables.

Time Differences

Paris, Berlin, Rome	1hr ahead of Britain
New York	5hr behind
Sydney	9hr ahead Apr-Sep, 10hr Oct, 11hr Nov-Mar
Los Angeles	8hr behind
Mumbai	5½hr ahead Nov-Feb, 4½hr Mar-Oct
Tokyo	9hr ahead Nov-Feb, 8hr Mar-Oct

Toilets

→ Public toilets in Britain are generally clean and modern, but cutbacks in public spending mean that many

---

PRACTICALITIES

Newspapers Tabloids include the *Sun, Express* and *Mirror*, and *Daily Record* (in Scotland); quality 'broadsheets' include (from right to left, politically) the *Telegraph, Times* and *Guardian*.

TV All TV in the UK is digital. The main broadcasters include the BBC, ITV and Channel 4. Satellite and cable TV providers include Sky and Virgin Media.

Radio Main BBC stations and wavelengths are Radio 1 (98–99.6MHz FM), Radio 2 (88–92MHz FM), Radio 3 (90–92.2 MHz FM), Radio 4 (92–94.4MHz FM) and Radio 5 Live (909 or 693 AM). National commercial stations include Virgin Radio (1215Hz MW) and non-highbrow classical specialist Classic FM (100–102MHz FM). All are available on digital.

DVD PAL format (incompatible with NTSC and Secam).

Weights & Measures Britain uses a mix of metric and imperial measures (eg petrol is sold by the litre but beer by the pint; mountain heights are in metres but road distances are in miles).

HERITAGE ORGANISATIONS

A highlight of a journey through Britain is visiting the numerous castles and historic sites that pepper the country. Membership of a heritage organisation gets you free admission (usually a good saving) as well as information handbooks and so on.

National Trust (NT; www.nationaltrust.org.uk) A charity protecting historic buildings and land with scenic importance across England and Wales. Annual membership is £69 (discounts for under-26s and families). A Touring Pass allows free entry to NT properties for one/two weeks (one person £31/36, two people £55/66, family £61/77). The National Trust for Scotland (www.nts.org.uk) is a similar organisation in Scotland; annual membership is £57.

English Heritage (EH; www.english-heritage.org.uk) A state-funded organisation responsible for numerous historic sites. Annual membership is £56 (couples and seniors get discounts). An Overseas Visitors Pass allows free entry to most sites for nine/16 days for £33/39 (couples £57/67, families £62/72). In Wales and Scotland the equivalent organisations are Cadw (www.cadw.wales.gov.uk) and Historic Environment Scotland (www.historicenvironment.scot). You can join at the first location you visit. If you join an English heritage organisation, it covers you for Wales and Scotland, and vice versa.

facilities have been closed down.

➡ Your best bet is to use the toilets in free-to-enter museums; those in railway and bus stations often charge a fee (from 20p to 50p).

➡ Most pubs and restaurants stipulate that their toilets are for customers only.

Tourist Information

Most British cities and towns, and some villages, have a tourist information centre or visitor information centre – for ease of reference Lonely Planet refers to all these places as 'tourist offices'.

Such places have helpful staff, books and maps for sale, leaflets to give away, and advice on things to see or do. Some can also assist with booking accommodation. Some are run by national parks and often have small exhibits about the area.

Most tourist offices keep regular business hours; in quiet areas they close from October to March, while in popular areas they open daily year-round. In recent years, cost-cutting has seen many smaller tourist offices close down; some have

been replaced with 'tourist information points' – racks of leaflets and maps in locations such as public libraries and town halls.

Before leaving home check the comprehensive website of Britain's official tourist board, **Visit Britain** (www.visitbritain.com), covering all angles of national tourism, with links to numerous other sites.

Visas

Due to the uncertainty surrounding the Brexit negotiations, this information is particularly prone to change, so it's worth double-checking the latest rules before you travel.

➡ If you're a citizen of the EEA (European Economic Area) nations or Switzerland, you don't need a visa to enter or work in Britain – you can enter using your national identity card.

➡ Visa regulations are always subject to change, and immigration restriction is currently big news in Britain, so it's essential to check with your local British embassy, high commission or consulate before leaving home.

➡ Currently, if you're a citizen of Australia, Canada,

New Zealand, Japan, Israel, the USA and several other countries, you can stay for up to six months (no visa required), but are not allowed to work.

➡ Nationals of many countries, including South Africa, will need to obtain a visa: for more info, see www.gov.uk/check-uk-visa.

➡ The Youth Mobility Scheme, for Australian, Canadian, Japanese, Hong Kong, Monégasque, New Zealand, South Korean and Taiwanese citizens aged 18 to 30, allows working visits of up to two years, but must be applied for in advance.

➡ Commonwealth citizens with a UK-born parent may be eligible for a Certificate of Entitlement to the Right of Abode, which entitles them to live and work in the UK.

➡ Commonwealth citizens with a UK-born grandparent could qualify for a UK Ancestry Employment Certificate, allowing them to work full time for up to five years in the UK.

➡ British immigration authorities have always been tough; dress neatly and carry proof that you have sufficient funds with which to support yourself. A credit card and/or an onward ticket will help.

Transport

GETTING THERE & AWAY

Most visitors reach Britain by air. As London is a global transport hub, it's easy to fly to Britain from just about anywhere. In recent years, the massive growth of budget ('no-frills') airlines has increased the number of routes – and reduced the fares – between Britain and other countries in Europe.

The other main option for travel between Britain and mainland Europe is ferry, either port-to-port or combined with a long-distance bus trip, although journeys can be long and financial savings not huge compared with budget airfares.

International trains are much more comfortable and a 'green' option; the Channel Tunnel allows direct rail services between Britain, France and Belgium, with onward connections to many other European destinations.

Flights, cars and tours can be booked online at lonelyplanet.com/bookings.

Air

Visitors to the UK arriving by air generally do so at one of London's two largest airports, Heathrow and Gatwick, which have a huge range of international flights to pretty much all corners of the globe. International flights also serve the capital's three other airports (Stansted, Luton and London City) and regional hubs such as Manchester, Bristol and Edinburgh.

Departure tax is included in the price of a ticket.

London Airports

The national carrier is **British Airways** (www.britishairways.com).

The main airports:

Heathrow (www.heathrowairport.com) Britain's main airport for international flights; often chaotic and crowded. About 15 miles west of central London.

Gatwick (www.gatwickairport.com) Britain's number-two airport, mainly for international flights, 30 miles south of central London.

Stansted (www.stanstedairport.com) About 35 miles north-east of central London, mainly handling charter and budget European flights.

Luton (www.london-luton.co.uk) Some 35 miles north of central London, well known as a holiday-flight airport.

London City (www.londoncityairport.com) A few miles east of central London, specialising in flights to/from European and other UK airports.

Regional Airports

Some planes on European and long-haul routes avoid London and use major regional airports including Manchester and Glasgow. Smaller regional airports such as Southampton, Cardiff and Birmingham

CLIMATE CHANGE & TRAVEL

Every form of transport that relies on carbon-based fuel generates CO_2, the main cause of human-induced climate change. Modern travel is dependent on aeroplanes, which might use less fuel per kilometre per person than most cars but travel much greater distances. The altitude at which aircraft emit gases (including CO_2) and particles also contributes to their climate change impact. Many websites offer 'carbon calculators' that allow people to estimate the carbon emissions generated by their journey and, for those who wish to do so, to offset the impact of the greenhouse gases emitted with contributions to portfolios of climate-friendly initiatives throughout the world. Lonely Planet offsets the carbon footprint of all staff and author travel.

are served by flights to and from continental Europe and Ireland.

Land

Bus & Coach

You can easily get between Britain and other European countries via long-distance bus or coach. The international network **Eurolines** (www.eurolines.com) connects a huge number of destinations; you can buy tickets online via one of the national operators.

Services to/from Britain are operated by **National Express** (www.nationalexpress. com). Sample journeys and times to/from London include Amsterdam (12 hours); Barcelona (24 hours); Dublin (12 hours); and Paris (eight hours).

If you book early, and can be flexible with timings (ie travel when few other people want to), you can get some very good deals. For example, between London and Paris or Amsterdam from about £25 one way (although paying £35 to £45 is more usual).

Train

CHANNEL TUNNEL PASSENGER SERVICE

High-speed **Eurostar** (www. eurostar.com) passenger services shuttle at least 10 times daily between London and Paris (2½ hours) or Brussels (two hours). Buy tickets from travel agencies, major train stations or the Eurostar website.

The normal one-way fare between London and Paris/ Brussels costs around £154; advance booking and off-peak travel gets cheaper fares, as low as £29 one way.

CHANNEL TUNNEL CAR SERVICE

Drivers use **Eurotunnel** (www.eurotunnel.com). At Folkestone in England or Calais in France, you drive onto a train, get carried through

the tunnel and drive off at the other end.

Trains run about four times an hour from 6am to 10pm, then hourly through the night. Loading and unloading takes an hour; the journey lasts 35 minutes.

Book in advance online or pay on the spot. The standard one-way fare for a car and up to nine passengers is between £75 and £100 depending on the time of day; promotional fares often bring it down to £59 or less.

TRAIN & FERRY CONNECTIONS TO EUROPE

As well as Eurostar, many 'normal' trains run between Britain and mainland Europe. You buy one ticket, but get off the train at the port, walk onto a ferry, then get another train on the other side. Routes include Amsterdam–London (via Hook of Holland and Harwich). Travelling between Ireland and Britain, the main train-ferry-train route is Dublin–London, via Dún Laoghaire and Holyhead. Ferries also run between Rosslare and Fishguard or Pembroke (Wales), with train connections on either side.

Sea

Ferry Routes

The main ferry routes between Great Britain and other European countries include the following:

➡ Dover–Calais (France)

➡ Dover–Boulogne (France)

➡ Newhaven–Dieppe (France)

➡ Liverpool–Dublin (Ireland)

➡ Holyhead–Dublin (Ireland)

➡ Fishguard–Rosslare (Ireland)

➡ Pembroke Dock–Rosslare (Ireland)

➡ Newcastle–Amsterdam (Netherlands)

➡ Harwich–Hook of Holland (Netherlands)

➡ Hull–Rotterdam (Netherlands)

➡ Hull–Zeebrugge (Belgium)

➡ Cairnryan–Larne (Northern Ireland)

➡ Portsmouth–Santander (Spain)

➡ Portsmouth–Bilbao (Spain)

Ferry Fares

Most ferry operators offer flexible fares, meaning great bargains at quiet times of day or year. For example, short cross-channel routes such as Dover to Calais or Boulogne can be as low as £45 for a car plus two passengers, although around £75 to £105 is more likely. If you're a foot passenger, or cycling, there's less need to book ahead; fares on short crossings cost about £30 to £50 each way.

Ferry Bookings

Book direct with one of the operators listed following, or use the very handy www. directferries.co.uk – a single site covering all sea-ferry routes, plus **Eurotunnel** (www.eurotunnel.com).

Brittany Ferries (www.brittany-ferries.com)

DFDS Seaways (www.dfdsseaways.co.uk)

Irish Ferries (www.irishferries.com)

P&O Ferries (www.poferries.com)

Stena Line (www.stenaline.com)

GETTING AROUND

Transport in Britain can be expensive compared to Continental Europe; bus and rail services are sparse in the more remote parts of the country. For timetables, check out www.traveline.info. Tourist offices can provide maps and information.

Car Useful for travelling at your own pace, or for visiting regions with minimal public transport.

Cars can be hired in every town or city.

Train Relatively expensive, with extensive coverage and frequent departures throughout most of the country.

Bus Cheaper and slower than trains, but useful in more remote regions that aren't serviced by rail.

Air

If you're really pushed for time, flights on longer routes across Britain (eg Exeter or Southampton to Newcastle, Edinburgh or Inverness), or to the Scottish islands, are handy, although you miss the glorious scenery in between. On some shorter routes (eg London to Newcastle, or Manchester to Newquay) trains compare favourably with planes on time, once airport downtime is factored in. On costs, you might get a bargain airfare, but trains can be cheaper if you buy tickets in advance. Some of Britain's domestic airline companies:

British Airways (www.british airways.com)

EasyJet (www.easyjet.com)

FlyBe (www.flybe.com)

Loganair (www.loganair.co.uk)

Ryanair (www.ryanair.com)

Bicycle

Britain is a compact region, and hiring a bike – for an hour or two, or a week or longer – is a great way to really see the country if you've got time to spare.

Bike Hire in London

London is famous for its **Santander Cycles** (✆0343 222 6666; www.tfl.gov.uk/modes/cycling/santander-cycles), known as 'Boris bikes' after the mayor that introduced them to the city. Bikes can be hired on the spot from automatic docking stations. For more information visit the website. Other rental options in the capital are listed at www.lcc.org.uk (under Advice/Bike Shops).

Bike Hire Elsewhere

The **nextbike** (www.nextbike.co.uk) bike-sharing scheme has stations in Exeter, Oxford, Coventry, Glasgow, Stirling and Bath as at the time of research, while tourist towns such as York and Cambridge have plentiful bike-rental options. Bikes can also be hired in national parks and forestry sites now primarily used for leisure activities, such as Kielder Water in Northumberland, Grizedale Forest in the Lake District and the Elan Valley in Mid-Wales. In some areas, disused railway lines are now bike routes, notably the Peak District in Derbyshire. Standard rental rates start at about £12 per day, or £20 and up for a quality machine.

Bikes on Trains

Bicycles can be taken free of charge on most local urban trains (although they may not be allowed at peak times when the trains are crowded with commuters) and on shorter trips in rural areas, on a first-come, first-served basis – though there may be space limits.

Bikes can be carried on long-distance train journeys free of charge, but advance booking is required for most conventional bikes. (Folding bikes can be carried on pretty much any train at any time.) In theory, this shouldn't be too much trouble as most long-distance rail trips are best bought in advance anyway, but you have to go a long way down the path of booking your seat before you start booking your bike – only to find space isn't available. A better course of action is to buy in advance at a major rail station, where the booking clerk can help you through the options.

A final warning: when railways are repaired, cancelled trains are replaced by buses – and they won't take bikes.

The **PlusBike** scheme provides all the information you need for travelling by train with a bike. Leaflets are available at major stations, or downloadable from www.nationalrail.co.uk/118390.aspx.

Boat

There are around 90 inhabited islands off the western and northern coasts of Scotland, which are linked to the mainland by a network of car and passenger ferries. There are two main ferry operators.

Caledonian MacBrayne (CalMac; ✆0800 066 5000; www.calmac.co.uk) Operates car ferry services to the Inner and Outer Hebrides and the islands in the Firth of Clyde.

Northlink Ferries (✆0845 600 0449; www.northlinkferries.co.uk) Operates car ferry services from Aberdeen and Scrabster to the Orkney and Shetland Islands.

Bus & Coach

If you're on a tight budget, long-distance buses (called coaches in Britain) are nearly always the cheapest way to get around, although they're also the slowest – sometimes by a considerable margin. Many towns have separate stations for local buses and long-distance

---

CROSS-BORDER BRITAIN

Travelling between Britain's three nations of England, Scotland and Wales is easy. The bus and train systems are fully integrated and in most cases you won't even know you've crossed the border; passports are not required.

coaches; make sure you go to the right one!

Long-Distance Buses

National Express (www.national express.com) is the main coach operator, with a wide network and frequent services between main centres. North of the border, services tie in with those of **Scottish Citylink** (www.citylink. co.uk), Scotland's leading coach company. Fares vary: they're cheaper if you book in advance and travel at quieter times, and more expensive if you buy your ticket on the spot and it's Friday afternoon. As a guide, a 200-mile trip (eg London to York) will cost £15 to £25 if you book a few days in advance.

Megabus (www.megabus.com) operates a budget coach service between about 30 destinations around the country. Go at a quiet time, book early and your ticket will be very cheap. Book later, for a busy time and... You get the picture.

Passes & Discounts

National Express offers discount passes to full-time students and under-26s, called Young Persons Coachcards. They cost £12.50 and give you 30% off standard adult fares. Also available are coachcards for people over 60, families and travellers with disabilities.

For those who aren't UK citizens, National Express offers Skimmer passes, allowing unlimited travel for seven/14/28 days (£69/119/199). You don't need to book journeys in advance: if the coach has a spare seat, you can take it.

Car & Motorcycle

Travelling by car or motorbike around Britain means you can be independent and flexible, and reach remote places. Downsides for drivers include traffic jams, the high price of fuel and high parking costs in cities.

Traffic drives on the left; steering wheels are on the

TRAVELINE

Traveline (www.traveline.info) is a very useful information service covering bus, coach, taxi and train services nationwide. The website offers access to online timetables, a journey planner, route maps and limited fares information.

right side of the car. Most rental cars have manual gears (stick shift).

Hire

CAMPERVAN

Hiring a motorhome or campervan (£650 to £1200 a week) is more expensive than hiring a car, but saves on accommodation costs and gives almost unlimited freedom. Sites to check include:

Just Go (www.justgo.uk.com)

Wicked Campers (www.wicked campers.co.uk)

Wild Horizon (www.wildhorizon. co.uk)

CAR

Compared with many countries (especially the USA), hire rates are expensive in Britain; the smallest cars start from about £130 per week, and it's around £190 and upwards per week for a medium car. All rates include insurance and unlimited mileage, and can rise at busy times (or drop at quiet times).

Some main players:

Avis (www.avis.co.uk)

Budget (www.budget.co.uk)

Europcar (www.europcar.co.uk)

Sixt (www.sixt.co.uk)

Thrifty (www.thrifty.co.uk)

Another option is to look online for small local car-hire companies in Britain that can undercut the international franchises. Generally those in cities are cheaper than in rural areas. Using a rental-broker or comparison site such as **UK Car Hire** (www. ukcarhire.net) or **Kayak** (www.kayak.com) can also help find bargains.

Motoring Organisations

Motoring organisations in Britain include the **Automobile Association** (www. theaa.com) and the **RAC** (www.rac.co.uk). For both, annual membership starts at around £40, including 24-hour roadside breakdown assistance.

Britannia (www.lv.com/ breakdown-cover) offers better value at £30 a year, while a greener alternative is the **Environmental Transport Association** (www.eta. co.uk); it provides breakdown assistance but doesn't campaign for more roads.

Insurance

It's illegal to drive a car or motorbike in Britain without (at least) third-party insurance. This will be included with all rental cars. If you're bringing a car from Europe, you'll need to arrange it.

Parking

Many cities have short-stay and long-stay car parks; the latter may be less convenient though. 'Park & Ride' systems allow you to park on the edge of the city then ride to the centre on frequent nonstop buses for an all-in-one price.

Yellow lines (single or double) along the edge of the road indicate parking restrictions. Nearby signs will spell out when you can and can't park. In London and other big cities, traffic wardens operate with efficiency; if you park on the yellow lines at the wrong time, your car will be clamped or towed away, and it'll cost you £130 or more to get driving again. In some cities there are also red lines, which mean no stopping at any time.

Also beware of other areas that may be restricted in some other way (eg for local residents or pass-holders only); these can sometimes be tricky to notice, but if you contravene the rules, the results will be the same: a parking ticket, wheel-clamping or towing away.

Roads

Motorways and main A-roads deliver you quickly from one end of the country to another. Lesser A-roads, B-roads and minor roads are much more scenic – ideal for car or motorcycle touring. You can't travel fast, but you won't care.

Speed limits are usually 30mph (48km/h) in built-up areas, 60mph (96km/h) on main roads and 70mph (112km/h) on motorways and most (but not all) dual carriageways.

Road Rules

A foreign driving licence is valid in Britain for up to 12 months.

Drink-driving is taken very seriously; you're allowed a maximum blood-alcohol level of 80mg/100mL (0.08%) in England and Wales, and 50mg/100mL (0.05%) in Scotland.

Some other important rules:

➡ drive on the left (!)

➡ wear fitted seatbelts in cars

➡ wear helmets on motorcycles

➡ give way to your right at junctions and roundabouts

➡ always use the left lane on motorways and dual carriageways unless overtaking (although so many people ignore this rule, you'd think it didn't exist)

➡ don't use a mobile phone while driving unless it's fully hands-free (another rule frequently flouted)

Hitching

Hitching is not as common as it used to be in Britain: maybe because more people have cars and maybe because few drivers give lifts any more. It's perfectly possible, however, if you don't mind long waits. Nevertheless, hitching is never entirely safe, and we don't recommend it. Travellers who hitch should understand that they are taking a small but potentially serious risk. If you decide to go by thumb, note that it's illegal to hitch on motorways; you must use approach roads or service stations.

However, it's all different in remote rural areas such as Mid-Wales or northwest Scotland, where hitching is a part of getting around – especially if you're a walker heading back to base after a hike on the hills. On some Scottish islands, local drivers may stop and offer a lift without you even asking.

Local Transport

Buses

There are good local bus networks year-round in cities and towns. Buses also run in some rural areas year-round, although timetables are designed to serve schools and businesses, so there aren't many midday and weekend services (and they may stop running during school holidays), or buses may link local villages to a market town on only one day each week.

In tourist areas (especially national parks), there are frequent services from Easter to September. However, it's always worth double-checking at a tourist office before planning your day's activities around a bus that may not actually be running.

If you're taking a few local bus rides in one area, day passes (with names like Day Rover, Wayfarer or Explorer) are cheaper than buying several single tickets. Often they can be bought on your first bus, and may include local rail services. It's always worth asking ticket clerks or bus drivers about your options.

Taxi

There are two sorts of taxi in Britain: those with meters that can be hailed in the street; and minicabs, which are cheaper but can only be called by phone. Unlicensed minicabs operate in some cities.

In London, most taxis are the famous 'black cabs' (some with advertising livery in other colours), which charge by distance and time. Depending on the time of day, a 1-mile journey takes five to 10 minutes and costs £6 to £9. Longer journeys are proportionally cheaper.

Black cabs also operate in some other large cities around Britain, with rates usually lower than in London.

In London, taxis are best flagged down in the street; a 'for hire' light on the roof indicates availability. In other cities, you can flag down a cab if you see one, but it's usually easier to go to a taxi rank.

Apps such as **Uber** (www.uber.com) and **Kabbee** (www.kabbee.com) allow you to book a minicab in double-quick time.

In rural areas, taxis need to be called by phone; the best place to find the local taxi's phone number is the local pub. Fares are £3 to £5 per mile.

Traintaxi (www.traintaxi.co.uk) is a portal site for journeys between the train station and your hotel or other final destination.

Train

For long-distance travel around Britain, trains are generally faster and more comfortable than coaches but can be more expensive, although with discount tickets they're competitive – and often take you through beautiful countryside. The British like to moan about their trains, but around 85% run on time. The other 15% that get delayed or cancelled mostly impact commuter services rather than long-distance journeys.

Train Operators

About 20 different companies operate train services in Britain, while Network Rail operates track and stations. For some passengers this system can be confusing at first, but information and ticket-buying services are mostly centralised. If you have to change trains, or use two or more train operators, you still buy one ticket – valid for the whole journey. The main railcards and passes are also accepted by all train operators.

Where more than one train operator services the same route, eg York to Edinburgh, a ticket purchased from one company may not be valid on trains run by another. So if you miss the train you originally booked, it's worth checking which later services your ticket will be valid for.

Tickets & Reservations

Your first stop should be **National Rail Enquiries** (www.nationalrail.co.uk), the nationwide timetable and fare information service. Its website advertises special offers and has real-time links to station departure boards and downloadable maps of the rail network.

BUYING TICKETS

Once you've found the journey you need on the National Rail Enquiries website, links take you to the relevant train operator to buy the ticket. This can be mailed to you (UK addresses only) or collected at the station on the day of travel from automatic machines. There's usually no booking fee on top of the ticket price.

You can also use a centralised ticketing service to buy your train ticket. These cover all train services in a single site, but they will charge a booking fee on top of every ticket price. The main players include:

QJump (www.qjump.co.uk)

Rail Easy (www.raileasy.co.uk)

Train Line (www.thetrainline.com)

To use operator or centralised ticketing websites, you always have to state a preferred time and day of travel, even if you don't mind when you go, but you can change it as you go through the process, and with a little delving around you can find some real bargains.

You can also buy train tickets on the spot at stations, which is fine for short journeys (under about 50 miles), but discount tickets for longer trips are usually not available and must be bought in advance by phone or online.

COSTS

For longer journeys, on-the-spot fares are always available, but tickets are much cheaper if bought in advance. The earlier you book, the cheaper it gets. You can also save if you travel off-peak. Advance purchase usually gets a reserved seat, too.

Whichever operator you travel with and wherever you buy tickets, these are the three main fare types:

Anytime Buy anytime, travel anytime – usually the most expensive option.

Off-peak Buy ticket any time, travel off-peak (what is off-peak depends on the journey).

Advance Buy ticket in advance, travel only on specific trains – usually the cheapest option.

For an idea of the (substantial) price differences, an Anytime single ticket from London to York will cost £127 or more, an Off-peak around £109, with an Advance around £44 to £55. The cheapest fares are usually nonrefundable, so if you miss your train you'll have to buy a new ticket.

TRAVEL FARES

When travelling by long-distance bus, coach or train in Britain, it's important to realise that there's no such thing as a standard fare. Prices vary according to demand and when you buy your ticket. Book long in advance and travel on Tuesday mid-morning and it's cheap. Buy your ticket on the spot late Friday afternoon and it'll be a lot more expensive. Ferries use similar systems.

Lonely Planet sample fares are somewhere in between the very cheapest and most expensive options. The price you pay will almost certainly be different.

To secure the cheapest fares, the two golden rules are: book as early in advance as you can, and be flexible with your travel times (off-peak times are always cheaper).

LONDON STATIONS

London has several main-line train stations, including Victoria, Paddington, King's Cross, Waterloo, Charing Cross and Liverpool St, positioned in a rough circle around the city's central area (and mostly linked by the Circle Underground line). The stations' proper names are London Victoria, London Paddington, London King's Cross and so on, and this is how you'll see them appear on official timetables, information boards and booking websites – although the British never use the full names in everyday speech.

Mobile train tickets are gradually becoming more common across the network, but it's a slow process – for now printed tickets are still the norm.

ONWARD TRAVEL

If the train doesn't get you all the way to your destination, you can add a **PlusBus** (www.plusbus.info) supplement when making your reservation to validate your train ticket for onward travel by bus. This is more convenient, and usually cheaper, than buying a separate bus ticket.

Train Classes

There are two classes of rail travel: first and standard. First class costs around 50% more than standard fare (up to double at busy periods) and gets you bigger seats, more leg-room, and usually a

more peaceful business-like atmosphere, plus extras such as complimentary drinks and newspapers. At weekends some train operators offer 'upgrades' to first class for an extra £5 to £25 on top of your standard class fare, payable on the spot.

Train Passes

DISCOUNT PASSES

If you're staying in Britain for a while, passes known as Railcards (www.railcard.co.uk) are worth considering:

16-25 Railcard For those aged 16 to 25, or full-time UK students.

Two Together Railcard For two specified people travelling together.

Senior Railcard For anyone over 60.

Family & Friends Railcard Covers up to four adults and four children travelling together.

Railcards cost £30 (valid for one year, available from major stations or online) and give a 33% discount on most train fares, except those already heavily discounted. With the Family card, adults get 33% and children get 60% discounts, so the fee is easily recouped in a couple of journeys.

LOCAL & REGIONAL PASSES

Local train passes usually cover rail networks around a city (many include bus travel too). If you're concentrating your travels on southeast England (eg London to Dover, Weymouth, Cambridge or Oxford), a **Network Railcard** (per year £30) covers up to four adults and up to four children travelling together outside peak times.

NATIONAL PASSES

For country-wide travel, **BritRail** (www.britrail.net) passes are available for visitors from overseas. They must be bought in your country of origin (not in Britain) from a specialist travel agency. They're available in seven different versions (eg England only; Scotland only; all of Britain; UK and Ireland) for periods from four to 30 days.

Glossary

almshouse – accommodation for the aged or needy

ap – prefix in a Welsh name meaning 'son of'

bag – originally to 'catch' – a shooting term – now used to mean 'reach the top of' (as in to 'bag a couple of peaks' or 'Munro bagging')

bailey – outermost wall of a castle

bar – gate (York, and some other northern cities)

beck – stream (northern England)

bill – the total you need to pay after eating in a restaurant ('check' to Americans)

billion – the British billion is a million million (unlike the American billion – a thousand million)

blackhouse – traditional low-walled stone cottage with thatch or turf roof and earth floors; shared by both humans and cattle and typical of the Outer Hebrides until the early 20th century (Scotland)

bloke – man (colloquial)

Blue Flag – an award given to beaches for their unpolluted sand and water

böd – once a simple trading booth used by fishing communities, today it refers to basic accommodation for walkers etc (used only in Shetland)

bothy – very simple hut or shelter, usually in mountain or wilderness area, used by walkers and hikers

brae – hill (Scotland)

bridleway – track for horse riders that can also be used by walkers and cyclists

broch – ancient defensive tower

burgh – town

burn – stream

bus – local bus; see also *coach*

Cadw – the Welsh historic monuments agency

cairn – pile of stones marking path, junction of paths or the summit of a mountain

CalMac – Caledonian Mac-Brayne, the main Scottish island ferry operator

canny – good, great, wise (northern England)

castell – castle (Welsh)

ceilidh – (*kay*-lee) a session of traditional music, song and dance; originally Scottish, now more widely used across Britain

Celtic high cross – a large, elaborately carved stone cross decorated with biblical scenes and Celtic interlace designs dating from the 8th to 10th centuries

cheers – goodbye; thanks (colloquial); also a drinking toast

chemist – pharmacist

chine – valley-like fissure leading to the sea (southern England)

chippy – fish-and-chip shop

circus – junction of several city streets, usually circular, and usually with a green or other feature at the centre

Clearances – eviction of Highland farmers from their land by *lairds* wanting to use it for grazing sheep

close – entrance to an alley

coach – long-distance bus

coasteering – adventurous activity that involves making your way around a rocky coastline by climbing, scrambling, jumping or swimming

cob – mixture of mud and straw for building

corrie – circular hollow on a hillside

cot – small bed for a baby ('crib' to Americans)

court – courtyard

craic – lively conversation; pronounced, and sometimes spelt, 'crack'

craig – exposed rock

crannog – an artificial island in a loch built for defensive purposes

croft – smallholding, usually in marginal agricultural area (Scotland); the activity is known as 'smallholding'

Cymraeg – Welsh language (Welsh); also Gymraeg

Cymru – Welsh word for Wales

dene – valley

dirk – dagger

DIY – do-it-yourself, ie home improvements

dram – a measure of whisky

dodgy – suspect, bad, dangerous (colloquial)

dolmen – chambered tomb (Wales)

dough – money (colloquial)

downs – rolling upland, characterised by lack of trees

duvet – quilt replacing sheets and blankets ('doona' to Australians)

EH – English Heritage; state-funded organisation responsible for historic sites

en suite room – hotel room with private attached bathroom (ie shower, basin and toilet)

eisteddfod – literally a gathering or session; festival in which competitions are held in music, poetry, drama and the fine arts; plural eisteddfodau (Welsh)

Evensong – daily evening service (Church of England)

fell race – tough running race through hills or moors

fen – drained or marshy low-lying flat land

firth – estuary

fiver – £5 note (colloquial)

flat – single dwelling in a larger building ('apartment' to Americans)

flip-flops – plastic sandals with a single strap over toes ('thongs' to Australians)

footpath – path through countryside and between houses, not beside a road (that's called a 'pavement')

gate – street (York, and some other northern cities)

graft – work (not corruption, as in American English; colloquial)

grand – 1000 (colloquial)

gutted – very disappointed (colloquial)

guv, guvner – from governor, a respectful term of address for owner or boss; can sometimes be used ironically

hart – deer

HI – Hostelling International (organisation)

hire – rent

Hogmanay – Scottish celebration of New Year's Eve

howff – pub or shelter (Scotland)

HS – Historic Scotland; organisation that manages historic sites in Scotland

inn – pub with accommodation

jumper – woollen item of clothing worn on torso ('sweater' to Americans)

ken – Scottish term for 'understand' or 'know', as in 'do you ken' = 'do you know'

kirk – church (northern England and Scotland)

knowe – burial mound (Scotland)

kyle – strait or channel (Scotland)

laird – estate owner (Scotland)

lass – young woman (northern England and Scotland)

lift – machine for carrying people up and down in large buildings ('elevator' to Americans)

linn – waterfall (Scotland)

loch – lake (Scotland)

lochan – small *loch*

lock – part of a canal or river that can be closed off and the water levels changed to raise or lower boats

lolly – money (colloquial); candy on a stick (possibly frozen)

lorry (s), lorries (pl) – truck

Mabinogion – key source of Welsh folk legends

machair – grass- and wildflower-covered sand dunes

mad – insane (not angry, as in American English)

Marches – borderlands between England and Wales or Scotland

menhir – standing stone

Mercat Cross – a symbol of the trading rights of a market town or village, usually found in the centre of town and usually a focal point for the community

mere – a body of water, usually shallow; technically a lake that has a large surface area relative to its depth

merthyr – burial place of a saint (Welsh)

midge – mosquito-like insect

motorway – major road linking cities (equivalent to 'interstate' or 'freeway')

motte – early Norman fortification consisting of a raised, flattened mound with

a keep on top; when attached to a *bailey* it is known as a motte-and-bailey

Munro – hill or mountain 3000ft (914m) or higher, especially in Scotland; those over 2500ft are called Corbetts

Munro bagger – a hill walker who tries to climb all the *Munros* in Scotland

naff – inferior, in poor taste (colloquial)

NCN – National Cycle Network

newydd – new (Welsh)

NNR – National Nature Reserve, managed by the Scottish Natural Heritage (SNH)

NT – National Trust; organisation that protects historic buildings and land with scenic importance in England and Wales

NTS – National Trust for Scotland; organisation dedicated to the preservation of historic sites and the environment in Scotland

oast house – building containing a kiln for drying hops

ogham – ancient Celtic script

oriel – gallery (Welsh)

OS – Ordnance Survey

p – (pronounced pee) pence; ie 2p is 'two p' not 'two pence' or 'tuppence'

pele – fortified house

Picts – early inhabitants of north and east Scotland (from Latin pictus, or 'painted', after their body-paint decorations)

pile – large imposing building (colloquial)

pissed – slang for drunk (not angry)

pissed off – angry (slang)

pitch – playing field

postbus – minibus delivering the mail, also carrying passengers in remote areas

provost – mayor

punter – customer (colloquial)

quid – pound (colloquial)

ramble – short easy walk

reiver – warrior or raider (historic term; northern England)

return ticket – round-trip ticket

RIB – rigid inflatable boat

rood – an old Scots word for a cross

RSPB – Royal Society for the Protection of Birds

RSPCA – Royal Society for the Prevention of Cruelty to Animals

sarsen – boulder, a geological remnant usually found in chalky areas (sometimes used in neolithic constructions, eg Stonehenge and Avebury)

Sassenach – from Gaelic 'Sasannach': anyone who is not a Highlander (including Lowland Scots)

sheila-na-gig – Celtic fertility symbol of a woman with exaggerated genitalia, often carved in stone on churches and castles; rare in England, found mainly in the *Marches*, along the border with Wales

single ticket – one-way ticket

SMC – Scottish Mountaineering Club

SNH – Scottish Natural Heritage, a government organisation directly responsible for safeguarding and improving Scotland's natural heritage

snickelway – narrow alley (York)

snug – usually a small separate room in a pub

sporran – purse worn around waist with the kilt (Scotland)

SSSI – Site of Special Scientific Interest

Sustrans – sustainable transport charity encouraging people to walk, cycle and use public transport; also responsible for instigating and developing the NCN (National Cycle Network)

SYHA – Scottish Youth Hostel Association

tarn – a small lake or pool, usually in mountain areas in England, often in a depression caused by glacial erosion

tenner – £10 note (colloquial)

TIC – Tourist Information Centre

ton – 100 (colloquial)

tor – pointed hill

torch – flashlight

Tory – Conservative (political party)

towpath – path running beside a river or canal, where horses once towed barges

twitcher – obsessive birdwatcher

Tube, the – London's underground railway system (colloquial)

Underground, the – London's underground railway system

wolds – open, rolling countryside

wynd – lane or narrow street (northern England and Scotland)

YHA – Youth Hostels Association

Behind the Scenes

SEND US YOUR FEEDBACK

We love to hear from travellers – your comments keep us on our toes and help make our books better. Our well-travelled team reads every word on what you loved or loathed about this book. Although we cannot reply individually to your submissions, we always guarantee that your feedback goes straight to the appropriate authors, in time for the next edition. Each person who sends us information is thanked in the next edition – the most useful submissions are rewarded with a selection of digital PDF chapters.

Visit **lonelyplanet.com/contact** to submit your updates and suggestions or to ask for help. Our award-winning website also features inspirational travel stories, news and discussions.

Note: We may edit, reproduce and incorporate your comments in Lonely Planet products such as guidebooks, websites and digital products, so let us know if you don't want your comments reproduced or your name acknowledged. For a copy of our privacy policy visit lonelyplanet.com/privacy.

WRITER THANKS

Oliver Berry

As always I've thoroughly enjoyed exploring my homeland for this update, and I'd like to extend a big thanks to everyone who's helped me along the way (you know who you are). I'd particularly like to thank all my co-authors for their hard work and help, and Cliff Wilkinson for sage advice, feedback and generally keeping the England ship on course. A special thanks also to Rosie Hillier for supporting me, putting up with long days and nights spent at the computer and providing emergency cups of tea when they were most needed.

Marc Di Duca

Huge thanks to Tanya at home in the Czech Republic for holding the fort, to Emy and David in Sandwich, to Gemma and Dave in Amesbury and to all the many employees at the various tourist offices across Kent and Sussex who helped me along the way.

Belinda Dixon

Researching and writing for Lonely Planet is a real joint effort – so huge thanks to the locals who share their time, knowledge and recommendations and to the random strangers who offer countless kindnesses. And thank you to Cliff for the gig, LP's behind the scenes teams (so much work!), and fellow writers for humour, wisdom and travellers' tales.

Damian Harper

Many thanks to Ann Harper, Jasmin Tonge, Kevin and Maki Fallows, Rosemary Hadow, Lily Greensmith, Antonia Mavromatidou, Arabella Sneddon, Bill Moran, Jim Peake, my ever-helpful co-authors and a big debt of gratitude again to Daisy, Tim and Emma.

Catherine Le Nevez

Cheers first and foremost to Julian, and to all of the locals, fellow travellers and tourism professionals throughout Northeast England, the Midlands and the Marches for insights, information and good times. Huge thanks too to Destination Editor Cliff Wilkinson and the Great Britain team, and everyone at LP. As ever, merci encore to my parents, brother, belle-sœur, neveu and nièce.

Hugh McNaughtan

Criss-crossing Wales in the golden summer of 2018 was a magical experience. For those who showered me with friendliness, generosity and inside tips along the way – thanks!; to Cliff and the LP team for editorial and technical guidance – thanks!; and to Tasmin, Maise and Willa for endless support and encouragement, thank you.

Lorna Parkes

Thanks to the many friendly folk of Yorkshire for their chats, advice and excellent beer-making. And to Rob, Austin and Lily for letting me drag them all over the Dales and east coast, come rain or shine (but mostly rain).

Andy Symington

It's always a huge pleasure to enjoy the very generous hospitality of Jenny Neil and Brendan Bolland, and to work with Neil Wilson, Cliff Wilkinson and the excellent LP team. Numerous other people have been very generous with time and information. I'd particularly like to thank Robin Mitchell, Maggie Maguire, Graeme Campbell, Jen Stewart and the staff at many tourist information offices, especially Judith and Janice at Bowmore, Sheona at John O'Groats, Susan at Callander and Neil at Kirkwall.

Greg Ward

Thanks to the many people who helped me as I pounded the streets of Oxford and criss-crossed the Cotswolds, and thanks especially to Adrian, Michael and Donald Ward for their Oxford memories and expertise. Thanks too to my editor Clifton Wilkinson for giving me this opportunity, and to my dear wife, Sam, for sharing so many adventures and late nights.

Neil Wilson

Thanks to the friendly and helpful tourist office staff all over the Highlands; to Steven Fallon, Keith Jeffrey, Fiona Garven, Derek McCrindle, Brendan Bolland, Jenny Neil, Tom and Christine Duffin, Steve Hall, Elaine Simpson, Peter Fallon and Duncan Pepper; and, as ever, to Carol Downie. Thanks also to James Smart and the editorial team at Lonely Planet.

ACKNOWLEDGEMENTS

Climate map data adapted from Peel MC, Finlayson BL & McMahon TA (2007) 'Updated World Map of the Köppen-Geiger Climate Classification', Hydrology and Earth System Sciences, 11, 1633–44.

Cover photograph: Neist Point, Isle of Skye, Colin Threlfall/Alamy ©

Illustrations: pp94–5, pp624–5, pp750–1, pp784–5 and pp830–1 by Javier Zarracina, pp74–5 by Javier Zarracina and Michael Weldon.

BEHIND THE SCENES

THIS BOOK

This 13th edition of Lonely Planet's *Great Britain* guidebook was curated by Oliver Berry, and researched and written by Oliver, Fionn Davenport, Marc Di Duca, Belinda Dixon, Damian Harper, Catherine Le Nevez, Hugh McNaughtan, Lorna Parkes, Andy Symington, Greg Ward and Neil Wilson. The previous edition was written by Oliver Berry, Fionn Davenport, Marc Di Duca, Belinda Dixon, Peter Dragicevich, Damian Harper,

Catherine Le Nevez, Hugh McNaughtan, Isabella Noble, Andy Symington and Neil Wilson. This guidebook was produced by the following:

Destination Editors James Smart, Clifton Wilkinson

Senior Product Editor Genna Patterson

Product Editor Kathryn Rowan

Senior Cartographer Mark Griffiths

Book Designer Clara Monitto

Assisting Editors Sarah Bailey, Andrew Bain, Judith Bamber, Michelle Bennett, Nigel Chin, Katie Connolly, Lucy Cowie, Michelle Coxall, Jacqueline Danam, Andrea Dobbin, Kellie Langdon, Lou McGregor, Kristin Odijk, Monique Perrin, Sarah Stewart

Cartographer Rachel Imeson

Cover Researcher Naomi Parker

Thanks to Ian Grundy, John Harper, Elizabeth Jones, Laura Manago, Alison Ridgway, Michael Weldon, Amanda Williamson

Index

Map Legend

Sights

- Beach
- Bird Sanctuary
- Buddhist
- Castle/Palace
- Christian
- Confucian
- Hindu
- Islamic
- Jain
- Jewish
- Monument
- Museum/Gallery/Historic Building
- Ruin
- Shinto
- Sikh
- Taoist
- Winery/Vineyard
- Zoo/Wildlife Sanctuary
- Other Sight

Activities, Courses & Tours

- Bodysurfing
- Diving
- Canoeing/Kayaking
- Course/Tour
- Sento Hot Baths/Onsen
- Skiing
- Snorkelling
- Surfing
- Swimming/Pool
- Walking
- Windsurfing
- Other Activity

Sleeping

- Sleeping
- Camping
- Hut/Shelter

Eating

- Eating

Drinking & Nightlife

- Drinking & Nightlife
- Cafe

Entertainment

- Entertainment

Shopping

- Shopping

Information

- Bank
- Embassy/Consulate
- Hospital/Medical
- Internet
- Police
- Post Office
- Telephone
- Toilet
- Tourist Information
- Other Information

Geographic

- Beach
- Gate
- Hut/Shelter
- Lighthouse
- Lookout
- Mountain/Volcano
- Oasis
- Park
- Pass
- Picnic Area
- Waterfall

Population

- Capital (National)
- Capital (State/Province)
- City/Large Town
- Town/Village

Transport

- Airport
- Border crossing
- Bus
- Cable car/Funicular
- Cycling
- Ferry
- Metro station
- Monorail
- Parking
- Petrol station
- S-Bahn/Subway station
- Taxi
- T-bane/Tunnelbana station
- Train station/Railway
- Tram
- Tube station
- U-Bahn/Underground station
- Other Transport

Routes

- Tollway
- Freeway
- Primary
- Secondary
- Tertiary
- Lane
- Unsealed road
- Road under construction
- Plaza/Mall
- Steps
- Tunnel
- Pedestrian overpass
- Walking Tour
- Walking Tour detour
- Path/Walking Trail

Boundaries

- International
- State/Province
- Disputed
- Regional/Suburb
- Marine Park
- Cliff
- Wall

Hydrography

- River, Creek
- Intermittent River
- Canal
- Water
- Dry/Salt/Intermittent Lake
- Reef

Areas

- Airport/Runway
- Beach/Desert
- Cemetery (Christian)
- Cemetery (Other)
- Glacier
- Mudflat
- Park/Forest
- Sight (Building)
- Sportsground
- Swamp/Mangrove

Note: Not all symbols displayed above appear on the maps in this book

Damian Harper

London With two degrees (one in modern and classical Chinese from SOAS), Damian has been writing for Lonely Planet for over two decades, contributing to titles as diverse as *China, Beijing, Shanghai, Vietnam, Thailand, Ireland, London, Mallorca, Malaysia, Singapore & Brunei, Hong Kong* and *Great Britain.* A seasoned guidebook writer, Damian has penned articles for numerous newspapers and magazines, including the *Guardian* and the *Daily Telegraph,* and currently makes Surrey, England, his home. Follow Damian on Instagram (damian.harper).

Catherine Le Nevez

Newcastle & Northeast England, Birmingham & the Midlands Catherine's wanderlust kicked in when she roadtripped across Europe from her Parisian base aged four, and she's been hitting the road at every opportunity since, travelling to around 60 countries and completing her Doctorate of Creative Arts in Writing, Masters in Professional Writing, and postgrad qualifications in Editing and Publishing along the way. Over the past dozen-plus years she's written scores of Lonely Planet guides and articles covering Paris, France, Europe and far beyond. Topping Catherine's list of travel tips is to travel without any expectations.

Hugh McNaughtan

Wales Hugh has been obsessed with Wales since a childhood steeped in books about castles and longbows. A former English lecturer who swapped grant applications for visa applications, turning his love of travel into a full-time thing, he's scoured Wales from end-to-end since 1994, yet always comes up with new things to wonder at.

Lorna Parkes

Yorkshire Londoner by birth, Melburnian by palate and ex-Lonely Planet staffer in both cities, Lorna has contributed to numerous Lonely Planet books and magazines. She's discovered she writes best on planes, and is most content when researching food and booze. Wineries and the tropics (not at the same time!) are her go-to happy places, but Yorkshire will always be special to her. Follow her @Lorna_Explorer.

Andy Symington

Glasgow & Southern Scotland, Inverness & the Northern Highlands & Islands Andy has written or worked on over a hundred books and other updates for Lonely Planet (especially in Europe and Latin America) and other publishing companies, and has published articles on numerous subjects for a variety of newspapers, magazines and websites. He part-owns and operates a rock bar, has written a novel and is currently working on several fiction and non-fiction writing projects. Originally from Australia, Andy moved to northern Spain many years ago.

Greg Ward

Oxford & the Cotswolds Since whetting his appetite for travel by following the hippy trail to India, and later living in northern Spain, Greg has written guides to destinations all over the world. As well as covering the USA from the Southwest to Hawaii, he has ranged on recent assignments from Corsica to the Cotswolds, and Japan to Corfu. See his website, www.gregward.info, for his favourite photos and memories.

Neil Wilson

Edinburgh, Stirling & Central Scotland, Inverness & the Northern Highlands & Islands Neil was born in Scotland and has lived there most of his life. Based in Perthshire, he has been a full-time writer since 1988, working on more than 80 guidebooks for various publishers, including the Lonely Planet guides to Scotland, England, Ireland and Prague. An outdoors enthusiast since childhood, Neil is an active hill-walker, mountain-biker, sailor, snowboarder, fly-fisher and rock-climber, and has climbed and tramped in four continents.

Contributing writers: Peter Dragicevich, Steve Fallon and Emilie Filou

OUR STORY

A beat-up old car, a few dollars in the pocket and a sense of adventure. In 1972 that's all Tony and Maureen Wheeler needed for the trip of a lifetime – across Europe and Asia overland to Australia. It took several months, and at the end – broke but inspired – they sat at their kitchen table writing and stapling together their first travel guide, *Across Asia on the Cheap*. Within a week they'd sold 1500 copies. Lonely Planet was born.

Today, Lonely Planet has offices in Franklin, London, Melbourne, Oakland, Dublin, Beijing and Delhi, with more than 600 staff and writers. We share Tony's belief that 'a great guidebook should do three things: inform, educate and amuse'.

OUR WRITERS

Oliver Berry

Curator, Southwest England, the Lake District & Cumbria Oliver is a writer and photographer from Cornwall. He has worked for Lonely Planet for more than a decade, covering destinations from Cornwall to the Cook Islands, and has worked on more than 30 guidebooks. He is also a regular contributor to many newspapers and magazines, including *Lonely Planet Traveller*. His writing has won several awards, including the Guardian Young Travel Writer of the Year and the TNT Magazine People's Choice Award. His latest work is published at www.oliverberry.com.

Fionn Davenport

Manchester, Liverpool & Northwest England Irish by birth and conviction, Fionn has spent the last two decades focusing on the country of his birth and his nearest neighbour, England, which he has written about extensively for Lonely Planet and others. In between writing gigs he's lived in Paris and New York, where he was an editor, actor, bartender and whatever else paid the rent; for the last 15 years or so he's also presented a series of radio programmes on Irish radio, most recently as host of Inside Culture on RTE Radio 1. Three years ago he moved to the northwest of England where he lives (and commutes from) with his partner, Laura, and their car, Trevor.

Marc Di Duca

Canterbury & Southeast England A travel author for over a decade, Marc has worked for Lonely Planet in Siberia, Slovakia, Bavaria, England, Ukraine, Austria, Poland, Croatia, Portugal, Madeira and on the Trans-Siberian Railway, as well as writing and updating tens of other guides for other publishers. When not on the road, Marc lives near Mariánské Lázně in the Czech Republic with his wife and two sons.

Belinda Dixon

Bath & Southwest England, Cambridge & East Anglia Only happy when her feet are suitably sandy, Belinda has been (gleefully) researching and writing for Lonely Planet since 2006. It's seen her marvelling at Stonehenge at sunrise, camping in Iceland, scrambling up Italian mountain paths, horse riding across Donegal's golden sands, kayaking down Devon rivers, gazing at Verona's frescoes and fossil hunting on Dorset's Jurassic Coast. Belinda is also an adventure writer and expedition media leader – which has seen her scale snowy Scottish mountains, paddle the Yukon, surf and swim in England's winter seas and sleep out under the stars. See her posts at https://belindadixon.com.

OVER PAGE MORE WRITERS

Published by Lonely Planet Global Limited
CRN 554153
13th edition – May 2019
ISBN 978 1 78657 806 8
© Lonely Planet 2019   Photographs © as indicated 2019
10 9 8 7 6 5 4 3 2 1
Printed in Singapore

Although the authors and Lonely Planet have taken all reasonable care in preparing this book, we make no warranty about the accuracy or completeness of its content and, to the maximum extent permitted, disclaim all liability arising from its use.